BRITISH RAILWAYS STEAM LOCOMOTIVE ALLOCATIONS

BRITISH RAILWAYS STEAM LOCOMOTIVE ALLOCATIONS

HUGH LONGWORTH

OPC
An imprint of
Ian Allan Publishing

Contents

Front cover: Inside North Blyth Shed on 14 May 1966 'J27' No 65801, 'K1' No 62005, and 'J27' No 65795 are being prepared for service. *P. K. King*

Half title: Bristol Barrow Road with GWR, LMS and BR Standard locomotives on shed. *Ivo Peters*

Title page: A Stanier Class 5 on the turntable at Patricroft MPD. *M. Dunnett*

First published 2011

ISBN 978 0 86093 642 8

Published by Oxford Publishing Co

an imprint of Ian Allan Publishing Ltd, Hersham, Surrey, KT12 4RG
Printed in England by Ian Allan Printing Ltd, Hersham, Surrey, KT12 4RG

Code: 1104/C

Distributed in the United States of America and Canada by BookMasters Distribution Services

Visit the Ian Allan Publishing website at www.ianallanpublishing.com

Preface

When I wrote my first book (British Railways Steam Locomotives 1948-1968) I was faced with some restrictions right from the beginning.

I decided early on not to include any information on allocations, as it would completely change the character of the book, as well as making it un-manageably large.

Another decision I had to make was to limit the number of photographs that I could include in the book. I was restricted to 180 photographs when I really needed nearly three times that number to cover all the classes.

Now with this volume I hope to set matters right. I've taken all the material left out after my last book and added a lot of the missing photographs. I've tried to be creative in my presentation of the information, and I hope you will enjoy the book.

I'd particularly like to thank Peter Waller at Ian Allan for again giving me the opportunity to present my work to you.

Hugh Longworth 2010

I would again like to express my thanks to my family – my wife Doris and my daughter Heppy. I have suffered a long period of illness over the past four years and they have faithfully stood by me and supported me through this time. I thank God for you both and I am eternally grateful to you.

I would also like to thank my parents Frank and Penny Longworth for all the support and freedom they gave me throughout my teenage years. Those were the years when I was travelling the country far and wide chasing trains. Being a parent myself now it scares me silly to think how much freedom they gave me, but chasing trains is far better than some of the other things I could have chased as a teenager!

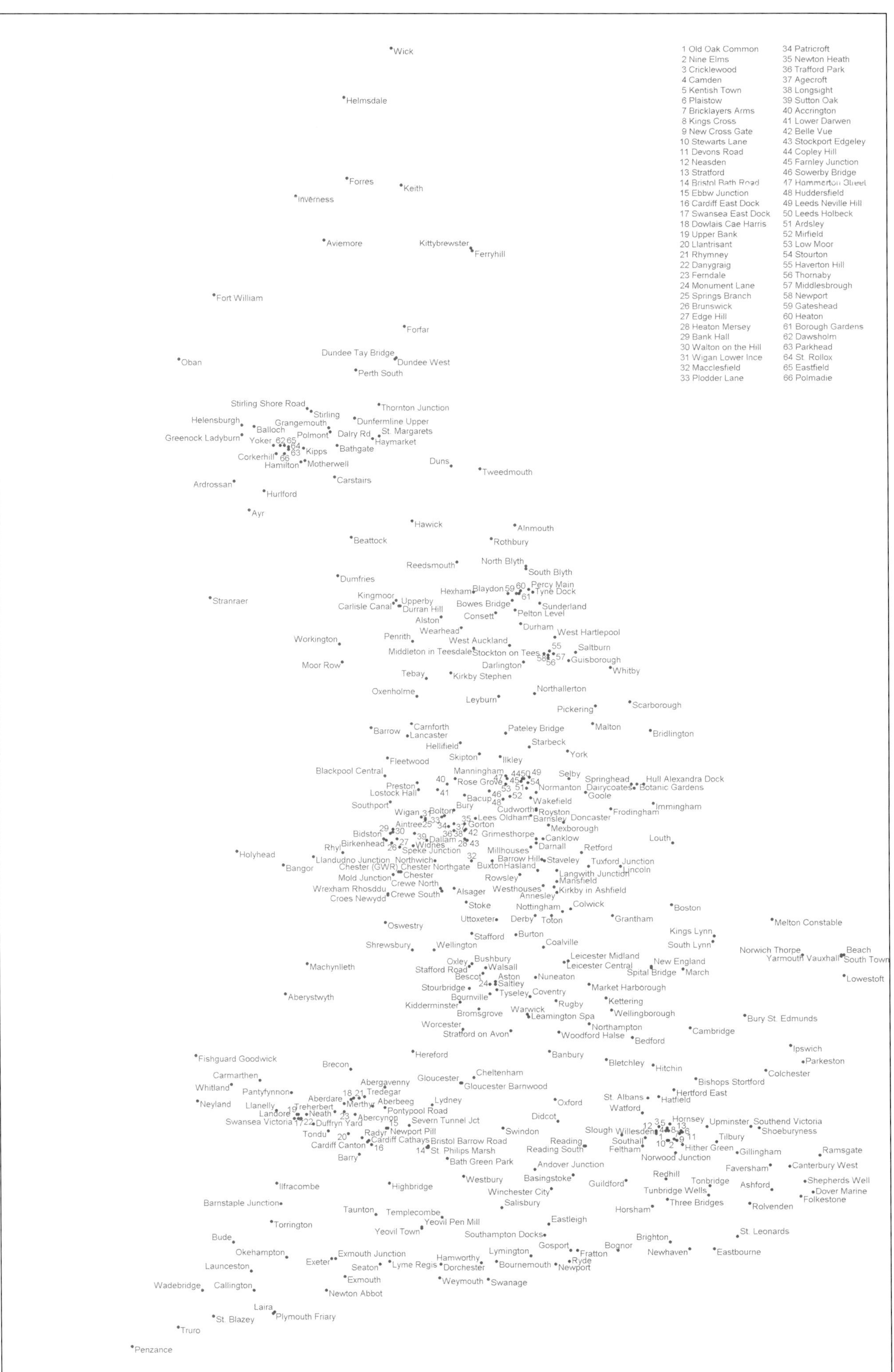

1 Old Oak Common
2 Nine Elms
3 Cricklewood
4 Camden
5 Kentish Town
6 Plaistow
7 Bricklayers Arms
8 Kings Cross
9 New Cross Gate
10 Stewarts Lane
11 Devons Road
12 Neasden
13 Stratford
14 Bristol Bath Road
15 Ebbw Junction
16 Cardiff East Dock
17 Swansea East Dock
18 Dowlais Cae Harris
19 Upper Bank
20 Llantrisant
21 Rhymney
22 Danygraig
23 Ferndale
24 Monument Lane
25 Springs Branch
26 Brunswick
27 Edge Hill
28 Heaton Mersey
29 Bank Hall
30 Walton on the Hill
31 Wigan Lower Ince
32 Macclesfield
33 Plodder Lane
34 Patricroft
35 Newton Heath
36 Trafford Park
37 Agecroft
38 Longsight
39 Sutton Oak
40 Accrington
41 Lower Darwen
42 Belle Vue
43 Stockport Edgeley
44 Copley Hill
45 Farnley Junction
46 Sowerby Bridge
47 Hammerton Street
48 Huddersfield
49 Leeds Neville Hill
50 Leeds Holbeck
51 Ardsley
52 Mirfield
53 Low Moor
54 Stourton
55 Haverton Hill
56 Thornaby
57 Middlesbrough
58 Newport
59 Gateshead
60 Heaton
61 Borough Gardens
62 Dawsholm
63 Parkhead
64 St. Rollox
65 Eastfield
66 Polmadie
Wick
Helmsdale
Forres
Keith
Inverness
Aviemore
Kittybrewster
Ferryhill
Fort William
Forfar
Dundee Tay Bridge
Dundee West
Oban
Perth South
Stirling Shore Road
Stirling
Thornton Junction
Helensburgh
Grangemouth
Dunfermline Upper
Balloch
Polmont
Dalry Rd
St. Margarets
Greenock Ladyburn
Yoker
Haymarket
Kipps
Bathgate
Corkerhill
Hamilton
Motherwell
Duns
Tweedmouth
Ardrossan
Carstairs
Hurlford
Ayr
Hawick
Alnmouth
Beattock
Rothbury
North Blyth
Reedsmouth
South Blyth
Dumfries
Percy Main
Hexham
Blaydon
Tyne Dock
Kingmoor
Upperby
Bowes Bridge
Sunderland
Stranraer
Carlisle Canal
Durran Hill
Consett
Pelton Level
Alston
Durham
Wearhead
West Hartlepool
Penrith
West Auckland
Workington
Saltburn
Middleton in Teesdale
Stockton on Tees
Guisborough
Darlington
Moor Row
Whitby
Tebay
Kirkby Stephen
Oxenholme
Northallerton
Leyburn
Pickering
Scarborough
Carnforth
Malton
Barrow
Lancaster
Pateley Bridge
Bridlington
Hellifield
Starbeck
York
Skipton
Ilkley
Fleetwood
Blackpool Central
Manningham
Selby
Springhead
Hull Alexandra Dock
Rose Grove
Dairycoates
Botanic Gardens
Preston
Normanton
Goole
Lostock Hall
Bacup
Wakefield
Southport
Bury
Immingham
Wigan
Bolton
Cudworth
Royston
Frodingham
Lees
Oldham
Barnsley
Doncaster
Aintree
Gorton
Mexborough
Bidston
Grimesthorpe
Dallam
Canklow
Louth
Rhyl
Birkenhead
Widnes
Darnall
Retford
Speke Junction
Millhouses
Holyhead
Llandudno Junction
Northwich
Barrow Hill
Staveley
Tuxford Junction
Bangor
Chester (GWR)
Chester Northgate
Buxton
Hasland
Langwith Junction
Lincoln
Chester
Rowsley
Mansfield
Mold Junction
Crewe North
Wrexham Rhosddu
Alsager
Westhouses
Kirkby in Ashfield
Crewe South
Annesley
Croes Newydd
Stoke
Nottingham
Colwick
Boston
Uttoxeter
Derby
Toton
Grantham
Melton Constable
Oswestry
Kings Lynn
Stafford
Burton
South Lynn
Shrewsbury
Wellington
Coalville
Norwich Thorpe
Beach
Yarmouth
Vauxhall
South Town
Leicester Midland
Oxley
Bushbury
New England
Machynlleth
Stafford Road
Walsall
Leicester Central
Spital Bridge
March
Bescot
Aston
Nuneaton
Lowestoft
Saltley
Stourbridge
Tyseley
Coventry
Market Harborough
Aberystwyth
Bournville
Kidderminster
Rugby
Kettering
Bromsgrove
Warwick
Wellingborough
Leamington Spa
Bury St. Edmunds
Worcester
Northampton
Stratford on Avon
Woodford Halse
Cambridge
Bedford
Hereford
Banbury
Ipswich
Fishguard Goodwick
Brecon
Bletchley
Hitchin
Parkeston
Cheltenham
Carmarthen
Gloucester
Colchester
Abergavenny
Gloucester Barnwood
Bishops Stortford
Whitland
Pantyfynnon
Tredegar
Hertford East
Aberdare
Aberbeeg
Lydney
St. Albans
Hatfield
Neyland
Llanelly
Merthyr
Oxford
Treherbert
Pontypool Road
Watford
Landore
Neath
Didcot
Hornsey
Upminster
Southend Victoria
Abercynon
Swansea Victoria
Duffryn Yard
Severn Tunnel Jct
Shoeburyness
Tondu
Radyr
Newport Pill
Swindon
Slough
Willesden
Tilbury
Cardiff Cathays
Bristol Barrow Road
Reading
Southall
Cardiff Canton
Reading South
Hither Green
Gillingham
Ramsgate
St. Philips Marsh
Feltham
Barry
Norwood Junction
Bath Green Park
Andover Junction
Faversham
Canterbury West
Redhill
Westbury
Basingstoke
Tonbridge
Shepherds Well
Ilfracombe
Highbridge
Guildford
Ashford
Tunbridge Wells
Dover Marine
Winchester City
Folkestone
Barnstaple Junction
Salisbury
Three Bridges
Horsham
Rolvenden
Taunton
Templecombe
Eastleigh
Torrington
Yeovil Pen Mill
Yeovil Town
Southampton Docks
St. Leonards
Bude
Brighton
Gosport
Bognor
Okehampton
Exmouth Junction
Lymington
Fratton
Newhaven
Eastbourne
Hamworthy
Ryde
Exeter
Launceston
Seaton
Lyme Regis
Dorchester
Bournemouth
Newport
Exmouth
Wadebridge
Callington
Weymouth
Swanage
Newton Abbot
Laira
St. Blazey
Plymouth Friary
Truro
Penzance

Introduction

While this book should function as a volume in its own right it is intended to build on the work in my first book (British Railways Steam Locomotives 1948-1968). In selecting the photographs to illustrate this book I have tried as far as possible to cover the gaps that were left in the first book.

I have used the same abbreviations for the classes that I used in the first book, so the books can be used together. This book does not provide class histories or individual engine histories as these were provided in the first book.

I am not the first person to try to publish a listing of locomotive allocations (see the bibliography for a list of others) and I suspect I will not be the last. There are several ways to attempt such a task.

- One way is to produce a list of locomotive allocations at a specific point in time somewhat like a locoshed book. This is helpful, but it is restricted to one date.
- This method can be further modified to show allocations on more than one date. This then runs into the problem of tracking depot code changes throughout the periods covered
- Another method is to give a complete listing of allocation changes over a period. This can be very interesting, but you can soon get bogged down in the vast amount of detail. Using this method it is hard to get a snapshot view of a particular class at a particular time.
- Another way of listing allocations is to provide a depot by depot list, showing all engines allocated there.

It seems obvious that to provide a flexible way of presenting the data a computer database is needed. This would allow you to use a number of different ways of accessing the information. In fact, over many years I have built up such a database myself, which is the underlying source of the data in this book. And yet, even for someone like myself who has been working in the IT industry for most of his working life, there is nothing to replace a book. A real paper and ink book – a heavy tome that you can pick up and flick through. Something that will allow you to follow your interests and head off in different directions every time you open it.

This has been my aim – I hope that I can go some way towards meeting these objectives.

Contents of the book

Opposite this page you will find a map of Great Britain showing the location of all the sheds in the country that had an allocation of steam locomotives during the period 1948-1968. In order to avoid this map becoming congested, sub-sheds are not shown, unless they had an allocation of their own. It might seem strange that sub-sheds could have an allocation, as normally the definition of a sub-shed is a shed that does not have a responsibility for any engines of its own – instead they are supplied by the main shed in that area. But in reality, the North Eastern Region, and to a lesser extent the Southern Region, *did* allocate engines to sub-sheds, as well as to main sheds, even though no shed code was allocated to the sub-shed. In the case of North and South Blyth, for example, both sheds were of similar size and importance. They were less than a mile apart and shared the same shed code, but as they were separated by the River Blyth, they maintained their own fleets of engines, and it was rare for an engine to be reallocated between the two.

One of the principles adopted in this book is to use a set of "key dates" to present the information in each section. These dates are the 1st January for the following years: 1948, 1951, 1954, 1957, 1960, 1963 and 1966. These dates have been deliberately chosen to be equally spaced (three years apart) for the whole period 1948-1968. These dates also happen to be different to the year-end dates chosen for some other published lists, thus expanding the information which is currently available in published form.

Steam sheds and sub-sheds

Following this introduction you will find a list of engine sheds in shed code order, for each of the key dates. In 1948, the pre-nationalisation codes are used (see next paragraph). Sub-sheds are listed under their main shed. Only steam sheds are shown, not diesel, electric or multiple unit sheds, even though these carried shed codes in the same series.

Shed Codes

The next section gives a list of all shed codes used, with the dates for each location. Before 1948, the LMS used the number and letter system which was eventually adopted by BR. The GWR had an alphabetic code for each shed (between two and five letters) which was painted on the frames of the engine. The LNER and the Southern Railway did not use shed codes, but enthusiasts' groups of the time (for example the RCTS and the SLS) had developed un-official codes which were widely used, and they are shown in this book. At the beginning of 1949 all Scottish Region sheds were allocated their new codes and at the beginning of 1950 the other regions started using new codes.

The main part of this book is split into five sections, one each for locomotives from each of the Big Four pre-nationalisation railway companies, and one for the BR Standard and ex-War Department engines. Each section contains *locomotive lists* and *class lists*.

Locomotive Lists
The first part of each of these sections is a full list of engines which came into BR stock. For each engine its class is given the classifications given are those in the first book, making it easy to look up the class histories. Then across the page is given the allocations for that engine on each of the key dates. For each allocation, not just the shed code is given, but also the shed name. This overcomes the problem of trying to keep track of the shed code changes. If an engine is allocated to a sub-shed, the main shed code is shown followed by the name of the relevant sub-shed.

Using these lists you can get a good overview of the allocation of engines over the whole BR period. In many cases you can see engines that stayed at the same shed throughout their life. However, do not make the mistake of thinking that because an engine is always shown at the same depot that it always stayed there. Engines often moved backwards and forwards, and while the allocations shown are accurate for the 1st January, these lists do not show where they were on the 1st December or the 1st February!

Class Lists
Following the numerical list for each section you will find the class list. Each individual class is described followed by a number of maps. Using the same key dates the map shows the spread of engine allocations at that date. Each dot on the map locates a depot with an allocation – the larger the dot, the larger the number of engines allocated there. Underneath each map you can see a full list of depots with an allocation and the number of engines based at each depot. As these maps are computer generated you should (within the restrictions of the scale) be able to locate each of the sheds and the relative sizes of their allocation on the map.

Shed Lists
This now just leaves one missing piece to enable you to track engines, and that is a depot-by-depot allocation listing. This is the last section of the book. Each depot (and other location where engines were based) is listed in alphabetical order. A map is given to show the location of each depot. Then for each of the key dates the depot code is given with a list of all the engines allocated there.

By skipping from section to section of the book you should be able to get a good overview of the chronological, geographical and taxonomical components that make up the allocation history of British Railways steam locomotives.

The devil is in the detail

Let me tell you a story. Many years ago I was in discussion with a respected railway publisher. He showed me the draft copy of a steam locomotive allocation listing that had been sent to him to be considered for publication. He turned the book down – why? Well he opened it up to a particular class of engine based at his local shed in the 1950s to see if it matched his memory of his local engines. Some were missing, so the book was scratched.

Many years later, by coincidence I was in correspondence with that same author. I was cross-checking some information in his book and I found out that he had missed out one week's reallocation details for one region, some eight years before the period in question. Yes, you've guessed it, those missing locomotives were re-allocated that week.

Let me state outright, I cannot guarantee this book to be 100% accurate. If your favourite engines are wrongly shown, then I'm sorry, please write and let me know. However I have spent many hundreds of hours checking and cross-checking and cross-checking again, so you should find the data dependable. (Before you ask, yes I do enjoy it!). As well as delving into the minute details of the book, take a step back and try and get an overview of the subject. It is amazing what you can discover just by looking through all the maps.

My sources are many and varied. Every time I come across a published allocation listing from whatever source I tear it apart and cross check it with my database. Some errors are copied from one publication to another. For my ultimate authority in solving disagreements, I have consulted the relevant Stephenson

Locomotive Society Journal and the Railway Correspondence and Travel Society's Railway Observer. In the rare event these disagree, I have based my information on that published in the Railway Observer.

You will notice that I have chosen not to give any scrapping details in this book. This area is currently the subject of a major research project being undertaken by the HSBT Project and if you are interested in this area you can check out their progress on *www.whatreallyhappenedtosteam.co.uk*.

In my professional career I have worked both as a computer programmer and as a technical author. It is those skills which I have been able to bring to use in this book, to hopefully throw some new light on an old subject.

Bibliography

- **British Railway Steam Locomotives 1948-1968.** Hugh Longworth. OPC. *www.ianallanpublishing.com*. My first book, and very much a companion to this book. Both books can stand alone, but they are designed to complement each other.
- **Ultimate Allocations 1948-1968**. Michael McManus. *www.ultimate-allocations.co.uk*. This is a self-published work in five volumes (plus a sixth for diesels and electrics). A complete listing of re-allocations for each locomotive from summer 1950 to 1968. If you want to find the missing re-allocations between the key dates in this book, then this is the place to look. Michael is also considering a computer database version of this work, and I have had some input into this to make sure that it is as accurate and user-friendly as possible. Check out his website for up-to-date information.
- **The Xpress Locomotive Register.** Xpress Publishing. Four volumes covering each of the Big Four groups. These books contain full listings of allocations and allocation changes for each engine from 1950-1960. The first book published was for the Southern Region, the final book for the Western Region. The main problem is that the style of publication changed as the series progressed, making the first book very hard to use, and the last book one of the very best of the allocation lists I have come across. It is a pity they end at 1960. However, well worth a look.
- **BR Steam Motive Power Depots.** Paul Bolger. Ian Allan. *www.ianallanpublishing.com*. A series of six books, one for each region. Contains a very helpful plan and photographs for each depot, together with a list of allocated locomotives for August 1950, March 1959 and May 1965. Recently reprinted by Booklaw Publications. *www.booklawco.uk*.
- **British Railways Steam Locomotive Allocations 1948-1968.** Jim Grindlay. Modelmaster Publications. *www.transportpublishing.com*. A series of five books covering each of the pre-grouping companies plus BR. (More books in the series cover diesels & electrics and DMUs.) A complete listing showing allocations at 1948, 1952, 1955, 1959, 1963 & 1966.
- **British Railways Locomotive Allocations 1948.** Jim Grindlay. Modelmaster Publications. *www.transportpublishing.com*. Lists all locomotives with allocations for January and July 1948.
- **British Railways Locomotives 1948** Chris Banks. OPC. *www.ianallanpublishing.com*.
- **British Railways Locomotives 1955** Chris Banks. OPC. *www.ianallanpublishing.com*.
- **British Railways Locomotives 1962** Chris Banks. OPC. *www.ianallanpublishing.com*. These three books are well designed and nicely illustrated. Each gives a full allocation listing for the relevant year, and a description of some of the happenings in that year.
- **Ian Allan Locoshed books.** Regularly produced by Ian Allan from 1950 onwards, these are the books that many of us took out train-spotting with us. Originals are getting harder to get (and more expensive), but you should be able to find recent reprints for 1950*, 1952, 1955*, 1959*, and 1960. (*included in a reprinted combined volume).
- **What Happened to Steam.** P.B. Hands. Fifty slim booklets listing all engines and their scrapping details. These have come under attack recently due to inaccuracies in some of the scrapping details. What should not be overlooked is that they give allocations for every January from 1957 to 1968, together with most reallocations between those dates. However, they are out of print and difficult to get hold of.
- **BR Steam Allocations.** P.B. Hands. Nine booklets, being companions to "What Happened to Steam". Depot listings with lists of engines and allocation dates. They cover the period 1957-1968, but again they are out of print and difficult to get hold of.
- **BR Steam Allocations**. Robin Summerhill. *www.br-steam-allocations.co.uk*. Described as an "electronic book" it is a CD-ROM based computer database covering May 1960-1968. If you are confident in playing around with spreadsheets, then this is well worth taking a look at.
- **Shed By Shed.** Tony Walmsley. *www.shedbyshed.com*. A series of six books currently being produced, one for each region. A complete listing of allocated locomotives for each depot from 1950-1968.

The End is Nigh. BR Standard Class 4MT No 75075 in front of the shed at Nine Elms on Sunday 9 July 1967. The last day of steam haulage on the Southern Region.
J. Seddon

Right: GWR Dean & Churchward 'Bulldog' '3300' class 4-4-0 No 3408 *Bombay.*

Below: SECR Stirling 'O1' class 0-6-0 No 31048.

Bottom: SDJR Sentinel 0-4-0T No 47191 at Gloucester on 22 June 1952. *L .Elsey*

Steam sheds and sub-sheds

1948

Code	Shed
1A	Willesden
1B	Camden
1C	Watford
2A	Rugby
	Market Harborough
	Seaton
2B	Bletchley
	Aylesbury
	Cambridge (LNWR)
	Leighton Buzzard
	Newport Pagnell
	Oxford (LMS)
2C	Northampton
2D	Nuneaton
2E	Warwick
2F	Coventry
3A	Bescot
3B	Bushbury
3C	Walsall
3D	Aston
3E	Monument Lane
	Tipton
4A	Shrewsbury
	Builth Road
	Clee Hill
	Coalport
	Craven Arms
	Knighton
	Ludlow
4B	Swansea Victoria
	Llandovery
4C	Upper Bank
	Brecon
	Gurnos
4D	Abergavenny
4E	Tredegar
5A	Crewe North
	Whitchurch
5B	Crewe South
5C	Stafford
5D	Stoke
5E	Alsager
5F	Uttoxeter
6A	Chester
6B	Mold Junction
6C	Birkenhead
7A	Llandudno Junction
7B	Bangor
7C	Holyhead
7D	Rhyl
	Denbigh
8A	Edge Hill
8B	Warrington Dallam
	Arpley
	Over & Wharton
8C	Speke Junction
8D	Widnes
9A	Longsight
9B	Stockport Edgeley
9C	Macclesfield
9D	Buxton
	Cromford
	Middleton Top
	Sheep Pasture
10A	Wigan Springs Branch
10B	Preston
10C	Patricroft
10D	Plodder Lane
10E	Sutton Oak
11A	Carnforth
11B	Barrow
	Coniston
	Lakeside
11D	Oxenholme
11E	Tebay
12A	Carlisle Kingmoor
	Durran Hill
12B	Carlisle Upperby
12C	Penrith
12D	Workington
12E	Moor Row
12F	Beattock
	Lockerbie
12G	Dumfries
	Kirkcudbright
12H	Stranraer
	Newton Stewart
13A	Plaistow
13B	Devons Road
13C	Tilbury
13D	Shoeburyness
13E	Upminster
14A	Cricklewood
14B	Kentish Town
14C	St. Albans
15A	Wellingborough
15B	Kettering
15C	Leicester Midland
15D	Bedford
16A	Nottingham
	Lincoln St. Marks
	Southwell
16B	Spital Bridge
16C	Kirkby in Ashfield
16D	Mansfield
17A	Derby
17B	Burton
	Horninglow
	Overseal
17C	Coalville
17D	Rowsley
18A	Toton
18B	Westhouses
18C	Hasland
	Clay Cross Works
	Morton Colliery
	Williamthorpe Colliery
18D	Staveley Barrow Hill
	Sheepbridge Works
	Staveley New Works
	Staveley Old Works
19A	Sheffield
	Grimesthorpe
19B	Millhouses
19C	Canklow
19D	Heaton Mersey
	Brunswick
	Gowhole
19E	Belle Vue
19F	York (LMS)
19G	Trafford Park
20A	Leeds Holbeck
20B	Stourton
20C	Royston
20D	Normanton
20E	Manningham
	Ilkley
20F	Skipton
	Ingleton
	Keighley
20G	Hellifield
20H	Lancaster
21A	Saltley
	Camp Hill
	Washwood Heath
	Water Orton
21B	Bournville
	Redditch
21C	Bromsgrove
21D	Stratford on Avon
22A	Bristol Barrow Road
22B	Gloucester
	Barnwood
	Dursley
	Tewkesbury
22C	Bath Green Park
	Branksome
	Radstock
22D	Templecombe
22E	Highbridge
	Wells (LMS)
23A	Bank Hall
23B	Aintree
23C	Southport
23D	Wigan
24A	Accrington
24B	Rose Grove
24C	Lostock Hall
24D	Lower Darwen
24E	Blackpool Central
	Blackpool North
24F	Fleetwood
25A	Wakefield
25B	Huddersfield
25C	Goole
25D	Mirfield
25E	Sowerby Bridge
25F	Low Moor
25G	Farnley Junction
26A	Newton Heath
26B	Agecroft
26C	Bolton
	Horwich
26D	Bury
26E	Bacup
26F	Lees Oldham
27A	Polmadie
	Paisley St. James
27B	Greenock Ladyburn
	Princes Pier
27C	Hamilton
28A	Motherwell
28B	Dalry Road
28C	Carstairs
29A	Perth
	Aberfeldy
	Alyth
	Blair Atholl
	Crieff
29B	Aberdeen Ferryhill
29C	Dundee West
29D	Forfar
	Arbroath
	Brechin
	Killin Loch Tay
30A	Corkerhill
30B	Hurlford
	Beith
	Muirkirk
30C	Ardrossan
30D	Ayr
31A	St. Rollox
31B	Stirling
31C	Oban
	Ballachulish
31D	Grangemouth
31E	Dawsholm
	Dumbarton
	Yoker
32A	Inverness
	Dingwall
	Dornoch
	Fortrose
	Helmsdale
	Kyle of Lochalsh
	Tain
	Thurso
	Wick
32B	Aviemore
32C	Forres
ABD	Aberdeen Ferryhill
ALN	Alnmouth
ALS	Alston
ANN	Annesley
	Kirkby Bentinck
	Nottingham Victoria
ARD	Ardsley
AUK	West Auckland
BFD	Bradford Hammerton St
BGT	Bathgate
	Morningside
BID	Bidston
BLA	Blaydon
BOR	Borough Gardens
BOS	Boston
BOW	Bowes Bridge
BRI	Bridlington
BRN	Barnsley
BSE	Bury St. Edmunds
	Sudbury
CAM	Cambridge
	Ely
	Huntingdon East
	Saffron Walden
	Thaxted
CAR	Carlisle Canal
	Silloth
CHR	Chester Northgate
CLK	Colwick
	Derby Friargate
COL	Colchester
	Braintree
	Clacton
	Kelvedon
	Maldon
	Walton on Naze
CON	Consett
COP	Copley Hill
CUD	Cudworth
DAR	Darlington
DEE	Dundee Tay Bridge
	Arbroath
	Montrose
	St. Andrews
	Tayport
DFU	Dunfermline Upper
	Kelty
	Loch Leven
DNS	Duns
DON	Doncaster
DUR	Durham
EFD	Eastfield
	Aberfoyle
	Arrochar
	Balloch
	Kilsyth
	Lennoxtown
	Stobcross
	Whiteinch
FRO	Frodingham
FW	Fort William
	Mallaig
GHD	Gateshead
GOR	Gorton
	Dinting
	Hayfield
	Macclesfield (GC)
GRA	Grantham
	Newark
	Sleaford
GUI	Guisborough
HAT	Hatfield
HAV	Haverton Hill
HAW	Hawick
	Jedburgh
	Kelso
	Riccarton Junction
	St. Boswells
HAY	Haymarket
HEX	Hexham
HIT	Hitchin
HLA	Hull Alexandra Dock
HLB	Hull Botanic Gardens
HLD	Hull Dairycoates
HLS	Hull Springhead
HSY	Hornsey
HTN	Heaton
ILK	Ilkley
IMM	Immingham
	Grimsby
	New Holland
IPS	Ipswich
	Aldeburgh
	Felixstowe Beach
	Framlingham
	Ipswich Docks
	Laxfield
	Stowmarket
KBY	Kirkby Stephen
KEI	Keith
	Banff
	Boat of Garten
	Elgin
KIT	Kittybrewster
	Alford
	Ballater
	Fraserburgh
	Inverurie
	Macduff
	Peterhead
KL	Kings Lynn
	Hunstanton
	Wisbech
KPS	Kipps
KX	Kings Cross
LEI	Leicester Central
	Leicester Belgrave Road
LEY	Leyburn
LIN	Lincoln
	Lincoln (GC)
LIV	Brunswick
	Birkenhead Shore Road
	Southport (CLC)
	Warrington Central
	Widnes (GC)
LNG	Langwith Junction
LOW	Lowestoft
LTH	Louth
MAL	Malton
MAR	March
MC	Melton Constable
	Cromer Beach
	Norwich City
MEX	Mexborough
MID	Middlesbrough
MIT	Middleton in Teesdale
NBH	North Blyth
NEA	Neasden
	Aylesbury
	Chesham
	Rickmansworth
NEV	Leeds Neville Hill
NLN	Northallerton
NMN	Normanton
NOR	Norwich Thorpe
	Cromer
	Dereham
	Swaffham
	Wells on Sea
	Wymondham
NPT	Newport
NTH	Northwich
NWE	New England
	Bourne
	Spalding
	Stamford
PAT	Pateley Bridge
PEL	Pelton Level
PKD	Parkhead
	Helensburgh
PKG	Pickering
PKS	Parkeston
PMN	Percy Main
POL	Polmont
	Kinniel
PTH	Perth South
RBY	Rothbury
RET	Retford
	Retford (GC)
RMH	Reedsmouth
SAL	Saltburn
SBH	South Blyth
SBK	Starbeck
SCA	Scarborough
SEL	Selby
SHF	Sheffield Darnall
SKN	Stockton on Tees
SL	South Lynn
STG	Stirling Shore Road
	Alloa
	Inverkeithing
STM	St. Margarets
	Dunbar
	Galashiels
	Granton
	Hardengreen
	Longniddry
	North Berwick
	North Leith
	Peebles
	Penicuick
	Polton
	Seafield
	South Leith
STP	Heaton Mersey
STR	Stratford
	Bishops Stortford
	Brentwood
	Buntingford
	Chelmsford
	Enfield Town
	Epping
	Hertford East
	Ongar
	Palace Gates
	Southend Victoria
	Southminster
	Spitalfields
	Ware
	Wickford
	Wood St. Walthamstow
STV	Staveley
SUN	Sunderland
TDK	Tyne Dock
TFD	Trafford Park
THJ	Thornton Junction
	Anstruther
	Burntisland
	Kirkcaldy
	Ladybank
	Methil
TUX	Tuxford Junction
TWD	Tweedmouth
	Seahouses
WAL	Walton on the Hill
WBY	Whitby
WFD	Woodford Halse
WHD	Wearhead
WHL	West Hartlepool
WIG	Wigan Lower Ince
WRX	Wrexham Rhosddu
YAR	Yarmouth South Town
	Yarmouth Vauxhall
YB	Yarmouth Beach
YK	York
	York South
3B	Three Bridges
9E	Nine Elms
AFD	Ashford
	Margate
AND	Andover Junction
BA	Bricklayers Arms
	Ewer Street
BAS	Basingstoke
BAT	Stewarts Lane
BM	Bournemouth
BOG	Bognor
BPL	Barnstaple Junction
BTN	Brighton
BUD	Bude
CAL	Callington
CAN	Canterbury West
DOR	Dorchester
DOV	Dover Marine
EBN	Eastbourne
EKR	Shepherds Well
ELH	Eastleigh
	Southampton Terminus
EXJ	Exmouth Junction
EXM	Exmouth
FAV	Faversham
FEL	Feltham
FOL	Folkestone Junction
FRA	Fratton
GFD	Guildford
GIL	Gillingham
GOS	Gosport
HAM	Hamworthy Junction
HIT	Hither Green
HOR	Horsham
ILF	Ilfracombe
KESR	Rolvenden
LCN	Launceston (SR)
LR	Lyme Regis
LYM	Lymington
NHN	Newhaven
NOR	Norwood Junction
NPT	Newport IOW
NX	New Cross Gate
OKE	Okehampton
PLY	Plymouth Friary
RAM	Ramsgate
RDG	Reading South
RED	Redhill
RYD	Ryde IOW
SAL	Salisbury
SEA	Seaton
SOT	Southampton Docks
	Southampton New Docks
STL	St. Leonards
SWE	Swanage
TEM	Templecombe Upper
TON	Tonbridge
TOR	Torrington
TWW	Tunbridge Wells West
WAD	Wadebridge
WEY	Weymouth
WIN	Winchester City
YEO	Yeovil Town
ABDR	Aberdare
ABEEG	Aberbeeg
ABH	Aberystwyth
	Aberystwyth (VoR)
AYN	Abercynon
BAN	Banbury
BCN	Brecon
	Builth Wells
BHD	Birkenhead
BRD	Bristol Bath Road
	Bath Spa
	Wells (GWR)
	Weston-super-Mare
	Yatton
BRY	Barry
CARM	Carmarthen
	Newcastle Emlyn
CDF	Cardiff Canton
CED	Cardiff East Dock
CH	Dowlais Cae Harris
CHEL	Cheltenham
	Brimscombe
	Chalford
	Cirencester
CHR	Chester (GWR)
CHYS	Cardiff Cathays
CNYD	Croes Newydd
	Bala
	Penmaenpool
	Trawsfynydd
DG	Danygraig
DID	Didcot
	Lambourn
	Newbury
	Wallingford
	Winchester Chesil
DYD	Duffryn Yard
	Glyncorrwg
EXE	Exeter
	Tiverton Junction
FDL	Ferndale
FGD	Fishguard Goodwick
GLO	Gloucester
HFD	Hereford
	Kington
	Ledbury
	Leominster
	Ross on Wye
KDR	Kidderminster
	Cleobury Mortimer
LA	Laira (Plymouth)
	Launceston
	Plymouth Docks
	Princetown
LDR	Landore
LLY	Llanelly
	Burry Port
	Pantyffynnon
LMTN	Leamington Spa
	Alcester
LTS	Llantrisant
LYD	Lydney
	Tetbury
MCH	Machynlleth
	Aberayron
	Corris
	Portmadoc
	Pwllheli
MTHR	Merthyr
NA	Newton Abbot
	Ashburton
	Kingsbridge
	Moreton-hampstead
NEA	Neath
	Glyn Neath
	Neath Riverside
NEY	Neyland
	Milford Haven
NPT	Ebbw Junction
OSW	Oswestry
	Llanfyllin
	Llanidloes
	Moat Lane
	Welshpool
	Welshpool (WLLR)
OXF	Oxford

Abingdon
Fairford
OXY Oxley
PDN Old Oak Common
PILL Newport Pill
PPRD Pontypool Road
Branches Fork
Pontrilas
PZ Penzance
Helston
St. Ives
RDG Reading
Basingstoke
Henley on Thames
RHY Rhymney
Dowlais Central
RYR Radyr
SALOP Shrewsbury
Ludlow
SBZ St. Blazey
Bodmin
Moorswater
SDN Swindon
Andover
Chippenham
Faringdon
Malmesbury
SED Swansea East Dock
SHL Southall
Staines
SLO Slough
Aylesbury
Marlow
Watlington
SPM St. Philips Marsh
SRD Stafford Road
STB Stourbridge
STJ Severn Tunnel Junction
TDU Tondu
Bridgend
THT Treherbert
Pwllyrhebog
TN Taunton
Barnstaple
Bridgwater
Minehead
TR Truro
TYS Tyseley
Stratford on Avon
WES Westbury
Frome
Salisbury (GWR)
WEY Weymouth
Bridport
WLN Wellington
Crewe Gresty Lane
Much Wenlock
WOS Worcester
Evesham
Honeybourne
Kingham
WTD Whitland
Cardigan
Pembroke Dock
YEO Yeovil Pen Mill

1951

1A Willesden
1B Camden
1C Watford
1D Devons Road
2A Rugby
Market Harborough
Seaton
2B Nuneaton
2C Warwick
2D Coventry
3A Bescot
3B Bushbury
3C Walsall
3D Aston
3E Monument Lane
Tipton
4A Bletchley
Aylesbury
Cambridge (LNWR)
Leighton Buzzard
Newport Pagnell
4B Northampton
5A Crewe North
Over & Wharton
Whitchurch
5B Crewe South
5C Stafford
5D Stoke
5E Alsager
5F Uttoxeter
6A Chester
6B Mold Junction
6C Birkenhead
6D Chester Northgate
6E Wrexham Rhosddu
6F Bidston
7A Llandudno Junction
7B Bangor
7C Holyhead
7D Rhyl
Denbigh
8A Edge Hill
8B Warrington Dallam
Arpley
8C Speke Junction
8D Widnes
8E Brunswick
Birkenhead Shore Road
Southport (CLC)
Warrington Central
Widnes (GC)
9A Longsight
9B Stockport Edgeley
9C Macclesfield
9D Buxton
9E Trafford Park
9F Heaton Mersey
Gowhole
9G Northwich
10A Wigan Springs Branch
10B Preston
10C Patricroft
10D Plodder Lane
10E Sutton Oak
10F Wigan Lower Ince
11A Carnforth
11B Barrow
Coniston
11C Oxenholme
11D Tebay
12A Carlisle Upperby
12B Carlisle Canal
Silloth
12C Penrith
12D Workington
12E Moor Row
14A Cricklewood
14B Kentish Town
14C St. Albans
15A Wellingborough
15B Kettering
15C Leicester Midland
15D Bedford
16A Nottingham
Lincoln St. Marks
Southwell
16C Kirkby in Ashfield
16D Mansfield
17A Derby
17B Burton
Horninglow
Overseal
17C Coalville
17D Rowsley
Cromford
Middleton Top
Sheep Pasture
18A Toton
18B Westhouses
18C Hasland
Clay Cross Works
Williamthorpe Colliery
18D Staveley Barrow Hill
Sheepbridge Works
Staveley New Works
Staveley Old Works
19A Sheffield
Grimesthorpe
19B Millhouses
19C Canklow
20A Leeds Holbeck
20B Stourton
20C Royston
20D Normanton
20E Manningham
Ilkley
21A Saltley
Camp Hill
Washwood Heath
Water Orton
21B Bournville
Redditch
21C Bromsgrove
21D Stratford on Avon
22A Bristol Barrow Road
22B Gloucester
Barnwood
Dursley
Tewkesbury
23A Skipton
Keighley
23B Hellifield
Ingleton
23C Lancaster
24A Accrington
24B Rose Grove
24C Lostock Hall
24D Lower Darwen
25A Wakefield
25B Huddersfield
25C Goole
25D Mirfield
25E Sowerby Bridge
25F Low Moor
25G Farnley Junction
26A Newton Heath
26B Agecroft
26C Bolton
26D Bury
26E Bacup
26F Lees Oldham
26G Belle Vue
27A Bank Hall
27B Aintree
27C Southport
27D Wigan
27E Walton on the Hill
28A Blackpool Central
Blackpool North
28B Fleetwood
30A Stratford
Brentwood
Chelmsford
Enfield Town
Epping
Palace Gates
Spitalfields
Ware
Wood St. Walthamstow
30B Hertford East
Buntingford
30C Bishops Stortford
30D Southend Victoria
Southminster
Wickford
30E Colchester
Braintree
Clacton
Kelvedon
Maldon
Walton on Naze
30F Parkeston
31A Cambridge
Ely
Huntingdon East
Saffron Walden
Thaxted
31B March
31C Kings Lynn
Hunstanton
Wisbech
31D South Lynn
31E Bury St. Edmunds
Sudbury
32A Norwich Thorpe
Cromer
Dereham
Swaffham
Wells on Sea
Wymondham
32B Ipswich
Aldeburgh
Felixstowe Beach
Framlingham
Ipswich Docks
Laxfield
Stowmarket
32C Lowestoft
32D Yarmouth South Town
32E Yarmouth Vauxhall
32F Yarmouth Beach
32G Melton Constable
Cromer Beach
Norwich City
33A Plaistow
Upminster
33B Tilbury
33C Shoeburyness
34A Kings Cross
34B Hornsey
34C Hatfield
34D Hitchin
34E Neasden
Aylesbury
Chesham
Rickmansworth
35A New England
Bourne
Spalding
Stamford
35B Grantham
35C Spital Bridge
36A Doncaster
36B Mexborough
36C Frodingham
36D Barnsley
36E Retford
Newark
Retford (GC)
37A Ardsley
37B Copley Hill
37C Bradford
Hammerton St
38A Colwick
Derby Friargate
38B Annesley
Kirkby Bentinck
Nottingham Victoria
38C Leicester Central
Leicester Belgrave Road
38D Staveley
38E Woodford Halse
39A Gorton
Dinting
Hayfield
39B Sheffield Darnall
40A Lincoln
Lincoln (GC)
40B Immingham
Grimsby
New Holland
40C Louth
40D Tuxford Junction
40E Langwith Junction
40F Boston
Sleaford
50A York
York (LMS)
York South
50B Leeds Neville Hill
50C Selby
50D Starbeck
Pateley Bridge
50E Scarborough
50F Malton
Pickering
50G Whitby
51A Darlington
Middleton in Teesdale
51B Newport
51C West Hartlepool
51D Middlesbrough
Guisborough
51E Stockton on Tees
51F West Auckland
Wearhead
51G Haverton Hill
51H Kirkby Stephen
51J Northallerton
Leyburn
51K Saltburn
52A Gateshead
Bowes Bridge
52B Heaton
52C Blaydon
Alston
Hexham
Reedsmouth
52D Tweedmouth
Alnmouth
Seahouses
52E Percy Main
52F North Blyth
Rothbury
South Blyth
53A Hull Dairycoates
53B Hull Botanic Gardens
53C Hull Springhead
Hull Alexandra Dock
53D Bridlington
53E Cudworth
54A Sunderland
Durham
54B Tyne Dock
Pelton Level
54C Borough Gardens
54D Consett
60A Inverness
Dingwall
Kyle of Lochalsh
60B Aviemore
Boat of Garten
60C Helmsdale
Dornoch
Tain
60D Wick
Thurso
60E Forres
61A Kittybrewster
Ballater
Fraserburgh
Inverurie
Macduff
Peterhead
61B Aberdeen Ferryhill
61C Keith
Banff
Elgin
62A Thornton Junction
Anstruther
Burntisland
Kirkcaldy
Ladybank
Methil
62B Dundee Tay Bridge
Arbroath
Dundee West
Montrose
St. Andrews
Tayport
62C Dunfermline Upper
Alloa
Inverkeithing
Kelty
Loch Leven
63A Perth
Aberfeldy
Alyth
Blair Atholl
Crieff
63B Stirling
Killin Loch Tay
Stirling Shore Road
63C Forfar
Brechin
63D Fort William
Mallaig
63E Oban
Ballachulish
64A St. Margarets
Dunbar
Galashiels
Granton
Hardengreen
Longniddry
North Berwick
North Leith
Peebles
Penicuick
Polton
Seafield
South Leith
64B Haymarket
64C Dalry Road
64D Carstairs
64E Polmont
Kinniel
64F Bathgate
64G Hawick
Kelso
Riccarton Junction
St. Boswells
65A Eastfield
Aberfoyle
Kilsyth
Lennoxtown
Whiteinch
65B St. Rollox
65C Parkhead
65D Dawsholm
Dumbarton
65E Kipps
65F Grangemouth
65G Yoker
65H Helensburgh
Arrochar
65I Balloch
66A Polmadie
Paisley St. James
66B Motherwell
Morningside
66C Hamilton
66D Greenock Ladyburn
Princes Pier
67A Corkerhill
67B Hurlford
Beith
Muirkirk
67C Ayr
67D Ardrossan
68A Carlisle Kingmoor
Durran Hill
68B Dumfries
Kirkcudbright
68C Stranraer
Newton Stewart
68D Beattock
Lockerbie
70A Nine Elms
70B Feltham
70C Guildford
70D Basingstoke
70E Reading South
71A Eastleigh
Andover Junction
Lymington
Southampton Terminus
Winchester City
71B Bournemouth
Hamworthy Junction
Swanage
71C Dorchester
71D Fratton
Gosport
71E Newport IOW
71F Ryde IOW
71G Bath Green Park
Branksome
Radstock
71H Templecombe
71I Southampton Docks
Southampton New Docks
71J Highbridge
Wells (LMS)
72A Exmouth Junction
Bude
Exmouth
Launceston (SR)
Lyme Regis
Okehampton
Seaton
72B Salisbury
72C Yeovil Town
Templecombe Upper
72D Plymouth Friary
Callington
72E Barnstaple Junction
Ilfracombe
Torrington
72F Wadebridge
73A Stewarts Lane
73B Bricklayers Arms
Ewer Street
New Cross Gate
73C Hither Green
73D Gillingham
73E Faversham
74A Ashford
Canterbury West
Margate
Rolvenden
74B Ramsgate
74C Dover Marine
Folkestone Junction
74D Tonbridge
74E St. Leonards
75A Brighton
Newhaven
75B Redhill
75C Norwood Junction
75D Horsham
Bognor
75E Three Bridges
75F Tunbridge Wells West
75G Eastbourne
81A Old Oak Common
81B Slough
Aylesbury
Marlow
Watlington
81C Southall
Staines
81D Reading
Henley on Thames
81E Didcot
Lambourn
Newbury
Wallingford
Winchester Chesil
81F Oxford
Abingdon
Fairford
82A Bristol Bath Road
Bath Spa
Wells (GWR)
Weston-super-Mare
Yatton
82B St. Philips Marsh
82C Swindon
Andover
Chippenham
Faringdon
Malmesbury
82D Westbury
Frome
82E Yeovil Pen Mill
82F Weymouth
Bridport
83A Newton Abbot
Ashburton
Kingsbridge
Moretonhampstead
83B Taunton
Barnstaple
Bridgwater
Minehead
83C Exeter
Tiverton Junction
83D Laira (Plymouth)
Launceston
Plymouth Docks
Princetown
83E St. Blazey
Bodmin
Moorswater
83F Truro
83G Penzance
Helston
St. Ives
84A Stafford Road
84B Oxley
84C Banbury
84D Leamington Spa
Alcester
84E Tyseley
Stratford on Avon
84F Stourbridge
84G Shrewsbury
Builth Road
Clee Hill
Coalport
Craven Arms
Knighton
84H Wellington
Crewe Gresty Lane
Much Wenlock

- 84J Croes Newydd
  - Bala
  - Penmaenpool
  - Trawsfynydd
- 84K Chester (GWR)
- 85A Worcester
  - Evesham
  - Honeybourne
  - Kingham
- 85B Gloucester
  - Brimscombe
  - Chalford
  - Cheltenham
  - Cirencester
  - Lydney
  - Tetbury
- 85C Hereford
  - Kington
  - Ledbury
  - Leominster
  - Ross on Wye
- 85D Kidderminster
  - Cleobury Mortimer
- 86A Ebbw Junction
- 86B Newport Pill
- 86C Cardiff Canton
- 86D Llantrisant
- 86E Severn Tunnel Junction
- 86F Tondu
- 86G Pontypool Road
  - Branches Fork
  - Pontrilas
- 86H Aberbeeg
- 86J Aberdare
- 86K Abergavenny
  - Tredegar
- 87A Neath
  - Glyn Neath
  - Neath Riverside
- 87B Duffryn Yard
  - Glyncorrwg
- 87C Danygraig
- 87D Swansea East Dock
- 87E Landore
- 87F Llanelly
  - Burry Port
  - Pantyffynnon
- 87G Carmarthen
  - Newcastle Emlyn
- 87H Neyland
  - Cardigan
  - Milford Haven
  - Pembroke Dock
  - Whitland
- 87J Fishguard Goodwick
- 87K Swansea Victoria
  - Gurnos
  - Llandovery
  - Upper Bank
- 88A Cardiff Cathays
  - Radyr
- 88B Cardiff East Dock
- 88C Barry
- 88D Merthyr
  - Dowlais Cae Harris
  - Dowlais Central
  - Rhymney
- 88E Abercynon
- 88F Treherbert
  - Ferndale
  - Pwllyrhebog
- 89A Oswestry
  - Llanfyllin
  - Llanidloes
  - Moat Lane
  - Welshpool
  - Welshpool (WLLR)
- 89B Brecon
  - Builth Wells
- 89C Machynlleth
  - Aberayron
  - Aberystwyth (VoR)
  - Aberystwyth
  - Portmadoc
  - Pwllheli

1954

- 1A Willesden
- 1B Camden
- 1C Watford
- 1D Devons Road
- 1E Bletchley
  - Leighton Buzzard
  - Newport Pagnell
- 2A Rugby
  - Market Harborough
  - Seaton
- 2B Nuneaton
- 2C Warwick
- 2D Coventry
- 2E Northampton
- 3A Bescot
- 3B Bushbury
- 3C Walsall
- 3D Aston
- 3E Monument Lane
  - Tipton
- 5A Crewe North
  - Over & Wharton
  - Whitchurch
- 5B Crewe South
- 5C Stafford
- 5D Stoke
- 5E Alsager
- 5F Uttoxeter
- 6A Chester
- 6B Mold Junction
- 6C Birkenhead
- 6D Chester Northgate
- 6E Wrexham Rhosddu
- 6F Bidston
  - Pwllheli
- 6G Llandudno Junction
- 6H Bangor
- 6J Holyhead
- 6K Rhyl
  - Denbigh
- 8A Edge Hill
- 8B Warrington Dallam
  - Arpley
- 8C Speke Junction
- 8D Widnes
- 8E Brunswick
  - Birkenhead Shore Road
  - Warrington Central
  - Widnes (GC)
- 9A Longsight
- 9B Stockport Edgeley
- 9C Macclesfield
- 9D Buxton
- 9E Trafford Park
- 9F Heaton Mersey
  - Gowhole
- 9G Northwich
- 10A Wigan Springs Branch
- 10B Preston
- 10C Patricroft
- 10D Plodder Lane
- 10E Sutton Oak
- 11A Carnforth
- 11B Barrow
  - Coniston
- 11C Oxenholme
- 11D Tebay
- 11E Lancaster
- 12A Carlisle Upperby
- 12C Penrith
- 12D Workington
- 12E Moor Row
- 14A Cricklewood
- 14B Kentish Town
- 14C St. Albans
- 15A Wellingborough
- 15B Kettering
- 15C Leicester Midland
- 15D Bedford
- 16A Nottingham
  - Lincoln St. Marks
  - Southwell
- 16C Kirkby in Ashfield
- 16D Mansfield
- 17A Derby
- 17B Burton
  - Horninglow
  - Overseal
- 17C Coalville
- 17D Rowsley
  - Cromford
  - Middleton Top
  - Sheep Pasture
- 18A Toton
- 18B Westhouses
- 18C Hasland
  - Clay Cross Works
  - Williamthorpe Colliery
- 18D Staveley Barrow Hill
  - Sheepbridge Works
  - Staveley New Works
  - Staveley Old Works
- 19A Sheffield
  - Grimesthorpe
- 19B Millhouses
- 19C Canklow
- 20A Leeds Holbeck
- 20B Stourton
- 20C Royston
- 20D Normanton
- 20E Manningham
  - Ilkley
- 20F Skipton
  - Keighley
- 20G Hellifield
  - Ingleton
- 21A Saltley
  - Camp Hill
  - Stratford on Avon
  - Washwood Heath
  - Water Orton
- 21B Bournville
  - Redditch
- 21C Bromsgrove
- 22A Bristol Barrow Road
- 22B Gloucester
  - Barnwood
  - Dursley
  - Tewkesbury
- 24A Accrington
- 24B Rose Grove
- 24C Lostock Hall
- 24D Lower Darwen
- 24E Blackpool Central
  - Blackpool North
- 24F Fleetwood
- 25A Wakefield
- 25B Huddersfield
- 25C Goole
- 25D Mirfield
- 25E Sowerby Bridge
- 25F Low Moor
- 25G Farnley Junction
- 26A Newton Heath
- 26B Agecroft
- 26C Bolton
- 26D Bury
- 26E Bacup
- 26F Lees Oldham
- 26G Belle Vue
- 27A Bank Hall
- 27B Aintree
- 27C Southport
- 27D Wigan
- 27E Walton on the Hill
- 30A Stratford
  - Brentwood
  - Chelmsford
  - Enfield Town
  - Epping
  - Palace Gates
  - Spitalfields
  - Ware
  - Wood St. Walthamstow
- 30B Hertford East
  - Buntingford
- 30C Bishops Stortford
- 30D Southend Victoria
  - Southminster
  - Wickford
- 30E Colchester
  - Braintree
  - Clacton
  - Maldon
  - Walton on Naze
- 30F Parkeston
- 31A Cambridge
  - Ely
  - Huntingdon East
  - Saffron Walden
- 31B March
- 31C Kings Lynn
  - Hunstanton
- 31D South Lynn
- 31E Bury St. Edmunds
  - Sudbury
- 32A Norwich Thorpe
  - Cromer
  - Dereham
  - Swaffham
  - Wells on Sea
  - Wymondham
- 32B Ipswich
  - Aldeburgh
  - Felixstowe Beach
  - Ipswich Docks
  - Stowmarket
- 32C Lowestoft
- 32D Yarmouth South Town
- 32E Yarmouth Vauxhall
- 32F Yarmouth Beach
- 32G Melton Constable
  - Cromer Beach
  - Norwich City
- 33A Plaistow
  - Upminster
- 33B Tilbury
- 33C Shoeburyness
- 34A Kings Cross
- 34B Hornsey
- 34C Hatfield
- 34D Hitchin
- 34E Neasden
  - Aylesbury
  - Chesham
  - Rickmansworth
- 35A New England
  - Spalding
  - Stamford
- 35B Grantham
- 35C Spital Bridge
- 36A Doncaster
- 36B Mexborough
- 36C Frodingham
- 36D Barnsley
- 36E Retford
  - Newark
  - Retford (GC)
- 37A Ardsley
- 37B Copley Hill
- 37C Bradford
  - Hammerton St
- 38A Colwick
  - Derby Friargate
- 38B Annesley
  - Kirkby Bentinck
  - Nottingham Victoria
- 38C Leicester Central
  - Leicester Belgrave Road
- 38D Staveley
- 38E Woodford Halse
- 39A Gorton
  - Dinting
  - Hayfield
- 39B Sheffield Darnall
- 40A Lincoln
  - Lincoln (GC)
- 40B Immingham
  - Grimsby
  - New Holland
- 40C Louth
- 40D Tuxford Junction
- 40E Langwith Junction
- 40F Boston
  - Sleaford
- 50A York
  - York (LMS)
  - York South
- 50B Leeds Neville Hill
- 50C Selby
- 50D Starbeck
- 50E Scarborough
- 50F Malton
  - Pickering
- 50G Whitby
- 51A Darlington
  - Middleton in Teesdale
- 51B Newport
- 51C West Hartlepool
- 51D Middlesbrough
  - Guisborough
- 51E Stockton on Tees
- 51F West Auckland
- 51G Haverton Hill
- 51H Kirkby Stephen
- 51J Northallerton
  - Leyburn
- 51K Saltburn
- 52A Gateshead
  - Bowes Bridge
- 52B Heaton
- 52C Blaydon
  - Alston
  - Hexham
- 52D Tweedmouth
  - Alnmouth
- 52E Percy Main
- 52F North Blyth
  - South Blyth
- 53A Hull Dairycoates
- 53B Hull Botanic Gardens
- 53C Hull Springhead
  - Hull Alexandra Dock
- 53D Bridlington
- 54A Sunderland
  - Durham
- 54B Tyne Dock
- 54C Borough Gardens
- 54D Consett
- 60A Inverness
  - Dingwall
  - Kyle of Lochalsh
- 60B Aviemore
  - Boat of Garten
- 60C Helmsdale
  - Dornoch
  - Tain
- 60D Wick
  - Thurso
- 60E Forres
- 61A Kittybrewster
  - Ballater
  - Fraserburgh
  - Inverurie
  - Peterhead
- 61B Aberdeen Ferryhill
- 61C Keith
  - Banff
  - Elgin
- 62A Thornton Junction
  - Anstruther
  - Burntisland
  - Kirkcaldy
  - Ladybank
  - Methil
- 62B Dundee Tay Bridge
  - Arbroath
  - Dundee West
  - Montrose
  - St. Andrews
- 62C Dunfermline Upper
  - Alloa
  - Inverkeithing
  - Kelty
- 63A Perth
  - Aberfeldy
  - Blair Atholl
  - Crieff
- 63B Stirling
  - Killin Loch Tay
  - Stirling Shore Road
- 63C Forfar
- 63D Fort William
  - Mallaig
- 63E Oban
  - Ballachulish
- 64A St. Margarets
  - Dunbar
  - Galashiels
  - Granton
  - Hardengreen
  - Longniddry
  - North Berwick
  - Peebles
  - Seafield
  - South Leith
- 64B Haymarket
- 64C Dalry Road
- 64D Carstairs
- 64E Polmont
- 64F Bathgate
- 64G Hawick
  - Kelso
  - Riccarton Junction
  - St. Boswells
- 65A Eastfield
- 65B St. Rollox
- 65C Parkhead
- 65D Dawsholm
  - Dumbarton
- 65E Kipps
- 65F Grangemouth
- 65G Yoker
- 65H Helensburgh
  - Arrochar
- 65I Balloch
- 66A Polmadie
- 66B Motherwell
  - Morningside
- 66C Hamilton
- 66D Greenock Ladyburn
  - Princes Pier
- 67A Corkerhill
- 67B Hurlford
  - Beith
  - Muirkirk
- 67C Ayr
- 67D Ardrossan
- 68A Carlisle Kingmoor
  - Durran Hill
- 68B Dumfries
  - Kirkcudbright
- 68C Stranraer
  - Newton Stewart
- 68D Beattock
- 68E Carlisle Canal
- 70A Nine Elms
- 70B Feltham
- 70C Guildford
- 70D Basingstoke
- 70E Reading South
- 71A Eastleigh
  - Andover Junction
  - Lymington
  - Southampton Terminus
  - Winchester City
- 71B Bournemouth
  - Branksome
  - Hamworthy Junction
  - Swanage
- 71C Dorchester
- 71D Fratton
- 71E Newport IOW
- 71F Ryde IOW
- 71G Bath Green Park
  - Radstock
- 71H Templecombe
- 71I Southampton Docks
  - Southampton New Docks
- 71J Highbridge
- 72A Exmouth Junction
  - Bude
  - Exmouth
  - Launceston (SR)
  - Lyme Regis
  - Okehampton
  - Seaton
- 72B Salisbury
- 72C Yeovil Town
- 72D Plymouth Friary
  - Callington
- 72E Barnstaple Junction
  - Ilfracombe
  - Torrington
- 72F Wadebridge
- 73A Stewarts Lane
- 73B Bricklayers Arms
  - Ewer Street
- 73C Hither Green
- 73D Gillingham
- 73E Faversham
- 74A Ashford
  - Canterbury West
  - Margate
  - Rolvenden
- 74B Ramsgate
- 74C Dover Marine
  - Folkestone Junction
- 74D Tonbridge
- 74E St. Leonards
- 75A Brighton
  - Eastbourne
  - Newhaven
- 75B Redhill
- 75C Norwood Junction
- 75D Horsham
- 75E Three Bridges
- 75F Tunbridge Wells West
- 81A Old Oak Common
- 81B Slough
  - Marlow
  - Watlington
- 81C Southall
- 81D Reading
  - Henley on Thames
- 81E Didcot
  - Lambourn
  - Newbury
  - Wallingford
- 81F Oxford
  - Abingdon
  - Fairford
- 82A Bristol Bath Road
  - Bath Spa
  - Wells (GWR)
  - Weston-super-Mare
  - Yatton
- 82B St. Philips Marsh
- 82C Swindon
  - Andover
  - Chippenham
- 82D Westbury
  - Frome
- 82E Yeovil Pen Mill
- 82F Weymouth
  - Bridport
- 83A Newton Abbot
  - Ashburton
  - Kingsbridge
  - Moreton-hampstead
- 83B Taunton
  - Bridgwater
  - Minehead
- 83C Exeter
  - Tiverton Junction
- 83D Laira (Plymouth)
  - Launceston
  - Plymouth Docks
  - Princetown
- 83E St. Blazey
  - Bodmin
  - Moorswater
- 83F Truro
- 83G Penzance
  - Helston
  - St. Ives
- 84A Stafford Road
- 84B Oxley
- 84C Banbury
- 84D Leamington Spa
- 84E Tyseley
  - Stratford on Avon
- 84F Stourbridge
- 84G Shrewsbury
  - Builth Road
  - Clee Hill
  - Craven Arms
  - Knighton
- 84H Wellington
  - Crewe Gresty Lane
- 84J Croes Newydd
  - Bala
  - Penmaenpool
  - Trawsfynydd
- 84K Chester (GWR)
- 85A Worcester
  - Evesham
  - Honeybourne
  - Kingham
- 85B Gloucester
  - Brimscombe
  - Cheltenham
  - Cirencester
  - Lydney
  - Tetbury
- 85C Hereford
  - Ledbury
  - Leominster
  - Ross on Wye
- 85D Kidderminster
  - Cleobury Mortimer
- 86A Ebbw Junction

86B Newport Pill
86C Cardiff Canton
86D Llantrisant
86E Severn Tunnel Junction
86F Tondu
86G Pontypool Road
86H Aberbeeg
86J Aberdare
86K Abergavenny
Tredegar
87A Neath
Glyn Neath
Neath Riverside
87B Duffryn Yard
Glyncorrwg
87C Danygraig
87D Swansea East Dock
87E Landore
87F Llanelly
Burry Port
Pantyffynnon
87G Carmarthen
87H Neyland
Cardigan
Milford Haven
Pembroke Dock
Whitland
87J Fishguard
Goodwick
87K Swansea Victoria
Gurnos
Llandovery
Upper Bank
88A Cardiff Cathays
Radyr
88B Cardiff East Dock
88C Barry
88D Merthyr
Dowlais Cae Harris
Dowlais Central
Rhymney
88E Abercynon
88F Treherbert
Ferndale
89A Oswestry
Llanidloes
Moat Lane
Welshpool
Welshpool (WLLR)
89B Brecon
Builth Wells
89C Machynlleth
Aberayron
Aberystwyth (VoR)
Aberystwyth
Portmadoc
Pwllheli

1957

1A Willesden
1B Camden
1C Watford
1D Devons Road
1E Bletchley
Leighton Buzzard
2A Rugby
2B Nuneaton
2C Warwick
2D Coventry
2E Northampton
2F Market Harborough
Seaton
3A Bescot
3B Bushbury
3C Walsall
3D Aston
3E Monument Lane
5A Crewe North
Over & Wharton
Whitchurch
5B Crewe South
5C Stafford
5D Stoke
5E Alsager
5F Uttoxeter
6A Chester
6B Mold Junction
6C Birkenhead
6D Chester Northgate
6E Wrexham Rhosddu
6F Bidston
6G Llandudno Junction
6H Bangor
6J Holyhead
6K Rhyl
8A Edge Hill
8B Warrington Dallam
Arpley
8C Speke Junction
8D Widnes
8E Brunswick
Birkenhead Shore Road
Warrington Central
9A Longsight
9B Stockport Edgeley
9C Macclesfield
9D Buxton
9G Northwich
10A Wigan Springs Branch
10B Preston
10C Patricroft
10D Sutton Oak
11A Carnforth
11B Barrow
Coniston
11C Oxenholme
11D Tebay
11E Lancaster
12A Carlisle Upperby
12B Penrith
12C Workington
14A Cricklewood
14B Kentish Town
14C St. Albans
15A Wellingborough
15B Kettering
15C Leicester Midland
15D Bedford
16A Nottingham
16B Kirkby in Ashfield
16C Mansfield
17A Derby
17B Burton
Horninglow
Overseal
17C Coalville
17D Rowsley
Cromford
Middleton Top
Sheep Pasture
17E Heaton Mersey
Gowhole
17F Trafford Park
18A Toton
18B Westhouses
18C Hasland
Williamthorpe Colliery
18D Staveley Barrow Hill
Sheepbridge Works
Staveley New Works
Staveley Old Works
19A Sheffield Grimesthorpe
19B Millhouses
19C Canklow
20F Skipton
20G Hellifield
21A Saltley
Camp Hill
Stratford on Avon
Washwood Heath
Water Orton
21B Bournville
Redditch
21C Bromsgrove
22A Bristol Barrow Road
22B Gloucester Barnwood
Dursley
Tewkesbury
24A Accrington
24B Rose Grove
24C Lostock Hall
24D Lower Darwen
24E Blackpool Central
Blackpool North
24F Fleetwood
26A Newton Heath
26B Agecroft
26C Bolton
26D Bury
26E Lees Oldham
27A Bank Hall
27B Aintree
27C Southport
27D Wigan
27E Walton on the Hill
30A Stratford
Chelmsford
Enfield Town
Epping
Spitalfields
Wood St. Walthamstow
30B Hertford East
Buntingford
Ware
30C Bishops Stortford
30D Southend Victoria
30E Colchester
Braintree
Clacton
Maldon
Walton on Naze
30F Parkeston
31A Cambridge
Ely
Huntingdon East
Saffron Walden
31B March
31C Kings Lynn
Hunstanton
31D South Lynn
31E Bury St. Edmunds
Sudbury
32A Norwich Thorpe
Swaffham
Wymondham
32B Ipswich
Felixstowe Beach
Stowmarket
32C Lowestoft
32D Yarmouth South Town
32E Yarmouth Vauxhall
32F Yarmouth Beach
32G Melton Constable
Cromer Beach
Norwich City
33A Plaistow
33B Tilbury
33C Shoeburyness
34A Kings Cross
34B Hornsey
34C Hatfield
34D Hitchin
34E Neasden
Aylesbury
Chesham
Rickmansworth
35A New England
Spalding
Stamford
35B Grantham
35C Spital Bridge
36A Doncaster
36B Mexborough
36C Frodingham
36D Barnsley
36E Retford
Newark
Retford (GC)
38A Colwick
38B Annesley
Kirkby Bentinck
Nottingham Victoria
38C Leicester Central
38D Staveley
38E Woodford Halse
39A Gorton
40A Lincoln
Lincoln (GC)
Lincoln St. Marks
40B Immingham
Grimsby
New Holland
40D Tuxford Junction
40E Langwith Junction
40F Boston
Sleaford
41A Sheffield Darnall
50A York
York (LMS)
York South
50B Leeds Neville Hill
50C Selby
50D Starbeck
50E Scarborough
50F Malton
Pickering
50G Whitby
51A Darlington
Middleton in Teesdale
51B Newport
51C West Hartlepool
51D Middlesbrough
51E Stockton on Tees
51F West Auckland
51G Haverton Hill
51H Kirkby Stephen
51J Northallerton
51K Saltburn
52A Gateshead
Bowes Bridge
52B Heaton
52C Blaydon
Alston
Hexham
52D Tweedmouth
Alnmouth
52E Percy Main
52F North Blyth
South Blyth
53A Hull Dairycoates
53B Hull Botanic Gardens
53C Hull Springhead
Hull Alexandra Dock
53D Bridlington
53E Goole
54A Sunderland
Durham
54B Tyne Dock
54C Borough Gardens
54D Consett
55A Leeds Holbeck
55B Stourton
55C Farnley Junction
55D Royston
55E Normanton
55F Manningham
Ilkley
Keighley
55G Huddersfield
56A Wakefield
56B Ardsley
56C Copley Hill
56D Mirfield
56E Sowerby Bridge
56F Low Moor
56G Bradford Hammerton St
60A Inverness
Dingwall
Kyle of Lochalsh
60B Aviemore
Boat of Garten
60C Helmsdale
Dornoch
Tain
60D Wick
Thurso
60E Forres
61A Kittybrewster
Ballater
Fraserburgh
Inverurie
Peterhead
61B Aberdeen Ferryhill
61C Keith
Banff
Elgin
62A Thornton Junction
Anstruther
Burntisland
Kirkcaldy
Ladybank
Methil
62B Dundee Tay Bridge
Arbroath
Dundee West
Montrose
St. Andrews
62C Dunfermline Upper
Alloa
Inverkeithing
Kelty
63A Perth
Aberfeldy
Blair Atholl
Crieff
63B Stirling
Killin Loch Tay
Stirling Shore Road
63C Forfar
63D Oban
Ballachulish
64A St. Margarets
Dunbar
Galashiels
Granton
Hardengreen
Longniddry
North Berwick
Seafield
South Leith
64B Haymarket
64C Dalry Road
64D Carstairs
64E Polmont
64F Bathgate
64G Hawick
Riccarton Junction
St. Boswells
65A Eastfield
Arrochar
65B St. Rollox
65C Parkhead
65D Dawsholm
Dumbarton
65E Kipps
65F Grangemouth
65G Yoker
65H Helensburgh
65I Balloch
65J Fort William
Mallaig
66A Polmadie
66B Motherwell
66C Hamilton
66D Greenock Ladyburn
Princes Pier
67A Corkerhill
67B Hurlford
Beith
Muirkirk
67C Ayr
67D Ardrossan
68A Carlisle Kingmoor
Durran Hill
68B Dumfries
68C Stranraer
Newton Stewart
68D Beattock
68E Carlisle Canal
70A Nine Elms
70B Feltham
70C Guildford
70D Basingstoke
70E Reading South
70F Fratton
70G Newport IOW
70H Ryde IOW
71A Eastleigh
Andover Junction
Lymington
Southampton Terminus
Winchester City
71B Bournemouth
Branksome
Dorchester
Swanage
71G Bath Green Park
Radstock
71H Templecombe
71I Southampton Docks
Southampton New Docks
71J Highbridge
72A Exmouth Junction
Bude
Exmouth
Launceston (SR)
Lyme Regis
Okehampton
Seaton
72B Salisbury
72C Yeovil Town
72D Plymouth Friary
Callington
72E Barnstaple Junction
Ilfracombe
Torrington
72F Wadebridge
73A Stewarts Lane
73B Bricklayers Arms
Ewer Street
73C Hither Green
73D Gillingham
73E Faversham
74A Ashford
Margate
74B Ramsgate
74C Dover Marine
Folkestone Junction
74D Tonbridge
74E St. Leonards
75A Brighton
Eastbourne
Newhaven
75B Redhill
75C Norwood Junction
75D Horsham
75E Three Bridges
75F Tunbridge Wells West
81A Old Oak Common
81B Slough
Marlow
Watlington
81C Southall
81D Reading
Henley on Thames
81E Didcot
Lambourn
Newbury
81F Oxford
Fairford
82A Bristol Bath Road
Bath Spa
Wells (GWR)
Weston-super-Mare
Yatton
82B St. Philips Marsh
82C Swindon
Andover
Chippenham
82D Westbury
Frome
82E Yeovil Pen Mill
82F Weymouth
Bridport
83A Newton Abbot
Ashburton
Kingsbridge
Moreton-hampstead
83B Taunton
Bridgwater
83C Exeter
Tiverton Junction
83D Laira (Plymouth)
Launceston
83E St. Blazey
Bodmin
Moorswater
83F Truro
83G Penzance
Helston
St. Ives
84A Stafford Road
84B Oxley
84C Banbury
84D Leamington Spa
84E Tyseley
Stratford on Avon
84F Stourbridge
84G Shrewsbury
Builth Road
Clee Hill
Craven Arms
Knighton
84H Wellington
Crewe Gresty Lane
84J Croes Newydd
Bala
Penmaenpool
Trawsfynydd
84K Chester (GWR)
85A Worcester
Evesham
Honeybourne
Kingham
85B Gloucester
Brimscombe
Cheltenham
Cirencester
Lydney
Tetbury
85C Hereford
Ledbury
Leominster
Ross on Wye
85D Kidderminster
Cleobury Mortimer
86A Ebbw Junction
86B Newport Pill
86C Cardiff Canton
86D Llantrisant
86E Severn Tunnel Junction
86F Tondu
86G Pontypool Road
86H Aberbeeg
86J Aberdare
86K Tredegar
Abergavenny
87A Neath
Glyn Neath
Neath Riverside
87B Duffryn Yard
Glyncorrwg
87C Danygraig
87D Swansea East Dock
87E Landore
87F Llanelly
Burry Port
Pantyffynnon
87G Carmarthen
87H Neyland
Cardigan
Milford Haven
Pembroke Dock
Whitland
87J Fishguard
Goodwick
87K Swansea Victoria
Gurnos
Llandovery
Upper Bank
88A Cardiff Cathays
Radyr
88B Cardiff East Dock
88C Barry
88D Merthyr
Dowlais Cae Harris
Dowlais Central
Rhymney
88E Abercynon
88F Treherbert
Ferndale
89A Oswestry
Llanidloes
Moat Lane
89B Brecon
Builth Wells
89C Machynlleth
Aberayron
Aberystwyth (VoR)
Aberystwyth
Portmadoc
Pwllheli

1960

Code	Shed
1A	Willesden
1B	Camden
1C	Watford
1E	Bletchley
	Leighton Buzzard
2A	Rugby
2B	Nuneaton
2E	Northampton
2F	Woodford Halse
3A	Bescot
3B	Bushbury
3C	Walsall
3D	Aston
3E	Monument Lane
5A	Crewe North
	Over & Wharton
5B	Crewe South
5C	Stafford
5D	Stoke
5E	Alsager
5F	Uttoxeter
6A	Chester
6B	Mold Junction
6C	Birkenhead
6D	Chester Northgate
6E	Chester (GWR)
6F	Bidston
6G	Llandudno Junction
6H	Bangor
6J	Holyhead
6K	Rhyl
8A	Edge Hill
8B	Warrington Dallam
	Arpley
8C	Speke Junction
8D	Widnes
8E	Northwich
8F	Wigan Springs Branch
8G	Sutton Oak
9A	Longsight
9B	Stockport Edgeley
9C	Macclesfield
9D	Buxton
9E	Trafford Park
9F	Heaton Mersey
	Gowhole
9G	Gorton
11A	Barrow
11B	Workington
11C	Oxenholme
11D	Tebay
12A	Carlisle Kingmoor
12B	Carlisle Upperby
	Penrith
12C	Carlisle Canal
12D	Kirkby Stephen
14A	Cricklewood
14B	Kentish Town
14C	St. Albans
14D	Neasden
	Aylesbury
	Chesham
	Rickmansworth
14E	Bedford
15A	Wellingborough
15B	Kettering
15C	Leicester Midland
15D	Coalville
15E	Leicester Central
15F	Market Harborough
	Seaton
16A	Nottingham
16B	Kirkby in Ashfield
16C	Mansfield
16D	Annesley
	Kirkby Bentinck
	Nottingham Victoria
17A	Derby
17B	Burton
	Horninglow
	Overseal
17C	Rowsley
	Cromford
	Middleton Top
	Sheep Pasture
18A	Toton
18B	Westhouses
18C	Hasland
	Williamthorpe Colliery
21A	Saltley
	Camp Hill
	Water Orton
21B	Bournville
24A	Accrington
24B	Rose Grove
24C	Lostock Hall
24D	Lower Darwen
24E	Blackpool Central
	Blackpool North
24F	Fleetwood
24G	Skipton
24H	Hellifield
24J	Lancaster
24K	Preston
24L	Carnforth
26A	Newton Heath
26B	Agecroft
26C	Bolton
26D	Bury
26E	Lees Oldham
26F	Patricroft
27A	Bank Hall
27B	Aintree
27C	Southport
27D	Wigan
27E	Walton on the Hill
27F	Brunswick
	Birkenhead Shore Road
	Warrington Central
30A	Stratford
	Chelmsford
	Enfield Town
	Hertford East
	Spitalfields
	Wood St. Walthamstow
	Maldon
	Walton on Naze
30F	Parkeston
31A	Cambridge
	Bishops Stortford
	Ely
31B	March
31C	Kings Lynn
31F	Spital Bridge
32A	Norwich Thorpe
	Cromer Beach
	Swaffham
	Stowmarket
32C	Lowestoft
33B	Tilbury
	Plaistow
33C	Shoeburyness
34A	Kings Cross
34B	Hornsey
34C	Hatfield
34D	Hitchin
34E	New England
34F	Grantham
36A	Doncaster
36C	Frodingham
36E	Retford
	Retford (GC)
40A	Lincoln
40B	Immingham
	Grimsby
	New Holland
40E	Colwick
40F	Boston
	Sleaford
	Spalding
41A	Sheffield Darnall
41B	Sheffield
	Grimesthorpe
41C	Millhouses
41D	Canklow
41E	Staveley Barrow Hill
	Sheepbridge Works
	Staveley New Works
	Staveley Old Works
41F	Mexborough
41G	Barnsley
41H	Staveley
41J	Langwith Junction
50A	York
	York (LMS)
	York South
50B	Leeds Neville Hill
50E	Scarborough
50F	Malton
51A	Darlington
51C	West Hartlepool
51F	West Auckland
51J	Northallerton
51L	Thornaby
52A	Gateshead
	Bowes Bridge
52B	Heaton
52C	Blaydon
52D	Tweedmouth
	Alnmouth
52E	Percy Main
52F	North Blyth
	South Blyth
52G	Sunderland
52H	Tyne Dock
52K	Consett
53A	Hull Dairycoates
53B	Hull Botanic Gardens
53C	Hull Alexandra Dock
53E	Goole
55A	Leeds Holbeck
55B	Stourton
55C	Farnley Junction
55D	Royston
55E	Normanton
55F	Manningham
	Keighley
55G	Huddersfield
56A	Wakefield
56B	Ardsley
56C	Copley Hill
56D	Mirfield
56E	Sowerby Bridge
56F	Low Moor
60A	Inverness
	Dingwall
	Kyle of Lochalsh
60B	Aviemore
60C	Helmsdale
	Dornoch
	Tain
60D	Wick
	Thurso
61A	Kittybrewster
	Fraserburgh
	Peterhead
61B	Aberdeen Ferryhill
61C	Keith
	Banff
	Elgin
62A	Thornton Junction
	Anstruther
62B	Dundee Tay Bridge
	Montrose
	St. Andrews
62C	Dunfermline Upper
	Alloa
	Inverkeithing
	Kelty
63A	Perth
	Aberfeldy
	Blair Atholl
	Crieff
	Forfar
63B	Stirling
	Killin Loch Tay
63C	Oban
	Ballachulish
64A	St. Margarets
	Dunbar
	Galashiels
	Granton
	Hardengreen
	Seafield
	South Leith
64B	Haymarket
64C	Dalry Road
64D	Carstairs
64E	Polmont
64F	Bathgate
64G	Hawick
64H	Leith Central
65A	Eastfield
65B	St. Rollox
65C	Parkhead
65D	Dawsholm
	Dumbarton
65E	Kipps
65F	Grangemouth
65G	Yoker
65H	Helensburgh
65I	Balloch
65J	Fort William
	Mallaig
66A	Polmadie
66B	Motherwell
66C	Hamilton
66D	Greenock Ladyburn
67A	Corkerhill
67B	Hurlford
	Beith
	Muirkirk
67C	Ayr
67D	Ardrossan
68B	Dumfries
68C	Stranraer
68D	Beattock
70A	Nine Elms
70B	Feltham
70C	Guildford
70D	Basingstoke
	Reading South
70H	Ryde IOW
71A	Eastleigh
	Andover Junction
	Lymington
	Southampton Terminus
	Winchester City
71B	Bournemouth
	Branksome
	Swanage
71G	Weymouth
71I	Southampton Docks
	Southampton New Docks
72A	Exmouth Junction
	Bude
	Callington
	Exmouth
	Launceston (SR)
	Lyme Regis
	Okehampton
	Seaton
72B	Salisbury
72C	Yeovil Town
72E	Barnstaple Junction
	Ilfracombe
72F	Wadebridge
73A	Stewarts Lane
73B	Bricklayers Arms
	Ewer Street
73C	Hither Green
73F	Ashford
	Gillingham
	Margate
	Ramsgate
73H	Dover Marine
	Folkestone Junction
73J	Tonbridge
75A	Brighton
	Eastbourne
	Newhaven
75B	Redhill
75C	Norwood Junction
75E	Three Bridges
	Horsham
75F	Tunbridge Wells West
81A	Old Oak Common
81B	Slough
	Marlow
81C	Southall
81D	Reading
81E	Didcot
	Lambourn
81F	Oxford
	Fairford
82A	Bristol Bath Road
	Bath Spa
	Wells (GWR)
	Weston-super-Mare
	Yatton
82B	St. Philips Marsh
82C	Swindon
	Chippenham
82D	Westbury
	Frome
82E	Bristol Barrow Road
82F	Bath Green Park
	Radstock
82G	Templecombe
	Highbridge
83A	Newton Abbot
	Kingsbridge
83B	Taunton
	Bridgwater
83C	Exeter
	Tiverton Junction
83D	Laira (Plymouth)
	Launceston
83E	St. Blazey
	Bodmin
	Moorswater
83F	Truro
83G	Penzance
	Helston
	St. Ives
83H	Plymouth Friary
84A	Stafford Road
84B	Oxley
84C	Banbury
84D	Leamington Spa
84E	Tyseley
	Stratford on Avon
84F	Stourbridge
84G	Shrewsbury
	Builth Road
	Clee Hill
	Craven Arms
	Knighton
84H	Wellington
	Crewe Gresty Lane
84J	Croes Newydd
	Bala
	Penmaenpool
	Trawsfynydd
84K	Wrexham Rhosddu
85A	Worcester
	Evesham
	Honeybourne
	Kingham
85B	Gloucester
	Brimscombe
	Cheltenham
	Cirencester
	Lydney
	Tetbury
85C	Hereford
	Ledbury
	Leominster
	Ross on Wye
85D	Kidderminster
	Cleobury Mortimer
85E	Gloucester
	Barnwood
	Dursley
	Tewkesbury
85F	Bromsgrove
	Redditch
86A	Ebbw Junction
86B	Newport Pill
86C	Cardiff Canton
86D	Llantrisant
86E	Severn Tunnel Junction
86F	Tondu
86G	Pontypool Road
86H	Aberbeeg
86J	Aberdare
86K	Tredegar
87A	Neath
	Glyn Neath
	Neath Riverside
87B	Duffryn Yard
	Glyncorrwg
87C	Danygraig
87D	Swansea East Dock
	Gurnos
	Upper Bank
87E	Landore
87F	Llanelly
	Burry Port
	Llandovery
	Pantyffynnon
87G	Carmarthen
87H	Neyland
	Cardigan
	Milford Haven
	Pembroke Dock
	Whitland
87J	Fishguard
	Goodwick
88A	Radyr
	Cardiff Cathays
88B	Cardiff East Dock
88C	Barry
88D	Merthyr
	Dowlais Cae Harris
	Dowlais Central
	Rhymney
88E	Abercynon
88F	Treherbert
	Ferndale
89A	Oswestry
	Brecon
	Llanidloes
	Moat Lane
89C	Machynlleth
	Aberayron
	Aberystwyth (VoR)
	Aberystwyth
	Portmadoc

1963

Code	Shed
1A	Willesden
1C	Watford
1E	Bletchley
2A	Rugby
2B	Nuneaton
2E	Northampton
2F	Woodford Halse
2H	Monument Lane
5A	Crewe North
	Over & Wharton
5B	Crewe South
5C	Stafford
5D	Stoke
5F	Uttoxeter
6A	Chester
6B	Mold Junction
6C	Birkenhead
6F	Bidston
6G	Llandudno Junction
6H	Bangor
6J	Holyhead
6K	Rhyl
8A	Edge Hill
8B	Warrington Dallam
	Arpley
8C	Speke Junction
8D	Widnes
8E	Northwich
8F	Wigan Springs Branch
8G	Sutton Oak
9A	Longsight
9B	Stockport Edgeley
9D	Buxton
9E	Trafford Park
9F	Heaton Mersey
	Gowhole
9G	Gorton
12A	Carlisle Kingmoor
12B	Carlisle Upperby
12C	Carlisle Canal
12E	Barrow
12F	Workington
12H	Tebay
14A	Cricklewood
14B	Kentish Town
14E	Bedford
15A	Wellingborough
	Market Harborough
15B	Kettering
15C	Leicester Midland
15D	Coalville
15E	Leicester Central
16A	Nottingham
16B	Kirkby in Ashfield
16D	Annesley
	Kirkby Bentinck
	Nottingham Victoria
17A	Derby
17B	Burton
	Overseal
17C	Rowsley
	Cromford
	Middleton Top
	Sheep Pasture
18A	Toton
18B	Westhouses
18C	Hasland
	Williamthorpe Colliery
21A	Saltley
	Walsall
	Camp Hill
	Water Orton
21B	Bescot
21C	Bushbury
21D	Aston
24B	Rose Grove
24C	Lostock Hall
24D	Lower Darwen
24E	Blackpool Central
	Blackpool North
24F	Fleetwood
24G	Skipton
24H	Hellifield
24J	Lancaster
24L	Carnforth
26A	Newton Heath
26B	Agecroft
26C	Bolton
26D	Bury
26E	Lees Oldham
26F	Patricroft
27A	Bank Hall
27B	Aintree
27C	Southport
27D	Wigan
27E	Walton on the Hill
31B	March
34A	Kings Cross
34E	New England
34F	Grantham
36A	Doncaster
36C	Frodingham
36E	Retford
	Retford (GC)
40A	Lincoln
40B	Immingham
40E	Colwick
40F	Boston
	Sleaford
41A	Sheffield Darnall
41D	Canklow
41E	Staveley Barrow Hill
	Sheepbridge Works
	Staveley New Works
	Staveley Old Works
41F	Mexborough
41H	Staveley
41J	Langwith Junction
50A	York
50B	Hull Dairycoates
50C	Hull Botanic Gardens
50D	Goole
50E	Scarborough
50F	Malton
51A	Darlington
51C	West Hartlepool
51F	West Auckland
51J	Northallerton
51L	Thornaby
52A	Gateshead
52B	Heaton
52C	Blaydon
52D	Tweedmouth
	Alnmouth
52E	Percy Main
52F	North Blyth
	South Blyth
52G	Sunderland
52H	Tyne Dock
52K	Consett
55A	Leeds Holbeck
55B	Stourton
55C	Farnley Junction
55D	Royston
55E	Normanton
55F	Manningham
55G	Huddersfield
55H	Leeds Neville Hill

56A	Wakefield
56B	Ardsley
56C	Copley Hill
56D	Mirfield
56E	Sowerby Bridge
56F	Low Moor
61B	Aberdeen Ferryhill
	Banff
62A	Thornton Junction
62B	Dundee Tay Bridge
	Montrose
62C	Dunfermline Upper
	Alloa
	Inverkeithing
	Kelty
63A	Perth
	Crieff
	Forfar
64A	St. Margarets
	Dunbar
	Granton
64B	Haymarket
64C	Dalry Road
64F	Bathgate
64G	Hawick
64H	Leith Central
65A	Eastfield
65B	St. Rollox
65C	Parkhead
65D	Dawsholm
	Dumbarton
65E	Kipps
65F	Grangemouth
65J	Stirling
	Killin Loch Tay
65K	Polmont
66A	Polmadie
66B	Motherwell
66D	Greenock Ladyburn
66E	Carstairs
66F	Beattock
67A	Corkerhill
67B	Hurlford
	Muirkirk
67C	Ayr
67D	Ardrossan
67E	Dumfries
67F	Stranraer
70A	Nine Elms
70B	Feltham
70C	Guildford
	Reading South
70D	Basingstoke
70E	Salisbury
70H	Ryde IOW
71A	Eastleigh
	Lymington
	Southampton Terminus
71B	Bournemouth
	Branksome
	Swanage
71G	Weymouth
71I	Southampton Docks
	Southampton New Docks
72A	Exmouth Junction
	Bude
	Callington
	Exmouth
	Launceston (SR)
	Lyme Regis
	Okehampton
	Seaton
72C	Yeovil Town
72E	Barnstaple Junction
	Ilfracombe
72F	Wadebridge
73F	Ashford
75A	Brighton
	Eastbourne
	Newhaven
75B	Redhill
75C	Norwood Junction
75D	Stewarts Lane
	Tonbridge
75E	Three Bridges
	Horsham
75F	Tunbridge Wells West
81A	Old Oak Common
81B	Slough
81C	Southall
81D	Reading
81E	Didcot
81F	Oxford
82B	St. Philips Marsh
	Wells (GWR)
82C	Swindon
	Chippenham
82D	Westbury
	Frome
82E	Bristol Barrow Road
82F	Bath Green Park
	Radstock
82G	Templecombe
	Highbridge
83A	Newton Abbot
83B	Taunton
83C	Exeter
	Tiverton Junction
83D	Laira (Plymouth)
83F	Truro
83H	Plymouth Friary
84A	Stafford Road
84B	Oxley
84C	Banbury
84D	Leamington Spa
84E	Tyseley
84F	Stourbridge
84G	Kidderminster
	Cleobury Mortimer
84H	Wellington
	Crewe Gresty Lane
85A	Worcester
	Honeybourne
	Ledbury
85B	Gloucester
	Brimscombe
	Cheltenham
	Cirencester
	Lydney
	Ross on Wye
	Tetbury
85C	Gloucester
	Barnwood
85D	Bromsgrove
	Redditch
86A	Ebbw Junction
86B	Newport Pill
86C	Hereford
86E	Severn Tunnel Junction
86F	Aberbeeg
86G	Pontypool Road
87A	Neath
	Glyn Neath
	Neath Riverside
87B	Duffryn Yard
	Glyncorrwg
87D	Swansea East Dock
	Upper Bank
87F	Llanelly
	Llandovery
	Pantyffynnon
87G	Carmarthen
87H	Neyland
	Pembroke Dock
	Whitland
87J	Fishguard
	Goodwick
88B	Radyr
88C	Barry
88D	Merthyr
	Dowlais Cae Harris
	Rhymney
88E	Abercynon
88F	Treherbert
	Ferndale
88G	Llantrisant
88H	Tondu
88J	Aberdare
88L	Cardiff East Dock
88M	Cardiff Cathays
89A	Shrewsbury
	Craven Arms
89B	Croes Newydd
	Bala
	Penmaenpool
89C	Machynlleth
	Aberystwyth (VoR)
	Aberystwyth
	Portmadoc
89D	Oswestry

1966

2A	Tyseley
2B	Oxley
2C	Stourbridge
2D	Banbury
2E	Saltley
	Camp Hill
	Water Orton
2F	Bescot
2G	Walsall
2H	Monument Lane
5B	Crewe South
5D	Stoke
5E	Nuneaton
6A	Chester
6B	Mold Junction
6C	Croes Newydd
6D	Shrewsbury
6F	Machynlleth
	Aberystwyth (VoR)
6G	Llandudno Junction
6J	Holyhead
8A	Edge Hill
8B	Warrington Dallam
8C	Speke Junction
8E	Northwich
8F	Wigan Springs Branch
8G	Sutton Oak
8H	Birkenhead
8K	Bank Hall
8L	Aintree
8M	Southport
9B	Stockport Edgeley
9D	Newton Heath
9E	Trafford Park
9F	Heaton Mersey
	Gowhole
9H	Patricroft
9J	Agecroft
9K	Bolton
9L	Buxton
	Middleton Top
10A	Carnforth
10C	Fleetwood
10D	Lostock Hall
10F	Rose Grove
10G	Skipton
10H	Lower Darwen
10J	Lancaster
12A	Carlisle Kingmoor
12B	Carlisle Upperby
12C	Barrow
12D	Workington
12E	Tebay
15A	Leicester Midland
15B	Wellingborough
16B	Annesley
	Kirkby Bentinck
	Nottingham Victoria
16C	Derby
	Cromford
	Sheep Pasture
	Williamthorpe Colliery
16E	Kirkby in Ashfield
16F	Burton
16G	Westhouses
36A	Doncaster
36C	Frodingham
40E	Colwick
41J	Langwith Junction
50A	York
50B	Hull Dairycoates
50C	Hull Botanic Gardens
50D	Goole
51A	Darlington
51C	West Hartlepool
52D	Tweedmouth
	Alnmouth
52F	North Blyth
	South Blyth
52G	Sunderland
52H	Tyne Dock
55A	Leeds Holbeck
55B	Stourton
55C	Farnley Junction
55D	Royston
55E	Normanton
55F	Manningham
55G	Huddersfield
55H	Leeds Neville Hill
56A	Wakefield
56D	Mirfield
56F	Low Moor
61B	Aberdeen Ferryhill
62A	Thornton Junction
62B	Dundee Tay Bridge
	Montrose
62C	Dunfermline Upper
	Alloa
	Inverkeithing
63A	Perth
64A	St. Margarets
64F	Bathgate
64G	Hawick
65A	Eastfield
65B	St. Rollox
65J	Stirling
66A	Polmadie
66B	Motherwell
66D	Greenock Ladyburn
66E	Carstairs
66F	Beattock
67A	Corkerhill
67B	Hurlford
67C	Ayr
67E	Dumfries
67F	Stranraer
70A	Nine Elms
70B	Feltham
70C	Guildford
70D	Eastleigh
	Southampton Terminus
70E	Salisbury
70F	Bournemouth
70G	Weymouth
70H	Ryde IOW
70I	Southampton Docks
	Southampton New Docks
81F	Oxford
82F	Bath Green Park
	Radstock
83G	Templecombe
	Highbridge
87H	Whitland

NBR Reid ‘C15’ class 4-4-2T No 67452.

Shed Codes

BR shed codes (ex-LMS system)

1A	Willesden	01/48	09/65
1B	Camden	01/48	09/63
1C	Watford	01/48	03/65
1D	Devons Road	01/49	08/58
1E	Bletchley	03/52	07/65
1F	Rugby	09/63	05/65
1G	Woodford Halse	09/63	06/65
1H	Northampton	09/63	09/65
2A	Rugby	01/48	09/63
2A	Tyseley	09/63	11/66
2B	Bletchley	01/48	01/50
2B	Nuneaton	01/50	09/63
2B	Oxley	09/63	03/67
2C	Northampton	01/48	01/50
2C	Warwick	01/50	11/58
2C	Stourbridge	09/63	07/66
2D	Nuneaton	01/48	01/50
2D	Coventry	01/50	11/58
2D	Banbury	09/63	10/66
2E	Warwick	01/48	01/50
2E	Northampton	03/52	09/63
2E	Saltley	09/63	03/67
2F	Coventry	01/48	01/50
2F	Market Harborough	10/55	04/58
2F	Woodford Halse	04/58	09/63
2F	Bescot	09/63	03/66
2G	Woodford Halse	02/58	04/48
2G	Walsall	09/63	04/67
2H	Monument Lane	09/63	04/67
2J	Aston	09/63	10/65
2K	Bushbury	09/63	04/65
2L	Leamington Spa	09/63	06/65
2M	Wellington	09/63	08/64
2P	Kidderminster	09/63	08/64
3A	Bescot	01/48	06/60
3B	Bushbury	01/48	06/60
3C	Walsall	01/48	06/60
3D	Aston	01/48	06/60
3E	Monument Lane	01/48	06/60
4A	Shrewsbury	01/48	01/50
4A	Bletchley	01/50	03/52
4B	Swansea Victoria	01/48	01/50
4B	Northampton	01/50	03/52
4C	Upper Bank	01/48	01/48
4D	Abergavenny	01/48	01/50
4E	Tredegar	01/48	01/50
5A	Crewe North	01/48	05/65
5B	Crewe South	01/48	11/67
5C	Stafford	01/48	07/65
5D	Stoke	01/48	08/67
5E	Alsager	01/48	06/62
5E	Nuneaton	09/63	06/66
5F	Uttoxeter	01/48	12/64
6A	Chester	01/48	06/67
6B	Mold Junction	01/48	04/66
6C	Birkenhead	01/48	09/63
6C	Croes Newydd	09/63	06/67
6D	Chester Northgate	01/50	01/60
6D	Shrewsbury	09/63	03/67
6E	Wrexham Rhosddu	01/50	02/58
6E	Chester (GWR)	02/58	04/60
6E	Oswestry	09/63	01/65
6F	Bidston	01/50	02/63
6F	Machynlleth	09/63	12/66
6G	Llandudno Junction	04/52	10/66
6H	Bangor	04/52	06/65
6J	Holyhead	04/52	12/66
6K	Rhyl	04/52	02/63
7A	Llandudno Junction	01/48	04/52
7B	Bangor	01/48	04/52
7C	Holyhead	01/48	04/52
7D	Rhyl	01/48	04/52
8A	Edge Hill	01/48	05/68
8B	Warrington Dallam	01/48	10/67
8C	Speke Junction	01/48	05/68
8D	Widnes	01/48	05/64
8E	Brunswick	05/50	04/58
8E	Northwich	04/58	03/68
8F	Wigan Springs Branch	02/58	12/67
8G	Sutton Oak	02/58	06/67
8H	Birkenhead	09/63	11/67
8K	Bank Hall	09/63	11/66
8L	Aintree	09/63	06/67
8M	Southport	09/63	06/66
8P	Wigan	09/63	04/64
8R	Walton on the Hill	09/63	12/63
9A	Longsight	01/48	02/65
9B	Stockport Edgeley	01/48	05/68
9C	Macclesfield	01/48	06/61
9D	Buxton	01/48	09/63
9D	Newton Heath	09/63	07/68
9E	Trafford Park	05/50	12/56
9E	Trafford Park	04/58	03/68
9F	Heaton Mersey	05/50	12/56
9F	Heaton Mersey	04/58	05/68
9G	Northwich	05/50	04/58
9G	Gorton	04/58	06/65
9H	Gorton	02/58	04/58
9H	Patricroft	09/63	07/68
9J	Agecroft	09/63	11/66
9K	Bolton	09/63	06/68
9L	Buxton	09/63	03/68
9M	Bury	09/63	04/65
9P	Lees Oldham	09/63	04/64
10A	Wigan Springs Branch	01/48	02/58
10A	Carnforth	09/63	08/68
10B	Preston	01/48	02/58
10B	Blackpool Central	09/63	11/64
10C	Patricroft	01/48	02/58
10C	Fleetwood	09/63	02/66
10D	Plodder Lane	01/48	10/54
10D	Sutton Oak	10/55	02/58
10D	Lostock Hall	09/63	08/68
10E	Sutton Oak	01/48	10/55
10F	Wigan Lower Ince	05/50	03/52
10F	Rose Grove	09/63	08/68
10G	Skipton	09/63	04/67
10H	Lower Darwen	09/63	02/66
10J	Lancaster	09/63	04/66
11A	Carnforth	01/48	04/58
11A	Barrow	04/58	09/60
11B	Barrow	01/48	04/58
11B	Workington	04/58	09/60
11C	Oxenholme	01/50	06/60
11D	Oxenholme	01/48	01/50
11D	Tebay	01/50	06/60
11E	Tebay	01/48	01/50
11E	Lancaster	10/51	03/57
12A	Carlisle Kingmoor	01/48	01/49
12A	Carlisle Upperby	01/50	02/58
12A	Carlisle Kingmoor	02/58	01/68
12B	Carlisle Upperby	01/48	01/50
12B	Carlisle Canal	01/50	10/51
12B	Penrith	10/55	12/55
12B	Carlisle Upperby	02/58	12/66
12C	Penrith	01/48	10/55
12C	Workington	10/55	04/58
12C	Carlisle Canal	04/58	06/63
12C	Barrow	09/63	12/66
12D	Workington	01/48	10/55
12D	Carlisle Canal	02/58	04/58
12D	Kirkby Stephen	04/58	11/61
12D	Workington	09/63	01/68
12E	Moor Row	01/48	07/54
12E	Kirkby Stephen	02/58	04/58
12E	Barrow	09/60	09/63
12E	Tebay	09/63	01/68
12F	Beattock	01/48	01/49
12F	Workington	09/60	09/63
12G	Dumfries	01/48	01/49
12G	Oxenholme	06/60	06/62
12H	Stranraer	01/48	01/49
12H	Tebay	06/60	09/63
13A	Plaistow	01/48	01/50
13A	Trafford Park	01/50	05/50
13B	Devons Road	01/48	01/50
13B	Belle Vue	01/50	05/50
13C	Tilbury	01/48	01/50
13C	Heaton Mersey	01/50	05/50
13D	Shoeburyness	01/48	01/50
13D	Northwich	01/50	05/50
13E	Upminster	01/48	01/50
13E	Brunswick	01/50	05/50
13F	Walton on the Hill	01/50	05/50
13G	Wigan Lower Ince	01/50	05/50
14A	Cricklewood	01/48	09/63
14A	Cricklewood	11/64	12/64
14B	Kentish Town	01/48	04/63
14B	Cricklewood	09/63	11/64
14C	St. Albans	01/48	02/60
14D	Neasden	02/58	06/62
14E	Bedford	04/58	08/63
15A	Wellingborough	01/48	09/63
15A	Leicester Midland	09/63	06/66
15B	Kettering	01/48	09/63
15B	Wellingborough	09/63	06/66
15C	Leicester Midland	01/48	09/63
15C	Kettering	09/63	06/65
15D	Bedford	01/48	04/58
15D	Coalville	04/58	09/63
15D	Leicester Central	09/63	07/64
15E	Leicester Central	02/58	09/63
15E	Coalville	09/63	10/65
15F	Market Harborough	04/58	12/65
16A	Nottingham	01/48	09/63
16A	Toton	09/63	11/66
16B	Spital Bridge	01/48	08/50
16B	Kirkby in Ashfield	10/55	09/63
16B	Annesley	09/63	01/66
16B	Colwick	01/66	07/67
16C	Kirkby in Ashfield	01/48	10/55
16C	Mansfield	10/55	04/60
16C	Derby	09/63	03/67
16D	Mansfield	01/48	10/55
16D	Annesley	02/58	09/63
16D	Nottingham	09/63	04/65
16E	Kirkby in Ashfield	09/63	10/66
16F	Burton	09/63	09/66
16G	Westhouses	09/63	10/66
16H	Hasland	09/63	10/64
16J	Rowsley	09/63	05/64
17A	Derby	01/48	09/63
17B	Burton	01/48	09/63
17C	Coalville	01/48	04/58
17C	Rowsley	04/58	09/63
17D	Rowsley	01/48	04/58
17E	Heaton Mersey	12/56	04/58
17F	Trafford Park	12/56	04/58
18A	Toton	01/48	09/63
18B	Westhouses	01/48	09/63
18C	Hasland	01/48	09/63
18D	Staveley Barrow Hill	01/48	02/58
19A	Sheffield Grimesthorpe	01/48	02/58
19B	Millhouses	01/48	02/58
19C	Canklow	01/48	02/58
19D	Heaton Mersey	01/48	01/50
19E	Belle Vue	01/48	01/50
19F	York (LMS)	01/48	01/50
19G	Trafford Park	01/48	01/50
20A	Leeds Holbeck	01/48	09/56
20B	Stourton	01/48	09/56
20C	Royston	01/48	09/56
20D	Normanton	01/48	09/56
20E	Manningham	01/48	09/56
20F	Skipton	01/48	01/50
20F	Skipton	10/51	03/57
20G	Hellifield	01/48	01/50
20G	Hellifield	10/51	03/57
20H	Lancaster	01/48	01/50
21A	Saltley	01/48	09/63
21B	Bournville	01/48	02/60
21B	Bescot	06/60	09/63
21C	Bromsgrove	01/48	02/58
21C	Bushbury	06/60	09/63
21D	Stratford on Avon	01/48	02/53
21D	Aston	06/60	09/63
21E	Monument Lane	06/60	09/63
21F	Walsall	06/60	09/63
22A	Bristol Barrow Road	01/48	02/58
22B	Gloucester Barnwood	01/48	02/58
22C	Bath Green Park	01/48	01/50
22D	Templecombe	01/48	01/50
22E	Highbridge	01/48	01/50
23A	Bank Hall	01/48	01/50
23A	Skipton	01/50	10/51
23B	Aintree	01/48	01/50
23B	Hellifield	01/50	10/51
23C	Southport	01/48	01/50
23C	Lancaster	01/50	10/51
23D	Wigan	01/48	01/50
24A	Accrington	01/48	03/61
24B	Rose Grove	01/48	09/63
24C	Lostock Hall	01/48	09/63
24D	Lower Darwen	01/48	09/63
24E	Blackpool Central	01/48	01/50
24E	Blackpool Central	04/52	09/63
24F	Fleetwood	01/48	01/50
24F	Fleetwood	04/52	09/63
24G	Skipton	03/57	09/63
24H	Hellifield	03/57	06/63
24J	Lancaster	03/57	09/63
24K	Preston	02/58	09/61
24L	Carnforth	04/58	09/63
25A	Wakefield	01/48	09/56
25B	Huddersfield	01/48	09/56
25C	Goole	01/48	09/56
25D	Mirfield	01/48	09/56
25E	Sowerby Bridge	01/48	09/56
25F	Low Moor	01/48	09/56
25G	Farnley Junction	01/48	09/56
26A	Newton Heath	01/48	09/63
26B	Agecroft	01/48	09/63
26C	Bolton	01/48	09/63
26D	Bury	01/48	09/63
26E	Bacup	01/48	10/54
26E	Lees Oldham	10/55	09/63
26F	Lees Oldham	01/48	10/55
26F	Belle Vue	10/55	04/56
26F	Patricroft	02/58	09/63
26G	Belle Vue	05/50	10/55
27A	Polmadie	01/48	01/49
27A	Bank Hall	01/50	09/63
27B	Greenock Ladyburn	01/48	01/49
27B	Aintree	01/50	09/63
27C	Hamilton	01/48	01/49
27C	Southport	01/50	09/63
27D	Wigan	01/50	09/63
27E	Walton on the Hill	05/50	09/63
27F	Brunswick	04/58	09/61
28A	Motherwell	01/48	01/49
28A	Blackpool Central	01/50	04/52
28B	Dalry Road	01/48	01/49
28B	Fleetwood	01/50	04/52
28C	Carstairs	01/48	01/49
29A	Perth	01/48	01/49
29B	Aberdeen Ferryhill	01/48	01/49
29C	Dundee West	01/48	01/49
29D	Forfar	01/48	01/49
30A	Corkerhill	01/48	01/49
30A	Stratford	01/50	09/62
30B	Hurlford	01/48	01/49
30B	Hertford East	01/50	11/60
30C	Ardrossan	01/48	01/49
30C	Bishops Stortford	01/50	11/60
30D	Ayr	01/48	01/49
30D	Southend Victoria	01/50	02/59
30E	Colchester	01/50	10/59
30F	Parkeston	01/50	01/61
31A	St. Rollox	01/48	01/49
31A	Cambridge	01/50	06/62
31B	Stirling	01/48	01/49
31B	March	01/50	11/63
31C	Oban	01/48	01/49
31C	Kings Lynn	01/50	07/62
31D	Grangemouth	01/48	01/49
31D	South Lynn	01/50	03/59
31E	Dawsholm	01/48	01/49
31E	Bury St. Edmunds	01/50	01/59
31F	Spital Bridge	04/58	01/60
32A	Inverness	01/48	01/49
32A	Norwich Thorpe	01/50	03/62
32B	Aviemore	01/48	01/49
32B	Ipswich	01/50	10/59
32C	Forres	01/48	01/49
32C	Lowestoft	01/50	12/60
32D	Yarmouth South Town	01/50	11/59
32E	Yarmouth Vauxhall	01/50	01/59
32F	Yarmouth Beach	01/50	03/59
32G	Melton Constable	01/50	03/59
33A	Plaistow	01/50	10/59
33B	Tilbury	01/50	06/62
33C	Shoeburyness	01/50	08/62
34A	Kings Cross	01/50	06/63
34B	Hornsey	01/50	07/61
34C	Hatfield	01/50	01/61
34D	Hitchin	01/50	06/61
34E	Neasden	01/50	02/58
34E	New England	04/58	01/65
34F	Grantham	04/58	09/63
35A	New England	01/50	04/58
35B	Grantham	01/50	04/58
35C	Spital Bridge	08/50	04/58
36A	Doncaster	01/50	06/66
36B	Mexborough	01/50	04/58
36C	Frodingham	01/50	02/66
36D	Barnsley	01/50	04/58
36E	Retford	01/50	06/65
37A	Ardsley	01/50	09/56
37B	Copley Hill	01/50	09/56
37C	Bradford Hammerton St	01/50	09/56
38A	Colwick	01/50	04/58
38B	Annesley	01/50	02/58
38C	Leicester Central	01/50	02/58
38D	Staveley	01/50	04/58
38E	Woodford Halse	01/50	02/58
39A	Gorton	01/50	02/58
39B	Sheffield Darnall	01/50	12/55
40A	Lincoln	01/50	01/64
40B	Immingham	01/50	02/66
40C	Louth	01/50	12/56
40D	Tuxford Junction	01/50	04/58
40E	Langwith Junction	01/50	04/58
40E	Colwick	04/58	01/66
40F	Boston	01/50	01/64
41A	Sheffield Darnall	12/55	04/64
41B	Sheffield Grimesthorpe	02/58	09/61
41C	Millhouses	02/58	01/62
41D	Canklow	02/58	06/65
41E	Staveley Barrow Hill	02/58	10/65
41F	Mexborough	04/58	03/64
41G	Barnsley	04/58	01/60
41H	Staveley	04/58	11/66
41J	Langwith Junction	04/58	02/66
41K	Tuxford Junction	04/58	02/59
50A	York	01/50	06/67
50B	Leeds Neville Hill	01/50	01/60
50B	Hull Dairycoates	01/60	06/67
50C	Selby	01/50	09/59
50C	Hull Botanic Gardens	01/60	11/67
50D	Starbeck	01/50	09/59
50D	Goole	01/60	07/67
50E	Scarborough	01/50	05/63
50F	Malton	01/50	04/63
50G	Whitby	01/50	04/59
51A	Darlington	01/50	03/66
51B	Newport	01/50	06/58
51C	West Hartlepool	01/50	09/67
51D	Middlesbrough	01/50	06/58
51E	Stockton on Tees	01/50	06/59
51F	West Auckland	01/50	02/64
51G	Haverton Hill	01/50	06/59
51H	Kirkby Stephen	01/50	02/58
51J	Northallerton	01/50	03/63
51K	Saltburn	01/50	01/58
51L	Thornaby	06/58	11/64
52A	Gateshead	01/50	10/65
52B	Heaton	01/50	06/63
52C	Blaydon	01/50	06/63
52D	Tweedmouth	01/50	06/66
52E	Percy Main	01/50	02/65
52F	North Blyth	01/50	09/67
52G	Sunderland	10/58	09/67
52H	Tyne Dock	10/58	07/67
52J	Borough Gardens	10/58	06/59
52K	Consett	10/58	05/65
53A	Hull Dairycoates	01/50	01/60
53B	Hull Botanic Gardens	01/50	01/60
53C	Hull Springhead	01/50	11/58
53C	Hull Alexandra Dock	11/58	01/60
53D	Bridlington	01/50	06/58
53E	Cudworth	01/50	07/51
53E	Goole	09/56	01/60
54A	Sunderland	01/50	10/58
54B	Tyne Dock	01/50	10/58
54C	Borough Gardens	01/50	10/58
54D	Consett	01/50	10/58
55A	Leeds Holbeck	09/56	10/67
55B	Stourton	09/56	01/67
55C	Farnley Junction	09/56	11/66
55D	Royston	09/56	11/67
55E	Normanton	09/56	01/68
55F	Manningham	09/56	04/67
55G	Huddersfield	09/56	01/67
55H	Leeds Neville Hill	01/60	06/66
56A	Wakefield	09/56	07/67
56B	Ardsley	09/56	11/65
56C	Copley Hill	09/56	09/64
56D	Mirfield	09/56	04/67

56E	Sowerby Bridge	*09/56*	*01/64*
56F	Low Moor	*09/56*	*10/67*
56G	Bradford Hammerton St	*09/56*	*03/68*
60A	Inverness	*01/49*	*07/62*
60B	Aviemore	*01/49*	*12/62*
60C	Helmsdale	*01/49*	*07/62*
60D	Wick	*01/49*	*07/62*
60E	Forres	*01/49*	*01/64*
61A	Kittybrewster	*01/49*	*06/61*
61B	Aberdeen Ferryhill	*01/49*	*03/67*
61C	Keith	*01/49*	*06/61*
62A	Thornton Junction	*01/49*	*04/67*
62B	Dundee Tay Bridge	*01/49*	*04/67*
62C	Dunfermline Upper	*01/49*	*05/67*
63A	Perth	*01/49*	*05/67*
83B	Stirling	*01/49*	*06/60*
63B	Fort William	*06/60*	*08/62*
63C	Forfar	*01/49*	*11/59*
63C	Oban	*11/59*	*05/63*
63D	Fort William	*01/49*	*05/55*
63D	Oban	*05/55*	*11/59*
63E	Oban	*01/49*	*05/55*
64A	St. Margarets	*01/49*	*05/67*
64B	Haymarket	*01/49*	*09/63*
64C	Dalry Road	*01/49*	*10/65*
64D	Carstairs	*01/49*	*06/60*
64E	Polmont	*01/49*	*06/60*
64F	Bathgate	*01/49*	*12/66*
64G	Hawick	*01/49*	*01/66*
64H	Leith Central	*12/59*	*11/63*
65A	Eastfield	*01/49*	*11/66*
65B	St. Rollox	*01/49*	*11/66*
65C	Parkhead	*01/49*	*10/65*
65D	Dawsholm	*01/49*	*10/64*
65E	Kipps	*01/49*	*12/62*
65F	Grangemouth	*01/49*	*10/65*
65G	Yoker	*01/49*	*12/64*
65H	Helensburgh	*01/49*	*11/61*
65I	Balloch	*01/50*	*03/61*
65J	Balloch	*01/49*	*01/50*
65J	Fort William	*05/55*	*06/60*
65J	Stirling	*06/60*	*12/66*
65K	Polmont	*06/60*	*05/64*
66A	Polmadie	*01/49*	*05/67*
66B	Motherwell	*01/49*	*05/67*
66C	Hamilton	*01/49*	*11/62*
66D	Greenock Ladyburn	*01/49*	*12/66*
66E	Carstairs	*06/60*	*03/67*
66F	Beattock	*09/62*	*05/67*
67A	Corkerhill	*01/49*	*05/67*
67B	Hurlford	*01/49*	*12/66*
67C	Ayr	*01/49*	*12/66*
67D	Ardrossan	*01/49*	*02/65*
67E	Dumfries	*09/62*	*05/66*
67F	Stranraer	*09/62*	*12/66*
68A	Carlisle Kingmoor	*01/49*	*02/58*
68B	Dumfries	*01/49*	*09/62*
68C	Stranraer	*01/49*	*09/62*
68D	Beattock	*01/49*	*09/62*
68E	Carlisle Canal	*10/51*	*04/58*
70A	Nine Elms	*01/50*	*07/67*
70B	Feltham	*01/50*	*06/67*
70C	Guildford	*01/50*	*07/67*
70D	Basingstoke	*01/50*	*10/63*
70D	Eastleigh	*09/63*	*07/67*
70E	Reading South	*01/50*	*12/62*
70E	Salisbury	*12/62*	*07/67*
70F	Fratton	*10/54*	*11/59*
70F	Salisbury	*09/63*	*07/67*
70G	Newport IOW	*10/54*	*11/57*
70G	Weymouth	*09/63*	*07/67*
70H	Ryde IOW	*10/54*	*03/67*
70I	Southampton Docks	*09/63*	*02/66*
71A	Eastleigh	*01/50*	*09/63*
71B	Bournemouth	*01/50*	*09/63*
71C	Dorchester	*01/50*	*11/56*
71D	Fratton	*01/50*	*10/54*
71E	Newport IOW	*01/50*	*10/54*
71F	Ryde IOW	*01/50*	*10/54*
71G	Bath Green Park	*01/50*	*02/58*
71G	Weymouth	*02/58*	*09/63*
71H	Templecombe	*01/50*	*02/58*
71H	Yeovil Pen Mill	*02/58*	*01/59*
71I	Southampton Docks	*01/50*	*09/63*
71J	Highbridge	*03/52*	*02/58*
72A	Exmouth Junction	*01/50*	*09/63*
72B	Salisbury	*01/50*	*12/62*
72C	Yeovil Town	*01/50*	*09/63*
72D	Plymouth Friary	*01/50*	*02/58*
72E	Barnstaple Junction	*01/50*	*09/63*
72F	Wadebridge	*01/50*	*09/63*
73A	Stewarts Lane	*01/50*	*06/62*
73B	Bricklayers Arms	*01/50*	*06/62*
73C	Hither Green	*01/50*	*10/61*
73D	Gillingham	*01/50*	*06/59*
73E	Faversham	*01/50*	*06/62*
73F	Ashford	*10/58*	*06/62*
73G	Ramsgate	*10/58*	*06/59*
73H	Dover Marine	*10/58*	*06/61*
73J	Tonbridge	*10/58*	*01/65*
74A	Ashford	*01/50*	*10/58*
74B	Ramsgate	*01/50*	*10/58*
74C	Dover Marine	*01/50*	*10/58*
74D	Tonbridge	*01/50*	*10/58*
74E	St. Leonards	*01/50*	*06/58*
75A	Brighton	*01/50*	*06/64*
75B	Redhill	*01/50*	*06/65*
75C	Norwood Junction	*01/50*	*01/64*
75D	Horsham	*01/50*	*07/59*
75D	Stewarts Lane	*06/62*	*09/63*
75E	Three Bridges	*01/50*	*01/64*
75F	Tunbridge Wells West	*01/50*	*09/63*
75G	Eastbourne	*01/50*	*10/52*
81A	Old Oak Common	*01/50*	*03/65*
81B	Slough	*01/50*	*06/64*
81C	Southall	*01/50*	*11/65*
81D	Reading	*01/50*	*01/65*
81E	Didcot	*01/50*	*06/65*
81F	Oxford	*01/50*	*01/66*
82A	Bristol Bath Road	*01/50*	*09/60*
82B	St. Philips Marsh	*01/50*	*06/64*
82C	Swindon	*01/50*	*12/64*
82D	Westbury	*01/50*	*10/63*
82E	Yeovil Pen Mill	*01/50*	*02/58*
82E	Bristol Barrow Road	*02/50*	*11/65*
82F	Weymouth	*01/50*	*02/58*
82F	Bath Green Park	*02/58*	*03/66*
82G	Templecombe	*02/58*	*10/63*
83A	Newton Abbot	*01/50*	*09/62*
83B	Taunton	*01/50*	*05/64*
83C	Exeter	*01/50*	*10/63*
83C	Westbury	*10/63*	*09/65*
83D	Laira (Plymouth)	*01/50*	*09/63*
83D	Exmouth Junction	*09/63*	*05/65*
83E	St. Blazey	*01/50*	*09/63*
83E	Yeovil Town	*09/63*	*09/65*
83F	Truro	*01/50*	*09/63*
83F	Barnstaple Junction	*09/63*	*11/64*
83G	Penzance	*01/50*	*09/62*
83G	Templecombe	*10/63*	*03/66*
83H	Plymouth Friary	*02/58*	*05/63*
84A	Stafford Road	*01/50*	*09/63*
84A	Laira (Plymouth)	*09/63*	*05/64*
84B	Oxley	*01/50*	*09/63*
84C	Banbury	*01/50*	*09/63*
84C	Truro	*09/63*	*10/65*
84D	Leamington Spa	*01/50*	*09/63*
84E	Tyseley	*01/50*	*09/63*
84E	Wadebridge	*09/63*	*11/64*
84F	Stourbridge	*01/50*	*09/63*
84G	Shrewsbury	*01/50*	*01/61*
84G	Kidderminster	*01/61*	*09/63*
84H	Wellington	*01/50*	*09/63*
84J	Croes Newydd	*01/50*	*01/61*
84K	Chester (GWR)	*01/50*	*02/58*
84K	Wrexham Rhosddu	*02/58*	*01/60*
85A	Worcester	*01/50*	*12/65*
85B	Gloucester	*01/50*	*12/65*
85C	Hereford	*01/50*	*01/61*
85C	Gloucester Barnwood	*01/61*	*05/64*
85D	Kidderminster	*01/50*	*01/61*
85D	Bromsgrove	*01/61*	*09/64*
85E	Gloucester Barnwood	*02/58*	*01/61*
85F	Bromsgrove	*02/58*	*01/61*
86A	Ebbw Junction	*01/50*	*09/63*
86B	Newport Pill	*01/50*	*06/63*
86B	Ebbw Junction	*09/63*	*10/65*
86C	Cardiff Canton	*01/50*	*01/61*
86C	Hereford	*01/61*	*11/64*
86D	Llantrisant	*01/50*	*01/61*
86E	Severn Tunnel Junction	*01/50*	*12/65*
86F	Tondu	*01/50*	*01/61*
86F	Aberbeeg	*01/61*	*12/64*
86G	Pontypool Road	*01/50*	*05/65*
86H	Aberbeeg	*01/50*	*01/61*
86J	Aberdare	*01/50*	*01/61*
86K	Abergavenny	*01/50*	*11/54*
86K	Tredegar	*11/54*	*06/60*
87A	Neath	*01/50*	*09/65*
87B	Duffryn Yard	*01/50*	*03/64*
87C	Danygraig	*01/50*	*03/64*
87D	Swansea East Dock	*01/50*	*07/64*
87E	Landore	*01/50*	*06/61*
87F	Llanelly	*01/50*	*10/65*
87G	Carmarthen	*01/50*	*04/64*
87H	Neyland	*01/50*	*12/63*
87H	Whitland	*10/63*	*01/66*
87J	Fishguard Goodwick	*01/50*	*12/63*
87K	Swansea Victoria	*01/50*	*09/59*
88A	Cardiff Cathays	*01/50*	*12/57*
88A	Radyr	*12/57*	*01/61*
88A	Cardiff Canton	*01/61*	*09/63*
88A	Cardiff East Dock	*09/63*	*08/65*
88B	Cardiff East Dock	*01/50*	*01/61*
88B	Cardiff Cathays	*01/61*	*03/62*
88B	Radyr	*03/62*	*07/65*
88C	Barry	*01/50*	*09/64*
88D	Merthyr	*01/50*	*10/64*
88D	Rhymney	*11/64*	*04/65*
88E	Abercynon	*01/50*	*11/64*
88F	Treherbert	*01/50*	*03/65*
88G	Llantrisant	*01/61*	*10/64*
88H	Tondu	*01/61*	*04/64*
88J	Aberdare	*01/61*	*03/65*
88K	Brecon	*01/61*	*12/62*
88L	Cardiff East Dock	*03/62*	*09/63*
88M	Cardiff Cathays	*03/62*	*11/64*
89A	Oswestry	*01/50*	*01/61*
89A	Shrewsbury	*01/61*	*09/63*
89B	Brecon	*01/50*	*11/59*
89B	Croes Newydd	*01/61*	*09/63*
89C	Machynlleth	*01/50*	*09/63*
89D	Oswestry	*01/61*	*09/63*

Below: GNR Ivatt 'J5' class 0-6-0 No 65497 on a Derby train at Nottingham Victoria on 13 September 1952. *J. F. Henton*

Below right: LBSCR Stroudley 'E1' class 0-6-0T No 32694 at Eastleigh on 1 May 1954. *R. Broughton*

Ex-LNER unofficial shed codes

Code	Shed	From	To
ABD	Aberdeen Ferryhill	01/48	01/49
ALN	Alnmouth	01/48	01/50
ALS	Alston	01/48	01/50
ANN	Annesley	01/48	01/50
ARD	Ardsley	01/48	01/50
AUK	West Auckland	01/48	01/50
BFD	Bradford Hammerton St	01/48	01/50
BGT	Bathgate	01/48	01/49
BID	Bidston	01/48	01/50
BLA	Blaydon	01/48	01/50
BOR	Borough Gardens	01/48	01/50
BOS	Boston	01/48	01/50
BOW	Bowes Bridge	01/48	01/50
BRI	Bridlington	01/48	01/50
BRN	Barnsley	01/48	01/50
BSE	Bury St. Edmunds	01/48	01/50
CAM	Cambridge	01/48	01/50
CAR	Carlisle Canal	01/48	01/50
CHR	Chester Northgate	01/48	01/50
CLK	Colwick	01/48	01/50
COL	Colchester	01/48	01/50
CON	Consett	01/48	01/50
COP	Copley Hill	01/48	01/50
CUD	Cudworth	01/48	01/50
DAR	Darlington	01/48	01/50
DEE	Dundee Tay Bridge	01/48	01/49
DFU	Dunfermline Upper	01/48	01/49
DNS	Duns	01/48	01/49
DON	Doncaster	01/48	01/50
DUR	Durham	01/48	01/50
EFD	Eastfield	01/48	01/49
FRO	Frodingham	01/48	01/50
FW	Fort William	01/48	01/49
GHD	Gateshead	01/48	01/50
GOR	Gorton	01/48	01/50
GRA	Grantham	01/48	01/50
GUI	Guisborough	01/48	01/50
HAT	Hatfield	01/48	01/50
HAV	Haverton Hill	01/48	01/50
HAW	Hawick	01/48	01/49
HAY	Haymarket	01/48	01/49
HEX	Hexham	01/48	01/50
HIT	Hitchin	01/48	01/50
HLA	Hull Alexandra Dock	01/48	01/50
HLB	Hull Botanic Gardens	01/48	01/50
HLD	Hull Dairycoates	01/48	01/50
HLS	Hull Springhead	01/48	01/50
HSY	Hornsey	01/48	01/50
HTN	Heaton	01/48	01/50
ILK	Ilkley	01/48	01/50
IMM	Immingham	01/48	01/50
IPS	Ipswich	01/48	01/50
KBY	Kirkby Stephen	01/48	01/50
KEI	Keith	01/48	01/49
KIT	Kittybrewster	01/48	01/49
KL	Kings Lynn	01/48	01/50
KPS	Kipps	01/48	01/49
KX	Kings Cross	01/48	01/50
LEI	Leicester Central	01/48	01/50
LEY	Leyburn	01/48	01/50
LIN	Lincoln	01/48	01/50
LIV	Brunswick	01/48	01/50
LNG	Langwith Junction	01/48	01/50
LOW	Lowestoft	01/48	01/50
LTH	Louth	01/48	01/50
MAL	Malton	01/48	01/50
MAR	March	01/48	01/50
MC	Melton Constable	01/48	01/50
MEX	Mexborough	01/48	01/50
MID	Middlesbrough	01/48	01/50
MIT	Middleton in Teesdale	01/48	01/50
NBH	North Blyth	01/48	01/50
NEA	Neasden	01/48	01/50
NEV	Leeds Neville Hill	01/48	01/50
NLN	Northallerton	01/48	01/50
NMN	Normanton	01/48	01/50
NOR	Norwich Thorpe	01/48	01/50
NPT	Newport	01/48	01/50
NTH	Northwich	01/48	01/50
NWE	New England	01/48	01/50
PAT	Pateley Bridge	01/48	01/50
PEL	Pelton Level	01/48	01/50
PKD	Parkhead	01/48	01/49
PKG	Pickering	01/48	01/50
PKS	Parkeston	01/48	01/50
PMN	Percy Main	01/48	01/50
POL	Polmont	01/48	01/49
PTH	Perth South	01/48	01/49
RBY	Rothbury	01/48	01/50
RET	Retford	01/48	01/50
RMH	Reedsmouth	01/48	01/50
SAL	Saltburn	01/48	01/50
SBH	South Blyth	01/48	01/50
SBK	Starbeck	01/48	01/50
SCA	Scarborough	01/48	01/50
SEL	Selby	01/48	01/50
SHF	Sheffield Darnall	01/48	01/50
SKN	Stockton on Tees	01/48	01/50
SL	South Lynn	01/48	01/50
STG	Stirling Shore Road	01/48	01/49
STM	St. Margarets	01/48	01/49
STP	Heaton Mersey	01/48	01/50
STR	Stratford	01/48	01/50
STV	Staveley	01/48	01/50
SUN	Sunderland	01/48	01/50
TDK	Tyne Dock	01/48	01/50
TFD	Trafford Park	01/48	01/50
THJ	Thornton Junction	01/48	01/49
TUX	Tuxford Junction	01/48	01/50
TWD	Tweedmouth	01/48	01/50
WAL	Walton on the Hill	01/48	01/50
WBY	Whitby	01/48	01/50
WFD	Woodford Halse	01/48	01/50
WHD	Wearhead	01/48	01/50
WHL	West Hartlepool	01/48	01/50
WIG	Wigan Lower Ince	01/48	01/50
WRX	Wrexham Rhosddu	01/48	01/50
YAR	Yarmouth South Town	01/48	01/50
YB	Yarmouth Beach	01/48	01/50
YK	York	01/48	01/50

Ex-SR unofficial shed codes

Code	Shed	From	To
3B	Three Bridges	01/48	01/50
9E	Nine Elms	01/48	01/50
AFD	Ashford	01/48	01/50
AND	Andover Junction	01/48	01/50
BA	Bricklayers Arms	01/48	01/50
BAS	Basingstoke	01/48	01/50
BAT	Stewarts Lane	01/48	01/50
BM	Bournemouth	01/48	01/50
BOG	Bognor	01/48	01/50
BPL	Barnstaple Junction	01/48	01/50
BTN	Brighton	01/48	01/50
BUD	Bude	01/48	01/50
CAL	Callington	01/48	01/50
CAN	Canterbury West	01/48	01/50
DOR	Dorchester	01/48	01/50
DOV	Dover Marine	01/48	01/50
EBN	Eastbourne	01/48	01/50
EKR	Shepherds Well	01/48	01/50
ELH	Eastleigh	01/48	01/50
EXJ	Exmouth Junction	01/48	01/50
EXM	Exmouth	01/48	01/50
FAV	Faversham	01/48	01/50
FEL	Feltham	01/48	01/50
FOL	Folkestone Junction	01/48	01/50
FRA	Fratton	01/48	01/50
GFD	Guildford	01/48	01/50
GIL	Gillingham	01/48	01/50
GOS	Gosport	01/48	01/50
HAM	Hamworthy Junction	01/48	01/50
HIT	Hither Green	01/48	01/50
HOR	Horsham	01/48	01/50
ILF	Ilfracombe	01/48	01/50
KESR	Rolvenden	01/48	01/50
LCN	Launceston (SR)	01/48	01/50
LR	Lyme Regis	01/48	01/50
LYM	Lymington	01/48	01/50
NHN	Newhaven	01/48	01/50
NOR	Norwood Junction	01/48	01/50
NPT	Newport IOW	01/48	01/50
NX	New Cross Gate	01/48	01/50
OKE	Okehampton	01/48	01/50
PLY	Plymouth Friary	01/48	01/50
RAM	Ramsgate	01/48	01/50
RDG	Reading South	01/48	01/50
RED	Redhill	01/48	01/50
RYD	Ryde IOW	01/48	01/50
SAL	Salisbury	01/48	01/50
SEA	Seaton	01/48	01/50
SOT	Southampton Docks	01/48	01/50
STL	St. Leonards	01/48	01/50
SWE	Swanage	01/48	01/50
TEM	Templecombe Upper	01/48	01/50
TON	Tonbridge	01/48	01/50
TOR	Torrington	01/48	01/50
TWW	Tunbridge Wells West	01/48	01/50
WAD	Wadebridge	01/48	01/50
WEY	Weymouth	01/48	01/50
WIN	Winchester City	01/48	01/50
YEO	Yeovil Town	01/48	01/50

Ex-GWR shed codes

Code	Shed	From	To
ABDR	Aberdare	01/48	01/50
ABEEG	Aberbeeg	01/48	01/50
ABH	Aberystwyth	01/48	01/50
AYN	Abercynon	01/48	01/50
BAN	Banbury	01/48	01/50
BCN	Brecon	01/48	01/50
BHD	Birkenhead	01/48	01/50
BRD	Bristol Bath Road	01/48	01/50
BRY	Barry	01/48	01/50
CARM	Carmarthen	01/48	01/50
CDF	Cardiff Canton	01/48	01/50
CED	Cardiff East Dock	01/48	01/50
CH	Dowlais Cae Harris	01/48	01/50
CHEL	Cheltenham	01/48	01/50
CHR	Chester (GWR)	01/48	01/50
CHYS	Cardiff Cathays	01/48	01/50
CNYD	Croes Newydd	01/48	01/50
DG	Danygraig	01/48	01/50
DID	Didcot	01/48	01/50
DYD	Duffryn Yard	01/48	01/50
EXE	Exeter	01/48	01/50
FDL	Ferndale	01/48	01/50
FGD	Fishguard Goodwick	01/48	01/50
GLO	Gloucester	01/48	01/50
HFD	Hereford	01/48	01/50
KDR	Kidderminster	01/48	01/50
LA	Laira (Plymouth)	01/48	01/50
LDR	Landore	01/48	01/50
LLY	Llanelly	01/48	01/50
LMTN	Leamington Spa	01/48	01/50
LTS	Llantrisant	01/48	01/50
LYD	Lydney	01/48	01/50
MCH	Machynlleth	01/48	01/50
MTHR	Merthyr	01/48	01/50
NA	Newton Abbot	01/48	01/50
NEA	Neath	01/48	01/50
NEY	Neyland	01/48	01/50
NPT	Ebbw Junction	01/48	01/50
OSW	Oswestry	01/48	01/50
OXF	Oxford	01/48	01/50
OXY	Oxley	01/48	01/50
PDN	Old Oak Common	01/48	01/50
PILL	Newport Pill	01/48	01/50
PPRD	Pontypool Road	01/48	01/50
PZ	Penzance	01/48	01/50
RDG	Reading	01/48	01/50
RHY	Rhymney	01/48	01/50
RYR	Radyr	01/48	01/50
SALOP	Shrewsbury	01/48	01/50
SBZ	St. Blazey	01/48	01/50
SDN	Swindon	01/48	01/50
SED	Swansea East Dock	01/48	01/50
SHL	Southall	01/48	01/50
SLO	Slough	01/48	01/50
SPM	St. Philips Marsh	01/48	01/50
SRD	Stafford Road	01/48	01/50
STB	Stourbridge	01/48	01/50
STJ	Severn Tunnel Junction	01/48	01/50
TDU	Tondu	01/48	01/50
THT	Treherbert	01/48	01/50
TN	Taunton	01/48	01/50
TR	Truro	01/48	01/50
TYS	Tyseley	01/48	01/50
WES	Westbury	01/48	01/50
WEY	Weymouth	01/48	01/50
WLN	Wellington	01/48	01/50
WOS	Worcester	01/48	01/50
WTD	Whitland	01/48	01/50
YEO	Yeovil Pen Mill	01/48	01/50

Above: Cleobury Mortimer & Ditton Priors Light Railway 0-6-0PT No 29 at its home depot of Kidderminster. It is fitted with a balloon type spark arrestor. *A. A. G. Delicata*

Below: Rhymney Railway 'AP' class 0-6-2T No 78 at Rhymney in June 1949 shortly before rebuilding with a GWR boiler. *P. Ransome-Wallis*

Right: A line-up of panner tanks at Old Oak Common on 16 August 1959. *R. C. Riley*

Former GWR Locomotives

Above: Rhymney Railway 'S' class 0-6-0T No 95 at 88B Cardiff East Dock on 5 May 1951. *H. C. Casserley*

Left: Cardiff Railway 0-6-2T No 155 carrying the GWR taper boiler it received in 1928. *F. W. Day*

Below: Barry Railway 'B1' class 0-6-2T No 261.

		1948		1951	1954	1957	1960	1963	1966
1	*YTW*	→		**87C** Danygraig	**87C** Danygraig				
3	*Cor*	**MCH**	Maespoeth						
4	*Cor*	**MCH**	Maespoeth						
5	*WCP*	**SPM**	St. Philips Marsh	**82C** Swindon	**82C** Swindon				
6	*WCP*	**SPM**	St. Philips Marsh						
7	*VoR*	**ABH**	Aberystwyth (VoR)	**89C** Aberystwyth (VoR)	**89C** Aberystwyth (VoR)	**89C** Aberystwyth (VoR)	**89C** Aberystwyth (VoR)	**89C** Aberystwyth (VoR)	**6F** Aberystwyth (VoR)
8	*VoR*	**ABH**	Aberystwyth (VoR)	**89C** Aberystwyth (VoR)	**89C** Aberystwyth (VoR)	**89C** Aberystwyth (VoR)	**89C** Aberystwyth (VoR)	**89C** Aberystwyth (VoR)	**6F** Aberystwyth (VoR)
9	*VoR*	**ABH**	Aberystwyth (VoR)	**89C** Aberystwyth (VoR)	**89C** Aberystwyth (VoR)	**89C** Aberystwyth (VoR)	**89C** Aberystwyth (VoR)	**89C** Aberystwyth (VoR)	**6F** Aberystwyth (VoR)
28	*CMDP*	**KDR**	Kidderminster	**85D** Kidderminster					
29	*CMDP*	**KDR**	Kidderminster	**85D** Kidderminster	**85D** Kidderminster				
30	*RR*[1]	**RYR**	Radyr						
31	*RR*[1]	**CED**	Cardiff East Dock	**88A** Cardiff Cathays					
32	*RR*[1]	**RYR**	Radyr						
33	*RR*[2]	**CED**	Cardiff East Dock	**88B** Cardiff East Dock					
34	*RR*[1]	**RYR**	Radyr						
35	*RR*[3]	**RYR**	Radyr	**88A** Cardiff Cathays	**88B** Cardiff East Dock				
36	*RR*[3]	**CED**	Cardiff East Dock	**88B** Cardiff East Dock	**88B** Cardiff East Dock	**88B** Cardiff East Dock			
37	*RR*[3]	**CED**	Cardiff East Dock	**88B** Cardiff East Dock	**88B** Cardiff East Dock				
38	*RR*[3]	**RYR**	Radyr	**88A** Cardiff Cathays	**88B** Cardiff East Dock	**88B** Cardiff East Dock			
39	*RR*[3]	**RHY**	Rhymney	**88B** Cardiff East Dock	**88B** Cardiff East Dock				
40	*RR*[3]	**RYR**	Radyr	**88A** Cardiff Cathays					
41	*RR*[3]	**RYR**	Radyr	**88A** Cardiff Cathays	**88B** Cardiff East Dock				
42	*RR*[3]	**RYR**	Radyr	**88A** Cardiff Cathays	**88A** Cardiff Cathays	**88B** Cardiff East Dock			
43	*RR*[3]	**RYR**	Radyr	**88A** Cardiff Cathays	**88A** Cardiff Cathays	**88B** Cardiff East Dock			
44	*RR*[3]	**RYR**	Radyr	**88A** Cardiff Cathays	**88A** Cardiff Cathays				
46	*RR*[1]	**RYR**	Radyr						
47	*RR*[2]	**CED**	Cardiff East Dock						
51	*RR*[2]	**CED**	Cardiff East Dock						
52	*RR*[4]	**CED**	Cardiff East Dock						
53	*RR*[4]	**CED**	Cardiff East Dock						
54	*RR*[4]	**CED**	Cardiff East Dock						
55	*RR*[4]	**CED**	Cardiff East Dock	**88B** Cardiff East Dock					
56	*RR*[4]	**RYR**	Radyr	**88A** Cardiff Cathays					
57	*RR*[4]	**BRY**	Barry	**88C** Barry					
58	*RR*[4]	**BRY**	Barry	**88C** Barry	**88B** Cardiff East Dock				
59	*RR*[4]	**BRY**	Barry	**88C** Barry	**88B** Cardiff East Dock				
60	*RR*[4]	**DG**	Danygraig	**87C** Danygraig					
61	*RR*[4]	**CED**	Cardiff East Dock						
62	*RR*[4]	**PILL**	Newport Pill						
63	*RR*[4]	**RYR**	Radyr	**88A** Cardiff Cathays					
64	*RR*[4]	**RYR**	Radyr						
65	*RR*[4]	**ABDR**	Aberdare	**86J** Aberdare	**88B** Cardiff East Dock				
66	*RR*[4]	**CED**	Cardiff East Dock	**88B** Cardiff East Dock	**88B** Cardiff East Dock				
67	*RR*[4]	**RHY**	Rhymney	**88B** Cardiff East Dock					
68	*RR*[4]	**CED**	Cardiff East Dock	**88B** Cardiff East Dock	**88B** Cardiff East Dock				
69	*RR*[4]	**DYD**	Duffryn Yard	**87B** Duffryn Yard	**87B** Duffryn Yard				
70	*RR*[4]	**DYD**	Duffryn Yard	**87B** Duffryn Yard	**87B** Duffryn Yard				
71	*RR*[4]	**DG**	Danygraig						
72	*RR*[4]	**CED**	Cardiff East Dock	**88B** Cardiff East Dock					
73	*RR*[4]	**CED**	Cardiff East Dock	**88B** Cardiff East Dock					
74	*RR*[4]	**CED**	Cardiff East Dock	**88B** Cardiff East Dock					
75	*RR*[4]	**NEA**	Neath	**87A** Neath					
76	*RR*[5]	**RHY**	Rhymney						
77	*RR*[5]	**RHY**	Rhymney	**88D** Merthyr					
78	*RR*[6]	**RHY**	Rhymney	**88D** Merthyr	**88D** Merthyr				
79	*RR*[6]	**RHY**	Rhymney	**88D** Merthyr	**88D** Merthyr				
80	*RR*[6]	**RHY**	Rhymney	**88D** Merthyr	**88A** Cardiff Cathays				
81	*RR*[6]	**RHY**	Rhymney	**88D** Merthyr	**88D** Merthyr				
82	*RR*[7]	**RHY**	Rhymney	**88D** Merthyr	**88B** Cardiff East Dock				
83	*RR*[7]	**CH**	Dowlais Cae Harris	**88D** Merthyr	**88B** Cardiff East Dock				
90	*RR*[8]	**CED**	Cardiff East Dock	**88B** Cardiff East Dock	**88B** Cardiff East Dock				
91	*RR*[8]	**CED**	Cardiff East Dock	**88B** Cardiff East Dock	**88B** Cardiff East Dock				
92	*RR*[8]	**CED**	Cardiff East Dock	**88B** Cardiff East Dock	**88B** Cardiff East Dock				
93	*RR*[9]	**CED**	Cardiff East Dock	**88B** Cardiff East Dock	**88B** Cardiff East Dock				
94	*RR*[9]	**CED**	Cardiff East Dock	**88B** Cardiff East Dock	**88B** Cardiff East Dock				
95	*RR*[9]	**CED**	Cardiff East Dock	**88B** Cardiff East Dock					
96	*RR*[9]	**CED**	Cardiff East Dock	**88B** Cardiff East Dock	**88B** Cardiff East Dock				
100 A1	*4073*	**PDN**	Old Oak Common						
111	*4073*	**PDN**	Old Oak Common	**83D** Laira (Plymouth)					
155	*Car*[1]	**CED**	Cardiff East Dock	**88B** Cardiff East Dock					
184	*PT*[1]	**DYD**	Duffryn Yard						
190	*AD*[1]	**PILL**	Newport Pill						
193	*TV*[1]	**THT**	Treherbert	**88F** Treherbert					
194	*TV*[1]	**THT**	Treherbert	**88F** Treherbert					
195	*TV*[1]	**THT**	Treherbert	**88F** Treherbert					
198	*BR*[1]	**RYR**	Radyr						
200	*TV*[2]	**CDF**	Cardiff Canton						
201	*TV*[2]	**CHYS**	Cardiff Cathays						
202	*TV*[2]	**THT**	Treherbert						
203	*TV*[2]	**CDF**	Cardiff Canton	**86C** Cardiff Canton					
204	*TV*[2]	**ABDR**	Aberdare	**86J** Aberdare	**88B** Cardiff East Dock				
205	*TV*[2]	**CDF**	Cardiff Canton	**86C** Cardiff Canton	**86C** Cardiff Canton				
206	*TV*[2]	**ABDR**	Aberdare						
207	*TV*[2]	**FDL**	Ferndale	**88F** Treherbert					
208	*TV*[2]	**CDF**	Cardiff Canton	**86C** Cardiff Canton	**86J** Aberdare				
209	*TV*[2]	**CDF**	Cardiff Canton	**86C** Cardiff Canton					
210	*TV*[2]	**CED**	Cardiff East Dock	**88F** Treherbert	**88B** Cardiff East Dock				
211	*TV*[2]	**CH**	Dowlais Cae Harris	**88D** Merthyr	**88B** Cardiff East Dock				
212	*BR*[1]	**CED**	Cardiff East Dock						
213	*BR*[1]	**BRY**	Barry						
215	*TV*[2]	**FDL**	Ferndale	**88F** Treherbert	**88B** Cardiff East Dock				
216	*TV*[2]	**FDL**	Ferndale	**88F** Treherbert	**88B** Cardiff East Dock				
217	*TV*[2]	**MTHR**	Merthyr	**88D** Merthyr					
218	*TV*[2]	**FDL**	Ferndale	**88E** Abercynon					
219	*TV*[2]	**AYN**	Abercynon	**88E** Abercynon					
220	*TV*[2]	**CDF**	Cardiff Canton	**86C** Cardiff Canton					
231	*BR*[1]	**BRY**	Barry						
236	*TV*[2]	**AYN**	Abercynon	**88E** Abercynon					
238	*BR*[2]	**CDF**	Cardiff Canton						
240	*BR*[2]	**RYR**	Radyr	**88C** Barry					
246	*BR*[2]	**RYR**	Radyr						
248	*BR*[2]	**BRY**	Barry						
258	*BR*[2]	**RYR**	Radyr						
259	*BR*[2]	**CED**	Cardiff East Dock						
261	*BR*[2]	**BRY**	Barry						
262	*BR*[2]	**BRY**	Barry						
263	*BR*[2]	**BRY**	Barry	**88C** Barry					
265	*BR*[2]	**BRY**	Barry						
267	*BR*[2]	**BRY**	Barry	**88C** Barry					
268	*BR*[2]	**BRY**	Barry						
269	*BR*[2]	**CED**	Cardiff East Dock						
270	*BR*[2]	**BRY**	Barry	**88C** Barry					
271	*BR*[2]	**BRY**	Barry	**88C** Barry					
272	*BR*[2]	**BRY**	Barry						

No.	Origin	1948	1951	1954	1957	1960	1963	1966
274	BR^2	**BRY** Barry	**88C** Barry					
275	BR^2	**BRY** Barry						
276	BR^2	**BRY** Barry	**88C** Barry					
277	BR^2	**BRY** Barry						
278	TV^2	**FDL** Ferndale	**88F** Treherbert					
279	TV^2	**FDL** Ferndale	**88F** Treherbert	**88B** Cardiff East Dock				
280	TV^2	**CDF** Cardiff Canton						
281	TV^2	**AYN** Abercynon						
282	TV^2	**ABDR** Aberdare	**86J** Aberdare	**86J** Aberdare				
283	TV^2	**FDL** Ferndale						
284	TV^2	**ABDR** Aberdare	**86J** Aberdare					
285	TV^2	**CED** Cardiff East Dock	**88F** Treherbert					
286	TV^2	**BRY** Barry						
287	TV^2	**AYN** Abercynon						
288	TV^2	**AYN** Abercynon						
289	TV^2	**SED** Swansea East Dock						
290	TV^2	**THT** Treherbert	**88F** Treherbert	**88B** Cardiff East Dock				
291	TV^2	**DYD** Duffryn Yard						
292	TV^2	**RHY** Rhymney	**88D** Merthyr					
293	TV^2	**RYR** Radyr	**88A** Cardiff Cathays					
294	TV^2	**DYD** Duffryn Yard						
295	TV^2	**AYN** Abercynon	**88E** Abercynon					
296	TV^2	**DYD** Duffryn Yard						
297	TV^2	**CED** Cardiff East Dock						
298	TV^2	**FDL** Ferndale						
299	TV^2	**FDL** Ferndale	**88F** Treherbert					
303	TV^3	**THT** Treherbert	**88F** Treherbert	**88C** Barry				
304	TV^3	**AYN** Abercynon	**88E** Abercynon	**88E** Abercynon	**88E** Abercynon			
305	TV^3	**CHYS** Cardiff Cathays	**88A** Cardiff Cathays	**88A** Cardiff Cathays	**88A** Cardiff Cathays			
306	TV^3	**BRY** Barry	**88C** Barry	**88C** Barry				
307	TV^3	**CHYS** Cardiff Cathays	**88A** Cardiff Cathays	**88A** Cardiff Cathays				
308	TV^3	**SED** Swansea East Dock	**87D** Swansea East Dock	**87D** Swansea East Dock				
309	TV^3	**SED** Swansea East Dock	**87D** Swansea East Dock					
312	TV^3	**BRY** Barry	**88C** Barry	**88C** Barry				
316	TV^3	**BRY** Barry	**88D** Merthyr	**88E** Abercynon				
322	TV^3	**BRY** Barry	**88C** Barry	**88E** Abercynon				
335	TV^3	**CDF** Cardiff Canton	**86C** Cardiff Canton	**88B** Cardiff East Dock				
337	TV^3	**AYN** Abercynon	**88E** Abercynon					
343	TV^3	**CHYS** Cardiff Cathays	**88A** Cardiff Cathays	**88A** Cardiff Cathays				
344	TV^3	**CHYS** Cardiff Cathays	**88A** Cardiff Cathays					
345	TV^3	**BRY** Barry	**88A** Cardiff Cathays	**88A** Cardiff Cathays				
346	TV^3	**CHYS** Cardiff Cathays	**88A** Cardiff Cathays	**88A** Cardiff Cathays				
347	TV^3	**CHYS** Cardiff Cathays	**88A** Cardiff Cathays	**88A** Cardiff Cathays				
348	TV^3	**CHYS** Cardiff Cathays	**88A** Cardiff Cathays	**88A** Cardiff Cathays				
349	TV^3	**PPRD** Pontypool Road	**86G** Pontypool Road	**86C** Cardiff Canton	**88E** Abercynon			
351	TV^3	**AYN** Abercynon	**88E** Abercynon	**88E** Abercynon				
352	TV^3	**THT** Treherbert	**88F** Treherbert	**88F** Treherbert				
356	TV^3	**AYN** Abercynon	**88E** Abercynon	**88E** Abercynon				
357	TV^3	**CDF** Cardiff Canton	**86C** Cardiff Canton	**88C** Barry				
359	LMM^1	**DG** Danygraig	**87C** Danygraig	**87C** Danygraig				
360	TV^3	**CHYS** Cardiff Cathays	**88A** Cardiff Cathays	**88A** Cardiff Cathays				
361	TV^3	**BRY** Barry	**88C** Barry	**88C** Barry	**88A** Cardiff Cathays			
362	TV^3	**ABDR** Aberdare	**86J** Aberdare	**88A** Cardiff Cathays				
364	TV^3	**CHYS** Cardiff Cathays	**88A** Cardiff Cathays	**88A** Cardiff Cathays	**88A** Cardiff Cathays			
365	TV^3	**THT** Treherbert	**88F** Treherbert	**88F** Treherbert				
366	TV^3	**THT** Treherbert	**88F** Treherbert	**88F** Treherbert				
367	TV^3	**CHYS** Cardiff Cathays	**88A** Cardiff Cathays	**88A** Cardiff Cathays				
368	TV^3	**THT** Treherbert	**88F** Treherbert	**88F** Treherbert				
370	TV^3	**RHY** Rhymney	**88D** Merthyr	**88E** Abercynon	**88E** Abercynon			
371	TV^3	**CHYS** Cardiff Cathays	**88A** Cardiff Cathays	**86C** Cardiff Canton				
372	TV^3	**BRY** Barry	**88C** Barry	**88C** Barry				
373	TV^3	**THT** Treherbert	**88C** Barry	**88C** Barry	**88E** Abercynon			
374	TV^3	**ABDR** Aberdare	**86J** Aberdare	**86C** Cardiff Canton				
375	TV^3	**RHY** Rhymney	**88D** Merthyr	**88C** Barry				
376	TV^3	**CHYS** Cardiff Cathays	**88A** Cardiff Cathays	**88B** Cardiff East Dock	**88A** Cardiff Cathays			
377	TV^3	**BRY** Barry	**88A** Cardiff Cathays	**88B** Cardiff East Dock				
378	TV^3	**THT** Treherbert	**88F** Treherbert	**88B** Cardiff East Dock				
379	TV^3	**BRY** Barry	**88C** Barry	**88E** Abercynon				
380	TV^3	**AYN** Abercynon	**88E** Abercynon	**88E** Abercynon				
381	TV^3	**CDF** Cardiff Canton	**86C** Cardiff Canton	**86C** Cardiff Canton	**88A** Cardiff Cathays			
382	TV^3	**BRY** Barry	**88C** Barry	**88C** Barry				
383	TV^3	**CHYS** Cardiff Cathays	**88A** Cardiff Cathays	**88A** Cardiff Cathays	**88A** Cardiff Cathays			
384	TV^3	**CHYS** Cardiff Cathays	**88A** Cardiff Cathays	**88A** Cardiff Cathays				
385	TV^3	**PPRD** Pontypool Road	**86G** Pontypool Road	**88E** Abercynon	**88A** Cardiff Cathays			
386	TV^3	**BRY** Barry	**88E** Abercynon	**88E** Abercynon				
387	TV^3	**BRY** Barry	**88C** Barry	**88C** Barry				
388	TV^3	**BRY** Barry	**88C** Barry	**88C** Barry				
389	TV^3	**BRY** Barry	**88C** Barry	**88C** Barry				
390	TV^3	**CHYS** Cardiff Cathays	**88A** Cardiff Cathays	**88C** Barry	**88E** Abercynon			
391	TV^3	**CHYS** Cardiff Cathays	**88A** Cardiff Cathays	**88A** Cardiff Cathays				
393	TV^3	**CHYS** Cardiff Cathays	**88A** Cardiff Cathays	**88C** Barry	**88E** Abercynon			
394	TV^3	**BRY** Barry	**88C** Barry	**88C** Barry				
397	TV^3	**AYN** Abercynon	**88E** Abercynon	**88E** Abercynon	**88E** Abercynon			
398	TV^3	**RHY** Rhymney	**88D** Merthyr	**88D** Merthyr	**88D** Merthyr			
399	TV^3	**THT** Treherbert	**88F** Treherbert	**88B** Cardiff East Dock				
410	TV^4	**CDF** Cardiff Canton						
411	TV^4	**CDF** Cardiff Canton						
421	BM^1	**PILL** Newport Pill						
422	BM^1	**STJ** Severn Tunnel Junction						
423	BM^1	**STJ** Severn Tunnel Junction						
424	BM^1	**PILL** Newport Pill						
425	BM^1	**PILL** Newport Pill	**86C** Cardiff Canton					
426	BM^1	**PILL** Newport Pill						
428	BM^1	**DYD** Duffryn Yard						
431	BM^2	**NPT** Ebbw Junction	**86A** Ebbw Junction					
432	BM^2	**NPT** Ebbw Junction	**86A** Ebbw Junction					
433	BM^2	**RYR** Radyr	**88A** Cardiff Cathays					
434	BM^2	**CHYS** Cardiff Cathays	**88A** Cardiff Cathays					
435	BM^2	**NPT** Ebbw Junction	**86A** Ebbw Junction	**86A** Ebbw Junction				
436	BM^2	**NPT** Ebbw Junction	**86A** Ebbw Junction	**86A** Ebbw Junction				
666	AD^2	**PILL** Newport Pill	**86B** Newport Pill	**86B** Newport Pill				
667	AD^2	**PILL** Newport Pill	**86B** Newport Pill	**86B** Newport Pill				
680	AD^3	**OSW** Oswestry						
681	Car^2	**CED** Cardiff East Dock	**88B** Cardiff East Dock	**88B** Cardiff East Dock				
682	Car^2	**CED** Cardiff East Dock	**88B** Cardiff East Dock					
683	Car^2	**CED** Cardiff East Dock	**88B** Cardiff East Dock	**88B** Cardiff East Dock				
684	Car^2	**CED** Cardiff East Dock	**88B** Cardiff East Dock	**88B** Cardiff East Dock				
783	BR^3	**BRY** Barry						
784	BR^3	**BRY** Barry						
803	LMM^2	**DG** Danygraig	**87C** Danygraig					
822	W&L	**OSW** Welshpool (WLLR)	**89A** Welshpool (WLLR)	**89A** Welshpool (WLLR)	**89A** Oswestry	**89A** Oswestry		
823	W&L	**OSW** Welshpool (WLLR)	**89A** Welshpool (WLLR)	**89A** Welshpool (WLLR)	**89A** Oswestry	**89A** Oswestry		
844	Cam^1	**OSW** Oswestry	**89A** Oswestry	**89A** Oswestry				
849	Cam^1	**OSW** Oswestry	**89A** Oswestry	**89C** Machynlleth				

		1948	1951	1954	1957	1960	1963	1966
855	*Cam[1]*	**OSW** Oswestry	**89A** Oswestry	**89A** Oswestry				
864	*Cam[1]*	**MCH** Machynlleth	**89C** Machynlleth					
873	*Cam[1]*	**OSW** Oswestry	**89A** Oswestry	**89A** Oswestry				
887	*Cam[1]*	**OSW** Oswestry	**89A** Oswestry					
892	*Cam[1]*	**OSW** Oswestry	**89C** Machynlleth					
893	*Cam[1]*	**OSW** Oswestry	**89A** Oswestry					
894	*Cam[1]*	**MCH** Machynlleth	**89C** Machynlleth					
895	*Cam[1]*	**OSW** Oswestry	**89A** Oswestry	**89A** Oswestry				
896	*Cam[1]*	**OSW** Oswestry	**89A** Oswestry					
906	*1854*	**NEA** Neath						
907	*1854*	**DID** Didcot	**81E** Didcot					
992	*1901*	**SDN** Swindon	**82C** Swindon					
1000	*1000*	**PDN** Old Oak Common	**81A** Old Oak Common	**84K** Chester (GWR)	**82A** Bristol Bath Road	**82A** Bristol Bath Road	**82B** St. Philips Marsh	
1001	*1000*	**NA** Newton Abbot	**87H** Neyland	**87H** Neyland	**87H** Neyland	**87H** Neyland	**87H** Neyland	
1002	*1000*	**BRD** Bristol Bath Road	**82A** Bristol Bath Road	**83G** Penzance	**83G** Penzance	**83G** Penzance	**89A** Shrewsbury	
1003	*1000*	**PDN** Old Oak Common	**81A** Old Oak Common	**84G** Shrewsbury	**84G** Shrewsbury	**84G** Shrewsbury		
1004	*1000*	**LA** Laira (Plymouth)	**83G** Penzance	**84A** Stafford Road	**82C** Swindon	**82C** Swindon		
1005	*1000*	**BRD** Bristol Bath Road	**82A** Bristol Bath Road	**82A** Bristol Bath Road	**82A** Bristol Bath Road	**82A** Bristol Bath Road	**82B** St. Philips Marsh	
1006	*1000*	**LA** Laira (Plymouth)	**83D** Laira (Plymouth)	**83D** Laira (Plymouth)	**83G** Penzance	**83G** Penzance	**82C** Swindon	
1007	*1000*	**BRD** Bristol Bath Road	**82A** Bristol Bath Road	**82A** Bristol Bath Road	**83F** Truro	**83C** Exeter		
1008	*1000*	**PDN** Old Oak Common	**81A** Old Oak Common	**84K** Chester (GWR)	**84K** Chester (GWR)	**83G** Penzance	**87H** Neyland	
1009	*1000*	**LA** Laira (Plymouth)	**87H** Neyland	**87H** Neyland	**82A** Bristol Bath Road	**82A** Bristol Bath Road	**82B** St. Philips Marsh	
1010	*1000*	**PDN** Old Oak Common	**81A** Old Oak Common	**83D** Laira (Plymouth)	**83D** Laira (Plymouth)	**82C** Swindon	**82C** Swindon	
1011	*1000*	**BRD** Bristol Bath Road	**82A** Bristol Bath Road	**82A** Bristol Bath Road	**82A** Bristol Bath Road	**82A** Bristol Bath Road	**82B** St. Philips Marsh	
1012	*1000*	**PDN** Old Oak Common	**81A** Old Oak Common	**83D** Laira (Plymouth)	**82C** Swindon	**82C** Swindon	**82C** Swindon	
1013	*1000*	**BRD** Bristol Bath Road	**83F** Truro	**84G** Shrewsbury	**84G** Shrewsbury	**84G** Shrewsbury	**89A** Shrewsbury	
1014	*1000*	**BRD** Bristol Bath Road	**82A** Bristol Bath Road	**82A** Bristol Bath Road	**82A** Bristol Bath Road	**82A** Bristol Bath Road	**87H** Neyland	
1015	*1000*	**PDN** Old Oak Common	**81A** Old Oak Common	**83D** Laira (Plymouth)	**83D** Laira (Plymouth)	**82C** Swindon		
1016	*1000*	**SRD** Stafford Road	**84A** Stafford Road	**84G** Shrewsbury	**84G** Shrewsbury	**84G** Shrewsbury	**89A** Shrewsbury	
1017	*1000*	**SRD** Stafford Road	**84A** Stafford Road	**84G** Shrewsbury	**84G** Shrewsbury	**84G** Shrewsbury		
1018	*1000*	**NA** Newton Abbot	**83A** Newton Abbot	**84A** Stafford Road	**83G** Penzance	**83G** Penzance		
1019	*1000*	**PZ** Penzance	**83A** Newton Abbot	**84A** Stafford Road	**82C** Swindon	**82C** Swindon	**89A** Shrewsbury	
1020	*1000*	**EXE** Exeter	**87H** Neyland	**87H** Neyland	**87H** Neyland	**87H** Neyland	**82B** St. Philips Marsh	
1021	*1000*	**PDN** Old Oak Common	**81A** Old Oak Common	**83D** Laira (Plymouth)	**83D** Laira (Plymouth)	**84G** Shrewsbury	**82B** St. Philips Marsh	
1022	*1000*	**PZ** Penzance	**83D** Laira (Plymouth)	**84K** Chester (GWR)	**84K** Chester (GWR)	**84G** Shrewsbury		
1023	*1000*	**TR** Truro	**83D** Laira (Plymouth)	**83F** Truro	**83F** Truro	**83C** Exeter	**89A** Shrewsbury	
1024	*1000*	**SRD** Stafford Road	**84G** Shrewsbury	**84K** Chester (GWR)	**84K** Chester (GWR)	**82A** Bristol Bath Road	**82B** St. Philips Marsh	
1025	*1000*	**SRD** Stafford Road	**84G** Shrewsbury	**84G** Shrewsbury	**84G** Shrewsbury	**84G** Shrewsbury	**89A** Shrewsbury	
1026	*1000*	**PDN** Old Oak Common	**81A** Old Oak Common	**82A** Bristol Bath Road	**84G** Shrewsbury	**84G** Shrewsbury		
1027	*1000*	**WES** Westbury	**87H** Neyland	**87H** Neyland	**87H** Neyland	**82A** Bristol Bath Road	**87H** Neyland	
1028	*1000*	**BRD** Bristol Bath Road	**82A** Bristol Bath Road	**82A** Bristol Bath Road	**82A** Bristol Bath Road	**82A** Bristol Bath Road	**82B** St. Philips Marsh	
1029	*1000*	**SRD** Stafford Road	**84A** Stafford Road	**87H** Neyland	**87H** Neyland	**87H** Neyland		
1101	*1101*	**DG** Danygraig	**87C** Danygraig	**87C** Danygraig	**87C** Danygraig			
1102	*1101*	**DG** Danygraig	**87C** Danygraig	**87C** Danygraig	**87C** Danygraig	**87C** Danygraig		
1103	*1101*	**DG** Danygraig	**87C** Danygraig	**87C** Danygraig	**87C** Danygraig	**87C** Danygraig		
1104	*1101*	**DG** Danygraig	**87C** Danygraig	**87C** Danygraig	**87C** Danygraig	**87C** Danygraig		
1105	*1101*	**DG** Danygraig	**87C** Danygraig	**87C** Danygraig	**87C** Danygraig	**87C** Danygraig		
1106	*1101*	**DG** Danygraig	**87C** Danygraig	**87C** Danygraig	**87C** Danygraig	**87C** Danygraig		
1140	*SHT[1]*	**SED** Swansea East Dock	**87D** Swansea East Dock	**87D** Swansea East Dock	**87D** Swansea East Dock			
1141	*SHT[2]*	**DG** Danygraig	**87C** Danygraig					
1142	*SHT[3]*	**DG** Danygraig	**87C** Danygraig	**87C** Danygraig	**87C** Danygraig			
1143	*SHT[2]*	**DG** Danygraig	**87C** Danygraig	**87C** Danygraig	**87C** Danygraig	**84G** Shrewsbury		
1144	*SHT[4]*	**SED** Swansea East Dock	**87D** Swansea East Dock	**87D** Swansea East Dock	**87D** Swansea East Dock	**87D** Swansea East Dock		
1145	*SHT[2]*	**DG** Danygraig	**87C** Danygraig	**87C** Danygraig	**87C** Danygraig			
1146	*SHT[5]*	**DG** Danygraig	**87D** Swansea East Dock					
1147	*SHT[5]*	**DG** Danygraig	**87C** Danygraig					
1150	*PM[1]*	**SED** Swansea East Dock	**87D** Swansea East Dock					
1151	*PM[1]*	**DG** Danygraig	**87C** Danygraig	**87C** Danygraig	**87C** Danygraig	**87D** Swansea East Dock	**87D** Swansea East Dock	
1152	*PM[1]*	**SED** Swansea East Dock	**87D** Swansea East Dock	**87D** Swansea East Dock	**87D** Swansea East Dock	**87D** Swansea East Dock		
1153	*PM[2]*	**DG** Danygraig	**87C** Danygraig	**81D** Reading				
1196	*Cam[2]*	**OSW** Oswestry						
1197	*Cam[2]*	**OSW** Oswestry						
1205	*AD[4]*	**LTS** Llantrisant	**86D** Llantrisant	**86C** Cardiff Canton				
1206	*AD[4]*	**HFD** Hereford	**85C** Hereford					
1308	*L&L*	**OSW** Oswestry						
1331	*W&C*	**OSW** Oswestry						
1334	*MSWJ*	**DID** Didcot	**81E** Didcot					
1335	*MSWJ*	**RDG** Reading	**81D** Reading					
1336	*MSWJ*	**RDG** Reading	**81D** Reading	**81D** Reading				
1338	*Car[3]*	**TN** Taunton	**83B** Taunton	**83B** Taunton	**83B** Taunton	**83B** Taunton	**87D** Swansea East Dock	
1358	*PT[2]*	**DG** Danygraig						
1361	*1361*	**LA** Laira (Plymouth)	**83D** Laira (Plymouth)	**83B** Taunton	**83D** Laira (Plymouth)	**83D** Laira (Plymouth)		
1362	*1361*	**NA** Newton Abbot	**83A** Newton Abbot	**83B** Taunton	**83B** Taunton	**83B** Taunton		
1363	*1361*	**LA** Laira (Plymouth)	**83D** Laira (Plymouth)	**83D** Laira (Plymouth)	**83D** Laira (Plymouth)	**83D** Laira (Plymouth)		
1364	*1361*	**LA** Laira (Plymouth)	**83D** Laira (Plymouth)	**83D** Laira (Plymouth)	**83D** Laira (Plymouth)	**83D** Laira (Plymouth)		
1365	*1361*	**LA** Laira (Plymouth)	**83D** Laira (Plymouth)	**83D** Laira (Plymouth)	**82C** Swindon	**82C** Swindon		
1366	*1366*	**SDN** Swindon	**82C** Swindon	**82C** Swindon	**83B** Taunton	**83B** Taunton		
1367	*1366*	**WEY** Weymouth	**82F** Weymouth	**82F** Weymouth	**82F** Weymouth	**71G** Weymouth	**72F** Wadebridge	
1368	*1366*	**WEY** Weymouth	**82F** Weymouth	**83B** Taunton	**82F** Weymouth	**71G** Weymouth	**72F** Wadebridge	
1369	*1366*	**SDN** Swindon	**82C** Swindon	**82C** Swindon	**82C** Swindon	**82C** Swindon	**72F** Wadebridge	
1370	*1366*	**WEY** Weymouth	**82F** Weymouth	**82F** Weymouth	**82F** Weymouth	**71G** Weymouth		
1371	*1366*	**SDN** Swindon	**82C** Swindon	**82C** Swindon	**82C** Swindon	**82C** Swindon		
1400	*1400*	**SDN** Swindon	**82C** Swindon	**82C** Swindon	**82C** Swindon			
1401	*1400*	**CNYD** Croes Newydd	**84C** Banbury	**85B** Gloucester	**85B** Gloucester			
1402	*1400*	**CHEL** Cheltenham	**85B** Gloucester	**85B** Gloucester				
1403	*1400*	**WEY** Weymouth	**82C** Swindon	**82F** Weymouth	**82F** Weymouth			
1404	*1400*	**HFD** Hereford	**85B** Gloucester	**85B** Gloucester				
1405	*1400*	**EXE** Exeter	**83C** Exeter	**83C** Exeter	**83C** Exeter			
1406	*1400*	**GLO** Gloucester	**85B** Gloucester	**85B** Gloucester	**85B** Gloucester			
1407	*1400*	**RDG** Reading	**81D** Reading	**81D** Reading	**81D** Reading	**81D** Reading		
1408	*1400*	**WOS** Worcester	**85A** Worcester	**85A** Worcester	**83D** Laira (Plymouth)			
1409	*1400*	**LYD** Lydney	**85B** Gloucester	**85B** Gloucester	**85B** Gloucester	**85B** Gloucester	**85B** Gloucester	
1410	*1400*	**STB** Stourbridge	**84F** Stourbridge	**84J** Croes Newydd	**82C** Swindon	**82C** Swindon		
1411	*1400*	**CNYD** Croes Newydd	**34E** Neasden	**34E** Neasden				
1412	*1400*	**OSW** Oswestry	**89A** Oswestry	**89A** Oswestry	**82A** Bristol Bath Road	**82A** Bristol Bath Road		
1413	*1400*	**GLO** Gloucester	**85B** Gloucester	**85B** Gloucester				
1414	*1400*	**STB** Stourbridge	**84F** Stourbridge		**84F** Stourbridge			
1415	*1400*	**BRD** Bristol Bath Road	**82A** Bristol Bath Road	**82A** Bristol Bath Road	**81C** Southall			
1416	*1400*	**CNYD** Croes Newydd	**84J** Croes Newydd	**84J** Croes Newydd				
1417	*1400*	**OSW** Oswestry	**6C** Birkenhead	**6C** Birkenhead	**6C** Birkenhead			
1418	*1400*	**WOS** Worcester	**85A** Worcester	**85A** Worcester	**85A** Worcester			
1419	*1400*	**FGD** Fishguard Goodwick	**83E** St. Blazey	**83E** St. Blazey	**83E** St. Blazey	**83E** St. Blazey		
1420	*1400*	**CHYS** Cardiff Cathays	**88A** Cardiff Cathays	**81F** Oxford	**81F** Oxford	**83D** Laira (Plymouth)	**86C** Hereford	
1421	*1400*	**NPT** Ebbw Junction	**86D** Llantrisant	**86A** Ebbw Junction	**86A** Ebbw Junction	**83D** Laira (Plymouth)	**83C** Exeter	
1422	*1400*	**PPRD** Pontypool Road	**86G** Pontypool Road	**86G** Pontypool Road	**82C** Swindon			
1423	*1400*	**FGD** Fishguard Goodwick	**87J** Fishguard Goodwick	**87J** Fishguard Goodwick	**87J** Fishguard Goodwick			
1424	*1400*	**GLO** Gloucester	**85B** Gloucester	**85B** Gloucester	**85B** Gloucester	**85B** Gloucester	**85B** Gloucester	
1425	*1400*	**CHYS** Cardiff Cathays	**88A** Cardiff Cathays	**81F** Oxford				
1426	*1400*	**SLO** Slough	**34E** Neasden	**81C** Southall	**81C** Southall	**85B** Gloucester		
1427	*1400*	**NA** Newton Abbot	**83A** Newton Abbot	**83A** Newton Abbot	**83A** Newton Abbot	**85B** Gloucester		
1428	*1400*	**CNYD** Croes Newydd	**89A** Oswestry	**87E** Landore	**85B** Gloucester			
1429	*1400*	**EXE** Exeter	**83C** Exeter	**83C** Exeter	**83C** Exeter			
1430	*1400*	**BRD** Bristol Bath Road	**82A** Bristol Bath Road	**82A** Bristol Bath Road	**85B** Gloucester			
1431	*1400*	**FGD** Fishguard Goodwick	**87J** Fishguard Goodwick	**87J** Fishguard Goodwick	**87J** Fishguard Goodwick	**81C** Southall		

No.	Class	1948	1951	1954	1957	1960	1963	1966
1432	*1400*	**OSW** Oswestry	**89A** Oswestry	**89A** Oswestry	**89A** Oswestry	**89A** Oswestry	**89D** Oswestry	
1433	*1400*	**SDN** Swindon	**82C** Swindon	**82C** Swindon	**82C** Swindon	**82C** Swindon		
1434	*1400*	**CHR** Chester (GWR)	**84K** Chester (GWR)	**84K** Chester (GWR)	**83D** Laira (Plymouth)	**83D** Laira (Plymouth)		
1435	*1400*	**EXE** Exeter	**83C** Exeter	**83C** Exeter	**83C** Exeter	**81F** Oxford		
1436	*1400*	**SDN** Swindon	**82C** Swindon	**82C** Swindon	**81C** Southall			
1437	*1400*	**SLO** Slough	**81B** Slough	**81B** Slough	**81F** Oxford			
1438	*1400*	**STB** Stourbridge	**84F** Stourbridge	**84F** Stourbridge	**84F** Stourbridge	**82C** Swindon		
1439	*1400*	**NA** Newton Abbot	**83A** Newton Abbot	**83A** Newton Abbot	**83A** Newton Abbot			
1440	*1400*	**EXE** Exeter	**83C** Exeter	**83C** Exeter	**83C** Exeter	**83C** Exeter	**84C** Banbury	
1441	*1400*	**LYD** Lydney	**85B** Gloucester	**85B** Gloucester	**85B** Gloucester	**85B** Gloucester		
1442	*1400*	**SLO** Slough	**81B** Slough	**81F** Oxford	**81F** Oxford	**81F** Oxford	**83C** Exeter	
1443	*1400*	**SHL** Southall	**81C** Southall	**81C** Southall	**81C** Southall			
1444	*1400*	**RDG** Reading	**81D** Reading	**81D** Reading	**81D** Reading	**81F** Oxford	**81F** Oxford	
1445	*1400*	**HFD** Hereford	**85C** Hereford	**85C** Hereford	**85C** Hereford	**85C** Hereford	**81B** Slough	
1446	*1400*	**SDN** Swindon	**82C** Swindon	**82C** Swindon	**81C** Southall			
1447	*1400*	**RDG** Reading	**81D** Reading	**81D** Reading	**81D** Reading	**81B** Slough	**86C** Hereford	
1448	*1400*	**OXF** Oxford	**81B** Slough	**81B** Slough	**81B** Slough	**81B** Slough		
1449	*1400*	**EXE** Exeter	**83C** Exeter	**83C** Exeter	**83C** Exeter	**89C** Machynlleth		
1450	*1400*	**OXF** Oxford	**81F** Oxford	**81B** Slough	**81B** Slough	**81F** Oxford	**83C** Exeter	
1451	*1400*	**EXE** Exeter	**83C** Exeter	**83C** Exeter	**83C** Exeter	**83C** Exeter	**83C** Exeter	
1452	*1400*	**FGD** Fishguard Goodwick	**87J** Fishguard Goodwick	**87J** Fishguard Goodwick	**87J** Fishguard Goodwick	**83C** Exeter		
1453	*1400*	**SDN** Swindon	**82F** Weymouth	**82F** Weymouth	**82F** Weymouth	**71G** Weymouth	**85B** Gloucester	
1454	*1400*	**WEY** Weymouth	**82F** Weymouth	**82A** Bristol Bath Road	**82A** Bristol Bath Road	**85B** Gloucester		
1455	*1400*	**HFD** Hereford	**85C** Hereford	**85C** Hereford	**85C** Hereford	**85C** Hereford	**84C** Banbury	
1456	*1400*	**LYD** Lydney	**85B** Gloucester	**87J** Fishguard Goodwick	**85C** Hereford			
1457	*1400*	**CNYD** Croes Newydd	**84J** Croes Newydd	**6C** Birkenhead	**6C** Birkenhead			
1458	*1400*	**BAN** Banbury	**84F** Stourbridge	**84F** Stourbridge	**84F** Stourbridge	**89A** Oswestry	**89D** Oswestry	
1459	*1400*	**OSW** Oswestry	**89A** Oswestry	**89A** Oswestry	**89A** Oswestry			
1460	*1400*	**HFD** Hereford	**85C** Hereford	**85C** Hereford				
1461	*1400*	**AYN** Abercynon	**88A** Cardiff Cathays	**85A** Worcester	**85A** Worcester			
1462	*1400*	**SHL** Southall	**81C** Southall	**81C** Southall	**82C** Swindon	**83C** Exeter		
1463	*1400*	**BRD** Bristol Bath Road	**82A** Bristol Bath Road	**82A** Bristol Bath Road	**82A** Bristol Bath Road	**82A** Bristol Bath Road		
1464	*1400*	**GLO** Gloucester	**85B** Gloucester	**85B** Gloucester	**85B** Gloucester	**82C** Swindon		
1465	*1400*	**MCH** Machynlleth	**89C** Machynlleth	**89C** Machynlleth	**84J** Croes Newydd			
1466	*1400*	**NA** Newton Abbot	**83A** Newton Abbot	**83A** Newton Abbot	**83A** Newton Abbot	**83A** Newton Abbot	**83C** Exeter	
1467	*1400*	**WEY** Weymouth	**82F** Weymouth	**82F** Weymouth	**82F** Weymouth			
1468	*1400*	**EXE** Exeter	**83C** Exeter	**83C** Exeter	**83C** Exeter	**83C** Exeter		
1469	*1400*	**EXE** Exeter	**83C** Exeter	**83C** Exeter	**83C** Exeter			
1470	*1400*	**NA** Newton Abbot	**83A** Newton Abbot	**83A** Newton Abbot	**83A** Newton Abbot	**83A** Newton Abbot		
1471	*1400*	**LTS** Llantrisant	**86D** Llantrisant	**86D** Llantrisant	**86D** Llantrisant	**83C** Exeter	**83C** Exeter	
1472	*1400*	**CARM** Carmarthen	**87G** Carmarthen	**87G** Carmarthen	**83A** Newton Abbot	**85B** Gloucester	**85B** Gloucester	
1473	*1400*	**BAN** Banbury	**84J** Croes Newydd	**34E** Neasden	**34E** Neasden	**14D** Neasden		
1474	*1400*	**MCH** Machynlleth	**89C** Machynlleth	**81C** Southall	**81C** Southall	**71G** Weymouth	**81B** Slough	
1500	*1500*	→	**81A** Old Oak Common	**81A** Old Oak Common	**81A** Old Oak Common	**81A** Old Oak Common	**81A** Old Oak Common	
1501	*1500*	→	**81C** Southall	**81C** Southall	**81C** Southall	**81C** Southall		
1502	*1500*	→	**81E** Didcot	**81E** Didcot	**81E** Didcot	**81E** Didcot		
1503	*1500*	→	**81A** Old Oak Common	**81A** Old Oak Common	**81A** Old Oak Common	**81A** Old Oak Common	**81A** Old Oak Common	
1504	*1500*	→	**81A** Old Oak Common	**81A** Old Oak Common	**81A** Old Oak Common	**81A** Old Oak Common	**81A** Old Oak Common	
1505	*1500*	→	**81A** Old Oak Common	**81A** Old Oak Common	**81A** Old Oak Common	**81A** Old Oak Common		
1506	*1500*	→	**86B** Newport Pill	**86B** Newport Pill	**86B** Newport Pill	**86A** Ebbw Junction	**81A** Old Oak Common	
1507	*1500*	→	**86B** Newport Pill	**86B** Newport Pill	**86B** Newport Pill	**86B** Newport Pill	**81A** Old Oak Common	
1508	*1500*	→	**86E** Severn Tunnel Junction	**86E** Severn Tunnel Junction	**86C** Cardiff Canton	**86C** Cardiff Canton		
1509	*1500*	→	**86A** Ebbw Junction	**86A** Ebbw Junction	**86A** Ebbw Junction			
1531	*1501*	**OXF** Oxford						
1532	*1501*	**CNYD** Croes Newydd						
1538	*1501*	**SPM** St. Philips Marsh						
1542	*1501*	**SDN** Swindon	**82C** Swindon					
1600	*1600*	→	**88C** Barry	**88C** Barry	**88C** Barry			
1601	*1600*	→	**87H** Neyland	**87H** Neyland	**87H** Neyland	**87H** Neyland		
1602	*1600*	→	**87H** Neyland	**87H** Neyland	**89A** Oswestry	**89A** Oswestry		
1603	*1600*	→	**89C** Machynlleth	**89C** Machynlleth	**89A** Oswestry			
1604	*1600*	→	**89A** Oswestry	**89A** Oswestry	**89A** Oswestry	**89A** Oswestry		
1605	*1600*	→	**81C** Southall	**85A** Worcester	**85A** Worcester	**85B** Gloucester		
1606	*1600*	→	**87H** Neyland	**87H** Neyland	**87F** Llanelly	**87F** Llanelly		
1607	*1600*	→	**87F** Llanelly	**87F** Llanelly	**87F** Llanelly	**87F** Llanelly	**87F** Llanelly	
1608	*1600*	→	**83A** Newton Abbot	**83A** Newton Abbot	**83A** Newton Abbot	**83A** Newton Abbot	**85B** Gloucester	
1609	*1600*	→	**87F** Llanelly	**87F** Llanelly	**87F** Llanelly	**87F** Llanelly		
1610	*1600*	→	**88E** Abercynon	**88E** Abercynon	**88E** Abercynon			
1611	*1600*	→	**87H** Neyland	**87H** Neyland	**87H** Neyland	**87F** Llanelly	**87F** Llanelly	
1612	*1600*	→	**85B** Gloucester	**85B** Gloucester	**87F** Llanelly	**88E** Abercynon	**88E** Abercynon	
1613	*1600*	→	**87G** Carmarthen	**87F** Llanelly	**87F** Llanelly	**87H** Neyland	**87H** Neyland	
1614	*1600*	→	**87F** Llanelly	**87F** Llanelly	**87F** Llanelly	**87F** Llanelly	**86A** Ebbw Junction	
1615	*1600*	→	**88C** Barry	**88C** Barry	**88C** Barry	**87F** Llanelly		
1616	*1600*	→	**85B** Gloucester	**85B** Gloucester	**85B** Gloucester			
1617	*1600*	→	**81F** Oxford	**85C** Hereford	**85C** Hereford	**85C** Hereford	**86C** Hereford	
1618	*1600*	→	**87F** Llanelly	**87F** Llanelly	**87F** Llanelly	**84K** Wrexham Rhosddu		
1619	*1600*	→	**84H** Wellington	**84F** Stourbridge	**84F** Stourbridge	**84F** Stourbridge	**84F** Stourbridge	
1620	*1600*	→	**88E** Abercynon	**88E** Abercynon	**88E** Abercynon	**88E** Abercynon		
1621	*1600*	→	**84F** Stourbridge	**84F** Stourbridge	**84F** Stourbridge	**84F** Stourbridge	**82C** Swindon	
1622	*1600*	→	**87K** Swansea Victoria	**87F** Llanelly	**87F** Llanelly	**87F** Llanelly	**81B** Slough	
1623	*1600*	→	**85B** Gloucester	**85B** Gloucester	**85B** Gloucester	**85B** Gloucester	**85B** Gloucester	
1624	*1600*	→	**84J** Croes Newydd	**83E** St. Blazey	**83E** St. Blazey	**83E** St. Blazey		
1625	*1600*	→	**85B** Gloucester	**85B** Gloucester	**85C** Hereford	**86C** Hereford		
1626	*1600*	→	**83E** St. Blazey	**83A** Newton Abbot	**83A** Newton Abbot	**83A** Newton Abbot		
1627	*1600*	→	**85B** Gloucester	**85B** Gloucester	**85B** Gloucester	**85B** Gloucester	**81F** Oxford	
1628	*1600*	→	**87H** Neyland	**87F** Llanelly	**87F** Llanelly	**89A** Oswestry	**89B** Croes Newydd	**6C** Croes Newydd
1629	*1600*	→	**88A** Cardiff Cathays	**85A** Worcester	**85A** Worcester	**85A** Worcester		
1630	*1600*	→	→	**85B** Gloucester	**85B** Gloucester	**85B** Gloucester	**81F** Oxford	
1631	*1600*	→	→	**85B** Gloucester	**85B** Gloucester	**85B** Gloucester	**85B** Gloucester	
1632	*1600*	→	→	**85B** Gloucester	**85B** Gloucester	**85B** Gloucester	**89B** Croes Newydd	
1633	*1600*	→	→	**87F** Llanelly	**87F** Llanelly	**87F** Llanelly		
1634	*1600*	→	→	**87C** Danygraig	**87C** Danygraig	**87C** Danygraig		
1635	*1600*	→	→	**84J** Croes Newydd	**84J** Croes Newydd			
1636	*1600*	→	→	**89A** Oswestry	**89C** Machynlleth	**89A** Oswestry	**81E** Didcot	
1637	*1600*	→	→	**87H** Neyland	**87H** Neyland	**87H** Neyland		
1638	*1600*	→	→	**87F** Llanelly	**87F** Llanelly	**87F** Llanelly	**89D** Oswestry	**6C** Croes Newydd
1639	*1600*	→	→	**85B** Gloucester	**85B** Gloucester	**85B** Gloucester	**85A** Worcester	
1640	*1600*	→	→	**87C** Danygraig	**87C** Danygraig	**87C** Danygraig		
1641	*1600*	→	→	**87D** Swansea East Dock	**87D** Swansea East Dock	**87D** Swansea East Dock	**88E** Abercynon	
1642	*1600*	→	→	**85B** Gloucester	**85B** Gloucester	**85B** Gloucester		
1643	*1600*	→	→	**87F** Llanelly	**87F** Llanelly	**87F** Llanelly	**87F** Llanelly	
1644	*1600*	→	→	**87F** Llanelly	**87F** Llanelly			
1645	*1600*	→	→	**87A** Neath	**87A** Neath	**87A** Neath		
1646	*1600*	→	→	**84J** Croes Newydd	**84J** Croes Newydd	**60C** Helmsdale		
1647	*1600*	→	→	**82C** Swindon	**87C** Danygraig	**87C** Danygraig		
1648	*1600*	→	→	**82C** Swindon	**87C** Danygraig	**87C** Danygraig	**87H** Neyland	
1649	*1600*	→	→	**82B** St. Philips Marsh	**82B** St. Philips Marsh	**60C** Helmsdale		
1650	*1600*	→	→	→	**83D** Laira (Plymouth)	**83D** Laira (Plymouth)	**85B** Gloucester	
1651	*1600*	→	→	→	**87F** Llanelly	**87F** Llanelly	**87F** Llanelly	
1652	*1600*	→	→	→	**87D** Swansea East Dock	**87D** Swansea East Dock		
1653	*1600*	→	→	→	**86A** Ebbw Junction	**86A** Ebbw Junction		
1654	*1600*	→	→	→	**87F** Llanelly	**87F** Llanelly	**81C** Southall	
1655	*1600*	→	→	→	**87F** Llanelly	**87F** Llanelly	**87F** Llanelly	
1656	*1600*	→	→	→	**86A** Ebbw Junction	**86A** Ebbw Junction	**86A** Ebbw Junction	

		1948	1951	1954	1957	1960	1963	1966
1657	*1600*	→	→	→	**85C** Hereford	**85C** Hereford	**86C** Hereford	
1658	*1600*	→	→	→	**82C** Swindon	**82C** Swindon	**82C** Swindon	
1659	*1600*	→	→	→	**87G** Carmarthen	**84J** Croes Newydd		
1660	*1600*	→	→	→	**84J** Croes Newydd	**84J** Croes Newydd	**89B** Croes Newydd	**6C** Croes Newydd
1661	*1600*	→	→	→	**85D** Kidderminster	**85A** Worcester	**85A** Worcester	
1662	*1600*	→	→	→	**85C** Hereford	**85C** Hereford	**86C** Hereford	
1663	*1600*	→	→	→	**84H** Wellington	**84K** Wrexham Rhosddu	**89D** Oswestry	
1664	*1600*	→	→	→	**83E** St. Blazey	**83E** St. Blazey	**82C** Swindon	
1665	*1600*	→	→	→	**87F** Llanelly	**87F** Llanelly	**87F** Llanelly	
1666	*1600*	→	→	→	**87F** Llanelly	**87F** Llanelly	**89D** Oswestry	
1667	*1600*	→	→	→	**85C** Hereford	**85C** Hereford	**86C** Hereford	
1668	*1600*	→	→	→	**83B** Taunton	**83B** Taunton	**89D** Oswestry	
1669	*1600*	→	→	→	**82B** St. Philips Marsh	**84K** Wrexham Rhosddu	**87A** Neath	
1705	*1854*	**CED** Cardiff East Dock						
1706	*1854*	**CNYD** Croes Newydd						
1709	*1854*	**PILL** Newport Pill						
1713	*1854*	**NPT** Ebbw Junction						
1715	*1854*	**NEA** Neath						
1720	*1854*	**NPT** Ebbw Junction						
1726	*1854*	**PILL** Newport Pill						
1730	*1854*	**TDU** Tondu						
1731	*1854*	**SDN** Swindon						
1742	*655*	**OXF** Oxford						
174[illegible]	*655*	**STB** Stourbridge						
1747	*655*	**CNYD** Croes Newydd						
1749	*655*	**STB** Stourbridge						
1752	*1854*	**STJ** Severn Tunnel Junction						
1753	*1854*	**TR** Truro						
1754	*1854*	**DYD** Duffryn Yard						
1758	*1854*	**SDN** Swindon						
1760	*1854*	**TN** Taunton						
1762	*1854*	**OXY** Oxley						
1764	*1854*	**PILL** Newport Pill						
1769	*1854*	**ABDR** Aberdare						
1773	*655*	**CNYD** Croes Newydd						
1780	*655*	**CNYD** Croes Newydd						
1782	*655*	**TR** Truro						
1789	*655*	**WEY** Weymouth						
1799	*1854*	**LA** Laira (Plymouth)						
1835	*1813*	**STB** Stourbridge						
1855	*1854*	**NEA** Neath						
1858	*1854*	**NEA** Neath						
1861	*1854*	**DID** Didcot	**81E** Didcot					
1862	*1854*	**NPT** Ebbw Junction						
1863	*1854*	**SRD** Stafford Road						
1867	*1854*	**DYD** Duffryn Yard						
1870	*1854*	**STJ** Severn Tunnel Junction						
1878	*1854*	**MTHR** Merthyr						
1884	*1854*	**CED** Cardiff East Dock						
1888	*1854*	**CED** Cardiff East Dock						
1889	*1854*	**CDF** Cardiff Canton						
1891	*1854*	**CDF** Cardiff Canton						
1894	*1854*	**NPT** Ebbw Junction						
1896	*1854*	**PILL** Newport Pill						
1897	*1854*	**CED** Cardiff East Dock						
1900	*1854*	**SBZ** St. Blazey						
1903	*1901*	**CARM** Carmarthen	**87G** Carmarthen					
1907	*1901*	**LLY** Llanelly						
1909	*1901*	**TN** Taunton						
1912	*1901*	**PDN** Old Oak Common						
1917	*1901*	**BHD** Birkenhead	**6C** Birkenhead					
1919	*1901*	**WOS** Worcester						
1925	*1901*	**SHL** Southall	**81D** Reading					
1930	*1901*	**SBZ** St. Blazey						
1935	*1901*	**OXF** Oxford	**81F** Oxford					
1941	*1901*	**CARM** Carmarthen	**87F** Llanelly					
1943	*1901*	**GLO** Gloucester	**85B** Gloucester					
1945	*1901*	**DG** Danygraig						
1949	*1901*	**BHD** Birkenhead						
1957	*1901*	**LLY** Llanelly	**87F** Llanelly					
1964	*1901*	**WTD** Whitland	**87B** Duffryn Yard					
1965	*1901*	**MCH** Machynlleth						
1967	*1901*	**LLY** Llanelly	**87F** Llanelly					
1968	*1901*	**BHD** Birkenhead	**6C** Birkenhead					
1969	*1901*	**SHL** Southall						
1973	*1901*	**LA** Laira (Plymouth)						
1979	*1901*	**WTD** Whitland						
1989	*1901*	**GLO** Gloucester						
1990	*1901*	**LA** Laira (Plymouth)						
1991	*1901*	**LLY** Llanelly	**87F** Llanelly					
1993	*1901*	**BRY** Barry	**88C** Barry					
1996	*1901*	**WTD** Whitland	**87A** Neath					
2000	*1901*	**AYN** Abercynon						
2001	*1901*	**WOS** Worcester	**85A** Worcester					
2002	*1901*	**LLY** Llanelly	**87F** Llanelly					
2004	*1901*	**BHD** Birkenhead	**6C** Birkenhead					
2006	*1901*	**BHD** Birkenhead						
2007	*1901*	**WOS** Worcester						
2008	*1901*	**CED** Cardiff East Dock	**88C** Barry	**6C** Birkenhead	**6C** Birkenhead			
2009	*1901*	**GLO** Gloucester	**85B** Gloucester					
2010	*1901*	**WTD** Whitland	**87H** Neyland					
2011	*1901*	**WTD** Whitland	**87B** Duffryn Yard	**6C** Birkenhead				
2012	*1901*	**LLY** Llanelly	**87F** Llanelly	**87F** Llanelly	**6C** Birkenhead			
2013	*1901*	**WTD** Whitland						
2014	*1901*	**SDN** Swindon	**82C** Swindon					
2016	*1901*	**WOS** Worcester	**85A** Worcester					
2017	*1901*	**SDN** Swindon	**82C** Swindon					
2018	*1901*	**WTD** Whitland						
2019	*1901*	**LLY** Llanelly						
2021	*2021*	**PPRD** Pontypool Road	**86G** Pontypool Road					
2022	*2021*	**CED** Cardiff East Dock						
2023	*2021*	**WES** Westbury	**82D** Westbury					
2025	*2021*	**LYD** Lydney	**85B** Gloucester					
2026	*2021*	**HFD** Hereford	**85C** Hereford					
2027	*2021*	**LLY** Llanelly	**87F** Llanelly	**87F** Llanelly	**87F** Llanelly			
2029	*2021*	**HFD** Hereford						
2030	*2021*	**WLN** Wellington	**84H** Wellington					
2031	*2021*	**SPM** St. Philips Marsh	**82B** St. Philips Marsh					
2032	*2021*	**OSW** Oswestry	**89A** Oswestry					
2033	*2021*	**PILL** Newport Pill	**86B** Newport Pill					
2034	*2021*	**LYD** Lydney	**85B** Gloucester	**85A** Worcester				
2035	*2021*	**PPRD** Pontypool Road	**86G** Pontypool Road	**86A** Ebbw Junction				
2037	*2021*	**WOS** Worcester						
2038	*2021*	**TN** Taunton	**83B** Taunton					

		1948	1951	1954	1957	1960	1963	1966
2039	*2021*	LYD Lydney						
2040	*2021*	HFD Hereford	**85C** Hereford	**85A** Worcester				
2042	*2021*	LLY Llanelly	**87F** Llanelly					
2043	*2021*	LYD Lydney	**85B** Gloucester	**6C** Birkenhead				
2044	*2021*	LYD Lydney	**85B** Gloucester					
2045	*2021*	LYD Lydney						
2047	*2021*	CARM Carmarthen						
2048	*2021*	CED Cardiff East Dock	**88B** Cardiff East Dock					
2050	*2021*	SBZ St. Blazey	**83E** St. Blazey					
2051	*2021*	WOS Worcester	**85D** Kidderminster					
2052	*2021*	BHD Birkenhead						
2053	*2021*	WES Westbury	**82D** Westbury	**82B** St. Philips Marsh				
2054	*2021*	OSW Oswestry	**89A** Oswestry					
2055	*2021*	SLO Slough	**87C** Danygraig					
2056	*2021*	CARM Carmarthen	**87G** Carmarthen					
2059	*2021*	LLY Llanelly						
2060	*2021*	SDN Swindon	**82C** Swindon	**82C** Swindon				
2061	*2021*	SRD Stafford Road	**84A** Stafford Road	**84H** Wellington				
2063	*2021*	NPT Ebbw Junction	**86A** Ebbw Junction					
2064	*2021*	SPM St. Philips Marsh						
2065	*2021*	BAN Banbury						
2066	*2021*	CHYS Cardiff Cathays	**88A** Cardiff Cathays					
2067	*2021*	SRD Stafford Road	**6C** Birkenhead					
2068	*2021*	OSW Oswestry	**89A** Oswestry					
2069	*2021*	CARM Carmarthen	**87G** Carmarthen	**87G** Carmarthen	**6C** Birkenhead			
2070	*2021*	SPM St. Philips Marsh	**82B** St. Philips Marsh	**82B** St. Philips Marsh				
2071	*2021*	TYS Tyseley						
2072	*2021*	BRD Bristol Bath Road	**82A** Bristol Bath Road	**82B** St. Philips Marsh				
2073	*2021*	NPT Ebbw Junction	**86A** Ebbw Junction					
2075	*2021*	OSW Oswestry	**89A** Oswestry					
2076	*2021*	RDG Reading	**81F** Oxford					
2079	*2021*	DYD Duffryn Yard	**87B** Duffryn Yard					
2080	*2021*	LYD Lydney	**85B** Gloucester					
2081	*2021*	LLY Llanelly	**87F** Llanelly	**87F** Llanelly				
2082	*2021*	DG Danygraig	**87C** Danygraig	**6C** Birkenhead				
2083	*2021*	LLY Llanelly	**87F** Llanelly					
2085	*2021*	LLY Llanelly	**87F** Llanelly					
2086	*2021*	CED Cardiff East Dock	**88B** Cardiff East Dock					
2088	*2021*	EXE Exeter	**83C** Exeter	**83B** Taunton				
2089	*2021*	BHD Birkenhead	**6C** Birkenhead					
2090	*2021*	STB Stourbridge	**84F** Stourbridge	**86A** Ebbw Junction				
2091	*2021*	LYD Lydney						
2092	*2021*	STB Stourbridge	**6C** Birkenhead	**6C** Birkenhead				
2093	*2021*	KDR Kidderminster	**85A** Worcester					
2094	*2021*	PPRD Pontypool Road	**86G** Pontypool Road					
2095	*2021*	SRD Stafford Road	**84A** Stafford Road					
2096	*2021*	HFD Hereford						
2097	*2021*	NA Newton Abbot	**83G** Penzance	**83D** Laira (Plymouth)				
2098	*2021*	LLY Llanelly	**87F** Llanelly					
2099	*2021*	HFD Hereford	**85C** Hereford	**6C** Birkenhead				
2100	*2021*	WOS Worcester	**85A** Worcester					
2101	*2021*	WOS Worcester	**85A** Worcester	**6C** Birkenhead				
2102	*2021*	LYD Lydney						
2104	*2021*	BHD Birkenhead	**6C** Birkenhead					
2106	*2021*	BHD Birkenhead	**6C** Birkenhead					
2107	*2021*	STB Stourbridge	**84F** Stourbridge	**6C** Birkenhead				
2108	*2021*	BHD Birkenhead	**6C** Birkenhead	**6C** Birkenhead				
2109	*2021*	SRD Stafford Road	**84A** Stafford Road					
2110	*2021*	SRD Stafford Road						
2111	*2021*	CARM Carmarthen	**87G** Carmarthen					
2112	*2021*	SLO Slough	**81B** Slough	**6C** Birkenhead				
2113	*2021*	PILL Newport Pill						
2114	*2021*	LYD Lydney						
2115	*2021*	WOS Worcester	**85A** Worcester					
2117	*2021*	ABDR Aberdare	**86G** Pontypool Road					
2121	*2021*	LYD Lydney	**85B** Gloucester					
2122	*2021*	NPT Ebbw Junction	**86A** Ebbw Junction					
2123	*2021*	CED Cardiff East Dock	**88B** Cardiff East Dock					
2124	*2021*	CED Cardiff East Dock						
2126	*2021*	LLY Llanelly						
2127	*2021*	TN Taunton	**83B** Taunton					
2129	*2021*	BHD Birkenhead	**6C** Birkenhead					
2130	*2021*	CED Cardiff East Dock						
2131	*2021*	LYD Lydney	**85B** Gloucester					
2132	*2021*	LYD Lydney						
2134	*2021*	DG Danygraig	**87C** Danygraig	**6C** Birkenhead	**6C** Birkenhead			
2135	*2021*	SPM St. Philips Marsh	**82B** St. Philips Marsh					
2136	*2021*	PILL Newport Pill	**86B** Newport Pill	**6C** Birkenhead				
2137	*2021*	LLY Llanelly						
2138	*2021*	HFD Hereford	**85C** Hereford	**85C** Hereford				
2140	*2021*	CED Cardiff East Dock	**88A** Cardiff Cathays					
2141	*2021*	CED Cardiff East Dock						
2144	*2021*	LYD Lydney	**85B** Gloucester	**85D** Kidderminster				
2146	*2021*	GLO Gloucester	**85B** Gloucester					
2147	*2021*	CED Cardiff East Dock	**88B** Cardiff East Dock					
2148	*2021*	PZ Penzance	**83D** Laira (Plymouth)					
2150	*2021*	LLY Llanelly	**87F** Llanelly					
2151	*2021*	MCH Machynlleth	**87C** Danygraig					
2152	*2021*	TYS Tyseley	**6C** Birkenhead					
2153	*2021*	LYD Lydney						
2154	*2021*	PILL Newport Pill	**86B** Newport Pill					
2155	*2021*	LYD Lydney						
2156	*2021*	SRD Stafford Road	**6C** Birkenhead					
2159	*2021*	PPRD Pontypool Road	**86J** Aberdare					
2160	*2021*	LYD Lydney	**85C** Hereford	**85C** Hereford	**6C** Birkenhead			
2162	*BPGV*[1]	LLY Llanelly	**87F** Llanelly	**87F** Llanelly				
2165	*BPGV*[1]	LLY Llanelly	**87F** Llanelly	**87F** Llanelly				
2166	*BPGV*[1]	SED Swansea East Dock	**87D** Swansea East Dock	**87D** Swansea East Dock				
2167	*BPGV*[1]	LLY Llanelly	**87F** Llanelly					
2168	*BPGV*[1]	LLY Llanelly	**87F** Llanelly	**87F** Llanelly				
2176	*BPGV*[2]	LLY Llanelly	**87F** Llanelly	**87F** Llanelly				
2181	*2181*	SBZ St. Blazey	**83A** Newton Abbot					
2182	*2181*	SBZ St. Blazey	**83E** St. Blazey	**83E** St. Blazey				
2183	*2181*	CNYD Croes Newydd	**83A** Newton Abbot	**83A** Newton Abbot				
2184	*2181*	CNYD Croes Newydd						
2185	*2181*	STB Stourbridge	**84F** Stourbridge					
2186	*2181*	STB Stourbridge	**84F** Stourbridge	**84J** Croes Newydd				
2187	*2181*	STB Stourbridge	**84F** Stourbridge					
2188	*2181*	CNYD Croes Newydd	**84J** Croes Newydd					
2189	*2181*	STB Stourbridge						
2190	*2181*	CNYD Croes Newydd	**84J** Croes Newydd					
2192	*BPGV*[3]	NEA Neath	**87A** Neath					
2193	*BPGV*[3]	LLY Llanelly	**87F** Llanelly					
2194	*BPGV*[4]	TN Taunton	**83B** Taunton					

No.	Class	1948	1951	1954	1957	1960	1963	1966
2195	*BPGV*[4]	**SDN** Swindon	**82C** Swindon					
2196	*BPGV*[5]	**LLY** Llanelly	**87F** Llanelly	**87F** Llanelly				
2197	*BPGV*[6]	**LLY** Llanelly	**87F** Llanelly					
2198	*BPGV*[7]	**LLY** Llanelly	**87F** Llanelly	**87F** Llanelly	**87F** Llanelly			
2200	*2251*	**ABH** Aberystwyth	**89C** Machynlleth	**89C** Machynlleth	**89C** Machynlleth	**89C** Machynlleth		
2201	*2251*	**OSW** Oswestry	**89C** Machynlleth	**85A** Worcester	**82B** St. Philips Marsh	**89C** Machynlleth	**81E** Didcot	
2202	*2251*	**DID** Didcot	**81E** Didcot	**84C** Banbury	**89C** Machynlleth	**89C** Machynlleth		
2203	*2251*	**TYS** Tyseley	**84E** Tyseley	**82A** Bristol Bath Road	**82C** Swindon	**82B** St. Philips Marsh		
2204	*2251*	**MCH** Machynlleth	**89C** Machynlleth	**89C** Machynlleth	**89C** Machynlleth	**89C** Machynlleth	**82G** Templecombe	
2205	*2251*	**WOS** Worcester	**85A** Worcester	**85A** Worcester	**85A** Worcester			
2206	*2251*	**TYS** Tyseley	**89C** Machynlleth	**84G** Shrewsbury	**85C** Hereford	**81D** Reading		
2207	*2251*	**WOS** Worcester	**85A** Worcester	**85D** Kidderminster	**85B** Gloucester	**85B** Gloucester		
2208	*2251*	**RDG** Reading	**81D** Reading	**83B** Taunton	**82D** Westbury			
2209	*2251*	**TYS** Tyseley	**84J** Croes Newydd	**84C** Banbury	**84J** Croes Newydd	**85A** Worcester		
2210	*2251*	**OSW** Oswestry	**89A** Oswestry	**89A** Oswestry	**89A** Oswestry	**81D** Reading	**84D** Leamington Spa	
2211	*2251*	**TN** Taunton	**83B** Taunton	**83B** Taunton	**83C** Exeter	**84E** Tyseley	**84D** Leamington Spa	
2212	*2251*	**TN** Taunton	**83B** Taunton	**83B** Taunton	**83B** Taunton	**81D** Reading		
2213	*2251*	**TN** Taunton	**83B** Taunton	**83B** Taunton	**82B** St. Philips Marsh	**82B** St. Philips Marsh		
2214	*2251*	**TN** Taunton	**83B** Taunton	**83B** Taunton	**81E** Didcot	**81E** Didcot	**89D** Oswestry	
2215	*2251*	**TN** Taunton	**82B** St. Philips Marsh	**82B** St. Philips Marsh	**82B** St. Philips Marsh	**82B** St. Philips Marsh		
2216	*2251*	**CARM** Carmarthen	**87G** Carmarthen	**87G** Carmarthen	**87G** Carmarthen	**87G** Carmarthen		
2217	*2251*	**CARM** Carmarthen	**87G** Carmarthen	**87G** Carmarthen	**89C** Machynlleth	**89C** Machynlleth	**82E** Bristol Barrow Road	
2218	*2251*	**NPT** Ebbw Junction	**86A** Ebbw Junction	**86A** Ebbw Junction	**86A** Ebbw Junction	**86A** Ebbw Junction	**86A** Ebbw Junction	
2219	*2251*	**MCH** Machynlleth	**89C** Machynlleth	**89A** Oswestry	**89A** Oswestry	**86A** Ebbw Junction	**83B** Taunton	
2220	*2251*	**SPM** St. Philips Marsh	**82B** St. Philips Marsh	**87H** Neyland	**87H** Neyland	**87H** Neyland		
2221	*2251*	**DID** Didcot	**81E** Didcot	**81D** Reading	**81E** Didcot	**81E** Didcot	**82E** Bristol Barrow Road	
2222	*2251*	**DID** Didcot	**81E** Didcot	**81A** Old Oak Common	**81A** Old Oak Common	**81A** Old Oak Common	**85A** Worcester	
2223	*2251*	**ABH** Aberystwyth	**89C** Machynlleth	**87J** Fishguard Goodwick	**87J** Fishguard Goodwick	**86A** Ebbw Junction		
2224	*2251*	**SDN** Swindon	**82C** Swindon	**82C** Swindon	**87G** Carmarthen	**82B** St. Philips Marsh	**82B** St. Philips Marsh	
2225	*2251*	**SPM** St. Philips Marsh	**82B** St. Philips Marsh	**85C** Hereford	**85C** Hereford			
2226	*2251*	**DID** Didcot	**81E** Didcot	**87H** Neyland	**87E** Landore			
2227	*2251*	**CNYD** Croes Newydd	**86A** Ebbw Junction	**86A** Ebbw Junction	**86A** Ebbw Junction	**86A** Ebbw Junction		
2228	*2251*	**SALOP** Shrewsbury	**84G** Shrewsbury	**87H** Neyland	**87H** Neyland			
2229	*2251*	**SALOP** Shrewsbury	**84G** Shrewsbury	**87H** Neyland	**87H** Neyland	**82E** Bristol Barrow Road		
2230	*2251*	**EXE** Exeter	**83C** Exeter	**83C** Exeter	**83C** Exeter	**82C** Swindon		
2231	*2251*	**SALOP** Shrewsbury	**84G** Shrewsbury	**84G** Shrewsbury	**86E** Severn Tunnel Junction	**86E** Severn Tunnel Junction	**86E** Severn Tunnel Junction	
2232	*2251*	**SRD** Stafford Road	**84J** Croes Newydd	**84G** Shrewsbury	**89C** Machynlleth	**89C** Machynlleth	**85B** Gloucester	
2233	*2251*	**SALOP** Shrewsbury	**84G** Shrewsbury	**89C** Machynlleth	**89C** Machynlleth	**89C** Machynlleth		
2234	*2251*	**SALOP** Shrewsbury	**84G** Shrewsbury	**84G** Shrewsbury	**84G** Shrewsbury	**81E** Didcot		
2235	*2251*	**SALOP** Shrewsbury	**84G** Shrewsbury	**84G** Shrewsbury	**89B** Brecon			
2236	*2251*	**CARM** Carmarthen	**87G** Carmarthen	**81F** Oxford	**81F** Oxford	**86A** Ebbw Junction	**89C** Machynlleth	
2237	*2251*	**WOS** Worcester	**85A** Worcester	**85A** Worcester	**89C** Machynlleth			
2238	*2251*	**TYS** Tyseley	**84E** Tyseley	**84E** Tyseley	**84E** Tyseley			
2239	*2251*	**NPT** Ebbw Junction	**86A** Ebbw Junction	**86A** Ebbw Junction	**89A** Oswestry	**89A** Oswestry		
2240	*2251*	**DID** Didcot	**81E** Didcot	**81E** Didcot	**81E** Didcot	**81E** Didcot		
2241	*2251*	**WOS** Worcester	**85A** Worcester	**85A** Worcester	**85A** Worcester	**85C** Hereford	**86C** Hereford	
2242	*2251*	**WOS** Worcester	**85A** Worcester	**85A** Worcester	**85A** Worcester	**85C** Hereford	**86C** Hereford	
2243	*2251*	**HFD** Hereford	**85C** Hereford	**81A** Old Oak Common	**81A** Old Oak Common	**85A** Worcester	**86A** Ebbw Junction	
2244	*2251*	**OSW** Oswestry	**89A** Oswestry	**84G** Shrewsbury	**89C** Machynlleth	**89C** Machynlleth	**82C** Swindon	
2245	*2251*	**RDG** Reading	**81D** Reading	**81D** Reading	**81D** Reading	**81D** Reading	**85B** Gloucester	
2246	*2251*	**STB** Stourbridge	**84F** Stourbridge	**84C** Banbury	**84C** Banbury	**81E** Didcot	**85A** Worcester	
2247	*2251*	**WOS** Worcester	**85A** Worcester	**85A** Worcester	**85A** Worcester	**85A** Worcester	**86A** Ebbw Junction	
2248	*2251*	**GLO** Gloucester	**85B** Gloucester	**85B** Gloucester	**85B** Gloucester	**85B** Gloucester	**87G** Carmarthen	
2249	*2251*	**OXF** Oxford	**81F** Oxford	**85C** Hereford	**85C** Hereford	**85C** Hereford	**86C** Hereford	
2250	*2251*	**SDN** Swindon	**82C** Swindon	**82B** St. Philips Marsh	**82B** St. Philips Marsh	**82C** Swindon		
2251	*2251*	**SPM** St. Philips Marsh	**82B** St. Philips Marsh	**82B** St. Philips Marsh	**82B** St. Philips Marsh	**87H** Neyland	**82E** Bristol Barrow Road	
2252	*2251*	**DID** Didcot	**81E** Didcot	**81E** Didcot	**81E** Didcot			
2253	*2251*	**SPM** St. Philips Marsh	**82B** St. Philips Marsh	**85A** Worcester	**81D** Reading	**85B** Gloucester	**85B** Gloucester	
2254	*2251*	**CARM** Carmarthen	**85B** Gloucester	**85B** Gloucester	**85B** Gloucester			
2255	*2251*	**OSW** Oswestry	**89A** Oswestry	**89A** Oswestry	**89C** Machynlleth	**89C** Machynlleth		
2256	*2251*	**BAN** Banbury	**84C** Banbury	**84C** Banbury	**84C** Banbury	**84C** Banbury		
2257	*2251*	**TYS** Tyseley	**84E** Tyseley	**84E** Tyseley	**84E** Tyseley	**84E** Tyseley	**81D** Reading	
2258	*2251*	**SPM** St. Philips Marsh	**82B** St. Philips Marsh	**85A** Worcester	**85A** Worcester			
2259	*2251*	**CNYD** Croes Newydd	**84J** Croes Newydd	**84C** Banbury	**84C** Banbury			
2260	*2251*	**ABH** Aberystwyth	**89C** Machynlleth	**89C** Machynlleth	**89C** Machynlleth	**89C** Machynlleth		
2261	*2251*	**TN** Taunton	**83B** Taunton	**82B** St. Philips Marsh	**82B** St. Philips Marsh	**82B** St. Philips Marsh	**81D** Reading	
2262	*2251*	**CHR** Chester (GWR)	**84J** Croes Newydd	**85A** Worcester	**81D** Reading			
2263	*2251*	**WOS** Worcester	**85A** Worcester	**85A** Worcester	**87H** Neyland			
2264	*2251*	**RDG** Reading	**81D** Reading	**81D** Reading	**89C** Machynlleth	**89C** Machynlleth		
2265	*2251*	**SPM** St. Philips Marsh	**82B** St. Philips Marsh	**82B** St. Philips Marsh	**82B** St. Philips Marsh	**82B** St. Philips Marsh		
2266	*2251*	**TN** Taunton	**83B** Taunton	**83B** Taunton	**85C** Hereford			
2267	*2251*	**TN** Taunton	**83B** Taunton	**83B** Taunton	**89C** Machynlleth	**84E** Tyseley		
2268	*2251*	**TN** Taunton	**83B** Taunton	**83B** Taunton	**82D** Westbury	**82D** Westbury	**82D** Westbury	
2269	*2251*	**SPM** St. Philips Marsh	**82B** St. Philips Marsh	**82B** St. Philips Marsh	**82B** St. Philips Marsh			
2270	*2251*	**STB** Stourbridge	**84F** Stourbridge	**84C** Banbury	**84C** Banbury			
2271	*2251*	**CARM** Carmarthen	**87G** Carmarthen	**87G** Carmarthen	**89C** Machynlleth	**87J** Fishguard Goodwick		
2272	*2251*	**CARM** Carmarthen	**87G** Carmarthen	**87G** Carmarthen	**87G** Carmarthen			
2273	*2251*	**LDR** Landore	**87E** Landore	**87G** Carmarthen	**87G** Carmarthen	**85A** Worcester	**82D** Westbury	
2274	*2251*	**WOS** Worcester	**85A** Worcester	**85C** Hereford	**85C** Hereford	**87G** Carmarthen		
2275	*2251*	**TN** Taunton	**83B** Taunton	**83B** Taunton	**89A** Oswestry	**89C** Machynlleth		
2276	*2251*	**PDN** Old Oak Common	**81A** Old Oak Common	**81A** Old Oak Common	**81A** Old Oak Common	**81A** Old Oak Common		
2277	*2251*	**WOS** Worcester	**85A** Worcester	**85A** Worcester	**85A** Worcester	**82B** St. Philips Marsh	**82E** Bristol Barrow Road	
2278	*2251*	**WOS** Worcester	**85A** Worcester	**85A** Worcester	**85B** Gloucester			
2279	*2251*	**STB** Stourbridge	**84F** Stourbridge	**84F** Stourbridge	**84E** Tyseley			
2280	*2251*	**NPT** Ebbw Junction	**86A** Ebbw Junction	**86A** Ebbw Junction	**86A** Ebbw Junction			
2281	*2251*	**STB** Stourbridge	**85C** Hereford	**85C** Hereford	**85C** Hereford			
2282	*2251*	**PDN** Old Oak Common	**81A** Old Oak Common	**81A** Old Oak Common	**81A** Old Oak Common	**81A** Old Oak Common		
2283	*2251*	**ABH** Aberystwyth	**89C** Machynlleth	**87H** Neyland	**87H** Neyland	**87H** Neyland	**87H** Neyland	
2284	*2251*	**CARM** Carmarthen	**87G** Carmarthen	**87E** Landore	**87E** Landore			
2285	*2251*	**SHL** Southall	**81C** Southall	**81C** Southall	**89C** Machynlleth			
2286	*2251*	**HFD** Hereford	**85C** Hereford	**89B** Brecon	**89C** Machynlleth	**89C** Machynlleth	**86C** Hereford	
2287	*2251*	**CNYD** Croes Newydd	**89B** Brecon	**89B** Brecon	**89B** Brecon	**89A** Oswestry	**87G** Carmarthen	
2288	*2251*	**WTD** Whitland	**87H** Neyland	**87H** Neyland	**87H** Neyland	**82B** St. Philips Marsh		
2289	*2251*	**DID** Didcot	**81E** Didcot	**81E** Didcot	**89C** Machynlleth	**89A** Oswestry	**84C** Banbury	
2290	*2251*	**WOS** Worcester	**85A** Worcester	**85A** Worcester	**87G** Carmarthen			
2291	*2251*	**CARM** Carmarthen	**85B** Gloucester	**85B** Gloucester	**85B** Gloucester	**82C** Swindon	**82C** Swindon	
2292	*2251*	**TYS** Tyseley	**89C** Machynlleth	**85B** Gloucester	**86E** Severn Tunnel Junction	**86E** Severn Tunnel Junction		
2293	*2251*	**SPM** St. Philips Marsh	**82B** St. Philips Marsh	**82B** St. Philips Marsh	**82C** Swindon			
2294	*2251*	**WOS** Worcester	**85A** Worcester	**85A** Worcester	**81F** Oxford	**89C** Machynlleth		
2295	*2251*	**BAN** Banbury	**84C** Banbury	**85B** Gloucester	**85C** Hereford	**85C** Hereford		
2296	*2251*	**TYS** Tyseley	**84E** Tyseley	**84E** Tyseley	**84J** Croes Newydd			
2297	*2251*	**TYS** Tyseley	**84J** Croes Newydd	**84C** Banbury	**84C** Banbury	**84C** Banbury		
2298	*2251*	**ABH** Aberystwyth	**89C** Machynlleth	**89C** Machynlleth	**89C** Machynlleth	**89C** Machynlleth	**86A** Ebbw Junction	
2299	*2251*	**RDG** Reading	**81D** Reading	**81D** Reading	**81D** Reading			
2322	*2301*	**SPM** St. Philips Marsh	**82B** St. Philips Marsh					
2323	*2301*	**MCH** Machynlleth	**89C** Machynlleth					
2327	*2301*	**OSW** Oswestry	**89A** Oswestry					
2339	*2301*	**WOS** Worcester	**85A** Worcester					
2340	*2301*	**SPM** St. Philips Marsh	**82B** St. Philips Marsh	**82D** Westbury				
2343	*2301*	**BCN** Brecon	**89B** Brecon					
2349	*2301*	**HFD** Hereford	**85C** Hereford					
2350	*2301*	**LYD** Lydney	**85B** Gloucester					
2351	*2301*	**BCN** Brecon	**89B** Brecon					
2354	*2301*	**OSW** Oswestry	**89A** Oswestry					

		1948	1951	1954	1957	1960	1963	1966
2356	*2301*	**MCH** Machynlleth						
2382	*2301*	**OSW** Oswestry						
2385	*2301*	**PPRD** Pontypool Road	**86G** Pontypool Road					
2386	*2301*	**OSW** Oswestry						
2401	*2301*	**BCN** Brecon	**89B** Brecon					
2407	*2301*	**NPT** Ebbw Junction	**86C** Cardiff Canton					
2408	*2301*	**BAN** Banbury	**89A** Oswestry					
2409	*2301*	**CARM** Carmarthen	**89A** Oswestry					
2411	*2301*	**CARM** Carmarthen	**87A** Neath	**82B** St. Philips Marsh				
2414	*2301*	**STJ** Severn Tunnel Junction	**86E** Severn Tunnel Junction					
2426	*2301*	**SPM** St. Philips Marsh	**82B** St. Philips Marsh					
2431	*2301*	**CARM** Carmarthen	**87G** Carmarthen					
2444	*2301*	**BRD** Bristol Bath Road	**82D** Westbury					
2445	*2301*	**WES** Westbury	**82B** St. Philips Marsh					
2449	*2301*	**OSW** Oswestry	**89A** Oswestry					
2452	*2301*	**BCN** Brecon	**89B** Brecon					
2458	*2301*	**WOS** Worcester	**85A** Worcester	**85A** Worcester				
2460	*2301*	**STJ** Severn Tunnel Junction	**86E** Severn Tunnel Junction	**86E** Severn Tunnel Junction				
2462	*2301*	**BRD** Bristol Bath Road	**82B** St. Philips Marsh					
2464	*2301*	**MCH** Machynlleth						
2468	*2301*	**BCN** Brecon	**89B** Brecon					
2474	*2301*	**CARM** Carmarthen	**87G** Carmarthen	**85C** Hereford				
2482	*2301*	**OSW** Oswestry	**89B** Brecon					
2483	*2301*	**OSW** Oswestry	**89B** Brecon					
2484	*2301*	**CDF** Cardiff Canton	**89A** Oswestry	**89A** Oswestry				
2513	*2301*	**CHR** Chester (GWR)	**84K** Chester (GWR)	**84K** Chester (GWR)				
2515	*2301*	**LYD** Lydney	**85C** Hereford					
2516	*2301*	**OSW** Oswestry	**89A** Oswestry	**81D** Reading				
2523	*2301*	**BCN** Brecon						
2532	*2301*	**DID** Didcot	**81E** Didcot	**81E** Didcot				
2534	*2301*	**SPM** St. Philips Marsh	**82A** Bristol Bath Road					
2537	*2301*	**CDF** Cardiff Canton	**86C** Cardiff Canton					
2538	*2301*	**CDF** Cardiff Canton	**89A** Oswestry	**89A** Oswestry	**89A** Oswestry			
2541	*2301*	**HFD** Hereford	**85C** Hereford	**85C** Hereford				
2543	*2301*	**OSW** Oswestry	**89A** Oswestry					
2551	*2301*	**WOS** Worcester	**85A** Worcester					
2556	*2301*	**OSW** Oswestry	**89A** Oswestry					
2568	*2301*	**SDN** Swindon	**82C** Swindon					
2569	*2301*	**BCN** Brecon						
2570	*2301*	**CDF** Cardiff Canton						
2572	*2301*	**MCH** Machynlleth	**89A** Oswestry					
2573	*2301*	**RDG** Reading	**81D** Reading					
2578	*2301*	**SPM** St. Philips Marsh	**82B** St. Philips Marsh					
2579	*2301*	**OXF** Oxford	**81E** Didcot	**81F** Oxford				
2612	*2600*	**BAN** Banbury						
2620	*2600*	**STB** Stourbridge						
2623	*2600*	**OXY** Oxley						
2643	*2600*	**BAN** Banbury						
2651	*2600*	**WOS** Worcester						
2655	*2600*	**STB** Stourbridge						
2656	*2600*	**GLO** Gloucester						
2662	*2600*	**CHR** Chester (GWR)						
2665	*2600*	**OXY** Oxley						
2667	*2600*	**CDF** Cardiff Canton						
2669	*2600*	**PPRD** Pontypool Road						
2680	*2600*	**HFD** Hereford						
2702	*655*	**SPM** St. Philips Marsh						
2704	*655*	**CNYD** Croes Newydd						
2706	*655*	**STB** Stourbridge						
2707	*655*	**LLY** Llanelly						
2708	*655*	**TN** Taunton						
2709	*655*	**SPM** St. Philips Marsh						
2712	*655*	**STB** Stourbridge						
2713	*655*	**CNYD** Croes Newydd						
2714	*655*	**HFD** Hereford						
2715	*655*	**DYD** Duffryn Yard						
2716	*655*	**CNYD** Croes Newydd						
2717	*655*	**CNYD** Croes Newydd						
2719	*655*	**TYS** Tyseley						
2721	*2721*	**DYD** Duffryn Yard						
2722	*2721*	**NEA** Neath						
2724	*2721*	**CED** Cardiff East Dock						
2728	*2721*	**PPRD** Pontypool Road						
2730	*2721*	**LLY** Llanelly						
2734	*2721*	**PILL** Newport Pill						
2738	*2721*	**PILL** Newport Pill						
2739	*2721*	**PPRD** Pontypool Road						
2743	*2721*	**WOS** Worcester						
2744	*2721*	**SALOP** Shrewsbury						
2745	*2721*	**SALOP** Shrewsbury						
2746	*2721*	**LLY** Llanelly						
2748	*2721*	**TN** Taunton						
2749	*2721*	**PPRD** Pontypool Road						
2751	*2721*	**LLY** Llanelly						
2752	*2721*	**PZ** Penzance						
2754	*2721*	**CED** Cardiff East Dock						
2755	*2721*	**TN** Taunton						
2756	*2721*	**GLO** Gloucester						
2757	*2721*	**SLO** Slough						
2760	*2721*	**MTHR** Merthyr						
2761	*2721*	**TDU** Tondu						
2764	*2721*	**PILL** Newport Pill						
2767	*2721*	**PPRD** Pontypool Road						
2769	*2721*	**TDU** Tondu						
2771	*2721*	**STB** Stourbridge						
2772	*2721*	**LMTN** Leamington Spa						
2774	*2721*	**WOS** Worcester						
2776	*2721*	**LA** Laira (Plymouth)						
2780	*2721*	**SBZ** St. Blazey						
2781	*2721*	**CED** Cardiff East Dock						
2785	*2721*	**NA** Newton Abbot						
2786	*2721*	**SPM** St. Philips Marsh						
2787	*2721*	**PANT** Pantyffynnon						
2789	*2721*	**SED** Swansea East Dock						
2790	*2721*	**SLO** Slough						
2791	*2721*	**SRD** Stafford Road						
2792	*2721*	**DYD** Duffryn Yard						
2793	*2721*	**PILL** Newport Pill						
2794	*2721*	**NPT** Ebbw Junction						
2795	*2721*	**NPT** Ebbw Junction						
2797	*2721*	**NEA** Neath						
2798	*2721*	**DG** Danygraig						
2799	*2721*	**WOS** Worcester						
2800	*2800*	**PPRD** Pontypool Road	**87B** Duffryn Yard	**87B** Duffryn Yard	**86A** Ebbw Junction			

		1948	1951	1954	1957	1960	1963	1966
2801	*2800*	**ABDR** Aberdare	**86G** Pontypool Road	**86G** Pontypool Road	**86G** Pontypool Road			
2802	*2800*	**PPRD** Pontypool Road	**86G** Pontypool Road	**86G** Pontypool Road	**86G** Pontypool Road			
2803	*2800*	**WES** Westbury	**87F** Llanelly	**86E** Severn Tunnel Junction	**86E** Severn Tunnel Junction			
2804	*2800*	**STJ** Severn Tunnel Junction	**86E** Severn Tunnel Junction	**84F** Stourbridge	**84F** Stourbridge			
2805	*2800*	**BAN** Banbury	**84C** Banbury	**86B** Newport Pill	**86C** Cardiff Canton	**83A** Newton Abbot		
2806	*2800*	**ABDR** Aberdare	**86C** Cardiff Canton	**86C** Cardiff Canton	**86E** Severn Tunnel Junction	**86E** Severn Tunnel Junction		
2807	*2800*	**HFD** Hereford	**85C** Hereford	**85A** Worcester	**85A** Worcester	**83A** Newton Abbot	**86E** Severn Tunnel Junction	
2808	*2800*	**ABDR** Aberdare	**86J** Aberdare	**86J** Aberdare	**87F** Llanelly			
2809	*2800*	**STJ** Severn Tunnel Junction	**83A** Newton Abbot	**83A** Newton Abbot	**85B** Gloucester	**83D** Laira (Plymouth)		
2810	*2800*	**ABDR** Aberdare	**84K** Chester (GWR)	**86J** Aberdare	**86J** Aberdare			
2811	*2800*	**ABDR** Aberdare	**86G** Pontypool Road	**86E** Severn Tunnel Junction	**82D** Westbury			
2812	*2800*	**CHR** Chester (GWR)	**84K** Chester (GWR)	**84C** Banbury	**84C** Banbury			
2813	*2800*	**PPRD** Pontypool Road	**86G** Pontypool Road	**87B** Duffryn Yard	**85A** Worcester	**86J** Aberdare		
2814	*2800*	**TN** Taunton	**83B** Taunton	**83B** Taunton	**86A** Ebbw Junction			
2815	*2800*	**STJ** Severn Tunnel Junction	**86A** Ebbw Junction	**86E** Severn Tunnel Junction	**86E** Severn Tunnel Junction			
2816	*2800*	**BAN** Banbury	**84C** Banbury	**84C** Banbury	**84C** Banbury			
2817	*2800*	**WEY** Weymouth	**86A** Ebbw Junction	**84C** Banbury	**84K** Chester (GWR)			
2818	*2800*	**WES** Westbury	**82B** St. Philips Marsh	**82C** Swindon	**82C** Swindon	**86A** Ebbw Junction	**86A** Ebbw Junction	
2819	*2800*	**STJ** Severn Tunnel Junction	**86A** Ebbw Junction	**81E** Didcot	**84B** Oxley	**81E** Didcot		
2820	*2800*	**CDF** Cardiff Canton	**86C** Cardiff Canton	**86C** Cardiff Canton	**86A** Ebbw Junction			
2821	*2800*	**CDF** Cardiff Canton	**86A** Ebbw Junction	**86G** Pontypool Road	**86C** Cardiff Canton	**86C** Cardiff Canton		
2822	*2800*	**ABDR** Aberdare	**84J** Croes Newydd	**84K** Chester (GWR)	**84C** Banbury	**83B** Taunton	**83B** Taunton	
2823	*2800*	**ABDR** Aberdare	**85B** Gloucester	**84C** Banbury	**84C** Banbury			
2824	*2800*	**STJ** Severn Tunnel Junction	**87F** Llanelly	**87F** Llanelly	**81D** Reading			
2825	*2800*	**OXY** Oxley	**81D** Reading	**85A** Worcester	**85A** Worcester			
2826	*2800*	**PDN** Old Oak Common	**81A** Old Oak Common	**84E** Tyseley	**86E** Severn Tunnel Junction			
2827	*2800*	**OXF** Oxford	**81F** Oxford	**84C** Banbury	**82D** Westbury			
2828	*2800*	**ABDR** Aberdare	**86J** Aberdare	**86J** Aberdare	**86J** Aberdare			
2829	*2800*	**STJ** Severn Tunnel Junction	**86E** Severn Tunnel Junction	**86E** Severn Tunnel Junction	**84F** Stourbridge			
2830	*2800*	**OXY** Oxley	**84B** Oxley	**84B** Oxley	**84B** Oxley			
2831	*2800*	**ABDR** Aberdare	**86J** Aberdare	**86J** Aberdare	**86J** Aberdare	**86J** Aberdare		
2832	*2800*	(4806)	**84B** Oxley	**84G** Shrewsbury	**86E** Severn Tunnel Junction			
2833	*2800*	**BHD** Birkenhead	**84B** Oxley	**84B** Oxley	**84B** Oxley			
2834	*2800*	(4808)	**86A** Ebbw Junction	**84C** Banbury	**84F** Stourbridge	**86C** Cardiff Canton		
2835	*2800*	**PDN** Old Oak Common	**81A** Old Oak Common	**84C** Banbury	**81D** Reading	**82C** Swindon		
2836	*2800*	**ABDR** Aberdare	**86J** Aberdare	**86J** Aberdare	**86J** Aberdare	**81E** Didcot	**81E** Didcot	
2837	*2800*	**CDF** Cardiff Canton	**86C** Cardiff Canton	**86C** Cardiff Canton	**86C** Cardiff Canton	**86E** Severn Tunnel Junction		
2838	*2800*	**STJ** Severn Tunnel Junction	**86E** Severn Tunnel Junction	**86E** Severn Tunnel Junction	**86E** Severn Tunnel Junction			
2839	*2800*	(4804)	**82B** St. Philips Marsh	**86E** Severn Tunnel Junction	**86E** Severn Tunnel Junction	**86G** Pontypool Road	**86G** Pontypool Road	
2840	*2800*	**PDN** Old Oak Common	**84J** Croes Newydd	**84J** Croes Newydd	**84J** Croes Newydd			
2841	*2800*	**ABDR** Aberdare	**84G** Shrewsbury	**84B** Oxley	**84B** Oxley	**81D** Reading	**81D** Reading	
2842	*2800*	**NPT** Ebbw Junction	**86A** Ebbw Junction	**86A** Ebbw Junction	**86A** Ebbw Junction	**86A** Ebbw Junction	**81E** Didcot	
2843	*2800*	**SHL** Southall	**81C** Southall	**83D** Laira (Plymouth)	**83D** Laira (Plymouth)			
2844	*2800*	**SPM** St. Philips Marsh	**82B** St. Philips Marsh	**86E** Severn Tunnel Junction	**86E** Severn Tunnel Junction	**81E** Didcot		
2845	*2800*	(4809)	**81D** Reading	**82B** St. Philips Marsh	**86A** Ebbw Junction	**86G** Pontypool Road	**84C** Banbury	
2846	*2800*	**SPM** St. Philips Marsh	**82B** St. Philips Marsh	**82B** St. Philips Marsh	**83A** Newton Abbot	**83A** Newton Abbot		
2847	*2800*	(4811)	**84C** Banbury	**84C** Banbury	**84C** Banbury	**86E** Severn Tunnel Junction		
2848	*2800*	(4807)	**84E** Tyseley	**84E** Tyseley	**84K** Chester (GWR)			
2849	*2800*	(4803)	**84E** Tyseley	**84E** Tyseley	**84E** Tyseley	**81E** Didcot		
2850	*2800*	**PDN** Old Oak Common	**87F** Llanelly	**84C** Banbury	**84B** Oxley	**84B** Oxley		
2851	*2800*	**NPT** Ebbw Junction	**86A** Ebbw Junction	**86A** Ebbw Junction	**84E** Tyseley	**83B** Taunton	**84C** Banbury	
2852	*2800*	**STB** Stourbridge	**84F** Stourbridge	**82C** Swindon	**82C** Swindon	**82C** Swindon	**81E** Didcot	
2853	*2800*	(4810)	**84C** Banbury	**84J** Croes Newydd	**81C** Southall	**81D** Reading		
2854	*2800*	(4801)	**84B** Oxley	**84B** Oxley	**85B** Gloucester	**85B** Gloucester	**86E** Severn Tunnel Junction	
2855	*2800*	**PDN** Old Oak Common	**87F** Llanelly	**85A** Worcester	**85A** Worcester	**84J** Croes Newydd		
2856	*2800*	**PDN** Old Oak Common	**84F** Stourbridge	**84E** Tyseley	**84E** Tyseley	**84F** Stourbridge	**84B** Oxley	
2857	*2800*	**LA** Laira (Plymouth)	**84F** Stourbridge	**84C** Banbury	**84E** Tyseley	**86G** Pontypool Road	**87A** Neath	
2858	*2800*	**SHL** Southall	**81F** Oxford	**81C** Southall	**86A** Ebbw Junction	**86A** Ebbw Junction	**86E** Severn Tunnel Junction	
2859	*2800*	**SPM** St. Philips Marsh	**82B** St. Philips Marsh	**86E** Severn Tunnel Junction	**86E** Severn Tunnel Junction	**86G** Pontypool Road	**86G** Pontypool Road	
2860	*2800*	**CDF** Cardiff Canton	**81F** Oxford	**86E** Severn Tunnel Junction	**86E** Severn Tunnel Junction	**86E** Severn Tunnel Junction		
2861	*2800*	**OXF** Oxford	**86A** Ebbw Junction	**86A** Ebbw Junction	**86A** Ebbw Junction	**86E** Severn Tunnel Junction	**86E** Severn Tunnel Junction	
2862	*2800*	(4802)	**86G** Pontypool Road	**86E** Severn Tunnel Junction	**86E** Severn Tunnel Junction	**86E** Severn Tunnel Junction	**86E** Severn Tunnel Junction	
2863	*2800*	(4805)	**84C** Banbury	**86J** Aberdare	**86J** Aberdare			
2864	*2800*	**CDF** Cardiff Canton	**86G** Pontypool Road	**86A** Ebbw Junction	**86E** Severn Tunnel Junction			
2865	*2800*	**NPT** Ebbw Junction	**86A** Ebbw Junction	**82C** Swindon	**82C** Swindon	**82C** Swindon	**86E** Severn Tunnel Junction	
2866	*2800*	**NPT** Ebbw Junction	**86A** Ebbw Junction	**86E** Severn Tunnel Junction	**86E** Severn Tunnel Junction	**86G** Pontypool Road	**84C** Banbury	
2867	*2800*	**LA** Laira (Plymouth)	**84E** Tyseley	**84E** Tyseley	**81D** Reading	**86G** Pontypool Road	**86A** Ebbw Junction	
2868	*2800*	**PDN** Old Oak Common	**81A** Old Oak Common	**82C** Swindon	**86A** Ebbw Junction			
2869	*2800*	**BAN** Banbury	**84K** Chester (GWR)	**83A** Newton Abbot	**86E** Severn Tunnel Junction			
2870	*2800*	**ABDR** Aberdare	**86J** Aberdare	**86J** Aberdare	**86J** Aberdare			
2871	*2800*	**BAN** Banbury	**84J** Croes Newydd	**84J** Croes Newydd	**84J** Croes Newydd	**84J** Croes Newydd	**83B** Taunton	
2872	*2800*	(4800)	**87F** Llanelly	**87B** Duffryn Yard	**86E** Severn Tunnel Junction	**86E** Severn Tunnel Junction	**86E** Severn Tunnel Junction	
2873	*2800*	**EXE** Exeter	**83A** Newton Abbot	**86E** Severn Tunnel Junction	**86E** Severn Tunnel Junction	**86J** Aberdare	**81C** Southall	
2874	*2800*	**BAN** Banbury	**84F** Stourbridge	**84F** Stourbridge	**86C** Cardiff Canton	**86C** Cardiff Canton	**87A** Neath	
2875	*2800*	**PDN** Old Oak Common	**83D** Laira (Plymouth)	**83A** Newton Abbot	**83A** Newton Abbot	**83A** Newton Abbot	**84C** Banbury	
2876	*2800*	**NPT** Ebbw Junction	**86A** Ebbw Junction	**86J** Aberdare	**86J** Aberdare	**86J** Aberdare	**88J** Aberdare	
2877	*2800*	**CDF** Cardiff Canton	**86C** Cardiff Canton	**86C** Cardiff Canton	**86C** Cardiff Canton	**86C** Cardiff Canton		
2878	*2800*	**BAN** Banbury	**84J** Croes Newydd	**84J** Croes Newydd	**84J** Croes Newydd			
2879	*2800*	**NPT** Ebbw Junction	**86A** Ebbw Junction	**82B** St. Philips Marsh	**82C** Swindon	**82C** Swindon	**82C** Swindon	
2880	*2800*	**ABDR** Aberdare	**86J** Aberdare	**81C** Southall	**81C** Southall			
2881	*2800*	**OXF** Oxford	**83A** Newton Abbot	**83A** Newton Abbot	**83A** Newton Abbot	**83A** Newton Abbot		
2882	*2800*	**BAN** Banbury	**84K** Chester (GWR)	**84B** Oxley	**84K** Chester (GWR)	**83B** Taunton	**83B** Taunton	
2883	*2800*	**CHR** Chester (GWR)	**84C** Banbury	**86E** Severn Tunnel Junction	**86E** Severn Tunnel Junction	**86G** Pontypool Road		
2884	*2884*	**STJ** Severn Tunnel Junction	**86G** Pontypool Road	**86G** Pontypool Road	**86G** Pontypool Road	**86A** Ebbw Junction	**86E** Severn Tunnel Junction	
2885	*2884*	**BAN** Banbury	**84F** Stourbridge	**84F** Stourbridge	**84F** Stourbridge	**84F** Stourbridge	**86A** Ebbw Junction	
2886	*2884*	**CHR** Chester (GWR)	**84C** Banbury	**84C** Banbury	**84C** Banbury	**84E** Tyseley	**82D** Westbury	
2887	*2884*	**STJ** Severn Tunnel Junction	**86E** Severn Tunnel Junction	**86E** Severn Tunnel Junction	**86E** Severn Tunnel Junction	**86E** Severn Tunnel Junction	**88L** Cardiff East Dock	
2888	*2884*	(4850)	**86G** Pontypool Road	**86E** Severn Tunnel Junction	**86E** Severn Tunnel Junction	**84F** Stourbridge	**84C** Banbury	
2889	*2884*	**CDF** Cardiff Canton	**86A** Ebbw Junction	**82B** St. Philips Marsh	**86E** Severn Tunnel Junction	**86C** Cardiff Canton	**81D** Reading	
2890	*2884*	**CDF** Cardiff Canton	**84K** Chester (GWR)	**84K** Chester (GWR)	**81C** Southall	**82C** Swindon	**82C** Swindon	
2891	*2884*	**CDF** Cardiff Canton	**86C** Cardiff Canton	**86C** Cardiff Canton	**86C** Cardiff Canton	**86C** Cardiff Canton	**86A** Ebbw Junction	
2892	*2884*	**STJ** Severn Tunnel Junction	**86C** Cardiff Canton	**86C** Cardiff Canton	**86C** Cardiff Canton	**86E** Severn Tunnel Junction	**86E** Severn Tunnel Junction	
2893	*2884*	**PPRD** Pontypool Road	**86G** Pontypool Road	**86E** Severn Tunnel Junction	**86E** Severn Tunnel Junction	**86A** Ebbw Junction	**81E** Didcot	
2894	*2884*	**NPT** Ebbw Junction	**86A** Ebbw Junction	**87B** Duffryn Yard	**86A** Ebbw Junction	**86A** Ebbw Junction	**86A** Ebbw Junction	
2895	*2884*	**BHD** Birkenhead	**81A** Old Oak Common	**86E** Severn Tunnel Junction	**86E** Severn Tunnel Junction	**86C** Cardiff Canton	**86E** Severn Tunnel Junction	
2896	*2884*	**NPT** Ebbw Junction	**86A** Ebbw Junction	**86A** Ebbw Junction	**86E** Severn Tunnel Junction	**86E** Severn Tunnel Junction	**86E** Severn Tunnel Junction	
2897	*2884*	**SALOP** Shrewsbury	**84C** Banbury	**84C** Banbury	**84E** Tyseley	**84F** Stourbridge	**86G** Pontypool Road	
2898	*2884*	**BAN** Banbury	**84C** Banbury	**82B** St. Philips Marsh	**84E** Tyseley	**86A** Ebbw Junction	**81E** Didcot	
2899	*2884*	**BAN** Banbury	**84C** Banbury	**81C** Southall	**81C** Southall	**83D** Laira (Plymouth)	**81C** Southall	
2902	*2900*	**LMTN** Leamington Spa						
2903	*2900*	**TYS** Tyseley						
2905	*2900*	**CDF** Cardiff Canton						
2906	*2900*	**CDF** Cardiff Canton	**86C** Cardiff Canton					
2908	*2900*	**SDN** Swindon						
2912	*2900*	**WEY** Weymouth	**82F** Weymouth					
2913	*2900*	**SDN** Swindon						
2915	*2900*	**CHR** Chester (GWR)						
2916	*2900*	**TYS** Tyseley						
2920	*2900*	**HFD** Hereford	**85C** Hereford					
2924	*2900*	**HFD** Hereford						
2926	*2900*	**CHR** Chester (GWR)	**84K** Chester (GWR)					
2927	*2900*	**SDN** Swindon	**82C** Swindon					
2928	*2900*	**WES** Westbury						
2929	*2900*	**BRD** Bristol Bath Road						

No.	Class	1948	1951	1954	1957	1960	1963	1966
2930	*2900*	**CHR** Chester (GWR)						
2931	*2900*	**BRD** Bristol Bath Road	**82A** Bristol Bath Road					
2932	*2900*	**HFD** Hereford	**84E** Tyseley					
2933	*2900*	**LMTN** Leamington Spa	**84D** Leamington Spa					
2934	*2900*	**SDN** Swindon	**82C** Swindon					
2935	*2900*	**SDN** Swindon						
2936	*2900*	**NPT** Ebbw Junction	**86A** Ebbw Junction					
2937	*2900*	**HFD** Hereford	**85C** Hereford					
2938	*2900*	**GLO** Gloucester	**85B** Gloucester					
2939	*2900*	**BRD** Bristol Bath Road						
2940	*2900*	**CDF** Cardiff Canton	**86C** Cardiff Canton					
2941	*2900*	**WES** Westbury						
2942	*2900*	**BRD** Bristol Bath Road						
2943	*2900*	**CDF** Cardiff Canton	**86C** Cardiff Canton					
2944	*2900*	**HFD** Hereford	**85C** Hereford					
2945	*2900*	**SDN** Swindon	**82C** Swindon					
2946	*2900*	**WES** Westbury						
2947	*2900*	**SDN** Swindon	**82C** Swindon					
2948	*2900*	**HFD** Hereford	**82A** Bristol Bath Road					
2949	*2900*	**SDN** Swindon	**82C** Swindon					
2950	*2900*	**BRD** Bristol Bath Road	**82A** Bristol Bath Road					
2951	*2900*	**HFD** Hereford	**85B** Gloucester					
2952	*2900*	**STJ** Severn Tunnel Junction	**86E** Severn Tunnel Junction					
2953	*2900*	**CHR** Chester (GWR)	**84K** Chester (GWR)					
2954	*2900*	**SDN** Swindon	**82C** Swindon					
2955	*2900*	**WEY** Weymouth						
2979	*2900*	**NPT** Ebbw Junction	**86A** Ebbw Junction					
2980	*2900*	**GLO** Gloucester						
2981	*2900*	**BAN** Banbury	**84C** Banbury					
2987	*2900*	**HFD** Hereford						
2988	*2900*	**TYS** Tyseley						
2989	*2900*	**CHR** Chester (GWR)						
3002	*ROD*	**PPRD** Pontypool Road						
3004	*ROD*	**CARM** Carmarthen						
3005	*ROD*	**TYS** Tyseley						
3006	*ROD*	**CARM** Carmarthen						
3008	*ROD*	**SRD** Stafford Road						
3009	*ROD*	**CARM** Carmarthen						
3010	*ROD*	**CARM** Carmarthen	**87G** Carmarthen	**87G** Carmarthen				
3011	*ROD*	**CARM** Carmarthen	**87G** Carmarthen	**87G** Carmarthen	**87G** Carmarthen			
3012	*ROD*	**PPRD** Pontypool Road	**86G** Pontypool Road	**86G** Pontypool Road				
3013	*ROD*	**SPM** St. Philips Marsh						
3014	*ROD*	**WES** Westbury	**82B** St. Philips Marsh	**82B** St. Philips Marsh				
3015	*ROD*	**CARM** Carmarthen	**87G** Carmarthen	**87G** Carmarthen	**87G** Carmarthen			
3016	*ROD*	**OXY** Oxley	**84E** Tyseley	**84B** Oxley				
3017	*ROD*	**SPM** St. Philips Marsh	**81A** Old Oak Common	**82B** St. Philips Marsh				
3018	*ROD*	**PPRD** Pontypool Road	**86G** Pontypool Road	**87G** Carmarthen	**87G** Carmarthen			
3019	*ROD*	**WES** Westbury						
3020	*ROD*	**SRD** Stafford Road	**84C** Banbury	**84C** Banbury				
3021	*ROD*	**WOS** Worcester						
3022	*ROD*	**SPM** St. Philips Marsh	**85A** Worcester	**85B** Gloucester				
3023	*ROD*	**PPRD** Pontypool Road	**86G** Pontypool Road	**86G** Pontypool Road				
3024	*ROD*	**OXY** Oxley	**81E** Didcot	**86C** Cardiff Canton	**87G** Carmarthen			
3025	*ROD*	**RDG** Reading	**81D** Reading	**87G** Carmarthen				
3026	*ROD*	**CNYD** Croes Newydd	**84J** Croes Newydd	**86C** Cardiff Canton				
3027	*ROD*	**WOS** Worcester						
3028	*ROD*	**CNYD** Croes Newydd	**84J** Croes Newydd	**84B** Oxley				
3029	*ROD*	**WOS** Worcester	**85A** Worcester	**84B** Oxley				
3030	*ROD*	**WOS** Worcester						
3031	*ROD*	**OXY** Oxley	**84B** Oxley	**84B** Oxley				
3032	*ROD*	**WES** Westbury	**82B** St. Philips Marsh	**82B** St. Philips Marsh				
3033	*ROD*	**OXY** Oxley	**84B** Oxley					
3034	*ROD*	**SPM** St. Philips Marsh	**82B** St. Philips Marsh					
3035	*ROD*	**WES** Westbury						
3036	*ROD*	**ABDR** Aberdare	**86C** Cardiff Canton	**86G** Pontypool Road	**87G** Carmarthen			
3037	*ROD*	**PPRD** Pontypool Road						
3038	*ROD*	**CDF** Cardiff Canton	**86G** Pontypool Road	**86G** Pontypool Road				
3039	*ROD*	**OXY** Oxley						
3040	*ROD*	**PPRD** Pontypool Road	**86G** Pontypool Road	**86G** Pontypool Road				
3041	*ROD*	**SPM** St. Philips Marsh	**82B** St. Philips Marsh	**84G** Shrewsbury	**87G** Carmarthen			
3042	*ROD*	**CDF** Cardiff Canton	**86G** Pontypool Road	**86G** Pontypool Road				
3043	*ROD*	**SRD** Stafford Road	**84C** Banbury	**86C** Cardiff Canton				
3044	*ROD*	**CDF** Cardiff Canton	**86G** Pontypool Road	**86G** Pontypool Road				
3046	*ROD*	**SPM** St. Philips Marsh						
3047	*ROD*	**RDG** Reading	**81D** Reading					
3048	*ROD*	**WOS** Worcester	**85A** Worcester	**85B** Gloucester				
3049	*ROD*	**TYS** Tyseley						
3100	*3100*	**TDU** Tondu	**86F** Tondu	**86F** Tondu	**86F** Tondu			
3101	*3100*	**TYS** Tyseley	**84E** Tyseley	**84E** Tyseley	**84E** Tyseley			
3102	*3100*	**OXY** Oxley	**84A** Stafford Road	**84A** Stafford Road	**84A** Stafford Road			
3103	*3100*	**NPT** Ebbw Junction	**86A** Ebbw Junction	**86A** Ebbw Junction	**86A** Ebbw Junction	**86A** Ebbw Junction		
3104	*3100*	**OXY** Oxley	**84A** Stafford Road	**84A** Stafford Road	**84A** Stafford Road			
3150	*3150*	**STJ** Severn Tunnel Junction	**86E** Severn Tunnel Junction	**86E** Severn Tunnel Junction	**86E** Severn Tunnel Junction			
3151	*3150*	**TYS** Tyseley	**84E** Tyseley					
3153	*3150*	**GLO** Gloucester	**85B** Gloucester					
3154	*3150*	**STJ** Severn Tunnel Junction						
3157	*3150*	**STJ** Severn Tunnel Junction	**86E** Severn Tunnel Junction					
3158	*3150*	**TYS** Tyseley						
3159	*3150*	**STJ** Severn Tunnel Junction						
3160	*3150*	**SRD** Stafford Road	**84A** Stafford Road					
3161	*3150*	**STJ** Severn Tunnel Junction	**86E** Severn Tunnel Junction					
3163	*3150*	**STJ** Severn Tunnel Junction	**85B** Gloucester	**85B** Gloucester	**85B** Gloucester			
3164	*3150*	**GLO** Gloucester	**85B** Gloucester	**85B** Gloucester				
3165	*3150*	**STJ** Severn Tunnel Junction						
3167	*3150*	**STJ** Severn Tunnel Junction	**86E** Severn Tunnel Junction					
3168	*3150*	**STJ** Severn Tunnel Junction						
3169	*3150*	**BHD** Birkenhead						
3170	*3150*	**STJ** Severn Tunnel Junction	**86E** Severn Tunnel Junction	**86E** Severn Tunnel Junction	**86A** Ebbw Junction			
3171	*3150*	**GLO** Gloucester	**85B** Gloucester	**85B** Gloucester	**85B** Gloucester			
3172	*3150*	**STJ** Severn Tunnel Junction	**86E** Severn Tunnel Junction	**86E** Severn Tunnel Junction	**86E** Severn Tunnel Junction			
3174	*3150*	**STJ** Severn Tunnel Junction	**86E** Severn Tunnel Junction	**86E** Severn Tunnel Junction	**86E** Severn Tunnel Junction			
3175	*3150*	**GLO** Gloucester						
3176	*3150*	**STJ** Severn Tunnel Junction	**86E** Severn Tunnel Junction	**86E** Severn Tunnel Junction	**86E** Severn Tunnel Junction			
3177	*3150*	**STJ** Severn Tunnel Junction	**86E** Severn Tunnel Junction	**86E** Severn Tunnel Junction	**86E** Severn Tunnel Junction			
3178	*3150*	**STJ** Severn Tunnel Junction	**83D** Laira (Plymouth)					
3180	*3150*	**TYS** Tyseley	**84E** Tyseley	**85B** Gloucester	**85B** Gloucester			
3182	*3150*	**STJ** Severn Tunnel Junction						
3183	*3150*	**STJ** Severn Tunnel Junction	**86E** Severn Tunnel Junction	**86E** Severn Tunnel Junction	**86E** Severn Tunnel Junction			
3184	*3150*	**STJ** Severn Tunnel Junction						
3185	*3150*	**STJ** Severn Tunnel Junction	**86E** Severn Tunnel Junction	**86E** Severn Tunnel Junction				
3186	*3150*	**LA** Laira (Plymouth)	**83D** Laira (Plymouth)	**83D** Laira (Plymouth)	**83D** Laira (Plymouth)			
3187	*3150*	**LA** Laira (Plymouth)	**83D** Laira (Plymouth)	**83D** Laira (Plymouth)	**83D** Laira (Plymouth)			
3188	*3150*	**STJ** Severn Tunnel Junction	**86E** Severn Tunnel Junction					
3189	*3150*	**STJ** Severn Tunnel Junction						

No.	Class	1948	1951	1954	1957	1960	1963	1966
3190	3150	**STJ** Severn Tunnel Junction	**86E** Severn Tunnel Junction	**86E** Severn Tunnel Junction	**86E** Severn Tunnel Junction			
3200	2251	**MCH** Machynlleth	**89C** Machynlleth	**89A** Oswestry	**89A** Oswestry	**89A** Oswestry	**89D** Oswestry	
3201	2251	**MCH** Machynlleth	**89C** Machynlleth	**89C** Machynlleth	**89A** Oswestry	**84J** Croes Newydd	**86A** Ebbw Junction	
3202	2251	**OSW** Oswestry	**89C** Machynlleth	**89C** Machynlleth	**89A** Oswestry	**89A** Oswestry		
3203	2251	**CNYD** Croes Newydd	**84J** Croes Newydd	**85B** Gloucester	**85B** Gloucester	**85B** Gloucester	**85B** Gloucester	
3204	2251	**GLO** Gloucester	**85B** Gloucester	**85B** Gloucester	**85A** Worcester	**84K** Wrexham Rhosddu	**89A** Shrewsbury	
3205	2251	**GLO** Gloucester	**85B** Gloucester	**85B** Gloucester	**85A** Worcester	**85A** Worcester	**89A** Shrewsbury	
3206	2251	**CNYD** Croes Newydd	**84J** Croes Newydd	**84F** Stourbridge	**81E** Didcot	**81E** Didcot	**82G** Templecombe	
3207	2251	**MCH** Machynlleth	**89C** Machynlleth	**89C** Machynlleth	**89A** Oswestry	**84G** Shrewsbury		
3208	2251	**OSW** Oswestry	**89A** Oswestry	**89A** Oswestry	**89A** Oswestry	**89A** Oswestry	**89D** Oswestry	
3209	2251	**HFD** Hereford	**85C** Hereford	**85C** Hereford	**85A** Worcester	**89A** Oswestry	**89B** Croes Newydd	
3210	2251	**DID** Didcot	**81E** Didcot	**81E** Didcot	**81E** Didcot	**81E** Didcot	**82G** Templecombe	
3211	2251	**DID** Didcot	**81E** Didcot	**81E** Didcot	**81E** Didcot	**81E** Didcot		
3212	2251	**DID** Didcot	**81E** Didcot	**81E** Didcot	**81E** Didcot	**82D** Westbury	**86E** Severn Tunnel Junction	
3213	2251	**GLO** Gloucester	**85B** Gloucester	**85B** Gloucester	**85A** Worcester	**85A** Worcester	**85A** Worcester	
3214	2251	**WOS** Worcester	**85A** Worcester	**85A** Worcester	**85A** Worcester	**85A** Worcester	**87H** Neyland	
3215	2251	**SDN** Swindon	**82B** St. Philips Marsh	**82B** St. Philips Marsh	**82B** St. Philips Marsh	**82B** St. Philips Marsh	**82G** Templecombe	
3216	2251	**BAN** Banbury	**84C** Banbury	**84F** Stourbridge	**85A** Worcester	**85A** Worcester	**82G** Templecombe	
3217	2251	**SALOP** Shrewsbury	**84G** Shrewsbury	**84F** Stourbridge	**85A** Worcester	**85A** Worcester	**84D** Leamington Spa	
3218	2251	→	**84C** Banbury	**84F** Stourbridge	**85A** Worcester	**85A** Worcester	**82E** Bristol Barrow Road	
3219	2251	→	**85A** Worcester	**81D** Reading	**81D** Reading	**81D** Reading	**81D** Reading	
3335	3300	**EXE** Exeter						
3341	3300	**NA** Newton Abbot						
3363	3300	**WES** Westbury						
0004	3300	**WES** Westbury						
3366	3300	**CHR** Chester (GWR)						
3376	3300	**DID** Didcot						
3377	3300	**SALOP** Shrewsbury	**85A** Worcester					
3379	3300	**GLO** Gloucester						
3382	3300	**WOS** Worcester						
3383	3300	**NA** Newton Abbot						
3386	3300	**RDG** Reading						
3391	3300	**LA** Laira (Plymouth)						
3393	3300	**WOS** Worcester						
3395	3300	**EXE** Exeter						
3396	3300	**DID** Didcot						
3400	3300	**NA** Newton Abbot						
3401	3300	**LA** Laira (Plymouth)						
3406	3300	**PPRD** Pontypool Road	**85C** Hereford					
3407	3300	**NA** Newton Abbot						
3408	3300	**DID** Didcot						
3417	3300	**WLN** Wellington						
3418	3300	**RDG** Reading						
3419	3300	**DID** Didcot						
3421	3300	**SDN** Swindon						
3426	3300	**RDG** Reading						
3430	3300	**NA** Newton Abbot						
3431	3300	**LA** Laira (Plymouth)						
3432	3300	**HFD** Hereford						
3438	3300	**WES** Westbury						
3440	3300	**WOS** Worcester						
3441	3300	**LA** Laira (Plymouth)						
3442	3300	**SALOP** Shrewsbury						
3443	3300	**TN** Taunton						
3444	3300	**TN** Taunton	**82C** Swindon					
3445	3300	**LA** Laira (Plymouth)						
3446	3300	**LA** Laira (Plymouth)						
3447	3300	**NEY** Neyland	**85A** Worcester					
3448	3300	**DID** Didcot						
3449	3300	**CHEL** Cheltenham	**82C** Swindon					
3450	3300	**STB** Stourbridge						
3451	3300	**EXE** Exeter	**82C** Swindon					
3452	3300	**SDN** Swindon						
3453	3300	**PPRD** Pontypool Road	**82C** Swindon					
3454	3300	**HFD** Hereford	**81D** Reading					
3455	3300	**NEA** Neath						
3400	9400	→	→	→	**88B** Cardiff East Dock	**84G** Shrewsbury	**88B** Radyr	
3401	9400	→	→	→	**88B** Cardiff East Dock	**88A** Radyr	**88B** Radyr	
3402	9400	→	→	→	**88B** Cardiff East Dock	**88A** Radyr	**88B** Radyr	
3403	9400	→	→	→	**88B** Cardiff East Dock	**88A** Radyr	**88B** Radyr	
3404	9400	→	→	→	**88B** Cardiff Fast Dock	**88A** Radyr		
3405	9400	→	→	·	**88B** Cardiff East Dock	**88A** Radyr	**88B** Radyr	
3406	9400	→	→	→	**88B** Cardiff East Dock	**88A** Radyr	**88B** Radyr	
3407	9400	→	→	→	**88B** Cardiff East Dock	**88A** Radyr		
3408	9400	→	→	→	**88B** Cardiff East Dock	**88A** Radyr		
3409	9400	→	→	→	**88B** Cardiff East Dock	**88A** Radyr	**88B** Radyr	
3440	City	→	→	→	→	**82C** Swindon		
3561	3500	**SDN** Swindon						
3562	3500	**SHL** Southall						
3574	3571	**WOS** Worcester						
3575	3571	**STJ** Severn Tunnel Junction						
3577	3571	**SED** Swansea East Dock						
3582	3500	**TN** Taunton						
3585	3500	**OXF** Oxford						
3586	3500	**LTS** Llantrisant						
3588	3500	**OXF** Oxford						
3589	3500	**OXF** Oxford						
3592	3500	**CARM** Carmarthen						
3597	3500	**CHYS** Cardiff Cathays						
3599	3500	**RYR** Radyr						
3600	5700	**PDN** Old Oak Common	**83A** Newton Abbot	**83A** Newton Abbot	**83A** Newton Abbot	**89A** Oswestry	**87A** Neath	
3601	5700	**HFD** Hereford	**85D** Kidderminster	**85D** Kidderminster	**85D** Kidderminster	**85D** Kidderminster	**84G** Kidderminster	
3602	5700	**SALOP** Shrewsbury	**84G** Shrewsbury	**84G** Shrewsbury	**84G** Shrewsbury	**84G** Shrewsbury		
3603	5700	**EXE** Exeter	**83C** Exeter	**83C** Exeter	**83C** Exeter	**86J** Aberdare	**88J** Aberdare	
3604	5700	**SPM** St. Philips Marsh	**82B** St. Philips Marsh	**82B** St. Philips Marsh	**82B** St. Philips Marsh	**82A** Bristol Bath Road	**82B** St. Philips Marsh	
3605	5700	**ABDR** Aberdare	**86J** Aberdare	**86J** Aberdare	**86J** Aberdare	**85A** Worcester	**84B** Oxley	**2B** Oxley
3606	5700	**EXE** Exeter	**83C** Exeter	**83C** Exeter	**83C** Exeter	**82E** Bristol Barrow Road		
3607	5700	**WOS** Worcester	**85A** Worcester	**85A** Worcester	**85A** Worcester	**85A** Worcester	**84G** Kidderminster	**2C** Stourbridge
3608	5700	**OXF** Oxford	**81F** Oxford	**81F** Oxford	**81F** Oxford	**81B** Slough	**81B** Slough	
3609	5700	**GLO** Gloucester	**85B** Gloucester	**85B** Gloucester	**85B** Gloucester	**85B** Gloucester		
3610	5700	**ABDR** Aberdare	**86J** Aberdare	**86J** Aberdare	**86J** Aberdare	**86J** Aberdare	**87B** Duffryn Yard	
3611	5700	**NEA** Neath	**87A** Neath	**87A** Neath	**87A** Neath	**87A** Neath		
3612	5700	**ABEEG** Aberbeeg	**86D** Llantrisant	**86D** Llantrisant	**86D** Llantrisant	**86D** Llantrisant	**88G** Llantrisant	
3613	5700	**TYS** Tyseley	**84H** Wellington	**84H** Wellington	**87B** Duffryn Yard	**87B** Duffryn Yard	**87B** Duffryn Yard	
3614	5700	**SPM** St. Philips Marsh	**82B** St. Philips Marsh	**82B** St. Philips Marsh	**82D** Westbury	**82D** Westbury		
3615	5700	**SRD** Stafford Road	**84A** Stafford Road	**84A** Stafford Road	**84A** Stafford Road	**84A** Stafford Road	**88C** Barry	
3616	5700	**ABEEG** Aberbeeg	**86F** Tondu	**86F** Tondu	**86F** Tondu	**86F** Tondu	**88H** Tondu	
3617	5700	**LTS** Llantrisant	**86D** Llantrisant	**86D** Llantrisant	**86D** Llantrisant	**86D** Llantrisant	**88G** Llantrisant	
3618	5700	**PDN** Old Oak Common	**81C** Southall	**81C** Southall	**81C** Southall	**81C** Southall	**81C** Southall	
3619	5700	**PDN** Old Oak Common	**84K** Chester (GWR)	**84D** Leamington Spa	**84D** Leamington Spa	**84D** Leamington Spa	**84G** Kidderminster	**2C** Stourbridge
3620	5700	**SHL** Southall	**81C** Southall	**81C** Southall	**81C** Southall	**81C** Southall	**81C** Southall	
3621	5700	**NEA** Neath	**87A** Neath	**87A** Neath	**87A** Neath	**87A** Neath	**87A** Neath	
3622	5700	**DID** Didcot	**81E** Didcot	**81E** Didcot	**81E** Didcot	**81E** Didcot	**81C** Southall	
3623	5700	**SPM** St. Philips Marsh	**82B** St. Philips Marsh	**82B** St. Philips Marsh	**82B** St. Philips Marsh	**82A** Bristol Bath Road		

No.	Class	1948	1951	1954	1957	1960	1963	1966
3624	5700	TYS Tyseley	84E Tyseley	84D Leamington Spa	84D Leamington Spa	84D Leamington Spa		
3625	5700	TYS Tyseley	84E Tyseley	84E Tyseley	84E Tyseley	84E Tyseley	84E Tyseley	2A Tyseley
3626	5700	BHD Birkenhead	6C Birkenhead	6C Birkenhead	6C Birkenhead	84H Wellington	87B Duffryn Yard	
3627	5700	TDU Tondu	86F Tondu	86F Tondu	86F Tondu	86F Tondu	88J Aberdare	
3628	5700	PPRD Pontypool Road	86G Pontypool Road	86G Pontypool Road	86G Pontypool Road	86G Pontypool Road	86G Pontypool Road	
3629	5700	LA Laira (Plymouth)	83D Laira (Plymouth)	83D Laira (Plymouth)	83D Laira (Plymouth)	82D Westbury	82D Westbury	
3630	5700	BAN Banbury	84C Banbury	84K Chester (GWR)	84K Chester (GWR)	6E Chester (GWR)		
3631	5700	LMTN Leamington Spa	84D Leamington Spa	84D Leamington Spa	84D Leamington Spa	84D Leamington Spa	84B Oxley	
3632	5700	SPM St. Philips Marsh	82B St. Philips Marsh	82B St. Philips Marsh	82B St. Philips Marsh	82B St. Philips Marsh		
3633	5700	SED Swansea East Dock	87D Swansea East Dock	87D Swansea East Dock	87C Danygraig	72A Exmouth Junction	71G Weymouth	
3634	5700	NPT Ebbw Junction	86A Ebbw Junction	86A Ebbw Junction	86A Ebbw Junction	86A Ebbw Junction	86A Ebbw Junction	
3635	5700	PDN Old Oak Common	83E St. Blazey	83E St. Blazey	83E St. Blazey	83E St. Blazey	87D Swansea East Dock	
3636	5700	NPT Ebbw Junction	86A Ebbw Junction	86A Ebbw Junction	86A Ebbw Junction	86A Ebbw Junction		
3637	5700	FGD Fishguard Goodwick	87J Fishguard Goodwick	87J Fishguard Goodwick	87J Fishguard Goodwick	87J Fishguard Goodwick		
3638	5700	BCN Brecon	89B Brecon	89B Brecon	89B Brecon	86A Ebbw Junction		
3639	5700	LA Laira (Plymouth)	83D Laira (Plymouth)	83D Laira (Plymouth)	83D Laira (Plymouth)	87H Neyland	87H Neyland	
3640	5700	ABEEG Aberbeeg	86H Aberbeeg	86G Pontypool Road	86G Pontypool Road	86G Pontypool Road		
3641	5700	SED Swansea East Dock	87D Swansea East Dock	87D Swansea East Dock	87D Swansea East Dock	87D Swansea East Dock		
3642	5700	LLY Llanelly	87F Llanelly	87F Llanelly	87G Carmarthen	87F Llanelly	87B Duffryn Yard	
3643	5700	SPM St. Philips Marsh	82B St. Philips Marsh	82B St. Philips Marsh	82B St. Philips Marsh	82B St. Philips Marsh	82E Bristol Barrow Road	
3644	5700	PDN Old Oak Common	86D Llantrisant	86D Llantrisant	86D Llantrisant	86D Llantrisant	88G Llantrisant	
3645	5700	SDN Swindon	82C Swindon	82C Swindon	82C Swindon	82C Swindon		
3646	5700	PDN Old Oak Common	84K Chester (GWR)	84K Chester (GWR)	84C Banbury	84C Banbury	81A Old Oak Common	
3647	5700	NPT Ebbw Junction	86A Ebbw Junction	86J Aberdare	86H Aberbeeg	86H Aberbeeg	86F Aberbeeg	
3648	5700	PDN Old Oak Common	81A Old Oak Common	81A Old Oak Common	81A Old Oak Common	81A Old Oak Common	88H Tondu	
3649	5700	STB Stourbridge	84F Stourbridge	84F Stourbridge	84F Stourbridge	84F Stourbridge		
3650	5700	TYS Tyseley	84E Tyseley	88B Cardiff East Dock	88E Abercynon	82B St. Philips Marsh	87A Neath	
3651	5700	PPRD Pontypool Road	86G Pontypool Road	86G Pontypool Road	86G Pontypool Road	86G Pontypool Road	86G Pontypool Road	
3652	5700	SLO Slough	86F Tondu	86F Tondu	86B Newport Pill	86B Newport Pill	87A Neath	
3653	5700	TYS Tyseley	84E Tyseley	81E Didcot	81E Didcot	81E Didcot	81F Oxford	
3654	5700	NEY Neyland	87H Neyland	87H Neyland	87H Neyland	87H Neyland	87H Neyland	
3655	5700	ABDR Aberdare	86J Aberdare	86J Aberdare	86J Aberdare	86J Aberdare		
3656	5700	LTS Llantrisant	86D Llantrisant	86D Llantrisant	86D Llantrisant	86D Llantrisant		
3657	5700	TYS Tyseley	84E Tyseley	87H Neyland	87H Neyland	87H Neyland		
3658	5700	PDN Old Oak Common	84E Tyseley	84F Stourbridge	84F Stourbridge	84F Stourbridge	84F Stourbridge	
3659	5700	PDN Old Oak Common	83A Newton Abbot	83A Newton Abbot	83A Newton Abbot	83A Newton Abbot	83C Exeter	
3660	5700	TYS Tyseley	84E Tyseley	84E Tyseley	84E Tyseley	84E Tyseley	84E Tyseley	
3661	5700	DG Danygraig	87F Llanelly	87F Llanelly	87F Llanelly	87D Swansea East Dock	88G Llantrisant	
3662	5700	NPT Ebbw Junction	86A Ebbw Junction	86A Ebbw Junction	86A Ebbw Junction	86A Ebbw Junction	86A Ebbw Junction	
3663	5700	RDG Reading	86B Newport Pill	86B Newport Pill	86B Newport Pill	86D Llantrisant		
3664	5700	TYS Tyseley	84E Tyseley	84A Stafford Road	84A Stafford Road	84A Stafford Road	88H Tondu	
3665	5700	CHR Chester (GWR)	84K Chester (GWR)	84K Chester (GWR)	84K Chester (GWR)	6E Chester (GWR)	81B Slough	
3666	5700	SDN Swindon	82C Swindon	82C Swindon	82C Swindon	82C Swindon		
3667	5700	STB Stourbridge	84F Stourbridge	84F Stourbridge	84F Stourbridge	84F Stourbridge		
3668	5700	TDU Tondu	86F Tondu	86F Tondu	86F Tondu	86F Tondu	88C Barry	
3669	5700	PDN Old Oak Common	83B Taunton	83B Taunton	83B Taunton	83B Taunton	83B Taunton	
3670	5700	ABEEG Aberbeeg	86C Cardiff Canton	86C Cardiff Canton	86C Cardiff Canton	86C Cardiff Canton		
3671	5700	YEO Yeovil Pen Mill	82E Yeovil Pen Mill	82E Yeovil Pen Mill	82E Yeovil Pen Mill	72C Yeovil Town	72C Yeovil Town	
3672	5700	PDN Old Oak Common	88A Cardiff Cathays	88A Cardiff Cathays	88A Cardiff Cathays	88A Radyr	88B Radyr	
3673	5700	TYS Tyseley	84E Tyseley	84E Tyseley	84E Tyseley	84E Tyseley	84E Tyseley	
3674	5700	TDU Tondu	86F Tondu	86F Tondu	86H Aberbeeg	86B Newport Pill		
3675	5700	LA Laira (Plymouth)	83D Laira (Plymouth)	83D Laira (Plymouth)	83D Laira (Plymouth)	83D Laira (Plymouth)	82E Bristol Barrow Road	
3676	5700	SPM St. Philips Marsh	82B St. Philips Marsh	82B St. Philips Marsh	82B St. Philips Marsh	6E Chester (GWR)		
3677	5700	SLO Slough	83C Exeter	83C Exeter	83C Exeter	82A Bristol Bath Road	82E Bristol Barrow Road	
3678	5700	LDR Landore	87E Landore	87E Landore	87E Landore	87E Landore	87F Llanelly	
3679	5700	SED Swansea East Dock	87D Swansea East Dock	87D Swansea East Dock	87C Danygraig	72A Exmouth Junction	72A Exmouth Junction	
3680	5700	ABEEG Aberbeeg	86H Aberbeeg	86J Aberdare	86D Llantrisant	86D Llantrisant	88G Llantrisant	
3681	5700	SLO Slough	88B Cardiff East Dock	88B Cardiff East Dock	88B Cardiff East Dock	86A Ebbw Junction	86A Ebbw Junction	82F Bath Green Park
3682	5700	SDN Swindon	82C Swindon	82C Swindon	82C Swindon	82C Swindon	87B Duffryn Yard	
3683	5700	ABEEG Aberbeeg	86G Pontypool Road	86G Pontypool Road	86G Pontypool Road	86H Aberbeeg	86G Pontypool Road	
3684	5700	SDN Swindon	82C Swindon	82C Swindon	82C Swindon	82C Swindon		
3685	5700	PDN Old Oak Common	81A Old Oak Common	81A Old Oak Common	86G Pontypool Road	86G Pontypool Road	86G Pontypool Road	
3686	5700	LA Laira (Plymouth)	83D Laira (Plymouth)	83D Laira (Plymouth)	83D Laira (Plymouth)	83D Laira (Plymouth)	86F Aberbeeg	
3687	5700	OXF Oxford	84H Wellington	87A Neath	87A Neath	87A Neath	87A Neath	
3688	5700	PDN Old Oak Common	81A Old Oak Common	81A Old Oak Common	81A Old Oak Common	81A Old Oak Common		
3689	5700	TYS Tyseley	84E Tyseley	84E Tyseley	84E Tyseley	84J Croes Newydd	88C Barry	
3690	5700	PPRD Pontypool Road	86G Pontypool Road	86F Tondu	86F Tondu	86F Tondu	88C Barry	
3691	5700	LTS Llantrisant	86D Llantrisant	86A Ebbw Junction	86A Ebbw Junction	86A Ebbw Junction	86A Ebbw Junction	
3692	5700	PPRD Pontypool Road	86G Pontypool Road	82F Weymouth	82A Bristol Bath Road	82B St. Philips Marsh	87B Duffryn Yard	
3693	5700	TYS Tyseley	84E Tyseley	84E Tyseley	84E Tyseley	84E Tyseley	87A Neath	
3694	5700	BAN Banbury	84C Banbury	84C Banbury	88B Cardiff East Dock	86A Ebbw Junction		
3695	5700	TDU Tondu	86F Tondu	86J Aberdare	86J Aberdare	86J Aberdare	88E Abercynon	
3696	5700	WES Westbury	82D Westbury	82D Westbury	82D Westbury	82D Westbury	82E Bristol Barrow Road	
3697	5700	RDG Reading	81B Slough	81B Slough	81B Slough	81B Slough		
3698	5700	LLY Llanelly	87F Llanelly	87F Llanelly	87F Llanelly	84B Oxley	84B Oxley	
3699	5700	TDU Tondu	86F Tondu	86J Aberdare	86J Aberdare	86J Aberdare	88J Aberdare	
3700	5700	NPT Ebbw Junction	86A Ebbw Junction	86A Ebbw Junction	86B Newport Pill	86K Tredegar	86A Ebbw Junction	
3701	5700	LDR Landore	87E Landore	87E Landore	87E Landore	87E Landore	87F Llanelly	
3702	5700	SALOP Shrewsbury	84G Shrewsbury	84G Shrewsbury	83F Truro	83F Truro	82E Bristol Barrow Road	
3703	5700	LTS Llantrisant	86G Pontypool Road	86G Pontypool Road	86G Pontypool Road	86G Pontypool Road		
3704	5700	SHL Southall	81C Southall	81C Southall	81C Southall	81C Southall		
3705	5700	LA Laira (Plymouth)	83D Laira (Plymouth)	83E St. Blazey	83E St. Blazey	83E St. Blazey	86B Newport Pill	
3706	5700	BCN Brecon	89B Brecon	89B Brecon	89B Brecon	86A Ebbw Junction	86A Ebbw Junction	
3707	5700	CED Cardiff East Dock	88B Cardiff East Dock	88B Cardiff East Dock	88E Abercynon	88E Abercynon	88E Abercynon	
3708	5700	CDF Cardiff Canton	86G Pontypool Road	86G Pontypool Road	86G Pontypool Road	86G Pontypool Road	86G Pontypool Road	
3709	5700	DID Didcot	81E Didcot	81E Didcot	81E Didcot	81E Didcot	89A Shrewsbury	6C Croes Newydd
3710	5700	PDN Old Oak Common	84F Stourbridge	84F Stourbridge	84F Stourbridge	84F Stourbridge	88C Barry	
3711	5700	PPRD Pontypool Road	86H Aberbeeg	86H Aberbeeg	86H Aberbeeg	82C Swindon	81A Old Oak Common	
3712	5700	NPT Ebbw Junction	86A Ebbw Junction	86A Ebbw Junction	86A Ebbw Junction	86K Tredegar	87H Neyland	
3713	5700	LDR Landore	87E Landore	87E Landore	87E Landore	87E Landore		
3714	5700	NPT Ebbw Junction	86A Ebbw Junction	86A Ebbw Junction	86A Ebbw Junction	86A Ebbw Junction	86A Ebbw Junction	
3715	5700	RDG Reading	81B Slough	81A Old Oak Common	87A Neath	81C Southall	81D Reading	
3716	5700	CDF Cardiff Canton	86H Aberbeeg	86H Aberbeeg	86J Aberdare	86J Aberdare	88B Radyr	
3717	5700	PPRD Pontypool Road	86G Pontypool Road	86G Pontypool Road	86G Pontypool Road	86G Pontypool Road	86G Pontypool Road	
3718	5700	DYD Duffryn Yard	87B Duffryn Yard	87B Duffryn Yard	87B Duffryn Yard	87B Duffryn Yard		
3719	5700	LLY Llanelly	87F Llanelly	87F Llanelly	87F Llanelly	87F Llanelly	87F Llanelly	
3720	5700	SPM St. Philips Marsh	82B St. Philips Marsh	82B St. Philips Marsh	82B St. Philips Marsh	82G Templecombe	82G Templecombe	
3721	5700	DID Didcot	81E Didcot	81E Didcot	81E Didcot	81E Didcot	85B Gloucester	
3722	5700	OXF Oxford	81F Oxford	81F Oxford	81F Oxford	81F Oxford		
3723	5700	PDN Old Oak Common	81D Reading	81D Reading	81D Reading	81D Reading		
3724	5700	SDN Swindon	82C Swindon	82C Swindon	82C Swindon	82C Swindon		
3725	5700	HFD Hereford	85A Worcester	85A Worcester	85A Worcester	85A Worcester	85A Worcester	
3726	5700	NPT Ebbw Junction	86A Ebbw Junction	86A Ebbw Junction	86A Ebbw Junction	82B St. Philips Marsh		
3727	5700	SHL Southall	81C Southall	81C Southall	81C Southall	88C Barry	88C Barry	
3728	5700	HFD Hereford	85C Hereford	85C Hereford	85C Hereford	85C Hereford	86C Hereford	
3729	5700	ABEEG Aberbeeg	86C Cardiff Canton	86C Cardiff Canton	84F Stourbridge	84F Stourbridge	86A Ebbw Junction	
3730	5700	PPRD Pontypool Road	86G Pontypool Road	86G Pontypool Road	88B Cardiff East Dock	88E Abercynon	88E Abercynon	
3731	5700	WES Westbury	82B St. Philips Marsh	82B St. Philips Marsh	82B St. Philips Marsh	82B St. Philips Marsh	87A Neath	
3732	5700	WLN Wellington	84H Wellington	84H Wellington	84H Wellington	84H Wellington		
3733	5700	YEO Yeovil Pen Mill	82E Yeovil Pen Mill	82E Yeovil Pen Mill	82E Yeovil Pen Mill	72C Yeovil Town	72C Yeovil Town	
3734	5700	PDN Old Oak Common	88A Cardiff Cathays	88A Cardiff Cathays	88B Cardiff East Dock	88E Abercynon	88E Abercynon	
3735	5700	WES Westbury	82D Westbury	82D Westbury	82D Westbury	82D Westbury	82D Westbury	
3736	5700	RDG Reading	83B Taunton	83B Taunton	83B Taunton	83B Taunton	83B Taunton	
3737	5700	SDN Swindon	82C Swindon	82C Swindon	82F Weymouth	71G Weymouth	71G Weymouth	

No.	Class	1948	1951	1954	1957	1960	1963	1966
3738	*5700*	**PDN** Old Oak Common	**81D** Reading	**81D** Reading	**81D** Reading	**81D** Reading	**88H** Tondu	
3739	*5700*	**SDN** Swindon	**82C** Swindon	**82C** Swindon	**82C** Swindon	**82C** Swindon	**82C** Swindon	
3740	*5700*	**STB** Stourbridge	**84F** Stourbridge	**81B** Slough	**85B** Gloucester			
3741	*5700*	**OXF** Oxford	**87A** Neath	**87A** Neath	**87A** Neath	**87A** Neath		
3742	*5700*	**BHD** Birkenhead	**6C** Birkenhead	**6C** Birkenhead	**6C** Birkenhead	**82F** Bath Green Park	**82F** Bath Green Park	
3743	*5700*	**TYS** Tyseley	**84E** Tyseley	**84F** Stourbridge	**84F** Stourbridge	**84F** Stourbridge		
3744	*5700*	**OXY** Oxley	**84B** Oxley	**84B** Oxley	**84H** Wellington	**84H** Wellington	**84H** Wellington	**2B** Oxley
3745	*5700*	**OXY** Oxley	**84B** Oxley	**84B** Oxley	**84F** Stourbridge	**84F** Stourbridge	**85B** Gloucester	
3746	*5700*	**SPM** St. Philips Marsh	**82B** St. Philips Marsh	**82C** Swindon	**82C** Swindon	**83C** Exeter	**83C** Exeter	
3747	*5700*	**ABDR** Aberdare	**86J** Aberdare	**86H** Aberbeeg	**86H** Aberbeeg	**86A** Ebbw Junction	**86A** Ebbw Junction	
3748	*5700*	**SDN** Swindon	**82C** Swindon	**82B** St. Philips Marsh	**82A** Bristol Bath Road	**82A** Bristol Bath Road	**88C** Barry	
3749	*5700*	**WLN** Wellington	**84H** Wellington	**84H** Wellington	**84H** Wellington	**84K** Wrexham Rhosddu	**89B** Croes Newydd	
3750	*5700*	**SHL** Southall	**81C** Southall	**81C** Southall	**81C** Southall	**81C** Southall		
3751	*5700*	**BAN** Banbury	**84E** Tyseley	**84F** Stourbridge	**81E** Didcot	**81E** Didcot	**81E** Didcot	
3752	*5700*	**LLY** Llanelly	**87F** Llanelly	**87F** Llanelly	**87F** Llanelly	**82E** Bristol Barrow Road	**82E** Bristol Barrow Road	
3753	*5700*	**ABDR** Aberdare	**86J** Aberdare	**86J** Aberdare	**86J** Aberdare	**86J** Aberdare	**88J** Aberdare	
3754	*5700*	**PDN** Old Oak Common	**81A** Old Oak Common	**81A** Old Oak Common	**81A** Old Oak Common	**81A** Old Oak Common	**81A** Old Oak Common	
3755	*5700*	**CDF** Cardiff Canton	**86C** Cardiff Canton	**86C** Cardiff Canton	**86C** Cardiff Canton	**86C** Cardiff Canton		
3756	*5700*	**SRD** Stafford Road	**84A** Stafford Road	**84A** Stafford Road	**84A** Stafford Road	**84A** Stafford Road	**88H** Tondu	
3757	*5700*	**NEA** Neath	**87A** Neath	**87A** Neath	**87A** Neath	**87A** Neath	**87A** Neath	
3758	*5700*	**WES** Westbury	**82D** Westbury	**82B** St. Philips Marsh	**82B** St. Philips Marsh	**82C** Swindon	**82C** Swindon	**82F** Bath Green Park
3759	*5700*	**SPM** St. Philips Marsh	**82B** St. Philips Marsh	**82B** St. Philips Marsh	**82A** Bristol Bath Road	**71G** Weymouth	**71G** Weymouth	
3760	*5700*	**SRD** Stafford Road	**84H** Wellington	**84H** Wellington	**84H** Wellington	**84K** Wrexham Rhosddu		
3761	*5700*	**LLY** Llanelly	**87F** Llanelly	**87F** Llanelly	**87F** Llanelly	**87F** Llanelly	**87F** Llanelly	
3762	*5700*	**CHR** Chester (GWR)	**84K** Chester (GWR)	**84K** Chester (GWR)	**84K** Chester (GWR)	**87B** Duffryn Yard	**87B** Duffryn Yard	
3763	*5700*	**SPM** St. Philips Marsh	**82B** St. Philips Marsh	**82B** St. Philips Marsh	**82C** Swindon	**82C** Swindon	**81E** Didcot	
3764	*5700*	**SPM** St. Philips Marsh	**82B** St. Philips Marsh	**82B** St. Philips Marsh	**82B** St. Philips Marsh	**82B** St. Philips Marsh	**86A** Ebbw Junction	
3765	*5700*	**SPM** St. Philips Marsh	**82B** St. Philips Marsh	**82B** St. Philips Marsh	**82B** St. Philips Marsh	**82B** St. Philips Marsh	**82E** Bristol Barrow Road	
3766	*5700*	**PDN** Old Oak Common	**87A** Neath	**87A** Neath	**87A** Neath	**87A** Neath	**87A** Neath	
3767	*5700*	**BCN** Brecon	**89B** Brecon	**89B** Brecon	**89B** Brecon	**86A** Ebbw Junction	**86A** Ebbw Junction	
3768	*5700*	**LDR** Landore	**87E** Landore	**87E** Landore	**87E** Landore	**87E** Landore	**87A** Neath	
3769	*5700*	**SLO** Slough	**84E** Tyseley	**84E** Tyseley	**84A** Stafford Road	**84G** Shrewsbury		
3770	*5700*	**RDG** Reading	**89B** Brecon	**89B** Brecon	**89B** Brecon	**89A** Oswestry	**89D** Oswestry	
3771	*5700*	**LLY** Llanelly	**87F** Llanelly	**87F** Llanelly	**87F** Llanelly	**87F** Llanelly	**87F** Llanelly	
3772	*5700*	**TDU** Tondu	**86F** Tondu	**86F** Tondu	**86F** Tondu	**86A** Ebbw Junction	**86A** Ebbw Junction	
3773	*5700*	**SPM** St. Philips Marsh	**82B** St. Philips Marsh	**82B** St. Philips Marsh	**82B** St. Philips Marsh	**82B** St. Philips Marsh		
3774	*5700*	**NEA** Neath	**87A** Neath	**87A** Neath	**87A** Neath	**87A** Neath		
3775	*5700*	**WLN** Wellington	**84H** Wellington	**85A** Worcester	**85A** Worcester	**85A** Worcester	**85B** Gloucester	
3776	*5700*	**ABEEG** Aberbeeg	**86H** Aberbeeg	**86D** Llantrisant	**86D** Llantrisant	**82B** St. Philips Marsh	**84H** Wellington	**2B** Oxley
3777	*5700*	**LLY** Llanelly	**87F** Llanelly	**87F** Llanelly	**87F** Llanelly	**87F** Llanelly	**87F** Llanelly	
3778	*5700*	**SRD** Stafford Road	**84A** Stafford Road	**84A** Stafford Road	**84A** Stafford Road	**84A** Stafford Road	**84A** Stafford Road	
3779	*5700*	**PPRD** Pontypool Road	**86G** Pontypool Road	**86G** Pontypool Road	**86G** Pontypool Road	**86G** Pontypool Road	**86G** Pontypool Road	
3780	*5700*	**SDN** Swindon	**82C** Swindon	**82C** Swindon	**82C** Swindon	**82C** Swindon		
3781	*5700*	**DG** Danygraig	**87C** Danygraig	**87C** Danygraig	**87C** Danygraig	**86F** Tondu	**87F** Llanelly	
3782	*5700*	**SALOP** Shrewsbury	**84G** Shrewsbury	**84G** Shrewsbury	**84G** Shrewsbury	**84G** Shrewsbury	**89A** Shrewsbury	**2B** Oxley
3783	*5700*	**RDG** Reading	**88B** Cardiff East Dock	**88B** Cardiff East Dock	**88B** Cardiff East Dock	**88E** Abercynon		
3784	*5700*	**SPM** St. Philips Marsh	**82B** St. Philips Marsh	**82B** St. Philips Marsh	**82B** St. Philips Marsh	**82B** St. Philips Marsh	**88L** Cardiff East Dock	
3785	*5700*	**LDR** Landore	**87E** Landore	**87E** Landore	**87E** Landore	**87E** Landore		
3786	*5700*	**CHR** Chester (GWR)	**84K** Chester (GWR)	**84K** Chester (GWR)	**84K** Chester (GWR)	**6E** Chester (GWR)	**86E** Severn Tunnel Junction	
3787	*5700*	**LA** Laira (Plymouth)	**83D** Laira (Plymouth)	**83D** Laira (Plymouth)	**83D** Laira (Plymouth)	**83D** Laira (Plymouth)	**82D** Westbury	
3788	*5700*	**SALOP** Shrewsbury	**84G** Shrewsbury	**84G** Shrewsbury	**84G** Shrewsbury	**84G** Shrewsbury	**89A** Shrewsbury	
3789	*5700*	**HFD** Hereford	**85C** Hereford	**85C** Hereford	**89A** Oswestry	**89A** Oswestry	**89B** Croes Newydd	
3790	*5700*	**LA** Laira (Plymouth)	**83D** Laira (Plymouth)	**83D** Laira (Plymouth)	**83D** Laira (Plymouth)	**83D** Laira (Plymouth)	**87A** Neath	
3791	*5700*	**DYD** Duffryn Yard	**87B** Duffryn Yard	**87B** Duffryn Yard	**87B** Duffryn Yard	**87B** Duffryn Yard	**87B** Duffryn Yard	
3792	*5700*	**OXY** Oxley	**84B** Oxley	**84A** Stafford Road	**84A** Stafford Road	**84A** Stafford Road	**84A** Stafford Road	
3793	*5700*	**OXY** Oxley	**84B** Oxley	**84A** Stafford Road	**84A** Stafford Road			
3794	*5700*	**EXE** Exeter	**83C** Exeter	**83C** Exeter	**83C** Exeter	**83C** Exeter	**83C** Exeter	
3795	*5700*	**SPM** St. Philips Marsh	**82B** St. Philips Marsh	**82B** St. Philips Marsh	**82B** St. Philips Marsh	**82B** St. Philips Marsh	**82E** Bristol Barrow Road	
3796	*5700*	**NPT** Ebbw Junction	**86A** Ebbw Junction	**83A** Newton Abbot	**83A** Newton Abbot	**83A** Newton Abbot	**83A** Newton Abbot	
3797	*5700*	**LDR** Landore	**87E** Landore	**87E** Landore	**87E** Landore	**87E** Landore	**87D** Swansea East Dock	
3798	*5700*	**SLO** Slough	**86A** Ebbw Junction	**86A** Ebbw Junction	**86A** Ebbw Junction	**86A** Ebbw Junction	**87A** Neath	
3799	*5700*	**SHL** Southall	**81C** Southall	**81C** Southall	**81C** Southall	**81C** Southall		
3800	*2884*	**NPT** Ebbw Junction	**86A** Ebbw Junction	**86A** Ebbw Junction	**86A** Ebbw Junction	**86E** Severn Tunnel Junction	**86A** Ebbw Junction	
3801	*2884*	**NPT** Ebbw Junction	**86A** Ebbw Junction	**86A** Ebbw Junction	**86C** Cardiff Canton	**86E** Severn Tunnel Junction	**86E** Severn Tunnel Junction	
3802	*2884*	**BAN** Banbury	**84C** Banbury	**84B** Oxley	**84B** Oxley	**84B** Oxley	**84E** Tyseley	
3803	*2884*	**BAN** Banbury	**81C** Southall	**86C** Cardiff Canton	**86C** Cardiff Canton	**85B** Gloucester	**86E** Severn Tunnel Junction	
3804	*2884*	**NPT** Ebbw Junction	**86A** Ebbw Junction	**86A** Ebbw Junction	**86A** Ebbw Junction	**86G** Pontypool Road	**88L** Cardiff East Dock	
3805	*2884*	**NPT** Ebbw Junction	**86A** Ebbw Junction	**86A** Ebbw Junction	**86A** Ebbw Junction	**86A** Ebbw Junction	**86A** Ebbw Junction	
3806	*2884*	**STJ** Severn Tunnel Junction	**86E** Severn Tunnel Junction	**86E** Severn Tunnel Junction	**86E** Severn Tunnel Junction	**86E** Severn Tunnel Junction	**84C** Banbury	
3807	*2884*	**NPT** Ebbw Junction	**86A** Ebbw Junction	**86A** Ebbw Junction	**86A** Ebbw Junction	**86A** Ebbw Junction	**86A** Ebbw Junction	
3808	*2884*	**STJ** Severn Tunnel Junction	**86E** Severn Tunnel Junction	**86E** Severn Tunnel Junction	**86A** Ebbw Junction	**86A** Ebbw Junction	**86A** Ebbw Junction	
3809	*2884*	**CDF** Cardiff Canton	**86C** Cardiff Canton	**86C** Cardiff Canton	**86C** Cardiff Canton	**86C** Cardiff Canton	**84C** Banbury	
3810	*2884*	**NPT** Ebbw Junction	**86A** Ebbw Junction	**86A** Ebbw Junction	**86C** Cardiff Canton	**86C** Cardiff Canton	**88L** Cardiff East Dock	
3811	*2884*	**LA** Laira (Plymouth)	**87F** Llanelly	**87F** Llanelly	**87F** Llanelly	**87F** Llanelly	**87F** Llanelly	
3812	*2884*	**CDF** Cardiff Canton	**86C** Cardiff Canton	**86C** Cardiff Canton	**86E** Severn Tunnel Junction	**86E** Severn Tunnel Junction	**86E** Severn Tunnel Junction	
3813	*2884*	(4855)	**81A** Old Oak Common	**84B** Oxley	**84B** Oxley	**84B** Oxley	**84B** Oxley	
3814	*2884*	**CDF** Cardiff Canton	**86C** Cardiff Canton	**86C** Cardiff Canton	**81C** Southall	**81F** Oxford	**81F** Oxford	
3815	*2884*	**STJ** Severn Tunnel Junction	**86E** Severn Tunnel Junction	**86E** Severn Tunnel Junction	**86E** Severn Tunnel Junction	**84J** Croes Newydd	**89B** Croes Newydd	
3816	*2884*	**NPT** Ebbw Junction	**86A** Ebbw Junction	**86A** Ebbw Junction	**86C** Cardiff Canton	**84C** Banbury	**88J** Aberdare	
3817	*2884*	**CDF** Cardiff Canton	**86C** Cardiff Canton	**86C** Cardiff Canton	**86C** Cardiff Canton	**86C** Cardiff Canton	**84C** Banbury	
3818	*2884*	(4852)	**86E** Severn Tunnel Junction	**86E** Severn Tunnel Junction	**86E** Severn Tunnel Junction	**86G** Pontypool Road	**86A** Ebbw Junction	
3819	*2884*	**BAN** Banbury	**84C** Banbury	**84C** Banbury	**84C** Banbury	**82D** Westbury	**81E** Didcot	
3820	*2884*	(4856)	**84C** Banbury	**84G** Shrewsbury	**84K** Chester (GWR)	**84B** Oxley	**81E** Didcot	
3821	*2884*	**BAN** Banbury	**84F** Stourbridge	**84F** Stourbridge	**84F** Stourbridge	**84F** Stourbridge	**84C** Banbury	
3822	*2884*	**PPRD** Pontypool Road	**86G** Pontypool Road	**86G** Pontypool Road	**86G** Pontypool Road	**86G** Pontypool Road	**87A** Neath	
3823	*2884*	**CDF** Cardiff Canton	**86C** Cardiff Canton	**86C** Cardiff Canton	**86E** Severn Tunnel Junction	**81F** Oxford	**81F** Oxford	
3824	*2884*	**CDF** Cardiff Canton	**86C** Cardiff Canton	**86C** Cardiff Canton	**86G** Pontypool Road	**86A** Ebbw Junction	**86A** Ebbw Junction	
3825	*2884*	**BAN** Banbury	**84J** Croes Newydd	**84B** Oxley	**84F** Stourbridge	**84F** Stourbridge	**84C** Banbury	
3826	*2884*	**PPRD** Pontypool Road	**86G** Pontypool Road	**86G** Pontypool Road	**86G** Pontypool Road	**86G** Pontypool Road	**86G** Pontypool Road	
3827	*2884*	**BAN** Banbury	**84F** Stourbridge	**84F** Stourbridge	**86A** Ebbw Junction	**86A** Ebbw Junction		
3828	*2884*	**PPRD** Pontypool Road	**86G** Pontypool Road	**86G** Pontypool Road	**86G** Pontypool Road	**84J** Croes Newydd	**84C** Banbury	
3829	*2884*	**BAN** Banbury	**84C** Banbury	**84E** Tyseley	**84C** Banbury	**84B** Oxley	**84E** Tyseley	
3830	*2884*	**NPT** Ebbw Junction	**86A** Ebbw Junction	**86A** Ebbw Junction	**86A** Ebbw Junction	**86A** Ebbw Junction	**86A** Ebbw Junction	
3831	*2884*	(4857)	**84C** Banbury	**84C** Banbury	**84C** Banbury	**84F** Stourbridge	**84B** Oxley	
3832	*2884*	**PDN** Old Oak Common	**83D** Laira (Plymouth)	**86E** Severn Tunnel Junction	**86E** Severn Tunnel Junction	**86A** Ebbw Junction	**86A** Ebbw Junction	
3833	*2884*	**NPT** Ebbw Junction	**86A** Ebbw Junction	**86A** Ebbw Junction	**86A** Ebbw Junction	**86A** Ebbw Junction	**86A** Ebbw Junction	
3834	*2884*	**EXE** Exeter	**83A** Newton Abbot	**83A** Newton Abbot	**83A** Newton Abbot	**87F** Llanelly	**81C** Southall	
3835	*2884*	**OXF** Oxford	**81F** Oxford	**81F** Oxford	**81D** Reading	**86C** Cardiff Canton	**86E** Severn Tunnel Junction	
3836	*2884*	**OXF** Oxford	**86A** Ebbw Junction	**86A** Ebbw Junction	**81C** Southall	**84G** Shrewsbury	**89A** Shrewsbury	
3837	*2884*	(4854)	**84E** Tyseley	**81E** Didcot	**84B** Oxley	**86A** Ebbw Junction	**86A** Ebbw Junction	
3838	*2884*	**OXF** Oxford	**86E** Severn Tunnel Junction	**86E** Severn Tunnel Junction	**86E** Severn Tunnel Junction	**86E** Severn Tunnel Junction	**86E** Severn Tunnel Junction	
3839	*2884*	(4853)	**85A** Worcester	**84E** Tyseley	**84E** Tyseley	**84F** Stourbridge	**88J** Aberdare	
3840	*2884*	**RDG** Reading	**81D** Reading	**83A** Newton Abbot	**83A** Newton Abbot	**83A** Newton Abbot	**81E** Didcot	
3841	*2884*	**RDG** Reading	**81D** Reading	**83A** Newton Abbot	**83A** Newton Abbot	**83A** Newton Abbot	**86G** Pontypool Road	
3842	*2884*	**WES** Westbury	**82B** St. Philips Marsh	**86C** Cardiff Canton	**86C** Cardiff Canton	**84B** Oxley	**82C** Swindon	
3843	*2884*	**RDG** Reading	**86E** Severn Tunnel Junction	**86C** Cardiff Canton	**86C** Cardiff Canton	**86C** Cardiff Canton	**88J** Aberdare	
3844	*2884*	**RDG** Reading	**86E** Severn Tunnel Junction	**86E** Severn Tunnel Junction	**86E** Severn Tunnel Junction	**86G** Pontypool Road	**86G** Pontypool Road	
3845	*2884*	**RDG** Reading	**81D** Reading	**81E** Didcot	**84B** Oxley	**86C** Cardiff Canton	**84C** Banbury	
3846	*2884*	**RDG** Reading	**81D** Reading	**86C** Cardiff Canton	**86C** Cardiff Canton	**84F** Stourbridge	**89B** Croes Newydd	
3847	*2884*	**OXF** Oxford	**81F** Oxford	**86E** Severn Tunnel Junction	**86E** Severn Tunnel Junction	**86E** Severn Tunnel Junction	**88J** Aberdare	
3848	*2884*	**OXF** Oxford	**85C** Hereford	**85A** Worcester	**85A** Worcester	**85B** Gloucester	**86E** Severn Tunnel Junction	
3849	*2884*	**WES** Westbury	**84C** Banbury	**86E** Severn Tunnel Junction	**86E** Severn Tunnel Junction	**86C** Cardiff Canton	**84C** Banbury	
3850	*2884*	**WES** Westbury	**86E** Severn Tunnel Junction	**86E** Severn Tunnel Junction	**86E** Severn Tunnel Junction	**86J** Aberdare	**88J** Aberdare	
3851	*2884*	**PDN** Old Oak Common	**87F** Llanelly	**87F** Llanelly	**87F** Llanelly	**87F** Llanelly	**87F** Llanelly	

		1948	1951	1954	1957	1960	1963	1966
3852	*2884*	**PDN** Old Oak Common	**81A** Old Oak Common	**86E** Severn Tunnel Junction	**86E** Severn Tunnel Junction	**86E** Severn Tunnel Junction	**84C** Banbury	
3853	*2884*	**PDN** Old Oak Common	**81A** Old Oak Common	**86E** Severn Tunnel Junction	**86E** Severn Tunnel Junction	**86A** Ebbw Junction	**88J** Aberdare	
3854	*2884*	**SHL** Southall	**81C** Southall	**82B** St. Philips Marsh	**81F** Oxford	**84B** Oxley	**81C** Southall	
3855	*2884*	**SHL** Southall	**81C** Southall	**86G** Pontypool Road	**86G** Pontypool Road	**86C** Cardiff Canton	**84C** Banbury	
3856	*2884*	**SHL** Southall	**81C** Southall	**81C** Southall	**81C** Southall	**86E** Severn Tunnel Junction	**86E** Severn Tunnel Junction	
3857	*2884*	**SHL** Southall	**81C** Southall	**81C** Southall	**81F** Oxford	**81F** Oxford	**84C** Banbury	
3858	*2884*	**SHL** Southall	**84K** Chester (GWR)	**84K** Chester (GWR)	**84K** Chester (GWR)	**81D** Reading	**81D** Reading	
3859	*2884*	**SHL** Southall	**84K** Chester (GWR)	**84C** Banbury	**84C** Banbury	**86G** Pontypool Road	**86E** Severn Tunnel Junction	
3860	*2884*	**SHL** Southall	**84K** Chester (GWR)	**84B** Oxley	**84B** Oxley	**86C** Cardiff Canton	**88J** Aberdare	
3861	*2884*	**BAN** Banbury	**84C** Banbury	**84F** Stourbridge	**84B** Oxley	**84B** Oxley	**86G** Pontypool Road	
3862	*2884*	**PPRD** Pontypool Road	**86G** Pontypool Road	**83D** Laira (Plymouth)	**83D** Laira (Plymouth)	**83D** Laira (Plymouth)	**88L** Cardiff East Dock	
3863	*2884*	**WES** Westbury	**84C** Banbury	**84B** Oxley	**84B** Oxley	**86E** Severn Tunnel Junction	**86E** Severn Tunnel Junction	
3864	*2884*	**LA** Laira (Plymouth)	**83D** Laira (Plymouth)	**83A** Newton Abbot	**83A** Newton Abbot	**83A** Newton Abbot	**86E** Severn Tunnel Junction	
3865	*2884*	(4851)	**84C** Banbury	**84B** Oxley	**84B** Oxley	**84B** Oxley	**84E** Tyseley	
3866	*2884*	**OXF** Oxford	**81F** Oxford	**86E** Severn Tunnel Junction	**86E** Severn Tunnel Junction	**86J** Aberdare	**88J** Aberdare	
3900	*4900*	**SPM** St. Philips Marsh	(4968)					
3901	*4900*	**LA** Laira (Plymouth)	(4971)					
3902	*4900*	**LA** Laira (Plymouth)	(4948)					
3903	*4900*	**PDN** Old Oak Common	(4907)					
3904	*4900*	**LA** Laira (Plymouth)	(4972)					
3950	*4900*	**BRD** Bristol Bath Road	(5955)					
3951	*4900*	**SPM** St. Philips Marsh	(5976)					
3952	*4900*	**PDN** Old Oak Common	(6957)					
3953	*4900*	**PDN** Old Oak Common	(6953)					
3954	*4900*	**PDN** Old Oak Common	(5986)					
3955	*4900*	**LA** Laira (Plymouth)	(6949)					
4000	*4073*	**SRD** Stafford Road	**84A** Stafford Road	**84A** Stafford Road	**87E** Landore			
4003	*4000*	**LDR** Landore	**87E** Landore					
4004	*4000*	**OXF** Oxford						
4007	*4000*	**WOS** Worcester	**85A** Worcester					
4012	*4000*	**NA** Newton Abbot						
4013	*4000*	**CHR** Chester (GWR)						
4015	*4000*	**SDN** Swindon	**82C** Swindon					
4016	*4073*	**NA** Newton Abbot	**81A** Old Oak Common					
4017	*4000*	**SDN** Swindon						
4018	*4000*	**SRD** Stafford Road	**84A** Stafford Road					
4019	*4000*	**BRD** Bristol Bath Road						
4020	*4000*	**BRD** Bristol Bath Road	**82A** Bristol Bath Road					
4021	*4000*	**OXF** Oxford	**81F** Oxford					
4022	*4000*	**SDN** Swindon	**82C** Swindon					
4023	*4000*	**LDR** Landore	**87E** Landore					
4025	*4000*	**SRD** Stafford Road						
4026	*4000*	**TN** Taunton						
4028	*4000*	**WES** Westbury	**82D** Westbury					
4030	*4000*	**BRD** Bristol Bath Road						
4031	*4000*	**SRD** Stafford Road	**84A** Stafford Road					
4032	*4073*	**LA** Laira (Plymouth)	**83B** Taunton					
4033	*4000*	**BRD** Bristol Bath Road	**82A** Bristol Bath Road					
4034	*4000*	**BRD** Bristol Bath Road	**82D** Westbury					
4035	*4000*	**BRD** Bristol Bath Road	**82A** Bristol Bath Road					
4036	*4000*	**SDN** Swindon	**82C** Swindon					
4037	*4073*	**PDN** Old Oak Common	**81A** Old Oak Common	**81A** Old Oak Common	**83A** Newton Abbot	**87E** Landore		
4038	*4000*	**WES** Westbury	**82D** Westbury					
4039	*4000*	**LDR** Landore						
4040	*4000*	**SALOP** Shrewsbury	**84G** Shrewsbury					
4041	*4000*	**BRD** Bristol Bath Road	**82A** Bristol Bath Road					
4042	*4000*	**BRD** Bristol Bath Road	**82A** Bristol Bath Road					
4043	*4000*	**BRD** Bristol Bath Road	**82A** Bristol Bath Road					
4044	*4000*	**SALOP** Shrewsbury	**84G** Shrewsbury					
4045	*4000*	**WES** Westbury						
4046	*4000*	**SALOP** Shrewsbury	**84G** Shrewsbury					
4047	*4000*	**BRD** Bristol Bath Road	**82A** Bristol Bath Road					
4048	*4000*	**LDR** Landore	**87E** Landore					
4049	*4000*	**OXF** Oxford	**84A** Stafford Road					
4050	*4000*	**LDR** Landore	**87E** Landore					
4051	*4000*	**WOS** Worcester						
4052	*4000*	**OXF** Oxford	**84G** Shrewsbury					
4053	*4000*	**SRD** Stafford Road	**84A** Stafford Road	**84A** Stafford Road				
4054	*4000*	**EXE** Exeter	**83D** Laira (Plymouth)					
4055	*4000*	**SDN** Swindon	**82C** Swindon					
4056	*4000*	**TN** Taunton	**82A** Bristol Bath Road	**82A** Bristol Bath Road	**82A** Bristol Bath Road			
4057	*4000*	**SDN** Swindon	**82C** Swindon					
4058	*4000*	**TYS** Tyseley	**84A** Stafford Road					
4059	*4000*	**GLO** Gloucester	**85B** Gloucester					
4060	*4000*	**SRD** Stafford Road	**82A** Bristol Bath Road					
4061	*4000*	**SALOP** Shrewsbury	**84A** Stafford Road	**84A** Stafford Road	**84A** Stafford Road			
4062	*4000*	**SDN** Swindon	**82C** Swindon	**82C** Swindon				
4073	*4073*	**PDN** Old Oak Common	**82A** Bristol Bath Road	**82A** Bristol Bath Road	**82A** Bristol Bath Road	**86C** Cardiff Canton		
4074	*4073*	**LDR** Landore	**87E** Landore	**87E** Landore	**87G** Carmarthen	**87E** Landore	**81A** Old Oak Common	
4075	*4073*	**PDN** Old Oak Common	**82A** Bristol Bath Road	**82A** Bristol Bath Road	**82A** Bristol Bath Road	**81A** Old Oak Common		
4076	*4073*	**PDN** Old Oak Common	**84K** Chester (GWR)	**84K** Chester (GWR)	**83A** Newton Abbot	**87E** Landore	**87F** Llanelly	
4077	*4073*	**NA** Newton Abbot	**83A** Newton Abbot	**83A** Newton Abbot	**83D** Laira (Plymouth)	**83A** Newton Abbot		
4078	*4073*	**LDR** Landore	**87E** Landore	**87E** Landore	**87E** Landore	**84C** Banbury		
4079	*4073*	**HFD** Hereford	**85B** Gloucester	**84A** Stafford Road	**84A** Stafford Road	**82A** Bristol Bath Road	**82C** Swindon	
4080	*4073*	**BRD** Bristol Bath Road	**82D** Westbury	**83A** Newton Abbot	**82A** Bristol Bath Road	**83A** Newton Abbot	**88L** Cardiff East Dock	
4081	*4073*	**LDR** Landore	**87E** Landore	**87E** Landore	**87E** Landore	**82A** Bristol Bath Road	**87G** Carmarthen	
4082	*4073*	**GLO** Gloucester	**85A** Worcester	(7013)				
4082	*4073*	(7013)	→	**85A** Worcester	**85A** Worcester	**85A** Worcester	**85A** Worcester	
4083	*4073*	**CDF** Cardiff Canton	**84G** Shrewsbury	**84A** Stafford Road	**84A** Stafford Road	**83A** Newton Abbot		
4084	*4073*	**BRD** Bristol Bath Road	**82A** Bristol Bath Road	**82A** Bristol Bath Road	**82A** Bristol Bath Road	**81D** Reading		
4085	*4073*	**RDG** Reading	**81D** Reading	**81D** Reading	**81D** Reading	**85B** Gloucester		
4086	*4073*	**WOS** Worcester	**85A** Worcester	**83D** Laira (Plymouth)	**83D** Laira (Plymouth)	**86C** Cardiff Canton		
4087	*4073*	**LA** Laira (Plymouth)	**83D** Laira (Plymouth)	**83G** Penzance	**83D** Laira (Plymouth)	**83D** Laira (Plymouth)	**83D** Laira (Plymouth)	
4088	*4073*	**LA** Laira (Plymouth)	**83D** Laira (Plymouth)	**83A** Newton Abbot	**83D** Laira (Plymouth)	**85A** Worcester	**82C** Swindon	
4089	*4073*	**BRD** Bristol Bath Road	**83D** Laira (Plymouth)	**83D** Laira (Plymouth)	**81A** Old Oak Common	**85A** Worcester	**81A** Old Oak Common	
4090	*4073*	**LA** Laira (Plymouth)	**83G** Penzance	**84A** Stafford Road	**81A** Old Oak Common	**87G** Carmarthen	**88L** Cardiff East Dock	
4091	*4073*	**PDN** Old Oak Common	**82A** Bristol Bath Road	**82A** Bristol Bath Road	**81A** Old Oak Common			
4092	*4073*	**WOS** Worcester	**84A** Stafford Road	**84A** Stafford Road	**84A** Stafford Road	**81D** Reading		
4093	*4073*	**BRD** Bristol Bath Road	**85A** Worcester	**87E** Landore	**87E** Landore	**87E** Landore	**87A** Neath	
4094	*4073*	**CDF** Cardiff Canton	**86C** Cardiff Canton	**82A** Bristol Bath Road	**84A** Stafford Road	**87E** Landore		
4095	*4073*	**LDR** Landore	**87E** Landore	**87E** Landore	**87E** Landore	**83G** Penzance		
4096	*4073*	**BRD** Bristol Bath Road	**82A** Bristol Bath Road	**82A** Bristol Bath Road	**82A** Bristol Bath Road	**81A** Old Oak Common	**81A** Old Oak Common	
4097	*4073*	**PZ** Penzance	**83D** Laira (Plymouth)	**81A** Old Oak Common	**81A** Old Oak Common	**87E** Landore		
4098	*4073*	**NA** Newton Abbot	**83A** Newton Abbot	**83A** Newton Abbot	**83A** Newton Abbot	**83A** Newton Abbot	**81A** Old Oak Common	
4099	*4073*	**NA** Newton Abbot	**83A** Newton Abbot	**83A** Newton Abbot	**83G** Penzance	**87E** Landore		
4100	*5101*	**WOS** Worcester	**85D** Kidderminster	**85D** Kidderminster	**85D** Kidderminster	**85B** Gloucester	**85B** Gloucester	
4101	*5101*	**TYS** Tyseley	**84E** Tyseley	**88D** Merthyr	**88A** Cardiff Cathays	**85B** Gloucester	**85B** Gloucester	
4102	*5101*	**LMTN** Leamington Spa	**84D** Leamington Spa	**84C** Banbury	**84K** Chester (GWR)	**82C** Swindon		
4103	*5101*	**SRD** Stafford Road	**84A** Stafford Road	**84A** Stafford Road	**84A** Stafford Road	**81F** Oxford	**82E** Bristol Barrow Road	
4104	*5101*	**STB** Stourbridge	**84F** Stourbridge	**84F** Stourbridge	**84F** Stourbridge	**84F** Stourbridge	**85A** Worcester	
4105	*5101*	**SRD** Stafford Road	**84A** Stafford Road	**84G** Shrewsbury	**83A** Newton Abbot	**83A** Newton Abbot	**84C** Banbury	
4106	*5101*	**TYS** Tyseley	**84E** Tyseley	**87E** Landore	**87E** Landore	**87E** Landore		
4107	*5101*	**TYS** Tyseley	**84E** Tyseley	**87E** Landore	**87E** Landore	**87E** Landore	**87H** Neyland	
4108	*5101*	**SRD** Stafford Road	**84A** Stafford Road	**84A** Stafford Road	**84A** Stafford Road	**83F** Truro	**88H** Tondu	

		1948	1951	1954	1957	1960	1963	1966
4109	5101	NA Newton Abbot	83A Newton Abbot	83A Newton Abbot	83A Newton Abbot	85A Worcester	85B Gloucester	
4110	5101	SRD Stafford Road	84E Tyseley	84E Tyseley	84H Wellington	84F Stourbridge	83B Taunton	
4111	5101	TYS Tyseley	84E Tyseley	84E Tyseley	84E Tyseley	84E Tyseley	84E Tyseley	
4112	5101	LMTN Leamington Spa	84D Leamington Spa	84D Leamington Spa	84D Leamington Spa	84D Leamington Spa		
4113	5101	TN Taunton	83B Taunton	85A Worcester	85A Worcester	85A Worcester	85A Worcester	
4114	5101	WOS Worcester	85A Worcester	85A Worcester	85D Kidderminster	85D Kidderminster	84G Kidderminster	
4115	5101	SRD Stafford Road	84A Stafford Road	84K Chester (GWR)	84K Chester (GWR)	85C Hereford	86C Hereford	
4116	5101	TYS Tyseley	84E Tyseley	84E Tyseley	84E Tyseley	85B Gloucester		
4117	5101	TN Taunton	83B Taunton	83B Taunton	83B Taunton	83C Exeter		
4118	5101	SALOP Shrewsbury	84G Shrewsbury	84G Shrewsbury	84D Leamington Spa	84D Leamington Spa		
4119	5101	STJ Severn Tunnel Junction	86E Severn Tunnel Junction	86E Severn Tunnel Junction	86A Ebbw Junction	86E Severn Tunnel Junction	86E Severn Tunnel Junction	
4120	5101	BHD Birkenhead	6C Birkenhead	6C Birkenhead	6C Birkenhead	84H Wellington	84D Leamington Spa	
4121	5101	BHD Birkenhead	86G Pontypool Road	86E Severn Tunnel Junction	86E Severn Tunnel Junction	86F Tondu	88H Tondu	
4122	5101	BHD Birkenhead	6C Birkenhead	6C Birkenhead	6C Birkenhead	87H Neyland	87H Neyland	
4123	5101	BHD Birkenhead	6C Birkenhead	6C Birkenhead	6C Birkenhead	85B Gloucester		
4124	5101	BHD Birkenhead	6C Birkenhead	6C Birkenhead	6C Birkenhead	85A Worcester	85A Worcester	
4125	5101	BHD Birkenhead	6C Birkenhead	6C Birkenhead	6C Birkenhead	81F Oxford	84D Leamington Spa	
4126	5101	BHD Birkenhead	6C Birkenhead	6C Birkenhead	6C Birkenhead	84E Tyseley		
4127	5101	BHD Birkenhead	6C Birkenhead	6C Birkenhead	6C Birkenhead	86E Severn Tunnel Junction	86E Severn Tunnel Junction	
4128	5101	BHD Birkenhead	6C Birkenhead	6C Birkenhead	6C Birkenhead	83B Taunton	86E Severn Tunnel Junction	
4129	5101	BHD Birkenhead	6C Birkenhead	6C Birkenhead	6C Birkenhead	82B St. Philips Marsh		
4130	5101	STJ Severn Tunnel Junction	86A Ebbw Junction	86B Newport Pill	86A Ebbw Junction	86E Severn Tunnel Junction	86E Severn Tunnel Junction	
4131	5101	PPRD Pontypool Road	86G Pontypool Road	86G Pontypool Road	82B St. Philips Marsh	82B St. Philips Marsh	82E Bristol Barrow Road	
4132	5101	NEA Neath	87H Neyland	87H Neyland	87H Neyland	87H Neyland	87H Neyland	
4133	5101	NA Newton Abbot	83A Newton Abbot	83A Newton Abbot	82F Weymouth	71G Weymouth	84D Leamington Spa	
4134	5101	LDR Landore	87E Landore	87G Carmarthen	87G Carmarthen	87G Carmarthen	87A Neath	
4135	5101	PPRD Pontypool Road	86G Pontypool Road	86G Pontypool Road	86G Pontypool Road	86G Pontypool Road	86C Hereford	
4136	5101	TN Taunton	83B Taunton	83B Taunton	83B Taunton	83G Penzance	86E Severn Tunnel Junction	
4137	5101	STJ Severn Tunnel Junction	86A Ebbw Junction	86E Severn Tunnel Junction	86E Severn Tunnel Junction	86E Severn Tunnel Junction	86E Severn Tunnel Junction	
4138	5101	PPRD Pontypool Road	86G Pontypool Road	86G Pontypool Road	86G Pontypool Road			
4139	5101	WOS Worcester	85A Worcester	82A Bristol Bath Road	82A Bristol Bath Road			
4140	5101	GLO Gloucester	85B Gloucester	85B Gloucester	84A Stafford Road	84F Stourbridge	84F Stourbridge	
4141	5101	CHEL Cheltenham	85B Gloucester	85B Gloucester	85B Gloucester	85B Gloucester	85B Gloucester	
4142	5101	BRD Bristol Bath Road	82A Bristol Bath Road	86G Pontypool Road	84H Wellington	85A Worcester	85B Gloucester	
4143	5101	BRD Bristol Bath Road	82A Bristol Bath Road	88D Merthyr	88D Merthyr	88A Radyr	83B Taunton	
4144	5101	STJ Severn Tunnel Junction	86E Severn Tunnel Junction	86E Severn Tunnel Junction	86E Severn Tunnel Junction	86F Tondu	86E Severn Tunnel Junction	
4145	5101	TDU Tondu	86C Cardiff Canton	86E Severn Tunnel Junction	83A Newton Abbot	83A Newton Abbot		
4146	5101	STB Stourbridge	84F Stourbridge	84F Stourbridge	84F Stourbridge	84B Oxley		
4147	5101	TYS Tyseley	84E Tyseley	81F Oxford	81F Oxford	81F Oxford	84G Kidderminster	
4148	5101	STJ Severn Tunnel Junction	86A Ebbw Junction	86A Ebbw Junction	85A Worcester	81F Oxford	84A Stafford Road	
4149	5101	STB Stourbridge	84C Banbury	84C Banbury	84C Banbury	84C Banbury	84C Banbury	
4150	5101	STB Stourbridge	84F Stourbridge	82F Weymouth	83A Newton Abbot	83A Newton Abbot	86E Severn Tunnel Junction	
4151	5101	BRD Bristol Bath Road	82A Bristol Bath Road	86E Severn Tunnel Junction	86E Severn Tunnel Junction	86E Severn Tunnel Junction	86E Severn Tunnel Junction	
4152	5101	BRD Bristol Bath Road	82A Bristol Bath Road	88D Merthyr	88D Merthyr	85A Worcester		
4153	5101	KDR Kidderminster	85D Kidderminster	85D Kidderminster	85D Kidderminster	85D Kidderminster	84G Kidderminster	
4154	5101	WLN Wellington	84H Wellington	85A Worcester	85A Worcester	85A Worcester	84C Banbury	
4155	5101	BRD Bristol Bath Road	82A Bristol Bath Road	84H Wellington	84E Tyseley	84E Tyseley	84E Tyseley	
4156	5101	STJ Severn Tunnel Junction	86A Ebbw Junction	86E Severn Tunnel Junction	86E Severn Tunnel Junction	86E Severn Tunnel Junction	86E Severn Tunnel Junction	
4157	5101	TYS Tyseley	84E Tyseley	82A Bristol Bath Road	83B Taunton	83B Taunton	82D Westbury	
4158	5101	STJ Severn Tunnel Junction	86G Pontypool Road	84H Wellington	84H Wellington	84H Wellington	84E Tyseley	
4159	5101	CHR Chester (GWR)	84E Tyseley	82A Bristol Bath Road	83B Taunton	83B Taunton	86E Severn Tunnel Junction	
4160	5101	→	88C Barry	88D Merthyr	88D Merthyr	88A Radyr	88B Radyr	
4161	5101	→	88C Barry	88D Merthyr	88D Merthyr	84F Stourbridge	85B Gloucester	
4162	5101	→	88F Treherbert	88D Merthyr	88D Merthyr	84D Leamington Spa		
4163	5101	→	88C Barry	88D Merthyr	88D Merthyr	88A Radyr		
4164	5101	→	87B Duffryn Yard	88D Merthyr	88D Merthyr	86E Severn Tunnel Junction		
4165	5101	→	84E Tyseley	84K Chester (GWR)	84K Chester (GWR)	85B Gloucester	84A Stafford Road	
4166	5101	→	84E Tyseley	82A Bristol Bath Road	82F Weymouth	71G Weymouth	88B Radyr	
4167	5101	→	83F Truro	83E St. Blazey	83E St. Blazey	83E St. Blazey	84E Tyseley	
4168	5101	→	86A Ebbw Junction	86A Ebbw Junction	86A Ebbw Junction	84F Stourbridge	84F Stourbridge	
4169	5101	→	87A Neath	87A Neath	87A Neath	87A Neath	87A Neath	
4170	5101	→	84E Tyseley	84E Tyseley	84E Tyseley	84E Tyseley		
4171	5101	→	84D Leamington Spa	84D Leamington Spa	84D Leamington Spa	84D Leamington Spa	84D Leamington Spa	
4172	5101	→	84E Tyseley	84E Tyseley	84E Tyseley	84E Tyseley	84E Tyseley	
4173	5101	→	84F Stourbridge	84F Stourbridge	84F Stourbridge	84F Stourbridge	84G Kidderminster	
4174	5101	→	85B Gloucester	85B Gloucester	83C Exeter	83D Laira (Plymouth)	82D Westbury	
4175	5101	→	85D Kidderminster	85D Kidderminster	85D Kidderminster	85D Kidderminster	84G Kidderminster	
4176	5101	→	83C Exeter	83C Exeter	83A Newton Abbot	83A Newton Abbot	84D Leamington Spa	
4177	5101	→	88C Barry	88C Barry	88A Cardiff Cathays	83A Newton Abbot	88B Radyr	
4178	5101	→	87G Carmarthen	84H Wellington	83A Newton Abbot	83A Newton Abbot	84D Leamington Spa	
4179	5101	→	83A Newton Abbot	83A Newton Abbot	83A Newton Abbot	83A Newton Abbot	84A Stafford Road	
4200	4200	STJ Severn Tunnel Junction	86E Severn Tunnel Junction	86E Severn Tunnel Junction	86H Aberbeeg			
4201	4200	PILL Newport Pill	86B Newport Pill	86B Newport Pill	86B Newport Pill			
4203	4200	NPT Ebbw Junction	86A Ebbw Junction	86A Ebbw Junction	86A Ebbw Junction	86A Ebbw Junction		
4206	4200	NPT Ebbw Junction	86A Ebbw Junction	83E St. Blazey	83E St. Blazey			
4207	4200	LDR Landore	87E Landore	86C Cardiff Canton	86C Cardiff Canton	86C Cardiff Canton		
4208	4200	LTS Llantrisant	86D Llantrisant	86D Llantrisant	86D Llantrisant			
4211	4200	PILL Newport Pill	86B Newport Pill	86B Newport Pill	86B Newport Pill			
4212	4200	LDR Landore	87B Duffryn Yard	87B Duffryn Yard	87B Duffryn Yard			
4213	4200	LLY Llanelly	87F Llanelly	87F Llanelly	87F Llanelly	87G Carmarthen	88H Tondu	
4214	4200	TDU Tondu	86H Aberbeeg	86H Aberbeeg	86B Newport Pill	86B Newport Pill	86B Newport Pill	
4215	4200	SBZ St. Blazey	83E St. Blazey	86H Aberbeeg	86E Severn Tunnel Junction			
4217	4200	ABEEG Aberbeeg	86H Aberbeeg	86F Tondu	86F Tondu			
4218	4200	TDU Tondu	86F Tondu	86F Tondu	86F Tondu	86F Tondu		
4221	4200	NEA Neath	87A Neath	87A Neath	87D Swansea East Dock			
4222	4200	ABEEG Aberbeeg	86C Cardiff Canton	86F Tondu	86F Tondu	86F Tondu	88H Tondu	
4223	4200	CARM Carmarthen	86H Aberbeeg	87F Llanelly	87F Llanelly			
4224	4200	NPT Ebbw Junction	86C Cardiff Canton	88C Barry	86F Tondu			
4225	4200	NPT Ebbw Junction	86A Ebbw Junction	86C Cardiff Canton	86C Cardiff Canton	86C Cardiff Canton	87F Llanelly	
4226	4200	PILL Newport Pill	86B Newport Pill	86C Cardiff Canton	86C Cardiff Canton			
4227	4200	CDF Cardiff Canton	86C Cardiff Canton	86H Aberbeeg	86A Ebbw Junction	86A Ebbw Junction	86A Ebbw Junction	
4228	4200	ABDR Aberdare	86J Aberdare	86J Aberdare	86J Aberdare	86J Aberdare	88H Tondu	
4229	4200	PILL Newport Pill	86B Newport Pill	86G Pontypool Road	86G Pontypool Road	86E Severn Tunnel Junction		
4230	4200	NPT Ebbw Junction	86A Ebbw Junction	86A Ebbw Junction	86G Pontypool Road	86C Cardiff Canton		
4231	4200	ABEEG Aberbeeg	86C Cardiff Canton	86C Cardiff Canton	86C Cardiff Canton			
4232	4200	NEA Neath	87A Neath	87A Neath	87D Swansea East Dock	87D Swansea East Dock	87D Swansea East Dock	
4233	4200	PILL Newport Pill	86B Newport Pill	86B Newport Pill	86B Newport Pill	86B Newport Pill	86B Newport Pill	
4235	4200	PILL Newport Pill	86B Newport Pill	86B Newport Pill	86B Newport Pill	86B Newport Pill		
4236	4200	CDF Cardiff Canton	86F Tondu	86F Tondu	86F Tondu	86F Tondu		
4237	4200	PILL Newport Pill	86B Newport Pill	86B Newport Pill	86B Newport Pill	86H Aberbeeg	86F Aberbeeg	
4238	4200	PPRD Pontypool Road	86H Aberbeeg	86H Aberbeeg	86H Aberbeeg	86B Newport Pill	86B Newport Pill	
4241	4200	TDU Tondu	86F Tondu	86F Tondu	86F Tondu	86E Severn Tunnel Junction	86E Severn Tunnel Junction	
4242	4200	NPT Ebbw Junction	86A Ebbw Junction	86A Ebbw Junction	87A Neath	87A Neath	88L Cardiff East Dock	
4243	4200	ABEEG Aberbeeg	86E Severn Tunnel Junction	87A Neath	87A Neath	86F Tondu	88H Tondu	
4246	4200	PILL Newport Pill	86B Newport Pill	86A Ebbw Junction	86A Ebbw Junction	86A Ebbw Junction		
4247	4200	NPT Ebbw Junction	86A Ebbw Junction	83E St. Blazey	83E St. Blazey	86A Ebbw Junction	88H Tondu	
4248	4200	NPT Ebbw Junction	86A Ebbw Junction	86A Ebbw Junction	86A Ebbw Junction	86A Ebbw Junction	86E Severn Tunnel Junction	
4250	4200	LDR Landore	87E Landore	86C Cardiff Canton	86H Aberbeeg	86H Aberbeeg		
4251	4200	TDU Tondu	86F Tondu	86F Tondu	86F Tondu	86F Tondu	88H Tondu	
4252	4200	NEA Neath	87A Neath	87A Neath	87A Neath	86D Llantrisant	88J Aberdare	
4253	4200	PILL Newport Pill	86B Newport Pill	86B Newport Pill	86B Newport Pill	86B Newport Pill	86B Newport Pill	
4254	4200	LLY Llanelly	87F Llanelly	82C Swindon	86C Cardiff Canton	86C Cardiff Canton	86B Newport Pill	
4255	4200	DYD Duffryn Yard	86C Cardiff Canton	86C Cardiff Canton	86J Aberdare	87A Neath	87A Neath	
4256	4200	LDR Landore	87B Duffryn Yard	87B Duffryn Yard	87B Duffryn Yard	87B Duffryn Yard	87B Duffryn Yard	

		1948	1951	1954	1957	1960	1963	1966
4257	4200	ABDR Aberdare	86J Aberdare	86J Aberdare	86J Aberdare	86J Aberdare	88J Aberdare	
4258	4200	PILL Newport Pill	86B Newport Pill	86B Newport Pill	86B Newport Pill	86B Newport Pill	86A Ebbw Junction	
4259	4200	NEA Neath	87A Neath	87D Swansea East Dock	86H Aberbeeg	86B Newport Pill	86B Newport Pill	
4260	4200	NPT Ebbw Junction	86F Tondu	87F Llanelly	87F Llanelly			
4261	4200	LTS Llantrisant	86D Llantrisant	86D Llantrisant	86D Llantrisant			
4262	4200	STJ Severn Tunnel Junction	82B St. Philips Marsh	82B St. Philips Marsh	82B St. Philips Marsh	86J Aberdare	88H Tondu	
4263	4200	NPT Ebbw Junction	86B Newport Pill	86B Newport Pill	86F Tondu	86F Tondu	88H Tondu	
4264	4200	ABDR Aberdare	86J Aberdare	86J Aberdare	87A Neath	87A Neath	86B Newport Pill	
4265	4200	LDR Landore	87B Duffryn Yard	87B Duffryn Yard	87B Duffryn Yard	87B Duffryn Yard	86A Ebbw Junction	
4266	4200	CARM Carmarthen	86C Cardiff Canton	86C Cardiff Canton	86C Cardiff Canton	86C Cardiff Canton		
4267	4200	ABEEG Aberbeeg	86H Aberbeeg	88C Barry	86A Ebbw Junction	86D Llantrisant		
4268	4200	NPT Ebbw Junction	86A Ebbw Junction	86C Cardiff Canton	86D Llantrisant	86D Llantrisant	88G Llantrisant	
4269	4200	PILL Newport Pill	86B Newport Pill	86B Newport Pill	86H Aberbeeg	86F Tondu		
4270	4200	NPT Ebbw Junction	86C Cardiff Canton	86C Cardiff Canton	86C Cardiff Canton	86C Cardiff Canton		
4271	4200	NPT Ebbw Junction	86H Aberbeeg	86A Ebbw Junction	86A Ebbw Junction	87D Swansea East Dock	86B Newport Pill	
4272	4200	NEA Neath	87A Neath	86J Aberdare	86J Aberdare	87F Llanelly	88L Cardiff East Dock	
4273	4200	TDU Tondu	86F Tondu	86F Tondu	86F Tondu	86D Llantrisant	88H Tondu	
4274	4200	NEA Neath	87A Neath	87A Neath	87A Neath	86F Tondu		
4275	4200	PPRD Pontypool Road	86C Cardiff Canton	86E Severn Tunnel Junction	87A Neath	87A Neath	87A Neath	
4276	4200	NPT Ebbw Junction	86F Tondu	86F Tondu	86F Tondu	86B Newport Pill		
4277	4200	DYD Duffryn Yard	86E Severn Tunnel Junction	86A Ebbw Junction	86H Aberbeeg	86H Aberbeeg	86F Aberbeeg	
4278	4200	LLY Llanelly	87F Llanelly	87F Llanelly	87F Llanelly	87B Duffryn Yard	87B Duffryn Yard	
4279	4200	NEA Neath	87A Neath	87A Neath	87A Neath	87A Neath	88J Aberdare	
4280	4200	PILL Newport Pill	86B Newport Pill	86B Newport Pill	86B Newport Pill	86B Newport Pill	86B Newport Pill	
4281	4200	LLY Llanelly	87F Llanelly	87A Neath	87A Neath	87A Neath		
4282	4200	SED Swansea East Dock	86E Severn Tunnel Junction	87A Neath	87A Neath	87A Neath	87A Neath	
4283	4200	SED Swansea East Dock	87F Llanelly	87F Llanelly	86A Ebbw Junction	86A Ebbw Junction	86A Ebbw Junction	
4284	4200	NEA Neath	87A Neath	87A Neath	87A Neath	87A Neath	87A Neath	
4285	4200	ABDR Aberdare	86C Cardiff Canton	86B Newport Pill	86B Newport Pill	86H Aberbeeg	86F Aberbeeg	
4286	4200	DYD Duffryn Yard	86E Severn Tunnel Junction	86E Severn Tunnel Junction	86A Ebbw Junction	87F Llanelly	87B Duffryn Yard	
4287	4200	ABEEG Aberbeeg	86C Cardiff Canton	86H Aberbeeg	86H Aberbeeg	86H Aberbeeg		
4288	4200	NEA Neath	87A Neath	87A Neath	87A Neath	87A Neath		
4289	4200	NPT Ebbw Junction	86A Ebbw Junction	86E Severn Tunnel Junction	86E Severn Tunnel Junction	86E Severn Tunnel Junction		
4290	4200	CDF Cardiff Canton	86G Pontypool Road	86A Ebbw Junction	86A Ebbw Junction	86A Ebbw Junction	86A Ebbw Junction	
4291	4200	PILL Newport Pill	86B Newport Pill	86B Newport Pill	86B Newport Pill	86H Aberbeeg		
4292	4200	DYD Duffryn Yard	87B Duffryn Yard	87B Duffryn Yard	87B Duffryn Yard	87F Llanelly	87F Llanelly	
4293	4200	NEA Neath	87A Neath	87A Neath	87A Neath	87B Duffryn Yard		
4294	4200	NPT Ebbw Junction	86A Ebbw Junction	86A Ebbw Junction	86A Ebbw Junction	83E St. Blazey	86B Newport Pill	
4295	4200	LDR Landore	87A Neath	87A Neath	87A Neath	87A Neath	87F Llanelly	
4296	4200	SED Swansea East Dock	87D Swansea East Dock	87B Duffryn Yard	87B Duffryn Yard	87B Duffryn Yard	87B Duffryn Yard	
4297	4200	ABDR Aberdare	86J Aberdare	86J Aberdare	86J Aberdare	86E Severn Tunnel Junction	86A Ebbw Junction	
4298	4200	SBZ St. Blazey	83E St. Blazey	86E Severn Tunnel Junction	86E Severn Tunnel Junction	86C Cardiff Canton	87F Llanelly	
4299	4200	DG Danygraig	87C Danygraig	87C Danygraig	87C Danygraig	87B Duffryn Yard	86A Ebbw Junction	
4303	4300	PPRD Pontypool Road	86G Pontypool Road					
4318	4300	DID Didcot	81E Didcot					
4320	4300	CHEL Cheltenham						
4326	4300	DID Didcot	81E Didcot	84F Stourbridge	84F Stourbridge			
4337	4300	BHD Birkenhead	84F Stourbridge					
4353	4300	BHD Birkenhead						
4358	4300	NEY Neyland	87H Neyland	87H Neyland	85B Gloucester			
4365	4300	WES Westbury						
4375	4300	CNYD Croes Newydd	84J Croes Newydd	84F Stourbridge	84F Stourbridge			
4377	4300	WES Westbury	82D Westbury	82D Westbury	89C Machynlleth			
4381	4300	SDN Swindon	82C Swindon					
4386	4300	BHD Birkenhead						
4400	4400	WLN Wellington	84H Wellington					
4401	4400	WLN Wellington	84H Wellington	83A Newton Abbot				
4402	4400	LA Laira (Plymouth)						
4403	4400	WLN Wellington	84H Wellington					
4404	4400	TDU Tondu	86F Tondu					
4405	4400	NA Newton Abbot	83A Newton Abbot	83A Newton Abbot				
4406	4400	WLN Wellington	84H Wellington	86F Tondu				
4407	4400	LA Laira (Plymouth)	83D Laira (Plymouth)					
4408	4400	TDU Tondu	86F Tondu					
4409	4400	WLN Wellington	83D Laira (Plymouth)					
4410	4400	EXE Exeter	83C Exeter	83D Laira (Plymouth)				
4500	4500	PZ Penzance	83G Penzance					
4501	4500	MCH Machynlleth	89C Machynlleth					
4502	4500	SDN Swindon	82C Swindon					
4503	4500	SBZ St. Blazey	83E St. Blazey					
4504	4500	WOS Worcester	83F Truro					
4505	4500	SBZ St. Blazey	83E St. Blazey	83E St. Blazey	83G Penzance			
4506	4500	WTD Whitland	87H Neyland	87H Neyland				
4507	4500	SDN Swindon	82F Weymouth	82E Yeovil Pen Mill	82F Weymouth	71G Weymouth	72C Yeovil Town	
4508	4500	WES Westbury	82D Westbury	83E St. Blazey	83F Truro			
4509	4500	PZ Penzance	83G Penzance					
4510	4500	SDN Swindon	82D Westbury					
4511	4500	MCH Machynlleth	81F Oxford					
4512	4500	MCH Machynlleth	89C Machynlleth					
4513	4500	MCH Machynlleth						
4514	4500	ABEEG Aberbeeg	86H Aberbeeg					
4515	4500	WTD Whitland	87H Neyland					
4516	4500	SBZ St. Blazey	83E St. Blazey					
4517	4500	LA Laira (Plymouth)	83E St. Blazey					
4518	4500	NPT Ebbw Junction	83D Laira (Plymouth)					
4519	4500	WTD Whitland	87H Neyland	87H Neyland	87H Neyland			
4520	4500	WES Westbury	82F Weymouth					
4521	4500	SDN Swindon	82C Swindon	85B Gloucester				
4522	4500	ABEEG Aberbeeg	86H Aberbeeg	86G Pontypool Road				
4523	4500	TR Truro	83F Truro	83E St. Blazey				
4524	4500	LA Laira (Plymouth)	83D Laira (Plymouth)	83D Laira (Plymouth)	82A Bristol Bath Road			
4525	4500	PZ Penzance	83G Penzance					
4526	4500	NA Newton Abbot	83E St. Blazey	83E St. Blazey	83E St. Blazey			
4527	4500	WEY Weymouth	82F Weymouth					
4528	4500	LA Laira (Plymouth)						
4529	4500	SBZ St. Blazey	83E St. Blazey					
4530	4500	EXE Exeter	89C Machynlleth	83D Laira (Plymouth)				
4531	4500	LA Laira (Plymouth)						
4532	4500	TR Truro	83A Newton Abbot	82A Bristol Bath Road				
4533	4500	PPRD Pontypool Road	86G Pontypool Road	86G Pontypool Road				
4534	4500	GLO Gloucester	85B Gloucester	83D Laira (Plymouth)				
4535	4500	BRD Bristol Bath Road	82A Bristol Bath Road	82A Bristol Bath Road				
4536	4500	BRD Bristol Bath Road	82C Swindon	82D Westbury	82D Westbury			
4537	4500	PZ Penzance	83G Penzance	83G Penzance				
4538	4500	SDN Swindon	82C Swindon	82C Swindon	82C Swindon			
4539	4500	BRD Bristol Bath Road	82A Bristol Bath Road	81D Reading				
4540	4500	PZ Penzance	83C Exeter	83C Exeter	83C Exeter			
4541	4500	PPRD Pontypool Road	86G Pontypool Road	87H Neyland				
4542	4500	LA Laira (Plymouth)	83D Laira (Plymouth)	83D Laira (Plymouth)				
4543	4500	SDN Swindon						
4544	4500	SDN Swindon	82C Swindon					
4545	4500	PZ Penzance	83G Penzance	83G Penzance	83G Penzance			
4546	4500	WOS Worcester	85A Worcester	89A Oswestry	89A Oswestry			
4547	4500	NA Newton Abbot	83A Newton Abbot	83A Newton Abbot	83G Penzance	83E St. Blazey		

		1948	1951	1954	1957	1960	1963	1966
4548	4500	PZ Penzance	83G Penzance	83G Penzance	83G Penzance			
4549	4500	MCH Machynlleth	89C Machynlleth	89C Machynlleth	89C Machynlleth	89C Machynlleth		
4550	4500	SDN Swindon	82C Swindon	82C Swindon	87H Neyland	87H Neyland		
4551	4500	SDN Swindon	82C Swindon	82D Westbury	82D Westbury			
4552	4500	SBZ St. Blazey	83E St. Blazey	83E St. Blazey	83E St. Blazey	83E St. Blazey		
4553	4500	WTD Whitland	87H Neyland	87H Neyland	85B Gloucester			
4554	4500	TR Truro	83F Truro	83F Truro	83F Truro			
4555	4500	MCH Machynlleth	89C Machynlleth	89C Machynlleth	89C Machynlleth	83A Newton Abbot	83D Laira (Plymouth)	
4556	4500	WTD Whitland	87H Neyland	87H Neyland	87H Neyland	87H Neyland		
4557	4500	TDU Tondu	86F Tondu	87H Neyland	87H Neyland	87H Neyland		
4558	4500	WOS Worcester	81F Oxford	82A Bristol Bath Road	87H Neyland	87H Neyland		
4559	4500	SBZ St. Blazey	83E St. Blazey	83E St. Blazey	83E St. Blazey	83E St. Blazey		
4560	4500	MCH Machynlleth	89C Machynlleth	89C Machynlleth	89C Machynlleth			
4561	4500	TR Truro	83F Truro	83F Truro	83F Truro	83A Newton Abbot		
4562	4500	WEY Weymouth	82F Weymouth	82F Weymouth	82F Weymouth	71G Weymouth		
4563	4500	BRD Bristol Bath Road	82A Bristol Bath Road	83B Taunton	83G Penzance	83G Penzance		
4564	4500	CHEL Cheltenham	85B Gloucester	85B Gloucester	85B Gloucester	84G Shrewsbury	89A Shrewsbury	
4565	4500	SBZ St. Blazey	83E St. Blazey	83E St. Blazey	83E St. Blazey	83E St. Blazey		
4566	4500	PZ Penzance	83G Penzance	83G Penzance	83G Penzance	83G Penzance		
4567	4500	CHEL Cheltenham	85B Gloucester	85A Worcester	85A Worcester	82D Westbury		
4568	4500	SBZ St. Blazey	83E St. Blazey	83E St. Blazey	83A Newton Abbot			
4569	4500	TR Truro	83E St. Blazey	83E St. Blazey	83E St. Blazey	83E St. Blazey	87H Neyland	
4570	4500	SBZ St. Blazey	83E St. Blazey	83F Truro	83G Penzance	83G Penzance	83D Laira (Plymouth)	
4571	4500	MCH Machynlleth	89C Machynlleth	85A Worcester	85A Worcester	83G Penzance		
4572	4500	WES Westbury	82D Westbury	82D Westbury	82D Westbury			
4573	4500	WES Westbury	82D Westbury	82C Swindon	85B Gloucester	85B Gloucester		
4574	4500	PZ Penzance	83G Penzance	83G Penzance	83G Penzance	83F Truro	83D Laira (Plymouth)	
4575	4575	MCH Machynlleth	89C Machynlleth	89C Machynlleth	89C Machynlleth	89C Machynlleth		
4576	4575	WTD Whitland	87H Neyland	87H Neyland	87H Neyland			
4577	4575	BRD Bristol Bath Road	82A Bristol Bath Road	82A Bristol Bath Road	82A Bristol Bath Road			
4578	4575	CHEL Cheltenham	85D Kidderminster	88C Barry	88C Barry			
4579	4575	WTD Whitland	87H Neyland	87H Neyland	87H Neyland			
4580	4575	BRD Bristol Bath Road	82A Bristol Bath Road	88A Cardiff Cathays	88A Cardiff Cathays			
4581	4575	TR Truro	89C Machynlleth	88A Cardiff Cathays	86F Tondu			
4582	4575	NA Newton Abbot	83A Newton Abbot	82A Bristol Bath Road	82A Bristol Bath Road			
4583	4575	LA Laira (Plymouth)	83D Laira (Plymouth)	83D Laira (Plymouth)	83D Laira (Plymouth)			
4584	4575	KDR Kidderminster	85D Kidderminster	83E St. Blazey	83E St. Blazey			
4585	4575	SDN Swindon	82C Swindon	83E St. Blazey	83E St. Blazey			
4586	4575	KDR Kidderminster	85D Kidderminster	85B Gloucester				
4587	4575	NA Newton Abbot	83A Newton Abbot	83G Penzance	83F Truro	83F Truro		
4588	4575	TR Truro	83F Truro	83F Truro	83F Truro	83G Penzance		
4589	4575	TR Truro	83F Truro	88A Cardiff Cathays	88A Cardiff Cathays	83C Exeter		
4590	4575	SDN Swindon	82C Swindon	83D Laira (Plymouth)	83D Laira (Plymouth)			
4591	4575	LA Laira (Plymouth)	83D Laira (Plymouth)	83D Laira (Plymouth)	83D Laira (Plymouth)	83D Laira (Plymouth)	83D Laira (Plymouth)	
4592	4575	SDN Swindon	82C Swindon	82A Bristol Bath Road	83D Laira (Plymouth)	83D Laira (Plymouth)		
4593	4575	NPT Ebbw Junction	86G Pontypool Road	86H Aberbeeg	86G Pontypool Road	82A Bristol Bath Road	83B Taunton	
4594	4575	KDR Kidderminster	85D Kidderminster	85A Worcester	87H Neyland	87H Neyland		
4595	4575	BRD Bristol Bath Road	82A Bristol Bath Road	82A Bristol Bath Road	82A Bristol Bath Road			
4596	4575	WOS Worcester	85A Worcester	85D Kidderminster	85D Kidderminster			
4597	4575	ABEEG Aberbeeg	86H Aberbeeg	82A Bristol Bath Road	82A Bristol Bath Road			
4598	4575	SBZ St. Blazey	83E St. Blazey	83F Truro				
4599	4575	NPT Ebbw Junction	85D Kidderminster	89C Machynlleth	89C Machynlleth			
4600	5700	HFD Hereford	85C Hereford	85C Hereford	86G Pontypool Road	86G Pontypool Road	86G Pontypool Road	
4601	5700	DID Didcot	88C Barry	88C Barry	88C Barry	73H Folkestone Junction		
4602	5700	SALOP Shrewsbury	84G Shrewsbury	84K Chester (GWR)	84K Chester (GWR)	6E Chester (GWR)	84F Stourbridge	
4603	5700	SPM St. Philips Marsh	82B St. Philips Marsh	82A Bristol Bath Road	82B St. Philips Marsh	82B St. Philips Marsh	86G Pontypool Road	
4604	5700	SHL Southall	83B Taunton	83B Taunton	83B Taunton	83B Taunton	86F Aberbeeg	
4605	5700	TYS Tyseley	84E Tyseley	84H Wellington	84H Wellington	84H Wellington		
4606	5700	PDN Old Oak Common	81D Reading	81D Reading	81D Reading	81B Slough	81E Didcot	
4607	5700	SPM St. Philips Marsh	82B St. Philips Marsh	82D Westbury	82D Westbury	82D Westbury	82D Westbury	
4608	5700	SHL Southall	81C Southall	81C Southall	81C Southall	81C Southall	81C Southall	
4609	5700	PDN Old Oak Common	81D Reading	81D Reading	81D Reading	81D Reading	81D Reading	
4610	5700	SHL Southall	81C Southall	81C Southall	81C Southall	73H Folkestone Junction	70B Feltham	
4611	5700	PPRD Pontypool Road	86G Pontypool Road	86A Ebbw Junction	86A Ebbw Junction	86A Ebbw Junction	86A Ebbw Junction	
4612	5700	SPM St. Philips Marsh	82C Swindon	82C Swindon	82C Swindon	82C Swindon	87A Neath	
4613	5700	WOS Worcester	85A Worcester	85A Worcester	85A Worcester	85A Worcester	85A Worcester	
4614	5700	WOS Worcester	85A Worcester	85D Kidderminster	85A Worcester	85A Worcester	85B Gloucester	
4615	5700	PDN Old Oak Common	81A Old Oak Common	81A Old Oak Common	81A Old Oak Common	81A Old Oak Common	81A Old Oak Common	
4616	5700	CHYS Cardiff Cathays	88B Cardiff East Dock	88D Merthyr	88D Merthyr	73H Folkestone Junction	71G Weymouth	
4617	5700	SLO Slough	84J Croes Newydd	84J Croes Newydd	84J Croes Newydd	84J Croes Newydd	89A Shrewsbury	
4618	5700	CED Cardiff East Dock	88A Cardiff Cathays	88A Cardiff Cathays	88A Cardiff Cathays	88C Barry	88C Barry	
4619	5700	SPM St. Philips Marsh	82B St. Philips Marsh	82B St. Philips Marsh	82B St. Philips Marsh	82A Bristol Bath Road	82E Bristol Barrow Road	
4620	5700	TYS Tyseley	86D Llantrisant	86D Llantrisant	86D Llantrisant	86D Llantrisant	88G Llantrisant	
4621	5700	NEA Neath	87A Neath	87A Neath	87A Neath	87A Neath	87A Neath	
4622	5700	CDF Cardiff Canton	86C Cardiff Canton	86C Cardiff Canton	86C Cardiff Canton	83F Truro	83B Taunton	
4623	5700	SALOP Shrewsbury	84G Shrewsbury	84G Shrewsbury	84G Shrewsbury	84G Shrewsbury	86C Hereford	
4624	5700	SPM St. Philips Marsh	82B St. Philips Marsh	82B St. Philips Marsh	82F Weymouth	71G Weymouth	71G Weymouth	
4625	5700	KDR Kidderminster	85D Kidderminster	85A Worcester	85A Worcester	85A Worcester		
4626	5700	SPM St. Philips Marsh	82B St. Philips Marsh	82B St. Philips Marsh	88B Cardiff East Dock	73H Folkestone Junction	70E Salisbury	
4627	5700	GLO Gloucester	85B Gloucester	85B Gloucester	85B Gloucester	86H Aberbeeg	86A Ebbw Junction	
4628	5700	GLO Gloucester	85B Gloucester	85B Gloucester	85B Gloucester	85B Gloucester	85A Worcester	
4629	5700	WOS Worcester	85A Worcester	85A Worcester	85A Worcester	85D Kidderminster	84G Kidderminster	
4630	5700	CED Cardiff East Dock	88B Cardiff East Dock	88D Merthyr	88D Merthyr	73H Folkestone Junction	70E Salisbury	
4631	5700	BAN Banbury	84C Banbury	84C Banbury	88B Cardiff East Dock	73H Folkestone Junction	72C Yeovil Town	
4632	5700	MTHR Merthyr	88D Merthyr	88D Merthyr	88D Merthyr	88D Merthyr		
4633	5700	CDF Cardiff Canton	86C Cardiff Canton	86C Cardiff Canton	86C Cardiff Canton	86C Cardiff Canton	88L Cardiff East Dock	
4634	5700	TDU Tondu	86F Tondu	86F Tondu	88A Cardiff Cathays	70A Nine Elms	70A Nine Elms	
4635	5700	MTHR Merthyr	88D Merthyr	88D Merthyr	88D Merthyr	88D Merthyr	88D Merthyr	2A Tyseley
4636	5700	WES Westbury	82D Westbury	82D Westbury	82D Westbury	82D Westbury	82D Westbury	
4637	5700	CDF Cardiff Canton	86H Aberbeeg	86D Llantrisant	86D Llantrisant	86D Llantrisant	88B Radyr	
4638	5700	STB Stourbridge	84F Stourbridge	81B Slough	81B Slough	81B Slough	81B Slough	
4639	5700	PPRD Pontypool Road	86G Pontypool Road	86G Pontypool Road	86G Pontypool Road	86G Pontypool Road	86G Pontypool Road	
4640	5700	DYD Duffryn Yard	87B Duffryn Yard	87B Duffryn Yard	87B Duffryn Yard	87B Duffryn Yard	87B Duffryn Yard	
4641	5700	KDR Kidderminster	85A Worcester	85D Kidderminster	85D Kidderminster	81D Reading		
4642	5700	PDN Old Oak Common	86G Pontypool Road	86G Pontypool Road	86G Pontypool Road	86G Pontypool Road	86G Pontypool Road	
4643	5700	TDU Tondu	86F Tondu	86H Aberbeeg	86H Aberbeeg	86B Newport Pill	86B Newport Pill	
4644	5700	PDN Old Oak Common	81A Old Oak Common	81A Old Oak Common	81A Old Oak Common	84G Shrewsbury	87J Fishguard Goodwick	
4645	5700	OXF Oxford	84J Croes Newydd	84J Croes Newydd	84J Croes Newydd	84J Croes Newydd	89B Croes Newydd	
4646	5700	BAN Banbury	84C Banbury	84F Stourbridge	84F Stourbridge	84F Stourbridge	84F Stourbridge	2C Stourbridge
4647	5700	SPM St. Philips Marsh	82D Westbury	82D Westbury	82D Westbury	82D Westbury		
4648	5700	TYS Tyseley	84E Tyseley	84E Tyseley	84E Tyseley	84E Tyseley	84E Tyseley	
4649	5700	RDG Reading	81E Didcot	81E Didcot	81E Didcot	81E Didcot	81F Oxford	
4650	5700	SLO Slough	81B Slough	81B Slough	81B Slough	81B Slough	86F Aberbeeg	
4651	5700	SDN Swindon	82C Swindon	82C Swindon	82C Swindon	82C Swindon	87B Duffryn Yard	
4652	5700	CDF Cardiff Canton	86H Aberbeeg	86H Aberbeeg	86H Aberbeeg	86H Aberbeeg	88H Tondu	
4653	5700	LA Laira (Plymouth)	83D Laira (Plymouth)	83D Laira (Plymouth)	83D Laira (Plymouth)	87A Neath	87A Neath	
4654	5700	NEY Neyland	87H Neyland	87H Neyland	87H Neyland	87H Neyland	87H Neyland	
4655	5700	WEY Weymouth	82B St. Philips Marsh	82B St. Philips Marsh	82B St. Philips Marsh	82B St. Philips Marsh	83B Taunton	
4656	5700	LA Laira (Plymouth)	83D Laira (Plymouth)	83D Laira (Plymouth)	83D Laira (Plymouth)	72C Yeovil Town		
4657	5700	HFD Hereford	85C Hereford	85C Hereford	85C Hereford	85C Hereford	86A Ebbw Junction	
4658	5700	LA Laira (Plymouth)	83D Laira (Plymouth)	83D Laira (Plymouth)	83D Laira (Plymouth)	83D Laira (Plymouth)	83D Laira (Plymouth)	
4659	5700	GLO Gloucester	85B Gloucester	85B Gloucester	85B Gloucester	85C Hereford	86C Hereford	
4660	5700	WEY Weymouth	82B St. Philips Marsh	82A Bristol Bath Road	82B St. Philips Marsh	82B St. Philips Marsh	87A Neath	
4661	5700	RDG Reading	81D Reading	81D Reading	81D Reading	81D Reading	81D Reading	

		1948	1951	1954	1957	1960	1963	1966
4662	5700	PILL Newport Pill	86F Tondu	86F Tondu	86D Llantrisant	86D Llantrisant	88G Llantrisant	
4663	5700	SHL Southall	83B Taunton	83B Taunton	83B Taunton	83B Taunton	88H Tondu	
4664	5700	WOS Worcester	85A Worcester	85A Worcester	85A Worcester	85A Worcester	85A Worcester	
4665	5700	PDN Old Oak Common	81D Reading	81D Reading	81D Reading	81D Reading	84F Stourbridge	
4666	5700	PDN Old Oak Common	87C Danygraig	87C Danygraig	87C Danygraig	72F Wadebridge	72F Wadebridge	
4667	5700	PDN Old Oak Common	88A Cardiff Cathays	88A Cardiff Cathays	88A Cardiff Cathays	88C Barry	88C Barry	
4668	5700	PPRD Pontypool Road	86G Pontypool Road	86G Pontypool Road	86G Pontypool Road	86G Pontypool Road	86G Pontypool Road	
4669	5700	TDU Tondu	86F Tondu	86F Tondu	86F Tondu	86F Tondu	88H Tondu	
4670	5700	RDG Reading	81D Reading	81D Reading	81D Reading	81D Reading	81D Reading	
4671	5700	NPT Ebbw Junction	86A Ebbw Junction	86A Ebbw Junction	86A Ebbw Junction	86A Ebbw Junction	86A Ebbw Junction	
4672	5700	SALOP Shrewsbury	84G Shrewsbury	84G Shrewsbury	84G Shrewsbury	70A Nine Elms	70A Nine Elms	
4673	5700	SHL Southall	81C Southall	81C Southall	81C Southall	81C Southall	83C Exeter	
4674	5700	LTS Llantrisant	86D Llantrisant	86D Llantrisant	86D Llantrisant	86D Llantrisant	88G Llantrisant	
4675	5700	TDU Tondu	86F Tondu	86F Tondu	86F Tondu	86F Tondu	88H Tondu	
4676	5700	OXF Oxford	81F Oxford	81F Oxford	81F Oxford	87F Llanelly	87F Llanelly	
4677	5700	CDF Cardiff Canton	86C Cardiff Canton	86C Cardiff Canton	87J Fishguard Goodwick	87J Fishguard Goodwick	87A Neath	
4678	5700	HFD Hereford	85C Hereford	85C Hereford	85C Hereford	85C Hereford	86G Pontypool Road	
4679	5700	LA Laira (Plymouth)	83D Laira (Plymouth)	83D Laira (Plymouth)	83D Laira (Plymouth)	83D Laira (Plymouth)	86A Ebbw Junction	
4680	5700	PDN Old Oak Common	81F Oxford	81B Slough	81B Slough	85A Worcester	85A Worcester	
4681	5700	DYD Duffryn Yard	87B Duffryn Yard	87B Duffryn Yard	87B Duffryn Yard	70A Nine Elms	70A Nine Elms	
4682	5700	ABEEG Aberbeeg	86H Aberbeeg	86H Aberbeeg	86H Aberbeeg	86B Newport Pill	87A Neath	
4683	5700	TYS Tyseley	84E Tyseley	84J Croes Newydd	84J Croes Newydd	84K Wrexham Rhosddu	89B Croes Newydd	
4684	5700	DYD Duffryn Yard	87B Duffryn Yard	87B Duffryn Yard	87B Duffryn Yard	87B Duffryn Yard	87B Duffryn Yard	
4685	5700	ABEEG Aberbeeg	86H Aberbeeg	86H Aberbeeg	86H Aberbeeg	86H Aberbeeg		
4686	5700	ABEEG Aberbeeg	86H Aberbeeg	86H Aberbeeg	88B Cardiff East Dock			
4687	5700	STB Stourbridge	84F Stourbridge	84F Stourbridge	84F Stourbridge	84F Stourbridge	84F Stourbridge	
4688	5700	RDG Reading	82B St. Philips Marsh	82B St. Philips Marsh	82B St. Philips Marsh	82B St. Philips Marsh	88J Aberdare	
4689	5700	YEO Yeovil Pen Mill	82E Yeovil Pen Mill	82E Yeovil Pen Mill	82E Yeovil Pen Mill	71G Weymouth	71G Weymouth	
4690	5700	RDG Reading	88D Merthyr	88D Merthyr	88D Merthyr	88D Merthyr	88D Merthyr	
4691	5700	PDN Old Oak Common	81B Slough	81B Slough	81B Slough	81B Slough	82G Templecombe	
4692	5700	RDG Reading	88C Barry	88C Barry	88C Barry	70A Nine Elms	70A Nine Elms	
4693	5700	LA Laira (Plymouth)	83D Laira (Plymouth)	83D Laira (Plymouth)	83D Laira (Plymouth)	84G Shrewsbury	86F Aberbeeg	
4694	5700	DG Danygraig	87C Danygraig	87C Danygraig	87C Danygraig	72F Wadebridge	72F Wadebridge	
4695	5700	SHL Southall	81C Southall	81C Southall	81C Southall	87B Duffryn Yard	87B Duffryn Yard	
4696	5700	STB Stourbridge	84F Stourbridge	84F Stourbridge	84F Stourbridge	84F Stourbridge	84F Stourbridge	2C Stourbridge
4697	5700	SDN Swindon	82C Swindon	82C Swindon	82C Swindon	82C Swindon	82C Swindon	
4698	5700	PDN Old Oak Common	81A Old Oak Common	81A Old Oak Common	88B Cardiff East Dock	70A Nine Elms	70A Nine Elms	
4699	5700	PDN Old Oak Common	81A Old Oak Common	81A Old Oak Common	87H Neyland	87H Neyland	87A Neath	
4700	4700	PDN Old Oak Common	81A Old Oak Common	81A Old Oak Common	81A Old Oak Common	81A Old Oak Common		
4701	4700	PDN Old Oak Common	81A Old Oak Common	81A Old Oak Common	81A Old Oak Common	81A Old Oak Common	81A Old Oak Common	
4702	4700	PDN Old Oak Common	81A Old Oak Common	81A Old Oak Common	81A Old Oak Common	81A Old Oak Common		
4703	4700	LA Laira (Plymouth)	83D Laira (Plymouth)	82B St. Philips Marsh	82B St. Philips Marsh	82B St. Philips Marsh	81A Old Oak Common	
4704	4700	BHD Birkenhead	6C Birkenhead	81A Old Oak Common	81A Old Oak Common	81A Old Oak Common	81A Old Oak Common	
4705	4700	PDN Old Oak Common	81A Old Oak Common	81A Old Oak Common	81A Old Oak Common	83D Laira (Plymouth)	81C Southall	
4706	4700	EXE Exeter	82B St. Philips Marsh	82B St. Philips Marsh	82B St. Philips Marsh	82B St. Philips Marsh	81C Southall	
4707	4700	PDN Old Oak Common	81A Old Oak Common	81A Old Oak Common	81C Southall	81C Southall	81C Southall	
4708	4700	OXY Oxley	84B Oxley	81A Old Oak Common	81A Old Oak Common	81A Old Oak Common		
4800	2800	LLY Llanelly	(2872)					
4801	2800	STJ Severn Tunnel Junction	(2854)					
4802	2800	LLY Llanelly	(2862)					
4803	2800	STJ Severn Tunnel Junction	(2849)					
4804	2800	SPM St. Philips Marsh	(2839)					
4805	2800	LLY Llanelly	(2863)					
4806	2800	LLY Llanelly	(2832)					
4807	2800	LA Laira (Plymouth)	(2848)					
4808	2800	LA Laira (Plymouth)	(2834)					
4809	2800	PDN Old Oak Common	(2845)					
4810	2800	SPM St. Philips Marsh	(2853)					
4811	2800	LA Laira (Plymouth)	(2847)					
4850	2884	LLY Llanelly	(2888)					
4851	2884	STJ Severn Tunnel Junction	(3865)					
4852	2884	STJ Severn Tunnel Junction	(3818)					
4853	2884	PDN Old Oak Common	(3839)					
4854	2884	PDN Old Oak Common	(3837)					
4855	2884	LA Laira (Plymouth)	(3813)					
4856	2884	PDN Old Oak Common	(3820)					
4857	2884	NPT Ebbw Junction	(3831)					
4900	4900	PDN Old Oak Common	81A Old Oak Common	85A Worcester	81A Old Oak Common			
4901	4900	CDF Cardiff Canton	86C Cardiff Canton	86C Cardiff Canton	86C Cardiff Canton	84A Stafford Road		
4902	4900	OXF Oxford	81F Oxford	81F Oxford	81F Oxford	84E Tyseley	81E Didcot	
4903	4900	OXF Oxford	81F Oxford	81F Oxford	81F Oxford	81A Old Oak Common	81A Old Oak Common	
4904	4900	OXY Oxley	84G Shrewsbury	84G Shrewsbury	84E Tyseley	83B Taunton	83B Taunton	
4905	4900	SDN Swindon	84K Chester (GWR)	85C Hereford	83A Newton Abbot	83A Newton Abbot	82B St. Philips Marsh	
4906	4900	TR Truro	83F Truro	83F Truro	83F Truro	83E St. Blazey		
4907	4900	(3903)	82B St. Philips Marsh	85C Hereford	81F Oxford	85A Worcester	86C Hereford	
4908	4900	LLY Llanelly	86E Severn Tunnel Junction	81C Southall	83G Penzance	83G Penzance	81E Didcot	
4909	4900	BAN Banbury	82B St. Philips Marsh	82A Bristol Bath Road	82B St. Philips Marsh	82B St. Philips Marsh		
4910	4900	CARM Carmarthen	87G Carmarthen	87G Carmarthen	87E Landore	87E Landore	81E Didcot	
4912	4900	PPRD Pontypool Road	82B St. Philips Marsh	82C Swindon	84A Stafford Road	84B Oxley		
4913	4900	CDF Cardiff Canton	86C Cardiff Canton	86C Cardiff Canton	86C Cardiff Canton	85C Hereford		
4914	4900	RDG Reading	82A Bristol Bath Road	82A Bristol Bath Road	82B St. Philips Marsh	82B St. Philips Marsh	82B St. Philips Marsh	
4915	4900	CARM Carmarthen	87G Carmarthen	87G Carmarthen	84G Shrewsbury	81E Didcot	81D Reading	
4916	4900	OXY Oxley	82B St. Philips Marsh	86A Ebbw Junction	86A Ebbw Junction	86G Pontypool Road	86C Hereford	
4917	4900	TYS Tyseley	81C Southall	83C Exeter	82D Westbury	82D Westbury		
4918	4900	CHR Chester (GWR)	84C Banbury	84B Oxley	82A Bristol Bath Road	84A Stafford Road	88L Cardiff East Dock	
4919	4900	SALOP Shrewsbury	84B Oxley	84B Oxley	81A Old Oak Common	81A Old Oak Common	81F Oxford	
4920	4900	RDG Reading	81D Reading	83B Taunton	83B Taunton	83A Newton Abbot	83D Laira (Plymouth)	
4921	4900	OXF Oxford	81F Oxford	81F Oxford	81F Oxford	81A Old Oak Common		
4922	4900	CARM Carmarthen	87G Carmarthen	87G Carmarthen	82B St. Philips Marsh	82A Bristol Bath Road	82B St. Philips Marsh	
4923	4900	OXY Oxley	81A Old Oak Common	81A Old Oak Common	87E Landore	87E Landore	84B Oxley	
4924	4900	TYS Tyseley	84E Tyseley	84B Oxley	82A Bristol Bath Road	83B Taunton	82C Swindon	
4925	4900	SDN Swindon	82C Swindon	82C Swindon	81A Old Oak Common	81C Southall		
4926	4900	WES Westbury	82D Westbury	84B Oxley	84A Stafford Road	86G Pontypool Road		
4927	4900	WES Westbury	82D Westbury	82D Westbury	82A Bristol Bath Road	86E Severn Tunnel Junction	87F Llanelly	
4928	4900	OXF Oxford	81F Oxford	81F Oxford	81A Old Oak Common	86C Cardiff Canton	87F Llanelly	
4929	4900	TR Truro	85B Gloucester	85B Gloucester	85B Gloucester	85B Gloucester	85B Gloucester	
4930	4900	TYS Tyseley	82F Weymouth	82D Westbury	82D Westbury	83B Taunton	82C Swindon	
4931	4900	RDG Reading	81D Reading	81C Southall	83G Penzance	86C Cardiff Canton		
4932	4900	PPRD Pontypool Road	82B St. Philips Marsh	83B Taunton	83B Taunton	83B Taunton	83B Taunton	
4933	4900	PPRD Pontypool Road	82D Westbury	81F Oxford	81E Didcot	82D Westbury	82B St. Philips Marsh	
4934	4900	TYS Tyseley	82B St. Philips Marsh	85B Gloucester	86C Cardiff Canton	81C Southall		
4935	4900	PDN Old Oak Common	81E Didcot	81E Didcot	81E Didcot	87G Carmarthen	81E Didcot	
4936	4900	TR Truro	83F Truro	83F Truro	83D Laira (Plymouth)	83A Newton Abbot	88L Cardiff East Dock	
4937	4900	NEY Neyland	87G Carmarthen	87G Carmarthen	87E Landore	86G Pontypool Road		
4938	4900	OXF Oxford	81F Oxford	81F Oxford	81F Oxford	84A Stafford Road		
4939	4900	TYS Tyseley	81D Reading	81C Southall	81E Didcot	81E Didcot	81E Didcot	
4940	4900	SBZ St. Blazey	83E St. Blazey	83B Taunton	83B Taunton			
4941	4900	NPT Ebbw Junction	86A Ebbw Junction	86E Severn Tunnel Junction	87F Llanelly	81D Reading		
4942	4900	BRD Bristol Bath Road	82A Bristol Bath Road	82A Bristol Bath Road	84C Banbury	84C Banbury	81E Didcot	
4943	4900	PDN Old Oak Common	81D Reading	81A Old Oak Common	81D Reading	86G Pontypool Road	86G Pontypool Road	
4944	4900	OXY Oxley	81C Southall	81C Southall	81C Southall	83C Exeter		
4945	4900	SDN Swindon	82C Swindon	81E Didcot	82D Westbury	82D Westbury		
4946	4900	PZ Penzance	83G Penzance	86C Cardiff Canton	86C Cardiff Canton	86C Cardiff Canton	89A Shrewsbury	
4947	4900	PZ Penzance	82B St. Philips Marsh	82B St. Philips Marsh	82A Bristol Bath Road	82B St. Philips Marsh		

No.	Class	1948		1951	1954	1957	1960	1963	1966
4948	*4900*	(3902)		**81D** Reading	**83C** Exeter	**83C** Exeter	**83C** Exeter		
4949	*4900*	**PZ**	Penzance	**83B** Taunton	**83B** Taunton	**83B** Taunton	**82B** St. Philips Marsh	**82B** St. Philips Marsh	
4950	*4900*	**SRD**	Stafford Road	**84B** Oxley	**83D** Laira (Plymouth)	**83D** Laira (Plymouth)	**81D** Reading	**81E** Didcot	
4951	*4900*	**PDN**	Old Oak Common	**82C** Swindon	**86A** Ebbw Junction	**86A** Ebbw Junction	**81D** Reading	**81F** Oxford	
4952	*4900*	**CDF**	Cardiff Canton	**86C** Cardiff Canton	**86E** Severn Tunnel Junction	**85C** Hereford	**86C** Cardiff Canton		
4953	*4900*	**CDF**	Cardiff Canton	**86C** Cardiff Canton	**86C** Cardiff Canton	**82C** Swindon	**82C** Swindon	**88L** Cardiff East Dock	
4954	*4900*	**TN**	Taunton	**82A** Bristol Bath Road	**83A** Newton Abbot	**81F** Oxford	**84A** Stafford Road	**84E** Tyseley	
4955	*4900*	**OXY**	Oxley	**84B** Oxley	**84B** Oxley	**83C** Exeter	**83B** Taunton	**83B** Taunton	
4956	*4900*	**SDN**	Swindon	**81C** Southall	**81C** Southall	**82A** Bristol Bath Road	**86C** Cardiff Canton	**82D** Westbury	
4957	*4900*	**NEY**	Neyland	**87H** Neyland	**86A** Ebbw Junction	**86A** Ebbw Junction	**84B** Oxley		
4958	*4900*	**PDN**	Old Oak Common	**81A** Old Oak Common	**82B** St. Philips Marsh	**82A** Bristol Bath Road	**86G** Pontypool Road	**86G** Pontypool Road	
4959	*4900*	**TYS**	Tyseley	**84E** Tyseley	**84B** Oxley	**82C** Swindon	**81E** Didcot	**81E** Didcot	
4960	*4900*	**SRD**	Stafford Road	**84C** Banbury	**81D** Reading	**81D** Reading	**82B** St. Philips Marsh		
4961	*4900*	**PDN**	Old Oak Common	**81A** Old Oak Common	**82A** Bristol Bath Road	**81D** Reading	**81D** Reading		
4962	*4900*	**PDN**	Old Oak Common	**81D** Reading	**81D** Reading	**81D** Reading	**81D** Reading	**87J** Fishguard Goodwick	
4963	*4900*	**WES**	Westbury	**86C** Cardiff Canton	**83D** Laira (Plymouth)	**84B** Oxley	**84B** Oxley		
4964	*4900*	**OXY**	Oxley	**84E** Tyseley	**84E** Tyseley	**86C** Cardiff Canton	**84C** Banbury	**86G** Pontypool Road	
4965	*4900*	**SPM**	St. Philips Marsh	**83G** Penzance	**83G** Penzance	**81D** Reading	**81E** Didcot		
4966	*4900*	**LA**	Laira (Plymouth)	**83D** Laira (Plymouth)	**83D** Laira (Plymouth)	**84B** Oxley	**84B** Oxley	**87A** Neath	
4967	*4900*	**TYS**	Tyseley	**82B** St. Philips Marsh	**81A** Old Oak Common	**83A** Newton Abbot	**83D** Laira (Plymouth)		
4968	*4900*	(3900)		**86C** Cardiff Canton	**86C** Cardiff Canton	**86C** Cardiff Canton	**82B** St. Philips Marsh		
4969	*4900*	**SPM**	St. Philips Marsh	**82B** St. Philips Marsh	**81F** Oxford	**81D** Reading	**81E** Didcot		
4970	*4900*	**PZ**	Penzance	**83B** Taunton	**83B** Taunton	**83B** Taunton	**83B** Taunton	**87B** Duffryn Yard	
4971	*4900*	(3901)		**83B** Taunton	**83B** Taunton	**83B** Taunton	**83B** Taunton		
4972	*4900*	(3904)		**83D** Laira (Plymouth)	**82A** Bristol Bath Road	**82C** Swindon	**82C** Swindon	**82D** Westbury	
4973	*4900*	**OXF**	Oxford	**82C** Swindon	**82C** Swindon	**86C** Cardiff Canton	**86C** Cardiff Canton		
4974	*4900*	**CDF**	Cardiff Canton	**86C** Cardiff Canton	**86C** Cardiff Canton	**86C** Cardiff Canton	**84E** Tyseley		
4975	*4900*	**CDF**	Cardiff Canton	**86C** Cardiff Canton	**85C** Hereford	**85C** Hereford	**83A** Newton Abbot	**81D** Reading	
4976	*4900*	**CHR**	Chester (GWR)	**84K** Chester (GWR)	**85C** Hereford	**83D** Laira (Plymouth)	**83D** Laira (Plymouth)	**81C** Southall	
4977	*4900*	**GLO**	Gloucester	**84B** Oxley	**84C** Banbury	**81A** Old Oak Common	**81D** Reading		
4978	*4900*	**PDN**	Old Oak Common	**81C** Southall	**83D** Laira (Plymouth)	**83B** Taunton	**83B** Taunton	**83D** Laira (Plymouth)	
4979	*4900*	**CDF**	Cardiff Canton	**86C** Cardiff Canton	**81C** Southall	**81E** Didcot	**81F** Oxford	**81F** Oxford	
4980	*4900*	**WOS**	Worcester	**84C** Banbury	**84C** Banbury	**82B** St. Philips Marsh	**82B** St. Philips Marsh	**82B** St. Philips Marsh	
4981	*4900*	**CARM**	Carmarthen	**87G** Carmarthen	**87E** Landore	**87J** Fishguard Goodwick	**87J** Fishguard Goodwick	**87J** Fishguard Goodwick	
4982	*4900*	**FGD**	Fishguard Goodwick	**87H** Neyland	**86A** Ebbw Junction	**86A** Ebbw Junction	**84E** Tyseley		
4983	*4900*	**NA**	Newton Abbot	**82C** Swindon	**82B** St. Philips Marsh	**82A** Bristol Bath Road	**86G** Pontypool Road	**87B** Duffryn Yard	
4984	*4900*	**CARM**	Carmarthen	**87G** Carmarthen	**87G** Carmarthen	**84B** Oxley	**84B** Oxley		
4985	*4900*	**PDN**	Old Oak Common	**82D** Westbury	**83B** Taunton	**83B** Taunton	**83B** Taunton	**83B** Taunton	
4986	*4900*	**SPM**	St. Philips Marsh	**82B** St. Philips Marsh	**81A** Old Oak Common	**84A** Stafford Road	**84A** Stafford Road		
4987	*4900*	**OXY**	Oxley	**84K** Chester (GWR)	**84C** Banbury	**81D** Reading	**81D** Reading		
4988	*4900*	**WEY**	Weymouth	**82F** Weymouth	**82F** Weymouth	**84E** Tyseley	**86E** Severn Tunnel Junction	**87F** Llanelly	
4989	*4900*	**RDG**	Reading	**81D** Reading	**81D** Reading	**81D** Reading	**85B** Gloucester	**81C** Southall	
4990	*4900*	**SPM**	St. Philips Marsh	**82B** St. Philips Marsh	**86G** Pontypool Road	**83G** Penzance	**85C** Hereford		
4991	*4900*	**OXY**	Oxley	**84B** Oxley	**86G** Pontypool Road	**83B** Taunton	**83B** Taunton	**82B** St. Philips Marsh	
4992	*4900*	**TYS**	Tyseley	**83D** Laira (Plymouth)	**83D** Laira (Plymouth)	**83D** Laira (Plymouth)	**83C** Exeter	**82B** St. Philips Marsh	
4993	*4900*	**TYS**	Tyseley	**85A** Worcester	**81D** Reading	**81D** Reading	**85A** Worcester	**82B** St. Philips Marsh	
4994	*4900*	**RDG**	Reading	**81D** Reading	**81E** Didcot	**81E** Didcot	**81E** Didcot	**81E** Didcot	
4995	*4900*	**RDG**	Reading	**81D** Reading	**81D** Reading	**81D** Reading	**81F** Oxford		
4996	*4900*	**OXY**	Oxley	**85B** Gloucester	**85B** Gloucester	**86C** Cardiff Canton	**85A** Worcester	**83B** Taunton	
4997	*4900*	**NEY**	Neyland	**87H** Neyland	**84A** Stafford Road	**84B** Oxley	**84B** Oxley		
4998	*4900*	**PDN**	Old Oak Common	**81D** Reading	**81D** Reading	**81D** Reading	**81D** Reading	**84C** Banbury	
4999	*4900*	**TYS**	Tyseley	**82B** St. Philips Marsh	**82B** St. Philips Marsh	**82B** St. Philips Marsh	**86C** Cardiff Canton		
5000	*4073*	**PDN**	Old Oak Common	**82A** Bristol Bath Road	**82A** Bristol Bath Road	**82C** Swindon	**82C** Swindon	**85B** Gloucester	
5001	*4073*	**CDF**	Cardiff Canton	**86C** Cardiff Canton	**86C** Cardiff Canton	**86C** Cardiff Canton	**84G** Shrewsbury	**81A** Old Oak Common	
5002	*4073*	**LDR**	Landore	**87E** Landore	**87E** Landore	**87E** Landore	**82C** Swindon	**82C** Swindon	
5003	*4073*	**TN**	Taunton	**83B** Taunton	**83C** Exeter	**83D** Laira (Plymouth)	**83A** Newton Abbot		
5004	*4073*	**PDN**	Old Oak Common	**81A** Old Oak Common	**81A** Old Oak Common	**84G** Shrewsbury	**87E** Landore		
5005	*4073*	**CDF**	Cardiff Canton	**86C** Cardiff Canton	**86C** Cardiff Canton	**86C** Cardiff Canton	**82C** Swindon		
5006	*4073*	**LDR**	Landore	**86C** Cardiff Canton	**86C** Cardiff Canton	**81A** Old Oak Common	**87G** Carmarthen		
5007	*4073*	**CDF**	Cardiff Canton	**86C** Cardiff Canton	**86C** Cardiff Canton	**86C** Cardiff Canton	**82C** Swindon		
5008	*4073*	**PDN**	Old Oak Common	**84A** Stafford Road	**84A** Stafford Road	**81A** Old Oak Common	**81A** Old Oak Common		
5009	*4073*	**LA**	Laira (Plymouth)	**82C** Swindon	**82C** Swindon	**82C** Swindon	**82C** Swindon		
5010	*4073*	**CDF**	Cardiff Canton	**84A** Stafford Road	**84A** Stafford Road	**84A** Stafford Road			
5011	*4073*	**NA**	Newton Abbot	**83A** Newton Abbot	**83A** Newton Abbot	**83A** Newton Abbot	**83A** Newton Abbot		
5012	*4073*	**EXE**	Exeter	**83D** Laira (Plymouth)	**81F** Oxford	**81F** Oxford	**81F** Oxford		
5013	*4073*	**LDR**	Landore	**87E** Landore	**87E** Landore	**87E** Landore	**87E** Landore		
5014	*4073*	**PDN**	Old Oak Common	**81A** Old Oak Common	**81A** Old Oak Common	**81A** Old Oak Common	**81A** Old Oak Common	**81A** Old Oak Common	
5015	*4073*	**SRD**	Stafford Road	**84A** Stafford Road	**84A** Stafford Road	**84A** Stafford Road	**82A** Bristol Bath Road	**88L** Cardiff East Dock	
5016	*4073*	**LDR**	Landore	**87E** Landore	**87E** Landore	**87E** Landore	**87E** Landore		
5017	*4073*	**WOS**	Worcester	**85A** Worcester	**85B** Gloucester	**85B** Gloucester	**85B** Gloucester		
5018	*4073*	**SRD**	Stafford Road	**82C** Swindon	**85B** Gloucester	**85B** Gloucester	**81D** Reading	**81D** Reading	
5019	*4073*	**BRD**	Bristol Bath Road	**82A** Bristol Bath Road	**82A** Bristol Bath Road	**82A** Bristol Bath Road	**84A** Stafford Road		
5020	*4073*	**CDF**	Cardiff Canton	**86C** Cardiff Canton	**86C** Cardiff Canton	**86C** Cardiff Canton	**83G** Penzance		
5021	*4073*	**SALOP**	Shrewsbury	**83D** Laira (Plymouth)	**83C** Exeter	**83C** Exeter	**86C** Cardiff Canton		
5022	*4073*	**PDN**	Old Oak Common	**84A** Stafford Road	**84A** Stafford Road	**84A** Stafford Road	**84A** Stafford Road	**84A** Stafford Road	
5023	*4073*	**PDN**	Old Oak Common	**83D** Laira (Plymouth)	**83G** Penzance	**83D** Laira (Plymouth)	**82C** Swindon	**82C** Swindon	
5024	*4073*	**BRD**	Bristol Bath Road	**83A** Newton Abbot	**83A** Newton Abbot	**83A** Newton Abbot	**83A** Newton Abbot		
5025	*4073*	**BRD**	Bristol Bath Road	**82A** Bristol Bath Road	**82A** Bristol Bath Road	**82C** Swindon	**81F** Oxford	**81F** Oxford	
5026	*4073*	**LA**	Laira (Plymouth)	**81F** Oxford	**81F** Oxford	**81F** Oxford	**84A** Stafford Road	**84A** Stafford Road	
5027	*4073*	**PDN**	Old Oak Common	**84K** Chester (GWR)	**84A** Stafford Road	**82A** Bristol Bath Road	**81A** Old Oak Common		
5028	*4073*	**NA**	Newton Abbot	**83A** Newton Abbot	**83A** Newton Abbot	**83D** Laira (Plymouth)	**83D** Laira (Plymouth)		
5029	*4073*	**PDN**	Old Oak Common	**81A** Old Oak Common	**81A** Old Oak Common	**81A** Old Oak Common	**83D** Laira (Plymouth)	**88L** Cardiff East Dock	
5030	*4073*	**CDF**	Cardiff Canton	**86C** Cardiff Canton	**86C** Cardiff Canton	**86C** Cardiff Canton	**87G** Carmarthen		
5031	*4073*	**SRD**	Stafford Road	**84A** Stafford Road	**84A** Stafford Road	**84A** Stafford Road	**84A** Stafford Road	**84A** Stafford Road	
5032	*4073*	**SALOP**	Shrewsbury	**84G** Shrewsbury	**84A** Stafford Road	**84A** Stafford Road	**83A** Newton Abbot		
5033	*4073*	**CHR**	Chester (GWR)	**84K** Chester (GWR)	**84K** Chester (GWR)	**84K** Chester (GWR)	**81F** Oxford		
5034	*4073*	**NA**	Newton Abbot	**81D** Reading	**81A** Old Oak Common	**81A** Old Oak Common	**81A** Old Oak Common		
5035	*4073*	**PDN**	Old Oak Common	**81A** Old Oak Common	**81A** Old Oak Common	**81A** Old Oak Common	**81A** Old Oak Common		
5036	*4073*	**PDN**	Old Oak Common	**81D** Reading	**81D** Reading	**81D** Reading	**81D** Reading		
5037	*4073*	**PDN**	Old Oak Common	**82A** Bristol Bath Road	**82A** Bristol Bath Road	**85A** Worcester	**85A** Worcester	**87A** Neath	
5038	*4073*	**PDN**	Old Oak Common	**81A** Old Oak Common	**81A** Old Oak Common	**81A** Old Oak Common	**84G** Shrewsbury	**81D** Reading	
5039	*4073*	**PDN**	Old Oak Common	**81A** Old Oak Common	**87G** Carmarthen	**87G** Carmarthen	**87E** Landore	**87G** Carmarthen	
5040	*4073*	**PDN**	Old Oak Common	**81A** Old Oak Common	**81A** Old Oak Common	**81A** Old Oak Common	**81A** Old Oak Common	**82B** St. Philips Marsh	
5041	*4073*	**LA**	Laira (Plymouth)	**83A** Newton Abbot	**83A** Newton Abbot	**87E** Landore	**87E** Landore	**81A** Old Oak Common	
5042	*4073*	**GLO**	Gloucester	**85B** Gloucester	**85B** Gloucester	**85B** Gloucester	**85A** Worcester	**83A** Newton Abbot	
5043	*4073*	**PDN**	Old Oak Common	**81A** Old Oak Common	**87G** Carmarthen	**81A** Old Oak Common	**81A** Old Oak Common	**88L** Cardiff East Dock	
5044	*4073*	**PDN**	Old Oak Common	**81A** Old Oak Common	**81A** Old Oak Common	**81A** Old Oak Common	**81A** Old Oak Common		
5045	*4073*	**PDN**	Old Oak Common	**84A** Stafford Road	**84A** Stafford Road	**84A** Stafford Road	**84A** Stafford Road		
5046	*4073*	**CDF**	Cardiff Canton	**86C** Cardiff Canton	**86C** Cardiff Canton	**86C** Cardiff Canton	**84A** Stafford Road		
5047	*4073*	**NA**	Newton Abbot	**83A** Newton Abbot	**83A** Newton Abbot	**84A** Stafford Road	**84A** Stafford Road		
5048	*4073*	**BRD**	Bristol Bath Road	**82A** Bristol Bath Road	**82A** Bristol Bath Road	**82A** Bristol Bath Road	**82A** Bristol Bath Road		
5049	*4073*	**CDF**	Cardiff Canton	**86C** Cardiff Canton	**86C** Cardiff Canton	**86C** Cardiff Canton	**83A** Newton Abbot	**82B** St. Philips Marsh	
5050	*4073*	**LA**	Laira (Plymouth)	**84G** Shrewsbury	**84G** Shrewsbury	**84G** Shrewsbury	**84G** Shrewsbury	**82B** St. Philips Marsh	
5051	*4073*	**LDR**	Landore	**87E** Landore	**87E** Landore	**87E** Landore	**87E** Landore	**87A** Neath	
5052	*4073*	**CDF**	Cardiff Canton	**86C** Cardiff Canton	**86C** Cardiff Canton	**86C** Cardiff Canton	**81A** Old Oak Common		
5053	*4073*	**SRD**	Stafford Road	**84A** Stafford Road	**84A** Stafford Road	**83A** Newton Abbot	**83D** Laira (Plymouth)		
5054	*4073*	**CDF**	Cardiff Canton	**86C** Cardiff Canton	**86C** Cardiff Canton	**86C** Cardiff Canton	**81A** Old Oak Common	**87A** Neath	
5055	*4073*	**PDN**	Old Oak Common	**81A** Old Oak Common	**81A** Old Oak Common	**81A** Old Oak Common	**83A** Newton Abbot	**83A** Newton Abbot	
5056	*4073*	**PDN**	Old Oak Common	**81A** Old Oak Common	**81A** Old Oak Common	**81A** Old Oak Common	**81A** Old Oak Common	**81A** Old Oak Common	
5057	*4073*	**LA**	Laira (Plymouth)	**83D** Laira (Plymouth)	**83D** Laira (Plymouth)	**82A** Bristol Bath Road	**84C** Banbury	**81A** Old Oak Common	
5058	*4073*	**NA**	Newton Abbot	**83D** Laira (Plymouth)	**83D** Laira (Plymouth)	**83D** Laira (Plymouth)	**83D** Laira (Plymouth)	**85B** Gloucester	
5059	*4073*	**EXE**	Exeter	**83C** Exeter	**83A** Newton Abbot	**83A** Newton Abbot	**84G** Shrewsbury		
5060	*4073*	**LA**	Laira (Plymouth)	**83D** Laira (Plymouth)	**81A** Old Oak Common	**81A** Old Oak Common	**81A** Old Oak Common	**81A** Old Oak Common	
5061	*4073*	**SALOP**	Shrewsbury	**84G** Shrewsbury	**84K** Chester (GWR)	**84K** Chester (GWR)	**86C** Cardiff Canton		

No.	Class	1948	1951	1954	1957	1960	1963	1966
5062	*4073*	**NA** Newton Abbot	**83C** Exeter	**82C** Swindon	**82C** Swindon	**82A** Bristol Bath Road		
5063	*4073*	**WOS** Worcester	**85A** Worcester	**85A** Worcester	**82A** Bristol Bath Road	**84A** Stafford Road	**84A** Stafford Road	
5064	*4073*	**SALOP** Shrewsbury	**82A** Bristol Bath Road	**82A** Bristol Bath Road	**82A** Bristol Bath Road	**82C** Swindon		
5065	*4073*	**PDN** Old Oak Common	**81A** Old Oak Common	**81A** Old Oak Common	**81A** Old Oak Common	**81A** Old Oak Common	**81A** Old Oak Common	
5066	*4073*	**PDN** Old Oak Common	**81A** Old Oak Common	**81A** Old Oak Common	**81A** Old Oak Common	**81A** Old Oak Common		
5067	*4073*	**SDN** Swindon	**82A** Bristol Bath Road	**82A** Bristol Bath Road	**82A** Bristol Bath Road	**87G** Carmarthen		
5068	*4073*	**SDN** Swindon	**82C** Swindon	**82C** Swindon	**82C** Swindon	**82C** Swindon		
5069	*4073*	**PDN** Old Oak Common	**81A** Old Oak Common	**82A** Bristol Bath Road	**83D** Laira (Plymouth)	**83D** Laira (Plymouth)		
5070	*4073*	**SRD** Stafford Road	**84A** Stafford Road	**84A** Stafford Road	**84A** Stafford Road	**84A** Stafford Road	**81A** Old Oak Common	
5071	*4073*	**NA** Newton Abbot	**83A** Newton Abbot	**83A** Newton Abbot	**83A** Newton Abbot	**85A** Worcester	**82B** St. Philips Marsh	
5072	*4073*	**LDR** Landore	**87E** Landore	**87E** Landore	**86C** Cardiff Canton	**84A** Stafford Road		
5073	*4073*	**SALOP** Shrewsbury	**84G** Shrewsbury	**84G** Shrewsbury	**84G** Shrewsbury	**82A** Bristol Bath Road	**88L** Cardiff East Dock	
5074	*4073*	**BRD** Bristol Bath Road	**82A** Bristol Bath Road	**82A** Bristol Bath Road	**86C** Cardiff Canton	**81A** Old Oak Common	**88L** Cardiff East Dock	
5075	*4073*	**SRD** Stafford Road	**84K** Chester (GWR)	**84K** Chester (GWR)	**84A** Stafford Road	**83C** Exeter		
5076	*4073*	**BRD** Bristol Bath Road	**82A** Bristol Bath Road	**82A** Bristol Bath Road	**82A** Bristol Bath Road	**82A** Bristol Bath Road	**81D** Reading	
5077	*4073*	**TN** Taunton	**86C** Cardiff Canton	**86C** Cardiff Canton	**87E** Landore	**87E** Landore		
5078	*4073*	**NA** Newton Abbot	**83A** Newton Abbot	**83A** Newton Abbot	**83A** Newton Abbot	**82A** Bristol Bath Road		
5079	*4073*	**LA** Laira (Plymouth)	**83A** Newton Abbot	**83A** Newton Abbot	**83A** Newton Abbot	**83A** Newton Abbot		
5080	*4073*	**CDF** Cardiff Canton	**86C** Cardiff Canton	**86C** Cardiff Canton	**87G** Carmarthen	**87G** Carmarthen	**87F** Llanelly	
5081	*4073*	**PDN** Old Oak Common	**81A** Old Oak Common	**81A** Old Oak Common	**85A** Worcester	**85A** Worcester	**88L** Cardiff East Dock	
5082	*4073*	**BRD** Bristol Bath Road	**82A** Bristol Bath Road	**81A** Old Oak Common	**81A** Old Oak Common	**81A** Old Oak Common		
5083	*4073*	**BRD** Bristol Bath Road	**82C** Swindon	**82C** Swindon	**85A** Worcester			
5084	*4073*	**BRD** Bristol Bath Road	**82C** Swindon	**82C** Swindon	**81A** Old Oak Common	**81A** Old Oak Common		
5085	*4073*	**PDN** Old Oak Common	**81A** Old Oak Common	**82A** Bristol Bath Road	**82A** Bristol Bath Road	**82A** Bristol Bath Road	**87A** Neath	
5086	*4073*	**SALOP** Shrewsbury	**85A** Worcester	**85A** Worcester	**85A** Worcester			
5087	*4073*	**PDN** Old Oak Common	**81A** Old Oak Common	**81A** Old Oak Common	**81A** Old Oak Common	**81A** Old Oak Common	**87F** Llanelly	
5088	*4073*	**SRD** Stafford Road	**84A** Stafford Road	**84A** Stafford Road	**84A** Stafford Road	**84A** Stafford Road		
5089	*4073*	**LDR** Landore	**86C** Cardiff Canton	**86C** Cardiff Canton	**83A** Newton Abbot	**84A** Stafford Road	**84A** Stafford Road	
5090	*4073*	**LA** Laira (Plymouth)	**83D** Laira (Plymouth)	**85A** Worcester	**85A** Worcester	**82A** Bristol Bath Road		
5091	*4073*	**BRD** Bristol Bath Road	**82C** Swindon	**84G** Shrewsbury	**84K** Chester (GWR)	**87E** Landore	**88L** Cardiff East Dock	
5092	*4073*	**WOS** Worcester	**85A** Worcester	**85A** Worcester	**81A** Old Oak Common	**82A** Bristol Bath Road	**88L** Cardiff East Dock	
5093	*4073*	**LDR** Landore	**87E** Landore	**81A** Old Oak Common	**81A** Old Oak Common	**81A** Old Oak Common	**81A** Old Oak Common	
5094	*4073*	**NA** Newton Abbot	**82A** Bristol Bath Road	**82A** Bristol Bath Road	**85B** Gloucester	**85B** Gloucester		
5095	*4073*	**LA** Laira (Plymouth)	**83D** Laira (Plymouth)	**81A** Old Oak Common	**81A** Old Oak Common	**86C** Cardiff Canton		
5096	*4073*	**BRD** Bristol Bath Road	**82A** Bristol Bath Road	**82A** Bristol Bath Road	**82A** Bristol Bath Road	**82A** Bristol Bath Road	**88L** Cardiff East Dock	
5097	*4073*	**SALOP** Shrewsbury	**84G** Shrewsbury	**84G** Shrewsbury	**84G** Shrewsbury	**82A** Bristol Bath Road	**88L** Cardiff East Dock	
5098	*4073*	**EXE** Exeter	**83D** Laira (Plymouth)	**83D** Laira (Plymouth)	**83D** Laira (Plymouth)	**83D** Laira (Plymouth)	**87G** Carmarthen	
5099	*4073*	**PDN** Old Oak Common	**86C** Cardiff Canton	**86C** Cardiff Canton	**86C** Cardiff Canton	**86C** Cardiff Canton	**85B** Gloucester	
5101	*5101*	**STB** Stourbridge	**84F** Stourbridge	**84F** Stourbridge	**84F** Stourbridge	**84D** Leamington Spa	**84D** Leamington Spa	
5102	*5101*	**TYS** Tyseley	**84E** Tyseley	**87A** Neath	**87A** Neath	**87A** Neath		
5103	*5101*	**SRD** Stafford Road	**84K** Chester (GWR)	**84K** Chester (GWR)	**84K** Chester (GWR)	**86G** Pontypool Road		
5104	*5101*	**LMTN** Leamington Spa	**84D** Leamington Spa	**84D** Leamington Spa	**84D** Leamington Spa	**82B** St. Philips Marsh		
5105	*5101*	**STB** Stourbridge	**84F** Stourbridge	**84F** Stourbridge	**84F** Stourbridge			
5106	*5101*	**TYS** Tyseley	**84E** Tyseley	**84A** Stafford Road	**84A** Stafford Road			
5107	*5101*	**STB** Stourbridge	**84F** Stourbridge	**84F** Stourbridge	**84F** Stourbridge	**83D** Laira (Plymouth)		
5108	*5101*	**NA** Newton Abbot	**83A** Newton Abbot	**83A** Newton Abbot	**83A** Newton Abbot			
5109	*5101*	**LMTN** Leamington Spa	**84H** Wellington	**84H** Wellington	**84F** Stourbridge			
5110	*5101*	**KDR** Kidderminster	**85D** Kidderminster	**85D** Kidderminster	**85D** Kidderminster	**85A** Worcester		
5111	*5101*	**SRD** Stafford Road						
5112	*5101*	**WOS** Worcester	**85B** Gloucester	**84A** Stafford Road				
5113	*5101*	**NA** Newton Abbot	**83A** Newton Abbot	**83A** Newton Abbot				
5114	*5101*	**WOS** Worcester						
5117	*5101*	**CHR** Chester (GWR)						
5119	*5101*	**SHL** Southall						
5121	*5101*	**TYS** Tyseley						
5122	*5101*	**STB** Stourbridge						
5125	*5101*	**TYS** Tyseley	**84H** Wellington					
5127	*5101*	**WLN** Wellington						
5128	*5101*	**RHY** Rhymney						
5129	*5101*	**TYS** Tyseley	**84K** Chester (GWR)					
5130	*5101*	**LMTN** Leamington Spa						
5131	*5101*	**STB** Stourbridge						
5132	*5101*	**NA** Newton Abbot	**83A** Newton Abbot					
5134	*5101*	**STB** Stourbridge	**84F** Stourbridge					
5135	*5101*	**WLN** Wellington						
5136	*5101*	**STB** Stourbridge	**84F** Stourbridge					
5137	*5101*	**WLN** Wellington	**84H** Wellington					
5138	*5101*	**STB** Stourbridge	**84H** Wellington					
5139	*5101*	**WLN** Wellington	**84H** Wellington					
5140	*5101*	**SBZ** St. Blazey	**83A** Newton Abbot					
5141	*5101*	**STB** Stourbridge	**84K** Chester (GWR)					
5142	*5101*	**NA** Newton Abbot	**83A** Newton Abbot					
5143	*5101*	**SRD** Stafford Road	**84A** Stafford Road					
5144	*5101*	**LMTN** Leamington Spa	**84D** Leamington Spa					
5146	*5101*	**STB** Stourbridge						
5147	*5101*	**STB** Stourbridge	**84F** Stourbridge					
5148	*5101*	**LA** Laira (Plymouth)	**83D** Laira (Plymouth)	**83D** Laira (Plymouth)	**83D** Laira (Plymouth)			
5150	*5101*	**NA** Newton Abbot	**83A** Newton Abbot	**83A** Newton Abbot	**83A** Newton Abbot	**83A** Newton Abbot		
5151	*5101*	**SRD** Stafford Road	**84A** Stafford Road	**84A** Stafford Road	**84A** Stafford Road	**84A** Stafford Road		
5152	*5101*	**TYS** Tyseley	**84E** Tyseley	**84E** Tyseley	**84C** Banbury	**84C** Banbury	**85A** Worcester	
5153	*5101*	**NA** Newton Abbot	**83A** Newton Abbot	**83A** Newton Abbot	**83A** Newton Abbot	**83A** Newton Abbot	**84G** Kidderminster	
5154	*5101*	**SALOP** Shrewsbury	**84G** Shrewsbury	**84G** Shrewsbury	**83A** Newton Abbot	**83A** Newton Abbot	**85B** Gloucester	
5155	*5101*	**STB** Stourbridge	**84F** Stourbridge	**86E** Severn Tunnel Junction	**86E** Severn Tunnel Junction	**86E** Severn Tunnel Junction		
5156	*5101*	**TYS** Tyseley	**84E** Tyseley	**84E** Tyseley	**84E** Tyseley			
5157	*5101*	**NA** Newton Abbot	**83A** Newton Abbot	**83B** Taunton	**85B** Gloucester			
5158	*5101*	**SBZ** St. Blazey	**83A** Newton Abbot	**83A** Newton Abbot	**83A** Newton Abbot	**83A** Newton Abbot		
5159	*5101*	**THT** Treherbert	**88F** Treherbert	**88F** Treherbert				
5160	*5101*	**STB** Stourbridge	**84F** Stourbridge	**84F** Stourbridge	**84K** Chester (GWR)			
5161	*5101*	**LMTN** Leamington Spa	**84D** Leamington Spa	**84D** Leamington Spa	**84D** Leamington Spa			
5162	*5101*	**TYS** Tyseley	**87E** Landore	**88F** Treherbert	**85B** Gloucester			
5163	*5101*	**LMTN** Leamington Spa	**84D** Leamington Spa	**84E** Tyseley	**84E** Tyseley			
5164	*5101*	**TYS** Tyseley	**84E** Tyseley	**84E** Tyseley	**83A** Newton Abbot	**83A** Newton Abbot	**86G** Pontypool Road	
5165	*5101*	**STB** Stourbridge	**84F** Stourbridge	**84F** Stourbridge	**84F** Stourbridge			
5166	*5101*	**TYS** Tyseley	**84E** Tyseley	**84E** Tyseley	**84E** Tyseley	**86E** Severn Tunnel Junction		
5167	*5101*	**STB** Stourbridge	**84F** Stourbridge	**84F** Stourbridge	**84H** Wellington	**84G** Shrewsbury		
5168	*5101*	**SALOP** Shrewsbury	**84G** Shrewsbury	**84G** Shrewsbury	**83A** Newton Abbot			
5169	*5101*	**BRD** Bristol Bath Road	**86E** Severn Tunnel Junction	**86E** Severn Tunnel Junction	**86E** Severn Tunnel Junction	**86E** Severn Tunnel Junction		
5170	*5101*	**STB** Stourbridge	**84F** Stourbridge	**84C** Banbury	**84C** Banbury			
5171	*5101*	**TYS** Tyseley	**84E** Tyseley	**87G** Carmarthen	**87G** Carmarthen			
5172	*5101*	**TN** Taunton	**83B** Taunton	**83B** Taunton	**83B** Taunton			
5173	*5101*	**WOS** Worcester	**85A** Worcester	**86A** Ebbw Junction	**86A** Ebbw Junction	**85B** Gloucester		
5174	*5101*	**CHR** Chester (GWR)	**84K** Chester (GWR)	**84K** Chester (GWR)	**84K** Chester (GWR)	**6E** Chester (GWR)		
5175	*5101*	**TYS** Tyseley	**84E** Tyseley	**83D** Laira (Plymouth)	**83D** Laira (Plymouth)	**83D** Laira (Plymouth)		
5176	*5101*	**CHR** Chester (GWR)	**6C** Birkenhead	**6C** Birkenhead	**6C** Birkenhead	**84F** Stourbridge		
5177	*5101*	**TYS** Tyseley	**84E** Tyseley	**84K** Chester (GWR)	**84K** Chester (GWR)	**85B** Gloucester		
5178	*5101*	**WLN** Wellington	**84H** Wellington	**84H** Wellington	**83A** Newton Abbot	**83A** Newton Abbot		
5179	*5101*	**CHR** Chester (GWR)	**84K** Chester (GWR)	**84K** Chester (GWR)	**84K** Chester (GWR)	**85A** Worcester		
5180	*5101*	**STB** Stourbridge	**84F** Stourbridge	**84F** Stourbridge	**84F** Stourbridge	**87G** Carmarthen		
5181	*5101*	**CHR** Chester (GWR)	**84K** Chester (GWR)	**84E** Tyseley	**84E** Tyseley	**86E** Severn Tunnel Junction		
5182	*5101*	**TYS** Tyseley	**84E** Tyseley	**82A** Bristol Bath Road	**85B** Gloucester	**85B** Gloucester		
5183	*5101*	**STJ** Severn Tunnel Junction	**88F** Treherbert	**88C** Barry	**83A** Newton Abbot	**83A** Newton Abbot		
5184	*5101*	**CHR** Chester (GWR)	**84K** Chester (GWR)	**84D** Leamington Spa	**84D** Leamington Spa	**84D** Leamington Spa	**85B** Gloucester	
5185	*5101*	**LMTN** Leamington Spa	**84D** Leamington Spa	**84D** Leamington Spa	**84D** Leamington Spa	**83B** Taunton		
5186	*5101*	**CHR** Chester (GWR)	**84K** Chester (GWR)	**84K** Chester (GWR)	**84F** Stourbridge			

		1948	1951	1954	1957	1960	1963	1966
5187	5101	LMTN Leamington Spa	84E Tyseley	84A Stafford Road	84A Stafford Road	84A Stafford Road		
5188	5101	TYS Tyseley	84E Tyseley	84A Stafford Road	84A Stafford Road	86A Ebbw Junction		
5189	5101	STB Stourbridge	84F Stourbridge	84F Stourbridge	84F Stourbridge			
5190	5101	TYS Tyseley	84E Tyseley	82F Weymouth	81F Oxford	81F Oxford		
5191	5101	STB Stourbridge	84F Stourbridge	84F Stourbridge	84F Stourbridge	86E Severn Tunnel Junction	86E Severn Tunnel Junction	
5192	5101	LMTN Leamington Spa	84D Leamington Spa	84D Leamington Spa	84E Tyseley	84E Tyseley	84F Stourbridge	
5193	5101	STB Stourbridge	84F Stourbridge	83E St. Blazey	83D Laira (Plymouth)	83E St. Blazey		
5194	5101	LMTN Leamington Spa	84D Leamington Spa	84D Leamington Spa	84D Leamington Spa	84D Leamington Spa		
5195	5101	BRY Barry	88C Barry	88F Treherbert	83A Newton Abbot	83A Newton Abbot		
5196	5101	STB Stourbridge	84F Stourbridge	83A Newton Abbot	83A Newton Abbot			
5197	5101	STB Stourbridge	84F Stourbridge	82A Bristol Bath Road	82A Bristol Bath Road	83A Newton Abbot		
5198	5101	TYS Tyseley	84E Tyseley	84E Tyseley	84E Tyseley	85B Gloucester		
5199	5101	TYS Tyseley	84F Stourbridge	84F Stourbridge	84F Stourbridge	84F Stourbridge	84A Stafford Road	
5200	4200	CDF Cardiff Canton	86B Newport Pill	86B Newport Pill	86B Newport Pill	86B Newport Pill	86B Newport Pill	
5201	4200	NPT Ebbw Junction	86A Ebbw Junction	86A Ebbw Junction	86A Ebbw Junction	86A Ebbw Junction	87F Llanelly	
5202	4200	TDU Tondu	86F Tondu	86H Aberbeeg	86B Newport Pill	86B Newport Pill	86F Aberbeeg	
5203	4200	LLY Llanelly	87F Llanelly	87F Llanelly	87F Llanelly	87A Neath	82E Bristol Barrow Road	
5204	4200	LLY Llanelly	87F Llanelly	87F Llanelly	87F Llanelly	87F Llanelly		
5205	5205	STJ Severn Tunnel Junction	86E Severn Tunnel Junction	86E Severn Tunnel Junction	86A Ebbw Junction	86A Ebbw Junction	85A Worcester	
5206	5205	NPT Ebbw Junction	86A Ebbw Junction	86A Ebbw Junction	86H Aberbeeg	86H Aberbeeg	86F Aberbeeg	
5207	5205	CARM Carmarthen	86H Aberbeeg	86C Cardiff Canton	86C Cardiff Canton	86C Cardiff Canton		
5208	5205	NPT Ebbw Junction	86A Ebbw Junction	86F Tondu	86F Tondu	86F Tondu	88H Tondu	
5209	5205	LLY Llanelly	87F Llanelly	87F Llanelly	87F Llanelly	87F Llanelly	87F Llanelly	
5210	5205	SED Swansea East Dock	87D Swansea East Dock	87D Swansea East Dock	87D Swansea East Dock	87D Swansea East Dock	87D Swansea East Dock	
5211	5205	LDR Landore	87E Landore	87D Swansea East Dock	87D Swansea East Dock	87D Swansea East Dock	87D Swansea East Dock	
5212	5205	LLY Llanelly	86A Ebbw Junction	86E Severn Tunnel Junction	86E Severn Tunnel Junction	86E Severn Tunnel Junction		
5213	5205	LLY Llanelly	87F Llanelly	87F Llanelly	87F Llanelly	87F Llanelly	86A Ebbw Junction	
5214	5205	SED Swansea East Dock	86E Severn Tunnel Junction	86E Severn Tunnel Junction	86E Severn Tunnel Junction	86E Severn Tunnel Junction	86E Severn Tunnel Junction	
5215	5205	LLY Llanelly	87F Llanelly	87F Llanelly	87F Llanelly	82B St. Philips Marsh	82E Bristol Barrow Road	
5216	5205	DYD Duffryn Yard	87B Duffryn Yard	87B Duffryn Yard	87B Duffryn Yard	87B Duffryn Yard	87B Duffryn Yard	
5217	5205	NPT Ebbw Junction	86A Ebbw Junction	86A Ebbw Junction	86A Ebbw Junction	86A Ebbw Junction	86A Ebbw Junction	
5218	5205	NPT Ebbw Junction	86A Ebbw Junction	86A Ebbw Junction	86C Cardiff Canton	86C Cardiff Canton	86F Aberbeeg	
5219	5205	LDR Landore	87E Landore	87F Llanelly	87F Llanelly	87F Llanelly		
5220	5205	LLY Llanelly	87B Duffryn Yard	87B Duffryn Yard	87B Duffryn Yard	87B Duffryn Yard	88L Cardiff East Dock	
5221	5205	SED Swansea East Dock	87D Swansea East Dock	87D Swansea East Dock	87D Swansea East Dock	87B Duffryn Yard	87A Neath	
5222	5205	NPT Ebbw Junction	86A Ebbw Junction	86A Ebbw Junction	87A Neath	87A Neath	87A Neath	
5223	5205	LLY Llanelly	87F Llanelly	87F Llanelly	87F Llanelly	87F Llanelly	87A Neath	
5224	5205	NPT Ebbw Junction	86A Ebbw Junction	86A Ebbw Junction	86E Severn Tunnel Junction	86E Severn Tunnel Junction	88L Cardiff East Dock	
5225	5205	NEA Neath	87A Neath	87A Neath	87A Neath	86C Cardiff Canton	88L Cardiff East Dock	
5226	5205	LLY Llanelly	86C Cardiff Canton	82C Swindon	85C Hereford	85F Bromsgrove	85A Worcester	
5227	5205	SED Swansea East Dock	87D Swansea East Dock	87D Swansea East Dock	86A Ebbw Junction	86A Ebbw Junction	86A Ebbw Junction	
5228	5205	LLY Llanelly	86E Severn Tunnel Junction	86A Ebbw Junction	86A Ebbw Junction	86A Ebbw Junction	86A Ebbw Junction	
5229	5205	NPT Ebbw Junction	86A Ebbw Junction	86A Ebbw Junction	86A Ebbw Junction	86A Ebbw Junction	86A Ebbw Junction	
5230	5205	LLY Llanelly	87F Llanelly	87F Llanelly	87F Llanelly	87D Swansea East Dock	87D Swansea East Dock	
5231	5205	CARM Carmarthen	86B Newport Pill	86B Newport Pill	86B Newport Pill	86B Newport Pill	86F Aberbeeg	
5232	5205	SED Swansea East Dock	87D Swansea East Dock	87D Swansea East Dock	87D Swansea East Dock	87D Swansea East Dock	87B Duffryn Yard	
5233	5205	NPT Ebbw Junction	86A Ebbw Junction	86A Ebbw Junction	86A Ebbw Junction	86A Ebbw Junction	86A Ebbw Junction	
5234	5205	NPT Ebbw Junction	86A Ebbw Junction	86A Ebbw Junction	86A Ebbw Junction	86A Ebbw Junction	86A Ebbw Junction	
5235	5205	PILL Newport Pill	86B Newport Pill	86B Newport Pill	86B Newport Pill	86B Newport Pill	86E Severn Tunnel Junction	
5236	5205	CDF Cardiff Canton	86H Aberbeeg	86A Ebbw Junction	86E Severn Tunnel Junction	86E Severn Tunnel Junction	86A Ebbw Junction	
5237	5205	ABDR Aberdare	86J Aberdare	86J Aberdare	86J Aberdare	86J Aberdare	88J Aberdare	
5238	5205	NPT Ebbw Junction	86A Ebbw Junction	86A Ebbw Junction	86A Ebbw Junction	86A Ebbw Junction	86A Ebbw Junction	
5239	5205	NEA Neath	87A Neath	87A Neath	87A Neath	87A Neath	87A Neath	
5240	5205	LLY Llanelly	87F Llanelly	82C Swindon	87D Swansea East Dock	87F Llanelly	88J Aberdare	
5241	5205	SPM St. Philips Marsh	86D Llantrisant	86H Aberbeeg	86H Aberbeeg	86H Aberbeeg	87F Llanelly	
5242	5205	NEA Neath	87A Neath	87A Neath	87A Neath	87A Neath	87F Llanelly	
5243	5205	NPT Ebbw Junction	86A Ebbw Junction	86A Ebbw Junction	85C Hereford	85C Hereford	88H Tondu	
5244	5205	PILL Newport Pill	86B Newport Pill	86B Newport Pill	86B Newport Pill	86B Newport Pill	86B Newport Pill	
5245	5205	ABDR Aberdare	86J Aberdare	86J Aberdare	86J Aberdare	85C Hereford	85A Worcester	
5246	5205	SED Swansea East Dock	87D Swansea East Dock	87D Swansea East Dock	87D Swansea East Dock	87D Swansea East Dock	87B Duffryn Yard	
5247	5205	LLY Llanelly	87F Llanelly	87F Llanelly	87F Llanelly	87F Llanelly	87F Llanelly	
5248	5205	LLY Llanelly	87F Llanelly	87F Llanelly	87F Llanelly	87F Llanelly	88G Llantrisant	
5249	5205	CDF Cardiff Canton	86C Cardiff Canton	87F Llanelly	87F Llanelly	86J Aberdare	88J Aberdare	
5250	5205	DYD Duffryn Yard	86B Newport Pill	86B Newport Pill	86B Newport Pill	86B Newport Pill	86B Newport Pill	
5251	5205	NPT Ebbw Junction	86A Ebbw Junction	86A Ebbw Junction	86A Ebbw Junction	86A Ebbw Junction	86A Ebbw Junction	
5252	5205	PILL Newport Pill	86B Newport Pill	86B Newport Pill	86B Newport Pill	86B Newport Pill	86F Aberbeeg	
5253	5205	SED Swansea East Dock	86E Severn Tunnel Junction	86E Severn Tunnel Junction	86E Severn Tunnel Junction	86E Severn Tunnel Junction	86E Severn Tunnel Junction	
5254	5205	NEA Neath	87A Neath	87B Duffryn Yard	87B Duffryn Yard	87B Duffryn Yard	87B Duffryn Yard	
5255	5205	NPT Ebbw Junction	86A Ebbw Junction	86A Ebbw Junction	86A Ebbw Junction	86A Ebbw Junction	86A Ebbw Junction	
5256	5205	NPT Ebbw Junction	86A Ebbw Junction	86A Ebbw Junction	86A Ebbw Junction	86B Newport Pill	86B Newport Pill	
5257	5205	DYD Duffryn Yard	87B Duffryn Yard	87B Duffryn Yard	86B Newport Pill	86H Aberbeeg	87B Duffryn Yard	
5258	5205	ABDR Aberdare	86J Aberdare	86J Aberdare	86J Aberdare	86J Aberdare		
5259	5205	ABEEG Aberbeeg	86A Ebbw Junction	86A Ebbw Junction	86A Ebbw Junction	86A Ebbw Junction	86A Ebbw Junction	
5260	5205	DYD Duffryn Yard	86B Newport Pill	86A Ebbw Junction	86E Severn Tunnel Junction	86C Cardiff Canton	86F Aberbeeg	
5261	5205	LLY Llanelly	87F Llanelly	87F Llanelly	87F Llanelly	86C Cardiff Canton	88L Cardiff East Dock	
5262	5205	STJ Severn Tunnel Junction	86E Severn Tunnel Junction	86E Severn Tunnel Junction	87D Swansea East Dock	87F Llanelly	87F Llanelly	
5263	5205	ABDR Aberdare	86J Aberdare	86J Aberdare	86J Aberdare	86J Aberdare	88J Aberdare	
5264	5205	NPT Ebbw Junction	86A Ebbw Junction	86A Ebbw Junction	86J Aberdare	87B Duffryn Yard	86F Aberbeeg	
5300	4300	OXY Oxley	84B Oxley					
5302	4300	BAN Banbury						
5303	4300	KDR Kidderminster	85A Worcester					
5305	4300	WEY Weymouth	82F Weymouth					
5306	4300	WES Westbury	82D Westbury	82B St. Philips Marsh	84C Banbury	86G Pontypool Road	86A Ebbw Junction	
5307	4300	CDF Cardiff Canton	84B Oxley	82B St. Philips Marsh				
5309	4300	WLN Wellington	84B Oxley					
5310	4300	NEY Neyland	87H Neyland	87G Carmarthen	87G Carmarthen			
5311	4300	WES Westbury	82A Bristol Bath Road	84K Chester (GWR)	84K Chester (GWR)	82B St. Philips Marsh		
5312	4300	GLO Gloucester	85B Gloucester	85B Gloucester	84B Oxley			
5313	4300	OXY Oxley	84B Oxley	84F Stourbridge	84B Oxley			
5314	4300	WEY Weymouth	82F Weymouth	82F Weymouth	82F Weymouth			
5315	4300	CNYD Croes Newydd	84J Croes Newydd	84J Croes Newydd	84K Chester (GWR)			
5316	4300	BHD Birkenhead	6C Birkenhead	6C Birkenhead				
5317	4300	BAN Banbury	84C Banbury	84C Banbury				
5318	4300	LA Laira (Plymouth)	83D Laira (Plymouth)	86G Pontypool Road	86A Ebbw Junction	86G Pontypool Road		
5319	4300	CNYD Croes Newydd	84J Croes Newydd	84J Croes Newydd	84J Croes Newydd			
5320	4300	RDG Reading						
5321	4300	EXE Exeter	83C Exeter	83B Taunton	83B Taunton			
5322	4300	SDN Swindon	82C Swindon	84E Tyseley	81E Didcot	86G Pontypool Road	86G Pontypool Road	
5323	4300	OXF Oxford	81F Oxford	81F Oxford	82B St. Philips Marsh			
5324	4300	BAN Banbury	84C Banbury	87H Neyland	87H Neyland	84G Shrewsbury		
5325	4300	BRD Bristol Bath Road	82A Bristol Bath Road	82B St. Philips Marsh	84E Tyseley			
5326	4300	WES Westbury	82D Westbury	84K Chester (GWR)	81D Reading	81E Didcot		
5327	4300	BRD Bristol Bath Road	82A Bristol Bath Road	82C Swindon				
5328	4300	WEY Weymouth	82F Weymouth	84G Shrewsbury	84G Shrewsbury			
5330	4300	DID Didcot	81E Didcot	81D Reading	81E Didcot	86G Pontypool Road	89B Croes Newydd	
5331	4300	OXY Oxley	84K Chester (GWR)	84K Chester (GWR)	84G Shrewsbury	84G Shrewsbury		
5332	4300	WLN Wellington	84C Banbury	84C Banbury	84C Banbury	87F Llanelly		
5333	4300	OXY Oxley	84E Tyseley	84E Tyseley	84E Tyseley	85D Kidderminster		
5334	4300	CNYD Croes Newydd	84J Croes Newydd	86G Pontypool Road	86C Cardiff Canton			
5335	4300	CDF Cardiff Canton	87F Llanelly	87F Llanelly	87F Llanelly			
5336	4300	GLO Gloucester	85B Gloucester	84B Oxley	83D Laira (Plymouth)	86E Severn Tunnel Junction	86E Severn Tunnel Junction	
5337	4300	WEY Weymouth	82F Weymouth	82F Weymouth	85A Worcester	81E Didcot		
5338	4300	WEY Weymouth	82F Weymouth	82D Westbury	82D Westbury			
5339	4300	CARM Carmarthen	87G Carmarthen	83A Newton Abbot	83A Newton Abbot	86E Severn Tunnel Junction		

		1948	1951	1954	1957	1960	1963	1966
5340	*4300*	**WEY** Weymouth						
5341	*4300*	**LDR** Landore	**84B** Oxley	**84B** Oxley	**84B** Oxley			
5343	*4300*	**BRD** Bristol Bath Road						
5344	*4300*	**CHR** Chester (GWR)	**84K** Chester (GWR)	**84K** Chester (GWR)	**83B** Taunton			
5345	*4300*	**CHEL** Cheltenham	**85B** Gloucester	**85B** Gloucester	**82B** St. Philips Marsh			
5346	*4300*	**TYS** Tyseley	**84E** Tyseley					
5347	*4300*	**GLO** Gloucester	**85B** Gloucester	**85B** Gloucester	**84G** Shrewsbury			
5348	*4300*	**HFD** Hereford	**85C** Hereford					
5349	*4300*	**BAN** Banbury						
5350	*4300*	**NA** Newton Abbot	**83A** Newton Abbot	**82B** St. Philips Marsh	**85A** Worcester			
5351	*4300*	**SPM** St. Philips Marsh	**82B** St. Philips Marsh	**82B** St. Philips Marsh	**82C** Swindon	**81E** Didcot		
5353	*4300*	**NEY** Neyland	**87H** Neyland	**87G** Carmarthen	**87G** Carmarthen	**87G** Carmarthen		
5355	*4300*	**PPRD** Pontypool Road	**86G** Pontypool Road	**86G** Pontypool Road	**85C** Hereford			
5356	*4300*	**RDG** Reading	**81C** Southall	**83D** Laira (Plymouth)	**83D** Laira (Plymouth)			
5357	*4300*	**NEY** Neyland	**87H** Neyland	**87H** Neyland	**87H** Neyland	**87H** Neyland		
5358	*4300*	**SPM** St. Philips Marsh	**82B** St. Philips Marsh	**82D** Westbury	**82D** Westbury	**82D** Westbury		
5359	*4300*	**WEY** Weymouth	**82F** Weymouth					
5360	*4300*	**SHL** Southall	**81C** Southall	**83A** Newton Abbot	**82B** St. Philips Marsh			
5361	*4300*	**BAN** Banbury	**84C** Banbury	**84C** Banbury	**84C** Banbury	**81E** Didcot		
5362	*4300*	**STJ** Severn Tunnel Junction	**86E** Severn Tunnel Junction	**83A** Newton Abbot	**84G** Shrewsbury			
5364	*4300*	**NPT** Ebbw Junction	**86A** Ebbw Junction					
5365	*4300*	**CNYD** Croes Newydd	**84J** Croes Newydd					
5367	*4300*	**SDN** Swindon	**82C** Swindon	**82B** St. Philips Marsh	**82B** St. Philips Marsh			
5368	*4300*	**NEY** Neyland	**87H** Neyland	**81D** Reading	**81D** Reading			
5369	*4300*	**TYS** Tyseley	**84E** Tyseley	**84E** Tyseley	**84E** Tyseley	**84E** Tyseley	**86G** Pontypool Road	
5370	*4300*	**TYS** Tyseley	**84E** Tyseley	**84E** Tyseley	**84E** Tyseley	**87F** Llanelly		
5371	*4300*	**SDN** Swindon	**82C** Swindon	**84F** Stourbridge	**84F** Stourbridge			
5372	*4300*	**NEY** Neyland	**87H** Neyland	**87H** Neyland	**87H** Neyland			
5373	*4300*	**BAN** Banbury						
5374	*4300*	**SPM** St. Philips Marsh						
5375	*4300*	**RDG** Reading	**81D** Reading	**84B** Oxley	**84B** Oxley			
5376	*4300*	**LA** Laira (Plymouth)	**83D** Laira (Plymouth)	**83D** Laira (Plymouth)	**83D** Laira (Plymouth)	**83F** Truro		
5377	*4300*	**HFD** Hereford	**85C** Hereford	**85C** Hereford	**85C** Hereford			
5378	*4300*	**CDF** Cardiff Canton	**87F** Llanelly	**84B** Oxley	**83E** St. Blazey			
5379	*4300*	**OXY** Oxley	**84B** Oxley	**84F** Stourbridge	**84C** Banbury			
5380	*4300*	**DID** Didcot	**81E** Didcot	**81E** Didcot	**81E** Didcot	**81E** Didcot	**81E** Didcot	
5381	*4300*	**DID** Didcot	**81E** Didcot	**84B** Oxley	**84B** Oxley			
5382	*4300*	**CDF** Cardiff Canton	**86C** Cardiff Canton	**86C** Cardiff Canton	**86A** Ebbw Junction			
5384	*4300*	**WEY** Weymouth	**82F** Weymouth	**82F** Weymouth	**82F** Weymouth	**71G** Weymouth		
5385	*4300*	**RDG** Reading	**82D** Westbury	**82D** Westbury	**82D** Westbury	**82B** St. Philips Marsh		
5386	*4300*	**OXY** Oxley	**84B** Oxley	**84E** Tyseley	**84E** Tyseley			
5388	*4300*	**CDF** Cardiff Canton	**86C** Cardiff Canton	**86C** Cardiff Canton	**86G** Pontypool Road			
5390	*4300*	**OXY** Oxley	**84B** Oxley	**84B** Oxley	**84B** Oxley			
5391	*4300*	**NA** Newton Abbot	**84C** Banbury	**84B** Oxley	**81D** Reading			
5392	*4300*	**NEY** Neyland	**87H** Neyland	**87H** Neyland	**87F** Llanelly			
5393	*4300*	(8393)	**6C** Birkenhead	**6C** Birkenhead	**6C** Birkenhead			
5394	*4300*	**GLO** Gloucester	**85B** Gloucester	**85B** Gloucester	**85D** Kidderminster			
5395	*4300*	**FGD** Fishguard Goodwick	**87J** Fishguard Goodwick	**89C** Machynlleth				
5396	*4300*	**SDN** Swindon	**82C** Swindon	**82C** Swindon	**85A** Worcester	**85A** Worcester		
5397	*4300*	**DID** Didcot	**81E** Didcot	**81E** Didcot	**81E** Didcot			
5398	*4300*	**GLO** Gloucester	**85B** Gloucester	**85B** Gloucester	**85B** Gloucester			
5399	*4300*	**CHR** Chester (GWR)	**84K** Chester (GWR)	**84C** Banbury	**84K** Chester (GWR)	**6E** Chester (GWR)		
5400	*5400*	**LDR** Landore	**87E** Landore	**87G** Carmarthen	**87G** Carmarthen			
5401	*5400*	**SHL** Southall	**81C** Southall	**89A** Oswestry	**89A** Oswestry			
5402	*5400*	**WES** Westbury	**82D** Westbury	**82D** Westbury	**82D** Westbury			
5403	*5400*	**WES** Westbury	**82D** Westbury	**82D** Westbury	**82D** Westbury			
5404	*5400*	**BAN** Banbury	**84C** Banbury	**84C** Banbury	**84C** Banbury			
5405	*5400*	**SHL** Southall	**81C** Southall	**89A** Oswestry	**89A** Oswestry			
5406	*5400*	**WES** Westbury	**82D** Westbury	**82D** Westbury	**82D** Westbury			
5407	*5400*	**BAN** Banbury	**84C** Banbury	**84C** Banbury	**84C** Banbury	**84C** Banbury		
5408	*5400*	**LDR** Landore	**87E** Landore	**85B** Gloucester				
5409	*5400*	**SHL** Southall	**81B** Slough	**81B** Slough	**34E** Neasden			
5410	*5400*	**SHL** Southall	**81C** Southall	**81C** Southall	**81C** Southall	**82D** Westbury	**82D** Westbury	
5411	*5400*	**SHL** Southall	**88A** Cardiff Cathays	**83B** Taunton	**83B** Taunton			
5412	*5400*	**LA** Laira (Plymouth)	**83B** Taunton	**83B** Taunton	**83C** Exeter	**83C** Exeter		
5413	*5400*	**SHL** Southall	**81F** Oxford	**81F** Oxford	**81F** Oxford			
5414	*5400*	**SHL** Southall	**81C** Southall	**81C** Southall	**86A** Ebbw Junction			
5415	*5400*	**SHL** Southall	**81C** Southall	**81C** Southall	**81C** Southall			
5416	*5400*	**SHL** Southall	**81C** Southall	**81C** Southall	**84J** Croes Newydd	**82D** Westbury	**82D** Westbury	
5417	*5400*	**SHL** Southall	**84C** Banbury	**85B** Gloucester	**85B** Gloucester	**14D** Neasden		
5418	*5400*	**SHL** Southall	**81C** Southall	**81C** Southall	**85B** Gloucester	**85B** Gloucester		
5419	*5400*	**WES** Westbury	**82D** Westbury	**82D** Westbury	**82D** Westbury			
5420	*5400*	**SHL** Southall	**81C** Southall	**81C** Southall	**81C** Southall	**84C** Banbury	**85B** Gloucester	
5421	*5400*	**SHL** Southall	**88E** Abercynon	**83B** Taunton	**83B** Taunton	**85B** Gloucester		
5422	*5400*	**WES** Westbury	**82D** Westbury	**82D** Westbury	**82D** Westbury	**89A** Oswestry		
5423	*5400*	**WES** Westbury	**82D** Westbury	**82D** Westbury	**82D** Westbury			
5424	*5400*	**BAN** Banbury	**84C** Banbury	**84C** Banbury	**84C** Banbury			
5500	*4575*	**TR** Truro	**83F** Truro	**83F** Truro	**83F** Truro			
5501	*4575*	**TN** Taunton	**83B** Taunton	**83B** Taunton	**83B** Taunton			
5502	*4575*	**SBZ** St. Blazey	**83E** St. Blazey	**83E** St. Blazey	**83E** St. Blazey			
5503	*4575*	**TN** Taunton	**83B** Taunton	**83B** Taunton	**83B** Taunton	**83B** Taunton		
5504	*4575*	**TN** Taunton	**83B** Taunton	**83B** Taunton	**83B** Taunton	**83B** Taunton		
5505	*4575*	**NA** Newton Abbot	**83A** Newton Abbot	**83F** Truro	**83F** Truro			
5506	*4575*	**BRD** Bristol Bath Road	**82A** Bristol Bath Road	**82A** Bristol Bath Road	**83D** Laira (Plymouth)			
5507	*4575*	**MCH** Machynlleth	**89C** Machynlleth	**89C** Machynlleth	**89C** Machynlleth			
5508	*4575*	**WES** Westbury	**82D** Westbury	**82D** Westbury	**82D** Westbury	**82D** Westbury	**87H** Neyland	
5509	*4575*	**WEY** Weymouth	**82D** Westbury	**82C** Swindon	**82C** Swindon	**82A** Bristol Bath Road		
5510	*4575*	**SDN** Swindon	**82C** Swindon	**82C** Swindon	**82C** Swindon	**82C** Swindon		
5511	*4575*	**BRD** Bristol Bath Road	**82A** Bristol Bath Road	**88A** Cardiff Cathays	**88A** Cardiff Cathays	**83D** Laira (Plymouth)		
5512	*4575*	**BRD** Bristol Bath Road	**82A** Bristol Bath Road	**82A** Bristol Bath Road	**82A** Bristol Bath Road			
5513	*4575*	**WTD** Whitland	**87H** Neyland	**87H** Neyland	**87H** Neyland			
5514	*4575*	**BRD** Bristol Bath Road	**82A** Bristol Bath Road	**82A** Bristol Bath Road	**85B** Gloucester	**85B** Gloucester		
5515	*4575*	**CHEL** Cheltenham	**83F** Truro	**83F** Truro	**83F** Truro	**83F** Truro		
5516	*4575*	**NPT** Ebbw Junction	**86G** Pontypool Road	**86G** Pontypool Road	**86G** Pontypool Road	**86H** Aberbeeg		
5517	*4575*	**MCH** Machynlleth	**89C** Machynlleth	**89C** Machynlleth	**89C** Machynlleth			
5518	*4575*	**KDR** Kidderminster	**85B** Gloucester	**85D** Kidderminster	**85D** Kidderminster	**85D** Kidderminster	**83E** St. Blazey	
5519	*4575*	**SBZ** St. Blazey	**83E** St. Blazey	**83E** St. Blazey	**83E** St. Blazey	**83D** Laira (Plymouth)		
5520	*4575*	**ABDR** Aberdare	**86H** Aberbeeg	**86H** Aberbeeg	**87H** Neyland	**87H** Neyland		
5521	*4575*	**TN** Taunton	**83B** Taunton	**83E** St. Blazey	**83E** St. Blazey	**83B** Taunton		
5522	*4575*	**TN** Taunton	**83B** Taunton	**83B** Taunton	**83B** Taunton			
5523	*4575*	**BRD** Bristol Bath Road	**82A** Bristol Bath Road	**82A** Bristol Bath Road	**82A** Bristol Bath Road	**83E** St. Blazey		
5524	*4575*	**MCH** Machynlleth	**89C** Machynlleth	**86F** Tondu	**86F** Tondu	**83C** Exeter		
5525	*4575*	**EXE** Exeter	**83C** Exeter	**82A** Bristol Bath Road	**82A** Bristol Bath Road	**83B** Taunton		
5526	*4575*	**TR** Truro	**83F** Truro	**83F** Truro	**83F** Truro	**82D** Westbury		
5527	*4575*	**BRD** Bristol Bath Road	**82A** Bristol Bath Road	**88C** Barry	**88C** Barry	**87H** Neyland		
5528	*4575*	**BRD** Bristol Bath Road	**82A** Bristol Bath Road	**82A** Bristol Bath Road	**82A** Bristol Bath Road			
5529	*4575*	**YEO** Yeovil Pen Mill	**82E** Yeovil Pen Mill	**88C** Barry	**88C** Barry	**82A** Bristol Bath Road		
5530	*4575*	**NA** Newton Abbot	**85B** Gloucester	**85B** Gloucester	**85B** Gloucester	**82A** Bristol Bath Road		
5531	*4575*	**SBZ** St. Blazey	**83D** Laira (Plymouth)	**83D** Laira (Plymouth)	**83D** Laira (Plymouth)	**83D** Laira (Plymouth)	**83E** St. Blazey	
5532	*4575*	**PPRD** Pontypool Road	**86G** Pontypool Road	**82A** Bristol Bath Road	**82A** Bristol Bath Road	**83D** Laira (Plymouth)		
5533	*4575*	**TN** Taunton	**83B** Taunton	**83B** Taunton	**83A** Newton Abbot			
5534	*4575*	**SDN** Swindon	**82C** Swindon	**88A** Cardiff Cathays	**88A** Cardiff Cathays	**86F** Tondu		
5535	*4575*	**BRD** Bristol Bath Road	**82A** Bristol Bath Road	**82A** Bristol Bath Road	**82A** Bristol Bath Road			
5536	*4575*	**BRD** Bristol Bath Road	**82A** Bristol Bath Road	**82C** Swindon	**83A** Newton Abbot	**82C** Swindon		

No.	Class	1948	1951	1954	1957	1960	1963	1966
5537	4575	TR Truro	83F Truro	83F Truro	83F Truro	83F Truro		
5538	4575	CHEL Cheltenham	85B Gloucester	85B Gloucester	85B Gloucester	85B Gloucester		
5539	4575	BRD Bristol Bath Road	82A Bristol Bath Road	83A Newton Abbot	86H Aberbeeg	83E St. Blazey		
5540	4575	LA Laira (Plymouth)	83D Laira (Plymouth)	82C Swindon	82C Swindon	89C Machynlleth		
5541	4575	MCH Machynlleth	89C Machynlleth	89C Machynlleth	89C Machynlleth	89C Machynlleth		
5542	4575	TN Taunton	83B Taunton	83A Newton Abbot	83B Taunton	82D Westbury		
5543	4575	TN Taunton	83B Taunton	83A Newton Abbot	83B Taunton	83B Taunton		
5544	4575	WOS Worcester	83A Newton Abbot	83A Newton Abbot	86H Aberbeeg	86H Aberbeeg		
5545	4575	NPT Ebbw Junction	86A Ebbw Junction	86F Tondu	86F Tondu	86F Tondu	87H Neyland	
5546	4575	BRD Bristol Bath Road	82A Bristol Bath Road	82A Bristol Bath Road	82A Bristol Bath Road	83F Truro		
5547	4575	BRD Bristol Bath Road	82A Bristol Bath Road	82A Bristol Bath Road	82A Bristol Bath Road	82C Swindon		
5548	4575	BRD Bristol Bath Road	82A Bristol Bath Road	82A Bristol Bath Road	82E Yeovil Pen Mill	72C Yeovil Town	72C Yeovil Town	
5549	4575	WTD Whitland	87H Neyland	87H Neyland	87H Neyland	87H Neyland		
5550	4575	NPT Ebbw Junction	86A Ebbw Junction	87H Neyland	87H Neyland	87H Neyland		
5551	4575	NA Newton Abbot	83A Newton Abbot	83A Newton Abbot	83D Laira (Plymouth)	83E St. Blazey		
5552	4575	NA Newton Abbot	83A Newton Abbot	83A Newton Abbot	83F Truro	83F Truro		
5553	4575	BRD Bristol Bath Road	82A Bristol Bath Road	82A Bristol Bath Road	82A Bristol Bath Road	89C Machynlleth		
5554	4575	WES Westbury	82D Westbury	82D Westbury	82D Westbury	83B Taunton	87H Neyland	
5555	4575	BRD Bristol Bath Road	82A Bristol Bath Road	86F Tondu	86F Tondu	86F Tondu	83C Exeter	
5556	4575	TDU Tondu	86F Tondu	89C Machynlleth	89C Machynlleth			
5557	4575	NA Newton Abbot	83A Newton Abbot	83A Newton Abbot	83E St. Blazey	83E St. Blazey		
5558	4575	BRD Bristol Bath Road	82A Bristol Bath Road	83B Taunton	83A Newton Abbot	83A Newton Abbot		
5559	4575	BRD Bristol Bath Road	82A Bristol Bath Road	82A Bristol Bath Road	82A Bristol Bath Road	83F Truro		
5560	4575	ABH Aberystwyth	89C Machynlleth	86F Tondu	86F Tondu	87H Neyland		
5561	4575	BRD Bristol Bath Road	82A Bristol Bath Road	82A Bristol Bath Road	82A Bristol Bath Road	82A Bristol Bath Road		
5562	4575	TR Truro	83F Truro	83F Truro	83F Truro	83F Truro		
5563	4575	SDN Swindon	82C Swindon	82E Yeovil Pen Mill	82E Yeovil Pen Mill	72C Yeovil Town	72C Yeovil Town	
5564	4575	BRD Bristol Bath Road	82A Bristol Bath Road	82C Swindon	86H Aberbeeg	84G Shrewsbury	83D Laira (Plymouth)	
5565	4575	YEO Yeovil Pen Mill	82E Yeovil Pen Mill	82A Bristol Bath Road	82A Bristol Bath Road	89C Machynlleth		
5566	4575	SDN Swindon	82C Swindon	82C Swindon	82C Swindon			
5567	4575	LA Laira (Plymouth)	83D Laira (Plymouth)	83D Laira (Plymouth)	83D Laira (Plymouth)	83D Laira (Plymouth)		
5568	4575	WTD Whitland	87H Neyland	88A Cardiff Cathays	88A Cardiff Cathays	86H Aberbeeg	83D Laira (Plymouth)	
5569	4575	LA Laira (Plymouth)	83D Laira (Plymouth)	83D Laira (Plymouth)	83D Laira (Plymouth)	83D Laira (Plymouth)	83D Laira (Plymouth)	
5570	4575	ABH Aberystwyth	89C Machynlleth	89C Machynlleth	89C Machynlleth	89C Machynlleth	82C Swindon	
5571	4575	TN Taunton	83B Taunton	83B Taunton	83B Taunton	83B Taunton	87H Neyland	
5572	4575	BRD Bristol Bath Road	82A Bristol Bath Road	88A Cardiff Cathays	88A Cardiff Cathays	83D Laira (Plymouth)		
5573	4575	KDR Kidderminster	85A Worcester	86G Pontypool Road	86G Pontypool Road	83A Newton Abbot	87H Neyland	
5574	4575	CHEL Cheltenham	85B Gloucester	86F Tondu	88A Cardiff Cathays			
5600	5600	FDL Ferndale	88F Treherbert	88F Treherbert	88F Treherbert	88F Treherbert		
5601	5600	THT Treherbert	88A Cardiff Cathays	88A Cardiff Cathays	88A Cardiff Cathays	88E Abercynon	88E Abercynon	
5602	5600	NPT Ebbw Junction	86A Ebbw Junction	86H Aberbeeg	86C Cardiff Canton	86C Cardiff Canton	87F Llanelly	
5603	5600	NPT Ebbw Junction	88D Merthyr	88D Merthyr	88D Merthyr	88D Merthyr	88D Merthyr	
5604	5600	LDR Landore	87E Landore	87E Landore	87E Landore	87B Duffryn Yard		
5605	5600	CHYS Cardiff Cathays	88D Merthyr	88D Merthyr	88D Merthyr	88D Merthyr	88D Merthyr	6C Croes Newydd
5606	5600	OXY Oxley	84F Stourbridge	84F Stourbridge	84F Stourbridge	84K Wrexham Rhosddu	84B Oxley	
5607	5600	THT Treherbert	88F Treherbert	88F Treherbert	88F Treherbert	88F Treherbert	88F Treherbert	
5608	5600	THT Treherbert	88F Treherbert	88F Treherbert	88F Treherbert	88F Treherbert	88F Treherbert	
5609	5600	BRY Barry	88C Barry	88C Barry	88C Barry	88C Barry	87D Swansea East Dock	
5610	5600	FDL Ferndale	88F Treherbert	88F Treherbert	88F Treherbert	88F Treherbert	88D Merthyr	
5611	5600	THT Treherbert	88F Treherbert	88F Treherbert	88F Treherbert	88F Treherbert	88F Treherbert	
5612	5600	DYD Duffryn Yard	87B Duffryn Yard	87F Llanelly	87F Llanelly	87F Llanelly	87F Llanelly	
5613	5600	THT Treherbert	88F Treherbert	88F Treherbert	88F Treherbert	88F Treherbert	88F Treherbert	
5614	5600	CHYS Cardiff Cathays	88C Barry	88C Barry	88C Barry	88C Barry	88E Abercynon	
5615	5600	THT Treherbert	88F Treherbert	88F Treherbert	88D Merthyr	88A Radyr	88E Abercynon	
5616	5600	OXF Oxford	87D Swansea East Dock	87D Swansea East Dock	87D Swansea East Dock	87D Swansea East Dock	87D Swansea East Dock	
5617	5600	CHYS Cardiff Cathays	88D Merthyr	88D Merthyr	88E Abercynon	88E Abercynon		
5618	5600	AYN Abercynon	88E Abercynon	88E Abercynon	88E Abercynon	88A Radyr	88D Merthyr	
5619	5600	AYN Abercynon	88C Barry	88C Barry	88C Barry	88C Barry	88C Barry	
5620	5600	STJ Severn Tunnel Junction	86G Pontypool Road	86G Pontypool Road	86E Severn Tunnel Junction	86E Severn Tunnel Junction	86G Pontypool Road	
5621	5600	BRY Barry	88C Barry	88C Barry	88C Barry	88C Barry	88C Barry	
5622	5600	BRY Barry	88D Merthyr	88D Merthyr	88D Merthyr	88D Merthyr	88D Merthyr	
5623	5600	CHYS Cardiff Cathays	88E Abercynon	88E Abercynon	88E Abercynon	88E Abercynon	87D Swansea East Dock	
5624	5600	CHYS Cardiff Cathays	84B Oxley	86F Tondu	86J Aberdare	86J Aberdare	88J Aberdare	
5625	5600	STJ Severn Tunnel Junction	86E Severn Tunnel Junction	86E Severn Tunnel Junction	86G Pontypool Road	86G Pontypool Road	88B Radyr	
5626	5600	STJ Severn Tunnel Junction	86E Severn Tunnel Junction	87B Duffryn Yard	88A Cardiff Cathays	88D Merthyr	88D Merthyr	
5627	5600	BRY Barry	88C Barry	88C Barry	88A Cardiff Cathays	88E Abercynon	88E Abercynon	
5628	5600	CDF Cardiff Canton	87D Swansea East Dock	87D Swansea East Dock	87D Swansea East Dock	87D Swansea East Dock	87D Swansea East Dock	
5629	5600	DYD Duffryn Yard	87B Duffryn Yard	81E Didcot	81E Didcot	86F Tondu	88H Tondu	
5630	5600	AYN Abercynon	88A Cardiff Cathays	88A Cardiff Cathays	88A Cardiff Cathays	88D Merthyr		
5631	5600	LDR Landore	87E Landore	87E Landore	87E Landore	87E Landore		
5632	5600	BRY Barry	88C Barry	88C Barry	88F Treherbert	88F Treherbert	88F Treherbert	
5633	5600	TDU Tondu	86F Tondu	86C Cardiff Canton	86C Cardiff Canton	86J Aberdare	88J Aberdare	
5634	5600	TYS Tyseley	84D Leamington Spa	84G Shrewsbury	84G Shrewsbury	84G Shrewsbury	87H Neyland	
5635	5600	RHY Rhymney	88D Merthyr	88D Merthyr	88D Merthyr	88D Merthyr	88B Radyr	
5636	5600	THT Treherbert	88A Cardiff Cathays	88A Cardiff Cathays	88A Cardiff Cathays	88D Merthyr		
5637	5600	AYN Abercynon	88E Abercynon	88E Abercynon	88A Cardiff Cathays	88F Treherbert	88C Barry	
5638	5600	NPT Ebbw Junction	86B Newport Pill	86G Pontypool Road	86G Pontypool Road	86G Pontypool Road	86G Pontypool Road	
5639	5600	DYD Duffryn Yard	87B Duffryn Yard	81E Didcot	81E Didcot	81E Didcot		
5640	5600	RYR Radyr	88A Cardiff Cathays	88D Merthyr	88D Merthyr	88A Radyr	84D Leamington Spa	
5641	5600	AYN Abercynon	88E Abercynon	88E Abercynon	88E Abercynon	88E Abercynon	88E Abercynon	
5642	5600	SALOP Shrewsbury	84G Shrewsbury	84F Stourbridge	82B St. Philips Marsh	86J Aberdare		
5643	5600	AYN Abercynon	88E Abercynon	88E Abercynon	88E Abercynon	88E Abercynon	88C Barry	
5644	5600	AYN Abercynon	88E Abercynon	86J Aberdare	86J Aberdare	88E Abercynon	88E Abercynon	
5645	5600	STJ Severn Tunnel Junction	86E Severn Tunnel Junction	86H Aberbeeg	86H Aberbeeg	86G Pontypool Road	83D Laira (Plymouth)	
5646	5600	CHYS Cardiff Cathays	87B Duffryn Yard	87H Neyland	88F Treherbert	88F Treherbert		
5647	5600	CHR Chester (GWR)	84K Chester (GWR)	84K Chester (GWR)	81E Didcot	81E Didcot	88J Aberdare	
5648	5600	BRY Barry	88C Barry	88C Barry	88C Barry	88A Radyr	88B Radyr	
5649	5600	PPRD Pontypool Road	86J Aberdare	86J Aberdare	86J Aberdare	86J Aberdare	88J Aberdare	
5650	5600	THT Treherbert	88E Abercynon	88A Cardiff Cathays	88D Merthyr	88D Merthyr	88D Merthyr	
5651	5600	CHYS Cardiff Cathays	84F Stourbridge	84F Stourbridge	84F Stourbridge	84K Wrexham Rhosddu	88B Radyr	
5652	5600	CH Dowlais Cae Harris	88D Merthyr	88D Merthyr	88D Merthyr	88D Merthyr		
5653	5600	CH Dowlais Cae Harris	88A Cardiff Cathays	88A Cardiff Cathays	88A Cardiff Cathays	88F Treherbert	88C Barry	
5654	5600	MTHR Merthyr	88A Cardiff Cathays	88A Cardiff Cathays	88A Cardiff Cathays	88F Treherbert	88F Treherbert	
5655	5600	RYR Radyr	88D Merthyr	88D Merthyr	88D Merthyr	88D Merthyr	88D Merthyr	
5656	5600	DYD Duffryn Yard	87E Landore	87E Landore	87E Landore	87F Llanelly	87D Swansea East Dock	
5657	5600	OXY Oxley	84B Oxley	87F Llanelly	86A Ebbw Junction	86A Ebbw Junction		
5658	5600	CHYS Cardiff Cathays	84F Stourbridge	84F Stourbridge	84F Stourbridge	84E Tyseley	84D Leamington Spa	
5659	5600	CHYS Cardiff Cathays	88D Merthyr	88A Cardiff Cathays	86G Pontypool Road	86G Pontypool Road	86G Pontypool Road	
5660	5600	RHY Rhymney	88D Merthyr	88E Abercynon	88D Merthyr	88D Merthyr	88D Merthyr	
5661	5600	CHYS Cardiff Cathays	88D Merthyr	88D Merthyr	88D Merthyr	88D Merthyr		
5662	5600	BRY Barry	88D Merthyr	88D Merthyr	88D Merthyr	88D Merthyr	88D Merthyr	
5663	5600	THT Treherbert	88F Treherbert	88A Cardiff Cathays	88A Cardiff Cathays	88A Radyr		
5664	5600	BRY Barry	88C Barry	88C Barry	88C Barry	88C Barry		
5665	5600	BRY Barry	88C Barry	88C Barry	88F Treherbert	88F Treherbert	88F Treherbert	
5666	5600	CH Dowlais Cae Harris	88D Merthyr	88D Merthyr	88D Merthyr	88D Merthyr	88D Merthyr	
5667	5600	BRY Barry	88C Barry	88C Barry	88C Barry	88C Barry	88C Barry	
5668	5600	FDL Ferndale	88F Treherbert	88F Treherbert	88F Treherbert	88F Treherbert	88C Barry	
5669	5600	AYN Abercynon	88A Cardiff Cathays	88A Cardiff Cathays	88A Cardiff Cathays	88A Radyr	88B Radyr	
5670	5600	OXY Oxley	88A Cardiff Cathays	88A Cardiff Cathays	88A Cardiff Cathays	87B Duffryn Yard	87B Duffryn Yard	
5671	5600	CH Dowlais Cae Harris	88D Merthyr	88D Merthyr	88D Merthyr	88D Merthyr	88D Merthyr	
5672	5600	CHYS Cardiff Cathays	88D Merthyr	88D Merthyr	88D Merthyr	88D Merthyr	88B Radyr	
5673	5600	SALOP Shrewsbury	84G Shrewsbury	87E Landore	87E Landore	87E Landore	87A Neath	
5674	5600	CH Dowlais Cae Harris	88D Merthyr	88D Merthyr	88D Merthyr	88D Merthyr	88F Treherbert	
5675	5600	LLY Llanelly	87F Llanelly	82B St. Philips Marsh	81E Didcot	87D Swansea East Dock	87D Swansea East Dock	

No.	Class	1948	1951	1954	1957	1960	1963	1966
5676	*5600*	**THT** Treherbert	**88F** Treherbert	**88F** Treherbert	**88F** Treherbert	**88F** Treherbert	**88F** Treherbert	
5677	*5600*	**MTHR** Merthyr	**88D** Merthyr	**88D** Merthyr	**88D** Merthyr	**88D** Merthyr	**88D** Merthyr	
5678	*5600*	**MTHR** Merthyr	**88A** Cardiff Cathays	**88A** Cardiff Cathays	**88F** Treherbert	**88F** Treherbert	**88F** Treherbert	
5679	*5600*	**CDF** Cardiff Canton	**86C** Cardiff Canton	**86C** Cardiff Canton	**86C** Cardiff Canton	**86G** Pontypool Road	**89B** Croes Newydd	
5680	*5600*	**THT** Treherbert	**88F** Treherbert	**88E** Abercynon	**88E** Abercynon	**88E** Abercynon	**88J** Aberdare	
5681	*5600*	**CHYS** Cardiff Cathays	**88A** Cardiff Cathays	**88A** Cardiff Cathays	**88D** Merthyr	**88D** Merthyr	**88D** Merthyr	
5682	*5600*	**AYN** Abercynon	**88E** Abercynon	**88E** Abercynon	**88E** Abercynon	**88E** Abercynon		
5683	*5600*	**RHY** Rhymney	**88A** Cardiff Cathays	**88A** Cardiff Cathays	**88A** Cardiff Cathays	**88A** Radyr	**88B** Radyr	
5684	*5600*	**OXY** Oxley	**84B** Oxley	**84B** Oxley	**84B** Oxley	**88F** Treherbert	**88F** Treherbert	
5685	*5600*	**CDF** Cardiff Canton	**86C** Cardiff Canton	**86C** Cardiff Canton	**86H** Aberbeeg	**86C** Cardiff Canton	**88E** Abercynon	
5686	*5600*	**AYN** Abercynon	**88E** Abercynon	**88E** Abercynon	**88E** Abercynon	**88E** Abercynon	**88E** Abercynon	
5687	*5600*	**CHYS** Cardiff Cathays	**88A** Cardiff Cathays	**88A** Cardiff Cathays	**88A** Cardiff Cathays	**88F** Treherbert	**88D** Merthyr	
5688	*5600*	**THT** Treherbert	**88F** Treherbert	**88F** Treherbert	**88F** Treherbert	**87B** Duffryn Yard	**88F** Treherbert	
5689	*5600*	**WES** Westbury	**82D** Westbury	**82D** Westbury	**82D** Westbury	**82D** Westbury	**82D** Westbury	
5690	*5600*	**CHR** Chester (GWR)	**84K** Chester (GWR)	**84K** Chester (GWR)	**84G** Shrewsbury	**84G** Shrewsbury	**88H** Tondu	
5691	*5600*	**THT** Treherbert	**88F** Treherbert	**88F** Treherbert	**88F** Treherbert	**88F** Treherbert	**88F** Treherbert	
5692	*5600*	**RHY** Rhymney	**88A** Cardiff Cathays	**88A** Cardiff Cathays	**88A** Cardiff Cathays	**88A** Radyr	**87F** Llanelly	
5693	*5600*	**BRY** Barry	**88F** Treherbert	**88F** Treherbert	**88F** Treherbert	**88F** Treherbert	**88F** Treherbert	
5694	*5600*	**CH** Dowlais Cae Harris	**88D** Merthyr	**88D** Merthyr	**88F** Treherbert	**88F** Treherbert	**88F** Treherbert	
5695	*5600*	**THT** Treherbert	**88F** Treherbert	**88F** Treherbert	**88F** Treherbert	**88F** Treherbert		
5696	*5600*	**RHY** Rhymney	**88D** Merthyr	**88D** Merthyr	**88D** Merthyr	**88D** Merthyr	**88D** Merthyr	
5697	*5600*	**GLO** Gloucester	**88A** Cardiff Cathays	**81E** Didcot	**81E** Didcot	**81F** Oxford	**88B** Radyr	
5698	*5600*	**CH** Dowlais Cae Harris	**88D** Merthyr	**86J** Aberdare	**86J** Aberdare	**86J** Aberdare		
5699	*5600*	**BRY** Barry	**88E** Abercynon	**88E** Abercynon	**88E** Abercynon	**88E** Abercynon	**88E** Abercynon	
5700	*5700*	**TYS** Tyseley	**84E** Tyseley	**89A** Oswestry				
5701	*5700*	**TYS** Tyseley	**84A** Stafford Road	**82D** Westbury	**82D** Westbury			
5702	*5700*	**LLY** Llanelly	**87F** Llanelly	**87F** Llanelly	**87F** Llanelly	**87F** Llanelly		
5703	*5700*	**NEA** Neath	**87A** Neath	**87C** Danygraig	**87F** Llanelly			
5704	*5700*	**SED** Swansea East Dock	**87D** Swansea East Dock	**87D** Swansea East Dock	**87C** Danygraig	**87C** Danygraig		
5705	*5700*	**LLY** Llanelly	**87F** Llanelly	**87F** Llanelly	**87F** Llanelly			
5706	*5700*	**STJ** Severn Tunnel Junction	**86E** Severn Tunnel Junction	**86B** Newport Pill	**86B** Newport Pill	**86F** Tondu		
5707	*5700*	**TDU** Tondu	**86F** Tondu	**86F** Tondu	**86F** Tondu			
5708	*5700*	**LTS** Llantrisant	**86D** Llantrisant	**86D** Llantrisant	**86D** Llantrisant			
5709	*5700*	**NPT** Ebbw Junction	**86A** Ebbw Junction	**86A** Ebbw Junction	**86A** Ebbw Junction	**86A** Ebbw Junction		
5710	*5700*	**DID** Didcot	**88B** Cardiff East Dock	**88B** Cardiff East Dock	**88A** Cardiff Cathays			
5711	*5700*	**MTHR** Merthyr	**88D** Merthyr	**88D** Merthyr	**88D** Merthyr			
5712	*5700*	**TYS** Tyseley	**84E** Tyseley	**84H** Wellington	**84H** Wellington			
5713	*5700*	**DYD** Duffryn Yard	**87B** Duffryn Yard	**87B** Duffryn Yard	**87B** Duffryn Yard	**87J** Fishguard Goodwick		
5714	*5700*	**STJ** Severn Tunnel Junction	**86B** Newport Pill	**86B** Newport Pill	**86B** Newport Pill			
5715	*5700*	**SLO** Slough	**81B** Slough	**81B** Slough	**81B** Slough			
5716	*5700*	**FGD** Fishguard Goodwick	**87J** Fishguard Goodwick	**87J** Fishguard Goodwick	**87J** Fishguard Goodwick			
5717	*5700*	**PDN** Old Oak Common	**81A** Old Oak Common	**81A** Old Oak Common	**81A** Old Oak Common	**81A** Old Oak Common		
5718	*5700*	**WES** Westbury	**82D** Westbury	**82D** Westbury	**82D** Westbury			
5719	*5700*	**STB** Stourbridge	**84F** Stourbridge	**84F** Stourbridge	**84F** Stourbridge			
5720	*5700*	**NEA** Neath	**87A** Neath	**87A** Neath	**87A** Neath	**87A** Neath		
5721	*5700*	**MTHR** Merthyr	**88D** Merthyr	**83B** Taunton	**83B** Taunton			
5722	*5700*	**LLY** Llanelly	**87F** Llanelly	**87F** Llanelly	**87F** Llanelly			
5723	*5700*	**CHR** Chester (GWR)	**84K** Chester (GWR)	**84K** Chester (GWR)	**84K** Chester (GWR)			
5724	*5700*	**BAN** Banbury	**84C** Banbury	**84C** Banbury	**88A** Cardiff Cathays			
5725	*5700*	**CHR** Chester (GWR)	**84K** Chester (GWR)	**84K** Chester (GWR)	**84K** Chester (GWR)			
5726	*5700*	**STB** Stourbridge	**84F** Stourbridge	**89A** Oswestry	**89A** Oswestry			
5727	*5700*	**SHL** Southall	**81C** Southall	**81C** Southall	**81C** Southall	**86C** Cardiff Canton		
5728	*5700*	**PPRD** Pontypool Road	**86G** Pontypool Road	**86G** Pontypool Road	**86G** Pontypool Road	**87B** Duffryn Yard		
5729	*5700*	**STJ** Severn Tunnel Junction	**86E** Severn Tunnel Junction	**86E** Severn Tunnel Junction	**86H** Aberbeeg			
5730	*5700*	**DG** Danygraig	**87C** Danygraig	**87C** Danygraig	**87C** Danygraig			
5731	*5700*	**DYD** Duffryn Yard	**87B** Duffryn Yard	**87D** Swansea East Dock	**87C** Danygraig	**87C** Danygraig		
5732	*5700*	**NPT** Ebbw Junction	**86A** Ebbw Junction	**86A** Ebbw Junction	**86A** Ebbw Junction			
5733	*5700*	**ABEEG** Aberbeeg	**86H** Aberbeeg	**86B** Newport Pill	**86B** Newport Pill			
5734	*5700*	**DYD** Duffryn Yard	**87B** Duffryn Yard	**87B** Duffryn Yard	**86B** Newport Pill			
5735	*5700*	**DID** Didcot	**81E** Didcot	**81E** Didcot	**81E** Didcot			
5736	*5700*	**BAN** Banbury	**84E** Tyseley	**84E** Tyseley	**86B** Newport Pill			
5737	*5700*	**SLO** Slough	**81B** Slough	**81E** Didcot	**81E** Didcot			
5738	*5700*	**TYS** Tyseley	**84E** Tyseley	**84E** Tyseley	**84E** Tyseley			
5739	*5700*	**SRD** Stafford Road	**84A** Stafford Road	**84A** Stafford Road	**84K** Chester (GWR)			
5740	*5700*	**PILL** Newport Pill	**86B** Newport Pill	**86B** Newport Pill	**86B** Newport Pill			
5741	*5700*	**NPT** Ebbw Junction	**86A** Ebbw Junction	**86J** Aberdare	**86B** Newport Pill			
5742	*5700*	**TYS** Tyseley	**84J** Croes Newydd	**84J** Croes Newydd	**84J** Croes Newydd			
5743	*5700*	**SED** Swansea East Dock	**87D** Swansea East Dock	**87D** Swansea East Dock	**87C** Danygraig			
5744	*5700*	**DID** Didcot	**81E** Didcot	**81E** Didcot	**81E** Didcot	**81E** Didcot		
5745	*5700*	**TYS** Tyseley	**84E** Tyseley	**84H** Wellington	**84E** Tyseley			
5746	*5700*	**NEA** Neath	**87A** Neath	**87A** Neath	**87A** Neath	**81E** Didcot		
5747	*5700*	**PILL** Newport Pill	**86B** Newport Pill	**86B** Newport Pill	**86B** Newport Pill			
5748	*5700*	**OXY** Oxley	**84B** Oxley	**84B** Oxley	**87H** Neyland	**87H** Neyland		
5749	*5700*	**CDF** Cardiff Canton	**86C** Cardiff Canton	**86C** Cardiff Canton	**86C** Cardiff Canton	**86C** Cardiff Canton	**88L** Cardiff East Dock	
5750	*5700*	**SHL** Southall	**86B** Newport Pill	**86H** Aberbeeg	**86G** Pontypool Road	**86G** Pontypool Road		
5751	*5700*	**RDG** Reading	**81C** Southall	**83B** Taunton	**83B** Taunton			
5752	*5700*	**DID** Didcot	**81E** Didcot	**81E** Didcot	**81E** Didcot			
5753	*5700*	**SHL** Southall	**81C** Southall	**81C** Southall	**81C** Southall			
5754	*5700*	**STB** Stourbridge	**84F** Stourbridge	**84F** Stourbridge	**84F** Stourbridge	**84F** Stourbridge		
5755	*5700*	**SHL** Southall	**81C** Southall	**81C** Southall	**81B** Slough	**81B** Slough		
5756	*5700*	**TDU** Tondu	**86F** Tondu	**86G** Pontypool Road	**86G** Pontypool Road	**86G** Pontypool Road		
5757	*5700*	**WES** Westbury	**82D** Westbury	**82D** Westbury	**82D** Westbury	**82D** Westbury		
5758	*5700*	**WLN** Wellington	**84H** Wellington	**84H** Wellington	**84H** Wellington	**86B** Newport Pill		
5759	*5700*	**LDR** Landore	**87E** Landore	**87E** Landore	**86G** Pontypool Road	**86G** Pontypool Road		
5760	*5700*	**EXE** Exeter	**83C** Exeter	**83C** Exeter	**83B** Taunton			
5761	*5700*	**RDG** Reading	**87B** Duffryn Yard	**87K** Swansea Victoria	**87K** Swansea Victoria	**87A** Neath		
5762	*5700*	**RDG** Reading	**81D** Reading	**81D** Reading				
5763	*5700*	**RDG** Reading	**81D** Reading	**81D** Reading	**81D** Reading	**85B** Gloucester		
5764	*5700*	**PDN** Old Oak Common	**81A** Old Oak Common	**81A** Old Oak Common	**81A** Old Oak Common	**81A** Old Oak Common		
5765	*5700*	**HFD** Hereford	**85C** Hereford	**85C** Hereford	**85C** Hereford			
5766	*5700*	**RDG** Reading	**81D** Reading	**81D** Reading	**81B** Slough	**81B** Slough		
5767	*5700*	**YEO** Yeovil Pen Mill	**82E** Yeovil Pen Mill	**82D** Westbury	**82D** Westbury			
5768	*5700*	**PPRD** Pontypool Road	**86G** Pontypool Road	**86G** Pontypool Road	**86G** Pontypool Road	**86B** Newport Pill		
5769	*5700*	**MTHR** Merthyr	**88D** Merthyr	**88D** Merthyr	**88D** Merthyr	**82B** St. Philips Marsh		
5770	*5700*	**ABDR** Aberdare	**86J** Aberdare	**87B** Duffryn Yard	**87B** Duffryn Yard	**87B** Duffryn Yard		
5771	*5700*	**WES** Westbury	**82D** Westbury	**82D** Westbury	**82D** Westbury	**82B** St. Philips Marsh		
5772	*5700*	**RDG** Reading	**81D** Reading	**81D** Reading	**86A** Ebbw Junction			
5773	*5700*	**DYD** Duffryn Yard	**87B** Duffryn Yard	**87K** Swansea Victoria	**87K** Swansea Victoria	**87A** Neath		
5774	*5700*	**SALOP** Shrewsbury	**84J** Croes Newydd	**84J** Croes Newydd	**84J** Croes Newydd	**84J** Croes Newydd		
5775	*5700*	**DG** Danygraig	**87C** Danygraig	**87G** Carmarthen	**86G** Pontypool Road	**86G** Pontypool Road	**86G** Pontypool Road	
5776	*5700*	**PILL** Newport Pill	**86C** Cardiff Canton	**86C** Cardiff Canton	**86C** Cardiff Canton	**86C** Cardiff Canton		
5777	*5700*	**LTS** Llantrisant	**86H** Aberbeeg	**86H** Aberbeeg	**86B** Newport Pill			
5778	*5700*	**NEA** Neath	**87A** Neath	**87A** Neath	**87A** Neath	**87A** Neath		
5779	*5700*	**TR** Truro	**83B** Taunton	**83B** Taunton	**83B** Taunton	**83B** Taunton		
5780	*5700*	**OXY** Oxley	**84A** Stafford Road	**84A** Stafford Road	**84A** Stafford Road	**83B** Taunton		
5781	*5700*	**WES** Westbury	**82D** Westbury	**82F** Weymouth	**82E** Yeovil Pen Mill			
5782	*5700*	**LLY** Llanelly	**87F** Llanelly	**87F** Llanelly	**87F** Llanelly			
5783	*5700*	**SLO** Slough	**81B** Slough	**81E** Didcot	**81E** Didcot	**81E** Didcot		
5784	*5700*	**SPM** St. Philips Marsh	**82B** St. Philips Marsh	**82B** St. Philips Marsh	**82C** Swindon			
5785	*5700*	**WES** Westbury	**82D** Westbury	**86H** Aberbeeg	**86H** Aberbeeg			
5786	*5700*	**ABEEG** Aberbeeg	**86C** Cardiff Canton	**86C** Cardiff Canton	**86C** Cardiff Canton			
5787	*5700*	**ABDR** Aberdare	**86J** Aberdare	**86J** Aberdare	**87B** Duffryn Yard	**87B** Duffryn Yard	**87B** Duffryn Yard	
5788	*5700*	**ABEEG** Aberbeeg	**86D** Llantrisant	**86D** Llantrisant	**86D** Llantrisant			
5789	*5700*	**ABEEG** Aberbeeg	**86H** Aberbeeg	**87B** Duffryn Yard	**87B** Duffryn Yard	**86G** Pontypool Road		

		1948	1951	1954	1957	1960	1963	1966
5790	*5700*	**TYS** Tyseley	**84E** Tyseley	**84E** Tyseley	**84E** Tyseley			
5791	*5700*	**CHR** Chester (GWR)	**84K** Chester (GWR)	**84K** Chester (GWR)	**84K** Chester (GWR)	**85D** Kidderminster		
5792	*5700*	**PPRD** Pontypool Road	**86G** Pontypool Road	**86G** Pontypool Road				
5793	*5700*	**GLO** Gloucester	**88D** Merthyr	**88D** Merthyr	**88A** Cardiff Cathays	**83B** Taunton		
5794	*5700*	**STB** Stourbridge	**84F** Stourbridge	**84F** Stourbridge	**86H** Aberbeeg			
5795	*5700*	**STB** Stourbridge	**84F** Stourbridge	**84F** Stourbridge	**84F** Stourbridge	**84F** Stourbridge		
5796	*5700*	**ABDR** Aberdare	**86J** Aberdare	**83A** Newton Abbot	**83A** Newton Abbot			
5797	*5700*	**TDU** Tondu	**86F** Tondu	**86J** Aberdare	**86J** Aberdare			
5798	*5700*	**NA** Newton Abbot	**83A** Newton Abbot	**83B** Taunton	**83B** Taunton	**83B** Taunton		
5799	*5700*	**SHL** Southall	**81C** Southall	**81C** Southall	**81C** Southall			
5800	*5800*	**SDN** Swindon	**82C** Swindon	**82C** Swindon	**82C** Swindon			
5801	*5800*	**BCN** Brecon	**89B** Brecon	**89B** Brecon	**89C** Machynlleth			
5802	*5800*	**SDN** Swindon	**82C** Swindon	**82C** Swindon	**82C** Swindon			
5803	*5800*	**BRD** Bristol Bath Road	**89A** Oswestry	**81F** Oxford	**89C** Machynlleth			
5804	*5800*	**SDN** Swindon	**82C** Swindon	**82C** Swindon	**82C** Swindon			
5805	*5800*	**SDN** Swindon	**82C** Swindon	**82C** Swindon	**82C** Swindon			
5806	*5800*	**OSW** Oswestry	**89A** Oswestry	**89A** Oswestry	**89A** Oswestry			
5807	*5800*	**HFD** Hereford	**85C** Hereford	**85C** Hereford	**85C** Hereford			
5808	*5800*	**HFD** Hereford	**85C** Hereford	**81F** Oxford	**81F** Oxford			
5809	*5800*	**BRD** Bristol Bath Road	**82A** Bristol Bath Road	**82A** Bristol Bath Road	**89C** Machynlleth			
5810	*5800*	**CNYD** Croes Newydd	**84J** Croes Newydd	**84J** Croes Newydd	**84J** Croes Newydd			
5811	*5800*	**CNYD** Croes Newydd	**84J** Croes Newydd	**84J** Croes Newydd	**84J** Croes Newydd			
5812	*5800*	**TN** Taunton	**89A** Oswestry	**89A** Oswestry	**89A** Oswestry			
5813	*5800*	**BRD** Bristol Bath Road	**82A** Bristol Bath Road	**82A** Bristol Bath Road	**82A** Bristol Bath Road			
5814	*5800*	**HFD** Hereford	**85C** Hereford	**85C** Hereford	**85C** Hereford			
5815	*5800*	**WOS** Worcester	**85A** Worcester	**85A** Worcester	**85A** Worcester	**82C** Swindon		
5816	*5800*	**WOS** Worcester	**85A** Worcester	**85A** Worcester	**85A** Worcester			
5817	*5800*	**HFD** Hereford	**85C** Hereford	**85C** Hereford	**85C** Hereford			
5818	*5800*	**PPRD** Pontypool Road	**86G** Pontypool Road	**85C** Hereford	**85A** Worcester			
5819	*5800*	**CARM** Carmarthen	**87G** Carmarthen	**87G** Carmarthen	**87G** Carmarthen			
5900	*4900*	**WES** Westbury	**82D** Westbury	**84E** Tyseley	**84A** Stafford Road	**84A** Stafford Road	**82B** St. Philips Marsh	
5901	*4900*	**RDG** Reading	**81D** Reading	**81D** Reading	**81D** Reading	**81D** Reading	**81D** Reading	
5902	*4900*	**EXE** Exeter	**83C** Exeter	**86E** Severn Tunnel Junction	**87F** Llanelly	**87F** Llanelly		
5903	*4900*	**DID** Didcot	**81E** Didcot	**81E** Didcot	**87H** Neyland	**87F** Llanelly	**87F** Llanelly	
5904	*4900*	**OXF** Oxford	**81F** Oxford	**82A** Bristol Bath Road	**82B** St. Philips Marsh	**82D** Westbury	**82B** St. Philips Marsh	
5905	*4900*	**FGD** Fishguard Goodwick	**87J** Fishguard Goodwick	**87J** Fishguard Goodwick	**87J** Fishguard Goodwick	**87J** Fishguard Goodwick	**87J** Fishguard Goodwick	
5906	*4900*	**NPT** Ebbw Junction	**86A** Ebbw Junction	**81A** Old Oak Common	**81D** Reading	**81D** Reading		
5907	*4900*	**TYS** Tyseley	**84E** Tyseley	**85B** Gloucester	**85B** Gloucester	**81A** Old Oak Common		
5908	*4900*	**LLY** Llanelly	**87J** Fishguard Goodwick	**87J** Fishguard Goodwick	**87J** Fishguard Goodwick	**87J** Fishguard Goodwick	**82B** St. Philips Marsh	
5909	*4900*	**SRD** Stafford Road	**84E** Tyseley	**84E** Tyseley	**85A** Worcester	**87F** Llanelly		
5910	*4900*	**CDF** Cardiff Canton	**86C** Cardiff Canton	**86C** Cardiff Canton	**82A** Bristol Bath Road	**86C** Cardiff Canton		
5911	*4900*	**NPT** Ebbw Junction	**86C** Cardiff Canton	**86C** Cardiff Canton	**86C** Cardiff Canton	**86C** Cardiff Canton		
5912	*4900*	**CHR** Chester (GWR)	**84K** Chester (GWR)	**84E** Tyseley	**84E** Tyseley	**84E** Tyseley		
5913	*4900*	**LDR** Landore	**87E** Landore	**83D** Laira (Plymouth)	**87E** Landore	**87E** Landore		
5914	*4900*	**WOS** Worcester	**85A** Worcester	**85A** Worcester	**85A** Worcester	**85B** Gloucester	**81D** Reading	
5915	*4900*	**PZ** Penzance	**83G** Penzance	**83G** Penzance	**81D** Reading	**81D** Reading		
5916	*4900*	**OXY** Oxley	**84E** Tyseley	**86G** Pontypool Road	**86A** Ebbw Junction	**84B** Oxley		
5917	*4900*	**WOS** Worcester	**85A** Worcester	**85A** Worcester	**85A** Worcester	**85A** Worcester		
5918	*4900*	**OXY** Oxley	**81C** Southall	**81C** Southall	**81C** Southall	**81E** Didcot		
5919	*4900*	**SRD** Stafford Road	**82B** St. Philips Marsh	**82A** Bristol Bath Road	**82A** Bristol Bath Road	**84B** Oxley	**81A** Old Oak Common	
5920	*4900*	**OXY** Oxley	**83A** Newton Abbot	**83A** Newton Abbot	**83A** Newton Abbot	**83A** Newton Abbot		
5921	*4900*	**OXY** Oxley	**84B** Oxley	**86A** Ebbw Junction	**86A** Ebbw Junction	**84C** Banbury		
5922	*4900*	**PDN** Old Oak Common	**82C** Swindon	**82C** Swindon	**82C** Swindon	**82C** Swindon	**81F** Oxford	
5923	*4900*	**CHR** Chester (GWR)	**84K** Chester (GWR)	**86E** Severn Tunnel Junction	**86C** Cardiff Canton	**81A** Old Oak Common	**81F** Oxford	
5924	*4900*	**WES** Westbury	**82B** St. Philips Marsh	**82B** St. Philips Marsh	**82B** St. Philips Marsh	**82B** St. Philips Marsh	**82B** St. Philips Marsh	
5925	*4900*	**WES** Westbury	**82D** Westbury	**86C** Cardiff Canton	**86C** Cardiff Canton	**81C** Southall		
5926	*4900*	**SBZ** St. Blazey	**83E** St. Blazey	**83E** St. Blazey	**83E** St. Blazey	**84A** Stafford Road		
5927	*4900*	**SRD** Stafford Road	**84E** Tyseley	**84E** Tyseley	**84E** Tyseley	**84E** Tyseley	**84E** Tyseley	
5928	*4900*	**FGD** Fishguard Goodwick	**87J** Fishguard Goodwick	**87J** Fishguard Goodwick	**87J** Fishguard Goodwick	**87J** Fishguard Goodwick		
5929	*4900*	**NEY** Neyland	**87E** Landore	**87E** Landore	**87E** Landore	**81A** Old Oak Common	**81C** Southall	
5930	*4900*	**BAN** Banbury	**84C** Banbury	**84C** Banbury	**84C** Banbury	**84E** Tyseley		
5931	*4900*	**PDN** Old Oak Common	**81A** Old Oak Common	**81A** Old Oak Common	**81A** Old Oak Common	**81A** Old Oak Common		
5932	*4900*	**PDN** Old Oak Common	**81A** Old Oak Common	**81A** Old Oak Common	**81A** Old Oak Common	**81A** Old Oak Common	**81A** Old Oak Common	
5933	*4900*	**RDG** Reading	**81D** Reading	**81D** Reading	**81D** Reading	**81C** Southall	**81F** Oxford	
5934	*4900*	**SDN** Swindon	**82C** Swindon	**82A** Bristol Bath Road	**83D** Laira (Plymouth)	**82A** Bristol Bath Road	**82B** St. Philips Marsh	
5935	*4900*	**DID** Didcot	**81E** Didcot	**81E** Didcot	**81E** Didcot	**82D** Westbury		
5936	*4900*	**PDN** Old Oak Common	**81A** Old Oak Common	**81A** Old Oak Common	**81A** Old Oak Common	**81D** Reading	**81D** Reading	
5937	*4900*	**PDN** Old Oak Common	**81A** Old Oak Common	**87G** Carmarthen	**87G** Carmarthen	**87G** Carmarthen	**88L** Cardiff East Dock	
5938	*4900*	**PDN** Old Oak Common	**81A** Old Oak Common	**87G** Carmarthen	**87G** Carmarthen	**87G** Carmarthen	**87G** Carmarthen	
5939	*4900*	**PDN** Old Oak Common	**81A** Old Oak Common	**81A** Old Oak Common	**81A** Old Oak Common	**81A** Old Oak Common	**82C** Swindon	
5940	*4900*	**PDN** Old Oak Common	**81A** Old Oak Common	**81A** Old Oak Common	**81A** Old Oak Common	**82A** Bristol Bath Road		
5941	*4900*	**PDN** Old Oak Common	**81A** Old Oak Common	**81A** Old Oak Common	**81A** Old Oak Common	**82A** Bristol Bath Road		
5942	*4900*	**SRD** Stafford Road	**84B** Oxley	**81D** Reading	**81D** Reading	**84G** Shrewsbury	**89A** Shrewsbury	
5943	*4900*	**SDN** Swindon	**85A** Worcester	**85A** Worcester	**81E** Didcot	**81E** Didcot	**82C** Swindon	
5944	*4900*	**SRD** Stafford Road	**84B** Oxley	**84B** Oxley	**84B** Oxley	**84B** Oxley	**85B** Gloucester	
5945	*4900*	**OXY** Oxley	**84B** Oxley	**84B** Oxley	**81A** Old Oak Common	**82C** Swindon	**81F** Oxford	
5946	*4900*	**CDF** Cardiff Canton	**86C** Cardiff Canton	**86C** Cardiff Canton	**86C** Cardiff Canton	**86C** Cardiff Canton		
5947	*4900*	**OXY** Oxley	**81A** Old Oak Common	**84C** Banbury	**84C** Banbury	**87J** Fishguard Goodwick		
5948	*4900*	**RDG** Reading	**85B** Gloucester	**86G** Pontypool Road	**86G** Pontypool Road	**86G** Pontypool Road	**86G** Pontypool Road	
5949	*4900*	**BRD** Bristol Bath Road	**82B** St. Philips Marsh	**82A** Bristol Bath Road	**82A** Bristol Bath Road	**82A** Bristol Bath Road		
5950	*4900*	**TYS** Tyseley	**84E** Tyseley	**84C** Banbury	**82A** Bristol Bath Road	**82B** St. Philips Marsh		
5951	*4900*	**GLO** Gloucester	**85B** Gloucester	**85B** Gloucester	**85B** Gloucester	**85B** Gloucester	**85B** Gloucester	
5952	*4900*	**PDN** Old Oak Common	**81C** Southall	**81C** Southall	**85A** Worcester	**85C** Hereford	**86C** Hereford	
5953	*4900*	**CDF** Cardiff Canton	**86C** Cardiff Canton	**81C** Southall	**81C** Southall	**87G** Carmarthen		
5954	*4900*	**BAN** Banbury	**84D** Leamington Spa	**84C** Banbury	**81A** Old Oak Common	**82B** St. Philips Marsh	**82B** St. Philips Marsh	
5955	*4900*	(3950)	**87E** Landore	**87E** Landore	**87E** Landore	**87E** Landore	**81F** Oxford	
5956	*4900*	**RDG** Reading	**81D** Reading	**81D** Reading	**85A** Worcester	**85A** Worcester	**81F** Oxford	
5957	*4900*	**OXY** Oxley	**81D** Reading	**81D** Reading	**81D** Reading	**81F** Oxford	**81F** Oxford	
5958	*4900*	**CDF** Cardiff Canton	**86C** Cardiff Canton	**82B** St. Philips Marsh	**84B** Oxley	**81A** Old Oak Common	**82B** St. Philips Marsh	
5959	*4900*	**RDG** Reading	**81D** Reading	**81D** Reading	**83C** Exeter	**84E** Tyseley		
5960	*4900*	**OXF** Oxford	**81F** Oxford	**81F** Oxford	**81F** Oxford	**81F** Oxford		
5961	*4900*	**WES** Westbury	**82D** Westbury	**83D** Laira (Plymouth)	**87F** Llanelly	**87F** Llanelly	**87A** Neath	
5962	*4900*	**PDN** Old Oak Common	**81A** Old Oak Common	**84G** Shrewsbury	**84K** Chester (GWR)	**86C** Cardiff Canton	**88L** Cardiff East Dock	
5963	*4900*	**CARM** Carmarthen	**87G** Carmarthen	**87G** Carmarthen	**82D** Westbury	**82D** Westbury	**82D** Westbury	
5964	*4900*	**SPM** St. Philips Marsh	**83D** Laira (Plymouth)	**83D** Laira (Plymouth)	**82F** Weymouth	**82C** Swindon		
5965	*4900*	**GLO** Gloucester	**81F** Oxford	**81F** Oxford	**81F** Oxford	**84B** Oxley		
5966	*4900*	**CHR** Chester (GWR)	**84K** Chester (GWR)	**84B** Oxley	**81F** Oxford	**81F** Oxford		
5967	*4900*	**BAN** Banbury	**84C** Banbury	**84C** Banbury	**83A** Newton Abbot	**83A** Newton Abbot	**81A** Old Oak Common	
5968	*4900*	**WEY** Weymouth	**82F** Weymouth	**84K** Chester (GWR)	**84G** Shrewsbury	**84G** Shrewsbury		
5969	*4900*	**WEY** Weymouth	**83G** Penzance	**83G** Penzance	**81F** Oxford	**87J** Fishguard Goodwick		
5970	*4900*	**CDF** Cardiff Canton	**86C** Cardiff Canton	**86C** Cardiff Canton	**86C** Cardiff Canton	**86G** Pontypool Road	**86C** Hereford	
5971	*4900*	**WES** Westbury	**85A** Worcester	**85A** Worcester	**85A** Worcester	**84G** Shrewsbury	**81C** Southall	
5972	*4900*	**CARM** Carmarthen	**87G** Carmarthen	**84B** Oxley	**83G** Penzance	**86E** Severn Tunnel Junction	**87J** Fishguard Goodwick	
5973	*4900*	**RDG** Reading	**81D** Reading	**81D** Reading	**81D** Reading	**81D** Reading		
5974	*4900*	**WES** Westbury	**82D** Westbury	**82D** Westbury	**82D** Westbury	**82D** Westbury	**82D** Westbury	
5975	*4900*	**PPRD** Pontypool Road	**82D** Westbury	**82C** Swindon	**82B** St. Philips Marsh	**82D** Westbury	**82B** St. Philips Marsh	
5976	*4900*	(3951)	**83C** Exeter	**83C** Exeter	**83C** Exeter	**81A** Old Oak Common	**87F** Llanelly	
5977	*4900*	**CDF** Cardiff Canton	**86C** Cardiff Canton	**86C** Cardiff Canton	**85C** Hereford	**85B** Gloucester	**81D** Reading	
5978	*4900*	**SDN** Swindon	**82F** Weymouth	**82F** Weymouth	**82F** Weymouth	**82C** Swindon	**82C** Swindon	
5979	*4900*	**OXY** Oxley	**81D** Reading	**81D** Reading	**81D** Reading	**81D** Reading	**81D** Reading	
5980	*4900*	**GLO** Gloucester	**85B** Gloucester	**85B** Gloucester	**85B** Gloucester	**86E** Severn Tunnel Junction		
5981	*4900*	**SALOP** Shrewsbury	**84G** Shrewsbury	**84G** Shrewsbury	**82B** St. Philips Marsh	**82C** Swindon		
5982	*4900*	**TN** Taunton	**82B** St. Philips Marsh	**82B** St. Philips Marsh	**82B** St. Philips Marsh	**81D** Reading		
5983	*4900*	**WOS** Worcester	**81C** Southall	**81C** Southall	**81C** Southall	**82C** Swindon	**84E** Tyseley	

		1948	1951	1954	1957	1960	1963	1966
5984	4900	SPM St. Philips Marsh	87G Carmarthen	87G Carmarthen	85A Worcester	87F Llanelly	81A Old Oak Common	
5985	4900	WES Westbury	82D Westbury	83F Truro	83G Penzance	84B Oxley	81C Southall	
5986	4900	(3954)	81A Old Oak Common	81A Old Oak Common	84G Shrewsbury	82C Swindon	82D Westbury	
5987	4900	PDN Old Oak Common	81A Old Oak Common	81A Old Oak Common	81A Old Oak Common	81E Didcot	81E Didcot	
5988	4900	GLO Gloucester	85B Gloucester	87E Landore	87E Landore	87E Landore	81A Old Oak Common	
5989	4900	OXY Oxley	81C Southall	81C Southall	81C Southall	84C Banbury		
5990	4900	GLO Gloucester	85B Gloucester	85B Gloucester	87E Landore	87E Landore	84C Banbury	
5991	4900	BAN Banbury	84B Oxley	84B Oxley	84B Oxley	84B Oxley	89A Shrewsbury	
5992	4900	BAN Banbury	82B St. Philips Marsh	83B Taunton	83B Taunton	83B Taunton	83B Taunton	
5993	4900	TYS Tyseley	84E Tyseley	81D Reading	81D Reading	81D Reading	81D Reading	
5994	4900	SALOP Shrewsbury	81A Old Oak Common	82C Swindon	85A Worcester	85A Worcester	89A Shrewsbury	
5995	4900	SRD Stafford Road	84B Oxley	84B Oxley	84B Oxley	84B Oxley	84B Oxley	
5996	4900	PDN Old Oak Common	81A Old Oak Common	81A Old Oak Common	81A Old Oak Common	85A Worcester		
5997	4900	TYS Tyseley	84E Tyseley	82C Swindon	82F Weymouth	82C Swindon		
5998	4900	LA Laira (Plymouth)	83D Laira (Plymouth)	83D Laira (Plymouth)	85C Hereford	85C Hereford	86C Hereford	
5999	4900	TN Taunton	83B Taunton	83B Taunton	83B Taunton	83B Taunton		
6000	6000	LA Laira (Plymouth)	82A Bristol Bath Road	81A Old Oak Common	81A Old Oak Common	81A Old Oak Common		
6001	6000	PDN Old Oak Common	81A Old Oak Common	81A Old Oak Common	84A Stafford Road	84A Stafford Road		
6002	6000	LA Laira (Plymouth)	81A Old Oak Common	81A Old Oak Common	81A Old Oak Common	81A Old Oak Common		
6003	6000	PDN Old Oak Common	81A Old Oak Common	81A Old Oak Common	81A Old Oak Common	81A Old Oak Common		
6004	6000	LA Laira (Plymouth)	84A Stafford Road	84A Stafford Road	83D Laira (Plymouth)	81A Old Oak Common		
6005	6000	SRD Stafford Road	84A Stafford Road	84A Stafford Road	84A Stafford Road	84A Stafford Road		
6006	6000	SRD Stafford Road	84A Stafford Road	84A Stafford Road	84A Stafford Road	84A Stafford Road		
6007	6000	PDN Old Oak Common	81A Old Oak Common	81A Old Oak Common	81A Old Oak Common	84A Stafford Road		
6008	6000	SRD Stafford Road	84A Stafford Road	83D Laira (Plymouth)	83D Laira (Plymouth)	84A Stafford Road		
6009	6000	PDN Old Oak Common	81A Old Oak Common	81A Old Oak Common	81A Old Oak Common	81A Old Oak Common		
6010	6000	LA Laira (Plymouth)	83D Laira (Plymouth)	83D Laira (Plymouth)	83D Laira (Plymouth)	81A Old Oak Common		
6011	6000	SRD Stafford Road	84A Stafford Road	84A Stafford Road	84A Stafford Road	84A Stafford Road		
6012	6000	LA Laira (Plymouth)	83D Laira (Plymouth)	83D Laira (Plymouth)	81A Old Oak Common	81A Old Oak Common		
6013	6000	PDN Old Oak Common	81A Old Oak Common	81A Old Oak Common	81A Old Oak Common	83D Laira (Plymouth)		
6014	6000	PDN Old Oak Common	81A Old Oak Common	83D Laira (Plymouth)	84A Stafford Road	84A Stafford Road		
6015	6000	PDN Old Oak Common	81A Old Oak Common	81A Old Oak Common	81A Old Oak Common	81A Old Oak Common		
6016	6000	LA Laira (Plymouth)	83D Laira (Plymouth)	84A Stafford Road	81A Old Oak Common	83D Laira (Plymouth)		
6017	6000	LA Laira (Plymouth)	81A Old Oak Common	83D Laira (Plymouth)	83D Laira (Plymouth)	84A Stafford Road		
6018	6000	NA Newton Abbot	81A Old Oak Common	81A Old Oak Common	81A Old Oak Common	81A Old Oak Common		
6019	6000	LA Laira (Plymouth)	81A Old Oak Common	81A Old Oak Common	81A Old Oak Common	81A Old Oak Common		
6020	6000	LA Laira (Plymouth)	84A Stafford Road	84A Stafford Road	84A Stafford Road	84A Stafford Road		
6021	6000	PDN Old Oak Common	81A Old Oak Common	81A Old Oak Common	83D Laira (Plymouth)	81A Old Oak Common		
6022	6000	LA Laira (Plymouth)	83D Laira (Plymouth)	83D Laira (Plymouth)	81A Old Oak Common	84A Stafford Road		
6023	6000	NA Newton Abbot	83D Laira (Plymouth)	83D Laira (Plymouth)	81A Old Oak Common	81A Old Oak Common		
6024	6000	NA Newton Abbot	83D Laira (Plymouth)	83D Laira (Plymouth)	81A Old Oak Common	81A Old Oak Common		
6025	6000	PDN Old Oak Common	83D Laira (Plymouth)	83D Laira (Plymouth)	83D Laira (Plymouth)	81A Old Oak Common		
6026	6000	LA Laira (Plymouth)	83D Laira (Plymouth)	83D Laira (Plymouth)	83D Laira (Plymouth)	83D Laira (Plymouth)		
6027	6000	NA Newton Abbot	83D Laira (Plymouth)	83D Laira (Plymouth)	83D Laira (Plymouth)	81A Old Oak Common		
6028	6000	NA Newton Abbot	81A Old Oak Common	81A Old Oak Common	83D Laira (Plymouth)	81A Old Oak Common		
6029	6000	LA Laira (Plymouth)	83D Laira (Plymouth)	83D Laira (Plymouth)	83D Laira (Plymouth)	81A Old Oak Common		
6100	6100	SLO Slough	81D Reading	81D Reading	81D Reading			
6101	6100	SLO Slough	81D Reading	81D Reading	81D Reading	81D Reading		
6102	6100	SHL Southall	82A Bristol Bath Road	86A Ebbw Junction	86A Ebbw Junction			
6103	6100	OXF Oxford	81D Reading	81D Reading	81D Reading	81D Reading	81D Reading	
6104	6100	SLO Slough	81B Slough	81D Reading	81D Reading	81D Reading		
6105	6100	SLO Slough	81D Reading	84E Tyseley	84E Tyseley	81E Didcot		
6106	6100	SLO Slough	81B Slough	81F Oxford	81F Oxford	81F Oxford	81F Oxford	
6107	6100	SLO Slough	82A Bristol Bath Road	86A Ebbw Junction	82A Bristol Bath Road	81D Reading	81D Reading	
6108	6100	SLO Slough	81B Slough	81B Slough	81B Slough	81A Old Oak Common	81C Southall	
6109	6100	RDG Reading	81F Oxford	81A Old Oak Common	81C Southall	81B Slough		
6110	6100	SHL Southall	81C Southall	81A Old Oak Common	81A Old Oak Common	81C Southall	81C Southall	
6111	6100	SLO Slough	81F Oxford	81F Oxford	81F Oxford	81F Oxford	81F Oxford	
6112	6100	PDN Old Oak Common	81E Didcot	81F Oxford	81F Oxford	81D Reading	81E Didcot	
6113	6100	SLO Slough	81B Slough	81F Oxford	81F Oxford	81A Old Oak Common	83B Taunton	
6114	6100	SLO Slough	81B Slough	86A Ebbw Junction	86A Ebbw Junction	87E Landore	87G Carmarthen	
6115	6100	RDG Reading	81B Slough	81B Slough	81B Slough	81B Slough	86G Pontypool Road	
6116	6100	SLO Slough	81B Slough	84E Tyseley	84E Tyseley	84E Tyseley	87J Fishguard Goodwick	
6117	6100	RDG Reading	81A Old Oak Common	81D Reading	81D Reading	81B Slough	81B Slough	
6118	6100	SHL Southall	81E Didcot	84E Tyseley	84E Tyseley	86E Severn Tunnel Junction	87G Carmarthen	
6119	6100	SLO Slough	81B Slough	81B Slough	86E Severn Tunnel Junction	81D Reading	81D Reading	
6120	6100	PDN Old Oak Common	81A Old Oak Common	81A Old Oak Common	81A Old Oak Common	81A Old Oak Common		
6121	6100	RDG Reading	81A Old Oak Common	81A Old Oak Common	81A Old Oak Common	81A Old Oak Common		
6122	6100	OXF Oxford	81F Oxford	81F Oxford	81B Slough	81D Reading	81D Reading	
6123	6100	SLO Slough	81B Slough	81B Slough	81D Reading	81B Slough		
6124	6100	SLO Slough	81B Slough	81B Slough	81B Slough	81E Didcot	81F Oxford	
6125	6100	SHL Southall	81C Southall	81C Southall	81C Southall	81D Reading	81A Old Oak Common	
6126	6100	SLO Slough	81C Southall	81C Southall	81D Reading	81B Slough	81E Didcot	
6127	6100	SLO Slough	81B Slough	81B Slough	81B Slough	81B Slough		
6128	6100	SHL Southall	81C Southall	81C Southall	81C Southall	81C Southall	81B Slough	
6129	6100	PDN Old Oak Common	34E Neasden	81D Reading	81D Reading	81D Reading	84C Banbury	
6130	6100	RDG Reading	81D Reading	81D Reading	81D Reading	81D Reading	81E Didcot	
6131	6100	RDG Reading	81B Slough	81B Slough	81B Slough	81D Reading	81D Reading	
6132	6100	PDN Old Oak Common	81E Didcot	81B Slough	81A Old Oak Common	81A Old Oak Common	81C Southall	
6133	6100	SLO Slough	81B Slough	81B Slough	81B Slough	81F Oxford	81C Southall	
6134	6100	PDN Old Oak Common	81E Didcot	84E Tyseley	84E Tyseley	81D Reading	81D Reading	
6135	6100	PDN Old Oak Common	81A Old Oak Common	81A Old Oak Common	81A Old Oak Common	81A Old Oak Common	81A Old Oak Common	
6136	6100	RDG Reading	81B Slough	81B Slough	81B Slough	81B Slough	81E Didcot	
6137	6100	PDN Old Oak Common	81A Old Oak Common	81A Old Oak Common	82A Bristol Bath Road	85B Gloucester	85B Gloucester	
6138	6100	OXF Oxford	81F Oxford	81F Oxford	81F Oxford	81F Oxford	81D Reading	
6139	6100	SHL Southall	81C Southall	84E Tyseley	84E Tyseley	81F Oxford	81E Didcot	
6140	6100	RDG Reading	81B Slough	81B Slough	81B Slough	86E Severn Tunnel Junction	86E Severn Tunnel Junction	
6141	6100	PDN Old Oak Common	81A Old Oak Common	81A Old Oak Common	81A Old Oak Common	81A Old Oak Common	81A Old Oak Common	
6142	6100	PDN Old Oak Common	81A Old Oak Common	81A Old Oak Common	81A Old Oak Common	81A Old Oak Common	81A Old Oak Common	
6143	6100	SLO Slough	81B Slough	81B Slough	81B Slough	81B Slough	81B Slough	
6144	6100	PDN Old Oak Common	81A Old Oak Common	81A Old Oak Common	81A Old Oak Common	81A Old Oak Common	81F Oxford	
6145	6100	SLO Slough	81D Reading	81D Reading	81D Reading	81A Old Oak Common	81A Old Oak Common	
6146	6100	SLO Slough	81B Slough	81B Slough	81B Slough	81B Slough		
6147	6100	SHL Southall	81C Southall	81C Southall	81C Southall	81C Southall	82E Bristol Barrow Road	
6148	6100	SHL Southall	81C Southall	81C Southall	81C Southall	81C Southall	83B Taunton	
6149	6100	PDN Old Oak Common	81A Old Oak Common	81A Old Oak Common	81A Old Oak Common	81C Southall	81F Oxford	
6150	6100	SLO Slough	81B Slough	81B Slough	81B Slough	81B Slough	81F Oxford	
6151	6100	SLO Slough	81B Slough	81B Slough	81B Slough	81B Slough	87G Carmarthen	
6152	6100	SLO Slough	81B Slough	81B Slough	81B Slough	81B Slough		
6153	6100	SLO Slough	81D Reading	81B Slough	81D Reading	81D Reading		
6154	6100	RDG Reading	81B Slough	81B Slough	81B Slough	81B Slough	81F Oxford	
6155	6100	PDN Old Oak Common	81A Old Oak Common	81A Old Oak Common	86E Severn Tunnel Junction	86E Severn Tunnel Junction	85A Worcester	
6156	6100	SHL Southall	81C Southall	81C Southall	81C Southall	81C Southall	81F Oxford	
6157	6100	SLO Slough	81B Slough	81B Slough	81B Slough	81A Old Oak Common		
6158	6100	PDN Old Oak Common	81A Old Oak Common	81A Old Oak Common	81A Old Oak Common	81A Old Oak Common	86E Severn Tunnel Junction	
6159	6100	PDN Old Oak Common	81A Old Oak Common	81A Old Oak Common	81A Old Oak Common	81C Southall	81E Didcot	
6160	6100	SLO Slough	81B Slough	81B Slough	81B Slough	84E Tyseley	81B Slough	
6161	6100	SLO Slough	81B Slough	81D Reading	81D Reading	81D Reading	81D Reading	
6162	6100	RDG Reading	81D Reading	81D Reading	81D Reading	81D Reading		
6163	6100	RDG Reading	81D Reading	81D Reading	82A Bristol Bath Road	81F Oxford	81A Old Oak Common	
6164	6100	SLO Slough	81B Slough	81B Slough	81B Slough	81E Didcot	81D Reading	
6165	6100	SHL Southall	81C Southall	81C Southall	81C Southall	81C Southall	81C Southall	
6166	6100	PDN Old Oak Common	34E Neasden	84E Tyseley	84E Tyseley	83D Laira (Plymouth)		
6167	6100	SLO Slough	81E Didcot	81E Didcot	81E Didcot	81E Didcot	81E Didcot	

No.	Class	1948	1951	1954	1957	1960	1963	1966
6168	6100	PDN Old Oak Common	81A Old Oak Common	81A Old Oak Common	81A Old Oak Common	81A Old Oak Common		
6169	6100	SHL Southall	81C Southall	81C Southall	81C Southall	81C Southall	81A Old Oak Common	
6300	4300	OXF Oxford	81F Oxford	83E St. Blazey	83F Truro	83F Truro		
6301	4300	EXE Exeter	83C Exeter	83C Exeter	83D Laira (Plymouth)	83D Laira (Plymouth)		
6302	4300	RDG Reading	81D Reading	81D Reading	81D Reading	81E Didcot		
6303	4300	CNYD Croes Newydd	84J Croes Newydd	84J Croes Newydd	84J Croes Newydd			
6304	4300	LDR Landore	87G Carmarthen	87G Carmarthen	81E Didcot	85B Gloucester	85B Gloucester	
6305	4300	TN Taunton	83B Taunton	83E St. Blazey	83E St. Blazey			
6306	4300	WOS Worcester	85A Worcester	85A Worcester	82B St. Philips Marsh	87H Neyland		
6307	4300	SALOP Shrewsbury	84G Shrewsbury	84E Tyseley	84E Tyseley	84J Croes Newydd		
6308	4300	CHR Chester (GWR)	84K Chester (GWR)	85C Hereford	86C Cardiff Canton			
6309	4300	GLO Gloucester	85B Gloucester	85B Gloucester	82C Swindon	82C Swindon	81E Didcot	
6310	4300	CARM Carmarthen	87G Carmarthen	87G Carmarthen	87G Carmarthen	87F Llanelly		
6311	4300	CHR Chester (GWR)	84J Croes Newydd	84J Croes Newydd	84J Croes Newydd	84C Banbury		
6312	4300	RDG Reading	81D Reading	81D Reading	82B St. Philips Marsh	82B St. Philips Marsh		
6313	4300	RDG Reading	81F Oxford	81E Didcot	81C Southall	81E Didcot		
6314	4300	WES Westbury	82D Westbury	82C Swindon	85C Hereford	85D Kidderminster	84G Kidderminster	
6316	4300	CNYD Croes Newydd	84J Croes Newydd	84J Croes Newydd	84J Croes Newydd	84J Croes Newydd		
6317	4300	TN Taunton	83B Taunton	86G Pontypool Road	84G Shrewsbury	84F Stourbridge	84C Banbury	
6318	4300	PZ Penzance	83G Penzance	83C Exeter	86A Ebbw Junction			
6319	4300	LA Laira (Plymouth)	83D Laira (Plymouth)	83D Laira (Plymouth)	83D Laira (Plymouth)	83C Exeter	82D Westbury	
6320	4300	SDN Swindon	82C Swindon	82C Swindon	82D Westbury	82D Westbury	86E Severn Tunnel Junction	
6321	4300	SRD Stafford Road	84A Stafford Road	84E Tyseley				
6322	4300	SDN Swindon	82C Swindon	82B St. Philips Marsh	83C Exeter			
6323	4300	TN Taunton	83B Taunton	83B Taunton	83B Taunton	82E Bristol Barrow Road		
6324	4300	WOS Worcester	85A Worcester	85A Worcester	84B Oxley	81D Reading		
6325	4300	SHL Southall	81C Southall	87F Llanelly	86G Pontypool Road			
6326	4300	CHEL Cheltenham	85C Hereford	85C Hereford	85D Kidderminster	86C Cardiff Canton	88L Cardiff East Dock	
6327	4300	CNYD Croes Newydd	84J Croes Newydd	84F Stourbridge	82B St. Philips Marsh	82B St. Philips Marsh	83B Taunton	
6328	4300	TN Taunton	83B Taunton	83B Taunton	83D Laira (Plymouth)			
6329	4300	DID Didcot	81E Didcot	81E Didcot	87G Carmarthen	87G Carmarthen		
6330	4300	SBZ St. Blazey	83E St. Blazey	85B Gloucester	85B Gloucester	85B Gloucester		
6331	4300	CARM Carmarthen	87G Carmarthen	84K Chester (GWR)	84C Banbury			
6332	4300	OXY Oxley	84F Stourbridge	84F Stourbridge	84F Stourbridge	84F Stourbridge		
6333	4300	PPRD Pontypool Road	86G Pontypool Road	86C Cardiff Canton	86C Cardiff Canton	81D Reading		
6334	4300	RDG Reading	81D Reading	85A Worcester	85A Worcester			
6335	4300	OXY Oxley	84B Oxley	84B Oxley	89C Machynlleth	89C Machynlleth	86G Pontypool Road	
6336	4300	TYS Tyseley	84E Tyseley	84E Tyseley	81F Oxford	82C Swindon		
6337	4300	CHR Chester (GWR)	84K Chester (GWR)	84K Chester (GWR)	83B Taunton	83B Taunton	81D Reading	
6338	4300	SALOP Shrewsbury	84G Shrewsbury	85C Hereford	82D Westbury	86E Severn Tunnel Junction	86E Severn Tunnel Junction	
6339	4300	CHR Chester (GWR)	84K Chester (GWR)	84G Shrewsbury	84J Croes Newydd	84J Croes Newydd		
6340	4300	SDN Swindon	81E Didcot	81E Didcot	81E Didcot	84F Stourbridge		
6341	4300	CHEL Cheltenham	85B Gloucester	85B Gloucester	85B Gloucester	82B St. Philips Marsh		
6342	4300	OXY Oxley	84C Banbury	84E Tyseley	84E Tyseley	89A Oswestry		
6343	4300	TN Taunton	83B Taunton	83B Taunton	83B Taunton	83B Taunton		
6344	4300	CARM Carmarthen	87G Carmarthen	84K Chester (GWR)	84K Chester (GWR)	71G Weymouth	85B Gloucester	
6345	4300	NA Newton Abbot	83A Newton Abbot	84K Chester (GWR)	84K Chester (GWR)	87F Llanelly	88L Cardiff East Dock	
6346	4300	BHD Birkenhead	6C Birkenhead	6C Birkenhead	6C Birkenhead	82E Bristol Barrow Road	83C Exeter	
6347	4300	NEY Neyland	87H Neyland	87H Neyland	87H Neyland	87J Fishguard Goodwick	87F Llanelly	
6348	4300	SALOP Shrewsbury	84G Shrewsbury	82C Swindon	85A Worcester	86A Ebbw Junction		
6349	4300	HFD Hereford	85C Hereford	85B Gloucester	85B Gloucester	84F Stourbridge	87F Llanelly	
6350	4300	BHD Birkenhead	6C Birkenhead	6C Birkenhead	6C Birkenhead	82E Bristol Barrow Road	81E Didcot	
6351	4300	WES Westbury	82A Bristol Bath Road	82A Bristol Bath Road	82B St. Philips Marsh	82B St. Philips Marsh		
6352	4300	HFD Hereford	85C Hereford	85C Hereford	86C Cardiff Canton	86C Cardiff Canton		
6353	4300	CDF Cardiff Canton	86C Cardiff Canton	86C Cardiff Canton	86C Cardiff Canton	84B Oxley	82D Westbury	
6354	4300	PZ Penzance	84C Banbury	85A Worcester	85A Worcester			
6355	4300	NEY Neyland	87H Neyland	85B Gloucester	82C Swindon			
6356	4300	SBZ St. Blazey	83E St. Blazey	83A Newton Abbot	82B St. Philips Marsh	82B St. Philips Marsh	82D Westbury	
6357	4300	SDN Swindon	82C Swindon	82C Swindon	85A Worcester	84J Croes Newydd	87F Llanelly	
6358	4300	SDN Swindon	82C Swindon	82D Westbury	82D Westbury			
6359	4300	DID Didcot	81E Didcot	85A Worcester	85C Hereford			
6360	4300	SDN Swindon	82C Swindon	82C Swindon	82A Bristol Bath Road	87C Danygraig		
6361	4300	OXY Oxley	84B Oxley	86G Pontypool Road	86J Aberdare	86J Aberdare	88J Aberdare	
6362	4300	OXY Oxley	84B Oxley	85C Hereford	84C Banbury	86E Severn Tunnel Junction		
6363	4300	RDG Reading	81D Reading	82B St. Philips Marsh	82B St. Philips Marsh	85B Gloucester	81E Didcot	
6364	4300	TN Taunton	83B Taunton	83B Taunton	83B Taunton	84C Banbury	84G Kidderminster	
6365	4300	WES Westbury	82D Westbury	82D Westbury	85B Gloucester	85B Gloucester	85B Gloucester	
6366	4300	RDG Reading	81D Reading	81D Reading	81D Reading	82C Swindon		
6367	4300	CARM Carmarthen	87G Carmarthen	84K Chester (GWR)	84K Chester (GWR)	84F Stourbridge	84C Banbury	
6368	4300	WES Westbury	82D Westbury	82C Swindon	86G Pontypool Road	85B Gloucester	89C Machynlleth	
6369	4300	WES Westbury	82D Westbury	86E Severn Tunnel Junction	86E Severn Tunnel Junction	86E Severn Tunnel Junction	86E Severn Tunnel Junction	
6370	4300	PPRD Pontypool Road	86G Pontypool Road	82B St. Philips Marsh	86A Ebbw Junction	86A Ebbw Junction	86G Pontypool Road	
6371	4300	NEY Neyland	87H Neyland	89C Machynlleth	89C Machynlleth	89C Machynlleth		
6372	4300	TN Taunton	83B Taunton	83B Taunton	83B Taunton	83B Taunton	83B Taunton	
6373	4300	TR Truro	83F Truro	85B Gloucester	85B Gloucester	85B Gloucester	86E Severn Tunnel Junction	
6374	4300	SDN Swindon	82C Swindon	82B St. Philips Marsh	82B St. Philips Marsh	82B St. Philips Marsh		
6375	4300	WES Westbury	82D Westbury	86E Severn Tunnel Junction	83B Taunton	83B Taunton	89A Shrewsbury	
6376	4300	BHD Birkenhead	6C Birkenhead	6C Birkenhead	6C Birkenhead	82E Bristol Barrow Road		
6377	4300	TN Taunton	83B Taunton	83B Taunton	83B Taunton	87G Carmarthen		
6378	4300	WOS Worcester	85A Worcester	85A Worcester	89C Machynlleth	89C Machynlleth	89C Machynlleth	
6379	4300	DID Didcot	81D Reading	81D Reading	81D Reading	81E Didcot	81D Reading	
6380	4300	CHR Chester (GWR)	84K Chester (GWR)	84K Chester (GWR)	84K Chester (GWR)	6E Chester (GWR)	89A Shrewsbury	
6381	4300	GLO Gloucester	85B Gloucester	85B Gloucester	85B Gloucester	85B Gloucester	85B Gloucester	
6382	4300	WOS Worcester	85D Kidderminster	85A Worcester	85D Kidderminster	85D Kidderminster		
6383	4300	RDG Reading	81D Reading	89C Machynlleth				
6384	4300	SDN Swindon	82C Swindon	82C Swindon	86E Severn Tunnel Junction	86E Severn Tunnel Junction	86E Severn Tunnel Junction	
6385	4300	WOS Worcester	85B Gloucester	85B Gloucester	83C Exeter	81D Reading	81D Reading	
6386	4300	STJ Severn Tunnel Junction	86E Severn Tunnel Junction	86E Severn Tunnel Junction	86E Severn Tunnel Junction	86E Severn Tunnel Junction		
6387	4300	SDN Swindon	82C Swindon	82C Swindon	84C Banbury	84C Banbury		
6388	4300	SHL Southall	81C Southall	85A Worcester	85A Worcester	85D Kidderminster		
6389	4300	NEY Neyland	87H Neyland	85A Worcester	87F Llanelly	87H Neyland		
6390	4300	BAN Banbury	84C Banbury	83B Taunton	83B Taunton	83B Taunton		
6391	4300	SRD Stafford Road	84F Stourbridge	84F Stourbridge	82B St. Philips Marsh	82C Swindon		
6392	4300	CHR Chester (GWR)	84K Chester (GWR)	84K Chester (GWR)	84K Chester (GWR)	89C Machynlleth		
6393	4300	RDG Reading	81D Reading	86G Pontypool Road	84F Stourbridge	86G Pontypool Road		
6394	4300	TN Taunton	83B Taunton	84E Tyseley	81D Reading	85B Gloucester	85B Gloucester	
6395	4300	HFD Hereford	85C Hereford	85C Hereford	85A Worcester	84G Shrewsbury	87F Llanelly	
6396	4300	WOS Worcester	85A Worcester	85A Worcester	87F Llanelly			
6397	4300	EXE Exeter	83C Exeter	83E St. Blazey	83E St. Blazey			
6398	4300	TN Taunton	83B Taunton	83B Taunton	83B Taunton	83B Taunton		
6399	4300	WES Westbury	82D Westbury	82D Westbury	82D Westbury			
6400	6400	PPRD Pontypool Road	86G Pontypool Road	86G Pontypool Road	86G Pontypool Road	83D Laira (Plymouth)	83D Laira (Plymouth)	
6401	6400	AYN Abercynon	88E Abercynon	88E Abercynon	86A Ebbw Junction	84F Stourbridge		
6402	6400	CHYS Cardiff Cathays	88A Cardiff Cathays	88A Cardiff Cathays	88A Cardiff Cathays			
6403	6400	PPRD Pontypool Road	86G Pontypool Road	86G Pontypool Road	86G Pontypool Road	84F Stourbridge	84F Stourbridge	
6404	6400	BHD Birkenhead	84J Croes Newydd	84J Croes Newydd	84J Croes Newydd			
6405	6400	BHD Birkenhead	84J Croes Newydd	84J Croes Newydd	84J Croes Newydd			
6406	6400	LA Laira (Plymouth)	83D Laira (Plymouth)	83D Laira (Plymouth)	83D Laira (Plymouth)	83D Laira (Plymouth)		
6407	6400	SHL Southall	83D Laira (Plymouth)	83D Laira (Plymouth)	83D Laira (Plymouth)			
6408	6400	MTHR Merthyr	88D Merthyr	88D Merthyr	88D Merthyr	83D Laira (Plymouth)		
6409	6400	NPT Ebbw Junction	86B Newport Pill	86B Newport Pill	86A Ebbw Junction			
6410	6400	ABDR Aberdare	86J Aberdare	86J Aberdare	86J Aberdare	83D Laira (Plymouth)		
6411	6400	AYN Abercynon	88E Abercynon	88E Abercynon	88E Abercynon	88A Radyr		
6412	6400	LDR Landore	87E Landore	87E Landore	86A Ebbw Junction	86A Ebbw Junction	86A Ebbw Junction	

		1948	1951	1954	1957	1960	1963	1966
6413	6400	ABDR Aberdare	86J Aberdare	86J Aberdare	86J Aberdare	83D Laira (Plymouth)		
6414	6400	LA Laira (Plymouth)	83D Laira (Plymouth)	83D Laira (Plymouth)	83D Laira (Plymouth)			
6415	6400	NPT Ebbw Junction	86A Ebbw Junction	86A Ebbw Junction	86A Ebbw Junction	85B Gloucester		
6416	6400	CHYS Cardiff Cathays	88A Cardiff Cathays	88A Cardiff Cathays	88A Cardiff Cathays	88D Merthyr	88D Merthyr	
6417	6400	LA Laira (Plymouth)	83D Laira (Plymouth)	86J Aberdare	86J Aberdare			
6418	6400	SRD Stafford Road	84C Banbury	84A Stafford Road	84A Stafford Road	84A Stafford Road		
6419	6400	LA Laira (Plymouth)	83D Laira (Plymouth)	83D Laira (Plymouth)	83D Laira (Plymouth)	83D Laira (Plymouth)	88H Tondu	
6420	6400	SBZ St. Blazey	83D Laira (Plymouth)	83D Laira (Plymouth)	83D Laira (Plymouth)			
6421	6400	LA Laira (Plymouth)	83D Laira (Plymouth)	83D Laira (Plymouth)	83D Laira (Plymouth)	83D Laira (Plymouth)	83D Laira (Plymouth)	
6422	6400	SRD Stafford Road	84J Croes Newydd	84A Stafford Road	84A Stafford Road	84A Stafford Road		
6423	6400	CHYS Cardiff Cathays	88A Cardiff Cathays	88A Cardiff Cathays	88D Merthyr			
6424	6400	PPRD Pontypool Road	86G Pontypool Road	86G Pontypool Road	86G Pontypool Road	86E Severn Tunnel Junction	84F Stourbridge	
6425	6400	LDR Landore	87E Landore	87E Landore	86A Ebbw Junction	86A Ebbw Junction		
6426	6400	NPT Ebbw Junction	86A Ebbw Junction	86A Ebbw Junction	86A Ebbw Junction	86A Ebbw Junction		
6427	6400	MTHR Merthyr	88D Merthyr	88D Merthyr	88D Merthyr			
6428	6400	NPT Ebbw Junction	86A Ebbw Junction	86A Ebbw Junction	86A Ebbw Junction			
6429	6400	PPRD Pontypool Road	86G Pontypool Road	86G Pontypool Road	86G Pontypool Road	84C Banbury		
6430	6400	PPRD Pontypool Road	86G Pontypool Road	86G Pontypool Road	86A Ebbw Junction	86E Severn Tunnel Junction	83D Laira (Plymouth)	
6431	6400	LDR Landore	87E Landore	87E Landore	86J Aberdare	86J Aberdare	88H Tondu	
6432	6400	PPRD Pontypool Road	86G Pontypool Road	86G Pontypool Road	86G Pontypool Road			
6433	6400	CHYS Cardiff Cathays	88A Cardiff Cathays	88D Merthyr	88D Merthyr	88D Merthyr	88D Merthyr	
6434	6400	MTHR Merthyr	88D Merthyr	88D Merthyr	88D Merthyr	88A Radyr	86A Ebbw Junction	
6435	6400	CHYS Cardiff Cathays	88A Cardiff Cathays	88D Merthyr	88A Cardiff Cathays	88E Abercynon	88H Tondu	
6436	6400	CHYS Cardiff Cathays	88A Cardiff Cathays	88D Merthyr	88D Merthyr	88D Merthyr		
6437	6400	ABDR Aberdare	86J Aberdare	86J Aberdare	86J Aberdare	86J Aberdare	85B Gloucester	
6438	6400	AYN Abercynon	88E Abercynon	88E Abercynon	88E Abercynon	88E Abercynon		
6439	6400	NPT Ebbw Junction	86A Ebbw Junction	86D Llantrisant	86K Tredegar	86K Tredegar		
6600	5600	OXY Oxley	84B Oxley	86C Cardiff Canton	86C Cardiff Canton	86D Llantrisant		
6601	5600	SPM St. Philips Marsh	82B St. Philips Marsh	82B St. Philips Marsh	82B St. Philips Marsh	82B St. Philips Marsh		
6602	5600	BRY Barry	87H Neyland	86C Cardiff Canton	87B Duffryn Yard	87B Duffryn Yard	87D Swansea East Dock	
6603	5600	RYR Radyr	88A Cardiff Cathays	88A Cardiff Cathays	88A Cardiff Cathays	88A Radyr	88B Radyr	
6604	5600	LDR Landore	87E Landore	87E Landore	87E Landore	84F Stourbridge	89B Croes Newydd	
6605	5600	ABDR Aberdare	86J Aberdare	86J Aberdare	86J Aberdare	86J Aberdare	88J Aberdare	
6606	5600	SALOP Shrewsbury	84G Shrewsbury	84G Shrewsbury	88A Cardiff Cathays	88A Radyr	88B Radyr	
6607	5600	RYR Radyr	88A Cardiff Cathays	88A Cardiff Cathays	88A Cardiff Cathays	88A Radyr	88B Radyr	
6608	5600	RYR Radyr	88A Cardiff Cathays	88A Cardiff Cathays	88A Cardiff Cathays	88A Radyr	88B Radyr	
6609	5600	OXY Oxley	84B Oxley	84F Stourbridge	84F Stourbridge	84F Stourbridge	84E Tyseley	
6610	5600	OXY Oxley	84B Oxley	84B Oxley	84B Oxley	84K Wrexham Rhosddu	87H Neyland	
6611	5600	TYS Tyseley	84E Tyseley	84J Croes Newydd	84J Croes Newydd	84J Croes Newydd	89B Croes Newydd	
6612	5600	NPT Ebbw Junction	88A Cardiff Cathays	88A Cardiff Cathays	88A Cardiff Cathays	88A Radyr	88B Radyr	
6613	5600	NEA Neath	87D Swansea East Dock	87D Swansea East Dock	87D Swansea East Dock	87D Swansea East Dock	87D Swansea East Dock	
6614	5600	BRY Barry	88C Barry	84E Tyseley	88A Cardiff Cathays	88A Radyr	88B Radyr	
6615	5600	CHYS Cardiff Cathays	88C Barry	88C Barry	88C Barry	84J Croes Newydd	89B Croes Newydd	
6616	5600	DYD Duffryn Yard	87B Duffryn Yard	87B Duffryn Yard	87B Duffryn Yard	87B Duffryn Yard		
6617	5600	STB Stourbridge	84F Stourbridge	84J Croes Newydd	84J Croes Newydd	84J Croes Newydd		
6618	5600	RYR Radyr	88A Cardiff Cathays	88A Cardiff Cathays	88A Cardiff Cathays	88A Radyr	84D Leamington Spa	
6619	5600	BRY Barry	88C Barry	88C Barry	88F Treherbert	88F Treherbert	88C Barry	
6620	5600	BRY Barry	88C Barry	84E Tyseley	87B Duffryn Yard	87B Duffryn Yard	87B Duffryn Yard	
6621	5600	ABEEG Aberbeeg	86F Tondu	86C Cardiff Canton	86C Cardiff Canton	86H Aberbeeg	88B Radyr	
6622	5600	CDF Cardiff Canton	86J Aberdare	86J Aberdare	86J Aberdare	86J Aberdare	88J Aberdare	
6623	5600	GLO Gloucester	87B Duffryn Yard	87B Duffryn Yard	87B Duffryn Yard	87B Duffryn Yard	87H Neyland	
6624	5600	CHR Chester (GWR)	84K Chester (GWR)	84D Leamington Spa	84D Leamington Spa	88A Radyr	88B Radyr	
6625	5600	LMTN Leamington Spa	84D Leamington Spa	82D Westbury	82D Westbury	82D Westbury	89B Croes Newydd	
6626	5600	CHYS Cardiff Cathays	88A Cardiff Cathays	88A Cardiff Cathays	88A Cardiff Cathays	88A Radyr	88B Radyr	
6627	5600	CHYS Cardiff Cathays	88D Merthyr	81D Reading	81D Reading	87H Neyland	87H Neyland	
6628	5600	ABDR Aberdare	86J Aberdare	86J Aberdare	86J Aberdare	86J Aberdare	88J Aberdare	
6629	5600	DYD Duffryn Yard	87B Duffryn Yard	87B Duffryn Yard	87B Duffryn Yard	86H Aberbeeg		
6630	5600	TYS Tyseley	84E Tyseley	87F Llanelly	82B St. Philips Marsh	82B St. Philips Marsh		
6631	5600	HFD Hereford	85B Gloucester	85B Gloucester	85B Gloucester	84E Tyseley	84B Oxley	
6632	5600	LMTN Leamington Spa	84D Leamington Spa	84J Croes Newydd	84J Croes Newydd	84J Croes Newydd	89B Croes Newydd	
6633	5600	SALOP Shrewsbury	84G Shrewsbury	84G Shrewsbury	88A Cardiff Cathays	88A Radyr	86E Severn Tunnel Junction	
6634	5600	PPRD Pontypool Road	88A Cardiff Cathays	86G Pontypool Road	86G Pontypool Road	86G Pontypool Road	86G Pontypool Road	
6635	5600	CHYS Cardiff Cathays	88A Cardiff Cathays	88A Cardiff Cathays	88A Cardiff Cathays	88A Radyr	88B Radyr	
6636	5600	PPRD Pontypool Road	86G Pontypool Road	86G Pontypool Road	86G Pontypool Road	86G Pontypool Road	86G Pontypool Road	
6637	5600	BRY Barry	88C Barry	88C Barry	88C Barry	88C Barry	88B Radyr	
6638	5600	OXY Oxley	84B Oxley	86H Aberbeeg	88A Cardiff Cathays	88A Radyr	88B Radyr	
6639	5600	STJ Severn Tunnel Junction	86E Severn Tunnel Junction	86E Severn Tunnel Junction	82C Swindon	82C Swindon	88G Llantrisant	
6640	5600	OXY Oxley	84B Oxley	84B Oxley	84B Oxley	84B Oxley		
6641	5600	BRY Barry	88C Barry	88C Barry	88C Barry	82B St. Philips Marsh		
6642	5600	TDU Tondu	86H Aberbeeg	86A Ebbw Junction	86E Severn Tunnel Junction	86E Severn Tunnel Junction	86E Severn Tunnel Junction	
6643	5600	BRY Barry	88C Barry	88C Barry	88C Barry	88C Barry	88C Barry	
6644	5600	LMTN Leamington Spa	87B Duffryn Yard	87D Swansea East Dock	86C Cardiff Canton	86H Aberbeeg	84B Oxley	
6645	5600	OXY Oxley	84B Oxley	84B Oxley	84B Oxley	84B Oxley		
6646	5600	STB Stourbridge	84F Stourbridge	84F Stourbridge	84F Stourbridge	84F Stourbridge	84F Stourbridge	
6647	5600	BRY Barry	88A Cardiff Cathays	88A Cardiff Cathays	88A Cardiff Cathays	88A Radyr		
6648	5600	CHYS Cardiff Cathays	88F Treherbert	88F Treherbert	88A Cardiff Cathays	88A Radyr	88B Radyr	
6649	5600	NPT Ebbw Junction	86F Tondu	86J Aberdare	86J Aberdare	87E Landore	87A Neath	
6650	5600	LMTN Leamington Spa	87B Duffryn Yard	87B Duffryn Yard	87B Duffryn Yard	87A Neath	87D Swansea East Dock	
6651	5600	PPRD Pontypool Road	86J Aberdare	86J Aberdare	86J Aberdare	86J Aberdare	88J Aberdare	
6652	5600	ABDR Aberdare	86J Aberdare	86J Aberdare	86J Aberdare	86J Aberdare	87F Llanelly	
6653	5600	BRY Barry	88C Barry	86G Pontypool Road	86G Pontypool Road	87F Llanelly	87F Llanelly	
6654	5600	NPT Ebbw Junction	86A Ebbw Junction	81E Didcot	81C Southall	81D Reading	88F Treherbert	
6655	5600	CHYS Cardiff Cathays	88F Treherbert	81C Southall	81C Southall	81B Slough	88C Barry	
6656	5600	SPM St. Philips Marsh	82B St. Philips Marsh	82B St. Philips Marsh	82B St. Philips Marsh	86A Ebbw Junction	88B Radyr	
6657	5600	LMTN Leamington Spa	84D Leamington Spa	84D Leamington Spa	84D Leamington Spa	84D Leamington Spa	88B Radyr	
6658	5600	BRY Barry	88C Barry	88C Barry	88C Barry	88C Barry	88D Merthyr	
6659	5600	CHYS Cardiff Cathays	88A Cardiff Cathays	88A Cardiff Cathays	88A Cardiff Cathays	88A Radyr	88B Radyr	
6660	5600	CHYS Cardiff Cathays	88A Cardiff Cathays	88A Cardiff Cathays	88A Cardiff Cathays	88A Radyr	88B Radyr	
6661	5600	CHYS Cardiff Cathays	88E Abercynon	86J Aberdare	86J Aberdare	86J Aberdare	88J Aberdare	
6662	5600	BRY Barry	87D Swansea East Dock	87D Swansea East Dock	87D Swansea East Dock	87D Swansea East Dock	87D Swansea East Dock	
6663	5600	NPT Ebbw Junction	86G Pontypool Road	86H Aberbeeg	86H Aberbeeg	86H Aberbeeg	84D Leamington Spa	
6664	5600	RYR Radyr	88A Cardiff Cathays	81C Southall	81B Slough	81F Oxford	88J Aberdare	
6665	5600	STB Stourbridge	88A Cardiff Cathays	88A Cardiff Cathays	88A Cardiff Cathays	88A Radyr	88B Radyr	
6666	5600	STJ Severn Tunnel Junction	86E Severn Tunnel Junction	86E Severn Tunnel Junction	86E Severn Tunnel Junction	86E Severn Tunnel Junction	86E Severn Tunnel Junction	
6667	5600	STB Stourbridge	84F Stourbridge	84F Stourbridge	84F Stourbridge	84F Stourbridge	84F Stourbridge	
6668	5600	BRY Barry	88C Barry	84E Tyseley	84E Tyseley	84E Tyseley	84D Leamington Spa	
6669	5600	BRY Barry	88C Barry	84E Tyseley	84E Tyseley	85B Gloucester		
6670	5600	SPM St. Philips Marsh	82B St. Philips Marsh	82B St. Philips Marsh	82B St. Philips Marsh	82B St. Philips Marsh	88G Llantrisant	
6671	5600	SPM St. Philips Marsh	82B St. Philips Marsh	82B St. Philips Marsh	82B St. Philips Marsh	82B St. Philips Marsh	84D Leamington Spa	
6672	5600	NPT Ebbw Junction	86A Ebbw Junction	86E Severn Tunnel Junction	86E Severn Tunnel Junction	86E Severn Tunnel Junction	86E Severn Tunnel Junction	
6673	5600	STJ Severn Tunnel Junction	86E Severn Tunnel Junction	86E Severn Tunnel Junction	86F Tondu	86F Tondu	88J Aberdare	
6674	5600	STB Stourbridge	84F Stourbridge	84F Stourbridge	84F Stourbridge	84J Croes Newydd	89B Croes Newydd	
6675	5600	TDU Tondu	86F Tondu	86G Pontypool Road	86G Pontypool Road	86G Pontypool Road	86G Pontypool Road	
6676	5600	STJ Severn Tunnel Junction	86E Severn Tunnel Junction	86E Severn Tunnel Junction	86F Tondu	86G Pontypool Road	86G Pontypool Road	
6677	5600	STB Stourbridge	84F Stourbridge	84F Stourbridge	84F Stourbridge	84F Stourbridge	84F Stourbridge	
6678	5600	STB Stourbridge	84F Stourbridge	84F Stourbridge	84F Stourbridge	84F Stourbridge	84F Stourbridge	
6679	5600	LDR Landore	86F Tondu	86F Tondu	85D Kidderminster	85D Kidderminster	84G Kidderminster	
6680	5600	LDR Landore	87E Landore	87E Landore	87E Landore	87E Landore	87B Duffryn Yard	
6681	5600	GLO Gloucester	85C Hereford	84F Stourbridge	84F Stourbridge	82B St. Philips Marsh	88L Cardiff East Dock	
6682	5600	OXF Oxford	88A Cardiff Cathays	88A Cardiff Cathays	88A Cardiff Cathays	88A Radyr	88B Radyr	
6683	5600	SALOP Shrewsbury	84G Shrewsbury	84F Stourbridge	84F Stourbridge	84F Stourbridge	84F Stourbridge	
6684	5600	STB Stourbridge	88A Cardiff Cathays	88A Cardiff Cathays	88A Cardiff Cathays	88A Radyr	88B Radyr	
6685	5600	TDU Tondu	86H Aberbeeg	86G Pontypool Road	86G Pontypool Road	86G Pontypool Road	86G Pontypool Road	
6686	5600	DYD Duffryn Yard	87B Duffryn Yard	87B Duffryn Yard	87B Duffryn Yard	87B Duffryn Yard	87B Duffryn Yard	

		1948	1951	1954	1957	1960	1963	1966
6687	*5600*	**PPRD** Pontypool Road	**86G** Pontypool Road	**86J** Aberdare	**86J** Aberdare	**86J** Aberdare		
6688	*5600*	**DYD** Duffryn Yard	**87F** Llanelly	**87E** Landore	**87E** Landore	**87E** Landore	**88B** Radyr	
6689	*5600*	**STJ** Severn Tunnel Junction	**86E** Severn Tunnel Junction	**86E** Severn Tunnel Junction	**88A** Cardiff Cathays	**88A** Radyr	**88B** Radyr	
6690	*5600*	**WES** Westbury	**82D** Westbury	**85B** Gloucester	**85B** Gloucester	**85B** Gloucester	**88J** Aberdare	
6691	*5600*	**CDF** Cardiff Canton	**87B** Duffryn Yard	**87B** Duffryn Yard	**87B** Duffryn Yard	**87B** Duffryn Yard	**87B** Duffryn Yard	
6692	*5600*	**ABDR** Aberdare	**86J** Aberdare	**84F** Stourbridge	**84F** Stourbridge	**84F** Stourbridge	**84F** Stourbridge	
6693	*5600*	**ABDR** Aberdare	**86J** Aberdare	**86G** Pontypool Road	**86G** Pontypool Road	**86G** Pontypool Road	**86G** Pontypool Road	
6694	*5600*	**CNYD** Croes Newydd	**84J** Croes Newydd	**84J** Croes Newydd	**84J** Croes Newydd	**84J** Croes Newydd	**89B** Croes Newydd	
6695	*5600*	**LDR** Landore	**87E** Landore	**87E** Landore	**87E** Landore	**87E** Landore	**87A** Neath	
6696	*5600*	**BAN** Banbury	**84C** Banbury	**84J** Croes Newydd	**84J** Croes Newydd	**84J** Croes Newydd	**88C** Barry	
6697	*5600*	**LMTN** Leamington Spa	**84D** Leamington Spa	**84D** Leamington Spa	**84D** Leamington Spa	**84D** Leamington Spa	**88C** Barry	**6C** Croes Newydd
6698	*5600*	**CNYD** Croes Newydd	**84J** Croes Newydd	**84F** Stourbridge	**84F** Stourbridge	**84G** Shrewsbury	**89B** Croes Newydd	
6699	*5600*	**WES** Westbury	**82D** Westbury	**82D** Westbury	**82C** Swindon	**88A** Radyr	**88B** Radyr	
6700	*6700*	**CED** Cardiff East Dock	**88B** Cardiff East Dock	**88B** Cardiff East Dock	**88B** Cardiff East Dock	**87D** Swansea East Dock		
6701	*6700*	**CED** Cardiff East Dock	**88B** Cardiff East Dock	**88B** Cardiff East Dock	**88B** Cardiff East Dock			
6702	*6700*	**CED** Cardiff East Dock	**88B** Cardiff East Dock	**88B** Cardiff East Dock	**88B** Cardiff East Dock	**87D** Swansea East Dock		
6703	*6700*	**CED** Cardiff East Dock	**88B** Cardiff East Dock	**88B** Cardiff East Dock	**88B** Cardiff East Dock			
6704	*6700*	**CED** Cardiff East Dock	**88B** Cardiff East Dock	**88B** Cardiff East Dock	**88B** Cardiff East Dock			
6705	*6700*	**CED** Cardiff East Dock	**88B** Cardiff East Dock	**88B** Cardiff East Dock	**88B** Cardiff East Dock			
6706	*6700*	**CED** Cardiff East Dock	**88B** Cardiff East Dock	**88B** Cardiff East Dock	**88B** Cardiff East Dock			
6707	*6700*	**CED** Cardiff East Dock	**88B** Cardiff East Dock	**88B** Cardiff East Dock	**88B** Cardiff East Dock			
6708	*6700*	**CED** Cardiff East Dock	**88B** Cardiff East Dock	**88B** Cardiff East Dock	**88B** Cardiff East Dock			
6709	*6700*	**CED** Cardiff East Dock	**88B** Cardiff East Dock	**88B** Cardiff East Dock	**88B** Cardiff East Dock			
6710	*6700*	**PILL** Newport Pill	**86B** Newport Pill	**86B** Newport Pill	**86B** Newport Pill			
6711	*6700*	**PILL** Newport Pill	**86B** Newport Pill	**86B** Newport Pill	**86B** Newport Pill			
6712	*6700*	**BRY** Barry	**88C** Barry	**88C** Barry	**88C** Barry	**87D** Swansea East Dock		
6713	*6700*	**DG** Danygraig	**87C** Danygraig	**87C** Danygraig	**87K** Swansea Victoria			
6714	*6700*	**SED** Swansea East Dock	**87D** Swansea East Dock	**87D** Swansea East Dock	**87K** Swansea Victoria	**87D** Swansea East Dock	**87D** Swansea East Dock	
6715	*6700*	**DYD** Duffryn Yard	**87B** Duffryn Yard	**87B** Duffryn Yard	**87B** Duffryn Yard			
6716	*6700*	**SDN** Swindon	**82C** Swindon	**82C** Swindon	**82C** Swindon			
6717	*6700*	**DYD** Duffryn Yard	**87B** Duffryn Yard	**87B** Duffryn Yard	**87B** Duffryn Yard			
6718	*6700*	**DYD** Duffryn Yard	**87B** Duffryn Yard	**87B** Duffryn Yard	**87B** Duffryn Yard			
6719	*6700*	**DYD** Duffryn Yard	**87B** Duffryn Yard	**87B** Duffryn Yard	**87C** Danygraig	**87C** Danygraig		
6720	*6700*	**DYD** Duffryn Yard	**87B** Duffryn Yard	**87K** Swansea Victoria	**87K** Swansea Victoria	**87D** Swansea East Dock		
6721	*6700*	**CED** Cardiff East Dock	**88B** Cardiff East Dock	**88B** Cardiff East Dock	**87K** Swansea Victoria			
6722	*6700*	**BRY** Barry	**88C** Barry	**88C** Barry	**88C** Barry			
6723	*6700*	**BRY** Barry	**88C** Barry	**88C** Barry	**88C** Barry			
6724	*6700*	**BRY** Barry	**88C** Barry	**88C** Barry	**88C** Barry	**86B** Newport Pill	**87D** Swansea East Dock	
6725	*6700*	**PILL** Newport Pill	**86B** Newport Pill	**86B** Newport Pill	**86B** Newport Pill			
6726	*6700*	**PILL** Newport Pill	**86B** Newport Pill	**86B** Newport Pill	**86B** Newport Pill			
6727	*6700*	**PILL** Newport Pill	**86B** Newport Pill	**86B** Newport Pill	**86B** Newport Pill			
6728	*6700*	**PILL** Newport Pill	**86B** Newport Pill	**86B** Newport Pill	**86B** Newport Pill	**86B** Newport Pill		
6729	*6700*	**PILL** Newport Pill	**86B** Newport Pill	**86B** Newport Pill	**86B** Newport Pill			
6730	*6700*	**PILL** Newport Pill	**86B** Newport Pill	**86B** Newport Pill	**86B** Newport Pill			
6731	*6700*	**PILL** Newport Pill	**86B** Newport Pill	**86B** Newport Pill	**86B** Newport Pill			
6732	*6700*	**PILL** Newport Pill	**86B** Newport Pill	**86B** Newport Pill	**86B** Newport Pill			
6733	*6700*	**BRY** Barry	**88C** Barry	**88C** Barry	**88C** Barry			
6734	*6700*	**DG** Danygraig	**87C** Danygraig	**87K** Swansea Victoria	**87K** Swansea Victoria			
6735	*6700*	**PILL** Newport Pill	**86B** Newport Pill	**86B** Newport Pill	**86B** Newport Pill			
6736	*6700*	**BRY** Barry	**88C** Barry	**88C** Barry	**88B** Cardiff East Dock			
6737	*6700*	**SDN** Swindon	**82C** Swindon	**82C** Swindon	**82C** Swindon			
6738	*6700*	**BRY** Barry	**88C** Barry	**88C** Barry	**88C** Barry	**87D** Swansea East Dock		
6739	*6700*	**SDN** Swindon	**82C** Swindon	**82C** Swindon	**86B** Newport Pill	**86B** Newport Pill		
6740	*6700*	**BRY** Barry	**88C** Barry	**88C** Barry	**88C** Barry			
6741	*6700*	**SDN** Swindon	**82C** Swindon	**82C** Swindon	**82C** Swindon	**82C** Swindon	**87D** Swansea East Dock	
6742	*6700*	**PPRD** Pontypool Road	**86G** Pontypool Road	**86B** Newport Pill	**86B** Newport Pill	**86B** Newport Pill	**87D** Swansea East Dock	
6743	*6700*	**PILL** Newport Pill	**86B** Newport Pill	**86B** Newport Pill	**86B** Newport Pill			
6744	*6700*	**CED** Cardiff East Dock	**88B** Cardiff East Dock	**88B** Cardiff East Dock	**88B** Cardiff East Dock			
6745	*6700*	**BRY** Barry	**88C** Barry	**88C** Barry	**88C** Barry			
6746	*6700*	**BRY** Barry	**88C** Barry	**88C** Barry	**88C** Barry			
6747	*6700*	**BRY** Barry	**88C** Barry	**88C** Barry	**88C** Barry			
6748	*6700*	**BRY** Barry	**88C** Barry	**88C** Barry	**88C** Barry			
6749	*6700*	**DYD** Duffryn Yard	**87B** Duffryn Yard	**87B** Duffryn Yard	**87B** Duffryn Yard	**87D** Swansea East Dock		
6750	*6700*	**BRY** Barry	**88C** Barry	**88C** Barry	**88C** Barry	**86J** Aberdare		
6751	*6700*	**CED** Cardiff East Dock	**88B** Cardiff East Dock	**88B** Cardiff East Dock	**88B** Cardiff East Dock	**86B** Newport Pill		
6752	*6700*	**BRY** Barry	**88C** Barry	**88C** Barry	**88C** Barry	**88C** Barry		
6753	*6700*	**BRY** Barry	**88C** Barry	**88C** Barry	**88C** Barry	**87D** Swansea East Dock		
6754	*6700*	**BRY** Barry	**88C** Barry	**88C** Barry	**88C** Barry	**88C** Barry		
6755	*6700*	**PILL** Newport Pill	**86B** Newport Pill	**86B** Newport Pill	**86B** Newport Pill	**86B** Newport Pill		
6756	*6700*	**PILL** Newport Pill	**86B** Newport Pill	**86B** Newport Pill	**86B** Newport Pill	**86B** Newport Pill		
6757	*6700*	**STJ** Severn Tunnel Junction	**86B** Newport Pill	**86B** Newport Pill	**86B** Newport Pill	**86B** Newport Pill		
6758	*6700*	**BRY** Barry	**88C** Barry	**88C** Barry	**88C** Barry	**82C** Swindon		
6759	*6700*	**PILL** Newport Pill	**86B** Newport Pill	**86B** Newport Pill	**86B** Newport Pill	**86B** Newport Pill		
6760	*6700*	→	**86B** Newport Pill	**86B** Newport Pill	**86B** Newport Pill	**86B** Newport Pill	**87D** Swansea East Dock	
6761	*6700*	→	**87B** Duffryn Yard	**87B** Duffryn Yard	**87B** Duffryn Yard	**87B** Duffryn Yard		
6762	*6700*	→	**87C** Danygraig	**87C** Danygraig	**87C** Danygraig	**87D** Swansea East Dock	**87D** Swansea East Dock	
6763	*6700*	→	**87C** Danygraig	**87C** Danygraig	**87K** Swansea Victoria	**87D** Swansea East Dock	**87D** Swansea East Dock	
6764	*6700*	→	**86B** Newport Pill	**86B** Newport Pill	**86B** Newport Pill	**86B** Newport Pill	**87D** Swansea East Dock	
6765	*6700*	→	**88B** Cardiff East Dock	**88B** Cardiff East Dock	**88B** Cardiff East Dock	**88C** Barry	**87D** Swansea East Dock	
6766	*6700*	→	**87C** Danygraig	**87C** Danygraig	**87C** Danygraig	**87B** Duffryn Yard		
6767	*6700*	→	**88B** Cardiff East Dock	**88B** Cardiff East Dock	**88B** Cardiff East Dock	**87D** Swansea East Dock		
6768	*6700*	→	**87B** Duffryn Yard	**87B** Duffryn Yard	**87K** Swansea Victoria	**87D** Swansea East Dock	**87D** Swansea East Dock	
6769	*6700*	→	**88C** Barry	**88C** Barry	**88B** Cardiff East Dock	**82C** Swindon	**82C** Swindon	
6770	*6700*	→	**88B** Cardiff East Dock	**88B** Cardiff East Dock	**88B** Cardiff East Dock	**87D** Swansea East Dock		
6771	*6700*	→	**88B** Cardiff East Dock	**88B** Cardiff East Dock	**88B** Cardiff East Dock			
6772	*6700*	→	**86B** Newport Pill	**86B** Newport Pill	**86B** Newport Pill	**86B** Newport Pill	**87D** Swansea East Dock	
6773	*6700*	→	**88B** Cardiff East Dock	**88B** Cardiff East Dock	**88B** Cardiff East Dock			
6774	*6700*	→	**88C** Barry	**88C** Barry	**88B** Cardiff East Dock			
6775	*6700*	→	**88C** Barry	**88C** Barry	**88B** Cardiff East Dock	**88C** Barry		
6776	*6700*	→	**87A** Neath	**87B** Duffryn Yard	**87B** Duffryn Yard	**87D** Swansea East Dock		
6777	*6700*	→	**87B** Duffryn Yard	**87B** Duffryn Yard	**87B** Duffryn Yard	**87D** Swansea East Dock	**87D** Swansea East Dock	
6778	*6700*	→	**88B** Cardiff East Dock	**88B** Cardiff East Dock	**88B** Cardiff East Dock	**87D** Swansea East Dock		
6779	*6700*	→	**88B** Cardiff East Dock	**88B** Cardiff East Dock	**87K** Swansea Victoria			
6800	*6800*	**LDR** Landore	**83G** Penzance	**83G** Penzance	**83G** Penzance	**83G** Penzance	**86A** Ebbw Junction	
6801	*6800*	**PZ** Penzance	**83G** Penzance	**83G** Penzance	**83G** Penzance	**83G** Penzance		
6802	*6800*	**RDG** Reading	**81D** Reading	**83D** Laira (Plymouth)	**83D** Laira (Plymouth)	**86G** Pontypool Road		
6803	*6800*	**BAN** Banbury	**84C** Banbury	**84F** Stourbridge	**84F** Stourbridge	**84F** Stourbridge	**84B** Oxley	
6804	*6800*	**WES** Westbury	**82B** St. Philips Marsh	**82B** St. Philips Marsh	**82B** St. Philips Marsh	**82B** St. Philips Marsh	**87F** Llanelly	
6805	*6800*	**CDF** Cardiff Canton	**82B** St. Philips Marsh	**82C** Swindon	**82C** Swindon	**83F** Truro		
6806	*6800*	**LDR** Landore	**83G** Penzance	**83G** Penzance	**84B** Oxley	**84B** Oxley	**85A** Worcester	
6807	*6800*	**WOS** Worcester	**85A** Worcester	**85A** Worcester	**85A** Worcester	**85A** Worcester	**85A** Worcester	
6808	*6800*	**PZ** Penzance	**83G** Penzance	**83G** Penzance	**83G** Penzance	**83G** Penzance	**88L** Cardiff East Dock	
6809	*6800*	**SHL** Southall	**83G** Penzance	**83G** Penzance	**83G** Penzance	**82B** St. Philips Marsh	**81C** Southall	
6810	*6800*	**CDF** Cardiff Canton	**87F** Llanelly	**87F** Llanelly	**87F** Llanelly	**87F** Llanelly	**86G** Pontypool Road	
6811	*6800*	**CDF** Cardiff Canton	**82B** St. Philips Marsh	**82B** St. Philips Marsh	**82B** St. Philips Marsh	**82B** St. Philips Marsh	**84F** Stourbridge	
6812	*6800*	**SRD** Stafford Road	**84A** Stafford Road	**86A** Ebbw Junction	**86G** Pontypool Road	**86G** Pontypool Road	**81D** Reading	
6813	*6800*	**NA** Newton Abbot	**83A** Newton Abbot	**83A** Newton Abbot	**83A** Newton Abbot	**83A** Newton Abbot	**86A** Ebbw Junction	
6814	*6800*	**NA** Newton Abbot	**83A** Newton Abbot	**83A** Newton Abbot	**83A** Newton Abbot	**83E** St. Blazey	**82B** St. Philips Marsh	
6815	*6800*	**STJ** Severn Tunnel Junction	**83B** Taunton	**83B** Taunton	**83B** Taunton	**83B** Taunton	**87F** Llanelly	
6816	*6800*	**BAN** Banbury	**84C** Banbury	**83D** Laira (Plymouth)	**83D** Laira (Plymouth)	**83G** Penzance	**82B** St. Philips Marsh	
6817	*6800*	**CDF** Cardiff Canton	**83G** Penzance	**83G** Penzance	**84K** Chester (GWR)	**84B** Oxley	**85A** Worcester	
6818	*6800*	**CARM** Carmarthen	**87G** Carmarthen	**87F** Llanelly	**87F** Llanelly	**87F** Llanelly	**87F** Llanelly	
6819	*6800*	**BHD** Birkenhead	**84C** Banbury	**86G** Pontypool Road	**86G** Pontypool Road	**86G** Pontypool Road	**86G** Pontypool Road	
6820	*6800*	**PPRD** Pontypool Road	**86A** Ebbw Junction	**86A** Ebbw Junction	**83C** Exeter	**85A** Worcester	**86A** Ebbw Junction	

No.	Class	1948	1951	1954	1957	1960	1963	1966
6821	*6800*	**NPT** Ebbw Junction	**86A** Ebbw Junction	**83D** Laira (Plymouth)	**83D** Laira (Plymouth)	**86G** Pontypool Road	**86G** Pontypool Road	
6822	*6800*	**NA** Newton Abbot	**83A** Newton Abbot	**83A** Newton Abbot	**82D** Westbury	**81F** Oxford	**86G** Pontypool Road	
6823	*6800*	**FGD** Fishguard Goodwick	**87J** Fishguard Goodwick	**84F** Stourbridge	**84K** Chester (GWR)	**83F** Truro	**84B** Oxley	
6824	*6800*	**CARM** Carmarthen	**87F** Llanelly	**83G** Penzance	**83G** Penzance	**83G** Penzance	**81E** Didcot	
6825	*6800*	**PZ** Penzance	**83G** Penzance	**83G** Penzance	**83G** Penzance	**83G** Penzance	**81D** Reading	
6826	*6800*	**SHL** Southall	**83G** Penzance	**83G** Penzance	**83G** Penzance	**83G** Penzance	**81D** Reading	
6827	*6800*	**CDF** Cardiff Canton	**82B** St. Philips Marsh	**82B** St. Philips Marsh	**82B** St. Philips Marsh	**82B** St. Philips Marsh	**84F** Stourbridge	
6828	*6800*	**LDR** Landore	**84F** Stourbridge	**84F** Stourbridge	**84F** Stourbridge	**83F** Truro	**84B** Oxley	
6829	*6800*	**NA** Newton Abbot	**83A** Newton Abbot	**83A** Newton Abbot	**83A** Newton Abbot	**83A** Newton Abbot	**86A** Ebbw Junction	
6830	*6800*	**SPM** St. Philips Marsh	**82B** St. Philips Marsh	**82B** St. Philips Marsh	**82B** St. Philips Marsh	**82B** St. Philips Marsh	**84B** Oxley	
6831	*6800*	**TYS** Tyseley	**6C** Birkenhead	**6C** Birkenhead	**6C** Birkenhead	**82B** St. Philips Marsh	**84B** Oxley	
6832	*6800*	**BAN** Banbury	**82B** St. Philips Marsh	**82C** Swindon	**82C** Swindon	**86C** Cardiff Canton	**87A** Neath	
6833	*6800*	**TYS** Tyseley	**84D** Leamington Spa	**84K** Chester (GWR)	**82B** St. Philips Marsh	**82B** St. Philips Marsh	**84B** Oxley	
6834	*6800*	**STJ** Severn Tunnel Junction	**86A** Ebbw Junction	**81D** Reading	**82B** St. Philips Marsh	**82B** St. Philips Marsh	**81C** Southall	
6835	*6800*	**BAN** Banbury	**84C** Banbury	**84K** Chester (GWR)	**82B** St. Philips Marsh	**82B** St. Philips Marsh	**82B** St. Philips Marsh	
6836	*6800*	**SPM** St. Philips Marsh	**82B** St. Philips Marsh	**83G** Penzance	**83A** Newton Abbot	**83A** Newton Abbot	**86G** Pontypool Road	
6837	*6800*	**NPT** Ebbw Junction	**86C** Cardiff Canton	**83G** Penzance	**83G** Penzance	**83G** Penzance	**87F** Llanelly	
6838	*6800*	**PZ** Penzance	**83G** Penzance	**83D** Laira (Plymouth)	**86A** Ebbw Junction	**86A** Ebbw Junction	**86G** Pontypool Road	
6839	*6800*	**BAN** Banbury	**84C** Banbury	**84C** Banbury	**84B** Oxley	**84B** Oxley	**84B** Oxley	
6840	*6800*	**PPRD** Pontypool Road	**86G** Pontypool Road	**86G** Pontypool Road	**86G** Pontypool Road	**86G** Pontypool Road	**86G** Pontypool Road	
6841	*6800*	**BAN** Banbury	**6C** Birkenhead	**6C** Birkenhead	**6C** Birkenhead	**82B** St. Philips Marsh	**81C** Southall	
6842	*6800*	**SPM** St. Philips Marsh	**82B** St. Philips Marsh	**82B** St. Philips Marsh	**82B** St. Philips Marsh	**82B** St. Philips Marsh	**84F** Stourbridge	
6843	*6800*	**TYS** Tyseley	**84E** Tyseley	**84E** Tyseley	**87F** Llanelly	**87F** Llanelly	**87F** Llanelly	
6844	*6800*	**SRD** Stafford Road	**6C** Birkenhead	**87F** Llanelly	**87F** Llanelly	**87F** Llanelly	**87F** Llanelly	
6845	*6800*	**WES** Westbury	**82B** St. Philips Marsh	**82B** St. Philips Marsh	**83G** Penzance	**83G** Penzance	**84E** Tyseley	
6846	*6800*	**SPM** St. Philips Marsh	**82B** St. Philips Marsh	**82B** St. Philips Marsh	**82B** St. Philips Marsh	**82B** St. Philips Marsh	**82B** St. Philips Marsh	
6847	*6800*	**TYS** Tyseley	**84E** Tyseley	**86A** Ebbw Junction	**86A** Ebbw Junction	**86C** Cardiff Canton	**88L** Cardiff East Dock	
6848	*6800*	**SRD** Stafford Road	**84A** Stafford Road	**87F** Llanelly	**83D** Laira (Plymouth)	**86G** Pontypool Road	**86G** Pontypool Road	
6849	*6800*	**BAN** Banbury	**86G** Pontypool Road	**86G** Pontypool Road	**86A** Ebbw Junction	**83G** Penzance	**81E** Didcot	
6850	*6800*	**SPM** St. Philips Marsh	**82B** St. Philips Marsh	**82C** Swindon	**82C** Swindon	**86A** Ebbw Junction	**86A** Ebbw Junction	
6851	*6800*	**WOS** Worcester	**85A** Worcester	**85A** Worcester	**85A** Worcester	**85A** Worcester	**84B** Oxley	
6852	*6800*	**SPM** St. Philips Marsh	**82B** St. Philips Marsh	**82B** St. Philips Marsh	**82B** St. Philips Marsh	**82B** St. Philips Marsh	**86A** Ebbw Junction	
6853	*6800*	**TYS** Tyseley	**84E** Tyseley	**84E** Tyseley	**84E** Tyseley	**84E** Tyseley	**84E** Tyseley	
6854	*6800*	**BAN** Banbury	**84C** Banbury	**84B** Oxley	**81F** Oxford	**81F** Oxford	**84B** Oxley	
6855	*6800*	**TYS** Tyseley	**83D** Laira (Plymouth)	**83D** Laira (Plymouth)	**83D** Laira (Plymouth)	**84F** Stourbridge	**84B** Oxley	
6856	*6800*	**OXY** Oxley	**84B** Oxley	**84B** Oxley	**83B** Taunton	**85A** Worcester	**85A** Worcester	
6857	*6800*	**LDR** Landore	**84F** Stourbridge	**84F** Stourbridge	**84K** Chester (GWR)	**84B** Oxley	**84B** Oxley	
6858	*6800*	**TYS** Tyseley	**84E** Tyseley	**84E** Tyseley	**83D** Laira (Plymouth)	**81F** Oxford	**84B** Oxley	
6859	*6800*	**CHR** Chester (GWR)	**6C** Birkenhead	**6C** Birkenhead	**6C** Birkenhead	**86C** Cardiff Canton	**88L** Cardiff East Dock	
6860	*6800*	**TYS** Tyseley	**6C** Birkenhead	**83G** Penzance	**83G** Penzance	**83G** Penzance	**82B** St. Philips Marsh	
6861	*6800*	**SPM** St. Philips Marsh	**86G** Pontypool Road	**84B** Oxley	**84E** Tyseley	**84E** Tyseley	**84E** Tyseley	
6862	*6800*	**OXY** Oxley	**84B** Oxley	**84B** Oxley	**84B** Oxley	**84B** Oxley	**84B** Oxley	
6863	*6800*	**SPM** St. Philips Marsh	**82B** St. Philips Marsh	**82B** St. Philips Marsh	**82B** St. Philips Marsh	**83D** Laira (Plymouth)	**81D** Reading	
6864	*6800*	**RDG** Reading	**81D** Reading	**81D** Reading	**81F** Oxford	**86C** Cardiff Canton	**84B** Oxley	
6865	*6800*	**PDN** Old Oak Common	**81D** Reading	**81D** Reading	**86A** Ebbw Junction	**82B** St. Philips Marsh		
6866	*6800*	**TYS** Tyseley	**84E** Tyseley	**84E** Tyseley	**84E** Tyseley	**84E** Tyseley	**84E** Tyseley	
6867	*6800*	**SPM** St. Philips Marsh	**82B** St. Philips Marsh	**82B** St. Philips Marsh	**82B** St. Philips Marsh	**86G** Pontypool Road	**86G** Pontypool Road	
6868	*6800*	**NPT** Ebbw Junction	**83B** Taunton	**83B** Taunton	**83B** Taunton	**83B** Taunton	**81E** Didcot	
6869	*6800*	**PDN** Old Oak Common	**83G** Penzance	**83D** Laira (Plymouth)	**82B** St. Philips Marsh	**87J** Fishguard Goodwick	**81C** Southall	
6870	*6800*	**NPT** Ebbw Junction	**86A** Ebbw Junction	**86A** Ebbw Junction	**82B** St. Philips Marsh	**83G** Penzance	**84B** Oxley	
6871	*6800*	**STJ** Severn Tunnel Junction	**86E** Severn Tunnel Junction	**86G** Pontypool Road	**83F** Truro	**84E** Tyseley	**84B** Oxley	
6872	*6800*	**LDR** Landore	**86E** Severn Tunnel Junction	**86G** Pontypool Road	**86G** Pontypool Road	**86G** Pontypool Road	**86G** Pontypool Road	
6873	*6800*	**STJ** Severn Tunnel Junction	**83D** Laira (Plymouth)	**83D** Laira (Plymouth)	**83D** Laira (Plymouth)	**83D** Laira (Plymouth)	**82B** St. Philips Marsh	
6874	*6800*	**NPT** Ebbw Junction	**86A** Ebbw Junction	**83B** Taunton	**83B** Taunton	**83B** Taunton	**81E** Didcot	
6875	*6800*	**PPRD** Pontypool Road	**83B** Taunton	**83B** Taunton	**83B** Taunton	**83G** Penzance	**88L** Cardiff East Dock	
6876	*6800*	**SPM** St. Philips Marsh	**82B** St. Philips Marsh	**82B** St. Philips Marsh	**82B** St. Philips Marsh	**86A** Ebbw Junction	**86G** Pontypool Road	
6877	*6800*	**WOS** Worcester	**85A** Worcester	**85A** Worcester	**85A** Worcester	**85A** Worcester	**85A** Worcester	
6878	*6800*	**BHD** Birkenhead	**6C** Birkenhead	**6C** Birkenhead	**6C** Birkenhead	**82B** St. Philips Marsh	**82B** St. Philips Marsh	
6879	*6800*	**OXY** Oxley	**84B** Oxley	**84B** Oxley	**84B** Oxley	**84F** Stourbridge	**84E** Tyseley	
6900	*4900*	**PDN** Old Oak Common	**81A** Old Oak Common	**82A** Bristol Bath Road	**82A** Bristol Bath Road	**82B** St. Philips Marsh	**87J** Fishguard Goodwick	
6901	*4900*	**SRD** Stafford Road	**84C** Banbury	**84K** Chester (GWR)	**84K** Chester (GWR)	**86G** Pontypool Road	**86G** Pontypool Road	
6902	*4900*	**SDN** Swindon	**82F** Weymouth	**82F** Weymouth	**82C** Swindon	**82C** Swindon		
6903	*4900*	**LDR** Landore	**87E** Landore	**87E** Landore	**87E** Landore	**86G** Pontypool Road	**86G** Pontypool Road	
6904	*4900*	**TYS** Tyseley	**84E** Tyseley	**84E** Tyseley	**84E** Tyseley	**83A** Newton Abbot	**84C** Banbury	
6905	*4900*	**HFD** Hereford	**85C** Hereford	**87E** Landore	**87E** Landore	**86E** Severn Tunnel Junction	**87A** Neath	
6906	*4900*	**BAN** Banbury	**84C** Banbury	**84C** Banbury	**84C** Banbury	**84C** Banbury	**84C** Banbury	
6907	*4900*	**LA** Laira (Plymouth)	**83D** Laira (Plymouth)	**83D** Laira (Plymouth)	**84B** Oxley	**84B** Oxley	**84B** Oxley	
6908	*4900*	**SRD** Stafford Road	**82B** St. Philips Marsh	**82B** St. Philips Marsh	**82A** Bristol Bath Road	**82B** St. Philips Marsh	**82B** St. Philips Marsh	
6909	*4900*	**SPM** St. Philips Marsh	**82B** St. Philips Marsh	**87J** Fishguard Goodwick	**87F** Llanelly	**87J** Fishguard Goodwick	**81E** Didcot	
6910	*4900*	**PDN** Old Oak Common	**81E** Didcot	**81E** Didcot	**81E** Didcot	**81E** Didcot	**81F** Oxford	
6911	*4900*	**PZ** Penzance	**83G** Penzance	**83G** Penzance	**83F** Truro	**84C** Banbury	**84C** Banbury	
6912	*4900*	**SPM** St. Philips Marsh	**82F** Weymouth	**83D** Laira (Plymouth)	**82C** Swindon	**86E** Severn Tunnel Junction	**88L** Cardiff East Dock	
6913	*4900*	**LA** Laira (Plymouth)	**83D** Laira (Plymouth)	**83D** Laira (Plymouth)	**83D** Laira (Plymouth)	**83D** Laira (Plymouth)	**81D** Reading	
6914	*4900*	**TYS** Tyseley	**82B** St. Philips Marsh	**82D** Westbury	**82D** Westbury	**83B** Taunton	**83B** Taunton	
6915	*4900*	**OXY** Oxley	**82C** Swindon	**82C** Swindon	**82A** Bristol Bath Road	**81E** Didcot	**89A** Shrewsbury	
6916	*4900*	**WOS** Worcester	**85C** Hereford	**85C** Hereford	**85C** Hereford	**84G** Shrewsbury	**89A** Shrewsbury	
6917	*4900*	**GLO** Gloucester	**85B** Gloucester	**85B** Gloucester	**85B** Gloucester	**85B** Gloucester	**84B** Oxley	
6918	*4900*	**LDR** Landore	**87E** Landore	**87E** Landore	**87E** Landore	**87E** Landore	**88L** Cardiff East Dock	
6919	*4900*	**CARM** Carmarthen	**87G** Carmarthen	**87G** Carmarthen	**82F** Weymouth	**82A** Bristol Bath Road	**82B** St. Philips Marsh	
6920	*4900*	**HFD** Hereford	**84B** Oxley	**81F** Oxford	**81F** Oxford	**81A** Old Oak Common	**87B** Duffryn Yard	
6921	*4900*	**WOS** Worcester	**85B** Gloucester	**85B** Gloucester	**83D** Laira (Plymouth)	**83D** Laira (Plymouth)	**83D** Laira (Plymouth)	
6922	*4900*	**SPM** St. Philips Marsh	**82B** St. Philips Marsh	**82D** Westbury	**81F** Oxford	**84G** Shrewsbury	**89A** Shrewsbury	
6923	*4900*	**DID** Didcot	**81D** Reading	**81D** Reading	**81D** Reading	**81D** Reading	**81D** Reading	
6924	*4900*	**SRD** Stafford Road	**84D** Leamington Spa	**84B** Oxley	**81F** Oxford	**81D** Reading	**81D** Reading	
6925	*4900*	**OXF** Oxford	**81F** Oxford	**82B** St. Philips Marsh	**84B** Oxley	**84B** Oxley	**84B** Oxley	
6926	*4900*	**NPT** Ebbw Junction	**81A** Old Oak Common	**84B** Oxley	**84B** Oxley	**84A** Stafford Road	**84E** Tyseley	
6927	*4900*	**NPT** Ebbw Junction	**86A** Ebbw Junction	**81D** Reading	**81D** Reading	**81F** Oxford	**81F** Oxford	
6928	*4900*	**CDF** Cardiff Canton	**86C** Cardiff Canton	**86C** Cardiff Canton	**86C** Cardiff Canton	**86G** Pontypool Road	**86G** Pontypool Road	
6929	*4900*	**BAN** Banbury	**84C** Banbury	**84C** Banbury	**84C** Banbury	**84C** Banbury	**84C** Banbury	
6930	*4900*	**WOS** Worcester	**85A** Worcester	**85A** Worcester	**85A** Worcester	**84A** Stafford Road	**84E** Tyseley	
6931	*4900*	**TR** Truro	**83F** Truro	**83F** Truro	**83F** Truro	**83E** St. Blazey	**88L** Cardiff East Dock	
6932	*4900*	**OXY** Oxley	**81A** Old Oak Common	**86C** Cardiff Canton	**86C** Cardiff Canton	**86C** Cardiff Canton	**88L** Cardiff East Dock	
6933	*4900*	**OXF** Oxford	**81F** Oxford	**83D** Laira (Plymouth)	**83A** Newton Abbot	**87E** Landore	**84B** Oxley	
6934	*4900*	**NA** Newton Abbot	**83A** Newton Abbot	**81C** Southall	**84B** Oxley	**84B** Oxley	**89A** Shrewsbury	
6935	*4900*	**SDN** Swindon	**82D** Westbury	**82D** Westbury	**87G** Carmarthen	**86C** Cardiff Canton	**88L** Cardiff East Dock	
6936	*4900*	**WOS** Worcester	**85C** Hereford	**82B** St. Philips Marsh	**82A** Bristol Bath Road	**86C** Cardiff Canton	**88L** Cardiff East Dock	
6937	*4900*	**OXF** Oxford	**81F** Oxford	**81F** Oxford	**81F** Oxford	**81F** Oxford	**81E** Didcot	
6938	*4900*	**WOS** Worcester	**85A** Worcester	**85B** Gloucester	**83A** Newton Abbot	**83D** Laira (Plymouth)	**81D** Reading	
6939	*4900*	**OXY** Oxley	**86C** Cardiff Canton	**86C** Cardiff Canton	**86C** Cardiff Canton	**86C** Cardiff Canton	**88L** Cardiff East Dock	
6940	*4900*	**GLO** Gloucester	**85B** Gloucester	**83D** Laira (Plymouth)	**83D** Laira (Plymouth)	**83A** Newton Abbot	**82C** Swindon	
6941	*4900*	**CHR** Chester (GWR)	**84K** Chester (GWR)	**84K** Chester (GWR)	**83D** Laira (Plymouth)	**83D** Laira (Plymouth)	**83B** Taunton	
6942	*4900*	**OXY** Oxley	**84B** Oxley	**84B** Oxley	**83E** St. Blazey	**81A** Old Oak Common	**81A** Old Oak Common	
6943	*4900*	**HFD** Hereford	**86C** Cardiff Canton	**86C** Cardiff Canton	**86C** Cardiff Canton	**86C** Cardiff Canton	**85B** Gloucester	
6944	*4900*	**SPM** St. Philips Marsh	**81A** Old Oak Common	**81A** Old Oak Common	**84G** Shrewsbury	**84G** Shrewsbury	**88L** Cardiff East Dock	
6945	*4900*	**WEY** Weymouth	**82F** Weymouth	**82F** Weymouth	**82F** Weymouth	**83G** Penzance	**88L** Cardiff East Dock	
6946	*4900*	**CDF** Cardiff Canton	**86C** Cardiff Canton	**86C** Cardiff Canton	**86C** Cardiff Canton	**86G** Pontypool Road	**86G** Pontypool Road	
6947	*4900*	**WOS** Worcester	**85A** Worcester	**85A** Worcester	**85A** Worcester	**85A** Worcester	**85B** Gloucester	
6948	*4900*	**CDF** Cardiff Canton	**86C** Cardiff Canton	**86C** Cardiff Canton	**86C** Cardiff Canton	**85A** Worcester	**85B** Gloucester	
6949	*4900*	(3955)	**83D** Laira (Plymouth)	**82C** Swindon	**84A** Stafford Road	**84C** Banbury		
6950	*4900*	**WOS** Worcester	**85A** Worcester	**85A** Worcester	**85A** Worcester	**85A** Worcester	**88L** Cardiff East Dock	
6951	*4900*	**WOS** Worcester	**85C** Hereford	**86C** Cardiff Canton	**82A** Bristol Bath Road	**82D** Westbury	**85A** Worcester	
6952	*4900*	**DID** Didcot	**81E** Didcot	**81E** Didcot	**81E** Didcot	**81E** Didcot	**84C** Banbury	
6953	*4900*	(3953)	**81F** Oxford	**81F** Oxford	**81D** Reading	**81D** Reading	**81D** Reading	
6954	*4900*	**SPM** St. Philips Marsh	**82A** Bristol Bath Road	**82B** St. Philips Marsh	**82A** Bristol Bath Road	**82B** St. Philips Marsh	**82B** St. Philips Marsh	

		1948	1951	1954	1957	1960	1963	1966
6955	4900	WES Westbury	82D Westbury	82D Westbury	82D Westbury	82D Westbury	82D Westbury	
6956	4900	OXY Oxley	84A Stafford Road	84G Shrewsbury	84A Stafford Road	84G Shrewsbury	85B Gloucester	
6957	4900	(3952)	82B St. Philips Marsh	82B St. Philips Marsh	82A Bristol Bath Road	82B St. Philips Marsh	88L Cardiff East Dock	
6958	4900	BRD Bristol Bath Road	82A Bristol Bath Road	82B St. Philips Marsh	82A Bristol Bath Road	86G Pontypool Road	86G Pontypool Road	
6959	6959	PDN Old Oak Common	81A Old Oak Common	81A Old Oak Common	81A Old Oak Common	81A Old Oak Common	81A Old Oak Common	
6960	6959	PDN Old Oak Common	81A Old Oak Common	81D Reading	81D Reading	81D Reading	81D Reading	
6961	6959	PDN Old Oak Common	81C Southall	81A Old Oak Common	81A Old Oak Common	81A Old Oak Common	81A Old Oak Common	
6962	6959	PDN Old Oak Common	81A Old Oak Common	81A Old Oak Common	81A Old Oak Common	81A Old Oak Common	81A Old Oak Common	
6963	6959	SALOP Shrewsbury	84G Shrewsbury	84K Chester (GWR)	84K Chester (GWR)	86C Cardiff Canton	81A Old Oak Common	
6964	6959	SRD Stafford Road	84A Stafford Road	84A Stafford Road	84A Stafford Road	84G Shrewsbury	89A Shrewsbury	
6965	6959	SDN Swindon	82A Bristol Bath Road	83D Laira (Plymouth)	83D Laira (Plymouth)	83C Exeter	87G Carmarthen	
6966	6959	WES Westbury	82D Westbury	84C Banbury	82C Swindon	81A Old Oak Common	81A Old Oak Common	
6967	6959	OXY Oxley	84B Oxley	82C Swindon	82F Weymouth	81C Southall	81C Southall	
6968	6959	RDG Reading	81D Reading	81D Reading	81D Reading	81D Reading	87J Fishguard Goodwick	
6969	6959	CDF Cardiff Canton	86C Cardiff Canton	86C Cardiff Canton	86C Cardiff Canton	81E Didcot	81E Didcot	
6970	6959	OXY Oxley	81F Oxford	81F Oxford	81F Oxford	81F Oxford	81F Oxford	
6971	6959	BRD Bristol Bath Road	84E Tyseley	84E Tyseley	84E Tyseley	84E Tyseley	84E Tyseley	
6972	6959	BRD Bristol Bath Road	82A Bristol Bath Road	82A Bristol Bath Road	82A Bristol Bath Road	82A Bristol Bath Road	82B St. Philips Marsh	
6973	6959	PDN Old Oak Common	81A Old Oak Common	81A Old Oak Common	81A Old Oak Common	81A Old Oak Common	81A Old Oak Common	
6974	6959	PDN Old Oak Common	81A Old Oak Common	81A Old Oak Common	81A Old Oak Common	81A Old Oak Common	81C Southall	
6975	6959	OXY Oxley	84B Oxley	84B Oxley	84B Oxley	84B Oxley	87A Neath	
6976	6959	SALOP Shrewsbury	84G Shrewsbury	84C Banbury	84C Banbury	84C Banbury	84C Banbury	
6977	6959	PDN Old Oak Common	82A Bristol Bath Road	82A Bristol Bath Road	82A Bristol Bath Road	82A Bristol Bath Road	82D Westbury	
6978	6959	WES Westbury	82D Westbury	83D Laira (Plymouth)	83D Laira (Plymouth)	81A Old Oak Common	81A Old Oak Common	
6979	6959	BAN Banbury	84C Banbury	84C Banbury	84C Banbury	84C Banbury	84C Banbury	
6980	6959	SALOP Shrewsbury	84G Shrewsbury	84G Shrewsbury	84G Shrewsbury	84B Oxley	84B Oxley	
6981	6959	→	82A Bristol Bath Road	82A Bristol Bath Road	82A Bristol Bath Road	82A Bristol Bath Road	82B St. Philips Marsh	
6982	6959	→	82D Westbury	82A Bristol Bath Road	82B St. Philips Marsh	82A Bristol Bath Road	82B St. Philips Marsh	
6983	6959	→	81A Old Oak Common	81E Didcot	81E Didcot	81E Didcot	81E Didcot	
6984	6959	→	85C Hereford	85C Hereford	85C Hereford	85A Worcester	85A Worcester	
6985	6959	→	85B Gloucester	85B Gloucester	85B Gloucester	85B Gloucester	85B Gloucester	
6986	6959	→	82B St. Philips Marsh	82B St. Philips Marsh	82A Bristol Bath Road	82B St. Philips Marsh	81C Southall	
6987	6959	→	85B Gloucester	85A Worcester	85A Worcester	84A Stafford Road	88L Cardiff East Dock	
6988	6959	→	82F Weymouth	82F Weymouth	83D Laira (Plymouth)	82A Bristol Bath Road	83D Laira (Plymouth)	
6989	6959	→	85C Hereford	85C Hereford	85A Worcester	85A Worcester	85B Gloucester	
6990	6959	→	81F Oxford	81A Old Oak Common	81A Old Oak Common	81A Old Oak Common	81A Old Oak Common	
6991	6959	→	82D Westbury	82D Westbury	81C Southall	81C Southall	81C Southall	
6992	6959	→	85B Gloucester	85C Hereford	85C Hereford	85A Worcester	85A Worcester	
6993	6959	→	82F Weymouth	82F Weymouth	82C Swindon	82C Swindon	85B Gloucester	
6994	6959	→	83C Exeter	83C Exeter	82D Westbury	82D Westbury	81C Southall	
6995	6959	→	83B Taunton	83B Taunton	83B Taunton	83B Taunton	88L Cardiff East Dock	
6996	6959	→	81D Reading	81A Old Oak Common	83B Taunton	81E Didcot	81E Didcot	
6997	6959	→	82A Bristol Bath Road	82A Bristol Bath Road	82A Bristol Bath Road	82A Bristol Bath Road	82B St. Philips Marsh	
6998	6959	→	86C Cardiff Canton	86C Cardiff Canton	86C Cardiff Canton	84G Shrewsbury	81A Old Oak Common	
6999	6959	→	86C Cardiff Canton	86C Cardiff Canton	86C Cardiff Canton	86C Cardiff Canton	82D Westbury	
7000	4073	NA Newton Abbot	83A Newton Abbot	83A Newton Abbot	83A Newton Abbot	85B Gloucester	85B Gloucester	
7001	4073	CDF Cardiff Canton	81A Old Oak Common	81A Old Oak Common	81A Old Oak Common	81A Old Oak Common	84A Stafford Road	
7002	4073	LDR Landore	87E Landore	87E Landore	87G Carmarthen	85A Worcester	85A Worcester	
7003	4073	LDR Landore	87E Landore	87E Landore	87E Landore	82A Bristol Bath Road	85B Gloucester	
7004	4073	GLO Gloucester	81A Old Oak Common	81A Old Oak Common	81A Old Oak Common	81A Old Oak Common	85A Worcester	
7005	4073	WOS Worcester	85A Worcester	85A Worcester	85A Worcester	85A Worcester	85A Worcester	
7006	4073	SALOP Shrewsbury	85B Gloucester	85B Gloucester	85B Gloucester	86C Cardiff Canton	81A Old Oak Common	
7007	4073	SRD Stafford Road	85A Worcester	85A Worcester	85A Worcester	85A Worcester	85A Worcester	
7008	4073	→	81F Oxford	81F Oxford	81A Old Oak Common	81A Old Oak Common	81A Old Oak Common	
7009	4073	→	87E Landore	87E Landore	87E Landore	87E Landore	81A Old Oak Common	
7010	4073	→	81F Oxford	81A Old Oak Common	81A Old Oak Common	81A Old Oak Common	81A Old Oak Common	
7011	4073	→	82A Bristol Bath Road	82A Bristol Bath Road	82A Bristol Bath Road	84C Banbury	85A Worcester	
7012	4073	→	87E Landore	87E Landore	87E Landore	87G Carmarthen	84A Stafford Road	
7013	4073	→	81A Old Oak Common	(4082)				
7013	4073	(4082)	→	81A Old Oak Common	81A Old Oak Common	81A Old Oak Common	85A Worcester	
7014	4073	→	82A Bristol Bath Road	82A Bristol Bath Road	82A Bristol Bath Road	82A Bristol Bath Road	84A Stafford Road	
7015	4073	→	82C Swindon	82C Swindon	82A Bristol Bath Road	84G Shrewsbury	81A Old Oak Common	
7016	4073	→	86C Cardiff Canton	86C Cardiff Canton	87E Landore	87G Carmarthen		
7017	4073	→	86C Cardiff Canton	86C Cardiff Canton	81A Old Oak Common	81A Old Oak Common	81A Old Oak Common	
7018	4073	→	87E Landore	87E Landore	82A Bristol Bath Road	82A Bristol Bath Road	81A Old Oak Common	
7019	4073	→	82A Bristol Bath Road	82A Bristol Bath Road	82A Bristol Bath Road	82A Bristol Bath Road	84A Stafford Road	
7020	4073	→	86C Cardiff Canton	86C Cardiff Canton	86C Cardiff Canton	81A Old Oak Common	81A Old Oak Common	
7021	4073	→	87E Landore	87E Landore	87E Landore	87E Landore	81A Old Oak Common	
7022	4073	→	86C Cardiff Canton	86C Cardiff Canton	86C Cardiff Canton	83D Laira (Plymouth)	83D Laira (Plymouth)	
7023	4073	→	86C Cardiff Canton	86C Cardiff Canton	86C Cardiff Canton	86C Cardiff Canton	85A Worcester	
7024	4073	→	81A Old Oak Common	81A Old Oak Common	81A Old Oak Common	81A Old Oak Common	84A Stafford Road	
7025	4073	→	81A Old Oak Common	81A Old Oak Common	81A Old Oak Common	81A Old Oak Common	85A Worcester	
7026	4073	→	84A Stafford Road	84A Stafford Road	84A Stafford Road	84A Stafford Road	84A Stafford Road	
7027	4073	→	83D Laira (Plymouth)	81A Old Oak Common	81A Old Oak Common	81A Old Oak Common	85A Worcester	
7028	4073	→	87E Landore	87E Landore	87G Carmarthen	87E Landore	87F Llanelly	
7029	4073	→	83A Newton Abbot	83A Newton Abbot	83D Laira (Plymouth)	83A Newton Abbot	81A Old Oak Common	
7030	4073	→	81A Old Oak Common	81A Old Oak Common	81A Old Oak Common	81A Old Oak Common	81A Old Oak Common	
7031	4073	→	83D Laira (Plymouth)	83D Laira (Plymouth)	83D Laira (Plymouth)	82C Swindon	85A Worcester	
7032	4073	→	81A Old Oak Common	81A Old Oak Common	81A Old Oak Common	81A Old Oak Common	81A Old Oak Common	
7033	4073	→	81A Old Oak Common	81A Old Oak Common	81A Old Oak Common	81A Old Oak Common	81A Old Oak Common	
7034	4073	→	82A Bristol Bath Road	82A Bristol Bath Road	82A Bristol Bath Road	82A Bristol Bath Road	85B Gloucester	
7035	4073	→	84G Shrewsbury	85B Gloucester	82A Bristol Bath Road	87E Landore	81F Oxford	
7036	4073	→	81A Old Oak Common	81A Old Oak Common	81A Old Oak Common	81A Old Oak Common	81A Old Oak Common	
7037	4073	→	82C Swindon	82C Swindon	82C Swindon	82C Swindon	82C Swindon	
7200	7200	NA Newton Abbot	83A Newton Abbot	87E Landore	87E Landore	87E Landore	87F Llanelly	
7201	7200	CDF Cardiff Canton	86C Cardiff Canton	82B St. Philips Marsh	86G Pontypool Road	86G Pontypool Road	86G Pontypool Road	
7202	7200	STJ Severn Tunnel Junction	88A Cardiff Cathays	88A Cardiff Cathays	88A Cardiff Cathays	88A Radyr	88C Barry	
7203	7200	NPT Ebbw Junction	86A Ebbw Junction	86A Ebbw Junction	87F Llanelly	86J Aberdare	87A Neath	
7204	7200	DID Didcot	87A Neath	85C Hereford	86G Pontypool Road	86A Ebbw Junction	87A Neath	
7205	7200	ABDR Aberdare	88A Cardiff Cathays	88A Cardiff Cathays	88A Cardiff Cathays	88A Radyr	88B Radyr	
7206	7200	PPRD Pontypool Road	86G Pontypool Road	86G Pontypool Road	86G Pontypool Road	86E Severn Tunnel Junction	86E Severn Tunnel Junction	
7207	7200	OXY Oxley	84B Oxley	87E Landore	87E Landore	87E Landore	84C Banbury	
7208	7200	SPM St. Philips Marsh	84D Leamington Spa	86E Severn Tunnel Junction	86E Severn Tunnel Junction	86E Severn Tunnel Junction	88C Barry	
7209	7200	STJ Severn Tunnel Junction	83A Newton Abbot	87E Landore	87E Landore	87E Landore	88J Aberdare	
7210	7200	STJ Severn Tunnel Junction	86C Cardiff Canton	86A Ebbw Junction	86A Ebbw Junction	86G Pontypool Road	86G Pontypool Road	
7211	7200	SED Swansea East Dock	87E Landore	87F Llanelly	87F Llanelly	86A Ebbw Junction	87F Llanelly	
7212	7200	NPT Ebbw Junction	86E Severn Tunnel Junction	81F Oxford	86A Ebbw Junction	86A Ebbw Junction	86E Severn Tunnel Junction	
7213	7200	ABDR Aberdare	86J Aberdare	86J Aberdare	86G Pontypool Road	86G Pontypool Road	84B Oxley	
7214	7200	DID Didcot	86A Ebbw Junction	86A Ebbw Junction	86A Ebbw Junction	86J Aberdare	88J Aberdare	
7215	7200	SPM St. Philips Marsh	86A Ebbw Junction	87F Llanelly	87F Llanelly	87D Swansea East Dock	87D Swansea East Dock	
7216	7200	STJ Severn Tunnel Junction	86E Severn Tunnel Junction	86J Aberdare	86J Aberdare	86J Aberdare	87B Duffryn Yard	
7217	7200	NPT Ebbw Junction	86A Ebbw Junction	87E Landore	87E Landore	86A Ebbw Junction	86E Severn Tunnel Junction	
7218	7200	LMTN Leamington Spa	84D Leamington Spa	86A Ebbw Junction	86A Ebbw Junction	86A Ebbw Junction	84C Banbury	
7219	7200	CDF Cardiff Canton	86C Cardiff Canton	86A Ebbw Junction	86A Ebbw Junction	86A Ebbw Junction	86A Ebbw Junction	
7220	7200	NA Newton Abbot	83A Newton Abbot	87A Neath	86G Pontypool Road	86G Pontypool Road	86G Pontypool Road	
7221	7200	ABDR Aberdare	86J Aberdare	86J Aberdare	86J Aberdare	86J Aberdare	88C Barry	
7222	7200	OXY Oxley	85A Worcester	85C Hereford	86A Ebbw Junction	86A Ebbw Junction	87B Duffryn Yard	
7223	7200	STJ Severn Tunnel Junction	86E Severn Tunnel Junction	86E Severn Tunnel Junction	86E Severn Tunnel Junction	86E Severn Tunnel Junction	86A Ebbw Junction	
7224	7200	STJ Severn Tunnel Junction	86E Severn Tunnel Junction	87D Swansea East Dock	87D Swansea East Dock	86J Aberdare		
7225	7200	LDR Landore	87E Landore	87F Llanelly	87F Llanelly	87D Swansea East Dock	87D Swansea East Dock	
7226	7200	OXY Oxley	84B Oxley	87D Swansea East Dock	87D Swansea East Dock	87D Swansea East Dock	87D Swansea East Dock	
7227	7200	OXY Oxley	84B Oxley	86A Ebbw Junction	86A Ebbw Junction	86G Pontypool Road	86G Pontypool Road	
7228	7200	DID Didcot	87F Llanelly	87F Llanelly	87F Llanelly	87F Llanelly	88C Barry	
7229	7200	STJ Severn Tunnel Junction	86E Severn Tunnel Junction	86E Severn Tunnel Junction	86A Ebbw Junction	86A Ebbw Junction	87B Duffryn Yard	

No.	Class	1948	1951	1954	1957	1960	1963	1966
7230	7200	PPRD Pontypool Road	86E Severn Tunnel Junction	86E Severn Tunnel Junction	88C Barry	87E Landore	89B Croes Newydd	
7231	7200	NPT Ebbw Junction	86A Ebbw Junction	86A Ebbw Junction	86A Ebbw Junction	86A Ebbw Junction	88C Barry	
7232	7200	PPRD Pontypool Road	86C Cardiff Canton	86A Ebbw Junction	86A Ebbw Junction	87F Llanelly	87F Llanelly	
7233	7200	PPRD Pontypool Road	86G Pontypool Road	86G Pontypool Road	86G Pontypool Road	86A Ebbw Junction	86A Ebbw Junction	
7234	7200	SPM St. Philips Marsh	86G Pontypool Road	86G Pontypool Road	86G Pontypool Road	86A Ebbw Junction	88J Aberdare	
7235	7200	PPRD Pontypool Road	86G Pontypool Road	86G Pontypool Road	86G Pontypool Road	87F Llanelly	87F Llanelly	
7236	7200	OXY Oxley	85A Worcester	87E Landore	87E Landore	87E Landore	84C Banbury	
7237	7200	SPM St. Philips Marsh	84D Leamington Spa	86E Severn Tunnel Junction	86E Severn Tunnel Junction	86J Aberdare	87F Llanelly	
7238	7200	OXY Oxley	84B Oxley	81F Oxford	81F Oxford	81F Oxford	86A Ebbw Junction	
7239	7200	STJ Severn Tunnel Junction	86E Severn Tunnel Junction	81F Oxford	81F Oxford	81F Oxford	87F Llanelly	
7240	7200	OXY Oxley	85A Worcester	87F Llanelly	87F Llanelly	86A Ebbw Junction	86A Ebbw Junction	
7241	7200	NPT Ebbw Junction	86A Ebbw Junction	86A Ebbw Junction	88C Barry	88C Barry		
7242	7200	ABDR Aberdare	86J Aberdare	88A Cardiff Cathays	88A Cardiff Cathays	88A Radyr	88B Radyr	
7243	7200	OXY Oxley	84B Oxley	86A Ebbw Junction	86A Ebbw Junction	86A Ebbw Junction	87A Neath	
7244	7200	LDR Landore	87E Landore	87B Duffryn Yard	87B Duffryn Yard	87B Duffryn Yard	87F Llanelly	
7245	7200	NPT Ebbw Junction	86A Ebbw Junction	86A Ebbw Junction	86A Ebbw Junction	86A Ebbw Junction	86A Ebbw Junction	
7246	7200	STJ Severn Tunnel Junction	86E Severn Tunnel Junction	86E Severn Tunnel Junction	86A Ebbw Junction	86G Pontypool Road	86G Pontypool Road	
7247	7200	NPT Ebbw Junction	86A Ebbw Junction	86A Ebbw Junction	84B Oxley	84B Oxley	88J Aberdare	
7248	7200	OXY Oxley	85A Worcester	87D Swansea East Dock	87E Landore	87D Swansea East Dock	87A Neath	
7249	7200	NPT Ebbw Junction	86A Ebbw Junction	86A Ebbw Junction	87B Duffryn Yard	87B Duffryn Yard	87B Duffryn Yard	
7250	7200	NA Newton Abbot	83A Newton Abbot	82B St. Philips Marsh	82B St. Philips Marsh	86A Ebbw Junction	88B Radyr	
7251	7200	STJ Severn Tunnel Junction	86E Severn Tunnel Junction	86E Severn Tunnel Junction	86A Ebbw Junction	86G Pontypool Road	86G Pontypool Road	
7252	7200	DID Didcot	86A Ebbw Junction	86A Ebbw Junction	88C Barry	88A Radyr	88B Radyr	
7253	7200	NPT Ebbw Junction	86A Ebbw Junction	86A Ebbw Junction	86A Ebbw Junction	86A Ebbw Junction	86A Ebbw Junction	
7300	4300	WES Westbury	82D Westbury	82D Westbury	82D Westbury	82D Westbury		
7301	4300	WOS Worcester	85A Worcester	85D Kidderminster	85C Hereford	82B St. Philips Marsh		
7302	4300	WES Westbury	82D Westbury	82D Westbury	82D Westbury	82D Westbury		
7303	4300	CHEL Cheltenham	85B Gloucester	82B St. Philips Marsh	82B St. Philips Marsh	71G Weymouth	88L Cardiff East Dock	
7304	4300	TN Taunton	83B Taunton	83B Taunton	83B Taunton	83B Taunton	83B Taunton	
7305	4300	CNYD Croes Newydd	84J Croes Newydd	84J Croes Newydd	84B Oxley	84C Banbury		
7306	4300	NEY Neyland	87H Neyland	87H Neyland	87H Neyland	87H Neyland	87G Carmarthen	
7307	4300	OXY Oxley	85C Hereford	85C Hereford	87F Llanelly	87F Llanelly	87F Llanelly	
7308	4300	WOS Worcester	85C Hereford	85C Hereford	85C Hereford	84C Banbury	86E Severn Tunnel Junction	
7309	4300	WES Westbury	81C Southall	84A Stafford Road	84G Shrewsbury	84G Shrewsbury		
7310	4300	CNYD Croes Newydd	84J Croes Newydd	84J Croes Newydd	84J Croes Newydd	84J Croes Newydd	89B Croes Newydd	
7311	4300	OXY Oxley	84B Oxley	83B Taunton	83B Taunton	83C Exeter		
7312	4300	CHEL Cheltenham	85B Gloucester	85B Gloucester	85B Gloucester	85B Gloucester	87F Llanelly	
7313	4300	CHR Chester (GWR)	84J Croes Newydd	84J Croes Newydd	84J Croes Newydd	84J Croes Newydd		
7314	4300	TN Taunton	85C Hereford	85C Hereford	87F Llanelly	87F Llanelly	89A Shrewsbury	
7315	4300	SRD Stafford Road	84A Stafford Road	84C Banbury	84C Banbury	84C Banbury	87F Llanelly	
7316	4300	EXE Exeter	83C Exeter	83C Exeter	83C Exeter	83C Exeter		
7317	4300	OXY Oxley	84E Tyseley	84E Tyseley	84E Tyseley	84E Tyseley	88L Cardiff East Dock	
7318	4300	RDG Reading	81D Reading	87F Llanelly	87H Neyland	87H Neyland	87H Neyland	
7319	4300	SALOP Shrewsbury	84G Shrewsbury	86A Ebbw Junction	86A Ebbw Junction	85B Gloucester	87F Llanelly	
7320	4300	RDG Reading	81D Reading	87F Llanelly	87F Llanelly	87H Neyland	87H Neyland	
7321	4300	SDN Swindon	82C Swindon	82C Swindon	85A Worcester	87F Llanelly		
7322	4300	(9300)	→	→	→	86E Severn Tunnel Junction		
7323	4300	(9301)	→	→	82B St. Philips Marsh	82B St. Philips Marsh		
7324	4300	(9302)	→	→	→	81E Didcot		
7325	4300	(9303)	→	→	→	86G Pontypool Road	86E Severn Tunnel Junction	
7326	4300	(9304)	→	→	→	85C Hereford	83B Taunton	
7327	4300	(9305)	→	→	→	81E Didcot	81E Didcot	
7328	4300	(9306)	→	→	→	86E Severn Tunnel Junction		
7329	4300	(9307)	→	→	84B Oxley	84G Shrewsbury	89A Shrewsbury	
7330	4300	(9308)	→	→	→	84G Shrewsbury		
7331	4300	(9309)	→	→	→	81D Reading		
7332	4300	(9310)	→	→	→	86C Cardiff Canton	82D Westbury	
7333	4300	(9311)	→	→	→	83D Laira (Plymouth)	83B Taunton	
7334	4300	(9312)	→	→	→	86G Pontypool Road		
7335	4300	(9313)	→	→	→	83D Laira (Plymouth)	85B Gloucester	
7336	4300	(9314)	→	→	→	84G Shrewsbury		
7337	4300	(9315)	→	→	→	82C Swindon	83B Taunton	
7338	4300	(9316)	→	→	→	85B Gloucester		
7339	4300	(9317)	→	→	84B Oxley	84B Oxley	89B Croes Newydd	
7340	4300	(9318)	→	→	→	87H Neyland	81E Didcot	
7341	4300	(9319)	→	→	→	84J Croes Newydd		
7400	7400	CARM Carmarthen	87G Carmarthen	87G Carmarthen	87G Carmarthen	87G Carmarthen		
7401	7400	CARM Carmarthen	87G Carmarthen	87G Carmarthen	87G Carmarthen			
7402	7400	STB Stourbridge	84F Stourbridge	89C Machynlleth	87G Carmarthen	87G Carmarthen		
7403	7400	CNYD Croes Newydd	84J Croes Newydd	84J Croes Newydd	84J Croes Newydd	84J Croes Newydd	86E Severn Tunnel Junction	
7404	7400	OXF Oxford	81F Oxford	81F Oxford	81F Oxford	81F Oxford	81F Oxford	
7405	7400	OSW Oswestry	89A Oswestry	89A Oswestry	89A Oswestry	89A Oswestry	87G Carmarthen	
7406	7400	ABH Aberystwyth	89C Machynlleth	89C Machynlleth	89C Machynlleth	89C Machynlleth		
7407	7400	CARM Carmarthen	87G Carmarthen	87G Carmarthen	87G Carmarthen	87G Carmarthen	87G Carmarthen	
7408	7400	WEY Weymouth	82F Weymouth	82F Weymouth	87K Swansea Victoria	87D Swansea East Dock		
7409	7400	CNYD Croes Newydd	84J Croes Newydd	84J Croes Newydd	84J Croes Newydd	84J Croes Newydd		
7410	7400	OSW Oswestry	89A Oswestry	89A Oswestry	89A Oswestry	89A Oswestry		
7411	7400	OXF Oxford	81F Oxford	81F Oxford	81F Oxford			
7412	7400	OXF Oxford	81F Oxford	81F Oxford	81F Oxford	81F Oxford	81F Oxford	
7413	7400	FGD Fishguard Goodwick	87H Neyland	87H Neyland	82C Swindon	82C Swindon	86C Hereford	
7414	7400	CNYD Croes Newydd	84J Croes Newydd	84J Croes Newydd	84J Croes Newydd	84J Croes Newydd	89B Croes Newydd	
7415	7400	SDN Swindon	82C Swindon	82C Swindon	82C Swindon			
7416	7400	WOS Worcester	85C Hereford	85C Hereford	85C Hereford			
7417	7400	WTD Whitland	89C Machynlleth	89C Machynlleth	89C Machynlleth	89C Machynlleth		
7418	7400	SDN Swindon	82C Swindon	82C Swindon	82C Swindon	85C Hereford	89B Croes Newydd	
7419	7400	CARM Carmarthen	87G Carmarthen	87G Carmarthen	87G Carmarthen	87G Carmarthen		
7420	7400	HFD Hereford	85C Hereford	85C Hereford	84F Stourbridge			
7421	7400	TN Taunton	83B Taunton	82F Weymouth	82C Swindon	82C Swindon		
7422	7400	TR Truro	83F Truro	83F Truro	83F Truro	87G Carmarthen		
7423	7400	ABDR Aberdare	86J Aberdare	86J Aberdare	86J Aberdare	86J Aberdare	88J Aberdare	
7424	7400	SDN Swindon	82C Swindon	82C Swindon	82C Swindon	84E Tyseley	84E Tyseley	
7425	7400	CARM Carmarthen	87G Carmarthen	87G Carmarthen	87G Carmarthen	87G Carmarthen		
7426	7400	PPRD Pontypool Road	86G Pontypool Road	86G Pontypool Road	86E Severn Tunnel Junction	85C Hereford	84E Tyseley	
7427	7400	NA Newton Abbot	83A Newton Abbot	83A Newton Abbot	83A Newton Abbot	82C Swindon	86E Severn Tunnel Junction	
7428	7400	STB Stourbridge	84F Stourbridge	84F Stourbridge	84F Stourbridge	84J Croes Newydd		
7429	7400	STJ Severn Tunnel Junction	84F Stourbridge	84F Stourbridge	84F Stourbridge	84F Stourbridge		
7430	7400	→	84F Stourbridge	84F Stourbridge	84F Stourbridge	84F Stourbridge	84F Stourbridge	
7431	7400	→	84J Croes Newydd	84J Croes Newydd	84J Croes Newydd	84J Croes Newydd	89B Croes Newydd	
7432	7400	→	84J Croes Newydd	84F Stourbridge	84F Stourbridge	84F Stourbridge	84F Stourbridge	
7433	7400	→	84J Croes Newydd	84J Croes Newydd	84J Croes Newydd	84J Croes Newydd		
7434	7400	→	89A Oswestry	89A Oswestry	89A Oswestry	89C Machynlleth		
7435	7400	→	84F Stourbridge	84F Stourbridge	84F Stourbridge	84F Stourbridge	84F Stourbridge	
7436	7400	→	81F Oxford	81F Oxford	81F Oxford	83B Taunton	83B Taunton	
7437	7400	→	85A Worcester	85C Hereford	85C Hereford	85C Hereford	86C Hereford	
7438	7400	→	84E Tyseley	84E Tyseley	84E Tyseley			
7439	7400	→	87K Swansea Victoria	87K Swansea Victoria	87G Carmarthen	87C Danygraig	87G Carmarthen	
7440	7400	→	84J Croes Newydd	84J Croes Newydd	84J Croes Newydd	84J Croes Newydd		
7441	7400	→	81B Slough	84F Stourbridge	84F Stourbridge	84F Stourbridge	84F Stourbridge	
7442	7400	→	81B Slough	84J Croes Newydd	84J Croes Newydd	84J Croes Newydd	89B Croes Newydd	
7443	7400	→	84J Croes Newydd	84J Croes Newydd	84J Croes Newydd	84J Croes Newydd	89B Croes Newydd	
7444	7400	→	87G Carmarthen	87G Carmarthen	87G Carmarthen	87G Carmarthen	87G Carmarthen	
7445	7400	→	88A Cardiff Cathays	88A Cardiff Cathays	88A Cardiff Cathays	81F Oxford	87G Carmarthen	
7446	7400	→	83E St. Blazey	83E St. Blazey	83E St. Blazey	83E St. Blazey	89D Oswestry	
7447	7400	→	84J Croes Newydd	84J Croes Newydd	84F Stourbridge			

		1948	1951	1954	1957	1960	1963	1966
7448	*7400*	→	**84F** Stourbridge	**84F** Stourbridge	**84F** Stourbridge	**84F** Stourbridge	**87G** Carmarthen	
7449	*7400*	→	**84F** Stourbridge	**84F** Stourbridge	**84F** Stourbridge	**84F** Stourbridge	**84F** Stourbridge	
7700	*5700*	**KDR** Kidderminster	**85D** Kidderminster	**85D** Kidderminster	**85B** Gloucester	**85B** Gloucester		
7701	*5700*	**NEA** Neath	**87A** Neath	**87A** Neath	**87A** Neath	**87A** Neath		
7702	*5700*	**LMTN** Leamington Spa	**84D** Leamington Spa	**84D** Leamington Spa	**84D** Leamington Spa	**84D** Leamington Spa		
7703	*5700*	**ABEEG** Aberbeeg	**86H** Aberbeeg	**86H** Aberbeeg	**86H** Aberbeeg	**86B** Newport Pill		
7704	*5700*	**SED** Swansea East Dock	**87D** Swansea East Dock	**87D** Swansea East Dock	**87D** Swansea East Dock	**87D** Swansea East Dock		
7705	*5700*	**STB** Stourbridge	**84F** Stourbridge	**84F** Stourbridge	**84F** Stourbridge			
7706	*5700*	**DYD** Duffryn Yard	**87B** Duffryn Yard	**87B** Duffryn Yard	**87B** Duffryn Yard	**87B** Duffryn Yard		
7707	*5700*	**HFD** Hereford	**85C** Hereford	**85C** Hereford	**85A** Worcester	**85A** Worcester		
7708	*5700*	**RDG** Reading	**81D** Reading	**81D** Reading	**81D** Reading	**81D** Reading		
7709	*5700*	**SBZ** St. Blazey	**83E** St. Blazey	**83E** St. Blazey	**83E** St. Blazey	**83E** St. Blazey		
7710	*5700*	**DID** Didcot	**81E** Didcot	**81E** Didcot	**81E** Didcot			
7711	*5700*	**SPM** St. Philips Marsh	**82B** St. Philips Marsh	**83C** Exeter				
7712	*5700*	**NPT** Ebbw Junction	**86B** Newport Pill	**86B** Newport Pill	**86B** Newport Pill	**86G** Pontypool Road		
7713	*5700*	**PDN** Old Oak Common	**84E** Tyseley	**84E** Tyseley	**84E** Tyseley	**83B** Taunton		
7714	*5700*	**BHD** Birkenhead	**6C** Birkenhead	**6C** Birkenhead	**6C** Birkenhead			
7715	*5700*	**SBZ** St. Blazey	**83E** St. Blazey	**83E** St. Blazey	**83E** St. Blazey	**83E** St. Blazey	**87B** Duffryn Yard	
7716	*5700*	**EXE** Exeter	**83C** Exeter	**83C** Exeter	**83C** Exeter			
7717	*5700*	**MTHR** Merthyr	**88D** Merthyr	**88D** Merthyr	**88D** Merthyr	**88C** Barry		
7718	*5700*	**SPM** St. Philips Marsh	**82B** St. Philips Marsh	**82B** St. Philips Marsh	**87F** Llanelly	**87F** Llanelly		
7719	*5700*	**SPM** St. Philips Marsh	**82B** St. Philips Marsh	**82B** St. Philips Marsh	**82B** St. Philips Marsh	**85C** Hereford		
7720	*5700*	**ABEEG** Aberbeeg	**86J** Aberdare	**86J** Aberdare	**86J** Aberdare	**86J** Aberdare		
7721	*5700*	**LTS** Llantrisant	**86H** Aberbeeg	**86B** Newport Pill	**86B** Newport Pill	**86K** Tredegar		
7722	*5700*	**THT** Treherbert	**88F** Treherbert	**88B** Cardiff East Dock	**88B** Cardiff East Dock	**81A** Old Oak Common		
7723	*5700*	**GLO** Gloucester	**85B** Gloucester	**85B** Gloucester	**85B** Gloucester	**85E** Gloucester Barnwood		
7724	*5700*	**PPRD** Pontypool Road	**86G** Pontypool Road	**86G** Pontypool Road	**86G** Pontypool Road	**86G** Pontypool Road		
7725	*5700*	**TDU** Tondu	**86F** Tondu	**86F** Tondu	**86F** Tondu	**86F** Tondu		
7726	*5700*	**SPM** St. Philips Marsh	**82B** St. Philips Marsh	**88A** Cardiff Cathays	**88A** Cardiff Cathays	**88E** Abercynon		
7727	*5700*	**WES** Westbury	**82D** Westbury	**82D** Westbury	**82D** Westbury	**82D** Westbury		
7728	*5700*	**SPM** St. Philips Marsh	**82B** St. Philips Marsh	**82B** St. Philips Marsh	**82B** St. Philips Marsh	**82B** St. Philips Marsh		
7729	*5700*	**SPM** St. Philips Marsh	**82B** St. Philips Marsh	**82B** St. Philips Marsh	**82B** St. Philips Marsh	**82B** St. Philips Marsh		
7730	*5700*	**SHL** Southall	**81C** Southall	**81C** Southall	**81C** Southall			
7731	*5700*	**SHL** Southall	**81C** Southall	**81C** Southall	**81C** Southall			
7732	*5700*	**SHL** Southall	**81C** Southall	**81C** Southall	**86F** Tondu	**86F** Tondu		
7733	*5700*	**DYD** Duffryn Yard	**87B** Duffryn Yard	**87B** Duffryn Yard	**88E** Abercynon	**88E** Abercynon		
7734	*5700*	**PDN** Old Oak Common	**81A** Old Oak Common	**81A** Old Oak Common	**81A** Old Oak Common			
7735	*5700*	**TYS** Tyseley	**84E** Tyseley	**84E** Tyseley	**84E** Tyseley			
7736	*5700*	**NPT** Ebbw Junction	**86A** Ebbw Junction	**86A** Ebbw Junction	**86A** Ebbw Junction	**86K** Tredegar		
7737	*5700*	**NEA** Neath	**87A** Neath	**87A** Neath	**87A** Neath	**87A** Neath		
7738	*5700*	**PDN** Old Oak Common	**88A** Cardiff Cathays	**88A** Cardiff Cathays	**88B** Cardiff East Dock			
7739	*5700*	**NEA** Neath	**87A** Neath	**87A** Neath	**87A** Neath	**87A** Neath		
7740	*5700*	**ABEEG** Aberbeeg	**86G** Pontypool Road	**86G** Pontypool Road	**86G** Pontypool Road	**86G** Pontypool Road		
7741	*5700*	**GLO** Gloucester	**85B** Gloucester	**85B** Gloucester	**85B** Gloucester	**85B** Gloucester		
7742	*5700*	**NEA** Neath	**87A** Neath	**87A** Neath	**87A** Neath			
7743	*5700*	**NEA** Neath	**87A** Neath	**87A** Neath	**87A** Neath			
7744	*5700*	**DYD** Duffryn Yard	**87B** Duffryn Yard	**87B** Duffryn Yard	**88E** Abercynon	**88E** Abercynon		
7745	*5700*	**LLY** Llanelly	**87F** Llanelly	**87F** Llanelly	**87F** Llanelly	**87F** Llanelly		
7746	*5700*	**TDU** Tondu	**86F** Tondu	**86F** Tondu	**86F** Tondu			
7747	*5700*	**FGD** Fishguard Goodwick	**87J** Fishguard Goodwick	**87J** Fishguard Goodwick	**87J** Fishguard Goodwick	**87J** Fishguard Goodwick		
7748	*5700*	**ABDR** Aberdare	**86J** Aberdare	**82D** Westbury	**82D** Westbury	**82D** Westbury		
7749	*5700*	**SPM** St. Philips Marsh	**82B** St. Philips Marsh	**82B** St. Philips Marsh	**82B** St. Philips Marsh	**82B** St. Philips Marsh		
7750	*5700*	**WOS** Worcester	**85A** Worcester	**85A** Worcester	**85A** Worcester			
7751	*5700*	**CED** Cardiff East Dock	**88B** Cardiff East Dock	**88B** Cardiff East Dock	**88A** Cardiff Cathays			
7752	*5700*	**TDU** Tondu	**86F** Tondu	**86F** Tondu	**86F** Tondu			
7753	*5700*	**NPT** Ebbw Junction	**86A** Ebbw Junction	**86F** Tondu	**86F** Tondu	**86F** Tondu		
7754	*5700*	**PDN** Old Oak Common	**84H** Wellington	**84H** Wellington	**84H** Wellington			
7755	*5700*	**LLY** Llanelly	**87F** Llanelly	**87G** Carmarthen	**86A** Ebbw Junction	**86H** Aberbeeg		
7756	*5700*	**SED** Swansea East Dock	**87D** Swansea East Dock	**87D** Swansea East Dock	**87D** Swansea East Dock	**85E** Gloucester Barnwood		
7757	*5700*	**NEA** Neath	**87A** Neath	**87A** Neath	**87A** Neath	**87A** Neath		
7758	*5700*	**TYS** Tyseley	**84E** Tyseley	**84E** Tyseley	**84E** Tyseley	**87B** Duffryn Yard		
7759	*5700*	**OXY** Oxley	**84B** Oxley	**84B** Oxley	**84B** Oxley	**84B** Oxley		
7760	*5700*	**PDN** Old Oak Common	**81F** Oxford	**81F** Oxford	**81F** Oxford	**81F** Oxford		
7761	*5700*	**EXE** Exeter	**83C** Exeter	**83C** Exeter	**83C** Exeter	**84C** Banbury		
7762	*5700*	**LA** Laira (Plymouth)	**83D** Laira (Plymouth)	**83D** Laira (Plymouth)	**83D** Laira (Plymouth)	**6E** Chester (GWR)		
7763	*5700*	**BAN** Banbury	**84C** Banbury	**84C** Banbury	**84E** Tyseley			
7764	*5700*	**STJ** Severn Tunnel Junction	**86E** Severn Tunnel Junction	**86E** Severn Tunnel Junction	**86E** Severn Tunnel Junction	**86E** Severn Tunnel Junction		
7765	*5700*	**LLY** Llanelly	**87F** Llanelly	**87F** Llanelly	**87F** Llanelly	**87F** Llanelly		
7766	*5700*	**MTHR** Merthyr	**88D** Merthyr	**88D** Merthyr	**88D** Merthyr	**88C** Barry		
7767	*5700*	**NEA** Neath	**87A** Neath	**87A** Neath	**87A** Neath	**87A** Neath		
7768	*5700*	**NPT** Ebbw Junction	**86A** Ebbw Junction	**86A** Ebbw Junction	**86A** Ebbw Junction			
7769	*5700*	**NEA** Neath	**87A** Neath	**87A** Neath	**87A** Neath			
7770	*5700*	**TDU** Tondu	**86F** Tondu	**86F** Tondu	**86F** Tondu			
7771	*5700*	**NPT** Ebbw Junction	**86A** Ebbw Junction	**86A** Ebbw Junction	**86A** Ebbw Junction	**86K** Tredegar		
7772	*5700*	**MTHR** Merthyr	**88D** Merthyr	**88D** Merthyr	**88A** Cardiff Cathays	**81E** Didcot		
7773	*5700*	**ABDR** Aberdare	**86J** Aberdare	**86J** Aberdare	**86J** Aberdare			
7774	*5700*	**PILL** Newport Pill	**86B** Newport Pill	**86B** Newport Pill	**86H** Aberbeeg			
7775	*5700*	**TDU** Tondu	**86H** Aberbeeg	**86H** Aberbeeg	**86C** Cardiff Canton	**86C** Cardiff Canton		
7776	*5700*	**LLY** Llanelly	**87F** Llanelly	**87F** Llanelly	**87F** Llanelly	**87F** Llanelly		
7777	*5700*	**RDG** Reading	**81D** Reading	**81D** Reading	**85A** Worcester	**85A** Worcester		
7778	*5700*	**ABEEG** Aberbeeg	**86H** Aberbeeg	**86F** Tondu	**86F** Tondu			
7779	*5700*	**SPM** St. Philips Marsh	**82B** St. Philips Marsh	**88A** Cardiff Cathays	**88A** Cardiff Cathays			
7780	*5700*	**SPM** St. Philips Marsh	**82B** St. Philips Marsh	**82B** St. Philips Marsh	**82B** St. Philips Marsh	**71G** Weymouth	**71G** Weymouth	
7781	*5700*	**NPT** Ebbw Junction	**86A** Ebbw Junction	**86A** Ebbw Junction	**86A** Ebbw Junction	**86A** Ebbw Junction		
7782	*5700*	**SPM** St. Philips Marsh	**82B** St. Philips Marsh	**82A** Bristol Bath Road	**82F** Weymouth	**71G** Weymouth	**71G** Weymouth	
7783	*5700*	**SPM** St. Philips Marsh	**82B** St. Philips Marsh	**82B** St. Philips Marsh	**82B** St. Philips Marsh	**82B** St. Philips Marsh		
7784	*5700*	**WES** Westbury	**82D** Westbury	**82D** Westbury	**82D** Westbury	**82D** Westbury		
7785	*5700*	**LLY** Llanelly	**87F** Llanelly	**87F** Llanelly	**87F** Llanelly	**87F** Llanelly		
7786	*5700*	**NEA** Neath	**87A** Neath	**87A** Neath	**87A** Neath	**87A** Neath		
7787	*5700*	**LDR** Landore	**87E** Landore	**87E** Landore	**86A** Ebbw Junction	**86K** Tredegar		
7788	*5700*	**RDG** Reading	**81D** Reading	**81D** Reading	**81D** Reading	**81D** Reading		
7789	*5700*	**ABEEG** Aberbeeg	**86B** Newport Pill	**86E** Severn Tunnel Junction	**86E** Severn Tunnel Junction			
7790	*5700*	**SPM** St. Philips Marsh	**82B** St. Philips Marsh	**82B** St. Philips Marsh	**82B** St. Philips Marsh	**82B** St. Philips Marsh		
7791	*5700*	**PDN** Old Oak Common	**81A** Old Oak Common	**81A** Old Oak Common	**81A** Old Oak Common			
7792	*5700*	**SDN** Swindon	**82C** Swindon	**82C** Swindon	**82C** Swindon			
7793	*5700*	**SPM** St. Philips Marsh	**82B** St. Philips Marsh	**82B** St. Philips Marsh	**82B** St. Philips Marsh	**87C** Danygraig		
7794	*5700*	**SDN** Swindon	**82C** Swindon	**82C** Swindon	**82C** Swindon	**86A** Ebbw Junction		
7795	*5700*	**SPM** St. Philips Marsh	**82B** St. Philips Marsh	**82B** St. Philips Marsh	**82B** St. Philips Marsh			
7796	*5700*	**OXY** Oxley	**84B** Oxley	**84B** Oxley	**86G** Pontypool Road	**86G** Pontypool Road		
7797	*5700*	**OXY** Oxley	**84B** Oxley	**84B** Oxley	**84G** Shrewsbury			
7798	*5700*	**TDU** Tondu	**86F** Tondu	**86F** Tondu	**86F** Tondu	**86F** Tondu		
7799	*5700*	**NEA** Neath	**87A** Neath	**87A** Neath	**87A** Neath	**87A** Neath		
7800	*7800*	**BAN** Banbury	**84C** Banbury	**84K** Chester (GWR)	**84K** Chester (GWR)	**89A** Oswestry	**89D** Oswestry	
7801	*7800*	**SPM** St. Philips Marsh	**83D** Laira (Plymouth)	**84K** Chester (GWR)	**84K** Chester (GWR)	**89A** Oswestry	**89D** Oswestry	
7802	*7800*	**ABH** Aberystwyth	**89C** Machynlleth	**89C** Machynlleth	**89C** Machynlleth	**89C** Machynlleth	**84E** Tyseley	
7803	*7800*	**ABH** Aberystwyth	**89C** Machynlleth	**89C** Machynlleth	**89C** Machynlleth	**89C** Machynlleth	**89B** Croes Newydd	
7804	*7800*	**SPM** St. Philips Marsh	**83D** Laira (Plymouth)	**83D** Laira (Plymouth)	**87G** Carmarthen	**87G** Carmarthen	**87F** Llanelly	
7805	*7800*	**BAN** Banbury	**83A** Newton Abbot	**85C** Hereford	**85C** Hereford	**86C** Cardiff Canton	**88L** Cardiff East Dock	
7806	*7800*	**BAN** Banbury	**83G** Penzance	**83A** Newton Abbot	**89C** Machynlleth	**83E** St. Blazey	**84B** Oxley	
7807	*7800*	**OSW** Oswestry	**89A** Oswestry	**84K** Chester (GWR)	**84K** Chester (GWR)	**89A** Oswestry	**89D** Oswestry	
7808	*7800*	**OSW** Oswestry	**89A** Oswestry	**82B** St. Philips Marsh	**85B** Gloucester	**83A** Newton Abbot	**81D** Reading	
7809	*7800*	**BRD** Bristol Bath Road	**83D** Laira (Plymouth)	**83D** Laira (Plymouth)	**83D** Laira (Plymouth)	**89A** Oswestry	**89D** Oswestry	
7810	*7800*	**LMTN** Leamington Spa	**84G** Shrewsbury	**84G** Shrewsbury	**85B** Gloucester	**89A** Oswestry	**89D** Oswestry	
7811	*7800*	**BAN** Banbury	**84C** Banbury	**84G** Shrewsbury	**84G** Shrewsbury	**84G** Shrewsbury	**89B** Croes Newydd	

No.	Class	1948	1951	1954	1957	1960	1963	1966
7812	*7800*	BRD Bristol Bath Road	**83A** Newton Abbot	**83A** Newton Abbot	**83D** Laira (Plymouth)	**83F** Truro	**89B** Croes Newydd	
7813	*7800*	OXY Oxley	**83A** Newton Abbot	**83A** Newton Abbot	**83A** Newton Abbot	**83F** Truro	**81D** Reading	
7814	*7800*	BRD Bristol Bath Road	**83D** Laira (Plymouth)	**83D** Laira (Plymouth)	**83A** Newton Abbot	**89C** Machynlleth	**89C** Machynlleth	
7815	*7800*	GLO Gloucester	**85B** Gloucester	**83D** Laira (Plymouth)	**85A** Worcester	**89C** Machynlleth	**87G** Carmarthen	
7816	*7800*	NEY Neyland	**87H** Neyland	**83E** St. Blazey	**83E** St. Blazey	**83E** St. Blazey	**81D** Reading	
7817	*7800*	CNYD Croes Newydd	**84J** Croes Newydd	**84J** Croes Newydd	**84J** Croes Newydd	**84J** Croes Newydd	**81D** Reading	
7818	*7800*	CHEL Cheltenham	**85B** Gloucester	**84E** Tyseley	**84E** Tyseley	**83A** Newton Abbot	**89C** Machynlleth	
7819	*7800*	OSW Oswestry	**89A** Oswestry	**89A** Oswestry	**89A** Oswestry	**89A** Oswestry	**89D** Oswestry	
7820	*7800*	→	**89A** Oswestry	**84K** Chester (GWR)	**83D** Laira (Plymouth)	**83F** Truro	**88L** Cardiff East Dock	
7821	*7800*	→	**89A** Oswestry	**84E** Tyseley	**84E** Tyseley	**83A** Newton Abbot	**89B** Croes Newydd	
7822	*7800*	→	**89A** Oswestry	**89A** Oswestry	**84K** Chester (GWR)	**89A** Oswestry	**89D** Oswestry	
7823	*7800*	→	**84C** Banbury	**84C** Banbury	**83F** Truro	**89C** Machynlleth	**84E** Tyseley	
7824	*7800*	→	**85B** Gloucester	**83D** Laira (Plymouth)	**83D** Laira (Plymouth)	**84E** Tyseley	**84B** Oxley	
7825	*7800*	→	**84J** Croes Newydd	**87G** Carmarthen	**87G** Carmarthen	**87G** Carmarthen	**87H** Neyland	
7826	*7800*	→	**84J** Croes Newydd	**87G** Carmarthen	**87G** Carmarthen	**87G** Carmarthen	**87G** Carmarthen	
7827	*7800*	→	**84K** Chester (GWR)	**84K** Chester (GWR)	**84K** Chester (GWR)	**89A** Oswestry	**89D** Oswestry	
7828	*7800*	→	**87A** Neath	**84G** Shrewsbury	**84G** Shrewsbury	**84G** Shrewsbury	**89B** Croes Newydd	
7829	*7800*	→	**87A** Neath	**87G** Carmarthen	**87G** Carmarthen	**87G** Carmarthen	**87G** Carmarthen	
7900	*6959*	→	**82B** St. Philips Marsh	**81F** Oxford	**81F** Oxford	**81F** Oxford	**81F** Oxford	
7901	*6959*	→	**82A** Bristol Bath Road	**82A** Bristol Bath Road	**82A** Bristol Bath Road	**82A** Bristol Bath Road	**82B** St. Philips Marsh	
7902	*6959*	→	**81A** Old Oak Common	**81A** Old Oak Common	**81A** Old Oak Common	**81A** Old Oak Common	**81A** Old Oak Common	
7903	*6959*	→	**81A** Old Oak Common	**81A** Old Oak Common	**81A** Old Oak Common	**81A** Old Oak Common	**81A** Old Oak Common	
7904	*6959*	→	**81A** Old Oak Common	**81A** Old Oak Common	**81A** Old Oak Common	**81A** Old Oak Common	**81A** Old Oak Common	
7905	*6959*	→	**83D** Laira (Plymouth)	**83D** Laira (Plymouth)	**83D** Laira (Plymouth)	**84C** Banbury	**84C** Banbury	
7906	*6959*	→	**81D** Reading	**81D** Reading	**81D** Reading	**81D** Reading	**81D** Reading	
7907	*6959*	→	**82B** St. Philips Marsh	**82A** Bristol Bath Road	**82A** Bristol Bath Road	**82A** Bristol Bath Road	**82B** St. Philips Marsh	
7908	*6959*	→	**82B** St. Philips Marsh	**82B** St. Philips Marsh	**84E** Tyseley	**84E** Tyseley	**84E** Tyseley	
7909	*6959*	→	**83D** Laira (Plymouth)	**83D** Laira (Plymouth)	**83D** Laira (Plymouth)	**82D** Westbury	**83B** Taunton	
7910	*6959*	→	**81C** Southall	**81C** Southall	**81C** Southall	**81C** Southall	**81C** Southall	
7911	*6959*	→	**81A** Old Oak Common	**81F** Oxford	**81F** Oxford	**81F** Oxford	**81F** Oxford	
7912	*6959*	→	**84E** Tyseley	**84E** Tyseley	**84E** Tyseley	**84E** Tyseley	**84C** Banbury	
7913	*6959*	→	**84E** Tyseley	**84E** Tyseley	**84E** Tyseley	**86C** Cardiff Canton	**88L** Cardiff East Dock	
7914	*6959*	→	**82C** Swindon	**82C** Swindon	**81D** Reading	**81D** Reading	**81D** Reading	
7915	*6959*	→	**84A** Stafford Road	**84B** Oxley	**84B** Oxley	**84B** Oxley	**84E** Tyseley	
7916	*6959*	→	**83E** St. Blazey	**83A** Newton Abbot	**83A** Newton Abbot	**83A** Newton Abbot	**83D** Laira (Plymouth)	
7917	*6959*	→	**82D** Westbury	**82D** Westbury	**82D** Westbury	**82D** Westbury	**82D** Westbury	
7918	*6959*	→	**84E** Tyseley	**84E** Tyseley	**84E** Tyseley	**84E** Tyseley	**84E** Tyseley	
7919	*6959*	→	**81D** Reading	**81D** Reading	**81D** Reading	**81D** Reading	**81D** Reading	
7920	*6959*	→	**85B** Gloucester	**85A** Worcester	**85A** Worcester	**85A** Worcester	**85A** Worcester	
7921	*6959*	→	**84K** Chester (GWR)	**84K** Chester (GWR)	**84K** Chester (GWR)	**83D** Laira (Plymouth)	**81A** Old Oak Common	
7922	*6959*	→	**84K** Chester (GWR)	**84K** Chester (GWR)	**84K** Chester (GWR)	**84G** Shrewsbury	**81C** Southall	
7923	*6959*	→	**82C** Swindon	**82C** Swindon	**82C** Swindon	**81C** Southall	**81C** Southall	
7924	*6959*	→	**82D** Westbury	**82D** Westbury	**82D** Westbury	**83B** Taunton	**82B** St. Philips Marsh	
7925	*6959*	→	**83G** Penzance	**83G** Penzance	**83G** Penzance	**86C** Cardiff Canton	**88L** Cardiff East Dock	
7926	*6959*		**85B** Gloucester	**85B** Gloucester	**85B** Gloucester	**85B** Gloucester	**85A** Worcester	
7927	*6959*	→	**81D** Reading	**81D** Reading	**81D** Reading	**81A** Old Oak Common	**88L** Cardiff East Dock	
7928	*6959*	→	**85A** Worcester	**85A** Worcester	**85A** Worcester	**85A** Worcester	**85A** Worcester	
7929	*6959*	→	**84E** Tyseley	**84E** Tyseley	**82B** St. Philips Marsh	**82B** St. Philips Marsh	**84E** Tyseley	
8100	*8100*	LMTN Leamington Spa	**84D** Leamington Spa	**84D** Leamington Spa	**84D** Leamington Spa	**84D** Leamington Spa		
8101	*8100*	KDR Kidderminster	**85D** Kidderminster	**85D** Kidderminster	**85D** Kidderminster	**85D** Kidderminster		
8102	*8100*	WTD Whitland	**87H** Neyland	**87H** Neyland	**87H** Neyland	**87G** Carmarthen	**87A** Neath	
8103	*8100*	OSW Oswestry	**89A** Oswestry	**87G** Carmarthen	**87G** Carmarthen	**87G** Carmarthen	**87F** Llanelly	
8104	*8100*	NEA Neath	**87A** Neath	**87A** Neath	**87A** Neath	**87A** Neath	**85A** Worcester	
8105	*8100*	SPM St. Philips Marsh	**82B** St. Philips Marsh	**85A** Worcester	**85A** Worcester			
8106	*8100*	WOS Worcester	**85A** Worcester	**85A** Worcester	**85A** Worcester	**85A** Worcester	**85A** Worcester	
8107	*8100*	WTD Whitland	**87H** Neyland	**87H** Neyland	**87H** Neyland	**87H** Neyland		
8108	*8100*	TYS Tyseley	**84E** Tyseley	**84E** Tyseley	**84E** Tyseley	**84E** Tyseley		
8109	*8100*	LMTN Leamington Spa	**84D** Leamington Spa	**84D** Leamington Spa	**84D** Leamington Spa	**84D** Leamington Spa	**84E** Tyseley	
8393	*8300*	BHD Birkenhead	(5393)					
8400	*9400*	→	**84C** Banbury	**84C** Banbury	**21C** Bromsgrove	**85F** Bromsgrove	**85D** Bromsgrove	
8401	*9400*	→	**86E** Severn Tunnel Junction	**86E** Severn Tunnel Junction	**21C** Bromsgrove	**85F** Bromsgrove	**85D** Bromsgrove	
8402	*9400*	→	**86H** Aberbeeg	**86H** Aberbeeg	**21C** Bromsgrove	**85F** Bromsgrove	**85D** Bromsgrove	
8403	*9400*	→	**83A** Newton Abbot	**83A** Newton Abbot	**21C** Bromsgrove	**85F** Bromsgrove	**85D** Bromsgrove	
8404	*9400*	→	**83F** Truro	**83F** Truro	**21C** Bromsgrove	**85F** Bromsgrove		
8405	*9400*	→	**84C** Banbury	**84C** Banbury	**21C** Bromsgrove	**85F** Bromsgrove	**85D** Bromsgrove	
8406	*9400*	→	**86A** Ebbw Junction	**86A** Ebbw Junction	**86A** Ebbw Junction	**85F** Bromsgrove		
8407	*9400*	→	**84C** Banbury	**84C** Banbury	**87B** Duffryn Yard	**87B** Duffryn Yard		
8408	*9400*	→	**87C** Danygraig	**87C** Danygraig	**87D** Swansea East Dock			
8409	*9400*	→	**83G** Penzance	**83G** Penzance	**83G** Penzance	**83E** St. Blazey	**85D** Bromsgrove	
8410	*9400*	→	**84E** Tyseley	**87B** Duffryn Yard	**87B** Duffryn Yard	**87B** Duffryn Yard		
8411	*9400*	→	**84A** Stafford Road	**84A** Stafford Road	**84A** Stafford Road	**84A** Stafford Road		
8412	*9400*	→	**83F** Truro	**83F** Truro	**83F** Truro			
8413	*9400*	→	**82B** St. Philips Marsh	**82B** St. Philips Marsh	**82B** St. Philips Marsh	**81C** Southall		
8414	*9400*	→	**88B** Cardiff East Dock	**88B** Cardiff East Dock	**88B** Cardiff East Dock	**87D** Swansea East Dock	**87D** Swansea East Dock	
8415	*9400*	→	**84E** Tyseley	**84E** Tyseley	**84E** Tyseley	**84E** Tyseley	**85A** Worcester	
8416	*9400*	→	**88B** Cardiff East Dock	**88B** Cardiff East Dock	**88B** Cardiff East Dock	**87B** Duffryn Yard		
8417	*9400*	→	**84B** Oxley	**84B** Oxley	**84B** Oxley			
8418	*9400*	→	**84F** Stourbridge	**87B** Duffryn Yard	**87B** Duffryn Yard	**87A** Neath	**87A** Neath	
8419	*9400*	→	**84F** Stourbridge	**84F** Stourbridge	**88F** Treherbert	**88C** Barry		
8420	*9400*	→	**87A** Neath	**88F** Treherbert	**88F** Treherbert	**88A** Radyr	**81A** Old Oak Common	
8421	*9400*	→	**83C** Exeter	**83F** Truro	**83F** Truro			
8422	*9400*	→	**83A** Newton Abbot	**83D** Laira (Plymouth)	**83D** Laira (Plymouth)	**83D** Laira (Plymouth)		
8423	*9400*	→	**84A** Stafford Road	**87B** Duffryn Yard	**87B** Duffryn Yard			
8424	*9400*	→	**87F** Llanelly	**88F** Treherbert	**88B** Cardiff East Dock	**81F** Oxford		
8425	*9400*	→	→	**83D** Laira (Plymouth)	**83D** Laira (Plymouth)	**84A** Stafford Road	**88L** Cardiff East Dock	
8426	*9400*	→	→	**83D** Laira (Plymouth)	**83D** Laira (Plymouth)	**84A** Stafford Road	**84A** Stafford Road	
8427	*9400*	→	→	**85A** Worcester	**85A** Worcester	**85A** Worcester		
8428	*9400*	→	→	**84B** Oxley	**84B** Oxley	**84B** Oxley		
8429	*9400*	→	→	**88B** Cardiff East Dock	**88B** Cardiff East Dock	**86H** Aberbeeg		
8430	*9400*	→	→	**81D** Reading	**81D** Reading	**81D** Reading	**81D** Reading	
8431	*9400*	→	→	**87D** Swansea East Dock	**87D** Swansea East Dock	**87D** Swansea East Dock	**87D** Swansea East Dock	
8432	*9400*	→	→	**81A** Old Oak Common	**81F** Oxford			
8433	*9400*	→	→	**81A** Old Oak Common	**82C** Swindon	**82C** Swindon	**82C** Swindon	
8434	*9400*	→	→	**81A** Old Oak Common	**81A** Old Oak Common			
8435	*9400*	→	→	**81E** Didcot	**81E** Didcot	**81E** Didcot		
8436	*9400*	→	→	**86H** Aberbeeg	**86H** Aberbeeg	**86H** Aberbeeg	**81A** Old Oak Common	
8437	*9400*	→	→	**84F** Stourbridge	**88B** Cardiff East Dock	**86H** Aberbeeg	**86F** Aberbeeg	
8438	*9400*	→	→	**84F** Stourbridge	**89B** Brecon	**88A** Radyr		
8439	*9400*	→	→	**86C** Cardiff Canton	**86H** Aberbeeg	**87E** Landore		
8440	*9400*	→	→	→	**86A** Ebbw Junction	**86G** Pontypool Road		
8441	*9400*	→	→	→	**88B** Cardiff East Dock	**86C** Cardiff Canton		
8442	*9400*	→	→	→	**87A** Neath			
8443	*9400*	→	→	→	**87D** Swansea East Dock			
8444	*9400*	→	→	→	**86J** Aberdare	**86H** Aberbeeg	**86F** Aberbeeg	
8445	*9400*	→	→	→	**86J** Aberdare	**86J** Aberdare		
8446	*9400*	→	→	→	**88C** Barry	**88C** Barry	**88C** Barry	
8447	*9400*	→	→	→	**86C** Cardiff Canton			
8448	*9400*	→	→	→	**86F** Tondu			
8449	*9400*	→	→	→	**84B** Oxley	**84G** Shrewsbury		
8450	*9400*	→	**86E** Severn Tunnel Junction	**86E** Severn Tunnel Junction	**88C** Barry			
8451	*9400*	→	**88C** Barry	**83A** Newton Abbot	**83A** Newton Abbot	**81C** Southall		
8452	*9400*	→	**84E** Tyseley	**84C** Banbury	**84C** Banbury	**84C** Banbury	**88L** Cardiff East Dock	
8453	*9400*	→	**86A** Ebbw Junction	**86A** Ebbw Junction	**86A** Ebbw Junction	**86F** Tondu		
8454	*9400*	→	**84D** Leamington Spa	**87B** Duffryn Yard	**87B** Duffryn Yard	**87B** Duffryn Yard		

		1948	1951	1954	1957	1960	1963	1966
8455	*9400*	→	**88B** Cardiff East Dock	**88C** Barry	**88F** Treherbert	**88A** Radyr		
8456	*9400*	→	**83C** Exeter	**83C** Exeter	**83C** Exeter	**81C** Southall	**81C** Southall	
8457	*9400*	→	**88B** Cardiff East Dock	**88B** Cardiff East Dock	**88B** Cardiff East Dock	**86C** Cardiff Canton		
8458	*9400*	→	**88C** Barry	**85A** Worcester	**81E** Didcot	**81E** Didcot	**81A** Old Oak Common	
8459	*9400*	→	**84C** Banbury	**84C** Banbury	**88C** Barry	**81A** Old Oak Common	**81A** Old Oak Common	
8460	*9400*	→	**88C** Barry	**88F** Treherbert	**88F** Treherbert	**85A** Worcester		
8461	*9400*	→	**88C** Barry	**82C** Swindon	**82C** Swindon	**84A** Stafford Road	**86G** Pontypool Road	
8462	*9400*	→	**84A** Stafford Road	**84A** Stafford Road	**84A** Stafford Road			
8463	*9400*	→	**84E** Tyseley	**87E** Landore	**87E** Landore	**87E** Landore		
8464	*9400*	→	**87B** Duffryn Yard	**88B** Cardiff East Dock	**88B** Cardiff East Dock	**84B** Oxley	**84B** Oxley	
8465	*9400*	→	**87B** Duffryn Yard	**88F** Treherbert	**88C** Barry	**82C** Swindon	**81C** Southall	
8466	*9400*	→	**87A** Neath	**87B** Duffryn Yard	**83A** Newton Abbot	**86C** Cardiff Canton	**88L** Cardiff East Dock	
8467	*9400*	→	→	**87F** Llanelly	**87F** Llanelly	**87F** Llanelly		
8468	*9400*	→	→	**84E** Tyseley	**84E** Tyseley	**84E** Tyseley		
8469	*9400*	→	→	**88F** Treherbert	**88A** Cardiff Cathays	**88A** Radyr	**88B** Radyr	
8470	*9400*	→	→	**88A** Cardiff Cathays	**88A** Cardiff Cathays	**88A** Radyr		
8471	*9400*	→	→	**88A** Cardiff Cathays	**88A** Cardiff Cathays	**88A** Radyr	**88L** Cardiff East Dock	
8472	*9400*	→	→	**82C** Swindon	**82C** Swindon	**82C** Swindon	**81A** Old Oak Common	
8473	*9400*	→	→	**83A** Newton Abbot	**83G** Penzance	**83G** Penzance		
8474	*9400*	→	→	**87F** Llanelly	**87F** Llanelly	**87F** Llanelly	**87F** Llanelly	
8475	*9400*	→	→	**87C** Danygraig	**87D** Swansea East Dock	**87D** Swansea East Dock	**87D** Swansea East Dock	
8476	*9400*	→	→	**87C** Danygraig	**87D** Swansea East Dock	**87D** Swansea East Dock		
8477	*9400*	→	→	**87F** Llanelly	**87F** Llanelly	**87F** Llanelly		
8478	*9400*	→	→	**88A** Cardiff Cathays	**88A** Cardiff Cathays	**88A** Radyr	**88B** Radyr	
8479	*9400*	→	→	**82D** Westbury	**82D** Westbury	**82D** Westbury	**88B** Radyr	
8480	*9400*	→	→	**85A** Worcester	**85A** Worcester	**85A** Worcester	**87A** Neath	
8481	*9400*	→	→	**88A** Cardiff Cathays	**88A** Cardiff Cathays	**88A** Radyr	**88C** Barry	
8482	*9400*	→	→	**88A** Cardiff Cathays	**88A** Cardiff Cathays	**82D** Westbury		
8483	*9400*	→	→	**87C** Danygraig	**87D** Swansea East Dock	**87D** Swansea East Dock		
8484	*9400*	→	→	**88A** Cardiff Cathays	**88A** Cardiff Cathays	**86C** Cardiff Canton	**88L** Cardiff East Dock	
8485	*9400*	→	→	**83F** Truro	**83F** Truro			
8486	*9400*	→	→	**83F** Truro	**83F** Truro	**83F** Truro	**81B** Slough	
8487	*9400*	→	→	**85B** Gloucester	**85B** Gloucester	**85B** Gloucester	**81A** Old Oak Common	
8488	*9400*	→	→	**85B** Gloucester	**85B** Gloucester	**85B** Gloucester	**87D** Swansea East Dock	
8489	*9400*	→	→	**88F** Treherbert	**88A** Cardiff Cathays	**86H** Aberbeeg		
8490	*9400*	→	→	**87B** Duffryn Yard	**87B** Duffryn Yard	**87B** Duffryn Yard		
8491	*9400*	→	→	**82B** St. Philips Marsh	**82A** Bristol Bath Road	**85B** Gloucester	**85B** Gloucester	
8492	*9400*	→	→	**82B** St. Philips Marsh	**82B** St. Philips Marsh			
8493	*9400*	→	→	**86H** Aberbeeg	**86A** Ebbw Junction	**86G** Pontypool Road	**86G** Pontypool Road	
8494	*9400*	→	→	**86H** Aberbeeg	**86H** Aberbeeg	**81F** Oxford		
8495	*9400*	→	→	**88A** Cardiff Cathays	**88A** Cardiff Cathays	**86G** Pontypool Road	**86G** Pontypool Road	
8496	*9400*	→	→	**85A** Worcester	**85A** Worcester	**85A** Worcester	**81D** Reading	
8497	*9400*	→	→	**86F** Tondu	**86F** Tondu	**86F** Tondu	**88B** Radyr	
8498	*9400*	→	→	**86F** Tondu	**86F** Tondu	**84C** Banbury	**84A** Stafford Road	
8499	*9400*	→	→	**86A** Ebbw Junction	**86A** Ebbw Junction	**86B** Newport Pill		
8700	*5700*	TYS Tyseley	**84E** Tyseley	**84E** Tyseley	**84E** Tyseley	**84E** Tyseley		
8701	*5700*	GLO Gloucester	**85B** Gloucester	**85C** Hereford	**85C** Hereford	**85B** Gloucester	**85B** Gloucester	
8702	*5700*	SPM St. Philips Marsh	**82B** St. Philips Marsh	**82B** St. Philips Marsh	**83E** St. Blazey	**83E** St. Blazey	**86A** Ebbw Junction	
8703	*5700*	SPM St. Philips Marsh	**82B** St. Philips Marsh	**82B** St. Philips Marsh	**82B** St. Philips Marsh			
8704	*5700*	STB Stourbridge	**84F** Stourbridge	**84F** Stourbridge	**84F** Stourbridge	**84F** Stourbridge		
8705	*5700*	SRD Stafford Road	**84A** Stafford Road	**84A** Stafford Road	**86H** Aberbeeg	**86H** Aberbeeg		
8706	*5700*	LLY Llanelly	**87F** Llanelly	**87K** Swansea Victoria	**87K** Swansea Victoria	**87F** Llanelly		
8707	*5700*	PDN Old Oak Common	**81A** Old Oak Common	**81A** Old Oak Common	**86G** Pontypool Road	**86G** Pontypool Road	**86G** Pontypool Road	
8708	*5700*	LLY Llanelly	**87F** Llanelly	**87F** Llanelly	**87F** Llanelly	**87F** Llanelly		
8709	*5700*	LA Laira (Plymouth)	**83D** Laira (Plymouth)	**83D** Laira (Plymouth)	**83D** Laira (Plymouth)	**6E** Chester (GWR)		
8710	*5700*	NPT Ebbw Junction	**86A** Ebbw Junction	**86A** Ebbw Junction	**86A** Ebbw Junction	**86F** Tondu	**88H** Tondu	
8711	*5700*	NPT Ebbw Junction	**86A** Ebbw Junction	**86A** Ebbw Junction	**86A** Ebbw Junction	**86K** Tredegar		
8712	*5700*	TDU Tondu	**86F** Tondu	**86F** Tondu	**86F** Tondu	**86F** Tondu	**88H** Tondu	
8713	*5700*	SPM St. Philips Marsh	**82B** St. Philips Marsh	**82B** St. Philips Marsh	**84E** Tyseley	**84E** Tyseley		
8714	*5700*	SPM St. Philips Marsh	**82B** St. Philips Marsh	**82B** St. Philips Marsh	**82A** Bristol Bath Road	**82B** St. Philips Marsh	**87B** Duffryn Yard	
8715	*5700*	NEA Neath	**87A** Neath	**87A** Neath	**87A** Neath	**87A** Neath		
8716	*5700*	PPRD Pontypool Road	**86G** Pontypool Road	**86G** Pontypool Road	**86G** Pontypool Road	**86G** Pontypool Road	**86G** Pontypool Road	
8717	*5700*	GLO Gloucester	**85B** Gloucester	**85B** Gloucester	**85B** Gloucester	**85B** Gloucester	**88E** Abercynon	
8718	*5700*	KDR Kidderminster	**85D** Kidderminster	**85D** Kidderminster	**85D** Kidderminster	**85D** Kidderminster	**84G** Kidderminster	**2C** Stourbridge
8719	*5700*	LA Laira (Plymouth)	**83D** Laira (Plymouth)	**83D** Laira (Plymouth)	**83D** Laira (Plymouth)	**83E** St. Blazey		
8720	*5700*	DG Danygraig	**87C** Danygraig	**87C** Danygraig	**87C** Danygraig	**81E** Didcot	**81E** Didcot	
8721	*5700*	TDU Tondu	**86F** Tondu	**86F** Tondu	**86F** Tondu	**86F** Tondu		
8722	*5700*	SPM St. Philips Marsh	**81B** Slough	**81B** Slough	**88B** Cardiff East Dock	**85C** Hereford		
8723	*5700*	ABEEG Aberbeeg	**86C** Cardiff Canton	**86C** Cardiff Canton	**86C** Cardiff Canton	**86C** Cardiff Canton	**88D** Merthyr	
8724	*5700*	ABEEG Aberbeeg	**86H** Aberbeeg	**86J** Aberdare	**87C** Danygraig	**87B** Duffryn Yard		
8725	*5700*	BHD Birkenhead	**6C** Birkenhead	**6C** Birkenhead	**6C** Birkenhead	**82E** Bristol Barrow Road		
8726	*5700*	SRD Stafford Road	**84A** Stafford Road	**84A** Stafford Road	**84A** Stafford Road	**84A** Stafford Road		
8727	*5700*	KDR Kidderminster	**85D** Kidderminster	**85D** Kidderminster	**85D** Kidderminster	**84J** Croes Newydd		
8728	*5700*	CDF Cardiff Canton	**86C** Cardiff Canton	**86C** Cardiff Canton	**86C** Cardiff Canton	**86C** Cardiff Canton	**88C** Barry	
8729	*5700*	BAN Banbury	**84C** Banbury	**84K** Chester (GWR)	**84K** Chester (GWR)	**6E** Chester (GWR)		
8730	*5700*	SPM St. Philips Marsh	**82B** St. Philips Marsh	**82B** St. Philips Marsh	**84K** Chester (GWR)	**6E** Chester (GWR)		
8731	*5700*	GLO Gloucester	**85B** Gloucester	**85D** Kidderminster	**85B** Gloucester	**85B** Gloucester		
8732	*5700*	LLY Llanelly	**87F** Llanelly	**87F** Llanelly	**87F** Llanelly	**87A** Neath	**87A** Neath	
8733	*5700*	SDN Swindon	**82C** Swindon	**83E** St. Blazey	**83E** St. Blazey	**83E** St. Blazey		
8734	*5700*	SRD Stafford Road	**84A** Stafford Road	**84A** Stafford Road	**84A** Stafford Road	**84K** Wrexham Rhosddu		
8735	*5700*	PDN Old Oak Common	**88C** Barry	**88C** Barry	**88C** Barry	**88E** Abercynon		
8736	*5700*	MTHR Merthyr	**88D** Merthyr	**88D** Merthyr	**88D** Merthyr	**87F** Llanelly		
8737	*5700*	SPM St. Philips Marsh	**82B** St. Philips Marsh	**82B** St. Philips Marsh	**82B** St. Philips Marsh	**83E** St. Blazey		
8738	*5700*	PDN Old Oak Common	**87F** Llanelly	**87K** Swansea Victoria	**87H** Neyland	**87H** Neyland	**87H** Neyland	
8739	*5700*	ABEEG Aberbeeg	**86D** Llantrisant	**86D** Llantrisant	**87H** Neyland	**87H** Neyland	**87J** Fishguard Goodwick	
8740	*5700*	CDF Cardiff Canton	**86F** Tondu	**86F** Tondu	**86F** Tondu	**86F** Tondu		
8741	*5700*	SPM St. Philips Marsh	**82B** St. Philips Marsh	**82B** St. Philips Marsh	**82B** St. Philips Marsh	**82A** Bristol Bath Road		
8742	*5700*	STB Stourbridge	**84F** Stourbridge	**84F** Stourbridge	**84F** Stourbridge	**84F** Stourbridge		
8743	*5700*	CED Cardiff East Dock	**88B** Cardiff East Dock	**88B** Cardiff East Dock	**88B** Cardiff East Dock	**85B** Gloucester	**85B** Gloucester	
8744	*5700*	WES Westbury	**82D** Westbury	**82D** Westbury	**82D** Westbury	**82D** Westbury		
8745	*5700*	WES Westbury	**82E** Yeovil Pen Mill	**82E** Yeovil Pen Mill	**82E** Yeovil Pen Mill	**72C** Yeovil Town	**72C** Yeovil Town	
8746	*5700*	SPM St. Philips Marsh	**82B** St. Philips Marsh	**82B** St. Philips Marsh	**82B** St. Philips Marsh	**82B** St. Philips Marsh		
8747	*5700*	SPM St. Philips Marsh	**82B** St. Philips Marsh	**82B** St. Philips Marsh	**82A** Bristol Bath Road	**82B** St. Philips Marsh	**87A** Neath	
8748	*5700*	TDU Tondu	**86F** Tondu	**86F** Tondu	**86F** Tondu	**86F** Tondu		
8749	*5700*	LLY Llanelly	**87F** Llanelly	**87F** Llanelly	**87F** Llanelly	**87F** Llanelly	**87F** Llanelly	
8750	*5700*	PDN Old Oak Common	**81A** Old Oak Common	**81C** Southall	**81C** Southall	**81C** Southall		
8751	*5700*	PDN Old Oak Common	**81A** Old Oak Common	**81A** Old Oak Common	**81A** Old Oak Common	**81A** Old Oak Common		
8752	*5700*	SHL Southall	**81C** Southall	**81C** Southall	**81C** Southall	**81C** Southall	**81C** Southall	
8753	*5700*	SHL Southall	**81A** Old Oak Common	**81A** Old Oak Common	**81A** Old Oak Common	**81A** Old Oak Common		
8754	*5700*	PDN Old Oak Common	**81A** Old Oak Common	**81A** Old Oak Common	**81A** Old Oak Common	**81A** Old Oak Common		
8755	*5700*	PPRD Pontypool Road	**86G** Pontypool Road	**86G** Pontypool Road	**81A** Old Oak Common			
8756	*5700*	PDN Old Oak Common	**81A** Old Oak Common	**81A** Old Oak Common	**81A** Old Oak Common	**81A** Old Oak Common		
8757	*5700*	PDN Old Oak Common	**81A** Old Oak Common	**81A** Old Oak Common	**81A** Old Oak Common	**81A** Old Oak Common		
8758	*5700*	SHL Southall	**81C** Southall	**81C** Southall	**81C** Southall			
8759	*5700*	PDN Old Oak Common	**81A** Old Oak Common	**81A** Old Oak Common	**81A** Old Oak Common	**81A** Old Oak Common	**81A** Old Oak Common	
8760	*5700*	PDN Old Oak Common	**81A** Old Oak Common	**81A** Old Oak Common	**81A** Old Oak Common	**81A** Old Oak Common		
8761	*5700*	PDN Old Oak Common	**81A** Old Oak Common	**81A** Old Oak Common	**81A** Old Oak Common	**81C** Southall		
8762	*5700*	PDN Old Oak Common	**81A** Old Oak Common	**81A** Old Oak Common	**81A** Old Oak Common	**81A** Old Oak Common		
8763	*5700*	PDN Old Oak Common	**81A** Old Oak Common	**81A** Old Oak Common	**81A** Old Oak Common	**81A** Old Oak Common		
8764	*5700*	SHL Southall	**81A** Old Oak Common	**81A** Old Oak Common	**81A** Old Oak Common	**81A** Old Oak Common		
8765	*5700*	PDN Old Oak Common	**81A** Old Oak Common	**81A** Old Oak Common	**81A** Old Oak Common	**81A** Old Oak Common		
8766	*5700*	SPM St. Philips Marsh	**82B** St. Philips Marsh	**82B** St. Philips Marsh	**86A** Ebbw Junction	**86A** Ebbw Junction	**86A** Ebbw Junction	
8767	*5700*	PDN Old Oak Common	**81A** Old Oak Common	**81A** Old Oak Common	**81A** Old Oak Common	**81A** Old Oak Common	**81A** Old Oak Common	**2B** Oxley
8768	*5700*	PDN Old Oak Common	**81A** Old Oak Common	**81A** Old Oak Common	**81A** Old Oak Common	**81A** Old Oak Common	**81A** Old Oak Common	

		1948	1951	1954	1957	1960	1963	1966
8769	*5700*	PDN Old Oak Common	**81A** Old Oak Common	**81A** Old Oak Common	**81A** Old Oak Common	**81C** Southall		
8770	*5700*	PDN Old Oak Common	**81A** Old Oak Common	**81A** Old Oak Common	**81A** Old Oak Common	**81A** Old Oak Common		
8771	*5700*	PDN Old Oak Common	**81A** Old Oak Common	**81A** Old Oak Common	**81A** Old Oak Common	**81A** Old Oak Common		
8772	*5700*	PDN Old Oak Common	**81A** Old Oak Common	**81A** Old Oak Common	**81A** Old Oak Common	**81A** Old Oak Common		
8773	*5700*	PDN Old Oak Common	**81A** Old Oak Common	**81A** Old Oak Common	**81A** Old Oak Common	**81A** Old Oak Common		
8774	*5700*	SHL Southall	**81C** Southall	**81C** Southall	**81C** Southall	**81C** Southall		
8775	*5700*	NEA Neath	**87A** Neath	**87A** Neath	**87A** Neath	**87A** Neath		
8776	*5700*	ABEEG Aberbeeg	**86H** Aberbeeg	**86C** Cardiff Canton	**86C** Cardiff Canton	**86C** Cardiff Canton		
8777	*5700*	TDU Tondu	**86F** Tondu	**86G** Pontypool Road	**87G** Carmarthen	**87G** Carmarthen		
8778	*5700*	NPT Ebbw Junction	**86A** Ebbw Junction	**86A** Ebbw Junction	**86H** Aberbeeg	**86H** Aberbeeg		
8779	*5700*	SDN Swindon	**82C** Swindon	**82C** Swindon	**82C** Swindon	**82C** Swindon		
8780	*5700*	PDN Old Oak Common	**88A** Cardiff Cathays	**88A** Cardiff Cathays	**88A** Cardiff Cathays	**88A** Radyr		
8781	*5700*	GLO Gloucester	**85B** Gloucester	**85B** Gloucester	**85B** Gloucester	**85C** Hereford		
8782	*5700*	NEA Neath	**87A** Neath	**87A** Neath	**87A** Neath	**87A** Neath		
8783	*5700*	SBZ St. Blazey	**83E** St. Blazey	**82C** Swindon	**82C** Swindon	**82C** Swindon	**83D** Taunton	
8784	*5700*	TYS Tyseley	**84E** Tyseley	**87A** Neath	**87A** Neath	**87A** Neath		
8785	*5700*	LLY Llanelly	**87F** Llanelly	**87F** Llanelly	**87F** Llanelly	**87F** Llanelly	**87F** Llanelly	
8786	*5700*	NPT Ebbw Junction	**86G** Pontypool Road	**86H** Aberbeeg	**86H** Aberbeeg	**86H** Aberbeeg	**86F** Aberbeeg	
8787	*5700*	BAN Banbury	**84C** Banbury	**84C** Banbury	**88B** Cardiff East Dock	**85C** Hereford		
8788	*5700*	PPRD Pontypool Road	**86G** Pontypool Road	**86G** Pontypool Road	**87E** Landore	**87E** Landore		
8789	*5700*	LDR Landore	**87E** Landore	**87E** Landore	**87E** Landore	**87E** Landore		
8790	*5700*	SPM St. Philips Marsh	**82B** St. Philips Marsh	**82B** St. Philips Marsh	**82B** St. Philips Marsh	**82B** St. Philips Marsh		
8791	*5700*	STB Stourbridge	**84F** Stourbridge	**84F** Stourbridge	**84J** Croes Newydd	**84J** Croes Newydd	**87A** Neath	
8792	*5700*	STB Stourbridge	**84F** Stourbridge	**84F** Stourbridge	**84F** Stourbridge	**84F** Stourbridge		
8793	*5700*	SPM St. Philips Marsh	**82C** Swindon	**82C** Swindon	**82C** Swindon	**82C** Swindon	**82C** Swindon	
8794	*5700*	ABEEG Aberbeeg	**86H** Aberbeeg	**86A** Ebbw Junction	**87E** Landore	**87E** Landore	**87D** Swansea East Dock	
8795	*5700*	SPM St. Philips Marsh	**82B** St. Philips Marsh	**82B** St. Philips Marsh	**82A** Bristol Bath Road	**82B** St. Philips Marsh	**82E** Bristol Barrow Road	
8796	*5700*	NPT Ebbw Junction	**86B** Newport Pill	**86B** Newport Pill	**86B** Newport Pill	**84A** Stafford Road		
8797	*5700*	STB Stourbridge	**84F** Stourbridge	**84F** Stourbridge	**84F** Stourbridge	**84F** Stourbridge		
8798	*5700*	OXY Oxley	**84B** Oxley	**84A** Stafford Road	**84A** Stafford Road	**84A** Stafford Road		
8799	*5700*	STJ Severn Tunnel Junction	**86E** Severn Tunnel Junction	**86E** Severn Tunnel Junction	**82F** Weymouth	**71G** Weymouth		
9000	*9000*	MCH Machynlleth	**89C** Machynlleth	**89C** Machynlleth				
9001	*9000*	OSW Oswestry	**89A** Oswestry	**89A** Oswestry				
9002	*9000*	ABH Aberystwyth	**89C** Machynlleth	**89C** Machynlleth				
9003	*9000*	OSW Oswestry	**89A** Oswestry	**89A** Oswestry				
9004	*9000*	MCH Machynlleth	**89C** Machynlleth	**89C** Machynlleth	**89C** Machynlleth	**84J** Croes Newydd		
9005	*9000*	MCH Machynlleth	**89C** Machynlleth	**89C** Machynlleth	**89A** Oswestry			
9006	*9000*	DID Didcot						
9007	*9000*	TYS Tyseley						
9008	*9000*	TYS Tyseley	**84E** Tyseley	**87G** Carmarthen	**89C** Machynlleth			
9009	*9000*	MCH Machynlleth	**89C** Machynlleth	**89C** Machynlleth	**89C** Machynlleth			
9010	*9000*	TYS Tyseley	**84E** Tyseley	**87G** Carmarthen	**89A** Oswestry			
9011	*9000*	SDN Swindon	**82C** Swindon	**82C** Swindon	**82C** Swindon			
9012	*9000*	MCH Machynlleth	**89C** Machynlleth	**89C** Machynlleth	**89C** Machynlleth			
9013	*9000*	ABH Aberystwyth	**89C** Machynlleth	**89C** Machynlleth	**89C** Machynlleth			
9014	*9000*	MCH Machynlleth	**89C** Machynlleth	**89C** Machynlleth	**89C** Machynlleth	**84J** Croes Newydd		
9015	*9000*	DID Didcot	**81E** Didcot	**81F** Oxford	**89C** Machynlleth	**89C** Machynlleth		
9016	*9000*	OSW Oswestry	**89A** Oswestry	**82A** Bristol Bath Road	**89C** Machynlleth			
9017	*9000*	ABH Aberystwyth	**89C** Machynlleth	**89C** Machynlleth	**89C** Machynlleth	**89C** Machynlleth		
9018	*9000*	SDN Swindon	**82C** Swindon	**89C** Machynlleth	**89C** Machynlleth	**89A** Oswestry		
9019	*9000*	TYS Tyseley						
9020	*9000*	OSW Oswestry	**89A** Oswestry	**82A** Bristol Bath Road	**89C** Machynlleth			
9021	*9000*	ABH Aberystwyth	**89C** Machynlleth	**89C** Machynlleth	**89C** Machynlleth			
9022	*9000*	OSW Oswestry	**89A** Oswestry	**89A** Oswestry	**89C** Machynlleth			
9023	*9000*	SDN Swindon	**82C** Swindon	**82C** Swindon	**82C** Swindon			
9024	*9000*	SALOP Shrewsbury	**89C** Machynlleth	**89C** Machynlleth	**89C** Machynlleth			
9025	*9000*	ABH Aberystwyth	**89C** Machynlleth	**89C** Machynlleth	**89C** Machynlleth			
9026	*9000*	OSW Oswestry	**89A** Oswestry	**82A** Bristol Bath Road	**89A** Oswestry			
9027	*9000*	MCH Machynlleth	**89C** Machynlleth	**89C** Machynlleth	**89A** Oswestry			
9028	*9000*	OSW Oswestry	**89A** Oswestry	**84J** Croes Newydd	**84J** Croes Newydd			
9054	*3252*	MCH Machynlleth						
9064	*3252*	GLO Gloucester						
9065	*3252*	OSW Oswestry						
9072	*3252*	MCH Machynlleth						
9073	*3252*	SALOP Shrewsbury						
9076	*3252*	SALOP Shrewsbury						
9083	*3252*	DID Didcot						
9084	*3252*	STB Stourbridge	**89A** Oswestry					
9087	*3252*	ABH Aberystwyth						
9089	*3252*	GLO Gloucester	**82C** Swindon					
9091	*3252*	MCH Machynlleth						
9300	*9300*	SHL Southall	**81C** Southall	**81C** Southall	**86C** Cardiff Canton	(7322)		
9301	*9300*	SHL Southall	**81C** Southall	**81C** Southall	(7323)			
9302	*9300*	PDN Old Oak Common	**81A** Old Oak Common	**81F** Oxford	**81F** Oxford	(7324)		
9303	*9300*	RDG Reading	**81D** Reading	**84E** Tyseley	**84C** Banbury	(7325)		
9304	*9300*	RDG Reading	**81A** Old Oak Common	**81C** Southall	**85C** Hereford	(7326)		
9305	*9300*	RDG Reading	**81D** Reading	**81D** Reading	**81C** Southall	(7327)		
9306	*9300*	PDN Old Oak Common	**81A** Old Oak Common	**81D** Reading	**86C** Cardiff Canton	(7328)		
9307	*9300*	RDG Reading	**81D** Reading	**84B** Oxley	(7329)			
9308	*9300*	PDN Old Oak Common	**81A** Old Oak Common	**81D** Reading	**84G** Shrewsbury	(7330)		
9309	*9300*	RDG Reading	**81A** Old Oak Common	**81C** Southall	**81D** Reading	(7331)		
9310	*9300*	PDN Old Oak Common	**81C** Southall	**81C** Southall	**87G** Carmarthen	(7332)		
9311	*9300*	SHL Southall	**81C** Southall	**81F** Oxford	**83F** Truro	(7333)		
9312	*9300*	OXY Oxley	**84B** Oxley	**84B** Oxley	**84C** Banbury	(7334)		
9313	*9300*	RDG Reading	**81D** Reading	**81D** Reading	**82B** St. Philips Marsh	(7335)		
9314	*9300*	OXY Oxley	**84B** Oxley	**84B** Oxley	**84B** Oxley	(7336)		
9315	*9300*	RDG Reading	**81A** Old Oak Common	**81D** Reading	**82C** Swindon	(7337)		
9316	*9300*	OXF Oxford	**81F** Oxford	**81F** Oxford	**85A** Worcester	(7338)		
9317	*9300*	OXF Oxford	**81F** Oxford	**84B** Oxley	(7339)			
9318	*9300*	RDG Reading	**81D** Reading	**84B** Oxley	**87H** Neyland	(7340)		
9319	*9300*	RDG Reading	**81D** Reading	**84E** Tyseley	**84B** Oxley	(7341)		
9400	*9400*	SDN Swindon	**82C** Swindon	**82C** Swindon	**81A** Old Oak Common			
9401	*9400*	PDN Old Oak Common	**81A** Old Oak Common	**81D** Reading	**81D** Reading	**85A** Worcester	**85D** Bromsgrove	
9402	*9400*	PDN Old Oak Common	**81A** Old Oak Common	**81D** Reading	**81D** Reading			
9403	*9400*	PDN Old Oak Common	**81A** Old Oak Common	**81F** Oxford	**81F** Oxford			
9404	*9400*	PDN Old Oak Common	**81A** Old Oak Common	**81D** Reading	**81D** Reading	**81D** Reading	**81D** Reading	
9405	*9400*	PDN Old Oak Common	**81A** Old Oak Common	**81D** Reading	**81D** Reading	**81A** Old Oak Common	**81A** Old Oak Common	
9406	*9400*	PDN Old Oak Common	**81A** Old Oak Common	**81B** Slough	**81B** Slough	**81B** Slough	**81B** Slough	
9407	*9400*	PDN Old Oak Common	**81C** Southall	**81C** Southall	**81E** Didcot	**81E** Didcot		
9408	*9400*	OXY Oxley	**84B** Oxley	**84B** Oxley	**84B** Oxley	**84B** Oxley	**87F** Llanelly	
9409	*9400*	PDN Old Oak Common	**81C** Southall	**81C** Southall	**81C** Southall	**81C** Southall		
9410	*9400*	→	**81D** Reading	**81A** Old Oak Common	**81A** Old Oak Common	**81A** Old Oak Common		
9411	*9400*	→	**81D** Reading	**81A** Old Oak Common	**81A** Old Oak Common	**81A** Old Oak Common	**81A** Old Oak Common	
9412	*9400*	→	**81D** Reading	**81A** Old Oak Common	**81A** Old Oak Common	**81A** Old Oak Common	**87A** Neath	
9413	*9400*	→	**81E** Didcot	**81E** Didcot	**81C** Southall	**81C** Southall	**81C** Southall	
9414	*9400*	→	**81B** Slough	**81A** Old Oak Common	**81A** Old Oak Common	**81A** Old Oak Common		
9415	*9400*	→	**81B** Slough	**81B** Slough	**81B** Slough	**81B** Slough	**81C** Southall	
9416	*9400*	→	**81F** Oxford	**81F** Oxford	**81A** Old Oak Common	**81A** Old Oak Common		
9417	*9400*	→	**81E** Didcot	**81E** Didcot	**81C** Southall			
9418	*9400*	→	**81A** Old Oak Common	**81A** Old Oak Common	**81A** Old Oak Common	**81A** Old Oak Common	**81A** Old Oak Common	
9419	*9400*	→	**81A** Old Oak Common	**81A** Old Oak Common	**81A** Old Oak Common	**81A** Old Oak Common	**81A** Old Oak Common	
9420	*9400*	→	**81D** Reading	**81A** Old Oak Common	**81A** Old Oak Common	**81A** Old Oak Common	**81A** Old Oak Common	
9421	*9400*	→	**81B** Slough	**81B** Slough	**81B** Slough	**81B** Slough		
9422	*9400*	→	**81A** Old Oak Common	**81A** Old Oak Common	**81A** Old Oak Common	**81C** Southall	**81B** Slough	

		1948	1951	1954	1957	1960	1963	1966
9423	*9400*	→	**81D** Reading	**81A** Old Oak Common	**81A** Old Oak Common	**81A** Old Oak Common	**81A** Old Oak Common	
9424	*9400*	→	**81B** Slough	**81B** Slough	**81B** Slough	**81B** Slough		
9425	*9400*	→	**84K** Chester (GWR)	**84C** Banbury	**88F** Treherbert	**88C** Barry	**88C** Barry	
9426	*9400*	→	**84C** Banbury	**84C** Banbury	**86C** Cardiff Canton	**86C** Cardiff Canton	**88L** Cardiff East Dock	
9427	*9400*	→	**84F** Stourbridge	**86H** Aberbeeg	**86A** Ebbw Junction			
9428	*9400*	→	**84A** Stafford Road	**84A** Stafford Road	**84A** Stafford Road	**84A** Stafford Road		
9429	*9400*	→	**85A** Worcester	**85A** Worcester	**85A** Worcester	**85A** Worcester	**87F** Llanelly	
9430	*9400*	→	**87A** Neath	**87A** Neath	**87A** Neath	**87A** Neath	**85D** Bromsgrove	
9431	*9400*	→	**87B** Duffryn Yard	**87B** Duffryn Yard	**87B** Duffryn Yard	**87D** Swansea East Dock	**87D** Swansea East Dock	
9432	*9400*	→	**84E** Tyseley	**84E** Tyseley	**84E** Tyseley			
9433	*9400*	→	**83D** Laira (Plymouth)	**83D** Laira (Plymouth)	**83D** Laira (Plymouth)	**83D** Laira (Plymouth)		
9434	*9400*	→	→	**83F** Truro	**83F** Truro	**83G** Penzance		
9435	*9400*	→	→	**84A** Stafford Road	**84A** Stafford Road	**84A** Stafford Road	**84A** Stafford Road	
9436	*9400*	→	→	**87A** Neath	**87E** Landore	**87E** Landore		
9437	*9400*	→	→	**87B** Duffryn Yard	**88B** Cardiff East Dock	**86C** Cardiff Canton	**88L** Cardiff East Dock	
9438	*9400*	→	→	**84C** Banbury	**85B** Gloucester			
9439	*9400*	→	→	**83C** Exeter	**83C** Exeter			
9440	*9400*	→	→	**83A** Newton Abbot	**83A** Newton Abbot	**83A** Newton Abbot	**81A** Old Oak Common	
9441	*9400*	→	→	**85B** Gloucester	**85B** Gloucester	**85B** Gloucester	**87D** Swansea East Dock	
9442	*9400*	→	→	**87A** Neath	**87A** Neath	**87A** Neath	**87A** Neath	
9443	*9400*	→	→	**87F** Llanelly	**88B** Cardiff East Dock			
9444	*9400*	→	→	**87B** Duffryn Yard	**87B** Duffryn Yard	**87B** Duffryn Yard	**86F** Aberbeeg	
9445	*9400*	→	→	**85B** Gloucester	**85B** Gloucester	**85B** Gloucester		
9446	*9400*	→	→	**87A** Neath	**87B** Duffryn Yard	**87B** Duffryn Yard	**87A** Neath	
9447	*9400*	→	→	**87B** Duffryn Yard	**87B** Duffryn Yard	**81D** Reading		
9448	*9400*	→	→	**87A** Neath	**87A** Neath	**87A** Neath		
9449	*9400*	→	→	**84C** Banbury	**84C** Banbury	**84C** Banbury		
9450	*9400*	→	→	**86H** Aberbeeg	**86H** Aberbeeg	**81F** Oxford	**81D** Reading	
9451	*9400*	→	→	**87A** Neath	**86F** Tondu	**86F** Tondu		
9452	*9400*	→	→	**87H** Neyland	**87A** Neath	**87A** Neath	**87A** Neath	
9453	*9400*	→	→	**82B** St. Philips Marsh	**88C** Barry	**86C** Cardiff Canton	**85B** Gloucester	
9454	*9400*	→	→	**87B** Duffryn Yard	**87B** Duffryn Yard	**87B** Duffryn Yard		
9455	*9400*	→	→	**87B** Duffryn Yard	**87B** Duffryn Yard	**85A** Worcester	**81A** Old Oak Common	
9456	*9400*	→	→	**87B** Duffryn Yard	**87B** Duffryn Yard	**87B** Duffryn Yard	**87B** Duffryn Yard	
9457	*9400*	→	→	**87B** Duffryn Yard	**87B** Duffryn Yard	**87B** Duffryn Yard	**87B** Duffryn Yard	
9458	*9400*	→	→	**86A** Ebbw Junction	**86H** Aberbeeg	**86H** Aberbeeg		
9459	*9400*	→	→	**86H** Aberbeeg	**86C** Cardiff Canton			
9460	*9400*	→	→	**86H** Aberbeeg	**86H** Aberbeeg	**86H** Aberbeeg		
9461	*9400*	→	→	**87B** Duffryn Yard	**86C** Cardiff Canton	**86C** Cardiff Canton	**88L** Cardiff East Dock	
9462	*9400*	→	→	**83A** Newton Abbot	**83A** Newton Abbot	**83A** Newton Abbot		
9463	*9400*	→	→	**83G** Penzance	**83G** Penzance	**84G** Shrewsbury	**89A** Shrewsbury	
9464	*9400*	→	→	**85B** Gloucester	**85B** Gloucester	**85B** Gloucester	**87B** Duffryn Yard	
9465	*9400*	→	→	**87F** Llanelly	**87F** Llanelly	**87F** Llanelly		
9466	*9400*	→	→	**85A** Worcester	**85A** Worcester	**85A** Worcester	**88H** Tondu	
9467	*9400*	→	→	**83D** Laira (Plymouth)	**83D** Laira (Plymouth)	**83D** Laira (Plymouth)		
9468	*9400*	→	→	**87F** Llanelly	**86A** Ebbw Junction	**86A** Ebbw Junction		
9469	*9400*	→	→	**87F** Llanelly	**81C** Southall	**81A** Old Oak Common		
9470	*9400*	→	→	**88C** Barry	**84G** Shrewsbury	**84G** Shrewsbury	**84A** Stafford Road	
9471	*9400*	→	→	**85B** Gloucester	**85B** Gloucester	**85B** Gloucester	**85B** Gloucester	
9472	*9400*	→	→	**87F** Llanelly	**87F** Llanelly	**84G** Shrewsbury	**88C** Barry	
9473	*9400*	→	→	**87A** Neath	**87A** Neath	**87A** Neath	**87A** Neath	
9474	*9400*	→	→	**87F** Llanelly	**87F** Llanelly	**83C** Exeter		
9475	*9400*	→	→	**85B** Gloucester	**85B** Gloucester	**85B** Gloucester	**87B** Duffryn Yard	
9476	*9400*	→	→	**82C** Swindon	**82C** Swindon	**82C** Swindon		
9477	*9400*	→	→	**84F** Stourbridge	**88B** Cardiff East Dock	**85B** Gloucester	**81A** Old Oak Common	
9478	*9400*	→	→	**87A** Neath	**87A** Neath	**87A** Neath		
9479	*9400*	→	→	**87F** Llanelly	**87F** Llanelly	**81A** Old Oak Common	**81A** Old Oak Common	
9480	*9400*	→	→	**85A** Worcester	**85A** Worcester	**85A** Worcester	**88B** Radyr	
9481	*9400*	→	→	**82B** St. Philips Marsh	**82B** St. Philips Marsh	**82A** Bristol Bath Road		
9482	*9400*	→	→	**86A** Ebbw Junction	**86A** Ebbw Junction	**86A** Ebbw Junction	**86F** Aberbeeg	
9483	*9400*	→	→	**87B** Duffryn Yard	**87B** Duffryn Yard	**87B** Duffryn Yard	**87B** Duffryn Yard	
9484	*9400*	→	→	**87E** Landore	**87E** Landore	**87E** Landore	**87D** Swansea East Dock	
9485	*9400*	→	→	**87C** Danygraig	**87D** Swansea East Dock	**87F** Llanelly	**87F** Llanelly	
9486	*9400*	→	→	**87F** Llanelly	**87F** Llanelly	**85A** Worcester		
9487	*9400*	→	→	**87B** Duffryn Yard	**83A** Newton Abbot	**83A** Newton Abbot		
9488	*9400*	→	→	**82B** St. Philips Marsh	**82B** St. Philips Marsh	**82B** St. Philips Marsh	**86A** Ebbw Junction	
9489	*9400*	→	→	**87D** Swansea East Dock	**87D** Swansea East Dock	**87D** Swansea East Dock	**87D** Swansea East Dock	
9490	*9400*	→	→	→	**86A** Ebbw Junction	**81C** Southall	**85A** Worcester	
9491	*9400*	→	→	→	**87D** Swansea East Dock			
9492	*9400*	→	→	→	**87D** Swansea East Dock			
9493	*9400*	→	→	→	**86C** Cardiff Canton	**86C** Cardiff Canton	**85D** Bromsgrove	
9494	*9400*	→	→	→	**86C** Cardiff Canton	**86C** Cardiff Canton	**86F** Aberbeeg	
9495	*9400*	→	→	→	**82B** St. Philips Marsh	**82B** St. Philips Marsh	**81A** Old Oak Common	
9496	*9400*	→	→	→	**84A** Stafford Road			
9497	*9400*	→	→	→	**83C** Exeter	**83C** Exeter		
9498	*9400*	→	→	→	**84E** Tyseley	**84G** Shrewsbury	**89A** Shrewsbury	
9499	*9400*	→	→	→	**86A** Ebbw Junction			
9600	*5700*	SDN Swindon	**82C** Swindon	**82C** Swindon	**82C** Swindon	**82C** Swindon	**88J** Aberdare	
9601	*5700*	YEO Yeovil Pen Mill	**82E** Yeovil Pen Mill	**82E** Yeovil Pen Mill	**82F** Weymouth	**82B** St. Philips Marsh	**82B** St. Philips Marsh	
9602	*5700*	FGD Fishguard Goodwick	**87J** Fishguard Goodwick	**87J** Fishguard Goodwick	**87J** Fishguard Goodwick	**87J** Fishguard Goodwick	**87J** Fishguard Goodwick	
9603	*5700*	FGD Fishguard Goodwick	**87J** Fishguard Goodwick	**87J** Fishguard Goodwick	**86C** Cardiff Canton	**86C** Cardiff Canton	**88C** Barry	
9604	*5700*	SPM St. Philips Marsh	**82B** St. Philips Marsh	**82A** Bristol Bath Road	**82C** Swindon	**82C** Swindon		
9605	*5700*	SPM St. Philips Marsh	**82B** St. Philips Marsh	**82B** St. Philips Marsh	**82C** Swindon	**82C** Swindon	**82C** Swindon	
9606	*5700*	SPM St. Philips Marsh	**82B** St. Philips Marsh	**82B** St. Philips Marsh	**87C** Danygraig	**87G** Carmarthen	**87G** Carmarthen	
9607	*5700*	ABDR Aberdare	**86J** Aberdare	**86J** Aberdare	**86J** Aberdare	**86J** Aberdare	**88J** Aberdare	
9608	*5700*	TYS Tyseley	**84E** Tyseley	**84E** Tyseley	**84E** Tyseley	**83B** Taunton	**89B** Croes Newydd	**2C** Stourbridge
9609	*5700*	ABDR Aberdare	**86J** Aberdare	**86J** Aberdare	**86J** Aberdare	**86F** Tondu	**88H** Tondu	
9610	*5700*	TYS Tyseley	**84E** Tyseley	**82A** Bristol Bath Road	**82A** Bristol Bath Road	**84K** Wrexham Rhosddu	**89B** Croes Newydd	**6C** Croes Newydd
9611	*5700*	OXF Oxford	**81F** Oxford	**81F** Oxford	**81F** Oxford	**81F** Oxford	**88E** Abercynon	
9612	*5700*	WES Westbury	**82D** Westbury	**82D** Westbury	**82D** Westbury	**82D** Westbury	**82D** Westbury	
9613	*5700*	STB Stourbridge	**84F** Stourbridge	**84F** Stourbridge	**84F** Stourbridge	**84F** Stourbridge	**84F** Stourbridge	
9614	*5700*	BCN Brecon	**84E** Tyseley	**84E** Tyseley	**84E** Tyseley	**84D** Leamington Spa	**84F** Stourbridge	**2C** Stourbridge
9615	*5700*	WES Westbury	**82D** Westbury	**82D** Westbury	**82D** Westbury	**82D** Westbury	**87B** Duffryn Yard	
9616	*5700*	LTS Llantrisant	**86A** Ebbw Junction	**86A** Ebbw Junction	**86A** Ebbw Junction	**86A** Ebbw Junction	**86A** Ebbw Junction	
9617	*5700*	DYD Duffryn Yard	**87B** Duffryn Yard	**87B** Duffryn Yard	**87B** Duffryn Yard	**87B** Duffryn Yard	**87B** Duffryn Yard	
9618	*5700*	MTHR Merthyr	**88D** Merthyr	**88D** Merthyr	**88D** Merthyr	**88D** Merthyr	**88D** Merthyr	
9619	*5700*	HFD Hereford	**85C** Hereford	**85C** Hereford	**85C** Hereford	**86E** Severn Tunnel Junction	**86E** Severn Tunnel Junction	
9620	*5700*	SPM St. Philips Marsh	**82F** Weymouth	**82F** Weymouth	**82F** Weymouth	**71G** Weymouth	**71G** Weymouth	
9621	*5700*	SRD Stafford Road	**84A** Stafford Road	**84A** Stafford Road	**84A** Stafford Road	**84H** Wellington	**87F** Llanelly	
9622	*5700*	MTHR Merthyr	**88D** Merthyr	**88D** Merthyr	**88C** Barry	**88E** Abercynon	**88E** Abercynon	
9623	*5700*	NA Newton Abbot	**83A** Newton Abbot	**83A** Newton Abbot	**82A** Bristol Bath Road	**82A** Bristol Bath Road	**82E** Bristol Barrow Road	
9624	*5700*	WLN Wellington	**84H** Wellington	**84H** Wellington	**84F** Stourbridge	**84F** Stourbridge	**84F** Stourbridge	
9625	*5700*	SED Swansea East Dock	**87D** Swansea East Dock	**87D** Swansea East Dock	**87D** Swansea East Dock	**87D** Swansea East Dock	**87A** Neath	
9626	*5700*	SPM St. Philips Marsh	**82B** St. Philips Marsh	**82B** St. Philips Marsh	**82B** St. Philips Marsh	**82A** Bristol Bath Road	**82E** Bristol Barrow Road	
9627	*5700*	NEA Neath	**87A** Neath	**87A** Neath	**87A** Neath	**87A** Neath		
9628	*5700*	WES Westbury	**82D** Westbury	**82D** Westbury	**82D** Westbury	**82D** Westbury	**82D** Westbury	
9629	*5700*	CDF Cardiff Canton	**86C** Cardiff Canton	**83C** Exeter	**83C** Exeter	**83C** Exeter	**88L** Cardiff East Dock	
9630	*5700*	WLN Wellington	**84H** Wellington	**84H** Wellington	**84H** Wellington	**84H** Wellington	**84H** Wellington	**6C** Croes Newydd
9631	*5700*	BRY Barry	**88C** Barry	**88C** Barry	**88C** Barry	**88D** Merthyr	**88D** Merthyr	
9632	*5700*	NPT Ebbw Junction	**86A** Ebbw Junction	**86A** Ebbw Junction	**87G** Carmarthen	**72C** Yeovil Town	**87G** Carmarthen	
9633	*5700*	NA Newton Abbot	**83A** Newton Abbot	**83A** Newton Abbot	**83A** Newton Abbot	**83A** Newton Abbot	**87B** Duffryn Yard	
9634	*5700*	DYD Duffryn Yard	**87B** Duffryn Yard	**87B** Duffryn Yard	**87B** Duffryn Yard	**87B** Duffryn Yard	**87B** Duffryn Yard	
9635	*5700*	TYS Tyseley	**84E** Tyseley	**84E** Tyseley	**84E** Tyseley	**84E** Tyseley	**83C** Exeter	
9636	*5700*	STB Stourbridge	**84F** Stourbridge	**84F** Stourbridge	**84F** Stourbridge	**84F** Stourbridge	**84H** Wellington	

		1948	1951	1954	1957	1960	1963	1966
9637	*5700*	**NPT** Ebbw Junction	**86A** Ebbw Junction	**86A** Ebbw Junction	**87E** Landore	**87E** Landore	**87F** Llanelly	
9638	*5700*	**MTHR** Merthyr	**88D** Merthyr	**88D** Merthyr	**88D** Merthyr	**88D** Merthyr	**88D** Merthyr	
9639	*5700*	**WLN** Wellington	**84H** Wellington	**84H** Wellington	**84H** Wellington	**84H** Wellington	**84H** Wellington	
9640	*5700*	**SLO** Slough	**81F** Oxford	**81F** Oxford	**81F** Oxford	**81F** Oxford	**81A** Old Oak Common	**2B** Oxley
9641	*5700*	**SHL** Southall	**81C** Southall	**81C** Southall	**81C** Southall	**81C** Southall	**81C** Southall	**2C** Stourbridge
9642	*5700*	**WEY** Weymouth	**82F** Weymouth	**82F** Weymouth	**88E** Abercynon	**81C** Southall	**81C** Southall	
9643	*5700*	**MTHR** Merthyr	**88D** Merthyr	**88D** Merthyr	**88D** Merthyr	**88D** Merthyr		
9644	*5700*	**NPT** Ebbw Junction	**86A** Ebbw Junction	**86A** Ebbw Junction	**86A** Ebbw Junction	**86A** Ebbw Junction	**86A** Ebbw Junction	
9645	*5700*	**SED** Swansea East Dock	**87D** Swansea East Dock	**87D** Swansea East Dock	**87D** Swansea East Dock	**87G** Carmarthen	**87J** Fishguard Goodwick	
9646	*5700*	**EXE** Exeter	**83B** Taunton	**83B** Taunton	**83B** Taunton	**83B** Taunton	**84F** Stourbridge	
9647	*5700*	**EXE** Exeter	**83C** Exeter	**83B** Taunton	**83B** Taunton	**83B** Taunton	**83B** Taunton	
9648	*5700*	**CDF** Cardiff Canton	**86C** Cardiff Canton	**86C** Cardiff Canton	**86C** Cardiff Canton	**86C** Cardiff Canton	**88C** Barry	
9649	*5700*	**TDU** Tondu	**86F** Tondu	**86F** Tondu	**86F** Tondu	**86F** Tondu	**88H** Tondu	
9650	*5700*	**PPRD** Pontypool Road	**86G** Pontypool Road	**86G** Pontypool Road	**86G** Pontypool Road	**86G** Pontypool Road	**86G** Pontypool Road	
9651	*5700*	**BHD** Birkenhead	**6C** Birkenhead	**6C** Birkenhead	**6C** Birkenhead	**82B** St. Philips Marsh	**88L** Cardiff East Dock	
9652	*5700*	**NEY** Neyland	**87H** Neyland	**87H** Neyland	**87H** Neyland	**87F** Llanelly	**87F** Llanelly	
9653	*5700*	**SLO** Slough	**81B** Slough	**81F** Oxford	**81F** Oxford	**81F** Oxford	**81F** Oxford	
9654	*5700*	**OXF** Oxford	**81F** Oxford	**81F** Oxford	**81F** Oxford	**81F** Oxford	**81F** Oxford	
9655	*5700*	**SBZ** St. Blazey	**83E** St. Blazey	**83E** St. Blazey	**83E** St. Blazey	**83E** St. Blazey	**86G** Pontypool Road	
9656	*5700*	**CNYD** Croes Newydd	**84G** Shrewsbury	**84G** Shrewsbury	**84G** Shrewsbury	**84G** Shrewsbury	**87B** Duffryn Yard	
9657	*5700*	**SALOP** Shrewsbury	**84G** Shrewsbury	**84G** Shrewsbury	**84G** Shrewsbury	**84G** Shrewsbury	**89A** Shrewsbury	**6D** Shrewsbury
9658	*5700*	**PDN** Old Oak Common	**81A** Old Oak Common	**81A** Old Oak Common	**81A** Old Oak Common	**81A** Old Oak Common	**81A** Old Oak Common	**2B** Oxley
9659	*5700*	**PDN** Old Oak Common	**81A** Old Oak Common	**81A** Old Oak Common	**81A** Old Oak Common	**81A** Old Oak Common	**81A** Old Oak Common	
9660	*5700*	**TDU** Tondu	**86F** Tondu	**86F** Tondu	**86F** Tondu	**86F** Tondu	**88H** Tondu	
9661	*5700*	**PDN** Old Oak Common	**81A** Old Oak Common	**81A** Old Oak Common	**81A** Old Oak Common	**81A** Old Oak Common	**81A** Old Oak Common	
9662	*5700*	→	**86A** Ebbw Junction	**86A** Ebbw Junction	**86A** Ebbw Junction	**86K** Tredegar	**86A** Ebbw Junction	
9663	*5700*	→	**83B** Taunton	**83B** Taunton	**83B** Taunton	**83B** Taunton	**83B** Taunton	
9664	*5700*	→	**86A** Ebbw Junction	**86A** Ebbw Junction	**86A** Ebbw Junction	**86A** Ebbw Junction	**86A** Ebbw Junction	
9665	*5700*	→	**82B** St. Philips Marsh	**82B** St. Philips Marsh	**85C** Hereford	**85C** Hereford	**86C** Hereford	
9666	*5700*	→	**87A** Neath	**87G** Carmarthen	**87G** Carmarthen	**87J** Fishguard Goodwick	**87J** Fishguard Goodwick	
9667	*5700*	→	**86A** Ebbw Junction	**86A** Ebbw Junction	**86A** Ebbw Junction	**86A** Ebbw Junction	**86A** Ebbw Junction	
9668	*5700*	→	**83A** Newton Abbot	**83A** Newton Abbot	**83A** Newton Abbot	**82D** Westbury	**88E** Abercynon	
9669	*5700*	→	**84J** Croes Newydd	**84J** Croes Newydd	**84J** Croes Newydd	**84J** Croes Newydd	**89B** Croes Newydd	**6C** Croes Newydd
9670	*5700*	→	**83B** Taunton	**83B** Taunton	**83B** Taunton	**83B** Taunton	**83B** Taunton	
9671	*5700*	→	**83D** Laira (Plymouth)	**83D** Laira (Plymouth)	**83B** Taunton	**83B** Taunton	**87B** Duffryn Yard	
9672	*5700*	→	**84G** Shrewsbury	**84G** Shrewsbury	**82C** Swindon	**82C** Swindon	**82C** Swindon	
9673	*5700*	→	**83D** Laira (Plymouth)	**83E** St. Blazey	**83E** St. Blazey	**83E** St. Blazey		
9674	*5700*	→	**86F** Tondu	**86A** Ebbw Junction	**86A** Ebbw Junction	**86A** Ebbw Junction	**82D** Westbury	
9675	*5700*	→	**88D** Merthyr	**88D** Merthyr	**88D** Merthyr	**88D** Merthyr	**88D** Merthyr	
9676	*5700*	→	**88C** Barry	**88C** Barry	**88C** Barry	**88D** Merthyr	**88D** Merthyr	
9677	*5700*	→	**88B** Cardiff East Dock	**88B** Cardiff East Dock	**88B** Cardiff East Dock	**87J** Fishguard Goodwick	**87J** Fishguard Goodwick	
9678	*5700*	→	**6C** Birkenhead	**83A** Newton Abbot	**83A** Newton Abbot	**83A** Newton Abbot	**88H** Tondu	
9679	*5700*	→	**88B** Cardiff East Dock	**88B** Cardiff East Dock	**88B** Cardiff East Dock	**88D** Merthyr	**88D** Merthyr	
9680	*5700*	→	**84E** Tyseley	**84E** Tyseley	**84E** Tyseley	**84E** Tyseley	**82C** Swindon	
9681	*5700*	→	**86F** Tondu	**86F** Tondu	**89A** Oswestry	**89A** Oswestry	**88C** Barry	
9682	*5700*	→	**84E** Tyseley	**84E** Tyseley	**84E** Tyseley	**84E** Tyseley	**86F** Aberbeeg	
9700	*9700*	**PDN** Old Oak Common	**81A** Old Oak Common	**81A** Old Oak Common	**81A** Old Oak Common	**81A** Old Oak Common	**81A** Old Oak Common	
9701	*9700*	**PDN** Old Oak Common	**81A** Old Oak Common	**81A** Old Oak Common	**81A** Old Oak Common	**81A** Old Oak Common		
9702	*9700*	**PDN** Old Oak Common	**81A** Old Oak Common	**81A** Old Oak Common	**81A** Old Oak Common	**81A** Old Oak Common		
9703	*9700*	**PDN** Old Oak Common	**81A** Old Oak Common	**81A** Old Oak Common	**81A** Old Oak Common	**81A** Old Oak Common		
9704	*9700*	**PDN** Old Oak Common	**81A** Old Oak Common	**81A** Old Oak Common	**81A** Old Oak Common	**81A** Old Oak Common	**81A** Old Oak Common	
9705	*9700*	**PDN** Old Oak Common	**81A** Old Oak Common	**81A** Old Oak Common	**81A** Old Oak Common	**81A** Old Oak Common		
9706	*9700*	**PDN** Old Oak Common	**81A** Old Oak Common	**81A** Old Oak Common	**81A** Old Oak Common	**81A** Old Oak Common	**81A** Old Oak Common	
9707	*9700*	**PDN** Old Oak Common	**81A** Old Oak Common	**81A** Old Oak Common	**81A** Old Oak Common	**81A** Old Oak Common	**81A** Old Oak Common	
9708	*9700*	**PDN** Old Oak Common	**81A** Old Oak Common	**81A** Old Oak Common	**81A** Old Oak Common			
9709	*9700*	**PDN** Old Oak Common	**81A** Old Oak Common	**81A** Old Oak Common	**81A** Old Oak Common	**81A** Old Oak Common		
9710	*9700*	**PDN** Old Oak Common	**81A** Old Oak Common	**81A** Old Oak Common	**81A** Old Oak Common	**81A** Old Oak Common	**81A** Old Oak Common	
9711	*5700*	**LA** Laira (Plymouth)	**83D** Laira (Plymouth)	**83D** Laira (Plymouth)	**83D** Laira (Plymouth)	**83D** Laira (Plymouth)	**88B** Radyr	
9712	*5700*	**ABDR** Aberdare	**86J** Aberdare	**86J** Aberdare	**86J** Aberdare	**86J** Aberdare		
9713	*5700*	**CDF** Cardiff Canton	**86C** Cardiff Canton	**86C** Cardiff Canton	**86C** Cardiff Canton	**86C** Cardiff Canton	**88C** Barry	
9714	*5700*	**OXY** Oxley	**84B** Oxley	**84B** Oxley	**87H** Neyland	**87H** Neyland		
9715	*5700*	**OXY** Oxley	**84B** Oxley	**84B** Oxley	**87E** Landore	**87E** Landore	**87B** Duffryn Yard	
9716	*5700*	**LA** Laira (Plymouth)	**83D** Laira (Plymouth)	**83D** Laira (Plymouth)	**83D** Laira (Plymouth)	**83D** Laira (Plymouth)	**87A** Neath	
9717	*5700*	**NA** Newton Abbot	**83G** Penzance	**83G** Penzance	**85C** Hereford	**85C** Hereford		
9718	*5700*	**TN** Taunton	**83B** Taunton	**83B** Taunton	**83B** Taunton	**83B** Taunton		
9719	*5700*	**SALOP** Shrewsbury	**84G** Shrewsbury	**84F** Stourbridge	**84F** Stourbridge	**84F** Stourbridge		
9720	*5700*	**SDN** Swindon	**82C** Swindon	**82C** Swindon	**82C** Swindon	**82C** Swindon		
9721	*5700*	**SDN** Swindon	**82C** Swindon	**82C** Swindon	**82C** Swindon	**82C** Swindon		
9722	*5700*	**RDG** Reading	**81B** Slough	**81B** Slough	**81B** Slough	**81B** Slough		
9723	*5700*	**ABEEG** Aberbeeg	**86C** Cardiff Canton	**86C** Cardiff Canton	**86C** Cardiff Canton	**86C** Cardiff Canton		
9724	*5700*	**TYS** Tyseley	**84E** Tyseley	**84E** Tyseley	**84E** Tyseley	**84E** Tyseley	**84E** Tyseley	**2C** Stourbridge
9725	*5700*	**PDN** Old Oak Common	**81A** Old Oak Common	**81A** Old Oak Common	**81A** Old Oak Common	**81A** Old Oak Common		
9726	*5700*	**PDN** Old Oak Common	**81C** Southall	**81C** Southall	**81C** Southall	**81C** Southall	**81C** Southall	
9727	*5700*	**GLO** Gloucester	**85B** Gloucester	**85B** Gloucester	**84E** Tyseley	**84E** Tyseley		
9728	*5700*	**CHR** Chester (GWR)	**84K** Chester (GWR)	**84K** Chester (GWR)	**84K** Chester (GWR)	**6E** Chester (GWR)		
9729	*5700*	**SPM** St. Philips Marsh	**82B** St. Philips Marsh	**82B** St. Philips Marsh	**82A** Bristol Bath Road	**82B** St. Philips Marsh	**82B** St. Philips Marsh	
9730	*5700*	**OXY** Oxley	**84B** Oxley	**84B** Oxley	**86G** Pontypool Road	**86G** Pontypool Road	**86G** Pontypool Road	
9731	*5700*	**NPT** Ebbw Junction	**86A** Ebbw Junction	**86J** Aberdare	**86J** Aberdare	**86J** Aberdare	**88J** Aberdare	
9732	*5700*	**SPM** St. Philips Marsh	**82E** Yeovil Pen Mill	**82E** Yeovil Pen Mill	**82E** Yeovil Pen Mill	**72C** Yeovil Town	**72C** Yeovil Town	
9733	*5700*	**TYS** Tyseley	**84E** Tyseley	**84E** Tyseley	**84E** Tyseley	**84D** Leamington Spa	**84F** Stourbridge	
9734	*5700*	**NEA** Neath	**87A** Neath	**87A** Neath	**87A** Neath	**87A** Neath	**87A** Neath	
9735	*5700*	**DYD** Duffryn Yard	**87B** Duffryn Yard	**87B** Duffryn Yard	**87B** Duffryn Yard	**87B** Duffryn Yard		
9736	*5700*	**DYD** Duffryn Yard	**87B** Duffryn Yard	**87B** Duffryn Yard	**87B** Duffryn Yard	**87B** Duffryn Yard		
9737	*5700*	**DYD** Duffryn Yard	**87B** Duffryn Yard	**87B** Duffryn Yard	**87B** Duffryn Yard	**87B** Duffryn Yard		
9738	*5700*	**LDR** Landore	**87E** Landore	**87E** Landore	**87E** Landore	**87E** Landore		
9739	*5700*	**OXY** Oxley	**84B** Oxley	**84B** Oxley	**84B** Oxley	**84B** Oxley		
9740	*5700*	**LMTN** Leamington Spa	**84D** Leamington Spa	**84G** Shrewsbury	**82C** Swindon	**82C** Swindon		
9741	*5700*	**STB** Stourbridge	**84F** Stourbridge	**84H** Wellington	**84H** Wellington	**84H** Wellington		
9742	*5700*	**OXY** Oxley	**84B** Oxley	**84H** Wellington	**84H** Wellington	**87B** Duffryn Yard	**87B** Duffryn Yard	
9743	*5700*	**LLY** Llanelly	**87F** Llanelly	**87F** Llanelly	**87F** Llanelly	**87F** Llanelly	**87A** Neath	
9744	*5700*	**SED** Swansea East Dock	**87D** Swansea East Dock	**87D** Swansea East Dock	**87C** Danygraig	**87C** Danygraig	**87D** Swansea East Dock	
9745	*5700*	**STJ** Severn Tunnel Junction	**86E** Severn Tunnel Junction	**86E** Severn Tunnel Junction	**86E** Severn Tunnel Junction	**86A** Ebbw Junction		
9746	*5700*	**LTS** Llantrisant	**86D** Llantrisant	**86D** Llantrisant	**86A** Ebbw Junction	**86A** Ebbw Junction	**87D** Swansea East Dock	
9747	*5700*	**OXY** Oxley	**84B** Oxley	**84B** Oxley	**88D** Merthyr	**88D** Merthyr	**88D** Merthyr	
9748	*5700*	**TYS** Tyseley	**84E** Tyseley	**83G** Penzance	**83G** Penzance	**83G** Penzance	**87A** Neath	
9749	*5700*	**RDG** Reading	**81D** Reading	**81D** Reading	**81D** Reading	**81D** Reading		
9750	*5700*	**NEA** Neath	**87A** Neath	**87A** Neath	**87A** Neath	**87A** Neath		
9751	*5700*	**PDN** Old Oak Common	**81A** Old Oak Common	**81A** Old Oak Common	**81A** Old Oak Common	**81A** Old Oak Common		
9752	*5700*	**OXY** Oxley	**84B** Oxley	**84B** Oxley	**84B** Oxley	**84B** Oxley	**87D** Swansea East Dock	
9753	*5700*	**TYS** Tyseley	**84E** Tyseley	**84E** Tyseley	**84E** Tyseley	**84E** Tyseley	**84E** Tyseley	
9754	*5700*	**PDN** Old Oak Common	**81A** Old Oak Common	**81A** Old Oak Common	**81A** Old Oak Common	**81A** Old Oak Common	**82C** Swindon	
9755	*5700*	**SHL** Southall	**83E** St. Blazey	**83E** St. Blazey	**83E** St. Blazey	**83E** St. Blazey	**81A** Old Oak Common	
9756	*5700*	**NEA** Neath	**87A** Neath	**87A** Neath	**87A** Neath	**72A** Exmouth Junction		
9757	*5700*	**TN** Taunton	**83B** Taunton	**83B** Taunton	**83B** Taunton	**83B** Taunton		
9758	*5700*	**PDN** Old Oak Common	**81A** Old Oak Common	**81A** Old Oak Common	**81A** Old Oak Common	**81A** Old Oak Common		
9759	*5700*	**CDF** Cardiff Canton	**86C** Cardiff Canton	**86C** Cardiff Canton	**86C** Cardiff Canton	**86C** Cardiff Canton		
9760	*5700*	**FGD** Fishguard Goodwick	**87J** Fishguard Goodwick	**87J** Fishguard Goodwick	**87J** Fishguard Goodwick	**87J** Fishguard Goodwick	**87J** Fishguard Goodwick	
9761	*5700*	**LDR** Landore	**87E** Landore	**87E** Landore	**87A** Neath	**87A** Neath		
9762	*5700*	**WES** Westbury	**82D** Westbury	**82D** Westbury	**82D** Westbury	**82D** Westbury		
9763	*5700*	**RDG** Reading	**81D** Reading	**81D** Reading	**81D** Reading	**81D** Reading	**81D** Reading	
9764	*5700*	**SPM** St. Philips Marsh	**82B** St. Philips Marsh	**82E** Yeovil Pen Mill	**82E** Yeovil Pen Mill	**72C** Yeovil Town	**72C** Yeovil Town	
9765	*5700*	**LA** Laira (Plymouth)	**83D** Laira (Plymouth)	**83C** Exeter	**83C** Exeter	**83C** Exeter		
9766	*5700*	**DYD** Duffryn Yard	**87B** Duffryn Yard	**87B** Duffryn Yard	**87B** Duffryn Yard	**87B** Duffryn Yard	**87B** Duffryn Yard	
9767	*5700*	**STB** Stourbridge	**84F** Stourbridge	**84F** Stourbridge	**84F** Stourbridge	**84F** Stourbridge		

No	Class	1948	1951	1954	1957	1960	1963	1966
9768	*5700*	**OXY** Oxley	**84B** Oxley	**84B** Oxley	**84B** Oxley	**84B** Oxley	**84B** Oxley	
9769	*5700*	**OXY** Oxley	**84B** Oxley	**84B** Oxley	**88B** Cardiff East Dock	**82B** St. Philips Marsh	**82D** Westbury	
9770	*5700*	**LA** Laira (Plymouth)	**83D** Laira (Plymouth)	**83D** Laira (Plymouth)	**83D** Laira (Plymouth)	**70A** Nine Elms	**70A** Nine Elms	
9771	*5700*	**YEO** Yeovil Pen Mill	**82E** Yeovil Pen Mill	**82B** St. Philips Marsh	**82A** Bristol Bath Road	**82A** Bristol Bath Road		
9772	*5700*	**SDN** Swindon	**82C** Swindon	**82C** Swindon	**82C** Swindon			
9773	*5700*	**SDN** Swindon	**82C** Swindon	**82C** Swindon	**82C** Swindon	**82C** Swindon	**82C** Swindon	
9774	*5700*	**CHR** Chester (GWR)	**84K** Chester (GWR)	**84H** Wellington	**84H** Wellington	**84H** Wellington	**84H** Wellington	**2A** Tyseley
9775	*5700*	**LDR** Landore	**87E** Landore	**87E** Landore	**87E** Landore	**87E** Landore		
9776	*5700*	**GLO** Gloucester	**88C** Barry	**88B** Cardiff East Dock	**88B** Cardiff East Dock	**88D** Merthyr	**88D** Merthyr	**2B** Oxley
9777	*5700*	**LDR** Landore	**87E** Landore	**87E** Landore	**87E** Landore	**87E** Landore	**87A** Neath	
9778	*5700*	**CDF** Cardiff Canton	**83A** Newton Abbot	**86C** Cardiff Canton	**86C** Cardiff Canton	**86C** Cardiff Canton	**88G** Llantrisant	
9779	*5700*	**NEA** Neath	**87A** Neath	**87A** Neath	**87A** Neath	**87A** Neath	**87A** Neath	
9780	*5700*	**LTS** Llantrisant	**86D** Llantrisant	**86D** Llantrisant	**86D** Llantrisant	**86D** Llantrisant	**88C** Barry	
9781	*5700*	**SLO** Slough	**81B** Slough	**81B** Slough	**81B** Slough	**81B** Slough		
9782	*5700*	**BAN** Banbury	**84C** Banbury	**84F** Stourbridge	**84F** Stourbridge	**84F** Stourbridge	**84F** Stourbridge	
9783	*5700*	**NEA** Neath	**87A** Neath	**87A** Neath	**87A** Neath	**87A** Neath		
9784	*5700*	**PDN** Old Oak Common	**81A** Old Oak Common	**81A** Old Oak Common	**81A** Old Oak Common	**81A** Old Oak Common	**81A** Old Oak Common	
9785	*5700*	**DYD** Duffryn Yard	**87B** Duffryn Yard	**87B** Duffryn Yard	**87B** Duffryn Yard	**87B** Duffryn Yard		
9786	*5700*	**NEA** Neath	**87A** Neath	**87A** Neath	**87A** Neath	**87A** Neath	**87A** Neath	
9787	*5700*	**LLY** Llanelly	**87F** Llanelly	**87F** Llanelly	**87F** Llanelly	**87G** Carmarthen	**87G** Carmarthen	
9788	*5700*	**LLY** Llanelly	**87F** Llanelly	**87F** Llanelly	**87F** Llanelly	**87F** Llanelly	**87B** Duffryn Yard	
9789	*5700*	**SLO** Slough	**81B** Slough	**81B** Slough	**81C** Southall	**81C** Southall	**81D** Reading	
9790	*5700*	**SDN** Swindon	**82C** Swindon	**82C** Swindon	**82C** Swindon	**82C** Swindon	**82C** Swindon	
9791	*5700*	**RDG** Reading	**81D** Reading	**81D** Reading	**81D** Reading	**81C** Southall	**81E** Didcot	
9792	*5700*	**NEA** Neath	**87A** Neath	**87A** Neath	**87A** Neath	**87A** Neath	**87A** Neath	
9793	*5700*	**TYS** Tyseley	**84E** Tyseley	**84J** Croes Newydd	**84J** Croes Newydd	**84J** Croes Newydd	**89B** Croes Newydd	
9794	*5700*	**CHR** Chester (GWR)	**84K** Chester (GWR)	**84K** Chester (GWR)	**84K** Chester (GWR)	**6E** Chester (GWR)	**88C** Barry	
9795	*5700*	**SDN** Swindon	**82C** Swindon	**82C** Swindon	**82C** Swindon	**82C** Swindon		
9796	*5700*	**CDF** Cardiff Canton	**86H** Aberbeeg	**86G** Pontypool Road	**86G** Pontypool Road	**86G** Pontypool Road	**86G** Pontypool Road	
9797	*5700*	**PPRD** Pontypool Road	**86G** Pontypool Road	**86G** Pontypool Road	**86G** Pontypool Road	**86G** Pontypool Road		
9798	*5700*	**TYS** Tyseley	**84E** Tyseley	**84E** Tyseley	**84E** Tyseley	**84E** Tyseley	**84E** Tyseley	
9799	*5700*	**DYD** Duffryn Yard	**87B** Duffryn Yard	**87B** Duffryn Yard	**87B** Duffryn Yard	**87B** Duffryn Yard	**87B** Duffryn Yard	

Llanelly & Mynydd Mawr Railway 0-6-0ST No 359 *Hilda* at Swansea East Dock on 6 September 1936. *R. J .Buckley*

Top: Brecon & Merthyr Railway '4ft 6in' 0-6-2T No 425. It carries the code PILL for Newport Pill on the edge of the running plate and carries an original boiler. *P. Ransome-Wallis*

Above: Alexandra Docks Railway 0-6-0T No 667. *Brian Morrison*

Right: Cardiff Railway 0-6-0PT No 682. *P. Ransome-Wallis*

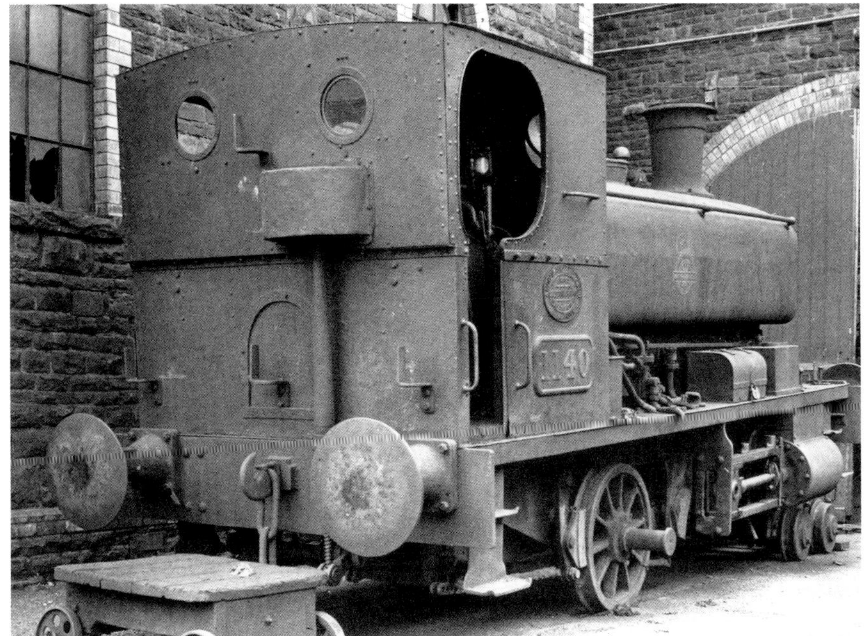

Left: Swansea Harbour Trust Barclay 0-4-0ST No 1140 at Danygraig. *Brian Morrison*

Right: Swansea Harbour Trust Hudswell Clarke 0-4-0ST No 1142 at Danygraig.

Left: Swansea Harbour Trust Peckett 0-4-0ST No 1143 at Danygraig. *P. J. Sharpe*

Right: Swansea Harbour Trust Hawthorn Leslie 0-4-0ST No 1144 at Swansea East Dock Shed on 22 August 1959. *N. Preedy*

Below: Swansea Harbour Trust Peckett 0-6-0ST No 1085 (later renumbered 1146) at Danygraig on 28 May 1939. *A. B. Crompton*

Bottom: Powlesland & Mason Peckett 0-4-0ST No 1151 at Swansea Victoria on 27 July 1962. *Leslie Sandler*

Left: Powlesland & Mason Hawthorn Leslie 0-4-0ST No 942 (formerly named *Dorothy*, later renumbered 1153) at Danygraig on 28 May 1939. *A. B. Crompton*

Below: Alexandra Docks Railway 2-6-2T No 1205. *P. Ransome-Wallis*

Bottom: Cardiff Railway Kitson 0-4-0ST No 1338 at Swansea in 1961. *G. T. Storer*

Above: Port Talbot Railway 0-8-2T No 1358.

Left: Burry Port & Gwendraeth Valley Railway 0-6-0T No 2165.

Below: Burry Port & Gwendraeth Valley Railway 0-6-0ST No 2176.

Above: GWR Churchward 'Saint' '2900' class 4-6-0 No 2938 *Corsham Court* at Gloucester in October 1951.

Below: ROD Robinson 2-8-0 No 3048 allocated to WOS (Worcester), but seen at Reading in September 1948. *G. G. S. Delicata*

Right: GWR Churchward '3100' class 2-6-2T No 3103.

Below: GWR Churchward '3150' class 2-6-2T No 3187.

Bottom: GWR Dean '3500' class 2-4-0T No 3589 of OXF (Oxford) shed at Cowley in 1947.

Above: GWR Churchward 'Star' '4000' class 4-6-0 No 4052 *Princess Beatrice* at Cardiff Canton shed on 10 September 1950. Fitted with later type of outside steam pipes. *P. M. Alexander*

Left: GWR Churchward '4200' class 2-8-0T No 4257 from 86J Aberdare at Gloucester Shed in June 1952.

Below: GWR Collett '4575' class 2-6-2T No 5527 at 88C Barry on 26 June 1955. *D. Marriott*

Left: GWR Collett '5800' class 0-4-2T No 5811 at Oxford MPD 10 May 1957. It is probably making its way to Swindon Works as it was withdrawn and scrapped that same month. *F. J. Bullock*

Right: GWR Churchward '4300' class 2-6-0 No 6378 of 85A Worcester is seen at its home shed in April 1953. *T. J. Edgington*

Below: GWR Collett '6400' class 0-6-0PT No 6434 at 88A Radyr on 23 May 1959. R. A. *Panting*

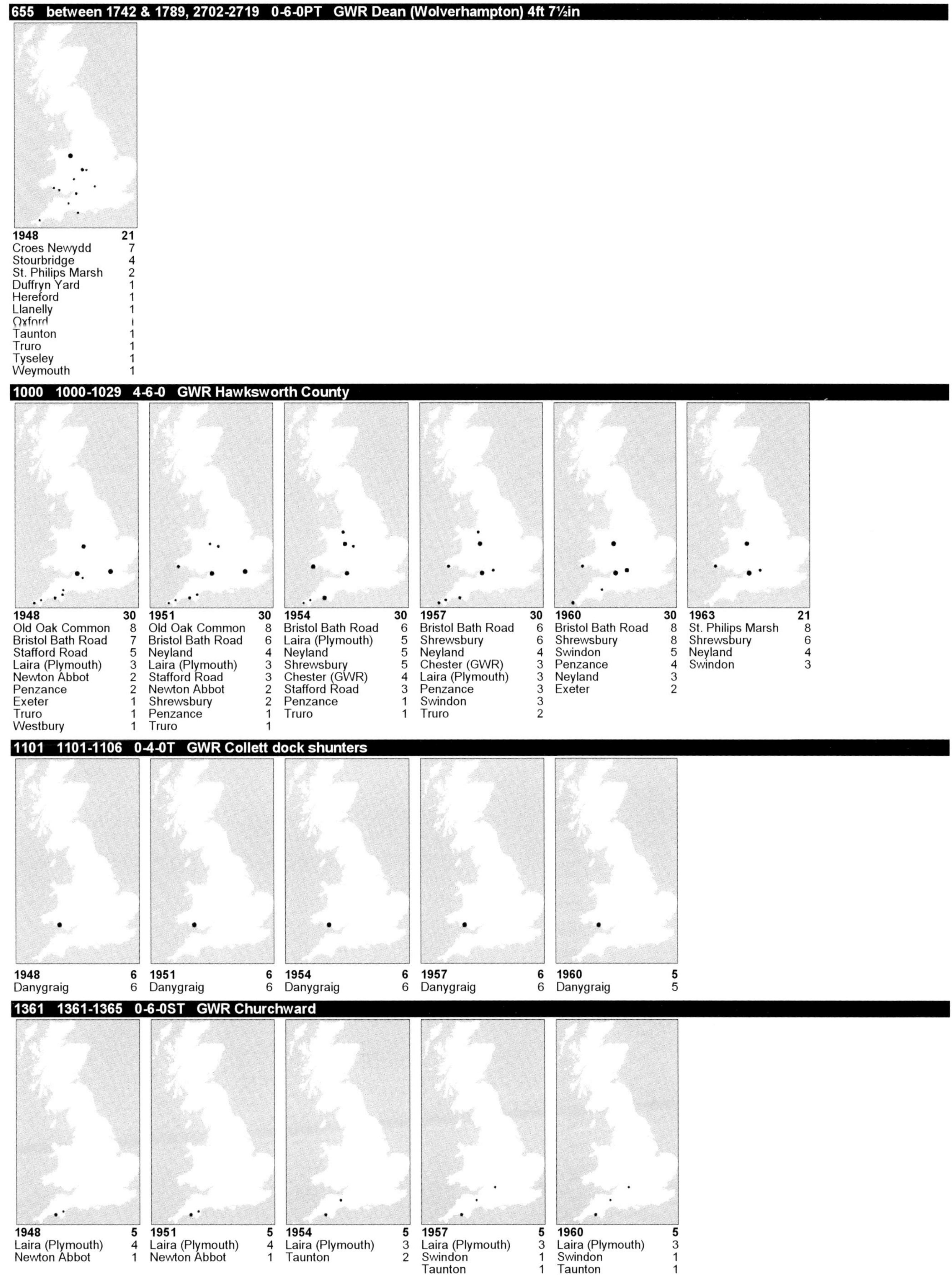

655 between 1742 & 1789, 2702-2719 0-6-0PT GWR Dean (Wolverhampton) 4ft 7½in

1948	21
Croes Newydd	7
Stourbridge	4
St. Philips Marsh	2
Duffryn Yard	1
Hereford	1
Llanelly	1
Oxford	1
Taunton	1
Truro	1
Tyseley	1
Weymouth	1

1000 1000-1029 4-6-0 GWR Hawksworth County

1948	30
Old Oak Common	8
Bristol Bath Road	7
Stafford Road	5
Laira (Plymouth)	3
Newton Abbot	2
Penzance	2
Exeter	1
Truro	1
Westbury	1

1951	30
Old Oak Common	8
Bristol Bath Road	6
Neyland	4
Laira (Plymouth)	3
Stafford Road	3
Newton Abbot	2
Shrewsbury	2
Penzance	1
Truro	1

1954	30
Bristol Bath Road	6
Laira (Plymouth)	5
Neyland	5
Shrewsbury	5
Chester (GWR)	4
Stafford Road	3
Penzance	1
Truro	1

1957	30
Bristol Bath Road	6
Shrewsbury	6
Neyland	4
Chester (GWR)	3
Laira (Plymouth)	3
Penzance	3
Swindon	3
Truro	2

1960	30
Bristol Bath Road	8
Shrewsbury	8
Swindon	5
Penzance	4
Neyland	3
Exeter	2

1963	21
St. Philips Marsh	8
Shrewsbury	6
Neyland	4
Swindon	3

1101 1101-1106 0-4-0T GWR Collett dock shunters

1948	6
Danygraig	6

1951	6
Danygraig	6

1954	6
Danygraig	6

1957	6
Danygraig	6

1960	5
Danygraig	5

1361 1361-1365 0-6-0ST GWR Churchward

1948	5
Laira (Plymouth)	4
Newton Abbot	1

1951	5
Laira (Plymouth)	4
Newton Abbot	1

1954	5
Laira (Plymouth)	3
Taunton	2

1957	5
Laira (Plymouth)	3
Swindon	1
Taunton	1

1960	5
Laira (Plymouth)	3
Swindon	1
Taunton	1

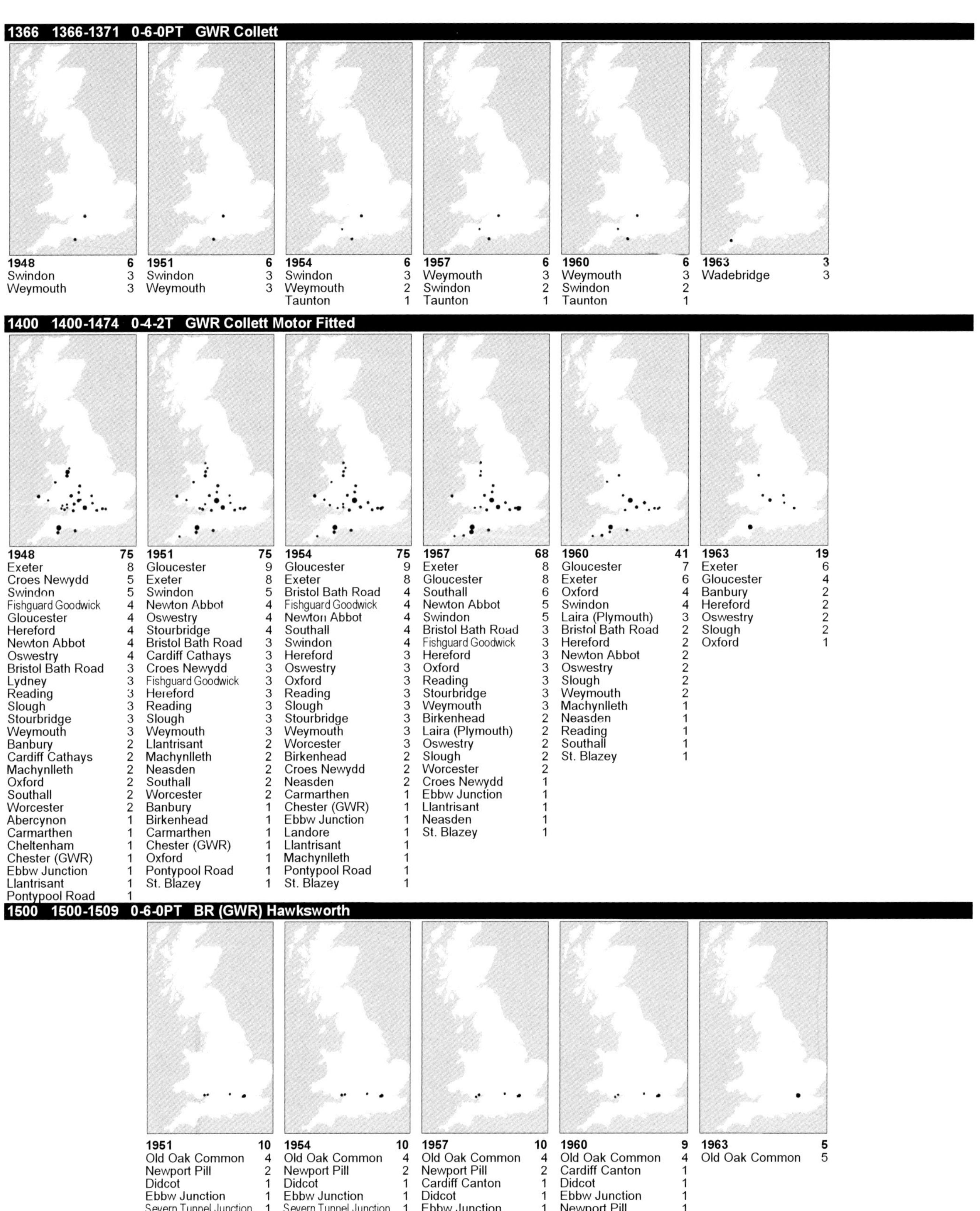

1366 1366-1371 0-6-0PT GWR Collett

1948	6	1951	6	1954	6	1957	6	1960	6	1963	3
Swindon	3	Swindon	3	Swindon	3	Weymouth	3	Weymouth	3	Wadebridge	3
Weymouth	3	Weymouth	3	Weymouth	2	Swindon	2	Swindon	2		
				Taunton	1	Taunton	1	Taunton	1		

1400 1400-1474 0-4-2T GWR Collett Motor Fitted

1948	75	1951	75	1954	75	1957	68	1960	41	1963	19
Exeter	8	Gloucester	9	Gloucester	9	Exeter	8	Gloucester	7	Exeter	6
Croes Newydd	5	Exeter	8	Exeter	8	Gloucester	8	Exeter	6	Gloucester	4
Swindon	5	Swindon	5	Bristol Bath Road	4	Southall	6	Oxford	4	Banbury	2
Fishguard Goodwick	4	Newton Abbot	4	Fishguard Goodwick	4	Newton Abbot	5	Swindon	4	Hereford	2
Gloucester	4	Oswestry	4	Newton Abbot	4	Swindon	5	Laira (Plymouth)	3	Oswestry	2
Hereford	4	Stourbridge	4	Southall	4	Bristol Bath Road	3	Bristol Bath Road	2	Slough	2
Newton Abbot	4	Bristol Bath Road	3	Swindon	4	Fishguard Goodwick	3	Hereford	2	Oxford	1
Oswestry	4	Cardiff Cathays	3	Hereford	3	Hereford	3	Newton Abbot	2		
Bristol Bath Road	3	Croes Newydd	3	Oswestry	3	Oxford	3	Oswestry	2		
Lydney	3	Fishguard Goodwick	3	Oxford	3	Reading	3	Slough	2		
Reading	3	Hereford	3	Reading	3	Stourbridge	3	Weymouth	2		
Slough	3	Reading	3	Slough	3	Weymouth	3	Machynlleth	1		
Stourbridge	3	Slough	3	Stourbridge	3	Birkenhead	2	Neasden	1		
Weymouth	3	Weymouth	3	Weymouth	3	Laira (Plymouth)	2	Reading	1		
Banbury	2	Llantrisant	2	Worcester	3	Oswestry	2	Southall	1		
Cardiff Cathays	2	Machynlleth	2	Birkenhead	2	Slough	2	St. Blazey	1		
Machynlleth	2	Neasden	2	Croes Newydd	2	Worcester	2				
Oxford	2	Southall	2	Neasden	2	Croes Newydd	1				
Southall	2	Worcester	2	Carmarthen	1	Ebbw Junction	1				
Worcester	2	Banbury	1	Chester (GWR)	1	Llantrisant	1				
Abercynon	1	Birkenhead	1	Ebbw Junction	1	Neasden	1				
Carmarthen	1	Carmarthen	1	Landore	1	St. Blazey	1				
Cheltenham	1	Chester (GWR)	1	Llantrisant	1						
Chester (GWR)	1	Oxford	1	Machynlleth	1						
Ebbw Junction	1	Pontypool Road	1	Pontypool Road	1						
Llantrisant	1	St. Blazey	1	St. Blazey	1						
Pontypool Road	1										

1500 1500-1509 0-6-0PT BR (GWR) Hawksworth

1951	10	1954	10	1957	10	1960	9	1963	5
Old Oak Common	4	Old Oak Common	4	Old Oak Common	4	Old Oak Common	4	Old Oak Common	5
Newport Pill	2	Newport Pill	2	Newport Pill	2	Cardiff Canton	1		
Didcot	1	Didcot	1	Cardiff Canton	1	Didcot	1		
Ebbw Junction	1	Ebbw Junction	1	Didcot	1	Ebbw Junction	1		
Severn Tunnel Junction	1	Severn Tunnel Junction	1	Ebbw Junction	1	Newport Pill	1		
Southall	1	Southall	1	Southall	1	Southall	1		

1501 1531-1542 0-6-0PT GWR Armstrong (Wolverhampton) 4ft 7½in

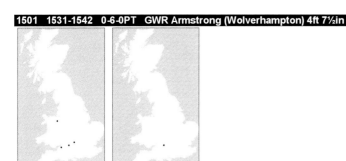

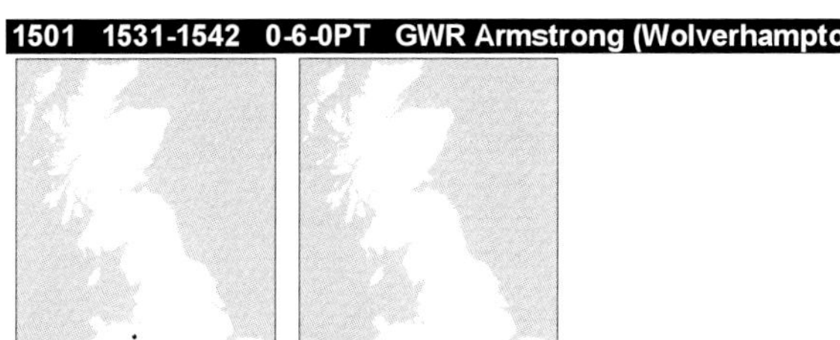

1948	4
Croes Newydd	1
Oxford	1
St. Philips Marsh	1
Swindon	1

1951	1
Swindon	1

1600 1600-1669 0-6-0PT BR (GWR) Hawksworth

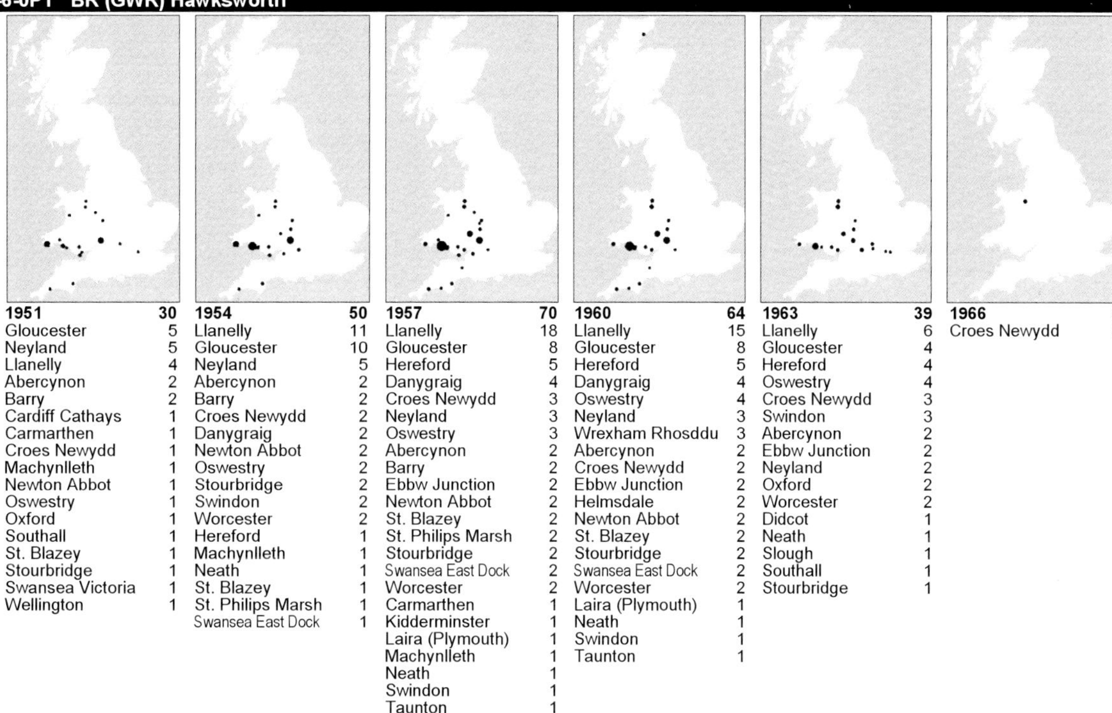

1951	30
Gloucester	5
Neyland	5
Llanelly	4
Abercynon	2
Barry	2
Cardiff Cathays	1
Carmarthen	1
Croes Newydd	1
Machynlleth	1
Newton Abbot	1
Oswestry	1
Oxford	1
Southall	1
St. Blazey	1
Stourbridge	1
Swansea Victoria	1
Wellington	1

1954	50
Llanelly	11
Gloucester	10
Neyland	5
Abercynon	2
Barry	2
Croes Newydd	2
Danygraig	2
Newton Abbot	2
Oswestry	2
Stourbridge	2
Swindon	2
Worcester	2
Hereford	1
Machynlleth	1
Neath	1
St. Blazey	1
St. Philips Marsh	1
Swansea East Dock	1

1957	70
Llanelly	18
Gloucester	8
Hereford	5
Danygraig	4
Croes Newydd	3
Neyland	3
Oswestry	3
Abercynon	2
Barry	2
Ebbw Junction	2
Newton Abbot	2
St. Blazey	2
St. Philips Marsh	2
Stourbridge	2
Swansea East Dock	2
Worcester	2
Carmarthen	1
Kidderminster	1
Laira (Plymouth)	1
Machynlleth	1
Neath	1
Swindon	1
Taunton	1
Wellington	1

1960	64
Llanelly	15
Gloucester	8
Hereford	5
Danygraig	4
Oswestry	4
Neyland	3
Wrexham Rhosddu	3
Abercynon	2
Croes Newydd	2
Ebbw Junction	2
Helmsdale	2
Newton Abbot	2
St. Blazey	2
Stourbridge	2
Swansea East Dock	2
Worcester	2
Laira (Plymouth)	1
Neath	1
Swindon	1
Taunton	1

1963	39
Llanelly	6
Gloucester	4
Hereford	4
Oswestry	4
Croes Newydd	3
Swindon	3
Abercynon	2
Ebbw Junction	2
Neyland	2
Oxford	2
Worcester	2
Didcot	1
Neath	1
Slough	1
Southall	1
Stourbridge	1

1966	3
Croes Newydd	3

1813 1835 0-6-0PT GWR Dean (Swindon) 4ft 7½in ex-Side Tank

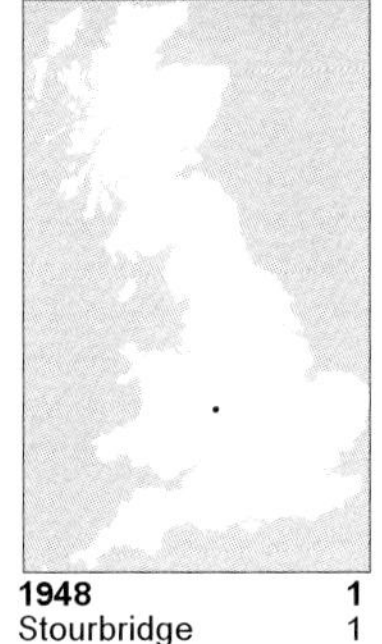

1948	1
Stourbridge	1

BR (GWR) Hawksworth '1600' class 0-6-0PT No 1603 at Oswestry.
J. Davenport

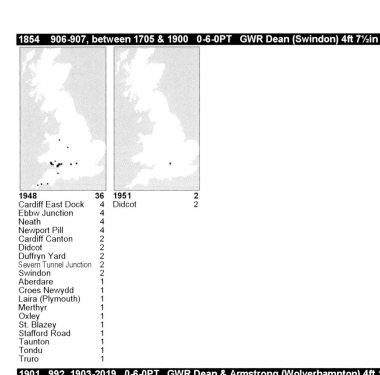

1854 906-907, between 1705 & 1900 0-6-0PT GWR Dean (Swindon) 4ft 7½in

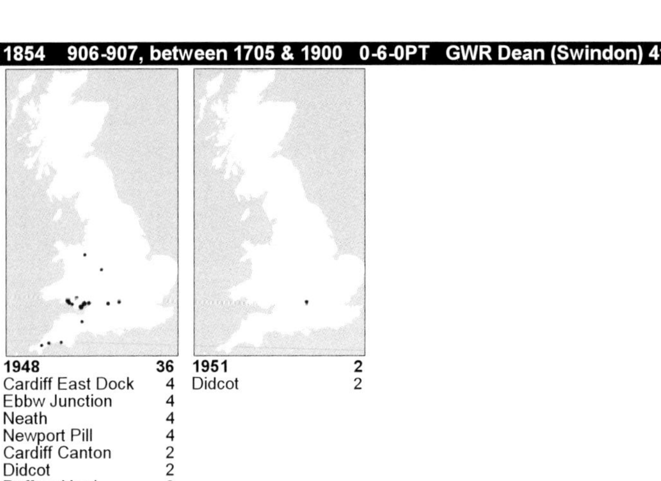

1948	36	1951	2
Cardiff East Dock	4	Didcot	2
Ebbw Junction	4		
Neath	4		
Newport Pill	4		
Cardiff Canton	2		
Didcot	2		
Duffryn Yard	2		
Severn Tunnel Junction	2		
Swindon	2		
Aberdare	1		
Croes Newydd	1		
Laira (Plymouth)	1		
Merthyr	1		
Oxley	1		
St. Blazey	1		
Stafford Road	1		
Taunton	1		
Tondu	1		
Truro	1		

1901 992, 1903-2019 0-6-0PT GWR Dean & Armstrong (Wolverhampton) 4ft 1½in

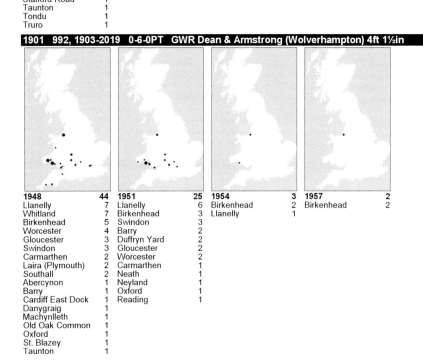

1948	44	1951	25	1954	3	1957	2
Llanelly	7	Llanelly	6	Birkenhead	2	Birkenhead	2
Whitland	7	Birkenhead	3	Llanelly	1		
Birkenhead	5	Swindon	3				
Worcester	4	Barry	2				
Gloucester	3	Duffryn Yard	2				
Swindon	3	Gloucester	2				
Carmarthen	2	Worcester	2				
Laira (Plymouth)	2	Carmarthen	1				
Southall	2	Neath	1				
Abercynon	1	Neyland	1				
Barry	1	Oxford	1				
Cardiff East Dock	1	Reading	1				
Danygraig	1						
Machynlleth	1						
Old Oak Common	1						
Oxford	1						
St. Blazey	1						
Taunton	1						

Didcot based GWR Dean '1854' class 0-6-0PT No 907 at Old Oak Common.
P. L. Melville

2021 2021-2160 0-6-0PT GWR Dean Wolverhampton 4ft 1½in

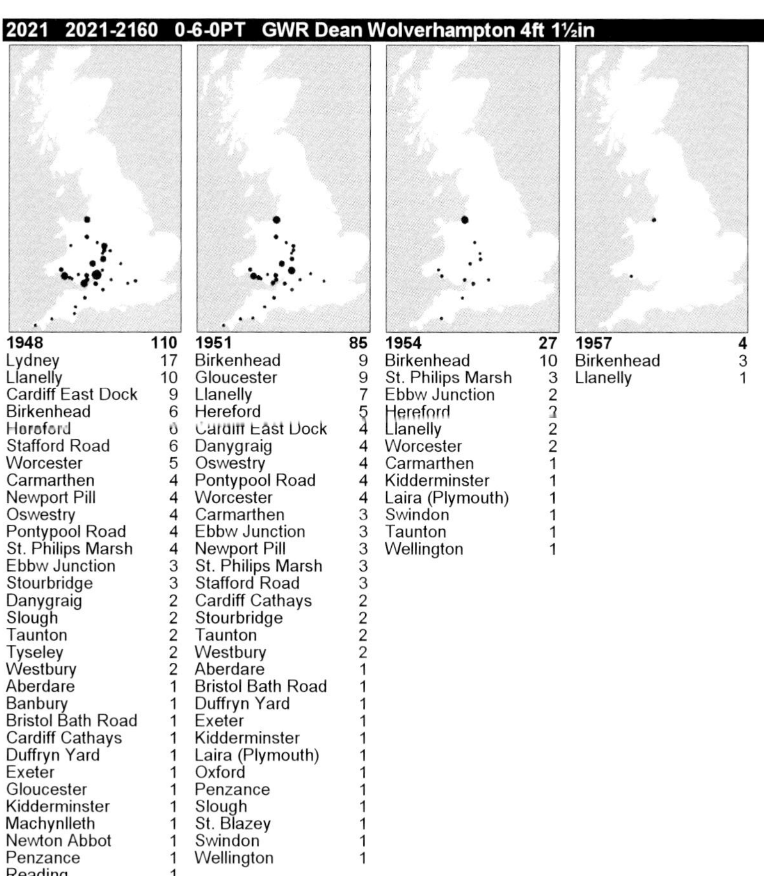

1948	110
Lydney	17
Llanelly	10
Cardiff East Dock	9
Birkenhead	6
Hereford	6
Stafford Road	6
Worcester	5
Carmarthen	4
Newport Pill	4
Oswestry	4
Pontypool Road	4
St. Philips Marsh	4
Ebbw Junction	3
Stourbridge	3
Danygraig	2
Slough	2
Taunton	2
Tyseley	2
Westbury	2
Aberdare	1
Banbury	1
Bristol Bath Road	1
Cardiff Cathays	1
Duffryn Yard	1
Exeter	1
Gloucester	1
Kidderminster	1
Machynlleth	1
Newton Abbot	1
Penzance	1
Reading	1
St. Blazey	1
Swindon	1
Wellington	1

1951	85
Birkenhead	9
Gloucester	9
Llanelly	7
Hereford	5
Cardiff East Dock	4
Danygraig	4
Oswestry	4
Pontypool Road	4
Worcester	4
Carmarthen	3
Ebbw Junction	3
Newport Pill	3
St. Philips Marsh	3
Stafford Road	3
Cardiff Cathays	2
Stourbridge	2
Taunton	2
Westbury	2
Aberdare	1
Bristol Bath Road	1
Duffryn Yard	1
Exeter	1
Kidderminster	1
Laira (Plymouth)	1
Oxford	1
Penzance	1
Slough	1
St. Blazey	1
Swindon	1
Wellington	1

1954	27
Birkenhead	10
St. Philips Marsh	3
Ebbw Junction	2
Hereford	2
Llanelly	2
Worcester	2
Carmarthen	1
Kidderminster	1
Laira (Plymouth)	1
Swindon	1
Taunton	1
Wellington	1

1957	4
Birkenhead	3
Llanelly	1

2181 2181-2190 0-6-0PT GWR 2021 with modified brakes 4ft 1½in

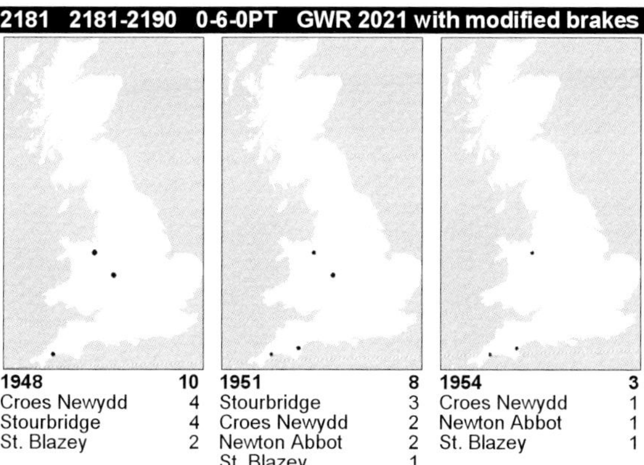

1948	10
Croes Newydd	4
Stourbridge	4
St. Blazey	2

1951	8
Stourbridge	3
Croes Newydd	2
Newton Abbot	2
St. Blazey	1

1954	3
Croes Newydd	1
Newton Abbot	1
St. Blazey	1

GWR Dean '2021' class 0-6-0PT No 2031.

2251 2200-2299, 3200-3219 0-6-0 GWR Collett

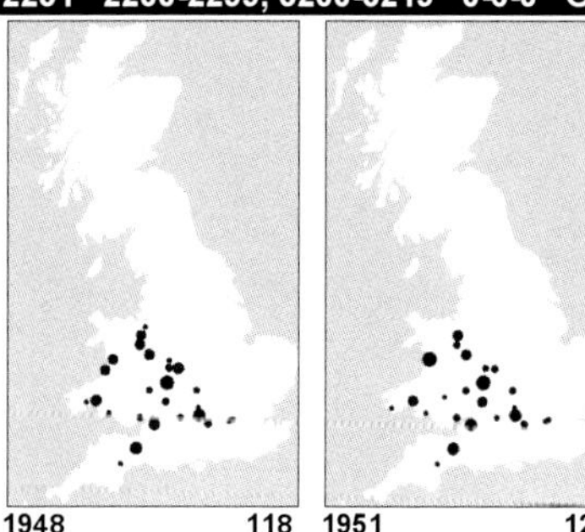
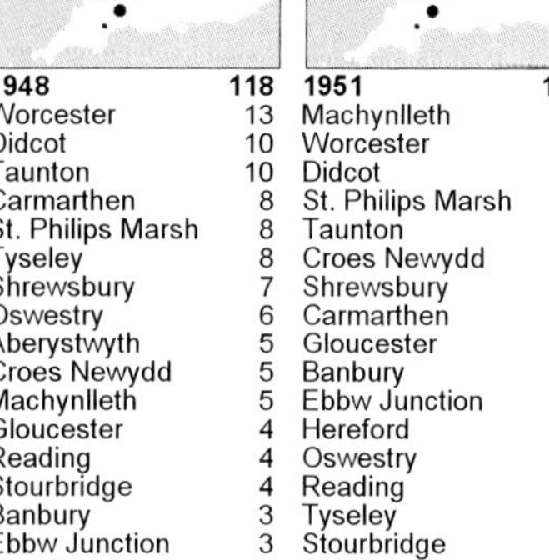

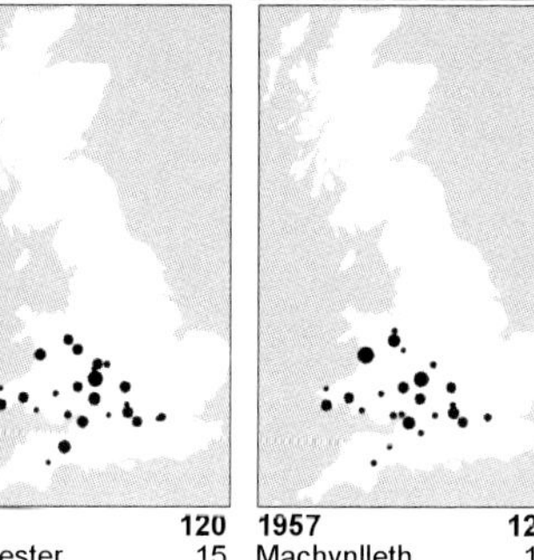
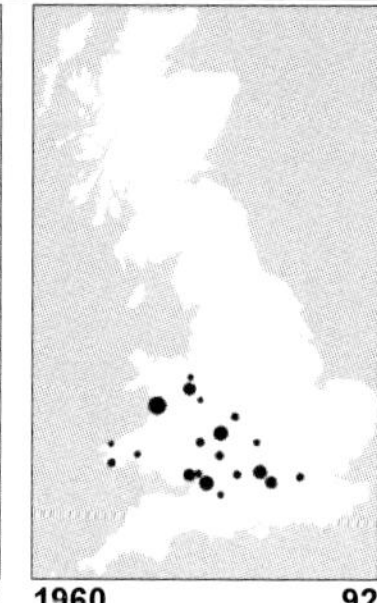
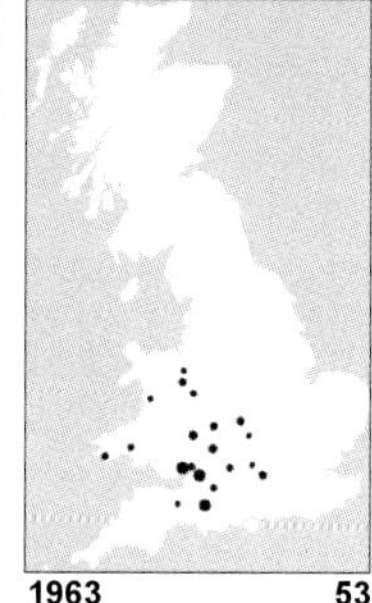

1948	118
Worcester	13
Didcot	10
Taunton	10
Carmarthen	8
St. Philips Marsh	8
Tyseley	8
Shrewsbury	7
Oswestry	6
Aberystwyth	5
Croes Newydd	5
Machynlleth	5
Gloucester	4
Reading	4
Stourbridge	4
Banbury	3
Ebbw Junction	3
Hereford	3
Swindon	3
Old Oak Common	2
Chester (GWR)	1
Exeter	1
Landore	1
Oxford	1
Southall	1
Stafford Road	1
Whitland	1

1951	120
Machynlleth	14
Worcester	14
Didcot	10
St. Philips Marsh	10
Taunton	9
Croes Newydd	7
Shrewsbury	7
Carmarthen	6
Gloucester	6
Banbury	4
Ebbw Junction	4
Hereford	4
Oswestry	4
Reading	4
Tyseley	4
Stourbridge	3
Old Oak Common	2
Swindon	2
Brecon	1
Exeter	1
Landore	1
Neyland	1
Oxford	1
Southall	1

1954	120
Worcester	15
Gloucester	9
Taunton	9
Machynlleth	8
St. Philips Marsh	8
Banbury	7
Didcot	6
Neyland	6
Shrewsbury	6
Carmarthen	5
Hereford	5
Oswestry	5
Reading	5
Stourbridge	5
Ebbw Junction	4
Old Oak Common	4
Tyseley	3
Brecon	2
Bristol Bath Road	1
Exeter	1
Fishguard Goodwick	1
Kidderminster	1
Landore	1
Oxford	1
Southall	1
Swindon	1

1957	120
Machynlleth	17
Worcester	14
Oswestry	9
St. Philips Marsh	9
Didcot	8
Hereford	7
Gloucester	6
Neyland	6
Banbury	5
Carmarthen	5
Reading	5
Old Oak Common	4
Ebbw Junction	3
Tyseley	3
Brecon	2
Croes Newydd	2
Exeter	2
Landore	2
Oxford	2
Severn Tunnel Junction	2
Swindon	2
Westbury	2
Fishguard Goodwick	1
Shrewsbury	1
Taunton	1

1960	92
Machynlleth	15
Worcester	10
St. Philips Marsh	9
Didcot	8
Oswestry	7
Ebbw Junction	5
Reading	5
Gloucester	4
Hereford	4
Neyland	3
Old Oak Common	3
Swindon	3
Tyseley	3
Banbury	2
Carmarthen	2
Severn Tunnel Junction	2
Westbury	2
Bristol Barrow Road	1
Croes Newydd	1
Fishguard Goodwick	1
Shrewsbury	1
Wrexham Rhosddu	1

1963	53
Bristol Barrow Road	5
Ebbw Junction	5
Templecombe	5
Gloucester	4
Hereford	4
Leamington Spa	3
Oswestry	3
Reading	3
Worcester	3
Carmarthen	2
Neyland	2
Severn Tunnel Junction	2
Shrewsbury	2
Swindon	2
Westbury	2
Banbury	1
Croes Newydd	1
Didcot	1
Machynlleth	1
St. Philips Marsh	1
Taunton	1

2301 2322-2579 0-6-0 GWR Dean Goods

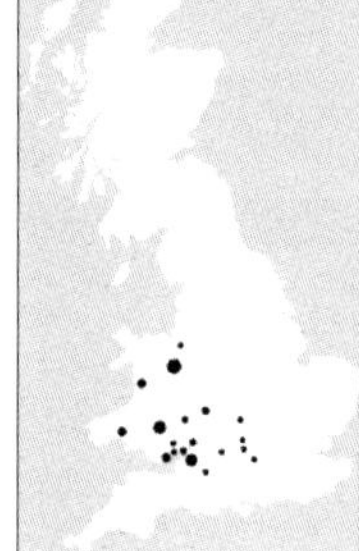
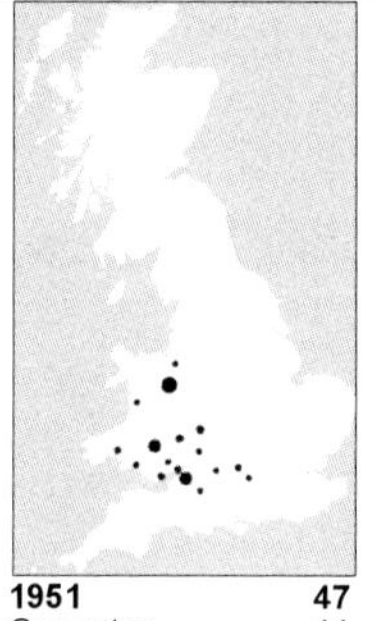

1948	54
Oswestry	10
Brecon	7
St. Philips Marsh	5
Cardiff Canton	4
Carmarthen	4
Machynlleth	4
Worcester	3
Bristol Bath Road	2
Hereford	2
Lydney	2
Severn Tunnel Junction	2
Banbury	1
Chester (GWR)	1
Didcot	1
Ebbw Junction	1
Oxford	1
Pontypool Road	1
Reading	1
Swindon	1
Westbury	1

1951	47
Oswestry	11
Brecon	7
St. Philips Marsh	6
Hereford	3
Worcester	3
Cardiff Canton	2
Carmarthen	2
Didcot	2
Severn Tunnel Junction	2
Bristol Bath Road	1
Chester (GWR)	1
Gloucester	1
Machynlleth	1
Neath	1
Pontypool Road	1
Reading	1
Swindon	1
Westbury	1

1954	12
Hereford	2
Oswestry	2
Chester (GWR)	1
Didcot	1
Oxford	1
Reading	1
Severn Tunnel Junction	1
St. Philips Marsh	1
Westbury	1
Worcester	1

1957	1
Oswestry	1

GWR 'Dean Goods' '2301' class 0-6-0 No 2407 at Oswestry. *J. Davenport*

2600 2612-2680 2-6-0 GWR Dean Aberdare

1948	12
Banbury	2
Oxley	2
Stourbridge	2
Cardiff Canton	1
Chester (GWR)	1
Gloucester	1
Hereford	1
Pontypool Road	1
Worcester	1

2721 2721-2799 0-6-0PT GWR Dean (Swindon) 4ft 7½in

1948	44
Newport Pill	4
Pontypool Road	4
Cardiff East Dock	3
Llanelly	3
Worcester	3
Duffryn Yard	2
Ebbw Junction	2
Neath	2
Shrewsbury	2
Slough	2
Taunton	2
Tondu	2
Danygraig	1
Gloucester	1
Laira (Plymouth)	1
Leamington Spa	1
Merthyr	1
Newton Abbot	1
Pantyffynnon	1
Penzance	1
St. Blazey	1
St. Philips Marsh	1
Stafford Road	1
Stourbridge	1
Swansea East Dock	1

Below: GWR Dean '2721' class 0-6-0PT No 2761, fitted with an open cab. It is stencilled OSW for Oswestry in this photograph. On the side of the cab is chalked 'Cond' which dates this photograph between March and May 1950.
P. Ransome-Wallis

2800 2800-2883, (4800-4811) 2-8-0 GWR Churchward

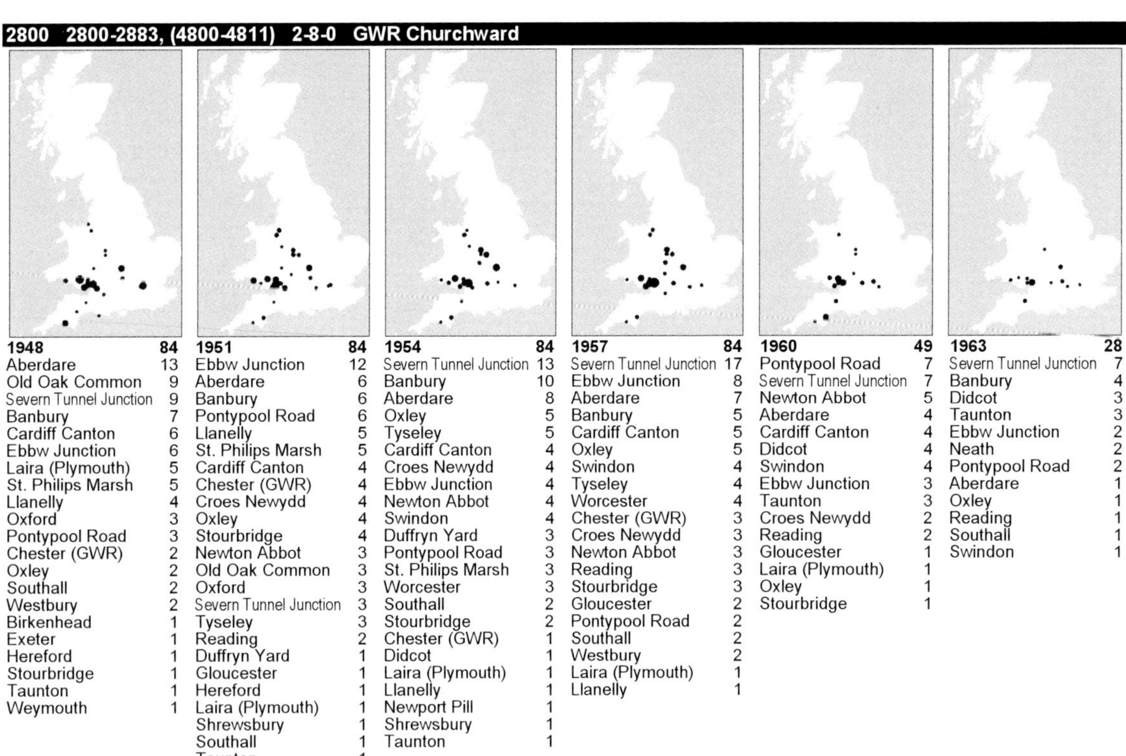

1948	84
Aberdare	13
Old Oak Common	9
Severn Tunnel Junction	9
Banbury	7
Cardiff Canton	6
Ebbw Junction	6
Laira (Plymouth)	5
St. Philips Marsh	5
Llanelly	4
Oxford	3
Pontypool Road	3
Chester (GWR)	2
Oxley	2
Southall	2
Westbury	2
Birkenhead	1
Exeter	1
Hereford	1
Stourbridge	1
Taunton	1
Weymouth	1

1951	84
Ebbw Junction	12
Aberdare	6
Banbury	6
Pontypool Road	6
Llanelly	5
St. Philips Marsh	5
Cardiff Canton	4
Chester (GWR)	4
Croes Newydd	4
Oxley	4
Stourbridge	4
Newton Abbot	3
Old Oak Common	3
Oxford	3
Severn Tunnel Junction	3
Tyseley	3
Reading	2
Duffryn Yard	1
Gloucester	1
Hereford	1
Laira (Plymouth)	1
Shrewsbury	1
Southall	1
Taunton	1

1954	84
Severn Tunnel Junction	13
Banbury	10
Aberdare	8
Oxley	5
Tyseley	5
Cardiff Canton	4
Croes Newydd	4
Ebbw Junction	4
Newton Abbot	4
Swindon	4
Duffryn Yard	3
Pontypool Road	3
St. Philips Marsh	3
Worcester	3
Southall	2
Stourbridge	2
Chester (GWR)	1
Didcot	1
Laira (Plymouth)	1
Llanelly	1
Newport Pill	1
Shrewsbury	1
Taunton	1

1957	84
Severn Tunnel Junction	17
Ebbw Junction	8
Aberdare	7
Banbury	5
Cardiff Canton	5
Oxley	5
Swindon	4
Tyseley	4
Worcester	4
Chester (GWR)	3
Croes Newydd	3
Newton Abbot	3
Reading	3
Stourbridge	3
Gloucester	2
Pontypool Road	2
Southall	2
Westbury	2
Laira (Plymouth)	1
Llanelly	1

1960	49
Pontypool Road	7
Severn Tunnel Junction	7
Newton Abbot	5
Aberdare	4
Cardiff Canton	4
Didcot	4
Swindon	4
Ebbw Junction	3
Taunton	3
Croes Newydd	2
Reading	2
Gloucester	1
Laira (Plymouth)	1
Oxley	1
Stourbridge	1

1963	28
Severn Tunnel Junction	7
Banbury	4
Didcot	3
Taunton	3
Ebbw Junction	2
Neath	2
Pontypool Road	2
Aberdare	1
Oxley	1
Reading	1
Southall	1
Swindon	1

2884 2884-2899, 3800-3866, (4850-4857) 2-8-0 GWR Modified 2800 class with side window cabs

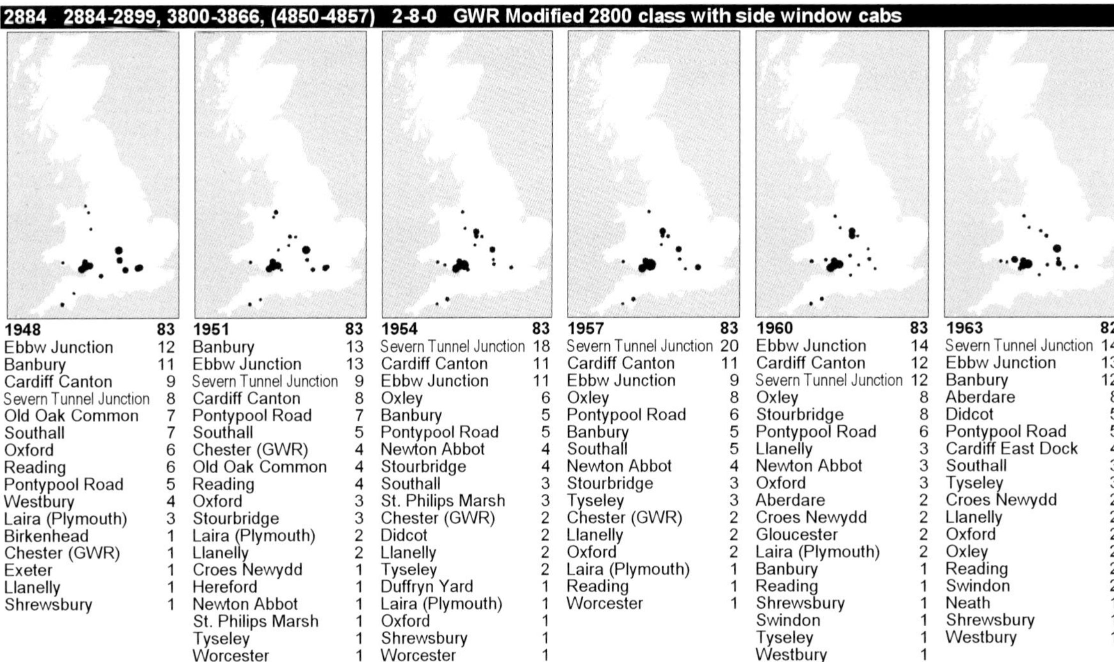

1948	83
Ebbw Junction	12
Banbury	11
Cardiff Canton	9
Severn Tunnel Junction	8
Old Oak Common	7
Southall	7
Oxford	6
Reading	6
Pontypool Road	5
Westbury	4
Laira (Plymouth)	3
Birkenhead	1
Chester (GWR)	1
Exeter	1
Llanelly	1
Shrewsbury	1

1951	83
Banbury	13
Ebbw Junction	13
Severn Tunnel Junction	9
Cardiff Canton	8
Pontypool Road	7
Southall	5
Chester (GWR)	4
Old Oak Common	4
Reading	4
Oxford	3
Stourbridge	3
Laira (Plymouth)	2
Llanelly	2
Croes Newydd	1
Hereford	1
Newton Abbot	1
St. Philips Marsh	1
Tyseley	1
Worcester	1

1954	83
Severn Tunnel Junction	18
Cardiff Canton	11
Ebbw Junction	11
Oxley	6
Banbury	5
Pontypool Road	5
Newton Abbot	4
Stourbridge	4
Southall	3
St. Philips Marsh	3
Chester (GWR)	2
Didcot	2
Llanelly	2
Tyseley	2
Duffryn Yard	1
Laira (Plymouth)	1
Oxford	1
Shrewsbury	1
Worcester	1

1957	83
Severn Tunnel Junction	20
Cardiff Canton	11
Ebbw Junction	9
Oxley	8
Pontypool Road	6
Banbury	5
Southall	5
Newton Abbot	4
Stourbridge	3
Tyseley	3
Chester (GWR)	2
Llanelly	2
Oxford	2
Laira (Plymouth)	1
Reading	1
Worcester	1

1960	83
Ebbw Junction	14
Cardiff Canton	12
Severn Tunnel Junction	12
Oxley	8
Stourbridge	8
Pontypool Road	6
Llanelly	3
Newton Abbot	3
Oxford	3
Aberdare	2
Croes Newydd	2
Gloucester	2
Laira (Plymouth)	2
Banbury	1
Reading	1
Shrewsbury	1
Swindon	1
Tyseley	1
Westbury	1

1963	82
Severn Tunnel Junction	14
Ebbw Junction	13
Banbury	12
Aberdare	8
Didcot	5
Pontypool Road	5
Cardiff East Dock	4
Southall	3
Tyseley	3
Croes Newydd	2
Llanelly	2
Oxford	2
Oxley	2
Reading	2
Swindon	2
Neath	1
Shrewsbury	1
Westbury	1

Right: GWR Collett '2884' class 2-8-0 No 2886 at Cardiff Canton Shed on 25 February 1962. *R. J. Henly*

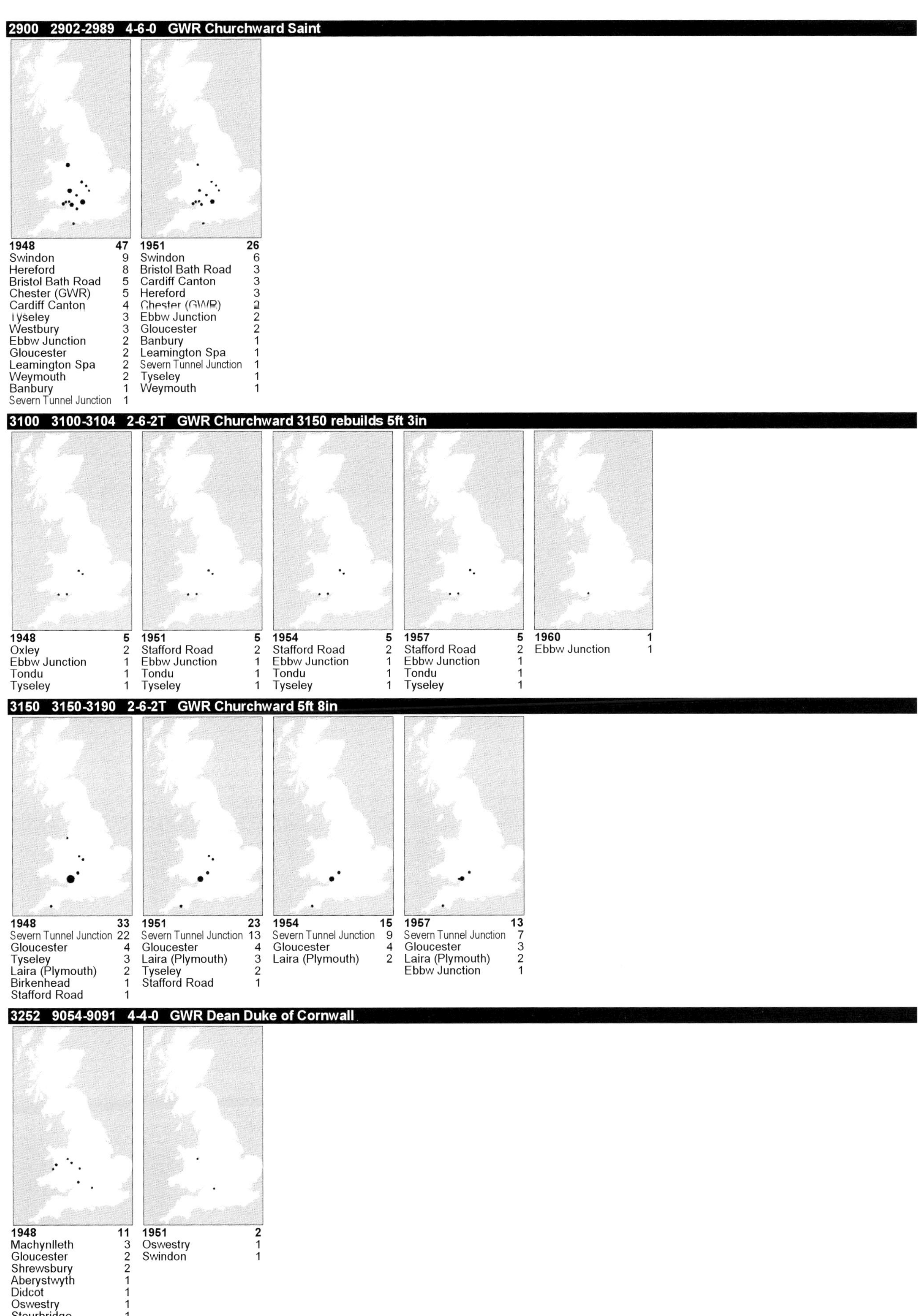

2900 2902-2989 4-6-0 GWR Churchward Saint

1948	47	1951	26
Swindon	9	Swindon	6
Hereford	8	Bristol Bath Road	3
Bristol Bath Road	5	Cardiff Canton	3
Chester (GWR)	5	Hereford	3
Cardiff Canton	4	Chester (GWR)	2
Tyseley	3	Ebbw Junction	2
Westbury	3	Gloucester	2
Ebbw Junction	2	Banbury	1
Gloucester	2	Leamington Spa	1
Leamington Spa	2	Severn Tunnel Junction	1
Weymouth	2	Tyseley	1
Banbury	1	Weymouth	1
Severn Tunnel Junction	1		

3100 3100-3104 2-6-2T GWR Churchward 3150 rebuilds 5ft 3in

1948	5	1951	5	1954	5	1957	5	1960	1
Oxley	2	Stafford Road	2	Stafford Road	2	Stafford Road	2	Ebbw Junction	1
Ebbw Junction	1	Ebbw Junction	1	Ebbw Junction	1	Ebbw Junction	1		
Tondu	1	Tondu	1	Tondu	1	Tondu	1		
Tyseley	1	Tyseley	1	Tyseley	1	Tyseley	1		

3150 3150-3190 2-6-2T GWR Churchward 5ft 8in

1948	33	1951	23	1954	15	1957	13
Severn Tunnel Junction	22	Severn Tunnel Junction	13	Severn Tunnel Junction	9	Severn Tunnel Junction	7
Gloucester	4	Gloucester	4	Gloucester	4	Gloucester	3
Tyseley	3	Laira (Plymouth)	3	Laira (Plymouth)	2	Laira (Plymouth)	2
Laira (Plymouth)	2	Tyseley	2			Ebbw Junction	1
Birkenhead	1	Stafford Road	1				
Stafford Road	1						

3252 9054-9091 4-4-0 GWR Dean Duke of Cornwall

1948	11	1951	2
Machynlleth	3	Oswestry	1
Gloucester	2	Swindon	1
Shrewsbury	2		
Aberystwyth	1		
Didcot	1		
Oswestry	1		
Stourbridge	1		

3300 3335-3455 4-4-0 GWR Dean & Churchward Bulldog

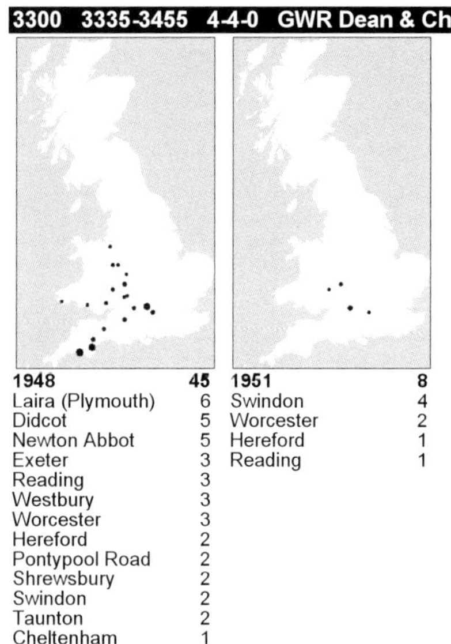

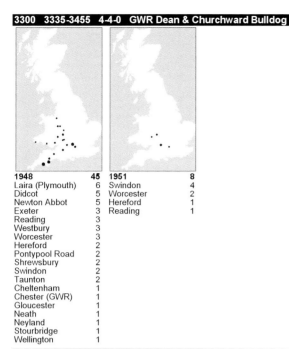

1948	45
Laira (Plymouth)	6
Didcot	5
Newton Abbot	5
Exeter	3
Reading	3
Westbury	3
Worcester	3
Hereford	2
Pontypool Road	2
Shrewsbury	2
Swindon	2
Taunton	2
Cheltenham	1
Chester (GWR)	1
Gloucester	1
Neath	1
Neyland	1
Stourbridge	1
Wellington	1

1951	8
Swindon	4
Worcester	2
Hereford	1
Reading	1

3500 3561-3562, 3582-3599 2-4-0T GWR Dean Metropolitan Tanks

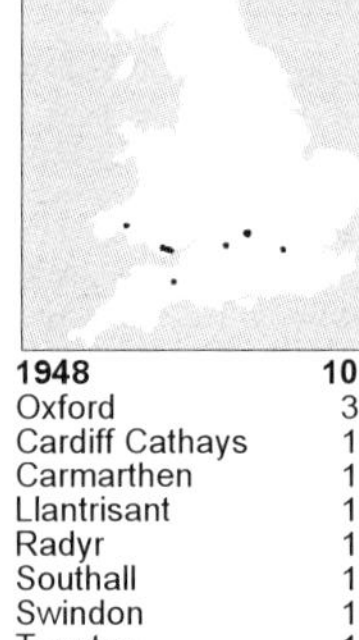

1948	10
Oxford	3
Cardiff Cathays	1
Carmarthen	1
Llantrisant	1
Radyr	1
Southall	1
Swindon	1
Taunton	1

3571 3574-3577 0-4-2T GWR Armstrong & Dean 3571 class (also known as 1159 or 517 class)

1948	3
Severn Tunnel Junction	1
Swansea East Dock	1
Worcester	1

GWR Armstrong & Dean '1159' class 0-4-2T No 3573 on a West Kirby branch service. Withdrawn from Swindon in December 1945. *R. C. Anthony*

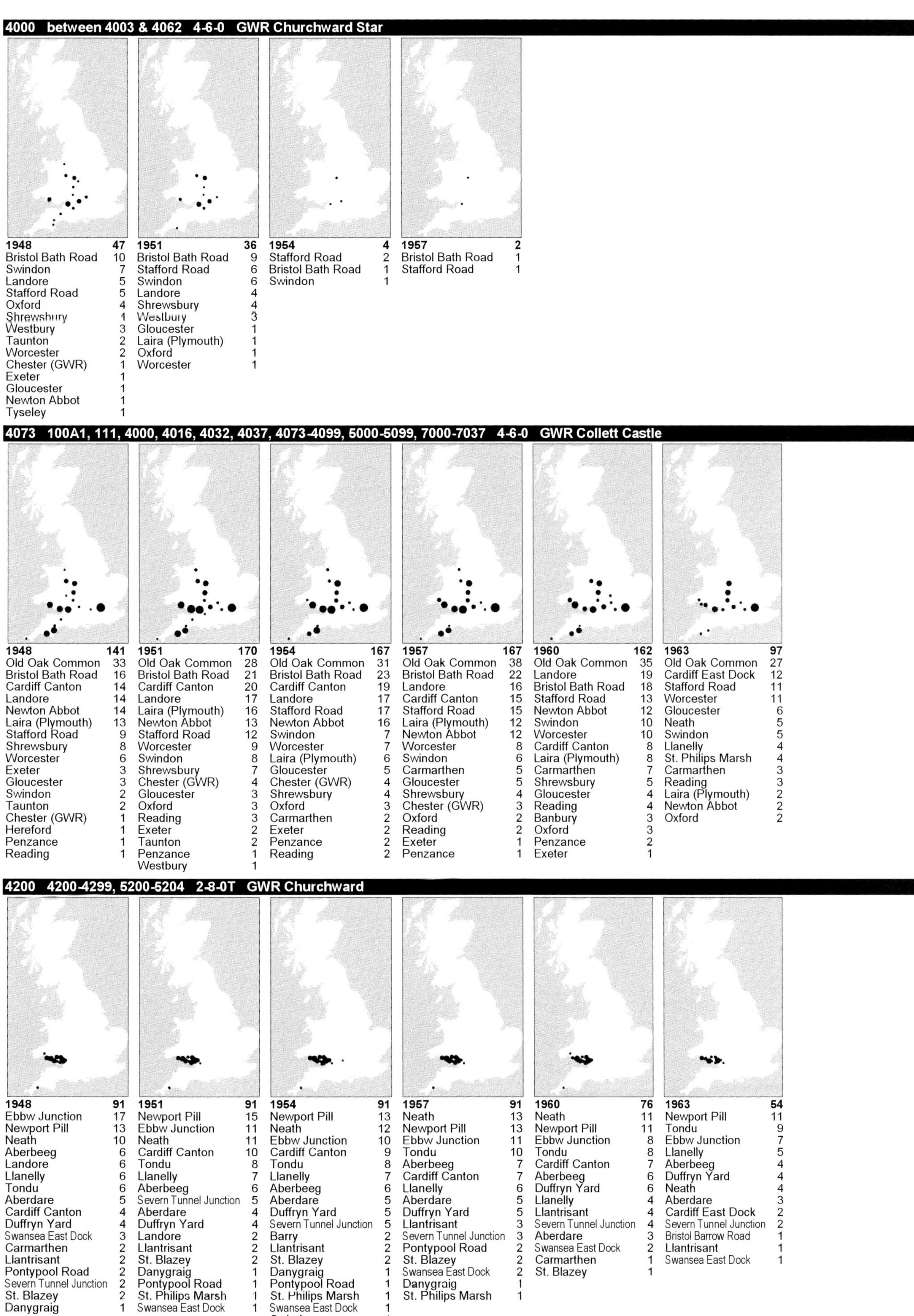

4000 between 4003 & 4062 4-6-0 GWR Churchward Star

1948	47
Bristol Bath Road	10
Swindon	7
Landore	5
Stafford Road	5
Oxford	4
Shrewsbury	1
Westbury	3
Taunton	2
Worcester	2
Chester (GWR)	1
Exeter	1
Gloucester	1
Newton Abbot	1
Tyseley	1

1951	36
Bristol Bath Road	9
Stafford Road	6
Swindon	6
Landore	4
Shrewsbury	4
Westbury	3
Gloucester	1
Laira (Plymouth)	1
Oxford	1
Worcester	1

1954	4
Stafford Road	2
Bristol Bath Road	1
Swindon	1

1957	2
Bristol Bath Road	1
Stafford Road	1

4073 100A1, 111, 4000, 4016, 4032, 4037, 4073-4099, 5000-5099, 7000-7037 4-6-0 GWR Collett Castle

1948	141
Old Oak Common	33
Bristol Bath Road	16
Cardiff Canton	14
Landore	14
Newton Abbot	14
Laira (Plymouth)	13
Stafford Road	9
Shrewsbury	8
Worcester	6
Exeter	3
Gloucester	3
Swindon	2
Taunton	2
Chester (GWR)	1
Hereford	1
Penzance	1
Reading	1

1951	170
Old Oak Common	28
Bristol Bath Road	21
Cardiff Canton	20
Landore	17
Laira (Plymouth)	16
Newton Abbot	13
Stafford Road	12
Worcester	9
Swindon	8
Shrewsbury	7
Chester (GWR)	4
Gloucester	3
Oxford	3
Reading	3
Exeter	2
Taunton	2
Penzance	1
Westbury	1

1954	167
Old Oak Common	31
Bristol Bath Road	23
Cardiff Canton	19
Landore	17
Stafford Road	17
Newton Abbot	16
Swindon	7
Worcester	7
Laira (Plymouth)	6
Gloucester	5
Chester (GWR)	4
Shrewsbury	4
Oxford	3
Carmarthen	2
Exeter	2
Penzance	2
Reading	2

1957	167
Old Oak Common	38
Bristol Bath Road	22
Landore	16
Cardiff Canton	15
Stafford Road	15
Laira (Plymouth)	12
Newton Abbot	12
Worcester	8
Swindon	6
Carmarthen	5
Gloucester	5
Shrewsbury	4
Chester (GWR)	3
Oxford	2
Reading	2
Exeter	1
Penzance	1

1960	162
Old Oak Common	35
Landore	19
Bristol Bath Road	18
Stafford Road	13
Newton Abbot	12
Swindon	10
Worcester	10
Cardiff Canton	8
Laira (Plymouth)	8
Carmarthen	7
Shrewsbury	5
Gloucester	4
Reading	4
Banbury	3
Oxford	3
Penzance	2
Exeter	1

1963	97
Old Oak Common	27
Cardiff East Dock	12
Stafford Road	11
Worcester	11
Gloucester	6
Neath	5
Swindon	5
Llanelly	4
St. Philips Marsh	4
Carmarthen	3
Reading	3
Laira (Plymouth)	2
Newton Abbot	2
Oxford	2

4200 4200-4299, 5200-5204 2-8-0T GWR Churchward

1948	91
Ebbw Junction	17
Newport Pill	13
Neath	10
Aberbeeg	6
Landore	6
Llanelly	6
Tondu	6
Aberdare	5
Cardiff Canton	4
Duffryn Yard	4
Swansea East Dock	3
Carmarthen	2
Llantrisant	2
Pontypool Road	2
Severn Tunnel Junction	2
St. Blazey	2
Danygraig	1

1951	91
Newport Pill	15
Ebbw Junction	11
Neath	11
Cardiff Canton	10
Tondu	8
Llanelly	7
Aberbeeg	6
Severn Tunnel Junction	5
Aberdare	4
Duffryn Yard	4
Landore	2
Llantrisant	2
St. Blazey	2
Danygraig	1
Pontypool Road	1
St. Philips Marsh	1
Swansea East Dock	1

1954	91
Newport Pill	13
Neath	12
Ebbw Junction	10
Cardiff Canton	9
Tondu	8
Llanelly	7
Aberbeeg	6
Aberdare	5
Duffryn Yard	5
Severn Tunnel Junction	5
Barry	2
Llantrisant	2
St. Blazey	2
Danygraig	1
Pontypool Road	1
St. Philips Marsh	1
Swansea East Dock	1
Swindon	1

1957	91
Neath	13
Newport Pill	13
Ebbw Junction	11
Tondu	10
Aberbeeg	7
Cardiff Canton	7
Llanelly	6
Aberdare	5
Duffryn Yard	5
Llantrisant	3
Severn Tunnel Junction	3
Pontypool Road	2
St. Blazey	2
Swansea East Dock	2
Danygraig	1
St. Philips Marsh	1

1960	76
Neath	11
Newport Pill	11
Ebbw Junction	8
Tondu	8
Cardiff Canton	7
Aberbeeg	6
Duffryn Yard	6
Llanelly	4
Llantrisant	4
Severn Tunnel Junction	4
Aberdare	3
Swansea East Dock	2
Carmarthen	1
St. Blazey	1

1963	54
Newport Pill	11
Tondu	9
Ebbw Junction	7
Llanelly	5
Aberbeeg	4
Duffryn Yard	4
Neath	4
Aberdare	3
Cardiff East Dock	2
Severn Tunnel Junction	2
Bristol Barrow Road	1
Llantrisant	1
Swansea East Dock	1

4300 4303-4386, 5300-5399, 6300-6399, 7300-7341 2-6-0 GWR Churchward

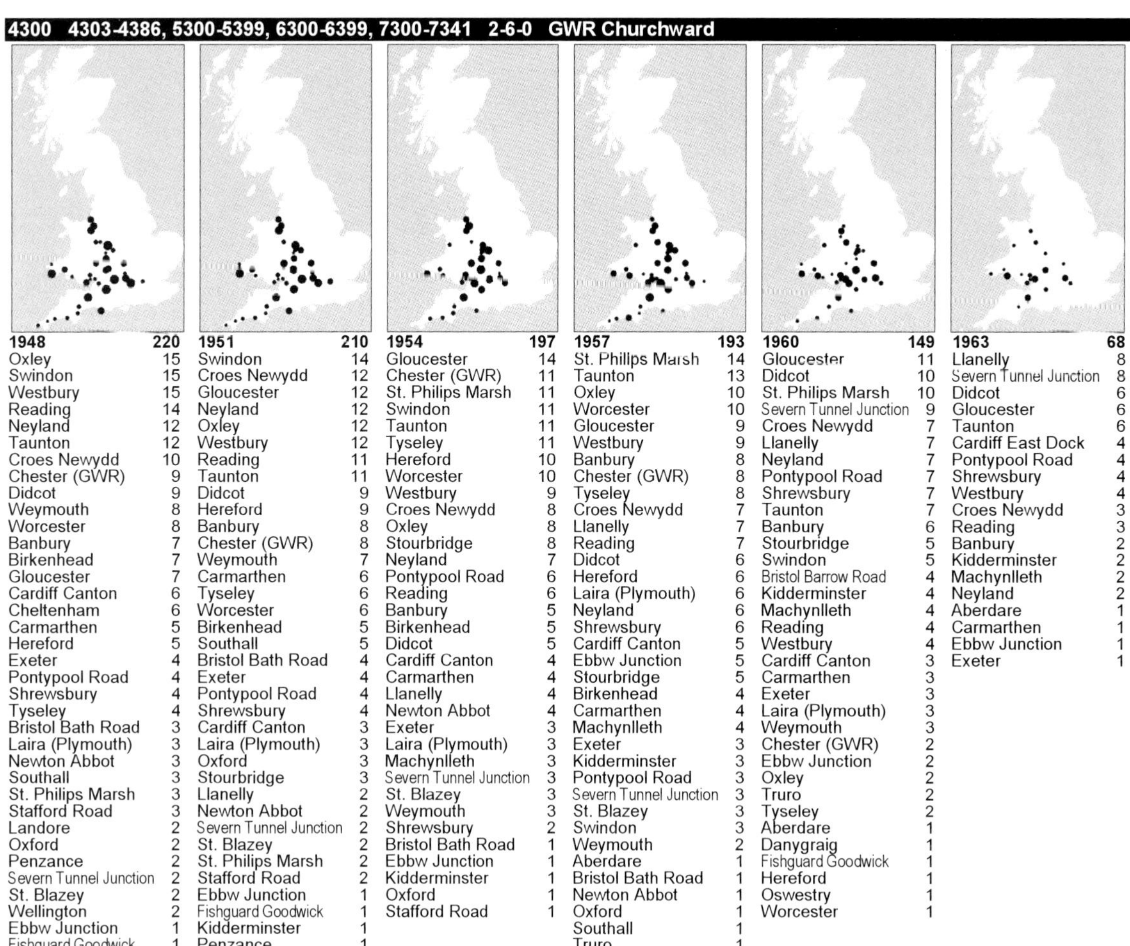

1948	220
Oxley	15
Swindon	15
Westbury	15
Reading	14
Neyland	12
Taunton	12
Croes Newydd	10
Chester (GWR)	9
Didcot	9
Weymouth	8
Worcester	8
Banbury	7
Birkenhead	7
Gloucester	7
Cardiff Canton	6
Cheltenham	6
Carmarthen	5
Hereford	5
Exeter	4
Pontypool Road	4
Shrewsbury	4
Tyseley	4
Bristol Bath Road	3
Laira (Plymouth)	3
Newton Abbot	3
Southall	3
St. Philips Marsh	3
Stafford Road	3
Landore	2
Oxford	2
Penzance	2
Severn Tunnel Junction	2
St. Blazey	2
Wellington	2
Ebbw Junction	1
Fishguard Goodwick	1
Kidderminster	1
Truro	1

1951	210
Swindon	14
Croes Newydd	12
Gloucester	12
Neyland	12
Oxley	12
Westbury	12
Reading	11
Taunton	11
Didcot	9
Hereford	9
Banbury	8
Chester (GWR)	8
Weymouth	7
Carmarthen	6
Tyseley	6
Worcester	6
Birkenhead	5
Southall	5
Bristol Bath Road	4
Exeter	4
Pontypool Road	4
Shrewsbury	4
Cardiff Canton	3
Laira (Plymouth)	3
Oxford	3
Stourbridge	3
Llanelly	2
Newton Abbot	2
Severn Tunnel Junction	2
St. Blazey	2
St. Philips Marsh	2
Stafford Road	2
Ebbw Junction	1
Fishguard Goodwick	1
Kidderminster	1
Penzance	1
Truro	1

1954	197
Gloucester	14
Chester (GWR)	11
St. Philips Marsh	11
Swindon	11
Taunton	11
Tyseley	11
Hereford	10
Worcester	10
Westbury	9
Croes Newydd	8
Oxley	8
Stourbridge	8
Neyland	7
Pontypool Road	6
Reading	6
Banbury	5
Birkenhead	5
Didcot	5
Cardiff Canton	4
Carmarthen	4
Llanelly	4
Newton Abbot	4
Exeter	3
Laira (Plymouth)	3
Machynlleth	3
Severn Tunnel Junction	3
St. Blazey	3
Weymouth	3
Shrewsbury	2
Bristol Bath Road	1
Ebbw Junction	1
Kidderminster	1
Oxford	1
Stafford Road	1

1957	193
St. Phillps Marsh	14
Taunton	13
Oxley	10
Worcester	10
Gloucester	9
Westbury	9
Banbury	8
Chester (GWR)	8
Tyseley	8
Croes Newydd	7
Llanelly	7
Reading	7
Didcot	6
Hereford	6
Laira (Plymouth)	6
Neyland	6
Shrewsbury	6
Cardiff Canton	5
Ebbw Junction	5
Stourbridge	5
Birkenhead	4
Carmarthen	4
Machynlleth	4
Exeter	3
Kidderminster	3
Pontypool Road	3
Severn Tunnel Junction	3
St. Blazey	3
Swindon	3
Weymouth	2
Aberdare	1
Bristol Bath Road	1
Newton Abbot	1
Oxford	1
Southall	1
Truro	1

1960	149
Gloucester	11
Didcot	10
St. Philips Marsh	10
Severn Tunnel Junction	9
Croes Newydd	7
Llanelly	7
Neyland	7
Pontypool Road	7
Shrewsbury	7
Taunton	7
Banbury	6
Stourbridge	5
Swindon	5
Bristol Barrow Road	4
Kidderminster	4
Machynlleth	4
Reading	4
Westbury	4
Cardiff Canton	3
Carmarthen	3
Exeter	3
Laira (Plymouth)	3
Weymouth	3
Chester (GWR)	2
Ebbw Junction	2
Oxley	2
Truro	2
Tyseley	2
Aberdare	1
Danygraig	1
Fishguard Goodwick	1
Hereford	1
Oswestry	1
Worcester	1

1963	68
Llanelly	8
Severn Tunnel Junction	8
Didcot	6
Gloucester	6
Taunton	6
Cardiff East Dock	4
Pontypool Road	4
Shrewsbury	4
Westbury	4
Croes Newydd	3
Reading	3
Banbury	2
Kidderminster	2
Machynlleth	2
Neyland	2
Aberdare	1
Carmarthen	1
Ebbw Junction	1
Exeter	1

4400 4400-4410 2-6-2T GWR Churchward 4ft 1½in

1948	11
Wellington	5
Laira (Plymouth)	2
Tondu	2
Exeter	1
Newton Abbot	1

1951	10
Wellington	4
Laira (Plymouth)	2
Tondu	2
Exeter	1
Newton Abbot	1

1954	4
Newton Abbot	2
Laira (Plymouth)	1
Tondu	1

Right: GWR Churchward '4400' class 2-6-2T No 4406 at its home shed 86F Tondu on 9 September 1951.
H. C. Casserley

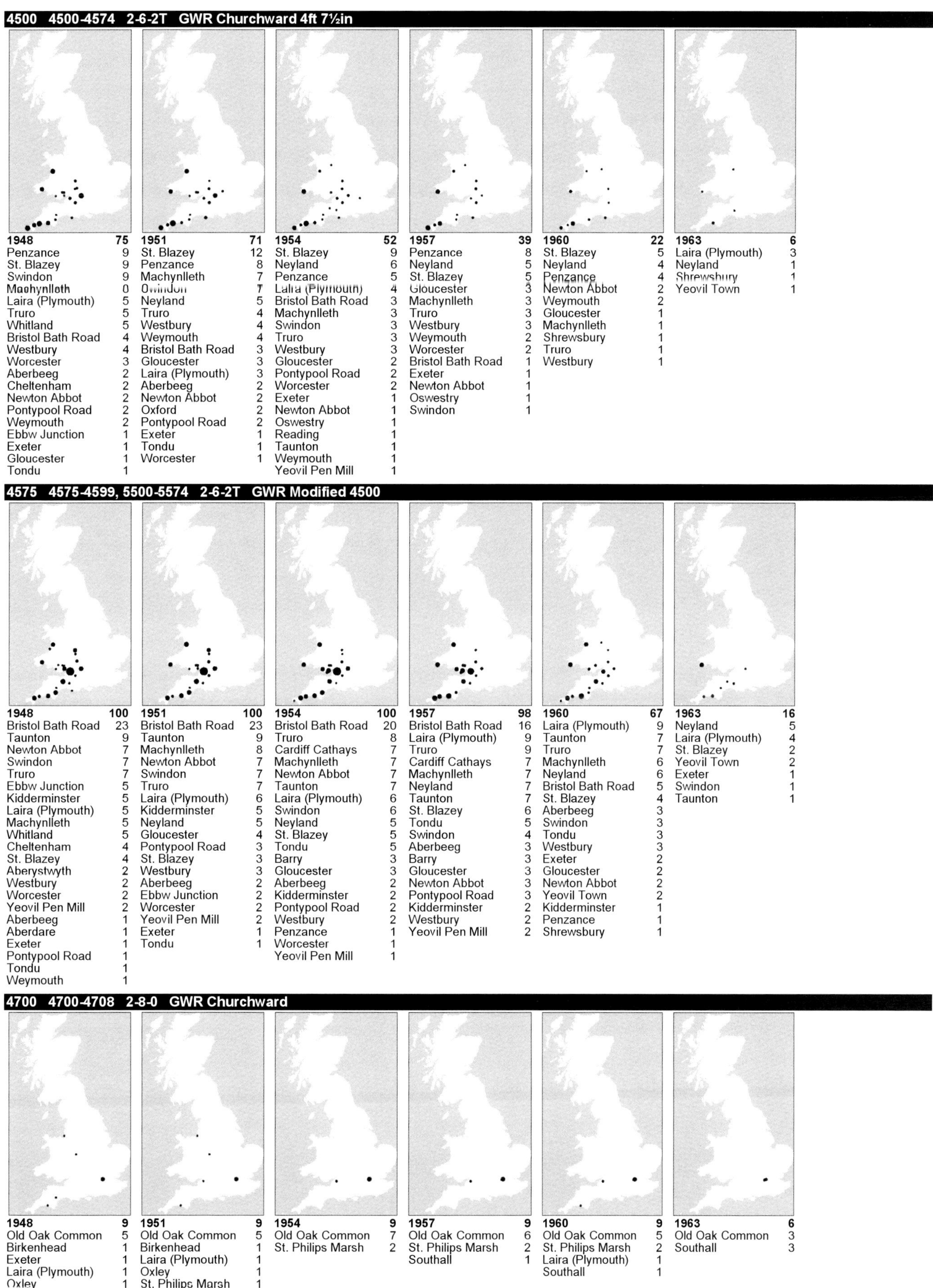

4500 4500-4574 2-6-2T GWR Churchward 4ft 7½in

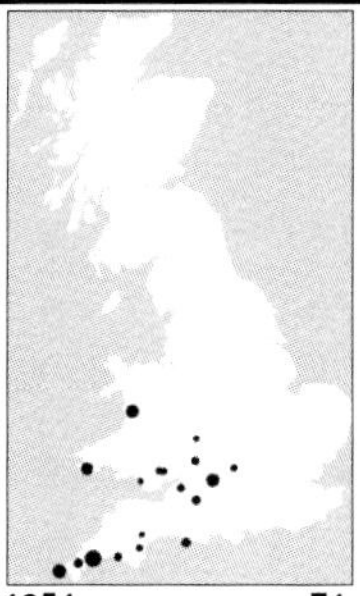
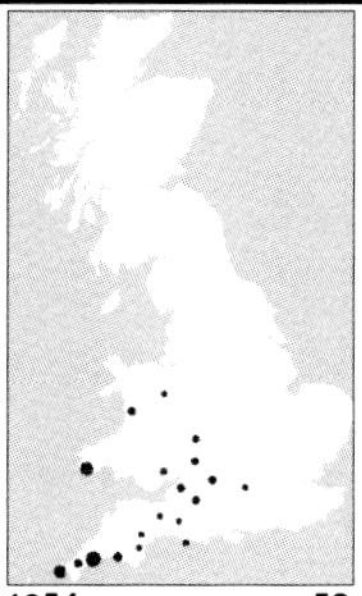
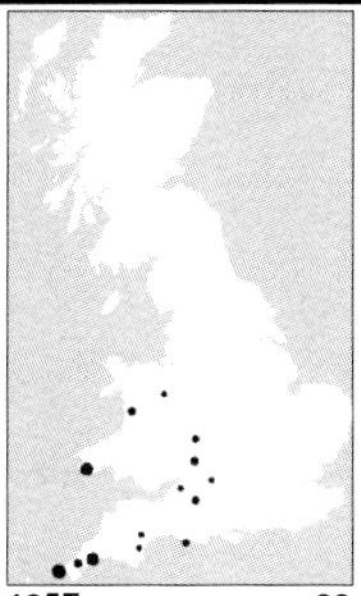

1948	75
Penzance	9
St. Blazey	9
Swindon	9
Machynlleth	0
Laira (Plymouth)	5
Truro	5
Whitland	5
Bristol Bath Road	4
Westbury	4
Worcester	3
Aberbeeg	2
Cheltenham	2
Newton Abbot	2
Pontypool Road	2
Weymouth	2
Ebbw Junction	1
Exeter	1
Gloucester	1
Tondu	1

1951	71
St. Blazey	12
Penzance	8
Machynlleth	7
Swindon	7
Neyland	5
Truro	4
Westbury	4
Weymouth	4
Bristol Bath Road	3
Gloucester	3
Laira (Plymouth)	3
Aberbeeg	2
Newton Abbot	2
Oxford	2
Pontypool Road	2
Exeter	1
Tondu	1
Worcester	1

1954	52
St. Blazey	9
Neyland	6
Penzance	5
Laira (Plymouth)	4
Bristol Bath Road	3
Machynlleth	3
Swindon	3
Truro	3
Westbury	3
Gloucester	2
Pontypool Road	2
Worcester	2
Exeter	1
Newton Abbot	1
Oswestry	1
Reading	1
Taunton	1
Weymouth	1
Yeovil Pen Mill	1

1957	39
Penzance	8
Neyland	5
St. Blazey	5
Gloucester	3
Machynlleth	3
Truro	3
Westbury	3
Weymouth	2
Worcester	2
Bristol Bath Road	1
Exeter	1
Newton Abbot	1
Oswestry	1
Swindon	1

1960	22
St. Blazey	5
Neyland	4
Penzance	4
Newton Abbot	2
Weymouth	2
Gloucester	1
Machynlleth	1
Shrewsbury	1
Truro	1
Westbury	1

1963	6
Laira (Plymouth)	3
Neyland	1
Shrewsbury	1
Yeovil Town	1

4575 4575-4599, 5500-5574 2-6-2T GWR Modified 4500

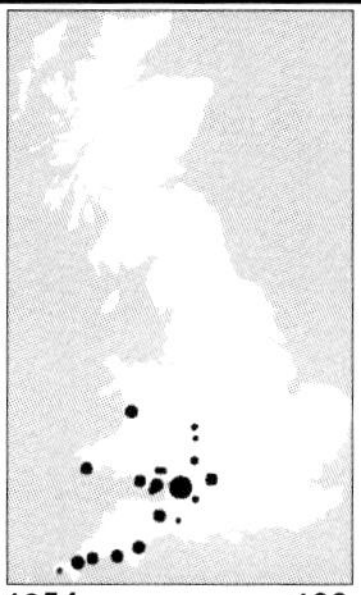
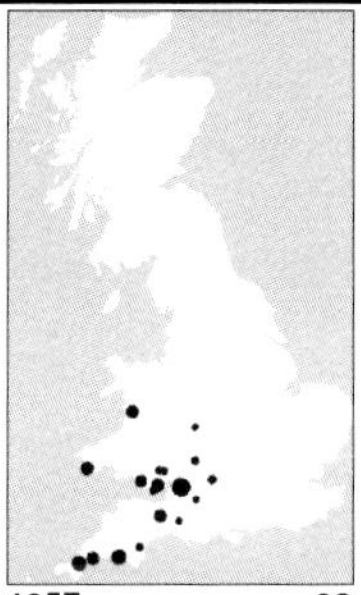

1948	100
Bristol Bath Road	23
Taunton	9
Newton Abbot	7
Swindon	7
Truro	7
Ebbw Junction	5
Kidderminster	5
Laira (Plymouth)	5
Machynlleth	5
Whitland	5
Cheltenham	4
St. Blazey	4
Aberystwyth	2
Westbury	2
Worcester	2
Yeovil Pen Mill	2
Aberbeeg	1
Aberdare	1
Exeter	1
Pontypool Road	1
Tondu	1
Weymouth	1

1951	100
Bristol Bath Road	23
Taunton	9
Machynlleth	8
Newton Abbot	7
Swindon	7
Truro	7
Laira (Plymouth)	6
Kidderminster	5
Neyland	5
Gloucester	4
Pontypool Road	3
St. Blazey	3
Westbury	3
Aberbeeg	2
Ebbw Junction	2
Worcester	2
Yeovil Pen Mill	2
Exeter	1
Tondu	1

1954	100
Bristol Bath Road	20
Truro	8
Cardiff Cathays	7
Machynlleth	7
Newton Abbot	7
Taunton	7
Laira (Plymouth)	6
Swindon	6
Neyland	5
St. Blazey	5
Tondu	5
Barry	3
Gloucester	3
Aberbeeg	2
Kidderminster	2
Pontypool Road	2
Westbury	2
Penzance	1
Worcester	1
Yeovil Pen Mill	1

1957	98
Bristol Bath Road	16
Laira (Plymouth)	9
Truro	9
Cardiff Cathays	7
Machynlleth	7
Neyland	7
Taunton	7
St. Blazey	6
Tondu	5
Swindon	4
Aberbeeg	3
Barry	3
Gloucester	3
Newton Abbot	3
Pontypool Road	3
Kidderminster	2
Westbury	2
Yeovil Pen Mill	2

1960	67
Laira (Plymouth)	9
Taunton	7
Truro	7
Machynlleth	6
Neyland	6
Bristol Bath Road	5
St. Blazey	4
Aberbeeg	3
Swindon	3
Tondu	3
Westbury	3
Exeter	2
Gloucester	2
Newton Abbot	2
Yeovil Town	2
Kidderminster	1
Penzance	1
Shrewsbury	1

1963	16
Neyland	5
Laira (Plymouth)	4
St. Blazey	2
Yeovil Town	2
Exeter	1
Swindon	1
Taunton	1

4700 4700-4708 2-8-0 GWR Churchward

1948	9
Old Oak Common	5
Birkenhead	1
Exeter	1
Laira (Plymouth)	1
Oxley	1

1951	9
Old Oak Common	5
Birkenhead	1
Laira (Plymouth)	1
Oxley	1
St. Philips Marsh	1

1954	9
Old Oak Common	7
St. Philips Marsh	2

1957	9
Old Oak Common	6
St. Philips Marsh	2
Southall	1

1960	9
Old Oak Common	5
St. Philips Marsh	2
Laira (Plymouth)	1
Southall	1

1963	6
Old Oak Common	3
Southall	3

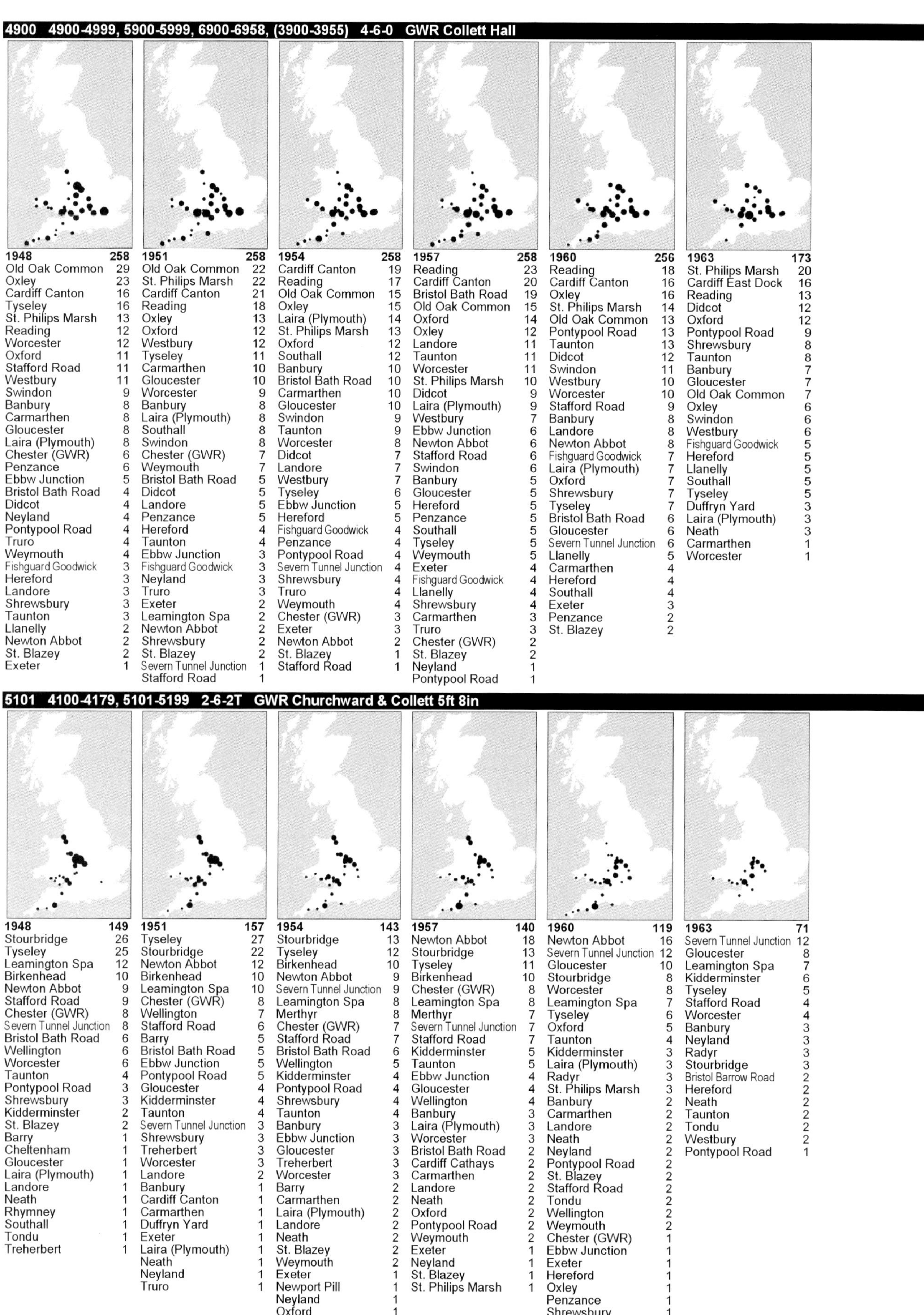

4900 4900-4999, 5900-5999, 6900-6958, (3900-3955) 4-6-0 GWR Collett Hall

1948	258
Old Oak Common	29
Oxley	23
Cardiff Canton	16
Tyseley	16
St. Philips Marsh	13
Reading	12
Worcester	12
Oxford	11
Stafford Road	11
Westbury	11
Swindon	9
Banbury	8
Carmarthen	8
Gloucester	8
Laira (Plymouth)	8
Chester (GWR)	6
Penzance	6
Ebbw Junction	5
Bristol Bath Road	4
Didcot	4
Neyland	4
Pontypool Road	4
Truro	4
Weymouth	4
Fishguard Goodwick	3
Hereford	3
Landore	3
Shrewsbury	3
Taunton	3
Llanelly	2
Newton Abbot	2
St. Blazey	2
Exeter	1

1951	258
Old Oak Common	22
St. Philips Marsh	22
Cardiff Canton	21
Reading	18
Oxley	13
Oxford	12
Westbury	12
Tyseley	11
Carmarthen	10
Gloucester	10
Worcester	9
Banbury	8
Laira (Plymouth)	8
Southall	8
Swindon	8
Chester (GWR)	7
Weymouth	7
Bristol Bath Road	5
Didcot	5
Landore	5
Penzance	5
Hereford	4
Taunton	4
Ebbw Junction	3
Fishguard Goodwick	3
Neyland	3
Truro	3
Exeter	2
Leamington Spa	2
Newton Abbot	2
Shrewsbury	2
St. Blazey	2
Severn Tunnel Junction	1
Stafford Road	1

1954	258
Cardiff Canton	19
Reading	17
Old Oak Common	15
Oxley	15
Laira (Plymouth)	14
St. Philips Marsh	13
Oxford	12
Southall	12
Banbury	10
Bristol Bath Road	10
Carmarthen	10
Gloucester	10
Swindon	9
Taunton	9
Worcester	8
Didcot	7
Landore	7
Westbury	7
Tyseley	6
Ebbw Junction	5
Hereford	5
Fishguard Goodwick	4
Penzance	4
Pontypool Road	4
Severn Tunnel Junction	4
Shrewsbury	4
Truro	4
Weymouth	4
Chester (GWR)	3
Exeter	3
Newton Abbot	2
St. Blazey	1
Stafford Road	1

1957	258
Reading	23
Cardiff Canton	20
Bristol Bath Road	19
Old Oak Common	15
Oxford	14
Oxley	12
Landore	11
Taunton	11
Worcester	11
St. Philips Marsh	10
Didcot	9
Laira (Plymouth)	9
Westbury	7
Ebbw Junction	6
Newton Abbot	6
Stafford Road	6
Swindon	6
Banbury	5
Gloucester	5
Hereford	5
Penzance	5
Southall	5
Tyseley	5
Weymouth	5
Exeter	4
Fishguard Goodwick	4
Llanelly	4
Shrewsbury	4
Carmarthen	3
Truro	3
Chester (GWR)	2
St. Blazey	2
Neyland	1
Pontypool Road	1

1960	256
Reading	18
Cardiff Canton	16
Oxley	16
St. Philips Marsh	14
Old Oak Common	13
Pontypool Road	13
Taunton	13
Didcot	12
Swindon	11
Westbury	10
Worcester	10
Stafford Road	9
Banbury	8
Landore	8
Newton Abbot	8
Fishguard Goodwick	7
Laira (Plymouth)	7
Oxford	7
Shrewsbury	7
Tyseley	7
Bristol Bath Road	6
Gloucester	6
Severn Tunnel Junction	6
Llanelly	5
Carmarthen	4
Hereford	4
Southall	4
Exeter	3
Penzance	2
St. Blazey	2

1963	173
St. Philips Marsh	20
Cardiff East Dock	16
Reading	13
Didcot	12
Oxford	12
Pontypool Road	9
Shrewsbury	8
Taunton	8
Banbury	7
Gloucester	7
Old Oak Common	7
Oxley	6
Swindon	6
Westbury	6
Fishguard Goodwick	5
Hereford	5
Llanelly	5
Southall	5
Tyseley	5
Duffryn Yard	3
Laira (Plymouth)	3
Neath	3
Carmarthen	1
Worcester	1

5101 4100-4179, 5101-5199 2-6-2T GWR Churchward & Collett 5ft 8in

1948	149
Stourbridge	26
Tyseley	25
Leamington Spa	12
Birkenhead	10
Newton Abbot	9
Stafford Road	9
Chester (GWR)	8
Severn Tunnel Junction	8
Bristol Bath Road	6
Wellington	6
Worcester	6
Taunton	4
Pontypool Road	3
Shrewsbury	3
Kidderminster	2
St. Blazey	2
Barry	1
Cheltenham	1
Gloucester	1
Laira (Plymouth)	1
Landore	1
Neath	1
Rhymney	1
Southall	1
Tondu	1
Treherbert	1

1951	157
Tyseley	27
Stourbridge	22
Newton Abbot	12
Birkenhead	10
Leamington Spa	10
Chester (GWR)	8
Wellington	7
Stafford Road	6
Barry	5
Bristol Bath Road	5
Ebbw Junction	5
Pontypool Road	5
Gloucester	4
Kidderminster	4
Taunton	4
Severn Tunnel Junction	3
Shrewsbury	3
Treherbert	3
Worcester	3
Landore	2
Banbury	1
Cardiff Canton	1
Carmarthen	1
Duffryn Yard	1
Exeter	1
Laira (Plymouth)	1
Neath	1
Neyland	1
Truro	1

1954	143
Stourbridge	13
Tyseley	12
Birkenhead	10
Newton Abbot	9
Severn Tunnel Junction	9
Leamington Spa	8
Merthyr	8
Chester (GWR)	7
Stafford Road	7
Bristol Bath Road	6
Wellington	5
Kidderminster	4
Pontypool Road	4
Shrewsbury	4
Taunton	4
Banbury	3
Ebbw Junction	3
Gloucester	3
Treherbert	3
Worcester	3
Barry	2
Carmarthen	2
Laira (Plymouth)	2
Landore	2
Neath	2
St. Blazey	2
Weymouth	2
Exeter	1
Newport Pill	1
Neyland	1
Oxford	1

1957	140
Newton Abbot	18
Stourbridge	13
Tyseley	11
Birkenhead	10
Chester (GWR)	8
Leamington Spa	8
Merthyr	7
Severn Tunnel Junction	7
Stafford Road	7
Kidderminster	5
Taunton	5
Ebbw Junction	4
Gloucester	4
Wellington	4
Banbury	3
Laira (Plymouth)	3
Worcester	3
Bristol Bath Road	2
Cardiff Cathays	2
Carmarthen	2
Landore	2
Neath	2
Oxford	2
Pontypool Road	2
Weymouth	2
Exeter	1
Neyland	1
St. Blazey	1
St. Philips Marsh	1

1960	119
Newton Abbot	16
Severn Tunnel Junction	12
Gloucester	10
Stourbridge	8
Worcester	8
Leamington Spa	7
Tyseley	6
Oxford	5
Taunton	4
Kidderminster	3
Laira (Plymouth)	3
Radyr	3
St. Philips Marsh	3
Banbury	2
Carmarthen	2
Landore	2
Neath	2
Neyland	2
Pontypool Road	2
St. Blazey	2
Stafford Road	2
Tondu	2
Wellington	2
Weymouth	2
Chester (GWR)	1
Ebbw Junction	1
Exeter	1
Hereford	1
Oxley	1
Penzance	1
Shrewsbury	1
Swindon	1
Truro	1

1963	71
Severn Tunnel Junction	12
Gloucester	8
Leamington Spa	7
Kidderminster	6
Tyseley	5
Stafford Road	4
Worcester	4
Banbury	3
Neyland	3
Radyr	3
Stourbridge	3
Bristol Barrow Road	2
Hereford	2
Neath	2
Taunton	2
Tondu	2
Westbury	2
Pontypool Road	1

5205 5205-5264 2-8-0T GWR 4200 with enlarged cylinders

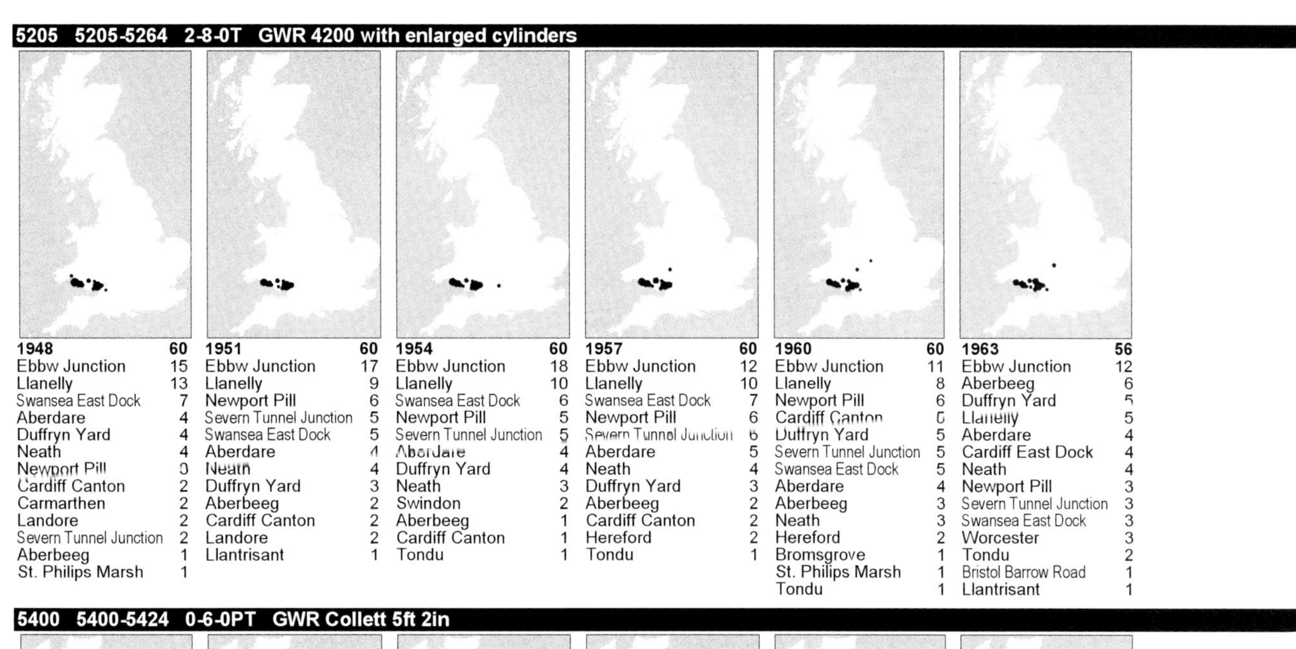

1948	60
Ebbw Junction	15
Llanelly	13
Swansea East Dock	7
Aberdare	4
Duffryn Yard	4
Neath	4
Newport Pill	3
Cardiff Canton	2
Carmarthen	2
Landore	2
Severn Tunnel Junction	2
Aberbeeg	1
St. Philips Marsh	1

1951	60
Ebbw Junction	17
Llanelly	9
Newport Pill	6
Severn Tunnel Junction	5
Swansea East Dock	5
Aberdare	4
Neath	4
Duffryn Yard	3
Aberbeeg	2
Cardiff Canton	2
Landore	2
Llantrisant	1

1954	60
Ebbw Junction	18
Llanelly	10
Swansea East Dock	6
Newport Pill	5
Severn Tunnel Junction	5
Aberdare	4
Duffryn Yard	4
Neath	3
Swindon	2
Aberbeeg	1
Cardiff Canton	1
Tondu	1

1957	60
Ebbw Junction	12
Llanelly	10
Swansea East Dock	7
Newport Pill	6
Severn Tunnel Junction	6
Aberdare	5
Neath	4
Duffryn Yard	3
Aberbeeg	2
Cardiff Canton	2
Hereford	2
Tondu	1

1960	60
Ebbw Junction	11
Llanelly	8
Newport Pill	6
Cardiff Canton	5
Duffryn Yard	5
Severn Tunnel Junction	5
Swansea East Dock	5
Aberdare	4
Aberbeeg	3
Neath	3
Hereford	2
Bromsgrove	1
St. Philips Marsh	1
Tondu	1

1963	56
Ebbw Junction	12
Aberbeeg	6
Duffryn Yard	5
Llanelly	5
Aberdare	4
Cardiff East Dock	4
Neath	4
Newport Pill	3
Severn Tunnel Junction	3
Swansea East Dock	3
Worcester	3
Tondu	2
Bristol Barrow Road	1
Llantrisant	1

5400 5400-5424 0-6-0PT GWR Collett 5ft 2in

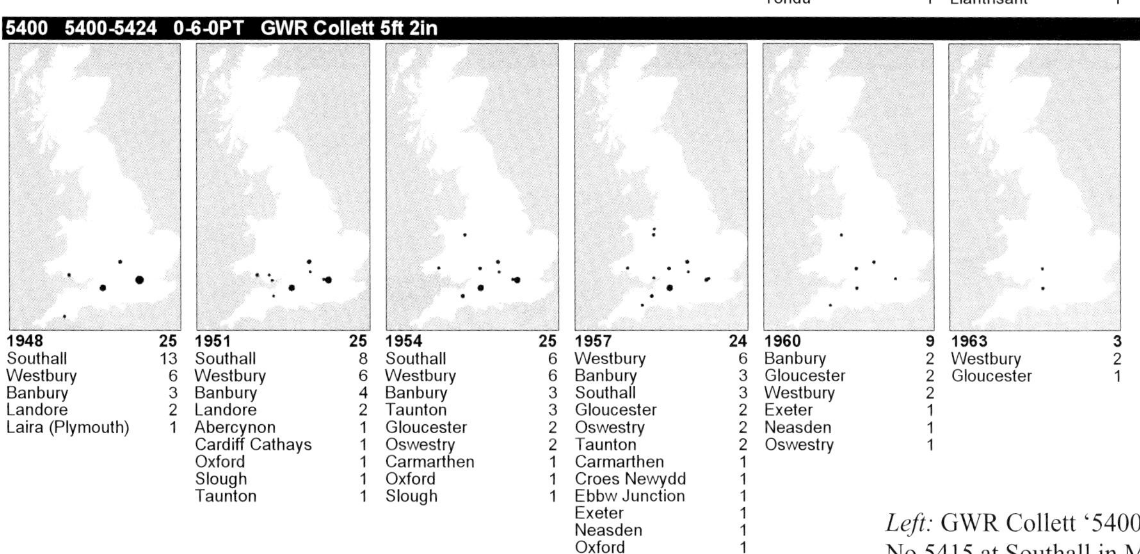

1948	25
Southall	13
Westbury	6
Banbury	3
Landore	2
Laira (Plymouth)	1

1951	25
Southall	8
Westbury	6
Banbury	4
Landore	2
Abercynon	1
Cardiff Cathays	1
Oxford	1
Slough	1
Taunton	1

1954	25
Southall	6
Westbury	6
Banbury	3
Taunton	3
Gloucester	2
Oswestry	2
Carmarthen	1
Oxford	1
Slough	1

1957	24
Westbury	6
Banbury	3
Southall	3
Gloucester	2
Oswestry	2
Taunton	2
Carmarthen	1
Croes Newydd	1
Ebbw Junction	1
Exeter	1
Neasden	1
Oxford	1

1960	9
Banbury	2
Gloucester	2
Westbury	2
Exeter	1
Neasden	1
Oswestry	1

1963	3
Westbury	2
Gloucester	1

Left: GWR Collett '5400' class 0-6-0PT No 5415 at Southall in May 1956. *Brian Morrison*

5600 5600-5699, 6600-6699 0-6-2T GWR Collett

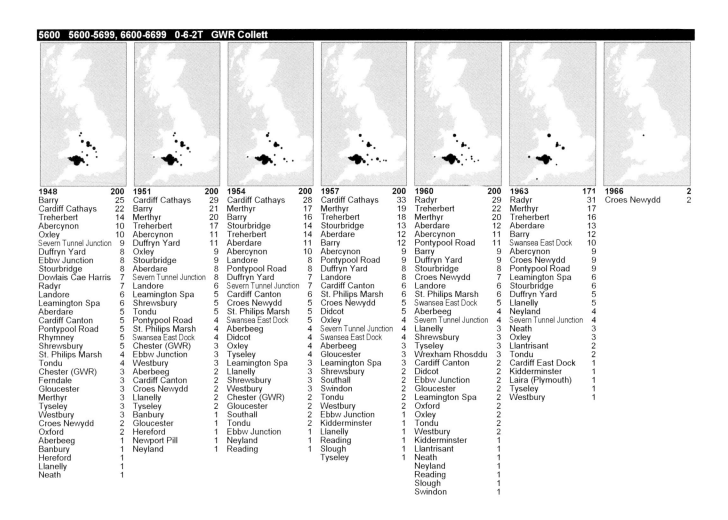

1948	200
Barry	25
Cardiff Cathays	22
Treherbert	14
Abercynon	10
Oxley	10
Severn Tunnel Junction	9
Duffryn Yard	8
Ebbw Junction	8
Stourbridge	8
Dowlais Cae Harris	7
Radyr	7
Landore	6
Leamington Spa	6
Aberdare	5
Cardiff Canton	5
Pontypool Road	5
Rhymney	5
Shrewsbury	5
St. Philips Marsh	4
Tondu	4
Chester (GWR)	3
Ferndale	3
Gloucester	3
Merthyr	3
Tyseley	3
Westbury	3
Croes Newydd	2
Oxford	2
Aberbeeg	1
Banbury	1
Hereford	1
Llanelly	1
Neath	1

1951	200
Cardiff Cathays	29
Barry	21
Merthyr	20
Treherbert	17
Abercynon	11
Duffryn Yard	11
Oxley	9
Stourbridge	9
Aberdare	8
Severn Tunnel Junction	8
Landore	6
Leamington Spa	5
Shrewsbury	5
Tondu	5
Pontypool Road	4
St. Philips Marsh	4
Swansea East Dock	4
Chester (GWR)	3
Ebbw Junction	3
Westbury	3
Aberbeeg	2
Cardiff Canton	2
Croes Newydd	2
Llanelly	2
Tyseley	2
Banbury	1
Gloucester	1
Hereford	1
Newport Pill	1
Neyland	1

1954	200
Cardiff Cathays	28
Merthyr	17
Barry	16
Stourbridge	14
Treherbert	14
Aberdare	11
Abercynon	10
Landore	8
Pontypool Road	8
Duffryn Yard	7
Severn Tunnel Junction	7
Cardiff Canton	6
Croes Newydd	5
St. Philips Marsh	5
Swansea East Dock	5
Aberbeeg	4
Didcot	4
Oxley	4
Tyseley	4
Leamington Spa	3
Llanelly	3
Shrewsbury	3
Westbury	3
Chester (GWR)	2
Gloucester	2
Southall	2
Tondu	2
Ebbw Junction	1
Neyland	1
Reading	1

1957	200
Cardiff Cathays	33
Merthyr	19
Treherbert	18
Stourbridge	13
Aberdare	12
Barry	12
Abercynon	9
Pontypool Road	9
Duffryn Yard	8
Landore	8
Cardiff Canton	6
St. Philips Marsh	6
Croes Newydd	5
Didcot	5
Oxley	4
Severn Tunnel Junction	4
Swansea East Dock	4
Aberbeeg	3
Gloucester	3
Leamington Spa	3
Shrewsbury	2
Southall	2
Swindon	2
Tondu	2
Westbury	2
Ebbw Junction	1
Kidderminster	1
Llanelly	1
Reading	1
Slough	1
Tyseley	1

1960	200
Radyr	29
Treherbert	22
Merthyr	20
Aberdare	12
Abercynon	11
Pontypool Road	11
Barry	9
Duffryn Yard	9
Stourbridge	8
Croes Newydd	7
Landore	6
St. Philips Marsh	6
Swansea East Dock	5
Aberbeeg	4
Severn Tunnel Junction	4
Llanelly	3
Shrewsbury	3
Tyseley	3
Wrexham Rhosddu	3
Cardiff Canton	2
Didcot	2
Ebbw Junction	2
Gloucester	2
Leamington Spa	2
Oxford	2
Oxley	2
Tondu	2
Westbury	2
Kidderminster	1
Llantrisant	1
Neath	1
Neyland	1
Reading	1
Slough	1
Swindon	1

1963	171
Radyr	31
Merthyr	17
Treherbert	16
Aberdare	13
Barry	12
Swansea East Dock	10
Abercynon	9
Croes Newydd	9
Pontypool Road	9
Leamington Spa	6
Stourbridge	6
Duffryn Yard	5
Llanelly	5
Neyland	4
Severn Tunnel Junction	4
Neath	3
Oxley	3
Llantrisant	2
Tondu	2
Cardiff East Dock	1
Kidderminster	1
Laira (Plymouth)	1
Tyseley	1
Westbury	1

1966	2
Croes Newydd	2

Collett-designed 0-6-2T No 6664. *Ian Allan Library*

5700 3600-3799, 4600-4699, 5700-5799, 7700-7799, 8700-8799, 9600-9682, 9711-9799 0-6-0PT GWR Collett 4ft 7½in

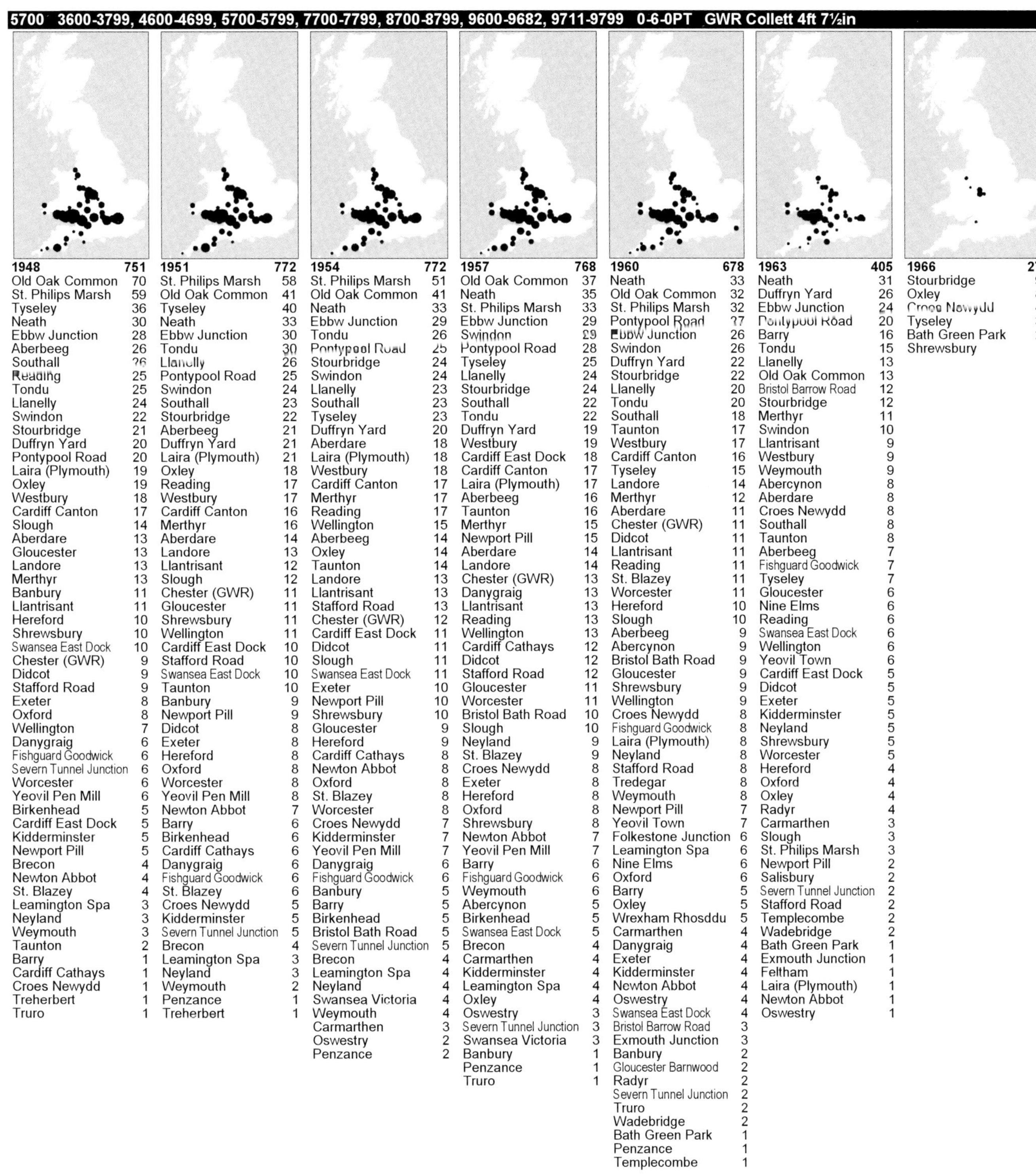

1948	751
Old Oak Common	70
St. Philips Marsh	59
Tyseley	36
Neath	30
Ebbw Junction	28
Aberbeeg	26
Southall	26
Reading	25
Tondu	25
Llanelly	24
Swindon	22
Stourbridge	21
Duffryn Yard	20
Pontypool Road	20
Laira (Plymouth)	19
Oxley	19
Westbury	18
Cardiff Canton	17
Slough	14
Aberdare	13
Gloucester	13
Landore	13
Merthyr	13
Banbury	11
Llantrisant	11
Hereford	10
Shrewsbury	10
Swansea East Dock	10
Chester (GWR)	9
Didcot	9
Stafford Road	9
Exeter	8
Oxford	8
Wellington	7
Danygraig	6
Fishguard Goodwick	6
Severn Tunnel Junction	6
Worcester	6
Yeovil Pen Mill	6
Birkenhead	5
Cardiff East Dock	5
Kidderminster	5
Newport Pill	5
Brecon	4
Newton Abbot	4
St. Blazey	4
Leamington Spa	3
Neyland	3
Weymouth	3
Taunton	2
Barry	1
Cardiff Cathays	1
Croes Newydd	1
Treherbert	1
Truro	1

1951	772
St. Philips Marsh	58
Old Oak Common	41
Tyseley	40
Neath	33
Ebbw Junction	30
Tondu	30
Llanelly	26
Pontypool Road	25
Swindon	24
Southall	23
Stourbridge	22
Aberbeeg	21
Duffryn Yard	21
Laira (Plymouth)	21
Oxley	18
Reading	17
Westbury	17
Cardiff Canton	16
Merthyr	16
Aberdare	14
Landore	13
Llantrisant	12
Slough	12
Chester (GWR)	11
Gloucester	11
Shrewsbury	11
Wellington	11
Cardiff East Dock	10
Stafford Road	10
Swansea East Dock	10
Taunton	10
Banbury	9
Newport Pill	9
Didcot	8
Exeter	8
Hereford	8
Oxford	8
Worcester	8
Yeovil Pen Mill	8
Newton Abbot	7
Barry	6
Birkenhead	6
Cardiff Cathays	6
Danygraig	6
Fishguard Goodwick	6
St. Blazey	6
Croes Newydd	5
Kidderminster	5
Severn Tunnel Junction	5
Brecon	4
Leamington Spa	3
Neyland	3
Weymouth	2
Penzance	1
Treherbert	1

1954	772
St. Philips Marsh	51
Old Oak Common	41
Neath	33
Ebbw Junction	29
Tondu	26
Pontypool Road	25
Stourbridge	24
Swindon	24
Llanelly	23
Southall	23
Tyseley	23
Duffryn Yard	20
Aberdare	18
Laira (Plymouth)	18
Westbury	18
Cardiff Canton	17
Merthyr	17
Reading	17
Wellington	15
Aberbeeg	14
Oxley	14
Taunton	14
Landore	13
Llantrisant	13
Stafford Road	13
Chester (GWR)	12
Cardiff East Dock	11
Didcot	11
Slough	11
Swansea East Dock	11
Exeter	10
Newport Pill	10
Shrewsbury	10
Gloucester	9
Hereford	9
Cardiff Cathays	8
Newton Abbot	8
Oxford	8
St. Blazey	8
Worcester	8
Croes Newydd	7
Kidderminster	7
Yeovil Pen Mill	7
Danygraig	6
Fishguard Goodwick	6
Banbury	5
Barry	5
Birkenhead	5
Bristol Bath Road	5
Severn Tunnel Junction	5
Brecon	4
Leamington Spa	4
Neyland	4
Swansea Victoria	4
Weymouth	4
Carmarthen	3
Oswestry	2
Penzance	2

1957	768
Old Oak Common	37
Neath	35
St. Philips Marsh	33
Ebbw Junction	29
Swindon	29
Pontypool Road	28
Tyseley	25
Llanelly	24
Stourbridge	24
Southall	23
Tondu	22
Duffryn Yard	19
Westbury	19
Cardiff East Dock	18
Cardiff Canton	17
Laira (Plymouth)	17
Aberbeeg	16
Taunton	16
Merthyr	15
Newport Pill	15
Aberdare	14
Landore	14
Chester (GWR)	13
Danygraig	13
Llantrisant	13
Reading	13
Wellington	13
Cardiff Cathays	12
Didcot	12
Stafford Road	12
Gloucester	11
Worcester	11
Bristol Bath Road	10
Slough	10
Neyland	9
St. Blazey	9
Croes Newydd	8
Exeter	8
Hereford	8
Oxford	8
Shrewsbury	8
Newton Abbot	7
Yeovil Pen Mill	7
Barry	6
Fishguard Goodwick	6
Weymouth	6
Abercynon	5
Birkenhead	5
Swansea East Dock	5
Brecon	4
Carmarthen	4
Kidderminster	4
Leamington Spa	4
Oxley	4
Oswestry	3
Severn Tunnel Junction	3
Swansea Victoria	3
Banbury	1
Penzance	1
Truro	1

1960	678
Neath	33
Old Oak Common	32
St. Philips Marsh	32
Pontypool Road	27
Ebbw Junction	26
Swindon	26
Duffryn Yard	22
Stourbridge	22
Llanelly	20
Tondu	20
Southall	18
Taunton	17
Westbury	17
Cardiff Canton	16
Tyseley	15
Landore	14
Merthyr	12
Aberdare	11
Chester (GWR)	11
Didcot	11
Llantrisant	11
Reading	11
St. Blazey	11
Worcester	11
Hereford	10
Slough	10
Aberbeeg	9
Abercynon	9
Bristol Bath Road	9
Gloucester	9
Shrewsbury	9
Wellington	9
Croes Newydd	8
Fishguard Goodwick	8
Laira (Plymouth)	8
Neyland	8
Stafford Road	8
Tredegar	8
Weymouth	8
Newport Pill	7
Yeovil Town	7
Folkestone Junction	6
Leamington Spa	6
Nine Elms	6
Oxford	6
Barry	5
Oxley	5
Wrexham Rhosddu	5
Carmarthen	4
Danygraig	4
Exeter	4
Kidderminster	4
Newton Abbot	4
Oswestry	4
Swansea East Dock	4
Bristol Barrow Road	3
Exmouth Junction	3
Banbury	2
Gloucester Barnwood	2
Radyr	2
Severn Tunnel Junction	2
Truro	2
Wadebridge	2
Bath Green Park	1
Penzance	1
Templecombe	1

1963	405
Neath	31
Duffryn Yard	26
Ebbw Junction	24
Pontypool Road	20
Barry	16
Tondu	15
Llanelly	13
Old Oak Common	13
Bristol Barrow Road	12
Stourbridge	12
Merthyr	11
Swindon	10
Llantrisant	9
Westbury	9
Weymouth	9
Abercynon	8
Aberdare	8
Croes Newydd	8
Southall	8
Taunton	8
Aberbeeg	7
Fishguard Goodwick	7
Tyseley	7
Gloucester	6
Nine Elms	6
Reading	6
Swansea East Dock	6
Wellington	6
Yeovil Town	6
Cardiff East Dock	5
Didcot	5
Exeter	5
Kidderminster	5
Neyland	5
Shrewsbury	5
Worcester	5
Hereford	4
Oxford	4
Oxley	4
Radyr	4
Carmarthen	3
Slough	3
St. Philips Marsh	3
Newport Pill	2
Salisbury	2
Severn Tunnel Junction	2
Stafford Road	2
Templecombe	2
Wadebridge	2
Bath Green Park	1
Exmouth Junction	1
Feltham	1
Laira (Plymouth)	1
Newton Abbot	1
Oswestry	1

1966	27
Stourbridge	9
Oxley	8
Croes Newydd	4
Tyseley	3
Bath Green Park	2
Shrewsbury	1

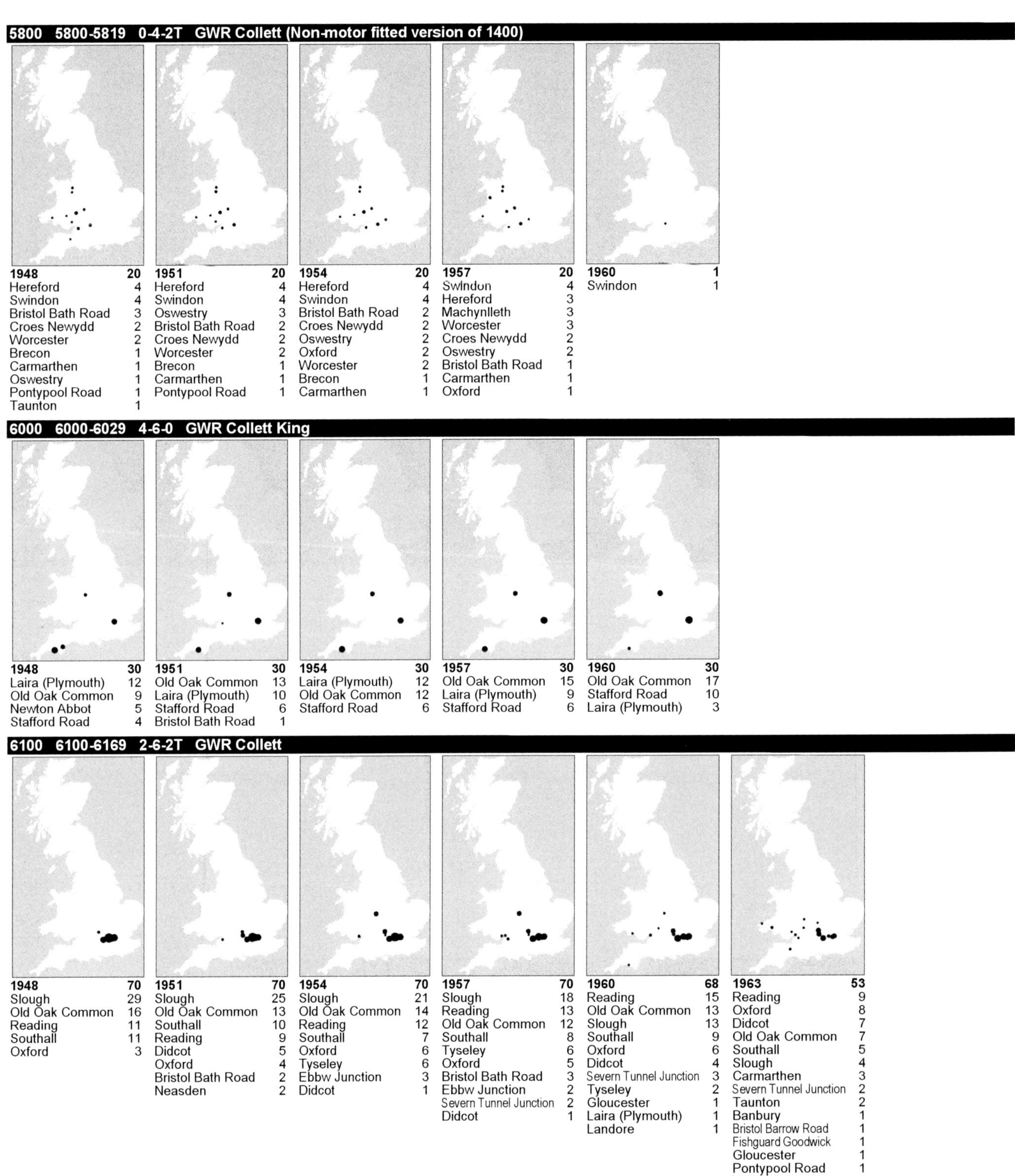

5800 5800-5819 0-4-2T GWR Collett (Non-motor fitted version of 1400)

1948	20
Hereford	4
Swindon	4
Bristol Bath Road	3
Croes Newydd	2
Worcester	2
Brecon	1
Carmarthen	1
Oswestry	1
Pontypool Road	1
Taunton	1

1951	20
Hereford	4
Swindon	4
Oswestry	3
Bristol Bath Road	2
Croes Newydd	2
Worcester	2
Brecon	1
Carmarthen	1
Pontypool Road	1

1954	20
Hereford	4
Swindon	4
Bristol Bath Road	2
Croes Newydd	2
Oswestry	2
Oxford	2
Worcester	2
Brecon	1
Carmarthen	1

1957	20
Swindon	4
Hereford	3
Machynlleth	3
Worcester	3
Croes Newydd	2
Oswestry	2
Bristol Bath Road	1
Carmarthen	1
Oxford	1

1960	1
Swindon	1

6000 6000-6029 4-6-0 GWR Collett King

1948	30
Laira (Plymouth)	12
Old Oak Common	9
Newton Abbot	5
Stafford Road	4

1951	30
Old Oak Common	13
Laira (Plymouth)	10
Stafford Road	6
Bristol Bath Road	1

1954	30
Laira (Plymouth)	12
Old Oak Common	12
Stafford Road	6

1957	30
Old Oak Common	15
Laira (Plymouth)	9
Stafford Road	6

1960	30
Old Oak Common	17
Stafford Road	10
Laira (Plymouth)	3

6100 6100-6169 2-6-2T GWR Collett

1948	70
Slough	29
Old Oak Common	16
Reading	11
Southall	11
Oxford	3

1951	70
Slough	25
Old Oak Common	13
Southall	10
Reading	9
Didcot	5
Oxford	4
Bristol Bath Road	2
Neasden	2

1954	70
Slough	21
Old Oak Common	14
Reading	12
Southall	7
Oxford	6
Tyseley	6
Ebbw Junction	3
Didcot	1

1957	70
Slough	18
Reading	13
Old Oak Common	12
Southall	8
Tyseley	6
Oxford	5
Bristol Bath Road	3
Ebbw Junction	2
Severn Tunnel Junction	2
Didcot	1

1960	68
Reading	15
Old Oak Common	13
Slough	13
Southall	9
Oxford	6
Didcot	4
Severn Tunnel Junction	3
Tyseley	2
Gloucester	1
Laira (Plymouth)	1
Landore	1

1963	53
Reading	9
Oxford	8
Didcot	7
Old Oak Common	7
Southall	5
Slough	4
Carmarthen	3
Severn Tunnel Junction	2
Taunton	2
Banbury	1
Bristol Barrow Road	1
Fishguard Goodwick	1
Gloucester	1
Pontypool Road	1
Worcester	1

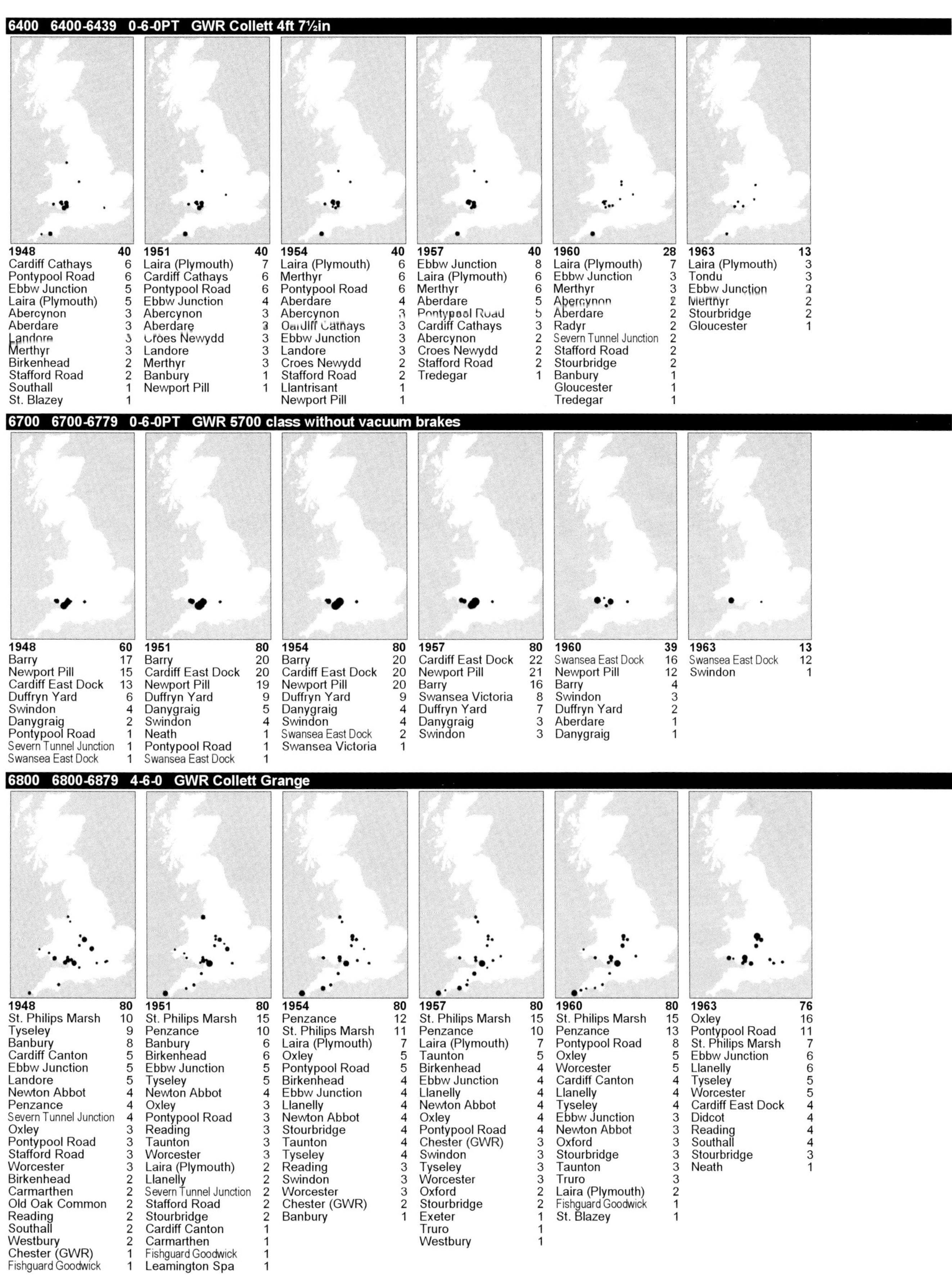

6400 6400-6439 0-6-0PT GWR Collett 4ft 7½in

1948	40	1951	40	1954	40	1957	40	1960	28	1963	13
Cardiff Cathays	6	Laira (Plymouth)	7	Laira (Plymouth)	6	Ebbw Junction	8	Laira (Plymouth)	7	Laira (Plymouth)	3
Pontypool Road	6	Cardiff Cathays	6	Merthyr	6	Laira (Plymouth)	6	Ebbw Junction	3	Tondu	3
Ebbw Junction	5	Pontypool Road	6	Pontypool Road	6	Merthyr	6	Merthyr	3	Ebbw Junction	2
Laira (Plymouth)	5	Ebbw Junction	4	Aberdare	4	Aberdare	5	Abercynon	2	Merthyr	2
Abercynon	3	Abercynon	3	Abercynon	3	Pontypool Road	5	Aberdare	2	Stourbridge	2
Aberdare	3	Aberdare	3	Cardiff Cathays	3	Cardiff Cathays	3	Radyr	2	Gloucester	1
Landore	3	Croes Newydd	3	Ebbw Junction	3	Abercynon	2	Severn Tunnel Junction	2		
Merthyr	3	Landore	3	Landore	3	Croes Newydd	2	Stafford Road	2		
Birkenhead	2	Merthyr	3	Croes Newydd	2	Stafford Road	2	Stourbridge	2		
Stafford Road	2	Banbury	1	Stafford Road	2	Tredegar	1	Banbury	1		
Southall	1	Newport Pill	1	Llantrisant	1			Gloucester	1		
St. Blazey	1			Newport Pill	1			Tredegar	1		

6700 6700-6779 0-6-0PT GWR 5700 class without vacuum brakes

1948	60	1951	80	1954	80	1957	80	1960	39	1963	13
Barry	17	Barry	20	Barry	20	Cardiff East Dock	22	Swansea East Dock	16	Swansea East Dock	12
Newport Pill	15	Cardiff East Dock	20	Cardiff East Dock	20	Newport Pill	21	Newport Pill	12	Swindon	1
Cardiff East Dock	13	Newport Pill	19	Newport Pill	20	Barry	16	Barry	4		
Duffryn Yard	6	Duffryn Yard	9	Duffryn Yard	9	Swansea Victoria	8	Swindon	3		
Swindon	4	Danygraig	5	Danygraig	4	Duffryn Yard	7	Duffryn Yard	2		
Danygraig	2	Swindon	4	Swindon	4	Danygraig	3	Aberdare	1		
Pontypool Road	1	Neath	1	Swansea East Dock	2	Swindon	3	Danygraig	1		
Severn Tunnel Junction	1	Pontypool Road	1	Swansea Victoria	1						
Swansea East Dock	1	Swansea East Dock	1								

6800 6800-6879 4-6-0 GWR Collett Grange

1948	80	1951	80	1954	80	1957	80	1960	80	1963	76
St. Philips Marsh	10	St. Philips Marsh	15	Penzance	12	St. Philips Marsh	15	St. Philips Marsh	15	Oxley	16
Tyseley	9	Penzance	10	St. Philips Marsh	11	Penzance	10	Penzance	13	Pontypool Road	11
Banbury	8	Banbury	6	Laira (Plymouth)	7	Laira (Plymouth)	7	Pontypool Road	8	St. Philips Marsh	7
Cardiff Canton	5	Birkenhead	6	Oxley	5	Taunton	5	Oxley	5	Ebbw Junction	6
Ebbw Junction	5	Ebbw Junction	5	Pontypool Road	5	Birkenhead	4	Worcester	5	Llanelly	6
Landore	5	Tyseley	5	Birkenhead	4	Ebbw Junction	4	Cardiff Canton	4	Tyseley	5
Newton Abbot	4	Newton Abbot	4	Ebbw Junction	4	Llanelly	4	Llanelly	4	Worcester	5
Penzance	4	Oxley	3	Llanelly	4	Newton Abbot	4	Tyseley	4	Cardiff East Dock	4
Severn Tunnel Junction	4	Pontypool Road	3	Newton Abbot	4	Oxley	4	Ebbw Junction	3	Didcot	4
Oxley	3	Reading	3	Stourbridge	4	Pontypool Road	4	Newton Abbot	3	Reading	4
Pontypool Road	3	Taunton	3	Taunton	4	Chester (GWR)	3	Oxford	3	Southall	4
Stafford Road	3	Worcester	3	Tyseley	4	Swindon	3	Stourbridge	3	Stourbridge	3
Worcester	3	Laira (Plymouth)	2	Reading	3	Tyseley	3	Taunton	3	Neath	1
Birkenhead	2	Llanelly	2	Swindon	3	Worcester	3	Truro	3		
Carmarthen	2	Severn Tunnel Junction	2	Worcester	3	Oxford	2	Laira (Plymouth)	2		
Old Oak Common	2	Stafford Road	2	Chester (GWR)	2	Stourbridge	2	Fishguard Goodwick	1		
Reading	2	Stourbridge	2	Banbury	1	Exeter	1	St. Blazey	1		
Southall	2	Cardiff Canton	1			Truro	1				
Westbury	2	Carmarthen	1			Westbury	1				
Chester (GWR)	1	Fishguard Goodwick	1								
Fishguard Goodwick	1	Leamington Spa	1								

6959 6959-6999, 7900-7929 4-6-0 GWR Hawksworth Modified Hall

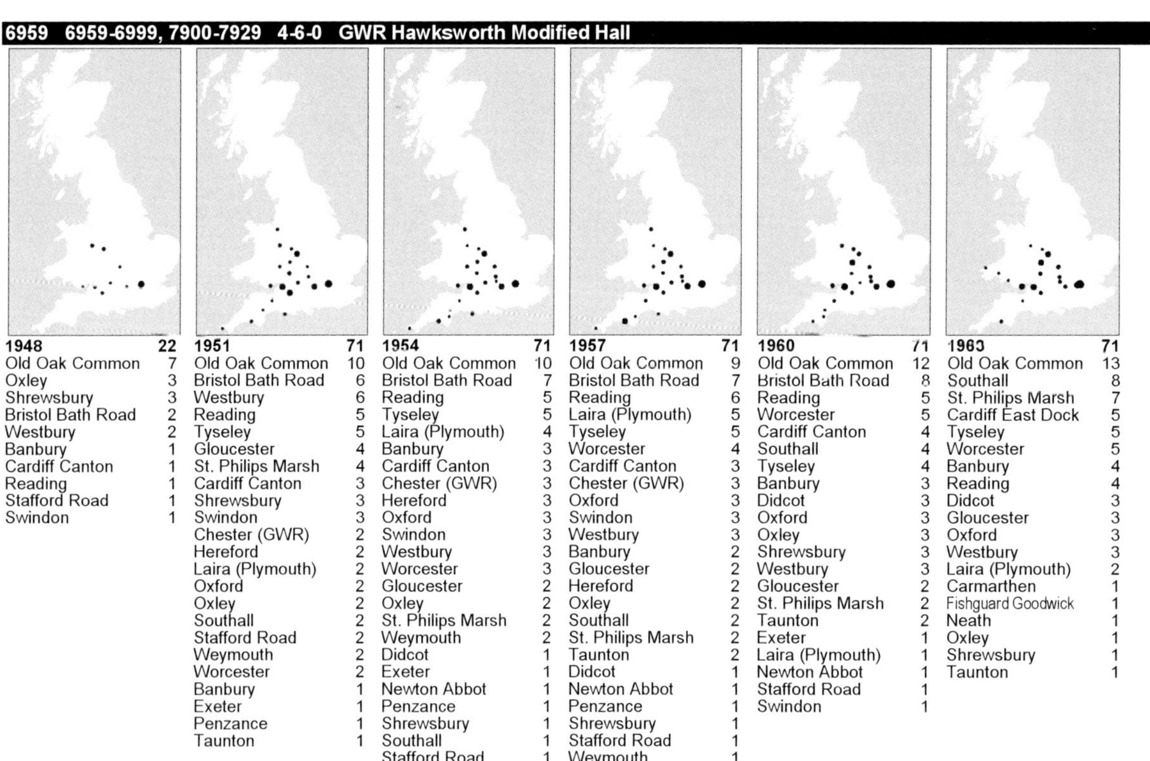

1948	22
Old Oak Common	7
Oxley	3
Shrewsbury	3
Bristol Bath Road	2
Westbury	2
Banbury	1
Cardiff Canton	1
Reading	1
Stafford Road	1
Swindon	1

1951	71
Old Oak Common	10
Bristol Bath Road	6
Westbury	6
Reading	5
Tyseley	5
Gloucester	4
St. Philips Marsh	4
Cardiff Canton	3
Shrewsbury	3
Swindon	3
Chester (GWR)	2
Hereford	2
Laira (Plymouth)	2
Oxford	2
Oxley	2
Southall	2
Stafford Road	2
Weymouth	2
Worcester	2
Banbury	1
Exeter	1
Penzance	1
Taunton	1

1954	71
Old Oak Common	10
Bristol Bath Road	7
Reading	5
Tyseley	5
Laira (Plymouth)	4
Banbury	3
Cardiff Canton	3
Chester (GWR)	3
Hereford	3
Oxford	3
Swindon	3
Westbury	3
Worcester	3
Gloucester	2
Oxley	2
St. Philips Marsh	2
Weymouth	2
Didcot	1
Exeter	1
Newton Abbot	1
Penzance	1
Shrewsbury	1
Southall	1
Stafford Road	1
Taunton	1

1957	71
Old Oak Common	9
Bristol Bath Road	7
Reading	6
Laira (Plymouth)	5
Tyseley	5
Worcester	4
Cardiff Canton	3
Chester (GWR)	3
Oxford	3
Swindon	3
Westbury	3
Banbury	2
Gloucester	2
Hereford	2
Oxley	2
Southall	2
St. Philips Marsh	2
Taunton	2
Didcot	1
Newton Abbot	1
Penzance	1
Shrewsbury	1
Stafford Road	1
Weymouth	1

1960	71
Old Oak Common	12
Bristol Bath Road	8
Reading	5
Worcester	5
Cardiff Canton	4
Southall	4
Tyseley	4
Banbury	3
Didcot	3
Oxford	3
Oxley	3
Shrewsbury	3
Westbury	3
Gloucester	2
St. Philips Marsh	2
Taunton	2
Exeter	1
Laira (Plymouth)	1
Newton Abbot	1
Stafford Road	1
Swindon	1

1963	71
Old Oak Common	13
Southall	8
St. Philips Marsh	7
Cardiff East Dock	5
Tyseley	5
Worcester	5
Banbury	4
Reading	4
Didcot	3
Gloucester	3
Oxford	3
Westbury	3
Laira (Plymouth)	2
Carmarthen	1
Fishguard Goodwick	1
Neath	1
Oxley	1
Shrewsbury	1
Taunton	1

7200 7200-7253 2-8-2T GWR rebuilt from 5205 & 4200 classes

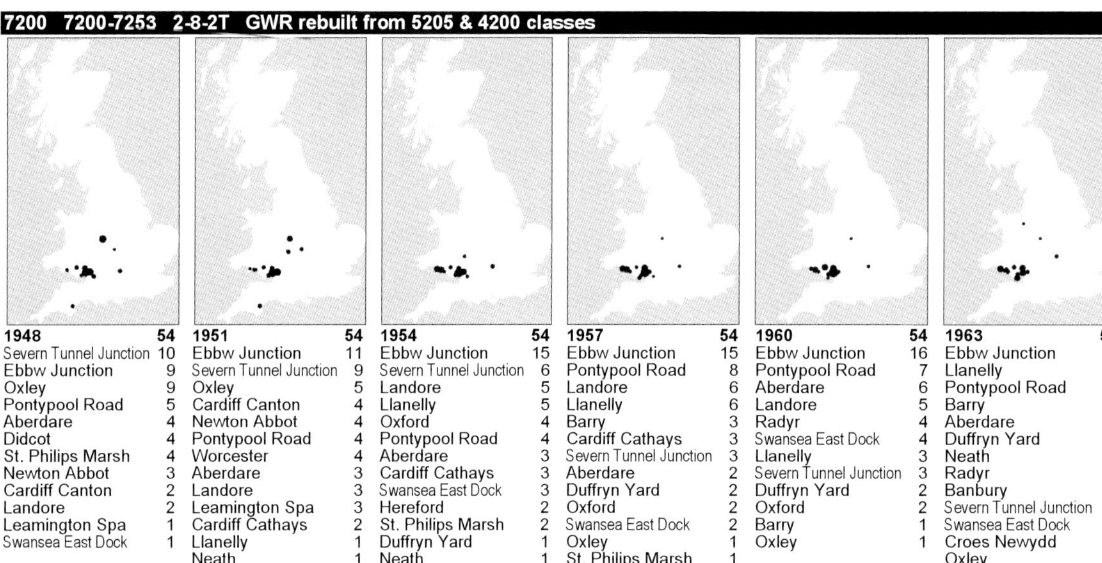

1948	54
Severn Tunnel Junction	10
Ebbw Junction	9
Oxley	9
Pontypool Road	5
Aberdare	4
Didcot	4
St. Philips Marsh	4
Newton Abbot	3
Cardiff Canton	2
Landore	2
Leamington Spa	1
Swansea East Dock	1

1951	54
Ebbw Junction	11
Severn Tunnel Junction	9
Oxley	5
Cardiff Canton	4
Newton Abbot	4
Pontypool Road	4
Worcester	4
Aberdare	3
Landore	3
Leamington Spa	3
Cardiff Cathays	2
Llanelly	1
Neath	1

1954	54
Ebbw Junction	15
Severn Tunnel Junction	6
Landore	5
Llanelly	5
Oxford	4
Pontypool Road	4
Aberdare	3
Cardiff Cathays	3
Swansea East Dock	3
Hereford	2
St. Philips Marsh	2
Duffryn Yard	1
Neath	1

1957	54
Ebbw Junction	15
Pontypool Road	8
Landore	6
Llanelly	6
Barry	3
Cardiff Cathays	3
Severn Tunnel Junction	3
Aberdare	2
Duffryn Yard	2
Oxford	2
Swansea East Dock	2
Oxley	1
St. Philips Marsh	1

1960	54
Ebbw Junction	16
Pontypool Road	7
Aberdare	6
Landore	5
Radyr	4
Swansea East Dock	4
Llanelly	3
Severn Tunnel Junction	3
Duffryn Yard	2
Oxford	2
Barry	1
Oxley	1

1963	52
Ebbw Junction	7
Llanelly	7
Pontypool Road	6
Barry	5
Aberdare	4
Duffryn Yard	4
Neath	4
Radyr	4
Banbury	3
Severn Tunnel Junction	3
Swansea East Dock	3
Croes Newydd	1
Oxley	1

Left: GWR Collett '7200' class 2-8-2T No 7251 from 86G Pontypool Road at Carmarthen MPD on 21 June 1959. *D. A. Idle*

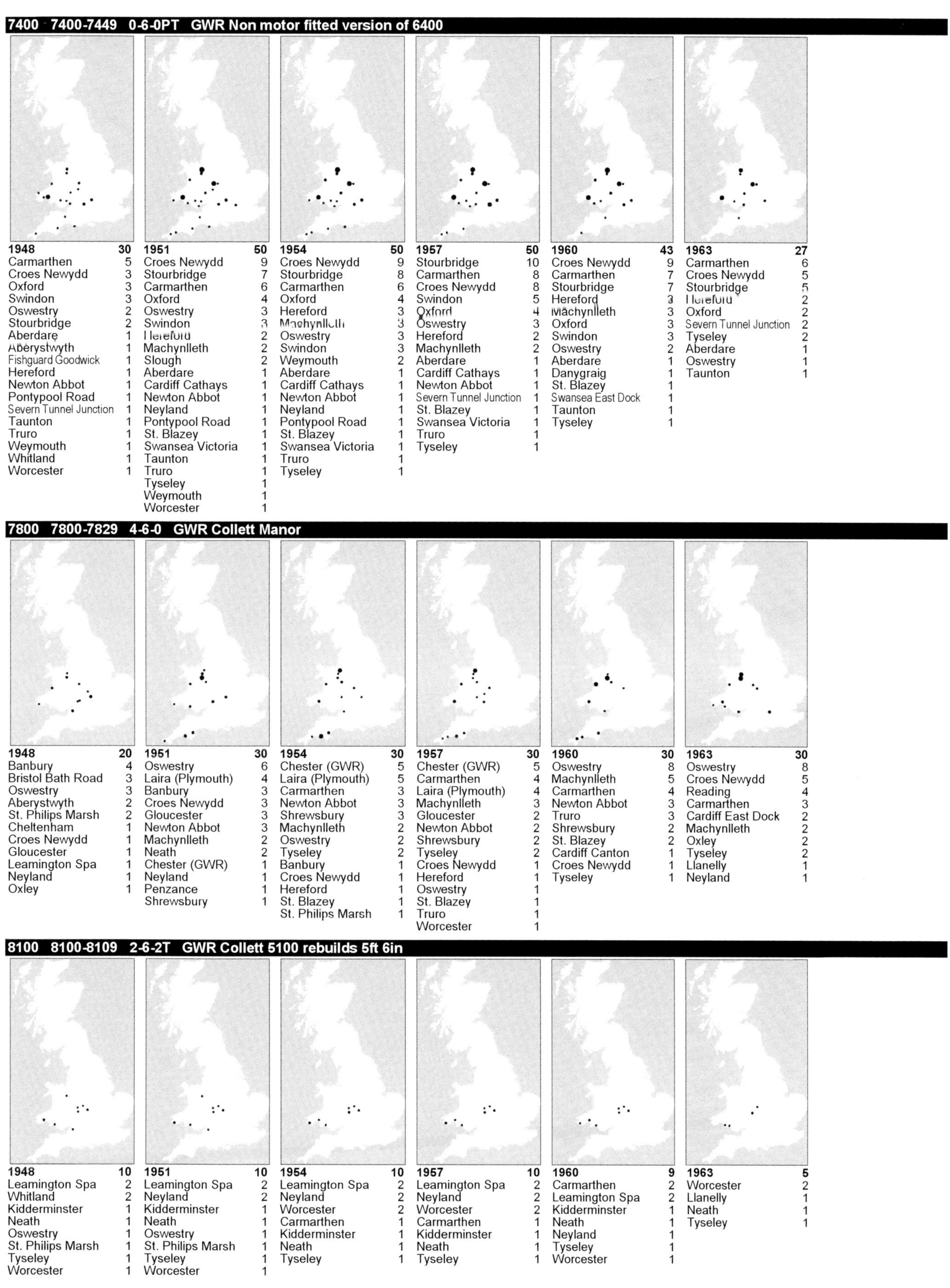

7400 7400-7449 0-6-0PT GWR Non motor fitted version of 6400

1948	30
Carmarthen	5
Croes Newydd	3
Oxford	3
Swindon	3
Oswestry	2
Stourbridge	2
Aberdare	1
Aberystwyth	1
Fishguard Goodwick	1
Hereford	1
Newton Abbot	1
Pontypool Road	1
Severn Tunnel Junction	1
Taunton	1
Truro	1
Weymouth	1
Whitland	1
Worcester	1

1951	50
Croes Newydd	9
Stourbridge	7
Carmarthen	6
Oxford	4
Oswestry	3
Swindon	3
Hereford	2
Machynlleth	2
Slough	2
Aberdare	1
Cardiff Cathays	1
Newton Abbot	1
Neyland	1
Pontypool Road	1
St. Blazey	1
Swansea Victoria	1
Taunton	1
Truro	1
Tyseley	1
Weymouth	1
Worcester	1

1954	50
Croes Newydd	9
Stourbridge	8
Carmarthen	6
Oxford	4
Hereford	3
Machynlleth	3
Oswestry	3
Swindon	3
Weymouth	2
Aberdare	1
Cardiff Cathays	1
Newton Abbot	1
Neyland	1
Pontypool Road	1
St. Blazey	1
Swansea Victoria	1
Truro	1
Tyseley	1

1957	50
Stourbridge	10
Carmarthen	8
Croes Newydd	8
Swindon	5
Oxford	4
Oswestry	3
Hereford	2
Machynlleth	2
Aberdare	1
Cardiff Cathays	1
Newton Abbot	1
Severn Tunnel Junction	1
St. Blazey	1
Swansea Victoria	1
Truro	1
Tyseley	1

1960	43
Croes Newydd	9
Carmarthen	7
Stourbridge	7
Hereford	3
Machynlleth	3
Oxford	3
Swindon	3
Oswestry	2
Aberdare	1
Danygraig	1
St. Blazey	1
Swansea East Dock	1
Taunton	1
Tyseley	1

1963	27
Carmarthen	6
Croes Newydd	5
Stourbridge	5
Hereford	2
Oxford	2
Severn Tunnel Junction	2
Tyseley	2
Aberdare	1
Oswestry	1
Taunton	1

7800 7800-7829 4-6-0 GWR Collett Manor

1948	20
Banbury	4
Bristol Bath Road	3
Oswestry	3
Aberystwyth	2
St. Philips Marsh	2
Cheltenham	1
Croes Newydd	1
Gloucester	1
Leamington Spa	1
Neyland	1
Oxley	1

1951	30
Oswestry	6
Laira (Plymouth)	4
Banbury	3
Croes Newydd	3
Gloucester	3
Newton Abbot	3
Machynlleth	2
Neath	2
Chester (GWR)	1
Neyland	1
Penzance	1
Shrewsbury	1

1954	30
Chester (GWR)	5
Laira (Plymouth)	5
Carmarthen	3
Newton Abbot	3
Shrewsbury	3
Machynlleth	2
Oswestry	2
Tyseley	2
Banbury	1
Croes Newydd	1
Hereford	1
St. Blazey	1
St. Philips Marsh	1

1957	30
Chester (GWR)	5
Carmarthen	4
Laira (Plymouth)	4
Machynlleth	3
Gloucester	2
Newton Abbot	2
Shrewsbury	2
Tyseley	2
Croes Newydd	1
Hereford	1
Oswestry	1
St. Blazey	1
Truro	1
Worcester	1

1960	30
Oswestry	8
Machynlleth	5
Carmarthen	4
Newton Abbot	3
Truro	3
Shrewsbury	2
St. Blazey	2
Cardiff Canton	1
Croes Newydd	1
Tyseley	1

1963	30
Oswestry	8
Croes Newydd	5
Reading	4
Carmarthen	3
Cardiff East Dock	2
Machynlleth	2
Oxley	2
Tyseley	2
Llanelly	1
Neyland	1

8100 8100-8109 2-6-2T GWR Collett 5100 rebuilds 5ft 6in

1948	10
Leamington Spa	2
Whitland	2
Kidderminster	1
Neath	1
Oswestry	1
St. Philips Marsh	1
Tyseley	1
Worcester	1

1951	10
Leamington Spa	2
Neyland	2
Kidderminster	1
Neath	1
Oswestry	1
St. Philips Marsh	1
Tyseley	1
Worcester	1

1954	10
Leamington Spa	2
Neyland	2
Worcester	2
Carmarthen	1
Kidderminster	1
Neath	1
Tyseley	1

1957	10
Leamington Spa	2
Neyland	2
Worcester	2
Carmarthen	1
Kidderminster	1
Neath	1
Tyseley	1

1960	9
Carmarthen	2
Leamington Spa	2
Kidderminster	1
Neath	1
Neyland	1
Tyseley	1
Worcester	1

1963	5
Worcester	2
Llanelly	1
Neath	1
Tyseley	1

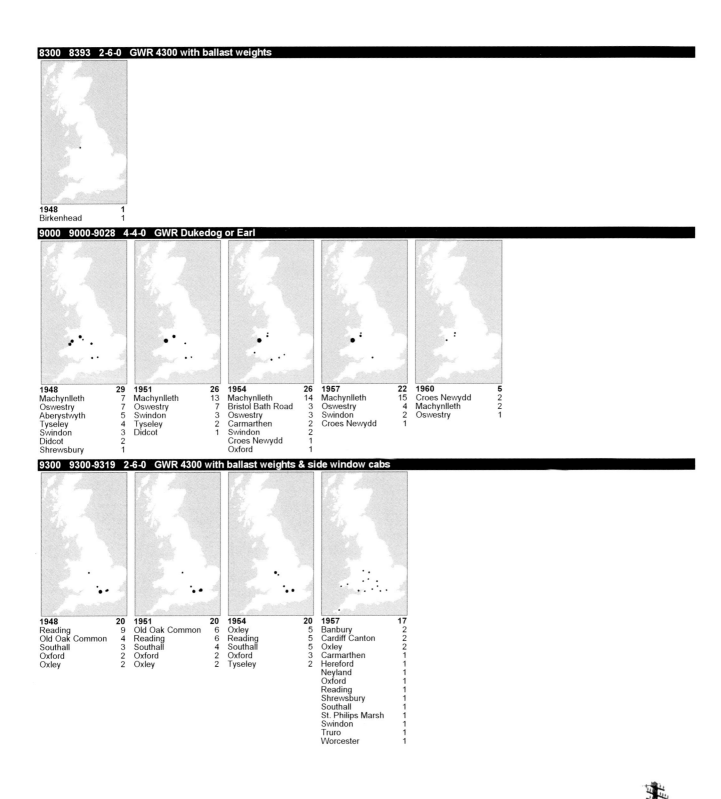

8300 8393 2-6-0 GWR 4300 with ballast weights

1948	1
Birkenhead	1

9000 9000-9028 4-4-0 GWR Dukedog or Earl

1948	29
Machynlleth	7
Oswestry	7
Aberystwyth	5
Tyseley	4
Swindon	3
Didcot	2
Shrewsbury	1

1951	26
Machynlleth	13
Oswestry	7
Swindon	3
Tyseley	2
Didcot	1

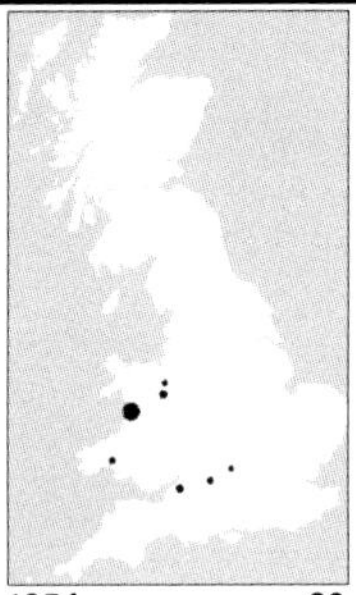

1954	26
Machynlleth	14
Bristol Bath Road	3
Oswestry	3
Carmarthen	2
Swindon	2
Croes Newydd	1
Oxford	1

1957	22
Machynlleth	15
Oswestry	4
Swindon	2
Croes Newydd	1

1960	5
Croes Newydd	2
Machynlleth	2
Oswestry	1

9300 9300-9319 2-6-0 GWR 4300 with ballast weights & side window cabs

1948	20
Reading	9
Old Oak Common	4
Southall	3
Oxford	2
Oxley	2

1951	20
Old Oak Common	6
Reading	6
Southall	4
Oxford	2
Oxley	2

1954	20
Oxley	5
Reading	5
Southall	5
Oxford	3
Tyseley	2

1957	17
Banbury	2
Cardiff Canton	2
Oxley	2
Carmarthen	1
Hereford	1
Neyland	1
Oxford	1
Reading	1
Shrewsbury	1
Southall	1
St. Philips Marsh	1
Swindon	1
Truro	1
Worcester	1

Right: GWR Churchward '9300' class 2-6-0 No 9316 (later rebuilt to '4300' class No 7338). Note the extra ballast weight behind the front buffer beam compared with the photograph of No 6378 on page 72. *R. H. G. Simpson*

9400 3400-3409, 8400-8499, 9400-9499 0-6-0PT GWR Hawksworth 4ft 7½in

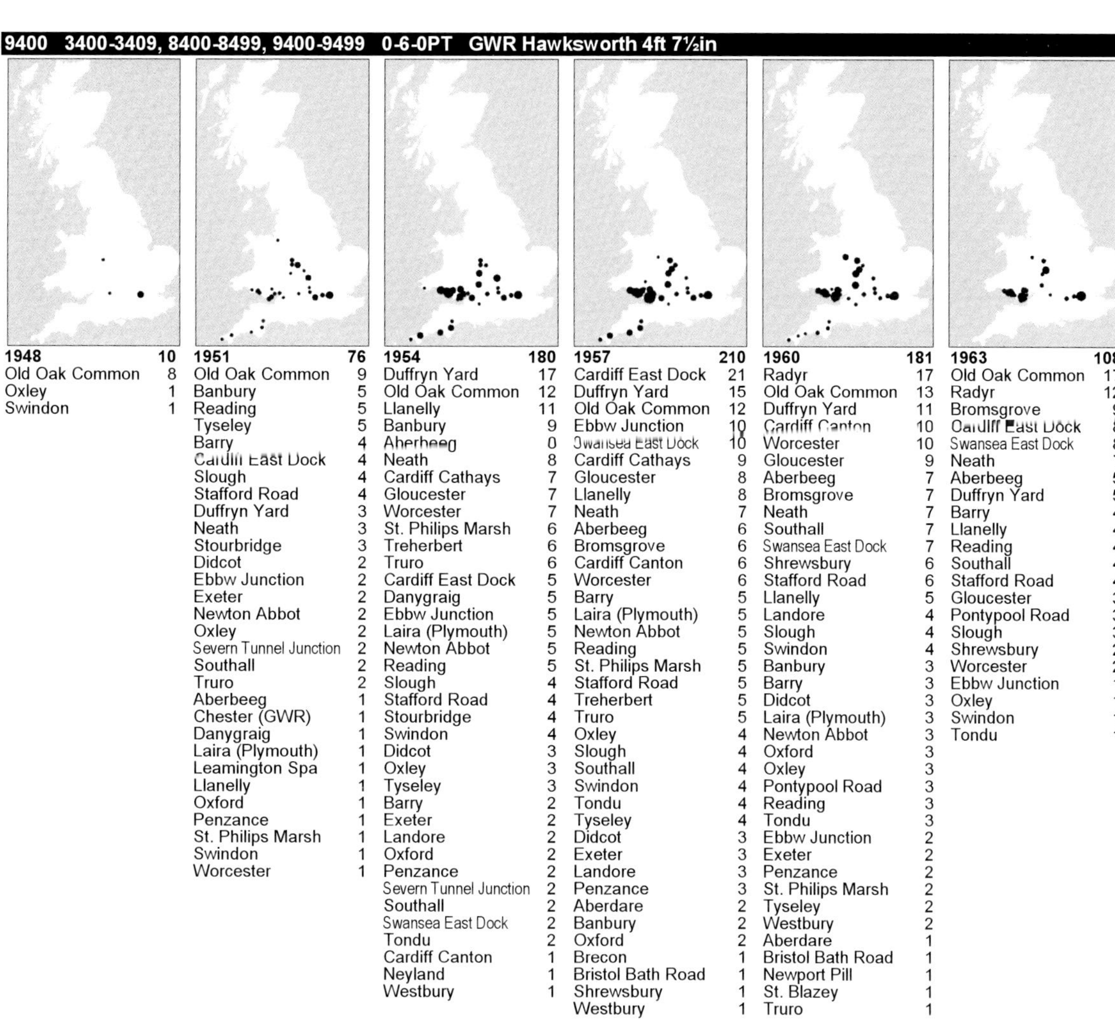

1948	10
Old Oak Common	8
Oxley	1
Swindon	1

1951	76
Old Oak Common	9
Banbury	5
Reading	5
Tyseley	5
Barry	4
Cardiff East Dock	4
Slough	4
Stafford Road	4
Duffryn Yard	3
Neath	3
Stourbridge	3
Didcot	2
Ebbw Junction	2
Exeter	2
Newton Abbot	2
Oxley	2
Severn Tunnel Junction	2
Southall	2
Truro	2
Aberbeeg	1
Chester (GWR)	1
Danygraig	1
Laira (Plymouth)	1
Leamington Spa	1
Llanelly	1
Oxford	1
Penzance	1
St. Philips Marsh	1
Swindon	1
Worcester	1

1954	180
Duffryn Yard	17
Old Oak Common	12
Llanelly	11
Banbury	9
Aberbeeg	0
Neath	8
Cardiff Cathays	7
Gloucester	7
Worcester	7
St. Philips Marsh	6
Treherbert	6
Truro	6
Cardiff East Dock	5
Danygraig	5
Ebbw Junction	5
Laira (Plymouth)	5
Newton Abbot	5
Reading	5
Slough	4
Stafford Road	4
Stourbridge	4
Swindon	4
Didcot	3
Oxley	3
Tyseley	3
Barry	2
Exeter	2
Landore	2
Oxford	2
Penzance	2
Severn Tunnel Junction	2
Southall	2
Swansea East Dock	2
Tondu	2
Cardiff Canton	1
Neyland	1
Westbury	1

1957	210
Cardiff East Dock	21
Duffryn Yard	15
Old Oak Common	12
Ebbw Junction	10
Swansea East Dock	10
Cardiff Cathays	9
Gloucester	8
Llanelly	8
Neath	7
Aberbeeg	6
Bromsgrove	6
Cardiff Canton	6
Worcester	6
Barry	5
Laira (Plymouth)	5
Newton Abbot	5
Reading	5
St. Philips Marsh	5
Stafford Road	5
Treherbert	5
Truro	5
Oxley	4
Slough	4
Southall	4
Swindon	4
Tondu	4
Tyseley	4
Didcot	3
Exeter	3
Landore	3
Penzance	3
Aberdare	2
Banbury	2
Oxford	2
Brecon	1
Bristol Bath Road	1
Shrewsbury	1
Westbury	1

1960	181
Radyr	17
Old Oak Common	13
Duffryn Yard	11
Cardiff Canton	10
Worcester	10
Gloucester	9
Aberbeeg	7
Bromsgrove	7
Neath	7
Southall	7
Swansea East Dock	7
Shrewsbury	6
Stafford Road	6
Llanelly	5
Landore	4
Slough	4
Swindon	4
Banbury	3
Barry	3
Didcot	3
Laira (Plymouth)	3
Newton Abbot	3
Oxford	3
Oxley	3
Pontypool Road	3
Reading	3
Tondu	3
Ebbw Junction	2
Exeter	2
Penzance	2
St. Philips Marsh	2
Tyseley	2
Westbury	2
Aberdare	1
Bristol Bath Road	1
Newport Pill	1
St. Blazey	1
Truro	1

1963	108
Old Oak Common	17
Radyr	12
Bromsgrove	9
Cardiff East Dock	8
Swansea East Dock	8
Neath	7
Aberbeeg	5
Duffryn Yard	5
Barry	4
Llanelly	4
Reading	4
Southall	4
Stafford Road	4
Gloucester	3
Pontypool Road	3
Slough	3
Shrewsbury	2
Worcester	2
Ebbw Junction	1
Oxley	1
Swindon	1
Tondu	1

9700 9700-9710 0-6-0PT GWR 5700 class with condensing apparatus

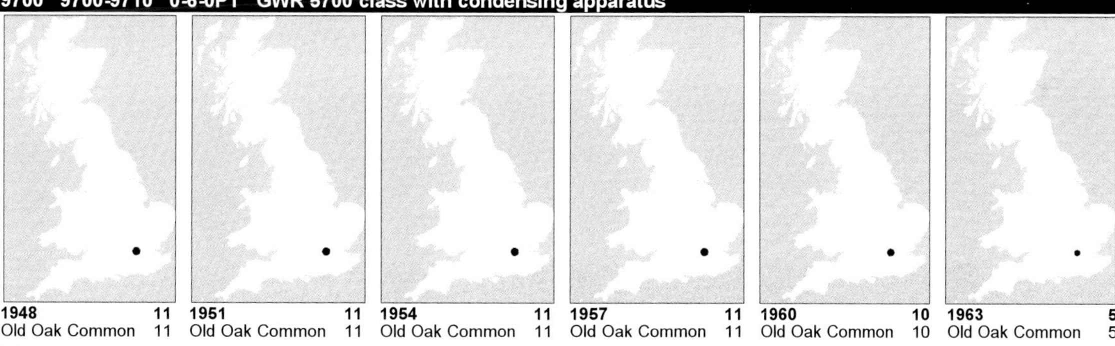

1948	11	1951	11	1954	11	1957	11	1960	10	1963	5
Old Oak Common	11	Old Oak Common	11	Old Oak Common	11	Old Oak Common	11	Old Oak Common	10	Old Oak Common	5

AD[1] 190 0-6-2ST Alexandra Docks

1948	1
Newport Pill	1

Right: Alexandra Docks Railway 0-6-0ST No 680 (see p96).

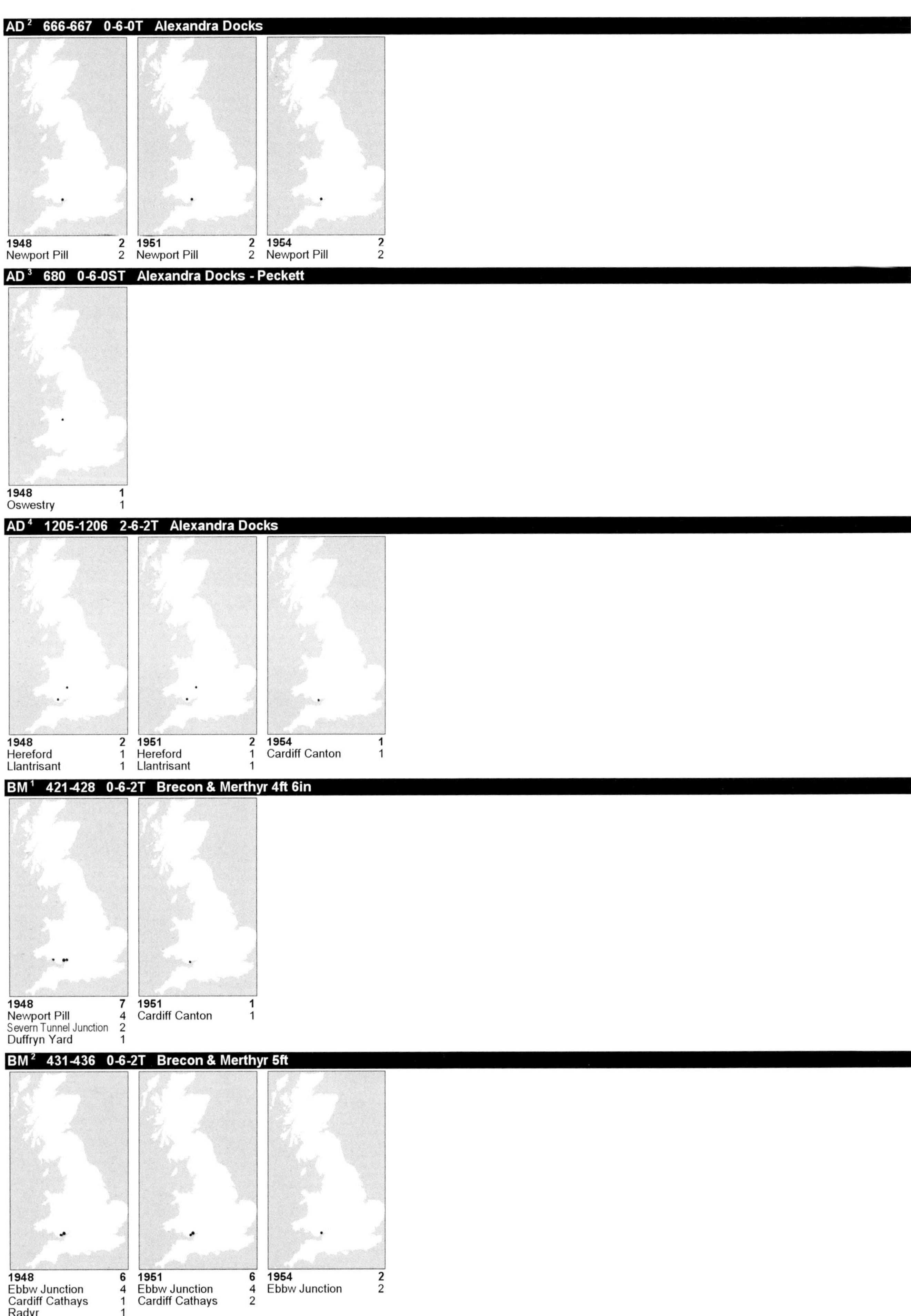

AD[2] 666-667 0-6-0T Alexandra Docks

1948	2	1951	2	1954	2
Newport Pill	2	Newport Pill	2	Newport Pill	2

AD[3] 680 0-6-0ST Alexandra Docks - Peckett

1948	1
Oswestry	1

AD[4] 1205-1206 2-6-2T Alexandra Docks

1948	2	1951	2	1954	1
Hereford	1	Hereford	1	Cardiff Canton	1
Llantrisant	1	Llantrisant	1		

BM[1] 421-428 0-6-2T Brecon & Merthyr 4ft 6in

1948	7	1951	1
Newport Pill	4	Cardiff Canton	1
Severn Tunnel Junction	2		
Duffryn Yard	1		

BM[2] 431-436 0-6-2T Brecon & Merthyr 5ft

1948	6	1951	6	1954	2
Ebbw Junction	4	Ebbw Junction	4	Ebbw Junction	2
Cardiff Cathays	1	Cardiff Cathays	2		
Radyr	1				

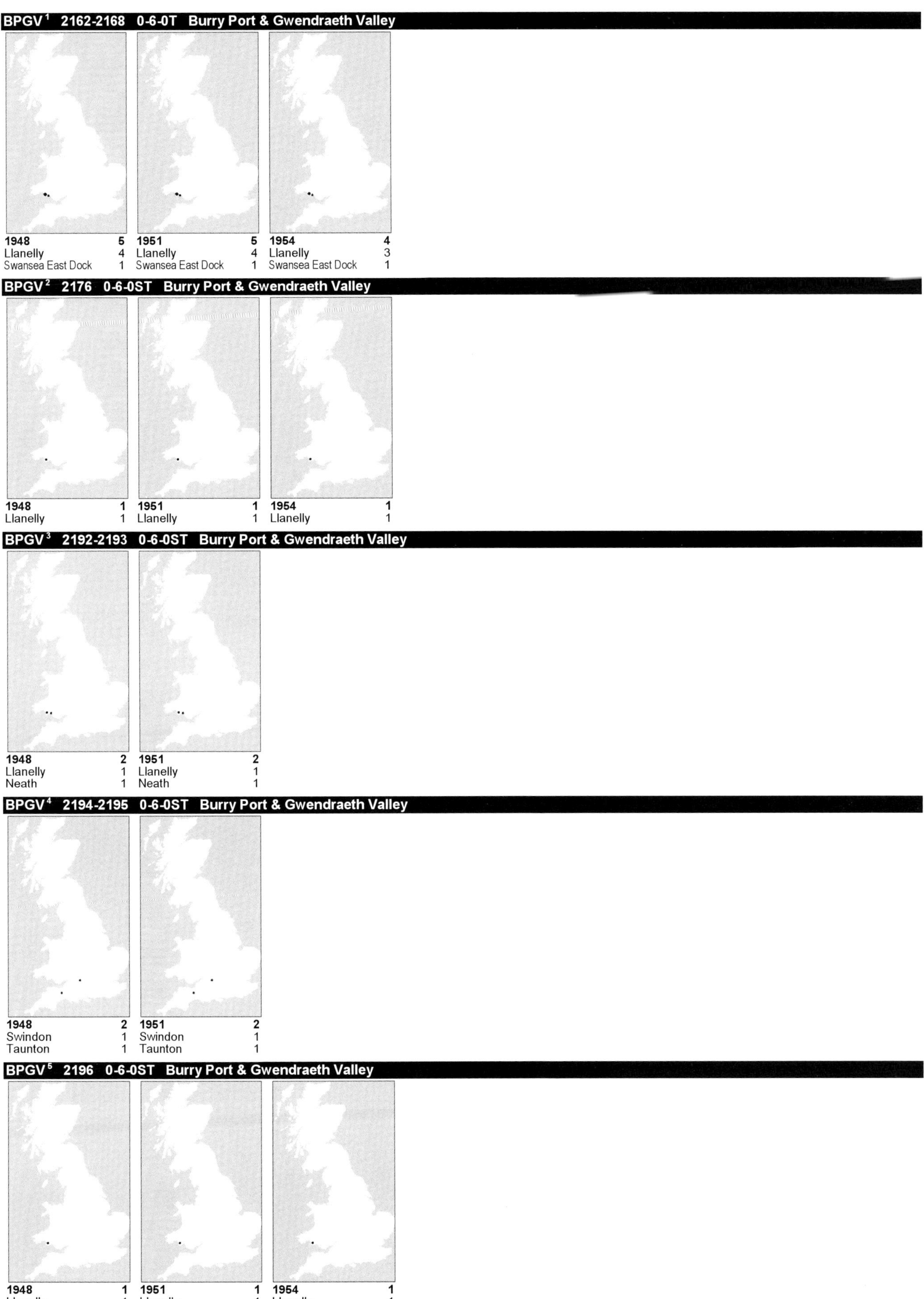

BPGV[1] 2162-2168 0-6-0T Burry Port & Gwendraeth Valley

1948	5	1951	5	1954	4
Llanelly	4	Llanelly	4	Llanelly	3
Swansea East Dock	1	Swansea East Dock	1	Swansea East Dock	1

BPGV[2] 2176 0-6-0ST Burry Port & Gwendraeth Valley

1948	1	1951	1	1954	1
Llanelly	1	Llanelly	1	Llanelly	1

BPGV[3] 2192-2193 0-6-0ST Burry Port & Gwendraeth Valley

1948	2	1951	2
Llanelly	1	Llanelly	1
Neath	1	Neath	1

BPGV[4] 2194-2195 0-6-0ST Burry Port & Gwendraeth Valley

1948	2	1951	2
Swindon	1	Swindon	1
Taunton	1	Taunton	1

BPGV[5] 2196 0-6-0ST Burry Port & Gwendraeth Valley

1948	1	1951	1	1954	1
Llanelly	1	Llanelly	1	Llanelly	1

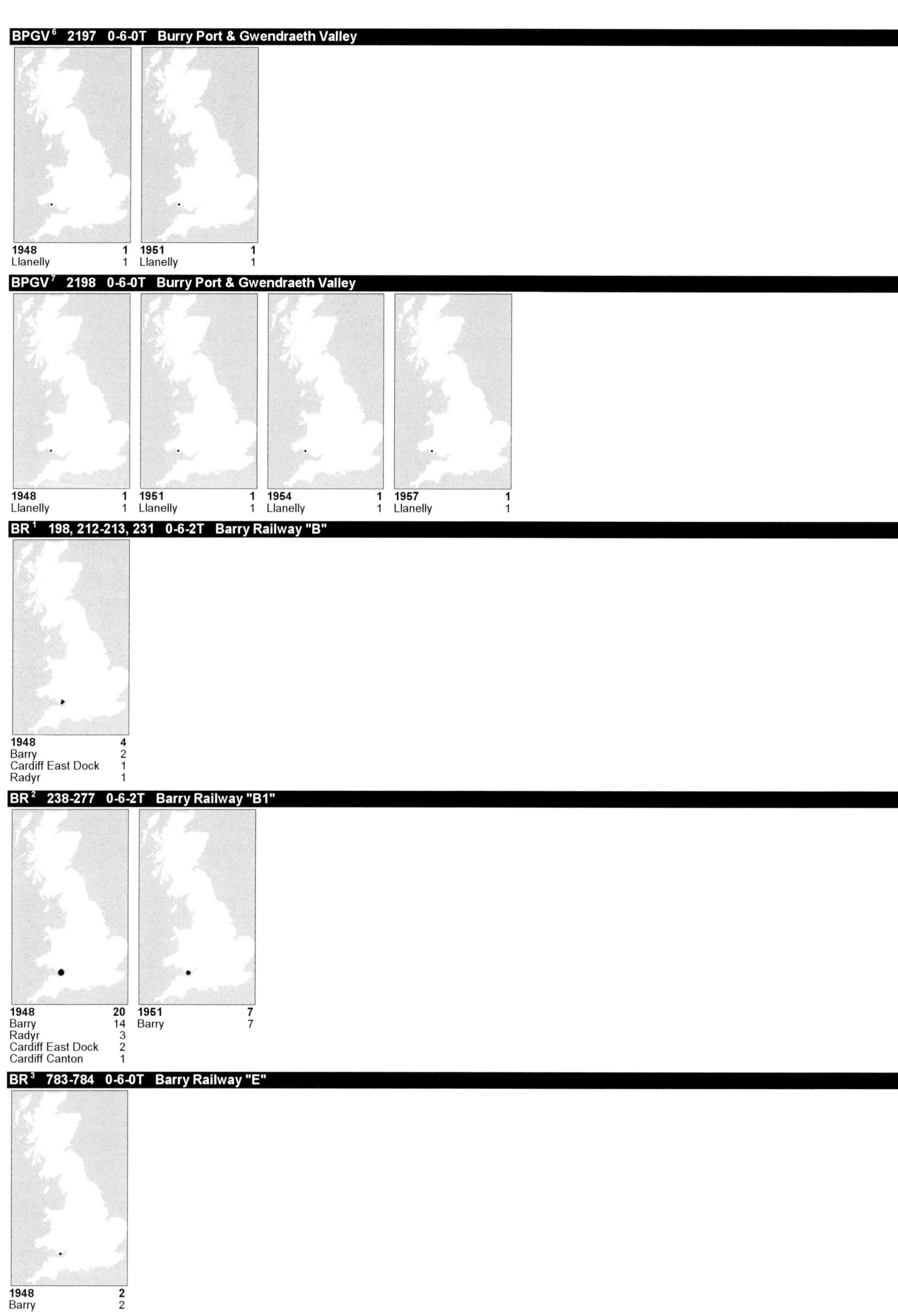

BPGV[6] 2197 0-6-0T Burry Port & Gwendraeth Valley
1948 1
Llanelly 1
1951 1
Llanelly 1
BPGV[7] 2198 0-6-0T Burry Port & Gwendraeth Valley
1948 1
Llanelly 1
1951 1
Llanelly 1
1954 1
Llanelly 1
1957 1
Llanelly 1
BR[1] 198, 212-213, 231 0-6-2T Barry Railway "B"
1948 4
Barry 2
Cardiff East Dock 1
Radyr 1
BR[2] 238-277 0-6-2T Barry Railway "B1"
1948 20
Barry 14
Radyr 3
Cardiff East Dock 2
Cardiff Canton 1
1951 7
Barry 7
BR[3] 783-784 0-6-0T Barry Railway "E"
1948 2
Barry 2

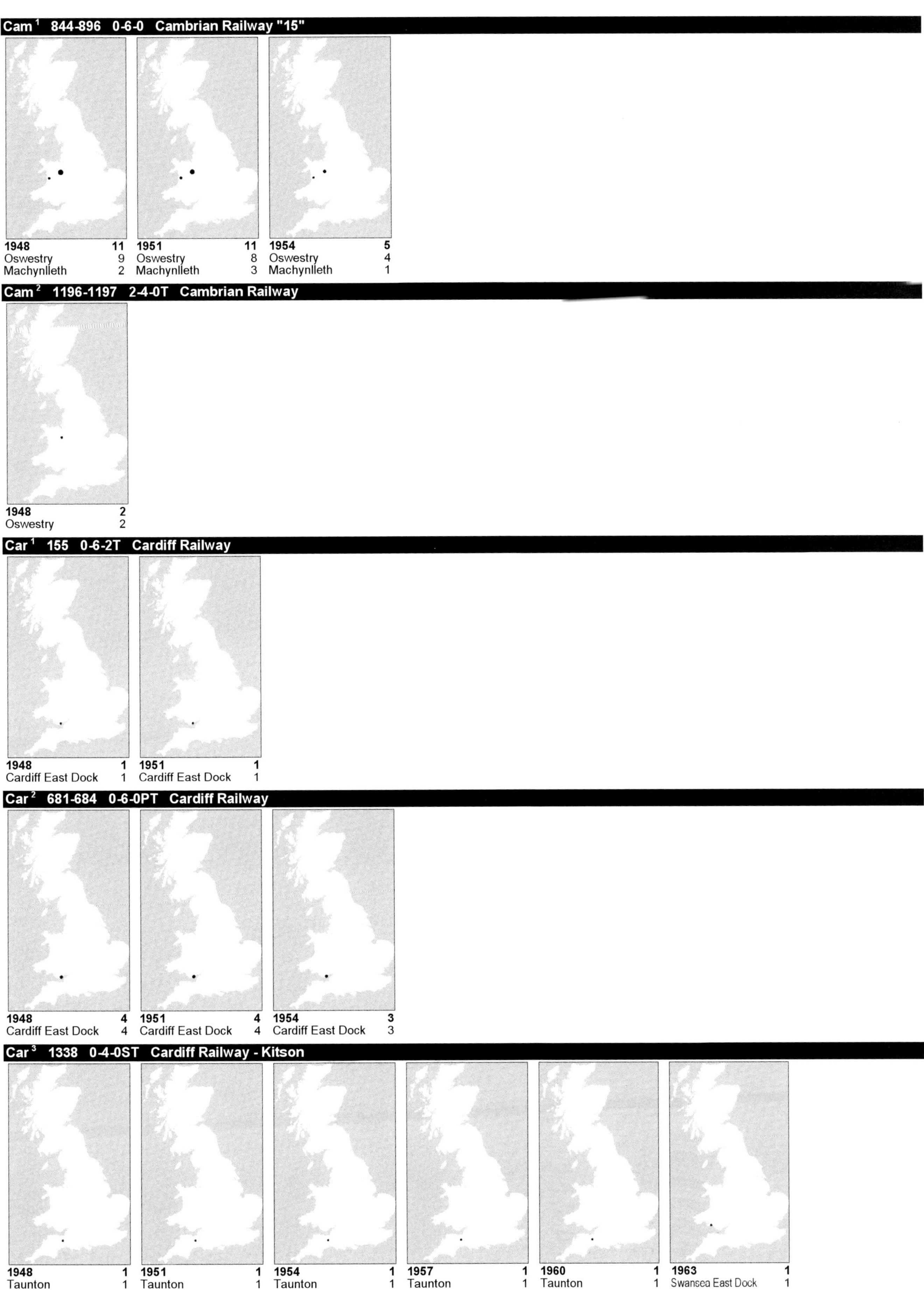

Cam 1 844-896 0-6-0 Cambrian Railway "15"
1948 11
Oswestry 9
Machynlleth 2
1951 11
Oswestry 8
Machynlleth 3
1954 5
Oswestry 4
Machynlleth 1
Cam 2 1196-1197 2-4-0T Cambrian Railway
1948 2
Oswestry 2
Car 1 155 0-6-2T Cardiff Railway
1948 1
Cardiff East Dock 1
1951 1
Cardiff East Dock 1
Car 2 681-684 0-6-0PT Cardiff Railway
1948 4
Cardiff East Dock 4
1951 4
Cardiff East Dock 4
1954 3
Cardiff East Dock 3
Car 3 1338 0-4-0ST Cardiff Railway - Kitson
1948 1
Taunton 1
1951 1
Taunton 1
1954 1
Taunton 1
1957 1
Taunton 1
1960 1
Taunton 1
1963 1
Swansea East Dock 1

City 3440 4-4-0 GWR City Class Preserved

1960	1
Swindon	1

CMDP 28-29 0-6-0PT Cleobury Mortimer & Ditton Priors

1948	2	1951	2	1954	1
Kidderminster	2	Kidderminster	2	Kidderminster	1

Cor 3-4 0-4-2ST Corris Railway (Narrow Gauge)

1948	2
Maespoeth	2

L&L 1308 2-4-0T Liskeard & Looe

1948	1
Oswestry	1

LMM[1] 359 0-6-0ST Llanelly & Mynydd Mawr

1948	1	1951	1	1954	1
Danygraig	1	Danygraig	1	Danygraig	1

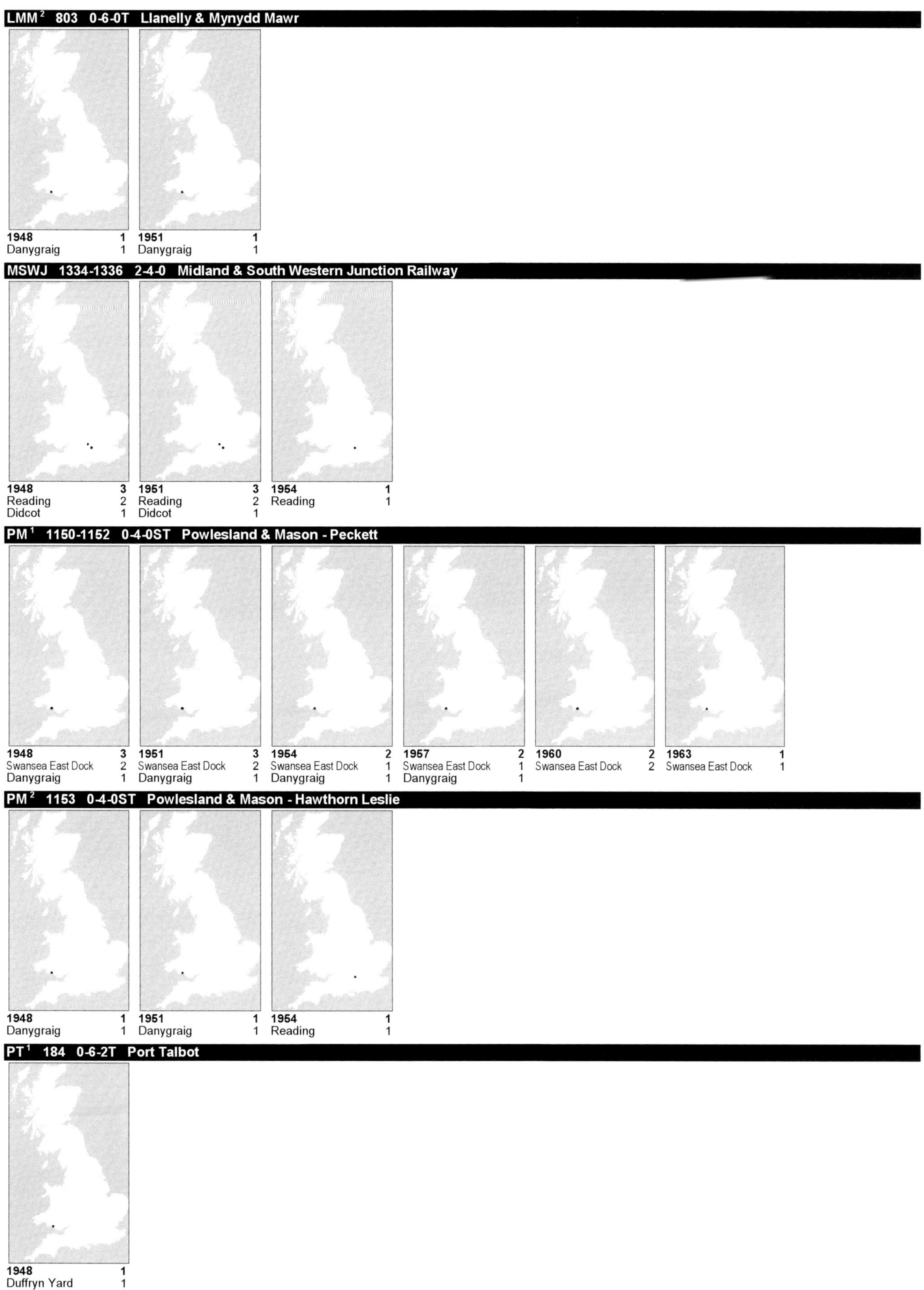
LMM[2] 803 0-6-0T Llanelly & Mynydd Mawr
1948 1
Danygraig 1
1951 1
Danygraig 1
MSWJ 1334-1336 2-4-0 Midland & South Western Junction Railway
1948 3
Reading 2
Didcot 1
1951 3
Reading 2
Didcot 1
1954 1
Reading 1
PM[1] 1150-1152 0-4-0ST Powlesland & Mason - Peckett
1948 3
Swansea East Dock 2
Danygraig 1
1951 3
Swansea East Dock 2
Danygraig 1
1954 2
Swansea East Dock 1
Danygraig 1
1957 2
Swansea East Dock 1
Danygraig 1
1960 2
Swansea East Dock 2
1963 1
Swansea East Dock 1
PM[2] 1153 0-4-0ST Powlesland & Mason - Hawthorn Leslie
1948 1
Danygraig 1
1951 1
Danygraig 1
1954 1
Reading 1
PT[1] 184 0-6-2T Port Talbot
1948 1
Duffryn Yard 1

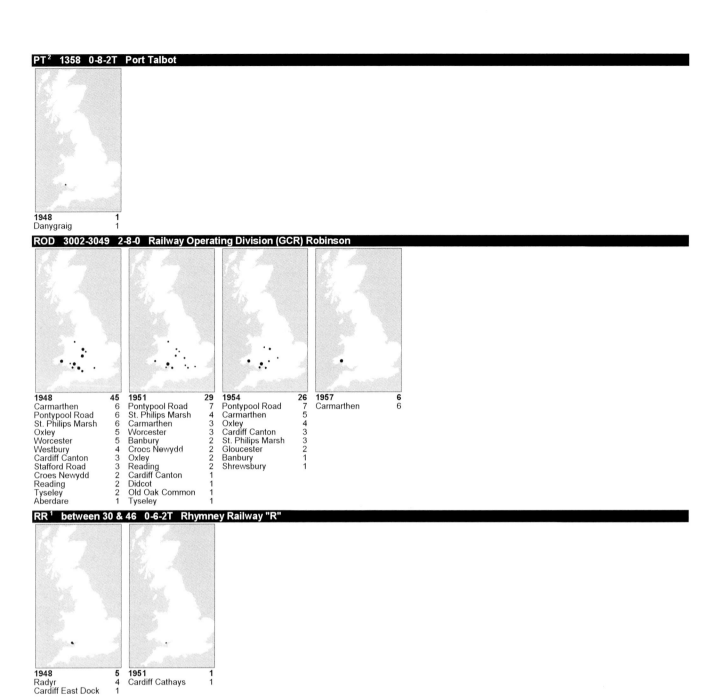

PT[2] 1358 0-8-2T Port Talbot

1948	1
Danygraig	1

ROD 3002-3049 2-8-0 Railway Operating Division (GCR) Robinson

1948	45	1951	29	1954	26	1957	6
Carmarthen	6	Pontypool Road	7	Pontypool Road	7	Carmarthen	6
Pontypool Road	6	St. Philips Marsh	4	Carmarthen	5		
St. Philips Marsh	6	Carmarthen	3	Oxley	4		
Oxley	5	Worcester	3	Cardiff Canton	3		
Worcester	5	Banbury	2	St. Philips Marsh	3		
Westbury	4	Croes Newydd	2	Gloucester	2		
Cardiff Canton	3	Oxley	2	Banbury	1		
Stafford Road	3	Reading	2	Shrewsbury	1		
Croes Newydd	2	Cardiff Canton	1				
Reading	2	Didcot	1				
Tyseley	2	Old Oak Common	1				
Aberdare	1	Tyseley	1				

RR[1] between 30 & 46 0-6-2T Rhymney Railway "R"

1948	5	1951	1
Radyr	4	Cardiff Cathays	1
Cardiff East Dock	1		

RR[2] between 33 & 51 0-6-2T Rhymney Railway "M"

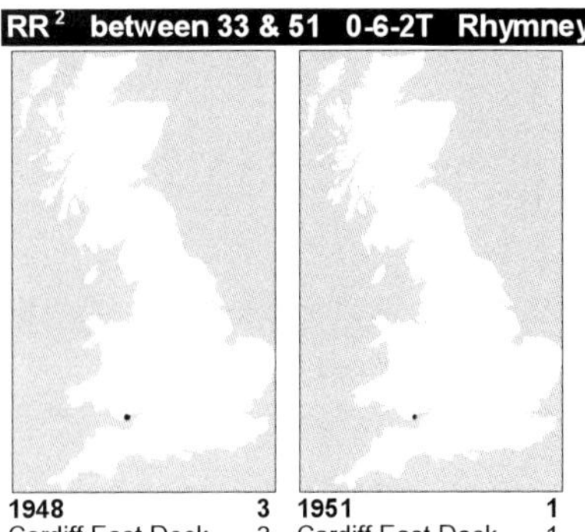

1948	3	1951	1
Cardiff East Dock	3	Cardiff East Dock	1

Rhymney Railway 'M' class 0-6-2T No 33 fitted with an original Belpaire boiler. *T. J. Saunders*

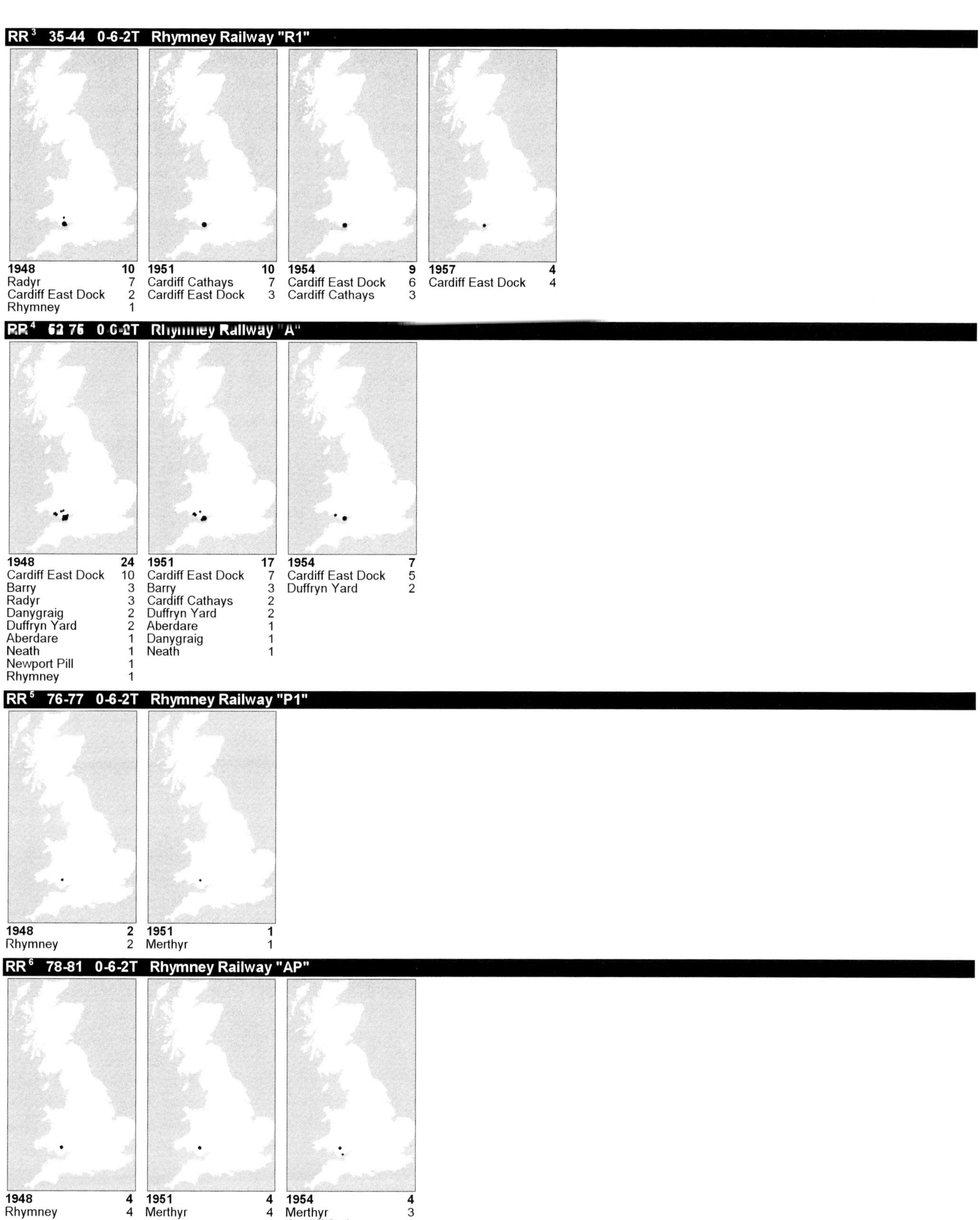
RR[3] 35-44 0-6-2T Rhymney Railway "R1"
1948 10
Radyr 7
Cardiff East Dock 2
Rhymney 1
1951 10
Cardiff Cathays 7
Cardiff East Dock 3
1954 9
Cardiff East Dock 6
Cardiff Cathays 3
1957 4
Cardiff East Dock 4
RR[4] 62-76 0-6-2T Rhymney Railway "A"
1948 24
Cardiff East Dock 10
Barry 3
Radyr 3
Danygraig 2
Duffryn Yard 2
Aberdare 1
Neath 1
Newport Pill 1
Rhymney 1
1951 17
Cardiff East Dock 7
Barry 3
Cardiff Cathays 2
Duffryn Yard 2
Aberdare 1
Danygraig 1
Neath 1
1954 7
Cardiff East Dock 5
Duffryn Yard 2
RR[5] 76-77 0-6-2T Rhymney Railway "P1"
1948 2
Rhymney 2
1951 1
Merthyr 1
RR[6] 78-81 0-6-2T Rhymney Railway "AP"
1948 4
Rhymney 4
1951 4
Merthyr 4
1954 4
Merthyr 3
Cardiff Cathays 1

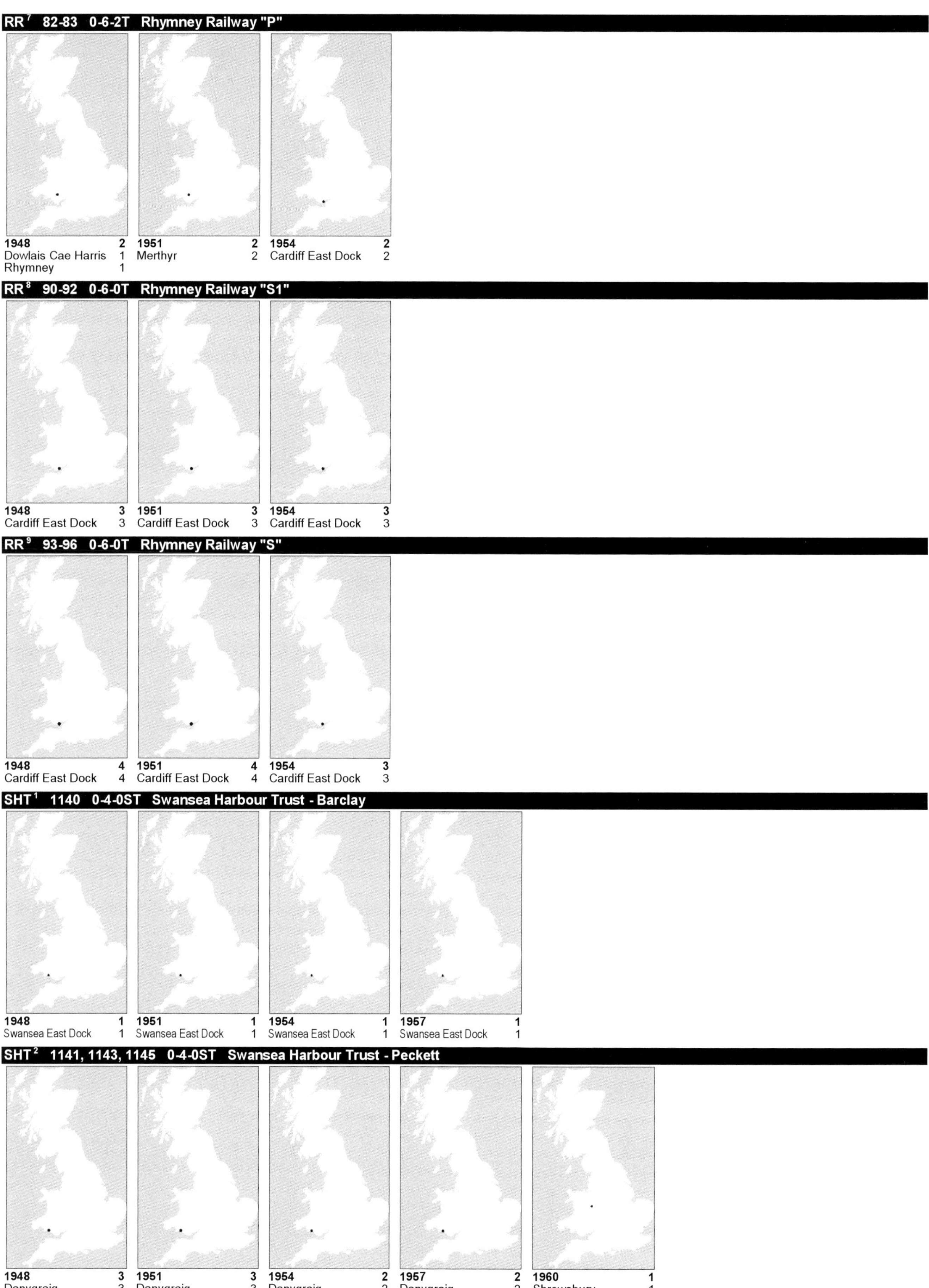

RR[7] 82-83 0-6-2T Rhymney Railway "P"

1948	2	1951	2	1954	2
Dowlais Cae Harris	1	Merthyr	2	Cardiff East Dock	2
Rhymney	1				

RR[8] 90-92 0-6-0T Rhymney Railway "S1"

1948	3	1951	3	1954	3
Cardiff East Dock	3	Cardiff East Dock	3	Cardiff East Dock	3

RR[9] 93-96 0-6-0T Rhymney Railway "S"

1948	4	1951	4	1954	3
Cardiff East Dock	4	Cardiff East Dock	4	Cardiff East Dock	3

SHT[1] 1140 0-4-0ST Swansea Harbour Trust - Barclay

1948	1	1951	1	1954	1	1957	1
Swansea East Dock	1	Swansea East Dock	1	Swansea East Dock	1	Swansea East Dock	1

SHT[2] 1141, 1143, 1145 0-4-0ST Swansea Harbour Trust - Peckett

1948	3	1951	3	1954	2	1957	2	1960	1
Danygraig	3	Danygraig	3	Danygraig	2	Danygraig	2	Shrewsbury	1

SHT[3] 1142 0-4-0ST Swansea Harbour Trust - Hudswell Clarke

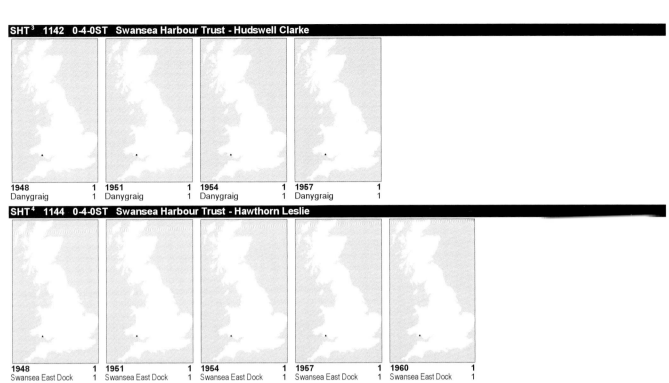

1948	1	1951	1	1954	1	1957	1
Danygraig	1	Danygraig	1	Danygraig	1	Danygraig	1

SHT[4] 1144 0-4-0ST Swansea Harbour Trust - Hawthorn Leslie

1948	1	1951	1	1954	1	1957	1	1960	1
Swansea East Dock	1	Swansea East Dock	1	Swansea East Dock	1	Swansea East Dock	1	Swansea East Dock	1

SHT[5] 1146-1147 0-6-0ST Swansea Harbour Trust - Peckett

1948	2	1951	2
Danygraig	2	Danygraig	1
		Swansea East Dock	1

TV[1] 193-195 0-6-0T Taff Vale "H"

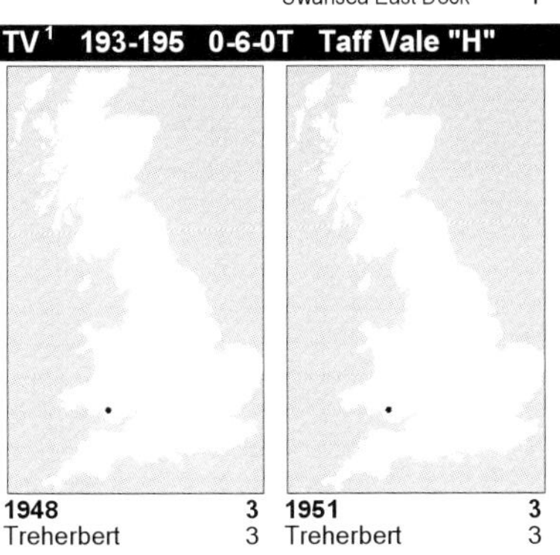

1948	3	1951	3
Treherbert	3	Treherbert	3

Right: Taff Vale Railway 'H' class 0-6-2T No 194 showing the specially designed taper boiler to allow the class to work on the Pwllyrhebog incline.

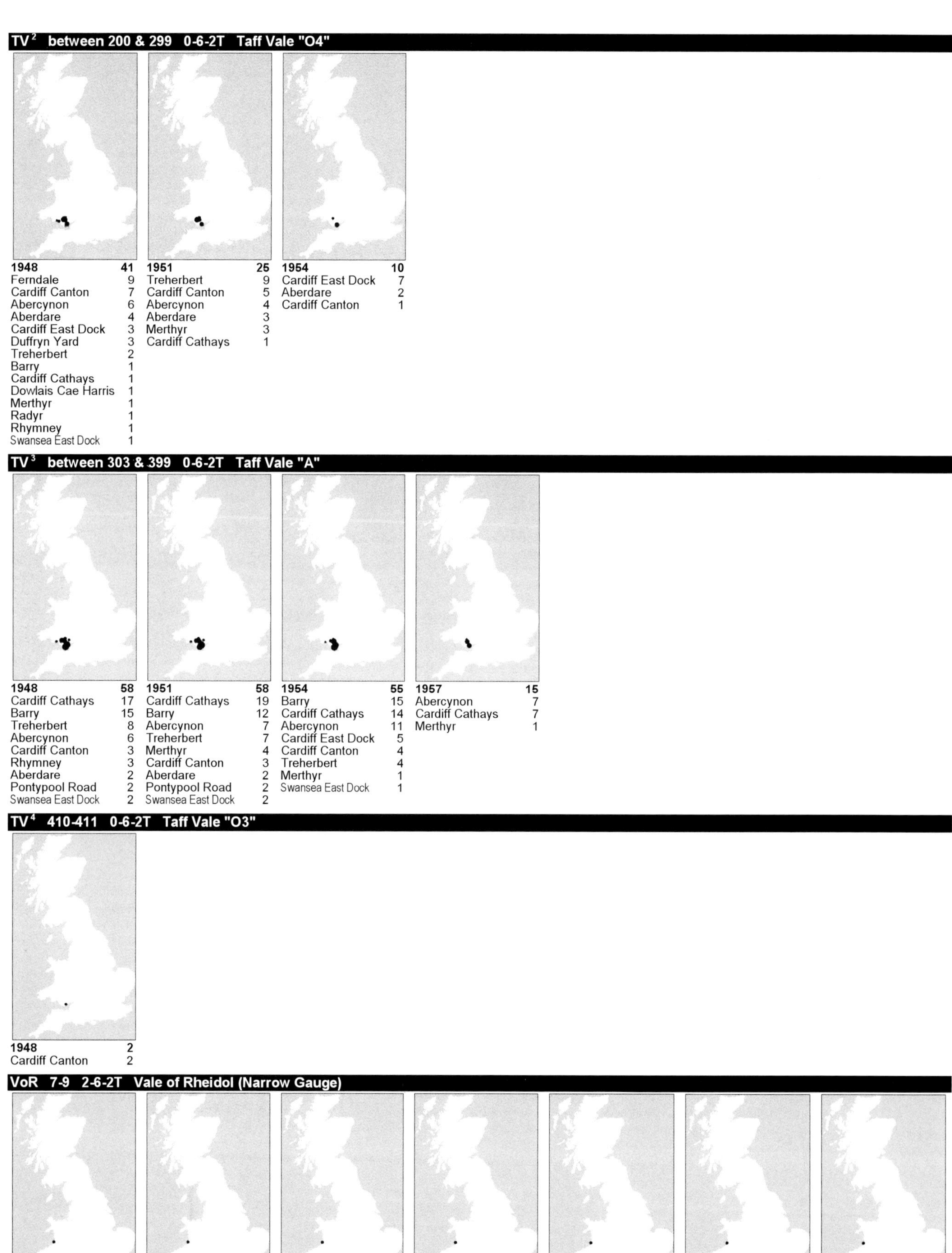

TV[2] between 200 & 299 0-6-2T Taff Vale "O4"

1948	41
Ferndale	9
Cardiff Canton	7
Abercynon	6
Aberdare	4
Cardiff East Dock	3
Duffryn Yard	3
Treherbert	2
Barry	1
Cardiff Cathays	1
Dowlais Cae Harris	1
Merthyr	1
Radyr	1
Rhymney	1
Swansea East Dock	1

1951	25
Treherbert	9
Cardiff Canton	5
Abercynon	4
Aberdare	3
Merthyr	3
Cardiff Cathays	1

1954	10
Cardiff East Dock	7
Aberdare	2
Cardiff Canton	1

TV[3] between 303 & 399 0-6-2T Taff Vale "A"

1948	58
Cardiff Cathays	17
Barry	15
Treherbert	8
Abercynon	6
Cardiff Canton	3
Rhymney	3
Aberdare	2
Pontypool Road	2
Swansea East Dock	2

1951	58
Cardiff Cathays	19
Barry	12
Abercynon	7
Treherbert	7
Merthyr	4
Cardiff Canton	3
Aberdare	2
Pontypool Road	2
Swansea East Dock	2

1954	55
Barry	15
Cardiff Cathays	14
Abercynon	11
Cardiff East Dock	5
Cardiff Canton	4
Treherbert	4
Merthyr	1
Swansea East Dock	1

1957	15
Abercynon	7
Cardiff Cathays	7
Merthyr	1

TV[4] 410-411 0-6-2T Taff Vale "O3"

1948	2
Cardiff Canton	2

VoR 7-9 2-6-2T Vale of Rheidol (Narrow Gauge)

1948	3
Aberystwyth (VoR)	3

1951	3
Aberystwyth (VoR)	3

1954	3
Aberystwyth (VoR)	3

1957	3
Aberystwyth (VoR)	3

1960	3
Aberystwyth (VoR)	3

1963	3
Aberystwyth (VoR)	3

1966	3
Aberystwyth (VoR)	3

W&C 1331 0-6-0ST Whitland & Cardigan

W&L 822-823 0-6-0T Welshpool & Llanfair (Narrow Gauge)

WCP 5-6 0-6-0T Weston Clevedon & Portishead Stroudley "Terrier"

YTW 1 0-4-0ST Ystalyfera Tin Works – Peckett

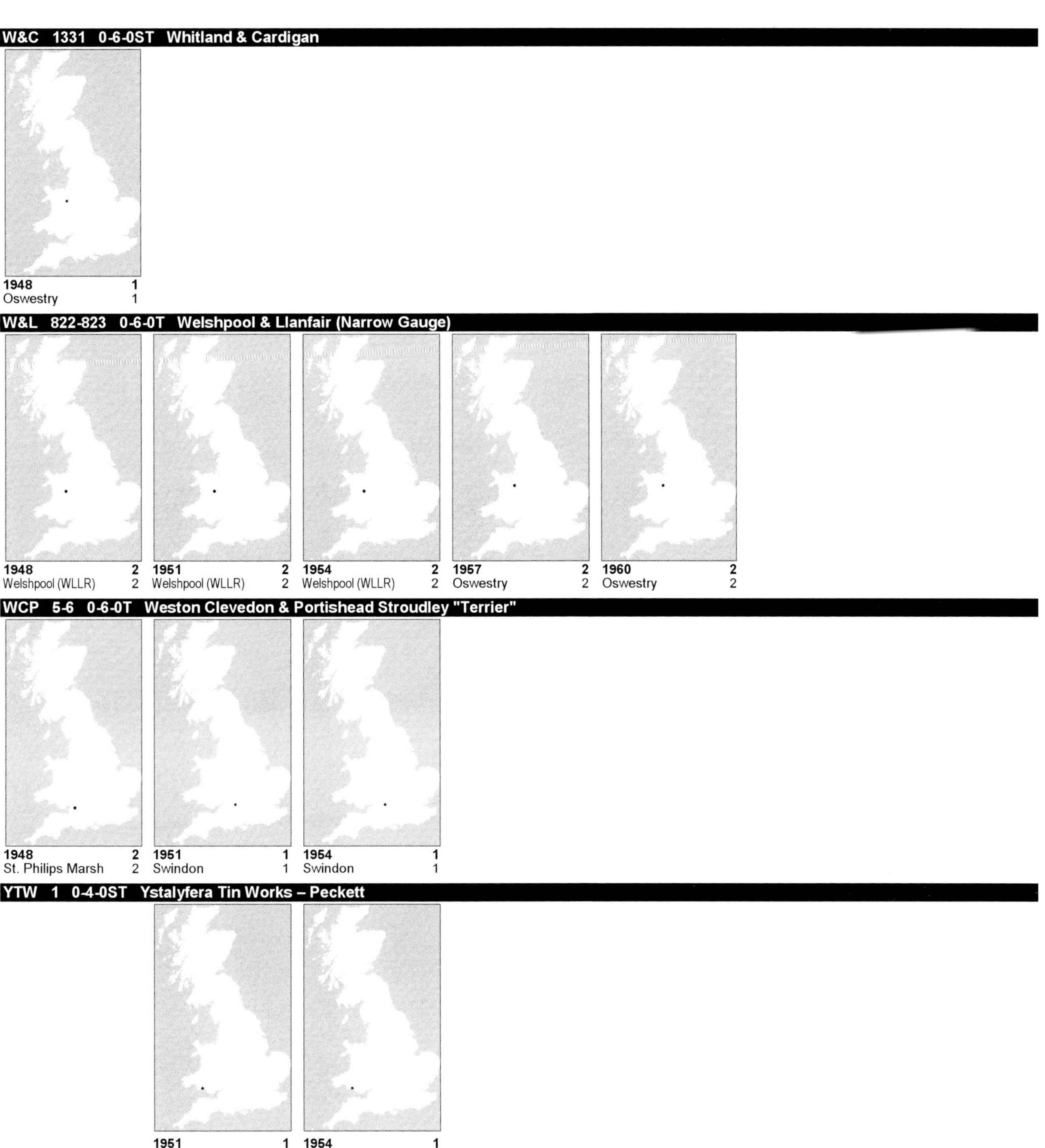

Above: GWR Collett '6700' class 0-6-0PT No 6707 at 88B Cardiff East Dock Shed on 11 August 1957. *B. K. B. Green*

Below: GWR Collett '8100' class 2-6-2T No 8109 at Swindon on 14 April 1963. Painted in plain unlined black livery. *G. H. Wheeler*

Right: Cleaners at Nine Elms giving 'Battle of Britain' class No 34088 *213 Squadron* the final once over before it departs to work a Royal Train.

Former SR Locomotives

Above: LSWR Urie 'G16' class 4-8-0T No 30495 in store at 70B Feltham on 14 October 1956. *A. W. Martin*

Below: LSWR Adams '0415' class 4-4-2T No 30583 at Axminster in May 1959. *K. R. Pirt*

No.	Class	1948	1951	1954	1957	1960	1963	1966
30001	T1	ELH Eastleigh						
30002	T1	ELH Eastleigh						
30003	T1	PLY Plymouth Friary						
30005	T1	ELH Eastleigh						
30007	T1	PLY Plymouth Friary	72D Plymouth Friary					
30008	T1	ELH Eastleigh						
30009	T1	FEL Feltham						
30010	T1	SAL Salisbury						
30013	T1	SAL Salisbury						
30020	T1	FRA Fratton	71D Fratton					
30021	M7	BM Bournemouth	70C Guildford	72A Exmouth Junction	72A Exmouth Junction	72A Exmouth Junction	70E Salisbury	
30022	M7	GFD Guildford	70C Guildford	70E Reading South	70F Fratton			
30023	M7	BPL Barnstaple Junction	72B Salisbury	72A Exmouth Junction	72A Exmouth Junction	72A Exmouth Junction		
30024	M7	EXJ Exmouth Junction	72A Exmouth Junction	72A Exmouth Junction	72A Exmouth Junction	72A Exmouth Junction	71B Bournemouth	
30025	M7	EXJ Exmouth Junction	72A Exmouth Junction	72A Exmouth Junction	72B Salisbury	72B Salisbury	72B Salisbury	
30026	M7	GFD Guildford	70C Guildford	70C Guildford	70C Guildford			
30027	M7	FRA Fratton	75D Horsham	70C Guildford	70C Guildford			
30028	M7	BM Bournemouth	71B Bournemouth	70C Guildford	71A Eastleigh	71A Eastleigh		
30029	M7	ELH Eastleigh	71A Eastleigh	71A Eastleigh	71A Eastleigh	71A Eastleigh	71A Eastleigh	
30030	M7	EXJ Exmouth Junction	72A Exmouth Junction	71A Eastleigh	71A Eastleigh			
30031	M7	FEL Feltham	71A Eastleigh	71A Eastleigh	75A Brighton	70B Feltham	(30128)	
30031	M7	(30128)	→	→	→	→	71D Bournemouth	
30032	M7	EXJ Exmouth Junction	71A Eastleigh	71A Eastleigh	71A Eastleigh	70B Feltham	70B Feltham	
30033	M7	9E Nine Elms	71A Eastleigh	71A Eastleigh	71A Eastleigh	72E Barnstaple Junction		
30034	M7	EXJ Exmouth Junction	72A Exmouth Junction	72D Plymouth Friary	72D Plymouth Friary	83H Plymouth Friary	70E Salisbury	
30035	M7	PLY Plymouth Friary	72D Plymouth Friary	72D Plymouth Friary	72D Plymouth Friary	83H Plymouth Friary	70B Feltham	
30036	M7	BPL Barnstaple Junction	72E Barnstaple Junction	72D Plymouth Friary	72D Plymouth Friary	83H Plymouth Friary	71A Eastleigh	
30037	M7	EXJ Exmouth Junction	72D Plymouth Friary	72D Plymouth Friary	72D Plymouth Friary			
30038	M7	9E Nine Elms	70A Nine Elms	70B Feltham	70B Feltham			
30039	M7	EXJ Exmouth Junction	72A Exmouth Junction	72D Plymouth Friary	70F Fratton	71A Eastleigh	70A Nine Elms	
30040	M7	BM Bournemouth	71B Bournemouth	72D Plymouth Friary	71B Bournemouth	71B Bournemouth		
30041	M7	SAL Salisbury	72B Salisbury	72A Exmouth Junction	70B Feltham			
30042	M7	BPL Barnstaple Junction	72E Barnstaple Junction	72A Exmouth Junction	70B Feltham			
30043	M7	GFD Guildford	70B Feltham	70B Feltham	70B Feltham	70B Feltham		
30044	M7	BPL Barnstaple Junction	72E Barnstaple Junction	72A Exmouth Junction	72A Exmouth Junction	72A Exmouth Junction		
30045	M7	FRA Fratton	71D Fratton	72A Exmouth Junction	72A Exmouth Junction	72A Exmouth Junction		
30046	M7	EXJ Exmouth Junction	72A Exmouth Junction	72A Exmouth Junction	72A Exmouth Junction			
30047	M7	BM Bournemouth	75D Horsham	75D Horsham	75D Horsham	75A Brighton		
30048	M7	ELH Eastleigh	71A Eastleigh	75D Horsham	75D Horsham	72A Exmouth Junction	72A Exmouth Junction	
30049	M7	EXJ Exmouth Junction	72A Exmouth Junction	75D Horsham	75D Horsham	75A Brighton		
30050	M7	BM Bournemouth	71D Fratton	75D Horsham	75D Horsham	75A Brighton		
30051	M7	BM Bournemouth	71B Bournemouth	75D Horsham	75D Horsham	75A Brighton		
30052	M7	BM Bournemouth	71B Bournemouth	75A Brighton	75A Brighton	75E Three Bridges	72C Yeovil Town	
30053	M7	ELH Eastleigh	71D Fratton	75A Brighton	75A Brighton	71A Eastleigh	71A Eastleigh	
30054	M7	FRA Fratton	71D Fratton	71D Fratton	75A Brighton			
30055	M7	EXJ Exmouth Junction	72A Exmouth Junction	71D Fratton	75A Brighton	75E Three Bridges	70C Guildford	
30056	M7	GFD Guildford	70C Guildford	71B Bournemouth	75A Brighton	75A Brighton	71B Bournemouth	
30057	M7	BM Bournemouth	71B Bournemouth	71B Bournemouth	71B Bournemouth	71B Bournemouth	71B Bournemouth	
30058	M7	YEO Yeovil Town	72C Yeovil Town	71B Bournemouth	71B Bournemouth	71B Bournemouth		
30059	M7	BM Bournemouth	71B Bournemouth	71B Bournemouth	71B Bournemouth	71B Bournemouth		
30060	M7	GFD Guildford	70C Guildford	71B Bournemouth	71B Bournemouth	71B Bournemouth		
30061	USA	SOT Southampton Docks	71I Southampton Docks	71I Southampton Docks	71I Southampton Docks	71I Southampton Docks	(DS233)	
30062	USA	SOT Southampton Docks	71I Southampton Docks	71I Southampton Docks	71I Southampton Docks	71I Southampton Docks	(DS234)	
30063	USA	SOT Southampton Docks	71I Southampton Docks	71I Southampton Docks	71I Southampton Docks	71I Southampton Docks		
30064	USA	SOT Southampton Docks	71I Southampton Docks	71I Southampton Docks	71I Southampton Docks	71I Southampton Docks	71I Southampton Docks	70D Eastleigh
30065	USA	SOT Southampton Docks	71I Southampton Docks	71I Southampton Docks	71I Southampton Docks	71I Southampton Docks	(DS237)	
30066	USA	SOT Southampton Docks	71I Southampton Docks	71I Southampton Docks	71I Southampton Docks	71I Southampton Docks	(DS235)	
30067	USA	SOT Southampton Docks	71I Southampton Docks	71I Southampton Docks	71I Southampton Docks	71I Southampton Docks	71I Southampton Docks	70D Eastleigh
30068	USA	SOT Southampton Docks	71I Southampton Docks	71I Southampton Docks	71I Southampton Docks	71I Southampton Docks	71I Southampton Docks	
30069	USA	SOT Southampton Docks	71I Southampton Docks	71I Southampton Docks	71I Southampton Docks	71I Southampton Docks	71I Southampton Docks	70D Eastleigh
30070	USA	SOT Southampton Docks	71I Southampton Docks	71I Southampton Docks	71I Southampton Docks	71I Southampton Docks	(DS238)	
30071	USA	SOT Southampton Docks	71I Southampton Docks	71I Southampton Docks	71I Southampton Docks	71I Southampton Docks	71I Southampton Docks	70D Eastleigh
30072	USA	SOT Southampton Docks	71I Southampton Docks	71I Southampton Docks	71I Southampton Docks	71I Southampton Docks	71I Southampton Docks	70C Guildford
30073	USA	SOT Southampton Docks	71I Southampton Docks	71I Southampton Docks	71I Southampton Docks	71I Southampton Docks	71I Southampton Docks	70D Eastleigh
30074	USA	SOT Southampton Docks	71I Southampton Docks	71I Southampton Docks	71I Southampton Docks	71I Southampton Docks	71I Southampton Docks	(DS236)
30081	B4[1]	SOT Southampton Docks						
30082	B4[1]	ELH Eastleigh	71A Eastleigh	71A Eastleigh	71A Eastleigh			
30083	B4[1]	DOV Dover Marine	71A Eastleigh	71A Eastleigh	71A Eastleigh			
30084	B4[1]	PLY Plymouth Friary	72D Plymouth Friary	74C Dover Marine	74C Dover Marine			
30085	B4[1]	SOT Southampton Docks						
30086	B4[1]	BAT Stewarts Lane	71B Bournemouth	71B Bournemouth	70C Guildford			
30087	B4[1]	ELH Eastleigh	71B Bournemouth	71B Bournemouth	71B Bournemouth			
30088	B4[1]	ELH Eastleigh	72D Plymouth Friary	72D Plymouth Friary	72D Plymouth Friary			
30089	B4[1]	SOT Southampton Docks	71A Eastleigh	72D Plymouth Friary	72D Plymouth Friary	70C Guildford	70C Guildford	
30090	B4[1]	BAT Stewarts Lane						
30091	B4[1]	PLY Plymouth Friary						
30092	B4[1]	BM Bournemouth						
30093	B4[1]	BM Bournemouth	71B Bournemouth	71B Bournemouth	71B Bournemouth	71B Bournemouth		
30094	B4[1]	PLY Plymouth Friary	72D Plymouth Friary	72D Plymouth Friary	72D Plymouth Friary			
30095	B4[1]	PLY Plymouth Friary						
30096	B4[1]	ELH Eastleigh	71A Eastleigh	71A Eastleigh	71A Eastleigh	71A Eastleigh	71A Eastleigh	
30097	B4[1]	SOT Southampton Docks						
30098	B4[1]	SOT Southampton Docks						
30099	B4[1]	BM Bournemouth						
30100	B4[1]	BM Bournemouth						
30101	B4[1]	SOT Southampton Docks						
30102	B4[1]	ELH Eastleigh	72D Plymouth Friary	72D Plymouth Friary	72D Plymouth Friary	71B Bournemouth	71A Eastleigh	
30103	B4[1]	PLY Plymouth Friary						
30104	M7	BM Bournemouth	71B Bournemouth	70E Reading South	71B Bournemouth	71B Bournemouth		
30105	M7	EXJ Exmouth Junction	72A Exmouth Junction	71B Bournemouth	71B Bournemouth	71B Bournemouth	71B Bournemouth	
30106	M7	BM Bournemouth	71B Bournemouth	71B Bournemouth	71B Bournemouth	71B Bournemouth	(30667)	
30107	M7	BM Bournemouth	72D Plymouth Friary	71B Bournemouth	71B Bournemouth	71B Bournemouth	71B Bournemouth	
30108	M7	GFD Guildford	70C Guildford	75D Horsham	71B Bournemouth	71B Bournemouth	71B Bournemouth	
30109	M7	ELH Eastleigh	71A Eastleigh	70C Guildford	70C Guildford	75E Three Bridges		
30110	M7	GFD Guildford	70C Guildford	70C Guildford	70C Guildford	75A Brighton	71B Bournemouth	
30111	M7	BM Bournemouth	71B Bournemouth	71B Bournemouth	71B Bournemouth	71B Bournemouth	71B Bournemouth	
30112	M7	BM Bournemouth	71B Bournemouth	71B Bournemouth	71B Bournemouth	71B Bournemouth	70C Guildford	
30113	T9	FRA Fratton	71D Fratton					
30114	T9	FRA Fratton	71D Fratton					
30115	T9	FRA Fratton	71D Fratton					
30116	T9	PLY Plymouth Friary	71C Dorchester					
30117	T9	SAL Salisbury	72C Yeovil Town	71A Eastleigh	71A Eastleigh	71A Eastleigh		
30118	T9	FRA Fratton	71D Fratton					
30119	T9	9E Nine Elms	70A Nine Elms					
30120	T9	ELH Eastleigh	71D Fratton	71A Eastleigh	71A Eastleigh	71A Eastleigh	(120)	
30121	T9	ELH Eastleigh	71A Eastleigh					
30122	T9	SAL Salisbury	72B Salisbury					
30123	M7	9E Nine Elms	70A Nine Elms	75B Redhill	70A Nine Elms			
30124	M7	EXJ Exmouth Junction	72A Exmouth Junction	70A Nine Elms	70C Guildford	70C Guildford		
30125	M7	ELH Eastleigh	71A Eastleigh	71A Eastleigh	71A Eastleigh	71A Eastleigh		
30127	M7	SAL Salisbury	71A Eastleigh	71A Eastleigh	71B Bournemouth	71B Bournemouth	71B Bournemouth	
30128	M7	ELH Eastleigh	71A Eastleigh	71B Bournemouth	71B Bournemouth	71B Bournemouth	(30031)	
30129	M7	YEO Yeovil Town	72C Yeovil Town	75A Brighton	72C Yeovil Town	72C Yeovil Town	72C Yeovil Town	
30130	M7	9E Nine Elms	70A Nine Elms	70A Nine Elms	71A Eastleigh			

		1948		1951	1954	1957	1960	1963	1966
30131	*M7*	**BM**	Bournemouth	**71B** Bournemouth	**72C** Yeovil Town	**72C** Yeovil Town	**72C** Yeovil Town		
30132	*M7*	**9E**	Nine Elms	**70A** Nine Elms	**70A** Nine Elms	**70A** Nine Elms	**70C** Guildford		
30133	*M7*	**EXJ**	Exmouth Junction	**72A** Exmouth Junction	**71A** Eastleigh	**70A** Nine Elms	**70A** Nine Elms	**71A** Eastleigh	
30134	*L11*	**YEO**	Yeovil Town	**72C** Yeovil Town					
30135	*K10*	**EXJ**	Exmouth Junction						
30137	*K10*	**EXJ**	Exmouth Junction						
30139	*K10*	**FEL**	Feltham						
30140	*K10*	**FEL**	Feltham						
30141	*K10*	**GFD**	Guildford						
30142	*K10*	**9E**	Nine Elms						
30143	*K10*	**YEO**	Yeovil Town						
30144	*K10*	**FEL**	Feltham						
30145	*K10*	**YEO**	Yeovil Town						
30146	*K10*	**DOR**	Dorchester						
30147	*D4*[1]	**SOT**	Southampton Docks						
30148	*L11*	**ELH**	Eastleigh	**71A** Eastleigh					
30150	*K10*	**ELH**	Eastleigh						
30151	*K10*	**ELH**	Eastleigh						
30152	*K10*	**YEO**	Yeovil Town						
30153	*K10*	**FEL**	Feltham						
30154	*L11*	**ELH**	Eastleigh	**71A** Eastleigh					
30155	*L11*	**ELH**	Eastleigh	**71A** Eastleigh					
30156	*L11*	**DOR**	Dorchester	**71A** Eastleigh					
30157	*L11*	**ELH**	Eastleigh	**71A** Eastleigh					
30158	*L11*	**FEL**	Feltham						
30159	*L11*	**ELH**	Eastleigh	**71A** Eastleigh					
30160	*G6*	**9E**	Nine Elms	**70A** Nine Elms	**70E** Reading South	**70D** Basingstoke			
30161	*L11*	**BM**	Bournemouth						
30162	*G6*	**DOR**	Dorchester	**71C** Dorchester	**71C** Dorchester	**72D** Plymouth Friary			
30163	*L11*	**YEO**	Yeovil Town	**70A** Nine Elms					
30164	*L11*	**FRA**	Fratton	**70B** Feltham					
30165	*L11*	**ELH**	Eastleigh	**70A** Nine Elms					
30166	*L11*	**FRA**	Fratton						
30167	*L11*	**FEL**	Feltham						
30168	*L11*	**BM**	Bournemouth						
30169	*L11*	**BM**	Bournemouth						
30170	*L11*	**FRA**	Fratton	**71D** Fratton					
30171	*L11*	**ELH**	Eastleigh	**71A** Eastleigh					
30172	*L11*	**FRA**	Fratton	**71D** Fratton					
30173	*L11*	**BM**	Bournemouth	**71A** Eastleigh					
30174	*L11*	**FEL**	Feltham	**70B** Feltham					
30175	*L11*	**ELH**	Eastleigh	**71A** Eastleigh					
30176	*B4*[1]	**SOT**	Southampton Docks						
30177	*O2*	**DOR**	Dorchester	**71C** Dorchester	**71A** Eastleigh	**70B** Feltham			
30179	*O2*	**9E**	Nine Elms	**71C** Dorchester	**70A** Nine Elms	**70B** Feltham			
30181	*O2*	**WAD**	Wadebridge	(W35)					
30182	*O2*	**PLY**	Plymouth Friary	**72D** Plymouth Friary	**72C** Yeovil Town	**72C** Yeovil Town	**72A** Exmouth Junction		
30183	*O2*	**PLY**	Plymouth Friary	**72D** Plymouth Friary	**72D** Plymouth Friary	**72A** Exmouth Junction	**83H** Plymouth Friary		
30192	*O2*	**EXJ**	Exmouth Junction	**72A** Exmouth Junction	**72D** Plymouth Friary	**72D** Plymouth Friary	**83H** Plymouth Friary		
30193	*O2*	**EXJ**	Exmouth Junction	**72A** Exmouth Junction	**70B** Feltham	**72A** Exmouth Junction	**83H** Plymouth Friary		
30197	*O2*	**PLY**	Plymouth Friary	**71C** Dorchester					
30198	*O2*	**ELH**	Eastleigh	(W36)					
30199	*O2*	**EXJ**	Exmouth Junction	**72A** Exmouth Junction	**72A** Exmouth Junction	**72A** Exmouth Junction	**72A** Exmouth Junction		
30200	*O2*	**ELH**	Eastleigh	**72F** Wadebridge	**72F** Wadebridge	**72F** Wadebridge	**72F** Wadebridge		
30203	*O2*	**WAD**	Wadebridge	**72F** Wadebridge	**72F** Wadebridge				
30204	*O2*	**9E**	Nine Elms	**71B** Bournemouth					
30207	*O2*	**EXJ**	Exmouth Junction	**72D** Plymouth Friary	**71D** Fratton	**70F** Fratton			
30212	*O2*	**9E**	Nine Elms	**71B** Bournemouth	**71B** Bournemouth	**71A** Eastleigh			
30213	*O2*	**ELH**	Eastleigh	**71A** Eastleigh					
30216	*O2*	**PLY**	Plymouth Friary	**72D** Plymouth Friary	**72D** Plymouth Friary	**72D** Plymouth Friary			
30221	*O2*	**DOR**	Dorchester	**70A** Nine Elms					
30223	*O2*	**DOR**	Dorchester	**71C** Dorchester	**71B** Bournemouth	**71A** Eastleigh	**71A** Eastleigh		
30224	*O2*	**EXJ**	Exmouth Junction	**72A** Exmouth Junction	**70A** Nine Elms	**70A** Nine Elms			
30225	*O2*	**ELH**	Eastleigh	**71A** Eastleigh	**71A** Eastleigh	**72D** Plymouth Friary	**83H** Plymouth Friary		
30229	*O2*	**DOR**	Dorchester	**71C** Dorchester	**71A** Eastleigh	**71A** Eastleigh	**71A** Eastleigh		
30230	*O2*	**EXJ**	Exmouth Junction	**72A** Exmouth Junction	**70B** Feltham				
30231	*O2*	**ELH**	Eastleigh	**71C** Dorchester					
30232	*O2*	**EXJ**	Exmouth Junction	**72A** Exmouth Junction	**72A** Exmouth Junction	**72A** Exmouth Junction			
30233	*O2*	**DOR**	Dorchester	**71A** Eastleigh	**71A** Eastleigh	**71A** Eastleigh			
30236	*O2*	**PLY**	Plymouth Friary	**72D** Plymouth Friary	**72D** Plymouth Friary	**72F** Wadebridge	**72F** Wadebridge		
30237	*G6*	**SAL**	Salisbury						
30238	*G6*	**YEO**	Yeovil Town	**70C** Guildford	**70C** Guildford	**70C** Guildford	**70C** Guildford	(DS682)	
30239	*G6*	**BM**	Bournemouth						
30240	*G6*	**ELH**	Eastleigh						
30241	*M7*	**9E**	Nine Elms	**70A** Nine Elms	**70A** Nine Elms	**70A** Nine Elms	**70A** Nine Elms	**70E** Salisbury	
30242	*M7*	**ELH**	Eastleigh	**71A** Eastleigh	**70A** Nine Elms	**70A** Nine Elms			
30243	*M7*	**SAL**	Salisbury	**71A** Eastleigh	**70A** Nine Elms	**70A** Nine Elms			
30244	*M7*	**9E**	Nine Elms	**70A** Nine Elms	**70A** Nine Elms	**70A** Nine Elms			
30245	*M7*	**EXJ**	Exmouth Junction	**72A** Exmouth Junction	**75B** Redhill	**70A** Nine Elms	**70A** Nine Elms		
30246	*M7*	**GFD**	Guildford	**70C** Guildford	**70C** Guildford	**70C** Guildford	**70C** Guildford		
30247	*M7*	**BPL**	Barnstaple Junction	**72E** Barnstaple Junction	**72E** Barnstaple Junction	**72E** Barnstaple Junction	**72E** Barnstaple Junction		
30248	*M7*	**9E**	Nine Elms	**70A** Nine Elms	**70A** Nine Elms	**70A** Nine Elms	**70A** Nine Elms		
30249	*M7*	**9E**	Nine Elms	**70A** Nine Elms	**70A** Nine Elms	**70A** Nine Elms	**70A** Nine Elms	**70A** Nine Elms	
30250	*M7*	**BPL**	Barnstaple Junction	**72E** Barnstaple Junction	**72E** Barnstaple Junction	**72E** Barnstaple Junction			
30251	*M7*	**BM**	Bournemouth	**71B** Bournemouth	**72E** Barnstaple Junction	**72E** Barnstaple Junction	**72E** Barnstaple Junction	**72E** Barnstaple Junction	
30252	*M7*	**EXJ**	Exmouth Junction	**72A** Exmouth Junction	**72E** Barnstaple Junction	**72E** Barnstaple Junction			
30253	*M7*	**EXJ**	Exmouth Junction	**72A** Exmouth Junction	**70B** Feltham	**72E** Barnstaple Junction	**72E** Barnstaple Junction		
30254	*M7*	**FEL**	Feltham	**70B** Feltham	**72E** Barnstaple Junction	**72E** Barnstaple Junction	**72E** Barnstaple Junction	**72E** Barnstaple Junction	
30255	*M7*	**EXJ**	Exmouth Junction	**72A** Exmouth Junction	**72E** Barnstaple Junction	**72E** Barnstaple Junction	**72E** Barnstaple Junction		
30256	*M7*	**EXJ**	Exmouth Junction	**72A** Exmouth Junction	**72E** Barnstaple Junction	**72E** Barnstaple Junction			
30257	*G6*	**9E**	Nine Elms						
30258	*G6*	**RDG**	Reading South	**70D** Basingstoke	**70D** Basingstoke	**70D** Basingstoke	**70D** Basingstoke		
30259	*G6*	**9E**	Nine Elms						
30260	*G6*	**RDG**	Reading South	**71B** Bournemouth	**71B** Bournemouth	**71B** Bournemouth			
30261	*G6*	**ELH**	Eastleigh						
30262	*G6*	**GFD**	Guildford						
30263	*G6*	**9E**	Nine Elms						
30264	*G6*	**ELH**	Eastleigh						
30265	*G6*	**BAS**	Basingstoke						
30266	*G6*	**9E**	Nine Elms	**70D** Basingstoke	**70D** Basingstoke	**72B** Salisbury	**72B** Salisbury		
30267	*G6*	**ELH**	Eastleigh						
30268	*G6*	**GFD**	Guildford						
30269	*G6*	**GFD**	Guildford						
30270	*G6*	**GFD**	Guildford	**70E** Reading South	**72B** Salisbury	**72B** Salisbury			
30271	*G6*	**9E**	Nine Elms						
30272	*G6*	**ELH**	Eastleigh	(DS3152)					
30273	*G6*	**9E**	Nine Elms						
30274	*G6*	**ELH**	Eastleigh	**71H** Templecombe	**71H** Templecombe	**71H** Templecombe	**71B** Bournemouth		
30275	*G6*	**ELH**	Eastleigh						
30276	*G6*	**YEO**	Yeovil Town						
30277	*G6*	**ELH**	Eastleigh	**71H** Templecombe	**70C** Guildford	**70C** Guildford	**70C** Guildford		
30278	*G6*	**BAS**	Basingstoke						
30279	*G6*	**SAL**	Salisbury						
30280	*T9*	**FRA**	Fratton	**71D** Fratton					

No.	Class	1948	1951	1954	1957	1960	1963	1966
30281	*T9*	**DOR** Dorchester	**70C** Guildford					
30282	*T9*	**EXJ** Exmouth Junction	**71A** Eastleigh	**71A** Eastleigh				
30283	*T9*	**EXJ** Exmouth Junction	**72A** Exmouth Junction	**71A** Eastleigh	**71A** Eastleigh			
30284	*T9*	**DOR** Dorchester	**71C** Dorchester	**71A** Eastleigh	**71A** Eastleigh			
30285	*T9*	**SAL** Salisbury	**71A** Eastleigh	**71A** Eastleigh	**71A** Eastleigh			
30286	*T9*	**ELH** Eastleigh	**71A** Eastleigh					
30287	*T9*	**FRA** Fratton	**71A** Eastleigh	**71A** Eastleigh	**71A** Eastleigh	**71A** Eastleigh		
30288	*T9*	**SAL** Salisbury	**72B** Salisbury	**71A** Eastleigh	**71A** Eastleigh	**71A** Eastleigh		
30289	*T9*	**PLY** Plymouth Friary	**72B** Salisbury	**71A** Eastleigh	**71A** Eastleigh			
30300	*T9*	**DOR** Dorchester	**72B** Salisbury	**71A** Eastleigh	**71A** Eastleigh	**71A** Eastleigh		
30301	*T9*	**EXJ** Exmouth Junction	**72B** Salisbury	**72B** Salisbury	**72B** Salisbury			
30302	*T9*	**ELH** Eastleigh	**70D** Basingstoke					
30303	*T9*	**FRA** Fratton	**71D** Fratton					
30304	*T9*	**FRA** Fratton	**71A** Eastleigh	**72B** Salisbury	**72B** Salisbury			
30305	*T9*	**FRA** Fratton	**71D** Fratton					
30306	*700*	**ELH** Eastleigh	**71A** Eastleigh	**71A** Eastleigh	**71B** Bournemouth	**71A** Eastleigh		
30307	*T9*	**BAS** Basingstoke	**71C** Dorchester					
30308	*700*	**GFD** Guildford	**70C** Guildford	**70C** Guildford	**70C** Guildford	**70C** Guildford		
30309	*700*	**GFD** Guildford	**70B** Feltham	**70C** Guildford	**72B** Salisbury	**72B** Salisbury		
30310	*T9*	**YEO** Yeovil Town	**71D** Fratton	**71A** Eastleigh	**71A** Eastleigh			
30311	*T9*	**GFD** Guildford	**70C** Guildford					
30312	*T9*	**SAL** Salisbury	**70C** Guildford					
30313	*T9*	**ELH** Eastleigh	**71A** Eastleigh	**70C** Guildford	**72B** Salisbury	**72A** Exmouth Junction		
30314	*T9*	**FRA** Fratton	**71D** Fratton					
30315	*700*	**SAL** Salisbury	**72B** Salisbury	**72B** Salisbury	**72A** Exmouth Junction	**72B** Salisbury		
30316	*700*	**ELH** Eastleigh	**71A** Eastleigh	**71A** Eastleigh	**71A** Eastleigh	**71A** Eastleigh		
30317	*700*	**SAL** Salisbury	**72B** Salisbury	**72B** Salisbury	**72B** Salisbury	**72A** Exmouth Junction		
30318	*M7*	**BM** Bournemouth	**71B** Bournemouth	**71B** Bournemouth	**71B** Bournemouth			
30319	*M7*	**9E** Nine Elms	**70A** Nine Elms	**70A** Nine Elms	**70A** Nine Elms	**70A** Nine Elms		
30320	*M7*	**EXJ** Exmouth Junction	**72A** Exmouth Junction	**70A** Nine Elms	**70A** Nine Elms	**70A** Nine Elms	**70A** Nine Elms	
30321	*M7*	**BPL** Barnstaple Junction	**72E** Barnstaple Junction	**70A** Nine Elms	**70A** Nine Elms	**70A** Nine Elms		
30322	*M7*	**9E** Nine Elms	**70A** Nine Elms	**70A** Nine Elms	**70A** Nine Elms			
30323	*M7*	**EXJ** Exmouth Junction	**72A** Exmouth Junction	**72A** Exmouth Junction	**72A** Exmouth Junction			
30324	*M7*	**GFD** Guildford	**70C** Guildford	**70C** Guildford	**71B** Bournemouth			
30325	*700*	**GFD** Guildford	**70C** Guildford	**70C** Guildford	**70C** Guildford	**70C** Guildford		
30326	*700*	**GFD** Guildford	**70C** Guildford	**70C** Guildford	**70C** Guildford	**70C** Guildford		
30327	*700*	**GFD** Guildford	**70C** Guildford	**70C** Guildford	**72B** Salisbury	**72A** Exmouth Junction		
30328	*M7*	**GFD** Guildford	**70C** Guildford	**70C** Guildford	**71A** Eastleigh	**71A** Eastleigh	**71B** Bournemouth	
30329	*K10*	**EXJ** Exmouth Junction						
30330	*H15*	**SAL** Salisbury	**72B** Salisbury	**72B** Salisbury	**72B** Salisbury			
30331	*H15*	**SAL** Salisbury	**72B** Salisbury	**72B** Salisbury	**72B** Salisbury	**72B** Salisbury		
30332	*H15*	**SAL** Salisbury	**72B** Salisbury	**72B** Salisbury				
30333	*H15*	**SAL** Salisbury	**72B** Salisbury	**72B** Salisbury	**72B** Salisbury			
30334	*H15*	**SAL** Salisbury	**72B** Salisbury	**72B** Salisbury	**72B** Salisbury			
30335	*H15*	**SAL** Salisbury	**72B** Salisbury	**72B** Salisbury	**72B** Salisbury			
30336	*T9*	**ELH** Eastleigh	**70C** Guildford					
30337	*T9*	**BM** Bournemouth	**72C** Yeovil Town	**70C** Guildford	**70C** Guildford			
30338	*T9*	**FRA** Fratton	**71C** Dorchester	**70C** Guildford	**70A** Nine Elms	**72A** Exmouth Junction		
30339	*700*	**9E** Nine Elms	**70A** Nine Elms	**70B** Feltham	**70B** Feltham	**70B** Feltham		
30340	*K10*	**YEO** Yeovil Town						
30341	*K10*	**ELH** Eastleigh						
30343	*K10*	**GFD** Guildford						
30345	*K10*	**ELH** Eastleigh						
30346	*700*	**GFD** Guildford	**70B** Feltham	**70B** Feltham	**70B** Feltham	**70B** Feltham		
30348	*G6*	**BAS** Basingstoke						
30349	*G6*	**GFD** Guildford	**70C** Guildford	**70C** Guildford	**70C** Guildford	**70C** Guildford		
30350	*700*	**ELH** Eastleigh	**71A** Eastleigh	**70C** Guildford	**70C** Guildford	**70C** Guildford		
30351	*G6*	**ELH** Eastleigh						
30352	*700*	**GFD** Guildford	**70B** Feltham	**70B** Feltham	**70B** Feltham			
30353	*G6*	**9E** Nine Elms	**70A** Nine Elms					
30354	*G6*	**9E** Nine Elms						
30355	*700*	**SAL** Salisbury	**70D** Basingstoke	**70B** Feltham	**70B** Feltham	**70B** Feltham		
30356	*M7*	**EXJ** Exmouth Junction	**72D** Plymouth Friary	**71D** Fratton	**71A** Eastleigh			
30357	*M7*	**ELH** Eastleigh	**71A** Eastleigh	**71D** Fratton	**70F** Fratton	**71A** Eastleigh		
30361	*T1*	**SAL** Salisbury						
30363	*T1*	**BM** Bournemouth						
30366	*T1*	**ELH** Eastleigh						
30367	*T1*	**ELH** Eastleigh	**71A** Eastleigh					
30368	*700*	**BAS** Basingstoke	**70D** Basingstoke	**70D** Basingstoke	**70D** Basingstoke	**70D** Basingstoke		
30374	*M7*	**EXJ** Exmouth Junction	**72A** Exmouth Junction	**70E** Reading South	**72B** Salisbury			
30375	*M7*	**EXJ** Exmouth Junction	**72D** Plymouth Friary	**71A** Eastleigh	**71A** Eastleigh	**71A** Eastleigh		
30376	*M7*	**EXJ** Exmouth Junction	**72A** Exmouth Junction	**71A** Eastleigh	**71A** Eastleigh			
30377	*M7*	**EXJ** Exmouth Junction	**72A** Exmouth Junction	**75B** Redhill	**71A** Eastleigh	**71A** Eastleigh		
30378	*M7*	**GFD** Guildford	**71A** Eastleigh	**71A** Eastleigh	**71A** Eastleigh	**70C** Guildford		
30379	*M7*	**BM** Bournemouth	**71B** Bournemouth	**71A** Eastleigh	**71A** Eastleigh	**71A** Eastleigh	**71B** Bournemouth	
30380	*K10*	**9E** Nine Elms						
30382	*K10*	**SAL** Salisbury						
30383	*K10*	**FEL** Feltham						
30384	*K10*	**FRA** Fratton	**70C** Guildford					
30385	*K10*	**FEL** Feltham						
30386	*K10*	**9E** Nine Elms						
30389	*K10*	**SAL** Salisbury	**72C** Yeovil Town					
30390	*K10*	**9E** Nine Elms						
30391	*K10*	**9E** Nine Elms						
30392	*K10*	**9E** Nine Elms						
30393	*K10*	**ELH** Eastleigh						
30394	*K10*	**ELH** Eastleigh						
30395	*S11*	**ELH** Eastleigh	**71D** Fratton					
30396	*S11*	**FRA** Fratton	**71D** Fratton					
30397	*S11*	**ELH** Eastleigh	**71D** Fratton					
30398	*S11*	**BM** Bournemouth	**71B** Bournemouth					
30399	*S11*	**BM** Bournemouth	**71C** Dorchester					
30400	*S11*	**FRA** Fratton	**71D** Fratton	**70C** Guildford				
30401	*S11*	**FRA** Fratton	**71A** Eastleigh					
30402	*S11*	**FRA** Fratton	**71D** Fratton					
30403	*S11*	**FRA** Fratton	**71B** Bournemouth					
30404	*S11*	**FRA** Fratton	**71B** Bournemouth					
30405	*L11*	**SAL** Salisbury	**70A** Nine Elms					
30406	*L11*	**9E** Nine Elms	**70A** Nine Elms					
30407	*L11*	**BAS** Basingstoke						
30408	*L11*	**EXJ** Exmouth Junction	**72A** Exmouth Junction					
30409	*L11*	**EXJ** Exmouth Junction	**72A** Exmouth Junction					
30410	*L11*	**DOR** Dorchester						
30411	*L11*	**ELH** Eastleigh	**71A** Eastleigh					
30412	*L11*	**YEO** Yeovil Town						
30413	*L11*	**FRA** Fratton	**70A** Nine Elms					
30414	*L11*	**FRA** Fratton	**71A** Eastleigh					
30415	*L12*	**BM** Bournemouth	**71C** Dorchester					
30416	*L12*	**GFD** Guildford	**71D** Fratton					
30417	*L12*	**FRA** Fratton	**71D** Fratton					
30418	*L12*	**BAS** Basingstoke	**70D** Basingstoke					
30419	*L12*	**GFD** Guildford	**71D** Fratton					
30420	*L12*	**ELH** Eastleigh	**70C** Guildford					
30421	*L12*	**SAL** Salisbury	**71A** Eastleigh					

No.	Class	1948	1951	1954	1957	1960	1963	1966
30422	L12	ELH Eastleigh	71A Eastleigh					
30423	L12	ELH Eastleigh	71A Eastleigh					
30424	L12	FRA Fratton	70C Guildford					
30425	L12	FRA Fratton	70C Guildford					
30426	L12	BAS Basingstoke	71D Fratton					
30427	L12	9E Nine Elms	71D Fratton					
30428	L12	ELH Eastleigh	70C Guildford					
30429	L12	BM Bournemouth	71A Eastleigh					
30430	L12	ELH Eastleigh	71A Eastleigh					
30431	L12	9E Nine Elms	71A Eastleigh					
30432	L12	SAL Salisbury	70C Guildford					
30433	L12	GFD Guildford	70C Guildford					
30434	L12	GFD Guildford	70C Guildford	70C Guildford				
30435	L11	9E Nine Elms						
30436	L11	EXJ Exmouth Junction	70C Guildford					
30437	L11	ELH Eastleigh	71A Eastleigh					
30438	L11	GFD Guildford	70B Feltham					
30439	L11	EXJ Exmouth Junction						
30440	L11	9E Nine Elms						
30441	L11	FRA Fratton	71D Fratton					
30442	L11	9E Nine Elms	70C Guildford					
30443	T14	9E Nine Elms						
30444	T14	9E Nine Elms						
30445	T14	9E Nine Elms						
30446	T14	9E Nine Elms	70A Nine Elms					
30447	T14	9E Nine Elms						
30448	N15	SAL Salisbury	72B Salisbury	72B Salisbury	72B Salisbury	72B Salisbury		
30449	N15	SAL Salisbury	72B Salisbury	72B Salisbury	72B Salisbury			
30450	N15	SAL Salisbury	72B Salisbury	72B Salisbury	72B Salisbury	72B Salisbury		
30451	N15	SAL Salisbury	72B Salisbury	72B Salisbury	72B Salisbury	72B Salisbury		
30452	N15	SAL Salisbury	72B Salisbury	72B Salisbury	72B Salisbury			
30453	N15	SAL Salisbury	72B Salisbury	72B Salisbury	72B Salisbury	72B Salisbury		
30454	N15	SAL Salisbury	72B Salisbury	72B Salisbury	72B Salisbury			
30455	N15	SAL Salisbury	72B Salisbury	70A Nine Elms	70A Nine Elms			
30456	N15	SAL Salisbury	72B Salisbury	70A Nine Elms	70A Nine Elms	70D Basingstoke		
30457	N15	SAL Salisbury	72B Salisbury	70A Nine Elms	70A Nine Elms	70A Nine Elms		
30458	458	GFD Guildford	70C Guildford	70C Guildford				
30459	T14	9E Nine Elms						
30460	T14	9E Nine Elms						
30461	T14	9E Nine Elms	70A Nine Elms					
30462	T14	9E Nine Elms						
30463	D15	ELH Eastleigh	71A Eastleigh					
30464	D15	ELH Eastleigh	71A Eastleigh	70A Nine Elms				
30465	D15	ELH Eastleigh	71A Eastleigh	71D Fratton				
30466	D15	ELH Eastleigh	71A Eastleigh					
30467	D15	ELH Eastleigh	71A Eastleigh	71A Eastleigh				
30468	D15	ELH Eastleigh	71A Eastleigh					
30469	D15	ELH Eastleigh	71A Eastleigh					
30470	D15	ELH Eastleigh	71A Eastleigh					
30471	D15	ELH Eastleigh	71A Eastleigh	71D Fratton				
30472	D15	ELH Eastleigh	71A Eastleigh					
30473	H15	ELH Eastleigh	71A Eastleigh	71A Eastleigh	71A Eastleigh			
30474	H15	ELH Eastleigh	71A Eastleigh	71A Eastleigh	71A Eastleigh	71A Eastleigh		
30475	H15	SAL Salisbury	71A Eastleigh	71A Eastleigh	71A Eastleigh	71A Eastleigh		
30476	H15	SAL Salisbury	71A Eastleigh	71A Eastleigh	71A Eastleigh	71A Eastleigh		
30477	H15	9E Nine Elms	71A Eastleigh	71A Eastleigh	71A Eastleigh			
30478	H15	ELH Eastleigh	71A Eastleigh	71A Eastleigh	70A Nine Elms			
30479	M7	ELH Eastleigh	71A Eastleigh	71A Eastleigh	71A Eastleigh	71A Eastleigh		
30480	M7	FRA Fratton	71D Fratton	71A Eastleigh	71A Eastleigh	71A Eastleigh	71A Eastleigh	
30481	M7	GFD Guildford	70C Guildford	71A Eastleigh	71A Eastleigh			
30482	H15	9E Nine Elms	70A Nine Elms	70A Nine Elms	70A Nine Elms			
30483	H15	9E Nine Elms	70A Nine Elms	70A Nine Elms	70A Nine Elms			
30484	H15	9E Nine Elms	70A Nine Elms	70A Nine Elms	70A Nine Elms			
30485	H15	9E Nine Elms	70A Nine Elms	70A Nine Elms				
30486	H15	9E Nine Elms	70A Nine Elms	70A Nine Elms	70A Nine Elms			
30487	H15	9E Nine Elms	70A Nine Elms	70A Nine Elms	70A Nine Elms			
30488	H15	9E Nine Elms	70A Nine Elms	70A Nine Elms	70A Nine Elms			
30489	H15	9E Nine Elms	70A Nine Elms	70A Nine Elms	70A Nine Elms	70A Nine Elms		
30490	H15	9E Nine Elms	70A Nine Elms	70A Nine Elms				
30491	H15	9E Nine Elms	70A Nine Elms	70A Nine Elms	70A Nine Elms	70A Nine Elms		
30492	G16	FEL Feltham	70B Feltham	70B Feltham	70B Feltham			
30493	G16	FEL Feltham	70B Feltham	70B Feltham	70B Feltham			
30494	G16	FEL Feltham	70B Feltham	70B Feltham	70B Feltham	70B Feltham		
30495	G16	FEL Feltham	70B Feltham	70B Feltham	70B Feltham	70B Feltham		
30496	S15	FEL Feltham	70B Feltham	70B Feltham	70B Feltham	70B Feltham	70B Feltham	
30497	S15	FEL Feltham	70B Feltham	70B Feltham	70B Feltham	70B Feltham	70B Feltham	
30498	S15	FEL Feltham	70B Feltham	70B Feltham	70B Feltham	70B Feltham	70B Feltham	
30499	S15	FEL Feltham	70B Feltham	70B Feltham	70B Feltham	70B Feltham	70B Feltham	
30500	S15	FEL Feltham	70B Feltham	70B Feltham	70B Feltham	70B Feltham	70B Feltham	
30501	S15	FEL Feltham	70B Feltham	70B Feltham	70B Feltham	70B Feltham	70B Feltham	
30502	S15	FEL Feltham	70B Feltham	70B Feltham	70B Feltham	70B Feltham		
30503	S15	FEL Feltham	70B Feltham	70B Feltham	70B Feltham	70B Feltham	70B Feltham	
30504	S15	FEL Feltham	70B Feltham	70B Feltham	70B Feltham	70B Feltham		
30505	S15	FEL Feltham	70B Feltham	70B Feltham	70B Feltham	70B Feltham		
30506	S15	FEL Feltham	70B Feltham	70B Feltham	70B Feltham	70B Feltham	70B Feltham	
30507	S15	FEL Feltham	70B Feltham	70B Feltham	70B Feltham	70B Feltham	70B Feltham	
30508	S15	FEL Feltham	70B Feltham	70B Feltham	70B Feltham	70B Feltham	70B Feltham	
30509	S15	FEL Feltham	70B Feltham	70B Feltham	70B Feltham	70B Feltham	70B Feltham	
30510	S15	FEL Feltham	70B Feltham	70B Feltham	70B Feltham	70B Feltham	70B Feltham	
30511	S15	FEL Feltham	70B Feltham	70B Feltham	70B Feltham	70B Feltham	70B Feltham	
30512	S15	FEL Feltham	70B Feltham	70B Feltham	70B Feltham	70B Feltham	70B Feltham	
30513	S15	FEL Feltham	70B Feltham	70B Feltham	70B Feltham	70B Feltham	70B Feltham	
30514	S15	FEL Feltham	70B Feltham	70B Feltham	70B Feltham	70B Feltham	70B Feltham	
30515	S15	FEL Feltham	70B Feltham	70B Feltham	70B Feltham	70B Feltham	70B Feltham	
30516	H16	FEL Feltham	70B Feltham	70B Feltham	70B Feltham	70B Feltham		
30517	H16	FEL Feltham	70B Feltham	70B Feltham	70B Feltham	70B Feltham		
30518	H16	FEL Feltham	70B Feltham	70B Feltham	70B Feltham	70B Feltham		
30519	H16	FEL Feltham	70B Feltham	70B Feltham	70B Feltham	70B Feltham		
30520	H16	FEL Feltham	70B Feltham	70B Feltham	70B Feltham	70B Feltham		
30521	H15	ELH Eastleigh	70A Nine Elms	70A Nine Elms	70A Nine Elms	70A Nine Elms		
30522	H15	ELH Eastleigh	71A Eastleigh	70A Nine Elms	70A Nine Elms	72B Salisbury		
30523	H15	ELH Eastleigh	71A Eastleigh	70A Nine Elms	70A Nine Elms	72B Salisbury		
30524	H15	ELH Eastleigh	71A Eastleigh	70A Nine Elms	70A Nine Elms	72B Salisbury		
30530	Q	ELH Eastleigh	71A Eastleigh	71A Eastleigh	71A Eastleigh	71A Eastleigh	72A Exmouth Junction	
30531	Q	TWW Tunbridge Wells West	71A Eastleigh	71A Eastleigh	71A Eastleigh	71A Eastleigh	72A Exmouth Junction	
30532	Q	ELH Eastleigh	71A Eastleigh	71A Eastleigh	71A Eastleigh	71A Eastleigh	70E Salisbury	
30533	Q	RED Redhill	75C Norwood Junction	75C Norwood Junction	75C Norwood Junction	75C Norwood Junction	75D Stewarts Lane	
30534	Q	TWW Tunbridge Wells West	75C Norwood Junction	75C Norwood Junction	75C Norwood Junction	75C Norwood Junction		
30535	Q	ELH Eastleigh	71A Eastleigh	71A Eastleigh	71A Eastleigh	71A Eastleigh	71B Bournemouth	
30536	Q	ELH Eastleigh	71A Eastleigh	71A Eastleigh	71A Eastleigh	71A Eastleigh	71A Eastleigh	
30537	Q	RED Redhill	75C Norwood Junction	75C Norwood Junction	75C Norwood Junction	75C Norwood Junction		
30538	Q	RED Redhill	75C Norwood Junction	75C Norwood Junction	75C Norwood Junction	75C Norwood Junction	75D Stewarts Lane	
30539	Q	RED Redhill	75C Norwood Junction	75C Norwood Junction	71B Bournemouth	71B Bournemouth	71B Bournemouth	
30540	Q	HOR Horsham	75E Three Bridges	75C Norwood Junction	75C Norwood Junction	75C Norwood Junction		

No.	Class	1948	1951	1954	1957	1960	1963	1966
30541	Q	3B Three Bridges	75E Three Bridges	71B Bournemouth	71B Bournemouth	71B Bournemouth	71B Bournemouth	
30542	Q	3B Three Bridges	71A Eastleigh	71A Eastleigh	71A Eastleigh	71A Eastleigh	70C Guildford	
30543	Q	HOR Horsham	71A Eastleigh	71A Eastleigh	71A Eastleigh	71A Eastleigh	75D Stewarts Lane	
30544	Q	HOR Horsham	71A Eastleigh	75D Horsham	75D Horsham	75E Three Bridges	75D Stewarts Lane	
30545	Q	RED Redhill	75D Horsham	75D Horsham	75D Horsham	75E Three Bridges	75E Three Bridges	
30546	Q	RED Redhill	75D Horsham	75D Horsham	75D Horsham	75E Three Bridges	75E Three Bridges	
30547	Q	RED Redhill	75C Norwood Junction	75C Norwood Junction	75D Horsham	75E Three Bridges	75E Three Bridges	
30548	Q	BM Bournemouth	71B Bournemouth	71B Bournemouth	71B Bournemouth	71B Bournemouth	71B Bournemouth	
30549	Q	BM Bournemouth	71B Bournemouth	71B Bournemouth	75C Norwood Junction	75C Norwood Junction	75E Three Bridges	
30564	0395	EXJ Exmouth Junction	72A Exmouth Junction	72A Exmouth Junction	72A Exmouth Junction			
30565	0395	GFD Guildford	71A Eastleigh					
30566	0395	ELH Eastleigh	71A Eastleigh	71A Eastleigh	71A Eastleigh			
30567	0395	FEL Feltham	70B Feltham	70B Feltham	70B Feltham			
30568	0395	GFD Guildford	70C Guildford	70B Feltham	70B Feltham			
30569	0395	FEL Feltham	70B Feltham	70B Feltham				
30570	0395	FEL Feltham	70B Feltham	70B Feltham				
30571	0395	ELH Eastleigh	71A Eastleigh					
30572	0395	FEL Feltham	70B Feltham	70B Feltham	70B Feltham			
30573	0395	FEL Feltham	70B Feltham	70B Feltham				
30574	0395	GFD Guildford	70C Guildford	70C Guildford	70C Guildford			
30575	0395	GFD Guildford	70C Guildford	72A Exmouth Junction	70C Guildford			
30576	0395	on loan Kent & East Sussex Railway						
30577	0395	SAL Salisbury	70C Guildford	70C Guildford				
30578	0395	GFD Guildford	70C Guildford	70C Guildford	70C Guildford			
30579	0395	FEL Feltham	70B Feltham	70C Guildford				
30580	0395	GFD Guildford	70C Guildford	72A Exmouth Junction	70C Guildford			
30581	0395	ELH Eastleigh	72A Exmouth Junction					
30582	0415	EXJ Exmouth Junction	72A Exmouth Junction	72A Exmouth Junction	72A Exmouth Junction	72A Exmouth Junction		
30583	0415	EXJ Exmouth Junction	72A Exmouth Junction	72A Exmouth Junction	72A Exmouth Junction	72A Exmouth Junction		
30584	0415	EXJ Exmouth Junction	72A Exmouth Junction	72A Exmouth Junction	72A Exmouth Junction	72A Exmouth Junction		
30585	0298	WAD Wadebridge	72F Wadebridge	72F Wadebridge	72F Wadebridge	72F Wadebridge		
30586	0298	WAD Wadebridge	72F Wadebridge	72F Wadebridge	72F Wadebridge	72F Wadebridge		
30587	0298	WAD Wadebridge	72F Wadebridge	72F Wadebridge	72F Wadebridge	72F Wadebridge		
30588	C14	ELH Eastleigh	71A Eastleigh	71A Eastleigh	71A Eastleigh			
30589	C14	ELH Eastleigh	71A Eastleigh	71A Eastleigh	71A Eastleigh			
30618	A12	GFD Guildford						
30627	A12	ELH Eastleigh						
30629	A12	ELH Eastleigh						
30636	A12	ELH Eastleigh						
30667	M7	9E Nine Elms	71A Eastleigh	70E Reading South	72A Exmouth Junction	72A Exmouth Junction		
30667	M7	(30106)	→	→	→	→	72A Exmouth Junction	
30668	M7	EXJ Exmouth Junction	72A Exmouth Junction	72A Exmouth Junction	72A Exmouth Junction	72A Exmouth Junction		
30669	M7	EXJ Exmouth Junction	72A Exmouth Junction	72A Exmouth Junction	72A Exmouth Junction	72A Exmouth Junction		
30670	M7	BPL Barnstaple Junction	72E Barnstaple Junction	72A Exmouth Junction	72A Exmouth Junction	72A Exmouth Junction	72E Barnstaple Junction	
30671	M7	EXJ Exmouth Junction	72A Exmouth Junction	72A Exmouth Junction	72E Barnstaple Junction			
30672	M7	9E Nine Elms						
30673	M7	9E Nine Elms	71A Eastleigh	72B Salisbury	72B Salisbury	72B Salisbury		
30674	M7	ELH Eastleigh	71A Eastleigh	72B Salisbury	72B Salisbury	72B Salisbury		
30675	M7	SAL Salisbury	72B Salisbury	70C Guildford	70C Guildford			
30676	M7	9E Nine Elms	70A Nine Elms	72A Exmouth Junction	72A Exmouth Junction	72A Exmouth Junction		
30687	700	FEL Feltham	70B Feltham	70B Feltham	70B Feltham	70B Feltham		
30688	700	FEL Feltham	70B Feltham	70B Feltham	70B Feltham			
30689	700	FEL Feltham	70B Feltham	70B Feltham	70B Feltham	70B Feltham		
30690	700	SAL Salisbury	72B Salisbury	72B Salisbury	71B Bournemouth	71B Bournemouth		
30691	700	SAL Salisbury	72B Salisbury	72B Salisbury	72A Exmouth Junction	72A Exmouth Junction		
30692	700	9E Nine Elms	70A Nine Elms	70A Nine Elms	70A Nine Elms	72B Salisbury		
30693	700	BAS Basingstoke	70D Basingstoke	70C Guildford	70C Guildford	70C Guildford		
30694	700	9E Nine Elms	70A Nine Elms	70A Nine Elms	70A Nine Elms	70A Nine Elms		
30695	700	DOR Dorchester	71B Bournemouth	71B Bournemouth	71B Bournemouth	71B Bournemouth		
30696	700	BM Bournemouth	70B Feltham	70B Feltham	70B Feltham	70B Feltham		
30697	700	FEL Feltham	70B Feltham	70A Nine Elms	70C Guildford	70C Guildford		
30698	700	FEL Feltham	70B Feltham	70A Nine Elms	70C Guildford	70C Guildford		
30699	700	9E Nine Elms	70A Nine Elms	70A Nine Elms	70A Nine Elms	70A Nine Elms		
30700	700	BM Bournemouth	71A Eastleigh	70A Nine Elms	70C Guildford	70C Guildford		
30701	700	9E Nine Elms	70A Nine Elms	70A Nine Elms	70A Nine Elms	70A Nine Elms		
30702	T9	YEO Yeovil Town	72A Exmouth Junction	72B Salisbury	72B Salisbury			
30703	T9	WAD Wadebridge	72A Exmouth Junction					
30704	T9	GFD Guildford	72C Yeovil Town					
30705	T9	ELH Eastleigh	71B Bournemouth	70D Basingstoke	70C Guildford			
30706	T9	BAS Basingstoke	72A Exmouth Junction	72C Yeovil Town	71B Bournemouth			
30707	T9	ELH Eastleigh	72A Exmouth Junction	72C Yeovil Town	71A Eastleigh	71B Bournemouth		
30708	T9	BAS Basingstoke	71B Bournemouth	72A Exmouth Junction	72A Exmouth Junction			
30709	T9	SAL Salisbury	72B Salisbury	72A Exmouth Junction	72A Exmouth Junction	72A Exmouth Junction		
30710	T9	YEO Yeovil Town	70C Guildford	72A Exmouth Junction	72A Exmouth Junction			
30711	T9	PLY Plymouth Friary	71D Fratton	72A Exmouth Junction	72A Exmouth Junction			
30712	T9	YEO Yeovil Town	70D Basingstoke	72A Exmouth Junction	72A Exmouth Junction			
30713	T9	ELH Eastleigh	71A Eastleigh					
30714	T9	YEO Yeovil Town	72A Exmouth Junction					
30715	T9	SAL Salisbury	72A Exmouth Junction	72A Exmouth Junction	72A Exmouth Junction	72A Exmouth Junction		
30716	T9	YEO Yeovil Town	72A Exmouth Junction					
30717	T9	WAD Wadebridge	72A Exmouth Junction	72A Exmouth Junction	72A Exmouth Junction	72A Exmouth Junction		
30718	T9	9E Nine Elms	70A Nine Elms	70A Nine Elms	70A Nine Elms	72A Exmouth Junction		
30719	T9	BM Bournemouth	72B Salisbury	70A Nine Elms	70A Nine Elms	72A Exmouth Junction		
30721	T9	SAL Salisbury	70A Nine Elms	72B Salisbury	72B Salisbury			
30722	T9	ELH Eastleigh	71A Eastleigh					
30723	T9	EXJ Exmouth Junction	72A Exmouth Junction					
30724	T9	EXJ Exmouth Junction	72B Salisbury	70D Basingstoke	70D Basingstoke			
30725	T9	EXJ Exmouth Junction	72B Salisbury					
30726	T9	GFD Guildford	71A Eastleigh	71D Fratton	70F Fratton			
30727	T9	SAL Salisbury	72B Salisbury	72A Exmouth Junction	71B Bournemouth			
30728	T9	BM Bournemouth	71B Bournemouth	71B Bournemouth				
30729	T9	SAL Salisbury	71A Eastleigh	71B Bournemouth	70F Fratton	72B Salisbury		
30730	T9	EXJ Exmouth Junction	72B Salisbury	71D Fratton	70F Fratton			
30731	T9	FRA Fratton	71D Fratton					
30732	T9	FRA Fratton	70B Feltham	71D Fratton	70F Fratton			
30733	T9	FRA Fratton	71B Bournemouth					
30736	N15	BM Bournemouth	71B Bournemouth	71B Bournemouth				
30737	N15	ELH Eastleigh	71B Bournemouth	71B Bournemouth				
30738	N15	9E Nine Elms	71B Bournemouth	71B Bournemouth	71B Bournemouth			
30739	N15	ELH Eastleigh	71B Bournemouth	71B Bournemouth	71B Bournemouth			
30740	N15	ELH Eastleigh	71B Bournemouth	71B Bournemouth				
30741	N15	ELH Eastleigh	71B Bournemouth	71B Bournemouth				
30742	N15	9E Nine Elms	71B Bournemouth	71B Bournemouth	71B Bournemouth			
30743	N15	BM Bournemouth	71B Bournemouth	71B Bournemouth				
30744	N15	SAL Salisbury	71A Eastleigh	70A Nine Elms				
30745	N15	ELH Eastleigh	71A Eastleigh	70D Basingstoke				
30746	N15	SAL Salisbury	71A Eastleigh	71A Eastleigh				
30747	N15	EXJ Exmouth Junction	71A Eastleigh	70A Nine Elms				
30748	N15	ELH Eastleigh	71A Eastleigh	71A Eastleigh	71A Eastleigh			
30749	N15	ELH Eastleigh	71A Eastleigh	70D Basingstoke	70D Basingstoke			
30750	N15	ELH Eastleigh	71A Eastleigh	70A Nine Elms	70A Nine Elms			
30751	N15	ELH Eastleigh	71A Eastleigh	70A Nine Elms	70D Basingstoke			
30752	N15	ELH Eastleigh	71A Eastleigh	70A Nine Elms				
30753	N15	9E Nine Elms	71A Eastleigh	70D Basingstoke	70D Basingstoke			

		1948		1951	1954	1957	1960	1963	1966
30754	*N15*	**ELH**	Eastleigh	**71A** Eastleigh					
30755	*N15*	**9E**	Nine Elms	**70A** Nine Elms	**70A** Nine Elms	**70D** Basingstoke			
30756	*756*	**ELH**	Eastleigh	**73A** Stewarts Lane					
30757	*757*	**PLY**	Plymouth Friary	**72D** Plymouth Friary	**72D** Plymouth Friary	**71A** Eastleigh			
30758	*757*	**PLY**	Plymouth Friary	**72D** Plymouth Friary	**72D** Plymouth Friary				
30763	*N15*	**BAT**	Stewarts Lane	**73A** Stewarts Lane	**73A** Stewarts Lane	**71A** Eastleigh	**70A** Nine Elms		
30764	*N15*	**BAT**	Stewarts Lane	**73A** Stewarts Lane	**73A** Stewarts Lane	**71B** Bournemouth	**71B** Bournemouth		
30765	*N15*	**BAT**	Stewarts Lane	**70A** Nine Elms	**73A** Stewarts Lane	**71B** Bournemouth	**70D** Basingstoke		
30766	*N15*	**9E**	Nine Elms	**73A** Stewarts Lane	**73A** Stewarts Lane	**73A** Stewarts Lane			
30767	*N15*	**DOV**	Dover Marine	**74C** Dover Marine	**73A** Stewarts Lane	**73A** Stewarts Lane			
30768	*N15*	**DOV**	Dover Marine	**74C** Dover Marine	**73A** Stewarts Lane	**73A** Stewarts Lane	**71A** Eastleigh		
30769	*N15*	**DOV**	Dover Marine	**74C** Dover Marine	**73A** Stewarts Lane	**73A** Stewarts Lane	**71A** Eastleigh		
30770	*N15*	**DOV**	Dover Marine	**74C** Dover Marine	**73A** Stewarts Lane	**71A** Eastleigh	**71A** Eastleigh		
30771	*N15*	**DOV**	Dover Marine	**74C** Dover Marine	**73A** Stewarts Lane	**71B** Bournemouth	**71B** Bournemouth		
30772	*N15*	**BM**	Bournemouth	**73A** Stewarts Lane	**73A** Stewarts Lane	**73C** Hither Green	**71B** Bournemouth		
30773	*N15*	**9E**	Nine Elms	**73A** Stewarts Lane	**73A** Stewarts Lane	**70A** Nine Elms	**71A** Eastleigh		
30774	*N15*	**9E**	Nine Elms	**73A** Stewarts Lane	**73A** Stewarts Lane	**70A** Nine Elms	**70A** Nine Elms		
30775	*N15*	**BAT**	Stewarts Lane	**73A** Stewarts Lane	**74C** Dover Marine	**74C** Dover Marine	**70B** Feltham		
30776	*N15*	**BAT**	Stewarts Lane	**73A** Stewarts Lane	**74C** Dover Marine	**74C** Dover Marine			
30777	*N15*	**ELH**	Eastleigh	**71A** Eastleigh	**74C** Dover Marine	**74C** Dover Marine	**70B** Feltham		
30778	*N15*	**BAT**	Stewarts Lane	**71A** Eastleigh	**70A** Nine Elms	**70A** Nine Elms			
30779	*N15*	**9E**	Nine Elms	**71A** Eastleigh	**70A** Nine Elms	**70A** Nine Elms			
30780	*N15*	**BAT**	Stewarts Lane	**71A** Eastleigh	**70A** Nine Elms	**71B** Bournemouth			
30781	*N15*	**BAT**	Stewarts Lane	**74C** Dover Marine	**70A** Nine Elms	**71B** Bournemouth	**71B** Bournemouth		
30782	*N15*	**9E**	Nine Elms	**70A** Nine Elms	**71B** Bournemouth	**71B** Bournemouth	**71B** Bournemouth		
30783	*N15*	**9E**	Nine Elms	**70A** Nine Elms	**71B** Bournemouth	**71B** Bournemouth	**71B** Bournemouth		
30784	*N15*	**ELH**	Eastleigh	**70A** Nine Elms	**71A** Eastleigh	**71A** Eastleigh			
30785	*N15*	**ELH**	Eastleigh	**70A** Nine Elms	**71A** Eastleigh	**71A** Eastleigh			
30786	*N15*	**9E**	Nine Elms	**70A** Nine Elms	**71A** Eastleigh	**71A** Eastleigh			
30787	*N15*	**BM**	Bournemouth	**70A** Nine Elms	**71A** Eastleigh	**71A** Eastleigh			
30788	*N15*	**9E**	Nine Elms	**70A** Nine Elms	**71A** Eastleigh	**71A** Eastleigh	**71A** Eastleigh		
30789	*N15*	**BM**	Bournemouth	**70D** Basingstoke	**71A** Eastleigh	**71A** Eastleigh			
30790	*N15*	**BM**	Bournemouth	**70D** Basingstoke	**71A** Eastleigh	**71A** Eastleigh	**71A** Eastleigh		
30791	*N15*	**9E**	Nine Elms	**73A** Stewarts Lane	**73A** Stewarts Lane	**71A** Eastleigh	**71A** Eastleigh		
30792	*N15*	**9E**	Nine Elms	**73A** Stewarts Lane	**73A** Stewarts Lane	**73A** Stewarts Lane			
30793	*N15*	**BAT**	Stewarts Lane	**73A** Stewarts Lane	**73A** Stewarts Lane	**73A** Stewarts Lane	**70B** Feltham		
30794	*N15*	**BAT**	Stewarts Lane	**74C** Dover Marine	**73A** Stewarts Lane	**73A** Stewarts Lane	**70D** Basingstoke		
30795	*N15*	**BAT**	Stewarts Lane	**74C** Dover Marine	**73A** Stewarts Lane	**73A** Stewarts Lane	**70B** Feltham		
30796	*N15*	**BAT**	Stewarts Lane	**74C** Dover Marine	**74C** Dover Marine	**74B** Ramsgate	**72B** Salisbury		
30797	*N15*	**BAT**	Stewarts Lane	**73C** Hither Green	**74C** Dover Marine	**74C** Dover Marine			
30798	*N15*	**BA**	Bricklayers Arms	**73B** Bricklayers Arms	**74C** Dover Marine	**74C** Dover Marine	**72B** Salisbury		
30799	*N15*	**BA**	Bricklayers Arms	**73B** Bricklayers Arms	**73B** Bricklayers Arms	**73B** Bricklayers Arms	**72B** Salisbury		
30800	*N15*	**HIT**	Hither Green	**73B** Bricklayers Arms	**73B** Bricklayers Arms	**73B** Bricklayers Arms	**71A** Eastleigh		
30801	*N15*	**AFD**	Ashford	**74A** Ashford	**73B** Bricklayers Arms	**73B** Bricklayers Arms			
30802	*N15*	**AFD**	Ashford	**74A** Ashford	**74A** Ashford	**74A** Ashford	**71A** Eastleigh		
30803	*N15*	**AFD**	Ashford	**74A** Ashford	**74A** Ashford	**74A** Ashford	**71A** Eastleigh		
30804	*N15*	**AFD**	Ashford	**74A** Ashford	**74A** Ashford	**74A** Ashford	**71A** Eastleigh		
30805	*N15*	**AFD**	Ashford	**74A** Ashford	**74A** Ashford	**74A** Ashford			
30806	*N15*	**AFD**	Ashford	**74C** Dover Marine	**73C** Hither Green	**73C** Hither Green	**71A** Eastleigh		
30823	*S15*	**EXJ**	Exmouth Junction	**72A** Exmouth Junction	**72B** Salisbury	**72B** Salisbury	**72B** Salisbury	**70E** Salisbury	
30824	*S15*	**EXJ**	Exmouth Junction	**72A** Exmouth Junction	**72B** Salisbury	**72B** Salisbury	**72B** Salisbury	**70E** Salisbury	
30825	*S15*	**EXJ**	Exmouth Junction	**72A** Exmouth Junction	**72B** Salisbury	**72B** Salisbury	**72B** Salisbury	**70E** Salisbury	
30826	*S15*	**EXJ**	Exmouth Junction	**72B** Salisbury	**72B** Salisbury	**72B** Salisbury	**72B** Salisbury		
30827	*S15*	**EXJ**	Exmouth Junction	**72B** Salisbury	**72B** Salisbury	**72B** Salisbury	**72B** Salisbury	**70E** Salisbury	
30828	*S15*	**SAL**	Salisbury	**72B** Salisbury	**72B** Salisbury	**72B** Salisbury	**72B** Salisbury	**70E** Salisbury	
30829	*S15*	**SAL**	Salisbury	**72B** Salisbury	**72B** Salisbury	**72B** Salisbury	**72B** Salisbury	**70E** Salisbury	
30830	*S15*	**SAL**	Salisbury	**72B** Salisbury	**72B** Salisbury	**72B** Salisbury	**72B** Salisbury	**70E** Salisbury	
30831	*S15*	**SAL**	Salisbury	**72B** Salisbury	**72B** Salisbury	**72B** Salisbury	**72B** Salisbury	**70E** Salisbury	
30832	*S15*	**SAL**	Salisbury	**72B** Salisbury	**72B** Salisbury	**72B** Salisbury	**72B** Salisbury	**70E** Salisbury	
30833	*S15*	**FEL**	Feltham	**70B** Feltham	**70B** Feltham	**70B** Feltham	**70B** Feltham	**70B** Feltham	
30834	*S15*	**FEL**	Feltham	**70B** Feltham	**70B** Feltham	**70B** Feltham	**70B** Feltham	**70B** Feltham	
30835	*S15*	**FEL**	Feltham	**70B** Feltham	**75B** Redhill	**75B** Redhill	**75B** Redhill	**75B** Redhill	
30836	*S15*	**FEL**	Feltham	**70B** Feltham	**75B** Redhill	**75B** Redhill	**75B** Redhill	**75B** Redhill	
30837	*S15*	**FEL**	Feltham	**70B** Feltham	**75B** Redhill	**75B** Redhill	**75B** Redhill	**70B** Feltham	
30838	*S15*	**FEL**	Feltham	**70B** Feltham	**70B** Feltham	**70B** Feltham	**70B** Feltham	**70B** Feltham	
30839	*S15*	**FEL**	Feltham	**70B** Feltham	**70B** Feltham	**70B** Feltham	**70B** Feltham	**70B** Feltham	
30840	*S15*	**FEL**	Feltham	**70B** Feltham	**70B** Feltham	**70B** Feltham	**70B** Feltham	**70B** Feltham	
30841	*S15*	**FEL**	Feltham	**72A** Exmouth Junction	**72A** Exmouth Junction	**72A** Exmouth Junction	**72A** Exmouth Junction	**72A** Exmouth Junction	
30842	*S15*	**FEL**	Feltham	**72A** Exmouth Junction	**72A** Exmouth Junction	**72A** Exmouth Junction	**72A** Exmouth Junction	**72A** Exmouth Junction	
30843	*S15*	**EXJ**	Exmouth Junction	**72A** Exmouth Junction	**72A** Exmouth Junction	**72A** Exmouth Junction	**72A** Exmouth Junction	**72A** Exmouth Junction	
30844	*S15*	**EXJ**	Exmouth Junction	**72A** Exmouth Junction	**72A** Exmouth Junction	**72A** Exmouth Junction	**72A** Exmouth Junction	**72A** Exmouth Junction	
30845	*S15*	**EXJ**	Exmouth Junction	**72A** Exmouth Junction	**72A** Exmouth Junction	**72A** Exmouth Junction	**72A** Exmouth Junction	**72A** Exmouth Junction	
30846	*S15*	**EXJ**	Exmouth Junction	**72A** Exmouth Junction	**72A** Exmouth Junction	**72A** Exmouth Junction	**72A** Exmouth Junction	**72A** Exmouth Junction	
30847	*S15*	**EXJ**	Exmouth Junction	**72A** Exmouth Junction	**72B** Salisbury	**72B** Salisbury	**75B** Redhill	**75B** Redhill	
30850	*LN*	**BM**	Bournemouth	**71A** Eastleigh	**71A** Eastleigh	**71A** Eastleigh	**71A** Eastleigh		
30851	*LN*	**BM**	Bournemouth	**71A** Eastleigh	**71A** Eastleigh	**71A** Eastleigh	**71A** Eastleigh		
30852	*LN*	**BM**	Bournemouth	**71A** Eastleigh	**71A** Eastleigh	**71A** Eastleigh	**71A** Eastleigh		
30853	*LN*	**BM**	Bournemouth	**71A** Eastleigh	**71A** Eastleigh	**71A** Eastleigh	**71A** Eastleigh		
30854	*LN*	**BM**	Bournemouth	**71A** Eastleigh	**71A** Eastleigh	**71A** Eastleigh	**71A** Eastleigh		
30855	*LN*	**BM**	Bournemouth	**71A** Eastleigh	**71A** Eastleigh	**71A** Eastleigh	**71A** Eastleigh		
30856	*LN*	**9E**	Nine Elms	**71A** Eastleigh	**71A** Eastleigh	**71A** Eastleigh	**71A** Eastleigh		
30857	*LN*	**9E**	Nine Elms	**71A** Eastleigh	**71A** Eastleigh	**71A** Eastleigh	**71A** Eastleigh		
30858	*LN*	**9E**	Nine Elms	**70A** Nine Elms	**70A** Nine Elms	**70A** Nine Elms	**71A** Eastleigh		
30859	*LN*	**9E**	Nine Elms	**70A** Nine Elms	**70A** Nine Elms	**70A** Nine Elms	**71A** Eastleigh		
30860	*LN*	**9E**	Nine Elms	**70A** Nine Elms	**70A** Nine Elms	**70A** Nine Elms	**71A** Eastleigh		
30861	*LN*	**9E**	Nine Elms	**71B** Bournemouth	**71B** Bournemouth	**71A** Eastleigh	**71A** Eastleigh		
30862	*LN*	**BM**	Bournemouth	**71B** Bournemouth	**71B** Bournemouth	**71A** Eastleigh	**71A** Eastleigh		
30863	*LN*	**BM**	Bournemouth	**71B** Bournemouth	**71B** Bournemouth	**71A** Eastleigh	**71A** Eastleigh		
30864	*LN*	**BM**	Bournemouth	**71B** Bournemouth	**71B** Bournemouth	**71B** Bournemouth	**71A** Eastleigh		
30865	*LN*	**BM**	Bournemouth	**71B** Bournemouth	**71B** Bournemouth	**71B** Bournemouth	**71A** Eastleigh		
30900	*V*	**STL**	St. Leonards	**74E** St. Leonards	**74E** St. Leonards	**74E** St. Leonards	**75A** Brighton		
30901	*V*	**STL**	St. Leonards	**74E** St. Leonards	**74E** St. Leonards	**74E** St. Leonards	**75A** Brighton		
30902	*V*	**STL**	St. Leonards	**74E** St. Leonards	**74E** St. Leonards	**74E** St. Leonards	**70A** Nine Elms		
30903	*V*	**STL**	St. Leonards	**74E** St. Leonards	**74E** St. Leonards	**74E** St. Leonards	**70A** Nine Elms		
30904	*V*	**STL**	St. Leonards	**74E** St. Leonards	**74E** St. Leonards	**74E** St. Leonards	**70D** Basingstoke		
30905	*V*	**STL**	St. Leonards	**74E** St. Leonards	**74E** St. Leonards	**74E** St. Leonards	**70D** Basingstoke		
30906	*V*	**STL**	St. Leonards	**74E** St. Leonards	**74E** St. Leonards	**74E** St. Leonards	**70A** Nine Elms		
30907	*V*	**STL**	St. Leonards	**74E** St. Leonards	**74E** St. Leonards	**74E** St. Leonards	**70A** Nine Elms		
30908	*V*	**STL**	St. Leonards	**74E** St. Leonards	**74E** St. Leonards	**74E** St. Leonards	**70D** Basingstoke		
30909	*V*	**STL**	St. Leonards	**74E** St. Leonards	**74E** St. Leonards	**74E** St. Leonards	**70A** Nine Elms		
30910	*V*	**STL**	St. Leonards	**74E** St. Leonards	**74E** St. Leonards	**74E** St. Leonards	**70A** Nine Elms		
30911	*V*	**RAM**	Ramsgate	**74B** Ramsgate	**74B** Ramsgate	**74B** Ramsgate	**70A** Nine Elms		
30912	*V*	**RAM**	Ramsgate	**74B** Ramsgate	**74B** Ramsgate	**74B** Ramsgate	**70A** Nine Elms		
30913	*V*	**RAM**	Ramsgate	**74B** Ramsgate	**74B** Ramsgate	**74B** Ramsgate	**70A** Nine Elms		
30914	*V*	**RAM**	Ramsgate	**74B** Ramsgate	**74B** Ramsgate	**74B** Ramsgate	**75A** Brighton		
30915	*V*	**RAM**	Ramsgate	**74B** Ramsgate	**73A** Stewarts Lane	**74B** Ramsgate	**75A** Brighton		
30916	*V*	**RAM**	Ramsgate	**74B** Ramsgate	**74B** Ramsgate	**74B** Ramsgate	**75A** Brighton		
30917	*V*	**RAM**	Ramsgate	**74B** Ramsgate	**74B** Ramsgate	**74B** Ramsgate	**75A** Brighton		
30918	*V*	**RAM**	Ramsgate	**74B** Ramsgate	**74C** Dover Marine	**74B** Ramsgate	**70A** Nine Elms		
30919	*V*	**RAM**	Ramsgate	**73B** Bricklayers Arms	**74C** Dover Marine	**74C** Dover Marine	**70A** Nine Elms		
30920	*V*	**RAM**	Ramsgate	**73B** Bricklayers Arms	**74C** Dover Marine	**74E** St. Leonards	**73A** Stewarts Lane		
30921	*V*	**BA**	Bricklayers Arms	**73B** Bricklayers Arms	**74C** Dover Marine	**74C** Dover Marine	**73A** Stewarts Lane		
30922	*V*	**BA**	Bricklayers Arms	**74E** St. Leonards	**74B** Ramsgate	**74B** Ramsgate	**73A** Stewarts Lane		
30923	*V*	**BA**	Bricklayers Arms	**74E** St. Leonards	**74C** Dover Marine	**74E** St. Leonards	**73A** Stewarts Lane		

No.	Class	1948		1951	1954	1957	1960	1963	1966
30924	*V*	DOV	Dover Marine	**74C** Dover Marine	**73B** Bricklayers Arms	**73B** Bricklayers Arms	**73B** Bricklayers Arms		
30925	*V*	DOV	Dover Marine	**74C** Dover Marine	**73B** Bricklayers Arms	**73B** Bricklayers Arms	**73B** Bricklayers Arms		
30926	*V*	DOV	Dover Marine	**74C** Dover Marine	**73B** Bricklayers Arms	**73B** Bricklayers Arms	**73B** Bricklayers Arms		
30927	*V*	DOV	Dover Marine	**74C** Dover Marine	**73B** Bricklayers Arms	**73B** Bricklayers Arms	**73B** Bricklayers Arms		
30928	*V*	BA	Bricklayers Arms	**73B** Bricklayers Arms	**73B** Bricklayers Arms	**73B** Bricklayers Arms	**73B** Bricklayers Arms		
30929	*V*	BA	Bricklayers Arms	**73B** Bricklayers Arms	**73B** Bricklayers Arms	**73B** Bricklayers Arms	**73B** Bricklayers Arms		
30930	*V*	BA	Bricklayers Arms	**73B** Bricklayers Arms	**73B** Bricklayers Arms	**74E** St. Leonards	**73B** Bricklayers Arms		
30931	*V*	BA	Bricklayers Arms	**73B** Bricklayers Arms	**73B** Bricklayers Arms	**73B** Bricklayers Arms	**73B** Bricklayers Arms		
30932	*V*	BA	Bricklayers Arms	**73B** Bricklayers Arms	**73B** Bricklayers Arms	**73B** Bricklayers Arms	**73F** Ashford		
30933	*V*	BA	Bricklayers Arms	**73B** Bricklayers Arms	**73B** Bricklayers Arms	**73B** Bricklayers Arms	**73F** Ashford		
30934	*V*	BA	Bricklayers Arms	**73B** Bricklayers Arms	**73B** Bricklayers Arms	**73B** Bricklayers Arms	**73F** Ashford		
30935	*V*	BA	Bricklayers Arms	**74E** St. Leonards	**73B** Bricklayers Arms	**73B** Bricklayers Arms	**73F** Ashford		
30936	*V*	BA	Bricklayers Arms	**73B** Bricklayers Arms	**73B** Bricklayers Arms	**73B** Bricklayers Arms	**73F** Ashford		
30937	*V*	BA	Bricklayers Arms	**73B** Bricklayers Arms	**73B** Bricklayers Arms	**73B** Bricklayers Arms	**73F** Ashford		
30938	*V*	BA	Bricklayers Arms	**73B** Bricklayers Arms	**73B** Bricklayers Arms	**73B** Bricklayers Arms	**73H** Dover Marine		
30939	*V*	BA	Bricklayers Arms	**73B** Bricklayers Arms	**73B** Bricklayers Arms	**73B** Bricklayers Arms	**73H** Dover Marine		
30948	*EKR*		East Kent Railway						
30949	*KESR*	9E	Nine Elms						
30950	*Z*	HIT	Hither Green	**71A** Eastleigh	**75A** Brighton	**72A** Exmouth Junction	**72A** Exmouth Junction		
30951	*Z*	HIT	Hither Green	**73D** Gillingham	**75E** Three Bridges	**74A** Ashford	**72A** Exmouth Junction		
30952	*Z*	ELH	Eastleigh	**71A** Eastleigh	**71A** Eastleigh	**74A** Ashford	**72A** Exmouth Junction		
30953	*Z*	HIT	Hither Green	**74A** Ashford	**74A** Ashford	**71H** Templecombe	**72A** Exmouth Junction		
30954	*Z*	EXJ	Exmouth Junction	**72A** Exmouth Junction	**72A** Exmouth Junction	**72B** Salisbury	**72A** Exmouth Junction		
30955	*Z*	HIT	Hither Green	**70A** Nine Elms	**71A** Eastleigh	**74A** Ashford	**72A** Exmouth Junction		
30956	*Z*	HIT	Hither Green	**71A** Eastleigh	**71A** Eastleigh	**72A** Exmouth Junction	**72A** Exmouth Junction		
30957	*Z*	SAL	Salisbury	**72B** Salisbury	**72B** Salisbury	**72B** Salisbury	**72A** Exmouth Junction		
31002	*F1*	GIL	Gillingham						
31003	*O1*	GIL	Gillingham						
31004	*C*	RAM	Ramsgate	**74B** Ramsgate	**74B** Ramsgate	**74B** Ramsgate	**70A** Nine Elms		
31005	*H*	BAT	Stewarts Lane	**73A** Stewarts Lane	**73A** Stewarts Lane	**74A** Ashford	**73F** Ashford	**75F** Tunbridge Wells West	
31007	*O1*	GIL	Gillingham						
31010	*R1*[1]	AFD	Ashford	**74A** Ashford	**74A** Ashford	**74E** St. Leonards			
31013	*B1*	GIL	Gillingham						
31014	*O1*	GIL	Gillingham						
31016	*H*	RAM	Ramsgate	**75F** Tunbridge Wells West					
31018	*C*	HIT	Hither Green	**73C** Hither Green	**73C** Hither Green	**73C** Hither Green			
31019	*E1*[1]	BAT	Stewarts Lane	**73A** Stewarts Lane	**73A** Stewarts Lane	**73A** Stewarts Lane	**72B** Salisbury		
31027	*P*	DOV	Dover Marine	**74C** Dover Marine	**74C** Dover Marine	**74C** Dover Marine	**73H** Dover Marine		
31028	*F1*	HIT	Hither Green						
31031	*F1*	HIT	Hither Green						
31033	*C*	BA	Bricklayers Arms	**73B** Bricklayers Arms	**73C** Hither Green	**73C** Hither Green	**70B** Feltham		
31036	*E*	BA	Bricklayers Arms	**73B** Bricklayers Arms					
31037	*C*	STL	St. Leonards	**74E** St. Leonards	**74D** Tonbridge	**74A** Ashford	**70C** Guildford		
31038	*C*	STL	St. Leonards	**74E** St. Leonards	**74D** Tonbridge				
31039	*O1*	GIL	Gillingham						
31041	*O1*	STL	St. Leonards	**74A** Ashford					
31042	*F1*	RDG	Reading South						
31044	*O1*	HIT	Hither Green	**73B** Bricklayers Arms					
31046	*O1*	FAV	Faversham						
31047	*R1*[1]	FOL	Folkestone Junction	**74C** Folkestone Junction	**74C** Folkestone Junction	**74C** Folkestone Junction	**70A** Nine Elms		
31048	*O1*	TON	Tonbridge	**74A** Ashford	**74A** Ashford	**74A** Ashford	**70A** Nine Elms		
31051	*O1*	GIL	Gillingham						
31054	*C*	HIT	Hither Green	**73C** Hither Green	**73C** Hither Green	**73C** Hither Green	**70C** Guildford		
31057	*D*	TON	Tonbridge	**70E** Reading South					
31059	*C*	HIT	Hither Green	**73C** Hither Green	**73C** Hither Green	**73C** Hither Green			
31061	*C*	HIT	Hither Green	**73C** Hither Green	**73C** Hither Green	**73C** Hither Green	**70A** Nine Elms		
31063	*C*	TON	Tonbridge	**74C** Dover Marine	**73C** Hither Green				
31064	*O1*	GIL	Gillingham	**73B** Bricklayers Arms	**74A** Ashford	**74A** Ashford			
31065	*O1*	DOV	Dover Marine	**74B** Ramsgate	**74A** Ashford	**74C** Dover Marine	**73H** Dover Marine		
31066	*O1*	GIL	Gillingham	**73B** Bricklayers Arms					
31067	*E1*[1]	BAT	Stewarts Lane	**73A** Stewarts Lane	**73A** Stewarts Lane	**73A** Stewarts Lane	**72B** Salisbury		
31068	*C*	HIT	Hither Green	**73B** Bricklayers Arms	**73B** Bricklayers Arms	**73B** Bricklayers Arms	**73B** Bricklayers Arms		
31069	*R1*[1]	AFD	Ashford	**74A** Ashford	**74C** Folkestone Junction	**74C** Folkestone Junction			
31071	*C*	HIT	Hither Green	**73B** Bricklayers Arms	**73B** Bricklayers Arms	**73B** Bricklayers Arms			
31075	*D*	STL	St. Leonards	**70E** Reading South	**70E** Reading South				
31078	*F1*	RDG	Reading South						
31080	*O1*	RAM	Ramsgate						
31086	*C*	TON	Tonbridge	**73D** Gillingham	**73B** Bricklayers Arms	**73B** Bricklayers Arms	**73B** Bricklayers Arms		
31090	*C*	BA	Bricklayers Arms	**73D** Gillingham					
31092	*D*	GIL	Gillingham	**73D** Gillingham					
31093	*O1*	BA	Bricklayers Arms	**74B** Ramsgate					
31102	*C*	BA	Bricklayers Arms	**73B** Bricklayers Arms	**73B** Bricklayers Arms	**73B** Bricklayers Arms	**73B** Bricklayers Arms		
31105	*F1*	GIL	Gillingham						
31106	*O1*	FAV	Faversham						
31107	*R1*[1]	FOL	Folkestone Junction	**74C** Folkestone Junction	**74C** Folkestone Junction	**74C** Folkestone Junction			
31108	*O1*	DOV	Dover Marine	**74C** Dover Marine					
31109	*O1*	HIT	Hither Green						
31112	*C*	GIL	Gillingham	**73D** Gillingham	**73D** Gillingham	**73D** Gillingham	**73H** Dover Marine		
31113	*C*	HIT	Hither Green	**74C** Dover Marine	**74C** Dover Marine	**74C** Dover Marine	**73H** Dover Marine		
31123	*O1*	AFD	Ashford						
31127	*R1*[1]	FOL	Folkestone Junction						
31128	*R1*[1]	FOL	Folkestone Junction	**74C** Folkestone Junction	**74C** Folkestone Junction	**74C** Folkestone Junction			
31145	*D1*[1]	BAT	Stewarts Lane	**73A** Stewarts Lane	**74C** Dover Marine	**70C** Guildford	**70A** Nine Elms		
31147	*R1*[1]	AFD	Ashford	**74C** Folkestone Junction	**74A** Ashford	**74C** Folkestone Junction			
31150	*C*	TON	Tonbridge	**73C** Hither Green	**74C** Dover Marine	**74C** Dover Marine	**73H** Dover Marine		
31151	*F1*	RAM	Ramsgate						
31154	*R1*[1]	FOL	Folkestone Junction	**74C** Folkestone Junction	**74C** Folkestone Junction				
31157	*E*	HOR	Horsham	**73E** Faversham					
31158	*H*	AFD	Ashford	**75F** Tunbridge Wells West	**73D** Gillingham				
31159	*E*	BA	Bricklayers Arms	**73C** Hither Green					
31160	*E1*[1]	BAT	Stewarts Lane	**73B** Bricklayers Arms					
31161	*H*	DOV	Dover Marine	**74A** Ashford	**74E** St. Leonards	**73D** Gillingham	**75E** Three Bridges		
31162	*H*	BA	Bricklayers Arms	**73B** Bricklayers Arms	**74E** St. Leonards	**74E** St. Leonards	**75F** Tunbridge Wells West		
31163	*E1*[1]	BAT	Stewarts Lane						
31164	*H*	RAM	Ramsgate	**74E** St. Leonards	**74D** Tonbridge	**74D** Tonbridge			
31165	*E1*[1]	BAT	Stewarts Lane	**73A** Stewarts Lane	**73B** Bricklayers Arms	**73B** Bricklayers Arms			
31166	*E*	BA	Bricklayers Arms	**73B** Bricklayers Arms	**74D** Tonbridge				
31174	*R1*[1]	STL	St. Leonards	**74E** St. Leonards	**74E** St. Leonards	**74E** St. Leonards			
31175	*E*	BA	Bricklayers Arms	**73B** Bricklayers Arms					
31176	*E*	BA	Bricklayers Arms	**73B** Bricklayers Arms					
31177	*H*	BAT	Stewarts Lane	**73A** Stewarts Lane	**74D** Tonbridge	**74D** Tonbridge	**73J** Tonbridge		
31178	*P*	BTN	Brighton	**75A** Brighton	**74C** Dover Marine	**74C** Dover Marine			
31179	*E1*[1]	BAT	Stewarts Lane						
31182	*H*	RAM	Ramsgate	**75F** Tunbridge Wells West					
31184	*H*	BAT	Stewarts Lane	**73A** Stewarts Lane	**74D** Tonbridge	**74D** Tonbridge			
31191	*C*	HIT	Hither Green	**74C** Dover Marine	**74C** Dover Marine	**74C** Dover Marine			
31193	*H*	TON	Tonbridge	**74D** Tonbridge	**74D** Tonbridge	**74D** Tonbridge	**73J** Tonbridge		
31215	*F1*	GIL	Gillingham						
31217	*B1*	RDG	Reading South						
31218	*C*	AFD	Ashford	**74A** Ashford	**74A** Ashford	**74A** Ashford	**73F** Ashford		
31219	*C*	TON	Tonbridge	**74D** Tonbridge	**74D** Tonbridge	**74A** Ashford			
31221	*C*	TON	Tonbridge	**73D** Gillingham	**73D** Gillingham	**74A** Ashford			
31223	*C*	BA	Bricklayers Arms	**73D** Gillingham	**73D** Gillingham	**74A** Ashford	**73F** Ashford		
31225	*C*	TON	Tonbridge	**73D** Gillingham	**73D** Gillingham				

		1948		1951	1954	1957	1960	1963	1966
31227	C	TON	Tonbridge	**73B** Bricklayers Arms	**73D** Gillingham	**73D** Gillingham			
31229	C	FAV	Faversham	**73E** Faversham	**73D** Gillingham	**73D** Gillingham	**70A** Nine Elms		
31231	F1	FAV	Faversham						
31234	C	GIL	Gillingham	**73A** Stewarts Lane					
31238	O1	GIL	Gillingham						
31239	H	AFD	Ashford	**74A** Ashford	**74D** Tonbridge	**74D** Tonbridge	**73J** Tonbridge		
31242	C	FAV	Faversham	**73E** Faversham	**73D** Gillingham	**73E** Faversham	**70A** Nine Elms		
31243	C	HIT	Hither Green	**74C** Dover Marine	**74C** Dover Marine	**74C** Dover Marine			
31244	C	HIT	Hither Green	**74D** Tonbridge	**74D** Tonbridge	**74D** Tonbridge	**73J** Tonbridge		
31245	C	HIT	Hither Green	**73C** Hither Green	**74B** Ramsgate	**74B** Ramsgate			
31246	D1[1]	DOV	Dover Marine	**74D** Tonbridge	**74C** Dover Marine	**74A** Ashford	**70A** Nine Elms		
31247	D1[1]	BAT	Stewarts Lane	**74C** Dover Marine	**73E** Faversham	**70C** Guildford	**70A** Nine Elms		
31248	O1	HIT	Hither Green	**73C** Hither Green					
31252	C	DOV	Dover Marine	**74B** Ramsgate	**74B** Ramsgate	**74B** Ramsgate			
31253	C	HIT	Hither Green	**73B** Bricklayers Arms	**73E** Faversham	**73A** Stewarts Lane			
31255	C	DOV	Dover Marine	**73D** Gillingham	**73E** Faversham	**73E** Faversham	**73F** Ashford		
31256	C	GIL	Gillingham	**73D** Gillingham	**73E** Faversham	**73E** Faversham	**73F** Ashford		
31257	C	HIT	Hither Green						
31258	O1	HIT	Hither Green	**73C** Hither Green	**74C** Dover Marine	**74C** Dover Marine	**73H** Dover Marine		
31259	H	BAT	Stewarts Lane	**73E** Faversham	**74D** Tonbridge	**74D** Tonbridge			
31260	C	FAV	Faversham	**74A** Ashford					
31261	H	AFD	Ashford	**73A** Stewarts Lane	**74D** Tonbridge	**73A** Stewarts Lane	**73A** Stewarts Lane		
31263	H	BAT	Stewarts Lane	**73A** Stewarts Lane	**73A** Stewarts Lane	**74A** Ashford	**73F** Ashford	**75F** Tunbridge Wells West	
31265	H	RAM	Ramsgate	**74D** Tonbridge	**73A** Stewarts Lane	**73A** Stewarts Lane	**73A** Stewarts Lane		
31266	H	BAT	Stewarts Lane	**73A** Stewarts Lane	**73A** Stewarts Lane	**73A** Stewarts Lane	**75F** Tunbridge Wells West		
31267	C	GIL	Gillingham	**73D** Gillingham	**73E** Faversham	**73B** Bricklayers Arms	**73B** Bricklayers Arms		
31268	C	AFD	Ashford	**73E** Faversham	**73E** Faversham	**73E** Faversham	**70A** Nine Elms		
31269	H	AFD	Ashford	**74A** Ashford	**74E** St. Leonards	**74E** St. Leonards			
31270	C	HIT	Hither Green	**73C** Hither Green	**74D** Tonbridge	**74D** Tonbridge			
31271	C	AFD	Ashford	**74A** Ashford	**74B** Ramsgate	**74B** Ramsgate	**70A** Nine Elms	Ashford Works	(DS240)
31272	C	TON	Tonbridge	**74D** Tonbridge	**74D** Tonbridge	**74D** Tonbridge			
31273	E	HOR	Horsham	**73B** Bricklayers Arms					
31274	H	AFD	Ashford	**74A** Ashford	**74E** St. Leonards	**74E** St. Leonards			
31275	E	BA	Bricklayers Arms	**73B** Bricklayers Arms					
31276	H	DOV	Dover Marine	**74C** Dover Marine	**74A** Ashford	**74A** Ashford	**75A** Brighton		
31277	C	BA	Bricklayers Arms	**74D** Tonbridge	**74D** Tonbridge				
31278	H	GIL	Gillingham	**73B** Bricklayers Arms	**74C** Dover Marine	**75F** Tunbridge Wells West	**75F** Tunbridge Wells West		
31279	H	FAV	Faversham	**74E** St. Leonards	**74E** St. Leonards	**74E** St. Leonards			
31280	C	BA	Bricklayers Arms	**73B** Bricklayers Arms	**73B** Bricklayers Arms	**73B** Bricklayers Arms	**73J** Tonbridge	Ashford Works	
31287	C	BA	Bricklayers Arms	**73D** Gillingham	**73B** Bricklayers Arms	**73B** Bricklayers Arms	**73C** Hither Green		
31291	C	DOV	Dover Marine	**74C** Dover Marine					
31293	C	BAT	Stewarts Lane	**73B** Bricklayers Arms	**73B** Bricklayers Arms	**73B** Bricklayers Arms	**73B** Bricklayers Arms		
31294	C	BA	Bricklayers Arms	**73B** Bricklayers Arms	**73B** Bricklayers Arms				
31295	H	BAT	Stewarts Lane	**73A** Stewarts Lane	**74E** St. Leonards	**74E** St. Leonards			
31297	C	BA	Bricklayers Arms	**73B** Bricklayers Arms	**73B** Bricklayers Arms	**73B** Bricklayers Arms			
31298	C	HIT	Hither Green	**74B** Ramsgate	**74B** Ramsgate	**74B** Ramsgate	**70A** Nine Elms		
31302	1302	BAT	Stewarts Lane						
31305	H	AFD	Ashford	**74A** Ashford	**73E** Faversham	**73B** Bricklayers Arms	**73B** Bricklayers Arms		
31306	H	AFD	Ashford	**74C** Dover Marine	**73D** Gillingham	**73B** Bricklayers Arms	**75F** Tunbridge Wells West		
31307	H	BAT	Stewarts Lane	**73A** Stewarts Lane	**73D** Gillingham	**74A** Ashford	**73F** Ashford		
31308	H	GIL	Gillingham	**73D** Gillingham	**73D** Gillingham	**73D** Gillingham	**75A** Brighton		
31309	H	FAV	Faversham	**73B** Bricklayers Arms	**75B** Redhill				
31310	H	FAV	Faversham	**74E** St. Leonards	**75A** Brighton	**75F** Tunbridge Wells West	**75F** Tunbridge Wells West		
31311	H	BAT	Stewarts Lane	**73A** Stewarts Lane	**75B** Redhill				
31315	E	BA	Bricklayers Arms	**73B** Bricklayers Arms	**73A** Stewarts Lane				
31316	O1	RAM	Ramsgate						
31317	C	GIL	Gillingham	**73D** Gillingham	**74C** Dover Marine	**74C** Dover Marine	**73A** Stewarts Lane		
31319	H	BAT	Stewarts Lane	**74E** St. Leonards	**75A** Brighton	**74A** Ashford	**73J** Tonbridge		
31320	H	TON	Tonbridge	**74D** Tonbridge	**75A** Brighton				
31321	H	BAT	Stewarts Lane	**73A** Stewarts Lane	**73A** Stewarts Lane	**73A** Stewarts Lane			
31322	H	AFD	Ashford	**74A** Ashford	**75F** Tunbridge Wells West	**73D** Gillingham	**73J** Tonbridge		
31323	P	FOL	Folkestone Junction	**74C** Dover Marine	**74C** Dover Marine	**74C** Dover Marine	**73H** Dover Marine		
31324	H	BA	Bricklayers Arms	**73B** Bricklayers Arms	**74B** Ramsgate	**74B** Ramsgate	**70A** Nine Elms		
31325	P	DOV	Dover Marine	**71A** Eastleigh	**75A** Brighton	**75A** Brighton	**75A** Brighton		
31326	H	BA	Bricklayers Arms	**73B** Bricklayers Arms	**74B** Ramsgate	**74B** Ramsgate	**73H** Dover Marine		
31327	H	TON	Tonbridge	**74D** Tonbridge	**74A** Ashford	**75F** Tunbridge Wells West			
31328	H	BA	Bricklayers Arms	**74E** St. Leonards	**74C** Dover Marine	**74C** Dover Marine	**73H** Dover Marine		
31329	H	BAT	Stewarts Lane	**73A** Stewarts Lane	**74C** Dover Marine	**75F** Tunbridge Wells West			
31335	R1[1]	STL	St. Leonards	**74E** St. Leonards	**74E** St. Leonards				
31337	R1[1]	FOL	Folkestone Junction	**74C** Folkestone Junction	**74C** Folkestone Junction	**74C** Folkestone Junction	**70A** Nine Elms		
31339	R1[1]	AFD	Ashford	**74A** Ashford	**74A** Ashford	**74C** Folkestone Junction			
31340	R1[1]	FOL	Folkestone Junction	**74C** Folkestone Junction	**74C** Folkestone Junction	**74C** Folkestone Junction			
31369	O1	FAV	Faversham	**73E** Faversham					
31370	O1	TON	Tonbridge	**74A** Ashford	**74A** Ashford	**74A** Ashford	**70A** Nine Elms		
31371	O1	on loan	East Kent Railway						
31372	O1	on loan	East Kent Railway						
31373	O1	DOV	Dover Marine	**74C** Dover Marine					
31374	O1	HIT	Hither Green						
31377	O1	HIT	Hither Green						
31378	O1	GIL	Gillingham						
31379	O1	FAV	Faversham	**74A** Ashford					
31380	O1	TON	Tonbridge						
31381	O1	DOV	Dover Marine	**74C** Dover Marine					
31383	O1	on loan	East Kent Railway	**74C** Dover Marine					
31384	O1	GIL	Gillingham						
31385	O1	HIT	Hither Green						
31386	O1	HIT	Hither Green						
31388	O1	BA	Bricklayers Arms						
31389	O1	BA	Bricklayers Arms						
31390	O1	AFD	Ashford	**74B** Ramsgate					
31391	O1	GIL	Gillingham	**73C** Hither Green					
31395	O1	BA	Bricklayers Arms	**73B** Bricklayers Arms					
31396	O1	TON	Tonbridge						
31397	O1	BA	Bricklayers Arms						
31398	O1	BA	Bricklayers Arms						
31400	N	AFD	Ashford	**74A** Ashford	**74A** Ashford	**74A** Ashford	**73F** Ashford	**75A** Brighton	
31401	N	AFD	Ashford	**74A** Ashford	**74A** Ashford	**74A** Ashford	**73F** Ashford	**75A** Brighton	
31402	N	AFD	Ashford	**74A** Ashford	**74A** Ashford	**74A** Ashford	**73F** Ashford	**75A** Brighton	
31403	N	AFD	Ashford	**74A** Ashford	**74A** Ashford	**74A** Ashford	**73F** Ashford	**75A** Brighton	
31404	N	AFD	Ashford	**74A** Ashford	**74A** Ashford	**74A** Ashford	**73F** Ashford	**70E** Salisbury	
31405	N	BAT	Stewarts Lane	**74A** Ashford	**74A** Ashford	**74A** Ashford	**73F** Ashford	**71G** Weymouth	**70C** Guildford
31406	N	RED	Redhill	**74A** Ashford	**74A** Ashford	**74A** Ashford	**73F** Ashford	**72A** Exmouth Junction	
31407	N	EXJ	Exmouth Junction	**72A** Exmouth Junction	**74A** Ashford	**74A** Ashford	**73F** Ashford	**71G** Weymouth	
31408	N	EXJ	Exmouth Junction	**72A** Exmouth Junction	**73B** Bricklayers Arms	**73A** Stewarts Lane	**73F** Ashford	**70E** Salisbury	**70C** Guildford
31409	N	EXJ	Exmouth Junction	**73A** Stewarts Lane	**73A** Stewarts Lane	**73A** Stewarts Lane	**73F** Ashford		
31410	N	BAT	Stewarts Lane	**73A** Stewarts Lane	**73A** Stewarts Lane	**73A** Stewarts Lane	**73A** Stewarts Lane	**75D** Stewarts Lane	
31411	N	BAT	Stewarts Lane	**73A** Stewarts Lane	**73A** Stewarts Lane	**73A** Stewarts Lane	**73A** Stewarts Lane	**75D** Stewarts Lane	**70C** Guildford
31412	N	BAT	Stewarts Lane	**73A** Stewarts Lane	**73A** Stewarts Lane	**73A** Stewarts Lane	**73A** Stewarts Lane	**75D** Stewarts Lane	
31413	N	BAT	Stewarts Lane	**73A** Stewarts Lane	**73A** Stewarts Lane	**73A** Stewarts Lane	**73H** Dover Marine	**71A** Eastleigh	
31414	N	BAT	Stewarts Lane	**73A** Stewarts Lane	**73A** Stewarts Lane	**73A** Stewarts Lane	**73H** Dover Marine		
31425	O1	BA	Bricklayers Arms	**74C** Dover Marine	**74C** Dover Marine	**74C** Dover Marine			
31426	O1	AFD	Ashford						
31428	O1	BA	Bricklayers Arms						
31429	O1	BA	Bricklayers Arms						

		1948		1951	1954	1957	1960	1963	1966
31430	*O1*	GIL	Gillingham	**74C** Dover Marine	**74C** Dover Marine	**74C** Dover Marine			
31432	*O1*	STL	St. Leonards	**73C** Hither Green					
31434	*O1*	AFD	Ashford	**74C** Dover Marine	**74C** Dover Marine	**74C** Dover Marine			
31437	*O1*	TON	Tonbridge						
31438	*O1*	FAV	Faversham						
31439	*O1*	GIL	Gillingham						
31440	*B1*	FAV	Faversham						
31443	*B1*	DOV	Dover Marine	**70E** Reading South					
31445	*B1*	BAT	Stewarts Lane						
31446	*B1*	RDG	Reading South						
31448	*B1*	FAV	Faversham						
31449	*B1*	GIL	Gillingham						
31450	*B1*	DOV	Dover Marine						
31451	*B1*	RAM	Ramsgate						
31452	*B1*	RAM	Ramsgate						
31453	*B1*	RAM	Ramsgate						
31454	*B1*	BAT	Stewarts Lane						
31455	*B1*	HIT	Hither Green						
31457	*B1*	HIT	Hither Green						
31459	*B1*	RDG	Reading South						
31460	*C*	BA	Bricklayers Arms						
31461	*C*	TON	Tonbridge	**74D** Tonbridge	**73A** Stewarts Lane	**73A** Stewarts Lane			
31470	*D1*[1]	DOV	Dover Marine	**74C** Dover Marine	**73E** Faversham	**74D** Tonbridge			
31477	*D*	AFD	Ashford	**74A** Ashford					
31480	*C*	HIT	Hither Green	**73C** Hither Green	**73C** Hither Green	**73C** Hither Green	**73B** Bricklayers Arms		
31481	*C*	FAV	Faversham	**73E** Faversham	**73E** Faversham	**73E** Faversham	**73H** Dover Marine		
31486	*C*	HIT	Hither Green	**73C** Hither Green					
31487	*D1*[1]	FAV	Faversham	**73A** Stewarts Lane	**73E** Faversham	**74D** Tonbridge	**73J** Tonbridge		
31488	*D*	TON	Tonbridge	**75B** Redhill	**70E** Reading South				
31489	*D1*[1]	FAV	Faversham	**73E** Faversham	**73E** Faversham	**74D** Tonbridge	**73J** Tonbridge		
31490	*D*	TON	Tonbridge	**75B** Redhill					
31491	*E*	BA	Bricklayers Arms	**73B** Bricklayers Arms					
31492	*D1*[1]	BAT	Stewarts Lane	**73D** Gillingham	**73E** Faversham	**74D** Tonbridge	**73J** Tonbridge		
31493	*D*	FAV	Faversham	**74E** St. Leonards	**74E** St. Leonards				
31494	*D1*[1]	BAT	Stewarts Lane	**73D** Gillingham	**73E** Faversham	**73E** Faversham	**70A** Nine Elms		
31495	*C*	FAV	Faversham	**73E** Faversham	**73D** Gillingham	**73D** Gillingham	**70A** Nine Elms		
31496	*D*	FAV	Faversham	**74D** Tonbridge	**70E** Reading South				
31497	*E1*[1]	BAT	Stewarts Lane	**73A** Stewarts Lane	**73B** Bricklayers Arms	**73B** Bricklayers Arms	**72B** Salisbury		
31498	*C*	BAT	Stewarts Lane	**73D** Gillingham	**73D** Gillingham	**73C** Hither Green	**73C** Hither Green		
31500	*H*	BA	Bricklayers Arms	**73A** Stewarts Lane	**74A** Ashford	**74B** Ramsgate	**73J** Tonbridge		
31501	*D*	FAV	Faversham	**73D** Gillingham					
31502	*D1*[1]	FAV	Faversham	**73E** Faversham					
31503	*H*	TON	Tonbridge	**74C** Dover Marine	**73E** Faversham	**73E** Faversham			
31504	*E1*[1]	BAT	Stewarts Lane	**73A** Stewarts Lane	**73A** Stewarts Lane	**73A** Stewarts Lane			
31505	*D1*[1]	FAV	Faversham	**73E** Faversham	**73E** Faversham	**73E** Faversham	**70A** Nine Elms		
31506	*E1*[1]	BAT	Stewarts Lane	**73A** Stewarts Lane	**73A** Stewarts Lane	**73A** Stewarts Lane			
31507	*E1*[1]	BAT	Stewarts Lane	**73B** Bricklayers Arms	**73B** Bricklayers Arms	**73B** Bricklayers Arms	**72B** Salisbury		
31508	*C*	BAT	Stewarts Lane	**73B** Bricklayers Arms	**73D** Gillingham	**73D** Gillingham			
31509	*D1*[1]	FAV	Faversham	**74D** Tonbridge	**73D** Gillingham	**73E** Faversham	**70A** Nine Elms		
31510	*C*	GIL	Gillingham	**73D** Gillingham	**73D** Gillingham	**73D** Gillingham	**70A** Nine Elms		
31511	*E1*[1]	BAT	Stewarts Lane						
31512	*H*	DOV	Dover Marine	**74C** Dover Marine	**74A** Ashford	**73D** Gillingham	**73J** Tonbridge		
31513	*C*	TON	Tonbridge	**74A** Ashford	**74A** Ashford				
31514	*E*	BAT	Stewarts Lane	**74A** Ashford					
31515	*E*	BAT	Stewarts Lane	**70E** Reading South					
31516	*E*	BAT	Stewarts Lane	**73D** Gillingham					
31517	*H*	DOV	Dover Marine	**74D** Tonbridge	**75F** Tunbridge Wells West	**74D** Tonbridge	**73J** Tonbridge		
31518	*H*	TON	Tonbridge	**74C** Dover Marine	**73D** Gillingham	**73D** Gillingham	**73J** Tonbridge	**75F** Tunbridge Wells West	
31519	*H*	TON	Tonbridge	**74B** Ramsgate	**74E** St. Leonards	**74E** St. Leonards	**73J** Tonbridge		
31520	*H*	DOV	Dover Marine	**74A** Ashford	**75F** Tunbridge Wells West	**74E** St. Leonards	**73J** Tonbridge		
31521	*H*	RAM	Ramsgate	**74B** Ramsgate	**74A** Ashford	**75E** Three Bridges	**75E** Three Bridges		
31522	*H*	RAM	Ramsgate	**74B** Ramsgate	**74A** Ashford	**74A** Ashford	**75F** Tunbridge Wells West	**75F** Tunbridge Wells West	
31523	*H*	RAM	Ramsgate	**74D** Tonbridge	**74D** Tonbridge	**74D** Tonbridge			
31530	*H*	DOV	Dover Marine	**74C** Dover Marine	**74D** Tonbridge	**75E** Three Bridges	**75A** Brighton		
31531	*H*	DOV	Dover Marine	**74C** Dover Marine	**74C** Dover Marine				
31532	*H*	DOV	Dover Marine	**73E** Faversham					
31533	*H*	BA	Bricklayers Arms	**73B** Bricklayers Arms	**73B** Bricklayers Arms	**73B** Bricklayers Arms	**73B** Bricklayers Arms		
31540	*H*	TON	Tonbridge	**74C** Dover Marine	**73B** Bricklayers Arms	**73B** Bricklayers Arms	**73B** Bricklayers Arms		
31541	*H*	BA	Bricklayers Arms	**73B** Bricklayers Arms					
31542	*H*	BA	Bricklayers Arms	**73B** Bricklayers Arms	**73B** Bricklayers Arms	**74C** Dover Marine	**73H** Dover Marine		
31543	*H*	TON	Tonbridge	**73B** Bricklayers Arms	**74D** Tonbridge	**74D** Tonbridge	**75A** Brighton	**75F** Tunbridge Wells West	
31544	*H*	9E	Nine Elms	**73B** Bricklayers Arms	**73B** Bricklayers Arms	**75F** Tunbridge Wells West	**75F** Tunbridge Wells West	**75F** Tunbridge Wells West	
31545	*D1*[1]	DOV	Dover Marine	**74C** Dover Marine	**73D** Gillingham	**73A** Stewarts Lane	**70A** Nine Elms		
31546	*H*	BA	Bricklayers Arms	**73B** Bricklayers Arms					
31547	*E*	BA	Bricklayers Arms	**74A** Ashford					
31548	*H*	DOV	Dover Marine	**74D** Tonbridge	**74D** Tonbridge	**74D** Tonbridge			
31549	*D*	AFD	Ashford	**74D** Tonbridge	**74A** Ashford				
31550	*H*	BA	Bricklayers Arms	**74D** Tonbridge	**75B** Redhill	**73A** Stewarts Lane	**73A** Stewarts Lane		
31551	*H*	9E	Nine Elms	**70A** Nine Elms	**75B** Redhill	**73A** Stewarts Lane	**73A** Stewarts Lane	**75F** Tunbridge Wells West	
31552	*H*	9E	Nine Elms	**70A** Nine Elms	**74D** Tonbridge	**73A** Stewarts Lane	**70A** Nine Elms		
31553	*H*	9E	Nine Elms	**70A** Nine Elms	**73B** Bricklayers Arms	**73B** Bricklayers Arms	**70A** Nine Elms		
31554	*H*	BAT	Stewarts Lane	**70A** Nine Elms	**74D** Tonbridge	**74D** Tonbridge			
31555	*P*	DOV	Dover Marine	**74C** Dover Marine	**73A** Stewarts Lane				
31556	*P*	DOV	Dover Marine	**75A** Brighton	**75A** Brighton	**75A** Brighton	**75A** Brighton		
31557	*P*	BTN	Brighton	**74C** Dover Marine	**73A** Stewarts Lane	**73A** Stewarts Lane			
31558	*P*	FOL	Folkestone Junction	**73A** Stewarts Lane	**71A** Eastleigh	**73A** Stewarts Lane	**73A** Stewarts Lane		
31572	*C*	HIT	Hither Green	**74A** Ashford	**74A** Ashford				
31573	*C*	GIL	Gillingham	**73D** Gillingham	**73A** Stewarts Lane	**73A** Stewarts Lane	**73C** Hither Green		
31574	*D*	AFD	Ashford	**74D** Tonbridge	**74A** Ashford				
31575	*C*	BAT	Stewarts Lane	**73A** Stewarts Lane	**73A** Stewarts Lane	**73A** Stewarts Lane	**73A** Stewarts Lane		
31576	*C*	BAT	Stewarts Lane	**73A** Stewarts Lane	**73A** Stewarts Lane	**73A** Stewarts Lane			
31577	*D*	AFD	Ashford	**74A** Ashford	**74A** Ashford				
31578	*C*	BAT	Stewarts Lane	**73A** Stewarts Lane	**73A** Stewarts Lane	**73A** Stewarts Lane	**73A** Stewarts Lane		
31579	*C*	GIL	Gillingham	**73D** Gillingham	**73A** Stewarts Lane	**73A** Stewarts Lane	**70A** Nine Elms		
31580	*C*	TON	Tonbridge	**74D** Tonbridge					
31581	*C*	HIT	Hither Green	**73C** Hither Green	**73A** Stewarts Lane	**73A** Stewarts Lane	**73A** Stewarts Lane		
31582	*C*	BAT	Stewarts Lane	**73A** Stewarts Lane	**73A** Stewarts Lane	**73A** Stewarts Lane			
31583	*C*	GIL	Gillingham	**73D** Gillingham	**73A** Stewarts Lane	**74D** Tonbridge	**73A** Stewarts Lane		
31584	*C*	BA	Bricklayers Arms	**73B** Bricklayers Arms	**73A** Stewarts Lane	**73A** Stewarts Lane	**73A** Stewarts Lane		
31585	*C*	GIL	Gillingham	**73D** Gillingham	**74D** Tonbridge	**74D** Tonbridge			
31586	*D*	TON	Tonbridge	**73D** Gillingham	**70E** Reading South				
31587	*E*	RED	Redhill	**74E** St. Leonards					
31588	*C*	GIL	Gillingham	**73D** Gillingham	**74D** Tonbridge	**74D** Tonbridge	**73J** Tonbridge		
31589	*C*	AFD	Ashford	**74A** Ashford	**74A** Ashford	**74A** Ashford	**73F** Ashford		
31590	*C*	TON	Tonbridge	**74D** Tonbridge	**74D** Tonbridge	**74D** Tonbridge	**73J** Tonbridge		
31591	*D*	TON	Tonbridge	**74A** Ashford	**75B** Redhill				
31592	*C*	RAM	Ramsgate	**74B** Ramsgate	**74B** Ramsgate	**74B** Ramsgate	**70A** Nine Elms	Ashford Works	(DS239)
31593	*C*	TON	Tonbridge	**74D** Tonbridge	**73D** Gillingham	**74A** Ashford			
31595	*J*	AFD	Ashford	**74A** Ashford					
31596	*J*	AFD	Ashford	**74A** Ashford					
31597	*J*	AFD	Ashford						
31598	*J*	AFD	Ashford						
31599	*J*	AFD	Ashford						
31602	*T*	BAT	Stewarts Lane	**70E** Reading South					

		1948	1951	1954	1957	1960	1963	1966
31604	T	BAT Stewarts Lane						
31610	U	RDG Reading South	70E Reading South	70E Reading South	72C Yeovil Town	72C Yeovil Town		
31611	U	RDG Reading South	70E Reading South	70E Reading South	70F Fratton	70D Basingstoke	70D Basingstoke	
31612	U	SAL Salisbury	71D Fratton	70E Reading South	70C Guildford	70C Guildford	70A Nine Elms	
31613	U	9E Nine Elms	70A Nine Elms	71A Eastleigh	71A Eastleigh	72C Yeovil Town	70A Nine Elms	
31614	U	GFD Guildford	70E Reading South	70E Reading South	71B Bournemouth	70C Guildford	72C Yeovil Town	
31615	U	RDG Reading South	70E Reading South	70E Reading South	71B Bournemouth	70C Guildford	70C Guildford	
31616	U	9E Nine Elms	73C Hither Green	70E Reading South	70C Guildford	70C Guildford	75C Norwood Junction	
31617	U	9E Nine Elms	73C Hither Green	70E Reading South	70A Nine Elms	70A Nine Elms	70A Nine Elms	
31618	U	SAL Salisbury	72B Salisbury	71C Dorchester	71A Eastleigh	71A Eastleigh	70D Basingstoke	
31619	U	9E Nine Elms	70A Nine Elms	70E Reading South	71A Eastleigh	71A Eastleigh	75C Norwood Junction	
31620	U	RDG Reading South	70C Guildford	70C Guildford	71A Eastleigh	71A Eastleigh	75C Norwood Junction	
31621	U	GFD Guildford	70A Nine Elms	71A Eastleigh	70A Nine Elms	70A Nine Elms	70A Nine Elms	
31622	U	BM Bournemouth	71B Bournemouth	71C Dorchester	70C Guildford	70C Guildford	70C Guildford	
31623	U	GFD Guildford	73A Stewarts Lane	72C Yeovil Town	72C Yeovil Town	72C Yeovil Town	70C Guildford	
31624	U	BM Bournemouth	70C Guildford	70C Guildford	70A Nine Elms	70A Nine Elms	70A Nine Elms	
31625	U	EXJ Exmouth Junction	70A Nine Elms	70C Guildford	70C Guildford	70C Guildford	70C Guildford	
31626	U	SAL Salisbury	72B Salisbury	71A Eastleigh	72C Yeovil Town	72C Yeovil Town	75C Norwood Junction	
31627	U	BAS Basingstoke	70C Guildford	70C Guildford	70C Guildford	70C Guildford	70C Guildford	
31628	U	RDG Reading South	70C Guildford	70C Guildford	70C Guildford	70C Guildford	70C Guildford	
31629	U	BAS Basingstoke	70C Guildford	70C Guildford	71A Eastleigh	71A Eastleigh	75C Norwood Junction	
31630	U	SAL Salisbury	70C Guildford	70C Guildford	70C Guildford	70C Guildford		
31631	U	FAV Faversham	73E Faversham	71C Dorchester	70C Guildford	70C Guildford	70C Guildford	
31632	U	BAS Basingstoke	71C Dorchester	71C Dorchester	71B Bournemouth	71A Eastleigh	72C Yeovil Town	
31633	U	BAS Basingstoke	70D Basingstoke	70D Basingstoke	70D Basingstoke	72C Yeovil Town	70C Guildford	
31634	U	BAS Basingstoke	72C Yeovil Town	70D Basingstoke	70A Nine Elms	70A Nine Elms	70A Nine Elms	
31635	U	EXJ Exmouth Junction	70C Guildford	72B Salisbury	70C Guildford	70C Guildford	70C Guildford	
31636	U	SAL Salisbury	72C Yeovil Town	72B Salisbury	70C Guildford	70C Guildford	70A Nine Elms	
31637	U	9E Nine Elms	70A Nine Elms	71D Fratton	70F Fratton	70C Guildford	72C Yeovil Town	
31638	U	EXJ Exmouth Junction	73E Faversham	71D Fratton	70F Fratton	70C Guildford	70C Guildford	
31639	U	FAV Faversham	73C Hither Green	72B Salisbury	71A Eastleigh	71A Eastleigh	75C Norwood Junction	70C Guildford
31658	R	GIL Gillingham	73D Gillingham					
31659	R	GIL Gillingham	73D Gillingham					
31660	R	GIL Gillingham	73A Stewarts Lane					
31661	R	BAT Stewarts Lane	73E Faversham	74C Dover Marine				
31662	R	GIL Gillingham	73D Gillingham					
31663	R	GIL Gillingham	73D Gillingham					
31665	R	GIL Gillingham	73D Gillingham					
31666	R	GIL Gillingham	73D Gillingham	74D Tonbridge				
31667	R	FAV Faversham	74D Tonbridge					
31670	R	TON Tonbridge	74D Tonbridge					
31671	R	TON Tonbridge	74D Tonbridge	73D Gillingham				
31672	R	TON Tonbridge						
31673	R	DOV Dover Marine	74C Dover Marine					
31674	R	FAV Faversham	73E Faversham					
31675	R	TON Tonbridge	74D Tonbridge					
31681	C	BAT Stewarts Lane	73A Stewarts Lane	73D Gillingham	73D Gillingham			
31682	C	GIL Gillingham	73D Gillingham	73D Gillingham	73D Gillingham	70A Nine Elms		
31683	C	BAT Stewarts Lane	73A Stewarts Lane	73D Gillingham	73D Gillingham			
31684	C	GIL Gillingham	74D Tonbridge	73D Gillingham	73D Gillingham	73J Tonbridge		
31685	S	BA Bricklayers Arms	74A Ashford					
31686	C	TON Tonbridge	74D Tonbridge	73C Hither Green	73C Hither Green	73C Hither Green		
31687	C	BA Bricklayers Arms	73B Bricklayers Arms	73C Hither Green				
31688	C	GIL Gillingham	73D Gillingham	73C Hither Green	73C Hither Green	73C Hither Green		
31689	C	HIT Hither Green	73C Hither Green	73C Hither Green	73C Hither Green	73C Hither Green		
31690	C	BAT Stewarts Lane	74B Ramsgate	73C Hither Green	73C Hither Green	73C Hither Green		
31691	C	FAV Faversham	73E Faversham	73C Hither Green	73C Hither Green	73C Hither Green		
31692	C	FAV Faversham	73E Faversham	73C Hither Green	73C Hither Green	73C Hither Green		
31693	C	BA Bricklayers Arms	73D Gillingham	73C Hither Green	73C Hither Green	73C Hither Green		
31694	C	BAT Stewarts Lane	73C Hither Green	73C Hither Green	73C Hither Green	73C Hither Green		
31695	C	HIT Hither Green	73C Hither Green	73C Hither Green	73C Hither Green	73C Hither Green		
31696	R1[2]	FEL Feltham	73E Faversham					
31697	R1[2]	GIL Gillingham	73D Gillingham					
31698	R1[2]	FEL Feltham	73E Faversham	74D Tonbridge				
31699	R1[2]	FAV Faversham						
31700	R1[2]	TON Tonbridge	74D Tonbridge					
31703	R1[2]	TON Tonbridge	74D Tonbridge	74D Tonbridge				
31704	R1[2]	TON Tonbridge	74D Tonbridge	74D Tonbridge				
31705	R1[2]	DOV Dover Marine	73E Faversham					
31706	R1[2]	BAT Stewarts Lane	74D Tonbridge					
31707	R1[2]	TON Tonbridge						
31708	R1[2]	DOV Dover Marine	74C Dover Marine					
31709	R1[2]	FAV Faversham						
31710	R1[2]	BAT Stewarts Lane	74A Ashford					
31711	C	AFD Ashford	74A Ashford	74A Ashford	73D Gillingham			
31712	C	BAT Stewarts Lane	73D Gillingham	73D Gillingham	73D Gillingham			
31713	C	GIL Gillingham	73D Gillingham	73D Gillingham				
31714	C	BAT Stewarts Lane	73A Stewarts Lane	73E Faversham	73E Faversham	73A Stewarts Lane		
31715	C	FAV Faversham	73E Faversham	73E Faversham	73E Faversham	73A Stewarts Lane		
31716	C	BAT Stewarts Lane	73A Stewarts Lane	74D Tonbridge	74D Tonbridge	73J Tonbridge		
31717	C	BAT Stewarts Lane	73A Stewarts Lane	74D Tonbridge	75C Norwood Junction	73B Bricklayers Arms		
31718	C	BAT Stewarts Lane	73A Stewarts Lane	73A Stewarts Lane				
31719	C	BAT Stewarts Lane	73A Stewarts Lane	73A Stewarts Lane	75C Norwood Junction	73A Stewarts Lane		
31720	C	HIT Hither Green	73C Hither Green	73B Bricklayers Arms	73E Faversham	73H Dover Marine		
31721	C	AFD Ashford	74A Ashford	74E St. Leonards	73C Hither Green	73C Hither Green		
31722	C	BAT Stewarts Lane	73A Stewarts Lane	73B Bricklayers Arms	70C Guildford	70C Guildford		
31723	C	BA Bricklayers Arms	73B Bricklayers Arms	73B Bricklayers Arms	70C Guildford	70C Guildford		
31724	C	BA Bricklayers Arms	73D Gillingham	73B Bricklayers Arms	75A Brighton	75A Brighton		
31725	C	BA Bricklayers Arms	73B Bricklayers Arms	73B Bricklayers Arms	75A Brighton	75A Brighton		
31727	D1[1]	DOV Dover Marine	73E Faversham	74D Tonbridge	74A Ashford	70A Nine Elms		
31728	D	RED Redhill	74D Tonbridge					
31729	D	RED Redhill	73D Gillingham	74D Tonbridge				
31730	D	HOR Horsham	74D Tonbridge					
31731	D	TON Tonbridge	74D Tonbridge					
31732	D	TON Tonbridge	73C Hither Green					
31733	D	TON Tonbridge	74D Tonbridge					
31734	D	TON Tonbridge	73E Faversham	74D Tonbridge				
31735	D1[1]	DOV Dover Marine	74C Dover Marine	73B Bricklayers Arms	73B Bricklayers Arms	71A Eastleigh		
31736	D1[1]	BAT Stewarts Lane						
31737	D	STL St. Leonards	74B Ramsgate	70E Reading South				
31738	D	STL St. Leonards						
31739	D1[1]	FAV Faversham	73E Faversham	73B Bricklayers Arms	73B Bricklayers Arms	73B Bricklayers Arms		
31740	D	STL St. Leonards	70E Reading South					
31741	D1[1]	FAV Faversham	73D Gillingham	73B Bricklayers Arms	73B Bricklayers Arms			
31743	D1[1]	BAT Stewarts Lane	73A Stewarts Lane	73A Stewarts Lane	73A Stewarts Lane	73B Bricklayers Arms		
31744	D	STL St. Leonards	70E Reading South					
31745	D1[1]	BAT Stewarts Lane	74D Tonbridge					
31746	D	GIL Gillingham	74D Tonbridge	70E Reading South				
31748	D	AFD Ashford	74B Ramsgate					
31749	D1[1]	BAT Stewarts Lane	73A Stewarts Lane	73A Stewarts Lane	73A Stewarts Lane	73B Bricklayers Arms		
31750	D	GIL Gillingham	70E Reading South					
31753	L1	DOV Dover Marine	74C Dover Marine	74C Dover Marine	74C Dover Marine	70A Nine Elms		
31754	L1	DOV Dover Marine	74C Dover Marine	74C Dover Marine	74C Dover Marine	70A Nine Elms		
31755	L1	DOV Dover Marine	74C Dover Marine	74C Dover Marine	74C Dover Marine			

No.	Class	1948	1951	1954	1957	1960	1963	1966
31756	*L1*	**DOV** Dover Marine	**74C** Dover Marine	**74A** Ashford	**74A** Ashford	**70A** Nine Elms		
31757	*L1*	**DOV** Dover Marine	**74C** Dover Marine	**74A** Ashford	**74A** Ashford	**70A** Nine Elms		
31758	*L1*	**BA** Bricklayers Arms	**73B** Bricklayers Arms	**74A** Ashford	**74A** Ashford			
31759	*L1*	**BA** Bricklayers Arms	**73B** Bricklayers Arms	**74A** Ashford	**74A** Ashford	**70A** Nine Elms		
31760	*L*	**BAT** Stewarts Lane	**74D** Tonbridge	**74D** Tonbridge	**74D** Tonbridge	**70A** Nine Elms		
31761	*L*	**TON** Tonbridge	**74D** Tonbridge	**74D** Tonbridge				
31762	*L*	**TON** Tonbridge	**74A** Ashford	**74D** Tonbridge	**74D** Tonbridge	**70A** Nine Elms		
31763	*L*	**TON** Tonbridge	**74A** Ashford	**74D** Tonbridge	**74D** Tonbridge	**70A** Nine Elms		
31764	*L*	**BAT** Stewarts Lane	**74A** Ashford	**74D** Tonbridge	**74B** Ramsgate	**70A** Nine Elms		
31765	*L*	**BAT** Stewarts Lane	**74D** Tonbridge	**74D** Tonbridge	**73E** Faversham	**70A** Nine Elms		
31766	*L*	**STL** St. Leonards	**74E** St. Leonards	**74D** Tonbridge	**73E** Faversham	**70A** Nine Elms		
31767	*L*	**STL** St. Leonards	**74C** Dover Marine	**74E** St. Leonards	**73E** Faversham			
31768	*L*	**STL** St. Leonards	**74E** St. Leonards	**74E** St. Leonards	**73E** Faversham	**70A** Nine Elms		
31769	*L*	**BAT** Stewarts Lane	**74E** St. Leonards	**74E** St. Leonards				
31770	*L*	**AFD** Ashford	**74A** Ashford	**74D** Tonbridge	**74D** Tonbridge			
31771	*L*	**AFD** Ashford	**74A** Ashford	**74D** Tonbridge	**74D** Tonbridge	**70A** Nine Elms		
31772	*L*	**AFD** Ashford	**74A** Ashford	**74A** Ashford	**74A** Ashford			
31773	*L*	**AFD** Ashford	**74A** Ashford	**74D** Tonbridge	**74D** Tonbridge			
31774	*L*	**AFD** Ashford	**74A** Ashford	**74A** Ashford	**74A** Ashford			
31775	*L*	**AFD** Ashford	**74A** Ashford	**74A** Ashford	**74A** Ashford			
31776	*L*	**AFD** Ashford	**74B** Ramsgate	**74A** Ashford	**75A** Brighton	**70A** Nine Elms		
31777	*L*	**RAM** Ramsgate	**74B** Ramsgate	**74A** Ashford	**75A** Brighton			
31778	*L*	**RAM** Ramsgate	**74D** Tonbridge	**74A** Ashford	**75A** Brighton			
31779	*L*	**RAM** Ramsgate	**74D** Tonbridge	**74B** Ramsgate	**74B** Ramsgate			
31780	*L*	**RAM** Ramsgate	**74B** Ramsgate	**74B** Ramsgate	**74B** Ramsgate	**70A** Nine Elms		
31781	*L*	**RAM** Ramsgate	**74B** Ramsgate	**74B** Ramsgate	**74B** Ramsgate			
31782	*L1*	**BA** Bricklayers Arms	**73B** Bricklayers Arms	**74A** Ashford	**74A** Ashford	**70A** Nine Elms		
31783	*L1*	**BA** Bricklayers Arms	**73B** Bricklayers Arms	**73B** Bricklayers Arms	**73B** Bricklayers Arms	**70A** Nine Elms		
31784	*L1*	**BA** Bricklayers Arms	**73B** Bricklayers Arms	**73B** Bricklayers Arms	**73B** Bricklayers Arms	**70A** Nine Elms		
31785	*L1*	**BA** Bricklayers Arms	**73B** Bricklayers Arms	**73B** Bricklayers Arms	**73D** Gillingham	**70A** Nine Elms		
31786	*L1*	**BA** Bricklayers Arms	**73B** Bricklayers Arms	**71A** Eastleigh	**73D** Gillingham	**70A** Nine Elms		
31787	*L1*	**BA** Bricklayers Arms	**73B** Bricklayers Arms	**71A** Eastleigh	**73D** Gillingham	**70A** Nine Elms		
31788	*L1*	**BA** Bricklayers Arms	**74B** Ramsgate	**71A** Eastleigh	**74C** Dover Marine	**70A** Nine Elms		
31789	*L1*	**BA** Bricklayers Arms	**74B** Ramsgate	**71A** Eastleigh	**74C** Dover Marine	**70A** Nine Elms		
31790	*U*	**YEO** Yeovil Town	**72C** Yeovil Town	**72C** Yeovil Town	**72C** Yeovil Town	**72C** Yeovil Town	**70C** Guildford	
31791	*U*	**YEO** Yeovil Town	**72C** Yeovil Town	**72C** Yeovil Town	**72C** Yeovil Town	**72C** Yeovil Town	**71A** Eastleigh	**70C** Guildford
31792	*U*	**YEO** Yeovil Town	**72C** Yeovil Town	**72C** Yeovil Town	**72C** Yeovil Town	**71A** Eastleigh	**72C** Yeovil Town	
31793	*U*	**YEO** Yeovil Town	**72C** Yeovil Town	**72C** Yeovil Town	**72C** Yeovil Town	**71A** Eastleigh	**71A** Eastleigh	
31794	*U*	**YEO** Yeovil Town	**70E** Reading South	**72C** Yeovil Town	**72C** Yeovil Town	**71A** Eastleigh	**71A** Eastleigh	
31795	*U*	**YEO** Yeovil Town	**71B** Bournemouth	**72C** Yeovil Town	**72C** Yeovil Town	**71A** Eastleigh	**71A** Eastleigh	
31796	*U*	**BM** Bournemouth	**70E** Reading South	**72C** Yeovil Town	**72C** Yeovil Town	**70A** Nine Elms	**70A** Nine Elms	
31797	*U*	**FRA** Fratton	**70E** Reading South	**70C** Guildford	**70C** Guildford	**70C** Guildford	**70C** Guildford	
31798	*U*	**GFD** Guildford	**70C** Guildford	**70C** Guildford	**70C** Guildford	**70C** Guildford	**72C** Yeovil Town	
31799	*U*	**GFD** Guildford	**70E** Reading South	**70C** Guildford	**70C** Guildford	**70C** Guildford	**75C** Norwood Junction	
31800	*U*	**GFD** Guildford	**70C** Guildford	**70C** Guildford	**70C** Guildford	**70C** Guildford	**70C** Guildford	
31801	*U*	**GFD** Guildford	**70C** Guildford	**71A** Eastleigh	**71A** Eastleigh	**71A** Eastleigh	**71A** Eastleigh	
31802	*U*	**GFD** Guildford	**70C** Guildford	**70C** Guildford	**71A** Eastleigh	**71A** Eastleigh	**72C** Yeovil Town	
31803	*U*	**GFD** Guildford	**70C** Guildford	**73E** Faversham	**71A** Eastleigh	**71A** Eastleigh	**71A** Eastleigh	**70C** Guildford
31804	*U*	**GFD** Guildford	**70C** Guildford	**73E** Faversham	**72A** Exmouth Junction	**71A** Eastleigh	**71A** Eastleigh	
31805	*U*	**GFD** Guildford	**71D** Fratton	**71D** Fratton	**70F** Fratton	**70C** Guildford	**72C** Yeovil Town	
31806	*U*	**GFD** Guildford	**73E** Faversham	**73E** Faversham	**70D** Basingstoke	**70D** Basingstoke	**70D** Basingstoke	
31807	*U*	**RDG** Reading South	**70A** Nine Elms	**71D** Fratton	**70F** Fratton	**70C** Guildford	**75C** Norwood Junction	
31808	*U*	**FAV** Faversham	**73E** Faversham	**71D** Fratton	**70F** Fratton	**71A** Eastleigh	**71A** Eastleigh	
31809	*U*	**GFD** Guildford	**71D** Fratton	**71D** Fratton	**70F** Fratton	**71A** Eastleigh	**71A** Eastleigh	**70C** Guildford
31810	*N*	**BAT** Stewarts Lane	**73A** Stewarts Lane	**73A** Stewarts Lane	**73A** Stewarts Lane	**73H** Dover Marine	**71A** Eastleigh	
31811	*N*	**BAT** Stewarts Lane	**73A** Stewarts Lane	**73A** Stewarts Lane	**73A** Stewarts Lane	**70C** Guildford	**70C** Guildford	
31812	*N*	**BAT** Stewarts Lane	**73A** Stewarts Lane	**73A** Stewarts Lane	**73A** Stewarts Lane	**70C** Guildford	**70C** Guildford	
31813	*N*	**BAT** Stewarts Lane	**73A** Stewarts Lane	**72B** Salisbury	**72B** Salisbury	**72B** Salisbury	**70E** Salisbury	
31814	*N*	**NOR** Norwood Junction	**73A** Stewarts Lane	**72B** Salisbury	**72B** Salisbury	**72B** Salisbury	**70E** Salisbury	
31815	*N*	**RED** Redhill	**73A** Stewarts Lane	**73A** Stewarts Lane	**73D** Gillingham	**70C** Guildford	**70C** Guildford	
31816	*N*	**RED** Redhill	**73A** Stewarts Lane	**73A** Stewarts Lane	**73D** Gillingham	**73C** Hither Green	**71A** Eastleigh	**70C** Guildford
31817	*N*	**RED** Redhill	**73A** Stewarts Lane	**74C** Dover Marine	**75B** Redhill	**75B** Redhill	**75B** Redhill	
31818	*N*	**RED** Redhill	**73A** Stewarts Lane	**74C** Dover Marine	**74C** Dover Marine	**73H** Dover Marine	**72A** Exmouth Junction	
31819	*N*	**DOV** Dover Marine	**74C** Dover Marine	**74C** Dover Marine	**74C** Dover Marine	**73H** Dover Marine	**70C** Guildford	
31820	*N*	**DOV** Dover Marine	**74C** Dover Marine	**74C** Dover Marine	**74C** Dover Marine	**73H** Dover Marine	**70C** Guildford	
31821	*N*	**DOV** Dover Marine	**74C** Dover Marine	**74C** Dover Marine	**74C** Dover Marine	**73H** Dover Marine	**70C** Guildford	
31822	*N1*	**STL** St. Leonards	**73C** Hither Green	**73C** Hither Green	**73C** Hither Green	**73J** Tonbridge		
31823	*N*	**DOV** Dover Marine	**74C** Dover Marine	**73B** Bricklayers Arms	**73B** Bricklayers Arms	**73B** Bricklayers Arms	**75D** Stewarts Lane	
31824	*N*	**BA** Bricklayers Arms	**73B** Bricklayers Arms	**73B** Bricklayers Arms	**73B** Bricklayers Arms	**73B** Bricklayers Arms	**75D** Stewarts Lane	
31825	*N*	**BA** Bricklayers Arms	**73B** Bricklayers Arms	**73B** Bricklayers Arms	**73B** Bricklayers Arms	**73B** Bricklayers Arms	**75D** Stewarts Lane	
31826	*N*	**BA** Bricklayers Arms	**73B** Bricklayers Arms	**73B** Bricklayers Arms	**73B** Bricklayers Arms	**73B** Bricklayers Arms	**75D** Stewarts Lane	
31827	*N*	**ELH** Eastleigh	**73B** Bricklayers Arms	**73B** Bricklayers Arms	**73B** Bricklayers Arms	**73B** Bricklayers Arms	**75A** Brighton	
31828	*N*	**EXJ** Exmouth Junction	**72A** Exmouth Junction	**73B** Bricklayers Arms	**73B** Bricklayers Arms	**73B** Bricklayers Arms	**75A** Brighton	
31829	*N*	**ELH** Eastleigh	**72A** Exmouth Junction	**73B** Bricklayers Arms	**73B** Bricklayers Arms	**73B** Bricklayers Arms	**75A** Brighton	
31830	*N*	**TON** Tonbridge	**72A** Exmouth Junction	**72A** Exmouth Junction	**72A** Exmouth Junction	**72A** Exmouth Junction	**75A** Brighton	
31831	*N*	**FRA** Fratton	**72A** Exmouth Junction	**72A** Exmouth Junction	**72A** Exmouth Junction	**72A** Exmouth Junction	**75A** Brighton	
31832	*N*	**EXJ** Exmouth Junction	**72A** Exmouth Junction	**72A** Exmouth Junction	**72A** Exmouth Junction	**72A** Exmouth Junction	**75A** Brighton	
31833	*N*	**EXJ** Exmouth Junction	**72A** Exmouth Junction	**72A** Exmouth Junction	**72A** Exmouth Junction	**72A** Exmouth Junction	**75A** Brighton	
31834	*N*	**EXJ** Exmouth Junction	**72A** Exmouth Junction	**72A** Exmouth Junction	**72A** Exmouth Junction	**72A** Exmouth Junction	**72A** Exmouth Junction	
31835	*N*	**EXJ** Exmouth Junction	**72A** Exmouth Junction	**72A** Exmouth Junction	**72A** Exmouth Junction	**72A** Exmouth Junction	**72A** Exmouth Junction	
31836	*N*	**EXJ** Exmouth Junction	**72A** Exmouth Junction	**72A** Exmouth Junction	**72A** Exmouth Junction	**72A** Exmouth Junction	**72A** Exmouth Junction	
31837	*N*	**EXJ** Exmouth Junction	**72A** Exmouth Junction	**72A** Exmouth Junction	**72A** Exmouth Junction	**72A** Exmouth Junction	**72A** Exmouth Junction	
31838	*N*	**EXJ** Exmouth Junction	**72A** Exmouth Junction	**72A** Exmouth Junction	**72A** Exmouth Junction	**72A** Exmouth Junction	**72A** Exmouth Junction	
31839	*N*	**EXJ** Exmouth Junction	**72A** Exmouth Junction	**72A** Exmouth Junction	**72A** Exmouth Junction	**72A** Exmouth Junction	**72A** Exmouth Junction	
31840	*N*	**EXJ** Exmouth Junction	**72A** Exmouth Junction	**72A** Exmouth Junction	**72A** Exmouth Junction	**72A** Exmouth Junction	**72A** Exmouth Junction	
31841	*N*	**EXJ** Exmouth Junction	**72A** Exmouth Junction	**72A** Exmouth Junction	**72A** Exmouth Junction	**72A** Exmouth Junction	**72A** Exmouth Junction	
31842	*N*	**EXJ** Exmouth Junction	**72E** Barnstaple Junction	**72A** Exmouth Junction	**72A** Exmouth Junction	**72A** Exmouth Junction	**72A** Exmouth Junction	
31843	*N*	**RED** Redhill	**75B** Redhill	**72E** Barnstaple Junction	**72A** Exmouth Junction	**72A** Exmouth Junction	**72A** Exmouth Junction	
31844	*N*	**NOR** Norwood Junction	**75B** Redhill	**72A** Exmouth Junction	**72A** Exmouth Junction	**72A** Exmouth Junction	**72A** Exmouth Junction	
31845	*N*	**EXJ** Exmouth Junction	**72A** Exmouth Junction	**72A** Exmouth Junction	**72A** Exmouth Junction	**72A** Exmouth Junction	**72A** Exmouth Junction	
31846	*N*	**SAL** Salisbury	**72A** Exmouth Junction	**72A** Exmouth Junction	**72A** Exmouth Junction	**72A** Exmouth Junction	**72A** Exmouth Junction	
31847	*N*	**EXJ** Exmouth Junction	**72A** Exmouth Junction	**72A** Exmouth Junction	**72A** Exmouth Junction	**72A** Exmouth Junction	**72A** Exmouth Junction	
31848	*N*	**SAL** Salisbury	**75B** Redhill	**72A** Exmouth Junction	**74A** Ashford	**73F** Ashford	**72A** Exmouth Junction	
31849	*N*	**RED** Redhill	**75B** Redhill	**72A** Exmouth Junction	**72A** Exmouth Junction	**72A** Exmouth Junction	**72A** Exmouth Junction	
31850	*N*	**RDG** Reading South	**73E** Faversham	**73E** Faversham	**73E** Faversham	**75B** Redhill	**75B** Redhill	
31851	*N*	**RED** Redhill	**75B** Redhill	**72A** Exmouth Junction	**73B** Bricklayers Arms	**75B** Redhill	**75B** Redhill	
31852	*N*	**RED** Redhill	**75B** Redhill	**73E** Faversham	**73E** Faversham	**75B** Redhill	**75B** Redhill	
31853	*N*	**EXJ** Exmouth Junction	**72A** Exmouth Junction	**73B** Bricklayers Arms	**73B** Bricklayers Arms	**72A** Exmouth Junction	**72A** Exmouth Junction	
31854	*N*	**RDG** Reading South	**73E** Faversham	**73E** Faversham	**73C** Hither Green	**73F** Ashford	**75D** Stewarts Lane	
31855	*N*	**EXJ** Exmouth Junction	**72A** Exmouth Junction	**73B** Bricklayers Arms	**73C** Hither Green	**73C** Hither Green	**72A** Exmouth Junction	
31856	*N*	**EXJ** Exmouth Junction	**72A** Exmouth Junction	**73C** Hither Green	**73C** Hither Green	**73C** Hither Green	**72A** Exmouth Junction	
31857	*N*	**RDG** Reading South	**75B** Redhill	**73C** Hither Green	**73C** Hither Green	**73C** Hither Green	**70C** Guildford	
31858	*N*	**RED** Redhill	**75B** Redhill	**73C** Hither Green	**73C** Hither Green	**70C** Guildford	**70C** Guildford	
31859	*N*	**TON** Tonbridge	**74C** Dover Marine	**73C** Hither Green	**73C** Hither Green	**73C** Hither Green	**70C** Guildford	
31860	*N*	**RDG** Reading South	**74A** Ashford	**73C** Hither Green	**73C** Hither Green	**72A** Exmouth Junction	**72A** Exmouth Junction	
31861	*N*	**RDG** Reading South	**74A** Ashford	**73C** Hither Green	**73C** Hither Green	**75B** Redhill	**75B** Redhill	
31862	*N*	**TON** Tonbridge	**75B** Redhill	**75B** Redhill	**75B** Redhill	**75B** Redhill	**75B** Redhill	
31863	*N*	**RED** Redhill	**75B** Redhill	**75B** Redhill	**75B** Redhill	**75B** Redhill	**75B** Redhill	
31864	*N*	**RED** Redhill	**75B** Redhill	**75B** Redhill	**75B** Redhill	**75B** Redhill	**75B** Redhill	
31865	*N*	**BA** Bricklayers Arms	**75B** Redhill	**75B** Redhill	**75B** Redhill	**75B** Redhill	**75B** Redhill	
31866	*N*	**ELH** Eastleigh	**72A** Exmouth Junction	**75B** Redhill	**75B** Redhill	**75B** Redhill	**75B** Redhill	**70C** Guildford
31867	*N*	**ELH** Eastleigh	**72A** Exmouth Junction	**75B** Redhill	**75B** Redhill	**75B** Redhill	**75B** Redhill	
31868	*N*	**RDG** Reading South	**73E** Faversham	**75B** Redhill	**75B** Redhill	**75B** Redhill	**75B** Redhill	
31869	*N*	**EXJ** Exmouth Junction	**72A** Exmouth Junction	**75B** Redhill	**75B** Redhill	**75B** Redhill	**75B** Redhill	

		1948	1951	1954	1957	1960	1963	1966
31870	*N*	**ELH** Eastleigh	**75A** Brighton	**73B** Bricklayers Arms	**73B** Bricklayers Arms	**75B** Redhill	**75B** Redhill	
31871	*N*	**EXJ** Exmouth Junction	**75A** Brighton	**73B** Bricklayers Arms	**73B** Bricklayers Arms	**75B** Redhill	**75B** Redhill	
31872	*N*	**SAL** Salisbury	**72B** Salisbury	**73B** Bricklayers Arms	**73B** Bricklayers Arms	**75B** Redhill	**75B** Redhill	
31873	*N*	**SAL** Salisbury	**72B** Salisbury	**73B** Bricklayers Arms	**73B** Bricklayers Arms	**73B** Bricklayers Arms	**75A** Brighton	**70C** Guildford
31874	*N*	**EXJ** Exmouth Junction	**72B** Salisbury	**73B** Bricklayers Arms	**73B** Bricklayers Arms	**73B** Bricklayers Arms	**72A** Exmouth Junction	
31875	*N*	**EXJ** Exmouth Junction	**72B** Salisbury	**73B** Bricklayers Arms	**73B** Bricklayers Arms	**73B** Bricklayers Arms	**72A** Exmouth Junction	
31876	*N1*	**STL** St. Leonards	**73C** Hither Green	**73C** Hither Green	**73C** Hither Green	**73J** Tonbridge		
31877	*N1*	**STL** St. Leonards	**73C** Hither Green	**73C** Hither Green	**73C** Hither Green	**73J** Tonbridge		
31878	*N1*	**HIT** Hither Green	**73C** Hither Green	**73C** Hither Green	**73C** Hither Green	**73J** Tonbridge		
31879	*N1*	**HIT** Hither Green	**73C** Hither Green	**73C** Hither Green	**73C** Hither Green	**73J** Tonbridge		
31880	*N1*	**HIT** Hither Green	**73C** Hither Green	**73C** Hither Green	**73C** Hither Green	**73J** Tonbridge		
31890	*U1*	**BTN** Brighton	**75A** Brighton	**73B** Bricklayers Arms	**73B** Bricklayers Arms	**75A** Brighton	**75A** Brighton	
31891	*U1*	**BTN** Brighton	**75A** Brighton	**73B** Bricklayers Arms	**73B** Bricklayers Arms	**75A** Brighton	**75A** Brighton	
31892	*U1*	**BTN** Brighton	**75A** Brighton	**73C** Hither Green	**73E** Faversham	**70B** Feltham		
31893	*U1*	**BTN** Brighton	**75A** Brighton	**73C** Hither Green	**73E** Faversham	**70B** Feltham		
31894	*U1*	**BTN** Brighton	**75A** Brighton	**75B** Redhill	**73A** Stewarts Lane	**73A** Stewarts Lane		
31895	*U1*	**RED** Redhill	**75B** Redhill	**75B** Redhill	**73A** Stewarts Lane	**73A** Stewarts Lane		
31896	*U1*	**RED** Redhill	**75B** Redhill	**75B** Redhill	**73A** Stewarts Lane	**73A** Stewarts Lane		
31897	*U1*	**RED** Redhill	**75B** Redhill	**75B** Redhill	**73A** Stewarts Lane	**73A** Stewarts Lane		
31898	*U1*	**RED** Redhill	**75B** Redhill	**75B** Redhill	**73A** Stewarts Lane	**73A** Stewarts Lane		
31899	*U1*	**RED** Redhill	**73B** Bricklayers Arms	**75B** Redhill	**73B** Bricklayers Arms	**73A** Stewarts Lane		
31900	*U1*	**BTN** Brighton	**73B** Bricklayers Arms	**75B** Redhill	**73B** Bricklayers Arms	**73A** Stewarts Lane		
31901	*U1*	**BA** Bricklayers Arms	**73B** Bricklayers Arms	**73A** Stewarts Lane	**73B** Bricklayers Arms	**73J** Tonbridge	**75A** Brighton	
31902	*U1*	**BA** Bricklayers Arms	**73B** Bricklayers Arms	**73A** Stewarts Lane	**73B** Bricklayers Arms	**73J** Tonbridge		
31903	*U1*	**BAT** Stewarts Lane	**73A** Stewarts Lane	**73A** Stewarts Lane	**73E** Faversham	**73J** Tonbridge		
31904	*U1*	**BAT** Stewarts Lane	**73A** Stewarts Lane	**73A** Stewarts Lane	**73A** Stewarts Lane	**73J** Tonbridge		
31905	*U1*	**BAT** Stewarts Lane	**73A** Stewarts Lane	**73A** Stewarts Lane	**73A** Stewarts Lane	**73J** Tonbridge		
31906	*U1*	**BAT** Stewarts Lane	**73A** Stewarts Lane	**73A** Stewarts Lane	**73A** Stewarts Lane	**73J** Tonbridge		
31907	*U1*	**BAT** Stewarts Lane	**73A** Stewarts Lane	**70A** Nine Elms	**73A** Stewarts Lane	**73J** Tonbridge		
31908	*U1*	**BAT** Stewarts Lane	**73A** Stewarts Lane	**70A** Nine Elms	**74D** Tonbridge	**73J** Tonbridge		
31909	*U1*	**BAT** Stewarts Lane	**73A** Stewarts Lane	**70A** Nine Elms	**74D** Tonbridge	**73J** Tonbridge		
31910	*U1*	**BAT** Stewarts Lane	**73A** Stewarts Lane	**70A** Nine Elms	**74D** Tonbridge	**73J** Tonbridge	**75A** Brighton	
31911	*W*	**HIT** Hither Green	**73C** Hither Green	**73C** Hither Green	**73C** Hither Green	**73C** Hither Green	**72A** Exmouth Junction	
31912	*W*	**BAT** Stewarts Lane	**73A** Stewarts Lane	**73C** Hither Green	**73C** Hither Green	**73C** Hither Green	**72A** Exmouth Junction	
31913	*W*	**HIT** Hither Green	**73C** Hither Green	**73C** Hither Green	**73C** Hither Green	**73C** Hither Green	**72A** Exmouth Junction	
31914	*W*	**BAT** Stewarts Lane	**73A** Stewarts Lane	**73A** Stewarts Lane	**73A** Stewarts Lane	**73A** Stewarts Lane	**72A** Exmouth Junction	
31915	*W*	**BAT** Stewarts Lane	**73A** Stewarts Lane	**73A** Stewarts Lane	**73A** Stewarts Lane	**73A** Stewarts Lane	**72A** Exmouth Junction	
31916	*W*	**NOR** Norwood Junction	**75C** Norwood Junction	**73C** Hither Green	**73C** Hither Green	**73C** Hither Green	**72A** Exmouth Junction	
31917	*W*	**NOR** Norwood Junction	**75C** Norwood Junction	**75C** Norwood Junction	**75C** Norwood Junction	**75C** Norwood Junction	**72A** Exmouth Junction	
31918	*W*	**NOR** Norwood Junction	**75C** Norwood Junction	**75C** Norwood Junction	**75C** Norwood Junction	**75C** Norwood Junction	**75C** Norwood Junction	
31919	*W*	**NOR** Norwood Junction	**75C** Norwood Junction	**75C** Norwood Junction	**75C** Norwood Junction	**75C** Norwood Junction	**75C** Norwood Junction	
31920	*W*	**NOR** Norwood Junction	**75C** Norwood Junction	**75C** Norwood Junction	**75C** Norwood Junction	**75C** Norwood Junction	**75C** Norwood Junction	
31921	*W*	**HIT** Hither Green	**73C** Hither Green	**73C** Hither Green	**73A** Stewarts Lane	**73A** Stewarts Lane	**75C** Norwood Junction	
31922	*W*	**HIT** Hither Green	**73C** Hither Green	**73C** Hither Green	**73C** Hither Green	**73C** Hither Green	**70B** Feltham	
31923	*W*	**HIT** Hither Green	**73C** Hither Green	**73C** Hither Green	**73C** Hither Green	**73C** Hither Green	**70B** Feltham	
31924	*W*	**HIT** Hither Green	**73C** Hither Green	**73C** Hither Green	**73C** Hither Green	**73C** Hither Green	**72A** Exmouth Junction	
31925	*W*	**HIT** Hither Green	**73C** Hither Green	**73C** Hither Green	**73C** Hither Green	**73C** Hither Green	**75C** Norwood Junction	
32001	*I1X*	**TWW** Tunbridge Wells West						
32002	*I1X*	**3B** Three Bridges	**75A** Brighton					
32003	*I1X*	**TWW** Tunbridge Wells West						
32004	*I1X*	**TWW** Tunbridge Wells West						
32005	*I1X*	**EBN** Eastbourne	**75A** Brighton					
32006	*I1X*	**TWW** Tunbridge Wells West						
32007	*I1X*	**3B** Three Bridges						
32008	*I1X*	**EBN** Eastbourne	**73B** New Cross Gate					
32009	*I1X*	**EBN** Eastbourne	**75G** Eastbourne					
32010	*I1X*	**EBN** Eastbourne						
32021	*I3*	**TWW** Tunbridge Wells West	**75F** Tunbridge Wells West					
32022	*I3*	**TWW** Tunbridge Wells West	**75F** Tunbridge Wells West					
32023	*I3*	**TWW** Tunbridge Wells West	**75F** Tunbridge Wells West					
32025	*I3*	**TWW** Tunbridge Wells West						
32026	*I3*	**TWW** Tunbridge Wells West	**75F** Tunbridge Wells West					
32027	*I3*	**TWW** Tunbridge Wells West	**75F** Tunbridge Wells West					
32028	*I3*	**TWW** Tunbridge Wells West	**75F** Tunbridge Wells West					
32029	*I3*	**TWW** Tunbridge Wells West	**75E** Three Bridges					
32030	*I3*	**TWW** Tunbridge Wells West	**75G** Eastbourne					
32037	*H1*	**BTN** Brighton	**75A** Newhaven					
32038	*H1*	**BTN** Brighton	**75A** Newhaven					
32039	*H1*	**BTN** Brighton	**75A** Brighton					
32043	*B4X*	**BTN** Brighton	**75G** Eastbourne					
32044	*B4*^{2}	**EBN** Eastbourne						
32045	*B4X*	**HOR** Horsham	**70D** Basingstoke					
32050	*B4X*	**EBN** Eastbourne	**73B** Bricklayers Arms					
32051	*B4*^{2}	**HOR** Horsham						
32052	*B4X*	**EBN** Eastbourne	**70D** Basingstoke					
32054	*B4*^{2}	**EBN** Eastbourne	**75G** Eastbourne					
32055	*B4X*	**HOR** Horsham	**75G** Eastbourne					
32056	*B4X*	**BTN** Brighton	**73B** Bricklayers Arms					
32060	*B4X*	**BTN** Brighton	**75G** Eastbourne					
32062	*B4*^{2}	**EBN** Eastbourne	**75G** Eastbourne					
32063	*B4*^{2}	**EBN** Eastbourne	**75G** Eastbourne					
32067	*B4X*	**HOR** Horsham	**70D** Basingstoke					
32068	*B4*^{2}	**EBN** Eastbourne	**75G** Eastbourne					
32070	*B4X*	**EBN** Eastbourne	**73B** Bricklayers Arms					
32071	*B4X*	**BTN** Brighton	**75G** Eastbourne					
32072	*B4X*	**BTN** Brighton	**75G** Eastbourne					
32073	*B4X*	**EBN** Eastbourne	**75G** Eastbourne					
32074	*B4*^{2}	**HOR** Horsham						
32075	*I3*	**BA** Bricklayers Arms	**73B** Bricklayers Arms					
32076	*I3*	**BA** Bricklayers Arms						
32077	*I3*	**BA** Bricklayers Arms	**75G** Eastbourne					
32078	*I3*	**3B** Three Bridges	**75E** Three Bridges					
32079	*I3*	**3B** Three Bridges						
32080	*I3*	**3B** Three Bridges						
32081	*I3*	**3B** Three Bridges	**75G** Eastbourne					
32082	*I3*	**3B** Three Bridges	**75E** Three Bridges					
32083	*I3*	**EBN** Eastbourne	**75G** Eastbourne					
32084	*I3*	**BTN** Brighton	**75E** Three Bridges					
32085	*I3*	**BA** Bricklayers Arms						
32086	*I3*	**BTN** Brighton	**75A** Brighton					
32087	*I3*	**BA** Bricklayers Arms						
32088	*I3*	**BTN** Brighton						
32089	*I3*	**BA** Bricklayers Arms	**75G** Eastbourne					
32090	*I3*	**EBN** Eastbourne						
32091	*I3*	**EBN** Eastbourne	**75E** Three Bridges					
32094	*E1R*	**BPL** Barnstaple Junction	**72D** Plymouth Friary	**72D** Plymouth Friary				
32095	*E1R*	**BPL** Barnstaple Junction	**72E** Barnstaple Junction	**72D** Plymouth Friary				
32096	*E1R*	**BPL** Barnstaple Junction	**72E** Barnstaple Junction	**72E** Barnstaple Junction				
32097	*E1*^{2}	**BA** Bricklayers Arms						
32100	*E2*	**BAT** Stewarts Lane	**73A** Stewarts Lane	**73A** Stewarts Lane	**73A** Stewarts Lane	**73A** Stewarts Lane		
32101	*E2*	**BAT** Stewarts Lane	**73A** Stewarts Lane	**73A** Stewarts Lane	**73A** Stewarts Lane	**71I** Southampton Docks		
32102	*E2*	**BAT** Stewarts Lane	**73A** Stewarts Lane	**73A** Stewarts Lane	**73A** Stewarts Lane	**73A** Stewarts Lane		
32103	*E2*	**BAT** Stewarts Lane	**73A** Stewarts Lane	**73A** Stewarts Lane	**73A** Stewarts Lane	**73A** Stewarts Lane		
32104	*E2*	**BAT** Stewarts Lane	**73A** Stewarts Lane	**73A** Stewarts Lane	**73A** Stewarts Lane	**75C** Norwood Junction	**71I** Southampton Docks	

No.	Class	1948	1951	1954	1957	1960	1963	1966
32105	*E2*	**BAT** Stewarts Lane	**73A** Stewarts Lane	**73A** Stewarts Lane	**73A** Stewarts Lane	**75C** Norwood Junction		
32106	*E2*	**BAT** Stewarts Lane	**73A** Stewarts Lane	**73A** Stewarts Lane	**73A** Stewarts Lane	**73A** Stewarts Lane		
32107	*E2*	**BAT** Stewarts Lane	**73A** Stewarts Lane	**73A** Stewarts Lane	**73A** Stewarts Lane	**75E** Three Bridges		
32108	*E2*	**DOV** Dover Marine	**74C** Dover Marine	**74C** Dover Marine	**71A** Eastleigh	**71I** Southampton Docks		
32109	*E2*	**DOV** Dover Marine	**74C** Dover Marine	**74C** Dover Marine	**71A** Eastleigh	**71I** Southampton Docks	**71I** Southampton Docks	
32112	$E1^2$	**SOT** Southampton Docks						
32113	$E1^2$	**TON** Tonbridge	**73B** Bricklayers Arms	**71A** Eastleigh	**71I** Southampton Docks			
32122	$E1^2$	**BTN** Brighton						
32124	*E1R*	**EXJ** Exmouth Junction	**72A** Exmouth Junction	**72A** Exmouth Junction	**72A** Exmouth Junction			
32127	$E1^2$	**BTN** Brighton						
32128	$E1^2$	**BA** Bricklayers Arms	**73A** Stewarts Lane					
32129	$E1^2$	**TON** Tonbridge	**71D** Fratton					
32133	$E1^2$	**ELH** Eastleigh	**71A** Eastleigh					
32135	*E1R*	**EXJ** Exmouth Junction	**72A** Exmouth Junction	**72A** Exmouth Junction	**72A** Exmouth Junction			
32138	$E1^2$	**TON** Tonbridge	**70A** Nine Elms	**71D** Fratton				
32139	$E1^2$	**BTN** Brighton	**71D** Fratton	**71D** Fratton	**70F** Fratton			
32141	$E1^2$	**BA** Bricklayers Arms						
32142	$E1^2$	**BA** Bricklayers Arms						
32145	$E1^2$	**TON** Tonbridge	**75A** Brighton					
32147	$E1^2$	**ELH** Eastleigh	**71A** Eastleigh					
32151	$E1^2$	**BA** Bricklayers Arms	**73B** Bricklayers Arms	**71A** Eastleigh	**71I** Southampton Docks	**71I** Southampton Docks		
32153	$E1^2$	**FRA** Fratton						
32156	$E1^2$	**SOT** Southampton Docks	**71I** Southampton Docks					
32160	$E1^2$	**ELH** Eastleigh	**70C** Guildford					
32162	$E1^2$	**SOT** Southampton Docks						
32164	$E1^2$	**TON** Tonbridge						
32165	*E3*	**BA** Bricklayers Arms	**73B** Bricklayers Arms	**75A** Brighton	**75A** Brighton			
32166	*E3*	**BA** Bricklayers Arms	**73B** Bricklayers Arms	**75A** Brighton	**75A** Brighton			
32167	*E3*	**NOR** Norwood Junction	**74D** Tonbridge	**75A** Brighton				
32168	*E3*	**BA** Bricklayers Arms	**73B** Bricklayers Arms	**70E** Reading South				
32169	*E3*	**NOR** Norwood Junction	**74D** Tonbridge	**75A** Brighton				
32170	*E3*	**BA** Bricklayers Arms	**73B** Bricklayers Arms	**75A** Brighton	**70E** Reading South			
32215	*D1/M*	**TWW** Tunbridge Wells West						
32234	*D1/M*	**EBN** Eastbourne						
32235	*D1/M*	**BTN** Brighton						
32239	*D1/M*	**ELH** Eastleigh						
32252	*D1/M*	**HOR** Horsham						
32253	*D1/M*	**TWW** Tunbridge Wells West						
32259	*D1/M*	**ELH** Eastleigh						
32269	*D1/M*	**FRA** Fratton						
32274	*D1/M*	**EBN** Eastbourne						
32283	*D1/M*	**HOR** Horsham						
32286	$D1^2$	**HOR** Horsham						
32289	*D1/M*	**HOR** Horsham						
32299	*D1/M*	**AFD** Ashford						
32300	*C3*	**HOR** Horsham	**71D** Fratton					
32301	*C3*	**HOR** Horsham	**71D** Fratton					
32302	*C3*	**NOR** Norwood Junction	**71D** Fratton					
32303	*C3*	**3B** Three Bridges	**71D** Fratton					
32306	*C3*	**HOR** Horsham	**71D** Fratton					
32307	*C3*	**HOR** Horsham						
32308	*C3*	**HOR** Horsham						
32309	*C3*	**NOR** Norwood Junction						
32325	*J1*	**TWW** Tunbridge Wells West	**75A** Brighton					
32326	*J2*	**TWW** Tunbridge Wells West	**75A** Brighton					
32327	*N15X*	**BAS** Basingstoke	**70D** Basingstoke	**70D** Basingstoke				
32328	*N15X*	**BAS** Basingstoke	**70D** Basingstoke	**70D** Basingstoke				
32329	*N15X*	**BAS** Basingstoke	**70D** Basingstoke	**70D** Basingstoke				
32330	*N15X*	**BAS** Basingstoke	**70D** Basingstoke	**70D** Basingstoke				
32331	*N15X*	**BAS** Basingstoke	**70D** Basingstoke	**70D** Basingstoke	**70D** Basingstoke			
32332	*N15X*	**BAS** Basingstoke	**70D** Basingstoke	**70D** Basingstoke				
32333	*N15X*	**BAS** Basingstoke	**70D** Basingstoke	**70D** Basingstoke				
32337	*K*	**FRA** Fratton	**75A** Brighton	**75A** Brighton	**70F** Fratton	**75E** Three Bridges		
32338	*K*	**FRA** Fratton	**71D** Fratton	**75A** Brighton	**75A** Brighton	**75A** Brighton		
32339	*K*	**BTN** Brighton	**75A** Brighton	**75A** Brighton	**75A** Brighton	**75A** Brighton		
32340	*K*	**BTN** Brighton	**71D** Fratton	**75A** Brighton	**75A** Brighton	**75A** Brighton		
32341	*K*	**BTN** Brighton	**75A** Brighton	**75A** Brighton	**75A** Brighton	**75A** Brighton		
32342	*K*	**BTN** Brighton	**75A** Brighton	**75A** Brighton	**75A** Brighton	**75A** Brighton		
32343	*K*	**BTN** Brighton	**75A** Brighton	**75A** Brighton	**75A** Brighton	**75A** Brighton		
32344	*K*	**BTN** Brighton	**75A** Brighton	**75A** Brighton	**75E** Three Bridges	**75E** Three Bridges		
32345	*K*	**BTN** Brighton	**75A** Brighton	**75E** Three Bridges	**75E** Three Bridges	**75E** Three Bridges		
32346	*K*	**BTN** Brighton	**75A** Brighton	**75E** Three Bridges	**75E** Three Bridges	**75E** Three Bridges		
32347	*K*	**BTN** Brighton	**75E** Three Bridges	**75E** Three Bridges	**75E** Three Bridges	**75E** Three Bridges		
32348	*K*	**EBN** Eastbourne	**75A** Brighton	**75E** Three Bridges	**75E** Three Bridges	**75E** Three Bridges		
32349	*K*	**EBN** Eastbourne	**75E** Three Bridges	**71D** Fratton	**70F** Fratton	**75E** Three Bridges		
32350	*K*	**NOR** Norwood Junction	**75E** Three Bridges	**75E** Three Bridges	**75E** Three Bridges	**75E** Three Bridges		
32351	*K*	**NOR** Norwood Junction	**75E** Three Bridges	**75E** Three Bridges	**75E** Three Bridges	**75E** Three Bridges		
32352	*K*	**3B** Three Bridges	**75E** Three Bridges	**75E** Three Bridges	**75E** Three Bridges	**75E** Three Bridges		
32353	*K*	**3B** Three Bridges	**75E** Three Bridges	**75E** Three Bridges	**75E** Three Bridges	**75E** Three Bridges		
32358	*D1/M*	**EBN** Eastbourne						
32359	$D1^2$	**DOV** Dover Marine	**74C** Dover Marine					
32361	*D1/M*	**ELH** Eastleigh						
32364	*D3*	**AFD** Ashford	**75D** Horsham					
32365	*D3*	**AFD** Ashford	**75D** Horsham					
32366	*D3*	**HOR** Horsham						
32367	*D3*	**TON** Tonbridge						
32368	*D3*	**BTN** Brighton	**75A** Brighton					
32370	*D3*	**TON** Tonbridge						
32371	*D3*	**STL** St. Leonards						
32372	*D3*	**BTN** Brighton	**75A** Brighton					
32373	*D3*	**HOR** Horsham						
32374	*D3*	**TON** Tonbridge						
32376	*D3*	**BTN** Brighton	**75A** Brighton					
32377	*D3*	**EBN** Eastbourne						
32378	*D3*	**TON** Tonbridge	**74E** St. Leonards					
32379	*D3*	**STL** St. Leonards	**75D** Horsham					
32380	*D3*	**AFD** Ashford	**75D** Horsham					
32383	*D3*	**STL** St. Leonards						
32384	*D3*	**HOR** Horsham	**75D** Horsham					
32385	*D3*	**BTN** Brighton	**75G** Eastbourne					
32386	*D3*	**BTN** Brighton	**75A** Brighton					
32387	*D3*	**HOR** Horsham						
32388	*D3*	**AFD** Ashford	**74E** St. Leonards					
32389	*D3*	**HOR** Horsham						
32390	*D3*	**TWW** Tunbridge Wells West	**74E** St. Leonards	**75A** Brighton				
32391	*D3*	**EBN** Eastbourne	**74E** St. Leonards					
32393	*D3*	**TWW** Tunbridge Wells West	**75A** Brighton					
32394	*D3*	**STL** St. Leonards	**75G** Eastbourne					
32395	*D3*	**EBN** Eastbourne						
32397	*D3X*	**BTN** Brighton						
32398	*D3*	**TWW** Tunbridge Wells West						
32399	*E5*	**HOR** Horsham	**71D** Fratton					
32400	*E5*	**3B** Three Bridges	**75A** Brighton					
32401	*E5X*	**HOR** Horsham	**75D** Horsham	**75A** Brighton				

		1948		1951	1954	1957	1960	1963	1966
32402	*E5*	**EBN**	Eastbourne	**75G** Eastbourne					
32404	*E5*	**NOR**	Norwood Junction	**75G** Eastbourne					
32405	*E5*	**3B**	Three Bridges	**75G** Eastbourne					
32406	*E5*	**EBN**	Eastbourne	**75A** Brighton					
32407	*E6X*	**NOR**	Norwood Junction	**75C** Norwood Junction	**75C** Norwood Junction	**75C** Norwood Junction			
32408	*E6*	**BAS**	Basingstoke	**73B** Bricklayers Arms	**73B** Bricklayers Arms	**73B** Bricklayers Arms	**73B** Bricklayers Arms		
32409	*E6*	**ELH**	Eastleigh	**71A** Eastleigh	**73B** Bricklayers Arms	**73B** Bricklayers Arms			
32410	*E6*	**BA**	Bricklayers Arms	**73B** Bricklayers Arms	**73B** Bricklayers Arms	**73B** Bricklayers Arms	**73B** Bricklayers Arms		
32411	*E6X*	**NOR**	Norwood Junction	**75C** Norwood Junction	**75C** Norwood Junction	**75C** Norwood Junction			
32412	*E6*	**BA**	Bricklayers Arms	**71A** Eastleigh	**73B** Bricklayers Arms	**73B** Bricklayers Arms			
32413	*E6*	**BA**	Bricklayers Arms	**73B** Bricklayers Arms	**75C** Norwood Junction	**75C** Norwood Junction			
32414	*E6*	**NOR**	Norwood Junction	**75C** Norwood Junction	**75C** Norwood Junction	**75C** Norwood Junction			
32415	*E6*	**BA**	Bricklayers Arms	**73B** Bricklayers Arms	**73B** Bricklayers Arms	**73B** Bricklayers Arms	**73B** Bricklayers Arms		
32416	*E6*	**NOR**	Norwood Junction	**71A** Eastleigh	**75C** Norwood Junction	**75C** Norwood Junction	**73B** Bricklayers Arms		
32417	*E6*	**NOR**	Norwood Junction	**75C** Norwood Junction	**75C** Norwood Junction	**75C** Norwood Junction	**73B** Bricklayers Arms		
32418	*E6*	**NOR**	Norwood Junction	**75C** Norwood Junction	**75C** Norwood Junction	**75C** Norwood Junction	**73B** Bricklayers Arms		
32421	*H2*	**NHN**	Newhaven	**75A** Newhaven	**75A** Brighton				
32422	*H2*	**NHN**	Newhaven	**75A** Newhaven	**75A** Newhaven				
32423	*H2*	**NHN**	Newhaven						
32424	*H2*	**NHN**	Newhaven	**75A** Newhaven	**75A** Newhaven	**75A** Brighton			
32425	*H2*	**NHN**	Newhaven	**75A** Brighton	**75A** Brighton				
32426	*H2*	**NHN**	Newhaven	**75A** Brighton	**75A** Brighton				
32434	*C2X*	**NHN**	Newhaven	**75A** Brighton	**75A** Brighton	**75A** Brighton			
32435	*C2*	**RED**	Redhill						
32436	*C2*	**3B**	Three Bridges						
32437	*C2X*	**BTN**	Brighton	**75A** Newhaven	**75A** Newhaven	**75A** Brighton			
32438	*C2X*	**BTN**	Brighton	**75A** Brighton	**75A** Brighton	**75E** Three Bridges	**70B** Feltham		
32440	*C2X*	**NOR**	Norwood Junction	**75C** Norwood Junction	**75A** Brighton	**75A** Brighton			
32441	*C2X*	**3B**	Three Bridges	**75E** Three Bridges	**75A** Brighton	**75A** Brighton	**75A** Brighton		
32442	*C2X*	**BA**	Bricklayers Arms	**73B** Bricklayers Arms	**75A** Brighton	**75A** Brighton	**75A** Brighton		
32443	*C2X*	**BTN**	Brighton	**75A** Brighton	**75C** Norwood Junction	**75C** Norwood Junction	**75C** Norwood Junction		
32444	*C2X*	**NOR**	Norwood Junction	**75C** Norwood Junction	**75C** Norwood Junction	**75C** Norwood Junction	**75C** Norwood Junction		
32445	*C2X*	**3B**	Three Bridges	**75E** Three Bridges	**75C** Norwood Junction	**75C** Norwood Junction	**75C** Norwood Junction		
32446	*C2X*	**BA**	Bricklayers Arms	**73B** Bricklayers Arms	**75C** Norwood Junction	**75C** Norwood Junction	**75C** Norwood Junction		
32447	*C2X*	**NOR**	Norwood Junction	**75C** Norwood Junction	**75C** Norwood Junction	**75C** Norwood Junction	**75C** Norwood Junction		
32448	*C2X*	**BA**	Bricklayers Arms	**73B** Bricklayers Arms	**75B** Redhill	**73A** Stewarts Lane	**75C** Norwood Junction		
32449	*C2X*	**HOR**	Horsham	**75B** Redhill	**75B** Redhill	**75A** Brighton	**75A** Brighton		
32450	*C2X*	**RED**	Redhill	**75B** Redhill	**75B** Redhill	**75B** Redhill	**75B** Redhill		
32451	*C2X*	**3B**	Three Bridges	**75E** Three Bridges	**75B** Redhill	**75B** Redhill	**75B** Redhill		
32453	*E3*	**BA**	Bricklayers Arms	**73B** Bricklayers Arms	**73B** Bricklayers Arms				
32454	*E3*	**BA**	Bricklayers Arms	**74D** Tonbridge	**74D** Tonbridge	**74D** Tonbridge			
32455	*E3*	**NOR**	Norwood Junction	**74D** Tonbridge	**73B** Bricklayers Arms	**73A** Stewarts Lane			
32456	*E3*	**NOR**	Norwood Junction	**74D** Tonbridge	**74D** Tonbridge	**74D** Tonbridge			
32457	*E3*	**NOR**	Norwood Junction						
32458	*E3*	**BA**	Bricklayers Arms	**73B** Bricklayers Arms	**73B** Bricklayers Arms	**73B** Bricklayers Arms			
32459	*E3*	**BA**	Bricklayers Arms	**73B** Bricklayers Arms	**73B** Bricklayers Arms				
32460	*E3*	**BA**	Bricklayers Arms	**73B** Bricklayers Arms	**73B** Bricklayers Arms				
32461	*E3*	**BA**	Bricklayers Arms	**73B** Bricklayers Arms	**73B** Bricklayers Arms	**73B** Bricklayers Arms			
32462	*E3*	**BA**	Bricklayers Arms	**73B** Bricklayers Arms	**73B** Bricklayers Arms	**73B** Bricklayers Arms			
32463	*E4*	**BA**	Bricklayers Arms	**73B** Bricklayers Arms	**75D** Horsham	**75D** Horsham			
32464	*E4*	**HOR**	Horsham	**75D** Horsham	**75D** Horsham				
32465	*E4*	**3B**	Three Bridges	**75E** Three Bridges	**75D** Horsham				
32466	*E4X*	**NOR**	Norwood Junction	**75C** Norwood Junction	**75C** Norwood Junction	**75C** Norwood Junction			
32467	*E4*	**BA**	Bricklayers Arms	**73B** Bricklayers Arms	**75D** Horsham	**75A** Brighton			
32468	*E4*	**BA**	Bricklayers Arms	**70A** Nine Elms	**75D** Horsham	**75A** Brighton	**75A** Brighton	**75A** Brighton	
32469	*E4*	**BA**	Bricklayers Arms	**73B** Bricklayers Arms	**75D** Horsham	**75D** Horsham	**75E** Three Bridges		
32470	*E4*	**BTN**	Brighton	**75A** Brighton	**75D** Horsham	**75D** Horsham	**75E** Three Bridges		
32471	*E4*	**BTN**	Brighton	**75A** Brighton	**73B** Bricklayers Arms	**73B** Bricklayers Arms			
32472	*E4*	**BA**	Bricklayers Arms	**73B** Bricklayers Arms	**73B** Bricklayers Arms	**73B** Bricklayers Arms	**73B** Bricklayers Arms		
32473	*E4*	**NOR**	Norwood Junction	**73B** Bricklayers Arms	**73B** Bricklayers Arms	**73B** Bricklayers Arms	**73B** Bricklayers Arms		
32474	*E4*	**BA**	Bricklayers Arms	**73B** Bricklayers Arms	**73B** Bricklayers Arms	**73B** Bricklayers Arms	**73B** Bricklayers Arms	**75A** Brighton	
32475	*E4*	**NHN**	Newhaven	**75A** Newhaven	**75A** Newhaven	**75A** Brighton	**75A** Brighton		
32476	*E4*	**NOR**	Norwood Junction	**75C** Norwood Junction	**70A** Nine Elms	**70A** Nine Elms			
32477	*E4X*	**NOR**	Norwood Junction	**75C** Norwood Junction	**75C** Norwood Junction	**75C** Norwood Junction			
32478	*E4X*	**NOR**	Norwood Junction	**75C** Norwood Junction	**75C** Norwood Junction				
32479	*E4*	**NOR**	Norwood Junction	**75C** Norwood Junction	**71D** Fratton	**70F** Fratton	**75C** Norwood Junction	**75A** Brighton	
32480	*E4*	**3B**	Three Bridges	**75E** Three Bridges	**75E** Three Bridges	**75D** Horsham			
32481	*E4*	**NOR**	Norwood Junction	**73B** Bricklayers Arms	**75E** Three Bridges	**75A** Brighton			
32482	*E4*	**NHN**	Newhaven	**75D** Horsham	**75E** Three Bridges				
32484	*E4*	**3B**	Three Bridges	**75E** Three Bridges	**75E** Three Bridges	**75A** Brighton	**75A** Brighton		
32485	*E4*	**EBN**	Eastbourne	**75G** Eastbourne	**75A** Brighton	**75A** Brighton			
32486	*E4*	**BTN**	Brighton	**75A** Brighton	**72B** Salisbury	**70A** Nine Elms			
32487	*E4*	**GFD**	Guildford	**70C** Guildford	**70C** Guildford	**70C** Guildford	**70A** Nine Elms		
32488	*E4*	**TON**	Tonbridge	**74D** Tonbridge	**74D** Tonbridge	**74D** Tonbridge			
32489	*E4X*	**NOR**	Norwood Junction	**75C** Norwood Junction	**75C** Norwood Junction				
32490	*E4*	**FRA**	Fratton	**70C** Guildford	**70C** Guildford				
32491	*E4*	**BTN**	Brighton	**71A** Eastleigh	**71A** Eastleigh	**71A** Eastleigh	**71A** Eastleigh		
32492	*E4*	**NHN**	Newhaven	**71A** Eastleigh	**71A** Eastleigh	**70A** Nine Elms			
32493	*E4*	**NOR**	Norwood Junction	**70A** Nine Elms	**70A** Nine Elms	**70A** Nine Elms			
32494	*E4*	**NHN**	Newhaven	**75A** Newhaven	**75A** Newhaven	**75A** Brighton			
32495	*E4*	**NOR**	Norwood Junction	**75C** Norwood Junction	**71D** Fratton	**70F** Fratton	**75C** Norwood Junction		
32496	*E4*	**HOR**	Horsham	**75A** Newhaven	**75A** Newhaven				
32497	*E4*	**3B**	Three Bridges	**75E** Three Bridges	**70A** Nine Elms	**70A** Nine Elms			
32498	*E4*	**NOR**	Norwood Junction	**70A** Nine Elms	**70A** Nine Elms	**70A** Nine Elms	**70A** Nine Elms		
32499	*E4*	**NHN**	Newhaven	**70A** Nine Elms	**70A** Nine Elms	**70A** Nine Elms			
32500	*E4*	**GFD**	Guildford	**70A** Nine Elms	**70A** Nine Elms	**70A** Nine Elms	**70A** Nine Elms		
32501	*E4*	**HOR**	Horsham	**70A** Nine Elms	**70E** Reading South				
32502	*E4*	**NOR**	Norwood Junction	**70A** Nine Elms	**70E** Reading South	**75A** Brighton			
32503	*E4*	**TON**	Tonbridge	**74D** Tonbridge	**74D** Tonbridge	**75A** Brighton	**75A** Brighton	**75A** Brighton	
32504	*E4*	**GFD**	Guildford	**75A** Newhaven	**75A** Newhaven	**75A** Brighton	**75A** Brighton		
32505	*E4*	**BTN**	Brighton	**75A** Brighton	**71D** Fratton	**70C** Guildford	**70C** Guildford		
32506	*E4*	**NOR**	Norwood Junction	**75C** Norwood Junction	**72B** Salisbury	**70C** Guildford	**70C** Guildford		
32507	*E4*	**RED**	Redhill	**75B** Redhill	**75B** Redhill	**75B** Redhill			
32508	*E4*	**NHN**	Newhaven	**75A** Newhaven	**75A** Brighton	**75A** Brighton	**75A** Brighton		
32509	*E4*	**FRA**	Fratton	**75A** Brighton	**71D** Fratton	**70F** Fratton	**75C** Norwood Junction		
32510	*E4*	**NPT**	Newport IOW	**71A** Eastleigh	**71A** Eastleigh	**71A** Eastleigh	**71A** Eastleigh		
32511	*E4*	**HOR**	Horsham	**75D** Horsham	**75A** Brighton				
32512	*E4*	**TWW**	Tunbridge Wells West	**75B** Redhill	**75B** Redhill	**75A** Brighton	**75A** Brighton		
32513	*E4*	**BTN**	Brighton	**75A** Brighton	**75A** Brighton				
32514	*E4*	**BTN**	Brighton	**75A** Brighton	**75A** Brighton				
32515	*E4*	**HOR**	Horsham	**75D** Horsham	**75A** Brighton	**75A** Brighton	**75A** Brighton		
32516	*E4*	**3B**	Three Bridges	**75E** Three Bridges	**75E** Three Bridges				
32517	*E4*	**RED**	Redhill	**75B** Redhill	**75F** Tunbridge Wells West	**75F** Tunbridge Wells West			
32518	*E4*	**EBN**	Eastbourne	**75G** Eastbourne	**75A** Brighton				
32519	*E4*	**3B**	Three Bridges	**75E** Three Bridges	**75E** Three Bridges	**75E** Three Bridges			
32520	*E4*	**3B**	Three Bridges	**75E** Three Bridges	**75E** Three Bridges	**75E** Three Bridges			
32521	*C2X*	**HOR**	Horsham	**75D** Horsham	**75D** Horsham	**75A** Brighton	**75C** Norwood Junction		
32522	*C2X*	**3B**	Three Bridges	**75E** Three Bridges	**75D** Horsham	**75D** Horsham	**75E** Three Bridges		
32523	*C2X*	**BTN**	Brighton	**75A** Brighton	**75D** Horsham	**75D** Horsham	**75E** Three Bridges		
32524	*C2X*	**BA**	Bricklayers Arms	**73B** Bricklayers Arms	**73B** Bricklayers Arms	**73B** Bricklayers Arms			
32525	*C2X*	**BA**	Bricklayers Arms	**73B** Bricklayers Arms	**73B** Bricklayers Arms	**73B** Bricklayers Arms	**73B** Bricklayers Arms		
32526	*C2X*	**NOR**	Norwood Junction	**75C** Norwood Junction	**75E** Three Bridges	**75E** Three Bridges	**75E** Three Bridges		
32527	*C2X*	**3B**	Three Bridges	**75E** Three Bridges	**75E** Three Bridges	**75E** Three Bridges	**75E** Three Bridges		
32528	*C2X*	**BTN**	Brighton	**75A** Brighton	**75E** Three Bridges	**75E** Three Bridges	**75E** Three Bridges		

No.	Class	1948	1951	1954	1957	1960	1963	1966
32529	C2X	3B Three Bridges	75E Three Bridges	75E Three Bridges	75E Three Bridges			
32532	C2X	3B Three Bridges	75E Three Bridges	75E Three Bridges	75E Three Bridges	75E Three Bridges		
32533	C2	NHN Newhaven						
32534	C2X	NHN Newhaven	75A Brighton	75E Three Bridges	75E Three Bridges	75E Three Bridges		
32535	C2X	NOR Norwood Junction	75C Norwood Junction	75E Three Bridges	75E Three Bridges	75E Three Bridges		
32536	C2X	NOR Norwood Junction	75C Norwood Junction	75E Three Bridges	75A Brighton	75E Three Bridges		
32537	C2X	FRA Fratton	75A Newhaven	75E Three Bridges	73B Bricklayers Arms			
32538	C2X	EBN Eastbourne	75A Brighton	75E Three Bridges	73B Bricklayers Arms	73B Bricklayers Arms		
32539	C2X	BTN Brighton	75D Horsham	75A Brighton	73B Bricklayers Arms	73B Bricklayers Arms		
32540	C2X	NOR Norwood Junction	75B Redhill	75A Brighton	75A Brighton			
32541	C2X	RED Redhill	75B Redhill	75D Horsham	75D Horsham	75C Norwood Junction		
32543	C2X	BTN Brighton	75A Brighton	75C Norwood Junction	75C Norwood Junction	75C Norwood Junction		
32544	C2X	NOR Norwood Junction	75D Horsham	75C Norwood Junction	75C Norwood Junction	75C Norwood Junction		
32545	C2X	3B Three Bridges	75E Three Bridges	75C Norwood Junction	75C Norwood Junction	75C Norwood Junction		
32546	C2X	BTN Brighton	75C Norwood Junction	75C Norwood Junction	75C Norwood Junction	75C Norwood Junction		
32547	C2X	NOR Norwood Junction	75C Norwood Junction	75C Norwood Junction	75C Norwood Junction	73A Stewarts Lane		
32548	C2X	FRA Fratton	75D Horsham	71D Fratton	70F Fratton	75C Norwood Junction		
32549	C2X	BA Bricklayers Arms	73B Bricklayers Arms	71D Fratton	70F Fratton	75C Norwood Junction		
32550	C2X	HOR Horsham	75B Redhill	71D Fratton	70F Fratton	75C Norwood Junction		
32551	C2X	BA Bricklayers Arms	73B Bricklayers Arms	73B Bricklayers Arms	73B Bricklayers Arms	73B Bricklayers Arms		
32552	C2X	3B Three Bridges	75E Three Bridges	73B Bricklayers Arms	73B Bricklayers Arms	73B Bricklayers Arms		
32553	C2X	3B Three Bridges	75E Three Bridges	73B Bricklayers Arms	73B Bricklayers Arms	73B Bricklayers Arms		
32554	C2X	FRA Fratton	73B Bricklayers Arms	73B Bricklayers Arms	73B Bricklayers Arms	73B Bricklayers Arms		
32556	E4	HOR Horsham	75D Horsham	71A Eastleigh	71A Eastleigh	71A Eastleigh		
32557	E4	HOR Horsham	71A Eastleigh	71A Eastleigh	71A Eastleigh	73B Bricklayers Arms		
32558	E4	BTN Brighton	71A Eastleigh	71A Eastleigh				
32559	E4	FRA Fratton	71A Eastleigh	71A Eastleigh	71A Eastleigh	71A Eastleigh		
32560	E4	RED Redhill	75B Redhill	75B Redhill	75B Redhill			
32561	E4	NOR Norwood Junction	75B Redhill	75B Redhill				
32562	E4	FRA Fratton	71A Eastleigh	71A Eastleigh	75A Brighton	75A Brighton		
32563	E4	NOR Norwood Junction	71A Eastleigh	71A Eastleigh	70A Nine Elms	70A Nine Elms		
32564	E4	BA Bricklayers Arms	73B Bricklayers Arms	73B Bricklayers Arms	73B Bricklayers Arms	73B Bricklayers Arms		
32565	E4	BA Bricklayers Arms	73B Bricklayers Arms	73B Bricklayers Arms	73B Bricklayers Arms	73B Bricklayers Arms		
32566	E4	BTN Brighton	75A Brighton	75A Brighton	75A Brighton			
32567	E5	BTN Brighton						
32568	E5	RED Redhill	75B Redhill	70D Basingstoke				
32570	E5X	HOR Horsham	75D Horsham	75D Horsham				
32571	E5	HOR Horsham	75B Redhill	75E Three Bridges				
32572	E5	3B Three Bridges						
32573	E5	HOR Horsham	75A Brighton					
32574	E5	EBN Eastbourne	75G Eastbourne					
32575	E5	EBN Eastbourne	75A Brighton					
32576	E5X	BTN Brighton	75A Brighton	75D Horsham				
32577	E4	BTN Brighton	75A Brighton	75A Brighton	75A Brighton			
32578	E4	BA Bricklayers Arms	75C Norwood Junction	74D Tonbridge	74D Tonbridge	73J Tonbridge		
32579	E4	NOR Norwood Junction	71A Eastleigh	71A Eastleigh	71A Eastleigh			
32580	E4	TON Tonbridge	74D Tonbridge	74D Tonbridge	74D Tonbridge	75A Brighton		
32581	E4	TWW Tunbridge Wells West	74D Tonbridge	75F Tunbridge Wells West	75F Tunbridge Wells West	75F Tunbridge Wells West		
32582	E4	TWW Tunbridge Wells West	75E Three Bridges	75F Tunbridge Wells West				
32583	E5	BTN Brighton	75A Brighton	75A Brighton				
32584	E5	HOR Horsham	75E Three Bridges					
32585	E5	3B Three Bridges	73B Bricklayers Arms	75A Brighton				
32586	E5X	RED Redhill	75D Horsham	75A Brighton				
32587	E5	BTN Brighton	73B Bricklayers Arms	70D Basingstoke				
32588	E5	EBN Eastbourne	75A Brighton					
32589	E5	TWW Tunbridge Wells West						
32590	E5	TWW Tunbridge Wells West	73B Bricklayers Arms					
32591	E5	TWW Tunbridge Wells West	75E Three Bridges	70D Basingstoke				
32592	E5	RED Redhill	75C Norwood Junction					
32593	E5	3B Three Bridges	75B Redhill	74C Dover Marine				
32594	E5	HOR Horsham	75A Brighton					
32595	I1X	EBN Eastbourne	75A Brighton					
32596	I1X	EBN Eastbourne	73B New Cross Gate					
32598	I1X	3B Three Bridges						
32599	I1X	3B Three Bridges						
32601	I1X	3B Three Bridges						
32602	I1X	3B Three Bridges	73B Bricklayers Arms					
32603	I1X	TWW Tunbridge Wells West	75G Eastbourne					
32604	I1X	3B Three Bridges						
32605	D1/M	EBN Eastbourne						
32606	E1[2]	BTN Brighton	71I Southampton Docks	71I Southampton Docks				
32608	E1R	BPL Barnstaple Junction	72E Barnstaple Junction	72E Barnstaple Junction	72E Barnstaple Junction			
32609	E1[2]	ELH Eastleigh						
32610	E1R	BPL Barnstaple Junction	72E Barnstaple Junction	72E Barnstaple Junction				
32635	A1X	(DS377)	→	→	→	75A Brighton	75A Brighton	
32636	A1X	NHN Newhaven	75A Newhaven	75A Newhaven	74E St. Leonards	71A Eastleigh	75A Brighton	
32640	A1X	FRA Fratton	74A Ashford	75A Newhaven	70F Fratton	71A Eastleigh	71A Eastleigh	
32644	A1X	FRA Fratton	74A Ashford					
32646	A1X	(W8)	71D Fratton	71D Fratton	70F Fratton	71A Eastleigh	71A Eastleigh	
32647	A1X	NHN Newhaven	75A Newhaven					
32650	A1X	(DS515)	→	71D Fratton	70F Fratton	71A Eastleigh	71A Eastleigh	
32655	A1X	FRA Fratton	71D Fratton	74A Ashford	75A Brighton	75A Brighton		
32659	A1X	FRA Fratton	74A Ashford	(DS681)				
32661	A1X	FRA Fratton	71D Fratton	71D Fratton	70F Fratton	71A Eastleigh	71A Eastleigh	
32662	A1X	FRA Fratton	71D Fratton	75A Newhaven	75A Brighton	75A Brighton	75A Brighton	
32670	A1X	KESR Rolvenden	74A Ashford	74A Ashford	74E St. Leonards	75A Brighton	75A Brighton	
32677	A1X	(W13)	71D Fratton	71D Fratton	70F Fratton			
32678	A1X	KESR Rolvenden	74A Ashford	74A Ashford	74E St. Leonards	71A Eastleigh	71A Eastleigh	
32689	E1[2]	SOT Southampton Docks	75A Brighton	71I Southampton Docks	71I Southampton Docks	71I Southampton Docks		
32690	E1[2]	FRA Fratton						
32691	E1[2]	FRA Fratton	71D Fratton					
32694	E1[2]	FRA Fratton	71D Fratton	71D Fratton	70F Fratton	71I Southampton Docks		
32695	E1R	EXJ Exmouth Junction	72A Exmouth Junction	72A Exmouth Junction	72A Exmouth Junction			
32696	E1R	BPL Barnstaple Junction	72E Barnstaple Junction	72E Barnstaple Junction				
32697	E1R	EXJ Exmouth Junction	72A Exmouth Junction	72A Exmouth Junction	72A Exmouth Junction			
32699	D1/M	ELH Eastleigh						
33001	Q1	GFD Guildford	70C Guildford	70C Guildford	70C Guildford	73J Tonbridge	70B Feltham	
33002	Q1	GFD Guildford	70C Guildford	70C Guildford	70C Guildford	73J Tonbridge	70B Feltham	
33003	Q1	GFD Guildford	70C Guildford	70C Guildford	70C Guildford	73J Tonbridge	70B Feltham	
33004	Q1	GFD Guildford	70C Guildford	70C Guildford	70C Guildford	73J Tonbridge	70B Feltham	
33005	Q1	GFD Guildford	70C Guildford	70C Guildford	70C Guildford	70C Guildford	70C Guildford	
33006	Q1	GFD Guildford	70B Feltham	70B Feltham	70B Feltham	70B Feltham	70B Feltham	70C Guildford
33007	Q1	GFD Guildford	70B Feltham	70B Feltham	70B Feltham	70B Feltham	70B Feltham	
33008	Q1	GFD Guildford	70B Feltham	70B Feltham	70B Feltham	70B Feltham	70B Feltham	
33009	Q1	GFD Guildford	70B Feltham	70B Feltham	70B Feltham	70B Feltham	70B Feltham	
33010	Q1	GFD Guildford	70B Feltham	70B Feltham	70B Feltham	70B Feltham	70B Feltham	
33011	Q1	GFD Guildford	70B Feltham	70B Feltham	70B Feltham	70B Feltham	70B Feltham	
33012	Q1	GFD Guildford	70B Feltham	70B Feltham	70B Feltham	70B Feltham	70B Feltham	
33013	Q1	GFD Guildford	70B Feltham	70B Feltham	70B Feltham	70B Feltham	70B Feltham	
33014	Q1	ELH Eastleigh	70C Guildford	73C Hither Green	73C Hither Green	73J Tonbridge	75E Three Bridges	
33015	Q1	ELH Eastleigh	70C Guildford	73C Hither Green	70A Nine Elms	70A Nine Elms	75E Three Bridges	
33016	Q1	ELH Eastleigh	70C Guildford	73C Hither Green	70B Feltham	70B Feltham	75E Three Bridges	
33017	Q1	ELH Eastleigh	71A Eastleigh	71A Eastleigh	70A Nine Elms	70A Nine Elms	75E Three Bridges	
33018	Q1	ELH Eastleigh	71A Eastleigh	73C Hither Green	70B Feltham	70B Feltham	75E Three Bridges	

		1948	1951	1954	1957	1960	1963	1966
33019	*Q1*	**ELH** Eastleigh	**71A** Eastleigh	**70C** Guildford	**70C** Guildford	**70C** Guildford	**70C** Guildford	
33020	*Q1*	**ELH** Eastleigh	**71A** Eastleigh	**71A** Eastleigh	**71A** Eastleigh	**71A** Eastleigh	**71A** Eastleigh	**70C** Guildford
33021	*Q1*	**ELH** Eastleigh	**71A** Eastleigh	**71A** Eastleigh	**71A** Eastleigh	**71A** Eastleigh	**71A** Eastleigh	
33022	*Q1*	**ELH** Eastleigh	**71A** Eastleigh	**70C** Guildford	**70C** Guildford	**70C** Guildford	**70C** Guildford	
33023	*Q1*	**ELH** Eastleigh	**71A** Eastleigh	**71A** Eastleigh	**71A** Eastleigh	**71A** Eastleigh	**71A** Eastleigh	
33024	*Q1*	**ELH** Eastleigh	**71A** Eastleigh	**74D** Tonbridge	**74D** Tonbridge	**73J** Tonbridge	**75E** Three Bridges	
33025	*Q1*	**ELH** Eastleigh	**71A** Eastleigh	**71A** Eastleigh	**70C** Guildford	**70C** Guildford	**70C** Guildford	
33026	*Q1*	**TON** Tonbridge	**73D** Gillingham	**70B** Feltham	**70B** Feltham	**70B** Feltham	**75E** Three Bridges	
33027	*Q1*	**TON** Tonbridge	**74D** Tonbridge	**70B** Feltham	**70B** Feltham	**70B** Feltham	**70B** Feltham	**70C** Guildford
33028	*Q1*	**TON** Tonbridge	**74D** Tonbridge	**74D** Tonbridge	**74D** Tonbridge	**73J** Tonbridge	**75E** Three Bridges	
33029	*Q1*	**TON** Tonbridge	**74D** Tonbridge	**74D** Tonbridge	**74D** Tonbridge	**73J** Tonbridge	**75E** Three Bridges	
33030	*Q1*	**TON** Tonbridge	**74D** Tonbridge	**74D** Tonbridge	**74D** Tonbridge	**73J** Tonbridge	**75E** Three Bridges	
33031	*Q1*	**FEL** Feltham	**74D** Tonbridge	**74D** Tonbridge	**74D** Tonbridge	**73J** Tonbridge	**75E** Three Bridges	
33032	*Q1*	**FEL** Feltham	**74D** Tonbridge	**74D** Tonbridge	**74D** Tonbridge	**73J** Tonbridge	**70C** Guildford	
33033	*Q1*	**FEL** Feltham	**74D** Tonbridge	**74D** Tonbridge	**74D** Tonbridge	**73J** Tonbridge	**70C** Guildford	
33034	*Q1*	**FEL** Feltham	**74D** Tonbridge	**74D** Tonbridge	**74D** Tonbridge	**73J** Tonbridge	**70C** Guildford	
33035	*Q1*	**FEL** Feltham	**74D** Tonbridge	**74D** Tonbridge	**74D** Tonbridge	**73J** Tonbridge	**70C** Guildford	
33036	*Q1*	**FEL** Feltham	**74D** Tonbridge	**74D** Tonbridge	**74D** Tonbridge	**73J** Tonbridge	**70C** Guildford	
33037	*Q1*	**FEL** Feltham	**74D** Tonbridge	**73C** Hither Green	**73C** Hither Green	**73J** Tonbridge	**71A** Eastleigh	
33038	*Q1*	**FEL** Feltham	**74D** Tonbridge	**71A** Eastleigh	**70A** Nine Elms	**70A** Nine Elms	**70B** Feltham	
33039	*Q1*	**FEL** Feltham	**74E** St. Leonards	**74E** St. Leonards	**74E** St. Leonards	**73J** Tonbridge	**71A** Eastleigh	
33040	*Q1*	**FEL** Feltham	**74E** St. Leonards	**74E** St. Leonards	**74E** St. Leonards	**73J** Tonbridge	**70B** Feltham	
34001	*WC*	**EXJ** Exmouth Junction	**72A** Exmouth Junction	**72A** Exmouth Junction	**72A** Exmouth Junction	**73B** Bricklayers Arms	**70A** Nine Elms	**70A** Nine Elms
34002	*WC*	**EXJ** Exmouth Junction	**72A** Exmouth Junction	**72A** Exmouth Junction	**72A** Exmouth Junction	**72A** Exmouth Junction	**72A** Exmouth Junction	**70A** Nine Elms
34003	*WC*	**EXJ** Exmouth Junction	**72A** Exmouth Junction	**72A** Exmouth Junction	**72A** Exmouth Junction	**73B** Bricklayers Arms	**70E** Salisbury	
34004	*WC*	**EXJ** Exmouth Junction	**72A** Exmouth Junction	**72A** Exmouth Junction	**72A** Exmouth Junction	**73B** Bricklayers Arms	**71A** Eastleigh	**70F** Bournemouth
34005	*WC*	**EXJ** Exmouth Junction	**72A** Exmouth Junction	**70A** Nine Elms	**70A** Nine Elms	**73B** Bricklayers Arms	**70E** Salisbury	**70F** Bournemouth
34006	*WC*	**EXJ** Exmouth Junction	**72A** Exmouth Junction	**70A** Nine Elms	**70A** Nine Elms	**70A** Nine Elms	**70A** Nine Elms	**70E** Salisbury
34007	*WC*	**EXJ** Exmouth Junction	**72A** Exmouth Junction	**70A** Nine Elms	**70A** Nine Elms	**70A** Nine Elms	**70A** Nine Elms	
34008	*WC*	**EXJ** Exmouth Junction	**72A** Exmouth Junction	**70A** Nine Elms	**70A** Nine Elms	**75A** Brighton	**71A** Eastleigh	**70D** Eastleigh
34009	*WC*	**EXJ** Exmouth Junction	**72A** Exmouth Junction	**70A** Nine Elms	**70A** Nine Elms	**70A** Nine Elms	**70A** Nine Elms	**70D** Eastleigh
34010	*WC*	**EXJ** Exmouth Junction	**72A** Exmouth Junction	**70A** Nine Elms	**70A** Nine Elms	**70A** Nine Elms	**70A** Nine Elms	
34011	*WC*	**EXJ** Exmouth Junction	**72D** Plymouth Friary	**70A** Nine Elms	**70A** Nine Elms	**72A** Exmouth Junction	**72A** Exmouth Junction	
34012	*WC*	**EXJ** Exmouth Junction	**72D** Plymouth Friary	**70A** Nine Elms	**70A** Nine Elms	**73B** Bricklayers Arms	**75A** Brighton	**70F** Bournemouth
34013	*WC*	**EXJ** Exmouth Junction	**72D** Plymouth Friary	**72A** Exmouth Junction	**72A** Exmouth Junction	**73B** Bricklayers Arms	**75A** Brighton	**70E** Salisbury
34014	*WC*	**EXJ** Exmouth Junction	**72A** Exmouth Junction	**72A** Exmouth Junction	**72A** Exmouth Junction	**73B** Bricklayers Arms	**75A** Brighton	
34015	*WC*	**EXJ** Exmouth Junction	**72A** Exmouth Junction	**72A** Exmouth Junction	**72A** Exmouth Junction	**72A** Exmouth Junction	**72A** Exmouth Junction	**70E** Salisbury
34016	*WC*	**EXJ** Exmouth Junction	**72A** Exmouth Junction	**72A** Exmouth Junction	**72A** Exmouth Junction	**73B** Bricklayers Arms	**71A** Eastleigh	
34017	*WC*	**EXJ** Exmouth Junction	**72A** Exmouth Junction	**72A** Exmouth Junction	**73A** Stewarts Lane	**73B** Bricklayers Arms	**70A** Nine Elms	**70D** Eastleigh
34018	*WC*	**EXJ** Exmouth Junction	**72A** Exmouth Junction	**70A** Nine Elms	**70A** Nine Elms	**70A** Nine Elms	**70A** Nine Elms	**70D** Eastleigh
34019	*WC*	**EXJ** Exmouth Junction	**72A** Exmouth Junction	**70A** Nine Elms	**70A** Nine Elms	**75A** Brighton	**75A** Brighton	**70D** Eastleigh
34020	*WC*	**EXJ** Exmouth Junction	**72A** Exmouth Junction	**70A** Nine Elms	**70A** Nine Elms	**70A** Nine Elms	**72A** Exmouth Junction	
34021	*WC*	**EXJ** Exmouth Junction	**72A** Exmouth Junction	**72A** Exmouth Junction	**72A** Exmouth Junction	**73B** Bricklayers Arms	**71A** Eastleigh	**70A** Nine Elms
34022	*WC*	**9E** Nine Elms	**72B** Salisbury	**72A** Exmouth Junction	**72A** Exmouth Junction	**73B** Bricklayers Arms	**71A** Eastleigh	
34023	*WC*	**9E** Nine Elms	**72B** Salisbury	**72A** Exmouth Junction	**72A** Exmouth Junction	**72A** Exmouth Junction	**72A** Exmouth Junction	**70D** Eastleigh
34024	*WC*	**EXJ** Exmouth Junction	**72A** Exmouth Junction	**72A** Exmouth Junction	**72A** Exmouth Junction	**72A** Exmouth Junction	**72A** Exmouth Junction	**70F** Bournemouth
34025	*WC*	**EXJ** Exmouth Junction	**72A** Exmouth Junction	**72A** Exmouth Junction	**72A** Exmouth Junction	**73B** Bricklayers Arms	**71A** Eastleigh	**70F** Bournemouth
34026	*WC*	**EXJ** Exmouth Junction	**72A** Exmouth Junction	**72A** Exmouth Junction	**72A** Exmouth Junction	**73B** Bricklayers Arms	**70E** Salisbury	**70E** Salisbury
34027	*WC*	**EXJ** Exmouth Junction	**72A** Exmouth Junction	**72A** Exmouth Junction	**72A** Exmouth Junction	**73B** Bricklayers Arms	**75A** Brighton	
34028	*WC*	**EXJ** Exmouth Junction	**72A** Exmouth Junction	**72A** Exmouth Junction	**72A** Exmouth Junction	**71B** Bournemouth	**71A** Eastleigh	
34029	*WC*	**EXJ** Exmouth Junction	**72A** Exmouth Junction	**72A** Exmouth Junction	**72A** Exmouth Junction	**71B** Bournemouth	**71B** Bournemouth	
34030	*WC*	**RAM** Ramsgate	**72A** Exmouth Junction	**72A** Exmouth Junction	**72A** Exmouth Junction	**72A** Exmouth Junction	**72A** Exmouth Junction	
34031	*WC*	**RAM** Ramsgate	**70A** Nine Elms	**72A** Exmouth Junction	**72A** Exmouth Junction	**70A** Nine Elms	**70A** Nine Elms	
34032	*WC*	**RAM** Ramsgate	**72B** Salisbury	**72A** Exmouth Junction	**72A** Exmouth Junction	**72A** Exmouth Junction	**72A** Exmouth Junction	**70E** Salisbury
34033	*WC*	**BAT** Stewarts Lane	**73A** Stewarts Lane	**72A** Exmouth Junction	**72A** Exmouth Junction	**72A** Exmouth Junction	**72A** Exmouth Junction	
34034	*WC*	**BAT** Stewarts Lane	**72D** Plymouth Friary	**72A** Exmouth Junction	**72A** Exmouth Junction	**72A** Exmouth Junction	**71A** Eastleigh	**70D** Eastleigh
34035	*WC*	**BAT** Stewarts Lane	**72D** Plymouth Friary	**72D** Plymouth Friary	**72D** Plymouth Friary	**72A** Exmouth Junction	**72A** Exmouth Junction	
34036	*WC*	**BAT** Stewarts Lane	**72D** Plymouth Friary	**72D** Plymouth Friary	**72D** Plymouth Friary	**72A** Exmouth Junction	**72A** Exmouth Junction	**70D** Eastleigh
34037	*WC*	**BAT** Stewarts Lane	**75A** Brighton	**72D** Plymouth Friary	**72D** Plymouth Friary	**73B** Bricklayers Arms	**71A** Eastleigh	**70D** Eastleigh
34038	*WC*	**BAT** Stewarts Lane	**75A** Brighton	**72D** Plymouth Friary	**72D** Plymouth Friary	**72A** Exmouth Junction	**71A** Eastleigh	**70A** Nine Elms
34039	*WC*	**BAT** Stewarts Lane	**75A** Brighton	**75A** Brighton	**75A** Brighton	**71B** Bournemouth	**71A** Eastleigh	
34040	*WC*	**BAT** Stewarts Lane	**75A** Brighton	**71G** Bath Green Park	**71B** Bournemouth	**71B** Bournemouth	**71B** Bournemouth	**70F** Bournemouth
34041	*WC*	**EXJ** Exmouth Junction	**75A** Brighton	**71G** Bath Green Park	**71B** Bournemouth	**71B** Bournemouth	**71B** Bournemouth	**70D** Eastleigh
34042	*WC*	**EXJ** Exmouth Junction	**72B** Salisbury	**71G** Bath Green Park	**71B** Bournemouth	**71B** Bournemouth	**71B** Bournemouth	
34043	*WC*	**EXJ** Exmouth Junction	**72B** Salisbury	**71B** Bournemouth	**71B** Bournemouth	**71B** Bournemouth	**71B** Bournemouth	
34044	*WC*	**EXJ** Exmouth Junction	**72A** Exmouth Junction	**71B** Bournemouth	**71B** Bournemouth	**71B** Bournemouth	**71B** Bournemouth	**70F** Bournemouth
34045	*WC*	**EXJ** Exmouth Junction	**72A** Exmouth Junction	**75A** Brighton	**75A** Brighton	**71B** Bournemouth	**71B** Bournemouth	
34046	*WC*	**EXJ** Exmouth Junction	**72A** Exmouth Junction	**75A** Brighton	**75A** Brighton	**71B** Bournemouth	**71B** Bournemouth	
34047	*WC*	**EXJ** Exmouth Junction	**72A** Exmouth Junction	**75A** Brighton	**75A** Brighton	**71B** Bournemouth	**71B** Bournemouth	**70F** Bournemouth
34048	*WC*	**SAL** Salisbury	**72A** Exmouth Junction	**75A** Brighton	**75A** Brighton	**71B** Bournemouth	**70E** Salisbury	**70E** Salisbury
34049	*BB*	**SAL** Salisbury	**70A** Nine Elms	**72B** Salisbury	**72B** Salisbury	**72B** Salisbury	**70E** Salisbury	
34050	*BB*	**SAL** Salisbury	**70A** Nine Elms	**72B** Salisbury	**72B** Salisbury	**72B** Salisbury	**70A** Nine Elms	
34051	*BB*	**SAL** Salisbury	**70A** Nine Elms	**72B** Salisbury	**72B** Salisbury	**72B** Salisbury	**70E** Salisbury	
34052	*BB*	**SAL** Salisbury	**70A** Nine Elms	**72B** Salisbury	**72B** Salisbury	**72B** Salisbury	**70E** Salisbury	**70E** Salisbury
34053	*BB*	**SAL** Salisbury	**70A** Nine Elms	**72B** Salisbury	**72B** Salisbury	**72B** Salisbury	**71B** Bournemouth	
34054	*BB*	**BAT** Stewarts Lane	**70A** Nine Elms	**72B** Salisbury	**72B** Salisbury	**72B** Salisbury	**70E** Salisbury	
34055	*BB*	**BAT** Stewarts Lane	**70A** Nine Elms	**72B** Salisbury	**72B** Salisbury	**72B** Salisbury	**75A** Brighton	
34056	*BB*	**DOV** Dover Marine	**70A** Nine Elms	**72A** Exmouth Junction	**72A** Exmouth Junction	**72A** Exmouth Junction	**72A** Exmouth Junction	**70E** Salisbury
34057	*BB*	**DOV** Dover Marine	**70A** Nine Elms	**72A** Exmouth Junction	**72A** Exmouth Junction	**72A** Exmouth Junction	**75A** Brighton	**70E** Salisbury
34058	*BB*	**9E** Nine Elms	**70A** Nine Elms	**72A** Exmouth Junction	**72A** Exmouth Junction	**72A** Exmouth Junction	**72A** Exmouth Junction	
34059	*BB*	**9E** Nine Elms	**70A** Nine Elms	**72A** Exmouth Junction	**72B** Salisbury	**72B** Salisbury	**70E** Salisbury	**70E** Salisbury
34060	*BB*	**9E** Nine Elms	**70A** Nine Elms	**72A** Exmouth Junction	**72A** Exmouth Junction	**72A** Exmouth Junction	**72A** Exmouth Junction	**70D** Eastleigh
34061	*BB*	**9E** Nine Elms	**70A** Nine Elms	**72A** Exmouth Junction	**72A** Exmouth Junction	**72A** Exmouth Junction	**71A** Eastleigh	
34062	*BB*	**RAM** Ramsgate	**70A** Nine Elms	**72A** Exmouth Junction	**72A** Exmouth Junction	**72A** Exmouth Junction	**72A** Exmouth Junction	
34063	*BB*	**RAM** Ramsgate	**70A** Nine Elms	**70A** Nine Elms	**70A** Nine Elms	**72A** Exmouth Junction	**72A** Exmouth Junction	
34064	*BB*	**9E** Nine Elms	**70A** Nine Elms	**70A** Nine Elms	**70A** Nine Elms	**72A** Exmouth Junction	**70A** Nine Elms	**70E** Salisbury
34065	*BB*	**RAM** Ramsgate	**70A** Nine Elms	**70A** Nine Elms	**70A** Nine Elms	**72A** Exmouth Junction	**72A** Exmouth Junction	
34066	*BB*	**RAM** Ramsgate	**73A** Stewarts Lane	**73A** Stewarts Lane	**73A** Stewarts Lane	**73A** Stewarts Lane	**72A** Exmouth Junction	**70E** Salisbury
34067	*BB*	**RAM** Ramsgate	**73A** Stewarts Lane	**73A** Stewarts Lane	**73A** Stewarts Lane	**73A** Stewarts Lane	**70E** Salisbury	
34068	*BB*	**RAM** Ramsgate	**73A** Stewarts Lane	**73A** Stewarts Lane	**73A** Stewarts Lane	**73A** Stewarts Lane	**70E** Salisbury	
34069	*BB*	**RAM** Ramsgate	**73A** Stewarts Lane	**73A** Stewarts Lane	**72A** Exmouth Junction	**72A** Exmouth Junction	**72A** Exmouth Junction	
34070	*BB*	**RAM** Ramsgate	**73A** Stewarts Lane	**73A** Stewarts Lane	**74C** Dover Marine	**73H** Dover Marine	**72A** Exmouth Junction	
34071	*BB*	→	**73A** Stewarts Lane	**73A** Stewarts Lane	**74C** Dover Marine	**73H** Dover Marine	**70A** Nine Elms	**70D** Eastleigh
34072	*BB*	→	**74C** Dover Marine	**74C** Dover Marine	**74C** Dover Marine	**72A** Exmouth Junction	**72A** Exmouth Junction	
34073	*BB*	→	**74C** Dover Marine	**74C** Dover Marine	**74C** Dover Marine	**73H** Dover Marine	**70A** Nine Elms	
34074	*BB*	→	**73A** Stewarts Lane	**74C** Dover Marine	**74C** Dover Marine	**72A** Exmouth Junction	**72A** Exmouth Junction	
34075	*BB*	→	**73A** Stewarts Lane	**74B** Ramsgate	**74B** Ramsgate	**72A** Exmouth Junction	**72A** Exmouth Junction	
34076	*BB*	→	**73A** Stewarts Lane	**74B** Ramsgate	**74B** Ramsgate	**72A** Exmouth Junction	**72A** Exmouth Junction	**70E** Salisbury
34077	*BB*	→	**74B** Ramsgate	**74B** Ramsgate	**74B** Ramsgate	**73A** Stewarts Lane	**70A** Nine Elms	**70D** Eastleigh
34078	*BB*	→	**74B** Ramsgate	**74B** Ramsgate	**74B** Ramsgate	**73B** Bricklayers Arms	**72A** Exmouth Junction	
34079	*BB*	→	**74B** Ramsgate	**74B** Ramsgate	**74B** Ramsgate	**72A** Exmouth Junction	**72A** Exmouth Junction	**70D** Eastleigh
34080	*BB*	→	**74B** Ramsgate	**74B** Ramsgate	**74B** Ramsgate	**72A** Exmouth Junction	**72A** Exmouth Junction	
34081	*BB*	→	**74B** Ramsgate	**74B** Ramsgate	**74B** Ramsgate	**72A** Exmouth Junction	**72A** Exmouth Junction	
34082	*BB*	→	**74B** Ramsgate	**74B** Ramsgate	**74B** Ramsgate	**73H** Dover Marine	**70A** Nine Elms	**70D** Eastleigh
34083	*BB*	→	**73A** Stewarts Lane	**74B** Ramsgate	**74B** Ramsgate	**73H** Dover Marine	**72A** Exmouth Junction	
34084	*BB*	→	**73A** Stewarts Lane	**74B** Ramsgate	**74B** Ramsgate	**73H** Dover Marine	**72A** Exmouth Junction	
34085	*BB*	→	**73A** Stewarts Lane	**74B** Ramsgate	**74B** Ramsgate	**73A** Stewarts Lane	**71B** Bournemouth	
34086	*BB*	→	**74B** Ramsgate	**74B** Ramsgate	**74B** Ramsgate	**73A** Stewarts Lane	**72A** Exmouth Junction	**70D** Eastleigh
34087	*BB*	→	**74B** Ramsgate	**73A** Stewarts Lane	**73A** Stewarts Lane	**73A** Stewarts Lane	**70A** Nine Elms	**70D** Eastleigh
34088	*BB*	→	**74B** Ramsgate	**73A** Stewarts Lane	**73A** Stewarts Lane	**73A** Stewarts Lane	**70A** Nine Elms	**70D** Eastleigh
34089	*BB*	→	**74B** Ramsgate	**73A** Stewarts Lane	**73A** Stewarts Lane	**73A** Stewarts Lane	**75A** Brighton	**70E** Salisbury
34090	*BB*	→	**74B** Ramsgate	**73A** Stewarts Lane	**73A** Stewarts Lane	**70A** Nine Elms	**70A** Nine Elms	**70D** Eastleigh
34091	*WC*	→	**73A** Stewarts Lane	**73A** Stewarts Lane	**73A** Stewarts Lane	**73A** Stewarts Lane	**70E** Salisbury	
34092	*WC*	→	**73A** Stewarts Lane	**73A** Stewarts Lane	**73A** Stewarts Lane	**73A** Stewarts Lane	**70E** Salisbury	

		1948	1951	1954	1957	1960	1963	1966
34093	WC	→	71B Bournemouth	71B Bournemouth	71B Bournemouth	70A Nine Elms	70A Nine Elms	70D Eastleigh
34094	WC	→	71B Bournemouth	71B Bournemouth	71B Bournemouth	70A Nine Elms	70A Nine Elms	
34095	WC	→	71B Bournemouth	71B Bournemouth	70A Nine Elms	70A Nine Elms	70A Nine Elms	70D Eastleigh
34096	WC	→	74B Ramsgate	74B Ramsgate	74B Ramsgate	72A Exmouth Junction	72A Exmouth Junction	
34097	WC	→	74B Ramsgate	74B Ramsgate	74B Ramsgate	75A Brighton	71A Eastleigh	70D Eastleigh
34098	WC	→	74B Ramsgate	74B Ramsgate	74B Ramsgate	75A Brighton	71A Eastleigh	70D Eastleigh
34099	WC	→	74B Ramsgate	74B Ramsgate	74B Ramsgate	75A Brighton	70E Salisbury	
34100	WC	→	74B Ramsgate	74B Ramsgate	74B Ramsgate	73A Stewarts Lane	75A Brighton	70E Salisbury
34101	WC	→	73A Stewarts Lane	73A Stewarts Lane	73A Stewarts Lane	73A Stewarts Lane	75A Brighton	70D Eastleigh
34102	WC	→	73A Stewarts Lane	73A Stewarts Lane	73A Stewarts Lane	71B Bournemouth	71B Bournemouth	70D Eastleigh
34103	WC	→	73A Stewarts Lane	73A Stewarts Lane	74C Dover Marine	73H Dover Marine	71B Bournemouth	
34104	WC	→	73A Stewarts Lane	73A Stewarts Lane	74C Dover Marine	72A Exmouth Junction	71A Eastleigh	70D Eastleigh
34105	WC	→	71B Bournemouth	71B Bournemouth	71B Bournemouth	71B Bournemouth	71B Bournemouth	
34106	WC	→	71B Bournemouth	71B Bournemouth	71B Bournemouth	72A Exmouth Junction	72A Exmouth Junction	
34107	WC	→	71B Bournemouth	71B Bournemouth	71B Bournemouth	72A Exmouth Junction	72A Exmouth Junction	
34108	WC	→	71B Bournemouth	71B Bournemouth	71B Bournemouth	72A Exmouth Junction	72A Exmouth Junction	70E Salisbury
34109	BB	→	71B Bournemouth	71B Bournemouth	71B Bournemouth	72A Exmouth Junction	72A Exmouth Junction	
34110	BB	→	→	71B Bournemouth	71B Bournemouth	72A Exmouth Junction	72A Exmouth Junction	
35001	MN	EXJ Exmouth Junction	72A Exmouth Junction	72A Exmouth Junction	72A Exmouth Junction	70A Nine Elms	70A Nine Elms	
35002	MN	EXJ Exmouth Junction	72A Exmouth Junction	72A Exmouth Junction	72A Exmouth Junction	71B Bournemouth	71B Bournemouth	
35003	MN	EXJ Exmouth Junction	72A Exmouth Junction	72A Exmouth Junction	72A Exmouth Junction	72A Exmouth Junction	72A Exmouth Junction	70F Bournemouth
35004	MN	EXJ Exmouth Junction	72A Exmouth Junction	72A Exmouth Junction	72A Exmouth Junction	72B Salisbury	70E Salisbury	
35005	MN	EXJ Exmouth Junction	70A Nine Elms	72A Exmouth Junction	70A Nine Elms	71B Bournemouth	71B Bournemouth	
35006	MN	SAL Salisbury	72B Salisbury	72B Salisbury	72B Salisbury	72B Salisbury	70E Salisbury	
35007	MN	SAL Salisbury	72B Salisbury	72B Salisbury	72B Salisbury	72B Salisbury	70E Salisbury	70G Weymouth
35008	MN	SAL Salisbury	72B Salisbury	72B Salisbury	72A Exmouth Junction	72A Exmouth Junction	71B Bournemouth	70F Bournemouth
35009	MN	SAL Salisbury	72B Salisbury	72B Salisbury	72B Salisbury	72A Exmouth Junction	72A Exmouth Junction	
35010	MN	SAL Salisbury	70A Nine Elms	70A Nine Elms	71B Bournemouth	71B Bournemouth	72A Exmouth Junction	70F Bournemouth
35011	MN	9E Nine Elms	70A Nine Elms	70A Nine Elms	70A Nine Elms	72A Exmouth Junction	71B Bournemouth	70F Bournemouth
35012	MN	9E Nine Elms	70A Nine Elms	70A Nine Elms	70A Nine Elms	70A Nine Elms	70A Nine Elms	70G Weymouth
35013	MN	9E Nine Elms	70A Nine Elms	70A Nine Elms	72A Exmouth Junction	72A Exmouth Junction	72A Exmouth Junction	70F Bournemouth
35014	MN	9E Nine Elms	70A Nine Elms	70A Nine Elms	70A Nine Elms	70A Nine Elms	70A Nine Elms	70G Weymouth
35015	MN	9E Nine Elms	70A Nine Elms	70A Nine Elms	73A Stewarts Lane	70A Nine Elms	70A Nine Elms	
35016	MN	9E Nine Elms	70A Nine Elms	70A Nine Elms	70A Nine Elms	70A Nine Elms	70A Nine Elms	
35017	MN	9E Nine Elms	70A Nine Elms	70A Nine Elms	70A Nine Elms	70A Nine Elms	70A Nine Elms	70G Weymouth
35018	MN	9E Nine Elms	70A Nine Elms	70A Nine Elms	70A Nine Elms	70A Nine Elms	70A Nine Elms	
35019	MN	9E Nine Elms	70A Nine Elms	70A Nine Elms	70A Nine Elms	70A Nine Elms	70A Nine Elms	
35020	MN	9E Nine Elms	70A Nine Elms	70A Nine Elms	70A Nine Elms	70A Nine Elms	70A Nine Elms	
35021	MN	→	72A Exmouth Junction	70A Nine Elms	70A Nine Elms	71B Bournemouth	71B Bournemouth	
35022	MN	→	72A Exmouth Junction	Rugby Testing Station	71B Bournemouth	71B Bournemouth	72A Exmouth Junction	70G Weymouth
35023	MN	→	72A Exmouth Junction	72A Exmouth Junction	72A Exmouth Junction	72A Exmouth Junction	71B Bournemouth	70F Bournemouth
35024	MN	→	72A Exmouth Junction	72A Exmouth Junction	72A Exmouth Junction	71B Bournemouth	70A Nine Elms	
35025	MN	→	73A Stewarts Lane	72A Exmouth Junction	71B Bournemouth	71B Bournemouth	72A Exmouth Junction	
35026	MN	→	73A Stewarts Lane	73A Stewarts Lane	73A Stewarts Lane	72A Exmouth Junction	72A Exmouth Junction	70G Weymouth
35027	MN	→	73A Stewarts Lane	73A Stewarts Lane	71B Bournemouth	71B Bournemouth	71B Bournemouth	70F Bournemouth
35028	MN	→	73A Stewarts Lane	73A Stewarts Lane	73A Stewarts Lane	70A Nine Elms	70A Nine Elms	70G Weymouth
35029	MN	→	74C Dover Marine	74C Dover Marine	70A Nine Elms	70A Nine Elms	70A Nine Elms	70G Weymouth
35030	MN	→	74C Dover Marine	74C Dover Marine	70A Nine Elms	70A Nine Elms	70A Nine Elms	70G Weymouth
KESR 4	0330	KESR Rolvenden						
W1	E1^2	NPT Newport IOW	71E Newport IOW	71E Newport IOW	70G Newport IOW			
W2	E1^2	NPT Newport IOW	71E Newport IOW	71E Newport IOW				
W3	E1^2	NPT Newport IOW	71E Newport IOW	71E Newport IOW	70G Newport IOW			
W4	E1^2	NPT Newport IOW	71E Newport IOW	71E Newport IOW	70G Newport IOW	70H Ryde IOW		
W8	A1X	NPT Newport IOW	(32646)					
W13	A1X	NPT Newport IOW	(32677)					
W14	O2	RYD Ryde IOW	71F Ryde IOW	71F Ryde IOW	70H Ryde IOW	70H Ryde IOW	70H Ryde IOW	70H Ryde IOW
W15	O2	RYD Ryde IOW	71F Ryde IOW	71F Ryde IOW				
W16	O2	RYD Ryde IOW	71F Ryde IOW	71F Ryde IOW	70H Ryde IOW	70H Ryde IOW	70H Ryde IOW	70H Ryde IOW
W17	O2	RYD Ryde IOW	71F Ryde IOW	71F Ryde IOW	70H Ryde IOW	70H Ryde IOW	70H Ryde IOW	70H Ryde IOW
W18	O2	RYD Ryde IOW	71F Ryde IOW	71F Ryde IOW	70H Ryde IOW	70H Ryde IOW	70H Ryde IOW	
W19	O2	RYD Ryde IOW	71F Ryde IOW	71F Ryde IOW				
W20	O2	RYD Ryde IOW	71F Ryde IOW	71F Ryde IOW	70H Ryde IOW	70H Ryde IOW	70H Ryde IOW	70H Ryde IOW
W21	O2	RYD Ryde IOW	71F Ryde IOW	71F Ryde IOW	70H Ryde IOW	70H Ryde IOW	70H Ryde IOW	70H Ryde IOW
W22	O2	RYD Ryde IOW	71F Ryde IOW	71F Ryde IOW	70H Ryde IOW	70H Ryde IOW	70H Ryde IOW	70H Ryde IOW
W23	O2	RYD Ryde IOW	71F Ryde IOW	71F Ryde IOW				
W24	O2	RYD Ryde IOW	71F Ryde IOW	71F Ryde IOW	70H Ryde IOW	70H Ryde IOW	70H Ryde IOW	70H Ryde IOW
W25	O2	NPT Newport IOW	71F Ryde IOW	71F Ryde IOW	70H Ryde IOW	70H Ryde IOW		
W26	O2	NPT Newport IOW	71E Newport IOW	71E Newport IOW	70G Newport IOW	70H Ryde IOW	70H Ryde IOW	70H Ryde IOW
W27	O2	NPT Newport IOW	71E Newport IOW	71E Newport IOW	70G Newport IOW	70H Ryde IOW	70H Ryde IOW	70H Ryde IOW
W28	O2	NPT Newport IOW	71E Newport IOW	71E Newport IOW	70G Newport IOW	70H Ryde IOW	70H Ryde IOW	70H Ryde IOW
W29	O2	NPT Newport IOW	71E Newport IOW	71E Newport IOW	70G Newport IOW	70H Ryde IOW	70H Ryde IOW	70H Ryde IOW
W30	O2	NPT Newport IOW	71E Newport IOW	71E Newport IOW	70G Newport IOW	70H Ryde IOW	70H Ryde IOW	
W31	O2	NPT Newport IOW	71E Newport IOW	71E Newport IOW	70G Newport IOW	70H Ryde IOW	70H Ryde IOW	70H Ryde IOW
W32	O2	NPT Newport IOW	71E Newport IOW	71E Newport IOW	70G Newport IOW	70H Ryde IOW	70H Ryde IOW	
W33	O2	NPT Newport IOW	71E Newport IOW	71E Newport IOW	70G Newport IOW	70H Ryde IOW	70H Ryde IOW	70H Ryde IOW
W34	O2	NPT Newport IOW	71E Newport IOW	71E Newport IOW				
W35	O2	(30181)	71E Newport IOW	71E Newport IOW	70G Newport IOW	70H Ryde IOW	70H Ryde IOW	70H Ryde IOW
W36	O2	(30198)	71E Newport IOW	71E Newport IOW	70G Newport IOW	70H Ryde IOW	70H Ryde IOW	
77S	C14	Redbridge Sleeper Depot	Redbridge Sleeper Depot	Redbridge Sleeper Depot	Redbridge Sleeper Depot			
DS233	USA	(30061)	→	→	→	→	Redbridge Sleeper Depot	Redbridge Sleeper Depot
DS234	USA	(30062)	→	→	→	→	Meldon Quarry	Meldon Quarry
DS235	USA	(30066)	→	→	→	→	Lancing Carriage Works	
DS236	USA	(30074)						
DS237	USA	(30065)	→	→	→	→	→	Ashford Carriage Works
DS238	USA	(30070)	→	→	→	→	→	Ashford Carriage Works
DS239	C	(31592)	→	→	→	→	→	Ashford Carriage Works
DS240	C	(31271)	→	→	→	→	→	Ashford Carriage Works
DS377	A1X	Brighton Works	Brighton Works	Brighton Works	Brighton Works	(32635)		
500S	T	Meldon Quarry						
DS515	A1X	Lancing Carriage Works	Lancing Carriage Works	(32650)				
DS680	A1	Lancing Carriage Works	Lancing Carriage Works	Lancing Carriage Works	Lancing Carriage Works	Lancing Carriage Works		
DS681	A1X	(32659)	→	Lancing Carriage Works	Lancing Carriage Works	Lancing Carriage Works	Lancing Carriage Works	
DS682	G6	(30238)						
700S	D1/M	Eastleigh						
701S	D1/M	Fratton	Fratton					
DS3152	G6	(30272)	Meldon Quarry	Meldon Quarry	Meldon Quarry	Meldon Quarry		
DS3191	A12	Eastleigh						
120	T9	(30120)	→	→	→	→	71A Eastleigh	

Left: LSWR Beattie '0298' class 2-4-0WT No 30587. *D. Penney*

Below: Plymouth, Devonport & South Western Junction Railway '756' class 0-6-0T No 756 *A. S. Harris*. Allocated number 30756.

Bottom: Plymouth, Devonport & South Western Junction Railway '757' class 0-6-2T No 30757 *Earl of Mount Edgcumbe* at Eastleigh on 22 May 1957. *H. C. Casserley*

Above: SR Maunsell 'Lord Nelson' (LN) class 4-6-0 No 30850 *Lord Nelson* at Eastleigh on 5 March 1961. *Alan G. Coombs*

Below: SR Maunsell 'Schools' (V) class 4-4-0 No 30927 *Clifton* at Nine Elms on 7 May 1961. *P. H. Wells*

Right: SECR Stirling 'F1' class 4-4-0 No 1231 awaiting scrap at Ashford in 1949. Allocated number 31231. *P. Ransome-Wallis*

Below: SECR Stirling 'B1' class 4-4-0 No 1443 working a Redhill-Reading train on 7 September 1949. Allocated number 31443.

Bottom: SECR Wainwright 'D' class 4-4-0 No 31574 at Ashford on 22 August 1954.

Above: London Chatham & Dover Railway Kirtley 'R' class 0-4-4T No 31662 based at 73D Gillingham. *P. Ransome-Wallis*

Right: SECR Kirtley/Wainwright 'R1' class 0-4-4T No 31703 at Ashford on 15 July 1950. *H. C. Casserley*

Below: SECR Wainwright 'L' class 4-4-0 No 31760 at its home depot 74D Tonbridge on 24 May 1958. *J. Scrace*

Above: SR Maunsell 'L1' class 4-4-0 No 31788 at Bricklayers Arms on 2 April 1955. *A. R. Carpenter*

Left: SR Maunsell 'U1' class 3-cylinder 2-6-0 No 31910 at Guildford on 10 June 1961. *R. S. Greenwood*

Below: LBSCR Marsh 'H1' class Atlantic No 2038 *Portland Bill* at New Cross Gate on 1 September 1946 in wartime black livery. It was the only 'H1' to be painted in Malachite Green in September 1947, and was later renumbered 32038. *R. C. Riley*

Top: LBSCR Billinton 'E2' class 0-6-0T No 32103 at Stewarts Lane on 25 June 1954. *F. W. Dixon*

Above: Later LBSCR Marsh 'H2' class Atlantic No 32424 *Beachy Head* at Brighton. *B. K. B. Green*

Below: A line of LBSCR and SECR engines are awaiting scrapping at Horley on 7 April 1950. From the front is 'C2' class 0-6-0 No 2436, 'R1' class 0-4-4T No 1699, 'O1' class 0-6-0s Nos 1377 and 1123, and 'B4' class 4-4-0 No 2074.

Top: Two LBSCR Marsh 'E4X' class 0-6-2Ts, Nos 32466 and 32477 at Norwood Junction on 18 May 1957. *F. J. Saunders*

Above: LBSCR Marsh 'E5X' class 0-6-2T No 32570.

Below: LBSCR Billinton 'E5' class 0-6-2T No 32591 at Brighton. *L. Elsey*

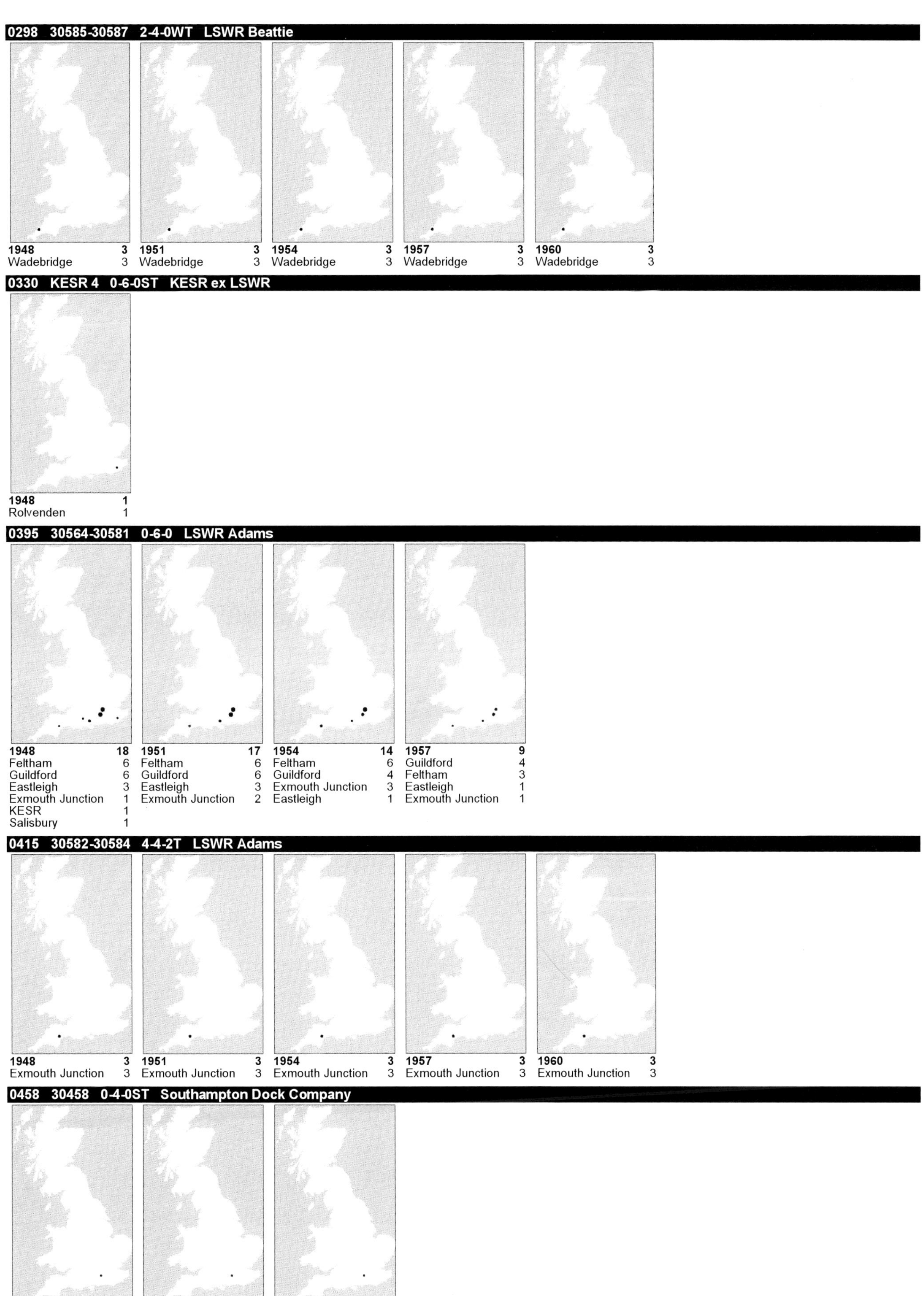
0298 30585-30587 2-4-0WT LSWR Beattie
1948 3
Wadebridge 3
1951 3
Wadebridge 3
1954 3
Wadebridge 3
1957 3
Wadebridge 3
1960 3
Wadebridge 3
0330 KESR 4 0-6-0ST KESR ex LSWR
1948 1
Rolvenden 1
0395 30564-30581 0-6-0 LSWR Adams
1948 18
Feltham 6
Guildford 6
Eastleigh 3
Exmouth Junction 1
KESR 1
Salisbury 1
1951 17
Feltham 6
Guildford 6
Eastleigh 3
Exmouth Junction 2
1954 14
Feltham 6
Guildford 4
Exmouth Junction 3
Eastleigh 1
1957 9
Guildford 4
Feltham 3
Eastleigh 1
Exmouth Junction 1
0415 30582-30584 4-4-2T LSWR Adams
1948 3
Exmouth Junction 3
1951 3
Exmouth Junction 3
1954 3
Exmouth Junction 3
1957 3
Exmouth Junction 3
1960 3
Exmouth Junction 3
0458 30458 0-4-0ST Southampton Dock Company
1948 1
Guildford 1
1951 1
Guildford 1
1954 1
Guildford 1

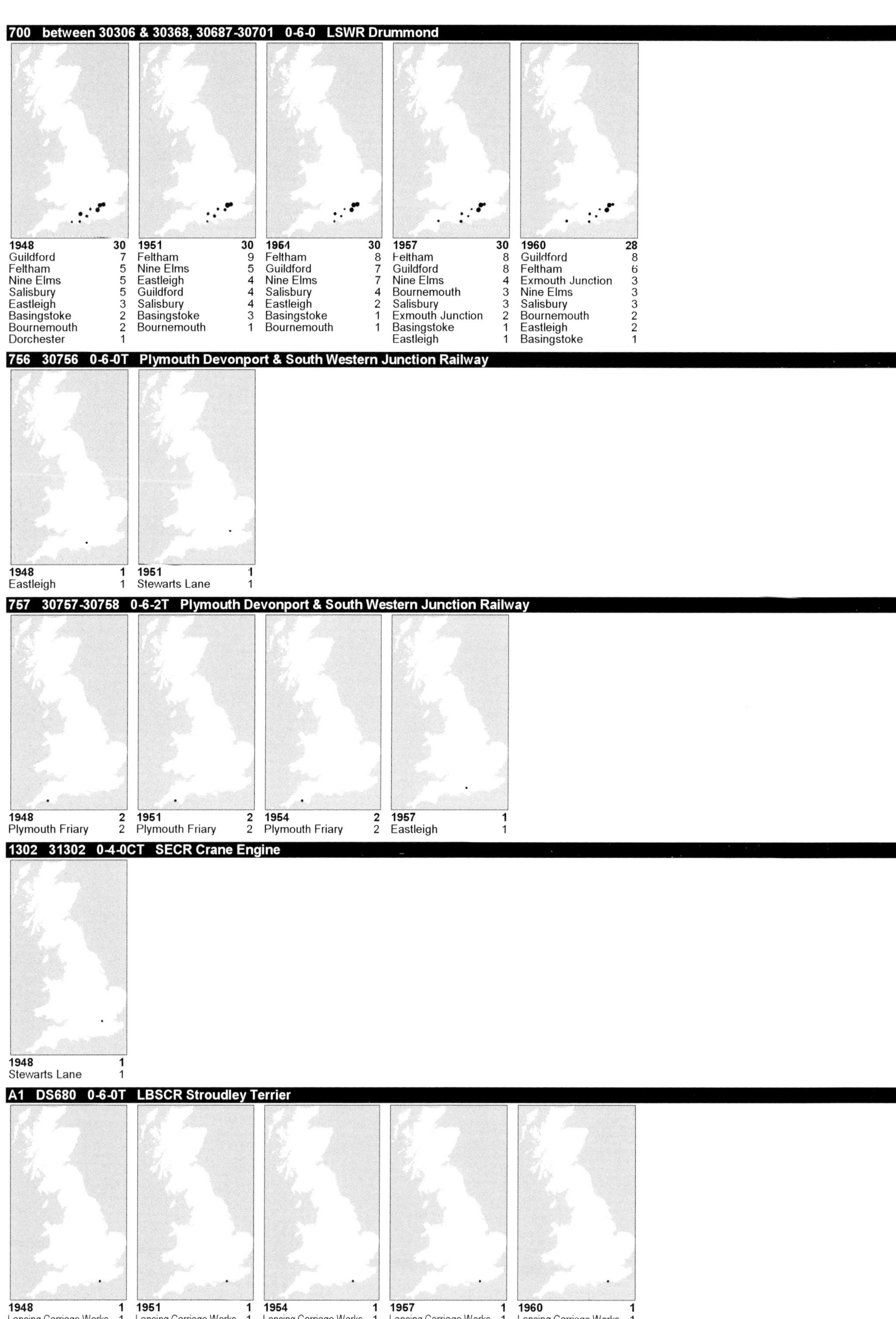

700 between 30306 & 30368, 30687-30701 0-6-0 LSWR Drummond

1948	30	1951	30	1954	30	1957	30	1960	28
Guildford	7	Feltham	9	Feltham	8	Feltham	8	Guildford	8
Feltham	5	Nine Elms	5	Guildford	7	Guildford	8	Feltham	6
Nine Elms	5	Eastleigh	4	Nine Elms	7	Nine Elms	4	Exmouth Junction	3
Salisbury	5	Guildford	4	Salisbury	4	Bournemouth	3	Nine Elms	3
Eastleigh	3	Salisbury	4	Eastleigh	2	Salisbury	3	Salisbury	3
Basingstoke	2	Basingstoke	3	Basingstoke	1	Exmouth Junction	2	Bournemouth	2
Bournemouth	2	Bournemouth	1	Bournemouth	1	Basingstoke	1	Eastleigh	2
Dorchester	1					Eastleigh	1	Basingstoke	1

756 30756 0-6-0T Plymouth Devonport & South Western Junction Railway

1948	1	1951	1
Eastleigh	1	Stewarts Lane	1

757 30757-30758 0-6-2T Plymouth Devonport & South Western Junction Railway

1948	2	1951	2	1954	2	1957	1
Plymouth Friary	2	Plymouth Friary	2	Plymouth Friary	2	Eastleigh	1

1302 31302 0-4-0CT SECR Crane Engine

1948	1
Stewarts Lane	1

A1 DS680 0-6-0T LBSCR Stroudley Terrier

1948	1	1951	1	1954	1	1957	1	1960	1
Lancing Carriage Works	1	Lancing Carriage Works	1	Lancing Carriage Works	1	Lancing Carriage Works	1	Lancing Carriage Works	1

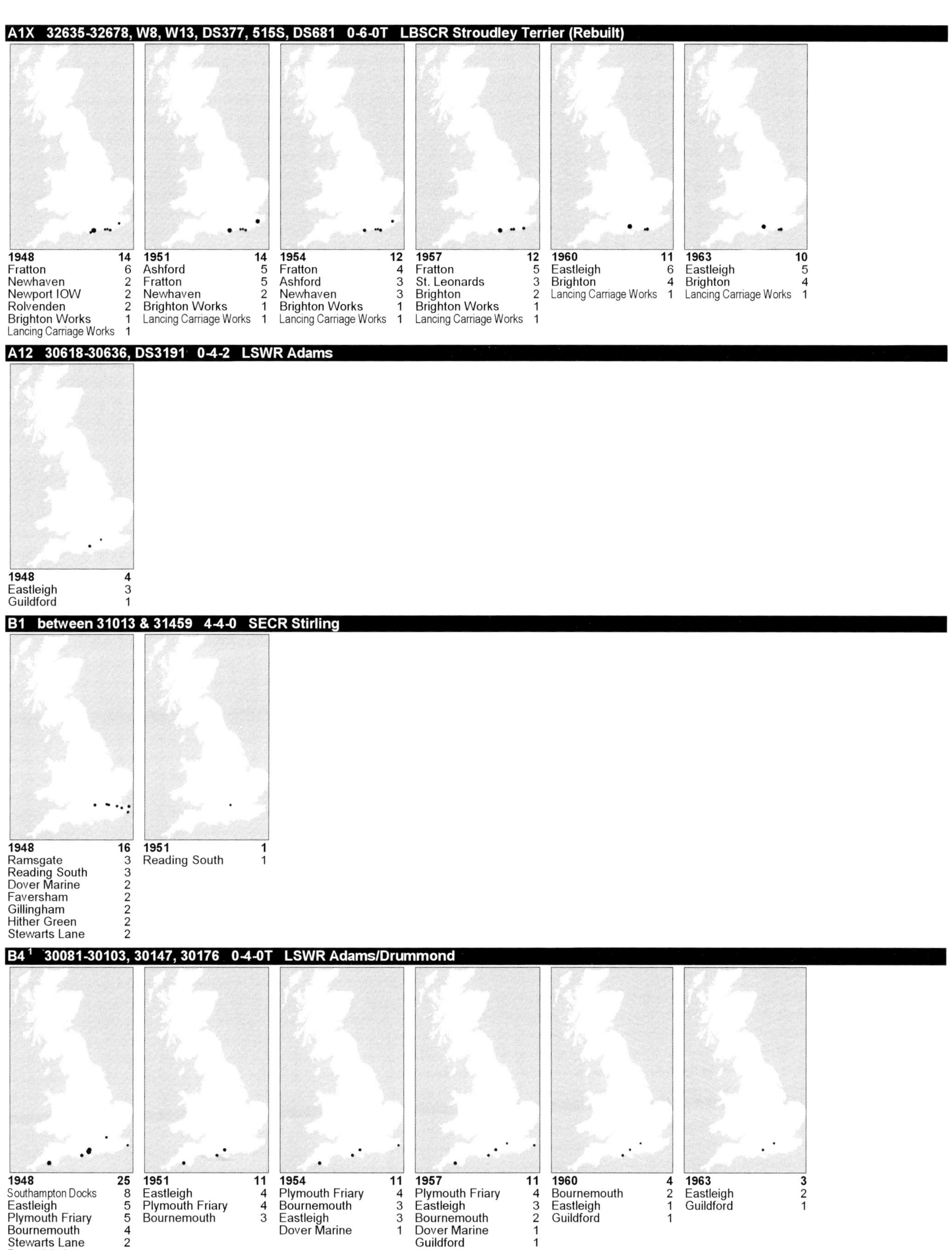

A1X 32635-32678, W8, W13, DS377, 515S, DS681 0-6-0T LBSCR Stroudley Terrier (Rebuilt)

1948	14
Fratton	6
Newhaven	2
Newport IOW	2
Rolvenden	2
Brighton Works	1
Lancing Carriage Works	1

1951	14
Ashford	5
Fratton	5
Newhaven	2
Brighton Works	1
Lancing Carriage Works	1

1954	12
Fratton	4
Ashford	3
Newhaven	3
Brighton Works	1
Lancing Carriage Works	1

1957	12
Fratton	5
St. Leonards	3
Brighton	2
Brighton Works	1
Lancing Carriage Works	1

1960	11
Eastleigh	6
Brighton	4
Lancing Carriage Works	1

1963	10
Eastleigh	5
Brighton	4
Lancing Carriage Works	1

A12 30618-30636, DS3191 0-4-2 LSWR Adams

1948	4
Eastleigh	3
Guildford	1

B1 between 31013 & 31459 4-4-0 SECR Stirling

1948	16
Ramsgate	3
Reading South	3
Dover Marine	2
Faversham	2
Gillingham	2
Hither Green	2
Stewarts Lane	2

1951	1
Reading South	1

B4 [1] 30081-30103, 30147, 30176 0-4-0T LSWR Adams/Drummond

1948	25
Southampton Docks	8
Eastleigh	5
Plymouth Friary	5
Bournemouth	4
Stewarts Lane	2
Dover Marine	1

1951	11
Eastleigh	4
Plymouth Friary	4
Bournemouth	3

1954	11
Plymouth Friary	4
Bournemouth	3
Eastleigh	3
Dover Marine	1

1957	11
Plymouth Friary	4
Eastleigh	3
Bournemouth	2
Dover Marine	1
Guildford	1

1960	4
Bournemouth	2
Eastleigh	1
Guildford	1

1963	3
Eastleigh	2
Guildford	1

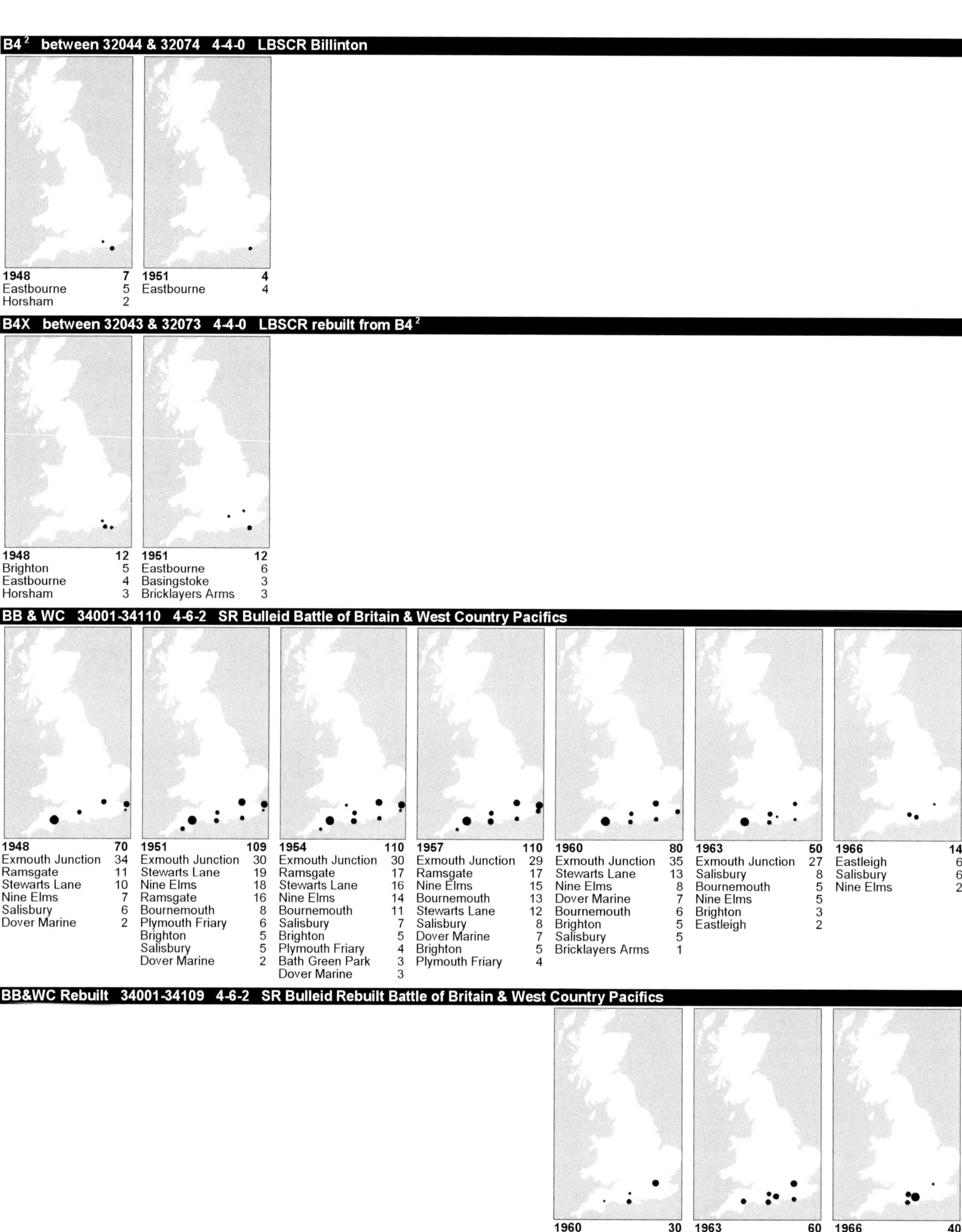

B4[2] between 32044 & 32074 4-4-0 LBSCR Billinton

1948	7	1951	4
Eastbourne	5	Eastbourne	4
Horsham	2		

B4X between 32043 & 32073 4-4-0 LBSCR rebuilt from B4[2]

1948	12	1951	12
Brighton	5	Eastbourne	6
Eastbourne	4	Basingstoke	3
Horsham	3	Bricklayers Arms	3

BB & WC 34001-34110 4-6-2 SR Bulleid Battle of Britain & West Country Pacifics

1948	70	1951	109	1954	110	1957	110
Exmouth Junction	34	Exmouth Junction	30	Exmouth Junction	30	Exmouth Junction	29
Ramsgate	11	Stewarts Lane	19	Ramsgate	17	Ramsgate	17
Stewarts Lane	10	Nine Elms	18	Stewarts Lane	16	Nine Elms	15
Nine Elms	7	Ramsgate	16	Nine Elms	14	Bournemouth	13
Salisbury	6	Bournemouth	8	Bournemouth	11	Stewarts Lane	12
Dover Marine	2	Plymouth Friary	6	Salisbury	7	Salisbury	8
		Brighton	5	Brighton	5	Dover Marine	7
		Salisbury	5	Plymouth Friary	4	Brighton	5
		Dover Marine	2	Bath Green Park	3	Plymouth Friary	4
				Dover Marine	3		

1960	80	1963	50	1966	14
Exmouth Junction	35	Exmouth Junction	27	Eastleigh	6
Stewarts Lane	13	Salisbury	8	Salisbury	6
Nine Elms	8	Bournemouth	5	Nine Elms	2
Dover Marine	7	Nine Elms	5		
Bournemouth	6	Brighton	3		
Brighton	5	Eastleigh	2		
Salisbury	5				
Bricklayers Arms	1				

BB&WC Rebuilt 34001-34109 4-6-2 SR Bulleid Rebuilt Battle of Britain & West Country Pacifics

1960	30	1963	60	1966	40
Bricklayers Arms	15	Nine Elms	15	Eastleigh	20
Bournemouth	8	Eastleigh	13	Salisbury	10
Nine Elms	3	Exmouth Junction	10	Bournemouth	8
Salisbury	3	Bournemouth	9	Nine Elms	2
Exmouth Junction	1	Brighton	7		
		Salisbury	6		

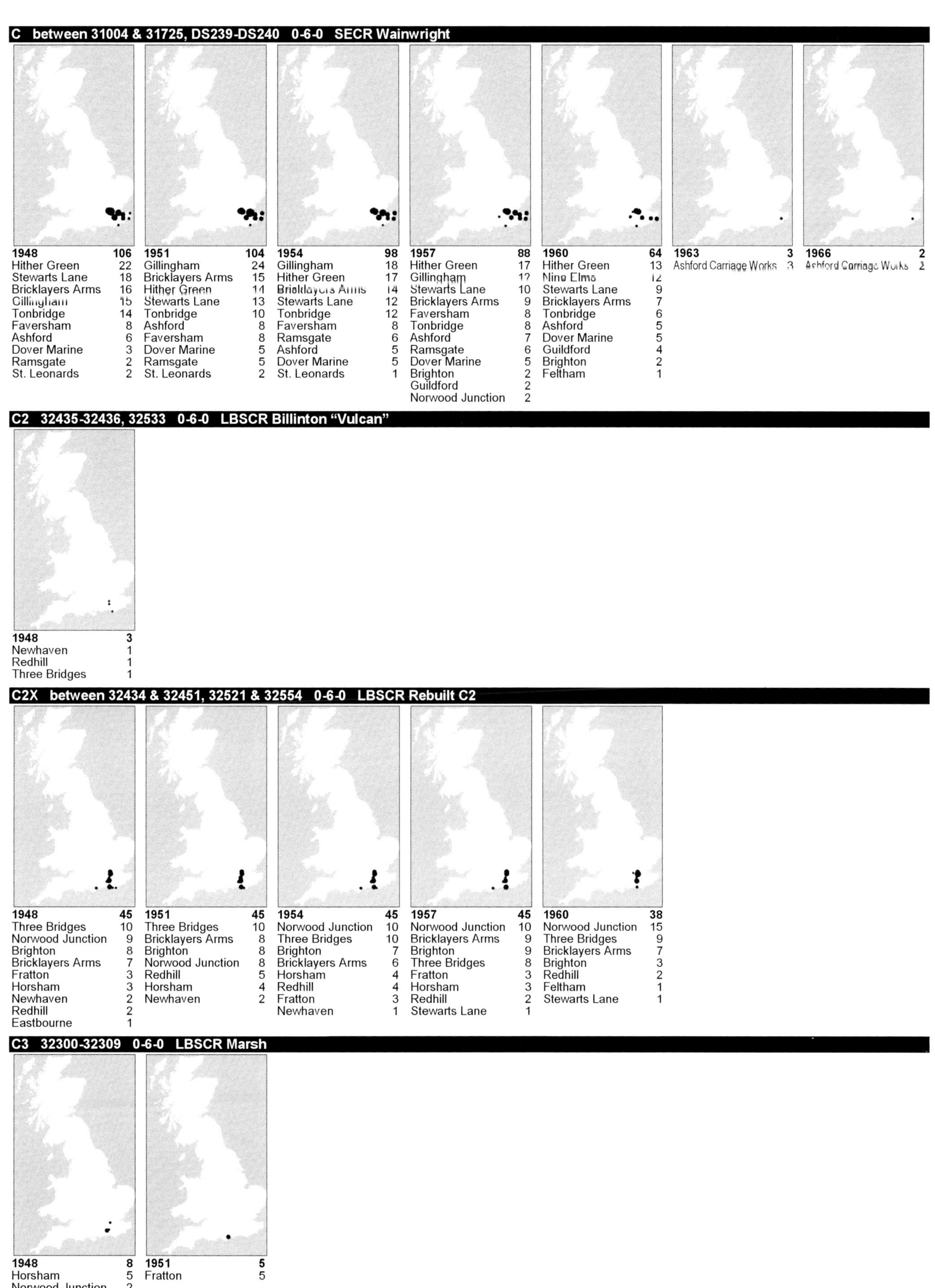

C between 31004 & 31725, DS239-DS240 0-6-0 SECR Wainwright

1948	106
Hither Green	22
Stewarts Lane	18
Bricklayers Arms	16
Gillingham	15
Tonbridge	14
Faversham	8
Ashford	6
Dover Marine	3
Ramsgate	2
St. Leonards	2

1951	104
Gillingham	24
Bricklayers Arms	15
Hither Green	14
Stewarts Lane	13
Tonbridge	10
Ashford	8
Faversham	8
Dover Marine	5
Ramsgate	5
St. Leonards	2

1954	98
Gillingham	18
Hither Green	17
Bricklayers Arms	14
Stewarts Lane	12
Tonbridge	12
Faversham	8
Ramsgate	6
Ashford	5
Dover Marine	5
St. Leonards	1

1957	88
Hither Green	17
Gillingham	12
Stewarts Lane	10
Bricklayers Arms	9
Faversham	8
Tonbridge	8
Ashford	7
Ramsgate	6
Dover Marine	5
Brighton	2
Guildford	2
Norwood Junction	2

1960	64
Hither Green	13
Nine Elms	12
Stewarts Lane	9
Bricklayers Arms	7
Tonbridge	6
Ashford	5
Dover Marine	5
Guildford	4
Brighton	2
Feltham	1

1963	3
Ashford Carriage Works	3

1966	2
Ashford Carriage Works	2

C2 32435-32436, 32533 0-6-0 LBSCR Billinton "Vulcan"

1948	3
Newhaven	1
Redhill	1
Three Bridges	1

C2X between 32434 & 32451, 32521 & 32554 0-6-0 LBSCR Rebuilt C2

1948	45
Three Bridges	10
Norwood Junction	9
Brighton	8
Bricklayers Arms	7
Fratton	3
Horsham	3
Newhaven	2
Redhill	2
Eastbourne	1

1951	45
Three Bridges	10
Bricklayers Arms	8
Brighton	8
Norwood Junction	8
Redhill	5
Horsham	4
Newhaven	2

1954	45
Norwood Junction	10
Three Bridges	10
Brighton	7
Bricklayers Arms	6
Horsham	4
Redhill	4
Fratton	3
Newhaven	1

1957	45
Norwood Junction	10
Bricklayers Arms	9
Brighton	9
Three Bridges	8
Fratton	3
Horsham	3
Redhill	2
Stewarts Lane	1

1960	38
Norwood Junction	15
Three Bridges	9
Bricklayers Arms	7
Brighton	3
Redhill	2
Feltham	1
Stewarts Lane	1

C3 32300-32309 0-6-0 LBSCR Marsh

1948	8
Horsham	5
Norwood Junction	2
Three Bridges	1

1951	5
Fratton	5

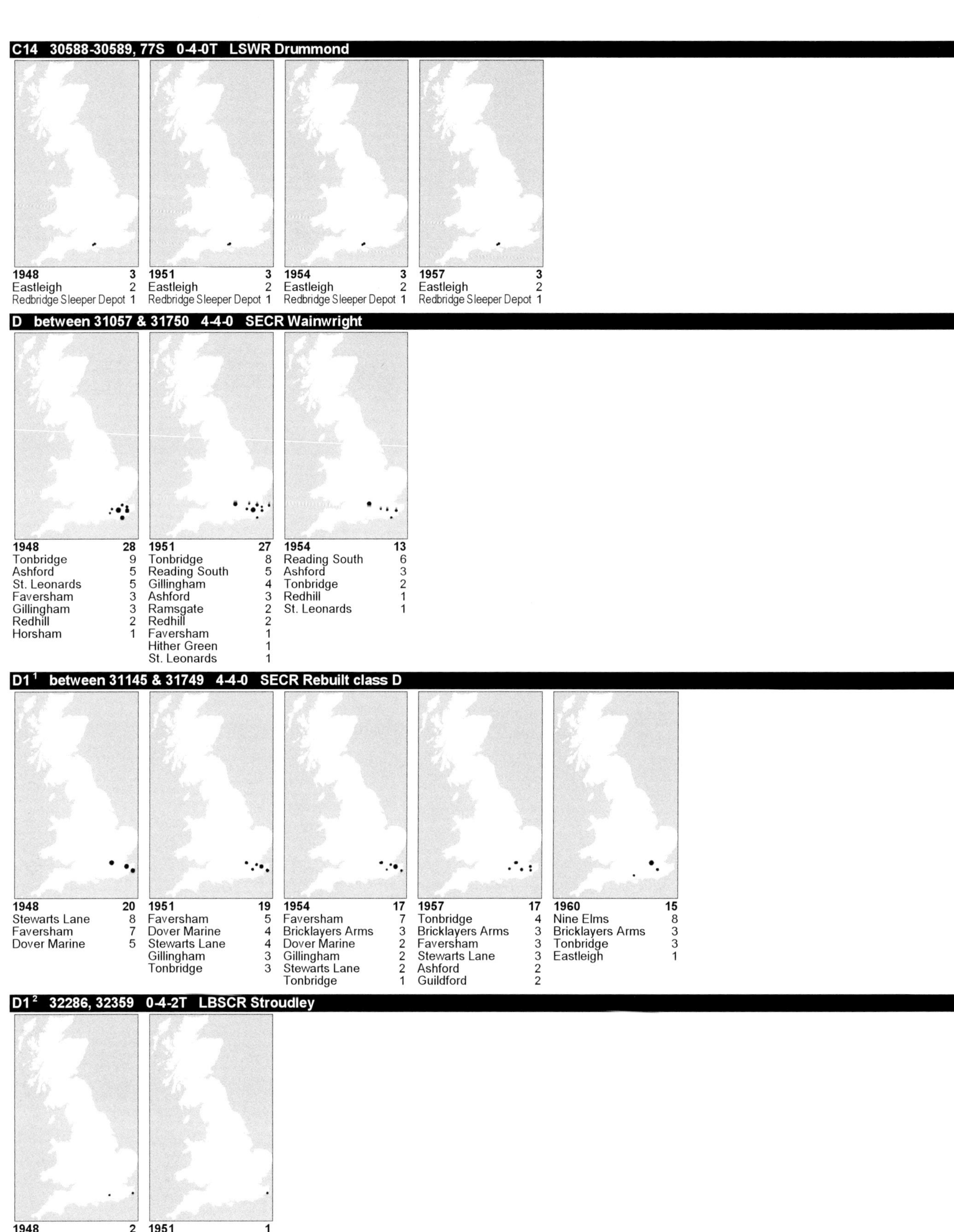

C14 30588-30589, 77S 0-4-0T LSWR Drummond

1948	3	1951	3	1954	3	1957	3
Eastleigh	2	Eastleigh	2	Eastleigh	2	Eastleigh	2
Redbridge Sleeper Depot	1	Redbridge Sleeper Depot	1	Redbridge Sleeper Depot	1	Redbridge Sleeper Depot	1

D between 31057 & 31750 4-4-0 SECR Wainwright

1948	28	1951	27	1954	13
Tonbridge	9	Tonbridge	8	Reading South	6
Ashford	5	Reading South	5	Ashford	3
St. Leonards	5	Gillingham	4	Tonbridge	2
Faversham	3	Ashford	3	Redhill	1
Gillingham	3	Ramsgate	2	St. Leonards	1
Redhill	2	Redhill	2		
Horsham	1	Faversham	1		
		Hither Green	1		
		St. Leonards	1		

D1[1] between 31145 & 31749 4-4-0 SECR Rebuilt class D

1948	20	1951	19	1954	17	1957	17	1960	15
Stewarts Lane	8	Faversham	5	Faversham	7	Tonbridge	4	Nine Elms	8
Faversham	7	Dover Marine	4	Bricklayers Arms	3	Bricklayers Arms	3	Bricklayers Arms	3
Dover Marine	5	Stewarts Lane	4	Dover Marine	2	Faversham	3	Tonbridge	3
		Gillingham	3	Gillingham	2	Stewarts Lane	3	Eastleigh	1
		Tonbridge	3	Stewarts Lane	2	Ashford	2		
				Tonbridge	1	Guildford	2		

D1[2] 32286, 32359 0-4-2T LBSCR Stroudley

1948	2	1951	1
Dover Marine	1	Dover Marine	1
Horsham	1		

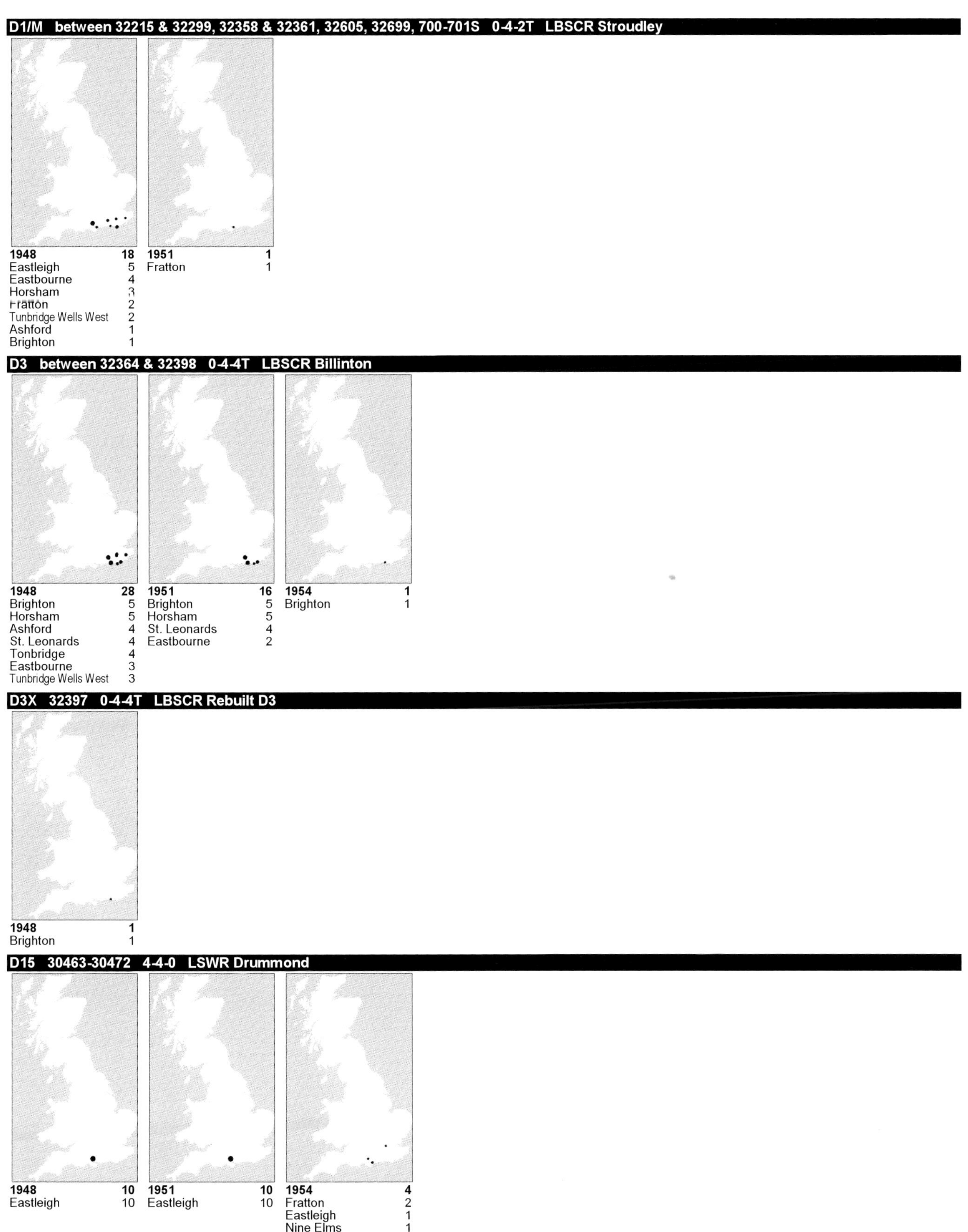

D1/M between 32215 & 32299, 32358 & 32361, 32605, 32699, 700-701S 0-4-2T LBSCR Stroudley

1948	18
Eastleigh	5
Eastbourne	4
Horsham	3
Fratton	2
Tunbridge Wells West	2
Ashford	1
Brighton	1

1951	1
Fratton	1

D3 between 32364 & 32398 0-4-4T LBSCR Billinton

1948	28
Brighton	5
Horsham	5
Ashford	4
St. Leonards	4
Tonbridge	4
Eastbourne	3
Tunbridge Wells West	3

1951	16
Brighton	5
Horsham	5
St. Leonards	4
Eastbourne	2

1954	1
Brighton	1

D3X 32397 0-4-4T LBSCR Rebuilt D3

1948	1
Brighton	1

D15 30463-30472 4-4-0 LSWR Drummond

1948	10
Eastleigh	10

1951	10
Eastleigh	10

1954	4
Fratton	2
Eastleigh	1
Nine Elms	1

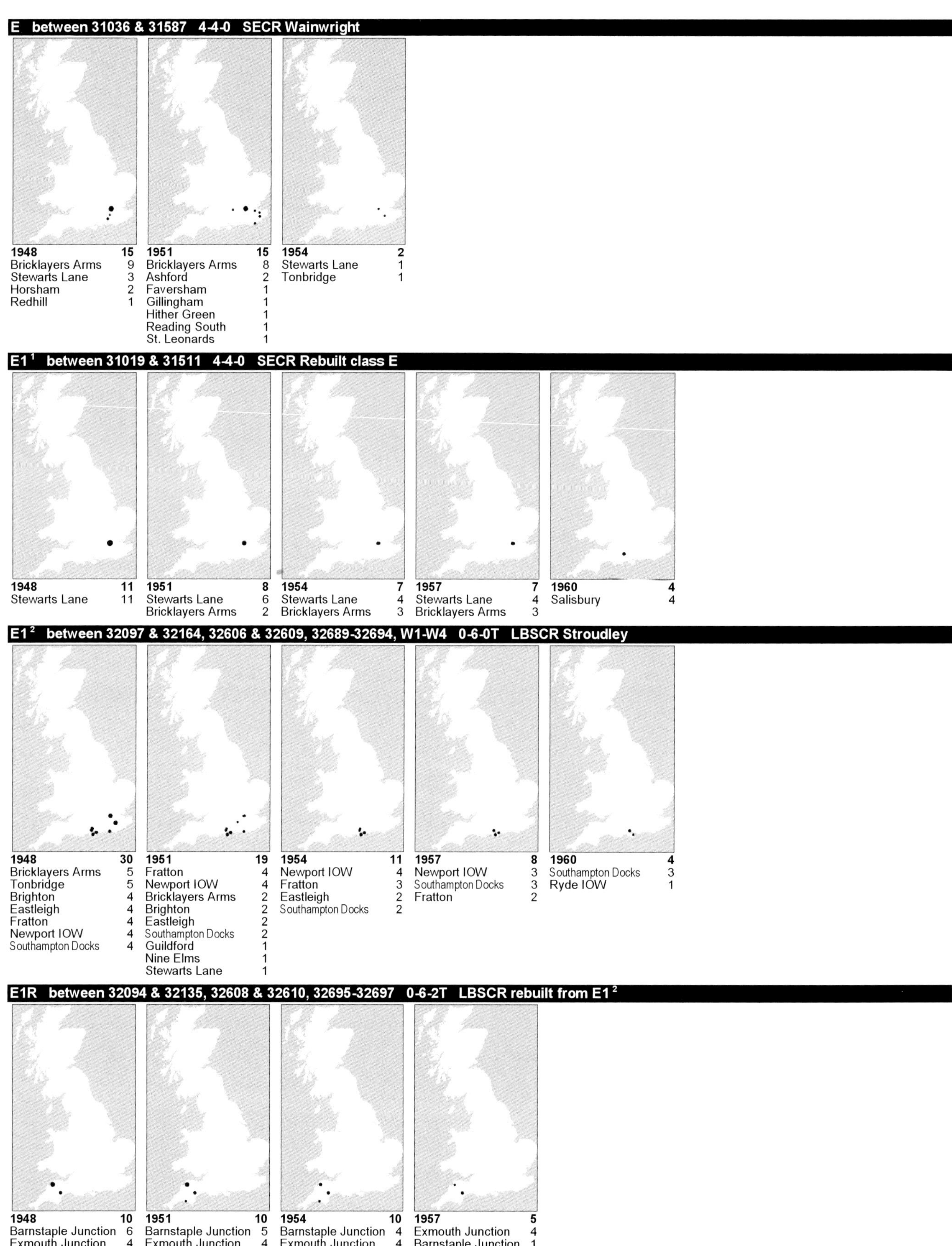
E between 31036 & 31587 4-4-0 SECR Wainwright
1948 15
Bricklayers Arms 9
Stewarts Lane 3
Horsham 2
Redhill 1
1951 15
Bricklayers Arms 8
Ashford 2
Faversham 1
Gillingham 1
Hither Green 1
Reading South 1
St. Leonards 1
1954 2
Stewarts Lane 1
Tonbridge 1
E1[1] between 31019 & 31511 4-4-0 SECR Rebuilt class E
1948 11
Stewarts Lane 11
1951 8
Stewarts Lane 6
Bricklayers Arms 2
1954 7
Stewarts Lane 4
Bricklayers Arms 3
1957 7
Stewarts Lane 4
Bricklayers Arms 3
1960 4
Salisbury 4
E1[2] between 32097 & 32164, 32606 & 32609, 32689-32694, W1-W4 0-6-0T LBSCR Stroudley
1948 30
Bricklayers Arms 5
Tonbridge 5
Brighton 4
Eastleigh 4
Fratton 4
Newport IOW 4
Southampton Docks 4
1951 19
Fratton 4
Newport IOW 4
Bricklayers Arms 2
Brighton 2
Eastleigh 2
Southampton Docks 2
Guildford 1
Nine Elms 1
Stewarts Lane 1
1954 11
Newport IOW 4
Fratton 3
Eastleigh 2
Southampton Docks 2
1957 8
Newport IOW 3
Southampton Docks 3
Fratton 2
1960 4
Southampton Docks 3
Ryde IOW 1
E1R between 32094 & 32135, 32608 & 32610, 32695-32697 0-6-2T LBSCR rebuilt from E1[2]
1948 10
Barnstaple Junction 6
Exmouth Junction 4
1951 10
Barnstaple Junction 5
Exmouth Junction 4
Plymouth Friary 1
1954 10
Barnstaple Junction 4
Exmouth Junction 4
Plymouth Friary 2
1957 5
Exmouth Junction 4
Barnstaple Junction 1

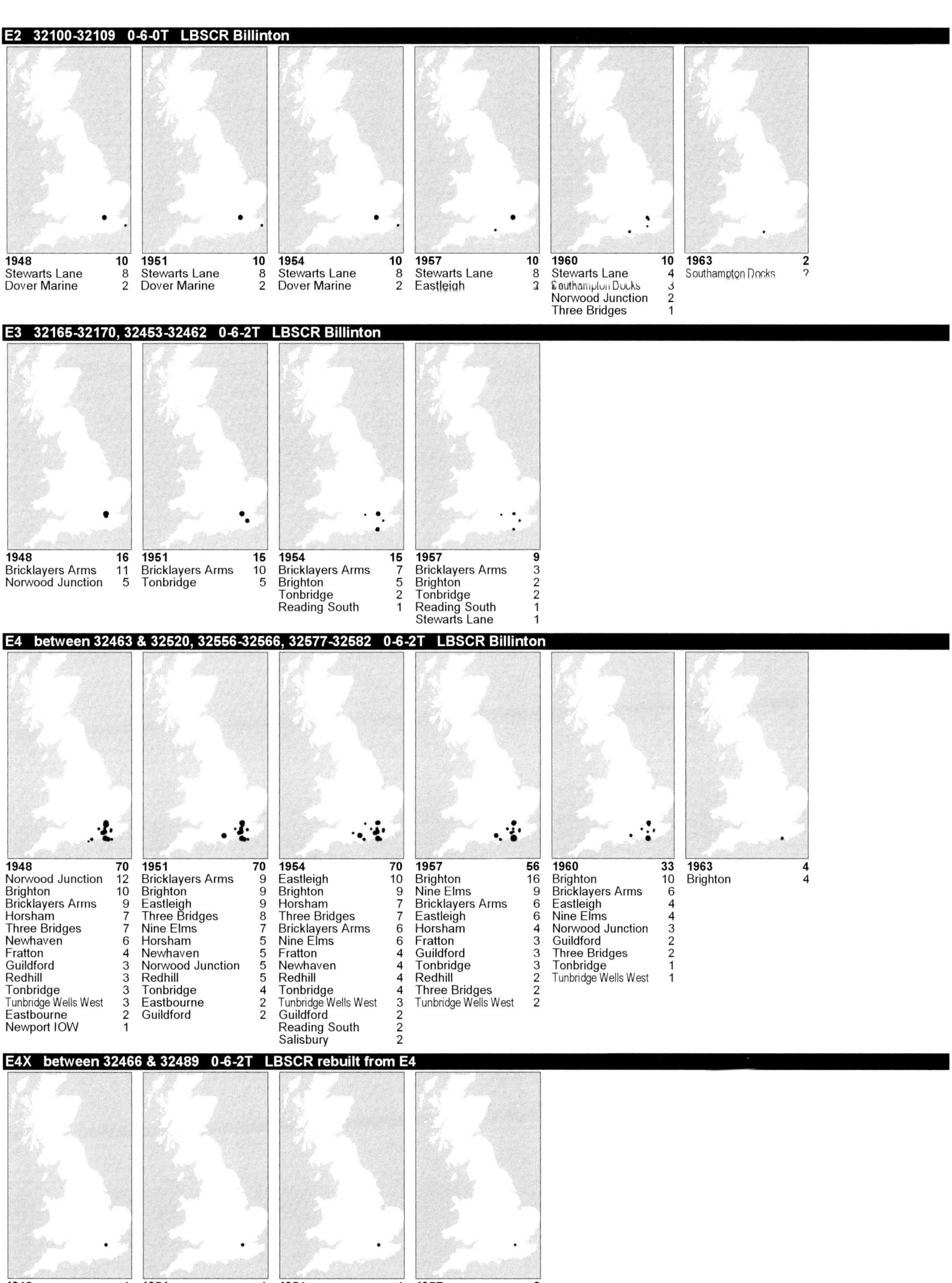

E2 32100-32109 0-6-0T LBSCR Billinton
1948 10
Stewarts Lane 8
Dover Marine 2
1951 10
Stewarts Lane 8
Dover Marine 2
1954 10
Stewarts Lane 8
Dover Marine 2
1957 10
Stewarts Lane 8
Eastleigh 2
1960 10
Stewarts Lane 4
Southampton Docks 3
Norwood Junction 2
Three Bridges 1
1963 2
Southampton Docks 2
E3 32165-32170, 32453-32462 0-6-2T LBSCR Billinton
1948 16
Bricklayers Arms 11
Norwood Junction 5
1951 15
Bricklayers Arms 10
Tonbridge 5
1954 15
Bricklayers Arms 7
Brighton 5
Tonbridge 2
Reading South 1
1957 9
Bricklayers Arms 3
Brighton 2
Tonbridge 2
Reading South 1
Stewarts Lane 1
E4 between 32463 & 32520, 32556-32566, 32577-32582 0-6-2T LBSCR Billinton
1948 70
Norwood Junction 12
Brighton 10
Bricklayers Arms 9
Horsham 7
Three Bridges 7
Newhaven 6
Fratton 4
Guildford 3
Redhill 3
Tonbridge 3
Tunbridge Wells West 3
Eastbourne 2
Newport IOW 1
1951 70
Bricklayers Arms 9
Brighton 9
Eastleigh 9
Three Bridges 8
Nine Elms 7
Horsham 5
Newhaven 5
Norwood Junction 5
Redhill 5
Tonbridge 4
Eastbourne 2
Guildford 2
1954 70
Eastleigh 10
Brighton 9
Horsham 7
Three Bridges 7
Bricklayers Arms 6
Nine Elms 6
Fratton 4
Newhaven 4
Redhill 4
Tonbridge 4
Tunbridge Wells West 3
Guildford 2
Reading South 2
Salisbury 2
1957 56
Brighton 16
Nine Elms 9
Bricklayers Arms 6
Eastleigh 6
Horsham 4
Fratton 3
Guildford 3
Tonbridge 3
Redhill 2
Three Bridges 2
Tunbridge Wells West 2
1960 33
Brighton 10
Bricklayers Arms 6
Eastleigh 4
Nine Elms 4
Norwood Junction 3
Guildford 2
Three Bridges 2
Tonbridge 1
Tunbridge Wells West 1
1963 4
Brighton 4
E4X between 32466 & 32489 0-6-2T LBSCR rebuilt from E4
1948 4
Norwood Junction 4
1951 4
Norwood Junction 4
1954 4
Norwood Junction 4
1957 2
Norwood Junction 2

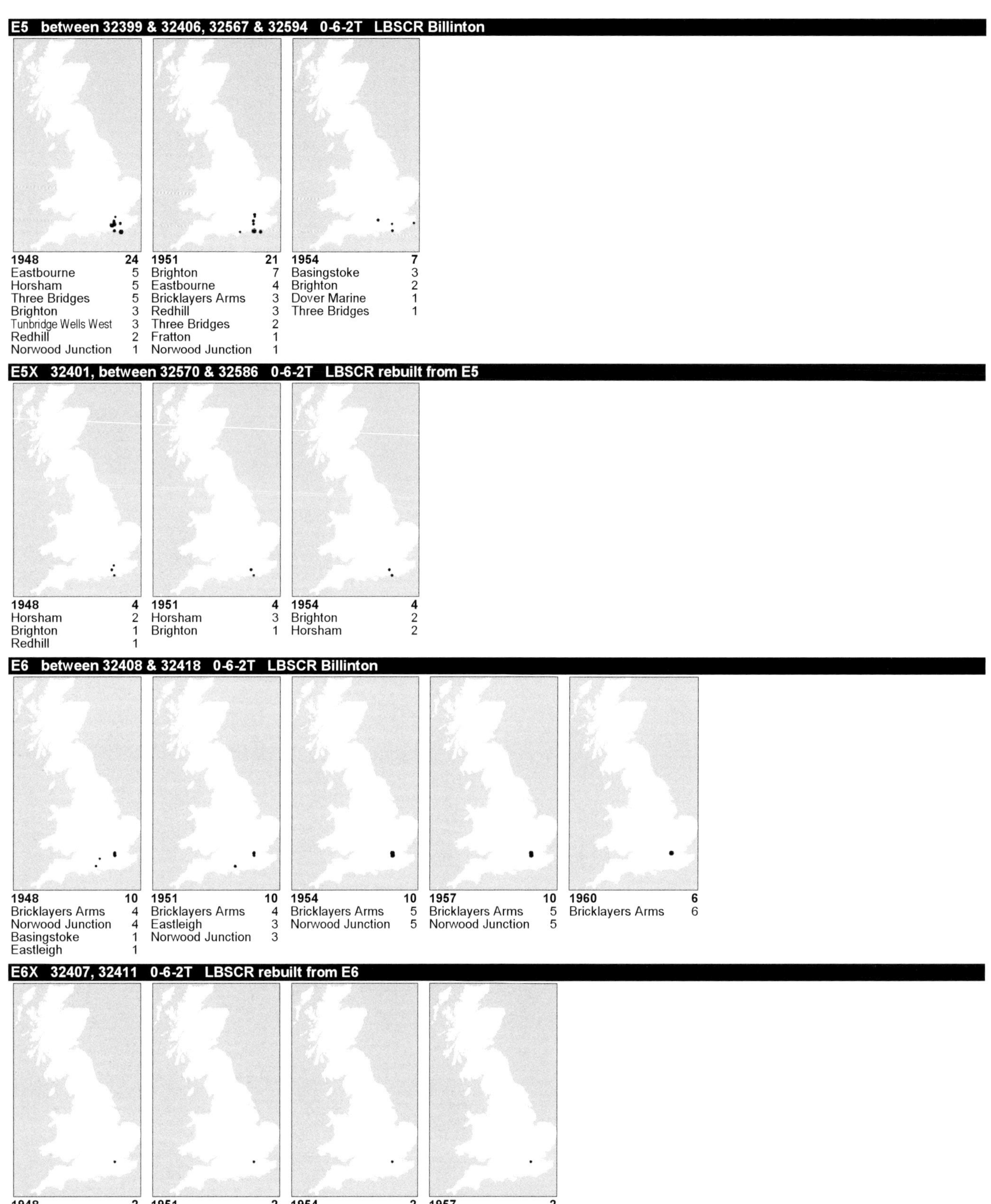

E5 between 32399 & 32406, 32567 & 32594 0-6-2T LBSCR Billinton

1948	24	1951	21	1954	7
Eastbourne	5	Brighton	7	Basingstoke	3
Horsham	5	Eastbourne	4	Brighton	2
Three Bridges	5	Bricklayers Arms	3	Dover Marine	1
Brighton	3	Redhill	3	Three Bridges	1
Tunbridge Wells West	3	Three Bridges	2		
Redhill	2	Fratton	1		
Norwood Junction	1	Norwood Junction	1		

E5X 32401, between 32570 & 32586 0-6-2T LBSCR rebuilt from E5

1948	4	1951	4	1954	4
Horsham	2	Horsham	3	Brighton	2
Brighton	1	Brighton	1	Horsham	2
Redhill	1				

E6 between 32408 & 32418 0-6-2T LBSCR Billinton

1948	10	1951	10	1954	10	1957	10	1960	6
Bricklayers Arms	4	Bricklayers Arms	4	Bricklayers Arms	5	Bricklayers Arms	5	Bricklayers Arms	6
Norwood Junction	4	Eastleigh	3	Norwood Junction	5	Norwood Junction	5		
Basingstoke	1	Norwood Junction	3						
Eastleigh	1								

E6X 32407, 32411 0-6-2T LBSCR rebuilt from E6

1948	2	1951	2	1954	2	1957	2
Norwood Junction	2	Norwood Junction	2	Norwood Junction	2	Norwood Junction	2

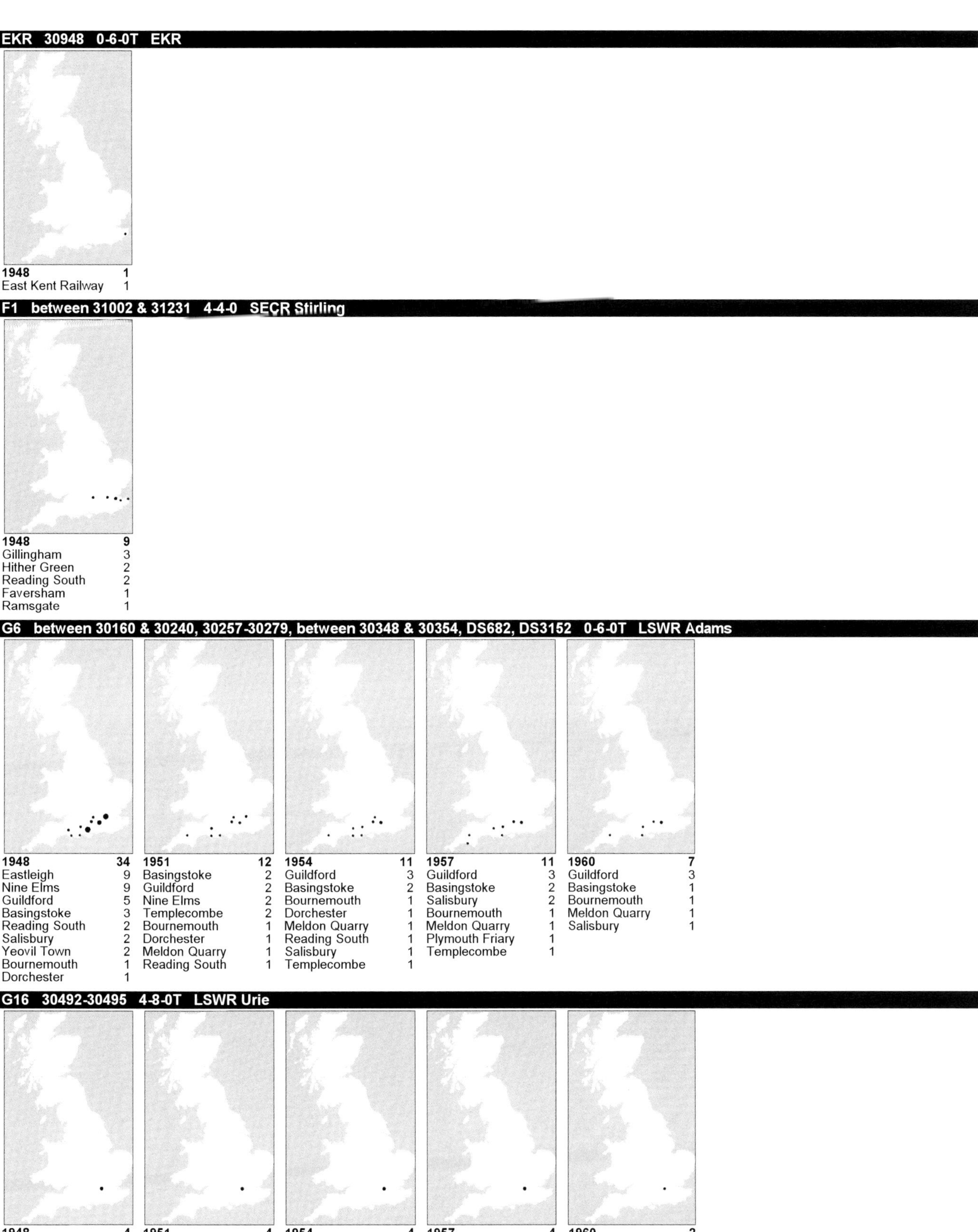

EKR 30948 0-6-0T EKR

1948	1
East Kent Railway	1

F1 between 31002 & 31231 4-4-0 SECR Stirling

1948	9
Gillingham	3
Hither Green	2
Reading South	2
Faversham	1
Ramsgate	1

G6 between 30160 & 30240, 30257-30279, between 30348 & 30354, DS682, DS3152 0-6-0T LSWR Adams

1948	34	1951	12	1954	11	1957	11	1960	7
Eastleigh	9	Basingstoke	2	Guildford	3	Guildford	3	Guildford	3
Nine Elms	9	Guildford	2	Basingstoke	2	Basingstoke	2	Basingstoke	1
Guildford	5	Nine Elms	2	Bournemouth	1	Salisbury	2	Bournemouth	1
Basingstoke	3	Templecombe	2	Dorchester	1	Bournemouth	1	Meldon Quarry	1
Reading South	2	Bournemouth	1	Meldon Quarry	1	Meldon Quarry	1	Salisbury	1
Salisbury	2	Dorchester	1	Reading South	1	Plymouth Friary	1		
Yeovil Town	2	Meldon Quarry	1	Salisbury	1	Templecombe	1		
Bournemouth	1	Reading South	1	Templecombe	1				
Dorchester	1								

G16 30492-30495 4-8-0T LSWR Urie

1948	4	1951	4	1954	4	1957	4	1960	2
Feltham	4	Feltham	4	Feltham	4	Feltham	4	Feltham	2

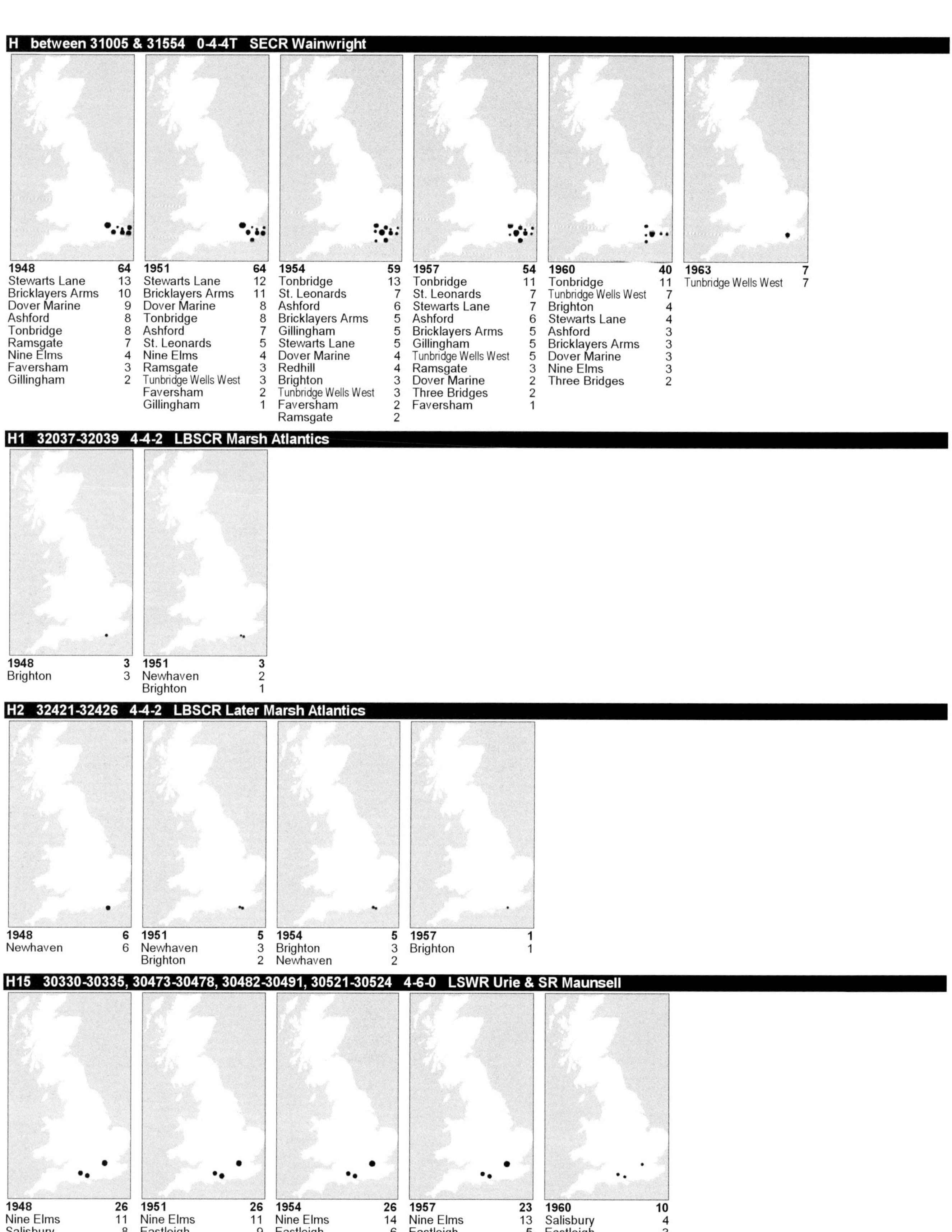

H between 31005 & 31554 0-4-4T SECR Wainwright

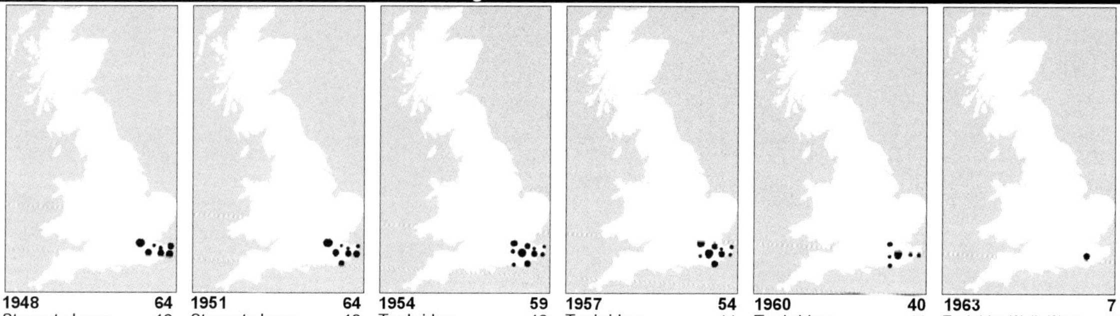

1948	64
Stewarts Lane	13
Bricklayers Arms	10
Dover Marine	9
Ashford	8
Tonbridge	8
Ramsgate	7
Nine Elms	4
Faversham	3
Gillingham	2

1951	64
Stewarts Lane	12
Bricklayers Arms	11
Dover Marine	8
Tonbridge	8
Ashford	7
St. Leonards	5
Nine Elms	4
Ramsgate	3
Tunbridge Wells West	3
Faversham	2
Gillingham	1

1954	59
Tonbridge	13
St. Leonards	7
Ashford	6
Bricklayers Arms	5
Gillingham	5
Stewarts Lane	5
Dover Marine	4
Redhill	4
Brighton	3
Tunbridge Wells West	3
Faversham	2
Ramsgate	2

1957	54
Tonbridge	11
St. Leonards	7
Stewarts Lane	7
Ashford	6
Bricklayers Arms	5
Gillingham	5
Tunbridge Wells West	5
Ramsgate	3
Dover Marine	2
Three Bridges	2
Faversham	1

1960	40
Tonbridge	11
Tunbridge Wells West	7
Brighton	4
Stewarts Lane	4
Ashford	3
Bricklayers Arms	3
Dover Marine	3
Nine Elms	3
Three Bridges	2

1963	7
Tunbridge Wells West	7

H1 32037-32039 4-4-2 LBSCR Marsh Atlantics

1948	3
Brighton	3

1951	3
Newhaven	2
Brighton	1

H2 32421-32426 4-4-2 LBSCR Later Marsh Atlantics

1948	6
Newhaven	6

1951	5
Newhaven	3
Brighton	2

1954	5
Brighton	3
Newhaven	2

1957	1
Brighton	1

H15 30330-30335, 30473-30478, 30482-30491, 30521-30524 4-6-0 LSWR Urie & SR Maunsell

1948	26
Nine Elms	11
Salisbury	8
Eastleigh	7

1951	26
Nine Elms	11
Eastleigh	9
Salisbury	6

1954	26
Nine Elms	14
Eastleigh	6
Salisbury	6

1957	23
Nine Elms	13
Eastleigh	5
Salisbury	5

1960	10
Salisbury	4
Eastleigh	3
Nine Elms	3

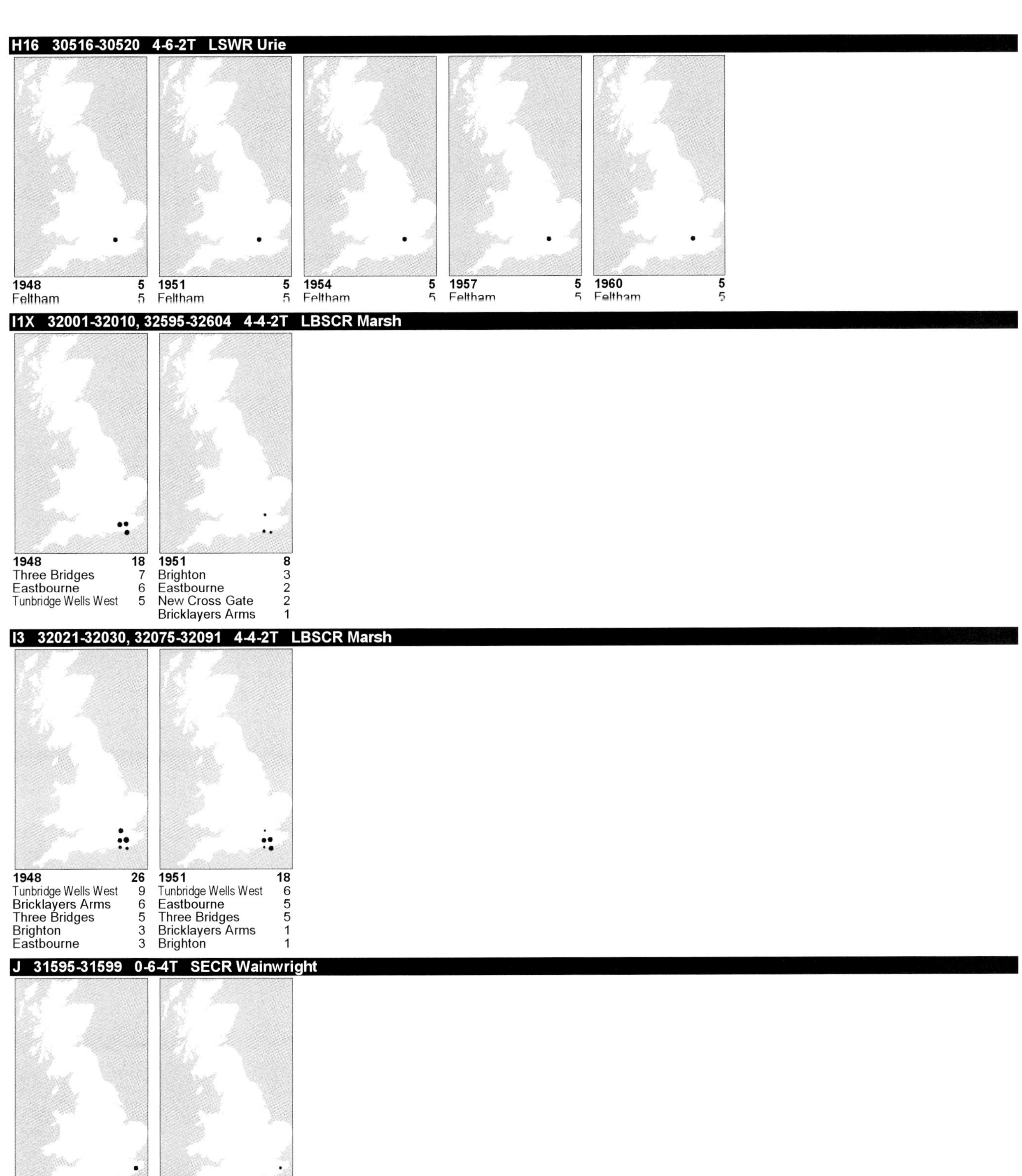

H16 30516-30520 4-6-2T LSWR Urie
1948 5
Feltham 5
1951 5
Feltham 5
1954 5
Feltham 5
1957 5
Feltham 5
1960 5
Feltham 5
I1X 32001-32010, 32595-32604 4-4-2T LBSCR Marsh
1948 18
Three Bridges 7
Eastbourne 6
Tunbridge Wells West 5
1951 8
Brighton 3
Eastbourne 2
New Cross Gate 2
Bricklayers Arms 1
I3 32021-32030, 32075-32091 4-4-2T LBSCR Marsh
1948 26
Tunbridge Wells West 9
Bricklayers Arms 6
Three Bridges 5
Brighton 3
Eastbourne 3
1951 18
Tunbridge Wells West 6
Eastbourne 5
Three Bridges 5
Bricklayers Arms 1
Brighton 1
J 31595-31599 0-6-4T SECR Wainwright
1948 5
Ashford 5
1951 2
Ashford 2

J1 32325 4-6-2T LBSCR Marsh

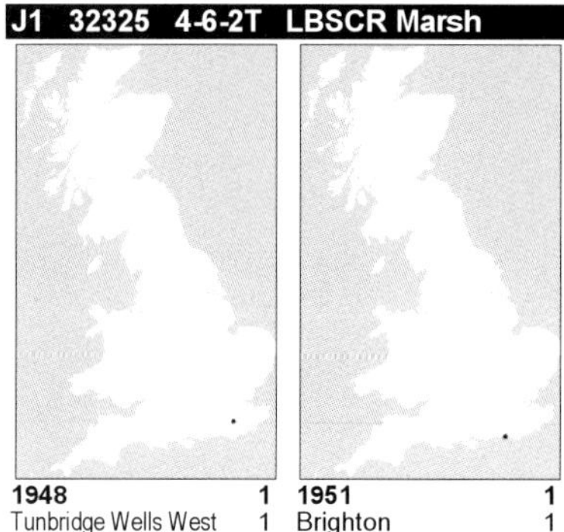

1948	1	1951	1
Tunbridge Wells West	1	Brighton	1

J2 32326 4-6-2T LBSCR Marsh

1948	1	1951	1
Tunbridge Wells West	1	Brighton	1

K 32337-32353 2-6-0 LBSCR Billinton

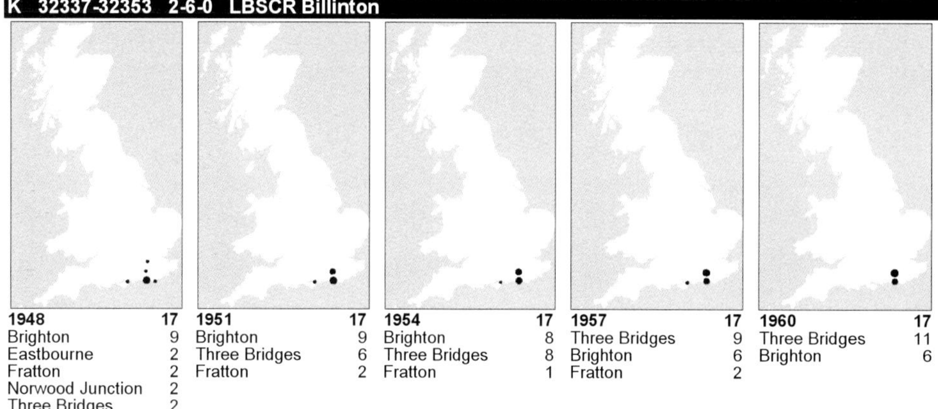

1948	17	1951	17	1954	17	1957	17	1960	17
Brighton	9	Brighton	9	Brighton	8	Three Bridges	9	Three Bridges	11
Eastbourne	2	Three Bridges	6	Three Bridges	8	Brighton	6	Brighton	6
Fratton	2	Fratton	2	Fratton	1	Fratton	2		
Norwood Junction	2								
Three Bridges	2								

K10 between 30135 & 30153, 30329 & 30345, 30380-30394 4-4-0 LSWR Drummond

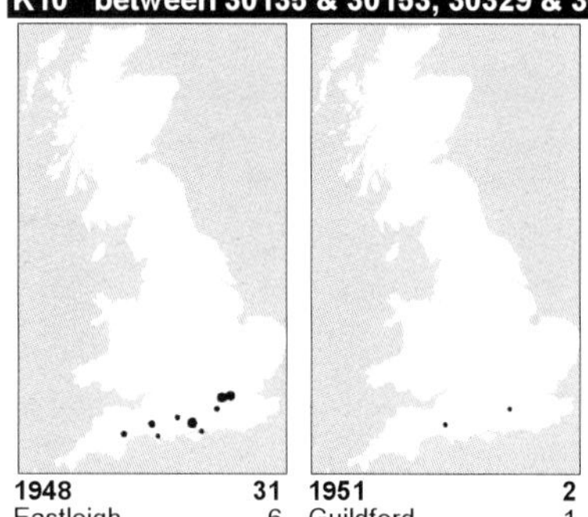

1948	31	1951	2
Eastleigh	6	Guildford	1
Feltham	6	Yeovil Town	1
Nine Elms	6		
Yeovil Town	4		
Exmouth Junction	3		
Guildford	2		
Salisbury	2		
Dorchester	1		
Fratton	1		

Below: LBSCR Marsh 'J1' class 4-6-2T No 32325 (formerly named *Abergavenny*).

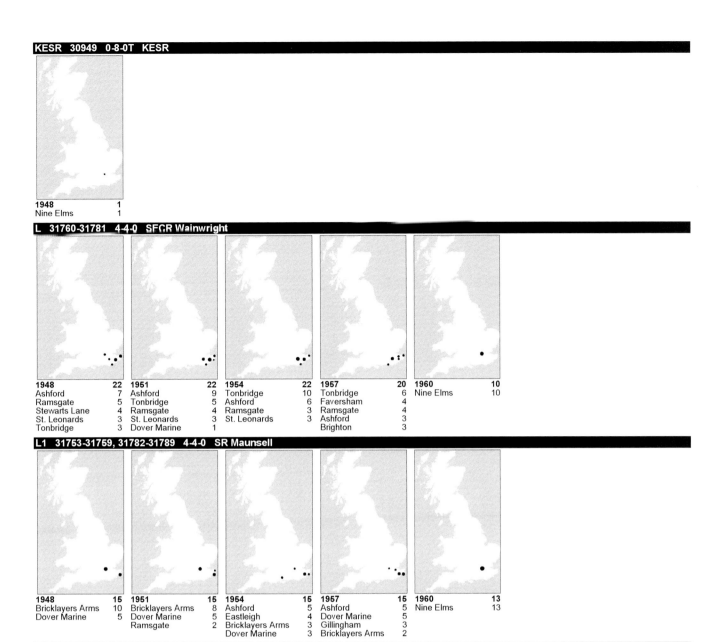

KESR 30949 0-8-0T KESR

1948	1
Nine Elms	1

L 31760-31781 4-4-0 SECR Wainwright

1948	22	1951	22	1954	22	1957	20	1960	10
Ashford	7	Ashford	9	Tonbridge	10	Tonbridge	6	Nine Elms	10
Ramsgate	5	Tonbridge	5	Ashford	6	Faversham	4		
Stewarts Lane	4	Ramsgate	4	Ramsgate	3	Ramsgate	4		
St. Leonards	3	St. Leonards	3	St. Leonards	3	Ashford	3		
Tonbridge	3	Dover Marine	1			Brighton	3		

L1 31753-31759, 31782-31789 4-4-0 SR Maunsell

1948	15	1951	15	1954	15	1957	15	1960	13
Bricklayers Arms	10	Bricklayers Arms	8	Ashford	5	Ashford	5	Nine Elms	13
Dover Marine	5	Dover Marine	5	Eastleigh	4	Dover Marine	5		
		Ramsgate	2	Bricklayers Arms	3	Gillingham	3		
				Dover Marine	3	Bricklayers Arms	2		

L11 between 30134 & 30175, 30405-30414, 30435-30442 4-4-0 LSWR Drummond

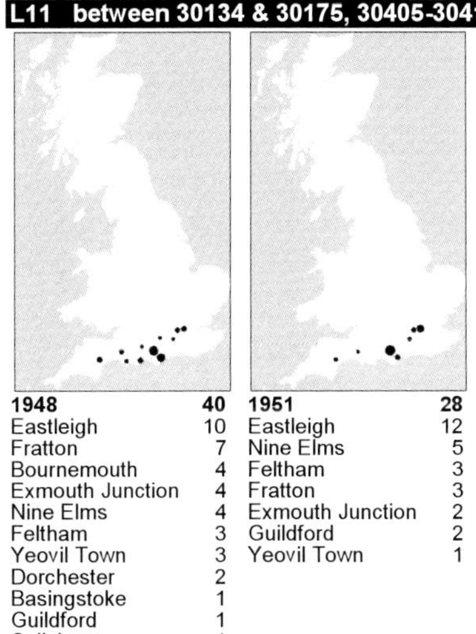

1948	40	1951	28
Eastleigh	10	Eastleigh	12
Fratton	7	Nine Elms	5
Bournemouth	4	Feltham	3
Exmouth Junction	4	Fratton	3
Nine Elms	4	Exmouth Junction	2
Feltham	3	Guildford	2
Yeovil Town	3	Yeovil Town	1
Dorchester	2		
Basingstoke	1		
Guildford	1		
Salisbury	1		

Below: Kent & East Sussex Railway 0-8-0T No 949 *Hecate* at Nine Elms. Allocated the number 30949, but not carried. *C. R. L. Coles*

L12 30415-30434 4-4-0 LSWR Drummond

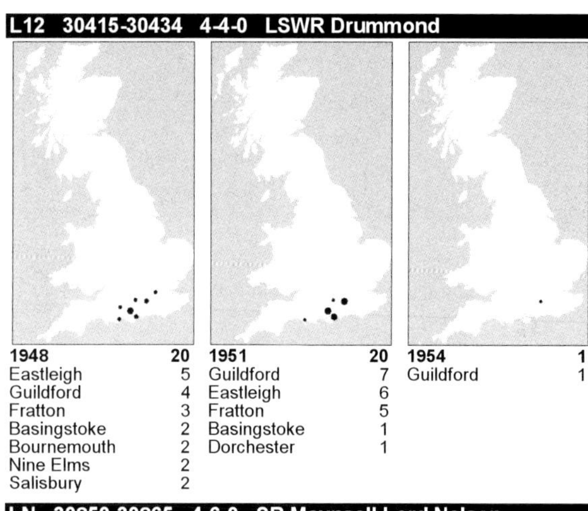

1948	20
Eastleigh	5
Guildford	4
Fratton	3
Basingstoke	2
Bournemouth	2
Nine Elms	2
Salisbury	2

1951	20
Guildford	7
Eastleigh	6
Fratton	5
Basingstoke	1
Dorchester	1

1954	1
Guildford	1

LN 30850-30865 4-6-0 SR Maunsell Lord Nelson

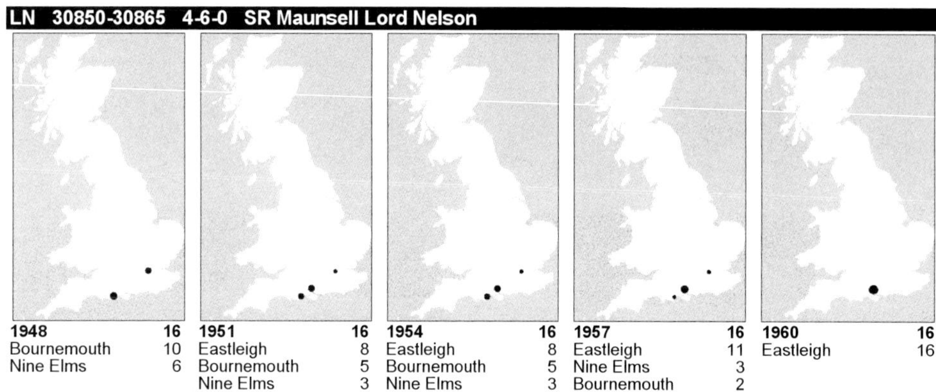

1948	16
Bournemouth	10
Nine Elms	6

1951	16
Eastleigh	8
Bournemouth	5
Nine Elms	3

1954	16
Eastleigh	8
Bournemouth	5
Nine Elms	3

1957	16
Eastleigh	11
Nine Elms	3
Bournemouth	2

1960	16
Eastleigh	16

M7 30021-30060, between 30104 & 30481, 30667-30676 0-4-4T LSWR Drummond

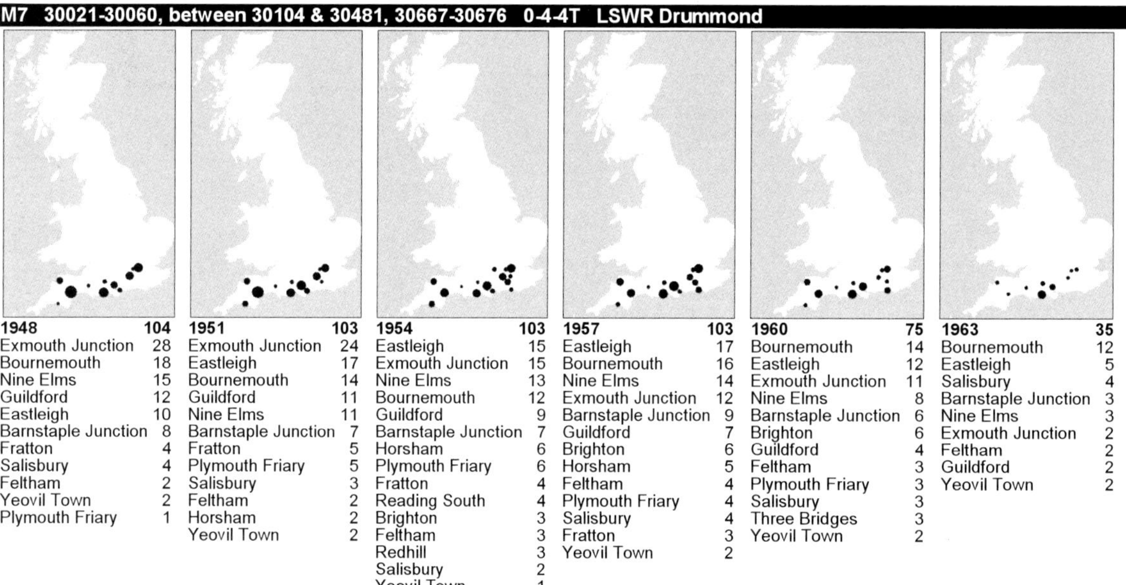

1948	104
Exmouth Junction	28
Bournemouth	18
Nine Elms	15
Guildford	12
Eastleigh	10
Barnstaple Junction	8
Fratton	4
Salisbury	4
Feltham	2
Yeovil Town	2
Plymouth Friary	1

1951	103
Exmouth Junction	24
Eastleigh	17
Bournemouth	14
Guildford	11
Nine Elms	11
Barnstaple Junction	7
Fratton	5
Plymouth Friary	5
Salisbury	3
Feltham	2
Horsham	2
Yeovil Town	2

1954	103
Eastleigh	15
Exmouth Junction	15
Nine Elms	13
Bournemouth	12
Guildford	9
Barnstaple Junction	7
Horsham	6
Plymouth Friary	6
Fratton	4
Reading South	4
Brighton	3
Feltham	3
Redhill	3
Salisbury	2
Yeovil Town	1

1957	103
Eastleigh	17
Bournemouth	16
Nine Elms	14
Exmouth Junction	12
Barnstaple Junction	9
Guildford	7
Brighton	6
Horsham	5
Feltham	4
Plymouth Friary	4
Salisbury	4
Fratton	3
Yeovil Town	2

1960	75
Bournemouth	14
Eastleigh	12
Exmouth Junction	11
Nine Elms	8
Barnstaple Junction	6
Brighton	6
Guildford	4
Feltham	3
Plymouth Friary	3
Salisbury	3
Three Bridges	3
Yeovil Town	2

1963	35
Bournemouth	12
Eastleigh	5
Salisbury	4
Barnstaple Junction	3
Nine Elms	3
Exmouth Junction	2
Feltham	2
Guildford	2
Yeovil Town	2

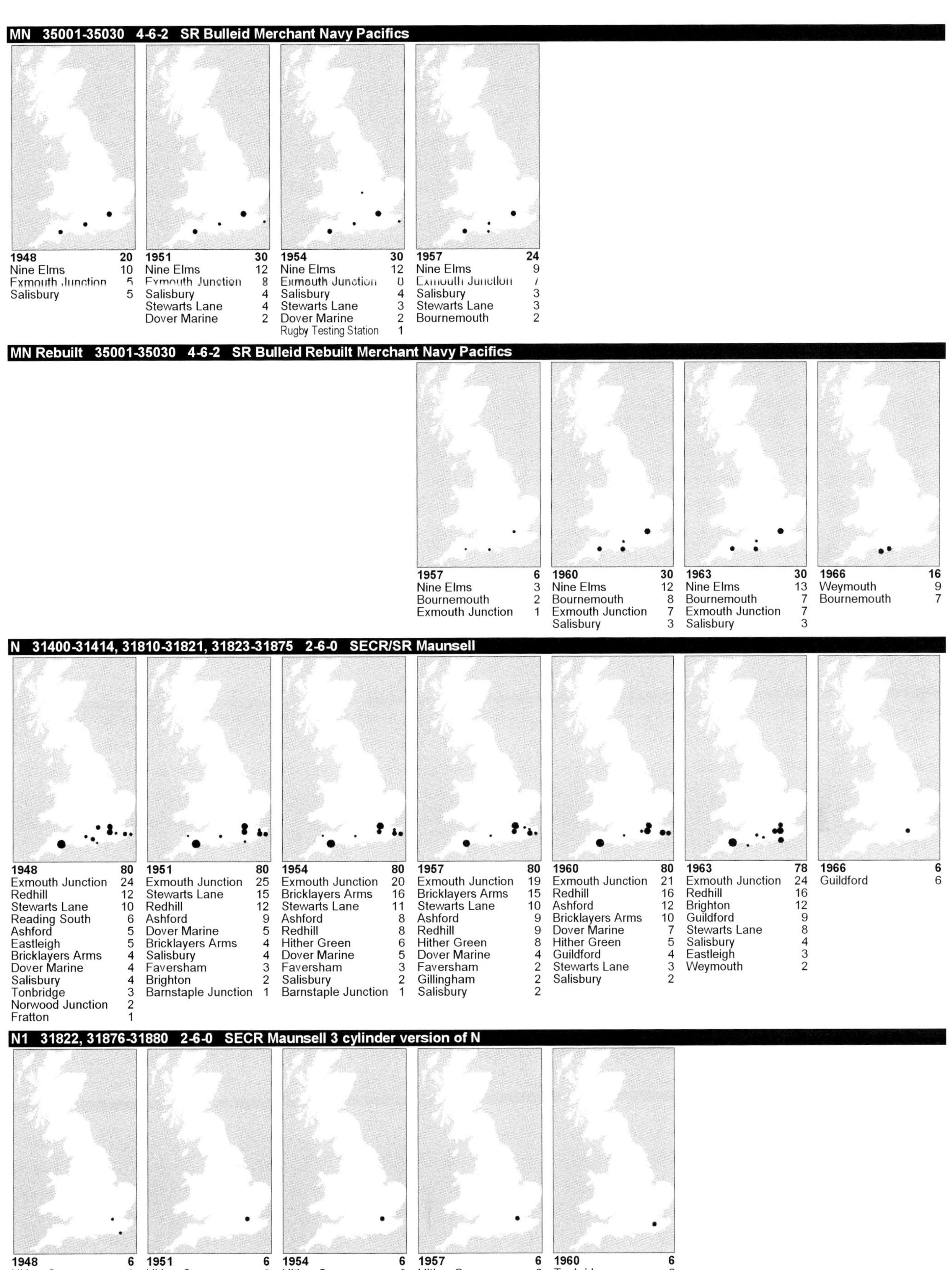

MN 35001-35030 4-6-2 SR Bulleid Merchant Navy Pacifics
1948 20
Nine Elms 10
Exmouth Junction 5
Salisbury 5
1951 30
Nine Elms 12
Exmouth Junction 8
Salisbury 4
Stewarts Lane 4
Dover Marine 2
1954 30
Nine Elms 12
Exmouth Junction 8
Salisbury 4
Stewarts Lane 3
Dover Marine 2
Rugby Testing Station 1
1957 24
Nine Elms 9
Exmouth Junction 7
Salisbury 3
Stewarts Lane 3
Bournemouth 2
MN Rebuilt 35001-35030 4-6-2 SR Bulleid Rebuilt Merchant Navy Pacifics
1957 6
Nine Elms 3
Bournemouth 2
Exmouth Junction 1
1960 30
Nine Elms 12
Bournemouth 8
Exmouth Junction 7
Salisbury 3
1963 30
Nine Elms 13
Bournemouth 7
Exmouth Junction 7
Salisbury 3
1966 16
Weymouth 9
Bournemouth 7
N 31400-31414, 31810-31821, 31823-31875 2-6-0 SECR/SR Maunsell
1948 80
Exmouth Junction 24
Redhill 12
Stewarts Lane 10
Reading South 6
Ashford 5
Eastleigh 5
Bricklayers Arms 4
Dover Marine 4
Salisbury 4
Tonbridge 3
Norwood Junction 2
Fratton 1
1951 80
Exmouth Junction 25
Stewarts Lane 15
Redhill 12
Ashford 9
Dover Marine 5
Bricklayers Arms 4
Salisbury 4
Faversham 3
Brighton 2
Barnstaple Junction 1
1954 80
Exmouth Junction 20
Bricklayers Arms 16
Stewarts Lane 11
Ashford 8
Redhill 8
Hither Green 6
Dover Marine 5
Faversham 3
Salisbury 2
Barnstaple Junction 1
1957 80
Exmouth Junction 19
Bricklayers Arms 15
Stewarts Lane 10
Ashford 9
Redhill 9
Hither Green 8
Dover Marine 4
Faversham 2
Gillingham 2
Salisbury 2
1960 80
Exmouth Junction 21
Redhill 16
Ashford 12
Bricklayers Arms 10
Dover Marine 7
Hither Green 5
Guildford 4
Stewarts Lane 3
Salisbury 2
1963 78
Exmouth Junction 24
Redhill 16
Brighton 12
Guildford 9
Stewarts Lane 8
Salisbury 4
Eastleigh 3
Weymouth 2
1966 6
Guildford 6
N1 31822, 31876-31880 2-6-0 SECR Maunsell 3 cylinder version of N
1948 6
Hither Green 3
St. Leonards 3
1951 6
Hither Green 6
1954 6
Hither Green 6
1957 6
Hither Green 6
1960 6
Tonbridge 6

Left: The original SECR Maunsell 'N1' class 3-cylinder 2-6-0 No 31822 working an up return excursion from Ramsgate to Victoria near Reculver in August 1958. *P. Ransome-Wallis*

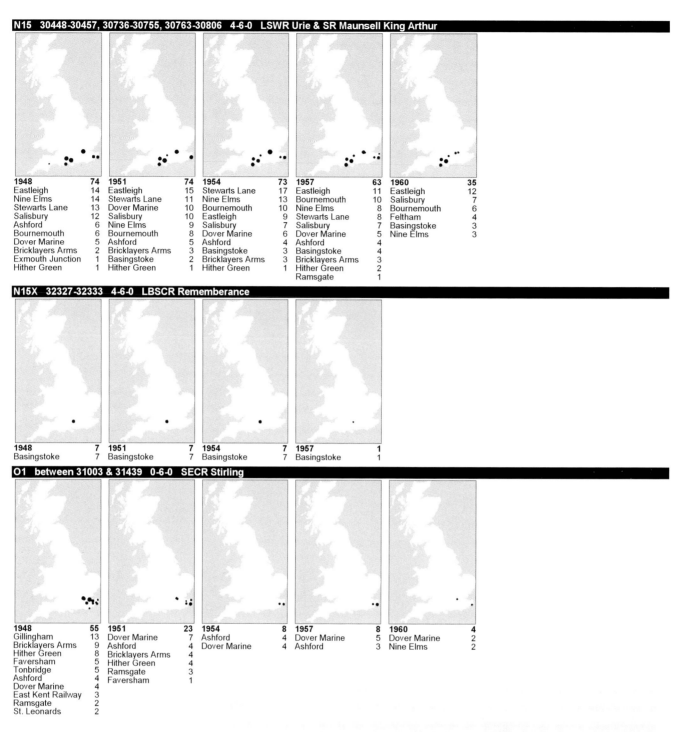

N15 30448-30457, 30736-30755, 30763-30806 4-6-0 LSWR Urie & SR Maunsell King Arthur

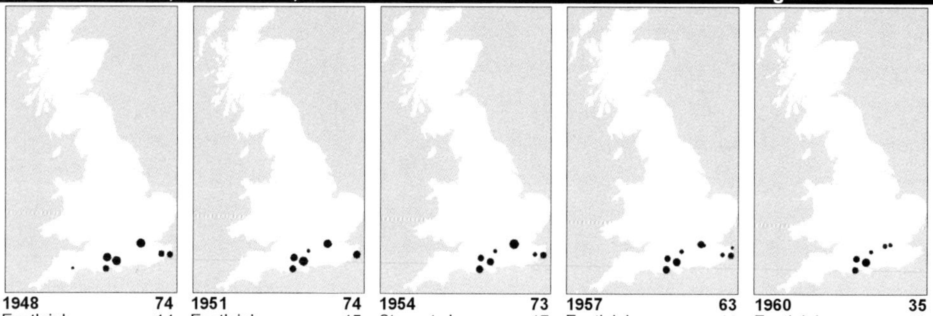

1948	74	1951	74	1954	73	1957	63	1960	35
Eastleigh	14	Eastleigh	15	Stewarts Lane	17	Eastleigh	11	Eastleigh	12
Nine Elms	14	Stewarts Lane	11	Nine Elms	13	Bournemouth	10	Salisbury	7
Stewarts Lane	13	Dover Marine	10	Bournemouth	10	Nine Elms	8	Bournemouth	6
Salisbury	12	Salisbury	10	Eastleigh	9	Stewarts Lane	8	Feltham	4
Ashford	6	Nine Elms	9	Salisbury	7	Salisbury	7	Basingstoke	3
Bournemouth	6	Bournemouth	8	Dover Marine	6	Dover Marine	5	Nine Elms	3
Dover Marine	5	Ashford	5	Ashford	4	Ashford	4		
Bricklayers Arms	2	Bricklayers Arms	3	Basingstoke	3	Basingstoke	4		
Exmouth Junction	1	Basingstoke	2	Bricklayers Arms	3	Bricklayers Arms	3		
Hither Green	1	Hither Green	1	Hither Green	1	Hither Green	2		
						Ramsgate	1		

N15X 32327-32333 4-6-0 LBSCR Rememberance

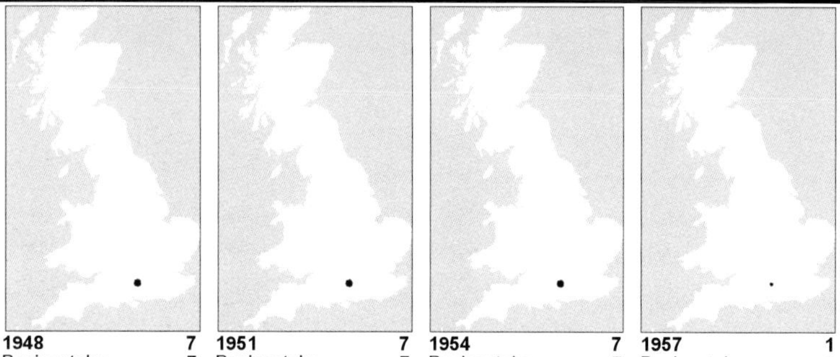

1948	7	1951	7	1954	7	1957	1
Basingstoke	7	Basingstoke	7	Basingstoke	7	Basingstoke	1

O1 between 31003 & 31439 0-6-0 SECR Stirling

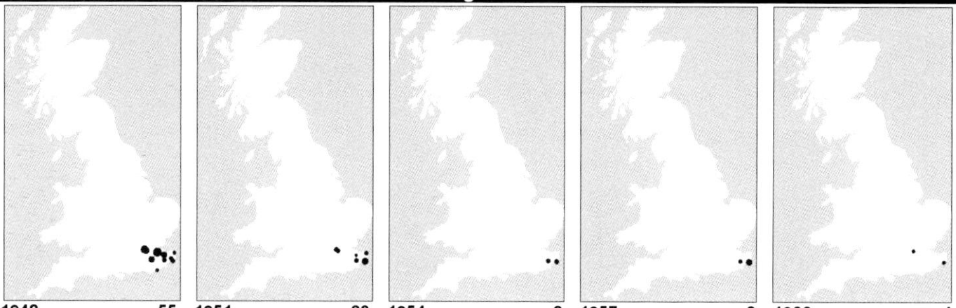

1948	55	1951	23	1954	8	1957	8	1960	4
Gillingham	13	Dover Marine	7	Ashford	4	Dover Marine	5	Dover Marine	2
Bricklayers Arms	9	Ashford	4	Dover Marine	4	Ashford	3	Nine Elms	2
Hither Green	8	Bricklayers Arms	4						
Faversham	5	Hither Green	4						
Tonbridge	5	Ramsgate	3						
Ashford	4	Faversham	1						
Dover Marine	4								
East Kent Railway	3								
Ramsgate	2								
St. Leonards	2								

Right: LBSCR Billinton 'N15X' Remembrance class 4-6-0 No 32329 *Stephenson* at Basingstoke in August 1952. *J. Davenport*

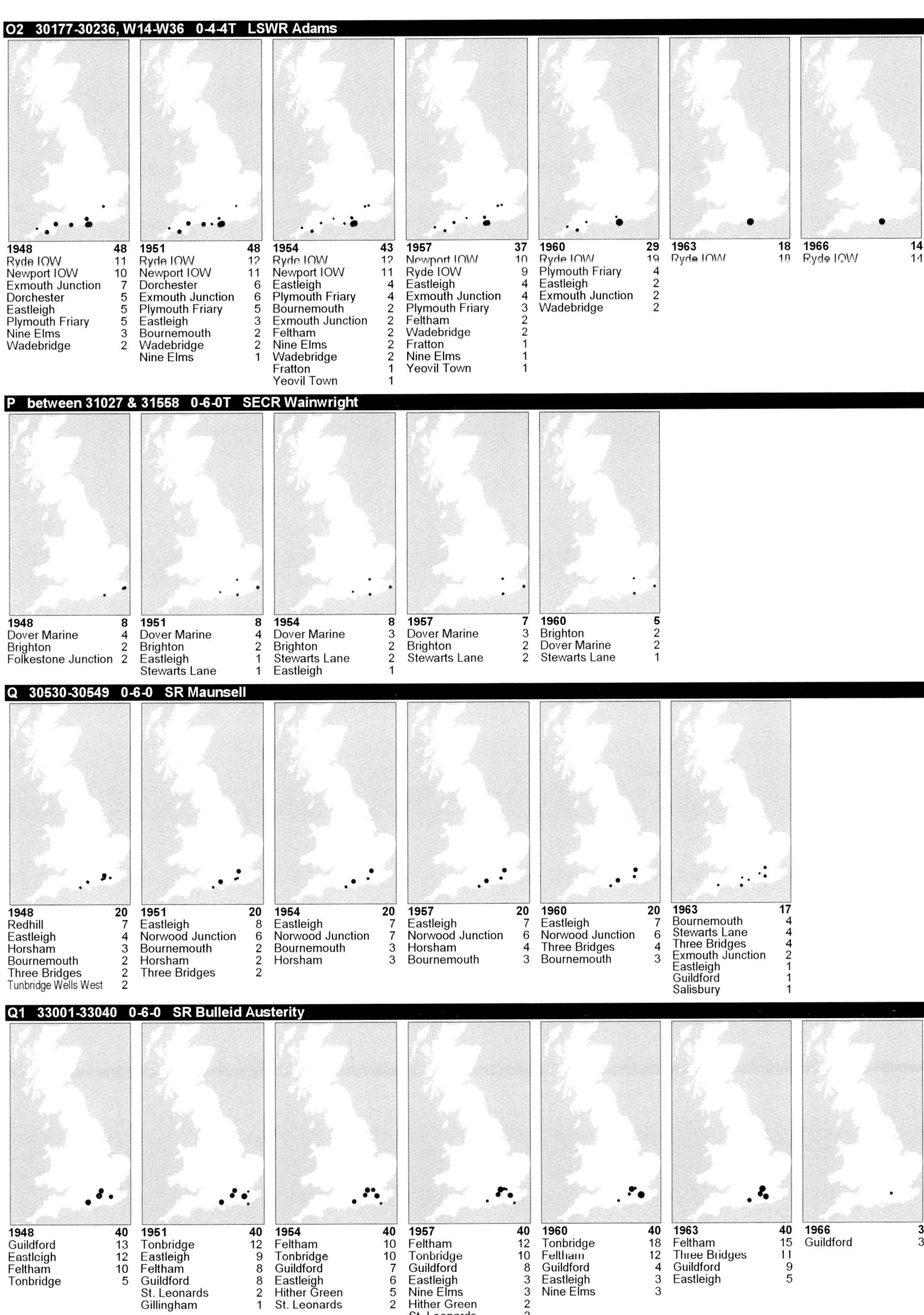
O2 30177-30236, W14-W36 0-4-4T LSWR Adams
1948 48
Ryde IOW 11
Newport IOW 10
Exmouth Junction 7
Dorchester 5
Eastleigh 5
Plymouth Friary 5
Nine Elms 3
Wadebridge 2
1951 48
Ryde IOW 12
Newport IOW 11
Dorchester 6
Exmouth Junction 6
Plymouth Friary 5
Eastleigh 3
Bournemouth 2
Wadebridge 2
Nine Elms 1
1954 43
Ryde IOW 12
Newport IOW 11
Eastleigh 4
Plymouth Friary 4
Bournemouth 2
Exmouth Junction 2
Feltham 2
Nine Elms 2
Wadebridge 2
Fratton 1
Yeovil Town 1
1957 37
Newport IOW 10
Ryde IOW 9
Eastleigh 4
Exmouth Junction 4
Plymouth Friary 3
Feltham 2
Wadebridge 2
Fratton 1
Nine Elms 1
Yeovil Town 1
1960 29
Ryde IOW 19
Plymouth Friary 4
Eastleigh 2
Exmouth Junction 2
Wadebridge 2
1963 18
Ryde IOW 18
1966 14
Ryde IOW 14
P between 31027 & 31558 0-6-0T SECR Wainwright
1948 8
Dover Marine 4
Brighton 2
Folkestone Junction 2
1951 8
Dover Marine 4
Brighton 2
Eastleigh 1
Stewarts Lane 1
1954 8
Dover Marine 3
Brighton 2
Stewarts Lane 2
Eastleigh 1
1957 7
Dover Marine 3
Brighton 2
Stewarts Lane 2
1960 5
Brighton 2
Dover Marine 2
Stewarts Lane 1
Q 30530-30549 0-6-0 SR Maunsell
1948 20
Redhill 7
Eastleigh 4
Horsham 3
Bournemouth 2
Three Bridges 2
Tunbridge Wells West 2
1951 20
Eastleigh 8
Norwood Junction 6
Bournemouth 2
Horsham 2
Three Bridges 2
1954 20
Eastleigh 7
Norwood Junction 7
Bournemouth 3
Horsham 3
1957 20
Eastleigh 7
Norwood Junction 6
Horsham 4
Bournemouth 3
1960 20
Eastleigh 7
Norwood Junction 6
Three Bridges 4
Bournemouth 3
1963 17
Bournemouth 4
Stewarts Lane 4
Three Bridges 4
Exmouth Junction 2
Eastleigh 1
Guildford 1
Salisbury 1
Q1 33001-33040 0-6-0 SR Bulleid Austerity
1948 40
Guildford 13
Eastleigh 12
Feltham 10
Tonbridge 5
1951 40
Tonbridge 12
Eastleigh 9
Feltham 8
Guildford 8
St. Leonards 2
Gillingham 1
1954 40
Feltham 10
Tonbridge 10
Guildford 7
Eastleigh 6
Hither Green 5
St. Leonards 2
1957 40
Feltham 12
Tonbridge 10
Guildford 8
Eastleigh 3
Nine Elms 3
Hither Green 2
St. Leonards 2
1960 40
Tonbridge 18
Feltham 12
Guildford 4
Eastleigh 3
Nine Elms 3
1963 40
Feltham 15
Three Bridges 11
Guildford 9
Eastleigh 5
1966 3
Guildford 3

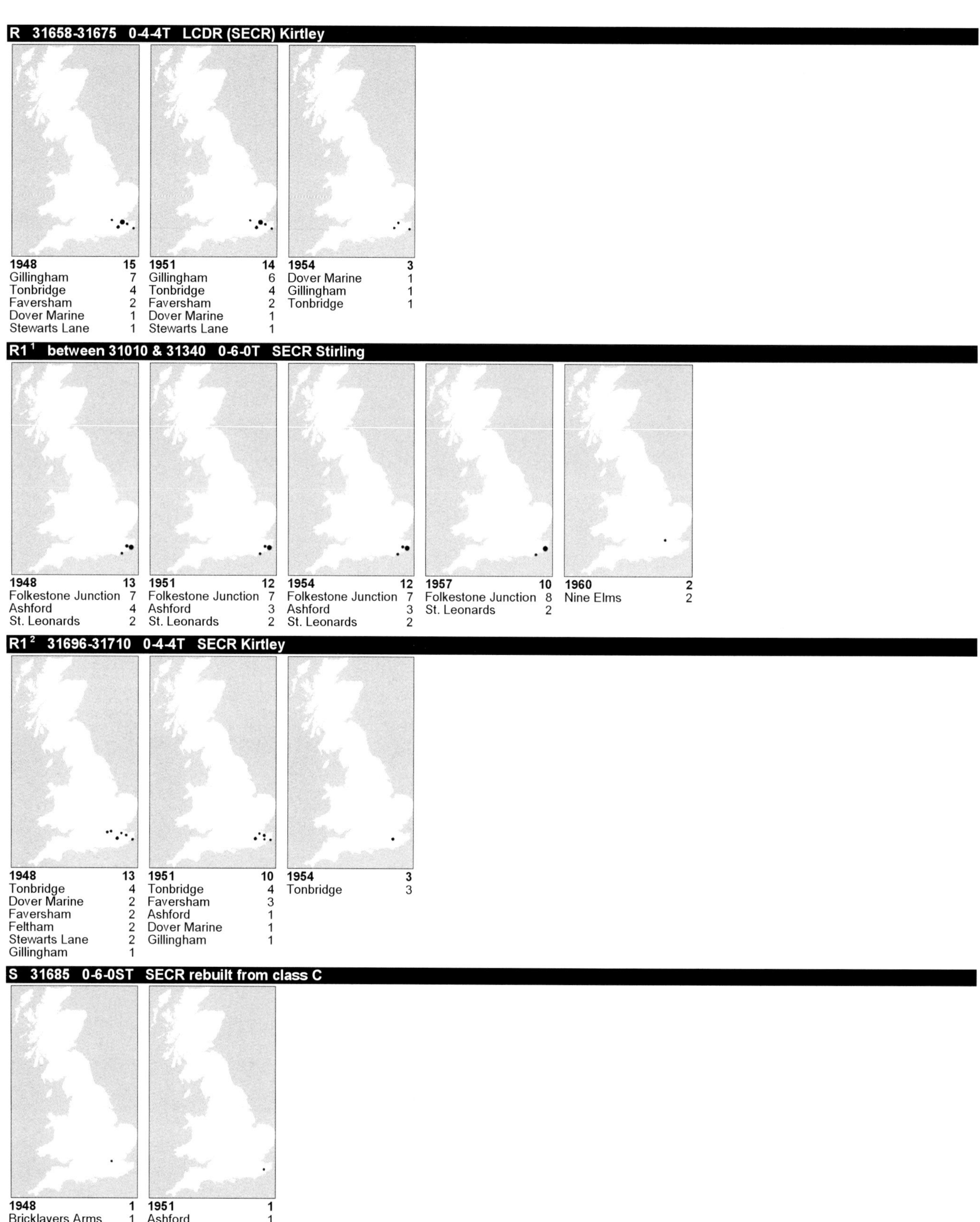

R 31658-31675 0-4-4T LCDR (SECR) Kirtley

1948	15	1951	14	1954	3
Gillingham	7	Gillingham	6	Dover Marine	1
Tonbridge	4	Tonbridge	4	Gillingham	1
Faversham	2	Faversham	2	Tonbridge	1
Dover Marine	1	Dover Marine	1		
Stewarts Lane	1	Stewarts Lane	1		

R1 [1] between 31010 & 31340 0-6-0T SECR Stirling

1948	13	1951	12	1954	12	1957	10	1960	2
Folkestone Junction	7	Folkestone Junction	7	Folkestone Junction	7	Folkestone Junction	8	Nine Elms	2
Ashford	4	Ashford	3	Ashford	3	St. Leonards	2		
St. Leonards	2	St. Leonards	2	St. Leonards	2				

R1 [2] 31696-31710 0-4-4T SECR Kirtley

1948	13	1951	10	1954	3
Tonbridge	4	Tonbridge	4	Tonbridge	3
Dover Marine	2	Faversham	3		
Faversham	2	Ashford	1		
Feltham	2	Dover Marine	1		
Stewarts Lane	2	Gillingham	1		
Gillingham	1				

S 31685 0-6-0ST SECR rebuilt from class C

1948	1	1951	1
Bricklayers Arms	1	Ashford	1

S11 30395-30404 4-4-0 LSWR Drummond

1948	10	1951	10	1954	1
Fratton	6	Fratton	5	Guildford	1
Bournemouth	2	Bournemouth	3		
Eastleigh	2	Eastleigh	1		
		Dorchester	1		

S15 30496-30515, 30823-30847 4-6-0 LSWR Urie & SR Maunsell

1948	45	1951	45	1954	45	1957	45	1960	45	1963	41
Feltham	30	Feltham	28	Feltham	25	Feltham	25	Feltham	25	Feltham	23
Exmouth Junction	10	Exmouth Junction	10	Salisbury	11	Salisbury	11	Salisbury	10	Salisbury	9
Salisbury	5	Salisbury	7	Exmouth Junction	6	Exmouth Junction	6	Exmouth Junction	6	Exmouth Junction	6
				Redhill	3	Redhill	3	Redhill	4	Redhill	3

T 31602-31604, 500S 0-6-0T LCDR (SECR) Kirtley

1948	3	1951	1
Stewarts Lane	2	Reading South	1
Meldon Quarry	1		

T1 30001-30020, 30361-30367 0-4-4T LSWR Adams

1948	14	1951	3
Eastleigh	6	Eastleigh	1
Salisbury	3	Fratton	1
Plymouth Friary	2	Plymouth Friary	1
Bournemouth	1		
Feltham	1		
Fratton	1		

LSWR Adams 'T1' class 0-4-4T No 367 (allocated the number 30367 but not carried).

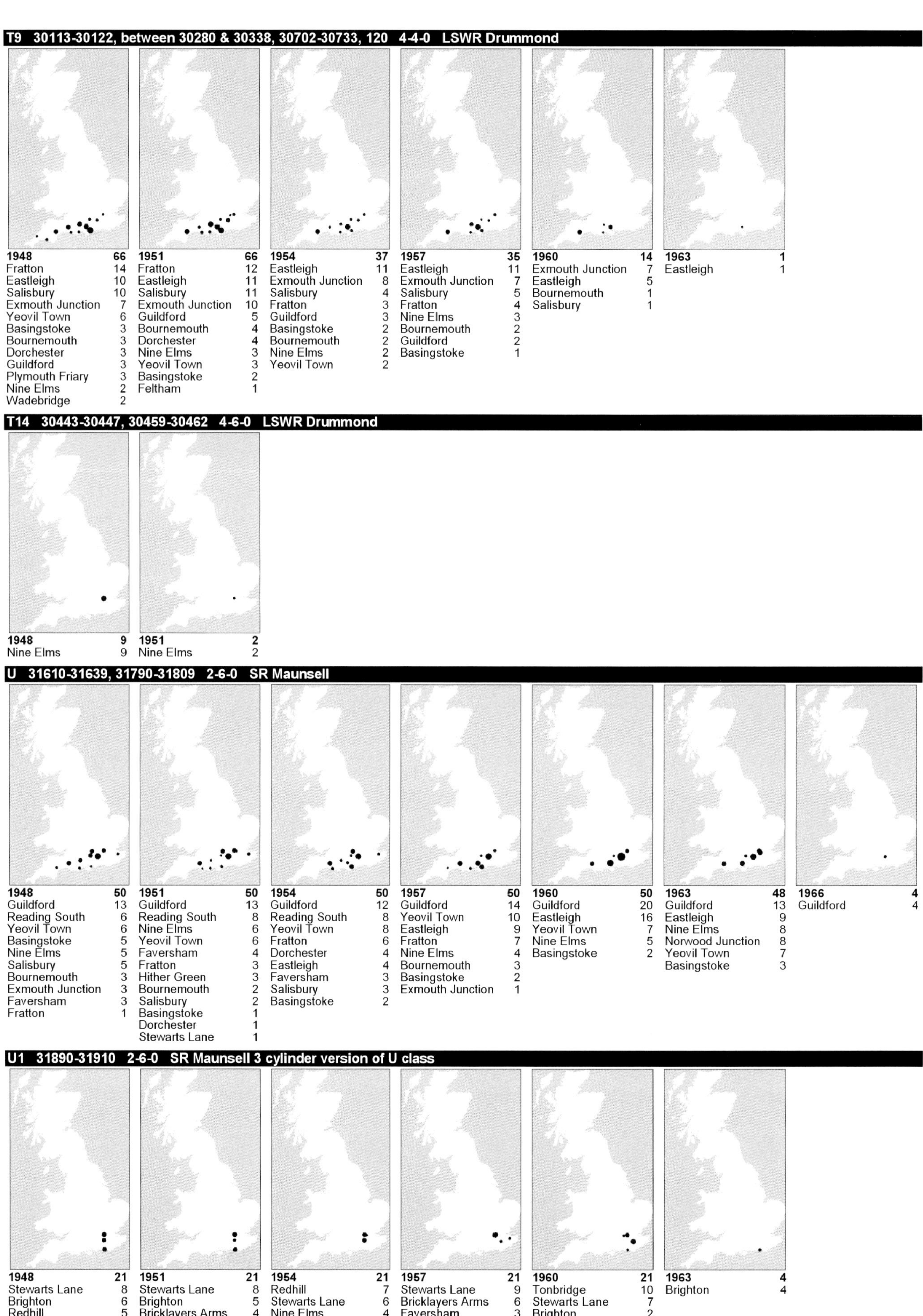

T9 30113-30122, between 30280 & 30338, 30702-30733, 120 4-4-0 LSWR Drummond

1948	66
Fratton	14
Eastleigh	10
Salisbury	10
Exmouth Junction	7
Yeovil Town	6
Basingstoke	3
Bournemouth	3
Dorchester	3
Guildford	3
Plymouth Friary	3
Nine Elms	2
Wadebridge	2

1951	66
Fratton	12
Eastleigh	11
Salisbury	11
Exmouth Junction	10
Guildford	5
Bournemouth	4
Dorchester	4
Nine Elms	3
Yeovil Town	3
Basingstoke	2
Feltham	1

1954	37
Eastleigh	11
Exmouth Junction	8
Salisbury	4
Fratton	3
Guildford	3
Basingstoke	2
Bournemouth	2
Nine Elms	2
Yeovil Town	2

1957	35
Eastleigh	11
Exmouth Junction	7
Salisbury	5
Fratton	4
Nine Elms	3
Bournemouth	2
Guildford	2
Basingstoke	1

1960	14
Exmouth Junction	7
Eastleigh	5
Bournemouth	1
Salisbury	1

1963	1
Eastleigh	1

T14 30443-30447, 30459-30462 4-6-0 LSWR Drummond

1948	9
Nine Elms	9

1951	2
Nine Elms	2

U 31610-31639, 31790-31809 2-6-0 SR Maunsell

1948	50
Guildford	13
Reading South	6
Yeovil Town	6
Basingstoke	5
Nine Elms	5
Salisbury	5
Bournemouth	3
Exmouth Junction	3
Faversham	3
Fratton	1

1951	50
Guildford	13
Reading South	8
Nine Elms	6
Yeovil Town	6
Faversham	4
Fratton	3
Hither Green	3
Bournemouth	2
Salisbury	2
Basingstoke	1
Dorchester	1
Stewarts Lane	1

1954	50
Guildford	12
Reading South	8
Yeovil Town	8
Fratton	6
Dorchester	4
Eastleigh	4
Faversham	3
Salisbury	3
Basingstoke	2

1957	50
Guildford	14
Yeovil Town	10
Eastleigh	9
Fratton	7
Nine Elms	4
Bournemouth	3
Basingstoke	2
Exmouth Junction	1

1960	50
Guildford	20
Eastleigh	16
Yeovil Town	7
Nine Elms	5
Basingstoke	2

1963	48
Guildford	13
Eastleigh	9
Nine Elms	8
Norwood Junction	8
Yeovil Town	7
Basingstoke	3

1966	4
Guildford	4

U1 31890-31910 2-6-0 SR Maunsell 3 cylinder version of U class

1948	21
Stewarts Lane	8
Brighton	6
Redhill	5
Bricklayers Arms	2

1951	21
Stewarts Lane	8
Brighton	5
Bricklayers Arms	4
Redhill	4

1954	21
Redhill	7
Stewarts Lane	6
Nine Elms	4
Bricklayers Arms	2
Hither Green	2

1957	21
Stewarts Lane	9
Bricklayers Arms	6
Faversham	3
Tonbridge	3

1960	21
Tonbridge	10
Stewarts Lane	7
Brighton	2
Feltham	2

1963	4
Brighton	4

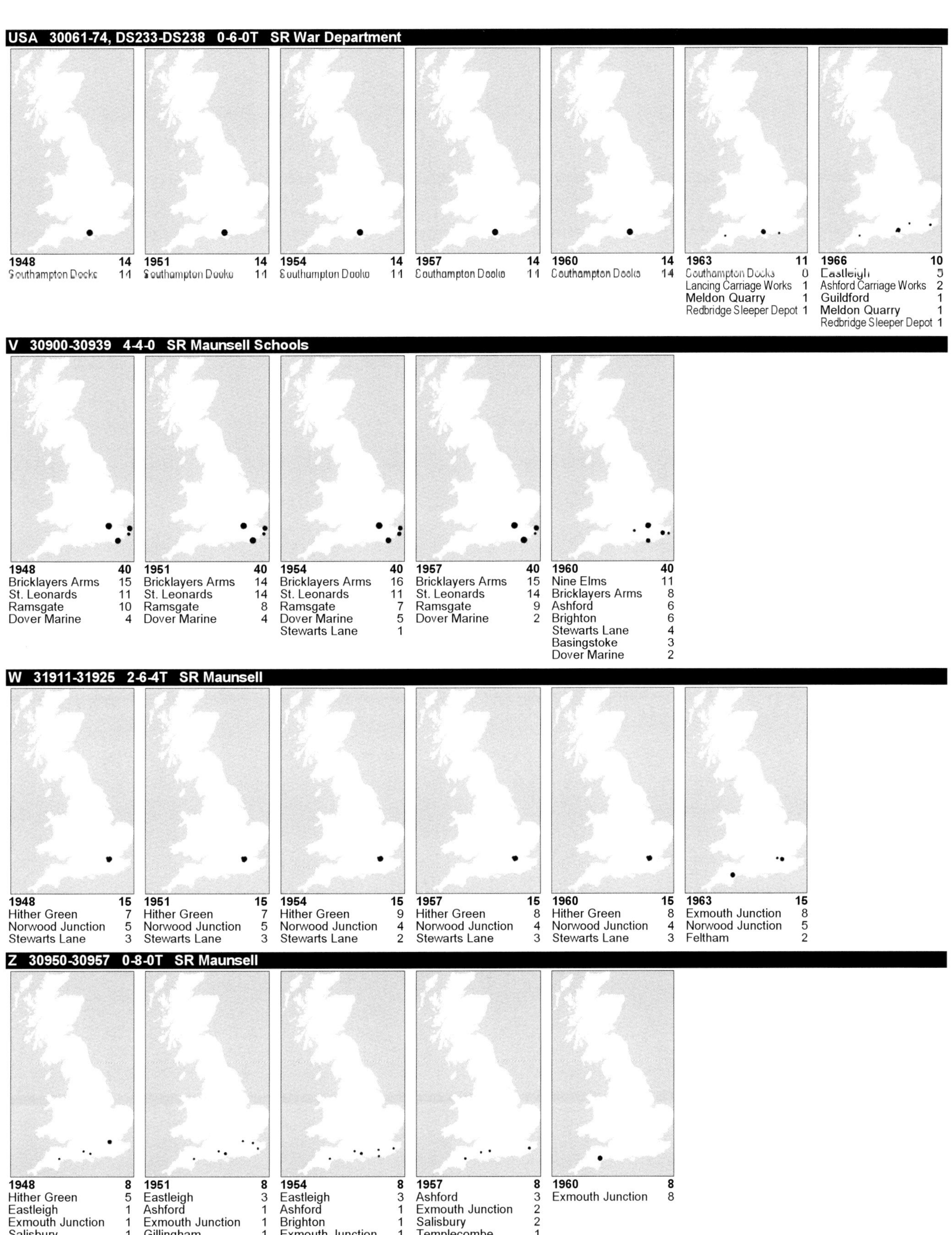
USA 30061-74, DS233-DS238 0-6-0T SR War Department
1948 14
Southampton Docks 14
1951 14
Southampton Docks 14
1954 14
Southampton Docks 14
1957 14
Southampton Docks 14
1960 14
Southampton Docks 14
1963 11
Southampton Docks 0
Lancing Carriage Works 1
Meldon Quarry 1
Redbridge Sleeper Depot 1
1966 10
Eastleigh 5
Ashford Carriage Works 2
Guildford 1
Meldon Quarry 1
Redbridge Sleeper Depot 1
V 30900-30939 4-4-0 SR Maunsell Schools
1948 40
Bricklayers Arms 15
St. Leonards 11
Ramsgate 10
Dover Marine 4
1951 40
Bricklayers Arms 14
St. Leonards 14
Ramsgate 8
Dover Marine 4
1954 40
Bricklayers Arms 16
St. Leonards 11
Ramsgate 7
Dover Marine 5
Stewarts Lane 1
1957 40
Bricklayers Arms 15
St. Leonards 14
Ramsgate 9
Dover Marine 2
1960 40
Nine Elms 11
Bricklayers Arms 8
Ashford 6
Brighton 6
Stewarts Lane 4
Basingstoke 3
Dover Marine 2
W 31911-31925 2-6-4T SR Maunsell
1948 15
Hither Green 7
Norwood Junction 5
Stewarts Lane 3
1951 15
Hither Green 7
Norwood Junction 5
Stewarts Lane 3
1954 15
Hither Green 9
Norwood Junction 4
Stewarts Lane 2
1957 15
Hither Green 8
Norwood Junction 4
Stewarts Lane 3
1960 15
Hither Green 8
Norwood Junction 4
Stewarts Lane 3
1963 15
Exmouth Junction 8
Norwood Junction 5
Feltham 2
Z 30950-30957 0-8-0T SR Maunsell
1948 8
Hither Green 5
Eastleigh 1
Exmouth Junction 1
Salisbury 1
1951 8
Eastleigh 3
Ashford 1
Exmouth Junction 1
Gillingham 1
Nine Elms 1
Salisbury 1
1954 8
Eastleigh 3
Ashford 1
Brighton 1
Exmouth Junction 1
Salisbury 1
Three Bridges 1
1957 8
Ashford 3
Exmouth Junction 2
Salisbury 2
Templecombe 1
1960 8
Exmouth Junction 8

Above: LCDR Kirtley 'T' class 0-6-0T service locomotive No 500S which was based at the Engineer's Department at Meldon Quarry was awaiting scrap in December 1949.
J. Macartney Robbins

Below: Unrebuilt LBSCR Stroudley 'A1' class 'Terrier' 0-6-0T number DS680, based at the Carriage & Wagon Department at Lancing Works.
C. P. Boocock

Right: LMS 'Jubilee' class 4-6-0 No 45593 *Kolhapur* inside Leeds Holbeck shed, 13 February 1967.
J. H. Cooper-Smith

Former LMS Locomotives

Top: Midland Railway Johnson '3P' class 4-4-0 No 40758 at Leeds on 30 April 1949. *H. C. Casserley*

Above: Midland Railway Deeley '4P' class Compound 4-4-0 No 41000 is seen in its pre-preservation days. *F. W. Day*

Left: LMS Stanier '2P' class 0-4-4T No 41908 at Watford in May 1958. *F. J. Saunders*

		1948	1951	1954	1957	1960	1963	1966
40001	3MT[1]	11A Carnforth	8A Edge Hill	1A Willesden	17E Heaton Mersey	9F Heaton Mersey		
40002	3MT[1]	7A Llandudno Junction	2C Warwick	1A Willesden	6D Chester Northgate			
40003	3MT[1]	2A Rugby	8A Edge Hill	2B Nuneaton	6H Bangor	1A Willesden		
40004	3MT[1]	1C Watford	1A Willesden	1A Willesden	6D Chester Northgate			
40005	3MT[1]	4A Shrewsbury	84G Shrewsbury	84G Shrewsbury	84G Shrewsbury			
40006	3MT[1]	8A Edge Hill	1A Willesden	1A Willesden	1A Willesden	Wolverton Works		
40007	3MT[1]	8A Edge Hill	8A Edge Hill	1A Willesden	1A Willesden	1A Willesden		
40008	3MT[1]	4A Shrewsbury	84G Shrewsbury	84G Shrewsbury	84G Shrewsbury			
40009	3MT[1]	2E Warwick	1A Willesden	9E Trafford Park	17F Trafford Park	9E Trafford Park		
40010	3MT[1]	1C Watford	1C Watford	1C Watford	1C Watford	1A Willesden		
40011	3MT[1]	3C Walsall	3C Walsall	11A Carnforth	11A Carnforth	24L Carnforth		
40012	3MT[1]	26F Lees Oldham	26F Lees Oldham	26F Lees Oldham	2A Rugby	14E Bedford		
40013	3MT[1]	26A Newton Heath	26A Newton Heath	26A Newton Heath	26A Newton Heath			
40014	3MT[1]	26A Newton Heath	26F Lees Oldham	26F Lees Oldham	26A Newton Heath	26A Newton Heath		
40015	3MT[1]	26A Newton Heath	26A Newton Heath	26A Newton Heath	26A Newton Heath	26A Newton Heath		
40016	3MT[1]	11E Tebay	2C Warwick	1A Willesden	1A Willesden	1A Willesden		
40017	3MT[1]	3C Walsall	1A Willesden	9E Trafford Park	2A Rugby			
40018	3MT[1]	2D Nuneaton	1A Willesden	1A Willesden	17F Trafford Park	9E Trafford Park		
40019	3MT[1]	3C Walsall	3C Walsall	1A Willesden	1A Willesden			
40020	3MT[1]	1C Watford	1C Watford	1C Watford	1C Watford	14E Bedford		
40021	3MT[1]	20G Hellifield	23B Hellifield	68D Beattock	14B Kentish Town			
40022	3MT[1]	14B Kentish Town	14C St. Albans	14C St. Albans	14C St. Albans	14C St. Albans		
40023	3MT[1]	14A Cricklewood	14A Cricklewood	14A Cricklewood	14A Cricklewood			
40024	3MT[1]	14C St. Albans	14C St. Albans	14C St. Albans	14C St. Albans	14C St. Albans		
40025	3MT[1]	14A Cricklewood	14A Cricklewood	14A Cricklewood	14A Cricklewood			
40026	3MT[1]	14A Cricklewood	14C St. Albans	14C St. Albans	14C St. Albans	14C St. Albans		
40027	3MT[1]	14B Kentish Town	14B Kentish Town	14B Kentish Town	14B Kentish Town			
40028	3MT[1]	14B Kentish Town	14B Kentish Town	14B Kentish Town	14B Kentish Town	14B Kentish Town		
40029	3MT[1]	14A Cricklewood	14B Kentish Town	14B Kentish Town	14B Kentish Town	14B Kentish Town		
40030	3MT[1]	14A Cricklewood	14A Cricklewood	68D Beattock	14A Cricklewood			
40031	3MT[1]	14A Cricklewood	14B Kentish Town	14B Kentish Town	14B Kentish Town	14B Kentish Town		
40032	3MT[1]	14A Cricklewood	14B Kentish Town	14B Kentish Town	14B Kentish Town	14B Kentish Town		
40033	3MT[1]	14A Cricklewood	14B Kentish Town	14B Kentish Town	14B Kentish Town	14B Kentish Town		
40034	3MT[1]	14C St. Albans	14B Kentish Town	14B Kentish Town	14B Kentish Town	14B Kentish Town		
40035	3MT[1]	14B Kentish Town	14B Kentish Town	14B Kentish Town	14B Kentish Town	14B Kentish Town		
40036	3MT[1]	14B Kentish Town	14B Kentish Town	14B Kentish Town	14B Kentish Town	14B Kentish Town		
40037	3MT[1]	14B Kentish Town	14B Kentish Town	14B Kentish Town	14C St. Albans	14C St. Albans		
40038	3MT[1]	14A Cricklewood	14B Kentish Town	14B Kentish Town	14B Kentish Town	14B Kentish Town		
40039	3MT[1]	14C St. Albans	14C St. Albans	14C St. Albans	14C St. Albans			
40040	3MT[1]	14B Kentish Town	22B Gloucester Barnwood	14B Kentish Town	14B Kentish Town			
40041	3MT[1]	11A Carnforth	11A Carnforth	11A Carnforth	11A Carnforth	24L Carnforth		
40042	3MT[1]	3C Walsall	8B Warrington Dallam	1A Willesden	1A Willesden	1A Willesden		
40043	3MT[1]	1C Watford	1C Watford	1C Watford	1C Watford			
40044	3MT[1]	2E Warwick	1A Willesden	1A Willesden	1A Willesden			
40045	3MT[1]	3C Walsall	3C Walsall	1A Willesden	2A Rugby			
40046	3MT[1]	1C Watford	1A Willesden	1A Willesden	1A Willesden			
40047	3MT[1]	3B Bushbury	3C Walsall	1A Willesden	1A Willesden			
40048	3MT[1]	4A Shrewsbury	84G Shrewsbury	84G Shrewsbury	84G Shrewsbury			
40049	3MT[1]	3B Bushbury	3B Bushbury	1A Willesden	1A Willesden	1A Willesden		
40050	3MT[1]	8A Edge Hill	1A Willesden	1A Willesden	1A Willesden	16C Mansfield		
40051	3MT[1]	9A Longsight	3D Aston	1A Willesden	1A Willesden	1A Willesden		
40052	3MT[1]	2A Rugby	1A Willesden	1A Willesden	17F Trafford Park			
40053	3MT[1]	3B Bushbury	3B Bushbury	1A Willesden	1A Willesden	14B Kentish Town		
40054	3MT[1]	3B Bushbury	1A Willesden	1A Willesden	1A Willesden	16C Mansfield		
40055	3MT[1]	9B Stockport Edgeley	1A Willesden	1A Willesden	17F Trafford Park			
40056	3MT[1]	26F Lees Oldham	26F Lees Oldham	26F Lees Oldham	2A Rugby			
40057	3MT[1]	26F Lees Oldham	26F Lees Oldham	26F Lees Oldham	2A Rugby	9F Heaton Mersey		
40058	3MT[1]	4A Shrewsbury	84G Shrewsbury	84G Shrewsbury	84G Shrewsbury			
40059	3MT[1]	26F Lees Oldham	26F Lees Oldham	26F Lees Oldham	2A Rugby			
40060	3MT[1]	26F Lees Oldham	26F Lees Oldham	26F Lees Oldham	2A Rugby			
40061	3MT[1]	26F Lees Oldham	26F Lees Oldham	26F Lees Oldham	2A Rugby			
40062	3MT[1]	26F Lees Oldham	26F Lees Oldham	26F Lees Oldham	26A Newton Heath	26A Newton Heath		
40063	3MT[1]	26A Newton Heath	26A Newton Heath	26A Newton Heath	26A Newton Heath	26A Newton Heath		
40064	3MT[1]	20G Hellifield	23B Hellifield	11D Tebay	1A Willesden	14B Kentish Town		
40065	3MT[1]	26A Newton Heath	26A Newton Heath	26A Newton Heath	26A Newton Heath			
40066	3MT[1]	3B Bushbury	3B Bushbury	1A Willesden	1A Willesden			
40067	3MT[1]	11B Barrow	11D Tebay	11D Tebay	17E Heaton Mersey			
40068	3MT[1]	11B Barrow	11A Carnforth	1A Willesden	1A Willesden			
40069	3MT[1]	3C Walsall	20E Manningham	1A Willesden	6D Chester Northgate			
40070	3MT[1]	11E Tebay	11A Carnforth	11A Carnforth	6D Chester Northgate	1A Willesden		
40071	3MT[2]	9A Longsight	9B Stockport Edgeley	9B Stockport Edgeley	9B Stockport Edgeley	6H Bangor		
40072	3MT[2]	7B Bangor	1C Watford	6C Birkenhead	24E Blackpool Central	24E Blackpool Central		
40073	3MT[2]	7B Bangor	1A Willesden	3C Walsall	6E Wrexham Rhosddu	16C Mansfield		
40074	3MT[2]	19G Trafford Park	20C Royston	20E Manningham	55F Manningham	56C Copley Hill		
40075	3MT[2]	19B Millhouses	20A Leeds Holbeck	20D Normanton	55E Normanton	55E Normanton		
40076	3MT[2]	5D Stoke	2C Warwick	2C Warwick	2C Warwick	6C Birkenhead		
40077	3MT[2]	9B Stockport Edgeley	9A Longsight	9A Longsight	9A Longsight	9A Longsight		
40078	3MT[2]	5D Stoke	2C Warwick	2C Warwick	2C Warwick	6C Birkenhead		
40079	3MT[2]	14B Kentish Town	14B Kentish Town	16D Mansfield	16C Mansfield	16C Mansfield		
40080	3MT[2]	8B Warrington Dallam	10E Sutton Oak	3C Walsall	3C Walsall	3A Bescot		
40081	3MT[2]	8B Warrington Dallam	1A Willesden	9B Stockport Edgeley	9B Stockport Edgeley	24L Carnforth		
40082	3MT[2]	19B Millhouses	19B Millhouses	20A Leeds Holbeck	55D Royston	55D Royston		
40083	3MT[2]	7B Bangor	7A Llandudno Junction	6G Llandudno Junction	6G Llandudno Junction	3A Bescot		
40084	3MT[2]	8B Warrington Dallam	10E Sutton Oak	3C Walsall	9A Longsight			
40085	3MT[2]	5F Uttoxeter	8E Brunswick	3C Walsall	6E Wrexham Rhosddu	84K Wrexham Rhosddu		
40086	3MT[2]	5F Uttoxeter	5F Uttoxeter	6G Llandudno Junction	6E Wrexham Rhosddu	84K Wrexham Rhosddu		
40087	3MT[2]	7A Llandudno Junction	1A Willesden	2B Nuneaton	2B Nuneaton	2B Nuneaton		
40088	3MT[2]	19G Trafford Park	5D Stoke	6C Birkenhead	17F Trafford Park	9E Trafford Park		
40089	3MT[2]	19G Trafford Park	9F Heaton Mersey	9F Heaton Mersey	17E Heaton Mersey	9F Heaton Mersey		
40090	3MT[2]	19D Heaton Mersey	20A Leeds Holbeck	20E Manningham	27C Southport	27C Southport		
40091	3MT[2]	14C St. Albans	14B Kentish Town	86K Abergavenny	86G Pontypool Road	24E Blackpool Central		
40092	3MT[2]	14B Kentish Town	14B Kentish Town	14B Kentish Town	14B Kentish Town	14B Kentish Town		
40093	3MT[2]	19D Heaton Mersey	9E Trafford Park	8E Brunswick	9A Longsight	9A Longsight		
40094	3MT[2]	19D Heaton Mersey	9E Trafford Park	9F Heaton Mersey	17E Heaton Mersey	9F Heaton Mersey		
40095	3MT[2]	19D Heaton Mersey	7A Llandudno Junction	6G Llandudno Junction	6G Llandudno Junction	6G Llandudno Junction		
40096	3MT[2]	14B Kentish Town	14B Kentish Town	14B Kentish Town	16C Mansfield			
40097	3MT[2]	21A Saltley	21A Saltley	86K Abergavenny	87K Swansea Victoria	9E Trafford Park		
40098	3MT[2]	14B Kentish Town	14B Kentish Town	86K Abergavenny	86K Tredegar	86K Tredegar		
40099	3MT[2]	14B Kentish Town	14B Kentish Town	21A Saltley	24E Blackpool Central	24E Blackpool Central		
40100	3MT[2]	14B Kentish Town	14B Kentish Town	14B Kentish Town	14B Kentish Town	14B Kentish Town		
40101	3MT[2]	6C Birkenhead	6C Birkenhead	6C Birkenhead	6C Birkenhead	6C Birkenhead		
40102	3MT[2]	6C Birkenhead	6C Birkenhead	6H Bangor	6C Birkenhead	6C Birkenhead		
40103	3MT[2]	11A Carnforth	8A Edge Hill	6C Birkenhead	24E Blackpool Central	24E Blackpool Central		
40104	3MT[2]	6C Birkenhead	6C Birkenhead	2B Nuneaton	2B Nuneaton	2B Nuneaton		
40105	3MT[2]	21B Bournville	21B Bournville	86K Abergavenny	87K Swansea Victoria	9E Trafford Park		
40106	3MT[2]	9A Longsight	9B Stockport Edgeley	9B Stockport Edgeley	6E Wrexham Rhosddu	6E Chester (GWR)		
40107	3MT[2]	9A Longsight	9A Longsight	9A Longsight	9A Longsight	9A Longsight		
40108	3MT[2]	9A Longsight	10E Sutton Oak	3C Walsall	3E Monument Lane	3E Monument Lane		
40109	3MT[2]	2E Warwick	1A Willesden	2B Nuneaton	24E Blackpool Central	24E Blackpool Central		
40110	3MT[2]	6C Birkenhead	6C Birkenhead	6C Birkenhead	6E Wrexham Rhosddu	84K Wrexham Rhosddu		
40111	3MT[2]	14B Kentish Town	14B Kentish Town	14B Kentish Town	14B Kentish Town	14B Kentish Town		
40112	3MT[2]	14B Kentish Town	14B Kentish Town	20E Manningham	55F Manningham	56C Copley Hill		
40113	3MT[2]	19D Heaton Mersey	9F Heaton Mersey	9F Heaton Mersey	17E Heaton Mersey	9F Heaton Mersey		
40114	3MT[2]	14B Kentish Town	14B Kentish Town	14B Kentish Town	55F Manningham	56C Copley Hill		

		1948	1951	1954	1957	1960	1963	1966
40115	$3MT^{2}$	21A Saltley	21A Saltley	21A Saltley	21A Saltley	16C Mansfield		
40116	$3MT^{2}$	15C Leicester Midland	22A Bristol Barrow Road	22A Bristol Barrow Road	22A Bristol Barrow Road	6C Birkenhead		
40117	$3MT^{2}$	21A Saltley	21A Saltley	20E Manningham	55F Manningham	56A Wakefield		
40118	$3MT^{2}$	19G Trafford Park	9F Heaton Mersey	8E Brunswick	3E Monument Lane	8D Widnes		
40119	$3MT^{2}$	22A Bristol Barrow Road	14B Kentish Town	14B Kentish Town	14B Kentish Town	14B Kentish Town		
40120	$3MT^{2}$	15C Leicester Midland	16A Nottingham	22A Bristol Barrow Road	20G Hellifield	24D Lower Darwen		
40121	$3MT^{2}$	6C Birkenhead	6C Birkenhead	6C Birkenhead	6C Birkenhead	6C Birkenhead		
40122	$3MT^{2}$	5D Stoke	5D Stoke	3B Bushbury	2B Nuneaton	9A Longsight		
40123	$3MT^{2}$	7A Llandudno Junction	7A Llandudno Junction	6G Llandudno Junction	6G Llandudno Junction	6G Llandudno Junction		
40124	$3MT^{2}$	7B Bangor	9F Heaton Mersey	9F Heaton Mersey	17E Heaton Mersey	9F Heaton Mersey		
40125	$3MT^{2}$	5D Stoke	8D Widnes	3B Bushbury	1A Willesden			
40126	$3MT^{2}$	5D Stoke	5D Stoke	2C Warwick	6E Wrexham Rhosddu	84K Wrexham Rhosddu		
40127	$3MT^{2}$	5D Stoke	8E Brunswick	8E Brunswick	8E Brunswick			
40128	$3MT^{2}$	5D Stoke	5D Stoke	6C Birkenhead	6E Wrexham Rhosddu	6G Llandudno Junction		
40129	$3MT^{2}$	6C Birkenhead	6C Birkenhead	3E Monument Lane	3C Walsall	3E Monument Lane		
40130	$3MT^{2}$	6A Chester	7A Llandudno Junction	6G Llandudno Junction	6G Llandudno Junction	6G Llandudno Junction		
40131	$3MT^{2}$	6C Birkenhead	6C Birkenhead	6C Birkenhead	6C Birkenhead	6C Birkenhead		
40132	$3MT^{2}$	6C Birkenhead	6C Birkenhead	6C Birkenhead	6H Bangor	6H Bangor		
40133	$3MT^{2}$	7B Bangor	7A Llandudno Junction	6G Llandudno Junction	6G Llandudno Junction	6G Llandudno Junction		
40134	$3MT^{2}$	7A Llandudno Junction	7B Bangor	8D Widnes	8D Widnes	8D Widnes		
40135	$3MT^{2}$	2E Warwick	1A Willesden	2B Nuneaton	6C Birkenhead	2B Nuneaton		
40136	$3MT^{2}$	6C Birkenhead	9A Longsight	9A Longsight	9A Longsight	6H Bangor		
40137	$3MT^{2}$	7A Llandudno Junction	2B Nuneaton	8D Widnes	8D Widnes	8D Widnes		
40138	$3MT^{2}$	9A Longsight	9B Stockport Edgeley	9B Stockport Edgeley	2B Nuneaton	2B Nuneaton		
40139	$3MT^{2}$	19B Millhouses	19B Millhouses	20C Royston	55F Manningham			
40140	$3MT^{2}$	16A Nottingham	16A Nottingham	20C Royston	55A Leeds Holbeck	55A Leeds Holbeck		
40141	$3MT^{2}$	15C Leicester Midland	15D Bedford	86K Abergavenny	87K Swansea Victoria	9E Trafford Park		
40142	$3MT^{2}$	22C Bath Green Park	14B Kentish Town	14B Kentish Town	14B Kentish Town	14B Kentish Town		
40143	$3MT^{2}$	2D Nuneaton	7B Bangor	8B Warrington Dallam	8B Warrington Dallam	8D Widnes		
40144	$3MT^{2}$	2A Rugby	8A Edge Hill	6C Birkenhead	6C Birkenhead	21B Bournville		
40145	$3MT^{2}$	15C Leicester Midland	15C Leicester Midland	86G Pontypool Road	86G Pontypool Road	27C Southport		
40146	$3MT^{2}$	15C Leicester Midland	15C Leicester Midland	15C Leicester Midland	16C Mansfield	16C Mansfield		
40147	$3MT^{2}$	19G Trafford Park	20C Royston	20E Manningham	55F Manningham	56E Sowerby Bridge		
40148	$3MT^{2}$	14B Kentish Town	14B Kentish Town	20A Leeds Holbeck	19B Millhouses	55D Royston		
40149	$3MT^{2}$	14B Kentish Town	14B Kentish Town	20E Manningham	21A Saltley	21A Saltley		
40150	$3MT^{2}$	27C Hamilton	66C Hamilton	66C Hamilton	60D Wick	60D Wick		
40151	$3MT^{2}$	27C Hamilton	66C Hamilton	66C Hamilton	60B Aviemore	67B Hurlford		
40152	$3MT^{2}$	27C Hamilton	65D Dawsholm	65D Dawsholm	65D Dawsholm	65D Dawsholm		
40153	$3MT^{2}$	27C Hamilton	65D Dawsholm	65D Dawsholm	65D Dawsholm	65D Dawsholm		
40154	$3MT^{2}$	27C Hamilton	65D Dawsholm	65D Dawsholm	65D Dawsholm	65D Dawsholm		
40155	$3MT^{2}$	14B Kentish Town	14B Kentish Town	20E Manningham	55F Manningham	56A Wakefield		
40156	$3MT^{2}$	5F Uttoxeter	5F Uttoxeter	2C Warwick	2B Nuneaton	16C Mansfield		
40157	$3MT^{2}$	5D Stoke	5D Stoke	2C Warwick	2B Nuneaton	2B Nuneaton		
40158	$3MT^{2}$	27C Hamilton	65D Dawsholm	65D Dawsholm	65D Dawsholm	65D Dawsholm		
40159	$3MT^{2}$	28A Motherwell	63A Perth	66C Hamilton	65D Dawsholm	65D Dawsholm		
40160	$3MT^{2}$	14B Kentish Town	14B Kentish Town	14B Kentish Town	14B Kentish Town			
40161	$3MT^{2}$	14B Kentish Town	14B Kentish Town	86K Abergavenny	86K Tredegar	86K Tredegar		
40162	$3MT^{2}$	21B Bournville	23B Hellifield	20G Hellifield	20G Hellifield	24D Lower Darwen		
40163	$3MT^{2}$	16A Nottingham	22A Bristol Barrow Road	22A Bristol Barrow Road	20G Hellifield			
40164	$3MT^{2}$	14B Kentish Town	22A Bristol Barrow Road	22A Bristol Barrow Road	24E Blackpool Central	24E Blackpool Central		
40165	$3MT^{2}$	15C Leicester Midland	15D Bedford	15D Bedford	15D Bedford	15E Leicester Central		
40166	$3MT^{2}$	14B Kentish Town	14B Kentish Town	14B Kentish Town	27A Bank Hall	24E Blackpool Central		
40167	$3MT^{2}$	14B Kentish Town	14B Kentish Town	14B Kentish Town	14B Kentish Town	15E Leicester Central		
40168	$3MT^{2}$	21B Bournville	21B Bournville	16D Mansfield	16C Mansfield	16C Mansfield		
40169	$3MT^{2}$	20C Royston	20A Leeds Holbeck	20A Leeds Holbeck	55A Leeds Holbeck			
40170	$3MT^{2}$	12G Dumfries	68B Dumfries	68B Dumfries	68B Dumfries	68B Dumfries		
40171	$3MT^{2}$	14B Kentish Town	21A Saltley	86K Abergavenny	86K Tredegar	86K Tredegar		
40172	$3MT^{2}$	14B Kentish Town	14B Kentish Town	14B Kentish Town	14B Kentish Town			
40173	$3MT^{2}$	21B Bournville	15C Leicester Midland	3C Walsall	3C Walsall	3A Bescot		
40174	$3MT^{2}$	22A Bristol Barrow Road	22A Bristol Barrow Road	22A Bristol Barrow Road	24E Blackpool Central	24E Blackpool Central		
40175	$3MT^{2}$	21A Saltley	21A Saltley	16D Mansfield	16C Mansfield	16C Mansfield		
40176	$3MT^{2}$	31E Dawsholm	65D Dawsholm	65D Dawsholm	65D Dawsholm	65D Dawsholm		
40177	$3MT^{2}$	31E Dawsholm	65D Dawsholm	65D Dawsholm	65D Dawsholm	65D Dawsholm		
40178	$3MT^{2}$	16A Nottingham	16A Nottingham	20E Manningham	55F Manningham	27C Southport		
40179	$3MT^{2}$	21B Bournville	20D Normanton	20D Normanton	55E Normanton	55E Normanton		
40180	$3MT^{2}$	16B Spital Bridge	8E Brunswick	3C Walsall	3D Aston	3D Aston		
40181	$3MT^{2}$	20C Royston	20C Royston	20C Royston	55D Royston	55D Royston		
40182	$3MT^{2}$	15C Leicester Midland	15C Leicester Midland	15C Leicester Midland	15C Leicester Midland	15E Leicester Central		
40183	$3MT^{2}$	20G Hellifield	23B Hellifield	20G Hellifield	20G Hellifield	24C Lostock Hall		
40184	$3MT^{2}$	20G Hellifield	23B Hellifield	20G Hellifield	16C Mansfield	16C Mansfield		
40185	$3MT^{2}$	31E Dawsholm	65D Dawsholm	68B Dumfries	68A Carlisle Kingmoor	2B Nuneaton		
40186	$3MT^{2}$	31E Dawsholm	65D Dawsholm	65D Dawsholm	65D Dawsholm	65D Dawsholm		
40187	$3MT^{2}$	31E Dawsholm	65D Dawsholm	65D Dawsholm	65D Dawsholm	65D Dawsholm		
40188	$3MT^{2}$	31E Dawsholm	65D Dawsholm	65D Dawsholm	65D Dawsholm	65D Dawsholm		
40189	$3MT^{2}$	31E Dawsholm	65D Dawsholm	65D Dawsholm	65D Dawsholm	65D Dawsholm		
40190	$3MT^{2}$	24C Lostock Hall	27C Southport	27C Southport	27C Southport	56E Sowerby Bridge		
40191	$3MT^{2}$	24C Lostock Hall	27C Southport	27C Southport	27C Southport	27C Southport		
40192	$3MT^{2}$	24C Lostock Hall	27C Southport	27C Southport	27C Southport	24C Lostock Hall		
40193	$3MT^{2}$	16A Nottingham	20C Royston	20C Royston	55A Leeds Holbeck	55A Leeds Holbeck		
40194	$3MT^{2}$	24C Lostock Hall	27C Southport	27C Southport	27C Southport	27C Southport		
40195	$3MT^{2}$	25G Farnley Junction	27C Southport	27C Southport	27C Southport	27C Southport		
40196	$3MT^{2}$	25G Farnley Junction	27C Southport	27C Southport	27C Southport	27C Southport		
40197	$3MT^{2}$	25G Farnley Junction	27C Southport	27C Southport	27C Southport	27C Southport		
40198	$3MT^{2}$	24C Lostock Hall	27C Southport	27C Southport	27C Southport	27C Southport		
40199	$3MT^{2}$	24C Lostock Hall	27D Wigan	27D Wigan	27D Wigan	27D Wigan		
40200	$3MT^{2}$	28A Motherwell	63A Perth	66B Motherwell	65D Dawsholm	65D Dawsholm		
40201	$3MT^{2}$	2D Nuneaton	2B Nuneaton	8D Widnes	8D Widnes	8D Widnes		
40202	$3MT^{2}$	2D Nuneaton	2B Nuneaton	8B Warrington Dallam	8B Warrington Dallam	6C Birkenhead		
40203	$3MT^{2}$	2E Warwick	8E Brunswick	8E Brunswick	2C Warwick	14B Kentish Town		
40204	$3MT^{2}$	2D Nuneaton	1A Willesden	2B Nuneaton	2B Nuneaton			
40205	$3MT^{2}$	2D Nuneaton	2B Nuneaton	2C Warwick	6E Wrexham Rhosddu	84K Wrexham Rhosddu		
40206	$3MT^{2}$	2D Nuneaton	1A Willesden	3D Aston	3D Aston	3D Aston		
40207	$3MT^{2}$	8B Warrington Dallam	7A Llandudno Junction	3B Bushbury	2B Nuneaton	2B Nuneaton		
40208	$3MT^{2}$	2D Nuneaton	7A Llandudno Junction	6G Llandudno Junction	17F Trafford Park	9E Trafford Park		
40209	$3MT^{2}$	7A Llandudno Junction	6C Birkenhead	6C Birkenhead	6C Birkenhead	6C Birkenhead		
40322	$2P^{1}$	5A Crewe North	5C Stafford					
40323	$2P^{1}$	20F Skipton	20A Leeds Holbeck	20A Leeds Holbeck				
40324	$2P^{1}$	19A Sheffield Grimesthorpe	7D Rhyl					
40325	$2P^{1}$	17A Derby	17B Burton					
40326	$2P^{1}$	22D Templecombe	20A Leeds Holbeck	17A Derby				
40332	$2P^{2}$	10C Patricroft	5A Crewe North	5A Crewe North	5A Crewe North			
40337	$2P^{2}$	18C Hasland	18C Hasland	18C Hasland	18C Hasland			
40351	$2P^{2}$	20A Leeds Holbeck	20A Leeds Holbeck					
40353	$2P^{2}$	15A Wellingborough	15A Wellingborough					
40356	$2P^{2}$	10B Preston	12A Carlisle Upperby	12A Carlisle Upperby	12A Carlisle Upperby			
40359	$2P^{2}$	20A Leeds Holbeck	18C Hasland	18C Hasland				
40362	$2P^{2}$	20C Royston	23C Lancaster	11E Lancaster				
40364	$2P^{2}$	17B Burton	17B Burton	17B Burton				
40370	$2P^{2}$	18C Hasland	18A Toton					
40377	$2P^{2}$	5C Stafford	7D Rhyl	6A Chester				
40383	$2P^{2}$	17A Derby	17A Derby					
40385	$2P^{2}$	21A Saltley						
40391	$2P^{2}$	20E Manningham						
40394	$2P^{2}$	16A Nottingham						

		1948	1951	1954	1957	1960	1963	1966
40395	$2P^2$	17B Burton	17B Burton	16A Nottingham				
40396	$2P^2$	7A Llandudno Junction	7D Rhyl	6K Rhyl	12A Carlisle Upperby	17B Burton		
40397	$2P^2$	10A Wigan Springs Branch	8E Brunswick					
40400	$2P^2$	15C Leicester Midland						
40401	$2P^2$	19A Sheffield Grimesthorpe	35C Spital Bridge					
40402	$2P^2$	5B Crewe South	5A Crewe North	18A Toton	5A Crewe North	15C Leicester Midland		
40403	$2P^2$	12B Carlisle Upperby						
40404	$2P^2$	17A Derby	17A Derby	17A Derby	17A Derby			
40405	$2P^2$	5B Crewe South	5C Stafford	9A Longsight				
40406	$2P^2$	20F Skipton	20D Normanton					
40407	$2P^2$	17A Derby	17A Derby	17A Derby	17A Derby			
40408	$2P^2$	16B Spital Bridge						
40409	$2P^2$	20F Skipton	18C Hasland	15C Leicester Midland	20F Skipton			
40410	$2P^2$	16B Spital Bridge	35C Spital Bridge					
40411	$2P^2$	17A Derby	17A Derby	15D Bedford	16A Nottingham	16A Nottingham		
40412	$2P^2$	2C Northampton	4B Northampton	2E Northampton	12A Carlisle Upperby			
40413	$2P^2$	3C Walsall	2B Nuneaton	5A Crewe North	5A Crewe North			
40414	$2P^2$	20F Skipton	23A Skipton	20F Skipton	17B Burton			
40415	$2P^2$	16A Nottingham	16A Nottingham					
40416	$2P^2$	17A Derby	17A Derby	17A Derby	17A Derby			
40417	$2P^2$	16A Nottingham	16A Nottingham					
40418	$2P^2$	17A Derby	17A Derby	17A Derby	17A Derby			
40419	$2P^2$	16A Nottingham	16A Nottingham	5A Crewe North				
40420	$2P^2$	2C Northampton	4B Northampton	2E Northampton	6K Rhyl			
40421	$2P^2$	2C Northampton	4B Northampton	2E Northampton	3C Walsall	16A Nottingham		
40422	$2P^2$	20F Skipton	23A Skipton					
40423	$2P^2$	22A Bristol Barrow Road	22A Bristol Barrow Road					
40424	$2P^2$	16D Mansfield	16D Mansfield					
40425	$2P^2$	2A Rugby	5A Crewe North					
40426	$2P^2$	17A Derby	17A Derby	22A Bristol Barrow Road	22A Bristol Barrow Road			
40427	$2P^2$	16A Nottingham						
40430	$2P^2$	2D Nuneaton	6A Chester					
40432	$2P^2$	17B Burton	17B Burton					
40433	$2P^2$	2D Nuneaton	7D Rhyl	9D Buxton	9A Longsight			
40434	$2P^2$	10C Patricroft	10C Patricroft	10C Patricroft				
40436	$2P^2$	17B Burton	17B Burton	17B Burton				
40437	$2P^2$	22B Gloucester Barnwood						
40438	$2P^2$	9D Buxton	2B Nuneaton	10C Patricroft				
40439	$2P^2$	21B Bournville	21B Bournville	21B Bournville	21B Bournville	21B Bournville		
40443	$2P^2$	5C Stafford	5C Stafford	5C Stafford	5C Stafford	21A Saltley		
40444	$2P^2$	20C Royston	20C Royston					
40446	$2P^2$	12B Carlisle Upperby						
40447	$2P^2$	2D Nuneaton	2B Nuneaton	5A Crewe North	5A Crewe North			
40448	$2P^2$	5B Crewe South	12A Carlisle Upperby	12A Carlisle Upperby				
40450	$2P^2$	2A Rugby	10C Patricroft	10C Patricroft	10C Patricroft			
40452	$2P^2$	20F Skipton	16A Nottingham	16A Nottingham	15C Leicester Midland	15C Leicester Midland		
40453	$2P^2$	15D Bedford	17B Burton	17B Burton	17B Burton	17B Burton		
40454	$2P^2$	15B Kettering	16D Mansfield	16A Nottingham	16A Nottingham	16A Nottingham		
40455	$2P^2$	20A Leeds Holbeck	20E Manningham	20E Manningham				
40456	$2P^2$	17B Burton						
40458	$2P^2$	16A Nottingham	16A Nottingham	16A Nottingham	16A Nottingham			
40459	$2P^2$	20G Hellifield						
40461	$2P^2$	5C Stafford	5C Stafford	5C Stafford	5C Stafford			
40462	$2P^2$	3C Walsall	3C Walsall					
40463	$2P^2$	21A Saltley	21B Bournville	21B Bournville				
40464	$2P^2$	2D Nuneaton	8E Brunswick	2E Northampton	2E Northampton			
40466	$2P^2$	18C Hasland						
40468	$2P^2$	15C Leicester Midland						
40470	$2P^2$	20G Hellifield	23B Hellifield					
40471	$2P^2$	5A Crewe North	5C Stafford					
40472	$2P^2$	18C Hasland	18C Hasland	20F Skipton				
40477	$2P^2$	14B Kentish Town	14B Kentish Town					
40478	$2P^2$	16A Nottingham						
40479	$2P^2$	9D Buxton						
40480	$2P^2$	20C Royston	20D Normanton	20D Normanton				
40482	$2P^2$	17A Derby	35C Spital Bridge	9A Longsight	9A Longsight			
40483	$2P^2$	9D Buxton						
40484	$2P^2$	20F Skipton	23A Skipton					
40485	$2P^2$	15C Leicester Midland	15C Leicester Midland	15C Leicester Midland	15C Leicester Midland			
40486	$2P^2$	21A Saltley	21A Saltley	22A Bristol Barrow Road	22A Bristol Barrow Road			
40487	$2P^2$	19B Millhouses	19B Millhouses	16A Nottingham	16A Nottingham	16A Nottingham		
40488	$2P^2$	20H Lancaster						
40489	$2P^2$	20E Manningham	20E Manningham	22B Gloucester Barnwood	22B Gloucester Barnwood	85E Gloucester Barnwood		
40490	$2P^2$	18C Hasland						
40491	$2P^2$	18C Hasland	18C Hasland	18C Hasland	55A Leeds Holbeck	55A Leeds Holbeck		
40492	$2P^2$	5A Crewe North						
40493	$2P^2$	21A Saltley	19B Millhouses	16A Nottingham	16A Nottingham			
40494	$2P^2$	7D Rhyl						
40495	$2P^2$	8A Edge Hill	7D Rhyl	6K Rhyl	6K Rhyl			
40496	$2P^2$	16A Nottingham						
40497	$2P^2$	16B Spital Bridge	35C Spital Bridge					
40498	$2P^2$	16A Nottingham						
40499	$2P^2$	17D Rowsley	17D Rowsley					
40500	$2P^2$	17B Burton						
40501	$2P^2$	3C Walsall	3C Walsall	3C Walsall	3C Walsall	82E Bristol Barrow Road		
40502	$2P^2$	16A Nottingham	19B Millhouses	18C Hasland	18C Hasland	16A Nottingham		
40503	$2P^2$	16D Mansfield	18C Hasland					
40504	$2P^2$	16A Nottingham	16A Nottingham	16A Nottingham	16A Nottingham	16A Nottingham		
40505	$2P^2$	22C Bath Green Park	71G Bath Green Park					
40506	$2P^2$	18C Hasland						
40507	$2P^2$	10C Patricroft	5C Stafford					
40508	$2P^2$	2D Nuneaton	2B Nuneaton					
40509	$2P^2$	22D Templecombe	71H Templecombe	71H Templecombe	71G Bath Green Park			
40510	$2P^2$	15A Wellingborough						
40511	$2P^2$	21A Saltley	21A Saltley	21A Saltley	21A Saltley	21A Saltley		
40512	$2P^2$	21A Saltley						
40513	$2P^2$	17A Derby	17A Derby	17A Derby	17A Derby			
40514	$2P^2$	20C Royston	20A Leeds Holbeck					
40515	$2P^2$	2A Rugby						
40516	$2P^2$	17A Derby						
40517	$2P^2$	21B Bournville						
40518	$2P^2$	19B Millhouses	19B Millhouses	20A Leeds Holbeck				
40519	$2P^2$	20A Leeds Holbeck	17B Burton	17B Burton	17B Burton			
40520	$2P^2$	17D Rowsley	17D Rowsley	17D Rowsley	55D Royston			
40521	$2P^2$	20A Leeds Holbeck	20C Royston	20C Royston				
40522	$2P^2$	2A Rugby	8E Brunswick	5C Stafford				
40523	$2P^2$	22B Gloucester Barnwood	22B Gloucester Barnwood					
40524	$2P^2$	7A Llandudno Junction	7B Bangor	10B Preston				
40525	$2P^2$	17B Burton	17B Burton	17B Burton	17B Burton			
40526	$2P^2$	17B Burton	17B Burton	17B Burton				
40527	$2P^2$	8D Widnes	4B Northampton	71H Templecombe				
40528	$2P^2$	5C Stafford	2B Nuneaton					
40529	$2P^2$	5A Crewe North	8E Brunswick	5A Crewe North				
40530	$2P^2$	22B Gloucester Barnwood	22B Gloucester Barnwood					

		1948	1951	1954	1957	1960	1963	1966
40531	$2P^2$	**9A** Longsight	**4B** Northampton	**3C** Walsall				
40532	$2P^2$	**16B** Spital Bridge	**35C** Spital Bridge					
40533	$2P^2$	**16B** Spital Bridge						
40534	$2P^2$	**2C** Northampton	**4B** Northampton	**2E** Northampton	**2E** Northampton			
40535	$2P^2$	**16A** Nottingham	**16A** Nottingham	**16A** Nottingham				
40536	$2P^2$	**15C** Leicester Midland	**15C** Leicester Midland	**9D** Buxton	**12A** Carlisle Upperby			
40537	$2P^2$	**15B** Kettering	**18C** Hasland	**18C** Hasland	**16A** Nottingham	**82E** Bristol Barrow Road		
40538	$2P^2$	**15C** Leicester Midland	**15C** Leicester Midland	**19B** Millhouses	**19B** Millhouses			
40539	$2P^2$	**9A** Longsight	**9A** Longsight	**9A** Longsight				
40540	$2P^2$	**16A** Nottingham	**16A** Nottingham	**22B** Gloucester Barnwood	**22B** Gloucester Barnwood	**85E** Gloucester Barnwood		
40541	$2P^2$	**15C** Leicester Midland	**15C** Leicester Midland	**22B** Gloucester Barnwood	**22B** Gloucester Barnwood			
40542	$2P^2$	**15C** Leicester Midland	**15C** Leicester Midland	**15C** Leicester Midland	**16A** Nottingham			
40543	$2P^2$	**15C** Leicester Midland	**15C** Leicester Midland	**15C** Leicester Midland	**15C** Leicester Midland	**15C** Leicester Midland		
40544	$2P^2$	**19B** Millhouses						
40545	$2P^2$	**19B** Millhouses						
40546	$2P^2$	**16A** Nottingham	**16A** Nottingham					
40547	$2P^2$	**14B** Kentish Town	**14B** Kentish Town					
40548	$2P^2$	**15A** Wellingborough	**18C** Hasland	**6G** Llandudno Junction	**6G** Llandudno Junction	**14B** Kentish Town		
40549	$2P^2$	**15C** Leicester Midland	**19B** Millhouses					
40550	$2P^2$	**15B** Kettering	**15B** Kettering	**16A** Nottingham	**18C** Hasland			
40551	$2P^2$	**15D** Bedford	**15D** Bedford					
40552	$2P^2$	**16B** Spital Bridge	**16A** Nottingham	**16A** Nottingham	**55A** Leeds Holbeck	**55A** Leeds Holbeck		
40553	$2P^2$	**16A** Nottingham	**16A** Nottingham	**16A** Nottingham	**16A** Nottingham			
40554	$2P^2$	**10B** Preston						
40555	$2P^2$	**18C** Hasland						
40556	$2P^2$	**18C** Hasland	**18C** Hasland	**18C** Hasland				
40557	$2P^2$	**18C** Hasland	**18C** Hasland	**18C** Hasland	**16A** Nottingham	**16A** Nottingham		
40558	$2P^2$	**16B** Spital Bridge	**35C** Spital Bridge					
40559	$2P^2$	**16A** Nottingham	**35C** Spital Bridge	**6G** Llandudno Junction	**6A** Chester			
40560	$2P^2$	**16A** Nottingham	**16A** Nottingham					
40561	$2P^2$	**10A** Wigan Springs Branch						
40562	$2P^2$	**20E** Manningham	**20E** Manningham	**20E** Manningham				
40563	$2P^3$	**22D** Templecombe	**71H** Templecombe	**71H** Templecombe	**71H** Templecombe	**82G** Templecombe		
40564	$2P^3$	**22D** Templecombe	**71H** Templecombe	**71H** Templecombe	**71H** Templecombe	**82G** Templecombe		
40565	$2P^3$	**20H** Lancaster	**10B** Preston	**10B** Preston	**10B** Preston			
40566	$2P^3$	**28C** Carstairs	**67B** Hurlford	**67B** Hurlford	**67B** Hurlford	**68C** Stranraer		
40567	$2P^3$	**20E** Manningham	**20E** Manningham	**5A** Crewe North	**5A** Crewe North			
40568	$2P^3$	**22C** Bath Green Park	**71G** Bath Green Park	**71H** Templecombe	**71H** Templecombe			
40569	$2P^3$	**22C** Bath Green Park	**71G** Bath Green Park	**71H** Templecombe	**71H** Templecombe	**82G** Templecombe		
40570	$2P^3$	**30B** Hurlford	**67B** Hurlford	**67B** Hurlford	**67B** Hurlford	**67B** Hurlford		
40571	$2P^3$	**30B** Hurlford	**67B** Hurlford	**67B** Hurlford	**67B** Hurlford	**67B** Hurlford		
40572	$2P^3$	**30B** Hurlford	**67B** Hurlford	**67B** Hurlford	**67B** Hurlford	**67B** Hurlford		
40573	$2P^3$	**30B** Hurlford	**67B** Hurlford	**67B** Hurlford	**67B** Hurlford			
40574	$2P^3$	**30D** Ayr	**67C** Ayr	**67C** Ayr	**67C** Ayr	**67B** Hurlford		
40575	$2P^3$	**30D** Ayr	**67C** Ayr	**67C** Ayr	**67C** Ayr	**67B** Hurlford		
40576	$2P^3$	**12G** Dumfries	**68B** Dumfries	**68B** Dumfries	**68B** Dumfries			
40577	$2P^3$	**12G** Dumfries	**68B** Dumfries	**68B** Dumfries	**68B** Dumfries	**68B** Dumfries		
40578	$2P^3$	**30C** Ardrossan	**67D** Ardrossan	**67D** Ardrossan	**67D** Ardrossan	**67D** Ardrossan		
40579	$2P^3$	**30C** Ardrossan	**67D** Ardrossan	**67D** Ardrossan	**67D** Ardrossan	**67D** Ardrossan		
40580	$2P^3$	**26E** Bacup	**27D** Wigan	**6K** Rhyl	**6A** Chester	**14B** Kentish Town		
40581	$2P^3$	**23A** Bank Hall	**27A** Bank Hall	**27A** Bank Hall	**55C** Farnley Junction	**55D** Royston		
40582	$2P^3$	**26A** Newton Heath	**27A** Bank Hall	**12A** Carlisle Upperby	**12C** Workington			
40583	$2P^3$	**23A** Bank Hall	**8E** Brunswick	**2B** Nuneaton	**5C** Stafford	**5C** Stafford		
40584	$2P^3$	**26A** Newton Heath	**27A** Bank Hall	**27A** Bank Hall	**55C** Farnley Junction	**55C** Farnley Junction		
40585	$2P^3$	**25C** Goole	**27A** Bank Hall	**26C** Bolton	**15C** Leicester Midland	**16A** Nottingham		
40586	$2P^3$	**25C** Goole	**25C** Goole	**26D** Bury	**26C** Bolton	**24G** Skipton		
40587	$2P^3$	**26E** Bacup	**27D** Wigan	**27D** Wigan	**27D** Wigan			
40588	$2P^3$	**26A** Newton Heath	**24D** Lower Darwen	**27A** Bank Hall	**27A** Bank Hall	**27A** Bank Hall		
40589	$2P^3$	**25C** Goole	**25C** Goole	**6K** Rhyl	**6K** Rhyl			
40590	$2P^3$	**30D** Ayr	**67C** Ayr	**67C** Ayr	**67C** Ayr			
40592	$2P^3$	**28C** Carstairs	**67A** Corkerhill	**67B** Hurlford	**67B** Hurlford	**67B** Hurlford		
40593	$2P^3$	**30B** Hurlford	**67B** Hurlford	**67B** Hurlford	**67B** Hurlford	**67B** Hurlford		
40594	$2P^3$	**30A** Corkerhill	**67A** Corkerhill	**67A** Corkerhill	**67A** Corkerhill			
40595	$2P^3$	**30A** Corkerhill	**67A** Corkerhill	**67A** Corkerhill	**67A** Corkerhill	**67B** Hurlford		
40596	$2P^3$	**30A** Corkerhill	**67A** Corkerhill	**67A** Corkerhill	**67A** Corkerhill	**67A** Corkerhill		
40597	$2P^3$	**30B** Hurlford	**67B** Hurlford	**67B** Hurlford	**67B** Hurlford	**67B** Hurlford		
40598	$2P^3$	**30A** Corkerhill	**67A** Corkerhill	**67A** Corkerhill	**67A** Corkerhill			
40599	$2P^3$	**30A** Corkerhill	**67A** Corkerhill	**67A** Corkerhill	**67A** Corkerhill			
40600	$2P^3$	**12H** Stranraer	**68C** Stranraer	**62B** Dundee Tay Bridge	**61C** Keith			
40601	$2P^3$	**22C** Bath Green Park	**71G** Bath Green Park	**71H** Templecombe	**71G** Bath Green Park			
40602	$2P^3$	**12A** Carlisle Kingmoor	**68A** Carlisle Kingmoor	**68A** Carlisle Kingmoor	**68A** Carlisle Kingmoor	**12A** Carlisle Kingmoor		
40603	$2P^3$	**30A** Corkerhill	**61A** Kittybrewster	**61A** Kittybrewster	**61A** Kittybrewster	**61C** Keith		
40604	$2P^3$	**30A** Corkerhill	**67A** Corkerhill	**67A** Corkerhill	**61A** Kittybrewster	**61C** Keith		
40605	$2P^3$	**28C** Carstairs	**67B** Hurlford	**67B** Hurlford	**67B** Hurlford			
40606	$2P^3$	**30C** Ardrossan	**67D** Ardrossan	**67D** Ardrossan	**67D** Ardrossan			
40607	$2P^3$	**30C** Ardrossan	**67D** Ardrossan	**67D** Ardrossan	**67D** Ardrossan			
40608	$2P^3$	**30C** Ardrossan	**67D** Ardrossan	**67D** Ardrossan	**67D** Ardrossan			
40609	$2P^3$	**30C** Ardrossan	**67D** Ardrossan	**67D** Ardrossan	**67D** Ardrossan	**67B** Hurlford		
40610	$2P^3$	**30D** Ayr	**67C** Ayr	**67C** Ayr	**67C** Ayr			
40611	$2P^3$	**12H** Stranraer	**68C** Stranraer	**68C** Stranraer	**68C** Stranraer			
40612	$2P^3$	**30B** Hurlford	**67B** Hurlford	**67B** Hurlford	**67B** Hurlford	**67B** Hurlford		
40613	$2P^3$	**12A** Carlisle Kingmoor	**68A** Carlisle Kingmoor	**68A** Carlisle Kingmoor	**68A** Carlisle Kingmoor	**12A** Carlisle Kingmoor		
40614	$2P^3$	**12G** Dumfries	**68B** Dumfries	**68B** Dumfries	**68B** Dumfries	**68B** Dumfries		
40615	$2P^3$	**12A** Carlisle Kingmoor	**68A** Carlisle Kingmoor	**68A** Carlisle Kingmoor	**68A** Carlisle Kingmoor	**12A** Carlisle Kingmoor		
40616	$2P^3$	**12H** Stranraer	**68C** Stranraer	**68C** Stranraer	**68C** Stranraer			
40617	$2P^3$	**30B** Hurlford	**67B** Hurlford	**67B** Hurlford	**67B** Hurlford			
40618	$2P^3$	**30B** Hurlford	**67B** Hurlford	**67B** Hurlford	**67B** Hurlford	**61C** Keith		
40619	$2P^3$	**28C** Carstairs	**67B** Hurlford	**67B** Hurlford	**67B** Hurlford	**67B** Hurlford		
40620	$2P^3$	**30A** Corkerhill	**67A** Corkerhill	**67A** Corkerhill	**67A** Corkerhill	**67A** Corkerhill		
40621	$2P^3$	**30A** Corkerhill	**67A** Corkerhill	**67A** Corkerhill	**67A** Corkerhill	**67A** Corkerhill		
40622	$2P^3$	**30A** Corkerhill	**61A** Kittybrewster	**61A** Kittybrewster	**61C** Keith	**61C** Keith		
40623	$2P^3$	**12H** Stranraer	**68C** Stranraer	**68C** Stranraer	**68C** Stranraer	**68C** Stranraer		
40624	$2P^3$	**30C** Ardrossan	**67D** Ardrossan	**67D** Ardrossan	**67D** Ardrossan	**67D** Ardrossan		
40625	$2P^3$	**30C** Ardrossan	**67D** Ardrossan	**67D** Ardrossan	**67D** Ardrossan	**67D** Ardrossan		
40626	$2P^3$	**30C** Ardrossan	**67D** Ardrossan	**67D** Ardrossan	**67D** Ardrossan	**67B** Hurlford		
40627	$2P^3$	**30A** Corkerhill	**67A** Corkerhill	**67A** Corkerhill	**67A** Corkerhill	**67A** Corkerhill		
40628	$2P^3$	**8A** Edge Hill	**10C** Patricroft	**10C** Patricroft	**12A** Carlisle Upperby	**12B** Carlisle Upperby		
40629	$2P^3$	**7D** Rhyl	**7D** Rhyl	**6K** Rhyl	**12A** Carlisle Upperby	**12B** Carlisle Upperby		
40630	$2P^3$	**16D** Mansfield	**20D** Normanton	**20D** Normanton	**55E** Normanton	**55E** Normanton		
40631	$2P^3$	**17B** Burton	**10B** Preston	**10B** Preston	**10B** Preston	**26F** Patricroft		
40632	$2P^3$	**17A** Derby	**17A** Derby	**20G** Hellifield	**16A** Nottingham	**16A** Nottingham		
40633	$2P^3$	**17B** Burton	**17B** Burton	**17B** Burton	**17B** Burton			
40634	$2P^3$	**22D** Templecombe	**71H** Templecombe	**71H** Templecombe	**71H** Templecombe	**82G** Templecombe		
40635	$2P^3$	**10C** Patricroft	**10C** Patricroft	**10C** Patricroft	**10C** Patricroft	**6G** Llandudno Junction		
40636	$2P^3$	**30A** Corkerhill	**67A** Corkerhill	**67A** Corkerhill	**67A** Corkerhill			
40637	$2P^3$	**30A** Corkerhill	**67A** Corkerhill	**67A** Corkerhill	**67A** Corkerhill	**67A** Corkerhill		
40638	$2P^3$	**30D** Ayr	**67C** Ayr	**67C** Ayr	**67D** Ardrossan	**67D** Ardrossan		
40640	$2P^3$	**30D** Ayr	**67C** Ayr	**67C** Ayr	**67C** Ayr	**67C** Ayr		
40641	$2P^3$	**30A** Corkerhill	**67A** Corkerhill	**67A** Corkerhill	**67A** Corkerhill	**68C** Stranraer		
40642	$2P^3$	**30A** Corkerhill	**67A** Corkerhill	**67A** Corkerhill	**67A** Corkerhill	**68C** Stranraer		
40643	$2P^3$	**30B** Hurlford	**67B** Hurlford	**67B** Hurlford	**67B** Hurlford	**67B** Hurlford		
40644	$2P^3$	**30B** Hurlford	**67B** Hurlford	**67B** Hurlford	**67B** Hurlford			
40645	$2P^3$	**30B** Hurlford	**67B** Hurlford	**67B** Hurlford	**67B** Hurlford	**67B** Hurlford		
40646	$2P^3$	**7D** Rhyl	**7D** Rhyl	**5C** Stafford	**5C** Stafford	**5C** Stafford		

		1948	1951	1954	1957	1960	1963	1966
40647	2P^{3}	**30D** Ayr	**67C** Ayr	**67C** Ayr	**67A** Corkerhill	**67B** Hurlford		
40648	2P^{3}	**30D** Ayr	**67C** Ayr	**67C** Ayr	**61A** Kittybrewster	**61A** Kittybrewster		
40649	2P^{3}	**30A** Corkerhill	**67A** Corkerhill	**67A** Corkerhill	**67A** Corkerhill			
40650	2P^{3}	**30A** Corkerhill	**61A** Kittybrewster	**61A** Kittybrewster	**61A** Kittybrewster	**61A** Kittybrewster		
40651	2P^{3}	**30A** Corkerhill	**67A** Corkerhill	**67A** Corkerhill	**68A** Carlisle Kingmoor	**12A** Carlisle Kingmoor		
40652	2P^{3}	**12B** Carlisle Upperby	**12A** Carlisle Upperby	**12A** Carlisle Upperby	**12A** Carlisle Upperby	**82G** Templecombe		
40653	2P^{3}	**2C** Northampton	**4B** Northampton	**2E** Northampton	**2E** Northampton			
40654	2P^{3}	**12B** Carlisle Upperby	**11B** Barrow	**11B** Barrow	**11B** Barrow			
40655	2P^{3}	**2A** Rugby	**9D** Buxton	**9D** Buxton	**12A** Carlisle Upperby			
40656	2P^{3}	**12D** Workington	**12D** Workington	**12D** Workington	**12A** Carlisle Upperby			
40657	2P^{3}	**2C** Northampton	**4B** Northampton	**2E** Northampton	**12A** Carlisle Upperby	**24K** Preston		
40658	2P^{3}	**7A** Llandudno Junction	**6A** Chester	**6A** Chester	**6A** Chester			
40659	2P^{3}	**5A** Crewe North	**5A** Crewe North	**5A** Crewe North	**5A** Crewe North	**1C** Watford		
40660	2P^{3}	**5A** Crewe North	**5A** Crewe North	**5A** Crewe North	**5A** Crewe North			
40661	2P^{3}	**30B** Hurlford	**67B** Hurlford	**67B** Hurlford	**67B** Hurlford	**67B** Hurlford		
40662	2P^{3}	**30B** Hurlford	**67B** Hurlford	**67B** Hurlford				
40663	2P^{3}	**30B** Hurlford	**67B** Hurlford	**67B** Hurlford	**61A** Kittybrewster	**61A** Kittybrewster		
40664	2P^{3}	**30D** Ayr	**67C** Ayr	**67C** Ayr	**67C** Ayr	**67C** Ayr		
40665	2P^{3}	**30B** Hurlford	**67B** Hurlford	**67B** Hurlford	**67B** Hurlford	**67B** Hurlford		
40666	2P^{3}	**28C** Carstairs	**67B** Hurlford	**67B** Hurlford	**67D** Ardrossan			
40667	2P^{3}	**30C** Ardrossan	**67D** Ardrossan	**67D** Ardrossan	**67D** Ardrossan			
40668	2P^{3}	**30C** Ardrossan	**67D** Ardrossan	**67D** Ardrossan	**67D** Ardrossan	**67D** Ardrossan		
40669	2P^{3}	**30C** Ardrossan	**67D** Ardrossan	**67D** Ardrossan	**67D** Ardrossan	**67D** Ardrossan		
40670	2P^{3}	**30D** Ayr	**67C** Ayr	**67C** Ayr	**67C** Ayr	**68B** Dumfries		
40671	2P^{3}	**7A** Llandudno Junction	**7D** Rhyl	**6K** Rhyl	**10B** Preston	**26F** Patricroft		
40672	2P^{3}	**1C** Watford	**1C** Watford	**1C** Watford	**1C** Watford	**1C** Watford		
40673	2P^{3}	**12B** Carlisle Upperby	**12A** Carlisle Upperby	**10B** Preston	**10B** Preston			
40674	2P^{3}	**9A** Longsight	**9A** Longsight	**9A** Longsight	**9A** Longsight			
40675	2P^{3}	**7A** Llandudno Junction	**7D** Rhyl	**6K** Rhyl	**6A** Chester			
40676	2P^{3}	**24A** Accrington	**24A** Accrington	**2B** Nuneaton	**10C** Patricroft			
40677	2P^{3}	**24D** Lower Darwen	**24A** Accrington	**2B** Nuneaton	**2E** Northampton			
40678	2P^{3}	**23D** Wigan	**27D** Wigan	**5C** Stafford	**5C** Stafford	**3A** Bescot		
40679	2P^{3}	**23D** Wigan	**8E** Brunswick	**6K** Rhyl	**6A** Chester			
40680	2P^{3}	**23D** Wigan	**24A** Accrington	**27D** Wigan	**27D** Wigan			
40681	2P^{3}	**26E** Bacup	**24A** Accrington	**24D** Lower Darwen	**26C** Bolton	**27D** Wigan		
40682	2P^{3}	**24A** Accrington	**26A** Newton Heath	**26C** Bolton	**17A** Derby	**16A** Nottingham		
40683	2P^{3}	**24A** Accrington	**8E** Brunswick	**2E** Northampton	**2E** Northampton	**24K** Preston		
40684	2P^{3}	**24D** Lower Darwen	**27D** Wigan	**27A** Bank Hall	**27A** Bank Hall	**27A** Bank Hall		
40685	2P^{3}	**25C** Goole	**25C** Goole	**26C** Bolton	**20G** Hellifield	**24H** Hellifield		
40686	2P^{3}	**30B** Hurlford	**67B** Hurlford	**67B** Hurlford	**67B** Hurlford	**67B** Hurlford		
40687	2P^{3}	**30B** Hurlford	**67B** Hurlford	**67B** Hurlford	**67B** Hurlford	**67B** Hurlford		
40688	2P^{3}	**30B** Hurlford	**67B** Hurlford	**67B** Hurlford	**67B** Hurlford			
40689	2P^{3}	**30B** Hurlford	**67B** Hurlford	**67B** Hurlford	**67B** Hurlford	**67B** Hurlford		
40690	2P^{3}	**24D** Lower Darwen	**27E** Walton on the Hill	**26D** Bury	**55A** Leeds Holbeck	**55A** Leeds Holbeck		
40691	2P^{3}	**26E** Bacup	**26A** Newton Heath	**25G** Farnley Junction	**18C** Hasland	**16A** Nottingham		
40692	2P^{3}	**2C** Northampton	**9D** Buxton	**9D** Buxton	**12A** Carlisle Upperby	**3A** Bescot		
40693	2P^{3}	**9D** Buxton	**9A** Longsight	**9A** Longsight	**9A** Longsight			
40694	2P^{3}	**12D** Workington	**12D** Workington	**12D** Workington	**10B** Preston	**24K** Preston		
40695	2P^{3}	**12D** Workington	**12D** Workington	**12D** Workington	**12A** Carlisle Upperby	**11A** Barrow		
40696	2P^{3}	**22C** Bath Green Park	**71G** Bath Green Park	**71G** Bath Green Park	**71G** Bath Green Park	**82F** Bath Green Park		
40697	2P^{3}	**22C** Bath Green Park	**71G** Bath Green Park	**71G** Bath Green Park	**71G** Bath Green Park	**82F** Bath Green Park		
40698	2P^{3}	**22C** Bath Green Park	**71G** Bath Green Park	**71G** Bath Green Park	**71G** Bath Green Park	**82F** Bath Green Park		
40699	2P^{3}	**12B** Carlisle Upperby	**12A** Carlisle Upperby	**12A** Carlisle Upperby	**12A** Carlisle Upperby			
40700	2P^{3}	**22C** Bath Green Park	**71G** Bath Green Park	**71G** Bath Green Park	**71G** Bath Green Park	**82F** Bath Green Park		
40711	3P^{1}	**17A** Derby						
40715	3P^{1}	**21A** Saltley						
40720	3P^{1}	**20A** Leeds Holbeck						
40726	3P^{1}	**19C** Canklow	**19C** Canklow					
40727	3P^{1}	**19C** Canklow						
40728	3P^{1}	**19A** Sheffield Grimesthorpe	**19A** Sheffield Grimesthorpe					
40729	3P^{1}	**19A** Sheffield Grimesthorpe	**19A** Sheffield Grimesthorpe					
40731	3P^{1}	**19B** Millhouses						
40734	3P^{1}	**17A** Derby						
40735	3P^{1}	**17A** Derby						
40736	3P^{1}	**20A** Leeds Holbeck						
40739	3P^{1}	**16A** Nottingham						
40740	3P^{1}	**15C** Leicester Midland						
40741	3P^{1}	**22A** Bristol Barrow Road	**22A** Bristol Barrow Road					
40743	3P^{1}	**17C** Coalville	**20A** Leeds Holbeck					
40745	3P^{1}	**21A** Saltley						
40747	3P^{1}	**16A** Nottingham	**20A** Leeds Holbeck					
40748	3P^{1}	**20A** Leeds Holbeck						
40756	3P^{1}	**17A** Derby						
40757	3P^{1}	**16A** Nottingham						
40758	3P^{1}	**20A** Leeds Holbeck	**20A** Leeds Holbeck					
40762	3P^{1}	**15D** Bedford	**15D** Bedford					
40900	4P^{1}	**6A** Chester	**9E** Trafford Park	**16A** Nottingham				
40901	4P^{1}	**28C** Carstairs	**64D** Carstairs	**64D** Carstairs				
40902	4P^{1}	**12G** Dumfries	**68B** Dumfries	**68B** Dumfries				
40903	4P^{1}	**28C** Carstairs	**64D** Carstairs	**64D** Carstairs				
40904	4P^{1}	**12G** Dumfries	**68B** Dumfries	**64D** Carstairs	**64D** Carstairs			
40905	4P^{1}	**30A** Corkerhill	**67A** Corkerhill					
40906	4P^{1}	**30A** Corkerhill	**67A** Corkerhill	**67A** Corkerhill				
40907	4P^{1}	**28C** Carstairs	**64D** Carstairs	**19B** Millhouses	**19B** Millhouses	**41C** Millhouses		
40908	4P^{1}	**30D** Ayr	**67C** Ayr	**67A** Corkerhill				
40909	4P^{1}	**30A** Corkerhill	**67A** Corkerhill	**67A** Corkerhill				
40910	4P^{1}	**20A** Leeds Holbeck	**9E** Trafford Park	**9E** Trafford Park				
40911	4P^{1}	**28B** Dalry Road	**64C** Dalry Road					
40912	4P^{1}	**12G** Dumfries	**68B** Dumfries	**68B** Dumfries				
40913	4P^{1}	**30A** Corkerhill	**63B** Stirling	**63A** Perth				
40914	4P^{1}	**30A** Corkerhill	**67A** Corkerhill	**67A** Corkerhill				
40915	4P^{1}	**28C** Carstairs	**67A** Corkerhill	**67A** Corkerhill				
40916	4P^{1}	**27A** Polmadie	**66A** Polmadie	**66A** Polmadie				
40917	4P^{1}	**21B** Bournville	**21B** Bournville	**21B** Bournville				
40918	4P^{1}	**31A** St. Rollox	**65B** St. Rollox					
40919	4P^{1}	**30A** Corkerhill	**67A** Corkerhill	**67A** Corkerhill				
40920	4P^{1}	**30A** Corkerhill	**67C** Ayr	**67C** Ayr	**68C** Stranraer			
40921	4P^{1}	**29A** Perth	**63A** Perth	**63A** Perth				
40922	4P^{1}	**29A** Perth	**63A** Perth					
40923	4P^{1}	**29A** Perth	**63A** Perth	**63A** Perth				
40924	4P^{1}	**29A** Perth	**63B** Stirling	**63A** Perth				
40925	4P^{1}	**7A** Llandudno Junction	**7A** Llandudno Junction	**6G** Llandudno Junction	**6G** Llandudno Junction			
40926	4P^{1}	**6A** Chester	**8E** Brunswick	**5A** Crewe North	**5A** Crewe North			
40927	4P^{1}	**20A** Leeds Holbeck	**17A** Derby	**17A** Derby	**17A** Derby			
40928	4P^{1}	**21A** Saltley	**21A** Saltley	**21A** Saltley	**21A** Saltley			
40929	4P^{1}	**16A** Nottingham	**16A** Nottingham	**17D** Rowsley				
40930	4P^{1}	**17A** Derby	**14B** Kentish Town	**22B** Gloucester Barnwood	**22B** Gloucester Barnwood			
40931	4P^{1}	**20H** Lancaster	**16A** Nottingham	**17D** Rowsley	**17D** Rowsley			
40932	4P^{1}	**20G** Hellifield	**14B** Kentish Town	**22B** Gloucester Barnwood				
40933	4P^{1}	**6A** Chester	**5A** Crewe North	**3E** Monument Lane	**3E** Monument Lane			
40934	4P^{1}	**21B** Bournville	**17A** Derby	**22B** Gloucester Barnwood	**22B** Gloucester Barnwood			
40935	4P^{1}	**22A** Bristol Barrow Road	**22A** Bristol Barrow Road	**16A** Nottingham	**16A** Nottingham			
40936	4P^{1}	**7A** Llandudno Junction	**9E** Trafford Park	**3E** Monument Lane	**3E** Monument Lane	**3E** Monument Lane		
40937	4P^{1}	**23A** Bank Hall	**27E** Walton on the Hill	**24A** Accrington	**27A** Bank Hall			

		1948	1951	1954	1957	1960	1963	1966
40938	4P[1]	**29A** Perth	**63A** Perth	**63B** Stirling				
40939	4P[1]	**29A** Perth	**63A** Perth	**63C** Forfar				
41000	4P[2]	**17A** Derby	**17A** Derby			(1000)		
41001	4P[2]	**22B** Gloucester Barnwood	**22B** Gloucester Barnwood					
41002	4P[2]	**16A** Nottingham						
41003	4P[2]	**17A** Derby	**17A** Derby					
41004	4P[2]	**20E** Manningham	**20E** Manningham					
41005	4P[2]	**20H** Lancaster	**23C** Lancaster					
41006	4P[2]	**20G** Hellifield	**15C** Leicester Midland					
41007	4P[2]	**15D** Bedford	**15D** Bedford					
41008	4P[2]	**15C** Leicester Midland						
41009	4P[2]	**15D** Bedford	**15D** Bedford					
41010	4P[2]	**15B** Kettering						
41011	4P[2]	**15C** Leicester Midland	**15C** Leicester Midland					
41012	4P[2]	**16A** Nottingham	**22A** Bristol Barrow Road					
41013	4P[2]	**15D** Bedford						
41014	4P[2]	**19B** Millhouses	**17A** Derby					
41015	4P[2]	**16A** Nottingham	**16A** Nottingham					
41016	4P[2]	**19B** Millhouses	**19B** Millhouses					
41017	4P[2]	**15D** Bedford						
41018	4P[2]	**14B** Kentish Town						
41019	4P[2]	**22B** Gloucester Barnwood	**16A** Nottingham					
41020	4P[2]	**20A** Leeds Holbeck	**14B** Kentish Town					
41021	4P[2]	**19B** Millhouses	**19B** Millhouses					
41022	4P[2]	**20H** Lancaster						
41023	4P[2]	**14B** Kentish Town	**17A** Derby					
41024	4P[2]	**19B** Millhouses						
41025	4P[2]	**22B** Gloucester Barnwood	**22B** Gloucester Barnwood					
41026	4P[2]	**19B** Millhouses						
41027	4P[2]	**22B** Gloucester Barnwood						
41028	4P[2]	**22A** Bristol Barrow Road	**22A** Bristol Barrow Road					
41029	4P[2]	**21A** Saltley						
41030	4P[2]	**22A** Bristol Barrow Road	**22A** Bristol Barrow Road					
41031	4P[2]	**15C** Leicester Midland						
41032	4P[2]	**16A** Nottingham	**16A** Nottingham					
41033	4P[2]	**17A** Derby						
41034	4P[2]	**15D** Bedford						
41035	4P[2]	**21A** Saltley	**21A** Saltley					
41036	4P[2]	**17A** Derby						
41037	4P[2]	**19B** Millhouses	**19B** Millhouses					
41038	4P[2]	**15D** Bedford	**15D** Bedford					
41039	4P[2]	**22B** Gloucester Barnwood						
41040	4P[2]	**20A** Leeds Holbeck	**20A** Leeds Holbeck					
41041	4P[2]	**15C** Leicester Midland	**15C** Leicester Midland					
41042	4P[2]	**15D** Bedford						
41043	4P[2]	**20E** Manningham	**17A** Derby					
41044	4P[2]	**15D** Bedford	**15D** Bedford					
41045	4P[1]	**20H** Lancaster	**23C** Lancaster	**11E** Lancaster	**11E** Lancaster			
41046	4P[1]	**21A** Saltley	**21A** Saltley					
41047	4P[1]	**15B** Kettering	**22B** Gloucester Barnwood	**22B** Gloucester Barnwood				
41048	4P[1]	**20A** Leeds Holbeck	**20A** Leeds Holbeck	**15D** Bedford	**15A** Wellingborough			
41049	4P[1]	**17D** Rowsley	**17D** Rowsley	**15D** Bedford	**22B** Gloucester Barnwood			
41050	4P[1]	**14B** Kentish Town	**14B** Kentish Town	**14B** Kentish Town				
41051	4P[1]	**14B** Kentish Town	**14B** Kentish Town	**14B** Kentish Town				
41052	4P[1]	**19G** Trafford Park	**9E** Trafford Park					
41053	4P[1]	**20H** Lancaster	**15C** Leicester Midland	**15C** Leicester Midland				
41054	4P[1]	**14B** Kentish Town	**14B** Kentish Town	**15D** Bedford				
41055	4P[1]	**17A** Derby	**9E** Trafford Park					
41056	4P[1]	**20G** Hellifield	**15D** Bedford					
41057	4P[1]	**17A** Derby	**17A** Derby					
41058	4P[1]	**22B** Gloucester Barnwood	**22B** Gloucester Barnwood	**19B** Millhouses				
41059	4P[1]	**17A** Derby	**17A** Derby	**15C** Leicester Midland				
41060	4P[1]	**17A** Derby	**17A** Derby	**5A** Crewe North	**5A** Crewe North			
41061	4P[1]	**21B** Bournville	**21B** Bournville	**20E** Manningham				
41062	4P[1]	**19B** Millhouses	**19B** Millhouses	**19B** Millhouses	**19B** Millhouses			
41063	4P[1]	**19B** Millhouses	**19B** Millhouses	**19B** Millhouses	**55F** Manningham	**55F** Manningham		
41064	4P[1]	**21B** Bournville	**21B** Bournville	**21B** Bournville	**21B** Bournville			
41065	4P[1]	**20H** Lancaster	**23C** Lancaster	**11E** Lancaster				
41066	4P[1]	**19G** Trafford Park	**9E** Trafford Park	**9E** Trafford Park	**17F** Trafford Park			
41067	4P[1]	**20E** Manningham	**20E** Manningham	**20E** Manningham				
41068	4P[1]	**20A** Leeds Holbeck	**20A** Leeds Holbeck	**20A** Leeds Holbeck	**55A** Leeds Holbeck			
41069	4P[1]	**20A** Leeds Holbeck	**20E** Manningham	**17A** Derby				
41070	4P[1]	**15D** Bedford	**15D** Bedford	**19B** Millhouses				
41071	4P[1]	**15B** Kettering	**14B** Kentish Town	**19B** Millhouses	**55A** Leeds Holbeck			
41072	4P[1]	**19B** Millhouses	**19B** Millhouses	**19B** Millhouses				
41073	4P[1]	**21B** Bournville	**21B** Bournville	**21B** Bournville	**21B** Bournville			
41074	4P[1]	**22B** Gloucester Barnwood	**22B** Gloucester Barnwood	**14B** Kentish Town				
41075	4P[1]	**19B** Millhouses	**15C** Leicester Midland	**15C** Leicester Midland	**55F** Manningham			
41076	4P[1]	**19G** Trafford Park	**9E** Trafford Park	**5A** Crewe North				
41077	4P[1]	**14B** Kentish Town	**14B** Kentish Town	**14B** Kentish Town	**17D** Rowsley			
41078	4P[1]	**22C** Bath Green Park	**22B** Gloucester Barnwood	**22B** Gloucester Barnwood	**15C** Leicester Midland			
41079	4P[1]	**19B** Millhouses	**19B** Millhouses	**15D** Bedford				
41080	4P[1]	**20G** Hellifield	**20E** Manningham	**20E** Manningham				
41081	4P[1]	**20H** Lancaster	**23C** Lancaster	**11E** Lancaster				
41082	4P[1]	**16A** Nottingham	**16A** Nottingham	**16A** Nottingham				
41083	4P[1]	**17A** Derby	**14B** Kentish Town	**14B** Kentish Town	**17A** Derby			
41084	4P[1]	**17A** Derby	**17A** Derby	**17A** Derby				
41085	4P[1]	**23C** Southport	**26C** Bolton	**24A** Accrington	**27A** Bank Hall			
41086	4P[1]	**7A** Llandudno Junction	**7A** Llandudno Junction	**6G** Llandudno Junction	**6J** Holyhead			
41087	4P[1]	**20A** Leeds Holbeck	**20A** Leeds Holbeck	**20A** Leeds Holbeck				
41088	4P[1]	**15C** Leicester Midland	**17A** Derby	**17A** Derby				
41089	4P[1]	**25C** Goole	**15C** Leicester Midland	**15C** Leicester Midland	**15C** Leicester Midland			
41090	4P[1]	**2A** Rugby	**2A** Rugby	**3E** Monument Lane	**3E** Monument Lane			
41091	4P[1]	**15D** Bedford	**15D** Bedford	**15D** Bedford				
41092	4P[1]	**12H** Stranraer	**68C** Stranraer					
41093	4P[1]	**7A** Llandudno Junction	**7A** Llandudno Junction	**6G** Llandudno Junction	**6G** Llandudno Junction			
41094	4P[1]	**16A** Nottingham	**15D** Bedford	**15C** Leicester Midland	**55A** Leeds Holbeck			
41095	4P[1]	**20H** Lancaster	**15C** Leicester Midland	**15C** Leicester Midland	**15C** Leicester Midland			
41096	4P[1]	**16A** Nottingham	**16A** Nottingham	**16A** Nottingham				
41097	4P[1]	**22B** Gloucester Barnwood	**22B** Gloucester Barnwood	**15C** Leicester Midland				
41098	4P[1]	**6A** Chester	**6A** Chester	**9E** Trafford Park	**11E** Lancaster			
41099	4P[1]	**29A** Perth	**68C** Stranraer					
41100	4P[1]	**24A** Accrington	**26B** Agecroft	**20A** Leeds Holbeck	**55A** Leeds Holbeck			
41101	4P[1]	**24A** Accrington	**27D** Wigan	**26C** Bolton	**27A** Bank Hall			
41102	4P[1]	**24A** Accrington	**27D** Wigan	**27B** Aintree	**24E** Blackpool Central			
41103	4P[1]	**26C** Bolton	**26C** Bolton	**20A** Leeds Holbeck	**17A** Derby			
41104	4P[1]	**26C** Bolton	**26C** Bolton	**20A** Leeds Holbeck				
41105	4P[1]	**2A** Rugby	**2A** Rugby	**2A** Rugby	**2A** Rugby			
41106	4P[1]	**6A** Chester	**6A** Chester	**6A** Chester	**6A** Chester			
41107	4P[1]	**6A** Chester	**6A** Chester	**11E** Lancaster				
41108	4P[1]	**6A** Chester	**6A** Chester	**6A** Chester	**11E** Lancaster			
41109	4P[1]	**12G** Dumfries	**68B** Dumfries					
41110	4P[1]	**30A** Corkerhill	**67B** Hurlford	**67B** Hurlford				
41111	4P[1]	**3E** Monument Lane	**9E** Trafford Park	**6G** Llandudno Junction	**6G** Llandudno Junction			

No.	Class	1948	1951	1954	1957	1960	1963	1966
41112	4P[1]	5A Crewe North	5A Crewe North	9E Trafford Park	11E Lancaster			
41113	4P[1]	9A Longsight	9A Longsight	2A Rugby	2A Rugby			
41114	4P[1]	7C Holyhead	7A Llandudno Junction	6G Llandudno Junction	17F Trafford Park			
41115	4P[1]	5A Crewe North	8E Brunswick	6J Holyhead				
41116	4P[1]	3E Monument Lane	8E Brunswick	8E Brunswick	17F Trafford Park			
41117	4P[1]	14B Kentish Town	14B Kentish Town	21B Bournville				
41118	4P[1]	7A Llandudno Junction	8E Brunswick	8E Brunswick	17F Trafford Park			
41119	4P[1]	7A Llandudno Junction	7A Llandudno Junction	6G Llandudno Junction	6G Llandudno Junction			
41120	4P[1]	6A Chester	6A Chester	6A Chester	6A Chester			
41121	4P[1]	6A Chester	6A Chester	6A Chester	8A Edge Hill			
41122	4P[1]	9A Longsight	2A Rugby	2A Rugby	2A Rugby			
41123	4P[1]	7C Holyhead	7A Llandudno Junction	6G Llandudno Junction	17F Trafford Park			
41124	4P[1]	7C Holyhead	7A Llandudno Junction	6G Llandudno Junction				
41125	4P[1]	29A Perth	63A Perth					
41126	4P[1]	31A St. Rollox	65B St. Rollox	65B St. Rollox				
41127	4P[1]	30A Corkerhill	68C Stranraer	68C Stranraer				
41128	4P[1]	31A St. Rollox	65B St. Rollox	65B St. Rollox				
41129	4P[1]	12A Carlisle Kingmoor	68A Carlisle Kingmoor	68C Stranraer				
41130	4P[1]	28C Carstairs	64D Carstairs	64D Carstairs				
41131	4P[1]	27A Polmadie	66A Polmadie	66A Polmadie				
41132	4P[1]	30D Ayr	67C Ayr	67C Ayr				
41133	4P[1]	30D Ayr	67C Ayr	67A Corkerhill				
41134	4P[1]	29B Aberdeen Ferryhill	61B Aberdeen Ferryhill	67A Corkerhill				
41135	4P[1]	12G Dumfries	68B Dumfries	68C Stranraer				
41136	4P[1]	28C Carstairs	64D Carstairs	11E Lancaster				
41137	4P[1]	20A Leeds Holbeck	20A Leeds Holbeck	20A Leeds Holbeck				
41138	4P[1]	30D Ayr	67C Ayr	67C Ayr				
41139	4P[1]	12A Carlisle Kingmoor	68A Carlisle Kingmoor	67A Corkerhill				
41140	4P[1]	12A Carlisle Kingmoor	68A Carlisle Kingmoor	21A Saltley	21A Saltley			
41141	4P[1]	12A Carlisle Kingmoor	68A Carlisle Kingmoor	68A Carlisle Kingmoor				
41142	4P[1]	12A Carlisle Kingmoor	68A Carlisle Kingmoor	67A Corkerhill				
41143	4P[1]	12A Carlisle Kingmoor	68A Carlisle Kingmoor	17A Derby	16A Nottingham			
41144	4P[1]	20A Leeds Holbeck	20A Leeds Holbeck	16A Nottingham	16A Nottingham			
41145	4P[1]	28C Carstairs	64D Carstairs					
41146	4P[1]	12A Carlisle Kingmoor	68A Carlisle Kingmoor	68A Carlisle Kingmoor				
41147	4P[1]	28C Carstairs	64D Carstairs	64C Dalry Road				
41148	4P[1]	30A Corkerhill	66D Greenock Ladyburn					
41149	4P[1]	30A Corkerhill	66D Greenock Ladyburn	66D Greenock Ladyburn				
41150	4P[1]	7A Llandudno Junction	7A Llandudno Junction	6G Llandudno Junction	17F Trafford Park			
41151	4P[1]	5C Stafford	5A Crewe North	8E Brunswick	11E Lancaster			
41152	4P[1]	2A Rugby	2A Rugby	11E Lancaster	11E Lancaster			
41153	4P[1]	3E Monument Lane	6A Chester	6A Chester	6A Chester			
41154	4P[1]	3E Monument Lane	9E Trafford Park	9E Trafford Park				
41155	4P[1]	30D Ayr	67C Ayr	67C Ayr	68C Stranraer			
41156	4P[1]	7A Llandudno Junction	8E Brunswick	21B Bournville	21B Bournville			
41157	4P[1]	6A Chester	6A Chester	6A Chester	6A Chester	17A Derby		
41158	4P[1]	6A Chester	6A Chester	6A Chester	6A Chester			
41159	4P[1]	9A Longsight	9A Longsight	9A Longsight	9A Longsight			
41160	4P[1]	5A Crewe North	5A Crewe North	5A Crewe North				
41161	4P[1]	7A Llandudno Junction	7A Llandudno Junction	9E Trafford Park				
41162	4P[1]	6A Chester	8E Brunswick	2A Rugby	2A Rugby	2A Rugby		
41163	4P[1]	6A Chester	6A Chester	6A Chester	17F Trafford Park			
41164	4P[1]	6A Chester	6A Chester	6A Chester	6A Chester			
41165	4P[1]	2A Rugby	2A Rugby	2A Rugby	2A Rugby			
41166	4P[1]	9A Longsight	8E Brunswick	6A Chester				
41167	4P[1]	5A Crewe North	5A Crewe North	5A Crewe North	5A Crewe North			
41168	4P[1]	9A Longsight	9A Longsight	9A Longsight	9A Longsight	3E Monument Lane		
41169	4P[1]	6A Chester	6A Chester	6A Chester				
41170	4P[1]	6A Chester	6A Chester	8E Brunswick				
41171	4P[1]	12G Dumfries	68B Dumfries					
41172	4P[1]	3E Monument Lane	2A Rugby	2A Rugby	2A Rugby			
41173	4P[1]	5A Crewe North	7A Llandudno Junction	9E Trafford Park	17F Trafford Park			
41174	4P[1]	2A Rugby	2A Rugby	2A Rugby				
41175	4P[1]	12G Dumfries	68B Dumfries	68B Dumfries				
41176	4P[1]	29B Aberdeen Ferryhill	61B Aberdeen Ferryhill	61B Aberdeen Ferryhill				
41177	4P[1]	28B Dalry Road	64C Dalry Road	64C Dalry Road				
41178	4P[1]	28B Dalry Road	64C Dalry Road					
41179	4P[1]	12G Dumfries	68B Dumfries	68B Dumfries	68B Dumfries			
41180	4P[1]	28C Carstairs	64D Carstairs	21A Saltley	21A Saltley			
41181	4P[1]	19G Trafford Park	9E Trafford Park	16A Nottingham	15C Leicester Midland			
41182	4P[1]	30A Corkerhill	66D Greenock Ladyburn					
41183	4P[1]	30D Ayr	67C Ayr	67C Ayr				
41184	4P[1]	29B Aberdeen Ferryhill	61B Aberdeen Ferryhill					
41185	4P[1]	24A Accrington	26C Bolton	16A Nottingham	17D Rowsley			
41186	4P[1]	25F Low Moor	26C Bolton	27B Aintree	27C Southport			
41187	4P[1]	24A Accrington	27A Bank Hall	27B Aintree				
41188	4P[1]	23A Bank Hall	27E Walton on the Hill	27B Aintree				
41189	4P[1]	25F Low Moor	26B Agecroft	26C Bolton	24E Blackpool Central			
41190	4P[1]	26C Bolton	26C Bolton	19B Millhouses	19B Millhouses			
41191	4P[1]	26C Bolton	26B Agecroft	19B Millhouses				
41192	4P[1]	24E Blackpool Central	28A Blackpool Central	17A Derby	17A Derby			
41193	4P[1]	23C Southport	27A Bank Hall	27A Bank Hall	24E Blackpool Central			
41194	4P[1]	24A Accrington	27E Walton on the Hill	21B Bournville	21B Bournville			
41195	4P[1]	24E Blackpool Central	28A Blackpool Central	22B Gloucester Barnwood	22B Gloucester Barnwood			
41196	4P[1]	23C Southport	26B Agecroft	11E Lancaster	11E Lancaster			
41197	4P[1]	24E Blackpool Central	20E Manningham	11E Lancaster	11E Lancaster			
41198	4P[1]	24A Accrington	15D Bedford	15C Leicester Midland				
41199	4P[1]	26C Bolton	14B Kentish Town	15D Bedford	19B Millhouses			
41200	2MT[1]	7B Bangor	7B Bangor	6H Bangor	6H Bangor	6H Bangor	6H Bangor	
41201	2MT[1]	7B Bangor	86K Abergavenny	86K Abergavenny	86K Tredegar	84H Wellington	84H Wellington	
41202	2MT[1]	4D Abergavenny	86K Abergavenny	86K Abergavenny	82A Bristol Bath Road	82A Bristol Bath Road	89A Shrewsbury	9B Stockport Edgeley
41203	2MT[1]	4D Abergavenny	86K Abergavenny	86K Abergavenny	82A Bristol Bath Road	82A Bristol Bath Road	89A Shrewsbury	
41204	2MT[1]	4E Tredegar	86K Abergavenny	86K Abergavenny	86K Tredegar	89A Oswestry	84H Wellington	9B Stockport Edgeley
41205	2MT[1]	20G Hellifield	23B Hellifield	20G Hellifield	20F Skipton	24F Fleetwood	27A Bank Hall	
41206	2MT[1]	20G Hellifield	23B Hellifield	20G Hellifield	20G Hellifield	27A Bank Hall	83H Plymouth Friary	83G Templecombe
41207	2MT[1]	14B Kentish Town	14A Cricklewood	14A Cricklewood	22A Bristol Barrow Road	82E Bristol Barrow Road	82E Bristol Barrow Road	10J Lancaster
41208	2MT[1]	14B Kentish Town	14A Cricklewood	14A Cricklewood	22A Bristol Barrow Road	82E Bristol Barrow Road	82E Bristol Barrow Road	
41209	2MT[1]	15D Bedford	15D Bedford	19B Millhouses	19B Millhouses	41C Millhouses	89A Shrewsbury	
41210	2MT[1]	→	10D Plodder Lane	10D Plodder Lane	8B Warrington Dallam	8B Warrington Dallam	71A Eastleigh	
41211	2MT[1]	→	10D Plodder Lane	2B Nuneaton	8B Warrington Dallam	8G Sutton Oak	8B Warrington Dallam	8K Bank Hall
41212	2MT[1]	→	10D Plodder Lane	6H Bangor	8B Warrington Dallam	5A Crewe North	5A Crewe North	
41213	2MT[1]	→	10D Plodder Lane	2B Nuneaton	3C Walsall	8B Warrington Dallam	71A Eastleigh	
41214	2MT[1]	→	10D Plodder Lane	10D Plodder Lane	2A Rugby	2A Rugby	83H Plymouth Friary	
41215	2MT[1]	→	10D Plodder Lane	6D Chester Northgate	6D Chester Northgate	6D Chester Northgate	24J Lancaster	
41216	2MT[1]	→	10D Plodder Lane	6D Chester Northgate	6K Rhyl	6K Rhyl	83H Plymouth Friary	83G Templecombe
41217	2MT[1]	→	10D Plodder Lane	11B Barrow	11B Barrow	9A Longsight	8B Warrington Dallam	12B Carlisle Upperby
41218	2MT[1]	→	4B Northampton	2E Northampton	2E Northampton	2E Northampton	2E Northampton	
41219	2MT[1]	→	4B Northampton	2E Northampton	2E Northampton	2E Northampton	2E Northampton	
41220	2MT[1]	→	1C Watford	1C Watford	1C Watford	5A Crewe North	5A Crewe North	9B Stockport Edgeley
41221	2MT[1]	→	11B Barrow	11B Barrow	11B Barrow	9A Longsight	24J Lancaster	
41222	2MT[1]	→	4A Bletchley	1E Bletchley	1E Bletchley	1E Bletchley	1E Bletchley	12B Carlisle Upperby
41223	2MT[1]	→	7B Bangor	6H Bangor	3C Walsall	1C Watford	75A Brighton	83G Templecombe
41224	2MT[1]	→	7B Bangor	6K Rhyl	3C Walsall	14E Bedford	15A Wellingborough	70F Bournemouth
41225	2MT[1]	→	3B Bushbury	3B Bushbury	3B Bushbury	14E Bedford	15C Leicester Midland	

		1948	1951	1954	1957	1960	1963	1966
41226	2MT[1]	→	3C Walsall	3C Walsall	2B Nuneaton	6C Birkenhead	6H Bangor	
41227	2MT[1]	→	2C Warwick	2C Warwick	2C Warwick	2A Rugby	15A Wellingborough	
41228	2MT[1]	→	2C Warwick	2C Warwick	2C Warwick	84D Leamington Spa	15C Leicester Midland	
41229	2MT[1]	→	5A Crewe North	5A Crewe North	5A Crewe North	5A Crewe North	5A Crewe North	12B Carlisle Upperby
41230	2MT[1]	→	17B Burton	6H Bangor	6H Bangor	6H Bangor	75A Brighton	70F Bournemouth
41231	2MT[1]	→	7D Rhyl	6K Rhyl	6E Wrexham Rhosddu	84K Wrexham Rhosddu	84D Leamington Spa	
41232	2MT[1]	→	7A Llandudno Junction	6G Llandudno Junction	6E Wrexham Rhosddu	84K Wrexham Rhosddu	84H Wellington	
41233	2MT[1]	→	7B Bangor	6H Bangor	6H Bangor	6H Bangor	6H Bangor	9B Stockport Edgeley
41234	2MT[1]	→	2B Nuneaton	6D Chester Northgate	6H Bangor	6H Bangor	6H Bangor	8G Sutton Oak
41235	2MT[1]	→	2B Nuneaton	6D Chester Northgate	6E Wrexham Rhosddu	6G Llandudno Junction		
41236	2MT[1]	→	2B Nuneaton	6G Llandudno Junction	6G Llandudno Junction	6G Llandudno Junction		
41237	2MT[1]	→	2B Nuneaton	6G Llandudno Junction	6E Wrexham Rhosddu	6H Bangor	27A Bank Hall	
41238	2MT[1]	→	2B Nuneaton	6G Llandudno Junction	6G Llandudno Junction	6G Llandudno Junction	72A Exmouth Junction	
41239	2MT[1]	→	2C Warwick	6D Chester Northgate	6H Bangor	6H Bangor	1B Camden	
41240	2MT[1]	→	71G Bath Green Park	22A Bristol Barrow Road	22A Bristol Barrow Road	82E Bristol Barrow Road	89A Shrewsbury	
41241	2MT[1]	→	71G Bath Green Park	71G Bath Green Park	71G Bath Green Park	84H Wellington	84H Wellington	10G Skipton
41242	2MT[1]	→	71G Bath Green Park	71G Bath Green Park	71G Bath Green Park	82F Bath Green Park	82G Templecombe	
41243	2MT[1]	→	71G Bath Green Park	71G Bath Green Park	71G Bath Green Park	82F Bath Green Park	82G Templecombe	
41244	2MT[1]	→	15A Wellingborough	6K Rhyl	6E Wrexham Rhosddu	6H Bangor	6G Llandudno Junction	8K Bank Hall
41245	2MT[1]	→	19B Millhouses	19B Millhouses	19B Millhouses	41C Millhouses	82E Bristol Barrow Road	
41246	2MT[1]	→	19B Millhouses	19B Millhouses	19B Millhouses	41C Millhouses		
41247	2MT[1]	→	17A Derby	17A Derby	55F Manningham	50F Malton		
41248	2MT[1]	→	14B Kentish Town	71H Templecombe	71H Templecombe	82G Templecombe	82E Bristol Barrow Road	
41249	2MT[1]	→	14B Kentish Town	71H Templecombe	71H Templecombe	82A Bristol Bath Road	82E Bristol Barrow Road	83G Templecombe
41250	2MT[1]	→	25A Wakefield	25A Wakefield	56F Low Moor	56F Low Moor	56F Low Moor	
41251	2MT[1]	→	25A Wakefield	25A Wakefield	56A Wakefield	50F Malton	50F Malton	10J Lancaster
41252	2MT[1]	→	25A Wakefield	25A Wakefield	56A Wakefield	50B Leeds Neville Hill		
41253	2MT[1]	→	25A Wakefield	25A Wakefield	56A Wakefield	56F Low Moor	55F Manningham	
41254	2MT[1]	→	25A Wakefield	25A Wakefield	55C Farnley Junction	55C Farnley Junction		
41255	2MT[1]	→	25G Farnley Junction	25G Farnley Junction	55C Farnley Junction	55C Farnley Junction		
41256	2MT[1]	→	25G Farnley Junction	25G Farnley Junction	55C Farnley Junction	55C Farnley Junction		
41257	2MT[1]	→	25G Farnley Junction	25G Farnley Junction	55C Farnley Junction	55F Manningham		
41258	2MT[1]	→	25G Farnley Junction	25G Farnley Junction	55C Farnley Junction	55C Farnley Junction		
41259	2MT[1]	→	25G Farnley Junction	25A Wakefield	55C Farnley Junction	55C Farnley Junction		
41260	2MT[1]	→	28B Fleetwood	24F Fleetwood	24F Fleetwood	24F Fleetwood	75A Brighton	
41261	2MT[1]	→	28B Fleetwood	24F Fleetwood	24F Fleetwood	24F Fleetwood	75A Brighton	
41262	2MT[1]	→	28B Fleetwood	24F Fleetwood	56F Low Moor	56F Low Moor	50B Hull Dairycoates	
41263	2MT[1]	→	28A Blackpool Central	24E Blackpool Central	56F Low Moor	56F Low Moor		
41264	2MT[1]	→	28A Blackpool Central	24E Blackpool Central	56F Low Moor	56D Mirfield	56F Low Moor	12B Carlisle Upperby
41265	2MT[1]	→	20E Manningham	20E Manningham	55F Manningham	50F Malton		
41266	2MT[1]	→	20E Manningham	20E Manningham	55F Manningham	55F Manningham		
41267	2MT[1]	→	20A Leeds Holbeck	20A Leeds Holbeck	55A Leeds Holbeck	55A Leeds Holbeck		
41268	2MT[1]	→	15C Leicester Midland	15C Leicester Midland	15C Leicester Midland	27A Bank Hall	27A Bank Hall	
41269	2MT[1]	→	15D Bedford	15D Bedford	15D Bedford	27A Bank Hall		
41270	2MT[1]	→	15D Bedford	15D Bedford	15D Bedford	14D Neasden	72A Exmouth Junction	
41271	2MT[1]	→	15D Bedford	15D Bedford	15D Bedford	14E Bedford		
41272	2MT[1]	→	15D Bedford	15D Bedford	15D Bedford	14D Neasden	72A Exmouth Junction	
41273	2MT[1]	→	20C Royston	20C Royston	55F Manningham	55F Manningham	55F Manningham	
41274	2MT[1]	→	20C Royston	20C Royston	55D Royston	56F Low Moor	56F Low Moor	
41275	2MT[1]	→	4A Bletchley	1E Bletchley	1E Bletchley	1E Bletchley	83H Plymouth Friary	
41276	2MT[1]	→	7D Rhyl	6K Rhyl	6K Rhyl	6K Rhyl	75A Brighton	
41277	2MT[1]	→	7D Rhyl	15A Wellingborough	15A Wellingborough	17B Burton		
41278	2MT[1]	→	2A Rugby	2A Rugby	2A Rugby	2E Northampton		
41279	2MT[1]	→	3C Walsall	3C Walsall	3C Walsall	3B Bushbury	15C Leicester Midland	
41280	2MT[1]	→	28B Fleetwood	24F Fleetwood	26E Lees Oldham	14E Bedford		
41281	2MT[1]	→	28B Fleetwood	24F Fleetwood	55D Royston	50B Leeds Neville Hill	55C Farnley Junction	
41282	2MT[1]	→	28B Fleetwood	24F Fleetwood	55D Royston	50B Leeds Neville Hill	55C Farnley Junction	
41283	2MT[1]	→	25A Wakefield	27B Aintree	27A Bank Hall	26F Patricroft	75A Brighton	83G Templecombe
41284	2MT[1]	→	25A Wakefield	27B Aintree	27A Bank Hall	14D Neasden	72A Exmouth Junction	70G Weymouth
41285	2MT[1]	→	10E Sutton Oak	2C Warwick	2C Warwick	84K Wrexham Rhosddu	84D Leamington Spa	12B Carlisle Upperby
41286	2MT[1]	→	10E Sutton Oak	10E Sutton Oak	10D Sutton Oak	8G Sutton Oak	8G Sutton Oak	8G Sutton Oak
41287	2MT[1]	→	10E Sutton Oak	6H Bangor	10C Patricroft	26F Patricroft	75A Brighton	70D Eastleigh
41288	2MT[1]	→	5A Crewe North	10E Sutton Oak	10D Sutton Oak	8G Sutton Oak		
41289	2MT[1]	→	5A Crewe North	10E Sutton Oak	10D Sutton Oak	8G Sutton Oak	1E Bletchley	
41290	2MT[1]	→	→	73A Stewarts Lane	73A Stewarts Lane	73A Stewarts Lane	72E Barnstaple Junction	83G Templecombe
41291	2MT[1]	→	→	73A Stewarts Lane	73A Stewarts Lane	73A Stewarts Lane	75A Brighton	83G Templecombe
41292	2MT[1]	→	→	73A Stewarts Lane	73A Stewarts Lane	73A Stewarts Lane	72A Exmouth Junction	
41293	2MT[1]	→	→	71A Eastleigh	71A Eastleigh	71A Eastleigh	71A Eastleigh	
41294	2MT[1]	→	→	73A Stewarts Lane	74A Ashford	72E Barnstaple Junction	72E Barnstaple Junction	70D Eastleigh
41295	2MT[1]	→	→	73A Stewarts Lane	72E Barnstaple Junction	72E Barnstaple Junction	83H Plymouth Friary	70F Bournemouth
41296	2MT[1]	→	→	73A Stewarts Lane	72E Barnstaple Junction	82G Templecombe	82G Templecombe	83G Templecombe
41297	2MT[1]	→	→	75E Three Bridges	72E Barnstaple Junction	72E Barnstaple Junction	72E Barnstaple Junction	
41298	2MT[1]	→	→	72E Barnstaple Junction	72E Barnstaple Junction	72E Barnstaple Junction	72E Barnstaple Junction	70G Weymouth
41299	2MT[1]	→	→	73B Bricklayers Arms	73B Bricklayers Arms	73B Bricklayers Arms	72A Exmouth Junction	70D Eastleigh
41300	2MT[1]	→	→	73B Bricklayers Arms	73B Bricklayers Arms	73B Bricklayers Arms	75A Brighton	
41301	2MT[1]	→	→	73B Bricklayers Arms	74B Ramsgate	73B Bricklayers Arms	75A Brighton	70G Weymouth
41302	2MT[1]	→	→	73B Bricklayers Arms	73B Bricklayers Arms	83H Plymouth Friary	83H Plymouth Friary	
41303	2MT[1]	→	→	75E Three Bridges	74A Ashford	73B Bricklayers Arms	75A Brighton	
41304	2MT[1]	→	→	71A Eastleigh	74B Ramsgate	82E Bristol Barrow Road	82E Bristol Barrow Road	8K Bank Hall
41305	2MT[1]	→	→	71A Eastleigh	71A Eastleigh	71A Eastleigh	71A Eastleigh	
41306	2MT[1]	→	→	75E Three Bridges	72A Exmouth Junction	72A Exmouth Junction	72A Exmouth Junction	
41307	2MT[1]	→	→	75E Three Bridges	72A Exmouth Junction	72A Exmouth Junction	72A Exmouth Junction	83G Templecombe
41308	2MT[1]	→	→	73E Faversham	73E Faversham	73F Ashford	72A Exmouth Junction	
41309	2MT[1]	→	→	73E Faversham	73E Faversham	73F Ashford	72A Exmouth Junction	
41310	2MT[1]	→	→	73E Faversham	73E Faversham	73F Ashford	72E Barnstaple Junction	
41311	2MT[1]	→	→	73E Faversham	73E Faversham	73F Ashford	71A Eastleigh	
41312	2MT[1]	→	→	73E Faversham	73E Faversham	73F Ashford	72E Barnstaple Junction	70F Bournemouth
41313	2MT[1]	→	→	72A Exmouth Junction	73E Faversham	73F Ashford	72E Barnstaple Junction	
41314	2MT[1]	→	→	72A Exmouth Junction	72D Plymouth Friary	72E Barnstaple Junction	72E Barnstaple Junction	
41315	2MT[1]	→	→	72D Plymouth Friary	72D Plymouth Friary	83H Plymouth Friary	83H Plymouth Friary	
41316	2MT[1]	→	→	75F Tunbridge Wells West	72D Plymouth Friary	83H Plymouth Friary	83H Plymouth Friary	70F Bournemouth
41317	2MT[1]	→	→	75F Tunbridge Wells West	74A Ashford	83H Plymouth Friary	83H Plymouth Friary	
41318	2MT[1]	→	→	75F Tunbridge Wells West	74B Ramsgate	72A Exmouth Junction	72A Exmouth Junction	
41319	2MT[1]	→	→	75F Tunbridge Wells West	74B Ramsgate	71A Eastleigh	71A Eastleigh	70D Eastleigh
41320	2MT[1]	→	→	5A Crewe North	1C Watford	16D Annesley	72A Exmouth Junction	70F Bournemouth
41321	2MT[1]	→	→	8B Warrington Dallam	2C Warwick	9G Gorton	72A Exmouth Junction	
41322	2MT[1]	→	→	8B Warrington Dallam	2B Nuneaton	6C Birkenhead	72A Exmouth Junction	
41323	2MT[1]	→	→	8B Warrington Dallam	2B Nuneaton	6D Chester Northgate	72A Exmouth Junction	
41324	2MT[1]	→	→	6K Rhyl	6E Wrexham Rhosddu	8B Warrington Dallam	75A Brighton	
41325	2MT[1]	→	→	20F Skipton	20F Skipton	55F Manningham	75A Brighton	
41326	2MT[1]	→	→	20F Skipton	20F Skipton	55F Manningham	75A Brighton	
41327	2MT[1]	→	→	20F Skipton	20F Skipton	24G Skipton	75A Brighton	
41328	2MT[1]	→	→	15A Wellingborough	15A Wellingborough	17B Burton	71A Eastleigh	
41329	2MT[1]	→	→	15D Bedford	15D Bedford	14D Neasden	71A Eastleigh	
41509	0F[1]	Derby Works						
41516	0F[1]	17B Burton	17B Burton	17B Burton				
41518	0F[1]	18C Hasland	18C Hasland	18C Hasland	18D Staveley Barrow Hill			
41523	0F[1]	17B Burton	17B Burton	17B Burton				
41528	0F[2]	18D Staveley Barrow Hill	18D Staveley Barrow Hill	18D Staveley Barrow Hill	18D Staveley Barrow Hill	41E Staveley Barrow Hill	41E Staveley Barrow Hill	41J Langwith Junction
41529	0F[2]	18D Staveley Barrow Hill	18D Staveley Barrow Hill	18D Staveley Barrow Hill	18D Staveley Barrow Hill	41E Staveley Barrow Hill		
41530	0F[2]	22B Gloucester Barnwood	22B Gloucester Barnwood	22B Gloucester Barnwood	22B Gloucester Barnwood			
41531	0F[2]	18C Hasland	18C Hasland	18C Hasland	18D Staveley Barrow Hill	41E Staveley Barrow Hill	41E Staveley Barrow Hill	
41532	0F[2]	18C Hasland	18C Hasland	18C Hasland	17B Burton	17B Burton		
41533	0F[2]	17B Burton	18D Staveley Barrow Hill	18D Staveley Barrow Hill	18D Staveley Barrow Hill	41E Staveley Barrow Hill	41E Staveley Barrow Hill	41J Langwith Junction

		1948	1951	1954	1957	1960	1963	1966
41534	$0F^{2}$	**18D** Staveley Barrow Hill	**18D** Staveley Barrow Hill	**18D** Staveley Barrow Hill	**17A** Derby			
41535	$0F^{2}$	**17A** Derby	**17A** Derby	**17A** Derby	**17A** Derby	**85E** Gloucester Barnwood	**85C** Gloucester Barnwood	
41536	$0F^{2}$	**17B** Burton	**17B** Burton	**17B** Burton	**17B** Burton	**17B** Burton		
41537	$0F^{2}$	**22B** Gloucester Barnwood	**22B** Gloucester Barnwood	**22B** Gloucester Barnwood	**22B** Gloucester Barnwood	**85E** Gloucester Barnwood	**85C** Gloucester Barnwood	
41660	$1F^{1}$	**14B** Kentish Town	**19A** Sheffield Grimesthorpe					
41661	$1F^{1}$	**14B** Kentish Town	**14B** Kentish Town	**20D** Normanton	**55B** Stourton			
41664	$1F^{1}$	**14B** Kentish Town	**14B** Kentish Town					
41666	$1F^{1}$	**16A** Nottingham	**20B** Stourton					
41668	$1F^{1}$	**14B** Kentish Town						
41671	$1F^{1}$	**14B** Kentish Town	**14B** Kentish Town	**14B** Kentish Town				
41672	$1F^{1}$	**14B** Kentish Town	**14B** Kentish Town	**14C** St. Albans				
41674	$1F^{1}$	**14B** Kentish Town						
41676	$1F^{1}$	**4B** Swansea Victoria						
41682	$1F^{1}$	**16A** Nottingham	**16A** Nottingham	**16A** Nottingham				
41686	$1F^{1}$	**16A** Nottingham	**16A** Nottingham	**40A** Lincoln				
41690	$1F^{1}$	**19E** Belle Vue	**26G** Belle Vue					
41695	$1F^{1}$	**17A** Derby	**14A** Cricklewood					
41699	$1F^{1}$	**21A** Saltley	**21A** Saltley	**87K** Swansea Victoria	**17B** Burton			
41702	$1F^{1}$	**19E** Belle Vue	**26G** Belle Vue	**26G** Belle Vue	**39A** Gorton	**9G** Gorton		
41706	$1F^{1}$	**22A** Bristol Barrow Road	**22A** Bristol Barrow Road	**22A** Bristol Barrow Road	**18D** Staveley Barrow Hill			
41708	$1F^{1}$	**18D** Staveley Barrow Hill	**18D** Staveley Barrow Hill	**18D** Staveley Barrow Hill	**18D** Staveley Barrow Hill	**41E** Staveley Barrow Hill	**41E** Staveley Barrow Hill	**41J** Langwith Junction
41710	$1F^{1}$	**18D** Staveley Barrow Hill	**18D** Staveley Barrow Hill	**18D** Staveley Barrow Hill	**17A** Derby			
41711	$1F^{1}$	**18D** Staveley Barrow Hill	**18D** Staveley Barrow Hill	**18D** Staveley Barrow Hill				
41712	$1F^{1}$	**14A** Cricklewood	**14A** Cricklewood	**14A** Cricklewood	**16A** Nottingham	**16C** Mansfield	**16B** Kirkby in Ashfield	
41713	$1F^{1}$	**14B** Kentish Town	**14B** Kentish Town	**14B** Kentish Town				
41714	$1F^{1}$	**6C** Birkenhead						
41718	$1F^{1}$	**17B** Burton						
41720	$1F^{1}$	**22B** Gloucester Barnwood	**22B** Gloucester Barnwood	**22B** Gloucester Barnwood				
41724	$1F^{1}$	**14A** Cricklewood	**14B** Kentish Town	**14B** Kentish Town	**17A** Derby			
41725	$1F^{1}$	**4A** Shrewsbury	**84G** Shrewsbury	**84G** Shrewsbury				
41726	$1F^{1}$	**17A** Derby	**17A** Derby	**17A** Derby	**17A** Derby			
41727	$1F^{1}$	**22B** Gloucester Barnwood	**22B** Gloucester Barnwood					
41734	$1F^{1}$	**6C** Birkenhead	**6C** Birkenhead	**6C** Birkenhead	**6C** Birkenhead	**41E** Staveley Barrow Hill	**41E** Staveley Barrow Hill	**41J** Langwith Junction
41739	$1F^{1}$	**20B** Stourton	**20B** Stourton	**20B** Stourton	**18D** Staveley Barrow Hill	**41E** Staveley Barrow Hill	**41E** Staveley Barrow Hill	
41745	$1F^{1}$	**20A** Leeds Holbeck	**20A** Leeds Holbeck					
41747	$1F^{1}$	**18D** Staveley Barrow Hill	**17A** Derby	**17A** Derby				
41748	$1F^{1}$	**20F** Skipton	**17B** Burton	**22B** Gloucester Barnwood	**22B** Gloucester Barnwood			
41749	$1F^{1}$	**18D** Staveley Barrow Hill	**18D** Staveley Barrow Hill	**18D** Staveley Barrow Hill				
41752	$1F^{1}$	**18D** Staveley Barrow Hill	**18D** Staveley Barrow Hill	**18D** Staveley Barrow Hill	**18D** Staveley Barrow Hill			
41753	$1F^{1}$	**18D** Staveley Barrow Hill	**18D** Staveley Barrow Hill	**6C** Birkenhead	**6C** Birkenhead			
41754	$1F^{1}$	**17A** Derby	**17A** Derby	**17A** Derby	**17A** Derby			
41756	$1F^{1}$	**19E** Belle Vue						
41759	$1F^{1}$	**20B** Stourton						
41762	$1F^{1}$	**16A** Nottingham						
41763	$1F^{1}$	**18D** Staveley Barrow Hill	**18D** Staveley Barrow Hill	**18D** Staveley Barrow Hill	**18D** Staveley Barrow Hill	**41E** Staveley Barrow Hill	**41E** Staveley Barrow Hill	**41J** Langwith Junction
41767	$1F^{1}$	**20F** Skipton	**23A** Skipton					
41768	$1F^{1}$	**19A** Sheffield Grimesthorpe						
41769	$1F^{1}$	**4C** Upper Bank	**87K** Swansea Victoria	**87K** Swansea Victoria	**87K** Swansea Victoria	**41E** Staveley Barrow Hill		
41770	$1F^{1}$	**17B** Burton	**17B** Burton					
41773	$1F^{1}$	**17A** Derby	**17A** Derby	**17A** Derby	**17A** Derby	**17A** Derby		
41777	$1F^{1}$	**21A** Saltley	**18D** Staveley Barrow Hill	**18D** Staveley Barrow Hill				
41779	$1F^{1}$	**17A** Derby	**17A** Derby	**16A** Nottingham	**36A** Doncaster			
41780	$1F^{1}$	**6C** Birkenhead	**6C** Birkenhead					
41781	$1F^{1}$	**20F** Skipton	**19A** Sheffield Grimesthorpe					
41788	$1F^{1}$	**17A** Derby						
41793	$1F^{1}$	**20D** Normanton	**20D** Normanton					
41794	$1F^{1}$	**20B** Stourton	**20B** Stourton					
41795	$1F^{1}$	**17A** Derby	**17A** Derby	**17A** Derby	**19A** Sheffield Grimesthorpe			
41797	$1F^{1}$	**19C** Canklow	**19C** Canklow	**20B** Stourton	**55B** Stourton			
41803	$1F^{1}$	**18D** Staveley Barrow Hill	**18D** Staveley Barrow Hill	**18D** Staveley Barrow Hill	**18D** Staveley Barrow Hill			
41804	$1F^{1}$	**18D** Staveley Barrow Hill	**18D** Staveley Barrow Hill	**18D** Staveley Barrow Hill	**18D** Staveley Barrow Hill	**41E** Staveley Barrow Hill	**41E** Staveley Barrow Hill	**41J** Langwith Junction
41805	$1F^{1}$	**20F** Skipton	**19C** Canklow	**19C** Canklow				
41811	$1F^{1}$	**14A** Cricklewood	**14A** Cricklewood	**20B** Stourton				
41813	$1F^{1}$	**19C** Canklow	**18C** Hasland	**18C** Hasland				
41814	$1F^{1}$	**19E** Belle Vue	**26G** Belle Vue	**26G** Belle Vue				
41818	$1F^{1}$	**6C** Birkenhead						
41820	$1F^{1}$	**20F** Skipton	**23A** Skipton					
41824	$1F^{1}$	**4C** Upper Bank	**87K** Swansea Victoria					
41826	$1F^{1}$	**16A** Nottingham	**14B** Kentish Town	**14A** Cricklewood				
41829	$1F^{1}$	**14A** Cricklewood	**18C** Hasland					
41833	$1F^{1}$	**17A** Derby	**17A** Derby					
41835	$1F^{1}$	**19C** Canklow	**19C** Canklow	**19C** Canklow	**19C** Canklow	**41D** Canklow	**41E** Staveley Barrow Hill	**41J** Langwith Junction
41838	$1F^{1}$	**20B** Stourton	**20B** Stourton	**20B** Stourton				
41839	$1F^{1}$	**17B** Burton	**17B** Burton	**17B** Burton				
41842	$1F^{1}$	**20B** Stourton						
41844	$1F^{1}$	**20D** Normanton	**20D** Normanton	**20D** Normanton	**16C** Mansfield	**16C** Mansfield	**16B** Kirkby in Ashfield	
41846	$1F^{1}$	**16B** Spital Bridge	**16A** Nottingham					
41847	$1F^{1}$	**17A** Derby	**17A** Derby	**17A** Derby	**17A** Derby	**17A** Derby		
41852	$1F^{1}$	**4C** Upper Bank	**87K** Swansea Victoria					
41853	$1F^{1}$	**6C** Birkenhead	**6C** Birkenhead	**6C** Birkenhead				
41854	$1F^{1}$	**14C** St. Albans	**14C** St. Albans					
41855	$1F^{1}$	**19A** Sheffield Grimesthorpe	**23A** Skipton	**20F** Skipton	**20F** Skipton	**53E** Goole		
41856	$1F^{1}$	**21A** Saltley	**21A** Saltley					
41857	$1F^{1}$	**19A** Sheffield Grimesthorpe	**19A** Sheffield Grimesthorpe	**19A** Sheffield Grimesthorpe	**19A** Sheffield Grimesthorpe			
41859	$1F^{1}$	**17B** Burton	**20B** Stourton	**20B** Stourton				
41860	$1F^{1}$	**4C** Upper Bank	**87K** Swansea Victoria	**87K** Swansea Victoria	**87K** Swansea Victoria			
41865	$1F^{1}$	**17B** Burton	**17B** Burton	**17B** Burton				
41869	$1F^{1}$	**19C** Canklow	**20B** Stourton					
41870	$1F^{1}$	**22B** Gloucester Barnwood						
41873	$1F^{1}$	**18C** Hasland						
41874	$1F^{1}$	**22A** Bristol Barrow Road						
41875	$1F^{1}$	**17D** Rowsley	**17D** Rowsley	**17D** Rowsley	**19C** Canklow	**41D** Canklow	**41E** Staveley Barrow Hill	
41878	$1F^{1}$	**17B** Burton	**17B** Burton	**17B** Burton	**17B** Burton			
41879	$1F^{1}$	**21A** Saltley	**21A** Saltley	**21A** Saltley	**22A** Bristol Barrow Road	**82E** Bristol Barrow Road		
41885	$1F^{1}$	**16D** Mansfield	**16D** Mansfield	**16D** Mansfield				
41889	$1F^{1}$	**15B** Kettering	**17A** Derby	**17A** Derby				
41890	$1F^{1}$	**20B** Stourton	**20B** Stourton					
41893	$1F^{1}$	**4C** Upper Bank						
41895	$1F^{1}$	**16A** Nottingham						
41900	$2P^{4}$	**22C** Bath Green Park	**23C** Lancaster	**11E** Lancaster	**9A** Longsight	**85E** Gloucester Barnwood		
41901	$2P^{4}$	**20H** Lancaster	**23C** Lancaster	**11E** Lancaster	**5A** Crewe North			
41902	$2P^{4}$	**22C** Bath Green Park	**23C** Lancaster	**11E** Lancaster	**2C** Warwick			
41903	$2P^{4}$	**22C** Bath Green Park	**17A** Derby	**11E** Lancaster	**11E** Lancaster			
41904	$2P^{4}$	**22C** Bath Green Park	**23C** Lancaster	**11E** Lancaster	**11E** Lancaster			
41905	$2P^{4}$	**9B** Stockport Edgeley	**9A** Longsight	**9A** Longsight	**9D** Buxton			
41906	$2P^{4}$	**9B** Stockport Edgeley	**9A** Longsight	**9A** Longsight	**9D** Buxton			
41907	$2P^{4}$	**9B** Stockport Edgeley	**9A** Longsight	**9A** Longsight	**9A** Longsight			
41908	$2P^{4}$	**1C** Watford	**1C** Watford	**1C** Watford	**9A** Longsight			
41909	$2P^{4}$	**1C** Watford	**1C** Watford	**1C** Watford	**2C** Warwick			
41910	$2P^{5}$	**18C** Hasland						
41911	$2P^{5}$	**16A** Nottingham	**18A** Toton					
41912	$2P^{5}$	**18C** Hasland.						
41913	$2P^{5}$	**18C** Hasland						
41914	$2P^{5}$	**16A** Nottingham						

		1948	1951	1954	1957	1960	1963	1966
41915	2P[5]	13C Tilbury	33A Plaistow					
41916	2P[5]	16A Nottingham	15A Wellingborough					
41917	2P[5]	19C Canklow	16A Nottingham					
41918	2P[5]	13C Tilbury						
41919	2P[5]	16A Nottingham	16A Nottingham					
41920	2P[5]	18C Hasland						
41921	2P[5]	16A Nottingham	16A Nottingham					
41922	2P[5]	16A Nottingham	16A Nottingham					
41923	2P[5]	13C Tilbury						
41924	2P[5]	13C Tilbury						
41925	2P[5]	18C Hasland	16A Nottingham					
41926	2P[5]	19C Canklow	16A Nottingham					
41928	3P[2]	13C Tilbury	33A Plaistow	33A Plaistow	33A Plaistow			
41929	3P[2]	13C Tilbury	33A Plaistow					
41930	3P[2]	13A Plaistow	33A Plaistow					
41931	3P[2]	13A Plaistow	33A Plaistow					
41932	3P[2]	13A Plaistow	33B Tilbury					
41933	3P[2]	13C Tilbury	33B Tilbury					
41934	3P[2]	13D Shoeburyness	33B Tilbury					
41935	3P[2]	13A Plaistow	33B Tilbury					
41936	3P[2]	13C Tilbury	33A Plaistow	33B Tilbury	30E Colchester			
41937	3P[2]	13D Shoeburyness	33A Plaistow					
41938	3P[2]	15C Leicester Midland	15C Leicester Midland	15C Leicester Midland				
41939	3P[2]	13C Tilbury	33A Plaistow	33A Plaistow	33A Plaistow			
41940	3P[2]	16D Mansfield	16D Mansfield	16D Mansfield				
41941	3P[2]	13D Shoeburyness	33A Plaistow	33A Plaistow	33A Plaistow			
41942	3P[2]	13A Plaistow	33A Plaistow	33A Plaistow				
41943	3P[2]	16D Mansfield	16D Mansfield	16D Mansfield				
41944	3P[2]	13A Plaistow	33A Plaistow	33C Shoeburyness				
41945	3P[2]	13A Plaistow	33A Plaistow	33B Tilbury	33A Plaistow			
41946	3P[2]	13C Tilbury	33B Tilbury	33B Tilbury	33A Plaistow			
41947	3P[2]	16D Mansfield	16D Mansfield	16D Mansfield	18A Toton	18A Toton		
41948	3P[2]	13A Plaistow	33A Plaistow	33A Plaistow	33A Plaistow			
41949	3P[2]	13A Plaistow	33B Tilbury	33B Tilbury	30E Colchester	31F Spital Bridge		
41950	3P[2]	13A Plaistow	33A Plaistow	33B Tilbury	33A Plaistow			
41951	3P[2]	13A Plaistow	33A Plaistow	33A Plaistow				
41952	3P[2]	13A Plaistow	33B Tilbury	30A Stratford				
41953	3P[2]	13C Tilbury	33B Tilbury					
41954	3P[2]	13A Plaistow	33B Tilbury					
41955	3P[2]	13C Tilbury	33B Tilbury					
41956	3P[2]	13C Tilbury	33A Plaistow					
41957	3P[2]	13A Plaistow	33B Tilbury					
41958	3P[2]	19C Canklow	16D Mansfield					
41959	3P[2]	13A Plaistow	33B Tilbury					
41960	3P[2]	13C Tilbury	33C Shoeburyness					
41961	3P[2]	16D Mansfield	16D Mansfield					
41962	3P[2]	19C Canklow	16D Mansfield					
41963	3P[2]	13A Plaistow	33C Shoeburyness					
41964	3P[2]	13C Tilbury	33C Shoeburyness					
41965	3P[2]	13C Tilbury	33A Plaistow					
41966	3P[2]	13C Tilbury	33C Shoeburyness	18A Toton				
41967	3P[2]	13A Plaistow	33A Plaistow					
41968	3P[2]	13D Shoeburyness	33A Plaistow					
41969	3P[2]	13A Plaistow	33A Plaistow	33B Tilbury	33C Shoeburyness	31B March		
41970	3P[2]	13A Plaistow	33A Plaistow	33B Tilbury				
41971	3P[2]	13D Shoeburyness	23A *(Carlisle Durran Hill)*	20F *(Carlisle Durran Hill)*				
41972	3P[2]	29C Dundee West	23A *(Carlisle Durran Hill)*	20F *(Carlisle Durran Hill)*				
41973	3P[2]	29C Dundee West	23A *(Carlisle Durran Hill)*	20F *(Carlisle Durran Hill)*				
41974	3P[2]	13A Plaistow	23A *(Carlisle Durran Hill)*	20F *(Carlisle Durran Hill)*				
41975	3P[2]	13A Plaistow	33A Plaistow	30A Stratford	30E Colchester			
41976	3P[2]	13A Plaistow	33A Plaistow	33A Plaistow				
41977	3P[2]	13C Tilbury	33A Plaistow	33A Plaistow	33A Plaistow			
41978	3P[2]	13D Shoeburyness	33A Plaistow	33A Plaistow	33A Plaistow			
41980	3F[1]	13C Tilbury	33B Tilbury	33A Plaistow	33A Plaistow			
41981	3F[1]	13A Plaistow	33A Plaistow	33A Plaistow	33A Plaistow	33B Tilbury		
41982	3F[1]	13A Plaistow	33A Plaistow	33B Tilbury	33A Plaistow			
41983	3F[1]	13A Plaistow	33A Plaistow	33A Plaistow	33A Plaistow			
41984	3F[1]	13A Plaistow	33A Plaistow	33A Plaistow	33A Plaistow			
41985	3F[1]	13A Plaistow	33A Plaistow	33A Plaistow	33A Plaistow			
41986	3F[1]	13A Plaistow	33A Plaistow	33A Plaistow	33A Plaistow			
41987	3F[1]	13A Plaistow	33A Plaistow	33A Plaistow	33A Plaistow			
41988	3F[1]	13A Plaistow	33A Plaistow	33A Plaistow	33A Plaistow			
41989	3F[1]	13A Plaistow	33A Plaistow	33A Plaistow	33A Plaistow			
41990	3F[1]	13A Plaistow	33A Plaistow	33C Shoeburyness	33A Plaistow			
41991	3F[1]	13D Shoeburyness	33C Shoeburyness	33A Plaistow	33A Plaistow			
41992	3F[1]	13D Shoeburyness	33C Shoeburyness	33A Plaistow	33A Plaistow			
41993	3F[1]	13A Plaistow	33A Plaistow	33B Tilbury	33A Plaistow			
42050	4MT[1]	→	21B Bournville	21B Bournville	17A Derby	9E Trafford Park	9E Trafford Park	
42051	4MT[1]	→	14B Kentish Town	14B Kentish Town	20G Hellifield	24H Hellifield	9E Trafford Park	
42052	4MT[1]	→	20E Manningham	20E Manningham	55F Manningham	55A Leeds Holbeck	55A Leeds Holbeck	55A Leeds Holbeck
42053	4MT[1]	→	21A Saltley	21A Saltley	21A Saltley	17C Rowsley	17C Rowsley	
42054	4MT[1]	→	21A Saltley	21A Saltley	21A Saltley	16A Nottingham	27E Walton on the Hill	
42055	4MT[1]	→	66A Polmadie	66A Polmadie	66A Polmadie	66E Carstairs	66E Carstairs	56F Low Moor
42056	4MT[1]	→	66A Polmadie	66A Polmadie	66A Polmadie	66A Polmadie	66A Polmadie	
42057	4MT[1]	→	66A Polmadie	66A Polmadie	66A Polmadie	66A Polmadie	66A Polmadie	
42058	4MT[1]	→	66A Polmadie	66A Polmadie	66A Polmadie	66A Polmadie	66A Polmadie	
42059	4MT[1]	→	66A Polmadie	66A Polmadie	66A Polmadie	66A Polmadie	66A Polmadie	66E Carstairs
42060	4MT[1]	→	66A Polmadie	66A Polmadie	66A Polmadie	66A Polmadie	66A Polmadie	
42061	4MT[1]	→	5D Stoke	1E Bletchley	2A Rugby	2A Rugby	27C Southport	
42062	4MT[1]	→	5D Stoke	1E Bletchley	2A Rugby	2A Rugby	2A Rugby	
42063	4MT[1]	→	5D Stoke	6A Chester	26A Newton Heath	27C Southport	27C Southport	
42064	4MT[1]	→	5D Stoke	9E Trafford Park	17F Trafford Park	9E Trafford Park	9E Trafford Park	
42065	4MT[1]	→	5D Stoke	9E Trafford Park	17F Trafford Park	9E Trafford Park	9E Trafford Park	
42066	4MT[1]	→	74B Ramsgate	75E Three Bridges	75E Three Bridges	1E Bletchley	5D Stoke	9E Trafford Park
42067	4MT[1]	→	74B Ramsgate	74B Ramsgate	75E Three Bridges	1E Bletchley	12C Carlisle Canal	
42068	4MT[1]	→	74B Ramsgate	75B Redhill	75E Three Bridges	1A Willesden	1A Willesden	
42069	4MT[1]	→	74B Ramsgate	74A Ashford	75E Three Bridges	1E Bletchley	5F Uttoxeter	9E Trafford Park
42070	4MT[1]	→	73A Stewarts Lane	74B Ramsgate	75E Three Bridges	1A Willesden	14A Cricklewood	
42071	4MT[1]	→	73A Stewarts Lane	74B Ramsgate	75E Three Bridges	1E Bletchley	1A Willesden	9E Trafford Park
42072	4MT[1]	→	73A Stewarts Lane	74B Ramsgate	52A Gateshead	55F Manningham	55F Manningham	55F Manningham
42073	4MT[1]	→	73A Stewarts Lane	74A Ashford	52A Gateshead	56A Wakefield	56C Copley Hill	56F Low Moor
42074	4MT[1]	→	73A Stewarts Lane	74C Dover Marine	74B Ramsgate	1A Willesden	6H Bangor	56F Low Moor
42075	4MT[1]	→	74C Dover Marine	74C Dover Marine	74C Dover Marine	1A Willesden	6H Bangor	
42076	4MT[1]	→	74C Dover Marine	74C Dover Marine	74C Dover Marine	1A Willesden	6H Bangor	9E Trafford Park
42077	4MT[1]	→	74C Dover Marine	75B Redhill	74C Dover Marine	6C Birkenhead	1A Willesden	
42078	4MT[1]	→	74C Dover Marine	74C Dover Marine	74C Dover Marine	6C Birkenhead	8C Speke Junction	8M Southport
42079	4MT[1]	→	→	74C Dover Marine	74C Dover Marine	1A Willesden	2A Rugby	9D Newton Heath
42080	4MT[1]	→	→	73B Bricklayers Arms	73B Bricklayers Arms	14D Neasden	16B Kirkby in Ashfield	12C Barrow
42081	4MT[1]	→	→	73B Bricklayers Arms	73B Bricklayers Arms	14D Neasden	12C Carlisle Canal	9E Trafford Park
42082	4MT[1]	→	→	73B Bricklayers Arms	73B Bricklayers Arms	14D Neasden	17B Burton	
42083	4MT[1]	→	→	51A Darlington	50G Whitby	56E Sowerby Bridge	55E Normanton	55E Normanton
42084	4MT[1]	→	→	51A Darlington	50E Scarborough	56F Low Moor	56F Low Moor	
42085	4MT[1]	→	→	51A Darlington	50E Scarborough	50A York	51A Darlington	55F Manningham
42086	4MT[1]	→	→	75A Brighton	73A Stewarts Lane	14D Neasden	14A Cricklewood	8H Birkenhead

		1948		1951	1954	1957	1960	1963	1966
42087	4MT[1]	→		→	**75A** Brighton	**73A** Stewarts Lane	**14D** Neasden	**15C** Leicester Midland	**9D** Newton Heath
42088	4MT[1]	→		→	**75A** Brighton	**73A** Stewarts Lane	**14D** Neasden		
42089	4MT[1]	→		→	**73A** Stewarts Lane	**73A** Stewarts Lane	**14D** Neasden	**16B** Kirkby in Ashfield	
42090	4MT[1]	→		→	**73A** Stewarts Lane	**73A** Stewarts Lane	**14D** Neasden	**14A** Cricklewood	
42091	4MT[1]	→		→	**73A** Stewarts Lane	**73A** Stewarts Lane	**14D** Neasden	**16A** Nottingham	
42092	4MT[1]	→		→	**75E** Three Bridges	**74A** Ashford	**14D** Neasden	**14A** Cricklewood	
42093	4MT[1]	→		→	**75E** Three Bridges	**52A** Gateshead	**55F** Manningham	**55F** Manningham	**55F** Manningham
42094	4MT[1]	→		→	**74A** Ashford	**52A** Gateshead	**56E** Sowerby Bridge		
42095	4MT[1]	→		→	**74A** Ashford	**74A** Ashford	**1C** Watford	**12C** Carlisle Canal	**12E** Tebay
42096	4MT[1]	→		**75F** Tunbridge Wells West	**74A** Ashford	**74A** Ashford	**1C** Watford	**1C** Watford	**10D** Lostock Hall
42097	4MT[1]	→		**75F** Tunbridge Wells West	**74A** Ashford	**74A** Ashford	**1C** Watford		
42098	4MT[1]	→		**75F** Tunbridge Wells West	**74A** Ashford	**74A** Ashford	**1C** Watford	**12C** Carlisle Canal	
42099	4MT[1]	→		**75F** Tunbridge Wells West	**75F** Tunbridge Wells West	**74A** Ashford	**1C** Watford	**1A** Willesden	
42100	4MT[1]	→		**75F** Tunbridge Wells West	**75F** Tunbridge Wells West	**74A** Ashford	**1C** Watford	**1C** Watford	
42101	4MT[1]	→		**75F** Tunbridge Wells West	**75F** Tunbridge Wells West	**75F** Tunbridge Wells West	**1C** Watford	**1A** Willesden	
42102	4MT[1]	→		**75F** Tunbridge Wells West	**75F** Tunbridge Wells West	**75F** Tunbridge Wells West	**1C** Watford	**1C** Watford	**8F** Wigan Springs Branch
42103	4MT[1]	→		**75F** Tunbridge Wells West	**75F** Tunbridge Wells West	**75F** Tunbridge Wells West	**1C** Watford	**2A** Rugby	
42104	4MT[1]	→		**75F** Tunbridge Wells West	**75A** Brighton	**75F** Tunbridge Wells West	**1C** Watford	**2A** Rugby	
42105	4MT[1]	→		**75F** Tunbridge Wells West	**75A** Brighton	**75F** Tunbridge Wells West	**1E** Bletchley	**1E** Bletchley	**10D** Lostock Hall
42106	4MT[1]	→		**74B** Ramsgate	**75E** Three Bridges	**75F** Tunbridge Wells West	**1E** Bletchley	**1E** Bletchley	
42107	4MT[1]	→		**25F** Low Moor	**25F** Low Moor	**56F** Low Moor	**56F** Low Moor	**56F** Low Moor	**56F** Low Moor
42108	4MT[1]	→		**25F** Low Moor	**25F** Low Moor	**56F** Low Moor	**56F** Low Moor	**56F** Low Moor	**56A** Wakefield
42109	4MT[1]	→		**25F** Low Moor	**25F** Low Moor	**56F** Low Moor	**56F** Low Moor	**56F** Low Moor	
42110	4MT[1]	→		**25F** Low Moor	**25B** Huddersfield	**24A** Accrington	**24A** Accrington	**24B** Rose Grove	**12E** Tebay
42111	4MT[1]	→		**25F** Low Moor	**27E** Walton on the Hill	**27E** Walton on the Hill	**9E** Trafford Park		
42112	4MT[1]	→		**25F** Low Moor	**27E** Walton on the Hill	**27E** Walton on the Hill	**27E** Walton on the Hill	**9E** Trafford Park	
42113	4MT[1]	→		**25F** Low Moor	**27E** Walton on the Hill	**27E** Walton on the Hill	**27E** Walton on the Hill	**9E** Trafford Park	
42114	4MT[1]	→		**25F** Low Moor	**26F** Lees Oldham	**26E** Lees Oldham	**26E** Lees Oldham	**26E** Lees Oldham	
42115	4MT[1]	→		**25F** Low Moor	**26F** Lees Oldham	**26E** Lees Oldham	**26E** Lees Oldham	**26E** Lees Oldham	**9D** Newton Heath
42116	4MT[1]	→		**25F** Low Moor	**25F** Low Moor	**56F** Low Moor	**56F** Low Moor	**56F** Low Moor	**56F** Low Moor
42117	4MT[1]	→		**1A** Willesden	**1A** Willesden	**1A** Willesden	**1A** Willesden		
42118	4MT[1]	→		**1A** Willesden	**1A** Willesden	**1A** Willesden	**1A** Willesden	**1A** Willesden	
42119	4MT[1]	→		**1C** Watford	**1C** Watford	**5D** Stoke	**11A** Barrow	**12E** Barrow	
42120	4MT[1]	→		**1C** Watford	**9B** Stockport Edgeley	**6C** Birkenhead	**11A** Barrow	**12E** Barrow	
42121	4MT[1]	→		**1C** Watford	**8A** Edge Hill	**8A** Edge Hill	**8A** Edge Hill	**8C** Speke Junction	**8H** Birkenhead
42122	4MT[1]	→		**67A** Corkerhill	**67A** Corkerhill	**67A** Corkerhill	**67C** Ayr		
42123	4MT[1]	→		**67A** Corkerhill	**67A** Corkerhill	**67A** Corkerhill	**67A** Corkerhill	**67D** Ardrossan	
42124	4MT[1]	→		**67A** Corkerhill	**67A** Corkerhill	**67A** Corkerhill	**67D** Ardrossan	**67D** Ardrossan	
42125	4MT[1]	→		**66B** Motherwell	**66B** Motherwell	**66B** Motherwell	**66B** Motherwell	**66B** Motherwell	**66E** Carstairs
42126	4MT[1]	→		**66B** Motherwell	**66B** Motherwell	**66B** Motherwell	**66B** Motherwell	**66B** Motherwell	
42127	4MT[1]	→		**66B** Motherwell	**66B** Motherwell	**66B** Motherwell	**66B** Motherwell	**66B** Motherwell	
42128	4MT[1]	→		**66C** Hamilton	**66C** Hamilton	**66C** Hamilton	**66C** Hamilton	**66A** Polmadie	**64A** St. Margarets
42129	4MT[1]	→		**66C** Hamilton	**66C** Hamilton	**66C** Hamilton	**66C** Hamilton	**66B** Motherwell	
42130	4MT[1]	→		**66C** Hamilton	**63A** Perth	**68D** Beattock	**68D** Beattock		
42131	4MT[1]	→		**67C** Ayr	**67C** Ayr	**67C** Ayr	**65D** Dawsholm	**65D** Dawsholm	
42132	4MT[1]	→		**14C** St. Albans	**14C** St. Albans	**20G** Hellifield	**24H** Hellifield	**27C** Southport	**8M** Southport
42133	4MT[1]	→		**14B** Kentish Town	**14B** Kentish Town	**14C** St. Albans	**14C** St. Albans	**9F** Heaton Mersey	**9K** Bolton
42134	4MT[1]	→		**14C** St. Albans	**14C** St. Albans	**14C** St. Albans	**14C** St. Albans	**9F** Heaton Mersey	**12C** Barrow
42135	4MT[1]	→		**23C** Lancaster	**11E** Lancaster	**11E** Lancaster	**24J** Lancaster	**24J** Lancaster	
42136	4MT[1]	→		**23C** Lancaster	**11E** Lancaster	**11E** Lancaster	**24J** Lancaster	**24J** Lancaster	
42137	4MT[1]	→		**15C** Leicester Midland	**15C** Leicester Midland	**15C** Leicester Midland	**15C** Leicester Midland	**6F** Uttoxeter	
42138	4MT[1]	→		**14B** Kentish Town	**14B** Kentish Town	**55F** Manningham	**55A** Leeds Holbeck	**55A** Leeds Holbeck	**55F** Manningham
42139	4MT[1]	→		**14B** Kentish Town	**14B** Kentish Town	**55F** Manningham	**55F** Manningham	**55F** Manningham	
42140	4MT[1]	→		**16A** Nottingham	**16A** Nottingham	**16A** Nottingham	**16A** Nottingham	**16A** Nottingham	
42141	4MT[1]	→		**21A** Saltley	**20D** Normanton	**55F** Manningham	**55F** Manningham	**55F** Manningham	**55G** Huddersfield
42142	4MT[1]	→		**20C** Royston	**64D** Carstairs	**64D** Carstairs	**64D** Carstairs	**66E** Carstairs	**56F** Low Moor
42143	4MT[1]	→		**20C** Royston	**66A** Polmadie	**66A** Polmadie	**66A** Polmadie	**66A** Polmadie	
42144	4MT[1]	→		**23C** Lancaster	**66A** Polmadie	**66A** Polmadie	**66A** Polmadie		
42145	4MT[1]	→		**20C** Royston	**64D** Carstairs	**64D** Carstairs	**64D** Carstairs	**66E** Carstairs	**55A** Leeds Holbeck
42146	4MT[1]	→		**16A** Nottingham	**16A** Nottingham	**17A** Derby	**17A** Derby		
42147	4MT[1]	→		**24D** Lower Darwen	**24D** Lower Darwen	**24D** Lower Darwen	**24D** Lower Darwen	**24C** Lostock Hall	
42148	4MT[1]	→		**28A** Blackpool Central	**24E** Blackpool Central	**24E** Blackpool Central	**24E** Blackpool Central	**24E** Blackpool Central	
42149	4MT[1]	→		**25E** Sowerby Bridge	**25E** Sowerby Bridge	**56E** Sowerby Bridge	**56E** Sowerby Bridge	**55E** Normanton	**55E** Normanton
42150	4MT[1]	→		**25E** Sowerby Bridge	**25E** Sowerby Bridge	**56E** Sowerby Bridge	**56E** Sowerby Bridge	**56A** Wakefield	**56A** Wakefield
42151	4MT[1]	→		**25E** Sowerby Bridge	**25E** Sowerby Bridge	**56E** Sowerby Bridge	**56E** Sowerby Bridge	**56F** Low Moor	
42152	4MT[1]	→		**25D** Mirfield	**25D** Mirfield	**56D** Mirfield	**56D** Mirfield	**56D** Mirfield	**55F** Manningham
42153	4MT[1]	→		**24A** Accrington	**24A** Accrington	**24A** Accrington	**24A** Accrington	**24E** Blackpool Central	
42154	4MT[1]	→		**24D** Lower Darwen	**24D** Lower Darwen	**24D** Lower Darwen	**24D** Lower Darwen	**24C** Lostock Hall	**10A** Carnforth
42155	4MT[1]	→		**5D** Stoke	**1E** Bletchley	**8A** Edge Hill	**8A** Edge Hill	**8A** Edge Hill	
42156	4MT[1]	→		**7B** Bangor	**6H** Bangor	**14B** Kentish Town	**14B** Kentish Town	**17C** Rowsley	**8H** Birkenhead
42157	4MT[1]	→		**7B** Bangor	**6H** Bangor	**14B** Kentish Town	**14B** Kentish Town	**2F** Woodford Halse	
42158	4MT[1]	→		**24C** Lostock Hall	**24C** Lostock Hall	**24C** Lostock Hall	**24C** Lostock Hall	**24C** Lostock Hall	
42159	4MT[1]	→		**1C** Watford	**6A** Chester	**14C** St. Albans	**14C** St. Albans	**9F** Heaton Mersey	**9K** Bolton
42160	4MT[1]	→		**14C** St. Albans	**17A** Derby	**15C** Leicester Midland	**15C** Leicester Midland	**5D** Stoke	
42161	4MT[1]	→		**14C** St. Albans	**14C** St. Albans	**16A** Nottingham	**16A** Nottingham	**16A** Nottingham	**51A** Darlington
42162	4MT[1]	→		**64D** Carstairs	**64D** Carstairs	**64D** Carstairs	**64D** Carstairs		
42163	4MT[1]	→		**64D** Carstairs	**64D** Carstairs	**64D** Carstairs	**64D** Carstairs	**66E** Carstairs	
42164	4MT[1]	→		**66C** Hamilton	**66C** Hamilton	**66C** Hamilton	**66C** Hamilton		
42165	4MT[1]	→		**66C** Hamilton	**66C** Hamilton	**66C** Hamilton	**66C** Hamilton	**66E** Carstairs	
42166	4MT[1]	→		**66C** Hamilton	**66C** Hamilton	**66C** Hamilton	**66C** Hamilton	**66A** Polmadie	
42167	4MT[1]	→		**66A** Polmadie	**66A** Polmadie	**66C** Hamilton	**66C** Hamilton	**66D** Greenock Ladyburn	
42168	4MT[1]	→		**66A** Polmadie	**66A** Polmadie	**63A** Perth	**63A** Perth	**64C** Dalry Road	
42169	4MT[1]	→		**66A** Polmadie	**66A** Polmadie	**63A** Perth	**63A** Perth	**66B** Motherwell	**66E** Carstairs
42170	4MT[1]	→		**66A** Polmadie	**66A** Polmadie	**66A** Polmadie	**66A** Polmadie	**66A** Polmadie	
42171	4MT[1]	→		**66A** Polmadie	**66A** Polmadie	**66A** Polmadie	**66A** Polmadie	**66A** Polmadie	
42172	4MT[1]	→		**66A** Polmadie	**66A** Polmadie	**66A** Polmadie	**66A** Polmadie		
42173	4MT[1]	→		**64D** Carstairs	**64D** Carstairs	**64D** Carstairs	**64D** Carstairs		
42174	4MT[1]	→		**17A** Derby	**17A** Derby	**17A** Derby	**17A** Derby	**15C** Leicester Midland	
42175	4MT[1]	→		**66D** Greenock Ladyburn	**66D** Greenock Ladyburn	**66D** Greenock Ladyburn	**66D** Greenock Ladyburn		
42176	4MT[1]	→		**66D** Greenock Ladyburn	**66D** Greenock Ladyburn	**66D** Greenock Ladyburn	**66D** Greenock Ladyburn	**66D** Greenock Ladyburn	**66D** Greenock Ladyburn
42177	4MT[1]	→		**64D** Carstairs	**64D** Carstairs	**64D** Carstairs	**64D** Carstairs	**66E** Carstairs	**56F** Low Moor
42178	4MT[1]	→		**1C** Watford	**1C** Watford	**14B** Kentish Town	**14B** Kentish Town	**2F** Woodford Halse	
42179	4MT[1]	→		**11B** Barrow	**11B** Barrow	**11B** Barrow	**11A** Barrow	**12E** Barrow	
42180	4MT[1]	→		**27D** Wigan	**27D** Wigan	**27D** Wigan	**27D** Wigan	**27D** Wigan	
42181	4MT[1]	→		**15C** Leicester Midland	**17A** Derby	**17A** Derby	**14C** St. Albans	**17A** Derby	**56A** Wakefield
42182	4MT[1]	→		**15C** Leicester Midland	**15C** Leicester Midland	**15C** Leicester Midland	**15C** Leicester Midland	**1A** Willesden	
42183	4MT[1]	→		**15C** Leicester Midland	**15C** Leicester Midland	**15C** Leicester Midland	**27F** Brunswick	**5A** Crewe North	**9K** Bolton
42184	4MT[1]	→		**16A** Nottingham	**16A** Nottingham	**17A** Derby	**17A** Derby	**15C** Leicester Midland	**55H** Leeds Neville Hill
42185	4MT[1]	→		**16A** Nottingham	**16A** Nottingham	**16A** Nottingham	**16A** Nottingham	**16A** Nottingham	
42186	4MT[1]	→		**21B** Bournville	**21B** Bournville	**21B** Bournville	**27F** Brunswick	**5C** Stafford	
42187	4MT[1]	**25F**	Low Moor	**24B** Rose Grove	**24B** Rose Grove	**24B** Rose Grove	**24C** Lostock Hall	**12H** Tebay	**10D** Lostock Hall
42188	4MT[1]	**25F**	Low Moor	**25F** Low Moor	**25F** Low Moor	**56F** Low Moor	**56F** Low Moor	**55H** Leeds Neville Hill	
42189	4MT[1]	**25F**	Low Moor	**25F** Low Moor	**25F** Low Moor	**56F** Low Moor	**56F** Low Moor	**55F** Manningham	**55F** Manningham
42190	4MT[1]	→		**67A** Corkerhill	**67A** Corkerhill	**67A** Corkerhill	**67A** Corkerhill	**67D** Ardrossan	
42191	4MT[1]	→		**67A** Corkerhill	**67A** Corkerhill	**67A** Corkerhill	**67A** Corkerhill		
42192	4MT[1]	→		**67A** Corkerhill	**68D** Beattock	**68D** Beattock	**68D** Beattock	**66F** Beattock	
42193	4MT[1]	→		**67A** Corkerhill	**67A** Corkerhill	**67A** Corkerhill	**67A** Corkerhill		
42194	4MT[1]	→		**67A** Corkerhill	**67A** Corkerhill	**67C** Ayr	**67D** Ardrossan	**67E** Dumfries	
42195	4MT[1]	→		**67A** Corkerhill	**67C** Ayr	**67C** Ayr	**65D** Dawsholm	**65D** Dawsholm	**66A** Polmadie
42196	4MT[1]	→		**67A** Corkerhill	**67C** Ayr	**67C** Ayr	**67C** Ayr	**67E** Dumfries	**55H** Leeds Neville Hill
42197	4MT[1]	→		**67A** Corkerhill	**67C** Ayr	**67C** Ayr	**65D** Dawsholm	**65D** Dawsholm	**66D** Greenock Ladyburn
42198	4MT[1]	→		**63B** Stirling	**63B** Stirling	**63B** Stirling	**63B** Stirling	**6H** Bangor	
42199	4MT[1]	→		**63B** Stirling	**63B** Stirling	**63B** Stirling	**63B** Stirling	**65D** Dawsholm	
42200	4MT[1]	**27A**	Polmadie	**66B** Motherwell	**66B** Motherwell	**66B** Motherwell	**66B** Motherwell	**66B** Motherwell	

		1948	1951	1954	1957	1960	1963	1966
42201	4MT[1]	27A Polmadie	66A Polmadie	67C Ayr	67C Ayr	65D Dawsholm	65D Dawsholm	
42202	4MT[1]	27A Polmadie	67C Ayr	67C Ayr	67C Ayr	60B Aviemore	6A Chester	
42203	4MT[1]	27A Polmadie	66B Motherwell	66B Motherwell	66B Motherwell	66B Motherwell		
42204	4MT[1]	27A Polmadie	66A Polmadie	64D Carstairs	64D Carstairs	64D Carstairs	66E Carstairs	56A Wakefield
42205	4MT[1]	27A Polmadie	66A Polmadie	63A Perth	68D Beattock	68D Beattock		
42206	4MT[1]	27A Polmadie	66A Polmadie	65B St. Rollox	65B St. Rollox	65B St. Rollox	24E Blackpool Central	
42207	4MT[1]	27A Polmadie	66A Polmadie	65B St. Rollox	65B St. Rollox	65B St. Rollox		
42208	4MT[1]	27A Polmadie	66B Motherwell	66B Motherwell	66B Motherwell	66B Motherwell	66B Motherwell	
42209	4MT[1]	30C Ardrossan	67D Ardrossan	67D Ardrossan	67D Ardrossan	67D Ardrossan	6A Chester	
42210	4MT[1]	30C Ardrossan	67D Ardrossan	67D Ardrossan	67D Ardrossan	67D Ardrossan	12C Carlisle Canal	12E Tebay
42211	4MT[1]	30C Ardrossan	67D Ardrossan	67D Ardrossan	67D Ardrossan	67A Corkerhill		
42212	4MT[1]	30C Ardrossan	67D Ardrossan	67D Ardrossan	67D Ardrossan	67D Ardrossan	6A Chester	
42213	4MT[1]	27A Polmadie	66A Polmadie	68D Beattock	68D Beattock	68D Beattock	6A Chester	55G Huddersfield
42214	4MT[1]	27A Polmadie	66A Polmadie	68D Beattock	68D Beattock	68D Beattock	66F Beattock	
42215	4MT[1]	27A Polmadie	66A Polmadie	68D Beattock	68D Beattock	68D Beattock		
42216	4MT[1]	27A Polmadie	66A Polmadie	64D Carstairs	64D Carstairs	64D Carstairs	66A Polmadie	66D Greenock Ladyburn
42217	4MT[1]	27C Hamilton	64D Carstairs	64D Carstairs	64D Carstairs	64D Carstairs		
42218	4MT[1]	13C Tilbury	33B Tilbury	33B Tilbury	33A Plaistow	33C Shoeburyness	1A Willesden	
42219	4MT[1]	13C Tilbury	33B Tilbury	33B Tilbury	33A Plaistow	33C Shoeburyness		
42220	4MT[1]	13C Tilbury	33B Tilbury	33B Tilbury	33A Plaistow	33C Shoeburyness		
42221	4MT[1]	13C Tilbury	33B Tilbury	33B Tilbury	33A Plaistow	33C Shoeburyness	1A Willesden	
42222	4MT[1]	13D Shoeburyness	33B Tilbury	33B Tilbury	34E Neasden	14D Neasden	16B Kirkby in Ashfield	
42223	4MT[1]	13D Shoeburyness	33B Tilbury	33B Tilbury	33A Plaistow	33C Shoeburyness		
42224	4MT[1]	13D Shoeburyness	33B Tilbury	33B Tilbury	33A Plaistow	33C Shoeburyness	5D Stoke	10C Fleetwood
42225	4MT[1]	13A Plaistow	33A Plaistow	33B Tilbury	34E Neasden	14D Neasden	17C Rowsley	12E Tebay
42226	4MT[1]	13A Plaistow	33A Plaistow	33A Plaistow	33A Plaistow	33C Shoeburyness	5D Stoke	
42227	4MT[1]	13A Plaistow	33A Plaistow	33A Plaistow	33A Plaistow	33C Shoeburyness		
42228	4MT[1]	16A Nottingham	16A Nottingham	16A Nottingham	17A Derby	17C Rowsley	17C Rowsley	
42229	4MT[1]	16A Nottingham	20E Manningham	67A Corkerhill	67A Corkerhill	67A Corkerhill	6A Chester	
42230	4MT[1]	14B Kentish Town	33C Shoeburyness	33A Plaistow	34E Neasden	14D Neasden	17C Rowsley	
42231	4MT[1]	5D Stoke	33A Plaistow	33A Plaistow	34E Neasden	14D Neasden	16B Kirkby in Ashfield	
42232	4MT[1]	5D Stoke	33A Plaistow	33A Plaistow	34E Neasden	14D Neasden	16B Kirkby in Ashfield	12E Tebay
42233	4MT[1]	5D Stoke	5D Stoke	5D Stoke	5D Stoke	11A Barrow	1E Bletchley	8M Southport
42234	4MT[1]	5D Stoke	5D Stoke	5D Stoke	5D Stoke	1A Willesden	1A Willesden	
42235	4MT[1]	5D Stoke	5D Stoke	5D Stoke	5D Stoke	8F Wigan Springs Branch	8F Wigan Springs Branch	8F Wigan Springs Branch
42236	4MT[1]	5D Stoke	5D Stoke	5D Stoke	66D Greenock Ladyburn	66D Greenock Ladyburn	6A Chester	12C Barrow
42237	4MT[1]	5D Stoke	14B Kentish Town	14B Kentish Town	14B Kentish Town	14B Kentish Town		
42238	4MT[1]	27A Polmadie	66A Polmadie	66A Polmadie	66D Greenock Ladyburn	67A Corkerhill	24L Carnforth	
42239	4MT[1]	27A Polmadie	66A Polmadie	66A Polmadie	66D Greenock Ladyburn	66A Polmadie	66E Carstairs	
42240	4MT[1]	27A Polmadie	66A Polmadie	66A Polmadie	66D Greenock Ladyburn	67A Corkerhill	6A Chester	9K Bolton
42241	4MT[1]	27A Polmadie	66A Polmadie	66A Polmadie	66D Greenock Ladyburn	66D Greenock Ladyburn	66D Greenock Ladyburn	
42242	4MT[1]	27A Polmadie	66A Polmadie	66A Polmadie	66A Polmadie	66A Polmadie	66D Greenock Ladyburn	
42243	4MT[1]	27A Polmadie	66A Polmadie	66A Polmadie	66A Polmadie	66A Polmadie	66A Polmadie	
42244	4MT[1]	27A Polmadie	66A Polmadie	66A Polmadie	66A Polmadie	66A Polmadie	66A Polmadie	
42245	4MT[1]	27A Polmadie	66A Polmadie	66A Polmadie	66A Polmadie	66A Polmadie	66D Greenock Ladyburn	
42246	4MT[1]	27A Polmadie	66A Polmadie	66A Polmadie	66A Polmadie	66A Polmadie	66A Polmadie	
42247	4MT[1]	27A Polmadie	66A Polmadie	5E Alsager	5E Alsager	67A Corkerhill	6A Chester	
42248	4MT[1]	13A Plaistow	33A Plaistow	33A Plaistow	34E Neasden	14D Neasden		
42249	4MT[1]	13A Plaistow	33A Plaistow	33A Plaistow	34E Neasden	14D Neasden	9G Gorton	9K Bolton
42250	4MT[1]	13A Plaistow	33A Plaistow	33A Plaistow	34E Neasden	14D Neasden	2F Woodford Halse	
42251	4MT[1]	13A Plaistow	33A Plaistow	33A Plaistow	34E Neasden	14D Neasden	2F Woodford Halse	10D Lostock Hall
42252	4MT[1]	13A Plaistow	33A Plaistow	33A Plaistow	34E Neasden	14D Neasden	2F Woodford Halse	9K Bolton
42253	4MT[1]	13A Plaistow	33A Plaistow	33A Plaistow	34E Neasden	14D Neasden	2F Woodford Halse	
42254	4MT[1]	13A Plaistow	33A Plaistow	33A Plaistow	33A Plaistow	33B Tilbury		
42255	4MT[1]	13A Plaistow	33A Plaistow	33A Plaistow	33A Plaistow	33B Tilbury		
42256	4MT[1]	13A Plaistow	33A Plaistow	33A Plaistow	34E Neasden	14D Neasden	9G Gorton	
42257	4MT[1]	13A Plaistow	33A Plaistow	33A Plaistow	33A Plaistow	33B Tilbury		
42258	4MT[1]	7B Bangor	7B Bangor	6H Bangor	66D Greenock Ladyburn	66D Greenock Ladyburn		
42259	4MT[1]	7B Bangor	7B Bangor	6H Bangor	66D Greenock Ladyburn	66D Greenock Ladyburn	66D Greenock Ladyburn	
42260	4MT[1]	7B Bangor	7B Bangor	6H Bangor	66D Greenock Ladyburn	66D Greenock Ladyburn	66D Greenock Ladyburn	66F Beattock
42261	4MT[1]	7B Bangor	7B Bangor	6H Bangor	66D Greenock Ladyburn	66D Greenock Ladyburn	66D Greenock Ladyburn	
42262	4MT[1]	3E Monument Lane	3E Monument Lane	3E Monument Lane	66D Greenock Ladyburn	66D Greenock Ladyburn	66D Greenock Ladyburn	
42263	4MT[1]	3E Monument Lane	3E Monument Lane	3E Monument Lane	66D Greenock Ladyburn	66D Greenock Ladyburn	66D Greenock Ladyburn	
42264	4MT[1]	3E Monument Lane	3E Monument Lane	3E Monument Lane	66D Greenock Ladyburn	66D Greenock Ladyburn	66D Greenock Ladyburn	66D Greenock Ladyburn
42265	4MT[1]	3E Monument Lane	3E Monument Lane	3E Monument Lane	66D Greenock Ladyburn	66D Greenock Ladyburn	66D Greenock Ladyburn	
42266	4MT[1]	5A Crewe North	10A Wigan Springs Branch	10A Wigan Springs Branch	66D Greenock Ladyburn	66D Greenock Ladyburn	66D Greenock Ladyburn	66D Greenock Ladyburn
42267	4MT[1]	11A Carnforth	3E Monument Lane	3E Monument Lane	3E Monument Lane	3E Monument Lane	5C Stafford	9E Trafford Park
42268	4MT[1]	28B Dalry Road	64C Dalry Road	64C Dalry Road	64C Dalry Road	66A Polmadie		
42269	4MT[1]	28B Dalry Road	64C Dalry Road	64C Dalry Road	64C Dalry Road	60B Aviemore	67E Dumfries	56A Wakefield
42270	4MT[1]	28B Dalry Road	64C Dalry Road	64C Dalry Road	64C Dalry Road	67A Corkerhill	6A Chester	
42271	4MT[1]	28B Dalry Road	64C Dalry Road	64C Dalry Road	64C Dalry Road	64D Carstairs	66E Carstairs	55A Leeds Holbeck
42272	4MT[1]	28B Dalry Road	64C Dalry Road	64C Dalry Road	64C Dalry Road	64C Dalry Road		
42273	4MT[1]	28B Dalry Road	64C Dalry Road	64C Dalry Road	64C Dalry Road	64C Dalry Road	64C Dalry Road	64A St. Margarets
42274	4MT[1]	27A Polmadie	66A Polmadie	66A Polmadie	66A Polmadie	66A Polmadie	66A Polmadie	66E Carstairs
42275	4MT[1]	30A Corkerhill	66A Polmadie	66A Polmadie	66A Polmadie	66A Polmadie	66A Polmadie	
42276	4MT[1]	30A Corkerhill	66A Polmadie	66A Polmadie	66A Polmadie	66A Polmadie		
42277	4MT[1]	30A Corkerhill	66A Polmadie	66A Polmadie	66A Polmadie	66A Polmadie	66A Polmadie	66A Polmadie
42278	4MT[1]	26A Newton Heath	26A Newton Heath	26A Newton Heath	26A Newton Heath	24H Hellifield	12H Tebay	
42279	4MT[1]	26A Newton Heath	26A Newton Heath	26A Newton Heath	26A Newton Heath	14D Neasden	15C Leicester Midland	
42280	4MT[1]	26A Newton Heath	26A Newton Heath	26A Newton Heath	26A Newton Heath	24B Rose Grove	26A Newton Heath	
42281	4MT[1]	26A Newton Heath	26A Newton Heath	26A Newton Heath	26A Newton Heath	14D Neasden	2F Woodford Halse	
42282	4MT[1]	26A Newton Heath	26A Newton Heath	26A Newton Heath	26A Newton Heath	14D Neasden	6H Bangor	
42283	4MT[1]	26A Newton Heath	26A Newton Heath	26A Newton Heath	26A Newton Heath	14D Neasden	6H Bangor	9D Newton Heath
42284	4MT[1]	26A Newton Heath	26A Newton Heath	26A Newton Heath	26A Newton Heath	14D Neasden	17C Rowsley	
42285	4MT[1]	26A Newton Heath	26A Newton Heath	26A Newton Heath	56D Mirfield	56D Mirfield	56F Low Moor	
42286	4MT[1]	26A Newton Heath	26A Newton Heath	26A Newton Heath	26A Newton Heath	24C Lostock Hall	24C Lostock Hall	
42287	4MT[1]	26A Newton Heath	26A Newton Heath	26A Newton Heath	26A Newton Heath	26B Agecroft	26E Lees Oldham	9E Trafford Park
42288	4MT[1]	26A Newton Heath	26A Newton Heath	26A Newton Heath	26A Newton Heath	26A Newton Heath	26A Newton Heath	
42289	4MT[1]	26A Newton Heath	26A Newton Heath	26A Newton Heath	26C Bolton	26C Bolton	26C Bolton	
42290	4MT[1]	26A Newton Heath	26A Newton Heath	26A Newton Heath	26A Newton Heath	27C Southport		
42291	4MT[1]	23C Southport	27C Southport	27C Southport	27C Southport	14D Neasden	17C Rowsley	
42292	4MT[1]	23C Southport	27C Southport	27C Southport	27C Southport	27C Southport	27C Southport	
42293	4MT[1]	23C Southport	27C Southport	27C Southport	27C Southport	27C Southport	27C Southport	
42294	4MT[1]	23C Southport	27C Southport	24A Accrington	24A Accrington	24A Accrington	24E Blackpool Central	
42295	4MT[1]	24A Accrington	24A Accrington	24A Accrington	24A Accrington	24A Accrington	24B Rose Grove	
42296	4MT[1]	25F Low Moor	24C Lostock Hall	24C Lostock Hall	24C Lostock Hall	87E Landore	24C Lostock Hall	
42297	4MT[1]	25F Low Moor	27D Wigan	27D Wigan	27D Wigan	27D Wigan	27D Wigan	10D Lostock Hall
42298	4MT[1]	25F Low Moor	24C Lostock Hall	24C Lostock Hall	24C Lostock Hall	24C Lostock Hall		
42299	4MT[1]	25F Low Moor	27D Wigan	27D Wigan	27D Wigan	27D Wigan	27D Wigan	
42300	4MT[2]	14C St. Albans	14C St. Albans	14C St. Albans	14C St. Albans	14C St. Albans		
42301	4MT[2]	11D Oxenholme	11C Oxenholme	11C Oxenholme	11C Oxenholme	11C Oxenholme	12A Carlisle Kingmoor	
42302	4MT[2]	14C St. Albans	14C St. Albans	14C St. Albans	14C St. Albans	14C St. Albans		
42303	4MT[2]	10A Wigan Springs Branch	4A Bletchley	5D Stoke	6C Birkenhead	6D Chester Northgate		
42304	4MT[2]	1C Watford	1C Watford	5F Uttoxeter	9A Longsight	9A Longsight		
42305	4MT[2]	9C Macclesfield	87K Swansea Victoria	87K Swansea Victoria	87K Swansea Victoria	87E Landore		
42306	4MT[2]	9D Buxton	9D Buxton	9D Buxton	9D Buxton	9D Buxton		
42307	4MT[2]	4B Swansea Victoria	87K Swansea Victoria	87K Swansea Victoria	87K Swansea Victoria	87E Landore		
42308	4MT[2]	11E Tebay	5A Crewe North	5A Crewe North	6C Birkenhead			
42309	4MT[2]	5A Crewe North	5C Stafford	5C Stafford	5C Stafford	5C Stafford	6H Bangor	
42310	4MT[2]	25B Huddersfield	25B Huddersfield	25B Huddersfield	55G Huddersfield	55G Huddersfield	55G Huddersfield	
42311	4MT[2]	25B Huddersfield	25B Huddersfield	25B Huddersfield	53E Goole	56F Low Moor	56F Low Moor	
42312	4MT[2]	25B Huddersfield	25B Huddersfield	25B Huddersfield	55G Huddersfield			
42313	4MT[2]	11D Oxenholme	11C Oxenholme	11C Oxenholme	11C Oxenholme	11C Oxenholme	12A Carlisle Kingmoor	
42314	4MT[2]	11D Oxenholme	11C Oxenholme	11C Oxenholme	11C Oxenholme	11C Oxenholme		

		1948		1951	1954	1957	1960	1963	1966
42315	4MT^{2}	9D	Buxton	9D Buxton	6A Chester	6A Chester	5D Stoke		
42316	4MT^{2}	1A	Willesden	1A Willesden	1A Willesden	2C Warwick	9B Stockport Edgeley	9B Stockport Edgeley	
42317	4MT^{2}	11D	Oxenholme	11C Oxenholme	11C Oxenholme	11C Oxenholme	6D Chester Northgate	55G Huddersfield	
42318	4MT^{2}	9D	Buxton	5A Crewe North	9C Macclesfield	9C Macclesfield	9C Macclesfield		
42319	4MT^{2}	9C	Macclesfield	9C Macclesfield	9C Macclesfield	9A Longsight	8E Northwich	24L Carnforth	
42320	4MT^{2}	5D	Stoke	5C Stafford	5C Stafford	11B Barrow	11A Barrow		
42321	4MT^{2}	11B	Barrow	11B Barrow	11B Barrow	5A Crewe North			
42322	4MT^{2}	9A	Longsight	9A Longsight	9A Longsight	9A Longsight	9B Stockport Edgeley	24L Carnforth	
42323	4MT^{2}	9C	Macclesfield	5D Stoke	5D Stoke	5D Stoke	5D Stoke		
42324	4MT^{2}	25B	Huddersfield	25D Mirfield	25D Mirfield	53E Goole	56D Mirfield		
42325	4MT^{2}	14B	Kentish Town	14B Kentish Town	14B Kentish Town	14B Kentish Town	14B Kentish Town		
42326	4MT^{2}	21A	Saltley	21A Saltley	21A Saltley	21A Saltley	9G Gorton		
42327	4MT^{2}	21B	Bournville	21B Bournville	21A Saltley	21A Saltley	21A Saltley	8F Wigan Springs Branch	
42328	4MT^{2}	16A	Nottingham	33A Plaistow	33A Plaistow	34D Hitchin	9G Gorton		
42329	4MT^{2}	14B	Kentish Town	14B Kentish Town	14B Kentish Town	14B Kentish Town	14B Kentish Town		
42330	4MT^{2}	15C	Leicester Midland	15C Leicester Midland	15C Leicester Midland	15C Leicester Midland	15C Leicester Midland		
42331	4MT^{2}	14B	Kentish Town	15C Leicester Midland	15C Leicester Midland	15C Leicester Midland	15C Leicester Midland		
42332	4MT^{2}	9B	Stockport Edgeley	9B Stockport Edgeley	9B Stockport Edgeley	11B Barrow	11A Barrow		
42333	4MT^{2}	16A	Nottingham	16A Nottingham	16A Nottingham	16A Nottingham	16D Annesley	15C Leicester Midland	
42334	4MT^{2}	15C	Leicester Midland	14C St. Albans	14C St. Albans	21B Bournville	14B Kentish Town	15C Leicester Midland	
42335	4MT^{2}	14C	St. Albans	14C St. Albans	14C St. Albans	14C St. Albans	2F Woodford Halse	17A Derby	
42336	4MT^{2}	17B	Burton	17B Burton	17A Derby	16A Nottingham	2F Woodford Halse		
42337	4MT^{2}	21A	Saltley	21A Saltley	21A Saltley	21A Saltley	21A Saltley	9B Stockport Edgeley	
42338	4MT^{2}	21B	Bournville	21B Bournville	21B Bournville	21B Bournville	14B Kentish Town	15C Leicester Midland	
42339	4MT^{2}	21B	Bournville	16A Nottingham	16A Nottingham	16A Nottingham	16D Annesley	17A Derby	
42340	4MT^{2}	17A	Derby	17A Derby	17A Derby	21B Bournville	21A Saltley		
42341	4MT^{2}	17A	Derby	17A Derby	14C St. Albans	14C St. Albans			
42342	4MT^{2}	21B	Bournville	21B Bournville	17A Derby	16A Nottingham	14B Kentish Town		
42343	4MT^{2}	5D	Stoke	5D Stoke	5D Stoke	12A Carlisle Upperby	9B Stockport Edgeley	9B Stockport Edgeley	
42344	4MT^{2}	5D	Stoke	5D Stoke	5D Stoke	5D Stoke	5D Stoke		
42345	4MT^{2}	5C	Stafford	5C Stafford	5C Stafford	5C Stafford	11C Oxenholme		
42346	4MT^{2}	5C	Stafford	5C Stafford	5C Stafford	5C Stafford	5D Stoke		
42347	4MT^{2}	5C	Stafford	5C Stafford	5C Stafford	5C Stafford	9C Macclesfield		
42348	4MT^{2}	5E	Alsager	4A Bletchley	5D Stoke	5D Stoke	9C Macclesfield		
42349	4MT^{2}	9C	Macclesfield	5D Stoke	8E Brunswick	8E Brunswick	2F Woodford Halse		
42350	4MT^{2}	9A	Longsight	9A Longsight	9A Longsight	9A Longsight	1A Willesden	1A Willesden	
42351	4MT^{2}	9A	Longsight	9A Longsight	9A Longsight	9A Longsight	1A Willesden		
42352	4MT^{2}	9B	Stockport Edgeley	9B Stockport Edgeley	8E Brunswick	8E Brunswick	17A Derby		
42353	4MT^{2}	9B	Stockport Edgeley	9B Stockport Edgeley	9B Stockport Edgeley	9B Stockport Edgeley	2E Northampton	6H Bangor	
42354	4MT^{2}	9B	Stockport Edgeley	9B Stockport Edgeley	9B Stockport Edgeley	9B Stockport Edgeley			
42355	4MT^{2}	9C	Macclesfield	9C Macclesfield	9C Macclesfield	9C Macclesfield	9C Macclesfield	15C Leicester Midland	
42356	4MT^{2}	9C	Macclesfield	9C Macclesfield	9C Macclesfield	9C Macclesfield	8E Northwich		
42357	4MT^{2}	9C	Macclesfield	9C Macclesfield	9C Macclesfield	9C Macclesfield	9B Stockport Edgeley	9A Longsight	
42358	4MT^{2}	5F	Uttoxeter	5F Uttoxeter	5F Uttoxeter	5F Uttoxeter	5F Uttoxeter		
42359	4MT^{2}	11B	Barrow	11B Barrow	11B Barrow	11B Barrow	8E Northwich	24L Carnforth	
42360	4MT^{2}	5D	Stoke	9C Macclesfield	5D Stoke	5D Stoke	1A Willesden		
42361	4MT^{2}	16A	Nottingham	16A Nottingham	16A Nottingham	16A Nottingham	16D Annesley	9G Gorton	
42362	4MT^{2}	23D	Wigan	9C Macclesfield	9C Macclesfield	9C Macclesfield	5D Stoke		
42363	4MT^{2}	5F	Uttoxeter	9C Macclesfield	9C Macclesfield	9C Macclesfield	9C Macclesfield		
42364	4MT^{2}	5D	Stoke	5D Stoke	11B Barrow	11B Barrow	11A Barrow		
42365	4MT^{2}	9D	Buxton	9D Buxton	9D Buxton	9D Buxton	8E Northwich		
42366	4MT^{2}	9D	Buxton	9D Buxton	9D Buxton	5D Stoke	1A Willesden	6A Chester	
42367	4MT^{2}	9D	Buxton	9D Buxton	9D Buxton	5D Stoke	1A Willesden		
42368	4MT^{2}	9D	Buxton	9D Buxton	9D Buxton	9D Buxton	1A Willesden	6H Bangor	
42369	4MT^{2}	9C	Macclesfield	9C Macclesfield	9C Macclesfield	9C Macclesfield	9A Longsight	12A Carlisle Kingmoor	
42370	4MT^{2}	9D	Buxton	9D Buxton	9D Buxton	9D Buxton	9D Buxton		
42371	4MT^{2}	9D	Buxton	9D Buxton	9D Buxton	9D Buxton	9D Buxton		
42372	4MT^{2}	1A	Willesden	11B Barrow	11B Barrow	11B Barrow	9B Stockport Edgeley		
42373	4MT^{2}	21B	Bournville	16A Nottingham	16A Nottingham	16A Nottingham	9G Gorton		
42374	4MT^{2}	14C	St. Albans	33A Plaistow	33A Plaistow	34D Hitchin	9G Gorton	9G Gorton	
42375	4MT^{2}	5D	Stoke	5D Stoke	5F Uttoxeter	5F Uttoxeter	5F Uttoxeter		
42376	4MT^{2}	5D	Stoke	5D Stoke	11B Barrow	11B Barrow	11A Barrow		
42377	4MT^{2}	20E	Manningham	20E Manningham	20E Manningham	55A Leeds Holbeck	55A Leeds Holbeck		
42378	4MT^{2}	5D	Stoke	4A Bletchley	5D Stoke	5D Stoke	5D Stoke	24L Carnforth	
42379	4MT^{2}	10A	Wigan Springs Branch	9B Stockport Edgeley	9B Stockport Edgeley	9B Stockport Edgeley	9B Stockport Edgeley	9D Buxton	
42380	4MT^{2}	20E	Manningham	20E Manningham	20E Manningham	55F Manningham	56E Sowerby Bridge		
42381	4MT^{2}	23D	Wigan	9C Macclesfield	9C Macclesfield	9A Longsight	9A Longsight	5D Stoke	
42382	4MT^{2}	9C	Macclesfield	9C Macclesfield	9C Macclesfield	9C Macclesfield	9C Macclesfield		
42383	4MT^{2}	14B	Kentish Town	14B Kentish Town	14B Kentish Town	21A Saltley	21A Saltley		
42384	4MT^{2}	25B	Huddersfield	25B Huddersfield	25B Huddersfield	55G Huddersfield	55G Huddersfield	55G Huddersfield	
42385	4MT^{2}	4B	Swansea Victoria	87K Swansea Victoria	87K Swansea Victoria	87K Swansea Victoria	87E Landore		
42386	4MT^{2}	11B	Barrow	9C Macclesfield	9C Macclesfield	9C Macclesfield	8E Northwich		
42387	4MT^{2}	4B	Swansea Victoria	87K Swansea Victoria	87K Swansea Victoria	87K Swansea Victoria	87E Landore		
42388	4MT^{2}	4B	Swansea Victoria	87K Swansea Victoria	87K Swansea Victoria	87K Swansea Victoria	87E Landore		
42389	4MT^{2}	1C	Watford	1C Watford	1C Watford	5D Stoke	5C Stafford	8C Speke Junction	
42390	4MT^{2}	4B	Swansea Victoria	87K Swansea Victoria	87K Swansea Victoria	87K Swansea Victoria	87E Landore		
42391	4MT^{2}	5C	Stafford	5C Stafford	9A Longsight	9B Stockport Edgeley	9B Stockport Edgeley	9D Buxton	
42392	4MT^{2}	11B	Barrow	11B Barrow	11B Barrow	11B Barrow	11A Barrow	5D Stoke	
42393	4MT^{2}	11B	Barrow	11B Barrow	11C Oxenholme	11D Tebay	8E Northwich		
42394	4MT^{2}	4B	Swansea Victoria	87K Swansea Victoria	87K Swansea Victoria	87K Swansea Victoria	87E Landore	6C Birkenhead	55A Leeds Holbeck
42395	4MT^{2}	9A	Longsight	11B Barrow	11B Barrow	11B Barrow	11A Barrow		
42396	4MT^{2}	9A	Longsight	11D Tebay	11D Tebay	11D Tebay	11D Tebay		
42397	4MT^{2}	9A	Longsight	9A Longsight	9A Longsight	9A Longsight	11A Barrow		
42398	4MT^{2}	9A	Longsight	9A Longsight	9A Longsight	9A Longsight	9A Longsight		
42399	4MT^{2}	9A	Longsight	9A Longsight	9A Longsight	9A Longsight	9A Longsight		
42400	4MT^{2}	27B	Greenock Ladyburn	66D Greenock Ladyburn	66D Greenock Ladyburn	5D Stoke	5C Stafford	21A Saltley	
42401	4MT^{2}	9A	Longsight	11B Barrow	11B Barrow	11B Barrow	11A Barrow	12E Barrow	
42402	4MT^{2}	9A	Longsight	11B Barrow	11B Barrow	11B Barrow	11A Barrow		
42403	4MT^{2}	11E	Tebay	11D Tebay	11D Tebay	11D Tebay	11D Tebay		
42404	4MT^{2}	11E	Tebay	11D Tebay	11D Tebay	11D Tebay	11D Tebay		
42405	4MT^{2}	25D	Mirfield	25D Mirfield	25D Mirfield	56D Mirfield	56E Sowerby Bridge	51A Darlington	
42406	4MT^{2}	25F	Low Moor	25D Mirfield	25D Mirfield	56D Mirfield	56D Mirfield	56D Mirfield	
42407	4MT^{2}	25F	Low Moor	25D Mirfield	25D Mirfield	53E Goole	56D Mirfield		
42408	4MT^{2}	25B	Huddersfield	25B Huddersfield	25B Huddersfield	55G Huddersfield	55D Royston	55A Leeds Holbeck	
42409	4MT^{2}	25F	Low Moor	25B Huddersfield	25B Huddersfield	55G Huddersfield	55A Leeds Holbeck	55A Leeds Holbeck	
42410	4MT^{2}	25B	Huddersfield	25B Huddersfield	25B Huddersfield	55G Huddersfield	55G Huddersfield	55G Huddersfield	55G Huddersfield
42411	4MT^{2}	25B	Huddersfield	25D Mirfield	25D Mirfield	53E Goole	56E Sowerby Bridge	56C Copley Hill	
42412	4MT^{2}	25B	Huddersfield	25B Huddersfield	25B Huddersfield	55G Huddersfield	55G Huddersfield		
42413	4MT^{2}	25B	Huddersfield	25B Huddersfield	25B Huddersfield	55G Huddersfield	55G Huddersfield	55G Huddersfield	
42414	4MT^{2}	25B	Huddersfield	25B Huddersfield	25B Huddersfield	55G Huddersfield	55G Huddersfield	12H Tebay	
42415	4MT^{2}	27B	Greenock Ladyburn	66D Greenock Ladyburn	66D Greenock Ladyburn	6H Bangor	9B Stockport Edgeley		
42416	4MT^{2}	27B	Greenock Ladyburn	66D Greenock Ladyburn	66D Greenock Ladyburn	6H Bangor	9A Longsight	21A Saltley	
42417	4MT^{2}	27B	Greenock Ladyburn	66D Greenock Ladyburn	66D Greenock Ladyburn	6D Chester Northgate	6D Chester Northgate	21A Saltley	
42418	4MT^{2}	27B	Greenock Ladyburn	66D Greenock Ladyburn	66D Greenock Ladyburn	5C Stafford	5D Stoke		
42419	4MT^{2}	27B	Greenock Ladyburn	66D Greenock Ladyburn	66D Greenock Ladyburn	17F Trafford Park	9E Trafford Park	21A Saltley	
42420	4MT^{2}	27B	Greenock Ladyburn	66D Greenock Ladyburn	66D Greenock Ladyburn	5D Stoke	5D Stoke		
42421	4MT^{2}	27B	Greenock Ladyburn	66D Greenock Ladyburn	66D Greenock Ladyburn	5C Stafford	5D Stoke	21A Saltley	
42422	4MT^{2}	27B	Greenock Ladyburn	66D Greenock Ladyburn	66D Greenock Ladyburn	3E Monument Lane	1A Willesden		
42423	4MT^{2}	27B	Greenock Ladyburn	66D Greenock Ladyburn	66D Greenock Ladyburn	10C Patricroft	27F Brunswick		
42424	4MT^{2}	11E	Tebay	11D Tebay	11D Tebay	11D Tebay	11D Tebay	12H Tebay	
42425	4MT^{3}	6A	Chester	6A Chester	6A Chester	5C Stafford	6H Bangor	9A Longsight	
42426	4MT^{3}	8A	Edge Hill	8A Edge Hill	8A Edge Hill	8A Edge Hill	12B Carlisle Upperby	8F Wigan Springs Branch	
42427	4MT^{3}	11B	Barrow	9A Longsight	9A Longsight	11B Barrow	11A Barrow		
42428	4MT^{3}	11A	Carnforth	11A Carnforth	11A Carnforth	3B Bushbury	15C Leicester Midland		

No.	Class	1948	1951	1954	1957	1960	1963	1966
42429	4MT[3]	11A Carnforth	11A Carnforth	11A Carnforth	3B Bushbury	9G Gorton		
42430	4MT[3]	11B Barrow	9A Longsight	9A Longsight	9A Longsight	1A Willesden	1A Willesden	
42431	4MT[3]	11A Carnforth	5D Stoke	5D Stoke	5D Stoke	6A Chester	6A Chester	10C Fleetwood
42432	4MT[3]	11A Carnforth	11A Carnforth	11A Carnforth	11A Carnforth	11A Barrow	12E Barrow	
42433	4MT[3]	24A Accrington	24A Accrington	24A Accrington	24A Accrington	24A Accrington		
42434	4MT[3]	24C Lostock Hall	24C Lostock Hall	24C Lostock Hall	24C Lostock Hall	24C Lostock Hall	9E Trafford Park	
42435	4MT[3]	24C Lostock Hall	24C Lostock Hall	24C Lostock Hall	24C Lostock Hall	27C Southport	27C Southport	
42436	4MT[3]	24C Lostock Hall	24C Lostock Hall	24C Lostock Hall	24C Lostock Hall	24C Lostock Hall	24C Lostock Hall	10D Lostock Hall
42437	4MT[3]	24C Lostock Hall	24A Accrington	24A Accrington	24A Accrington	14D Neasden	15E Leicester Central	
42438	4MT[3]	24B Rose Grove	24B Rose Grove	24B Rose Grove	24B Rose Grove	24B Rose Grove		
42439	4MT[3]	24B Rose Grove	24D Lower Darwen	24B Rose Grove	24B Rose Grove	24B Rose Grove	26F Patricroft	
42440	4MT[3]	3D Aston	5D Stoke	5D Stoke	5D Stoke	11A Barrow	12C Carlisle Canal	
42441	4MT[3]	3D Aston	3D Aston	3D Aston	3C Walsall	6C Birkenhead	6C Birkenhead	
42442	4MT[3]	2B Bletchley	10A Wigan Springs Branch	10A Wigan Springs Branch	10C Patricroft	26F Patricroft	26F Patricroft	
42443	4MT[3]	1A Willesden	5D Stoke	5D Stoke	5D Stoke	5D Stoke		
42444	4MT[3]	3C Walsall	3C Walsall	6H Bangor	26D Bury	26D Bury	26C Bolton	
42445	4MT[3]	1C Watford	6D Stoke	6D Stoke	6A Chester	9E Trafford Park	8C Speke Junction	
42446	4MT[3]	1C Watford	4A Bletchley	2A Rugby	2F Market Harborough	15F Market Harborough	6H Bangor	
42447	4MT[3]	5E Alsager	5E Alsager	5A Crewe North	6C Birkenhead	6C Birkenhead	12C Carlisle Canal	
42448	4MT[3]	3C Walsall	3C Walsall	8E Brunswick	8E Brunswick	27F Brunswick		
42449	4MT[3]	3D Aston	5D Stoke	5D Stoke	5D Stoke	12A Carlisle Kingmoor	12C Carlisle Canal	
42450	4MT[3]	3E Monument Lane	6A Chester	6A Chester	26A Newton Heath	14D Neasden		
42451	4MT[3]	3E Monument Lane	6A Chester	6A Chester	26A Newton Heath	27C Southport	27C Southport	
42452	4MT[3]	3C Walsall	3C Walsall	9E Trafford Park	17F Trafford Park	9E Trafford Park		
42453	4MT[3]	8A Edge Hill	10A Wigan Springs Branch	10A Wigan Springs Branch	14B Kentish Town	14D Neasden	15E Leicester Central	
42454	4MT[3]	10C Patricroft	10A Wigan Springs Branch	10A Wigan Springs Branch	10A Wigan Springs Branch	5D Stoke		
42455	4MT[3]	10A Wigan Springs Branch	6A Chester	6H Bangor	26D Bury	24E Blackpool Central	24E Blackpool Central	9E Trafford Park
42456	4MT[3]	10A Wigan Springs Branch	10A Wigan Springs Branch	10A Wigan Springs Branch	10A Wigan Springs Branch	8F Wigan Springs Branch	8F Wigan Springs Branch	
42457	4MT[3]	11D Oxenholme	11C Oxenholme	11C Oxenholme	11C Oxenholme	11C Oxenholme		
42458	4MT[3]	2B Bletchley	5D Stoke	5D Stoke	5D Stoke	26F Patricroft	26F Patricroft	
42459	4MT[3]	8A Edge Hill	8A Edge Hill	8A Edge Hill	8A Edge Hill	1A Willesden	6C Birkenhead	
42460	4MT[3]	7B Bangor	7B Bangor	6H Bangor	26D Bury	26D Bury	26C Bolton	
42461	4MT[3]	9A Longsight	9A Longsight	6A Chester	26A Newton Heath	26B Agecroft	24E Blackpool Central	
42462	4MT[3]	11B Barrow	11B Barrow	10A Wigan Springs Branch	10A Wigan Springs Branch	8F Wigan Springs Branch	8F Wigan Springs Branch	8F Wigan Springs Branch
42463	4MT[3]	9B Stockport Edgeley	9B Stockport Edgeley	9B Stockport Edgeley	9B Stockport Edgeley	1A Willesden	6A Chester	
42464	4MT[3]	11D Oxenholme	11C Oxenholme	11C Oxenholme	11C Oxenholme	11C Oxenholme	24L Carnforth	
42465	4MT[3]	10A Wigan Springs Branch	10A Wigan Springs Branch	10A Wigan Springs Branch	10A Wigan Springs Branch	8F Wigan Springs Branch	8F Wigan Springs Branch	
42466	4MT[3]	3C Walsall	3C Walsall	8E Brunswick	8E Brunswick	9E Trafford Park	9E Trafford Park	
42467	4MT[3]	9A Longsight	9A Longsight	9A Longsight	9G Northwich	2E Northampton		
42468	4MT[3]	5F Uttoxeter	1C Watford	5F Uttoxeter	5F Uttoxeter	26F Patricroft	26F Patricroft	
42469	4MT[3]	5D Stoke	3C Walsall	9E Trafford Park	17F Trafford Park	9E Trafford Park	9F Heaton Mersey	
42470	4MT[3]	3D Aston	3D Aston	3D Aston	3D Aston	3D Aston		
42471	4MT[3]	5E Alsager	5E Alsager	5E Alsager	5E Alsager	8F Wigan Springs Branch		
42472	4MT[3]	23D Wigan	26C Bolton	26C Bolton	26C Bolton	9G Gorton		
42473	4MT[3]	26D Bury	26D Bury	24E Blackpool Central	27D Wigan	27D Wigan		
42474	4MT[3]	26D Bury	26D Bury	24E Blackpool Central	24B Rose Grove	24B Rose Grove	26B Agecroft	
42475	4MT[3]	24B Rose Grove	24B Rose Grove	24B Rose Grove	24B Rose Grove	27D Wigan		
42476	4MT[3]	26D Bury	26D Bury	24E Blackpool Central	24C Lostock Hall	24C Lostock Hall		
42477	4MT[3]	26A Newton Heath	25C Goole	25C Goole	56D Mirfield	50A York	51A Darlington	
42478	4MT[3]	9A Longsight	9A Longsight	9A Longsight	9A Longsight	11A Barrow	1A Willesden	
42479	4MT[3]	14C St. Albans	5D Stoke	8E Brunswick	8E Brunswick	9E Trafford Park		
42480	4MT[3]	24C Lostock Hall	24C Lostock Hall	24C Lostock Hall	24C Lostock Hall	24C Lostock Hall	24C Lostock Hall	
42481	4MT[3]	24C Lostock Hall	24C Lostock Hall	24C Lostock Hall	24C Lostock Hall	24C Lostock Hall	24C Lostock Hall	
42482	4MT[3]	1C Watford	3C Walsall	3C Walsall	3C Walsall	6A Chester	6A Chester	
42483	4MT[3]	24D Lower Darwen	24D Lower Darwen	24D Lower Darwen	24D Lower Darwen	24D Lower Darwen		
42484	4MT[3]	24D Lower Darwen	24D Lower Darwen	24D Lower Darwen	24D Lower Darwen	24H Hellifield	24H Hellifield	9K Bolton
42485	4MT[3]	24D Lower Darwen	24D Lower Darwen	24D Lower Darwen	24D Lower Darwen	24D Lower Darwen	27C Southport	
42486	4MT[3]	26A Newton Heath	26A Newton Heath	26A Newton Heath	26A Newton Heath	17C Rowsley	17C Rowsley	
42487	4MT[3]	2A Rugby	2A Rugby	2A Rugby	1A Willesden	6H Bangor	6H Bangor	
42488	4MT[3]	3E Monument Lane	3C Walsall	3C Walsall	3C Walsall	3E Monument Lane	5C Stafford	
42489	4MT[3]	3E Monument Lane	3E Monument Lane	3D Aston	2A Rugby	6H Bangor	6H Bangor	
42490	4MT[3]	24A Accrington	24D Lower Darwen	24D Lower Darwen	24D Lower Darwen	27F Brunswick		
42491	4MT[3]	26A Newton Heath	24C Lostock Hall	24C Lostock Hall	24C Lostock Hall	24H Hellifield	24H Hellifield	
42492	4MT[3]	26A Newton Heath	24C Lostock Hall	24C Lostock Hall	24C Lostock Hall	24H Hellifield	24H Hellifield	
42493	4MT[3]	11B Barrow	11B Barrow	11B Barrow	6C Birkenhead	6C Birkenhead	6C Birkenhead	
42494	4MT[3]	5D Stoke	5D Stoke	5D Stoke	5D Stoke	26F Patricroft	27D Wigan	
42500	4MT[4]	13D Shoeburyness	33C Shoeburyness	33C Shoeburyness	33C Shoeburyness	33C Shoeburyness		
42501	4MT[4]	13D Shoeburyness	33C Shoeburyness	33C Shoeburyness	33C Shoeburyness	33C Shoeburyness		
42502	4MT[4]	13D Shoeburyness	33C Shoeburyness	33C Shoeburyness	33C Shoeburyness	33C Shoeburyness		
42503	4MT[4]	13D Shoeburyness	33C Shoeburyness	33C Shoeburyness	33C Shoeburyness	33C Shoeburyness		
42504	4MT[4]	13D Shoeburyness	33C Shoeburyness	33C Shoeburyness	33C Shoeburyness	33C Shoeburyness		
42505	4MT[4]	13D Shoeburyness	33C Shoeburyness	33C Shoeburyness	33C Shoeburyness	33C Shoeburyness		
42506	4MT[4]	13D Shoeburyness	33C Shoeburyness	33C Shoeburyness	33C Shoeburyness	33C Shoeburyness		
42507	4MT[4]	13D Shoeburyness	33C Shoeburyness	33C Shoeburyness	33C Shoeburyness	33C Shoeburyness		
42508	4MT[4]	13D Shoeburyness	33C Shoeburyness	33C Shoeburyness	33C Shoeburyness	33C Shoeburyness		
42509	4MT[4]	13D Shoeburyness	33C Shoeburyness	33C Shoeburyness	33C Shoeburyness	33C Shoeburyness		
42510	4MT[4]	13D Shoeburyness	33C Shoeburyness	33C Shoeburyness	33C Shoeburyness	33C Shoeburyness		
42511	4MT[4]	13D Shoeburyness	33C Shoeburyness	33C Shoeburyness	33C Shoeburyness	33C Shoeburyness		
42512	4MT[4]	13D Shoeburyness	33C Shoeburyness	33C Shoeburyness	33C Shoeburyness	33C Shoeburyness		
42513	4MT[4]	13D Shoeburyness	33C Shoeburyness	33C Shoeburyness	33C Shoeburyness	33C Shoeburyness		
42514	4MT[4]	13D Shoeburyness	33C Shoeburyness	33C Shoeburyness	33C Shoeburyness	33C Shoeburyness		
42515	4MT[4]	13D Shoeburyness	33C Shoeburyness	33C Shoeburyness	33C Shoeburyness	33C Shoeburyness		
42516	4MT[4]	13D Shoeburyness	33C Shoeburyness	33C Shoeburyness	33C Shoeburyness	33C Shoeburyness		
42517	4MT[4]	13D Shoeburyness	33C Shoeburyness	33C Shoeburyness	33C Shoeburyness	33C Shoeburyness		
42518	4MT[4]	13D Shoeburyness	33C Shoeburyness	33C Shoeburyness	33C Shoeburyness	33C Shoeburyness		
42519	4MT[4]	13D Shoeburyness	33C Shoeburyness	33C Shoeburyness	33C Shoeburyness	33C Shoeburyness		
42520	4MT[4]	13D Shoeburyness	33C Shoeburyness	33C Shoeburyness	33C Shoeburyness	33C Shoeburyness		
42521	4MT[4]	13D Shoeburyness	33C Shoeburyness	33C Shoeburyness	33C Shoeburyness	33C Shoeburyness		
42522	4MT[4]	13A Plaistow	33C Shoeburyness	33C Shoeburyness	33C Shoeburyness	33C Shoeburyness		
42523	4MT[4]	13A Plaistow	33C Shoeburyness	33C Shoeburyness	33C Shoeburyness	33C Shoeburyness		
42524	4MT[4]	13A Plaistow	33C Shoeburyness	33C Shoeburyness	33C Shoeburyness	33C Shoeburyness		
42525	4MT[4]	13A Plaistow	33C Shoeburyness	33C Shoeburyness	33C Shoeburyness	33C Shoeburyness		
42526	4MT[4]	13A Plaistow	33C Shoeburyness	33C Shoeburyness	33C Shoeburyness	33C Shoeburyness		
42527	4MT[4]	13A Plaistow	33C Shoeburyness	33C Shoeburyness	33C Shoeburyness	33C Shoeburyness		
42528	4MT[4]	13A Plaistow	33C Shoeburyness	33C Shoeburyness	33C Shoeburyness	33C Shoeburyness		
42529	4MT[4]	13A Plaistow	33C Shoeburyness	33C Shoeburyness	33C Shoeburyness	33C Shoeburyness		
42530	4MT[4]	13A Plaistow	33A Plaistow	33C Shoeburyness	33C Shoeburyness	33C Shoeburyness		
42531	4MT[4]	13A Plaistow	33A Plaistow	33C Shoeburyness	33C Shoeburyness	33C Shoeburyness		
42532	4MT[4]	13A Plaistow	33A Plaistow	33A Plaistow	33C Shoeburyness	33C Shoeburyness		
42533	4MT[4]	13A Plaistow	33A Plaistow	33A Plaistow	33C Shoeburyness	33C Shoeburyness		
42534	4MT[4]	13A Plaistow	33A Plaistow	33A Plaistow	33C Shoeburyness	33C Shoeburyness		
42535	4MT[4]	13A Plaistow	33A Plaistow	33A Plaistow	33C Shoeburyness	33C Shoeburyness		
42536	4MT[4]	13A Plaistow	33A Plaistow	33A Plaistow	33C Shoeburyness	33C Shoeburyness		
42537	4MT[3]	23D Wigan	27D Wigan	27D Wigan	27C Southport	27C Southport		
42538	4MT[3]	3D Aston	3D Aston	3C Walsall	5C Stafford	1A Willesden		
42539	4MT[3]	10A Wigan Springs Branch	10A Wigan Springs Branch	10A Wigan Springs Branch	10A Wigan Springs Branch	12B Carlisle Upperby		
42540	4MT[3]	6A Chester	6A Chester	6A Chester	14B Kentish Town	14D Neasden		
42541	4MT[3]	1C Watford	2A Rugby	2A Rugby	2A Rugby	2A Rugby		
42542	4MT[3]	10C Patricroft	9A Longsight	9A Longsight	11A Carnforth	12A Carlisle Kingmoor	6C Birkenhead	
42543	4MT[3]	5D Stoke	5D Stoke	5D Stoke	5D Stoke	5D Stoke	5D Stoke	
42544	4MT[3]	11A Carnforth	11A Carnforth	11A Carnforth	12A Carlisle Upperby	6H Bangor		
42545	4MT[3]	26C Bolton	26C Bolton	26C Bolton	26C Bolton	26C Bolton		
42546	4MT[3]	24B Rose Grove	24B Rose Grove	24B Rose Grove	24B Rose Grove	24B Rose Grove	24B Rose Grove	10D Lostock Hall
42547	4MT[3]	24B Rose Grove	24B Rose Grove	24B Rose Grove	24B Rose Grove	24B Rose Grove	24B Rose Grove	

		1948	1951	1954	1957	1960	1963	1966
42548	4MT^3	24A Accrington	24A Accrington	24A Accrington	24A Accrington	26A Newton Heath	26A Newton Heath	9D Newton Heath
42549	4MT^3	26A Newton Heath	24A Accrington	24A Accrington	24A Accrington	26A Newton Heath		
42550	4MT^3	26F Lees Oldham	26A Newton Heath	26A Newton Heath	26A Newton Heath	26D Bury	26C Bolton	
42551	4MT^3	26A Newton Heath	26A Newton Heath	26F Lees Oldham	26E Lees Oldham	24D Lower Darwen	27C Southport	
42552	4MT^3	3D Aston	3D Aston	3D Aston	3E Monument Lane	3D Aston		
42553	4MT^3	25D Mirfield	25C Goole	25C Goole	56D Mirfield	50A York		
42554	4MT^3	23D Wigan	27D Wigan	27D Wigan	27D Wigan	27D Wigan	27D Wigan	
42555	4MT^3	24B Rose Grove	24B Rose Grove	24B Rose Grove	24B Rose Grove	24B Rose Grove	27D Wigan	
42556	4MT^3	24C Lostock Hall	24C Lostock Hall	24C Lostock Hall	24C Lostock Hall	14D Neasden	15E Leicester Central	
42557	4MT^3	23D Wigan	27D Wigan	27D Wigan	27D Wigan	27D Wigan	27D Wigan	
42558	4MT^3	24B Rose Grove	24D Lower Darwen	24D Lower Darwen	24D Lower Darwen	24D Lower Darwen	24E Blackpool Central	
42559	4MT^3	24D Lower Darwen	24D Lower Darwen	24D Lower Darwen	24D Lower Darwen	24D Lower Darwen	24E Blackpool Central	
42560	4MT^3	10C Patricroft	10C Patricroft	10C Patricroft	10C Patricroft	9G Gorton	9E Trafford Park	
42561	4MT^3	10C Patricroft	10C Patricroft	10C Patricroft	10C Patricroft	26F Patricroft	26F Patricroft	
42562	4MT^3	3C Walsall	3C Walsall	3C Walsall	5C Stafford	14D Neasden	1A Willesden	
42563	4MT^3	10A Wigan Springs Branch	10A Wigan Springs Branch	10C Patricroft	10C Patricroft	26F Patricroft	26C Bolton	
42564	4MT^3	8A Edge Hill	8A Edge Hill	8A Edge Hill	8A Edge Hill	8A Edge Hill	5F Uttoxeter	
42565	4MT^3	26C Bolton	26C Bolton	26C Bolton	26C Bolton	26C Bolton	26C Bolton	
42566	4MT^3	2B Bletchley	4A Bletchley	5A Crewe North	5A Crewe North	84D Leamington Spa	1A Willesden	
42567	4MT^3	3E Monument Lane	5D Stoke	5D Stoke	5D Stoke	14D Neasden	6H Bangor	
42568	4MT^3	6A Chester	6A Chester	6A Chester	26A Newton Heath	14D Neasden		
42569	4MT^3	23D Wigan	27D Wigan	27D Wigan	27D Wigan	27D Wigan	27D Wigan	
42570	4MT^3	11B Barrow	8A Edge Hill	8A Edge Hill	8A Edge Hill	8A Edge Hill		
42571	4MT^3	11B Barrow	11B Barrow	11B Barrow	11B Barrow	8F Wigan Springs Branch	24L Carnforth	
42572	4MT^3	10A Wigan Springs Branch	10A Wigan Springs Branch	10A Wigan Springs Branch	10A Wigan Springs Branch	8F Wigan Springs Branch	8F Wigan Springs Branch	
42573	4MT^3	11B Barrow	11A Carnforth	11A Carnforth	2A Rugby	2A Rugby	1A Willesden	
42574	4MT^3	10C Patricroft	10C Patricroft	10C Patricroft	10C Patricroft	26F Patricroft	26F Patricroft	9E Trafford Park
42575	4MT^3	9A Longsight	9A Longsight	9A Longsight	9G Northwich	5A Crewe North		
42576	4MT^3	2A Rugby	2A Rugby	2A Rugby	2A Rugby	1A Willesden		
42577	4MT^3	2A Rugby	2A Rugby	2A Rugby	2A Rugby	2A Rugby	1A Willesden	8F Wigan Springs Branch
42578	4MT^3	3D Aston	3D Aston	3C Walsall	5C Stafford	5A Crewe North		
42579	4MT^3	3E Monument Lane	3E Monument Lane	3E Monument Lane	3E Monument Lane	1A Willesden		
42580	4MT^3	9A Longsight	9A Longsight	9A Longsight	8E Brunswick	27F Brunswick		
42581	4MT^3	11B Barrow	11B Barrow	11B Barrow	11B Barrow	11A Barrow	1A Willesden	8H Birkenhead
42582	4MT^3	1C Watford	5D Stoke	1E Bletchley	5D Stoke	3B Bushbury	21C Bushbury	
42583	4MT^3	8B Warrington Dallam	8A Edge Hill	8A Edge Hill	8A Edge Hill	1A Willesden	6C Birkenhead	9E Trafford Park
42584	4MT^3	5D Stoke	6A Chester	8E Brunswick	8E Brunswick	27F Brunswick	8C Speke Junction	
42585	4MT^3	5D Stoke	2A Rugby	2A Rugby	2A Rugby	1A Willesden		
42586	4MT^3	3C Walsall	3C Walsall	3C Walsall	3C Walsall	1A Willesden	1E Bletchley	
42587	4MT^3	6A Chester	6A Chester	6A Chester	14B Kentish Town	14C St. Albans	16A Nottingham	8F Wigan Springs Branch
42588	4MT^3	10A Wigan Springs Branch	7B Bangor	6H Bangor	26D Bury	14D Neasden	16A Nottingham	
42589	4MT^3	1C Watford	1C Watford	11E Lancaster	11E Lancaster	24J Lancaster	24J Lancaster	
42590	4MT^3	1C Watford	1C Watford	5D Stoke	5D Stoke	5D Stoke	5D Stoke	
42591	4MT^3	2B Bletchley	4A Bletchley	10C Patricroft	11A Carnforth	11A Barrow		
42592	4MT^3	23D Wigan	27D Wigan	27D Wigan	27D Wigan	27D Wigan	27D Wigan	
42593	4MT^3	1C Watford	1C Watford	5D Stoke	5D Stoke	5D Stoke		
42594	4MT^3	11B Barrow	9A Longsight	9A Longsight	9A Longsight	12B Carlisle Upperby	24L Carnforth	
42595	4MT^3	11D Oxenholme	6A Chester	6A Chester	14B Kentish Town	14D Neasden	17C Rowsley	
42596	4MT^3	10C Patricroft	8A Edge Hill	8A Edge Hill	8E Brunswick	27F Brunswick		
42597	4MT^3	8A Edge Hill	8A Edge Hill	8E Brunswick	6C Birkenhead	14D Neasden	6C Birkenhead	
42598	4MT^3	1C Watford	1C Watford	8E Brunswick	8E Brunswick	27F Brunswick	8C Speke Junction	
42599	4MT^3	9A Longsight	9A Longsight	9A Longsight	6C Birkenhead	6C Birkenhead		
42600	4MT^3	2B Bletchley	4A Bletchley	5D Stoke	5D Stoke	5D Stoke		
42601	4MT^3	11A Carnforth	11A Carnforth	11A Carnforth	3E Monument Lane	14D Neasden	6H Bangor	
42602	4MT^3	11B Barrow	8A Edge Hill	8A Edge Hill	8A Edge Hill	6C Birkenhead	6C Birkenhead	
42603	4MT^3	5D Stoke	5D Stoke	5D Stoke	5D Stoke	5D Stoke	5D Stoke	
42604	4MT^3	3C Walsall	3C Walsall	3C Walsall	3C Walsall	1A Willesden	1A Willesden	
42605	4MT^3	5D Stoke	5D Stoke	5F Uttoxeter	5F Uttoxeter	5F Uttoxeter	5F Uttoxeter	
42606	4MT^3	8B Warrington Dallam	8B Warrington Dallam	8B Warrington Dallam	8B Warrington Dallam	8B Warrington Dallam	6C Birkenhead	8H Birkenhead
42607	4MT^3	5D Stoke	8B Warrington Dallam	8B Warrington Dallam	8B Warrington Dallam	8B Warrington Dallam	8F Wigan Springs Branch	
42608	4MT^3	9A Longsight	9A Longsight	9A Longsight	6C Birkenhead	6C Birkenhead	6C Birkenhead	
42609	4MT^3	5D Stoke	5D Stoke	5D Stoke	5D Stoke	5D Stoke	5D Stoke	
42610	4MT^3	1C Watford	10A Wigan Springs Branch	10A Wigan Springs Branch	14B Kentish Town	14B Kentish Town	17C Rowsley	12C Barrow
42611	4MT^3	5E Alsager	5E Alsager	5E Alsager	5E Alsager	1A Willesden	1A Willesden	8F Wigan Springs Branch
42612	4MT^3	8A Edge Hill	8A Edge Hill	8E Brunswick	8E Brunswick	27F Brunswick	8C Speke Junction	
42613	4MT^3	11A Carnforth	11C Oxenholme	11C Oxenholme	11C Oxenholme	11C Oxenholme	24L Carnforth	10A Carnforth
42614	4MT^3	23D Wigan	27D Wigan	27D Wigan	27D Wigan	27D Wigan	26A Newton Heath	
42615	4MT^3	11A Carnforth	2A Rugby	2A Rugby	2A Rugby	2E Northampton		
42616	4MT^3	3D Aston	3D Aston	3D Aston	3D Aston	1A Willesden	1C Watford	10A Carnforth
42617	4MT^3	6A Chester	7B Bangor	6H Bangor	14B Kentish Town	14B Kentish Town	27E Walton on the Hill	
42618	4MT^3	26A Newton Heath	26A Newton Heath	26A Newton Heath	26A Newton Heath	14D Neasden	16B Kirkby in Ashfield	
42619	4MT^3	26A Newton Heath	26E Bacup	26E Bacup	24A Accrington	24A Accrington	26A Newton Heath	
42620	4MT^3	26A Newton Heath	26E Bacup	26E Bacup	24A Accrington	24A Accrington	26A Newton Heath	
42621	4MT^3	26A Newton Heath	26A Newton Heath	26A Newton Heath	26A Newton Heath	27D Wigan		
42622	4MT^3	26A Newton Heath	26A Newton Heath	26A Newton Heath	56F Low Moor	56A Wakefield	56F Low Moor	55A Leeds Holbeck
42623	4MT^3	26A Newton Heath	26A Newton Heath	26A Newton Heath	26A Newton Heath	26A Newton Heath	26A Newton Heath	
42624	4MT^3	26A Newton Heath	26A Newton Heath	26A Newton Heath	26A Newton Heath	26A Newton Heath		
42625	4MT^3	26A Newton Heath	26A Newton Heath	26A Newton Heath	24E Blackpool Central	24E Blackpool Central	24E Blackpool Central	10D Lostock Hall
42626	4MT^3	26A Newton Heath	26A Newton Heath	26C Bolton	26C Bolton	26C Bolton	26C Bolton	
42627	4MT^3	3C Walsall	3C Walsall	3C Walsall	3C Walsall	1A Willesden		
42628	4MT^3	7B Bangor	7B Bangor	6H Bangor	8E Brunswick	9E Trafford Park	16A Nottingham	
42629	4MT^3	26D Bury	26D Bury	24E Blackpool Central	26C Bolton	14D Neasden	16B Kirkby in Ashfield	
42630	4MT^3	26A Newton Heath	26A Newton Heath	26C Bolton	26C Bolton	26C Bolton	26C Bolton	
42631	4MT^3	23D Wigan	27D Wigan	27D Wigan	27D Wigan	27D Wigan	27D Wigan	
42632	4MT^3	23D Wigan	27D Wigan	27D Wigan	27D Wigan	27D Wigan	26A Newton Heath	
42633	4MT^3	26C Bolton	26C Bolton	26C Bolton	26C Bolton	26C Bolton	26C Bolton	
42634	4MT^3	24A Accrington	24A Accrington	24A Accrington	24A Accrington	24C Lostock Hall	12C Carlisle Canal	
42635	4MT^3	24B Rose Grove	26A Newton Heath	26C Bolton	26C Bolton	26C Bolton		
42636	4MT^3	24E Blackpool Central	28A Blackpool Central	24E Blackpool Central	24E Blackpool Central	16A Nottingham	16A Nottingham	
42637	4MT^3	24E Blackpool Central	28A Blackpool Central	24E Blackpool Central	24E Blackpool Central	27C Southport		
42638	4MT^3	24E Blackpool Central	28A Blackpool Central	24E Blackpool Central	24E Blackpool Central	24E Blackpool Central		
42639	4MT^3	23A Bank Hall	25E Sowerby Bridge	25E Sowerby Bridge	56E Sowerby Bridge	50A York	51A Darlington	
42640	4MT^3	23D Wigan	27D Wigan	27D Wigan	27D Wigan	27D Wigan	26A Newton Heath	
42641	4MT^3	23D Wigan	27D Wigan	27D Wigan	27D Wigan	27D Wigan		
42642	4MT^3	23D Wigan	27D Wigan	27D Wigan	27D Wigan	27D Wigan		
42643	4MT^3	23A Bank Hall	24A Accrington	24A Accrington	24A Accrington	24A Accrington	24E Blackpool Central	
42644	4MT^3	25F Low Moor	27D Wigan	27D Wigan	27D Wigan	27D Wigan	27D Wigan	9E Trafford Park
42645	4MT^3	26B Agecroft	26B Agecroft	26B Agecroft	26B Agecroft	87E Landore	27C Southport	
42646	4MT^3	26B Agecroft	26B Agecroft	26B Agecroft	26B Agecroft	26B Agecroft		
42647	4MT^3	26B Agecroft	26B Agecroft	26B Agecroft	26B Agecroft	26B Agecroft	26B Agecroft	8F Wigan Springs Branch
42648	4MT^3	26B Agecroft	26B Agecroft	26B Agecroft	26B Agecroft	24H Hellifield		
42649	4MT^3	26E Bacup	26E Bacup	26E Bacup	56F Low Moor	56C Copley Hill	56A Wakefield	
42650	4MT^3	26E Bacup	26E Bacup	26E Bacup	56F Low Moor	56C Copley Hill	56A Wakefield	56A Wakefield
42651	4MT^3	26E Bacup	26E Bacup	26E Bacup	26A Newton Heath	87E Landore	26A Newton Heath	
42652	4MT^3	26C Bolton	26C Bolton	26C Bolton	26D Bury	26C Bolton	26C Bolton	
42653	4MT^3	26C Bolton	26C Bolton	26C Bolton	26C Bolton	26C Bolton		
42654	4MT^3	26C Bolton	26C Bolton	26C Bolton	26C Bolton	26C Bolton	26C Bolton	
42655	4MT^3	26C Bolton	26C Bolton	26C Bolton	26C Bolton	26C Bolton	26C Bolton	
42656	4MT^3	26C Bolton	26C Bolton	26C Bolton	26C Bolton	26C Bolton	26C Bolton	9D Newton Heath
42657	4MT^3	26C Bolton	26C Bolton	26C Bolton	26E Lees Oldham	24E Blackpool Central	24E Blackpool Central	
42658	4MT^3	8A Edge Hill	3D Aston	3D Aston	3E Monument Lane	3D Aston		
42659	4MT^3	3E Monument Lane	4A Bletchley	1E Bletchley	5D Stoke	3B Bushbury	21C Bushbury	
42660	4MT^3	3C Walsall	6A Chester	6A Chester	26A Newton Heath	26A Newton Heath	26F Patricroft	
42661	4MT^3	24C Lostock Hall	24A Accrington	24A Accrington	24A Accrington	24A Accrington		

No.	Class	1948	1951	1954	1957	1960	1963	1966
42662	4MT[3]	10C Patricroft	10C Patricroft	10C Patricroft	10C Patricroft	26F Patricroft	27C Southport	
42663	4MT[3]	5D Stoke	6F Uttoxeter	10A Wigan Springs Branch	10A Wigan Springs Branch	5D Stoke	5D Stoke	10A Carnforth
42664	4MT[3]	5D Stoke	5D Stoke	8E Brunswick	8A Edge Hill	12B Carlisle Upperby	8F Wigan Springs Branch	56F Low Moor
42665	4MT[3]	5D Stoke	5F Uttoxeter	5F Uttoxeter	5F Uttoxeter	5F Uttoxeter	5F Uttoxeter	8M Southport
42666	4MT[3]	5D Stoke	4A Bletchley	10A Wigan Springs Branch	10A Wigan Springs Branch	11A Barrow		
42667	4MT[3]	5D Stoke	5D Stoke	5D Stoke	5D Stoke	5D Stoke	5D Stoke	
42668	4MT[3]	5D Stoke	5D Stoke	5D Stoke	5D Stoke	5D Stoke	5D Stoke	
42669	4MT[3]	5D Stoke	4A Bletchley	1E Bletchley	2A Rugby	2A Rugby		
42670	4MT[3]	5D Stoke	5D Stoke	5D Stoke	5D Stoke	5D Stoke	9B Stockport Edgeley	
42671	4MT[3]	5D Stoke	2C Warwick	5D Stoke	5D Stoke	5D Stoke		
42672	4MT[3]	5D Stoke	5D Stoke	5D Stoke	5D Stoke	5D Stoke		
42673	4MT[1]	5D Stoke	2A Rugby	2A Rugby	2A Rugby	1A Willesden	12E Barrow	
42674	4MT[1]	5D Stoke	2C Warwick	2C Warwick	2C Warwick	14D Neasden		
42675	4MT[1]	5D Stoke	26G Belle Vue	5F Uttoxeter	17F Trafford Park	9E Trafford Park	9E Trafford Park	
42676	4MT[1]	5D Stoke	5D Stoke	9E Trafford Park	17F Trafford Park	9E Trafford Park	9E Trafford Park	9D Newton Heath
42677	4MT[1]	6A Chester	7B Bangor	5A Crewe North	6A Crewe North	5A Crewe North		
42678	4MT[1]	16A Nottingham	33A Plaistow	33A Plaistow	33C Shoeburyness	33C Shoeburyness		
42679	4MT[1]	16A Nottingham	33A Plaistow	33A Plaistow	33C Shoeburyness	33C Shoeburyness		
42680	4MT[1]	16A Nottingham	16A Nottingham	16A Nottingham	14C St. Albans	14C St. Albans	14E Bedford	
42681	4MT[1]	14C St. Albans	33A Plaistow	33A Plaistow	33C Shoeburyness	33C Shoeburyness	6A Chester	
42682	4MT[1]	20E Manningham	20E Manningham	20E Manningham	14B Kentish Town	14B Kentish Town	14E Bedford	
42683	4MT[1]	14B Kentish Town	5D Stoke	9E Trafford Park	17F Trafford Park	9E Trafford Park		
42684	4MT[1]	14C St. Albans	33A Plaistow	33A Plaistow	33C Shoeburyness	33C Shoeburyness		
42685	4MT[1]	21A Saltley	21A Saltley	21A Saltley	14B Kentish Town	14B Kentish Town		
42686	4MT[1]	16A Nottingham	16A Nottingham	16A Nottingham	14C St. Albans	14C St. Albans	14E Bedford	
42687	4MT[1]	14B Kentish Town	33A Plaistow	33A Plaistow	33C Shoeburyness	33C Shoeburyness		
42688	4MT[1]	27A Polmadie	66A Polmadie	66A Polmadie	68D Beattock	68D Beattock	66F Beattock	
42689	4MT[1]	27A Polmadie	66A Polmadie	66B Motherwell	66B Motherwell	66B Motherwell	67E Dumfries	55G Huddersfield
42690	4MT[1]	27A Polmadie	66A Polmadie	66A Polmadie	62B Dundee Tay Bridge	63B Stirling	65B St. Rollox	66A Polmadie
42691	4MT[1]	27A Polmadie	66A Polmadie	66D Greenock Ladyburn	62B Dundee Tay Bridge	62B Dundee Tay Bridge	66D Greenock Ladyburn	64A St. Margarets
42692	4MT[1]	27A Polmadie	66A Polmadie	66A Polmadie	62B Dundee Tay Bridge	62B Dundee Tay Bridge		
42693	4MT[1]	27A Polmadie	66A Polmadie	66A Polmadie	62B Dundee Tay Bridge	63B Stirling	66F Beattock	68D Beattock
42694	4MT[1]	27A Polmadie	66A Polmadie	66A Polmadie	65B St. Rollox	65D Dawsholm	65D Dawsholm	66E Carstairs
42695	4MT[1]	27A Polmadie	66A Polmadie	66A Polmadie	64C Dalry Road	66A Polmadie	66B Motherwell	
42696	4MT[1]	27A Polmadie	66A Polmadie	66A Polmadie	66B Motherwell	66B Motherwell	26A Newton Heath	
42697	4MT[1]	27B Greenock Ladyburn	66D Greenock Ladyburn	66D Greenock Ladyburn	67D Ardrossan	67D Ardrossan	26A Newton Heath	12C Barrow
42698	4MT[1]	27A Polmadie	66A Polmadie	66D Greenock Ladyburn	66D Greenock Ladyburn	66D Greenock Ladyburn	26A Newton Heath	
42699	4MT[1]	27A Polmadie	66A Polmadie	66A Polmadie	66B Motherwell	66B Motherwell	67E Dumfries	55H Leeds Neville Hill
42700	5MT[1]	26A Newton Heath	25D Mirfield	25G Farnley Junction	26D Bury	26D Bury	26D Bury	8H Birkenhead
42701	5MT[1]	26A Newton Heath	26A Newton Heath	26A Newton Heath	26A Newton Heath	26A Newton Heath	26A Newton Heath	
42702	5MT[1]	26A Newton Heath	26A Newton Heath	26A Newton Heath	55C Farnley Junction	55F Manningham	55E Normanton	67C Ayr
42703	5MT[1]	26A Newton Heath	26A Newton Heath	26A Newton Heath	26A Newton Heath	26A Newton Heath	24B Rose Grove	
42704	5MT[1]	26A Newton Heath	26A Newton Heath	26A Newton Heath	26A Newton Heath	26A Newton Heath	26C Bolton	
42705	5MT[1]	26A Newton Heath	26A Newton Heath	26A Newton Heath	26A Newton Heath	26A Newton Heath	26C Bolton	
42706	5MT[1]	26A Newton Heath	24B Rose Grove	24B Rose Grove	24B Rose Grove	24B Rose Grove	24B Rose Grove	
42707	5MT[1]	26A Newton Heath	26A Newton Heath	26A Newton Heath	26A Newton Heath	26A Newton Heath	21A Saltley	
42708	5MT[1]	26A Newton Heath	26A Newton Heath	26A Newton Heath	26A Newton Heath	26A Newton Heath	26C Bolton	
42709	5MT[1]	26A Newton Heath	26A Newton Heath	26A Newton Heath	26A Newton Heath	26A Newton Heath	26A Newton Heath	
42710	5MT[1]	26A Newton Heath	26A Newton Heath	26A Newton Heath	26A Newton Heath	26A Newton Heath	26A Newton Heath	
42711	5MT[1]	26A Newton Heath	26A Newton Heath	26A Newton Heath	26A Newton Heath	27B Aintree	27D Wigan	
42712	5MT[1]	24F Fleetwood	25D Mirfield	25G Farnley Junction	26D Bury	26D Bury	26D Bury	9B Stockport Edgeley
42713	5MT[1]	26A Newton Heath	26A Newton Heath	26A Newton Heath	55C Farnley Junction	55C Farnley Junction		
42714	5MT[1]	26A Newton Heath	26A Newton Heath	26A Newton Heath	26A Newton Heath	26A Newton Heath		
42715	5MT[1]	26B Agecroft	26A Newton Heath	26A Newton Heath	26A Newton Heath	26A Newton Heath	27D Wigan	9B Stockport Edgeley
42716	5MT[1]	26B Agecroft	24A Accrington	24B Rose Grove	24B Rose Grove	24B Rose Grove	24B Rose Grove	
42717	5MT[1]	26B Agecroft	24A Accrington	64A St. Margarets	24B Rose Grove	24B Rose Grove	24B Rose Grove	
42718	5MT[1]	26B Agecroft	24A Accrington	24D Lower Darwen	24D Lower Darwen	24D Lower Darwen	26B Agecroft	
42719	5MT[1]	26B Agecroft	25D Mirfield	25G Farnley Junction	26D Bury	26D Bury	26D Bury	
42720	5MT[1]	26B Agecroft	68A Carlisle Kingmoor	68A Carlisle Kingmoor	68A Carlisle Kingmoor	12A Carlisle Kingmoor		
42721	5MT[1]	26B Agecroft	26B Agecroft	26B Agecroft	26B Agecroft	27B Aintree	27D Wigan	
42722	5MT[1]	26B Agecroft	26B Agecroft	26B Agecroft	26B Agecroft	24D Lower Darwen	24F Fleetwood	
42723	5MT[1]	26B Agecroft	26B Agecroft	26B Agecroft	26B Agecroft	26B Agecroft	26B Agecroft	
42724	5MT[1]	26B Agecroft	26B Agecroft	26B Agecroft	26B Agecroft	26B Agecroft		
42725	5MT[1]	26B Agecroft	26B Agecroft	26B Agecroft	26B Agecroft	26B Agecroft	26C Bolton	
42726	5MT[1]	25F Low Moor	27B Aintree	27B Aintree	26A Newton Heath	26A Newton Heath		
42727	5MT[1]	25F Low Moor	27B Aintree	27B Aintree	26A Newton Heath	27B Aintree	27B Aintree	9B Stockport Edgeley
42728	5MT[1]	25F Low Moor	27B Aintree	27B Aintree	26A Newton Heath	26A Newton Heath	24D Lower Darwen	
42729	5MT[1]	25G Farnley Junction	24A Accrington	24D Lower Darwen	24D Lower Darwen	24D Lower Darwen	24D Lower Darwen	
42730	5MT[1]	25G Farnley Junction	26B Agecroft	26B Agecroft	26B Agecroft	26D Bury	27B Aintree	
42731	5MT[1]	25G Farnley Junction	25D Mirfield	25G Farnley Junction	26D Bury	26D Bury	27D Wigan	
42732	5MT[1]	25F Low Moor	25F Low Moor	27B Aintree	26A Newton Heath	24F Fleetwood	24D Lower Darwen	
42733	5MT[1]	25B Huddersfield	24B Rose Grove	62B Dundee Tay Bridge	26A Newton Heath	26A Newton Heath	26A Newton Heath	
42734	5MT[1]	26B Agecroft	26B Agecroft	26B Agecroft	26B Agecroft	26B Agecroft	27D Wigan	8H Birkenhead
42735	5MT[1]	27C Hamilton	66C Hamilton	66C Hamilton	66C Hamilton	66C Hamilton	67B Hurlford	
42736	5MT[1]	31D Grangemouth	65F Grangemouth	65F Grangemouth	65F Grangemouth	65F Grangemouth	67C Ayr	67B Hurlford
42737	5MT[1]	31D Grangemouth	65F Grangemouth	65F Grangemouth	65F Grangemouth	65F Grangemouth	67C Ayr	67C Ayr
42738	5MT[1]	29D Forfar	63C Forfar	63C Forfar	63C Forfar	66A Polmadie	67F Stranraer	
42739	5MT[1]	30D Ayr	67C Ayr	67C Ayr	67C Ayr	67B Hurlford	67B Hurlford	67B Hurlford
42740	5MT[1]	27C Hamilton	66C Hamilton	66C Hamilton	66C Hamilton	66D Greenock Ladyburn	67D Ardrossan	67C Ayr
42741	5MT[1]	27C Hamilton	66C Hamilton	66C Hamilton	66C Hamilton	66D Greenock Ladyburn	67B Hurlford	
42742	5MT[1]	12A Carlisle Kingmoor	63A Perth	67D Ardrossan	67D Ardrossan	67D Ardrossan		
42743	5MT[1]	12A Carlisle Kingmoor	63A Perth	67B Hurlford	67B Hurlford	67B Hurlford		
42744	5MT[1]	12A Carlisle Kingmoor	67B Hurlford	67B Hurlford	67B Hurlford	67B Hurlford		
42745	5MT[1]	12A Carlisle Kingmoor	67B Hurlford	67B Hurlford	67C Ayr	67C Ayr		
42746	5MT[1]	12A Carlisle Kingmoor	65B St. Rollox	65B St. Rollox	65B St. Rollox	66C Hamilton	67B Hurlford	
42747	5MT[1]	1A Willesden	1A Willesden	1A Willesden	5B Crewe South	1A Willesden	6C Birkenhead	
42748	5MT[1]	12A Carlisle Kingmoor	68A Carlisle Kingmoor	68A Carlisle Kingmoor	68A Carlisle Kingmoor	9G Gorton	9G Gorton	
42749	5MT[1]	12A Carlisle Kingmoor	68A Carlisle Kingmoor	68C Stranraer	68C Stranraer	68C Stranraer		
42750	5MT[1]	26B Agecroft	26A Newton Heath	26A Newton Heath	26A Newton Heath	26A Newton Heath	26A Newton Heath	
42751	5MT[1]	12A Carlisle Kingmoor	68A Carlisle Kingmoor	68A Carlisle Kingmoor	68A Carlisle Kingmoor	12A Carlisle Kingmoor	8F Wigan Springs Branch	
42752	5MT[1]	12A Carlisle Kingmoor	68A Carlisle Kingmoor	68A Carlisle Kingmoor	68A Carlisle Kingmoor	12A Carlisle Kingmoor		
42753	5MT[1]	26B Agecroft	26B Agecroft	26B Agecroft	26B Agecroft	26B Agecroft	26B Agecroft	
42754	5MT[1]	21A Saltley	21A Saltley	17B Burton	21A Saltley	9G Gorton	9G Gorton	
42755	5MT[1]	26B Agecroft	26B Agecroft	26B Agecroft	26B Agecroft	26B Agecroft	26B Agecroft	
42756	5MT[1]	17D Rowsley	17B Burton	17B Burton	17B Burton	17B Burton	16A Nottingham	
42757	5MT[1]	17B Burton	68A Carlisle Kingmoor	68A Carlisle Kingmoor	68A Carlisle Kingmoor	12A Carlisle Kingmoor	9G Gorton	
42758	5MT[1]	21A Saltley	21A Saltley	21A Saltley	21A Saltley	21A Saltley	9G Gorton	
42759	5MT[1]	20B Stourton	14A Cricklewood	14A Cricklewood	14A Cricklewood	17B Burton	9G Gorton	
42760	5MT[1]	17D Rowsley	17D Rowsley	17D Rowsley	17D Rowsley	9G Gorton	9G Gorton	
42761	5MT[1]	19A Sheffield Grimesthorpe	17B Burton	17B Burton	21A Saltley	21A Saltley	9G Gorton	
42762	5MT[1]	20E Manningham	20E Manningham	20E Manningham	55F Manningham	55F Manningham	55D Royston	
42763	5MT[1]	17B Burton	17B Burton	17B Burton	17B Burton	17B Burton	16A Nottingham	
42764	5MT[1]	21A Saltley	21A Saltley	21A Saltley	21A Saltley	21A Saltley		
42765	5MT[1]	19E Belle Vue	24B Rose Grove	24F Fleetwood	24F Fleetwood	24F Fleetwood	24F Fleetwood	8H Birkenhead
42766	5MT[1]	26A Newton Heath	26A Newton Heath	26A Newton Heath	55C Farnley Junction	55C Farnley Junction		
42767	5MT[1]	17B Burton	17B Burton	17B Burton	17B Burton	9G Gorton	9G Gorton	
42768	5MT[1]	17B Burton	17D Rowsley	17D Rowsley	17D Rowsley	9G Gorton	9G Gorton	
42769	5MT[1]	19A Sheffield Grimesthorpe	19A Sheffield Grimesthorpe	16A Nottingham	16A Nottingham	16D Annesley	9G Gorton	
42770	5MT[1]	20G Hellifield	23B Hellifield	20G Hellifield	55F Manningham	55F Manningham	55D Royston	
42771	5MT[1]	20B Stourton	14A Cricklewood	14A Cricklewood	55A Leeds Holbeck	55A Leeds Holbeck	55A Leeds Holbeck	
42772	5MT[1]	9B Stockport Edgeley	9A Longsight	9A Longsight	9A Longsight	9A Longsight	9D Buxton	
42773	5MT[1]	9B Stockport Edgeley	5B Crewe South	9B Stockport Edgeley	9B Stockport Edgeley	9B Stockport Edgeley		
42774	5MT[1]	17D Rowsley	14A Cricklewood	14A Cricklewood	55A Leeds Holbeck	55C Farnley Junction	55F Manningham	
42775	5MT[1]	9A Longsight	9A Longsight	9F Heaton Mersey	17E Heaton Mersey	9G Gorton		

No.	Class	1948	1951	1954	1957	1960	1963	1966
42776	5MT[1]	9A Longsight	9A Longsight	9A Longsight	5B Crewe South	5A Crewe North	24J Lancaster	
42777	5MT[1]	2D Nuneaton	2B Nuneaton	5B Crewe South	5B Crewe South	2A Rugby	8F Wigan Springs Branch	
42778	5MT[1]	9A Longsight	9A Longsight	9A Longsight	6C Birkenhead	6C Birkenhead	24J Lancaster	
42779	5MT[1]	3A Bescot	3A Bescot	3A Bescot	3A Bescot	9B Stockport Edgeley		
42780	5MT[1]	12A Carlisle Kingmoor	68A Carlisle Kingmoor	68A Carlisle Kingmoor	65F Grangemouth	65F Grangemouth	67C Ayr	
42781	5MT[1]	2D Nuneaton	2B Nuneaton	2B Nuneaton	2B Nuneaton	2B Nuneaton		
42782	5MT[1]	3D Aston	3D Aston	3D Aston	3D Aston	2A Rugby	5D Stoke	8H Birkenhead
42783	5MT[1]	2D Nuneaton	2B Nuneaton	2B Nuneaton	2B Nuneaton	2B Nuneaton	6C Birkenhead	
42784	5MT[1]	21A Saltley	23B Hellifield	20G Hellifield	16A Nottingham	16D Annesley		
42785	5MT[1]	5B Crewe South	5B Crewe South	5B Crewe South	5B Crewe South	1A Willesden	6C Birkenhead	
42786	5MT[1]	1A Willesden	8C Speke Junction	8C Speke Junction	8C Speke Junction	9A Longsight		
42787	5MT[1]	1A Willesden	1A Willesden	1A Willesden	1A Willesden	2A Rugby	5D Stoke	
42788	5MT[1]	8C Speke Junction	9A Longsight	9F Heaton Mersey	17E Heaton Mersey	9G Gorton	9G Gorton	
42789	5MT[1]	26A Newton Heath	26A Newton Heath	26A Newton Heath	55C Farnley Junction	55C Farnley Junction	55F Manningham	67C Ayr
42790	5MT[1]	21A Saltley	21A Saltley	21A Saltley	21A Saltley	21A Saltley	21A Saltley	
42791	5MT[1]	20E Manningham	14B Kentish Town	17B Burton	21A Saltley	21A Saltley	9G Gorton	
42792	5MT[1]	15C Leicester Midland	15C Leicester Midland	17D Rowsley	17D Rowsley	9G Gorton	9G Gorton	
42793	5MT[1]	21A Saltley	68A Carlisle Kingmoor	68A Carlisle Kingmoor	68A Carlisle Kingmoor	12A Carlisle Kingmoor	9G Gorton	
42794	5MT[1]	14A Cricklewood	14A Cricklewood	14A Cricklewood	19A Sheffield Grimesthorpe	41B Sheffield Grimesthorpe	27D Wigan	
42795	5MT[1]	20B Stourton	20A Leeds Holbeck	20A Leeds Holbeck	55A Leeds Holbeck	55C Farnley Junction	55D Royston	67B Hurlford
42796	5MT[1]	26B Agecroft	24A Accrington	24D Lower Darwen	24D Lower Darwen	24D Lower Darwen	24D Lower Darwen	
42797	5MT[1]	19A Sheffield Grimesthorpe	19A Sheffield Grimesthorpe	14A Cricklewood	19A Sheffield Grimesthorpe	41B Sheffield Grimesthorpe		
42798	5MT[1]	20B Stourton	20A Leeds Holbeck	20A Leeds Holbeck	55A Leeds Holbeck	55A Leeds Holbeck	55A Leeds Holbeck	
42799	5MT[1]	21A Saltley	17B Burton	17B Burton	17B Burton	17B Burton	16A Nottingham	
42800	5MT[1]	29D Forfar	63C Forfar	63C Forfar	63C Forfar	67C Ayr	67C Ayr	
42801	5MT[1]	29D Forfar	63C Forfar	63C Forfar	63C Forfar	67C Ayr	67C Ayr	67C Ayr
42802	5MT[1]	12A Carlisle Kingmoor	68A Carlisle Kingmoor	68A Carlisle Kingmoor	65F Grangemouth	65F Grangemouth	67B Hurlford	
42803	5MT[1]	12A Carlisle Kingmoor	68A Carlisle Kingmoor	68A Carlisle Kingmoor	65F Grangemouth	65F Grangemouth	67C Ayr	67C Ayr
42804	5MT[1]	28B Dalry Road	64C Dalry Road	64C Dalry Road	68A Carlisle Kingmoor	12A Carlisle Kingmoor		
42805	5MT[1]	30D Ayr	67C Ayr	67C Ayr	67C Ayr	67C Ayr	67C Ayr	
42806	5MT[1]	30D Ayr	67C Ayr	67A Corkerhill	67D Ardrossan	67D Ardrossan	67D Ardrossan	
42807	5MT[1]	28B Dalry Road	64C Dalry Road	64C Dalry Road	64C Dalry Road	64C Dalry Road		
42808	5MT[1]	30D Ayr	67C Ayr	67C Ayr	67C Ayr	67C Ayr		
42809	5MT[1]	30D Ayr	67C Ayr	67C Ayr	67C Ayr	67C Ayr		
42810	5MT[1]	8C Speke Junction	5B Crewe South	2B Nuneaton	11E Lancaster	24J Lancaster	6C Birkenhead	
42811	5MT[1]	3D Aston	5B Crewe South	5B Crewe South	5B Crewe South	2B Nuneaton		
42812	5MT[1]	1A Willesden	1A Willesden	1A Willesden	1A Willesden	1A Willesden	24J Lancaster	8H Birkenhead
42813	5MT[1]	9A Longsight	2B Nuneaton	5B Crewe South	5B Crewe South	9G Gorton	9G Gorton	
42814	5MT[1]	2D Nuneaton	2B Nuneaton	2B Nuneaton	2B Nuneaton	2B Nuneaton	6C Birkenhead	
42815	5MT[1]	8C Speke Junction	5B Crewe South	5B Crewe South	5B Crewe South	5A Crewe North	8A Edge Hill	
42816	5MT[1]	20B Stourton	20A Leeds Holbeck	20A Leeds Holbeck	21A Saltley	9G Gorton	9G Gorton	
42817	5MT[1]	1A Willesden	1A Willesden	2B Nuneaton	2B Nuneaton	3D Aston	9B Stockport Edgeley	
42818	5MT[1]	21A Saltley	21A Saltley	21A Saltley	17B Burton	17B Burton		
42819	5MT[1]	26B Agecroft	26B Agecroft	26B Agecroft	26B Agecroft	26B Agecroft	26B Agecroft	
42820	5MT[1]	26A Newton Heath	26A Newton Heath	26A Newton Heath	26D Bury	26D Bury	26D Bury	
42821	5MT[1]	25G Farnley Junction	24B Rose Grove	24D Lower Darwen	24D Lower Darwen	24D Lower Darwen	27D Wigan	
42822	5MT[1]	21A Saltley	21A Saltley	21A Saltley	17B Burton	17B Burton		
42823	5MT[1]	16A Nottingham	16A Nottingham	16A Nottingham	21A Saltley	21A Saltley	21A Saltley	
42824	5MT[1]	21A Saltley	21A Saltley	21A Saltley	17B Burton	17B Burton		
42825	5MT[1]	21A Saltley	21A Saltley	21A Saltley	17B Burton	17B Burton		
42826	5MT[1]	21A Saltley	21A Saltley	17B Burton	17B Burton	17B Burton	16A Nottingham	
42827	5MT[1]	21A Saltley	21A Saltley	21A Saltley	21A Saltley	21A Saltley	21A Saltley	
42828	5MT[1]	25F Low Moor	24B Rose Grove	24B Rose Grove	24B Rose Grove	24B Rose Grove	6C Birkenhead	
42829	5MT[1]	21A Saltley	21A Saltley	21A Saltley	17B Burton	17B Burton		
42830	5MT[1]	12A Carlisle Kingmoor	64C Dalry Road	64C Dalry Road	68A Carlisle Kingmoor	12A Carlisle Kingmoor		
42831	5MT[1]	12A Carlisle Kingmoor	68A Carlisle Kingmoor	68A Carlisle Kingmoor	68A Carlisle Kingmoor	12A Carlisle Kingmoor	9G Gorton	
42832	5MT[1]	12A Carlisle Kingmoor	68A Carlisle Kingmoor	68A Carlisle Kingmoor	68A Carlisle Kingmoor	12A Carlisle Kingmoor	12A Carlisle Kingmoor	
42833	5MT[1]	12A Carlisle Kingmoor	68A Carlisle Kingmoor	68A Carlisle Kingmoor	68A Carlisle Kingmoor	12A Carlisle Kingmoor		
42834	5MT[1]	12A Carlisle Kingmoor	68A Carlisle Kingmoor	68A Carlisle Kingmoor	68A Carlisle Kingmoor	12A Carlisle Kingmoor		
42835	5MT[1]	12A Carlisle Kingmoor	68A Carlisle Kingmoor	68A Carlisle Kingmoor	68A Carlisle Kingmoor	12A Carlisle Kingmoor		
42836	5MT[1]	12A Carlisle Kingmoor	68A Carlisle Kingmoor	68A Carlisle Kingmoor	68A Carlisle Kingmoor	12A Carlisle Kingmoor		
42837	5MT[1]	12A Carlisle Kingmoor	68A Carlisle Kingmoor	68A Carlisle Kingmoor	68A Carlisle Kingmoor	12A Carlisle Kingmoor		
42838	5MT[1]	26B Agecroft	26B Agecroft	26B Agecroft	26B Agecroft	26B Agecroft	26B Agecroft	
42839	5MT[1]	14B Kentish Town	14A Cricklewood	14A Cricklewood	14A Cricklewood	17B Burton	16A Nottingham	
42840	5MT[1]	24F Fleetwood	28B Fleetwood	24F Fleetwood	24F Fleetwood	24F Fleetwood	24F Fleetwood	
42841	5MT[1]	24F Fleetwood	28B Fleetwood	24F Fleetwood	24F Fleetwood	24F Fleetwood	24F Fleetwood	
42842	5MT[1]	24F Fleetwood	28B Fleetwood	24F Fleetwood	24F Fleetwood	24F Fleetwood	24F Fleetwood	
42843	5MT[1]	25F Low Moor	24A Accrington	24F Fleetwood	24F Fleetwood	24F Fleetwood	24F Fleetwood	
42844	5MT[1]	25G Farnley Junction	28B Fleetwood	24F Fleetwood	24F Fleetwood	24F Fleetwood	24F Fleetwood	
42845	5MT[1]	17D Rowsley	26A Newton Heath	25B Huddersfield	26B Agecroft	27B Aintree	27B Aintree	
42846	5MT[1]	17B Burton	17B Burton	17B Burton	21A Saltley	21A Saltley	9G Gorton	
42847	5MT[1]	17A Derby	17A Derby	17A Derby	17A Derby	16D Annesley		
42848	5MT[1]	9A Longsight	9A Longsight	9A Longsight	9A Longsight	9B Stockport Edgeley	8A Edge Hill	
42849	5MT[1]	9A Longsight	8C Speke Junction	8C Speke Junction	8C Speke Junction	8C Speke Junction	9B Stockport Edgeley	
42850	5MT[1]	21A Saltley	66C Hamilton	66C Hamilton	66C Hamilton	66A Polmadie		
42851	5MT[1]	3A Bescot	3A Bescot	5B Crewe South	11E Lancaster	24J Lancaster	8A Edge Hill	
42852	5MT[1]	9A Longsight	8C Speke Junction	2B Nuneaton	1A Willesden	1A Willesden	6C Birkenhead	
42853	5MT[1]	3A Bescot	3A Bescot	3A Bescot	3A Bescot	2B Nuneaton	6C Birkenhead	
42854	5MT[1]	9A Longsight	9A Longsight	2B Nuneaton	2B Nuneaton	9B Stockport Edgeley	6C Birkenhead	
42855	5MT[1]	14A Cricklewood	14A Cricklewood	14A Cricklewood	14A Cricklewood	17B Burton	16A Nottingham	
42856	5MT[1]	5B Crewe South	5B Crewe South	5B Crewe South	5B Crewe South	6C Birkenhead	5D Stoke	
42857	5MT[1]	21A Saltley	21A Saltley	21A Saltley	21A Saltley	21A Saltley		
42858	5MT[1]	9A Longsight	9A Longsight	9A Longsight	9A Longsight	9A Longsight	5D Stoke	
42859	5MT[1]	9B Stockport Edgeley	9B Stockport Edgeley	9B Stockport Edgeley	9B Stockport Edgeley	1A Willesden	6C Birkenhead	8H Birkenhead
42860	5MT[1]	26B Agecroft	26B Agecroft	26B Agecroft	26B Agecroft	26B Agecroft	26B Agecroft	
42861	5MT[1]	25B Huddersfield	25B Huddersfield	25B Huddersfield	56A Wakefield	56A Wakefield	56A Wakefield	67C Ayr
42862	5MT[1]	25B Huddersfield	25B Huddersfield	25B Huddersfield	56A Wakefield	56A Wakefield		
42863	5MT[1]	25B Huddersfield	25B Huddersfield	25B Huddersfield	56A Wakefield	56A Wakefield	56A Wakefield	67C Ayr
42864	5MT[1]	26B Agecroft	26B Agecroft	26B Agecroft	26B Agecroft	27B Aintree		
42865	5MT[1]	25F Low Moor	25D Mirfield	64A St. Margarets	55C Farnley Junction	55C Farnley Junction	55E Normanton	
42866	5MT[1]	25B Huddersfield	25B Huddersfield	62B Dundee Tay Bridge	55C Farnley Junction	55C Farnley Junction		
42867	5MT[1]	24F Fleetwood	28B Fleetwood	24F Fleetwood	24F Fleetwood	24F Fleetwood	9G Gorton	
42868	5MT[1]	26B Agecroft	26B Agecroft	26B Agecroft	26B Agecroft	26B Agecroft		
42869	5MT[1]	25B Huddersfield	25B Huddersfield	24B Rose Grove	24B Rose Grove	24B Rose Grove	24B Rose Grove	
42870	5MT[1]	1A Willesden	1A Willesden	1A Willesden	1A Willesden	1A Willesden	6C Birkenhead	
42871	5MT[1]	26A Newton Heath	26A Newton Heath	26A Newton Heath	26A Newton Heath	26A Newton Heath	26A Newton Heath	
42872	5MT[1]	17A Derby	17A Derby	17A Derby	17A Derby	16D Annesley	16A Nottingham	
42873	5MT[1]	17D Rowsley	17D Rowsley	17D Rowsley	17D Rowsley	9G Gorton	9G Gorton	
42874	5MT[1]	17D Rowsley	17D Rowsley	17D Rowsley	17D Rowsley	9G Gorton		
42875	5MT[1]	12A Carlisle Kingmoor	68A Carlisle Kingmoor	68A Carlisle Kingmoor	68A Carlisle Kingmoor	12A Carlisle Kingmoor		
42876	5MT[1]	12A Carlisle Kingmoor	68A Carlisle Kingmoor	68A Carlisle Kingmoor	68A Carlisle Kingmoor	12A Carlisle Kingmoor		
42877	5MT[1]	12A Carlisle Kingmoor	68A Carlisle Kingmoor	68A Carlisle Kingmoor	68A Carlisle Kingmoor	12A Carlisle Kingmoor		
42878	5MT[1]	12A Carlisle Kingmoor	26A Newton Heath	26A Newton Heath	26A Newton Heath	27B Aintree	27B Aintree	
42879	5MT[1]	30D Ayr	67C Ayr	67C Ayr	67C Ayr	67C Ayr	67B Hurlford	
42880	5MT[1]	12A Carlisle Kingmoor	66C Hamilton	66C Hamilton	66C Hamilton	66C Hamilton	67B Hurlford	
42881	5MT[1]	12A Carlisle Kingmoor	68A Carlisle Kingmoor	68A Carlisle Kingmoor	68A Carlisle Kingmoor	12A Carlisle Kingmoor		
42882	5MT[1]	12A Carlisle Kingmoor	68A Carlisle Kingmoor	68A Carlisle Kingmoor	68A Carlisle Kingmoor	12A Carlisle Kingmoor		
42883	5MT[1]	12A Carlisle Kingmoor	68A Carlisle Kingmoor	68A Carlisle Kingmoor	68A Carlisle Kingmoor	12A Carlisle Kingmoor		
42884	5MT[1]	12A Carlisle Kingmoor	68A Carlisle Kingmoor	68A Carlisle Kingmoor	68A Carlisle Kingmoor	12A Carlisle Kingmoor		
42885	5MT[1]	1A Willesden	1A Willesden	1A Willesden	1A Willesden	1A Willesden	6C Birkenhead	
42886	5MT[1]	9A Longsight	9A Longsight	9A Longsight	9A Longsight	9B Stockport Edgeley	8A Edge Hill	
42887	5MT[1]	9A Longsight	9A Longsight	9A Longsight	9A Longsight	9A Longsight		
42888	5MT[1]	2D Nuneaton	2B Nuneaton	2B Nuneaton	11E Lancaster	6C Birkenhead	5D Stoke	
42889	5MT[1]	9A Longsight	9A Longsight	9A Longsight	9A Longsight	9A Longsight		

		1948	1951	1954	1957	1960	1963	1966
42890	5MT[1]	21A Saltley	21A Saltley	17B Burton	21A Saltley	21A Saltley	9G Gorton	
42891	5MT[1]	3D Aston	3A Bescot	2B Nuneaton	2B Nuneaton	2B Nuneaton		
42892	5MT[1]	3D Aston	8C Speke Junction	8C Speke Junction	8C Speke Junction	8C Speke Junction	6C Birkenhead	
42893	5MT[1]	20G Hellifield	23C Lancaster	11E Lancaster	11E Lancaster	24J Lancaster		
42894	5MT[1]	3D Aston	3A Bescot	5B Crewe South	5B Crewe South	6C Birkenhead	8F Wigan Springs Branch	
42895	5MT[1]	20H Lancaster	23C Lancaster	11E Lancaster	11E Lancaster	24J Lancaster	24J Lancaster	
42896	5MT[1]	19E Belle Vue	17B Burton	17B Burton	17B Burton	17B Burton	16A Nottingham	
42897	5MT[1]	17A Derby	17A Derby	17A Derby	17A Derby	16D Annesley	16A Nottingham	
42898	5MT[1]	17B Burton	24B Rose Grove	24B Rose Grove	24B Rose Grove	24B Rose Grove	24B Rose Grove	
42899	5MT[1]	16A Nottingham	68A Carlisle Kingmoor	68A Carlisle Kingmoor	68A Carlisle Kingmoor	12A Carlisle Kingmoor		
42900	5MT[1]	21A Saltley	21A Saltley	21A Saltley	21A Saltley	21A Saltley	21A Saltley	
42901	5MT[1]	26A Newton Heath	26A Newton Heath	64A St. Margarets	26A Newton Heath	26A Newton Heath	26B Agecroft	
42902	5MT[1]	17D Rowsley	17D Rowsley	17D Rowsley	17D Rowsley	9G Gorton	9G Gorton	
42903	5MT[1]	21A Saltley	21A Saltley	21A Saltley	21A Saltley	21A Saltley		
42904	5MT[1]	19A Sheffield Grimesthorpe	19A Sheffield Grimesthorpe	19A Sheffield Grimesthorpe	19A Sheffield Grimesthorpe	41B Sheffield Grimesthorpe	9B Stockport Edgeley	
42905	5MT[1]	12A Carlisle Kingmoor	68A Carlisle Kingmoor	68A Carlisle Kingmoor	68A Carlisle Kingmoor	12A Carlisle Kingmoor	12A Carlisle Kingmoor	
42906	5MT[1]	12A Carlisle Kingmoor	68A Carlisle Kingmoor	68A Carlisle Kingmoor	68A Carlisle Kingmoor	12A Carlisle Kingmoor		
42907	5MT[1]	12A Carlisle Kingmoor	68A Carlisle Kingmoor	68A Carlisle Kingmoor	68A Carlisle Kingmoor	12A Carlisle Kingmoor	12A Carlisle Kingmoor	
42908	5MT[1]	12G Dumfries	68B Dumfries	68B Dumfries	68B Dumfries	68B Dumfries	67E Dumfries	67C Ayr
42909	5MT[1]	12G Dumfries	68B Dumfries	68B Dumfries	68B Dumfries	68B Dumfries	67E Dumfries	67C Ayr
42910	5MT[1]	30A Corkerhill	67B Hurlford	67B Hurlford	67C Ayr	67C Ayr	67C Ayr	
42911	5MT[1]	30A Corkerhill	67A Corkerhill	67D Ardrossan	67D Ardrossan	67D Ardrossan	67D Ardrossan	
42912	5MT[1]	30A Corkerhill	67B Hurlford	67B Hurlford	67D Ardrossan	67C Ayr	67C Ayr	
42913	5MT[1]	30A Corkerhill	68A Carlisle Kingmoor	68A Carlisle Kingmoor	68A Carlisle Kingmoor	12A Carlisle Kingmoor	67E Dumfries	67C Ayr
42914	5MT[1]	30A Corkerhill	67A Corkerhill	67A Corkerhill	67C Ayr	67C Ayr	67E Dumfries	
42915	5MT[1]	30A Corkerhill	68B Dumfries	68B Dumfries	68B Dumfries	68B Dumfries		
42916	5MT[1]	30A Corkerhill	67A Corkerhill	67A Corkerhill	67C Ayr	67C Ayr	67C Ayr	
42917	5MT[1]	30A Corkerhill	67A Corkerhill	67A Corkerhill	67C Ayr	67C Ayr	67C Ayr	67C Ayr
42918	5MT[1]	12G Dumfries	68B Dumfries	68B Dumfries	68B Dumfries	68B Dumfries		
42919	5MT[1]	12G Dumfries	68B Dumfries	68B Dumfries	68B Dumfries	68B Dumfries	67E Dumfries	67C Ayr
42920	5MT[1]	5B Crewe South	5B Crewe South	5B Crewe South	5B Crewe South	3D Aston	8A Edge Hill	
42921	5MT[1]	3D Aston	3D Aston	3D Aston	3D Aston	3D Aston	9B Stockport Edgeley	
42922	5MT[1]	22B Gloucester Barnwood	17B Burton	17B Burton	17B Burton	17B Burton	16A Nottingham	
42923	5MT[1]	9A Longsight	9A Longsight	9A Longsight	9A Longsight	9A Longsight	6C Birkenhead	
42924	5MT[1]	9A Longsight	9A Longsight	9A Longsight	9A Longsight	9A Longsight	8A Edge Hill	8H Birkenhead
42925	5MT[1]	9A Longsight	9A Longsight	9A Longsight	9A Longsight	9A Longsight	8A Edge Hill	
42926	5MT[1]	8C Speke Junction	5B Crewe South	5B Crewe South	5B Crewe South	2B Nuneaton	9D Buxton	
42927	5MT[1]	30D Ayr	67C Ayr	67C Ayr	67C Ayr	67C Ayr		
42928	5MT[1]	20H Lancaster	23C Lancaster	11E Lancaster	11E Lancaster	24J Lancaster	24J Lancaster	
42929	5MT[1]	3D Aston	3A Bescot	3A Bescot	3A Bescot	3D Aston		
42930	5MT[1]	9A Longsight	9A Longsight	9A Longsight	9A Longsight	9A Longsight		
42931	5MT[1]	1A Willesden	1A Willesden	1A Willesden	1A Willesden	1A Willesden	24J Lancaster	
42932	5MT[1]	2D Nuneaton	2B Nuneaton	9A Longsight	5B Crewe South	9B Stockport Edgeley	9B Stockport Edgeley	
42933	5MT[1]	8C Speke Junction	2B Nuneaton	5B Crewe South	5B Crewe South	2B Nuneaton	6A Chester	
42934	5MT[1]	8C Speke Junction	9B Stockport Edgeley	9B Stockport Edgeley	9B Stockport Edgeley	9A Longsight	6A Chester	
42935	5MT[1]	9A Longsight	9A Longsight	9A Longsight	9A Longsight	2B Nuneaton	6C Birkenhead	
42936	5MT[1]	9A Longsight	9A Longsight	9A Longsight	9A Longsight	9A Longsight	6C Birkenhead	
42937	5MT[1]	9A Longsight	9A Longsight	9A Longsight	1A Willesden	9B Stockport Edgeley	5D Stoke	
42938	5MT[1]	9B Stockport Edgeley	9A Longsight	9A Longsight	9A Longsight	9A Longsight	24J Lancaster	
42939	5MT[1]	5B Crewe South	5B Crewe South	5B Crewe South	5B Crewe South	2B Nuneaton		
42940	5MT[1]	1A Willesden	1A Willesden	6B Mold Junction	5B Crewe South	5A Crewe North	9D Buxton	
42941	5MT[1]	2D Nuneaton	2B Nuneaton	6B Mold Junction	6C Birkenhead	6C Birkenhead	9B Stockport Edgeley	
42942	5MT[1]	9D Buxton	9D Buxton	9D Buxton	9D Buxton	9D Buxton	9B Stockport Edgeley	9B Stockport Edgeley
42943	5MT[1]	9D Buxton	9D Buxton	9D Buxton	9D Buxton	9D Buxton	6C Birkenhead	
42944	5MT[1]	5B Crewe South	2B Nuneaton	2B Nuneaton	5B Crewe South	1A Willesden	6C Birkenhead	
42945	5MT[2]	6B Mold Junction	6B Mold Junction	6B Mold Junction	6B Mold Junction	6B Mold Junction	2B Nuneaton	9F Heaton Mersey
42946	5MT[2]	8C Speke Junction	3D Aston	3D Aston	3D Aston	5B Crewe South	2B Nuneaton	
42947	5MT[2]	5B Crewe South	3D Aston	3D Aston	3D Aston	3D Aston	2B Nuneaton	
42948	5MT[2]	7B Bangor	3D Aston	3D Aston	5B Crewe South	5B Crewe South	5D Stoke	
42949	5MT[2]	2B Bletchley	8E Brunswick	8E Brunswick	8E Brunswick	5B Crewe South	5D Stoke	
42950	5MT[2]	5B Crewe South	5B Crewe South	5B Crewe South	5B Crewe South	5B Crewe South	2B Nuneaton	
42951	5MT[2]	7B Bangor	3D Aston	3D Aston	3D Aston	3D Aston	2B Nuneaton	9F Heaton Mersey
42952	5MT[2]	5B Crewe South	5B Crewe South	5B Crewe South	5B Crewe South	5B Crewe South	5D Stoke	
42953	5MT[2]	6C Birkenhead	6C Birkenhead	5B Crewe South	5B Crewe South	5B Crewe South	5D Stoke	8F Wigan Springs Branch
42954	5MT[2]	7A Llandudno Junction	3D Aston	3D Aston	3D Aston	5A Crewe North	2B Nuneaton	8F Wigan Springs Branch
42955	5MT[2]	5B Crewe South	5B Crewe South	5B Crewe South	5A Crewe North	5B Crewe South	2B Nuneaton	9F Heaton Mersey
42956	5MT[2]	5B Crewe South	5B Crewe South	5B Crewe South	5B Crewe South	5B Crewe South	5D Stoke	
42957	5MT[2]	2B Bletchley	3D Aston	3D Aston	3D Aston	3D Aston	21B Bescot	9F Heaton Mersey
42958	5MT[2]	2D Nuneaton	3D Aston	3D Aston	3D Aston	5A Crewe North	2B Nuneaton	
42959	5MT[2]	2D Nuneaton	6B Mold Junction	6B Mold Junction	6B Mold Junction	5B Crewe South	5D Stoke	
42960	5MT[2]	5B Crewe South	2B Nuneaton	9A Longsight	9A Longsight	6B Mold Junction	2B Nuneaton	9F Heaton Mersey
42961	5MT[2]	5B Crewe South	6C Birkenhead	6C Birkenhead	5A Crewe North	5B Crewe South	5D Stoke	
42962	5MT[2]	5B Crewe South	8C Speke Junction	5B Crewe South	5B Crewe South	5B Crewe South	2B Nuneaton	
42963	5MT[2]	3D Aston	3D Aston	3D Aston	5A Crewe North	5A Crewe North	5D Stoke	8F Wigan Springs Branch
42964	5MT[2]	2D Nuneaton	8C Speke Junction	6C Birkenhead	6B Mold Junction	5B Crewe South	2B Nuneaton	
42965	5MT[2]	6B Mold Junction	8C Speke Junction	6B Mold Junction	6B Mold Junction	6B Mold Junction	5D Stoke	
42966	5MT[2]	3D Aston	3D Aston	3D Aston	5B Crewe South	5A Crewe North	21C Bushbury	
42967	5MT[2]	6C Birkenhead	6C Birkenhead	6C Birkenhead	6C Birkenhead	6B Mold Junction	2B Nuneaton	9F Heaton Mersey
42968	5MT[2]	5B Crewe South	5B Crewe South	5B Crewe South	5B Crewe South	5A Crewe North	2B Nuneaton	9F Heaton Mersey
42969	5MT[2]	6C Birkenhead	6C Birkenhead	6C Birkenhead	6C Birkenhead	6C Birkenhead	2B Nuneaton	
42970	5MT[2]	6C Birkenhead	6C Birkenhead	6C Birkenhead	6C Birkenhead	6C Birkenhead	2B Nuneaton	
42971	5MT[2]	7A Llandudno Junction	8C Speke Junction	6B Mold Junction	6B Mold Junction	6B Mold Junction	2B Nuneaton	
42972	5MT[2]	8C Speke Junction	5B Crewe South	5B Crewe South	5B Crewe South	5B Crewe South	5D Stoke	
42973	5MT[2]	2D Nuneaton	6C Birkenhead	6B Mold Junction	6B Mold Junction	6B Mold Junction	2B Nuneaton	
42974	5MT[2]	8C Speke Junction	3D Aston	3D Aston	3D Aston	3D Aston	21B Bescot	
42975	5MT[2]	6B Mold Junction	6B Mold Junction	6B Mold Junction	6B Mold Junction	3D Aston	2B Nuneaton	9F Heaton Mersey
42976	5MT[2]	6B Mold Junction	6B Mold Junction	6B Mold Junction	6B Mold Junction	3A Bescot	2B Nuneaton	
42977	5MT[2]	5B Crewe South	8C Speke Junction	6C Birkenhead	6C Birkenhead	6C Birkenhead	5D Stoke	9F Heaton Mersey
42978	5MT[2]	8C Speke Junction	9A Longsight	6C Birkenhead	6C Birkenhead	6C Birkenhead	2B Nuneaton	9F Heaton Mersey
42979	5MT[2]	6B Mold Junction	9A Longsight	3D Aston	3D Aston	3D Aston	21B Bescot	
42980	5MT[2]	5B Crewe South	5B Crewe South	5B Crewe South	5B Crewe South	5B Crewe South	5D Stoke	9F Heaton Mersey
42981	5MT[2]	2D Nuneaton	6C Birkenhead	6C Birkenhead	6C Birkenhead	6B Mold Junction	2B Nuneaton	9F Heaton Mersey
42982	5MT[2]	5B Crewe South	8C Speke Junction	6B Mold Junction	6B Mold Junction	6B Mold Junction	2B Nuneaton	
42983	5MT[2]	5B Crewe South	5B Crewe South	5B Crewe South	5B Crewe South	5B Crewe South	5B Crewe South	9F Heaton Mersey
42984	5MT[2]	7B Bangor	5B Crewe South	5B Crewe South	5B Crewe South	5B Crewe South	5B Crewe South	
43000	4MT[5]	5B Crewe South	4A Bletchley	1D Devons Road	1D Devons Road	2B Nuneaton	12C Carlisle Canal	12A Carlisle Kingmoor
43001	4MT[5]	5B Crewe South	4A Bletchley	1D Devons Road	1D Devons Road	2B Nuneaton	21B Bescot	5B Crewe South
43002	4MT[5]	5B Crewe South	4A Bletchley	2B Nuneaton	2B Nuneaton	2B Nuneaton	21B Bescot	2F Bescot
43003	4MT[5]	→	4A Bletchley	2B Nuneaton	2B Nuneaton	2B Nuneaton	21B Bescot	5D Stoke
43004	4MT[5]	→	12D Workington	12D Workington	12C Workington	11B Workington	12F Workington	12A Carlisle Kingmoor
43005	4MT[5]	→	4A Bletchley	2B Nuneaton	12C Workington	2B Nuneaton	21B Bescot	
43006	4MT[5]	→	12D Workington	12D Workington	12C Workington	11B Workington	12F Workington	12D Workington
43007	4MT[5]	→	12D Workington	12D Workington	12C Workington	24J Lancaster	1C Watford	5D Stoke
43008	4MT[5]	→	12D Workington	12D Workington	12C Workington	11B Workington	12F Workington	12D Workington
43009	4MT[5]	→	12D Workington	12D Workington	12C Workington	11B Workington	12H Tebay	12E Tebay
43010	4MT[5]	→	17A Derby	17A Derby	21A Saltley	14D Neasden	15A Wellingborough	12D Workington
43011	4MT[5]	→	21A Saltley	2B Nuneaton	2B Nuneaton	11D Tebay	12C Carlisle Canal	12D Workington
43012	4MT[5]	→	22A Bristol Barrow Road	22A Bristol Barrow Road	19A Sheffield Grimesthorpe	21B Bournville	15A Wellingborough	9F Heaton Mersey
43013	4MT[5]	→	71G Bath Green Park	21A Saltley	21A Saltley	21A Saltley	15A Wellingborough	
43014	4MT[5]	→	21A Saltley	20B Stourton	55B Stourton	50A York	50A York	55F Manningham
43015	4MT[5]	→	19A Sheffield Grimesthorpe	53A Hull Dairycoates	51C West Hartlepool	51C West Hartlepool	51C West Hartlepool	51C West Hartlepool
43016	4MT[5]	→	20A Leeds Holbeck	52B Heaton	52B Heaton	55F Manningham	55F Manningham	55F Manningham
43017	4MT[5]	→	71G Bath Green Park	21A Saltley	21A Saltley	21A Saltley	21A Saltley	12D Workington
43018	4MT[5]	→	16A Nottingham	15C Leicester Midland	15C Leicester Midland	24J Lancaster	1C Watford	5D Stoke

		1948	1951	1954	1957	1960	1963	1966
43019	$4MT^{5}$	→	16A Nottingham	14A Cricklewood	14A Cricklewood	14A Cricklewood	15A Wellingborough	10H Lower Darwen
43020	$4MT^{5}$	→	2B Nuneaton	1D Devons Road	1D Devons Road	2B Nuneaton	5B Crewe South	5B Crewe South
43021	$4MT^{5}$	→	2B Nuneaton	1D Devons Road	1D Devons Road	24J Lancaster	1C Watford	5D Stoke
43022	$4MT^{5}$	→	2B Nuneaton	1D Devons Road	1D Devons Road	2B Nuneaton	5B Crewe South	5D Stoke
43023	$4MT^{5}$	→	2B Nuneaton	2B Nuneaton	2B Nuneaton	2B Nuneaton	12A Carlisle Kingmoor	12A Carlisle Kingmoor
43024	$4MT^{5}$	→	2B Nuneaton	1D Devons Road	1D Devons Road	2B Nuneaton	5B Crewe South	5B Crewe South
43025	$4MT^{5}$	→	10E Sutton Oak	10E Sutton Oak	10D Sutton Oak	11B Workington	12F Workington	
43026	$4MT^{5}$	→	10E Sutton Oak	10E Sutton Oak	10D Sutton Oak	2B Nuneaton	5B Crewe South	5B Crewe South
43027	$4MT^{5}$	→	2B Nuneaton	17A Derby	17A Derby	21A Saltley	12A Carlisle Kingmoor	10A Carnforth
43028	$4MT^{5}$	→	10E Sutton Oak	10E Sutton Oak	10D Sutton Oak	11D Tebay	12C Carlisle Canal	12A Carlisle Kingmoor
43029	$4MT^{5}$	→	10E Sutton Oak	10E Sutton Oak	10D Sutton Oak	11D Tebay	12H Tebay	12E Tebay
43030	$4MT^{5}$	→	20A Leeds Holbeck	52B Heaton	52B Heaton	55F Manningham	55F Manningham	55F Manningham
43031	$4MT^{5}$	→	17A Derby	14A Cricklewood	14A Cricklewood	14A Cricklewood	15A Wellingborough	9F Heaton Mersey
43032	$4MT^{5}$	→	19A Sheffield Grimesthorpe	19B Millhouses	19B Millhouses	41C Millhouses	40E Colwick	
43033	$4MT^{5}$	→	16A Nottingham	16A Nottingham	16A Nottingham	21B Bournville	9E Trafford Park	12E Tebay
43034	$4MT^{5}$	→	23C Lancaster	11E Lancaster	2B Nuneaton	2B Nuneaton	5B Crewe South	5B Crewe South
43035	$4MT^{5}$	→	23C Lancaster	11E Lancaster	10D Sutton Oak	11D Tebay	12H Tebay	
43036	$4MT^{5}$	→	71G Bath Green Park	21A Saltley	21A Saltley	21A Saltley	9E Trafford Park	12D Workington
43037	$4MT^{5}$	→	19C Canklow	19C Canklow	19C Canklow	41D Canklow	36E Retford	
43038	$4MT^{5}$	→	19A Sheffield Grimesthorpe	53A Hull Dairycoates	51D Middlesbrough	55B Stourton	55B Stourton	
43039	$4MT^{5}$	→	20A Leeds Holbeck	20A Leeds Holbeck	55A Leeds Holbeck	55A Leeds Holbeck	55A Leeds Holbeck	55A Leeds Holbeck
43040	$4MT^{5}$		16A Nottingham	16A Nottingham	16A Nottingham	21A Saltley	9E Trafford Park	12A Carlisle Kingmoor
43041	$4MT^{5}$	→	19A Sheffield Grimesthorpe	19A Sheffield Grimesthorpe	17A Derby	21A Saltley	9E Trafford Park	10H Lower Darwen
43042	$4MT^{5}$	→	19A Sheffield Grimesthorpe	19A Sheffield Grimesthorpe	19A Sheffield Grimesthorpe	15B Kettering	9F Heaton Mersey	9F Heaton Mersey
43043	$4MT^{5}$	→	21A Saltley	52B Heaton	52B Heaton	55A Leeds Holbeck	55A Leeds Holbeck	55E Normanton
43044	$4MT^{5}$	→	21A Saltley	20B Stourton	55B Stourton	55B Stourton	55B Stourton	55B Stourton
43045	$4MT^{5}$	→	15C Leicester Midland	15C Leicester Midland	15C Leicester Midland	24J Lancaster	12C Carlisle Canal	12D Workington
43046	$4MT^{5}$	→	22A Bristol Barrow Road	21A Saltley	21A Saltley	21A Saltley	9F Heaton Mersey	10H Lower Darwen
43047	$4MT^{5}$	→	22A Bristol Barrow Road	21A Saltley	21A Saltley	21A Saltley	15A Wellingborough	9F Heaton Mersey
43048	$4MT^{5}$	→	21A Saltley	21A Saltley	21A Saltley	15B Kettering	9F Heaton Mersey	9F Heaton Mersey
43049	$4MT^{5}$	→	17A Derby	17A Derby	21A Saltley	21A Saltley	9F Heaton Mersey	12A Carlisle Kingmoor
43050	$4MT^{5}$	→	51D Middlesbrough	51D Middlesbrough	51A Darlington	51A Darlington	51A Darlington	51A Darlington
43051	$4MT^{5}$	→	51D Middlesbrough	51D Middlesbrough	51D Middlesbrough	50B Leeds Neville Hill	55H Leeds Neville Hill	55F Manningham
43052	$4MT^{5}$	→	50E Scarborough	50C Selby	50C Selby	2B Nuneaton	5B Crewe South	5B Crewe South
43053	$4MT^{5}$	→	53A Hull Dairycoates	53A Hull Dairycoates	53A Hull Dairycoates	51C West Hartlepool	51C West Hartlepool	
43054	$4MT^{5}$	→	51D Middlesbrough	51D Middlesbrough	51K Saltburn	50B Leeds Neville Hill	55H Leeds Neville Hill	55H Leeds Neville Hill
43055	$4MT^{5}$	→	51A Darlington	51C West Hartlepool	52B Heaton	50A York	50A York	51A Darlington
43056	$4MT^{5}$	→	51A Darlington	51A Darlington	52B Heaton	50A York	51A Darlington	51A Darlington
43057	$4MT^{5}$	→	51A Darlington	51A Darlington	52D Tweedmouth	50A York	51L Thornaby	51C West Hartlepool
43058	$4MT^{5}$	→	35A New England	35B Grantham	35A New England	40F Boston	40F Boston	
43059	$4MT^{5}$	→	35A New England	35A New England	35A New England	40F Boston	40F Boston	
43060	$4MT^{5}$	→	35A New England	35A New England	35A New England	40A Lincoln	40E Colwick	
43061	$4MT^{5}$	→	35A New England	35A New England	35A New England	40F Boston	40F Boston	
43062	$4MT^{5}$	→	35A New England	35A New England	35A New England	40F Boston	40F Boston	
43063	$4MT^{5}$	→	35A New England	35A New England	38E Woodford Halse	2F Woodford Halse	9F Heaton Mersey	9F Heaton Mersey
43064	$4MT^{5}$	→	35C Spital Bridge	35C Spital Bridge	35A New England	40F Boston	40F Boston	
43065	$4MT^{5}$	→	35A New England	34E Neasden	35A New England	40F Boston	40F Boston	
43066	$4MT^{5}$	→	35A New England	34E Neasden	35A New England	40F Boston	40F Boston	10A Carnforth
43067	$4MT^{5}$	→	35A New England	34E Neasden	35A New England	34E New England	34E New England	
43068	$4MT^{5}$	→	35A New England	34E Neasden	31D South Lynn	40F Boston	40F Boston	
43069	$4MT^{5}$	→	35A New England	53A Hull Dairycoates	53A Hull Dairycoates	53A Hull Dairycoates	50B Hull Dairycoates	55A Leeds Holbeck
43070	$4MT^{5}$	→	52B Heaton	52B Heaton	52B Heaton	50A York	56A Wakefield	56A Wakefield
43071	$4MT^{5}$	→	51A Darlington	51A Darlington	52D Tweedmouth	50A York	50A York	50A York
43072	$4MT^{5}$	→	51A Darlington	51D Middlesbrough	51D Middlesbrough	51L Thornaby	56F Low Moor	
43073	$4MT^{5}$	→	51A Darlington	51D Middlesbrough	51D Middlesbrough	24J Lancaster	5B Crewe South	12D Workington
43074	$4MT^{5}$	→	51A Darlington	51D Middlesbrough	51D Middlesbrough	55E Normanton	55F Manningham	55F Manningham
43075	$4MT^{5}$	→	51A Darlington	51A Darlington	52B Heaton	56A Wakefield	51L Thornaby	
43076	$4MT^{5}$	→	53A Hull Dairycoates	53A Hull Dairycoates	53A Hull Dairycoates	53A Hull Dairycoates	50B Hull Dairycoates	55D Royston
43077	$4MT^{5}$	→	53A Hull Dairycoates	53A Hull Dairycoates	53A Hull Dairycoates	53A Hull Dairycoates	50B Hull Dairycoates	55D Royston
43078	$4MT^{5}$	→	53A Hull Dairycoates	53A Hull Dairycoates	53A Hull Dairycoates	53A Hull Dairycoates	50B Hull Dairycoates	55D Royston
43079	$4MT^{5}$	→	53A Hull Dairycoates	53A Hull Dairycoates	53A Hull Dairycoates	53A Hull Dairycoates	50B Hull Dairycoates	55D Royston
43080	$4MT^{5}$	→	35A New England	35A New England	35A New England	40F Boston	40F Boston	
43081	$4MT^{5}$	→	35A New England	35A New England	35A New England	34E New England	34E New England	
43082	$4MT^{5}$	→	35A New England	35A New England	35A New England	34E New England	34E New England	
43083	$4MT^{5}$	→	35A New England	35A New England	35A New England	40F Boston	40F Boston	
43084	$4MT^{5}$	→	35A New England	35A New England	35A New England	34E New England	34E New England	55B Stourton
43085	$4MT^{5}$	→	35A New England	35A New England	35A New England	40F Boston	40F Boston	
43086	$4MT^{5}$	→	35A New England	35A New England	35A New England	34E New England	40A Lincoln	
43087	$4MT^{5}$	→	35A New England	35A New England	35A New England	31C Kings Lynn	34F Grantham	
43088	$4MT^{5}$	→	35A New England	35A New England	35A New England	34E New England	34E New England	5B Crewe South
43089	$4MT^{5}$	→	35A New England	34E Neasden	31A Cambridge	31C Kings Lynn	34E New England	
43090	$4MT^{5}$	→	31D South Lynn	31D South Lynn	31D South Lynn	31C Kings Lynn	34F Grantham	
43091	$4MT^{5}$	→	31D South Lynn	31D South Lynn	31D South Lynn	40F Boston	40F Boston	
43092	$4MT^{5}$	→	31D South Lynn	31D South Lynn	31D South Lynn	40F Boston	40F Boston	
43093	$4MT^{5}$	→	31D South Lynn	31D South Lynn	31D South Lynn	40F Boston	40F Boston	
43094	$4MT^{5}$	→	31D South Lynn	31D South Lynn	31D South Lynn	31C Kings Lynn	34E New England	
43095	$4MT^{5}$	→	31D South Lynn	31D South Lynn	31D South Lynn	40A Lincoln	40A Lincoln	10A Carnforth
43096	$4MT^{5}$	→	50C Selby	50C Selby	50C Selby	50A York	56B Ardsley	55B Stourton
43097	$4MT^{5}$	→	→	50C Selby	50C Selby	53E Goole	50A York	50A York
43098	$4MT^{5}$	→	→	50C Selby	50C Selby	53E Goole	50D Goole	55E Normanton
43099	$4MT^{5}$	→	→	53A Hull Dairycoates	53A Hull Dairycoates	51A Darlington	51A Darlington	55E Normanton
43100	$4MT^{5}$	→	→	53A Hull Dairycoates	53A Hull Dairycoates	51C West Hartlepool	51C West Hartlepool	51C West Hartlepool
43101	$4MT^{5}$	→	→	51D Middlesbrough	52B Heaton	56A Wakefield	56A Wakefield	52F North Blyth
43102	$4MT^{5}$	→	→	51D Middlesbrough	51D Middlesbrough	51L Thornaby	51A Darlington	55B Stourton
43103	$4MT^{5}$	→	→	53A Hull Dairycoates	53A Hull Dairycoates	21A Saltley	12A Carlisle Kingmoor	10A Carnforth
43104	$4MT^{5}$	→	→	31D South Lynn	31D South Lynn	40A Lincoln	40A Lincoln	
43105	$4MT^{5}$	→	→	31D South Lynn	31D South Lynn	30A Stratford	40A Lincoln	10A Carnforth
43106	$4MT^{5}$	→	→	31D South Lynn	38E Woodford Halse	2F Woodford Halse	15A Wellingborough	9F Heaton Mersey
43107	$4MT^{5}$	→	→	34E Neasden	31D South Lynn	40F Boston	40F Boston	
43108	$4MT^{5}$	→	→	31D South Lynn	31D South Lynn	40E Colwick	40F Boston	
43109	$4MT^{5}$	→	→	31D South Lynn	31D South Lynn	40F Boston	40F Boston	
43110	$4MT^{5}$	→	→	31D South Lynn	31D South Lynn	40F Boston	40F Boston	
43111	$4MT^{5}$	→	→	31D South Lynn	31D South Lynn	41B Sheffield Grimesthorpe	34F Grantham	
43112	$4MT^{5}$	→	→	20F Skipton	20F Skipton	24J Lancaster	21B Bescot	5D Stoke
43113	$4MT^{5}$	→	→	20F Skipton	20F Skipton	24J Lancaster	5B Crewe South	5B Crewe South
43114	$4MT^{5}$	→	→	19A Sheffield Grimesthorpe	55E Normanton	55E Normanton	55E Normanton	
43115	$4MT^{5}$	→	→	19A Sheffield Grimesthorpe	19A Sheffield Grimesthorpe	24J Lancaster	21B Bescot	5D Stoke
43116	$4MT^{5}$	→	→	20A Leeds Holbeck	55E Normanton	55E Normanton	55E Normanton	55E Normanton
43117	$4MT^{5}$	→	→	20A Leeds Holbeck	55A Leeds Holbeck	55A Leeds Holbeck	55A Leeds Holbeck	55B Stourton
43118	$4MT^{5}$	→	→	14A Cricklewood	14A Cricklewood	14A Cricklewood	15A Wellingborough	10H Lower Darwen
43119	$4MT^{5}$	→	→	16A Nottingham	14C St. Albans	14C St. Albans	15A Wellingborough	10H Lower Darwen
43120	$4MT^{5}$	→	→	14A Cricklewood	14A Cricklewood	14A Cricklewood	15A Wellingborough	12A Carlisle Kingmoor
43121	$4MT^{5}$	→	→	14A Cricklewood	14A Cricklewood	14A Cricklewood	15A Wellingborough	12A Carlisle Kingmoor
43122	$4MT^{5}$	→	→	53A Hull Dairycoates	53A Hull Dairycoates	21A Saltley	21A Saltley	12D Workington
43123	$4MT^{5}$	→	→	50C Selby	50C Selby	53A Hull Dairycoates	51C West Hartlepool	51C West Hartlepool
43124	$4MT^{5}$	→	→	53A Hull Dairycoates	51A Darlington	55A Leeds Holbeck	55A Leeds Holbeck	55A Leeds Holbeck
43125	$4MT^{5}$	→	→	52B Heaton	50C Selby	53E Goole	50D Goole	55E Normanton
43126	$4MT^{5}$	→	→	52C Blaydon	52B Heaton	52B Heaton	50A York	50A York
43127	$4MT^{5}$	→	→	34E Neasden	35C Spital Bridge	31F Spital Bridge	36E Retford	
43128	$4MT^{5}$	→	→	52C Blaydon	51C West Hartlepool	51C West Hartlepool	51C West Hartlepool	
43129	$4MT^{5}$	→	→	52B Heaton	52B Heaton	51A Darlington	51A Darlington	51A Darlington
43130	$4MT^{5}$	→	→	53A Hull Dairycoates	51A Darlington	55A Leeds Holbeck	55A Leeds Holbeck	55A Leeds Holbeck
43131	$4MT^{5}$	→	→	53A Hull Dairycoates	53A Hull Dairycoates	53A Hull Dairycoates	50B Hull Dairycoates	
43132	$4MT^{5}$	→	→	65A Eastfield	65E Kipps	65E Kipps	67B Hurlford	52F North Blyth

No.	Class	1948	1951	1954	1957	1960	1963	1966
43133	4MT^{5}	→	→	65A Eastfield	65E Kipps	65E Kipps	67B Hurlford	50A York
43134	4MT^{5}	→	→	65A Eastfield	65E Kipps	65E Kipps	66D Greenock Ladyburn	
43135	4MT^{5}	→	→	65A Eastfield	65A Eastfield	65A Eastfield	65D Dawsholm	55B Stourton
43136	4MT^{5}	→	→	65A Eastfield	65A Eastfield	65A Eastfield	65D Dawsholm	
43137	4MT^{5}	→	→	65A Eastfield	65A Eastfield	65A Eastfield	65F Grangemouth	56A Wakefield
43138	4MT^{5}	→	→	65A Eastfield	64F Bathgate	64F Bathgate	64G Hawick	50A York
43139	4MT^{5}	→	→	68E Carlisle Canal	68E Carlisle Canal	12C Carlisle Canal	12C Carlisle Canal	12A Carlisle Kingmoor
43140	4MT^{5}	→	→	64E Polmont	64E Polmont	65B St. Rollox	65D Dawsholm	55B Stourton
43141	4MT^{5}	→	→	64E Polmont	64E Polmont	64G Hawick	66A Polmadie	55E Normanton
43142	4MT^{5}	→	→	31D South Lynn	31D South Lynn	40F Boston	40F Boston	
43143	4MT^{5}	→	→	31D South Lynn	31D South Lynn	40F Boston	40F Boston	
43144	4MT^{5}	→	→	34E Neasden	31D South Lynn	30A Stratford	40F Boston	
43145	4MT^{5}	→	→	32G Melton Constable	32G Melton Constable	32A Norwich Thorpe	40E Colwick	
43146	4MT^{5}	→	→	32G Melton Constable	32G Melton Constable	32A Norwich Thorpe	34E New England	
43147	4MT^{5}	→	→	32G Melton Constable	32G Melton Constable	40F Boston	40F Boston	
43148	4MT^{5}	→	→	32G Melton Constable	32G Melton Constable	30A Stratford	40F Boston	
43149	4MT^{5}		→	32G Melton Constable	32G Melton Constable	30A Stratford	40A Lincoln	
43150	4MT^{5}	→	→	32G Melton Constable	32G Melton Constable	30A Stratford	34E New England	
43151	4MT^{5}	→	→	32G Melton Constable	32G Melton Constable	30A Stratford	34E New England	5B Crewe South
43152	4MT^{5}	→	→	32G Melton Constable	32G Melton Constable	30A Stratford	40E Colwick	
43153	4MT^{5}	→	→	32G Melton Constable	32G Melton Constable	30A Stratford	34E New England	
43154	4MT^{5}	→	→	32G Melton Constable	32G Melton Constable	40A Lincoln	40E Colwick	
43155	4MT^{5}	→	→	32G Melton Constable	32G Melton Constable	40E Colwick	40E Colwick	
43156	4MT^{5}	→	→	32G Melton Constable	32G Melton Constable	32A Norwich Thorpe	40E Colwick	
43157	4MT^{5}	→	→	32F Yarmouth Beach	32F Yarmouth Beach	40F Boston	36E Retford	
43158	4MT^{5}	→	→	32F Yarmouth Beach	32F Yarmouth Beach	40A Lincoln	40F Boston	
43159	4MT^{5}	→	→	32F Yarmouth Beach	32F Yarmouth Beach	41B Sheffield Grimesthorpe	34F Grantham	
43160	4MT^{5}	→	→	32F Yarmouth Beach	32F Yarmouth Beach	32A Norwich Thorpe	40E Colwick	
43161	4MT^{5}	→	→	34E Neasden	32F Yarmouth Beach	32A Norwich Thorpe	40E Colwick	
43137	3F^{2}	20G Hellifield	17A Derby	(43750)				
43174	3F^{2}	15D Bedford	15D Bedford	15D Bedford	15D Bedford	41B Sheffield Grimesthorpe		
43178	3F^{2}	22A Bristol Barrow Road	20E Manningham	20E Manningham	20F Skipton	55F Manningham		
43180	3F^{2}	19C Canklow	19C Canklow	19C Canklow	19C Canklow			
43181	3F^{2}	19C Canklow	19C Canklow	19C Canklow	19A Sheffield Grimesthorpe			
43183	3F^{2}	15C Leicester Midland	15C Leicester Midland	20D Normanton	55E Normanton			
43185	3F^{2}	15D Bedford	17A Derby	17A Derby	17A Derby	8G Sutton Oak		
43186	3F^{2}	20G Hellifield	21C Bromsgrove	21C Bromsgrove	21C Bromsgrove			
43187	3F^{2}	20H Lancaster	23C Lancaster	5D Crewe South	3E Monument Lane	9G Gorton		
43188	3F^{2}	17B Burton	17B Burton	17B Burton	17B Burton	17B Burton		
43189	3F^{2}	11A Carnforth	5B Crewe South	5B Crewe South	5B Crewe South	3A Bescot		
43191	3F^{3}	17A Derby	17A Derby	17A Derby				
43192	3F^{3}	16A Nottingham	16A Nottingham	16A Nottingham	16A Nottingham			
43193	3F^{3}	16D Mansfield	15A Wellingborough	17B Burton	18B Westhouses			
43194	3F^{3}	22E Highbridge	71H Templecombe	71H Templecombe	71H Templecombe	82G Templecombe		
43200	3F^{3}	17A Derby	17A Derby	17A Derby	17A Derby	17A Derby		
43201	3F^{3}	21A Saltley	21A Saltley	71J Highbridge	71J Highbridge			
43203	3F^{3}	21A Saltley	21B Bournville	21B Bournville	21B Bournville	41B Sheffield Grimesthorpe		
43204	3F^{3}	22A Bristol Barrow Road	71J Highbridge	71J Highbridge				
43205	3F^{3}	15C Leicester Midland	15C Leicester Midland	15C Leicester Midland	15C Leicester Midland			
43207	3F^{3}	8B Warrington Dallam	5B Crewe South	5B Crewe South	5B Crewe South	9G Gorton		
43208	3F^{3}	19C Canklow	19C Canklow	19C Canklow	19C Canklow			
43210	3F^{3}	21A Saltley	21A Saltley	21A Saltley	21A Saltley			
43211	3F^{3}	18C Hasland	18C Hasland	18C Hasland	18C Hasland	9E Trafford Park		
43212	3F^{3}	18C Hasland	18C Hasland	18C Hasland	18C Hasland	9F Heaton Mersey		
43213	3F^{3}	22B Gloucester Barnwood	22B Gloucester Barnwood	22B Gloucester Barnwood	22B Gloucester Barnwood	8G Sutton Oak		
43214	3F^{3}	17B Burton	21A Saltley	21A Saltley	21A Saltley	21A Saltley		
43216	3F^{3}	22E Highbridge	71H Templecombe	71H Templecombe	71H Templecombe	82G Templecombe		
43218	3F^{3}	22E Highbridge	71H Templecombe	71H Templecombe	71H Templecombe	82G Templecombe		
43219	3F^{3}	18C Hasland	18C Hasland	21A Saltley	21A Saltley			
43222	3F^{3}	15D Bedford	15D Bedford	15D Bedford	15D Bedford			
43223	3F^{3}	21A Saltley	21A Saltley	21A Saltley	21A Saltley			
43224	3F^{3}	18D Staveley Barrow Hill	18D Staveley Barrow Hill	18D Staveley Barrow Hill	18D Staveley Barrow Hill			
43225	3F^{3}	21A Saltley	21A Saltley	19C Canklow	19C Canklow	41D Canklow		
43226	3F^{3}	20G Hellifield	17A Derby	17A Derby				
43228	3F^{3}	22A Bristol Barrow Road	71H Templecombe					
43231	3F^{3}	20G Hellifield	3E Monument Lane	3E Monument Lane	3E Monument Lane			
43232	3F^{3}	15C Leicester Midland	15C Leicester Midland	15C Leicester Midland				
43233	3F^{3}	20C Royston	20C Royston	20C Royston	55D Royston			
43234	3F^{3}	18D Staveley Barrow Hill	18D Staveley Barrow Hill	18D Staveley Barrow Hill	18D Staveley Barrow Hill	41B Sheffield Grimesthorpe		
43235	3F^{3}	18B Westhouses	18B Westhouses	18B Westhouses	18B Westhouses	9G Gorton		
43237	3F^{3}	11A Carnforth	8B Warrington Dallam	8B Warrington Dallam	8B Warrington Dallam			
43239	3F^{3}	16D Mansfield	16D Mansfield	16D Mansfield	16C Mansfield			
43240	3F^{3}	18D Staveley Barrow Hill	16A Nottingham	16A Nottingham	16A Nottingham	12A Carlisle Kingmoor		
43241	3F^{3}	19A Sheffield Grimesthorpe	19A Sheffield Grimesthorpe	68A Carlisle Kingmoor	68A Carlisle Kingmoor			
43242	3F^{3}	18D Staveley Barrow Hill	16C Kirkby in Ashfield	16C Kirkby in Ashfield	16B Kirkby in Ashfield	21A Saltley		
43243	3F^{3}	19C Canklow	19C Canklow	19C Canklow	19A Sheffield Grimesthorpe	41B Sheffield Grimesthorpe		
43244	3F^{3}	17B Burton	17B Burton	15B Kettering	15C Leicester Midland			
43245	3F^{3}	14C St. Albans	14C St. Albans	14C St. Albans	14C St. Albans	9F Heaton Mersey		
43246	3F^{3}	14A Cricklewood	21A Saltley	21A Saltley				
43247	3F^{3}	17B Burton	17B Burton	17B Burton	17B Burton			
43248	3F^{3}	22D Templecombe	71H Templecombe	71H Templecombe	71H Templecombe			
43249	3F^{3}	16A Nottingham	16A Nottingham	16A Nottingham	16A Nottingham			
43250	3F^{3}	20C Royston	20C Royston	20C Royston	55D Royston	17C Rowsley		
43251	3F^{3}	20F Skipton	16D Mansfield	18A Toton	18A Toton			
43252	3F^{3}	18D Staveley Barrow Hill	18D Staveley Barrow Hill	19A Sheffield Grimesthorpe				
43253	3F^{3}	16B Spital Bridge	18B Westhouses	18B Westhouses	18B Westhouses			
43254	3F^{3}	18B Westhouses	18B Westhouses	18B Westhouses	19A Sheffield Grimesthorpe	41B Sheffield Grimesthorpe		
43256	3F^{3}	17B Burton	17B Burton	17B Burton	17B Burton	17B Burton		
43257	3F^{3}	22B Gloucester Barnwood	21A Saltley	20F Skipton	20F Skipton	8B Warrington Dallam		
43258	3F^{3}	22B Gloucester Barnwood	22B Gloucester Barnwood	22B Gloucester Barnwood	22B Gloucester Barnwood			
43259	3F^{3}	18A Toton	17A Derby	17A Derby	17A Derby			
43260	3F^{3}	22D Templecombe						
43261	3F^{3}	14A Cricklewood	14A Cricklewood	14A Cricklewood	14A Cricklewood	14E Bedford		
43263	3F^{3}	22B Gloucester Barnwood	21B Bournville	21B Bournville	21B Bournville	21A Saltley		
43265	3F^{3}	14A Cricklewood						
43266	3F^{3}	18B Westhouses	18B Westhouses	18B Westhouses	18B Westhouses	18B Westhouses		
43267	3F^{3}	20B Stourton	20B Stourton	20C Royston	55D Royston	55D Royston		
43268	3F^{3}	9D Buxton	9D Buxton	9D Buxton	9D Buxton	9D Buxton		
43269	3F^{3}	9D Buxton						
43271	3F^{3}	9D Buxton	9D Buxton	9D Buxton	11E Lancaster			
43273	3F^{3}	17A Derby	17D Rowsley	17D Rowsley				
43274	3F^{3}	9D Buxton	9D Buxton	9D Buxton	9D Buxton			
43275	3F^{3}	9A Longsight	9A Longsight	9A Longsight				
43277	3F^{3}	21D Stratford on Avon	21D Stratford on Avon	84G Shrewsbury	84G Shrewsbury	15C Leicester Midland		
43278	3F^{3}	9D Buxton	9D Buxton	9D Buxton	9D Buxton			
43281	3F^{3}	9B Stockport Edgeley	9B Stockport Edgeley	9B Stockport Edgeley				
43282	3F^{3}	9D Buxton	8B Warrington Dallam	8B Warrington Dallam	8B Warrington Dallam	8B Warrington Dallam		
43283	3F^{3}	8B Warrington Dallam	8B Warrington Dallam					
43284	3F^{3}	21A Saltley	21A Saltley	21A Saltley	21A Saltley	21A Saltley		
43286	3F^{3}	17B Burton	17B Burton	17B Burton	17B Burton			
43287	3F^{3}	18A Toton	16C Kirkby in Ashfield	16C Kirkby in Ashfield	16B Kirkby in Ashfield			
43290	3F^{3}	17D Rowsley	17D Rowsley	17D Rowsley	17D Rowsley			
43292	3F^{3}	18D Staveley Barrow Hill	18D Staveley Barrow Hill	18D Staveley Barrow Hill	17A Derby			
43293	3F^{3}	20H Lancaster	23C Lancaster					

No.	Class	1948	1951	1954	1957	1960	1963	1966
43294	$3F^3$	**18D** Staveley Barrow Hill	**18D** Staveley Barrow Hill	**18D** Staveley Barrow Hill	**17A** Derby			
43295	$3F^3$	**20F** Skipton	**23A** Skipton	**20F** Skipton	**20F** Skipton	**8B** Warrington Dallam		
43296	$3F^3$	**9D** Buxton	**9D** Buxton	**9D** Buxton				
43297	$3F^3$	**18D** Staveley Barrow Hill						
43298	$3F^3$	**18D** Staveley Barrow Hill	**18D** Staveley Barrow Hill	**18D** Staveley Barrow Hill				
43299	$3F^3$	**18D** Staveley Barrow Hill	**18D** Staveley Barrow Hill	**18D** Staveley Barrow Hill				
43300	$3F^3$	**19C** Canklow	**16A** Nottingham	**16A** Nottingham	**9D** Buxton			
43301	$3F^3$	**20D** Normanton	**20D** Normanton	**68A** Carlisle Kingmoor	**68A** Carlisle Kingmoor			
43305	$3F^3$	**18A** Toton	**16C** Kirkby in Ashfield	**16C** Kirkby in Ashfield	**16B** Kirkby in Ashfield	**9B** Stockport Edgeley		
43306	$3F^3$	**17B** Burton	**17B** Burton	**17B** Burton	**17B** Burton	**17A** Derby		
43307	$3F^3$	**20H** Lancaster	**14A** Cricklewood	**14A** Cricklewood	**14A** Cricklewood	**41B** Sheffield Grimesthorpe		
43308	$3F^3$	**17A** Derby	**3D** Aston	**3D** Aston	**2B** Nuneaton			
43309	$3F^3$	**18D** Staveley Barrow Hill	**18D** Staveley Barrow Hill	**18A** Toton	**18A** Toton	**21A** Saltley		
43310	$3F^3$	**18D** Staveley Barrow Hill	**18D** Staveley Barrow Hill	**18D** Staveley Barrow Hill				
43312	$3F^3$	**17A** Derby	**17A** Derby	**17B** Burton	**17A** Derby			
43313	$3F^3$	**14A** Cricklewood	**14A** Cricklewood	**14A** Cricklewood				
43314	$3F^3$	**8B** Warrington Dallam	**8B** Warrington Dallam	**8B** Warrington Dallam	**8B** Warrington Dallam	**8B** Warrington Dallam		
43315	$3F^3$	**17A** Derby	**17A** Derby	**17A** Derby	**17A** Derby			
43317	$3F^3$	**16B** Spital Bridge	**18B** Westhouses	**18B** Westhouses				
43318	$3F^3$	**17A** Derby	**17A** Derby	**17A** Derby	**17A** Derby			
43319	$3F^3$	**16B** Spital Bridge						
43321	$3F^3$	**21A** Saltley	**21A** Saltley	**20C** Royston	**55E** Normanton	**21A** Saltley		
43323	$3F^3$	**17A** Derby	**17A** Derby	**17A** Derby	**17D** Rowsley			
43324	$3F^3$	**17A** Derby	**17A** Derby	**17A** Derby	**17A** Derby			
43325	$3F^3$	**19C** Canklow	**19C** Canklow	**19C** Canklow	**9A** Longsight	**1C** Watford		
43326	$3F^3$	**15C** Leicester Midland	**15C** Leicester Midland	**15C** Leicester Midland	**15C** Leicester Midland	**15C** Leicester Midland		
43327	$3F^3$	**18A** Toton	**16D** Mansfield	**17B** Burton	**17B** Burton			
43329	$3F^3$	**11A** Carnforth	**8B** Warrington Dallam	**8B** Warrington Dallam	**8B** Warrington Dallam	**9D** Buxton		
43330	$3F^3$	**20H** Lancaster	**23C** Lancaster	**5B** Crewe South	**5B** Crewe South	**2F** Woodford Halse		
43331	$3F^3$	**18B** Westhouses	**18B** Westhouses	**18B** Westhouses				
43332	$3F^3$	**20C** Royston	**20C** Royston	**20C** Royston	**19A** Sheffield Grimesthorpe			
43333	$3F^3$	**15C** Leicester Midland	**15C** Leicester Midland	**15C** Leicester Midland	**15C** Leicester Midland	**14E** Bedford		
43334	$3F^3$	**19A** Sheffield Grimesthorpe	**19A** Sheffield Grimesthorpe	**19A** Sheffield Grimesthorpe				
43335	$3F^3$	**20G** Hellifield	**19A** Sheffield Grimesthorpe	**19A** Sheffield Grimesthorpe	**19A** Sheffield Grimesthorpe			
43336	$3F^3$	**21A** Saltley	**21A** Saltley					
43337	$3F^3$	**20F** Skipton	**22B** Gloucester Barnwood	**22B** Gloucester Barnwood	**22B** Gloucester Barnwood	**85E** Gloucester Barnwood		
43338	$3F^3$	**17D** Rowsley						
43339	$3F^3$	**21A** Saltley	**21A** Saltley	**21A** Saltley	**21A** Saltley			
43340	$3F^3$	**17B** Burton	**17B** Burton	**17B** Burton	**17B** Burton	**17B** Burton		
43341	$3F^3$	**16D** Mansfield	**19B** Millhouses	**19A** Sheffield Grimesthorpe	**19A** Sheffield Grimesthorpe			
43342	$3F^3$	**17D** Rowsley	**17D** Rowsley	**17D** Rowsley	**17D** Rowsley	**17C** Rowsley	**14E** Bedford	
43344	$3F^3$	**22B** Gloucester Barnwood	**22B** Gloucester Barnwood	**22B** Gloucester Barnwood	**22A** Bristol Barrow Road	**82E** Bristol Barrow Road		
43351	$3F^3$	**20E** Manningham	**20E** Manningham	**68A** Carlisle Kingmoor				
43355	$3F^3$	**21B** Bournville	**21B** Bournville	**21B** Bournville	**21B** Bournville			
43356	$3F^3$	**22D** Templecombe	**71H** Templecombe	**71H** Templecombe	**71H** Templecombe			
43357	$3F^3$	**8B** Warrington Dallam	**84G** Shrewsbury	**9B** Stockport Edgeley	**9B** Stockport Edgeley			
43359	$3F^3$	**21B** Bournville	**21B** Bournville	**21B** Bournville	**21B** Bournville	**21A** Saltley		
43361	$3F^3$	**19E** Belle Vue	**17A** Derby	**17A** Derby	**17B** Burton	**41B** Sheffield Grimesthorpe		
43364	$3F^3$	**17A** Derby	**17A** Derby					
43367	$3F^3$	**15A** Wellingborough	**15A** Wellingborough	**15A** Wellingborough	**15B** Kettering			
43368	$3F^3$	**17A** Derby	**17A** Derby	**17A** Derby	**17A** Derby	**17A** Derby		
43369	$3F^3$	**16A** Nottingham	**16A** Nottingham	**16A** Nottingham	**16A** Nottingham			
43370	$3F^3$	**17A** Derby	**17D** Rowsley	**17D** Rowsley	**17D** Rowsley			
43371	$3F^3$	**16B** Spital Bridge	**16A** Nottingham	**16A** Nottingham	**16A** Nottingham	**41D** Canklow		
43373	$3F^3$	**22B** Gloucester Barnwood	**22B** Gloucester Barnwood	**22B** Gloucester Barnwood	**22B** Gloucester Barnwood	**14E** Bedford		
43374	$3F^3$	**21A** Saltley	**21A** Saltley	**21A** Saltley	**21A** Saltley	**15C** Leicester Midland		
43378	$3F^3$	**16A** Nottingham	**16A** Nottingham	**16A** Nottingham	**16A** Nottingham			
43379	$3F^3$	**18B** Westhouses	**18B** Westhouses	**17A** Derby	**17A** Derby			
43381	$3F^3$	**21D** Stratford on Avon	**21D** Stratford on Avon	**21A** Saltley	**21A** Saltley			
43386	$3F^3$	**18D** Staveley Barrow Hill	**18D** Staveley Barrow Hill	**18D** Staveley Barrow Hill	**18D** Staveley Barrow Hill	**41E** Staveley Barrow Hill		
43387	$3F^3$	**9D** Buxton	**9D** Buxton	**9D** Buxton	**9D** Buxton			
43388	$3F^3$	**17B** Burton	**17B** Burton	**17B** Burton	**19A** Sheffield Grimesthorpe			
43389	$3F^3$	**8B** Warrington Dallam	**8B** Warrington Dallam	**3D** Aston	**3D** Aston	**21A** Saltley		
43392	$3F^3$	**20B** Stourton	**20B** Stourton	**20B** Stourton	**55B** Stourton			
43394	$3F^3$	**4A** Shrewsbury	**84G** Shrewsbury	**84G** Shrewsbury	**84G** Shrewsbury	**2F** Woodford Halse		
43395	$3F^3$	**17B** Burton	**17B** Burton	**17B** Burton	**17B** Burton	**41B** Sheffield Grimesthorpe		
43396	$3F^3$	**7D** Rhyl	**7D** Rhyl	**6K** Rhyl	**6K** Rhyl			
43398	$3F^3$	**8B** Warrington Dallam	**8B** Warrington Dallam	**8B** Warrington Dallam	**8B** Warrington Dallam			
43399	$3F^3$	**16A** Nottingham	**16A** Nottingham	**16A** Nottingham	**2E** Northampton	**2E** Northampton		
43400	$3F^3$	**14A** Cricklewood	**14A** Cricklewood	**17D** Rowsley	**17D** Rowsley	**9E** Trafford Park		
43401	$3F^3$	**20A** Leeds Holbeck	**16A** Nottingham	**16A** Nottingham	**16A** Nottingham			
43402	$3F^3$	**17A** Derby	**17A** Derby	**17A** Derby	**17A** Derby			
43405	$3F^3$	**18A** Toton	**18A** Toton	**18A** Toton	**18A** Toton	**15C** Leicester Midland		
43406	$3F^3$	**17A** Derby	**17A** Derby	**17B** Burton	**17B** Burton	**41B** Sheffield Grimesthorpe		
43408	$3F^3$	**14A** Cricklewood						
43410	$3F^3$	**3C** Walsall	**3C** Walsall	**3C** Walsall	**3C** Walsall	**9B** Stockport Edgeley		
43411	$3F^3$	**15C** Leicester Midland	**15C** Leicester Midland	**15C** Leicester Midland	**15C** Leicester Midland	**15C** Leicester Midland		
43419	$3F^3$	**22A** Bristol Barrow Road	**71J** Highbridge	**71J** Highbridge	**71J** Highbridge			
43427	$3F^3$	**22B** Gloucester Barnwood	**22A** Bristol Barrow Road	**22A** Bristol Barrow Road	**22A** Bristol Barrow Road	**82G** Templecombe		
43428	$3F^3$	**15D** Bedford	**15D** Bedford	**15D** Bedford	**15D** Bedford	**14E** Bedford		
43429	$3F^3$	**17C** Coalville	**17C** Coalville	**17C** Coalville	**17D** Rowsley	**17C** Rowsley		
43431	$3F^3$	**16D** Mansfield	**16D** Mansfield	**16D** Mansfield	**16C** Mansfield	**41B** Sheffield Grimesthorpe		
43433	$3F^3$	**21A** Saltley	**21A** Saltley	**21A** Saltley	**21A** Saltley			
43435	$3F^3$	**21A** Saltley	**21A** Saltley	**21A** Saltley	**21A** Saltley	**17A** Derby		
43436	$3F^3$	**22A** Bristol Barrow Road	**22A** Bristol Barrow Road	**71H** Templecombe	**71H** Templecombe	**82G** Templecombe		
43439	$3F^3$	**22A** Bristol Barrow Road						
43440	$3F^3$	**14A** Cricklewood	**14A** Cricklewood	**14A** Cricklewood	**14A** Cricklewood			
43441	$3F^3$	**21A** Saltley	**21A** Saltley	**21A** Saltley	**21A** Saltley			
43443	$3F^3$	**21A** Saltley	**21A** Saltley	**21A** Saltley	**21A** Saltley			
43444	$3F^3$	**22A** Bristol Barrow Road	**22A** Bristol Barrow Road	**21A** Saltley	**22A** Bristol Barrow Road	**82E** Bristol Barrow Road		
43446	$3F^3$	**20C** Royston	**20C** Royston	**20C** Royston	**55D** Royston	**55D** Royston		
43448	$3F^3$	**14A** Cricklewood	**14A** Cricklewood	**14A** Cricklewood				
43449	$3F^3$	**20B** Stourton	**20B** Stourton	**20D** Normanton	**55E** Normanton	**14E** Bedford		
43453	$3F^3$	**18A** Toton	**18A** Toton	**18A** Toton	**18A** Toton	**21A** Saltley	**14E** Bedford	
43454	$3F^3$	**20A** Leeds Holbeck	**15C** Leicester Midland	**15D** Bedford				
43456	$3F^3$	**20B** Stourton	**20B** Stourton	**20B** Stourton	**55B** Stourton	**14E** Bedford		
43457	$3F^3$	**9A** Longsight	**9A** Longsight	**9A** Longsight	**9A** Longsight	**9G** Gorton		
43458	$3F^3$	**16A** Nottingham						
43459	$3F^3$	**17A** Derby	**17A** Derby	**17A** Derby	**17A** Derby	**17A** Derby		
43462	$3F^3$	**22D** Templecombe	**22A** Bristol Barrow Road	**22A** Bristol Barrow Road				
43463	$3F^3$	**19B** Millhouses	**19A** Sheffield Grimesthorpe	**19C** Canklow	**19C** Canklow			
43464	$3F^3$	**22A** Bristol Barrow Road	**22A** Bristol Barrow Road	**22A** Bristol Barrow Road	**22A** Bristol Barrow Road	**5B** Crewe South		
43468	$3F^3$	**19A** Sheffield Grimesthorpe	**16C** Kirkby in Ashfield	**16C** Kirkby in Ashfield	**16B** Kirkby in Ashfield	**21A** Saltley		
43469	$3F^3$	**17A** Derby	**17A** Derby	**17A** Derby	**17B** Burton			
43474	$3F^3$	**15D** Bedford	**15D** Bedford	**15D** Bedford	**15D** Bedford	**14E** Bedford		
43476	$3F^3$	**20B** Stourton	**20B** Stourton	**20C** Royston	**55D** Royston			
43482	$3F^3$	**17A** Derby	**17A** Derby	**17A** Derby	**21A** Saltley	**21A** Saltley		
43484	$3F^3$	**21A** Saltley	**21A** Saltley	**21A** Saltley	**21A** Saltley	**21A** Saltley		
43490	$3F^3$	**21A** Saltley	**21A** Saltley	**21A** Saltley	**21A** Saltley			
43491	$3F^3$	**21A** Saltley	**21A** Saltley	**84G** Shrewsbury	**84G** Shrewsbury			
43494	$3F^3$	**16C** Kirkby in Ashfield	**16C** Kirkby in Ashfield	**16D** Mansfield				
43496	$3F^3$	**17A** Derby	**17A** Derby	**17D** Rowsley	**17D** Rowsley	**17C** Rowsley		
43497	$3F^3$	**20D** Normanton	**20D** Normanton	**20D** Normanton				
43499	$3F^3$	**18A** Toton	**18A** Toton	**18A** Toton	**18A** Toton	**15B** Kettering		

		1948	1951	1954	1957	1960	1963	1966
43502	3F^3	**3C** Walsall	**3C** Walsall	**3C** Walsall	**11E** Lancaster			
43506	3F^3	**22B** Gloucester Barnwood	**22B** Gloucester Barnwood	**22B** Gloucester Barnwood	**22B** Gloucester Barnwood			
43507	3F^3	**22B** Gloucester Barnwood	**21A** Saltley	**21A** Saltley	**21A** Saltley	**21A** Saltley		
43509	3F^3	**20C** Royston	**20D** Normanton	**20D** Normanton	**55E** Normanton	**55E** Normanton		
43510	3F^3	**17A** Derby	**17A** Derby	**17A** Derby	**17A** Derby	**17A** Derby		
43514	3F^3	**20D** Normanton	**20D** Normanton	**68A** Carlisle Kingmoor	**68A** Carlisle Kingmoor	**12A** Carlisle Kingmoor		
43515	3F^3	**18D** Staveley Barrow Hill	**18D** Staveley Barrow Hill	**18D** Staveley Barrow Hill	**18D** Staveley Barrow Hill	**41E** Staveley Barrow Hill		
43520	3F^3	**21D** Stratford on Avon	**21D** Stratford on Avon	**21A** Saltley	**22B** Gloucester Barnwood			
43521	3F^3	**21D** Stratford on Avon	**21D** Stratford on Avon	**21B** Bournville	**21B** Bournville	**21B** Bournville	**14E** Bedford	
43522	3F^3	**16D** Mansfield	**16D** Mansfield	**16D** Mansfield	**16C** Mansfield			
43523	3F^3	**21D** Stratford on Avon	**21D** Stratford on Avon	**21A** Saltley	**21A** Saltley	**21A** Saltley		
43524	3F^3	**18D** Staveley Barrow Hill	**18D** Staveley Barrow Hill	**18D** Staveley Barrow Hill				
43529	3F^3	**16D** Mansfield	**16D** Mansfield	**16D** Mansfield	**15D** Bedford	**14E** Bedford		
43531	3F^3	**21A** Saltley	**21A** Saltley	**15A** Wellingborough	**15D** Bedford			
43538	3F^3	**16A** Nottingham	**16A** Nottingham	**9G** Northwich	**9G** Northwich			
43540	3F^3	**21A** Saltley	**21A** Saltley					
43544	3F^3	**21A** Saltley	**21A** Saltley	**21A** Saltley				
43546	3F^3	**18D** Staveley Barrow Hill	**18D** Staveley Barrow Hill	**18D** Staveley Barrow Hill				
43548	3F^3	**17A** Derby	**17A** Derby	**17A** Derby	**17A** Derby	**17A** Derby		
43550	3F^3	**17A** Derby	**17A** Derby	**17A** Derby				
43553	3F^3	**20C** Royston	**20C** Royston	**20C** Royston	**55F** Manningham			
43558	3F^3	**16D** Mansfield	**16A** Nottingham	**16A** Nottingham	**21A** Saltley			
43562	3F^3	**21B** Bournville	**9D** Buxton	**5B** Crewe South	**5B** Crewe South	**9D** Buxton		
43565	3F^3	**14A** Cricklewood	**14A** Cricklewood	**14C** St. Albans	**14C** St. Albans	**14E** Bedford		
43568	3F^3	**21D** Stratford on Avon	**21D** Stratford on Avon	**21A** Saltley				
43570	3F^3	**11A** Carnforth	**84G** Shrewsbury	**84G** Shrewsbury	**84G** Shrewsbury	**17B** Burton		
43572	3F^3	**17A** Derby	**17A** Derby	**17A** Derby	**17A** Derby	**9E** Trafford Park		
43573	3F^3	**4A** Shrewsbury						
43574	3F^3	**17A** Derby	**17A** Derby	**17B** Burton	**17B** Burton	**17B** Burton		
43575	3F^3	**18D** Staveley Barrow Hill	**18D** Staveley Barrow Hill	**18D** Staveley Barrow Hill	**18D** Staveley Barrow Hill			
43578	3F^3	**17A** Derby	**17A** Derby	**17A** Derby	**17A** Derby			
43579	3F^3	**20B** Stourton	**20B** Stourton	**20B** Stourton	**55B** Stourton	**56A** Wakefield		
43580	3F^3	**18B** Westhouses	**18B** Westhouses	**18B** Westhouses	**18B** Westhouses	**9E** Trafford Park		
43581	3F^3	**4A** Shrewsbury	**84G** Shrewsbury	**84G** Shrewsbury				
43582	3F^3	**17B** Burton	**17B** Burton					
43583	3F^3	**21B** Bournville	**21B** Bournville	**21B** Bournville	**21B** Bournville	**21B** Bournville		
43584	3F^3	**17A** Derby	**17A** Derby	**17A** Derby	**17A** Derby			
43585	3F^3	**20G** Hellifield	**23B** Hellifield	**20G** Hellifield	**20G** Hellifield	**24H** Hellifield		
43586	3F^3	**20G** Hellifield	**23B** Hellifield	**20G** Hellifield	**55F** Manningham	**55F** Manningham		
43587	3F^3	**16D** Mansfield	**16D** Mansfield	**19C** Canklow	**17B** Burton			
43593	3F^3	**22A** Bristol Barrow Road	**22A** Bristol Barrow Road	**22A** Bristol Barrow Road	**22A** Bristol Barrow Road	**82E** Bristol Barrow Road		
43594	3F^3	**21A** Saltley	**21A** Saltley	**21A** Saltley	**21A** Saltley	**21A** Saltley		
43595	3F^3	**19A** Sheffield Grimesthorpe	**19A** Sheffield Grimesthorpe	**19A** Sheffield Grimesthorpe	**19A** Sheffield Grimesthorpe			
43596	3F^3	**19A** Sheffield Grimesthorpe	**16C** Kirkby in Ashfield	**16C** Kirkby in Ashfield	**16B** Kirkby in Ashfield			
43598	3F^3	**17A** Derby	**17A** Derby	**17A** Derby				
43599	3F^3	**18A** Toton	**18A** Toton	**21A** Saltley	**21A** Saltley	**21A** Saltley		
43600	3F^3	**4A** Shrewsbury	**84G** Shrewsbury	**84G** Shrewsbury				
43604	3F^3	**22B** Gloucester Barnwood	**19A** Sheffield Grimesthorpe					
43605	3F^3	**19A** Sheffield Grimesthorpe	**19A** Sheffield Grimesthorpe	**18D** Staveley Barrow Hill	**18D** Staveley Barrow Hill	**41E** Staveley Barrow Hill		
43607	3F^3	**19A** Sheffield Grimesthorpe	**19A** Sheffield Grimesthorpe	**19A** Sheffield Grimesthorpe				
43608	3F^3	**17B** Burton	**17B** Burton	**17B** Burton	**17B** Burton	**17B** Burton		
43612	3F^3	**19E** Belle Vue	**26G** Belle Vue	**26G** Belle Vue	**39A** Gorton			
43615	3F^3	**8B** Warrington Dallam	**8B** Warrington Dallam	**8B** Warrington Dallam	**8B** Warrington Dallam	**8B** Warrington Dallam		
43618	3F^3	**4A** Shrewsbury	**8B** Warrington Dallam	**8B** Warrington Dallam	**8B** Warrington Dallam	**6K** Rhyl		
43619	3F^3	**17B** Burton	**17B** Burton	**17B** Burton	**17B** Burton			
43620	3F^3	**21A** Saltley	**21A** Saltley	**21A** Saltley	**21A** Saltley	**21A** Saltley	**17A** Derby	
43621	3F^3	**21A** Saltley	**21A** Saltley	**84G** Shrewsbury	**84G** Shrewsbury	**17B** Burton		
43622	3F^3	**18C** Hasland	**18C** Hasland	**68A** Carlisle Kingmoor	**68A** Carlisle Kingmoor			
43623	3F^3	**17B** Burton	**17B** Burton	**17B** Burton	**17B** Burton			
43624	3F^3	**21A** Saltley	**21A** Saltley	**21A** Saltley	**15A** Wellingborough	**15B** Kettering		
43627	3F^3	**21A** Saltley	**21A** Saltley	**21A** Saltley	**21A** Saltley	**21A** Saltley		
43629	3F^3	**14A** Cricklewood	**14A** Cricklewood	**15C** Leicester Midland	**15C** Leicester Midland			
43630	3F^3	**19E** Belle Vue	**26G** Belle Vue	**26G** Belle Vue	**39A** Gorton			
43631	3F^3	**18A** Toton	**18A** Toton	**18A** Toton	**18D** Staveley Barrow Hill			
43633	3F^3	**18A** Toton	**8B** Warrington Dallam	**8B** Warrington Dallam				
43634	3F^3	**16D** Mansfield	**16D** Mansfield	**16D** Mansfield	**16C** Mansfield	**41B** Sheffield Grimesthorpe		
43636	3F^3	**19A** Sheffield Grimesthorpe	**19A** Sheffield Grimesthorpe	**68A** Carlisle Kingmoor				
43637	3F^3	**16A** Nottingham	**16A** Nottingham	**16A** Nottingham	**19A** Sheffield Grimesthorpe	**41B** Sheffield Grimesthorpe	**17A** Derby	
43638	3F^3	**19E** Belle Vue	**26G** Belle Vue	**26G** Belle Vue	**39A** Gorton			
43639	3F^3	**20D** Normanton	**20D** Normanton	**20D** Normanton	**55E** Normanton	**21A** Saltley		
43644	3F^3	**21A** Saltley	**21A** Saltley	**21A** Saltley	**21A** Saltley	**21A** Saltley		
43645	3F^3	**22B** Gloucester Barnwood	**22B** Gloucester Barnwood	**22B** Gloucester Barnwood	**22B** Gloucester Barnwood	**85E** Gloucester Barnwood		
43650	3F^3	**18A** Toton	**18A** Toton	**18A** Toton	**18A** Toton	**9E** Trafford Park		
43651	3F^3	**16B** Spital Bridge	**35C** Spital Bridge	**9G** Northwich	**9G** Northwich			
43652	3F^3	**16B** Spital Bridge	**17B** Burton	**17B** Burton	**17B** Burton	**17B** Burton		
43653	3F^3	**15C** Leicester Midland	**15C** Leicester Midland					
43656	3F^3	**20D** Normanton	**20D** Normanton	**20D** Normanton	**55E** Normanton			
43657	3F^3	**8B** Warrington Dallam	**8B** Warrington Dallam	**8B** Warrington Dallam	**8B** Warrington Dallam	**8B** Warrington Dallam		
43658	3F^3	**17A** Derby	**17A** Derby	**17D** Rowsley	**17A** Derby	**17A** Derby	**17A** Derby	
43660	3F^3	**19C** Canklow	**19C** Canklow	**19C** Canklow	**19C** Canklow			
43661	3F^3	**19A** Sheffield Grimesthorpe	**19A** Sheffield Grimesthorpe	**19A** Sheffield Grimesthorpe				
43662	3F^3	**19A** Sheffield Grimesthorpe	**19A** Sheffield Grimesthorpe					
43664	3F^3	**19C** Canklow	**19C** Canklow	**19C** Canklow	**19C** Canklow	**41D** Canklow		
43665	3F^3	**20A** Leeds Holbeck	**20A** Leeds Holbeck	**15D** Bedford	**15D** Bedford			
43667	3F^3	**21A** Saltley	**21C** Bromsgrove	**21C** Bromsgrove				
43668	3F^3	**21B** Bournville	**21B** Bournville	**21B** Bournville	**21B** Bournville	**21B** Bournville		
43669	3F^3	**19C** Canklow	**19C** Canklow	**19C** Canklow	**19A** Sheffield Grimesthorpe	**41B** Sheffield Grimesthorpe	**17A** Derby	
43673	3F^3	**21A** Saltley	**21A** Saltley	**21A** Saltley	**21A** Saltley	**21A** Saltley		
43674	3F^3	**21A** Saltley	**21A** Saltley	**21A** Saltley	**21A** Saltley			
43675	3F^3	**21B** Bournville	**21B** Bournville	**21B** Bournville	**21B** Bournville			
43676	3F^3	**15C** Leicester Midland	**15C** Leicester Midland	**15C** Leicester Midland				
43678	3F^3	**20B** Stourton	**20B** Stourton	**68A** Carlisle Kingmoor	**68A** Carlisle Kingmoor			
43679	3F^3	**4A** Shrewsbury	**84G** Shrewsbury	**84G** Shrewsbury	**84G** Shrewsbury	**17B** Burton		
43680	3F^3	**21A** Saltley	**21A** Saltley	**21A** Saltley	**21A** Saltley	**21A** Saltley		
43681	3F^3	**20B** Stourton	**20B** Stourton	**20B** Stourton	**55B** Stourton	**55B** Stourton		
43682	3F^3	**17C** Coalville	**17C** Coalville	**17C** Coalville	**71J** Highbridge	**82G** Templecombe		
43683	3F^3	**19A** Sheffield Grimesthorpe	**19A** Sheffield Grimesthorpe	**19A** Sheffield Grimesthorpe				
43684	3F^3	**21A** Saltley	**21A** Saltley	**21A** Saltley	**21A** Saltley			
43686	3F^3	**21A** Saltley	**21C** Bromsgrove	**20E** Manningham				
43687	3F^3	**21B** Bournville	**21B** Bournville	**21B** Bournville	**21B** Bournville	**21B** Bournville		
43690	3F^3	**21A** Saltley	**21A** Saltley	**21A** Saltley	**21A** Saltley			
43693	3F^3	**21D** Stratford on Avon	**21D** Stratford on Avon	**21A** Saltley	**21A** Saltley			
43698	3F^3	**21A** Saltley	**21A** Saltley	**21A** Saltley				
43705	3F^3	**20B** Stourton	**20B** Stourton	**20C** Royston	**55D** Royston	**56A** Wakefield		
43709	3F^3	**17B** Burton	**17B** Burton	**17B** Burton	**17B** Burton	**17B** Burton		
43710	3F^3	**15C** Leicester Midland	**15C** Leicester Midland	**15C** Leicester Midland	**15C** Leicester Midland			
43711	3F^3	**16A** Nottingham	**16A** Nottingham	**16D** Mansfield	**18D** Staveley Barrow Hill			
43712	3F^3	**22A** Bristol Barrow Road	**22A** Bristol Barrow Road	**22A** Bristol Barrow Road	**22A** Bristol Barrow Road			
43714	3F^3	**20D** Normanton	**20D** Normanton	**20D** Normanton	**55E** Normanton	**55E** Normanton		
43715	3F^3	**19A** Sheffield Grimesthorpe	**19A** Sheffield Grimesthorpe	**19A** Sheffield Grimesthorpe	**19A** Sheffield Grimesthorpe	**41B** Sheffield Grimesthorpe		
43717	3F^3	**9A** Longsight	**9A** Longsight	**9A** Longsight	**9A** Longsight			
43721	3F^3	**15D** Bedford	**15D** Bedford	**15D** Bedford	**15D** Bedford	**15B** Kettering		
43723	3F^3	**19E** Belle Vue	**16A** Nottingham	**18C** Hasland				
43724	3F^3	**16A** Nottingham	**16A** Nottingham					

No.	Class	1948	1951	1954	1957	1960	1963	1966
43727	$3F^3$	16D Mansfield	16D Mansfield	16D Mansfield	16C Mansfield			
43728	$3F^3$	15C Leicester Midland	15C Leicester Midland	15C Leicester Midland	15C Leicester Midland			
43729	$3F^3$	16A Nottingham	16A Nottingham	16A Nottingham	16A Nottingham	41F Mexborough		
43731	$3F^3$	19A Sheffield Grimesthorpe	19A Sheffield Grimesthorpe	19A Sheffield Grimesthorpe	19A Sheffield Grimesthorpe			
43734	$3F^3$	22A Bristol Barrow Road	22A Bristol Barrow Road	22A Bristol Barrow Road	22A Bristol Barrow Road	82G Templecombe		
43735	$3F^3$	17A Derby	17A Derby	17A Derby	17A Derby	17A Derby		
43737	$3F^3$	20B Stourton	20B Stourton	20B Stourton	55B Stourton	55B Stourton		
43742	$3F^3$	20D Normanton	20E Manningham	20E Manningham	55F Manningham			
43745	$3F^3$	17A Derby	17A Derby	17A Derby	19A Sheffield Grimesthorpe			
43747	$3F^3$	19C Canklow	19C Canklow					
43748	$3F^3$	15C Leicester Midland	15C Leicester Midland	15C Leicester Midland				
43749	$3F^3$	19A Sheffield Grimesthorpe	19A Sheffield Grimesthorpe	19A Sheffield Grimesthorpe	19A Sheffield Grimesthorpe	41B Sheffield Grimesthorpe		
43750	$3F^2$	(43137)	→	17A Derby	17D Rowsley			
43751	$3F^3$	18D Staveley Barrow Hill	18D Staveley Barrow Hill	18A Toton	18A Toton	41B Sheffield Grimesthorpe		
43753	$3F^3$	15C Leicester Midland	15C Leicester Midland	15C Leicester Midland	15C Leicester Midland			
43754	$3F^3$	22B Gloucester Barnwood	22B Gloucester Barnwood	22B Gloucester Barnwood	22B Gloucester Barnwood	85E Gloucester Barnwood		
43755	$3F^3$	19A Sheffield Grimesthorpe	19A Sheffield Grimesthorpe	19A Sheffield Grimesthorpe				
43756	$3F^3$	19E Belle Vue	26G Belle Vue	26G Belle Vue	26A Newton Heath	24H Hellifield		
43757	$3F^3$	11A Carnforth	84G Shrewsbury	84G Shrewsbury	84G Shrewsbury			
43759	$3F^3$	17A Derby	21A Saltley	17D Rowsley	17D Rowsley			
43760	$3F^3$	11A Carnforth	84G Shrewsbury	84G Shrewsbury	84G Shrewsbury	3A Bescot		
43762	$3F^3$	16D Mansfield	21A Saltley	21A Saltley	21C Bromsgrove	85F Bromsgrove		
43763	$3F^3$	17A Derby	17A Derby	17A Derby	17A Derby	9G Gorton		
43765	$3F^4$	16D Mansfield	20C Royston					
43766	$3F^4$	15D Bedford	15D Bedford	15D Bedford	15D Bedford	14E Bedford		
43767	$3F^4$	21D Stratford on Avon	18A Toton					
43769	$3F^4$	18C Hasland						
43770	$3F^4$	20B Stourton	20E Manningham	20E Manningham				
43771	$3F^4$	18C Hasland	18C Hasland	21A Saltley	21A Saltley			
43772	$3F^4$	19A Sheffield Grimesthorpe						
43773	$3F^4$	16C Kirkby in Ashfield	16C Kirkby in Ashfield	16C Kirkby in Ashfield	16B Kirkby in Ashfield	9G Gorton		
43775	$3F^4$	19A Sheffield Grimesthorpe	19A Sheffield Grimesthorpe	19A Sheffield Grimesthorpe				
43776	$3F^4$	17A Derby	17A Derby	17D Rowsley	17D Rowsley			
43777	$3F^4$	15D Bedford	15D Bedford					
43778	$3F^4$	18A Toton	18A Toton	18A Toton	17B Burton	17A Derby		
43779	$3F^4$	17C Coalville	17C Coalville	16C Kirkby in Ashfield				
43781	$3F^4$	20G Hellifield	20B Stourton	20B Stourton				
43782	$3F^4$	14A Cricklewood	14C St. Albans	14C St. Albans				
43783	$3F^4$	20E Manningham						
43784	$3F^4$	20F Skipton	23A Skipton	20F Skipton	55F Manningham	55F Manningham		
43785	$3F^4$	15D Bedford	15D Bedford	15D Bedford	15D Bedford			
43786	$3F^4$	3C Walsall	3C Walsall	2B Nuneaton	2B Nuneaton			
43787	$3F^4$	18A Toton	8B Warrington Dallam	8B Warrington Dallam	8B Warrington Dallam			
43789	$3F^4$	20C Royston	20C Royston	20C Royston	55D Royston	17B Burton		
43790	$3F^4$	15C Leicester Midland	15C Leicester Midland	15C Leicester Midland				
43791	$3F^4$	22B Gloucester Barnwood	21A Saltley	21A Saltley				
43792	$3F^4$	22D Templecombe	71J Highbridge					
43793	$3F^4$	18A Toton	18A Toton	18A Toton	18A Toton	15C Leicester Midland		
43795	$3F^4$	18A Toton	18A Toton	18A Toton	18A Toton			
43796	$3F^4$	15A Wellingborough						
43797	$3F^4$	15A Wellingborough	15A Wellingborough					
43798	$3F^4$	18A Toton	18A Toton	21A Saltley	21A Saltley			
43799	$3F^4$	18A Toton	18A Toton	15C Leicester Midland	15C Leicester Midland			
43800	$3F^4$	14A Cricklewood	21A Saltley	19A Sheffield Grimesthorpe	19A Sheffield Grimesthorpe	41B Sheffield Grimesthorpe		
43801	$3F^4$	14C St. Albans	14C St. Albans					
43802	$3F^4$	16D Mansfield						
43803	$3F^4$	18A Toton	18A Toton	21A Saltley				
43804	$3F^4$	18A Toton	18A Toton					
43805	$3F^4$	18A Toton						
43806	$3F^4$	14A Cricklewood	15C Leicester Midland	15C Leicester Midland	15C Leicester Midland			
43807	$3F^4$	15C Leicester Midland	15C Leicester Midland					
43808	$3F^4$	15A Wellingborough	15A Wellingborough	15A Wellingborough	15D Bedford	14E Bedford		
43809	$3F^4$	18D Staveley Barrow Hill	17C Coalville	17C Coalville	17C Coalville	15D Coalville		
43810	$3F^4$	18A Toton	18A Toton	18A Toton				
43811	$3F^4$	19D Heaton Mersey	9F Heaton Mersey					
43812	$3F^4$	21A Saltley	21A Saltley	21A Saltley	21A Saltley	21A Saltley		
43813	$3F^4$	19C Canklow						
43814	$3F^4$	19C Canklow	19C Canklow	19C Canklow	19C Canklow	41D Canklow		
43815	$3F^4$	17B Burton	17B Burton	17B Burton	17B Burton			
43817	$3F^4$	18A Toton	18A Toton	21A Saltley				
43818	$3F^4$	18A Toton						
43819	$3F^4$	18A Toton	18A Toton	18A Toton				
43820	$3F^4$	18A Toton	18A Toton					
43821	$3F^4$	18A Toton		18A Toton				
43822	$3F^4$	21D Stratford on Avon	21D Stratford on Avon	84G Shrewsbury	84G Shrewsbury	3A Bescot		
43823	$3F^4$	18A Toton	18A Toton	18A Toton	18A Toton			
43824	$3F^4$	18A Toton	18A Toton					
43825	$3F^4$	18A Toton	18A Toton	18A Toton	18B Westhouses	18B Westhouses		
43826	$3F^4$	18A Toton	18A Toton	18A Toton	18A Toton	9G Gorton		
43827	$3F^4$	18A Toton						
43828	$3F^4$	18A Toton	18A Toton	18A Toton	18A Toton	41E Staveley Barrow Hill		
43829	$3F^4$	15C Leicester Midland	15C Leicester Midland	15C Leicester Midland	15D Bedford			
43830	$3F^4$	15A Wellingborough						
43831	$3F^4$	18A Toton						
43832	$3F^4$	18A Toton	18A Toton	18A Toton	18A Toton	9F Heaton Mersey		
43833	$3F^4$	18A Toton	18A Toton					
43835	$4F^1$	17C Coalville	17C Coalville	17C Coalville				
43836	$4F^1$	19E Belle Vue	9F Heaton Mersey	6B Mold Junction	9D Buxton			
43837	$4F^1$	17B Burton	17B Burton	22B Gloucester Barnwood	21B Bournville			
43838	$4F^1$	17A Derby	17A Derby	17A Derby				
43839	$4F^1$	17A Derby	17A Derby	17A Derby	17B Burton	17B Burton		
43840	$4F^1$	17A Derby	17A Derby	17A Derby	17A Derby	5D Stoke		
43841	$4F^1$	2B Bletchley	4A Bletchley	1E Bletchley	1E Bletchley			
43842	$4F^1$	9D Buxton	9D Buxton	9D Buxton	9D Buxton			
43843	$4F^1$	21A Saltley	21A Saltley	21A Saltley	15C Leicester Midland	17B Burton		
43844	$4F^1$	19A Sheffield Grimesthorpe	19A Sheffield Grimesthorpe	19A Sheffield Grimesthorpe	19A Sheffield Grimesthorpe	41B Sheffield Grimesthorpe		
43845	$4F^1$	21A Saltley	21A Saltley	21A Saltley	18A Toton	18A Toton	18A Toton	
43846	$4F^1$	22B Gloucester Barnwood	22B Gloucester Barnwood	22B Gloucester Barnwood	17B Burton	14C St. Albans		
43847	$4F^1$	17B Burton	17A Derby	17A Derby	17A Derby			
43848	$4F^1$	31A St. Rollox	65B St. Rollox	65B St. Rollox	65B St. Rollox	66A Polmadie		
43849	$4F^1$	31A St. Rollox	65B St. Rollox	65B St. Rollox	65B St. Rollox	66A Polmadie		
43850	$4F^1$	18B Westhouses	18B Westhouses	18B Westhouses	18B Westhouses	18B Westhouses	18B Westhouses	
43851	$4F^1$	20B Stourton	20D Normanton	20B Stourton	55B Stourton			
43852	$4F^1$	20B Stourton	20D Normanton	20D Normanton	66E Normanton			
43853	$4F^1$	22A Bristol Barrow Road	22A Bristol Barrow Road	22B Gloucester Barnwood	22B Gloucester Barnwood	85E Gloucester Barnwood	85C Gloucester Barnwood	
43854	$4F^1$	16B Spital Bridge	35C Spital Bridge	9F Heaton Mersey	17E Heaton Mersey	15D Coalville	15D Coalville	
43855	$4F^1$	20B Stourton	21A Saltley	21A Saltley	17A Derby	21A Saltley	17A Derby	
43856	$4F^1$	18C Hasland	18C Hasland	18B Westhouses	16A Nottingham	16A Nottingham	9G Gorton	
43857	$4F^1$	18D Staveley Barrow Hill	18D Staveley Barrow Hill	18D Staveley Barrow Hill	19C Canklow			
43858	$4F^1$	21A Saltley	21A Saltley	21A Saltley	17B Burton			
43859	$4F^1$	16B Spital Bridge	17A Derby	17A Derby	16B Kirkby in Ashfield	16A Nottingham		
43860	$4F^1$	18B Westhouses	18B Westhouses	18B Westhouses	18B Westhouses			
43861	$4F^1$	15A Wellingborough	15A Wellingborough	15A Wellingborough	15A Wellingborough	15A Wellingborough	18A Toton	
43862	$4F^1$	18D Staveley Barrow Hill	17A Derby	21A Saltley				

		1948	1951	1954	1957	1960	1963	1966
43863	4F[1]	18D Staveley Barrow Hill	18D Staveley Barrow Hill	18D Staveley Barrow Hill	18D Staveley Barrow Hill	41E Staveley Barrow Hill		
43864	4F[1]	16B Spital Bridge	35C Spital Bridge	8E Brunswick	5D Stoke			
43865	4F[1]	17C Coalville	17C Coalville	21A Saltley	18A Toton	18A Toton	18A Toton	
43866	4F[1]	18B Westhouses	18B Westhouses	18B Westhouses	18B Westhouses			
43867	4F[1]	18B Westhouses	18B Westhouses	18B Westhouses				
43868	4F[1]	12A Carlisle Kingmoor	68A Carlisle Kingmoor	68A Carlisle Kingmoor	68A Carlisle Kingmoor	11B Workington		
43869	4F[1]	16A Nottingham	21A Saltley	21A Saltley	18D Staveley Barrow Hill	41E Staveley Barrow Hill		
43870	4F[1]	15A Wellingborough	15C Leicester Midland	15C Leicester Midland	15C Leicester Midland	16A Nottingham	16A Nottingham	
43871	4F[1]	20B Stourton	20B Stourton	20B Stourton	55B Stourton	55B Stourton	55B Stourton	
43872	4F[1]	17C Coalville	17C Coalville	19C Canklow	19C Canklow	41B Sheffield Grimesthorpe		
43873	4F[1]	21D Stratford on Avon	21D Stratford on Avon	15D Bedford	15D Bedford			
43874	4F[1]	16D Mansfield	16D Mansfield	16C Kirkby in Ashfield				
43875	4F[1]	22C Bath Green Park	71G Bath Green Park	21A Saltley				
43876	4F[1]	15A Wellingborough	15C Leicester Midland	15C Leicester Midland	15C Leicester Midland	15D Coalville		
43877	4F[1]	7A Llandudno Junction	7A Llandudno Junction	6G Llandudno Junction	6E Wrexham Rhosddu			
43878	4F[1]	20A Leeds Holbeck	20B Stourton	21A Saltley	21A Saltley			
43879	4F[1]	21A Saltley	21A Saltley	21A Saltley	17A Derby			
43880	4F[1]	18B Westhouses	18B Westhouses	18B Westhouses	18B Westhouses	26D Bury	26D Bury	
43881	4F[1]	17A Derby	17D Rowsley	17D Rowsley	17A Derby			
43882	4F[1]	18B Westhouses	17C Coalville	19A Sheffield Grimesthorpe	19A Sheffield Grimesthorpe	41B Sheffield Grimesthorpe	41E Staveley Barrow Hill	
43883	4F[1]	31D Grangemouth	65D Dawsholm	66B Motherwell	66B Motherwell	66B Motherwell		
43884	4F[1]	28A Motherwell	63B Stirling	63B Stirling	63B Stirling	66A Polmadie		
43885	4F[1]	18A Toton	18B Westhouses	18B Westhouses	17C Coalville	16B Kirkby in Ashfield	16B Kirkby in Ashfield	
43886	4F[1]	18D Staveley Barrow Hill	18D Staveley Barrow Hill	18D Staveley Barrow Hill	18D Staveley Barrow Hill			
43887	4F[1]	22B Gloucester Barnwood	22B Gloucester Barnwood	22B Gloucester Barnwood	22B Gloucester Barnwood	85E Gloucester Barnwood	85C Gloucester Barnwood	
43888	4F[1]	15D Bedford	15D Bedford	15D Bedford	16A Nottingham	16A Nottingham	16A Nottingham	
43889	4F[1]	15B Kettering	15B Kettering	15B Kettering	18D Staveley Barrow Hill			
43890	4F[1]	18C Hasland	23C Lancaster	11E Lancaster	11E Lancaster			
43891	4F[1]	21A Saltley	21A Saltley	18C Hasland	18C Hasland			
43892	4F[1]	17B Burton	17B Burton	17B Burton	17B Burton			
43893	4F[1]	20F Skipton	23A Skipton	20F Skipton	20F Skipton	24G Skipton	24G Skipton	
43894	4F[1]	16C Kirkby in Ashfield	17C Coalville	17C Coalville				
43895	4F[1]	16C Kirkby in Ashfield	16C Kirkby in Ashfield	16C Kirkby in Ashfield				
43896	4F[1]	19G Trafford Park	9E Trafford Park	12A Carlisle Upperby	12A Carlisle Upperby			
43897	4F[1]	24D Lower Darwen	24D Lower Darwen	24D Lower Darwen	24D Lower Darwen	24D Lower Darwen		
43898	4F[1]	16B Spital Bridge	15B Kettering	15B Kettering	15D Bedford			
43899	4F[1]	30B Hurlford	67A Corkerhill	67A Corkerhill	67A Corkerhill	67A Corkerhill		
43900	4F[1]	18A Toton	18D Staveley Barrow Hill	18D Staveley Barrow Hill	18D Staveley Barrow Hill	41E Staveley Barrow Hill		
43901	4F[1]	14A Cricklewood	14A Cricklewood	14A Cricklewood	14A Cricklewood			
43902	4F[1]	12A Carlisle Kingmoor	68A Carlisle Kingmoor	68A Carlisle Kingmoor	68A Carlisle Kingmoor	12A Carlisle Kingmoor		
43903	4F[1]	20D Normanton	16C Kirkby in Ashfield	16C Kirkby in Ashfield	16B Kirkby in Ashfield	16B Kirkby in Ashfield	16B Kirkby in Ashfield	
43904	4F[1]	20F Skipton	23C Lancaster	6B Mold Junction	11B Barrow			
43905	4F[1]	13A Plaistow	14A Cricklewood	14A Cricklewood	14A Cricklewood	14A Cricklewood		
43906	4F[1]	19C Canklow	19C Canklow	20C Royston	55D Royston	55D Royston	55D Royston	
43907	4F[1]	16C Kirkby in Ashfield	16C Kirkby in Ashfield	16C Kirkby in Ashfield	16B Kirkby in Ashfield			
43908	4F[1]	19D Heaton Mersey	9E Trafford Park	6B Mold Junction	6B Mold Junction	24L Carnforth	12B Carlisle Upperby	
43909	4F[1]	15A Wellingborough	14B Kentish Town	21A Saltley				
43910	4F[1]	15D Bedford	15D Bedford	16A Nottingham	16A Nottingham			
43911	4F[1]	21A Saltley	21A Saltley	21A Saltley	21A Saltley	21A Saltley		
43912	4F[1]	21A Saltley	21A Saltley	21A Saltley	21A Saltley			
43913	4F[1]	20D Normanton	23A Skipton	20F Skipton	20F Skipton	24G Skipton	26D Bury	
43914	4F[1]	18A Toton	18D Staveley Barrow Hill	18D Staveley Barrow Hill	55D Royston	55D Royston		
43915	4F[1]	2B Bletchley	5D Stoke	5F Uttoxeter	8E Brunswick	27F Brunswick	9G Gorton	
43916	4F[1]	17B Burton	17B Burton	20F Skipton	20F Skipton			
43917	4F[1]	17B Burton	23A Skipton	16A Nottingham	16A Nottingham	16A Nottingham	18B Westhouses	
43918	4F[1]	17D Rowsley	17D Rowsley	17D Rowsley	16A Nottingham	16A Nottingham	16A Nottingham	
43919	4F[1]	17B Burton	17B Burton	17B Burton	14B Kentish Town			
43920	4F[1]	16B Spital Bridge	18D Staveley Barrow Hill	18D Staveley Barrow Hill	18D Staveley Barrow Hill	41E Staveley Barrow Hill		
43921	4F[1]	17C Coalville	17C Coalville	17C Coalville	17C Coalville	18A Toton		
43922	4F[1]	12A Carlisle Kingmoor	68A Carlisle Kingmoor	68A Carlisle Kingmoor	68A Carlisle Kingmoor	12A Carlisle Kingmoor		
43923	4F[1]	18A Toton	15D Bedford	15D Bedford	17C Coalville	14A Cricklewood	16B Kirkby in Ashfield	
43924	4F[1]	22B Gloucester Barnwood	22B Gloucester Barnwood	22B Gloucester Barnwood	22B Gloucester Barnwood	85E Gloucester Barnwood	82E Bristol Barrow Road	
43925	4F[1]	17D Rowsley	17D Rowsley	17A Derby	17A Derby	17A Derby	9G Gorton	
43926	4F[1]	14A Cricklewood	22A Bristol Barrow Road	22A Bristol Barrow Road	22A Bristol Barrow Road			
43927	4F[1]	19E Belle Vue	26G Belle Vue	26G Belle Vue	39A Gorton			
43928	4F[1]	22A Bristol Barrow Road	22A Bristol Barrow Road	22A Bristol Barrow Road	16A Nottingham	16A Nottingham	16A Nottingham	
43929	4F[1]	17D Rowsley	17D Rowsley	17D Rowsley	15A Wellingborough	15A Wellingborough	9G Gorton	
43930	4F[1]	17B Burton	15A Wellingborough	15A Wellingborough	15C Leicester Midland			
43931	4F[1]	20B Stourton	20A Leeds Holbeck	20B Stourton	55B Stourton	55B Stourton	55B Stourton	
43932	4F[1]	22B Gloucester Barnwood	22B Gloucester Barnwood	22A Bristol Barrow Road	21B Bournville	21A Saltley		
43933	4F[1]	16A Nottingham	23C Lancaster	18A Toton	17C Coalville	16B Kirkby in Ashfield		
43934	4F[1]	14A Cricklewood	14A Cricklewood	14A Cricklewood	14A Cricklewood			
43935	4F[1]	14B Kentish Town	14A Cricklewood	14A Cricklewood	14A Cricklewood	14A Cricklewood	14E Bedford	
43936	4F[1]	18C Hasland	18C Hasland	18C Hasland				
43937	4F[1]	15C Leicester Midland	15C Leicester Midland	15C Leicester Midland	15C Leicester Midland	15C Leicester Midland	9G Gorton	
43938	4F[1]	17B Burton	17B Burton	21A Saltley	21A Saltley	21A Saltley		
43939	4F[1]	18A Toton	21A Saltley	21A Saltley	21A Saltley			
43940	4F[1]	21A Saltley	21A Saltley	21A Saltley	21A Saltley	21A Saltley	21A Saltley	
43941	4F[1]	21A Saltley	21A Saltley	21A Saltley	18A Toton			
43942	4F[1]	20C Royston	20C Royston	20C Royston	55D Royston	55D Royston	55D Royston	
43943	4F[1]	18A Toton	18A Toton	18A Toton				
43944	4F[1]	20F Skipton	23A Skipton	20F Skipton	55F Manningham	55F Manningham		
43945	4F[1]	19D Heaton Mersey	9F Heaton Mersey	9F Heaton Mersey	17E Heaton Mersey	9F Heaton Mersey	9F Heaton Mersey	
43946	4F[1]	21A Saltley	21A Saltley	21A Saltley	18A Toton			
43947	4F[1]	14A Cricklewood	14A Cricklewood	14A Cricklewood	14A Cricklewood	14A Cricklewood	15B Kettering	
43948	4F[1]	16A Nottingham	17B Burton	17B Burton	17B Burton	21A Saltley		
43949	4F[1]	21A Saltley	21A Saltley	21A Saltley	21A Saltley		21A Saltley	
43950	4F[1]	19C Canklow	19C Canklow	19C Canklow	19C Canklow	17C Rowsley	9G Gorton	
43951	4F[1]	21A Saltley	21A Saltley	21A Saltley	21A Saltley	21A Saltley	21A Saltley	
43952	4F[1]	19E Belle Vue	26G Belle Vue	27D Wigan	27D Wigan	27D Wigan	26A Newton Heath	
43953	4F[1]	22A Bristol Barrow Road	20A Leeds Holbeck	20A Leeds Holbeck	17B Burton	16A Nottingham	9G Gorton	
43954	4F[1]	16A Nottingham	16A Nottingham	16A Nottingham	16A Nottingham	16A Nottingham	16A Nottingham	
43955	4F[1]	17A Derby	17A Derby	17A Derby	17A Derby	17A Derby	17A Derby	
43956	4F[1]	16A Nottingham	16A Nottingham	16A Nottingham	16A Nottingham			
43957	4F[1]	16B Spital Bridge	35C Spital Bridge	35C Spital Bridge	35C Spital Bridge	31F Spital Bridge	Crewe Works	
43958	4F[1]	16A Nottingham	16A Nottingham	16A Nottingham	16A Nottingham	16A Nottingham	21A Saltley	
43959	4F[1]	18C Hasland	18C Hasland	18C Hasland	18C Hasland			
43960	4F[1]	20F Skipton	23A Skipton	20F Skipton	20F Skipton	24G Skipton	24G Skipton	
43961	4F[1]	18A Toton	18A Toton	18A Toton	18A Toton			
43962	4F[1]	16A Nottingham	16A Nottingham	16A Nottingham	16A Nottingham	16A Nottingham		
43963	4F[1]	20B Stourton	20B Stourton	21A Saltley	21A Saltley	21A Saltley	21A Saltley	
43964	4F[1]	14B Kentish Town	14B Kentish Town	14B Kentish Town	14B Kentish Town	14B Kentish Town	14A Cricklewood	
43965	4F[1]	15C Leicester Midland	17B Burton	17B Burton	17B Burton			
43966	4F[1]	18B Westhouses	18B Westhouses	18B Westhouses	18B Westhouses			
43967	4F[1]	15D Bedford	15D Bedford	15D Bedford	15D Bedford	18C Hasland	18C Hasland	
43968	4F[1]	21B Bournville	21A Saltley	20A Leeds Holbeck	55A Leeds Holbeck	55B Stourton	55B Stourton	
43969	4F[1]	16A Nottingham	18A Toton	18A Toton	17A Derby	15C Leicester Midland	15C Leicester Midland	
43970	4F[1]	18A Toton	18C Hasland	16C Kirkby in Ashfield	16B Kirkby in Ashfield			
43971	4F[1]	15D Bedford	15D Bedford	15D Bedford	15D Bedford	14C St. Albans	18A Toton	
43972	4F[1]	17B Burton	17B Burton	16A Nottingham	16A Nottingham	16C Mansfield	9G Gorton	
43973	4F[1]	12A Carlisle Kingmoor	68A Carlisle Kingmoor	68A Carlisle Kingmoor	68A Carlisle Kingmoor	5E Alsager		
43974	4F[1]	18A Toton	18A Toton	18A Toton				
43975	4F[1]	18A Toton	15A Wellingborough	15A Wellingborough	14B Kentish Town	15D Coalville	16B Kirkby in Ashfield	
43976	4F[1]	17B Burton	17B Burton	17B Burton	17B Burton	26F Patricroft	24D Lower Darwen	

No.	Class	1948	1951	1954	1957	1960	1963	1966
43977	$4F^1$	15C Leicester Midland	15C Leicester Midland	15A Wellingborough	15A Wellingborough	15A Wellingborough	2B Nuneaton	
43978	$4F^1$	22B Gloucester Barnwood	22B Gloucester Barnwood	19C Canklow	19C Canklow			
43979	$4F^1$	18A Toton	18A Toton	15A Wellingborough	15A Wellingborough	15A Wellingborough	21A Saltley	
43980	$4F^1$	16B Spital Bridge	35C Spital Bridge	5D Stoke	11D Tebay			
43981	$4F^1$	16B Spital Bridge	35C Spital Bridge	6E Wrexham Rhosddu	6G Llandudno Junction	6K Rhyl	12A Carlisle Kingmoor	
43982	$4F^1$	15A Wellingborough	16A Nottingham	16A Nottingham	17D Rowsley	18B Westhouses	18C Hasland	
43983	$4F^1$	16D Mansfield	16D Mansfield	16D Mansfield	55D Royston	55D Royston	55D Royston	
43984	$4F^1$	20F Skipton	23A Skipton	11E Lancaster	11E Lancaster			
43985	$4F^1$	19E Belle Vue	21A Saltley	21A Saltley	21A Saltley	21A Saltley		
43986	$4F^1$	21A Saltley	21A Saltley	21A Saltley	21A Saltley	21A Saltley	18C Hasland	
43987	$4F^1$	20B Stourton	20B Stourton	20B Stourton	55B Stourton	55B Stourton	55B Stourton	
43988	$4F^1$	18A Toton	18A Toton	18A Toton	18A Toton	27E Walton on the Hill	15C Leicester Midland	
43989	$4F^1$	20B Stourton	20B Stourton	20B Stourton	21B Bournville	17B Burton		
43990	$4F^1$	18A Toton	18A Toton	18A Toton	18A Toton			
43991	$4F^1$	17B Burton	17B Burton	17A Derby	17A Derby	17A Derby	15D Coalville	
43992	$4F^1$	18B Westhouses	18B Westhouses	17B Burton	20F Skipton			
43993	$4F^1$	18D Staveley Barrow Hill	18D Staveley Barrow Hill	18D Staveley Barrow Hill	18D Staveley Barrow Hill			
43994	$4F^1$	16A Nottingham	18A Toton	18A Toton	18A Toton	18A Toton	18A Toton	
43995	$4F^1$	18A Toton	18A Toton	18A Toton	15C Leicester Midland	15A Wellingborough	15D Coalville	
43996	$4F^1$	12A Carlisle Kingmoor	67B Hurlford	67A Corkerhill	67A Corkerhill	67A Corkerhill		
43997	$4F^1$	10D Mansfield	10D Mansfield	16C Kirkby in Ashfield	16B Kirkby in Ashfield			
43998	$4F^1$	20B Stourton	18B Westhouses	18B Westhouses	18B Westhouses			
43999	$4F^1$	20F Skipton	23A Skipton	20F Skipton	20F Skipton	24G Skipton	24G Skipton	
44000	$4F^1$	20F Skipton	23A Skipton	20F Skipton	20F Skipton			
44001	$4F^1$	12A Carlisle Kingmoor	67B Hurlford	67A Corkerhill	67A Corkerhill	67A Corkerhill		
44002	$4F^1$	17B Burton	17B Burton	19C Canklow	19C Canklow	41D Canklow		
44003	$4F^1$	20C Royston	20C Royston	20C Royston	55D Royston	55B Stourton	55B Stourton	
44004	$4F^1$	16D Mansfield	16D Mansfield	21A Saltley	21A Saltley	21A Saltley		
44005	$4F^1$	16C Kirkby in Ashfield	16C Kirkby in Ashfield	16C Kirkby in Ashfield	16B Kirkby in Ashfield			
44006	$4F^1$	19A Sheffield Grimesthorpe	18D Staveley Barrow Hill	18D Staveley Barrow Hill				
44007	$4F^1$	20F Skipton	23A Skipton	20F Skipton	20F Skipton	24G Skipton	24G Skipton	
44008	$4F^1$	12A Carlisle Kingmoor	68A Carlisle Kingmoor	68A Carlisle Kingmoor	68A Carlisle Kingmoor	12A Carlisle Kingmoor		
44009	$4F^1$	12A Carlisle Kingmoor	68A Carlisle Kingmoor	68A Carlisle Kingmoor	68A Carlisle Kingmoor	12A Carlisle Kingmoor	12A Carlisle Kingmoor	
44010	$4F^1$	19D Heaton Mersey	21A Saltley	18D Staveley Barrow Hill	18D Staveley Barrow Hill	41E Staveley Barrow Hill	41E Staveley Barrow Hill	
44011	$4F^1$	28A Motherwell	63B Stirling	63B Stirling	63B Stirling	66D Greenock Ladyburn		
44012	$4F^1$	18A Toton	18A Toton	18A Toton	18A Toton	18A Toton	18A Toton	
44013	$4F^1$	19C Canklow	19C Canklow	19C Canklow	19C Canklow	21A Saltley	15C Leicester Midland	
44014	$4F^1$	18B Westhouses	18B Westhouses	18B Westhouses	18B Westhouses			
44015	$4F^1$	19C Canklow	19C Canklow	19C Canklow	22A Bristol Barrow Road	9G Gorton	9G Gorton	
44016	$4F^1$	12A Carlisle Kingmoor	68A Carlisle Kingmoor	68A Carlisle Kingmoor	68A Carlisle Kingmoor	12B Carlisle Upperby		
44017	$4F^1$	17D Rowsley	17D Rowsley	17D Rowsley	17A Derby			
44018	$4F^1$	17D Rowsley	17D Rowsley	17D Rowsley	16A Nottingham			
44019	$4F^1$	9D Buxton	26G Belle Vue	25A Wakefield	56A Wakefield	56A Wakefield		
44020	$4F^1$	20B Stourton	20B Stourton	18A Toton	17A Derby	17A Derby		
44021	$4F^1$	16C Kirkby in Ashfield	16C Kirkby in Ashfield	16C Kirkby in Ashfield	16A Nottingham			
44022	$4F^1$	19E Belle Vue	26G Belle Vue	26G Belle Vue	26A Newton Heath	26A Newton Heath	26A Newton Heath	
44023	$4F^1$	17A Derby	21A Saltley	21A Saltley	16B Kirkby in Ashfield	27E Walton on the Hill	17A Derby	
44024	$4F^1$	17D Rowsley	17D Rowsley	5D Stoke	5F Uttoxeter			
44025	$4F^1$	19E Belle Vue	26G Belle Vue	26G Belle Vue	39A Gorton	9G Gorton	9G Gorton	
44026	$4F^1$	21A Saltley	21A Saltley	21A Saltley	21A Saltley	21A Saltley	18A Toton	
44027	$4F^2$	3B Bushbury	3B Bushbury	3B Bushbury	3B Bushbury	3A Bescot	21B Bescot	
44028	$4F^2$	14A Cricklewood	14A Cricklewood	17D Rowsley	55B Stourton	55B Stourton	55B Stourton	
44029	$4F^2$	14A Cricklewood	14A Cricklewood	14A Cricklewood	14A Cricklewood	14A Cricklewood		
44030	$4F^2$	16A Nottingham	16A Nottingham	16A Nottingham	16A Nottingham	16A Nottingham	15C Leicester Midland	
44031	$4F^2$	17A Derby	17A Derby	17A Derby	17A Derby	17A Derby		
44032	$4F^2$	20H Lancaster	23C Lancaster	11E Lancaster	5D Stoke			
44033	$4F^2$	15A Wellingborough	14A Cricklewood	16A Nottingham	16A Nottingham	16A Nottingham		
44034	$4F^2$	15C Leicester Midland	15C Leicester Midland	15C Leicester Midland	15C Leicester Midland	15C Leicester Midland	15C Leicester Midland	
44035	$4F^2$	17B Burton	22B Gloucester Barnwood	22B Gloucester Barnwood	22B Gloucester Barnwood	85E Gloucester Barnwood	12F Workington	
44036	$4F^2$	19C Canklow	19C Canklow	19C Canklow	19C Canklow	41B Sheffield Grimesthorpe		
44037	$4F^2$	20B Stourton	15A Wellingborough	19C Canklow	19C Canklow	41D Canklow		
44038	$4F^2$	25E Sowerby Bridge	27E Walton on the Hill	27E Walton on the Hill	27E Walton on the Hill	27E Walton on the Hill	21A Saltley	
44039	$4F^2$	16A Nottingham	16A Nottingham	16A Nottingham	19A Sheffield Grimesthorpe	41B Sheffield Grimesthorpe	55F Manningham	
44040	$4F^2$	19E Belle Vue	26G Belle Vue	26G Belle Vue	27E Walton on the Hill	27E Walton on the Hill	21A Saltley	
44041	$4F^2$	20F Skipton	23A Skipton	20F Skipton	20F Skipton	24G Skipton	24G Skipton	
44042	$4F^2$	25E Sowerby Bridge	25D Mirfield	26G Belle Vue	17A Derby	17C Rowsley	17C Rowsley	
44043	$4F^2$	18A Toton	15B Kettering	15D Bedford	15D Bedford	14C St. Albans	18A Toton	
44044	$4F^2$	20A Leeds Holbeck	20A Leeds Holbeck	20A Leeds Holbeck	55A Leeds Holbeck	55B Stourton	55B Stourton	
44045	$4F^2$	22B Gloucester Barnwood	22B Gloucester Barnwood	22B Gloucester Barnwood	22B Gloucester Barnwood	85E Gloucester Barnwood	85C Gloucester Barnwood	
44046	$4F^2$	17B Burton	17D Rowsley	17D Rowsley	17D Rowsley	17C Rowsley	17C Rowsley	
44047	$4F^2$	17B Burton	17B Burton	18A Toton	17B Burton	16A Nottingham	21A Saltley	
44048	$4F^2$	17B Burton	17B Burton	17B Burton	17A Derby	17A Derby	5F Uttoxeter	
44049	$4F^2$	21A Saltley	21A Saltley	21A Saltley	17A Derby	17A Derby	17A Derby	
44050	$4F^2$	17D Rowsley	17D Rowsley	17D Rowsley	17D Rowsley			
44051	$4F^2$	14A Cricklewood	14A Cricklewood	14A Cricklewood	14A Cricklewood	14A Cricklewood	15B Kettering	
44052	$4F^2$	14B Kentish Town	14B Kentish Town	14B Kentish Town	14B Kentish Town	14B Kentish Town		
44053	$4F^2$	18C Hasland	18C Hasland	18C Hasland	18C Hasland	18C Hasland	18C Hasland	
44054	$4F^2$	18C Hasland	18C Hasland	18C Hasland	18C Hasland	18C Hasland	18C Hasland	
44055	$4F^2$	16A Nottingham	16A Nottingham	17B Burton	55A Leeds Holbeck	55F Manningham	56E Sowerby Bridge	
44056	$4F^2$	23C Southport	25D Mirfield	25D Mirfield	56D Mirfield	56D Mirfield	56D Mirfield	
44057	$4F^2$	3E Monument Lane	3E Monument Lane	3E Monument Lane	3E Monument Lane	3E Monument Lane	21B Bescot	
44058	$4F^2$	3D Aston	2A Rugby	6E Wrexham Rhosddu	6E Wrexham Rhosddu			
44059	$4F^2$	11B Barrow	11B Barrow	11B Barrow	9B Stockport Edgeley	9D Buxton	9D Buxton	
44060	$4F^2$	11A Carnforth	11A Carnforth	12A Carlisle Upperby	12A Carlisle Upperby	12B Carlisle Upperby	12A Carlisle Kingmoor	
44061	$4F^2$	3A Bescot	4B Northampton	2E Northampton	2E Northampton	5E Alsager	8B Warrington Dallam	
44062	$4F^2$	23C Southport	25D Mirfield	25D Mirfield	56D Mirfield	56F Low Moor		
44063	$4F^2$	5E Alsager	5E Alsager	5E Alsager	5E Alsager	5E Alsager	8B Warrington Dallam	
44064	$4F^2$	12D Workington	12D Workington	2A Rugby	2A Rugby			
44065	$4F^2$	6B Mold Junction	6B Mold Junction	6B Mold Junction	6B Mold Junction	6B Mold Junction	12F Workington	
44066	$4F^2$	18D Staveley Barrow Hill	18D Staveley Barrow Hill	18D Staveley Barrow Hill	18D Staveley Barrow Hill	41E Staveley Barrow Hill	41E Staveley Barrow Hill	
44067	$4F^2$	5D Stoke	5D Stoke	1C Watford	1A Willesden	5E Alsager		
44068	$4F^2$	5D Stoke	5D Stoke	5D Stoke	5D Stoke	5D Stoke	5D Stoke	
44069	$4F^2$	3C Walsall	9B Stockport Edgeley	9A Longsight	9A Longsight	8F Wigan Springs Branch	8F Wigan Springs Branch	
44070	$4F^2$	18D Staveley Barrow Hill	18D Staveley Barrow Hill	18D Staveley Barrow Hill	18D Staveley Barrow Hill	41E Staveley Barrow Hill		
44071	$4F^2$	19C Canklow	19C Canklow	19C Canklow	19C Canklow	41D Canklow	41E Staveley Barrow Hill	
44072	$4F^2$	2B Bletchley	4B Northampton	2A Rugby	1E Bletchley			
44073	$4F^2$	6B Mold Junction	6B Mold Junction	6B Mold Junction	6B Mold Junction			
44074	$4F^2$	9B Stockport Edgeley	9B Stockport Edgeley	5D Stoke	5D Stoke	5D Stoke	5D Stoke	
44075	$4F^2$	12D Workington	11A Carnforth	9B Stockport Edgeley	9B Stockport Edgeley	6H Bangor	8G Sutton Oak	
44076	$4F^2$	2C Northampton	4B Northampton	2E Northampton	2E Northampton	2E Northampton	8F Wigan Springs Branch	
44077	$4F^2$	3D Aston	5D Stoke	5D Stoke	5D Stoke	5D Stoke		
44078	$4F^2$	9A Longsight	3C Walsall	3C Walsall	3C Walsall	9E Trafford Park	9G Gorton	
44079	$4F^2$	10D Plodder Lane	5B Crewe South	5E Alsager	5E Alsager	5E Alsager	5D Stoke	
44080	$4F^2$	9D Buxton	9F Heaton Mersey	9F Heaton Mersey	17F Trafford Park	9E Trafford Park	17C Rowsley	
44081	$4F^2$	12B Carlisle Upperby	12A Carlisle Upperby	12A Carlisle Upperby	12A Carlisle Upperby	12B Carlisle Upperby	24L Carnforth	
44082	$4F^2$	16C Kirkby in Ashfield	16C Kirkby in Ashfield	16C Kirkby in Ashfield	19C Canklow	41D Canklow		
44083	$4F^2$	11E Tebay	11D Tebay	11D Tebay	11D Tebay	24L Carnforth	9D Buxton	
44084	$4F^2$	21A Saltley	21A Saltley	21A Saltley	21A Saltley			
44085	$4F^2$	17C Coalville	17C Coalville	17C Coalville	17C Coalville	15D Coalville	15D Coalville	
44086	$4F^2$	12B Carlisle Upperby	11B Barrow	11B Barrow	11B Barrow	11A Barrow	8G Sutton Oak	
44087	$4F^2$	17C Coalville	22B Gloucester Barnwood	22B Gloucester Barnwood	22B Gloucester Barnwood	41B Sheffield Grimesthorpe		
44088	$4F^2$	21A Saltley	21A Saltley	18A Toton	16B Kirkby in Ashfield	41E Staveley Barrow Hill		
44089	$4F^2$	18A Toton	19C Canklow	19C Canklow	19C Canklow	41D Canklow	41E Staveley Barrow Hill	
44090	$4F^2$	19D Heaton Mersey	9F Heaton Mersey	9F Heaton Mersey	17E Heaton Mersey	9F Heaton Mersey		

		1948	1951	1954	1957	1960	1963	1966
44091	4F[2]	**18A** Toton	**18A** Toton	**18A** Toton	**18A** Toton	**21A** Saltley	**16B** Kirkby in Ashfield	
44092	4F[2]	**21A** Saltley	**21A** Saltley	**21A** Saltley	**21A** Saltley	**21A** Saltley	**21A** Saltley	
44093	4F[2]	**5D** Stoke	**5D** Stoke	**5D** Stoke	**5D** Stoke	**5D** Stoke		
44094	4F[2]	**20B** Stourton	**20B** Stourton	**20B** Stourton	**55B** Stourton	**55B** Stourton	**56E** Sowerby Bridge	
44095	4F[2]	**16A** Nottingham	**16A** Nottingham	**16A** Nottingham	**16A** Nottingham			
44096	4F[2]	**22C** Bath Green Park	**71G** Bath Green Park	**71G** Bath Green Park	**71G** Bath Green Park	**82F** Bath Green Park	**26D** Bury	
44097	4F[2]	**16B** Spital Bridge	**35C** Spital Bridge	**35C** Spital Bridge	**35C** Spital Bridge	**31F** Spital Bridge	**55F** Manningham	
44098	4F[2]	**20D** Normanton	**20D** Normanton	**20D** Normanton	**55E** Normanton	**55E** Normanton	**55D** Royston	
44099	4F[2]	**20D** Normanton	**20D** Normanton	**20D** Normanton	**55E** Normanton	**55E** Normanton	**55D** Royston	
44100	4F[2]	**17B** Burton	**17B** Burton	**17B** Burton	**17B** Burton	**17B** Burton	**17B** Burton	
44101	4F[2]	**17A** Derby	**17A** Derby	**17D** Rowsley	**17D** Rowsley	**17C** Rowsley	**17C** Rowsley	
44102	4F[2]	**22D** Templecombe	**71H** Templecombe	**71H** Templecombe	**71H** Templecombe	**82G** Templecombe	**82G** Templecombe	
44103	4F[2]	**17C** Coalville	**17C** Coalville	**17C** Coalville	**17C** Coalville			
44104	4F[2]	**18D** Staveley Barrow Hill	**18D** Staveley Barrow Hill	**18D** Staveley Barrow Hill	**18D** Staveley Barrow Hill	**41E** Staveley Barrow Hill		
44105	4F[2]	**25C** Goole	**24D** Lower Darwen	**27D** Wigan	**27D** Wigan	**24G** Skipton		
44106	4F[2]	**18A** Toton	**18A** Toton	**18A** Toton	**18A** Toton	**18A** Toton	**18A** Toton	
44107	4F[2]	**18C** Hasland	**18C** Hasland	**18C** Hasland	**55D** Royston	**55B** Stourton		
44108	4F[2]	**21A** Saltley	**21A** Saltley	**21A** Saltley	**21A** Saltley			
44109	4F[2]	**17C** Coalville	**17C** Coalville	**17C** Coalville	**17C** Coalville	**15D** Coalville	**15D** Coalville	
44110	4F[2]	**19D** Heaton Mersey	**35C** Spital Bridge	**35C** Spital Bridge	**35C** Spital Bridge	**31F** Spital Bridge	**9D** Buxton	
44111	4F[2]	**19D** Heaton Mersey	**19C** Canklow	**19C** Canklow	**19C** Canklow	**41D** Canklow		
44112	4F[2]	**22A** Bristol Barrow Road	**21A** Saltley	**17A** Derby	**17A** Derby	**17A** Derby	**21A** Saltley	
44113	4F[2]	**16C** Kirkby in Ashfield	**16A** Nottingham	**16A** Nottingham	**17C** Coalville	**15D** Coalville	**15D** Coalville	**16G** Westhouses
44114	4F[2]	**19E** Belle Vue	**26G** Belle Vue	**26G** Belle Vue	**39A** Gorton	**9G** Gorton	**9G** Gorton	
44115	4F[2]	**3C** Walsall	**3C** Walsall	**3C** Walsall	**3C** Walsall	**5D** Stoke	**5D** Stoke	
44116	4F[2]	**1A** Willesden	**1A** Willesden	**1A** Willesden	**1A** Willesden			
44117	4F[2]	**19D** Heaton Mersey	**35C** Spital Bridge	**6B** Mold Junction	**6B** Mold Junction	**1E** Bletchley	**8G** Sutton Oak	
44118	4F[2]	**11A** Carnforth	**5D** Stoke	**18B** Westhouses	**18B** Westhouses	**18B** Westhouses	**18A** Toton	
44119	4F[2]	**10D** Plodder Lane	**26G** Belle Vue	**26G** Belle Vue	**26A** Newton Heath	**24G** Skipton	**24D** Lower Darwen	
44120	4F[2]	**11B** Barrow	**5D** Stoke	**3D** Aston	**3D** Aston			
44121	4F[2]	**12B** Carlisle Upperby	**12A** Carlisle Upperby	**12A** Carlisle Upperby	**12A** Carlisle Upperby	**12B** Carlisle Upperby	**8F** Wigan Springs Branch	
44122	4F[2]	**18D** Staveley Barrow Hill	**18D** Staveley Barrow Hill	**18D** Staveley Barrow Hill	**15B** Kettering	**18C** Hasland		
44123	4F[2]	**15C** Leicester Midland	**22B** Gloucester Barnwood	**22B** Gloucester Barnwood	**22B** Gloucester Barnwood	**85E** Gloucester Barnwood	**85C** Gloucester Barnwood	
44124	4F[2]	**17B** Burton	**17B** Burton	**17B** Burton	**17B** Burton	**17B** Burton	**9G** Gorton	
44125	4F[2]	**10E** Sutton Oak	**5B** Crewe South	**5E** Alsager	**5E** Alsager	**5E** Alsager	**8F** Wigan Springs Branch	
44126	4F[2]	**11A** Carnforth	**5E** Alsager	**5E** Alsager	**12A** Carlisle Upperby	**12B** Carlisle Upperby	**5D** Stoke	
44127	4F[2]	**19C** Canklow	**19C** Canklow	**19C** Canklow	**19C** Canklow	**27F** Brunswick	**8G** Sutton Oak	
44128	4F[2]	**19C** Canklow	**19C** Canklow	**19C** Canklow	**19C** Canklow	**41D** Canklow		
44129	4F[2]	**18D** Staveley Barrow Hill	**18D** Staveley Barrow Hill	**18D** Staveley Barrow Hill	**18D** Staveley Barrow Hill	**41E** Staveley Barrow Hill		
44130	4F[2]	**18B** Westhouses	**18B** Westhouses	**18B** Westhouses	**18B** Westhouses	**18B** Westhouses	**18B** Westhouses	
44131	4F[2]	**16A** Nottingham	**16A** Nottingham	**16A** Nottingham	**16A** Nottingham	**16A** Nottingham	**21A** Saltley	
44132	4F[2]	**16A** Nottingham	**16A** Nottingham	**16A** Nottingham	**16A** Nottingham	**16A** Nottingham	**16A** Nottingham	
44133	4F[2]	**18A** Toton	**18A** Toton	**18A** Toton	**18A** Toton	**18A** Toton	**18A** Toton	
44134	4F[2]	**17D** Rowsley	**17D** Rowsley	**17D** Rowsley	**17D** Rowsley	**17C** Rowsley	**17C** Rowsley	
44135	4F[2]	**22A** Bristol Barrow Road	**22A** Bristol Barrow Road	**22A** Bristol Barrow Road	**22A** Bristol Barrow Road	**82E** Bristol Barrow Road	**82E** Bristol Barrow Road	
44136	4F[2]	**18A** Toton	**18A** Toton	**18A** Toton	**18C** Hasland			
44137	4F[2]	**21A** Saltley	**21A** Saltley	**21A** Saltley	**21A** Saltley	**21A** Saltley	**21A** Saltley	
44138	4F[2]	**21B** Bournville	**21B** Bournville	**21A** Saltley	**21A** Saltley	**9E** Trafford Park		
44139	4F[2]	**21A** Saltley	**14A** Cricklewood	**16A** Nottingham	**16A** Nottingham	**16A** Nottingham	**16A** Nottingham	
44140	4F[2]	**16C** Kirkby in Ashfield	**16C** Kirkby in Ashfield	**16C** Kirkby in Ashfield	**18A** Toton			
44141	4F[2]	**20C** Royston	**20C** Royston	**20C** Royston	**55D** Royston	**55D** Royston		
44142	4F[2]	**17A** Derby	**17A** Derby	**17A** Derby	**17A** Derby			
44143	4F[2]	**17B** Burton	**17B** Burton	**17B** Burton	**14B** Kentish Town	**21A** Saltley		
44144	4F[2]	**19D** Heaton Mersey	**9F** Heaton Mersey	**9F** Heaton Mersey	**17E** Heaton Mersey			
44145	4F[2]	**21A** Saltley	**21A** Saltley	**18A** Toton	**18A** Toton			
44146	4F[2]	**22D** Templecombe	**71H** Templecombe	**71H** Templecombe	**71H** Templecombe	**82F** Bath Green Park	**82F** Bath Green Park	
44147	4F[2]	**18D** Staveley Barrow Hill	**18D** Staveley Barrow Hill	**18D** Staveley Barrow Hill	**18D** Staveley Barrow Hill	**41E** Staveley Barrow Hill		
44148	4F[2]	**17C** Coalville	**17C** Coalville	**17C** Coalville	**17C** Coalville	**15D** Coalville		
44149	4F[2]	**20G** Hellifield	**23B** Hellifield	**20G** Hellifield	**20G** Hellifield		**24H** Hellifield	
44150	4F[2]	**18A** Toton	**21A** Saltley	**21A** Saltley	**18B** Westhouses	**15D** Coalville	**15D** Coalville	
44151	4F[2]	**20A** Leeds Holbeck	**20D** Normanton	**16A** Nottingham	**16A** Nottingham	**16A** Nottingham	**9G** Gorton	
44152	4F[2]	**16B** Spital Bridge	**35C** Spital Bridge	**35C** Spital Bridge	**35C** Spital Bridge	**31F** Spital Bridge		
44153	4F[2]	**20D** Normanton	**20B** Stourton	**20B** Stourton	**55B** Stourton	**55B** Stourton	**56E** Sowerby Bridge	
44154	4F[2]	**18D** Staveley Barrow Hill	**18D** Staveley Barrow Hill	**18A** Toton	**18A** Toton	**18B** Westhouses		
44155	4F[2]	**16B** Spital Bridge	**35C** Spital Bridge	**9G** Northwich	**9G** Northwich	**8E** Northwich	**8E** Northwich	
44156	4F[2]	**17B** Burton	**17C** Coalville	**17C** Coalville	**17C** Coalville	**15D** Coalville	**15D** Coalville	
44157	4F[2]	**18A** Toton	**18A** Toton	**18A** Toton	**2B** Nuneaton	**12C** Carlisle Canal	**12F** Workington	
44158	4F[2]	**16A** Nottingham	**16A** Nottingham	**16A** Nottingham	**16A** Nottingham	**16A** Nottingham		
44159	4F[2]	**30B** Hurlford	**67A** Corkerhill	**67B** Hurlford	**67B** Hurlford	**67A** Corkerhill		
44160	4F[2]	**15A** Wellingborough	**15C** Leicester Midland	**15C** Leicester Midland	**21A** Saltley	**21A** Saltley	**21A** Saltley	
44161	4F[2]	**20C** Royston	**20C** Royston	**18A** Toton	**18A** Toton			
44162	4F[2]	**18C** Hasland	**18C** Hasland	**18C** Hasland	**18C** Hasland	**18A** Toton	**18A** Toton	
44163	4F[2]	**17D** Rowsley	**17D** Rowsley	**17D** Rowsley	**17D** Rowsley	**17C** Rowsley		
44164	4F[2]	**16A** Nottingham	**17A** Derby	**6B** Mold Junction	**17A** Derby	**17A** Derby	**9G** Gorton	
44165	4F[2]	**19A** Sheffield Grimesthorpe	**21A** Saltley	**21A** Saltley	**21A** Saltley	**21A** Saltley	**21A** Saltley	
44166	4F[2]	**17B** Burton	**17B** Burton	**17B** Burton	**17C** Coalville	**15D** Coalville		
44167	4F[2]	**22B** Gloucester Barnwood	**22B** Gloucester Barnwood	**22B** Gloucester Barnwood	**22B** Gloucester Barnwood	**85E** Gloucester Barnwood	**82G** Templecombe	
44168	4F[2]	**17D** Rowsley	**17D** Rowsley	**17D** Rowsley	**17D** Rowsley	**21A** Saltley	**21A** Saltley	
44169	4F[2]	**22A** Bristol Barrow Road	**22A** Bristol Barrow Road	**22A** Bristol Barrow Road	**17A** Derby	**17A** Derby	**9G** Gorton	
44170	4F[2]	**17B** Burton	**17B** Burton	**20D** Normanton	**55E** Normanton	**55E** Normanton	**55H** Leeds Neville Hill	
44171	4F[2]	**17B** Burton	**17B** Burton	**20D** Normanton	**21A** Saltley	**21A** Saltley	**14E** Bedford	
44172	4F[2]	**17D** Rowsley	**17D** Rowsley	**17D** Rowsley	**17D** Rowsley	**17C** Rowsley	**17C** Rowsley	
44173	4F[2]	**19C** Canklow	**19C** Canklow	**18B** Westhouses	**18B** Westhouses			
44174	4F[2]	**17D** Rowsley	**17D** Rowsley	**19A** Sheffield Grimesthorpe	**19A** Sheffield Grimesthorpe	**41B** Sheffield Grimesthorpe	**41E** Staveley Barrow Hill	
44175	4F[2]	**22B** Gloucester Barnwood	**22B** Gloucester Barnwood	**22B** Gloucester Barnwood	**15C** Leicester Midland			
44176	4F[2]	**21A** Saltley	**21A** Saltley	**21A** Saltley	**17A** Derby	**17A** Derby	**17A** Derby	
44177	4F[2]	**17A** Derby	**17A** Derby	**17A** Derby	**17A** Derby	**18B** Westhouses	**27E** Walton on the Hill	
44178	4F[2]	**19D** Heaton Mersey	**9F** Heaton Mersey	**9F** Heaton Mersey	**17E** Heaton Mersey	**18A** Toton	**18A** Toton	
44179	4F[2]	**20D** Normanton	**21A** Saltley	**21A** Saltley	**21A** Saltley	**21A** Saltley	**21A** Saltley	
44180	4F[2]	**16A** Nottingham	**17C** Coalville	**17C** Coalville	**17C** Coalville	**15D** Coalville	**21A** Saltley	
44181	4F[2]	**12A** Carlisle Kingmoor	**68A** Carlisle Kingmoor	**68A** Carlisle Kingmoor	**68A** Carlisle Kingmoor	**12A** Carlisle Kingmoor	**12A** Carlisle Kingmoor	
44182	4F[2]	**18D** Staveley Barrow Hill	**18D** Staveley Barrow Hill	**18D** Staveley Barrow Hill	**15A** Wellingborough	**15A** Wellingborough	**15C** Leicester Midland	
44183	4F[2]	**12A** Carlisle Kingmoor	**68A** Carlisle Kingmoor	**68A** Carlisle Kingmoor	**68A** Carlisle Kingmoor	**12A** Carlisle Kingmoor	**12A** Carlisle Kingmoor	
44184	4F[2]	**21A** Saltley	**21A** Saltley	**21A** Saltley	**15C** Leicester Midland	**21A** Saltley	**21A** Saltley	
44185	4F[2]	**21A** Saltley	**21A** Saltley	**21A** Saltley	**21A** Saltley	**21A** Saltley	**21A** Saltley	
44186	4F[2]	**21A** Saltley	**21D** Stratford on Avon	**2E** Northampton	**5B** Crewe South	**5D** Stoke	**12E** Barrow	
44187	4F[2]	**18A** Toton	**21A** Saltley	**21A** Saltley	**21A** Saltley	**21A** Saltley		
44188	4F[2]	**18B** Westhouses	**18B** Westhouses	**18B** Westhouses	**18B** Westhouses	**27E** Walton on the Hill	**27E** Walton on the Hill	
44189	4F[2]	**12A** Carlisle Kingmoor	**68A** Carlisle Kingmoor	**68A** Carlisle Kingmoor	**67A** Corkerhill	**67A** Corkerhill		
44190	4F[2]	**21A** Saltley	**21A** Saltley	**18A** Toton	**17C** Coalville	**16A** Nottingham	**9G** Gorton	
44191	4F[2]	**18B** Westhouses	**18B** Westhouses	**18B** Westhouses	**18B** Westhouses	**18B** Westhouses	**18B** Westhouses	
44192	4F[2]	**12D** Workington	**11A** Carnforth	**11A** Carnforth	**11A** Carnforth	**8G** Sutton Oak	**8G** Sutton Oak	
44193	4F[2]	**29A** Perth	**63A** Perth	**63A** Perth	**63A** Perth	**66A** Polmadie		
44194	4F[2]	**31A** St. Rollox	**63A** Perth	**63A** Perth	**63A** Perth	**63A** Perth		
44195	4F[2]	**17A** Derby	**14A** Cricklewood	**16A** Nottingham	**16A** Nottingham	**16A** Nottingham	**9G** Gorton	
44196	4F[2]	**29A** Perth	**66A** Polmadie	**66A** Polmadie	**66A** Polmadie	**66B** Motherwell		
44197	4F[2]	**20F** Skipton	**23A** Skipton	**20F** Skipton	**20F** Skipton	**24G** Skipton	**24G** Skipton	
44198	4F[2]	**30B** Hurlford	**67A** Corkerhill	**67A** Corkerhill	**67A** Corkerhill	**67A** Corkerhill		
44199	4F[2]	**12A** Carlisle Kingmoor	**68A** Carlisle Kingmoor	**68B** Dumfries	**65B** St. Rollox	**65B** St. Rollox		
44200	4F[2]	**21A** Saltley	**21A** Saltley	**18A** Toton	**18A** Toton	**18A** Toton	**18A** Toton	
44201	4F[2]	**20H** Lancaster	**21A** Saltley	**21A** Saltley	**21A** Saltley			
44202	4F[2]	**16C** Kirkby in Ashfield	**16C** Kirkby in Ashfield	**16C** Kirkby in Ashfield	**16B** Kirkby in Ashfield	**16B** Kirkby in Ashfield	**16B** Kirkby in Ashfield	
44203	4F[2]	**21A** Saltley	**21A** Saltley	**21A** Saltley	**21A** Saltley	**21A** Saltley	**14E** Bedford	**16G** Westhouses
44204	4F[2]	**21D** Stratford on Avon	**21D** Stratford on Avon	**21A** Saltley	**18B** Westhouses			

		1948	1951	1954	1957	1960	1963	1966
44205	$4F^2$	**16C** Kirkby in Ashfield	**16C** Kirkby in Ashfield	**16C** Kirkby in Ashfield	**18D** Staveley Barrow Hill	**41E** Staveley Barrow Hill	**41E** Staveley Barrow Hill	
44206	$4F^2$	**16C** Kirkby in Ashfield	**16C** Kirkby in Ashfield	**16C** Kirkby in Ashfield	**19C** Canklow	**41D** Canklow		
44207	$4F^2$	**21A** Saltley	**20A** Leeds Holbeck	**20A** Leeds Holbeck	**55A** Leeds Holbeck	**55B** Stourton	**55B** Stourton	
44208	$4F^2$	**1A** Willesden	**1A** Willesden	**1A** Willesden	**1A** Willesden	**1A** Willesden	**5D** Stoke	
44209	$4F^2$	**17D** Rowsley	**17D** Rowsley	**22B** Gloucester Barnwood	**22B** Gloucester Barnwood	**85E** Gloucester Barnwood	**82E** Bristol Barrow Road	
44210	$4F^2$	**14A** Cricklewood	**14B** Kentish Town	**14B** Kentish Town	**14B** Kentish Town	**14B** Kentish Town	**14A** Cricklewood	
44211	$4F^2$	**19A** Sheffield Grimesthorpe	**19A** Sheffield Grimesthorpe	**21A** Saltley	**21A** Saltley	**21A** Saltley	**21A** Saltley	
44212	$4F^2$	**19A** Sheffield Grimesthorpe	**19A** Sheffield Grimesthorpe	**19A** Sheffield Grimesthorpe	**19A** Sheffield Grimesthorpe	**41B** Sheffield Grimesthorpe	**41E** Staveley Barrow Hill	
44213	$4F^2$	**21A** Saltley	**21A** Saltley	**21A** Saltley	**21A** Saltley	**21A** Saltley	**18A** Toton	
44214	$4F^2$	**17A** Derby	**17A** Derby	**17A** Derby	**17A** Derby	**17A** Derby	**17A** Derby	
44215	$4F^2$	**16A** Nottingham	**16A** Nottingham	**16A** Nottingham	**16A** Nottingham	**16A** Nottingham	**16A** Nottingham	
44216	$4F^2$	**20D** Normanton	**20E** Manningham	**20E** Manningham	**55F** Manningham	**55F** Manningham		
44217	$4F^2$	**20D** Normanton	**20D** Normanton	**20D** Normanton	**18A** Toton			
44218	$4F^2$	**16B** Spital Bridge	**35C** Spital Bridge	**27E** Walton on the Hill	**27E** Walton on the Hill	**27E** Walton on the Hill	**21A** Saltley	**16G** Westhouses
44219	$4F^2$	**3D** Aston	**3D** Aston	**3D** Aston	**2E** Northampton	**2E** Northampton	**8B** Warrington Dallam	
44220	$4F^2$	**23B** Aintree	**24D** Lower Darwen	**27D** Wigan	**27D** Wigan	**24G** Skipton	**24G** Skipton	
44221	$4F^2$	**25C** Goole	**27E** Walton on the Hill	**27D** Wigan	**27D** Wigan	**27D** Wigan	**26A** Newton Heath	
44222	$4F^2$	**20F** Skipton	**23A** Skipton	**20F** Skipton	**20F** Skipton	**24G** Skipton	**27D** Wigan	
44223	$4F^2$	**16A** Nottingham	**16A** Nottingham	**16A** Nottingham	**16A** Nottingham	**16A** Nottingham	**16A** Nottingham	
44224	$4F^2$	**21A** Saltley	**21A** Saltley	**21A** Saltley	**18A** Toton	**18A** Toton		
44225	$4F^2$	**21D** Lower Darwen	**24D** Lower Darwen	**27D** Wigan	**27D** Wigan			
44226	$4F^2$	**17B** Burton	**17B** Burton	**21A** Saltley	**21A** Saltley	**21A** Saltley	**21A** Saltley	
44227	$4F^2$	**17C** Coalville	**17C** Coalville	**21A** Saltley	**21A** Saltley			
44228	$4F^2$	**13A** Plaistow	**33A** Plaistow	**14A** Cricklewood	**14A** Cricklewood	**14A** Cricklewood		
44229	$4F^2$	**22B** Gloucester Barnwood	**18B** Westhouses	**18B** Westhouses	**18B** Westhouses	**18B** Westhouses	**18B** Westhouses	
44230	$4F^2$	**16A** Nottingham	**16A** Nottingham	**16D** Mansfield	**21A** Saltley			
44231	$4F^2$	**15C** Leicester Midland	**15C** Leicester Midland	**15C** Leicester Midland	**15C** Leicester Midland	**15C** Leicester Midland	**15C** Leicester Midland	
44232	$4F^2$	**19C** Canklow	**19C** Canklow	**19C** Canklow	**19C** Canklow	**27F** Brunswick	**8B** Warrington Dallam	
44233	$4F^2$	**18A** Toton	**18A** Toton	**18A** Toton	**18B** Westhouses	**18B** Westhouses	**18B** Westhouses	
44234	$4F^2$	**27A** Polmadie	**65B** St. Rollox	**65B** St. Rollox	**65B** St. Rollox	**65F** Grangemouth		
44235	$4F^2$	**22B** Gloucester Barnwood	**71G** Bath Green Park	**21A** Saltley	**21A** Saltley	**14B** Kentish Town	**18A** Toton	
44236	$4F^2$	**19G** Trafford Park	**9E** Trafford Park	**9E** Trafford Park	**17E** Heaton Mersey	**9G** Gorton	**9G** Gorton	
44237	$4F^2$	**19D** Heaton Mersey	**10D** Plodder Lane	**10D** Plodder Lane	**8B** Warrington Dallam	**8B** Warrington Dallam	**8B** Warrington Dallam	
44238	$4F^2$	**16B** Spital Bridge	**35C** Spital Bridge	**20B** Stourton	**55B** Stourton	**55B** Stourton	**55B** Stourton	
44239	$4F^2$	**16B** Spital Bridge	**35C** Spital Bridge	**35C** Spital Bridge	**35C** Spital Bridge	**31F** Spital Bridge	**8B** Warrington Dallam	
44240	$4F^2$	**24D** Lower Darwen	**24D** Lower Darwen	**27D** Wigan	**27D** Wigan	**27D** Wigan	**27D** Wigan	
44241	$4F^2$	**18A** Toton	**20C** Royston	**20B** Stourton	**17D** Rowsley	**17B** Burton	**17A** Derby	
44242	$4F^2$	**15A** Wellingborough	**15A** Wellingborough	**2E** Northampton	**2E** Northampton	**2E** Northampton	**5D** Stoke	
44243	$4F^2$	**14A** Cricklewood	**14B** Kentish Town	**14B** Kentish Town	**14B** Kentish Town	**14B** Kentish Town	**15A** Wellingborough	
44244	$4F^2$	**18C** Hasland	**18C** Hasland	**18C** Hasland	**18C** Hasland	**18C** Hasland	**18B** Westhouses	
44245	$4F^2$	**20B** Stourton	**20B** Stourton	**20G** Hellifield	**19C** Canklow	**41D** Canklow		
44246	$4F^2$	**17D** Rowsley	**17D** Rowsley	**5D** Stoke	**5D** Stoke	**5D** Stoke	**8F** Wigan Springs Branch	
44247	$4F^2$	**16A** Nottingham	**16A** Nottingham	**35C** Spital Bridge	**35C** Spital Bridge	**31F** Spital Bridge	**9D** Buxton	
44248	$4F^2$	**21A** Saltley	**21A** Saltley	**21A** Saltley	**21A** Saltley	**16A** Nottingham	**16A** Nottingham	
44249	$4F^2$	**17D** Rowsley	**15A** Wellingborough	**15A** Wellingborough	**18D** Staveley Barrow Hill	**41E** Staveley Barrow Hill		
44250	$4F^2$	**18A** Toton	**18A** Toton	**18A** Toton	**17D** Rowsley	**9F** Heaton Mersey	**9F** Heaton Mersey	
44251	$4F^2$	**29A** Perth	**63A** Perth	**63A** Perth	**63A** Perth	**66A** Polmadie		
44252	$4F^2$	**17C** Coalville	**17C** Coalville	**17C** Coalville	**15C** Leicester Midland	**16C** Mansfield	**16B** Kirkby in Ashfield	
44253	$4F^2$	**31A** St. Rollox	**63A** Perth	**63A** Perth	**63A** Perth	**63A** Perth		
44254	$4F^2$	**31A** St. Rollox	**63A** Perth	**63A** Perth	**63A** Perth	**63A** Perth		
44255	$4F^2$	**31A** St. Rollox	**65B** St. Rollox	**65B** St. Rollox	**65B** St. Rollox	**65J** Fort William		
44256	$4F^2$	**31A** St. Rollox	**65B** St. Rollox	**65B** St. Rollox	**65B** St. Rollox	**66A** Polmadie		
44257	$4F^2$	**31A** St. Rollox	**63A** Perth	**63A** Perth	**63A** Perth	**63A** Perth		
44258	$4F^2$	**29A** Perth	**63A** Perth	**63A** Perth	**63A** Perth	**63A** Perth		
44259	$4F^2$	**13C** Tilbury	**14A** Cricklewood	**14A** Cricklewood	**14A** Cricklewood	**14A** Cricklewood	**14A** Cricklewood	
44260	$4F^2$	**17C** Coalville	**17C** Coalville	**17C** Coalville	**17C** Coalville	**15D** Coalville	**15D** Coalville	
44261	$4F^2$	**19E** Belle Vue	**10D** Plodder Lane	**10D** Plodder Lane	**17E** Heaton Mersey	**9F** Heaton Mersey	**18C** Hasland	
44262	$4F^2$	**17D** Rowsley	**17D** Rowsley	**17D** Rowsley	**17D** Rowsley	**17C** Rowsley	**17C** Rowsley	
44263	$4F^2$	**17A** Derby	**21A** Saltley	**21A** Saltley	**21A** Saltley	**21A** Saltley	**21A** Saltley	
44264	$4F^2$	**16A** Nottingham	**16A** Nottingham	**16A** Nottingham	**16A** Nottingham	**16A** Nottingham	**82E** Bristol Barrow Road	
44265	$4F^2$	**17B** Burton	**17B** Burton	**17B** Burton	**19A** Sheffield Grimesthorpe	**41B** Sheffield Grimesthorpe	**41E** Staveley Barrow Hill	
44266	$4F^2$	**22A** Bristol Barrow Road	**22A** Bristol Barrow Road	**22A** Bristol Barrow Road	**15D** Bedford	**8G** Sutton Oak	**8G** Sutton Oak	
44267	$4F^2$	**16A** Nottingham	**22A** Bristol Barrow Road	**18D** Staveley Barrow Hill	**18D** Staveley Barrow Hill	**41E** Staveley Barrow Hill		
44268	$4F^2$	**16C** Kirkby in Ashfield	**16C** Kirkby in Ashfield	**16C** Kirkby in Ashfield	**16B** Kirkby in Ashfield	**16B** Kirkby in Ashfield	**16B** Kirkby in Ashfield	
44269	$4F^2$	**22B** Gloucester Barnwood	**22A** Bristol Barrow Road	**22A** Bristol Barrow Road	**22A** Bristol Barrow Road	**82E** Bristol Barrow Road	**82E** Bristol Barrow Road	
44270	$4F^2$	**17B** Burton	**17B** Burton	**17B** Burton	**14B** Kentish Town	**14B** Kentish Town	**18A** Toton	
44271	$4F^2$	**19D** Heaton Mersey	**9A** Longsight	**9B** Stockport Edgeley	**9B** Stockport Edgeley	**5D** Stoke	**9D** Buxton	
44272	$4F^2$	**22B** Gloucester Barnwood	**22B** Gloucester Barnwood	**22B** Gloucester Barnwood	**22B** Gloucester Barnwood	**85E** Gloucester Barnwood	**82G** Templecombe	
44273	$4F^2$	**16B** Spital Bridge	**35C** Spital Bridge	**35C** Spital Bridge	**35C** Spital Bridge	**31F** Spital Bridge		
44274	$4F^2$	**18C** Hasland	**18C** Hasland	**18C** Hasland	**55D** Royston	**55D** Royston	**55D** Royston	
44275	$4F^2$	**16A** Nottingham	**17B** Burton	**9E** Trafford Park	**17F** Trafford Park	**9G** Gorton	**9G** Gorton	
44276	$4F^2$	**20F** Skipton	**23B** Hellifield	**20G** Hellifield	**20G** Hellifield	**24H** Hellifield	**24H** Hellifield	
44277	$4F^2$	**20F** Skipton	**23A** Skipton	**20F** Skipton	**20F** Skipton	**24G** Skipton	**24G** Skipton	
44278	$4F^2$	**15B** Kettering	**15B** Kettering	**15B** Kettering	**15B** Kettering	**15D** Coalville	**18A** Toton	**16G** Westhouses
44279	$4F^2$	**17C** Coalville	**17C** Coalville	**17C** Coalville	**17C** Coalville	**15D** Coalville	**15D** Coalville	
44280	$4F^2$	**20H** Lancaster	**23C** Lancaster	**10E** Sutton Oak	**10D** Sutton Oak	**8F** Wigan Springs Branch	**8F** Wigan Springs Branch	
44281	$4F^2$	**27A** Polmadie	**67B** Hurlford	**67B** Hurlford	**67B** Hurlford	**67B** Hurlford		
44282	$4F^2$	**20G** Hellifield	**23B** Hellifield	**20G** Hellifield	**20G** Hellifield	**24H** Hellifield	**24H** Hellifield	
44283	$4F^2$	**31B** Stirling	**63B** Stirling	**66A** Polmadie	**66A** Polmadie	**66A** Polmadie		
44284	$4F^2$	**19A** Sheffield Grimesthorpe	**19A** Sheffield Grimesthorpe	**19A** Sheffield Grimesthorpe	**18B** Westhouses	**18A** Toton	**16A** Nottingham	
44285	$4F^2$	**19A** Sheffield Grimesthorpe	**19A** Sheffield Grimesthorpe	**19A** Sheffield Grimesthorpe	**18B** Westhouses			
44286	$4F^2$	**19D** Heaton Mersey	**9F** Heaton Mersey	**9F** Heaton Mersey	**17E** Heaton Mersey	**9F** Heaton Mersey	**9F** Heaton Mersey	
44287	$4F^2$	**15A** Wellingborough	**15C** Leicester Midland	**19A** Sheffield Grimesthorpe	**19A** Sheffield Grimesthorpe	**41B** Sheffield Grimesthorpe	**41E** Staveley Barrow Hill	
44288	$4F^2$	**18C** Hasland	**18C** Hasland	**18C** Hasland	**18C** Hasland	**18C** Hasland	**18C** Hasland	
44289	$4F^2$	**21B** Bournville	**21A** Saltley	**18A** Toton	**18A** Toton	**18B** Westhouses	**9F** Heaton Mersey	
44290	$4F^2$	**20D** Normanton	**20C** Royston	**20C** Royston	**55D** Royston	**55D** Royston	**55D** Royston	
44291	$4F^2$	**24D** Lower Darwen	**24D** Lower Darwen	**27D** Wigan	**27E** Walton on the Hill			
44292	$4F^2$	**11E** Tebay	**11D** Tebay	**11D** Tebay	**11D** Tebay	**11B** Workington	**12F** Workington	
44293	$4F^2$	**16B** Spital Bridge	**35C** Spital Bridge	**22B** Gloucester Barnwood	**22B** Gloucester Barnwood			
44294	$4F^2$	**18C** Hasland	**18C** Hasland	**18C** Hasland	**18C** Hasland	**14B** Kentish Town	**14A** Cricklewood	
44295	$4F^2$	**17B** Burton	**17B** Burton	**17A** Derby	**17A** Derby	**18A** Toton	**18A** Toton	
44296	$4F^2$	**16B** Spital Bridge	**35C** Spital Bridge	**22A** Bristol Barrow Road	**22A** Bristol Barrow Road	**85E** Gloucester Barnwood	**85C** Gloucester Barnwood	
44297	$4F^2$	**13A** Plaistow	**14A** Cricklewood	**14A** Cricklewood	**14A** Cricklewood	**14A** Cricklewood	**15A** Wellingborough	
44298	$4F^2$	**14A** Cricklewood	**14A** Cricklewood	**14B** Kentish Town	**14B** Kentish Town			
44299	$4F^2$	**20F** Skipton	**18D** Staveley Barrow Hill	**18D** Staveley Barrow Hill	**18D** Staveley Barrow Hill	**27E** Walton on the Hill	**5D** Stoke	
44300	$4F^2$	**5B** Crewe South	**5E** Alsager	**5E** Alsager	**10D** Sutton Oak	**8G** Sutton Oak	**8G** Sutton Oak	
44301	$4F^2$	**5E** Alsager	**5B** Crewe South	**5B** Crewe South	**5B** Crewe South	**5B** Crewe South	**8F** Wigan Springs Branch	
44302	$4F^2$	**3D** Aston	**3D** Aston	**3D** Aston	**3D** Aston	**3D** Aston	**21B** Bescot	
44303	$4F^2$	**9A** Longsight	**9A** Longsight	**10E** Sutton Oak	**10D** Sutton Oak	**8F** Wigan Springs Branch	**8F** Wigan Springs Branch	
44304	$4F^2$	**21A** Saltley	**14A** Cricklewood	**17A** Derby	**17A** Derby	**16A** Nottingham	**16A** Nottingham	
44305	$4F^2$	**7B** Bangor	**7B** Bangor	**6H** Bangor	**6H** Bangor	**24L** Carnforth	**12A** Carlisle Kingmoor	
44306	$4F^2$	**11B** Barrow	**12C** Penrith	**11A** Carnforth	**11A** Carnforth			
44307	$4F^2$	**5F** Uttoxeter	**5F** Uttoxeter	**5F** Uttoxeter	**6E** Wrexham Rhosddu	**5D** Stoke		
44308	$4F^2$	**9A** Longsight	**8E** Brunswick	**5D** Stoke	**5D** Stoke	**5D** Stoke	**5D** Stoke	
44309	$4F^2$	**9D** Buxton	**5D** Stoke	**5D** Stoke	**5D** Stoke	**5D** Stoke	**5D** Stoke	
44310	$4F^2$	**5D** Stoke	**5D** Stoke	**5D** Stoke	**5D** Stoke	**5D** Stoke	**5D** Stoke	**12D** Workington
44311	$4F^2$	**26A** Newton Heath	**26A** Newton Heath	**26A** Newton Heath	**26A** Newton Heath	**26A** Newton Heath	**26D** Bury	**12C** Barrow
44312	$4F^2$	**30B** Hurlford	**67B** Hurlford	**67B** Hurlford	**67B** Hurlford	**67B** Hurlford		
44313	$4F^2$	**16A** Nottingham	**16A** Nottingham	**16A** Nottingham	**16A** Nottingham			
44314	$4F^2$	**29A** Perth	**63A** Perth	**63A** Perth	**63C** Forfar	**63A** Perth		
44315	$4F^2$	**12A** Carlisle Kingmoor	**68A** Carlisle Kingmoor	**68A** Carlisle Kingmoor	**68A** Carlisle Kingmoor	**5D** Stoke	**9D** Buxton	
44316	$4F^2$	**17B** Burton	**17B** Burton	**17B** Burton	**17B** Burton			
44317	$4F^2$	**21A** Saltley	**21A** Saltley	**22A** Bristol Barrow Road	**15D** Bedford			
44318	$4F^2$	**28B** Dalry Road	**63A** Perth	**63C** Forfar	**63B** Stirling	**66A** Polmadie		

		1948	1951	1954	1957	1960	1963	1966
44319	4F^2	**30B** Hurlford	**67B** Hurlford	**67B** Hurlford	**67B** Hurlford	**67A** Corkerhill		
44320	4F^2	**31D** Grangemouth	**65F** Grangemouth	**65F** Grangemouth	**65F** Grangemouth	**65F** Grangemouth		
44321	4F^2	**18B** Westhouses	**18B** Westhouses	**18B** Westhouses	**18B** Westhouses	**18B** Westhouses	**18B** Westhouses	
44322	4F^2	**29A** Perth	**63B** Stirling	**63B** Stirling	**63B** Stirling	**66A** Polmadie		
44323	4F^2	**30B** Hurlford	**67B** Hurlford	**67B** Hurlford	**67C** Ayr	**67C** Ayr		
44324	4F^2	**12A** Carlisle Kingmoor	**68A** Carlisle Kingmoor	**68A** Carlisle Kingmoor	**68A** Carlisle Kingmoor	**12A** Carlisle Kingmoor		
44325	4F^2	**30B** Hurlford	**67B** Hurlford	**67B** Hurlford	**67B** Hurlford	**67B** Hurlford		
44326	4F^2	**12A** Carlisle Kingmoor	**68A** Carlisle Kingmoor	**68A** Carlisle Kingmoor	**68A** Carlisle Kingmoor			
44327	4F^2	**17D** Rowsley	**17D** Rowsley	**17D** Rowsley	**17D** Rowsley	**17C** Rowsley	**17C** Rowsley	
44328	4F^2	**29A** Perth	**63A** Perth	**63A** Perth	**63A** Perth	**63A** Perth		
44329	4F^2	**30B** Hurlford	**67A** Corkerhill	**67A** Corkerhill	**67A** Corkerhill	**67C** Ayr		
44330	4F^2	**31B** Stirling	**63B** Stirling	**63B** Stirling	**67C** Ayr	**67A** Corkerhill		
44331	4F^2	**31B** Stirling	**63B** Stirling	**63B** Stirling	**67C** Ayr	**67C** Ayr		
44332	4F^2	**15A** Wellingborough	**17B** Burton	**17B** Burton	**17B** Burton	**17B** Burton	**17B** Burton	
44333	4F^2	**21B** Bournville	**21B** Bournville	**21A** Saltley	**21A** Saltley	**21A** Saltley	**17A** Derby	
44334	4F^2	**19A** Sheffield Grimesthorpe	**19A** Sheffield Grimesthorpe	**19A** Sheffield Grimesthorpe	**17A** Derby	**17A** Derby	**17C** Rowsley	
44335	4F^2	**20D** Normanton	**20B** Stourton	**20B** Stourton	**55B** Stourton	**55B** Stourton	**55B** Stourton	
44336	4F^2	**20D** Normanton	**20D** Normanton	**20D** Normanton	**55E** Normanton	**55E** Normanton	**55E** Normanton	
44337	4F^2	**20D** Normanton	**20D** Normanton	**20D** Normanton	**55E** Normanton	**55E** Normanton	**55E** Normanton	
44338	4F^2	**20D** Normanton	**20D** Normanton	**20D** Normanton	**55E** Normanton	**55E** Normanton		
44339	4F^2	**3C** Walsall	**9D** Buxton	**9D** Buxton	**9D** Buxton	**9D** Buxton	**9D** Buxton	
44340	4F^2	**9B** Stockport Edgeley	**9B** Stockport Edgeley	**9B** Stockport Edgeley	**9B** Stockport Edgeley	**1A** Willesden		
44341	4F^2	**10D** Plodder Lane	**5B** Crewe South	**9G** Northwich	**9G** Northwich	**8E** Northwich	**12A** Carlisle Kingmoor	
44342	4F^2	**5B** Crewe South	**5E** Alsager	**5E** Alsager	**5E** Alsager	**5E** Alsager	**5D** Stoke	
44343	4F^2	**5D** Stoke	**5D** Stoke	**1C** Watford	**1C** Watford	**11B** Workington		
44344	4F^2	**5B** Crewe South	**5B** Crewe South	**5B** Crewe South	**5B** Crewe South	**5D** Stoke	**5D** Stoke	
44345	4F^2	**3C** Walsall	**3C** Walsall	**3C** Walsall	**3C** Walsall	**24L** Carnforth	**12E** Barrow	
44346	4F^2	**12B** Carlisle Upperby	**12A** Carlisle Upperby	**12A** Carlisle Upperby	**12A** Carlisle Upperby	**12B** Carlisle Upperby	**12B** Carlisle Upperby	
44347	4F^2	**11B** Barrow	**11B** Barrow	**11B** Barrow	**11B** Barrow	**11A** Barrow	**12E** Barrow	
44348	4F^2	**1A** Willesden	**1D** Devons Road	**1D** Devons Road	**1D** Devons Road	**1C** Watford	**21B** Bescot	
44349	4F^2	**5D** Stoke	**9A** Longsight	**9A** Longsight	**9A** Longsight	**5E** Alsager	**5D** Stoke	
44350	4F^2	**3D** Aston	**3D** Aston	**9E** Trafford Park	**10D** Sutton Oak	**8G** Sutton Oak	**8G** Sutton Oak	
44351	4F^2	**11B** Barrow	**11B** Barrow	**11B** Barrow	**11B** Barrow	**11A** Barrow	**12E** Barrow	
44352	4F^2	**10D** Plodder Lane	**1E** Bletchley	**1E** Bletchley	**1E** Bletchley	**5E** Alsager	**5D** Stoke	
44353	4F^2	**5D** Stoke	**5D** Stoke	**5D** Stoke	**5D** Stoke	**2E** Northampton	**8B** Warrington Dallam	
44354	4F^2	**2A** Rugby	**2A** Rugby	**3D** Aston	**5E** Alsager	**5E** Alsager	**5D** Stoke	
44355	4F^2	**19A** Sheffield Grimesthorpe	**71G** Bath Green Park	**71G** Bath Green Park	**71G** Bath Green Park	**6H** Bangor	**5F** Uttoxeter	
44356	4F^2	**10D** Plodder Lane	**10D** Plodder Lane	**10D** Plodder Lane	**8B** Warrington Dallam	**8B** Warrington Dallam	**8B** Warrington Dallam	
44357	4F^2	**9A** Longsight	**9A** Longsight	**9A** Longsight	**9A** Longsight			
44358	4F^2	**10E** Sutton Oak	**5D** Stoke	**5D** Stoke	**5D** Stoke	**5D** Stoke	**21B** Bescot	
44359	4F^2	**5B** Crewe South	**5E** Alsager	**5B** Crewe South	**5B** Crewe South	**5B** Crewe South	**6B** Mold Junction	
44360	4F^2	**9D** Buxton	**3C** Walsall	**3D** Aston	**3D** Aston	**11B** Workington		
44361	4F^2	**11B** Barrow	**3E** Monument Lane	**3E** Monument Lane	**17E** Heaton Mersey			
44362	4F^2	**15D** Bedford	**21A** Saltley	**18A** Toton	**18A** Toton	**18B** Westhouses	**18B** Westhouses	
44363	4F^2	**5D** Stoke	**5D** Stoke	**1C** Watford	**1C** Watford	Crewe Works	Crewe Works	
44364	4F^2	**12D** Workington	**12D** Workington	**1E** Bletchley	**1E** Bletchley	**1E** Bletchley	**9D** Buxton	
44365	4F^2	**9D** Buxton	**12D** Workington	**12D** Workington	**12C** Workington			
44366	4F^2	**2C** Northampton	**21B** Bournville	**21B** Bournville	**11B** Barrow	**11A** Barrow		
44367	4F^2	**6B** Mold Junction	**6B** Mold Junction	**6K** Rhyl	**6K** Rhyl	**6K** Rhyl	**12E** Barrow	
44368	4F^2	**11B** Barrow	**11B** Barrow	**11B** Barrow	**11B** Barrow	**55B** Stourton		
44369	4F^2	**5D** Stoke	**5D** Stoke	**17A** Derby	**17A** Derby			
44370	4F^2	**1A** Willesden	**1D** Devons Road	**1A** Willesden	**1A** Willesden	**1E** Bletchley	**5D** Stoke	
44371	4F^2	**19E** Belle Vue	**18A** Toton	**18D** Staveley Barrow Hill	**18D** Staveley Barrow Hill	**41E** Staveley Barrow Hill		
44372	4F^2	**1A** Willesden	**1A** Willesden	**1A** Willesden	**1A** Willesden			
44373	4F^2	**5D** Stoke	**5D** Stoke	**5D** Stoke	**5D** Stoke	Crewe Works	Crewe Works	
44374	4F^2	**11A** Carnforth	**11A** Carnforth	**5D** Stoke	**5D** Stoke	Crewe Works	Crewe Works	
44375	4F^2	**11A** Carnforth	**5D** Stoke	**5D** Stoke	**5D** Stoke	**9D** Buxton		
44376	4F^2	**18A** Toton	**18A** Toton	**18A** Toton	**18A** Toton	**18A** Toton	**18A** Toton	
44377	4F^2	**5D** Stoke	**5D** Stoke	**5D** Stoke	**5D** Stoke	**5D** Stoke	**8B** Warrington Dallam	Crewe Works
44378	4F^2	**5D** Stoke	**5D** Stoke	**17A** Derby	**17A** Derby	**9F** Heaton Mersey	**9E** Trafford Park	
44379	4F^2	**10D** Plodder Lane	**10E** Sutton Oak	**9F** Heaton Mersey	**17E** Heaton Mersey	**9F** Heaton Mersey	**9F** Heaton Mersey	
44380	4F^2	**5D** Stoke	**5D** Stoke	**17A** Derby	**17A** Derby	**17B** Burton	**17B** Burton	
44381	4F^2	**1A** Willesden	**1A** Willesden	**1A** Willesden	**1D** Devons Road	**14B** Kentish Town	**14A** Cricklewood	
44382	4F^2	**9D** Buxton	**9D** Buxton	**9D** Buxton	**9B** Stockport Edgeley			
44383	4F^2	**5D** Stoke	**5D** Stoke	**5D** Stoke	**5D** Stoke			
44384	4F^2	**5E** Alsager	**10D** Plodder Lane	**10D** Plodder Lane	**8B** Warrington Dallam	**8B** Warrington Dallam	**8B** Warrington Dallam	
44385	4F^2	**12D** Workington	**11A** Carnforth	**5D** Stoke	**5B** Crewe South			
44386	4F^2	**10D** Plodder Lane	**5E** Alsager	**5E** Alsager	**5E** Alsager	**5E** Alsager	**12F** Workington	
44387	4F^2	**5B** Crewe South	**11B** Barrow	**11B** Barrow	**17E** Heaton Mersey	**9F** Heaton Mersey	**18B** Westhouses	
44388	4F^2	**5D** Stoke	**5D** Stoke	**5D** Stoke	**2F** Market Harborough	**16F** Market Harborough		
44389	4F^2	**7A** Llandudno Junction	**7A** Llandudno Junction	**6G** Llandudno Junction	**6G** Llandudno Junction	**6G** Llandudno Junction	**6G** Llandudno Junction	
44390	4F^2	**12B** Carlisle Upperby	**12A** Carlisle Upperby	**12C** Penrith	**12C** Workington	**11B** Workington	**24L** Carnforth	
44391	4F^2	**5D** Stoke	**5D** Stoke	**2E** Northampton	**2E** Northampton	**2E** Northampton		
44392	4F^2	**2A** Rugby	**8E** Brunswick	**9E** Trafford Park	**17F** Trafford Park	**9E** Trafford Park	**9E** Trafford Park	
44393	4F^2	**5D** Stoke	**5D** Stoke	**5D** Stoke	**5D** Stoke	**5D** Stoke		
44394	4F^2	**16D** Mansfield	**16D** Mansfield	**16D** Mansfield	**16C** Mansfield	**16A** Nottingham	**9F** Heaton Mersey	**12C** Barrow
44395	4F^2	**2A** Rugby	**2A** Rugby	**2A** Rugby	**2A** Rugby	**5D** Stoke	**5D** Stoke	
44396	4F^2	**1C** Watford	**5D** Stoke	**8E** Brunswick	**8E** Brunswick	**27F** Brunswick	**9E** Trafford Park	
44397	4F^2	**1A** Willesden	**14B** Kentish Town	**1A** Willesden	**1A** Willesden	**1E** Bletchley		
44398	4F^2	**24D** Lower Darwen	**24D** Lower Darwen	**24D** Lower Darwen	**24D** Lower Darwen	**24D** Lower Darwen	**24D** Lower Darwen	
44399	4F^2	**12D** Workington	**11A** Carnforth	**11A** Carnforth	**11A** Carnforth	**24L** Carnforth	**12B** Carlisle Upperby	
44400	4F^2	**20E** Manningham	**20E** Manningham	**20E** Manningham	**55F** Manningham	**55F** Manningham	**55F** Manningham	
44401	4F^2	**16A** Nottingham	**16A** Nottingham	**16A** Nottingham	**16A** Nottingham	**16A** Nottingham	**16A** Nottingham	
44402	4F^2	**17A** Derby	**17A** Derby	**17A** Derby	**17A** Derby	**9E** Trafford Park	**9E** Trafford Park	
44403	4F^2	**15C** Leicester Midland	**15C** Leicester Midland	**15C** Leicester Midland	**15C** Leicester Midland	**15C** Leicester Midland	**15C** Leicester Midland	
44404	4F^2	**20A** Leeds Holbeck	**20A** Leeds Holbeck	**20A** Leeds Holbeck	**18D** Staveley Barrow Hill	**41E** Staveley Barrow Hill		
44405	4F^2	**20H** Lancaster	**23C** Lancaster	**5D** Stoke	**5D** Stoke	**5E** Alsager	**5B** Crewe South	Crewe Works
44406	4F^2	**21A** Saltley	**21A** Saltley	**21A** Saltley	**21A** Saltley	**21A** Saltley		
44407	4F^2	**19D** Heaton Mersey	**9F** Heaton Mersey	**9F** Heaton Mersey	**17E** Heaton Mersey	**9F** Heaton Mersey		
44408	4F^2	**16A** Nottingham	**16A** Nottingham	**16A** Nottingham	**55E** Normanton	**55E** Normanton	**55E** Normanton	
44409	4F^2	**17A** Derby	**17A** Derby	**17A** Derby	**17A** Derby	**14B** Kentish Town		
44410	4F^2	**18C** Hasland	**18C** Hasland	**18C** Hasland	**18C** Hasland	**18C** Hasland		
44411	4F^2	**22A** Bristol Barrow Road	**22A** Bristol Barrow Road	**22A** Bristol Barrow Road	**22A** Bristol Barrow Road	**82E** Bristol Barrow Road	**82F** Bath Green Park	
44412	4F^2	**16A** Nottingham	**16A** Nottingham	**16A** Nottingham	**16A** Nottingham	**16A** Nottingham		
44413	4F^2	**21A** Saltley	**21A** Saltley	**21A** Saltley	**21A** Saltley	**9E** Trafford Park	**21A** Saltley	
44414	4F^2	**16A** Nottingham	**16A** Nottingham	**16A** Nottingham	**16A** Nottingham	**16A** Nottingham	**15C** Leicester Midland	
44415	4F^2	**16C** Kirkby in Ashfield	**16D** Mansfield	**16D** Mansfield	**16C** Mansfield	**16C** Mansfield		
44416	4F^2	**16A** Nottingham	**16D** Mansfield	**16D** Mansfield	**16C** Mansfield	**16C** Mansfield	**16B** Kirkby in Ashfield	
44417	4F^2	**22D** Templecombe	**71H** Templecombe	**71H** Templecombe	**71H** Templecombe	**82G** Templecombe		
44418	4F^2	**19A** Sheffield Grimesthorpe	**21A** Saltley	**21A** Saltley	**15B** Kettering	**16A** Nottingham	**16B** Kirkby in Ashfield	
44419	4F^2	**17A** Derby	**17A** Derby	**17A** Derby	**17A** Derby	**17A** Derby	**21A** Saltley	
44420	4F^2	**17A** Derby	**17A** Derby	**17A** Derby	**17A** Derby	**17A** Derby	**17A** Derby	
44421	4F^2	**19D** Heaton Mersey	**8E** Brunswick	**5D** Stoke	**17E** Heaton Mersey	**9F** Heaton Mersey	**17C** Rowsley	
44422	4F^2	**22C** Bath Green Park	**71G** Bath Green Park	**71G** Bath Green Park	**71G** Bath Green Park	**82F** Bath Green Park	**82G** Templecombe	
44423	4F^2	**15C** Leicester Midland	**15C** Leicester Midland	**15C** Leicester Midland	**15C** Leicester Midland			
44424	4F^2	**22A** Bristol Barrow Road	**22A** Bristol Barrow Road	**22A** Bristol Barrow Road	**22A** Bristol Barrow Road	**5D** Stoke	**5D** Stoke	
44425	4F^2	**14A** Cricklewood	**16A** Nottingham	**16A** Nottingham	**17A** Derby	**17A** Derby	**9G** Gorton	
44426	4F^2	**19A** Sheffield Grimesthorpe	**19A** Sheffield Grimesthorpe	**19A** Sheffield Grimesthorpe	**19A** Sheffield Grimesthorpe	**41B** Sheffield Grimesthorpe	**41E** Staveley Barrow Hill	
44427	4F^2	**21A** Saltley	**21A** Saltley	**21A** Saltley	**18A** Toton	**18A** Toton		
44428	4F^2	**17B** Burton	**17B** Burton	**17A** Derby	**17A** Derby	**17A** Derby	**17C** Rowsley	
44429	4F^2	**17B** Burton	**17D** Rowsley	**17D** Rowsley	**17D** Rowsley	**17C** Rowsley	**17C** Rowsley	
44430	4F^2	**17A** Derby	**18B** Westhouses	**18B** Westhouses	**18B** Westhouses	**18B** Westhouses		
44431	4F^2	**20A** Leeds Holbeck	**20A** Leeds Holbeck	**20F** Skipton	**20F** Skipton	**24G** Skipton	**26A** Newton Heath	
44432	4F^2	**17A** Derby	**17A** Derby	**5D** Stoke	**5D** Stoke	**5D** Stoke	**5D** Stoke	

No.	Class	1948	1951	1954	1957	1960	1963	1966
44433	$4F^2$	**17B** Burton	**17B** Burton	**17B** Burton	**17B** Burton	**17B** Burton	**14E** Bedford	
44434	$4F^2$	**17B** Burton	**17B** Burton	**17B** Burton	**17B** Burton	**17B** Burton	**17B** Burton	
44435	$4F^2$	**17B** Burton	**17B** Burton	**17B** Burton	**17B** Burton	**17B** Burton		
44436	$4F^2$	**17B** Burton	**17B** Burton	**17B** Burton	**17B** Burton	**17B** Burton	**17B** Burton	
44437	$4F^2$	**19A** Sheffield Grimesthorpe	**19A** Sheffield Grimesthorpe	**19A** Sheffield Grimesthorpe	**19A** Sheffield Grimesthorpe	**41B** Sheffield Grimesthorpe	**41E** Staveley Barrow Hill	
44438	$4F^2$	**2B** Bletchley	**5D** Stoke	**8E** Brunswick	**10D** Sutton Oak	**8F** Wigan Springs Branch		
44439	$4F^2$	**3B** Bushbury	**3B** Bushbury	**3B** Bushbury	**3B** Bushbury	**3D** Aston	**12F** Workington	
44440	$4F^2$	**1A** Willesden	**14B** Kentish Town	**1A** Willesden	**1A** Willesden	**1C** Watford	**21B** Bescot	
44441	$4F^2$	**1A** Willesden	**1C** Watford	**1D** Devons Road	**1D** Devons Road	**16C** Mansfield	**18A** Toton	
44442	$4F^2$	**1A** Willesden	**1A** Willesden	**1A** Willesden	**1C** Watford	**1C** Watford	**21B** Bescot	
44443	$4F^2$	**1C** Watford	**1C** Watford	**1C** Watford	**11B** Barrow	**11A** Barrow	**12E** Barrow	
44444	$4F^2$	**9B** Stockport Edgeley	**9B** Stockport Edgeley	**9B** Stockport Edgeley	**3C** Walsall	**3E** Monument Lane	**8F** Wigan Springs Branch	
44445	$4F^2$	**7B** Bangor	**7B** Bangor	**6H** Bangor	**6H** Bangor	**6B** Mold Junction	**9B** Stockport Edgeley	
44446	$4F^2$	**20C** Royston	**20C** Royston	**20C** Royston	**55D** Royston	**55D** Royston	**55D** Royston	
44447	$4F^2$	**2B** Bletchley	**4A** Bletchley	**1E** Bletchley	**1E** Bletchley	**1E** Bletchley	**12E** Barrow	
44448	$4F^2$	**5D** Stoke	**4B** Northampton	**3C** Walsall	**3C** Walsall	**3A** Bescot	**21B** Bescot	
44449	$4F^2$	**12D** Workington	**12D** Workington	**12D** Workington	**12C** Workington	**11B** Workington	**12F** Workington	
44450	$4F^2$	**5E** Alsager	**5E** Alsager	**5E** Alsager	**5E** Alsager	**5E** Alsager	**5B** Crewe South	
44451	$4F^2$	**1A** Willesden	**1A** Willesden	**1A** Willesden	**1A** Willesden	**1A** Willesden	**12A** Carlisle Kingmoor	
44452	$4F^2$	**5E** Alsager	**5E** Alsager	**17B** Burton	**17B** Burton	**17B** Burton	**12B** Carlisle Upperby	
44453	$4F^2$	**5B** Crewe South	**5E** Alsager	**5E** Alsager	**5E** Alsager	**5E** Alsager		
44454	$4F^2$	**3C** Walsall	**10D** Plodder Lane	**12D** Workington	**11A** Carnforth	**24L** Carnforth	**17A** Derby	
44455	$4F^2$	**2A** Rugby	**5D** Stoke	**5D** Stoke	**5D** Stoke	**5D** Stoke	**5D** Stoke	
44456	$4F^2$	**2A** Rugby	**2A** Rugby	**9G** Northwich	**9G** Northwich	**8E** Northwich	**8E** Northwich	
44457	$4F^2$	**19C** Canklow	**19C** Canklow	**19A** Sheffield Grimesthorpe	**19A** Sheffield Grimesthorpe	**41B** Sheffield Grimesthorpe	**55E** Normanton	
44458	$4F^2$	**16B** Spital Bridge	**35C** Spital Bridge	**35C** Spital Bridge	**55E** Normanton	**55E** Normanton	**55E** Normanton	
44459	$4F^2$	**19E** Belle Vue	**11D** Tebay	**11D** Tebay	**11D** Tebay	**5D** Stoke		
44460	$4F^2$	**24A** Accrington	**24D** Lower Darwen	**24D** Lower Darwen	**24D** Lower Darwen	**24D** Lower Darwen	**24D** Lower Darwen	
44461	$4F^2$	**5B** Crewe South	**12E** Moor Row	**12E** Moor Row	**12C** Workington	**11B** Workington	**12F** Workington	
44462	$4F^2$	**23B** Aintree	**25D** Mirfield	**25D** Mirfield	**27E** Walton on the Hill	**27E** Walton on the Hill	**27E** Walton on the Hill	
44463	$4F^2$	**16C** Kirkby in Ashfield	**16C** Kirkby in Ashfield	**16C** Kirkby in Ashfield	**21A** Saltley	**21B** Bournville	**18C** Hasland	
44464	$4F^2$	**25E** Sowerby Bridge	**27E** Walton on the Hill	**27D** Wigan	**27D** Wigan	**27D** Wigan	**27D** Wigan	
44465	$4F^2$	**15B** Kettering	**15B** Kettering	**15B** Kettering	**15B** Kettering	**17A** Derby	**18A** Toton	
44466	$4F^2$	**22A** Bristol Barrow Road	**22A** Bristol Barrow Road	**22A** Bristol Barrow Road	**22A** Bristol Barrow Road	**82E** Bristol Barrow Road	**82E** Bristol Barrow Road	
44467	$4F^2$	**20B** Stourton	**20B** Stourton	**20B** Stourton	**55B** Stourton	**55B** Stourton	**55B** Stourton	
44468	$4F^2$	**20H** Lancaster	**23A** Skipton	**20F** Skipton	**20F** Skipton	**24G** Skipton	**24G** Skipton	
44469	$4F^2$	**11E** Tebay	**11D** Tebay	**11D** Tebay	**11D** Tebay	**24L** Carnforth	**12B** Carlisle Upperby	
44470	$4F^2$	**18A** Toton	**16C** Kirkby in Ashfield	**16C** Kirkby in Ashfield	**16B** Kirkby in Ashfield	**16B** Kirkby in Ashfield	**16B** Kirkby in Ashfield	
44471	$4F^2$	**23C** Southport	**25D** Mirfield	**25D** Mirfield	**27E** Walton on the Hill	**27E** Walton on the Hill		
44472	$4F^2$	**16C** Kirkby in Ashfield	**16A** Nottingham	**16A** Nottingham	**16A** Nottingham	**16A** Nottingham	**16A** Nottingham	
44473	$4F^2$	**10E** Sutton Oak	**10D** Plodder Lane	**10D** Plodder Lane	**1A** Willesden	**5D** Stoke		
44474	$4F^2$	**23C** Southport	**25D** Mirfield	**25D** Mirfield	**56D** Mirfield	**56D** Mirfield		
44475	$4F^2$	**21A** Saltley	**21A** Saltley	**18D** Staveley Barrow Hill	**18D** Staveley Barrow Hill	**41E** Staveley Barrow Hill	**41E** Staveley Barrow Hill	
44476	$4F^2$	**16B** Spital Bridge	**35C** Spital Bridge	**35C** Spital Bridge	**35C** Spital Bridge	**31F** Spital Bridge	**14E** Bedford	
44477	$4F^2$	**19C** Canklow	**19A** Sheffield Grimesthorpe	**19A** Sheffield Grimesthorpe	**19A** Sheffield Grimesthorpe	**41B** Sheffield Grimesthorpe		
44478	$4F^2$	**5D** Stoke	**5D** Stoke	**5D** Stoke	**5D** Stoke	**5D** Stoke	**6H** Bangor	
44479	$4F^2$	**24A** Accrington	**24D** Lower Darwen	**24D** Lower Darwen	**24D** Lower Darwen	**24D** Lower Darwen	**24D** Lower Darwen	
44480	$4F^2$	**16A** Nottingham	**16A** Nottingham	**16A** Nottingham	**16A** Nottingham	**16A** Nottingham		
44481	$4F^2$	**23B** Aintree	**27E** Walton on the Hill	**27E** Walton on the Hill	**27E** Walton on the Hill	**27E** Walton on the Hill	**27E** Walton on the Hill	
44482	$4F^2$	**17B** Burton	**18B** Westhouses	**18B** Westhouses	**18B** Westhouses	**41E** Staveley Barrow Hill		
44483	$4F^2$	**24D** Lower Darwen	**24D** Lower Darwen	**24D** Lower Darwen	**24D** Lower Darwen	**24D** Lower Darwen		
44484	$4F^2$	**5D** Stoke	**5D** Stoke	**5D** Stoke	**5D** Stoke	**5D** Stoke	**21B** Bescot	
44485	$4F^2$	**25C** Goole	**25D** Mirfield	**25D** Mirfield	**56D** Mirfield	**56D** Mirfield	**55B** Stourton	
44486	$4F^2$	**25C** Goole	**26G** Belle Vue	**26G** Belle Vue	**27D** Wigan	**27D** Wigan	**27D** Wigan	
44487	$4F^2$	**11B** Barrow	**11B** Barrow	**11B** Barrow	**11B** Barrow	**11A** Barrow		
44488	$4F^2$	**3C** Walsall	**3C** Walsall	**3C** Walsall	**3C** Walsall	**3A** Bescot		
44489	$4F^2$	**5D** Stoke	**5D** Stoke	**8E** Brunswick	**8E** Brunswick	**27F** Brunswick	**9E** Trafford Park	
44490	$4F^2$	**3D** Aston	**3D** Aston	**3E** Monument Lane	**3E** Monument Lane	**3E** Monument Lane	**8F** Wigan Springs Branch	
44491	$4F^2$	**2C** Northampton	**4B** Northampton	**2E** Northampton	**1A** Willesden	**2E** Northampton		
44492	$4F^2$	**3B** Bushbury	**3B** Bushbury	**3B** Bushbury	**1A** Willesden	**3D** Aston	**8F** Wigan Springs Branch	
44493	$4F^2$	**6B** Mold Junction	**6B** Mold Junction	**6B** Mold Junction	**6B** Mold Junction	**6B** Mold Junction	**8G** Sutton Oak	
44494	$4F^2$	**5E** Alsager	**8E** Brunswick	**8E** Brunswick	**8E** Brunswick	**27F** Brunswick	**8B** Warrington Dallam	
44495	$4F^2$	**12D** Workington	**12D** Workington	**12D** Workington	**12C** Workington	**11B** Workington		
44496	$4F^2$	**5D** Stoke	**5D** Stoke	**5D** Stoke	**5D** Stoke	**5D** Stoke		
44497	$4F^2$	**1A** Willesden	**1A** Willesden	**1A** Willesden	**1A** Willesden	**1A** Willesden	**9D** Buxton	
44498	$4F^2$	**5D** Stoke	**5D** Stoke	**5D** Stoke	**5D** Stoke	**5D** Stoke		
44499	$4F^2$	**5D** Stoke	**5D** Stoke	**5D** Stoke	**5D** Stoke	**5D** Stoke	**5D** Stoke	
44500	$4F^2$	**5D** Stoke	**5D** Stoke	**5D** Stoke	**5D** Stoke	**5D** Stoke	**5D** Stoke	**12C** Barrow
44501	$4F^2$	**20A** Leeds Holbeck	**20A** Leeds Holbeck	**20C** Royston	**17A** Derby	**9F** Heaton Mersey	**9F** Heaton Mersey	
44502	$4F^2$	**5D** Stoke	**5D** Stoke	**5D** Stoke	**5D** Stoke	**5D** Stoke		
44503	$4F^2$	**5D** Stoke	**5D** Stoke	**5E** Alsager	**5E** Alsager	**5E** Alsager		
44504	$4F^2$	**5F** Uttoxeter	**5F** Uttoxeter	**5F** Uttoxeter	**5F** Uttoxeter	**5F** Uttoxeter	**6H** Bangor	
44505	$4F^2$	**12D** Workington	**12D** Workington	**12D** Workington	**12C** Workington	**11B** Workington	**12F** Workington	
44506	$4F^2$	**3C** Walsall	**3E** Monument Lane	**3E** Monument Lane	**3E** Monument Lane	**3E** Monument Lane		
44507	$4F^2$	**1A** Willesden	**5D** Stoke	**5D** Stoke	**5D** Stoke	**5D** Stoke		
44508	$4F^2$	**5D** Stoke	**5D** Stoke	**5D** Stoke	**5D** Stoke	**5D** Stoke		
44509	$4F^2$	**16B** Spital Bridge	**35C** Spital Bridge	**35C** Spital Bridge	**35C** Spital Bridge	**31F** Spital Bridge		
44510	$4F^2$	**11A** Carnforth	**11A** Carnforth	**11A** Carnforth	**11A** Carnforth	**24L** Carnforth		
44511	$4F^2$	**2A** Rugby	**11B** Barrow	**11B** Barrow	**11B** Barrow	**11A** Barrow		
44512	$4F^2$	**3C** Walsall	**3C** Walsall	**3E** Monument Lane	**3C** Walsall	**3A** Bescot	**21B** Bescot	
44513	$4F^2$	**5D** Stoke	**5D** Stoke	**5D** Stoke	**5D** Stoke	**5D** Stoke		
44514	$4F^2$	**3E** Monument Lane	**3E** Monument Lane	**3E** Monument Lane	**3E** Monument Lane	**3E** Monument Lane	**8F** Wigan Springs Branch	
44515	$4F^2$	**21A** Saltley	**21A** Saltley	**21A** Saltley	**21A** Saltley	**21A** Saltley		
44516	$4F^2$	**21A** Saltley	**21A** Saltley	**21A** Saltley	**21A** Saltley	**21B** Bournville	**21A** Saltley	
44517	$4F^2$	**3D** Aston	**3D** Aston	**3D** Aston	**3D** Aston	**5D** Stoke	**17A** Derby	
44518	$4F^2$	**16B** Spital Bridge	**35C** Spital Bridge	**35C** Spital Bridge	**35C** Spital Bridge	**31F** Spital Bridge		
44519	$4F^2$	**16B** Spital Bridge	**35C** Spital Bridge	**35C** Spital Bridge	**35C** Spital Bridge	**31F** Spital Bridge	**15C** Leicester Midland	
44520	$4F^2$	**21A** Saltley	**21A** Saltley	**21A** Saltley	**21A** Saltley	**21A** Saltley	**21A** Saltley	
44521	$4F^2$	**16B** Spital Bridge	**35C** Spital Bridge	**35C** Spital Bridge	**35C** Spital Bridge	**31F** Spital Bridge		
44522	$4F^2$	**16B** Spital Bridge	**35C** Spital Bridge	**35C** Spital Bridge	**35C** Spital Bridge	**31F** Spital Bridge	**8B** Warrington Dallam	
44523	$4F^2$	**22C** Bath Green Park	**71G** Bath Green Park	**71G** Bath Green Park	**71G** Bath Green Park	**82F** Bath Green Park	**82E** Bristol Barrow Road	
44524	$4F^2$	**21A** Saltley	**21D** Stratford on Avon	**2E** Northampton	**2E** Northampton	**2E** Northampton	**9D** Buxton	
44525	$4F^2$	**21A** Saltley	**21A** Saltley	**3D** Aston	**6G** Llandudno Junction	**6G** Llandudno Junction	**6G** Llandudno Junction	Crewe Works
44526	$4F^2$	**17B** Burton	**17B** Burton	**17B** Burton	**17B** Burton	**17B** Burton	**17B** Burton	
44527	$4F^2$	**17B** Burton	**17B** Burton	**17B** Burton	**17B** Burton	**17B** Burton	**17B** Burton	
44528	$4F^2$	**17B** Burton	**17B** Burton	**17B** Burton	**17B** Burton	**17B** Burton	**17B** Burton	
44529	$4F^2$	**14B** Kentish Town	**14A** Cricklewood	**14A** Cricklewood	**14A** Cricklewood	**14A** Cricklewood	**14A** Cricklewood	
44530	$4F^2$	**13A** Plaistow	**33A** Plaistow	**14A** Cricklewood	**14A** Cricklewood	**14A** Cricklewood	**15C** Leicester Midland	
44531	$4F^2$	**14B** Kentish Town	**14B** Kentish Town	**14B** Kentish Town	**14B** Kentish Town	**14B** Kentish Town	**14A** Cricklewood	
44532	$4F^2$	**14B** Kentish Town	**14B** Kentish Town	**14B** Kentish Town	**14B** Kentish Town	**14B** Kentish Town	**14A** Cricklewood	
44533	$4F^2$	**16A** Nottingham	**16A** Nottingham	**16A** Nottingham	**16A** Nottingham	**16A** Nottingham	**9E** Trafford Park	
44534	$4F^2$	**22A** Bristol Barrow Road	**22A** Bristol Barrow Road	**22A** Bristol Barrow Road	**22A** Bristol Barrow Road	**82E** Bristol Barrow Road	**82E** Bristol Barrow Road	
44535	$4F^2$	**22C** Bath Green Park	**71G** Bath Green Park	**15B** Kettering	**15B** Kettering	**41B** Sheffield Grimesthorpe	**41E** Staveley Barrow Hill	
44536	$4F^2$	**22A** Bristol Barrow Road	**22A** Bristol Barrow Road	**22A** Bristol Barrow Road	**22A** Bristol Barrow Road	**5D** Stoke	**5D** Stoke	
44537	$4F^2$	**22A** Bristol Barrow Road	**22A** Bristol Barrow Road	**22A** Bristol Barrow Road	**22A** Bristol Barrow Road	**11A** Barrow		
44538	$4F^2$	**21A** Saltley	**21A** Saltley	**21A** Saltley	**17B** Burton	**17B** Burton	**17B** Burton	
44539	$4F^2$	**17C** Coalville	**17C** Coalville	**17C** Coalville	**17C** Coalville	**15D** Coalville	**15D** Coalville	
44540	$4F^2$	**17D** Rowsley	**17D** Rowsley	**17A** Derby	**17A** Derby	**17A** Derby	**14E** Bedford	
44541	$4F^2$	**23B** Aintree	**27E** Walton on the Hill	**27E** Walton on the Hill	**27E** Walton on the Hill	**17B** Burton	**17B** Burton	
44542	$4F^2$	**17A** Derby	**17A** Derby	**17A** Derby	**17B** Burton	**17B** Burton	**17B** Burton	
44543	$4F^2$	**26A** Newton Heath	**26A** Newton Heath	**26A** Newton Heath	**26A** Newton Heath	**26A** Newton Heath	**26A** Newton Heath	
44544	$4F^2$	**26A** Newton Heath	**27E** Walton on the Hill	**27D** Wigan	**27D** Wigan	**27D** Wigan	**27D** Wigan	
44545	$4F^2$	**21A** Saltley	**21A** Saltley	**17A** Derby	**17A** Derby	**17A** Derby	**17A** Derby	
44546	$4F^2$	**16A** Nottingham	**16A** Nottingham	**16A** Nottingham	**16A** Nottingham	**16A** Nottingham		

Loco	Class	1948	1951	1954	1957	1960	1963	1966
44547	$4F^2$	18A Toton	16C Kirkby in Ashfield	16C Kirkby in Ashfield	19A Sheffield Grimesthorpe	41B Sheffield Grimesthorpe		
44548	$4F^2$	9D Buxton	5D Stoke	5D Stoke	5D Stoke	5D Stoke	5D Stoke	
44549	$4F^2$	2B Bletchley	12E Moor Row	12D Workington	12C Workington	11B Workington	12F Workington	
44550	$4F^2$	19A Sheffield Grimesthorpe	19A Sheffield Grimesthorpe	19A Sheffield Grimesthorpe	55D Royston	55D Royston		
44551	$4F^2$	17B Burton	17B Burton	17B Burton	17B Burton	17B Burton	17B Burton	
44552	$4F^2$	18A Toton	16C Kirkby in Ashfield	17B Burton	17B Burton	17B Burton	17B Burton	
44553	$4F^2$	22B Gloucester Barnwood	22A Bristol Barrow Road	22A Bristol Barrow Road	22A Bristol Barrow Road	82E Bristol Barrow Road		
44554	$4F^2$	20H Lancaster	17C Coalville	17C Coalville	17C Coalville	9F Heaton Mersey	9F Heaton Mersey	
44555	$4F^2$	20G Hellifield	17A Derby	17A Derby	16A Nottingham	16A Nottingham		
44556	$4F^2$	20H Lancaster	19A Sheffield Grimesthorpe	19A Sheffield Grimesthorpe	17D Rowsley	17C Rowsley	17C Rowsley	
44557	$4F^2$	22C Bath Green Park	71G Bath Green Park	71G Bath Green Park	71G Bath Green Park	82G Templecombe		
44558	$4F^2$	22C Bath Green Park	71G Bath Green Park	71G Bath Green Park	71G Bath Green Park	82F Bath Green Park	82F Bath Green Park	
44559	$4F^2$	22C Bath Green Park	71G Bath Green Park	71G Bath Green Park	71G Bath Green Park	82F Bath Green Park	82F Bath Green Park	
44560	$4F^2$	22C Bath Green Park	71G Bath Green Park	71G Bath Green Park	71G Bath Green Park	82F Bath Green Park	82G Templecombe	
44561	$4F^2$	22C Bath Green Park	71G Bath Green Park	71G Bath Green Park	71G Bath Green Park	82F Bath Green Park		
44562	$4F^2$	20D Normanton	20B Stourton	20B Stourton	17B Burton	17B Burton	17B Burton	
44563	$4F^2$	14B Kentish Town	14B Kentish Town	14B Kentish Town	14B Kentish Town	14B Kentish Town		
44564	$4F^2$	17D Rowsley	17D Rowsley	17D Rowsley	17D Rowsley	17C Rowsley	9E Trafford Park	
44565	$4F^2$	17A Derby	17A Derby	17D Rowsley	17D Rowsley	17C Rowsley	9E Trafford Park	
44566	$4F^2$	17A Derby	17A Derby	17D Rowsley	17D Rowsley	17C Rowsley	9E Trafford Park	
44567	$4F^2$	21A Saltley	21A Saltley	22B Gloucester Barnwood	22B Gloucester Barnwood	85E Gloucester Barnwood	26D Bury	
44568	$4F^2$	19A Sheffield Grimesthorpe	19A Sheffield Grimesthorpe	19A Sheffield Grimesthorpe	19A Sheffield Grimesthorpe	41B Sheffield Grimesthorpe	41E Staveley Barrow Hill	
44569	$4F^2$	22A Bristol Barrow Road	22A Bristol Barrow Road	22A Bristol Barrow Road	22A Bristol Barrow Road	82E Bristol Barrow Road	82E Bristol Barrow Road	
44570	$4F^2$	20D Normanton	20E Manningham	20B Stourton	55B Stourton	55B Stourton	55B Stourton	
44571	$4F^2$	21A Saltley	21A Saltley	21A Saltley	21A Saltley	21B Bournville	21A Saltley	
44572	$4F^2$	19A Sheffield Grimesthorpe	17C Coalville	17C Coalville	17C Coalville	14B Kentish Town	14A Cricklewood	
44573	$4F^2$	19A Sheffield Grimesthorpe	19A Sheffield Grimesthorpe	19A Sheffield Grimesthorpe	19A Sheffield Grimesthorpe	41B Sheffield Grimesthorpe		
44574	$4F^2$	15A Wellingborough	15A Wellingborough	15A Wellingborough	15A Wellingborough	15A Wellingborough	18A Toton	
44575	$4F^2$	15A Wellingborough	15A Wellingborough	15A Wellingborough	15A Wellingborough	15A Wellingborough	15A Wellingborough	
44576	$4F^2$	22B Gloucester Barnwood	19C Canklow	19C Canklow	19C Canklow	41D Canklow		
44577	$4F^2$	16A Nottingham	16A Nottingham	16A Nottingham	16A Nottingham	16A Nottingham	16A Nottingham	
44578	$4F^2$	16A Nottingham	16A Nottingham	16A Nottingham	16A Nottingham	16A Nottingham	14E Bedford	
44579	$4F^2$	20G Hellifield	23B Hellifield	20G Hellifield	20G Hellifield	24H Hellifield		
44580	$4F^2$	21A Saltley	21A Saltley	21A Saltley	21A Saltley	21A Saltley	21A Saltley	
44581	$4F^2$	14A Cricklewood	14A Cricklewood	14A Cricklewood	14A Cricklewood	14A Cricklewood	15D Coalville	
44582	$4F^2$	15D Bedford	17B Burton	20A Leeds Holbeck	55D Royston	55D Royston	55D Royston	
44583	$4F^2$	21A Saltley	15C Leicester Midland	15C Leicester Midland	21A Saltley	21A Saltley	21A Saltley	
44584	$4F^2$	21A Saltley	20A Leeds Holbeck	20B Stourton	55B Stourton	55B Stourton	55B Stourton	
44585	$4F^2$	22C Bath Green Park	16A Nottingham	16A Nottingham	16A Nottingham	16A Nottingham		
44586	$4F^2$	20D Normanton	20D Normanton	20B Stourton	55B Stourton	55B Stourton	55B Stourton	
44587	$4F^2$	21D Stratford on Avon	21D Stratford on Avon	22B Gloucester Barnwood	22B Gloucester Barnwood	27F Brunswick	9E Trafford Park	
44588	$4F^2$	17D Rowsley	17D Rowsley	17D Rowsley	17D Rowsley	17C Rowsley	17C Rowsley	
44589	$4F^2$	16C Kirkby in Ashfield	16C Kirkby in Ashfield	16C Kirkby in Ashfield	17A Derby	27F Brunswick	8B Warrington Dallam	
44590	$4F^2$	18D Staveley Barrow Hill	18D Staveley Barrow Hill	18D Staveley Barrow Hill	18D Staveley Barrow Hill	41E Staveley Barrow Hill		
44591	$4F^2$	21A Saltley	21A Saltley	21A Saltley	17B Burton	17B Burton	17B Burton	
44592	$4F^2$	3E Monument Lane	3E Monument Lane	3E Monument Lane	5B Crewe South	5B Crewe South	5B Crewe South	
44593	$4F^2$	12D Workington	9F Heaton Mersey	1E Bletchley	1E Bletchley	5D Stoke	5D Stoke	
44594	$4F^2$	11B Barrow	11B Barrow	11B Barrow	11B Barrow	11A Barrow		
44595	$4F^2$	5E Alsager	5E Alsager	5B Crewe South	5B Crewe South	5B Crewe South	6B Mold Junction	
44596	$4F^2$	2C Northampton	5D Stoke	5D Stoke	12A Carlisle Upperby	12B Carlisle Upperby	8G Sutton Oak	
44597	$4F^2$	17B Burton	17B Burton	17B Burton	17B Burton	17B Burton	17B Burton	
44598	$4F^2$	16A Nottingham	16A Nottingham	18B Westhouses	18B Westhouses	18B Westhouses	18B Westhouses	
44599	$4F^2$	17B Burton	17B Burton	17B Burton	17B Burton	17B Burton	17B Burton	
44600	$4F^2$	17B Burton	17B Burton	17B Burton	17B Burton	17B Burton		
44601	$4F^2$	17A Derby	17A Derby	17A Derby	17A Derby	11A Barrow	12E Barrow	
44602	$4F^2$	17A Derby	17A Derby	17A Derby	17D Rowsley	17C Rowsley	9G Gorton	
44603	$4F^2$	20D Normanton	20D Normanton	18C Hasland	18C Hasland	18C Hasland	18C Hasland	
44604	$4F^2$	20D Normanton	20D Normanton	20D Normanton	55E Normanton	55E Normanton	55E Normanton	
44605	$4F^2$	17A Derby	18B Westhouses	18B Westhouses	18B Westhouses	27E Walton on the Hill	21A Saltley	
44606	$4F^2$	21D Stratford on Avon	21D Stratford on Avon	18D Staveley Barrow Hill	18D Staveley Barrow Hill	41E Staveley Barrow Hill		
44658	$5MT^3$	→	14B Kentish Town	14B Kentish Town	14B Kentish Town	14B Kentish Town	16A Nottingham	8B Warrington Dallam
44659	$5MT^3$	→	21A Saltley	21A Saltley	21A Saltley	21A Saltley	21A Saltley	16B Annesley
44660	$5MT^3$	→	21A Saltley	21A Saltley	21A Saltley	21A Saltley	21A Saltley	
44661	$5MT^3$	→	21A Saltley	21A Saltley	19B Millhouses	6J Holyhead	6G Llandudno Junction	2A Tyseley
44662	$5MT^3$	→	20A Leeds Holbeck	20A Leeds Holbeck	55A Leeds Holbeck	55A Leeds Holbeck	55A Leeds Holbeck	55A Leeds Holbeck
44663	$5MT^3$	→	15C Leicester Midland	15C Leicester Midland	15C Leicester Midland	21A Saltley	21A Saltley	2A Tyseley
44664	$5MT^3$	→	19B Millhouses	19B Millhouses	21A Saltley	16A Nottingham	17A Derby	9K Bolton
44665	$5MT^3$	→	19B Millhouses	19B Millhouses	19B Millhouses	9E Trafford Park	16D Annesley	16B Annesley
44666	$5MT^3$	→	21A Saltley	21A Saltley	21A Saltley	21A Saltley	21A Saltley	2A Tyseley
44667	$5MT^3$	→	17A Derby	17A Derby	17A Derby	15C Leicester Midland	2F Woodford Halse	10J Lancaster
44668	$5MT^3$	→	68A Carlisle Kingmoor	68A Carlisle Kingmoor	68A Carlisle Kingmoor	12A Carlisle Kingmoor	12A Carlisle Kingmoor	12A Carlisle Kingmoor
44669	$5MT^3$	→	68A Carlisle Kingmoor	68A Carlisle Kingmoor	68A Carlisle Kingmoor	12A Carlisle Kingmoor	12A Carlisle Kingmoor	12A Carlisle Kingmoor
44670	$5MT^3$	→	68A Carlisle Kingmoor	68A Carlisle Kingmoor	68A Carlisle Kingmoor	12A Carlisle Kingmoor	12A Carlisle Kingmoor	12A Carlisle Kingmoor
44671	$5MT^3$	→	68A Carlisle Kingmoor	68A Carlisle Kingmoor	68A Carlisle Kingmoor	12A Carlisle Kingmoor	12A Carlisle Kingmoor	12A Carlisle Kingmoor
44672	$5MT^3$	→	68A Carlisle Kingmoor	68A Carlisle Kingmoor	68A Carlisle Kingmoor	12A Carlisle Kingmoor	12A Carlisle Kingmoor	12A Carlisle Kingmoor
44673	$5MT^3$	→	68A Carlisle Kingmoor	68A Carlisle Kingmoor	68A Carlisle Kingmoor	12A Carlisle Kingmoor	12A Carlisle Kingmoor	
44674	$5MT^3$	→	68A Carlisle Kingmoor	68A Carlisle Kingmoor	68A Carlisle Kingmoor	12A Carlisle Kingmoor	12A Carlisle Kingmoor	12A Carlisle Kingmoor
44675	$5MT^3$	→	68A Carlisle Kingmoor	68A Carlisle Kingmoor	68A Carlisle Kingmoor	12A Carlisle Kingmoor	12A Carlisle Kingmoor	12A Carlisle Kingmoor
44676	$5MT^3$	→	68A Carlisle Kingmoor	68A Carlisle Kingmoor	68A Carlisle Kingmoor	12A Carlisle Kingmoor	12A Carlisle Kingmoor	
44677	$5MT^3$	→	68A Carlisle Kingmoor	65B St. Rollox	65B St. Rollox	65B St. Rollox	12A Carlisle Kingmoor	12A Carlisle Kingmoor
44678	$5MT^3$	→	5A Crewe North	6J Holyhead	12A Carlisle Upperby	5A Crewe North	5A Crewe North	8C Speke Junction
44679	$5MT^3$	→	5A Crewe North	5A Crewe North	5A Crewe North	5A Crewe North	5A Crewe North	8C Speke Junction
44680	$5MT^3$	→	5A Crewe North	5A Crewe North	5A Crewe North	5A Crewe North	5A Crewe North	5B Crewe South
44681	$5MT^3$	→	5A Crewe North	6J Holyhead	6J Holyhead	5A Crewe North	5A Crewe North	5B Crewe South
44682	$5MT^3$	→	5A Crewe North	5A Crewe North	5A Crewe North	24K Preston	2E Northampton	5D Stoke
44683	$5MT^3$	→	5A Crewe North	5A Crewe North	5A Crewe North	5A Crewe North	5A Crewe North	5B Crewe South
44684	$5MT^3$	→	5A Crewe North	5A Crewe North	5A Crewe North	5A Crewe North	5A Crewe North	5B Crewe South
44685	$5MT^3$	→	5A Crewe North	5A Crewe North	5A Crewe North	5A Crewe North	5A Crewe North	5B Crewe South
44686	$5MT^3$	→	→	9A Longsight	9A Longsight	9A Longsight	6G Llandudno Junction	
44687	$5MT^3$	→	→	9A Longsight	9A Longsight	9A Longsight	6G Llandudno Junction	8M Southport
44688	$5MT^3$	→	27A Bank Hall	27A Bank Hall	27A Bank Hall	9E Trafford Park	2F Woodford Halse	8A Edge Hill
44689	$5MT^3$	→	27A Bank Hall	27A Bank Hall	24A Accrington	24A Accrington	27C Southport	12A Carlisle Kingmoor
44690	$5MT^3$	→	27A Bank Hall	27A Bank Hall	27A Bank Hall	15C Leicester Midland	15E Leicester Central	16C Derby
44691	$5MT^3$	→	27A Bank Hall	27A Bank Hall	27A Bank Hall	14D Neasden	2F Woodford Halse	2B Oxley
44692	$5MT^3$	→	27A Bank Hall	27A Bank Hall	24A Accrington	24A Accrington	27B Aintree	12A Carlisle Kingmoor
44693	$5MT^3$	→	25F Low Moor	25F Low Moor	56F Low Moor	56F Low Moor	56F Low Moor	56D Mirfield
44694	$5MT^3$	→	25F Low Moor	25F Low Moor	56F Low Moor	56F Low Moor	56F Low Moor	56D Mirfield
44695	$5MT^3$	→	25F Low Moor	25F Low Moor	56F Low Moor	56F Low Moor	56F Low Moor	56D Mirfield
44696	$5MT^3$	→	26A Newton Heath	26A Newton Heath	26A Newton Heath	26A Newton Heath	26A Newton Heath	9D Newton Heath
44697	$5MT^3$	→	26A Newton Heath	26A Newton Heath	26A Newton Heath	26A Newton Heath	26A Newton Heath	9D Newton Heath
44698	$5MT^3$	→	63A Perth	63A Perth	63A Perth	63A Perth	63A Perth	63A Perth
44699	$5MT^3$	→	63A Perth	63A Perth	63A Perth	63A Perth	67A Corkerhill	67E Dumfries
44700	$5MT^3$	→	64D Carstairs	64D Carstairs	64D Carstairs	64D Carstairs	66E Carstairs	66E Carstairs
44701	$5MT^3$	→	64D Carstairs	64D Carstairs	64D Carstairs	64D Carstairs	66E Carstairs	
44702	$5MT^3$	→	65B St. Rollox	65B St. Rollox	65B St. Rollox	65A Eastfield	65A Eastfield	
44703	$5MT^3$	→	65B St. Rollox	68A Carlisle Kingmoor	61B Aberdeen Ferryhill	61B Aberdeen Ferryhill	61B Aberdeen Ferryhill	61B Aberdeen Ferryhill
44704	$5MT^3$	→	63A Perth	63A Perth	63A Perth	63A Perth	63A Perth	63A Perth
44705	$5MT^3$	→	63A Perth	63A Perth	63A Perth	63A Perth	63A Perth	63A Perth
44706	$5MT^3$	→	67A Corkerhill	67A Corkerhill	67A Corkerhill	67A Corkerhill	67A Corkerhill	
44707	$5MT^3$	→	66A Polmadie	66A Polmadie	65A Eastfield	65A Eastfield	65A Eastfield	66E Carstairs
44708	$5MT^3$	→	5B Crewe South	10C Patricroft	10C Patricroft	26F Patricroft	26F Patricroft	9E Trafford Park
44709	$5MT^3$	→	11A Carnforth	11A Carnforth	11A Carnforth	24L Carnforth	24L Carnforth	10A Carnforth
44710	$5MT^3$	→	2A Rugby	6A Chester	6A Chester	6A Chester	21D Aston	2D Banbury
44711	$5MT^3$	→	2A Rugby	2A Rugby	2A Rugby	2A Rugby	2A Rugby	6J Holyhead

No.	Class	1948	1951	1954	1957	1960	1963	1966
44712	5MT^3	→	**2A** Rugby	**2A** Rugby	**2A** Rugby	**2E** Northampton	**2A** Rugby	**6J** Holyhead
44713	5MT^3	→	**2A** Rugby	**2A** Rugby	**1A** Willesden	**5B** Crewe South	**2E** Northampton	**5D** Stoke
44714	5MT^3	→	**2A** Rugby	**2A** Rugby	**12A** Carlisle Upperby	**5A** Crewe North	**5A** Crewe North	**5D** Stoke
44715	5MT^3	→	**2A** Rugby	**2A** Rugby	**2A** Rugby	**2A** Rugby	**2A** Rugby	**5B** Crewe South
44716	5MT^3	→	**2A** Rugby	**2A** Rugby	**2A** Rugby	**2A** Rugby	**2A** Rugby	
44717	5MT^3	→	**5A** Crewe North	**9E** Trafford Park	**17F** Trafford Park	**9E** Trafford Park	**16D** Annesley	**8A** Edge Hill
44718	5MT^3	→	**68A** Carlisle Kingmoor	**60A** Inverness	**60A** Inverness	**60A** Inverness	**67B** Hurlford	**65B** St. Rollox
44719	5MT^3	→	**68A** Carlisle Kingmoor	**60A** Inverness	**60A** Inverness	**60A** Inverness	**60A** Inverness	
44720	5MT^3	→	**68A** Carlisle Kingmoor	**63A** Perth	**63A** Perth	**63A** Perth	**63A** Perth	**63A** Perth
44721	5MT^3	→	**68A** Carlisle Kingmoor	**63A** Perth	**63A** Perth	**63A** Perth	**63A** Perth	
44722	5MT^3	→	**68A** Carlisle Kingmoor	**60A** Inverness	**60A** Inverness	**60A** Inverness	**63A** Perth	**63A** Perth
44723	5MT^3	→	**68A** Carlisle Kingmoor	**60A** Inverness	**60A** Inverness	**60A** Inverness	**67A** Corkerhill	**67E** Dumfries
44724	5MT^3	→	**68A** Carlisle Kingmoor	**60A** Inverness	**60A** Inverness	**60A** Inverness	**63A** Perth	**67C** Ayr
44725	5MT^3	→	**68A** Carlisle Kingmoor	**68A** Carlisle Kingmoor	**68A** Carlisle Kingmoor	**12A** Carlisle Kingmoor	**12A** Carlisle Kingmoor	**8C** Speke Junction
44726	5MT^3	→	**68A** Carlisle Kingmoor	**68A** Carlisle Kingmoor	**68A** Carlisle Kingmoor	**12A** Carlisle Kingmoor	**12A** Carlisle Kingmoor	**12A** Carlisle Kingmoor
44727	5MT^3	→	**68A** Carlisle Kingmoor	**68A** Carlisle Kingmoor	**68A** Carlisle Kingmoor	**12A** Carlisle Kingmoor	**12A** Carlisle Kingmoor	**12A** Carlisle Kingmoor
44728	5MT^3	→	**27C** Southport	**27C** Southport	**27C** Southport	**27C** Southport	**24E** Blackpool Central	**9K** Bolton
44729	5MT^3	→	**27C** Southport	**27C** Southport	**27C** Southport	**27C** Southport	**27B** Aintree	**10C** Fleetwood
44730	5MT^3	→	**28A** Blackpool Central	**24E** Blackpool Central	**24E** Blackpool Central	**24E** Blackpool Central	**24E** Blackpool Central	**8B** Warrington Dallam
44731	5MT^3	→	**28A** Blackpool Central	**24E** Blackpool Central	**24E** Blackpool Central	**24E** Blackpool Central	**24E** Blackpool Central	**8B** Warrington Dallam
44732	5MT^3	→	**28A** Blackpool Central	**24E** Blackpool Central	**24E** Blackpool Central	**24E** Blackpool Central	**24E** Blackpool Central	**8C** Speke Junction
44733	5MT^3	→	**28A** Blackpool Central	**24E** Blackpool Central	**24E** Blackpool Central	**24E** Blackpool Central	**24E** Blackpool Central	**10A** Carnforth
44734	5MT^3		**26A** Newton Heath	**26A** Newton Heath	**26A** Newton Heath	**26A** Newton Heath	**26A** Newton Heath	**9D** Newton Heath
44735	5MT^3	→	**26A** Newton Heath	**26A** Newton Heath	**26A** Newton Heath	**26A** Newton Heath	**26A** Newton Heath	**9E** Trafford Park
44736	5MT^3	→	**26A** Newton Heath	**26A** Newton Heath	**26A** Newton Heath	**26A** Newton Heath	**26A** Newton Heath	**9K** Bolton
44737	5MT^3	→	**27C** Southport	**24E** Blackpool Central	**24E** Blackpool Central	**24E** Blackpool Central	**24E** Blackpool Central	**9K** Bolton
44738	5MT^3	→	**7A** Llandudno Junction	**6G** Llandudno Junction	**6G** Llandudno Junction	**6G** Llandudno Junction	**6G** Llandudno Junction	
44739	5MT^3	→	**7A** Llandudno Junction	**6G** Llandudno Junction	**6G** Llandudno Junction	**6G** Llandudno Junction	**6G** Llandudno Junction	
44740	5MT^3	→	**7A** Llandudno Junction	**6G** Llandudno Junction	**6G** Llandudno Junction	**6G** Llandudno Junction	**6G** Llandudno Junction	
44741	5MT^3	→	**7A** Llandudno Junction	**9A** Longsight	**9A** Longsight	**9A** Longsight	**8C** Speke Junction	
44742	5MT^3	→	**7A** Llandudno Junction	**9A** Longsight	**9A** Longsight	**9A** Longsight	**27C** Southport	
44743	5MT^3	→	**22A** Bristol Barrow Road	**22A** Bristol Barrow Road	**22A** Bristol Barrow Road	**27A** Bank Hall	**27C** Southport	**8C** Speke Junction
44744	5MT^3	→	**22A** Bristol Barrow Road	**20A** Leeds Holbeck	**22A** Bristol Barrow Road	**27A** Bank Hall	**27C** Southport	
44745	5MT^3	→	**22A** Bristol Barrow Road	**22A** Bristol Barrow Road	**22A** Bristol Barrow Road	**27A** Bank Hall	**27C** Southport	
44746	5MT^3	→	**22A** Bristol Barrow Road	**20A** Leeds Holbeck	**22A** Bristol Barrow Road	**9A** Longsight	**26C** Bolton	
44747	5MT^3	→	**22A** Bristol Barrow Road	**22A** Bristol Barrow Road	**22A** Bristol Barrow Road	**9A** Longsight	**9A** Longsight	
44748	5MT^3	→	**9A** Longsight	**9A** Longsight	**9A** Longsight	**9A** Longsight	**9A** Longsight	
44749	5MT^3	→	**9A** Longsight	**9A** Longsight	**9A** Longsight	**9A** Longsight	**8C** Speke Junction	
44750	5MT^3	→	**9A** Longsight	**9A** Longsight	**9A** Longsight	**9A** Longsight	**8C** Speke Junction	
44751	5MT^3	→	**9A** Longsight	**9A** Longsight	**9A** Longsight	**9A** Longsight	**8C** Speke Junction	
44752	5MT^3	→	**9A** Longsight	**9A** Longsight	**9A** Longsight	**9A** Longsight	**9B** Stockport Edgeley	
44753	5MT^3	→	**20A** Leeds Holbeck	**20A** Leeds Holbeck	**55A** Leeds Holbeck	**55A** Leeds Holbeck	**55A** Leeds Holbeck	
44754	5MT^3	→	**20A** Leeds Holbeck	**20A** Leeds Holbeck	**55A** Leeds Holbeck	**55A** Leeds Holbeck	**8C** Speke Junction	
44755	5MT^3	→	**20A** Leeds Holbeck	**20A** Leeds Holbeck	**55A** Leeds Holbeck	**55A** Leeds Holbeck	**9B** Stockport Edgeley	
44756	5MT^3	→	**20A** Leeds Holbeck	**20A** Leeds Holbeck	**55A** Leeds Holbeck	**55A** Leeds Holbeck	**55A** Leeds Holbeck	
44757	5MT^3	→	**20A** Leeds Holbeck	**20A** Leeds Holbeck	**55A** Leeds Holbeck	**55A** Leeds Holbeck	**55A** Leeds Holbeck	
44758	5MT^3	**5A** Crewe North	**5A** Crewe North	**5A** Crewe North	**5A** Crewe North	**8F** Wigan Springs Branch	**24J** Lancaster	**10J** Lancaster
44759	5MT^3	**5A** Crewe North	**9A** Longsight	**5A** Crewe North	**5A** Crewe North	**5A** Crewe North	**5A** Crewe North	**5B** Crewe South
44760	5MT^3	**5A** Crewe North	**9A** Longsight	**9A** Longsight	**9A** Longsight	**2E** Northampton	**6G** Llandudno Junction	**2A** Tyseley
44761	5MT^3	**5A** Crewe North	**5A** Crewe North	**5A** Crewe North	**5A** Crewe North	**5A** Crewe North	**5A** Crewe North	**5B** Crewe South
44762	5MT^3	**5A** Crewe North	**5A** Crewe North	**5A** Crewe North	**5A** Crewe North	**5A** Crewe North	**5A** Crewe North	**2A** Tyseley
44763	5MT^3	**5A** Crewe North	**5A** Crewe North	**5A** Crewe North	**5A** Crewe North	**5A** Crewe North	**5A** Crewe North	
44764	5MT^3	**5A** Crewe North	**5A** Crewe North	**5A** Crewe North	**5A** Crewe North	**5A** Crewe North	**5A** Crewe North	
44765	5MT^3	**5A** Crewe North	**5A** Crewe North	**5A** Crewe North	**5A** Crewe North	**5A** Crewe North	**5A** Crewe North	**5B** Crewe South
44766	5MT^3	**5A** Crewe North	**5A** Crewe North	**5A** Crewe North	**5A** Crewe North	**3E** Monument Lane	**21B** Bescot	**2F** Bescot
44767	5MT^3	**5A** Crewe North	**27A** Bank Hall	**27A** Bank Hall	**27A** Bank Hall	**27A** Bank Hall	**27C** Southport	**12A** Carlisle Kingmoor
44768	5MT^3	**29A** Perth	**8A** Edge Hill	**8A** Edge Hill	**8A** Edge Hill	**8A** Edge Hill	**8A** Edge Hill	**8A** Edge Hill
44769	5MT^3	**29A** Perth	**8A** Edge Hill	**8A** Edge Hill	**8A** Edge Hill	**8A** Edge Hill	**8A** Edge Hill	
44770	5MT^3	**29A** Perth	**5A** Crewe North	**5A** Crewe North	**12A** Carlisle Upperby	**12B** Carlisle Upperby	**5A** Crewe North	**6J** Holyhead
44771	5MT^3	**32A** Inverness	**5A** Crewe North	**1A** Willesden	**1A** Willesden	**2A** Rugby	**2A** Rugby	**5E** Nuneaton
44772	5MT^3	**32A** Inverness	**8A** Edge Hill	**8A** Edge Hill	**8A** Edge Hill	**8A** Edge Hill	**8A** Edge Hill	**8A** Edge Hill
44773	5MT^3	**32A** Inverness	**8A** Edge Hill	**8A** Edge Hill	**8A** Edge Hill	**8A** Edge Hill	**8A** Edge Hill	**8A** Edge Hill
44774	5MT^3	**20A** Leeds Holbeck	**20A** Leeds Holbeck	**20A** Leeds Holbeck	**14A** Cricklewood	**14A** Cricklewood	**14E** Bedford	**2A** Tyseley
44775	5MT^3	**20A** Leeds Holbeck	**20A** Leeds Holbeck	**21A** Saltley	**21A** Saltley	**21A** Saltley	**21A** Saltley	**6D** Shrewsbury
44776	5MT^3	**14B** Kentish Town	**17A** Derby	**21A** Saltley	**21A** Saltley	**21A** Saltley	**17A** Derby	**2A** Tyseley
44777	5MT^3	**14B** Kentish Town	**14B** Kentish Town	**20A** Leeds Holbeck	**14A** Cricklewood	**14A** Cricklewood	**17A** Derby	**2A** Tyseley
44778	5MT^3	**24E** Blackpool Central	**28A** Blackpool Central	**24E** Blackpool Central	**24E** Blackpool Central	**24E** Blackpool Central	**24E** Blackpool Central	**10A** Carnforth
44779	5MT^3	**24E** Blackpool Central	**28A** Blackpool Central	**24E** Blackpool Central	**24E** Blackpool Central	**24E** Blackpool Central	**24E** Blackpool Central	**8B** Warrington Dallam
44780	5MT^3	**25A** Wakefield	**25B** Huddersfield	**25B** Huddersfield	**24B** Rose Grove	**8F** Wigan Springs Branch	**6G** Llandudno Junction	**2A** Tyseley
44781	5MT^3	**26A** Newton Heath	**26B** Agecroft	**26B** Agecroft	**26B** Agecroft	**26B** Agecroft	**26B** Agecroft	**9J** Agecroft
44782	5MT^3	**26A** Newton Heath	**26B** Agecroft	**26B** Agecroft	**26B** Agecroft	**26B** Agecroft	**26B** Agecroft	**9J** Agecroft
44783	5MT^3	**12B** Carlisle Upperby	**60A** Inverness	**60A** Inverness	**60A** Inverness	**60A** Inverness	**60A** Inverness	
44784	5MT^3	**12B** Carlisle Upperby	**60A** Inverness	**60A** Inverness	**60A** Inverness	**60A** Inverness	**67A** Corkerhill	
44785	5MT^3	**12B** Carlisle Upperby	**60A** Inverness	**60A** Inverness	**60A** Inverness	**60A** Inverness	**67A** Corkerhill	
44786	5MT^3	**12B** Carlisle Upperby	**65B** St. Rollox	**65B** St. Rollox	**65B** St. Rollox	**65B** St. Rollox	**66B** Motherwell	**66B** Motherwell
44787	5MT^3	**12B** Carlisle Upperby	**66A** Polmadie	**66A** Polmadie	**65A** Eastfield	**65A** Eastfield	**65A** Eastfield	
44788	5MT^3	**5A** Crewe North	**60A** Inverness	**60A** Inverness	**60A** Inverness	**60A** Inverness	**65F** Grangemouth	**67C** Ayr
44789	5MT^3	**5A** Crewe North	**60A** Inverness	**60A** Inverness	**60A** Inverness	**60A** Inverness	**67F** Stranraer	
44790	5MT^3	**5A** Crewe North	**66A** Polmadie	**68A** Carlisle Kingmoor	**68A** Carlisle Kingmoor	**12A** Carlisle Kingmoor	**12A** Carlisle Kingmoor	**12A** Carlisle Kingmoor
44791	5MT^3	**28A** Motherwell	**65C** Parkhead	**67A** Corkerhill	**67A** Corkerhill	**67A** Corkerhill	**67A** Corkerhill	**66E** Carstairs
44792	5MT^3	**28A** Motherwell	**66A** Polmadie	**68A** Carlisle Kingmoor	**68A** Carlisle Kingmoor	**12A** Carlisle Kingmoor	**12A** Carlisle Kingmoor	**12A** Carlisle Kingmoor
44793	5MT^3	**27A** Polmadie	**66A** Polmadie	**66A** Polmadie	**64D** Carstairs	**64D** Carstairs	**66E** Carstairs	
44794	5MT^3	**27A** Polmadie	**66A** Polmadie	**66A** Polmadie	**61B** Aberdeen Ferryhill	**61B** Aberdeen Ferryhill	**61B** Aberdeen Ferryhill	**61B** Aberdeen Ferryhill
44795	5MT^3	**12A** Carlisle Kingmoor	**68A** Carlisle Kingmoor	**68A** Carlisle Kingmoor	**68A** Carlisle Kingmoor	**12A** Carlisle Kingmoor	**12A** Carlisle Kingmoor	**12A** Carlisle Kingmoor
44796	5MT^3	**29A** Perth	**63A** Perth	**63A** Perth	**63A** Perth	**63A** Perth	**63A** Perth	**66A** Polmadie
44797	5MT^3	**29A** Perth	**63A** Perth	**63A** Perth	**63A** Perth	**63A** Perth	**63A** Perth	**63A** Perth
44798	5MT^3	**32A** Inverness	**60A** Inverness	**60A** Inverness	**60A** Inverness	**60A** Inverness	**67A** Corkerhill	**67A** Corkerhill
44799	5MT^3	**32A** Inverness	**60A** Inverness	**60A** Inverness	**60A** Inverness	**60A** Inverness	**63A** Perth	
44800	5MT^3	**6B** Mold Junction	**6B** Mold Junction	**6B** Mold Junction	**6B** Mold Junction	**6B** Mold Junction	**6B** Mold Junction	**6B** Mold Junction
44801	5MT^3	**5A** Crewe North	**63A** Perth	**63A** Perth	**63A** Perth	**63A** Perth	**67A** Corkerhill	
44802	5MT^3	**19E** Belle Vue	**19A** Sheffield Grimesthorpe	**19A** Sheffield Grimesthorpe	**19A** Sheffield Grimesthorpe	**6J** Holyhead	**12A** Carlisle Kingmoor	**12A** Carlisle Kingmoor
44803	5MT^3	**19E** Belle Vue	**26G** Belle Vue	**26G** Belle Vue	**26A** Newton Heath	**26A** Newton Heath	**26A** Newton Heath	**9D** Newton Heath
44804	5MT^3	**22A** Bristol Barrow Road	**21A** Saltley	**21A** Saltley	**21A** Saltley	**21A** Saltley	**21A** Saltley	**9E** Trafford Park
44805	5MT^3	**21A** Saltley	**21A** Saltley	**21A** Saltley	**21A** Saltley	**21A** Saltley	**21A** Saltley	**2B** Oxley
44806	5MT^3	**21A** Saltley	**15C** Leicester Midland	**15C** Leicester Midland	**14B** Kentish Town	**16A** Nottingham	**16A** Nottingham	**8C** Speke Junction
44807	5MT^3	**5A** Crewe North	**5B** Crewe South	**5A** Crewe North	**5A** Crewe North	**3E** Monument Lane	**6J** Holyhead	**6J** Holyhead
44808	5MT^3	**5A** Crewe North	**7A** Llandudno Junction	**10C** Patricroft	**10C** Patricroft	**26F** Patricroft	**26F** Patricroft	**2B** Oxley
44809	5MT^3	**17A** Derby	**17A** Derby	**17A** Derby	**17A** Derby	**9E** Trafford Park	**9E** Trafford Park	**8M** Southport
44810	5MT^3	**21A** Saltley	**21A** Saltley	**21A** Saltley	**21A** Saltley	**21A** Saltley	**21A** Saltley	**5D** Stoke
44811	5MT^3	**21A** Saltley	**21B** Bournville	**21B** Bournville	**17B** Burton	**15C** Leicester Midland	**15C** Leicester Midland	**16B** Annesley
44812	5MT^3	**22A** Bristol Barrow Road	**15C** Leicester Midland	**15C** Leicester Midland	**14B** Kentish Town	**21A** Saltley	**21A** Saltley	**2B** Oxley
44813	5MT^3	**21A** Saltley	**21A** Saltley	**21A** Saltley	**21A** Saltley	**21A** Saltley	**21A** Saltley	**5D** Stoke
44814	5MT^3	**21A** Saltley	**21A** Saltley	**21A** Saltley	**21A** Saltley	**21A** Saltley	**21A** Saltley	**6D** Shrewsbury
44815	5MT^3	**17A** Derby	**17A** Derby	**17A** Derby	**17A** Derby	**15C** Leicester Midland	**15C** Leicester Midland	**9E** Trafford Park
44816	5MT^3	**14B** Kentish Town	**14B** Kentish Town	**14B** Kentish Town	**14B** Kentish Town	**14A** Cricklewood	**17B** Burton	**9K** Bolton
44817	5MT^3	**14A** Cricklewood	**14B** Kentish Town	**14B** Kentish Town	**14B** Kentish Town	**14B** Kentish Town	**17B** Burton	**9J** Agecroft
44818	5MT^3	**17A** Derby	**17A** Derby	**17A** Derby	**17A** Derby	**21A** Saltley	**17B** Burton	**9D** Newton Heath
44819	5MT^3	**17A** Derby	**17A** Derby	**17A** Derby	**17A** Derby	**14D** Neasden	**17A** Derby	**8B** Warrington Dallam
44820	5MT^3	**20A** Leeds Holbeck	**17A** Derby	**64A** St. Margarets	**63A** Perth	**63A** Perth	**66B** Motherwell	**66B** Motherwell
44821	5MT^3	**20A** Leeds Holbeck	**20A** Leeds Holbeck	**20A** Leeds Holbeck	**21A** Saltley	**14B** Kentish Town	**15E** Leicester Central	**6D** Shrewsbury
44822	5MT^3	**14B** Kentish Town	**14B** Kentish Town	**14B** Kentish Town	**14B** Kentish Town	**14B** Kentish Town	**17B** Burton	**9D** Newton Heath
44823	5MT^3	**20A** Leeds Holbeck	**26B** Agecroft	**26B** Agecroft	**26B** Agecroft	**26B** Agecroft	**26B** Agecroft	
44824	5MT^3	**20A** Leeds Holbeck	**25B** Huddersfield	**25B** Huddersfield	**55G** Huddersfield	**55A** Leeds Holbeck	**55A** Leeds Holbeck	**55A** Leeds Holbeck
44825	5MT^3	**16A** Nottingham	**16A** Nottingham	**14B** Kentish Town	**14B** Kentish Town	**21A** Saltley	**17B** Burton	**16B** Annesley

No.	Class	1948	1951	1954	1957	1960	1963	1966
44826	5MT[3]	**22C** Bath Green Park	**71G** Bath Green Park	**20A** Leeds Holbeck	**55A** Leeds Holbeck	**55A** Leeds Holbeck	**55A** Leeds Holbeck	**55C** Farnley Junction
44827	5MT[3]	**5B** Crewe South	**5B** Crewe South	**5A** Crewe North	**5B** Crewe South	**24K** Preston	**8C** Speke Junction	
44828	5MT[3]	**20A** Leeds Holbeck	**20A** Leeds Holbeck	**20A** Leeds Holbeck	**55A** Leeds Holbeck	**55A** Leeds Holbeck	**55A** Leeds Holbeck	**55A** Leeds Holbeck
44829	5MT[3]	**18A** Toton	**3E** Monument Lane	**3B** Bushbury	**3B** Bushbury	**3B** Bushbury	**21C** Bushbury	**5B** Crewe South
44830	5MT[3]	**22C** Bath Green Park	**71G** Bath Green Park	**19B** Millhouses	**19B** Millhouses	**14D** Neasden	**15E** Leicester Central	**16B** Annesley
44831	5MT[3]	**2A** Rugby	**2A** Rugby	**2A** Rugby	**2A** Rugby	**2A** Rugby	**2A** Rugby	**5E** Nuneaton
44832	5MT[3]	**5A** Crewe North	**5B** Crewe South	**5B** Crewe South	**5B** Crewe South	**5B** Crewe South	**5B** Crewe South	**5B** Crewe South
44833	5MT[3]	**5A** Crewe North	**2A** Rugby	**2A** Rugby	**2A** Rugby	**2A** Rugby	**2A** Rugby	**5B** Crewe South
44834	5MT[3]	**5A** Crewe North	**9A** Longsight	**5B** Crewe South	**5B** Crewe South	**5B** Crewe South	**5B** Crewe South	**5B** Crewe South
44835	5MT[3]	**5A** Crewe North	**84G** Shrewsbury	**84G** Shrewsbury	**84G** Shrewsbury	**84G** Shrewsbury	**89A** Shrewsbury	**16B** Annesley
44836	5MT[3]	**5A** Crewe North	**2A** Rugby	**2A** Rugby	**2A** Rugby	**2A** Rugby	**2A** Rugby	**9B** Stockport Edgeley
44837	5MT[3]	**5A** Crewe North	**9A** Longsight	**2A** Rugby	**2A** Rugby	**11A** Barrow	**21D** Aston	**8A** Edge Hill
44838	5MT[3]	**5A** Crewe North	**9A** Longsight	**1A** Willesden	**1A** Willesden	**1A** Willesden	**8A** Edge Hill	**8A** Edge Hill
44839	5MT[3]	**17A** Derby	**71G** Bath Green Park	**17A** Derby	**17A** Derby	**21A** Saltley	**17B** Burton	**16B** Annesley
44840	5MT[3]	**21A** Saltley	**6A** Chester	**5A** Crewe North	**9A** Longsight	**3E** Monument Lane	**21B** Bescot	**2F** Bescot
44841	5MT[3]	**16A** Nottingham	**16A** Nottingham	**21A** Saltley	**21A** Saltley	**21A** Saltley	**21A** Saltley	**2B** Oxley
44842	5MT[3]	**21A** Saltley	**21A** Saltley	**21A** Saltley	**21A** Saltley	**9E** Trafford Park	**6B** Mold Junction	**6B** Mold Junction
44843	5MT[3]	**22A** Bristol Barrow Road	**20A** Leeds Holbeck	**20A** Leeds Holbeck	**17B** Burton	**15C** Leicester Midland	**15C** Leicester Midland	**2B** Oxley
44844	5MT[3]	**5B** Crewe South	**6A** Chester	**3D** Aston	**3D** Aston	**5A** Crewe North	**1A** Willesden	**5B** Crewe South
44845	5MT[3]	**19E** Belle Vue	**26G** Belle Vue	**26G** Belle Vue	**26A** Newton Heath	**26A** Newton Heath	**26A** Newton Heath	**9D** Newton Heath
44846	5MT[3]	**14B** Kentish Town	**14B** Kentish Town	**14B** Kentish Town	**14B** Kentish Town	**14B** Kentish Town	**2F** Woodford Halse	**9D** Newton Heath
44847	5MT[3]	**20A** Leeds Holbeck	**17A** Derby	**17A** Derby	**19B** Millhouses	**14D** Neasden	**15E** Leicester Central	**16B** Annesley
44848	5MT[3]	**20A** Leeds Holbeck	**17A** Derby	**19B** Millhouses	**17A** Derby	**15C** Leicester Midland	**15E** Leicester Central	**16B** Annesley
44849	5MT[3]	**20A** Leeds Holbeck	**20A** Leeds Holbeck	**20A** Leeds Holbeck	**55A** Leeds Holbeck	**55A** Leeds Holbeck	**55A** Leeds Holbeck	
44850	5MT[3]	**20A** Leeds Holbeck	**20A** Leeds Holbeck	**66B** Motherwell	**66B** Motherwell	**66B** Motherwell	**66B** Motherwell	**66B** Motherwell
44851	5MT[3]	**17A** Derby	**17A** Derby	**19B** Millhouses	**17A** Derby	**17A** Derby	**16A** Nottingham	**16F** Burton
44852	5MT[3]	**21A** Saltley	**21B** Bournville	**20A** Leeds Holbeck	**55A** Leeds Holbeck	**55A** Leeds Holbeck	**55A** Leeds Holbeck	**55A** Leeds Holbeck
44853	5MT[3]	**20A** Leeds Holbeck	**20A** Leeds Holbeck	**20A** Leeds Holbeck	**55A** Leeds Holbeck	**55A** Leeds Holbeck	**55A** Leeds Holbeck	**55A** Leeds Holbeck
44854	5MT[3]	**20A** Leeds Holbeck	**20A** Leeds Holbeck	**20A** Leeds Holbeck	**55A** Leeds Holbeck	**55A** Leeds Holbeck	**55A** Leeds Holbeck	**55A** Leeds Holbeck
44855	5MT[3]	**22A** Bristol Barrow Road	**22A** Bristol Barrow Road	**19A** Sheffield Grimesthorpe	**14B** Kentish Town	**14B** Kentish Town	**8A** Edge Hill	**9E** Trafford Park
44856	5MT[3]	**20A** Leeds Holbeck	**20A** Leeds Holbeck	**17A** Derby	**17A** Derby	**21A** Saltley	**16A** Nottingham	**2B** Oxley
44857	5MT[3]	**20A** Leeds Holbeck	**20A** Leeds Holbeck	**20A** Leeds Holbeck	**55A** Leeds Holbeck	**55A** Leeds Holbeck	**55A** Leeds Holbeck	**55A** Leeds Holbeck
44858	5MT[3]	**19A** Sheffield Grimesthorpe	**19A** Sheffield Grimesthorpe	**19A** Sheffield Grimesthorpe	**19A** Sheffield Grimesthorpe	**21A** Saltley	**17B** Burton	**16C** Derby
44859	5MT[3]	**19B** Millhouses	**19B** Millhouses	**16A** Nottingham	**21A** Saltley	**21A** Saltley	**21A** Saltley	**2A** Tyseley
44860	5MT[3]	**7A** Llandudno Junction	**2A** Rugby	**2A** Rugby	**2A** Rugby	**2A** Rugby	**2A** Rugby	**2D** Banbury
44861	5MT[3]	**16A** Nottingham	**16A** Nottingham	**16A** Nottingham	**16A** Nottingham	**16A** Nottingham	**16A** Nottingham	**9D** Newton Heath
44862	5MT[3]	**5A** Crewe North	**2A** Rugby	**2A** Rugby	**2A** Rugby	**2A** Rugby	**2A** Rugby	**12A** Carlisle Kingmoor
44863	5MT[3]	**5A** Crewe North	**2A** Rugby	**2A** Rugby	**2A** Rugby	**2A** Rugby	**2A** Rugby	**8A** Edge Hill
44864	5MT[3]	**5A** Crewe North	**4A** Bletchley	**1E** Bletchley	**6G** Llandudno Junction	**6G** Llandudno Junction	**8C** Speke Junction	**8A** Edge Hill
44865	5MT[3]	**5A** Crewe North	**4A** Bletchley	**1E** Bletchley	**6G** Llandudno Junction	**6G** Llandudno Junction	**21D** Aston	**2A** Tyseley
44866	5MT[3]	**2A** Rugby	**2A** Rugby	**2A** Rugby	**2A** Rugby	**2A** Rugby	**2A** Rugby	**5E** Nuneaton
44867	5MT[3]	**2A** Rugby	**2A** Rugby	**2A** Rugby	**2A** Rugby	**2A** Rugby	**9B** Stockport Edgeley	**9B** Stockport Edgeley
44868	5MT[3]	**12B** Carlisle Upperby	**7C** Holyhead	**6J** Holyhead	**5B** Crewe South	**5B** Crewe South	**9B** Stockport Edgeley	**9B** Stockport Edgeley
44869	5MT[3]	**12B** Carlisle Upperby	**12A** Carlisle Upperby	**1A** Willesden	**1A** Willesden	**1A** Willesden	**2E** Northampton	**2D** Banbury
44870	5MT[3]	**9A** Longsight	**2A** Rugby	**2A** Rugby	**2A** Rugby	**2A** Rugby	**2A** Rugby	**10F** Rose Grove
44871	5MT[3]	**9A** Longsight	**12A** Carlisle Upperby	**5D** Stoke	**5D** Stoke	**5B** Crewe South	**9B** Stockport Edgeley	**9B** Stockport Edgeley
44872	5MT[3]	**3D** Aston	**3D** Aston	**3D** Aston	**3D** Aston	**3D** Aston	**21D** Aston	**2D** Banbury
44873	5MT[3]	**3C** Walsall	**3C** Walsall	**3C** Walsall	**3C** Walsall	**3A** Bescot	**21B** Bescot	**8F** Wigan Springs Branch
44874	5MT[3]	**5A** Crewe North	**11A** Carnforth	**11A** Carnforth	**11A** Carnforth	**24L** Carnforth	**24L** Carnforth	**10A** Carnforth
44875	5MT[3]	**5A** Crewe North	**1A** Willesden	**1A** Willesden	**1A** Willesden	**1A** Willesden	**21B** Bescot	**2F** Bescot
44876	5MT[3]	**12B** Carlisle Upperby	**12A** Carlisle Upperby	**3D** Aston	**3D** Aston	**3D** Aston	**21D** Aston	**2B** Oxley
44877	5MT[3]	**12A** Carlisle Kingmoor	**68A** Carlisle Kingmoor	**68A** Carlisle Kingmoor	**68A** Carlisle Kingmoor	**12A** Carlisle Kingmoor	**24J** Lancaster	**8C** Speke Junction
44878	5MT[3]	**12A** Carlisle Kingmoor	**68A** Carlisle Kingmoor	**68A** Carlisle Kingmoor	**68A** Carlisle Kingmoor	**12A** Carlisle Kingmoor	**12A** Carlisle Kingmoor	**12A** Carlisle Kingmoor
44879	5MT[3]	**12A** Carlisle Kingmoor	**63A** Perth	**63A** Perth	**63A** Perth	**63A** Perth	**63A** Perth	**63A** Perth
44880	5MT[3]	**31A** St. Rollox	**65B** St. Rollox	**65B** St. Rollox	**65B** St. Rollox	**65B** St. Rollox	**65B** St. Rollox	**66B** Motherwell
44881	5MT[3]	**31A** St. Rollox	**65B** St. Rollox	**65B** St. Rollox	**65B** St. Rollox	**65B** St. Rollox	**65B** St. Rollox	**66B** Motherwell
44882	5MT[3]	**12A** Carlisle Kingmoor	**68A** Carlisle Kingmoor	**68A** Carlisle Kingmoor	**68A** Carlisle Kingmoor	**12A** Carlisle Kingmoor	**12E** Barrow	**12C** Barrow
44883	5MT[3]	**12A** Carlisle Kingmoor	**68A** Carlisle Kingmoor	**68A** Carlisle Kingmoor	**68A** Carlisle Kingmoor	**12A** Carlisle Kingmoor	**12A** Carlisle Kingmoor	**12A** Carlisle Kingmoor
44884	5MT[3]	**12A** Carlisle Kingmoor	**68A** Carlisle Kingmoor	**68A** Carlisle Kingmoor	**68A** Carlisle Kingmoor	**12A** Carlisle Kingmoor	**12C** Carlisle Canal	**12A** Carlisle Kingmoor
44885	5MT[3]	**29A** Perth	**63A** Perth	**63A** Perth	**63A** Perth	**63A** Perth	**67E** Dumfries	
44886	5MT[3]	**12A** Carlisle Kingmoor	**68A** Carlisle Kingmoor	**68A** Carlisle Kingmoor	**68A** Carlisle Kingmoor	**12A** Carlisle Kingmoor	**12A** Carlisle Kingmoor	**12A** Carlisle Kingmoor
44887	5MT[3]	**23C** Southport	**27C** Southport	**27C** Southport	**27C** Southport	**27C** Southport	**27B** Aintree	**12A** Carlisle Kingmoor
44888	5MT[3]	**26A** Newton Heath	**21A** Saltley	**21A** Saltley	**21A** Saltley	**21A** Saltley	**21A** Saltley	**9E** Trafford Park
44889	5MT[3]	**26A** Newton Heath	**26A** Newton Heath	**24E** Blackpool Central	**24A** Accrington	**24A** Accrington	**24F** Fleetwood	**10J** Lancaster
44890	5MT[3]	**26A** Newton Heath	**26A** Newton Heath	**26A** Newton Heath	**26A** Newton Heath	**26A** Newton Heath	**26A** Newton Heath	**9D** Newton Heath
44891	5MT[3]	**26A** Newton Heath	**26A** Newton Heath	**26A** Newton Heath	**26A** Newton Heath	**26A** Newton Heath	**26A** Newton Heath	**9D** Newton Heath
44892	5MT[3]	**10A** Wigan Springs Branch	**10B** Preston	**11A** Carnforth	**11A** Carnforth	**24L** Carnforth	**24L** Carnforth	**10A** Carnforth
44893	5MT[3]	**26A** Newton Heath	**26A** Newton Heath	**26A** Newton Heath	**26A** Newton Heath	**26A** Newton Heath	**26A** Newton Heath	**9K** Bolton
44894	5MT[3]	**26A** Newton Heath	**26A** Newton Heath	**26A** Newton Heath	**26A** Newton Heath	**26A** Newton Heath	**24F** Fleetwood	**10A** Carnforth
44895	5MT[3]	**26A** Newton Heath	**26A** Newton Heath	**26A** Newton Heath	**26A** Newton Heath	**26A** Newton Heath	**26A** Newton Heath	**9E** Trafford Park
44896	5MT[3]	**25G** Farnley Junction	**25G** Farnley Junction	**25G** Farnley Junction	**55C** Farnley Junction	**55C** Farnley Junction	**55C** Farnley Junction	**55C** Farnley Junction
44897	5MT[3]	**8B** Warrington Dallam	**8B** Warrington Dallam	**3D** Aston	**3D** Aston	**3D** Aston	**2A** Rugby	**6B** Mold Junction
44898	5MT[3]	**12A** Carlisle Kingmoor	**68A** Carlisle Kingmoor	**68A** Carlisle Kingmoor	**68A** Carlisle Kingmoor	**12A** Carlisle Kingmoor	**12A** Carlisle Kingmoor	**12A** Carlisle Kingmoor
44899	5MT[3]	**12A** Carlisle Kingmoor	**68A** Carlisle Kingmoor	**68A** Carlisle Kingmoor	**68A** Carlisle Kingmoor	**12A** Carlisle Kingmoor	**12A** Carlisle Kingmoor	**12A** Carlisle Kingmoor
44900	5MT[3]	**12A** Carlisle Kingmoor	**68A** Carlisle Kingmoor	**68A** Carlisle Kingmoor	**68A** Carlisle Kingmoor	**12A** Carlisle Kingmoor	**12A** Carlisle Kingmoor	**12A** Carlisle Kingmoor
44901	5MT[3]	**12A** Carlisle Kingmoor	**68A** Carlisle Kingmoor	**68A** Carlisle Kingmoor	**68A** Carlisle Kingmoor	**12A** Carlisle Kingmoor	**12A** Carlisle Kingmoor	
44902	5MT[3]	**12A** Carlisle Kingmoor	**68A** Carlisle Kingmoor	**68A** Carlisle Kingmoor	**68A** Carlisle Kingmoor	**12A** Carlisle Kingmoor	**12A** Carlisle Kingmoor	**12A** Carlisle Kingmoor
44903	5MT[3]	**12A** Carlisle Kingmoor	**68A** Carlisle Kingmoor	**68A** Carlisle Kingmoor	**68A** Carlisle Kingmoor	**12A** Carlisle Kingmoor	**12A** Carlisle Kingmoor	**12A** Carlisle Kingmoor
44904	5MT[3]	**8A** Edge Hill	**11A** Carnforth	**11A** Carnforth	**11A** Carnforth	**24L** Carnforth	**24L** Carnforth	
44905	5MT[3]	**12B** Carlisle Upperby	**11A** Carnforth	**11A** Carnforth	**11A** Carnforth	**24L** Carnforth	**24L** Carnforth	**10A** Carnforth
44906	5MT[3]	**12B** Carlisle Upperby	**8A** Edge Hill	**8A** Edge Hill	**8A** Edge Hill	**8A** Edge Hill	**8A** Edge Hill	**8A** Edge Hill
44907	5MT[3]	**12B** Carlisle Upperby	**8A** Edge Hill	**8A** Edge Hill	**8A** Edge Hill	**8A** Edge Hill	**8A** Edge Hill	**8A** Edge Hill
44908	5MT[3]	**5A** Crewe North	**84G** Shrewsbury	**65A** Eastfield	**65A** Eastfield	**65A** Eastfield	**65A** Eastfield	**66B** Motherwell
44909	5MT[3]	**2A** Rugby	**2A** Rugby	**2A** Rugby	**2A** Rugby	**2A** Rugby	**2A** Rugby	**10F** Rose Grove
44910	5MT[3]	**2A** Rugby	**2A** Rugby	**6A** Chester	**6A** Chester	**6A** Chester	**21B** Bescot	**8L** Aintree
44911	5MT[3]	**7A** Llandudno Junction	**5B** Crewe South	**5A** Crewe North	**34A** Kings Cross	**6A** Chester	**9B** Stockport Edgeley	**12A** Carlisle Kingmoor
44912	5MT[3]	**25F** Low Moor	**25F** Low Moor	**25F** Low Moor	**56F** Low Moor	**56F** Low Moor	**56C** Copley Hill	**55D** Royston
44913	5MT[3]	**3A** Bescot	**7B** Bangor	**6H** Bangor	**6H** Bangor	**6H** Bangor	**6H** Bangor	**6A** Chester
44914	5MT[3]	**3A** Bescot	**3A** Bescot	**3A** Bescot	**3A** Bescot	**3A** Bescot	**21B** Bescot	**2F** Bescot
44915	5MT[3]	**2C** Northampton	**2A** Rugby	**2A** Rugby	**2A** Rugby	**2A** Rugby	**2A** Rugby	**10D** Lostock Hall
44916	5MT[3]	**2B** Bletchley	**4A** Bletchley	**1A** Willesden	**1A** Willesden	**1A** Willesden	**9A** Longsight	**9B** Stockport Edgeley
44917	5MT[3]	**14B** Kentish Town	**17A** Derby	**71G** Bath Green Park	**71G** Bath Green Park	**6B** Mold Junction	**6B** Mold Junction	**6B** Mold Junction
44918	5MT[3]	**16A** Nottingham	**16A** Nottingham	**16A** Nottingham	**16A** Nottingham	**16A** Nottingham	**16A** Nottingham	**9E** Trafford Park
44919	5MT[3]	**21A** Saltley	**21A** Saltley	**21A** Saltley	**21A** Saltley	**21A** Saltley	**21A** Saltley	**2B** Oxley
44920	5MT[3]	**21A** Saltley	**21A** Saltley	**21A** Saltley	**21A** Saltley	**21A** Saltley	**21A** Saltley	**16B** Annesley
44921	5MT[3]	**19A** Sheffield Grimesthorpe	**24A** Accrington	**68A** Carlisle Kingmoor	**63A** Perth	**63A** Perth	**63A** Perth	
44922	5MT[3]	**31A** St. Rollox	**65B** St. Rollox	**65B** St. Rollox	**65B** St. Rollox	**65B** St. Rollox	**65B** St. Rollox	
44923	5MT[3]	**31A** St. Rollox	**65B** St. Rollox	**65B** St. Rollox	**65B** St. Rollox	**65B** St. Rollox	**65B** St. Rollox	
44924	5MT[3]	**29A** Perth	**63A** Perth	**63A** Perth	**63A** Perth	**63A** Perth	**63A** Perth	
44925	5MT[3]	**29A** Perth	**63A** Perth	**63A** Perth	**63A** Perth	**63A** Perth	**63A** Perth	**64A** St. Margarets
44926	5MT[3]	**23C** Southport	**27C** Southport	**24E** Blackpool Central	**24E** Blackpool Central	**24E** Blackpool Central	**24E** Blackpool Central	**9D** Newton Heath
44927	5MT[3]	**24E** Blackpool Central	**28A** Blackpool Central	**24E** Blackpool Central	**24E** Blackpool Central	**24E** Blackpool Central	**24E** Blackpool Central	**9K** Bolton
44928	5MT[3]	**24E** Blackpool Central	**28A** Blackpool Central	**25A** Wakefield	**27A** Bank Hall	**27A** Bank Hall	**26B** Agecroft	**9J** Agecroft
44929	5MT[3]	**24E** Blackpool Central	**28A** Blackpool Central	**24E** Blackpool Central	**24E** Blackpool Central	**26B** Agecroft	**26B** Agecroft	**9J** Agecroft
44930	5MT[3]	**24E** Blackpool Central	**28A** Blackpool Central	**24E** Blackpool Central	**24E** Blackpool Central	**24E** Blackpool Central	**24E** Blackpool Central	**8B** Warrington Dallam
44931	5MT[3]	**28B** Dalry Road	**63A** Perth	**63A** Perth	**63A** Perth	**63A** Perth	**63A** Perth	
44932	5MT[3]	**24E** Blackpool Central	**28A** Blackpool Central	**24A** Accrington	**24A** Accrington	**15E** Leicester Central	**16D** Annesley	**16C** Derby
44933	5MT[3]	**26A** Newton Heath	**26A** Newton Heath	**26A** Newton Heath	**26A** Newton Heath	**26A** Newton Heath	**26A** Newton Heath	**9D** Newton Heath
44934	5MT[3]	**26A** Newton Heath	**26A** Newton Heath	**26A** Newton Heath	**26A** Newton Heath	**26A** Newton Heath	**26A** Newton Heath	**9D** Newton Heath
44935	5MT[3]	**8A** Edge Hill	**9A** Longsight	**6J** Holyhead	**9A** Longsight	**6B** Mold Junction	**12A** Carlisle Kingmoor	**8B** Warrington Dallam
44936	5MT[3]	**12B** Carlisle Upperby	**12A** Carlisle Upperby	**12A** Carlisle Upperby	**12A** Carlisle Upperby	**12B** Carlisle Upperby	**2E** Northampton	**2D** Banbury
44937	5MT[3]	**9A** Longsight	**9A** Longsight	**9A** Longsight	**9A** Longsight	**9A** Longsight	**12B** Carlisle Upperby	**12B** Carlisle Upperby
44938	5MT[3]	**9A** Longsight	**9E** Trafford Park	**9E** Trafford Park	**9A** Longsight	**2A** Rugby	**2A** Rugby	**9D** Newton Heath
44939	5MT[3]	**12B** Carlisle Upperby	**12A** Carlisle Upperby	**12A** Carlisle Upperby	**12A** Carlisle Upperby	**12B** Carlisle Upperby	**12B** Carlisle Upperby	

		1948	1951	1954	1957	1960	1963	1966
44940	$5MT^3$	26A Newton Heath	26A Newton Heath	24B Rose Grove	24B Rose Grove	24B Rose Grove	24B Rose Grove	10C Fleetwood
44941	$5MT^3$	8A Edge Hill	7A Llandudno Junction	9A Longsight	9A Longsight	14A Cricklewood	17B Burton	16B Annesley
44942	$5MT^3$	3A Bescot	3D Aston	3E Monument Lane	3D Aston	3D Aston	21D Aston	2D Banbury
44943	$5MT^3$	20A Leeds Holbeck	20A Leeds Holbeck	20A Leeds Holbeck	55A Leeds Holbeck	55A Leeds Holbeck	55A Leeds Holbeck	55C Farnley Junction
44944	$5MT^3$	19G Trafford Park	19A Sheffield Grimesthorpe	19A Sheffield Grimesthorpe	19A Sheffield Grimesthorpe	21A Saltley	21A Saltley	2B Oxley
44945	$5MT^3$	22C Bath Green Park	71G Bath Green Park	17A Derby	21A Saltley	21A Saltley	21A Saltley	2B Oxley
44946	$5MT^3$	23A Bank Hall	25F Low Moor	25F Low Moor	56F Low Moor	56F Low Moor	56F Low Moor	56D Mirfield
44947	$5MT^3$	24E Blackpool Central	28A Blackpool Central	24E Blackpool Central	24E Blackpool Central	24E Blackpool Central	24E Blackpool Central	9K Bolton
44948	$5MT^3$	24F Fleetwood	28B Fleetwood	24F Fleetwood	24B Rose Grove	24B Rose Grove	24B Rose Grove	10A Carnforth
44949	$5MT^3$	25A Wakefield	25B Huddersfield	25B Huddersfield	24B Rose Grove	24B Rose Grove	24B Rose Grove	9D Newton Heath
44950	$5MT^3$	24E Blackpool Central	28A Blackpool Central	24E Blackpool Central	24E Blackpool Central	24E Blackpool Central	24E Blackpool Central	8C Speke Junction
44951	$5MT^3$	26A Newton Heath	25F Low Moor	25F Low Moor	56F Low Moor	56F Low Moor	56F Low Moor	56D Mirfield
44952	$5MT^3$	5A Crewe North	64D Carstairs	64D Carstairs	64D Carstairs	64D Carstairs	66E Carstairs	66E Carstairs
44953	$5MT^3$	28C Carstairs	64D Carstairs	64D Carstairs	64D Carstairs	64D Carstairs	66E Carstairs	66E Carstairs
44954	$5MT^3$	5A Crewe North	62B Dundee Tay Bridge	62B Dundee Tay Bridge	62B Dundee Tay Bridge	62B Dundee Tay Bridge	66E Carstairs	66E Carstairs
44955	$5MT^3$	28C Carstairs	64D Carstairs	64D Carstairs	64D Carstairs	64D Carstairs	66E Carstairs	
44956	$5MT^3$	31A St. Rollox	65B St. Rollox	65B St. Rollox	65A Eastfield	65A Eastfield	65A Eastfield	66E Carstairs
44957	$5MT^3$	31A St. Rollox	65B St. Rollox	65B St. Rollox	65A Eastfield	65A Eastfield	65A Eastfield	
44958	$5MT^3$	29A Perth	63A Perth	68A Carlisle Kingmoor	68A Carlisle Kingmoor	12A Carlisle Kingmoor	12A Carlisle Kingmoor	10D Lostock Hall
44959	$5MT^3$	29A Perth	63A Perth	63A Perth	63A Perth	63A Perth	63A Perth	
44960	$5MT^3$	29A Perth	63A Perth	63A Perth	63A Perth	63A Perth	63B Fort William	63A Perth
44961	$5MT^3$	29A Perth	63A Perth	63A Perth	63A Perth	63A Perth	63A Perth	
44962	$5MT^3$	17A Derby	19B Millhouses	21A Saltley	21A Saltley	21A Saltley	21A Saltley	16F Burton
44963	$5MT^3$	19B Millhouses	19B Millhouses	17A Derby	21A Saltley	21A Saltley	21A Saltley	8B Warrington Dallam
44964	$5MT^3$	19B Millhouses	19B Millhouses	19B Millhouses	21A Saltley	9E Trafford Park	9E Trafford Park	8A Edge Hill
44965	$5MT^3$	19B Millhouses	19B Millhouses	17A Derby	21A Saltley	21A Saltley	21A Saltley	2B Oxley
44966	$5MT^3$	21A Saltley	21A Saltley	21A Saltley	22A Bristol Barrow Road	21A Saltley	21A Saltley	6D Shrewsbury
44967	$5MT^3$	5A Crewe North	65B St. Rollox	65B St. Rollox	65B St. Rollox	65A Eastfield	65A Eastfield	
44968	$5MT^3$	2B Bletchley	67A Corkerhill	67A Corkerhill	65A Eastfield	65A Eastfield	65A Eastfield	
44969	$5MT^3$	9A Longsight	66B Motherwell	66B Motherwell	66B Motherwell	66B Motherwell	66B Motherwell	
44970	$5MT^3$	9A Longsight	65B St. Rollox	65B St. Rollox	65B St. Rollox	65A Eastfield	65A Eastfield	
44971	$5MT^3$	19B Millhouses	7A Llandudno Junction	5B Crewe South	6B Mold Junction	6B Mold Junction	6B Mold Junction	6B Mold Junction
44972	$5MT^3$	29A Perth	63A Perth	63A Perth	65J Fort William	65J Fort William	66A Polmadie	67B Hurlford
44973	$5MT^3$	29A Perth	63A Perth	63A Perth	65J Fort William	65J Fort William	66A Polmadie	
44974	$5MT^3$	29A Perth	63A Perth	63A Perth	65J Fort William	65J Fort William	66A Polmadie	67C Ayr
44975	$5MT^3$	29A Perth	63A Perth	63A Perth	65J Fort William	65J Fort William	64C Dalry Road	
44976	$5MT^3$	29A Perth	63A Perth	63A Perth	65J Fort William	65J Fort William	64C Dalry Road	
44977	$5MT^3$	29A Perth	63A Perth	63A Perth	65J Fort William	65J Fort William	67C Ayr	67C Ayr
44978	$5MT^3$	27A Polmadie	63A Perth	63A Perth	63A Perth	63A Perth	63A Perth	
44979	$5MT^3$	27A Polmadie	63A Perth	63A Perth	63A Perth	63A Perth	63A Perth	
44980	$5MT^3$	27A Polmadie	63A Perth	63A Perth	63A Perth	63A Perth	63A Perth	
44981	$5MT^3$	14A Cricklewood	14B Kentish Town	14B Kentish Town	21B Bournville	21A Saltley	21A Saltley	6D Shrewsbury
44982	$5MT^3$	23A Bank Hall	27A Bank Hall	24E Blackpool Central	24E Blackpool Central	24E Blackpool Central	24F Fleetwood	12A Carlisle Kingmoor
44983	$5MT^3$	20A Leeds Holbeck	20A Leeds Holbeck	20A Leeds Holbeck	55A Leeds Holbeck	55A Leeds Holbeck	55A Leeds Holbeck	55A Leeds Holbeck
44984	$5MT^3$	14B Kentish Town	14B Kentish Town	14B Kentish Town	15D Bedford	14E Bedford	15E Leicester Central	16B Annesley
44985	$5MT^3$	14B Kentish Town	14B Kentish Town	14B Kentish Town	14B Kentish Town	14B Kentish Town	14E Bedford	2A Tyseley
44986	$5MT^3$	20A Leeds Holbeck	19B Millhouses	19B Millhouses	19B Millhouses	6J Holyhead	12A Carlisle Kingmoor	12A Carlisle Kingmoor
44987	$5MT^3$	26A Newton Heath	26A Newton Heath	26B Agecroft	26B Agecroft	26B Agecroft	26B Agecroft	9J Agecroft
44988	$5MT^3$	24E Blackpool Central	28A Blackpool Central	24E Blackpool Central	24E Blackpool Central	24E Blackpool Central	24F Fleetwood	10C Fleetwood
44989	$5MT^3$	23C Southport	27C Southport	27C Southport	27C Southport	27C Southport	27C Southport	12A Carlisle Kingmoor
44990	$5MT^3$	23A Bank Hall	25F Low Moor	25F Low Moor	56F Low Moor	56F Low Moor	56F Low Moor	56D Mirfield
44991	$5MT^3$	32A Inverness	60A Inverness	60A Inverness	60A Inverness	60A Inverness	66B Motherwell	66B Motherwell
44992	$5MT^3$	32A Inverness	60A Inverness	60A Inverness	60A Inverness	60A Inverness	67B Hurlford	67B Hurlford
44993	$5MT^3$	12A Carlisle Kingmoor	68A Carlisle Kingmoor	68A Carlisle Kingmoor	68A Carlisle Kingmoor	12A Carlisle Kingmoor	12A Carlisle Kingmoor	12A Carlisle Kingmoor
44994	$5MT^3$	12A Carlisle Kingmoor	68A Carlisle Kingmoor	64C Dalry Road	64C Dalry Road	64C Dalry Road	64C Dalry Road	
44995	$5MT^3$	31A St. Rollox	65B St. Rollox	65B St. Rollox	68B Dumfries	68B Dumfries	67E Dumfries	67E Dumfries
44996	$5MT^3$	31A St. Rollox	65B St. Rollox	65B St. Rollox	65A Eastfield	65A Eastfield	65A Eastfield	
44997	$5MT^3$	2A Rugby	63A Perth	63A Perth	63A Perth	63A Perth	63A Perth	63A Perth
44998	$5MT^3$	2A Rugby	63A Perth	63A Perth	63A Perth	63A Perth	63A Perth	63A Perth
44999	$5MT^3$	2A Rugby	63A Perth	63A Perth	63A Perth	63A Perth	63A Perth	67F Stranraer
45000	$5MT^3$	2A Rugby	2A Rugby	2A Rugby	5B Crewe South	5B Crewe South	5B Crewe South	6A Chester
45001	$5MT^3$	8B Warrington Dallam	8B Warrington Dallam	6B Mold Junction	6B Mold Junction	5B Crewe South	5B Crewe South	5E Nuneaton
45002	$5MT^3$	2A Rugby	2A Rugby	2A Rugby	6B Mold Junction	5B Crewe South	5B Crewe South	
45003	$5MT^3$	2A Rugby	2A Rugby	1A Willesden	5B Crewe South	5A Crewe North	5D Stoke	5D Stoke
45004	$5MT^3$	2A Rugby	11A Carnforth	10A Wigan Springs Branch	1E Bletchley	5A Crewe North	5B Crewe South	6G Llandudno Junction
45005	$5MT^3$	12A Carlisle Kingmoor	8A Edge Hill	10C Patricroft	8A Edge Hill	8A Edge Hill	8A Edge Hill	8A Edge Hill
45006	$5MT^3$	12A Carlisle Kingmoor	5B Crewe South	5A Crewe North	17F Trafford Park	14D Neasden	21A Saltley	2B Oxley
45007	$5MT^3$	28A Motherwell	63A Perth	68A Carlisle Kingmoor	68A Carlisle Kingmoor	67A Corkerhill	67B Hurlford	
45008	$5MT^3$	28A Motherwell	66B Motherwell	66B Motherwell	66B Motherwell	66B Motherwell	66B Motherwell	
45009	$5MT^3$	12A Carlisle Kingmoor	66B Motherwell	66B Motherwell	66B Motherwell	66B Motherwell	66B Motherwell	
45010	$5MT^3$	29A Perth	65A Eastfield	67B Hurlford	67B Hurlford	67B Hurlford	67B Hurlford	
45011	$5MT^3$	29A Perth	63A Perth	65F Grangemouth	64D Carstairs	64D Carstairs	66E Carstairs	
45012	$5MT^3$	28A Motherwell	60A Inverness	68A Carlisle Kingmoor	68A Carlisle Kingmoor	12A Carlisle Kingmoor	12B Carlisle Upperby	12A Carlisle Kingmoor
45013	$5MT^3$	12A Carlisle Kingmoor	5B Crewe South	68A Carlisle Kingmoor	68A Carlisle Kingmoor	12A Carlisle Kingmoor	12A Carlisle Kingmoor	12A Carlisle Kingmoor
45014	$5MT^3$	12A Carlisle Kingmoor	12B Carlisle Canal	2E Northampton	11A Carnforth	24L Carnforth	24J Lancaster	10J Lancaster
45015	$5MT^3$	12A Carlisle Kingmoor	3B Bushbury	3B Bushbury	3B Bushbury	3B Bushbury	8A Edge Hill	8A Edge Hill
45016	$5MT^3$	28A Motherwell	63B Stirling	63B Stirling	63B Stirling	63B Stirling	65J Stirling	67C Ayr
45017	$5MT^3$	12A Carlisle Kingmoor	8A Edge Hill	11A Carnforth	11A Carnforth	8F Wigan Springs Branch	8F Wigan Springs Branch	10A Carnforth
45018	$5MT^3$	28A Motherwell	60B Aviemore	68A Carlisle Kingmoor	68A Carlisle Kingmoor	12A Carlisle Kingmoor	8B Warrington Dallam	12A Carlisle Kingmoor
45019	$5MT^3$	10A Wigan Springs Branch	10A Wigan Springs Branch	11A Carnforth	11A Carnforth	8F Wigan Springs Branch	8F Wigan Springs Branch	8F Wigan Springs Branch
45020	$5MT^3$	2A Rugby	2A Rugby	8A Edge Hill	1E Bletchley	1E Bletchley	1A Willesden	
45021	$5MT^3$	10B Preston	4B Northampton	2E Northampton	2E Northampton	5A Crewe North	5A Crewe North	5B Crewe South
45022	$5MT^3$	12A Carlisle Kingmoor	64C Dalry Road	64C Dalry Road	64C Dalry Road	64C Dalry Road	64C Dalry Road	
45023	$5MT^3$	12A Carlisle Kingmoor	64C Dalry Road	64C Dalry Road	64C Dalry Road	64C Dalry Road	64C Dalry Road	
45024	$5MT^3$	1A Willesden	1A Willesden	1A Willesden	1A Willesden	1A Willesden	8F Wigan Springs Branch	8F Wigan Springs Branch
45025	$5MT^3$	2B Bletchley	1A Willesden	1A Willesden	1A Willesden	12B Carlisle Upperby	12B Carlisle Upperby	10J Lancaster
45026	$5MT^3$	8B Warrington Dallam	10A Wigan Springs Branch	10A Wigan Springs Branch	10A Wigan Springs Branch	8F Wigan Springs Branch	8F Wigan Springs Branch	
45027	$5MT^3$	1A Willesden	1A Willesden	1A Willesden	1A Willesden	1A Willesden	6B Mold Junction	9B Stockport Edgeley
45028	$5MT^3$	5B Crewe South	5B Crewe South	5B Crewe South	6B Mold Junction	6B Mold Junction	12B Carlisle Upperby	12A Carlisle Kingmoor
45029	$5MT^3$	28B Dalry Road	64C Dalry Road	66B Motherwell	66B Motherwell	66B Motherwell	66B Motherwell	66B Motherwell
45030	$5MT^3$	10A Wigan Springs Branch	5B Crewe South	66A Polmadie	64C Dalry Road	64C Dalry Road		
45031	$5MT^3$	19E Belle Vue	26G Belle Vue	26G Belle Vue	26A Newton Heath	26A Newton Heath	6B Mold Junction	6A Chester
45032	$5MT^3$	8B Warrington Dallam	8B Warrington Dallam	8B Warrington Dallam	8B Warrington Dallam	8A Edge Hill	8C Speke Junction	
45033	$5MT^3$	2A Rugby	2A Rugby	5A Crewe North	5A Crewe North	5A Crewe North	5B Crewe South	5B Crewe South
45034	$5MT^3$	2A Rugby	2A Rugby	2A Rugby	3E Monument Lane	3E Monument Lane	8C Speke Junction	8C Speke Junction
45035	$5MT^3$	8B Warrington Dallam	8B Warrington Dallam	8B Warrington Dallam	8B Warrington Dallam	8B Warrington Dallam	8B Warrington Dallam	
45036	$5MT^3$	29A Perth	66A Polmadie	66A Polmadie	64C Dalry Road	64C Dalry Road		
45037	$5MT^3$	10C Patricroft	10C Patricroft	10C Patricroft	11A Carnforth	9A Longsight	1A Willesden	
45038	$5MT^3$	5B Crewe South	5B Crewe South	5B Crewe South	3D Aston	3E Monument Lane	21D Aston	2A Tyseley
45039	$5MT^3$	11A Carnforth	11A Carnforth	8A Edge Hill	8A Edge Hill	8A Edge Hill	8A Edge Hill	8A Edge Hill
45040	$5MT^3$	20A Leeds Holbeck	21A Saltley	21A Saltley	22A Bristol Barrow Road	21A Saltley	21A Saltley	2B Oxley
45041	$5MT^3$	5B Crewe South	5B Crewe South	5B Crewe South	5B Crewe South	6A Chester	8A Edge Hill	8B Warrington Dallam
45042	$5MT^3$	6A Chester	10C Patricroft	10C Patricroft	10C Patricroft	6B Mold Junction	6B Mold Junction	6B Mold Junction
45043	$5MT^3$	20A Leeds Holbeck	28A Blackpool Central	6A Chester	6B Mold Junction	6B Mold Junction	6B Mold Junction	6B Mold Junction
45044	$5MT^3$	5B Crewe South	5B Crewe South	5B Crewe South	5B Crewe South	5D Stoke	1A Willesden	6A Chester
45045	$5MT^3$	8A Edge Hill	6A Chester	6J Holyhead	5B Crewe South	5B Crewe South	6J Holyhead	6C Croes Newydd
45046	$5MT^3$	12B Carlisle Upperby	11B Barrow	11B Barrow	11A Carnforth	9A Longsight	5A Crewe North	9B Stockport Edgeley
45047	$5MT^3$	30A Corkerhill	67A Corkerhill	67C Ayr	63A Perth	63A Perth	63A Perth	64A St. Margarets
45048	$5MT^3$	5B Crewe South	5B Crewe South	5B Crewe South	5B Crewe South	5B Crewe South	5B Crewe South	2F Bescot
45049	$5MT^3$	30A Corkerhill	67A Corkerhill	67C Ayr	63B Stirling	63B Stirling	65J Stirling	
45050	$5MT^3$	11A Carnforth	11A Carnforth	2A Rugby	2E Northampton	2E Northampton	2E Northampton	5D Stoke
45051	$5MT^3$	3D Aston	3D Aston	3E Monument Lane	3A Bescot	3D Aston	2E Northampton	2A Tyseley
45052	$5MT^3$	2A Rugby	3D Aston	3D Aston	3D Aston	3E Monument Lane	21D Aston	2A Tyseley
45053	$5MT^3$	32A Inverness	60A Inverness	63A Perth	63A Perth	67A Corkerhill	64C Dalry Road	64A St. Margarets

		1948	1951	1954	1957	1960	1963	1966
45054	5MT^{3}	**8A** Edge Hill	**11B** Barrow	**11A** Carnforth	**11A** Carnforth	**24L** Carnforth	**24L** Carnforth	**10A** Carnforth
45055	5MT^{3}	**10C** Patricroft	**10C** Patricroft	**10A** Wigan Springs Branch	**6B** Mold Junction	**6B** Mold Junction	**8F** Wigan Springs Branch	**8M** Southport
45056	5MT^{3}	**22C** Bath Green Park	**19A** Sheffield Grimesthorpe	**19A** Sheffield Grimesthorpe	**19B** Millhouses	**6J** Holyhead	**2A** Rugby	**5B** Crewe South
45057	5MT^{3}	**2A** Rugby	**4A** Bletchley	**10C** Patricroft	**10A** Wigan Springs Branch	**8F** Wigan Springs Branch	**8F** Wigan Springs Branch	**8C** Speke Junction
45058	5MT^{3}	**3D** Aston	**3D** Aston	**3D** Aston	**3D** Aston	**3D** Aston	**21D** Aston	**6D** Shrewsbury
45059	5MT^{3}	**16A** Nottingham	**16A** Nottingham	**19A** Sheffield Grimesthorpe	**14A** Cricklewood	**14A** Cricklewood	**17B** Burton	**8C** Speke Junction
45060	5MT^{3}	**5B** Crewe South	**5B** Crewe South	**5B** Crewe South	**5B** Crewe South	**5D** Stoke	**5D** Stoke	**5D** Stoke
45061	5MT^{3}	**23C** Southport	**27C** Southport	**24E** Blackpool Central	**27C** Southport	**27C** Southport	**27B** Aintree	**12A** Carlisle Kingmoor
45062	5MT^{3}	**25F** Low Moor	**19A** Sheffield Grimesthorpe	**19A** Sheffield Grimesthorpe	**19A** Sheffield Grimesthorpe	**14A** Cricklewood	**17B** Burton	**9J** Agecroft
45063	5MT^{3}	**25G** Farnley Junction	**25G** Farnley Junction	**25G** Farnley Junction	**55C** Farnley Junction	**55C** Farnley Junction	**55C** Farnley Junction	**55A** Leeds Holbeck
45064	5MT^{3}	**5B** Crewe South	**1A** Willesden	**1A** Willesden	**1A** Willesden	**1A** Willesden	**2E** Northampton	**2F** Bescot
45065	5MT^{3}	**20A** Leeds Holbeck	**12A** Carlisle Upperby	**3D** Aston	**3D** Aston	**3D** Aston	**21D** Aston	**5E** Nuneaton
45066	5MT^{3}	**32A** Inverness	**60A** Inverness	**60A** Inverness	**60A** Inverness	**60A** Inverness	**66A** Polmadie	
45067	5MT^{3}	**5B** Crewe South	**5B** Crewe South	**5B** Crewe South	**5B** Crewe South	**5B** Crewe South	**5B** Crewe South	**2F** Bescot
45068	5MT^{3}	**20A** Leeds Holbeck	**27A** Bank Hall	**27A** Bank Hall	**24A** Accrington	**24A** Accrington	**24B** Rose Grove	
45069	5MT^{3}	**5B** Crewe South	**3A** Bescot	**8A** Edge Hill	**8A** Edge Hill	**8A** Edge Hill	**8C** Speke Junction	**8A** Edge Hill
45070	5MT^{3}	**1A** Willesden	**7C** Holyhead	**12A** Carlisle Upperby	**10C** Patricroft	**12B** Carlisle Upperby	**8F** Wigan Springs Branch	**8B** Warrington Dallam
45071	5MT^{3}	**1A** Willesden	**1A** Willesden	**5A** Crewe North	**12A** Carlisle Upperby	**3E** Monument Lane	**8C** Speke Junction	**8C** Speke Junction
45072	5MT^{3}	**5B** Crewe South	**11A** Carnforth	**11A** Carnforth	**11A** Carnforth	**24L** Carnforth	**12B** Carlisle Upperby	**10A** Carnforth
45073	5MT^{3}	**5B** Crewe South	**5B** Crewe South	**5B** Crewe South	**5B** Crewe South	**5A** Crewe North	**8F** Wigan Springs Branch	**9E** Trafford Park
45074	5MT^{3}	**5B** Crewe South	**5B** Crewe South	**5B** Crewe South	**5B** Crewe South	**5B** Crewe South	**5D** Stoke	
45075	5MT^{3}	**25G** Farnley Junction	**25G** Farnley Junction	**25G** Farnley Junction	**55C** Farnley Junction	**55C** Farnley Junction	**55C** Farnley Junction	**55A** Leeds Holbeck
45076	5MT^{3}	**25G** Farnley Junction	**25G** Farnley Junction	**25G** Farnley Junction	**26A** Newton Heath	**26A** Newton Heath	**26A** Newton Heath	**9D** Newton Heath
45077	5MT^{3}	**25G** Farnley Junction	**28A** Blackpool Central	**24E** Blackpool Central	**27A** Bank Hall	**24E** Blackpool Central	**24E** Blackpool Central	
45078	5MT^{3}	**25G** Farnley Junction	**25G** Farnley Junction	**27C** Southport	**24A** Accrington	**24A** Accrington	**24E** Blackpool Central	
45079	5MT^{3}	**26A** Newton Heath	**25G** Farnley Junction	**25G** Farnley Junction	**55C** Farnley Junction	**55C** Farnley Junction	**55C** Farnley Junction	**55A** Leeds Holbeck
45080	5MT^{3}	**25G** Farnley Junction	**25G** Farnley Junction	**25G** Farnley Junction	**55C** Farnley Junction	**55C** Farnley Junction	**55C** Farnley Junction	**55C** Farnley Junction
45081	5MT^{3}	**12A** Carlisle Kingmoor	**68A** Carlisle Kingmoor	**68A** Carlisle Kingmoor	**68A** Carlisle Kingmoor	**12A** Carlisle Kingmoor	**12B** Carlisle Upperby	
45082	5MT^{3}	**12A** Carlisle Kingmoor	**68A** Carlisle Kingmoor	**68A** Carlisle Kingmoor	**68A** Carlisle Kingmoor	**12A** Carlisle Kingmoor	**12B** Carlisle Upperby	**12A** Carlisle Kingmoor
45083	5MT^{3}	**12A** Carlisle Kingmoor	**68A** Carlisle Kingmoor	**68A** Carlisle Kingmoor	**68A** Carlisle Kingmoor	**12A** Carlisle Kingmoor	**12B** Carlisle Upperby	**9D** Newton Heath
45084	5MT^{3}	**12A** Carlisle Kingmoor	**68A** Carlisle Kingmoor	**63B** Stirling	**63B** Stirling	**63B** Stirling	**65J** Stirling	**65J** Stirling
45085	5MT^{3}	**29A** Perth	**64C** Dalry Road	**66B** Motherwell	**66B** Motherwell	**66B** Motherwell		
45086	5MT^{3}	**29A** Perth	**63A** Perth	**64C** Dalry Road	**64C** Dalry Road	**64C** Dalry Road		
45087	5MT^{3}	**29A** Perth	**64D** Carstairs	**64D** Carstairs	**64D** Carstairs	**64D** Carstairs	**66E** Carstairs	
45088	5MT^{3}	**17A** Derby	**15C** Leicester Midland	**16A** Nottingham	**16A** Nottingham	**21A** Saltley	**21A** Saltley	
45089	5MT^{3}	**5B** Crewe South	**1A** Willesden	**1A** Willesden	**1A** Willesden	**1E** Bletchley	**1E** Bletchley	**2D** Banbury
45090	5MT^{3}	**32A** Inverness	**60A** Inverness	**60A** Inverness	**60A** Inverness	**60A** Inverness	**66A** Polmadie	
45091	5MT^{3}	**10B** Preston	**4B** Northampton	**2E** Northampton	**2E** Northampton	**2E** Northampton	**8A** Edge Hill	**8F** Wigan Springs Branch
45092	5MT^{3}	**20A** Leeds Holbeck	**1A** Willesden	**11A** Carnforth	**11A** Carnforth	**8F** Wigan Springs Branch	**12B** Carlisle Upperby	**10A** Carnforth
45093	5MT^{3}	**5B** Crewe South	**5B** Crewe South	**5B** Crewe South	**5B** Crewe South	**5A** Crewe North	**5A** Crewe North	
45094	5MT^{3}	**8A** Edge Hill	**3D** Aston	**3D** Aston	**3D** Aston	**3D** Aston	**8A** Edge Hill	**8A** Edge Hill
45095	5MT^{3}	**8B** Warrington Dallam	**6A** Chester	**10C** Patricroft	**10C** Patricroft	**26F** Patricroft	**26F** Patricroft	**10A** Carnforth
45096	5MT^{3}	**12A** Carlisle Kingmoor	**12B** Carlisle Canal	**10B** Preston	**10B** Preston	**26F** Patricroft	**26F** Patricroft	**9J** Agecroft
45097	5MT^{3}	**5B** Crewe South	**1A** Willesden	**1A** Willesden	**11A** Carnforth	**24L** Carnforth	**12A** Carlisle Kingmoor	**12A** Carlisle Kingmoor
45098	5MT^{3}	**32A** Inverness	**60A** Inverness	**60A** Inverness	**60A** Inverness	**60A** Inverness		
45099	5MT^{3}	**25B** Huddersfield	**25B** Huddersfield	**66B** Motherwell	**66B** Motherwell	**66B** Motherwell	**66B** Motherwell	
45100	5MT^{3}	**12A** Carlisle Kingmoor	**68A** Carlisle Kingmoor	**68A** Carlisle Kingmoor	**68A** Carlisle Kingmoor	**12A** Carlisle Kingmoor	**12A** Carlisle Kingmoor	
45101	5MT^{3}	**24A** Accrington	**25A** Wakefield	**25A** Wakefield	**26A** Newton Heath	**26A** Newton Heath	**26A** Newton Heath	**9D** Newton Heath
45102	5MT^{3}	**26A** Newton Heath	**26A** Newton Heath	**26A** Newton Heath	**26A** Newton Heath	**26A** Newton Heath	**24E** Blackpool Central	
45103	5MT^{3}	**26A** Newton Heath	**26A** Newton Heath	**26A** Newton Heath	**26A** Newton Heath	**26A** Newton Heath	**26B** Agecroft	
45104	5MT^{3}	**26B** Agecroft	**26A** Newton Heath	**26A** Newton Heath	**26A** Newton Heath	**26A** Newton Heath	**26A** Newton Heath	**9K** Bolton
45105	5MT^{3}	**26A** Newton Heath	**26A** Newton Heath	**26A** Newton Heath	**26A** Newton Heath	**26A** Newton Heath	**27C** Southport	**12A** Carlisle Kingmoor
45106	5MT^{3}	**12B** Carlisle Upperby	**12A** Carlisle Upperby	**12A** Carlisle Upperby	**12A** Carlisle Upperby	**12B** Carlisle Upperby	**12B** Carlisle Upperby	**12A** Carlisle Kingmoor
45107	5MT^{3}	**24F** Fleetwood	**28B** Fleetwood	**24F** Fleetwood	**24F** Fleetwood	**24F** Fleetwood	**24F** Fleetwood	**10C** Fleetwood
45108	5MT^{3}	**5B** Crewe South	**5B** Crewe South	**5B** Crewe South	**5B** Crewe South	**8F** Wigan Springs Branch	**8F** Wigan Springs Branch	
45109	5MT^{3}	**8B** Warrington Dallam	**8B** Warrington Dallam	**9A** Longsight	**9A** Longsight	**8F** Wigan Springs Branch	**8F** Wigan Springs Branch	**8B** Warrington Dallam
45110	5MT^{3}	**7C** Holyhead	**7C** Holyhead	**6J** Holyhead	**6J** Holyhead	**6J** Holyhead	**6J** Holyhead	**9K** Bolton
45111	5MT^{3}	**7C** Holyhead	**7C** Holyhead	**8A** Edge Hill	**5B** Crewe South	**9A** Longsight	**1A** Willesden	**6B** Mold Junction
45112	5MT^{3}	**7A** Llandudno Junction	**84G** Shrewsbury	**68A** Carlisle Kingmoor	**68A** Carlisle Kingmoor	**12A** Carlisle Kingmoor	**12A** Carlisle Kingmoor	**12A** Carlisle Kingmoor
45113	5MT^{3}	**7C** Holyhead	**8A** Edge Hill	**8A** Edge Hill	**5A** Crewe North	**3E** Monument Lane	**2A** Rugby	
45114	5MT^{3}	**5D** Stoke	**5D** Stoke	**3D** Aston	**3D** Aston	**3D** Aston	**21D** Aston	**2D** Banbury
45115	5MT^{3}	**31A** St. Rollox	**65B** St. Rollox	**65B** St. Rollox	**65B** St. Rollox	**65B** St. Rollox	**65B** St. Rollox	**67E** Dumfries
45116	5MT^{3}	**31A** St. Rollox	**65B** St. Rollox	**65B** St. Rollox	**65B** St. Rollox	**15E** Leicester Central	**16D** Annesley	**6B** Mold Junction
45117	5MT^{3}	**31A** St. Rollox	**66A** Polmadie	**63A** Perth	**63A** Perth	**60A** Inverness	**67B** Hurlford	
45118	5MT^{3}	**12A** Carlisle Kingmoor	**63A** Perth	**68A** Carlisle Kingmoor	**68A** Carlisle Kingmoor	**12A** Carlisle Kingmoor	**12A** Carlisle Kingmoor	**12A** Carlisle Kingmoor
45119	5MT^{3}	**12A** Carlisle Kingmoor	**63A** Perth	**65F** Grangemouth	**65B** St. Rollox	**65B** St. Rollox		
45120	5MT^{3}	**28A** Motherwell	**60A** Inverness	**68A** Carlisle Kingmoor	**68A** Carlisle Kingmoor	**12A** Carlisle Kingmoor	**12A** Carlisle Kingmoor	**12A** Carlisle Kingmoor
45121	5MT^{3}	**28A** Motherwell	**66B** Motherwell	**66B** Motherwell	**66B** Motherwell	**66B** Motherwell	**66B** Motherwell	
45122	5MT^{3}	**32A** Inverness	**60A** Inverness	**68A** Carlisle Kingmoor	**68A** Carlisle Kingmoor	**12A** Carlisle Kingmoor	**12A** Carlisle Kingmoor	
45123	5MT^{3}	**32A** Inverness	**60A** Inverness	**60A** Inverness	**60A** Inverness	**60A** Inverness	**67B** Hurlford	
45124	5MT^{3}	**32A** Inverness	**60A** Inverness	**60A** Inverness	**60A** Inverness	**60A** Inverness	**67B** Hurlford	**67B** Hurlford
45125	5MT^{3}	**29A** Perth	**63A** Perth	**63A** Perth	**63A** Perth	**65B** St. Rollox		
45126	5MT^{3}	**12A** Carlisle Kingmoor	**68A** Carlisle Kingmoor	**68A** Carlisle Kingmoor	**68A** Carlisle Kingmoor	**12A** Carlisle Kingmoor	**12A** Carlisle Kingmoor	**12A** Carlisle Kingmoor
45127	5MT^{3}	**12A** Carlisle Kingmoor	**63A** Perth	**64C** Dalry Road	**64C** Dalry Road	**64C** Dalry Road	**64C** Dalry Road	**64A** St. Margarets
45128	5MT^{3}	**5B** Crewe South	**5B** Crewe South	**5B** Crewe South	**5B** Crewe South	**5B** Crewe South	**5B** Crewe South	**8F** Wigan Springs Branch
45129	5MT^{3}	**12B** Carlisle Upperby	**12A** Carlisle Upperby	**12A** Carlisle Upperby	**10C** Patricroft	**26F** Patricroft	**26F** Patricroft	**8B** Warrington Dallam
45130	5MT^{3}	**2B** Bletchley	**4A** Bletchley	**6B** Mold Junction	**6B** Mold Junction	**5B** Crewe South	**2A** Rugby	**6C** Croes Newydd
45131	5MT^{3}	**5B** Crewe South	**5B** Crewe South	**5B** Crewe South	**5B** Crewe South	**5B** Crewe South	**8C** Speke Junction	**8C** Speke Junction
45132	5MT^{3}	**3D** Aston	**6B** Mold Junction	**6A** Chester	**3D** Aston	**5A** Crewe North	**5A** Crewe North	**6D** Shrewsbury
45133	5MT^{3}	**12B** Carlisle Upperby	**11A** Carnforth	**11A** Carnforth	**6G** Llandudno Junction	**26F** Patricroft	**26F** Patricroft	**9D** Newton Heath
45134	5MT^{3}	**5B** Crewe South	**5B** Crewe South	**5B** Crewe South	**5B** Crewe South	**5B** Crewe South	**2E** Northampton	**2A** Tyseley
45135	5MT^{3}	**10C** Patricroft	**10C** Patricroft	**10A** Wigan Springs Branch	**10A** Wigan Springs Branch	**8F** Wigan Springs Branch	**8F** Wigan Springs Branch	**12A** Carlisle Kingmoor
45136	5MT^{3}	**32A** Inverness	**60A** Inverness	**60B** Aviemore	**60A** Inverness	**60B** Aviemore	**63A** Perth	
45137	5MT^{3}	**10C** Patricroft	**10C** Patricroft	**10C** Patricroft	**15D** Bedford	**14E** Bedford	**8C** Speke Junction	**8C** Speke Junction
45138	5MT^{3}	**32A** Inverness	**60A** Inverness	**68A** Carlisle Kingmoor	**68A** Carlisle Kingmoor	**12A** Carlisle Kingmoor	**12A** Carlisle Kingmoor	**12A** Carlisle Kingmoor
45139	5MT^{3}	**12B** Carlisle Upperby	**12A** Carlisle Upperby	**12A** Carlisle Upperby	**15D** Bedford	**14E** Bedford	**8A** Edge Hill	**9B** Stockport Edgeley
45140	5MT^{3}	**1A** Willesden	**1A** Willesden	**12A** Carlisle Upperby	**12A** Carlisle Upperby	**12B** Carlisle Upperby	**8F** Wigan Springs Branch	**8F** Wigan Springs Branch
45141	5MT^{3}	**10A** Wigan Springs Branch	**10A** Wigan Springs Branch	**11B** Barrow	**11B** Barrow	**11A** Barrow	**12E** Barrow	**12C** Barrow
45142	5MT^{3}	**10B** Preston	**10C** Patricroft	**10C** Patricroft	**6B** Mold Junction	**5B** Crewe South	**5B** Crewe South	
45143	5MT^{3}	**5B** Crewe South	**84G** Shrewsbury	**84G** Shrewsbury	**84G** Shrewsbury	**84G** Shrewsbury	**89A** Shrewsbury	
45144	5MT^{3}	**3A** Bescot	**7B** Bangor	**6H** Bangor	**6H** Bangor	**6H** Bangor	**6H** Bangor	
45145	5MT^{3}	**5B** Crewe South	**84G** Shrewsbury	**84G** Shrewsbury	**84G** Shrewsbury	**84G** Shrewsbury	**89A** Shrewsbury	**6D** Shrewsbury
45146	5MT^{3}	**5B** Crewe South	**1A** Willesden	**12A** Carlisle Upperby	**9A** Longsight	**1A** Willesden	**21B** Bescot	
45147	5MT^{3}	**10C** Patricroft	**10C** Patricroft	**10C** Patricroft	**1A** Willesden	**2E** Northampton	**1E** Bletchley	**8L** Aintree
45148	5MT^{3}	**5B** Crewe South	**5B** Crewe South	**5A** Crewe North	**5A** Crewe North	**5A** Crewe North	**12A** Carlisle Kingmoor	
45149	5MT^{3}	**8B** Warrington Dallam	**8B** Warrington Dallam	**5D** Stoke	**5D** Stoke	**5B** Crewe South	**6G** Llandudno Junction	**6G** Llandudno Junction
45150	5MT^{3}	**2C** Northampton	**2A** Rugby	**2A** Rugby	**5A** Crewe North	**24K** Preston	**8B** Warrington Dallam	**9E** Trafford Park
45151	5MT^{3}	**12A** Carlisle Kingmoor	**66B** Motherwell	**66B** Motherwell	**66B** Motherwell	**66B** Motherwell		
45152	5MT^{3}	**12A** Carlisle Kingmoor	**66B** Motherwell	**66B** Motherwell	**66B** Motherwell	**66B** Motherwell		
45153	5MT^{3}	**31A** St. Rollox	**65B** St. Rollox	**65B** St. Rollox	**65B** St. Rollox	**65B** St. Rollox	**65B** St. Rollox	
45154	5MT^{3}	**31A** St. Rollox	**65B** St. Rollox	**65B** St. Rollox	**65B** St. Rollox	**26A** Newton Heath	**26A** Newton Heath	**8C** Speke Junction
45155	5MT^{3}	**31A** St. Rollox	**65B** St. Rollox	**65B** St. Rollox	**65B** St. Rollox	**64C** Dalry Road	**64C** Dalry Road	
45156	5MT^{3}	**31A** St. Rollox	**65B** St. Rollox	**65B** St. Rollox	**65B** St. Rollox	**26A** Newton Heath	**26C** Bolton	**8A** Edge Hill
45157	5MT^{3}	**31A** St. Rollox	**65B** St. Rollox	**65B** St. Rollox	**65B** St. Rollox	**65B** St. Rollox		
45158	5MT^{3}	**31A** St. Rollox	**65B** St. Rollox	**65B** St. Rollox	**65B** St. Rollox	**65B** St. Rollox	**65B** St. Rollox	
45159	5MT^{3}	**31A** St. Rollox	**65B** St. Rollox	**65B** St. Rollox	**65B** St. Rollox	**65B** St. Rollox		
45160	5MT^{3}	**32A** Inverness	**60A** Inverness	**67A** Corkerhill	**67A** Corkerhill	**67C** Ayr	**67C** Ayr	**67C** Ayr
45161	5MT^{3}	**29A** Perth	**64D** Carstairs	**64C** Dalry Road	**64C** Dalry Road	**64D** Carstairs	**66E** Carstairs	**67C** Ayr
45162	5MT^{3}	**29A** Perth	**63A** Perth	**66A** Polmadie	**61B** Aberdeen Ferryhill	**61B** Aberdeen Ferryhill	**61B** Aberdeen Ferryhill	**64A** St. Margarets
45163	5MT^{3}	**29A** Perth	**67A** Corkerhill	**68A** Carlisle Kingmoor	**68A** Carlisle Kingmoor	**12A** Carlisle Kingmoor	**12A** Carlisle Kingmoor	
45164	5MT^{3}	**29A** Perth	**63A** Perth	**66A** Polmadie	**62B** Dundee Tay Bridge	**62B** Dundee Tay Bridge	**67C** Ayr	**67C** Ayr
45165	5MT^{3}	**29A** Perth	**63A** Perth	**63A** Perth	**63A** Perth	**63A** Perth		
45166	5MT^{3}	**29A** Perth	**63A** Perth	**67A** Corkerhill	**64D** Carstairs	**64D** Carstairs	**66E** Carstairs	
45167	5MT^{3}	**29A** Perth	**63A** Perth	**63A** Perth	**61B** Aberdeen Ferryhill	**61B** Aberdeen Ferryhill	**67D** Ardrossan	**67C** Ayr

		1948	1951	1954	1957	1960	1963	1966
45168	*5MT*^{3}	**30A** Corkerhill	**67A** Corkerhill	**63A** Perth	**63A** Perth	**63A** Perth	**66B** Motherwell	**64A** St. Margarets
45169	*5MT*^{3}	**12A** Carlisle Kingmoor	**63A** Perth	**68B** Dumfries	**68B** Dumfries	**68B** Dumfries		
45170	*5MT*^{3}	**29A** Perth	**63A** Perth	**63A** Perth	**63A** Perth	**63A** Perth	**64C** Dalry Road	
45171	*5MT*^{3}	**29A** Perth	**63A** Perth	**63A** Perth	**63A** Perth	**63A** Perth	**67A** Corkerhill	
45172	*5MT*^{3}	**29A** Perth	**63A** Perth	**63A** Perth	**63A** Perth	**63A** Perth	**66E** Carstairs	
45173	*5MT*^{3}	**29A** Perth	**63A** Perth	**66A** Polmadie	**64D** Carstairs	**64D** Carstairs	**66E** Carstairs	
45174	*5MT*^{3}	**29A** Perth	**67A** Corkerhill	**67A** Corkerhill	**64D** Carstairs	**64D** Carstairs		
45175	*5MT*^{3}	**29A** Perth	**63A** Perth	**63A** Perth	**64D** Carstairs	**64D** Carstairs	**66E** Carstairs	
45176	*5MT*^{3}	**31A** St. Rollox	**66B** Motherwell	**66B** Motherwell	**66B** Motherwell	**66B** Motherwell	**66B** Motherwell	**66B** Motherwell
45177	*5MT*^{3}	**31A** St. Rollox	**65B** St. Rollox	**65B** St. Rollox	**65B** St. Rollox	**65B** St. Rollox	**65F** Grangemouth	**67C** Ayr
45178	*5MT*^{3}	**31A** St. Rollox	**65B** St. Rollox	**65B** St. Rollox	**65B** St. Rollox	**65B** St. Rollox	**65F** Grangemouth	
45179	*5MT*^{3}	**31A** St. Rollox	**60A** Inverness	**60A** Inverness	**60A** Inverness	**60A** Inverness		
45180	*5MT*^{3}	**4A** Shrewsbury	**84G** Shrewsbury	**6A** Chester	**5B** Crewe South	**6G** Llandudno Junction	**21B** Bescot	
45181	*5MT*^{3}	**5B** Crewe South	**8A** Edge Hill	**8A** Edge Hill	**8A** Edge Hill	**8A** Edge Hill	**8C** Speke Junction	**8C** Speke Junction
45182	*5MT*^{3}	**10C** Patricroft	**10C** Patricroft	**10C** Patricroft	**10C** Patricroft	**26F** Patricroft	**26F** Patricroft	**12C** Barrow
45183	*5MT*^{3}	**5B** Crewe South	**84G** Shrewsbury	**64C** Dalry Road	**64C** Dalry Road	**64C** Dalry Road	**64C** Dalry Road	
45184	*5MT*^{3}	**12B** Carlisle Upperby	**64C** Dalry Road	**64C** Dalry Road	**12A** Carlisle Upperby	**2A** Rugby	**2A** Rugby	
45185	*5MT*^{3}	**10B** Preston	**5B** Crewe South	**5B** Crewe South	**5D** Stoke	**12B** Carlisle Upperby	**12B** Carlisle Upperby	**12A** Carlisle Kingmoor
45186	*5MT*^{3}	**21A** Saltley	**21A** Saltley	**17A** Derby	**21A** Saltley	**21A** Saltley	**21A** Saltley	**2B** Oxley
45187	*5MT*^{3}	**20A** Leeds Holbeck	**2A** Rugby	**2A** Rugby	**1A** Willesden	**1A** Willesden	**8A** Edge Hill	**8A** Edge Hill
45188	*5MT*^{3}	**10C** Patricroft	**10C** Patricroft	**10C** Patricroft	**5B** Crewe South	**5B** Crewe South	**8F** Wigan Springs Branch	**8C** Speke Junction
45189	*5MT*^{3}	**5B** Crewe South	**5B** Crewe South	**5B** Crewe South	**5B** Crewe South	**5A** Crewe North	**5A** Crewe North	
45190	*5MT*^{3}	**4A** Shrewsbury	**84G** Shrewsbury	**84G** Shrewsbury	**84G** Shrewsbury	**84G** Shrewsbury	**89A** Shrewsbury	**16B** Annesley
45191	*5MT*^{3}	**2C** Northampton	**4B** Northampton	**2E** Northampton	**2E** Northampton	**2E** Northampton	**5D** Stoke	**5D** Stoke
45192	*5MT*^{3}	**32A** Inverness	**60A** Inverness	**60A** Inverness	**60A** Inverness	**60A** Inverness	**67B** Hurlford	
45193	*5MT*^{3}	**12B** Carlisle Upperby	**11A** Carnforth	**11A** Carnforth	**11A** Carnforth	**24L** Carnforth	**24J** Lancaster	**10J** Lancaster
45194	*5MT*^{3}	**30A** Corkerhill	**67A** Corkerhill	**67A** Corkerhill	**67A** Corkerhill	**67C** Ayr	**67C** Ayr	
45195	*5MT*^{3}	**5B** Crewe South	**5B** Crewe South	**5B** Crewe South	**1E** Bletchley	**26F** Patricroft	**26B** Agecroft	**12A** Carlisle Kingmoor
45196	*5MT*^{3}	**8B** Warrington Dallam	**8B** Warrington Dallam	**8B** Warrington Dallam	**8B** Warrington Dallam	**8B** Warrington Dallam	**8A** Edge Hill	**10F** Rose Grove
45197	*5MT*^{3}	**5B** Crewe South	**12A** Carlisle Upperby	**12A** Carlisle Upperby	**12A** Carlisle Upperby	**12B** Carlisle Upperby	**6G** Llandudno Junction	**10D** Lostock Hall
45198	*5MT*^{3}	**5B** Crewe South	**5B** Crewe South	**5B** Crewe South	**5B** Crewe South	**5B** Crewe South	**1A** Willesden	**6C** Croes Newydd
45199	*5MT*^{3}	**10C** Patricroft	**10C** Patricroft	**10C** Patricroft	**10C** Patricroft	**26F** Patricroft	**26C** Bolton	
45200	*5MT*^{3}	**23C** Southport	**27C** Southport	**24E** Blackpool Central	**24E** Blackpool Central	**24E** Blackpool Central	**24E** Blackpool Central	**10C** Fleetwood
45201	*5MT*^{3}	**25F** Low Moor	**25F** Low Moor	**25A** Wakefield	**27A** Bank Hall	**24E** Blackpool Central	**24E** Blackpool Central	**8C** Speke Junction
45202	*5MT*^{3}	**26A** Newton Heath	**26A** Newton Heath	**26A** Newton Heath	**26A** Newton Heath	**26A** Newton Heath	**26A** Newton Heath	**9D** Newton Heath
45203	*5MT*^{3}	**26A** Newton Heath	**26A** Newton Heath	**26A** Newton Heath	**26A** Newton Heath	**26A** Newton Heath	**26A** Newton Heath	**9D** Newton Heath
45204	*5MT*^{3}	**25A** Wakefield	**25A** Wakefield	**25A** Wakefield	**55C** Farnley Junction	**55C** Farnley Junction	**55C** Farnley Junction	**55A** Leeds Holbeck
45205	*5MT*^{3}	**25A** Wakefield	**25A** Wakefield	**24B** Rose Grove	**24B** Rose Grove	**24B** Rose Grove	**24B** Rose Grove	**10F** Rose Grove
45206	*5MT*^{3}	**25A** Wakefield	**25A** Wakefield	**24F** Fleetwood	**24F** Fleetwood	**24F** Fleetwood	**24F** Fleetwood	**9D** Newton Heath
45207	*5MT*^{3}	**25F** Low Moor	**25F** Low Moor	**25F** Low Moor	**56F** Low Moor	**56F** Low Moor	**56F** Low Moor	**55D** Royston
45208	*5MT*^{3}	**25F** Low Moor	**25F** Low Moor	**25F** Low Moor	**56F** Low Moor	**56F** Low Moor	**56F** Low Moor	**56D** Mirfield
45209	*5MT*^{3}	**25F** Low Moor	**25A** Wakefield	**24B** Rose Grove	**24B** Rose Grove	**24B** Rose Grove	**24B** Rose Grove	**10A** Carnforth
45210	*5MT*^{3}	**25F** Low Moor	**25F** Low Moor	**25F** Low Moor	**27A** Bank Hall	**27A** Bank Hall	**27B** Aintree	**12A** Carlisle Kingmoor
45211	*5MT*^{3}	**25F** Low Moor	**25G** Farnley Junction	**25G** Farnley Junction	**55C** Farnley Junction	**55C** Farnley Junction	**55C** Farnley Junction	**55A** Leeds Holbeck
45212	*5MT*^{3}	**24F** Fleetwood	**28B** Fleetwood	**24F** Fleetwood	**24F** Fleetwood	**24F** Fleetwood	**24F** Fleetwood	**12A** Carlisle Kingmoor
45213	*5MT*^{3}	**29A** Perth	**63A** Perth	**63A** Perth	**63B** Stirling	**63B** Stirling	**65J** Stirling	**65J** Stirling
45214	*5MT*^{3}	**24F** Fleetwood	**28B** Fleetwood	**65A** Eastfield	**63B** Stirling	**63B** Stirling	**65J** Stirling	**65J** Stirling
45215	*5MT*^{3}	**25B** Huddersfield	**25B** Huddersfield	**25B** Huddersfield	**55G** Huddersfield	**14D** Neasden	**16D** Annesley	**10F** Rose Grove
45216	*5MT*^{3}	**23A** Bank Hall	**27A** Bank Hall	**27A** Bank Hall	**27A** Bank Hall	**27A** Bank Hall	**24B** Rose Grove	**10F** Rose Grove
45217	*5MT*^{3}	**23A** Bank Hall	**5A** Crewe North	**8E** Brunswick	**8E** Brunswick	**27F** Brunswick	**16D** Annesley	**12A** Carlisle Kingmoor
45218	*5MT*^{3}	**25B** Huddersfield	**25B** Huddersfield	**25A** Wakefield	**27C** Southport	**27C** Southport	**27C** Southport	**12A** Carlisle Kingmoor
45219	*5MT*^{3}	**26B** Agecroft	**25F** Low Moor	**25F** Low Moor	**56F** Low Moor	**56F** Low Moor	**56C** Copley Hill	**55D** Royston
45220	*5MT*^{3}	**26B** Agecroft	**26A** Newton Heath	**26A** Newton Heath	**26A** Newton Heath	**26A** Newton Heath	**26A** Newton Heath	**9E** Trafford Park
45221	*5MT*^{3}	**25F** Low Moor	**14B** Kentish Town	**15C** Leicester Midland	**15C** Leicester Midland	**14E** Bedford	**21A** Saltley	**8B** Warrington Dallam
45222	*5MT*^{3}	**26A** Newton Heath	**25B** Huddersfield	**25B** Huddersfield	**55G** Huddersfield	**2E** Northampton	**1E** Bletchley	**2F** Bescot
45223	*5MT*^{3}	**26B** Agecroft	**26A** Newton Heath	**26A** Newton Heath	**26A** Newton Heath	**15E** Leicester Central	**15E** Leicester Central	**6J** Holyhead
45224	*5MT*^{3}	**26A** Newton Heath	**26A** Newton Heath	**26A** Newton Heath	**26A** Newton Heath	**26A** Newton Heath	**26C** Bolton	**16C** Derby
45225	*5MT*^{3}	**23A** Bank Hall	**26A** Newton Heath	**26A** Newton Heath	**26A** Newton Heath	**26A** Newton Heath	**9B** Stockport Edgeley	**9B** Stockport Edgeley
45226	*5MT*^{3}	**23A** Bank Hall	**26G** Belle Vue	**24A** Accrington	**24A** Accrington	**24A** Accrington	**24F** Fleetwood	**10D** Lostock Hall
45227	*5MT*^{3}	**23A** Bank Hall	**27A** Bank Hall	**27A** Bank Hall	**24A** Accrington	**24A** Accrington	**24E** Blackpool Central	**10A** Carnforth
45228	*5MT*^{3}	**23A** Bank Hall	**27A** Bank Hall	**27A** Bank Hall	**27C** Southport	**27C** Southport	**27B** Aintree	**12A** Carlisle Kingmoor
45229	*5MT*^{3}	**23A** Bank Hall	**27A** Bank Hall	**27A** Bank Hall	**24B** Rose Grove	**24B** Rose Grove	**24B** Rose Grove	
45230	*5MT*^{3}	**12B** Carlisle Upperby	**12A** Carlisle Upperby	**12A** Carlisle Upperby	**11A** Carnforth	**24L** Carnforth	**24L** Carnforth	
45231	*5MT*^{3}	**10C** Patricroft	**10C** Patricroft	**10C** Patricroft	**3D** Aston	**3D** Aston	**21D** Aston	**6A** Chester
45232	*5MT*^{3}	**26A** Newton Heath	**26A** Newton Heath	**26A** Newton Heath	**26A** Newton Heath	**26A** Newton Heath	**26C** Bolton	**16F** Burton
45233	*5MT*^{3}	**26A** Newton Heath	**26A** Newton Heath	**26A** Newton Heath	**26A** Newton Heath	**26A** Newton Heath	**26A** Newton Heath	**9E** Trafford Park
45234	*5MT*^{3}	**26A** Newton Heath	**26A** Newton Heath	**26A** Newton Heath	**26B** Agecroft	**15E** Leicester Central	**16D** Annesley	**10F** Rose Grove
45235	*5MT*^{3}	**5B** Crewe South	**10A** Wigan Springs Branch	**5A** Crewe North	**5A** Crewe North	**5A** Crewe North	**12A** Carlisle Kingmoor	**12A** Carlisle Kingmoor
45236	*5MT*^{3}	**5B** Crewe South	**21B** Bournville	**21B** Bournville	**21B** Bournville	**12B** Carlisle Upperby	**12B** Carlisle Upperby	**12A** Carlisle Kingmoor
45237	*5MT*^{3}	**25B** Huddersfield	**25B** Huddersfield	**25B** Huddersfield	**55G** Huddersfield	**5A** Crewe North	**6B** Mold Junction	
45238	*5MT*^{3}	**25B** Huddersfield	**19A** Sheffield Grimesthorpe	**19A** Sheffield Grimesthorpe	**14B** Kentish Town	**14A** Cricklewood	**2F** Woodford Halse	**8B** Warrington Dallam
45239	*5MT*^{3}	**5B** Crewe South	**5B** Crewe South	**9E** Trafford Park	**17F** Trafford Park	**9E** Trafford Park	**9E** Trafford Park	**9K** Bolton
45240	*5MT*^{3}	**5B** Crewe South	**5B** Crewe South	**5A** Crewe North	**5A** Crewe North	**5A** Crewe North	**5D** Stoke	**5D** Stoke
45241	*5MT*^{3}	**12A** Carlisle Kingmoor	**11A** Carnforth	**11A** Carnforth	**11A** Carnforth	**24L** Carnforth	**5A** Crewe North	**5D** Stoke
45242	*5MT*^{3}	**5B** Crewe South	**8A** Edge Hill	**8A** Edge Hill	**8A** Edge Hill	**8A** Edge Hill	**8A** Edge Hill	**8A** Edge Hill
45243	*5MT*^{3}	**12B** Carlisle Upperby	**8A** Edge Hill	**8A** Edge Hill	**8A** Edge Hill	**5A** Crewe North	**5A** Crewe North	**5B** Crewe South
45244	*5MT*^{3}	**12B** Carlisle Upperby	**12A** Carlisle Upperby	**12A** Carlisle Upperby	**12A** Carlisle Upperby	**12B** Carlisle Upperby	**12B** Carlisle Upperby	
45245	*5MT*^{3}	**4A** Shrewsbury	**84G** Shrewsbury	**61B** Aberdeen Ferryhill	**63A** Perth	**64D** Carstairs	**66E** Carstairs	
45246	*5MT*^{3}	**12B** Carlisle Upperby	**12A** Carlisle Upperby	**12A** Carlisle Upperby	**12A** Carlisle Upperby	**12B** Carlisle Upperby	**12B** Carlisle Upperby	**9D** Newton Heath
45247	*5MT*^{3}	**6A** Chester	**6A** Chester	**6A** Chester	**6B** Mold Junction	**6B** Mold Junction	**6H** Bangor	**6J** Holyhead
45248	*5MT*^{3}	**5B** Crewe South	**8A** Edge Hill	**12A** Carlisle Upperby	**12A** Carlisle Upperby	**24K** Preston	**5B** Crewe South	**5B** Crewe South
45249	*5MT*^{3}	**7C** Holyhead	**7C** Holyhead	**8A** Edge Hill	**8A** Edge Hill	**8A** Edge Hill	**8A** Edge Hill	**8A** Edge Hill
45250	*5MT*^{3}	**2A** Rugby	**2A** Rugby	**8A** Edge Hill	**8A** Edge Hill	**5A** Crewe North	**5A** Crewe North	**6A** Chester
45251	*5MT*^{3}	**30A** Corkerhill	**67A** Corkerhill	**67A** Corkerhill	**67A** Corkerhill	**67D** Ardrossan	**67D** Ardrossan	
45252	*5MT*^{3}	**8B** Warrington Dallam	**8B** Warrington Dallam	**8B** Warrington Dallam	**8B** Warrington Dallam	**26F** Patricroft	**26F** Patricroft	**9K** Bolton
45253	*5MT*^{3}	**7A** Llandudno Junction	**14B** Kentish Town	**14B** Kentish Town	**14B** Kentish Town	**21A** Saltley	**17A** Derby	**12A** Carlisle Kingmoor
45254	*5MT*^{3}	**5B** Crewe South	**5B** Crewe South	**5A** Crewe North	**5A** Crewe North	**5A** Crewe North	**12A** Carlisle Kingmoor	**12A** Carlisle Kingmoor
45255	*5MT*^{3}	**5B** Crewe South	**8B** Warrington Dallam	**8B** Warrington Dallam	**8B** Warrington Dallam	**26F** Patricroft	**26A** Newton Heath	**9D** Newton Heath
45256	*5MT*^{3}	**8A** Edge Hill	**8A** Edge Hill	**8A** Edge Hill	**8A** Edge Hill	**8B** Warrington Dallam	**9A** Longsight	**8B** Warrington Dallam
45257	*5MT*^{3}	**5D** Stoke	**5D** Stoke	**5D** Stoke	**5D** Stoke	**5A** Crewe North	**5A** Crewe North	
45258	*5MT*^{3}	**12B** Carlisle Upperby	**12A** Carlisle Upperby	**12A** Carlisle Upperby	**12A** Carlisle Upperby	**12B** Carlisle Upperby	**12E** Barrow	**9K** Bolton
45259	*5MT*^{3}	**10C** Patricroft	**10C** Patricroft	**10C** Patricroft	**12A** Carlisle Upperby	**12B** Carlisle Upperby	**12B** Carlisle Upperby	**12A** Carlisle Kingmoor
45260	*5MT*^{3}	**20A** Leeds Holbeck	**19B** Millhouses	**16A** Nottingham	**17A** Derby	**14D** Neasden	**21A** Saltley	**9K** Bolton
45261	*5MT*^{3}	**17A** Derby	**25A** Wakefield	**25A** Wakefield	**27A** Bank Hall	**26B** Agecroft	**26B** Agecroft	**9B** Stockport Edgeley
45262	*5MT*^{3}	**19A** Sheffield Grimesthorpe	**19A** Sheffield Grimesthorpe	**19A** Sheffield Grimesthorpe	**17B** Burton	**27F** Brunswick	**17A** Derby	**16C** Derby
45263	*5MT*^{3}	**19B** Millhouses	**15C** Leicester Midland	**15C** Leicester Midland	**17A** Derby	**21A** Saltley	**21A** Saltley	**2B** Oxley
45264	*5MT*^{3}	**14A** Cricklewood	**19B** Millhouses	**17A** Derby	**17B** Burton	**15C** Leicester Midland	**15C** Leicester Midland	**2A** Tyseley
45265	*5MT*^{3}	**21A** Saltley	**21A** Saltley	**21A** Saltley	**21A** Saltley	**21A** Saltley		
45266	*5MT*^{3}	**12A** Carlisle Kingmoor	**63A** Perth	**67B** Hurlford	**67B** Hurlford	**67B** Hurlford		
45267	*5MT*^{3}	**14B** Kentish Town	**14B** Kentish Town	**14B** Kentish Town	**15D** Bedford	**14E** Bedford	**16D** Annesley	**16B** Annesley
45268	*5MT*^{3}	**21A** Saltley	**21A** Saltley	**21A** Saltley	**21A** Saltley	**21A** Saltley	**21A** Saltley	**5D** Stoke
45269	*5MT*^{3}	**21A** Saltley	**21A** Saltley	**21A** Saltley	**21A** Saltley	**21A** Saltley	**21A** Saltley	**9E** Trafford Park
45270	*5MT*^{3}	**5B** Crewe South	**5B** Crewe South	**5B** Crewe South	**5B** Crewe South	**5B** Crewe South	**5A** Crewe North	**5D** Stoke
45271	*5MT*^{3}	**5B** Crewe South	**5B** Crewe South	**8B** Warrington Dallam	**8B** Warrington Dallam	**8B** Warrington Dallam	**8B** Warrington Dallam	**9D** Newton Heath
45272	*5MT*^{3}	**22A** Bristol Barrow Road	**20A** Leeds Holbeck	**17A** Derby	**21A** Saltley	**21A** Saltley	**21A** Saltley	
45273	*5MT*^{3}	**21A** Saltley	**21A** Saltley	**21A** Saltley	**55A** Leeds Holbeck	**55A** Leeds Holbeck	**55C** Farnley Junction	**55A** Leeds Holbeck
45274	*5MT*^{3}	**21A** Saltley	**21B** Bournville	**21A** Saltley	**55A** Leeds Holbeck	**14A** Cricklewood	**17A** Derby	**12A** Carlisle Kingmoor
45275	*5MT*^{3}	**6A** Chester	**6B** Mold Junction	**6B** Mold Junction	**6B** Mold Junction	**6B** Mold Junction	**6B** Mold Junction	**6B** Mold Junction
45276	*5MT*^{3}	**20A** Leeds Holbeck	**8A** Edge Hill	**8A** Edge Hill	**8A** Edge Hill	**8B** Warrington Dallam	**1A** Willesden	**5D** Stoke
45277	*5MT*^{3}	**14A** Cricklewood	**14B** Kentish Town	**14B** Kentish Town	**14B** Kentish Town	**14B** Kentish Town	**15E** Leicester Central	**6G** Llandudno Junction
45278	*5MT*^{3}	**5D** Stoke	**5D** Stoke	**5D** Stoke	**1A** Willesden	**1A** Willesden	**8F** Wigan Springs Branch	**8F** Wigan Springs Branch
45279	*5MT*^{3}	**14B** Kentish Town	**14B** Kentish Town	**14B** Kentish Town	**14B** Kentish Town	**14B** Kentish Town	**17B** Burton	**6G** Llandudno Junction
45280	*5MT*^{3}	**20A** Leeds Holbeck	**15C** Leicester Midland	**15C** Leicester Midland	**22A** Bristol Barrow Road	**21A** Saltley	**21A** Saltley	**6J** Holyhead
45281	*5MT*^{3}	**4A** Shrewsbury	**84G** Shrewsbury	**68A** Carlisle Kingmoor	**68A** Carlisle Kingmoor	**8A** Edge Hill	**8F** Wigan Springs Branch	**8F** Wigan Springs Branch

No.	Class	1948	1951	1954	1957	1960	1963	1966
45282	5MT^3	2C Northampton	2A Rugby	2A Rugby	5A Crewe North	5A Crewe North	6J Holyhead	6G Llandudno Junction
45283	5MT^3	4A Shrewsbury	84G Shrewsbury	84G Shrewsbury	84G Shrewsbury	84G Shrewsbury	89A Shrewsbury	2B Oxley
45284	5MT^3	19E Belle Vue	26G Belle Vue	26G Belle Vue	26A Newton Heath	26A Newton Heath	8A Edge Hill	8A Edge Hill
45285	5MT^3	17A Derby	14B Kentish Town	14B Kentish Town	14B Kentish Town	14B Kentish Town	2F Woodford Halse	6D Shrewsbury
45286	5MT^3	6B Mold Junction	6B Mold Junction	12A Carlisle Upperby	12A Carlisle Upperby	12B Carlisle Upperby	12B Carlisle Upperby	
45287	5MT^3	3B Bushbury	3B Bushbury	3B Bushbury	3B Bushbury	3B Bushbury	2E Northampton	2A Tyseley
45288	5MT^3	6B Mold Junction	6B Mold Junction	12A Carlisle Upperby	1A Willesden	1A Willesden	1A Willesden	2D Banbury
45289	5MT^3	20A Leeds Holbeck	10A Wigan Springs Branch	10A Wigan Springs Branch	5A Crewe North	5A Crewe North	6G Llandudno Junction	16C Derby
45290	5MT^3	10C Patricroft	10C Patricroft	10C Patricroft	15D Bedford	26A Newton Heath	26C Bolton	9K Bolton
45291	5MT^3	11A Carnforth	11B Barrow	11B Barrow	11A Carnforth	5B Crewe South	9B Stockport Edgeley	
45292	5MT^3	4A Shrewsbury	7A Llandudno Junction	6J Holyhead	2E Northampton	2E Northampton	1E Bletchley	2A Tyseley
45293	5MT^3	12B Carlisle Upperby	12A Carlisle Upperby	12A Carlisle Upperby	12A Carlisle Upperby	12B Carlisle Upperby	12B Carlisle Upperby	
45294	5MT^3	9A Longsight	5B Crewe South	10C Patricroft	10C Patricroft	26F Patricroft	26F Patricroft	12C Barrow
45295	5MT^3	12B Carlisle Upperby	12A Carlisle Upperby	12A Carlisle Upperby	12A Carlisle Upperby	12B Carlisle Upperby	12B Carlisle Upperby	12A Carlisle Kingmoor
45296	5MT^3	12B Carlisle Upperby	12A Carlisle Upperby	12A Carlisle Upperby	12A Carlisle Upperby	12B Carlisle Upperby	12B Carlisle Upperby	8F Wigan Springs Branch
45297	5MT^3	6A Chester	19B Millhouses	17A Derby	19B Millhouses	12B Carlisle Upperby	5B Crewe South	5B Crewe South
45298	5MT^3	8A Edge Hill	84G Shrewsbury	84G Shrewsbury	84G Shrewsbury	84G Shrewsbury	89A Shrewsbury	6G Llandudno Junction
45299	5MT^3	12B Carlisle Upperby	12A Carlisle Upperby	12A Carlisle Upperby	9A Longsight	5B Crewe South	5B Crewe South	2D Banbury
45300	5MT^3	5B Crewe South	5B Crewe South	5A Crewe North	5A Crewe North	5B Crewe South	5B Crewe South	
45301	5MT^3	7A Llandudno Junction	5B Crewe South	5A Crewe North	5B Crewe South	3E Monument Lane	1A Willesden	
45302	5MT^3	10C Patricroft	10C Patricroft	10C Patricroft	5A Crewe North	24K Preston	2E Northampton	2A Tyseley
45303	5MT^3	7A Llandudno Junction	8A Edge Hill	8A Edge Hill	8A Edge Hill	24L Carnforth	24L Carnforth	8B Warrington Dallam
45304	5MT^3	10C Patricroft	10C Patricroft	10C Patricroft	12A Carlisle Upperby	26F Patricroft	26C Bolton	9K Bolton
45305	5MT^3	5B Crewe South	5A Crewe North	8A Edge Hill	5B Crewe South	5A Crewe North	1A Willesden	8F Wigan Springs Branch
45306	5MT^3	11A Carnforth	11A Carnforth	11A Carnforth	11A Carnforth	24L Carnforth	24L Carnforth	
45307	5MT^3	12B Carlisle Upperby	6A Chester	5A Crewe North	1E Bletchley	2E Northampton	8A Edge Hill	8A Edge Hill
45308	5MT^3	3C Walsall	3C Walsall	3C Walsall	3E Monument Lane	3E Monument Lane	2E Northampton	2D Banbury
45309	5MT^3	27A Polmadie	63A Perth	66B Motherwell	66B Motherwell	66B Motherwell	66B Motherwell	66E Carstairs
45310	5MT^3	1A Willesden	3A Bescot	3A Bescot	3B Bushbury	3B Bushbury	21C Bushbury	5E Nuneaton
45311	5MT^3	12B Carlisle Upperby	12A Carlisle Upperby	12A Carlisle Upperby	5B Crewe South	5A Crewe North	6G Llandudno Junction	6D Shrewsbury
45312	5MT^3	10C Patricroft	10C Patricroft	10C Patricroft	6A Chester	6A Chester	8C Speke Junction	8A Edge Hill
45313	5MT^3	7C Holyhead	10A Wigan Springs Branch	10A Wigan Springs Branch	10A Wigan Springs Branch	8F Wigan Springs Branch	8F Wigan Springs Branch	
45314	5MT^3	2B Bletchley	4A Bletchley	10A Wigan Springs Branch	10A Wigan Springs Branch	8F Wigan Springs Branch	8F Wigan Springs Branch	
45315	5MT^3	10C Patricroft	6B Mold Junction	12A Carlisle Upperby	12A Carlisle Upperby	12B Carlisle Upperby	5B Crewe South	
45316	5MT^3	2B Bletchley	4A Bletchley	12A Carlisle Upperby	12A Carlisle Upperby	12B Carlisle Upperby	12B Carlisle Upperby	9E Trafford Park
45317	5MT^3	5B Crewe South	11B Barrow	11B Barrow	12A Carlisle Upperby	12B Carlisle Upperby	12B Carlisle Upperby	
45318	5MT^3	4A Shrewsbury	84G Shrewsbury	24E Blackpool Central	24E Blackpool Central	24E Blackpool Central	24E Blackpool Central	9K Bolton
45319	5MT^3	32A Inverness	60A Inverness	60A Inverness	60A Inverness	60A Inverness	66F Grangemouth	66E Carstairs
45320	5MT^3	32A Inverness	60A Inverness	60A Inverness	60A Inverness	60A Inverness	66A Polmadie	
45321	5MT^3	8B Warrington Dallam	8B Warrington Dallam	8B Warrington Dallam	8B Warrington Dallam	8B Warrington Dallam	8B Warrington Dallam	8F Wigan Springs Branch
45322	5MT^3	3A Bescot	3D Aston	3D Aston	3D Aston	3D Aston	21D Aston	5D Stoke
45323	5MT^3	12B Carlisle Upperby	12A Carlisle Upperby	12A Carlisle Upperby	12A Carlisle Upperby	12B Carlisle Upperby	12B Carlisle Upperby	8B Warrington Dallam
45324	5MT^3	5D Stoke	5D Stoke	5D Stoke	1A Willesden	1A Willesden	2A Rugby	2F Bescot
45325	5MT^3	5D Stoke	5D Stoke	2A Rugby	6B Mold Junction	6B Mold Junction	6B Mold Junction	6B Mold Junction
45326	5MT^3	5D Stoke	5D Stoke	11A Carnforth	11A Carnforth	24L Carnforth	24L Carnforth	10A Carnforth
45327	5MT^3	12B Carlisle Upperby	10C Patricroft	9A Longsight	11A Carnforth	3D Aston	8A Edge Hill	
45328	5MT^3	6B Mold Junction	8B Warrington Dallam	8B Warrington Dallam	8B Warrington Dallam	8B Warrington Dallam	8B Warrington Dallam	10A Carnforth
45329	5MT^3	10C Patricroft	10C Patricroft	10C Patricroft	12A Carlisle Upperby	12A Carlisle Kingmoor	8C Speke Junction	8C Speke Junction
45330	5MT^3	4A Shrewsbury	84G Shrewsbury	68A Carlisle Kingmoor	68A Carlisle Kingmoor	12A Carlisle Kingmoor	12A Carlisle Kingmoor	8L Aintree
45331	5MT^3	2B Bletchley	4B Northampton	6G Llandudno Junction	1E Bletchley	1E Bletchley	1E Bletchley	2D Banbury
45332	5MT^3	8A Edge Hill	10B Preston	10B Preston	10B Preston	24K Preston	8C Speke Junction	8C Speke Junction
45333	5MT^3	11A Carnforth	8A Edge Hill	8E Brunswick	8E Brunswick	15C Leicester Midland	15C Leicester Midland	16B Annesley
45334	5MT^3	23C Southport	27C Southport	68A Carlisle Kingmoor	68A Carlisle Kingmoor	12A Carlisle Kingmoor	12A Carlisle Kingmoor	
45335	5MT^3	23A Bank Hall	19A Sheffield Grimesthorpe	19A Sheffield Grimesthorpe	14A Cricklewood	14A Cricklewood	2F Woodford Halse	
45336	5MT^3	23A Bank Hall	26A Newton Heath	26A Newton Heath	26A Newton Heath	26A Newton Heath	26A Newton Heath	9D Newton Heath
45337	5MT^3	26B Agecroft	26B Agecroft	26B Agecroft	26B Agecroft	26B Agecroft	26B Agecroft	
45338	5MT^3	26B Agecroft	26B Agecroft	26B Agecroft	26B Agecroft	26B Agecroft	26B Agecroft	8C Speke Junction
45339	5MT^3	25A Wakefield	25A Wakefield	25A Wakefield	55G Huddersfield	9A Longsight	26A Newton Heath	9D Newton Heath
45340	5MT^3	25G Farnley Junction	25B Huddersfield	25B Huddersfield	55G Huddersfield	8F Wigan Springs Branch	24L Carnforth	12B Carlisle Upperby
45341	5MT^3	25G Farnley Junction	25G Farnley Junction	25G Farnley Junction	26A Newton Heath	26A Newton Heath	26A Newton Heath	9D Newton Heath
45342	5MT^3	14A Cricklewood	15C Leicester Midland	15C Leicester Midland	15D Bedford	14E Bedford	2F Woodford Halse	10A Carnforth
45343	5MT^3	11A Carnforth	8A Edge Hill	8A Edge Hill	8A Edge Hill	8B Warrington Dallam	8B Warrington Dallam	9D Newton Heath
45344	5MT^3	8A Edge Hill	3C Walsall	3C Walsall	3C Walsall	12B Carlisle Upperby	5A Crewe North	6C Croes Newydd
45345	5MT^3	10B Preston	12A Carlisle Upperby	12A Carlisle Upperby	6B Mold Junction	6B Mold Junction	6H Bangor	6G Llandudno Junction
45346	5MT^3	7A Llandudno Junction	7C Holyhead	8E Brunswick	8E Brunswick	27F Brunswick	17A Derby	9E Trafford Park
45347	5MT^3	8A Edge Hill	8A Edge Hill	9E Trafford Park	10A Wigan Springs Branch	8F Wigan Springs Branch	8F Wigan Springs Branch	10C Fleetwood
45348	5MT^3	12B Carlisle Upperby	12A Carlisle Upperby	12A Carlisle Upperby	12A Carlisle Upperby	5A Crewe North	6G Llandudno Junction	6D Shrewsbury
45349	5MT^3	3D Aston	3D Aston	3D Aston	3D Aston	3D Aston	21D Aston	2A Tyseley
45350	5MT^3	8A Edge Hill	8A Edge Hill	1A Willesden	1A Willesden	1A Willesden	5D Stoke	5D Stoke
45351	5MT^3	8A Edge Hill	12A Carlisle Upperby	12A Carlisle Upperby	12A Carlisle Upperby	12B Carlisle Upperby	12B Carlisle Upperby	
45352	5MT^3	5D Stoke	8A Edge Hill	10C Patricroft	10C Patricroft	26F Patricroft	26F Patricroft	9E Trafford Park
45353	5MT^3	1A Willesden	4A Bletchley	5B Crewe South	5B Crewe South	3D Aston	21D Aston	6A Chester
45354	5MT^3	12B Carlisle Upperby	8B Warrington Dallam	8B Warrington Dallam	8B Warrington Dallam	8B Warrington Dallam	8B Warrington Dallam	
45355	5MT^3	31A St. Rollox	65B St. Rollox	65B St. Rollox	65B St. Rollox	65B St. Rollox		
45356	5MT^3	31A St. Rollox	65B St. Rollox	65B St. Rollox	65B St. Rollox	65B St. Rollox	66B Motherwell	
45357	5MT^3	29A Perth	63A Perth	63A Perth	63B Stirling	63B Stirling	65J Stirling	65J Stirling
45358	5MT^3	31A St. Rollox	63B Stirling	63B Stirling	65B St. Rollox	65B St. Rollox	65B St. Rollox	
45359	5MT^3	31A St. Rollox	63B Stirling	63B Stirling	63B Stirling	63B Stirling	65J Stirling	65J Stirling
45360	5MT^3	32A Inverness	60A Inverness	60A Inverness	60A Inverness	60A Inverness	64C Dalry Road	
45361	5MT^3	32A Inverness	60A Inverness	60A Inverness	60A Inverness	60A Inverness	67A Corkerhill	
45362	5MT^3	31A St. Rollox	64C Dalry Road	67A Corkerhill	67A Corkerhill	67A Corkerhill	67A Corkerhill	
45363	5MT^3	12A Carlisle Kingmoor	68A Carlisle Kingmoor	68A Carlisle Kingmoor	68A Carlisle Kingmoor	12A Carlisle Kingmoor	12A Carlisle Kingmoor	12A Carlisle Kingmoor
45364	5MT^3	12A Carlisle Kingmoor	68A Carlisle Kingmoor	68A Carlisle Kingmoor	68A Carlisle Kingmoor	12A Carlisle Kingmoor	12F Workington	12A Carlisle Kingmoor
45365	5MT^3	29A Perth	63A Perth	63A Perth	63A Perth	63A Perth	67A Corkerhill	67C Ayr
45366	5MT^3	29A Perth	63A Perth	63A Perth	63A Perth	63A Perth	67A Corkerhill	
45367	5MT^3	24A Accrington	24A Accrington	61B Aberdeen Ferryhill	63A Perth	63A Perth	64C Dalry Road	
45368	5MT^3	12B Carlisle Upperby	12A Carlisle Upperby	12A Carlisle Upperby	12A Carlisle Upperby	12B Carlisle Upperby	12B Carlisle Upperby	9J Agecroft
45369	5MT^3	5A Crewe North	5B Crewe South	5B Crewe South	5A Crewe North	5A Crewe North	6G Llandudno Junction	6B Mold Junction
45370	5MT^3	7A Llandudno Junction	8B Warrington Dallam	3D Aston	3D Aston	5B Crewe South	8C Speke Junction	8C Speke Junction
45371	5MT^3	12B Carlisle Upperby	12A Carlisle Upperby	2A Rugby	12A Carlisle Upperby	12B Carlisle Upperby	12B Carlisle Upperby	12B Carlisle Upperby
45372	5MT^3	2A Rugby	2A Rugby	2A Rugby	1A Willesden	8F Wigan Springs Branch	8F Wigan Springs Branch	8F Wigan Springs Branch
45373	5MT^3	10B Preston	10C Patricroft	10C Patricroft	5A Crewe North	8F Wigan Springs Branch	8F Wigan Springs Branch	10J Lancaster
45374	5MT^3	5A Crewe North	1A Willesden	1A Willesden	1A Willesden	1A Willesden	21D Aston	10A Carnforth
45375	5MT^3	2A Rugby	2A Rugby	2A Rugby	1A Willesden	1A Willesden	8C Speke Junction	8B Warrington Dallam
45376	5MT^3	8A Edge Hill	7C Holyhead	8A Edge Hill	8A Edge Hill	8A Edge Hill	8A Edge Hill	8A Edge Hill
45377	5MT^3	10C Patricroft	10C Patricroft	10C Patricroft	10C Patricroft	26F Patricroft	24E Blackpool Central	9K Bolton
45378	5MT^3	12B Carlisle Upperby	10C Patricroft	10C Patricroft	10C Patricroft	26F Patricroft	26C Bolton	
45379	5MT^3	2A Rugby	2A Rugby	2A Rugby	5A Crewe North	5A Crewe North	5A Crewe North	
45380	5MT^3	8A Edge Hill	8A Edge Hill	8A Edge Hill	8A Edge Hill	8B Warrington Dallam	8B Warrington Dallam	
45381	5MT^3	5D Stoke	5D Stoke	5D Stoke	1A Willesden	1A Willesden	8B Warrington Dallam	9K Bolton
45382	5MT^3	6A Chester	7C Holyhead	6J Holyhead	12A Carlisle Upperby	6J Holyhead	9B Stockport Edgeley	9D Newton Heath
45383	5MT^3	6B Mold Junction	11B Barrow	11B Barrow	11B Barrow	11A Barrow	12E Barrow	12C Barrow
45384	5MT^3	4A Shrewsbury	84G Shrewsbury	62B Dundee Tay Bridge	62B Dundee Tay Bridge	62B Dundee Tay Bridge	67C Ayr	
45385	5MT^3	6B Mold Junction	6A Chester	6J Holyhead	6J Holyhead	3A Bescot	9A Longsight	8F Wigan Springs Branch
45386	5MT^3	10C Patricroft	11B Barrow	11B Barrow	11B Barrow	11A Barrow	8C Speke Junction	8C Speke Junction
45387	5MT^3	8A Edge Hill	9A Longsight	1A Willesden	1A Willesden	1A Willesden	21B Bescot	
45388	5MT^3	12B Carlisle Upperby	12A Carlisle Upperby	8A Edge Hill	1E Bletchley	1E Bletchley	8F Wigan Springs Branch	8C Speke Junction
45389	5MT^3	29A Perth	63A Perth	63A Perth	63A Perth	63B Stirling	65J Stirling	
45390	5MT^3	3D Aston	3E Monument Lane	3E Monument Lane	5B Crewe South	5B Crewe South	24L Carnforth	10A Carnforth
45391	5MT^3	2A Rugby	2A Rugby	2A Rugby	5B Crewe South	5B Crewe South	5B Crewe South	5B Crewe South
45392	5MT^3	11A Carnforth	11A Carnforth	11A Carnforth	2E Northampton	2E Northampton	2E Northampton	2D Banbury
45393	5MT^3	12B Carlisle Upperby	8A Edge Hill	8A Edge Hill	1E Bletchley	1E Bletchley	1E Bletchley	5B Crewe South
45394	5MT^3	2A Rugby	2A Rugby	2A Rugby	12A Carlisle Upperby	12B Carlisle Upperby	24L Carnforth	10J Lancaster
45395	5MT^3	3C Walsall	3C Walsall	3C Walsall	3C Walsall	3D Aston	5D Stoke	6B Mold Junction

		1948	1951	1954	1957	1960	1963	1966
45396	5MT[3]	**24A** Accrington	**24A** Accrington	**65F** Grangemouth	**63B** Stirling	**63B** Stirling	**65J** Stirling	**65J** Stirling
45397	5MT[3]	**3D** Aston	**3D** Aston	**3D** Aston	**3D** Aston	**12B** Carlisle Upperby	**12B** Carlisle Upperby	**10F** Rose Grove
45398	5MT[3]	**8A** Edge Hill	**8A** Edge Hill	**8A** Edge Hill	**8A** Edge Hill	**8B** Warrington Dallam	**2E** Northampton	
45399	5MT[3]	**8A** Edge Hill	**8A** Edge Hill	**8A** Edge Hill	**8A** Edge Hill	**8A** Edge Hill	**24L** Carnforth	**10A** Carnforth
45400	5MT[3]	**8A** Edge Hill	**84G** Shrewsbury	**65A** Eastfield	**63B** Stirling	**63B** Stirling	**65J** Stirling	
45401	5MT[3]	**10C** Patricroft	**10C** Patricroft	**10C** Patricroft	**8A** Edge Hill	**8A** Edge Hill		
45402	5MT[3]	**10C** Patricroft	**6B** Mold Junction	**3A** Bescot	**12A** Carlisle Upperby	**12B** Carlisle Upperby	**12B** Carlisle Upperby	**10D** Lostock Hall
45403	5MT[3]	**6A** Chester	**10C** Patricroft	**2A** Rugby	**3B** Bushbury	**5B** Crewe South	**5B** Crewe South	**6A** Chester
45404	5MT[3]	**2A** Rugby	**2A** Rugby	**1A** Willesden	**1A** Willesden	**1A** Willesden	**8C** Speke Junction	**9E** Trafford Park
45405	5MT[3]	**3B** Bushbury	**3B** Bushbury	**3B** Bushbury	**3B** Bushbury	**3B** Bushbury	**21C** Bushbury	**5E** Nuneaton
45406	5MT[3]	**4A** Shrewsbury	**84G** Shrewsbury	**84G** Shrewsbury	**84G** Shrewsbury	**84G** Shrewsbury	**89A** Shrewsbury	**16B** Annesley
45407	5MT[3]	**19A** Sheffield Grimesthorpe	**19A** Sheffield Grimesthorpe	**19A** Sheffield Grimesthorpe	**14B** Kentish Town	**14B** Kentish Town	**17B** Burton	**8C** Speke Junction
45408	5MT[3]	**10C** Patricroft	**10C** Patricroft	**10A** Wigan Springs Branch	**10A** Wigan Springs Branch	**8F** Wigan Springs Branch	**8F** Wigan Springs Branch	**8F** Wigan Springs Branch
45409	5MT[3]	**12B** Carlisle Upperby	**12A** Carlisle Upperby	**12A** Carlisle Upperby	**12A** Carlisle Upperby	**26F** Patricroft	**26F** Patricroft	**9K** Bolton
45410	5MT[3]	**8A** Edge Hill	**10C** Patricroft	**10C** Patricroft	**8A** Edge Hill	**8B** Warrington Dallam	**21B** Bescot	**2F** Bescot
45411	5MT[3]	**10C** Patricroft	**10C** Patricroft	**10C** Patricroft	**10C** Patricroft	**26F** Patricroft	**26F** Patricroft	**9K** Bolton
45412	5MT[3]	**5A** Crewe North	**12A** Carlisle Upperby	**12A** Carlisle Upperby	**12A** Carlisle Upperby	**12B** Carlisle Upperby	**8C** Speke Junction	**8C** Speke Junction
45413	5MT[3]	**10A** Wigan Springs Branch	**10A** Wigan Springs Branch	**8A** Edge Hill	**8A** Edge Hill	**8A** Edge Hill	**8C** Speke Junction	
45414	5MT[3]	**12B** Carlisle Upperby	**12A** Carlisle Upperby	**12A** Carlisle Upperby	**12A** Carlisle Upperby	**12B** Carlisle Upperby	**8B** Warrington Dallam	
45415	5MT[3]	**23C** Southport	**27C** Southport	**10C** Patricroft	**24A** Accrington	**24A** Accrington	**24E** Blackpool Central	**9K** Bolton
45416	5MT[3]	**12B** Carlisle Upperby	**12A** Carlisle Upperby	**12A** Carlisle Upperby	**3D** Aston	**14D** Neasden	**14E** Bedford	
45417	5MT[3]	**3A** Bescot	**3A** Bescot	**6H** Bangor	**6H** Bangor	**6H** Bangor	**6H** Bangor	**8C** Speke Junction
45418	5MT[3]	**3A** Bescot	**3E** Monument Lane	**3D** Aston	**3D** Aston	**3D** Aston	**21D** Aston	**2D** Banbury
45419	5MT[3]	**2A** Rugby	**2A** Rugby	**2A** Rugby	**2A** Rugby	**3A** Bescot	**2A** Rugby	**6A** Chester
45420	5MT[3]	**10C** Patricroft	**10C** Patricroft	**10C** Patricroft	**10C** Patricroft	**26F** Patricroft	**26F** Patricroft	**9D** Newton Heath
45421	5MT[3]	**10C** Patricroft	**10C** Patricroft	**8A** Edge Hill	**8A** Edge Hill	**8A** Edge Hill	**12A** Carlisle Kingmoor	**10C** Fleetwood
45422	5MT[3]	**5A** Crewe North	**84G** Shrewsbury	**84G** Shrewsbury	**84G** Shrewsbury	**84G** Shrewsbury	**89A** Shrewsbury	**5D** Stoke
45423	5MT[3]	**31A** St. Rollox	**65B** St. Rollox	**65B** St. Rollox	**63B** Stirling	**63B** Stirling	**65J** Stirling	**67C** Ayr
45424	5MT[3]	**10C** Patricroft	**10C** Patricroft	**10C** Patricroft	**10C** Patricroft	**26F** Patricroft	**26F** Patricroft	**9J** Agecroft
45425	5MT[3]	**10A** Wigan Springs Branch	**10A** Wigan Springs Branch	**10A** Wigan Springs Branch	**10A** Wigan Springs Branch	**8F** Wigan Springs Branch	**8F** Wigan Springs Branch	**8F** Wigan Springs Branch
45426	5MT[3]	**10C** Patricroft	**10C** Patricroft	**10C** Patricroft	**5B** Crewe South	**9A** Longsight	**5A** Crewe North	**2D** Banbury
45427	5MT[3]	**11A** Carnforth	**11A** Carnforth	**11A** Carnforth	**11A** Carnforth	**24L** Carnforth	**1A** Willesden	**6A** Chester
45428	5MT[3]	**12B** Carlisle Upperby	**10C** Patricroft	**10C** Patricroft	**55A** Leeds Holbeck	**55C** Farnley Junction	**55C** Farnley Junction	**55C** Farnley Junction
45429	5MT[3]	**12A** Carlisle Kingmoor	**2A** Rugby	**2A** Rugby	**2A** Rugby	**6J** Holyhead	**5A** Crewe North	
45430	5MT[3]	**2A** Rugby	**2A** Rugby	**2A** Rugby	**1A** Willesden	**3D** Aston	**21D** Aston	**6D** Shrewsbury
45431	5MT[3]	**1A** Willesden	**2A** Rugby	**2A** Rugby	**12A** Carlisle Upperby	**8F** Wigan Springs Branch	**8F** Wigan Springs Branch	**8F** Wigan Springs Branch
45432	5MT[3]	**12A** Carlisle Kingmoor	**68A** Carlisle Kingmoor	**68A** Carlisle Kingmoor	**68A** Carlisle Kingmoor	**68B** Dumfries	**67E** Dumfries	**67E** Dumfries
45433	5MT[3]	**3A** Bescot	**3A** Bescot	**66B** Motherwell	**66C** Hamilton	**66B** Motherwell	**66B** Motherwell	**66B** Motherwell
45434	5MT[3]	**3B** Bushbury	**3B** Bushbury	**5A** Crewe North	**5A** Crewe North	**5A** Crewe North	**1A** Willesden	**5B** Crewe South
45435	5MT[3]	**23C** Southport	**27C** Southport	**25A** Wakefield	**26A** Newton Heath	**26A** Newton Heath	**26A** Newton Heath	**9D** Newton Heath
45436	5MT[3]	**5A** Crewe North	**84G** Shrewsbury	**24E** Blackpool Central	**24E** Blackpool Central	**24E** Blackpool Central	**24E** Blackpool Central	**8B** Warrington Dallam
45437	5MT[3]	**3B** Bushbury	**3B** Bushbury	**3A** Bescot	**6G** Llandudno Junction	**12B** Carlisle Upperby	**12B** Carlisle Upperby	**12A** Carlisle Kingmoor
45438	5MT[3]	**10C** Patricroft	**10C** Patricroft	**12A** Carlisle Upperby	**12A** Carlisle Upperby	**12B** Carlisle Upperby	**6B** Mold Junction	**6A** Chester
45439	5MT[3]	**12B** Carlisle Upperby	**12A** Carlisle Upperby	**3A** Bescot	**3B** Bushbury	**3B** Bushbury	**21C** Bushbury	
45440	5MT[3]	**22C** Bath Green Park	**71G** Bath Green Park	**71G** Bath Green Park	**71G** Bath Green Park	**6C** Birkenhead	**8A** Edge Hill	**8A** Edge Hill
45441	5MT[3]	**2A** Rugby	**2A** Rugby	**2A** Rugby	**6A** Chester	**6J** Holyhead	**8C** Speke Junction	**8C** Speke Junction
45442	5MT[3]	**10C** Patricroft	**10C** Patricroft	**10C** Patricroft	**10C** Patricroft	**26F** Patricroft	**24E** Blackpool Central	**12A** Carlisle Kingmoor
45443	5MT[3]	**12A** Carlisle Kingmoor	**65B** St. Rollox	**65B** St. Rollox	**65B** St. Rollox	**65B** St. Rollox	**65B** St. Rollox	
45444	5MT[3]	**10C** Patricroft	**10C** Patricroft	**10C** Patricroft	**14B** Kentish Town	**27F** Brunswick	**16D** Annesley	**10C** Fleetwood
45445	5MT[3]	**4A** Shrewsbury	**12A** Carlisle Upperby	**12A** Carlisle Upperby	**12A** Carlisle Upperby	**12B** Carlisle Upperby	**12E** Barrow	**10J** Lancaster
45446	5MT[3]	**3D** Aston	**3D** Aston	**5A** Crewe North	**5A** Crewe North	**5A** Crewe North	**5A** Crewe North	**5B** Crewe South
45447	5MT[3]	**21A** Saltley	**21A** Saltley	**20A** Leeds Holbeck	**14B** Kentish Town	**21A** Saltley	**21A** Saltley	**6J** Holyhead
45448	5MT[3]	**2A** Rugby	**3D** Aston	**3D** Aston	**3D** Aston	**3D** Aston	**21D** Aston	**5E** Nuneaton
45449	5MT[3]	**10A** Wigan Springs Branch	**10A** Wigan Springs Branch	**10A** Wigan Springs Branch	**10A** Wigan Springs Branch	**8F** Wigan Springs Branch	**8F** Wigan Springs Branch	**8F** Wigan Springs Branch
45450	5MT[3]	**12B** Carlisle Upperby	**26G** Belle Vue	**26G** Belle Vue	**26B** Agecroft	**15E** Leicester Central	**16D** Annesley	**10D** Lostock Hall
45451	5MT[3]	**12B** Carlisle Upperby	**12A** Carlisle Upperby	**12A** Carlisle Upperby	**12A** Carlisle Upperby	**12B** Carlisle Upperby	**12B** Carlisle Upperby	**12B** Carlisle Upperby
45452	5MT[3]	**29A** Perth	**63A** Perth	**63A** Perth	**63A** Perth	**64D** Carstairs		
45453	5MT[3]	**28A** Motherwell	**60A** Inverness	**60A** Inverness	**60A** Inverness	**60A** Inverness		
45454	5MT[3]	**12A** Carlisle Kingmoor	**12B** Carlisle Canal	**10A** Wigan Springs Branch	**10A** Wigan Springs Branch	**24K** Preston	**2E** Northampton	**2D** Banbury
45455	5MT[3]	**12A** Carlisle Kingmoor	**68A** Carlisle Kingmoor	**68A** Carlisle Kingmoor	**68A** Carlisle Kingmoor	**12A** Carlisle Kingmoor	**12A** Carlisle Kingmoor	**12A** Carlisle Kingmoor
45456	5MT[3]	**29A** Perth	**63A** Perth	**63A** Perth	**63A** Perth	**67D** Ardrossan	**67D** Ardrossan	
45457	5MT[3]	**29A** Perth	**63A** Perth	**63A** Perth	**63A** Perth	**67D** Ardrossan	**67D** Ardrossan	
45458	5MT[3]	**29A** Perth	**63A** Perth	**63A** Perth	**63A** Perth	**66A** Polmadie		
45459	5MT[3]	**29A** Perth	**63A** Perth	**63A** Perth	**63A** Perth	**66A** Polmadie	**66A** Polmadie	
45460	5MT[3]	**29A** Perth	**63A** Perth	**63A** Perth	**63A** Perth	**60A** Inverness	**67C** Ayr	
45461	5MT[3]	**28A** Motherwell	**60A** Inverness	**60A** Inverness	**60A** Inverness	**60A** Inverness	**63A** Perth	**63A** Perth
45462	5MT[3]	**28A** Motherwell	**66B** Motherwell	**66B** Motherwell	**66B** Motherwell	**66B** Motherwell	**66B** Motherwell	
45463	5MT[3]	**29A** Perth	**63A** Perth	**63A** Perth	**63A** Perth	**63A** Perth	**67D** Ardrossan	**67E** Dumfries
45464	5MT[3]	**29A** Perth	**63A** Perth	**63A** Perth	**63A** Perth	**24E** Blackpool Central	**24E** Blackpool Central	**16B** Annesley
45465	5MT[3]	**29A** Perth	**63A** Perth	**63A** Perth	**63A** Perth	**63A** Perth	**63A** Perth	
45466	5MT[3]	**29A** Perth	**63A** Perth	**68A** Carlisle Kingmoor	**68A** Carlisle Kingmoor	**12A** Carlisle Kingmoor	**12A** Carlisle Kingmoor	**8C** Speke Junction
45467	5MT[3]	**29A** Perth	**63A** Perth	**63A** Perth	**63A** Perth	**63A** Perth	**67A** Corkerhill	**67C** Ayr
45468	5MT[3]	**31A** St. Rollox	**65B** St. Rollox	**65B** St. Rollox	**65B** St. Rollox	**65B** St. Rollox	**65B** St. Rollox	
45469	5MT[3]	**29A** Perth	**63A** Perth	**63A** Perth	**61B** Aberdeen Ferryhill	**61B** Aberdeen Ferryhill	**64C** Dalry Road	**64A** St. Margarets
45470	5MT[3]	**29A** Perth	**63A** Perth	**63A** Perth	**63A** Perth	**63A** Perth	**67F** Stranraer	
45471	5MT[3]	**31A** St. Rollox	**65B** St. Rollox	**65B** St. Rollox	**65B** St. Rollox	**65B** St. Rollox	**65B** St. Rollox	
45472	5MT[3]	**29A** Perth	**63A** Perth	**63A** Perth	**63A** Perth	**63A** Perth	**63A** Perth	**63A** Perth
45473	5MT[3]	**29A** Perth	**63A** Perth	**63A** Perth	**63A** Perth	**63A** Perth	**63A** Perth	**63A** Perth
45474	5MT[3]	**29A** Perth	**63A** Perth	**63A** Perth	**63A** Perth	**63A** Perth	**63A** Perth	**67C** Ayr
45475	5MT[3]	**29A** Perth	**63A** Perth	**63A** Perth	**63A** Perth	**63A** Perth	**63A** Perth	**63A** Perth
45476	5MT[3]	**32A** Inverness	**60A** Inverness	**60A** Inverness	**60A** Inverness	**60A** Inverness	**64C** Dalry Road	
45477	5MT[3]	**32A** Inverness	**60A** Inverness	**60A** Inverness	**60A** Inverness	**60A** Inverness	**64C** Dalry Road	**64A** St. Margarets
45478	5MT[3]	**32A** Inverness	**60A** Inverness	**60A** Inverness	**60A** Inverness	**60A** Inverness	**66A** Polmadie	**66E** Carstairs
45479	5MT[3]	**32A** Inverness	**60A** Inverness	**60A** Inverness	**60A** Inverness	**60A** Inverness	**67D** Ardrossan	
45480	5MT[3]	**31A** St. Rollox	**65B** St. Rollox	**68B** Dumfries	**68B** Dumfries	**68B** Dumfries	**67E** Dumfries	**67E** Dumfries
45481	5MT[3]	**31A** St. Rollox	**65B** St. Rollox	**68A** Carlisle Kingmoor	**68A** Carlisle Kingmoor	**12A** Carlisle Kingmoor	**12A** Carlisle Kingmoor	**12A** Carlisle Kingmoor
45482	5MT[3]	**12A** Carlisle Kingmoor	**65B** St. Rollox	**65B** St. Rollox	**65B** St. Rollox	**65B** St. Rollox	**65F** Grangemouth	
45483	5MT[3]	**28A** Motherwell	**63A** Perth	**63A** Perth	**63A** Perth	**63A** Perth	**64C** Dalry Road	**64A** St. Margarets
45484	5MT[3]	**27A** Polmadie	**66A** Polmadie	**66A** Polmadie	**66B** Motherwell	**66B** Motherwell	**66B** Motherwell	
45485	5MT[3]	**27A** Polmadie	**66A** Polmadie	**66A** Polmadie	**66B** Motherwell	**66B** Motherwell	**67F** Stranraer	
45486	5MT[3]	**27A** Polmadie	**66A** Polmadie	**64A** St. Margarets	**62B** Dundee Tay Bridge	**62B** Dundee Tay Bridge	**67C** Ayr	
45487	5MT[3]	**27A** Polmadie	**66A** Polmadie	**64A** St. Margarets	**63A** Perth	**63A** Perth	**65F** Grangemouth	
45488	5MT[3]	**28A** Motherwell	**63A** Perth	**63A** Perth	**63A** Perth	**63A** Perth	**67A** Corkerhill	**67A** Corkerhill
45489	5MT[3]	**30A** Corkerhill	**67A** Corkerhill	**67A** Corkerhill	**67A** Corkerhill	**67A** Corkerhill	**67B** Hurlford	**67B** Hurlford
45490	5MT[3]	**30A** Corkerhill	**67A** Corkerhill	**67A** Corkerhill	**67A** Corkerhill	**67D** Ardrossan	**67C** Ayr	**67B** Hurlford
45491	5MT[3]	**30A** Corkerhill	**67A** Corkerhill	**68A** Carlisle Kingmoor	**68A** Carlisle Kingmoor	**12A** Carlisle Kingmoor	**12A** Carlisle Kingmoor	
45492	5MT[3]	**4A** Shrewsbury	**63A** Perth	**63A** Perth	**63A** Perth	**63A** Perth	**66B** Motherwell	**66E** Carstairs
45493	5MT[3]	**5A** Crewe North	**2A** Rugby	**2A** Rugby	**2A** Rugby	**2A** Rugby	**2A** Rugby	**2D** Banbury
45494	5MT[3]	**12B** Carlisle Upperby	**12A** Carlisle Upperby	**12A** Carlisle Upperby	**12A** Carlisle Upperby	**5B** Crewe South	**5B** Crewe South	**5B** Crewe South
45495	5MT[3]	**3E** Monument Lane	**8B** Warrington Dallam	**8B** Warrington Dallam	**8B** Warrington Dallam	**8B** Warrington Dallam	**8B** Warrington Dallam	**10A** Carnforth
45496	5MT[3]	**28A** Motherwell	**63A** Perth	**63A** Perth	**63A** Perth	**63A** Perth	**65F** Grangemouth	
45497	5MT[3]	**28A** Motherwell	**63A** Perth	**63A** Perth	**63A** Perth	**63A** Perth	**67C** Ayr	
45498	5MT[3]	**28A** Motherwell	**66B** Motherwell	**66B** Motherwell	**66B** Motherwell	**66B** Motherwell	**66B** Motherwell	
45499	5MT[3]	**28A** Motherwell	**65B** St. Rollox	**65B** St. Rollox	**65B** St. Rollox	**65B** St. Rollox	**65B** St. Rollox	
45500	6P5F[1]	**8A** Edge Hill	**9A** Longsight	**9A** Longsight	**12A** Carlisle Upperby	**24L** Carnforth		
45501	6P5F[1]	**8A** Edge Hill	**9A** Longsight	**9A** Longsight	**9A** Longsight	**24L** Carnforth		
45502	6P5F[1]	**10B** Preston	**5A** Crewe North	**12A** Carlisle Upperby	**12A** Carlisle Upperby	**24K** Preston		
45503	6P5F[1]	**5A** Crewe North	**5A** Crewe North	**5A** Crewe North	**5A** Crewe North	**8B** Warrington Dallam		
45504	6P5F[1]	**5A** Crewe North	**5A** Crewe North	**5A** Crewe North	**12A** Carlisle Upperby	**82E** Bristol Barrow Road		
45505	6P5F[1]	**10B** Preston	**12A** Carlisle Upperby	**12A** Carlisle Upperby	**9A** Longsight	**9A** Longsight		
45506	6P5F[1]	**12B** Carlisle Upperby	**5A** Crewe North	**5A** Crewe North	**12A** Carlisle Upperby	**82E** Bristol Barrow Road		
45507	6P5F[1]	**5A** Crewe North	**5A** Crewe North	**5A** Crewe North	**5A** Crewe North	**24K** Preston		
45508	6P5F[1]	**5A** Crewe North	**10B** Preston	**12A** Carlisle Upperby	**12A** Carlisle Upperby	**24K** Preston		
45509	6P5F[1]	**1A** Willesden	**1A** Willesden	**17A** Derby	**17A** Derby	**26A** Newton Heath		

No.	Class	1948	1951	1954	1957	1960	1963	1966
45510	6P5F[1]	**1A** Willesden	**5A** Crewe North	**5A** Crewe North	**1A** Willesden	**24L** Carnforth		
45511	6P5F[1]	**5A** Crewe North	**5A** Crewe North	**1A** Willesden	**1A** Willesden	**24L** Carnforth		
45512	6P5F[1]/7P[1]	**5A** Crewe North	**12A** Carlisle Upperby	**12A** Carlisle Upperby	**12A** Carlisle Upperby	**12B** Carlisle Upperby	**12B** Carlisle Upperby	
45513	6P5F[1]	**10B** Preston	**5A** Crewe North	**5A** Crewe North	**12A** Carlisle Upperby	**12B** Carlisle Upperby		
45514	7P[1]	**3B** Bushbury	**1B** Camden	**1B** Camden	**1B** Camden	**1B** Camden		
45515	6P5F[1]	**10B** Preston	**8A** Edge Hill	**8A** Edge Hill	**8A** Edge Hill	**8A** Edge Hill		
45516	6P5F[1]	**10B** Preston	**10B** Preston	**5A** Crewe North	**8A** Edge Hill	**8A** Edge Hill		
45517	6P5F[1]	**8A** Edge Hill	**12A** Carlisle Upperby	**1A** Willesden	**1A** Willesden	**27A** Bank Hall		
45518	6P5F[1]	**12B** Carlisle Upperby	**12A** Carlisle Upperby	**8A** Edge Hill	**8A** Edge Hill	**8A** Edge Hill		
45519	6P5F[1]	**10B** Preston	**10B** Preston	**10B** Preston	**9A** Longsight	**82E** Bristol Barrow Road		
45520	6P5F[1]	**8A** Edge Hill	**9A** Longsight	**9A** Longsight	**9A** Longsight	**9A** Longsight		
45521	7P[1]	**8A** Edge Hill	**8B** Warrington Dallam	**8B** Warrington Dallam	**8A** Edge Hill	**8A** Edge Hill	**8F** Wigan Springs Branch	
45522	6P5F[1]/7P[1]	**5A** Crewe North	**1B** Camden	**1B** Camden	**1B** Camden	**14B** Kentish Town	**26A** Newton Heath	
45523	6P5F[1]/7P[1]	**8A** Edge Hill	**5A** Crewe North	**1B** Camden	**1B** Camden	**1B** Camden	**1A** Willesden	
45524	6P5F[1]	**10B** Preston	**3B** Bushbury	**5A** Crewe North	**12A** Carlisle Upperby	**12B** Carlisle Upperby		
45525	6P5F[1]/7P[1]	**1A** Willesden	**5A** Crewe North	**8A** Edge Hill	**8A** Edge Hill	**8A** Edge Hill	**6G** Llandudno Junction	
45526	7P[1]	**8A** Edge Hill	**12A** Carlisle Upperby	**12A** Carlisle Upperby	**12A** Carlisle Upperby	**12B** Carlisle Upperby	**12B** Carlisle Upperby	
45527	6P5F[1]/7P[1]	**8A** Edge Hill	**8A** Edge Hill	**8A** Edge Hill	**8A** Edge Hill	**8A** Edge Hill	**6J** Holyhead	
45528	7P[1]	**3B** Bushbury	**5A** Crewe North	**5A** Crewe North	**5A** Crewe North	**5A** Crewe North	**1A** Willesden	
45529	7P[1]	**3B** Bushbury	**5A** Crewe North	**1B** Camden	**5A** Crewe North	**5A** Crewe North	**1A** Willesden	
45530	7P[1]	**9A** Longsight	**9A** Longsight	**9A** Longsight	**9A** Longsight	**9A** Longsight	**1A** Willesden	
45531	7P[1]	**3B** Bushbury	**8A** Edge Hill	**8A** Edge Hill	**8A** Edge Hill	**8A** Edge Hill	**8A** Edge Hill	
45532	6P5F[1]/7P[1]	**5A** Crewe North	**1B** Camden	**1B** Camden	**1B** Camden	**16A** Nottingham	**12B** Carlisle Upperby	
45533	6P5F[1]	**8A** Edge Hill	**8A** Edge Hill	**8A** Edge Hill	**8A** Edge Hill	**2A** Rugby		
45534	6P5F[1]/7P[1]	**20A** Leeds Holbeck	**9A** Longsight	**8A** Edge Hill	**8A** Edge Hill	**6G** Llandudno Junction	**6G** Llandudno Junction	
45535	6P5F[1]/7P[1]	**20A** Leeds Holbeck	**5A** Crewe North	**5A** Crewe North	**8A** Edge Hill	**8A** Edge Hill	**12A** Carlisle Kingmoor	
45536	6P5F[1]/7P[1]	**10B** Preston	**9A** Longsight	**9A** Longsight	**9A** Longsight	**9A** Longsight		
45537	6P5F[1]	**10B** Preston	**10B** Preston	**12A** Carlisle Upperby	**12A** Carlisle Upperby	**2A** Rugby		
45538	6P5F[1]	**20A** Leeds Holbeck	**8A** Edge Hill	**8A** Edge Hill	**8A** Edge Hill	**1A** Willesden		
45539	6P5F[1]	**5A** Crewe North	**9A** Longsight	**9A** Longsight	**8A** Edge Hill	**24L** Carnforth		
45540	7P[1]	**3B** Bushbury	**9A** Longsight	**9A** Longsight	**9A** Longsight	**3B** Bushbury	**12B** Carlisle Upperby	
45541	6P5F[1]	**12B** Carlisle Upperby	**1B** Camden	**1B** Camden	**1B** Camden	**2A** Rugby		
45542	6P5F[1]	**5A** Crewe North	**12A** Carlisle Upperby	**12A** Carlisle Upperby	**12A** Carlisle Upperby	**24K** Preston		
45543	6P5F[1]	**8A** Edge Hill	**5A** Crewe North	**5A** Crewe North	**12A** Carlisle Upperby	**9A** Longsight		
45544	6P5F[1]	**10B** Preston	**10B** Preston	**5A** Crewe North	**8A** Edge Hill	**12B** Carlisle Upperby		
45545	6P5F[1]/7P[1]	**8A** Edge Hill	**1B** Camden	**1B** Camden	**5A** Crewe North	**5A** Crewe North	**12B** Carlisle Upperby	
45546	6P5F[1]	**5A** Crewe North	**1A** Willesden	**1A** Willesden	**12A** Carlisle Upperby	**24L** Carnforth		
45547	6P5F[1]	**8A** Edge Hill	**8A** Edge Hill	**5A** Crewe North	**1A** Willesden	**1A** Willesden		
45548	6P5F[1]	**5A** Crewe North	**5A** Crewe North	**5A** Crewe North	**5A** Crewe North	**24L** Carnforth		
45549	6P5F[1]	**5A** Crewe North	**12A** Carlisle Upperby	**12A** Carlisle Upperby	**12A** Carlisle Upperby	**8B** Warrington Dallam		
45550	6P5F[1]	**12B** Carlisle Upperby	**12A** Carlisle Upperby	**8A** Edge Hill	**8A** Edge Hill	**8B** Warrington Dallam		
45551	6P5F[1]	**5A** Crewe North	**12A** Carlisle Upperby	**12A** Carlisle Upperby	**12A** Carlisle Upperby	**12B** Carlisle Upperby		
45552	6P5F[2]	**9A** Longsight	**12A** Carlisle Upperby	**12A** Carlisle Upperby	**8A** Edge Hill	**8A** Edge Hill	**5A** Crewe North	
45553	6P5F[2]	**12B** Carlisle Upperby	**9E** Trafford Park	**9A** Longsight	**12A** Carlisle Upperby	**5A** Crewe North	**5A** Crewe North	
45554	6P5F[2]	**16A** Nottingham	**16A** Nottingham	**16A** Nottingham	**16A** Nottingham	**8A** Edge Hill	**5A** Crewe North	
45555	6P5F[2]	**5A** Crewe North	**12A** Carlisle Upperby	**9A** Longsight	**3B** Bushbury	**12B** Carlisle Upperby	**5B** Crewe South	
45556	6P5F[2]	**9A** Longsight	**9A** Longsight	**9A** Longsight	**5A** Crewe North	**5A** Crewe North	**5A** Crewe North	
45557	6P5F[2]	**14B** Kentish Town	**14B** Kentish Town	**14B** Kentish Town	**14B** Kentish Town	**17A** Derby	**17B** Burton	
45558	6P5F[2]	**5A** Crewe North	**10C** Patricroft	**10C** Patricroft	**10C** Patricroft	**26F** Patricroft	**26F** Patricroft	
45559	6P5F[2]	**10C** Patricroft	**10C** Patricroft	**10C** Patricroft	**10C** Patricroft	**17A** Derby		
45560	6P5F[2]	**30A** Corkerhill	**67A** Corkerhill	**16A** Nottingham	**16A** Nottingham	**8A** Edge Hill	**5A** Crewe North	
45561	6P5F[2]	**22A** Bristol Barrow Road	**22A** Bristol Barrow Road	**22A** Bristol Barrow Road	**22A** Bristol Barrow Road	**14B** Kentish Town	**17B** Burton	
45562	6P5F[2]	**20A** Leeds Holbeck	**20A** Leeds Holbeck	**20A** Leeds Holbeck	**55A** Leeds Holbeck	**55A** Leeds Holbeck	**55A** Leeds Holbeck	**55C** Farnley Junction
45563	6P5F[2]	**12B** Carlisle Upperby	**10C** Patricroft	**10C** Patricroft	**10C** Patricroft	**26F** Patricroft	**26F** Patricroft	
45564	6P5F[2]	**12A** Carlisle Kingmoor	**63A** Perth	**20A** Leeds Holbeck	**55A** Leeds Holbeck	**55A** Leeds Holbeck	**55A** Leeds Holbeck	
45565	6P5F[2]	**20A** Leeds Holbeck	**20A** Leeds Holbeck	**20A** Leeds Holbeck	**55A** Leeds Holbeck	**55A** Leeds Holbeck	**56F** Low Moor	**56F** Low Moor
45566	6P5F[2]	**20A** Leeds Holbeck	**20A** Leeds Holbeck	**20A** Leeds Holbeck	**55A** Leeds Holbeck	**55A** Leeds Holbeck		
45567	6P5F[2]	**8A** Edge Hill	**8A** Edge Hill	**8A** Edge Hill	**8A** Edge Hill	**8A** Edge Hill	**6C** Birkenhead	
45568	6P5F[2]	**20A** Leeds Holbeck	**20A** Leeds Holbeck	**20A** Leeds Holbeck	**55A** Leeds Holbeck	**55A** Leeds Holbeck	**55A** Leeds Holbeck	
45569	6P5F[2]	**20A** Leeds Holbeck	**20A** Leeds Holbeck	**20A** Leeds Holbeck	**55A** Leeds Holbeck	**55A** Leeds Holbeck	**55A** Leeds Holbeck	
45570	6P5F[2]	**22A** Bristol Barrow Road	**22A** Bristol Barrow Road	**17A** Derby	**17A** Derby	**41C** Millhouses		
45571	6P5F[2]	**24E** Blackpool Central	**28A** Blackpool Central	**24E** Blackpool Central	**24E** Blackpool Central	**24E** Blackpool Central	**24E** Blackpool Central	
45572	6P5F[2]	**22A** Bristol Barrow Road	**22A** Bristol Barrow Road	**22A** Bristol Barrow Road	**22A** Bristol Barrow Road	**82E** Bristol Barrow Road	**89A** Shrewsbury	
45573	6P5F[2]	**20A** Leeds Holbeck	**20A** Leeds Holbeck	**20A** Leeds Holbeck	**55A** Leeds Holbeck	**55A** Leeds Holbeck	**55A** Leeds Holbeck	
45574	6P5F[2]	**24E** Blackpool Central	**28A** Blackpool Central	**24E** Blackpool Central	**24E** Blackpool Central	**24E** Blackpool Central	**24E** Blackpool Central	**55A** Leeds Holbeck
45575	6P5F[2]	**30A** Corkerhill	**63A** Perth	**14B** Kentish Town	**14B** Kentish Town	**14B** Kentish Town	**17B** Burton	
45576	6P5F[2]	**30A** Corkerhill	**67A** Corkerhill	**19B** Millhouses	**19B** Millhouses	**41C** Millhouses		
45577	6P5F[2]	**12A** Carlisle Kingmoor	**68A** Carlisle Kingmoor	**22A** Bristol Barrow Road	**22A** Bristol Barrow Road	**82E** Bristol Barrow Road	**89A** Shrewsbury	
45578	6P5F[2]	**5A** Crewe North	**12A** Carlisle Upperby	**9A** Longsight	**9A** Longsight	**8A** Edge Hill	**26A** Newton Heath	
45579	6P5F[2]	**12A** Carlisle Kingmoor	**66A** Polmadie	**14B** Kentish Town	**14B** Kentish Town	**14B** Kentish Town	**17B** Burton	
45580	6P5F[2]	**12A** Carlisle Kingmoor	**68A** Carlisle Kingmoor	**24E** Blackpool Central	**24E** Blackpool Central	**24E** Blackpool Central	**24E** Blackpool Central	
45581	6P5F[2]	**12A** Carlisle Kingmoor	**68A** Carlisle Kingmoor	**25G** Farnley Junction	**55C** Farnley Junction	**55C** Farnley Junction	**55C** Farnley Junction	
45582	6P5F[2]	**12A** Carlisle Kingmoor	**68A** Carlisle Kingmoor	**10B** Preston	**10B** Preston	**24K** Preston		**55C** Farnley Junction
45583	6P5F[2]	**27A** Polmadie	**66A** Polmadie	**12A** Carlisle Upperby	**8A** Edge Hill	**8A** Edge Hill	**8B** Warrington Dallam	
45584	6P5F[2]	**27A** Polmadie	**66A** Polmadie	**24E** Blackpool Central	**24E** Blackpool Central	**24E** Blackpool Central	**24E** Blackpool Central	
45585	6P5F[2]	**17A** Derby	**17A** Derby	**17A** Derby	**17A** Derby	**14B** Kentish Town	**17B** Burton	
45586	6P5F[2]	**8A** Edge Hill	**5A** Crewe North	**5A** Crewe North	**5A** Crewe North	**8A** Edge Hill	**5B** Crewe South	
45587	6P5F[2]	**20A** Leeds Holbeck	**20A** Leeds Holbeck	**9A** Longsight	**9A** Longsight	**9A** Longsight		
45588	6P5F[2]	**24E** Blackpool Central	**28A** Blackpool Central	**24E** Blackpool Central	**24E** Blackpool Central	**12B** Carlisle Upperby	**12A** Carlisle Kingmoor	
45589	6P5F[2]	**20A** Leeds Holbeck	**20A** Leeds Holbeck	**20A** Leeds Holbeck	**55A** Leeds Holbeck	**55A** Leeds Holbeck	**55A** Leeds Holbeck	
45590	6P5F[2]	**19B** Millhouses	**19B** Millhouses	**19B** Millhouses	**19B** Millhouses	**41C** Millhouses	**26B** Agecroft	
45591	6P5F[2]	**1A** Willesden	**1A** Willesden	**1A** Willesden	**5A** Crewe North	**5A** Crewe North	**5A** Crewe North	
45592	6P5F[2]	**8A** Edge Hill	**5A** Crewe North	**1B** Camden	**1B** Camden	**1B** Camden	**24L** Carnforth	
45593	6P5F[2]	**9A** Longsight	**9A** Longsight	**12A** Carlisle Upperby	**12A** Carlisle Upperby	**12B** Carlisle Upperby	**21D** Aston	**55A** Leeds Holbeck
45594	6P5F[2]	**19B** Millhouses	**19B** Millhouses	**19B** Millhouses	**19B** Millhouses	**41C** Millhouses		
45595	6P5F[2]	**12B** Carlisle Upperby	**12A** Carlisle Upperby	**9A** Longsight	**9A** Longsight	**5A** Crewe North	**5A** Crewe North	
45596	6P5F[2]	**5A** Crewe North	**8A** Edge Hill	**8A** Edge Hill	**8A** Edge Hill	**8A** Edge Hill	**9B** Stockport Edgeley	**9B** Stockport Edgeley
45597	6P5F[2]	**20A** Leeds Holbeck	**20A** Leeds Holbeck	**20A** Leeds Holbeck	**55A** Leeds Holbeck	**55A** Leeds Holbeck	**55A** Leeds Holbeck	
45598	6P5F[2]	**14B** Kentish Town	**14B** Kentish Town	**14B** Kentish Town	**14B** Kentish Town	**17A** Derby	**17B** Burton	
45599	6P5F[2]	**12B** Carlisle Upperby	**10B** Preston	**12A** Carlisle Upperby	**12A** Carlisle Upperby	**1A** Willesden	**2B** Nuneaton	
45600	6P5F[2]	**5A** Crewe North	**10C** Patricroft	**10C** Patricroft	**10C** Patricroft	**26F** Patricroft	**26F** Patricroft	
45601	6P5F[2]	**1B** Camden	**1B** Camden	**1B** Camden	**1B** Camden	**1A** Willesden	**26A** Newton Heath	
45602	6P5F[2]	**17A** Derby	**14B** Kentish Town	**22A** Bristol Barrow Road	**17A** Derby	**41C** Millhouses	**26A** Newton Heath	
45603	6P5F[2]	**5A** Crewe North	**9A** Longsight	**1B** Camden	**1A** Willesden	**1A** Willesden		
45604	6P5F[2]	**20A** Leeds Holbeck	**20A** Leeds Holbeck	**5A** Crewe North	**5A** Crewe North	**5A** Crewe North	**24L** Carnforth	
45605	6P5F[2]	**20A** Leeds Holbeck	**20A** Leeds Holbeck	**20A** Leeds Holbeck	**55A** Leeds Holbeck	**55A** Leeds Holbeck	**55A** Leeds Holbeck	
45606	6P5F[2]	**1B** Camden	**5A** Crewe North	**8A** Edge Hill	**1B** Camden	**1B** Camden	**24L** Carnforth	
45607	6P5F[2]	**19B** Millhouses	**19B** Millhouses	**19B** Millhouses	**19B** Millhouses	**41C** Millhouses		
45608	6P5F[2]	**20A** Leeds Holbeck	**20A** Leeds Holbeck	**20A** Leeds Holbeck	**55A** Leeds Holbeck	**55A** Leeds Holbeck		
45609	6P5F[2]	**14B** Kentish Town	**19B** Millhouses	**19B** Millhouses	**19B** Millhouses	**41C** Millhouses	**55A** Leeds Holbeck	
45610	6P5F[2]	**17A** Derby	**17A** Derby	**17A** Derby	**17A** Derby	**17A** Derby	**17B** Burton	
45611	6P5F[2]	**20A** Leeds Holbeck	**16A** Nottingham	**16A** Nottingham	**16A** Nottingham	**16A** Nottingham	**17B** Burton	
45612	6P5F[2]	**14B** Kentish Town	**14B** Kentish Town	**14B** Kentish Town	**14B** Kentish Town	**17A** Derby	**17B** Burton	
45613	6P5F[2]	**8A** Edge Hill	**8A** Edge Hill	**8A** Edge Hill	**12A** Carlisle Upperby	**8A** Edge Hill	**24L** Carnforth	
45614	6P5F[2]	**14B** Kentish Town	**14B** Kentish Town	**14B** Kentish Town	**14B** Kentish Town	**14B** Kentish Town	**17B** Burton	
45615	6P5F[2]	**14B** Kentish Town	**14B** Kentish Town	**14B** Kentish Town	**14B** Kentish Town	**14B** Kentish Town		
45616	6P5F[2]	**14B** Kentish Town	**14B** Kentish Town	**14B** Kentish Town	**14B** Kentish Town	**16A** Nottingham		
45617	6P5F[2]	**1B** Camden	**9A** Longsight	**5A** Crewe North	**5A** Crewe North	**12B** Carlisle Upperby	**5A** Crewe North	
45618	6P5F[2]	**19G** Trafford Park	**9E** Trafford Park	**9E** Trafford Park	**17F** Trafford Park	**17A** Derby	**17B** Burton	
45619	6P5F[2]	**20A** Leeds Holbeck	**20A** Leeds Holbeck	**20A** Leeds Holbeck	**55A** Leeds Holbeck	**55A** Leeds Holbeck		
45620	6P5F[2]	**20A** Leeds Holbeck	**16A** Nottingham	**16A** Nottingham	**16A** Nottingham	**16A** Nottingham	**17B** Burton	
45621	6P5F[2]	**19B** Millhouses	**19B** Millhouses	**67A** Corkerhill	**67A** Corkerhill	**63A** Perth		
45622	6P5F[2]	**19G** Trafford Park	**9E** Trafford Park	**9E** Trafford Park	**17F** Trafford Park	**14B** Kentish Town	**14B** Kentish Town	
45623	6P5F[2]	**8A** Edge Hill	**8A** Edge Hill	**8A** Edge Hill	**8A** Edge Hill	**5A** Crewe North	**26A** Newton Heath	

		1948	1951	1954	1957	1960	1963	1966
45624	$6P5F^2$	**12B** Carlisle Upperby	**12A** Carlisle Upperby	**9A** Longsight	**9A** Longsight	**1A** Willesden	**2B** Nuneaton	
45625	$6P5F^2$	**1A** Willesden	**1A** Willesden	**1A** Willesden	**5A** Crewe North	**5A** Crewe North	**24L** Carnforth	
45626	$6P5F^2$	**19B** Millhouses	**20A** Leeds Holbeck	**17A** Derby	**17A** Derby	**17A** Derby	**16D** Annesley	
45627	$6P5F^2$	**14B** Kentish Town	**14B** Kentish Town	**14B** Kentish Town	**14B** Kentish Town	**17A** Derby	**27A** Bank Hall	**8K** Bank Hall
45628	$6P5F^2$	**19G** Trafford Park	**9E** Trafford Park	**9E** Trafford Park	**17F** Trafford Park	**14B** Kentish Town		
45629	$6P5F^2$	**19G** Trafford Park	**9E** Trafford Park	**9E** Trafford Park	**9A** Longsight	**5A** Crewe North	**24L** Carnforth	
45630	$6P5F^2$	**5A** Crewe North	**12A** Carlisle Upperby	**12A** Carlisle Upperby	**5A** Crewe North	**5A** Crewe North		
45631	$6P5F^2$	**9A** Longsight	**9A** Longsight	**9A** Longsight	**9A** Longsight	**9A** Longsight	**5A** Crewe North	
45632	$6P5F^2$	**5A** Crewe North	**9A** Longsight	**9A** Longsight	**9A** Longsight	**1B** Camden	**9B** Stockport Edgeley	
45633	$6P5F^2$	**9A** Longsight	**9A** Longsight	**10B** Preston	**10B** Preston	**24K** Preston	**24L** Carnforth	
45634	$6P5F^2$	**8A** Edge Hill	**5A** Crewe North	**5A** Crewe North	**5A** Crewe North	**5A** Crewe North	**5B** Crewe South	
45635	$6P5F^2$	**26A** Newton Heath	**26A** Newton Heath	**26A** Newton Heath	**26A** Newton Heath	**26A** Newton Heath	**26A** Newton Heath	
45636	$6P5F^2$	**16A** Nottingham	**16A** Nottingham	**16A** Nottingham	**16A** Nottingham	**16A** Nottingham		
45637	$6P5F^2$	**5A** Crewe North	**8A** Edge Hill					
45638	$6P5F^2$	**9A** Longsight	**9A** Longsight	**9A** Longsight	**9A** Longsight	**9A** Longsight	**8B** Warrington Dallam	
45639	$6P5F^2$	**17A** Derby	**17A** Derby	**20A** Leeds Holbeck	**55A** Leeds Holbeck	**55A** Leeds Holbeck	**55A** Leeds Holbeck	
45640	$6P5F^2$	**16A** Nottingham	**16A** Nottingham	**68A** Carlisle Kingmoor	**68A** Carlisle Kingmoor	**12A** Carlisle Kingmoor	**12A** Carlisle Kingmoor	
45641	$6P5F^2$	**14B** Kentish Town	**14B** Kentish Town	**14B** Kentish Town	**14B** Kentish Town	**16A** Nottingham	**17B** Burton	
45642	$6P5F^2$	**26A** Newton Heath	**26A** Newton Heath	**26A** Newton Heath	**26A** Newton Heath	**26A** Newton Heath	**26A** Newton Heath	
45643	$6P5F^2$	**30A** Corkerhill	**67A** Corkerhill	**12A** Carlisle Upperby	**9A** Longsight	**5A** Crewe North	**2B** Nuneaton	**55A** Leeds Holbeck
45644	$6P5F^2$	**30A** Corkerhill	**63A** Perth	**9A** Longsight	**9A** Longsight	**9A** Longsight	**5B** Crewe South	
45645	$6P5F^2$	**30A** Corkerhill	**67A** Corkerhill	**10C** Patricroft	**10C** Patricroft	**26F** Patricroft	**26F** Patricroft	
45646	$6P5F^2$	**30A** Corkerhill	**67A** Corkerhill	**25G** Farnley Junction	**55C** Farnley Junction	**55C** Farnley Junction	**55C** Farnley Junction	
45647	$6P5F^2$	**5A** Crewe North	**5A** Crewe North	**3B** Bushbury	**3B** Bushbury	**3B** Bushbury	**5A** Crewe North	**55C** Farnley Junction
45648	$6P5F^2$	**14B** Kentish Town	**14B** Kentish Town	**14B** Kentish Town	**14B** Kentish Town	**17A** Derby	**17B** Burton	
45649	$6P5F^2$	**14B** Kentish Town	**14B** Kentish Town	**14B** Kentish Town	**14B** Kentish Town	**17A** Derby	**17B** Burton	
45650	$6P5F^2$	**14B** Kentish Town	**14B** Kentish Town	**14B** Kentish Town	**14B** Kentish Town	**16A** Nottingham	**17B** Burton	
45651	$6P5F^2$	**20A** Leeds Holbeck	**20A** Leeds Holbeck	**22A** Bristol Barrow Road	**22A** Bristol Barrow Road	**82E** Bristol Barrow Road		
45652	$6P5F^2$	**19G** Trafford Park	**9E** Trafford Park	**9E** Trafford Park	**17F** Trafford Park	**14B** Kentish Town	**26A** Newton Heath	
45653	$6P5F^2$	**24E** Blackpool Central	**28A** Blackpool Central	**24E** Blackpool Central	**24E** Blackpool Central	**24E** Blackpool Central	**24E** Blackpool Central	
45654	$6P5F^2$	**14B** Kentish Town	**19B** Millhouses	**19B** Millhouses	**19B** Millhouses	**41C** Millhouses	**26B** Agecroft	**9D** Newton Heath
45655	$6P5F^2$	**19G** Trafford Park	**9A** Longsight	**9E** Trafford Park	**9A** Longsight	**5A** Crewe North	**8B** Warrington Dallam	
45656	$6P5F^2$	**17A** Derby	**17A** Derby	**19B** Millhouses	**19B** Millhouses	**41C** Millhouses		
45657	$6P5F^2$	**14B** Kentish Town	**14B** Kentish Town	**68A** Carlisle Kingmoor	**68A** Carlisle Kingmoor	**12A** Carlisle Kingmoor	**27A** Bank Hall	
45658	$6P5F^2$	**20A** Leeds Holbeck	**20A** Leeds Holbeck	**20A** Leeds Holbeck	**55A** Leeds Holbeck	**55A** Leeds Holbeck	**55A** Leeds Holbeck	
45659	$6P5F^2$	**20A** Leeds Holbeck	**20A** Leeds Holbeck	**20A** Leeds Holbeck	**55A** Leeds Holbeck	**55A** Leeds Holbeck	**55A** Leeds Holbeck	
45660	$6P5F^2$	**20A** Leeds Holbeck	**22A** Bristol Barrow Road	**22A** Bristol Barrow Road	**22A** Bristol Barrow Road	**82E** Bristol Barrow Road	**89A** Shrewsbury	**55A** Leeds Holbeck
45661	$6P5F^2$	**26A** Newton Heath	**26A** Newton Heath	**26A** Newton Heath	**26A** Newton Heath	**26A** Newton Heath	**26A** Newton Heath	
45662	$6P5F^2$	**22A** Bristol Barrow Road	**22A** Bristol Barrow Road	**22A** Bristol Barrow Road	**22A** Bristol Barrow Road	**82E** Bristol Barrow Road		
45663	$6P5F^2$	**22A** Bristol Barrow Road	**22A** Bristol Barrow Road	**22A** Bristol Barrow Road	**22A** Bristol Barrow Road	**26F** Patricroft	**26F** Patricroft	
45664	$6P5F^2$	**19G** Trafford Park	**19B** Millhouses	**19B** Millhouses	**19B** Millhouses	**41C** Millhouses	**26B** Agecroft	
45665	$6P5F^2$	**14B** Kentish Town	**14B** Kentish Town	**67A** Corkerhill	**67A** Corkerhill	**66A** Polmadie		
45666	$6P5F^2$	**8A** Edge Hill	**5A** Crewe North	**12A** Carlisle Upperby	**12A** Carlisle Upperby	**5A** Crewe North	**5A** Crewe North	
45667	$6P5F^2$	**17C** Coalville	**17A** Derby	**16A** Nottingham	**16A** Nottingham	**16A** Nottingham	**17B** Burton	
45668	$6P5F^2$	**10C** Patricroft	**10C** Patricroft	**10C** Patricroft	**10C** Patricroft	**17A** Derby	**17B** Burton	
45669	$6P5F^2$	**1B** Camden	**1B** Camden	**1B** Camden	**1B** Camden	**1A** Willesden	**2B** Nuneaton	
45670	$6P5F^2$	**10C** Patricroft	**8A** Edge Hill	**8A** Edge Hill	**8A** Edge Hill	**8A** Edge Hill	**2A** Rugby	
45671	$6P5F^2$	**25G** Farnley Junction	**26A** Newton Heath	**26A** Newton Heath	**26A** Newton Heath	**9A** Longsight	**8B** Warrington Dallam	
45672	$6P5F^2$	**8A** Edge Hill	**1B** Camden	**1B** Camden	**1B** Camden	**12B** Carlisle Upperby	**2A** Rugby	
45673	$6P5F^2$	**8A** Edge Hill	**8A** Edge Hill	**63A** Perth	**63A** Perth	**63A** Perth		
45674	$6P5F^2$	**5A** Crewe North	**5A** Crewe North	**5A** Crewe North	**5A** Crewe North	**5A** Crewe North	**5A** Crewe North	
45675	$6P5F^2$	**5A** Crewe North	**20A** Leeds Holbeck	**20A** Leeds Holbeck	**55A** Leeds Holbeck	**55A** Leeds Holbeck	**55A** Leeds Holbeck	**55A** Leeds Holbeck
45676	$6P5F^2$	**5A** Crewe North	**1B** Camden	**1B** Camden	**1B** Camden	**1B** Camden	**5A** Crewe North	
45677	$6P5F^2$	**12B** Carlisle Upperby	**12A** Carlisle Upperby	**66A** Polmadie	**67A** Corkerhill	**63A** Perth		
45678	$6P5F^2$	**12B** Carlisle Upperby	**5A** Crewe North	**5A** Crewe North	**5A** Crewe North	**8A** Edge Hill		
45679	$6P5F^2$	**19B** Millhouses	**19B** Millhouses	**68A** Carlisle Kingmoor	**68A** Carlisle Kingmoor	**5A** Crewe North		
45680	$6P5F^2$	**9A** Longsight	**9A** Longsight	**9A** Longsight	**9A** Longsight	**9A** Longsight	**12A** Carlisle Kingmoor	
45681	$6P5F^2$	**8A** Edge Hill	**8A** Edge Hill	**8A** Edge Hill	**8A** Edge Hill	**8A** Edge Hill	**24E** Blackpool Central	
45682	$6P5F^2$	**22A** Bristol Barrow Road	**22A** Bristol Barrow Road	**22A** Bristol Barrow Road	**22A** Bristol Barrow Road	**82E** Bristol Barrow Road	**82E** Bristol Barrow Road	
45683	$6P5F^2$	**19B** Millhouses	**19B** Millhouses	**19B** Millhouses	**19B** Millhouses	**41C** Millhouses		
45684	$6P5F^2$	**5A** Crewe North	**5A** Crewe North	**5A** Crewe North	**5A** Crewe North	**5A** Crewe North	**2A** Rugby	
45685	$6P5F^2$	**22A** Bristol Barrow Road	**22A** Bristol Barrow Road	**22A** Bristol Barrow Road	**22A** Bristol Barrow Road	**82E** Bristol Barrow Road	**82E** Bristol Barrow Road	
45686	$6P5F^2$	**5A** Crewe North	**5A** Crewe North	**1B** Camden	**1B** Camden	**1B** Camden		
45687	$6P5F^2$	**5A** Crewe North	**12A** Carlisle Upperby	**67A** Corkerhill	**67A** Corkerhill	**67A** Corkerhill		
45688	$6P5F^2$	**5A** Crewe North	**9A** Longsight	**3B** Bushbury	**3B** Bushbury	**12B** Carlisle Upperby		
45689	$6P5F^2$	**5A** Crewe North	**5A** Crewe North	**9A** Longsight	**9A** Longsight	**5A** Crewe North	**5A** Crewe North	
45690	$6P5F^2$	**22A** Bristol Barrow Road	**22A** Bristol Barrow Road	**22A** Bristol Barrow Road	**22A** Bristol Barrow Road	**82E** Bristol Barrow Road	**82E** Bristol Barrow Road	
45691	$6P5F^2$	**27A** Polmadie	**66A** Polmadie	**66A** Polmadie	**68A** Carlisle Kingmoor	**12A** Carlisle Kingmoor		
45692	$6P5F^2$	**27A** Polmadie	**66A** Polmadie	**66A** Polmadie	**63A** Perth	**63A** Perth		
45693	$6P5F^2$	**30A** Corkerhill	**67A** Corkerhill	**67A** Corkerhill	**67A** Corkerhill	**67A** Corkerhill		
45694	$6P5F^2$	**22A** Bristol Barrow Road	**20A** Leeds Holbeck	**20A** Leeds Holbeck	**55A** Leeds Holbeck	**55A** Leeds Holbeck	**56F** Low Moor	**56A** Wakefield
45695	$6P5F^2$	**24E** Blackpool Central	**28A** Blackpool Central	**25G** Farnley Junction	**55C** Farnley Junction	**55C** Farnley Junction	**55C** Farnley Junction	
45696	$6P5F^2$	**19B** Millhouses	**17A** Derby	**66A** Polmadie	**68A** Carlisle Kingmoor	**5A** Crewe North	**24L** Carnforth	
45697	$6P5F^2$	**24E** Blackpool Central	**28A** Blackpool Central	**68A** Carlisle Kingmoor	**68A** Carlisle Kingmoor	**12A** Carlisle Kingmoor	**24E** Blackpool Central	**55A** Leeds Holbeck
45698	$6P5F^2$	**23A** Bank Hall	**27A** Bank Hall	**27A** Bank Hall	**27A** Bank Hall	**27A** Bank Hall	**27A** Bank Hall	
45699	$6P5F^2$	**20A** Leeds Holbeck	**22A** Bristol Barrow Road	**22A** Bristol Barrow Road	**22A** Bristol Barrow Road	**82E** Bristol Barrow Road	**89A** Shrewsbury	
45700	$6P5F^2$	**26A** Newton Heath	**26A** Newton Heath	**26A** Newton Heath	**26A** Newton Heath	**26A** Newton Heath	**26A** Newton Heath	
45701	$6P5F^2$	**26A** Newton Heath	**26A** Newton Heath	**26A** Newton Heath	**26A** Newton Heath	**26A** Newton Heath	**26A** Newton Heath	
45702	$6P5F^2$	**25G** Farnley Junction	**26A** Newton Heath	**26A** Newton Heath	**26A** Newton Heath	**26A** Newton Heath	**26A** Newton Heath	
45703	$6P5F^2$	**9A** Longsight	**5A** Crewe North	**3B** Bushbury	**5A** Crewe North	**12B** Carlisle Upperby	**24E** Blackpool Central	
45704	$6P5F^2$	**25G** Farnley Junction	**25G** Farnley Junction	**68A** Carlisle Kingmoor	**68A** Carlisle Kingmoor	**8A** Edge Hill	**2A** Rugby	
45705	$6P5F^2$	**25G** Farnley Junction	**25G** Farnley Junction	**25G** Farnley Junction	**24E** Blackpool Central	**24E** Blackpool Central	**24E** Blackpool Central	
45706	$6P5F^2$	**26A** Newton Heath	**26A** Newton Heath	**26A** Newton Heath	**26A** Newton Heath	**26A** Newton Heath	**26A** Newton Heath	
45707	$6P5F^2$	**24E** Blackpool Central	**28A** Blackpool Central	**66A** Polmadie	**67A** Corkerhill	**66A** Polmadie		
45708	$6P5F^2$	**25G** Farnley Junction	**25G** Farnley Junction	**25G** Farnley Junction	**55C** Farnley Junction	**55C** Farnley Junction	**55C** Farnley Junction	
45709	$6P5F^2$	**5A** Crewe North	**9A** Longsight	**9A** Longsight	**3B** Bushbury	**3B** Bushbury	**5A** Crewe North	
45710	$6P5F^2$	**26A** Newton Heath	**26A** Newton Heath	**26A** Newton Heath	**26A** Newton Heath	**26A** Newton Heath	**26A** Newton Heath	
45711	$6P5F^2$	**26A** Newton Heath	**25G** Farnley Junction	**67A** Corkerhill	**67A** Corkerhill	**66A** Polmadie		
45712	$6P5F^2$	**26A** Newton Heath	**26A** Newton Heath	**26A** Newton Heath	**26A** Newton Heath	**14B** Kentish Town	**17B** Burton	
45713	$6P5F^2$	**12A** Carlisle Kingmoor	**68A** Carlisle Kingmoor	**68A** Carlisle Kingmoor	**68A** Carlisle Kingmoor	**12A** Carlisle Kingmoor		
45714	$6P5F^2$	**12A** Carlisle Kingmoor	**68A** Carlisle Kingmoor	**68A** Carlisle Kingmoor	**68A** Carlisle Kingmoor	**12A** Carlisle Kingmoor	**24L** Carnforth	
45715	$6P5F^2$	**12A** Carlisle Kingmoor	**68A** Carlisle Kingmoor	**68A** Carlisle Kingmoor	**68A** Carlisle Kingmoor	**12A** Carlisle Kingmoor		
45716	$6P5F^2$	**12A** Carlisle Kingmoor	**68A** Carlisle Kingmoor	**68A** Carlisle Kingmoor	**68A** Carlisle Kingmoor	**12A** Carlisle Kingmoor	**26B** Agecroft	
45717	$6P5F^2$	**26A** Newton Heath	**27A** Bank Hall	**27A** Bank Hall	**27A** Bank Hall	**27A** Bank Hall	**27A** Bank Hall	
45718	$6P5F^2$	**12B** Carlisle Upperby	**12A** Carlisle Upperby	**68A** Carlisle Kingmoor	**68A** Carlisle Kingmoor	**12A** Carlisle Kingmoor		
45719	$6P5F^2$	**26A** Newton Heath	**26A** Newton Heath	**27A** Bank Hall	**27A** Bank Hall	**27A** Bank Hall	**27A** Bank Hall	
45720	$6P5F^2$	**10C** Patricroft	**10C** Patricroft	**67A** Corkerhill	**67A** Corkerhill	**66A** Polmadie		
45721	$6P5F^2$	**1A** Willesden	**8A** Edge Hill	**8A** Edge Hill	**5A** Crewe North	**12B** Carlisle Upperby	**5A** Crewe North	
45722	$6P5F^2$	**5A** Crewe North	**12A** Carlisle Upperby	**12A** Carlisle Upperby	Rugby Testing Station	**1A** Willesden		
45723	$6P5F^2$	**9A** Longsight	**9A** Longsight	**9A** Longsight	**9A** Longsight	**12B** Carlisle Upperby	**2B** Nuneaton	
45724	$6P5F^2$	**8A** Edge Hill	**5A** Crewe North	**68A** Carlisle Kingmoor	**68A** Carlisle Kingmoor	**12A** Carlisle Kingmoor		
45725	$6P5F^2$	**8A** Edge Hill	**19B** Millhouses	**19B** Millhouses	**19B** Millhouses	**41C** Millhouses		
45726	$6P5F^2$	**10C** Patricroft	**8A** Edge Hill	**5A** Crewe North	**5A** Crewe North	**5A** Crewe North	**5A** Crewe North	
45727	$6P5F^2$	**12A** Carlisle Kingmoor	**68A** Carlisle Kingmoor	**63A** Perth	**63A** Perth	**63A** Perth		
45728	$6P5F^2$	**12A** Carlisle Kingmoor	**68A** Carlisle Kingmoor	**68A** Carlisle Kingmoor	**68A** Carlisle Kingmoor	**12A** Carlisle Kingmoor		
45729	$6P5F^2$	**12A** Carlisle Kingmoor	**68A** Carlisle Kingmoor	**68A** Carlisle Kingmoor	**68A** Carlisle Kingmoor	**12A** Carlisle Kingmoor		
45730	$6P5F^2$	**12A** Carlisle Kingmoor	**68A** Carlisle Kingmoor	**68A** Carlisle Kingmoor	**68A** Carlisle Kingmoor	**12A** Carlisle Kingmoor	**24L** Carnforth	
45731	$6P5F^2$	**12A** Carlisle Kingmoor	**68A** Carlisle Kingmoor	**68A** Carlisle Kingmoor	**68A** Carlisle Kingmoor	**12A** Carlisle Kingmoor		
45732	$6P5F^2$	**12A** Carlisle Kingmoor	**68A** Carlisle Kingmoor	**68A** Carlisle Kingmoor	**68A** Carlisle Kingmoor	**12A** Carlisle Kingmoor	**24E** Blackpool Central	
45733	$6P5F^2$	**3B** Bushbury	**5A** Crewe North	**3B** Bushbury	**3B** Bushbury	**8A** Edge Hill	**2A** Rugby	
45734	$6P5F^2$	**3B** Bushbury	**9A** Longsight	**3B** Bushbury	**3B** Bushbury	**12B** Carlisle Upperby	**12A** Carlisle Kingmoor	
45735	$7P^2$	**1B** Camden	**1B** Camden	**1B** Camden	**1B** Camden	**24K** Preston	**1A** Willesden	
45736	$7P^2$	**1B** Camden	**1B** Camden	**1B** Camden	**5A** Crewe North	**5A** Crewe North	**6J** Holyhead	
45737	$6P5F^2$	**5A** Crewe North	**8A** Edge Hill	**3B** Bushbury	**3B** Bushbury	**3B** Bushbury	**26A** Newton Heath	

No.	Class	1948	1951	1954	1957	1960	1963	1966
45738	$6P5F^2$	**3B** Bushbury	**5A** Crewe North	**3B** Bushbury	**3B** Bushbury	**12B** Carlisle Upperby	**12A** Carlisle Kingmoor	
45739	$6P5F^2$	**1A** Willesden	**20A** Leeds Holbeck	**20A** Leeds Holbeck	**55A** Leeds Holbeck	**55A** Leeds Holbeck	**55A** Leeds Holbeck	**56A** Wakefield
45740	$6P5F^2$	**9A** Longsight	**9A** Longsight	**1B** Camden	**1A** Willesden	**1A** Willesden	**21D** Aston	
45741	$6P5F^2$	**5A** Crewe North	**3B** Bushbury	**3B** Bushbury	**3B** Bushbury	**12B** Carlisle Upperby	**12A** Carlisle Kingmoor	
45742	$6P5F^2$	**3B** Bushbury	**9A** Longsight	**3B** Bushbury	**3B** Bushbury	**12B** Carlisle Upperby	**12A** Carlisle Kingmoor	
46004	5XP	**8A** Edge Hill						
46100	$7P^3$	**1B** Camden	**1B** Camden	**1B** Camden	**1B** Camden	**16A** Nottingham		
46101	$7P^3$	**1B** Camden	**5A** Crewe North	**5A** Crewe North	**5A** Crewe North	**1B** Camden	**1A** Willesden	
46102	$7P^3$	**27A** Polmadie	**66A** Polmadie	**66A** Polmadie	**66A** Polmadie	**66A** Polmadie		
46103	$7P^3$	**20A** Leeds Holbeck	**20A** Leeds Holbeck	**20A** Leeds Holbeck	**55A** Leeds Holbeck	**14B** Kentish Town		
46104	$7P^3$	**27A** Polmadie	**66A** Polmadie	**66A** Polmadie	**66A** Polmadie	**66A** Polmadie		
46105	$7P^3$	**27A** Polmadie	**66A** Polmadie	**66A** Polmadie	**66A** Polmadie	**66A** Polmadie		
46106	$7P^3$	**8A** Edge Hill	**8A** Edge Hill	**5A** Crewe North	**5A** Crewe North	**9A** Longsight		
46107	$7P^3$	**27A** Polmadie	**66A** Polmadie	**66A** Polmadie	**66A** Polmadie	**66A** Polmadie		
46108	$7P^3$	**20A** Leeds Holbeck	**20A** Leeds Holbeck	**20A** Leeds Holbeck	**55A** Leeds Holbeck	**24K** Preston	**12B** Carlisle Upperby	
46109	$7P^3$	**20A** Leeds Holbeck	**20A** Leeds Holbeck	**20A** Leeds Holbeck	**55A** Leeds Holbeck	**55A** Leeds Holbeck		
46110	$7P^3$	**12B** Carlisle Upperby	**3B** Bushbury	**6J** Holyhead	**5A** Crewe North	**5A** Crewe North	**8A** Edge Hill	
46111	$7P^3$	**8A** Edge Hill	**8A** Edge Hill	**9A** Longsight	**9A** Longsight	**9A** Longsight	**1A** Willesden	
46112	$7P^3$	**7C** Holyhead	**7C** Holyhead	**20A** Leeds Holbeck	**55A** Leeds Holbeck	**16A** Nottingham	**16D** Annesley	
46113	$7P^3$	**5A** Crewe North	**5A** Crewe North	**20A** Leeds Holbeck	**55A** Leeds Holbeck	**55A** Leeds Holbeck		
46114	$7P^3$	**9A** Longsight	**9A** Longsight	**9A** Longsight	**8A** Edge Hill	**8A** Edge Hill	**6J** Holyhead	
46115	$7P^3$	**5A** Crewe North	**9A** Longsight	**9A** Longsight	**9A** Longsight	**9A** Longsight	**9A** Longsight	
46116	$7P^3$	**1B** Camden	**1B** Camden	**1B** Camden	**12A** Carlisle Upperby	**5A** Crewe North	**12A** Carlisle Kingmoor	
46117	$7P^3$	**20A** Leeds Holbeck	**20A** Leeds Holbeck	**20A** Leeds Holbeck	**55A** Leeds Holbeck	**55A** Leeds Holbeck		
46118	$7P^3$	**1B** Camden	**5A** Crewe North	**5A** Crewe North	**5A** Crewe North	**1B** Camden	**12B** Carlisle Upperby	
46119	$7P^3$	**1B** Camden	**7C** Holyhead	**5A** Crewe North	**5A** Crewe North	**8A** Edge Hill	**8A** Edge Hill	
46120	$7P^3$	**9A** Longsight	**9A** Longsight	**9A** Longsight	**5A** Crewe North	**5A** Crewe North	**6G** Llandudno Junction	
46121	$7P^3$	**9A** Longsight	**66A** Polmadie	**66A** Polmadie	**66A** Polmadie	**66A** Polmadie		
46122	$7P^3$	**9A** Longsight	**9A** Longsight	**9A** Longsight	**9A** Longsight	**3B** Bushbury	**16D** Annesley	
46123	$7P^3$	**1B** Camden	**8A** Edge Hill	**8A** Edge Hill	**8A** Edge Hill	**14B** Kentish Town		
46124	$7P^3$	**8A** Edge Hill	**8A** Edge Hill	**8A** Edge Hill	**8A** Edge Hill	**8A** Edge Hill		
46125	$7P^3$	**5A** Crewe North	**8A** Edge Hill	**5A** Crewe North	**5A** Crewe North	**5A** Crewe North	**6J** Holyhead	
46126	$7P^3$	**5A** Crewe North	**1B** Camden	**1B** Camden	**12A** Carlisle Upperby	**24K** Preston	**16D** Annesley	
46127	$7P^3$	**7C** Holyhead	**7C** Holyhead	**6J** Holyhead	**5A** Crewe North	**6J** Holyhead		
46128	$7P^3$	**12B** Carlisle Upperby	**5A** Crewe North	**5A** Crewe North	**5A** Crewe North	**5A** Crewe North	**12A** Carlisle Kingmoor	
46129	$7P^3$	**9A** Longsight	**9A** Longsight	**6J** Holyhead	**5A** Crewe North	**6J** Holyhead	**9A** Longsight	
46130	$7P^3$	**1B** Camden	**5A** Crewe North	**9A** Longsight	**12A** Carlisle Upperby	**55A** Leeds Holbeck		
46131	$7P^3$	**9A** Longsight	**9A** Longsight	**9A** Longsight	**9A** Longsight	**9A** Longsight		
46132	$7P^3$	**7C** Holyhead	**7C** Holyhead	**6J** Holyhead	**8A** Edge Hill	**14B** Kentish Town	**12B** Carlisle Upperby	
46133	$7P^3$	**20A** Leeds Holbeck	**20A** Leeds Holbeck	**20A** Leeds Holbeck	**55A** Leeds Holbeck	**14B** Kentish Town	**26A** Newton Heath	
46134	$7P^3$	**8A** Edge Hill	**8A** Edge Hill	**5A** Crewe North	**5A** Crewe North	**5A** Crewe North		
46135	$7P^3$	**8A** Edge Hill	**8A** Edge Hill	**8A** Edge Hill	**9A** Longsight	**5A** Crewe North		
46136	$7P^3$	**8A** Edge Hill	**12A** Carlisle Upperby	**12A** Carlisle Upperby	**12A** Carlisle Upperby	**24K** Preston	**12B** Carlisle Upperby	
46137	$7P^3$	**12B** Carlisle Upperby	**8A** Edge Hill	**5A** Crewe North	**9A** Longsight	**9A** Longsight		
46138	$7P^3$	**8A** Edge Hill	**8A** Edge Hill	**5A** Crewe North	**5A** Crewe North	**6G** Llandudno Junction	**12B** Carlisle Upperby	
46139	$7P^3$	**1B** Camden	**1B** Camden	**1B** Camden	**1B** Camden	**14B** Kentish Town		
46140	$7P^3$	**1B** Camden	**3B** Bushbury	**5A** Crewe North	**9A** Longsight	**14B** Kentish Town	**26A** Newton Heath	
46141	$7P^3$	**1B** Camden	**1B** Camden	**1B** Camden	**12A** Carlisle Upperby	**3B** Bushbury	**12B** Carlisle Upperby	
46142	$7P^3$	**1B** Camden	**1B** Camden	**1B** Camden	**8A** Edge Hill	**14B** Kentish Town	**26A** Newton Heath	
46143	$7P^3$	**27A** Polmadie	**9A** Longsight	**9A** Longsight	**9A** Longsight	**3B** Bushbury	**16D** Annesley	
46144	$7P^3$	**8A** Edge Hill	**8A** Edge Hill	**1B** Camden	**1B** Camden	**1B** Camden	**6G** Llandudno Junction	
46145	$7P^3$	**9A** Longsight	**9A** Longsight	**20A** Leeds Holbeck	**55A** Leeds Holbeck	**55A** Leeds Holbeck		
46146	$7P^3$	**5A** Crewe North	**5A** Crewe North	**1B** Camden	**1B** Camden	**1B** Camden		
46147	$7P^3$	**5A** Crewe North	**12A** Carlisle Upperby	**1B** Camden	**6J** Holyhead	**5A** Crewe North		
46148	$7P^3$	**1B** Camden	**3B** Bushbury	**5A** Crewe North	**5A** Crewe North	**12B** Carlisle Upperby	**6G** Llandudno Junction	
46149	$7P^3$	**9A** Longsight	**9A** Longsight	**8A** Edge Hill	**6J** Holyhead	**6J** Holyhead	**9A** Longsight	
46150	$7P^3$	**9A** Longsight	**9A** Longsight	**6J** Holyhead	**5A** Crewe North	**6G** Llandudno Junction	**6J** Holyhead	
46151	$7P^3$	**1B** Camden	**3B** Bushbury	**5A** Crewe North	**5A** Crewe North	**9A** Longsight		
46152	$7P^3$	**1B** Camden	**1B** Camden	**8A** Edge Hill	**8A** Edge Hill	**5A** Crewe North	**6J** Holyhead	
46153	$7P^3$	**1B** Camden	**8A** Edge Hill	**8A** Edge Hill	**9A** Longsight	**3B** Bushbury		
46154	$7P^3$	**5A** Crewe North	**1B** Camden	**1B** Camden	**1B** Camden	**24K** Preston		
46155	$7P^3$	**5A** Crewe North	**5A** Crewe North	**5A** Crewe North	**5A** Crewe North	**5A** Crewe North	**6G** Llandudno Junction	
46156	$7P^3$	**8A** Edge Hill	**8A** Edge Hill	**5A** Crewe North	**5A** Crewe North	**6G** Llandudno Junction	**6J** Holyhead	
46157	$7P^3$	**7C** Holyhead	**5A** Crewe North	**6J** Holyhead	**8A** Edge Hill	**16A** Nottingham	**12B** Carlisle Upperby	
46158	$7P^3$	**12B** Carlisle Upperby	**3B** Bushbury	**8A** Edge Hill	**9A** Longsight	**3B** Bushbury	**16D** Annesley	
46159	$7P^3$	**1B** Camden	**1B** Camden	**5A** Crewe North	**5A** Crewe North	**5A** Crewe North		
46160	$7P^3$	**9A** Longsight	**9A** Longsight	**9A** Longsight	**9A** Longsight	**14B** Kentish Town	**12B** Carlisle Upperby	
46161	$7P^3$	**5A** Crewe North	**7C** Holyhead	**9A** Longsight	**5A** Crewe North	**24K** Preston		
46162	$7P^3$	**5A** Crewe North	**1B** Camden	**1B** Camden	**1B** Camden	**14B** Kentish Town	**12B** Carlisle Upperby	
46163	$7P^3$	**5A** Crewe North	**3B** Bushbury	**5A** Crewe North	**5A** Crewe North	**24K** Preston	**1A** Willesden	
46164	$7P^3$	**8A** Edge Hill	**8A** Edge Hill	**8A** Edge Hill	**8A** Edge Hill	**5A** Crewe North		
46165	$7P^3$	**5A** Crewe North	**3B** Bushbury	**12A** Carlisle Upperby	**12A** Carlisle Upperby	**24K** Preston	**6G** Llandudno Junction	
46166	$7P^3$	**5A** Crewe North	**7C** Holyhead	**5A** Crewe North	**5A** Crewe North	**9A** Longsight	**12B** Carlisle Upperby	
46167	$7P^3$	**5A** Crewe North	**9A** Longsight	**5A** Crewe North	**12A** Carlisle Upperby	**24K** Preston	**6J** Holyhead	
46168	$7P^3$	**1B** Camden	**1B** Camden	**1B** Camden	**1B** Camden	**24K** Preston	**8F** Wigan Springs Branch	
46169	$7P^3$	**9A** Longsight	**9A** Longsight	**9A** Longsight	**9A** Longsight	**5A** Crewe North	**1A** Willesden	
46170	$7P^3$	**1B** Camden	**1B** Camden	**1B** Camden	**1B** Camden	**24K** Preston		
46200	$8P^1$	**5A** Crewe North	**8A** Edge Hill	**8A** Edge Hill	**8A** Edge Hill	**5A** Crewe North		
46201	$8P^1$	**5A** Crewe North	**8A** Edge Hill	**5A** Crewe North	**5A** Crewe North	**66A** Polmadie		
46202	$8P^1$	**1B** Camden	**1B** Camden	**5A** *(Crewe Works)*				
46203	$8P^1$	**5A** Crewe North	**8A** Edge Hill	**5A** Crewe North	**5A** Crewe North	**8A** Edge Hill		
46204	$8P^1$	**5A** Crewe North	**8A** Edge Hill	**8A** Edge Hill	**8A** Edge Hill	**8A** Edge Hill		
46205	$8P^1$	**5A** Crewe North	**8A** Edge Hill	**8A** Edge Hill	**8A** Edge Hill	**5A** Crewe North		
46206	$8P^1$	**5A** Crewe North	**5A** Crewe North	**5A** Crewe North	**5A** Crewe North	**5A** Crewe North		
46207	$8P^1$	**5A** Crewe North	**5A** Crewe North	**8A** Edge Hill	**8A** Edge Hill	**1B** Camden		
46208	$8P^1$	**5A** Crewe North	**5A** Crewe North	**8A** Edge Hill	**8A** Edge Hill	**8A** Edge Hill		
46209	$8P^1$	**5A** Crewe North	**5A** Crewe North	**5A** Crewe North	**5A** Crewe North	**5A** Crewe North		
46210	$8P^1$	**5A** Crewe North	**5A** Crewe North	**5A** Crewe North	**8A** Edge Hill	**66A** Polmadie		
46211	$8P^1$	**5A** Crewe North	**5A** Crewe North	**5A** Crewe North	**5A** Crewe North	**8A** Edge Hill		
46212	$8P^1$	**5A** Crewe North	**5A** Crewe North	**5A** Crewe North	**5A** Crewe North	**5A** Crewe North		
46220	$8P^2$	**27A** Polmadie	**66A** Polmadie	**66A** Polmadie	**66A** Polmadie	**5A** Crewe North	**12B** Carlisle Upperby	
46221	$8P^2$	**27A** Polmadie	**66A** Polmadie	**66A** Polmadie	**66A** Polmadie	**1B** Camden	**12B** Carlisle Upperby	
46222	$8P^2$	**27A** Polmadie	**66A** Polmadie	**66A** Polmadie	**66A** Polmadie	**66A** Polmadie	**66A** Polmadie	
46223	$8P^2$	**27A** Polmadie	**66A** Polmadie	**66A** Polmadie	**66A** Polmadie	**66A** Polmadie	**66A** Polmadie	
46224	$8P^2$	**27A** Polmadie	**66A** Polmadie	**66A** Polmadie	**66A** Polmadie	**66A** Polmadie	**66A** Polmadie	
46225	$8P^2$	**1B** Camden	**12A** Carlisle Upperby	**5A** Crewe North	**5A** Crewe North	**12B** Carlisle Upperby	**12B** Carlisle Upperby	
46226	$8P^2$	**12B** Carlisle Upperby	**12A** Carlisle Upperby	**8A** Edge Hill	**12A** Carlisle Upperby	**12B** Carlisle Upperby	**12A** Carlisle Kingmoor	
46227	$8P^2$	**5A** Crewe North	**66A** Polmadie	**66A** Polmadie	**66A** Polmadie	**66A** Polmadie		
46228	$8P^2$	**12B** Carlisle Upperby	**12A** Carlisle Upperby	**12A** Carlisle Upperby	**12A** Carlisle Upperby	**5A** Crewe North	**5A** Crewe North	
46229	$8P^2$	**5A** Crewe North	**12A** Carlisle Upperby	**1B** Camden	**1B** Camden	**1B** Camden	**8A** Edge Hill	
46230	$8P^2$	**27A** Polmadie	**66A** Polmadie	**66A** Polmadie	**66A** Polmadie	**66A** Polmadie	**66A** Polmadie	
46231	$8P^2$	**27A** Polmadie	**66A** Polmadie	**66A** Polmadie	**66A** Polmadie	**66A** Polmadie		
46232	$8P^2$	**27A** Polmadie	**66A** Polmadie	**66A** Polmadie	**66A** Polmadie	**66A** Polmadie		
46233	$8P^2$	**5A** Crewe North	**5A** Crewe North	**5A** Crewe North	**5A** Crewe North	**5A** Crewe North	**8A** Edge Hill	
46234	$8P^2$	**5A** Crewe North	**5A** Crewe North	**5A** Crewe North	**5A** Crewe North	**12B** Carlisle Upperby	**12B** Carlisle Upperby	
46235	$8P^2$	**5A** Crewe North	**5A** Crewe North	**5A** Crewe North	**5A** Crewe North	**5A** Crewe North	**5A** Crewe North	
46236	$8P^2$	**5A** Crewe North	**5A** Crewe North	**1B** Camden	**1B** Camden	**12B** Carlisle Upperby	**12A** Carlisle Kingmoor	
46237	$8P^2$	**1B** Camden	**1B** Camden	**1B** Camden	**1B** Camden	**12B** Carlisle Upperby	**12B** Carlisle Upperby	
46238	$8P^2$	**12B** Carlisle Upperby	**12A** Carlisle Upperby	**12A** Carlisle Upperby	**12A** Carlisle Upperby	**12B** Carlisle Upperby	**12B** Carlisle Upperby	
46239	$8P^2$	**1B** Camden	**1B** Camden	**1B** Camden	**1B** Camden	**1B** Camden	**1B** Camden	
46240	$8P^2$	**1B** Camden	**1B** Camden	**1B** Camden	**1B** Camden	**1B** Camden	**1B** Camden	
46241	$8P^2$	**1B** Camden	**1B** Camden	**1B** Camden	**1B** Camden	**5A** Crewe North	**8A** Edge Hill	
46242	$8P^2$	**27A** Polmadie	**1B** Camden	**5A** Crewe North	**1B** Camden	**1B** Camden	**66A** Polmadie	
46243	$8P^2$	**1B** Camden	**5A** Crewe North	**5A** Crewe North	**5A** Crewe North	**5A** Crewe North	**8A** Edge Hill	

		1948	1951	1954	1957	1960	1963	1966
46244	8P[2]	1B Camden	1B Camden	1B Camden	1B Camden	12B Carlisle Upperby	12A Carlisle Kingmoor	
46245	8P[2]	1B Camden	1B Camden	1B Camden	1B Camden	1B Camden	1B Camden	
46246	8P[2]	1B Camden	5A Crewe North	5A Crewe North	5A Crewe North	5A Crewe North	1B Camden	
46247	8P[2]	1B Camden	1B Camden	1B Camden	1B Camden	1B Camden	12A Carlisle Kingmoor	
46248	8P[2]	1B Camden	5A Crewe North	5A Crewe North	5A Crewe North	5A Crewe North	5A Crewe North	
46249	8P[2]	12B Carlisle Upperby	1B Camden	1B Camden	5A Crewe North	5A Crewe North	66A Polmadie	
46250	8P[2]	12B Carlisle Upperby	1B Camden	1B Camden	1B Camden	12B Carlisle Upperby	12B Carlisle Upperby	
46251	8P[2]	12B Carlisle Upperby	12A Carlisle Upperby	12A Carlisle Upperby	5A Crewe North	5A Crewe North	5A Crewe North	
46252	8P[2]	5A Crewe North	5A Crewe North	5A Crewe North	5A Crewe North	5A Crewe North	1B Camden	
46253	8P[2]	1B Camden	12A Carlisle Upperby	1B Camden	1B Camden	5A Crewe North	5A Crewe North	
46254	8P[2]	1B Camden	12A Carlisle Upperby	1B Camden	1B Camden	1B Camden	5A Crewe North	
46255	8P[2]	1B Camden	12A Carlisle Upperby	12A Carlisle Upperby	12A Carlisle Upperby	12B Carlisle Upperby	12A Carlisle Kingmoor	
46256	8P[2]	5A Crewe North	1B Camden	1B Camden	1B Camden	12B Carlisle Upperby	5A Crewe North	
46257	8P[2]	→	1B Camden	1B Camden	1B Camden	12B Carlisle Upperby	12A Carlisle Kingmoor	
46400	2MT[2]	15B Kettering	15B Kettering	15B Kettering	19B Millhouses	41C Millhouses	12E Barrow	10A Carnforth
46401	2MT[2]	15B Kettering	15B Kettering	15B Kettering	22B Gloucester Barnwood	89A Oswestry	89D Oswestry	9L Buxton
46402	2MT[2]	15B Kettering	15B Kettering	15B Kettering	15C Leicester Midland	17A Derby	17A Derby	9L Buxton
46403	2MT[2]	15B Kettering	15B Kettering	15B Kettering	15B Kettering	15B Kettering	15B Kettering	
46404	2MT[2]	15B Kettering	15B Kettering	15B Kettering	15B Kettering	15B Kettering	15B Kettering	
46405	2MT[2]	25G Farnley Junction	25C Goole	25C Goole	27B Aintree	27B Aintree	26D Bury	8K Bank Hall
46406	2MT[2]	25G Farnley Junction	27A Bank Hall	27A Bank Hall	26D Bury	26D Bury	26D Bury	9D Newton Heath
46407	2MT[2]	25C Goole	25C Goole	25C Goole	53E Goole	53E Goole		
46408	2MT[2]	25C Goole	25C Goole	25C Goole	53E Goole	53E Goole		
46409	2MT[2]	25A Wakefield	25C Goole	25C Goole	53E Goole	53E Goole	50D Goole	
46410	2MT[2]	24E Blackpool Central	28A Blackpool Central	26A Newton Heath	26A Newton Heath	24J Lancaster	24J Lancaster	8C Speke Junction
46411	2MT[2]	24E Blackpool Central	28A Blackpool Central	26A Newton Heath	26A Newton Heath	26A Newton Heath	26A Newton Heath	9D Newton Heath
46412	2MT[2]	24E Blackpool Central	28A Blackpool Central	26B Agecroft	27B Aintree	27B Aintree	26D Bury	9D Newton Heath
46413	2MT[2]	24E Blackpool Central	28A Blackpool Central	24E Blackpool Central	56A Wakefield	56F Low Moor	50F Malton	
46414	2MT[2]	4B Swansea Victoria	27A Bank Hall	27A Bank Hall	26D Bury	26D Bury	26D Bury	8K Bank Hall
46415	2MT[2]	4B Swansea Victoria	27A Bank Hall	25A Wakefield	56A Wakefield	53E Goole		
46416	2MT[2]	23A Bank Hall	27A Bank Hall	27A Bank Hall	26D Bury	26D Bury	26D Bury	9K Bolton
46417	2MT[2]	23A Bank Hall	27A Bank Hall	27A Bank Hall	26D Bury	26D Bury	26D Bury	9K Bolton
46418	2MT[2]	26A Newton Heath	26A Newton Heath	26A Newton Heath	26A Newton Heath	26A Newton Heath	26A Newton Heath	9D Newton Heath
46419	2MT[2]	26A Newton Heath	26A Newton Heath	26A Newton Heath	26A Newton Heath	26A Newton Heath	26E Lees Oldham	8F Wigan Springs Branch
46420	2MT[2]	→	8D Widnes	8D Widnes	2D Coventry	2A Rugby	2B Nuneaton	
46421	2MT[2]	→	8D Widnes	8D Widnes	3A Bescot	3A Bescot	21B Bescot	2F Bescot
46422	2MT[2]	→	8D Widnes	8D Widnes	10A Wigan Springs Branch	8F Wigan Springs Branch	24J Lancaster	10J Lancaster
46423	2MT[2]	→	8D Widnes	8D Widnes	6K Rhyl	3D Aston	1C Watford	
46424	2MT[2]	→	8D Widnes	8D Widnes	1A Willesden	1A Willesden	1A Willesden	12D Workington
46425	2MT[2]	→	3A Bescot	3A Bescot	3A Bescot	3A Bescot	21B Bescot	
46426	2MT[2]	→	3A Bescot	3A Bescot	11E Lancaster	24J Lancaster	24J Lancaster	12B Carlisle Upperby
46427	2MT[2]	→	3E Monument Lane	3D Aston	3D Aston	3D Aston	21D Aston	2F Bescot
46428	2MT[2]	→	10B Preston	10A Wigan Springs Branch	10A Wigan Springs Branch	8F Wigan Springs Branch	21C Bushbury	2A Tyseley
46429	2MT[2]	→	10B Preston	10B Preston	5D Stoke	5D Stoke	21B Bescot	2F Bescot
46430	2MT[2]	→	10B Preston	10B Preston	5D Stoke	5D Stoke	21B Bescot	
46431	2MT[2]	→	1A Willesden	1A Willesden	1A Willesden	1C Watford	1C Watford	10J Lancaster
46432	2MT[2]	→	1A Willesden	10A Wigan Springs Branch	6K Rhyl	11B Workington	12F Workington	12D Workington
46433	2MT[2]	→	1A Willesden	1A Willesden	6K Rhyl	11B Workington	12F Workington	10J Lancaster
46434	2MT[2]	→	8D Widnes	10A Wigan Springs Branch	10A Wigan Springs Branch	8F Wigan Springs Branch	12B Carlisle Upperby	12B Carlisle Upperby
46435	2MT[2]	→	28A Blackpool Central	27A Bank Hall	56A Wakefield	56F Low Moor	56F Low Moor	
46436	2MT[2]	→	25C Goole	25C Goole	26D Bury	26D Bury	26D Bury	9K Bolton
46437	2MT[2]	→	25C Goole	25C Goole	26A Newton Heath	26A Newton Heath	26A Newton Heath	9D Newton Heath
46438	2MT[2]	→	25A Wakefield	25A Wakefield	56A Wakefield	56E Sowerby Bridge	56A Wakefield	
46439	2MT[2]	→	25A Wakefield	25A Wakefield	27B Aintree	27B Aintree	26D Bury	8L Aintree
46440	2MT[2]	→	23A Skipton	20F Skipton	18A Toton	17A Derby	17A Derby	8C Speke Junction
46441	2MT[2]	→	23C Lancaster	11E Lancaster	11E Lancaster	24J Lancaster	24J Lancaster	10J Lancaster
46442	2MT[2]	→	23A Skipton	20F Skipton	20F Skipton	24G Skipton	2A Rugby	2A Tyseley
46443	2MT[2]	→	17A Derby	17A Derby	17A Derby	17A Derby	21A Saltley	2E Saltley
46444	2MT[2]	→	17A Derby	15B Kettering	15B Kettering	15B Kettering	15B Kettering	
46445	2MT[2]	→	2D Coventry	2D Coventry	6K Rhyl	2A Rugby	2A Rugby	2F Bescot
46446	2MT[2]	→	2D Coventry	2D Coventry	2D Coventry	2A Rugby	2A Rugby	6F Machynlleth
46447	2MT[2]	→	12D Workington	12D Workington	12C Workington	8F Wigan Springs Branch	2B Nuneaton	8F Wigan Springs Branch
46448	2MT[2]	→	12D Workington	12D Workington	10A Wigan Springs Branch	8F Wigan Springs Branch	21C Bushbury	2E Saltley
46449	2MT[2]	→	12C Penrith	12C Penrith	12A Carlisle Upperby	12B Carlisle Upperby	24C Lostock Hall	9D Newton Heath
46450	2MT[2]	→	19A Sheffield Grimesthorpe	19A Sheffield Grimesthorpe	19A Sheffield Grimesthorpe	41B Sheffield Grimesthorpe	67E Dumfries	67E Dumfries
46451	2MT[2]	→	19A Sheffield Grimesthorpe	19A Sheffield Grimesthorpe	19A Sheffield Grimesthorpe	41B Sheffield Grimesthorpe	67B Hurlford	67B Hurlford
46452	2MT[2]	→	20E Manningham	20F Skipton	20F Skipton	24G Skipton	24C Lostock Hall	12D Workington
46453	2MT[2]	→	20E Manningham	20E Manningham	55A Leeds Holbeck	55A Leeds Holbeck		
46454	2MT[2]	→	17A Derby	17A Derby	17A Derby	15C Leicester Midland	21A Saltley	2E Saltley
46455	2MT[2]	→	12C Penrith	12C Penrith	12C Workington	11B Workington	12B Carlisle Upperby	12B Carlisle Upperby
46456	2MT[2]	→	12D Workington	12D Workington	12C Workington	11B Workington	21B Bescot	
46457	2MT[2]	→	12D Workington	12D Workington	12C Workington	12B Carlisle Upperby	21B Bescot	2A Tyseley
46458	2MT[2]	→	12D Workington	12D Workington	1A Willesden	1A Willesden	12B Carlisle Upperby	12B Carlisle Upperby
46459	2MT[2]	→	12C Penrith	12C Penrith	3A Bescot	3A Bescot	21B Bescot	
46460	2MT[2]	→	64A St. Margarets	61A Kittybrewster	61A Kittybrewster	61A Kittybrewster	63C Oban	67C Ayr
46461	2MT[2]	→	64A St. Margarets	64A St. Margarets	64A St. Margarets	64A St. Margarets	64A St. Margarets	
46462	2MT[2]	→	64A St. Margarets	64A St. Margarets	64A St. Margarets	64A St. Margarets	64A St. Margarets	64A St. Margarets
46463	2MT[2]	→	62B Dundee Tay Bridge	62B Dundee Tay Bridge	62B Dundee Tay Bridge	62B Dundee Tay Bridge	62B Dundee Tay Bridge	66B Motherwell
46464	2MT[2]	→	64A St. Margarets	62B Dundee Tay Bridge	62B Dundee Tay Bridge	62B Dundee Tay Bridge	62B Dundee Tay Bridge	62B Dundee Tay Bridge
46465	2MT[2]	→	→	31A Cambridge	31A Cambridge	31A Cambridge	9D Buxton	9L Buxton
46466	2MT[2]	→	→	31A Cambridge	31A Cambridge	31A Cambridge		
46467	2MT[2]	→	→	31A Cambridge	31A Cambridge	31A Cambridge	67B Hurlford	
46468	2MT[2]	→	→	30E Colchester	30E Colchester	30F Parkeston	63A Perth	
46469	2MT[2]	→	→	30E Colchester	30E Colchester	30F Parkeston		
46470	2MT[2]	→	→	51F West Auckland	51H Kirkby Stephen	12D Kirkby Stephen	1C Watford	2A Tyseley
46471	2MT[2]	→	→	51H Kirkby Stephen	51F West Auckland	51J Northallerton		
46472	2MT[2]	→	→	51A Darlington	51H Kirkby Stephen	2A Rugby	1A Willesden	
46473	2MT[2]	→	→	51F West Auckland	51A Darlington	51A Darlington	50F Malton	
46474	2MT[2]	→	→	51H Kirkby Stephen	51A Darlington	51A Darlington	52D Tweedmouth	
46475	2MT[2]	→	→	51A Darlington	51A Darlington	51A Darlington	52D Tweedmouth	
46476	2MT[2]	→	→	51H Kirkby Stephen	51A Darlington	52D Tweedmouth		
46477	2MT[2]	→	→	51H Kirkby Stephen	51A Darlington	51A Darlington		
46478	2MT[2]	→	→	51H Kirkby Stephen	51A Darlington	51L Thornaby		
46479	2MT[2]	→	→	51F West Auckland	51A Darlington	51A Darlington	52D Tweedmouth	
46480	2MT[2]	→	→	51H Kirkby Stephen	51F West Auckland	50A York	9D Buxton	9L Buxton
46481	2MT[2]	→	→	51H Kirkby Stephen	51F West Auckland	50A York		
46482	2MT[2]	→	→	51F West Auckland	51F West Auckland	52D Tweedmouth	51A Darlington	
46483	2MT[2]	→	→	27A Bank Hall	56A Wakefield	56E Sowerby Bridge	56A Wakefield	
46484	2MT[2]	→	→	26A Newton Heath	26A Newton Heath	26A Newton Heath	26E Lees Oldham	9L Buxton
46485	2MT[2]	→	→	26B Agecroft	26B Agecroft	26B Agecroft	26E Lees Oldham	12D Workington
46486	2MT[2]	→	→	24E Blackpool Central	26B Agecroft	26B Agecroft	26E Lees Oldham	10J Lancaster
46487	2MT[2]	→	→	25C Goole	26A Newton Heath	26A Newton Heath	26A Newton Heath	8F Wigan Springs Branch
46488	2MT[2]	→	→	12D Workington	12C Workington	12B Carlisle Upperby	12F Workington	
46489	2MT[2]	→	→	10A Wigan Springs Branch	12C Workington	12B Carlisle Upperby	12B Carlisle Upperby	
46490	2MT[2]	→	→	3A Bescot	3A Bescot	3A Bescot	21B Bescot	2F Bescot
46491	2MT[2]	→	→	12D Workington	12C Workington	11B Workington	12F Workington	12D Workington
46492	2MT[2]	→	→	3D Aston	3D Aston	3D Aston	21D Aston	2E Saltley
46493	2MT[2]	→	→	20A Leeds Holbeck	55A Leeds Holbeck	55A Leeds Holbeck		
46494	2MT[2]	→	→	17B Burton	19B Millhouses	41C Millhouses		
46495	2MT[2]	→	→	15B Kettering	15B Kettering	15B Kettering	17A Derby	5E Nuneaton
46496	2MT[2]	→	→	15B Kettering	15B Kettering	15B Kettering	15B Kettering	8K Bank Hall
46497	2MT[2]	→	→	20A Leeds Holbeck	18C Hasland	17A Derby	17A Derby	
46498	2MT[2]	→	→	20A Leeds Holbeck	55A Leeds Holbeck	55A Leeds Holbeck	55A Leeds Holbeck	
46499	2MT[2]	→	→	18C Hasland	18C Hasland	17A Derby	17A Derby	10A Carnforth

No.	Class	1948	1951	1954	1957	1960	1963	1966
46500	*2MT*[2]	→	→	**18C** Hasland	**18C** Hasland	**17A** Derby	**17A** Derby	**8L** Aintree
46501	*2MT*[2]	→	→	**16D** Mansfield	**16C** Mansfield	**16C** Mansfield	**24C** Lostock Hall	**9D** Newton Heath
46502	*2MT*[2]	→	→	**16A** Nottingham	**16A** Nottingham	**17A** Derby	**17A** Derby	**8L** Aintree
46503	*2MT*[2]	→	→	**89A** Oswestry	**89A** Oswestry	**89A** Oswestry	**89D** Oswestry	**8C** Speke Junction
46504	*2MT*[2]	→	→	**89A** Oswestry	**89A** Oswestry	**89A** Oswestry	**89D** Oswestry	**9K** Bolton
46505	*2MT*[2]	→	→	**89A** Oswestry	**89A** Oswestry	**89A** Oswestry	**89D** Oswestry	**2E** Saltley
46506	*2MT*[2]	→	→	**89A** Oswestry	**82B** St. Philips Marsh	**89A** Oswestry	**84F** Stourbridge	**9K** Bolton
46507	*2MT*[2]	→	→	**89A** Oswestry	**89A** Oswestry	**89A** Oswestry	**89D** Oswestry	
46508	*2MT*[2]	→	→	**89A** Oswestry	**89B** Brecon	**89A** Oswestry	**89D** Oswestry	**6C** Croes Newydd
46509	*2MT*[2]	→	→	**89A** Oswestry	**89A** Oswestry	**89A** Oswestry	**89D** Oswestry	**2A** Tyseley
46510	*2MT*[2]	→	→	**89A** Oswestry	**89A** Oswestry	**89A** Oswestry	**89D** Oswestry	
46511	*2MT*[2]	→	→	**89A** Oswestry	**89A** Oswestry	**89A** Oswestry	**89D** Oswestry	
46512	*2MT*[2]	→	→	**89A** Oswestry	**89A** Oswestry	**89A** Oswestry	**89D** Oswestry	**5E** Nuneaton
46513	*2MT*[2]	→	→	**89A** Oswestry	**89A** Oswestry	**89A** Oswestry	**89D** Oswestry	**12B** Carlisle Upperby
46514	*2MT*[2]	→	→	**89A** Oswestry	**89A** Oswestry	**89A** Oswestry	**89D** Oswestry	**10J** Lancaster
46515	*2MT*[2]	→	→	**89A** Oswestry	**89A** Oswestry	**89A** Oswestry	**89D** Oswestry	**8C** Speke Junction
46516	*2MT*[2]	→	→	**89B** Brecon	**89B** Brecon	**89A** Oswestry	**89D** Oswestry	**8C** Speke Junction
46517	*2MT*[2]	→	→	**89B** Brecon	**89B** Brecon	**82B** St. Philips Marsh	**84F** Stourbridge	**8F** Wigan Springs Branch
46518	*2MT*[2]	→	→	**89B** Brecon	**89B** Brecon	**89A** Oswestry	**89D** Oswestry	**8C** Speke Junction
46519	*2MT*[2]	→	→	**89A** Oswestry	**89A** Oswestry	**89A** Oswestry	**89D** Oswestry	**5E** Nuneaton
46520	*2MT*[2]	→	→	**89A** Oswestry	**89A** Oswestry	**89A** Oswestry	**89D** Oswestry	**5E** Nuneaton
46521	*2MT*[2]	→	→	**89B** Brecon	**89B** Brecon	**89A** Oswestry	**89D** Oswestry	**6F** Machynlleth
46522	*2MT*[2]	→	→	**89B** Brecon	**89B** Brecon	**89A** Oswestry	**89D** Oswestry	**2F** Bescot
46523	*2MT*[2]	→	→	**89B** Brecon	**89A** Oswestry	**89A** Oswestry	**89D** Oswestry	**8L** Aintree
46524	*2MT*[2]	→	→	**89B** Brecon	**89B** Brecon	**89A** Oswestry	**89D** Oswestry	
46525	*2MT*[2]	→	→	**82B** St. Philips Marsh	**82B** St. Philips Marsh	**82B** St. Philips Marsh	**89D** Oswestry	
46526	*2MT*[2]	→	→	**82B** St. Philips Marsh	**89A** Oswestry	**89A** Oswestry	**89D** Oswestry	**2E** Saltley
46527	*2MT*[2]	→	→	**82B** St. Philips Marsh	**82A** Bristol Bath Road	**89A** Oswestry	**89D** Oswestry	
46601	*1P*[1]	**4A** Shrewsbury	**4A** Bletchley					
46603	*1P*[1]	**8B** Warrington Dallam	**8B** Warrington Dallam					
46604	*1P*[1]	**2B** Bletchley	**7A** Llandudno Junction	**2A** Rugby				
46605	*1P*[1]	**5A** Crewe North						
46616	*1P*[1]	**2C** Northampton	**9D** Buxton	**87K** Swansea Victoria				
46620	*1P*[1]	**4B** Swansea Victoria	**87K** Swansea Victoria					
46628	*1P*[1]	**10E** Sutton Oak	**10E** Sutton Oak					
46632	*1P*[1]	**7D** Rhyl						
46635	*1P*[1]	**12G** Dumfries						
46637	*1P*[1]	**10E** Sutton Oak						
46639	*1P*[1]	**12G** Dumfries						
46643	*1P*[1]	**7B** Bangor	**10E** Sutton Oak					
46654	*1P*[1]	**3B** Bushbury	**8B** Warrington Dallam					
46656	*1P*[1]	**27C** Hamilton	**68D** Beattock					
46658	*1P*[1]	**7D** Rhyl						
46661	*1P*[1]	**3C** Walsall						
46663	*1P*[1]	**8B** Warrington Dallam						
46666	*1P*[1]	**2C** Northampton	**4B** Northampton	**2E** Northampton				
46669	*1P*[1]	**2E** Warwick						
46673	*1P*[1]	**2E** Warwick						
46676	*1P*[1]	**10E** Sutton Oak						
46679	*1P*[1]	**3C** Walsall						
46680	*1P*[1]	**5A** Crewe North	**5A** Crewe North					
46681	*1P*[1]	**7A** Llandudno Junction						
46682	*1P*[1]	**10E** Sutton Oak						
46683	*1P*[1]	**2E** Warwick	**2C** Warwick					
46686	*1P*[1]	**1C** Watford						
46687	*1P*[1]	**7D** Rhyl						
46688	*1P*[1]	**8B** Warrington Dallam	**8B** Warrington Dallam					
46691	*1P*[1]	**7D** Rhyl						
46692	*1P*[1]	**10E** Sutton Oak						
46701	*1P*[1]	**7D** Rhyl	**8B** Warrington Dallam					
46710	*1P*[1]	**8B** Warrington Dallam						
46711	*1P*[1]	**5A** Crewe North						
46712	*1P*[1]	**7D** Rhyl	**3C** Walsall	**3C** Walsall				
46718	*1P*[1]	**8B** Warrington Dallam						
46727	*1P*[1]	**7D** Rhyl	**8B** Warrington Dallam					
46738	*1P*[1]	**9D** Buxton						
46740	*1P*[1]	**4B** Swansea Victoria						
46742	*1P*[1]	**2C** Northampton						
46747	*1P*[1]	**7A** Llandudno Junction						
46749	*1P*[1]	**2E** Warwick	**2C** Warwick					
46757	*1P*[1]	**3C** Walsall	**10E** Sutton Oak					
46762	*2P*[6]	**10B** Preston	**10B** Preston					
46876	*2P*[7]	**5C** Stafford						
46878	*2P*[7]	**3E** Monument Lane						
46881	*2P*[7]	**3B** Bushbury						
46883	*2P*[7]	**12B** Carlisle Upperby						
46899	*2P*[7]	**7C** Holyhead	**7B** Bangor					
46900	*2P*[7]	**8A** Edge Hill	**3E** Monument Lane					
46906	*2P*[7]	**8B** Warrington Dallam	**7B** Bangor					
46909	*2P*[7]	**2B** Bletchley						
46912	*2P*[7]	**2B** Bletchley	**3E** Monument Lane					
46917	*2P*[7]	**8A** Edge Hill						
46920	*2P*[7]	**8B** Warrington Dallam						
46922	*2P*[7]	**3E** Monument Lane	**3E** Monument Lane					
46924	*2P*[7]	**8B** Warrington Dallam						
46926	*2P*[7]	**7B** Bangor						
46931	*2P*[7]	**3B** Bushbury						
47000	*0F*[3]	**17B** Burton	**17B** Burton	**17D** Rowsley	**17D** Rowsley	**17A** Derby	**17A** Derby	**16C** Derby
47001	*0F*[3]	**23A** Bank Hall	**27A** Bank Hall	**27A** Bank Hall	**27A** Bank Hall	**27A** Bank Hall	**27A** Bank Hall	**41J** Langwith Junction
47002	*0F*[3]	**23A** Bank Hall	**27A** Bank Hall	**27A** Bank Hall	**27A** Bank Hall	**27A** Bank Hall	**24C** Lostock Hall	
47003	*0F*[3]	**18C** Hasland	**18C** Hasland	**18C** Hasland	**18C** Hasland	**18C** Hasland	**18C** Hasland	
47004	*0F*[3]	**18C** Hasland	**18C** Hasland	**18C** Hasland	**18C** Hasland	**18C** Hasland	**18C** Hasland	
47005	*0F*[3]	→	→	**6C** Birkenhead	**6C** Birkenhead	**6C** Birkenhead	**6C** Birkenhead	**41J** Langwith Junction
47006	*0F*[3]	→	→	**6C** Birkenhead	**6C** Birkenhead	**17A** Derby	**17A** Derby	**16C** Derby
47007	*0F*[3]	→	→	**6C** Birkenhead	**1D** Devons Road	**17C** Rowsley	**17C** Rowsley	
47008	*0F*[3]	→	→	**10B** Preston	**10B** Preston	**24K** Preston	**24C** Lostock Hall	
47009	*0F*[3]	→	→	→	**6C** Birkenhead	**6C** Birkenhead	**6C** Birkenhead	
47160	*2F*[1]	**6C** Birkenhead	**6C** Birkenhead	**6F** Bidston	**6F** Bidston	**8C** Speke Junction	**6F** Bidston	
47161	*2F*[1]	**24F** Fleetwood	**28B** Fleetwood	**24F** Fleetwood	**24F** Fleetwood	**24F** Fleetwood	**24F** Fleetwood	
47162	*2F*[1]	**28B** Dalry Road	**64A** St. Margarets	**64A** St. Margarets	**64A** St. Margarets			
47163	*2F*[1]	**28B** Dalry Road	**64C** Dalry Road	**64C** Dalry Road	**64C** Dalry Road	**64C** Dalry Road		
47164	*2F*[1]	**6C** Birkenhead	**6C** Birkenhead	**6F** Bidston	**1D** Devons Road	**8C** Speke Junction	**6F** Bidston	
47165	*2F*[1]	**24F** Fleetwood	**28B** Fleetwood	**24F** Fleetwood	**24F** Fleetwood	**24F** Fleetwood	**26C** Bolton	
47166	*2F*[1]	**6C** Birkenhead	**6C** Birkenhead	**6F** Bidston	**6F** Bidston	**6F** Bidston	**8A** Edge Hill	
47167	*2F*[1]	**27B** Greenock Ladyburn	**66D** Greenock Ladyburn	**66D** Greenock Ladyburn	**66D** Greenock Ladyburn	**66D** Greenock Ladyburn		
47168	*2F*[1]	**27B** Greenock Ladyburn	**66D** Greenock Ladyburn	**66D** Greenock Ladyburn	**66D** Greenock Ladyburn	**66D** Greenock Ladyburn		
47169	*2F*[1]	**27B** Greenock Ladyburn	**66D** Greenock Ladyburn	**66D** Greenock Ladyburn	**66D** Greenock Ladyburn			
47180	*Sentinel*[1]	**10E** Sutton Oak	**10E** Sutton Oak					
47181	*Sentinel*[1]	**4A** Shrewsbury	**10E** Sutton Oak	**10E** Sutton Oak				
47182	*Sentinel*[1]	**30D** Ayr	**67C** Ayr	**67C** Ayr				
47183	*Sentinel*[1]	**10E** Sutton Oak	**84G** Shrewsbury	**84G** Shrewsbury				
47184	*Sentinel*[2]	**10E** Sutton Oak	**6E** Wrexham Rhosddu	**5B** Crewe South				
47190	*Sentinel*[3]	**22A** Bristol Barrow Road	**22A** Bristol Barrow Road	**71G** Bath Green Park	**71G** Bath Green Park	**82F** Bath Green Park		
47191	*Sentinel*[3]	**22C** Bath Green Park	**71G** Bath Green Park	**71G** Bath Green Park	**71G** Bath Green Park			

No.	Class	1948	1951	1954	1957	1960	1963	1966
47200	3F[5]	14A Cricklewood	14B Kentish Town	14B Kentish Town	14B Kentish Town	14B Kentish Town		
47201	3F[5]	14A Cricklewood	23C Lancaster	11E Lancaster	11E Lancaster	24A Accrington	24B Rose Grove	10G Skipton
47202	3F[5]	16B Spital Bridge	14B Kentish Town	14B Kentish Town	14B Kentish Town	14B Kentish Town	14A Cricklewood	9J Agecroft
47203	3F[5]	14A Cricklewood	14A Cricklewood	14A Cricklewood	14A Cricklewood	14B Kentish Town		
47204	3F[5]	14A Cricklewood	14A Cricklewood	14B Kentish Town	14B Kentish Town	14B Kentish Town		
47205	3F[5]	14A Cricklewood	14A Cricklewood	14B Kentish Town	14B Kentish Town			
47206	3F[5]	14A Cricklewood	14A Cricklewood	14A Cricklewood	14A Cricklewood			
47207	3F[5]	14A Cricklewood	14A Cricklewood	14A Cricklewood	14A Cricklewood	26A Newton Heath	26A Newton Heath	
47208	3F[5]	14A Cricklewood	14A Cricklewood	14A Cricklewood	15A Wellingborough			
47209	3F[5]	14A Cricklewood	14A Cricklewood	14A Cricklewood	14B Kentish Town	14B Kentish Town		
47210	3F[5]	14A Cricklewood	14A Cricklewood	14A Cricklewood	14A Cricklewood			
47211	3F[5]	14A Cricklewood	14A Cricklewood	14A Cricklewood	14A Cricklewood	14A Cricklewood	9G Gorton	
47212	3F[5]	14A Cricklewood	14A Cricklewood	14A Cricklewood	14B Kentish Town	14B Kentish Town		
47213	3F[5]	14A Cricklewood	14A Cricklewood	14A Cricklewood	14A Cricklewood	14A Cricklewood		
47214	3F[5]	14A Cricklewood	14A Cricklewood	14A Cricklewood	14A Cricklewood			
47215	3F[5]	14A Cricklewood	14A Cricklewood	14A Cricklewood				
47216	3F[5]	14A Cricklewood	14A Cricklewood	14A Cricklewood	14A Cricklewood			
47217	3F[5]	14A Cricklewood	14A Cricklewood	14A Cricklewood	14A Cricklewood	26A Newton Heath		
47218	3F[5]	14A Cricklewood	14A Cricklewood	14A Cricklewood	18C Hasland	18C Hasland		
47219	3F[5]	14A Cricklewood	14A Cricklewood	14A Cricklewood	14A Cricklewood			
47220	3F[5]	14A Cricklewood	14A Cricklewood	14A Cricklewood				
47221	3F[5]	14A Cricklewood	14A Cricklewood	14A Cricklewood	18D Staveley Barrow Hill	41E Staveley Barrow Hill		
47222	3F[5]	14A Cricklewood	20E Manningham	20E Manningham	55F Manningham			
47223	3F[5]	14A Cricklewood	15D Bedford	15D Bedford	18A Toton	14A Cricklewood	14A Cricklewood	
47224	3F[5]	14A Cricklewood	14A Cricklewood	14A Cricklewood	14A Cricklewood	26B Agecroft		
47225	3F[5]	14A Cricklewood	14A Cricklewood	21A Saltley	21A Saltley	27E Walton on the Hill	27E Walton on the Hill	
47226	3F[5]	14A Cricklewood	14A Cricklewood	14A Cricklewood	14A Cricklewood			
47227	3F[5]	14A Cricklewood	14A Cricklewood	15C Leicester Midland	15C Leicester Midland			
47228	3F[5]	14A Cricklewood	14A Cricklewood	19A Sheffield Grimesthorpe	19A Sheffield Grimesthorpe	27E Walton on the Hill	27E Walton on the Hill	
47229	3F[5]	14B Kentish Town	14B Kentish Town	14B Kentish Town	14B Kentish Town	14B Kentish Town		
47230	3F[5]	4C Upper Bank	87K Swansea Victoria	87K Swansea Victoria	87K Swansea Victoria	27A Bank Hall	26B Agecroft	
47231	3F[5]	17B Burton	17B Burton	17B Burton	17B Burton	15C Leicester Midland	18A Toton	16G Westhouses
47232	3F[5]	4C Upper Bank	87K Swansea Victoria	87K Swansea Victoria				
47233	3F[5]	17B Burton	17B Burton	17B Burton				
47234	3F[5]	21C Bromsgrove	21C Bromsgrove	18A Toton	18A Toton			
47235	3F[5]	19A Sheffield Grimesthorpe	19A Sheffield Grimesthorpe	19A Sheffield Grimesthorpe	19A Sheffield Grimesthorpe	27E Walton on the Hill		
47236	3F[5]	19A Sheffield Grimesthorpe	19A Sheffield Grimesthorpe	19A Sheffield Grimesthorpe	17B Burton	17B Burton	17A Derby	
47237	3F[5]	22B Gloucester Barnwood	22B Gloucester Barnwood	22B Gloucester Barnwood				
47238	3F[5]	15A Wellingborough	15A Wellingborough	19C Canklow	19C Canklow	24G Skipton		
47239	3F[5]	20B Stourton	20D Normanton	20D Normanton	55E Normanton	50A York		
47240	3F[5]	14A Cricklewood	14A Cricklewood	14A Cricklewood	14A Cricklewood			
47241	3F[5]	14B Kentish Town	14B Kentish Town	14B Kentish Town	14B Kentish Town	14B Kentish Town		
47242	3F[5]	14B Kentish Town	14B Kentish Town	14B Kentish Town	14B Kentish Town			
47243	3F[5]	14A Cricklewood	14A Cricklewood	14B Kentish Town	14B Kentish Town			
47244	3F[5]	14B Kentish Town	14B Kentish Town	14B Kentish Town				
47245	3F[5]	14B Kentish Town	14B Kentish Town	14B Kentish Town				
47246	3F[5]	14B Kentish Town	14B Kentish Town	14B Kentish Town	14B Kentish Town			
47247	3F[5]	18A Toton	18A Toton	18D Staveley Barrow Hill	18A Toton			
47248	3F[5]	14A Cricklewood	14A Cricklewood	14A Cricklewood	14A Cricklewood	14A Cricklewood	9G Gorton	
47249	3F[5]	18A Toton	20B Stourton	20B Stourton	55B Stourton			
47250	3F[5]	14A Cricklewood	17A Derby	17A Derby	17A Derby	15C Leicester Midland	18B Westhouses	
47251	3F[5]	14A Cricklewood	14A Cricklewood	14A Cricklewood	14A Cricklewood			
47252	3F[5]	15D Bedford	15D Bedford	15D Bedford				
47253	3F[5]	17B Burton	17B Burton	17B Burton				
47254	3F[5]	20A Leeds Holbeck	20A Leeds Holbeck	20A Leeds Holbeck	55A Leeds Holbeck	50A York		
47255	3F[5]	20E Manningham	20E Manningham	20E Manningham	55F Manningham	56F Low Moor		
47256	3F[5]	4C Upper Bank	87K Swansea Victoria	87K Swansea Victoria				
47257	3F[5]	17B Burton	17B Burton	21C Bromsgrove	17B Burton	15C Leicester Midland	15A Wellingborough	
47258	3F[5]	4C Upper Bank	87K Swansea Victoria	87K Swansea Victoria	87K Swansea Victoria			
47259	3F[5]	4C Upper Bank	87K Swansea Victoria	87K Swansea Victoria	87K Swansea Victoria	27B Aintree		
47260	3F[6]	14B Kentish Town	14B Kentish Town	14B Kentish Town	14B Kentish Town	14B Kentish Town		
47261	3F[6]	14C St. Albans	14C St. Albans	14C St. Albans	14C St. Albans	14C St. Albans		
47262	3F[6]	14B Kentish Town	14B Kentish Town	33A Plaistow	33A Plaistow	33B Tilbury		
47263	3F[6]	14B Kentish Town	18D Staveley Barrow Hill	18D Staveley Barrow Hill	18D Staveley Barrow Hill	41E Staveley Barrow Hill		
47264	3F[6]	15A Wellingborough	15A Wellingborough	15A Wellingborough	15D Bedford	14E Bedford	14E Bedford	
47265	3F[6]	15A Wellingborough	15A Wellingborough	15A Wellingborough	15A Wellingborough	15A Wellingborough		
47266	3F[6]	5B Crewe South	5B Crewe South	5B Crewe South	56E Sowerby Bridge	56D Mirfield	56A Wakefield	6J Holyhead
47267	3F[6]	9A Longsight	9A Longsight	9A Longsight	9A Longsight	6H Bangor	6H Bangor	
47268	3F[6]	8B Warrington Dallam	8B Warrington Dallam	8B Warrington Dallam	8B Warrington Dallam	8B Warrington Dallam		
47269	3F[6]	16B Spital Bridge	35C Spital Bridge	2A Rugby	2A Rugby	6B Mold Junction		
47270	3F[6]	16B Spital Bridge	35C Spital Bridge	5D Stoke	5D Stoke	5D Stoke		
47271	3F[6]	20B Stourton	20B Stourton	20B Stourton	55B Stourton	56A Wakefield		
47272	3F[6]	18C Hasland	18C Hasland	18C Hasland	18C Hasland	18C Hasland	18C Hasland	8H Birkenhead
47273	3F[6]	21A Saltley	15A Wellingborough	15A Wellingborough	15A Wellingborough	15A Wellingborough	15A Wellingborough	5D Stoke
47274	3F[6]	15C Leicester Midland	15C Leicester Midland	15C Leicester Midland	15C Leicester Midland			
47275	3F[6]	22C Bath Green Park	71G Bath Green Park	71G Bath Green Park	71G Bath Green Park	82F Bath Green Park		
47276	3F[6]	21A Saltley	21C Bromsgrove	21C Bromsgrove	21C Bromsgrove	85F Bromsgrove	85D Bromsgrove	82F Bath Green Park
47277	3F[6]	16A Nottingham	16A Nottingham	16A Nottingham	16A Nottingham	16A Nottingham		
47278	3F[6]	18C Hasland	18C Hasland	18C Hasland	18C Hasland	18C Hasland	18C Hasland	
47279	3F[6]	15A Wellingborough	15A Wellingborough	15A Wellingborough	15A Wellingborough	14E Bedford	14E Bedford	8L Aintree
47280	3F[6]	5B Crewe South	5B Crewe South	5B Crewe South	5B Crewe South	5B Crewe South	5D Stoke	5D Stoke
47281	3F[6]	1A Willesden	5D Stoke	5D Stoke	5D Stoke	5D Stoke	12A Carlisle Kingmoor	
47282	3F[6]	14B Kentish Town	14B Kentish Town	33A Plaistow	35C Spital Bridge	30A Stratford		
47283	3F[6]	14B Kentish Town	14B Kentish Town	14B Kentish Town	14B Kentish Town	14B Kentish Town	18A Toton	
47284	3F[6]	8C Speke Junction	8C Speke Junction	8C Speke Junction	6E Wrexham Rhosddu	26F Patricroft	26A Newton Heath	
47285	3F[6]	2D Nuneaton	2B Nuneaton	2B Nuneaton	2B Nuneaton	8A Edge Hill	8A Edge Hill	
47286	3F[6]	2D Nuneaton	2B Nuneaton	2B Nuneaton	2B Nuneaton	Wolverton Works	2E Northampton	
47287	3F[6]	11B Barrow	11B Barrow	11B Barrow	11B Barrow	11A Barrow	12E Barrow	
47288	3F[6]	2B Bletchley	4A Bletchley	1E Bletchley	10D Sutton Oak	12B Carlisle Upperby	12B Carlisle Upperby	
47289	3F[6]	9B Stockport Edgeley	9B Stockport Edgeley	9B Stockport Edgeley	9B Stockport Edgeley	8A Edge Hill	8A Edge Hill	8L Aintree
47290	3F[6]	12D Workington	12D Workington	12D Workington	12C Workington	11B Workington		
47291	3F[6]	10B Preston	10B Preston	10B Preston	10B Preston			
47292	3F[6]	12D Workington	12D Workington	12D Workington	12A Carlisle Upperby	12B Carlisle Upperby		
47293	3F[6]	10B Preston	10B Preston	10B Preston	10B Preston	24K Preston	24C Lostock Hall	10D Lostock Hall
47294	3F[6]	5C Stafford	3A Bescot	3A Bescot	3A Bescot	3A Bescot	Wolverton Works	
47295	3F[6]	12B Carlisle Upperby	12A Carlisle Upperby	12A Carlisle Upperby	12A Carlisle Upperby	12B Carlisle Upperby	12B Carlisle Upperby	
47296	3F[6]	10B Preston	10B Preston	3C Walsall	3C Walsall			
47297	3F[6]	6A Chester	6A Chester	6A Chester	6A Chester	6A Chester	6A Chester	
47298	3F[6]	2B Bletchley	4A Bletchley	1E Bletchley	10D Sutton Oak	8G Sutton Oak	8G Sutton Oak	8G Sutton Oak
47299	3F[6]	2C Northampton	4B Northampton	2E Northampton	56E Sowerby Bridge			
47300	3F[6]	13A Plaistow	33A Plaistow	33A Plaistow	35B Grantham	31F Spital Bridge	26A Newton Heath	
47301	3F[6]	21C Bromsgrove	21C Bromsgrove	21C Bromsgrove	26A Newton Heath			
47302	3F[6]	13B Devons Road	1D Devons Road	1D Devons Road	1D Devons Road	1A Willesden		
47303	3F[6]	21C Bromsgrove	21C Bromsgrove	21C Bromsgrove	26A Newton Heath	27A Bank Hall		
47304	3F[6]	13B Devons Road	1D Devons Road	1D Devons Road	1D Devons Road	1A Willesden		
47305	3F[6]	21C Bromsgrove	21C Bromsgrove	21C Bromsgrove	26A Newton Heath	27B Aintree	27B Aintree	
47306	3F[6]	13B Devons Road	1D Devons Road	33A Plaistow	35C Spital Bridge	30A Stratford	27A Bank Hall	
47307	3F[6]	13B Devons Road	1D Devons Road	1D Devons Road	1D Devons Road	1C Watford	1A Willesden	5D Stoke
47308	3F[6]	21C Bromsgrove	21C Bromsgrove	21C Bromsgrove	21C Bromsgrove	85F Bromsgrove	85D Bromsgrove	
47309	3F[6]	8A Edge Hill	8E Brunswick	8E Brunswick	10C Patricroft			
47310	3F[6]	13B Devons Road	1D Devons Road	1D Devons Road	1D Devons Road	8C Speke Junction		
47311	3F[6]	13A Plaistow	33A Plaistow	33A Plaistow	35C Spital Bridge	30A Stratford		
47312	3F[6]	13B Devons Road	1D Devons Road	33A Plaistow	33A Plaistow	33B Tilbury		
47313	3F[6]	21C Bromsgrove	21A Saltley	21A Saltley	21A Saltley	15C Leicester Midland	17B Burton	16F Burton

		1948	1951	1954	1957	1960	1963	1966
47314	3F^6	13B Devons Road	1D Devons Road	1D Devons Road	1D Devons Road	8C Speke Junction	8F Wigan Springs Branch	8F Wigan Springs Branch
47315	3F^6	13B Devons Road	1D Devons Road	1D Devons Road	1D Devons Road			
47316	3F^6	22C Bath Green Park	71G Bath Green Park	71G Bath Green Park	71G Bath Green Park	82F Bath Green Park		
47317	3F^6	11A Carnforth	11A Carnforth	11A Carnforth	11A Carnforth	24L Carnforth	24J Lancaster	10C Fleetwood
47318	3F^6	2C Northampton	4B Northampton	2E Northampton	2E Northampton	2E Northampton	Wolverton Works	Wolverton Works
47319	3F^6	10B Preston	10B Preston	10B Preston	10B Preston	24K Preston		
47320	3F^6	5D Stoke	8E Brunswick	8E Brunswick	8E Brunswick	27F Brunswick	16A Nottingham	
47321	3F^6	7C Holyhead	7C Holyhead	6J Holyhead	6J Holyhead	6J Holyhead	6J Holyhead	
47322	3F^6	11B Barrow	11B Barrow	11B Barrow	11B Barrow	11A Barrow	24L Carnforth	
47323	3F^6	11B Barrow	11B Barrow	11B Barrow	11B Barrow	11A Barrow		
47324	3F^6	6C Birkenhead	6C Birkenhead	6C Birkenhead	6C Birkenhead	6C Birkenhead	6C Birkenhead	8H Birkenhead
47325	3F^6	8A Edge Hill	8A Edge Hill	8A Edge Hill	8E Brunswick	27F Brunswick	17A Derby	
47326	3F^6	12B Carlisle Upperby	12A Carlisle Upperby	12A Carlisle Upperby	12A Carlisle Upperby	12B Carlisle Upperby	12B Carlisle Upperby	12A Carlisle Kingmoor
47327	3F^6	1A Willesden	8E Brunswick	8E Brunswick	8E Brunswick	27F Brunswick	27A Bank Hall	8L Aintree
47328	3F^6	13A Plaistow	33A Plaistow	33A Plaistow	33A Plaistow	33B Tilbury		
47329	3F^6	30A Corkerhill	67A Corkerhill	67A Corkerhill	67A Corkerhill			
47330	3F^6	5B Crewe South	5B Crewe South	5B Crewe South	5B Crewe South	5B Crewe South	5B Crewe South	
47331	3F^6	27A Polmadie	66A Polmadie	66A Polmadie	66C Hamilton			
47332	3F^6	27A Polmadie	66A Polmadie	66A Polmadie	68A Carlisle Kingmoor	12A Carlisle Kingmoor		
47333	3F^6	15A Wellingborough	15A Wellingborough	15A Wellingborough	22A Bristol Barrow Road	82E Bristol Barrow Road	24B Rose Grove	
47334	3F^6	20D Normanton	20D Normanton	20D Normanton	55E Normanton	50A York		
47335	3F^6	20D Normanton	20D Normanton	20D Normanton	55E Normanton	56D Mirfield		
47336	3F^6	19E Belle Vue	26G Belle Vue	26G Belle Vue	39A Gorton	8A Edge Hill	8A Edge Hill	10D Lostock Hall
47337	3F^6	12E Moor Row	12E Moor Row	12E Moor Row	12C Workington			
47338	3F^6	5D Stoke	5D Stoke	5B Crewe South	2D Coventry	6C Birkenhead	5B Crewe South	
47339	3F^6	11A Carnforth	11A Carnforth	11A Carnforth	11A Carnforth			
47340	3F^6	12B Carlisle Upperby	12A Carlisle Upperby	12A Carlisle Upperby	12A Carlisle Upperby	12B Carlisle Upperby		
47341	3F^6	9A Longsight	9A Longsight	9A Longsight	9A Longsight	9A Longsight	1A Willesden	Wolverton Works
47342	3F^6	1A Willesden	1A Willesden	1A Willesden	1A Willesden	12B Carlisle Upperby		
47343	3F^6	9A Longsight	9A Longsight	9A Longsight	9A Longsight	6F Bidston	6F Bidston	
47344	3F^6	5B Crewe South	5B Crewe South	5D Stoke	5D Stoke	5D Stoke	12F Workington	
47345	3F^6	9A Longsight	9A Longsight	9A Longsight	9A Longsight	11A Barrow	12B Carlisle Upperby	
47346	3F^6	9B Stockport Edgeley	9B Stockport Edgeley	9B Stockport Edgeley	9B Stockport Edgeley			
47347	3F^6	9A Longsight	9A Longsight	9A Longsight	9A Longsight	24J Lancaster		
47348	3F^6	13B Devons Road	1D Devons Road	1D Devons Road	1D Devons Road	1E Bletchley		
47349	3F^6	13B Devons Road	1D Devons Road	1D Devons Road	1D Devons Road	3A Bescot	8D Widnes	
47350	3F^6	13B Devons Road	1D Devons Road	1B Camden	6K Rhyl	6K Rhyl	6K Rhyl	
47351	3F^6	13A Plaistow	33A Plaistow	33A Plaistow	33A Plaistow	33B Tilbury		
47352	3F^6	8B Warrington Dallam	8B Warrington Dallam	8B Warrington Dallam	8B Warrington Dallam	8B Warrington Dallam		
47353	3F^6	6B Mold Junction	8A Edge Hill	8A Edge Hill	8A Edge Hill	8A Edge Hill		
47354	3F^6	1B Camden	1B Camden	1B Camden	1B Camden	3A Bescot	5B Crewe South	
47355	3F^6	1A Willesden	1C Watford	1C Watford	1C Watford	1C Watford	1C Watford	
47356	3F^6	1B Camden	1B Camden	1B Camden	1B Camden	11A Barrow		
47357	3F^6	1A Willesden	8A Edge Hill	8A Edge Hill	8A Edge Hill	8A Edge Hill	8A Edge Hill	8A Edge Hill
47358	3F^6	1B Camden	1B Camden	1B Camden	1B Camden	12A Carlisle Kingmoor		
47359	3F^6	1B Camden	1B Camden	1B Camden	5C Stafford	5C Stafford	5C Stafford	
47360	3F^6	2A Rugby	2A Rugby	10B Preston	10B Preston	24K Preston	24C Lostock Hall	
47361	3F^6	1A Willesden	1A Willesden	1A Willesden	1A Willesden	11B Workington	6G Llandudno Junction	
47362	3F^6	1A Willesden	8C Speke Junction	8B Warrington Dallam	8B Warrington Dallam	8B Warrington Dallam	8B Warrington Dallam	
47363	3F^6	3D Aston	3D Aston	3B Bushbury	3B Bushbury			
47364	3F^6	3D Aston	3D Aston	10C Patricroft	10C Patricroft			
47365	3F^6	3D Aston	3D Aston	10C Patricroft	10C Patricroft	26F Patricroft	26F Patricroft	
47366	3F^6	3D Aston	3D Aston	10E Sutton Oak	10D Sutton Oak	8G Sutton Oak		
47367	3F^6	2D Nuneaton	2B Nuneaton	2B Nuneaton	8E Brunswick	27F Brunswick	18A Toton	8L Aintree
47368	3F^6	7C Holyhead	7C Holyhead	6J Holyhead	6J Holyhead	6J Holyhead	6J Holyhead	
47369	3F^6	9A Longsight	9A Longsight	9A Longsight	9A Longsight	24J Lancaster		
47370	3F^6	5D Stoke	5D Stoke	5D Stoke	5D Stoke			
47371	3F^6	6B Mold Junction	6B Mold Junction	6B Mold Junction	6B Mold Junction	6A Chester	6A Chester	
47372	3F^6	6B Mold Junction	6B Mold Junction	6B Mold Junction	6B Mold Junction	6C Birkenhead	6C Birkenhead	
47373	3F^6	6A Chester	8C Speke Junction	8C Speke Junction	11A Carnforth	11A Barrow	12F Workington	12D Workington
47374	3F^6	6A Chester	6A Chester	6A Chester	6A Chester	6A Chester		
47375	3F^6	6A Chester	6A Chester	6A Chester	6A Chester	6A Chester	24J Lancaster	
47376	3F^6	8B Warrington Dallam	8B Warrington Dallam	8B Warrington Dallam	8B Warrington Dallam	8G Sutton Oak		
47377	3F^6	12B Carlisle Upperby	12A Carlisle Upperby	12A Carlisle Upperby	12A Carlisle Upperby	12B Carlisle Upperby	12B Carlisle Upperby	8G Sutton Oak
47378	3F^6	2A Rugby	2A Rugby	1A Willesden	1A Willesden	26F Patricroft	26F Patricroft	
47379	3F^6	2A Rugby	2A Rugby	2A Rugby	56E Sowerby Bridge	56E Sowerby Bridge	56A Wakefield	
47380	3F^6	1A Willesden	1A Willesden	1A Willesden	1A Willesden	1A Willesden	Crewe Works	
47381	3F^6	20H Lancaster	23C Lancaster	11E Lancaster	11E Lancaster	24J Lancaster		
47382	3F^6	3A Bescot	3A Bescot	3A Bescot	3A Bescot			
47383	3F^6	6A Chester	6A Chester	6A Chester	6A Chester	6A Chester	12C Carlisle Canal	10F Rose Grove
47384	3F^6	5B Crewe South	5B Crewe South	5B Crewe South	5B Crewe South	5B Crewe South	5B Crewe South	Crewe Works
47385	3F^6	8A Edge Hill	8A Edge Hill	8A Edge Hill	8A Edge Hill	3A Bescot	Wolverton Works	
47386	3F^6	24B Rose Grove	24B Rose Grove	24B Rose Grove	24B Rose Grove	24B Rose Grove	24C Lostock Hall	
47387	3F^6	8B Warrington Dallam	8B Warrington Dallam	8B Warrington Dallam	8B Warrington Dallam			
47388	3F^6	8C Speke Junction	8C Speke Junction	8C Speke Junction	8C Speke Junction	8C Speke Junction	12C Carlisle Canal	9D Newton Heath
47389	3F^6	6C Birkenhead	6A Chester	6A Chester	6A Chester	6A Chester	6A Chester	6A Chester
47390	3F^6	12E Moor Row	12E Moor Row	12E Moor Row	12C Workington	11B Workington	12F Workington	
47391	3F^6	12B Carlisle Upperby	12A Carlisle Upperby	12A Carlisle Upperby	12A Carlisle Upperby	5B Crewe South	5B Crewe South	5B Crewe South
47392	3F^6	5E Alsager	8A Edge Hill	8A Edge Hill	8A Edge Hill	8B Warrington Dallam		
47393	3F^6	10E Sutton Oak	10E Sutton Oak	10E Sutton Oak	10D Sutton Oak	8G Sutton Oak	8G Sutton Oak	8G Sutton Oak
47394	3F^6	9A Longsight	7A Llandudno Junction	6G Llandudno Junction	6G Llandudno Junction			
47395	3F^6	1A Willesden	9A Longsight	9A Longsight	9A Longsight	9A Longsight	8F Wigan Springs Branch	
47396	3F^6	3A Bescot	3A Bescot	3A Bescot	3A Bescot	3A Bescot	2B Nuneaton	Wolverton Works
47397	3F^6	3B Bushbury	3B Bushbury	3B Bushbury	3B Bushbury	3B Bushbury	5B Crewe South	5B Crewe South
47398	3F^6	3B Bushbury	3B Bushbury	3B Bushbury	3B Bushbury	3B Bushbury		
47399	3F^6	3B Bushbury	3B Bushbury	3B Bushbury	10C Patricroft	3B Bushbury	5B Crewe South	
47400	3F^6	9A Longsight	9A Longsight	9A Longsight	9A Longsight	9A Longsight	5B Crewe South	
47401	3F^6	10D Plodder Lane	10D Plodder Lane	10D Plodder Lane	10C Patricroft	8B Warrington Dallam		
47402	3F^6	8A Edge Hill	8A Edge Hill	8A Edge Hill	8A Edge Hill	8A Edge Hill		
47403	3F^6	12B Carlisle Upperby	12A Carlisle Upperby	12A Carlisle Upperby	55G Huddersfield	50E Scarborough		
47404	3F^6	8A Edge Hill	8A Edge Hill	8A Edge Hill	8A Edge Hill	8A Edge Hill		
47405	3F^6	20D Normanton	20D Normanton	20D Normanton	55E Normanton	56F Low Moor		
47406	3F^6	11A Carnforth	11A Carnforth	11A Carnforth	11A Carnforth	24L Carnforth	12F Workington	8A Edge Hill
47407	3F^6	11A Carnforth	8A Edge Hill	8A Edge Hill	8A Edge Hill			
47408	3F^6	12B Carlisle Upperby	12A Carlisle Upperby	12A Carlisle Upperby	12A Carlisle Upperby	12B Carlisle Upperby	12B Carlisle Upperby	
47409	3F^6	11A Carnforth	11A Carnforth	11A Carnforth	11A Carnforth			
47410	3F^6	11A Carnforth	11A Carnforth	11A Carnforth	11A Carnforth	24L Carnforth	6B Mold Junction	6J Holyhead
47411	3F^6	13B Devons Road	1D Devons Road	8A Edge Hill	8A Edge Hill			
47412	3F^6	1A Willesden	1A Willesden	1A Willesden	1A Willesden	8A Edge Hill	8A Edge Hill	
47413	3F^6	3B Bushbury	3C Walsall	10B Preston	10B Preston	24K Preston	24C Lostock Hall	
47414	3F^6	5B Crewe South	5B Crewe South	5B Crewe South	5B Crewe South	5B Crewe South		
47415	3F^6	12B Carlisle Upperby	12A Carlisle Upperby	12A Carlisle Upperby	12A Carlisle Upperby	12B Carlisle Upperby	12B Carlisle Upperby	8A Edge Hill
47416	3F^6	5B Crewe South	8A Edge Hill	8A Edge Hill	8A Edge Hill	8A Edge Hill	8A Edge Hill	8A Edge Hill
47417	3F^6	17A Derby	17A Derby	17A Derby	22B Gloucester Barnwood	85E Gloucester Barnwood		
47418	3F^6	20A Leeds Holbeck	20A Leeds Holbeck	20A Leeds Holbeck	55A Leeds Holbeck	50A York		
47419	3F^6	20E Manningham	20E Manningham	20E Manningham	55F Manningham	55F Manningham	55C Farnley Junction	
47420	3F^6	20B Stourton	20A Leeds Holbeck	20A Leeds Holbeck	55A Leeds Holbeck	55A Leeds Holbeck		
47421	3F^6	20C Royston	20C Royston	20C Royston	55D Royston	50A York		
47422	3F^6	16A Nottingham	16A Nottingham	16A Nottingham	22B Gloucester Barnwood	85E Gloucester Barnwood		
47423	3F^6	18C Hasland	18C Hasland	18C Hasland	18C Hasland	18C Hasland	18C Hasland	
47424	3F^6	18D Staveley Barrow Hill	18D Staveley Barrow Hill	18D Staveley Barrow Hill	18D Staveley Barrow Hill	41E Staveley Barrow Hill		
47425	3F^6	21C Bromsgrove	21C Bromsgrove	21C Bromsgrove	26A Newton Heath	27B Aintree		
47426	3F^6	18C Hasland	18D Staveley Barrow Hill	18D Staveley Barrow Hill	18D Staveley Barrow Hill	41E Staveley Barrow Hill		
47427	3F^6	14B Kentish Town	23A Skipton	20F Skipton	20F Skipton	24G Skipton	24G Skipton	10G Skipton

		1948	1951	1954	1957	1960	1963	1966
47428	$3F^{6}$	**14B** Kentish Town	**14B** Kentish Town	**20F** Skipton	**20F** Skipton	**24G** Skipton	**26B** Agecroft	
47429	$3F^{6}$	**14B** Kentish Town	**14B** Kentish Town	**33A** Plaistow	**35B** Grantham	**17A** Derby	Horwich Works	
47430	$3F^{6}$	**1A** Willesden	**1A** Willesden	**10C** Patricroft	**10C** Patricroft	**26F** Patricroft	**26F** Patricroft	
47431	$3F^{6}$	**5B** Crewe South	**5B** Crewe South	**5B** Crewe South	**5B** Crewe South	**9B** Stockport Edgeley		
47432	$3F^{6}$	**14B** Kentish Town	**19A** Sheffield Grimesthorpe	**19A** Sheffield Grimesthorpe	**19A** Sheffield Grimesthorpe	**14A** Cricklewood	**14A** Cricklewood	
47433	$3F^{6}$	**14A** Cricklewood	**14A** Cricklewood	**14A** Cricklewood	**14A** Cricklewood	**14A** Cricklewood		
47434	$3F^{6}$	**14A** Cricklewood	**14A** Cricklewood	**14A** Cricklewood	**14A** Cricklewood	**14A** Cricklewood	**14A** Cricklewood	
47435	$3F^{6}$	**14A** Cricklewood	**14A** Cricklewood	**14A** Cricklewood	**14A** Cricklewood	**14A** Cricklewood	**14A** Cricklewood	Wolverton Works
47436	$3F^{6}$	**18A** Toton	**18A** Toton	**20A** Leeds Holbeck	**55A** Leeds Holbeck	**50A** York		
47437	$3F^{6}$	**15B** Kettering	**15B** Kettering	**14B** Kentish Town	**14B** Kentish Town	**14B** Kentish Town	**14A** Cricklewood	**6A** Chester
47438	$3F^{6}$	**16A** Nottingham	**16A** Nottingham	**20C** Royston	**55D** Royston	**53E** Goole		
47439	$3F^{6}$	**8C** Speke Junction	**8C** Speke Junction	**8C** Speke Junction	**6J** Holyhead	**6J** Holyhead	**6J** Holyhead	
47440	$3F^{6}$	**19E** Belle Vue	**26G** Belle Vue	**26G** Belle Vue	**26A** Newton Heath			
47441	$3F^{6}$	**15C** Leicester Midland	**15C** Leicester Midland	**15C** Leicester Midland	**15C** Leicester Midland	**15C** Leicester Midland	**17A** Derby	
47442	$3F^{6}$	**15C** Leicester Midland	**15C** Leicester Midland	**15C** Leicester Midland	**15C** Leicester Midland	**15E** Leicester Central	**18A** Toton	
47443	$3F^{6}$	**20B** Stourton	**20B** Stourton	**20B** Stourton	**55B** Stourton	**56D** Mirfield		
47444	$3F^{6}$	**5B** Crewe South	**10E** Sutton Oak	**10E** Sutton Oak	**10D** Sutton Oak	**8G** Sutton Oak	**8F** Wigan Springs Branch	**8F** Wigan Springs Branch
47445	$3F^{6}$	**5B** Crewe South	**5E** Alsager	**5E** Alsager	**5E** Alsager	**5E** Alsager	**5B** Crewe South	**5B** Crewe South
47446	$3F^{6}$	**15A** Wellingborough	**15A** Wellingborough	**15A** Wellingborough	**55E** Normanton	**56F** Low Moor		
47447	$3F^{6}$	**14A** Cricklewood	**17D** Rowsley	**17D** Rowsley	**17D** Rowsley	**17C** Rowsley	**17C** Rowsley	**8H** Birkenhead
47448	$3F^{6}$	**20C** Royston	**20C** Royston	**20C** Royston	**55D** Royston	**50A** York		
47449	$3F^{6}$	**17C** Coalville	**17C** Coalville	**17C** Coalville	**17C** Coalville	**14B** Kentish Town	**18A** Toton	
47450	$3F^{6}$	**6C** Birkenhead	**5B** Crewe South	**5B** Crewe South	**5B** Crewe South	**5B** Crewe South	**5B** Crewe South	**5B** Crewe South
47451	$3F^{6}$	**5B** Crewe South	**10E** Sutton Oak	**5D** Stoke	**5D** Stoke	**5D** Stoke	**5C** Stafford	
47452	$3F^{6}$	**2B** Bletchley	**4A** Bletchley	**1E** Bletchley	**10D** Sutton Oak	**8G** Sutton Oak	**8G** Sutton Oak	
47453	$3F^{6}$	**10E** Sutton Oak	**10E** Sutton Oak	**10E** Sutton Oak	**10D** Sutton Oak	**8G** Sutton Oak	**8G** Sutton Oak	**8L** Aintree
47454	$3F^{6}$	**18A** Toton	**18A** Toton	**20F** Skipton	**20F** Skipton	**24G** Skipton	**24G** Skipton	
47455	$3F^{6}$	**18D** Staveley Barrow Hill	**18D** Staveley Barrow Hill	**18D** Staveley Barrow Hill	**18D** Staveley Barrow Hill	**41E** Staveley Barrow Hill		
47457	$3F^{6}$	**17D** Rowsley	**17D** Rowsley	**17D** Rowsley	**17D** Rowsley	**17C** Rowsley		
47458	$3F^{6}$	**13A** Plaistow	**33A** Plaistow	**33A** Plaistow	**35B** Grantham	**17B** Burton	**26F** Patricroft	
47459	$3F^{6}$	**17D** Rowsley	**17D** Rowsley	**17D** Rowsley	**17D** Rowsley	**17C** Rowsley	**17C** Rowsley	
47460	$3F^{6}$	**17D** Rowsley	**17D** Rowsley	**17D** Rowsley	**17D** Rowsley	**17C** Rowsley	**17C** Rowsley	
47461	$3F^{6}$	**17D** Rowsley	**17D** Rowsley	**17D** Rowsley	**17D** Rowsley	**17C** Rowsley	**17C** Rowsley	
47462	$3F^{6}$	**20C** Royston	**20C** Royston	**20C** Royston	**55D** Royston	**53E** Goole		
47463	$3F^{6}$	**20B** Stourton	**20B** Stourton	**20B** Stourton	**55B** Stourton	**56A** Wakefield		
47464	$3F^{6}$	**17B** Burton	**17B** Burton	**17B** Burton	**17B** Burton	**17B** Burton	**17B** Burton	
47465	$3F^{6}$	**22C** Bath Green Park	**71G** Bath Green Park	**71G** Bath Green Park	**71G** Bath Green Park	**82F** Bath Green Park	**82F** Bath Green Park	
47466	$3F^{6}$	**18B** Westhouses	**18B** Westhouses	**18B** Westhouses	**18B** Westhouses	**18B** Westhouses		
47467	$3F^{6}$	**1B** Camden	**1B** Camden	**1B** Camden	**1B** Camden	**5B** Crewe South	**5B** Crewe South	
47468	$3F^{6}$	**20H** Lancaster	**23C** Lancaster	**11E** Lancaster	**11E** Lancaster	**24J** Lancaster	**24J** Lancaster	
47469	$3F^{6}$	**20H** Lancaster	**23C** Lancaster	**11E** Lancaster	**11E** Lancaster	**24J** Lancaster	**24J** Lancaster	
47470	$3F^{6}$	**20H** Lancaster	**23C** Lancaster	**11E** Lancaster	**11E** Lancaster	**24J** Lancaster		
47471	$3F^{6}$	**20H** Lancaster	**23C** Lancaster	**11E** Lancaster	**11E** Lancaster	**24J** Lancaster	**12A** Carlisle Kingmoor	**12A** Carlisle Kingmoor
47472	$3F^{6}$	**6C** Birkenhead	**6C** Birkenhead	**10B** Preston	**10B** Preston	**24K** Preston	**24C** Lostock Hall	**10D** Lostock Hall
47473	$3F^{6}$	**3B** Bushbury	**3B** Bushbury	**3B** Bushbury	**3B** Bushbury	**3B** Bushbury		
47474	$3F^{6}$	**1A** Willesden	**1A** Willesden	**1A** Willesden	**1A** Willesden	**3E** Monument Lane		
47475	$3F^{6}$	**1A** Willesden	**1A** Willesden	**1A** Willesden	**1A** Willesden	**5C** Stafford		
47476	$3F^{6}$	**7C** Holyhead	**7C** Holyhead	**6J** Holyhead	**6J** Holyhead	**6J** Holyhead	**6J** Holyhead	
47477	$3F^{6}$	**4C** Upper Bank	**87K** Swansea Victoria	**87K** Swansea Victoria	**87K** Swansea Victoria			
47478	$3F^{6}$	**4C** Upper Bank	**87K** Swansea Victoria	**87K** Swansea Victoria	**87K** Swansea Victoria	Wolverton Works	**2B** Nuneaton	
47479	$3F^{6}$	**4C** Upper Bank	**87K** Swansea Victoria	**87K** Swansea Victoria	**87K** Swansea Victoria	Wolverton Works		
47480	$3F^{6}$	**4C** Upper Bank	**87K** Swansea Victoria	**87K** Swansea Victoria	**87K** Swansea Victoria	**27A** Bank Hall	**27B** Aintree	
47481	$3F^{6}$	**4C** Upper Bank	**87K** Swansea Victoria	**87K** Swansea Victoria	**87K** Swansea Victoria	**24J** Lancaster	**24J** Lancaster	
47482	$3F^{6}$	**13B** Devons Road	**1D** Devons Road	**1D** Devons Road	**1D** Devons Road	**1A** Willesden	**5B** Crewe South	**5B** Crewe South
47483	$3F^{6}$	**13B** Devons Road	**1D** Devons Road	**1D** Devons Road	**1D** Devons Road	**1A** Willesden		
47484	$3F^{6}$	**13A** Plaistow	**33A** Plaistow	**33A** Plaistow	**33A** Plaistow	**33B** Tilbury		
47485	$3F^{6}$	**16A** Nottingham	**16A** Nottingham	**17B** Burton	**17B** Burton	**17B** Burton	**14E** Bedford	
47486	$3F^{6}$	**13B** Devons Road	**1D** Devons Road	**1D** Devons Road	**1D** Devons Road	**1A** Willesden		
47487	$3F^{6}$	**13B** Devons Road	**1D** Devons Road	**8A** Edge Hill	**8A** Edge Hill	**8A** Edge Hill	**8A** Edge Hill	
47488	$3F^{6}$	**13B** Devons Road	**1D** Devons Road	**1D** Devons Road	**1D** Devons Road	**8A** Edge Hill		
47489	$3F^{6}$	**13B** Devons Road	**1D** Devons Road	**8A** Edge Hill	**8A** Edge Hill			
47490	$3F^{6}$	**13B** Devons Road	**1D** Devons Road	**8C** Speke Junction	**8D** Widnes	**8D** Widnes	**8G** Sutton Oak	
47491	$3F^{6}$	**13B** Devons Road	**1A** Willesden	**1A** Willesden	**6E** Wrexham Rhosddu	**26F** Patricroft		
47492	$3F^{6}$	**13B** Devons Road	**1D** Devons Road	**1A** Willesden	**1A** Willesden	**12A** Carlisle Kingmoor	**12A** Carlisle Kingmoor	
47493	$3F^{6}$	**13B** Devons Road	**1D** Devons Road	**1D** Devons Road	**8C** Speke Junction	**8C** Speke Junction	**8F** Wigan Springs Branch	**8A** Edge Hill
47494	$3F^{6}$	**13B** Devons Road	**1D** Devons Road	**1D** Devons Road	**1D** Devons Road	**3E** Monument Lane	**5B** Crewe South	**5B** Crewe South
47495	$3F^{6}$	**13B** Devons Road	**1D** Devons Road	**1D** Devons Road	**1D** Devons Road	**1B** Camden	**6F** Bidston	
47496	$3F^{6}$	**22C** Bath Green Park	**71G** Bath Green Park	**71G** Bath Green Park	**71G** Bath Green Park	**82F** Bath Green Park	**82F** Bath Green Park	
47497	$3F^{6}$	**13B** Devons Road	**1D** Devons Road	**1D** Devons Road	**1D** Devons Road	**6C** Birkenhead		
47498	$3F^{6}$	**13B** Devons Road	**1D** Devons Road	**8A** Edge Hill	**8A** Edge Hill	**8A** Edge Hill		
47499	$3F^{6}$	**13B** Devons Road	**1D** Devons Road	**1D** Devons Road	**1D** Devons Road	**2E** Northampton	**2E** Northampton	
47500	$3F^{6}$	**13B** Devons Road	**1D** Devons Road	**1D** Devons Road	**1E** Bletchley	Wolverton Works	**1E** Bletchley	
47501	$3F^{6}$	**13B** Devons Road	**1D** Devons Road	**1D** Devons Road	**1D** Devons Road	**1A** Willesden	**1A** Willesden	
47502	$3F^{6}$	**13B** Devons Road	**18D** Staveley Barrow Hill	**21C** Bromsgrove	**21C** Bromsgrove	**17B** Burton	**9G** Gorton	
47503	$3F^{6}$	**11A** Carnforth	**11C** Oxenholme	**11C** Oxenholme	**11C** Oxenholme	**11A** Barrow	**12E** Barrow	
47504	$3F^{6}$	**6A** Chester	**6A** Chester	**6A** Chester	**6A** Chester	**6A** Chester		
47505	$3F^{6}$	**13B** Devons Road	**1A** Willesden	**1A** Willesden	**1A** Willesden	**11A** Barrow	**5B** Crewe South	
47506	$3F^{6}$	**13B** Devons Road	**1D** Devons Road	**1D** Devons Road	**22B** Gloucester Barnwood	**85E** Gloucester Barnwood	**85C** Gloucester Barnwood	**82F** Bath Green Park
47507	$3F^{6}$	**6C** Birkenhead	**6C** Birkenhead	**6C** Birkenhead	**6C** Birkenhead	**6C** Birkenhead	**6K** Rhyl	**6G** Llandudno Junction
47508	$3F^{6}$	**25E** Sowerby Bridge	**25E** Sowerby Bridge	**25E** Sowerby Bridge	**56E** Sowerby Bridge	**56E** Sowerby Bridge		
47509	$3F^{6}$	**25E** Sowerby Bridge	**25E** Sowerby Bridge	**25E** Sowerby Bridge	**56E** Sowerby Bridge	**56E** Sowerby Bridge		
47510	$3F^{6}$	**25E** Sowerby Bridge	**25A** Wakefield	**25A** Wakefield	**56A** Wakefield	**56A** Wakefield		
47511	$3F^{6}$	**13B** Devons Road	**1D** Devons Road	**1D** Devons Road	**1D** Devons Road	**6H** Bangor	**6H** Bangor	
47512	$3F^{6}$	**13A** Plaistow	**33A** Plaistow	**33A** Plaistow	**33A** Plaistow	**33B** Tilbury	**27B** Aintree	
47513	$3F^{6}$	**19A** Sheffield Grimesthorpe	**19A** Sheffield Grimesthorpe	**19A** Sheffield Grimesthorpe	**19A** Sheffield Grimesthorpe	**41B** Sheffield Grimesthorpe		
47514	$3F^{6}$	**13B** Devons Road	**1D** Devons Road	**1D** Devons Road	**1D** Devons Road	**1B** Camden		
47515	$3F^{6}$	**13B** Devons Road	**1D** Devons Road	**1D** Devons Road	**1D** Devons Road	**12A** Carlisle Kingmoor	**12A** Carlisle Kingmoor	
47516	$3F^{6}$	**13B** Devons Road	**1D** Devons Road	**8C** Speke Junction	**5B** Crewe South	**5B** Crewe South		
47517	$3F^{6}$	**13B** Devons Road	**1D** Devons Road	**1D** Devons Road	**1D** Devons Road	**11A** Barrow	**8F** Wigan Springs Branch	
47518	$3F^{6}$	**13B** Devons Road	**1D** Devons Road	**1D** Devons Road	**1D** Devons Road	**11A** Barrow	**5C** Stafford	
47519	$3F^{6}$	**3A** Bescot	**8A** Edge Hill	**8A** Edge Hill	**8A** Edge Hill	**8A** Edge Hill	**8A** Edge Hill	
47520	$3F^{6}$	**1A** Willesden	**1A** Willesden	**1A** Willesden	**1A** Willesden	**11A** Barrow	**12C** Carlisle Canal	
47521	$3F^{6}$	**2B** Bletchley	**4A** Bletchley	**1E** Bletchley	**1E** Bletchley	**1E** Bletchley	**1E** Bletchley	**5B** Crewe South
47522	$3F^{6}$	**1B** Camden	**1B** Camden	**1B** Camden	**1B** Camden	**1B** Camden		
47523	$3F^{6}$	**5B** Crewe South	**5B** Crewe South	**5B** Crewe South	**5B** Crewe South	**5B** Crewe South		
47524	$3F^{6}$	**5B** Crewe South	**5B** Crewe South	**5B** Crewe South	**5B** Crewe South	**5B** Crewe South	**5B** Crewe South	
47525	$3F^{6}$	**12E** Moor Row	**12E** Moor Row	**12E** Moor Row	**12C** Workington	**11B** Workington		
47526	$3F^{6}$	**5B** Crewe South	**5B** Crewe South	**5B** Crewe South	**5B** Crewe South	**5B** Crewe South		
47527	$3F^{6}$	**1B** Camden	**1B** Camden	**1B** Camden	**1B** Camden	**12A** Carlisle Kingmoor		
47528	$3F^{6}$	**9A** Longsight	**9A** Longsight	**9A** Longsight	**9A** Longsight	**9A** Longsight		
47529	$3F^{6}$	**1B** Camden	**1B** Camden	**1B** Camden	**1B** Camden	**1B** Camden		
47530	$3F^{6}$	**6C** Birkenhead	**6C** Birkenhead	**6C** Birkenhead	**6C** Birkenhead	**6C** Birkenhead	**5B** Crewe South	**5B** Crewe South
47531	$3F^{6}$	**1A** Willesden	**1A** Willesden	**1A** Willesden	**1A** Willesden	**11A** Barrow	**12E** Barrow	**12D** Workington
47532	$3F^{6}$	**20H** Lancaster	**23C** Lancaster	**11E** Lancaster	**11E** Lancaster	**24J** Lancaster	**24J** Lancaster	
47533	$3F^{6}$	**15C** Leicester Midland	**15C** Leicester Midland	**15C** Leicester Midland	**15C** Leicester Midland	**15C** Leicester Midland	**16A** Nottingham	**8H** Birkenhead
47534	$3F^{6}$	**15C** Leicester Midland	**15C** Leicester Midland	**15C** Leicester Midland	**15C** Leicester Midland	**15C** Leicester Midland	**17A** Derby	**16G** Westhouses
47535	$3F^{6}$	**18C** Hasland	**18C** Hasland	**18C** Hasland	**18C** Hasland	**18C** Hasland	**18C** Hasland	**16G** Westhouses
47536	$3F^{6}$	**27A** Polmadie	**66A** Polmadie	**66A** Polmadie	**66A** Polmadie	**66A** Polmadie		
47537	$3F^{6}$	**27A** Polmadie	**66A** Polmadie	**66A** Polmadie	**68A** Carlisle Kingmoor	**12A** Carlisle Kingmoor		
47538	$3F^{6}$	**20B** Stourton	**20B** Stourton	**20B** Stourton	**55B** Stourton			
47539	$3F^{6}$	**16A** Nottingham	**16A** Nottingham	**16A** Nottingham	**22B** Gloucester Barnwood	**85E** Gloucester Barnwood	**82F** Bath Green Park	
47540	$3F^{6}$	**27A** Polmadie	**66A** Polmadie	**66A** Polmadie	**68A** Carlisle Kingmoor	**12A** Carlisle Kingmoor		
47541	$3F^{6}$	**32A** Inverness	**66A** Polmadie	**66A** Polmadie	**66A** Polmadie	**66A** Polmadie		
47542	$3F^{6}$	**22C** Bath Green Park	**71G** Bath Green Park	**71G** Bath Green Park	**71G** Bath Green Park	**82G** Templecombe		

		1948	1951	1954	1957	1960	1963	1966
47543	$3F^{6}$	15A Wellingborough	15A Wellingborough	15A Wellingborough	15A Wellingborough	15C Leicester Midland	14A Cricklewood	
47544	$3F^{6}$	22A Bristol Barrow Road	22A Bristol Barrow Road	22A Bristol Barrow Road	22A Bristol Barrow Road	82E Bristol Barrow Road	82F Bath Green Park	
47545	$3F^{6}$	19A Sheffield Grimesthorpe	18A Toton	18D Staveley Barrow Hill	18D Staveley Barrow Hill	41E Staveley Barrow Hill		
47546	$3F^{6}$	19C Canklow	19C Canklow	19C Canklow	19C Canklow	26A Newton Heath		
47547	$3F^{6}$	19C Canklow	19C Canklow	19C Canklow	19C Canklow	26A Newton Heath	26A Newton Heath	
47548	$3F^{6}$	14A Cricklewood	19A Sheffield Grimesthorpe	19A Sheffield Grimesthorpe	19A Sheffield Grimesthorpe	41B Sheffield Grimesthorpe		
47549	$3F^{6}$	15D Bedford	15D Bedford	15D Bedford	15D Bedford	14E Bedford	14E Bedford	
47550	$3F^{6}$	22A Bristol Barrow Road	22A Bristol Barrow Road	22A Bristol Barrow Road	22A Bristol Barrow Road	27A Bank Hall	Horwich Works	
47551	$3F^{6}$	18A Toton	18A Toton	18A Toton	18A Toton	18A Toton	18A Toton	
47552	$3F^{6}$	16A Nottingham	16A Nottingham	22A Bristol Barrow Road	22A Bristol Barrow Road	82G Templecombe		
47554	$3F^{6}$	15A Wellingborough	15A Wellingborough	15A Wellingborough	14C St. Albans	14C St. Albans		
47555	$3F^{6}$	18A Toton	18A Toton	33A Plaistow	33A Plaistow	33B Tilbury		
47556	$3F^{6}$	12B Carlisle Upperby	12A Carlisle Upperby	12A Carlisle Upperby	55G Huddersfield	50A York		
47557	$3F^{6}$	22C Bath Green Park	71G Bath Green Park	71G Bath Green Park	71G Bath Green Park	82F Bath Green Park	82F Bath Green Park	
47558	$3F^{6}$	13B Devons Road	1D Devons Road	1D Devons Road	1D Devons Road	6G Llandudno Junction	6G Llandudno Junction	
47559	$3F^{6}$	13B Devons Road	1D Devons Road	1D Devons Road	1D Devons Road	1A Willesden		
47560	$3F^{6}$	13B Devons Road	1D Devons Road	1D Devons Road	1D Devons Road	8C Speke Junction		
47561	$3F^{6}$	13B Devons Road	1D Devons Road	1D Devons Road	1D Devons Road	3E Monument Lane		
47562	$3F^{6}$	13B Devons Road	23A Skipton	20F Skipton	20F Skipton	24A Accrington		
47563	$3F^{6}$	13B Devons Road	19A Sheffield Grimesthorpe	19A Sheffield Grimesthorpe	17A Derby	17A Derby		
47564	$3F^{6}$	13B Devons Road	1D Devons Road	1D Devons Road	1D Devons Road	11A Barrow	12E Barrow	
47565	$3F^{6}$	21C Bromsgrove	21C Bromsgrove	21C Bromsgrove	21C Bromsgrove	6C Birkenhead	6C Birkenhead	5B Crewe South
47566	$3F^{6}$	16B Spital Bridge	35C Spital Bridge	8E Brunswick	8A Edge Hill	8A Edge Hill	8A Edge Hill	8L Aintree
47567	$3F^{6}$	25G Farnley Junction	25G Farnley Junction	25G Farnley Junction	55C Farnley Junction	56A Wakefield		
47568	$3F^{6}$	25G Farnley Junction	25G Farnley Junction	25G Farnley Junction	55C Farnley Junction	55C Farnley Junction		
47569	$3F^{6}$	25G Farnley Junction	25G Farnley Junction	25G Farnley Junction	55C Farnley Junction	55C Farnley Junction		
47570	$3F^{6}$	25G Farnley Junction	25G Farnley Junction	25G Farnley Junction	55C Farnley Junction	55C Farnley Junction		
47571	$3F^{6}$	25G Farnley Junction	25G Farnley Junction	25G Farnley Junction	55C Farnley Junction	56A Wakefield		
47572	$3F^{6}$	26B Agecroft	25A Wakefield	25A Wakefield	56A Wakefield	56A Wakefield		
47573	$3F^{6}$	26B Agecroft	25A Wakefield	25A Wakefield	56A Wakefield	56A Wakefield		
47574	$3F^{6}$	26B Agecroft	26B Agecroft	26B Agecroft	26B Agecroft	26B Agecroft		
47575	$3F^{6}$	24B Rose Grove	24B Rose Grove	24B Rose Grove	24B Rose Grove	24B Rose Grove		
47576	$3F^{6}$	24B Rose Grove	24B Rose Grove	24B Rose Grove	24B Rose Grove	24B Rose Grove		
47577	$3F^{6}$	26E Bacup	26A Newton Heath	26A Newton Heath	24B Rose Grove	24B Rose Grove	24G Skipton	
47578	$3F^{6}$	26B Agecroft	26B Agecroft	26B Agecroft	26B Agecroft	26B Agecroft	26B Agecroft	
47579	$3F^{6}$	26B Agecroft	26B Agecroft	26B Agecroft	26B Agecroft	26B Agecroft	26B Agecroft	
47580	$3F^{6}$	26E Bacup	25A Wakefield	25A Wakefield	56A Wakefield	56D Mirfield		
47581	$3F^{6}$	20C Royston	20C Royston	20C Royston	55D Royston	53E Goole	55C Farnley Junction	
47582	$3F^{6}$	26E Bacup	25A Wakefield	25A Wakefield	56A Wakefield	56A Wakefield	26A Newton Heath	
47583	$3F^{6}$	26B Agecroft	26B Agecroft	26B Agecroft	26B Agecroft	27A Bank Hall	27A Bank Hall	
47584	$3F^{6}$	26B Agecroft	26B Agecroft	26B Agecroft	26D Bury	26D Bury	26D Bury	
47585	$3F^{6}$	26B Agecroft	26B Agecroft	26B Agecroft	26B Agecroft	26B Agecroft		
47586	$3F^{6}$	26A Newton Heath	26A Newton Heath	26A Newton Heath	24B Rose Grove	24B Rose Grove		
47587	$3F^{6}$	5D Stoke	5D Stoke	5D Stoke	5D Stoke	5D Stoke	5D Stoke	
47588	$3F^{6}$	5C Stafford	5C Stafford	5C Stafford	5C Stafford	5C Stafford		
47589	$3F^{6}$	*(France)*	20B Stourton	20B Stourton	55B Stourton	56B Ardsley	55C Farnley Junction	
47590	$3F^{6}$	5B Crewe South	5B Crewe South	5C Stafford	5C Stafford	5C Stafford	5C Stafford	5B Crewe South
47591	$3F^{6}$	8B Warrington Dallam	8B Warrington Dallam	8B Warrington Dallam	8B Warrington Dallam	8B Warrington Dallam		
47592	$3F^{6}$	Crewe Works	Crewe Works	Crewe Works	Crewe Works	Crewe Works	Crewe Works	Crewe Works
47593	$3F^{6}$	12D Workington	12D Workington	12D Workington	12C Workington	11B Workington		
47594	$3F^{6}$	2D Nuneaton	2B Nuneaton	2B Nuneaton	2B Nuneaton	8A Edge Hill	8A Edge Hill	
47595	$3F^{6}$	5E Alsager	5E Alsager	5E Alsager	5E Alsager	5E Alsager		
47596	$3F^{6}$	5D Stoke	5D Stoke	5D Stoke	5D Stoke	5D Stoke	5D Stoke	
47597	$3F^{6}$	8A Edge Hill	8A Edge Hill	8A Edge Hill	8A Edge Hill	8A Edge Hill	Crewe Works	
47598	$3F^{6}$	5C Stafford	5C Stafford	5E Alsager	5E Alsager	5E Alsager	5C Stafford	6B Mold Junction
47599	$3F^{6}$	5D Stoke	5D Stoke	5D Stoke	5D Stoke	5D Stoke	24J Lancaster	10C Fleetwood
47600	$3F^{6}$	6A Chester	6A Chester	6A Chester	6A Chester	6A Chester		
47601	$3F^{6}$	9B Stockport Edgeley	9B Stockport Edgeley	9B Stockport Edgeley	9B Stockport Edgeley	8D Widnes		
47602	$3F^{6}$	5B Crewe South	5E Alsager	5B Crewe South	12A Carlisle Upperby	12B Carlisle Upperby	12B Carlisle Upperby	10G Skipton
47603	$3F^{6}$	8A Edge Hill	8B Warrington Dallam	8B Warrington Dallam	8B Warrington Dallam	8B Warrington Dallam	8F Wigan Springs Branch	8F Wigan Springs Branch
47604	$3F^{6}$	12D Workington	12E Moor Row	12D Workington	12C Workington	11B Workington		
47605	$3F^{6}$	11A Carnforth	11A Carnforth	11A Carnforth	11B Barrow	11A Barrow		
47606	$3F^{6}$	5C Stafford	5C Stafford	5C Stafford	5C Stafford	5E Alsager	1C Watford	
47607	$3F^{6}$	*(France)*	22B Gloucester Barnwood	22B Gloucester Barnwood	55E Normanton	50A York		
47608	$3F^{6}$	5B Crewe South	5E Alsager	5E Alsager	5E Alsager	5B Crewe South		
47609	$3F^{6}$	5D Stoke	5D Stoke	5D Stoke	5D Stoke	5D Stoke	5D Stoke	
47610	$3F^{6}$	5D Stoke	5D Stoke	5D Stoke	5D Stoke	5D Stoke		
47611	$3F^{6}$	*(France)*	19A Sheffield Grimesthorpe	19A Sheffield Grimesthorpe	17B Burton	27F Brunswick	14B Kentish Town	16G Westhouses
47612	$3F^{6}$	2C Northampton	4B Northampton	2E Northampton	2E Northampton	8C Speke Junction	12F Workington	12D Workington
47614	$3F^{6}$	12B Carlisle Upperby	12A Carlisle Upperby	12A Carlisle Upperby	12A Carlisle Upperby	12B Carlisle Upperby	12B Carlisle Upperby	
47615	$3F^{6}$	6B Mold Junction	6B Mold Junction	6B Mold Junction	6B Mold Junction	6B Mold Junction	5B Crewe South	Crewe Works
47616	$3F^{6}$	5B Crewe South	5E Alsager	5B Crewe South	8D Widnes	8D Widnes	8D Widnes	
47618	$3F^{6}$	12B Carlisle Upperby	12A Carlisle Upperby	12A Carlisle Upperby	12A Carlisle Upperby	5B Crewe South	Crewe Works	
47619	$3F^{6}$	22B Gloucester Barnwood	22B Gloucester Barnwood	22B Gloucester Barnwood	18D Staveley Barrow Hill	41E Staveley Barrow Hill		
47620	$3F^{6}$	22B Gloucester Barnwood	22B Gloucester Barnwood	22B Gloucester Barnwood	18D Staveley Barrow Hill	41D Canklow		
47621	$3F^{6}$	14A Cricklewood	35C Spital Bridge	10C Patricroft	10C Patricroft	26F Patricroft		
47622	$3F^{6}$	16B Spital Bridge	35C Spital Bridge	2A Rugby	6F Bidston	6F Bidston	6F Bidston	
47623	$3F^{6}$	18A Toton	16A Nottingham	16A Nottingham	22B Gloucester Barnwood	85E Gloucester Barnwood	85C Gloucester Barnwood	
47624	$3F^{6}$	19A Sheffield Grimesthorpe	19A Sheffield Grimesthorpe	19A Sheffield Grimesthorpe	19A Sheffield Grimesthorpe	41B Sheffield Grimesthorpe		
47625	$3F^{6}$	18D Staveley Barrow Hill	18D Staveley Barrow Hill	18D Staveley Barrow Hill	18D Staveley Barrow Hill	41E Staveley Barrow Hill		
47626	$3F^{6}$	18D Staveley Barrow Hill	18D Staveley Barrow Hill	18D Staveley Barrow Hill	18D Staveley Barrow Hill	41E Staveley Barrow Hill		
47627	$3F^{6}$	18D Staveley Barrow Hill	6C Birkenhead	6F Bidston	6J Holyhead	6C Birkenhead	6C Birkenhead	8H Birkenhead
47628	$3F^{6}$	18D Staveley Barrow Hill	6C Birkenhead	6F Bidston	6F Bidston	6F Bidston	6F Bidston	
47629	$3F^{6}$	16A Nottingham	16A Nottingham	17A Derby	17A Derby	17A Derby	17C Rowsley	16F Burton
47630	$3F^{6}$	18A Toton	18A Toton	18A Toton	18D Staveley Barrow Hill	41E Staveley Barrow Hill		
47631	$3F^{6}$	16A Nottingham	16A Nottingham	16A Nottingham	16A Nottingham	6G Llandudno Junction	26B Agecroft	10F Rose Grove
47632	$3F^{6}$	16A Nottingham	16A Nottingham	20B Stourton	55B Stourton	56D Mirfield		
47633	$3F^{6}$	5B Crewe South	5B Crewe South	5E Alsager	5E Alsager	5E Alsager		
47634	$3F^{6}$	20C Royston	20C Royston	20C Royston	55D Royston	53E Goole		
47635	$3F^{6}$	22B Gloucester Barnwood	22B Gloucester Barnwood	22B Gloucester Barnwood	55E Normanton	56F Low Moor		
47636	$3F^{6}$	15A Wellingborough	15A Wellingborough	15A Wellingborough	19A Sheffield Grimesthorpe	41B Sheffield Grimesthorpe		
47637	$3F^{6}$	16A Nottingham	16A Nottingham	18D Staveley Barrow Hill	18D Staveley Barrow Hill	41E Staveley Barrow Hill		
47638	$3F^{6}$	21A Saltley	21A Saltley	21A Saltley	21A Saltley	17B Burton	18B Westhouses	
47639	$3F^{6}$	21A Saltley	23C Lancaster	11E Lancaster	11E Lancaster	24J Lancaster		
47640	$3F^{6}$	14B Kentish Town	20B Stourton	20B Stourton	55B Stourton	56B Ardsley	26A Newton Heath	
47641	$3F^{6}$	17B Burton	17B Burton	17B Burton	17B Burton	17B Burton	9G Gorton	12A Carlisle Kingmoor
47642	$3F^{6}$	15A Wellingborough	15A Wellingborough	15A Wellingborough	14B Kentish Town	14B Kentish Town		
47643	$3F^{6}$	17B Burton	17B Burton	17B Burton	17B Burton	17B Burton	17B Burton	16F Burton
47644	$3F^{6}$	14B Kentish Town	14B Kentish Town	14B Kentish Town	14B Kentish Town	14B Kentish Town		
47645	$3F^{6}$	14B Kentish Town	14B Kentish Town	14B Kentish Town	14B Kentish Town	14B Kentish Town	18A Toton	
47646	$3F^{6}$	6B Mold Junction	6B Mold Junction	6B Mold Junction	6B Mold Junction	6B Mold Junction	6B Mold Junction	
47647	$3F^{6}$	5D Stoke	5D Stoke	5D Stoke	5D Stoke	5D Stoke	12F Workington	
47648	$3F^{6}$	5D Stoke	5D Stoke	5D Stoke	5D Stoke	5D Stoke	5B Crewe South	
47649	$3F^{6}$	5C Stafford	5C Stafford	5C Stafford	5C Stafford	5C Stafford	5C Stafford	5B Crewe South
47650	$3F^{6}$	6B Mold Junction	6B Mold Junction	6B Mold Junction	6B Mold Junction	6B Mold Junction		
47651	$3F^{6}$	8A Edge Hill	8C Speke Junction	8C Speke Junction	8C Speke Junction	8C Speke Junction	8C Speke Junction	
47652	$3F^{6}$	8B Warrington Dallam	8B Warrington Dallam	8B Warrington Dallam	8B Warrington Dallam	8B Warrington Dallam		
47653	$3F^{6}$	5C Stafford	5C Stafford	5C Stafford	5C Stafford	5C Stafford	2B Nuneaton	
47654	$3F^{6}$	8B Warrington Dallam	8B Warrington Dallam	8B Warrington Dallam	8B Warrington Dallam	8B Warrington Dallam	8B Warrington Dallam	
47655	$3F^{6}$	4C Upper Bank	87K Swansea Victoria	87K Swansea Victoria	87K Swansea Victoria	27E Walton on the Hill	27B Aintree	
47656	$3F^{6}$	6B Mold Junction	6B Mold Junction	6B Mold Junction	6B Mold Junction	8A Edge Hill	8A Edge Hill	
47657	$3F^{6}$	8B Warrington Dallam	8B Warrington Dallam	8B Warrington Dallam	8B Warrington Dallam	8B Warrington Dallam	8B Warrington Dallam	
47658	$3F^{6}$	5D Stoke	5D Stoke	5D Stoke	5D Stoke	5D Stoke	Crewe Works	Crewe Works
47659	$3F^{6}$	*(France)*	35C Spital Bridge	10B Preston	10B Preston	8B Warrington Dallam	6C Birkenhead	8H Birkenhead

		1948	1951	1954	1957	1960	1963	1966
47660	3F^{6}	(France)	**17A** Derby	**17A** Derby	**17A** Derby	**17A** Derby	**24B** Rose Grove	
47661	3F^{6}	**5E** Alsager	**5B** Crewe South	**5B** Crewe South	**5B** Crewe South	**5B** Crewe South	Crewe Works	Crewe Works
47662	3F^{6}	**5E** Alsager	**5B** Crewe South	**5B** Crewe South	**5B** Crewe South	**11B** Workington	**24J** Lancaster	**9H** Patricroft
47664	3F^{6}	**12B** Carlisle Upperby	**12A** Carlisle Upperby	**12A** Carlisle Upperby	**12A** Carlisle Upperby	**6B** Crewe South	**5D** Stoke	
47665	3F^{6}	**5B** Crewe South	**5C** Stafford	**5C** Stafford	**5C** Stafford	**5C** Stafford	**5C** Stafford	
47666	3F^{6}	**12B** Carlisle Upperby	**12A** Carlisle Upperby	**12A** Carlisle Upperby	**12A** Carlisle Upperby	**12B** Carlisle Upperby	**12B** Carlisle Upperby	
47667	3F^{6}	**1B** Camden	**1B** Camden	**1B** Camden	**1B** Camden	**12A** Carlisle Kingmoor	**12B** Carlisle Upperby	**12A** Carlisle Kingmoor
47668	3F^{6}	**1B** Camden	**1B** Camden	**1B** Camden	**1B** Camden	**1B** Camden	**8G** Sutton Oak	**8G** Sutton Oak
47669	3F^{6}	**1B** Camden	**1B** Camden	**1B** Camden	**1B** Camden	**1B** Camden	**6K** Rhyl	
47670	3F^{6}	**5C** Stafford	**5B** Crewe South	**5B** Crewe South	**5B** Crewe South	**5B** Crewe South		
47671	3F^{6}	**1B** Camden	**1B** Camden	**1B** Camden	**1B** Camden	**1B** Camden	**8F** Wigan Springs Branch	**8F** Wigan Springs Branch
47672	3F^{6}	**6C** Birkenhead	**6C** Birkenhead	**6F** Bidston	**10C** Patricroft	**26F** Patricroft		
47673	3F^{6}	**9A** Longsight	**9A** Longsight	**9A** Longsight	**9A** Longsight	**9A** Longsight	**6B** Mold Junction	**6G** Llandudno Junction
47674	3F^{6}	**6C** Birkenhead	**6C** Birkenhead	**6F** Bidston	**6F** Bidston	**6C** Birkenhead	**6F** Bidston	**8H** Birkenhead
47675	3F^{6}	**1A** Willesden	**1A** Willesden	**1A** Willesden	**1A** Willesden	**11A** Barrow	**12E** Barrow	**12C** Barrow
47676	3F^{6}	**1A** Willesden	**1A** Willesden	**1A** Willesden	**1A** Willesden	**11A** Barrow	**12F** Workington	
47677	3F^{6}	**2A** Rugby	**2A** Rugby	**2A** Rugby	**2A** Rugby	**6C** Birkenhead	**5B** Crewe South	
47678	3F^{6}	**22A** Bristol Barrow Road	**22A** Bristol Barrow Road	**22A** Bristol Barrow Road	**22A** Bristol Barrow Road	**82E** Bristol Barrow Road		
47679	3F^{6}	**17D** Rowsley	**17D** Rowsley	**17D** Rowsley	**17D** Rowsley	**17C** Rowsley	**17C** Rowsley	
47680	3F^{6}	**5B** Crewe South	**5B** Crewe South	**5B** Crewe South	**5B** Crewe South	**5B** Crewe South	**5B** Crewe South	
47681	3F^{6}	**5B** Crewe South	**87K** Swansea Victoria	**87K** Swansea Victoria	**87K** Swansea Victoria	**27E** Walton on the Hill	**27E** Walton on the Hill	
47862	1F^{2}	Crewe Works	Crewe Works	Crewe Works				
47865	1F^{2}	Crewe Works	Crewe Works					
[illegible]	6F^{1}	**8C** Speke Junction						
47877	6F^{1}	**8C** Speke Junction	**10A** Wigan Springs Branch					
47881	6F^{1}	**8C** Speke Junction	**10A** Wigan Springs Branch					
47884	6F^{1}	**8C** Speke Junction	**10A** Wigan Springs Branch					
47885	6F^{1}	**10A** Wigan Springs Branch						
47887	6F^{1}	**10C** Patricroft						
47888	6F^{1}	**10A** Wigan Springs Branch						
47892	6F^{1}	**10C** Patricroft						
47896	6F^{1}	**10A** Wigan Springs Branch						
47930	7F^{1}	**8A** Edge Hill						
47931	7F^{1}	**4B** Swansea Victoria	**8A** Edge Hill					
47932	7F^{1}	**4B** Swansea Victoria						
47933	7F^{1}	**8A** Edge Hill						
47936	7F^{1}	**9D** Buxton						
47937	7F^{1}	**4B** Swansea Victoria						
47938	7F^{1}	**8A** Edge Hill						
47939	7F^{1}	**4E** Tredegar						
47948	7F^{1}	**4B** Swansea Victoria						
47951	7F^{1}	**8A** Edge Hill						
47954	7F^{1}	**9D** Buxton						
47956	7F^{1}	**8A** Edge Hill						
47958	7F^{1}	**8A** Edge Hill						
47959	7F^{1}	**8A** Edge Hill						
47967	Garratt	**18A** Toton	**18A** Toton	**18A** Toton	**18C** Hasland			
47968	Garratt	**18C** Hasland	**18C** Hasland	**18C** Hasland	**18C** Hasland			
47969	Garratt	**18A** Toton	**18A** Toton	**18A** Toton	**18C** Hasland			
47970	Garratt	**18A** Toton	**18A** Toton	**18A** Toton				
47971	Garratt	**18C** Hasland	**18C** Hasland	**18C** Hasland				
47972	Garratt	**18A** Toton	**18A** Toton	**18A** Toton	**18C** Hasland			
47973	Garratt	**18C** Hasland	**18C** Hasland	**18C** Hasland	**18C** Hasland			
47974	Garratt	**18A** Toton	**18A** Toton	**15A** Wellingborough				
47975	Garratt	**18A** Toton	**18A** Toton	**18A** Toton				
47976	Garratt	**18A** Toton	**18A** Toton	**18A** Toton				
47977	Garratt	**18A** Toton	**18A** Toton	**15A** Wellingborough				
47978	Garratt	**18A** Toton	**18A** Toton	**18A** Toton	**18C** Hasland			
47979	Garratt	**18A** Toton	**18A** Toton	**18A** Toton	**18C** Hasland			
47980	Garratt	**18C** Hasland	**18C** Hasland	**18C** Hasland	**18C** Hasland			
47981	Garratt	**18A** Toton	**18A** Toton	**18A** Toton				
47982	Garratt	**18A** Toton	**18A** Toton	**15A** Wellingborough	**18C** Hasland			
47983	Garratt	**18C** Hasland	**18C** Hasland	**18C** Hasland				
47984	Garratt	**18C** Hasland	**18C** Hasland	**18C** Hasland				
47985	Garratt	**18A** Toton	**18A** Toton	**18A** Toton				
47986	Garratt	**18A** Toton	**18A** Toton	**18A** Toton	**18C** Hasland			
47987	Garratt	**18A** Toton	**18A** Toton	**18A** Toton	**18A** Toton			
47988	Garratt	**18A** Toton	**18A** Toton	**18A** Toton				
47989	Garratt	**18A** Toton	**18A** Toton	**18A** Toton				
47990	Garratt	**18C** Hasland	**18C** Hasland	**18C** Hasland				
47991	Garratt	**18A** Toton	**18A** Toton	**18A** Toton				
47992	Garratt	**18C** Hasland	**18C** Hasland	**18C** Hasland				
47993	Garratt	**18C** Hasland	**18C** Hasland	**18A** Toton				
47994	Garratt	**18A** Toton	**18A** Toton	**15A** Wellingborough	**18C** Hasland			
47995	Garratt	**18A** Toton	**18A** Toton	**15A** Wellingborough	**18A** Toton			
47996	Garratt	**18A** Toton	**18A** Toton	**18A** Toton				
47997	Garratt	**18C** Hasland	**18A** Toton	**18A** Toton				
47998	Garratt	**18A** Toton	**18A** Toton	**18A** Toton				
47999	Garratt	**18A** Toton	**18A** Toton	**18A** Toton				
48000	8F	**16C** Kirkby in Ashfield	**16C** Kirkby in Ashfield	**16C** Kirkby in Ashfield	**16B** Kirkby in Ashfield	**16A** Nottingham	**16A** Nottingham	**16B** Annesley
48001	8F	**20A** Leeds Holbeck	**23C** Lancaster	**20A** Leeds Holbeck	**16C** Mansfield	**16C** Mansfield	**16B** Kirkby in Ashfield	
48002	8F	**18A** Toton	**18A** Toton	**17B** Burton	**17B** Burton	**17A** Derby	**16D** Annesley	**10D** Lostock Hall
48003	8F	**16A** Nottingham	**16C** Kirkby in Ashfield	**16C** Kirkby in Ashfield	**16B** Kirkby in Ashfield	**16B** Kirkby in Ashfield	**16B** Kirkby in Ashfield	**16E** Kirkby in Ashfield
48004	8F	**18A** Toton	**16C** Kirkby in Ashfield	**16C** Kirkby in Ashfield	**16B** Kirkby in Ashfield	**16B** Kirkby in Ashfield	**16B** Kirkby in Ashfield	
48005	8F	**20G** Hellifield	**23A** Skipton	**20B** Stourton	**17A** Derby	**17A** Derby	**17C** Rowsley	**10C** Fleetwood
48006	8F	**16C** Kirkby in Ashfield	**16C** Kirkby in Ashfield	**16C** Kirkby in Ashfield	**16B** Kirkby in Ashfield	**16B** Kirkby in Ashfield	**16B** Kirkby in Ashfield	
48007	8F	**16C** Kirkby in Ashfield	**18A** Toton	**18A** Toton	**15C** Leicester Midland	**15C** Leicester Midland	**16D** Annesley	
48008	8F	**17C** Coalville	**15A** Wellingborough	**15A** Wellingborough	**16B** Kirkby in Ashfield	**17C** Rowsley	**15B** Kettering	
48009	8F	**16C** Kirkby in Ashfield	**16C** Kirkby in Ashfield	**16C** Kirkby in Ashfield	**16B** Kirkby in Ashfield	**16B** Kirkby in Ashfield		
48010	8F	**21A** Saltley	**15A** Wellingborough	**15A** Wellingborough	**15C** Leicester Midland	**15C** Leicester Midland	**15A** Wellingborough	**1A** Willesden
48011	8F	**18B** Westhouses	**9G** Northwich	**17A** Derby	**19C** Canklow	**41D** Canklow	**16D** Annesley	**9J** Agecroft
48012	8F	(WD 70577)	**2C** Warwick	**2C** Warwick	**2C** Warwick	**2A** Rugby	**2A** Rugby	**5D** Stoke
48016	8F	(WD 70591)	**2B** Nuneaton	**2B** Nuneaton	**2B** Nuneaton	**2B** Nuneaton	**2B** Nuneaton	
48017	8F	**19A** Sheffield Grimesthorpe	**6B** Mold Junction	**8D** Widnes	**8D** Widnes	**8E** Northwich	**8E** Northwich	**8L** Aintree
48018	8F	(WD 70582)	**2C** Warwick	**2C** Warwick	**2C** Warwick	**2A** Rugby	**2A** Rugby	**5D** Stoke
48020	8F	(WD 70579)	**2B** Nuneaton	**2B** Nuneaton	**2B** Nuneaton	**2B** Nuneaton	**2B** Nuneaton	
48024	8F	**15A** Wellingborough	**15A** Wellingborough	**15B** Kettering	**16C** Mansfield	**16A** Nottingham	**16D** Annesley	**10F** Rose Grove
48026	8F	**19C** Canklow	**19C** Canklow	**19C** Canklow	**19C** Canklow	**41D** Canklow	**41E** Staveley Barrow Hill	**9J** Agecroft
48027	8F	**16C** Kirkby in Ashfield	**21A** Saltley	**21A** Saltley	**21A** Saltley	**21A** Saltley	**15A** Wellingborough	
48029	8F	**16C** Kirkby in Ashfield	**16C** Kirkby in Ashfield	**16C** Kirkby in Ashfield	**16B** Kirkby in Ashfield	**16B** Kirkby in Ashfield	**41E** Staveley Barrow Hill	**8C** Speke Junction
48033	8F	**18A** Toton	**18A** Toton	**18D** Staveley Barrow Hill	**18D** Staveley Barrow Hill	**18A** Toton	**18B** Westhouses	**8G** Sutton Oak
48035	8F	**16D** Mansfield	**15A** Wellingborough	**15B** Kettering	**21A** Saltley	**2A** Rugby	**2A** Rugby	**2F** Bescot
48036	8F	**16C** Kirkby in Ashfield	**1A** Willesden	**1A** Willesden	**1A** Willesden	**1A** Willesden	**1A** Willesden	**5B** Crewe South
48037	8F	**18A** Toton	**18A** Toton	**18A** Toton	**18D** Staveley Barrow Hill	**41E** Staveley Barrow Hill	**26F** Patricroft	
48039	8F	(WD 70588)	**2A** Rugby	**8C** Speke Junction	**8C** Speke Junction	**8C** Speke Junction	**8E** Northwich	
48045	8F	(WD 70573)	**9G** Northwich	**9G** Northwich	**9G** Northwich	**8E** Northwich	**8C** Speke Junction	**16E** Kirkby in Ashfield
48046	8F	(WD 70599)	**9G** Northwich	**9G** Northwich	**9G** Northwich	**6G** Llandudno Junction	**8C** Speke Junction	**16G** Westhouses
48050	8F	**15A** Wellingborough	**15A** Wellingborough	**15A** Wellingborough	**15B** Kettering	**15B** Kettering	**15B** Kettering	**8L** Aintree
48053	8F	**18D** Staveley Barrow Hill	**18A** Toton	**20C** Royston	**16A** Nottingham	**15D** Coalville	**15D** Coalville	**10F** Rose Grove
48054	8F	**18D** Staveley Barrow Hill	**8C** Speke Junction	**8C** Speke Junction	**8C** Speke Junction	**6B** Mold Junction	**2B** Nuneaton	**5E** Nuneaton
48055	8F	**20H** Lancaster	**19C** Canklow	**19C** Canklow	**55E** Normanton	**55B** Stourton	**56D** Mirfield	**56D** Mirfield
48056	8F	**18B** Westhouses	**18B** Westhouses	**18B** Westhouses	**18B** Westhouses	**18C** Hasland	**18A** Toton	**16F** Burton
48057	8F	**18B** Westhouses	**18B** Westhouses	**18B** Westhouses	**18B** Westhouses	**18B** Westhouses	**16D** Annesley	**8E** Northwich
48060	8F	**18B** Westhouses	**18B** Westhouses	**18B** Westhouses	**18B** Westhouses	**18A** Toton	**17A** Derby	**16B** Annesley

		1948	1951	1954	1957	1960	1963	1966
48061	8F	(WD 70614)	2B Nuneaton	15B Kettering	15C Leicester Midland	15C Leicester Midland	15A Wellingborough	2F Bescot
48062	8F	20C Royston	20C Royston	14A Cricklewood	14A Cricklewood	18A Toton	9D Buxton	10F Rose Grove
48063	8F	18B Westhouses	18B Westhouses	18B Westhouses	18B Westhouses	16B Kirkby in Ashfield	16B Kirkby in Ashfield	16E Kirkby in Ashfield
48064	8F	16A Nottingham	16A Nottingham	16A Nottingham	16A Nottingham	16A Nottingham	16D Annesley	16F Burton
48065	8F	19C Canklow	19C Canklow	19C Canklow	18C Hasland	18C Hasland	17B Burton	15A Leicester Midland
48067	8F	15B Kettering	20A Leeds Holbeck	20A Leeds Holbeck	55A Leeds Holbeck	55A Leeds Holbeck	55D Royston	55D Royston
48069	8F	15B Kettering	15B Kettering	15B Kettering	15B Kettering	15B Kettering	15B Kettering	
48070	8F	18A Toton	20A Leeds Holbeck	20A Leeds Holbeck	55D Royston	55D Royston	55D Royston	55D Royston
48073	8F	20A Leeds Holbeck	16C Kirkby in Ashfield	16C Kirkby in Ashfield	16B Kirkby in Ashfield	16B Kirkby in Ashfield	16B Kirkby in Ashfield	16G Westhouses
48074	8F	16C Kirkby in Ashfield	12B Carlisle Canal	1A Willesden	1A Willesden	6B Mold Junction	2A Rugby	5E Nuneaton
48075	8F	18A Toton	18A Toton	18A Toton	19C Canklow	56B Ardsley	55B Stourton	55D Royston
48076	8F	18B Westhouses	18B Westhouses	20D Normanton	55E Normanton	55B Stourton	55D Royston	55C Farnley Junction
48077	8F	(WD 70611)	2B Nuneaton	2B Nuneaton	2B Nuneaton	2B Nuneaton	1A Willesden	10J Lancaster
48078	8F	20C Royston	20C Royston	20C Royston	55D Royston	55D Royston	8A Edge Hill	
48079	8F	20C Royston	17A Derby	17A Derby	17A Derby	17A Derby	16D Annesley	10J Lancaster
48080	8F	20C Royston	20C Royston	20C Royston	55D Royston	56F Low Moor	55B Stourton	55C Farnley Junction
48081	8F	20F Skipton	16C Kirkby in Ashfield	16C Kirkby in Ashfield	16B Kirkby in Ashfield	17C Rowsley	17C Rowsley	10F Rose Grove
48082	8F	15A Wellingborough	15A Wellingborough	15A Wellingborough	18C Hasland	18C Hasland	18A Toton	15A Leicester Midland
48083	8F	18B Westhouses	18B Westhouses	19C Canklow	17A Derby	17A Derby	17A Derby	16C Derby
48084	8F	20D Normanton	20D Normanton	20D Normanton	55E Normanton	55B Stourton	55B Stourton	55B Stourton
48085	8F	20C Royston	2A Rugby	2A Rugby	2A Rugby	2A Rugby	1E Bletchley	2E Saltley
48088	8F	16D Mansfield	16D Mansfield	16D Mansfield	16C Mansfield	16C Mansfield	16B Kirkby in Ashfield	9L Buxton
48089	8F	19D Heaton Mersey	9F Heaton Mersey	9F Heaton Mersey	17E Heaton Mersey	18C Hasland	9F Heaton Mersey	9F Heaton Mersey
48090	8F	20A Leeds Holbeck	9D Buxton	2E Northampton	2E Northampton	2E Northampton	2E Northampton	6B Mold Junction
48092	8F	16C Kirkby in Ashfield	16C Kirkby in Ashfield	16C Kirkby in Ashfield	16B Kirkby in Ashfield	16B Kirkby in Ashfield	16B Kirkby in Ashfield	16E Kirkby in Ashfield
48093	8F	21A Saltley	20C Royston	20C Royston	55D Royston	55D Royston	55D Royston	55B Stourton
48094	8F	(WD 70606)	6B Mold Junction	8C Speke Junction	8B Warrington Dallam	8B Warrington Dallam	6C Birkenhead	
48095	8F	20C Royston	20C Royston	20C Royston	18C Hasland	18C Hasland	18A Toton	
48096	8F	16C Kirkby in Ashfield	16C Kirkby in Ashfield	16C Kirkby in Ashfield	16B Kirkby in Ashfield	16B Kirkby in Ashfield	16B Kirkby in Ashfield	
48097	8F	16C Kirkby in Ashfield	16C Kirkby in Ashfield	16C Kirkby in Ashfield	16B Kirkby in Ashfield	16B Kirkby in Ashfield	16B Kirkby in Ashfield	
48098	8F	16C Kirkby in Ashfield	16C Kirkby in Ashfield	16C Kirkby in Ashfield	16B Kirkby in Ashfield	16B Kirkby in Ashfield	16B Kirkby in Ashfield	16E Kirkby in Ashfield
48099	8F	19D Heaton Mersey	9F Heaton Mersey	9F Heaton Mersey	17E Heaton Mersey	18A Toton	16D Annesley	
48100	8F	16C Kirkby in Ashfield	16C Kirkby in Ashfield	16C Kirkby in Ashfield	16B Kirkby in Ashfield	16B Kirkby in Ashfield	16B Kirkby in Ashfield	16E Kirkby in Ashfield
48101	8F	16C Kirkby in Ashfield	16C Kirkby in Ashfield	16C Kirkby in Ashfield	16B Kirkby in Ashfield	21A Saltley	21A Saltley	2F Bescot
48102	8F	18B Westhouses	16A Nottingham	16A Nottingham	16B Kirkby in Ashfield	16B Kirkby in Ashfield	16B Kirkby in Ashfield	
48103	8F	20C Royston	20C Royston	20C Royston	18D Staveley Barrow Hill	41E Staveley Barrow Hill	26F Patricroft	16C Derby
48104	8F	16C Kirkby in Ashfield	20A Leeds Holbeck	20A Leeds Holbeck	55A Leeds Holbeck	55A Leeds Holbeck	55A Leeds Holbeck	55A Leeds Holbeck
48105	8F	19A Sheffield Grimesthorpe	23B Hellifield	20G Hellifield	20G Hellifield	21A Saltley	16B Kirkby in Ashfield	16E Kirkby in Ashfield
48106	8F	17C Coalville	6C Birkenhead	6B Mold Junction	6C Birkenhead	8B Warrington Dallam	8B Warrington Dallam	9K Bolton
48107	8F	17C Coalville	15A Wellingborough	15A Wellingborough	15C Leicester Midland	15C Leicester Midland	15B Kettering	16B Annesley
48108	8F	16C Kirkby in Ashfield	16C Kirkby in Ashfield	16A Nottingham	16A Nottingham	16A Nottingham	16A Nottingham	8L Aintree
48109	8F	16C Kirkby in Ashfield	14A Cricklewood	14A Cricklewood	14A Cricklewood	18A Toton	21A Saltley	2E Saltley
48110	8F	20A Leeds Holbeck	84G Shrewsbury	84G Shrewsbury	84G Shrewsbury	84G Shrewsbury	82E Bristol Barrow Road	5D Stoke
48111	8F	18D Staveley Barrow Hill	15A Wellingborough	15A Wellingborough	16A Nottingham	2B Nuneaton	2B Nuneaton	5E Nuneaton
48112	8F	18A Toton	18A Toton	18A Toton	18B Westhouses	18B Westhouses	18B Westhouses	
48113	8F	20C Royston	20C Royston	20C Royston	55D Royston	55D Royston	55D Royston	55D Royston
48114	8F	16C Kirkby in Ashfield	16C Kirkby in Ashfield	16C Kirkby in Ashfield	16B Kirkby in Ashfield	16B Kirkby in Ashfield	16D Kirkby in Ashfield	8F Wigan Springs Branch
48115	8F	18B Westhouses	18B Westhouses	18B Westhouses	18B Westhouses	26A Newton Heath	26A Newton Heath	9F Heaton Mersey
48116	8F	19A Sheffield Grimesthorpe	19A Sheffield Grimesthorpe	19A Sheffield Grimesthorpe	19A Sheffield Grimesthorpe	18C Hasland	18C Hasland	
48117	8F	18A Toton	18A Toton	18A Toton	16A Nottingham	16A Nottingham	16D Annesley	16F Burton
48118	8F	18B Westhouses	18B Westhouses	18B Westhouses	18B Westhouses	18A Toton	8E Northwich	8E Northwich
48119	8F	18A Toton	16D Mansfield	16D Mansfield	16C Mansfield	16C Mansfield	16B Kirkby in Ashfield	16E Kirkby in Ashfield
48120	8F	18D Staveley Barrow Hill	3A Bescot	3A Bescot	3A Bescot	2A Rugby	2A Rugby	6B Mold Junction
48121	8F	20A Leeds Holbeck	17A Derby	17A Derby	17A Derby	17A Derby	17A Derby	2C Stourbridge
48122	8F	18D Staveley Barrow Hill	1A Willesden	1A Willesden	1A Willesden	1A Willesden	2A Rugby	6C Croes Newydd
48123	8F	20D Normanton	20B Stourton	20B Stourton	55B Stourton	55D Royston	55D Royston	55D Royston
48124	8F	15B Kettering	15B Kettering	15B Kettering	15B Kettering	17A Derby	17A Derby	16E Kirkby in Ashfield
48125	8F	18B Westhouses	18B Westhouses	18B Westhouses	18B Westhouses	18C Hasland	15A Wellingborough	8F Wigan Springs Branch
48126	8F	20A Leeds Holbeck	20B Stourton	20B Stourton	55B Stourton	55B Stourton	55B Stourton	55B Stourton
48127	8F	20A Leeds Holbeck	9F Heaton Mersey	9F Heaton Mersey	17E Heaton Mersey	18A Toton	15B Kettering	16G Westhouses
48128	8F	15A Wellingborough	15A Wellingborough	18A Toton	18A Toton	18A Toton	17B Burton	16F Burton
48129	8F	20A Leeds Holbeck	1A Willesden	1A Willesden	1A Willesden	1A Willesden	8D Widnes	8A Edge Hill
48130	8F	20D Normanton	20D Normanton	20D Normanton	55E Normanton	55D Royston	55D Royston	55B Stourton
48131	8F	20D Normanton	15A Wellingborough	15B Kettering	15B Kettering	2A Rugby	6C Birkenhead	5D Stoke
48132	8F	15C Leicester Midland	14A Cricklewood	14A Cricklewood	14A Cricklewood	18A Toton	15B Kettering	16B Annesley
48133	8F	18A Toton	15A Wellingborough	15B Kettering	15C Leicester Midland	15C Leicester Midland	16A Nottingham	2E Saltley
48134	8F	18D Staveley Barrow Hill	9F Heaton Mersey	1A Willesden	1A Willesden	1A Willesden	1A Willesden	6C Croes Newydd
48135	8F	19D Heaton Mersey	9G Northwich	9F Heaton Mersey	6D Chester Northgate	8E Northwich	8E Northwich	
48136	8F	18B Westhouses	18B Westhouses	16A Nottingham	16A Nottingham	2A Rugby	8D Widnes	9D Newton Heath
48137	8F	20A Leeds Holbeck	16C Kirkby in Ashfield	16C Kirkby in Ashfield	16B Kirkby in Ashfield	16B Kirkby in Ashfield	16B Kirkby in Ashfield	16B Annesley
48138	8F	20A Leeds Holbeck	16C Kirkby in Ashfield	16C Kirkby in Ashfield	19C Canklow	56B Ardsley	56D Mirfield	
48139	8F	16C Kirkby in Ashfield	16C Kirkby in Ashfield	18A Toton	18B Westhouses	8E Northwich	8D Widnes	8L Aintree
48140	8F	20B Stourton	19C Canklow	19C Canklow	19C Canklow	41D Canklow	41D Canklow	
48141	8F	15B Kettering	15B Kettering	15B Kettering	15B Kettering	15A Wellingborough	16D Annesley	10D Lostock Hall
48142	8F	18A Toton	6B Mold Junction	8B Warrington Dallam	15B Kettering	14A Cricklewood	16D Annesley	16B Annesley
48143	8F	20A Leeds Holbeck	15B Kettering	15B Kettering	15B Kettering	15A Wellingborough	16B Kirkby in Ashfield	16G Westhouses
48144	8F	18A Toton	18A Toton	19A Sheffield Grimesthorpe	19A Sheffield Grimesthorpe	41B Sheffield Grimesthorpe	41E Staveley Barrow Hill	
48145	8F	20G Hellifield	23A Skipton	20A Leeds Holbeck	18A Toton	18A Toton	17C Rowsley	
48146	8F	20D Normanton	20D Normanton	20D Normanton	55D Royston	55D Royston	55D Royston	55B Stourton
48147	8F	31D Grangemouth	1A Willesden	1A Willesden	2E Northampton	2E Northampton	2E Northampton	6C Croes Newydd
48148	8F	31D Grangemouth	23C Lancaster	9F Heaton Mersey	17E Heaton Mersey	26A Newton Heath	26A Newton Heath	
48149	8F	31D Grangemouth	20B Stourton	20B Stourton	15C Leicester Midland	15C Leicester Midland	18A Toton	16G Westhouses
48150	8F	31D Grangemouth	15A Wellingborough	15A Wellingborough	19C Canklow	41D Canklow	41E Staveley Barrow Hill	
48151	8F	31D Grangemouth	15A Wellingborough	15A Wellingborough	19C Canklow	41D Canklow	41D Canklow	8A Edge Hill
48152	8F	31D Grangemouth	18A Toton	18A Toton	21A Saltley	8A Edge Hill	8A Edge Hill	8A Edge Hill
48153	8F	31E Dawsholm	17A Derby	17A Derby	17A Derby	17A Derby	17A Derby	16C Derby
48154	8F	19D Heaton Mersey	9F Heaton Mersey	2B Nuneaton	2B Nuneaton	2B Nuneaton	6C Birkenhead	10F Rose Grove
48155	8F	31E Dawsholm	9F Heaton Mersey	9G Northwich	9G Northwich	8E Northwich	8E Northwich	8E Northwich
48156	8F	28A Motherwell	16D Mansfield	16D Mansfield	16C Mansfield	16C Mansfield	16B Kirkby in Ashfield	
48157	8F	17A Derby	20A Leeds Holbeck	20A Leeds Holbeck	55A Leeds Holbeck	55A Leeds Holbeck	55A Leeds Holbeck	55A Leeds Holbeck
48158	8F	16A Nottingham	20A Leeds Holbeck	20A Leeds Holbeck	55A Leeds Holbeck	55A Leeds Holbeck	55A Leeds Holbeck	55A Leeds Holbeck
48159	8F	20D Normanton	20A Leeds Holbeck	20A Leeds Holbeck	55A Leeds Holbeck	55A Leeds Holbeck	55D Royston	55D Royston
48160	8F	20D Normanton	20D Normanton	20D Normanton	55E Normanton	55B Stourton	55B Stourton	55B Stourton
48161	8F	20C Royston	23C Lancaster	9F Heaton Mersey	17E Heaton Mersey	9F Heaton Mersey	9F Heaton Mersey	9F Heaton Mersey
48162	8F	20C Royston	20C Royston	20C Royston	55D Royston	55D Royston	55D Royston	55D Royston
48163	8F	28B Dalry Road	14A Cricklewood	14A Cricklewood	14A Cricklewood	18A Toton	15B Kettering	8C Speke Junction
48164	8F	20D Normanton	20D Normanton	18B Westhouses	18D Staveley Barrow Hill	41E Staveley Barrow Hill	26F Patricroft	9J Agecroft
48165	8F	4A Shrewsbury	2A Rugby	2A Rugby	9D Buxton	9A Longsight	9D Buxton	15A Leicester Midland
48166	8F	16C Kirkby in Ashfield	9D Buxton	9D Buxton	9D Buxton	6B Mold Junction	8E Northwich	9K Bolton
48167	8F	15A Wellingborough	15A Wellingborough	18D Staveley Barrow Hill	18D Staveley Barrow Hill	18A Toton	18A Toton	16B Annesley
48168	8F	18A Toton	18A Toton	18A Toton	17A Derby	17A Derby	16D Annesley	9H Patricroft
48169	8F	20C Royston	20C Royston	20C Royston	55D Royston	55D Royston	55D Royston	55D Royston
48170	8F	16A Nottingham	16A Nottingham	16A Nottingham	16A Nottingham	16A Nottingham	16A Nottingham	16B Annesley
48171	8F	1A Willesden	1A Willesden	1A Willesden	1A Willesden	1A Willesden	1A Willesden	9L Buxton
48172	8F	1A Willesden	84G Shrewsbury	84G Shrewsbury	84G Shrewsbury	84G Shrewsbury	85C Gloucester Barnwood	
48173	8F	1A Willesden	2A Rugby	2A Rugby	2A Rugby	2A Rugby	2A Rugby	
48174	8F	1A Willesden	1A Willesden	1A Willesden	6B Mold Junction	5B Crewe South	5C Stafford	9D Newton Heath
48175	8F	4B Swansea Victoria	3A Bescot	3A Bescot	3A Bescot	6B Mold Junction	6B Mold Junction	6B Mold Junction
48176	8F	20A Leeds Holbeck	18A Toton	18A Toton	19C Canklow	41D Canklow	41E Staveley Barrow Hill	9F Heaton Mersey
48177	8F	15D Bedford	15D Bedford	15D Bedford	15D Bedford	16B Kirkby in Ashfield	18B Westhouses	16G Westhouses
48178	8F	18A Toton	18A Toton	18A Toton	18A Toton	41B Sheffield Grimesthorpe	26F Patricroft	9E Trafford Park
48179	8F	19D Heaton Mersey	19A Sheffield Grimesthorpe	19A Sheffield Grimesthorpe	19A Sheffield Grimesthorpe	41B Sheffield Grimesthorpe	41D Canklow	
48180	8F	15A Wellingborough	15A Wellingborough	15A Wellingborough	14A Cricklewood	15B Kettering	15B Kettering	16B Annesley
48181	8F	15A Wellingborough	15A Wellingborough	15A Wellingborough	19C Canklow	41D Canklow	26F Patricroft	9H Patricroft

		1948	1951	1954	1957	1960	1963	1966
48182	*8F*	**18A** Toton	**18A** Toton	**18A** Toton	**18A** Toton	**17B** Burton	**17B** Burton	**9B** Stockport Edgeley
48183	*8F*	**28A** Motherwell	**15A** Wellingborough	**15A** Wellingborough	**18A** Toton	**18A** Toton	**15B** Kettering	
48184	*8F*	**28A** Motherwell	**18A** Toton	**18A** Toton	**18A** Toton	**18A** Toton	**16A** Nottingham	
48185	*8F*	**28A** Motherwell	**18A** Toton	**18A** Toton	**18A** Toton	**18A** Toton	**16A** Nottingham	**15A** Leicester Midland
48186	*8F*	**28A** Motherwell	**18A** Toton	**18A** Toton	**18A** Toton	**18A** Toton	**18A** Toton	**16E** Kirkby in Ashfield
48187	*8F*	**28A** Motherwell	**18A** Toton	**18A** Toton	**18A** Toton	**18C** Hasland	**18C** Hasland	**8F** Wigan Springs Branch
48188	*8F*	**28A** Motherwell	**26G** Belle Vue	**8B** Warrington Dallam	**8B** Warrington Dallam	**8B** Warrington Dallam	**8A** Edge Hill	**8A** Edge Hill
48189	*8F*	**20G** Hellifield	**23B** Hellifield	**20G** Hellifield	**20G** Hellifield	**24H** Hellifield	**41E** Staveley Barrow Hill	
48190	*8F*	**19D** Heaton Mersey	**9F** Heaton Mersey	**9F** Heaton Mersey	**17E** Heaton Mersey	**9F** Heaton Mersey	**9F** Heaton Mersey	**9L** Buxton
48191	*8F*	**5B** Crewe South	**15A** Wellingborough	**15A** Wellingborough	**15A** Wellingborough	**9F** Heaton Mersey	**9F** Heaton Mersey	**9F** Heaton Mersey
48192	*8F*	**15A** Wellingborough	**15A** Wellingborough	**15A** Wellingborough	**17D** Rowsley	**16B** Kirkby in Ashfield	**16B** Kirkby in Ashfield	**16B** Annesley
48193	*8F*	**16C** Kirkby in Ashfield	**16C** Kirkby in Ashfield	**16C** Kirkby in Ashfield	**16B** Kirkby in Ashfield	**16A** Nottingham	**16A** Nottingham	**16B** Annesley
48194	*8F*	**18A** Toton	**18A** Toton	**18A** Toton	**18A** Toton	**18A** Toton	**17B** Burton	**16F** Burton
48195	*8F*	**18D** Staveley Barrow Hill	**18A** Toton	**18A** Toton	**18A** Toton	**18A** Toton	**18B** Westhouses	**16G** Westhouses
48196	*8F*	**18A** Toton	**18A** Toton	**18A** Toton	**18A** Toton	**18A** Toton	**18B** Westhouses	**16G** Westhouses
48197	*8F*	**18A** Toton	**18A** Toton	**18A** Toton	**18A** Toton	**18A** Toton	**18B** Westhouses	**16B** Annesley
48198	*8F*	**15A** Wellingborough	**15A** Wellingborough	**15A** Wellingborough	**15A** Wellingborough	**17A** Derby	**17A** Derby	
48199	*8F*	**18A** Toton	**18A** Toton	**18A** Toton	**18D** Staveley Barrow Hill	**41E** Staveley Barrow Hill	**41E** Staveley Barrow Hill	**10C** Fleetwood
48200	*8F*	**18A** Toton	**18A** Toton	**18A** Toton	**18A** Toton	**41E** Staveley Barrow Hill	**41E** Staveley Barrow Hill	**8A** Edge Hill
48201	*8F*	**18A** Toton	**18A** Toton	**18A** Toton	**18A** Toton	**18A** Toton	**18A** Toton	**16E** Kirkby in Ashfield
48202	*8F*	**18A** Toton	**18A** Toton	**20D** Normanton	**55E** Normanton	**56D** Mirfield	**56D** Mirfield	**56D** Mirfield
48203	*8F*	**18A** Toton	**18A** Toton	**18A** Toton	**18A** Toton	**2A** Rugby	**1E** Bletchley	**2F** Bescot
48204	*8F*	**18A** Toton	**18A** Toton	**18A** Toton	**18A** Toton	**18B** Westhouses	**18A** Toton	**16G** Westhouses
48205	*8F*	**18A** Toton	**18A** Toton	**18A** Toton	**18A** Toton	**18C** Hasland	**18C** Hasland	**9K** Bolton
48206	*8F*	**16A** Nottingham	**16A** Nottingham	**16A** Nottingham	**16A** Nottingham	**8D** Widnes	**2B** Nuneaton	**5E** Nuneaton
48207	*8F*	**16A** Nottingham	**4A** Bletchley	**1E** Bletchley	**1E** Bletchley	**1E** Bletchley	**1E** Bletchley	**5D** Stoke
48208	*8F*	**19D** Heaton Mersey	**9F** Heaton Mersey	**9F** Heaton Mersey	**17E** Heaton Mersey	**9F** Heaton Mersey	**9F** Heaton Mersey	**9F** Heaton Mersey
48209	*8F*	**19C** Canklow	**19C** Canklow	**19C** Canklow	**19C** Canklow	**41D** Canklow	**41E** Staveley Barrow Hill	
48210	*8F*	**18D** Staveley Barrow Hill	**18D** Staveley Barrow Hill	**18D** Staveley Barrow Hill	**18D** Staveley Barrow Hill	**41E** Staveley Barrow Hill	**41E** Staveley Barrow Hill	
48211	*8F*	**15C** Leicester Midland	**15C** Leicester Midland	**15C** Leicester Midland	**15C** Leicester Midland	**15C** Leicester Midland	**16A** Nottingham	**10J** Lancaster
48212	*8F*	**18B** Westhouses	**18B** Westhouses	**18B** Westhouses	**18C** Hasland	**18C** Hasland	**18A** Toton	**16B** Annesley
48213	*8F*	**18D** Staveley Barrow Hill	**18D** Staveley Barrow Hill	**18D** Staveley Barrow Hill	**18D** Staveley Barrow Hill	**41E** Staveley Barrow Hill	**26F** Patricroft	**9H** Patricroft
48214	*8F*	**16C** Kirkby in Ashfield	**16C** Kirkby in Ashfield	**16C** Kirkby in Ashfield	**16B** Kirkby in Ashfield	**16B** Kirkby in Ashfield	**16B** Kirkby in Ashfield	**16G** Westhouses
48215	*8F*	**16C** Kirkby in Ashfield	**16C** Kirkby in Ashfield	**16C** Kirkby in Ashfield	**16B** Kirkby in Ashfield	**16B** Kirkby in Ashfield	**16B** Kirkby in Ashfield	**16E** Kirkby in Ashfield
48216	*8F*	**19A** Sheffield Grimesthorpe	**19A** Sheffield Grimesthorpe	**19C** Canklow	**19C** Canklow	**41D** Canklow	**41E** Staveley Barrow Hill	
48217	*8F*	**16A** Nottingham	**16A** Nottingham	**16A** Nottingham	**16A** Nottingham	**16A** Nottingham	**16A** Nottingham	
48218	*8F*	**16A** Nottingham	**16A** Nottingham	**16A** Nottingham	**16A** Nottingham	**16A** Nottingham	**16A** Nottingham	**10F** Rose Grove
48219	*8F*	**19A** Sheffield Grimesthorpe	**19A** Sheffield Grimesthorpe	**14A** Cricklewood	**18A** Toton	**16C** Mansfield	**16B** Kirkby in Ashfield	**16G** Westhouses
48220	*8F*	**19D** Heaton Mersey	**9F** Heaton Mersey	**9F** Heaton Mersey	**17E** Heaton Mersey	**21A** Saltley	**21A** Saltley	**2E** Saltley
48221	*8F*	**18A** Toton	**18A** Toton	**18A** Toton	**18A** Toton	**18A** Toton	**18A** Toton	**8F** Wigan Springs Branch
48222	*8F*	**15A** Wellingborough	**15A** Wellingborough	**15A** Wellingborough	**55D** Royston	**55D** Royston	**55D** Royston	**55D** Royston
48223	*8F*	**16C** Kirkby in Ashfield	**16C** Kirkby in Ashfield	**16C** Kirkby in Ashfield	**16B** Kirkby in Ashfield	**16B** Kirkby in Ashfield	**16B** Kirkby in Ashfield	**10C** Fleetwood
48224	*8F*	**16C** Kirkby in Ashfield	**16C** Kirkby in Ashfield	**16C** Kirkby in Ashfield	**16B** Kirkby in Ashfield	**16B** Kirkby in Ashfield	**16B** Kirkby in Ashfield	**9J** Agecroft
48225	*8F*	**16C** Kirkby in Ashfield	**16C** Kirkby in Ashfield	**16C** Kirkby in Ashfield	**16B** Kirkby in Ashfield	**16B** Kirkby in Ashfield	**16B** Kirkby in Ashfield	**16E** Kirkby in Ashfield
48246	*8F*	(WD 70300)	**6B** Mold Junction	**6B** Mold Junction	**6B** Mold Junction	**6B** Mold Junction	**6G** Llandudno Junction	**5D** Stoke
48247	*8F*	(WD 70301)	**6C** Birkenhead	**6B** Mold Junction	**8B** Warrington Dallam	**8C** Speke Junction	**1A** Willesden	**5E** Nuneaton
48248	*8F*	(WD 70311)	**5B** Crewe South	**2A** Rugby	**5B** Crewe South	**5B** Crewe South	**5B** Crewe South	
48249	*8F*	(WD 70314)	**5B** Crewe South	**6C** Birkenhead	**6C** Birkenhead	**8A** Edge Hill	**8A** Edge Hill	**8A** Edge Hill
48250	*8F*	(WD 70318)	**5B** Crewe South	**3A** Bescot	**3A** Bescot	**3A** Bescot	**8C** Speke Junction	**9J** Agecroft
48251	*8F*	(WD 70332)	**5B** Crewe South	**5B** Crewe South	**5B** Crewe South	**2B** Nuneaton	**2B** Nuneaton	**8G** Sutton Oak
48252	*8F*	(WD 70363)	**5B** Crewe South	**5B** Crewe South	**5B** Crewe South	**2A** Rugby	**1A** Willesden	**6C** Croes Newydd
48253	*8F*	(WD 70376)	**5B** Crewe South	**5B** Crewe South	**6F** Bidston	**6G** Llandudno Junction	**6B** Mold Junction	**6B** Mold Junction
48254	*8F*	(WD 70378)	**9G** Northwich	**9G** Northwich	**9G** Northwich	**8E** Northwich	**8E** Northwich	**16F** Burton
48255	*8F*	(WD 70384)	**5B** Crewe South	**5B** Crewe South	**5B** Crewe South	**5B** Crewe South	**5B** Crewe South	**5B** Crewe South
48256	*8F*	(WD 70394)	**5B** Crewe South	**5B** Crewe South	**5B** Crewe South	**5B** Crewe South	**21B** Bescot	**2F** Bescot
48257	*8F*	(WD 70395)	**5B** Crewe South	**5B** Crewe South	**5B** Crewe South	**5B** Crewe South	**6C** Birkenhead	**10F** Rose Grove
48258	*8F*	(WD 70398)	**5B** Crewe South	**5B** Crewe South	**2B** Nuneaton	**2B** Nuneaton	**6C** Birkenhead	**16B** Annesley
48259	*8F*	(WD 70504)	**5B** Crewe South	**6B** Mold Junction	**6B** Mold Junction	**6B** Mold Junction	**6B** Mold Junction	
48260	*8F*	(WD 70518)	**5B** Crewe South	**8A** Edge Hill	**8A** Edge Hill	**6C** Birkenhead	**6C** Birkenhead	
48261	*8F*	(WD 70544)	**5B** Crewe South	**11E** Lancaster	**11E** Lancaster	**16A** Nottingham	**16A** Nottingham	**8F** Wigan Springs Branch
48262	*8F*	(WD 70576)	**5B** Crewe South	**5B** Crewe South	**5B** Crewe South	**5B** Crewe South	**6C** Birkenhead	
48263	*8F*	(WD 70584)	**5B** Crewe South	**5B** Crewe South	**5C** Stafford	**2B** Nuneaton	**2B** Nuneaton	**5E** Nuneaton
48264	*8F*	**15A** Wellingborough	**15A** Wellingborough	**15A** Wellingborough	**15A** Wellingborough	**6B** Mold Junction	**2B** Nuneaton	**5E** Nuneaton
48265	*8F*	**17C** Coalville	**15A** Wellingborough	**15A** Wellingborough	**55D** Royston	**56D** Mirfield	**56D** Mirfield	**56D** Mirfield
48266	*8F*	**20D** Normanton	**20D** Normanton	**20A** Leeds Holbeck	**15C** Leicester Midland	**15C** Leicester Midland	**15A** Wellingborough	**16F** Burton
48267	*8F*	**16C** Kirkby in Ashfield	**16C** Kirkby in Ashfield	**16C** Kirkby in Ashfield	**16B** Kirkby in Ashfield	**16B** Kirkby in Ashfield	**16B** Kirkby in Ashfield	**16E** Kirkby in Ashfield
48268	*8F*	**16C** Kirkby in Ashfield	**16C** Kirkby in Ashfield	**16C** Kirkby in Ashfield	**16B** Kirkby in Ashfield	**8C** Speke Junction	**8B** Warrington Dallam	**8L** Aintree
48269	*8F*	**15A** Wellingborough	**15A** Wellingborough	**15A** Wellingborough	**21A** Saltley	**2E** Northampton	**21B** Bescot	**6B** Mold Junction
48270	*8F*	**16C** Kirkby in Ashfield	**16C** Kirkby in Ashfield	**16C** Kirkby in Ashfield	**16B** Kirkby in Ashfield	**17A** Derby	**17A** Derby	**16C** Derby
48271	*8F*	**20D** Normanton	**20D** Normanton	**18A** Toton	**18A** Toton	**18A** Toton	**18A** Toton	**16F** Burton
48272	*8F*	**16C** Kirkby in Ashfield	**16C** Kirkby in Ashfield	**16D** Mansfield	**16C** Mansfield	**16C** Mansfield	**16B** Kirkby in Ashfield	**16E** Kirkby in Ashfield
48273	*8F*	**5B** Crewe South	**18A** Toton	**18A** Toton	**18A** Toton	**9E** Trafford Park	**9E** Trafford Park	
48274	*8F*	**20D** Normanton	**20D** Normanton	**20D** Normanton	**55E** Normanton	**56D** Mirfield	**55B** Stourton	**55B** Stourton
48275	*8F*	**19D** Heaton Mersey	**9F** Heaton Mersey	**9F** Heaton Mersey	**9A** Longsight	**9A** Longsight	**9D** Buxton	**8F** Wigan Springs Branch
48276	*8F*	**20B** Stourton	**20B** Stourton	**20B** Stourton	**55B** Stourton	**55B** Stourton	**56D** Mirfield	**56D** Mirfield
48277	*8F*	**20B** Stourton	**16D** Mansfield	**16D** Mansfield	**16C** Mansfield	**16C** Mansfield	**16B** Kirkby in Ashfield	**16E** Kirkby in Ashfield
48278	*8F*	**1A** Willesden	**9D** Buxton	**9D** Buxton	**9D** Buxton	**9D** Buxton	**9D** Buxton	**8F** Wigan Springs Branch
48279	*8F*	**16A** Nottingham	**16A** Nottingham	**16A** Nottingham	**16A** Nottingham	**16A** Nottingham	**16A** Nottingham	**16B** Annesley
48280	*8F*	**18B** Westhouses	**18B** Westhouses	**18B** Westhouses	**18B** Westhouses	**8A** Edge Hill	**8A** Edge Hill	**8A** Edge Hill
48281	*8F*	**15A** Wellingborough	**15A** Wellingborough	**15A** Wellingborough	**55D** Royston	**55D** Royston	**55D** Royston	**55D** Royston
48282	*8F*	**16A** Nottingham	**16C** Kirkby in Ashfield	**16A** Nottingham	**16A** Nottingham	**16C** Mansfield	**16B** Kirkby in Ashfield	**16B** Annesley
48283	*8F*	**16C** Kirkby in Ashfield	**20A** Leeds Holbeck	**20A** Leeds Holbeck	**55A** Leeds Holbeck	**55A** Leeds Holbeck	**55A** Leeds Holbeck	**55A** Leeds Holbeck
48284	*8F*	**19A** Sheffield Grimesthorpe	**19A** Sheffield Grimesthorpe	**18A** Toton	**18A** Toton	**18C** Hasland	**18A** Toton	**16E** Kirkby in Ashfield
48285	*8F*	**15B** Kettering	**15B** Kettering	**15B** Kettering	**15B** Kettering	**15B** Kettering	**15B** Kettering	
48286	*8F*	(WD 70401)	**5B** Crewe South	**11E** Lancaster	**11E** Lancaster	**16A** Nottingham	**16A** Nottingham	**16G** Westhouses
48287	*8F*	(WD 70402)	**5B** Crewe South	**5B** Crewe South	**5B** Crewe South	**2B** Nuneaton	**2A** Rugby	**6C** Croes Newydd
48288	*8F*	(WD 70403)	**5B** Crewe South	**5B** Crewe South	**17F** Trafford Park	**9E** Trafford Park	**9E** Trafford Park	**9E** Trafford Park
48289	*8F*	(WD 70413)	**5B** Crewe South	**5B** Crewe South	**5B** Crewe South	**2B** Nuneaton	**2B** Nuneaton	**5E** Nuneaton
48290	*8F*	(WD 70438)	**5B** Crewe South	**1A** Willesden	**1A** Willesden	**2E** Northampton	**6C** Birkenhead	
48291	*8F*	(WD 70440)	**5B** Crewe South	**5B** Crewe South	**5B** Crewe South	**2B** Nuneaton	**2B** Nuneaton	**5D** Stoke
48292	*8F*	(WD 70442)	**5B** Crewe South	**5B** Crewe South	**5B** Crewe South	**5B** Crewe South	**5B** Crewe South	**8C** Speke Junction
48293	*8F*	**16A** Nottingham	**16A** Nottingham	**16A** Nottingham	**17A** Derby	**17A** Derby	**16D** Annesley	**8A** Edge Hill
48294	*8F*	(WD 70443)	**5B** Crewe South	**5B** Crewe South	**5B** Crewe South	**5B** Crewe South	**8C** Speke Junction	**8C** Speke Junction
48295	*8F*	(WD 70446)	**5B** Crewe South	**5B** Crewe South	**5B** Crewe South	**8E** Northwich	**8E** Northwich	
48296	*8F*	(WD 70447)	**5B** Crewe South	**5B** Crewe South	**6D** Chester Northgate	**8B** Warrington Dallam	**8D** Widnes	**8C** Speke Junction
48297	*8F*	(WD 70449)	**5B** Crewe South	**3A** Bescot	**3A** Bescot	**5B** Crewe South	**8C** Speke Junction	
48301	*8F*	**28C** Carstairs	**15B** Kettering	**15B** Kettering	**15B** Kettering	**14A** Cricklewood	**15A** Wellingborough	**8L** Aintree
48302	*8F*	**28C** Carstairs	**17A** Derby	**17A** Derby	**17A** Derby	**17A** Derby	**9F** Heaton Mersey	**10D** Lostock Hall
48303	*8F*	**28C** Carstairs	**18A** Toton	**18A** Toton	**18A** Toton	**18A** Toton	**17B** Burton	**16E** Kirkby in Ashfield
48304	*8F*	**18A** Toton	**18A** Toton	**18A** Toton	**18A** Toton	**14A** Cricklewood	**16D** Annesley	**16E** Kirkby in Ashfield
48305	*8F*	**15A** Wellingborough	**15A** Wellingborough	**15A** Wellingborough	**15A** Wellingborough	**2E** Northampton	**5B** Crewe South	**8C** Speke Junction
48306	*8F*	**20A** Leeds Holbeck	**15C** Leicester Midland	**15C** Leicester Midland	**15C** Leicester Midland	**14A** Cricklewood	**18A** Toton	
48307	*8F*	**4A** Shrewsbury	**84G** Shrewsbury	**84G** Shrewsbury	**84G** Shrewsbury	**84G** Shrewsbury	**87F** Llanelly	**10D** Lostock Hall
48308	*8F*	**4A** Shrewsbury	**84G** Shrewsbury	**84G** Shrewsbury	**84G** Shrewsbury	**8D** Widnes	**8D** Widnes	**8C** Speke Junction
48309	*8F*	**2A** Rugby	**84G** Shrewsbury	**84G** Shrewsbury	**87K** Swansea Victoria	**87F** Llanelly	**87F** Llanelly	**82F** Bath Green Park
48310	*8F*	**5B** Crewe South	**1A** Willesden	**3A** Bescot	**3A** Bescot	**3A** Bescot	**9A** Longsight	**10C** Fleetwood
48311	*8F*	**18A** Toton	**20B** Stourton	**20B** Stourton	**55B** Stourton	**55B** Stourton	**55B** Stourton	**55B** Stourton
48312	*8F*	**24B** Rose Grove	**1A** Willesden	**1A** Willesden	**2B** Nuneaton	**2B** Nuneaton	**6C** Birkenhead	
48313	*8F*	**18A** Toton	**18A** Toton	**20D** Normanton	**15B** Kettering	**14A** Cricklewood	**18A** Toton	**16B** Annesley
48314	*8F*	**19A** Sheffield Grimesthorpe	**19A** Sheffield Grimesthorpe	**20B** Stourton	**18A** Toton	**18A** Toton	**18A** Toton	
48315	*8F*	**19D** Heaton Mersey	**9F** Heaton Mersey	**9F** Heaton Mersey	**17E** Heaton Mersey	**21A** Saltley	**15D** Coalville	**16B** Annesley
48316	*8F*	**19D** Heaton Mersey	**9F** Heaton Mersey	**9F** Heaton Mersey	**17E** Heaton Mersey	**9F** Heaton Mersey	**9F** Heaton Mersey	**9F** Heaton Mersey
48317	*8F*	**20F** Skipton	**21A** Saltley	**21A** Saltley	**21A** Saltley	**16B** Kirkby in Ashfield	**16B** Kirkby in Ashfield	**16E** Kirkby in Ashfield
48318	*8F*	**5B** Crewe South	**3A** Bescot	**3A** Bescot	**3A** Bescot	**8A** Edge Hill	**8A** Edge Hill	**9D** Newton Heath

		1948	1951	1954	1957	1960	1963	1966
48319	*8F*	**24B** Rose Grove	**24B** Rose Grove	**24B** Rose Grove	**18A** Toton	**18A** Toton	**18A** Toton	**10C** Fleetwood
48320	*8F*	**5B** Crewe South	**2A** Rugby	**2B** Nuneaton	**2B** Nuneaton	**2B** Nuneaton	**2B** Nuneaton	**5E** Nuneaton
48321	*8F*	**28B** Dalry Road	**68A** Carlisle Kingmoor	**68A** Carlisle Kingmoor	**68A** Carlisle Kingmoor	**12A** Carlisle Kingmoor	**12A** Carlisle Kingmoor	**9D** Newton Heath
48322	*8F*	**17A** Derby	**9D** Buxton	**9D** Buxton	**9D** Buxton	**9D** Buxton	**9D** Buxton	**9F** Heaton Mersey
48323	*8F*	**18A** Toton	**12B** Carlisle Canal	**8C** Speke Junction	**8C** Speke Junction	**6B** Mold Junction	**8A** Edge Hill	**10F** Rose Grove
48324	*8F*	**18A** Toton	**18A** Toton	**18A** Toton	**18A** Toton	**14A** Cricklewood	**16D** Annesley	**9H** Patricroft
48325	*8F*	**4B** Swansea Victoria	**1A** Willesden	**1A** Willesden	**1A** Willesden	**1A** Willesden	**1A** Willesden	**6C** Croes Newydd
48326	*8F*	**9D** Buxton	**9D** Buxton	**9D** Buxton	**9D** Buxton	**8D** Widnes	**6C** Birkenhead	**8G** Sutton Oak
48327	*8F*	**4A** Shrewsbury	**6C** Birkenhead	**9F** Heaton Mersey	**17E** Heaton Mersey	**9F** Heaton Mersey	**9F** Heaton Mersey	**9L** Buxton
48328	*8F*	**4A** Shrewsbury	**84G** Shrewsbury	**84G** Shrewsbury	**84G** Shrewsbury	**87F** Llanelly	**87F** Llanelly	
48329	*8F*	**19D** Heaton Mersey	**9F** Heaton Mersey	**9F** Heaton Mersey	**17E** Heaton Mersey	**9F** Heaton Mersey	**9F** Heaton Mersey	**9F** Heaton Mersey
48330	*8F*	**19E** Belle Vue	**87K** Swansea Victoria	**87K** Swansea Victoria	**87K** Swansea Victoria	**87F** Llanelly	**84F** Stourbridge	
48331	*8F*	**28C** Carstairs	**18A** Toton	**21A** Saltley	**18D** Staveley Barrow Hill	**41E** Staveley Barrow Hill	**41E** Staveley Barrow Hill	**9D** Newton Heath
48332	*8F*	**18D** Staveley Barrow Hill	**18D** Staveley Barrow Hill	**18A** Toton	**18A** Toton	**18A** Toton	**17B** Burton	**16F** Burton
48333	*8F*	**18B** Westhouses	**18B** Westhouses	**18B** Westhouses	**18B** Westhouses	**18A** Toton	**16D** Annesley	
48334	*8F*	**15A** Wellingborough	**15A** Wellingborough	**15A** Wellingborough	**16B** Kirkby in Ashfield	**16B** Kirkby in Ashfield	**16B** Kirkby in Ashfield	**16E** Kirkby in Ashfield
48335	*8F*	**4B** Swansea Victoria	**3A** Bescot	**3A** Bescot	**3A** Bescot	**1A** Willesden	**1A** Willesden	**2F** Bescot
48336	*8F*	**21A** Saltley	**21A** Saltley	**21A** Saltley	**21A** Saltley	**21A** Saltley	**15B** Kettering	**2F** Bescot
48337	*8F*	**21A** Saltley	**20C** Royston	**20C** Royston	**55D** Royston	**55D** Royston	**55D** Royston	**55D** Royston
48338	*8F*	**15A** Wellingborough	**15A** Wellingborough	**15A** Wellingborough	**21A** Saltley	**18A** Toton	**9F** Heaton Mersey	**10C** Fleetwood
48339	*8F*	**24B** Rose Grove	**21A** Saltley	**21A** Saltley	**21A** Saltley	**21A** Saltley	**21A** Saltley	**2E** Saltley
48340	*8F*	**5B** Crewe South	**9G** Northwich	**9G** Northwich	**9G** Northwich	**8E** Northwich	**8E** Northwich	**8L** Aintree
48341	*8F*	**18D** Staveley Barrow Hill	**18D** Staveley Barrow Hill	**18D** Staveley Barrow Hill	**18D** Staveley Barrow Hill	**41E** Staveley Barrow Hill	**41E** Staveley Barrow Hill	
48342	*8F*	**18B** Westhouses	**6B** Mold Junction	**9D** Buxton	**11E** Lancaster	**21A** Saltley	**16B** Kirkby in Ashfield	**16B** Annesley
48343	*8F*	**4B** Swansea Victoria	**2A** Rugby	**2B** Nuneaton	**2B** Nuneaton	**2B** Nuneaton	**2B** Nuneaton	**5E** Nuneaton
48344	*8F*	**4B** Swansea Victoria	**84G** Shrewsbury	**84G** Shrewsbury	**84G** Shrewsbury	**9E** Trafford Park	**9E** Trafford Park	**9E** Trafford Park
48345	*8F*	**5B** Crewe South	**2B** Nuneaton	**2B** Nuneaton	**2B** Nuneaton	**2A** Rugby	**2A** Rugby	**6B** Mold Junction
48346	*8F*	**18D** Staveley Barrow Hill	**18D** Staveley Barrow Hill	**18D** Staveley Barrow Hill	**18D** Staveley Barrow Hill	**41E** Staveley Barrow Hill	**26F** Patricroft	**16E** Kirkby in Ashfield
48347	*8F*	**4A** Shrewsbury	**84G** Shrewsbury	**84G** Shrewsbury	**84G** Shrewsbury	**84G** Shrewsbury	**89A** Shrewsbury	**5B** Crewe South
48348	*8F*	**19E** Belle Vue	**26G** Belle Vue	**8B** Warrington Dallam	**8B** Warrington Dallam	**6C** Birkenhead	**6B** Mold Junction	**10F** Rose Grove
48349	*8F*	**19E** Belle Vue	**26G** Belle Vue	**8B** Warrington Dallam	**8B** Warrington Dallam	**6C** Birkenhead	**2E** Northampton	**5D** Stoke
48350	*8F*	**18A** Toton	**18A** Toton	**18A** Toton	**18A** Toton	**18A** Toton	**18A** Toton	**16C** Derby
48351	*8F*	**21A** Saltley	**21A** Saltley	**21A** Saltley	**21A** Saltley	**21A** Saltley	**21A** Saltley	**2E** Saltley
48352	*8F*	**20D** Normanton	**20D** Normanton	**20D** Normanton	**55E** Normanton	**55B** Stourton	**55B** Stourton	**55D** Royston
48353	*8F*	**18B** Westhouses	**18B** Westhouses	**18B** Westhouses	**18B** Westhouses	**18B** Westhouses	**18B** Westhouses	**5D** Stoke
48354	*8F*	**20B** Stourton	**84G** Shrewsbury	**84G** Shrewsbury	**84G** Shrewsbury	**84G** Shrewsbury	**89A** Shrewsbury	**5D** Stoke
48355	*8F*	**15B** Kettering	**15B** Kettering	**15B** Kettering	**15B** Kettering	**15B** Kettering	**15B** Kettering	
48356	*8F*	**15B** Kettering	**15B** Kettering	**15B** Kettering	**15B** Kettering	**15B** Kettering	**15B** Kettering	**9E** Trafford Park
48357	*8F*	**20D** Normanton	**20D** Normanton	**20D** Normanton	**55E** Normanton	**56D** Mirfield	**56D** Mirfield	**56D** Mirfield
48358	*8F*	**18B** Westhouses	**18B** Westhouses	**20B** Stourton	**55B** Stourton	**55B** Stourton	**56D** Mirfield	**56D** Mirfield
48359	*8F*	**15A** Wellingborough	**15A** Wellingborough	**15A** Wellingborough	**15A** Wellingborough	**18C** Hasland	**18C** Hasland	**16C** Derby
48360	*8F*	**15A** Wellingborough	**15A** Wellingborough	**15A** Wellingborough	**15A** Wellingborough	**2E** Northampton	**1E** Bletchley	
48361	*8F*	**18A** Toton	**18A** Toton	**18A** Toton	**18A** Toton	**18A** Toton	**18A** Toton	**16B** Annesley
48362	*8F*	**18A** Toton	**18A** Toton	**18A** Toton	**18A** Toton	**18A** Toton	**18A** Toton	**16E** Kirkby in Ashfield
48363	*8F*	**15A** Wellingborough	**15A** Wellingborough	**15A** Wellingborough	**15A** Wellingborough	**18A** Toton	**18A** Toton	**8L** Aintree
48364	*8F*	**15A** Wellingborough	**14A** Cricklewood	**15A** Wellingborough	**15A** Wellingborough	**17C** Rowsley	**17C** Rowsley	**16E** Kirkby in Ashfield
48365	*8F*	**15A** Wellingborough	**15A** Wellingborough	**15A** Wellingborough	**15A** Wellingborough	**2A** Rugby	**2A** Rugby	**9F** Heaton Mersey
48366	*8F*	**4B** Swansea Victoria	**8B** Warrington Dallam	**3A** Bescot	**3A** Bescot	**3A** Bescot	**5C** Stafford	
48367	*8F*	**18A** Toton	**18A** Toton	**18A** Toton	**18A** Toton	**14A** Cricklewood	**14A** Cricklewood	**16F** Burton
48368	*8F*	**1A** Willesden	**1A** Willesden	**1A** Willesden	**9G** Northwich	**8E** Northwich	**1A** Willesden	**16F** Burton
48369	*8F*	**4A** Shrewsbury	**84G** Shrewsbury	**84G** Shrewsbury	**84G** Shrewsbury	**84G** Shrewsbury	**89A** Shrewsbury	**9D** Newton Heath
48370	*8F*	**18A** Toton	**18A** Toton	**18A** Toton	**18A** Toton	**18A** Toton	**16A** Nottingham	**16C** Derby
48371	*8F*	**15A** Wellingborough	**15A** Wellingborough	**15A** Wellingborough	**18C** Hasland	**18C** Hasland	**18C** Hasland	**9E** Trafford Park
48372	*8F*	**1A** Willesden	**2A** Rugby	**2B** Nuneaton	**2B** Nuneaton	**26A** Newton Heath	**26A** Newton Heath	**9D** Newton Heath
48373	*8F*	**4A** Shrewsbury	**4A** Bletchley	**8C** Speke Junction	**8C** Speke Junction	**8B** Warrington Dallam	**6C** Birkenhead	**9B** Stockport Edgeley
48374	*8F*	**15A** Wellingborough	**15A** Wellingborough	**15A** Wellingborough	**15A** Wellingborough	**15A** Wellingborough	**15A** Wellingborough	**8C** Speke Junction
48375	*8F*	**4A** Shrewsbury	**3A** Bescot	**3A** Bescot	**3A** Bescot	**3A** Bescot	**21B** Bescot	**2F** Bescot
48376	*8F*	**20C** Royston	**15A** Wellingborough	**15A** Wellingborough	**15A** Wellingborough	**15B** Kettering	**15B** Kettering	**16G** Westhouses
48377	*8F*	**20C** Royston	**20C** Royston	**16A** Nottingham	**16A** Nottingham	**16A** Nottingham	**16A** Nottingham	**10C** Fleetwood
48378	*8F*	**16C** Kirkby in Ashfield	**15A** Wellingborough	**15A** Wellingborough	**15A** Wellingborough	**14A** Cricklewood	**16D** Annesley	
48379	*8F*	**16C** Kirkby in Ashfield	**16C** Kirkby in Ashfield	**16C** Kirkby in Ashfield	**16B** Kirkby in Ashfield	**16B** Kirkby in Ashfield	**16B** Kirkby in Ashfield	**8F** Wigan Springs Branch
48380	*8F*	**16A** Nottingham	**16A** Nottingham	**15B** Kettering	**15B** Kettering	**15B** Kettering	**15B** Kettering	**16B** Annesley
48381	*8F*	**16A** Nottingham	**16A** Nottingham	**16A** Nottingham	**14A** Cricklewood	**15A** Wellingborough	**15A** Wellingborough	**15A** Leicester Midland
48382	*8F*	**16C** Kirkby in Ashfield	**16C** Kirkby in Ashfield	**16C** Kirkby in Ashfield	**16B** Kirkby in Ashfield	**15A** Wellingborough	**15D** Coalville	**16B** Annesley
48383	*8F*	**16C** Kirkby in Ashfield	**16C** Kirkby in Ashfield	**16C** Kirkby in Ashfield	**16B** Kirkby in Ashfield	**16B** Kirkby in Ashfield	**16B** Kirkby in Ashfield	**16E** Kirkby in Ashfield
48384	*8F*	**18A** Toton	**18A** Toton	**18A** Toton	**18A** Toton	**18A** Toton	**18A** Toton	**16B** Annesley
48385	*8F*	**23B** Aintree	**15A** Wellingborough	**15A** Wellingborough	**15A** Wellingborough	**15A** Wellingborough	**15A** Wellingborough	**2E** Saltley
48386	*8F*	**25A** Wakefield	**15A** Wellingborough	**15A** Wellingborough	**15A** Wellingborough	**15A** Wellingborough	**15A** Wellingborough	**10F** Rose Grove
48387	*8F*	**18A** Toton	**18A** Toton	**18A** Toton	**18A** Toton	**18A** Toton	**18A** Toton	
48388	*8F*	**18A** Toton	**21A** Saltley	**21A** Saltley	**21A** Saltley	**21A** Saltley	**15B** Kettering	**16B** Annesley
48389	*8F*	**21A** Saltley	**9A** Longsight	**9A** Longsight	**9A** Longsight	**9A** Longsight	**9D** Buxton	
48390	*8F*	**17A** Derby	**17A** Derby	**17A** Derby	**17A** Derby	**17A** Derby	**9F** Heaton Mersey	**9F** Heaton Mersey
48391	*8F*	**18B** Westhouses	**15B** Kettering	**19C** Canklow	**19C** Canklow	**41D** Canklow	**41D** Canklow	
48392	*8F*	**16C** Kirkby in Ashfield	**16C** Kirkby in Ashfield	**16C** Kirkby in Ashfield	**16B** Kirkby in Ashfield	**16B** Kirkby in Ashfield	**16B** Kirkby in Ashfield	**9B** Stockport Edgeley
48393	*8F*	**16C** Kirkby in Ashfield	**16C** Kirkby in Ashfield	**16C** Kirkby in Ashfield	**16B** Kirkby in Ashfield	**16A** Nottingham	**16A** Nottingham	**16B** Annesley
48394	*8F*	**20D** Normanton	**20D** Normanton	**20D** Normanton	**55E** Normanton	**56F** Low Moor	**55B** Stourton	**55B** Stourton
48395	*8F*	**20D** Normanton	**20D** Normanton	**20D** Normanton	**18A** Toton	**16B** Kirkby in Ashfield	**16B** Kirkby in Ashfield	**16E** Kirkby in Ashfield
48396	*8F*	**20D** Normanton	**20D** Normanton	**20D** Normanton	**19C** Canklow	**41D** Canklow	**41D** Canklow	
48397	*8F*	**15C** Leicester Midland	**15C** Leicester Midland	**19C** Canklow	**19C** Canklow	**41D** Canklow	**26F** Patricroft	**9J** Agecroft
48398	*8F*	**15C** Leicester Midland	**2A** Rugby	**2A** Rugby	**2B** Nuneaton	**2B** Nuneaton	**2B** Nuneaton	**8E** Northwich
48399	*8F*	**15C** Leicester Midland	**20A** Leeds Holbeck	**20A** Leeds Holbeck	**55A** Leeds Holbeck	**55A** Leeds Holbeck	**55A** Leeds Holbeck	**55A** Leeds Holbeck
48400	*8F*	**21A** Saltley	**18A** Toton	**18A** Toton	**18A** Toton	**87F** Llanelly	**87F** Llanelly	**10D** Lostock Hall
48401	*8F*	**21A** Saltley	**14A** Cricklewood	**17B** Burton	**17B** Burton	**18A** Toton	**16A** Nottingham	
48402	*8F*	**21A** Saltley	**16A** Nottingham	**19C** Canklow	**84G** Shrewsbury	**84E** Tyseley	**84F** Stourbridge	**2C** Stourbridge
48403	*8F*	**21A** Saltley	**16C** Kirkby in Ashfield	**16C** Kirkby in Ashfield	**17A** Derby	**17A** Derby	**9F** Heaton Mersey	
48404	*8F*	**17A** Derby	**17A** Derby	**20A** Leeds Holbeck	**82B** St. Philips Marsh	**82B** St. Philips Marsh	**89A** Shrewsbury	**6D** Shrewsbury
48405	*8F*	**21A** Saltley	**16C** Kirkby in Ashfield	**16D** Mansfield	**16C** Mansfield	**16C** Mansfield	**16B** Kirkby in Ashfield	**16E** Kirkby in Ashfield
48406	*8F*	**19D** Heaton Mersey	**9F** Heaton Mersey	**9F** Heaton Mersey	**17E** Heaton Mersey	**9F** Heaton Mersey	**9F** Heaton Mersey	
48407	*8F*	**19C** Canklow	**19C** Canklow	**19C** Canklow	**19C** Canklow	**41D** Canklow	**41E** Staveley Barrow Hill	
48408	*8F*	**24B** Rose Grove	**16C** Kirkby in Ashfield	**16C** Kirkby in Ashfield	**16B** Kirkby in Ashfield	**3A** Bescot	**1E** Bletchley	**8E** Northwich
48409	*8F*	**16C** Kirkby in Ashfield	**16C** Kirkby in Ashfield	**16A** Nottingham	**16A** Nottingham	**87F** Llanelly	**87F** Llanelly	
48410	*8F*	**14A** Cricklewood	**14A** Cricklewood	**14A** Cricklewood	**82B** St. Philips Marsh	**82B** St. Philips Marsh	**84F** Stourbridge	**2C** Stourbridge
48411	*8F*	**19G** Trafford Park	**9E** Trafford Park	**9E** Trafford Park	**5B** Crewe South	**2A** Rugby	**2A** Rugby	**6C** Croes Newydd
48412	*8F*	**20C** Royston	**20C** Royston	**18A** Toton	**84C** Banbury	**82B** St. Philips Marsh	**84D** Leamington Spa	**2C** Stourbridge
48413	*8F*	**16C** Kirkby in Ashfield	**16C** Kirkby in Ashfield	**16C** Kirkby in Ashfield	**16B** Kirkby in Ashfield	**16B** Kirkby in Ashfield	**16B** Kirkby in Ashfield	
48414	*8F*	**14A** Cricklewood	**14A** Cricklewood	**14A** Cricklewood	**14A** Cricklewood	**18A** Toton	**18A** Toton	**16B** Annesley
48415	*8F*	**14A** Cricklewood	**14A** Cricklewood	**14A** Cricklewood	**86G** Pontypool Road	**84E** Tyseley	**84F** Stourbridge	**2B** Oxley
48416	*8F*	**24A** Accrington	**1A** Willesden	**1A** Willesden	**1A** Willesden	**1A** Willesden	**1A** Willesden	
48417	*8F*	**21A** Saltley	**21A** Saltley	**21A** Saltley	**86G** Pontypool Road	**84E** Tyseley	**84F** Stourbridge	**2C** Stourbridge
48418	*8F*	**18A** Toton	**18A** Toton	**18A** Toton	**86G** Pontypool Road	**84E** Tyseley	**89A** Shrewsbury	**6D** Shrewsbury
48419	*8F*	**20C** Royston	**20C** Royston	**18A** Toton	**84C** Banbury	**87F** Llanelly	**87F** Llanelly	
48420	*8F*	**21A** Saltley	**21A** Saltley	**21A** Saltley	**82B** St. Philips Marsh	**82B** St. Philips Marsh	**85C** Gloucester Barnwood	
48421	*8F*	**16C** Kirkby in Ashfield	**9D** Buxton	**9D** Buxton	**9D** Buxton	**9D** Buxton	**9D** Buxton	**8L** Aintree
48422	*8F*	**2C** Northampton	**4B** Northampton	**2E** Northampton	**2E** Northampton	**2E** Northampton	**6C** Birkenhead	**8G** Sutton Oak
48423	*8F*	**2C** Northampton	**4B** Northampton	**2E** Northampton	**2E** Northampton	**2A** Rugby	**6C** Birkenhead	**10H** Lower Darwen
48424	*8F*	**21A** Saltley	**21A** Saltley	**21A** Saltley	**86G** Pontypool Road	**84E** Tyseley	**84F** Stourbridge	**2C** Stourbridge
48425	*8F*	**26B** Agecroft	**9A** Longsight	**9A** Longsight	**9A** Longsight	**8D** Widnes	**8A** Edge Hill	**8C** Speke Junction
48426	*8F*	**2C** Northampton	**4B** Northampton	**9G** Northwich	**9G** Northwich	**8E** Northwich	**8E** Northwich	**9D** Newton Heath
48427	*8F*	**4B** Swansea Victoria	**2A** Rugby	**2A** Rugby	**2A** Rugby	**2A** Rugby	**1E** Bletchley	
48428	*8F*	**5B** Crewe South	**9A** Longsight	**9A** Longsight	**9A** Longsight	**9A** Longsight	**9D** Buxton	**9F** Heaton Mersey
48429	*8F*	**25C** Goole	**9A** Longsight	**9F** Heaton Mersey	**17E** Heaton Mersey	**9F** Heaton Mersey	**9F** Heaton Mersey	
48430	*8F*	**19C** Canklow	**18B** Westhouses	**18B** Westhouses	**82B** St. Philips Marsh	**84E** Tyseley	**84F** Stourbridge	
48431	*8F*	**20C** Royston	**20C** Royston	**20C** Royston	**82B** St. Philips Marsh	**82B** St. Philips Marsh	**82E** Bristol Barrow Road	
48432	*8F*	**17A** Derby	**17A** Derby	**17A** Derby	**17D** Rowsley	**16B** Kirkby in Ashfield	**16B** Kirkby in Ashfield	**16B** Annesley

		1948	1951	1954	1957	1960	1963	1966
48433	*8F*	**1A** Willesden	**1A** Willesden	**1A** Willesden	**8A** Edge Hill	**8A** Edge Hill	**8A** Edge Hill	**8A** Edge Hill
48434	*8F*	**19C** Canklow	**19C** Canklow	**19C** Canklow	**82B** St. Philips Marsh	**82B** St. Philips Marsh	**87F** Llanelly	
48435	*8F*	**24B** Rose Grove	**24B** Rose Grove	**24B** Rose Grove	**24B** Rose Grove	**24B** Rose Grove	**1A** Willesden	**10F** Rose Grove
48436	*8F*	**24D** Lower Darwen	**8B** Warrington Dallam	**20C** Royston	**82B** St. Philips Marsh	**82B** St. Philips Marsh	**89A** Shrewsbury	**6D** Shrewsbury
48437	*8F*	**26C** Bolton	**2A** Rugby	**2A** Rugby	**2A** Rugby	**2A** Rugby	**9B** Stockport Edgeley	**9B** Stockport Edgeley
48438	*8F*	**1A** Willesden	**84G** Shrewsbury	**84G** Shrewsbury	**84G** Shrewsbury	**87F** Llanelly	**87F** Llanelly	**10D** Lostock Hall
48439	*8F*	**20C** Royston	**20C** Royston	**20C** Royston	**55D** Royston	**55D** Royston	**55D** Royston	**55D** Royston
48440	*8F*	**19G** Trafford Park	**9E** Trafford Park	**1A** Willesden	**1A** Willesden	**1A** Willesden	**1A** Willesden	**6C** Croes Newydd
48441	*8F*	**25C** Goole	**18D** Staveley Barrow Hill	**2E** Northampton	**8B** Warrington Dallam	**6C** Birkenhead	**6C** Birkenhead	**10H** Lower Darwen
48442	*8F*	**16C** Kirkby in Ashfield	**16C** Kirkby in Ashfield	**16D** Mansfield	**16C** Mansfield	**16C** Mansfield	**16B** Kirkby in Ashfield	**16E** Kirkby in Ashfield
48443	*8F*	**20C** Royston	**20C** Royston	**20C** Royston	**55B** Stourton	**55A** Leeds Holbeck	**55D** Royston	**55D** Royston
48444	*8F*	**26B** Agecroft	**6B** Mold Junction	**18B** Westhouses	**86G** Pontypool Road	**84E** Tyseley	**87F** Llanelly	**82F** Bath Green Park
48445	*8F*	**2C** Northampton	**4B** Northampton	**2E** Northampton	**2E** Northampton	**2E** Northampton	**1A** Willesden	**5E** Nuneaton
48446	*8F*	**26B** Agecroft	**6B** Mold Junction	**2E** Northampton	**1E** Bletchley	**1E** Bletchley	**6C** Birkenhead	
48447	*8F*	**25B** Huddersfield	**6B** Mold Junction	**19A** Sheffield Grimesthorpe	**16C** Mansfield	**16B** Kirkby in Ashfield	**16B** Kirkby in Ashfield	**9B** Stockport Edgeley
48448	*8F*	**24A** Accrington	**6C** Birkenhead	**6C** Birkenhead	**6C** Birkenhead	**6C** Birkenhead	**6C** Birkenhead	**10F** Rose Grove
48449	*8F*	**25C** Goole	**25C** Goole	**2B** Nuneaton	**2B** Nuneaton	**2B** Nuneaton	**2B** Nuneaton	**2F** Bescot
48450	*8F*	**19C** Canklow	**19C** Canklow	**19C** Canklow	**82B** St. Philips Marsh	**82B** St. Philips Marsh	**84F** Stourbridge	**2C** Stourbridge
48451	*8F*	**9D** Buxton	**9D** Buxton	**9D** Buxton	**9D** Buxton	**9D** Buxton	**9D** Buxton	**10F** Rose Grove
48452	*8F*	**25B** Huddersfield	**6B** Mold Junction	**19A** Sheffield Grimesthorpe	**19A** Sheffield Grimesthorpe	**87F** Llanelly	**87F** Llanelly	**5D** Stoke
48453	*8F*	**26C** Bolton	**26C** Bolton	**3A** Bescot	**3A** Bescot	**3A** Bescot	**5C** Stafford	**5D** Stoke
48454	*8F*	**4A** Shrewsbury	**20A** Leeds Holbeck	**20A** Leeds Holbeck	**20A** Leeds Holbeck	**55A** Leeds Holbeck	**55A** Leeds Holbeck	**55A** Leeds Holbeck
48455	*8F*	**25B** Huddersfield	**6C** Birkenhead	**6C** Birkenhead	**6C** Birkenhead	**6C** Birkenhead	**6B** Mold Junction	
48456	*8F*	**24B** Rose Grove	**25G** Farnley Junction	**25G** Farnley Junction	**2B** Nuneaton	**2B** Nuneaton	**2B** Nuneaton	**5E** Nuneaton
48457	*8F*	**5B** Crewe South	**8A** Edge Hill	**8A** Edge Hill	**8A** Edge Hill	**8A** Edge Hill	**8A** Edge Hill	**8C** Speke Junction
48458	*8F*	**24B** Rose Grove	**6B** Mold Junction	**6B** Mold Junction	**6B** Mold Junction	**6B** Mold Junction	**6B** Mold Junction	**6B** Mold Junction
48459	*8F*	**24B** Rose Grove	**6B** Mold Junction	**20C** Royston	**82B** St. Philips Marsh	**82B** St. Philips Marsh	**84F** Stourbridge	**2C** Stourbridge
48460	*8F*	**26A** Newton Heath	**18D** Staveley Barrow Hill	**18D** Staveley Barrow Hill	**86G** Pontypool Road	**86C** Cardiff Canton	**84F** Stourbridge	**2C** Stourbridge
48461	*8F*	**23B** Aintree	**18A** Toton	**18A** Toton	**82B** St. Philips Marsh	**87F** Llanelly	**87F** Llanelly	
48462	*8F*	**26A** Newton Heath	**8D** Widnes	**8D** Widnes	**8D** Widnes	**8E** Northwich	**8E** Northwich	**8E** Northwich
48463	*8F*	**24B** Rose Grove	**18A** Toton	**18A** Toton	**18A** Toton	**87F** Llanelly	**85C** Gloucester Barnwood	
48464	*8F*	**9D** Buxton	**68A** Carlisle Kingmoor	**68A** Carlisle Kingmoor	**68A** Carlisle Kingmoor	**12A** Carlisle Kingmoor	**12A** Carlisle Kingmoor	**9F** Heaton Mersey
48465	*8F*	**5B** Crewe South	**9D** Buxton	**9D** Buxton	**9D** Buxton	**8E** Northwich	**9D** Buxton	**9L** Buxton
48466	*8F*	**5B** Crewe South	**8B** Warrington Dallam	**20C** Royston	**55D** Royston	**55D** Royston	**55D** Royston	**55D** Royston
48467	*8F*	**5B** Crewe South	**6B** Mold Junction	**15B** Kettering	**15B** Kettering	**15B** Kettering	**15B** Kettering	**15A** Leicester Midland
48468	*8F*	**26C** Bolton	**84G** Shrewsbury	**84G** Shrewsbury	**84G** Shrewsbury	**84G** Shrewsbury	**82F** Bath Green Park	**2C** Stourbridge
48469	*8F*	**23B** Aintree	**8B** Warrington Dallam	**20C** Royston	**55D** Royston	**55D** Royston	**8A** Edge Hill	**9K** Bolton
48470	*8F*	**24B** Rose Grove	**6B** Mold Junction	**19C** Canklow	**86G** Pontypool Road	**87F** Llanelly	**87F** Llanelly	**10D** Lostock Hall
48471	*8F*	**24B** Rose Grove	**16B** Kettering	**15B** Kettering	**84C** Banbury	**84E** Tyseley	**89A** Shrewsbury	**6D** Shrewsbury
48472	*8F*	**24D** Lower Darwen	**68A** Carlisle Kingmoor	**68A** Carlisle Kingmoor	**68A** Carlisle Kingmoor	**12A** Carlisle Kingmoor	**12A** Carlisle Kingmoor	**9L** Buxton
48473	*8F*	**4B** Swansea Victoria	**8B** Warrington Dallam	**20C** Royston	**55D** Royston	**55D** Royston	**55D** Royston	**55B** Stourton
48474	*8F*	**4A** Shrewsbury	**84G** Shrewsbury	**84G** Shrewsbury	**84G** Shrewsbury	**84G** Shrewsbury	**84F** Stourbridge	**2B** Oxley
48475	*8F*	**24B** Rose Grove	**15A** Wellingborough	**15A** Wellingborough	**82B** St. Philips Marsh	**84E** Tyseley	**84F** Stourbridge	**2B** Oxley
48476	*8F*	**1A** Willesden	**1A** Willesden	**1A** Willesden	**1A** Willesden	**1A** Willesden	**6C** Birkenhead	**8C** Speke Junction
48477	*8F*	**5B** Crewe South	**6B** Mold Junction	**3A** Bescot	**3A** Bescot	**3A** Bescot	**21B** Bescot	**2F** Bescot
48478	*8F*	**5B** Crewe South	**84G** Shrewsbury	**84G** Shrewsbury	**84G** Shrewsbury	**84G** Shrewsbury	**84F** Stourbridge	
48479	*8F*	**24A** Accrington	**2A** Rugby	**6C** Birkenhead	**9D** Buxton	**8A** Edge Hill	**1A** Willesden	**8G** Sutton Oak
48490	*8F*	**18A** Toton	**18A** Toton	**18A** Toton	**18A** Toton	**18A** Toton	**16A** Nottingham	
48491	*8F*	**15B** Kettering	**6C** Birkenhead	**6C** Birkenhead	**8B** Warrington Dallam	**26A** Newton Heath	**26A** Newton Heath	**9H** Patricroft
48492	*8F*	**15A** Wellingborough	**15A** Wellingborough	**15A** Wellingborough	**15A** Wellingborough	**15A** Wellingborough	**15A** Wellingborough	**15A** Leicester Midland
48493	*8F*	**18D** Staveley Barrow Hill	**18D** Staveley Barrow Hill	**18D** Staveley Barrow Hill	**18D** Staveley Barrow Hill	**41E** Staveley Barrow Hill	**1A** Willesden	**8C** Speke Junction
48494	*8F*	**18B** Westhouses	**18B** Westhouses	**18B** Westhouses	**18B** Westhouses	**18C** Hasland	**18A** Toton	**8F** Wigan Springs Branch
48495	*8F*	**18B** Westhouses	**18B** Westhouses	**18B** Westhouses	**18B** Westhouses	**15A** Wellingborough	**15A** Wellingborough	**9L** Buxton
48500	*8F*	**25A** Wakefield	**9A** Longsight	**9A** Longsight	**9A** Longsight	**9A** Longsight	**8C** Speke Junction	
48501	*8F*	**25A** Wakefield	**9A** Longsight	**9A** Longsight	**17E** Heaton Mersey	**9F** Heaton Mersey	**9F** Heaton Mersey	**9F** Heaton Mersey
48502	*8F*	**25A** Wakefield	**26A** Wakefield	**25A** Wakefield	**56A** Wakefield	**8D** Widnes	**5B** Crewe South	**9H** Patricroft
48503	*8F*	**25A** Wakefield	**9F** Heaton Mersey	**9F** Heaton Mersey	**17E** Heaton Mersey	**9F** Heaton Mersey	**9F** Heaton Mersey	**9F** Heaton Mersey
48504	*8F*	**25A** Wakefield	**25A** Wakefield	**25A** Wakefield	**56A** Wakefield	**2B** Nuneaton	**2B** Nuneaton	**5E** Nuneaton
48505	*8F*	**25A** Wakefield	**2A** Rugby	**11E** Lancaster	**5B** Crewe South	**9D** Buxton	**5B** Crewe South	**5B** Crewe South
48506	*8F*	**25A** Wakefield	**25A** Wakefield	**25A** Wakefield	**9G** Northwich	**8C** Speke Junction	**1A** Willesden	**10F** Rose Grove
48507	*8F*	**25A** Wakefield	**20D** Normanton	**18A** Toton	**15C** Leicester Midland	**18A** Toton	**18B** Westhouses	**16B** Annesley
48508	*8F*	**25A** Wakefield	**19C** Canklow	**19C** Canklow	**19C** Canklow	**41D** Canklow	**41E** Staveley Barrow Hill	
48509	*8F*	**25A** Wakefield	**2A** Rugby	**2A** Rugby	**8A** Edge Hill	**8A** Edge Hill	**8A** Edge Hill	**8C** Speke Junction
48510	*8F*	**25A** Wakefield	**8A** Edge Hill	**17A** Derby	**17A** Derby	**17A** Derby	**17A** Derby	**16B** Annesley
48511	*8F*	**25A** Wakefield	**25A** Wakefield	**25A** Wakefield	**56A** Wakefield	**3A** Bescot	**8E** Northwich	**9K** Bolton
48512	*8F*	**25A** Wakefield	**8A** Edge Hill	**8A** Edge Hill	**8A** Edge Hill	**8A** Edge Hill	**8A** Edge Hill	**8A** Edge Hill
48513	*8F*	**25A** Wakefield	**8A** Edge Hill	**8A** Edge Hill	**8A** Edge Hill	**8A** Edge Hill	**8A** Edge Hill	**8A** Edge Hill
48514	*8F*	**25A** Wakefield	**25A** Wakefield	**3A** Bescot	**3A** Bescot	**3A** Bescot	**21B** Bescot	**2F** Bescot
48515	*8F*	**25A** Wakefield	**27B** Aintree	**18D** Staveley Barrow Hill	**18D** Staveley Barrow Hill	**41E** Staveley Barrow Hill	**41E** Staveley Barrow Hill	**9F** Heaton Mersey
48516	*8F*	**25A** Wakefield	**9A** Longsight	**9A** Longsight	**9A** Longsight	**5B** Crewe South	**5B** Crewe South	**5D** Stoke
48517	*8F*	**25A** Wakefield	**15C** Leicester Midland	**15C** Leicester Midland	**15C** Leicester Midland	**14A** Cricklewood	**14A** Cricklewood	**2F** Bescot
48518	*8F*	**25A** Wakefield	**1A** Willesden	**1A** Willesden	**1A** Willesden	**1A** Willesden	**1A** Willesden	
48519	*8F*	**25A** Wakefield	**9D** Buxton	**9D** Buxton	**9D** Buxton	**9D** Buxton	**9D** Buxton	**10A** Carnforth
48520	*8F*	**25A** Wakefield	**8C** Speke Junction	**8B** Warrington Dallam	**8B** Warrington Dallam	**8B** Warrington Dallam	**8C** Speke Junction	**8C** Speke Junction
48521	*8F*	**25A** Wakefield	**8C** Speke Junction	**9G** Northwich	**9G** Northwich	**8E** Northwich	**8E** Northwich	**9J** Agecroft
48522	*8F*	**25A** Wakefield	**8C** Speke Junction	**8C** Speke Junction	**8C** Speke Junction	**8C** Speke Junction	**21B** Bescot	**2F** Bescot
48523	*8F*	**24B** Rose Grove	**27B** Aintree	**21B** Bournville	**21B** Bournville	**21A** Saltley	**9F** Heaton Mersey	**9K** Bolton
48524	*8F*	**24B** Rose Grove	**87K** Swansea Victoria	**87K** Swansea Victoria	**87K** Swansea Victoria	**87F** Llanelly	**87F** Llanelly	
48525	*8F*	**24B** Rose Grove	**87K** Swansea Victoria	**87K** Swansea Victoria	**87K** Swansea Victoria	**87F** Llanelly	**87F** Llanelly	
48526	*8F*	**24C** Lostock Hall	**2B** Nuneaton	**2B** Nuneaton	**2B** Nuneaton	**2A** Rugby	**2A** Rugby	**2C** Stourbridge
48527	*8F*	**24C** Lostock Hall	**9F** Heaton Mersey	**9F** Heaton Mersey	**17E** Heaton Mersey	**18C** Hasland	**18C** Hasland	**5D** Stoke
48528	*8F*	**24C** Lostock Hall	**8C** Speke Junction	**9F** Heaton Mersey	**17E** Heaton Mersey	**16B** Kirkby in Ashfield	**16B** Kirkby in Ashfield	**15A** Leicester Midland
48529	*8F*	**24C** Lostock Hall	**8C** Speke Junction	**5B** Crewe South	**5B** Crewe South	**2E** Northampton	**21B** Bescot	**2F** Bescot
48530	*8F*	**16C** Kirkby in Ashfield	**16C** Kirkby in Ashfield	**16C** Kirkby in Ashfield	**18A** Toton	**18A** Toton	**17A** Derby	**15A** Leicester Midland
48531	*8F*	**15C** Leicester Midland	**26G** Belle Vue	**8B** Warrington Dallam	**8B** Warrington Dallam	**8C** Speke Junction	**1A** Willesden	**2C** Stourbridge
48532	*8F*	**20C** Royston	**20C** Royston	**20C** Royston	**55D** Royston	**55D** Royston	**8A** Edge Hill	**9L** Buxton
48533	*8F*	**14A** Cricklewood	**15A** Wellingborough	**15A** Wellingborough	**18D** Staveley Barrow Hill	**41E** Staveley Barrow Hill	**41E** Staveley Barrow Hill	**9D** Newton Heath
48534	*8F*	**18B** Westhouses	**18B** Westhouses	**2E** Northampton	**2E** Northampton	**2E** Northampton	**1E** Bletchley	**5E** Nuneaton
48535	*8F*	**18B** Westhouses	**4A** Bletchley	**1E** Bletchley	**1E** Bletchley	**8C** Speke Junction	**8C** Speke Junction	**9E** Trafford Park
48536	*8F*	**18B** Westhouses	**68A** Carlisle Kingmoor	**68A** Carlisle Kingmoor	**68A** Carlisle Kingmoor	**12A** Carlisle Kingmoor	**12A** Carlisle Kingmoor	**9J** Agecroft
48537	*8F*	**18D** Staveley Barrow Hill	**20A** Leeds Holbeck	**20A** Leeds Holbeck	**55B** Stourton	**55D** Royston	**55D** Royston	**55B** Stourton
48538	*8F*	**18D** Staveley Barrow Hill	**18A** Toton	**18A** Toton	**18A** Toton	**18A** Toton	**15A** Wellingborough	**16G** Westhouses
48539	*8F*	**18D** Staveley Barrow Hill	**18D** Staveley Barrow Hill	**18D** Staveley Barrow Hill	**18D** Staveley Barrow Hill	**41E** Staveley Barrow Hill	**41E** Staveley Barrow Hill	**9J** Agecroft
48540	*8F*	**20C** Royston	**20C** Royston	**20C** Royston	**55D** Royston	**55D** Royston	**55D** Royston	**55D** Royston
48541	*8F*	**14A** Cricklewood	**14A** Cricklewood	**14A** Cricklewood	**16C** Mansfield	**16C** Mansfield	**16B** Kirkby in Ashfield	**16E** Kirkby in Ashfield
48542	*8F*	**20C** Royston	**20C** Royston	**20C** Royston	**55D** Royston	**55D** Royston	**55C** Farnley Junction	**55A** Leeds Holbeck
48543	*8F*	**17C** Coalville	**15A** Wellingborough	**18A** Toton	**18A** Toton	**9F** Heaton Mersey	**9F** Heaton Mersey	**9D** Newton Heath
48544	*8F*	**18D** Staveley Barrow Hill	**12B** Carlisle Canal	**1E** Bletchley	**1E** Bletchley	**1E** Bletchley	**1E** Bletchley	**5B** Crewe South
48545	*8F*	**20C** Royston	**18D** Staveley Barrow Hill	**18D** Staveley Barrow Hill	**18D** Staveley Barrow Hill	**18A** Toton	**15B** Kettering	**15A** Leicester Midland
48546	*8F*	**20C** Royston	**18D** Staveley Barrow Hill	**18D** Staveley Barrow Hill	**18D** Staveley Barrow Hill	**41E** Staveley Barrow Hill	**26F** Patricroft	**9F** Heaton Mersey
48547	*8F*	**20C** Royston	**20D** Normanton	**17B** Burton	**17B** Burton	**18C** Hasland	**18C** Hasland	**9K** Bolton
48548	*8F*	**19C** Canklow	**19C** Canklow	**19C** Canklow	**19C** Canklow	**5B** Crewe South	**5B** Crewe South	**5D** Stoke
48549	*8F*	**18B** Westhouses	**4A** Bletchley	**1E** Bletchley	**1E** Bletchley	**1E** Bletchley	**1E** Bletchley	**9B** Stockport Edgeley
48550	*8F*	**2C** Northampton	**4A** Bletchley	**1E** Bletchley	**1E** Bletchley	**1E** Bletchley	**1E** Bletchley	**2C** Stourbridge
48551	*8F*	**4B** Swansea Victoria	**1A** Willesden	**1A** Willesden	**1A** Willesden	**1A** Willesden	**1A** Willesden	**5B** Crewe South
48552	*8F*	**16C** Kirkby in Ashfield	**16C** Kirkby in Ashfield	**16C** Kirkby in Ashfield	**16B** Kirkby in Ashfield	**16B** Kirkby in Ashfield	**16B** Kirkby in Ashfield	**16B** Annesley
48553	*8F*	**5B** Crewe South	**18A** Toton	**18A** Toton	**18A** Toton	**26A** Newton Heath	**26A** Newton Heath	**9H** Patricroft
48554	*8F*	**1A** Willesden	**8D** Widnes	**8D** Widnes	**8D** Widnes	**8D** Widnes	**6C** Birkenhead	**5B** Crewe South
48555	*8F*	**5B** Crewe South	**9G** Northwich	**9G** Northwich	**9G** Northwich	**8E** Northwich	**5B** Crewe South	**5D** Stoke
48556	*8F*	**4A** Shrewsbury	**3A** Bescot	**3A** Bescot	**3A** Bescot	**3A** Bescot	**21B** Bescot	**2F** Bescot
48557	*8F*	**2C** Northampton	**9F** Heaton Mersey	**9F** Heaton Mersey	**17E** Heaton Mersey	**9F** Heaton Mersey	**9F** Heaton Mersey	**9D** Newton Heath
48558	*8F*	**9D** Buxton	**8D** Widnes	**8D** Widnes	**8D** Widnes	**8D** Widnes	**9D** Buxton	
48559	*8F*	**5B** Crewe South	**2A** Rugby	**2A** Rugby	**2A** Rugby	**2A** Rugby	**2A** Rugby	**5B** Crewe South
48600	*8F*	**1A** Willesden	**1A** Willesden	**1A** Willesden	**1A** Willesden	**1A** Willesden	**1A** Willesden	**16G** Westhouses

		1948	1951	1954	1957	1960	1963	1966
48601	8F	1A Willesden	1A Willesden	1A Willesden	1A Willesden	1A Willesden	1A Willesden	
48602	8F	1A Willesden	1A Willesden	3A Bescot	3A Bescot	3A Bescot	21B Bescot	9D Newton Heath
48603	8F	1A Willesden	1A Willesden	1A Willesden	1A Willesden	1A Willesden	1A Willesden	2E Saltley
48604	8F	18D Staveley Barrow Hill	18D Staveley Barrow Hill	18D Staveley Barrow Hill	18D Staveley Barrow Hill	18A Toton	16A Nottingham	16C Derby
48605	8F	1A Willesden	9G Northwich	9G Northwich	9G Northwich	8E Northwich	8E Northwich	8L Aintree
48606	8F	18A Toton	18A Toton	18A Toton	18A Toton	18A Toton	18A Toton	16F Burton
48607	8F	18A Toton	18A Toton	18A Toton	18A Toton	18A Toton	15B Kettering	
48608	8F	16C Kirkby in Ashfield	23B Hellifield	20C Royston	55D Royston	55D Royston	56D Mirfield	56D Mirfield
48609	8F	18D Staveley Barrow Hill	23A Skipton	15B Kettering	15B Kettering	15B Kettering	15B Kettering	15A Leicester Midland
48610	8F	1A Willesden	1A Willesden	1A Willesden	1A Willesden	1E Bletchley	1E Bletchley	
48611	8F	18A Toton	15B Kettering	15B Kettering	15B Kettering	15B Kettering	15B Kettering	
48612	8F	1A Willesden	68A Carlisle Kingmoor	68A Carlisle Kingmoor	68A Carlisle Kingmoor	12A Carlisle Kingmoor	12A Carlisle Kingmoor	9D Newton Heath
48613	8F	4A Shrewsbury	9G Northwich	9G Northwich	9G Northwich	9F Heaton Mersey	9F Heaton Mersey	9F Heaton Mersey
48614	8F	16A Nottingham	16A Nottingham	16A Nottingham	16A Nottingham	16A Nottingham	16A Nottingham	16B Annesley
48615	8F	18A Toton	18A Toton	18A Toton	18A Toton	18A Toton	16D Annesley	8E Northwich
48616	8F	16C Kirkby in Ashfield	23B Hellifield	20G Hellifield	20G Hellifield	14A Cricklewood		
48617	8F	15A Wellingborough	15A Wellingborough	15A Wellingborough	15A Wellingborough	15A Wellingborough	15A Wellingborough	16B Annesley
48618	8F	18A Toton	18A Toton	18A Toton	18A Toton	41E Staveley Barrow Hill	41E Staveley Barrow Hill	10D Lostock Hall
48619	8F	15C Leicester Midland	15A Wellingborough	15C Leicester Midland	16C Leicester Midland	15D Coalville	15D Coalville	16G Westhouses
48620	8F	18B Westhouses	18B Westhouses	18B Westhouses	18B Westhouses	18A Toton	18B Westhouses	16G Westhouses
48621	8F	16D Mansfield	16D Mansfield	16D Mansfield	16C Mansfield	16C Mansfield	16B Kirkby in Ashfield	16E Kirkby in Ashfield
48622	8F	16D Mansfield	20B Stourton	20B Stourton	55B Stourton	55B Stourton	55B Stourton	55B Stourton
48623	8F	18B Westhouses	18B Westhouses	18B Westhouses	18B Westhouses	2B Nuneaton	2B Nuneaton	8G Sutton Oak
48624	8F	1A Willesden	1A Willesden	1A Willesden	1A Willesden	1A Willesden	1A Willesden	
48625	8F	15A Wellingborough	15A Wellingborough	15A Wellingborough	15A Wellingborough	15A Wellingborough	18B Westhouses	15A Leicester Midland
48626	8F	1A Willesden	1A Willesden	1A Willesden	5B Crewe South	5B Crewe South	1E Bletchley	9B Stockport Edgeley
48627	8F	15A Wellingborough	15A Wellingborough	15A Wellingborough	15A Wellingborough	15A Wellingborough	14A Cricklewood	16E Kirkby in Ashfield
48628	8F	1A Willesden	1A Willesden	1A Willesden	1A Willesden	1A Willesden	1A Willesden	2B Oxley
48629	8F	1A Willesden	1A Willesden	1A Willesden	1A Willesden	1A Willesden	1A Willesden	2E Saltley
48630	8F	1A Willesden	8C Speke Junction	8C Speke Junction	5B Crewe South	5B Crewe South	5B Crewe South	
48631	8F	4A Shrewsbury	8C Speke Junction	8C Speke Junction	8C Speke Junction	8C Speke Junction	8E Northwich	8E Northwich
48632	8F	1A Willesden	1A Willesden	1A Willesden	1A Willesden	8E Northwich	1A Willesden	6C Croes Newydd
48633	8F	1A Willesden	9A Longsight	9A Longsight	9A Longsight	5B Crewe South	5B Crewe South	5B Crewe South
48634	8F	1A Willesden	1A Willesden	1A Willesden	17E Heaton Mersey	9F Heaton Mersey	9F Heaton Mersey	
48635	8F	16A Nottingham	16A Nottingham	16A Nottingham	16A Nottingham	16A Nottingham	18A Toton	16F Burton
48636	8F	18A Toton	18A Toton	18A Toton	18A Toton	18A Toton	17A Derby	9H Patricroft
48637	8F	18A Toton	18A Toton	18A Toton	18A Toton	18A Toton	18A Toton	15A Leicester Midland
48638	8F	18A Toton	18A Toton	18A Toton	18A Toton	18A Toton	16A Nottingham	16G Westhouses
48639	8F	16A Nottingham	16A Nottingham	16A Nottingham	16A Nottingham	16A Nottingham	16A Nottingham	8E Northwich
48640	8F	17A Derby	17A Derby	18A Toton	18D Staveley Barrow Hill	18A Toton	16A Nottingham	8E Northwich
48641	8F	16C Kirkby in Ashfield	20B Stourton	20B Stourton	55B Stourton	55B Stourton	55B Stourton	55B Stourton
48642	8F	19A Sheffield Grimesthorpe	19A Sheffield Grimesthorpe	19A Sheffield Grimesthorpe	19A Sheffield Grimesthorpe	41B Sheffield Grimesthorpe	41E Staveley Barrow Hill	
48643	8F	16D Mansfield	16D Mansfield	16D Mansfield	16C Mansfield	16C Mansfield	16B Kirkby in Ashfield	16E Kirkby in Ashfield
48644	8F	15A Wellingborough	15A Wellingborough	15A Wellingborough	15A Wellingborough	15D Coalville	15D Coalville	16G Westhouses
48645	8F	15B Kettering	15B Kettering	15B Kettering	15B Kettering	15B Kettering	15B Kettering	16B Annesley
48646	8F	15A Wellingborough	19C Canklow	19C Canklow	19C Canklow	2A Rugby	1E Bletchley	2E Saltley
48647	8F	17A Derby	17A Derby	21A Saltley	21A Saltley	21A Saltley	18A Toton	8G Sutton Oak
48648	8F	1A Willesden	1A Willesden	1A Willesden	1A Willesden	1A Willesden	6C Birkenhead	8L Aintree
48649	8F	2A Rugby	1A Willesden	1A Willesden	1A Willesden	1A Willesden	1A Willesden	
48650	8F	18B Westhouses	18B Westhouses	18B Westhouses	18B Westhouses	18B Westhouses	18A Toton	5E Nuneaton
48651	8F	15A Wellingborough	15A Wellingborough	15A Wellingborough	15A Wellingborough	15A Wellingborough	15A Wellingborough	16F Burton
48652	8F	18D Staveley Barrow Hill	20B Stourton	20B Stourton	55B Stourton	55B Stourton	8A Edge Hill	9K Bolton
48653	8F	16A Nottingham	16A Nottingham	16A Nottingham	16A Nottingham	16A Nottingham	16A Nottingham	
48654	8F	17A Derby	17A Derby	17A Derby	17D Rowsley	17C Rowsley	17C Rowsley	
48655	8F	18A Toton	18A Toton	18A Toton	18A Toton	5B Crewe South	6B Mold Junction	6B Mold Junction
48656	8F	1A Willesden	1A Willesden	1A Willesden	1A Willesden	1A Willesden	1E Bletchley	
48657	8F	1A Willesden	1A Willesden	1A Willesden	1A Willesden	1A Willesden	1E Bletchley	
48658	8F	1A Willesden	1A Willesden	1A Willesden	2B Nuneaton	2B Nuneaton	2E Northampton	
48659	8F	2A Rugby	1A Willesden	1A Willesden	1A Willesden	5B Crewe South	5B Crewe South	2F Bescot
48660	8F	1A Willesden	84G Shrewsbury	84G Shrewsbury	84G Shrewsbury	84G Shrewsbury	82F Bath Green Park	
48661	8F	18B Westhouses	18B Westhouses	18B Westhouses	18B Westhouses	18B Westhouses	18A Toton	
48662	8F	18A Toton	18A Toton	18A Toton	18A Toton	17B Burton	17B Burton	16F Burton
48663	8F	18D Staveley Barrow Hill	18D Staveley Barrow Hill	18D Staveley Barrow Hill	18D Staveley Barrow Hill	41E Staveley Barrow Hill	26F Patricroft	9H Patricroft
48664	8F	4B Swansea Victoria	8B Warrington Dallam	20C Royston	55D Royston	55D Royston	55C Farnley Junction	55C Farnley Junction
48665	8F	4B Swansea Victoria	1A Willesden	1A Willesden	1A Willesden	1A Willesden	1A Willesden	6C Croes Newydd
48666	8F	16A Nottingham	16A Nottingham	16A Nottingham	16A Nottingham	16A Nottingham	16A Nottingham	16C Derby
48667	8F	19D Heaton Mersey	9G Northwich	9G Northwich	6F Bidston	6G Llandudno Junction	6B Mold Junction	6B Mold Junction
48668	8F	15C Leicester Midland	15A Wellingborough	15A Wellingborough	21A Saltley	2A Rugby	1E Bletchley	10F Rose Grove
48669	8F	21A Saltley	21A Saltley	21A Saltley	21A Saltley	21A Saltley	21A Saltley	2E Saltley
48670	8F	20D Normanton	20D Normanton	20D Normanton	55D Royston	55D Royston	55D Royston	55B Stourton
48671	8F	15A Wellingborough	15A Wellingborough	15A Wellingborough	15A Wellingborough	15A Wellingborough	15A Wellingborough	15A Leicester Midland
48672	8F	18A Toton	18A Toton	18A Toton	18A Toton	18A Toton	18A Toton	16F Burton
48673	8F	4B Swansea Victoria	6C Birkenhead	6C Birkenhead	18A Toton	16B Kirkby in Ashfield	16B Kirkby in Ashfield	16E Kirkby in Ashfield
48674	8F	4A Shrewsbury	3A Bescot	3A Bescot	3A Bescot	3A Bescot	21B Bescot	2F Bescot
48675	8F	16A Nottingham	16A Nottingham	16A Nottingham	16A Nottingham	16A Nottingham	16A Nottingham	8F Wigan Springs Branch
48676	8F	19D Heaton Mersey	9F Heaton Mersey	9F Heaton Mersey	17E Heaton Mersey	9F Heaton Mersey	9F Heaton Mersey	8L Aintree
48677	8F	17A Derby	17A Derby	9F Heaton Mersey	17E Heaton Mersey	9F Heaton Mersey	9F Heaton Mersey	9F Heaton Mersey
48678	8F	15A Wellingborough	15A Wellingborough	15A Wellingborough	15A Wellingborough	14A Cricklewood	14A Cricklewood	16E Kirkby in Ashfield
48679	8F	1A Willesden	1A Willesden	1A Willesden	9D Buxton	9D Buxton	9D Buxton	10D Lostock Hall
48680	8F	19G Trafford Park	9E Trafford Park	9E Trafford Park	9A Longsight	9A Longsight	21B Bescot	2F Bescot
48681	8F	18A Toton	18A Toton	18A Toton	18A Toton	18A Toton	18A Toton	16F Burton
48682	8F	19C Canklow	9F Heaton Mersey	9F Heaton Mersey	17E Heaton Mersey	9F Heaton Mersey	9F Heaton Mersey	
48683	8F	19D Heaton Mersey	9F Heaton Mersey	9F Heaton Mersey	8B Warrington Dallam	8A Edge Hill	8E Northwich	8E Northwich
48684	8F	1A Willesden	6C Birkenhead	6C Birkenhead	6C Birkenhead	6C Birkenhead	6C Birkenhead	10H Lower Darwen
48685	8F	18A Toton	18A Toton	18A Toton	18A Toton	18A Toton	18A Toton	15A Leicester Midland
48686	8F	18D Staveley Barrow Hill	2A Rugby	2A Rugby	2B Nuneaton	2B Nuneaton	2B Nuneaton	5E Nuneaton
48687	8F	21A Saltley	21A Saltley	21A Saltley	21A Saltley	21A Saltley	15D Coalville	16B Annesley
48688	8F	4A Shrewsbury	4A Bletchley	1E Bletchley	1E Bletchley	1E Bletchley	1E Bletchley	
48689	8F	4A Shrewsbury	8B Warrington Dallam	20C Royston	55D Royston	55D Royston	55C Farnley Junction	
48690	8F	18A Toton	18A Toton	15B Kettering	15B Kettering	15B Kettering	15B Kettering	16F Burton
48691	8F	4B Swansea Victoria	6C Birkenhead	6C Birkenhead	6C Birkenhead	6C Birkenhead	6C Birkenhead	10H Lower Darwen
48692	8F	15A Wellingborough	15A Wellingborough	15A Wellingborough	21A Saltley	5B Crewe South	8C Speke Junction	8C Speke Junction
48693	8F	2C Northampton	4A Bletchley	1E Bletchley	8B Warrington Dallam	5B Crewe South	8E Northwich	8E Northwich
48694	8F	15A Wellingborough	18A Toton	18A Toton	18A Toton	17B Burton	17B Burton	16E Kirkby in Ashfield
48695	8F	15A Wellingborough	15A Wellingborough	15A Wellingborough	15A Wellingborough	9F Heaton Mersey	9F Heaton Mersey	9F Heaton Mersey
48696	8F	16A Nottingham	16A Nottingham	16A Nottingham	16A Nottingham	16A Nottingham	16A Nottingham	16B Annesley
48697	8F	19D Heaton Mersey	9G Northwich	9G Northwich	9G Northwich	6B Mold Junction	6C Birkenhead	6C Croes Newydd
48698	8F	19G Trafford Park	9E Trafford Park	9E Trafford Park	17F Trafford Park	18A Toton	18A Toton	16B Annesley
48699	8F	15A Wellingborough	15A Wellingborough	15A Wellingborough	15A Wellingborough	15A Wellingborough	15A Wellingborough	16B Annesley
48700	8F	20C Royston	21A Saltley	21A Saltley	21A Saltley	21A Saltley	16D Annesley	16F Burton
48701	8F	16D Mansfield	16D Mansfield	16D Mansfield	16C Mansfield	16C Mansfield	16B Kirkby in Ashfield	9F Heaton Mersey
48702	8F	20D Normanton	20D Normanton	20D Normanton	55E Normanton	56F Low Moor	8A Edge Hill	9K Bolton
48703	8F	18A Toton	20B Stourton	20B Stourton	55B Stourton	55B Stourton	55B Stourton	55B Stourton
48704	8F	15B Kettering	15B Kettering	15B Kettering	15B Kettering	15B Kettering	15B Kettering	
48705	8F	24A Accrington	26A Newton Heath	3A Bescot	3A Bescot	3A Bescot	21B Bescot	2F Bescot
48706	8F	23B Aintree	87K Swansea Victoria	87K Swansea Victoria	87K Swansea Victoria	87F Llanelly	87F Llanelly	82F Bath Green Park
48707	8F	23B Aintree	26A Newton Heath	84G Shrewsbury	84G Shrewsbury	87F Llanelly	87F Llanelly	10D Lostock Hall
48708	8F	5B Crewe South	8D Widnes	68A Carlisle Kingmoor	68A Carlisle Kingmoor	12A Carlisle Kingmoor	12A Carlisle Kingmoor	9J Agecroft
48709	8F	15C Leicester Midland	15C Leicester Midland	16A Nottingham	16A Nottingham	8D Widnes	8D Widnes	8C Speke Junction
48710	8F	24B Rose Grove	26C Bolton	20C Royston	55D Royston	55D Royston	55D Royston	55D Royston
48711	8F	24B Rose Grove	26C Bolton	9G Northwich	9G Northwich	8E Northwich	8C Speke Junction	8C Speke Junction
48712	8F	9D Buxton	9D Buxton	9D Buxton	9D Buxton	9D Buxton	9D Buxton	10A Carnforth
48713	8F	24B Rose Grove	27B Aintree	3A Bescot	3A Bescot	3A Bescot	21B Bescot	2F Bescot
48714	8F	24B Rose Grove	26G Belle Vue	8B Warrington Dallam	8B Warrington Dallam	8C Speke Junction	8C Speke Junction	9H Patricroft

No.	Class	1948	1951	1954	1957	1960	1963	1966
48715	8F	**24B** Rose Grove	**26G** Belle Vue	**8B** Warrington Dallam	**8B** Warrington Dallam	**8B** Warrington Dallam	**8B** Warrington Dallam	**8F** Wigan Springs Branch
48716	8F	**5B** Crewe South	**2B** Nuneaton	**2B** Nuneaton	**2B** Nuneaton	**26A** Newton Heath	**26A** Newton Heath	
48717	8F	**4B** Swansea Victoria	**9G** Northwich	**9G** Northwich	**9G** Northwich	**8E** Northwich	**8E** Northwich	**8E** Northwich
48718	8F	**24B** Rose Grove	**26A** Newton Heath	**6C** Birkenhead	**6C** Birkenhead	**3D** Aston	**21D** Aston	**5E** Nuneaton
48719	8F	**24C** Lostock Hall	**6C** Birkenhead	**6C** Birkenhead	**6C** Birkenhead	**3D** Aston	**21D** Aston	
48720	8F	**24C** Lostock Hall	**26A** Newton Heath	**8D** Widnes	**8D** Widnes	**26A** Newton Heath	**26A** Newton Heath	**9H** Patricroft
48721	8F	**24D** Lower Darwen	**15A** Wellingborough	**20B** Stourton	**55B** Stourton	**55B** Stourton	**55B** Stourton	**55B** Stourton
48722	8F	**25A** Wakefield	**26A** Newton Heath	**3A** Bescot	**3A** Bescot	**3A** Bescot	**8C** Speke Junction	**8C** Speke Junction
48723	8F	**5B** Crewe South	**2B** Nuneaton	**2B** Nuneaton	**2B** Nuneaton	**2B** Nuneaton	**2B** Nuneaton	**6B** Mold Junction
48724	8F	**25A** Wakefield	**87K** Swansea Victoria	**87K** Swansea Victoria	**84G** Shrewsbury	**84G** Shrewsbury	**84F** Stourbridge	**2F** Bescot
48725	8F	**25A** Wakefield	**26A** Newton Heath	**3A** Bescot	**3A** Bescot	**3A** Bescot	**21B** Bescot	**2F** Bescot
48726	8F	**25A** Wakefield	**6C** Birkenhead	**6C** Birkenhead	**6C** Birkenhead	**3D** Aston	**21B** Bescot	**2F** Bescot
48727	8F	**25A** Wakefield	**26A** Newton Heath	**3A** Bescot	**5C** Stafford	**3A** Bescot	**9D** Buxton	**8G** Sutton Oak
48728	8F	**15C** Leicester Midland	**15C** Leicester Midland	**15C** Leicester Midland	**15C** Leicester Midland	**17B** Burton	**17B** Burton	**16F** Burton
48729	8F	**5B** Crewe South	**2A** Rugby	**2A** Rugby	**1A** Willesden	**12A** Carlisle Kingmoor	**1E** Bletchley	**2F** Bescot
48730	8F	**25A** Wakefield	**87K** Swansea Victoria	**87K** Swansea Victoria	**87K** Swansea Victoria	**87F** Llanelly	**87F** Llanelly	**10D** Lostock Hall
48731	8F	**5B** Crewe South	**9D** Buxton	**9A** Longsight	**17E** Heaton Mersey	**9F** Heaton Mersey	**9F** Heaton Mersey	**9F** Heaton Mersey
48732	8F	**25A** Wakefield	**87K** Swansea Victoria	**87K** Swansea Victoria	**87K** Swansea Victoria	**87F** Llanelly	**87F** Llanelly	
48733	8F	**25B** Huddersfield	**26A** Newton Heath	**3A** Bescot	**3A** Bescot	**3A** Bescot	**21B** Bescot	
48734	8F	**5B** Crewe South	**9D** Buxton	**9D** Buxton	**5B** Crewe South	**5B** Crewe South	**21B** Bescot	
48735	8F	**25G** Farnley Junction	**84G** Shrewsbury	**87K** Swansea Victoria	**87K** Swansea Victoria	**87F** Llanelly	**87F** Llanelly	**8E** Northwich
48736	8F	**4A** Shrewsbury	**2A** Rugby	**5B** Crewe South	**5B** Crewe South	**2E** Northampton	**5B** Crewe South	**5B** Crewe South
48737	8F	**25B** Huddersfield	**87K** Swansea Victoria	**87K** Swansea Victoria	**87K** Swansea Victoria	**84G** Shrewsbury	**82F** Bath Green Park	
48738	8F	**25D** Mirfield	**87K** Swansea Victoria	**84G** Shrewsbury	**84G** Shrewsbury	**84G** Shrewsbury	**89A** Shrewsbury	**5D** Stoke
48739	8F	**25G** Farnley Junction	**87K** Swansea Victoria	**84G** Shrewsbury	**84G** Shrewsbury	**84G** Shrewsbury	**89A** Shrewsbury	**10A** Carnforth
48740	8F	**5B** Crewe South	**9D** Buxton	**9D** Buxton	**9D** Buxton	**9D** Buxton	**8E** Northwich	**9K** Bolton
48741	8F	**5B** Crewe South	**9D** Buxton	**9E** Trafford Park	**17F** Trafford Park	**9E** Trafford Park	**9E** Trafford Park	**9E** Trafford Park
48742	8F	**5B** Crewe South	**9D** Buxton	**9D** Buxton	**9G** Northwich	**8E** Northwich	**8A** Edge Hill	**8A** Edge Hill
48743	8F	**4A** Shrewsbury	**8C** Speke Junction	**5B** Crewe South	**5B** Crewe South	**5B** Crewe South	**5B** Crewe South	**9J** Agecroft
48744	8F	**5B** Crewe South	**6B** Mold Junction	**9A** Longsight	**9A** Longsight	**9A** Longsight	**9B** Stockport Edgeley	**9D** Newton Heath
48745	8F	**5B** Crewe South	**9D** Buxton	**9D** Buxton	**9D** Buxton	**26A** Newton Heath	**26A** Newton Heath	**9H** Patricroft
48746	8F	**5B** Crewe South	**9D** Buxton	**9D** Buxton	**9D** Buxton	**8B** Warrington Dallam	**8A** Edge Hill	**8A** Edge Hill
48747	8F	**5B** Crewe South	**8C** Speke Junction	**8C** Speke Junction	**8C** Speke Junction	**8C** Speke Junction	**21B** Bescot	**2F** Bescot
48748	8F	**5B** Crewe South	**8C** Speke Junction	**16A** Nottingham	**16A** Nottingham	**16A** Nottingham	**16A** Nottingham	**9L** Buxton
48749	8F	**5B** Crewe South	**9D** Buxton	**9D** Buxton	**6B** Mold Junction	**6B** Mold Junction	**6B** Mold Junction	**6B** Mold Junction
48750	8F	**5B** Crewe South	**6B** Mold Junction	**20A** Leeds Holbeck	**14A** Cricklewood	**18A** Toton	**18B** Westhouses	**16B** Annesley
48751	8F	**25D** Mirfield	**5B** Crewe South	**2B** Nuneaton	**2B** Nuneaton	**2B** Nuneaton	**2B** Nuneaton	**5E** Nuneaton
48752	8F	**25D** Mirfield	**26A** Newton Heath	**3A** Bescot	**3A** Bescot	**3D** Aston	**21D** Aston	**2F** Bescot
48753	8F	**5B** Crewe South	**8D** Widnes	**8D** Widnes	**8D** Widnes	**6B** Mold Junction	**2B** Nuneaton	**5E** Nuneaton
48754	8F	**25G** Farnley Junction	**5B** Crewe South	**1E** Bletchley	**1E** Bletchley	**6B** Mold Junction	**2A** Rugby	**6B** Mold Junction
48755	8F	**25G** Farnley Junction	**26A** Newton Heath	**3A** Bescot	**3A** Bescot	**3A** Bescot	**1E** Bletchley	**2E** Saltley
48756	8F	**26A** Newton Heath	**5B** Crewe South	**68A** Carlisle Kingmoor	**68A** Carlisle Kingmoor	**12A** Carlisle Kingmoor	**12A** Carlisle Kingmoor	**9D** Newton Heath
48757	8F	**5B** Crewe South	**5B** Crewe South	**2A** Rugby	**2A** Rugby	**2A** Rugby	**5B** Crewe South	**2C** Stourbridge
48758	8F	**5B** Crewe South	**1A** Willesden	**68A** Carlisle Kingmoor	**68A** Carlisle Kingmoor	**12A** Carlisle Kingmoor	**12A** Carlisle Kingmoor	**9D** Newton Heath
48759	8F	**26A** Newton Heath	**15B** Kettering	**15B** Kettering	**15B** Kettering	**15B** Kettering	**15B** Kettering	
48760	8F	**26A** Newton Heath	**84G** Shrewsbury	**84G** Shrewsbury	**84G** Shrewsbury	**87F** Llanelly	**87F** Llanelly	**82F** Bath Green Park
48761	8F	**26A** Newton Heath	**87K** Swansea Victoria	**87K** Swansea Victoria	**87K** Swansea Victoria	**87F** Llanelly	**87F** Llanelly	
48762	8F	**26A** Newton Heath	**26C** Bolton	**3A** Bescot	**3A** Bescot	**3A** Bescot	**21B** Bescot	**2E** Saltley
48763	8F	**26A** Newton Heath	**21A** Saltley	**21A** Saltley	**16A** Nottingham	**16A** Nottingham	**16A** Nottingham	**16G** Westhouses
48764	8F	**5B** Crewe South	**8D** Widnes	**6C** Birkenhead	**6C** Birkenhead	**8E** Northwich	**8E** Northwich	**8F** Wigan Springs Branch
48765	8F	**26A** Newton Heath	**26C** Bolton	**19A** Sheffield Grimesthorpe	**19A** Sheffield Grimesthorpe	**41B** Sheffield Grimesthorpe	**41E** Staveley Barrow Hill	**9B** Stockport Edgeley
48766	8F	**26B** Agecroft	**26A** Newton Heath	**3A** Bescot	**3A** Bescot	**3A** Bescot	**21B** Bescot	**2F** Bescot
48767	8F	**26C** Bolton	**26C** Bolton	**3A** Bescot	**3A** Bescot	**3A** Bescot	**21B** Bescot	**2F** Bescot
48768	8F	**26D** Bury	**87K** Swansea Victoria	**87K** Swansea Victoria	**87K** Swansea Victoria	**84G** Shrewsbury	**89A** Shrewsbury	**5D** Stoke
48769	8F	**26D** Bury	**26A** Newton Heath	**3A** Bescot	**3A** Bescot	**3A** Bescot	**21B** Bescot	
48770	8F	**5B** Crewe South	**6B** Mold Junction	**20A** Leeds Holbeck	**16B** Kirkby in Ashfield	**18A** Toton	**16D** Annesley	**9H** Patricroft
48771	8F	**5B** Crewe South	**8D** Widnes	**8D** Widnes	**8D** Widnes	**6B** Mold Junction	**6G** Llandudno Junction	
48772	8F	**5B** Crewe South	**8D** Widnes	**15A** Wellingborough	**18A** Toton	**41E** Staveley Barrow Hill	**41D** Canklow	
48773	8F	(WD 500)	→	→	→	**66A** Polmadie	(Polmadie)	**9K** Bolton
48774	8F	(WD 501)	→	→	→	**66A** Polmadie	(Polmadie)	
48775	8F	(WD 512)	→	→	→	**66A** Polmadie	(Polmadie)	**9D** Newton Heath
48801	4F[3]	**10C** Patricroft						
48824	4F[3]	**10A** Wigan Springs Branch						
48834	4F[3]	**10A** Wigan Springs Branch						
48892	6F[2]	**2F** Coventry						
48893	7F[2]	**4B** Swansea Victoria	**87K** Swansea Victoria	**84G** Shrewsbury				
48894	6F[2]	**2B** Bletchley						
48895	7F[2]	**4A** Shrewsbury	**10A** Wigan Springs Branch	**10A** Wigan Springs Branch	**10A** Wigan Springs Branch	**8F** Wigan Springs Branch	**21C** Bushbury	
48896	7F[2]	**2D** Nuneaton						
48897	7F[2]	**2E** Warwick						
48898	7F[2]	**8A** Edge Hill	**8A** Edge Hill	**1E** Bletchley	**1E** Bletchley	**1E** Bletchley		
48899	7F[2]	**4D** Abergavenny	**86K** Abergavenny	**86K** Abergavenny				
48901	7F[2]	**2A** Rugby	**84G** Shrewsbury					
48902	6F[2]	**2B** Bletchley	**3B** Bushbury					
48903	7F[2]	**10C** Patricroft						
48904	6F[2]	**8C** Speke Junction						
48905	7F[2]	**3A** Bescot	**3A** Bescot	**3C** Walsall	**3C** Walsall			
48906	6F[2]	**5B** Crewe South						
48907	7F[2]	**8D** Widnes	**3A** Bescot	**3C** Walsall	**3C** Walsall			
48908	6F[2]	**8A** Edge Hill						
48909	7F[2]	**3A** Bescot						
48910	6F[2]	**2E** Warwick						
48911	6F[2]	**2D** Nuneaton						
48912	6F[2]	**10C** Patricroft						
48913	6F[2]	**2B** Bletchley						
48914	7F[2]	**2C** Northampton	**4B** Northampton	**2A** Rugby	**2A** Rugby			
48915	7F[2]	**1C** Watford	**1C** Watford	**1C** Watford	**10A** Wigan Springs Branch	**8F** Wigan Springs Branch		
48917	7F[2]	**3A** Bescot	**3A** Bescot	**3C** Walsall	**3C** Walsall			
48918	6F[2]	**10E** Sutton Oak						
48920	7F[2]	**10C** Patricroft	**10C** Patricroft					
48921	7F[2]	**4E** Tredegar	**86K** Abergavenny	**86K** Abergavenny	**86K** Tredegar			
48922	7F[2]	**2E** Warwick	**5C** Stafford	**3C** Walsall	**5C** Stafford			
48924	6F[2]	**2E** Warwick						
48925	7F[2]	**2B** Bletchley						
48926	7F[2]	**2A** Rugby	**10C** Patricroft	**10C** Patricroft	**10C** Patricroft			
48927	7F[2]	**8A** Edge Hill	**2B** Nuneaton	**2B** Nuneaton	**2B** Nuneaton	**2B** Nuneaton		
48929	6F[2]	**2C** Northampton						
48930	7F[2]	**10A** Wigan Springs Branch	**3A** Bescot	**3A** Bescot	**3A** Bescot	**3A** Bescot		
48931	6F[2]	**2B** Bletchley						
48932	7F[2]	**4D** Abergavenny	**8A** Edge Hill	**8A** Edge Hill	**3C** Walsall	**9D** Buxton		
48933	7F[2]	**8A** Edge Hill						
48934	7F[2]	**11A** Carnforth						
48935	6F[2]	**2B** Bletchley						
48936	7F[2]	**2C** Northampton	**4B** Northampton					
48939	6F[2]	**8D** Widnes						
48940	7F[2]	**5C** Stafford	**3B** Bushbury	**3B** Bushbury	**3B** Bushbury			
48941	7F[2]	**10C** Patricroft						
48942	7F[2]	**8C** Speke Junction	**8C** Speke Junction	**8C** Speke Junction	**8C** Speke Junction	**8F** Wigan Springs Branch		
48943	7F[2]	**1A** Willesden	**3C** Walsall	**3C** Walsall	**3C** Walsall			
48944	7F[2]	**8B** Warrington Dallam	**8C** Speke Junction	**8C** Speke Junction	**8C** Speke Junction			
48945	7F[2]	**4A** Shrewsbury	**84G** Shrewsbury	**84G** Shrewsbury	**84G** Shrewsbury			
48948	7F[2]	**4D** Abergavenny						
48950	7F[2]	**6B** Mold Junction	**3A** Bescot	**3A** Bescot	**3A** Bescot	**3B** Bushbury		
48951	7F[2]	**2B** Bletchley	**4A** Bletchley	**1E** Bletchley	**1E** Bletchley			

		1948	1951	1954	1957	1960	1963	1966
48952	$7F^2$	**2B** Bletchley	**4A** Bletchley	**1E** Bletchley	**1E** Bletchley			
48953	$7F^2$	**1A** Willesden	**3A** Bescot	**1E** Bletchley	**1E** Bletchley	**1E** Bletchley		
48954	$7F^2$	**10E** Sutton Oak						
48962	$6F^2$	**5B** Crewe South						
48964	$7F^2$	**1C** Watford	**10A** Wigan Springs Branch	**3A** Bescot	**3A** Bescot	**3A** Bescot		
48966	$7F^2$	**8A** Edge Hill						
49002	$7F^2$	**9A** Longsight	**9B** Stockport Edgeley	**2B** Nuneaton	**2B** Nuneaton	**2B** Nuneaton		
49003	$7F^2$	**3C** Walsall						
49004	$7F^2$	**2C** Northampton						
49005	$7F^2$	**2B** Bletchley	**4A** Bletchley	**1E** Bletchley	**1E** Bletchley			
49006	$7F^2$	**4D** Abergavenny	**86K** Abergavenny					
49007	$7F^2$	**2B** Bletchley	**4A** Bletchley	**10A** Wigan Springs Branch	**10A** Wigan Springs Branch	**8F** Wigan Springs Branch		
49008	$7F^2$	**8B** Warrington Dallam	**8B** Warrington Dallam	**8B** Warrington Dallam	**8B** Warrington Dallam	**8F** Wigan Springs Branch		
49009	$7F^2$	**9D** Buxton	**3A** Bescot	**3A** Bescot	**3A** Bescot			
49010	$7F^2$	**9D** Stockport Edgeley	**9B** Stockport Edgeley	**9B** Stockport Edgeley	**9B** Stockport Edgeley			
49011	$6F^2$	**3D** Aston						
49012	$6F^2$	**1A** Willesden						
49013	$6F^2$	**2A** Rugby						
49014	$7F^2$	**10A** Wigan Springs Branch	**4A** Bletchley					
49015	$6F^2$	**3C** Walsall						
49016	$7F^2$	**8A** Edge Hill						
49017	$6F^2$	**3D** Aston	**3D** Aston					
49018	$7F^2$	**20B** Stourton	**10A** Wigan Springs Branch	**10A** Wigan Springs Branch	**10A** Wigan Springs Branch			
49019	$7F^2$	**4D** Abergavenny						
49020	$7F^2$	**8D** Widnes	**8D** Widnes	**3C** Walsall	**3C** Walsall	**8F** Wigan Springs Branch		
49021	$7F^2$	**1A** Willesden	**1A** Willesden	**3A** Bescot	**3A** Bescot	**3A** Bescot		
49022	$7F^2$	**3A** Bescot	**3A** Bescot					
49023	$7F^2$	**10A** Wigan Springs Branch	**10A** Wigan Springs Branch	**10A** Wigan Springs Branch	**10A** Wigan Springs Branch	**8F** Wigan Springs Branch		
49024	$7F^2$	**10A** Wigan Springs Branch	**9B** Stockport Edgeley	**8B** Warrington Dallam	**2C** Warwick			
49025	$7F^2$	**3A** Bescot	**3A** Bescot	**10A** Wigan Springs Branch	**5B** Crewe South	**8F** Wigan Springs Branch		
49026	$7F^2$	**10A** Wigan Springs Branch						
49027	$7F^2$	**8C** Speke Junction	**10C** Patricroft	**10C** Patricroft	**10C** Patricroft			
49028	$7F^2$	**4A** Shrewsbury	**86K** Abergavenny	**86K** Abergavenny				
49029	$7F^2$	**10A** Wigan Springs Branch						
49030	$6F^2$	**10A** Wigan Springs Branch	**10A** Wigan Springs Branch					
49031	$7F^2$	**3C** Walsall	**3C** Walsall					
49032	$6F^2$	**8A** Edge Hill						
49033	$7F^2$	**4B** Swansea Victoria	**87K** Swansea Victoria	**87K** Swansea Victoria	**87K** Swansea Victoria			
49034	$7F^2$	**3A** Bescot	**10D** Plodder Lane	**10D** Plodder Lane	**10C** Patricroft	**26F** Patricroft		
49035	$7F^2$	**4B** Swansea Victoria	**87K** Swansea Victoria	**87K** Swansea Victoria	**87K** Swansea Victoria			
49036	$7F^2$	**3A** Bescot						
49037	$7F^2$	**2B** Bletchley	**3B** Bushbury	**3B** Bushbury	**3B** Bushbury	**3B** Bushbury		
49038	$6F^2$	**8D** Widnes						
49039	$7F^2$	**3A** Bescot						
49040	$6F^2$	**3C** Walsall						
49041	$7F^2$	**1A** Willesden						
49042	$7F^2$	**2C** Northampton						
49043	$6F^2$	**10A** Wigan Springs Branch						
49044	$7F^2$	**3A** Bescot	**3B** Bushbury	**3B** Bushbury	**3B** Bushbury			
49045	$7F^2$	**3A** Bescot	**3A** Bescot	**3A** Bescot	**3A** Bescot	**3A** Bescot		
49046	$7F^2$	**4A** Shrewsbury	**86K** Abergavenny	**86K** Abergavenny	**85C** Hereford			
49047	$7F^2$	**6B** Mold Junction	**5C** Stafford	**5C** Stafford	**5C** Stafford			
49048	$7F^2$	**3C** Walsall	**3C** Walsall	**3C** Walsall	**5C** Stafford			
49049	$7F^2$	**2A** Rugby	**4A** Bletchley	**1E** Bletchley	**2A** Rugby	**8F** Wigan Springs Branch		
49050	$7F^2$	**3A** Bescot						
49051	$7F^2$	**4D** Abergavenny	**86K** Abergavenny	**86K** Abergavenny	**84G** Shrewsbury			
49052	$6F^2$	**6B** Mold Junction						
49053	$6F^2$	**10A** Wigan Springs Branch						
49054	$6F^2$	**9A** Longsight						
49055	$7F^2$	**19C** Canklow						
49056	$6F^2$	**3C** Walsall						
49057	$7F^2$	**8C** Speke Junction	**9D** Buxton	**9D** Buxton	**9D** Buxton			
49058	$6F^2$	**8D** Widnes						
49059	$6F^2$	**9D** Buxton						
49060	$6F^2$	**8C** Speke Junction						
49061	$7F^2$	**2A** Rugby	**4A** Bletchley	**1E** Bletchley	**1E** Bletchley	**1E** Bletchley		
49062	$7F^2$	**1A** Willesden	**1A** Willesden					
49063	$7F^2$	**3A** Bescot	**3A** Bescot	**3A** Bescot	**3A** Bescot			
49064	$7F^2$	**4E** Tredegar	**86K** Abergavenny	**86K** Abergavenny	**86K** Tredegar	**8A** Edge Hill		
49065	$7F^2$	**8C** Speke Junction						
49066	$7F^2$	**8C** Speke Junction	**3C** Walsall	**3C** Walsall	**3C** Walsall			
49067	$6F^2$	**8D** Widnes						
49068	$7F^2$	**2D** Nuneaton	**2B** Nuneaton	**2B** Nuneaton	**2B** Nuneaton			
49069	$7F^2$	**2A** Rugby						
49070	$7F^2$	**2A** Rugby	**4A** Bletchley	**1A** Willesden	**1A** Willesden	**1A** Willesden		
49071	$6F^2$	**8D** Widnes	**3A** Bescot					
49072	$7F^2$	**6B** Mold Junction						
49073	$7F^2$	**8D** Widnes	**8D** Widnes	**8D** Widnes	**10A** Wigan Springs Branch			
49074	$7F^2$	**8D** Widnes						
49075	$6F^2$	**8B** Warrington Dallam						
49076	$6F^2$	**2B** Bletchley						
49077	$7F^2$	**6B** Mold Junction	**3A** Bescot	**3A** Bescot	**3A** Bescot	**3A** Bescot		
49078	$7F^2$	**3A** Bescot	**1C** Watford	**1A** Willesden	**1A** Willesden	**1A** Willesden		
49079	$7F^2$	**8D** Widnes	**8D** Widnes	**8D** Widnes	**8D** Widnes	**2B** Nuneaton		
49080	$7F^2$	**2D** Nuneaton						
49081	$7F^2$	**3A** Bescot	**3A** Bescot	**8D** Widnes	**8D** Widnes	**5C** Stafford		
49082	$7F^2$	**2D** Nuneaton	**8A** Edge Hill	**8A** Edge Hill	**85C** Hereford	**8A** Edge Hill		
49083	$6F^2$	**3A** Bescot						
49084	$7F^2$	**3A** Bescot						
49085	$6F^2$	**8B** Warrington Dallam						
49086	$7F^2$	**8C** Speke Junction						
49087	$7F^2$	**20B** Stourton	**10C** Patricroft	**10C** Patricroft	**10C** Patricroft	**26F** Patricroft		
49088	$7F^2$	**11E** Tebay	**3A** Bescot	**1A** Willesden	**1A** Willesden			
49089	$6F^2$	**3A** Bescot	**3A** Bescot	**3D** Aston				
49090	$7F^2$	**10A** Wigan Springs Branch						
49091	$6F^2$	**5C** Stafford						
49092	$6F^2$	**9B** Stockport Edgeley	**10A** Wigan Springs Branch					
49093	$7F^2$	**2B** Bletchley	**3A** Bescot	**8B** Warrington Dallam	**10A** Wigan Springs Branch	**1E** Bletchley		
49094	$7F^2$	**6C** Birkenhead	**10C** Patricroft	**10C** Patricroft	**1E** Bletchley	**1E** Bletchley		
49095	$6F^2$	**10C** Patricroft						
49096	$7F^2$	**3A** Bescot	**3A** Bescot					
49097	$7F^2$	**3A** Bescot						
49098	$6F^2$	**5C** Stafford	**3A** Bescot					
49099	$7F^2$	**3A** Bescot	**3A** Bescot	**3A** Bescot	**3A** Bescot	**3A** Bescot		
49100	$6F^2$	**2B** Bletchley						
49101	$7F^2$	**6C** Birkenhead						
49102	$6F^2$	**10B** Preston						
49103	$6F^2$	**2C** Northampton						
49104	$7F^2$	**11E** Tebay	**10B** Preston	**10B** Preston	**10B** Preston	**24K** Preston		
49105	$7F^2$	**6B** Mold Junction	**4B** Northampton	**2E** Northampton	**2E** Northampton			
49106	$7F^2$	**3A** Bescot	**3A** Bescot	**3A** Bescot	**3A** Bescot	**3A** Bescot		
49107	$6F^2$	**2A** Rugby						
49108	$7F^2$	**9B** Stockport Edgeley	**9B** Stockport Edgeley	**3C** Walsall	**3C** Walsall			
49109	$7F^2$	**11A** Carnforth	**11A** Carnforth	**11A** Carnforth	**8C** Speke Junction			

		1948	1951	1954	1957	1960	1963	1966
49110	7F^2	**3B** Bushbury						
49111	7F^2	**9B** Stockport Edgeley						
49112	7F^2	**6B** Mold Junction	**11A** Carnforth	**2B** Nuneaton	**2B** Nuneaton			
49113	7F^2	**4D** Abergavenny	**86K** Abergavenny	**86K** Abergavenny	**86G** Pontypool Road			
49114	7F^2	**2D** Nuneaton	**3A** Bescot	**2A** Rugby	**2A** Rugby	**3A** Bescot		
49115	7F^2	**6B** Mold Junction	**5C** Stafford	**5C** Stafford	**5C** Stafford			
49116	7F^2	**5B** Crewe South	**8D** Widnes	**8D** Widnes	**8D** Widnes			
49117	7F^2	**2B** Bletchley	**1A** Willesden	**87K** Swansea Victoria	**87K** Swansea Victoria			
49119	7F^2	**10B** Preston	**8B** Warrington Dallam	**8B** Warrington Dallam	**8B** Warrington Dallam	**26F** Patricroft		
49120	7F^2	**6B** Mold Junction	**8C** Speke Junction	**2C** Warwick	**2B** Nuneaton			
49121	7F^2	**15A** Wellingborough	**86K** Abergavenny	**86K** Abergavenny	**86K** Tredegar			
49122	7F^2	**15B** Kettering	**1A** Willesden	**1A** Willesden	**1A** Willesden	**1A** Willesden		
49123	7F^2	**15A** Wellingborough						
49124	6F^2	**10A** Wigan Springs Branch						
49125	7F^2	**10A** Wigan Springs Branch	**8C** Speke Junction	**3B** Bushbury	**3A** Bescot	**3A** Bescot		
49126	7F^2	**15B** Kettering	**8A** Edge Hill	**8D** Widnes	**8D** Widnes	**5C** Stafford		
49127	7F^2	**2B** Bletchley						
49128	6F^2	**1A** Willesden						
49129	7F^2	**10A** Wigan Springs Branch	**10A** Wigan Springs Branch	**10A** Wigan Springs Branch	**10A** Wigan Springs Branch	**8F** Wigan Springs Branch		
49130	7F^2	**8A** Edge Hill	**11A** Carnforth	**11A** Carnforth	**11A** Carnforth	**5B** Crewe South		
49131	6F^2	**3A** Bescot						
49132	7F^2	**9D** Buxton	**9D** Buxton	**9D** Buxton	**9D** Buxton			
49133	7F^2	**2A** Rugby						
49134	7F^2	**10A** Wigan Springs Branch	**10B** Preston	**8C** Speke Junction	**8C** Speke Junction	**2B** Nuneaton		
49135	6F^2	**2F** Coventry						
49136	6F^2	**8B** Warrington Dallam						
49137	7F^2	**2A** Rugby	**8A** Edge Hill	**8A** Edge Hill	**8A** Edge Hill	**8A** Edge Hill		
49138	7F^2	**4A** Shrewsbury	**84G** Shrewsbury					
49139	7F^2	**1A** Willesden	**1A** Willesden	**1A** Willesden	**1A** Willesden	**8F** Wigan Springs Branch		
49140	6F^2	**8C** Speke Junction	**CME** Crewe	**CME** Crewe				
49141	7F^2	**10A** Wigan Springs Branch	**10B** Preston	**10B** Preston	**10B** Preston	**8F** Wigan Springs Branch		
49142	7F^2	**3A** Bescot	**3A** Bescot	**2B** Nuneaton	**2B** Nuneaton	**2B** Nuneaton		
49143	7F^2	**6B** Mold Junction	**8C** Speke Junction	**8C** Speke Junction	**8C** Speke Junction			
49144	7F^2	**5C** Stafford	**4A** Bletchley	**11A** Carnforth	**10A** Wigan Springs Branch	**2B** Nuneaton		
49145	7F^2	**1C** Watford	**1C** Watford	**1C** Watford	**10A** Wigan Springs Branch			
49146	7F^2	**4D** Abergavenny	**86K** Abergavenny	**86K** Abergavenny	**85C** Hereford			
49147	7F^2	**10D** Plodder Lane	**10D** Plodder Lane	**10D** Plodder Lane	**10C** Patricroft	**26F** Patricroft		
49148	7F^2	**4D** Abergavenny	**87K** Swansea Victoria	**87K** Swansea Victoria	**87K** Swansea Victoria			
49149	7F^2	**10A** Wigan Springs Branch	**8B** Warrington Dallam	**10D** Plodder Lane	**10C** Patricroft			
49150	7F^2	**2D** Nuneaton	**10B** Preston	**10B** Preston	**10B** Preston			
49151	6F^2	**11A** Carnforth	**11A** Carnforth					
49152	6F^2	**10E** Sutton Oak						
49153	7F^2	**2C** Northampton	**8C** Speke Junction	**8C** Speke Junction	**8C** Speke Junction			
49154	7F^2	**2B** Bletchley	**4A** Bletchley	**10A** Wigan Springs Branch	**10A** Wigan Springs Branch	**8F** Wigan Springs Branch		
49155	7F^2	**8A** Edge Hill	**4A** Bletchley	**8C** Speke Junction	**10A** Wigan Springs Branch	**8F** Wigan Springs Branch		
49156	6F^2	**9B** Stockport Edgeley	**9B** Stockport Edgeley					
49157	7F^2	**2C** Northampton	**1C** Watford	**84G** Shrewsbury	**84G** Shrewsbury			
49158	7F^2	**2C** Northampton	**5C** Stafford	**5C** Stafford	**5C** Stafford	**5B** Crewe South		
49159	6F^2	**10A** Wigan Springs Branch						
49160	7F^2	**3A** Bescot	**10B** Preston	**10A** Wigan Springs Branch	**10A** Wigan Springs Branch			
49161	7F^2	**4E** Tredegar	**86K** Abergavenny	**86K** Abergavenny	**86K** Tredegar			
49162	6F^2	**2A** Rugby	**3B** Bushbury					
49163	7F^2	**1A** Willesden	**10A** Wigan Springs Branch					
49164	7F^2	**1A** Willesden	**1A** Willesden	**1A** Willesden	**1A** Willesden	**1A** Willesden		
49165	6F^2	**3A** Bescot						
49166	6F^2	**6B** Mold Junction						
49167	7F^2	**2F** Coventry	**3B** Bushbury	**3B** Bushbury	**3B** Bushbury			
49168	7F^2	**4E** Tredegar	**86K** Abergavenny	**86K** Abergavenny	**86G** Pontypool Road			
49169	7F^2	**2C** Northampton						
49170	7F^2	**8D** Widnes						
49171	6F^2	**9A** Longsight	**3C** Walsall					
49172	7F^2	**6C** Birkenhead	**8C** Speke Junction	**2B** Nuneaton	**2B** Nuneaton			
49173	7F^2	**2B** Bletchley	**8A** Edge Hill	**8A** Edge Hill	**8A** Edge Hill	**8A** Edge Hill	**21B** Bescot	
49174	7F^2	**4E** Tredegar	**86K** Abergavenny	**86K** Abergavenny	**86G** Pontypool Road			
49175	6F^2	**3A** Bescot						
49176	7F^2	**10A** Wigan Springs Branch						
49177	7F^2	**3A** Bescot	**87K** Swansea Victoria	**87K** Swansea Victoria	**87K** Swansea Victoria			
49178	7F^2	**8B** Warrington Dallam	**10C** Patricroft					
49179	6F^2	**2B** Bletchley						
49180	7F^2	**3A** Bescot	**3A** Bescot	**1A** Willesden	**1A** Willesden			
49181	7F^2	**2D** Nuneaton	**2B** Nuneaton	**2B** Nuneaton	**2B** Nuneaton			
49183	6F^2	**9A** Longsight						
49184	6F^2	**5B** Crewe South						
49185	7F^2	**9B** Stockport Edgeley						
49186	7F^2	**9B** Stockport Edgeley	**2B** Nuneaton	**2B** Nuneaton	**3D** Aston			
49187	6F^2	**9B** Stockport Edgeley	**9B** Stockport Edgeley					
49188	7F^2	**11A** Carnforth						
49189	7F^2	**3A** Bescot	**3A** Bescot	**3D** Aston	**3D** Aston			
49190	6F^2	**2D** Nuneaton						
49191	7F^2	**2D** Nuneaton	**10B** Preston	**10B** Preston	**10B** Preston	**9B** Stockport Edgeley		
49192	7F^2	**10A** Wigan Springs Branch						
49193	6F^2	**2B** Bletchley	**3C** Walsall					
49194	6F^2	**5C** Stafford						
49195	6F^2	**3A** Bescot						
49196	7F^2	**3B** Bushbury	**3B** Bushbury	**10B** Preston	**10B** Preston	**24K** Preston		
49197	6F^2	**10A** Wigan Springs Branch						
49198	7F^2	**5E** Alsager	**3C** Walsall	**3C** Walsall	**5C** Stafford			
49199	7F^2	**10C** Patricroft	**10C** Patricroft	**10C** Patricroft	**10C** Patricroft	**26F** Patricroft		
49200	7F^2	**2A** Rugby	**8A** Edge Hill	**8A** Edge Hill	**8A** Edge Hill			
49201	6F^2	**2B** Bletchley						
49202	7F^2	**3A** Bescot	**3A** Bescot	**3A** Bescot	**3A** Bescot			
49203	7F^2	**2C** Northampton	**4B** Northampton	**2E** Northampton	**10A** Wigan Springs Branch			
49204	6F^2	**3B** Bushbury	**3B** Bushbury					
49205	7F^2	**2C** Northampton	**10E** Sutton Oak					
49207	7F^2	**10A** Wigan Springs Branch						
49208	6F^2	**2B** Bletchley	**3C** Walsall					
49209	7F^2	**5B** Crewe South	**10C** Patricroft	**10C** Patricroft	**10C** Patricroft	**26F** Patricroft		
49210	7F^2	**5B** Crewe South	**5B** Crewe South	**9D** Buxton	**9D** Buxton	**9D** Buxton		
49211	6F^2→7F^2	**3A** Bescot						
49212	7F^2	**9D** Buxton	**3A** Bescot	**2B** Nuneaton				
49213	6F^2	**2B** Bletchley	**3C** Walsall					
49214	7F^2	**9D** Buxton	**9D** Buxton	**9D** Buxton	**9D** Buxton			
49216	7F^2	**9D** Buxton	**3A** Bescot	**3A** Bescot	**3A** Bescot	**3A** Bescot		
49217	7F^2	**15A** Wellingborough						
49218	7F^2	**8C** Speke Junction	**8C** Speke Junction					
49219	7F^2	**8C** Speke Junction						
49220	7F^2	**6B** Mold Junction						
49221	6F^2	**10A** Wigan Springs Branch						
49222	6F^2	**3C** Walsall	**3C** Walsall					
49223	7F^2	**15A** Wellingborough	**3A** Bescot	**3A** Bescot	**3A** Bescot			
49224	7F^2	**9D** Buxton	**8A** Edge Hill	**8A** Edge Hill	**8A** Edge Hill	**8A** Edge Hill		
49225	6F^2	**9D** Buxton						
49226	7F^2	**4D** Abergavenny	**86K** Abergavenny	**86K** Abergavenny	**85C** Hereford			
49227	7F^2	**9A** Longsight						

No.	Class	1948	1951	1954	1957	1960	1963	1966
49228	$7F^2$	6B Mold Junction	10A Wigan Springs Branch	10A Wigan Springs Branch	10A Wigan Springs Branch			
49229	$7F^2$	2A Rugby	5C Stafford	5C Stafford	5C Stafford	3B Bushbury		
49230	$7F^2$	5B Crewe South	5B Crewe South	5B Crewe South	5B Crewe South			
49231	$6F^2$	10B Preston						
49232	$6F^2$	5B Crewe South						
49233	$6F^2$	3B Bushbury						
49234	$7F^2$	10C Patricroft	10C Patricroft	10C Patricroft	10C Patricroft	5C Stafford		
49235	$7F^2$	6B Mold Junction						
49236	$6F^2$	3C Walsall						
49237	$7F^2$	2B Bletchley						
49238	$7F^2$	10C Patricroft						
49239	$7F^2$	8A Edge Hill	8A Edge Hill	10E Sutton Oak	10D Sutton Oak			
49240	$7F^2$	9D Buxton	3B Bushbury	3B Bushbury	3B Bushbury	3B Bushbury		
49241	$6F^2$	5B Crewe South	11A Carnforth					
49242	$7F^2$	8A Edge Hill						
49243	$7F^2$	4D Abergavenny	86K Abergavenny	86K Abergavenny	84G Shrewsbury	8A Edge Hill		
49244	$7F^2$	6C Birkenhead	8C Speke Junction					
49245	$7F^2$	3A Bescot	3A Bescot	3A Bescot	2A Rugby			
49246	$7F^2$	6C Birkenhead	3A Bescot	3A Bescot	3A Bescot	3A Bescot		
49247	$7F^2$	8B Warrington Dallam	8B Warrington Dallam	3B Bushbury	3B Bushbury			
49248	$6F^2$	3C Walsall						
49249	$7F^2$	1C Watford	8C Speke Junction	8B Warrington Dallam	2A Rugby			
49250	$6F^2$	10B Preston						
49251	$6F^2$	6B Mold Junction						
49252	$7F^2$	11E Tebay	11A Carnforth	11A Carnforth	11A Carnforth			
49253	$7F^2$	8C Speke Junction	8C Speke Junction					
49254	$7F^2$	10C Patricroft	10C Patricroft	10C Patricroft	10C Patricroft			
49255	$6F^2$	10C Patricroft						
49256	$7F^2$	6C Birkenhead						
49257	$7F^2$	10A Wigan Springs Branch						
49258	$7F^2$	6C Birkenhead	3C Walsall					
49259	$6F^2$	3A Bescot						
49260	$7F^2$	4B Swansea Victoria	87K Swansea Victoria	84G Shrewsbury	84G Shrewsbury			
49261	$6F^2$	6B Mold Junction	3D Aston					
49262	$7F^2$	1C Watford	10E Sutton Oak	10E Sutton Oak	10D Sutton Oak	8G Sutton Oak		
49263	$6F^2$	5B Crewe South						
49264	$7F^2$	2D Nuneaton	10A Wigan Springs Branch					
49265	$7F^2$	3A Bescot	3A Bescot					
49266	$7F^2$	3A Bescot	3A Bescot	3A Bescot	8C Speke Junction			
49267	$7F^2$	5B Crewe South	10B Preston	10B Preston	10B Preston	8F Wigan Springs Branch		
49268	$7F^2$	2D Nuneaton	10A Wigan Springs Branch	10A Wigan Springs Branch	10A Wigan Springs Branch			
49269	$6F^2$	11A Carnforth						
49270	$7F^2$	2C Northampton	4B Northampton	2E Northampton	2E Northampton			
49271	$7F^2$	2C Northampton	4B Northampton	3C Walsall	3C Walsall			
49272	$6F^2$	5B Crewe South						
49273	$6F^2$	10C Patricroft						
49274	$6F^2$	3A Bescot						
49275	$7F^2$	5B Crewe South	1A Willesden	1A Willesden	3A Bescot	3A Bescot		
49276	$7F^2$	4D Abergavenny	84G Shrewsbury	84G Shrewsbury	84G Shrewsbury			
49277	$7F^2$	1A Willesden	1A Willesden	1A Willesden	1A Willesden	9D Buxton		
49278	$7F^2$	2F Coventry	6B Mold Junction	3D Aston	3D Aston			
49279	$6F^2$	3A Bescot						
49280	$7F^2$	6B Mold Junction						
49281	$7F^2$	8C Speke Junction	9B Stockport Edgeley	9B Stockport Edgeley	10D Sutton Oak	9D Buxton		
49282	$7F^2$	3A Bescot	3A Bescot					
49283	$6F^2$	3C Walsall						
49284	$7F^2$	9A Longsight						
49285	$6F^2$	9A Longsight						
49286	$6F^2$	3A Bescot						
49287	$7F^2$	8A Edge Hill	4A Bletchley	1E Bletchley	1E Bletchley	1E Bletchley		
49288	$7F^2$	15A Wellingborough	4A Bletchley	10E Sutton Oak	10D Sutton Oak	8G Sutton Oak		
49289	$7F^2$	15A Wellingborough	4A Bletchley	1E Bletchley	1E Bletchley			
49290	$7F^2$	15A Wellingborough						
49291	$7F^2$	6B Mold Junction						
49292	$7F^2$	15A Wellingborough	4A Bletchley					
49293	$7F^2$	8C Speke Junction	2B Nuneaton	2B Nuneaton	2B Nuneaton	2B Nuneaton		
49294	$7F^2$	3A Bescot						
49295	$6F^2$	3B Bushbury						
49296	$7F^2$	5B Crewe South	1A Willesden					
49297	$6F^2$	8C Speke Junction						
49298	$7F^2$	9A Longsight						
49299	$7F^2$	10B Preston						
49300	$7F^2$	2B Bletchley	3C Walsall					
49301	$7F^2$	3A Bescot	8A Edge Hill	3C Walsall	3C Walsall			
49302	$7F^2$	8B Warrington Dallam	8C Speke Junction					
49303	$6F^2$	10E Sutton Oak						
49304	$7F^2$	10C Patricroft	2B Nuneaton	2B Nuneaton	9G Northwich			
49305	$6F^2$	9D Buxton						
49306	$7F^2$	10A Wigan Springs Branch	10A Wigan Springs Branch	10A Wigan Springs Branch	10A Wigan Springs Branch			
49307	$7F^2$	2B Bletchley						
49308	$7F^2$	3A Bescot	3A Bescot	3A Bescot	3A Bescot			
49309	$6F^2$	3D Aston						
49310	$7F^2$	10A Wigan Springs Branch	10A Wigan Springs Branch	1E Bletchley	1E Bletchley	1E Bletchley		
49311	$7F^2$	10A Wigan Springs Branch	10A Wigan Springs Branch	10A Wigan Springs Branch	10A Wigan Springs Branch			
49312	$7F^2$	10E Sutton Oak	10E Sutton Oak					
49313	$7F^2$	3A Bescot	3A Bescot	3A Bescot	3A Bescot	3A Bescot		
49314	$7F^2$	11A Carnforth	11A Carnforth	8A Edge Hill	2B Nuneaton	2B Nuneaton		
49315	$7F^2$	9D Buxton	10D Plodder Lane	10D Plodder Lane	10A Wigan Springs Branch			
49316	$7F^2$	6B Mold Junction	86K Abergavenny	86K Abergavenny	86K Tredegar			
49317	$7F^2$	10E Sutton Oak						
49318	$7F^2$	2D Nuneaton	2B Nuneaton	5B Crewe South	10D Sutton Oak			
49319	$7F^2$	2A Rugby						
49320	$6F^2$	5C Stafford						
49321	$7F^2$	2C Northampton	4B Northampton	2E Northampton	2E Northampton	8F Wigan Springs Branch		
49322	$7F^2$	6B Mold Junction	3C Walsall	10A Wigan Springs Branch				
49323	$7F^2$	1C Watford	1C Watford	1C Watford	8B Warrington Dallam	26F Patricroft		
49324	$6F^2$	2C Northampton						
49325	$7F^2$	3C Walsall						
49326	$6F^2$	9D Buxton	3C Walsall					
49327	$7F^2$	3A Bescot	3A Bescot	3A Bescot	3A Bescot			
49328	$7F^2$	3A Bescot	3A Bescot	3A Bescot	3A Bescot	3A Bescot		
49329	$7F^2$	21A Saltley						
49330	$7F^2$	10C Patricroft	2D Coventry	2D Coventry	1E Bletchley			
49331	$7F^2$	9D Buxton						
49332	$6F^2$	2B Bletchley						
49333	$7F^2$	8A Edge Hill						
49334	$6F^2$	1A Willesden						
49335	$7F^2$	3A Bescot	10C Patricroft	10C Patricroft	10C Patricroft	26F Patricroft		
49337	$6F^2 \rightarrow 7F^2$	2A Rugby						
49338	$6F^2$	8B Warrington Dallam						
49339	$7F^2$	6C Birkenhead	2B Nuneaton	2B Nuneaton				
49340	$7F^2$	2F Coventry	10C Patricroft	10C Patricroft	10C Patricroft			
49341	$7F^2$	8C Speke Junction	10A Wigan Springs Branch	10A Wigan Springs Branch	10A Wigan Springs Branch			
49342	$7F^2$	2D Nuneaton	1A Willesden	2B Nuneaton	2B Nuneaton	2B Nuneaton		

No.	Class	1948	1951	1954	1957	1960	1963	1966
49343	$7F^2$	9A Longsight	8D Widnes	8D Widnes	8D Widnes	3A Bescot		
49344	$7F^2$	1C Watford	1A Willesden	1A Willesden	1A Willesden	1A Willesden		
49345	$7F^2$	2D Nuneaton	86K Abergavenny	86K Abergavenny	84G Shrewsbury			
49346	$6F^2$	2D Nuneaton	3B Bushbury					
49347	$7F^2$	9D Buxton	9D Buxton					
49348	$7F^2$	10B Preston	9D Buxton	9D Buxton	9D Buxton			
49349	$6F^2$	3C Walsall						
49350	$7F^2$	2D Nuneaton	2B Nuneaton	2B Nuneaton	2B Nuneaton	2B Nuneaton		
49351	$7F^2$	2D Nuneaton						
49352	$7F^2$	2D Nuneaton	10A Wigan Springs Branch	10A Wigan Springs Branch	10A Wigan Springs Branch	8G Sutton Oak		
49353	$6F^2$	10C Patricroft						
49354	$7F^2$	3A Bescot	3A Bescot	3C Walsall				
49355	$7F^2$	8A Edge Hill	8A Edge Hill	8A Edge Hill	8A Edge Hill			
49356	$7F^2$	3B Bushbury						
49357	$7F^2$	5B Crewe South	4B Northampton	2E Northampton	2E Northampton	5C Stafford		
49358	$7F^2$	4B Swansea Victoria	87K Swansea Victoria	87K Swansea Victoria	87K Swansea Victoria			
49359	$6F^2$	2B Bletchley	3A Bescot					
49360	$7F^2$	21A Saltley						
49361	$7F^2$	3A Bescot	3A Bescot	3A Bescot	3A Bescot	3A Bescot	21B Bescot	
49362	$6F^2$	3D Aston						
49363	$7F^2$	9A Longsight						
49364	$6F^2$	3C Walsall						
49365	$7F^2$	8C Speke Junction						
49366	$7F^2$	2D Nuneaton	4B Northampton	2E Northampton	8D Widnes			
49367	$7F^2$	3A Bescot	3A Bescot	3A Bescot	3A Bescot			
49368	$7F^2$	2F Coventry	2B Nuneaton	8A Edge Hill	8C Speke Junction			
49369	$7F^2$	5B Crewe South						
49370	$6F^2$	5B Crewe South	3D Aston					
49371	$6F^2$	2B Bletchley	3A Bescot					
49372	$7F^2$	2B Bletchley						
49373	$7F^2$	5B Crewe South	3C Walsall	3C Walsall	3C Walsall	3A Bescot		
49375	$7F^2$	1C Watford	1C Watford	8A Edge Hill	8A Edge Hill	8A Edge Hill		
49376	$7F^2$	9D Buxton	87K Swansea Victoria	87K Swansea Victoria	87K Swansea Victoria			
49377	$7F^2$	21A Saltley	10E Sutton Oak	10E Sutton Oak	2A Rugby	5C Stafford		
49378	$7F^2$	10D Plodder Lane	10A Wigan Springs Branch	10A Wigan Springs Branch	10A Wigan Springs Branch			
49379	$7F^2$	25G Farnley Junction						
49381	$7F^2$	25B Huddersfield	10A Wigan Springs Branch	10A Wigan Springs Branch	10A Wigan Springs Branch	8F Wigan Springs Branch		
49382	$7F^2$	25G Farnley Junction	10B Preston	10B Preston	10B Preston	24K Preston		
49383	$6F^2$	6B Mold Junction						
49384	$6F^2$	2E Warwick						
49385	$7F^2$	8A Edge Hill	2B Nuneaton	10A Wigan Springs Branch	10A Wigan Springs Branch			
49386	$7F^2$	9D Buxton	10C Patricroft	10C Patricroft	10C Patricroft			
49387	$7F^2$	25B Huddersfield	9D Buxton	9D Buxton	9D Buxton			
49388	$7F^2$	3C Walsall	3C Walsall					
49389	$7F^2$	25G Farnley Junction	10E Sutton Oak	10E Sutton Oak				
49390	$7F^2$	25G Farnley Junction	10B Preston	10B Preston	10B Preston			
49391	$7F^2$	2B Bletchley	4A Bletchley	10B Preston	10B Preston	9D Buxton		
49392	$7F^2$	25G Farnley Junction	8A Edge Hill	8A Edge Hill	8A Edge Hill	8A Edge Hill		
49393	$7F^2$	1A Willesden	10A Wigan Springs Branch	10A Wigan Springs Branch	10A Wigan Springs Branch			
49394	$7F^2$	25G Farnley Junction	8A Edge Hill	8A Edge Hill	8A Edge Hill	8A Edge Hill		
49395	$7F^3$	2C Northampton	8C Speke Junction	8C Speke Junction	8C Speke Junction			
49396	$7F^3$	5B Crewe South	8C Speke Junction	10B Preston	10B Preston			
49397	$7F^3$	2A Rugby	2B Nuneaton	2A Rugby	2A Rugby			
49398	$7F^3$	1A Willesden	8C Speke Junction	8C Speke Junction	8C Speke Junction			
49399	$7F^3$	2A Rugby	8A Edge Hill	8A Edge Hill	8A Edge Hill	8A Edge Hill		
49400	$7F^3$	2D Nuneaton	10C Patricroft	10C Patricroft	10C Patricroft			
49401	$7F^3$	2B Bletchley	2A Rugby	10A Wigan Springs Branch	10A Wigan Springs Branch	8F Wigan Springs Branch		
49402	$7F^3$	3A Bescot	10A Wigan Springs Branch	10A Wigan Springs Branch	10A Wigan Springs Branch	8F Wigan Springs Branch		
49403	$7F^3$	4D Abergavenny	86K Abergavenny	86K Abergavenny	86G Pontypool Road	1E Bletchley		
49404	$7F^3$	2A Rugby	8A Edge Hill	8A Edge Hill	8A Edge Hill	8A Edge Hill		
49405	$7F^3$	10C Patricroft	2D Coventry	9G Northwich	2A Rugby	8A Edge Hill		
49406	$7F^3$	2B Bletchley	4A Bletchley	8C Speke Junction	8C Speke Junction	9D Buxton	21B Bescot	
49407	$7F^3$	4B Swansea Victoria	5B Crewe South	5B Crewe South	5B Crewe South	5B Crewe South	21C Bushbury	
49408	$7F^3$	2A Rugby	10A Wigan Springs Branch	10A Wigan Springs Branch	10A Wigan Springs Branch	8F Wigan Springs Branch		
49409	$7F^3$	4E Tredegar	86K Abergavenny	86K Abergavenny	86K Tredegar			
49410	$7F^3$	2A Rugby	5C Stafford	5C Stafford	5C Stafford			
49411	$7F^3$	8B Warrington Dallam	2A Rugby	2A Rugby	2D Coventry	3A Bescot		
49412	$7F^3$	2D Nuneaton	8A Edge Hill	8A Edge Hill	8A Edge Hill	8A Edge Hill		
49413	$7F^3$	2A Rugby	2A Rugby	2A Rugby	2A Rugby	1A Willesden		
49414	$7F^3$	2C Northampton	2B Nuneaton	2B Nuneaton	2B Nuneaton	2B Nuneaton		
49415	$7F^3$	5B Crewe South	2A Rugby	2D Coventry	2D Coventry	2B Nuneaton		
49416	$7F^3$	2B Bletchley	2A Rugby	8D Widnes	8D Widnes	8A Edge Hill		
49417	$7F^3$	10B Preston	4A Bletchley	2A Rugby	2A Rugby			
49418	$7F^3$	4B Swansea Victoria	2B Nuneaton	9B Stockport Edgeley	9B Stockport Edgeley			
49419	$7F^3$	10B Preston	8A Edge Hill	8A Edge Hill	8A Edge Hill			
49420	$7F^3$	10B Preston	8C Speke Junction	8C Speke Junction	8C Speke Junction			
49421	$7F^3$	10B Preston	10C Patricroft	10C Patricroft	10C Patricroft	26F Patricroft		
49422	$7F^3$	10A Wigan Springs Branch	86K Abergavenny	86K Abergavenny	86G Pontypool Road	8F Wigan Springs Branch		
49423	$7F^3$	2F Coventry	2A Rugby	8A Edge Hill	8A Edge Hill	9D Buxton		
49424	$7F^3$	10A Wigan Springs Branch	2B Nuneaton	2B Nuneaton	84G Shrewsbury			
49425	$7F^3$	3A Bescot	2A Rugby	2D Coventry	2D Coventry	2B Nuneaton		
49426	$7F^3$	2C Northampton	10C Patricroft	10C Patricroft	10C Patricroft	26F Patricroft		
49427	$7F^3$	2B Bletchley	4A Bletchley	1E Bletchley	1E Bletchley			
49428	$7F^3$	2D Nuneaton	9A Longsight	9A Longsight	9A Longsight	24L Carnforth		
49429	$7F^3$	2D Nuneaton	8A Edge Hill	8A Edge Hill	8A Edge Hill			
49430	$7F^3$	2D Nuneaton	2C Warwick	2B Nuneaton	2B Nuneaton	2B Nuneaton	21B Bescot	
49431	$7F^3$	3A Bescot	2A Rugby	2A Rugby	2F Market Harborough	2B Nuneaton		
49432	$7F^3$	2D Nuneaton	2B Nuneaton	2B Nuneaton	2B Nuneaton	2B Nuneaton		
49433	$7F^3$	2A Rugby	2A Rugby	2A Rugby	2A Rugby	9D Buxton		
49434	$7F^3$	2A Rugby	2B Nuneaton	8A Edge Hill	8A Edge Hill	8A Edge Hill		
49435	$7F^3$	2D Nuneaton	2B Nuneaton	9G Northwich	2A Rugby			
49436	$7F^3$	2D Nuneaton	2B Nuneaton	10A Wigan Springs Branch	10A Wigan Springs Branch			
49437	$7F^3$	2D Nuneaton	8A Edge Hill	8A Edge Hill	8A Edge Hill	8A Edge Hill		
49438	$7F^3$	1A Willesden	11A Carnforth	11A Carnforth	11A Carnforth	8F Wigan Springs Branch		
49439	$7F^3$	2D Nuneaton	9A Longsight	9A Longsight	9A Longsight	5B Crewe South		
49440	$7F^3$	2F Coventry	84G Shrewsbury	84G Shrewsbury	84G Shrewsbury	2B Nuneaton		
49441	$7F^3$	2A Rugby	2D Coventry	2D Coventry	2D Coventry	2B Nuneaton		
49442	$7F^3$	10B Preston	2D Coventry	2D Coventry	2D Coventry			
49443	$7F^3$	2B Bletchley	4A Bletchley	1E Bletchley	1E Bletchley	1E Bletchley		
49444	$7F^3$	2C Northampton	2D Coventry	2A Rugby	2F Market Harborough	15F Market Harborough		
49445	$7F^3$	4A Shrewsbury	8A Edge Hill	8A Edge Hill	8A Edge Hill			
49446	$7F^3$	2A Rugby	2D Coventry	2D Coventry	2F Market Harborough	5C Stafford	21C Bushbury	
49447	$7F^3$	6B Mold Junction	2A Rugby	2A Rugby	2F Market Harborough	15F Market Harborough		
49448	$7F^3$	1A Willesden	4A Bletchley	86K Abergavenny	5B Crewe South	8G Sutton Oak	5B Crewe South	
49449	$7F^3$	8A Edge Hill	8A Edge Hill	11A Carnforth	11A Carnforth	24L Carnforth		
49450	$7F^3$	5B Crewe South	9D Buxton	9D Buxton	9D Buxton			
49451	$7F^3$	10B Preston	8C Speke Junction	8C Speke Junction	8C Speke Junction	8F Wigan Springs Branch		
49452	$7F^3$	2A Rugby	2A Rugby	2A Rugby	2A Rugby	3B Bushbury		
49453	$7F^3$	1A Willesden	2B Nuneaton	9B Stockport Edgeley	9B Stockport Edgeley	9B Stockport Edgeley		
49454	$7F^3$	1A Willesden	9D Buxton	5B Crewe South	5B Crewe South	5B Crewe South	5B Crewe South	
49500	$7F^4$	25D Mirfield						
49501	$7F^4$	25B Huddersfield						
49502	$7F^4$	24C Lostock Hall	26B Agecroft					
49503	$7F^4$	24C Lostock Hall	27B Aintree	27B Aintree				

		1948	1951	1954	1957	1960	1963	1966
49504	$7F^4$	**25A** Wakefield						
49505	$7F^4$	**25A** Wakefield	**27B** Aintree	**27B** Aintree	**26E** Lees Oldham	**26B** Agecroft		
49506	$7F^4$	**25A** Wakefield	**27B** Aintree					
49507	$7F^4$	**25E** Sowerby Bridge						
49508	$7F^4$	**25E** Sowerby Bridge	**26D** Bury	**26A** Newton Heath	**26A** Newton Heath	**26A** Newton Heath		
49509	$7F^4$	**26F** Lees Oldham	**26F** Lees Oldham	**26F** Lees Oldham	**26E** Lees Oldham			
49510	$7F^4$	**26A** Newton Heath	**27B** Aintree					
49511	$7F^4$	**26A** Newton Heath	**26B** Agecroft	**25E** Sowerby Bridge	**26A** Newton Heath			
49512	$7F^4$	**26A** Newton Heath						
49513	$7F^4$	**25A** Wakefield						
49514	$7F^4$	**25A** Wakefield						
49515	$7F^4$	**25A** Wakefield	**27B** Aintree	**27B** Aintree	**26A** Newton Heath			
49516	$7F^4$	**25A** Wakefield						
49517	$7F^4$	**25A** Wakefield						
49518	$7F^4$	**25A** Wakefield						
49519	$7F^4$	**25A** Wakefield						
49520	$7F^4$	**26A** Newton Heath						
49521	$7F^4$	**23B** Aintree						
49522	$7F^4$	**25D** Mirfield						
49523	$7F^4$	**24C** Lostock Hall	**27B** Aintree					
49524	$7F^4$	**24C** Lostock Hall	**27B** Aintree					
49525	$7F^4$	**25A** Wakefield						
49526	$7F^4$	**25A** Wakefield						
49527	$7F^4$	**25E** Sowerby Bridge						
49528	$7F^4$	**25E** Sowerby Bridge						
49529	$7F^4$	**25A** Wakefield						
49530	$7F^4$	**25A** Wakefield						
49531	$7F^4$	**25A** Wakefield						
49532	$7F^4$	**25A** Wakefield	**26B** Agecroft	**26C** Bolton				
49533	$7F^4$	**26A** Newton Heath						
49534	$7F^4$	**24C** Lostock Hall						
49535	$7F^4$	**23B** Aintree						
49536	$7F^4$	**25B** Huddersfield	**26A** Newton Heath	**26F** Lees Oldham	**26E** Lees Oldham			
49537	$7F^4$	**25G** Farnley Junction						
49538	$7F^4$	**25G** Farnley Junction	**26B** Agecroft	**26C** Bolton	**26C** Bolton			
49539	$7F^4$	**25G** Farnley Junction						
49540	$7F^4$	**25G** Farnley Junction	**25E** Sowerby Bridge					
49541	$7F^4$	**25A** Wakefield						
49542	$7F^4$	**26C** Bolton						
49543	$7F^4$	**25A** Wakefield						
49544	$7F^4$	**25B** Huddersfield	**26B** Agecroft	**26C** Bolton	**26C** Bolton	**26C** Bolton		
49545	$7F^4$	**25A** Wakefield	**27B** Aintree	**27B** Aintree	**27B** Aintree			
49546	$7F^4$	**25A** Wakefield						
49547	$7F^4$	**25G** Farnley Junction	**27B** Aintree	**27B** Aintree	**27B** Aintree			
49548	$7F^4$	**26F** Lees Oldham	**26F** Lees Oldham					
49549	$7F^4$	**24B** Rose Grove						
49550	$7F^4$	**25A** Wakefield						
49551	$7F^4$	**25G** Farnley Junction						
49552	$7F^4$	**25G** Farnley Junction	**27B** Aintree	**27B** Aintree				
49553	$7F^4$	**25G** Farnley Junction						
49554	$7F^4$	**26A** Newton Heath	**27B** Aintree	**27B** Aintree				
49555	$7F^4$	**25D** Mirfield	**26B** Agecroft	**26B** Agecroft	**26B** Agecroft			
49556	$7F^4$	**26A** Newton Heath						
49557	$7F^4$	**26D** Bury	**26D** Bury	**26A** Newton Heath				
49558	$7F^4$	**25A** Wakefield	**26A** Newton Heath					
49559	$7F^4$	**25A** Wakefield						
49560	$7F^4$	**26A** Newton Heath	**26A** Newton Heath	**26A** Newton Heath	**26A** Newton Heath			
49561	$7F^4$	**25A** Wakefield						
49562	$7F^4$	**25A** Wakefield						
49563	$7F^4$	**25B** Huddersfield	**27B** Aintree					
49564	$7F^4$	**23B** Aintree						
49565	$7F^4$	**26A** Newton Heath						
49566	$7F^4$	**23B** Aintree	**27B** Aintree	**27B** Aintree	**27B** Aintree			
49567	$7F^4$	**23B** Aintree						
49568	$7F^4$	**25E** Sowerby Bridge	**27D** Wigan					
49569	$7F^4$	**25E** Sowerby Bridge						
49570	$7F^4$	**25A** Wakefield	**26A** Newton Heath	**26A** Newton Heath				
49571	$7F^4$	**23B** Aintree	**27B** Aintree					
49572	$7F^4$	**25B** Huddersfield						
49573	$7F^4$	**26C** Bolton						
49574	$7F^4$	**25A** Wakefield						
49575	$7F^4$	**25A** Wakefield						
49576	$7F^4$	**25A** Wakefield						
49577	$7F^4$	**25A** Wakefield						
49578	$7F^4$	**25A** Wakefield	**26B** Agecroft	**26B** Agecroft	**26E** Lees Oldham			
49579	$7F^4$	**25D** Mirfield						
49580	$7F^4$	**25B** Huddersfield	**26A** Newton Heath					
49581	$7F^4$	**23B** Aintree						
49582	$7F^4$	**25C** Goole	**27B** Aintree	**27B** Aintree	**27B** Aintree			
49583	$7F^4$	**25B** Huddersfield						
49584	$7F^4$	**25A** Wakefield						
49585	$7F^4$	**24C** Lostock Hall	**27D** Wigan					
49586	$7F^4$	**23B** Aintree	**27B** Aintree	**27B** Aintree	**27B** Aintree			
49587	$7F^4$	**23B** Aintree	**27D** Wigan					
49588	$7F^4$	**25A** Wakefield						
49589	$7F^4$	**25A** Wakefield	**27B** Aintree					
49590	$7F^4$	**26D** Bury	**26F** Lees Oldham					
49591	$7F^4$	**26D** Bury	**26D** Bury					
49592	$7F^4$	**23B** Aintree	**27B** Aintree	**27D** Wigan	**56E** Sowerby Bridge			
49593	$7F^4$	**26F** Lees Oldham	**26F** Lees Oldham					
49594	$7F^4$	**26D** Bury	**26D** Bury					
49595	$7F^4$	**23B** Aintree	**27B** Aintree					
49596	$7F^4$	**25B** Huddersfield						
49597	$7F^4$	**23B** Aintree						
49598	$7F^4$	**25G** Farnley Junction	**25D** Mirfield	**27D** Wigan	**27D** Wigan			
49599	$7F^4$	**26B** Agecroft						
49600	$7F^4$	**25C** Goole	**27B** Aintree					
49601	$7F^4$	**25D** Mirfield						
49602	$7F^4$	**25D** Mirfield	**25D** Mirfield	**25E** Sowerby Bridge				
49603	$7F^4$	**25A** Wakefield	**27B** Aintree	**26B** Agecroft				
49604	$7F^4$	**25A** Wakefield						
49605	$7F^4$	**25A** Wakefield						
49606	$7F^4$	**25E** Sowerby Bridge						
49607	$7F^4$	**26A** Newton Heath						
49608	$7F^4$	**26A** Newton Heath	**26A** Newton Heath					
49609	$7F^4$	**25A** Wakefield						
49610	$7F^4$	**24B** Rose Grove	**27D** Wigan					
49611	$7F^4$	**24C** Lostock Hall						
49612	$7F^4$	**24C** Lostock Hall	**27D** Wigan					
49613	$7F^4$	**23B** Aintree						
49614	$7F^4$	**24C** Lostock Hall						
49615	$7F^4$	**24C** Lostock Hall						
49616	$7F^4$	**24C** Lostock Hall						
49617	$7F^4$	**24C** Lostock Hall	**27B** Aintree					

		1948	1951	1954	1957	1960	1963	1966
49618	*7F*[4]	**25D** Mirfield	**25D** Mirfield	**26F** Lees Oldham	**26E** Lees Oldham	**26C** Bolton		
49619	*7F*[4]	**25D** Mirfield						
49620	*7F*[4]	**25D** Mirfield	**25D** Mirfield	**27B** Aintree				
49621	*7F*[4]	**25A** Wakefield						
49622	*7F*[4]	**25A** Wakefield						
49623	*7F*[4]	**25A** Wakefield	**27B** Aintree					
49624	*7F*[4]	**25G** Farnley Junction	**27B** Aintree	**25E** Sowerby Bridge	**26A** Newton Heath	**26A** Newton Heath		
49625	*7F*[4]	**25A** Wakefield	**27D** Wigan					
49626	*7F*[4]	**25A** Wakefield						
49627	*7F*[4]	**25A** Wakefield	**26B** Agecroft	**26B** Agecroft	**26B** Agecroft	**26B** Agecroft		
49628	*7F*[4]	**25E** Sowerby Bridge						
49629	*7F*[4]	**25A** Wakefield						
49630	*7F*[4]	**25A** Wakefield						
49631	*7F*[4]	**26B** Agecroft	**27B** Aintree					
49632	*7F*[4]	**25A** Wakefield						
49633	*7F*[4]	**25A** Wakefield						
49634	*7F*[4]	**25A** Wakefield						
49635	*7F*[4]	**25A** Wakefield						
49636	*7F*[4]	**26A** Newton Heath						
49637	*7F*[4]	**26A** Newton Heath	**26A** Newton Heath	**27B** Aintree	**27D** Wigan	**27D** Wigan		
49638	*7F*[4]	**25A** Wakefield	**27D** Wigan	**27B** Aintree				
49639	*7F*[4]	**26A** Newton Heath						
49640	*7F*[4]	**24C** Lostock Hall	**27B** Aintree	**27B** Aintree	**27B** Aintree			
49641	*7F*[4]	**26C** Bolton						
49642	*7F*[4]	**26A** Newton Heath						
49643	*7F*[4]	**25A** Wakefield						
49644	*7F*[4]	**25A** Wakefield						
49645	*7F*[4]	**25A** Wakefield						
49646	*7F*[4]	**25A** Wakefield						
49647	*7F*[4]	**25A** Wakefield						
49648	*7F*[4]	**25A** Wakefield	**25B** Huddersfield	**25B** Huddersfield	**26B** Agecroft			
49649	*7F*[4]	**24C** Lostock Hall						
49650	*7F*[4]	**26A** Newton Heath	**25E** Sowerby Bridge					
49651	*7F*[4]	**26A** Newton Heath						
49652	*7F*[4]	**26A** Newton Heath						
49653	*7F*[4]	**26A** Newton Heath						
49654	*7F*[4]	**26A** Newton Heath						
49655	*7F*[4]	**26A** Newton Heath						
49656	*7F*[4]	**26A** Newton Heath						
49657	*7F*[4]	**26A** Newton Heath	**25E** Sowerby Bridge	**25E** Sowerby Bridge	**56E** Sowerby Bridge			
49658	*7F*[4]	**25D** Mirfield						
49659	*7F*[4]	**25D** Mirfield	**27D** Wigan	**27B** Aintree	**27B** Aintree			
49660	*7F*[4]	**25D** Mirfield	**25D** Mirfield					
49661	*7F*[4]	**25D** Mirfield	**25E** Sowerby Bridge					
49662	*7F*[4]	**25D** Mirfield	**25E** Sowerby Bridge	**26F** Lees Oldham	**26E** Lees Oldham			
49663	*7F*[4]	**25D** Mirfield	**25E** Sowerby Bridge					
49664	*7F*[4]	**26C** Bolton	**26C** Bolton	**27B** Aintree	**27B** Aintree			
49665	*7F*[4]	**26D** Bury						
49666	*7F*[4]	**26D** Bury	**26D** Bury	**26A** Newton Heath				
49667	*7F*[4]	**26D** Bury	**26D** Bury	**26A** Newton Heath	**26A** Newton Heath			
49668	*7F*[4]	**26F** Lees Oldham	**26F** Lees Oldham	**26F** Lees Oldham	**26E** Lees Oldham	**27B** Aintree		
49669	*7F*[4]	**25A** Wakefield						
49670	*7F*[4]	**25A** Wakefield						
49671	*7F*[4]	**25A** Wakefield	**27B** Aintree					
49672	*7F*[4]	**25G** Farnley Junction	**27B** Aintree	**27B** Aintree	**27B** Aintree			
49673	*7F*[4]	**25G** Farnley Junction	**25E** Sowerby Bridge					
49674	*7F*[4]	**23A** Bank Hall	**25E** Sowerby Bridge	**25E** Sowerby Bridge	**26C** Bolton	**26B** Agecroft		
50412	*5P*	**24E** Blackpool Central						
50423	*5P*	**24E** Blackpool Central						
50429	*5P*	**24E** Blackpool Central						
50432	*5P*	**24E** Blackpool Central						
50442	*5P*	**24E** Blackpool Central						
50448	*5P*	**24E** Blackpool Central						
50455	*5P*	**24E** Blackpool Central	**28A** Blackpool Central					
50617	*Rail Motor*[1]	**26C** Bolton						
50621	*2P*[8]	**20D** Normanton	**20D** Normanton	**20D** Normanton				
50622	*2P*[8]	**20A** Leeds Holbeck	**20E** Manningham					
50623	*2P*[8]	**20F** Skipton	**20E** Manningham					
50625	*2P*[8]	**20G** Hellifield	**23B** Hellifield					
50630	*2P*[8]	**20E** Manningham						
50631	*2P*[8]	**20E** Manningham						
50633	*2P*[8]	**20E** Manningham	**20E** Manningham					
50634	*2P*[8]	**20E** Manningham	**20E** Manningham					
50636	*2P*[8]	**20E** Manningham	**20E** Manningham	**20E** Manningham	**55F** Manningham			
50639	*2P*[8]	**10B** Preston	**10B** Preston					
50640	*2P*[8]	**24F** Fleetwood	**28B** Fleetwood					
50642	*2P*[8]	**26C** Bolton	**28B** Fleetwood					
50643	*2P*[8]	**11B** Barrow	**11B** Barrow	**8B** Warrington Dallam	**8B** Warrington Dallam			
50644	*2P*[8]	**11B** Barrow	**10D** Plodder Lane	**8B** Warrington Dallam	**8B** Warrington Dallam			
50646	*2P*[8]	**26C** Bolton	**28B** Fleetwood	**26C** Bolton	**15D** Bedford			
50647	*2P*[8]	**25A** Wakefield	**26C** Bolton	**26E** Bacup	**26C** Bolton			
50648	*2P*[8]	**23B** Aintree	**27B** Aintree	**24B** Rose Grove				
50650	*2P*[8]	**25A** Wakefield	**26E** Bacup	**26C** Bolton				
50651	*2P*[8]	**26E** Bacup	**26E** Bacup	**24B** Rose Grove				
50652	*2P*[8]	**26E** Bacup	**26E** Bacup	**24B** Rose Grove				
50653	*2P*[8]	**24B** Rose Grove	**24B** Rose Grove	**24B** Rose Grove				
50654	*2P*[8]	**24B** Rose Grove	**24B** Rose Grove					
50655	*2P*[8]	**23B** Aintree	**27B** Aintree	**24B** Rose Grove				
50656	*2P*[8]	**25A** Wakefield	**26E** Bacup	**24B** Rose Grove				
50660	*2P*[8]	**23B** Aintree	**26C** Bolton	**26C** Bolton	**26C** Bolton			
50665	*2P*[8]	**25F** Low Moor						
50667	*2P*[8]	**25A** Wakefield						
50670	*2P*[8]	**25D** Mirfield						
50671	*2P*[8]	**20F** Skipton	**20E** Manningham					
50675	*2P*[8]	**24F** Fleetwood						
50676	*2P*[8]	**10B** Preston						
50678	*2P*[8]	**23C** Southport	**10B** Preston					
50681	*2P*[8]	**20E** Manningham	**20E** Manningham					
50686	*2P*[8]	**20G** Hellifield	**23B** Hellifield	**20E** Manningham				
50687	*2P*[8]	**23C** Southport	**8B** Warrington Dallam					
50689	*2P*[8]	**20A** Leeds Holbeck	**20E** Manningham					
50692	*2P*[8]	**23D** Wigan						
50695	*2P*[8]	**25A** Wakefield	**10B** Preston					
50696	*2P*[8]	**23C** Southport						
50697	*2P*[8]	**26C** Bolton	**8B** Warrington Dallam					
50703	*2P*[8]	**24F** Fleetwood	**8B** Warrington Dallam					
50705	*2P*[8]	**24F** Fleetwood	**8B** Warrington Dallam	**8B** Warrington Dallam	**8B** Warrington Dallam			
50711	*2P*[8]	**25E** Sowerby Bridge						
50712	*2P*[8]	**25D** Mirfield	**25E** Sowerby Bridge	**24C** Lostock Hall	**27C** Southport			
50714	*2P*[8]	**20E** Manningham	**20E** Manningham					
50715	*2P*[8]	**25F** Low Moor	**25A** Wakefield	**25E** Sowerby Bridge				
50720	*2P*[8]	**24F** Fleetwood	**28B** Fleetwood					
50721	*2P*[8]	**24E** Blackpool Central	**28A** Blackpool Central	**27C** Southport	**27C** Southport	**27A** Bank Hall		
50725	*2P*[8]	**24E** Blackpool Central	**28A** Blackpool Central	**24C** Lostock Hall	**55G** Huddersfield			

		1948	1951	1954	1957	1960	1963	1966
50728	$2P^8$	**23C** Southport						
50731	$2P^8$	**25D** Mirfield	**25B** Huddersfield	**26C** Bolton				
50732	$2P^8$	**24F** Fleetwood						
50735	$2P^8$	**24D** Lower Darwen	**25B** Huddersfield					
50736	$2P^8$	**26A** Newton Heath	**25B** Huddersfield					
50738	$2P^8$	**26A** Newton Heath						
50743	$2P^8$	**23C** Southport						
50746	$2P^8$	**23C** Southport	**28A** Blackpool Central	**24D** Lower Darwen	**27C** Southport	**27C** Southport		
50748	$2P^8$	**25A** Wakefield						
50749	$2P^8$	**24E** Blackpool Central	**28A** Blackpool Central					
50750	$2P^8$	**24E** Blackpool Central						
50752	$2P^8$	**23C** Southport	**28A** Blackpool Central	**25E** Sowerby Bridge	**56E** Sowerby Bridge			
50755	$2P^8$	**25A** Wakefield						
50757	$2P^8$	**23D** Wigan	**28A** Blackpool Central	**25E** Sowerby Bridge	**56F** Low Moor			
50762	$2P^8$	**25F** Low Moor	**25A** Wakefield					
50764	$2P^8$	**25A** Wakefield	**24C** Lostock Hall	**25F** Low Moor				
50765	$2P^8$	**24F** Fleetwood	**25E** Sowerby Bridge	**26C** Bolton				
50766	$2P^8$	**24E** Blackpool Central	**28B** Fleetwood					
50777	$2P^8$	**25A** Wakefield	**28A** Blackpool Central	**27C** Southport	**56E** Sowerby Bridge			
50778	$2P^8$	**23C** Southport	**28B** Fleetwood					
50781	$2P^8$	**24D** Lower Darwen	**24C** Lostock Hall	**27C** Southport	**27C** Southport	**27E** Walton on the Hill		
50788	$2P^8$	**25F** Low Moor	**26C** Bolton	**24F** Fleetwood				
50793	$2P^8$	**10B** Preston						
50795	$2P^8$	**20F** Skipton	**20E** Manningham	**20E** Manningham	**55F** Manningham			
50798	$2P^8$	**25D** Mirfield						
50799	$2P^8$	**24E** Blackpool Central	**25A** Wakefield					
50800	$2P^8$	**25A** Wakefield						
50801	$2P^8$	**25A** Wakefield						
50802	$2P^8$	**24F** Fleetwood	**28B** Fleetwood					
50804	$2P^8$	**25A** Wakefield						
50806	$2P^8$	**25A** Wakefield	**28A** Blackpool Central					
50807	$2P^8$	**26C** Bolton	**26C** Bolton	**25F** Low Moor				
50812	$2P^8$	**24F** Fleetwood	**28B** Fleetwood					
50813	$2P^8$	**25A** Wakefield						
50815	$2P^8$	**26C** Bolton	**26C** Bolton					
50818	$2P^8$	**26A** Newton Heath	**26C** Bolton	**25F** Low Moor	**56E** Sowerby Bridge			
50823	$2P^8$	**26D** Bury						
50829	$2P^8$	**25D** Mirfield	**26C** Bolton	**26E** Bacup	**26C** Bolton			
50831	$2P^8$	**26C** Bolton	**26C** Bolton	**25F** Low Moor	**56F** Low Moor			
50835	$3P^3$	**25E** Sowerby Bridge						
50840	$2P^8$	**25F** Low Moor	**28B** Fleetwood					
50842	$2P^8$	**20G** Hellifield	**20E** Manningham					
50844	$2P^8$	**23D** Wigan						
50849	$2P^8$	**23C** Southport						
50850	$2P^8$	**25D** Mirfield	**28B** Fleetwood	**26C** Bolton	**26C** Bolton	**26C** Bolton		
50852	$2P^8$	**25A** Wakefield	**24C** Lostock Hall					
50855	$2P^8$	**25F** Low Moor	**26A** Newton Heath	**26C** Bolton	**56F** Low Moor			
50859	$2P^8$	**26C** Bolton	**26A** Newton Heath					
50865	$2P^8$	**23C** Southport	**26C** Bolton	**25B** Huddersfield	**55G** Huddersfield			
50869	$2P^8$	**25A** Wakefield	**25A** Wakefield	**25F** Low Moor				
50872	$2P^8$	**26D** Bury	**26C** Bolton					
50873	$2P^8$	**25D** Mirfield	**25A** Wakefield					
50875	$2P^8$	**26D** Bury						
50880	$2P^8$	**20A** Leeds Holbeck						
50886	$2P^8$	**25F** Low Moor	**25A** Wakefield					
50887	$2P^8$	**23D** Wigan	**25B** Huddersfield	**26C** Bolton	**26C** Bolton			
50889	$2P^8$	**24E** Blackpool Central						
50891	$3P^3$	**25E** Sowerby Bridge						
50892	$2P^8$	**26D** Bury	**25E** Sowerby Bridge					
50893	$3P^3$	**24D** Lower Darwen						
50896	$2P^8$	**20G** Hellifield						
50898	$2P^8$	**25D** Mirfield	**25E** Sowerby Bridge					
50899	$2P^8$	**20G** Hellifield						
50901	$3P^3$	**20D** Normanton						
50903	$3P^3$	**20A** Leeds Holbeck						
50909	$3P^3$	**25F** Low Moor	**25F** Low Moor					
50925	$3P^3$	**25E** Sowerby Bridge	**25E** Sowerby Bridge					
50934	$3P^3$	**25E** Sowerby Bridge						
50943	$3P^3$	**25E** Sowerby Bridge						
50945	$3P^3$	**24D** Lower Darwen						
50950	$3P^3$	**24D** Lower Darwen						
50951	$3P^3$	**24D** Lower Darwen						
50952	$3P^3$	**25F** Low Moor						
50953	$3P^3$	**24D** Lower Darwen						
51202	$0F^4$	**22C** Bath Green Park	**71G** Bath Green Park	**22A** Bristol Barrow Road	**22A** Bristol Barrow Road			
51204	$0F^4$	**10E** Sutton Oak	**5B** Crewe South	**5B** Crewe South	**8D** Widnes	**26B** Agecroft		
51206	$0F^4$	**23A** Bank Hall	**27A** Bank Hall	**27A** Bank Hall	**27A** Bank Hall	**27A** Bank Hall		
51207	$0F^4$	**25C** Goole	**25C** Goole	**26B** Agecroft	**26B** Agecroft	**26B** Agecroft		
51212	$0F^4$	**22A** Bristol Barrow Road	**22A** Bristol Barrow Road	**22A** Bristol Barrow Road	**22A** Bristol Barrow Road			
51216	$0F^4$	**23A** Bank Hall	**27A** Bank Hall	**27A** Bank Hall				
51217	$0F^4$	**17B** Burton	**17B** Burton	**17A** Derby	**17A** Derby	**82E** Bristol Barrow Road		
51218	$0F^4$	**10B** Preston	**5B** Crewe South	**5B** Crewe South	**5B** Crewe South	**82E** Bristol Barrow Road	**87D** Swansea East Dock	
51221	$0F^4$	**5B** Crewe South	**5B** Crewe South	**5B** Crewe South	**6H** Bangor	**82E** Bristol Barrow Road		
51222	$0F^4$	**26A** Newton Heath	**25C** Goole	**25C** Goole	**53E** Goole	**53E** Goole		
51227	$0F^4$	**23A** Bank Hall	**27A** Bank Hall	**27A** Bank Hall	**27A** Bank Hall	**27A** Bank Hall		
51229	$0F^4$	**23A** Bank Hall	**27A** Bank Hall	**27A** Bank Hall	**27A** Bank Hall	**27A** Bank Hall		
51230	$0F^4$	**26B** Agecroft	**26B** Agecroft	**26B** Agecroft	**26B** Agecroft			
51231	$0F^4$	**23A** Bank Hall	**27A** Bank Hall	**27A** Bank Hall	**27A** Bank Hall			
51232	$0F^4$	**23A** Bank Hall	**27A** Bank Hall	**27A** Bank Hall	**27A** Bank Hall	**27A** Bank Hall	**26B** Agecroft	
51234	$0F^4$	**26A** Newton Heath	**27A** Bank Hall	**27A** Bank Hall	**27A** Bank Hall			
51235	$0F^4$	**17B** Burton	**17A** Derby	**17A** Derby	**50A** York			
51237	$0F^4$	**23A** Bank Hall	**27A** Bank Hall	**27A** Bank Hall	**27A** Bank Hall	**27A** Bank Hall	**26B** Agecroft	
51240	$0F^4$	**26B** Agecroft	**27A** Bank Hall	**27A** Bank Hall	**53E** Goole			
51241	$0F^4$	**25C** Goole	**25C** Goole	**25C** Goole	**26B** Agecroft	**53E** Goole		
51244	$0F^4$	**25C** Goole	**25C** Goole	**25C** Goole	**53E** Goole	**53E** Goole		
51246	$0F^4$	**23A** Bank Hall	**27A** Bank Hall	**27A** Bank Hall	**27A** Bank Hall	**27A** Bank Hall		
51253	$0F^4$	**23A** Bank Hall	**27A** Bank Hall	**27A** Bank Hall	**27A** Bank Hall	**27A** Bank Hall	**8C** Speke Junction	
51307	$2F^2$	**23A** Bank Hall	**27A** Bank Hall	**27A** Bank Hall	**27A** Bank Hall			
51313	$2F^2$	**6C** Birkenhead	**6C** Birkenhead	**8A** Edge Hill				
51316	$2F^2$	**10E** Sutton Oak	**10E** Sutton Oak	**10E** Sutton Oak	**10D** Sutton Oak			
51318	$2F^2$	**8A** Edge Hill						
51319	$2F^2$	**10E** Sutton Oak	**10E** Sutton Oak	**10E** Sutton Oak	**10D** Sutton Oak			
51320	$2F^2$	**25D** Mirfield						
51321	$2F^2$	**24F** Fleetwood	**28B** Fleetwood	**24F** Fleetwood	**24F** Fleetwood			
51323	$2F^2$	**25C** Goole	**25C** Goole	**25C** Goole				
51325	$2F^2$	**23A** Bank Hall						
51336	$2F^2$	**24D** Lower Darwen	**24B** Rose Grove	**24B** Rose Grove	**26A** Newton Heath	**24F** Fleetwood		
51338	$2F^2$	**26D** Bury	**26A** Newton Heath	**27E** Walton on the Hill	**17B** Burton			
51342	$2F^2$	**8C** Speke Junction						
51343	$2F^2$	**23B** Aintree	**27B** Aintree	**27B** Aintree	**27B** Aintree	**26A** Newton Heath		
51345	$2F^2$	**24C** Lostock Hall	**24C** Lostock Hall	**24C** Lostock Hall				
51348	$2F^2$	**26C** Bolton	**25E** Sowerby Bridge					
51353	$2F^2$	**8A** Edge Hill	**8A** Edge Hill	**8A** Edge Hill	**8A** Edge Hill			
51358	$2F^2$	**25A** Wakefield	**25D** Mirfield	**25D** Mirfield	**56D** Mirfield			

		1948	1951	1954	1957	1960	1963	1966
51361	$2F^2$	**24A** Accrington	**25C** Goole	**25C** Goole				
51371	$2F^2$	**23A** Bank Hall	**27A** Bank Hall	**27A** Bank Hall	**27A** Bank Hall	**26A** Newton Heath		
51375	$2F^2$	**23A** Bank Hall	**27A** Bank Hall	**27A** Bank Hall				
51376	$2F^2$	**24F** Fleetwood	**26D** Bury	**26D** Bury				
51379	$2F^2$	**26A** Newton Heath	**25C** Goole	**25C** Goole				
51381	$2F^2$	**25E** Sowerby Bridge	**25E** Sowerby Bridge	**25E** Sowerby Bridge	**26A** Newton Heath			
51390	$2F^2$	**25A** Wakefield	**24A** Accrington	**24A** Accrington				
51396	$2F^2$	**23A** Bank Hall	**27A** Bank Hall	**27A** Bank Hall				
51397	$2F^2$	**8C** Speke Junction	**10E** Sutton Oak	**10E** Sutton Oak	**27B** Aintree			
51400	$2F^2$	**26A** Newton Heath						
51404	$2F^2$	**26A** Newton Heath	**25F** Low Moor	**25F** Low Moor	**56F** Low Moor			
51405	$2F^2$	**8C** Speke Junction						
51408	$2F^2$	**25B** Huddersfield	**25B** Huddersfield	**25B** Huddersfield	**26C** Bolton	**26C** Bolton		
51410	$2F^2$	**24B** Rose Grove	**24A** Accrington	**24A** Accrington				
51412	$2F^2$	Crewe Works	Crewe Works	Crewe Works	Crewe Works	Crewe Works		
51413	$2F^2$	**23B** Aintree	**27B** Aintree	**27B** Aintree	**27B** Aintree	**26B** Agecroft		
51415	$2F^2$	**25A** Wakefield	**24D** Lower Darwen	**24D** Lower Darwen	**24D** Lower Darwen			
51419	$2F^2$	**26D** Bury	**26D** Bury	**26D** Bury	**24F** Fleetwood	**24F** Fleetwood		
51423	$2F^2$	**24C** Lostock Hall	**28B** Fleetwood	**24C** Lostock Hall	**24C** Lostock Hall			
51424	$2F^2$	**26A** Newton Heath	**26A** Newton Heath	**25D** Mirfield	**56D** Mirfield			
51425	$2F^2$	**26A** Newton Heath	**26A** Newton Heath	**27C** Southport				
51427	$2F^2$	**8C** Speke Junction						
51429	$2F^2$	**25E** Sowerby Bridge	**26A** Newton Heath	Horwich Works	Horwich Works	Horwich Works		
51432	$2F^2$	**25C** Goole	**25C** Goole	**25C** Goole	**53E** Goole			
51436	$2F^2$	**26A** Newton Heath	**26A** Newton Heath	**26A** Newton Heath				
51438	$2F^2$	**26A** Newton Heath						
51439	$2F^2$	**8A** Edge Hill	**8C** Speke Junction	**8C** Speke Junction				
51441	$2F^2$	**8C** Speke Junction	**6C** Birkenhead	**10E** Sutton Oak	**10D** Sutton Oak	**8G** Sutton Oak		
51443	$2F^2$	**25C** Goole						
51444	$2F^2$	**8C** Speke Junction	Crewe Works	Crewe Works	Crewe Works	Crewe Works		
51445	$2F^2$	**8A** Edge Hill	**8A** Edge Hill	**8A** Edge Hill	**8A** Edge Hill	**8A** Edge Hill		
51446	$2F^2$	Crewe Works	Crewe Works	Crewe Works	Crewe Works	Crewe Works		
51447	$2F^2$	**25B** Huddersfield	**25A** Wakefield	**26A** Newton Heath	**26A** Newton Heath			
51453	$2F^2$	**25D** Mirfield	**25D** Mirfield	**25D** Mirfield	**56D** Mirfield			
51457	$2F^2$	**25A** Wakefield	**26A** Newton Heath	**26A** Newton Heath	**26A** Newton Heath			
51458	$2F^2$	**25C** Goole	**26A** Newton Heath	**26A** Newton Heath	**26A** Newton Heath			
51460	$2F^2$	**23B** Aintree	**27B** Aintree	**27B** Aintree				
51462	$2F^2$	**23B** Aintree	**27B** Aintree	**27B** Aintree				
51464	$2F^2$	**26B** Agecroft	**26B** Agecroft	**24A** Accrington				
51467	$2F^2$	**24D** Lower Darwen						
51468	$2F^2$	**25A** Wakefield						
51469	$2F^2$	**8C** Speke Junction						
51470	$2F^2$	**26A** Newton Heath	**26A** Newton Heath	**26A** Newton Heath				
51471	$2F^2$	**10E** Sutton Oak	**10E** Sutton Oak	**10E** Sutton Oak				
51472	$2F^2$	**26A** Newton Heath	**26A** Newton Heath	**26A** Newton Heath				
51474	$2F^2$	**26B** Agecroft	**27D** Wigan	**27D** Wigan	**27D** Wigan			
51475	$2F^2$	**23B** Aintree						
51477	$2F^2$	**24F** Fleetwood	**28B** Fleetwood	**24F** Fleetwood				
51479	$2F^2$	**25E** Sowerby Bridge	**25E** Sowerby Bridge	**25C** Goole				
51481	$2F^2$	**26D** Bury	**28B** Fleetwood	**24F** Fleetwood	**27A** Bank Hall			
51482	$2F^2$	**25E** Sowerby Bridge						
51484	$2F^2$	**25A** Wakefield	**26G** Belle Vue	**26G** Belle Vue	**39A** Gorton			
51486	$2F^2$	**26D** Bury	**26D** Bury	**26D** Bury	**26C** Bolton	**26C** Bolton		
51487	$2F^2$	**26D** Bury						
51488	$2F^2$	**26A** Newton Heath	**25E** Sowerby Bridge	**25E** Sowerby Bridge				
51489	$2F^2$	**26D** Bury	**26D** Bury	**26D** Bury				
51490	$2F^2$	**23C** Southport	**27C** Southport					
51491	$2F^2$	**10E** Sutton Oak	**10E** Sutton Oak	**10E** Sutton Oak	**10D** Sutton Oak			
51492	$2F^2$	**24B** Rose Grove						
51495	$2F^2$	**10E** Sutton Oak						
51496	$2F^2$	**26A** Newton Heath	**26A** Newton Heath	**26A** Newton Heath	**26A** Newton Heath	**26B** Agecroft		
51497	$2F^2$	**24B** Rose Grove	**24B** Rose Grove	**24B** Rose Grove	**24A** Accrington			
51498	$2F^2$	**24F** Fleetwood	**28B** Fleetwood	**24F** Fleetwood	**24D** Lower Darwen	**26C** Bolton		
51499	$2F^2$	**24D** Lower Darwen	**24D** Lower Darwen	**24D** Lower Darwen	**26B** Agecroft			
51500	$2F^2$	**25A** Wakefield	**26B** Agecroft	**26B** Agecroft	**26B** Agecroft			
51503	$2F^2$	**25A** Wakefield	**25E** Sowerby Bridge	**25C** Goole	**53E** Goole			
51504	$2F^2$	**26D** Bury	**26D** Bury	**26D** Bury				
51506	$2F^2$	**24D** Lower Darwen	**24D** Lower Darwen	**24D** Lower Darwen	**24D** Lower Darwen			
51510	$2F^2$	**26A** Newton Heath	**26A** Newton Heath	**26G** Belle Vue				
51511	$2F^2$	**26C** Bolton	**26C** Bolton	**26C** Bolton				
51512	$2F^2$	**26B** Agecroft	**26B** Agecroft	**26B** Agecroft	**39A** Gorton			
51513	$2F^2$	**26C** Bolton	**26C** Bolton	**26C** Bolton				
51514	$2F^2$	**24F** Fleetwood	**24A** Accrington					
51516	$2F^2$	**25C** Goole	**25C** Goole	**25C** Goole				
51519	$2F^2$	**26C** Bolton	**26C** Bolton	**26C** Bolton				
51521	$2F^2$	**25C** Goole	**25C** Goole	**25C** Goole				
51524	$2F^2$	**25B** Huddersfield	**25B** Huddersfield	**25B** Huddersfield	**24F** Fleetwood	**24F** Fleetwood		
51526	$2F^2$	**24C** Lostock Hall	**24C** Lostock Hall	**24C** Lostock Hall	**24C** Lostock Hall			
51530	$2F^2$	**23B** Aintree	**27B** Aintree	**27B** Aintree				
51535	$1F^3$	**23A** Bank Hall	**27A** Bank Hall	**27B** Aintree				
51536	$1F^3$	**23A** Bank Hall	**27A** Bank Hall					
51537	$1F^3$	**23A** Bank Hall	**27A** Bank Hall	**27B** Aintree	**27B** Aintree	**27B** Aintree		
51544	$1F^3$	**23B** Aintree	**27B** Aintree	**27B** Aintree	**27A** Bank Hall			
51546	$1F^3$	**23A** Bank Hall	**27A** Bank Hall	**27A** Bank Hall	**27A** Bank Hall			
52016	$2F^3$	**10B** Preston	**10C** Patricroft	**10C** Patricroft				
52019	$2F^3$	**10C** Patricroft						
52021	$2F^3$	**10A** Wigan Springs Branch	**10A** Wigan Springs Branch	**10A** Wigan Springs Branch				
52022	$2F^3$	**10A** Wigan Springs Branch						
52023	$2F^3$	**10A** Wigan Springs Branch						
52024	$2F^3$	**10A** Wigan Springs Branch	**10C** Patricroft	**10C** Patricroft				
52030	$2F^3$	**10C** Patricroft	**10C** Patricroft					
52031	$2F^3$	**10C** Patricroft	**10C** Patricroft	**10C** Patricroft				
52032	$2F^3$	**10A** Wigan Springs Branch						
52034	$2F^3$	**10B** Preston	**10C** Patricroft					
52036	$2F^3$	**10C** Patricroft						
52037	$2F^3$	**25C** Goole	**25A** Wakefield					
52041	$2F^3$	**25C** Goole						
52043	$2F^3$	**25C** Goole	**25A** Wakefield					
52044	$2F^3$	**25C** Goole	**25A** Wakefield	**25A** Wakefield	**56A** Wakefield			
52045	$2F^3$	**10A** Wigan Springs Branch	**10A** Wigan Springs Branch	**10C** Patricroft				
52046	$2F^3$	**25A** Wakefield						
52047	$2F^3$	**25A** Wakefield						
52049	$2F^3$	**10C** Patricroft						
52051	$2F^3$	**10B** Preston	**10A** Wigan Springs Branch	**10A** Wigan Springs Branch				
52053	$2F^3$	**10A** Wigan Springs Branch	**10A** Wigan Springs Branch	**25A** Wakefield				
52056	$2F^3$	**25C** Goole	**25A** Wakefield					
52059	$2F^3$	**10C** Patricroft	**10C** Patricroft					
52063	$2F^3$	**10A** Wigan Springs Branch						
52064	$2F^3$	**10A** Wigan Springs Branch						
52088	$3F^7$	**8C** Speke Junction	**8B** Warrington Dallam					
52089	$3F^7$	**20D** Normanton	**20D** Normanton	**26A** Newton Heath	**26A** Newton Heath	**56D** Mirfield		
52091	$3F^7$	**10E** Sutton Oak	**10E** Sutton Oak					
52092	$3F^7$	**25A** Wakefield	**25F** Low Moor					
52093	$3F^7$	**23D** Wigan	**27B** Aintree	Crewe Works	Crewe Works	Crewe Works		

		1948	1951	1954	1957	1960	1963	1966
52094	3F[7]	**23B** Aintree	**26A** Newton Heath	**26D** Bury	**26D** Bury			
52095	3F[7]	**20D** Normanton	**20C** Royston	**27D** Wigan	**24B** Rose Grove			
52098	3F[7]	**12E** Moor Row	**10A** Wigan Springs Branch					
52099	3F[7]	**25E** Sowerby Bridge	**26F** Lees Oldham	**26F** Lees Oldham				
52100	3F[7]	**8B** Warrington Dallam	**8C** Speke Junction					
52102	3F[7]	**23A** Bank Hall	**26A** Newton Heath					
52103	3F[7]	**4A** Shrewsbury						
52104	3F[7]	**25F** Low Moor	**25F** Low Moor	**25F** Low Moor				
52105	3F[7]	**4A** Shrewsbury	**10B** Preston					
52107	3F[7]	**2D** Nuneaton	**10A** Wigan Springs Branch					
52108	3F[7]	**20C** Royston	**20C** Royston	**26A** Newton Heath	**26A** Newton Heath			
52110	3F[7]	**12E** Moor Row						
52111	3F[7]	**8A** Edge Hill	**8A** Edge Hill					
52112	3F[7]	**23B** Aintree	**27B** Aintree					
52118	3F[7]	**8B** Warrington Dallam	**8A** Edge Hill	**10A** Wigan Springs Branch				
52119	3F[7]	**4A** Shrewsbury	**7B** Bangor	**6H** Bangor	**6H** Bangor	**6K** Rhyl		
52120	3F[7]	**26A** Newton Heath	**25A** Wakefield	**25A** Wakefield	**56F** Low Moor			
52121	3F[7]	**16A** Nottingham	**16A** Nottingham	**25C** Goole	**56D** Mirfield	**56D** Mirfield		
52123	3F[7]	**16A** Nottingham	**16A** Nottingham	**26C** Bolton	**27C** Southport			
52124	3F[7]	**26A** Newton Heath	**25D** Mirfield	**26B** Agecroft				
52125	3F[7]	**7D** Rhyl	**7D** Rhyl	**10E** Sutton Oak	**10D** Sutton Oak			
52126	3F[7]	**10E** Sutton Oak	**10A** Wigan Springs Branch					
52127	3F[7]	**25F** Low Moor						
52129	3F[7]	**26D** Bury	**26D** Bury	**26D** Bury	**26D** Bury	**26D** Bury		
52132	3F[7]	**26A** Newton Heath	**26A** Newton Heath	**26C** Bolton	**26C** Bolton			
52133	3F[7]	**25C** Goole	**25A** Wakefield	**25A** Wakefield	**56A** Wakefield	**56A** Wakefield		
52135	3F[7]	**16A** Nottingham	**16A** Nottingham	**27B** Aintree	**27B** Aintree			
52136	3F[7]	**26A** Newton Heath	**26C** Bolton	**27B** Aintree	**27B** Aintree			
52137	3F[7]	**26B** Agecroft	**26A** Newton Heath	**26A** Newton Heath				
52138	3F[7]	**26A** Newton Heath	**28A** Blackpool Central	**24B** Rose Grove				
52139	3F[7]	**26D** Bury	**26A** Newton Heath	**26C** Bolton	**56D** Mirfield	**56D** Mirfield		
52140	3F[7]	**8B** Warrington Dallam	**26B** Agecroft	**8A** Edge Hill	**8A** Edge Hill	**26A** Newton Heath		
52141	3F[7]	**2D** Nuneaton	**2B** Nuneaton	**2B** Nuneaton	**26A** Newton Heath	**26A** Newton Heath		
52143	3F[7]	**8C** Speke Junction	**8C** Speke Junction	**10A** Wigan Springs Branch	**10A** Wigan Springs Branch			
52150	3F[7]	**25A** Wakefield	**25A** Wakefield	**25A** Wakefield				
52152	3F[7]	**23D** Wigan						
52154	3F[7]	**25A** Wakefield	**25A** Wakefield	**25E** Sowerby Bridge	**53E** Goole	**53E** Goole		
52156	3F[7]	**26A** Newton Heath	**26A** Newton Heath					
52157	3F[7]	**26C** Bolton	**28A** Blackpool Central					
52159	3F[7]	**26D** Bury	**26D** Bury	**26A** Newton Heath	**26A** Newton Heath			
52160	3F[7]	**24C** Lostock Hall	**24C** Lostock Hall	**24D** Lower Darwen	**24D** Lower Darwen			
52161	3F[7]	**23C** Southport	**27C** Southport	**27C** Southport	**27C** Southport	**26A** Newton Heath		
52162	3F[7]	**26B** Agecroft	**27C** Southport	**6K** Rhyl	**6K** Rhyl	**6K** Rhyl		
52163	3F[7]	**8C** Speke Junction	**8C** Speke Junction	**8C** Speke Junction	**8C** Speke Junction			
52164	3F[7]	**26D** Bury	**26D** Bury	**26D** Bury				
52165	3F[7]	**26D** Bury	**26D** Bury	**26A** Newton Heath	**26A** Newton Heath			
52166	3F[7]	**25D** Mirfield	**25D** Mirfield	**25F** Low Moor				
52167	3F[7]	**7D** Rhyl	**7D** Rhyl	**6K** Rhyl				
52169	3F[7]	**23D** Wigan	**27D** Wigan					
52170	3F[7]	**8A** Edge Hill						
52171	3F[7]	**24C** Lostock Hall	**24C** Lostock Hall	**27B** Aintree	**27B** Aintree	**27B** Aintree		
52172	3F[7]	**10A** Wigan Springs Branch	**7D** Rhyl	**6K** Rhyl	**6K** Rhyl			
52174	3F[7]	**24E** Blackpool Central	**28A** Blackpool Central	**24C** Lostock Hall				
52175	3F[7]	**8B** Warrington Dallam	**8C** Speke Junction	**8C** Speke Junction	**8C** Speke Junction			
52176	3F[7]	**7B** Bangor	**7B** Bangor					
52177	3F[7]	**10E** Sutton Oak	**10E** Sutton Oak	**10E** Sutton Oak				
52179	3F[7]	**23B** Aintree	**27B** Aintree	**26D** Bury	**24B** Rose Grove	**24B** Rose Grove		
52181	3F[7]	**25C** Goole						
52182	3F[7]	**25A** Wakefield	**28A** Blackpool Central	**24C** Lostock Hall	**24C** Lostock Hall	**24C** Lostock Hall		
52183	3F[7]	**24B** Rose Grove	**27C** Southport	**27C** Southport	**27C** Southport			
52184	3F[7]	**12E** Moor Row						
52186	3F[7]	**25A** Wakefield	**25A** Wakefield	**25A** Wakefield	**56A** Wakefield			
52189	3F[7]	**23D** Wigan	**25E** Sowerby Bridge	**25D** Mirfield				
52191	3F[7]	**25D** Mirfield	**25C** Goole					
52192	3F[7]	**25D** Mirfield						
52194	3F[7]	**24E** Blackpool Central	**28A** Blackpool Central	**24D** Lower Darwen				
52196	3F[7]	**23B** Aintree	**27B** Aintree	**10E** Sutton Oak	**10D** Sutton Oak			
52197	3F[7]	**23C** Southport	**27D** Wigan	**27D** Wigan				
52201	3F[7]	**12E** Moor Row	**12E** Moor Row	**12E** Moor Row	**2B** Nuneaton	**26D** Bury		
52203	3F[7]	**26B** Agecroft	**24D** Lower Darwen	**24C** Lostock Hall	**24C** Lostock Hall			
52207	3F[7]	**26A** Newton Heath	**26A** Newton Heath	Crewe Works	Crewe Works	**26D** Bury		
52208	3F[7]	**10A** Wigan Springs Branch						
52212	3F[7]	**26C** Bolton	**26C** Bolton	Crewe Works	Crewe Works			
52215	3F[7]	**24E** Blackpool Central	**28A** Blackpool Central	**24E** Blackpool Central				
52216	3F[7]	**24A** Accrington	**24C** Lostock Hall	**24D** Lower Darwen	**24D** Lower Darwen			
52217	3F[7]	**25F** Low Moor	**25E** Sowerby Bridge	**25E** Sowerby Bridge	**56E** Sowerby Bridge			
52218	3F[7]	**23B** Aintree	**27B** Aintree	Crewe Works	Crewe Works	Crewe Works		
52219	3F[7]	**8C** Speke Junction	**26B** Agecroft					
52220	3F[7]	**24B** Rose Grove	**24C** Lostock Hall	**24D** Lower Darwen				
52225	3F[7]	**6C** Birkenhead	**6C** Birkenhead	**8B** Warrington Dallam	**8B** Warrington Dallam	**8B** Warrington Dallam		
52229	3F[7]	**26A** Newton Heath						
52230	3F[7]	**7B** Bangor	**7B** Bangor	**6H** Bangor	**6H** Bangor	**26A** Newton Heath		
52231	3F[7]	**25D** Mirfield	**26C** Bolton					
52232	3F[7]	**6C** Birkenhead	**6C** Birkenhead	**6C** Birkenhead	**8C** Speke Junction			
52233	3F[7]	**4A** Shrewsbury	**7D** Rhyl					
52235	3F[7]	**25D** Mirfield	**25A** Wakefield	**25A** Wakefield	**56F** Low Moor			
52236	3F[7]	**26C** Bolton	**26C** Bolton	**25D** Mirfield	**56D** Mirfield			
52237	3F[7]	**25F** Low Moor	**25F** Low Moor	**26D** Bury	**26C** Bolton			
52238	3F[7]	**24A** Accrington	**24C** Lostock Hall					
52239	3F[7]	**26A** Newton Heath	**26A** Newton Heath	**26D** Bury				
52240	3F[7]	**24F** Fleetwood	**28B** Fleetwood	**24E** Blackpool Central	**24E** Blackpool Central	**26E** Lees Oldham		
52243	3F[7]	**25E** Sowerby Bridge	**25E** Sowerby Bridge					
52244	3F[7]	**24C** Lostock Hall	**27B** Aintree	**25A** Wakefield	**53E** Goole	**53E** Goole		
52245	3F[7]	**26D** Bury	**26D** Bury	**26D** Bury				
52246	3F[7]	**26D** Bury	**26D** Bury					
52248	3F[7]	**26F** Lees Oldham	**26F** Lees Oldham	**26F** Lees Oldham	**26E** Lees Oldham	**26E** Lees Oldham		
52250	3F[7]	**8B** Warrington Dallam	**10A** Wigan Springs Branch					
52252	3F[7]	**20C** Royston	**20C** Royston	**25C** Goole	**53E** Goole	**53E** Goole		
52253	3F[7]	**24D** Lower Darwen						
52255	3F[7]	**25F** Low Moor	**25D** Mirfield					
52256	3F[7]	**23C** Southport						
52258	3F[7]	**20C** Royston	**20C** Royston	**27B** Aintree				
52260	3F[7]	**24D** Lower Darwen	**24D** Lower Darwen	**24D** Lower Darwen	**24D** Lower Darwen	**27B** Aintree		
52262	3F[7]	**24B** Rose Grove	**24D** Lower Darwen					
52266	3F[7]	**26A** Newton Heath	**26A** Newton Heath					
52268	3F[7]	**24B** Rose Grove	**24D** Lower Darwen	**26D** Bury	**26D** Bury			
52269	3F[7]	**10A** Wigan Springs Branch	**7B** Bangor	**6H** Bangor	**6H** Bangor			
52270	3F[7]	**6C** Birkenhead	**6C** Birkenhead	**6C** Birkenhead	**6C** Birkenhead	**26A** Newton Heath		
52271	3F[7]	**23C** Southport	**26D** Bury	**26A** Newton Heath	**26A** Newton Heath	**26A** Newton Heath		
52272	3F[7]	**23C** Southport	**24C** Lostock Hall	**24D** Lower Darwen				
52273	3F[7]	**25D** Mirfield	**25C** Goole	**25C** Goole				
52275	3F[7]	**24E** Blackpool Central	**28A** Blackpool Central	**27D** Wigan	**26A** Newton Heath	**26A** Newton Heath		
52278	3F[7]	**24B** Rose Grove	**27C** Southport	**27B** Aintree	**26A** Newton Heath			
52279	3F[7]	**26A** Newton Heath	**26B** Agecroft					

		1948	1951	1954	1957	1960	1963	1966
52280	3F[7]	**10E** Sutton Oak	**10E** Sutton Oak					
52284	3F[7]	**25A** Wakefield	**25A** Wakefield					
52285	3F[7]	**12E** Moor Row	**12E** Moor Row					
52288	3F[7]	**24A** Accrington	**27D** Wigan					
52289	3F[7]	**24D** Lower Darwen	**24D** Lower Darwen	**27D** Wigan	**26D** Bury			
52290	3F[7]	**23D** Wigan	**28B** Fleetwood	**24F** Fleetwood	**24C** Lostock Hall	**24C** Lostock Hall		
52293	3F[7]	**26B** Agecroft	**26B** Agecroft	**26B** Agecroft	**26E** Lees Oldham			
52294	3F[7]	**2D** Nuneaton						
52296	3F[7]	**24C** Lostock Hall	**24C** Lostock Hall					
52299	3F[7]	**26E** Bacup	**26E** Bacup	**27B** Aintree				
52300	3F[7]	**26A** Newton Heath	**26A** Newton Heath	**24D** Lower Darwen				
52304	3F[7]	**26B** Agecroft	**26A** Newton Heath					
52305	3F[7]	**25A** Wakefield	**25A** Wakefield	**25C** Goole	**53E** Goole	**53E** Goole		
52309	3F[7]	**24B** Rose Grove	**25F** Low Moor	**25C** Goole				
52311	3F[7]	**25D** Mirfield	**26C** Bolton	**27B** Aintree	**27B** Aintree	**27B** Aintree		
52312	3F[7]	**23D** Wigan	**27B** Aintree	**26C** Bolton	Crewe Works	Crewe Works		
52317	3F[7]	**24C** Lostock Hall	**24C** Lostock Hall	**24C** Lostock Hall				
52319	3F[7]	**25A** Wakefield	**25A** Wakefield	**24B** Rose Grove	**24B** Rose Grove	**53E** Goole		
52321	3F[7]	**2D** Nuneaton	**8A** Edge Hill	**8A** Edge Hill				
52322	3F[7]	**2D** Nuneaton	**2B** Nuneaton	**10A** Wigan Springs Branch	**10D** Sutton Oak	**26E** Lees Oldham		
52326	3F[7]	**26F** Lees Oldham						
52328	3F[7]	**23B** Aintree	**26D** Bury	**26C** Bolton	**26A** Newton Heath			
52330	3F[7]	**8B** Warrington Dallam	**8A** Edge Hill					
52331	3F[7]	**25D** Mirfield	**25C** Goole	**25C** Goole				
52333	3F[7]	**23B** Aintree	**26B** Agecroft					
52334	3F[7]	**24C** Lostock Hall	**28A** Blackpool Central	**26A** Newton Heath				
52336	3F[7]	**24C** Lostock Hall	**24C** Lostock Hall	**25D** Mirfield	**56D** Mirfield			
52337	3F[7]	**23B** Aintree						
52338	3F[7]	**7D** Rhyl	**7D** Rhyl	**10E** Sutton Oak	**10D** Sutton Oak			
52341	3F[7]	**10B** Preston	**10A** Wigan Springs Branch	**10A** Wigan Springs Branch	**26A** Newton Heath	**26A** Newton Heath		
52343	3F[7]	**26A** Newton Heath	**26A** Newton Heath	**25F** Low Moor				
52345	3F[7]	**26A** Newton Heath	**25A** Wakefield	Crewe Works	Crewe Works	**26C** Bolton		
52348	3F[7]	**26C** Bolton	**26C** Bolton	**26C** Bolton	**26C** Bolton			
52349	3F[7]	**10E** Sutton Oak	**10E** Sutton Oak	**10E** Sutton Oak				
52350	3F[7]	**26C** Bolton	**26C** Bolton	**26C** Bolton	**26D** Bury			
52351	3F[7]	**25B** Huddersfield	**25A** Wakefield	**25F** Low Moor	**56E** Sowerby Bridge	**56E** Sowerby Bridge		
52353	3F[7]	**26B** Agecroft	**25A** Wakefield					
52355	3F[7]	**26A** Newton Heath	**26A** Newton Heath	**25F** Low Moor	**56F** Low Moor	**56A** Wakefield		
52356	3F[7]	**7D** Rhyl	**7D** Rhyl	**6K** Rhyl	**6K** Rhyl			
52357	3F[7]	**26C** Bolton	**28A** Blackpool Central					
52358	3F[7]	**26A** Newton Heath	**26A** Newton Heath	**26A** Newton Heath				
52360	3F[7]	**23D** Wigan	**27D** Wigan	**26A** Newton Heath	**26C** Bolton			
52362	3F[7]	**23B** Aintree	**27B** Aintree					
52363	3F[7]	**24D** Lower Darwen	**24D** Lower Darwen					
52365	3F[7]	**26C** Bolton	**26F** Lees Oldham	**26F** Lees Oldham				
52366	3F[7]	**10E** Sutton Oak	**10E** Sutton Oak	**10E** Sutton Oak	**10D** Sutton Oak			
52368	3F[7]	**24C** Lostock Hall	**24C** Lostock Hall	**24C** Lostock Hall	**24C** Lostock Hall			
52369	3F[7]	**25A** Wakefield	**25A** Wakefield	**24B** Rose Grove				
52374	3F[7]	**4A** Shrewsbury						
52376	3F[7]	**25E** Sowerby Bridge	**25E** Sowerby Bridge	**25A** Wakefield	**56A** Wakefield			
52378	3F[7]	**26F** Lees Oldham	**26F** Lees Oldham	**27B** Aintree	**27B** Aintree	**27B** Aintree		
52379	3F[7]	**23B** Aintree	**27D** Wigan	**27B** Aintree	**27B** Aintree			
52381	3F[7]	**23C** Southport	**27B** Aintree	**27B** Aintree				
52382	3F[7]	**26D** Bury	**26D** Bury					
52386	3F[7]	**25A** Wakefield	**25A** Wakefield					
52387	3F[7]	**26F** Lees Oldham	**26F** Lees Oldham	**27D** Wigan	**26D** Bury			
52388	3F[7]	**26E** Bacup	**24D** Lower Darwen	**24D** Lower Darwen	**26E** Lees Oldham			
52389	3F[7]	**26F** Lees Oldham	**26F** Lees Oldham	**26A** Newton Heath	**26C** Bolton			
52390	3F[7]	**23B** Aintree	**27D** Wigan	**26A** Newton Heath				
52393	3F[7]	**10E** Sutton Oak	**10E** Sutton Oak	**10E** Sutton Oak	**10A** Wigan Springs Branch	**26C** Bolton		
52397	3F[7]	**10E** Sutton Oak	**10E** Sutton Oak	**10E** Sutton Oak				
52399	3F[7]	**24C** Lostock Hall	**24C** Lostock Hall	**24D** Lower Darwen	**56E** Sowerby Bridge			
52400	3F[7]	**23C** Southport	**25E** Sowerby Bridge	**25E** Sowerby Bridge	**56E** Sowerby Bridge	**56E** Sowerby Bridge		
52401	3F[7]	**23B** Aintree						
52403	3F[7]	**25F** Low Moor						
52404	3F[7]	**26C** Bolton	**26C** Bolton					
52405	3F[7]	**23B** Aintree	**27B** Aintree	**26D** Bury				
52407	3F[7]	**7B** Bangor	**7B** Bangor					
52408	3F[7]	**25D** Mirfield	**25D** Mirfield	**25E** Sowerby Bridge				
52410	3F[7]	**25F** Low Moor	**25F** Low Moor	**25E** Sowerby Bridge	**26E** Lees Oldham	**26E** Lees Oldham		
52411	3F[7]	**26B** Agecroft	**25F** Low Moor	**25A** Wakefield	**56E** Sowerby Bridge	**56E** Sowerby Bridge		
52412	3F[7]	**24A** Accrington	**27B** Aintree	**27B** Aintree	**27B** Aintree			
52413	3F[7]	**23D** Wigan	**27D** Wigan	**26C** Bolton	**24D** Lower Darwen	**56F** Low Moor		
52414	3F[7]	**4A** Shrewsbury	**84G** Shrewsbury					
52415	3F[7]	**24E** Blackpool Central	**28A** Blackpool Central	**24E** Blackpool Central	**24E** Blackpool Central	**26C** Bolton		
52416	3F[7]	**25E** Sowerby Bridge	**26E** Bacup	**27B** Aintree				
52417	3F[7]	**6A** Chester						
52418	3F[7]	**12E** Moor Row	**12E** Moor Row	**12E** Moor Row	**12C** Workington			
52422	3F[7]	**25F** Low Moor						
52427	3F[7]	**25F** Low Moor	**26C** Bolton	**26F** Lees Oldham	**26E** Lees Oldham			
52428	3F[7]	**4A** Shrewsbury	**84G** Shrewsbury					
52429	3F[7]	**4A** Shrewsbury	**2B** Nuneaton	**2B** Nuneaton	**10D** Sutton Oak	**24C** Lostock Hall		
52430	3F[7]	**24E** Blackpool Central	**28A** Blackpool Central					
52431	3F[7]	**24D** Lower Darwen	**24D** Lower Darwen	**24D** Lower Darwen	**24D** Lower Darwen			
52432	3F[7]	**12B** Carlisle Upperby	**6C** Birkenhead	**8B** Warrington Dallam	**8B** Warrington Dallam			
52433	3F[7]	**25A** Wakefield	**25A** Wakefield					
52435	3F[7]	**25A** Wakefield	**25A** Wakefield	**25A** Wakefield				
52437	3F[7]	**26A** Newton Heath	**27E** Walton on the Hill	**24E** Blackpool Central				
52438	3F[7]	**8C** Speke Junction	**8C** Speke Junction	**8C** Speke Junction	**8C** Speke Junction	**6K** Rhyl		
52439	3F[7]	**24F** Fleetwood						
52440	3F[7]	**26E** Bacup	**26E** Bacup					
52441	3F[7]	**24A** Accrington	**24D** Lower Darwen	Crewe Works	Crewe Works	Crewe Works		
52442	3F[7]	**26E** Bacup						
52443	3F[7]	**26A** Newton Heath	**26E** Bacup	**26E** Bacup	**26D** Bury			
52444	3F[7]	**24D** Lower Darwen	**24D** Lower Darwen					
52445	3F[7]	**26E** Bacup	**24D** Lower Darwen	**24D** Lower Darwen	**24C** Lostock Hall	**24C** Lostock Hall		
52446	3F[7]	**26C** Bolton	**26C** Bolton					
52447	3F[7]	**24E** Blackpool Central	**28A** Blackpool Central	**24D** Lower Darwen				
52448	3F[7]	**25D** Mirfield	**25C** Goole					
52449	3F[7]	**10E** Sutton Oak	**10E** Sutton Oak	**10A** Wigan Springs Branch	**10A** Wigan Springs Branch			
52450	3F[7]	**23A** Bank Hall	**27D** Wigan	**27D** Wigan				
52452	3F[7]	**24A** Accrington	**25E** Sowerby Bridge	**25D** Mirfield	**56E** Sowerby Bridge	**56E** Sowerby Bridge		
52453	3F[7]	**10E** Sutton Oak	**7D** Rhyl	**6K** Rhyl				
52454	3F[7]	**25C** Goole						
52455	3F[7]	**26D** Bury	**26A** Newton Heath	**26A** Newton Heath	**26A** Newton Heath			
52456	3F[7]	**23B** Aintree	**24C** Lostock Hall	**24C** Lostock Hall	**24C** Lostock Hall	**24C** Lostock Hall		
52457	3F[7]	**4A** Shrewsbury						
52458	3F[7]	**24F** Fleetwood	**28B** Fleetwood	**24C** Lostock Hall	**24C** Lostock Hall			
52459	3F[7]	**24E** Blackpool Central	**28A** Blackpool Central	Crewe Works	Crewe Works	Crewe Works		
52460	3F[7]	**24C** Lostock Hall	**24D** Lower Darwen					
52461	3F[7]	**26B** Agecroft	**25F** Low Moor	**25F** Low Moor	**26C** Bolton	**56F** Low Moor		
52464	3F[7]	**26F** Lees Oldham	**26F** Lees Oldham	Crewe Works	Crewe Works	Crewe Works		
52465	3F[7]	**6C** Birkenhead	**2B** Nuneaton	**2B** Nuneaton				
52466	3F[7]	**26A** Newton Heath	**28A** Blackpool Central	**24E** Blackpool Central	**24E** Blackpool Central	**26E** Lees Oldham		

No.	Class	1948	1951	1954	1957	1960	1963	1966
52467	3F[7]	**24C** Lostock Hall						
52494	3F[8]	**12E** Moor Row	**12E** Moor Row	**12E** Moor Row				
52499	3F[8]	**12E** Moor Row	**12D** Workington	**12D** Workington	**12C** Workington			
52501	3F[8]	**12D** Workington	**12D** Workington	**12D** Workington	**11A** Carnforth			
52508	3F[8]	**12D** Workington						
52509	3F[8]	**12D** Workington	**12D** Workington	**12E** Moor Row				
52510	3F[8]	**12E** Moor Row	**12E** Moor Row	**12E** Moor Row	**12C** Workington			
52515	3F[7]	**25B** Huddersfield	**25D** Mirfield	**25F** Low Moor	**56F** Low Moor	**56D** Mirfield		
52517	3F[7]	**26A** Newton Heath	**26A** Newton Heath	Crewe Works	Crewe Works			
52518	3F[7]	**26A** Newton Heath						
52521	3F[7]	**25D** Mirfield	**25A** Wakefield	**25F** Low Moor	**56F** Low Moor			
52522	3F[7]	**24C** Lostock Hall	**24C** Lostock Hall	**24D** Lower Darwen				
52523	3F[7]	**23C** Southport	**24C** Lostock Hall	**24C** Lostock Hall	**24E** Blackpool Central	**26C** Bolton		
52524	3F[7]	**24A** Accrington	**24C** Lostock Hall	**24C** Lostock Hall				
52525	3F[7]	**4A** Shrewsbury	**84G** Shrewsbury					
52526	3F[7]	**24D** Lower Darwen	**24D** Lower Darwen	**24D** Lower Darwen	**24D** Lower Darwen	**24B** Rose Grove		
52527	3F[7]	**23B** Aintree	**24C** Lostock Hall	**24B** Rose Grove	**24E** Blackpool Central			
52528	3F[9]	**26C** Bolton						
52529	3F[7]	**24B** Rose Grove	**24D** Lower Darwen	**24B** Rose Grove	**24B** Rose Grove			
52541	3F[9]	**24C** Lostock Hall						
52542	3F[9]	**24E** Blackpool Central						
52545	3F[9]	**26F** Lees Oldham						
52549	3F[9]	**26B** Agecroft	**27D** Wigan	**26E** Bacup				
52551	3F[9]	**12E** Moor Row	**84G** Shrewsbury	**10A** Wigan Springs Branch	**10A** Wigan Springs Branch			
52554	3F[9]	**26D** Bury	**26D** Bury					
52557	3F[9]	**23B** Aintree	**27B** Aintree					
52558	3F[9]	**24E** Blackpool Central	**26A** Newton Heath	**25E** Sowerby Bridge				
52559	3F[9]	**20C** Royston	**20C** Royston					
52561	3F[9]	**25A** Wakefield	**25A** Wakefield	**25F** Low Moor				
52568	3F[9]	**25A** Wakefield						
52569	3F[9]	**26F** Lees Oldham	**26A** Newton Heath	**26F** Lees Oldham				
52572	3F[9]	**24E** Blackpool Central	**28A** Blackpool Central					
52574	3F[9]	**25E** Sowerby Bridge						
52575	3F[9]	**25E** Sowerby Bridge	**25E** Sowerby Bridge	**26C** Bolton				
52576	3F[9]	**25A** Wakefield	**25A** Wakefield	**25A** Wakefield	**56D** Mirfield			
52578	3F[9]	**26A** Newton Heath						
52579	3F[9]	**26D** Bury	**24D** Lower Darwen					
52580	3F[9]	**26D** Bury	**26D** Bury	**24B** Rose Grove				
52581	3F[9]	**26D** Bury	**26D** Bury					
52582	3F[9]	**23B** Aintree	**27C** Southport	**27C** Southport				
52583	3F[9]	**25D** Mirfield	**26A** Newton Heath					
52586	3F[9]	**26F** Lees Oldham						
52587	3F[9]	**25E** Sowerby Bridge	**25E** Sowerby Bridge					
52588	3F[9]	**23D** Wigan	**28B** Fleetwood					
52590	3F[9]	**25E** Sowerby Bridge	**25F** Low Moor					
52592	3F[9]	**25C** Goole	**25C** Goole	**25D** Mirfield				
52598	3F[9]	**23D** Wigan	**10C** Patricroft					
52602	3F[9]	**23D** Wigan						
52607	3F[9]	**26F** Lees Oldham						
52608	3F[9]	**26D** Bury	**7D** Rhyl	**6K** Rhyl				
52609	3F[9]	**26C** Bolton						
52615	3F[9]	**26D** Bury	**26D** Bury					
52616	3F[9]	**25E** Sowerby Bridge	**27D** Wigan					
52618	3F[9]	**10B** Preston						
52619	3F[9]	**10B** Preston	**10B** Preston					
52727	6F[3]	**23D** Wigan						
52782	6F[3]	**23B** Aintree						
52806	6F[3]	**23D** Wigan						
52821	6F[3]	**24A** Accrington						
52822	6F[3]	**24A** Accrington						
52825	6F[3]	**24A** Accrington						
52827	6F[3]	**23D** Wigan						
52828	6F[3]	**23D** Wigan						
52831	6F[3]	**24A** Accrington	**27D** Wigan					
52834	6F[3]	**23D** Wigan						
52837	6F[3]	**23D** Wigan						
52839	6F[3]	**23D** Wigan						
52841	7F[5]	**24B** Rose Grove						
52856	7F[5]	**23B** Aintree						
52857	7F[5]	**23B** Aintree	**25F** Low Moor					
52870	7F[5]	**23B** Aintree	**27D** Wigan					
52873	7F[5]	**24B** Rose Grove						
52877	7F[5]	**23B** Aintree						
52886	7F[5]	**24B** Rose Grove						
52906	7F[5]	**24B** Rose Grove						
52910	7F[5]	**23B** Aintree						
52913	7F[5]	**24B** Rose Grove						
52916	7F[5]	**24B** Rose Grove						
52935	7F[5]	**23B** Aintree						
52945	7F[5]	**24B** Rose Grove	**27D** Wigan					
52952	7F[5]	**24B** Rose Grove						
52956	7F[5]	**23B** Aintree						
52962	7F[5]	**23B** Aintree						
52971	7F[5]	**23B** Aintree						
53800	7F[6]	**22C** Bath Green Park	**71G** Bath Green Park	**71G** Bath Green Park	**71G** Bath Green Park			
53801	7F[6]	**22C** Bath Green Park	**71G** Bath Green Park	**71G** Bath Green Park	**71G** Bath Green Park	**82F** Bath Green Park		
53802	7F[6]	**22C** Bath Green Park	**71G** Bath Green Park	**71G** Bath Green Park	**71G** Bath Green Park	**82F** Bath Green Park		
53803	7F[6]	**22C** Bath Green Park	**71G** Bath Green Park	**71G** Bath Green Park	**71G** Bath Green Park	**82F** Bath Green Park		
53804	7F[6]	**22C** Bath Green Park	**71G** Bath Green Park	**71G** Bath Green Park	**71G** Bath Green Park	**82F** Bath Green Park		
53805	7F[6]	**22C** Bath Green Park	**71G** Bath Green Park	**71G** Bath Green Park	**71G** Bath Green Park	**82F** Bath Green Park		
53806	7F[6]	**22C** Bath Green Park	**71G** Bath Green Park	**71G** Bath Green Park	**71G** Bath Green Park	**82F** Bath Green Park	**82F** Bath Green Park	
53807	7F[6]	**22C** Bath Green Park	**71G** Bath Green Park	**71G** Bath Green Park	**71G** Bath Green Park	**82F** Bath Green Park	**82F** Bath Green Park	
53808	7F[6]	**22C** Bath Green Park	**71G** Bath Green Park	**71G** Bath Green Park	**71G** Bath Green Park	**82F** Bath Green Park	**82F** Bath Green Park	
53809	7F[6]	**22C** Bath Green Park	**71G** Bath Green Park	**71G** Bath Green Park	**71G** Bath Green Park	**82F** Bath Green Park	**82F** Bath Green Park	
53810	7F[6]	**22C** Bath Green Park	**71G** Bath Green Park	**71G** Bath Green Park	**71G** Bath Green Park	**82F** Bath Green Park	**82F** Bath Green Park	
54363	2P[9]	**32B** Aviemore						
54379	2P[10]	**32B** Aviemore						
54385	2P[10]	**32C** Forres						
54397	2P[11]	**32A** Inverness						
54398	2P[11]	**32B** Aviemore	**60D** Wick					
54399	2P[11]	**32A** Inverness	**60D** Wick					
54401	2P[11]	**32A** Inverness						
54403	2P[11]	**32A** Inverness						
54404	2P[11]	**32A** Inverness						
54409	2P[11]	**32A** Inverness						
54410	2P[11]	**32C** Forres						
54415	2P[11]	**32A** Inverness						
54416	2P[11]	**32A** Inverness						
54434	3P[4]	**32B** Aviemore						
54438	3P[5]	**28C** Carstairs	**64D** Carstairs	**68B** Dumfries				
54439	3P[5]	**28C** Carstairs	**60A** Inverness	**60A** Inverness	**60D** Wick			
54440	3P[5]	**27B** Greenock Ladyburn	**66D** Greenock Ladyburn	**66D** Greenock Ladyburn	**66D** Greenock Ladyburn			
54441	3P[5]	**28A** Motherwell	**66B** Motherwell	**66D** Greenock Ladyburn	**66D** Greenock Ladyburn			
54443	3P[5]	**27B** Greenock Ladyburn	**68B** Dumfries	**68B** Dumfries				

		1948	1951	1954	1957	1960	1963	1966
54444	$3P^{5}$	**27B** Greenock Ladyburn	**68B** Dumfries					
54445	$3P^{5}$	**27B** Greenock Ladyburn	**60D** Wick					
54446	$3P^{5}$	**28C** Carstairs	**64D** Carstairs	**64D** Carstairs				
54447	$3P^{5}$	**29A** Perth	**63A** Perth					
54448	$3P^{5}$	**29A** Perth	**63A** Perth	**63A** Perth				
54449	$3P^{5}$	**28C** Carstairs	**64D** Carstairs					
54450	$3P^{5}$	**29D** Forfar	**63C** Forfar	**63C** Forfar				
54451	$3P^{5}$	**28B** Dalry Road	**64C** Dalry Road	**64C** Dalry Road				
54452	$3P^{5}$	**28B** Dalry Road	**64C** Dalry Road	**64C** Dalry Road	**64C** Dalry Road			
54453	$3P^{5}$	**28A** Motherwell	**66B** Motherwell	**66D** Greenock Ladyburn	**66D** Greenock Ladyburn			
54454	$3P^{5}$	**29D** Forfar	**63C** Forfar	**63C** Forfar				
54455	$3P^{5}$	**31B** Stirling	**60B** Aviemore	**60B** Aviemore				
54456	$3P^{5}$	**30B** Hurlford	**67B** Hurlford	**66D** Greenock Ladyburn	**66D** Greenock Ladyburn			
54457	$3P^{5}$	**27B** Greenock Ladyburn	**66D** Greenock Ladyburn	**66B** Motherwell				
54458	$3P^{5}$	**29A** Perth	**60A** Inverness	**60A** Inverness	**60A** Inverness			
54459	$3P^{5}$	**29A** Perth	**60A** Inverness	**60D** Wick				
54460	$3P^{5}$	**28A** Motherwell	**66B** Motherwell	**66B** Motherwell				
54461	$3P^{6}$	**28C** Carstairs	**64D** Carstairs	**64D** Carstairs	**64D** Carstairs			
54462	$3P^{6}$	**28A** Motherwell	**66B** Motherwell	**66B** Motherwell	**66B** Motherwell	**66B** Motherwell		
54463	$3P^{6}$	**28C** Carstairs	**60A** Inverness	**60A** Inverness	**60A** Inverness	**60A** Inverness		
54464	$3P^{6}$	**28A** Motherwell	**66B** Motherwell	**66B** Motherwell	**66B** Motherwell	**66B** Motherwell		
54465	$3P^{6}$	**28A** Motherwell	**66B** Motherwell	**66B** Motherwell	**66B** Motherwell	**66B** Motherwell		
54466	$3P^{6}$	**31B** Stirling	**60B** Aviemore	**60B** Aviemore	**60B** Aviemore	**60B** Aviemore		
54467	$3P^{6}$	**29A** Perth	**63A** Perth	**63A** Perth	**63C** Forfar			
54468	$3P^{6}$	**27B** Greenock Ladyburn	**66D** Greenock Ladyburn	**66D** Greenock Ladyburn	**66D** Greenock Ladyburn			
54469	$3P^{6}$	**29A** Perth	**63A** Perth	**63A** Perth	**63A** Perth			
54470	$3P^{6}$	**32A** Inverness	**60A** Inverness	**60A** Inverness	**60C** Helmsdale			
54471	$3P^{6}$	**32A** Inverness	**60A** Inverness	**60A** Inverness	**60E** Forres			
54472	$3P^{6}$	**32A** Inverness	**60A** Inverness	**60E** Forres	**60E** Forres			
54473	$3P^{6}$	**32C** Forres	**60E** Forres	**60E** Forres	**60E** Forres			
54474	$3P^{6}$	**31A** St. Rollox	**65B** St. Rollox	**65B** St. Rollox	**65B** St. Rollox			
54475	$3P^{6}$	**31A** St. Rollox	**65B** St. Rollox	**65B** St. Rollox	**65B** St. Rollox	**65B** St. Rollox		
54476	$3P^{6}$	**29A** Perth	**63A** Perth	**63A** Perth	**63A** Perth	**63B** Stirling		
54477	$3P^{6}$	**28C** Carstairs	**64D** Carstairs	**64D** Carstairs	**64D** Carstairs	**64D** Carstairs		
54478	$3P^{6}$	**28B** Dalry Road	**64C** Dalry Road	**64C** Dalry Road	**64C** Dalry Road	**64C** Dalry Road		
54479	$3P^{6}$	**27B** Greenock Ladyburn	**66D** Greenock Ladyburn	**66D** Greenock Ladyburn	**66D** Greenock Ladyburn			
54480	$3P^{6}$	**32A** Inverness	**60C** Helmsdale	**60C** Helmsdale	**60C** Helmsdale	**60C** Helmsdale		
54481	$3P^{6}$	**32C** Forres	**60E** Forres					
54482	$3P^{6}$	**32A** Inverness	**60E** Forres	**60E** Forres	**60E** Forres	**60B** Aviemore		
54483	$3P^{6}$	**31A** St. Rollox	**65F** Grangemouth	**65F** Grangemouth	**65B** St. Rollox	**65B** St. Rollox		
54484	$3P^{6}$	**32A** Inverness	**60A** Inverness	**60A** Inverness	**60A** Inverness			
54485	$3P^{6}$	**31B** Stirling	**63A** Perth	**63A** Perth	**63A** Perth	**63A** Perth		
54486	$3P^{6}$	**29D** Forfar	**63A** Perth	**63C** Forfar	**63C** Forfar	**63A** Perth		
54487	$3P^{6}$	**31A** St. Rollox	**60A** Inverness	**60A** Inverness	**60A** Inverness	**60A** Inverness		
54488	$3P^{6}$	**32A** Inverness	**60B** Aviemore	**60B** Aviemore	**60B** Aviemore	**60B** Aviemore		
54489	$3P^{6}$	**29A** Perth	**63A** Perth	**63A** Perth	**63A** Perth	**63A** Perth		
54490	$3P^{6}$	**28C** Carstairs	**64D** Carstairs	**64D** Carstairs	**64D** Carstairs	**64D** Carstairs		
54491	$3P^{6}$	**31B** Stirling	**60A** Inverness	**60D** Wick	**60D** Wick	**60D** Wick		
54492	$3P^{6}$	**27B** Greenock Ladyburn	**66D** Greenock Ladyburn	**66D** Greenock Ladyburn	**68C** Stranraer	**68C** Stranraer		
54493	$3P^{6}$	**32B** Aviemore	**60B** Aviemore	**60B** Aviemore	**60A** Inverness	**60A** Inverness		
54494	$3P^{6}$	**31A** St. Rollox	**63A** Perth	**63A** Perth	**63A** Perth	**63A** Perth		
54495	$3P^{6}$	**32A** Inverness	**60C** Helmsdale	**60C** Helmsdale	**60C** Helmsdale	**60C** Helmsdale		
54496	$3P^{6}$	**31B** Stirling	**60A** Inverness	**60A** Inverness	**60A** Inverness			
54497	$3P^{6}$	**27B** Greenock Ladyburn	**66D** Greenock Ladyburn	**66D** Greenock Ladyburn	**66D** Greenock Ladyburn			
54498	$3P^{6}$	**28A** Motherwell	**66D** Greenock Ladyburn	**66D** Greenock Ladyburn	**66D** Greenock Ladyburn	**66D** Greenock Ladyburn		
54499	$3P^{6}$	**29A** Perth	**63A** Perth	**63A** Perth	**63A** Perth	**63A** Perth		
54500	$3P^{6}$	**29A** Perth	**63A** Perth	**63A** Perth	**63A** Perth	**63A** Perth		
54501	$3P^{6}$	**29A** Perth	**63A** Perth	**65B** St. Rollox	**65B** St. Rollox	**65B** St. Rollox		
54502	$3P^{6}$	**29A** Perth	**63A** Perth	**68B** Dumfries	**68B** Dumfries	**68B** Dumfries		
54503	$3P^{6}$	**29A** Perth	**63A** Perth	**63A** Perth	**63A** Perth			
54504	$3P^{6}$	**30B** Hurlford	**67B** Hurlford	**67B** Hurlford	**63B** Stirling			
54505	$3P^{6}$	**28C** Carstairs	**64D** Carstairs	**64D** Carstairs	**64D** Carstairs	**64D** Carstairs		
54506	$3P^{6}$	**28A** Motherwell	**66D** Greenock Ladyburn	**66D** Greenock Ladyburn	**66D** Greenock Ladyburn	**66D** Greenock Ladyburn		
54507	$3P^{6}$	**28B** Dalry Road	**68B** Dumfries	**68B** Dumfries	**68B** Dumfries	**68B** Dumfries		
54508	$3P^{6}$	**27B** Greenock Ladyburn	**66D** Greenock Ladyburn	**66D** Greenock Ladyburn	**68C** Stranraer			
54630	$4P^{3}$	**28C** Carstairs	**66B** Motherwell					
54631	$4P^{3}$	**28A** Motherwell						
54634	$4P^{3}$	**28A** Motherwell	**66B** Motherwell					
54635	$4P^{3}$	**28A** Motherwell	**66B** Motherwell					
54636	$4P^{3}$	**28A** Motherwell	**66B** Motherwell					
54637	$4P^{3}$	**28A** Motherwell						
54638	$4P^{3}$	**27C** Hamilton	**66C** Hamilton					
54639	$4P^{3}$	**27C** Hamilton	**66C** Hamilton					
54640	$4P^{3}$	**28A** Motherwell	**66B** Motherwell					
54641	$4P^{3}$	**28A** Motherwell						
54642	$4P^{3}$	**28A** Motherwell						
54643	$4P^{3}$	**28A** Motherwell						
54644	$4P^{3}$	**28B** Dalry Road						
54645	$4P^{3}$	**28A** Motherwell						
54646	$4P^{3}$	**28A** Motherwell						
54647	$4P^{3}$	**28A** Motherwell	**66B** Motherwell					
54648	$4P^{3}$	**27C** Hamilton	**66B** Motherwell					
54649	$4P^{3}$	**28A** Motherwell	**66B** Motherwell					
54650	$4P^{3}$	**28A** Motherwell	**66B** Motherwell					
54651	$4P^{3}$	**28A** Motherwell						
54652	$4P^{3}$	**28A** Motherwell						
54653	$4P^{3}$	**28A** Motherwell						
54654	$4P^{3}$	**28A** Motherwell	**66B** Motherwell					
54764	$4P^{4}$	**32B** Aviemore						
54767	$4P^{4}$	**32B** Aviemore						
55051	$0P$	**32A** Inverness	**60C** Helmsdale	**60C** Helmsdale				
55053	$0P$	**32A** Inverness	**60C** Helmsdale	**60C** Helmsdale	**60C** Helmsdale			
55116	$2P^{12}$	**27A** Polmadie						
55117	$2P^{12}$	**31B** Stirling						
55119	$2P^{12}$	**31D** Grangemouth	**65F** Grangemouth					
55121	$2P^{12}$	**31A** St. Rollox	**65B** St. Rollox					
55122	$2P^{12}$	**31B** Stirling	**63B** Stirling					
55123	$2P^{12}$	**27A** Polmadie						
55124	$2P^{12}$	**31A** St. Rollox	**68B** Dumfries	**68B** Dumfries	**68B** Dumfries	**68B** Dumfries		
55125	$2P^{12}$	**28B** Dalry Road	**68C** Stranraer	**68C** Stranraer	**68C** Stranraer			
55126	$2P^{12}$	**31B** Stirling	**63B** Stirling	**63B** Stirling	**63B** Stirling	**63C** Oban		
55127	$2P^{12}$	**27A** Polmadie						
55129	$2P^{12}$	**31E** Dawsholm						
55130	$2P^{12}$	**20E** Manningham						
55132	$2P^{12}$	**30D** Ayr	**67C** Ayr					
55133	$2P^{12}$	**32B** Aviemore						
55134	$2P^{12}$	**28A** Motherwell	**CME** Law Junction					
55135	$2P^{12}$	**30A** Corkerhill	**67A** Corkerhill					
55136	$2P^{12}$	**31E** Dawsholm	**63C** Forfar					
55138	$2P^{12}$	**28A** Motherwell	**66B** Motherwell					
55139	$2P^{12}$	**28B** Dalry Road	**64C** Dalry Road					
55140	$2P^{12}$	**30A** Corkerhill	**67A** Corkerhill					
55141	$2P^{12}$	**27A** Polmadie	**66A** Polmadie	**66A** Polmadie	**66A** Polmadie			
55142	$2P^{12}$	**31D** Grangemouth	**65F** Grangemouth					

No.	Class	1948	1951	1954	1957	1960	1963	1966
55143	*2P[12]*	**30A** Corkerhill	**67A** Corkerhill					
55144	*2P[12]*	**29A** Perth	**63A** Perth					
55145	*2P[12]*	**31E** Dawsholm	**63B** Stirling	**63B** Stirling				
55146	*2P[12]*	**27C** Hamilton	**66C** Hamilton	**66A** Polmadie				
55159	*2P[13]*	**31A** St. Rollox						
55160	*2P[13]*	**29D** Forfar	**60A** Inverness	**60A** Inverness	**60A** Inverness			
55161	*2P[13]*	**29D** Forfar	**63C** Forfar					
55162	*2P[13]*	**29D** Forfar	**63C** Forfar	**62B** Dundee Tay Bridge				
55164	*2P[13]*	**12F** Beattock	**68B** Dumfries	**68B** Dumfries	**68B** Dumfries			
55165	*2P[13]*	**28B** Dalry Road	**64C** Dalry Road	**64C** Dalry Road	**64C** Dalry Road	**64C** Dalry Road		
55166	*2P[13]*	**28B** Dalry Road	**64C** Dalry Road					
55167	*2P[13]*	**27A** Polmadie	**66A** Polmadie	**66A** Polmadie	**66A** Polmadie	**66A** Polmadie		
55168	*2P[13]*	**31E** Dawsholm	**65D** Dawsholm	**65B** St. Rollox	**65B** St. Rollox			
55169	*2P[13]*	**20E** Manningham	**63C** Forfar	**62B** Dundee Tay Bridge	**66A** Polmadie	**66A** Polmadie		
55170	*2P[13]*	**27A** Polmadie	**66A** Polmadie					
55171	*2P[13]*	**29A** Perth	**63A** Perth					
55172	*2P[13]*	**29D** Forfar	**63C** Forfar					
55173	*2P[13]*	**29C** Dundee West	**62B** Dundee Tay Bridge	**62B** Dundee Tay Bridge	**60B** Aviemore	**60B** Aviemore		
55174	*2P[13]*	**31E** Dawsholm	**60B** Aviemore	**60B** Aviemore				
55175	*2P[13]*	**29A** Perth	**63A** Perth					
55176	*2P[13]*	**29A** Perth	**63A** Perth	**63C** Forfar	**63B** Stirling			
55177	*2P[13]*	**28B** Dalry Road	**64C** Dalry Road	**64C** Dalry Road				
55178	*2P[13]*	**31A** St. Rollox	**60E** Forres	**60E** Forres	**60E** Forres			
55179	*2P[13]*	**27A** Polmadie	**66A** Polmadie					
55180	*2P[13]*	**29C** Dundee West						
55181	*2P[13]*	**12F** Beattock	**68D** Beattock					
55182	*2P[13]*	**30A** Corkerhill	**67A** Corkerhill	**66C** Hamilton	**66C** Hamilton			
55183	*2P[13]*	**27A** Polmadie						
55184	*2P[13]*	**29D** Forfar						
55185	*2P[13]*	**29D** Forfar	**63C** Forfar	**61C** Keith	**61C** Keith	**61C** Keith		
55186	*2P[13]*	**29C** Dundee West	**62B** Dundee Tay Bridge					
55187	*2P[13]*	**31C** Oban	**63E** Oban	**68D** Beattock				
55188	*2P[13]*	**28A** Motherwell	**66B** Motherwell					
55189	*2P[13]*	**28B** Dalry Road	**64C** Dalry Road	**66A** Polmadie	**66A** Polmadie	**66A** Polmadie		
55190	*2P[13]*	**29D** Forfar						
55191	*2P[13]*	**28A** Motherwell						
55192	*2P[13]*	**20E** Manningham						
55193	*2P[13]*	**30A** Corkerhill	**63C** Forfar	**63C** Forfar				
55194	*2P[13]*	**29D** Forfar	**63C** Forfar	**63C** Forfar				
55195	*2P[13]*	**29D** Forfar	**63C** Forfar	**63E** Oban	**63B** Stirling	**63B** Stirling		
55196	*2P[13]*	**29C** Dundee West	**63E** Oban	**63E** Oban				
55197	*2P[13]*	**27A** Polmadie	**66A** Polmadie	**66A** Polmadie				
55198	*2P[13]*	**29D** Forfar	**63E** Oban	**63C** Forfar	**63C** Forfar	**60A** Inverness		
55199	*2P[13]*	**32A** Inverness	**60A** Inverness	**60A** Inverness	**60A** Inverness	**60A** Inverness		
55200	*2P[13]*	**29D** Forfar	**63C** Forfar	**63C** Forfar	**63D** Oban	**63A** Perth		
55201	*2P[13]*	**27A** Polmadie	**66A** Polmadie	**66A** Polmadie	**66A** Polmadie	**66A** Polmadie		
55202	*2P[13]*	**28B** Dalry Road	**64C** Dalry Road	**64C** Dalry Road	**64C** Dalry Road	**64C** Dalry Road		
55203	*2P[13]*	**30B** Hurlford	**67B** Hurlford	**67B** Hurlford	**67B** Hurlford	**67A** Corkerhill		
55204	*2P[13]*	**31A** St. Rollox	**65B** St. Rollox	**65B** St. Rollox	**65B** St. Rollox	**65F** Grangemouth		
55206	*2P[13]*	**30A** Corkerhill	**67A** Corkerhill	**67A** Corkerhill	**67A** Corkerhill	**67A** Corkerhill		
55207	*2P[13]*	**27A** Polmadie	**66A** Polmadie	**66A** Polmadie	**66A** Polmadie	**66A** Polmadie		
55208	*2P[13]*	**29A** Perth	**63A** Perth	**63A** Perth	**63D** Oban	**63C** Oban		
55209	*2P[13]*	**29A** Perth	**63A** Perth	**63A** Perth	**63A** Perth	**63A** Perth		
55210	*2P[13]*	**28B** Dalry Road	**64C** Dalry Road	**64C** Dalry Road	**64C** Dalry Road	**64C** Dalry Road		
55211	*2P[13]*	**30A** Corkerhill	**67A** Corkerhill	**67A** Corkerhill	**67A** Corkerhill	**67B** Hurlford		
55212	*2P[13]*	**31B** Stirling	**63A** Perth	**63A** Perth	**63A** Perth			
55213	*2P[13]*	**29A** Perth	**63A** Perth	**63A** Perth	**63A** Perth			
55214	*2P[13]*	**29D** Forfar	**63C** Forfar	**65F** Grangemouth	**65F** Grangemouth	**65F** Grangemouth		
55215	*2P[13]*	**31C** Oban	**63E** Oban	**63E** Oban	**63D** Oban	**63C** Oban		
55216	*2P[13]*	**29A** Perth	**63A** Perth	**60A** Inverness	**60A** Inverness	**60A** Inverness		
55217	*2P[13]*	**29C** Dundee West	**62B** Dundee Tay Bridge	**62B** Dundee Tay Bridge	**62A** Thornton Junction	**63A** Perth		
55218	*2P[13]*	**29A** Perth	**63A** Perth	**63A** Perth	**63A** Perth	**63A** Perth		
55219	*2P[13]*	**30A** Corkerhill	**67A** Corkerhill	**67A** Corkerhill	**67A** Corkerhill	**67A** Corkerhill		
55220	*2P[13]*	**29B** Aberdeen Ferryhill	**68D** Beattock	**68D** Beattock	**63C** Forfar	**63C** Oban		
55221	*2P[13]*	**27A** Polmadie	**66C** Hamilton	**61C** Keith	**61C** Keith	**61C** Keith		
55222	*2P[13]*	**31B** Stirling	**63B** Stirling	**63B** Stirling	**63B** Stirling	**63B** Stirling		
55223	*2P[13]*	**29C** Dundee West	**62B** Dundee Tay Bridge	**62B** Dundee Tay Bridge	**66A** Polmadie	**66A** Polmadie		
55224	*2P[13]*	**27A** Polmadie	**66A** Polmadie	**66A** Polmadie	**66A** Polmadie	**66A** Polmadie		
55225	*2P[13]*	**30A** Corkerhill	**67A** Corkerhill	**67A** Corkerhill	**67A** Corkerhill	**67A** Corkerhill		
55226	*2P[13]*	**29C** Dundee West	**62B** Dundee Tay Bridge	**63A** Perth	**63A** Perth	**63A** Perth		
55227	*2P[13]*	**20E** Manningham	**62B** Dundee Tay Bridge	**62B** Dundee Tay Bridge	**62B** Dundee Tay Bridge	**60A** Inverness		
55228	*2P[13]*	**27A** Polmadie	**66A** Polmadie	**66A** Polmadie	**66A** Polmadie	**66A** Polmadie		
55229	*2P[13]*	**28B** Dalry Road	**64C** Dalry Road	**64C** Dalry Road	**64C** Dalry Road	**64C** Dalry Road		
55230	*2P[13]*	**29D** Forfar	**63C** Forfar	**63C** Forfar	**63C** Forfar	**63A** Perth		
55231	*2P[13]*	**29C** Dundee West	**62B** Dundee Tay Bridge	**60A** Inverness	**67C** Ayr	**67C** Ayr		
55232	*2P[13]*	**12F** Beattock	**68D** Beattock	**68D** Beattock	**68D** Beattock	**68B** Dumfries		
55233	*2P[13]*	**28B** Dalry Road	**64C** Dalry Road	**64C** Dalry Road	**64C** Dalry Road	**64C** Dalry Road		
55234	*2P[13]*	**29B** Aberdeen Ferryhill	**68D** Beattock	**68D** Beattock	**68D** Beattock	**68D** Beattock		
55235	*2P[13]*	**30A** Corkerhill	**67A** Corkerhill	**67A** Corkerhill	**67A** Corkerhill	**67A** Corkerhill		
55236	*2P[13]*	**30B** Hurlford	**67B** Hurlford	**60D** Wick	**60C** Helmsdale	**60D** Wick		
55237	*2P[14]*	**12F** Beattock	**68D** Beattock	**68D** Beattock	**66A** Polmadie	**66A** Polmadie		
55238	*2P[14]*	**31D** Grangemouth	**65F** Grangemouth	**65F** Grangemouth	**65F** Grangemouth	**65F** Grangemouth		
55239	*2P[14]*	**12F** Beattock	**68D** Beattock	**66B** Motherwell	**66A** Polmadie	**66A** Polmadie		
55240	*2P[14]*	**31E** Dawsholm	**67C** Ayr	**67C** Ayr	**67C** Ayr	**68C** Stranraer		
55260	*2P[15]*	**30B** Hurlford	**67B** Hurlford	**68D** Beattock	**68D** Beattock	**68D** Beattock		
55261	*2P[15]*	**28C** Carstairs	**64D** Carstairs	**64D** Carstairs	**64D** Carstairs	**64D** Carstairs		
55262	*2P[15]*	**30D** Ayr	**67C** Ayr	**67C** Ayr	**67C** Ayr	**67C** Ayr		
55263	*2P[15]*	**31C** Oban	**63E** Oban	**63E** Oban	**63D** Oban	**63C** Oban		
55264	*2P[15]*	**30D** Ayr	**67C** Ayr	**67B** Hurlford	**67B** Hurlford	**67A** Corkerhill		
55265	*2P[15]*	**27A** Polmadie	**66A** Polmadie	**66A** Polmadie	**66A** Polmadie	**66A** Polmadie		
55266	*2P[15]*	**30A** Corkerhill	**67A** Corkerhill	**67A** Corkerhill	**67A** Corkerhill	**67A** Corkerhill		
55267	*2P[15]*	**27A** Polmadie	**66D** Greenock Ladyburn	**66D** Greenock Ladyburn	**66D** Greenock Ladyburn	**66D** Greenock Ladyburn		
55268	*2P[15]*	**27A** Polmadie	**66A** Polmadie	**66A** Polmadie	**66A** Polmadie	**66A** Polmadie		
55269	*2P[15]*	**30A** Corkerhill	**67A** Corkerhill	**67A** Corkerhill	**67A** Corkerhill	**60A** Inverness		
55350	*4P[5]*	**12F** Beattock	**68D** Beattock					
55351	*4P[5]*	**12F** Beattock						
55352	*4P[5]*	**12F** Beattock	**68D** Beattock					
55353	*4P[5]*	**12F** Beattock	**68D** Beattock					
55354	*4P[5]*	**12F** Beattock						
55355	*4P[5]*	**27B** Greenock Ladyburn						
55356	*4P[5]*	**12F** Beattock						
55359	*4P[5]*	**12F** Beattock	**68D** Beattock					
55360	*4P[5]*	**12F** Beattock	**68D** Beattock					
55361	*4P[5]*	**12F** Beattock	**68D** Beattock					
56010	*0F[5]*	**32A** Inverness						
56011	*0F[5]*	**32A** Inverness	**60A** Inverness	**60A** Inverness	**60A** Inverness			
56020	*0F[5]*	**17B** Burton	**17B** Burton	**21C** Bromsgrove				
56025	*0F[5]*	St Rollox Works	St. Rollox Works	St. Rollox Works	St. Rollox Works	St. Rollox Works		
56026	*0F[5]*	**31E** Dawsholm						
56027	*0F[5]*	**4A** Shrewsbury	**10B** Preston	**10B** Preston	**10B** Preston	Crewe Works		
56028	*0F[5]*	**28A** Motherwell	**66D** Greenock Ladyburn	**66D** Greenock Ladyburn	**66D** Greenock Ladyburn			
56029	*0F[5]*	**28A** Motherwell	**65D** Dawsholm	**65D** Dawsholm	**65D** Dawsholm	**65E** Kipps		
56030	*0F[5]*	**31E** Dawsholm	**65G** Yoker	**65G** Yoker	**65G** Yoker			
56031	*0F[5]*	**28A** Motherwell	**66D** Greenock Ladyburn	**66D** Greenock Ladyburn	**66D** Greenock Ladyburn	**67A** Corkerhill		

		1948	1951	1954	1957	1960	1963	1966
56032	0F[5]	Crewe Works	Crewe Works	Crewe Works	Crewe Works	Crewe Works		
56035	0F[5]	**27B** Greenock Ladyburn	**66D** Greenock Ladyburn	**66D** Greenock Ladyburn	**64A** St. Margarets	**66D** Greenock Ladyburn		
56038	0F[5]	**31E** Dawsholm	**60A** Inverness	**60A** Inverness	**60A** Inverness			
56039	0F[5]	**31E** Dawsholm	hire BWL Renfrew	**65G** Yoker	**65G** Yoker	**65G** Yoker		
56151	2F[4]	**31A** St. Rollox	**65B** St. Rollox	**65B** St. Rollox	**65B** St. Rollox	**65B** St. Rollox		
56152	2F[4]	**31D** Grangemouth	**65F** Grangemouth	**65F** Grangemouth	**65A** Eastfield			
56153	2F[4]	**27A** Polmadie	**66A** Polmadie	**66A** Polmadie	**66A** Polmadie			
56154	2F[4]	**31E** Dawsholm	**66A** Polmadie	**66A** Polmadie	**66A** Polmadie			
56155	2F[4]	**28A** Motherwell	**66B** Motherwell	**66A** Polmadie	**66A** Polmadie			
56156	2F[4]	**27B** Greenock Ladyburn	**66D** Greenock Ladyburn	**66D** Greenock Ladyburn	**66D** Greenock Ladyburn			
56157	2F[4]	**27B** Greenock Ladyburn	**66D** Greenock Ladyburn	**66D** Greenock Ladyburn	**66D** Greenock Ladyburn			
56158	2F[4]	**31E** Dawsholm	**65G** Yoker	**65G** Yoker	**65G** Yoker	**66A** Polmadie		
56159	2F[4]	**27A** Polmadie	**66A** Polmadie	**66A** Polmadie	**66A** Polmadie	**66A** Polmadie		
56160	2F[4]	**27A** Polmadie	**66A** Polmadie	**66A** Polmadie	**66A** Polmadie			
56161	2F[4]	**31E** Dawsholm	**65G** Yoker	**65G** Yoker	**65G** Yoker			
56162	2F[4]	**27A** Polmadie	**66A** Polmadie	**66A** Polmadie	**66A** Polmadie			
56163	2F[4]	**27B** Greenock Ladyburn	**66D** Greenock Ladyburn	**66D** Greenock Ladyburn	**66D** Greenock Ladyburn			
56164	2F[4]	**31D** Grangemouth	**65F** Grangemouth	**65F** Grangemouth	**65F** Grangemouth			
56165	2F[4]	**27B** Greenock Ladyburn	**66D** Greenock Ladyburn	**66D** Greenock Ladyburn	**66D** Greenock Ladyburn	**66D** Greenock Ladyburn		
56166	2F[4]	**27B** Greenock Ladyburn	**66D** Greenock Ladyburn	**66D** Greenock Ladyburn	**66D** Greenock Ladyburn			
56167	2F[4]	**27A** Polmadie	**66A** Polmadie	**66A** Polmadie	**65D** Dawsholm	**66D** Greenock Ladyburn		
56168	2F[4]	**31E** Dawsholm	**65G** Yoker	**65G** Yoker	**65G** Yoker	**65G** Yoker		
56169	2F[4]	**31E** Dawsholm	**65D** Dawsholm	**65B** St. Rollox	**65B** St. Rollox	**65B** St. Rollox		
56170	2F[4]	**31E** Dawsholm	**65G** Yoker	**65G** Yoker	**65G** Yoker	**66D** Greenock Ladyburn		
56171	2F[4]	**31E** Dawsholm	**65D** Dawsholm	**65D** Dawsholm	**65D** Dawsholm	**65D** Dawsholm		
56172	2F[4]	**27A** Polmadie	**66B** Motherwell	**65E** Kipps	**65E** Kipps	**66A** Polmadie		
56173	2F[4]	**27B** Greenock Ladyburn	**66D** Greenock Ladyburn	**66D** Greenock Ladyburn	**66D** Greenock Ladyburn	**66D** Greenock Ladyburn		
56230	3F[10]	**31D** Grangemouth	**65F** Grangemouth	**65F** Grangemouth	**65F** Grangemouth			
56231	3F[10]	**12A** Carlisle Kingmoor	**68A** Carlisle Kingmoor	**68A** Carlisle Kingmoor				
56232	3F[10]	**31D** Grangemouth	**63B** Stirling	**63B** Stirling	**63B** Stirling	**67C** Ayr		
56233	3F[10]	**31A** St. Rollox	**65B** St. Rollox	**65B** St. Rollox				
56234	3F[10]	**31A** St. Rollox	**68C** Stranraer	**68C** Stranraer	**68C** Stranraer			
56235	3F[10]	**12A** Carlisle Kingmoor	**68A** Carlisle Kingmoor	**68A** Carlisle Kingmoor	**68A** Carlisle Kingmoor			
56236	3F[10]	**28B** Dalry Road	**67B** Hurlford	**67B** Hurlford	**67B** Hurlford			
56237	3F[10]	**27C** Hamilton	**66C** Hamilton					
56238	3F[10]	**31E** Dawsholm	**65G** Yoker	**65G** Yoker	**65G** Yoker			
56239	3F[10]	**27A** Polmadie	**66A** Polmadie	**66A** Polmadie	**66A** Polmadie	**66A** Polmadie		
56240	3F[10]	**29B** Aberdeen Ferryhill	**61B** Aberdeen Ferryhill	**61B** Aberdeen Ferryhill	**61B** Aberdeen Ferryhill	**61B** Aberdeen Ferryhill		
56241	3F[10]	**28A** Motherwell	**66B** Motherwell	**66B** Motherwell	**66B** Motherwell	**66A** Polmadie		
56242	3F[10]	**27C** Hamilton	**66C** Hamilton	**66C** Hamilton	**66C** Hamilton	**66C** Hamilton		
56243	3F[10]	**31D** Grangemouth	**65F** Grangemouth	**65F** Grangemouth	**68B** Dumfries			
56244	3F[10]	**27A** Polmadie	**66A** Polmadie	**66A** Polmadie	**66A** Polmadie			
56245	3F[10]	**28A** Motherwell	**66B** Motherwell	**66B** Motherwell	**66B** Motherwell			
56246	3F[10]	**29A** Perth	**63A** Perth	**63A** Perth	**63A** Perth	**63A** Perth		
56247	3F[10]	**28A** Motherwell	**66B** Motherwell	**66B** Motherwell	**66B** Motherwell			
56248	3F[10]	**12A** Carlisle Kingmoor	**68A** Carlisle Kingmoor	**66A** Polmadie				
56249	3F[10]	**30A** Corkerhill	**67A** Corkerhill	**67A** Corkerhill				
56250	3F[10]	**31E** Dawsholm	**65G** Yoker	**65G** Yoker				
56251	3F[10]	**29B** Aberdeen Ferryhill	**61B** Aberdeen Ferryhill	**61B** Aberdeen Ferryhill	**61B** Aberdeen Ferryhill			
56252	3F[10]	**31A** St. Rollox	**65B** St. Rollox	**65B** St. Rollox	**65B** St. Rollox			
56253	3F[10]	**28B** Dalry Road	**64C** Dalry Road	**64C** Dalry Road	**64C** Dalry Road			
56254	3F[10]	**31B** Stirling	**63B** Stirling	**63B** Stirling	**63B** Stirling			
56255	3F[10]	**27C** Hamilton	**66C** Hamilton	**66C** Hamilton	**66C** Hamilton			
56256	3F[10]	**27C** Hamilton	**66C** Hamilton	**66C** Hamilton	**66C** Hamilton			
56257	3F[10]	**30D** Ayr	**67C** Ayr	**67C** Ayr	**67C** Ayr			
56258	3F[10]	**28A** Motherwell	**66B** Motherwell					
56259	3F[10]	**30C** Ardrossan	**67D** Ardrossan	**67D** Ardrossan	**67D** Ardrossan	**67D** Ardrossan		
56260	3F[10]	**27A** Polmadie	**66A** Polmadie	**66A** Polmadie	**66A** Polmadie	**66A** Polmadie		
56261	3F[10]	**27A** Polmadie	**66A** Polmadie	**66A** Polmadie				
56262	3F[10]	**32A** Inverness	**60A** Inverness	**60A** Inverness	**60A** Inverness			
56263	3F[10]	**27A** Polmadie	**66A** Polmadie	**66A** Polmadie				
56264	3F[10]	**28A** Motherwell	**66B** Motherwell	**66B** Motherwell	**66B** Motherwell			
56265	3F[10]	**28A** Motherwell	**66B** Motherwell	**66B** Motherwell	**66B** Motherwell			
56266	3F[10]	**12A** Carlisle Kingmoor	**68A** Carlisle Kingmoor	**66A** Polmadie	**66A** Polmadie			
56267	3F[10]	**31D** Grangemouth	**65F** Grangemouth	**65F** Grangemouth	**67A** Corkerhill			
56268	3F[10]	**28A** Motherwell	**66B** Motherwell					
56269	3F[10]	**28A** Motherwell	**66B** Motherwell	**66B** Motherwell	**66B** Motherwell			
56270	3F[10]	**28A** Motherwell						
56271	3F[10]	**28A** Motherwell	**66B** Motherwell	**66B** Motherwell				
56272	3F[10]	**30D** Ayr	**67C** Ayr	**67C** Ayr	**67C** Ayr			
56273	3F[10]	**30D** Ayr	**67C** Ayr	**67C** Ayr				
56274	3F[10]	**30D** Ayr	**67C** Ayr	**67C** Ayr	**67C** Ayr			
56275	3F[10]	**31D** Grangemouth	**65F** Grangemouth	**65F** Grangemouth	**65D** Dawsholm			
56276	3F[10]	**28A** Motherwell	**66B** Motherwell					
56277	3F[10]	**28A** Motherwell	**66B** Motherwell	**66B** Motherwell	**66B** Motherwell			
56278	3F[10]	**29B** Aberdeen Ferryhill	**61B** Aberdeen Ferryhill	**61B** Aberdeen Ferryhill	**61B** Aberdeen Ferryhill	**61B** Aberdeen Ferryhill		
56279	3F[10]	**30C** Ardrossan	**67D** Ardrossan	**67D** Ardrossan	**67D** Ardrossan	**67A** Corkerhill		
56280	3F[10]	**27A** Polmadie	**66A** Polmadie	**66A** Polmadie	**66A** Polmadie			
56281	3F[10]	**28A** Motherwell	**66A** Polmadie	**66A** Polmadie	**66A** Polmadie			
56282	3F[10]	**30C** Ardrossan	**67D** Ardrossan	**67D** Ardrossan	**67D** Ardrossan	**67D** Ardrossan		
56283	3F[10]	**28B** Dalry Road	**64C** Dalry Road	**64C** Dalry Road	**64C** Dalry Road			
56284	3F[10]	**27C** Hamilton	**66C** Hamilton	**66C** Hamilton	**66C** Hamilton			
56285	3F[10]	**28A** Motherwell	**66B** Motherwell	**66B** Motherwell	**66B** Motherwell			
56286	3F[10]	**27C** Hamilton	**66C** Hamilton	**66C** Hamilton	**66C** Hamilton			
56287	3F[10]	**27C** Hamilton	hire NCB Blantyre	**66C** Hamilton	**66C** Hamilton			
56288	3F[10]	**27B** Greenock Ladyburn	**66D** Greenock Ladyburn	**66D** Greenock Ladyburn	**66D** Greenock Ladyburn			
56289	3F[10]	**31A** St. Rollox	**65B** St. Rollox	**65B** St. Rollox	**65B** St. Rollox	**65B** St. Rollox		
56290	3F[10]	**29A** Perth	**63A** Perth	**63A** Perth	**63C** Forfar			
56291	3F[10]	**32A** Inverness	**60A** Inverness	**60A** Inverness	**60A** Inverness			
56292	3F[10]	**27A** Polmadie	**66A** Polmadie	**66A** Polmadie	**66A** Polmadie	**66A** Polmadie		
56293	3F[10]	**32A** Inverness	**60A** Inverness	**60A** Inverness	**60A** Inverness			
56294	3F[10]	**27A** Polmadie	**66A** Polmadie	**66A** Polmadie	**66C** Hamilton			
56295	3F[10]	**27A** Polmadie	**66A** Polmadie	**66A** Polmadie	**66A** Polmadie			
56296	3F[10]	**27C** Hamilton	**66C** Hamilton	**66C** Hamilton	**66C** Hamilton			
56297	3F[10]	**31E** Dawsholm	**65G** Yoker	**65G** Yoker	**65G** Yoker			
56298	3F[10]	**27A** Polmadie	**66A** Polmadie	**66A** Polmadie	**66A** Polmadie	**66A** Polmadie		
56299	3F[10]	**32A** Inverness	**60A** Inverness	**60A** Inverness	**60A** Inverness			
56300	3F[10]	**31D** Grangemouth	**65F** Grangemouth	**65F** Grangemouth	**65D** Dawsholm	**60A** Inverness		
56301	3F[10]	**32C** Forres	**60E** Forres	**60E** Forres	**60E** Forres			
56302	3F[10]	**31E** Dawsholm	**65D** Dawsholm	**65D** Dawsholm	**65D** Dawsholm	**68B** Dumfries		
56303	3F[10]	**27C** Hamilton	**66C** Hamilton	**66C** Hamilton				
56304	3F[10]	**27A** Polmadie	**66A** Polmadie	**66A** Polmadie	**66A** Polmadie	**66A** Polmadie		
56305	3F[10]	**27A** Polmadie	**66A** Polmadie	**66A** Polmadie	**60A** Inverness	**60A** Inverness		
56306	3F[10]	**27A** Polmadie	**66A** Polmadie	**66A** Polmadie	**66A** Polmadie			
56307	3F[10]	**27A** Polmadie	**66A** Polmadie	**66A** Polmadie				
56308	3F[10]	**27A** Polmadie	**66A** Polmadie	**66A** Polmadie	**66A** Polmadie	**66A** Polmadie		
56309	3F[10]	**27C** Hamilton	**66C** Hamilton	**66C** Hamilton	**66C** Hamilton	**66C** Hamilton		
56310	3F[10]	**12A** Carlisle Kingmoor	**65B** St. Rollox	**65B** St. Rollox	**65B** St. Rollox	**68B** Dumfries		
56311	3F[10]	**30C** Ardrossan	**67D** Ardrossan	**67D** Ardrossan	**67D** Ardrossan			
56312	3F[10]	**28B** Dalry Road	**64C** Dalry Road	**64C** Dalry Road	**64C** Dalry Road	**64C** Dalry Road		
56313	3F[10]	**28B** Dalry Road	**64C** Dalry Road	**64C** Dalry Road	**64C** Dalry Road	**64C** Dalry Road		
56314	3F[10]	**27A** Polmadie	**66A** Polmadie	**66A** Polmadie	**66A** Polmadie			
56315	3F[10]	**31E** Dawsholm	**65G** Yoker	**65G** Yoker	**65G** Yoker			
56316	3F[10]	**12A** Carlisle Kingmoor	**68A** Carlisle Kingmoor	**68A** Carlisle Kingmoor	**68A** Carlisle Kingmoor			

		1948	1951	1954	1957	1960	1963	1966
56317	3F[10]	12A Carlisle Kingmoor	68A Carlisle Kingmoor	68A Carlisle Kingmoor				
56318	3F[10]	27A Polmadie	66A Polmadie	66A Polmadie	66A Polmadie			
56319	3F[10]	27C Hamilton	66C Hamilton	66C Hamilton				
56320	3F[10]	27C Hamilton	66C Hamilton	66C Hamilton	66C Hamilton			
56321	3F[10]	27C Hamilton	66C Hamilton	66C Hamilton	66C Hamilton			
56322	3F[10]	27A Polmadie	66A Polmadie	66A Polmadie	66A Polmadie			
56323	3F[10]	29C Dundee West	62B Dundee Tay Bridge	62B Dundee Tay Bridge	62B Dundee Tay Bridge			
56324	3F[10]	27A Polmadie	66A Polmadie	66A Polmadie	66A Polmadie	66A Polmadie		
56325	3F[10]	29C Dundee West	62B Dundee Tay Bridge	62B Dundee Tay Bridge	62B Dundee Tay Bridge	61B Aberdeen Ferryhill		
56326	3F[10]	29B Aberdeen Ferryhill	61B Aberdeen Ferryhill	61B Aberdeen Ferryhill	61B Aberdeen Ferryhill	61B Aberdeen Ferryhill		
56327	3F[10]	12A Carlisle Kingmoor	68A Carlisle Kingmoor	68B Dumfries	68B Dumfries			
56328	3F[10]	29A Perth	63A Perth	63A Perth	63A Perth			
56329	3F[10]	28B Dalry Road	67A Corkerhill	67A Corkerhill	67A Corkerhill			
56330	3F[10]	31A St. Rollox	65B St. Rollox	65B St. Rollox	65B St. Rollox			
56331	3F[10]	29A Perth	63A Perth	63A Perth	63A Perth	63A Perth		
56332	3F[10]	12A Carlisle Kingmoor	68A Carlisle Kingmoor	68A Carlisle Kingmoor	68A Carlisle Kingmoor			
56333	3F[10]	12A Carlisle Kingmoor	68A Carlisle Kingmoor	68A Carlisle Kingmoor	68A Carlisle Kingmoor			
56334	3F[10]	28A Motherwell	66B Motherwell	66B Motherwell	66B Motherwell			
56335	3F[10]	28A Motherwell	66B Motherwell	66B Motherwell	66B Motherwell	66A Polmadie		
56336	3F[10]	31D Grangemouth	65F Grangemouth	65F Grangemouth	65F Grangemouth	65D Dawsholm		
56337	3F[10]	28A Motherwell	66B Motherwell	66B Motherwell	66B Motherwell	66B Motherwell		
56338	3F[10]	28A Motherwell	66B Motherwell	66B Motherwell	66B Motherwell	66B Motherwell		
56339	3F[10]	31E Dawsholm	65G Yoker	65G Yoker				
56340	3F[10]	12A Carlisle Kingmoor	68A Carlisle Kingmoor	68A Carlisle Kingmoor	68A Carlisle Kingmoor			
56341	3F[10]	32A Inverness	60A Inverness	60A Inverness	60A Inverness	60A Inverness		
56342	3F[10]	27A Polmadie	66A Polmadie	66A Polmadie	66A Polmadie			
56343	3F[10]	31B Stirling	63B Stirling	63B Stirling	63B Stirling	63B Stirling		
56344	3F[10]	31E Dawsholm	65D Dawsholm	65D Dawsholm	65D Dawsholm			
56345	3F[10]	28A Motherwell	66B Motherwell	66B Motherwell	66B Motherwell			
56346	3F[10]	27A Polmadie	66A Polmadie	66A Polmadie	66A Polmadie			
56347	3F[10]	29A Perth	63A Perth	63A Perth	63A Perth	63A Perth		
56348	3F[10]	29B Aberdeen Ferryhill	61B Aberdeen Ferryhill	61B Aberdeen Ferryhill	61B Aberdeen Ferryhill	61C Keith		
56349	3F[10]	27A Polmadie	66A Polmadie	66A Polmadie	66A Polmadie	66A Polmadie		
56350	3F[10]	30A Corkerhill	67A Corkerhill	67A Corkerhill	67A Corkerhill			
56351	3F[10]	12H Stranraer						
56352	3F[10]	29A Perth	63A Perth	63A Perth	63A Perth			
56353	3F[10]	29A Perth	63A Perth	63A Perth	63A Perth			
56354	3F[10]	12A Carlisle Kingmoor	68A Carlisle Kingmoor	66B Motherwell	66B Motherwell			
56355	3F[10]	12A Carlisle Kingmoor	68A Carlisle Kingmoor	68A Carlisle Kingmoor				
56356	3F[10]	28A Motherwell	66B Motherwell	66B Motherwell	66B Motherwell	66B Motherwell		
56357	3F[10]	28A Motherwell	66B Motherwell	66B Motherwell	66B Motherwell			
56358	3F[10]	28A Motherwell	66B Motherwell	66B Motherwell				
56359	3F[10]	29B Aberdeen Ferryhill	63A Perth	63A Perth	63A Perth			
56360	3F[10]	27C Hamilton	66C Hamilton	66C Hamilton	66C Hamilton	66C Hamilton		
56361	3F[10]	30A Corkerhill	67A Corkerhill	67A Corkerhill	67A Corkerhill	67A Corkerhill		
56362	3F[10]	27C Hamilton	66C Hamilton	66C Hamilton	66C Hamilton	66C Hamilton		
56363	3F[10]	30D Ayr	67C Ayr	67C Ayr	67C Ayr	67C Ayr		
56364	3F[10]	30C Ardrossan	67D Ardrossan	67D Ardrossan	67A Corkerhill	67A Corkerhill		
56365	3F[10]	31B Stirling	63B Stirling	63B Stirling	63B Stirling			
56366	3F[10]	31B Stirling	63B Stirling	63B Stirling				
56367	3F[10]	30D Ayr	67C Ayr	66B Motherwell	66B Motherwell	66B Motherwell		
56368	3F[10]	30B Hurlford	67B Hurlford	67B Hurlford	67B Hurlford	67B Hurlford		
56369	3F[10]	30A Corkerhill	67A Corkerhill	67A Corkerhill	67A Corkerhill			
56370	3F[10]	31A St. Rollox	65B St. Rollox	65B St. Rollox	65B St. Rollox	65B St. Rollox		
56371	3F[10]	27C Hamilton	66C Hamilton	66C Hamilton	66C Hamilton	66C Hamilton		
56372	3F[10]	12H Stranraer	68C Stranraer	68C Stranraer	68C Stranraer	67C Ayr		
56373	3F[10]	12A Carlisle Kingmoor	68A Carlisle Kingmoor	68A Carlisle Kingmoor	68A Carlisle Kingmoor			
56374	3F[10]	12A Carlisle Kingmoor	68A Carlisle Kingmoor	68A Carlisle Kingmoor	68A Carlisle Kingmoor			
56375	3F[10]	31D Grangemouth	65F Grangemouth	65F Grangemouth	63B Stirling			
56376	3F[10]	31D Grangemouth	65F Grangemouth	65F Grangemouth	65F Grangemouth	65F Grangemouth		
56905	3F[11]	12A Carlisle Kingmoor						
57230	2F[5]	12G Dumfries	66A Polmadie	66A Polmadie				
57231	2F[5]	28A Motherwell						
57232	2F[5]	31B Stirling	63B Stirling	63B Stirling	63B Stirling	63B Stirling		
57233	2F[5]	31B Stirling	63B Stirling	63B Stirling	63B Stirling	63B Stirling		
57234	2F[5]	30D Ayr	67C Ayr	67C Ayr	67C Ayr			
57235	2F[5]	30D Ayr	67C Ayr	67C Ayr				
57236	2F[5]	30B Hurlford	67B Hurlford	67B Hurlford	67B Hurlford	67B Hurlford		
57237	2F[5]	27C Hamilton	66C Hamilton	66C Hamilton	66B Motherwell	66B Motherwell		
57238	2F[5]	12G Dumfries	66A Polmadie	66A Polmadie	68C Stranraer	68C Stranraer		
57239	2F[5]	27A Polmadie	66A Polmadie	66A Polmadie	66A Polmadie	66A Polmadie		
57240	2F[5]	31A St. Rollox	65B St. Rollox	65B St. Rollox	65B St. Rollox	65B St. Rollox		
57241	2F[5]	30A Corkerhill	67A Corkerhill	67A Corkerhill	67A Corkerhill			
57242	2F[5]	27C Hamilton	66C Hamilton	66C Hamilton	66C Hamilton	66C Hamilton		
57243	2F[5]	31B Stirling	63B Stirling	63B Stirling	63B Stirling			
57244	2F[5]	27C Hamilton	66C Hamilton	66C Hamilton	66C Hamilton	66A Polmadie		
57245	2F[5]	31E Dawsholm	65D Dawsholm	65D Dawsholm	65D Dawsholm	65D Dawsholm		
57246	2F[5]	31B Stirling	63B Stirling	63B Stirling	63B Stirling	63B Stirling		
57247	2F[5]	28A Motherwell	66B Motherwell	66B Motherwell	66B Motherwell			
57249	2F[5]	30A Corkerhill	67A Corkerhill	67A Corkerhill	67A Corkerhill	67A Corkerhill		
57250	2F[5]	27C Hamilton	66C Hamilton	66C Hamilton	66C Hamilton	66A Polmadie		
57251	2F[5]	31A St. Rollox	65B St. Rollox	65B St. Rollox	65B St. Rollox	65B St. Rollox		
57252	2F[5]	31B Stirling	63B Stirling	63B Stirling	63B Stirling	63B Stirling		
57253	2F[5]	31A St. Rollox	65B St. Rollox	65B St. Rollox	65B St. Rollox	65B St. Rollox		
57254	2F[5]	31A St. Rollox	63E Oban	63E Oban	67D Ardrossan	67D Ardrossan		
57255	2F[5]	30A Corkerhill	67A Corkerhill					
57256	2F[5]	28A Motherwell	66B Motherwell	66B Motherwell	66B Motherwell	66B Motherwell		
57257	2F[5]	31B Stirling	63B Stirling	63B Stirling	63B Stirling	63B Stirling		
57258	2F[5]	31E Dawsholm	65D Dawsholm	65B St. Rollox	65B St. Rollox	65B St. Rollox		
57259	2F[5]	31E Dawsholm	65G Yoker	65G Yoker	65G Yoker	65G Yoker		
57260	2F[5]	27C Hamilton	66C Hamilton	66C Hamilton				
57261	2F[5]	30D Ayr	65B St. Rollox	65B St. Rollox	65B St. Rollox	65B St. Rollox	65J Stirling	
57262	2F[5]	30D Ayr	67C Ayr	67C Ayr	67C Ayr	67C Ayr		
57263	2F[5]	30C Ardrossan	67D Ardrossan	67D Ardrossan	67D Ardrossan	67D Ardrossan		
57264	2F[5]	31B Stirling	63B Stirling	63B Stirling	63B Stirling	63B Stirling		
57265	2F[5]	31D Grangemouth	65F Grangemouth	65F Grangemouth	65F Grangemouth	65F Grangemouth		
57266	2F[5]	30A Corkerhill	67A Corkerhill	67A Corkerhill	67D Ardrossan	67D Ardrossan		
57267	2F[5]	28A Motherwell	66B Motherwell	66B Motherwell	66B Motherwell	66B Motherwell		
57268	2F[5]	27A Polmadie	66A Polmadie	66A Polmadie	66A Polmadie	66A Polmadie		
57269	2F[5]	31A St. Rollox	65B St. Rollox	65B St. Rollox	65B St. Rollox	65B St. Rollox	65F Grangemouth	
57270	2F[5]	28A Motherwell	66B Motherwell	66B Motherwell	66B Motherwell	66B Motherwell	66B Motherwell	
57271	2F[5]	30D Ayr	66A Polmadie	66A Polmadie	66A Polmadie	66A Polmadie		
57272	2F[5]	28A Motherwell	66B Motherwell					
57273	2F[5]	28A Motherwell	65D Dawsholm	65D Dawsholm	65D Dawsholm	65D Dawsholm		
57274	2F[5]	30C Ardrossan	67D Ardrossan	67D Ardrossan	67D Ardrossan	67D Ardrossan		
57275	2F[5]	27A Polmadie	66A Polmadie	66A Polmadie	66A Polmadie	66A Polmadie		
57276	2F[5]	30C Ardrossan	67D Ardrossan	67D Ardrossan	63D Oban			
57277	2F[5]	30B Hurlford	67B Hurlford					
57278	2F[5]	28A Motherwell	66B Motherwell	66B Motherwell	66B Motherwell	66B Motherwell	66B Motherwell	
57279	2F[5]	30D Ayr	67C Ayr	67C Ayr	67C Ayr			
57280	2F[5]	27C Hamilton	66C Hamilton					
57282	2F[5]	30C Ardrossan	67D Ardrossan	67D Ardrossan				
57283	2F[5]	29B Aberdeen Ferryhill	63B Stirling					
57284	2F[5]	30D Ayr	67C Ayr	67C Ayr	67C Ayr	67B Hurlford		

		1948	1951	1954	1957	1960	1963	1966
57285	2F^{5}	**31D** Grangemouth	**65F** Grangemouth	**65F** Grangemouth	**65F** Grangemouth	**65F** Grangemouth		
57286	2F^{5}	**12G** Dumfries						
57287	2F^{5}	**31D** Grangemouth	**65F** Grangemouth	**65F** Grangemouth	**65F** Grangemouth	**65F** Grangemouth		
57288	2F^{5}	**12G** Dumfries	**66A** Polmadie	**66A** Polmadie	**66A** Polmadie	**66A** Polmadie		
57289	2F^{5}	**28A** Motherwell	**66B** Motherwell					
57290	2F^{5}	**28A** Motherwell						
57291	2F^{5}	**28A** Motherwell	**66B** Motherwell	**66B** Motherwell	**66B** Motherwell	**66B** Motherwell	**66B** Motherwell	
57292	2F^{5}	**27A** Polmadie	**66A** Polmadie	**66A** Polmadie	**66A** Polmadie	**66A** Polmadie		
57294	2F^{5}	**31D** Grangemouth						
57295	2F^{5}	**30D** Ayr	**67C** Ayr	**67C** Ayr	**67C** Ayr	**67B** Hurlford		
57296	2F^{5}	**31E** Dawsholm	**65D** Dawsholm	**65D** Dawsholm	**65D** Dawsholm	**65D** Dawsholm	**67E** Dumfries	
57298	2F^{5}	**28C** Carstairs						
57299	2F^{5}	**28A** Motherwell	**66B** Motherwell	**66B** Motherwell	**66B** Motherwell	**66B** Motherwell		
57300	2F^{5}	**30A** Corkerhill	**67A** Corkerhill	**67A** Corkerhill	**67A** Corkerhill	**67A** Corkerhill		
57301	2F^{5}	**28A** Motherwell						
57302	2F^{5}	**12G** Dumfries	**68B** Dumfries	**68B** Dumfries	**68B** Dumfries	**68B** Dumfries	**67E** Dumfries	
57303	2F^{5}	**28A** Motherwell	**66B** Motherwell	**66B** Motherwell	**66B** Motherwell	**66B** Motherwell		
57304	2F^{5}	**30C** Ardrossan						
57305	2F^{5}	**31A** St. Rollox						
57306	2F^{5}	**31E** Dawsholm	**65D** Dawsholm					
57307	2F^{5}	**27C** Hamilton	**66C** Hamilton	**66C** Hamilton	**66C** Hamilton			
57308	2F^{5}	**28A** Motherwell						
57309	2F^{5}	**30A** Corkerhill	**67A** Corkerhill	**67A** Corkerhill	**67D** Ardrossan	**67D** Ardrossan	**67D** Ardrossan	
57310	2F^{5}	**27A** Polmadie						
57311	2F^{5}	**31A** St. Rollox	**65B** St. Rollox	**65B** St. Rollox	**65B** St. Rollox	**65B** St. Rollox		
57312	2F^{5}	**30D** Ayr	**67C** Ayr					
57313	2F^{5}	**28A** Motherwell						
57314	2F^{5}	**31E** Dawsholm	**65D** Dawsholm	**65D** Dawsholm	**65D** Dawsholm	**65D** Dawsholm		
57315	2F^{5}	**30D** Ayr	**67C** Ayr	**67C** Ayr				
57316	2F^{5}	**27A** Polmadie						
57317	2F^{5}	**27A** Polmadie	**66A** Polmadie	**66A** Polmadie	**66A** Polmadie	**66A** Polmadie		
57318	2F^{5}	**31A** St. Rollox	**65B** St. Rollox					
57319	2F^{5}	**27A** Polmadie	**66A** Polmadie	**66A** Polmadie	**66A** Polmadie	**66A** Polmadie		
57320	2F^{5}	**27A** Polmadie	**66A** Polmadie	**66A** Polmadie				
57321	2F^{5}	**27A** Polmadie	**66A** Polmadie	**66A** Polmadie	**66A** Polmadie	**66C** Hamilton		
57322	2F^{5}	**31E** Dawsholm	**65D** Dawsholm					
57323	2F^{5}	**28C** Carstairs	**64D** Carstairs					
57324	2F^{5}	**29D** Forfar	**63C** Forfar	**63B** Stirling	**63B** Stirling	**63B** Stirling		
57325	2F^{5}	**28A** Motherwell	**66B** Motherwell	**66B** Motherwell	**66B** Motherwell	**66B** Motherwell		
57326	2F^{5}	**28A** Motherwell	**66B** Motherwell	**66B** Motherwell	**66B** Motherwell	**66B** Motherwell	**66B** Motherwell	
57327	2F^{5}	**28A** Motherwell						
57328	2F^{5}	**28A** Motherwell	**66B** Motherwell	**66B** Motherwell	**66B** Motherwell	**66B** Motherwell	**66B** Motherwell	
57329	2F^{5}	**12G** Dumfries	**68B** Dumfries	**68B** Dumfries	**68B** Dumfries	**68B** Dumfries		
57330	2F^{5}	**27A** Polmadie						
57331	2F^{5}	**30B** Hurlford	**67B** Hurlford	**67B** Hurlford	**67B** Hurlford	**67B** Hurlford		
57332	2F^{5}	**28A** Motherwell	**66B** Motherwell					
57333	2F^{5}	**31A** St. Rollox						
57334	2F^{5}	**31D** Grangemouth	**65F** Grangemouth					
57335	2F^{5}	**27A** Polmadie	**66B** Motherwell	**66C** Hamilton	**66C** Hamilton	**66C** Hamilton		
57336	2F^{5}	**31E** Dawsholm	**65D** Dawsholm	**65D** Dawsholm	**65D** Dawsholm	**66C** Hamilton	**67D** Ardrossan	
57337	2F^{5}	**12G** Dumfries	**68B** Dumfries					
57338	2F^{5}	**31D** Grangemouth	**65F** Grangemouth	**65F** Grangemouth	**65F** Grangemouth	**65F** Grangemouth		
57339	2F^{5}	**29B** Aberdeen Ferryhill	**63A** Perth	**63B** Stirling	**63B** Stirling			
57340	2F^{5}	**28C** Carstairs	**68C** Stranraer	**68C** Stranraer	**68C** Stranraer	**68C** Stranraer		
57341	2F^{5}	**31E** Dawsholm	**65D** Dawsholm	**65D** Dawsholm	**65D** Dawsholm	**65D** Dawsholm		
57342	2F^{5}	**28A** Motherwell						
57343	2F^{5}	**12G** Dumfries						
57344	2F^{5}	**28A** Motherwell	**68B** Dumfries					
57345	2F^{5}	**29B** Aberdeen Ferryhill	**63A** Perth	**63A** Perth	**63A** Perth	**63A** Perth		
57346	2F^{5}	**31E** Dawsholm	**65D** Dawsholm	**65D** Dawsholm	**65D** Dawsholm			
57347	2F^{5}	**27A** Polmadie	**66A** Polmadie	**66A** Polmadie	**66A** Polmadie	**66A** Polmadie		
57348	2F^{5}	**30C** Ardrossan	**67D** Ardrossan	**67D** Ardrossan	**67D** Ardrossan	**67D** Ardrossan	**67D** Ardrossan	
57349	2F^{5}	**12G** Dumfries	**68B** Dumfries	**68B** Dumfries	**68B** Dumfries	**68B** Dumfries		
57350	2F^{5}	**31A** St. Rollox	**65B** St. Rollox	**65B** St. Rollox	**65B** St. Rollox	**65B** St. Rollox		
57351	2F^{5}	**30D** Ayr						
57352	2F^{5}	**31A** St. Rollox	**65B** St. Rollox					
57353	2F^{5}	**30B** Hurlford	**67B** Hurlford	**67B** Hurlford	**67B** Hurlford	**67B** Hurlford		
57354	2F^{5}	**30D** Ayr	**67C** Ayr	**67C** Ayr	**67C** Ayr			
57355	2F^{5}	**30C** Ardrossan	**67D** Ardrossan	**67D** Ardrossan	**67D** Ardrossan	**67D** Ardrossan	**67F** Stranraer	
57356	2F^{5}	**30C** Ardrossan	**67D** Ardrossan	**67D** Ardrossan	**67D** Ardrossan	**67D** Ardrossan		
57357	2F^{5}	**30C** Ardrossan	**67D** Ardrossan	**67D** Ardrossan	**67D** Ardrossan	**67D** Ardrossan		
57358	2F^{5}	**28A** Motherwell						
57359	2F^{5}	**30A** Corkerhill	**67A** Corkerhill	**67A** Corkerhill	**67A** Corkerhill	**67A** Corkerhill		
57360	2F^{5}	**27A** Polmadie	**66A** Polmadie	**66A** Polmadie	**66A** Polmadie	**66A** Polmadie	**66B** Motherwell	
57361	2F^{5}	**27A** Polmadie	**66A** Polmadie	**66A** Polmadie	**66A** Polmadie			
57362	2F^{5}	**12G** Dumfries	**68B** Dumfries	**68B** Dumfries	**68B** Dumfries	**68B** Dumfries		
57363	2F^{5}	**28A** Motherwell	**66B** Motherwell	**66B** Motherwell	**66B** Motherwell	**66B** Motherwell		
57364	2F^{5}	**30D** Ayr	**67C** Ayr	**67C** Ayr	**67C** Ayr	**67C** Ayr		
57365	2F^{5}	**27A** Polmadie	**66A** Polmadie	**66A** Polmadie	**66A** Polmadie	**66A** Polmadie		
57366	2F^{5}	**31E** Dawsholm	**65F** Grangemouth	**65F** Grangemouth	**65F** Grangemouth	**65F** Grangemouth		
57367	2F^{5}	**27A** Polmadie	**66A** Polmadie	**66A** Polmadie	**66A** Polmadie	**66A** Polmadie		
57368	2F^{5}	**29B** Aberdeen Ferryhill	**63C** Forfar	**63C** Forfar	**63C** Forfar			
57369	2F^{5}	**27B** Greenock Ladyburn	**66D** Greenock Ladyburn	**66A** Polmadie	**66A** Polmadie	**66A** Polmadie		
57370	2F^{5}	**27A** Polmadie	**66A** Polmadie	**66A** Polmadie	**66A** Polmadie	**66B** Motherwell		
57371	2F^{5}	**31E** Dawsholm						
57372	2F^{5}	**31E** Dawsholm	**65D** Dawsholm					
57373	2F^{5}	**31D** Grangemouth	**65D** Dawsholm	**65B** St. Rollox	**65B** St. Rollox	**65B** St. Rollox		
57374	2F^{5}	**31A** St. Rollox						
57375	2F^{5}	**12H** Stranraer	**68C** Stranraer	**68C** Stranraer	**68C** Stranraer	**68C** Stranraer	**67F** Stranraer	
57377	2F^{5}	**28A** Motherwell	**66B** Motherwell	**66B** Motherwell	**66B** Motherwell	**66B** Motherwell		
57378	2F^{5}	**12G** Dumfries	**68B** Dumfries	**68B** Dumfries	**68B** Dumfries	**68B** Dumfries		
57379	2F^{5}	**28A** Motherwell	**66B** Motherwell					
57380	2F^{5}	**31A** St. Rollox						
57381	2F^{5}	**27A** Polmadie						
57382	2F^{5}	**27C** Hamilton						
57383	2F^{5}	**30B** Hurlford	**67B** Hurlford	**67B** Hurlford	**67B** Hurlford	**67B** Hurlford		
57384	2F^{5}	**27C** Hamilton	**66C** Hamilton	**66C** Hamilton	**66C** Hamilton	**66B** Motherwell	**66B** Motherwell	
57385	2F^{5}	**28C** Carstairs	**64D** Carstairs	**64D** Carstairs	**64D** Carstairs	**64D** Carstairs		
57386	2F^{5}	**28C** Carstairs	**64D** Carstairs	**64D** Carstairs	**64D** Carstairs	**64D** Carstairs		
57387	2F^{5}	**27A** Polmadie	**66A** Polmadie					
57388	2F^{5}	**27A** Polmadie	**66A** Polmadie					
57389	2F^{5}	**27A** Polmadie	**66A** Polmadie	**66A** Polmadie	**66A** Polmadie	**66A** Polmadie		
57390	2F^{5}	**30D** Ayr						
57391	2F^{5}	**12G** Dumfries						
57392	2F^{5}	**30D** Ayr	**67C** Ayr	**67C** Ayr	**67C** Ayr	**67C** Ayr		
57393	2F^{5}	**27C** Hamilton						
57394	2F^{5}	**31A** St. Rollox	**65D** Dawsholm					
57395	2F^{5}	**27C** Hamilton	**66C** Hamilton					
57396	2F^{5}	**31C** Oban	**63E** Oban	**63B** Stirling	**63B** Stirling			
57397	2F^{5}	**29A** Perth	**68B** Dumfries					
57398	2F^{5}	**27C** Hamilton	**66C** Hamilton	**66C** Hamilton	**66C** Hamilton	**66B** Motherwell		
57399	2F^{5}	**28C** Carstairs						
57400	2F^{5}	**29B** Aberdeen Ferryhill						
57401	2F^{5}	**27C** Hamilton						

		1948	1951	1954	1957	1960	1963	1966
57402	$2F^5$	**31B** Stirling						
57403	$2F^5$	**28A** Motherwell						
57404	$2F^5$	**28A** Motherwell	**66B** Motherwell	**66B** Motherwell	**66B** Motherwell	**66B** Motherwell		
57405	$2F^5$	**12G** Dumfries	**68B** Dumfries	**68B** Dumfries	**68B** Dumfries			
57406	$2F^5$	**28A** Motherwell						
57407	$2F^5$	**27C** Hamilton	**66C** Hamilton	**66C** Hamilton	**66C** Hamilton			
57408	$2F^5$	**27C** Hamilton						
57409	$2F^5$	**12G** Dumfries						
57410	$2F^5$	**27C** Hamilton	**66C** Hamilton					
57411	$2F^5$	**31C** Oban	**65B** St. Rollox	**65B** St. Rollox	**65B** St. Rollox	**65B** St. Rollox		
57412	$2F^5$	**27A** Polmadie	**66A** Polmadie	**66A** Polmadie				
57413	$2F^5$	**28A** Motherwell	**66C** Hamilton	**66C** Hamilton	**66C** Hamilton			
57414	$2F^5$	**28A** Motherwell	**66B** Motherwell	**66B** Motherwell	**66B** Motherwell			
57415	$2F^5$	**28A** Motherwell						
57416	$2F^5$	**28A** Motherwell	**66B** Motherwell	**66B** Motherwell	**66B** Motherwell	**66D** Greenock Ladyburn		
57417	$2F^5$	**28A** Motherwell	**66B** Motherwell	**66B** Motherwell	**66B** Motherwell	**66A** Polmadie		
57418	$2F^5$	**28A** Motherwell	**66B** Motherwell	**66B** Motherwell	**66B** Motherwell	**66A** Polmadie		
57419	$2F^5$	**28A** Motherwell	**66B** Motherwell	**66B** Motherwell	**66B** Motherwell			
57420	$2F^5$	**27C** Hamilton						
57421	$2F^5$	**12H** Stranraer						
57422	$2F^5$	**31B** Stirling						
57423	$2F^5$	**31B** Stirling	**63B** Stirling					
57424	$2F^5$	**31B** Stirling	**63B** Stirling	**63E** Oban	**63C** Forfar			
57425	$2F^5$	**31B** Stirling						
57426	$2F^5$	**31E** Dawsholm	**65D** Dawsholm	**65B** St. Rollox	**65B** St. Rollox	**65B** St. Rollox		
57427	$2F^5$	**31E** Dawsholm						
57429	$2F^5$	**31E** Dawsholm	**65D** Dawsholm	**65D** Dawsholm	**65D** Dawsholm	**65D** Dawsholm		
57430	$2F^5$	**27C** Hamilton	**66C** Hamilton	**66C** Hamilton	**66C** Hamilton			
57431	$2F^5$	**27C** Hamilton	**66C** Hamilton	**66C** Hamilton	**66C** Hamilton	**66B** Motherwell		
57432	$2F^5$	**27A** Polmadie	**66A** Polmadie	**66A** Polmadie	**66A** Polmadie	**66A** Polmadie		
57433	$2F^5$	**27A** Polmadie	**66A** Polmadie					
57434	$2F^5$	**31A** St. Rollox	**65B** St. Rollox	**65B** St. Rollox	**65B** St. Rollox	**65B** St. Rollox		
57435	$2F^5$	**28A** Motherwell	**66B** Motherwell	**66B** Motherwell	**66B** Motherwell	**66B** Motherwell		
57436	$2F^5$	**27A** Polmadie	**66B** Motherwell	**66B** Motherwell	**66B** Motherwell	**66B** Motherwell		
57437	$2F^5$	**28A** Motherwell	**66B** Motherwell	**66B** Motherwell	**66B** Motherwell			
57438	$2F^5$	**28C** Carstairs	**64D** Carstairs					
57439	$2F^5$	**27A** Polmadie	**66A** Polmadie					
57440	$2F^5$	**12H** Stranraer						
57441	$2F^5$	**29D** Forfar	**63C** Forfar	**63B** Stirling	**63B** Stirling	**63A** Perth		
57442	$2F^5$	**31D** Grangemouth						
57443	$2F^5$	**27A** Polmadie	**66A** Polmadie	**66A** Polmadie	**66A** Polmadie			
57444	$2F^5$	**27A** Polmadie	**66A** Polmadie	**66A** Polmadie	**66A** Polmadie			
57445	$2F^5$	**12H** Stranraer	**68C** Stranraer	**68C** Stranraer	**68C** Stranraer	**68C** Stranraer		
57446	$2F^5$	**27A** Polmadie	**66A** Polmadie	**66A** Polmadie	**66A** Polmadie	**66B** Motherwell		
57447	$2F^5$	**27A** Polmadie	**66A** Polmadie	**66A** Polmadie	**66A** Polmadie	**66C** Hamilton		
57448	$2F^5$	**27A** Polmadie	**66A** Polmadie	**66A** Polmadie	**66A** Polmadie	**66A** Polmadie		
57449	$2F^5$	**29A** Perth						
57450	$2F^5$	**29C** Dundee West	**63C** Forfar					
57451	$2F^5$	**28C** Carstairs	**64D** Carstairs	**64D** Carstairs	**64D** Carstairs	**64D** Carstairs		
57452	$2F^5$	**31E** Dawsholm						
57453	$2F^5$	**31A** St. Rollox						
57454	$2F^5$	**31A** St. Rollox	**65B** St. Rollox					
57455	$2F^5$	**31A** St. Rollox	**65B** St. Rollox					
57456	$2F^5$	**31E** Dawsholm	**65D** Dawsholm	**65D** Dawsholm				
57457	$2F^5$	**31A** St. Rollox	**65B** St. Rollox	**65B** St. Rollox				
57458	$2F^5$	**12H** Stranraer	**68C** Stranraer					
57459	$2F^5$	**27A** Polmadie	**66A** Polmadie	**66A** Polmadie				
57460	$2F^5$	**31B** Stirling	**63B** Stirling	**63B** Stirling	**63B** Stirling			
57461	$2F^5$	**28A** Motherwell	**66B** Motherwell	**66B** Motherwell	**66B** Motherwell	**66B** Motherwell		
57462	$2F^5$	**28A** Motherwell	**66B** Motherwell	**66B** Motherwell	**66B** Motherwell			
57463	$2F^5$	**27B** Greenock Ladyburn	**66A** Polmadie	**66A** Polmadie	**66A** Polmadie	**66A** Polmadie		
57464	$2F^5$	**27A** Polmadie	**66A** Polmadie					
57465	$2F^5$	**27A** Polmadie	**66A** Polmadie	**66A** Polmadie	**66A** Polmadie			
57466	$2F^5$	**31B** Stirling						
57467	$2F^5$	**27A** Polmadie						
57468	$2F^5$	**31B** Stirling	**63B** Stirling					
57469	$2F^5$	**31E** Dawsholm						
57470	$2F^5$	**31E** Dawsholm	**65D** Dawsholm	**65D** Dawsholm	**65D** Dawsholm	**65D** Dawsholm		
57471	$2F^5$	**31E** Dawsholm						
57472	$2F^5$	**31E** Dawsholm	**65D** Dawsholm	**65D** Dawsholm	**65D** Dawsholm	**65D** Dawsholm		
57473	$2F^5$	**29A** Perth	**63A** Perth	**63A** Perth	**63A** Perth	**63A** Perth		
57550	$3F^{12}$	**28B** Dalry Road	**64C** Dalry Road	**64C** Dalry Road	**64C** Dalry Road	**64C** Dalry Road		
57551	$3F^{12}$	**27B** Greenock Ladyburn						
57552	$3F^{12}$	**27B** Greenock Ladyburn	**66D** Greenock Ladyburn	**66D** Greenock Ladyburn	**66D** Greenock Ladyburn			
57553	$3F^{12}$	**28B** Dalry Road	**64C** Dalry Road	**66A** Polmadie	**66A** Polmadie			
57554	$3F^{12}$	**31A** St. Rollox	**65B** St. Rollox	**65D** Dawsholm	**65D** Dawsholm	**65D** Dawsholm		
57555	$3F^{12}$	**27A** Polmadie	**66A** Polmadie	**66A** Polmadie	**66A** Polmadie	**66A** Polmadie		
57556	$3F^{12}$	**27B** Greenock Ladyburn	**66D** Greenock Ladyburn	**66D** Greenock Ladyburn	**66D** Greenock Ladyburn			
57557	$3F^{12}$	**31A** St. Rollox	**65B** St. Rollox	**65B** St. Rollox	**65B** St. Rollox	**65B** St. Rollox		
57558	$3F^{12}$	**31A** St. Rollox	**65B** St. Rollox	**65B** St. Rollox	**65B** St. Rollox	**65B** St. Rollox		
57559	$3F^{12}$	**28B** Dalry Road	**64C** Dalry Road	**64C** Dalry Road	**64C** Dalry Road	**64C** Dalry Road		
57560	$3F^{12}$	**30A** Corkerhill	**67A** Corkerhill	**67A** Corkerhill	**67A** Corkerhill	**64C** Dalry Road		
57561	$3F^{12}$	**30A** Corkerhill						
57562	$3F^{12}$	**30A** Corkerhill	**67A** Corkerhill	**67A** Corkerhill	**67A** Corkerhill	**67B** Hurlford		
57563	$3F^{12}$	**12G** Dumfries	**68B** Dumfries	**66A** Polmadie	**66A** Polmadie	**66A** Polmadie		
57564	$3F^{12}$	**27A** Polmadie	**66A** Polmadie	**66A** Polmadie	**66A** Polmadie	**66A** Polmadie		
57565	$3F^{12}$	**28B** Dalry Road	**64C** Dalry Road	**64C** Dalry Road	**64C** Dalry Road	**64C** Dalry Road		
57566	$3F^{12}$	**30A** Corkerhill	**67A** Corkerhill	**67A** Corkerhill	**67A** Corkerhill	**67D** Ardrossan	**67D** Ardrossan	
57568	$3F^{12}$	**29C** Dundee West	**62B** Dundee Tay Bridge	**62B** Dundee Tay Bridge	**68D** Beattock	**68D** Beattock	**66B** Motherwell	
57569	$3F^{12}$	**30D** Ayr	**67C** Ayr	**67C** Ayr	**67C** Ayr	**67C** Ayr		
57570	$3F^{12}$	**30B** Hurlford	**67B** Hurlford	**67B** Hurlford	**67B** Hurlford	**67B** Hurlford		
57571	$3F^{12}$	**30B** Hurlford	**67B** Hurlford	**67B** Hurlford	**67B** Hurlford	**63C** Oban		
57572	$3F^{12}$	**30B** Hurlford	**67B** Hurlford	**67B** Hurlford	**67B** Hurlford	**67B** Hurlford	**67B** Hurlford	
57573	$3F^{12}$	**30B** Hurlford	**67B** Hurlford	**67B** Hurlford	**67B** Hurlford			
57574	$3F^{12}$	**30B** Hurlford						
57575	$3F^{12}$	**30A** Corkerhill	**67A** Corkerhill	**67A** Corkerhill	**67A** Corkerhill			
57576	$3F^{12}$	**28B** Dalry Road	**64C** Dalry Road	**64C** Dalry Road	**64C** Dalry Road	**63B** Stirling		
57577	$3F^{12}$	**30C** Ardrossan	**67D** Ardrossan	**67D** Ardrossan	**67D** Ardrossan	**67B** Hurlford		
57578	$3F^{12}$	**28B** Dalry Road						
57579	$3F^{12}$	**30C** Ardrossan	**67D** Ardrossan	**67A** Corkerhill	**67A** Corkerhill	**67D** Ardrossan		
57580	$3F^{12}$	**30A** Corkerhill	**67A** Corkerhill	**67A** Corkerhill	**67A** Corkerhill	**67C** Ayr		
57581	$3F^{12}$	**27A** Polmadie	**66A** Polmadie	**66A** Polmadie	**66A** Polmadie	**66A** Polmadie	**66A** Polmadie	
57582	$3F^{12}$	**28A** Motherwell	**66B** Motherwell	**66B** Motherwell	**66B** Motherwell			
57583	$3F^{12}$	**28C** Carstairs	**64D** Carstairs	**64D** Carstairs	**64D** Carstairs	**64D** Carstairs		
57584	$3F^{12}$	**28A** Motherwell						
57585	$3F^{12}$	**32A** Inverness	**60D** Wick	**60D** Wick	**60D** Wick	**60D** Wick		
57586	$3F^{12}$	**32A** Inverness	**60B** Aviemore	**60B** Aviemore	**60B** Aviemore	**60B** Aviemore		
57587	$3F^{12}$	**32A** Inverness	**60C** Helmsdale	**60C** Helmsdale	**60C** Helmsdale	**60C** Helmsdale		
57588	$3F^{12}$	**28A** Motherwell	**66B** Motherwell	**66B** Motherwell	**66B** Motherwell			
57589	$3F^{12}$	**30A** Corkerhill	**67A** Corkerhill	**67A** Corkerhill				
57590	$3F^{12}$	**30C** Ardrossan	**67D** Ardrossan	**67D** Ardrossan	**67D** Ardrossan	**67D** Ardrossan	**67D** Ardrossan	
57591	$3F^{12}$	**32C** Forres	**60A** Inverness	**60A** Inverness	**61C** Keith	**60B** Aviemore		
57592	$3F^{12}$	**12A** Carlisle Kingmoor	**65D** Dawsholm	**65D** Dawsholm	**65D** Dawsholm	**65D** Dawsholm	**65D** Dawsholm	
57593	$3F^{12}$	**28A** Motherwell	**66B** Motherwell	**66B** Motherwell	**66B** Motherwell	**66B** Motherwell		

No.	Class	1948	1951	1954	1957	1960	1963	1966
57594	3F[12]	30A Corkerhill	67C Ayr	67A Corkerhill	67A Corkerhill	60A Inverness		
57595	3F[12]	28A Motherwell	66B Motherwell	66B Motherwell	66B Motherwell			
57596	3F[12]	30A Corkerhill	67A Corkerhill	67A Corkerhill	67A Corkerhill	67C Ayr		
57597	3F[12]	32B Aviemore	60A Inverness	60A Inverness	60A Inverness	60B Aviemore		
57599	3F[12]	28A Motherwell	66B Motherwell	66B Motherwell	66B Motherwell			
57600	3F[12]	12G Dumfries	68B Dumfries	68B Dumfries	68B Dumfries	68B Dumfries	67E Dumfries	
57601	3F[12]	12G Dumfries	68B Dumfries	68B Dumfries	68B Dumfries	68B Dumfries		
57602	3F[12]	12G Dumfries	68B Dumfries	68B Dumfries	68B Dumfries	68B Dumfries		
57603	3F[12]	31D Grangemouth	64D Carstairs	66A Polmadie	66A Polmadie	66A Polmadie		
57604	3F[12]	28C Carstairs	64D Carstairs	64D Carstairs	64D Carstairs	64D Carstairs		
57605	3F[12]	12A Carlisle Kingmoor	65D Dawsholm	65D Dawsholm	65D Dawsholm	60A Inverness		
57606	3F[12]	28A Motherwell						
57607	3F[12]	31E Dawsholm	65D Dawsholm	65D Dawsholm	65D Dawsholm	65D Dawsholm	65D Dawsholm	
57608	3F[12]	28C Carstairs	64D Carstairs	64D Carstairs	64D Carstairs	64D Carstairs		
57609	3F[12]	27C Hamilton	66C Hamilton	66C Hamilton	66C Hamilton	66A Polmadie		
57611	3F[12]	30D Ayr	67C Ayr	67C Ayr	67C Ayr	67C Ayr		
57612	3F[12]	31E Dawsholm	65D Dawsholm	65D Dawsholm	65D Dawsholm	65F Grangemouth		
57613	3F[12]	28C Carstairs	64D Carstairs	64D Carstairs	64D Carstairs	64D Carstairs		
57614	3F[12]	30D Ayr	67C Ayr	67C Ayr	67C Ayr	67C Ayr		
57615	3F[12]	30D Ayr	67C Ayr	67C Ayr	67C Ayr	67C Ayr		
57616	3F[12]	30D Ayr						
57617	3F[12]	31A St. Rollox	65B St. Rollox	65B St. Rollox	65B St. Rollox	65B St. Rollox		
57618	3F[12]	28C Carstairs	64D Carstairs	64D Carstairs	64D Carstairs	64D Carstairs		
57619	3F[12]	27A Polmadie	66A Polmadie	66A Polmadie	66A Polmadie	66D Greenock Ladyburn		
57620	3F[12]	32C Forres	60E Forres	60E Forres	60E Forres	67A Corkerhill		
57621	3F[12]	12G Dumfries	68B Dumfries	68B Dumfries	68B Dumfries	68B Dumfries		
57622	3F[12]	32A Inverness	60D Wick	66A Polmadie	66A Polmadie	66A Polmadie		
57623	3F[12]	12G Dumfries	68B Dumfries	68B Dumfries	68B Dumfries	68B Dumfries		
57624	3F[12]	30A Corkerhill						
57625	3F[12]	32A Inverness	60B Aviemore	66A Polmadie	66A Polmadie	66A Polmadie	66A Polmadie	
57626	3F[12]	12A Carlisle Kingmoor	64D Carstairs	64D Carstairs	64D Carstairs	64D Carstairs		
57627	3F[12]	30C Ardrossan	67D Ardrossan	67D Ardrossan	67D Ardrossan	67D Ardrossan	67D Ardrossan	
57628	3F[12]	30D Ayr	67C Ayr	67C Ayr	67C Ayr	67C Ayr		
57629	3F[13]	32A Inverness						
57630	3F[13]	27C Hamilton	66C Hamilton	66C Hamilton	66C Hamilton	66C Hamilton	66A Polmadie	
57631	3F[13]	31A St. Rollox	65B St. Rollox	65B St. Rollox	65B St. Rollox	65B St. Rollox		
57632	3F[13]	27A Polmadie	68A Carlisle Kingmoor	66A Polmadie	60B Aviemore	60B Aviemore		
57633	3F[13]	30D Ayr	67C Ayr	67C Ayr	67C Ayr	67C Ayr		
57634	3F[13]	32B Aviemore	60A Inverness	60A Inverness	61C Keith	61C Keith	64C Dalry Road	
57635	3F[13]	28C Carstairs	64D Carstairs	64D Carstairs	64D Carstairs	64D Carstairs		
57636	3F[13]	12G Dumfries						
57637	3F[13]	30B Hurlford	67B Hurlford	67B Hurlford	67B Hurlford	67B Hurlford		
57638	3F[13]	28A Motherwell	66B Motherwell	66B Motherwell	66B Motherwell			
57639	3F[13]	27B Greenock Ladyburn						
57640	3F[13]	30D Ayr	67C Ayr	67C Ayr	67C Ayr	67C Ayr		
57641	3F[13]	27A Polmadie						
57642	3F[13]	29D Forfar	60A Inverness	60A Inverness	60A Inverness	63B Stirling		
57643	3F[13]	30B Hurlford	67B Hurlford	67B Hurlford	67B Hurlford	67B Hurlford		
57644	3F[13]	30D Ayr	67C Ayr	67C Ayr	67C Ayr	67C Ayr		
57645	3F[13]	28B Dalry Road	64C Dalry Road	64C Dalry Road	64C Dalry Road	64C Dalry Road		
57650	3F[14]	30B Hurlford	67B Hurlford	67B Hurlford	67B Hurlford	67B Hurlford		
57651	3F[14]	30B Hurlford	67B Hurlford	67B Hurlford	67B Hurlford	67B Hurlford		
57652	3F[14]	31E Dawsholm	65D Dawsholm	65D Dawsholm	65D Dawsholm	65D Dawsholm	65D Dawsholm	
57653	3F[14]	29C Dundee West	62B Dundee Tay Bridge	62B Dundee Tay Bridge	68A Carlisle Kingmoor	12A Carlisle Kingmoor		
57654	3F[14]	28B Dalry Road	64C Dalry Road	64C Dalry Road	64C Dalry Road	64C Dalry Road		
57655	3F[14]	28C Carstairs	64D Carstairs	64D Carstairs	64D Carstairs	64D Carstairs		
57658	3F[14]	31D Grangemouth	67C Ayr	67C Ayr	67C Ayr	67C Ayr		
57659	3F[14]	28B Dalry Road	66B Motherwell	66B Motherwell	66B Motherwell	66B Motherwell		
57661	3F[14]	27A Polmadie	66A Polmadie	66A Polmadie	60A Inverness	60A Inverness	67E Dumfries	
57663	3F[14]	27C Hamilton	66C Hamilton	66C Hamilton	66C Hamilton	66C Hamilton		
57665	3F[14]	27C Hamilton	66C Hamilton	66C Hamilton	66C Hamilton	66B Motherwell		
57666	3F[14]	28A Motherwell	66B Motherwell	66B Motherwell	66B Motherwell	66B Motherwell		
57667	3F[14]	31D Grangemouth	65F Grangemouth	65F Grangemouth	63D Oban	63C Oban		
57668	3F[14]	28A Motherwell	66B Motherwell	66B Motherwell	66B Motherwell	66B Motherwell	66B Motherwell	
57669	3F[14]	30C Ardrossan	67D Ardrossan	67D Ardrossan	67D Ardrossan	67D Ardrossan		
57670	3F[14]	28C Carstairs	64D Carstairs	64D Carstairs	64D Carstairs	64D Carstairs	66E Carstairs	
57671	3F[14]	30B Hurlford	67B Hurlford	67B Hurlford	67B Hurlford	67B Hurlford		
57672	3F[14]	30B Hurlford	67B Hurlford	67B Hurlford	67B Hurlford	67B Hurlford		
57673	3F[14]	30C Ardrossan	67D Ardrossan	67D Ardrossan	67D Ardrossan	67D Ardrossan		
57674	3F[14]	28B Dalry Road	66A Polmadie	66A Polmadie	66A Polmadie	66A Polmadie		
57679	3F[14]	28C Carstairs	64D Carstairs	64C Dalry Road	64C Dalry Road	63B Stirling	65J Stirling	
57681	3F[14]	28A Motherwell	66B Motherwell	66B Motherwell	66B Motherwell	66B Motherwell		
57682	3F[14]	27B Greenock Ladyburn	66D Greenock Ladyburn	66D Greenock Ladyburn	66D Greenock Ladyburn	66D Greenock Ladyburn		
57684	3F[14]	30D Ayr	67C Ayr	67C Ayr	67C Ayr	67C Ayr		
57686	3F[14]	31A St. Rollox	65B St. Rollox	65B St. Rollox	65B St. Rollox	65B St. Rollox		
57688	3F[14]	30B Hurlford	67B Hurlford	67B Hurlford	67B Hurlford	66B Motherwell	66B Motherwell	
57689	3F[14]	31D Grangemouth	65F Grangemouth	65F Grangemouth	65F Grangemouth	67B Hurlford	66B Motherwell	
57690	3F[14]	27A Polmadie	66A Polmadie	66D Greenock Ladyburn	66D Greenock Ladyburn	66D Greenock Ladyburn	66B Motherwell	
57691	3F[14]	31D Grangemouth	65F Grangemouth	65F Grangemouth	65F Grangemouth	65F Grangemouth		
57693	3F[15]	30A Corkerhill						
57694	3F[15]	30A Corkerhill						
57695	3F[15]	30A Corkerhill	67A Corkerhill					
57697	3F[15]	30D Ayr	67C Ayr					
57698	3F[15]	30A Corkerhill	67A Corkerhill					
57699	3F[15]	30A Corkerhill						
57702	3F[15]	30A Corkerhill						
57950	4F[4]	32A Inverness						
57951	4F[4]	32A Inverness	60A Inverness					
57953	4F[4]	32A Inverness						
57954	4F[4]	32A Inverness	60A Inverness					
57955	4F[4]	32A Inverness	60A Inverness					
57956	4F[4]	32A Inverness	60A Inverness					
58000	4P[6]	5C Stafford						
58001	4P[6]	5C Stafford						
25722	4P[6]	2B Bletchley						
58002	4P[6]	5C Stafford						
58003	4P[6]	5C Stafford						
25827	4P[6]	2B Bletchley						
58010	3P[7]	6A Chester						
25321	3P[8]	6A Chester						
58011	3P[8]	6A Chester						
58012	3P[8]	6A Chester						
58020	1P[2]	16A Nottingham						
58021	1P[3]	11B Barrow						
58022	1P[4]	15B Kettering						
58030	1P[5]	15A Wellingborough						
58031	1P[5]	15A Wellingborough						
58032	1P[5]	20A Leeds Holbeck						
58033	1P[5]	19B Millhouses						
58034	1P[5]	22B Gloucester Barnwood						
58035	1P[5]	17A Derby						
58036	1P[5]	20E Manningham						
58037	1P[5]	15D Bedford						
58038	1P[5]	13A Plaistow	33A Plaistow	33A Plaistow				

No.	Class	1948	1951	1954	1957	1960	1963	1966
58039	*1P^6*	**15D** Bedford						
58040	*1P^6*	**15D** Bedford	**23A** Skipton	**20C** Royston				
58041	*1P^6*	**20F** Skipton						
58042	*1P^6*	**9D** Buxton	**9D** Buxton					
58043	*1P^6*	**13A** Plaistow	**33A** Plaistow					
58044	*1P^6*	**13A** Plaistow						
58045	*1P^6*	**15D** Bedford	**33A** Plaistow					
58046	*1P^6*	**22E** Highbridge	**71J** Highbridge					
58047	*1P^6*	**22B** Gloucester Barnwood	**71J** Highbridge					
1307	*1P^6*	**22E** Highbridge						
58048	*1P^6*	**20A** Leeds Holbeck						
58049	*1P^6*	**22E** Highbridge						
58050	*1P^6*	**16A** Nottingham	**16A** Nottingham					
58051	*1P^6*	**15C** Leicester Midland	**22B** Gloucester Barnwood	**71J** Highbridge				
58052	*1P^6*	**20C** Royston	**20C** Royston					
58053	*1P^6*	**15D** Bedford	**15A** Wellingborough					
58054	*1P^6*	**16D** Mansfield	**22B** Gloucester Barnwood	**33A** Plaistow				
58055	*1P^6*	**20C** Royston						
58056	*1P^6*	**16A** Nottingham	**16A** Nottingham	**16A** Nottingham				
58057	*1P^6*	**17B** Burton						
58058	*1P^6*	**16D** Mansfield	**17A** Derby					
58059	*1P^6*	**22B** Gloucester Barnwood						
58060	*1P^6*	**17B** Burton	**20A** Leeds Holbeck					
58061	*1P^6*	**20F** Skipton						
58062	*1P^6*	**13A** Plaistow	**33A** Plaistow	**33A** Plaistow				
1361	*1P^6*	**20F** Skipton						
58063	*1P^6*	**22B** Gloucester Barnwood	**22B** Gloucester Barnwood					
58064	*1P^6*	**20F** Skipton						
58065	*1P^6*	**14A** Cricklewood	**33A** Plaistow	**33A** Plaistow	**36E** Retford			
58066	*1P^6*	**20C** Royston	**20C** Royston	**20G** Hellifield	**55D** Royston			
58067	*1P^6*	**19B** Millhouses	**19B** Millhouses					
58068	*1P^6*	**14B** Kentish Town	**19B** Millhouses					
58069	*1P^6*	**14A** Cricklewood	**20E** Manningham					
58070	*1P^6*	**14A** Cricklewood	**20E** Manningham					
58071	*1P^6*	**19B** Millhouses	**19B** Millhouses	**22B** Gloucester Barnwood				
58072	*1P^6*	**14B** Kentish Town	**15C** Leicester Midland	**71J** Highbridge				
58073	*1P^6*	**14B** Kentish Town	**15C** Leicester Midland	**71J** Highbridge				
1385	*1P^6*	**14A** Cricklewood						
58074	*1P^6*	**22A** Bristol Barrow Road						
58075	*1P^6*	**20C** Royston	**20C** Royston					
58076	*1P^6*	**19B** Millhouses	**19B** Millhouses					
58077	*1P^6*	**17A** Derby	**23A** Skipton	**19B** Millhouses				
58078	*1P^6*	**19B** Millhouses						
58079	*1P^6*	**22C** Bath Green Park						
58080	*1P^6*	**22A** Bristol Barrow Road	**17B** Burton	**19B** Millhouses				
58081	*1P^6*	**20E** Manningham						
58082	*1P^6*	**2A** Rugby						
58083	*1P^6*	**2A** Rugby	**2A** Rugby	**9D** Buxton	**9D** Buxton			
58084	*1P^6*	**9D** Buxton	**9D** Buxton	**9D** Buxton				
58085	*1P^6*	**15C** Leicester Midland	**15A** Wellingborough	**16A** Nottingham	**36E** Retford			
58086	*1P^6*	**14B** Kentish Town	**71J** Highbridge	**71J** Highbridge	**71J** Highbridge	**82F** Bath Green Park		
58087	*1P^6*	**17B** Burton	**17B** Burton	**17B** Burton				
58088	*1P^6*	**22E** Highbridge	**71J** Highbridge					
58089	*1P^6*	**13A** Plaistow	**33A** Plaistow	**33A** Plaistow				
58090	*1P^6*	**17A** Derby	**23A** Skipton					
58091	*1P^6*	**15D** Bedford	**15D** Bedford	**15A** Wellingborough				
58092	*1P^7*	**9D** Buxton	**9D** Buxton					
58100	*0-10-0*	**21C** Bromsgrove	**21C** Bromsgrove	**21C** Bromsgrove				
58110	*2F^6*	**21B** Bournville	**17A** Derby					
58111	*2F^7*	**21B** Bournville						
58112	*2F^7*	**21A** Saltley						
58113	*2F^7*	**21B** Bournville						
58114	*2F^8*	**19C** Canklow	**19C** Canklow	**19C** Canklow	**19C** Canklow			
58115	*2F^8*	**11B** Barrow	**11B** Barrow	**11B** Barrow	**11B** Barrow	**11A** Barrow		
58116	*2F^8*	**2D** Nuneaton	**3C** Walsall	**11B** Barrow	**11B** Barrow	**11A** Barrow		
58117	*2F^8*	**3E** Monument Lane	**3D** Aston	**3E** Monument Lane				
58118	*2F^8*	**2D** Nuneaton	**2B** Nuneaton	**2B** Nuneaton	**2B** Nuneaton	**3B** Bushbury		
58119	*2F^8*	**2A** Rugby	**3B** Bushbury	**3B** Bushbury	**3B** Bushbury			
58120	*2F^8*	**11B** Barrow	**11B** Barrow	**11B** Barrow	**11B** Barrow	**8F** Wigan Springs Branch		
58121	*2F^8*	**2C** Northampton	**11B** Barrow	**11B** Barrow	**11B** Barrow			
58122	*2F^8*	**3A** Bescot	**3A** Bescot	**3C** Walsall	**3C** Walsall	**3A** Bescot		
58123	*2F^8*	**3A** Bescot	**3C** Walsall	**3C** Walsall	**11B** Barrow	**8F** Wigan Springs Branch		
58124	*2F^8*	**3E** Monument Lane	**3E** Monument Lane	**3E** Monument Lane	**3E** Monument Lane	**3B** Bushbury		
58125	*2F^8*	**17A** Derby	**17A** Derby	**3C** Walsall				
58126	*2F^8*	**21B** Bournville	**21B** Bournville	**21B** Bournville				
58127	*2F^8*	**19C** Canklow	**19C** Canklow	**19C** Canklow				
58128	*2F^8*	**19D** Heaton Mersey	**9F** Heaton Mersey	**9F** Heaton Mersey	**26A** Newton Heath	**17B** Burton		
58129	*2F^8*	**13C** Tilbury	**33B** Tilbury	**33A** Plaistow				
58130	*2F^8*	**17B** Burton	**17B** Burton	**17B** Burton	**17B** Burton			
58131	*2F^8*	**15D** Bedford	**14B** Kentish Town	**14B** Kentish Town	**14B** Kentish Town	**14B** Kentish Town		
58132	*2F^8*	**17A** Derby	**17A** Derby	**17A** Derby	**17A** Derby			
58133	*2F^8*	**16D** Mansfield	**16A** Nottingham	**16A** Nottingham				
58134	*2F^8*	**20C** Royston						
58135	*2F^8*	**16D** Mansfield	**16A** Nottingham	**16A** Nottingham	**3A** Bescot	**3E** Monument Lane		
58136	*2F^8*	**20B** Stourton	**20B** Stourton	**20B** Stourton	**55B** Stourton			
58137	*2F^8*	**16C** Kirkby in Ashfield	**16C** Kirkby in Ashfield	**16A** Nottingham	**16A** Nottingham	**17C** Rowsley		
58138	*2F^8*	**21A** Saltley	**21B** Bournville	**21B** Bournville	**21B** Bournville	**21B** Bournville		
58139	*2F^8*	**19A** Sheffield Grimesthorpe	**19A** Sheffield Grimesthorpe	**11B** Barrow				
58140	*2F^8*	**19A** Sheffield Grimesthorpe	**19A** Sheffield Grimesthorpe	**19A** Sheffield Grimesthorpe	**19A** Sheffield Grimesthorpe			
58141	*2F^8*	**21B** Bournville						
58142	*2F^8*	**15C** Leicester Midland	**15C** Leicester Midland	**15C** Leicester Midland	**15C** Leicester Midland			
58143	*2F^8*	**21B** Bournville	**21B** Bournville	**21B** Bournville	**21B** Bournville	**21B** Bournville	**15D** Coalville	
58144	*2F^8*	**17A** Derby	**17A** Derby	**17A** Derby	**17A** Derby	**17A** Derby		
58145	*2F^8*	**17A** Derby	**17B** Burton					
58146	*2F^8*	**18A** Toton	**18A** Toton	**18A** Toton	**18A** Toton	**41E** Staveley Barrow Hill		
58147	*2F^8*	**19C** Canklow	**19C** Canklow					
58148	*2F^8*	**17A** Derby	**17A** Derby	**17A** Derby	**17B** Burton	**17B** Burton	**15D** Coalville	
58149	*2F^8*	**15D** Bedford	**15D** Bedford					
58150	*2F^8*	**19C** Canklow						
58151	*2F^8*	**19A** Sheffield Grimesthorpe	**19A** Sheffield Grimesthorpe					
58152	*2F^8*	**2A** Rugby	**3B** Bushbury	**3B** Bushbury				
58153	*2F^8*	**18A** Toton	**18A** Toton	**18C** Hasland	**18A** Toton	**18A** Toton		
58154	*2F^8*	**19C** Canklow	**20C** Royston	**20C** Royston				
58155	*2F^8*	**20E** Manningham						
58156	*2F^8*	**20C** Royston	**20C** Royston	**11B** Barrow	**11B** Barrow			
58157	*2F^8*	**3A** Bescot	**3C** Walsall	**3C** Walsall	**3C** Walsall			
58158	*2F^8*	**17A** Derby	**14B** Kentish Town	**14B** Kentish Town	**17A** Derby	**17A** Derby		
58159	*2F^8*	**18A** Toton	**18A** Toton	**18A** Toton				
58160	*2F^8*	**17B** Burton	**17B** Burton	**17B** Burton	**17B** Burton	**17B** Burton		
58161	*2F^8*	**14A** Cricklewood	**14A** Cricklewood					
58162	*2F^8*	**15B** Kettering	**15B** Kettering	**15B** Kettering				
58163	*2F^8*	**17C** Coalville	**17C** Coalville	**17C** Coalville	**17C** Coalville	**15D** Coalville		
58164	*2F^8*	**14B** Kentish Town	**15B** Kettering	**15B** Kettering				
58165	*2F^8*	**19A** Sheffield Grimesthorpe	**19A** Sheffield Grimesthorpe	**19A** Sheffield Grimesthorpe	**18A** Toton	**17B** Burton		

		1948	1951	1954	1957	1960	1963	1966
58166	$2F^8$	18A Toton	18B Westhouses	18B Westhouses	18A Toton	18A Toton		
58167	$2F^8$	21A Saltley	21A Saltley	21A Saltley	21B Bournville			
58168	$2F^8$	18B Westhouses	18B Westhouses	18B Westhouses	21A Saltley	21B Bournville		
58169	$2F^8$	18B Westhouses	18A Toton	3A Bescot	3C Walsall	3A Bescot		
58170	$2F^8$	19C Canklow	19C Canklow	19C Canklow	19C Canklow	41D Canklow		
58171	$2F^8$	20E Manningham	18A Toton	18A Toton	18A Toton			
58172	$2F^8$	15B Kettering	15B Kettering	15B Kettering				
58173	$2F^8$	18A Toton	18A Toton	18A Toton	18A Toton	18A Toton		
58174	$2F^8$	17C Coalville	17C Coalville	3A Bescot	3C Walsall	3A Bescot		
58175	$2F^8$	19C Canklow	19A Sheffield Grimesthorpe	19A Sheffield Grimesthorpe	16A Nottingham	16A Nottingham		
58176	$2F^8$	18A Toton	18A Toton	18C Hasland				
58177	$2F^8$	3E Monument Lane	3E Monument Lane	11B Barrow	11B Barrow	8G Sutton Oak		
58178	$2F^8$	3E Monument Lane	3E Monument Lane	3E Monument Lane	3E Monument Lane			
58179	$2F^8$	3E Monument Lane	3E Monument Lane	3E Monument Lane				
58180	$2F^8$	3D Aston	3D Aston					
58181	$2F^8$	2A Rugby	2A Rugby	2A Rugby	2A Rugby	3A Bescot		
58182	$2F^8$	3D Aston	3D Aston	3D Aston	3D Aston	8G Sutton Oak	12E Barrow	
58183	$2F^8$	15B Kettering	3B Bushbury	3B Bushbury	3B Bushbury	3B Bushbury		
58184	$2F^8$	13A Plaistow	33A Plaistow	33A Plaistow				
58185	$2F^8$	3D Aston	3D Aston	3E Monument Lane	3E Monument Lane	3E Monument Lane		
58186	$2F^8$	17B Burton	17B Burton	17B Burton	17B Burton	17B Burton		
23016	$2F^8$	14B Kentish Town						
58187	$2F^8$	2F Coventry	11B Barrow	11B Barrow	11B Barrow			
3021	$2F^9$	14D Kentish Town						
58188	$2F^9$	17A Derby	20C Royston	20C Royston	55D Royston			
58189	$2F^9$	17D Rowsley	17D Rowsley	17D Rowsley	17D Rowsley			
58190	$2F^9$	19A Sheffield Grimesthorpe	19A Sheffield Grimesthorpe	19A Sheffield Grimesthorpe	19A Sheffield Grimesthorpe			
58191	$2F^9$	13A Plaistow	33A Plaistow	33A Plaistow	33A Plaistow			
58192	$2F^9$	20F Skipton	19A Sheffield Grimesthorpe	19A Sheffield Grimesthorpe	19A Sheffield Grimesthorpe			
58193	$2F^9$	15B Kettering	15B Kettering	15B Kettering				
58194	$2F^9$	15C Leicester Midland	15C Leicester Midland	84G Shrewsbury				
58195	$2F^9$	15B Kettering	15B Kettering	15B Kettering				
58196	$2F^9$	18B Westhouses	18B Westhouses	5B Crewe South	5B Crewe South			
58197	$2F^9$	17D Rowsley	18A Toton	18A Toton	33A Plaistow	55D Royston		
58198	$2F^9$	19C Canklow	19C Canklow	19C Canklow	19C Canklow			
58199	$2F^9$	2F Coventry	11B Barrow	11B Barrow	11B Barrow			
58200	$2F^9$	14A Cricklewood	14B Kentish Town	33A Plaistow				
3050	$2F^9$	20C Royston						
58201	$2F^9$	16A Nottingham	16A Nottingham					
58202	$2F^9$	21A Saltley						
58203	$2F^9$	17D Rowsley	17A Derby	84G Shrewsbury	3C Walsall			
58204	$2F^9$	19C Canklow	19C Canklow	19C Canklow	3B Bushbury			
58205	$2F^9$	3A Bescot						
58206	$2F^9$	22B Gloucester Barnwood	22B Gloucester Barnwood	22B Gloucester Barnwood	22B Gloucester Barnwood			
58207	$2F^9$	20C Royston	17B Burton	84G Shrewsbury				
58208	$2F^9$	19A Sheffield Grimesthorpe						
58209	$2F^9$	19B Millhouses	19B Millhouses	19B Millhouses	17C Coalville	15D Coalville		
58210	$2F^9$	16A Nottingham						
58211	$2F^9$	2F Coventry	84G Shrewsbury					
58212	$2F^9$	20E Manningham	20B Stourton	20C Royston				
58213	$2F^9$	2D Nuneaton	84G Shrewsbury	84G Shrewsbury	84G Shrewsbury			
58214	$2F^9$	15B Kettering	15B Kettering	15B Kettering	15B Kettering	14E Bedford		
58215	$2F^9$	22A Bristol Barrow Road	14B Kentish Town	14B Kentish Town	15D Bedford	15B Kettering		
58216	$2F^9$	17A Derby	17A Derby	17A Derby	55D Royston			
58217	$2F^9$	2F Coventry	2D Coventry	2D Coventry	11B Barrow			
58218	$2F^9$	2C Northampton	4B Northampton	2A Rugby	2A Rugby	2A Rugby		
58219	$2F^9$	17D Rowsley	17D Rowsley	17A Derby	17A Derby	17A Derby		
58220	$2F^9$	19A Sheffield Grimesthorpe	19A Sheffield Grimesthorpe	19A Sheffield Grimesthorpe	3E Monument Lane	3E Monument Lane		
58221	$2F^9$	17B Burton	17B Burton	2B Nuneaton	11B Barrow	2A Rugby		
58222	$2F^9$	17B Burton						
58223	$2F^9$	17D Rowsley						
58224	$2F^9$	17D Rowsley	17D Rowsley	17D Rowsley				
58225	$2F^9$	19A Sheffield Grimesthorpe	19A Sheffield Grimesthorpe	19A Sheffield Grimesthorpe	19A Sheffield Grimesthorpe			
58226	$2F^9$	17D Rowsley	17D Rowsley					
58227	$2F^9$	17A Derby						
58228	$2F^9$	17D Rowsley	17D Rowsley	17D Rowsley	17D Rowsley	17C Rowsley		
58229	$2F^8$	14B Kentish Town	14B Kentish Town					
58230	$2F^8$	17A Derby	21A Saltley	21A Saltley				
58231	$2F^8$	21A Saltley	21A Saltley					
58232	$2F^8$	19A Sheffield Grimesthorpe	19A Sheffield Grimesthorpe	19A Sheffield Grimesthorpe				
58233	$2F^8$	19C Canklow	19C Canklow	19C Canklow				
58234	$2F^8$	14B Kentish Town	14B Kentish Town	14A Cricklewood				
58235	$2F^8$	14A Cricklewood	14A Cricklewood	14A Cricklewood				
58236	$2F^8$	17D Rowsley	17B Burton	17B Burton				
3153	$2F^8$	17D Rowsley						
58237	$2F^8$	20C Royston	20C Royston					
58238	$2F^8$	20D Normanton	19C Canklow	19C Canklow	19C Canklow			
58239	$2F^8$	15D Bedford						
58240	$2F^8$	2D Nuneaton	2B Nuneaton					
58241	$2F^8$	15D Bedford	15D Bedford	84G Shrewsbury				
58242	$2F^8$	15C Leicester Midland	15C Leicester Midland	15C Leicester Midland				
58243	$2F^8$	3D Aston						
58244	$2F^8$	19C Canklow	19C Canklow	19C Canklow				
58245	$2F^8$	20B Stourton						
58246	$2F^8$	17A Derby	17A Derby	17A Derby	17A Derby			
58247	$2F^8$	17C Coalville	17C Coalville	17C Coalville	17C Coalville			
58248	$2F^8$	16A Nottingham	16A Nottingham					
58249	$2F^9$	15C Leicester Midland	15C Leicester Midland					
3195	$2F^9$	15B Kettering						
58250	$2F^9$	3D Aston						
58251	$2F^9$	17C Coalville						
58252	$2F^9$	16A Nottingham	16A Nottingham					
58253	$2F^9$	17A Derby						
58254	$2F^9$	17D Rowsley	17D Rowsley					
58255	$2F^9$	21A Saltley						
58256	$2F^9$	17B Burton						
58257	$2F^9$	1A Willesden	3A Bescot	11B Barrow				
58258	$2F^9$	17B Burton	17B Burton	84G Shrewsbury				
58259	$2F^9$	13A Plaistow	33A Plaistow					
58260	$2F^9$	14A Cricklewood	20C Royston	20C Royston	55D Royston	55D Royston		
58261	$2F^9$	21C Bromsgrove	21A Saltley	21A Saltley	21A Saltley	21A Saltley		
3424	$2F^9$	16C Kirkby in Ashfield						
58262	$2F^9$	19A Sheffield Grimesthorpe	17B Burton					
58263	$2F^9$	17B Burton						
58264	$2F^9$	17C Coalville	17C Coalville	17C Coalville				
58265	$2F^9$	20C Royston	20C Royston	20C Royston				
58266	$2F^9$	19C Canklow						
3473	$2F^9$	1A Willesden						
58267	$2F^9$	20F Skipton						
58268	$2F^9$	17D Rowsley	18A Toton					
58269	$2F^9$	2A Rugby	2A Rugby	2A Rugby				
58270	$2F^9$	2C Northampton						
58271	$2F^9$	21C Bromsgrove	21A Saltley	16A Nottingham	5B Crewe South	3E Monument Lane		
58272	$2F^9$	1C Watford	2B Nuneaton	2B Nuneaton				

No.	Class	1948	1951	1954	1957	1960	1963	1966
58273	2F[9]	3E Monument Lane	3A Bescot	11B Barrow				
58274	2F[9]	14A Cricklewood	14A Cricklewood					
58275	2F[9]	16A Nottingham						
58276	2F[9]	19A Sheffield Grimesthorpe	19A Sheffield Grimesthorpe	19A Sheffield Grimesthorpe				
58277	2F[9]	1A Willesden	3A Bescot	3A Bescot				
58278	2F[9]	1A Willesden	2D Coventry	2D Coventry				
58279	2F[9]	1A Willesden	3D Aston	3C Walsall	10C Patricroft			
58280	2F[9]	1A Willesden	2A Rugby					
58281	2F[9]	1A Willesden	4B Northampton	2E Northampton	2B Nuneaton			
58282	2F[9]	19D Heaton Mersey						
58283	2F[9]	1A Willesden	3C Walsall	3C Walsall	3C Walsall	3A Bescot		
58284	2F[9]	17B Burton						
58285	2F[9]	1A Willesden	3B Bushbury					
58286	2F[9]	1A Willesden	3E Monument Lane	3E Monument Lane				
58287	2F[9]	1A Willesden	3B Bushbury	11B Barrow	11B Barrow	6K Rhyl		
58288	2F[9]	3A Bescot	3C Walsall	3C Walsall	3D Aston			
58289	2F[9]	13A Plaistow	33A Plaistow					
58290	2F[9]	1A Willesden	2C Warwick	2A Rugby				
58291	2F[9]	1A Willesden	11B Barrow	11B Barrow	11B Barrow	8G Sutton Oak		
58292	2F[9]	20E Manningham						
58293	2F[9]	2F Coventry	2D Coventry	2D Coventry	11B Barrow	11A Barrow		
58294	2F[9]	21A Saltley						
3602	2F[9]	16A Nottingham						
58295	2F[9]	1A Willesden	3D Aston	3D Aston	3D Aston	3B Bushbury		
58296	2F[9]	14A Cricklewood	18A Toton					
58297	2F[9]	17B Burton						
58298	2F[9]	15C Leicester Midland	15C Leicester Midland	15C Leicester Midland	15C Leicester Midland	15D Coalville		
58299	2F[9]	2C Northampton	11B Barrow	11B Barrow	11B Barrow			
58300	2F[9]	15C Leicester Midland	15C Leicester Midland	15C Leicester Midland				
58301	2F[9]	2F Coventry						
58302	2F[9]	1A Willesden	3C Walsall					
58303	2F[9]	1A Willesden	9F Heaton Mersey					
58304	2F[9]	17B Burton	17B Burton					
58305	2F[9]	15D Bedford	15D Bedford	15D Bedford	15C Leicester Midland	17B Burton		
58306	2F[9]	1A Willesden	2D Coventry	2D Coventry	3E Monument Lane			
58307	2F[9]	1A Willesden						
58308	2F[9]	2E Warwick	2C Warwick	2A Rugby	2A Rugby			
58309	2F[9]	1A Willesden	11B Barrow	11B Barrow				
58310	2F[9]	14B Kentish Town	14A Cricklewood	33B Tilbury				
58320	2F[10]	3C Walsall						
58321	2F[10]	Crewe Works	Crewe Works					
58322	2F[10]	3C Walsall	84G Shrewsbury					
28095	2F[10]	8D Widnes						
28097	2F[10]	3A Bescot						
58323	2F[10]	Crewe Works	Crewe Works					
58324	2F[10]	11B Barrow						
58325	2F[10]	3C Walsall						
58326	2F[10]	Crewe Works	Crewe Works					
58327	2F[10]	8D Widnes	84G Shrewsbury					
8108	2F[10]	(S&M)						
58328	2F[10]	Crewe Works	Crewe Works					
58329	2F[10]	11A Carnforth						
58330	2F[10]	11B Barrow	84G Shrewsbury					
58331	2F[10]	11B Barrow						
58332	2F[10]	Crewe Works	Crewe Works					
58333	2F[10]	3B Bushbury	84G Shrewsbury					
28153	2F[10]	4A Shrewsbury						
58334	2F[10]	11A Carnforth						
58335	2F[10]	11B Barrow	11B Barrow					
58336	2F[10]	Crewe Works	Crewe Works					
8182	2F[10]	(S&M)						
58337	2F[10]	11B Barrow						
58338	2F[10]	3A Bescot						
58339	2F[10]	11B Barrow						
58340	2F[10]	11B Barrow	11B Barrow					
58341	2F[10]	3B Bushbury						
58342	2F[10]	8D Widnes						
58343	2F[10]	Crewe Works	Crewe Works					
28230	2F[10]	3B Bushbury						
58344	2F[10]	11B Barrow						
58345	2F[10]	3B Bushbury						
8236	2F[10]	(S&M)						
58346	2F[10]	8D Widnes	11B Barrow					
58347	2F[10]	Crewe Works	Crewe Works					
58348	2F[10]	3C Walsall						
58349	2F[10]	3C Walsall	11B Barrow					
58350	2F[10]	3C Walsall	11B Barrow					
58351	2F[10]	8D Widnes						
58352	2F[10]	3C Walsall	11B Barrow					
58353	2F[10]	8D Widnes						
58354	2F[10]	11B Barrow	11B Barrow					
58355	2F[10]	4A Shrewsbury						
58356	2F[10]	11B Barrow						
58357	2F[10]	11B Barrow						
58358	2F[10]	4A Shrewsbury						
58359	2F[10]	3C Walsall						
58360	2F[10]	11B Barrow	11B Barrow					
58361	2F[10]	3C Walsall						
58362	2F[11]	12C Penrith	12D Workington					
58363	2F[11]	2D Nuneaton	8D Widnes					
58364	2F[11]	7A Llandudno Junction	7A Llandudno Junction					
58365	2F[11]	7A Llandudno Junction	7A Llandudno Junction					
58366	2F[11]	9B Stockport Edgeley						
58367	2F[11]	4A Shrewsbury						
58368	2F[11]	2D Nuneaton	10A Wigan Springs Branch					
28350	2F[11]	5A Crewe North						
58369	2F[11]	4A Shrewsbury						
58370	2F[11]	12D Workington						
58371	2F[11]	6C Birkenhead						
58372	2F[11]	7B Bangor						
58373	2F[11]	10A Wigan Springs Branch						
58374	2F[11]	7B Bangor						
58375	2F[11]	12D Workington	7B Bangor	6H Bangor				
28415	2F[11]	12D Workington						
58376	2F[11]	10A Wigan Springs Branch	12A Carlisle Upperby	5D Stoke				
58377	2F[11]	8D Widnes	9B Stockport Edgeley					
58378	2F[11]	3B Bushbury	10E Sutton Oak					
28441	2F[11]	12D Workington						
58379	2F[11]	5D Stoke						
58380	2F[11]	9B Stockport Edgeley						
58381	2F[11]	10A Wigan Springs Branch	7B Bangor					
58382	2F[11]	6B Mold Junction	5D Stoke	5D Stoke				
58383	2F[11]	8D Widnes	8D Widnes					
58384	2F[11]	5B Crewe South						

No.	Class	1948	1951	1954	1957	1960	1963	1966
58385	2F[11]	**5D** Stoke						
58386	2F[11]	**5B** Crewe South						
58387	2F[11]	**12D** Workington						
58388	2F[11]	**2E** Warwick						
58389	2F[11]	**12C** Penrith	**5D** Stoke					
58390	2F[11]	**10E** Sutton Oak						
58391	2F[11]	**12D** Workington						
58392	2F[11]	**7A** Llandudno Junction	**7D** Rhyl					
58393	2F[11]	**8D** Widnes	**8D** Widnes					
58394	2F[11]	**10E** Sutton Oak	**10E** Sutton Oak	**8D** Widnes				
58395	2F[11]	**5B** Crewe South						
58396	2F[11]	**5B** Crewe South	**12D** Workington					
58397	2F[11]	**4A** Shrewsbury						
58398	2F[11]	**12D** Workington	**7A** Llandudno Junction					
58399	2F[11]	**7D** Rhyl						
58400	2F[11]	**12D** Workington	**5D** Stoke					
58401	2F[11]	**12D** Workington						
58402	2F[11]	**8D** Widnes						
58403	2F[11]	**6C** Birkenhead						
58404	2F[11]	**2E** Warwick						
58405	2F[11]	**2D** Nuneaton						
28542	2F[11]	**12D** Workington						
58406	2F[11]	**4B** Swansea Victoria						
58407	2F[11]	**12D** Workington						
58408	2F[11]	**12D** Workington						
58409	2F[11]	**3D** Aston	**12C** Penrith	**12C** Penrith				
58410	2F[11]	**10E** Sutton Oak						
58411	2F[11]	**12C** Penrith						
58412	2F[11]	**7B** Bangor	**12C** Penrith	**12C** Penrith				
58413	2F[11]	**12D** Workington	**8D** Widnes	**8D** Widnes				
58414	2F[11]	**3B** Bushbury						
58415	2F[11]	**3D** Aston	**8D** Widnes					
58416	2F[11]	**12D** Workington						
58417	2F[11]	**12C** Penrith						
58418	2F[11]	**12C** Penrith	**10E** Sutton Oak					
58419	2F[11]	**10E** Sutton Oak	**12A** Carlisle Upperby					
58420	2F[11]	**8D** Widnes	**7D** Rhyl					
28586	2F[11]	**3D** Aston						
58421	2F[11]	**12C** Penrith	**12D** Workington					
58422	2F[11]	**10A** Wigan Springs Branch						
58423	2F[11]	**3C** Walsall						
28597	2F[11]	**3C** Walsall						
58424	2F[11]	**8D** Widnes						
58425	2F[11]	**4A** Shrewsbury						
58426	2F[11]	**2D** Nuneaton	**5B** Crewe South					
58427	2F[11]	**7D** Rhyl	**9B** Stockport Edgeley	**9B** Stockport Edgeley				
58428	2F[11]	**6A** Chester						
58429	2F[11]	**3E** Monument Lane	**5B** Crewe South					
58430	2F[11]	**4B** Swansea Victoria	**8D** Widnes	**8D** Widnes				
58850	2F[12]	**17D** Rowsley	**17D** Rowsley	**17D** Rowsley	**17D** Rowsley	**17C** Rowsley		
58851	2F[12]	**13B** Devons Road	**6C** Birkenhead	**1D** Devons Road				
58852	2F[12]	**13B** Devons Road	**1D** Devons Road	**1D** Devons Road				
58853	2F[12]	**13B** Devons Road	**1D** Devons Road	**1D** Devons Road				
58854	2F[12]	**6C** Birkenhead	**6C** Birkenhead	**1D** Devons Road				
58855	2F[12]	**13B** Devons Road	**1D** Devons Road	**1D** Devons Road				
58856	2F[12]	**17D** Rowsley	**17D** Rowsley	**17D** Rowsley	**17D** Rowsley			
58857	2F[12]	**6C** Birkenhead	**6C** Birkenhead	**1D** Devons Road	**1D** Devons Road			
58858	2F[12]	**13B** Devons Road	**1D** Devons Road					
58859	2F[12]	**6C** Birkenhead	**1D** Devons Road	**1D** Devons Road	**1D** Devons Road			
27525	2F[12]	**6C** Birkenhead						
58860	2F[12]	**13B** Devons Road	**17D** Rowsley	**17D** Rowsley	**17D** Rowsley			
58861	2F[12]	**6C** Birkenhead	**6C** Birkenhead					
58862	2F[12]	**17D** Rowsley	**17D** Rowsley	**17D** Rowsley				
58863	2F[12]	**6C** Birkenhead	**6C** Birkenhead					
58865	Crane	**13B** Devons Road	**1D** Devons Road					
58870	2F[13]	Crewe Works						
58880	2F[14]	**4E** Tredegar	**86K** Abergavenny	**87K** Swansea Victoria				
58881	2F[14]	**2B** Bletchley						
58882	2F[14]	**7D** Rhyl						
58883	2F[14]	**8C** Speke Junction						
58884	2F[14]	**7D** Rhyl						
58885	2F[14]	**4E** Tredegar						
58886	2F[14]	**3D** Aston						
58887	2F[14]	**8A** Edge Hill	**4A** Bletchley	**1E** Bletchley				
58888	2F[14]	**7B** Bangor	**86K** Abergavenny	**86K** Abergavenny				
58889	2F[14]	**7B** Bangor	**86K** Abergavenny					
58890	2F[14]	**10D** Plodder Lane						
58891	2F[14]	**4B** Swansea Victoria	**86K** Abergavenny	**86K** Abergavenny				
58892	2F[14]	**4B** Swansea Victoria	**87K** Swansea Victoria					
58893	2F[14]	**7D** Rhyl						
58894	2F[14]	**4A** Shrewsbury						
27648	2F[14]	**4E** Tredegar						
58895	2F[14]	**4E** Tredegar	**86K** Abergavenny					
58896	2F[14]	**3D** Aston						
58897	2F[14]	**8A** Edge Hill						
58898	2F[14]	**8A** Edge Hill						
58899	2F[14]	**10E** Sutton Oak	**86K** Abergavenny	**87K** Swansea Victoria				
58900	2F[14]	**8A** Edge Hill	**10E** Sutton Oak	**3E** Monument Lane				
7700	2F[14]	**4B** Swansea Victoria						
58901	2F[14]	**10A** Wigan Springs Branch						
58902	2F[14]	**4D** Abergavenny	**86K** Abergavenny	**86K** Abergavenny				
58903	2F[14]	**7D** Rhyl	**7B** Bangor	**6H** Bangor				
7715	2F[14]	**4B** Swansea Victoria						
58904	2F[14]	**10D** Plodder Lane	**84G** Shrewsbury	**84G** Shrewsbury				
58905	2F[14]	**4D** Abergavenny						
58906	2F[14]	**8C** Speke Junction						
58907	2F[14]	**4D** Abergavenny						
58908	2F[14]	**10D** Plodder Lane	**4A** Bletchley					
58909	2F[14]	**3E** Monument Lane						
58910	2F[14]	**4B** Swansea Victoria	**87K** Swansea Victoria					
58911	2F[14]	**4D** Abergavenny	**4A** Bletchley	**87K** Swansea Victoria				
58912	2F[14]	**8A** Edge Hill						
58913	2F[14]	**10E** Sutton Oak	**86K** Abergavenny					
58914	2F[14]	**10D** Plodder Lane						
58915	2F[14]	**8A** Edge Hill	**86K** Abergavenny	**86K** Abergavenny				
58916	2F[14]	**3E** Monument Lane						
58917	2F[11]	**10E** Sutton Oak						
58918	2F[14]	**10D** Plodder Lane						
58919	2F[14]	**2B** Bletchley	**86K** Abergavenny					
58920	2F[14]	**4E** Tredegar						
58921	2F[14]	**4E** Tredegar	**7D** Rhyl	**87K** Swansea Victoria				
58922	2F[14]	**8A** Edge Hill						
58923	2F[14]	**10D** Plodder Lane						
58924	2F[14]	**8A** Edge Hill	**86K** Abergavenny	**86K** Abergavenny				

		1948		1951	1954	1957	1960	1963	1966
58925	2F[14]	**8B**	Warrington Dallam	**86K** Abergavenny	**86K** Abergavenny				
7796	2F[14]	**7A**	Llandudno Junction						
58926	2F[14]	**10D**	Plodder Lane	**84G** Shrewsbury	**84G** Shrewsbury	**84G** Shrewsbury			
58927	2F[14]	**10D**	Plodder Lane						
58928	2F[14]	**8A**	Edge Hill	**3E** Monument Lane					
58929	2F[14]	**4D**	Abergavenny						
7812	2F[14]	**4D**	Abergavenny						
58930	2F[14]	**8A**	Edge Hill						
58931	2F[14]	**4E**	Tredegar						
58932	2F[14]	**7B**	Bangor	**10E** Sutton Oak					
58933	2F[14]	**4D**	Abergavenny	**86K** Abergavenny					
58934	2F[14]	**2B**	Bletchley						
58935	2F[14]	**8A**	Edge Hill	**86K** Abergavenny					
58936	2F[14]	**4A**	Shrewsbury						
58937	2F[14]	**4D**	Abergavenny						
7841	2F[14]	**4D**	Abergavenny						
CD3	2F[15]		Wolverton Works	Wolverton Works	Wolverton Works	Wolverton Works			
CD6	2F[15]		Wolverton Works	Wolverton Works	Wolverton Works	Wolverton Works			
CD7	2F[15]		Wolverton Works	Wolverton Works	Wolverton Works	Wolverton Works			
CD8	2F[15]		Wolverton Works	Wolverton Works	Wolverton Works	Wolverton Works			
3323	2F[15]		Crewe Works	Crewe Works	Crewe Works				
11304	2F[2]		Horwich Works	Horwich Works	Horwich Works	Horwich Works	Horwich Works		
11305	2F[2]		Horwich Works	Horwich Works	Horwich Works	Horwich Works	Horwich Works	Horwich Works	
11324	2F[2]		Horwich Works	Horwich Works	Horwich Works	Horwich Works	Horwich Works	Horwich Works	
11368	2F[2]		Horwich Works	Horwich Works	Horwich Works	Horwich Works	Horwich Works	Horwich Works	
11394	2F[2]		Horwich Works	Horwich Works	Horwich Works	Horwich Works	Horwich Works		
Wren	NG[1]		Horwich Works	Horwich Works	Horwich Works	Horwich Works	Horwich Works		
10	NG[2]		Beeston Creosote Works	Beeston Creosote Works	Beeston Creosote Works				
10897	2P[8]		Uttoxeter	Rugby Testing Station	Rugby Testing Station				
29988	Rail Motor[2]	**12F**	Beattock						
80	3P[2]								
103	*Jones Goods*			→	→	→	**65D** Dawsholm	**65D** Dawsholm	
123	*CR Single*			→	→	→	**65D** Dawsholm	**65D** Dawsholm	
1000	4P[2]	(41000)		→	→	→	**17A** Derby		

Right: LMS Stanier '4MT' class 2-6-4T No 42484 from 24H Hellifield at Crewe North MPD on 11 March 1962. *Ian G. Holt*

Left: LMS Stanier '5MT' class 2-6-0 No 42979 at its home shed 21B Bescot on 30 June 1963. *A. W. Martin*

Right: Midland Railway Johnson '3F' class 0-6-0 No 43186 (with 4ft 11in driving wheels) at Bromsgrove depot on 4 May 1958.

Left: SDJR Johnson '3F' class 0-6-0 No 43204 from 71J Highbridge at Derby on 25 March 1952. *R. J. Buckley*

Below: Midland Railway Deeley '3F' class 0-6-0 No 43791 at Derby 17 March 1950. *R. J. Buckley*

Above: LMS Fowler/Ivatt rebuilt 'Patriot' '7P' class 4-6-0 No 45526 *Morecambe & Heysham* at Carlisle Kingmoor just after withdrawal on 28 November 1964. *N. E. Preedy*

Left: LMS Stanier Rebuilt Jubilee '7P' class 4-6-0 No 45736 *Phoenix* based at 5A Crewe North shed. *J. E. Wilkinson*

Below: The last LNWR Bowen Cooke rebuilt 'Claughton '5XP' class 4-6-0 No 6004 at Edge Hill on 19 October 1946. It did not receive its allocated number 46004. *H. C. Casserley*

Above: LMS Stanier 'Princess Royal' '8P' class 4-6-2 No 46206 *Princess Marie Louise* at Patricroft on 13 August 1961. *J. R. Carter*

Below: LNWR Webb '2P' class 0-6-2T No 6876 at Birmingham New Street on 20 August 1938. Later allocated the number 46876, but never carried. *P. B. Whitehouse*

Above: LMS Fowler '2F' Dock Tank 0-6-0T No 47162 at Edinburgh St Margarets on 16 July 1953. *P. H. Wells*

Below: Condensing Midland Railway Johnson '3F' class 'Jinty' 0-6-0T No 47247 at Badnall Wharf. *J. B. Bucknall*

Above: LNWR Webb '1F' class 'Bissel Truck' 0-4-2PT No 47862 at Crewe Works on 18 August 1954.
Brian Morrison

Below: LNWR Beames '7F' class 0-8-4T No 7932 at 8A Edge Hill depot. Allocated number 47932.
P. Ransome-Wallis

Above: LMS Fowler '7F' class 0-8-0 No 49674 at 26C Bolton shed on 11 August 1956. *T. K. Widd*

Left: LYR Hughes '5P' class 4-6-0 No 50455 from 28A Blackpool working the SLS special from Blackpool to York, seen at Manchester Victoria on 1 July 1951.

Left: LYR Hughes '3P' class 2-4-2T No 50891 at Sowerby Bridge on 5 July 1949. *A. F. Cook*

Left: Two LYR Aspinall '0F' 'Pug' class 0-4-0STs Nos 51206 and 51246 at Bank Hall shed. *J. Davenport*

Right: LYR Barton Wright '2F' class 0-6-0 No 12034. Most of these engines were quickly renumbered to make space for newly built English Electric diesel shunters (later Class 11). This engine became 52034 in April 1948.

Below: LYR Hughes '3F' class 0-6-0 No 52551 at Horwich on 17 March 1957, the month of its withdrawal. *A. W. Martin*

Above: LYR Hughes '7F' class 0-8-0 No 52857 at Lostock Hall in June 1950. *J. Davenport*

Left: SDJR Fowler '7F' class 2-8-0 No 53807 fitted with a small boiler at Bath on 7 June 1964. *Carl Symes*

Right: Highland Railway Drummond '2P' class 'Small Ben' 4-4-0 No 14398 *Ben Alder*. Later it became 54398 and although set aside for preservation it was scrapped in 1966.

Above: Caledonian Railway McIntosh '3P' class 'Dunalastair IV' 4-4-0 No 54452 at Haymarket. *J. R. Paterson*

Right: LMS (Caledonian Railway) Pickersgill '4P' class 4-6-0 No 54640.

Left: Caledonian Railway McIntosh '2P' class 0-4-4T No 55126. *W. L. Sellar*

Right: Caledonian Railway Pickersgill '2P' class 0-4-4T No 55237 at Beattock Shed. Fitted with a stovepipe chimney. *E. Treacy*

Below: LMS (Caledonian Railway) Pickersgill '2P' class 0-4-4T No 55261 at Carstairs on 17 September 1956. *David A. Anderson*

Bottom: Caledonian Railway Pickersgill '4P' class 4-6-2T No 55359 at Kilmarnock in 1948. *P. Ransome-Wallis*

Top: Caledonian Railway Drummond '2F' class 'Jumbo' 0-6-0 No 57340 at Kingmoor shed on 23 April 1957. *R. E. Vincent*

Above: Caledonian Railway McIntosh '3F' class 0-6-0 No 57645 at Dalry Road on 16 August 1961. *J. C. Haydon*

Left: Caledonian Railway Pickersgill '3F' class 0-6-0 No 57688 entering Motherwell Shed on 8 February 1963. *S. Rickard*

Top: Highland Railway Drummond '3F' class 'Barney' 0-6-0 No 17695. Later renumbered 57695.

Above: Highland Railway Cummings '4F' class 'Clan Goods' 4-6-0 No 57954 *Clan Mackinnon* in the locomotive yard at Kyle of Lochalsh in September 1949. *C. C. B. Herbert*

Right: The last LNWR Bowen Cooke '4P' class 'Prince of Wales' 4-6-0 No 25752 awaiting scrapping at Crewe in July 1949. It did not receive its allocated number 58002. *BR*

Top: LNWR Whale '3P' class 'Precursor' 4-4-0 No 25297 *Sirocco*. Its allocated number 58010 was not carried.

Above: Midland Railway Johnson '1P' class 0-4-4T No 1251 at Bath Green Park 16th July 1936. It did not receive its allocated number 58034. *Rev A. G .Newman*

Left: LNWR Webb '1P' class 2-4-0T No 58092 at Middleton Quarries on the Cromford & High Peak Railway on 18 May 1951. *P. H. Wells*

Top: Midland Railway Fowler 0-10-0 Lickey Banker No 58100.

Above: Midland Railway Kirtley '2F' class 0-6-0 No 22853 in April 1950. It has recently been withdrawn and did not receive its allocated number 58112. *P. Ransome-Wallis*

Right: Midland Railway Johnson '2F' class 4ft 11in 0-6-0 No 58159 at its home depot 18A Toton on 11 September 1955. *A. R. Carpenter*

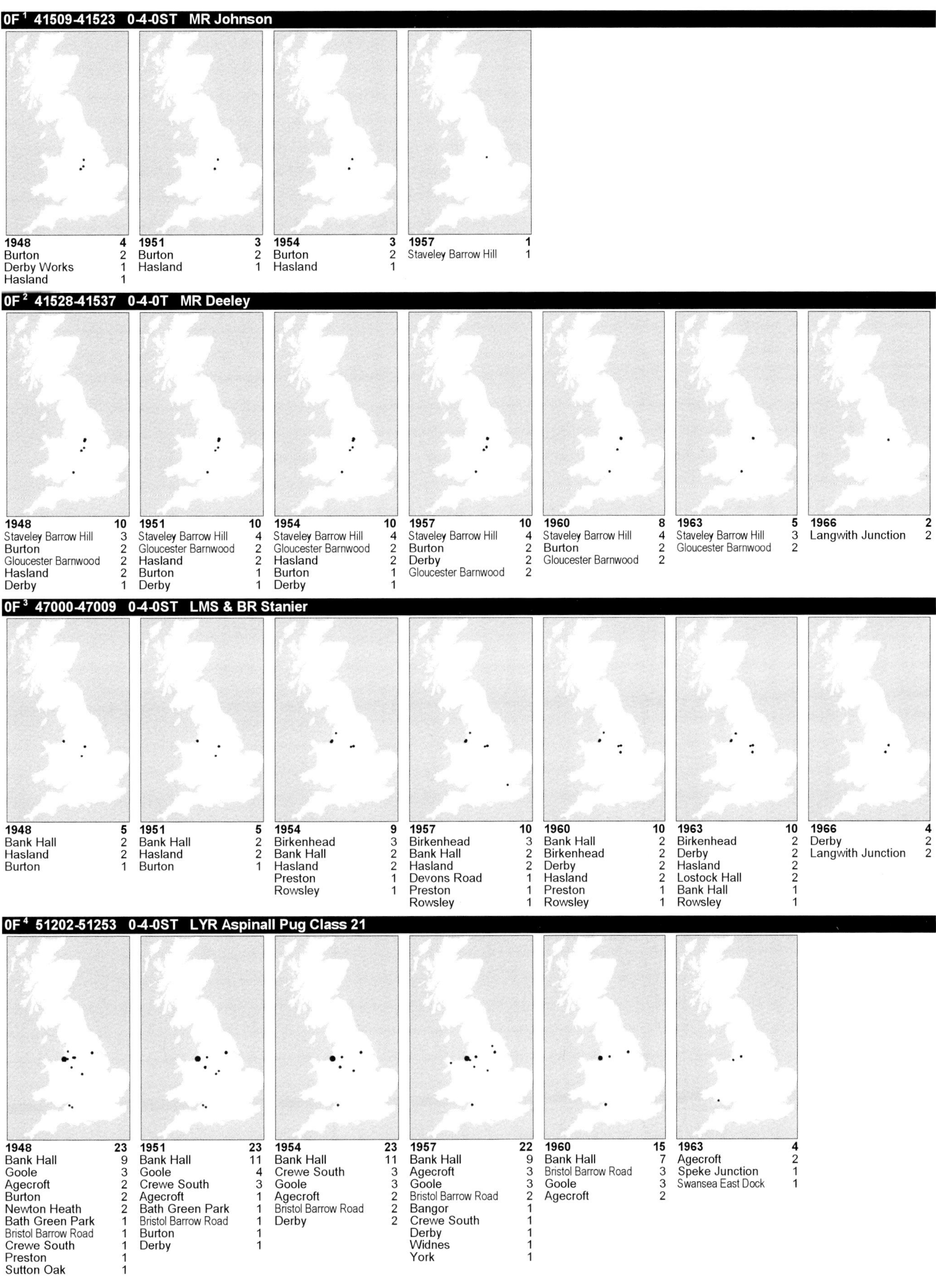

0F [1] 41509-41523 0-4-0ST MR Johnson

1948	4	1951	3	1954	3	1957	1
Burton	2	Burton	2	Burton	2	Staveley Barrow Hill	1
Derby Works	1	Hasland	1	Hasland	1		
Hasland	1						

0F [2] 41528-41537 0-4-0T MR Deeley

1948	10	1951	10	1954	10	1957	10	1960	8	1963	5	1966	2
Staveley Barrow Hill	3	Staveley Barrow Hill	4	Staveley Barrow Hill	4	Staveley Barrow Hill	4	Staveley Barrow Hill	4	Staveley Barrow Hill	3	Langwith Junction	2
Burton	2	Gloucester Barnwood	2	Gloucester Barnwood	2	Burton	2	Burton	2	Gloucester Barnwood	2		
Gloucester Barnwood	2	Hasland	2	Hasland	2	Derby	2	Gloucester Barnwood	2				
Hasland	2	Burton	1	Burton	1	Gloucester Barnwood	2						
Derby	1	Derby	1	Derby	1								

0F [3] 47000-47009 0-4-0ST LMS & BR Stanier

1948	5	1951	5	1954	9	1957	10	1960	10	1963	10	1966	4
Bank Hall	2	Bank Hall	2	Birkenhead	3	Birkenhead	3	Bank Hall	2	Birkenhead	2	Derby	2
Hasland	2	Hasland	2	Bank Hall	2	Bank Hall	2	Birkenhead	2	Derby	2	Langwith Junction	2
Burton	1	Burton	1	Hasland	2	Hasland	2	Derby	2	Hasland	2		
				Preston	1	Devons Road	1	Hasland	2	Lostock Hall	2		
				Rowsley	1	Preston	1	Preston	1	Bank Hall	1		
						Rowsley	1	Rowsley	1	Rowsley	1		

0F [4] 51202-51253 0-4-0ST LYR Aspinall Pug Class 21

1948	23	1951	23	1954	23	1957	22	1960	15	1963	4
Bank Hall	9	Bank Hall	11	Bank Hall	11	Bank Hall	9	Bank Hall	7	Agecroft	2
Goole	3	Goole	4	Crewe South	3	Agecroft	3	Bristol Barrow Road	3	Speke Junction	1
Agecroft	2	Crewe South	3	Goole	3	Goole	3	Goole	3	Swansea East Dock	1
Burton	2	Agecroft	1	Agecroft	2	Bristol Barrow Road	2	Agecroft	2		
Newton Heath	2	Bath Green Park	1	Bristol Barrow Road	2	Bangor	1				
Bath Green Park	1	Bristol Barrow Road	1	Derby	2	Crewe South	1				
Bristol Barrow Road	1	Burton	1			Derby	1				
Crewe South	1	Derby	1			Widnes	1				
Preston	1					York	1				
Sutton Oak	1										

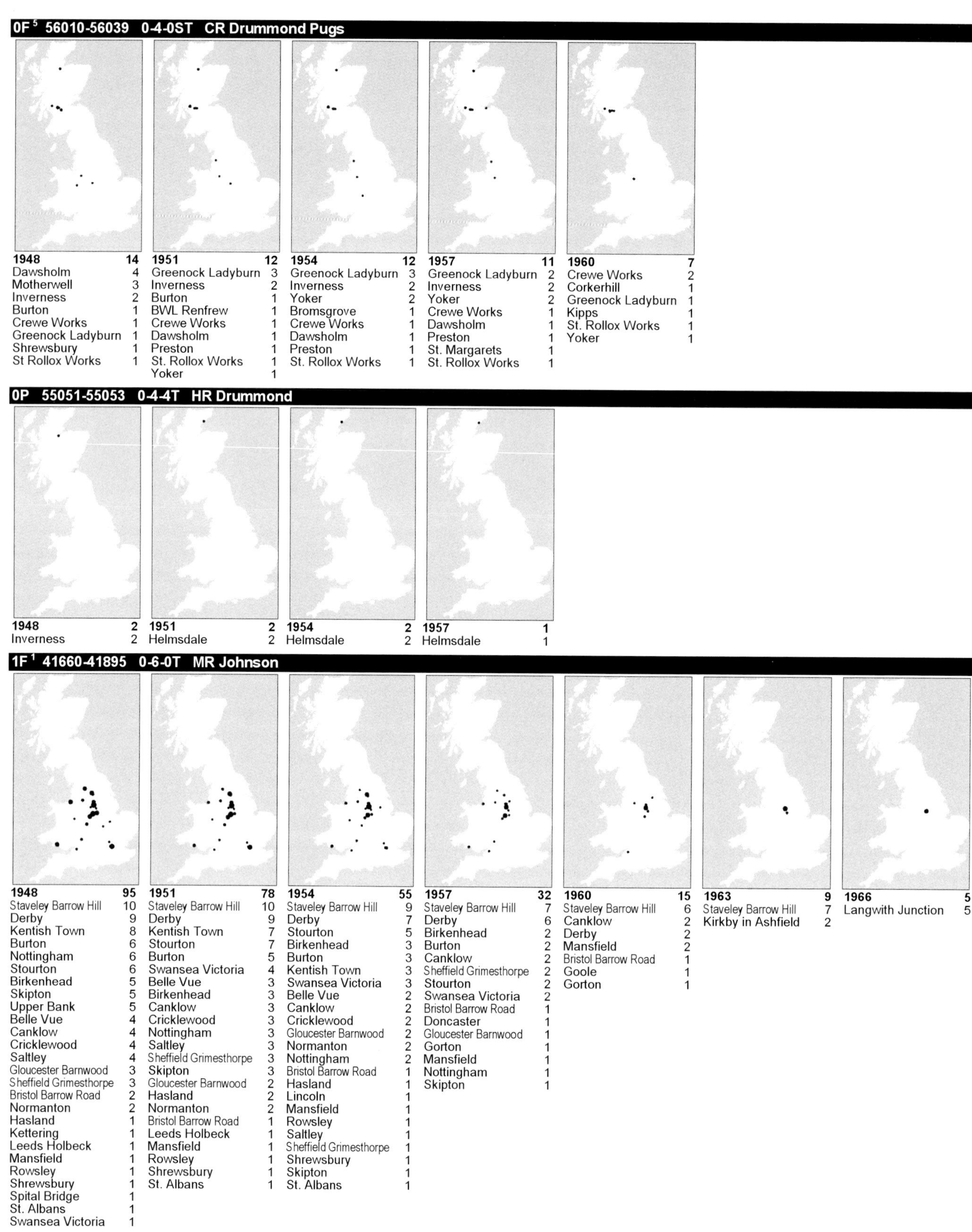

0F^5 56010-56039 0-4-0ST CR Drummond Pugs

1948	14
Dawsholm	4
Motherwell	3
Inverness	2
Burton	1
Crewe Works	1
Greenock Ladyburn	1
Shrewsbury	1
St Rollox Works	1

1951	12
Greenock Ladyburn	3
Inverness	2
Burton	1
BWL Renfrew	1
Crewe Works	1
Dawsholm	1
Preston	1
St. Rollox Works	1
Yoker	1

1954	12
Greenock Ladyburn	3
Inverness	2
Yoker	2
Bromsgrove	1
Crewe Works	1
Dawsholm	1
Preston	1
St. Rollox Works	1

1957	11
Greenock Ladyburn	2
Inverness	2
Yoker	2
Crewe Works	1
Dawsholm	1
Preston	1
St. Margarets	1
St. Rollox Works	1

1960	7
Crewe Works	2
Corkerhill	1
Greenock Ladyburn	1
Kipps	1
St. Rollox Works	1
Yoker	1

0P 55051-55053 0-4-4T HR Drummond

1948	2
Inverness	2

1951	2
Helmsdale	2

1954	2
Helmsdale	2

1957	1
Helmsdale	1

1F^1 41660-41895 0-6-0T MR Johnson

1948	95
Staveley Barrow Hill	10
Derby	9
Kentish Town	8
Burton	6
Nottingham	6
Stourton	6
Birkenhead	5
Skipton	5
Upper Bank	5
Belle Vue	4
Canklow	4
Cricklewood	4
Saltley	4
Gloucester Barnwood	3
Sheffield Grimesthorpe	3
Bristol Barrow Road	2
Normanton	2
Hasland	1
Kettering	1
Leeds Holbeck	1
Mansfield	1
Rowsley	1
Shrewsbury	1
Spital Bridge	1
St. Albans	1
Swansea Victoria	1

1951	78
Staveley Barrow Hill	10
Derby	9
Kentish Town	7
Stourton	7
Burton	5
Swansea Victoria	4
Belle Vue	3
Birkenhead	3
Canklow	3
Cricklewood	3
Nottingham	3
Saltley	3
Sheffield Grimesthorpe	3
Skipton	3
Gloucester Barnwood	2
Hasland	2
Normanton	2
Bristol Barrow Road	1
Leeds Holbeck	1
Mansfield	1
Rowsley	1
Shrewsbury	1
St. Albans	1

1954	55
Staveley Barrow Hill	9
Derby	7
Stourton	5
Birkenhead	3
Burton	3
Kentish Town	3
Swansea Victoria	3
Belle Vue	2
Canklow	2
Cricklewood	2
Gloucester Barnwood	2
Normanton	2
Nottingham	2
Bristol Barrow Road	1
Hasland	1
Lincoln	1
Mansfield	1
Rowsley	1
Saltley	1
Sheffield Grimesthorpe	1
Shrewsbury	1
Skipton	1
St. Albans	1

1957	32
Staveley Barrow Hill	7
Derby	6
Birkenhead	2
Burton	2
Canklow	2
Sheffield Grimesthorpe	2
Stourton	2
Swansea Victoria	2
Bristol Barrow Road	1
Doncaster	1
Gloucester Barnwood	1
Gorton	1
Mansfield	1
Nottingham	1
Skipton	1

1960	15
Staveley Barrow Hill	6
Canklow	2
Derby	2
Mansfield	2
Bristol Barrow Road	1
Goole	1
Gorton	1

1963	9
Staveley Barrow Hill	7
Kirkby in Ashfield	2

1966	5
Langwith Junction	5

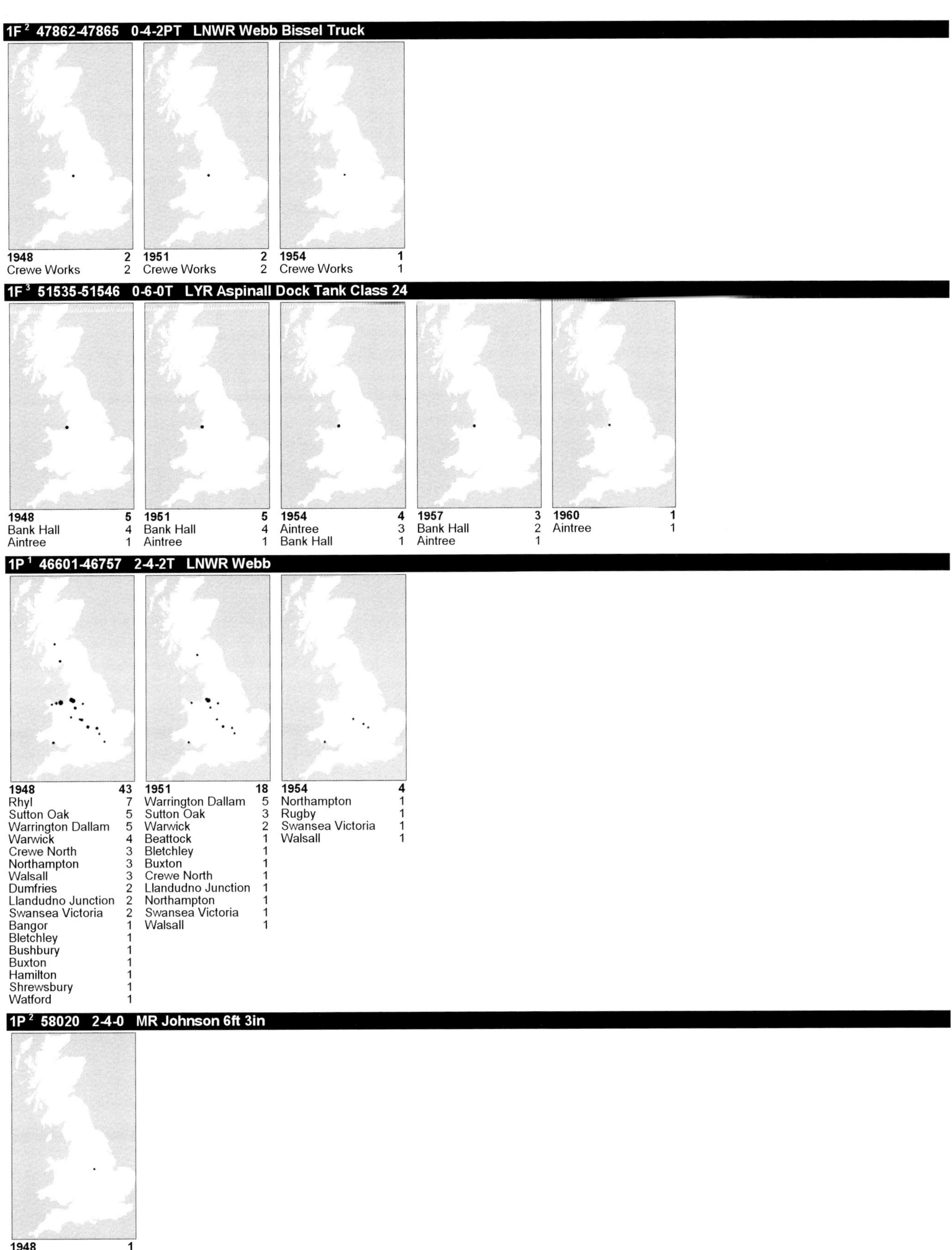

1F[2] 47862-47865 0-4-2PT LNWR Webb Bissel Truck

1948	2
Crewe Works	2

1951	2
Crewe Works	2

1954	1
Crewe Works	1

1F[3] 51535-51546 0-6-0T LYR Aspinall Dock Tank Class 24

1948	5
Bank Hall	4
Aintree	1

1951	5
Bank Hall	4
Aintree	1

1954	4
Aintree	3
Bank Hall	1

1957	3
Bank Hall	2
Aintree	1

1960	1
Aintree	1

1P[1] 46601-46757 2-4-2T LNWR Webb

1948	43
Rhyl	7
Sutton Oak	5
Warrington Dallam	5
Warwick	4
Crewe North	3
Northampton	3
Walsall	3
Dumfries	2
Llandudno Junction	2
Swansea Victoria	2
Bangor	1
Bletchley	1
Bushbury	1
Buxton	1
Hamilton	1
Shrewsbury	1
Watford	1

1951	18
Warrington Dallam	5
Sutton Oak	3
Warwick	2
Beattock	1
Bletchley	1
Buxton	1
Crewe North	1
Llandudno Junction	1
Northampton	1
Swansea Victoria	1
Walsall	1

1954	4
Northampton	1
Rugby	1
Swansea Victoria	1
Walsall	1

1P[2] 58020 2-4-0 MR Johnson 6ft 3in

1948	1
Nottingham	1

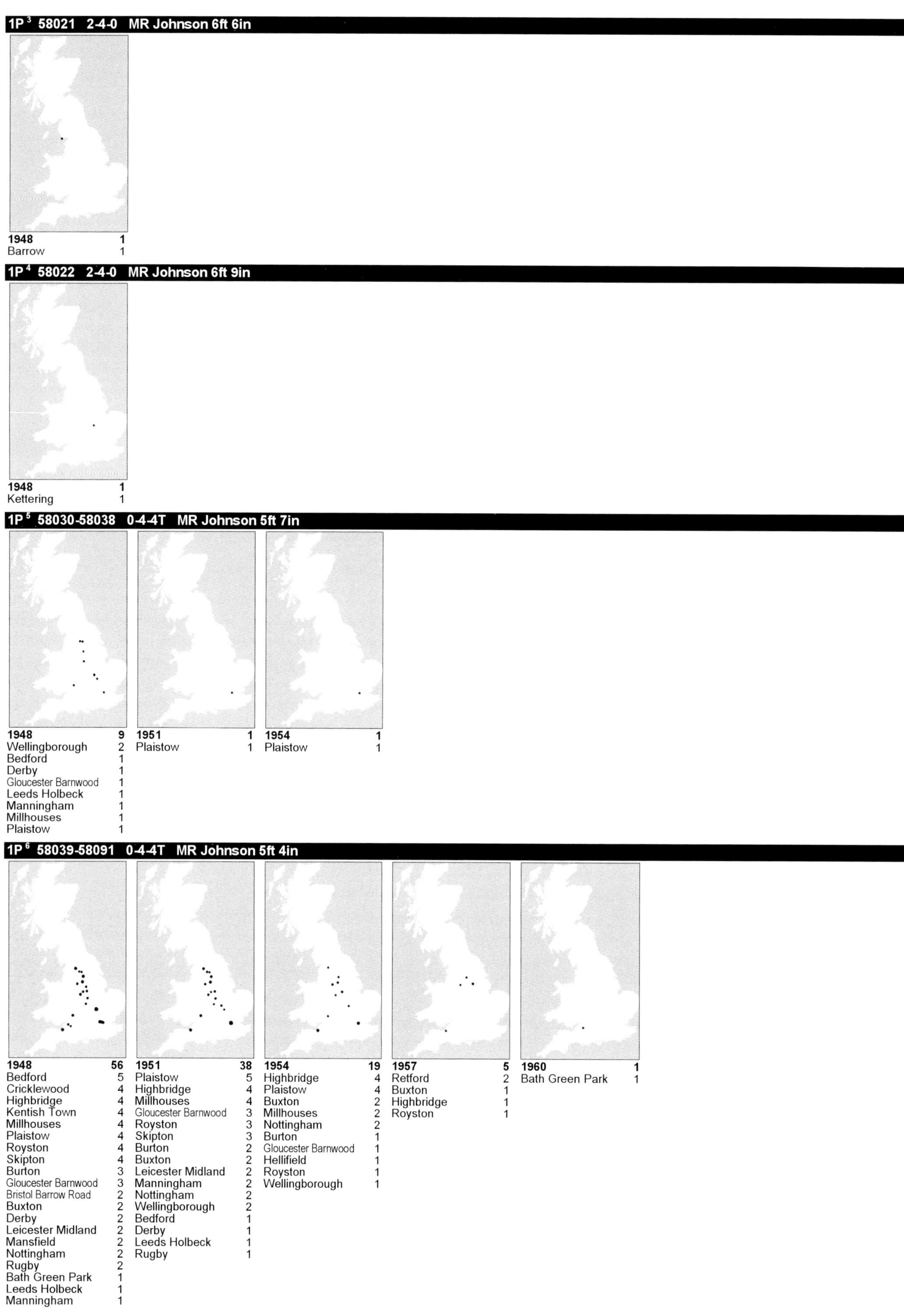

$1P^3$ 58021 2-4-0 MR Johnson 6ft 6in

1948	1
Barrow	1

$1P^4$ 58022 2-4-0 MR Johnson 6ft 9in

1948	1
Kettering	1

$1P^5$ 58030-58038 0-4-4T MR Johnson 5ft 7in

1948	9
Wellingborough	2
Bedford	1
Derby	1
Gloucester Barnwood	1
Leeds Holbeck	1
Manningham	1
Millhouses	1
Plaistow	1

1951	1
Plaistow	1

1954	1
Plaistow	1

$1P^6$ 58039-58091 0-4-4T MR Johnson 5ft 4in

1948	56
Bedford	5
Cricklewood	4
Highbridge	4
Kentish Town	4
Millhouses	4
Plaistow	4
Royston	4
Skipton	4
Burton	3
Gloucester Barnwood	3
Bristol Barrow Road	2
Buxton	2
Derby	2
Leicester Midland	2
Mansfield	2
Nottingham	2
Rugby	2
Bath Green Park	1
Leeds Holbeck	1
Manningham	1

1951	38
Plaistow	5
Highbridge	4
Millhouses	4
Gloucester Barnwood	3
Royston	3
Skipton	3
Burton	2
Buxton	2
Leicester Midland	2
Manningham	2
Nottingham	2
Wellingborough	2
Bedford	1
Derby	1
Leeds Holbeck	1
Rugby	1

1954	19
Highbridge	4
Plaistow	4
Buxton	2
Millhouses	2
Nottingham	2
Burton	1
Gloucester Barnwood	1
Hellifield	1
Royston	1
Wellingborough	1

1957	5
Retford	2
Buxton	1
Highbridge	1
Royston	1

1960	1
Bath Green Park	1

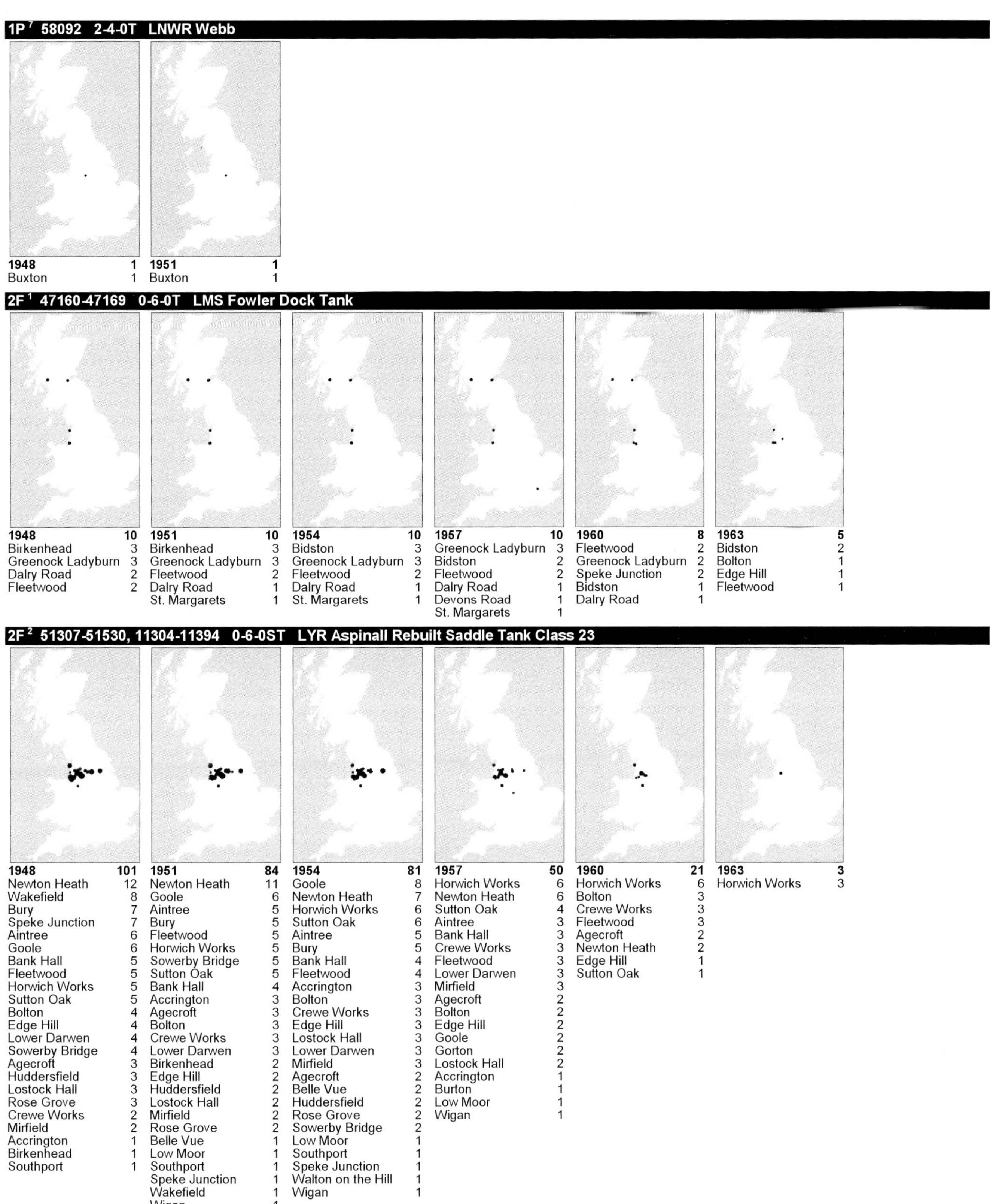

1P [7] 58092 2-4-0T LNWR Webb

1948	1
Buxton	1

1951	1
Buxton	1

2F [1] 47160-47169 0-6-0T LMS Fowler Dock Tank

1948	10
Birkenhead	3
Greenock Ladyburn	3
Dalry Road	2
Fleetwood	2

1951	10
Birkenhead	3
Greenock Ladyburn	3
Fleetwood	2
Dalry Road	1
St. Margarets	1

1954	10
Bidston	3
Greenock Ladyburn	3
Fleetwood	2
Dalry Road	1
St. Margarets	1

1957	10
Greenock Ladyburn	3
Bidston	2
Fleetwood	2
Dalry Road	1
Devons Road	1
St. Margarets	1

1960	8
Fleetwood	2
Greenock Ladyburn	2
Speke Junction	2
Bidston	1
Dalry Road	1

1963	5
Bidston	2
Bolton	1
Edge Hill	1
Fleetwood	1

2F [2] 51307-51530, 11304-11394 0-6-0ST LYR Aspinall Rebuilt Saddle Tank Class 23

1948	101
Newton Heath	12
Wakefield	8
Bury	7
Speke Junction	7
Aintree	6
Goole	6
Bank Hall	5
Fleetwood	5
Horwich Works	5
Sutton Oak	5
Bolton	4
Edge Hill	4
Lower Darwen	4
Sowerby Bridge	4
Agecroft	3
Huddersfield	3
Lostock Hall	3
Rose Grove	3
Crewe Works	2
Mirfield	2
Accrington	1
Birkenhead	1
Southport	1

1951	84
Newton Heath	11
Goole	6
Aintree	5
Bury	5
Fleetwood	5
Horwich Works	5
Sowerby Bridge	5
Sutton Oak	5
Bank Hall	4
Accrington	3
Agecroft	3
Bolton	3
Crewe Works	3
Lower Darwen	3
Birkenhead	2
Edge Hill	2
Huddersfield	2
Lostock Hall	2
Mirfield	2
Rose Grove	2
Belle Vue	1
Low Moor	1
Southport	1
Speke Junction	1
Wakefield	1
Wigan	1

1954	81
Goole	8
Newton Heath	7
Horwich Works	6
Sutton Oak	6
Aintree	5
Bury	5
Bank Hall	4
Fleetwood	4
Accrington	3
Bolton	3
Crewe Works	3
Edge Hill	3
Lostock Hall	3
Lower Darwen	3
Mirfield	3
Agecroft	2
Belle Vue	2
Huddersfield	2
Rose Grove	2
Sowerby Bridge	2
Low Moor	1
Southport	1
Speke Junction	1
Walton on the Hill	1
Wigan	1

1957	50
Horwich Works	6
Newton Heath	6
Sutton Oak	4
Aintree	3
Bank Hall	3
Crewe Works	3
Fleetwood	3
Lower Darwen	3
Mirfield	3
Agecroft	2
Bolton	2
Edge Hill	2
Goole	2
Gorton	2
Lostock Hall	2
Accrington	1
Burton	1
Low Moor	1
Wigan	1

1960	21
Horwich Works	6
Bolton	3
Crewe Works	3
Fleetwood	3
Agecroft	2
Newton Heath	2
Edge Hill	1
Sutton Oak	1

1963	3
Horwich Works	3

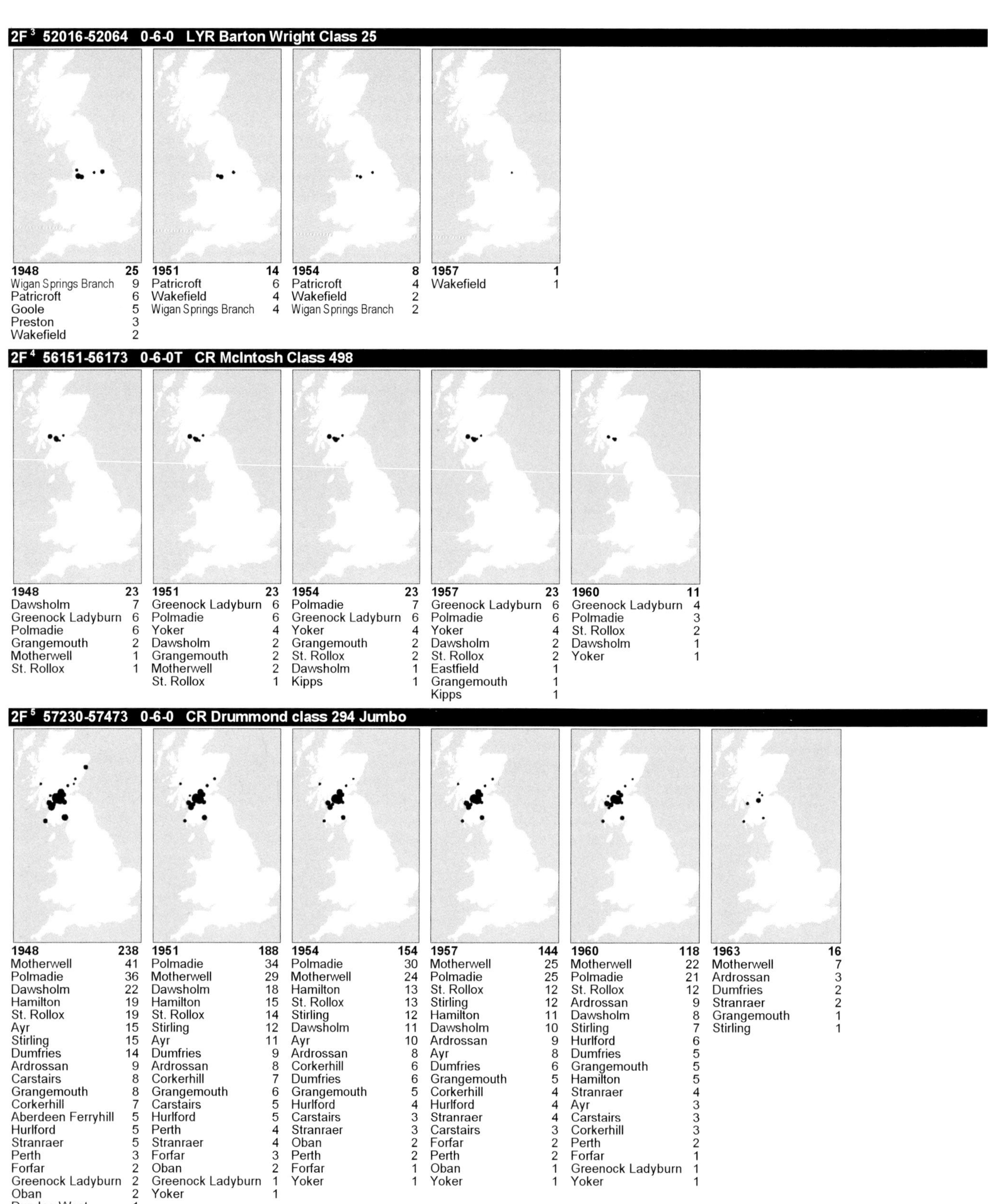

2F[3] 52016-52064 0-6-0 LYR Barton Wright Class 25

1948	25	1951	14	1954	8	1957	1
Wigan Springs Branch	9	Patricroft	6	Patricroft	4	Wakefield	1
Patricroft	6	Wakefield	4	Wakefield	2		
Goole	5	Wigan Springs Branch	4	Wigan Springs Branch	2		
Preston	3						
Wakefield	2						

2F[4] 56151-56173 0-6-0T CR McIntosh Class 498

1948	23	1951	23	1954	23	1957	23	1960	11
Dawsholm	7	Greenock Ladyburn	6	Polmadie	7	Greenock Ladyburn	6	Greenock Ladyburn	4
Greenock Ladyburn	6	Polmadie	6	Greenock Ladyburn	6	Polmadie	6	Polmadie	3
Polmadie	6	Yoker	4	Yoker	4	Yoker	4	St. Rollox	2
Grangemouth	2	Dawsholm	2	Grangemouth	2	Dawsholm	2	Dawsholm	1
Motherwell	1	Grangemouth	2	St. Rollox	2	St. Rollox	2	Yoker	1
St. Rollox	1	Motherwell	2	Dawsholm	1	Eastfield	1		
		St. Rollox	1	Kipps	1	Grangemouth	1		
						Kipps	1		

2F[5] 57230-57473 0-6-0 CR Drummond class 294 Jumbo

1948	238	1951	188	1954	154	1957	144	1960	118	1963	16
Motherwell	41	Polmadie	34	Polmadie	30	Motherwell	25	Motherwell	22	Motherwell	7
Polmadie	36	Motherwell	29	Motherwell	24	Polmadie	25	Polmadie	21	Ardrossan	3
Dawsholm	22	Dawsholm	18	Hamilton	13	St. Rollox	12	St. Rollox	12	Dumfries	2
Hamilton	19	Hamilton	15	St. Rollox	13	Stirling	12	Ardrossan	9	Stranraer	2
St. Rollox	19	St. Rollox	14	Stirling	12	Hamilton	11	Dawsholm	8	Grangemouth	1
Ayr	15	Stirling	12	Dawsholm	11	Dawsholm	10	Stirling	7	Stirling	1
Stirling	15	Ayr	11	Ayr	10	Ardrossan	9	Hurlford	6		
Dumfries	14	Dumfries	9	Ardrossan	8	Ayr	8	Dumfries	5		
Ardrossan	9	Ardrossan	8	Corkerhill	6	Dumfries	6	Grangemouth	5		
Carstairs	8	Corkerhill	7	Dumfries	6	Grangemouth	5	Hamilton	5		
Grangemouth	8	Grangemouth	6	Grangemouth	5	Corkerhill	4	Stranraer	4		
Corkerhill	7	Carstairs	5	Hurlford	4	Hurlford	4	Ayr	3		
Aberdeen Ferryhill	5	Hurlford	5	Carstairs	3	Stranraer	4	Carstairs	3		
Hurlford	5	Perth	4	Stranraer	3	Carstairs	3	Corkerhill	3		
Stranraer	5	Stranraer	4	Oban	2	Forfar	2	Perth	2		
Perth	3	Forfar	3	Perth	2	Perth	2	Forfar	1		
Forfar	2	Oban	2	Forfar	1	Oban	1	Greenock Ladyburn	1		
Greenock Ladyburn	2	Greenock Ladyburn	1	Yoker	1	Yoker	1	Yoker	1		
Oban	2	Yoker	1								
Dundee West	1										

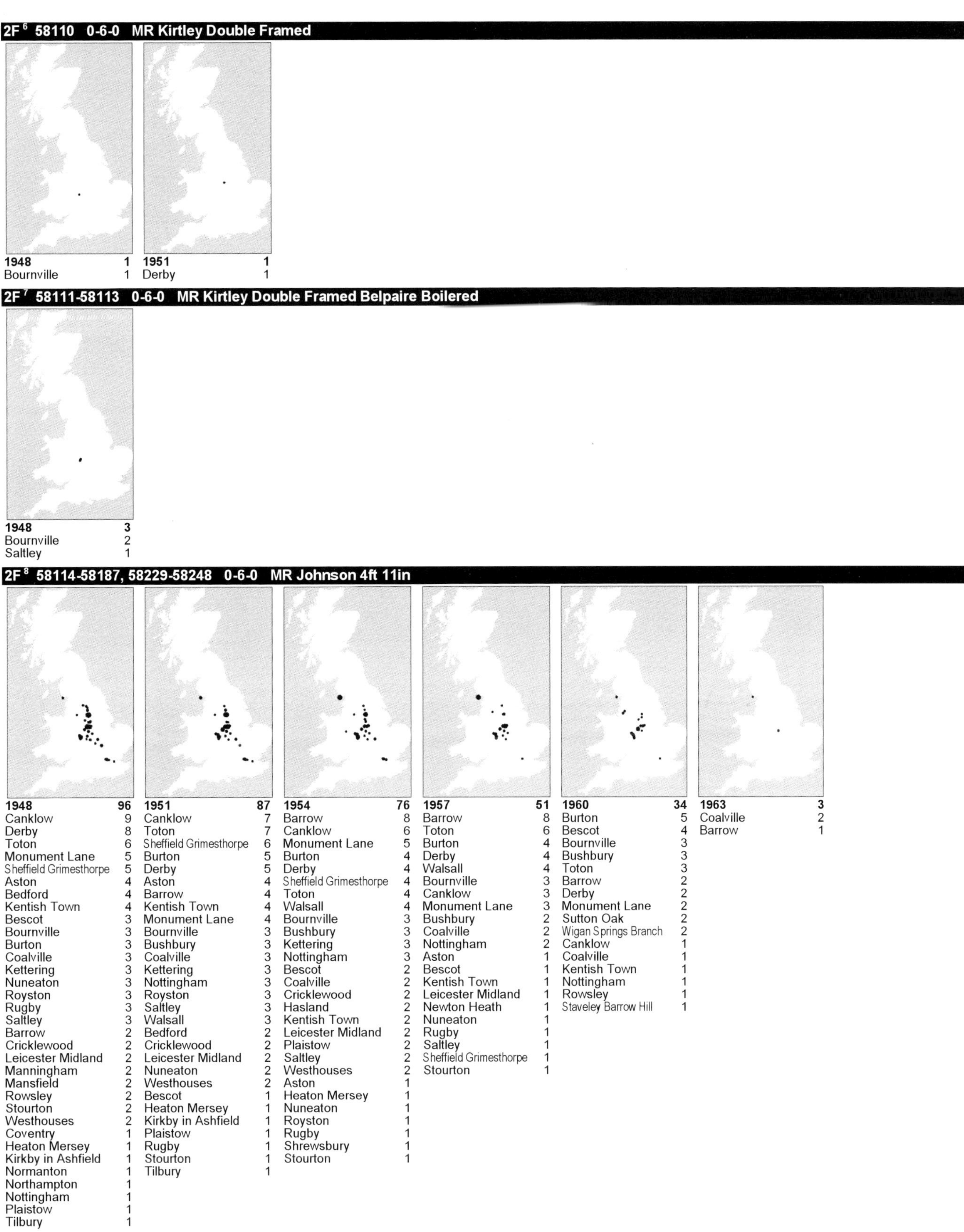

2F[6] 58110 0-6-0 MR Kirtley Double Framed

1948	1
Bournville	1

1951	1
Derby	1

2F[7] 58111-58113 0-6-0 MR Kirtley Double Framed Belpaire Boilered

1948	3
Bournville	2
Saltley	1

2F[8] 58114-58187, 58229-58248 0-6-0 MR Johnson 4ft 11in

1948	96
Canklow	9
Derby	8
Toton	6
Monument Lane	5
Sheffield Grimesthorpe	5
Aston	4
Bedford	4
Kentish Town	4
Bescot	3
Bournville	3
Burton	3
Coalville	3
Kettering	3
Nuneaton	3
Royston	3
Rugby	3
Saltley	3
Barrow	2
Cricklewood	2
Leicester Midland	2
Manningham	2
Mansfield	2
Rowsley	2
Stourton	2
Westhouses	2
Coventry	1
Heaton Mersey	1
Kirkby in Ashfield	1
Normanton	1
Northampton	1
Nottingham	1
Plaistow	1
Tilbury	1

1951	87
Canklow	7
Toton	7
Sheffield Grimesthorpe	6
Burton	5
Derby	5
Aston	4
Barrow	4
Kentish Town	4
Monument Lane	4
Bournville	3
Bushbury	3
Coalville	3
Kettering	3
Nottingham	3
Royston	3
Saltley	3
Walsall	3
Bedford	2
Cricklewood	2
Leicester Midland	2
Nuneaton	2
Westhouses	2
Bescot	1
Heaton Mersey	1
Kirkby in Ashfield	1
Plaistow	1
Rugby	1
Stourton	1
Tilbury	1

1954	76
Barrow	8
Canklow	6
Monument Lane	5
Burton	4
Derby	4
Sheffield Grimesthorpe	4
Toton	4
Walsall	4
Bournville	3
Bushbury	3
Kettering	3
Nottingham	3
Bescot	2
Coalville	2
Cricklewood	2
Hasland	2
Kentish Town	2
Leicester Midland	2
Plaistow	2
Saltley	2
Westhouses	2
Aston	1
Heaton Mersey	1
Nuneaton	1
Royston	1
Rugby	1
Shrewsbury	1
Stourton	1

1957	51
Barrow	8
Toton	6
Burton	4
Derby	4
Walsall	4
Bournville	3
Canklow	3
Monument Lane	3
Bushbury	2
Coalville	2
Nottingham	2
Aston	1
Bescot	1
Kentish Town	1
Leicester Midland	1
Newton Heath	1
Nuneaton	1
Rugby	1
Saltley	1
Sheffield Grimesthorpe	1
Stourton	1

1960	34
Burton	5
Bescot	4
Bournville	3
Bushbury	3
Toton	3
Barrow	2
Derby	2
Monument Lane	2
Sutton Oak	2
Wigan Springs Branch	2
Canklow	1
Coalville	1
Kentish Town	1
Nottingham	1
Rowsley	1
Staveley Barrow Hill	1

1963	3
Coalville	2
Barrow	1

2F^{9} 58188-58228, 58249-58310 0-6-0 MR Johnson 5ft 3in

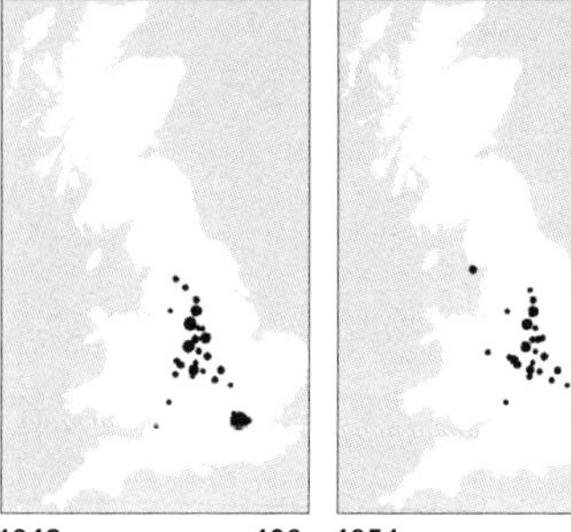

1948	109
Willesden	19
Rowsley	10
Burton	8
Sheffield Grimesthorpe	6
Coventry	5
Nottingham	5
Cricklewood	4
Derby	4
Kettering	4
Leicester Midland	4
Canklow	3
Northampton	3
Plaistow	3
Royston	3
Saltley	3
Bescot	2
Bromsgrove	2
Coalville	2
Kentish Town	2
Manningham	2
Skipton	2
Aston	1
Bedford	1
Bristol Barrow Road	1
Gloucester Barnwood	1
Heaton Mersey	1
Kirkby in Ashfield	1
Millhouses	1
Monument Lane	1
Nuneaton	1
Rugby	1
Warwick	1
Watford	1
Westhouses	1

1951	79
Rowsley	6
Burton	5
Sheffield Grimesthorpe	5
Barrow	4
Coventry	4
Leicester Midland	4
Bescot	3
Kettering	3
Plaistow	3
Royston	3
Toton	3
Walsall	3
Aston	2
Bushbury	2
Canklow	2
Cricklewood	2
Derby	2
Kentish Town	2
Northampton	2
Nottingham	2
Rugby	2
Saltley	2
Shrewsbury	2
Warwick	2
Bedford	1
Coalville	1
Gloucester Barnwood	1
Heaton Mersey	1
Millhouses	1
Monument Lane	1
Nuneaton	1
Stourton	1
Westhouses	1

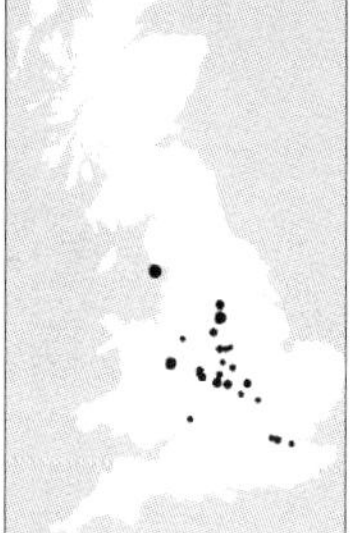

1954	62
Barrow	7
Sheffield Grimesthorpe	5
Shrewsbury	5
Coventry	4
Royston	4
Rugby	4
Kettering	3
Rowsley	3
Walsall	3
Canklow	2
Derby	2
Leicester Midland	2
Nuneaton	2
Plaistow	2
Aston	1
Bedford	1
Bescot	1
Coalville	1
Crewe South	1
Gloucester Barnwood	1
Kentish Town	1
Millhouses	1
Monument Lane	1
Northampton	1
Nottingham	1
Saltley	1
Tilbury	1
Toton	1

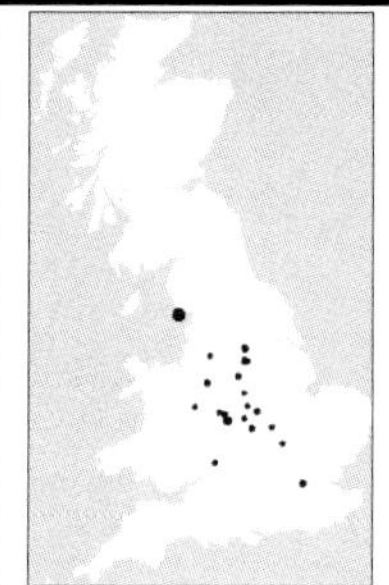

1957	40
Barrow	7
Royston	3
Sheffield Grimesthorpe	3
Aston	2
Crewe South	2
Leicester Midland	2
Monument Lane	2
Plaistow	2
Rowsley	2
Rugby	2
Walsall	2
Bedford	1
Bushbury	1
Canklow	1
Coalville	1
Derby	1
Gloucester Barnwood	1
Kettering	1
Nuneaton	1
Patricroft	1
Saltley	1
Shrewsbury	1

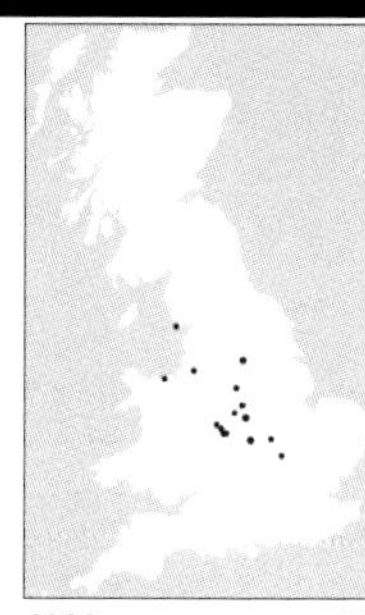

1960	19
Coalville	2
Monument Lane	2
Royston	2
Rugby	2
Barrow	1
Bedford	1
Bescot	1
Burton	1
Bushbury	1
Derby	1
Kettering	1
Rhyl	1
Rowsley	1
Saltley	1
Sutton Oak	1

2F^{10} 58320-58361 0-6-0 LNWR Webb Coal Engine

1948	46
Barrow	12
Walsall	9
Crewe Works	8
Widnes	6
Bushbury	4
Shrewsbury	3
Bescot	2
Carnforth	2

1951	20
Barrow	8
Crewe Works	8
Shrewsbury	4

LNWR Webb '2F' class 'Cauliflower' 0-6-0 No 58412 at Carlisle on 8 May 1950 (see p259). *D. J. Sutton*

2F 11 58362-58430 0-6-0 LNWR Webb 18in Goods "Cauliflower"

1948	75
Workington	14
Penrith	6
Widnes	6
Crewe South	4
Nuneaton	4
Shrewsbury	4
Sutton Oak	4
Wigan Springs Branch	4
Aston	3
Bangor	3
Llandudno Junction	3
Birkenhead	2
Bushbury	2
Rhyl	2
Stockport Edgeley	2
Stoke	2
Swansea Victoria	2
Walsall	2
Warwick	2
Chester	1
Crewe North	1
Mold Junction	1
Monument Lane	1

1951	31
Widnes	6
Llandudno Junction	3
Stoke	3
Sutton Oak	3
Workington	3
Bangor	2
Carlisle Upperby	2
Crewe South	2
Penrith	2
Rhyl	2
Stockport Edgeley	2
Wigan Springs Branch	1

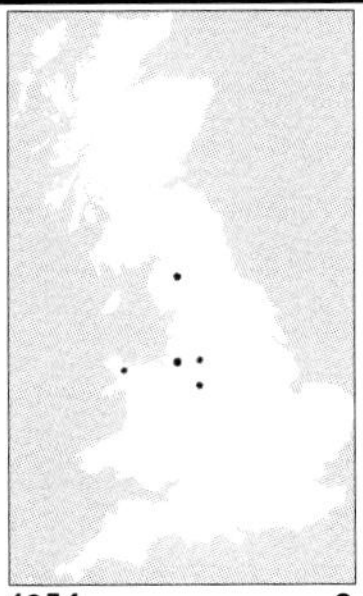

1954	9
Widnes	3
Penrith	2
Stoke	2
Bangor	1
Stockport Edgeley	1

2F 12 58850-58863 0-6-0T North London Railway (Park)

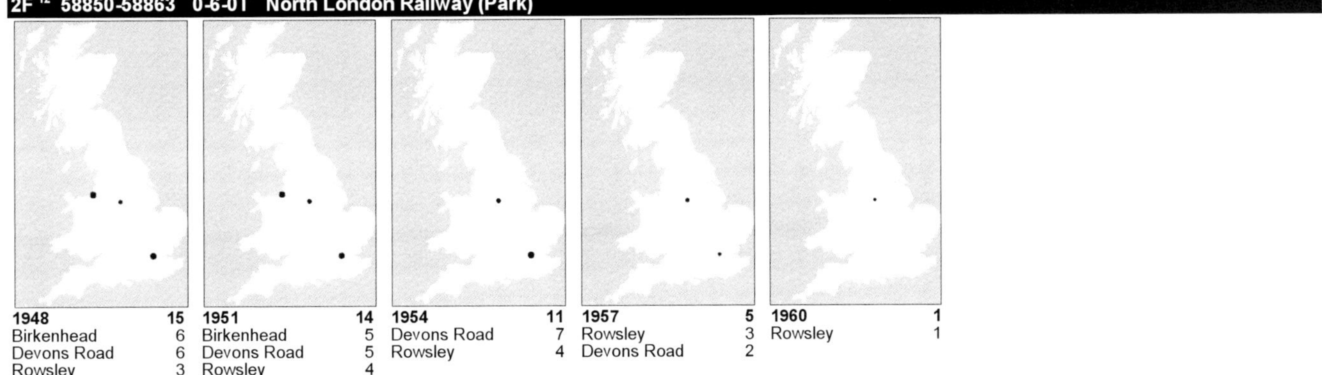

1948	15
Birkenhead	6
Devons Road	6
Rowsley	3

1951	14
Birkenhead	5
Devons Road	5
Rowsley	4

1954	11
Devons Road	7
Rowsley	4

1957	5
Rowsley	3
Devons Road	2

1960	1
Rowsley	1

2F 13 58870 0-6-0ST LNWR Webb Saddle Tank

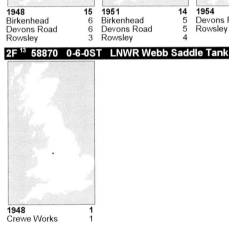

1948	1
Crewe Works	1

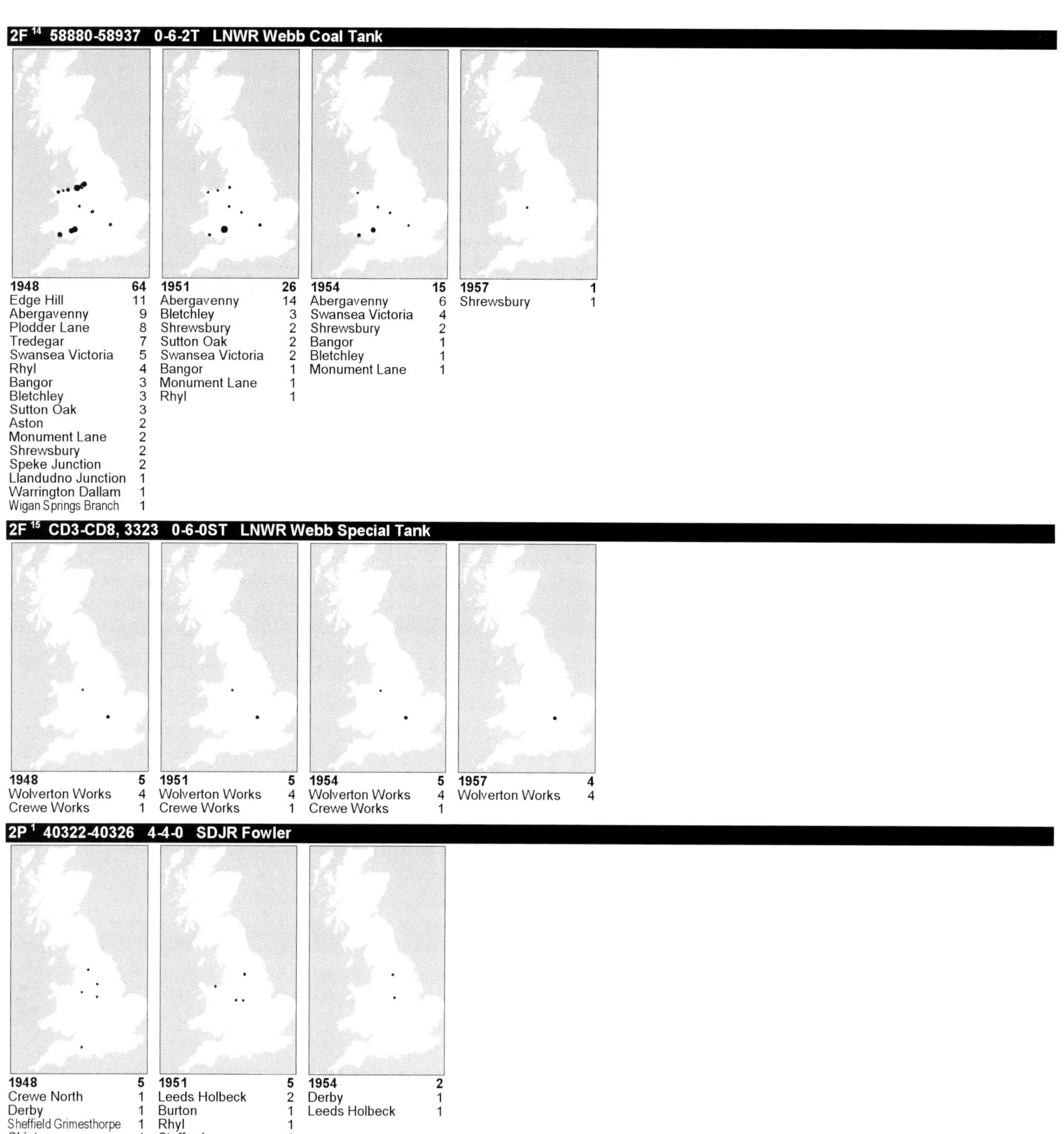

2F [14] 58880-58937 0-6-2T LNWR Webb Coal Tank

1948	64
Edge Hill	11
Abergavenny	9
Plodder Lane	8
Tredegar	7
Swansea Victoria	5
Rhyl	4
Bangor	3
Bletchley	3
Sutton Oak	3
Aston	2
Monument Lane	2
Shrewsbury	2
Speke Junction	2
Llandudno Junction	1
Warrington Dallam	1
Wigan Springs Branch	1

1951	26
Abergavenny	14
Bletchley	3
Shrewsbury	2
Sutton Oak	2
Swansea Victoria	2
Bangor	1
Monument Lane	1
Rhyl	1

1954	15
Abergavenny	6
Swansea Victoria	4
Shrewsbury	2
Bangor	1
Bletchley	1
Monument Lane	1

1957	1
Shrewsbury	1

2F [15] CD3-CD8, 3323 0-6-0ST LNWR Webb Special Tank

1948	5
Wolverton Works	4
Crewe Works	1

1951	5
Wolverton Works	4
Crewe Works	1

1954	5
Wolverton Works	4
Crewe Works	1

1957	4
Wolverton Works	4

2P [1] 40322-40326 4-4-0 SDJR Fowler

1948	5
Crewe North	1
Derby	1
Sheffield Grimesthorpe	1
Skipton	1
Templecombe	1

1951	5
Leeds Holbeck	2
Burton	1
Rhyl	1
Stafford	1

1954	2
Derby	1
Leeds Holbeck	1

2P[2] 40332-40562 4-4-0 MR Johnson/Fowler

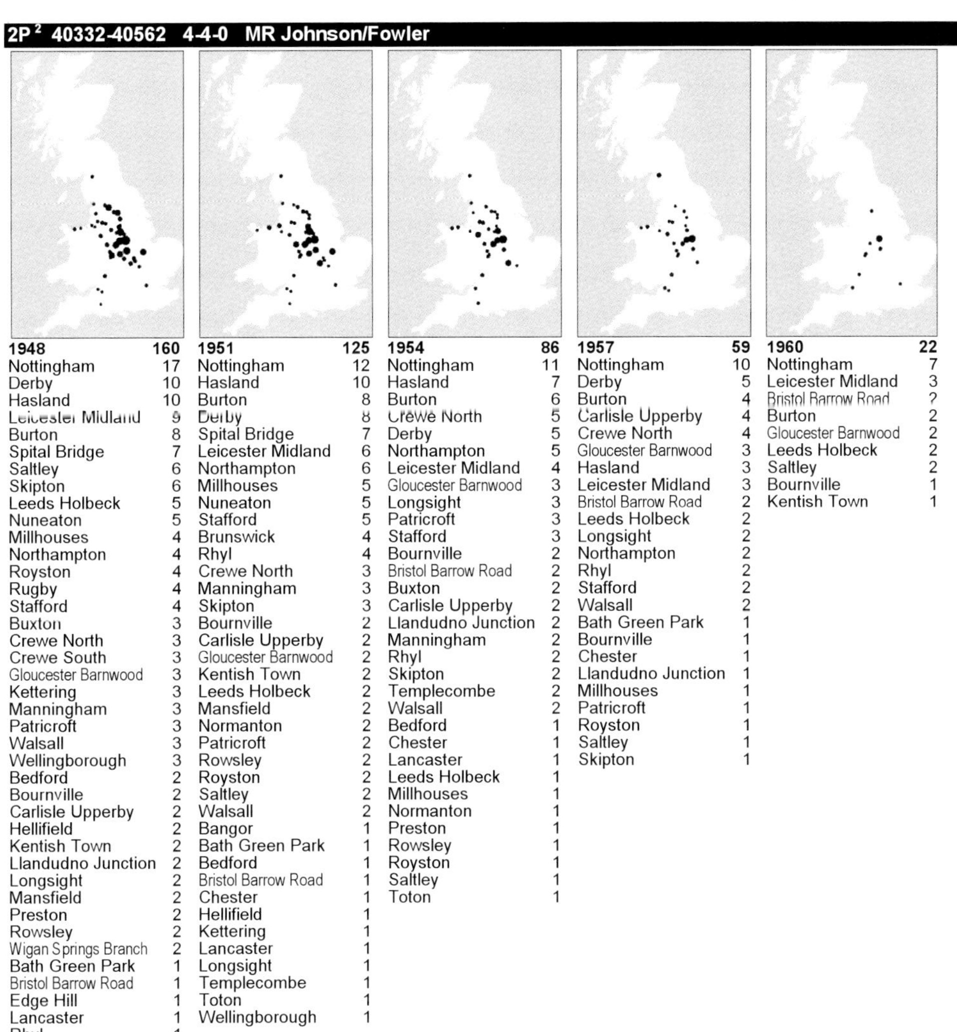

1948	160
Nottingham	17
Derby	10
Hasland	10
Leicester Midland	9
Burton	8
Spital Bridge	7
Saltley	6
Skipton	6
Leeds Holbeck	5
Nuneaton	5
Millhouses	4
Northampton	4
Royston	4
Rugby	4
Stafford	4
Buxton	3
Crewe North	3
Crewe South	3
Gloucester Barnwood	3
Kettering	3
Manningham	3
Patricroft	3
Walsall	3
Wellingborough	3
Bedford	2
Bournville	2
Carlisle Upperby	2
Hellifield	2
Kentish Town	2
Llandudno Junction	2
Longsight	2
Mansfield	2
Preston	2
Rowsley	2
Wigan Springs Branch	2
Bath Green Park	1
Bristol Barrow Road	1
Edge Hill	1
Lancaster	1
Rhyl	1
Sheffield Grimesthorpe	1
Templecombe	1
Widnes	1

1951	125
Nottingham	12
Hasland	10
Burton	8
Derby	8
Spital Bridge	7
Leicester Midland	6
Northampton	6
Millhouses	5
Nuneaton	5
Stafford	5
Brunswick	4
Rhyl	4
Crewe North	3
Manningham	3
Skipton	3
Bournville	2
Carlisle Upperby	2
Gloucester Barnwood	2
Kentish Town	2
Leeds Holbeck	2
Mansfield	2
Normanton	2
Patricroft	2
Rowsley	2
Royston	2
Saltley	2
Walsall	2
Bangor	1
Bath Green Park	1
Bedford	1
Bristol Barrow Road	1
Chester	1
Hellifield	1
Kettering	1
Lancaster	1
Longsight	1
Templecombe	1
Toton	1
Wellingborough	1

1954	86
Nottingham	11
Hasland	7
Burton	6
Crewe North	5
Derby	5
Northampton	5
Leicester Midland	4
Gloucester Barnwood	3
Longsight	3
Patricroft	3
Stafford	3
Bournville	2
Bristol Barrow Road	2
Buxton	2
Carlisle Upperby	2
Llandudno Junction	2
Manningham	2
Rhyl	2
Skipton	2
Templecombe	2
Walsall	2
Bedford	1
Chester	1
Lancaster	1
Leeds Holbeck	1
Millhouses	1
Normanton	1
Preston	1
Rowsley	1
Royston	1
Saltley	1
Toton	1

1957	59
Nottingham	10
Derby	5
Burton	4
Carlisle Upperby	4
Crewe North	4
Gloucester Barnwood	3
Hasland	3
Leicester Midland	3
Bristol Barrow Road	2
Leeds Holbeck	2
Longsight	2
Northampton	2
Rhyl	2
Stafford	2
Walsall	2
Bath Green Park	1
Bournville	1
Chester	1
Llandudno Junction	1
Millhouses	1
Patricroft	1
Royston	1
Saltley	1
Skipton	1

1960	22
Nottingham	7
Leicester Midland	3
Bristol Barrow Road	2
Burton	2
Gloucester Barnwood	2
Leeds Holbeck	2
Saltley	2
Bournville	1
Kentish Town	1

Midland Railway Fowler '2P' class 4-4-0 No 40522 on 7 May 1949 at Nottingham Victoria on a Northampton Train. *J. F. Henton*

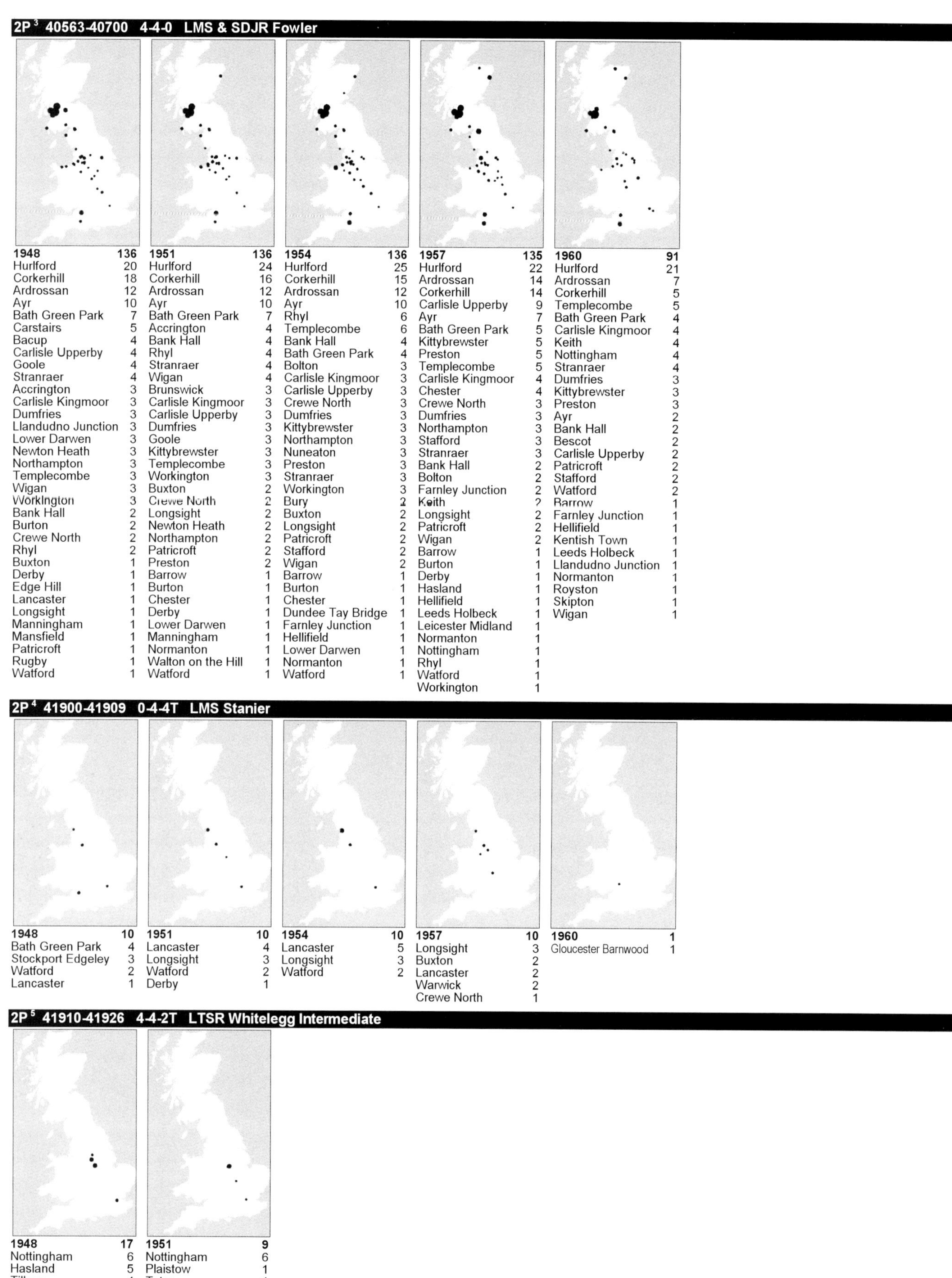

2P[3] 40563-40700 4-4-0 LMS & SDJR Fowler

1948	136
Hurlford	20
Corkerhill	18
Ardrossan	12
Ayr	10
Bath Green Park	7
Carstairs	5
Bacup	4
Carlisle Upperby	4
Goole	4
Stranraer	4
Accrington	3
Carlisle Kingmoor	3
Dumfries	3
Llandudno Junction	3
Lower Darwen	3
Newton Heath	3
Northampton	3
Templecombe	3
Wigan	3
Workington	3
Bank Hall	2
Burton	2
Crewe North	2
Rhyl	2
Buxton	1
Derby	1
Edge Hill	1
Lancaster	1
Longsight	1
Manningham	1
Mansfield	1
Patricroft	1
Rugby	1
Watford	1

1951	136
Hurlford	24
Corkerhill	16
Ardrossan	12
Ayr	10
Bath Green Park	7
Accrington	4
Bank Hall	4
Rhyl	4
Stranraer	4
Wigan	4
Brunswick	3
Carlisle Kingmoor	3
Carlisle Upperby	3
Dumfries	3
Goole	3
Kittybrewster	3
Templecombe	3
Workington	3
Buxton	2
Crewe North	2
Longsight	2
Newton Heath	2
Northampton	2
Patricroft	2
Preston	2
Barrow	1
Burton	1
Chester	1
Derby	1
Lower Darwen	1
Manningham	1
Normanton	1
Walton on the Hill	1
Watford	1

1954	136
Hurlford	25
Corkerhill	15
Ardrossan	12
Ayr	10
Rhyl	6
Templecombe	6
Bank Hall	4
Bath Green Park	4
Bolton	3
Carlisle Kingmoor	3
Carlisle Upperby	3
Crewe North	3
Dumfries	3
Kittybrewster	3
Northampton	3
Nuneaton	3
Preston	3
Stranraer	3
Workington	3
Bury	2
Buxton	2
Longsight	2
Patricroft	2
Stafford	2
Wigan	2
Barrow	1
Burton	1
Chester	1
Dundee Tay Bridge	1
Farnley Junction	1
Hellifield	1
Lower Darwen	1
Normanton	1
Watford	1

1957	135
Hurlford	22
Ardrossan	14
Corkerhill	14
Carlisle Upperby	9
Ayr	7
Bath Green Park	5
Kittybrewster	5
Preston	5
Templecombe	5
Carlisle Kingmoor	4
Chester	4
Crewe North	3
Dumfries	3
Northampton	3
Stafford	3
Stranraer	3
Bank Hall	2
Bolton	2
Farnley Junction	2
Keith	2
Longsight	2
Patricroft	2
Wigan	2
Barrow	1
Burton	1
Derby	1
Hasland	1
Hellifield	1
Leeds Holbeck	1
Leicester Midland	1
Normanton	1
Nottingham	1
Rhyl	1
Watford	1
Workington	1

1960	91
Hurlford	21
Ardrossan	7
Corkerhill	5
Templecombe	5
Bath Green Park	4
Carlisle Kingmoor	4
Keith	4
Nottingham	4
Stranraer	4
Dumfries	3
Kittybrewster	3
Preston	3
Ayr	2
Bank Hall	2
Bescot	2
Carlisle Upperby	2
Patricroft	2
Stafford	2
Watford	2
Barrow	1
Farnley Junction	1
Hellifield	1
Kentish Town	1
Leeds Holbeck	1
Llandudno Junction	1
Normanton	1
Royston	1
Skipton	1
Wigan	1

2P[4] 41900-41909 0-4-4T LMS Stanier

1948	10
Bath Green Park	4
Stockport Edgeley	3
Watford	2
Lancaster	1

1951	10
Lancaster	4
Longsight	3
Watford	2
Derby	1

1954	10
Lancaster	5
Longsight	3
Watford	2

1957	10
Longsight	3
Buxton	2
Lancaster	2
Warwick	2
Crewe North	1

1960	1
Gloucester Barnwood	1

2P[5] 41910-41926 4-4-2T LTSR Whitelegg Intermediate

1948	17
Nottingham	6
Hasland	5
Tilbury	4
Canklow	2

1951	9
Nottingham	6
Plaistow	1
Toton	1
Wellingborough	1

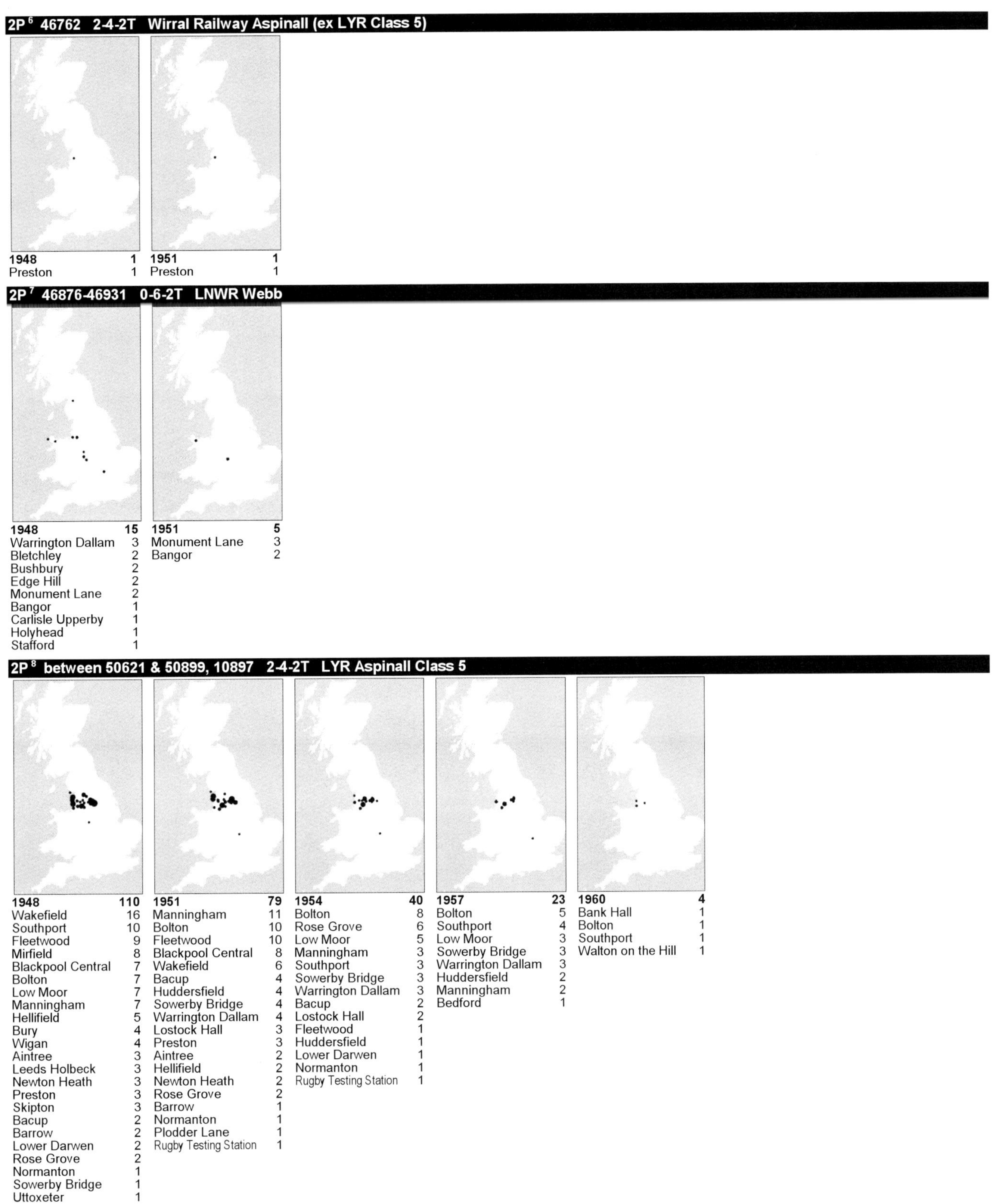

2P[6] 46762 2-4-2T Wirral Railway Aspinall (ex LYR Class 5)

1948	1
Preston	1

1951	1
Preston	1

2P[7] 46876-46931 0-6-2T LNWR Webb

1948	15
Warrington Dallam	3
Bletchley	2
Bushbury	2
Edge Hill	2
Monument Lane	2
Bangor	1
Carlisle Upperby	1
Holyhead	1
Stafford	1

1951	5
Monument Lane	3
Bangor	2

2P[8] between 50621 & 50899, 10897 2-4-2T LYR Aspinall Class 5

1948	110
Wakefield	16
Southport	10
Fleetwood	9
Mirfield	8
Blackpool Central	7
Bolton	7
Low Moor	7
Manningham	7
Hellifield	5
Bury	4
Wigan	4
Aintree	3
Leeds Holbeck	3
Newton Heath	3
Preston	3
Skipton	3
Bacup	2
Barrow	2
Lower Darwen	2
Rose Grove	2
Normanton	1
Sowerby Bridge	1
Uttoxeter	1

1951	79
Manningham	11
Bolton	10
Fleetwood	10
Blackpool Central	8
Wakefield	6
Bacup	4
Huddersfield	4
Sowerby Bridge	4
Warrington Dallam	4
Lostock Hall	3
Preston	3
Aintree	2
Hellifield	2
Newton Heath	2
Rose Grove	2
Barrow	1
Normanton	1
Plodder Lane	1
Rugby Testing Station	1

1954	40
Bolton	8
Rose Grove	6
Low Moor	5
Manningham	3
Southport	3
Sowerby Bridge	3
Warrington Dallam	3
Bacup	2
Lostock Hall	2
Fleetwood	1
Huddersfield	1
Lower Darwen	1
Normanton	1
Rugby Testing Station	1

1957	23
Bolton	5
Southport	4
Low Moor	3
Sowerby Bridge	3
Warrington Dallam	3
Huddersfield	2
Manningham	2
Bedford	1

1960	4
Bank Hall	1
Bolton	1
Southport	1
Walton on the Hill	1

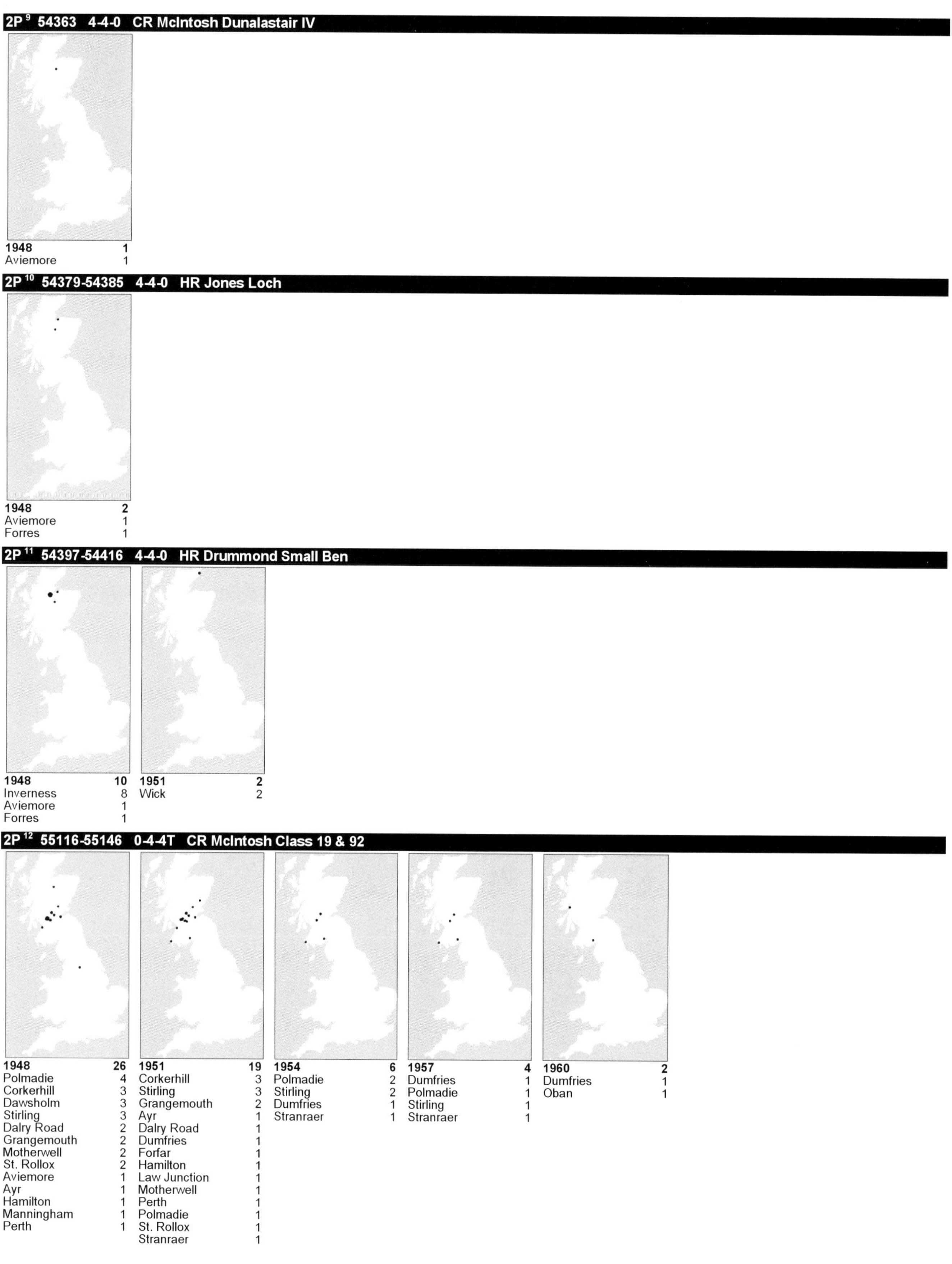

2P[9] 54363 4-4-0 CR McIntosh Dunalastair IV

1948	1
Aviemore	1

2P[10] 54379-54385 4-4-0 HR Jones Loch

1948	2
Aviemore	1
Forres	1

2P[11] 54397-54416 4-4-0 HR Drummond Small Ben

1948	10	1951	2
Inverness	8	Wick	2
Aviemore	1		
Forres	1		

2P[12] 55116-55146 0-4-4T CR McIntosh Class 19 & 92

1948	26	1951	19	1954	6	1957	4	1960	2
Polmadie	4	Corkerhill	3	Polmadie	2	Dumfries	1	Dumfries	1
Corkerhill	3	Stirling	3	Stirling	2	Polmadie	1	Oban	1
Dawsholm	3	Grangemouth	2	Dumfries	1	Stirling	1		
Stirling	3	Ayr	1	Stranraer	1	Stranraer	1		
Dalry Road	2	Dalry Road	1						
Grangemouth	2	Dumfries	1						
Motherwell	2	Forfar	1						
St. Rollox	2	Hamilton	1						
Aviemore	1	Law Junction	1						
Ayr	1	Motherwell	1						
Hamilton	1	Perth	1						
Manningham	1	Polmadie	1						
Perth	1	St. Rollox	1						
		Stranraer	1						

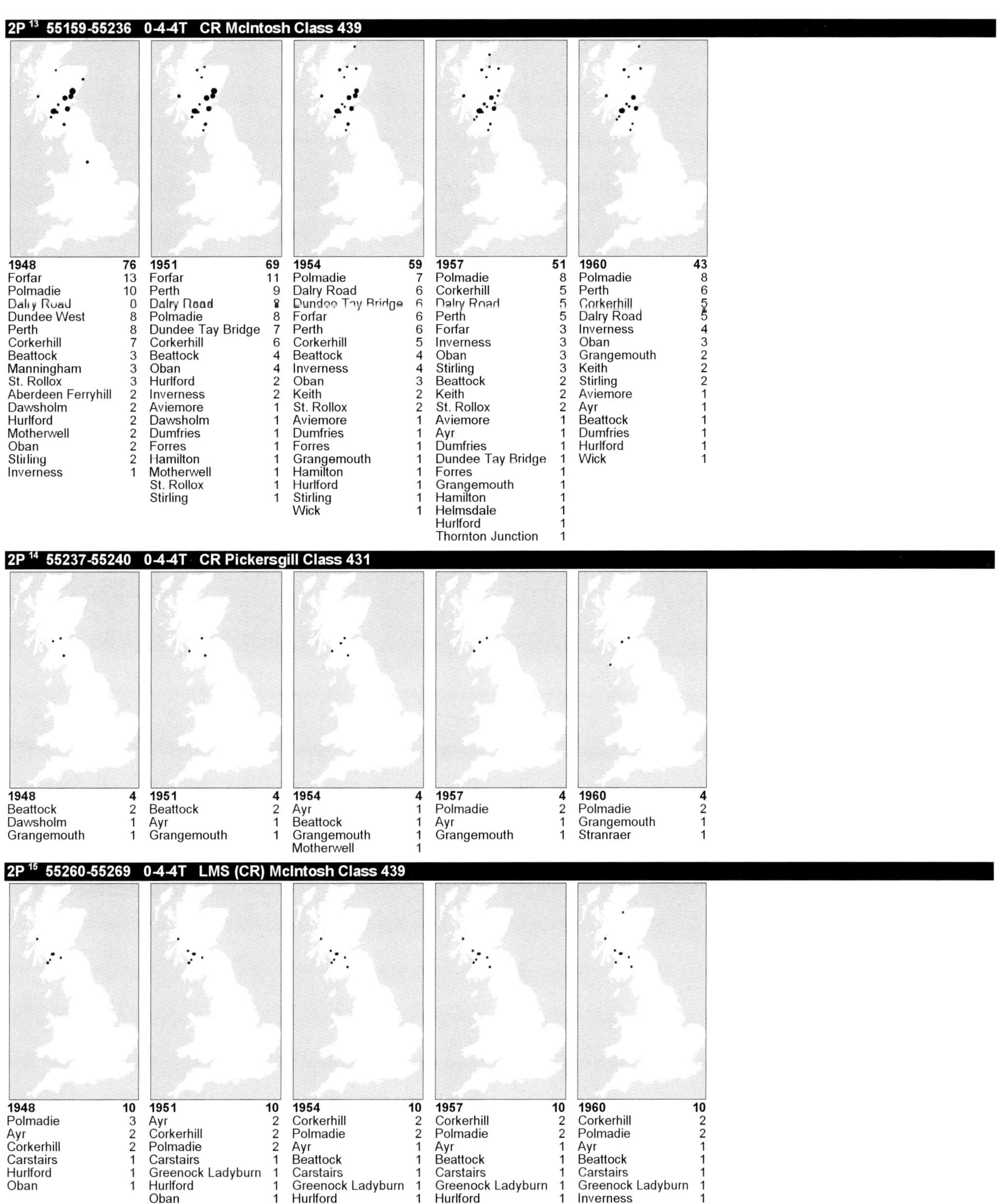

2P [13] 55159-55236 0-4-4T CR McIntosh Class 439

1948	76	1951	69	1954	59	1957	51	1960	43
Forfar	13	Forfar	11	Polmadie	7	Polmadie	8	Polmadie	8
Polmadie	10	Perth	9	Dalry Road	6	Corkerhill	5	Perth	6
Dalry Road	8	Dalry Road	8	Dundee Tay Bridge	6	Dalry Road	5	Corkerhill	5
Dundee West	8	Polmadie	8	Forfar	6	Perth	5	Dalry Road	5
Perth	8	Dundee Tay Bridge	7	Perth	6	Forfar	3	Inverness	4
Corkerhill	7	Corkerhill	6	Corkerhill	5	Inverness	3	Oban	3
Beattock	3	Beattock	4	Beattock	4	Oban	3	Grangemouth	2
Manningham	3	Oban	4	Inverness	4	Stirling	3	Keith	2
St. Rollox	3	Hurlford	2	Oban	3	Beattock	2	Stirling	2
Aberdeen Ferryhill	2	Inverness	2	Keith	2	Keith	2	Aviemore	1
Dawsholm	2	Aviemore	1	St. Rollox	2	St. Rollox	2	Ayr	1
Hurlford	2	Dawsholm	1	Aviemore	1	Aviemore	1	Beattock	1
Motherwell	2	Dumfries	1	Dumfries	1	Ayr	1	Dumfries	1
Oban	2	Forres	1	Forres	1	Dumfries	1	Hurlford	1
Stirling	2	Hamilton	1	Grangemouth	1	Dundee Tay Bridge	1	Wick	1
Inverness	1	Motherwell	1	Hamilton	1	Forres	1		
		St. Rollox	1	Hurlford	1	Grangemouth	1		
		Stirling	1	Stirling	1	Hamilton	1		
				Wick	1	Helmsdale	1		
						Hurlford	1		
						Thornton Junction	1		

2P [14] 55237-55240 0-4-4T CR Pickersgill Class 431

1948	4	1951	4	1954	4	1957	4	1960	4
Beattock	2	Beattock	2	Ayr	1	Polmadie	2	Polmadie	2
Dawsholm	1	Ayr	1	Beattock	1	Ayr	1	Grangemouth	1
Grangemouth	1	Grangemouth	1	Grangemouth	1	Grangemouth	1	Stranraer	1
				Motherwell	1				

2P [15] 55260-55269 0-4-4T LMS (CR) McIntosh Class 439

1948	10	1951	10	1954	10	1957	10	1960	10
Polmadie	3	Ayr	2	Corkerhill	2	Corkerhill	2	Corkerhill	2
Ayr	2	Corkerhill	2	Polmadie	2	Polmadie	2	Polmadie	2
Corkerhill	2	Polmadie	2	Ayr	1	Ayr	1	Ayr	1
Carstairs	1	Carstairs	1	Beattock	1	Beattock	1	Beattock	1
Hurlford	1	Greenock Ladyburn	1	Carstairs	1	Carstairs	1	Carstairs	1
Oban	1	Hurlford	1	Greenock Ladyburn	1	Greenock Ladyburn	1	Greenock Ladyburn	1
		Oban	1	Hurlford	1	Hurlford	1	Inverness	1
				Oban	1	Oban	1	Oban	1

2MT[1] 41200-41329 2-6-2T LMS Ivatt

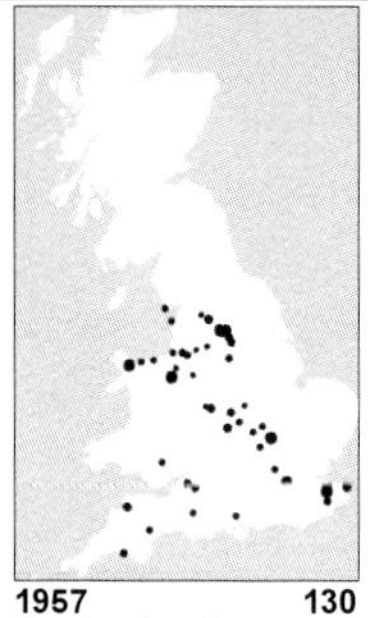
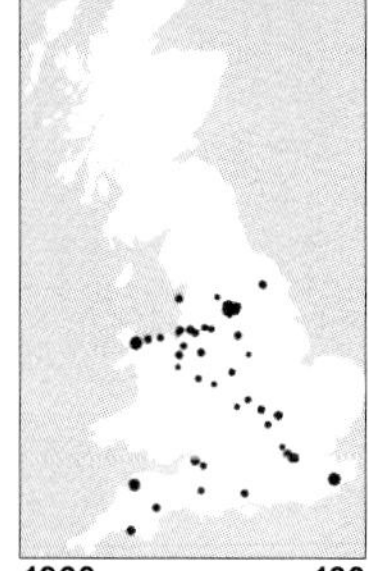
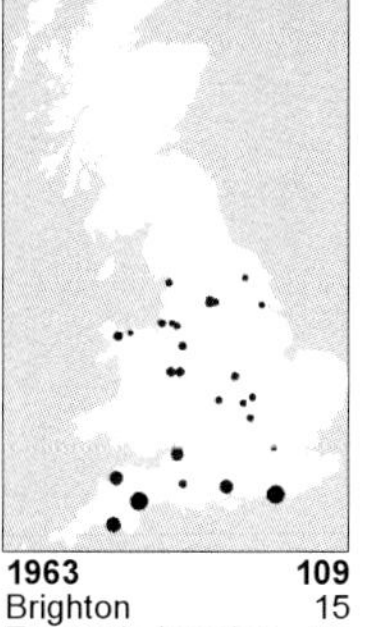
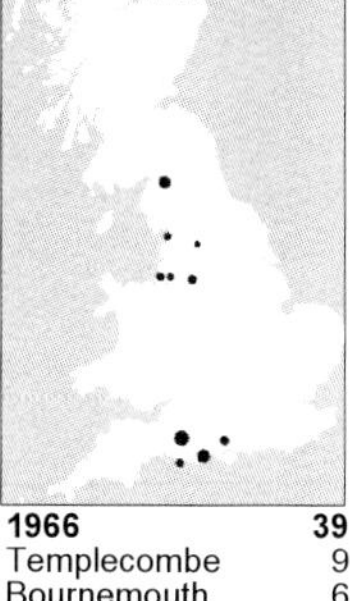

1948	10
Abergavenny	2
Bangor	2
Hellifield	2
Kentish Town	2
Bedford	1
Tredegar	1

1951	90
Plodder Lane	8
Wakefield	7
Fleetwood	6
Bedford	5
Farnley Junction	5
Nuneaton	5
Abergavenny	4
Bangor	4
Bath Green Park	4
Crewe North	3
Rhyl	3
Sutton Oak	3
Warwick	3
Blackpool Central	2
Bletchley	2
Cricklewood	2
Hellifield	2
Kentish Town	2
Manningham	2
Millhouses	2
Northampton	2
Royston	2
Walsall	2
Barrow	1
Burton	1
Bushbury	1
Derby	1
Leeds Holbeck	1
Leicester Midland	1
Llandudno Junction	1
Rugby	1
Watford	1
Wellingborough	1

1954	130
Bangor	6
Fleetwood	6
Stewarts Lane	6
Wakefield	6
Bedford	5
Chester Northgate	5
Faversham	5
Rhyl	5
Abergavenny	4
Bricklayers Arms	4
Farnley Junction	4
Llandudno Junction	4
Three Bridges	4
Tunbridge Wells West	4
Bath Green Park	3
Eastleigh	3
Millhouses	3
Skipton	3
Sutton Oak	3
Warrington Dallam	3
Warwick	3
Aintree	2
Barrow	2
Blackpool Central	2
Bletchley	2
Crewe North	2
Cricklewood	2
Exmouth Junction	2
Hellifield	2
Manningham	2
Northampton	2
Nuneaton	2
Plodder Lane	2
Royston	2
Templecombe	2
Walsall	2
Wellingborough	2
Barnstaple Junction	1
Bristol Barrow Road	1
Bushbury	1
Derby	1
Leeds Holbeck	1
Leicester Midland	1
Plymouth Friary	1
Rugby	1
Watford	1

1957	130
Farnley Junction	6
Faversham	6
Wrexham Rhosddu	6
Bangor	5
Bedford	5
Barnstaple Junction	4
Low Moor	4
Manningham	4
Ramsgate	4
Skipton	4
Walsall	4
Warwick	4
Ashford	3
Bath Green Park	3
Bricklayers Arms	3
Bristol Barrow Road	3
Eastleigh	3
Nuneaton	3
Plymouth Friary	3
Royston	3
Stewarts Lane	3
Sutton Oak	3
Wakefield	3
Warrington Dallam	3
Bank Hall	2
Barrow	2
Bletchley	2
Bristol Bath Road	2
Eastleigh	2
Exmouth Junction	2
Fleetwood	2
Llandudno Junction	2
Northampton	2
Rhyl	2
Rugby	2
Templecombe	2
Tredegar	2
Watford	2
Wellingborough	2
Bushbury	1
Chester Northgate	1
Crewe North	1
Hellifield	1
Leeds Holbeck	1
Lees Oldham	1
Leicester Midland	1
Patricroft	1

1960	130
Bangor	7
Ashford	6
Barnstaple Junction	5
Farnley Junction	5
Low Moor	5
Manningham	5
Bedford	4
Bricklayers Arms	4
Bristol Barrow Road	4
Neasden	4
Plymouth Friary	4
Sutton Oak	4
Bank Hall	3
Bristol Bath Road	3
Crewe North	3
Eastleigh	3
Exmouth Junction	3
Fleetwood	3
Leeds Neville Hill	3
Llandudno Junction	3
Malton	3
Millhouses	3
Northampton	3
Stewarts Lane	3
Warrington Dallam	3
Wrexham Rhosddu	3
Bath Green Park	2
Birkenhead	2
Bletchley	2
Burton	2
Chester Northgate	2
Longsight	2
Patricroft	2
Rhyl	2
Rugby	2
Templecombe	2
Wellington	2
Annesley	1
Bushbury	1
Gorton	1
Leamington Spa	1
Leeds Holbeck	1
Mirfield	1
Oswestry	1
Skipton	1
Watford	1

1963	109
Brighton	15
Exmouth Junction	15
Plymouth Friary	9
Barnstaple Junction	8
Eastleigh	8
Bristol Barrow Road	6
Bangor	4
Shrewsbury	4
Wellington	4
Bank Hall	3
Crewe North	3
Leicester Midland	3
Low Moor	3
Templecombe	3
Bletchley	2
Farnley Junction	2
Lancaster	2
Leamington Spa	2
Manningham	2
Northampton	2
Warrington Dallam	2
Wellingborough	2
Camden	1
Hull Dairycoates	1
Llandudno Junction	1
Malton	1
Sutton Oak	1

1966	39
Templecombe	9
Bournemouth	6
Carlisle Upperby	5
Eastleigh	4
Stockport Edgeley	4
Bank Hall	3
Weymouth	3
Lancaster	2
Sutton Oak	2
Skipton	1

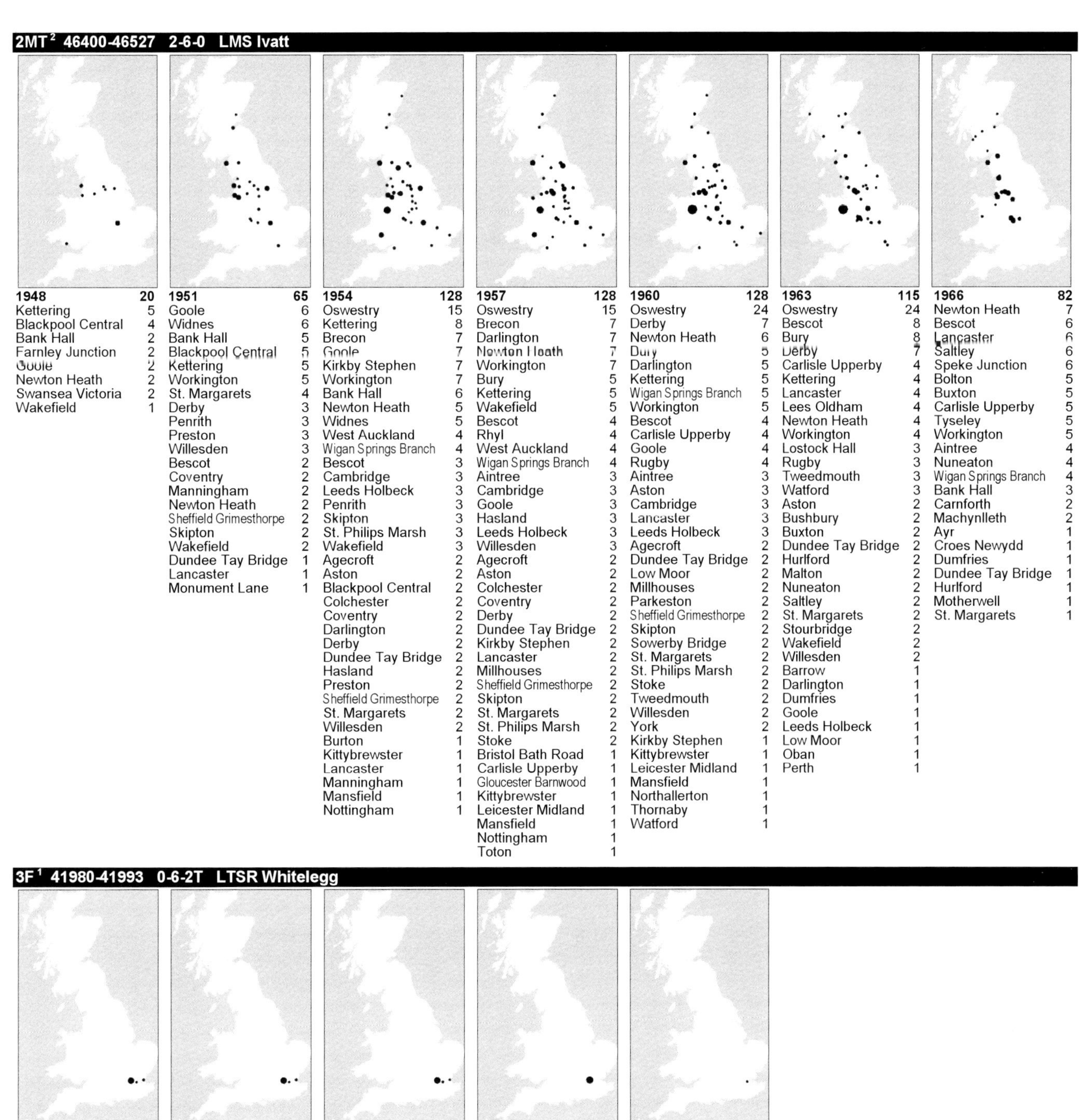

2MT[2] 46400-46527 2-6-0 LMS Ivatt

1948	20
Kettering	5
Blackpool Central	4
Bank Hall	2
Farnley Junction	2
Goole	2
Newton Heath	2
Swansea Victoria	2
Wakefield	1

1951	65
Goole	6
Widnes	6
Bank Hall	5
Blackpool Central	5
Kettering	5
Workington	5
St. Margarets	4
Derby	3
Penrith	3
Preston	3
Willesden	3
Bescot	2
Coventry	2
Manningham	2
Newton Heath	2
Sheffield Grimesthorpe	2
Skipton	2
Wakefield	2
Dundee Tay Bridge	1
Lancaster	1
Monument Lane	1

1954	128
Oswestry	15
Kettering	8
Brecon	7
Goole	7
Kirkby Stephen	7
Workington	7
Bank Hall	6
Newton Heath	5
Widnes	5
West Auckland	4
Wigan Springs Branch	4
Bescot	3
Cambridge	3
Leeds Holbeck	3
Penrith	3
Skipton	3
St. Philips Marsh	3
Wakefield	3
Agecroft	2
Aston	2
Blackpool Central	2
Colchester	2
Coventry	2
Darlington	2
Derby	2
Dundee Tay Bridge	2
Hasland	2
Preston	2
Sheffield Grimesthorpe	2
St. Margarets	2
Willesden	2
Burton	1
Kittybrewster	1
Lancaster	1
Manningham	1
Mansfield	1
Nottingham	1

1957	128
Oswestry	15
Brecon	7
Darlington	7
Newton Heath	7
Workington	7
Bury	5
Kettering	5
Wakefield	5
Bescot	4
Rhyl	4
West Auckland	4
Wigan Springs Branch	4
Aintree	3
Cambridge	3
Goole	3
Hasland	3
Leeds Holbeck	3
Willesden	3
Agecroft	2
Aston	2
Colchester	2
Coventry	2
Derby	2
Dundee Tay Bridge	2
Kirkby Stephen	2
Lancaster	2
Millhouses	2
Sheffield Grimesthorpe	2
Skipton	2
St. Margarets	2
St. Philips Marsh	2
Stoke	2
Bristol Bath Road	1
Carlisle Upperby	1
Gloucester Barnwood	1
Kittybrewster	1
Leicester Midland	1
Mansfield	1
Nottingham	1
Toton	1

1960	128
Oswestry	24
Derby	7
Newton Heath	6
Bury	5
Darlington	5
Kettering	5
Wigan Springs Branch	5
Workington	5
Bescot	4
Carlisle Upperby	4
Goole	4
Rugby	4
Aintree	3
Aston	3
Cambridge	3
Lancaster	3
Leeds Holbeck	3
Agecroft	2
Dundee Tay Bridge	2
Low Moor	2
Millhouses	2
Parkeston	2
Sheffield Grimesthorpe	2
Skipton	2
Sowerby Bridge	2
St. Margarets	2
St. Philips Marsh	2
Stoke	2
Tweedmouth	2
Willesden	2
York	2
Kirkby Stephen	1
Kittybrewster	1
Leicester Midland	1
Mansfield	1
Northallerton	1
Thornaby	1
Watford	1

1963	115
Oswestry	24
Bescot	8
Bury	8
Derby	7
Carlisle Upperby	4
Kettering	4
Lancaster	4
Lees Oldham	4
Newton Heath	4
Workington	4
Lostock Hall	3
Rugby	3
Tweedmouth	3
Watford	3
Aston	2
Bushbury	2
Buxton	2
Dundee Tay Bridge	2
Hurlford	2
Malton	2
Nuneaton	2
Saltley	2
St. Margarets	2
Stourbridge	2
Wakefield	2
Willesden	2
Barrow	1
Darlington	1
Dumfries	1
Goole	1
Leeds Holbeck	1
Low Moor	1
Oban	1
Perth	1

1966	82
Newton Heath	7
Bescot	6
Lancaster	6
Saltley	6
Speke Junction	6
Bolton	5
Buxton	5
Carlisle Upperby	5
Tyseley	5
Workington	5
Aintree	4
Nuneaton	4
Wigan Springs Branch	4
Bank Hall	3
Carnforth	2
Machynlleth	2
Ayr	1
Croes Newydd	1
Dumfries	1
Dundee Tay Bridge	1
Hurlford	1
Motherwell	1
St. Margarets	1

3F[1] 41980-41993 0-6-2T LTSR Whitelegg

1948	14
Plaistow	11
Shoeburyness	2
Tilbury	1

1951	14
Plaistow	11
Shoeburyness	2
Tilbury	1

1954	14
Plaistow	11
Tilbury	2
Shoeburyness	1

1957	14
Plaistow	14

1960	1
Tilbury	1

Left: LTSR Whitelegg '3F' class 0-6-2T No 1982. It had just been renumbered from 2182 (see smokebox numberplate) at Plaistow on 24 September 1947. This engine was later numbered 41982. *E. R. Wethersett*

3F[2] (43137), 43174-43189, 43750 0-6-0 MR Johnson 4ft 11in

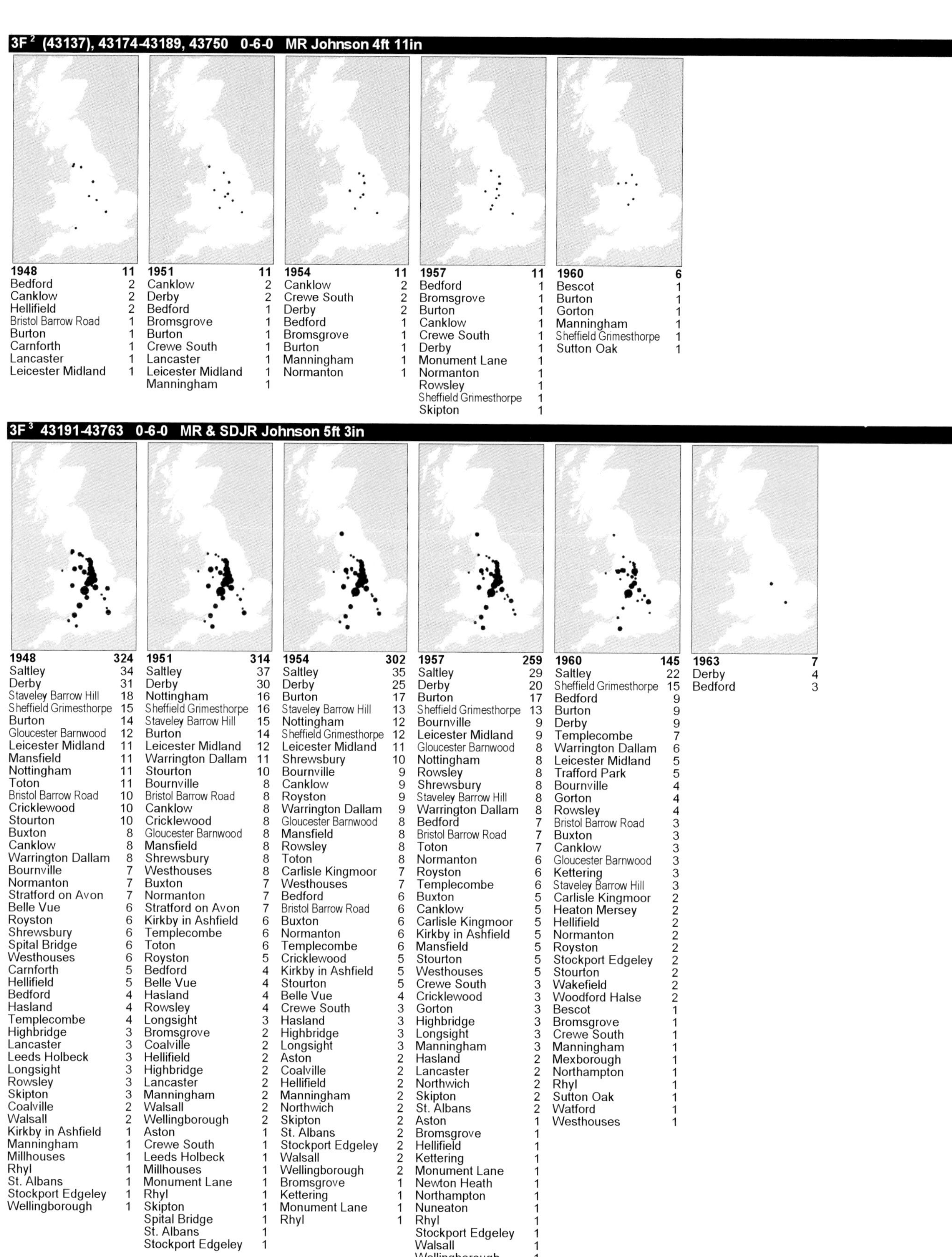

1948	11
Bedford	2
Canklow	2
Hellifield	2
Bristol Barrow Road	1
Burton	1
Carnforth	1
Lancaster	1
Leicester Midland	1

1951	11
Canklow	2
Derby	2
Bedford	1
Bromsgrove	1
Burton	1
Crewe South	1
Lancaster	1
Leicester Midland	1
Manningham	1

1954	11
Canklow	2
Crewe South	2
Derby	2
Bedford	1
Bromsgrove	1
Burton	1
Manningham	1
Normanton	1

1957	11
Bedford	1
Bromsgrove	1
Burton	1
Canklow	1
Crewe South	1
Derby	1
Monument Lane	1
Normanton	1
Rowsley	1
Sheffield Grimesthorpe	1
Skipton	1

1960	6
Bescot	1
Burton	1
Gorton	1
Manningham	1
Sheffield Grimesthorpe	1
Sutton Oak	1

3F[3] 43191-43763 0-6-0 MR & SDJR Johnson 5ft 3in

1948	324
Saltley	34
Derby	31
Staveley Barrow Hill	18
Sheffield Grimesthorpe	15
Burton	14
Gloucester Barnwood	12
Leicester Midland	11
Mansfield	11
Nottingham	11
Toton	11
Bristol Barrow Road	10
Cricklewood	10
Stourton	10
Buxton	8
Canklow	8
Warrington Dallam	8
Bournville	7
Normanton	7
Stratford on Avon	7
Belle Vue	6
Royston	6
Shrewsbury	6
Spital Bridge	6
Westhouses	6
Carnforth	5
Hellifield	5
Bedford	4
Hasland	4
Templecombe	4
Highbridge	3
Lancaster	3
Leeds Holbeck	3
Longsight	3
Rowsley	3
Skipton	3
Coalville	2
Walsall	2
Kirkby in Ashfield	1
Manningham	1
Millhouses	1
Rhyl	1
St. Albans	1
Stockport Edgeley	1
Wellingborough	1

1951	314
Saltley	37
Derby	30
Nottingham	16
Sheffield Grimesthorpe	16
Staveley Barrow Hill	15
Burton	14
Leicester Midland	12
Warrington Dallam	11
Stourton	10
Bournville	8
Bristol Barrow Road	8
Canklow	8
Cricklewood	8
Gloucester Barnwood	8
Mansfield	8
Shrewsbury	8
Westhouses	8
Buxton	7
Normanton	7
Stratford on Avon	7
Kirkby in Ashfield	6
Templecombe	6
Toton	6
Royston	5
Bedford	4
Belle Vue	4
Hasland	4
Rowsley	4
Longsight	3
Bromsgrove	2
Coalville	2
Hellifield	2
Highbridge	2
Lancaster	2
Manningham	2
Walsall	2
Wellingborough	2
Aston	1
Crewe South	1
Leeds Holbeck	1
Millhouses	1
Monument Lane	1
Rhyl	1
Skipton	1
Spital Bridge	1
St. Albans	1
Stockport Edgeley	1

1954	302
Saltley	35
Derby	25
Burton	17
Staveley Barrow Hill	13
Nottingham	12
Sheffield Grimesthorpe	12
Leicester Midland	11
Shrewsbury	10
Bournville	9
Canklow	9
Royston	9
Warrington Dallam	9
Gloucester Barnwood	8
Mansfield	8
Rowsley	8
Toton	8
Carlisle Kingmoor	7
Westhouses	7
Bedford	6
Bristol Barrow Road	6
Buxton	6
Normanton	6
Templecombe	6
Cricklewood	5
Kirkby in Ashfield	5
Stourton	5
Belle Vue	4
Crewe South	3
Hasland	3
Highbridge	3
Longsight	3
Aston	2
Coalville	2
Hellifield	2
Manningham	2
Northwich	2
Skipton	2
St. Albans	2
Stockport Edgeley	2
Walsall	2
Wellingborough	2
Bromsgrove	1
Kettering	1
Monument Lane	1
Rhyl	1

1957	259
Saltley	29
Derby	20
Burton	17
Sheffield Grimesthorpe	13
Bournville	9
Leicester Midland	9
Gloucester Barnwood	8
Nottingham	8
Rowsley	8
Shrewsbury	8
Staveley Barrow Hill	8
Warrington Dallam	8
Bedford	7
Bristol Barrow Road	7
Toton	7
Normanton	6
Royston	6
Templecombe	6
Buxton	5
Canklow	5
Carlisle Kingmoor	5
Kirkby in Ashfield	5
Mansfield	5
Stourton	5
Westhouses	5
Crewe South	3
Cricklewood	3
Gorton	3
Highbridge	3
Longsight	3
Manningham	3
Hasland	2
Lancaster	2
Northwich	2
Skipton	2
St. Albans	2
Aston	1
Bromsgrove	1
Hellifield	1
Kettering	1
Monument Lane	1
Newton Heath	1
Northampton	1
Nuneaton	1
Rhyl	1
Stockport Edgeley	1
Walsall	1
Wellingborough	1

1960	145
Saltley	22
Sheffield Grimesthorpe	15
Bedford	9
Burton	9
Derby	9
Templecombe	7
Warrington Dallam	6
Leicester Midland	5
Trafford Park	5
Bournville	4
Gorton	4
Rowsley	4
Bristol Barrow Road	3
Buxton	3
Canklow	3
Gloucester Barnwood	3
Kettering	3
Staveley Barrow Hill	3
Carlisle Kingmoor	2
Heaton Mersey	2
Hellifield	2
Normanton	2
Royston	2
Stockport Edgeley	2
Stourton	2
Wakefield	2
Woodford Halse	2
Bescot	1
Bromsgrove	1
Crewe South	1
Manningham	1
Mexborough	1
Northampton	1
Rhyl	1
Sutton Oak	1
Watford	1
Westhouses	1

1963	7
Derby	4
Bedford	3

3F[4] 43765-43833 0-6-0 MR Deeley

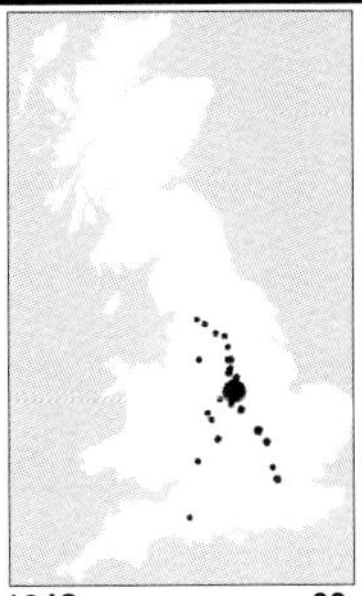

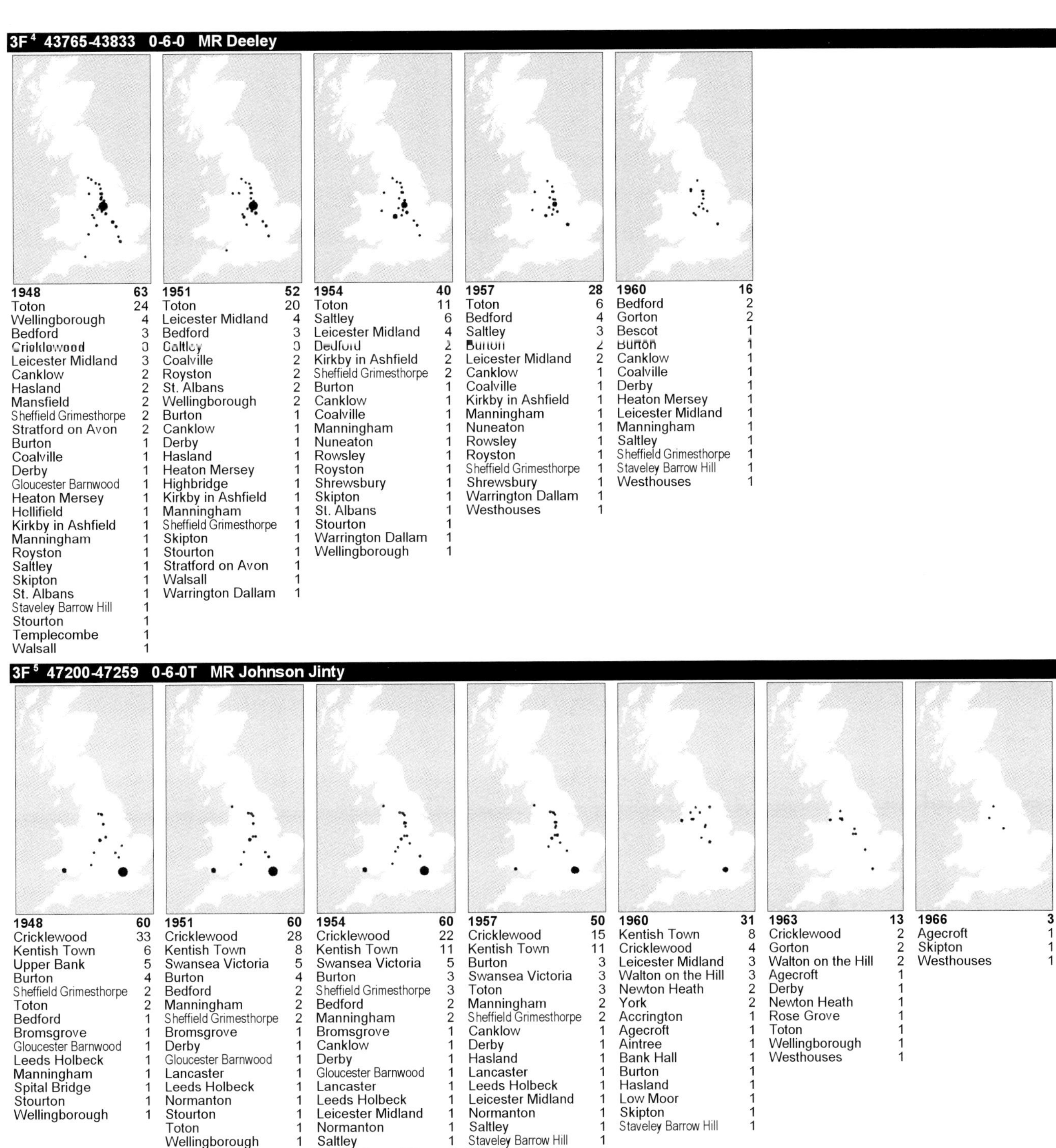

1948	63
Toton	24
Wellingborough	4
Bedford	3
Cricklewood	3
Leicester Midland	3
Canklow	2
Hasland	2
Mansfield	2
Sheffield Grimesthorpe	2
Stratford on Avon	2
Burton	1
Coalville	1
Derby	1
Gloucester Barnwood	1
Heaton Mersey	1
Hellifield	1
Kirkby in Ashfield	1
Manningham	1
Royston	1
Saltley	1
Skipton	1
St. Albans	1
Staveley Barrow Hill	1
Stourton	1
Templecombe	1
Walsall	1

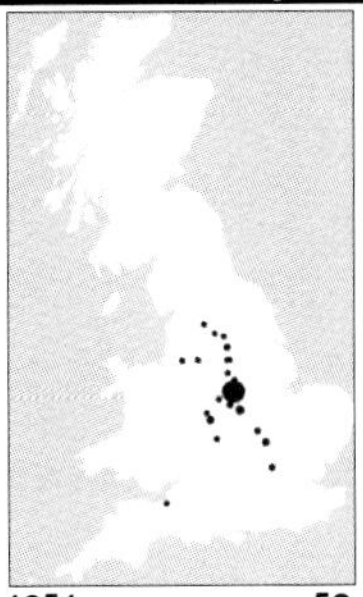

1951	52
Toton	20
Leicester Midland	4
Bedford	3
Saltley	3
Coalville	2
Royston	2
St. Albans	2
Wellingborough	2
Burton	1
Canklow	1
Derby	1
Hasland	1
Heaton Mersey	1
Highbridge	1
Kirkby in Ashfield	1
Manningham	1
Sheffield Grimesthorpe	1
Skipton	1
Stourton	1
Stratford on Avon	1
Walsall	1
Warrington Dallam	1

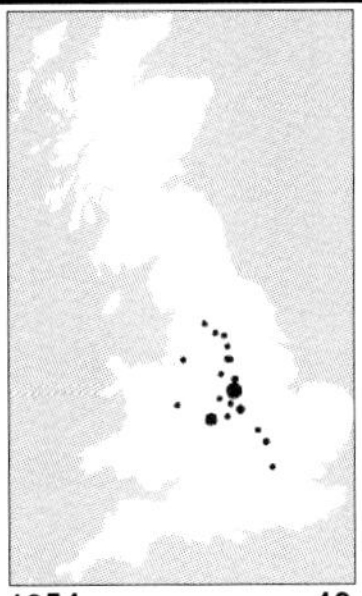

1954	40
Toton	11
Saltley	6
Leicester Midland	4
Bedford	2
Kirkby in Ashfield	2
Sheffield Grimesthorpe	2
Burton	1
Canklow	1
Coalville	1
Manningham	1
Nuneaton	1
Rowsley	1
Royston	1
Shrewsbury	1
Skipton	1
St. Albans	1
Stourton	1
Warrington Dallam	1
Wellingborough	1

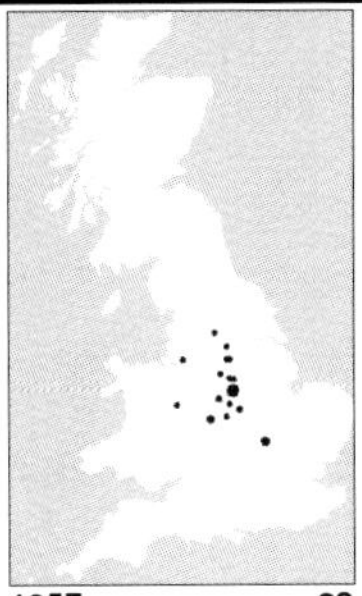

1957	28
Toton	6
Bedford	4
Saltley	3
Burton	2
Leicester Midland	2
Canklow	1
Coalville	1
Kirkby in Ashfield	1
Manningham	1
Nuneaton	1
Rowsley	1
Royston	1
Sheffield Grimesthorpe	1
Shrewsbury	1
Warrington Dallam	1
Westhouses	1

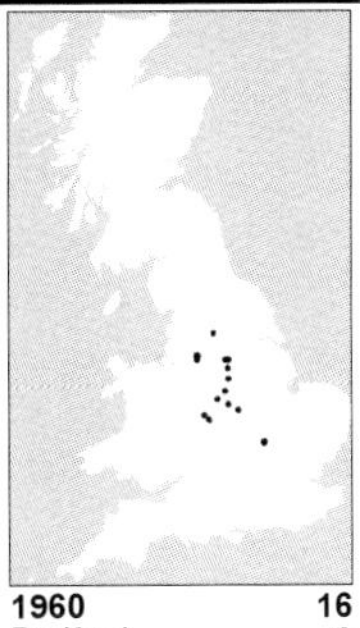

1960	16
Bedford	2
Gorton	2
Bescot	1
Burton	1
Canklow	1
Coalville	1
Derby	1
Heaton Mersey	1
Leicester Midland	1
Manningham	1
Saltley	1
Sheffield Grimesthorpe	1
Staveley Barrow Hill	1
Westhouses	1

3F[5] 47200-47259 0-6-0T MR Johnson Jinty

1948	60
Cricklewood	33
Kentish Town	6
Upper Bank	5
Burton	4
Sheffield Grimesthorpe	2
Toton	2
Bedford	1
Bromsgrove	1
Gloucester Barnwood	1
Leeds Holbeck	1
Manningham	1
Spital Bridge	1
Stourton	1
Wellingborough	1

1951	60
Cricklewood	28
Kentish Town	8
Swansea Victoria	5
Burton	4
Bedford	2
Manningham	2
Sheffield Grimesthorpe	2
Bromsgrove	1
Derby	1
Gloucester Barnwood	1
Lancaster	1
Leeds Holbeck	1
Normanton	1
Stourton	1
Toton	1
Wellingborough	1

1954	60
Cricklewood	22
Kentish Town	11
Swansea Victoria	5
Burton	3
Sheffield Grimesthorpe	3
Bedford	2
Manningham	2
Bromsgrove	1
Canklow	1
Derby	1
Gloucester Barnwood	1
Lancaster	1
Leeds Holbeck	1
Leicester Midland	1
Normanton	1
Saltley	1
Staveley Barrow Hill	1
Stourton	1
Toton	1

1957	50
Cricklewood	15
Kentish Town	11
Burton	3
Swansea Victoria	3
Toton	3
Manningham	2
Sheffield Grimesthorpe	2
Canklow	1
Derby	1
Hasland	1
Lancaster	1
Leeds Holbeck	1
Leicester Midland	1
Normanton	1
Saltley	1
Staveley Barrow Hill	1
Stourton	1
Wellingborough	1

1960	31
Kentish Town	8
Cricklewood	4
Leicester Midland	3
Walton on the Hill	3
Newton Heath	2
York	2
Accrington	1
Agecroft	1
Aintree	1
Bank Hall	1
Burton	1
Hasland	1
Low Moor	1
Skipton	1
Staveley Barrow Hill	1

1963	13
Cricklewood	2
Gorton	2
Walton on the Hill	2
Agecroft	1
Derby	1
Newton Heath	1
Rose Grove	1
Toton	1
Wellingborough	1
Westhouses	1

1966	3
Agecroft	1
Skipton	1
Westhouses	1

3F[6] 47260-47681 0-6-0T LMS & SDJR Fowler Jinty

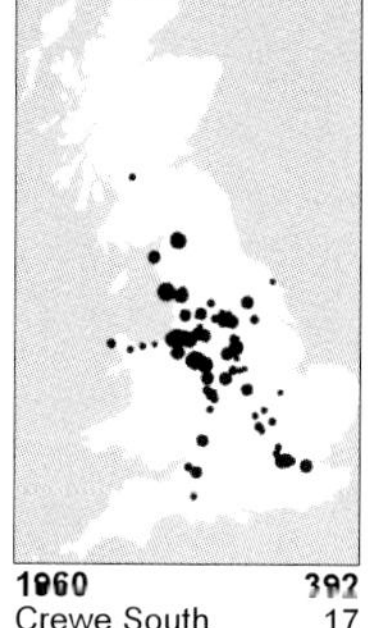

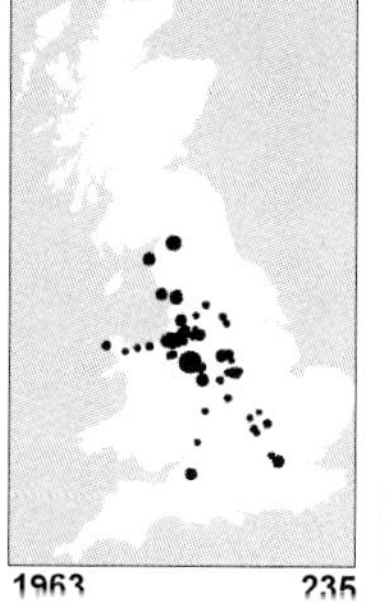

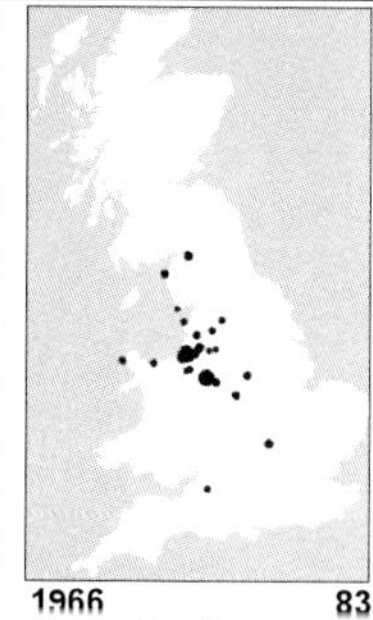

1948	412
Devons Road	45
Crewe South	22
Willesden	17
Carlisle Upperby	13
Camden	12
Kentish Town	12
Stoke	11
Longsight	10
Nottingham	10
Wellingborough	9
Agecroft	8
Birkenhead	8
Carnforth	8
Edge Hill	8
Warrington Dallam	8
Bromsgrove	7
Chester	7
Mold Junction	7
Plaistow	7
Stafford	7
Bath Green Park	6
Cricklewood	6
Lancaster	6
Staveley Barrow Hill	6
Toton	6
Upper Bank	6
Bushbury	5
Farnley Junction	5
Hasland	5
Leicester Midland	5
Polmadie	5
Rowsley	5
Royston	5
Stourton	5
Alsager	4
Aston	4
Bletchley	4
Nuneaton	4
Preston	4
Rugby	4
Saltley	4
Spital Bridge	4
Workington	4
Bacup	3
Barrow	3
Bescot	3
Bristol Barrow Road	3
Burton	3
Gloucester Barnwood	3
Holyhead	3
Moor Row	3
Normanton	3
Northampton	3
Rose Grove	3
Sheffield Grimesthorpe	3
Sowerby Bridge	3
Speke Junction	3
Stockport Edgeley	3
Belle Vue	2
Canklow	2
Sutton Oak	2
Bedford	1
Coalville	1
Corkerhill	1
Crewe Works	1
Derby	1
Inverness	1
Kettering	1
Leeds Holbeck	1
Manningham	1
Newton Heath	1
Plodder Lane	1
St. Albans	1
Westhouses	1

1951	417
Devons Road	40
Crewe South	17
Carlisle Upperby	13
Willesden	13
Camden	12
Edge Hill	11
Nottingham	11
Stoke	11
Longsight	10
Wellingborough	10
Warrington Dallam	9
Birkenhead	8
Kentish Town	8
Bromsgrove	7
Chester	7
Lancaster	7
Plaistow	7
Staveley Barrow Hill	7
Swansea Victoria	7
Agecroft	6
Bath Green Park	6
Carnforth	6
Mold Junction	6
Polmadie	6
Rowsley	6
Sheffield Grimesthorpe	6
Speke Junction	6
Spital Bridge	6
Stafford	6
Stourton	6
Toton	6
Alsager	5
Farnley Junction	5
Leicester Midland	5
Royston	5
Wakefield	5
Aston	4
Bletchley	4
Bushbury	4
Gloucester Barnwood	4
Hasland	4
Moor Row	4
Nuneaton	4
Preston	4
Rugby	4
Sutton Oak	4
Barrow	3
Bescot	3
Bristol Barrow Road	3
Brunswick	3
Burton	3
Cricklewood	3
Holyhead	3
Normanton	3
Northampton	3
Rose Grove	3
Stockport Edgeley	3
Workington	3
Belle Vue	2
Canklow	2
Derby	2
Leeds Holbeck	2
Newton Heath	2
Saltley	2
Skipton	2
Sowerby Bridge	2
Bedford	1
Coalville	1
Corkerhill	1
Crewe Works	1
Kettering	1
Llandudno Junction	1
Manningham	1
Oxenholme	1
Plodder Lane	1
St. Albans	1
Walsall	1
Watford	1
Westhouses	1

1954	417
Devons Road	30
Crewe South	17
Edge Hill	15
Willesden	14
Camden	13
Carlisle Upperby	13
Plaistow	13
Stoke	13
Longsight	10
Warrington Dallam	10
Wellingborough	10
Bromsgrove	8
Staveley Barrow Hill	8
Chester	7
Lancaster	7
Preston	7
Speke Junction	7
Stourton	7
Swansea Victoria	7
Agecroft	6
Bath Green Park	6
Carnforth	6
Mold Junction	6
Polmadie	6
Rowsley	6
Royston	6
Sheffield Grimesthorpe	6
Stafford	6
Alsager	5
Farnley Junction	5
Kentish Town	5
Leicester Midland	5
Nottingham	5
Patricroft	5
Wakefield	5
Bidston	4
Bletchley	4
Bristol Barrow Road	4
Brunswick	4
Burton	4
Bushbury	4
Gloucester Barnwood	4
Hasland	4
Nuneaton	4
Rugby	4
Skipton	4
Sutton Oak	4
Workington	4
Barrow	3
Bescot	3
Birkenhead	3
Cricklewood	3
Derby	3
Holyhead	3
Leeds Holbeck	3
Moor Row	3
Normanton	3
Northampton	3
Rose Grove	3
Stockport Edgeley	3
Belle Vue	2
Canklow	2
Newton Heath	2
Saltley	2
Sowerby Bridge	2
Toton	2
Bedford	1
Coalville	1
Corkerhill	1
Crewe Works	1
Llandudno Junction	1
Manningham	1
Oxenholme	1
Plodder Lane	1
St. Albans	1
Walsall	1
Watford	1
Westhouses	1

1957	417
Devons Road	27
Edge Hill	15
Crewe South	14
Carlisle Upperby	13
Stoke	13
Willesden	13
Camden	11
Staveley Barrow Hill	11
Longsight	10
Warrington Dallam	10
Patricroft	8
Chester	7
Lancaster	7
Plaistow	7
Preston	7
Stafford	7
Stourton	7
Sutton Oak	7
Swansea Victoria	7
Bath Green Park	6
Carnforth	6
Kentish Town	6
Mold Junction	6
Normanton	6
Rowsley	6
Royston	6
Workington	6
Agecroft	5
Alsager	5
Bristol Barrow Road	5
Burton	5
Farnley Junction	5
Gloucester Barnwood	5
Holyhead	5
Leicester Midland	5
Newton Heath	5
Rose Grove	5
Sheffield Grimesthorpe	5
Sowerby Bridge	5
Wakefield	5
Barrow	4
Bromsgrove	4
Brunswick	4
Bushbury	4
Hasland	4
Skipton	4
Wellingborough	4
Bescot	3
Bidston	3
Birkenhead	3
Carlisle Kingmoor	3
Cricklewood	3
Derby	3
Grantham	3
Leeds Holbeck	3
Nuneaton	3
Speke Junction	3
Spital Bridge	3
Stockport Edgeley	3
Bedford	2
Bletchley	2
Canklow	2
Huddersfield	2
Northampton	2
Nottingham	2
Polmadie	2
Rugby	2
Saltley	2
St. Albans	2
Widnes	2
Wrexham Rhosddu	2
Bury	1
Coalville	1
Corkerhill	1
Coventry	1
Crewe Works	1
Gorton	1
Hamilton	1
Llandudno Junction	1
Manningham	1
Oxenholme	1
Rhyl	1
Toton	1
Walsall	1
Watford	1
Westhouses	1

1960	392
Crewe South	17
Edge Hill	17
Barrow	16
Carlisle Upperby	12
Stoke	12
Warrington Dallam	11
Birkenhead	10
Lancaster	10
Staveley Barrow Hill	10
Carlisle Kingmoor	8
Chester	8
Wakefield	8
Willesden	8
Burton	7
Camden	7
Kentish Town	7
Patricroft	7
Speke Junction	7
Stafford	7
Sutton Oak	7
Tilbury	7
Workington	7
York	7
Rowsley	6
Alsager	5
Bath Green Park	5
Bescot	5
Brunswick	5
Gloucester Barnwood	5
Leicester Midland	5
Longsight	5
Mirfield	5
Preston	5
Rose Grove	5
Agecroft	4
Bank Hall	4
Bushbury	4
Cricklewood	4
Derby	4
Goole	4
Hasland	4
Holyhead	4
Mold Junction	4
Sheffield Grimesthorpe	4
Wolverton Works	4
Bedford	3
Bidston	3
Bristol Barrow Road	3
Carnforth	3
Farnley Junction	3
Low Moor	3
Monument Lane	3
Skipton	3
Sowerby Bridge	3
Stratford	3
Widnes	3
Aintree	2
Ardsley	2
Bangor	2
Bletchley	2
Bromsgrove	2
Llandudno Junction	2
Newton Heath	2
Northampton	2
Polmadie	2
St. Albans	2
Templecombe	2
Walton on the Hill	2
Watford	2
Wellingborough	2
Accrington	1
Bury	1
Canklow	1
Crewe Works	1
Leeds Holbeck	1
Leicester Central	1
Manningham	1
Nottingham	1
Rhyl	1
Scarborough	1
Spital Bridge	1
Stockport Edgeley	1
Toton	1
Westhouses	1

1963	235
Crewe South	20
Carlisle Upperby	11
Edge Hill	11
Lancaster	8
Stafford	7
Wigan Springs Branch	7
Workington	7
Crewe Works	6
Rowsley	6
Sutton Oak	6
Toton	6
Barrow	5
Bath Green Park	5
Bidston	5
Birkenhead	5
Cricklewood	5
Lostock Hall	5
Newton Heath	5
Stoke	5
Agecroft	4
Aintree	4
Bedford	4
Carlisle Kingmoor	4
Hasland	4
Holyhead	4
Patricroft	4
Bank Hall	3
Burton	3
Carlisle Canal	3
Chester	3
Derby	3
Farnley Junction	3
Mold Junction	3
Nuneaton	3
Rhyl	3
Skipton	3
Warrington Dallam	3
Willesden	3
Wolverton Works	3
Bangor	2
Bletchley	2
Bromsgrove	2
Gloucester Barnwood	2
Gorton	2
Horwich Works	2
Llandudno Junction	2
Northampton	2
Nottingham	2
Rose Grove	2
Wakefield	2
Watford	2
Widnes	2
Bury	1
Carnforth	1
Kentish Town	1
Speke Junction	1
Walton on the Hill	1
Wellingborough	1
Westhouses	1

1966	83
Crewe South	11
Birkenhead	7
Aintree	6
Crewe Works	5
Edge Hill	5
Carlisle Kingmoor	4
Sutton Oak	4
Wigan Springs Branch	4
Wolverton Works	4
Burton	3
Lostock Hall	3
Stoke	3
Westhouses	3
Workington	3
Bath Green Park	2
Chester	2
Fleetwood	2
Holyhead	2
Llandudno Junction	2
Rose Grove	2
Skipton	2
Barrow	1
Mold Junction	1
Newton Heath	1
Patricroft	1

3F[7] between 52088 & 52529 0-6-0 LYR Aspinall Class 27

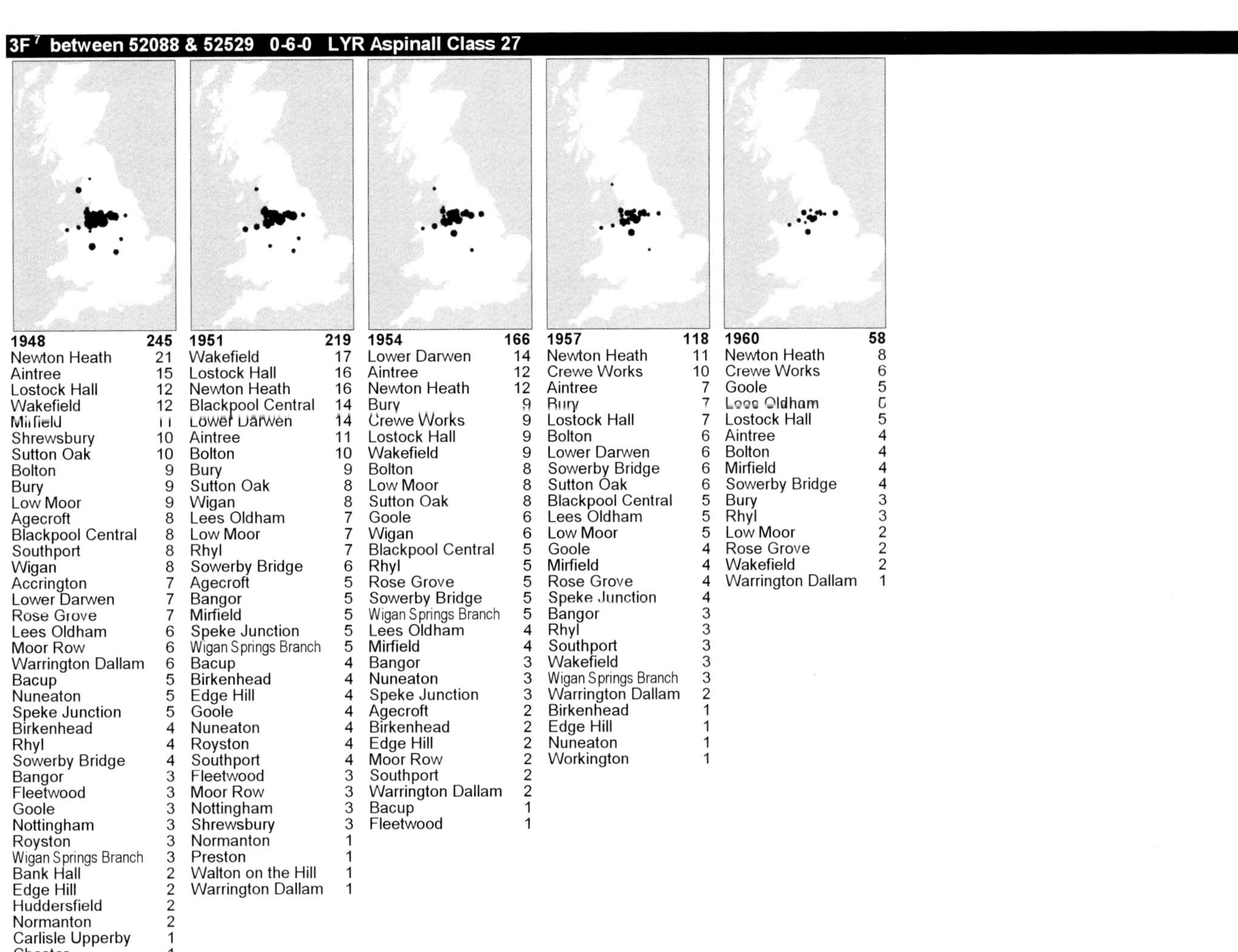

1948	245
Newton Heath	21
Aintree	15
Lostock Hall	12
Wakefield	12
Mirfield	11
Shrewsbury	10
Sutton Oak	10
Bolton	9
Bury	9
Low Moor	9
Agecroft	8
Blackpool Central	8
Southport	8
Wigan	8
Accrington	7
Lower Darwen	7
Rose Grove	7
Lees Oldham	6
Moor Row	6
Warrington Dallam	6
Bacup	5
Nuneaton	5
Speke Junction	5
Birkenhead	4
Rhyl	4
Sowerby Bridge	4
Bangor	3
Fleetwood	3
Goole	3
Nottingham	3
Royston	3
Wigan Springs Branch	3
Bank Hall	2
Edge Hill	2
Huddersfield	2
Normanton	2
Carlisle Upperby	1
Chester	1
Preston	1

1951	219
Wakefield	17
Lostock Hall	16
Newton Heath	16
Blackpool Central	14
Lower Darwen	14
Aintree	11
Bolton	10
Bury	9
Sutton Oak	8
Wigan	8
Lees Oldham	7
Low Moor	7
Rhyl	7
Sowerby Bridge	6
Agecroft	5
Bangor	5
Mirfield	5
Speke Junction	5
Wigan Springs Branch	5
Bacup	4
Birkenhead	4
Edge Hill	4
Goole	4
Nuneaton	4
Royston	4
Southport	4
Fleetwood	3
Moor Row	3
Nottingham	3
Shrewsbury	3
Normanton	1
Preston	1
Walton on the Hill	1
Warrington Dallam	1

1954	166
Lower Darwen	14
Aintree	12
Newton Heath	12
Bury	9
Crewe Works	9
Lostock Hall	9
Wakefield	9
Bolton	8
Low Moor	8
Sutton Oak	8
Goole	6
Wigan	6
Blackpool Central	5
Rhyl	5
Rose Grove	5
Sowerby Bridge	5
Wigan Springs Branch	5
Lees Oldham	4
Mirfield	4
Bangor	3
Nuneaton	3
Speke Junction	3
Agecroft	2
Birkenhead	2
Edge Hill	2
Moor Row	2
Southport	2
Warrington Dallam	2
Bacup	1
Fleetwood	1

1957	118
Newton Heath	11
Crewe Works	10
Aintree	7
Bury	7
Lostock Hall	7
Bolton	6
Lower Darwen	6
Sowerby Bridge	6
Sutton Oak	6
Blackpool Central	5
Lees Oldham	5
Low Moor	5
Goole	4
Mirfield	4
Rose Grove	4
Speke Junction	4
Bangor	3
Rhyl	3
Southport	3
Wakefield	3
Wigan Springs Branch	3
Warrington Dallam	2
Birkenhead	1
Edge Hill	1
Nuneaton	1
Workington	1

1960	58
Newton Heath	8
Crewe Works	6
Goole	5
Lees Oldham	5
Lostock Hall	5
Aintree	4
Bolton	4
Mirfield	4
Sowerby Bridge	4
Bury	3
Rhyl	3
Low Moor	2
Rose Grove	2
Wakefield	2
Warrington Dallam	1

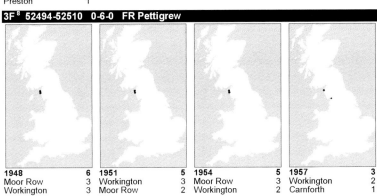

3F[8] 52494-52510 0-6-0 FR Pettigrew

1948	6
Moor Row	3
Workington	3

1951	5
Workington	3
Moor Row	2

1954	5
Moor Row	3
Workington	2

1957	3
Workington	2
Carnforth	1

3F[9] between 52528 & 52619 0-6-0 LYR Hughes Class 28

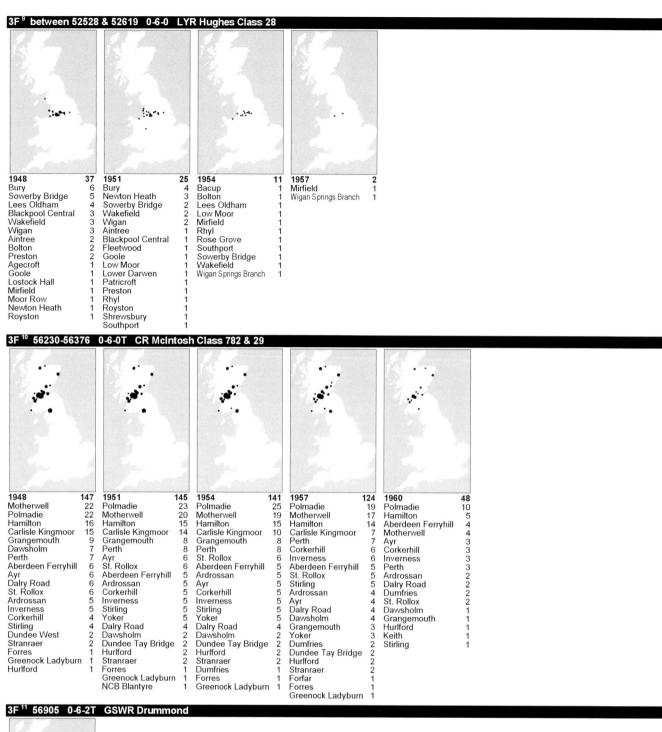

1948	37
Bury	6
Sowerby Bridge	5
Lees Oldham	4
Blackpool Central	3
Wakefield	3
Wigan	3
Aintree	2
Bolton	2
Preston	2
Agecroft	1
Goole	1
Lostock Hall	1
Mirfield	1
Moor Row	1
Newton Heath	1
Royston	1

1951	25
Bury	4
Newton Heath	3
Sowerby Bridge	2
Wakefield	2
Wigan	2
Aintree	1
Blackpool Central	1
Fleetwood	1
Goole	1
Low Moor	1
Lower Darwen	1
Patricroft	1
Preston	1
Rhyl	1
Royston	1
Shrewsbury	1
Southport	1

1954	11
Bacup	1
Bolton	1
Lees Oldham	1
Low Moor	1
Mirfield	1
Rhyl	1
Rose Grove	1
Southport	1
Sowerby Bridge	1
Wakefield	1
Wigan Springs Branch	1

1957	2
Mirfield	1
Wigan Springs Branch	1

3F[10] 56230-56376 0-6-0T CR McIntosh Class 782 & 29

1948	147
Motherwell	22
Polmadie	22
Hamilton	16
Carlisle Kingmoor	15
Grangemouth	9
Dawsholm	7
Perth	7
Aberdeen Ferryhill	6
Ayr	6
Dalry Road	6
St. Rollox	6
Ardrossan	5
Inverness	5
Corkerhill	4
Stirling	4
Dundee West	2
Stranraer	2
Forres	1
Greenock Ladyburn	1
Hurlford	1

1951	145
Polmadie	23
Motherwell	20
Hamilton	15
Carlisle Kingmoor	14
Grangemouth	8
Perth	8
Ayr	6
St. Rollox	6
Aberdeen Ferryhill	5
Ardrossan	5
Corkerhill	5
Inverness	5
Stirling	5
Yoker	5
Dalry Road	4
Dawsholm	2
Dundee Tay Bridge	2
Hurlford	2
Stranraer	2
Forres	1
Greenock Ladyburn	1
NCB Blantyre	1

1954	141
Polmadie	25
Motherwell	19
Hamilton	15
Carlisle Kingmoor	10
Grangemouth	8
Perth	8
St. Rollox	6
Aberdeen Ferryhill	5
Ardrossan	5
Ayr	5
Corkerhill	5
Inverness	5
Stirling	5
Yoker	5
Dalry Road	4
Dawsholm	2
Dundee Tay Bridge	2
Hurlford	2
Stranraer	2
Dumfries	1
Forres	1
Greenock Ladyburn	1

1957	124
Polmadie	19
Motherwell	17
Hamilton	14
Carlisle Kingmoor	7
Perth	7
Corkerhill	6
Inverness	6
Aberdeen Ferryhill	5
St. Rollox	5
Stirling	5
Ardrossan	4
Ayr	4
Dalry Road	4
Dawsholm	4
Grangemouth	3
Yoker	3
Dumfries	2
Dundee Tay Bridge	2
Hurlford	2
Stranraer	2
Forfar	1
Forres	1
Greenock Ladyburn	1

1960	48
Polmadie	10
Hamilton	5
Aberdeen Ferryhill	4
Motherwell	4
Ayr	3
Corkerhill	3
Inverness	3
Perth	3
Ardrossan	2
Dalry Road	2
Dumfries	2
St. Rollox	2
Dawsholm	1
Grangemouth	1
Hurlford	1
Keith	1
Stirling	1

3F[11] 56905 0-6-2T GSWR Drummond

1948	1
Carlisle Kingmoor	1

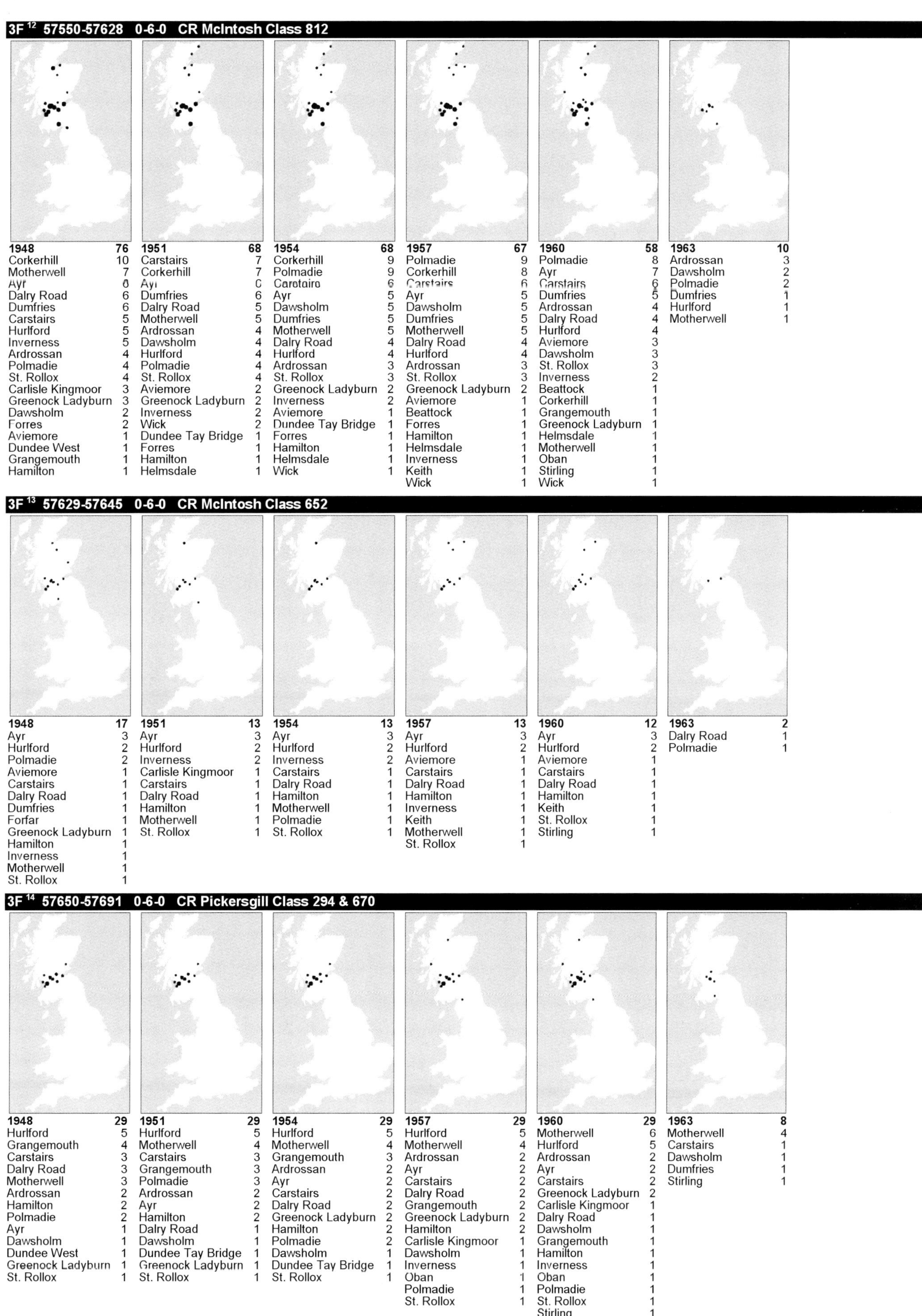

3F[12] 57550-57628 0-6-0 CR McIntosh Class 812

1948	76
Corkerhill	10
Motherwell	7
Ayr	6
Dalry Road	6
Dumfries	6
Carstairs	5
Hurlford	5
Inverness	5
Ardrossan	4
Polmadie	4
St. Rollox	4
Carlisle Kingmoor	3
Greenock Ladyburn	3
Dawsholm	2
Forres	2
Aviemore	1
Dundee West	1
Grangemouth	1
Hamilton	1

1951	68
Carstairs	7
Corkerhill	7
Ayr	6
Dumfries	6
Dalry Road	5
Motherwell	5
Ardrossan	4
Dawsholm	4
Hurlford	4
Polmadie	4
St. Rollox	4
Aviemore	2
Greenock Ladyburn	2
Inverness	2
Wick	2
Dundee Tay Bridge	1
Forres	1
Hamilton	1
Helmsdale	1

1954	68
Corkerhill	9
Polmadie	9
Carstairs	6
Ayr	5
Dawsholm	5
Dumfries	5
Motherwell	5
Dalry Road	4
Hurlford	4
Ardrossan	3
St. Rollox	3
Greenock Ladyburn	2
Inverness	2
Aviemore	1
Dundee Tay Bridge	1
Forres	1
Hamilton	1
Helmsdale	1
Wick	1

1957	67
Polmadie	9
Corkerhill	8
Carstairs	6
Ayr	5
Dawsholm	5
Dumfries	5
Motherwell	5
Dalry Road	4
Hurlford	4
Ardrossan	3
St. Rollox	3
Greenock Ladyburn	2
Aviemore	1
Beattock	1
Forres	1
Hamilton	1
Helmsdale	1
Inverness	1
Keith	1
Wick	1

1960	58
Polmadie	8
Ayr	7
Carstairs	6
Dumfries	5
Ardrossan	4
Dalry Road	4
Hurlford	4
Aviemore	3
Dawsholm	3
St. Rollox	3
Inverness	2
Beattock	1
Corkerhill	1
Grangemouth	1
Greenock Ladyburn	1
Helmsdale	1
Motherwell	1
Oban	1
Stirling	1
Wick	1

1963	10
Ardrossan	3
Dawsholm	2
Polmadie	2
Dumfries	1
Hurlford	1
Motherwell	1

3F[13] 57629-57645 0-6-0 CR McIntosh Class 652

1948	17
Ayr	3
Hurlford	2
Polmadie	2
Aviemore	1
Carstairs	1
Dalry Road	1
Dumfries	1
Forfar	1
Greenock Ladyburn	1
Hamilton	1
Inverness	1
Motherwell	1
St. Rollox	1

1951	13
Ayr	3
Hurlford	2
Inverness	2
Carlisle Kingmoor	1
Carstairs	1
Dalry Road	1
Hamilton	1
Motherwell	1
St. Rollox	1

1954	13
Ayr	3
Hurlford	2
Inverness	2
Carstairs	1
Dalry Road	1
Hamilton	1
Motherwell	1
Polmadie	1
St. Rollox	1

1957	13
Ayr	3
Hurlford	2
Aviemore	1
Carstairs	1
Dalry Road	1
Hamilton	1
Inverness	1
Keith	1
Motherwell	1
St. Rollox	1

1960	12
Ayr	3
Hurlford	2
Aviemore	1
Carstairs	1
Dalry Road	1
Hamilton	1
Keith	1
St. Rollox	1
Stirling	1

1963	2
Dalry Road	1
Polmadie	1

3F[14] 57650-57691 0-6-0 CR Pickersgill Class 294 & 670

1948	29
Hurlford	5
Grangemouth	4
Carstairs	3
Dalry Road	3
Motherwell	3
Ardrossan	2
Hamilton	2
Polmadie	2
Ayr	1
Dawsholm	1
Dundee West	1
Greenock Ladyburn	1
St. Rollox	1

1951	29
Hurlford	5
Motherwell	4
Carstairs	3
Grangemouth	3
Polmadie	3
Ardrossan	2
Ayr	2
Hamilton	2
Dalry Road	1
Dawsholm	1
Dundee Tay Bridge	1
Greenock Ladyburn	1
St. Rollox	1

1954	29
Hurlford	5
Motherwell	4
Grangemouth	3
Ardrossan	2
Ayr	2
Carstairs	2
Dalry Road	2
Greenock Ladyburn	2
Hamilton	2
Polmadie	2
Dawsholm	1
Dundee Tay Bridge	1
St. Rollox	1

1957	29
Hurlford	5
Motherwell	4
Ardrossan	2
Ayr	2
Carstairs	2
Dalry Road	2
Grangemouth	2
Greenock Ladyburn	2
Hamilton	2
Carlisle Kingmoor	1
Dawsholm	1
Inverness	1
Oban	1
Polmadie	1
St. Rollox	1

1960	29
Motherwell	6
Hurlford	5
Ardrossan	2
Ayr	2
Carstairs	2
Greenock Ladyburn	2
Carlisle Kingmoor	1
Dalry Road	1
Dawsholm	1
Grangemouth	1
Hamilton	1
Inverness	1
Oban	1
Polmadie	1
St. Rollox	1
Stirling	1

1963	8
Motherwell	4
Carstairs	1
Dawsholm	1
Dumfries	1
Stirling	1

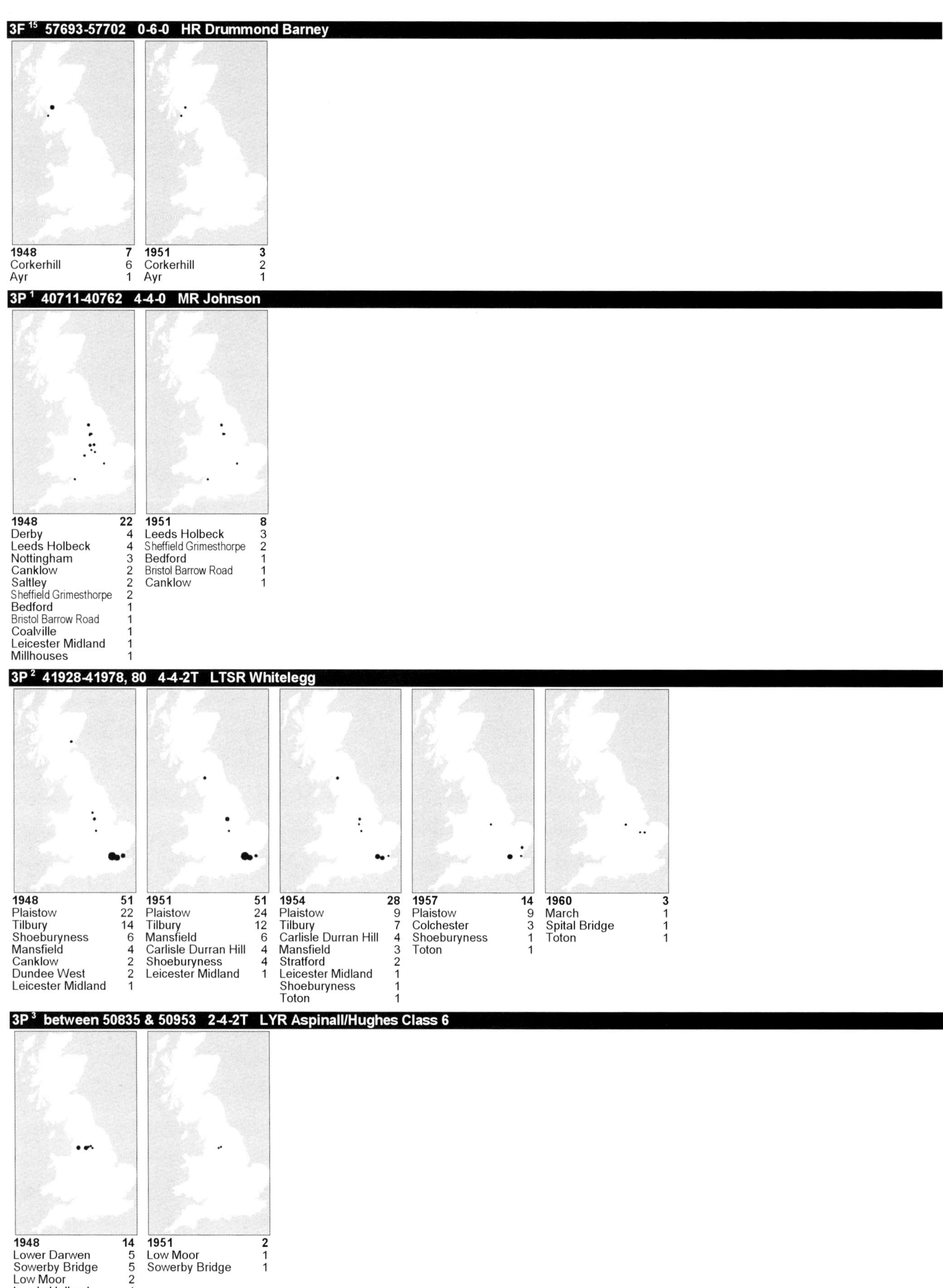

3F^{15} 57693-57702 0-6-0 HR Drummond Barney

1948	7	1951	3
Corkerhill	6	Corkerhill	2
Ayr	1	Ayr	1

3P^{1} 40711-40762 4-4-0 MR Johnson

1948	22	1951	8
Derby	4	Leeds Holbeck	3
Leeds Holbeck	4	Sheffield Grimesthorpe	2
Nottingham	3	Bedford	1
Canklow	2	Bristol Barrow Road	1
Saltley	2	Canklow	1
Sheffield Grimesthorpe	2		
Bedford	1		
Bristol Barrow Road	1		
Coalville	1		
Leicester Midland	1		
Millhouses	1		

3P^{2} 41928-41978, 80 4-4-2T LTSR Whitelegg

1948	51	1951	51	1954	28	1957	14	1960	3
Plaistow	22	Plaistow	24	Plaistow	9	Plaistow	9	March	1
Tilbury	14	Tilbury	12	Tilbury	7	Colchester	3	Spital Bridge	1
Shoeburyness	6	Mansfield	6	Carlisle Durran Hill	4	Shoeburyness	1	Toton	1
Mansfield	4	Carlisle Durran Hill	4	Mansfield	3	Toton	1		
Canklow	2	Shoeburyness	4	Stratford	2				
Dundee West	2	Leicester Midland	1	Leicester Midland	1				
Leicester Midland	1			Shoeburyness	1				
				Toton	1				

3P^{3} between 50835 & 50953 2-4-2T LYR Aspinall/Hughes Class 6

1948	14	1951	2
Lower Darwen	5	Low Moor	1
Sowerby Bridge	5	Sowerby Bridge	1
Low Moor	2		
Leeds Holbeck	1		
Normanton	1		

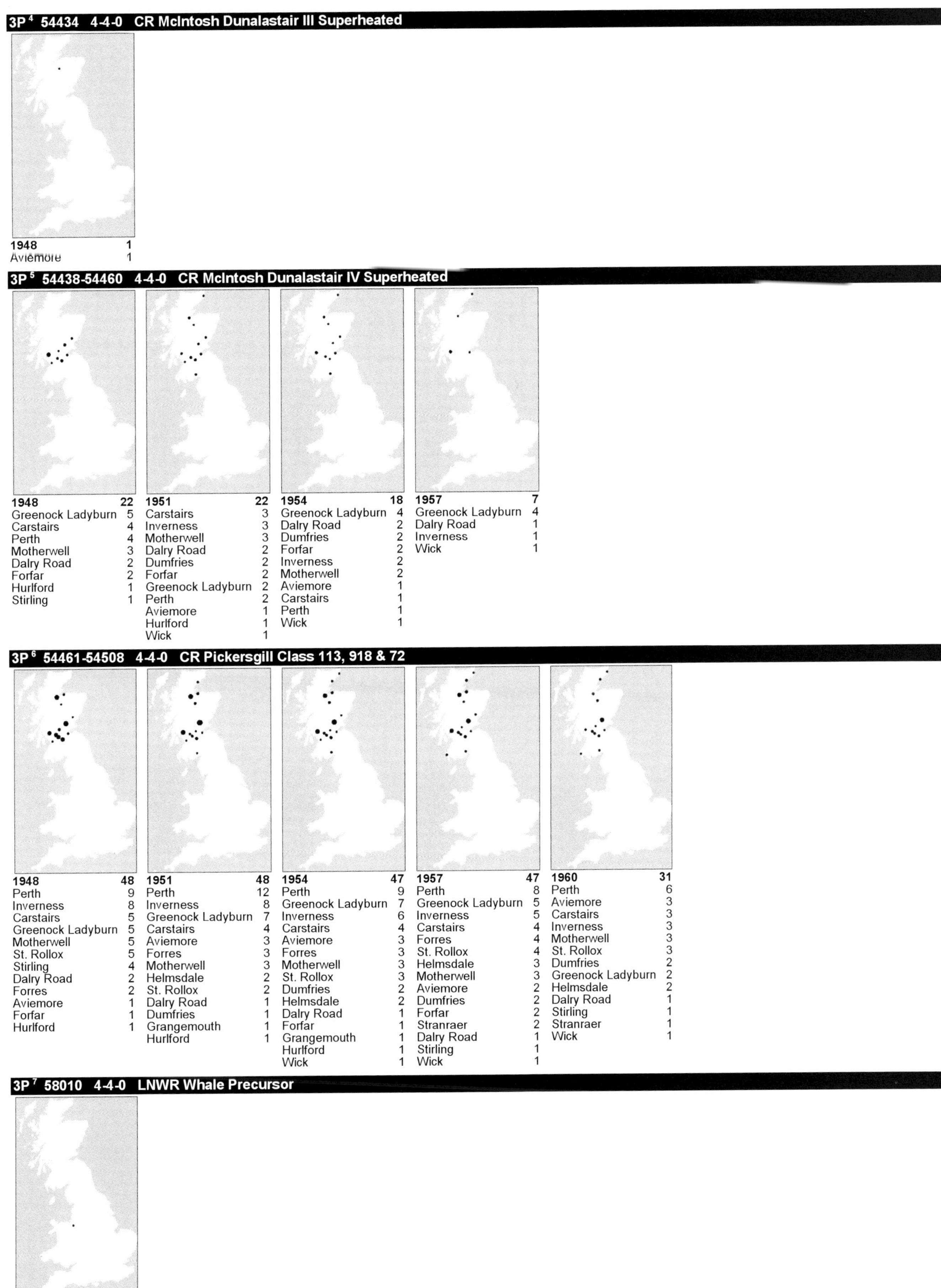

3P^{4} 54434 4-4-0 CR McIntosh Dunalastair III Superheated

1948	1
Aviemore	1

3P^{5} 54438-54460 4-4-0 CR McIntosh Dunalastair IV Superheated

1948	22
Greenock Ladyburn	5
Carstairs	4
Perth	4
Motherwell	3
Dalry Road	2
Forfar	2
Hurlford	1
Stirling	1

1951	22
Carstairs	3
Inverness	3
Motherwell	3
Dalry Road	2
Dumfries	2
Forfar	2
Greenock Ladyburn	2
Perth	2
Aviemore	1
Hurlford	1
Wick	1

1954	18
Greenock Ladyburn	4
Dalry Road	2
Dumfries	2
Forfar	2
Inverness	2
Motherwell	2
Aviemore	1
Carstairs	1
Perth	1
Wick	1

1957	7
Greenock Ladyburn	4
Dalry Road	1
Inverness	1
Wick	1

3P^{6} 54461-54508 4-4-0 CR Pickersgill Class 113, 918 & 72

1948	48
Perth	9
Inverness	8
Carstairs	5
Greenock Ladyburn	5
Motherwell	5
St. Rollox	5
Stirling	4
Dalry Road	2
Forres	2
Aviemore	1
Forfar	1
Hurlford	1

1951	48
Perth	12
Inverness	8
Greenock Ladyburn	7
Carstairs	4
Aviemore	3
Forres	3
Motherwell	3
Helmsdale	2
St. Rollox	2
Dalry Road	1
Dumfries	1
Grangemouth	1
Hurlford	1

1954	47
Perth	9
Greenock Ladyburn	7
Inverness	6
Carstairs	4
Aviemore	3
Forres	3
Motherwell	3
St. Rollox	3
Dumfries	2
Helmsdale	2
Dalry Road	1
Forfar	1
Grangemouth	1
Hurlford	1
Wick	1

1957	47
Perth	8
Greenock Ladyburn	5
Inverness	5
Carstairs	4
Forres	4
St. Rollox	4
Helmsdale	3
Motherwell	3
Aviemore	2
Dumfries	2
Forfar	2
Stranraer	2
Dalry Road	1
Stirling	1
Wick	1

1960	31
Perth	6
Aviemore	3
Carstairs	3
Inverness	3
Motherwell	3
St. Rollox	3
Dumfries	2
Greenock Ladyburn	2
Helmsdale	2
Dalry Road	1
Stirling	1
Stranraer	1
Wick	1

3P^{7} 58010 4-4-0 LNWR Whale Precursor

1948	1
Chester	1

3P[8] 58011-58012 4-4-0 LNWR Bowen Cooke George V

1948	3
Chester	3

3MT[1] 40001-40070 2-6-2T LMS Fowler

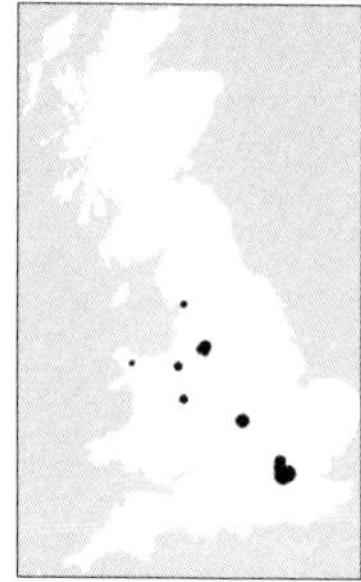

1948	70
Cricklewood	9
Kentish Town	7
Lees Oldham	7
Walsall	6
Bushbury	5
Newton Heath	5
Watford	5
Shrewsbury	4
Edge Hill	3
St. Albans	3
Barrow	2
Carnforth	2
Hellifield	2
Rugby	2
Tebay	2
Warwick	2
Llandudno Junction	1
Longsight	1
Nuneaton	1
Stockport Edgeley	1

1951	70
Kentish Town	11
Willesden	11
Lees Oldham	8
Newton Heath	4
Shrewsbury	4
St. Albans	4
Walsall	4
Bushbury	3
Carnforth	3
Cricklewood	3
Edge Hill	3
Watford	3
Hellifield	2
Warwick	2
Aston	1
Gloucester Barnwood	1
Manningham	1
Tebay	1
Warrington Dallam	1

1954	70
Willesden	23
Kentish Town	12
Lees Oldham	8
Newton Heath	4
Shrewsbury	4
St. Albans	4
Carnforth	3
Watford	3
Beattock	2
Cricklewood	2
Tebay	2
Trafford Park	2
Nuneaton	1

1957	70
Willesden	16
Kentish Town	12
Rugby	8
Newton Heath	6
St. Albans	5
Chester Northgate	4
Shrewsbury	4
Trafford Park	4
Cricklewood	3
Watford	3
Carnforth	2
Heaton Mersey	2
Bangor	1

1960	38
Kentish Town	11
Willesden	8
Newton Heath	4
St. Albans	4
Bedford	2
Carnforth	2
Heaton Mersey	2
Mansfield	2
Trafford Park	2
Wolverton Works	1

Below: LMS Fowler '3MT' 2-6-2T No 40043 at Derby in 1953.

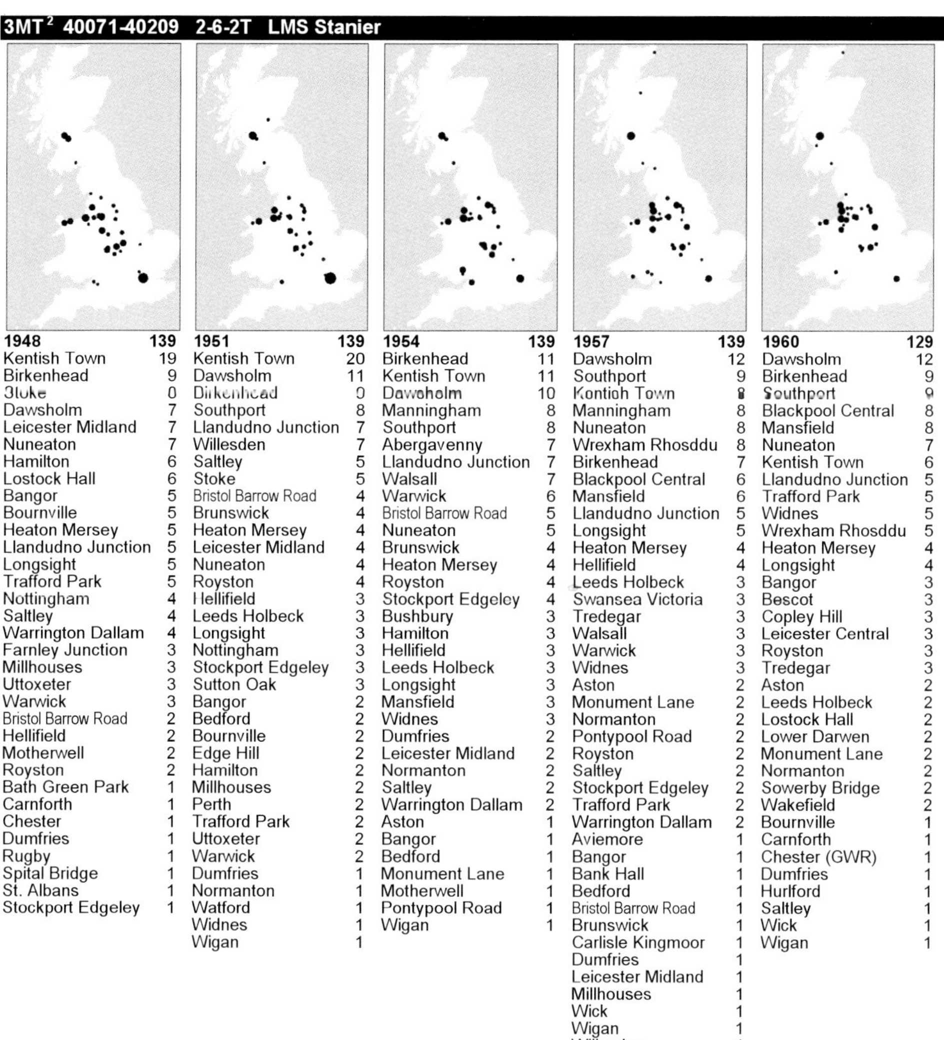

3MT² 40071-40209 2-6-2T LMS Stanier

1948	139	1951	139	1954	139	1957	139	1960	129
Kentish Town	19	Kentish Town	20	Birkenhead	11	Dawsholm	12	Dawsholm	12
Birkenhead	9	Dawsholm	11	Kentish Town	11	Southport	9	Birkenhead	9
Stoke	8	Birkenhead	9	Dawsholm	10	Kentish Town	8	Southport	9
Dawsholm	7	Southport	8	Manningham	8	Manningham	8	Blackpool Central	8
Leicester Midland	7	Llandudno Junction	7	Southport	8	Nuneaton	8	Mansfield	8
Nuneaton	7	Willesden	7	Abergavenny	7	Wrexham Rhosddu	8	Nuneaton	7
Hamilton	6	Saltley	5	Llandudno Junction	7	Birkenhead	7	Kentish Town	6
Lostock Hall	6	Stoke	5	Walsall	7	Blackpool Central	6	Llandudno Junction	5
Bangor	5	Bristol Barrow Road	4	Warwick	6	Mansfield	6	Trafford Park	5
Bournville	5	Brunswick	4	Bristol Barrow Road	5	Llandudno Junction	5	Widnes	5
Heaton Mersey	5	Heaton Mersey	4	Nuneaton	5	Longsight	5	Wrexham Rhosddu	5
Llandudno Junction	5	Leicester Midland	4	Brunswick	4	Heaton Mersey	4	Heaton Mersey	4
Longsight	5	Nuneaton	4	Heaton Mersey	4	Hellifield	4	Longsight	4
Trafford Park	5	Royston	4	Royston	4	Leeds Holbeck	3	Bangor	3
Nottingham	4	Hellifield	3	Stockport Edgeley	4	Swansea Victoria	3	Bescot	3
Saltley	4	Leeds Holbeck	3	Bushbury	3	Tredegar	3	Copley Hill	3
Warrington Dallam	4	Longsight	3	Hamilton	3	Walsall	3	Leicester Central	3
Farnley Junction	3	Nottingham	3	Hellifield	3	Warwick	3	Royston	3
Millhouses	3	Stockport Edgeley	3	Leeds Holbeck	3	Widnes	3	Tredegar	3
Uttoxeter	3	Sutton Oak	3	Longsight	3	Aston	2	Aston	2
Warwick	3	Bangor	2	Mansfield	3	Monument Lane	2	Leeds Holbeck	2
Bristol Barrow Road	2	Bedford	2	Widnes	3	Normanton	2	Lostock Hall	2
Hellifield	2	Bournville	2	Dumfries	2	Pontypool Road	2	Lower Darwen	2
Motherwell	2	Edge Hill	2	Leicester Midland	2	Royston	2	Monument Lane	2
Royston	2	Hamilton	2	Normanton	2	Saltley	2	Normanton	2
Bath Green Park	1	Millhouses	2	Saltley	2	Stockport Edgeley	2	Sowerby Bridge	2
Carnforth	1	Perth	2	Warrington Dallam	2	Trafford Park	2	Wakefield	2
Chester	1	Trafford Park	2	Aston	1	Warrington Dallam	2	Bournville	1
Dumfries	1	Uttoxeter	2	Bangor	1	Aviemore	1	Carnforth	1
Rugby	1	Warwick	2	Bedford	1	Bangor	1	Chester (GWR)	1
Spital Bridge	1	Dumfries	1	Monument Lane	1	Bank Hall	1	Dumfries	1
St. Albans	1	Normanton	1	Motherwell	1	Bedford	1	Hurlford	1
Stockport Edgeley	1	Watford	1	Pontypool Road	1	Bristol Barrow Road	1	Saltley	1
		Widnes	1	Wigan	1	Brunswick	1	Wick	1
		Wigan	1			Carlisle Kingmoor	1	Wigan	1
						Dumfries	1		
						Leicester Midland	1		
						Millhouses	1		
						Wick	1		
						Wigan	1		
						Willesden	1		

Below: LMS Stanier '3MT' 2-6-2T No 40184.

4F [1] 43835-44026 0-6-0 MR Fowler

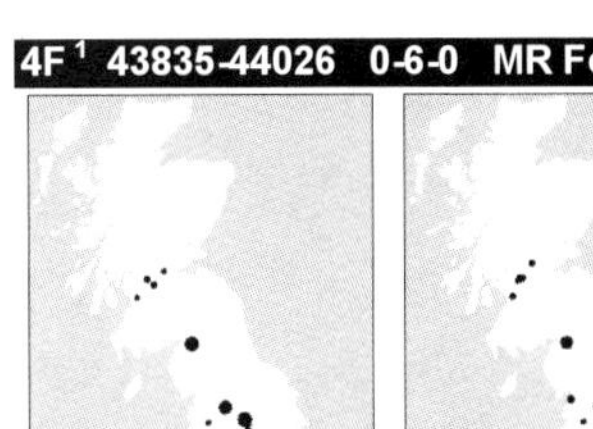
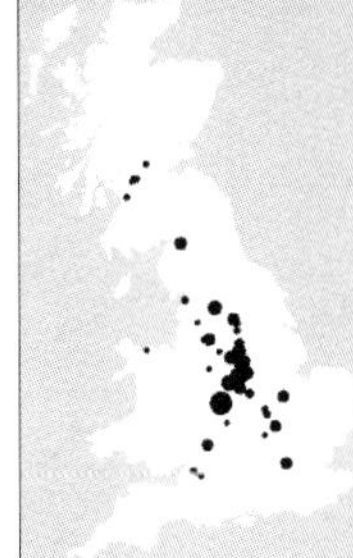
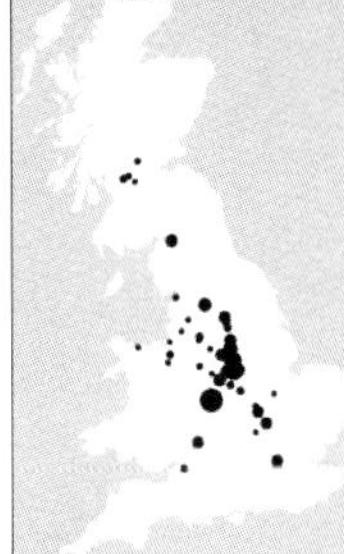

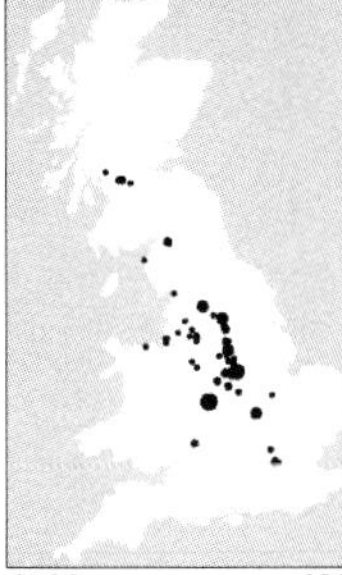
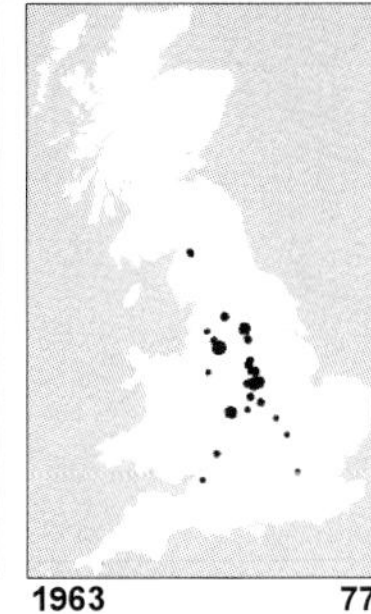

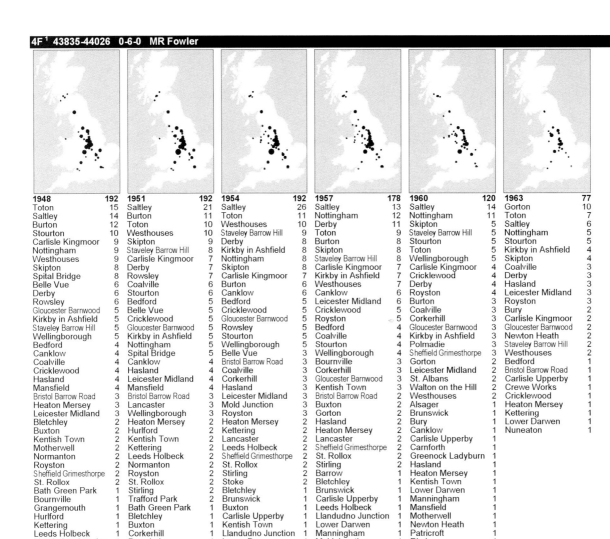

1948	192	1951	192	1954	192	1957	178	1960	120	1963	77
Toton	15	Saltley	21	Saltley	26	Saltley	13	Saltley	14	Gorton	10
Saltley	14	Burton	11	Toton	11	Nottingham	12	Nottingham	11	Toton	7
Burton	12	Toton	10	Westhouses	10	Derby	11	Skipton	5	Saltley	6
Stourton	10	Westhouses	10	Staveley Barrow Hill	9	Toton	9	Staveley Barrow Hill	5	Nottingham	5
Carlisle Kingmoor	9	Skipton	9	Derby	8	Burton	8	Stourton	5	Stourton	5
Nottingham	9	Staveley Barrow Hill	8	Kirkby in Ashfield	8	Skipton	8	Toton	5	Kirkby in Ashfield	4
Westhouses	9	Carlisle Kingmoor	7	Nottingham	8	Staveley Barrow Hill	8	Wellingborough	5	Skipton	4
Skipton	8	Derby	7	Skipton	8	Carlisle Kingmoor	7	Carlisle Kingmoor	4	Coalville	3
Spital Bridge	8	Rowsley	7	Carlisle Kingmoor	7	Kirkby in Ashfield	7	Cricklewood	4	Derby	3
Belle Vue	6	Coalville	6	Burton	6	Westhouses	7	Derby	4	Hasland	3
Derby	6	Stourton	6	Canklow	6	Canklow	6	Royston	4	Leicester Midland	3
Rowsley	6	Bedford	5	Bedford	5	Leicester Midland	6	Burton	3	Royston	3
Gloucester Barnwood	5	Belle Vue	5	Cricklewood	5	Cricklewood	5	Coalville	3	Bury	2
Kirkby in Ashfield	5	Cricklewood	5	Gloucester Barnwood	5	Royston	5	Corkerhill	3	Carlisle Kingmoor	2
Staveley Barrow Hill	5	Gloucester Barnwood	5	Rowsley	5	Bedford	4	Gloucester Barnwood	3	Gloucester Barnwood	2
Wellingborough	5	Kirkby in Ashfield	5	Stourton	5	Coalville	4	Kirkby in Ashfield	3	Newton Heath	2
Bedford	4	Nottingham	5	Wellingborough	5	Stourton	4	Polmadie	3	Staveley Barrow Hill	2
Canklow	4	Spital Bridge	5	Belle Vue	3	Wellingborough	4	Sheffield Grimesthorpe	3	Westhouses	2
Coalville	4	Canklow	4	Bristol Barrow Road	3	Bournville	3	Gorton	2	Bedford	1
Cricklewood	4	Hasland	4	Coalville	3	Corkerhill	3	Leicester Midland	2	Bristol Barrow Road	1
Hasland	4	Leicester Midland	4	Corkerhill	3	Gloucester Barnwood	3	St. Albans	2	Carlisle Upperby	1
Mansfield	4	Mansfield	4	Hasland	3	Kentish Town	3	Walton on the Hill	2	Crewe Works	1
Bristol Barrow Road	3	Bristol Barrow Road	3	Leicester Midland	3	Bristol Barrow Road	2	Westhouses	2	Cricklewood	1
Heaton Mersey	3	Lancaster	3	Mold Junction	3	Buxton	2	Alsager	1	Heaton Mersey	1
Leicester Midland	3	Wellingborough	3	Royston	3	Gorton	2	Brunswick	1	Kettering	1
Bletchley	2	Heaton Mersey	2	Heaton Mersey	2	Hasland	2	Bury	1	Lower Darwen	1
Buxton	2	Hurlford	2	Kettering	2	Heaton Mersey	2	Canklow	1	Nuneaton	1
Kentish Town	2	Kentish Town	2	Lancaster	2	Lancaster	2	Carlisle Upperby	1		
Motherwell	2	Kettering	2	Leeds Holbeck	2	Sheffield Grimesthorpe	2	Carnforth	1		
Normanton	2	Leeds Holbeck	2	Sheffield Grimesthorpe	2	St. Rollox	2	Greenock Ladyburn	1		
Royston	2	Normanton	2	St. Rollox	2	Stirling	2	Hasland	1		
Sheffield Grimesthorpe	2	Royston	2	Stirling	2	Barrow	1	Heaton Mersey	1		
St. Rollox	2	St. Rollox	2	Stoke	2	Bletchley	1	Kentish Town	1		
Bath Green Park	1	Stirling	2	Bletchley	1	Brunswick	1	Lower Darwen	1		
Bournville	1	Trafford Park	2	Brunswick	1	Carlisle Upperby	1	Manningham	1		
Grangemouth	1	Bath Green Park	1	Buxton	1	Leeds Holbeck	1	Mansfield	1		
Hurlford	1	Bletchley	1	Carlisle Upperby	1	Llandudno Junction	1	Motherwell	1		
Kettering	1	Buxton	1	Kentish Town	1	Lower Darwen	1	Newton Heath	1		
Leeds Holbeck	1	Corkerhill	1	Llandudno Junction	1	Manningham	1	Patricroft	1		
Llandudno Junction	1	Dawsholm	1	Lower Darwen	1	Mold Junction	1	Rhyl	1		
Lower Darwen	1	Llandudno Junction	1	Mansfield	1	Motherwell	1	Rowsley	1		
Plaistow	1	Lower Darwen	1	Motherwell	1	Newton Heath	1	Spital Bridge	1		
Stratford on Avon	1	Sheffield Grimesthorpe	1	Normanton	1	Normanton	1	Stoke	1		
Trafford Park	1	Stoke	1	Spital Bridge	1	Rowsley	1	Wakefield	1		
		Stratford on Avon	1	Uttoxeter	1	Spital Bridge	1	Wigan	1		
				Wakefield	1	Stoke	1	Workington	1		
				Wigan	1	Tebay	1				
				Wrexham Rhosddu	1	Uttoxeter	1				
						Wakefield	1				
						Wigan	1				
						Wrexham Rhosddu	1				

Midland Railway Fowler '4F' class 0-6-0 No 43914 based at 55D Royston. *J. B. Bucknall*

4F² 44027-44606 0-6-0 LMS & SDJR Fowler

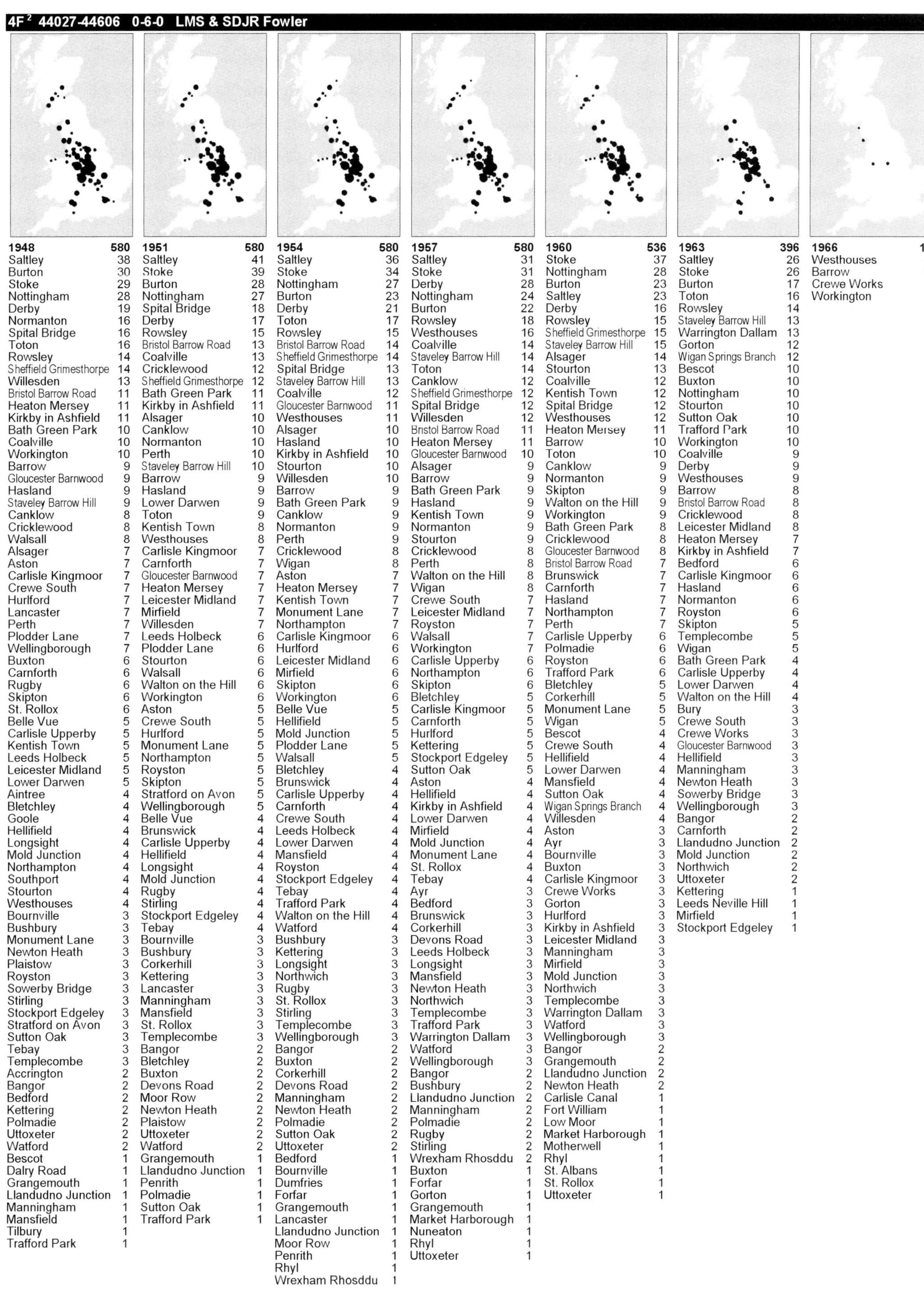

1948	580
Saltley	38
Burton	30
Stoke	29
Nottingham	28
Derby	19
Normanton	16
Spital Bridge	16
Toton	16
Rowsley	14
Sheffield Grimesthorpe	14
Willesden	13
Bristol Barrow Road	11
Heaton Mersey	11
Kirkby in Ashfield	11
Bath Green Park	10
Coalville	10
Workington	10
Barrow	9
Gloucester Barnwood	9
Hasland	9
Staveley Barrow Hill	9
Canklow	8
Cricklewood	8
Walsall	8
Alsager	7
Aston	7
Carlisle Kingmoor	7
Crewe South	7
Hurlford	7
Lancaster	7
Perth	7
Plodder Lane	7
Wellingborough	7
Buxton	6
Carnforth	6
Rugby	6
Skipton	6
St. Rollox	6
Belle Vue	5
Carlisle Upperby	5
Kentish Town	5
Leeds Holbeck	5
Leicester Midland	5
Lower Darwen	5
Aintree	4
Bletchley	4
Goole	4
Hellifield	4
Longsight	4
Mold Junction	4
Northampton	4
Southport	4
Stourton	4
Westhouses	4
Bournville	3
Bushbury	3
Monument Lane	3
Newton Heath	3
Plaistow	3
Royston	3
Sowerby Bridge	3
Stirling	3
Stockport Edgeley	3
Stratford on Avon	3
Sutton Oak	3
Tebay	3
Templecombe	3
Accrington	2
Bangor	2
Bedford	2
Kettering	2
Polmadie	2
Uttoxeter	2
Watford	2
Bescot	1
Dalry Road	1
Grangemouth	1
Llandudno Junction	1
Manningham	1
Mansfield	1
Tilbury	1
Trafford Park	1

1951	580
Saltley	41
Stoke	39
Burton	28
Nottingham	27
Spital Bridge	18
Derby	17
Rowsley	15
Bristol Barrow Road	13
Coalville	13
Cricklewood	12
Sheffield Grimesthorpe	12
Bath Green Park	11
Kirkby in Ashfield	11
Alsager	10
Canklow	10
Normanton	10
Perth	10
Staveley Barrow Hill	10
Barrow	9
Hasland	9
Lower Darwen	9
Toton	9
Kentish Town	8
Westhouses	8
Carlisle Kingmoor	7
Carnforth	7
Gloucester Barnwood	7
Heaton Mersey	7
Leicester Midland	7
Mirfield	7
Willesden	7
Leeds Holbeck	6
Plodder Lane	6
Stourton	6
Walsall	6
Walton on the Hill	6
Workington	6
Aston	5
Crewe South	5
Hurlford	5
Monument Lane	5
Northampton	5
Royston	5
Skipton	5
Stratford on Avon	5
Wellingborough	5
Belle Vue	4
Brunswick	4
Carlisle Upperby	4
Hellifield	4
Longsight	4
Mold Junction	4
Rugby	4
Stirling	4
Stockport Edgeley	4
Tebay	4
Bournville	3
Bushbury	3
Corkerhill	3
Kettering	3
Lancaster	3
Manningham	3
Mansfield	3
St. Rollox	3
Templecombe	3
Bangor	2
Bletchley	2
Buxton	2
Devons Road	2
Moor Row	2
Newton Heath	2
Plaistow	2
Uttoxeter	2
Watford	2
Grangemouth	1
Llandudno Junction	1
Penrith	1
Polmadie	1
Sutton Oak	1
Trafford Park	1

1954	580
Saltley	36
Stoke	34
Nottingham	27
Burton	23
Derby	21
Toton	17
Rowsley	15
Bristol Barrow Road	14
Sheffield Grimesthorpe	14
Spital Bridge	13
Staveley Barrow Hill	13
Coalville	12
Gloucester Barnwood	11
Westhouses	11
Alsager	10
Hasland	10
Kirkby in Ashfield	10
Stourton	10
Willesden	10
Barrow	9
Bath Green Park	9
Canklow	9
Normanton	9
Perth	9
Cricklewood	8
Wigan	8
Aston	7
Heaton Mersey	7
Kentish Town	7
Monument Lane	7
Northampton	7
Carlisle Kingmoor	6
Hurlford	6
Leicester Midland	6
Mirfield	6
Skipton	6
Workington	6
Belle Vue	5
Hellifield	5
Mold Junction	5
Plodder Lane	5
Walsall	5
Bletchley	4
Brunswick	4
Carlisle Upperby	4
Carnforth	4
Crewe South	4
Leeds Holbeck	4
Lower Darwen	4
Mansfield	4
Royston	4
Stockport Edgeley	4
Tebay	4
Trafford Park	4
Walton on the Hill	4
Watford	4
Bushbury	3
Kettering	3
Longsight	3
Northwich	3
Rugby	3
St. Rollox	3
Stirling	3
Templecombe	3
Wellingborough	3
Bangor	2
Buxton	2
Corkerhill	2
Devons Road	2
Manningham	2
Newton Heath	2
Polmadie	2
Sutton Oak	2
Uttoxeter	2
Bedford	1
Bournville	1
Dumfries	1
Forfar	1
Grangemouth	1
Lancaster	1
Llandudno Junction	1
Moor Row	1
Penrith	1
Rhyl	1
Wrexham Rhosddu	1

1957	580
Saltley	31
Stoke	31
Derby	28
Nottingham	24
Burton	22
Rowsley	18
Westhouses	16
Coalville	14
Staveley Barrow Hill	14
Toton	14
Canklow	12
Sheffield Grimesthorpe	12
Spital Bridge	12
Willesden	12
Bristol Barrow Road	11
Heaton Mersey	11
Gloucester Barnwood	10
Alsager	9
Barrow	9
Bath Green Park	9
Hasland	9
Kentish Town	9
Normanton	9
Stourton	9
Cricklewood	8
Perth	8
Walton on the Hill	8
Wigan	8
Crewe South	7
Leicester Midland	7
Royston	7
Walsall	7
Workington	7
Carlisle Upperby	6
Northampton	6
Skipton	6
Bletchley	5
Carlisle Kingmoor	5
Carnforth	5
Hurlford	5
Kettering	5
Stockport Edgeley	5
Sutton Oak	5
Aston	4
Hellifield	4
Kirkby in Ashfield	4
Lower Darwen	4
Mirfield	4
Mold Junction	4
Monument Lane	4
St. Rollox	4
Tebay	4
Ayr	3
Bedford	3
Brunswick	3
Corkerhill	3
Devons Road	3
Leeds Holbeck	3
Longsight	3
Mansfield	3
Newton Heath	3
Northwich	3
Templecombe	3
Trafford Park	3
Warrington Dallam	3
Watford	3
Wellingborough	3
Bangor	2
Bushbury	2
Llandudno Junction	2
Manningham	2
Polmadie	2
Rugby	2
Stirling	2
Wrexham Rhosddu	2
Buxton	1
Forfar	1
Gorton	1
Grangemouth	1
Market Harborough	1
Nuneaton	1
Rhyl	1
Uttoxeter	1

1960	536
Stoke	37
Nottingham	28
Burton	23
Saltley	23
Derby	16
Rowsley	15
Sheffield Grimesthorpe	15
Staveley Barrow Hill	15
Alsager	14
Stourton	13
Coalville	12
Kentish Town	12
Spital Bridge	12
Westhouses	12
Heaton Mersey	11
Barrow	10
Toton	10
Canklow	9
Normanton	9
Skipton	9
Walton on the Hill	9
Workington	9
Bath Green Park	8
Cricklewood	8
Gloucester Barnwood	8
Bristol Barrow Road	7
Brunswick	7
Carnforth	7
Hasland	7
Northampton	7
Perth	7
Carlisle Upperby	6
Polmadie	6
Royston	6
Trafford Park	6
Bletchley	5
Corkerhill	5
Monument Lane	5
Wigan	5
Bescot	4
Crewe South	4
Hellifield	4
Lower Darwen	4
Mansfield	4
Sutton Oak	4
Wigan Springs Branch	4
Willesden	4
Aston	3
Ayr	3
Bournville	3
Buxton	3
Carlisle Kingmoor	3
Crewe Works	3
Gorton	3
Hurlford	3
Kirkby in Ashfield	3
Leicester Midland	3
Manningham	3
Mirfield	3
Mold Junction	3
Northwich	3
Templecombe	3
Warrington Dallam	3
Watford	3
Wellingborough	3
Bangor	2
Grangemouth	2
Llandudno Junction	2
Newton Heath	2
Carlisle Canal	1
Fort William	1
Low Moor	1
Market Harborough	1
Motherwell	1
Rhyl	1
St. Albans	1
St. Rollox	1
Uttoxeter	1

1963	396
Saltley	26
Stoke	26
Burton	17
Toton	16
Rowsley	14
Staveley Barrow Hill	13
Warrington Dallam	13
Gorton	12
Wigan Springs Branch	12
Bescot	10
Buxton	10
Nottingham	10
Stourton	10
Sutton Oak	10
Trafford Park	10
Workington	10
Coalville	9
Derby	9
Westhouses	9
Barrow	8
Bristol Barrow Road	8
Cricklewood	8
Leicester Midland	8
Heaton Mersey	7
Kirkby in Ashfield	7
Bedford	6
Carlisle Kingmoor	6
Hasland	6
Normanton	6
Royston	6
Skipton	5
Templecombe	5
Wigan	5
Bath Green Park	4
Carlisle Upperby	4
Lower Darwen	4
Walton on the Hill	4
Bury	3
Crewe South	3
Crewe Works	3
Gloucester Barnwood	3
Hellifield	3
Manningham	3
Newton Heath	3
Sowerby Bridge	3
Wellingborough	3
Bangor	2
Carnforth	2
Llandudno Junction	2
Mold Junction	2
Northwich	2
Uttoxeter	2
Kettering	1
Leeds Neville Hill	1
Mirfield	1
Stockport Edgeley	1

1966	11
Westhouses	4
Barrow	3
Crewe Works	3
Workington	1

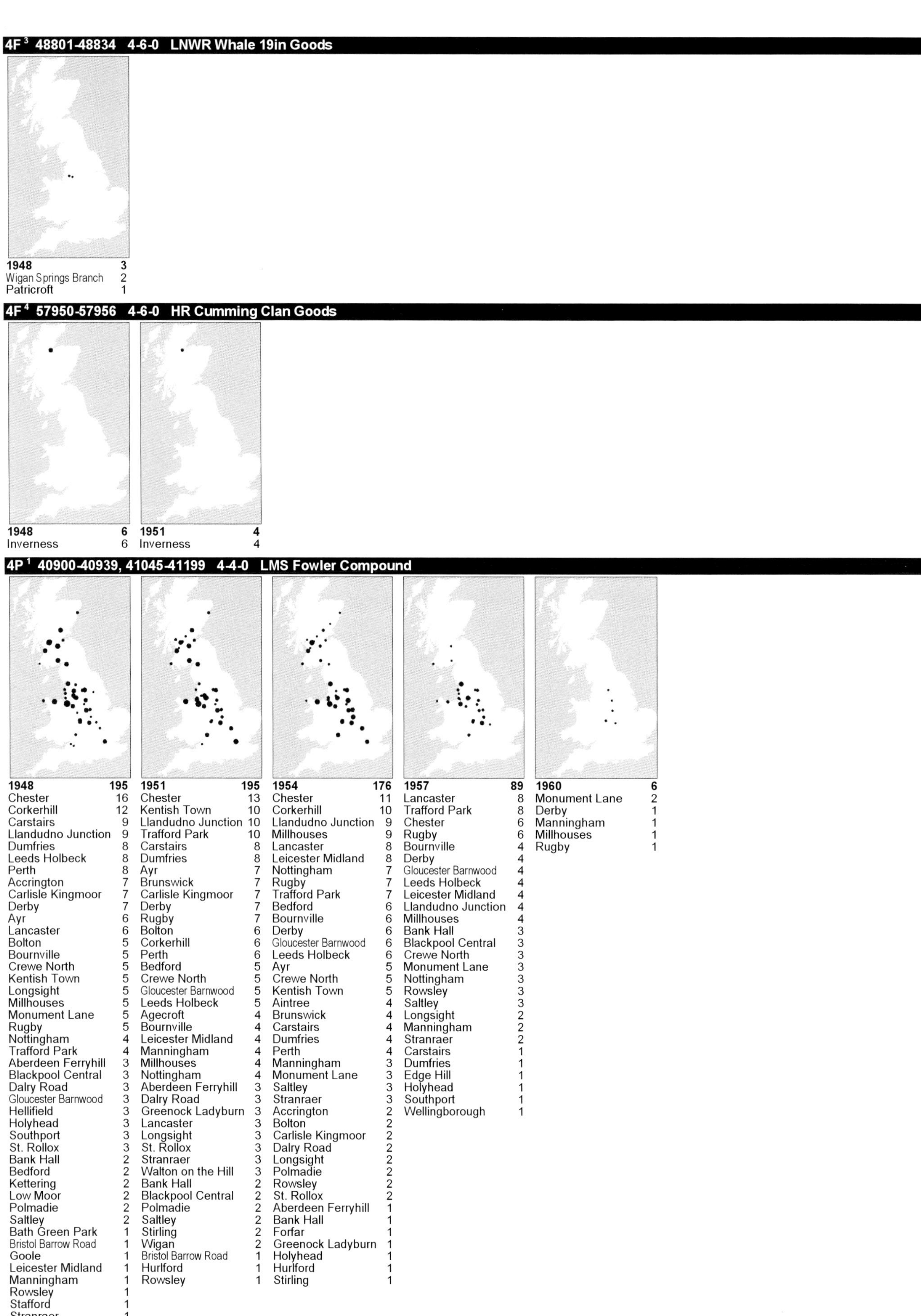

4F[3] 48801-48834 4-6-0 LNWR Whale 19in Goods

1948	3
Wigan Springs Branch	2
Patricroft	1

4F[4] 57950-57956 4-6-0 HR Cumming Clan Goods

1948	6
Inverness	6

1951	4
Inverness	4

4P[1] 40900-40939, 41045-41199 4-4-0 LMS Fowler Compound

1948	195
Chester	16
Corkerhill	12
Carstairs	9
Llandudno Junction	9
Dumfries	8
Leeds Holbeck	8
Perth	8
Accrington	7
Carlisle Kingmoor	7
Derby	7
Ayr	6
Lancaster	6
Bolton	5
Bournville	5
Crewe North	5
Kentish Town	5
Longsight	5
Millhouses	5
Monument Lane	5
Rugby	5
Nottingham	4
Trafford Park	4
Aberdeen Ferryhill	3
Blackpool Central	3
Dalry Road	3
Gloucester Barnwood	3
Hellifield	3
Holyhead	3
Southport	3
St. Rollox	3
Bank Hall	2
Bedford	2
Kettering	2
Low Moor	2
Polmadie	2
Saltley	2
Bath Green Park	1
Bristol Barrow Road	1
Goole	1
Leicester Midland	1
Manningham	1
Rowsley	1
Stafford	1
Stranraer	1

1951	195
Chester	13
Kentish Town	10
Llandudno Junction	10
Trafford Park	10
Carstairs	8
Dumfries	8
Ayr	7
Brunswick	7
Carlisle Kingmoor	7
Derby	7
Rugby	7
Bolton	6
Corkerhill	6
Perth	6
Bedford	5
Crewe North	5
Gloucester Barnwood	5
Leeds Holbeck	5
Agecroft	4
Bournville	4
Leicester Midland	4
Manningham	4
Millhouses	4
Nottingham	4
Aberdeen Ferryhill	3
Dalry Road	3
Greenock Ladyburn	3
Lancaster	3
Longsight	3
St. Rollox	3
Stranraer	3
Walton on the Hill	3
Bank Hall	2
Blackpool Central	2
Polmadie	2
Saltley	2
Stirling	2
Wigan	2
Bristol Barrow Road	1
Hurlford	1
Rowsley	1

1954	176
Chester	11
Corkerhill	10
Llandudno Junction	9
Millhouses	9
Lancaster	8
Leicester Midland	8
Nottingham	7
Rugby	7
Trafford Park	7
Bedford	6
Bournville	6
Derby	6
Gloucester Barnwood	6
Leeds Holbeck	6
Ayr	5
Crewe North	5
Kentish Town	5
Aintree	4
Brunswick	4
Carstairs	4
Dumfries	4
Perth	4
Manningham	3
Monument Lane	3
Saltley	3
Stranraer	3
Accrington	2
Bolton	2
Carlisle Kingmoor	2
Dalry Road	2
Longsight	2
Polmadie	2
Rowsley	2
St. Rollox	2
Aberdeen Ferryhill	1
Bank Hall	1
Forfar	1
Greenock Ladyburn	1
Holyhead	1
Hurlford	1
Stirling	1

1957	89
Lancaster	8
Trafford Park	8
Chester	6
Rugby	6
Bournville	4
Derby	4
Gloucester Barnwood	4
Leeds Holbeck	4
Leicester Midland	4
Llandudno Junction	4
Millhouses	4
Bank Hall	3
Blackpool Central	3
Crewe North	3
Monument Lane	3
Nottingham	3
Rowsley	3
Saltley	3
Longsight	2
Manningham	2
Stranraer	2
Carstairs	1
Dumfries	1
Edge Hill	1
Holyhead	1
Southport	1
Wellingborough	1

1960	6
Monument Lane	2
Derby	1
Manningham	1
Millhouses	1
Rugby	1

4P² 41000-41044, 1000 4-4-0 MR Deeley Compound

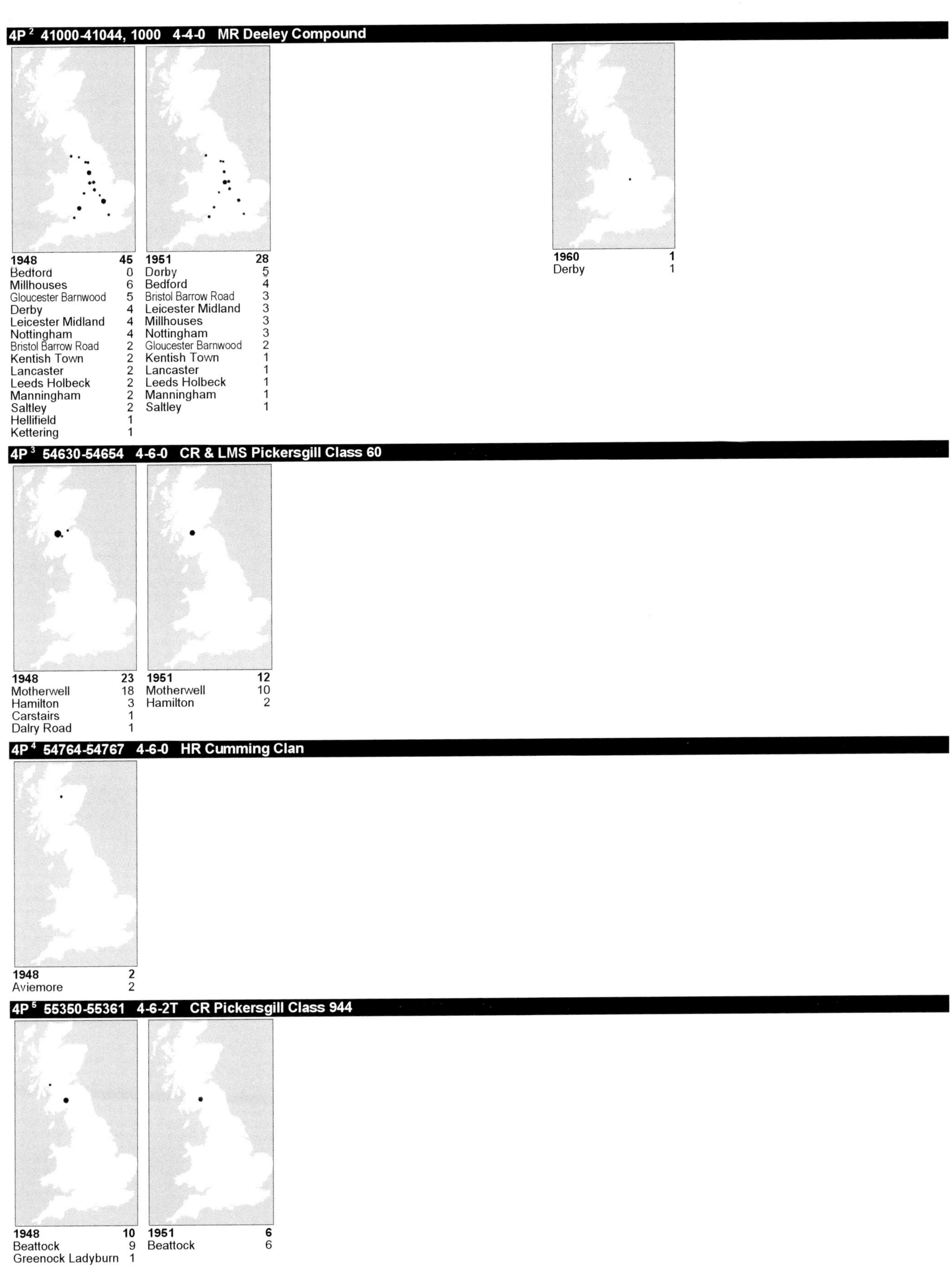

1948	45
Bedford	0
Millhouses	6
Gloucester Barnwood	5
Derby	4
Leicester Midland	4
Nottingham	4
Bristol Barrow Road	2
Kentish Town	2
Lancaster	2
Leeds Holbeck	2
Manningham	2
Saltley	2
Hellifield	1
Kettering	1

1951	28
Derby	5
Bedford	4
Bristol Barrow Road	3
Leicester Midland	3
Millhouses	3
Nottingham	3
Gloucester Barnwood	2
Kentish Town	1
Lancaster	1
Leeds Holbeck	1
Manningham	1
Saltley	1

1960	1
Derby	1

4P³ 54630-54654 4-6-0 CR & LMS Pickersgill Class 60

1948	23
Motherwell	18
Hamilton	3
Carstairs	1
Dalry Road	1

1951	12
Motherwell	10
Hamilton	2

4P⁴ 54764-54767 4-6-0 HR Cumming Clan

1948	2
Aviemore	2

4P⁵ 55350-55361 4-6-2T CR Pickersgill Class 944

1948	10
Beattock	9
Greenock Ladyburn	1

1951	6
Beattock	6

4P[6] 58000-58003 4-6-0 LNWR Bowen Cooke Prince of Wales

1948	6
Stafford	4
Bletchley	2

4MT[1] 42050-42299, 42673-42699 2-6-4T LMS Fairburn

1948	130
Polmadie	35
Newton Heath	13
Plaistow	13
Stoke	11
Low Moor	7
Dalry Road	6
Nottingham	6
Ardrossan	4
Bangor	4
Monument Lane	4
Southport	4
Tilbury	4
Corkerhill	3
Kentish Town	3
Shoeburyness	3
St. Albans	2
Accrington	1
Carnforth	1
Chester	1
Crewe North	1
Greenock Ladyburn	1
Hamilton	1
Manningham	1
Saltley	1

1951	260
Polmadie	46
Plaistow	20
Newton Heath	13
Low Moor	12
Stoke	12
Corkerhill	11
Tunbridge Wells West	10
Bangor	7
Nottingham	7
Tilbury	7
Dalry Road	6
Hamilton	6
Motherwell	6
Carstairs	5
Kentish Town	5
Monument Lane	5
Ramsgate	5
Stewarts Lane	5
Watford	5
Ardrossan	4
Dover Marine	4
Leicester Midland	4
Saltley	4
Southport	4
St. Albans	4
Greenock Ladyburn	3
Lancaster	3
Lostock Hall	3
Manningham	3
Royston	3
Sowerby Bridge	3
Wigan	3
Accrington	2
Ayr	2
Bournville	2
Lower Darwen	2
Stirling	2
Willesden	2
Barrow	1
Belle Vue	1
Blackpool Central	1
Derby	1
Mirfield	1
Rose Grove	1
Rugby	1
Shoeburyness	1
Warwick	1
Wigan Springs Branch	1

1954	277
Polmadie	35
Plaistow	20
Newton Heath	13
Carstairs	9
Corkerhill	8
Tilbury	8
Ashford	7
Motherwell	7
Nottingham	7
Ayr	6
Bangor	6
Dalry Road	6
Low Moor	6
Brighton	5
Dover Marine	5
Greenock Ladyburn	5
Hamilton	5
Kentish Town	5
Monument Lane	5
Tunbridge Wells West	5
Ardrossan	4
Beattock	4
Ramsgate	4
Stoke	4
Three Bridges	4
Trafford Park	4
Accrington	3
Bletchley	3
Bricklayers Arms	3
Darlington	3
Derby	3
Leicester Midland	3
Lostock Hall	3
Saltley	3
Southport	3
Sowerby Bridge	3
St. Albans	3
Stewarts Lane	3
Walton on the Hill	3
Wigan	3
Bournville	2
Chester	2
Lancaster	2
Lees Oldham	2
Lower Darwen	2
Manningham	2
Perth	2
Redhill	2
St. Rollox	2
Stirling	2
Watford	2
Willesden	2
Alsager	1
Barrow	1
Blackpool Central	1
Crewe North	1
Edge Hill	1
Huddersfield	1
Mirfield	1
Normanton	1
Rose Grove	1
Rugby	1
Stockport Edgeley	1
Uttoxeter	1
Warwick	1
Wigan Springs Branch	1

1957	277
Polmadie	20
Greenock Ladyburn	17
Neasden	12
Newton Heath	12
Plaistow	11
Carstairs	9
Motherwell	9
Ashford	7
Ayr	7
Beattock	7
Corkerhill	7
Dalry Road	7
Derby	6
Hamilton	6
Kentish Town	6
Low Moor	6
Stewarts Lane	6
Three Bridges	6
Tunbridge Wells West	6
Ardrossan	5
Dover Marine	5
Shoeburyness	5
St. Albans	5
Trafford Park	5
Accrington	4
Dundee Tay Bridge	4
Gateshead	4
Leicester Midland	4
Manningham	4
Stoke	4
Bricklayers Arms	3
Lostock Hall	3
Nottingham	3
Rugby	3
Southport	3
Sowerby Bridge	3
St. Rollox	3
Walton on the Hill	3
Wigan	3
Edge Hill	2
Hellifield	2
Lancaster	2
Lees Oldham	2
Lower Darwen	2
Mirfield	2
Perth	2
Saltley	2
Scarborough	2
Stirling	2
Willesden	2
Alsager	1
Barrow	1
Birkenhead	1
Blackpool Central	1
Bolton	1
Bournville	1
Crewe North	1
Monument Lane	1
Ramsgate	1
Rose Grove	1
Warwick	1
Whitby	1

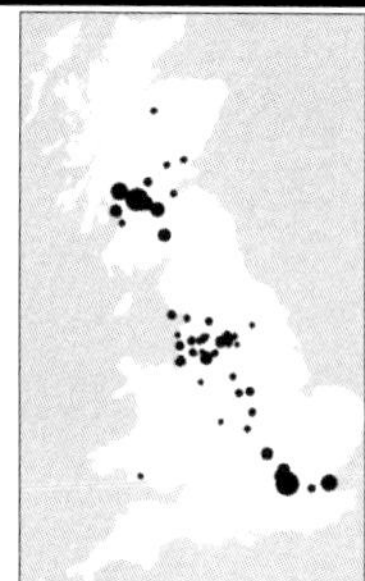

1960	277
Neasden	29
Polmadie	23
Greenock Ladyburn	14
Shoeburyness	13
Carstairs	10
Corkerhill	10
Watford	10
Willesden	10
Motherwell	9
Beattock	7
Low Moor	7
Trafford Park	7
Ardrossan	6
Bletchley	6
Hamilton	6
Kentish Town	6
St. Albans	6
Dawsholm	5
Sowerby Bridge	5
Accrington	4
Barrow	4
Lostock Hall	4
Manningham	4
Nottingham	4
Southport	4
Stirling	4
Derby	3
Hellifield	3
Leicester Midland	3
Tilbury	3
Wigan	3
Aviemore	2
Ayr	2
Birkenhead	2
Brunswick	2
Dalry Road	2
Dundee Tay Bridge	2
Edge Hill	2
Lancaster	2
Leeds Holbeck	2
Lees Oldham	2
Lower Darwen	2
Mirfield	2
Perth	2
Rowsley	2
Rugby	2
St. Rollox	2
Walton on the Hill	2
Agecroft	1
Blackpool Central	1
Bolton	1
Crewe North	1
Landore	1
Monument Lane	1
Newton Heath	1
Rose Grove	1
Wakefield	1
Wigan Springs Branch	1
York	1

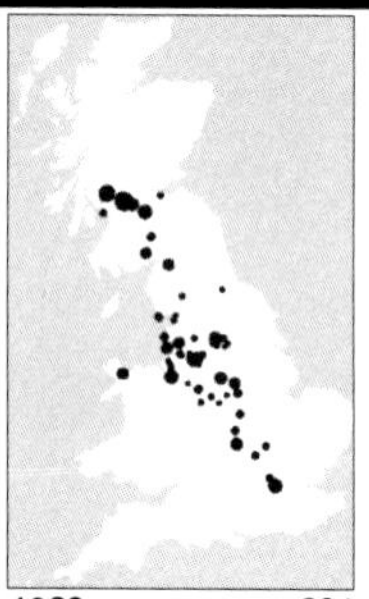

1963	231
Polmadie	17
Greenock Ladyburn	14
Chester	10
Willesden	10
Carstairs	9
Motherwell	8
Trafford Park	8
Low Moor	7
Rowsley	7
Woodford Halse	7
Bangor	6
Dawsholm	6
Carlisle Canal	5
Dumfries	5
Kirkby in Ashfield	5
Lostock Hall	5
Manningham	5
Newton Heath	5
Southport	5
Barrow	4
Beattock	4
Blackpool Central	4
Cricklewood	4
Leicester Midland	4
Nottingham	4
Rugby	4
Stoke	4
Ardrossan	3
Bedford	3
Bletchley	3
Heaton Mersey	3
Lees Oldham	3
Watford	3
Wigan	3
Dalry Road	2
Gorton	2
Lancaster	2
Leeds Holbeck	2
Normanton	2
Rose Grove	2
Speke Junction	2
Stafford	2
Tebay	2
Uttoxeter	2
Bolton	1
Burton	1
Carnforth	1
Copley Hill	1
Crewe North	1
Darlington	1
Derby	1
Edge Hill	1
Leeds Neville Hill	1
Mirfield	1
St. Rollox	1
Wakefield	1
Walton on the Hill	1
Wigan Springs Branch	1

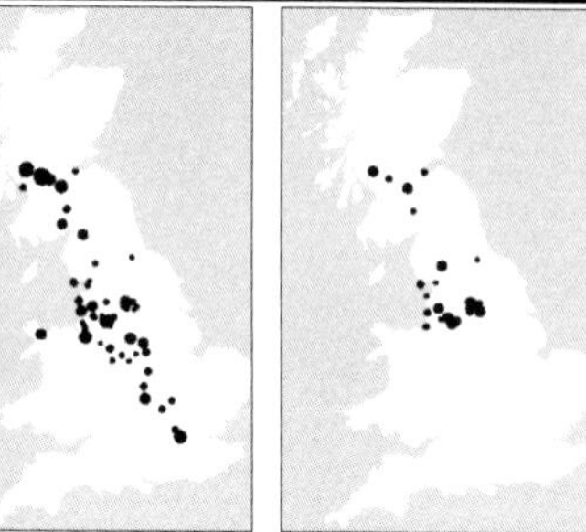

1966	90
Low Moor	7
Trafford Park	7
Bolton	6
Manningham	6
Carstairs	5
Greenock Ladyburn	5
Lostock Hall	5
Newton Heath	5
Tebay	5
Wakefield	5
Barrow	4
Birkenhead	3
Huddersfield	3
Leeds Holbeck	3
Leeds Neville Hill	3
Polmadie	3
Southport	3
St. Margarets	3
Beattock	2
Normanton	2
Wigan Springs Branch	2
Carnforth	1
Darlington	1
Fleetwood	1

4MT[2] 42300-42424 2-6-4T LMS Fowler

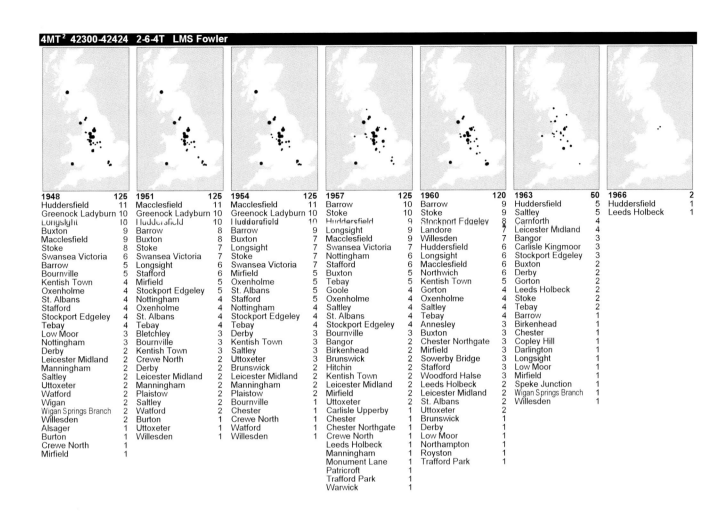

1948	125
Huddersfield	11
Greenock Ladyburn	10
Longsight	10
Buxton	9
Macclesfield	9
Stoke	8
Swansea Victoria	6
Barrow	5
Bournville	5
Kentish Town	4
Oxenholme	4
St. Albans	4
Stafford	4
Stockport Edgeley	4
Tebay	4
Low Moor	3
Nottingham	3
Derby	2
Leicester Midland	2
Manningham	2
Saltley	2
Uttoxeter	2
Watford	2
Wigan	2
Wigan Springs Branch	2
Willesden	2
Alsager	1
Burton	1
Crewe North	1
Mirfield	1

1951	125
Macclesfield	11
Greenock Ladyburn	10
Huddersfield	10
Barrow	8
Buxton	8
Stoke	7
Swansea Victoria	7
Longsight	6
Stafford	6
Mirfield	5
Stockport Edgeley	5
Nottingham	4
Oxenholme	4
St. Albans	4
Tebay	4
Bletchley	3
Bournville	3
Kentish Town	3
Crewe North	2
Derby	2
Leicester Midland	2
Manningham	2
Plaistow	2
Saltley	2
Watford	2
Burton	1
Uttoxeter	1
Willesden	1

1954	125
Macclesfield	11
Greenock Ladyburn	10
Huddersfield	10
Barrow	9
Buxton	7
Longsight	7
Stoke	7
Swansea Victoria	7
Mirfield	5
Oxenholme	5
St. Albans	5
Stafford	5
Nottingham	4
Stockport Edgeley	4
Tebay	4
Derby	3
Kentish Town	3
Saltley	3
Uttoxeter	3
Brunswick	2
Leicester Midland	2
Manningham	2
Plaistow	2
Bournville	1
Chester	1
Crewe North	1
Watford	1
Willesden	1

1957	125
Barrow	10
Stoke	10
Huddersfield	9
Longsight	9
Macclesfield	9
Swansea Victoria	7
Nottingham	6
Stafford	6
Buxton	5
Tebay	5
Goole	4
Oxenholme	4
Saltley	4
St. Albans	4
Stockport Edgeley	4
Bournville	3
Bangor	2
Birkenhead	2
Brunswick	2
Hitchin	2
Kentish Town	2
Leicester Midland	2
Mirfield	2
Uttoxeter	2
Carlisle Upperby	1
Chester	1
Chester Northgate	1
Crewe North	1
Leeds Holbeck	1
Manningham	1
Monument Lane	1
Patricroft	1
Trafford Park	1
Warwick	1

1960	120
Barrow	9
Stoke	9
Stockport Edgeley	8
Landore	7
Willesden	7
Huddersfield	6
Longsight	6
Macclesfield	6
Northwich	6
Kentish Town	5
Gorton	4
Oxenholme	4
Saltley	4
Tebay	4
Annesley	3
Buxton	3
Chester Northgate	3
Mirfield	3
Sowerby Bridge	3
Stafford	3
Woodford Halse	3
Leeds Holbeck	2
Leicester Midland	2
St. Albans	2
Uttoxeter	2
Brunswick	1
Derby	1
Low Moor	1
Northampton	1
Royston	1
Trafford Park	1

1963	50
Huddersfield	5
Saltley	5
Carnforth	4
Leicester Midland	4
Bangor	3
Carlisle Kingmoor	3
Stockport Edgeley	3
Buxton	2
Derby	2
Gorton	2
Leeds Holbeck	2
Stoke	2
Tebay	2
Barrow	1
Birkenhead	1
Chester	1
Copley Hill	1
Darlington	1
Longsight	1
Low Moor	1
Mirfield	1
Speke Junction	1
Wigan Springs Branch	1
Willesden	1

1966	2
Huddersfield	1
Leeds Holbeck	1

LMS Fowler '4MT' class 2-6-4T No 42346 at Stafford on 7 November 1953.
J. B. Bucknall

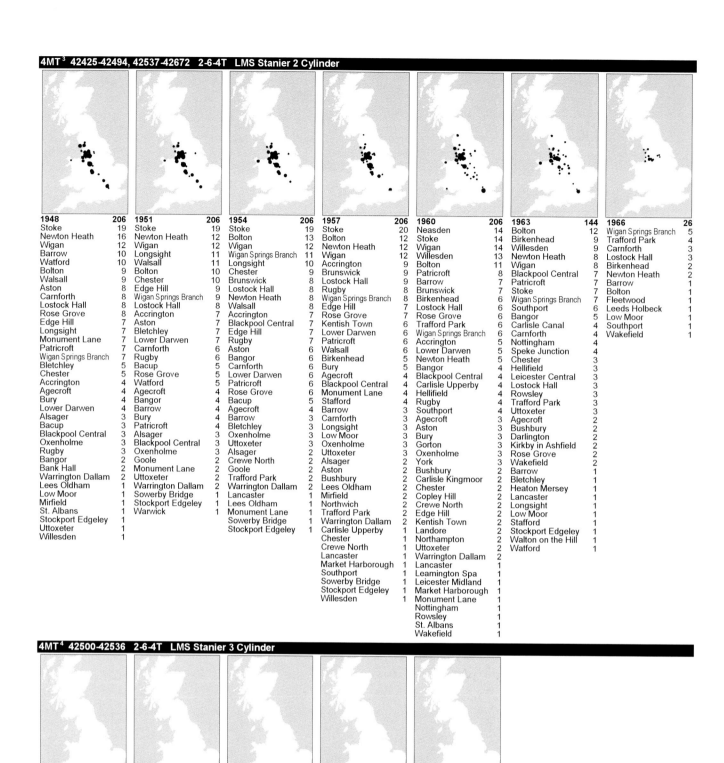

4MT[3] 42425-42494, 42537-42672 2-6-4T LMS Stanier 2 Cylinder

1948	206
Stoke	19
Newton Heath	16
Wigan	12
Barrow	10
Watford	10
Bolton	9
Walsall	9
Aston	8
Carnforth	8
Lostock Hall	8
Rose Grove	8
Edge Hill	7
Longsight	7
Monument Lane	7
Patricroft	7
Wigan Springs Branch	7
Bletchley	5
Chester	5
Accrington	4
Agecroft	4
Bury	4
Lower Darwen	4
Alsager	3
Bacup	3
Blackpool Central	3
Oxenholme	3
Rugby	3
Bangor	2
Bank Hall	2
Warrington Dallam	2
Lees Oldham	1
Low Moor	1
Mirfield	1
St. Albans	1
Stockport Edgeley	1
Uttoxeter	1
Willesden	1

1951	206
Stoke	19
Newton Heath	12
Wigan	12
Longsight	11
Walsall	11
Bolton	10
Chester	10
Edge Hill	9
Wigan Springs Branch	9
Lostock Hall	8
Accrington	7
Aston	7
Bletchley	7
Lower Darwen	7
Carnforth	6
Rugby	6
Bacup	5
Rose Grove	5
Watford	5
Agecroft	4
Bangor	4
Barrow	4
Bury	4
Patricroft	4
Alsager	3
Blackpool Central	3
Oxenholme	3
Goole	2
Monument Lane	2
Uttoxeter	2
Warrington Dallam	2
Sowerby Bridge	1
Stockport Edgeley	1
Warwick	1

1954	206
Stoke	19
Bolton	13
Wigan	12
Wigan Springs Branch	11
Longsight	10
Chester	9
Brunswick	8
Lostock Hall	8
Newton Heath	8
Walsall	8
Accrington	7
Blackpool Central	7
Edge Hill	7
Rugby	7
Aston	6
Bangor	6
Carnforth	6
Lower Darwen	6
Patricroft	6
Rose Grove	6
Bacup	5
Agecroft	4
Barrow	3
Bletchley	3
Oxenholme	3
Uttoxeter	3
Alsager	2
Crewe North	2
Goole	2
Trafford Park	2
Warrington Dallam	2
Lancaster	1
Lees Oldham	1
Monument Lane	1
Sowerby Bridge	1
Stockport Edgeley	1

1957	206
Stoke	20
Bolton	12
Newton Heath	12
Wigan	12
Accrington	9
Brunswick	9
Lostock Hall	9
Rugby	8
Wigan Springs Branch	8
Edge Hill	7
Rose Grove	7
Kentish Town	6
Lower Darwen	6
Patricroft	6
Walsall	6
Birkenhead	5
Bury	5
Agecroft	4
Blackpool Central	4
Monument Lane	4
Stafford	4
Barrow	3
Carnforth	3
Longsight	3
Low Moor	3
Oxenholme	3
Uttoxeter	3
Alsager	2
Aston	2
Bushbury	2
Lees Oldham	2
Mirfield	2
Northwich	2
Trafford Park	2
Warrington Dallam	2
Carlisle Upperby	1
Chester	1
Crewe North	1
Lancaster	1
Market Harborough	1
Southport	1
Sowerby Bridge	1
Stockport Edgeley	1
Willesden	1

1960	206
Neasden	14
Stoke	14
Wigan	14
Willesden	13
Bolton	11
Patricroft	8
Barrow	7
Brunswick	7
Birkenhead	6
Lostock Hall	6
Rose Grove	6
Trafford Park	6
Wigan Springs Branch	6
Accrington	5
Lower Darwen	5
Newton Heath	5
Bangor	4
Blackpool Central	4
Carlisle Upperby	4
Hellifield	4
Rugby	4
Southport	4
Agecroft	3
Aston	3
Bury	3
Gorton	3
Oxenholme	3
York	3
Bushbury	2
Carlisle Kingmoor	2
Chester	2
Copley Hill	2
Crewe North	2
Edge Hill	2
Kentish Town	2
Landore	2
Northampton	2
Uttoxeter	2
Warrington Dallam	2
Lancaster	1
Leamington Spa	1
Leicester Midland	1
Market Harborough	1
Monument Lane	1
Nottingham	1
Rowsley	1
St. Albans	1
Wakefield	1

1963	144
Bolton	12
Birkenhead	9
Willesden	9
Newton Heath	8
Wigan	8
Blackpool Central	7
Patricroft	7
Stoke	7
Wigan Springs Branch	7
Southport	6
Bangor	5
Carlisle Canal	4
Carnforth	4
Nottingham	4
Speke Junction	4
Chester	3
Hellifield	3
Leicester Central	3
Lostock Hall	3
Rowsley	3
Trafford Park	3
Uttoxeter	3
Agecroft	2
Bushbury	2
Darlington	2
Kirkby in Ashfield	2
Rose Grove	2
Wakefield	2
Barrow	1
Bletchley	1
Heaton Mersey	1
Lancaster	1
Longsight	1
Low Moor	1
Stafford	1
Stockport Edgeley	1
Walton on the Hill	1
Watford	1

1966	26
Wigan Springs Branch	5
Trafford Park	4
Carnforth	3
Lostock Hall	3
Birkenhead	2
Newton Heath	2
Barrow	1
Bolton	1
Fleetwood	1
Leeds Holbeck	1
Low Moor	1
Southport	1
Wakefield	1

4MT[4] 42500-42536 2-6-4T LMS Stanier 3 Cylinder

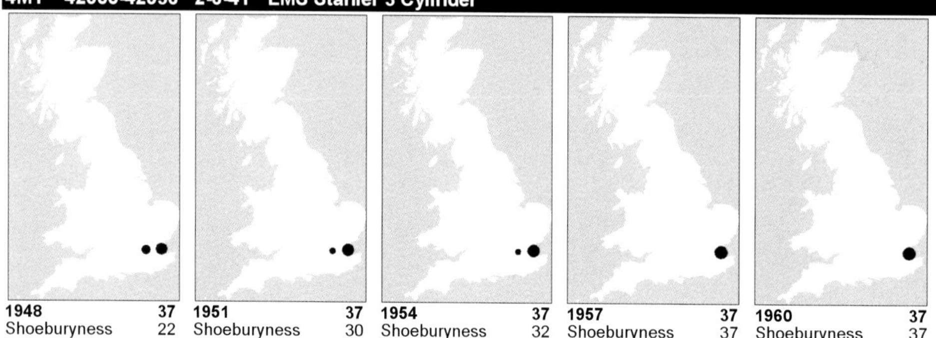

1948	37
Shoeburyness	22
Plaistow	15

1951	37
Shoeburyness	30
Plaistow	7

1954	37
Shoeburyness	32
Plaistow	5

1957	37
Shoeburyness	37

1960	37
Shoeburyness	37

4MT[5] 43000-43161 2-6-0 LMS Ivatt Mogul

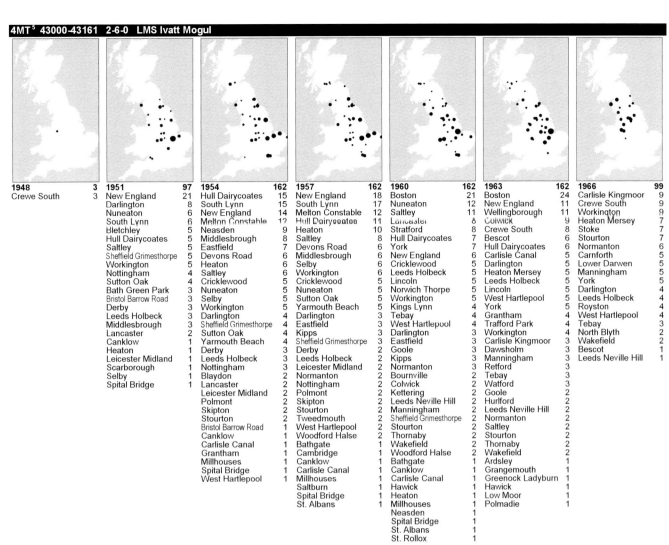

1948	3
Crewe South	3

1951	97
New England	21
Darlington	8
Nuneaton	6
South Lynn	6
Bletchley	5
Hull Dairycoates	5
Saltley	5
Sheffield Grimesthorpe	5
Workington	5
Nottingham	4
Sutton Oak	4
Bath Green Park	3
Bristol Barrow Road	3
Derby	3
Leeds Holbeck	3
Middlesbrough	3
Lancaster	2
Canklow	1
Heaton	1
Leicester Midland	1
Scarborough	1
Selby	1
Spital Bridge	1

1954	162
Hull Dairycoates	15
South Lynn	15
New England	14
Melton Constable	12
Neasden	9
Middlesbrough	8
Eastfield	7
Devons Road	6
Heaton	6
Saltley	6
Cricklewood	5
Nuneaton	5
Selby	5
Workington	5
Darlington	4
Sheffield Grimesthorpe	4
Sutton Oak	4
Yarmouth Beach	4
Derby	3
Leeds Holbeck	3
Nottingham	3
Blaydon	2
Lancaster	2
Leicester Midland	2
Polmont	2
Skipton	2
Stourton	2
Bristol Barrow Road	1
Canklow	1
Carlisle Canal	1
Grantham	1
Millhouses	1
Spital Bridge	1
West Hartlepool	1

1957	162
New England	18
South Lynn	17
Melton Constable	12
Hull Dairycoates	11
Heaton	10
Saltley	8
Devons Road	6
Middlesbrough	6
Selby	6
Workington	6
Cricklewood	5
Nuneaton	5
Sutton Oak	5
Yarmouth Beach	5
Darlington	3
Eastfield	3
Kipps	3
Sheffield Grimesthorpe	3
Derby	2
Leeds Holbeck	2
Leicester Midland	2
Normanton	2
Nottingham	2
Polmont	2
Skipton	2
Stourton	2
Tweedmouth	2
West Hartlepool	2
Woodford Halse	2
Bathgate	1
Cambridge	1
Canklow	1
Carlisle Canal	1
Millhouses	1
Saltburn	1
Spital Bridge	1
St. Albans	1

1960	162
Boston	21
Nuneaton	12
Saltley	11
Lancaster	8
Stratford	8
Hull Dairycoates	7
York	7
New England	6
Cricklewood	5
Leeds Holbeck	5
Lincoln	5
Norwich Thorpe	5
Workington	5
Kings Lynn	4
Tebay	4
West Hartlepool	4
Darlington	3
Eastfield	3
Goole	3
Kipps	3
Normanton	3
Bournville	2
Colwick	2
Kettering	2
Leeds Neville Hill	2
Manningham	2
Sheffield Grimesthorpe	2
Stourton	2
Thornaby	2
Wakefield	2
Woodford Halse	2
Bathgate	1
Canklow	1
Carlisle Canal	1
Hawick	1
Heaton	1
Millhouses	1
Neasden	1
Spital Bridge	1
St. Albans	1
St. Rollox	1

1963	162
Boston	24
New England	11
Wellingborough	11
Colwick	9
Crewe South	8
Bescot	6
Hull Dairycoates	6
Carlisle Canal	5
Darlington	5
Heaton Mersey	5
Leeds Holbeck	5
Lincoln	5
West Hartlepool	5
York	5
Grantham	4
Trafford Park	4
Workington	4
Carlisle Kingmoor	3
Dawsholm	3
Manningham	3
Retford	3
Tebay	3
Watford	3
Goole	2
Hurlford	2
Leeds Neville Hill	2
Normanton	2
Saltley	2
Stourton	2
Thornaby	2
Wakefield	2
Ardsley	1
Grangemouth	1
Greenock Ladyburn	1
Hawick	1
Low Moor	1
Polmadie	1

1966	99
Carlisle Kingmoor	9
Crewe South	9
Workington	9
Heaton Mersey	7
Stoke	7
Stourton	7
Normanton	6
Carnforth	5
Lower Darwen	5
Manningham	5
York	5
Darlington	4
Leeds Holbeck	4
Royston	4
West Hartlepool	4
Tebay	3
North Blyth	2
Wakefield	2
Bescot	1
Leeds Neville Hill	1

5P 50412-50455 4-6-0 LYR Hughes

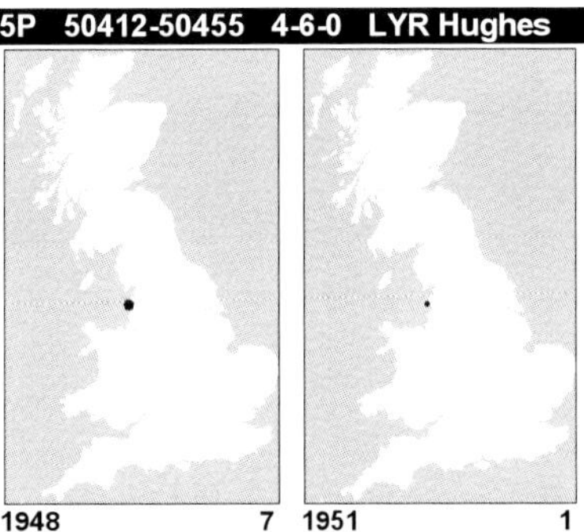

1948	7
Blackpool Central	7

1951	1
Blackpool Central	1

5XP 46004 4-6-0 LNWR Bowen Cooke Rebuilt Claughton

1948	1
Edge Hill	1

5MT[1] 42700-42944 2-6-0 LMS Hughes/Fowler Horwich Crab

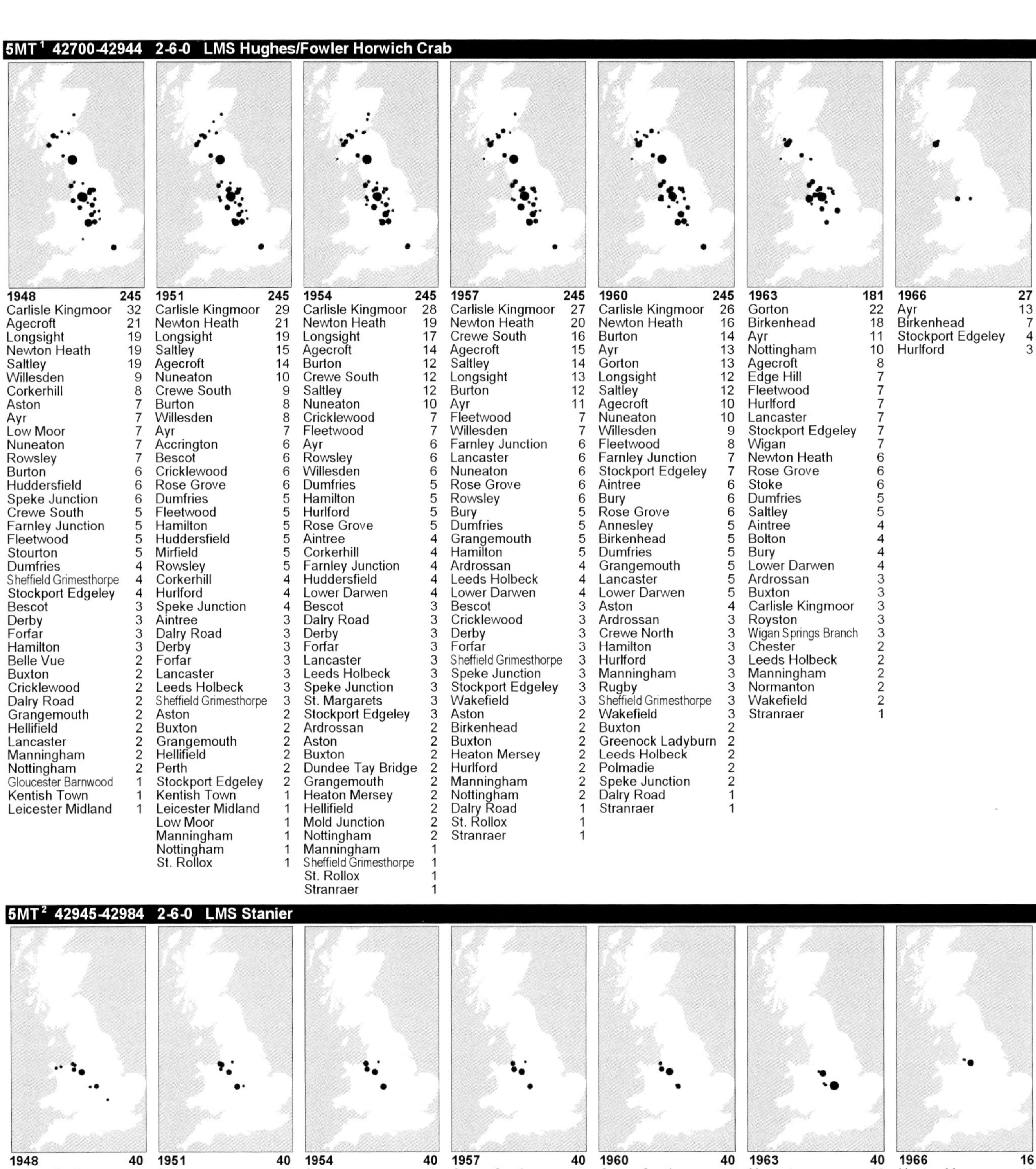

1948	245
Carlisle Kingmoor	32
Agecroft	21
Longsight	19
Newton Heath	19
Saltley	19
Willesden	9
Corkerhill	8
Aston	7
Ayr	7
Low Moor	7
Nuneaton	7
Rowsley	7
Burton	6
Huddersfield	6
Speke Junction	6
Crewe South	5
Farnley Junction	5
Fleetwood	5
Stourton	5
Dumfries	4
Sheffield Grimesthorpe	4
Stockport Edgeley	4
Bescot	3
Derby	3
Forfar	3
Hamilton	3
Belle Vue	2
Buxton	2
Cricklewood	2
Dalry Road	2
Grangemouth	2
Hellifield	2
Lancaster	2
Manningham	2
Nottingham	2
Gloucester Barnwood	1
Kentish Town	1
Leicester Midland	1

1951	245
Carlisle Kingmoor	29
Newton Heath	21
Longsight	19
Saltley	15
Agecroft	14
Nuneaton	10
Crewe South	9
Burton	8
Willesden	8
Ayr	7
Accrington	6
Bescot	6
Cricklewood	6
Rose Grove	6
Dumfries	5
Fleetwood	5
Hamilton	5
Huddersfield	5
Mirfield	5
Rowsley	5
Corkerhill	4
Hurlford	4
Speke Junction	4
Aintree	3
Dalry Road	3
Derby	3
Forfar	3
Lancaster	3
Leeds Holbeck	3
Sheffield Grimesthorpe	3
Aston	2
Buxton	2
Grangemouth	2
Hellifield	2
Perth	2
Stockport Edgeley	2
Kentish Town	1
Leicester Midland	1
Low Moor	1
Manningham	1
Nottingham	1
St. Rollox	1

1954	245
Carlisle Kingmoor	28
Newton Heath	19
Longsight	17
Agecroft	14
Burton	12
Crewe South	12
Saltley	12
Nuneaton	10
Cricklewood	7
Fleetwood	7
Ayr	6
Rowsley	6
Willesden	6
Dumfries	5
Hamilton	5
Hurlford	5
Rose Grove	5
Aintree	4
Corkerhill	4
Farnley Junction	4
Huddersfield	4
Lower Darwen	4
Bescot	3
Dalry Road	3
Derby	3
Forfar	3
Lancaster	3
Leeds Holbeck	3
Speke Junction	3
St. Margarets	3
Stockport Edgeley	3
Ardrossan	2
Aston	2
Buxton	2
Dundee Tay Bridge	2
Grangemouth	2
Heaton Mersey	2
Hellifield	2
Mold Junction	2
Nottingham	2
Manningham	1
Sheffield Grimesthorpe	1
St. Rollox	1
Stranraer	1

1957	245
Carlisle Kingmoor	27
Newton Heath	20
Crewe South	16
Agecroft	15
Saltley	14
Longsight	13
Burton	12
Ayr	11
Fleetwood	7
Willesden	7
Farnley Junction	6
Lancaster	6
Nuneaton	6
Rose Grove	6
Rowsley	6
Bury	5
Dumfries	5
Grangemouth	5
Hamilton	5
Ardrossan	4
Leeds Holbeck	4
Lower Darwen	4
Bescot	3
Cricklewood	3
Derby	3
Forfar	3
Sheffield Grimesthorpe	3
Speke Junction	3
Stockport Edgeley	3
Wakefield	3
Aston	2
Birkenhead	2
Buxton	2
Heaton Mersey	2
Hurlford	2
Manningham	2
Nottingham	2
Dalry Road	1
St. Rollox	1
Stranraer	1

1960	245
Carlisle Kingmoor	26
Newton Heath	16
Burton	14
Ayr	13
Gorton	13
Longsight	12
Saltley	12
Agecroft	10
Nuneaton	10
Willesden	9
Fleetwood	8
Farnley Junction	7
Stockport Edgeley	7
Aintree	6
Bury	6
Rose Grove	6
Annesley	5
Birkenhead	5
Dumfries	5
Grangemouth	5
Lancaster	5
Lower Darwen	5
Aston	4
Ardrossan	3
Crewe North	3
Hamilton	3
Hurlford	3
Manningham	3
Rugby	3
Sheffield Grimesthorpe	3
Wakefield	3
Buxton	2
Greenock Ladyburn	2
Leeds Holbeck	2
Polmadie	2
Speke Junction	2
Dalry Road	1
Stranraer	1

1963	181
Gorton	22
Birkenhead	18
Ayr	11
Nottingham	10
Agecroft	8
Edge Hill	7
Fleetwood	7
Hurlford	7
Lancaster	7
Stockport Edgeley	7
Wigan	7
Newton Heath	6
Rose Grove	6
Stoke	6
Dumfries	5
Saltley	5
Aintree	4
Bolton	4
Bury	4
Lower Darwen	4
Ardrossan	3
Buxton	3
Carlisle Kingmoor	3
Royston	3
Wigan Springs Branch	3
Chester	2
Leeds Holbeck	2
Manningham	2
Normanton	2
Wakefield	2
Stranraer	1

1966	27
Ayr	13
Birkenhead	7
Stockport Edgeley	4
Hurlford	3

5MT[2] 42945-42984 2-6-0 LMS Stanier

1948	40
Crewe South	13
Mold Junction	5
Nuneaton	5
Birkenhead	4
Speke Junction	4
Bangor	3
Aston	2
Bletchley	2
Llandudno Junction	2

1951	40
Aston	10
Crewe South	9
Birkenhead	7
Speke Junction	6
Mold Junction	4
Longsight	2
Brunswick	1
Nuneaton	1

1954	40
Aston	11
Crewe South	11
Birkenhead	8
Mold Junction	8
Brunswick	1
Longsight	1

1957	40
Crewe South	12
Mold Junction	9
Aston	8
Birkenhead	6
Crewe North	3
Brunswick	1
Longsight	1

1960	40
Crewe South	16
Mold Junction	8
Aston	6
Crewe North	5
Birkenhead	4
Bescot	1

1963	40
Nuneaton	22
Stoke	12
Bescot	3
Crewe South	2
Bushbury	1

1966	16
Heaton Mersey	13
Wigan Springs Branch	3

5MT^3 44658-45499 4-6-0 LMS Stanier Black Five

1948	742
Perth	60
Carlisle Kingmoor	48
Carlisle Upperby	48
Crewe South	44
Crewe North	39
St. Rollox	32
Patricroft	29
Leeds Holbeck	28
Rugby	28
Inverness	26
Newton Heath	25
Edge Hill	20
Saltley	19
Motherwell	18
Bank Hall	12
Shrewsbury	12
Warrington Dallam	11
Blackpool Central	10
Derby	10
Kentish Town	10
Polmadie	10
Farnley Junction	9
Low Moor	9
Aston	8
Bescot	8
Carnforth	8
Corkerhill	8
Llandudno Junction	8
Southport	8
Stoke	8
Willesden	8
Bletchley	7
Longsight	7
Wigan Springs Branch	7
Agecroft	6
Chester	6
Millhouses	6
Mold Junction	6
Preston	6
Wakefield	6
Bath Green Park	5
Belle Vue	5
Bristol Barrow Road	5
Cricklewood	5
Holyhead	5
Huddersfield	5
Nottingham	5
Bushbury	4
Fleetwood	4
Northampton	4
Sheffield Grimesthorpe	4
Accrington	3
Walsall	3
Carstairs	2
Dalry Road	2
Monument Lane	1
Toton	1
Trafford Park	1

1951	840
Perth	75
Carlisle Kingmoor	45
Rugby	41
Crewe South	30
Carlisle Upperby	34
Patricroft	34
St. Rollox	34
Inverness	33
Newton Heath	29
Edge Hill	25
Saltley	21
Crewe North	20
Leeds Holbeck	20
Shrewsbury	19
Blackpool Central	16
Kentish Town	15
Carnforth	14
Warrington Dallam	14
Longsight	13
Bank Hall	12
Corkerhill	12
Low Moor	12
Polmadie	12
Willesden	12
Aston	11
Derby	11
Millhouses	11
Southport	11
Farnley Junction	9
Huddersfield	9
Llandudno Junction	9
Motherwell	9
Sheffield Grimesthorpe	9
Wigan Springs Branch	9
Bletchley	8
Holyhead	8
Carstairs	7
Chester	7
Leicester Midland	7
Mold Junction	7
Stoke	7
Wakefield	7
Barrow	6
Belle Vue	6
Bristol Barrow Road	6
Dalry Road	6
Agecroft	5
Bath Green Park	5
Bescot	5
Bushbury	5
Nottingham	5
Bournville	5
Fleetwood	4
Northampton	4
Walsall	4
Accrington	3
Carlisle Canal	3
Monument Lane	3
Stirling	3
Bangor	2
Preston	2
Aviemore	1
Dundee Tay Bridge	1
Eastfield	1
Parkhead	1
Trafford Park	1

1954	842
Perth	65
Carlisle Kingmoor	56
Rugby	39
Carlisle Upperby	30
Patricroft	35
St. Rollox	32
Crewe North	31
Inverness	31
Edge Hill	29
Newton Heath	26
Crewe South	24
Saltley	24
Leeds Holbeck	22
Blackpool Central	21
Carnforth	17
Willesden	16
Aston	15
Derby	15
Motherwell	15
Kentish Town	14
Longsight	14
Bank Hall	11
Corkerhill	11
Low Moor	11
Polmadie	11
Sheffield Grimesthorpe	11
Wigan Springs Branch	11
Warrington Dallam	10
Holyhead	9
Dalry Road	8
Farnley Junction	8
Shrewsbury	8
Wakefield	8
Huddersfield	7
Leicester Midland	7
Millhouses	7
Agecroft	6
Barrow	6
Carstairs	6
Chester	6
Stoke	6
Belle Vue	5
Bescot	5
Nottingham	5
Southport	5
Bushbury	4
Fleetwood	4
Llandudno Junction	4
Mold Junction	4
Northampton	4
Stirling	4
Trafford Park	4
Walsall	4
Bangor	3
Bristol Barrow Road	3
Brunswick	3
Eastfield	3
Grangemouth	3
Monument Lane	3
Rose Grove	3
St. Margarets	3
Aberdeen Ferryhill	2
Accrington	2
Ayr	2
Bath Green Park	2
Bletchley	2
Bournville	2
Dumfries	2
Dundee Tay Bridge	2
Hurlford	2
Preston	2
Aviemore	1

1957	842
Perth	60
Carlisle Kingmoor	54
Carlisle Upperby	40
Newton Heath	33
Crewe South	32
Crewe North	31
Inverness	31
St. Rollox	29
Saltley	28
Edge Hill	26
Willesden	24
Carnforth	22
Aston	20
Rugby	19
Blackpool Central	18
Kentish Town	18
Leeds Holbeck	18
Longsight	18
Motherwell	16
Patricroft	16
Mold Junction	13
Carstairs	12
Derby	11
Bank Hall	10
Low Moor	10
Stirling	10
Warrington Dallam	10
Wigan Springs Branch	10
Accrington	9
Agecroft	8
Bristol Barrow Road	8
Corkerhill	8
Shrewsbury	8
Bletchley	7
Bushbury	7
Eastfield	7
Farnley Junction	7
Llandudno Junction	7
Millhouses	7
Rose Grove	7
Southport	7
Bedford	6
Fort William	6
Huddersfield	6
Northampton	6
Aberdeen Ferryhill	5
Burton	4
Chester	4
Cricklewood	4
Dundee Tay Bridge	4
Sheffield Grimesthorpe	4
Stoke	4
Bangor	3
Barrow	3
Brunswick	3
Dumfries	3
Fleetwood	3
Holyhead	3
Nottingham	3
Trafford Park	3
Walsall	3
Bath Green Park	2
Bescot	2
Bournville	2
Hurlford	2
Leicester Midland	2
Monument Lane	2
Preston	2
Aviemore	1
Hamilton	1
Kings Cross	1

1960	842
Carlisle Kingmoor	52
Perth	48
Crewe North	40
Saltley	40
Carlisle Upperby	36
Newton Heath	35
Inverness	33
Crewe South	29
St. Rollox	23
Patricroft	21
Blackpool Central	20
Wigan Springs Branch	20
Edge Hill	19
Aston	18
Rugby	18
Willesden	18
Leeds Holbeck	17
Longsight	17
Motherwell	17
Carnforth	16
Carstairs	15
Warrington Dallam	13
Mold Junction	12
Kentish Town	11
Stirling	11
Eastfield	10
Low Moor	10
Monument Lane	10
Northampton	10
Cricklewood	9
Dalry Road	9
Accrington	8
Agecroft	8
Farnley Junction	8
Holyhead	8
Leicester Midland	8
Neasden	8
Shrewsbury	8
Bank Hall	7
Preston	7
Southport	7
Trafford Park	7
Bedford	6
Bushbury	6
Corkerhill	6
Fort William	6
Llandudno Junction	6
Rose Grove	6
Aberdeen Ferryhill	5
Bletchley	5
Chester	5
Leicester Central	5
Ardrossan	4
Barrow	4
Bescot	4
Brunswick	4
Dumfries	4
Dundee Tay Bridge	4
Nottingham	4
Bangor	3
Fleetwood	3
Ayr	2
Hurlford	2
Polmadie	2
Stoke	2
Aviemore	1
Birkenhead	1
Derby	1

1963	820
Carlisle Kingmoor	51
Saltley	35
Perth	31
Carlisle Upperby	30
Crewe North	30
Newton Heath	26
Blackpool Central	25
Wigan Springs Branch	25
Edge Hill	24
Rugby	24
Speke Junction	24
Aston	19
Crewe South	19
Motherwell	19
Dalry Road	16
Carstairs	15
Corkerhill	15
Carnforth	14
Leeds Holbeck	14
Llandudno Junction	14
Northampton	14
Patricroft	14
Burton	12
Mold Junction	12
St. Rollox	12
Warrington Dallam	12
Willesden	12
Agecroft	11
Stirling	11
Annesley	10
Bescot	10
Eastfield	10
Ayr	9
Farnley Junction	9
Hurlford	9
Southport	9
Stockport Edgeley	9
Bolton	8
Derby	8
Fleetwood	8
Leicester Central	8
Low Moor	8
Polmadie	8
Rose Grove	8
Shrewsbury	8
Woodford Halse	8
Grangemouth	7
Stoke	7
Aintree	6
Ardrossan	6
Bletchley	6
Nottingham	6
Bangor	5
Barrow	5
Leicester Midland	5
Longsight	5
Bushbury	4
Dumfries	4
Holyhead	4
Lancaster	4
Aberdeen Ferryhill	3
Bedford	3
Stranraer	3
Trafford Park	3
Copley Hill	2
Inverness	2
Carlisle Canal	1
Fort William	1
Workington	1

1966	627
Carlisle Kingmoor	68
Newton Heath	33
Speke Junction	29
Edge Hill	26
Crewe South	25
Bolton	22
Carnforth	22
Tyseley	21
Warrington Dallam	19
Annesley	17
Banbury	17
Oxley	17
Stoke	17
Trafford Park	17
Wigan Springs Branch	17
Ayr	14
Leeds Holbeck	14
Perth	14
Mold Junction	13
Shrewsbury	12
Carstairs	11
Chester	11
Agecroft	10
Bescot	10
Motherwell	10
Stockport Edgeley	10
Lancaster	9
St. Margarets	9
Fleetwood	8
Holyhead	8
Nuneaton	8
Rose Grove	8
Dumfries	7
Llandudno Junction	7
Mirfield	7
Derby	6
Lostock Hall	6
Stirling	6
Barrow	5
Farnley Junction	5
Hurlford	5
Carlisle Upperby	4
Croes Newydd	4
Aintree	3
Burton	3
Royston	3
Southport	3
Aberdeen Ferryhill	2
Corkerhill	2
Polmadie	1
St. Rollox	1
Stranraer	1

6F[1] 47875-47896 0-8-2T LNWR Bowen Cooke

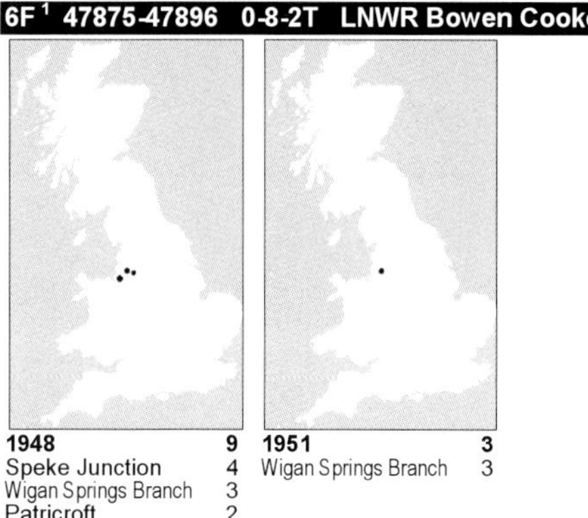

1948	9	1951	3
Speke Junction	4	Wigan Springs Branch	3
Wigan Springs Branch	3		
Patricroft	2		

6F[2] between 48892 & 49384 0-8-0 LNWR G1 Class

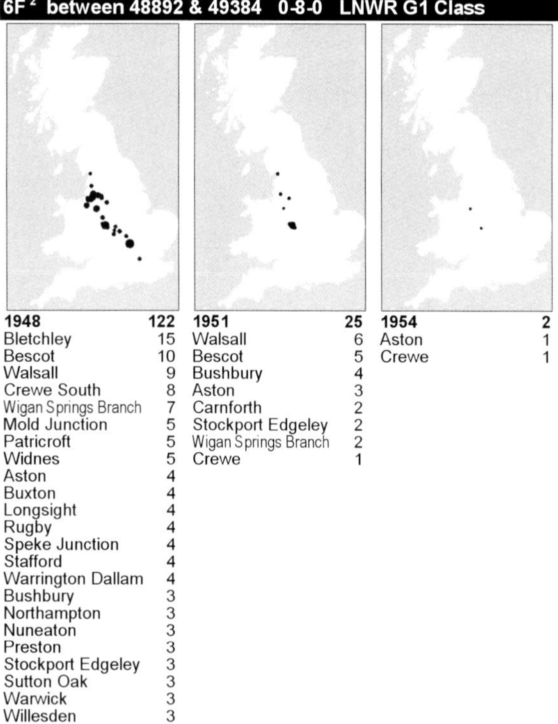

1948	122	1951	25	1954	2
Bletchley	15	Walsall	6	Aston	1
Bescot	10	Bescot	5	Crewe	1
Walsall	9	Bushbury	4		
Crewe South	8	Aston	3		
Wigan Springs Branch	7	Carnforth	2		
Mold Junction	5	Stockport Edgeley	2		
Patricroft	5	Wigan Springs Branch	2		
Widnes	5	Crewe	1		
Aston	4				
Buxton	4				
Longsight	4				
Rugby	4				
Speke Junction	4				
Stafford	4				
Warrington Dallam	4				
Bushbury	3				
Northampton	3				
Nuneaton	3				
Preston	3				
Stockport Edgeley	3				
Sutton Oak	3				
Warwick	3				
Willesden	3				
Carnforth	2				
Coventry	2				
Edge Hill	2				

6F[3] 52727-52839 0-8-0 LYR Aspinall Class 30

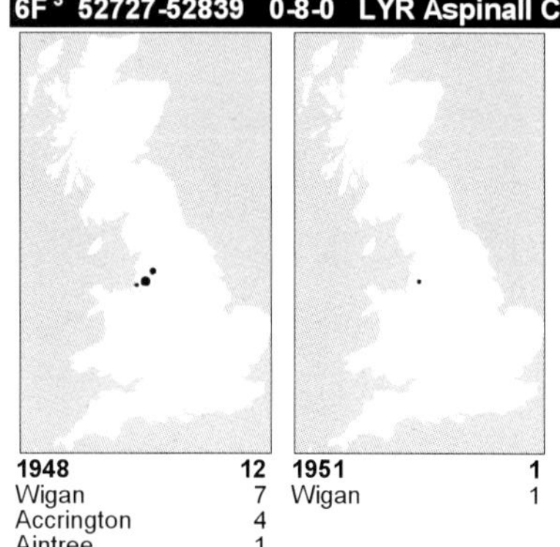

1948	12	1951	1
Wigan	7	Wigan	1
Accrington	4		
Aintree	1		

Below: LNWR '6F' 'G1' class 0-8-0 No 49371 at its home shed 3A Bescot on 20 May 1950. *P. B. Whitehouse*

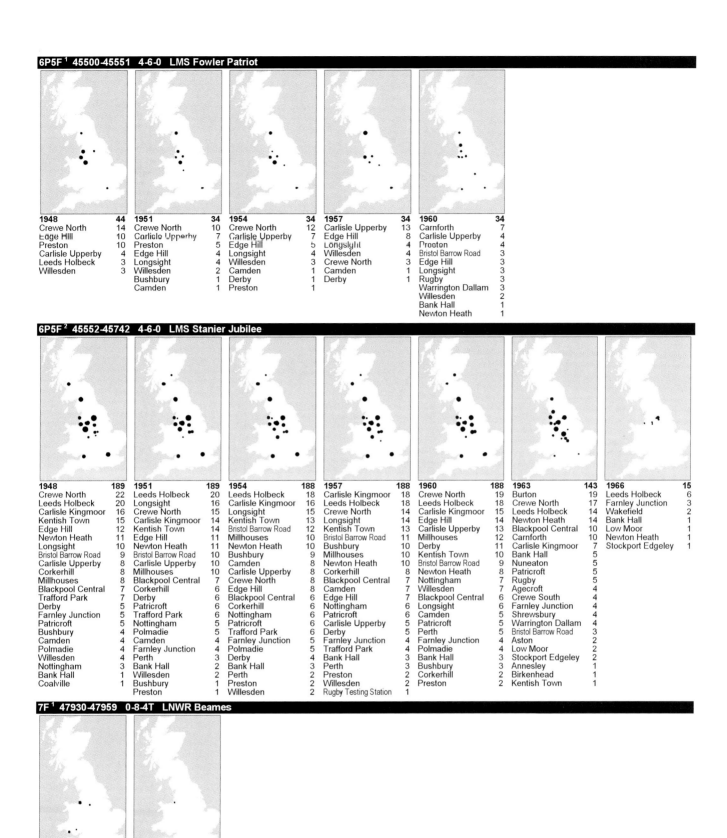

6P5F[1] 45500-45551 4-6-0 LMS Fowler Patriot

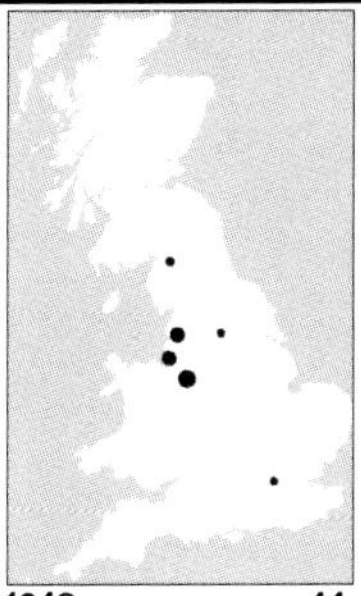

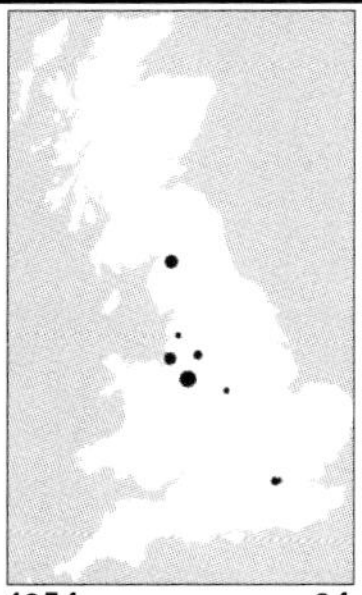

1948	44
Crewe North	14
Edge Hill	10
Preston	10
Carlisle Upperby	4
Leeds Holbeck	3
Willesden	3

1951	34
Crewe North	10
Carlisle Upperby	7
Preston	5
Edge Hill	4
Longsight	4
Willesden	2
Bushbury	1
Camden	1

1954	34
Crewe North	12
Carlisle Upperby	7
Edge Hill	5
Longsight	4
Willesden	3
Camden	1
Derby	1
Preston	1

1957	34
Carlisle Upperby	13
Edge Hill	8
Longsight	4
Willesden	4
Crewe North	3
Camden	1
Derby	1

1960	34
Carnforth	7
Carlisle Upperby	4
Preston	4
Bristol Barrow Road	3
Edge Hill	3
Longsight	3
Rugby	3
Warrington Dallam	3
Willesden	2
Bank Hall	1
Newton Heath	1

6P5F[2] 45552-45742 4-6-0 LMS Stanier Jubilee

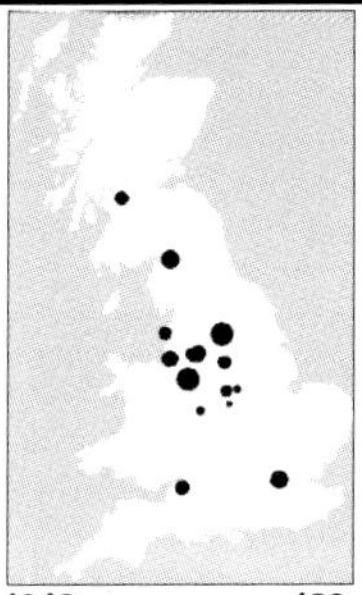

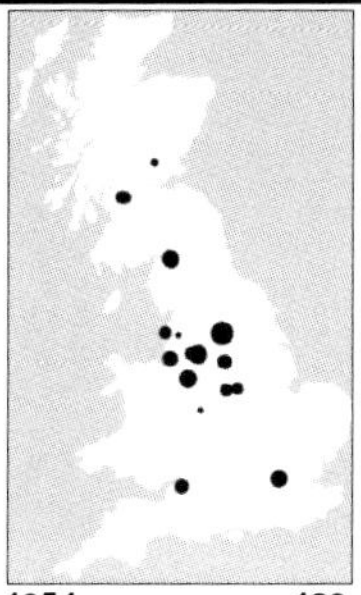

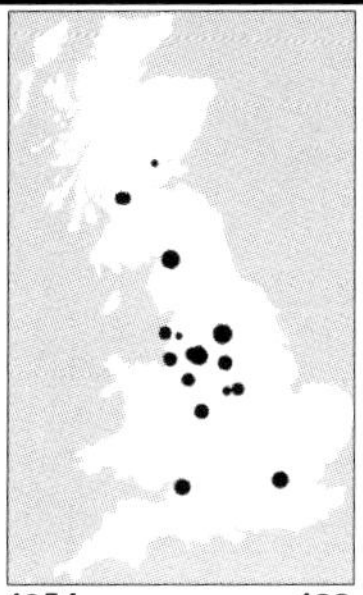

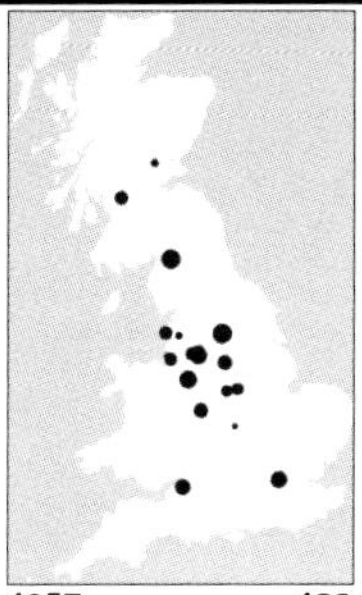

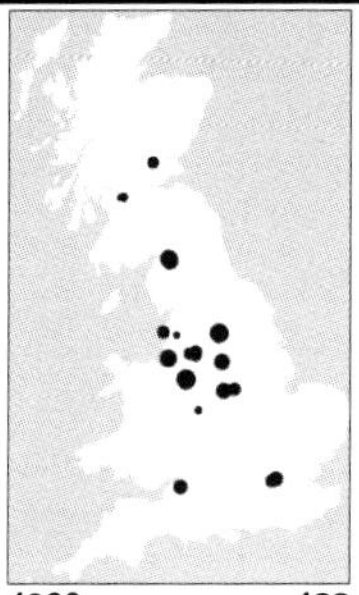

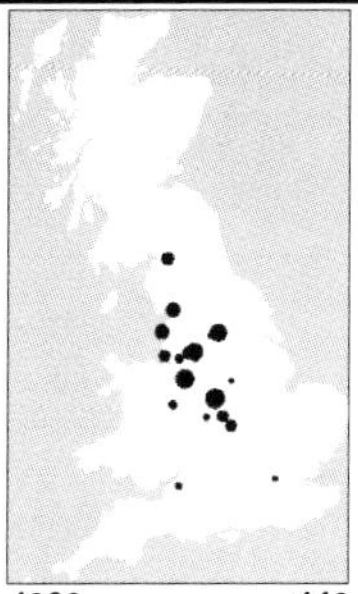

1948	189
Crewe North	22
Leeds Holbeck	20
Carlisle Kingmoor	16
Kentish Town	15
Edge Hill	12
Newton Heath	11
Longsight	10
Bristol Barrow Road	9
Carlisle Upperby	8
Corkerhill	8
Millhouses	8
Blackpool Central	7
Trafford Park	7
Derby	5
Farnley Junction	5
Patricroft	5
Bushbury	4
Camden	4
Polmadie	4
Willesden	4
Nottingham	3
Bank Hall	1
Coalville	1

1951	189
Leeds Holbeck	20
Longsight	16
Crewe North	15
Carlisle Kingmoor	14
Kentish Town	14
Edge Hill	11
Newton Heath	11
Bristol Barrow Road	10
Carlisle Upperby	10
Millhouses	10
Blackpool Central	7
Corkerhill	6
Derby	6
Patricroft	6
Trafford Park	6
Nottingham	5
Polmadie	5
Camden	4
Farnley Junction	4
Perth	3
Bank Hall	2
Willesden	2
Bushbury	1
Preston	1

1954	188
Leeds Holbeck	18
Carlisle Kingmoor	16
Longsight	15
Kentish Town	13
Bristol Barrow Road	12
Millhouses	10
Newton Heath	10
Bushbury	9
Camden	8
Carlisle Upperby	8
Crewe North	8
Edge Hill	8
Blackpool Central	6
Corkerhill	6
Nottingham	6
Patricroft	6
Trafford Park	6
Farnley Junction	5
Polmadie	5
Derby	4
Bank Hall	3
Perth	2
Preston	2
Willesden	2

1957	188
Carlisle Kingmoor	18
Leeds Holbeck	18
Crewe North	14
Longsight	14
Kentish Town	13
Bristol Barrow Road	11
Bushbury	10
Millhouses	10
Newton Heath	10
Corkerhill	8
Blackpool Central	7
Camden	7
Edge Hill	7
Nottingham	6
Patricroft	6
Carlisle Upperby	5
Derby	5
Farnley Junction	4
Trafford Park	4
Bank Hall	3
Perth	3
Preston	2
Willesden	2
Rugby Testing Station	1

1960	188
Crewe North	19
Leeds Holbeck	18
Carlisle Kingmoor	15
Edge Hill	14
Carlisle Upperby	13
Millhouses	12
Derby	11
Kentish Town	10
Bristol Barrow Road	9
Newton Heath	8
Nottingham	7
Willesden	7
Blackpool Central	6
Longsight	6
Camden	5
Patricroft	5
Perth	5
Farnley Junction	4
Polmadie	4
Bank Hall	3
Bushbury	3
Corkerhill	2
Preston	2

1963	143
Burton	19
Crewe North	17
Leeds Holbeck	14
Newton Heath	14
Blackpool Central	10
Carnforth	10
Carlisle Kingmoor	7
Bank Hall	5
Nuneaton	5
Patricroft	5
Rugby	5
Agecroft	4
Crewe South	4
Farnley Junction	4
Shrewsbury	4
Warrington Dallam	4
Bristol Barrow Road	3
Aston	2
Low Moor	2
Stockport Edgeley	2
Annesley	1
Birkenhead	1
Kentish Town	1

1966	15
Leeds Holbeck	6
Farnley Junction	3
Wakefield	2
Bank Hall	1
Low Moor	1
Newton Heath	1
Stockport Edgeley	1

7F[1] 47930-47959 0-8-4T LNWR Beames

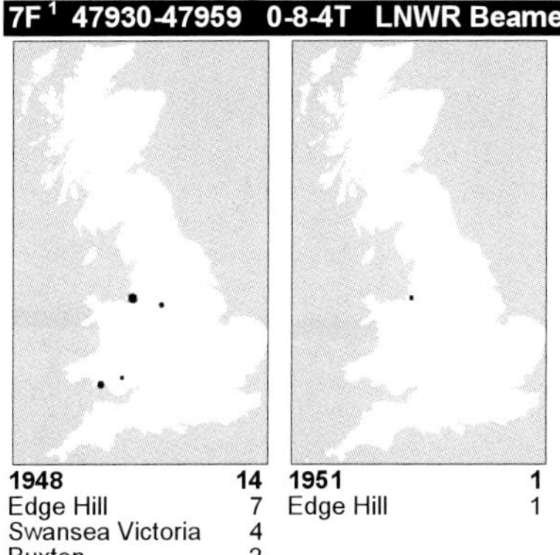

1948	14
Edge Hill	7
Swansea Victoria	4
Buxton	2
Tredegar	1

1951	1
Edge Hill	1

7F^{2} between 48893 & 49394 0-8-0 LNWR G2A Class

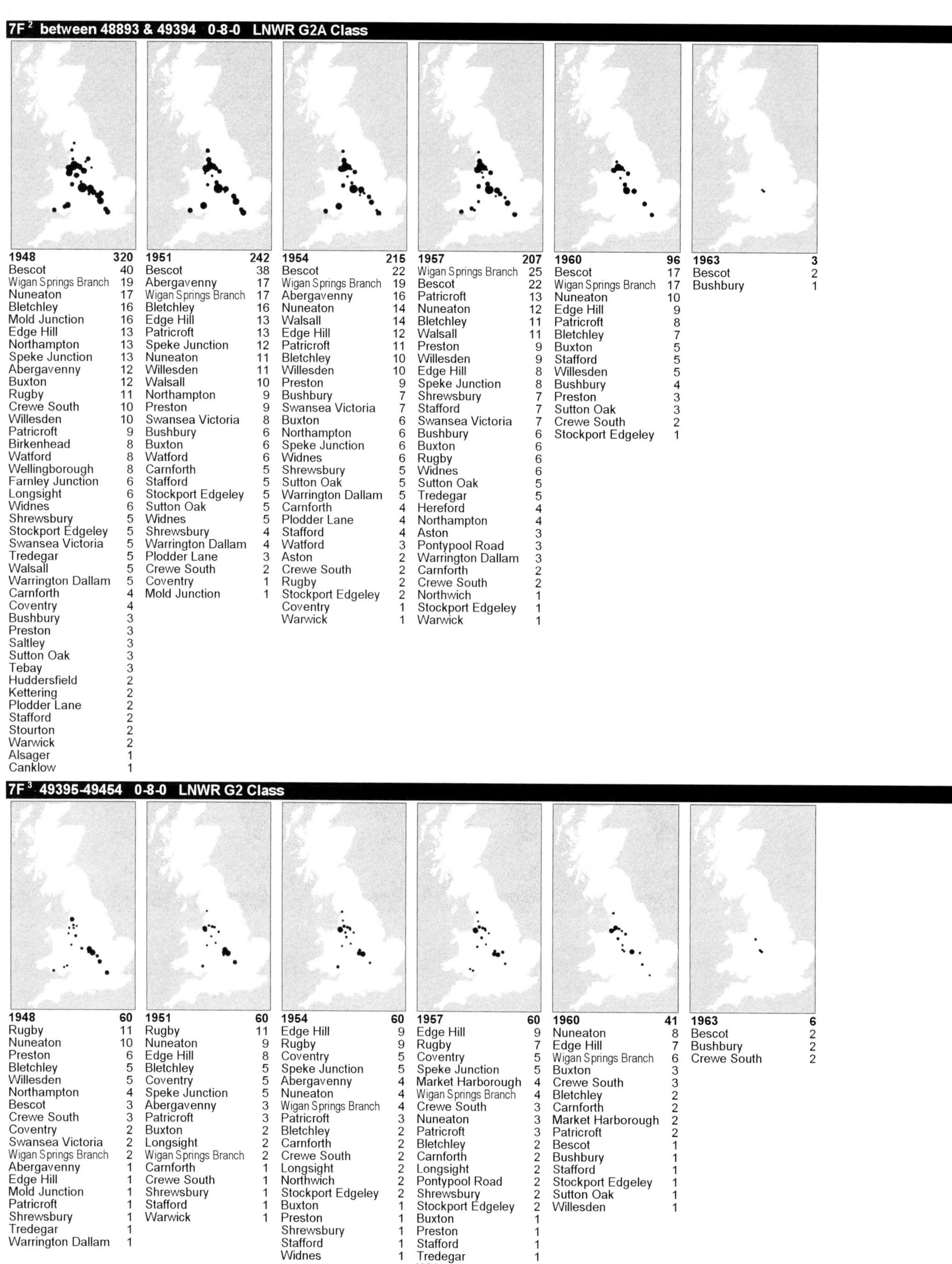

1948	320
Bescot	40
Wigan Springs Branch	19
Nuneaton	17
Bletchley	16
Mold Junction	16
Edge Hill	13
Northampton	13
Speke Junction	13
Abergavenny	12
Buxton	12
Rugby	11
Crewe South	10
Willesden	10
Patricroft	9
Birkenhead	8
Watford	8
Wellingborough	8
Farnley Junction	6
Longsight	6
Widnes	6
Shrewsbury	5
Stockport Edgeley	5
Swansea Victoria	5
Tredegar	5
Walsall	5
Warrington Dallam	5
Carnforth	4
Coventry	4
Bushbury	3
Preston	3
Saltley	3
Sutton Oak	3
Tebay	3
Huddersfield	2
Kettering	2
Plodder Lane	2
Stafford	2
Stourton	2
Warwick	2
Alsager	1
Canklow	1

1951	242
Bescot	38
Abergavenny	17
Wigan Springs Branch	17
Bletchley	16
Edge Hill	13
Patricroft	13
Speke Junction	12
Nuneaton	11
Willesden	11
Walsall	10
Northampton	9
Preston	9
Swansea Victoria	8
Bushbury	6
Buxton	6
Watford	6
Carnforth	5
Stafford	5
Stockport Edgeley	5
Sutton Oak	5
Widnes	5
Shrewsbury	4
Warrington Dallam	4
Plodder Lane	3
Crewe South	2
Coventry	1
Mold Junction	1

1954	215
Bescot	22
Wigan Springs Branch	19
Abergavenny	16
Nuneaton	14
Walsall	14
Edge Hill	12
Patricroft	11
Bletchley	10
Willesden	10
Preston	9
Bushbury	7
Swansea Victoria	7
Buxton	6
Northampton	6
Speke Junction	6
Widnes	6
Shrewsbury	5
Sutton Oak	5
Warrington Dallam	5
Carnforth	4
Plodder Lane	4
Stafford	4
Watford	3
Aston	2
Crewe South	2
Rugby	2
Stockport Edgeley	2
Coventry	1
Warwick	1

1957	207
Wigan Springs Branch	25
Bescot	22
Patricroft	13
Nuneaton	12
Bletchley	11
Walsall	11
Preston	9
Willesden	9
Edge Hill	8
Speke Junction	8
Shrewsbury	7
Stafford	7
Swansea Victoria	7
Bushbury	6
Buxton	6
Rugby	6
Widnes	6
Sutton Oak	5
Tredegar	5
Hereford	4
Northampton	4
Aston	3
Pontypool Road	3
Warrington Dallam	3
Carnforth	2
Crewe South	2
Northwich	1
Stockport Edgeley	1
Warwick	1

1960	96
Bescot	17
Wigan Springs Branch	17
Nuneaton	10
Edge Hill	9
Patricroft	8
Bletchley	7
Buxton	5
Stafford	5
Willesden	5
Bushbury	4
Preston	3
Sutton Oak	3
Crewe South	2
Stockport Edgeley	1

1963	3
Bescot	2
Bushbury	1

7F^{3} 49395-49454 0-8-0 LNWR G2 Class

1948	60
Rugby	11
Nuneaton	10
Preston	6
Bletchley	5
Willesden	5
Northampton	4
Bescot	3
Crewe South	3
Coventry	2
Swansea Victoria	2
Wigan Springs Branch	2
Abergavenny	1
Edge Hill	1
Mold Junction	1
Patricroft	1
Shrewsbury	1
Tredegar	1
Warrington Dallam	1

1951	60
Rugby	11
Nuneaton	9
Edge Hill	8
Bletchley	5
Coventry	5
Speke Junction	5
Abergavenny	3
Patricroft	3
Buxton	2
Longsight	2
Wigan Springs Branch	2
Carnforth	1
Crewe South	1
Shrewsbury	1
Stafford	1
Warwick	1

1954	60
Edge Hill	9
Rugby	9
Coventry	5
Speke Junction	5
Abergavenny	4
Nuneaton	4
Wigan Springs Branch	4
Patricroft	3
Bletchley	2
Carnforth	2
Crewe South	2
Longsight	2
Northwich	2
Stockport Edgeley	2
Buxton	1
Preston	1
Shrewsbury	1
Stafford	1
Widnes	1

1957	60
Edge Hill	9
Rugby	7
Coventry	5
Speke Junction	5
Market Harborough	4
Wigan Springs Branch	4
Crewe South	3
Nuneaton	3
Patricroft	3
Bletchley	2
Carnforth	2
Longsight	2
Pontypool Road	2
Shrewsbury	2
Stockport Edgeley	2
Buxton	1
Preston	1
Stafford	1
Tredegar	1
Widnes	1

1960	41
Nuneaton	8
Edge Hill	7
Wigan Springs Branch	6
Buxton	3
Crewe South	3
Bletchley	2
Carnforth	2
Market Harborough	2
Patricroft	2
Bescot	1
Bushbury	1
Stafford	1
Stockport Edgeley	1
Sutton Oak	1
Willesden	1

1963	6
Bescot	2
Bushbury	2
Crewe South	2

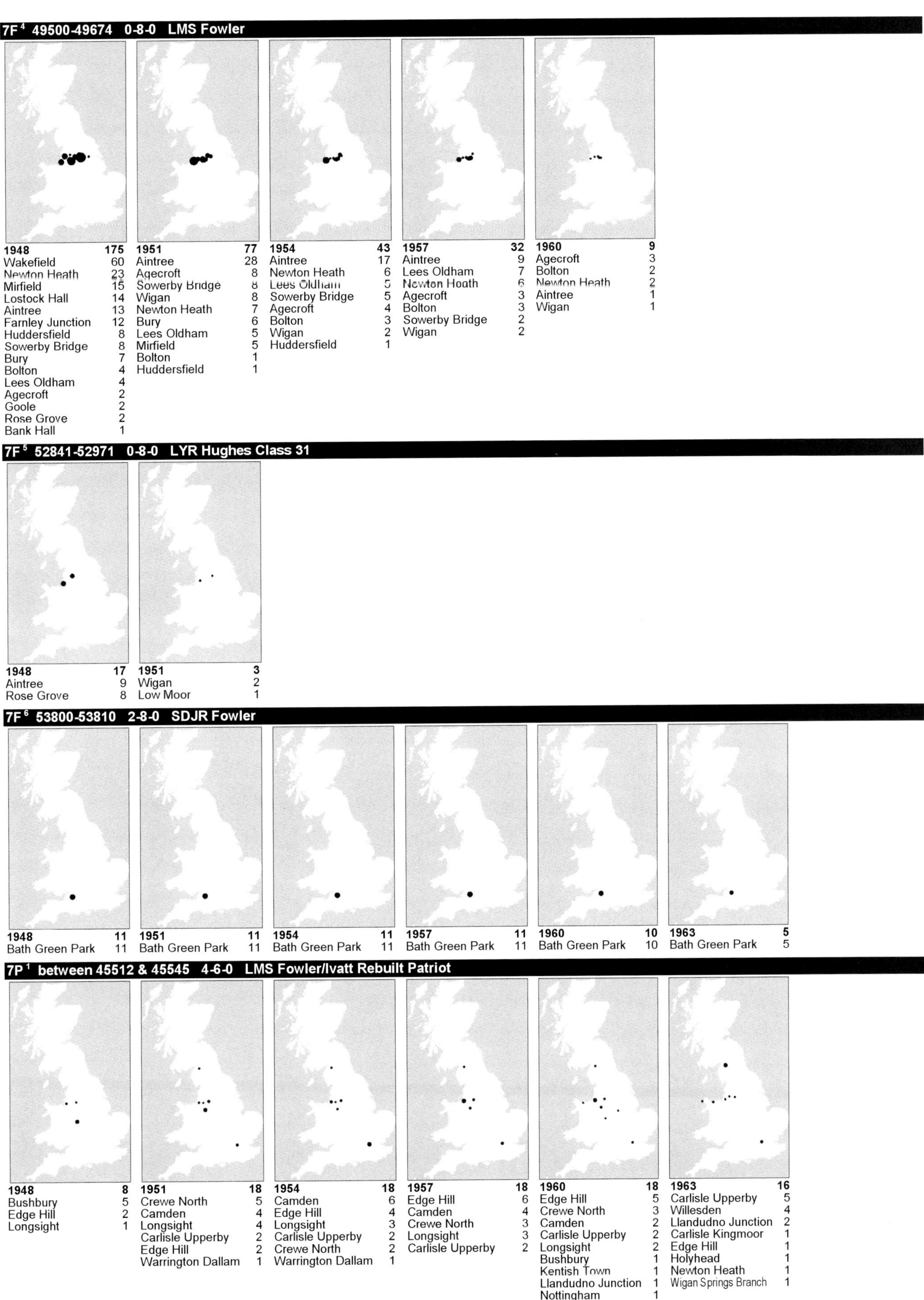

7F[4] 49500-49674 0-8-0 LMS Fowler

1948	175
Wakefield	60
Newton Heath	23
Mirfield	15
Lostock Hall	14
Aintree	13
Farnley Junction	12
Huddersfield	8
Sowerby Bridge	8
Bury	7
Bolton	4
Lees Oldham	4
Agecroft	2
Goole	2
Rose Grove	2
Bank Hall	1

1951	77
Aintree	28
Agecroft	8
Sowerby Bridge	8
Wigan	8
Newton Heath	7
Bury	6
Lees Oldham	5
Mirfield	5
Bolton	1
Huddersfield	1

1954	43
Aintree	17
Newton Heath	6
Lees Oldham	5
Sowerby Bridge	5
Agecroft	4
Bolton	3
Wigan	2
Huddersfield	1

1957	32
Aintree	9
Lees Oldham	7
Newton Heath	6
Agecroft	3
Bolton	3
Sowerby Bridge	2
Wigan	2

1960	9
Agecroft	3
Bolton	2
Newton Heath	2
Aintree	1
Wigan	1

7F[5] 52841-52971 0-8-0 LYR Hughes Class 31

1948	17
Aintree	9
Rose Grove	8

1951	3
Wigan	2
Low Moor	1

7F[6] 53800-53810 2-8-0 SDJR Fowler

1948	11
Bath Green Park	11

1951	11
Bath Green Park	11

1954	11
Bath Green Park	11

1957	11
Bath Green Park	11

1960	10
Bath Green Park	10

1963	5
Bath Green Park	5

7P[1] between 45512 & 45545 4-6-0 LMS Fowler/Ivatt Rebuilt Patriot

1948	8
Bushbury	5
Edge Hill	2
Longsight	1

1951	18
Crewe North	5
Camden	4
Longsight	4
Carlisle Upperby	2
Edge Hill	2
Warrington Dallam	1

1954	18
Camden	6
Edge Hill	4
Longsight	3
Carlisle Upperby	2
Crewe North	2
Warrington Dallam	1

1957	18
Edge Hill	6
Camden	4
Crewe North	3
Longsight	3
Carlisle Upperby	2

1960	18
Edge Hill	5
Crewe North	3
Camden	2
Carlisle Upperby	2
Longsight	2
Bushbury	1
Kentish Town	1
Llandudno Junction	1
Nottingham	1

1963	16
Carlisle Upperby	5
Willesden	4
Llandudno Junction	2
Carlisle Kingmoor	1
Edge Hill	1
Holyhead	1
Newton Heath	1
Wigan Springs Branch	1

7P^{2} 45735-45736 4-6-0 LMS Stanier Rebuilt Jubilee

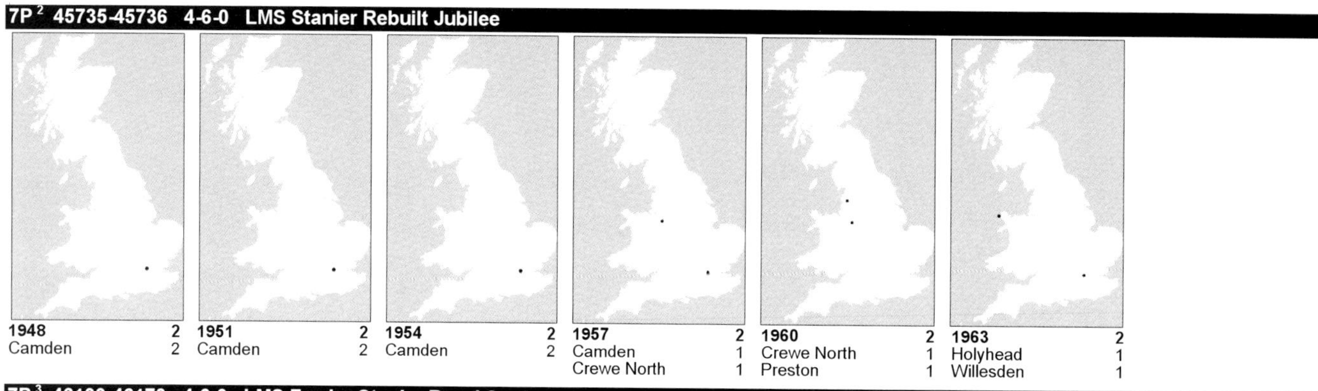

1948	2	1951	2	1954	2	1957	2	1960	2	1963	2
Camden	2	Camden	2	Camden	2	Camden	1	Crewe North	1	Holyhead	1
						Crewe North	1	Preston	1	Willesden	1

7P^{3} 46100-46170 4-6-0 LMS Fowler Stanier Royal Scot

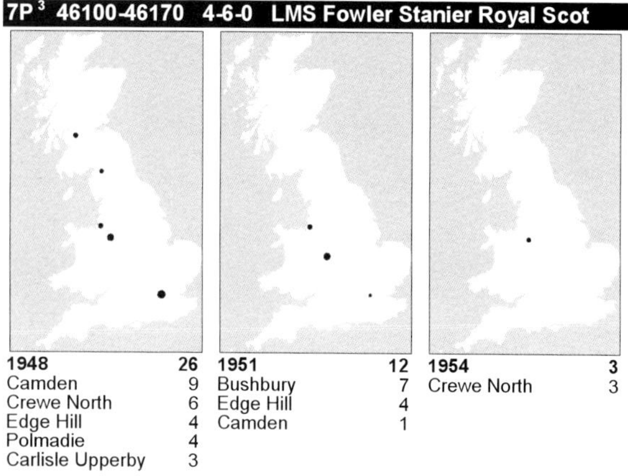

1948	26	1951	12	1954	3
Camden	9	Bushbury	7	Crewe North	3
Crewe North	6	Edge Hill	4		
Edge Hill	4	Camden	1		
Polmadie	4				
Carlisle Upperby	3				

7P^{3}Reb 46100-46170 4-6-0 LMS Fowler Stanier Rebuilt Royal Scot

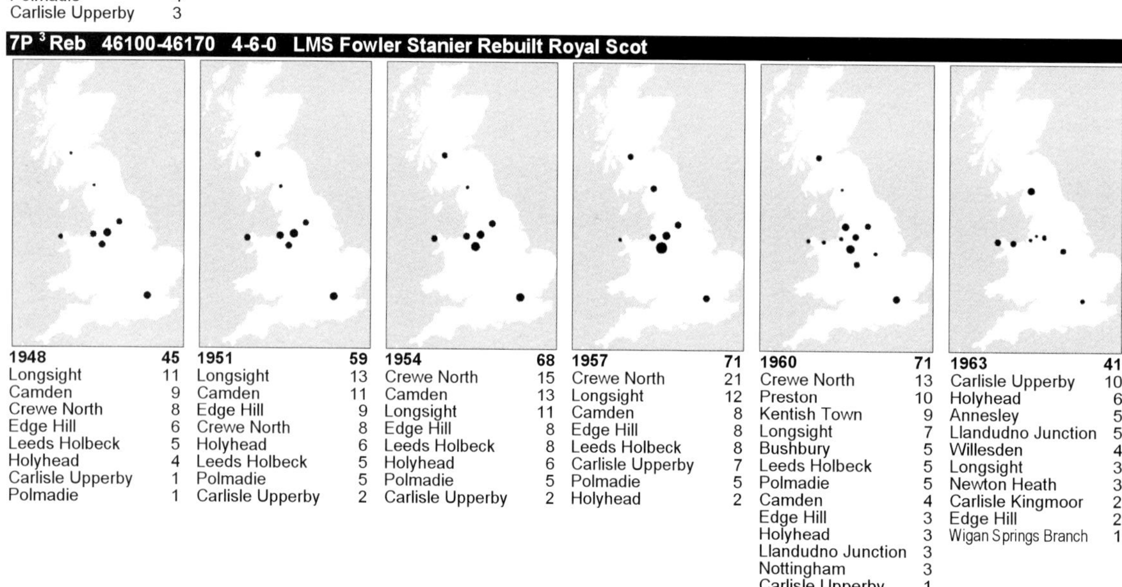

1948	45	1951	59	1954	68	1957	71	1960	71	1963	41
Longsight	11	Longsight	13	Crewe North	15	Crewe North	21	Crewe North	13	Carlisle Upperby	10
Camden	9	Camden	11	Camden	13	Longsight	12	Preston	10	Holyhead	6
Crewe North	8	Edge Hill	9	Longsight	11	Camden	8	Kentish Town	9	Annesley	5
Edge Hill	6	Crewe North	8	Edge Hill	8	Edge Hill	8	Longsight	7	Llandudno Junction	5
Leeds Holbeck	5	Holyhead	6	Leeds Holbeck	8	Leeds Holbeck	8	Bushbury	5	Willesden	4
Holyhead	4	Leeds Holbeck	5	Holyhead	6	Carlisle Upperby	7	Leeds Holbeck	5	Longsight	3
Carlisle Upperby	1	Polmadie	5	Polmadie	5	Polmadie	5	Polmadie	5	Newton Heath	3
Polmadie	1	Carlisle Upperby	2	Carlisle Upperby	2	Holyhead	2	Camden	4	Carlisle Kingmoor	2
								Edge Hill	3	Edge Hill	2
								Holyhead	3	Wigan Springs Branch	1
								Llandudno Junction	3		
								Nottingham	3		
								Carlisle Upperby	1		

LMS Fowler unrebuilt 'Royal Scot' '7P' class 4-6-0 No 46163 *Civil Service Rifleman* at Crewe. *J. Davenport*

8F 48000-48775 2-8-0 LMS & War Department Stanier

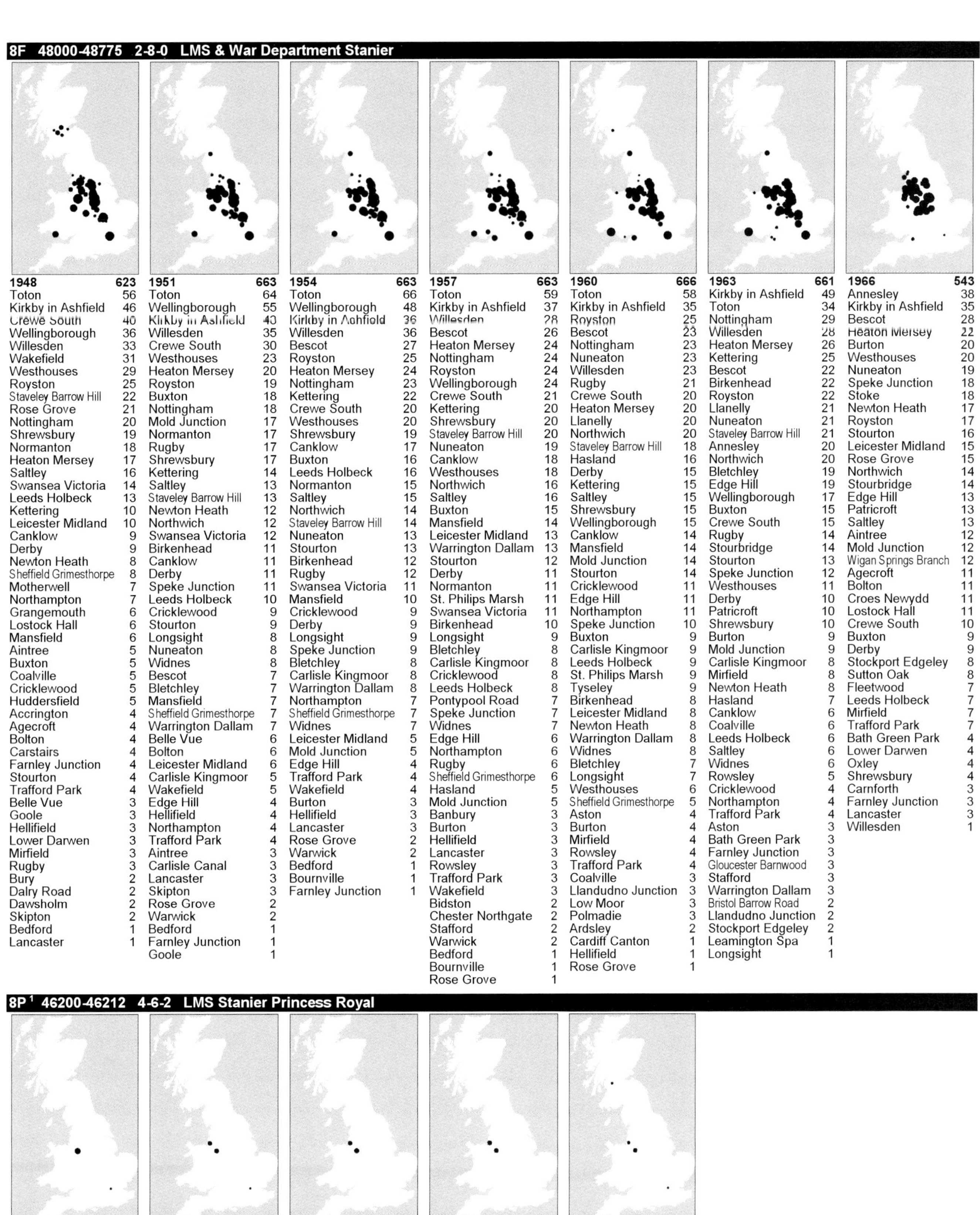

1948	623
Toton	56
Kirkby in Ashfield	46
Crewe South	40
Wellingborough	36
Willesden	33
Wakefield	31
Westhouses	29
Royston	25
Staveley Barrow Hill	22
Rose Grove	21
Nottingham	20
Shrewsbury	19
Normanton	18
Heaton Mersey	17
Saltley	16
Swansea Victoria	14
Leeds Holbeck	13
Kettering	10
Leicester Midland	10
Canklow	9
Derby	9
Newton Heath	8
Sheffield Grimesthorpe	8
Motherwell	7
Northampton	7
Grangemouth	6
Lostock Hall	6
Mansfield	6
Aintree	5
Buxton	5
Coalville	5
Cricklewood	5
Huddersfield	5
Accrington	4
Agecroft	4
Bolton	4
Carstairs	4
Farnley Junction	4
Stourton	4
Trafford Park	4
Belle Vue	3
Goole	3
Hellifield	3
Lower Darwen	3
Mirfield	3
Rugby	3
Bury	2
Dalry Road	2
Dawsholm	2
Skipton	2
Bedford	1
Lancaster	1

1951	663
Toton	64
Wellingborough	55
Kirkby in Ashfield	40
Willesden	35
Crewe South	30
Westhouses	23
Heaton Mersey	20
Royston	19
Buxton	18
Nottingham	18
Mold Junction	17
Normanton	17
Rugby	17
Shrewsbury	17
Kettering	14
Saltley	13
Staveley Barrow Hill	13
Newton Heath	12
Northwich	12
Swansea Victoria	12
Birkenhead	11
Canklow	11
Derby	11
Speke Junction	11
Leeds Holbeck	10
Cricklewood	9
Stourton	9
Longsight	8
Nuneaton	8
Widnes	8
Bescot	7
Bletchley	7
Mansfield	7
Sheffield Grimesthorpe	7
Warrington Dallam	7
Belle Vue	6
Bolton	6
Leicester Midland	6
Carlisle Kingmoor	5
Wakefield	5
Edge Hill	4
Hellifield	4
Northampton	4
Trafford Park	4
Aintree	3
Carlisle Canal	3
Lancaster	3
Skipton	3
Rose Grove	2
Warwick	2
Bedford	1
Farnley Junction	1
Goole	1

1954	663
Toton	66
Wellingborough	48
Kirkby in Ashfield	36
Willesden	36
Bescot	27
Royston	25
Heaton Mersey	24
Nottingham	23
Kettering	22
Crewe South	20
Westhouses	20
Shrewsbury	19
Canklow	17
Buxton	16
Leeds Holbeck	16
Normanton	15
Saltley	15
Northwich	14
Staveley Barrow Hill	14
Nuneaton	13
Stourton	13
Birkenhead	12
Rugby	12
Swansea Victoria	11
Mansfield	10
Cricklewood	9
Derby	9
Longsight	9
Speke Junction	9
Bletchley	8
Carlisle Kingmoor	8
Warrington Dallam	8
Northampton	7
Sheffield Grimesthorpe	7
Widnes	7
Leicester Midland	5
Mold Junction	5
Edge Hill	4
Trafford Park	4
Wakefield	4
Burton	3
Hellifield	3
Lancaster	3
Rose Grove	2
Warwick	2
Bedford	1
Bournville	1
Farnley Junction	1

1957	663
Toton	59
Kirkby in Ashfield	37
Willesden	28
Bescot	26
Heaton Mersey	24
Nottingham	24
Royston	24
Wellingborough	24
Crewe South	21
Kettering	20
Shrewsbury	20
Staveley Barrow Hill	20
Nuneaton	19
Canklow	18
Westhouses	18
Northwich	16
Saltley	16
Buxton	15
Mansfield	14
Leicester Midland	13
Warrington Dallam	13
Stourton	12
Derby	11
Normanton	11
St. Philips Marsh	11
Swansea Victoria	11
Birkenhead	10
Longsight	9
Bletchley	8
Carlisle Kingmoor	8
Cricklewood	8
Leeds Holbeck	8
Pontypool Road	7
Speke Junction	7
Widnes	7
Edge Hill	6
Northampton	6
Rugby	6
Sheffield Grimesthorpe	6
Hasland	5
Mold Junction	5
Banbury	3
Burton	3
Hellifield	3
Lancaster	3
Rowsley	3
Trafford Park	3
Wakefield	3
Bidston	2
Chester Northgate	2
Stafford	2
Warwick	2
Bedford	1
Bournville	1
Rose Grove	1

1960	666
Toton	58
Kirkby in Ashfield	35
Royston	25
Bescot	23
Nottingham	23
Nuneaton	23
Willesden	23
Rugby	21
Crewe South	20
Heaton Mersey	20
Llanelly	20
Northwich	20
Staveley Barrow Hill	18
Hasland	16
Derby	15
Kettering	15
Saltley	15
Shrewsbury	15
Wellingborough	15
Canklow	14
Mansfield	14
Mold Junction	14
Stourton	14
Cricklewood	11
Edge Hill	11
Northampton	11
Speke Junction	10
Buxton	9
Carlisle Kingmoor	9
Leeds Holbeck	9
St. Philips Marsh	9
Tyseley	9
Birkenhead	8
Leicester Midland	8
Newton Heath	8
Warrington Dallam	8
Widnes	8
Bletchley	7
Longsight	7
Westhouses	6
Sheffield Grimesthorpe	5
Aston	4
Burton	4
Mirfield	4
Rowsley	4
Trafford Park	4
Coalville	3
Llandudno Junction	3
Low Moor	3
Polmadie	3
Ardsley	2
Cardiff Canton	1
Hellifield	1
Rose Grove	1

1963	661
Kirkby in Ashfield	49
Toton	34
Nottingham	29
Willesden	28
Heaton Mersey	26
Kettering	25
Bescot	22
Birkenhead	22
Royston	22
Llanelly	21
Nuneaton	21
Staveley Barrow Hill	21
Annesley	20
Northwich	20
Bletchley	19
Edge Hill	19
Wellingborough	17
Buxton	15
Crewe South	15
Rugby	14
Stourbridge	14
Stourton	13
Speke Junction	12
Westhouses	11
Derby	10
Patricroft	10
Shrewsbury	10
Burton	9
Mold Junction	9
Carlisle Kingmoor	8
Mirfield	8
Newton Heath	8
Hasland	7
Canklow	6
Coalville	6
Leeds Holbeck	6
Saltley	6
Widnes	6
Rowsley	5
Cricklewood	4
Northampton	4
Trafford Park	4
Aston	3
Bath Green Park	3
Farnley Junction	3
Gloucester Barnwood	3
Stafford	3
Warrington Dallam	3
Bristol Barrow Road	2
Llandudno Junction	2
Stockport Edgeley	2
Leamington Spa	1
Longsight	1

1966	543
Annesley	38
Kirkby in Ashfield	35
Bescot	28
Heaton Mersey	22
Burton	20
Westhouses	20
Nuneaton	19
Speke Junction	18
Stoke	18
Newton Heath	17
Royston	17
Stourton	16
Leicester Midland	15
Rose Grove	15
Northwich	14
Stourbridge	14
Edge Hill	13
Patricroft	13
Saltley	13
Aintree	12
Mold Junction	12
Wigan Springs Branch	12
Agecroft	11
Bolton	11
Croes Newydd	11
Lostock Hall	11
Crewe South	10
Buxton	9
Derby	9
Stockport Edgeley	8
Sutton Oak	8
Fleetwood	7
Leeds Holbeck	7
Mirfield	7
Trafford Park	7
Bath Green Park	4
Lower Darwen	4
Oxley	4
Shrewsbury	4
Carnforth	3
Farnley Junction	3
Lancaster	3
Willesden	1

8P[1] 46200-46212 4-6-2 LMS Stanier Princess Royal

1948	13
Crewe North	12
Camden	1

1951	13
Crewe North	7
Edge Hill	5
Camden	1

1954	13
Crewe North	8
Edge Hill	5

1957	12
Crewe North	6
Edge Hill	6

1960	12
Crewe North	5
Edge Hill	4
Polmadie	2
Camden	1

8P[2] 46220-46257 4-6-2 LMS Stanier Princess Coronation or Duchess

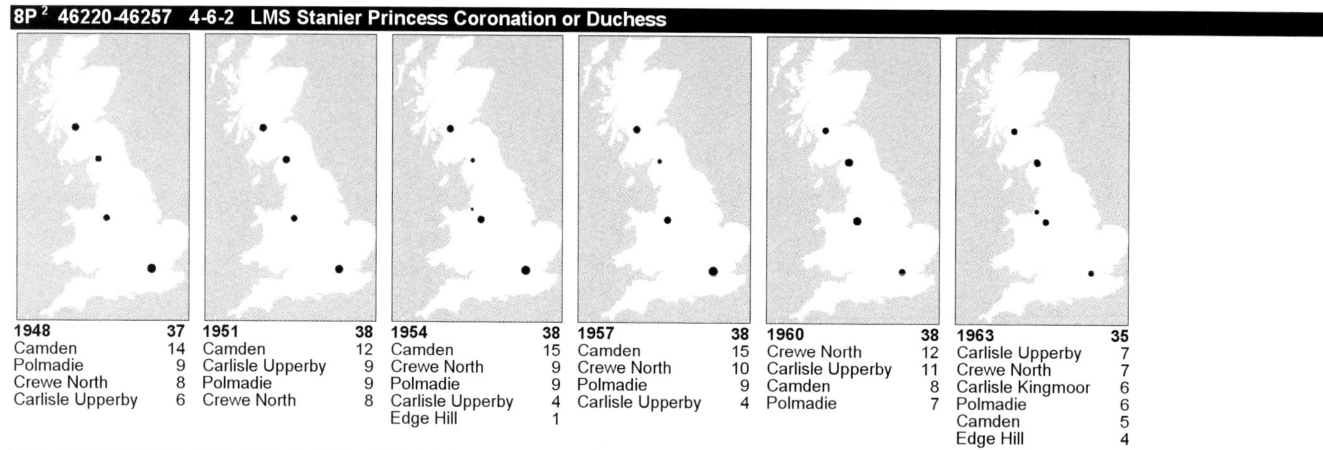

1948	37
Camden	14
Polmadie	9
Crewe North	8
Carlisle Upperby	6

1951	38
Camden	12
Carlisle Upperby	9
Polmadie	9
Crewe North	8

1954	38
Camden	15
Crewe North	9
Polmadie	9
Carlisle Upperby	4
Edge Hill	1

1957	38
Camden	15
Crewe North	10
Polmadie	9
Carlisle Upperby	4

1960	38
Crewe North	12
Carlisle Upperby	11
Camden	8
Polmadie	7

1963	35
Carlisle Upperby	7
Crewe North	7
Carlisle Kingmoor	6
Polmadie	6
Camden	5
Edge Hill	4

0-10-0 58100 0-10-0 MR Fowler "Lickey Banker"

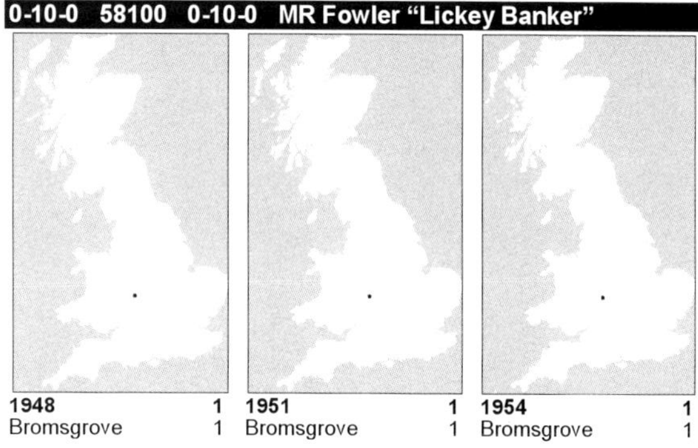

1948	1
Bromsgrove	1

1951	1
Bromsgrove	1

1954	1
Bromsgrove	1

CR Single 123 4-2-2 CR Preserved

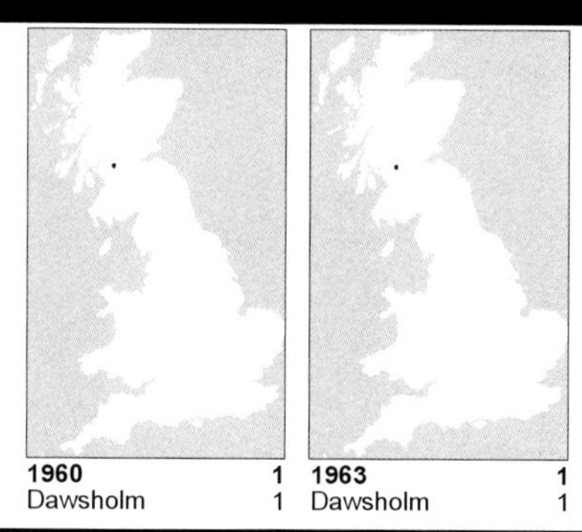

1960	1
Dawsholm	1

1963	1
Dawsholm	1

Crane 58865 0-4-2ST North London Railway Crane Tank

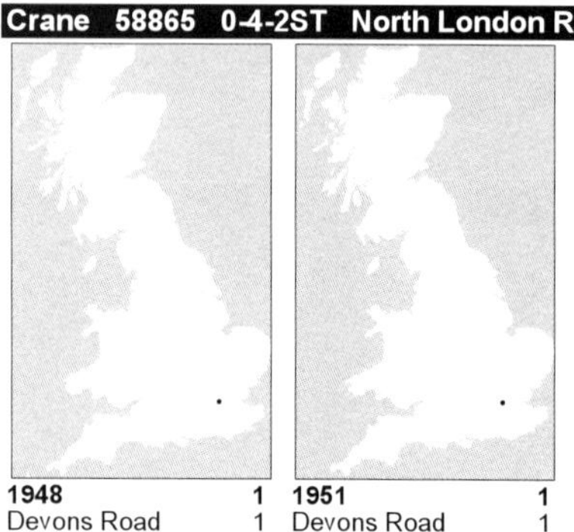

1948	1
Devons Road	1

1951	1
Devons Road	1

Garratt 47967-47999 2-6-6-2T LMS Fowler & Beyer Peacock

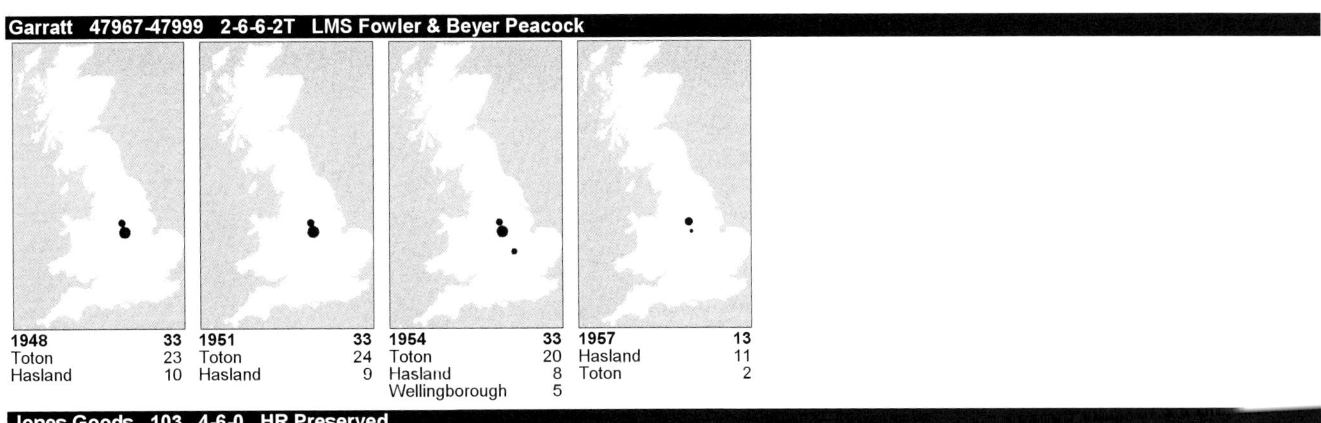

1948	33	1951	33	1954	33	1957	13
Toton	23	Toton	24	Toton	20	Hasland	11
Hasland	10	Hasland	9	Hasland	8	Toton	2
				Wellingborough	5		

Jones Goods 103 4-6-0 HR Preserved

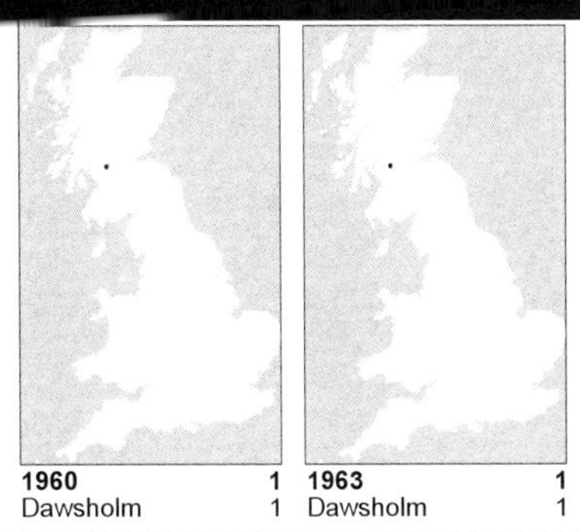

1960	1	1963	1
Dawsholm	1	Dawsholm	1

NG[1] Wren 0-4-0ST Horwich Works Narrow Gauge

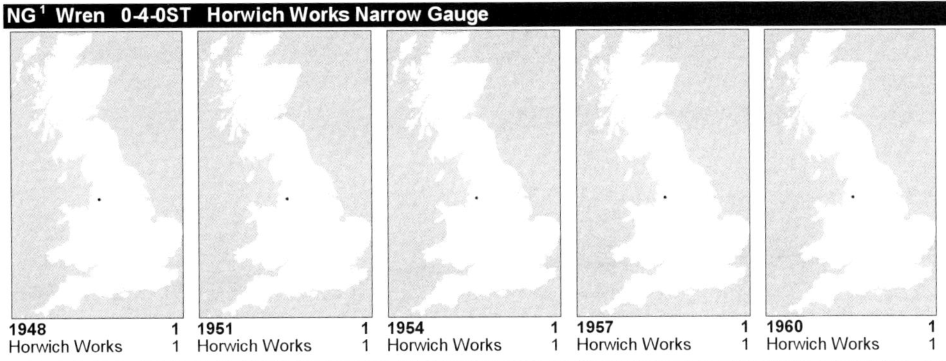

1948	1	1951	1	1954	1	1957	1	1960	1
Horwich Works	1	Horwich Works	1	Horwich Works	1	Horwich Works	1	Horwich Works	1

NG[2] 10 0-4-0ST Beeston Depot Narrow Gauge

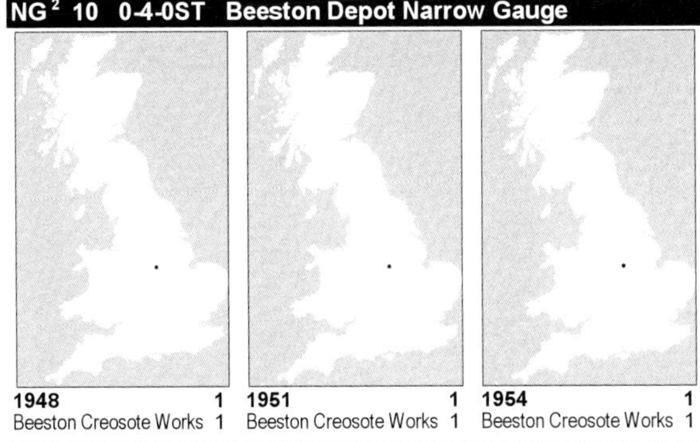

1948	1	1951	1	1954	1
Beeston Creosote Works	1	Beeston Creosote Works	1	Beeston Creosote Works	1

Rail Motor[1] 50617 0-4-0T LYR Hughes

1948	1
Bolton	1

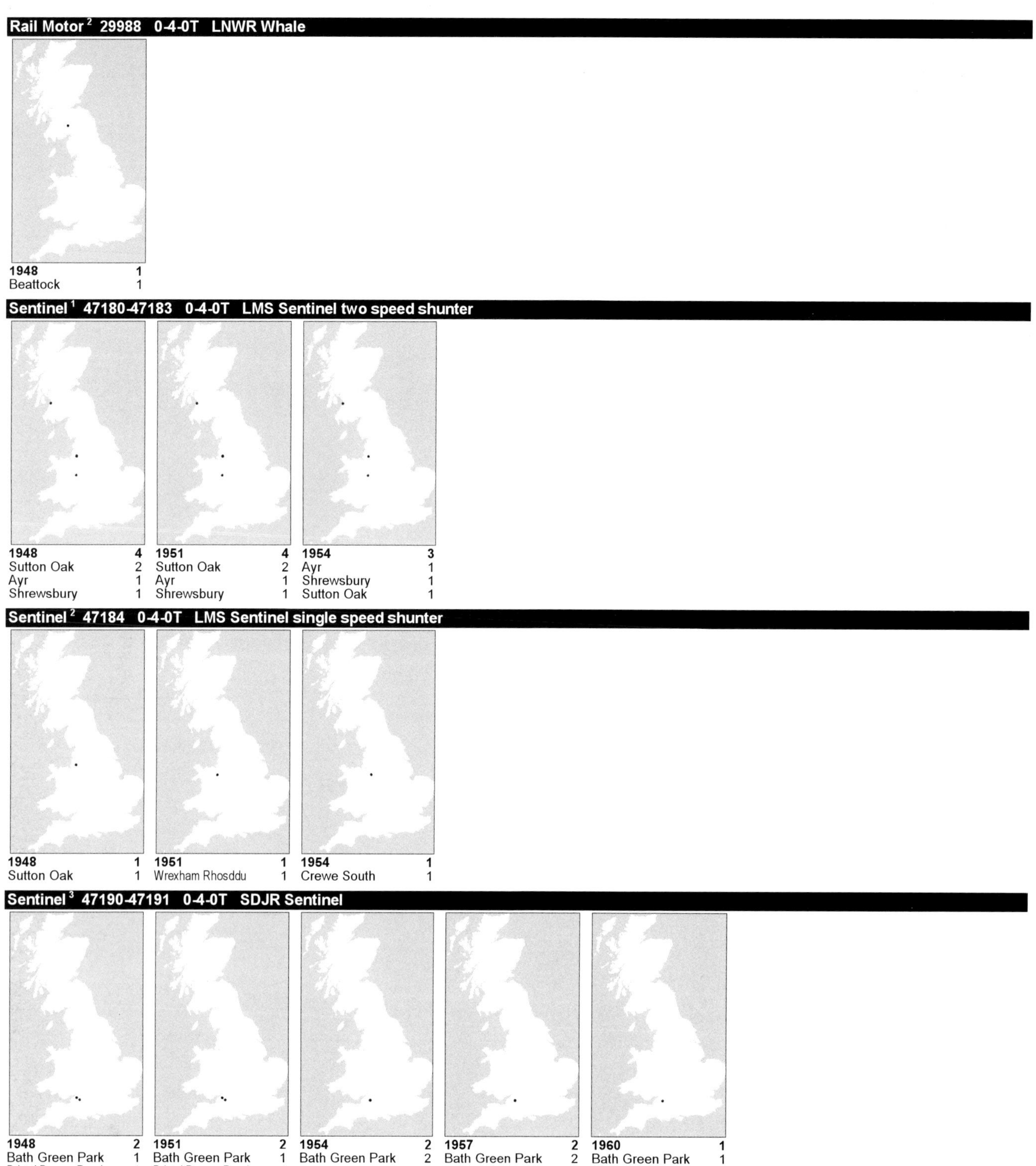

Right: Shafts of sunlight highlight 'B1' No 61199 inside York MPD on 1st May 1966. *P. Hocquard*

Former LNER Locomotives

Left: BR (LNER) Peppercorn 'A2' class 4-6-2 No 60530 *Sayajirao* at Doncaster Works on 8 April 1962. *John K. Morton*

Below: LNER Gresley 'W1' class 4-6-4 No 60700 working a Newcastle to Kings Cross Express. *E. R. Wethersett*

Bottom: LNER Gresley 'V2' class 2-6-2 No 60813 fitted with trough type smoke deflectors and a rimless chimney. At Craigentinny on 16 September 1961. *David C. Smith*

		1948	1951	1954	1957	1960	1963	1966
60001	*A4*	GHD Gateshead	**52A** Gateshead	**52A** Gateshead	**52A** Gateshead	**52A** Gateshead	**52A** Gateshead	
60002	*A4*	GHD Gateshead	**52A** Gateshead	**52A** Gateshead	**52A** Gateshead	**52A** Gateshead	**52A** Gateshead	
60003	*A4*	KX Kings Cross	**34A** Kings Cross	**34A** Kings Cross	**34A** Kings Cross	**34A** Kings Cross		
60004	*A4*	HAY Haymarket	**64B** Haymarket	**64B** Haymarket	**64B** Haymarket	**64B** Haymarket	**64B** Haymarket	**61B** Aberdeen Ferryhill
60005	*A4*	GHD Gateshead	**52A** Gateshead	**52A** Gateshead	**52A** Gateshead	**52A** Gateshead	**52A** Gateshead	
60006	*A4*	KX Kings Cross	**34A** Kings Cross	**34A** Kings Cross	**34A** Kings Cross	**34A** Kings Cross	**34A** Kings Cross	
60007	*A4*	GRA Grantham	**34A** Kings Cross	**34A** Kings Cross	**34A** Kings Cross	**34A** Kings Cross	**34A** Kings Cross	**61B** Aberdeen Ferryhill
60008	*A4*	GRA Grantham	**34A** Kings Cross	**34A** Kings Cross	**34A** Kings Cross	**34A** Kings Cross	**34A** Kings Cross	
60009	*A4*	HAY Haymarket	**64B** Haymarket	**64B** Haymarket	**64B** Haymarket	**64B** Haymarket	**61B** Aberdeen Ferryhill	**61B** Aberdeen Ferryhill
60010	*A4*	KX Kings Cross	**34A** Kings Cross	**34A** Kings Cross	**34A** Kings Cross	**34A** Kings Cross	**34A** Kings Cross	
60011	*A4*	HAY Haymarket	**64B** Haymarket	**64B** Haymarket	**64B** Haymarket	**64B** Haymarket	**61B** Aberdeen Ferryhill	
60012	*A4*	HAY Haymarket	**64B** Haymarket	**64B** Haymarket	**64B** Haymarket	**64B** Haymarket	**64B** Haymarket	
60013	*A4*	KX Kings Cross	**34A** Kings Cross	**34A** Kings Cross	**34A** Kings Cross	**34A** Kings Cross	**34A** Kings Cross	
60014	*A4*	GRA Grantham	**34A** Kings Cross	**34A** Kings Cross	**34A** Kings Cross	**34A** Kings Cross		
60015	*A4*	GRA Grantham	**35B** Grantham	**34A** Kings Cross	**34A** Kings Cross	**34A** Kings Cross	**34A** Kings Cross	
60016	*A4*	GHD Gateshead	**52A** Gateshead	**52A** Gateshead	**52A** Gateshead	**52A** Gateshead	**52A** Gateshead	
60017	*A4*	KX Kings Cross	**34A** Kings Cross	**34A** Kings Cross	**34A** Kings Cross	**34A** Kings Cross	**34A** Kings Cross	
60018	*A4*	GHD Gateshead	**52A** Gateshead	**52A** Gateshead	**52A** Gateshead	**52A** Gateshead	**52A** Gateshead	**61B** Aberdeen Ferryhill
60019	*A4*	GHD Gateshead	**52A** Gateshead	**52A** Gateshead	**52A** Gateshead	**52A** Gateshead	**52A** Gateshead	
60020	*A4*	GHD Gateshead	**52A** Gateshead	**52A** Gateshead	**52A** Gateshead	**52A** Gateshead	**52A** Gateshead	
60021	*A4*	KX Kings Cross	**34A** Kings Cross	**34A** Kings Cross	**34A** Kings Cross	**34A** Kings Cross	**34A** Kings Cross	
60022	*A4*	GRA Grantham	**34A** Kings Cross	**34A** Kings Cross	**34A** Kings Cross	**34A** Kings Cross	**34A** Kings Cross	
60023	*A4*	GHD Gateshead	**52A** Gateshead	**52A** Gateshead	**52A** Gateshead	**52A** Gateshead	**52A** Gateshead	
60024	*A4*	HAY Haymarket	**64B** Haymarket	**64B** Haymarket	**64B** Haymarket	**64B** Haymarket	**64B** Haymarket	**64A** St. Margarets
60025	*A4*	KX Kings Cross	**34A** Kings Cross	**34A** Kings Cross	**34A** Kings Cross	**34A** Kings Cross	**34A** Kings Cross	
60026	*A4*	KX Kings Cross	**35B** Grantham	**34A** Kings Cross	**34A** Kings Cross	**34A** Kings Cross	**34A** Kings Cross	
60027	*A4*	HAY Haymarket	**64B** Haymarket	**64B** Haymarket	**64B** Haymarket	**64B** Haymarket	**65B** St. Rollox	
60028	*A4*	GRA Grantham	**34A** Kings Cross	**34A** Kings Cross	**34A** Kings Cross	**34A** Kings Cross		
60029	*A4*	KX Kings Cross	**34A** Kings Cross	**34A** Kings Cross	**34A** Kings Cross	**34A** Kings Cross	**34A** Kings Cross	
60030	*A4*	GRA Grantham	**34A** Kings Cross	**34A** Kings Cross	**34A** Kings Cross	**34A** Kings Cross		
60031	*A4*	HAY Haymarket	**64B** Haymarket	**64B** Haymarket	**64B** Haymarket	**64B** Haymarket	**65B** St. Rollox	
60032	*A4*	GRA Grantham	**34A** Kings Cross	**34A** Kings Cross	**34A** Kings Cross	**34A** Kings Cross	**34A** Kings Cross	
60033	*A4*	GRA Grantham	**34A** Kings Cross	**34A** Kings Cross	**34A** Kings Cross	**34A** Kings Cross		
60034	*A4*	GRA Grantham	**34A** Kings Cross	**34A** Kings Cross	**34A** Kings Cross	**34A** Kings Cross	**34A** Kings Cross	**61B** Aberdeen Ferryhill
60035	*A3*	HAY Haymarket	**64B** Haymarket	**64B** Haymarket	**64B** Haymarket	**64B** Haymarket		
60036	*A3*	GHD Gateshead	**50B** Leeds Neville Hill	**50B** Leeds Neville Hill	**50B** Leeds Neville Hill	**50B** Leeds Neville Hill	**56B** Ardsley	
60037	*A3*	HAY Haymarket	**64B** Haymarket	**64B** Haymarket	**64B** Haymarket	**64B** Haymarket	**64A** St. Margarets	
60038	*A3*	GHD Gateshead	**52A** Gateshead	**52A** Gateshead	**51A** Darlington	**52A** Gateshead	**55A** Leeds Holbeck	
60039	*A3*	GRA Grantham	**34A** Kings Cross	**35B** Grantham	**38C** Leicester Central	**34A** Kings Cross	**34A** Kings Cross	
60040	*A3*	GHD Gateshead	**52A** Gateshead	**51A** Darlington	**52A** Gateshead	**51A** Darlington	**52B** Heaton	
60041	*A3*	HAY Haymarket	**64B** Haymarket	**64B** Haymarket	**64B** Haymarket	**64B** Haymarket	**64A** St. Margarets	
60042	*A3*	GHD Gateshead	**52A** Gateshead	**52A** Gateshead	**51A** Darlington	**52A** Gateshead	**52B** Heaton	
60043	*A3*	HAY Haymarket	**64B** Haymarket	**64B** Haymarket	**64B** Haymarket	**64B** Haymarket	**64A** St. Margarets	
60044	*A3*	GRA Grantham	**37B** Copley Hill	**38C** Leicester Central	**35B** Grantham	**34A** Kings Cross	**34A** Kings Cross	
60045	*A3*	GHD Gateshead	**52A** Gateshead	**52A** Gateshead	**52A** Gateshead	**52A** Gateshead	**51A** Darlington	
60046	*A3*	KX Kings Cross	**37B** Copley Hill	**36A** Doncaster	**36A** Doncaster	**34F** Grantham	**34E** New England	
60047	*A3*	KX Kings Cross	**36A** Doncaster	**35B** Grantham	**35B** Grantham	**34F** Grantham	**34E** New England	
60048	*A3*	DON Doncaster	**38C** Leicester Central	**36A** Doncaster	**36A** Doncaster	**34F** Grantham	**34E** New England	
60049	*A3*	DON Doncaster	**38C** Leicester Central	**38C** Leicester Central	**38C** Leicester Central	**34F** Grantham		
60050	*A3*	KX Kings Cross	**34E** Neasden	**34E** Neasden	**35B** Grantham	**34F** Grantham	**34E** New England	
60051	*A3*	KX Kings Cross	**34E** Neasden	**35B** Grantham	**56C** Copley Hill	**52A** Gateshead	**52B** Heaton	
60052	*A3*	NWE New England	**38C** Leicester Central	**38C** Leicester Central	**56C** Copley Hill	**52A** Gateshead	**51A** Darlington	**64A** St. Margarets
60053	*A3*	NWE New England	**35B** Grantham	**35B** Grantham	**56C** Copley Hill	**52A** Gateshead	**52B** Heaton	
60054	*A3*	NWE New England	**38C** Leicester Central	**38C** Leicester Central	**34A** Kings Cross	**34F** Grantham	**34F** Grantham	
60055	*A3*	KX Kings Cross	**36A** Doncaster	**36A** Doncaster	**34A** Kings Cross	**34A** Kings Cross		
60056	*A3*	KX Kings Cross	**37B** Copley Hill	**35B** Grantham	**35B** Grantham	**34F** Grantham	**34F** Grantham	
60057	*A3*	HAY Haymarket	**64B** Haymarket	**64B** Haymarket	**64B** Haymarket	**64B** Haymarket	**64A** St. Margarets	
60058	*A3*	DON Doncaster	**36A** Doncaster	**36A** Doncaster	**56C** Copley Hill	**52A** Gateshead	**52B** Heaton	
60059	*A3*	KX Kings Cross	**34A** Kings Cross	**38C** Leicester Central	**38C** Leicester Central	**34A** Kings Cross		
60060	*A3*	GHD Gateshead	**52A** Gateshead	**52A** Gateshead	**52A** Gateshead	**52A** Gateshead	**52B** Heaton	
60061	*A3*	NWE New England	**37B** Copley Hill	**35B** Grantham	**35B** Grantham	**34A** Kings Cross	**34A** Kings Cross	
60062	*A3*	KX Kings Cross	**37B** Copley Hill	**34A** Kings Cross	**34A** Kings Cross	**34A** Kings Cross	**34E** New England	
60063	*A3*	DON Doncaster	**34A** Kings Cross	**34E** Neasden	**35B** Grantham	**34F** Grantham	**34A** Kings Cross	
60064	*A3*	HAY Haymarket	**36A** Doncaster	**36A** Doncaster	**36A** Doncaster	**34F** Grantham		
60065	*A3*	HAY Haymarket	**34A** Kings Cross	**35B** Grantham	**35B** Grantham	**34F** Grantham	**34E** New England	
60066	*A3*	HAY Haymarket	**36A** Doncaster	**36A** Doncaster	**36A** Doncaster	**34A** Kings Cross	**34A** Kings Cross	
60067	*A3*	HAY Haymarket	**34A** Kings Cross	**36A** Doncaster	**36A** Doncaster	**34A** Kings Cross		
60068	*A10→A3*	CAR Carlisle Canal	**12B** Carlisle Canal	**68E** Carlisle Canal	**68E** Carlisle Canal	**12C** Carlisle Canal		
60069	*A3*	HTN Heaton	**52B** Heaton	**52B** Heaton	**52B** Heaton	**52D** Tweedmouth		
60070	*A3*	GHD Gateshead	**51A** Darlington	**51A** Darlington	**52A** Gateshead	**52A** Gateshead	**56B** Ardsley	
60071	*A3*	GHD Gateshead	**52A** Gateshead	**52A** Gateshead	**52A** Gateshead	**51A** Darlington	**52B** Heaton	
60072	*A3*	HTN Heaton	**52B** Heaton	**52B** Heaton	**52B** Heaton	**52D** Tweedmouth		
60073	*A3*	HTN Heaton	**52B** Heaton	**52B** Heaton	**52B** Heaton	**52B** Heaton	**52B** Heaton	
60074	*A3*	GHD Gateshead	**50B** Leeds Neville Hill	**50B** Leeds Neville Hill	**50B** Leeds Neville Hill	**50B** Leeds Neville Hill	**55H** Leeds Neville Hill	
60075	*A3*	GHD Gateshead	**52A** Gateshead	**52A** Gateshead	**52A** Gateshead	**52A** Gateshead	**52B** Heaton	
60076	*A3*	GHD Gateshead	**51A** Darlington	**52A** Gateshead	**52A** Gateshead	**52A** Gateshead		
60077	*A3*	HTN Heaton	**52B** Heaton	**52B** Heaton	**52B** Heaton	**52B** Heaton	**56B** Ardsley	
60078	*A3*	GHD Gateshead	**52A** Gateshead	**52A** Gateshead	**52A** Gateshead	**52A** Gateshead		
60079	*A3*	GHD Gateshead	**12B** Carlisle Canal	**68E** Carlisle Canal	**68E** Carlisle Canal	**12C** Carlisle Canal		
60080	*A3*	HTN Heaton	**52B** Heaton	**52B** Heaton	**52B** Heaton	**52B** Heaton	**56B** Ardsley	
60081	*A3*	GHD Gateshead	**50B** Leeds Neville Hill	**50B** Leeds Neville Hill	**50B** Leeds Neville Hill	**50B** Leeds Neville Hill		
60082	*A3*	HTN Heaton	**52A** Gateshead	**52A** Gateshead	**52B** Heaton	**52B** Heaton	**52B** Heaton	
60083	*A3*	HTN Heaton	**52B** Heaton	**52B** Heaton	**52B** Heaton	**52B** Heaton	**52B** Heaton	
60084	*A3*	GHD Gateshead	**50B** Leeds Neville Hill	**50B** Leeds Neville Hill	**50B** Leeds Neville Hill	**50B** Leeds Neville Hill	**55H** Leeds Neville Hill	
60085	*A3*	HTN Heaton	**52B** Heaton	**52B** Heaton	**52B** Heaton	**52B** Heaton	**52B** Heaton	
60086	*A3*	GHD Gateshead	**50B** Leeds Neville Hill	**50B** Leeds Neville Hill	**50B** Leeds Neville Hill	**50B** Leeds Neville Hill	**55H** Leeds Neville Hill	
60087	*A3*	HAY Haymarket	**64B** Haymarket	**64B** Haymarket	**64B** Haymarket	**64B** Haymarket	**64A** St. Margarets	
60088	*A3*	HTN Heaton	**52B** Heaton	**52B** Heaton	**52B** Heaton	**52B** Heaton	**52B** Heaton	
60089	*A3*	KX Kings Cross	**34A** Kings Cross	**64B** Haymarket	**64B** Haymarket	**64B** Haymarket	**64A** St. Margarets	
60090	*A3*	NWE New England	**64B** Haymarket	**64B** Haymarket	**64B** Haymarket	**64B** Haymarket	**65B** St. Rollox	
60091	*A3*	CAR Carlisle Canal	**52B** Heaton	**52B** Heaton	**52B** Heaton	**52A** Gateshead	**52B** Heaton	
60092	*A3*	HTN Heaton	**52B** Heaton	**52B** Heaton	**52B** Heaton	**52B** Heaton	**56B** Ardsley	
60093	*A3*	CAR Carlisle Canal	**12B** Carlisle Canal	**68E** Carlisle Canal	**68E** Carlisle Canal	**12C** Carlisle Canal		
60094	*A3*	HAY Haymarket	**64B** Haymarket	**64B** Haymarket	**64B** Haymarket	**64B** Haymarket	**65B** St. Rollox	
60095	*A3*	CAR Carlisle Canal	**12B** Carlisle Canal	**68E** Carlisle Canal	**68E** Carlisle Canal	**12C** Carlisle Canal		
60096	*A3*	KX Kings Cross	**64B** Haymarket	**64B** Haymarket	**64B** Haymarket	**64B** Haymarket	**64A** St. Margarets	
60097	*A3*	KX Kings Cross	**64B** Haymarket	**64B** Haymarket	**64B** Haymarket	**64B** Haymarket	**64A** St. Margarets	
60098	*A3*	KX Kings Cross	**64B** Haymarket	**64B** Haymarket	**64B** Haymarket	**64B** Haymarket	**64B** Haymarket	
60099	*A3*	HAY Haymarket	**64B** Haymarket	**64B** Haymarket	**64B** Haymarket	**64B** Haymarket	**64B** Haymarket	
60100	*A3*	HAY Haymarket	**64B** Haymarket	**64B** Haymarket	**64B** Haymarket	**64B** Haymarket	**64B** Haymarket	
60101	*A3*	HAY Haymarket	**64B** Haymarket	**64B** Haymarket	**64B** Haymarket	**64B** Haymarket	**64B** Haymarket	
60102	*A3*	GRA Grantham	**38C** Leicester Central	**38C** Leicester Central	**38C** Leicester Central	**34F** Grantham		
60103	*A3*	DON Doncaster	**38C** Leicester Central	**35B** Grantham	**35B** Grantham	**34A** Kings Cross	**34A** Kings Cross	
60104	*A3*	KX Kings Cross	**38C** Leicester Central	**38C** Leicester Central	**38C** Leicester Central			
60105	*A3*	KX Kings Cross	**34A** Kings Cross	**35B** Grantham	**35B** Grantham	**34F** Grantham	**34F** Grantham	
60106	*A3*	GRA Grantham	**35B** Grantham	**35B** Grantham	**38C** Leicester Central	**34F** Grantham	**34F** Grantham	
60107	*A3*	KX Kings Cross	**38C** Leicester Central	**38C** Leicester Central	**38C** Leicester Central	**34F** Grantham	**34A** Kings Cross	
60108	*A3*	KX Kings Cross	**34A** Kings Cross	**34E** Neasden	**34E** Neasden	**34A** Kings Cross	**34E** New England	
60109	*A3*	KX Kings Cross	**34A** Kings Cross	**36A** Doncaster	**36A** Doncaster	**34A** Kings Cross		
60110	*A3*	KX Kings Cross	**34A** Kings Cross	**35B** Grantham	**35B** Grantham	**34A** Kings Cross	**34A** Kings Cross	
60111	*A3*	NWE New England	**34E** Neasden	**34E** Neasden	**38C** Leicester Central	**34F** Grantham		
60112	*A3*	KX Kings Cross	**36A** Doncaster	**36A** Doncaster	**36A** Doncaster	**34F** Grantham	**34F** Grantham	
60113	*A1/1*	KX Kings Cross	**35A** New England	**35B** Grantham	**35B** Grantham	**36A** Doncaster		
60114	*A1*	→	**37B** Copley Hill	**35B** Grantham	**35B** Grantham	**36A** Doncaster	**36A** Doncaster	

No.	Class	1948		1951	1954	1957	1960	1963	1966
60115	A1	→		52A Gateshead	52A Gateshead	52A Gateshead	52A Gateshead		
60116	A1	→		52B Heaton	52B Heaton	52B Heaton	52B Heaton	52D Tweedmouth	
60117	A1	→		37B Copley Hill	37B Copley Hill	56C Copley Hill	56C Copley Hill	56C Copley Hill	
60118	A1	→		37B Copley Hill	37B Copley Hill	56C Copley Hill	56C Copley Hill	56B Ardsley	
60119	A1	→		37B Copley Hill	37B Copley Hill	35B Grantham	36A Doncaster	36A Doncaster	
60120	A1	→		37B Copley Hill	37B Copley Hill	56C Copley Hill	56C Copley Hill	56C Copley Hill	
60121	A1	→		50A York	50A York	50A York	50A York	50A York	
60122	A1	→		34A Kings Cross	37B Copley Hill	35B Grantham	36A Doncaster		
60123	A1	→		37B Copley Hill	37A Ardsley	56B Ardsley	56C Copley Hill		
60124	A1	→		52A Gateshead	52A Gateshead	52A Gateshead	52A Gateshead	50A York	51A Darlington
60125	A1	→		37B Copley Hill	37B Copley Hill	35B Grantham	36A Doncaster	36A Doncaster	
60126	A1	→		52B Heaton	52B Heaton	52B Heaton	52B Heaton	50A York	
60127	A1	→		52B Heaton	52B Heaton	52B Heaton	52B Heaton	52D Tweedmouth	
60128	A1	→		34A Kings Cross	35B Grantham	35B Grantham	36A Doncaster	36A Doncaster	
60129	A1	→		52A Gateshead	52A Gateshead	52A Gateshead	52A Gateshead	52D Tweedmouth	
60130	A1	→		34A Kings Cross	37A Ardsley	56B Ardsley	56C Copley Hill	56C Copley Hill	
60131	A1	→		34A Kings Cross	37B Copley Hill	56C Copley Hill	56C Copley Hill	56B Ardsley	
60132	A1	→		52A Gateshead	52A Gateshead	52A Gateshead	52A Gateshead	52D Tweedmouth	
60133	A1	→		37B Copley Hill	37B Copley Hill	56C Copley Hill	56C Copley Hill	56C Copley Hill	
60134	A1	→		37B Copley Hill	37B Copley Hill	56C Copley Hill	56C Copley Hill	56B Ardsley	
60135	A1	→		52A Gateshead	52A Gateshead	52A Gateshead	52A Gateshead		
60136	A1	→		34A Kings Cross	35B Grantham	35B Grantham	36A Doncaster	36A Doncaster	
60137	A1	→		52A Gateshead	52A Gateshead	52A Gateshead	52A Gateshead		
60138	A1	→		50A York	50A York	50A York	50A York	50A York	
60139	A1	→		34A Kings Cross	37B Copley Hill	35B Grantham	36A Doncaster	36A Doncaster	
60140	A1	→		50A York	50A York	50A York	50A York	50A York	
60141	A1	→		37B Copley Hill	37B Copley Hill	56C Copley Hill	56C Copley Hill	56C Copley Hill	
60142	A1	→		52A Gateshead	52A Gateshead	52A Gateshead	52A Gateshead	52D Tweedmouth	
60143	A1	→		52A Gateshead	52A Gateshead	52A Gateshead	52A Gateshead	52D Tweedmouth	
60144	A1	→		34A Kings Cross	35B Grantham	35B Grantham	36A Doncaster	36A Doncaster	
60145	A1	→		52A Gateshead	52A Gateshead	52A Gateshead	52A Gateshead	56C Copley Hill	50A York
60146	A1	→		50A York	50A York	50A York	50A York	50A York	
60147	A1	→		52A Gateshead	52A Gateshead	52A Gateshead	52A Gateshead	52D Tweedmouth	
60148	A1	→		34A Kings Cross	37B Copley Hill	56C Copley Hill	56C Copley Hill	56C Copley Hill	
60149	A1	→		34A Kings Cross	35B Grantham	34A Kings Cross	36A Doncaster	36A Doncaster	
60150	A1	→		52A Gateshead	52A Gateshead	52A Gateshead	52A Gateshead	50A York	
60151	A1	→		52A Gateshead	52A Gateshead	52A Gateshead	52A Gateshead	52D Tweedmouth	
60152	A1	→		64B Haymarket	64B Haymarket	64B Haymarket	64B Haymarket	64B Haymarket	
60153	A1	→		50A York	50A York	50A York	50A York		
60154	A1	→		52A Gateshead	52A Gateshead	52A Gateshead	52A Gateshead	50A York	
60155	A1	→		52A Gateshead	52A Gateshead	52A Gateshead	52A Gateshead	50A York	
60156	A1	→		34A Kings Cross	35B Grantham	34A Kings Cross	36A Doncaster	36A Doncaster	
60157	A1	→		34A Kings Cross	35B Grantham	34A Kings Cross	36A Doncaster	36A Doncaster	
60158	A1	→		34A Kings Cross	37B Copley Hill	35B Grantham	36A Doncaster	36A Doncaster	
60159	A1	→		64B Haymarket	64B Haymarket	64B Haymarket	64B Haymarket	64B Haymarket	
60160	A1	→		64B Haymarket	64B Haymarket	64B Haymarket	64B Haymarket	64B Haymarket	
60161	A1	→		64B Haymarket	64B Haymarket	64B Haymarket	64B Haymarket	64B Haymarket	
60162	A1	→		64B Haymarket	64B Haymarket	64B Haymarket	64B Haymarket	64B Haymarket	
60500	A2/3	KX	Kings Cross	35A New England	35A New England	35A New England	34E New England	34E New England	
60501	A2/2	ABD	Aberdeen Ferryhill	50A York	50A York	50A York	50A York		
60502	A2/2	ABD	Aberdeen Ferryhill	50A York	50A York	50A York	50A York		
60503	A2/2	HAY	Haymarket	50A York	50A York	50A York			
60504	A2/2	HAY	Haymarket	35A New England	35A New England	35A New England	34E New England		
60505	A2/2	HAY	Haymarket	35A New England	35A New England	35A New England			
60506	A2/2	HAY	Haymarket	35A New England	35A New England	35A New England	34E New England		
60507	A2/1	KX	Kings Cross	64B Haymarket	64B Haymarket	64B Haymarket	64B Haymarket		
60508	A2/1	KX	Kings Cross	35A New England	35A New England	35A New England	34E New England		
60509	A2/1	HAY	Haymarket	64B Haymarket	64B Haymarket	64B Haymarket	64B Haymarket		
60510	A2/1	HAY	Haymarket	64B Haymarket	64B Haymarket	64B Haymarket	64B Haymarket		
60511	A2/3	HTN	Heaton	52B Heaton	52B Heaton	52B Heaton	52B Heaton		
60512	A2/3	HTN	Heaton	52B Heaton	50A York	50A York	50A York	64A St. Margarets	
60513	A2/3	KX	Kings Cross	35A New England	35A New England	35A New England	34E New England	34E New England	
60514	A2/3	KX	Kings Cross	35A New England	35A New England	35A New England	34E New England		
60515	A2/3	HTN	Heaton	52B Heaton	50A York	50A York	50A York		
60516	A2/3	HTN	Heaton	52B Heaton	52A Gateshead	52A Gateshead	52A Gateshead		
60517	A2/3	HTN	Heaton	52B Heaton	52B Heaton	52B Heaton	52B Heaton		
60518	A2/3	GHD	Gateshead	52A Gateshead	52A Gateshead	52A Gateshead	52A Gateshead		
60519	A2/3	HAY	Haymarket	64B Haymarket	64B Haymarket	64B Haymarket	64B Haymarket		
60520	A2/3	DON	Doncaster	35A New England	35A New England	35A New England	34E New England	34E New England	
60521	A2/3	GHD	Gateshead	52A Gateshead	52A Gateshead	52A Gateshead	52A Gateshead		
60522	A2/3	YK	York	50A York	50A York	50A York	50A York	61B Aberdeen Ferryhill	
60523	A2/3	KX	Kings Cross	35A New England	35A New England	35A New England	34E New England	34E New England	
60524	A2/3	YK	York	50A York	50A York	50A York	50A York	64A St. Margarets	
60525	A2	DON	Doncaster	61B Aberdeen Ferryhill	61B Aberdeen Ferryhill	61B Aberdeen Ferryhill	61B Aberdeen Ferryhill	61B Aberdeen Ferryhill	
60526	A2	→		50A York	50A York	50A York	50A York		
60527	A2	→		62B Dundee Tay Bridge	62B Dundee Tay Bridge	62B Dundee Tay Bridge	62B Dundee Tay Bridge	61B Aberdeen Ferryhill	
60528	A2	→		62B Dundee Tay Bridge	62B Dundee Tay Bridge	62B Dundee Tay Bridge	62B Dundee Tay Bridge	62B Dundee Tay Bridge	62B Dundee Tay Bridge
60529	A2	→		64B Haymarket	64B Haymarket	64B Haymarket	64B Haymarket		
60530	A2	→		64B Haymarket	64B Haymarket	64B Haymarket	64B Haymarket	64A St. Margarets	62B Dundee Tay Bridge
60531	A2	→		61B Aberdeen Ferryhill	61B Aberdeen Ferryhill	61B Aberdeen Ferryhill	61B Aberdeen Ferryhill		
60532	A2	→		64B Haymarket	61B Aberdeen Ferryhill	61B Aberdeen Ferryhill	61B Aberdeen Ferryhill	62B Dundee Tay Bridge	62B Dundee Tay Bridge
60533	A2	→		35A New England	35A New England	35A New England	34E New England	34E New England	
60534	A2	→		64B Haymarket	64B Haymarket	64B Haymarket	64B Haymarket		
60535	A2	→		64B Haymarket	64B Haymarket	64B Haymarket	64B Haymarket	64A St. Margarets	
60536	A2	→		64B Haymarket	64B Haymarket	64B Haymarket	64B Haymarket		
60537	A2	→		61B Aberdeen Ferryhill	64B Haymarket	64B Haymarket	64B Haymarket		
60538	A2	→		52A Gateshead	52A Gateshead	52A Gateshead	52A Gateshead		
60539	A2	→		52B Heaton	52B Heaton	52B Heaton	52B Heaton		
60700	W1	KX	Kings Cross	34A Kings Cross	36A Doncaster	36A Doncaster			
60800	V2	KX	Kings Cross	34A Kings Cross	34A Kings Cross	34A Kings Cross	34A Kings Cross		
60801	V2	GHD	Gateshead	52B Heaton	52B Heaton	52D Tweedmouth	52D Tweedmouth		
60802	V2	HTN	Heaton	52B Heaton	52A Gateshead	52B Heaton	52B Heaton	52B Heaton	
60803	V2	NWE	New England	35A New England	31B March	31B March	31B March	34E New England	
60804	V2	DEE	Dundee Tay Bridge	62B Dundee Tay Bridge	62B Dundee Tay Bridge	62B Dundee Tay Bridge	62B Dundee Tay Bridge	62B Dundee Tay Bridge	
60805	V2	GHD	Gateshead	52B Heaton	52B Heaton	52D Tweedmouth	52A Gateshead	50A York	
60806	V2	GHD	Gateshead	52B Heaton	52B Heaton	52B Heaton	52B Heaton	51L Thornaby	51A Darlington
60807	V2	GHD	Gateshead	52B Heaton	52A Gateshead	52A Gateshead	52A Gateshead		
60808	V2	HTN	Heaton	52B Heaton	52D Tweedmouth	52D Tweedmouth	52B Heaton	51A Darlington	
60809	V2	GHD	Gateshead	52B Heaton	52A Gateshead	52B Heaton	52B Heaton	51A Darlington	
60810	V2	GHD	Gateshead	52B Heaton	52B Heaton	52B Heaton	52B Heaton	50A York	
60811	V2	GHD	Gateshead	52B Heaton	52B Heaton	52B Heaton	52B Heaton		
60812	V2	HTN	Heaton	52B Heaton	52B Heaton	52B Heaton	52B Heaton	52B Heaton	
60813	V2	KX	Kings Cross	34A Kings Cross	64A St. Margarets	64A St. Margarets	64A St. Margarets	64A St. Margarets	64A St. Margarets
60814	V2	KX	Kings Cross	34A Kings Cross	34A Kings Cross	34A Kings Cross	34A Kings Cross	34F Grantham	
60815	V2	DON	Doncaster	38E Woodford Halse	36A Doncaster	38E Woodford Halse	15E Leicester Central		
60816	V2	HAY	Haymarket	64B Haymarket	64B Haymarket	64B Haymarket	64A St. Margarets	64A St. Margarets	
60817	V2	KX	Kings Cross	38E Woodford Halse	38E Woodford Halse	38E Woodford Halse	36A Doncaster	34E New England	
60818	V2	KX	Kings Cross	38E Woodford Halse	64A St. Margarets	64A St. Margarets	64A St. Margarets	64A St. Margarets	62B Dundee Tay Bridge
60819	V2	ABD	Aberdeen Ferryhill	61B Aberdeen Ferryhill	61B Aberdeen Ferryhill	61B Aberdeen Ferryhill	64A St. Margarets		
60820	V2	KX	Kings Cross	38E Woodford Halse	38C Leicester Central	34E Neasden	34E New England		
60821	V2	KX	Kings Cross	34A Kings Cross	34A Kings Cross	35A New England	34E New England		
60822	V2	ABD	Aberdeen Ferryhill	62B Dundee Tay Bridge	62B Dundee Tay Bridge	62B Dundee Tay Bridge	62B Dundee Tay Bridge	62B Dundee Tay Bridge	
60823	V2	KX	Kings Cross	34A Kings Cross	64A St. Margarets	64A St. Margarets	64A St. Margarets		
60824	V2	ABD	Aberdeen Ferryhill	61B Aberdeen Ferryhill	61B Aberdeen Ferryhill	61B Aberdeen Ferryhill	64A St. Margarets	64A St. Margarets	64A St. Margarets

No.	Class	1948	1951	1954	1957	1960	1963	1966
60825	V2	ABD Aberdeen Ferryhill	64A St. Margarets	64A St. Margarets	64A St. Margarets	64A St. Margarets	64A St. Margarets	
60826	V2	DON Doncaster	38E Woodford Halse	37A Ardsley	35A New England	36A Doncaster		
60827	V2	ABD Aberdeen Ferryhill	61B Aberdeen Ferryhill	61B Aberdeen Ferryhill	61B Aberdeen Ferryhill	64A St. Margarets		
60828	V2	NWE New England	35A New England	35A New England	34A Kings Cross	50A York	50A York	
60829	V2	KX Kings Cross	35A New England	35A New England	35A New England	34E New England		
60830	V2	DON Doncaster	38E Woodford Halse	31B March	31B March	31B March	34F Grantham	
60831	V2	DON Doncaster	38E Woodford Halse	38E Woodford Halse	38E Woodford Halse	50A York	50A York	50A York
60832	V2	DON Doncaster	38E Woodford Halse	35A New England	35A New England	34E New England		
60833	V2	GHD Gateshead	52B Heaton	52B Heaton	52A Gateshead	52A Gateshead	50A York	
60834	V2	HAY Haymarket	62B Dundee Tay Bridge	62B Dundee Tay Bridge	62B Dundee Tay Bridge	62B Dundee Tay Bridge	62B Dundee Tay Bridge	
60835	V2	GHD Gateshead	52B Heaton	52B Heaton	52B Heaton	52B Heaton	52B Heaton	
60836	V2	HAY Haymarket	64A St. Margarets	64A St. Margarets	64A St. Margarets	64A St. Margarets	64A St. Margarets	62B Dundee Tay Bridge
60837	V2	YK York	50A York	50A York	50A York	50A York	50A York	
60838	V2	DEE Dundee Tay Bridge	62B Dundee Tay Bridge	62B Dundee Tay Bridge	62B Dundee Tay Bridge	62B Dundee Tay Bridge	62B Dundee Tay Bridge	
60839	V2	YK York	50A York	50A York	50A York	50A York		
60840	V2	DEE Dundee Tay Bridge	62B Dundee Tay Bridge	64A St. Margarets	64A St. Margarets	64A St. Margarets		
60841	V2	NWE New England	35A New England	35A New England	36A Doncaster	36A Doncaster	34E New England	
60842	V2	NWE New England	35A New England	35A New England	35A New England	50A York		
60843	V2	YK York	50A York	50A York	50A York	52D Tweedmouth	56B Ardsley	
60844	V2	DEE Dundee Tay Bridge	62B Dundee Tay Bridge	62B Dundee Tay Bridge	62B Dundee Tay Bridge	62B Dundee Tay Bridge	62B Dundee Tay Bridge	
60845	V2	DON Doncaster	38E Woodford Halse	35A New England	35A New England	34E New England		
60846	V2	DON Doncaster	36A Doncaster	37A Ardsley	56B Ardsley	52B Heaton	51L Thornaby	
60847	V2	YK York	50A York	50A York	50A York	50A York	50A York	
60848	V2	HAY Haymarket	64A St. Margarets	64A St. Margarets	52A Gateshead	51A Darlington		
60849	V2	DON Doncaster	36A Doncaster	36A Doncaster	36A Doncaster	36A Doncaster		
60850	V2	NWE New England	35A New England	35A New England	35A New England	36A Doncaster		
60851	V2	ABD Aberdeen Ferryhill	61B Aberdeen Ferryhill	61B Aberdeen Ferryhill	61B Aberdeen Ferryhill	61B Aberdeen Ferryhill		
60852	V2	DON Doncaster	36A Doncaster	36A Doncaster	36A Doncaster	36A Doncaster	36A Doncaster	
60853	V2	COP Copley Hill	38E Woodford Halse	35A New England	35A New England	34E New England	36A Doncaster	
60854	V2	NWE New England	35A New England	35A New England	35A New England	34A Kings Cross	34A Kings Cross	
60855	V2	NWE New England	35A New England	34A Kings Cross	34A Kings Cross	50A York	50A York	
60856	V2	YK York	50A York	50A York	50A York	50A York	50A York	
60857	V2	DON Doncaster	36A Doncaster	36A Doncaster	36A Doncaster	36A Doncaster		
60858	V2	NWE New England	35A New England	31B March	31B March	31B March	34E New England	
60859	V2	NWE New England	35A New England	38E Woodford Halse	56C Copley Hill	56C Copley Hill	51L Thornaby	
60860	V2	GHD Gateshead	52B Heaton	52D Tweedmouth	52D Tweedmouth	52A Gateshead		
60861	V2	DON Doncaster	36A Doncaster	37A Ardsley	56B Ardsley	56B Ardsley	56B Ardsley	
60862	V2	NWE New England	34A Kings Cross	34A Kings Cross	34A Kings Cross	34A Kings Cross	34A Kings Cross	
60863	V2	NWE New England	35A New England	38C Leicester Central	38C Leicester Central	15E Leicester Central		
60864	V2	DAR Darlington	50A York	50A York	50A York	50A York	50A York	
60865	V2	NWE New England	35A New England	37B Copley Hill	56C Copley Hill	52D Tweedmouth	52D Tweedmouth	
60866	V2	NWE New England	35A New England	35A New England	35A New England	36A Doncaster		
60867	V2	DON Doncaster	36A Doncaster	36A Doncaster	35A New England	34E New England		
60868	V2	GHD Gateshead	52B Heaton	52A Gateshead	52A Gateshead	52A Gateshead	52B Heaton	64A St. Margarets
60869	V2	NWE New England	35A New England	35A New England	35A New England	34E New England	34E New England	
60870	V2	DON Doncaster	36A Doncaster	36A Doncaster	36A Doncaster	36A Doncaster	36A Doncaster	
60871	V2	NWE New England	35A New England	38E Woodford Halse	34A Kings Cross	34A Kings Cross	34A Kings Cross	
60872	V2	DON Doncaster	36A Doncaster	36A Doncaster	36A Doncaster	36A Doncaster	36A Doncaster	
60873	V2	KX Kings Cross	34A Kings Cross	64A St. Margarets	64A St. Margarets	64A St. Margarets		
60874	V2	NWE New England	35A New England	35A New England	35A New England	34E New England		
60875	V2	DON Doncaster	36A Doncaster	36A Doncaster	35A New England	36A Doncaster		
60876	V2	NWE New England	35A New England	34A Kings Cross	34A Kings Cross	50A York	50A York	
60877	V2	DON Doncaster	36A Doncaster	36A Doncaster	34E Neasden	50A York	50A York	50A York
60878	V2	NWE New England	35A New England	38E Woodford Halse	38C Leicester Central	50A York		
60879	V2	NWE New England	35A New England	38E Woodford Halse	38E Woodford Halse	50A York		
60880	V2	DON Doncaster	36A Doncaster	36A Doncaster	36A Doncaster	36A Doncaster	34E New England	
60881	V2	DON Doncaster	36A Doncaster	36A Doncaster	36A Doncaster	36A Doncaster	34E New England	
60882	V2	HAY Haymarket	64B Haymarket	64A St. Margarets	64A St. Margarets	64A St. Margarets	64A St. Margarets	
60883	V2	GHD Gateshead	52A Gateshead	52A Gateshead	64A St. Margarets	64A St. Margarets	64A St. Margarets	
60884	V2	GHD Gateshead	52B Heaton	52D Tweedmouth	56B Ardsley	56B Ardsley	56B Ardsley	
60885	V2	GHD Gateshead	52B Heaton	52B Heaton	56C Copley Hill	51L Thornaby	51L Thornaby	
60886	V2	HTN Heaton	52B Heaton	52B Heaton	52B Heaton	52B Heaton	50A York	50A York
60887	V2	GHD Gateshead	52B Heaton	52B Heaton	52A Gateshead	50A York	50A York	
60888	V2	ABD Aberdeen Ferryhill	61B Aberdeen Ferryhill	61B Aberdeen Ferryhill	61B Aberdeen Ferryhill	61B Aberdeen Ferryhill		
60889	V2	DON Doncaster	36A Doncaster	36A Doncaster	36A Doncaster	36A Doncaster	36A Doncaster	
60890	V2	DON Doncaster	36A Doncaster	38E Woodford Halse	38E Woodford Halse	15E Leicester Central		
60891	V2	HTN Heaton	52B Heaton	52B Heaton	52B Heaton	52B Heaton	52B Heaton	
60892	V2	KX Kings Cross	34A Kings Cross	64A St. Margarets	64A St. Margarets	64A St. Margarets	64A St. Margarets	
60893	V2	NWE New England	35A New England	35A New England	35A New England	34E New England		
60894	V2	HAY Haymarket	64A St. Margarets	64A St. Margarets	64A St. Margarets	64A St. Margarets		
60895	V2	HTN Heaton	52B Heaton	50A York	50A York	50A York	50A York	
60896	V2	DON Doncaster	36A Doncaster	36A Doncaster	36A Doncaster	36A Doncaster		
60897	V2	NWE New England	35A New England	35A New England	35A New England	34E New England	36A Doncaster	
60898	V2	ABD Aberdeen Ferryhill	61B Aberdeen Ferryhill	61B Aberdeen Ferryhill	61B Aberdeen Ferryhill	61B Aberdeen Ferryhill	61B Aberdeen Ferryhill	
60899	V2	NWE New England	35A New England	31B March	31B March	36A Doncaster	36A Doncaster	
60900	V2	KX Kings Cross	34A Kings Cross	64A St. Margarets	64A St. Margarets	64A St. Margarets	64A St. Margarets	
60901	V2	YK York	50A York	50A York	52B Heaton	52B Heaton	51L Thornaby	
60902	V2	DON Doncaster	36A Doncaster	36A Doncaster	34A Kings Cross	34A Kings Cross	34A Kings Cross	
60903	V2	KX Kings Cross	34A Kings Cross	34A Kings Cross	34A Kings Cross	34A Kings Cross	34A Kings Cross	
60904	V2	YK York	50A York	50A York	50A York	52A Gateshead	52B Heaton	
60905	V2	NWE New England	35A New England	35A New England	36A Doncaster	36A Doncaster	36A Doncaster	
60906	V2	DON Doncaster	35A New England	35A New England	35A New England	34E New England	34E New England	
60907	V2	YK York	50A York	50A York	50A York	50A York		
60908	V2	NWE New England	35A New England	35A New England	35A New England	36A Doncaster		
60909	V2	KX Kings Cross	34A Kings Cross	34A Kings Cross	36A Doncaster	36A Doncaster		
60910	V2	GHD Gateshead	52B Heaton	52B Heaton	52B Heaton	52B Heaton	52B Heaton	
60911	V2	NWE New England	35A New England	35A New England	35A New England	51L Thornaby		
60912	V2	NWE New England	35A New England	35A New England	35A New England	36A Doncaster	34E New England	
60913	V2	NWE New England	35A New England	37B Copley Hill	56C Copley Hill	52D Tweedmouth	52D Tweedmouth	
60914	V2	KX Kings Cross	34A Kings Cross	34A Kings Cross	34A Kings Cross	34E New England		
60915	V2	KX Kings Cross	34A Kings Cross	38E Woodford Halse	38E Woodford Halse	51L Thornaby		
60916	V2	NWE New England	35A New England	35A New England	56B Ardsley	56B Ardsley	51A Darlington	
60917	V2	DON Doncaster	36A Doncaster	36A Doncaster	36A Doncaster	36A Doncaster		
60918	V2	YK York	50A York	50A York	50A York	50A York		
60919	V2	ABD Aberdeen Ferryhill	61B Aberdeen Ferryhill	61B Aberdeen Ferryhill	61B Aberdeen Ferryhill	61B Aberdeen Ferryhill	61B Aberdeen Ferryhill	62B Dundee Tay Bridge
60920	V2	DEE Dundee Tay Bridge	62B Dundee Tay Bridge	62B Dundee Tay Bridge	62B Dundee Tay Bridge	64A St. Margarets		
60921	V2	NWE New England	36A Doncaster	36A Doncaster	36A Doncaster	36A Doncaster	36A Doncaster	
60922	V2	KX Kings Cross	34A Kings Cross	64A St. Margarets	52B Heaton	52B Heaton	52B Heaton	
60923	V2	GHD Gateshead	52A Gateshead	52A Gateshead	52A Gateshead	52A Gateshead	56B Ardsley	
60924	V2	NWE New England	35A New England	35A New England	35A New England	34E New England	36A Doncaster	
60925	V2	YK York	50A York	50A York	50A York	50A York	50A York	
60926	V2	GHD Gateshead	52B Heaton	52D Tweedmouth	52D Tweedmouth	52D Tweedmouth		
60927	V2	HAY Haymarket	64B Haymarket	64B Haymarket	64B Haymarket	64B Haymarket		
60928	V2	DON Doncaster	36A Doncaster	36A Doncaster	36A Doncaster	36A Doncaster		
60929	V2	YK York	50A York	50A York	50A York	52A Gateshead	50A York	
60930	V2	DON Doncaster	36A Doncaster	36A Doncaster	36A Doncaster	36A Doncaster		
60931	V2	HAY Haymarket	62B Dundee Tay Bridge	62B Dundee Tay Bridge	62B Dundee Tay Bridge	64A St. Margarets	64A St. Margarets	
60932	V2	TWD Tweedmouth	52D Tweedmouth	52D Tweedmouth	52D Tweedmouth	52B Heaton	50A York	
60933	V2	YK York	50A York	64A St. Margarets	64A St. Margarets	64A St. Margarets		
60934	V2	YK York	50A York	50A York	50A York	52A Gateshead		
60935	V2	DON Doncaster	36A Doncaster	36A Doncaster	36A Doncaster	36A Doncaster	36A Doncaster	
60936	V2	NWE New England	35A New England	35A New England	35A New England	36A Doncaster		
60937	V2	DEE Dundee Tay Bridge	62B Dundee Tay Bridge	62B Dundee Tay Bridge	62B Dundee Tay Bridge	64A St. Margarets		
60938	V2	NWE New England	35A New England	31B March	31B March	31B March		

		1948	1951	1954	1957	1960	1963	1966
60939	*V2*	**HTN** Heaton	**52B** Heaton	**52B** Heaton	**52B** Heaton	**50A** York	**50A** York	
60940	*V2*	**GHD** Gateshead	**52A** Gateshead	**52A** Gateshead	**52A** Gateshead	**52B** Heaton	**52B** Heaton	
60941	*V2*	**YK** York	**50A** York	**50A** York	**50A** York	**50A** York	**50A** York	
60942	*V2*	**GHD** Gateshead	**52B** Heaton	**52B** Heaton	**52B** Heaton	**52A** Gateshead	**50A** York	
60943	*V2*	**DON** Doncaster	**36A** Doncaster	**36A** Doncaster	**34A** Kings Cross	**36A** Doncaster		
60944	*V2*	**HTN** Heaton	**52B** Heaton	**52B** Heaton	**52B** Heaton	**52B** Heaton	**52B** Heaton	
60945	*V2*	**NWE** New England	**52B** Heaton	**52B** Heaton	**52B** Heaton	**52B** Heaton	**50A** York	
60946	*V2*	**YK** York	**50A** York	**50A** York	**50A** York	**51L** Thornaby	**51L** Thornaby	
60947	*V2*	**HTN** Heaton	**52B** Heaton	**52A** Gateshead	**52A** Gateshead	**52A** Gateshead		
60948	*V2*	**DON** Doncaster	**36A** Doncaster	**31B** March	**31B** March	**31B** March		
60949	*V2*	**HTN** Heaton	**52B** Heaton	**52A** Gateshead	**52A** Gateshead	**52A** Gateshead	**34E** New England	
60950	*V2*	**NWE** New England	**35A** New England	**35A** New England	**34A** Kings Cross	**34A** Kings Cross	**34E** New England	
60951	*V2*	**HAY** Haymarket	**64B** Haymarket	**64B** Haymarket	**64B** Haymarket	**64B** Haymarket		
60952	*V2*	**GHD** Gateshead	**52B** Heaton	**52B** Heaton	**52B** Heaton	**52A** Gateshead	**56B** Ardsley	
60953	*V2*	**HAY** Haymarket	**64A** St. Margarets	**64A** St. Margarets	**64A** St. Margarets	**64A** St. Margarets		
60954	*V2*	**YK** York	**50A** York	**50A** York	**50A** York	**50A** York	**50A** York	
60955	*V2*	**HAY** Haymarket	**61B** Aberdeen Ferryhill	**61B** Aberdeen Ferryhill	**61B** Aberdeen Ferryhill	**61B** Aberdeen Ferryhill	**61B** Aberdeen Ferryhill	**64A** St. Margarets
60956	*V2*	**DON** Doncaster	**36A** Doncaster	**36A** Doncaster	**36A** Doncaster	**36A** Doncaster		
60957	*V2*	**HTN** Heaton	**52B** Heaton	**52A** Gateshead	**64A** St. Margarets	**64A** St. Margarets	**64B** Haymarket	
60958	*V2*	**HAY** Haymarket	**62B** Dundee Tay Bridge	**62B** Dundee Tay Bridge	**62B** Dundee Tay Bridge	**64A** St. Margarets		
60959	*V2*	**GHD** Gateshead	**64B** Haymarket	**64B** Haymarket	**64B** Haymarket	**64B** Haymarket	**64A** St. Margarets	
60960	*V2*	**YK** York	**50A** York	**50A** York	**50A** York	**51L** Thornaby		
60961	*V2*	**YK** York	**50A** York	**50A** York	**50A** York	**50A** York	**50A** York	
60962	*V2*	**YK** York	**50A** York	**50A** York	**52B** Heaton	**52B** Heaton	**52B** Heaton	
60963	*V2*	**DAR** Darlington	**50A** York	**50A** York	**50A** York	**50A** York	**50A** York	
60964	*V2*	**GHD** Gateshead	**52A** Gateshead	**52A** Gateshead	**52A** Gateshead	**52A** Gateshead	**52A** Gateshead	
60965	*V2*	**GHD** Gateshead	**52A** Gateshead	**64A** St. Margarets	**64A** St. Margarets	**64A** St. Margarets		
60966	*V2*	**HTN** Heaton	**35A** New England	**35A** New England	**35A** New England	**34E** New England	**36A** Doncaster	
60967	*V2*	**GHD** Gateshead	**52A** Gateshead	**52A** Gateshead	**52A** Gateshead	**52A** Gateshead	**50A** York	
60968	*V2*	**YK** York	**50A** York	**50A** York	**50A** York	**50A** York	**50A** York	
60969	*V2*	**DEE** Dundee Tay Bridge	**62B** Dundee Tay Bridge	**62B** Dundee Tay Bridge	**62B** Dundee Tay Bridge	**64A** St. Margarets	**64A** St. Margarets	
60970	*V2*	**ABD** Aberdeen Ferryhill	**61B** Aberdeen Ferryhill	**61B** Aberdeen Ferryhill	**61B** Aberdeen Ferryhill	**61B** Aberdeen Ferryhill	**63A** Perth	**64A** St. Margarets
60971	*V2*	**DEE** Dundee Tay Bridge	**62B** Dundee Tay Bridge	**61B** Aberdeen Ferryhill	**62B** Dundee Tay Bridge	**64A** St. Margarets		
60972	*V2*	**HAY** Haymarket	**64B** Haymarket	**62B** Dundee Tay Bridge	**61B** Aberdeen Ferryhill	**61B** Aberdeen Ferryhill	**61B** Aberdeen Ferryhill	
60973	*V2*	**ABD** Aberdeen Ferryhill	**61B** Aberdeen Ferryhill	**61B** Aberdeen Ferryhill	**61B** Aberdeen Ferryhill	**61B** Aberdeen Ferryhill	**62B** Dundee Tay Bridge	**62B** Dundee Tay Bridge
60974	*V2*	**YK** York	**50A** York	**50A** York	**50A** York	**50A** York	**50A** York	
60975	*V2*	**YK** York	**50A** York	**50A** York	**50A** York	**50A** York	**50A** York	
60976	*V2*	**YK** York	**50A** York	**50A** York	**50A** York	**52B** Heaton	**52B** Heaton	**64A** St. Margarets
60977	*V2*	**YK** York	**50A** York	**50A** York	**50A** York	**50A** York		
60978	*V2*	**YK** York	**50A** York	**50A** York	**52B** Heaton	**52B** Heaton		
60979	*V2*	**YK** York	**50A** York	**50A** York	**52B** Heaton	**52A** Gateshead		
60980	*V2*	**HAY** Haymarket	**64A** St. Margarets	**64A** St. Margarets	**64A** St. Margarets	**64A** St. Margarets		
60981	*V2*	**YK** York	**50A** York	**50A** York	**50A** York	**50A** York	**50A** York	
60982	*V2*	**YK** York	**50A** York	**50A** York	**50A** York	**50A** York	**50A** York	
60983	*V2*	**KX** Kings Cross	**34A** Kings Cross	**34A** Kings Cross	**34A** Kings Cross	**34A** Kings Cross		
61000	*B1*	**PKS** Parkeston	**30A** Stratford	**30A** Stratford	**30A** Stratford	**36A** Doncaster		
61001	*B1*	**PKS** Parkeston	**30A** Stratford	**34E** Neasden	**34E** Neasden	**36A** Doncaster	**36A** Doncaster	
61002	*B1*	**PTH** Perth South	**64A** St. Margarets	**50A** York	**50A** York	**50A** York	**50A** York	**50B** Hull Dairycoates
61003	*B1*	**PKS** Parkeston	**30F** Parkeston	**30F** Parkeston	**30F** Parkeston	**36A** Doncaster	**36A** Doncaster	
61004	*B1*	**PKS** Parkeston	**30F** Parkeston	**30F** Parkeston	**30F** Parkeston	**31B** March	**41D** Canklow	
61005	*B1*	**PKS** Parkeston	**30F** Parkeston	**30F** Parkeston	**35A** New England	**31B** March		
61006	*B1*	**PKS** Parkeston	**30F** Parkeston	**30F** Parkeston	**35A** New England	**31B** March	**40A** Lincoln	
61007	*B1*	**HAY** Haymarket	**64B** Haymarket	**64B** Haymarket	**64B** Haymarket	**64B** Haymarket	**64A** St. Margarets	
61008	*B1*	**PKS** Parkeston	**30A** Stratford	**30A** Stratford	**38C** Leicester Central	**26B** Agecroft	**2F** Woodford Halse	**65A** Eastfield
61009	*B1*	**STR** Stratford	**30A** Stratford	**34E** Neasden	**41A** Sheffield Darnall	**40A** Lincoln		
61010	*B1*	**HLB** Hull Botanic Gardens	**53B** Hull Botanic Gardens	**53B** Hull Botanic Gardens	**53B** Hull Botanic Gardens	**53A** Hull Dairycoates	**50B** Hull Dairycoates	
61011	*B1*	**GHD** Gateshead	**52A** Gateshead	**52A** Gateshead	**56B** Ardsley	**56D** Mirfield		
61012	*B1*	**GHD** Gateshead	**52A** Gateshead	**52A** Gateshead	**52A** Gateshead	**52A** Gateshead	**50B** Hull Dairycoates	**50B** Hull Dairycoates
61013	*B1*	**GHD** Gateshead	**52A** Gateshead	**52A** Gateshead	**56B** Ardsley	**56B** Ardsley	**56B** Ardsley	**56A** Wakefield
61014	*B1*	**GHD** Gateshead	**52A** Gateshead	**52A** Gateshead	**52D** Tweedmouth	**52A** Gateshead	**52H** Tyne Dock	**56F** Low Moor
61015	*B1*	**YK** York	**50A** York	**50B** Leeds Neville Hill	**51A** Darlington	**56A** Wakefield		
61016	*B1*	**YK** York	**50A** York	**50A** York	**50A** York	**50B** Leeds Neville Hill	**56C** Copley Hill	
61017	*B1*	**YK** York	**51E** Stockton on Tees	**50B** Leeds Neville Hill	**50A** York	**56A** Wakefield	**56B** Ardsley	**50A** York
61018	*B1*	**YK** York	**51E** Stockton on Tees	**51E** Stockton on Tees	**51E** Stockton on Tees	**51A** Darlington	**50A** York	
61019	*B1*	**HTN** Heaton	**52D** Tweedmouth	**52D** Tweedmouth	**52A** Gateshead	**52A** Gateshead	**52D** Alnmouth	**50A** York
61020	*B1*	**HTN** Heaton	**50A** York	**50B** Leeds Neville Hill	**51A** Darlington	**56A** Wakefield		
61021	*B1*	**HTN** Heaton	**51A** Darlington	**51A** Darlington	**51A** Darlington	**51A** Darlington	**50A** York	**50A** York
61022	*B1*	**HTN** Heaton	**51A** Darlington	**52A** Gateshead	**52A** Gateshead	**52A** Gateshead	**52D** Alnmouth	**56A** Wakefield
61023	*B1*	**HTN** Heaton	**51A** Darlington	**51A** Darlington	**51A** Darlington	**56B** Ardsley	**56C** Copley Hill	
61024	*B1*	**TWD** Tweedmouth	**52D** Tweedmouth	**51A** Darlington	**51A** Darlington	**51A** Darlington	**56B** Ardsley	**56A** Wakefield
61025	*B1*	**TWD** Tweedmouth	**52D** Tweedmouth	**52D** Tweedmouth	**52D** Tweedmouth	**52D** Tweedmouth		
61026	*B1*	**DON** Doncaster	**36A** Doncaster	**36A** Doncaster	**36A** Doncaster	**40B** Immingham	**40A** Lincoln	**40B** Immingham
61027	*B1*	**NWE** New England	**35A** New England	**34D** Hitchin	**34D** Hitchin	**41A** Sheffield Darnall		
61028	*B1*	**NEA** Neasden	**34E** Neasden	**34E** Neasden	**34E** Neasden	**2F** Woodford Halse		
61029	*B1*	**KX** Kings Cross	**37B** Copley Hill	**64A** St. Margarets	**64A** St. Margarets	**64A** St. Margarets	**64A** St. Margarets	**64A** St. Margarets
61030	*B1*	**SKN** Stockton on Tees	**51E** Stockton on Tees	**51E** Stockton on Tees	**51E** Stockton on Tees	**51A** Darlington	**56B** Ardsley	**56A** Wakefield
61031	*B1*	**COP** Copley Hill	**37A** Ardsley	**37C** Bradford Hammerton St	**56G** Bradford Hammerton St	**51L** Thornaby	**50A** York	
61032	*B1*	**SKN** Stockton on Tees	**51E** Stockton on Tees	**51E** Stockton on Tees	**51E** Stockton on Tees	**51A** Darlington	**51A** Darlington	**50B** Hull.Dairycoates
61033	*B1*	**COP** Copley Hill	**37B** Copley Hill	**38A** Colwick	**41A** Sheffield Darnall	**41A** Sheffield Darnall	**41D** Canklow	
61034	*B1*	**NEV** Leeds Neville Hill	**51E** Stockton on Tees	**51E** Stockton on Tees	**51E** Stockton on Tees	**51L** Thornaby	**56B** Ardsley	
61035	*B1*	**YK** York	**50B** Leeds Neville Hill	**50B** Leeds Neville Hill	**50B** Leeds Neville Hill	**50B** Leeds Neville Hill	**52C** Blaydon	**50A** York
61036	*B1*	**GOR** Gorton	**36A** Doncaster	**36A** Doncaster	**36A** Doncaster	**36A** Doncaster		
61037	*B1*	**DAR** Darlington	**51E** Stockton on Tees	**51E** Stockton on Tees	**51E** Stockton on Tees	**51L** Thornaby	**51A** Darlington	
61038	*B1*	**DAR** Darlington	**50A** York	**50A** York	**50A** York	**50B** Leeds Neville Hill	**52C** Blaydon	
61039	*B1*	**DAR** Darlington	**51A** Darlington	**51A** Darlington	**51A** Darlington	**56B** Ardsley	**9G** Gorton	
61040	*B1*	**NOR** Norwich Thorpe	**32A** Norwich Thorpe	**51A** Darlington	**51A** Darlington	**56D** Mirfield	**56A** Wakefield	**56A** Wakefield
61041	*B1*	**NOR** Norwich Thorpe	**32A** Norwich Thorpe	**39B** Sheffield Darnall	**41A** Sheffield Darnall	**41A** Sheffield Darnall	**41H** Staveley	
61042	*B1*	**NOR** Norwich Thorpe	**32A** Norwich Thorpe	**32A** Norwich Thorpe	**32A** Norwich Thorpe	**31B** March	**40A** Lincoln	**36A** Doncaster
61043	*B1*	**NOR** Norwich Thorpe	**32A** Norwich Thorpe	**32A** Norwich Thorpe	**32A** Norwich Thorpe	**32A** Norwich Thorpe		
61044	*B1*	**NOR** Norwich Thorpe	**32A** Norwich Thorpe	**39B** Sheffield Darnall	**41A** Sheffield Darnall	**41A** Sheffield Darnall	**41A** Sheffield Darnall	
61045	*B1*	**NOR** Norwich Thorpe	**32A** Norwich Thorpe	**32A** Norwich Thorpe	**32A** Norwich Thorpe	**32A** Norwich Thorpe		
61046	*B1*	**NOR** Norwich Thorpe	**32A** Norwich Thorpe	**32A** Norwich Thorpe	**32A** Norwich Thorpe	**32A** Norwich Thorpe		
61047	*B1*	**NOR** Norwich Thorpe	**32A** Norwich Thorpe	**35A** New England	**35C** Spital Bridge	**41A** Sheffield Darnall		
61048	*B1*	**NOR** Norwich Thorpe	**32A** Norwich Thorpe	**32A** Norwich Thorpe	**32A** Norwich Thorpe	**32A** Norwich Thorpe		
61049	*B1*	**NOR** Norwich Thorpe	**32A** Norwich Thorpe	**51A** Darlington	**51A** Darlington	**56D** Mirfield	**50A** York	
61050	*B1*	**NOR** Norwich Thorpe	**32A** Norwich Thorpe	**32A** Norwich Thorpe	**41A** Sheffield Darnall	**41A** Sheffield Darnall	**41A** Sheffield Darnall	**41J** Langwith Junction (30)
61051	*B1*	**NOR** Norwich Thorpe	**32A** Norwich Thorpe	**32A** Norwich Thorpe	**41A** Sheffield Darnall	**41A** Sheffield Darnall	**41A** Sheffield Darnall	**41J** Langwith Junction (31)
61052	*B1*	**NOR** Norwich Thorpe	**32B** Ipswich	**32B** Ipswich	**32B** Ipswich	**31B** March		
61053	*B1*	**IPS** Ipswich	**32B** Ipswich	**50A** York	**50A** York	**50A** York	**50A** York	
61054	*B1*	**IPS** Ipswich	**32B** Ipswich	**32B** Ipswich	**32B** Ipswich	**32A** Norwich Thorpe		
61055	*B1*	**IPS** Ipswich	**32B** Ipswich	**32B** Ipswich	**32B** Ipswich	**36A** Doncaster	**36E** Retford	**36A** Doncaster
61056	*B1*	**IPS** Ipswich	**32B** Ipswich	**38A** Colwick	**38A** Colwick	**31B** March	**40B** Immingham	
61057	*B1*	**IPS** Ipswich						
61058	*B1*	**IPS** Ipswich	**32B** Ipswich	**32B** Ipswich	**32B** Ipswich	**31B** March	**40A** Lincoln	**40B** Immingham
61059	*B1*	**IPS** Ipswich	**32B** Ipswich	**32B** Ipswich	**32B** Ipswich	**31B** March	**31B** March	(17)
61060	*B1*	**NEV** Leeds Neville Hill	**53A** Hull Dairycoates	**53A** Hull Dairycoates	**53A** Hull Dairycoates	**34E** New England		
61061	*B1*	**PTH** Perth South	**64A** St. Margarets	**51A** Darlington	**51A** Darlington	**51C** West Hartlepool	**56B** Ardsley	
61062	*B1*	**NEV** Leeds Neville Hill	**50B** Leeds Neville Hill	**50B** Leeds Neville Hill	**50B** Leeds Neville Hill	**51L** Thornaby	**50A** York	
61063	*B1*	**WFD** Woodford Halse	**38B** Annesley	**38B** Annesley	**38C** Leicester Central	**15E** Leicester Central		
61064	*B1*	**KEI** Keith	**65A** Eastfield	**65A** Eastfield	**68E** Carlisle Canal	**12C** Carlisle Canal		
61065	*B1*	**NEV** Leeds Neville Hill	**52B** Heaton	**50B** Leeds Neville Hill	**50B** Leeds Neville Hill	**53A** Hull Dairycoates	**50B** Hull Dairycoates	
61066	*B1*	**WFD** Woodford Halse	**38B** Annesley	**38B** Annesley	**38A** Colwick	**31A** Cambridge		
61067	*B1*	**KIT** Kittybrewster	**64A** St. Margarets	**65C** Parkhead	**65C** Parkhead	**65C** Parkhead		
61068	*B1*	**NEV** Leeds Neville Hill	**53A** Hull Dairycoates	**53A** Hull Dairycoates	**53B** Hull Botanic Gardens	**50E** Scarborough	**56B** Ardsley	

		1948	1951	1954	1957	1960	1963	1966
61069	B1	NEV Leeds Neville Hill	50B Leeds Neville Hill	50B Leeds Neville Hill	50B Leeds Neville Hill	50A York	50A York	
61070	B1	NWE New England	35A New England	35A New England	35A New England	34E New England	34E New England	
61071	B1	HLB Hull Botanic Gardens	50A York	50A York	50A York	50A York	50A York	
61072	B1	HAY Haymarket	62A Thornton Junction	62A Thornton Junction	62A Thornton Junction	62C Dunfermline Upper	62C Dunfermline Upper	62C Dunfermline Upper
61073	B1	NWE New England	35A New England	35A New England	35A New England	34E New England	34E New England	
61074	B1	HLB Hull Botanic Gardens	53A Hull Dairycoates	53A Hull Dairycoates	53A Hull Dairycoates	34E New England	34E New England	
61075	B1	NWE New England	35A New England	35A New England	34A Kings Cross	34A Kings Cross	34A Kings Cross	
61076	B1	HAY Haymarket	64B Haymarket	64B Haymarket	64B Haymarket	64B Haymarket	64A St. Margarets	
61077	B1	NEA Neasden	34E Neasden	34E Neasden	34E Neasden	14D Neasden		
61078	B1	WFD Woodford Halse	38A Colwick	38E Woodford Halse	38E Woodford Halse	2F Woodford Halse		
61079	B1	IMM Immingham	40B Immingham	40B Immingham	40B Immingham	40B Immingham		
61080	B1	HLB Hull Botanic Gardens	53A Hull Dairycoates	53A Hull Dairycoates	53A Hull Dairycoates	53A Hull Dairycoates	50B Hull Dairycoates	
61081	B1	HAY Haymarket	64B Haymarket	64B Haymarket	64B Haymarket	64B Haymarket	64B Haymarket	
61082	B1	IMM Immingham	40B Immingham	40B Immingham	40B Immingham	40B Immingham		
61083	B1	NEA Neasden	34E Neasden	34E Neasden	34E Neasden	41F Mexborough	41D Canklow	
61084	B1	HLB Hull Botanic Gardens	50A York	50A York	50A York	50A York	50A York	
61085	B1	NEA Neasden	37A Ardsley	35A New England	40A Lincoln	2F Woodford Halse		
61086	B1	LEI Leicester Central	36A Doncaster	50B Leeds Neville Hill	50B Leeds Neville Hill	50A York		
61087	B1	WFD Woodford Halse	36A Doncaster	36A Doncaster	36A Doncaster	36A Doncaster	36A Doncaster	
61088	B1	WFD Woodford Halse	38C Leicester Central	38C Leicester Central	38A Colwick	40E Colwick	40E Colwick	
61089	B1	HIT Hitchin	30A Stratford	30A Stratford	30A Stratford	30A Stratford	40A Lincoln	40E Colwick
61090	B1	HIT Hitchin	34D Hitchin	34D Hitchin	34D Hitchin	41F Mexborough	41F Mexborough	
61091	B1	HIT Hitchin	34D Hitchin	34D Hitchin	34D Hitchin	34D Hitchin		
61092	B1	HIT Hitchin	38C Leicester Central	38C Leicester Central	38A Colwick	40E Colwick	40E Colwick	40E Colwick
61093	B1	HIT Hitchin	34D Hitchin	34D Hitchin	34D Hitchin	41F Mexborough	41D Canklow	
61094	B1	HIT Hitchin	34D Hitchin	34D Hitchin	34D Hitchin	41A Sheffield Darnall	41A Sheffield Darnall	
61095	B1	HIT Hitchin	34D Hitchin	35A New England	35A New England	31F Spital Bridge	31B March	
61096	B1	HIT Hitchin	37A Ardsley	39B Sheffield Darnall	41A Sheffield Darnall	31F Spital Bridge		
61097	B1	HIT Hitchin	34D Hitchin	34D Hitchin	34D Hitchin	34D Hitchin	34E New England	
61098	B1	HIT Hitchin	30A Stratford	40B Immingham	40B Immingham	40B Immingham	40B Immingham	
61099	B1	HIT Hitchin	34D Hitchin	64A St. Margarets	64A St. Margarets	64A St. Margarets	64A St. Margarets	64A St. Margarets
61100	B1	GHD Gateshead	52A Gateshead	52A Gateshead	52A Gateshead	52A Gateshead		
61101	B1	DEE Dundee Tay Bridge	62B Dundee Tay Bridge	62B Dundee Tay Bridge	62C Dunfermline Upper	62C Dunfermline Upper	62C Dunfermline Upper	62C Dunfermline Upper
61102	B1	DEE Dundee Tay Bridge	62B Dundee Tay Bridge	62B Dundee Tay Bridge	62B Dundee Tay Bridge	62B Dundee Tay Bridge	62B Dundee Tay Bridge	62B Dundee Tay Bridge
61103	B1	THJ Thornton Junction	62A Thornton Junction	62A Thornton Junction	62A Thornton Junction	62A Thornton Junction	62A Thornton Junction	62A Thornton Junction
61104	B1	PKS Parkeston	30A Stratford	30A Stratford	30A Stratford	41F Mexborough	41D Canklow	
61105	B1	HIT Hitchin	34D Hitchin	34A Kings Cross	34D Hitchin	41A Sheffield Darnall	41A Sheffield Darnall	(27)
61106	B1	HIT Hitchin	38C Leicester Central	38C Leicester Central	38A Colwick	2F Woodford Halse		
61107	B1	HIT Hitchin	36A Doncaster	36A Doncaster	36A Doncaster	36A Doncaster	40A Lincoln	
61108	B1	WFD Woodford Halse	38C Leicester Central	64A St. Margarets	64A St. Margarets	64A St. Margarets		
61109	B1	NEA Neasden	30A Stratford	30A Stratford	30A Stratford	30A Stratford	41A Sheffield Darnall	
61110	B1	LEI Leicester Central	38A Colwick	37A Ardsley	56B Ardsley	56B Ardsley	56B Ardsley	
61111	B1	LEI Leicester Central	38A Colwick	38A Colwick	34E Neasden	41A Sheffield Darnall		
61112	B1	KX Kings Cross	40A Lincoln	36B Mexborough	36B Mexborough	41A Sheffield Darnall		
61113	B1	KX Kings Cross	34A Kings Cross	35A New England	35A New England	34E New England	40A Lincoln	
61114	B1	KX Kings Cross	39A Gorton	30A Stratford	36A Doncaster	40B Immingham		
61115	B1	YK York	50A York	50A York	50A York	56C Copley Hill	56C Copley Hill	56F Low Moor
61116	B1	EFD Eastfield	65A Eastfield	34E Neasden	34E Neasden	14D Neasden	2F Woodford Halse	65A Eastfield
61117	B1	EFD Eastfield	65A Eastfield	65A Eastfield	65C Parkhead	65C Parkhead	64A St. Margarets	
61118	B1	THJ Thornton Junction	62A Thornton Junction	62A Thornton Junction	62A Thornton Junction	62A Thornton Junction	62A Thornton Junction	
61119	B1	STR Stratford	30A Stratford	30A Stratford	30A Stratford	30A Stratford	31B March	
61120	B1	DON Doncaster	36A Doncaster	36A Doncaster	36A Doncaster	36E Retford	36E Retford	
61121	B1	KX Kings Cross	31A Cambridge	31A Cambridge	36A Doncaster	36A Doncaster	36A Doncaster	36A Doncaster
61122	B1	LEI Leicester Central	38A Colwick	35A New England	36A Doncaster	36A Doncaster	34E New England	
61123	B1	LEI Leicester Central	38A Colwick	37A Ardsley	56B Ardsley	56B Ardsley	56C Copley Hill	56A Wakefield
61124	B1	DON Doncaster	36A Doncaster	36A Doncaster	36A Doncaster	36A Doncaster		
61125	B1	DON Doncaster	36A Doncaster	36A Doncaster	36A Doncaster	36A Doncaster	36A Doncaster	
61126	B1	DON Doncaster	36E Retford	36E Retford	36E Retford	36E Retford	36E Retford	
61127	B1	DON Doncaster	36A Doncaster	36A Doncaster	36A Doncaster	36A Doncaster	36E Retford	
61128	B1	LEI Leicester Central	36A Doncaster	36A Doncaster	36A Doncaster	36A Doncaster		
61129	B1	KX Kings Cross	34A Kings Cross	37B Copley Hill	56C Copley Hill	56C Copley Hill	56C Copley Hill	
61130	B1	LEI Leicester Central	30A Stratford	40B Immingham	40B Immingham	40B Immingham		
61131	B1	WFD Woodford Halse	38A Colwick	37A Ardsley	56B Ardsley	56A Wakefield	56B Ardsley	56A Wakefield
61132	B1	KIT Kittybrewster	61B Aberdeen Ferryhill	62B Dundee Tay Bridge	62B Dundee Tay Bridge	62B Dundee Tay Bridge	62A Thornton Junction	62A Thornton Junction
61133	B1	KIT Kittybrewster	61B Aberdeen Ferryhill	65A Eastfield	62A Thornton Junction	62A Thornton Junction	62A Thornton Junction	62A Thornton Junction
61134	B1	KIT Kittybrewster	61A Kittybrewster	65A Eastfield	62A Thornton Junction	62A Thornton Junction	65A Eastfield	
61135	B1	PKS Parkeston	30F Parkeston	30F Parkeston	30F Parkeston	36A Doncaster	36A Doncaster	
61136	B1	KX Kings Cross	34A Kings Cross	34E Neasden	34E Neasden	14D Neasden		
61137	B1	KX Kings Cross	34A Kings Cross	36A Doncaster	36A Doncaster	15E Leicester Central		
61138	B1	KX Kings Cross	34A Kings Cross	35A New England	41A Sheffield Darnall	41C Millhouses	41F Mexborough	(26)
61139	B1	KX Kings Cross	34A Kings Cross	34A Kings Cross	34A Kings Cross	41A Sheffield Darnall		
61140	B1	NEA Neasden	34E Neasden	65A Eastfield	65A Eastfield	65A Eastfield	65A Eastfield	65A Eastfield
61141	B1	WFD Woodford Halse	38C Leicester Central	38C Leicester Central	38A Colwick	40E Colwick	40E Colwick	
61142	B1	IMM Immingham	40B Immingham	40B Immingham	40B Immingham	40E Colwick	40E Colwick	
61143	B1	NWE New England	35A New England	35A New England	40A Lincoln	40B Immingham	40B Immingham	
61144	B1	NWE New England	30A Stratford	40B Immingham	40B Immingham	40B Immingham	40B Immingham	
61145	B1	SHF Sheffield Darnall	39B Sheffield Darnall	36A Doncaster	36A Doncaster	36A Doncaster	36A Doncaster	40E Colwick
61146	B1	KIT Kittybrewster	62A Thornton Junction	62A Thornton Junction	62A Thornton Junction	62A Thornton Junction	62A Thornton Junction	
61147	B1	KIT Kittybrewster	62B Dundee Tay Bridge	62A Thornton Junction	62A Thornton Junction	62A Thornton Junction	62A Thornton Junction	
61148	B1	KIT Kittybrewster	62A Thornton Junction	62A Thornton Junction	62A Thornton Junction	62A Thornton Junction	62A Thornton Junction	62A Thornton Junction
61149	B1	PKS Parkeston	30F Parkeston	30F Parkeston	30F Parkeston	30F Parkeston		
61150	B1	SHF Sheffield Darnall	39B Sheffield Darnall	39B Sheffield Darnall	41A Sheffield Darnall	41A Sheffield Darnall		
61151	B1	SHF Sheffield Darnall	39B Sheffield Darnall	39B Sheffield Darnall	41A Sheffield Darnall	41A Sheffield Darnall		
61152	B1	SHF Sheffield Darnall	39B Sheffield Darnall	39B Sheffield Darnall	41A Sheffield Darnall	41C Millhouses	41A Sheffield Darnall	
61153	B1	SHF Sheffield Darnall	39B Sheffield Darnall	39B Sheffield Darnall	41A Sheffield Darnall	41A Sheffield Darnall	41A Sheffield Darnall	
61154	B1	SHF Sheffield Darnall	39B Sheffield Darnall	39B Sheffield Darnall	41A Sheffield Darnall	41A Sheffield Darnall		
61155	B1	GOR Gorton	39A Gorton	39A Gorton	36A Doncaster	36A Doncaster	41F Mexborough	
61156	B1	GOR Gorton	39A Gorton	39A Gorton	39A Gorton	31F Spital Bridge	31B March	
61157	B1	GOR Gorton	39A Gorton	36A Doncaster	36A Doncaster	36A Doncaster	36A Doncaster	
61158	B1	GOR Gorton	39A Gorton	36A Doncaster	36A Doncaster	36A Doncaster	36A Doncaster	36A Doncaster
61159	B1	GOR Gorton	39A Gorton	39A Gorton	40B Immingham	40B Immingham	40B Immingham	
61160	B1	GOR Gorton	39A Gorton	39A Gorton	38A Colwick	32C Lowestoft	40E Colwick	
61161	B1	GOR Gorton	39A Gorton	39A Gorton	39A Gorton	9G Gorton	56A Wakefield	56A Wakefield
61162	B1	GOR Gorton	39A Gorton	39A Gorton	36A Doncaster	41A Sheffield Darnall	41H Staveley	
61163	B1	NEA Neasden	34E Neasden	34E Neasden	38A Colwick	40E Colwick		
61164	B1	NEA Neasden	34E Neasden	34E Neasden	34E Neasden	41A Sheffield Darnall		
61165	B1	MEX Mexborough	36B Mexborough	36B Mexborough	36B Mexborough	41F Mexborough	41D Canklow	
61166	B1	MEX Mexborough	36B Mexborough	36B Mexborough	36B Mexborough	41F Mexborough		
61167	B1	MEX Mexborough	36B Mexborough	36B Mexborough	36B Mexborough	41F Mexborough	41F Mexborough	
61168	B1	MEX Mexborough	36B Mexborough	40B Immingham	40B Immingham	40B Immingham	40B Immingham	
61169	B1	NEA Neasden	39B Sheffield Darnall	39B Sheffield Darnall	41A Sheffield Darnall	41A Sheffield Darnall	41F Mexborough	
61170	B1	DON Doncaster	36A Doncaster	36A Doncaster	36A Doncaster	36A Doncaster		
61171	B1	GRA Grantham	30A Stratford	40A Lincoln	36A Doncaster	31A Cambridge		
61172	B1	EFD Eastfield	65A Eastfield	65A Eastfield	62B Dundee Tay Bridge	62B Dundee Tay Bridge	62B Dundee Tay Bridge	
61173	B1	DAR Darlington	51A Darlington	51E Stockton on Tees	51E Stockton on Tees	51L Thornaby	56B Ardsley	56A Wakefield
61174	B1	MEX Mexborough	36B Mexborough	39B Sheffield Darnall	41A Sheffield Darnall	34A Kings Cross	34E New England	
61175	B1	GRA Grantham	30A Stratford	40B Immingham	40B Immingham	40B Immingham	40E Colwick	
61176	B1	DAR Darlington	51A Darlington	50A York	51A Darlington	51A Darlington	51A Darlington	
61177	B1	GRA Grantham	30A Stratford	40A Lincoln	38A Colwick	40E Colwick	40E Colwick	
61178	B1	HAY Haymarket	64B Haymarket	64B Haymarket	64B Haymarket	64B Haymarket	64B Haymarket	
61179	B1	SHF Sheffield Darnall	39B Sheffield Darnall	39B Sheffield Darnall	41A Sheffield Darnall	34A Kings Cross	34A Kings Cross	
61180	B1	EFD Eastfield	65A Eastfield	65A Eastfield	62B Dundee Tay Bridge	62B Dundee Tay Bridge	62B Dundee Tay Bridge	62B Dundee Tay Bridge
61181	B1	SHF Sheffield Darnall	39B Sheffield Darnall	39B Sheffield Darnall	41A Sheffield Darnall	41A Sheffield Darnall	41A Sheffield Darnall	(18)
61182	B1	GOR Gorton	39A Gorton	39A Gorton	40B Immingham	31A Cambridge		

No.	Class	1948	1951	1954	1957	1960	1963	1966
61183	B1	SHF Sheffield Darnall	39B Sheffield Darnall	39B Sheffield Darnall	41A Sheffield Darnall	41A Sheffield Darnall		
61184	B1	GOR Gorton	39A Gorton	64A St. Margarets	64A St. Margarets	64A St. Margarets		
61185	B1	LEI Leicester Central	38C Leicester Central	38C Leicester Central	38A Colwick	40B Immingham	40B Immingham	
61186	B1	LEI Leicester Central	38C Leicester Central	38A Colwick	38A Colwick	2F Woodford Halse		
61187	B1	LEI Leicester Central	38C Leicester Central	38C Leicester Central	34E Neasden	2F Woodford Halse		
61188	B1	LEI Leicester Central	38C Leicester Central	38A Colwick	38A Colwick	40E Colwick	40E Colwick	
61189	B1	SKN Stockton on Tees	51E Stockton on Tees	51E Stockton on Tees	56B Ardsley	56C Copley Hill	56F Low Moor	56F Low Moor
61190	B1	DON Doncaster	40B Immingham	40B Immingham	40B Immingham	40B Immingham	40B Immingham	
61191	B1	DON Doncaster	40B Immingham	64A St. Margarets	64A St. Margarets	64A St. Margarets	64A St. Margarets	
61192	B1	LEI Leicester Central	30A Stratford	38A Colwick	38E Woodford Halse	2F Woodford Halse		
61193	B1	DON Doncaster	36A Doncaster	36A Doncaster	36A Doncaster	36A Doncaster		
61194	B1	DON Doncaster	36B Mexborough	36B Mexborough	36B Mexborough	41F Mexborough	41D Canklow	(28)
61195	B1	IMM Immingham	40B Immingham	40B Immingham	40B Immingham	40B Immingham	40B Immingham	
61196	B1	DON Doncaster	36A Doncaster	36A Doncaster	36A Doncaster	36A Doncaster	36A Doncaster	
61197	B1	EFD Eastfield	65A Eastfield	65A Eastfield	65A Eastfield	65A Eastfield	65A Eastfield	
61198	B1	TWD Tweedmouth	51A Darlington	51A Darlington	51A Darlington	50A York	50A York	
61199	B1	TWD Tweedmouth	52D Tweedmouth	52A Gateshead	52D Tweedmouth	52D Tweedmouth	52C Blaydon	50A York
61200	B1	KX Kings Cross	34A Kings Cross	34A Kings Cross	34A Kings Cross	34E New England		
61201	B1	DON Doncaster	32B Ipswich	38A Colwick	38A Colwick	26B Agecroft		
61202	B1	IMM Immingham	40B Immingham	40A Lincoln	40A Lincoln	40A Lincoln		
61203	B1	KX Kings Cross	34A Kings Cross	34A Kings Cross	34A Kings Cross	31A Cambridge		
61204	B1	IMM Immingham	40B Immingham	35A New England	35A New England	31F Spital Bridge	31B March	(19)
61205	B1	GRA Grantham	30A Stratford	35A New England	35A New England	31F Spital Bridge	31B March	(20)
61206	B1	NWE New England	35A New England	34E Neasden	34E Neasden	14D Neasden		
61207	B1	NWE New England	35A New England	35A New England	35A New England	34E New England	34E New England	
61208	B1	RET Retford	36E Retford	36E Retford	36E Retford	36E Retford	36E Retford	
61209	B1	NWE New England	38B Annesley	38B Annesley	38A Colwick	40E Colwick		
61210	B1	NWE New England	35A New England	35A New England	35A New England	34E New England	34E New England	36A Doncaster
61211	B1	RET Retford	36E Retford	36E Retford	36E Retford	36E Retford		
61212	B1	RET Retford	36E Retford	36E Retford	36E Retford	36E Retford	36E Retford	
61213	B1	RET Retford	36E Retford	36E Retford	36E Retford	36E Retford	36E Retford	
61214	B1	SKN Stockton on Tees	51E Stockton on Tees	51E Stockton on Tees	56C Copley Hill	56C Copley Hill	56C Copley Hill	
61215	B1	HLB Hull Botanic Gardens	53B Hull Botanic Gardens	53B Hull Botanic Gardens	53B Hull Botanic Gardens	53A Hull Dairycoates	56B Ardsley	
61216	B1	YK York	50B Leeds Neville Hill	50B Leeds Neville Hill	50B Leeds Neville Hill	50B Leeds Neville Hill	52B Heaton	50A York
61217	B1	CAR Carlisle Canal	12B Carlisle Canal	68E Carlisle Canal	68E Carlisle Canal	12C Carlisle Canal		
61218	B1	NEV Leeds Neville Hill	50B Leeds Neville Hill	50B Leeds Neville Hill	50B Leeds Neville Hill	50B Leeds Neville Hill	56B Ardsley	
61219	B1	CAR Carlisle Canal	12B Carlisle Canal	68E Carlisle Canal	68E Carlisle Canal	64B Haymarket	64A St. Margarets	
61220	B1	SKN Stockton on Tees	51E Stockton on Tees	51E Stockton on Tees	51E Stockton on Tees	51L Thornaby	51L Thornaby	
61221	B1	HAY Haymarket	64B Haymarket	64B Haymarket	64B Haymarket	64B Haymarket	64B Haymarket	
61222	B1	CAR Carlisle Canal	12B Carlisle Canal	68E Carlisle Canal	68E Carlisle Canal	12C Carlisle Canal		
61223	B1	GOR Gorton	39A Gorton	31A Cambridge	32A Norwich Thorpe	32A Norwich Thorpe	40A Lincoln	40B Immingham
61224	B1	HTN Heaton	51A Darlington	50A York	51A Darlington	51A Darlington	51A Darlington	56A Wakefield
61225	B1	GOR Gorton	39A Gorton	39B Sheffield Darnall	36A Doncaster	36A Doncaster	36E Retford	
61226	B1	STR Stratford	30F Parkeston	30F Parkeston	30F Parkeston	30F Parkeston		
61227	B1	GOR Gorton	30A Stratford	30A Stratford	30F Parkeston	30F Parkeston	40E Colwick	
61228	B1	GOR Gorton	39A Gorton	39A Gorton	32B Ipswich	32A Norwich Thorpe		
61229	B1	BFD Bradford Hammerton St	37C Bradford Hammerton St	37C Bradford Hammerton St	56G Bradford Hammerton St	50A York	50A York	
61230	B1	BFD Bradford Hammerton St	37C Bradford Hammerton St	37C Bradford Hammerton St	56G Bradford Hammerton St	56D Mirfield		
61231	B1	RET Retford	36E Retford	36E Retford	36E Retford	36E Retford		
61232	B1	STR Stratford	30F Parkeston	30F Parkeston	30F Parkeston	30F Parkeston	40E Colwick	40E Colwick
61233	B1	STR Stratford	30A Stratford	30A Stratford	30A Stratford	30A Stratford	31B March	(21)
61234	B1	STR Stratford	30A Stratford	30A Stratford	30A Stratford	41A Sheffield Darnall		
61235	B1	STR Stratford	30A Stratford	30A Stratford	30A Stratford	32A Norwich Thorpe		
61236	B1	STR Stratford	30A Stratford	30A Stratford	30A Stratford	31A Cambridge		
61237	B1	NEV Leeds Neville Hill	50B Leeds Neville Hill	50B Leeds Neville Hill	50B Leeds Neville Hill	50B Leeds Neville Hill	52C Blaydon	56A Wakefield
61238	B1	GHD Gateshead	52A Gateshead	52A Gateshead	52A Gateshead	52A Gateshead	52H Tyne Dock	50A York
61239	B1	YK York	50A York	68E Carlisle Canal	68E Carlisle Canal	12C Carlisle Canal		
61240	B1	YK York	50B Leeds Neville Hill	50B Leeds Neville Hill	50B Leeds Neville Hill	51L Thornaby	56B Ardsley	56A Wakefield
61241	B1	HTN Heaton	52D Tweedmouth	52D Tweedmouth	52D Tweedmouth	52D Tweedmouth		
61242	B1	KIT Kittybrewster	64A St. Margarets	61C Keith	61C Keith	61A Kittybrewster	64A St. Margarets	
61243	B1	EFD Eastfield	65A Eastfield	65A Eastfield	65A Eastfield	65A Eastfield	65A Eastfield	
61244	B1	HAY Haymarket	64B Haymarket	64B Haymarket	64B Haymarket	64B Haymarket	64A St. Margarets	
61245	B1	HAY Haymarket	64B Haymarket	64B Haymarket	64B Haymarket	64B Haymarket	64B Haymarket	
61246	B1	DON Doncaster	36A Doncaster	64A St. Margarets	64C Dalry Road	64A St. Margarets		
61247	B1	DON Doncaster	36A Doncaster	36A Doncaster	36A Doncaster	36A Doncaster		
61248	B1	DON Doncaster	36A Doncaster	36A Doncaster	40A Lincoln	40B Immingham	40B Immingham	
61249	B1	DON Doncaster	36A Doncaster	36A Doncaster	30A Stratford	41A Sheffield Darnall	41A Sheffield Darnall	
61250	B1	DON Doncaster	36A Doncaster	36A Doncaster	36A Doncaster	36A Doncaster	34E New England	40B Immingham
61251	B1	KX Kings Cross	34A Kings Cross	34A Kings Cross	34D Hitchin	34F Grantham	34F Grantham	
61252	B1	IPS Ipswich	32B Ipswich	32B Ipswich	32B Ipswich	31B March	31B March	(22)
61253	B1	IPS Ipswich	32B Ipswich	32B Ipswich	32B Ipswich	31B March		
61254	B1	NOR Norwich Thorpe	32B Ipswich	32B Ipswich	32B Ipswich	31B March		
61255	B1	HTN Heaton	51A Darlington	51A Darlington	51A Darlington	51L Thornaby	50B Hull Dairycoates	50B Hull Dairycoates
61256	B1	NEV Leeds Neville Hill	50B Leeds Neville Hill	50B Leeds Neville Hill	50B Leeds Neville Hill	53A Hull Dairycoates	50B Hull Dairycoates	
61257	B1	NEV Leeds Neville Hill	50B Leeds Neville Hill	50B Leeds Neville Hill	50B Leeds Neville Hill	51L Thornaby	51C West Hartlepool	
61258	B1	NEV Leeds Neville Hill	50B Leeds Neville Hill	40A Lincoln	40A Lincoln	40A Lincoln	40A Lincoln	
61259	B1	NEV Leeds Neville Hill	50B Leeds Neville Hill	50B Leeds Neville Hill	50B Leeds Neville Hill	50B Leeds Neville Hill	56B Ardsley	
61260	B1	EFD Eastfield	65A Eastfield	65A Eastfield	65A Eastfield	64A St. Margarets		
61261	B1	EFD Eastfield	65A Eastfield	65A Eastfield	65A Eastfield	65A Eastfield	65A Eastfield	62A Thornton Junction
61262	B1	THJ Thornton Junction	62A Thornton Junction	62A Thornton Junction	62A Thornton Junction	62A Thornton Junction	62B Dundee Tay Bridge	62B Dundee Tay Bridge
61263	B1	DEE Dundee Tay Bridge	62B Dundee Tay Bridge	62B Dundee Tay Bridge	62B Dundee Tay Bridge	62B Dundee Tay Bridge	62B Dundee Tay Bridge	62B Dundee Tay Bridge
61264	B1	PKS Parkeston	30F Parkeston	30F Parkeston	30F Parkeston	30F Parkeston	40E Colwick	(29)
61265	B1	DON Doncaster	36A Doncaster	36A Doncaster	39A Gorton	9G Gorton		
61266	B1	KX Kings Cross	34A Kings Cross	36A Doncaster	36A Doncaster	36A Doncaster		
61267	B1	ARD Ardsley	37C Bradford Hammerton St	37C Bradford Hammerton St	56G Bradford Hammerton St	51C West Hartlepool		
61268	B1	ARD Ardsley	37C Bradford Hammerton St	37C Bradford Hammerton St	56G Bradford Hammerton St	56A Wakefield	56B Ardsley	
61269	B1	LIN Lincoln	40A Lincoln	38A Colwick	38C Leicester Central	26B Agecroft	9G Gorton	
61270	B1	NOR Norwich Thorpe	32A Norwich Thorpe	32A Norwich Thorpe	32A Norwich Thorpe	36A Doncaster	36A Doncaster	
61271	B1	NOR Norwich Thorpe	32A Norwich Thorpe	38A Colwick	38A Colwick	2F Woodford Halse		
61272	B1	NOR Norwich Thorpe	32A Norwich Thorpe	38A Colwick	38A Colwick	34E New England	34E New England	(25)
61273	B1	DAR Darlington	51A Darlington	51A Darlington	51A Darlington	50A York	50A York	
61274	B1	→	51A Darlington	51A Darlington	51A Darlington	56F Low Moor	56A Wakefield	
61275	B1	→	51A Darlington	51E Stockton on Tees	51C West Hartlepool	51C West Hartlepool	51C West Hartlepool	
61276	B1	→	51A Darlington	51A Darlington	51A Darlington	50A York	50A York	
61277	B1	→	64A St. Margarets	65A Eastfield	65A Eastfield	62A Thornton Junction	62B Dundee Tay Bridge	
61278	B1	→	62B Dundee Tay Bridge	62B Dundee Tay Bridge	62B Dundee Tay Bridge	62B Dundee Tay Bridge	62B Dundee Tay Bridge	62B Dundee Tay Bridge
61279	B1	→	40A Lincoln	40A Lincoln	40A Lincoln	36A Doncaster	36A Doncaster	
61280	B1	→	40A Lincoln	30A Stratford	30A Stratford	31A Cambridge		
61281	B1	→	40A Lincoln	40A Lincoln	40B Immingham	40E Colwick	40E Colwick	40E Colwick
61282	B1	→	30A Stratford	35A New England	35A New England	34E New England		
61283	B1	→	38A Colwick	38A Colwick	38A Colwick	31A Cambridge		
61284	B1	→	40B Immingham	40B Immingham	40B Immingham	40A Lincoln		
61285	B1	→	31A Cambridge	31A Cambridge	36A Doncaster	36A Doncaster	40E Colwick	
61286	B1	→	31A Cambridge	31A Cambridge	31A Cambridge	31A Cambridge		
61287	B1	→	31A Cambridge	31A Cambridge	31A Cambridge	31A Cambridge		
61288	B1	→	50A York	50A York	50A York	50A York	50A York	
61289	B1	→	51A Darlington	51A Darlington	51A Darlington	53A Hull Dairycoates	50B Hull Dairycoates	50B Hull Dairycoates
61290	B1	→	51E Stockton on Tees	68E Carlisle Canal	68E Carlisle Canal	12C Carlisle Canal		
61291	B1	→	51A Darlington	51A Darlington	51A Darlington	50A York	56B Ardsley	
61292	B1	→	62B Dundee Tay Bridge	62B Dundee Tay Bridge	62B Dundee Tay Bridge	62B Dundee Tay Bridge	62B Dundee Tay Bridge	
61293	B1	→	62B Dundee Tay Bridge	62B Dundee Tay Bridge	62B Dundee Tay Bridge	62B Dundee Tay Bridge	62B Dundee Tay Bridge	62B Dundee Tay Bridge
61294	B1	→	37C Bradford Hammerton St	65A Eastfield	61A Kittybrewster	61A Kittybrewster	64A St. Margarets	
61295	B1	→	37B Copley Hill	37A Ardsley	56B Ardsley	56B Ardsley		
61296	B1	→	37C Bradford Hammerton St	37C Bradford Hammerton St	56G Bradford Hammerton St	56A Wakefield		

		1948	1951	1954	1957	1960	1963	1966
61297	*B1*	→	**37A** Ardsley	**37A** Ardsley	**56B** Ardsley	**56B** Ardsley		
61298	*B1*	→	**38C** Leicester Central	**38C** Leicester Central	**38C** Leicester Central	**26B** Agecroft		
61299	*B1*	→	**38C** Leicester Central	**38C** Leicester Central	**38C** Leicester Central	**40E** Colwick	**40E** Colwick	
61300	*B1*	→	**31A** Cambridge	**31A** Cambridge	**31A** Cambridge	**31B** March	**31B** March	(23)
61301	*B1*	→	**31A** Cambridge	**31A** Cambridge	**31A** Cambridge	**31A** Cambridge		
61302	*B1*	→	**31A** Cambridge	**31A** Cambridge	**35A** New England	**34E** New England	**34E** New England	**40E** Colwick
61303	*B1*	→	**51E** Stockton on Tees	**51E** Stockton on Tees	**51E** Stockton on Tees	**51L** Thornaby	**50B** Hull Dairycoates	**50A** York
61304	*B1*	→	**53B** Hull Botanic Gardens	**53B** Hull Botanic Gardens	**53B** Hull Botanic Gardens	**50E** Scarborough	**51A** Darlington	
61305	*B1*	→	**53B** Hull Botanic Gardens	**53B** Hull Botanic Gardens	**53B** Hull Botanic Gardens	**50E** Scarborough	**50B** Hull Dairycoates	
61306	*B1*	→	**53B** Hull Botanic Gardens	**53B** Hull Botanic Gardens	**53B** Hull Botanic Gardens	**53A** Hull Dairycoates	**50B** Hull Dairycoates	**50B** Hull Dairycoates
61307	*B1*	→	**61A** Kittybrewster	**61A** Kittybrewster	**61C** Keith	**64A** St. Margarets	**64A** St. Margarets	**64A** St. Margarets
61308	*B1*	→	**61C** Keith	**61C** Keith	**61C** Keith	**64A** St. Margarets	**64A** St. Margarets	**64A** St. Margarets
61309	*B1*	→	**37A** Ardsley	**37B** Copley Hill	**56C** Copley Hill	**56C** Copley Hill	**56C** Copley Hill	**56F** Low Moor
61310	*B1*	→	**37A** Ardsley	**37A** Ardsley	**56B** Ardsley	**56B** Ardsley	**56B** Ardsley	
61311	*B1*	→	**39B** Sheffield Darnall	**39B** Sheffield Darnall	**34A** Kings Cross	**30F** Parkeston		
61312	*B1*	→	**39B** Sheffield Darnall	**39B** Sheffield Darnall	**32A** Norwich Thorpe	**41H** Staveley	**41H** Staveley	
61313	*B1*	→	**39B** Sheffield Darnall	**39B** Sheffield Darnall	**41A** Sheffield Darnall	**41A** Sheffield Darnall	**41A** Sheffield Darnall	
61314	*B1*	→	**39B** Sheffield Darnall	**39B** Sheffield Darnall	**41A** Sheffield Darnall	**36A** Doncaster	**34E** New England	
61315	*B1*	→	**39B** Sheffield Darnall	**39B** Sheffield Darnall	**41A** Sheffield Darnall	**41A** Sheffield Darnall	**41A** Sheffield Darnall	**41J** Langwith Junction (32)
61316	*B1*	→	**39B** Sheffield Darnall	**00D** Sheffield Darnall	**41A** Sheffield Darnall	**41A** Sheffield Darnall		
61317	*B1*	→	**39B** Sheffield Darnall	**39B** Sheffield Darnall	**32A** Norwich Thorpe	**32A** Norwich Thorpe		
61318	*B1*	→	**40B** Immingham	**40B** Immingham	**40B** Immingham	**40B** Immingham	**40B** Immingham	
61319	*B1*	→	**54C** Borough Gardens	**54C** Borough Gardens	**54C** Borough Gardens	**50A** York	**50A** York	**50A** York
61320	*B1*	→	**54C** Borough Gardens	**54C** Borough Gardens	**56G** Bradford Hammerton St	**56C** Copley Hill	**56C** Copley Hill	
61321	*B1*	→	**54C** Borough Gardens	**54C** Borough Gardens	**54C** Borough Gardens	**51A** Darlington	**51A** Darlington	
61322	*B1*	→	**52D** Tweedmouth	**52D** Tweedmouth	**52D** Tweedmouth	**52D** Tweedmouth	**52B** Heaton	**50B** Hull Dairycoates
61323	*B1*	→	**61A** Kittybrewster	**61A** Kittybrewster	**61A** Kittybrewster	**31F** Spital Bridge	**31B** March	
61324	*B1*	→	**61A** Kittybrewster	**61A** Kittybrewster	**61A** Kittybrewster	**61A** Kittybrewster	**64A** St. Margarets	
61325	*B1*	→	**40B** Immingham	**40B** Immingham	**40B** Immingham	**40B** Immingham	**40B** Immingham	
61326	*B1*	→	**39A** Gorton	**39A** Gorton	**36A** Doncaster	**36A** Doncaster	**36A** Doncaster	**36A** Doncaster
61327	*B1*	→	**39B** Sheffield Darnall	**39B** Sheffield Darnall	**41A** Sheffield Darnall	**41A** Sheffield Darnall	**41D** Canklow	
61328	*B1*	→	**40B** Immingham	**40B** Immingham	**40B** Immingham	**40B** Immingham	**40B** Immingham	
61329	*B1*	→	**40A** Lincoln	**30A** Stratford	**30A** Stratford	**30A** Stratford	**36A** Doncaster	**36A** Doncaster
61330	*B1*	→	**35A** New England	**64A** St. Margarets	**64A** St. Margarets	**62A** Thornton Junction	**62A** Thornton Junction	**62A** Thornton Junction
61331	*B1*	→	**35A** New England	**34A** Kings Cross	**34A** Kings Cross	**34A** Kings Cross	**34E** New England	
61332	*B1*	→	**32A** Norwich Thorpe	**64A** St. Margarets	**64A** St. Margarets	**64A** St. Margarets		
61333	*B1*	→	**31A** Cambridge	**64A** St. Margarets	**61A** Kittybrewster	**65C** Parkhead		
61334	*B1*	→	**31A** Cambridge	**31A** Cambridge	**41A** Sheffield Darnall	**41C** Millhouses	**41D** Canklow	
61335	*B1*	→	**30A** Stratford	**30A** Stratford	**30A** Stratford	**30A** Stratford		
61336	*B1*	→	**30A** Stratford	**30A** Stratford	**30A** Stratford	**30F** Parkeston	**40E** Colwick	
61337	*B1*	→	**50A** York	**50A** York	**50A** York	**50A** York	**50A** York	**50A** York
61338	*B1*	→	**52B** Heaton	**50A** York	**51A** Darlington	**51A** Darlington	**51A** Darlington	
61339	*B1*	→	**50B** Leeds Neville Hill	**50A** York	**50A** York	**56C** Copley Hill		
61340	*B1*	→	**65A** Eastfield	**65A** Eastfield	**65A** Eastfield	**65A** Eastfield	**62B** Dundee Tay Bridge	**62B** Dundee Tay Bridge
61341	*B1*	→	**64A** St. Margarets	**64A** St. Margarets	**64A** St. Margarets	**64A** St. Margarets	**64A** St. Margarets	
61342	*B1*	→	**65A** Eastfield	**65A** Eastfield	**65A** Eastfield	**65A** Eastfield	**65A** Eastfield	**65A** Eastfield
61343	*B1*	→	**61A** Kittybrewster	**61A** Kittybrewster	**61A** Kittybrewster	**62A** Thornton Junction	**62A** Thornton Junction	**62A** Thornton Junction
61344	*B1*	→	**65A** Eastfield	**65A** Eastfield	**65A** Eastfield	**65C** Parkhead	**64A** St. Margarets	**64A** St. Margarets
61345	*B1*	→	**61A** Kittybrewster	**61A** Kittybrewster	**61A** Kittybrewster	**61A** Kittybrewster	**64A** St. Margarets	**64A** St. Margarets
61346	*B1*	→	**61A** Kittybrewster	**61A** Kittybrewster	**61A** Kittybrewster	**61A** Kittybrewster	**61B** Aberdeen Ferryhill	
61347	*B1*	→	**61A** Kittybrewster	**61A** Kittybrewster	**61A** Kittybrewster	**61A** Kittybrewster	**61B** Aberdeen Ferryhill	**64A** St. Margarets
61348	*B1*	→	**61A** Kittybrewster	**61A** Kittybrewster	**61A** Kittybrewster	**31F** Spital Bridge	**40A** Lincoln	
61349	*B1*	→	**61A** Kittybrewster	**61A** Kittybrewster	**61A** Kittybrewster	**64A** St. Margarets	**64A** St. Margarets	**64A** St. Margarets
61350	*B1*	→	**61A** Kittybrewster	**61A** Kittybrewster	**61A** Kittybrewster	**61A** Kittybrewster	**64A** St. Margarets	**64A** St. Margarets
61351	*B1*	→	**61A** Kittybrewster	**61A** Kittybrewster	**61A** Kittybrewster	**64A** St. Margarets	**64A** St. Margarets	
61352	*B1*	→	**61A** Kittybrewster	**61A** Kittybrewster	**61A** Kittybrewster	**61A** Kittybrewster		
61353	*B1*	→	Rugby Testing Station	**51A** Darlington	**51A** Darlington	**51A** Darlington	**51A** Darlington	
61354	*B1*	→	**64A** St. Margarets	**64A** St. Margarets	**64A** St. Margarets	**64A** St. Margarets	**64A** St. Margarets	**64A** St. Margarets
61355	*B1*	→	**64A** St. Margarets	**64A** St. Margarets	**64B** Haymarket	**65A** Eastfield	**65A** Eastfield	
61356	*B1*	→	**64A** St. Margarets	**64A** St. Margarets	**64A** St. Margarets	**64A** St. Margarets	**64A** St. Margarets	
61357	*B1*	→	**64A** St. Margarets	**64A** St. Margarets	**64A** St. Margarets	**64A** St. Margarets	**64A** St. Margarets	
61358	*B1*	→	**64A** St. Margarets	**64A** St. Margarets	**64A** St. Margarets	**62A** Thornton Junction	**62A** Thornton Junction	
61359	*B1*	→	**64A** St. Margarets	**64A** St. Margarets	**64A** St. Margarets	**64A** St. Margarets	**64A** St. Margarets	
61360	*B1*	→	**30A** Stratford	**30A** Stratford	**30A** Stratford	**36A** Doncaster	**36A** Doncaster	**36A** Doncaster
61361	*B1*	→	**30A** Stratford	**30A** Stratford	**30A** Stratford	**30F** Parkeston	**40E** Colwick	
61362	*B1*	→	**30A** Stratford	**30A** Stratford	**30A** Stratford	**30F** Parkeston		
61363	*B1*	→	**30A** Stratford	**30A** Stratford	**30A** Stratford	**31B** March		
61364	*B1*	→	**40A** Lincoln	**35A** New England	**34A** Kings Cross	**34A** Kings Cross		
61365	*B1*	→	**40B** Immingham	**36A** Doncaster	**36A** Doncaster	**36A** Doncaster	**36A** Doncaster	
61366	*B1*	→	**40B** Immingham	**40B** Immingham	**40B** Immingham	**40B** Immingham		
61367	*B1*	→	**38A** Colwick	**38A** Colwick	**38A** Colwick	**34F** Grantham	**34F** Grantham	
61368	*B1*	→	**38A** Colwick	**38E** Woodford Halse	**38E** Woodford Halse	**2F** Woodford Halse		
61369	*B1*	→	**38A** Colwick	**38C** Leicester Central	**38C** Leicester Central	**26B** Agecroft	**9G** Gorton	
61370	*B1*	→	**40A** Lincoln	**30A** Stratford	**30A** Stratford	**41A** Sheffield Darnall	**41D** Canklow	
61371	*B1*	→	**40A** Lincoln	**40A** Lincoln	**31A** Cambridge	**31A** Cambridge		
61372	*B1*	→	**40B** Immingham	**30A** Stratford	**30A** Stratford	**30F** Parkeston	**41A** Sheffield Darnall	
61373	*B1*	→	**40B** Immingham	**30A** Stratford	**30A** Stratford	**30F** Parkeston		
61374	*B1*	→	→	**40B** Immingham	**40B** Immingham	**40B** Immingham	**40B** Immingham	
61375	*B1*	→	→	**30A** Stratford	**30A** Stratford	**30A** Stratford	**31B** March	(24)
61376	*B1*	→	→	**38A** Colwick	**38A** Colwick	**15E** Leicester Central		
61377	*B1*	→	→	**37B** Copley Hill	**36A** Doncaster	**36A** Doncaster		
61378	*B1*	→	→	**30A** Stratford	**30A** Stratford	**30F** Parkeston	**31B** March	
61379	*B1*	→	→	**40B** Immingham	**40B** Immingham	**40B** Immingham		
61380	*B1*	→	→	**38C** Leicester Central	**38C** Leicester Central	**15E** Leicester Central		
61381	*B1*	→	→	**38E** Woodford Halse	**38C** Leicester Central	**15E** Leicester Central		
61382	*B1*	→	→	**37A** Ardsley	**56B** Ardsley	**51A** Darlington	**51A** Darlington	
61383	*B1*	→	→	**37A** Ardsley	**56B** Ardsley	**56F** Low Moor	**56F** Low Moor	
61384	*B1*	→	→	**30A** Stratford	**30F** Parkeston	**30F** Parkeston	**40A** Lincoln	**40B** Immingham
61385	*B1*	→	→	**37A** Ardsley	**56B** Ardsley	**56A** Wakefield	**56C** Copley Hill	
61386	*B1*	→	→	**37B** Copley Hill	**56C** Copley Hill	**56C** Copley Hill	**56F** Low Moor	**56F** Low Moor
61387	*B1*	→	→	**37B** Copley Hill	**56C** Copley Hill	**56F** Low Moor	**56A** Wakefield	
61388	*B1*	→	→	**37B** Copley Hill	**56C** Copley Hill	**50A** York	**56B** Ardsley	**56F** Low Moor
61389	*B1*	→	→	**35A** New England	**35A** New England	**34F** Grantham	**34F** Grantham	
61390	*B1*	→	→	**38A** Colwick	**40B** Immingham	**36A** Doncaster	**40E** Colwick	**40E** Colwick
61391	*B1*	→	→	**35A** New England	**35A** New England	**34E** New England		
61392	*B1*	→	→	**35A** New England	**35A** New England	**34F** Grantham	**34F** Grantham	
61393	*B1*	→	→	**34D** Hitchin	**34A** Kings Cross	**34E** New England	**34A** Kings Cross	
61394	*B1*	→	→	**34D** Hitchin	**34A** Kings Cross	**34A** Kings Cross	**34A** Kings Cross	
61395	*B1*	→	→	**68E** Carlisle Canal	**68E** Carlisle Canal	**12C** Carlisle Canal		
61396	*B1*	→	→	**65A** Eastfield	**65A** Eastfield	**65A** Eastfield	**65A** Eastfield	
61397	*B1*	→	→	**64A** St. Margarets	**64A** St. Margarets	**64A** St. Margarets	**64A** St. Margarets	
61398	*B1*	→	→	**64A** St. Margarets	**64A** St. Margarets	**64A** St. Margarets	**64A** St. Margarets	
61399	*B1*	→	→	**30A** Stratford	**30A** Stratford	**32A** Norwich Thorpe	**41D** Canklow	
61400	*B1*	→	**61A** Kittybrewster	**61A** Kittybrewster	**61A** Kittybrewster	**61A** Kittybrewster	**61B** Aberdeen Ferryhill	
61401	*B1*	→	**61A** Kittybrewster	**61A** Kittybrewster	**62A** Thornton Junction	**62A** Thornton Junction	**62A** Thornton Junction	
61402	*B1*	→	**62B** Dundee Tay Bridge	**62B** Dundee Tay Bridge	**62B** Dundee Tay Bridge	**62B** Dundee Tay Bridge	**62B** Dundee Tay Bridge	
61403	*B1*	→	**62B** Dundee Tay Bridge	**62B** Dundee Tay Bridge	**62A** Thornton Junction	**62A** Thornton Junction	**62C** Dunfermline Upper	**62B** Dundee Tay Bridge
61404	*B1*	→	**64B** Haymarket	**64B** Haymarket	**64B** Haymarket	**65C** Parkhead	**64A** St. Margarets	
61405	*B1*	→	**40A** Lincoln	**40A** Lincoln	**40A** Lincoln	**40A** Lincoln		
61406	*B1*	→	**40B** Immingham	**40B** Immingham	**40B** Immingham	**40B** Immingham	**40B** Immingham	**40B** Immingham
61407	*B1*	→	**40B** Immingham	**64A** St. Margarets	**64C** Dalry Road	**62C** Dunfermline Upper	**62C** Dunfermline Upper	**62C** Dunfermline Upper
61408	*B1*	→	**40B** Immingham	**40B** Immingham	**40B** Immingham	**40B** Immingham		
61409	*B1*	→	**40B** Immingham	**40B** Immingham	**40B** Immingham	**40A** Lincoln	**40A** Lincoln	
61353	*B8*	**SHF** Sheffield Darnall						

No.	Class	1948	1951	1954	1957	1960	1963	1966
61354	*B8*	**SHF** Sheffield Darnall						
61355	*B8*	**SHF** Sheffield Darnall						
61357	*B8*	**SHF** Sheffield Darnall						
61358	*B8*	**SHF** Sheffield Darnall						
61360	*B7*	**SHF** Sheffield Darnall						
61361	*B7*	**SHF** Sheffield Darnall						
61362	*B7*	**SHF** Sheffield Darnall						
61363	*B7*	**SHF** Sheffield Darnall						
61364	*B7*	**GOR** Gorton						
61365	*B7*	**SHF** Sheffield Darnall	(61702)					
61366	*B7*	**GOR** Gorton						
61367	*B7*	**GOR** Gorton	(61703)					
61368	*B7*	**GOR** Gorton						
61369	*B7*	**GOR** Gorton						
61370	*B7*	**GOR** Gorton						
61371	*B7*	**GOR** Gorton						
61372	*B7*	**SHF** Sheffield Darnall						
61373	*B7*	**GOR** Gorton						
61374	*B7*	**GOR** Gorton						
61375	*B7*	**GOR** Gorton	(61704)					
61376	*B7*	**GOR** Gorton						
61377	*B7*	**SHF** Sheffield Darnall	(61705)					
61378	*B7*	**SHF** Sheffield Darnall						
61379	*B7*	**SHF** Sheffield Darnall						
61380	*B7*	**GOR** Gorton						
61381	*B7*	**GOR** Gorton	(61706)					
61382	*B7*	**GOR** Gorton	(61707)					
61383	*B7*	**SHF** Sheffield Darnall						
61384	*B7*	**SHF** Sheffield Darnall						
61385	*B7*	**GOR** Gorton						
61386	*B7*	**SHF** Sheffield Darnall	(61708)					
61387	*B7*	**SHF** Sheffield Darnall	(61709)					
61388	*B7*	**GOR** Gorton	(61710)					
61389	*B7*	**GOR** Gorton						
61390	*B7*	**GOR** Gorton						
61391	*B7*	**GOR** Gorton	(61711)					
61392	*B7*	**GOR** Gorton	(61712)					
61393	*B7*	**GOR** Gorton						
61394	*B7*	**GOR** Gorton						
61395	*B7*	**GOR** Gorton						
61396	*B7*	**GOR** Gorton	(61713)					
61397	*B7*	**SHF** Sheffield Darnall						
61400	*B16/1*	**YK** York	(61469)					
61401	*B16/1*	**YK** York	(61470)					
61402	*B16/1*	**YK** York	(61471)					
61403	*B16/3*	**YK** York	(61472)					
61404	*B16/1*	**YK** York	(61473)					
61405	*B16/1*	**YK** York	(61474)					
61406	*B16/2*	**YK** York	(61475)					
61407	*B16/3*	**YK** York	(61476)					
61408	*B16/1*	**YK** York	(61477)					
61409	*B16/1*	**YK** York	(61478)					
61410	*B16/1*	**YK** York	**50B** Leeds Neville Hill	**50B** Leeds Neville Hill	**52B** Heaton	**50A** York		
61411	*B16/1*	**YK** York	**50B** Leeds Neville Hill	**50B** Leeds Neville Hill	**50B** Leeds Neville Hill	**50B** Leeds Neville Hill		
61412	*B16/1*	**YK** York	**50B** Leeds Neville Hill	**50B** Leeds Neville Hill	**50B** Leeds Neville Hill	**50B** Leeds Neville Hill		
61413	*B16/1*	**YK** York	**50B** Leeds Neville Hill	**50B** Leeds Neville Hill	**52B** Heaton	**50A** York		
61414	*B16/1*	**YK** York	**50B** Leeds Neville Hill	**50B** Leeds Neville Hill	**50B** Leeds Neville Hill	**50B** Leeds Neville Hill		
61415	*B16/1*	**YK** York	**50B** Leeds Neville Hill	**50B** Leeds Neville Hill	**50B** Leeds Neville Hill	**50B** Leeds Neville Hill		
61416	*B16/1*	**YK** York	**50A** York	**50A** York	**50A** York	**50A** York		
61417	*B16/3*	**YK** York	**50A** York	**50A** York	**50A** York	**50A** York		
61418	*B16/3*	**YK** York	**50A** York	**50A** York	**50A** York	**50A** York	**50B** Hull Dairycoates	
61419	*B16/1*	**YK** York	**50A** York	**50A** York	**50A** York	**50A** York		
61420	*B16/3*	**YK** York	**50A** York	**50A** York	**50A** York	**50A** York	**50B** Hull Dairycoates	
61421	*B16/2*	**YK** York	**50A** York	**50A** York	**50A** York	**50A** York	**50A** York	
61422	*B16/1*	**YK** York	**50A** York	**50C** Selby	**50A** York	**50A** York		
61423	*B16/1*	**YK** York	**50A** York	**50A** York	**50A** York	**50A** York		
61424	*B16/1*	**YK** York	**50A** York	**50A** York	**50A** York	**50A** York		
61425	*B16/1*	**YK** York	**50B** Leeds Neville Hill	**50B** Leeds Neville Hill	**50B** Leeds Neville Hill	**50B** Leeds Neville Hill		
61426	*B16/1*	**YK** York	**50A** York	**50A** York	**50A** York			
61427	*B16/1*	**YK** York	**50B** Leeds Neville Hill	**50B** Leeds Neville Hill	**50B** Leeds Neville Hill	**50B** Leeds Neville Hill		
61428	*B16/1*	**YK** York	**50B** Leeds Neville Hill	**50B** Leeds Neville Hill	**50B** Leeds Neville Hill	**50B** Leeds Neville Hill		
61429	*B16/1*	**YK** York	**50B** Leeds Neville Hill	**50B** Leeds Neville Hill	**50B** Leeds Neville Hill	**50B** Leeds Neville Hill		
61430	*B16/1*	**YK** York	**50A** York	**50A** York	**50A** York			
61431	*B16/1*	**YK** York	**50B** Leeds Neville Hill	**50B** Leeds Neville Hill	**50B** Leeds Neville Hill	**50B** Leeds Neville Hill		
61432	*B16/1*	**YK** York	**50B** Leeds Neville Hill	**50B** Leeds Neville Hill	**50B** Leeds Neville Hill	**50B** Leeds Neville Hill		
61433	*B16/1*	**YK** York	**50B** Leeds Neville Hill	**50B** Leeds Neville Hill	**50C** Selby			
61434	*B16/1→3*	**YK** York	**50A** York	**50A** York	**50A** York	**50A** York	**50A** York	
61435	*B16/2*	**YK** York	**50A** York	**50A** York	**50A** York	**50A** York	**50B** Hull Dairycoates	
61436	*B16/1*	**YK** York	**50A** York	**50A** York	**50A** York	**50A** York		
61437	*B16/2*	**YK** York	**50A** York	**50A** York	**50A** York	**50A** York	**50B** Hull Dairycoates	
61438	*B16/2*	**YK** York	**50A** York	**50A** York	**50A** York	**50A** York	**50B** Hull Dairycoates	
61439	*B16/3*	**YK** York	**50A** York	**50A** York	**50A** York	**50A** York		
61440	*B16/1*	**YK** York	**50B** Leeds Neville Hill	**50B** Leeds Neville Hill	**52B** Heaton	**50A** York		
61441	*B16/1*	**YK** York	**50A** York	**50A** York	**50A** York			
61442	*B16/1*	**YK** York	**50B** Leeds Neville Hill	**50D** Starbeck	**50B** Leeds Neville Hill	**50B** Leeds Neville Hill		
61443	*B16/1*	**YK** York	**50A** York	**50A** York	**50A** York	**50A** York		
61444	*B16/3*	**YK** York	**50A** York	**50A** York	**50A** York	**50A** York	**50B** Hull Dairycoates	
61445	*B16/1*	**YK** York	**50B** Leeds Neville Hill	**50E** Scarborough	**50E** Scarborough	**50E** Scarborough		
61446	*B16/1*	**YK** York	**50B** Leeds Neville Hill	**50B** Leeds Neville Hill	**50B** Leeds Neville Hill	**50B** Leeds Neville Hill		
61447	*B16/1*	**YK** York	**50B** Leeds Neville Hill	**50B** Leeds Neville Hill	**50B** Leeds Neville Hill	**50B** Leeds Neville Hill		
61448	*B16/3*	**YK** York	**50A** York	**50A** York	**50A** York	**50A** York	**50A** York	
61449	*B16/3*	**YK** York	**50A** York	**50A** York	**50A** York	**50A** York	**56D** Mirfield	
61450	*B16/1*	**YK** York	**50A** York	**50A** York	**50A** York	**50A** York		
61451	*B16/1*	**YK** York	**50A** York	**50A** York	**52B** Heaton	**50A** York		
61452	*B16/1*	**YK** York	**50A** York	**50A** York	**50A** York	**50A** York		
61453	*B16/3*	**YK** York	**50A** York	**50A** York	**50A** York	**50A** York	**50B** Hull Dairycoates	
61454	*B16/3*	**YK** York	**50A** York	**50A** York	**50A** York	**50A** York	**50A** York	
61455	*B16/2*	**YK** York	**50A** York	**50A** York	**50A** York	**50A** York	**50A** York	
61456	*B16/1*	**YK** York	**50A** York	**50A** York	**52B** Heaton	**50A** York		
61457	*B16/2*	**YK** York	**50A** York	**50A** York	**50A** York	**50A** York	**50A** York	
61458	*B16/1*	**YK** York	**50A** York	**50A** York	**52B** Heaton			
61459	*B16/1*	**YK** York	**50A** York	**50A** York	**50A** York	**50A** York		
61460	*B16/1*	**YK** York	**50A** York	**50A** York	**50A** York	**50A** York		
61461	*B16/1→3*	**YK** York	**50A** York	**50A** York	**50A** York	**50A** York	**56D** Mirfield	
61462	*B16/1*	**YK** York	**50A** York	**50A** York	**50A** York	**50A** York		
61463	*B16/3*	**YK** York	**50A** York	**50A** York	**50A** York	**50A** York	**50B** Hull Dairycoates	
61464	*B16/3*	**YK** York	**50A** York	**50A** York	**50A** York	**50A** York	**56D** Mirfield	
61465	*B16/1*	**YK** York	**50A** York	**50A** York	**50A** York	**50A** York		
61466	*B16/1*	**YK** York	**50A** York	**50A** York	**50A** York	**50A** York		
61467	*B16/3*	**YK** York	**50A** York	**50A** York	**50A** York	**50A** York	**50B** Hull Dairycoates	
61468	*B16/3*	**YK** York	**50A** York	**50A** York	**50A** York	**50A** York	**56D** Mirfield	
61469	*B16/1*	(61400)	**50B** Leeds Neville Hill	**50B** Leeds Neville Hill	**52B** Heaton	**50A** York		
61470	*B16/1*	(61401)	**50B** Leeds Neville Hill	**50B** Leeds Neville Hill	**50B** Leeds Neville Hill			
61471	*B16/1*	(61402)	**50B** Leeds Neville Hill	**50B** Leeds Neville Hill	**50B** Leeds Neville Hill	**50B** Leeds Neville Hill		

		1948		1951	1954	1957	1960	1963	1966
61472	*B16/3*	(61403)		**50A** York	**50A** York	**50A** York	**50A** York	**50B** Hull Dairycoates	
61473	*B16/1*	(61404)		**50A** York	**50A** York	**50A** York	**50A** York		
61474	*B16/1*	(61405)		**50A** York	**50A** York	**50C** Selby			
61475	*B16/2*	(61406)		**50A** York	**50A** York	**50A** York	**50A** York	**50A** York	
61476	*B16/3*	(61407)		**50A** York	**50A** York	**50A** York	**50A** York	**56D** Mirfield	
61477	*B16/1*	(61408)		**50A** York	**50A** York	**50A** York	**50A** York		
61478	*B16/1*	(61409)		**50B** Leeds Neville Hill	**50B** Leeds Neville Hill	**50D** Starbeck	**50A** York		
61469	*B9*	STP	Heaton Mersey						
61470	*B9*	LIV	Brunswick						
61475	*B9*	STP	Heaton Mersey						
61476	*B9*	TFD	Trafford Park						
61482	*B4*	ARD	Ardsley						
61483	*B4*	ARD	Ardsley						
61485	*B4*	ARD	Ardsley						
61488	*B4*	ARD	Ardsley						
61497	*B3*	IMM	Immingham						
61500	*B12/4*	KEI	Keith						
61501	*B12/1*	KEI	Keith	**61C** Keith					
61502	*B12/1*	KEI	Keith	**61C** Keith	**61C** Keith				
61503	*B12/1*	KEI	Keith	**61C** Keith					
61504	*B12/4*	KIT	Kittybrewster						
61505	*B12/4*	KIT	Kittybrewster	**61A** Kittybrewster					
61507	*B12/4*	KIT	Kittybrewster	**61A** Kittybrewster					
61508	*B12/4*	KIT	Kittybrewster	**61A** Kittybrewster					
61509	*B12/3*	IPS	Ipswich						
61510	*B12/3*	STR	Stratford						
61511	*B12/4*	KIT	Kittybrewster	**61A** Kittybrewster					
61512	*B12/3*	COL	Colchester	**30E** Colchester	**30A** Stratford	**30A** Stratford			
61513	*B12/1*	KIT	Kittybrewster	**61A** Kittybrewster					
61514	*B12/3*	STR	Stratford	**30A** Stratford	**32D** Yarmouth South Town	**32A** Norwich Thorpe			
61515	*B12/3*	STR	Stratford	**30A** Stratford					
61516	*B12/3*	IPS	Ipswich	**30A** Stratford	**30A** Stratford	**30A** Stratford			
61517	*B12/3*	STR	Stratford						
61519	*B12/3*	STR	Stratford	**30A** Stratford	**30A** Stratford	**30A** Stratford			
61520	*B12/3*	STR	Stratford	**32F** Yarmouth Beach	**32F** Yarmouth Beach	**32A** Norwich Thorpe			
61521	*B12/1*	KIT	Kittybrewster	**61A** Kittybrewster					
61523	*B12/3*	COL	Colchester	**30E** Colchester	**30A** Stratford				
61524	*B12/4*	KIT	Kittybrewster	**61A** Kittybrewster					
61525	*B12/3*	STR	Stratford	**30A** Stratford					
61526	*B12/4*	KIT	Kittybrewster	**61A** Kittybrewster					
61528	*B12/1*	KIT	Kittybrewster	**61A** Kittybrewster					
61529	*B12/1*	KIT	Kittybrewster						
61530	*B12/3*	STR	Stratford	**32B** Ipswich	**32A** Norwich Thorpe	**32F** Yarmouth Beach			
61532	*B12/4*	KIT	Kittybrewster	**61A** Kittybrewster					
61533	*B12/3*	STR	Stratford	**31D** South Lynn	**32D** Yarmouth South Town	**32B** Ipswich			
61535	*B12/3*	STR	Stratford	**32B** Ipswich	**32B** Ipswich	**32B** Ipswich			
61536	*B12/1*	KIT	Kittybrewster						
61537	*B12/3*	STR	Stratford	**31D** South Lynn	**31D** South Lynn	**32B** Ipswich			
61538	*B12/3*	STR	Stratford	**35B** Grantham	**35B** Grantham	**35C** Spital Bridge			
61539	*B12/1*	KIT	Kittybrewster	**61A** Kittybrewster	**61C** Keith				
61540	*B12/3*	STR	Stratford	**31D** South Lynn	**31D** South Lynn	**32A** Norwich Thorpe			
61541	*B12/3*	STR	Stratford	**35B** Grantham	**35B** Grantham	**35B** Grantham			
61542	*B12/3*	STR	Stratford	**30A** Stratford	**32D** Yarmouth South Town	**32A** Norwich Thorpe			
61543	*B12/1*	KIT	Kittybrewster	**61A** Kittybrewster					
61545	*B12/3*	STR	Stratford	**32A** Norwich Thorpe	**32F** Yarmouth Beach	**32F** Yarmouth Beach			
61546	*B12/3*	STR	Stratford	**30A** Stratford	**30A** Stratford	**30A** Stratford			
61547	*B12/3*	STR	Stratford	**31D** South Lynn	**31D** South Lynn	**32A** Norwich Thorpe			
61549	*B12/3*	STR	Stratford	**30A** Stratford	**30A** Stratford	**30A** Stratford			
61550	*B12/3*	STR	Stratford	**30A** Stratford	**30A** Stratford	**30A** Stratford			
61552	*B12/1*	KIT	Kittybrewster	**61A** Kittybrewster					
61553	*B12/3*	COL	Colchester	**35B** Grantham	**35B** Grantham	**35B** Grantham			
61554	*B12/3*	STR	Stratford	**35B** Grantham	**35B** Grantham	**35C** Spital Bridge			
61555	*B12/3*	STR	Stratford	**30E** Colchester	**30A** Stratford	**30E** Colchester			
61556	*B12/3*	STR	Stratford	**30E** Colchester	**30A** Stratford	**30E** Colchester			
61557	*B12/3*	STR	Stratford	**30E** Colchester	**30A** Stratford	**30E** Colchester			
61558	*B12/3*	STR	Stratford	**30E** Colchester	**30A** Stratford	**30E** Colchester			
61559	*B12/3*	STR	Stratford	**30A** Stratford					
61560	*B12/1*	KIT	Kittybrewster	**61A** Kittybrewster					
61561	*B12/3*	IPS	Ipswich	**32B** Ipswich	**32B** Ipswich	**32B** Ipswich			
61562	*B12/3*	IPS	Ipswich	**32B** Ipswich	**32B** Ipswich				
61563	*B12/1*	KIT	Kittybrewster	**61A** Kittybrewster					
61564	*B12/3*	IPS	Ipswich	**32B** Ipswich	**32B** Ipswich	**32B** Ipswich			
61565	*B12/3*	STR	Stratford	**35B** Grantham	**35B** Grantham	**35C** Spital Bridge			
61566	*B12/3*	IPS	Ipswich	**32B** Ipswich	**32B** Ipswich	**32B** Ipswich			
61567	*B12/3*	STR	Stratford	**30A** Stratford	**35B** Grantham	**35C** Spital Bridge			
61568	*B12/3*	STR	Stratford	**30A** Stratford	**32D** Yarmouth South Town	**32A** Norwich Thorpe			
61569	*B12/3*	IPS	Ipswich	**32B** Ipswich	**32B** Ipswich	**32B** Ipswich			
61570	*B12/3*	IPS	Ipswich	**32B** Ipswich	**32B** Ipswich	**32B** Ipswich			
61571	*B12/3*	STR	Stratford	**30A** Stratford	**32B** Ipswich	**32B** Ipswich			
61572	*B12/3*	STR	Stratford	**30A** Stratford	**32B** Ipswich	**32B** Ipswich	**32A** Norwich Thorpe		
61573	*B12/3*	STR	Stratford	**30A** Stratford	**30A** Stratford	**30A** Stratford			
61574	*B12/3*	STR	Stratford	**30A** Stratford	**35B** Grantham	**35B** Grantham			
61575	*B12/3*	STR	Stratford	**30A** Stratford	**30A** Stratford	**30A** Stratford			
61576	*B12/3*	STR	Stratford	**30A** Stratford	**30A** Stratford	**30A** Stratford			
61577	*B12/3*	IPS	Ipswich	**32B** Ipswich	**32B** Ipswich	**32B** Ipswich			
61578	*B12/3*	STR	Stratford	**30A** Stratford	**30A** Stratford	**30A** Stratford			
61579	*B12/3*	STR	Stratford	**30A** Stratford	**30A** Stratford	**30A** Stratford			
61580	*B12/3*	STR	Stratford	**30A** Stratford	**35B** Grantham	**35B** Grantham			
61600	*B17/1→6*	IPS	Ipswich	**32B** Ipswich	**30A** Stratford	**30A** Stratford			
61601	*B17/1*	IPS	Ipswich	**32B** Ipswich	**30A** Stratford	**30A** Stratford			
61602	*B17/1→6*	IPS	Ipswich	**30A** Stratford	**30A** Stratford	**30A** Stratford			
61603	*B2*	COL	Colchester	**30E** Colchester	**30E** Colchester	**31A** Cambridge			
61604	*B17/1→6*	IPS	Ipswich	**32B** Ipswich					
61605	*B17/1→6*	STR	Stratford	**30A** Stratford	**30A** Stratford	**30A** Stratford			
61606	*B17/1→6*	STR	Stratford	**30A** Stratford	**30A** Stratford	**30E** Colchester			
61607	*B2*	COL	Colchester	**30E** Colchester	**30E** Colchester	**31A** Cambridge			
61608	*B17/1→6*	CAM	Cambridge	**30A** Stratford	**30A** Stratford	**30E** Colchester	**31A** Cambridge		
61609	*B17/1→6*	STR	Stratford	**32A** Norwich Thorpe	**30A** Stratford	**30A** Stratford			
61610	*B17/1→6*	CAM	Cambridge	**30A** Stratford	**30A** Stratford	**30A** Stratford	**31A** Cambridge		
61611	*B17/1→6*	CAM	Cambridge	**30A** Stratford	**30A** Stratford	**30E** Colchester			
61612	*B17/1→6*	STR	Stratford	**30A** Stratford	**30A** Stratford	**30A** Stratford			
61613	*B17/1→6*	CAM	Cambridge	**30A** Stratford	**30A** Stratford	**30A** Stratford			
61614	*B2*	COL	Colchester	**30E** Colchester	**30E** Colchester	**31A** Cambridge			
61615	*B2*	COL	Colchester	**30E** Colchester	**30E** Colchester	**31A** Cambridge			
61616	*B2*	COL	Colchester	**30E** Colchester	**30E** Colchester	**31A** Cambridge			
61617	*B2*	CAM	Cambridge	**31A** Cambridge	**31A** Cambridge	**31A** Cambridge			
61618	*B17/1→6*	IPS	Ipswich	**32B** Ipswich	**30A** Stratford	**32B** Ipswich	**31A** Cambridge		
61619	*B17/1→6*	CAM	Cambridge	**31A** Cambridge	**31B** March	**31B** March			
61620	*B17/1→6*	CAM	Cambridge	**31A** Cambridge	**31B** March	**31B** March	**31C** Kings Lynn		
61621	*B17/1→6*	CAM	Cambridge	**30A** Stratford	**30A** Stratford	**31B** March			
61622	*B17/6*	CAM	Cambridge	**31A** Cambridge	**32D** Yarmouth South Town	**32D** Yarmouth South Town			
61623	*B17/1→6*	CAM	Cambridge	**31A** Cambridge	**31A** Cambridge	**31A** Cambridge			
61624	*B17/1*	CAM	Cambridge	**31A** Cambridge					
61625	*B17/1*	NOR	Norwich Thorpe	**31A** Cambridge	**32B** Ipswich	**32B** Ipswich			

No.	Class	Code	1948	1951	1954	1957	1960	1963	1966
61626	B17/1→6	NOR	Norwich Thorpe	**31B** March	**31B** March	**31B** March	**31A** Cambridge		
61627	B17/1→6	CAM	Cambridge	**31A** Cambridge	**31A** Cambridge	**31B** March			
61628	B17/1→6	CAM	Cambridge	**31A** Cambridge					
61629	B17/1	NOR	Norwich Thorpe	**32A** Norwich Thorpe	**32A** Norwich Thorpe	**32B** Ipswich			
61630	B17/1→6	MAR	March	**31B** March	**30A** Stratford	**30A** Stratford			
61631	B17/1→6	CAM	Cambridge	**31A** Cambridge	**32B** Ipswich	**32B** Ipswich			
61632	B2	COL	Colchester	**30E** Colchester	**30E** Colchester	**31A** Cambridge			
61633	B17/1→6	CAM	Cambridge	**31B** March	**31B** March	**31B** March			
61634	B17/1→6	IPS	Ipswich	**32B** Ipswich	**30E** Colchester	**31A** Cambridge			
61635	B17/1→6	MAR	March	**31B** March	**31B** March	**31B** March			
61636	B17/1→6	MAR	March	**31A** Cambridge	**31A** Cambridge	**31A** Cambridge			
61637	B17/1→6	CAM	Cambridge	**31A** Cambridge	**32B** Ipswich	**32B** Ipswich			
61638	B17/1→6	CAM	Cambridge	**31A** Cambridge	**31B** March	**31B** March			
61639	B2	STR	Stratford	**30E** Colchester	**30E** Colchester	**31A** Cambridge			
61640	B17/1→6	CAM	Cambridge	**31A** Cambridge	**31A** Cambridge	**31A** Cambridge			
61641	B17/1→6	CAM	Cambridge	**31B** March	**31B** March	**31B** March	**31B** March		
61642	B17/1→6	CAM	Cambridge	**31A** Cambridge	**31A** Cambridge	**31A** Cambridge			
61643	B17/1→6	CAM	Cambridge	**31A** Cambridge	**31B** March	**31B** March			
61644	B17/1→B2	NOR	Norwich Thorpe	**30E** Colchester	**30E** Colchester	**31A** Cambridge			
61645	B17/1→6	IPS	Ipswich	**32B** Ipswich	**30E** Colchester	**31B** March			
61646	B17/1→6	MAR	March	**31B** March	**30E** Colchester	**31A** Cambridge			
61647	B17/4→6	LIN	Lincoln	**32B** Ipswich	**32B** Ipswich	**32B** Ipswich			
61648	B17/4→6	MAR	March	**30A** Stratford	**30A** Stratford	**30A** Stratford			
61649	B17/4→6	IPS	Ipswich	**32B** Ipswich	**32B** Ipswich	**32B** Ipswich			
61650	B17/4→6	CLK	Colwick	**38E** Woodford Halse	**30E** Colchester	**30E** Colchester			
61651	B17/4→6	CLK	Colwick	**38E** Woodford Halse	**30E** Colchester	**30E** Colchester			
61652	B17/4→6	CLK	Colwick	**31A** Cambridge	**31A** Cambridge	**31A** Cambridge			
61653	B17/4→6	CLK	Colwick	**31A** Cambridge	**31A** Cambridge	**31A** Cambridge	**31B** March		
61654	B17/4→6	CAM	Cambridge	**30A** Stratford	**30A** Stratford	**30A** Stratford			
61655	B17/4→6	STR	Stratford	**31A** Cambridge	**30A** Stratford	**30A** Stratford			
61656	B17/4→6	MAR	March	**31B** March	**32A** Norwich Thorpe	**32D** Yarmouth South Town	**32A** Norwich Thorpe		
61657	B17/4→6	CLK	Colwick	**38A** Colwick	**31A** Cambridge	**31B** March	**31B** March		
61658	B17/1→6	STR	Stratford	**30A** Stratford	**31B** March	**30E** Colchester			
61659	B17/5→6	NOR	Norwich Thorpe	**32A** Norwich Thorpe	**32D** Yarmouth South Town	**32D** Yarmouth South Town	**32C** Lowestoft		
61660	B17/4	MAR	March	**31B** March	**30A** Stratford	**30A** Stratford	**32C** Lowestoft		
61661	B17/4→6	MAR	March	**32D** Yarmouth South Town	**30A** Stratford	**30A** Stratford			
61662	B17/4→6	CLK	Colwick	**38A** Colwick	**30E** Colchester	**30E** Colchester			
61663	B17/4→6	CAM	Cambridge	**31A** Cambridge	**30A** Stratford	**30A** Stratford	**30A** Stratford		
61664	B17/4→6	CLK	Colwick	**38E** Woodford Halse	**32A** Norwich Thorpe	**32D** Yarmouth South Town	**32C** Lowestoft		
61665	B17/4→6	CAM	Cambridge	**32D** Yarmouth South Town	**32A** Norwich Thorpe	**32D** Yarmouth South Town			
61666	B17/6	CAM	Cambridge	**31B** March	**30A** Stratford	**30E** Colchester	**30A** Stratford		
61667	B17/4	CLK	Colwick	**38E** Woodford Halse	**30E** Colchester	**30E** Colchester			
61668	B17/4→6	IPS	Ipswich	**32B** Ipswich	**30A** Stratford	**30A** Stratford	**30A** Stratford		
61669	B17/4→6	CLK	Colwick	**32B** Ipswich	**32B** Ipswich	**32B** Ipswich			
61670	B17/5→6	NOR	Norwich Thorpe	**32A** Norwich Thorpe	**32D** Yarmouth South Town	**32D** Yarmouth South Town	**32C** Lowestoft		
61671	B2	CAM	Cambridge	**31A** Cambridge	**31A** Cambridge	**31A** Cambridge			
61672	B17/4→6	MAR	March	**31B** March	**30A** Stratford	**30A** Stratford	**32C** Lowestoft		
61680	B5	MEX	Mexborough						
61681	B5	MEX	Mexborough						
61685	B5	MEX	Mexborough						
61686	B5	MEX	Mexborough						
61688	B5	MEX	Mexborough						
61689	B5	MEX	Mexborough						
61690	B5	MEX	Mexborough						
61699	B13	DAR	Darlington	Rugby Testing Station					
61700	V4	EFD	Eastfield	**65A** Eastfield	**65A** Eastfield	**61B** Aberdeen Ferryhill			
61701	V4	EFD	Eastfield	**65A** Eastfield	**65A** Eastfield	**61B** Aberdeen Ferryhill			
61702	B7	(61365)							
61703	B7	(61367)							
61704	B7	(61375)							
61705	B7	(61377)							
61706	B7	(61381)							
61707	B7	(61382)							
61708	B7	(61386)							
61709	B7	(61387)							
61710	B7	(61388)							
61711	B7	(61391)							
61712	B7	(61392)							
61713	B7	(61396)							
61720	K2	IMM	Immingham	**40B** Immingham	**40B** Immingham				
61721	K2	STR	Stratford	**30A** Stratford	**62C** Dunfermline Upper	**62C** Dunfermline Upper			
61722	K2	IMM	Immingham	**40B** Immingham	**65C** Parkhead				
61723	K2	CLK	Colwick	**38A** Colwick	**38A** Colwick	**38A** Colwick			
61724	K2	IMM	Immingham	**40B** Immingham	**40B** Immingham	**41A** Sheffield Darnall			
61725	K2	BOS	Boston	**40F** Boston	**40F** Boston	**40F** Boston			
61726	K2	CLK	Colwick	**38A** Colwick	**38A** Colwick	**38A** Colwick			
61727	K2	IMM	Immingham	**40B** Immingham	**40B** Immingham				
61728	K2	IMM	Immingham	**40B** Immingham	**40F** Boston	**41A** Sheffield Darnall	**41A** Sheffield Darnall		
61729	K2	PKD	Parkhead	**35B** Grantham	**38A** Colwick	**38A** Colwick			
61730	K2	STR	Stratford	**32A** Norwich Thorpe	**40B** Immingham	**40B** Immingham			
61731	K2	BOS	Boston	**40F** Boston	**62A** Thornton Junction	**40F** Boston			
61732	K2	CLK	Colwick	**38A** Colwick	**38A** Colwick	**38A** Colwick			
61733	K2	IMM	Immingham	**40B** Immingham	**65C** Parkhead	**65C** Parkhead			
61734	K2	STR	Stratford	**30A** Stratford	**61B** Aberdeen Ferryhill				
61735	K2	IMM	Immingham	**35A** New England	**65C** Parkhead	**65C** Parkhead			
61736	K2	NWE	New England	**35A** New England	**40B** Immingham	**40B** Immingham			
61737	K2	STR	Stratford	**30A** Stratford	**38A** Colwick				
61738	K2	SL	South Lynn	**31D** South Lynn	**38A** Colwick	**38A** Colwick			
61739	K2	IMM	Immingham	**35A** New England	**40B** Immingham	**41A** Sheffield Darnall			
61740	K2	STR	Stratford	**35A** New England	**40B** Immingham	**40B** Immingham	**40B** Immingham		
61741	K2	CLK	Colwick	**38A** Colwick	**65A** Eastfield	**65A** Eastfield	**61A** Kittybrewster		
61742	K2	SL	South Lynn	**31D** South Lynn	**40A** Lincoln	**40F** Boston	**40F** Boston		
61743	K2	SL	South Lynn	**31D** South Lynn	**40A** Lincoln	**40F** Boston			
61744	K2	BOS	Boston	**40F** Boston	**40F** Boston	**40F** Boston			
61745	K2	STR	Stratford	**30A** Stratford	**40F** Boston	**40F** Boston	**40B** Immingham		
61746	K2	STR	Stratford	**30A** Stratford	**40A** Lincoln	**40A** Lincoln			
61747	K2	NWE	New England	**32A** Norwich Thorpe	**38A** Colwick	**41A** Sheffield Darnall	**41A** Sheffield Darnall		
61748	K2	SL	South Lynn	**31D** South Lynn	**40A** Lincoln	**40F** Boston			
61749	K2	CLK	Colwick	**38A** Colwick	**38A** Colwick	**41A** Sheffield Darnall			
61750	K2	CLK	Colwick	**40F** Boston	**40F** Boston	**40F** Boston			
61751	K2	CLK	Colwick	**38A** Colwick	**38A** Colwick	**40A** Lincoln			
61752	K2	STR	Stratford	**30A** Stratford	**38A** Colwick	**38A** Colwick			
61753	K2	STR	Stratford	**30A** Stratford	**38A** Colwick	**38A** Colwick			
61754	K2	STR	Stratford	**30A** Stratford	**38A** Colwick	**38A** Colwick			
61755	K2	BOS	Boston	**40F** Boston	**62A** Thornton Junction	**62A** Thornton Junction			
61756	K2	CLK	Colwick	**40F** Boston	**40F** Boston	**40F** Boston	**40B** Immingham		
61757	K2	COL	Colchester	**31D** South Lynn	**40F** Boston	**40F** Boston			
61758	K2	CLK	Colwick	**38A** Colwick	**62C** Dunfermline Upper	**62C** Dunfermline Upper			
61759	K2	STR	Stratford	**30A** Stratford	**38A** Colwick	**40A** Lincoln	**34E** New England		
61760	K2	BOS	Boston	**40F** Boston	**40F** Boston	**41A** Sheffield Darnall	**41A** Sheffield Darnall		
61761	K2	STR	Stratford	**30A** Stratford	**40A** Lincoln	**41A** Sheffield Darnall	**41A** Sheffield Darnall		
61762	K2	BOS	Boston	**40F** Boston	**40F** Boston	**40F** Boston			
61763	K2	CLK	Colwick	**38A** Colwick	**38A** Colwick	**38A** Colwick	**34E** New England		
61764	K2	EFD	Eastfield	**65A** Eastfield	**65A** Eastfield	**65A** Eastfield	**65A** Eastfield		

No.	Class	1948	1951	1954	1957	1960	1963	1966
61765	*K2*	**STR** Stratford	**30A** Stratford	**40A** Lincoln	**40F** Boston			
61766	*K2*	**COL** Colchester	**31D** South Lynn	**40F** Boston	**40F** Boston	**40B** Immingham		
61767	*K2*	**STR** Stratford	**30A** Stratford	**40A** Lincoln	**40F** Boston	**40B** Immingham		
61768	*K2*	**CLK** Colwick	**38A** Colwick	**38A** Colwick	**38A** Colwick			
61769	*K2*	**CLK** Colwick	**38A** Colwick	**65C** Parkhead	**65C** Parkhead	**65C** Parkhead		
61770	*K2*	**CLK** Colwick	**40F** Boston	**62C** Dunfermline Upper	**62C** Dunfermline Upper			
61771	*K2*	**CLK** Colwick	**38A** Colwick	**38A** Colwick	**38A** Colwick	**40B** Immingham		
61772	*K2*	**EFD** Eastfield	**65C** Parkhead	**65C** Parkhead	**65C** Parkhead			
61773	*K2*	**CLK** Colwick	**38A** Colwick	**38A** Colwick	**38A** Colwick	**40B** Immingham		
61774	*K2*	**EFD** Eastfield	**65A** Eastfield	**65A** Eastfield	**65A** Eastfield			
61775	*K2*	**EFD** Eastfield	**65A** Eastfield	**65A** Eastfield	**65A** Eastfield			
61776	*K2*	**EFD** Eastfield	**65A** Eastfield	**65A** Eastfield	**65A** Eastfield			
61777	*K2*	**STR** Stratford	**30A** Stratford	**30A** Stratford	**38A** Colwick			
61778	*K2*	**STR** Stratford	**30A** Stratford	**40A** Lincoln	**40A** Lincoln			
61779	*K2*	**EFD** Eastfield	**65A** Eastfield	**61A** Kittybrewster	**61C** Keith	**61C** Keith		
61780	*K2*	**STR** Stratford	**30A** Stratford	**38A** Colwick	**38A** Colwick			
61781	*K2*	**EFD** Eastfield	**65A** Eastfield	**65A** Eastfield	**65A** Eastfield			
61782	*K2*	**FW** Fort William	**63D** Fort William	**61A** Kittybrewster	**61C** Keith	**61C** Keith		
61783	*K2*	**FW** Fort William	**63D** Fort William	**63D** Fort William	**61C** Keith			
61784	*K2*	**EFD** Eastfield	**65A** Eastfield	**65A** Eastfield	**65A** Eastfield	**65J** Fort William		
61785	*K2*	**EFD** Eastfield	**65A** Eastfield	**65A** Eastfield	**65A** Eastfield			
61786	*K2*	**EFD** Eastfield	**65A** Eastfield	**65A** Eastfield	**65A** Eastfield			
61787	*K2*	**FW** Fort William	**63D** Fort William	**63D** Fort William	**65A** Eastfield			
61788	*K2*	**FW** Fort William	**63D** Fort William	**63D** Fort William	**65A** Eastfield	**65A** Eastfield		
61789	*K2*	**FW** Fort William	**63D** Fort William	**65A** Eastfield	**65A** Eastfield			
61790	*K2*	**FW** Fort William	**63D** Fort William	**63D** Fort William	**61A** Kittybrewster			
61791	*K2*	**FW** Fort William	**63D** Fort William	**63D** Fort William	**65J** Fort William	**65J** Fort William		
61792	*K2*	**EFD** Eastfield	**65A** Eastfield	**61A** Kittybrewster	**61C** Keith	**61C** Keith		
61793	*K2*	**EFD** Eastfield	**65A** Eastfield	**61A** Kittybrewster	**61C** Keith			
61794	*K2*	**EFD** Eastfield	**65A** Eastfield	**65A** Eastfield	**65A** Eastfield	**65A** Eastfield		
61800	*K3*	**IMM** Immingham	**40B** Immingham	**40B** Immingham	**40B** Immingham	**36A** Doncaster		
61801	*K3*	**CLK** Colwick	**30A** Stratford	**30A** Stratford	**30A** Stratford	**31A** Cambridge		
61802	*K3*	**CLK** Colwick	**40B** Immingham	**40B** Immingham	**40A** Lincoln	**40A** Lincoln		
61803	*K3*	**IMM** Immingham	**40B** Immingham	**40B** Immingham	**40B** Immingham	**36A** Doncaster		
61804	*K3*	**NWE** New England	**35A** New England	**31B** March	**40A** Lincoln	**2F** Woodford Halse		
61805	*K3*	**MAR** March	**30A** Stratford	**30A** Stratford	**30A** Stratford	**34E** New England		
61806	*K3*	**IMM** Immingham	**40B** Immingham	**40B** Immingham	**40B** Immingham	**40A** Lincoln		
61807	*K3*	**LIN** Lincoln	**40A** Lincoln	**40A** Lincoln	**40A** Lincoln	**40A** Lincoln		
61808	*K3*	**CLK** Colwick	**39A** Gorton	**39A** Gorton	**39A** Gorton	**40E** Colwick		
61809	*K3*	**NWE** New England	**39A** Gorton	**39A** Gorton	**38A** Colwick	**2F** Woodford Halse		
61810	*K3*	**NWE** New England	**30A** Stratford	**30A** Stratford	**30A** Stratford	**31B** March		
61811	*K3*	**NWE** New England	**35A** New England	**31B** March	**31B** March	**31B** March		
61812	*K3*	**MAR** March	**38A** Colwick	**39A** Gorton	**32A** Norwich Thorpe	**36A** Doncaster		
61813	*K3*	**HLD** Hull Dairycoates	**53A** Hull Dairycoates	**53A** Hull Dairycoates	**53A** Hull Dairycoates	**53A** Hull Dairycoates		
61814	*K3*	**HLD** Hull Dairycoates	**53A** Hull Dairycoates	**53A** Hull Dairycoates	**53A** Hull Dairycoates	**53A** Hull Dairycoates		
61815	*K3*	**MAR** March	**30A** Stratford	**30A** Stratford	**30A** Stratford	**30A** Stratford		
61816	*K3*	**CLK** Colwick	**38A** Colwick	**31B** March	**31B** March	**41A** Sheffield Darnall		
61817	*K3*	**MAR** March	**30A** Stratford	**30A** Stratford	**30A** Stratford	**31A** Cambridge		
61818	*K3*	**HTN** Heaton	**52B** Heaton	**52B** Heaton	**52B** Heaton	**52B** Heaton		
61819	*K3*	**HLD** Hull Dairycoates	**53A** Hull Dairycoates	**53A** Hull Dairycoates	**53A** Hull Dairycoates	**53A** Hull Dairycoates		
61820	*K3*	**MAR** March	**30A** Stratford	**30A** Stratford	**30A** Stratford	**30A** Stratford		
61821	*K3*	**CLK** Colwick	**38A** Colwick	**38A** Colwick	**38A** Colwick	**40E** Colwick		
61822	*K3*	**LIN** Lincoln	**38A** Colwick	**31B** March	**31B** March	**31B** March		
61823	*K3*	**STM** St. Margarets	**64A** St. Margarets	**64A** St. Margarets	**64A** St. Margarets			
61824	*K3*	**CLK** Colwick	**38A** Colwick	**31B** March	**38A** Colwick	**2F** Woodford Halse		
61825	*K3*	**NWE** New England	**40B** Immingham	**40B** Immingham	**40B** Immingham	**41A** Sheffield Darnall		
61826	*K3*	**CLK** Colwick	**38A** Colwick	**31B** March	**31B** March	**32A** Norwich Thorpe		
61827	*K3*	**NWE** New England	**40B** Immingham	**40B** Immingham	**40B** Immingham	**40B** Immingham		
61828	*K3*	**NWE** New England	**39A** Gorton	**39A** Gorton	**40A** Lincoln	**40A** Lincoln		
61829	*K3*	**WFD** Woodford Halse	**39A** Gorton	**39A** Gorton	**32A** Norwich Thorpe	**36A** Doncaster		
61830	*K3*	**MAR** March	**30A** Stratford	**30A** Stratford	**30A** Stratford	**34E** New England		
61831	*K3*	**MAR** March	**30A** Stratford	**30A** Stratford	**30A** Stratford	**31B** March		
61832	*K3*	**NWE** New England	**39A** Gorton	**39A** Gorton	**39A** Gorton	**2F** Woodford Halse		
61833	*K3*	**NWE** New England	**38A** Colwick	**38A** Colwick	**38A** Colwick	**40E** Colwick		
61834	*K3*	**NWE** New England	**30A** Stratford	**30A** Stratford	**30A** Stratford	**31A** Cambridge		
61835	*K3*	**MAR** March	**30A** Stratford	**31B** March	**31B** March	**31B** March		
61836	*K3*	**IMM** Immingham	**40B** Immingham	**40B** Immingham	**40B** Immingham	**36A** Doncaster		
61837	*K3*	**IMM** Immingham	**40B** Immingham	**40B** Immingham	**40B** Immingham	**40E** Colwick		
61838	*K3*	**IMM** Immingham	**40B** Immingham	**40B** Immingham	**40B** Immingham	**2F** Woodford Halse		
61839	*K3*	**WFD** Woodford Halse	**39A** Gorton	**40B** Immingham	**40B** Immingham	**36A** Doncaster		
61840	*K3*	**NWE** New England	**30A** Stratford	**30A** Stratford	**30A** Stratford	**31B** March		
61841	*K3*	**NWE** New England	**35A** New England	**31B** March	**38E** Woodford Halse	**2F** Woodford Halse		
61842	*K3*	**IMM** Immingham	**40B** Immingham	**31B** March	**38E** Woodford Halse	**2F** Woodford Halse		
61843	*K3*	**NWE** New England	**35A** New England	**31B** March	**38E** Woodford Halse	**2F** Woodford Halse		
61844	*K3*	**NWE** New England	**31B** March	**53A** Hull Dairycoates	**52B** Heaton	**52B** Heaton		
61845	*K3*	**IMM** Immingham	**40B** Immingham	**31B** March	**31B** March	**31B** March		
61846	*K3*	**MAR** March	**31B** March	**53A** Hull Dairycoates	**53A** Hull Dairycoates	**53A** Hull Dairycoates		
61847	*K3*	**MAR** March	**31B** March	**53A** Hull Dairycoates	**53A** Hull Dairycoates	**53A** Hull Dairycoates		
61848	*K3*	**NWE** New England	**39A** Gorton	**39A** Gorton	**40A** Lincoln	**40A** Lincoln		
61849	*K3*	**MAR** March	**30A** Stratford	**30A** Stratford	**30A** Stratford	**31A** Cambridge		
61850	*K3*	**NWE** New England	**35A** New England	**31B** March	**36B** Mexborough	**36A** Doncaster		
61851	*K3*	**CAR** Carlisle Canal	**12B** Carlisle Canal	**68E** Carlisle Canal	**68E** Carlisle Canal	**31B** March		
61852	*K3*	**LIN** Lincoln	**39A** Gorton	**39A** Gorton	**40B** Immingham	**40E** Colwick		
61853	*K3*	**NWE** New England	**35A** New England	**31B** March	**38E** Woodford Halse	**56B** Ardsley		
61854	*K3*	**CAR** Carlisle Canal	**12B** Carlisle Canal	**68E** Carlisle Canal	**68E** Carlisle Canal	**52D** Tweedmouth		
61855	*K3*	**STM** St. Margarets	**64A** St. Margarets	**64A** St. Margarets	**64A** St. Margarets			
61856	*K3*	**DON** Doncaster	**39A** Gorton	**39A** Gorton	**38B** Annesley	**56B** Ardsley		
61857	*K3*	**STM** St. Margarets	**64A** St. Margarets	**64A** St. Margarets	**64A** St. Margarets	**53A** Hull Dairycoates		
61858	*K3*	**CAR** Carlisle Canal	**12B** Carlisle Canal	**68E** Carlisle Canal	**68E** Carlisle Canal	**12C** Carlisle Canal		
61859	*K3*	**LIN** Lincoln	**40A** Lincoln	**40A** Lincoln	**40A** Lincoln	**40A** Lincoln		
61860	*K3*	**MAR** March	**31B** March	**31B** March	**31B** March	**31B** March		
61861	*K3*	**DON** Doncaster	**36A** Doncaster	**31B** March	**31B** March	**31B** March		
61862	*K3*	**NWE** New England	**35A** New England	**30A** Stratford	**30A** Stratford	**30F** Parkeston		
61863	*K5*	**NWE** New England	**35A** New England	**30A** Stratford	**30A** Stratford	**30A** Stratford		
61864	*K3*	**NWE** New England	**38A** Colwick	**31B** March	**35A** New England	**34E** New England		
61865	*K3*	**CLK** Colwick	**39A** Gorton	**39A** Gorton	**39A** Gorton	**9G** Gorton		
61866	*K3*	**MAR** March	**31B** March	**31B** March	**38E** Woodford Halse	**40B** Immingham		
61867	*K3*	**NWE** New England	**35A** New England	**31B** March	**36B** Mexborough	**36A** Doncaster		
61868	*K3*	**NWE** New England	**35A** New England	**31B** March	**36B** Mexborough	**36A** Doncaster		
61869	*K3*	**NWE** New England	**31B** March	**53A** Hull Dairycoates	**52B** Heaton	**52B** Heaton		
61870	*K3*	**WFD** Woodford Halse	**39A** Gorton	**39A** Gorton	**38A** Colwick	**40E** Colwick		
61871	*K3*	**HLD** Hull Dairycoates	**53A** Hull Dairycoates	**53A** Hull Dairycoates	**53A** Hull Dairycoates	**53A** Hull Dairycoates		
61872	*K3*	**HLD** Hull Dairycoates	**53A** Hull Dairycoates	**53A** Hull Dairycoates	**53A** Hull Dairycoates	**53A** Hull Dairycoates		
61873	*K3*	**MAR** March	**31B** March	**31B** March	**38A** Colwick	**40E** Colwick		
61874	*K3*	**HLD** Hull Dairycoates	**53A** Hull Dairycoates	**53A** Hull Dairycoates	**53A** Hull Dairycoates	**53A** Hull Dairycoates		
61875	*K3*	**GHD** Gateshead	**52B** Heaton	**52B** Heaton	**52B** Heaton	**52B** Heaton		
61876	*K3*	**STM** St. Margarets	**64A** St. Margarets	**64A** St. Margarets	**64A** St. Margarets			
61877	*K3*	**NWE** New England	**39A** Gorton	**32A** Norwich Thorpe	**32A** Norwich Thorpe	**32A** Norwich Thorpe		
61878	*K3*	**GHD** Gateshead	**64A** St. Margarets	**64A** St. Margarets	**64A** St. Margarets			
61879	*K3*	**STM** St. Margarets	**64A** St. Margarets	**64A** St. Margarets	**64A** St. Margarets			
61880	*K3*	**NWE** New England	**30A** Stratford	**30A** Stratford	**30A** Stratford	**31A** Cambridge		
61881	*K3*	**GHD** Gateshead	**64A** St. Margarets	**64A** St. Margarets	**64A** St. Margarets	**64A** St. Margarets		
61882	*K3*	**CAR** Carlisle Canal	**12B** Carlisle Canal	**68E** Carlisle Canal	**68E** Carlisle Canal	**2F** Woodford Halse		
61883	*K3*	**HLD** Hull Dairycoates	**53A** Hull Dairycoates	**53A** Hull Dairycoates	**53A** Hull Dairycoates	**53A** Hull Dairycoates		

No.	Class	1948	1951	1954	1957	1960	1963	1966
61884	*K3*	**HTN** Heaton	**52B** Heaton	**53A** Hull Dairycoates	**53A** Hull Dairycoates	**52B** Heaton		
61885	*K3*	**STM** St. Margarets	**64A** St. Margarets	**64A** St. Margarets	**64A** St. Margarets			
61886	*K3*	**MAR** March	**31B** March	**31B** March	**31B** March	**31B** March		
61887	*K3*	**MAR** March	**31B** March	**31B** March	**36A** Doncaster	**36A** Doncaster		
61888	*K3*	**MAR** March	**31B** March	**31B** March	**38A** Colwick	**40E** Colwick		
61889	*K3*	**MAR** March	**31B** March	**31B** March	**40A** Lincoln	**40A** Lincoln		
61890	*K3*	**NWE** New England	**35A** New England	**31B** March	**31B** March	**31B** March		
61891	*K3*	**IMM** Immingham	**40B** Immingham	**40B** Immingham	**40B** Immingham	**40B** Immingham		
61892	*K3*	**HLD** Hull Dairycoates	**53A** Hull Dairycoates	**53A** Hull Dairycoates	**53A** Hull Dairycoates	**53A** Hull Dairycoates		
61893	*K3*	**MAR** March	**31B** March	**53A** Hull Dairycoates	**53A** Hull Dairycoates	**53A** Hull Dairycoates		
61894	*K3*	**CLK** Colwick	**40A** Lincoln	**40A** Lincoln	**40A** Lincoln	**40A** Lincoln		
61895	*K3*	**ANN** Annesley	**31B** March	**31B** March	**36A** Doncaster	**36A** Doncaster		
61896	*K3*	**NWE** New England	**39A** Gorton	**39A** Gorton	**38A** Colwick	**40E** Colwick		
61897	*K3*	**GHD** Gateshead	**64A** St. Margarets	**64A** St. Margarets	**64A** St. Margarets	**53A** Hull Dairycoates		
61898	*K3*	**CAR** Carlisle Canal	**12B** Carlisle Canal	**68E** Carlisle Canal	**68E** Carlisle Canal			
61899	*K3*	**HLD** Hull Dairycoates	**53A** Hull Dairycoates	**52D** Tweedmouth	**53A** Hull Dairycoates	**53A** Hull Dairycoates		
61900	*K3*	**STM** St. Margarets	**64A** St. Margarets	**64A** St. Margarets	**64A** St. Margarets	**64A** St. Margarets		
61901	*K3*	**HTN** Heaton	**52B** Heaton	**52D** Tweedmouth	**52D** Tweedmouth	**52D** Tweedmouth		
61902	*K3*	**HLD** Hull Dairycoates	**53A** Hull Dairycoates	**53A** Hull Dairycoates	**53A** Hull Dairycoates	**53A** Hull Dairycoates		
61903	*K3*	**HLD** Hull Dairycoates	**53A** Hull Dairycoates	**53A** Hull Dairycoates	**53A** Hull Dairycoates	**53A** Hull Dairycoates		
61904	*K3*	**GHD** Gateshead	**52B** Heaton	**52B** Heaton	**53A** Hull Dairycoates	**53A** Hull Dairycoates		
61905	*K3*	**CLK** Colwick	**40B** Immingham	**40B** Immingham	**40B** Immingham	**40B** Immingham		
61906	*K3*	**HTN** Heaton	**52B** Heaton	**52B** Heaton	**52B** Heaton	**52B** Heaton		
61907	*K3*	**DON** Doncaster	**36A** Doncaster	**31B** March	**41A** Sheffield Darnall	**40E** Colwick		
61908	*K3*	**WFD** Woodford Halse	**39A** Gorton	**32A** Norwich Thorpe	**32A** Norwich Thorpe	**32A** Norwich Thorpe		
61909	*K3*	**STM** St. Margarets	**64A** St. Margarets	**64A** St. Margarets	**64A** St. Margarets	**64A** St. Margarets		
61910	*K3*	**DON** Doncaster	**39A** Gorton	**39A** Gorton	**39A** Gorton	**9G** Gorton		
61911	*K3*	**STM** St. Margarets	**64A** St. Margarets	**64A** St. Margarets	**64A** St. Margarets			
61912	*K3*	**IMM** Immingham	**40B** Immingham	**40B** Immingham	**40B** Immingham	**40B** Immingham		
61913	*K3*	**WFD** Woodford Halse	**39A** Gorton	**39A** Gorton	**39A** Gorton	**2F** Woodford Halse		
61914	*K3*	**MAR** March	**39A** Gorton	**39A** Gorton	**38A** Colwick	**40E** Colwick		
61915	*K3*	**NWE** New England	**35A** New England	**31B** March	**31B** March	**31B** March		
61916	*K3*	**STM** St. Margarets	**64A** St. Margarets	**68E** Carlisle Canal	**68E** Carlisle Canal	**12C** Carlisle Canal		
61917	*K3*	**HTN** Heaton	**52B** Heaton	**52D** Tweedmouth	**52D** Tweedmouth	**52D** Tweedmouth		
61918	*K3*	**DON** Doncaster	**36A** Doncaster	**32A** Norwich Thorpe	**32A** Norwich Thorpe	**32A** Norwich Thorpe		
61919	*K3*	**MAR** March	**39A** Gorton	**39A** Gorton	**40A** Lincoln	**40A** Lincoln		
61920	*K3*	**HLD** Hull Dairycoates	**53A** Hull Dairycoates	**53A** Hull Dairycoates	**53A** Hull Dairycoates	**53A** Hull Dairycoates		
61921	*K3*	**NOR** Norwich Thorpe	**32A** Norwich Thorpe	**30A** Stratford	**30A** Stratford	**30F** Parkeston		
61922	*K3*	**HLD** Hull Dairycoates	**53A** Hull Dairycoates	**53A** Hull Dairycoates	**53A** Hull Dairycoates	**53A** Hull Dairycoates		
61923	*K3*	**HLD** Hull Dairycoates	**53A** Hull Dairycoates	**53A** Hull Dairycoates	**53A** Hull Dairycoates	**52B** Heaton		
61924	*K3*	**STM** St. Margarets	**64A** St. Margarets	**64A** St. Margarets	**64A** St. Margarets	**64A** St. Margarets		
61925	*K3*	**LIN** Lincoln	**40A** Lincoln	**40A** Lincoln	**40A** Lincoln	**36A** Doncaster		
61926	*K3*	**LOW** Lowestoft	**32C** Lowestoft	**32C** Lowestoft	**32C** Lowestoft	**32A** Norwich Thorpe		
61927	*K3*	**HLD** Hull Dairycoates	**53A** Hull Dairycoates	**52B** Heaton	**52B** Heaton	**52B** Heaton		
61928	*K3*	**GHD** Gateshead	**64A** St. Margarets	**64A** St. Margarets	**64A** St. Margarets	**64A** St. Margarets		
61929	*K3*	**NWE** New England	**35A** New England	**31B** March	**31B** March	**31B** March		
61930	*K3*	**GHD** Gateshead	**52B** Heaton	**52D** Tweedmouth	**52D** Tweedmouth	**52D** Tweedmouth		
61931	*K3*	**STM** St. Margarets	**64A** St. Margarets	**64A** St. Margarets	**64A** St. Margarets			
61932	*K3*	**HLD** Hull Dairycoates	**53A** Hull Dairycoates	**52D** Tweedmouth	**53A** Hull Dairycoates	**53A** Hull Dairycoates		
61933	*K3*	**STM** St. Margarets	**64A** St. Margarets	**64A** St. Margarets	**64A** St. Margarets	**64A** St. Margarets		
61934	*K3*	**HLD** Hull Dairycoates	**53A** Hull Dairycoates	**53A** Hull Dairycoates	**53A** Hull Dairycoates	**52D** Tweedmouth		
61935	*K3*	**HLD** Hull Dairycoates	**53A** Hull Dairycoates	**53A** Hull Dairycoates	**53A** Hull Dairycoates	**53A** Hull Dairycoates		
61936	*K3*	**CAR** Carlisle Canal	**12B** Carlisle Canal	**68E** Carlisle Canal	**68E** Carlisle Canal	**12C** Carlisle Canal		
61937	*K3*	**CAR** Carlisle Canal	**12B** Carlisle Canal	**68E** Carlisle Canal	**68E** Carlisle Canal	**31B** March		
61938	*K3*	**NWE** New England	**31B** March	**31B** March	**41A** Sheffield Darnall	**41A** Sheffield Darnall		
61939	*K3*	**NOR** Norwich Thorpe	**32A** Norwich Thorpe	**32A** Norwich Thorpe	**32A** Norwich Thorpe	**32A** Norwich Thorpe		
61940	*K3*	**MAR** March	**31B** March	**31B** March	**36A** Doncaster	**36A** Doncaster		
61941	*K3*	**HLD** Hull Dairycoates	**53A** Hull Dairycoates	**53A** Hull Dairycoates	**53A** Hull Dairycoates	**53A** Hull Dairycoates		
61942	*K3*	**NOR** Norwich Thorpe	**32A** Norwich Thorpe	**30A** Stratford	**30A** Stratford	**30F** Parkeston		
61943	*K3*	**WFD** Woodford Halse	**38B** Annesley	**31B** March	**40F** Boston	**40E** Colwick		
61944	*K3*	**LIN** Lincoln	**40A** Lincoln	**40A** Lincoln	**40A** Lincoln	**40A** Lincoln		
61945	*K3*	**HLD** Hull Dairycoates	**53A** Hull Dairycoates	**53A** Hull Dairycoates	**53A** Hull Dairycoates	**53A** Hull Dairycoates		
61946	*K3*	**NWE** New England	**31B** March	**31B** March	**31B** March	**31B** March		
61947	*K3*	**NOR** Norwich Thorpe	**32A** Norwich Thorpe	**31B** March	**38A** Colwick	**40E** Colwick		
61948	*K3*	**MAR** March	**31B** March	**31B** March	**31B** March	**31B** March		
61949	*K3*	**LOW** Lowestoft	**32C** Lowestoft	**32C** Lowestoft	**32C** Lowestoft	**32A** Norwich Thorpe		
61950	*K3*	**NWE** New England	**39A** Gorton	**39A** Gorton	**40B** Immingham	**40B** Immingham		
61951	*K3*	**NWE** New England	**35A** New England	**30A** Stratford	**30A** Stratford	**30F** Parkeston		
61952	*K3*	**HTN** Heaton	**52B** Heaton	**52D** Tweedmouth	**52D** Tweedmouth	**52D** Tweedmouth		
61953	*K3*	**NOR** Norwich Thorpe	**32A** Norwich Thorpe	**32C** Lowestoft	**32A** Norwich Thorpe	**32A** Norwich Thorpe		
61954	*K3*	**NWE** New England	**35A** New England	**31B** March	**41A** Sheffield Darnall	**31B** March		
61955	*K3*	**STM** St. Margarets	**64A** St. Margarets	**64A** St. Margarets	**64A** St. Margarets	**64A** St. Margarets		
61956	*K3*	**WFD** Woodford Halse	**39A** Gorton	**40B** Immingham	**40B** Immingham	**40B** Immingham		
61957	*K3*	**NOR** Norwich Thorpe	**32A** Norwich Thorpe	**32A** Norwich Thorpe	**32A** Norwich Thorpe	**32A** Norwich Thorpe		
61958	*K3*	**LOW** Lowestoft	**32C** Lowestoft	**32C** Lowestoft	**32C** Lowestoft	**32C** Lowestoft		
61959	*K3*	**LOW** Lowestoft	**32C** Lowestoft	**32C** Lowestoft	**32C** Lowestoft	**32C** Lowestoft		
61960	*K3*	**LIN** Lincoln	**40A** Lincoln	**40A** Lincoln	**40A** Lincoln	**40A** Lincoln		
61961	*K3*	**NWE** New England	**31B** March	**31B** March	**36A** Doncaster	**36A** Doncaster		
61962	*K3*	**HTN** Heaton	**52B** Heaton	**52D** Tweedmouth	**52D** Tweedmouth	**52B** Heaton		
61963	*K3*	**IMM** Immingham	**40B** Immingham	**30A** Stratford	**30A** Stratford	**30F** Parkeston		
61964	*K3*	**LIN** Lincoln	**40A** Lincoln	**40A** Lincoln	**40A** Lincoln	**36A** Doncaster		
61965	*K3*	**HLD** Hull Dairycoates	**53A** Hull Dairycoates	**53A** Hull Dairycoates	**53A** Hull Dairycoates	**53A** Hull Dairycoates		
61966	*K3*	**LIN** Lincoln	**40A** Lincoln	**39A** Gorton	**39A** Gorton	**40B** Immingham		
61967	*K3*	**NWE** New England	**35A** New England	**31B** March	**41A** Sheffield Darnall	**41A** Sheffield Darnall		
61968	*K3*	**STM** St. Margarets	**64A** St. Margarets	**64A** St. Margarets	**64A** St. Margarets	**64A** St. Margarets		
61969	*K3*	**HTN** Heaton	**52B** Heaton	**52D** Tweedmouth	**52D** Tweedmouth	**52D** Tweedmouth		
61970	*K3*	**NOR** Norwich Thorpe	**32A** Norwich Thorpe	**32A** Norwich Thorpe	**32A** Norwich Thorpe	**32A** Norwich Thorpe		
61971	*K3*	**NOR** Norwich Thorpe	**32A** Norwich Thorpe	**32A** Norwich Thorpe	**32A** Norwich Thorpe	**32A** Norwich Thorpe		
61972	*K3*	**NWE** New England	**35A** New England	**31B** March	**31B** March	**31B** March		
61973	*K3*	**NOR** Norwich Thorpe	**32C** Lowestoft	**32C** Lowestoft	**32C** Lowestoft	**32A** Norwich Thorpe		
61974	*K3*	**ANN** Annesley	**38B** Annesley	**38B** Annesley	**38A** Colwick	**40E** Colwick		
61975	*K3*	**ANN** Annesley	**38B** Annesley	**38B** Annesley	**38B** Annesley	**56B** Ardsley		
61976	*K3*	**ANN** Annesley	**38B** Annesley	**31B** March	**31B** March	**31B** March		
61977	*K3*	**ANN** Annesley	**38B** Annesley	**30A** Stratford	**30A** Stratford	**30F** Parkeston		
61978	*K3*	**DON** Doncaster	**36A** Doncaster	**31B** March	**35A** New England	**34E** New England		
61979	*K3*	**ANN** Annesley	**38B** Annesley	**31B** March	**35A** New England	**34E** New England		
61980	*K3*	**ANN** Annesley	**38B** Annesley	**38B** Annesley	**38B** Annesley	**56B** Ardsley		
61981	*K3*	**LOW** Lowestoft	**32A** Norwich Thorpe	**32A** Norwich Thorpe	**32A** Norwich Thorpe	**32A** Norwich Thorpe		
61982	*K3*	**LIN** Lincoln	**38A** Colwick	**31B** March	**38A** Colwick	**40E** Colwick		
61983	*K3*	**STM** St. Margarets	**64A** St. Margarets	**64A** St. Margarets	**64A** St. Margarets			
61984	*K3*	**HTN** Heaton	**52B** Heaton	**52B** Heaton	**52B** Heaton	**52B** Heaton		
61985	*K3*	**GHD** Gateshead	**52B** Heaton	**52D** Tweedmouth	**52D** Tweedmouth	**52D** Tweedmouth		
61986	*K3*	**GHD** Gateshead	**52B** Heaton	**52B** Heaton	**52B** Heaton	**52B** Heaton		
61987	*K3*	**HTN** Heaton	**52B** Heaton	**52B** Heaton	**52B** Heaton	**52B** Heaton		
61988	*K3*	**STM** St. Margarets	**64A** St. Margarets	**64A** St. Margarets	**64A** St. Margarets			
61989	*K3*	**NOR** Norwich Thorpe	**32A** Norwich Thorpe	**32C** Lowestoft	**32A** Norwich Thorpe	**32A** Norwich Thorpe		
61990	*K3*	**STM** St. Margarets	**64A** St. Margarets	**64A** St. Margarets	**64A** St. Margarets	**64A** St. Margarets		
61991	*K3*	**STM** St. Margarets	**64A** St. Margarets	**64A** St. Margarets	**64A** St. Margarets			
61992	*K3*	**STM** St. Margarets	**64A** St. Margarets	**64A** St. Margarets	**64A** St. Margarets	**64A** St. Margarets		
61993	*K4*	**EFD** Eastfield	**65A** Eastfield	**65A** Eastfield	**65A** Eastfield	**62A** Thornton Junction		
61994	*K4*	**EFD** Eastfield	**65A** Eastfield	**65A** Eastfield	**65A** Eastfield	**62C** Dunfermline Upper		
61995	*K4*	**FW** Fort William	**63D** Fort William	**63D** Fort William	**65A** Eastfield	**62C** Dunfermline Upper		
61996	*K4*	**FW** Fort William	**63D** Fort William	**63D** Fort William	**65A** Eastfield	**62A** Thornton Junction		
61997	*K1/1*	**NWE** New England	**65A** Eastfield	**65A** Eastfield	**65J** Fort William	**65J** Fort William		

No.	Class	1948	1951	1954	1957	1960	1963	1966
61998	*K4*	EFD Eastfield	**65A** Eastfield	**65A** Eastfield	**65A** Eastfield	**62C** Dunfermline Upper		
62000	*D3*	GRA Grantham	**35B** Grantham					
62001	*K1*	→	**51E** Stockton on Tees	**51A** Darlington	**51A** Darlington	**51L** Thornaby	**51L** Thornaby	**51A** Darlington
62002	*K1*	→	**52B** Heaton	**52C** Blaydon	**52C** Blaydon	**52C** Blaydon	**52K** Consett	**52F** South Blyth
62003	*K1*	→	**52B** Heaton	**51A** Darlington	**51A** Darlington	**51L** Thornaby	**51J** Northallerton	
62004	*K1*	→	**51A** Darlington	**51A** Darlington	**51A** Darlington	**51A** Darlington	**51A** Darlington	**51C** West Hartlepool
62005	*K1*	→	**52B** Heaton	**51A** Darlington	**51A** Darlington	**50A** York	**50A** York	**50A** York
62006	*K1*	→	**51A** Darlington	**51A** Darlington	**52C** Blaydon	**52C** Blaydon	**52D** Alnmouth	**52D** Alnmouth
62007	*K1*	→	**52B** Heaton	**51A** Darlington	**51A** Darlington	**51A** Darlington	**51A** Darlington	**52G** Sunderland
62008	*K1*	→	**51A** Darlington	**51A** Darlington	**51A** Darlington	**51A** Darlington	**51A** Darlington	**51A** Darlington
62009	*K1*	→	**51A** Darlington	**51A** Darlington	**51A** Darlington	**50A** York	**50A** York	
62010	*K1*	→	**52B** Heaton	**52C** Blaydon	**52C** Blaydon	**52C** Blaydon	**52A** Gateshead	
62011	*K1*	→	**31B** March	**63D** Fort William	**65J** Fort William	**65J** Fort William	**52D** Alnmouth	**52D** Alnmouth
62012	*K1*	→	**31B** March	**63D** Fort William	**65J** Fort William	**65J** Fort William	**52D** Alnmouth	**50A** York
62013	*K1*	→	**31B** March	**31B** March	**31B** March	**30A** Stratford	**36C** Frodingham	
62014	*K1*	→	**31B** March	**31B** March	**31B** March	**30A** Stratford	**36A** Doncaster	
62015	*K1*	→	**31B** March	**31B** March	**31B** March	**30A** Stratford	**36A** Doncaster	
62016	*K1*	→	**31B** March	**31B** March	**31B** March	**31B** March	**36C** Frodingham	
62017	*K1*	→	**31B** March	**31B** March	**31B** March	**31B** March	**36C** Frodingham	**52F** North Blyth
62018	*K1*	→	**31B** March	**31B** March	**31B** March	**31B** March	**36C** Frodingham	
62019	*K1*	→	**31B** March	**31B** March	**31B** March	**30A** Stratford	**36E** Retford	
62020	*K1*	→	**31B** March	**31B** March	**31B** March	**31B** March	**36C** Frodingham	
62021	*K1*	→	**52C** Blaydon	**52C** Blaydon	**52C** Blaydon	**52C** Blaydon	**52D** Alnmouth	**52D** Alnmouth
62022	*K1*	→	**52C** Blaydon	**52C** Blaydon	**52C** Blaydon	**52C** Blaydon	**52K** Consett	**52F** North Blyth
62023	*K1*	→	**52C** Blaydon	**52C** Blaydon	**52C** Blaydon	**52C** Blaydon	**52D** Alnmouth	**52D** Alnmouth
62024	*K1*	→	**52C** Blaydon	**52C** Blaydon	**52C** Blaydon	**52C** Blaydon	**52A** Gateshead	**52F** North Blyth
62025	*K1*	→	**52C** Blaydon	**52C** Blaydon	**52C** Blaydon	**52C** Blaydon	**52D** Alnmouth	**52D** Alnmouth
62026	*K1*	→	**52C** Blaydon	**52C** Blaydon	**52C** Blaydon	**52C** Blaydon	**52A** Gateshead	**52G** Sunderland
62027	*K1*	→	**52C** Blaydon	**52C** Blaydon	**52C** Blaydon	**52C** Blaydon	**52K** Consett	**52F** North Blyth
62028	*K1*	→	**52C** Blaydon	**52C** Blaydon	**52C** Blaydon	**52C** Blaydon	**52A** Gateshead	**50A** York
62029	*K1*	→	**52C** Blaydon	**52C** Blaydon	**52C** Blaydon	**52C** Blaydon	**52A** Gateshead	
62030	*K1*	→	**52C** Blaydon	**52C** Blaydon	**52C** Blaydon	**52C** Blaydon	**52D** Alnmouth	
62031	*K1*	→	**31B** March	**65A** Eastfield	**65J** Fort William	**65J** Fort William		
62032	*K1*	→	**31B** March	**31B** March	**31B** March	**31B** March	**36C** Frodingham	
62033	*K1*	→	**31B** March	**31B** March	**31B** March	**31B** March	**36C** Frodingham	
62034	*K1*	→	**31B** March	**65A** Eastfield	**65J** Fort William	**65J** Fort William		
62035	*K1*	→	**31B** March	**31B** March	**31B** March	**31B** March	**36C** Frodingham	
62036	*K1*	→	**31B** March	**31B** March	**31B** March	**30A** Stratford	**36A** Doncaster	
62037	*K1*	→	**31B** March	**31B** March	**31B** March	**31B** March	**36A** Doncaster	
62038	*K1*	→	**31B** March	**31B** March	**31B** March	**31B** March	**36A** Doncaster	
62039	*K1*	→	**31B** March	**31B** March	**31B** March	**31B** March	**36E** Retford	
62040	*K1*	→	**31B** March	**31B** March	**31B** March	**31B** March	**36A** Doncaster	
62041	*K1*	→	**51E** Stockton on Tees	**51E** Stockton on Tees	**51E** Stockton on Tees	**51A** Darlington	**51A** Darlington	**51A** Darlington
62042	*K1*	→	**51E** Stockton on Tees	**51E** Stockton on Tees	**51E** Stockton on Tees	**51L** Thornaby	**50A** York	**50A** York
62043	*K1*	→	**51E** Stockton on Tees	**51E** Stockton on Tees	**51E** Stockton on Tees	**51A** Darlington	**51A** Darlington	
62044	*K1*	→	**51A** Darlington	**51J** Northallerton	**51J** Northallerton	**51J** Northallerton	**51J** Northallerton	**51A** Darlington
62045	*K1*	→	**51A** Darlington	**51A** Darlington	**51A** Darlington	**51A** Darlington	**51A** Darlington	**51A** Darlington
62046	*K1*	→	**51A** Darlington	**51A** Darlington	**50A** York	**50A** York	**50A** York	**50A** York
62047	*K1*	→	**51A** Darlington	**51A** Darlington	**50A** York	**50A** York	**50A** York	
62048	*K1*	→	**52B** Heaton	**51G** Haverton Hill	**50A** York	**51A** Darlington	**51A** Darlington	**51A** Darlington
62049	*K1*	→	**52B** Heaton	**51A** Darlington	**50A** York	**50A** York	**50A** York	
62050	*K1*	→	**52B** Heaton	**51G** Haverton Hill	**50A** York	**52C** Blaydon	**52K** Consett	**52D** Alnmouth
62051	*K1*	→	**31B** March	**31B** March	**31B** March	**31B** March	**36A** Doncaster	
62052	*K1*	→	**31B** March	**65A** Eastfield	**65J** Fort William	**65J** Fort William		
62053	*K1*	→	**31B** March	**31B** March	**31B** March	**30A** Stratford	**36A** Doncaster	
62054	*K1*	→	**31B** March	**31B** March	**31B** March	**31B** March	**36E** Retford	
62055	*K1*	→	**31B** March	**31B** March	**31B** March	**31B** March	**36A** Doncaster	
62056	*K1*	→	**51A** Darlington	**51G** Haverton Hill	**50A** York	**50A** York	**50A** York	
62057	*K1*	→	**51A** Darlington	**51G** Haverton Hill	**50A** York	**50A** York	**50A** York	**50A** York
62058	*K1*	→	**51A** Darlington	**51G** Haverton Hill	**51G** Haverton Hill	**51A** Darlington	**51A** Darlington	
62059	*K1*	→	**51A** Darlington	**51G** Haverton Hill	**51G** Haverton Hill	**51A** Darlington	**51A** Darlington	**51A** Darlington
62060	*K1*	→	**51E** Stockton on Tees	**51E** Stockton on Tees	**51E** Stockton on Tees	**52C** Blaydon	**52K** Consett	**50A** York
62061	*K1*	→	**51A** Darlington	**51G** Haverton Hill	**50A** York	**50A** York	**50A** York	
62062	*K1*	→	**51A** Darlington	**51A** Darlington	**50A** York	**51A** Darlington	**51A** Darlington	**50A** York
62063	*K1*	→	**51E** Stockton on Tees	**51A** Darlington	**50A** York	**50A** York	**50A** York	
62064	*K1*	→	**51E** Stockton on Tees	**51E** Stockton on Tees	**51E** Stockton on Tees	**51A** Darlington	**51A** Darlington	
62065	*K1*	→	**51E** Stockton on Tees	**51E** Stockton on Tees	**51E** Stockton on Tees	**50A** York	**50A** York	**50A** York
62066	*K1*	→	**31B** March	**31B** March	**31B** March	**31B** March	**36A** Doncaster	
62067	*K1*	→	**31B** March	**31B** March	**31B** March	**31B** March	**36E** Retford	**52F** North Blyth
62068	*K1*	→	**31B** March	**31B** March	**31B** March	**31B** March	**36A** Doncaster	
62069	*K1*	→	**31B** March	**31B** March	**31B** March	**31B** March	**36A** Doncaster	
62070	*K1*	→	**31B** March	**31B** March	**31B** March	**30A** Stratford	**36E** Retford	
62059	*D31*	CAR Carlisle Canal	(62281)					
62060	*D31*	CAR Carlisle Canal	(62282)					
62062	*D31*	KIT Kittybrewster						
62064	*D31*	KIT Kittybrewster						
62065	*D31*	KIT Kittybrewster						
62066	*D31*	KIT Kittybrewster						
62072	*D31*	BGT Bathgate	(62283)					
62111	*D17*	YK York						
62112	*D17*	YK York						
62116	*D3*	CLK Colwick						
62122	*D3*	SL South Lynn						
62123	*D3*	CLK Colwick						
62124	*D3*	SL South Lynn						
62125	*D3*	CLK Colwick						
62126	*D3*	CLK Colwick						
62128	*D3*	NWE New England						
62131	*D3*	NWE New England						
62132	*D3*	IMM Immingham						
62133	*D3*	STV Staveley						
62135	*D3*	CLK Colwick						
62137	*D3*	SL South Lynn						
62139	*D3*	IMM Immingham						
62140	*D3*	CLK Colwick						
62143	*D3*	LTH Louth						
62144	*D3*	SL South Lynn						
62145	*D3*	SL South Lynn						
62148	*D3*	HIT Hitchin						
62150	*D2*	CLK Colwick						
62151	*D2*	CLK Colwick						
62152	*D2*	YB Yarmouth Beach						
62153	*D2*	CLK Colwick						
62154	*D2*	BOS Boston						
62155	*D2*	MC Melton Constable						
62156	*D2*	MC Melton Constable						
62157	*D2*	MC Melton Constable						
62160	*D2*	HIT Hitchin						
62161	*D2*	GRA Grantham						
62163	*D2*	HIT Hitchin						
62165	*D2*	NWE New England						
62167	*D2*	GRA Grantham						
62169	*D2*	CLK Colwick						
62172	*D2*	GRA Grantham	**38A** Colwick					

		1948	1951	1954	1957	1960	1963	1966
62173	*D2*	GRA Grantham						
62175	*D2*	YB Yarmouth Beach						
62177	*D2*	CLK Colwick						
62179	*D2*	BOS Boston						
62180	*D2*	BOS Boston						
62181	*D2*	BOS Boston						
62187	*D2*	CLK Colwick						
62188	*D2*	CLK Colwick						
62189	*D2*	MC Melton Constable						
62190	*D2*	NWE New England						
62193	*D2*	CLK Colwick						
62194	*D2*	CLK Colwick						
62195	*D2*	MC Melton Constable						
62197	*D2*	MC Melton Constable						
62198	*D2*	CLK Colwick						
62199	*D2*	CLK Colwick						
62203	*D1*	NOR Norwich Thorpe						
62205	*D1*	DFU Dunfermline Upper						
62207	*D1*	YB Yarmouth Beach						
62208	*D1*	HAW Hawick						
62209	*D1*	STG Stirling Shore Road						
62214	*D1*	HAY Haymarket						
62215	*D1*	PTH Perth South						
62225	*D41*	KIT Kittybrewster	**61C** Keith					
62227	*D41*	KIT Kittybrewster	**61C** Keith					
62228	*D41*	KIT Kittybrewster	**61A** Kittybrewster					
62229	*D41*	KIT Kittybrewster	**61A** Kittybrewster					
62230	*D41*	KIT Kittybrewster	**61C** Keith					
62231	*D41*	KIT Kittybrewster	**61C** Keith					
62232	*D41*	KIT Kittybrewster	**61C** Keith					
62234	*D41*	KEI Keith						
62235	*D41*	KEI Keith						
62238	*D41*	KEI Keith						
62240	*D41*	KEI Keith						
62241	*D41*	KIT Kittybrewster	**61A** Kittybrewster					
62242	*D41*	KIT Kittybrewster	**61C** Keith					
62243	*D41*	KEI Keith	**61C** Keith					
62246	*D41*	KEI Keith	**61C** Keith					
62247	*D41*	KEI Keith						
62248	*D41*	KEI Keith	**61C** Keith					
62249	*D41*	KEI Keith						
62251	*D41*	KEI Keith	**61C** Keith					
62252	*D41*	KEI Keith	**61C** Keith					
62255	*D41*	KEI Keith	**61C** Keith					
62256	*D41*	KEI Keith	**61C** Keith					
62260	*D40*	KIT Kittybrewster	**61A** Kittybrewster					
62261	*D40*	KIT Kittybrewster	**61A** Kittybrewster					
62262	*D40*	KEI Keith	**61C** Keith	**61C** Keith				
62264	*D40*	KEI Keith	**61C** Keith	**61C** Keith	**61C** Keith			
62265	*D40*	KIT Kittybrewster	**61A** Kittybrewster	**61C** Keith				
62267	*D40*	KEI Keith	**61C** Keith	**61C** Keith				
62268	*D40*	KIT Kittybrewster	**61A** Kittybrewster	**61C** Keith				
62269	*D40*	KIT Kittybrewster	**61C** Keith	**61C** Keith				
62270	*D40*	KIT Kittybrewster	**61A** Kittybrewster					
62271	*D40*	KIT Kittybrewster	**61C** Keith	**61C** Keith				
62272	*D40*	KIT Kittybrewster	**61A** Kittybrewster	**61C** Keith				
62273	*D40*	KIT Kittybrewster	**61A** Kittybrewster	**61C** Keith				
62274	*D40*	KIT Kittybrewster	**61A** Kittybrewster	**61C** Keith				
62275	*D40*	KIT Kittybrewster	**61A** Kittybrewster	**61C** Keith				
62276	*D40*	KIT Kittybrewster	**61A** Kittybrewster	**61A** Kittybrewster				
62277	*D40*	KIT Kittybrewster	**61A** Kittybrewster	**61C** Keith	**61C** Keith	(49)		
62278	*D40*	KIT Kittybrewster	**61A** Kittybrewster	**61A** Kittybrewster				
62279	*D40*	KIT Kittybrewster	**61A** Kittybrewster	**61A** Kittybrewster				
62281	*D31*	(62059)	**12B** Carlisle Canal					
62282	*D31*	(62060)						
62283	*D31*	(62072)	**64F** Bathgate					
62300	*D9*	TFD Trafford Park						
62301	*D9*	TFD Trafford Park						
62302	*D9*	LIV Brunswick						
62303	*D9*	LIV Brunswick						
62304	*D9*	LIV Brunswick						
62305	*D9*	TFD Trafford Park						
62306	*D9*	LIV Brunswick						
62307	*D9*	TFD Trafford Park						
62308	*D9*	LIV Brunswick						
62309	*D9*	LIV Brunswick						
62311	*D9*	WAL Walton on the Hill						
62312	*D9*	TFD Trafford Park						
62313	*D9*	TFD Trafford Park						
62314	*D9*	STP Heaton Mersey						
62315	*D9*	LIV Brunswick						
62317	*D9*	TFD Trafford Park						
62318	*D9*	LIV Brunswick						
62319	*D9*	LIV Brunswick						
62321	*D9*	LIV Brunswick						
62322	*D9*	STP Heaton Mersey						
62324	*D9*	LIV Brunswick						
62325	*D9*	TFD Trafford Park						
62329	*D9*	TFD Trafford Park						
62330	*D9*	TFD Trafford Park						
62332	*D9*	LIV Brunswick						
62333	*D9*	LIV Brunswick						
62340	*D20*	SEL Selby	**50C** Selby					
62341	*D20*	SEL Selby	**50C** Selby					
62342	*D20*	SBK Starbeck	**50C** Selby					
62343	*D20*	SBK Starbeck	**50C** Selby	**50A** York				
62344	*D20*	TWD Tweedmouth	**52D** Alnmouth					
62345	*D20*	BRI Bridlington	**53B** Hull Botanic Gardens	**50A** York				
62347	*D20*	ALN Alnmouth	**51J** Northallerton	**51J** Northallerton				
62348	*D20*	SEL Selby	**50C** Selby					
62349	*D20*	BLA Blaydon	**52D** Alnmouth	**52D** Alnmouth				
62351	*D20*	ALN Alnmouth	**52D** Alnmouth	**52D** Alnmouth				
62352	*D20*	ALN Alnmouth	**52D** Alnmouth	**52D** Alnmouth				
62353	*D20*	BRI Bridlington	**53D** Bridlington					
62354	*D20*	TWD Tweedmouth	**52D** Alnmouth					
62355	*D20*	HLB Hull Botanic Gardens	**53D** Bridlington	**52D** Alnmouth				
62357	*D20*	DNS Duns	**52D** Alnmouth					
62358	*D20*	TWD Tweedmouth	**52D** Alnmouth	**52D** Alnmouth				
62359	*D20*	WHL West Hartlepool	**51J** Northallerton	**51C** West Hartlepool				
62360	*D20*	BLA Blaydon	**52D** Alnmouth	**52A** Gateshead				
62361	*D20*	HLB Hull Botanic Gardens	**50C** Selby					
62362	*D20*	ALN Alnmouth	**52D** Alnmouth					
62363	*D20*	SBK Starbeck	**50C** Selby					
62365	*D20*	SKN Stockton on Tees	**52D** Alnmouth					

No.	Class	1948	1951	1954	1957	1960	1963	1966
62366	D20	SBK Starbeck	50C Selby					
62367	D20	HLB Hull Botanic Gardens						
62369	D20	HLB Hull Botanic Gardens	50D Starbeck					
62370	D20	SBK Starbeck	50D Starbeck					
62371	D20	BLA Blaydon	52D Alnmouth	52A Gateshead				
62372	D20	SEL Selby	51C West Hartlepool	51J Northallerton				
62373	D20	SBK Starbeck	50D Starbeck					
62374	D20	SEL Selby	50C Selby	50C Selby				
62375	D20	SBK Starbeck	53D Bridlington	52A Gateshead	52D Alnmouth			
62376	D20	SEL Selby	50C Selby					
62377	D20	ALN Alnmouth						
62378	D20	SEL Selby	50C Selby	50C Selby				
62379	D20	YK York	51C West Hartlepool					
62380	D20	ALN Alnmouth	52D Alnmouth	52D Alnmouth				
62381	D20	SEL Selby	50C Selby	50C Selby	53B Hull Botanic Gardens			
62382	D20	HLB Hull Botanic Gardens	50C Selby					
62383	D20	BRI Bridlington	53B Hull Botanic Gardens	52D Alnmouth	52D Alnmouth			
62384	D20	WHL West Hartlepool	50C Selby	50C Selby				
62386	D20	SEL Selby	50C Selby	50C Selby				
62387	D20	WHL West Hartlepool	52D Alnmouth	52B Heaton	50C Selby			
62388	D20	NLN Northallerton	51J Northallerton	51J Northallerton				
62389	D20	SBK Starbeck	50D Starbeck	50D Leeds Neville Hill				
62390	D20	SKN Stockton on Tees						
62391	D20	NLN Northallerton	51J Northallerton					
62392	D20	SBK Starbeck	50D Starbeck	50C Selby				
62395	D20	SBK Starbeck	50C Selby	50C Selby	50A York			
62396	D20	ALN Alnmouth	53B Hull Botanic Gardens	52D Alnmouth	53B Hull Botanic Gardens			
62397	D20	NLN Northallerton	50C Selby	50B Leeds Neville Hill	53D Bridlington			
62400	D29	STM St. Margarets						
62401	D29	THJ Thornton Junction						
62402	D29	STM St. Margarets						
62403	D29	HAY Haymarket						
62404	D29	STM St. Margarets						
62405	D29	STM St. Margarets	64B Haymarket					
62406	D29	THJ Thornton Junction						
62409	D29	DEE Dundee Tay Bridge						
62410	D29	DEE Dundee Tay Bridge	62A Thornton Junction					
62411	D29	POL Polmont	62A Thornton Junction					
62412	D29	DEE Dundee Tay Bridge						
62413	D29	HAY Haymarket						
62417	D30	HAW Hawick	64G Hawick					
62418	D30	DEE Dundee Tay Bridge	62A Thornton Junction	62A Thornton Junction	62A Thornton Junction			
62419	D30	THJ Thornton Junction	62A Thornton Junction	62A Thornton Junction	62A Thornton Junction			
62420	D30	STM St. Margarets	64G Hawick	64G Hawick	64G Hawick			
62421	D30	STM St. Margarets	64A St. Margarets	64A St. Margarets	64A St. Margarets	64A St. Margarets		
62422	D30	HAW Hawick	64G Hawick	64G Hawick	64G Hawick			
62423	D30	HAW Hawick	64G Hawick	64G Hawick	64G Hawick			
62424	D30	STM St. Margarets	64A St. Margarets	64A St. Margarets	64A St. Margarets			
62425	D30	HAW Hawick	64G Hawick	64G Hawick	64G Hawick			
62426	D30	PTH Perth South	63B Stirling	63B Stirling	63B Stirling	63B Stirling		
62427	D30	PTH Perth South	62B Dundee Tay Bridge	62C Dunfermline Upper	62C Dunfermline Upper			
62428	D30	HAW Hawick	64G Hawick	64G Hawick	64G Hawick			
62429	D30	THJ Thornton Junction	62A Thornton Junction	62A Thornton Junction	62A Thornton Junction			
62430	D30	THJ Thornton Junction	62A Thornton Junction	62A Thornton Junction	62A Thornton Junction			
62431	D30	THJ Thornton Junction	62A Thornton Junction	62A Thornton Junction	62A Thornton Junction			
62432	D30	HAW Hawick	64G Hawick	64G Hawick	64G Hawick			
62434	D30	DEE Dundee Tay Bridge	62B Dundee Tay Bridge	62B Dundee Tay Bridge	62B Dundee Tay Bridge			
62435	D30	STM St. Margarets	64A St. Margarets	64G Hawick	64G Hawick			
62436	D30	THJ Thornton Junction	62B Dundee Tay Bridge	62C Dunfermline Upper	62C Dunfermline Upper			
62437	D30	HAY Haymarket	64B Haymarket	64B Haymarket	64B Haymarket			
62438	D30	DEE Dundee Tay Bridge	62B Dundee Tay Bridge	62B Dundee Tay Bridge	62B Dundee Tay Bridge			
62439	D30	BGT Bathgate	64F Bathgate	64F Bathgate	64F Bathgate			
62440	D30	HAW Hawick	64G Hawick	64G Hawick	64G Hawick			
62441	D30	DFU Dunfermline Upper	62C Dunfermline Upper	62C Dunfermline Upper	62C Dunfermline Upper			
62442	D30	THJ Thornton Junction	62A Thornton Junction	62A Thornton Junction	62A Thornton Junction			
62443	D32	STM St. Margarets						
62444	D32	STM St. Margarets						
62445	D32	STM St. Margarets						
62446	D32	THJ Thornton Junction						
62448	D32	BLA Blaydon						
62449	D32	BLA Blaydon						
62450	D32	STM St. Margarets						
62451	D32	STM St. Margarets	64A St. Margarets					
62453	D32	STM St. Margarets						
62454	D32	STM St. Margarets						
62455	D33	DFU Dunfermline Upper						
62457	D33	PTH Perth South	62B Dundee Tay Bridge					
62458	D33	BGT Bathgate						
62459	D33	DFU Dunfermline Upper	62C Dunfermline Upper					
62460	D33	EFD Eastfield	65A Eastfield					
62461	D33	STG Stirling Shore Road	63B Stirling					
62462	D33	EFD Eastfield	65A Eastfield					
62463	D33	BGT Bathgate						
62464	D33	DFU Dunfermline Upper	62C Dunfermline Upper					
62466	D33	PTH Perth South	62C Dunfermline Upper					
62467	D34	THJ Thornton Junction	62A Thornton Junction	62A Thornton Junction	62A Thornton Junction	62A Thornton Junction		
62468	D34	THJ Thornton Junction	62A Thornton Junction	62A Thornton Junction	62A Thornton Junction			
62469	D34	EFD Eastfield	65A Eastfield	61A Kittybrewster	61C Keith	(256)		
62470	D34	FW Fort William	65A Eastfield	63A Perth	63A Perth			
62471	D34	STM St. Margarets	64A St. Margarets	64A St. Margarets	64A St. Margarets	64A St. Margarets		
62472	D34	EFD Eastfield	65A Eastfield	65A Eastfield	65A Eastfield			
62473	D34	EFD Eastfield						
62474	D34	EFD Eastfield	65A Eastfield	65A Eastfield	65A Eastfield	65A Eastfield		
62475	D34	THJ Thornton Junction	62A Thornton Junction	62A Thornton Junction	62A Thornton Junction			
62476	D34	POL Polmont						
62477	D34	EFD Eastfield	65A Eastfield	65A Eastfield	65A Eastfield			
62478	D34	THJ Thornton Junction	62A Thornton Junction	62A Thornton Junction	62A Thornton Junction			
62479	D34	EFD Eastfield	65A Eastfield	61A Kittybrewster	61A Kittybrewster	61A Kittybrewster		
62480	D34	FW Fort William	65A Eastfield	61A Kittybrewster	61A Kittybrewster			
62481	D34	EFD Eastfield						
62482	D34	EFD Eastfield	65A Eastfield	61A Kittybrewster	61A Kittybrewster	61A Kittybrewster		
62483	D34	STM St. Margarets	64A St. Margarets	64A St. Margarets	64A St. Margarets			
62484	D34	STM St. Margarets	64A St. Margarets	63A Perth	63A Perth	63A Perth		
62485	D34	DEE Dundee Tay Bridge	62B Dundee Tay Bridge	62B Dundee Tay Bridge	62B Dundee Tay Bridge	62C Dunfermline Upper		
62487	D34	STM St. Margarets	64A St. Margarets	64A St. Margarets	64A St. Margarets			
62488	D34	STM St. Margarets	64A St. Margarets	64A St. Margarets	64A St. Margarets	64G Hawick		
62489	D34	EFD Eastfield	65A Eastfield	61A Kittybrewster	61A Kittybrewster			
62490	D34	STM St. Margarets	64A St. Margarets	64A St. Margarets	64A St. Margarets			
62492	D34	THJ Thornton Junction	62A Thornton Junction	62A Thornton Junction	62A Thornton Junction			
62493	D34	EFD Eastfield	65A Eastfield	61A Kittybrewster	61A Kittybrewster	61A Kittybrewster		
62494	D34	STM St. Margarets	64A St. Margarets	64A St. Margarets	64A St. Margarets			
62495	D34	STM St. Margarets	64F Bathgate	64F Bathgate	64F Bathgate	64F Bathgate		
62496	D34	EFD Eastfield	65A Eastfield	65A Eastfield	65A Eastfield	65A Eastfield		
62497	D34	EFD Eastfield	65A Eastfield	65A Eastfield	65A Eastfield	65A Eastfield		

		1948		1951	1954	1957	1960	1963	1966
62498	D34	EFD	Eastfield	65A Eastfield	65A Eastfield	61A Kittybrewster	61A Kittybrewster		
62501	D15	KL	Kings Lynn	31C Kings Lynn					
62502	D15	KL	Kings Lynn	31C Kings Lynn					
62503	D15	BSE	Bury St. Edmunds	31E Bury St. Edmunds					
62504	D15	KL	Kings Lynn						
62505	D15	KL	Kings Lynn	31C Kings Lynn					
62506	D15	KL	Kings Lynn	31C Kings Lynn					
62507	D15	KL	Kings Lynn	31D South Lynn					
62508	D15	BSE	Bury St. Edmunds						
62509	D15	STR	Stratford	32G Melton Constable					
62510	D16/3	NOR	Norwich Thorpe	32A Norwich Thorpe	32A Norwich Thorpe	31A Cambridge			
62511	D16/3	NOR	Norwich Thorpe	32D Yarmouth South Town	32D Yarmouth South Town	32D Yarmouth South Town			
62512	D15	KL	Kings Lynn						
62513	D16/3	KL	Kings Lynn	31C Kings Lynn	31E Bury St. Edmunds	31E Bury St. Edmunds			
62514	D16/3	KL	Kings Lynn	31C Kings Lynn	31C Kings Lynn	31C Kings Lynn			
62515	D16/3	MC	Melton Constable	32G Melton Constable	32G Melton Constable	32G Melton Constable			
62516	D16/3	CAM	Cambridge	31A Cambridge	31C Kings Lynn	31C Kings Lynn			
62517	D16/3	YAR	Yarmouth South Town	32D Yarmouth South Town	32D Yarmouth South Town	32F Yarmouth Beach			
62518	D16/3	KL	Kings Lynn	31C Kings Lynn	31C Kings Lynn	31C Kings Lynn			
62519	D16/3	COL	Colchester	32G Melton Constable	32G Melton Constable	32G Melton Constable			
62520	D15	MC	Melton Constable	32G Melton Constable					
62521	D16/3	YAR	Yarmouth South Town	32D Yarmouth South Town	31A Cambridge	31A Cambridge			
62522	D16/3	NOR	Norwich Thorpe	32A Norwich Thorpe	32A Norwich Thorpe	31C Kings Lynn			
62523	D16/3	COL	Colchester	32G Melton Constable	32A Norwich Thorpe				
62524	D16/3	YAR	Yarmouth South Town	32D Yarmouth South Town	32D Yarmouth South Town	32D Yarmouth South Town	32A Norwich Thorpe		
62525	D16/3	CAM	Cambridge	31A Cambridge	31A Cambridge				
62526	D16/3	IPS	Ipswich	32B Ipswich	31B March	31B March			
62527	D16/3	CAM	Cambridge	31A Cambridge					
62528	D15	MC	Melton Constable	32G Melton Constable					
62529	D16/3	NOR	Norwich Thorpe	31B March	31B March	31B March			
62530	D16/3	CAM	Cambridge	31A Cambridge	31A Cambridge	31A Cambridge			
62531	D16/3	CAM	Cambridge	31A Cambridge	31A Cambridge				
62532	D16/3	STR	Stratford	9E Trafford Park	31A Cambridge				
62533	D16/3	MC	Melton Constable	32G Melton Constable	32G Melton Constable	32G Melton Constable			
62534	D16/3	SL	South Lynn	31D South Lynn	31C Kings Lynn	31C Kings Lynn			
62535	D16/3	NOR	Norwich Thorpe	9E Trafford Park	35C Spital Bridge	35C Spital Bridge			
62536	D16/3	CAM	Cambridge	9E Trafford Park	35C Spital Bridge				
62538	D15	STR	Stratford	32G Melton Constable					
62539	D16/3	MAR	March	31B March	31B March	31A Cambridge			
62540	D16/3	YAR	Yarmouth South Town	32A Norwich Thorpe	32A Norwich Thorpe	32A Norwich Thorpe			
62541	D16/3	NOR	Norwich Thorpe	32A Norwich Thorpe	31E Bury St. Edmunds				
62542	D16/3	MAR	March	31B March	31B March				
62543	D16/2→3	SL	South Lynn	31A Cambridge	31E Bury St. Edmunds	31E Bury St. Edmunds			
62544	D16/3	YAR	Yarmouth South Town	32D Yarmouth South Town	32D Yarmouth South Town	32D Yarmouth South Town			
62545	D16/3	NOR	Norwich Thorpe	32A Norwich Thorpe	31E Bury St. Edmunds	31C Kings Lynn			
62546	D16/3	YAR	Yarmouth South Town	32D Yarmouth South Town	32D Yarmouth South Town	32D Yarmouth South Town			
62547	D16/2	MAR	March	31B March					
62548	D16/3	MAR	March	31B March	31B March	31B March			
62549	D16/3	CAM	Cambridge	31A Cambridge	31A Cambridge				
62551	D16/3	CAM	Cambridge	31A Cambridge	31A Cambridge				
62552	D16/2→3	IPS	Ipswich	32A Norwich Thorpe	32A Norwich Thorpe				
62553	D16/2→3	YAR	Yarmouth South Town	32A Norwich Thorpe	32A Norwich Thorpe	31A Cambridge			
62554	D16/3	NOR	Norwich Thorpe	32A Norwich Thorpe	32A Norwich Thorpe				
62555	D16/3	NOR	Norwich Thorpe	32A Norwich Thorpe	32A Norwich Thorpe	32A Norwich Thorpe			
62556	D16/3	IPS	Ipswich	32C Lowestoft	32A Norwich Thorpe	32A Norwich Thorpe			
62557	D16/3	CAM	Cambridge	31A Cambridge	31A Cambridge				
62558	D16/2→3	SL	South Lynn	31D South Lynn	31A Cambridge	31C Kings Lynn			
62559	D16/3	SL	South Lynn	31C Kings Lynn	31C Kings Lynn				
62560	D16/3	IPS	Ipswich						
62561	D16/3	YB	Yarmouth Beach	32F Yarmouth Beach	32A Norwich Thorpe	32G Melton Constable			
62562	D16/3	MC	Melton Constable	32G Melton Constable	31A Cambridge	31B March			
62563	D16/3	NOR	Norwich Thorpe						
62564	D16/2→3	NOR	Norwich Thorpe	32F Yarmouth Beach	32A Norwich Thorpe	32A Norwich Thorpe			
62565	D16/3	COL	Colchester	30A Stratford	31C Kings Lynn	31C Kings Lynn			
62566	D16/3	BSE	Bury St. Edmunds	31E Bury St. Edmunds	31E Bury St. Edmunds	31E Bury St. Edmunds			
62567	D16/3	CAM	Cambridge	31A Cambridge	31A Cambridge				
62568	D16/3	NOR	Norwich Thorpe	9E Trafford Park	35C Spital Bridge	35C Spital Bridge			
62569	D16/2→3	KL	Kings Lynn	31C Kings Lynn	31C Kings Lynn				
62570	D16/2→3	NOR	Norwich Thorpe	32A Norwich Thorpe	31A Cambridge	31A Cambridge			
62571	D16/3	CAM	Cambridge	31A Cambridge	31A Cambridge	31A Cambridge			
62572	D16/3	SL	South Lynn	30A Stratford	31B March	31B March			
62573	D16/3	SL	South Lynn	31E Bury St. Edmunds	31C Kings Lynn				
62574	D16/3	CAM	Cambridge	31A Cambridge	31A Cambridge				
62575	D16/3	KL	Kings Lynn	31C Kings Lynn	31C Kings Lynn	31C Kings Lynn			
62576	D16/3	NOR	Norwich Thorpe	32D Yarmouth South Town	31A Cambridge	31E Bury St. Edmunds			
62577	D16/2→3	NOR	Norwich Thorpe	32A Norwich Thorpe	32A Norwich Thorpe				
62578	D16/3	MC	Melton Constable	32G Melton Constable	32G Melton Constable	32G Melton Constable			
62579	D16/3	MAR	March	31B March	31C Kings Lynn				
62580	D16/2→3	YAR	Yarmouth South Town	32D Yarmouth South Town	32D Yarmouth South Town	32D Yarmouth South Town			
62581	D16/3	NOR	Norwich Thorpe	32A Norwich Thorpe					
62582	D16/3	KL	Kings Lynn	31C Kings Lynn	31C Kings Lynn	31C Kings Lynn			
62583	D16/3	NOR	Norwich Thorpe						
62584	D16/3	MAR	March	32A Norwich Thorpe	32A Norwich Thorpe	31C Kings Lynn			
62585	D16/3	NOR	Norwich Thorpe	32A Norwich Thorpe	31A Cambridge				
62586	D16/3	YAR	Yarmouth South Town	32D Yarmouth South Town	32D Yarmouth South Town	32D Yarmouth South Town			
62587	D16/3	STR	Stratford	9E Trafford Park	35C Spital Bridge				
62588	D16/3	YAR	Yarmouth South Town	9E Trafford Park	31B March	31E Bury St. Edmunds			
62589	D16/3	MAR	March	31B March	31B March	31B March			
62590	D16/2	IPS	Ipswich	32B Ipswich					
62591	D16/2	YAR	Yarmouth South Town						
62592	D16/3	YB	Yarmouth Beach	32F Yarmouth Beach	32A Norwich Thorpe	32A Norwich Thorpe			
62593	D16/3	LOW	Lowestoft	32A Norwich Thorpe	32A Norwich Thorpe	32A Norwich Thorpe			
62594	D16/3	YAR	Yarmouth South Town						
62596	D16/3	YB	Yarmouth Beach	32F Yarmouth Beach	32G Melton Constable	32A Norwich Thorpe			
62597	D16/3	YAR	Yarmouth South Town	32D Yarmouth South Town	32D Yarmouth South Town	32F Yarmouth Beach	31F Spital Bridge		
62598	D16/3	COL	Colchester	30E Colchester					
62599	D16/3	NOR	Norwich Thorpe	9E Trafford Park	35C Spital Bridge	35C Spital Bridge			
62600	D16/3	NOR	Norwich Thorpe						
62601	D16/3	CAM	Cambridge	31C Kings Lynn	31C Kings Lynn	31C Kings Lynn			
62602	D16/3	STR	Stratford						
62603	D16/2	MAR	March	31A Cambridge					
62604	D16/3	YAR	Yarmouth South Town	32D Yarmouth South Town	32D Yarmouth South Town	32D Yarmouth South Town	32C Lowestoft		
62605	D16/3	MAR	March	31B March	31B March	31A Cambridge			
62606	D16/3	CAM	Cambridge	32A Norwich Thorpe	31C Kings Lynn	31C Kings Lynn			
62607	D16/3	CAM	Cambridge	31E Bury St. Edmunds	31E Bury St. Edmunds				
62608	D16/3	COL	Colchester	30E Colchester	32A Norwich Thorpe	31B March			
62609	D16/3	COL	Colchester	9E Trafford Park	35C Spital Bridge	35C Spital Bridge			
62610	D16/3	NOR	Norwich Thorpe	32A Norwich Thorpe	32A Norwich Thorpe	31A Cambridge			
62611	D16/3	IPS	Ipswich	32D Yarmouth South Town	32D Yarmouth South Town	32D Yarmouth South Town			
62612	D16/2→3	IPS	Ipswich	32A Norwich Thorpe	32A Norwich Thorpe	32B Ipswich			
62613	D16/2→3	YB	Yarmouth Beach	32D Yarmouth South Town	32D Yarmouth South Town	32D Yarmouth South Town	31F Spital Bridge		
62614	D16/3	KL	Kings Lynn	31C Kings Lynn	31C Kings Lynn	31C Kings Lynn			
62615	D16/3	BSE	Bury St. Edmunds	31E Bury St. Edmunds	31E Bury St. Edmunds	31E Bury St. Edmunds			
62616	D16/3	NOR	Norwich Thorpe	32A Norwich Thorpe					

No.	Class	1948		1951	1954	1957	1960	1963	1966
62617	*D16/3*	COL	Colchester	**32A** Norwich Thorpe	**32G** Melton Constable	**32G** Melton Constable			
62618	*D16/3*	CAM	Cambridge	**31A** Cambridge	**31A** Cambridge	**31A** Cambridge			
62619	*D16/3*	NOR	Norwich Thorpe	**32A** Norwich Thorpe	**32A** Norwich Thorpe	**32A** Norwich Thorpe			
62620	*D16/2→3*	NOR	Norwich Thorpe	**32G** Melton Constable	**32G** Melton Constable				
62650	*D10*	NTH	Northwich	**9G** Northwich	**9G** Northwich				
62651	*D10*	TFD	Trafford Park	**9E** Trafford Park					
62652	*D10*	NTH	Northwich	**9G** Northwich	**9G** Northwich				
62653	*D10*	LIV	Brunswick	**9E** Trafford Park	**9E** Trafford Park				
62654	*D10*	SHF	Sheffield Darnall	**9E** Trafford Park					
62655	*D10*	NTH	Northwich	**9G** Northwich					
62656	*D10*	TFD	Trafford Park	**9E** Trafford Park	**9G** Northwich				
62657	*D10*	SHF	Sheffield Darnall	**9E** Trafford Park					
62658	*D10*	LIV	Brunswick	**9E** Trafford Park	**9E** Trafford Park				
62659	*D10*	SHF	Sheffield Darnall	**9E** Trafford Park	**9G** Northwich				
62660	*D11*	IMM	Immingham	**40B** Immingham	**40A** Lincoln	**40A** Lincoln	**41A** Sheffield Darnall		
62661	*D11*	IMM	Immingham	**40B** Immingham	**9E** Trafford Park	**9G** Northwich	**41H** Staveley		
62662	*D11*	IMM	Immingham	**9E** Trafford Park	**9E** Trafford Park	**9G** Northwich	**41A** Sheffield Darnall		
62663	*D11*	IMM	Immingham	**9F** Heaton Mersey	**9F** Heaton Mersey	**40A** Lincoln	**41H** Staveley		
62664	*D11*	IMM	Immingham	**40B** Immingham	**9E** Trafford Park	**9G** Northwich	**41A** Sheffield Darnall		
62665	*D11*	IMM	Immingham	**9F** Heaton Mersey	**9F** Heaton Mersey	**9G** Northwich			
62666	*D11*	IMM	Immingham	**9E** Trafford Park	**40A** Lincoln	**40A** Lincoln	**41A** Sheffield Darnall		
62667	*D11*	IMM	Immingham	**40B** Immingham	**40A** Lincoln	**40A** Lincoln	**41A** Sheffield Darnall		
62668	*D11*	IMM	Immingham	**9E** Trafford Park	**9E** Trafford Park	**17F** Trafford Park	**41A** Sheffield Darnall		
62669	*D11*	IMM	Immingham	**9E** Trafford Park	**9G** Northwich	**9G** Northwich	**41A** Sheffield Darnall		
62670	*D11*	IMM	Immingham	**9E** Trafford Park	**40B** Immingham	**40A** Lincoln	**41A** Sheffield Darnall		
62671	*D11*	EFD	Eastfield	**65A** Eastfield	**65A** Eastfield	**65A** Eastfield	**65A** Eastfield		
62672	*D11*	EFD	Eastfield	**65A** Eastfield	**65A** Eastfield	**65A** Eastfield	**65A** Eastfield		
62673	*D11*	EFD	Eastfield	**65A** Eastfield	**65A** Eastfield	**65A** Eastfield			
62674	*D11*	EFD	Eastfield	**65A** Eastfield	**65A** Eastfield	**65A** Eastfield	**65A** Eastfield		
62675	*D11*	EFD	Eastfield	**65A** Eastfield	**65A** Eastfield	**65A** Eastfield			
62676	*D11*	EFD	Eastfield	**65A** Eastfield	**65A** Eastfield	**65A** Eastfield			
62677	*D11*	HAY	Haymarket	**64B** Haymarket	**64B** Haymarket	**64B** Haymarket			
62678	*D11*	HAY	Haymarket	**64B** Haymarket	**64B** Haymarket	**64B** Haymarket			
62679	*D11*	HAY	Haymarket	**64B** Haymarket	**64B** Haymarket	**64B** Haymarket			
62680	*D11*	EFD	Eastfield	**65A** Eastfield	**65A** Eastfield	**65A** Eastfield	**65A** Eastfield		
62681	*D11*	EFD	Eastfield	**65A** Eastfield	**65A** Eastfield	**65A** Eastfield	**65A** Eastfield		
62682	*D11*	EFD	Eastfield	**65A** Eastfield	**65A** Eastfield	**65A** Eastfield	**65A** Eastfield		
62683	*D11*	HAY	Haymarket	**64B** Haymarket	**64B** Haymarket	**64B** Haymarket			
62684	*D11*	EFD	Eastfield	**65A** Eastfield	**65A** Eastfield	**65A** Eastfield			
62685	*D11*	HAY	Haymarket	**64B** Haymarket	**64B** Haymarket	**64B** Haymarket	**64B** Haymarket		
62686	*D11*	EFD	Eastfield	**65A** Eastfield	**65A** Eastfield	**65A** Eastfield	**65A** Eastfield		
62687	*D11*	EFD	Eastfield	**65A** Eastfield	**65A** Eastfield	**65A** Eastfield	**65A** Eastfield		
62688	*D11*	EFD	Eastfield	**65A** Eastfield	**65A** Eastfield	**65A** Eastfield	**65A** Eastfield		
62689	*D11*	EFD	Eastfield	**65A** Eastfield	**65A** Eastfield	**65A** Eastfield	**65A** Eastfield		
62690	*D11*	HAY	Haymarket	**64B** Haymarket	**64B** Haymarket	**64B** Haymarket	**64B** Haymarket		
62691	*D11*	HAY	Haymarket	**64B** Haymarket	**64B** Haymarket	**64B** Haymarket	**64B** Haymarket		
62692	*D11*	HAY	Haymarket	**64B** Haymarket	**64B** Haymarket	**64B** Haymarket			
62693	*D11*	HAY	Haymarket	**64B** Haymarket	**64B** Haymarket	**64B** Haymarket	**64B** Haymarket		
62694	*D11*	HAY	Haymarket	**64B** Haymarket	**64B** Haymarket	**64B** Haymarket			
62700	*D49/1*	HLB	Hull Botanic Gardens	**53B** Hull Botanic Gardens	**53B** Hull Botanic Gardens	**53D** Bridlington			
62701	*D49/1*	HLB	Hull Botanic Gardens	**53D** Bridlington	**53D** Bridlington	**53D** Bridlington			
62702	*D49/1*	STM	St. Margarets	**64A** St. Margarets	**50A** York	**50A** York			
62703	*D49/1*	HLB	Hull Botanic Gardens	**53D** Bridlington	**53D** Bridlington	**53D** Bridlington			
62704	*D49/1*	THJ	Thornton Junction	**62A** Thornton Junction	**62A** Thornton Junction	**62A** Thornton Junction			
62705	*D49/1*	HAY	Haymarket	**64B** Haymarket	**64B** Haymarket	**64B** Haymarket			
62706	*D49/1*	HAY	Haymarket	**64B** Haymarket	**64B** Haymarket	**64B** Haymarket			
62707	*D49/1*	HLB	Hull Botanic Gardens	**53D** Bridlington	**53D** Bridlington	**53D** Bridlington			
62708	*D49/1*	THJ	Thornton Junction	**62A** Thornton Junction	**62A** Thornton Junction	**62A** Thornton Junction			
62709	*D49/1*	HAY	Haymarket	**64B** Haymarket	**64B** Haymarket	**64B** Haymarket	**64B** Haymarket		
62710	*D49/1*	HLB	Hull Botanic Gardens	**53B** Hull Botanic Gardens	**53B** Hull Botanic Gardens	**53B** Hull Botanic Gardens	**53A** Hull Dairycoates		
62711	*D49/1*	HAY	Haymarket	**64A** St. Margarets	**64A** St. Margarets	**64A** St. Margarets	**64A** St. Margarets		
62712	*D49/1*	HAY	Haymarket	**64A** St. Margarets	**64A** St. Margarets	**64A** St. Margarets	**62A** Thornton Junction		
62713	*D49/1*	DEE	Dundee Tay Bridge	**62A** Thornton Junction	**62A** Thornton Junction	**62A** Thornton Junction			
62714	*D49/1*	PTH	Perth South	**63A** Perth	**63B** Stirling	**63B** Stirling			
62715	*D49/1*	STM	St. Margarets	**64A** St. Margarets	**64A** St. Margarets	**64A** St. Margarets			
62716	*D49/1*	THJ	Thornton Junction	**62A** Thornton Junction	**62A** Thornton Junction	**62A** Thornton Junction	**62A** Thornton Junction		
62717	*D49/1*	THJ	Thornton Junction	**62A** Thornton Junction	**53B** Hull Botanic Gardens	**53B** Hull Botanic Gardens	**53A** Hull Dairycoates		
62718	*D49/1*	DEE	Dundee Tay Bridge	**62B** Dundee Tay Bridge	**64A** St. Margarets	**64A** St. Margarets	**64A** St. Margarets		
62719	*D49/1*	HAY	Haymarket	**64B** Haymarket	**64B** Haymarket	**64B** Haymarket	**64G** Hawick		
62720	*D49/1*	HLB	Hull Botanic Gardens	**53B** Hull Botanic Gardens	**53B** Hull Botanic Gardens	**53B** Hull Botanic Gardens			
62721	*D49/1*	HAY	Haymarket	**64A** St. Margarets	**64A** St. Margarets	**64A** St. Margarets			
62722	*D49/1*	HLB	Hull Botanic Gardens	**53B** Hull Botanic Gardens	**53B** Hull Botanic Gardens	**53B** Hull Botanic Gardens			
62723	*D49/1*	HLB	Hull Botanic Gardens	**53B** Hull Botanic Gardens	**53B** Hull Botanic Gardens	**53B** Hull Botanic Gardens	**53A** Hull Dairycoates		
62724	*D49/1*	HLB	Hull Botanic Gardens	**53B** Hull Botanic Gardens	**53B** Hull Botanic Gardens	**53B** Hull Botanic Gardens			
62725	*D49/1*	PTH	Perth South	**63A** Perth	**63B** Stirling	**63B** Stirling			
62726	*D49/2*	SBK	Starbeck	**50A** York	**50E** Scarborough	**50E** Scarborough			
62727	*D49/2*	HLB	Hull Botanic Gardens	**50D** Starbeck	**50D** Starbeck	**50D** Starbeck	**53A** Hull Dairycoates		
62728	*D49/1*	DEE	Dundee Tay Bridge	**62B** Dundee Tay Bridge	**62B** Dundee Tay Bridge	**62B** Dundee Tay Bridge			
62729	*D49/1*	THJ	Thornton Junction	**62A** Thornton Junction	**62A** Thornton Junction	**62A** Thornton Junction	**62A** Thornton Junction		
62730	*D49/1*	CAR	Carlisle Canal	**50A** York	**50A** York	**50A** York			
62731	*D49/1*	CAR	Carlisle Canal	**50A** York	**50A** York	**50A** York			
62732	*D49/1*	CAR	Carlisle Canal	**50A** York	**68E** Carlisle Canal	**68E** Carlisle Canal			
62733	*D49/1*	HAY	Haymarket	**64B** Haymarket	**64B** Haymarket	**64B** Haymarket	**62A** Thornton Junction		
62734	*D49/1*	CAR	Carlisle Canal	**50A** York	**68E** Carlisle Canal	**68E** Carlisle Canal	**12C** Carlisle Canal		
62735	*D49/1*	CAR	Carlisle Canal	**50A** York	**50A** York	**50E** Scarborough			
62736	*D49/2*	GHD	Gateshead	**50D** Starbeck	**50D** Starbeck	**50D** Starbeck			
62737	*D49/2*	HLB	Hull Botanic Gardens	**53B** Hull Botanic Gardens	**53B** Hull Botanic Gardens	**53B** Hull Botanic Gardens			
62738	*D49/2*	GHD	Gateshead	**50D** Starbeck	**50D** Starbeck	**50D** Starbeck			
62739	*D49/2*	GHD	Gateshead	**50B** Leeds Neville Hill	**50E** Scarborough	**50E** Scarborough	**50E** Scarborough		
62740	*D49/2*	YK	York	**50D** Starbeck	**50D** Starbeck	**50B** Leeds Neville Hill	**53A** Hull Dairycoates		
62741	*D49/2*	HLB	Hull Botanic Gardens	**53B** Hull Botanic Gardens	**53B** Hull Botanic Gardens	**53B** Hull Botanic Gardens			
62742	*D49/2*	GHD	Gateshead	**50B** Leeds Neville Hill	**50B** Leeds Neville Hill	**50B** Leeds Neville Hill			
62743	*D49/2*	HLB	Hull Botanic Gardens	**53B** Hull Botanic Gardens	**64B** Haymarket	**64B** Haymarket	**64B** Haymarket		
62744	*D49/2*	HLB	Hull Botanic Gardens	**50A** York	**62B** Dundee Tay Bridge	**62B** Dundee Tay Bridge	**62A** Thornton Junction		
62745	*D49/2*	GHD	Gateshead	**50A** York	**50A** York	**50A** York			
62746	*D49/2*	NEV	Leeds Neville Hill	**50B** Leeds Neville Hill	**50D** Starbeck	**50D** Starbeck			
62747	*D49/2*	GHD	Gateshead	**52C** Blaydon	**52C** Blaydon	**50A** York	**12C** Carlisle Canal		
62748	*D49/2*	NEV	Leeds Neville Hill	**50B** Leeds Neville Hill	**50B** Leeds Neville Hill	**50B** Leeds Neville Hill			
62749	*D49/2*	GHD	Gateshead	**50D** Starbeck	**50D** Starbeck	**50B** Leeds Neville Hill			
62750	*D49/2*	GHD	Gateshead	**53D** Bridlington	**53D** Bridlington	**53D** Bridlington			
62751	*D49/2*	YK	York	**50E** Scarborough	**50E** Scarborough	**50E** Scarborough			
62752	*D49/2*	SBK	Starbeck	**50D** Starbeck	**50D** Starbeck	**50D** Starbeck			
62753	*D49/2*	SBK	Starbeck	**50D** Starbeck	**50D** Starbeck	**50D** Starbeck			
62754	*D49/2*	HLB	Hull Botanic Gardens	**53B** Hull Botanic Gardens	**53B** Hull Botanic Gardens	**53B** Hull Botanic Gardens			
62755	*D49/2*	YK	York	**50D** Starbeck	**50D** Starbeck	**50C** Selby			
62756	*D49/2*	NEV	Leeds Neville Hill	**50B** Leeds Neville Hill	**50E** Scarborough	**50E** Scarborough			
62757	*D49/2*	HLB	Hull Botanic Gardens	**53B** Hull Botanic Gardens	**53B** Hull Botanic Gardens	**53B** Hull Botanic Gardens			
62758	*D49/2*	NEV	Leeds Neville Hill	**50D** Starbeck	**50D** Starbeck	**50D** Starbeck			
62759	*D49/2*	YK	York	**50A** York	**50A** York	**50D** Starbeck	**53A** Hull Dairycoates		
62760	*D49/2*	YK	York	**50A** York	**50A** York	**50A** York			
62761	*D49/2*	YK	York	**50D** Starbeck	**50D** Starbeck	**50C** Selby			
62762	*D49/2*	SBK	Starbeck	**50D** Starbeck	**50D** Starbeck	**50D** Starbeck	**50E** Scarborough		
62763	*D49/2*	YK	York	**50D** Starbeck	**50D** Starbeck	**50D** Starbeck	**53A** Hull Dairycoates		
62764	*D49/2*	GHD	Gateshead	**50E** Scarborough	**50B** Leeds Neville Hill	**50B** Leeds Neville Hill			

No.	Class	1948	1951	1954	1957	1960	1963	1966
62765	*D49/2*	**NEV** Leeds Neville Hill	**50D** Starbeck	**50D** Starbeck	**50D** Starbeck	**53A** Hull Dairycoates		
62766	*D49/2*	**GHD** Gateshead	**53D** Bridlington	**53D** Bridlington	**53B** Hull Botanic Gardens			
62767	*D49/2*	**HLB** Hull Botanic Gardens	**53B** Hull Botanic Gardens	**53B** Hull Botanic Gardens	**53B** Hull Botanic Gardens			
62768	*D49/4*	**SBK** Starbeck	**50D** Starbeck					
62769	*D49/2*	**NEV** Leeds Neville Hill	**50E** Scarborough	**50E** Scarborough	**50E** Scarborough			
62770	*D49/2*	**NEV** Leeds Neville Hill	**50E** Scarborough	**50E** Scarborough	**50E** Scarborough			
62771	*D49/2*	**GHD** Gateshead	**52C** Blaydon	**52C** Blaydon	**50A** York			
62772	*D49/2*	**NEV** Leeds Neville Hill	**50D** Starbeck	**50D** Starbeck	**50C** Selby			
62773	*D49/2*	**SBK** Starbeck	**50D** Starbeck	**50D** Starbeck	**50D** Starbeck			
62774	*D49/2*	**NEV** Leeds Neville Hill	**50F** Pickering	**50A** York	**50D** Starbeck			
62775	*D49/2*	**NEV** Leeds Neville Hill	**50B** Leeds Neville Hill	**50B** Leeds Neville Hill	**50C** Selby			
62780	*E4*	**CAM** Cambridge	**32A** Norwich Thorpe	**31A** Cambridge				
62781	*E4*	**CAM** Cambridge	**31A** Cambridge	**31A** Cambridge				
62782	*E4*	**NOR** Norwich Thorpe	**32A** Norwich Thorpe	**32A** Norwich Thorpe				
62783	*E4*	**CAM** Cambridge	**31A** Cambridge	**31A** Cambridge				
62784	*E4*	**CAM** Cambridge	**31A** Cambridge	**31A** Cambridge				
62785	*E4*	**BSE** Bury St. Edmunds	**31A** Cambridge	**31A** Cambridge	**34D** Hitchin			
62786	*E4*	**CAM** Cambridge	**31E** Bury St. Edmunds	**31A** Cambridge				
62787	*E4*	**NOR** Norwich Thorpe	**32A** Norwich Thorpe	**32A** Norwich Thorpe				
62788	*E4*	**CAM** Cambridge	**31A** Cambridge	**32A** Norwich Thorpe	**31A** Cambridge			
62789	*E4*	**NOR** Norwich Thorpe	**32A** Norwich Thorpe	**32A** Norwich Thorpe	**31A** Cambridge			
62790	*E4*	**CAM** Cambridge	**31C** Kings Lynn	**31A** Cambridge				
62791	*E4*	**CAM** Cambridge	**30A** Stratford	**31A** Cambridge				
62792	*E4*	**NOR** Norwich Thorpe	**32A** Norwich Thorpe	**32A** Norwich Thorpe				
62793	*E4*	**NOR** Norwich Thorpe	**32A** Norwich Thorpe	**32A** Norwich Thorpe				
62794	*E4*	**CAM** Cambridge	**31A** Cambridge	**31A** Cambridge				
62795	*E4*	**CAM** Cambridge	**31E** Bury St. Edmunds	**31A** Cambridge				
62796	*E4*	**CAM** Cambridge	**32A** Norwich Thorpe	**32A** Norwich Thorpe	**31A** Cambridge			
62797	*E4*	**NOR** Norwich Thorpe	**32A** Norwich Thorpe	**32A** Norwich Thorpe	**32C** Lowestoft			
62808	*C1*	**NWE** New England						
62810	*C1*	**GRA** Grantham						
62817	*C1*	**KX** Kings Cross						
62821	*C1*	**KX** Kings Cross						
62822	*C1*	**GRA** Grantham						
62828	*C1*	**ARD** Ardsley						
62829	*C1*	**ARD** Ardsley						
62839	*C1*	**NWE** New England						
62849	*C1*	**ARD** Ardsley						
62854	*C1*	**DON** Doncaster						
62870	*C1*	**GRA** Grantham						
62871	*C1*	**NWE** New England						
62875	*C1*	**COP** Copley Hill						
62876	*C1*	**GRA** Grantham						
62877	*C1*	**DON** Doncaster						
62881	*C1*	**COP** Copley Hill						
62885	*C1*	**DON** Doncaster						
62900	*C4*	**BOS** Boston						
62901	*C4*	**BOS** Boston						
62902	*C4*	**IMM** Immingham						
62903	*C4*	**IMM** Immingham						
62908	*C4*	**LIN** Lincoln						
62909	*C4*	**LIN** Lincoln						
62910	*C4*	**LIN** Lincoln						
62912	*C4*	**LIN** Lincoln						
62914	*C4*	**LIN** Lincoln						
62915	*C4*	**LIN** Lincoln						
62916	*C4*	**LIN** Lincoln						
62917	*C4*	**LIN** Lincoln						
62918	*C4*	**LIN** Lincoln						
62919	*C4*	**BOS** Boston						
62920	*C4*	**BOS** Boston						
62921	*C4*	**BOS** Boston						
62922	*C4*	**BOS** Boston						
62923	*C4*	**BOS** Boston						
62924	*C4*	**BOS** Boston						
62925	*C4*	**BOS** Boston						
62933	*C6*	**HLD** Hull Dairycoates						
62937	*C6*	**GHD** Gateshead						
62954	*C7*	**SCA** Scarborough						
62970	*C7*	**HLD** Hull Dairycoates						
62972	*C7*	**SCA** Scarborough						
62973	*C7*	**SCA** Scarborough						
62975	*C7*	**SCA** Scarborough						
62978	*C7*	**DAR** Darlington						
62981	*C7*	**DAR** Darlington						
62982	*C7*	**HLD** Hull Dairycoates						
62983	*C7*	**HLD** Hull Dairycoates						
62988	*C7*	**HLD** Hull Dairycoates						
62989	*C7*	**SCA** Scarborough						
62992	*C7*	**SCA** Scarborough						
62993	*C7*	**SCA** Scarborough						
62995	*C7*	**HLD** Hull Dairycoates						
63000	*O7*	**ANN** Annesley	(90000)					
63001	*O7*	**TWD** Tweedmouth	(90001)					
63002	*O7*	**ANN** Annesley	(90002)					
63003	*O7*	**MAR** March	(90003)					
63004	*O7*	**THJ** Thornton Junction	(90004)					
63005	*O7*	**IMM** Immingham	(90005)					
63006	*O7*	**TWD** Tweedmouth	(90006)					
63007	*O7*	**MEX** Mexborough	(90007)					
63008	*O7*	**CLK** Colwick	(90008)					
63009	*O7*	**MEX** Mexborough	(90009)					
63010	*O7*	**ANN** Annesley	(90010)					
63011	*O7*	**MEX** Mexborough	(90011)					
63012	*O7*	**HTN** Heaton	(90012)					
63013	*O7*	**MAR** March	(90013)					
63014	*O7*	**ANN** Annesley	(90014)					
63015	*O7*	**MAR** March	(90015)					
63016	*O7*	**NPT** Newport	(90016)					
63017	*O7*	**THJ** Thornton Junction	(90017)					
63018	*O7*	**MAR** March	(90018)					
63019	*O7*	**THJ** Thornton Junction	(90019)					
63020	*O7*	**EFD** Eastfield	(90020)					
63021	*O7*	**CLK** Colwick	(90021)					
63022	*O7*	**CLK** Colwick	(90022)					
63023	*O7*	**MAR** March	(90023)					
63024	*O7*	**MAR** March	(90024)					
63025	*O7*	**CLK** Colwick	(90025)					
63026	*O7*	**ANN** Annesley	(90026)					
63027	*O7*	**CLK** Colwick	(90027)					
63028	*O7*	**MAR** March	(90028)					
63029	*O7*	**MAR** March	(90029)					
63030	*O7*	**TWD** Tweedmouth	(90030)					
63031	*O7*	**NWE** New England	(90031)					

		1948		1951	1954	1957	1960	1963	1966
63032	*O7*	**IMM**	Immingham	(90032)					
63033	*O7*	**WFD**	Woodford Halse	(90033)					
63034	*O7*	**NWE**	New England	(90034)					
63035	*O7*	**MAR**	March	(90035)					
63036	*O7*	**CLK**	Colwick	(90036)					
63037	*O7*	**MAR**	March	(90037)					
63038	*O7*	**STM**	St. Margarets	(90038)					
63039	*O7*	**WFD**	Woodford Halse	(90039)					
63040	*O7*	**WFD**	Woodford Halse	(90040)					
63041	*O7*	**ABD**	Aberdeen Ferryhill	(90041)					
63042	*O7*	**MAR**	March	(90042)					
63043	*O7*	**WFD**	Woodford Halse	(90043)					
63044	*O7*	**NPT**	Newport	(90044)					
63045	*O7*	**HTN**	Heaton	(90045)					
63046	*O7*	**WFD**	Woodford Halse	(90046)					
63047	*O7*	**MEX**	Mexborough	(90047)					
63048	*O7*	**HTN**	Heaton	(90048)					
63049	*O7*	**THJ**	Thornton Junction	(90049)					
63050	*O7*	**CLK**	Colwick	(90050)					
63051	*O7*	**CLK**	Colwick	(90051)					
63052	*O7*	**MEX**	Mexborough	(90052)					
63053	*O7*	**MAR**	March	(90053)					
63054	*O7*	**NPT**	Newport	(90054)					
63055	*O7*	**NWE**	New England	(90055)					
63056	*O7*	**WFD**	Woodford Halse	(90056)					
63057	*O7*	**MEX**	Mexborough	(90057)					
63058	*O7*	**THJ**	Thornton Junction	(90058)					
63059	*O7*	**NWE**	New England	(90059)					
63060	*O7*	**NWE**	New England	(90060)					
63061	*O7*	**HTN**	Heaton	(90061)					
63062	*O7*	**NWE**	New England	(90062)					
63063	*O7*	**STM**	St. Margarets	(90063)					
63064	*O7*	**NWE**	New England	(90064)					
63065	*O7*	**WFD**	Woodford Halse	(90065)					
63066	*O7*	**NWE**	New England	(90066)					
63067	*O7*	**HTN**	Heaton	(90067)					
63068	*O7*	**CLK**	Colwick	(90068)					
63069	*O7*	**CLK**	Colwick	(90069)					
63070	*O7*	**NWE**	New England	(90070)					
63071	*O7*	**DEE**	Dundee Tay Bridge	(90071)					
63072	*O7*	**TWD**	Tweedmouth	(90072)					
63073	*O7*	**CLK**	Colwick	(90073)					
63074	*O7*	**NPT**	Newport	(90074)					
63075	*O7*	**NWE**	New England	(90075)					
63076	*O7*	**HTN**	Heaton	(90076)					
63077	*O7*	**DEE**	Dundee Tay Bridge	(90077)					
63078	*O7*	**HTN**	Heaton	(90078)					
63079	*O7*	**ANN**	Annesley	(90079)					
63080	*O7*	**WFD**	Woodford Halse	(90080)					
63081	*O7*	**NPT**	Newport	(90081)					
63082	*O7*	**HTN**	Heaton	(90082)					
63083	*O7*	**MAR**	March	(90083)					
63084	*O7*	**CLK**	Colwick	(90084)					
63085	*O7*	**MAR**	March	(90085)					
63086	*O7*	**HTN**	Heaton	(90086)					
63087	*O7*	**MAR**	March	(90087)					
63088	*O7*	**NWE**	New England	(90088)					
63089	*O7*	**STM**	St. Margarets	(90089)					
63090	*O7*	**STM**	St. Margarets	(90090)					
63091	*O7*	**NPT**	Newport	(90091)					
63092	*O7*	**HTN**	Heaton	(90092)					
63093	*O7*	**NWE**	New England	(90093)					
63094	*O7*	**MEX**	Mexborough	(90094)					
63095	*O7*	**WFD**	Woodford Halse	(90095)					
63096	*O7*	**MAR**	March	(90096)					
63097	*O7*	**ABD**	Aberdeen Ferryhill	(90097)					
63098	*O7*	**NPT**	Newport	(90098)					
63099	*O7*	**HTN**	Heaton	(90099)					
63100	*O7*	**CLK**	Colwick	(90100)					
63101	*O7*	**MAR**	March	(90422)					
63102	*O7*	**CLK**	Colwick	(90423)					
63103	*O7*	**HTN**	Heaton	(90424)					
63104	*O7*	**MAR**	March	(90425)					
63105	*O7*	**HTN**	Heaton	(90426)					
63106	*O7*	**TWD**	Tweedmouth	(90427)					
63107	*O7*	**MAR**	March	(90428)					
63108	*O7*	**MEX**	Mexborough	(90429)					
63109	*O7*	**HTN**	Heaton	(90430)					
63110	*O7*	**MAR**	March	(90431)					
63111	*O7*	**HTN**	Heaton	(90432)					
63112	*O7*	**MAR**	March	(90433)					
63113	*O7*	**HTN**	Heaton	(90434)					
63114	*O7*	**TWD**	Tweedmouth	(90435)					
63115	*O7*	**STM**	St. Margarets	(90436)					
63116	*O7*	**WFD**	Woodford Halse	(90437)					
63117	*O7*	**NWE**	New England	(90438)					
63118	*O7*	**NWE**	New England	(90439)					
63119	*O7*	**EFD**	Eastfield	(90440)					
63120	*O7*	**EFD**	Eastfield	(90441)					
63121	*O7*	**NWE**	New England	(90442)					
63122	*O7*	**MAR**	March	(90443)					
63123	*O7*	**DEE**	Dundee Tay Bridge	(90444)					
63124	*O7*	**HTN**	Heaton	(90445)					
63125	*O7*	**NPT**	Newport	(90446)					
63126	*O7*	**STM**	St. Margarets	(90447)					
63127	*O7*	**WFD**	Woodford Halse	(90448)					
63128	*O7*	**CLK**	Colwick	(90449)					
63129	*O7*	**CLK**	Colwick	(90450)					
63130	*O7*	**NPT**	Newport	(90451)					
63131	*O7*	**NPT**	Newport	(90452)					
63132	*O7*	**NWE**	New England	(90453)					
63133	*O7*	**MAR**	March	(90454)					
63134	*O7*	**ABD**	Aberdeen Ferryhill	(90455)					
63135	*O7*	**NWE**	New England	(90456)					
63136	*O7*	**CLK**	Colwick	(90457)					
63137	*O7*	**HTN**	Heaton	(90458)					
63138	*O7*	**CLK**	Colwick	(90459)					
63139	*O7*	**NWE**	New England	(90460)					
63140	*O7*	**NPT**	Newport	(90461)					
63141	*O7*	**HTN**	Heaton	(90462)					
63142	*O7*	**DEE**	Dundee Tay Bridge	(90463)					
63143	*O7*	**THJ**	Thornton Junction	(90464)					
63144	*O7*	**NPT**	Newport	(90465)					
63145	*O7*	**CLK**	Colwick	(90466)					

		1948	1951	1954	1957	1960	1963	1966
63146	*O7*	**HTN** Heaton	(90467)					
63147	*O7*	**STM** St. Margarets	(90468)					
63148	*O7*	**STM** St. Margarets	(90469)					
63149	*O7*	**MEX** Mexborough	(90470)					
63150	*O7*	**MAR** March	(90471)					
63151	*O7*	**THJ** Thornton Junction	(90472)					
63152	*O7*	**MAR** March	(90473)					
63153	*O7*	**NWE** New England	(90474)					
63154	*O7*	**NPT** Newport	(90475)					
63155	*O7*	**MAR** March	(90476)					
63156	*O7*	**MAR** March	(90477)					
63157	*O7*	**CLK** Colwick	(90478)					
63158	*O7*	**HTN** Heaton	(90479)					
63159	*O7*	**MAR** March	(90480)					
63160	*O7*	**NPT** Newport	(90481)					
63161	*O7*	**HTN** Heaton	(90482)					
63162	*O7*	**HTN** Heaton	(90483)					
63163	*O7*	**CLK** Colwick	(90484)					
63164	*O7*	**HTN** Heaton	(90485)					
63165	*O7*	**WFD** Woodford Halse	(90486)					
63166	*O7*	**HTN** Heaton	(90487)					
63167	*O7*	**HTN** Heaton	(90488)					
63168	*O7*	**THJ** Thornton Junction	(90489)					
63169	*O7*	**NWE** New England	(90490)					
63170	*O7*	**CLK** Colwick	(90491)					
63171	*O7*	**CLK** Colwick	(90492)					
63172	*O7*	**STM** St. Margarets	(90493)					
63173	*O7*	**NWE** New England	(90494)					
63174	*O7*	**NWE** New England	(90495)					
63175	*O7*	**STM** St. Margarets	(90496)					
63176	*O7*	**MEX** Mexborough	(90497)					
63177	*O7*	**THJ** Thornton Junction	(90498)					
63178	*O7*	**CLK** Colwick	(90499)					
63179	*O7*	**NPT** Newport	(90500)					
63180	*O7*	**STM** St. Margarets	(90501)					
63181	*O7*	**NWE** New England	(90502)					
63182	*O7*	**HTN** Heaton	(90503)					
63183	*O7*	**WFD** Woodford Halse	(90504)					
63184	*O7*	**CLK** Colwick	(90505)					
63185	*O7*	**MAR** March	(90506)					
63186	*O7*	**WFD** Woodford Halse	(90507)					
63187	*O7*	**MAR** March	(90508)					
63188	*O7*	**WFD** Woodford Halse	(90509)					
63189	*O7*	**NWE** New England	(90510)					
63190	*O7*	**TWD** Tweedmouth	(90511)					
63191	*O7*	**CLK** Colwick	(90512)					
63192	*O7*	**CLK** Colwick	(90513)					
63193	*O7*	**NWE** New England	(90514)					
63194	*O7*	**DEE** Dundee Tay Bridge	(90515)					
63195	*O7*	**WFD** Woodford Halse	(90516)					
63196	*O7*	**NPT** Newport	(90517)					
63197	*O7*	**HTN** Heaton	(90518)					
63198	*O7*	**NWE** New England	(90519)					
63199	*O7*	**WFD** Woodford Halse	(90520)					
63200	*Q4*	**ARD** Ardsley						
63201	*Q4*	**GRA** Grantham	**36D** Barnsley					
63202	*Q4*	**BRN** Barnsley	**37A** Ardsley					
63203	*Q4*	**BRN** Barnsley						
63204	*Q4*	**BRN** Barnsley	**37A** Ardsley					
63205	*Q4*	**ARD** Ardsley						
63206	*Q4*	**GRA** Grantham						
63207	*Q4*	**GRA** Grantham						
63210	*Q4*	**ARD** Ardsley						
63212	*Q4*	**BRN** Barnsley						
63213	*Q4*	**ARD** Ardsley						
63214	*Q4*	**BRN** Barnsley						
63216	*Q4*	**BRN** Barnsley						
63217	*Q4*	**BFD** Bradford Hammerton St	**37A** Ardsley					
63219	*Q4*	**BRN** Barnsley						
63220	*Q4*	**BRN** Barnsley	**36D** Barnsley					
63221	*Q4*	**ARD** Ardsley						
63223	*Q4*	**ARD** Ardsley	**37A** Ardsley					
63224	*Q4*	**ARD** Ardsley						
63225	*Q4*	**ARD** Ardsley	**37A** Ardsley					
63226	*Q4*	**ARD** Ardsley						
63227	*Q4*	**BRN** Barnsley	**37A** Ardsley					
63228	*Q4*	**GRA** Grantham						
63229	*Q4*	**GRA** Grantham						
63231	*Q4*	**ARD** Ardsley						
63232	*Q4*	**ARD** Ardsley						
63233	*Q4*	**BRN** Barnsley						
63234	*Q4*	**GRA** Grantham	**37A** Ardsley					
63235	*Q4*	**BRN** Barnsley	**36D** Barnsley					
63236	*Q4*	**ARD** Ardsley	**37A** Ardsley					
63238	*Q4*	**BRN** Barnsley						
63240	*Q4*	**GRA** Grantham	**37A** Ardsley					
63241	*Q4*	**ARD** Ardsley						
63243	*Q4*	**GRA** Grantham	**37A** Ardsley					
63250	*Q5*	**WHL** West Hartlepool						
63251	*Q5*	**BOR** Borough Gardens						
63252	*Q5*	**HAV** Haverton Hill						
63253	*Q5*	**WHL** West Hartlepool						
63254	*Q5*	**BOR** Borough Gardens						
63255	*Q5*	**DAR** Darlington						
63256	*Q5*	**WHL** West Hartlepool						
63257	*Q5*	**BOR** Borough Gardens						
63259	*Q5*	**BOR** Borough Gardens	**54C** Borough Gardens					
63260	*Q5*	**MID** Middlesbrough						
63261	*Q5*	**BOR** Borough Gardens						
63262	*Q5*	**SEL** Selby						
63263	*Q5*	**MID** Middlesbrough						
63264	*Q5*	**BOR** Borough Gardens						
63267	*Q5*	**BOR** Borough Gardens	**54C** Borough Gardens					
63268	*Q5*	**MID** Middlesbrough						
63270	*Q5*	**HAV** Haverton Hill	**50A** Normanton					
63271	*Q5*	**BOR** Borough Gardens						
63272	*Q5*	**CUD** Cudworth						
63273	*Q5*	**MID** Middlesbrough						
63274	*Q5*	**TDK** Tyne Dock						
63275	*Q5*	**BOR** Borough Gardens						
63276	*Q5*	**SEL** Selby						
63277	*Q5*	**DAR** Darlington						
63278	*Q5*	**DAR** Darlington						
63279	*Q5*	**SEL** Selby						

		1948	1951	1954	1957	1960	1963	1966
63280	Q5	SEL Selby						
63281	Q5	WHL West Hartlepool						
63282	Q5	BOR Borough Gardens						
63283	Q5	BOR Borough Gardens						
63284	Q5	BOR Borough Gardens	54C Borough Gardens					
63285	Q5	MID Middlesbrough						
63286	Q5	BOR Borough Gardens						
63287	Q5	BOR Borough Gardens						
63289	Q5	BOR Borough Gardens						
63290	Q5	SEL Selby						
63291	Q5	MID Middlesbrough						
63292	Q5	MID Middlesbrough						
63293	Q5	WHL West Hartlepool						
63294	Q5	WHL West Hartlepool						
63295	Q5	MID Middlesbrough						
63296	Q5	BOR Borough Gardens						
63297	Q5	WHL West Hartlepool						
63298	Q5	BOR Borough Gardens						
63299	Q5	HAV Haverton Hill						
63300	Q5	WHL West Hartlepool						
63301	Q5	HAV Haverton Hill						
63303	Q5	WHL West Hartlepool	54C Borough Gardens					
63305	Q5	MID Middlesbrough						
63306	Q5	HAV Haverton Hill						
63307	Q5	DAR Darlington						
63308	Q5	MID Middlesbrough						
63310	Q5	SEL Selby						
63311	Q5	CUD Cudworth	51G Haverton Hill					
63312	Q5	SEL Selby						
63313	Q5	SEL Selby						
63314	Q5	AUK West Auckland	51G Haverton Hill					
63315	Q5	AUK West Auckland						
63316	Q5	MID Middlesbrough						
63317	Q5	MID Middlesbrough						
63318	Q5	WHL West Hartlepool						
63319	Q5	MID Middlesbrough	50C Selby					
63321	Q5	BOR Borough Gardens						
63322	Q5	MID Middlesbrough						
63323	Q5	MID Middlesbrough						
63326	Q5	BOR Borough Gardens	54C Borough Gardens					
63327	Q5	NPT Newport						
63328	Q5	DAR Darlington	51D Middlesbrough					
63330	Q5	DAR Darlington						
63331	Q5	HAV Haverton Hill						
63332	Q5	CUD Cudworth						
63333	Q5	MID Middlesbrough						
63334	Q5	DAR Darlington						
63335	Q5	DAR Darlington						
63336	Q5	WHL West Hartlepool						
63338	Q5	NPT Newport						
63339	Q5	MID Middlesbrough						
63340	Q6	HAV Haverton Hill	51G Haverton Hill	51D Middlesbrough	51D Middlesbrough	51F West Auckland	51F West Auckland	
63341	Q6	NPT Newport	51B Newport	51B Newport	51G Haverton Hill	51L Thornaby	51F West Auckland	
63342	Q6	BOR Borough Gardens	54C Borough Gardens	54C Borough Gardens	54C Borough Gardens	52K Consett	52G Sunderland	
63343	Q6	NPT Newport	51B Newport	51B Newport	51G Haverton Hill	51L Thornaby	51F West Auckland	
63344	Q6	NPT Newport	51B Newport	51B Newport	51G Haverton Hill	51L Thornaby	51F West Auckland	55H Leeds Neville Hill
63345	Q6	NPT Newport	51B Newport	51B Newport	51G Haverton Hill	52K Consett	52G Sunderland	
63346	Q6	CON Consett	54D Consett	54D Consett	54C Borough Gardens	52K Consett	52K Consett	52G Sunderland
63347	Q6	NPT Newport	51B Newport	51B Newport	51G Haverton Hill	51L Thornaby	51F West Auckland	
63348	Q6	WHL West Hartlepool	50C Selby	50B Leeds Neville Hill	50B Leeds Neville Hill	50B Leeds Neville Hill	55H Leeds Neville Hill	
63349	Q6	NPT Newport	51D Middlesbrough	51D Middlesbrough	51D Middlesbrough	51L Thornaby	51L Thornaby	51C West Hartlepool
63350	Q6	NPT Newport	54C Borough Gardens	54C Borough Gardens	54C Borough Gardens	52H Tyne Dock	52H Tyne Dock	
63351	Q6	TDK Tyne Dock	51D Middlesbrough	51D Middlesbrough	51F West Auckland	51F West Auckland	51F West Auckland	
63352	Q6	TDK Tyne Dock	54B Tyne Dock	54B Tyne Dock	54B Tyne Dock	52C Blaydon	52F North Blyth	
63353	Q6	BLA Blaydon	52C Blaydon	52C Blaydon	52F North Blyth	51F West Auckland	51F West Auckland	
63354	Q6	NPT Newport	54C Borough Gardens	54C Borough Gardens	54C Borough Gardens	52K Consett	52F North Blyth	
63355	Q6	NPT Newport	51C West Hartlepool	51D Middlesbrough	51D Middlesbrough	51L Thornaby	51F West Auckland	
63356	Q6	BLA Blaydon	52C Blaydon	52C Blaydon	52C Blaydon	52C Blaydon	52F North Blyth	
63357	Q6	CON Consett	54D Consett	54D Consett	54D Consett	52K Consett	52K Consett	
63358	Q6	NPT Newport	54C Borough Gardens	54C Borough Gardens	54C Borough Gardens	52H Tyne Dock	52H Tyne Dock	
63359	Q6	CON Consett	54D Consett	54B Tyne Dock	54D Consett	52K Consett	52F North Blyth	
63360	Q6	NPT Newport	51B Newport	51B Newport	51B Newport	51L Thornaby	52H Tyne Dock	52H Tyne Dock
63361	Q6	CON Consett	54D Consett	54D Consett	54D Consett	51L Thornaby	51F West Auckland	
63362	Q6	TDK Tyne Dock	50C Selby	50C Selby	54B Tyne Dock	52C Blaydon	52C Blaydon	
63363	Q6	TDK Tyne Dock	50C Selby	52C Blaydon	52C Blaydon	52C Blaydon	52H Tyne Dock	52H Tyne Dock
63364	Q6	MID Middlesbrough	51D Middlesbrough	51D Middlesbrough	51D Middlesbrough	51L Thornaby	51L Thornaby	
63365	Q6	CON Consett	54D Consett	54D Consett	54D Consett	52K Consett	52G Sunderland	
63366	Q6	NPT Newport	54C Borough Gardens	54C Borough Gardens	54C Borough Gardens	52C Blaydon	52H Tyne Dock	52H Tyne Dock
63367	Q6	SKN Stockton on Tees	51G Haverton Hill	51G Haverton Hill	51G Haverton Hill	51L Thornaby	51L Thornaby	
63368	Q6	MID Middlesbrough	51D Middlesbrough	51D Middlesbrough	51D Middlesbrough	52C Blaydon	52K Consett	51C West Hartlepool
63369	Q6	SKN Stockton on Tees	51D Middlesbrough	51D Middlesbrough	51D Middlesbrough	51L Thornaby	51L Thornaby	
63370	Q6	NPT Newport	51B Newport	51B Newport	51B Newport	51L Thornaby	55H Leeds Neville Hill	
63371	Q6	NPT Newport	51B Newport	51B Newport	51B Newport	51L Thornaby	51L Thornaby	
63372	Q6	CON Consett	54D Consett	54D Consett	54D Consett	52K Consett		
63373	Q6	NPT Newport	51D Middlesbrough	51D Middlesbrough	51D Middlesbrough	51L Thornaby	51F West Auckland	
63374	Q6	HAV Haverton Hill	51G Haverton Hill	51G Haverton Hill	51G Haverton Hill	51L Thornaby	51F West Auckland	
63375	Q6	NPT Newport	51D Middlesbrough	51D Middlesbrough	51D Middlesbrough	51L Thornaby	51L Thornaby	
63376	Q6	BLA Blaydon	52C Blaydon	52C Blaydon	52C Blaydon	52C Blaydon	52G Sunderland	
63377	Q6	BOR Borough Gardens	54C Borough Gardens	54C Borough Gardens	54C Borough Gardens	52C Blaydon	52H Tyne Dock	52H Tyne Dock
63378	Q6	SEL Selby	50C Selby	50C Selby	50C Selby	52C Blaydon	52H Tyne Dock	
63379	Q6	CON Consett	54B Tyne Dock	54B Tyne Dock	54B Tyne Dock	52K Consett	52K Consett	52H Tyne Dock
63380	Q6	SKN Stockton on Tees	51D Middlesbrough	51D Middlesbrough	51D Middlesbrough	51L Thornaby	51C West Hartlepool	
63381	Q6	BLA Blaydon	52C Blaydon	52C Blaydon	52C Blaydon	52C Blaydon	52F North Blyth	52F North Blyth
63382	Q6	SEL Selby	50C Selby	50C Selby	50C Selby	51L Thornaby	51C West Hartlepool	
63383	Q6	WHL West Hartlepool	51C West Hartlepool	51C West Hartlepool	51C West Hartlepool	51C West Hartlepool	51C West Hartlepool	
63384	Q6	NPT Newport	54C Borough Gardens	54C Borough Gardens	54C Borough Gardens	52C Blaydon	52H Tyne Dock	52H Tyne Dock
63385	Q6	BLA Blaydon	52C Blaydon	52C Blaydon	52C Blaydon	52C Blaydon	52C Blaydon	
63386	Q6	NPT Newport	54C Borough Gardens	54C Borough Gardens	54C Borough Gardens	52C Blaydon	52F North Blyth	
63387	Q6	SEL Selby	50C Selby	54B Tyne Dock	54B Tyne Dock	52K Consett	52C Blaydon	55H Leeds Neville Hill
63388	Q6	BOR Borough Gardens	51B Newport	51B Newport	51B Newport	51L Thornaby	51L Thornaby	
63389	Q6	NPT Newport	51B Newport	51B Newport	51B Newport	51L Thornaby	52H Tyne Dock	
63390	Q6	BLA Blaydon	52C Blaydon	52C Blaydon	52C Blaydon	52C Blaydon	52C Blaydon	
63391	Q6	BLA Blaydon	52C Blaydon	52C Blaydon	52F North Blyth	51C West Hartlepool	51C West Hartlepool	
63392	Q6	WHL West Hartlepool	51C West Hartlepool	51C West Hartlepool	51C West Hartlepool	51C West Hartlepool	51C West Hartlepool	
63393	Q6	SKN Stockton on Tees	51D Middlesbrough	51D Middlesbrough	51D Middlesbrough	51L Thornaby	52H Tyne Dock	
63394	Q6	BLA Blaydon	52C Blaydon	52C Blaydon	52C Blaydon	52C Blaydon	52C Blaydon	51C West Hartlepool
63395	Q6	WHL West Hartlepool	50C Selby	50C Selby	50C Selby	51A Darlington	51A Darlington	52G Sunderland
63396	Q6	NPT Newport	51C West Hartlepool	51C West Hartlepool	51D Middlesbrough	51L Thornaby	51L Thornaby	
63397	Q6	NPT Newport	51C West Hartlepool	51C West Hartlepool	51C West Hartlepool	51C West Hartlepool	51C West Hartlepool	51C West Hartlepool
63398	Q6	BLA Blaydon	52C Blaydon	52C Blaydon	52F North Blyth	51F West Auckland	51F West Auckland	
63399	Q6	BLA Blaydon	52C Blaydon	52C Blaydon	52F North Blyth	51L Thornaby	52H Tyne Dock	
63400	Q6	BOR Borough Gardens	54C Borough Gardens	54C Borough Gardens	54C Borough Gardens	52C Blaydon	52C Blaydon	
63401	Q6	NPT Newport	51C West Hartlepool	51D Middlesbrough	51D Middlesbrough	51L Thornaby	51L Thornaby	
63402	Q6	BOR Borough Gardens	54C Borough Gardens	54C Borough Gardens	54C Borough Gardens	52C Blaydon	52C Blaydon	

		1948		1951	1954	1957	1960	1963	1966
63403	Q6	BLA	Blaydon	52C Blaydon	52C Blaydon	52F North Blyth	51F West Auckland	51F West Auckland	
63404	Q6	CON	Consett	54D Consett	54D Consett	54D Consett	52K Consett	52G Sunderland	
63405	Q6	NPT	Newport	51G Haverton Hill	51D Middlesbrough	51D Middlesbrough	51L Thornaby	51L Thornaby	52G Sunderland
63406	Q6	SEL	Selby	50C Selby	50C Selby	50C Selby	52K Consett	52K Consett	52G Sunderland
63407	Q6	SKN	Stockton on Tees	51G Haverton Hill	51G Haverton Hill	51G Haverton Hill	51F West Auckland	51F West Auckland	51C West Hartlepool
63408	Q6	SEL	Selby	50C Selby	54C Borough Gardens	54C Borough Gardens	52C Blaydon	52C Blaydon	
63409	Q6	NPT	Newport	51D Middlesbrough	51D Middlesbrough	51D Middlesbrough	51L Thornaby	52H Tyne Dock	52H Tyne Dock
63410	Q6	WHL	West Hartlepool	51C West Hartlepool	51C West Hartlepool	51C West Hartlepool	51C West Hartlepool	51C West Hartlepool	51C West Hartlepool
63411	Q6	NPT	Newport	51D Middlesbrough	51D Middlesbrough	51D Middlesbrough	51L Thornaby	52H Tyne Dock	
63412	Q6	BLA	Blaydon	52C Blaydon	52C Blaydon	52C Blaydon	51C West Hartlepool	51C West Hartlepool	51C West Hartlepool
63413	Q6	BLA	Blaydon	52C Blaydon	52C Blaydon	52C Blaydon	52C Blaydon	52F North Blyth	52F North Blyth
63414	Q6	WHL	West Hartlepool	51C West Hartlepool	51C West Hartlepool	51C West Hartlepool	51C West Hartlepool	51C West Hartlepool	
63415	Q6	NPT	Newport	51C West Hartlepool	51C West Hartlepool	51C West Hartlepool	51C West Hartlepool	51C West Hartlepool	
63416	Q6	HAV	Haverton Hill	51G Haverton Hill	51G Haverton Hill	51G Haverton Hill	51L Thornaby	51L Thornaby	
63417	Q6	NPT	Newport	51D Middlesbrough	51D Middlesbrough	51D Middlesbrough	51L Thornaby	55H Leeds Neville Hill	55H Leeds Neville Hill
63418	Q6	CON	Consett	54D Consett	54D Consett	54D Consett	52K Consett	52G Sunderland	
63419	Q6	NPT	Newport	51C West Hartlepool	51C West Hartlepool	51C West Hartlepool	51C West Hartlepool	51C West Hartlepool	
63420	Q6	NPT	Newport	51D Middlesbrough	51D Middlesbrough	51D Middlesbrough	51L Thornaby	55H Leeds Neville Hill	55H Leeds Neville Hill
63421	Q6	WHL	West Hartlepool	51C West Hartlepool	51C West Hartlepool	51C West Hartlepool	51C West Hartlepool	51C West Hartlepool	51C West Hartlepool
63422	Q6	WHL	West Hartlepool	51C West Hartlepool	51C West Hartlepool	51C West Hartlepool	51C West Hartlepool	51C West Hartlepool	
63423	Q6	NPT	Newport	50C Selby	50C Selby	50C Selby	51A Darlington	51A Darlington	
63424	Q6	WHL	West Hartlepool	51C West Hartlepool	51C West Hartlepool	51D Middlesbrough	51L Thornaby	55H Leeds Neville Hill	
63425	Q6	NPT	Newport	50C Selby	50C Selby	50C Selby	52H Tyne Dock	52H Tyne Dock	
63426	Q6	NPT	Newport	51B Newport	51B Newport	51B Newport	51L Thornaby	55H Leeds Neville Hill	55H Leeds Neville Hill
63427	Q6	WHL	West Hartlepool	51C West Hartlepool	54D Consett	54D Consett	52K Consett	52K Consett	
63428	Q6	BLA	Blaydon	52C Blaydon	52C Blaydon	52F North Blyth	51L Thornaby	51L Thornaby	
63429	Q6	SEL	Selby	50C Selby	50C Selby	50C Selby	52H Tyne Dock	52C Blaydon	52F North Blyth
63430	Q6	NPT	Newport	51B Newport	51B Newport	51B Newport	51L Thornaby	51L Thornaby	
63431	Q6	NPT	Newport	50C Selby	54C Borough Gardens	54C Borough Gardens	52C Blaydon	52C Blaydon	52H Tyne Dock
63432	Q6	BLA	Blaydon	52C Blaydon	52C Blaydon	52C Blaydon	51L Thornaby	51C West Hartlepool	
63433	Q6	CON	Consett	54D Consett	54D Consett	54D Consett	52K Consett	52K Consett	
63434	Q6	BOR	Borough Gardens	54C Borough Gardens	54C Borough Gardens	54C Borough Gardens	52C Blaydon	52C Blaydon	
63435	Q6	WHL	West Hartlepool	51C West Hartlepool	51D Middlesbrough	51D Middlesbrough	51L Thornaby	51L Thornaby	51C West Hartlepool
63436	Q6	SEL	Selby	50C Selby	50B Leeds Neville Hill	50B Leeds Neville Hill	50B Leeds Neville Hill	55H Leeds Neville Hill	52G Sunderland
63437	Q6	BLA	Blaydon	54B Tyne Dock	54B Tyne Dock	54B Tyne Dock	52K Consett	52C Blaydon	52G Sunderland
63438	Q6	NPT	Newport	51C West Hartlepool	51C West Hartlepool	51C West Hartlepool	51C West Hartlepool	51C West Hartlepool	
63439	Q6	CON	Consett	54D Consett	54D Consett	54D Consett	52K Consett	52K Consett	
63440	Q6	SEL	Selby	50C Selby	50C Selby	50C Selby	51C West Hartlepool	51C West Hartlepool	51C West Hartlepool
63441	Q6	BLA	Blaydon	52C Blaydon	52C Blaydon	52C Blaydon	52C Blaydon	52C Blaydon	
63442	Q6	NPT	Newport	51D Middlesbrough	51D Middlesbrough	51D Middlesbrough	51L Thornaby	51L Thornaby	
63443	Q6	NPT	Newport	51G Haverton Hill	51G Haverton Hill	51G Haverton Hill	51F West Auckland	51F West Auckland	
63444	Q6	BLA	Blaydon	54C Borough Gardens	54C Borough Gardens	54C Borough Gardens	52C Blaydon	52C Blaydon	
63445	Q6	NPT	Newport	51B Newport	51B Newport	51B Newport	51L Thornaby	55H Leeds Neville Hill	52G Sunderland
63446	Q6	NPT	Newport	51G Haverton Hill	51G Haverton Hill	51G Haverton Hill	51F West Auckland	51F West Auckland	51C West Hartlepool
63447	Q6	SEL	Selby	51B Newport	51B Newport	51B Newport	51L Thornaby	51L Thornaby	
63448	Q6	BLA	Blaydon	50C Selby	50C Selby	50C Selby	52K Consett	52K Consett	
63449	Q6	SEL	Selby	50C Selby	50C Selby	50C Selby	50B Leeds Neville Hill	55H Leeds Neville Hill	
63450	Q6	SEL	Selby	50B Leeds Neville Hill	50C Selby	50C Selby	51L Thornaby	51C West Hartlepool	51C West Hartlepool
63451	Q6	SEL	Selby	50C Selby	50C Selby	50C Selby	51L Thornaby	51C West Hartlepool	
63452	Q6	WHL	West Hartlepool	51C West Hartlepool	51D Middlesbrough	51D Middlesbrough	51L Thornaby	51L Thornaby	
63453	Q6	NPT	Newport	50C Selby	54B Tyne Dock	54B Tyne Dock	52C Blaydon	52C Blaydon	52H Tyne Dock
63454	Q6	WHL	West Hartlepool	51C West Hartlepool	51C West Hartlepool	51C West Hartlepool	51C West Hartlepool	51C West Hartlepool	51C West Hartlepool
63455	Q6	CON	Consett	54D Consett	54D Consett	54D Consett	52K Consett	52K Consett	52H Tyne Dock
63456	Q6	SEL	Selby	50C Selby	54C Borough Gardens	54C Borough Gardens	52K Consett	52G Sunderland	
63457	Q6	WHL	West Hartlepool	51C West Hartlepool	51C West Hartlepool	51C West Hartlepool	51C West Hartlepool		
63458	Q6	NPT	Newport	54C Borough Gardens	54C Borough Gardens	54C Borough Gardens	52C Blaydon	52C Blaydon	52G Sunderland
63459	Q6	NPT	Newport	51D Middlesbrough	51D Middlesbrough	51F West Auckland	51F West Auckland	51F West Auckland	52H Tyne Dock
63460	Q7	TDK	Tyne Dock	54B Tyne Dock	54B Tyne Dock	54B Tyne Dock	52H Tyne Dock		
63461	Q7	TDK	Tyne Dock	54B Tyne Dock	54B Tyne Dock	52C Blaydon	52H Tyne Dock		
63462	Q7	TDK	Tyne Dock	54B Tyne Dock	54B Tyne Dock	52C Blaydon	52H Tyne Dock		
63463	Q7	TDK	Tyne Dock	54B Tyne Dock	54B Tyne Dock	54B Tyne Dock	52H Tyne Dock		
63464	Q7	TDK	Tyne Dock	54B Tyne Dock	54B Tyne Dock	52C Blaydon	52H Tyne Dock		
63465	Q7	TDK	Tyne Dock	54B Tyne Dock	54B Tyne Dock	54B Tyne Dock	52H Tyne Dock		
63466	Q7	TDK	Tyne Dock	54B Tyne Dock	54B Tyne Dock	54A Sunderland	52H Tyne Dock		
63467	Q7	TDK	Tyne Dock	54B Tyne Dock	54B Tyne Dock	54A Sunderland	52G Sunderland		
63468	Q7	TDK	Tyne Dock	54B Tyne Dock	54B Tyne Dock	52C Blaydon	52H Tyne Dock		
63469	Q7	TDK	Tyne Dock	54B Tyne Dock	54B Tyne Dock	54B Tyne Dock	52G Sunderland		
63470	Q7	TDK	Tyne Dock	54B Tyne Dock	54B Tyne Dock	52C Blaydon	52H Tyne Dock		
63471	Q7	TDK	Tyne Dock	54B Tyne Dock	54B Tyne Dock	52C Blaydon	52H Tyne Dock		
63472	Q7	TDK	Tyne Dock	54B Tyne Dock	54B Tyne Dock	52C Blaydon	52H Tyne Dock		
63473	Q7	TDK	Tyne Dock	54B Tyne Dock	54B Tyne Dock	54B Tyne Dock	52H Tyne Dock		
63474	Q7	TDK	Tyne Dock	54B Tyne Dock	54B Tyne Dock	54A Sunderland	52G Sunderland		
63475	O3	FRO	Frodingham	36E Retford					
63476	O3	FRO	Frodingham	36A Doncaster					
63477	O3	FRO	Frodingham	36A Doncaster					
63478	O3	FRO	Frodingham	36E Retford					
63479	O3	FRO	Frodingham	36A Doncaster					
63480	O3	FRO	Frodingham	36A Doncaster					
63481	O3	FRO	Frodingham	36A Doncaster					
63482	O3	FRO	Frodingham	36E Retford					
63483	O3	FRO	Frodingham	36A Doncaster					
63484	O3	FRO	Frodingham	36A Doncaster					
63485	O3	FRO	Frodingham	36A Doncaster					
63486	O3	FRO	Frodingham	36A Doncaster					
63488	O3	FRO	Frodingham	36E Retford					
63489	O3	FRO	Frodingham						
63491	O3	FRO	Frodingham						
63493	O3	FRO	Frodingham	36A Doncaster					
63494	O3	FRO	Frodingham						
63570	O4/7	TUX	Tuxford Junction	40D Tuxford Junction	37A Ardsley	56B Ardsley	56B Ardsley		
63571	O4/1→O1	ANN	Annesley	38B Annesley	38B Annesley	38B Annesley	31B March	41H Staveley	
63572	O4/1	DON	Doncaster	36C Frodingham	36C Frodingham	36C Frodingham			
63573	O4/1→8	CLK	Colwick	39A Gorton	39A Gorton	39A Gorton	9G Gorton		
63574	O4/1	CLK	Colwick	39B Sheffield Darnall	39B Sheffield Darnall	41A Sheffield Darnall	41A Sheffield Darnall		
63575	O4/8	ANN	Annesley	39A Gorton	39A Gorton	39A Gorton	9G Gorton		
63576	O4/1	MEX	Mexborough	36C Frodingham	36C Frodingham	36C Frodingham	36C Frodingham	36C Frodingham	
63577	O4/1	MEX	Mexborough	40E Langwith Junction	40E Langwith Junction	40E Langwith Junction	41J Langwith Junction	41J Langwith Junction	
63578	O1	GOR	Gorton	38B Annesley	38B Annesley	38B Annesley	16D Annesley		
63579	O4/5→O1	SHF	Sheffield Darnall	38B Annesley	38B Annesley	38B Annesley	31B March		
63580	O4/1	ANN	Annesley	39A Gorton					
63581	O4/1	SHF	Sheffield Darnall	39B Sheffield Darnall	39B Sheffield Darnall	41A Sheffield Darnall			
63582	O4/7	ANN	Annesley	39A Gorton	39A Gorton	39A Gorton			
63583	O4/1	SHF	Sheffield Darnall	39B Sheffield Darnall	39B Sheffield Darnall	41A Sheffield Darnall			
63584	O4/1	FRO	Frodingham	36C Frodingham	39B Sheffield Darnall	56B Ardsley	56B Ardsley		
63585	O4/1	MEX	Mexborough	40E Langwith Junction	40E Langwith Junction	40E Langwith Junction	40E Colwick	40E Colwick	
63586	O4/1	DON	Doncaster	40B Immingham	36B Mexborough	36B Mexborough	41F Mexborough	36C Frodingham	
63587	O4/1	DON	Doncaster	36C Frodingham	38D Staveley	38A Colwick	40E Colwick		
63588	O4/7	SHF	Sheffield Darnall	40D Tuxford Junction	37A Ardsley	56B Ardsley	56A Wakefield		
63589	O4/5→O1	ANN	Annesley	38B Annesley	38B Annesley	38B Annesley	40E Colwick	40E Colwick	
63590	O1	GOR	Gorton	38B Annesley	38B Annesley	38B Annesley	41H Staveley	41H Staveley	
63591	O1	GOR	Gorton	38B Annesley	38B Annesley	38B Annesley	16D Annesley		
63592	O1	GOR	Gorton	38B Annesley	38B Annesley	38B Annesley	40E Colwick	40E Colwick	
63593	O4/1	DON	Doncaster	40B Immingham	36B Mexborough	36B Mexborough	41F Mexborough	36A Doncaster	
63594	O1	DON	Doncaster	38B Annesley	38B Annesley	38B Annesley	40E Colwick	40E Colwick	

		1948	1951	1954	1957	1960	1963	1966
63595	*O4/7*	**FRO** Frodingham	**36C** Frodingham	**36C** Frodingham	**36C** Frodingham	**36C** Frodingham		
63596	*O4/7→O1*	**ANN** Annesley	**38B** Annesley	**38B** Annesley	**38B** Annesley	**31B** March	**41H** Staveley	
63597	*O4/1*	**LNG** Langwith Junction	**40E** Langwith Junction	**40E** Langwith Junction	**40D** Tuxford Junction	**41J** Langwith Junction		
63598	*O4/1*	**DON** Doncaster	**39A** Gorton	**39A** Gorton	**39A** Gorton	**9G** Gorton		
63599	*O4/1*	**CLK** Colwick	**38A** Colwick	**38A** Colwick	**41A** Sheffield Darnall	**41A** Sheffield Darnall		
63600	*O4/7*	**DON** Doncaster	**39A** Gorton	**39A** Gorton	**39A** Gorton	**9G** Gorton		
63601	*O4/1*	**DON** Doncaster	**36C** Frodingham	**39A** Gorton	**36C** Frodingham	**36C** Frodingham	**36C** Frodingham	
63602	*O4/1→8*	**FRO** Frodingham	**36C** Frodingham	**38A** Colwick	**38A** Colwick	**36C** Frodingham		
63603	*O4/7*	**TDK** Tyne Dock	**53A** Hull Dairycoates	**40E** Langwith Junction	**40E** Langwith Junction	**41J** Langwith Junction		
63604	*O4/1→8*	**TUX** Tuxford Junction	**39B** Sheffield Darnall	**39B** Sheffield Darnall	**41A** Sheffield Darnall	**41A** Sheffield Darnall	**41H** Staveley	
63605	*O4/1*	**CLK** Colwick	**39B** Sheffield Darnall	**39B** Sheffield Darnall	**56B** Ardsley	**56B** Ardsley		
63606	*O4/1→8*	**FRO** Frodingham	**36C** Frodingham	**36C** Frodingham	**36C** Frodingham	**36C** Frodingham	**36C** Frodingham	
63607	*O4/1*	**DON** Doncaster	**40B** Immingham	**39B** Sheffield Darnall	**40D** Tuxford Junction	**41J** Langwith Junction	**40E** Colwick	
63608	*O4/1*	**RET** Retford	**36E** Retford	**36E** Retford	**36E** Retford	**36E** Retford		
63609	*O4/1*	**STV** Staveley	**39B** Sheffield Darnall	**39B** Sheffield Darnall	**41A** Sheffield Darnall	**41A** Sheffield Darnall		
63610	*O1*	**THJ** Thornton Junction	**38B** Annesley	**38B** Annesley	**38B** Annesley	**16D** Annesley		
63611	*O4/1*	**MEX** Mexborough	**36B** Mexborough	**36B** Mexborough	**36B** Mexborough	**41F** Mexborough	**41F** Mexborough	
63612	*O4/1→8*	**MEX** Mexborough	**36B** Mexborough	**36B** Mexborough	**36D** Barnsley	**41J** Langwith Junction	**41H** Staveley	
63613	*O4/8*	**STV** Staveley	**38D** Staveley	**38D** Staveley	**36A** Doncaster	**36A** Doncaster	**36A** Doncaster	
63614	*O4/1*	**ANN** Annesley	**39A** Gorton	**39A** Gorton	**38A** Colwick			
63615	*O4/7*	**LNG** Langwith Junction	**40E** Langwith Junction	**40E** Langwith Junction	**40B** Immingham	**40B** Immingham	**40E** Colwick	
63616	*O4/7*	**DON** Doncaster	**40B** Immingham	**40B** Immingham	**40B** Immingham	**40B** Immingham		
63617	*O4/1*	**DON** Doncaster	**36C** Frodingham	**36C** Frodingham	**36C** Frodingham	**36C** Frodingham		
63618	*O4/1*	**ANN** Annesley	**38A** Colwick	**38A** Colwick	**36A** Doncaster	**36A** Doncaster	**36A** Doncaster	
63619	*O1*	**GOR** Gorton	**38B** Annesley	**38B** Annesley	**38B** Annesley	**31B** March	**41H** Staveley	
63620	*O4/1*	**TDK** Tyne Dock	**53E** Cudworth	**39B** Sheffield Darnall	**41A** Sheffield Darnall			
63621	*O4/1*	**DON** Doncaster	**40B** Immingham	**39B** Sheffield Darnall	**41A** Sheffield Darnall	**41A** Sheffield Darnall		
63622	*O4/1*	**SHF** Sheffield Darnall	**39B** Sheffield Darnall	**39B** Sheffield Darnall	**40D** Tuxford Junction	**41G** Barnsley	**41J** Langwith Junction	
63623	*O4/1*	**DON** Doncaster	**36D** Barnsley	**36D** Barnsley	**36D** Barnsley	**41G** Barnsley		
63624	*O4/1→8*	**DON** Doncaster	**40B** Immingham	**39B** Sheffield Darnall	**41A** Sheffield Darnall	**41A** Sheffield Darnall		
63625	*O4/1*	**MEX** Mexborough	**36D** Barnsley	**36D** Barnsley	**36D** Barnsley			
63626	*O4/1*	**FRO** Frodingham	**36C** Frodingham	**36C** Frodingham	**36C** Frodingham	**36C** Frodingham		
63627	*O4/1*	**DON** Doncaster	**40E** Langwith Junction					
63628	*O4/5→8*	**HLD** Hull Dairycoates	**53A** Hull Dairycoates	**38A** Colwick	**36B** Mexborough	**41F** Mexborough	**36C** Frodingham	
63629	*O4/3*	**SHF** Sheffield Darnall	**39B** Sheffield Darnall	**39B** Sheffield Darnall	**41A** Sheffield Darnall			
63630	*O1*	**GOR** Gorton	**38B** Annesley	**38B** Annesley	**38B** Annesley	**31B** March	**41H** Staveley	
63631	*O4/1→8*	**ANN** Annesley	**39A** Gorton	**39A** Gorton	**39A** Gorton	**9G** Gorton		
63632	*O4/1*	**MEX** Mexborough	**40E** Langwith Junction	**40E** Langwith Junction	**40E** Langwith Junction	**41G** Barnsley	**36E** Retford	
63633	*O4/8*	**ANN** Annesley	**39A** Gorton	**37A** Ardsley	**56B** Ardsley	**56B** Ardsley		
63634	*O4/7*	**IMM** Immingham	**40D** Tuxford Junction	**40E** Langwith Junction	**40E** Langwith Junction	**41J** Langwith Junction		
63635	*O4/1*	**ANN** Annesley	**39A** Gorton	**39A** Gorton	**40D** Tuxford Junction	**41J** Langwith Junction		
63636	*O4/3→8*	**CLK** Colwick	**38A** Colwick	**40E** Langwith Junction	**40E** Langwith Junction	**41J** Langwith Junction	**41J** Langwith Junction	
63637	*O4/3*	**RET** Retford	**36E** Retford	**36E** Retford	**36E** Retford	**36E** Retford		
63638	*O4/3*	**ANN** Annesley	**39A** Gorton	**39A** Gorton	**38A** Colwick			
63639	*O4/3→8*	**CLK** Colwick	**38B** Annesley	**38A** Colwick	**38A** Colwick	**40E** Colwick	**40E** Colwick	
63640	*O4/1*	**FRO** Frodingham	**36C** Frodingham	**39B** Sheffield Darnall	**41A** Sheffield Darnall			
63641	*O4/3→8*	**CLK** Colwick	**39A** Gorton	**39A** Gorton	**39A** Gorton	**9G** Gorton		
63642	*O4/3*	**FRO** Frodingham	**36C** Frodingham	**36C** Frodingham	**36C** Frodingham			
63643	*O4/7*	**DON** Doncaster	**40E** Langwith Junction	**40E** Langwith Junction	**40D** Tuxford Junction	**41J** Langwith Junction		
63644	*O4/2→8*	**LNG** Langwith Junction	**40E** Langwith Junction	**40E** Langwith Junction	**40B** Immingham	**40B** Immingham	**40E** Colwick	**40E** Colwick
63645	*O4/3→8*	**FRO** Frodingham	**36C** Frodingham	**39B** Sheffield Darnall	**41A** Sheffield Darnall	**41A** Sheffield Darnall	**41A** Sheffield Darnall	
63646	*O1*	**GOR** Gorton	**38B** Annesley	**38B** Annesley	**38B** Annesley	**31B** March	**41H** Staveley	
63647	*O4/2→8*	**DON** Doncaster	**40B** Immingham	**38A** Colwick	**38A** Colwick	**36C** Frodingham	**36E** Retford	
63648	*O4/2*	**MEX** Mexborough	**40E** Langwith Junction	**38D** Staveley	**38D** Staveley	**41H** Staveley		
63649	*O4/3→8*	**FRO** Frodingham	**36C** Frodingham	**38A** Colwick	**39A** Gorton	**9G** Gorton		
63650	*O1*	**GOR** Gorton	**38B** Annesley	**38B** Annesley	**38B** Annesley	**31B** March	**41H** Staveley	
63651	*O4/8*	**LNG** Langwith Junction	**40B** Immingham	**40B** Immingham	**40B** Immingham	**40B** Immingham	**40E** Colwick	
63652	*O1*	**GOR** Gorton	**38B** Annesley	**38B** Annesley	**38B** Annesley	**31B** March	**40E** Colwick	
63653	*O4/8*	**MAR** March	**36C** Frodingham	**36C** Frodingham	**36C** Frodingham	**36C** Frodingham	**36C** Frodingham	**36A** Doncaster
63654	*O4/1*	**RET** Retford	**36E** Retford	**36E** Retford	**36E** Retford			
63655	*O4/7→8*	**FRO** Frodingham	**36C** Frodingham	**36C** Frodingham	**36E** Retford	**36E** Retford		
63656	*O4/3*	**MEX** Mexborough	**36D** Barnsley	**36D** Barnsley	**36D** Barnsley	**41G** Barnsley		
63657	*O4/3*	**DON** Doncaster	**40B** Immingham	**38A** Colwick	**38A** Colwick	**40E** Colwick		
63658	*O4/1*	**MAR** March	**40E** Langwith Junction	**38A** Colwick	**41A** Sheffield Darnall	**41A** Sheffield Darnall		
63659	*O4/3*	**DON** Doncaster	**36C** Frodingham	**36C** Frodingham	**36D** Barnsley	**41G** Barnsley		
63660	*O4/1*	**DON** Doncaster	**36C** Frodingham	**36C** Frodingham	**36C** Frodingham			
63661	*O4/7*	**SHF** Sheffield Darnall	**39B** Sheffield Darnall	**39B** Sheffield Darnall	**41A** Sheffield Darnall	**41A** Sheffield Darnall	**41A** Sheffield Darnall	
63662	*O4/7*	**ANN** Annesley	**39A** Gorton	**39A** Gorton	**36C** Frodingham	**36C** Frodingham		
63663	*O1*	**GOR** Gorton	**38B** Annesley	**38B** Annesley	**38B** Annesley	**41H** Staveley	**40E** Colwick	
63664	*O4/1*	**HLD** Hull Dairycoates	**53A** Hull Dairycoates	**40E** Langwith Junction	**40E** Langwith Junction	**41J** Langwith Junction		
63665	*O4/3*	**LNG** Langwith Junction	**40E** Langwith Junction	**40E** Langwith Junction	**40D** Tuxford Junction	**36C** Frodingham	**36E** Retford	
63666	*O4/3*	**MEX** Mexborough	**36B** Mexborough	**36B** Mexborough	**36B** Mexborough	**36C** Frodingham		
63667	*O4/3*	**TDK** Tyne Dock	**53E** Cudworth	**40E** Langwith Junction	**40E** Langwith Junction			
63668	*O4/3*	**DON** Doncaster	**36B** Mexborough	**36B** Mexborough	**36B** Mexborough			
63669	*O4/7*	**FRO** Frodingham	**36C** Frodingham	**36D** Barnsley	**36D** Barnsley	**41G** Barnsley		
63670	*O1*	**GOR** Gorton	**38B** Annesley	**38B** Annesley	**38B** Annesley	**31B** March	**41H** Staveley	
63671	*O4/1*	**DON** Doncaster	**36C** Frodingham	**36C** Frodingham	**36C** Frodingham	**36C** Frodingham	**36C** Frodingham	
63672	*O4/3→8*	**MEX** Mexborough	**36B** Mexborough	**36B** Mexborough	**36B** Mexborough	**41F** Mexborough	**36E** Retford	
63673	*O4/7*	**HLS** Hull Springhead	**53A** Hull Dairycoates	**38A** Colwick	**36B** Mexborough			
63674	*O4/2→8*	**ANN** Annesley	**38B** Annesley	**38A** Colwick	**38A** Colwick	**40E** Colwick	**40E** Colwick	**40E** Colwick
63675	*O4/7→8*	**STV** Staveley	**39B** Sheffield Darnall	**38D** Staveley	**38A** Colwick	**40E** Colwick	**40E** Colwick	**40E** Colwick
63676	*O1*	**TDK** Tyne Dock	**53A** Hull Dairycoates	**38B** Annesley	**38B** Annesley	**16D** Annesley		
63677	*O4/1*	**LNG** Langwith Junction	**40D** Tuxford Junction	**37A** Ardsley	**36B** Mexborough	**36A** Doncaster		
63678	*O1*	**GOR** Gorton	**38B** Annesley	**38B** Annesley	**38B** Annesley	**31B** March	**41H** Staveley	
63679	*O4/3→8*	**IMM** Immingham	**40E** Langwith Junction	**40E** Langwith Junction	**40E** Langwith Junction	**41J** Langwith Junction	**41J** Langwith Junction	
63680	*O4/2*	**SHF** Sheffield Darnall	**39B** Sheffield Darnall	**39B** Sheffield Darnall	**41A** Sheffield Darnall			
63681	*O4/3*	**ANN** Annesley	**39A** Gorton	**39A** Gorton	**39A** Gorton	**9G** Gorton		
63682	*O4/2*	**DON** Doncaster	**40E** Langwith Junction	**39B** Sheffield Darnall	**41A** Sheffield Darnall			
63683	*O4/1→8*	**ARD** Ardsley	**40E** Langwith Junction	**40E** Langwith Junction	**40D** Tuxford Junction	**41J** Langwith Junction	**41J** Langwith Junction	
63684	*O4/1*	**DON** Doncaster	**36C** Frodingham	**38A** Colwick	**36B** Mexborough	**41F** Mexborough	**41A** Sheffield Darnall	
63685	*O4/3*	**ANN** Annesley	**39B** Sheffield Darnall	**39B** Sheffield Darnall	**41A** Sheffield Darnall	**41A** Sheffield Darnall	**41A** Sheffield Darnall	
63686	*O4/3*	**SHF** Sheffield Darnall	**39A** Gorton	**39A** Gorton	**39A** Gorton	**9G** Gorton		
63687	*O1*	**GOR** Gorton	**38B** Annesley	**38B** Annesley	**38B** Annesley	**31B** March	**31B** March	
63688	*O4/3→8*	**RET** Retford	**36E** Retford	**36E** Retford	**36E** Retford	**36E** Retford	**36E** Retford	
63689	*O1*	**GOR** Gorton	**38B** Annesley	**38B** Annesley	**38B** Annesley	**16D** Annesley		
63690	*O4/2*	**FRO** Frodingham	**36C** Frodingham	**36C** Frodingham	**36C** Frodingham	**36C** Frodingham		
63691	*O4/3→8*	**TUX** Tuxford Junction	**40D** Tuxford Junction	**37A** Ardsley	**40D** Tuxford Junction	**41J** Langwith Junction	**41J** Langwith Junction	
63692	*O4/1*	**IMM** Immingham	**40B** Immingham	**40B** Immingham	**40B** Immingham	**40B** Immingham	**40E** Colwick	
63693	*O4/1*	**DON** Doncaster	**40B** Immingham	**36B** Mexborough	**36B** Mexborough	**36A** Doncaster		
63694	*O4/3*	**ANN** Annesley	**38D** Staveley	**38D** Staveley	**38A** Colwick			
63695	*O4/3*	**CLK** Colwick	**39A** Gorton	**39A** Gorton	**41A** Sheffield Darnall	**41A** Sheffield Darnall		
63696	*O4/3*	**FRO** Frodingham	**36C** Frodingham	**36C** Frodingham	**36C** Frodingham			
63697	*O4/3→8*	**DON** Doncaster	**36D** Barnsley	**36D** Barnsley	**36D** Barnsley	**41J** Langwith Junction	**41J** Langwith Junction	
63698	*O4/1*	**DON** Doncaster	**40B** Immingham	**36B** Mexborough	**36B** Mexborough	**36A** Doncaster		
63699	*O4/7*	**ANN** Annesley	**38A** Colwick	**38A** Colwick	**38A** Colwick			
63700	*O4/1*	**ANN** Annesley	**39A** Gorton	**39A** Gorton	**39A** Gorton	**9G** Gorton		
63701	*O4/3*	**MAR** March	**31B** March	**36B** Mexborough	**36B** Mexborough	**41F** Mexborough	**41H** Staveley	
63702	*O4/3*	**STV** Staveley	**39A** Gorton	**38D** Staveley	**38D** Staveley	**41H** Staveley	**36E** Retford	
63703	*O4/3→8*	**MEX** Mexborough	**40E** Langwith Junction	**40E** Langwith Junction	**40E** Langwith Junction	**41J** Langwith Junction	**41J** Langwith Junction	
63704	*O4/2→8*	**CAM** Cambridge	**31B** March	**36B** Mexborough	**36D** Barnsley	**41J** Langwith Junction	**36E** Retford	
63705	*O4/7→8*	**CAM** Cambridge	**39A** Gorton	**38D** Staveley	**38D** Staveley	**41H** Staveley	**41H** Staveley	
63706	*O4/7→8*	**ANN** Annesley	**39A** Gorton	**38D** Staveley	**38D** Staveley	**41H** Staveley	**41H** Staveley	
63707	*O4/1*	**MEX** Mexborough	**40E** Langwith Junction	**40E** Langwith Junction	**40E** Langwith Junction	**41J** Langwith Junction	**40E** Colwick	
63708	*O4/7*	**CAM** Cambridge	**39A** Gorton	**39A** Gorton	**40B** Immingham	**40B** Immingham		

No.	Class	1948		1951	1954	1957	1960	1963	1966
63709	O4/2→8	**MEX**	Mexborough	**40E** Langwith Junction	**39A** Gorton	**39A** Gorton	**9G** Gorton		
63710	O4/1	**SHF**	Sheffield Darnall	**39B** Sheffield Darnall	**39B** Sheffield Darnall	**41A** Sheffield Darnall			
63711	O1	**GOR**	Gorton	**38B** Annesley	**38B** Annesley	**38B** Annesley	**16D** Annesley		
63712	O1	**TDK**	Tyne Dock	**53A** Hull Dairycoates	**54B** Tyne Dock	**54B** Tyne Dock	**52H** Tyne Dock		
63713	O4/3	**CLK**	Colwick	**39A** Gorton	**39A** Gorton	**39A** Gorton	**9G** Gorton		
63714	O4/3	**SHF**	Sheffield Darnall	**39B** Sheffield Darnall	**39B** Sheffield Darnall	**41A** Sheffield Darnall			
63715	O4/3→8	**MEX**	Mexborough	**40E** Langwith Junction	**40E** Langwith Junction	**40E** Langwith Junction	**41J** Langwith Junction	**41J** Langwith Junction	
63716	O4/3	**ANN**	Annesley	**39A** Gorton	**39A** Gorton	**39A** Gorton	**9G** Gorton		
63717	O4/3→8	**MEX**	Mexborough	**40E** Langwith Junction	**40E** Langwith Junction	**40E** Langwith Junction	**41J** Langwith Junction	**41J** Langwith Junction	
63718	O4/3→8	**CAM**	Cambridge	**36C** Frodingham	**36D** Barnsley	**36D** Barnsley	**41J** Langwith Junction		
63719	O4/1	**DON**	Doncaster	**39A** Gorton	**39A** Gorton	**39A** Gorton	**9G** Gorton		
63720	O4/3→8	**ANN**	Annesley	**38D** Staveley	**38D** Staveley	**38D** Staveley	**41H** Staveley	**41J** Langwith Junction	
63721	O4/3→8	**CLK**	Colwick	**39A** Gorton	**39A** Gorton	**39A** Gorton	**9G** Gorton		
63722	O4/1	**ANN**	Annesley	**39A** Gorton	**39A** Gorton	**40D** Tuxford Junction	**41G** Barnsley	**41J** Langwith Junction	
63723	O4/1	**ANN**	Annesley	**38A** Colwick	**38A** Colwick	**36B** Mexborough			
63724	O4/3	**CAM**	Cambridge	**40E** Langwith Junction	**37A** Ardsley	**56B** Ardsley	**56B** Ardsley		
63725	O1	**GOR**	Gorton	**38B** Annesley	**38B** Annesley	**15A** Wellingborough	**31B** March	**31B** March	
63726	O4/5→8	**FRO**	Frodingham	**36C** Frodingham	**36D** Barnsley	**36D** Barnsley	**41G** Barnsley	**36E** Retford	
63727	O4/1	**MEX**	Mexborough	**36D** Barnsley	**36D** Barnsley	**36D** Barnsley	**41G** Barnsley	**36E** Retford	
63728	O4/3→8	**DON**	Doncaster	**36C** Frodingham	**36C** Frodingham	**36C** Frodingham	**36C** Frodingham	**36C** Frodingham	
63729	O4/3	**CLK**	Colwick	**38A** Colwick	**38A** Colwick	**38A** Colwick			
63730	O4/2→8	**CAM**	Cambridge	**31B** March	**36B** Mexborough	**36B** Mexborough	**36C** Frodingham	**36C** Frodingham	**36A** Doncaster
63731	O4/3→8	**DON**	Doncaster	**36C** Frodingham	**36D** Barnsley	**36D** Barnsley	**41J** Langwith Junction	**41J** Langwith Junction	
63732	O4/3→8	**HLS**	Hull Springhead	**53A** Hull Dairycoates	**40E** Langwith Junction	**40E** Langwith Junction	**41J** Langwith Junction	**41J** Langwith Junction	
63733	O4/3	**SHF**	Sheffield Darnall	**39B** Sheffield Darnall	**39B** Sheffield Darnall	**41A** Sheffield Darnall	**41A** Sheffield Darnall		
63734	O4/3→8	**STV**	Staveley	**39B** Sheffield Darnall	**39B** Sheffield Darnall	**41A** Sheffield Darnall	**41A** Sheffield Darnall	**41F** Mexborough	
63735	O4/3	**ANN**	Annesley	**38A** Colwick	**38A** Colwick	**38D** Staveley	**41H** Staveley		
63736	O4/1	**RET**	Retford	**36E** Retford	**36E** Retford	**36E** Retford	**36E** Retford	**36E** Retford	
63737	O4/3	**SHF**	Sheffield Darnall	**39B** Sheffield Darnall	**39B** Sheffield Darnall	**41A** Sheffield Darnall	**41A** Sheffield Darnall		
63738	O4/8	**DON**	Doncaster	**40B** Immingham	**40B** Immingham	**40B** Immingham	**40B** Immingham	**40E** Colwick	
63739	O4/3→8	**ANN**	Annesley	**39A** Gorton	**39A** Gorton	**40E** Langwith Junction	**41J** Langwith Junction	**41J** Langwith Junction	
63740	O1	**TDK**	Tyne Dock	**53A** Hull Dairycoates	**38B** Annesley	**38B** Annesley	**16D** Annesley		
63741	O4/3→8	**DON**	Doncaster	**36C** Frodingham	**36C** Frodingham	**36C** Frodingham	**36C** Frodingham	**36C** Frodingham	
63742	O4/3→8	**ANN**	Annesley	**39A** Gorton	**39A** Gorton	**41A** Sheffield Darnall	**41A** Sheffield Darnall	**41A** Sheffield Darnall	
63743	O4/1	**ANN**	Annesley	**39A** Gorton	**39A** Gorton	**39A** Gorton	**9G** Gorton		
63744	O4/3	**FRO**	Frodingham	**36C** Frodingham	**36C** Frodingham	**36C** Frodingham	**36C** Frodingham	**36C** Frodingham	
63745	O4/5	**DON**	Doncaster	**36C** Frodingham	**38A** Colwick	**36B** Mexborough			
63746	O4/3→O1	**STV**	Staveley	**38B** Annesley	**38B** Annesley	**38B** Annesley	**31B** March	**31B** March	
63747	O4/7	**MEX**	Mexborough	**36C** Frodingham	**36C** Frodingham	**36C** Frodingham	**36C** Frodingham		
63748	O4/7	**ANN**	Annesley	**39A** Gorton	**39A** Gorton	**41A** Sheffield Darnall	**36C** Frodingham		
63749	O4/7	**STV**	Staveley	**38D** Staveley	**38D** Staveley	**38D** Staveley			
63750	O4/3→8	**CLK**	Colwick	**40E** Langwith Junction	**40E** Langwith Junction	**40B** Immingham	**40B** Immingham	**40E** Colwick	
63751	O4/3	**TDK**	Tyne Dock	**53E** Cudworth	**38B** Annesley	**36B** Mexborough			
63752	O1	**GOR**	Gorton	**38B** Annesley	**38B** Annesley	**38B** Annesley	**16D** Annesley		
63753	O4/3	**TDK**	Tyne Dock	**53A** Hull Dairycoates	**36B** Mexborough	**36B** Mexborough			
63754	O4/3→8	**TDK**	Tyne Dock	**53E** Cudworth	**38A** Colwick	**38A** Colwick	**40E** Colwick	**40E** Colwick	
63755	O1	**TDK**	Tyne Dock	**53A** Hull Dairycoates	**54B** Tyne Dock	**54B** Tyne Dock	**52H** Tyne Dock		
63756	O4/3	**ANN**	Annesley	**38A** Colwick	**38A** Colwick	**36B** Mexborough			
63757	O4/1	**DON**	Doncaster	**36B** Mexborough	**36B** Mexborough	**36B** Mexborough	**41F** Mexborough		
63758	O4/7	**DON**	Doncaster	**40E** Langwith Junction	**40E** Langwith Junction	**40D** Tuxford Junction	**41J** Langwith Junction		
63759	O4/3	**ANN**	Annesley	**40E** Langwith Junction	**40E** Langwith Junction	**40B** Immingham	**40B** Immingham		
63760	O1	**TDK**	Tyne Dock	**53A** Hull Dairycoates	**54B** Tyne Dock	**54B** Tyne Dock	**52H** Tyne Dock		
63761	O4/7	**ANN**	Annesley	**39A** Gorton	**39A** Gorton	**36C** Frodingham			
63762	O4/1	**ANN**	Annesley	**38A** Colwick	**38D** Staveley	**38D** Staveley	**41H** Staveley		
63763	O4/3→8	**RET**	Retford	**36E** Retford	**36D** Barnsley	**36D** Barnsley	**41J** Langwith Junction	**41J** Langwith Junction	
63764	O4/3	**HLD**	Hull Dairycoates	**53A** Hull Dairycoates	**36A** Doncaster	**36B** Mexborough	**36C** Frodingham	**36E** Retford	**36A** Doncaster
63765	O4/3→8	**DON**	Doncaster	**40E** Langwith Junction	**40E** Langwith Junction	**40E** Langwith Junction	**41J** Langwith Junction	**41J** Langwith Junction	
63766	O4/3	**SHF**	Sheffield Darnall	**39B** Sheffield Darnall	**38A** Colwick	**39A** Gorton	**9G** Gorton		
63767	O4/3	**ANN**	Annesley	**38D** Staveley	**39A** Gorton	**39A** Gorton	**9G** Gorton		
63768	O1	**GOR**	Gorton	**38B** Annesley	**38B** Annesley	**38B** Annesley	**40E** Colwick	**40E** Colwick	
63769	O4/3	**TDK**	Tyne Dock	**53A** Hull Dairycoates	**36A** Doncaster	**36A** Doncaster			
63770	O4/7	**HLD**	Hull Dairycoates	**53A** Hull Dairycoates	**40B** Immingham	**40B** Immingham	**40E** Colwick	**40E** Colwick	
63771	O4/3	**SHF**	Sheffield Darnall	**39B** Sheffield Darnall	**39B** Sheffield Darnall	**41A** Sheffield Darnall	**41A** Sheffield Darnall		
63772	O4/7	**HLD**	Hull Dairycoates	**53A** Hull Dairycoates	**38D** Staveley	**38D** Staveley	**41H** Staveley	**41A** Sheffield Darnall	
63773	O1	**GOR**	Gorton	**38B** Annesley	**38B** Annesley	**38B** Annesley	**41H** Staveley	**41H** Staveley	
63774	O4/3	**RET**	Retford	**36B** Mexborough	**36B** Mexborough	**36B** Mexborough	**41F** Mexborough	**41A** Sheffield Darnall	
63775	O4/7	**RET**	Retford	**36B** Mexborough	**36B** Mexborough	**36B** Mexborough	**9G** Gorton		
63776	O4/3→8	**MEX**	Mexborough	**40E** Langwith Junction	**40E** Langwith Junction	**40E** Langwith Junction	**41J** Langwith Junction		
63777	O1	**GOR**	Gorton	**38B** Annesley	**38B** Annesley	**38B** Annesley	**16D** Annesley		
63778	O4/1	**FRO**	Frodingham	**36C** Frodingham					
63779	O4/3	**CAM**	Cambridge	**36B** Mexborough	**36B** Mexborough	**36B** Mexborough	**41F** Mexborough		
63780	O1	**GOR**	Gorton	**38B** Annesley	**38B** Annesley	**38B** Annesley	**31B** March	**31B** March	
63781	O4/3→8	**CLK**	Colwick	**39A** Gorton	**39A** Gorton	**36B** Mexborough	**36C** Frodingham	**36C** Frodingham	**36A** Doncaster
63782	O4/3	**RET**	Retford	**36E** Retford	**36E** Retford	**36E** Retford	**36E** Retford		
63783	O4/3	**SHF**	Sheffield Darnall	**39B** Sheffield Darnall	**39B** Sheffield Darnall	**41A** Sheffield Darnall	**41A** Sheffield Darnall		
63784	O1	**GOR**	Gorton	**38B** Annesley	**38B** Annesley	**38B** Annesley	**41H** Staveley	**41H** Staveley	
63785	O4/8	**RET**	Retford	**36E** Retford	**36E** Retford	**36E** Retford	**36E** Retford	**36E** Retford	**36A** Doncaster
63786	O1	**GOR**	Gorton	**38B** Annesley	**38B** Annesley	**38B** Annesley	**31B** March	**41H** Staveley	
63787	O4/3	**CLK**	Colwick	**39A** Gorton	**38D** Staveley	**38D** Staveley	**41H** Staveley		
63788	O4/5→8	**FRO**	Frodingham	**36C** Frodingham	**36C** Frodingham	**36C** Frodingham	**36C** Frodingham	**36C** Frodingham	**36A** Doncaster
63789	O1	**GOR**	Gorton	**38B** Annesley	**38B** Annesley	**38B** Annesley	**16D** Annesley		
63790	O4/3	**SHF**	Sheffield Darnall	**39B** Sheffield Darnall	**39B** Sheffield Darnall	**41A** Sheffield Darnall			
63791	O4/3→8	**MEX**	Mexborough	**36B** Mexborough	**36B** Mexborough	**36B** Mexborough	**41F** Mexborough	**36C** Frodingham	
63792	O1	**MAR**	March	**38B** Annesley	**38B** Annesley	**38B** Annesley	**16D** Annesley		
63793	O4/3→8	**FRO**	Frodingham	**36C** Frodingham	**36C** Frodingham	**36C** Frodingham	**36C** Frodingham	**36C** Frodingham	
63794	O4/7→8	**ANN**	Annesley	**39A** Gorton	**39A** Gorton	**39A** Gorton	**9G** Gorton		
63795	O1	**GOR**	Gorton	**38B** Annesley	**38B** Annesley	**38B** Annesley	**41H** Staveley	**41H** Staveley	
63796	O1	**GOR**	Gorton	**38B** Annesley	**38B** Annesley	**38B** Annesley	**31B** March		
63797	O4/1	**CLK**	Colwick	**39B** Sheffield Darnall	**39B** Sheffield Darnall	**41A** Sheffield Darnall			
63798	O4/3	**CLK**	Colwick	**38B** Annesley	**38A** Colwick	**36B** Mexborough	**41F** Mexborough		
63799	O4/1	**ANN**	Annesley	**39A** Gorton	**39A** Gorton	**36C** Frodingham	**36C** Frodingham		
63800	O4/3→8	**DON**	Doncaster	**40E** Langwith Junction	**40E** Langwith Junction	**40E** Langwith Junction	**41J** Langwith Junction	**41J** Langwith Junction	
63801	O4/3→8	**ANN**	Annesley	**38A** Colwick	**38D** Staveley	**38D** Staveley	**41J** Langwith Junction	**41J** Langwith Junction	
63802	O4/8	**FRO**	Frodingham	**40B** Immingham	**40B** Immingham	**40B** Immingham	**41G** Barnsley	**36C** Frodingham	
63803	O1	**GOR**	Gorton	**38B** Annesley	**38B** Annesley	**38B** Annesley	**31B** March	**31B** March	
63804	O4/3	**ANN**	Annesley	**38A** Colwick	**38A** Colwick	**38D** Staveley			
63805	O4/1→8	**ANN**	Annesley	**39A** Gorton	**39A** Gorton	**39A** Gorton	**9G** Gorton		
63806	O1	**THJ**	Thornton Junction	**38B** Annesley	**38B** Annesley	**38B** Annesley	**16D** Annesley		
63807	O4/3→8	**MEX**	Mexborough	**40E** Langwith Junction	**38A** Colwick	**36C** Frodingham	**36C** Frodingham	**36C** Frodingham	
63808	O1	**GOR**	Gorton	**38B** Annesley	**38B** Annesley	**38B** Annesley	**16D** Annesley		
63809	O4/1	**ANN**	Annesley	**40E** Langwith Junction					
63812	O4/3	**HLD**	Hull Dairycoates	**53A** Hull Dairycoates	**38A** Colwick	**36B** Mexborough			
63813	O4/3	**MEX**	Mexborough	**36B** Mexborough	**36B** Mexborough	**36B** Mexborough	**41F** Mexborough	**41F** Mexborough	
63816	O4/5→8	**HLD**	Hull Dairycoates	**53A** Hull Dairycoates	**38A** Colwick	**38A** Colwick	**40E** Colwick	**40E** Colwick	**40E** Colwick
63817	O1	**GOR**	Gorton	**38B** Annesley	**38B** Annesley	**38B** Annesley	**16D** Annesley		
63818	O4/8	**FRO**	Frodingham	**36C** Frodingham	**36C** Frodingham	**36C** Frodingham	**36E** Retford	**36A** Doncaster	**36A** Doncaster
63819	O4/8	**TUX**	Tuxford Junction	**40B** Immingham	**40B** Immingham	**40B** Immingham	**40E** Colwick	**40E** Colwick	
63821	O4/3	**SHF**	Sheffield Darnall	**39B** Sheffield Darnall	**39B** Sheffield Darnall	**41A** Sheffield Darnall	**41A** Sheffield Darnall		
63822	O4/3→8	**SHF**	Sheffield Darnall	**39B** Sheffield Darnall	**39B** Sheffield Darnall	**41A** Sheffield Darnall	**41A** Sheffield Darnall	**41A** Sheffield Darnall	
63823	O4/3→8	**HLD**	Hull Dairycoates	**53A** Hull Dairycoates	**37A** Ardsley	**56B** Ardsley	**56B** Ardsley		
63824	O4/7	**FRO**	Frodingham	**36C** Frodingham	**36D** Barnsley	**36D** Barnsley	**36C** Frodingham	**36E** Retford	
63827	O4/8	**CLK**	Colwick	**38D** Staveley	**38D** Staveley	**38D** Staveley	**41H** Staveley	**41H** Staveley	
63828	O4/8	**TDK**	Tyne Dock	**53A** Hull Dairycoates	**36B** Mexborough	**36B** Mexborough	**41F** Mexborough	**41J** Langwith Junction	
63829	O4/3→8	**ANN**	Annesley	**39A** Gorton	**39A** Gorton	**38A** Colwick	**41J** Langwith Junction	**41J** Langwith Junction	

		1948		1951	1954	1957	1960	1963	1966
63832	O4/3→8	**DON**	Doncaster	**36C** Frodingham	**38A** Colwick	**36B** Mexborough	**41F** Mexborough		
63833	O4/3	**MEX**	Mexborough	**40E** Langwith Junction	**40E** Langwith Junction	**40E** Langwith Junction	**41J** Langwith Junction		
63835	O4/3	**TDK**	Tyne Dock	**53A** Hull Dairycoates	**38A** Colwick	**36B** Mexborough			
63836	O4/8	**CAM**	Cambridge	**40B** Immingham	**40B** Immingham	**40B** Immingham	**36C** Frodingham	**36C** Frodingham	
63837	O4/3→8	**LNG**	Langwith Junction	**40E** Langwith Junction	**40E** Langwith Junction	**40B** Immingham	**40B** Immingham		
63838	O4/3→O1	**STV**	Staveley	**38B** Annesley	**38B** Annesley	**38B** Annesley	**16D** Annesley		
63839	O4/7	**CAM**	Cambridge	**39A** Gorton	**39A** Gorton	**38A** Colwick			
63840	O4/3→8	**MEX**	Mexborough	**40E** Langwith Junction	**40E** Langwith Junction	**40E** Langwith Junction	**41J** Langwith Junction	**41J** Langwith Junction	
63841	O4/3→8	**ANN**	Annesley	**39A** Gorton	**39A** Gorton	**36B** Mexborough	**41F** Mexborough	**41A** Sheffield Darnall	
63842	O4/3	**MEX**	Mexborough	**40E** Langwith Junction	**40E** Langwith Junction	**40E** Langwith Junction	**41J** Langwith Junction	**41J** Langwith Junction	
63843	O4/7	**HLD**	Hull Dairycoates	**53E** Cudworth	**36B** Mexborough	**36B** Mexborough	**41F** Mexborough	**41F** Mexborough	
63845	O4/3	**TDK**	Tyne Dock	**53E** Cudworth	**38A** Colwick	**38D** Staveley	**41H** Staveley		
63846	O4/3	**SHF**	Sheffield Darnall	**39B** Sheffield Darnall	**39B** Sheffield Darnall	**41A** Sheffield Darnall	**41A** Sheffield Darnall	**41A** Sheffield Darnall	
63847	O4/2	**DON**	Doncaster	**36C** Frodingham	**38D** Staveley	**38D** Staveley			
63848	O4/7	**CLK**	Colwick	**39A** Gorton	**39A** Gorton	**39A** Gorton	**9G** Gorton		
63849	O4/3	**HLS**	Hull Springhead	**53E** Cudworth					
63850	O4/3→8	**STV**	Staveley	**39B** Sheffield Darnall	**39B** Sheffield Darnall	**41A** Sheffield Darnall	**41A** Sheffield Darnall	**41A** Sheffield Darnall	
63851	O4/5	**ANN**	Annesley	**38B** Annesley	**38A** Colwick	**36B** Mexborough			
63852	O4/3→8	**TUX**	Tuxford Junction	**40D** Tuxford Junction	**37A** Ardsley	**41A** Sheffield Darnall	**41A** Sheffield Darnall	**41A** Sheffield Darnall	
63853	O4/8	**ANN**	Annesley	**39A** Gorton	**39A** Gorton	**36C** Frodingham	**41J** Langwith Junction	**41J** Langwith Junction	
63854	O1	**GOR**	Gorton	**38B** Annesley	**38B** Annesley	**38B** Annesley	**16D** Annesley		
63855	O4/3	**HLD**	Hull Dairycoates	**53A** Hull Dairycoates	**36A** Doncaster	**36A** Doncaster			
63856	O4/3→O1	**TDK**	Tyne Dock	**53A** Hull Dairycoates	**54B** Tyne Dock	**54B** Tyne Dock	**52H** Tyne Dock		
63857	O4/7	**TDK**	Tyne Dock	**53E** Cudworth	**37A** Ardsley	**56B** Ardsley	**56A** Wakefield		
63858	O4/3→8	**CLK**	Colwick	**39A** Gorton	**36A** Doncaster	**36A** Doncaster	**36A** Doncaster	**36A** Doncaster	**36A** Doncaster
63859	O4/3	**ANN**	Annesley	**39A** Gorton	**39A** Gorton	**38A** Colwick	**40E** Colwick	**40E** Colwick	
63860	O4/7	**SHF**	Sheffield Darnall	**39B** Sheffield Darnall	**39B** Sheffield Darnall	**40B** Immingham	**40B** Immingham		
63861	O4/3→8	**TUX**	Tuxford Junction	**40D** Tuxford Junction	**40E** Langwith Junction	**40E** Langwith Junction	**41J** Langwith Junction	**41J** Langwith Junction	
63862	O4/3→8	**ANN**	Annesley	**39A** Gorton	**39A** Gorton	**39A** Gorton	**9G** Gorton		
63863	O1	**GOR**	Gorton	**38B** Annesley	**38B** Annesley	**38B** Annesley	**40E** Colwick	**40E** Colwick	
63864	O4/3→8	**DON**	Doncaster	**39A** Gorton	**37A** Ardsley	**56B** Ardsley	**56A** Wakefield		
63865	O1	**GOR**	Gorton	**38B** Annesley	**38B** Annesley	**38B** Annesley	**16D** Annesley		
63867	O1	**MAR**	March	**38B** Annesley	**38B** Annesley	**38B** Annesley	**16D** Annesley		
63868	O1	**GOR**	Gorton	**38B** Annesley	**38B** Annesley	**38B** Annesley	**31B** March	**31B** March	
63869	O1	**GOR**	Gorton	**38B** Annesley	**38B** Annesley	**38B** Annesley	**16D** Annesley		
63870	O4/3	**MEX**	Mexborough	**40E** Langwith Junction	**40E** Langwith Junction	**40E** Langwith Junction	**41J** Langwith Junction		
63872	O1	**GOR**	Gorton	**38B** Annesley	**38B** Annesley	**38B** Annesley	**31B** March	**31B** March	
63873	O4/3→8	**ANN**	Annesley	**39A** Gorton	**39A** Gorton	**38A** Colwick	**40E** Colwick	**40E** Colwick	**40E** Colwick
63874	O1	**TDK**	Tyne Dock	**53A** Hull Dairycoates	**54B** Tyne Dock	**54B** Tyne Dock	**52H** Tyne Dock		
63876	O4/7	**ANN**	Annesley	**39A** Gorton	**39A** Gorton	**36B** Mexborough			
63877	O4/3→8	**RET**	Retford	**40E** Langwith Junction	**38A** Colwick	**38D** Staveley	**41H** Staveley	**41F** Mexborough	
63878	O4/3→8	**IMM**	Immingham	**40B** Immingham	**40B** Immingham	**40B** Immingham	**40B** Immingham	**40E** Colwick	
63879	O1	**GOR**	Gorton	**38B** Annesley	**38B** Annesley	**38B** Annesley	**31B** March	**31B** March	
63880	O4/7	**CAM**	Cambridge	**39A** Gorton	**39A** Gorton	**36C** Frodingham	**36C** Frodingham	**36C** Frodingham	
63881	O4/3→8	**TDK**	Tyne Dock	**53A** Hull Dairycoates	**38A** Colwick	**41A** Sheffield Darnall	**41A** Sheffield Darnall		
63882	O4/8	**SHF**	Sheffield Darnall	**39B** Sheffield Darnall	**39B** Sheffield Darnall	**41A** Sheffield Darnall	**41A** Sheffield Darnall	**41A** Sheffield Darnall	
63883	O4/3	**DON**	Doncaster	**36D** Barnsley	**36D** Barnsley	**36D** Barnsley	**41G** Barnsley		
63884	O4/7→8	**DON**	Doncaster	**40E** Langwith Junction	**38D** Staveley	**38D** Staveley	**41H** Staveley	**36C** Frodingham	
63885	O4/3→8	**TUX**	Tuxford Junction	**40D** Tuxford Junction	**37A** Ardsley	**56B** Ardsley	**56B** Ardsley		
63886	O1	**GOR**	Gorton	**38B** Annesley	**38B** Annesley	**38B** Annesley	**16D** Annesley		
63887	O1	**GOR**	Gorton	**38B** Annesley	**38B** Annesley	**38B** Annesley	**31B** March	**41H** Staveley	
63888	O4/3	**SHF**	Sheffield Darnall	**39B** Sheffield Darnall	**39B** Sheffield Darnall	**41A** Sheffield Darnall	**41A** Sheffield Darnall		
63889	O4/3	**STV**	Staveley	**39B** Sheffield Darnall	**39B** Sheffield Darnall	**41A** Sheffield Darnall			
63890	O1	**GOR**	Gorton	**38B** Annesley	**38B** Annesley	**38B** Annesley	**31B** March	**31B** March	
63891	O4/7	**DON**	Doncaster	**39A** Gorton	**39A** Gorton	**36B** Mexborough	**41F** Mexborough		
63893	O4/8	**ANN**	Annesley	**38A** Colwick	**40E** Langwith Junction	**40D** Tuxford Junction	**41J** Langwith Junction	**41J** Langwith Junction	
63894	O4/7	**ANN**	Annesley	**38A** Colwick	**38A** Colwick	**36B** Mexborough	**41F** Mexborough		
63895	O4/3→8	**CLK**	Colwick	**39A** Gorton	**39A** Gorton	**39A** Gorton	**9G** Gorton		
63897	O4/3→8	**CAM**	Cambridge	**31B** March	**36B** Mexborough	**36B** Mexborough	**41F** Mexborough	**36C** Frodingham	
63898	O4/3→8	**CAM**	Cambridge	**36B** Mexborough	**36B** Mexborough	**36B** Mexborough	**41F** Mexborough	**36C** Frodingham	
63899	O4/3→8	**ANN**	Annesley	**39A** Gorton	**38D** Staveley	**38D** Staveley	**41H** Staveley	**41H** Staveley	
63900	O4/3	**DON**	Doncaster	**40E** Langwith Junction	**40B** Immingham	**40B** Immingham	**40B** Immingham		
63901	O1	**GOR**	Gorton	**38B** Annesley	**38B** Annesley	**38B** Annesley	**16D** Annesley		
63902	O4/6	**IMM**	Immingham	**40E** Langwith Junction	**40E** Langwith Junction	**40E** Langwith Junction	**41J** Langwith Junction	**41J** Langwith Junction	
63904	O4/6	**CAM**	Cambridge	**36D** Barnsley	**36D** Barnsley	**36D** Barnsley	**41G** Barnsley		
63905	O4/6	**RET**	Retford	**36E** Retford	**36E** Retford	**36E** Retford			
63906	O4/6	**MEX**	Mexborough	**36C** Frodingham	**36C** Frodingham	**36C** Frodingham	**36C** Frodingham	**36C** Frodingham	
63907	O4/6	**RET**	Retford	**36E** Retford	**36D** Barnsley	**36D** Barnsley	**41G** Barnsley	**41F** Mexborough	
63908	O4/6	**RET**	Retford	**40E** Langwith Junction	**38A** Colwick	**36B** Mexborough	**41F** Mexborough	**36E** Retford	
63911	O4/6	**DON**	Doncaster	**36C** Frodingham	**36C** Frodingham	**36D** Barnsley	**41G** Barnsley		
63912	O4/6	**ANN**	Annesley	**39A** Gorton	**38A** Colwick	**40D** Tuxford Junction	**41J** Langwith Junction		
63913	O4/6	**CAM**	Cambridge	**36D** Barnsley	**36D** Barnsley	**36D** Barnsley	**41G** Barnsley	**41H** Staveley	
63914	O4/6→8	**RET**	Retford	**36E** Retford	**36E** Retford	**36E** Retford	**36E** Retford	**36E** Retford	
63915	O4/6→8	**DON**	Doncaster	**39A** Gorton	**40E** Langwith Junction	**39A** Gorton	**9G** Gorton		
63917	O4/6	**IMM**	Immingham	**36C** Frodingham	**36C** Frodingham	**36C** Frodingham	**36C** Frodingham		
63920	O4/6	**FRO**	Frodingham	**36C** Frodingham	**37C** Bradford Hammerton St	**56G** Bradford Hammerton St	**56A** Wakefield		
63921	O2	**LNG**	Langwith Junction						
63922	O2	**FRO**	Frodingham	**36C** Frodingham	**36C** Frodingham	**36A** Doncaster	**36A** Doncaster		
63923	O2	**LNG**	Langwith Junction	**35A** New England	**35B** Grantham	**35B** Grantham	**34F** Grantham		
63924	O2	**LNG**	Langwith Junction	**36B** Mexborough	**36E** Retford	**36E** Retford	**36E** Retford	**36E** Retford	
63925	O2	**LNG**	Langwith Junction	**36A** Doncaster	**36E** Retford	**36E** Retford	**36E** Retford	**36E** Retford	
63926	O2	**LNG**	Langwith Junction	**36A** Doncaster	**36E** Retford	**36E** Retford	**36E** Retford	**36E** Retford	
63927	O2	**LNG**	Langwith Junction	**36B** Mexborough	**36E** Retford	**36E** Retford	**36E** Retford	**36E** Retford	
63928	O2	**LNG**	Langwith Junction	**36A** Doncaster	**36A** Doncaster	**36A** Doncaster	**36A** Doncaster	**34F** Grantham	
63929	O2	**GRA**	Grantham	**35B** Grantham	**35B** Grantham	**35B** Grantham	**34F** Grantham		
63930	O2	**GRA**	Grantham	**35B** Grantham	**35B** Grantham	**35B** Grantham	**34F** Grantham		
63931	O2	**GRA**	Grantham	**35B** Grantham	**35B** Grantham	**35B** Grantham	**34F** Grantham	**34F** Grantham	
63932	O2	**GRA**	Grantham	**35B** Grantham	**35B** Grantham	**35B** Grantham	**34F** Grantham	**34F** Grantham	
63933	O2	**GRA**	Grantham	**35B** Grantham	**35B** Grantham	**35B** Grantham	**34F** Grantham		
63934	O2	**FRO**	Frodingham	**36C** Frodingham	**36C** Frodingham	**36A** Doncaster	**36A** Doncaster		
63935	O2	**GRA**	Grantham	**35B** Grantham	**36A** Doncaster	**36A** Doncaster	**36A** Doncaster	**36A** Doncaster	
63936	O2	**GRA**	Grantham	**35B** Grantham	**35B** Grantham	**35B** Grantham	**34F** Grantham	**36E** Retford	
63937	O2	**FRO**	Frodingham	**36C** Frodingham	**36E** Retford	**36E** Retford	**36E** Retford	**36E** Retford	
63938	O2	**GRA**	Grantham	**35B** Grantham	**35B** Grantham	**35B** Grantham	**34F** Grantham	**34F** Grantham	
63939	O2	**FRO**	Frodingham	**36C** Frodingham	**36C** Frodingham	**36A** Doncaster	**36A** Doncaster	**36E** Retford	
63940	O2	**GRA**	Grantham	**35B** Grantham	**35B** Grantham	**35B** Grantham	**34F** Grantham	**34F** Grantham	
63941	O2	**FRO**	Frodingham	**36A** Doncaster	**36A** Doncaster	**36A** Doncaster	**36A** Doncaster	**34F** Grantham	
63942	O2	**LNG**	Langwith Junction	**36A** Doncaster	**36A** Doncaster	**36A** Doncaster	**36A** Doncaster	**34F** Grantham	
63943	O2	**LNG**	Langwith Junction	**36A** Doncaster	**36A** Doncaster	**36A** Doncaster	**36A** Doncaster	**34F** Grantham	
63944	O2	**FRO**	Frodingham	**36C** Frodingham	**36C** Frodingham	**36A** Doncaster	**36E** Retford		
63945	O2	**LNG**	Langwith Junction	**36A** Doncaster	**36C** Frodingham	**36E** Retford	**36E** Retford	**36E** Retford	
63946	O2	**LNG**	Langwith Junction	**36A** Doncaster	**35B** Grantham	**35B** Grantham	**34F** Grantham	**36E** Retford	
63947	O2	**MAR**	March	**36A** Doncaster	**36A** Doncaster	**36A** Doncaster	**36E** Retford		
63948	O2	**MAR**	March	**35A** New England	**35B** Grantham	**35B** Grantham	**34F** Grantham		
63949	O2	**MAR**	March	**35B** Grantham	**36E** Retford	**36E** Retford	**36E** Retford	**34F** Grantham	
63950	O2	**MAR**	March	**35B** Grantham	**35B** Grantham	**35B** Grantham	**34F** Grantham		
63951	O2	**MAR**	March	**36A** Doncaster	**36A** Doncaster	**36A** Doncaster	**36A** Doncaster		
63952	O2	**MAR**	March	**36A** Doncaster	**36A** Doncaster	**36A** Doncaster	**36A** Doncaster		
63953	O2	**MAR**	March	**36A** Doncaster	**36A** Doncaster	**36A** Doncaster	**36A** Doncaster		
63954	O2	**MAR**	March	**36A** Doncaster	**36A** Doncaster	**36A** Doncaster	**36A** Doncaster		
63955	O2	**MAR**	March	**36A** Doncaster	**36A** Doncaster	**36A** Doncaster	**36A** Doncaster		
63956	O2	**MAR**	March	**36A** Doncaster	**36A** Doncaster	**36A** Doncaster	**36A** Doncaster	**34F** Grantham	
63957	O2	**MAR**	March	**36A** Doncaster	**36A** Doncaster	**36A** Doncaster	**34F** Grantham		
63958	O2	**MAR**	March	**36A** Doncaster	**36A** Doncaster	**36A** Doncaster	**36A** Doncaster		

No.	Class	1948	1951	1954	1957	1960	1963	1966
63959	*O2*	**MAR** March	**36A** Doncaster	**36A** Doncaster	**36A** Doncaster	**36E** Retford		
63960	*O2*	**MAR** March	**35B** Grantham	**35B** Grantham	**35B** Grantham	**34F** Grantham	**34F** Grantham	
63961	*O2*	**MAR** March	**36A** Doncaster	**36C** Frodingham	**36E** Retford	**36E** Retford		
63962	*O2*	**MAR** March	**36A** Doncaster	**36A** Doncaster	**36A** Doncaster	**36A** Doncaster	**36E** Retford	
63963	*O2*	**FRO** Frodingham	**36C** Frodingham	**36C** Frodingham	**36A** Doncaster	**34F** Grantham	**34F** Grantham	
63964	*O2*	**LNG** Langwith Junction	**36A** Doncaster	**36A** Doncaster	**36A** Doncaster	**36A** Doncaster	**36E** Retford	
63965	*O2*	**LNG** Langwith Junction	**35B** Grantham	**36E** Retford	**36E** Retford	**36E** Retford		
63966	*O2*	**LNG** Langwith Junction	**35B** Grantham	**35B** Grantham	**35B** Grantham	**34F** Grantham		
63967	*O2*	**LNG** Langwith Junction	**36A** Doncaster	**36A** Doncaster	**36A** Doncaster	**36A** Doncaster		
63968	*O2*	**LNG** Langwith Junction	**36A** Doncaster	**36A** Doncaster	**36A** Doncaster	**36A** Doncaster	**36E** Retford	
63969	*O2*	**LNG** Langwith Junction	**36B** Mexborough	**36A** Doncaster	**36A** Doncaster	**36A** Doncaster	**36E** Retford	
63970	*O2*	**LNG** Langwith Junction	**36B** Mexborough	**36E** Retford	**36E** Retford	**36E** Retford		
63971	*O2*	**LNG** Langwith Junction	**36B** Mexborough	**36A** Doncaster	**36A** Doncaster	**36E** Retford		
63972	*O2*	**LNG** Langwith Junction	**36B** Mexborough	**36E** Retford	**36E** Retford	**36E** Retford	**36E** Retford	
63973	*O2*	**LNG** Langwith Junction	**36A** Doncaster	**36A** Doncaster	**36A** Doncaster	**36A** Doncaster	**36E** Retford	
63974	*O2*	**LNG** Langwith Junction	**36A** Doncaster	**36A** Doncaster	**36A** Doncaster	**36A** Doncaster	**34F** Grantham	
63975	*O2*	**FRO** Frodingham	**36B** Mexborough	**36A** Doncaster	**36A** Doncaster	**36A** Doncaster	**36E** Retford	
63976	*O2*	**LNG** Langwith Junction	**36B** Mexborough	**36E** Retford	**36E** Retford	**36E** Retford	**36E** Retford	
63977	*O2*	**LNG** Langwith Junction	**36B** Mexborough	**36A** Doncaster	**36A** Doncaster	**36A** Doncaster	**36E** Retford	
63978	*O2*	**LNG** Langwith Junction	**36B** Mexborough	**36A** Doncaster	**36A** Doncaster	**36A** Doncaster	**36E** Retford	
63979	*O2*	**LNG** Langwith Junction	**36B** Mexborough	**36E** Retford	**36E** Retford	**36E** Retford		
63980	*O2*	**LNG** Langwith Junction	**36B** Mexborough	**36E** Retford	**36E** Retford	**36E** Retford	**36E** Retford	
63981	*O2*	**LNG** Langwith Junction	**36B** Mexborough	**36A** Doncaster	**36A** Doncaster	**36A** Doncaster	**34F** Grantham	
63982	*O2*	**LNG** Langwith Junction	**36B** Mexborough	**36E** Retford	**36E** Retford	**36E** Retford		
63983	*O2*	**LNG** Langwith Junction	**36B** Mexborough	**36C** Frodingham	**36A** Doncaster	**36A** Doncaster	**36E** Retford	
63984	*O2*	**LNG** Langwith Junction	**36B** Mexborough	**36C** Frodingham	**36A** Doncaster	**36A** Doncaster	**36E** Retford	
63985	*O2*	**LNG** Langwith Junction	**36B** Mexborough	**36C** Frodingham	**36A** Doncaster	**36A** Doncaster	**36E** Retford	
63986	*O2*	**LNG** Langwith Junction	**36A** Doncaster	**36E** Retford	**36E** Retford	**36E** Retford	**36E** Retford	
63987	*O2*	**LNG** Langwith Junction	**36A** Doncaster	**36E** Retford	**36E** Retford	**36E** Retford	**36E** Retford	
64105	*J3*	**HIT** Hitchin	**34D** Hitchin					
64106	*J3*	**NWE** New England						
64107	*J3*	**RET** Retford						
64109	*J4*	**NWE** New England						
64110	*J4*	**NWE** New England						
64112	*J4*	**NWE** New England	**35A** New England					
64114	*J3*	**HIT** Hitchin	**34D** Hitchin					
64115	*J3*	**BOS** Boston	**40F** Boston					
64116	*J3*	**ARD** Ardsley	**37A** Ardsley					
64117	*J3*	**HIT** Hitchin	**34D** Hitchin					
64118	*J3*	**NWE** New England	**35A** New England					
64119	*J3*	**ARD** Ardsley	**37A** Ardsley					
64120	*J4*	**NWE** New England						
64121	*J4*	**NWE** New England						
64122	*J3*	**HIT** Hitchin	**34D** Hitchin					
64123	*J3*	**NWE** New England	**35A** New England					
64124	*J3*	**RET** Retford	**36A** Doncaster					
64125	*J3*	**RET** Retford	**36E** Retford					
64127	*J3*	**ARD** Ardsley						
64128	*J3*	**NWE** New England						
64129	*J3*	**ARD** Ardsley	**37A** Ardsley					
64131	*J3*	**NWE** New England	**35A** New England	**40F** Boston				
64132	*J3*	**BOS** Boston	**40F** Boston	**36E** Retford				
64133	*J3*	**RET** Retford	**36E** Retford					
64135	*J3*	**NWE** New England	**35A** New England					
64136	*J3*	**NWE** New England						
64137	*J3*	**BOS** Boston	**40F** Boston					
64140	*J3*	**HIT** Hitchin	**34D** Hitchin	**36E** Retford				
64141	*J3*	**RET** Retford	**36E** Retford					
64142	*J3*	**ARD** Ardsley	**37A** Ardsley					
64145	*J3*	**HIT** Hitchin						
64148	*J3*	**RET** Retford	**36E** Retford					
64150	*J3*	**RET** Retford	**36E** Retford					
64151	*J3*	**NWE** New England	**35A** New England					
64152	*J3*	**RET** Retford						
64153	*J3*	**HIT** Hitchin	**34D** Hitchin					
64158	*J3*	**NWE** New England	**35A** New England					
64160	*J4*	**NWE** New England	**35A** New England					
64162	*J4*	**NWE** New England						
64163	*J3*	**SL** South Lynn						
64167	*J4*	**SL** South Lynn						
64170	*J6*	**BFD** Bradford Hammerton St	**37C** Bradford Hammerton St	**37C** Bradford Hammerton St	**56G** Bradford Hammerton St	**56F** Low Moor		
64171	*J6*	**NWE** New England	**35A** New England	**35A** New England	**35A** New England	**40F** Boston		
64172	*J6*	**GRA** Grantham	**35B** Grantham	**35A** New England	**35A** New England	**40F** Boston		
64173	*J6*	**COP** Copley Hill	**37B** Copley Hill	**37B** Copley Hill	**56C** Copley Hill	**56C** Copley Hill		
64174	*J6*	**ARD** Ardsley	**37A** Ardsley	**37A** Ardsley	**36E** Retford	**36E** Retford		
64175	*J6*	**GRA** Grantham	**34D** Hitchin	**34D** Hitchin	**34D** Hitchin	**34D** Hitchin		
64176	*J6*	**NWE** New England	**35A** New England	**35A** New England	**35A** New England			
64177	*J6*	**NWE** New England	**35A** New England	**35A** New England	**35A** New England	**34E** New England		
64178	*J6*	**GRA** Grantham	**35B** Grantham	**35B** Grantham	**35B** Grantham	**36E** Retford		
64179	*J6*	**DON** Doncaster	**36A** Doncaster	**36A** Doncaster	**36A** Doncaster	**36A** Doncaster		
64180	*J6*	**BOS** Boston	**40F** Boston	**40F** Boston	**40F** Boston	**34E** New England		
64181	*J6*	**BOS** Boston	**40F** Boston	**35A** New England	**35A** New England			
64182	*J6*	**ARD** Ardsley	**37A** Ardsley	**37A** Ardsley	**56B** Ardsley	**56B** Ardsley		
64183	*J6*	**DON** Doncaster	**36A** Doncaster	**38A** Colwick	**38A** Colwick			
64184	*J6*	**NWE** New England	**35A** New England	**35A** New England	**35A** New England			
64185	*J6*	**DON** Doncaster	**36A** Doncaster	**36A** Doncaster	**36A** Doncaster	**36A** Doncaster		
64186	*J6*	**NWE** New England	**35A** New England	**34D** Hitchin	**34D** Hitchin			
64187	*J6*	**NWE** New England	**35B** Grantham	**35B** Grantham	**35B** Grantham			
64188	*J6*	**HSY** Hornsey	**34B** Hornsey	**36E** Retford	**36E** Retford			
64189	*J6*	**NWE** New England	**35A** New England	**35A** New England	**35A** New England			
64190	*J6*	**BOS** Boston	**40F** Boston	**40F** Boston	**40F** Boston			
64191	*J6*	**NWE** New England	**35A** New England	**35A** New England	**35A** New England	**40F** Boston		
64192	*J6*	**NWE** New England	**35A** New England	**35A** New England	**35A** New England	**34E** New England		
64193	*J6*	**DON** Doncaster	**36A** Doncaster	**36A** Doncaster	**36A** Doncaster			
64194	*J6*	**CLK** Colwick	**38A** Colwick	**38A** Colwick				
64195	*J6*	**DON** Doncaster	**36A** Doncaster	**36A** Doncaster	**38A** Colwick			
64196	*J6*	**BOS** Boston	**40F** Boston	**34B** Hornsey	**34B** Hornsey	**34B** Hornsey		
64197	*J6*	**CLK** Colwick	**38A** Colwick	**34D** Hitchin	**34D** Hitchin			
64198	*J6*	**BOS** Boston	**40F** Boston	**35A** New England	**35A** New England			
64199	*J6*	**CLK** Colwick	**38A** Colwick	**38A** Colwick	**38A** Colwick			
64200	*J6*	**CLK** Colwick	**38A** Colwick	**38A** Colwick	**38A** Colwick			
64201	*J6*	**BOS** Boston	**40F** Boston	**40F** Boston	**40F** Boston			
64202	*J6*	**CLK** Colwick	**38A** Colwick	**38A** Colwick	**38A** Colwick			
64203	*J6*	**BFD** Bradford Hammerton St	**37C** Bradford Hammerton St	**37C** Bradford Hammerton St	**56G** Bradford Hammerton St	**56F** Low Moor		
64204	*J6*	**BOS** Boston	**40F** Boston	**40F** Boston	**40F** Boston			
64205	*J6*	**BFD** Bradford Hammerton St	**37C** Bradford Hammerton St	**37C** Bradford Hammerton St	**56B** Ardsley			
64206	*J6*	**GRA** Grantham	**35B** Grantham	**34D** Hitchin	**34D** Hitchin	**34D** Hitchin		
64207	*J6*	**NWE** New England	**35A** New England	**35A** New England	**35A** New England			
64208	*J6*	**ARD** Ardsley	**37A** Ardsley	**37A** Ardsley	**56B** Ardsley	**56B** Ardsley		
64209	*J6*	**DON** Doncaster	**36A** Doncaster	**36A** Doncaster	**36A** Doncaster	**36A** Doncaster		
64210	*J6*	**BOS** Boston	**40F** Boston	**35A** New England	**35A** New England			
64211	*J6*	**NWE** New England	**35A** New England	**35A** New England	**35A** New England			
64212	*J6*	**CLK** Colwick	**38A** Colwick	**38A** Colwick				
64213	*J6*	**CLK** Colwick	**38A** Colwick	**38A** Colwick	**38A** Colwick	**40E** Colwick		

		1948	1951	1954	1957	1960	1963	1966
64214	*J6*	**ARD** Ardsley	**37A** Ardsley	**40F** Boston	**40F** Boston			
64215	*J6*	**CLK** Colwick	**38A** Colwick	**38A** Colwick	**38A** Colwick			
64216	*J6*	**NWE** New England	**35A** New England	**35A** New England	**35A** New England			
64217	*J6*	**NWE** New England	**35A** New England	**35A** New England	**35A** New England			
64218	*J6*	**DON** Doncaster	**36A** Doncaster	**38A** Colwick	**38A** Colwick			
64219	*J6*	**DON** Doncaster	**36A** Doncaster	**35A** New England	**35A** New England	**40A** Lincoln		
64220	*J6*	**NWE** New England	**35A** New England	**35A** New England	**35A** New England			
64221	*J6*	**NWE** New England	**35A** New England	**34B** Hornsey	**38A** Colwick			
64222	*J6*	**CLK** Colwick	**38A** Colwick	**34B** Hornsey	**56B** Ardsley	**56B** Ardsley		
64223	*J6*	**CLK** Colwick	**38A** Colwick	**34B** Hornsey	**34B** Hornsey	**34B** Hornsey		
64224	*J6*	**CLK** Colwick	**38A** Colwick	**35A** New England	**35A** New England			
64225	*J6*	**NWE** New England	**35A** New England	**38A** Colwick	**38A** Colwick			
64226	*J6*	**BFD** Bradford Hammerton St	**37C** Bradford Hammerton St	**37C** Bradford Hammerton St	**56G** Bradford Hammerton St	**56F** Low Moor		
64227	*J6*	**GRA** Grantham	**35B** Grantham	**35B** Grantham	**35B** Grantham			
64228	*J6*	**NWE** New England	**35A** New England	**35A** New England	**35A** New England			
64229	*J6*	**BOS** Boston	**40F** Boston	**40F** Boston	**40F** Boston			
64230	*J6*	**CLK** Colwick	**38A** Colwick	**38A** Colwick	**38A** Colwick			
64231	*J6*	**CLK** Colwick	**38A** Colwick	**35A** New England	**35A** New England	**40F** Boston		
64232	*J6*	**DON** Doncaster	**36A** Doncaster	**36A** Doncaster	**36A** Doncaster	**36A** Doncaster		
64233	*J6*	**CLK** Colwick	**38A** Colwick	**34B** Hornsey	**34B** Hornsey	**34B** Hornsey		
64234	*J6*	**HSY** Hornsey	**34B** Hornsey	**36E** Retford	**36E** Retford			
64235	*J6*	**NWE** New England	**35A** New England	**38A** Colwick	**38A** Colwick			
64236	*J6*	**DON** Doncaster	**36A** Doncaster	**36A** Doncaster	**36E** Retford	**36E** Retford		
64237	*J6*	**GRA** Grantham	**35B** Grantham	**34D** Hitchin	**34D** Hitchin			
64238	*J6*	**NWE** New England	**35A** New England	**38E** Woodford Halse	**38E** Woodford Halse			
64239	*J6*	**HSY** Hornsey	**34B** Hornsey	**34B** Hornsey	**38A** Colwick			
64240	*J6*	**HIT** Hitchin	**34D** Hitchin	**34D** Hitchin	**34D** Hitchin	**34D** Hitchin		
64241	*J6*	**DON** Doncaster	**36E** Retford	**36E** Retford	**36E** Retford			
64242	*J6*	**BOS** Boston	**40F** Boston	**34B** Hornsey				
64243	*J6*	**DON** Doncaster	**36A** Doncaster	**36A** Doncaster	**36A** Doncaster			
64244	*J6*	**BOS** Boston	**40F** Boston	**40F** Boston	**40F** Boston			
64245	*J6*	**NWE** New England	**35A** New England	**36E** Retford	**36E** Retford	**36E** Retford		
64246	*J6*	**NWE** New England	**35A** New England	**35A** New England	**35A** New England			
64247	*J6*	**BOS** Boston	**40F** Boston	**40F** Boston	**40F** Boston			
64248	*J6*	**BOS** Boston	**40F** Boston	**40F** Boston	**38A** Colwick			
64249	*J6*	**NWE** New England	**35A** New England	**38A** Colwick	**38A** Colwick			
64250	*J6*	**COP** Copley Hill	**37B** Copley Hill	**40F** Boston	**40F** Boston			
64251	*J6*	**HSY** Hornsey	**34B** Hornsey	**34D** Hitchin	**34D** Hitchin	**34D** Hitchin		
64252	*J6*	**NWE** New England	**35A** New England	**36E** Retford	**36E** Retford			
64253	*J6*	**CLK** Colwick	**38A** Colwick	**34B** Hornsey	**34B** Hornsey	**34B** Hornsey		
64254	*J6*	**NWE** New England	**35A** New England	**35A** New England	**35A** New England			
64255	*J6*	**DON** Doncaster	**36A** Doncaster	**36A** Doncaster	**36E** Retford			
64256	*J6*	**HSY** Hornsey	**34B** Hornsey	**34B** Hornsey	**38A** Colwick	**9G** Gorton		
64257	*J6*	**NWE** New England	**35A** New England	**38A** Colwick	**38A** Colwick	**40E** Colwick		
64258	*J6*	**DON** Doncaster	**36A** Doncaster	**36A** Doncaster	**36A** Doncaster			
64259	*J6*	**DON** Doncaster	**36A** Doncaster	**35A** New England	**36E** Retford			
64260	*J6*	**COP** Copley Hill	**37B** Copley Hill	**40F** Boston	**40F** Boston	**34D** Hitchin		
64261	*J6*	**DON** Doncaster	**36A** Doncaster	**36A** Doncaster	**36A** Doncaster			
64262	*J6*	**DON** Doncaster	**36A** Doncaster	**37A** Ardsley	**36A** Doncaster			
64263	*J6*	**DON** Doncaster	**36A** Doncaster	**36A** Doncaster	**36A** Doncaster			
64264	*J6*	**DON** Doncaster	**36A** Doncaster	**36A** Doncaster	**36A** Doncaster			
64265	*J6*	**GRA** Grantham	**35A** New England	**35A** New England	**35A** New England	**34E** New England		
64266	*J6*	**NWE** New England	**35A** New England	**34B** Hornsey	**34B** Hornsey			
64267	*J6*	**ARD** Ardsley	**37A** Ardsley	**37A** Ardsley	**38A** Colwick			
64268	*J6*	**BFD** Bradford Hammerton St	**37C** Bradford Hammerton St	**37C** Bradford Hammerton St	**56B** Ardsley	**56C** Copley Hill		
64269	*J6*	**CLK** Colwick	**38A** Colwick	**38A** Colwick	**38A** Colwick			
64270	*J6*	**DON** Doncaster	**36A** Doncaster	**36A** Doncaster	**36A** Doncaster	**36A** Doncaster		
64271	*J6*	**BFD** Bradford Hammerton St	**37C** Bradford Hammerton St	**37A** Ardsley	**56B** Ardsley			
64272	*J6*	**ARD** Ardsley	**37A** Ardsley	**35A** New England	**35A** New England			
64273	*J6*	**NWE** New England	**35A** New England	**38A** Colwick	**38A** Colwick			
64274	*J6*	**BFD** Bradford Hammerton St	**37C** Bradford Hammerton St	**37A** Ardsley	**56B** Ardsley			
64275	*J6*	**NWE** New England	**36A** New England	**35A** New England	**35A** New England			
64276	*J6*	**BOS** Boston	**40F** Boston	**37B** Copley Hill	**56C** Copley Hill			
64277	*J6*	**ARD** Ardsley	**37A** Ardsley	**37B** Copley Hill	**56C** Copley Hill	**56C** Copley Hill		
64278	*J6*	**NWE** New England	**35A** New England	**35A** New England	**35A** New England	**40A** Lincoln		
64279	*J6*	**DON** Doncaster	**36A** Doncaster	**35A** New England	**35A** New England			
64280	*J11*	**RET** Retford	**36E** Retford	**36E** Retford	**36E** Retford			
64281	*J11*	**LNG** Langwith Junction	**40E** Langwith Junction	**40E** Langwith Junction	**40E** Langwith Junction			
64282	*J11*	**RET** Retford	**36E** Retford	**36E** Retford				
64283	*J11*	**MEX** Mexborough	**36B** Mexborough	**36B** Mexborough	**36E** Retford			
64284	*J11*	**IMM** Immingham	**40B** Immingham	**40B** Immingham	**40B** Immingham	**40B** Immingham		
64285	*J11*	**LIN** Lincoln	**36A** Doncaster	**36A** Doncaster	**36B** Mexborough			
64286	*J11*	**TUX** Tuxford Junction	**40E** Langwith Junction	**39B** Sheffield Darnall				
64287	*J11*	**RET** Retford	**36E** Retford	**36E** Retford	**36E** Retford			
64288	*J11*	**MEX** Mexborough	**36B** Mexborough	**35C** Spital Bridge	**39A** Gorton	**9G** Gorton		
64289	*J11*	**LNG** Langwith Junction	**40E** Langwith Junction	**40E** Langwith Junction				
64290	*J11*	**BRN** Barnsley	**36D** Barnsley	**36D** Barnsley	**36D** Barnsley			
64291	*J11*	**SHF** Sheffield Darnall	**39B** Sheffield Darnall	**39B** Sheffield Darnall				
64292	*J11*	**ANN** Annesley	**38B** Annesley	**38B** Annesley	**38D** Staveley	**41H** Staveley		
64293	*J11*	**TUX** Tuxford Junction	**40D** Tuxford Junction	**40E** Langwith Junction	**40E** Langwith Junction			
64294	*J11*	**ANN** Annesley	**39A** Gorton	**39A** Gorton	**39A** Gorton			
64295	*J11*	**RET** Retford	**36E** Retford	**36E** Retford	**36E** Retford			
64296	*J11*	**MEX** Mexborough	**36B** Mexborough	**36A** Doncaster	**36A** Doncaster			
64297	*J11*	**LNG** Langwith Junction	**40E** Langwith Junction	**40E** Langwith Junction	**40E** Langwith Junction			
64298	*J11*	**GOR** Gorton	**39A** Gorton	**39A** Gorton	**39A** Gorton			
64299	*J11*	**TUX** Tuxford Junction	**40D** Tuxford Junction	**40D** Tuxford Junction				
64300	*J11*	**ANN** Annesley	**38B** Annesley	**38B** Annesley	**38E** Woodford Halse			
64301	*J11*	**LIN** Lincoln	**38A** Colwick	**38A** Colwick				
64302	*J11*	**MEX** Mexborough	**36B** Mexborough	**36D** Barnsley	**36D** Barnsley			
64303	*J11*	**LIN** Lincoln	**40A** Lincoln	**40A** Lincoln	**40A** Lincoln			
64304	*J11*	**GOR** Gorton	**39A** Gorton	**39A** Gorton	**39A** Gorton			
64305	*J11*	**IMM** Immingham	**40B** Immingham	**40B** Immingham	**40B** Immingham	**40B** Immingham		
64306	*J11*	**RET** Retford	**36E** Retford	**39A** Gorton	**39A** Gorton			
64307	*J11*	**IMM** Immingham	**40B** Immingham	**40B** Immingham				
64308	*J11*	**FRO** Frodingham	**36C** Frodingham	**36C** Frodingham	**36C** Frodingham	**36C** Frodingham		
64309	*J11*	**FRO** Frodingham	**36C** Frodingham	**36A** Doncaster				
64310	*J11*	**TUX** Tuxford Junction	**40E** Langwith Junction	**40E** Langwith Junction	**40E** Langwith Junction	**9G** Gorton		
64311	*J11*	**GOR** Gorton	**39A** Gorton	**39A** Gorton	**39A** Gorton	**9G** Gorton		
64312	*J11*	**IMM** Immingham	**40B** Immingham	**40B** Immingham	**40B** Immingham			
64313	*J11*	**NEA** Neasden	**34E** Neasden	**38D** Staveley	**38D** Staveley	**41H** Staveley		
64314	*J11*	**IMM** Immingham	**40B** Immingham	**40B** Immingham	**40B** Immingham	**41J** Langwith Junction		
64315	*J11*	**LIN** Lincoln	**40A** Lincoln	**40A** Lincoln	**40A** Lincoln	**36E** Retford		
64316	*J11*	**GOR** Gorton	**39A** Gorton	**39A** Gorton	**39A** Gorton	**41J** Langwith Junction		
64317	*J11*	**CLK** Colwick	**38D** Staveley	**38D** Staveley	**39A** Gorton	**41J** Langwith Junction		
64318	*J11*	**ANN** Annesley	**38B** Annesley	**38B** Annesley	**38B** Annesley	**40A** Lincoln		
64319	*J11*	**MEX** Mexborough	**36B** Mexborough	**36A** Doncaster	**36C** Frodingham			
64320	*J11*	**IMM** Immingham	**40C** Louth	**40C** Louth	**40B** Immingham			
64321	*J11*	**LNG** Langwith Junction	**40E** Langwith Junction	**40E** Langwith Junction	**36E** Retford			
64322	*J11*	**GOR** Gorton	**39A** Gorton	**39A** Gorton	**39A** Gorton			
64323	*J11*	**IMM** Immingham	**40B** Immingham	**40B** Immingham				
64324	*J11*	**WFD** Woodford Halse	**38E** Woodford Halse	**38E** Woodford Halse	**38B** Annesley	**41J** Langwith Junction		
64325	*J11*	**IMM** Immingham	**40B** Immingham	**40B** Immingham	**40B** Immingham	**40B** Immingham		
64326	*J11*	**GOR** Gorton	**39A** Gorton	**39A** Gorton				
64327	*J11*	**WFD** Woodford Halse	**38E** Woodford Halse	**38E** Woodford Halse	**38E** Woodford Halse			

		1948	1951	1954	1957	1960	1963	1966
64328	*J11*	LTH Louth	**40C** Louth	**40C** Louth	**40C** Louth			
64329	*J11*	NEA Neasden	**34E** Neasden	**39B** Sheffield Darnall	**41A** Sheffield Darnall	**41A** Sheffield Darnall		
64330	*J11*	WFD Woodford Halse	**38E** Woodford Halse	**38E** Woodford Halse	**38E** Woodford Halse			
64331	*J11*	STV Staveley	**38D** Staveley	**38E** Woodford Halse	**38E** Woodford Halse	**9G** Gorton		
64332	*J11*	GOR Gorton	**39A** Gorton	**39A** Gorton	**39A** Gorton	**41J** Langwith Junction		
64333	*J11*	LNG Langwith Junction	**39A** Gorton	**39A** Gorton	**39A** Gorton	**41J** Langwith Junction		
64334	*J11*	MEX Mexborough	**36B** Mexborough	**36A** Doncaster				
64335	*J11*	RET Retford	**36E** Retford	**36E** Retford				
64336	*J11*	STV Staveley	**39B** Sheffield Darnall	**38D** Staveley	**38D** Staveley			
64337	*J11*	LIN Lincoln	**40D** Tuxford Junction	**40E** Langwith Junction	**40E** Langwith Junction	**9G** Gorton		
64338	*J11*	WRX Wrexham Rhosddu	**6E** Wrexham Rhosddu	**35C** Spital Bridge	**38A** Colwick			
64339	*J11*	FRO Frodingham	**36C** Frodingham	**36C** Frodingham				
64340	*J11*	RET Retford	**36E** Retford	**36E** Retford	**36E** Retford			
64341	*J11*	RET Retford	**36E** Retford	**36E** Retford	**36E** Retford	**9G** Gorton		
64342	*J11*	STV Staveley	**39A** Gorton	**39A** Gorton				
64343	*J11*	BRN Barnsley	**36D** Barnsley	**36D** Barnsley	**36D** Barnsley			
64344	*J11*	TUX Tuxford Junction	**40D** Tuxford Junction	**40D** Tuxford Junction	**40D** Tuxford Junction			
64345	*J11*	STV Staveley	**38D** Staveley	**38D** Staveley	**38A** Colwick			
64346	*J11*	GOR Gorton	**39A** Gorton	**39A** Gorton	**39A** Gorton	**40A** Lincoln		
64347	*J11*	RET Retford	**36E** Retford	**36E** Retford				
64348	*J11*	RET Retford	**36E** Retford	**36A** Doncaster	**36A** Doncaster	**40E** Colwick		
64349	*J11*	RET Retford	**36A** Doncaster	**36A** Doncaster	**39A** Gorton			
64350	*J11*	STV Staveley	**40A** Lincoln	**40A** Lincoln				
64351	*J11*	STV Staveley	**40A** Lincoln	**40A** Lincoln	**40A** Lincoln			
64352	*J11*	MEX Mexborough	**36B** Mexborough	**36B** Mexborough	**36B** Mexborough	**41J** Langwith Junction		
64353	*J11*	LIN Lincoln	**40D** Tuxford Junction	**40D** Tuxford Junction	**40D** Tuxford Junction			
64354	*J11*	ANN Annesley	**38B** Annesley	**38B** Annesley	**38B** Annesley	**41H** Staveley		
64355	*J11*	IMM Immingham	**40B** Immingham	**40B** Immingham	**40B** Immingham	**40B** Immingham		
64356	*J11*	MEX Mexborough	**36B** Mexborough	**36B** Mexborough				
64357	*J11*	GOR Gorton	**39A** Gorton	**39A** Gorton	**39A** Gorton	**9G** Gorton		
64358	*J11*	LNG Langwith Junction	**40E** Langwith Junction	**40E** Langwith Junction				
64359	*J11*	LIN Lincoln	**40A** Lincoln	**40A** Lincoln	**40A** Lincoln	**9G** Gorton		
64360	*J11*	SHF Sheffield Darnall	**39B** Sheffield Darnall	**39B** Sheffield Darnall				
64361	*J11*	LEI Leicester Central	**38B** Annesley	**38B** Annesley	**38D** Staveley			
64362	*J11*	FRO Frodingham	**36D** Barnsley	**36D** Barnsley	**36D** Barnsley	**40A** Lincoln		
64363	*J11*	GOR Gorton	**39A** Gorton	**39A** Gorton	**39A** Gorton	**9G** Gorton		
64364	*J11*	WFD Woodford Halse	**38E** Woodford Halse	**38E** Woodford Halse	**38B** Annesley	**41J** Langwith Junction		
64365	*J11*	ANN Annesley	**40A** Lincoln	**40A** Lincoln	**40A** Lincoln			
64366	*J11*	BRN Barnsley	**36D** Barnsley	**36D** Barnsley				
64367	*J11*	GOR Gorton	**9G** Northwich	**36A** Doncaster				
64368	*J11*	GOR Gorton	**39A** Gorton	**39A** Gorton	**39A** Gorton	**9G** Gorton		
64369	*J11*	WFD Woodford Halse	**38E** Woodford Halse	**38A** Colwick				
64370	*J11*	ANN Annesley	**38B** Annesley	**38B** Annesley				
64371	*J11*	STV Staveley	**40A** Lincoln	**40A** Lincoln	**40A** Lincoln	**36C** Frodingham		
64372	*J11*	IMM Immingham	**40B** Immingham	**40B** Immingham	**40B** Immingham			
64373	*J11*	STV Staveley	**39B** Sheffield Darnall	**39B** Sheffield Darnall	**41A** Sheffield Darnall	**41A** Sheffield Darnall		
64374	*J11*	MEX Mexborough	**36B** Mexborough	**36B** Mexborough				
64375	*J11*	ANN Annesley	**38E** Woodford Halse	**38A** Colwick	**38C** Leicester Central	**16D** Annesley		
64376	*J11*	LIV Brunswick	**9G** Northwich	**36A** Doncaster	**36A** Doncaster			
64377	*J11*	MEX Mexborough	**36B** Mexborough	**36B** Mexborough	**36B** Mexborough	**41F** Mexborough		
64378	*J11*	LNG Langwith Junction	**40E** Langwith Junction	**40E** Langwith Junction				
64379	*J11*	LNG Langwith Junction	**40E** Langwith Junction	**40E** Langwith Junction	**40E** Langwith Junction	**41J** Langwith Junction		
64380	*J11*	RET Retford	**36E** Retford	**36E** Retford				
64381	*J11*	WRX Wrexham Rhosddu	**6E** Wrexham Rhosddu	**40A** Lincoln	**40A** Lincoln			
64382	*J11*	GOR Gorton	**39A** Gorton	**39A** Gorton	**39A** Gorton			
64383	*J11*	GOR Gorton	**39A** Gorton	**39A** Gorton	**39A** Gorton	**9G** Gorton		
64384	*J11*	STV Staveley	**38D** Staveley	**38D** Staveley	**38D** Staveley	**41H** Staveley		
64385	*J11*	RET Retford	**36E** Retford	**36E** Retford	**36E** Retford	**36C** Frodingham		
64386	*J11*	ANN Annesley	**38D** Staveley	**38D** Staveley	**38B** Annesley	**40B** Immingham		
64387	*J11*	SHF Sheffield Darnall	**39B** Sheffield Darnall	**39B** Sheffield Darnall	**41A** Sheffield Darnall	**41A** Sheffield Darnall		
64388	*J11*	WFD Woodford Halse	**38E** Woodford Halse	**38E** Woodford Halse	**38E** Woodford Halse			
64389	*J11*	LNG Langwith Junction	**40E** Langwith Junction	**40E** Langwith Junction	**40E** Langwith Junction	**9G** Gorton		
64390	*J11*	WFD Woodford Halse	**38E** Woodford Halse	**38E** Woodford Halse				
64391	*J11*	BRN Barnsley	**36D** Barnsley	**36D** Barnsley				
64392	*J11*	TUX Tuxford Junction	**40D** Tuxford Junction	**40D** Tuxford Junction	**40D** Tuxford Junction			
64393	*J11*	RET Retford	**36E** Retford	**36E** Retford	**36B** Mexborough	**41F** Mexborough		
64394	*J11*	NEA Neasden	**34E** Neasden	**39B** Sheffield Darnall	**41A** Sheffield Darnall	**41A** Sheffield Darnall		
64395	*J11*	FRO Frodingham	**36C** Frodingham	**36C** Frodingham	**36E** Retford	**36C** Frodingham		
64396	*J11*	LIN Lincoln	**38D** Staveley	**38D** Staveley	**38D** Staveley	**41H** Staveley		
64397	*J11*	WAL Walton on the Hill	**27E** Walton on the Hill	**35C** Spital Bridge	**38A** Colwick	**40E** Colwick		
64398	*J11*	BRN Barnsley	**36D** Barnsley	**36D** Barnsley				
64399	*J11*	BRN Barnsley	**36D** Barnsley	**36D** Barnsley	**36D** Barnsley			
64400	*J11*	MEX Mexborough	**36B** Mexborough	**36B** Mexborough				
64401	*J11*	GOR Gorton	**39A** Gorton	**39A** Gorton	**39A** Gorton			
64402	*J11*	RET Retford	**36E** Retford	**36E** Retford	**36B** Mexborough	**41F** Mexborough		
64403	*J11*	MEX Mexborough	**36B** Mexborough	**36A** Doncaster	**36E** Retford	**41F** Mexborough		
64404	*J11*	MEX Mexborough	**36B** Mexborough	**36A** Doncaster	**36A** Doncaster	**36C** Frodingham		
64405	*J11*	LIV Brunswick	**8E** Brunswick	**40A** Lincoln	**40D** Tuxford Junction	**9G** Gorton		
64406	*J11*	LIV Brunswick	**38A** Colwick	**38B** Annesley	**38B** Annesley	**41F** Mexborough		
64407	*J11*	FRO Frodingham	**36C** Frodingham	**36C** Frodingham	**36C** Frodingham			
64408	*J11*	WFD Woodford Halse	**38E** Woodford Halse	**40E** Langwith Junction				
64409	*J11*	ANN Annesley	**39A** Gorton	**39A** Gorton	**39A** Gorton			
64410	*J11*	RET Retford	**36A** Doncaster	**36A** Doncaster				
64411	*J11*	IMM Immingham	**40B** Immingham	**40B** Immingham	**40B** Immingham			
64412	*J11*	SHF Sheffield Darnall	**39B** Sheffield Darnall	**39B** Sheffield Darnall	**41A** Sheffield Darnall			
64413	*J11*	RET Retford	**36E** Retford	**39A** Gorton				
64414	*J11*	LNG Langwith Junction	**40E** Langwith Junction	**40E** Langwith Junction	**40E** Langwith Junction			
64415	*J11*	GOR Gorton	**39A** Gorton	**39A** Gorton				
64416	*J11*	RET Retford	**36E** Retford	**36E** Retford	**36E** Retford			
64417	*J11*	LIV Brunswick	**38A** Colwick	**36D** Barnsley	**36D** Barnsley	**41G** Barnsley		
64418	*J11*	LNG Langwith Junction	**40E** Langwith Junction	**40E** Langwith Junction	**38E** Woodford Halse	**9G** Gorton		
64419	*J11*	SHF Sheffield Darnall	**39B** Sheffield Darnall	**39B** Sheffield Darnall	**41A** Sheffield Darnall	**41A** Sheffield Darnall		
64420	*J11*	LIV Brunswick	**8E** Brunswick	**38A** Colwick	**38A** Colwick	**16D** Annesley		
64421	*J11*	RET Retford	**36E** Retford	**36E** Retford	**36E** Retford			
64422	*J11*	RET Retford	**36E** Retford	**36E** Retford	**36E** Retford			
64423	*J11*	RET Retford	**36E** Retford	**36E** Retford	**36E** Retford	**36C** Frodingham		
64424	*J11*	TUX Tuxford Junction	**40D** Tuxford Junction	**40D** Tuxford Junction	**40D** Tuxford Junction			
64425	*J11*	RET Retford	**36D** Barnsley	**36D** Barnsley	**36D** Barnsley	**41G** Barnsley		
64426	*J11*	LNG Langwith Junction	**40E** Langwith Junction	**40E** Langwith Junction				
64427	*J11*	LNG Langwith Junction	**40E** Langwith Junction	**40E** Langwith Junction	**40E** Langwith Junction	**41J** Langwith Junction		
64428	*J11*	STV Staveley	**38D** Staveley	**38E** Woodford Halse	**38E** Woodford Halse			
64429	*J11*	FRO Frodingham	**36C** Frodingham	**36C** Frodingham	**36C** Frodingham			
64430	*J11*	LIN Lincoln	**40A** Lincoln	**40A** Lincoln	**40A** Lincoln			
64431	*J11*	ANN Annesley	**38B** Annesley	**38B** Annesley				
64432	*J11*	MEX Mexborough	**36B** Mexborough	**36B** Mexborough	**36B** Mexborough			
64433	*J11*	STV Staveley	**38D** Staveley	**38D** Staveley	**38D** Staveley	**41H** Staveley		
64434	*J11*	GOR Gorton	**39A** Gorton	**39A** Gorton	**39A** Gorton	**9G** Gorton		
64435	*J11*	GOR Gorton	**39A** Gorton	**39A** Gorton	**39A** Gorton	**9G** Gorton		
64436	*J11*	BRN Barnsley	**36D** Barnsley	**36D** Barnsley				
64437	*J11*	GOR Gorton	**39A** Gorton	**39A** Gorton	**39A** Gorton	**9G** Gorton		
64438	*J11*	WFD Woodford Halse	**38E** Woodford Halse	**38A** Colwick	**38E** Woodford Halse	**40E** Colwick		
64439	*J11*	LTH Louth	**40B** Immingham	**40B** Immingham	**40B** Immingham	**9G** Gorton		
64440	*J11*	GOR Gorton	**39A** Gorton	**39A** Gorton	**39A** Gorton	**9G** Gorton		
64441	*J11*	SHF Sheffield Darnall	**39B** Sheffield Darnall	**39B** Sheffield Darnall	**41A** Sheffield Darnall	**41A** Sheffield Darnall		

No.	Class	1948	1951	1954	1957	1960	1963	1966
64442	J11	MEX Mexborough	36B Mexborough	36B Mexborough	36D Barnsley	41G Barnsley		
64443	J11	SHF Sheffield Darnall	39B Sheffield Darnall	39B Sheffield Darnall	41A Sheffield Darnall	41A Sheffield Darnall		
64444	J11	STV Staveley	38D Staveley	38D Staveley	38D Staveley	41H Staveley		
64445	J11	SHF Sheffield Darnall	39B Sheffield Darnall	39B Sheffield Darnall	41A Sheffield Darnall	41A Sheffield Darnall		
64446	J11	IMM Immingham	40B Immingham	40B Immingham	40B Immingham	40B Immingham		
64447	J11	SHF Sheffield Darnall	39B Sheffield Darnall	39B Sheffield Darnall	41A Sheffield Darnall	41A Sheffield Darnall		
64448	J11	BRN Barnsley	36D Barnsley	36D Barnsley	36D Barnsley			
64449	J11	MEX Mexborough	36B Mexborough	36B Mexborough				
64450	J11	LNG Langwith Junction	39A Gorton	39A Gorton	39A Gorton	36E Retford		
64451	J11	RET Retford	36E Retford	36E Retford	36E Retford			
64452	J11	BRN Barnsley	36D Barnsley	36D Barnsley	36D Barnsley	41G Barnsley		
64453	J11	GOR Gorton	9G Northwich	36A Doncaster	38C Leicester Central			
64460	J35	KPS Kipps	65E Kipps	65E Kipps	65E Kipps			
64461	J35	STG Stirling Shore Road	63B Stirling	65C Parkhead	65C Parkhead	65C Parkhead		
64462	J35	STM St. Margarets	64A St. Margarets	64A St. Margarets	64A St. Margarets	64A St. Margarets		
64463	J35	HAW Hawick	64G Hawick	64G Hawick	64G Hawick	64A St. Margarets		
64464	J35	THJ Thornton Junction	62A Thornton Junction	62A Thornton Junction	62A Thornton Junction			
64466	J35	THJ Thornton Junction	62A Thornton Junction	62A Thornton Junction	62A Thornton Junction			
64468	J35	BGT Bathgate	64F Bathgate	64F Bathgate	64F Bathgate	64F Bathgate		
64470	J35	KPS Kipps	65E Kipps	65E Kipps	65E Kipps	65E Kipps		
64471	J35	STG Stirling Shore Road	63B Stirling	68E Carlisle Canal	66A Polmadie	66A Polmadie		
64472	J35	KPS Kipps	65E Kipps	65E Kipps	65E Kipps	65E Kipps		
64473	J35	KPS Kipps	65E Kipps	65E Kipps	65E Kipps			
64474	J35	THJ Thornton Junction	62A Thornton Junction	62A Thornton Junction	62A Thornton Junction	62A Thornton Junction		
64475	J35	DFU Dunfermline Upper	62C Dunfermline Upper	62C Dunfermline Upper	62C Dunfermline Upper			
64476	J35	DFU Dunfermline Upper	62C Dunfermline Upper	62C Dunfermline Upper	62C Dunfermline Upper	62C Dunfermline Upper		
64477	J35	THJ Thornton Junction	62A Thornton Junction	62A Thornton Junction	62A Thornton Junction	66A Polmadie		
64478	J35	CAR Carlisle Canal	12B Carlisle Canal	68E Carlisle Canal	68E Carlisle Canal	12C Carlisle Canal		
64479	J35	STM St. Margarets	64A St. Margarets	64A St. Margarets	64A St. Margarets	64A St. Margarets		
64480	J35	DFU Dunfermline Upper	62C Dunfermline Upper	62C Dunfermline Upper	62C Dunfermline Upper	62C Dunfermline Upper		
64482	J35	DEE Dundee Tay Bridge	62B Dundee Tay Bridge	61A Kittybrewster	61A Kittybrewster	64A St. Margarets		
64483	J35	DFU Dunfermline Upper	62C Dunfermline Upper	62C Dunfermline Upper	61B Aberdeen Ferryhill	64A St. Margarets		
64484	J35	POL Polmont	64E Polmont	64F Bathgate	64F Bathgate			
64485	J35	DEE Dundee Tay Bridge	62B Dundee Tay Bridge	61B Aberdeen Ferryhill	61B Aberdeen Ferryhill			
64486	J35	STM St. Margarets	64A St. Margarets	64A St. Margarets	64A St. Margarets			
64487	J35	DFU Dunfermline Upper	62C Dunfermline Upper	62C Dunfermline Upper	62C Dunfermline Upper	62C Dunfermline Upper		
64488	J35	THJ Thornton Junction	62A Thornton Junction	62A Thornton Junction	62A Thornton Junction	62A Thornton Junction		
64489	J35	STM St. Margarets	64A St. Margarets	64A St. Margarets	64A St. Margarets	64A St. Margarets		
64490	J35	POL Polmont	64E Polmont	64E Polmont	64E Polmont			
64491	J35	BGT Bathgate	64F Bathgate	64F Bathgate	64F Bathgate	64F Bathgate		
64492	J35	STM St. Margarets	64A St. Margarets	64A St. Margarets	64A St. Margarets			
64493	J35	DEE Dundee Tay Bridge	62C Dunfermline Upper	62C Dunfermline Upper	62C Dunfermline Upper	62C Dunfermline Upper		
64494	J35	HAW Hawick	64G Hawick	64G Hawick	64G Hawick	64G Hawick		
64495	J35	THJ Thornton Junction	62A Thornton Junction	64C Dalry Road	64C Dalry Road			
64496	J35	DFU Dunfermline Upper	62C Dunfermline Upper	62C Dunfermline Upper	62C Dunfermline Upper			
64497	J35	STG Stirling Shore Road	63B Stirling	63B Stirling	63B Stirling	64C Dalry Road		
64498	J35	KPS Kipps	65E Kipps	65E Kipps	65E Kipps			
64499	J35	CAR Carlisle Canal	12B Carlisle Canal	68E Carlisle Canal	68E Carlisle Canal	12C Carlisle Canal		
64500	J35	THJ Thornton Junction	62A Thornton Junction	64C Dalry Road	64C Dalry Road	64C Dalry Road		
64501	J35	STG Stirling Shore Road	63B Stirling	63B Stirling	63B Stirling			
64502	J35	POL Polmont	64E Polmont	64E Polmont	64E Polmont	64E Polmont		
64504	J35	BGT Bathgate	64F Bathgate	64F Bathgate	64F Bathgate	64F Bathgate		
64505	J35	DFU Dunfermline Upper	62C Dunfermline Upper	62C Dunfermline Upper	62C Dunfermline Upper	62C Dunfermline Upper		
64506	J35	DEE Dundee Tay Bridge	64A St. Margarets	64A St. Margarets	64A St. Margarets			
64507	J35	KPS Kipps	65E Kipps	65E Kipps	65E Kipps	65E Kipps		
64509	J35	HAW Hawick	64G Hawick	64G Hawick	64G Hawick			
64510	J35	BGT Bathgate	64F Bathgate	64F Bathgate	64F Bathgate	64F Bathgate		
64511	J35	CAR Carlisle Canal	12B Carlisle Canal	68E Carlisle Canal	66A Polmadie			
64512	J35	DEE Dundee Tay Bridge	64A St. Margarets	64F Bathgate	64F Bathgate	64F Bathgate		
64513	J35	DFU Dunfermline Upper	62C Dunfermline Upper	62C Dunfermline Upper	62C Dunfermline Upper			
64514	J35	THJ Thornton Junction	62A Thornton Junction	65C Parkhead	65C Parkhead	65C Parkhead		
64515	J35	STM St. Margarets	64A St. Margarets	64A St. Margarets	64A St. Margarets	64A St. Margarets		
64516	J35	THJ Thornton Junction	62A Thornton Junction	62A Thornton Junction	62C Dunfermline Upper			
64517	J35	STM St. Margarets	64A St. Margarets	64A St. Margarets	64C Dalry Road			
64518	J35	STM St. Margarets	64A St. Margarets	64A St. Margarets	64A St. Margarets	64A St. Margarets		
64519	J35	STM St. Margarets	64A St. Margarets	64A St. Margarets	64A St. Margarets	64A St. Margarets		
64520	J35	STG Stirling Shore Road	63B Stirling	63B Stirling	65D Dawsholm			
64521	J35	THJ Thornton Junction	62A Thornton Junction	62A Thornton Junction	62A Thornton Junction			
64522	J35	THJ Thornton Junction	62A Thornton Junction	62A Thornton Junction	62A Thornton Junction			
64523	J35	DEE Dundee Tay Bridge	64A St. Margarets	64A St. Margarets	64A St. Margarets	65C Parkhead		
64524	J35	STM St. Margarets	64A St. Margarets	64A St. Margarets	64A St. Margarets	64A St. Margarets		
64525	J35	STG Stirling Shore Road	62C Dunfermline Upper	62C Dunfermline Upper	62C Dunfermline Upper	62C Dunfermline Upper		
64526	J35	CAR Carlisle Canal	12B Carlisle Canal	68E Carlisle Canal	68E Carlisle Canal			
64527	J35	STM St. Margarets	64A St. Margarets	64A St. Margarets	64C Dalry Road	64C Dalry Road		
64528	J35	POL Polmont	64E Polmont	64E Polmont	64E Polmont			
64529	J35	BGT Bathgate	64F Bathgate	64F Bathgate	64F Bathgate	64F Bathgate		
64530	J35	DEE Dundee Tay Bridge	62B Dundee Tay Bridge	62B Dundee Tay Bridge	62B Dundee Tay Bridge			
64531	J35	POL Polmont	65E Kipps	65E Kipps	65E Kipps	65E Kipps		
64532	J35	STM St. Margarets	64A St. Margarets	64A St. Margarets	64A St. Margarets	64A St. Margarets		
64533	J35	STM St. Margarets	64A St. Margarets	64A St. Margarets	64A St. Margarets	64A St. Margarets		
64534	J35	BGT Bathgate	65E Kipps	65E Kipps	65E Kipps	65E Kipps		
64535	J35	STM St. Margarets	64A St. Margarets	64A St. Margarets	64A St. Margarets	64A St. Margarets		
64536	J37	PTH Perth South	64C Dalry Road	64C Dalry Road	64C Dalry Road			
64537	J37	DEE Dundee Tay Bridge	64E Polmont	64E Polmont	64E Polmont	64E Polmont	65K Polmont	
64538	J37	STM St. Margarets	64A St. Margarets	64A St. Margarets	64A St. Margarets			
64539	J37	HAW Hawick	64G Hawick	64G Hawick	64G Hawick	64A St. Margarets		
64540	J37	EFD Eastfield	65A Eastfield	65A Eastfield	65A Eastfield	65A Eastfield		
64541	J37	EFD Eastfield	65A Eastfield	65A Eastfield	65A Eastfield	65A Eastfield	67C Ayr	
64542	J37	STG Stirling Shore Road	63B Stirling	63B Stirling	63B Stirling	65E Kipps		
64543	J37	STM St. Margarets	64A St. Margarets	64A St. Margarets	64A St. Margarets	62C Dunfermline Upper		
64544	J37	STG Stirling Shore Road	63B Stirling	63B Stirling	63B Stirling	65E Kipps		
64545	J37	DFU Dunfermline Upper	62C Dunfermline Upper	62C Dunfermline Upper	62B Dundee Tay Bridge	62C Dunfermline Upper		
64546	J37	THJ Thornton Junction	62A Thornton Junction	62A Thornton Junction	62A Thornton Junction	62A Thornton Junction	62A Thornton Junction	
64547	J37	STM St. Margarets	64A St. Margarets	64A St. Margarets	64A St. Margarets	64A St. Margarets	64A St. Margarets	62B Dundee Tay Bridge
64548	J37	DEE Dundee Tay Bridge	65C Parkhead	65E Kipps	65E Kipps	65A Eastfield	65A Eastfield	
64549	J37	THJ Thornton Junction	62A Thornton Junction	62A Thornton Junction	62A Thornton Junction	62A Thornton Junction	62A Thornton Junction	
64550	J37	THJ Thornton Junction	62A Thornton Junction	62A Thornton Junction	62A Thornton Junction	62A Thornton Junction	62C Dunfermline Upper	
64551	J37	POL Polmont	64E Polmont	64E Polmont	64E Polmont	64E Polmont	65K Polmont	
64552	J37	STM St. Margarets	64A St. Margarets	64A St. Margarets	64A St. Margarets	64A St. Margarets	62C Dunfermline Upper	
64553	J37	THJ Thornton Junction	64E Polmont	64F Bathgate	64F Bathgate	64F Bathgate		
64554	J37	DFU Dunfermline Upper	62C Dunfermline Upper	62C Dunfermline Upper	64C Dalry Road	64C Dalry Road	64F Bathgate	
64555	J37	STM St. Margarets	64A St. Margarets	64A St. Margarets	64A St. Margarets	64A St. Margarets	64A St. Margarets	
64556	J37	STG Stirling Shore Road	62C Dunfermline Upper	62C Dunfermline Upper	62B Dundee Tay Bridge	62B Dundee Tay Bridge		
64557	J37	STM St. Margarets	64A St. Margarets	64A St. Margarets	64A St. Margarets	64A St. Margarets	64A St. Margarets	
64558	J37	EFD Eastfield	65A Eastfield	65A Eastfield	65A Eastfield	65A Eastfield	65A Eastfield	
64559	J37	PKD Parkhead	65C Parkhead	65C Parkhead	65C Parkhead	65C Parkhead	65C Parkhead	
64560	J37	DFU Dunfermline Upper	62C Dunfermline Upper	62C Dunfermline Upper	62C Dunfermline Upper	62C Dunfermline Upper		
64561	J37	DFU Dunfermline Upper	62C Dunfermline Upper	62C Dunfermline Upper	64C Dalry Road	64C Dalry Road	64A St. Margarets	
64562	J37	STM St. Margarets	64A St. Margarets	64A St. Margarets	64A St. Margarets	64A St. Margarets	64A St. Margarets	
64563	J37	PKD Parkhead	65C Parkhead	65C Parkhead	65C Parkhead	65C Parkhead	65C Parkhead	
64564	J37	THJ Thornton Junction	62A Thornton Junction	62A Thornton Junction	62A Thornton Junction	62A Thornton Junction	62A Thornton Junction	
64565	J37	THJ Thornton Junction	62A Thornton Junction	62A Thornton Junction	62A Thornton Junction	62A Thornton Junction		
64566	J37	STM St. Margarets	64A St. Margarets	64A St. Margarets	64A St. Margarets	64A St. Margarets		
64567	J37	DFU Dunfermline Upper	62C Dunfermline Upper	62C Dunfermline Upper	62C Dunfermline Upper	62C Dunfermline Upper		

No.	Class	1948		1951	1954	1957	1960	1963	1966
64568	*J37*	**DFU**	Dunfermline Upper	**62C** Dunfermline Upper	**62C** Dunfermline Upper	**62C** Dunfermline Upper	**62C** Dunfermline Upper	**62C** Dunfermline Upper	
64569	*J37*	**STG**	Stirling Shore Road	**63B** Stirling	**63B** Stirling	**63B** Stirling	**64C** Dalry Road	**64F** Bathgate	**62A** Thornton Junction
64570	*J37*	**POL**	Polmont	**64E** Polmont	**64E** Polmont	**64E** Polmont	**64E** Polmont	**65K** Polmont	**62A** Thornton Junction
64571	*J37*	**POL**	Polmont	**64E** Polmont	**64E** Polmont	**64E** Polmont	**64E** Polmont	**65K** Polmont	
64572	*J37*	**STM**	St. Margarets	**64A** St. Margarets	**64A** St. Margarets	**64A** St. Margarets	**64A** St. Margarets	**64A** St. Margarets	
64573	*J37*	**PKD**	Parkhead	**65C** Parkhead	**65C** Parkhead	**65C** Parkhead	**65C** Parkhead	**62C** Dunfermline Upper	
64574	*J37*	**DFU**	Dunfermline Upper	**62C** Dunfermline Upper	**62C** Dunfermline Upper	**64C** Dalry Road	**65E** Kipps		
64575	*J37*	**DEE**	Dundee Tay Bridge	**62B** Dundee Tay Bridge	**62B** Dundee Tay Bridge	**62B** Dundee Tay Bridge	**62B** Dundee Tay Bridge	**62B** Dundee Tay Bridge	
64576	*J37*	**STM**	St. Margarets	**64A** St. Margarets	**64A** St. Margarets	**64A** St. Margarets	**64A** St. Margarets	**64A** St. Margarets	**62B** Dundee Tay Bridge
64577	*J37*	**STM**	St. Margarets	**64A** St. Margarets	**64A** St. Margarets	**64A** St. Margarets	**64A** St. Margarets	**64A** St. Margarets	**62B** Dundee Tay Bridge
64578	*J37*	**EFD**	Eastfield	**65A** Eastfield	**65A** Eastfield	**65A** Eastfield	**65A** Eastfield		
64579	*J37*	**EFD**	Eastfield	**65A** Eastfield	**65E** Kipps	**65E** Kipps	**65E** Kipps	**62C** Dunfermline Upper	
64580	*J37*	**EFD**	Eastfield	**65A** Eastfield	**65A** Eastfield	**65A** Eastfield	**65A** Eastfield	**65A** Eastfield	
64581	*J37*	**EFD**	Eastfield	**65A** Eastfield	**65A** Eastfield	**65A** Eastfield	**65A** Eastfield		
64582	*J37*	**STM**	St. Margarets	**64A** St. Margarets	**64A** St. Margarets	**64A** St. Margarets	**64A** St. Margarets	**64A** St. Margarets	
64583	*J37*	**EFD**	Eastfield	**65A** Eastfield	**64F** Bathgate	**64F** Bathgate	**64F** Bathgate	**64F** Bathgate	
64584	*J37*	**PKD**	Parkhead	**65C** Parkhead	**65C** Parkhead	**65C** Parkhead			
64585	*J37*	**STG**	Stirling Shore Road	**63B** Stirling	**63B** Stirling	**63B** Stirling	**62B** Dundee Tay Bridge	**62C** Dunfermline Upper	
64586	*J37*	**STM**	St. Margarets	**64A** St. Margarets	**64A** St. Margarets	**64A** St. Margarets	**64A** St. Margarets	**64A** St. Margarets	
64587	*J37*	**DEE**	Dundee Tay Bridge	**62B** Dundee Tay Bridge	**62B** Dundee Tay Bridge	**62B** Dundee Tay Bridge	**62B** Dundee Tay Bridge	**62B** Dundee Tay Bridge	
64588	*J37*	**PTH**	Perth South	**64E** Polmont	**64E** Polmont	**64E** Polmont	**65C** Parkhead	**64A** St. Margarets	**62A** Thornton Junction
64589	*J37*	**POL**	Polmont	**64E** Polmont	**64E** Polmont	**64E** Polmont	**65F** Grangemouth	**65F** Grangemouth	
64590	*J37*	**DFU**	Dunfermline Upper	**62C** Dunfermline Upper	**64A** St. Margarets	**64A** St. Margarets	**64A** St. Margarets		
64591	*J37*	**PTH**	Perth South	**64C** Dalry Road	**64C** Dalry Road	**64C** Dalry Road	**64A** St. Margarets	**64A** St. Margarets	
64592	*J37*	**STM**	St. Margarets	**64E** Polmont	**64E** Polmont	**64E** Polmont	**65F** Grangemouth	**65K** Polmont	
64593	*J37*	**DEE**	Dundee Tay Bridge	**64E** Polmont	**64E** Polmont	**64E** Polmont	**65F** Grangemouth	**65E** Kipps	
64594	*J37*	**STM**	St. Margarets	**64A** St. Margarets	**64A** St. Margarets	**64A** St. Margarets	**64A** St. Margarets		
64595	*J37*	**STM**	St. Margarets	**64A** St. Margarets	**64A** St. Margarets	**64A** St. Margarets	**64A** St. Margarets	**64A** St. Margarets	**62A** Thornton Junction
64596	*J37*	**THJ**	Thornton Junction	**62A** Thornton Junction	**62A** Thornton Junction	**62A** Thornton Junction	**62A** Thornton Junction		
64597	*J37*	**THJ**	Thornton Junction	**62A** Thornton Junction	**64A** St. Margarets	**64A** St. Margarets	**62C** Dunfermline Upper	**62C** Dunfermline Upper	**62B** Dundee Tay Bridge
64598	*J37*	**THJ**	Thornton Junction	**62B** Dundee Tay Bridge	**62B** Dundee Tay Bridge	**62B** Dundee Tay Bridge	**62B** Dundee Tay Bridge		
64599	*J37*	**STM**	St. Margarets	**64A** St. Margarets	**64A** St. Margarets	**64A** St. Margarets	**64A** St. Margarets	**64A** St. Margarets	
64600	*J37*	**THJ**	Thornton Junction	**62A** Thornton Junction	**62A** Thornton Junction	**62A** Thornton Junction	**62B** Dundee Tay Bridge	**62B** Dundee Tay Bridge	
64601	*J37*	**EFD**	Eastfield	**65A** Eastfield	**64A** St. Margarets	**64A** St. Margarets	**64A** St. Margarets		
64602	*J37*	**THJ**	Thornton Junction	**62A** Thornton Junction	**62A** Thornton Junction	**62A** Thornton Junction	**62B** Dundee Tay Bridge	**62B** Dundee Tay Bridge	**62B** Dundee Tay Bridge
64603	*J37*	**STM**	St. Margarets	**64A** St. Margarets	**64A** St. Margarets	**64A** St. Margarets	**64A** St. Margarets	**64A** St. Margarets	
64604	*J37*	**DFU**	Dunfermline Upper	**62C** Dunfermline Upper	**62C** Dunfermline Upper	**62C** Dunfermline Upper	**62C** Dunfermline Upper		
64605	*J37*	**STM**	St. Margarets	**64A** St. Margarets	**64A** St. Margarets	**64A** St. Margarets	**64A** St. Margarets	**64A** St. Margarets	
64606	*J37*	**STM**	St. Margarets	**64A** St. Margarets	**64A** St. Margarets	**64A** St. Margarets	**64A** St. Margarets	**64A** St. Margarets	**62A** Thornton Junction
64607	*J37*	**STM**	St. Margarets	**64A** St. Margarets	**64A** St. Margarets	**64A** St. Margarets	**64A** St. Margarets		
64608	*J37*	**STM**	St. Margarets	**64A** St. Margarets	**64A** St. Margarets	**64A** St. Margarets	**64A** St. Margarets	**64A** St. Margarets	**62B** Dundee Tay Bridge
64609	*J37*	**PKD**	Parkhead	**65C** Parkhead	**65C** Parkhead	**65C** Parkhead	**65C** Parkhead		
64610	*J37*	**EFD**	Eastfield	**65C** Parkhead	**65C** Parkhead	**65C** Parkhead	**65C** Parkhead	**65C** Parkhead	**62C** Dunfermline Upper
64611	*J37*	**EFD**	Eastfield	**65A** Eastfield	**65A** Eastfield	**65A** Eastfield	**65A** Eastfield	**65K** Polmont	**62C** Dunfermline Upper
64612	*J37*	**THJ**	Thornton Junction	**62A** Thornton Junction	**62A** Thornton Junction	**64C** Dalry Road	**64A** St. Margarets		
64613	*J37*	**POL**	Polmont	**64E** Polmont	**64A** St. Margarets	**64A** St. Margarets	**64A** St. Margarets	**64A** St. Margarets	
64614	*J37*	**STM**	St. Margarets	**64A** St. Margarets	**64A** St. Margarets	**64A** St. Margarets	**64A** St. Margarets	**64A** St. Margarets	
64615	*J37*	**DEE**	Dundee Tay Bridge	**62B** Dundee Tay Bridge	**62B** Dundee Tay Bridge	**62B** Dundee Tay Bridge	**62B** Dundee Tay Bridge		
64616	*J37*	**THJ**	Thornton Junction	**62A** Thornton Junction	**62A** Thornton Junction	**62A** Thornton Junction	**62A** Thornton Junction	**62A** Thornton Junction	
64617	*J37*	**DFU**	Dunfermline Upper	**62C** Dunfermline Upper	**62C** Dunfermline Upper	**62C** Dunfermline Upper	**62C** Dunfermline Upper		
64618	*J37*	**THJ**	Thornton Junction	**62A** Thornton Junction	**62A** Thornton Junction	**62A** Thornton Junction	**62A** Thornton Junction	**62A** Thornton Junction	**62A** Thornton Junction
64619	*J37*	**DEE**	Dundee Tay Bridge	**62B** Dundee Tay Bridge	**62B** Dundee Tay Bridge	**62B** Dundee Tay Bridge	**62B** Dundee Tay Bridge	**62B** Dundee Tay Bridge	
64620	*J37*	**DEE**	Dundee Tay Bridge	**62B** Dundee Tay Bridge	**62B** Dundee Tay Bridge	**62B** Dundee Tay Bridge	**62B** Dundee Tay Bridge	**62B** Dundee Tay Bridge	**62B** Dundee Tay Bridge
64621	*J37*	**POL**	Polmont	**65C** Parkhead	**65C** Parkhead	**65C** Parkhead	**65C** Parkhead	**65C** Parkhead	
64622	*J37*	**EFD**	Eastfield	**65A** Eastfield	**65A** Eastfield	**65A** Eastfield	**65A** Eastfield		
64623	*J37*	**EFD**	Eastfield	**65A** Eastfield	**65A** Eastfield	**65A** Eastfield	**65A** Eastfield	**65A** Eastfield	**62C** Dunfermline Upper
64624	*J37*	**STM**	St. Margarets	**64A** St. Margarets	**64A** St. Margarets	**64A** St. Margarets	**64A** St. Margarets	**64A** St. Margarets	**62B** Dundee Tay Bridge
64625	*J37*	**STM**	St. Margarets	**64A** St. Margarets	**64A** St. Margarets	**64A** St. Margarets	**64A** St. Margarets	**64A** St. Margarets	
64626	*J37*	**PKD**	Parkhead	**65C** Parkhead	**65C** Parkhead	**65C** Parkhead	**65C** Parkhead	**67C** Ayr	
64627	*J37*	**DEE**	Dundee Tay Bridge	**62B** Dundee Tay Bridge	**62B** Dundee Tay Bridge	**62B** Dundee Tay Bridge	**62B** Dundee Tay Bridge	**62B** Dundee Tay Bridge	
64628	*J37*	**DFU**	Dunfermline Upper	**65A** Eastfield	**65A** Eastfield	**65A** Eastfield	**65E** Kipps		
64629	*J37*	**THJ**	Thornton Junction	**62A** Thornton Junction	**62A** Thornton Junction	**62A** Thornton Junction	**62A** Thornton Junction	**62A** Thornton Junction	
64630	*J37*	**DFU**	Dunfermline Upper	**62C** Dunfermline Upper	**62C** Dunfermline Upper	**62C** Dunfermline Upper	**62C** Dunfermline Upper		
64631	*J37*	**DEE**	Dundee Tay Bridge	**62B** Dundee Tay Bridge	**62B** Dundee Tay Bridge	**62B** Dundee Tay Bridge	**62B** Dundee Tay Bridge		
64632	*J37*	**EFD**	Eastfield	**65A** Eastfield	**65A** Eastfield	**65A** Eastfield	**65A** Eastfield	**65A** Eastfield	
64633	*J37*	**EFD**	Eastfield	**65A** Eastfield	**65A** Eastfield	**65A** Eastfield	**65A** Eastfield	**65A** Eastfield	
64634	*J37*	**DEE**	Dundee Tay Bridge	**62B** Dundee Tay Bridge	**62B** Dundee Tay Bridge	**64F** Bathgate	**64F** Bathgate	**64F** Bathgate	
64635	*J37*	**THJ**	Thornton Junction	**62A** Thornton Junction	**62A** Thornton Junction	**62A** Thornton Junction	**62A** Thornton Junction		
64636	*J37*	**STM**	St. Margarets	**64A** St. Margarets	**64E** Polmont	**64E** Polmont	**64E** Polmont	**65K** Polmont	
64637	*J37*	**STM**	St. Margarets	**64A** St. Margarets	**64A** St. Margarets	**64A** St. Margarets	**64A** St. Margarets		
64638	*J37*	**EFD**	Eastfield	**65A** Eastfield	**65A** Eastfield	**65A** Eastfield	**65A** Eastfield		
64639	*J37*	**EFD**	Eastfield	**65A** Eastfield	**65A** Eastfield	**65A** Eastfield	**65A** Eastfield		
64640	*J19*	**MAR**	March	**31C** Kings Lynn	**31B** March	**31B** March			
64641	*J19*	**MAR**	March	**31B** March	**31B** March	**31B** March	**32A** Norwich Thorpe		
64642	*J19*	**KL**	Kings Lynn	**31C** Kings Lynn	**31B** March	**31B** March	**31B** March		
64643	*J19*	**MAR**	March	**31B** March	**31B** March	**31B** March	**32A** Norwich Thorpe		
64644	*J19*	**MAR**	March	**32A** Norwich Thorpe	**32A** Norwich Thorpe	**32A** Norwich Thorpe			
64645	*J19*	**SL**	South Lynn	**31D** South Lynn	**30E** Colchester	**30E** Colchester			
64646	*J19*	**MAR**	March	**31D** South Lynn	**31D** South Lynn	**31A** Cambridge	**31A** Cambridge		
64647	*J19*	**MAR**	March	**31B** March	**30E** Colchester	**30E** Colchester	**31C** Kings Lynn		
64648	*J19*	**MAR**	March	**31B** March	**31B** March	**31B** March			
64649	*J19*	**CAM**	Cambridge	**31D** South Lynn	**30E** Colchester	**30E** Colchester			
64650	*J19*	**MAR**	March	**30A** Stratford	**30E** Colchester	**30E** Colchester	**30A** Stratford		
64651	*J19*	**MAR**	March	**30A** Stratford	**30E** Colchester	**30E** Colchester			
64652	*J19*	**MAR**	March	**30A** Stratford	**30E** Colchester	**30E** Colchester	**30F** Parkeston		
64653	*J19*	**MAR**	March	**31D** South Lynn	**30E** Colchester	**30E** Colchester	**30A** Stratford		
64654	*J19*	**MAR**	March	**31C** Kings Lynn	**31A** Cambridge	**31A** Cambridge	**31A** Cambridge		
64655	*J19*	**MAR**	March	**31B** March	**31B** March	**31B** March	**31C** Kings Lynn		
64656	*J19*	**MAR**	March	**31B** March	**30A** Stratford	**30A** Stratford	**30A** Stratford		
64657	*J19*	**MAR**	March	**30A** Stratford	**30A** Stratford	**30A** Stratford	**30A** Stratford		
64658	*J19*	**CAM**	Cambridge	**31D** South Lynn	**31A** Cambridge	**31A** Cambridge			
64659	*J19*	**MAR**	March	**31B** March	**30E** Colchester	**30E** Colchester	**32B** Ipswich		
64660	*J19*	**MAR**	March	**30A** Stratford	**30E** Colchester	**30E** Colchester	**30A** Stratford		
64661	*J19*	**MAR**	March	**31B** March	**31B** March	**31B** March			
64662	*J19*	**MAR**	March	**30A** Stratford	**30A** Stratford	**30A** Stratford			
64663	*J19*	**MAR**	March	**30A** Stratford	**30A** Stratford	**30A** Stratford	**30A** Stratford		
64664	*J19*	**MAR**	March	**30A** Stratford	**30A** Stratford	**30A** Stratford	**30A** Stratford		
64665	*J19*	**MAR**	March	**30A** Stratford	**30A** Stratford	**30A** Stratford			
64666	*J19*	**MAR**	March	**31B** March	**30E** Colchester	**30E** Colchester	**30A** Stratford		
64667	*J19*	**MAR**	March	**31B** March	**30E** Colchester	**30E** Colchester	**30A** Stratford		
64668	*J19*	**KL**	Kings Lynn	**31C** Kings Lynn	**31B** March	**31B** March			
64669	*J19*	**MAR**	March	**31B** March	**31B** March	**31B** March	**31B** March		
64670	*J19*	**KL**	Kings Lynn	**30A** Stratford	**30A** Stratford	**30A** Stratford			
64671	*J19*	**MAR**	March	**31B** March	**31B** March	**31B** March	**31B** March		
64672	*J19*	**MAR**	March	**31C** Kings Lynn	**31B** March	**31B** March			
64673	*J19*	**MAR**	March	**31D** South Lynn	**31A** Cambridge	**31A** Cambridge	**31C** Kings Lynn		
64674	*J19*	**MAR**	March	**32A** Norwich Thorpe	**32A** Norwich Thorpe	**32A** Norwich Thorpe	**32A** Norwich Thorpe		
64675	*J20*	**STR**	Stratford	**30A** Stratford	**30A** Stratford	**30A** Stratford			
64676	*J20*	**CAM**	Cambridge	**30A** Stratford	**30A** Stratford	**30A** Stratford	**30A** Stratford		
64677	*J20*	**STR**	Stratford	**30A** Stratford	**30A** Stratford	**30A** Stratford	**30A** Stratford		
64678	*J20*	**CAM**	Cambridge	**31A** Cambridge	**31B** March	**31B** March	**30F** Parkeston		
64679	*J20*	**CAM**	Cambridge	**31A** Cambridge	**31B** March	**31B** March	**30F** Parkeston		
64680	*J20*	**CAM**	Cambridge	**30A** Stratford	**30A** Stratford	**30A** Stratford	**30A** Stratford		
64681	*J20*	**STR**	Stratford	**30A** Stratford	**30A** Stratford	**30A** Stratford	**30A** Stratford		

No.	Class	1948	1951	1954	1957	1960	1963	1966
64682	*J20*	**STR** Stratford	**30A** Stratford	**30A** Stratford	**30A** Stratford	**30A** Stratford		
64683	*J20*	**CAM** Cambridge	**31A** Cambridge	**31A** Cambridge	**31A** Cambridge			
64684	*J20*	**CAM** Cambridge	**31A** Cambridge	**31B** March	**31B** March	**31A** Cambridge		
64685	*J20*	**STR** Stratford	**30A** Stratford	**30A** Stratford	**30A** Stratford	**30A** Stratford		
64686	*J20*	**STR** Stratford	**30A** Stratford	**30A** Stratford	**30A** Stratford	**30A** Stratford		
64687	*J20*	**CAM** Cambridge	**31A** Cambridge	**31B** March	**31B** March	**31B** March		
64688	*J20*	**MAR** March	**31B** March	**31A** Cambridge	**31A** Cambridge			
64689	*J20*	**MAR** March	**31B** March	**31A** Cambridge	**30A** Stratford	**30A** Stratford		
64690	*J20*	**MAR** March	**30A** Stratford	**30A** Stratford	**31B** March	**31B** March		
64691	*J20*	**STR** Stratford	**30A** Stratford	**30A** Stratford	**31B** March	**31B** March		
64692	*J20*	**MAR** March	**31B** March	**31B** March	**31B** March	**31B** March		
64693	*J20*	**MAR** March	**31B** March	**31B** March	**30A** Stratford	**30A** Stratford		
64694	*J20*	**MAR** March	**31B** March	**31B** March	**30A** Stratford	**30A** Stratford		
64695	*J20*	**STR** Stratford	**30A** Stratford	**31B** March	**31A** Cambridge	**31A** Cambridge		
64696	*J20*	**STR** Stratford	**30A** Stratford	**30A** Stratford	**31A** Cambridge	**31A** Cambridge		
64697	*J20*	**MAR** March	**31B** March	**31B** March	**31B** March	**31B** March		
64698	*J20*	**MAR** March	**31B** March	**31B** March	**31B** March	**31A** Cambridge		
64699	*J20*	**MAR** March	**31B** March	**31B** March	**31B** March	**31B** March		
64700	*J39*	**BLA** Blaydon	**52C** Blaydon	**54C** Borough Gardens	**54C** Borough Gardens	**52G** Sunderland		
64701	*J39*	**BLA** Blaydon	**52A** Gateshead	**52A** Gateshead	**52A** Gateshead	**52G** Sunderland		
64702	*J39*	**LIN** Lincoln	**40A** Lincoln	**40A** Lincoln	**40A** Lincoln			
64703	*J39*	**BLA** Blaydon	**52C** Blaydon	**52B** Heaton	**52B** Heaton	**52G** Sunderland		
64704	*J39*	**BLA** Blaydon	**52A** Gateshead	**52A** Gateshead	**52A** Gateshead	**52G** Sunderland		
64705	*J39*	**BLA** Blaydon	**52C** Blaydon	**52C** Blaydon	**52C** Blaydon	**56B** Ardsley		
64706	*J39*	**SBK** Starbeck	**50D** Starbeck	**50D** Starbeck	**50D** Starbeck	**51L** Thornaby		
64707	*J39*	**BLA** Blaydon	**52A** Gateshead	**54C** Borough Gardens	**54C** Borough Gardens	**52A** Gateshead		
64708	*J39*	**STR** Stratford	**30A** Stratford	**30A** Stratford	**30A** Stratford	**30A** Stratford		
64709	*J39*	**BLA** Blaydon	**52B** Heaton	**53A** Hull Dairycoates	**53A** Hull Dairycoates	**53A** Hull Dairycoates		
64710	*J39*	**DAR** Darlington	**50B** Leeds Neville Hill	**54C** Borough Gardens	**54C** Borough Gardens	**52G** Sunderland		
64711	*J39*	**BLA** Blaydon	**52D** Tweedmouth	**52D** Tweedmouth	**52D** Tweedmouth	**52D** Tweedmouth		
64712	*J39*	**GOR** Gorton	**39A** Gorton	**39A** Gorton	**40A** Lincoln	**40E** Colwick		
64713	*J39*	**DON** Doncaster	**36A** Doncaster	**54C** Borough Gardens	**54C** Borough Gardens	**52A** Gateshead		
64714	*J39*	**LIV** Brunswick	**39A** Gorton	**39A** Gorton	**40A** Lincoln			
64715	*J39*	**LIN** Lincoln	**40A** Lincoln	**40A** Lincoln	**38A** Colwick			
64716	*J39*	**CLK** Colwick	**38A** Colwick	**38A** Colwick	**38A** Colwick	**36A** Doncaster		
64717	*J39*	**GOR** Gorton	**39A** Gorton	**39A** Gorton	**39A** Gorton	**9G** Gorton		
64718	*J39*	**GOR** Gorton	**39A** Gorton	**39A** Gorton	**39A** Gorton	**9G** Gorton		
64719	*J39*	**CLK** Colwick	**38A** Colwick	**35C** Spital Bridge	**35C** Spital Bridge	**41A** Sheffield Darnall		
64720	*J39*	**CLK** Colwick	**38A** Colwick	**37A** Ardsley	**56B** Ardsley	**56B** Ardsley		
64721	*J39*	**DON** Doncaster	**36A** Doncaster	**36A** Doncaster	**36A** Doncaster	**36A** Doncaster		
64722	*J39*	**LIN** Lincoln	**40A** Lincoln	**40A** Lincoln	**40A** Lincoln	**36A** Doncaster		
64723	*J39*	**TFD** Trafford Park	**9E** Trafford Park	**35C** Spital Bridge	**35C** Spital Bridge	**36A** Doncaster		
64724	*J39*	**IPS** Ipswich	**32A** Norwich Thorpe	**32C** Lowestoft	**32B** Ipswich	**32B** Ipswich		
64725	*J39*	**SHF** Sheffield Darnall	**40A** Lincoln	**53A** Hull Dairycoates	**50C** Selby	**51L** Thornaby		
64726	*J39*	**NOR** Norwich Thorpe	**32A** Norwich Thorpe	**32A** Norwich Thorpe	**32B** Ipswich	**40A** Lincoln		
64727	*J39*	**PKS** Parkeston	**9F** Heaton Mersey	**68E** Carlisle Canal	**68E** Carlisle Canal	**9G** Gorton		
64728	*J39*	**LIN** Lincoln	**40A** Lincoln	**40A** Lincoln	**40A** Lincoln	**40F** Boston		
64729	*J39*	**NWE** New England	**38A** Colwick	**40D** Tuxford Junction	**31A** Cambridge	**40E** Colwick		
64730	*J39*	**STR** Stratford	**40A** Lincoln	**50B** Leeds Neville Hill	**50C** Selby	**51L** Thornaby		
64731	*J39*	**NOR** Norwich Thorpe	**32A** Norwich Thorpe	**32A** Norwich Thorpe	**32A** Norwich Thorpe			
64732	*J39*	**CLK** Colwick	**14A** Cricklewood	**37A** Ardsley	**56B** Ardsley	**56B** Ardsley		
64733	*J39*	**STR** Stratford	**9F** Heaton Mersey	**68E** Carlisle Canal	**68E** Carlisle Canal	**12C** Carlisle Canal		
64734	*J39*	**LIN** Lincoln	**40A** Lincoln	**40D** Tuxford Junction	**40A** Lincoln			
64735	*J39*	**CLK** Colwick	**38A** Colwick	**40D** Tuxford Junction	**38A** Colwick			
64736	*J39*	**LIN** Lincoln	**40A** Lincoln	**40A** Lincoln	**35C** Spital Bridge	**41A** Sheffield Darnall		
64737	*J39*	**DON** Doncaster	**36A** Doncaster	**36A** Doncaster	**36A** Doncaster			
64738	*J39*	**NWE** New England	**40A** Lincoln	**39A** Gorton	**41A** Sheffield Darnall	**9G** Gorton		
64739	*J39*	**CLK** Colwick	**38A** Colwick	**38A** Colwick	**38A** Colwick	**16D** Annesley		
64740	*J39*	**GOR** Gorton	**39A** Gorton	**39A** Gorton	**39A** Gorton	**9G** Gorton		
64741	*J39*	**GOR** Gorton	**39A** Gorton	**39A** Gorton	**38A** Colwick	**40A** Lincoln		
64742	*J39*	**GOR** Gorton	**39A** Gorton	**39A** Gorton	**39A** Gorton	**9G** Gorton		
64743	*J39*	**GOR** Gorton	**39A** Gorton	**39A** Gorton	**39A** Gorton	**9G** Gorton		
64744	*J39*	**GOR** Gorton	**39A** Gorton	**39A** Gorton	**41A** Sheffield Darnall	**9G** Gorton		
64745	*J39*	**GOR** Gorton	**39A** Gorton	**39A** Gorton	**39A** Gorton	**9G** Gorton		
64746	*J39*	**NWE** New England	**39B** Sheffield Darnall	**39B** Sheffield Darnall	**41A** Sheffield Darnall	**41A** Sheffield Darnall		
64747	*J39*	**CLK** Colwick	**38A** Colwick	**38A** Colwick	**38A** Colwick	**9G** Gorton		
64748	*J39*	**NWE** New England	**39A** Gorton	**39A** Gorton	**39A** Gorton	**9G** Gorton		
64749	*J39*	**COP** Copley Hill	**37A** Ardsley	**37A** Ardsley	**56B** Ardsley	**56B** Ardsley		
64750	*J39*	**CLK** Colwick	**38A** Colwick	**40D** Tuxford Junction	**30A** Stratford			
64751	*J39*	**ARD** Ardsley	**37A** Ardsley	**40D** Tuxford Junction	**31A** Cambridge			
64752	*J39*	**IPS** Ipswich	**32B** Ipswich	**32B** Ipswich	**32B** Ipswich			
64753	*J39*	**SHF** Sheffield Darnall	**39B** Sheffield Darnall	**39B** Sheffield Darnall	**41A** Sheffield Darnall			
64754	*J39*	**ARD** Ardsley	**37A** Ardsley	**37A** Ardsley	**56B** Ardsley	**56B** Ardsley		
64755	*J39*	**GOR** Gorton	**39A** Gorton	**39A** Gorton	**40A** Lincoln			
64756	*J39*	**DAR** Darlington	**51F** West Auckland	**51F** West Auckland	**51F** West Auckland	**51F** West Auckland		
64757	*J39*	**CLK** Colwick	**38A** Colwick	**37A** Ardsley	**56B** Ardsley	**56B** Ardsley		
64758	*J39*	**DON** Doncaster	**36A** Doncaster	**50B** Leeds Neville Hill	**50B** Leeds Neville Hill	**51L** Thornaby		
64759	*J39*	**RET** Retford	**36E** Retford	**36E** Retford	**36E** Retford	**36E** Retford		
64760	*J39*	**ARD** Ardsley	**37A** Ardsley	**37A** Ardsley	**56B** Ardsley	**56B** Ardsley		
64761	*J39*	**NOR** Norwich Thorpe	**32A** Norwich Thorpe	**32A** Norwich Thorpe	**32A** Norwich Thorpe			
64762	*J39*	**CLK** Colwick	**38A** Colwick	**38A** Colwick	**38A** Colwick			
64763	*J39*	**CLK** Colwick	**38A** Colwick	**40D** Tuxford Junction	**38A** Colwick			
64764	*J39*	**STR** Stratford	**30A** Stratford	**30A** Stratford	**30F** Parkeston	**31B** March		
64765	*J39*	**PKS** Parkeston	**30A** Stratford	**30A** Stratford	**30A** Stratford	**30A** Stratford		
64766	*J39*	**STR** Stratford	**30A** Stratford	**30A** Stratford	**30A** Stratford			
64767	*J39*	**STR** Stratford	**32B** Ipswich	**30A** Stratford	**30A** Stratford	**30A** Stratford		
64768	*J39*	**STR** Stratford	**30A** Stratford	**30A** Stratford	**30A** Stratford			
64769	*J39*	**STR** Stratford	**30A** Stratford	**30A** Stratford	**30A** Stratford	**31B** March		
64770	*J39*	**STR** Stratford	**30F** Parkeston	**30F** Parkeston	**30F** Parkeston	**31B** March		
64771	*J39*	**STR** Stratford	**32B** Ipswich	**30A** Stratford	**30F** Parkeston	**31B** March		
64772	*J39*	**STR** Stratford	**30A** Stratford	**30A** Stratford	**30A** Stratford	**31B** March		
64773	*J39*	**STR** Stratford	**32B** Ipswich	**30F** Parkeston	**30F** Parkeston			
64774	*J39*	**STR** Stratford	**30A** Stratford	**30A** Stratford	**30A** Stratford	**31B** March		
64775	*J39*	**STR** Stratford	**30A** Stratford	**30A** Stratford	**30A** Stratford	**30A** Stratford		
64776	*J39*	**STR** Stratford	**30A** Stratford	**30A** Stratford	**30F** Parkeston			
64777	*J39*	**STR** Stratford	**30F** Parkeston	**30F** Parkeston	**30F** Parkeston	**30A** Stratford		
64778	*J39*	**DAR** Darlington	**51F** West Auckland	**51F** West Auckland	**51F** West Auckland	**51F** West Auckland		
64779	*J39*	**STR** Stratford	**30F** Parkeston	**30A** Stratford	**30A** Stratford	**31B** March		
64780	*J39*	**STR** Stratford	**30A** Stratford	**30A** Stratford	**30A** Stratford	**30A** Stratford		
64781	*J39*	**STR** Stratford	**30A** Stratford	**30A** Stratford	**30A** Stratford	**30A** Stratford		
64782	*J39*	**STR** Stratford	**30A** Stratford	**30A** Stratford	**30A** Stratford	**31B** March		
64783	*J39*	**STR** Stratford	**30A** Stratford	**30A** Stratford	**30A** Stratford	**30A** Stratford		
64784	*J39*	**NOR** Norwich Thorpe	**32A** Norwich Thorpe	**30A** Stratford	**30A** Stratford	**30A** Stratford		
64785	*J39*	**IPS** Ipswich	**32B** Ipswich	**32B** Ipswich	**32B** Ipswich			
64786	*J39*	**DEE** Dundee Tay Bridge	**62B** Dundee Tay Bridge	**62B** Dundee Tay Bridge	**62B** Dundee Tay Bridge	**62B** Dundee Tay Bridge		
64787	*J39*	**STR** Stratford	**30F** Parkeston	**30F** Parkeston	**30F** Parkeston			
64788	*J39*	**PKS** Parkeston	**30F** Parkeston	**30F** Parkeston	**30F** Parkeston			
64789	*J39*	**STR** Stratford	**40A** Lincoln	**35C** Spital Bridge	**35C** Spital Bridge	**31F** Spital Bridge		
64790	*J39*	**DEE** Dundee Tay Bridge	**62B** Dundee Tay Bridge	**62B** Dundee Tay Bridge	**62B** Dundee Tay Bridge	**62A** Thornton Junction		
64791	*J39*	**DAR** Darlington	**50B** Leeds Neville Hill	**50B** Leeds Neville Hill	**50B** Leeds Neville Hill	**56F** Low Moor		
64792	*J39*	**DEE** Dundee Tay Bridge	**62B** Dundee Tay Bridge	**62B** Dundee Tay Bridge	**62B** Dundee Tay Bridge	**62A** Thornton Junction		
64793	*J39*	**IPS** Ipswich	**32B** Ipswich	**32B** Ipswich	**32B** Ipswich			
64794	*J39*	**ABD** Aberdeen Ferryhill	**64A** St. Margarets	**64F** Bathgate	**64A** St. Margarets	**64C** Dalry Road		
64795	*J39*	**ABD** Aberdeen Ferryhill	**61B** Aberdeen Ferryhill	**61B** Aberdeen Ferryhill	**61B** Aberdeen Ferryhill	**64A** St. Margarets		

No.	Class	1948	1951	1954	1957	1960	1963	1966
64796	J39	ARD Ardsley	37A Ardsley	37A Ardsley	56B Ardsley	56B Ardsley		
64797	J39	NOR Norwich Thorpe	32A Norwich Thorpe	32A Norwich Thorpe	32A Norwich Thorpe			
64798	J39	NOR Norwich Thorpe	38A Colwick	38A Colwick	38A Colwick	16D Annesley		
64799	J39	YAR Yarmouth South Town	37A Ardsley	40D Tuxford Junction	35A New England			
64800	J39	IPS Ipswich	32B Ipswich	32B Ipswich	32B Ipswich	31B March		
64801	J39	ARD Ardsley	37A Ardsley	37A Ardsley	56G Bradford Hammerton St	56F Low Moor		
64802	J39	NOR Norwich Thorpe	32A Norwich Thorpe	32A Norwich Thorpe	32A Norwich Thorpe	40E Colwick		
64803	J39	IPS Ipswich	32B Ipswich	30A Stratford	31A Cambridge			
64804	J39	PKS Parkeston	40A Lincoln	40A Lincoln	40A Lincoln	41A Sheffield Darnall		
64805	J39	CLK Colwick	38A Colwick	40D Tuxford Junction	35A New England			
64806	J39	ARD Ardsley	37A Ardsley	37A Ardsley	56B Ardsley	52B Heaton		
64807	J39	GOR Gorton	38A Colwick	40D Tuxford Junction	30A Stratford	41A Sheffield Darnall		
64808	J39	SHF Sheffield Darnall	39B Sheffield Darnall	39B Sheffield Darnall	41A Sheffield Darnall	41A Sheffield Darnall		
64809	J39	SHF Sheffield Darnall	39B Sheffield Darnall	39B Sheffield Darnall	41A Sheffield Darnall	9G Gorton		
64810	J39	GOR Gorton	39A Gorton	39A Gorton	36A Doncaster	36A Doncaster		
64811	J39	ARD Ardsley	37A Ardsley	37A Ardsley	56B Ardsley	56B Ardsley		
64812	J39	DAR Darlington	52C Blaydon	52C Blaydon	52C Blaydon	52A Gateshead		
64813	J39	BLA Blaydon	52D Tweedmouth	52D Tweedmouth	52D Tweedmouth	52D Tweedmouth		
64814	J39	BLA Blaydon	52C Blaydon	52C Blaydon	52C Blaydon	52A Gateshead		
64815	J39	ALN Alnmouth	52D Alnmouth	52D Alnmouth	52C Blaydon	52C Blaydon		
64816	J39	BLA Blaydon	52C Blaydon	52C Blaydon	52C Blaydon	52C Blaydon		
64817	J39	BLA Blaydon	51A Darlington	51C West Hartlepool	54A Sunderland	56F Low Moor		
64818	J39	SBK Starbeck	50D Starbeck	50D Starbeck	50D Starbeck	51L Thornaby		
64819	J39	DAR Darlington	50B Leeds Neville Hill	50B Leeds Neville Hill	53A Hull Dairycoates	53A Hull Dairycoates		
64820	J39	IPS Ipswich	32B Ipswich	37A Ardsley	56B Ardsley	56B Ardsley		
64821	J39	DAR Darlington	51D Middlesbrough	50D Starbeck	50D Starbeck	51L Thornaby		
64822	J39	DEE Dundee Tay Bridge	62B Dundee Tay Bridge	62B Dundee Tay Bridge	62B Dundee Tay Bridge	62B Dundee Tay Bridge		
64823	J39	TFD Trafford Park	9E Trafford Park	38A Colwick	38A Colwick	40E Colwick		
64824	J39	GOR Gorton	39A Gorton	39B Sheffield Darnall	41A Sheffield Darnall	9G Gorton		
64825	J39	ARD Ardsley	37A Ardsley	37A Ardsley	56B Ardsley	52G Sunderland		
64826	J39	IPS Ipswich	32B Ipswich	32B Ipswich	32B Ipswich	31B March		
64827	J39	CLK Colwick	38A Colwick	38A Colwick	38A Colwick	36A Doncaster		
64828	J39	CLK Colwick	38A Colwick	40D Tuxford Junction	36A Doncaster	41G Barnsley		
64829	J39	IPS Ipswich	32B Ipswich	32B Ipswich	32B Ipswich			
64830	J39	RET Retford	36E Retford	36E Retford	36E Retford	36E Retford		
64831	J39	CLK Colwick	38A Colwick	37A Ardsley	56B Ardsley	53A Hull Dairycoates		
64832	J39	CLK Colwick	38A Colwick	38A Colwick	38A Colwick			
64833	J39	NOR Norwich Thorpe	32A Norwich Thorpe	37A Ardsley	56B Ardsley	52G Sunderland		
64834	J39	IPS Ipswich	32B Ipswich	32B Ipswich	32B Ipswich			
64835	J39	DON Doncaster	36A Doncaster	50B Leeds Neville Hill	50B Leeds Neville Hill	51L Thornaby		
64836	J39	ARD Ardsley	37A Ardsley	37A Ardsley	56B Ardsley	56B Ardsley		
64837	J39	CLK Colwick	38A Colwick	37A Ardsley	56B Ardsley	52B Heaton		
64838	J39	NOR Norwich Thorpe	38A Colwick	40D Tuxford Junction	36A Doncaster	36A Doncaster		
64839	J39	STR Stratford	37A Ardsley	37A Ardsley	56B Ardsley	56B Ardsley		
64840	J39	STR Stratford	37A Ardsley	37A Ardsley	56B Ardsley	56B Ardsley		
64841	J39	IPS Ipswich	32B Ipswich	32B Ipswich	32B Ipswich			
64842	J39	BLA Blaydon	52C Blaydon	52C Blaydon	52C Blaydon	52C Blaydon		
64843	J39	BLA Blaydon	52D Tweedmouth	52D Tweedmouth	52D Tweedmouth	52D Tweedmouth		
64844	J39	BLA Blaydon	52D Tweedmouth	52D Tweedmouth	52D Tweedmouth	52D Tweedmouth		
64845	J39	SBK Starbeck	50D Starbeck	50D Starbeck	50D Starbeck	51L Thornaby		
64846	J39	BLA Blaydon	54C Borough Gardens	54C Borough Gardens	54C Borough Gardens	52A Gateshead		
64847	J39	DAR Darlington	51D Middlesbrough	50D Starbeck	50D Starbeck	52G Sunderland		
64848	J39	DAR Darlington	51F West Auckland	51F West Auckland	51F West Auckland	51F West Auckland		
64849	J39	BLA Blaydon	52C Blaydon	52C Blaydon	52C Blaydon	52C Blaydon		
64850	J39	DAR Darlington	50B Leeds Neville Hill	50B Leeds Neville Hill	50B Leeds Neville Hill	51L Thornaby		
64851	J39	DAR Darlington	52C Alston	54C Borough Gardens	54C Borough Gardens	52A Gateshead		
64852	J39	BLA Blaydon	52C Blaydon	52A Gateshead	52A Gateshead	52A Gateshead		
64853	J39	BLA Blaydon	52A Gateshead	52B Heaton	52B Heaton	52G Sunderland		
64854	J39	BLA Blaydon	52D Tweedmouth	54C Borough Gardens	54C Borough Gardens	52A Gateshead		
64855	J39	SBK Starbeck	50D Starbeck	50D Starbeck	50D Starbeck	51L Thornaby		
64856	J39	BLA Blaydon	52B Heaton	52B Heaton	52B Heaton	52B Heaton		
64857	J39	SBK Starbeck	50D Starbeck	50D Starbeck	50D Starbeck	51L Thornaby		
64858	J39	DAR Darlington	52C Blaydon	52C Blaydon	52C Blaydon	52C Blaydon		
64859	J39	SBK Starbeck	50D Starbeck	50D Starbeck	50D Starbeck	51L Thornaby		
64860	J39	SBK Starbeck	50D Starbeck	50D Starbeck	50C Selby	52A Gateshead		
64861	J39	SBK Starbeck	50D Starbeck	50D Starbeck	50D Starbeck	51L Thornaby		
64862	J39	DAR Darlington	51C West Hartlepool	51C West Hartlepool	51F West Auckland	51F West Auckland		
64863	J39	DAR Darlington	50B Leeds Neville Hill	50B Leeds Neville Hill	50B Leeds Neville Hill	50B Leeds Neville Hill		
64864	J39	DAR Darlington	54C Borough Gardens	52C Blaydon	53A Hull Dairycoates	52B Heaton		
64865	J39	DAR Darlington	52B Heaton	52A Gateshead	52A Gateshead	52A Gateshead		
64866	J39	SBK Starbeck	50D Starbeck	50D Starbeck	50D Starbeck	52B Heaton		
64867	J39	HLD Hull Dairycoates	53A Hull Dairycoates	50F Malton	50F Malton	50F Malton		
64868	J39	ALN Alnmouth	52D Alnmouth	52D Alnmouth	52D Alnmouth	52D Alnmouth		
64869	J39	DAR Darlington	52A Gateshead	52A Gateshead	52A Gateshead	52A Gateshead		
64870	J39	DAR Darlington	53A Hull Dairycoates	52C Blaydon	50B Leeds Neville Hill	51L Thornaby		
64871	J39	BLA Blaydon	52A Gateshead	52A Gateshead	52A Gateshead	52B Heaton		
64872	J39	IPS Ipswich	37A Ardsley	37A Ardsley	56B Ardsley	56F Low Moor		
64873	J39	STR Stratford	30F Parkeston	30F Parkeston	35A New England			
64874	J39	STR Stratford	30A Stratford	30F Parkeston	35A New England	36A Doncaster		
64875	J39	CAR Carlisle Canal	12B Carlisle Canal	68E Carlisle Canal	68E Carlisle Canal	9G Gorton		
64876	J39	STR Stratford	30A Stratford	30A Stratford	36A Doncaster			
64877	J39	CAR Carlisle Canal	12B Carlisle Canal	68E Carlisle Canal	68E Carlisle Canal	12C Carlisle Canal		
64878	J39	SHF Sheffield Darnall	39B Sheffield Darnall	39B Sheffield Darnall	41A Sheffield Darnall	41A Sheffield Darnall		
64879	J39	GOR Gorton	39A Gorton	37A Ardsley	56B Ardsley	56B Ardsley		
64880	J39	CAR Carlisle Canal	12B Carlisle Canal	68E Carlisle Canal	68E Carlisle Canal	12C Carlisle Canal		
64881	J39	LIN Lincoln	40A Lincoln	40D Tuxford Junction	40A Lincoln			
64882	J39	NOR Norwich Thorpe	32A Norwich Thorpe	32A Norwich Thorpe	32B Ipswich	36E Retford		
64883	J39	LIN Lincoln	40A Lincoln	35C Spital Bridge	35C Spital Bridge	36A Doncaster		
64884	J39	CAR Carlisle Canal	12B Carlisle Canal	68E Carlisle Canal	68E Carlisle Canal	12C Carlisle Canal		
64885	J39	DON Doncaster	36A Doncaster	36A Doncaster	36A Doncaster	36A Doncaster		
64886	J39	RET Retford	40A Lincoln	50B Leeds Neville Hill	50B Leeds Neville Hill	56F Low Moor		
64887	J39	RET Retford	40A Lincoln	40A Lincoln	40A Lincoln	40E Colwick		
64888	J39	CAR Carlisle Canal	12B Carlisle Canal	68E Carlisle Canal	68E Carlisle Canal	12C Carlisle Canal		
64889	J39	NOR Norwich Thorpe	32A Norwich Thorpe	32A Norwich Thorpe	32A Norwich Thorpe	40E Colwick		
64890	J39	SHF Sheffield Darnall	39B Sheffield Darnall	39B Sheffield Darnall	31A Cambridge	40A Lincoln		
64891	J39	DON Doncaster	36A Doncaster	35C Spital Bridge	35C Spital Bridge	31B March		
64892	J39	CAR Carlisle Canal	62B Dundee Tay Bridge	62B Dundee Tay Bridge	62B Dundee Tay Bridge	62B Dundee Tay Bridge		
64893	J39	DON Doncaster	36A Doncaster	36E Retford	36E Retford	36E Retford		
64894	J39	IPS Ipswich	32B Ipswich	32B Ipswich	32B Ipswich			
64895	J39	CAR Carlisle Canal	12B Carlisle Canal	68E Carlisle Canal	68E Carlisle Canal	12C Carlisle Canal		
64896	J39	ARD Ardsley	37A Ardsley	35C Spital Bridge	35C Spital Bridge	40A Lincoln		
64897	J39	DAR Darlington	53A Hull Dairycoates	52C Blaydon	52D Alnmouth	52D Alnmouth		
64898	J39	RET Retford	36E Retford	36E Retford	36E Retford	36E Retford		
64899	J39	CAR Carlisle Canal	12B Carlisle Canal	68E Carlisle Canal	68E Carlisle Canal	12C Carlisle Canal		
64900	J39	IPS Ipswich	32B Ipswich	32A Norwich Thorpe	32A Norwich Thorpe			
64901	J39	TFD Trafford Park	9E Trafford Park	35C Spital Bridge	35C Spital Bridge	31F Spital Bridge		
64902	J39	DON Doncaster	36A Doncaster	35C Spital Bridge	36D Barnsley	41G Barnsley		
64903	J39	SHF Sheffield Darnall	39B Sheffield Darnall	37C Bradford Hammerton St	56G Bradford Hammerton St	56F Low Moor		
64904	J39	LIN Lincoln	40A Lincoln	52B Heaton	50C Selby	53A Hull Dairycoates		
64905	J39	IPS Ipswich	32B Ipswich	32B Ipswich	32B Ipswich			
64906	J39	RET Retford	36E Retford	36E Retford	36E Retford	36E Retford		
64907	J39	STR Stratford	37A Ardsley	37C Bradford Hammerton St	56G Bradford Hammerton St	56F Low Moor		
64908	J39	RET Retford	36E Retford	36E Retford	36E Retford	36E Retford		
64909	J39	DON Doncaster	36A Doncaster	36A Doncaster	36A Doncaster	36A Doncaster		

No.	Class	1948	1951	1954	1957	1960	1963	1966
64910	*J39*	**DON** Doncaster	**36A** Doncaster	**51C** West Hartlepool	**53A** Hull Dairycoates	**53A** Hull Dairycoates		
64911	*J39*	**ARD** Ardsley	**37A** Ardsley	**37A** Ardsley	**56C** Copley Hill	**56C** Copley Hill		
64912	*J39*	**CAR** Carlisle Canal	**12B** Carlisle Canal	**68E** Carlisle Canal	**68E** Carlisle Canal			
64913	*J39*	**NOR** Norwich Thorpe	**32A** Norwich Thorpe	**32A** Norwich Thorpe	**32A** Norwich Thorpe			
64914	*J39*	**HLD** Hull Dairycoates	**53A** Hull Dairycoates	**53A** Hull Dairycoates	**53A** Hull Dairycoates	**53A** Hull Dairycoates		
64915	*J39*	**BLA** Blaydon	**52B** Heaton	**52B** Heaton	**52B** Heaton	**52B** Heaton		
64916	*J39*	**DAR** Darlington	**51C** West Hartlepool	**51C** West Hartlepool	**52D** Tweedmouth	**52D** Tweedmouth		
64917	*J39*	**BLA** Blaydon	**52D** Tweedmouth	**52D** Tweedmouth	**52D** Tweedmouth	**52D** Tweedmouth		
64918	*J39*	**GOR** Gorton	**14A** Cricklewood	**37A** Ardsley	**56B** Ardsley	**56B** Ardsley		
64919	*J39*	**DAR** Darlington	**50B** Leeds Neville Hill	**54A** Sunderland	**54A** Sunderland	**56F** Low Moor		
64920	*J39*	**BLA** Blaydon	**50B** Leeds Neville Hill	**50B** Leeds Neville Hill	**50B** Leeds Neville Hill	**50B** Leeds Neville Hill		
64921	*J39*	**DAR** Darlington	**50B** Leeds Neville Hill	**54C** Borough Gardens	**54C** Borough Gardens	**52A** Gateshead		
64922	*J39*	**SBK** Starbeck	**50B** Leeds Neville Hill	**50B** Leeds Neville Hill	**50B** Leeds Neville Hill	**50B** Leeds Neville Hill		
64923	*J39*	**BLA** Blaydon	**52B** Heaton	**52B** Heaton	**52B** Heaton	**52B** Heaton		
64924	*J39*	**ALN** Alnmouth	**52D** Alnmouth	**52D** Alnmouth	**52D** Alnmouth	**52D** Alnmouth		
64925	*J39*	**DAR** Darlington	**52D** Tweedmouth	**52D** Tweedmouth	**52D** Tweedmouth	**52D** Tweedmouth		
64926	*J39*	**BLA** Blaydon	**53A** Hull Dairycoates	**54C** Borough Gardens	**54C** Borough Gardens	**52B** Heaton		
64927	*J39*	**BLA** Blaydon	**53A** Hull Dairycoates	**54C** Borough Gardens	**51F** West Auckland	**51F** West Auckland		
64928	*J39*	**DAR** Darlington	**53A** Hull Dairycoates	**50F** Malton	**50F** Malton	**50F** Malton		
64929	*J39*	**DAR** Darlington	**54C** Borough Gardens	**52A** Gateshead	**52A** Gateshead	**52D** Alnmouth		
64930	*J39*	**CAR** Carlisle Canal	**12B** Carlisle Canal	**68E** Carlisle Canal	**68E** Carlisle Canal	**9G** Gorton		
64931	*J39*	**DAR** Darlington	**53A** Hull Dairycoates	**54C** Borough Gardens	**54C** Borough Gardens	**52B** Heaton		
64932	*J39*	**CAR** Carlisle Canal	**12B** Carlisle Canal	**68E** Carlisle Canal	**68E** Carlisle Canal	**12C** Carlisle Canal		
64933	*J39*	**DAR** Darlington	**50B** Leeds Neville Hill	**50B** Leeds Neville Hill	**50B** Leeds Neville Hill	**50B** Leeds Neville Hill		
64934	*J39*	**BLA** Blaydon	**50B** Leeds Neville Hill	**50B** Leeds Neville Hill	**50B** Leeds Neville Hill	**50B** Leeds Neville Hill		
64935	*J39*	**SBK** Starbeck	**50E** Scarborough	**50B** Leeds Neville Hill	**50B** Leeds Neville Hill	**50B** Leeds Neville Hill		
64936	*J39*	**DAR** Darlington	**54C** Borough Gardens	**54C** Borough Gardens	**54C** Borough Gardens	**52A** Gateshead		
64937	*J39*	**LIN** Lincoln	**40A** Lincoln	**40A** Lincoln	**40A** Lincoln	**40A** Lincoln		
64938	*J39*	**DAR** Darlington	**50D** Starbeck	**50D** Starbeck	**50F** Malton	**52A** Gateshead		
64939	*J39*	**DAR** Darlington	**54C** Borough Gardens	**54A** Sunderland	**53A** Hull Dairycoates	**52B** Heaton		
64940	*J39*	**DAR** Darlington	**51A** Darlington	**51F** West Auckland	**53A** Hull Dairycoates	**53A** Hull Dairycoates		
64941	*J39*	**BLA** Blaydon	**53A** Hull Dairycoates	**52D** Tweedmouth	**52D** Tweedmouth	**52D** Tweedmouth		
64942	*J39*	**DAR** Darlington	**50D** Starbeck	**50D** Starbeck	**50D** Starbeck	**50A** York		
64943	*J39*	**DAR** Darlington	**50B** Leeds Neville Hill	**50B** Leeds Neville Hill	**50B** Leeds Neville Hill	**53A** Hull Dairycoates		
64944	*J39*	**SBK** Starbeck	**50D** Starbeck	**50D** Starbeck	**50D** Starbeck	**50B** Leeds Neville Hill		
64945	*J39*	**DAR** Darlington	**52B** Heaton	**52B** Heaton	**52B** Heaton	**52B** Heaton		
64946	*J39*	**CAR** Carlisle Canal	**64A** St. Margarets	**64A** St. Margarets	**64A** St. Margarets	**64C** Dalry Road		
64947	*J39*	**BLA** Blaydon	**52B** Heaton	**53A** Hull Dairycoates	**50F** Malton	**53A** Hull Dairycoates		
64948	*J39*	**CAR** Carlisle Canal	**12B** Carlisle Canal	**68E** Carlisle Canal	**68E** Carlisle Canal	**12C** Carlisle Canal		
64949	*J39*	**DAR** Darlington	**50B** Leeds Neville Hill	**50B** Leeds Neville Hill	**53A** Hull Dairycoates	**52D** Alnmouth		
64950	*J39*	**DEE** Dundee Tay Bridge	**62B** Dundee Tay Bridge	**62B** Dundee Tay Bridge	**62B** Dundee Tay Bridge	**62B** Dundee Tay Bridge		
64951	*J39*	**DON** Doncaster	**36A** Doncaster	**35C** Spital Bridge	**35C** Spital Bridge	**33B** Tilbury		
64952	*J39*	**DON** Doncaster	**36A** Doncaster	**36A** Doncaster	**36A** Doncaster	**33B** Tilbury		
64953	*J39*	**STR** Stratford	**30F** Parkeston	**30F** Parkeston	**30F** Parkeston	**33B** Tilbury		
64954	*J39*	**LIV** Brunswick	**9E** Trafford Park	**35C** Spital Bridge	**35C** Spital Bridge	**33B** Tilbury		
64955	*J39*	**CLK** Colwick	**38A** Colwick	**38A** Colwick	**38A** Colwick	**16D** Annesley		
64956	*J39*	**RET** Retford	**36E** Retford	**36A** Doncaster	**36A** Doncaster	**33B** Tilbury		
64957	*J39*	**IPS** Ipswich	**32B** Ipswich	**32B** Ipswich	**32B** Ipswich	**33B** Tilbury		
64958	*J39*	**IPS** Ipswich	**32B** Ipswich	**30A** Stratford	**31A** Cambridge	**33B** Tilbury		
64959	*J39*	**NOR** Norwich Thorpe	**32A** Norwich Thorpe	**40A** Lincoln	**40A** Lincoln	**40A** Lincoln		
64960	*J39*	**SHF** Sheffield Darnall	**39B** Sheffield Darnall	**39B** Sheffield Darnall	**40A** Lincoln	**40A** Lincoln		
64961	*J39*	**RET** Retford	**36E** Retford	**36E** Retford	**36E** Retford			
64962	*J39*	**GOR** Gorton	**39A** Gorton	**39B** Sheffield Darnall	**41A** Sheffield Darnall	**33B** Tilbury		
64963	*J39*	**CAR** Carlisle Canal	**64A** St. Margarets	**64A** St. Margarets	**64A** St. Margarets	**64C** Dalry Road		
64964	*J39*	**CAR** Carlisle Canal	**12B** Carlisle Canal	**68E** Carlisle Canal	**68E** Carlisle Canal	**12C** Carlisle Canal		
64965	*J39*	**NWE** New England	**38A** Colwick	**35C** Spital Bridge	**35C** Spital Bridge	**33B** Tilbury		
64966	*J39*	**GOR** Gorton	**14A** Cricklewood	**37A** Ardsley	**36A** Doncaster	**40A** Lincoln		
64967	*J39*	**DON** Doncaster	**36A** Doncaster	**36A** Doncaster	**36A** Doncaster	**36A** Doncaster		
64968	*J39*	**NOR** Norwich Thorpe	**32A** Norwich Thorpe	**32A** Norwich Thorpe	**32B** Ipswich	**33B** Tilbury		
64969	*J39*	**NWE** New England	**39B** Sheffield Darnall	**37A** Ardsley	**56B** Ardsley	**56B** Ardsley		
64970	*J39*	**RET** Retford	**36E** Retford	**36E** Retford	**36E** Retford	**36E** Retford		
64971	*J39*	**LIN** Lincoln	**40A** Lincoln	**53A** Hull Dairycoates	**53A** Hull Dairycoates	**53A** Hull Dairycoates		
64972	*J39*	**GOR** Gorton	**39A** Gorton	**37A** Ardsley	**36A** Doncaster			
64973	*J39*	**SHF** Sheffield Darnall	**39B** Sheffield Darnall	**39B** Sheffield Darnall	**30A** Stratford			
64974	*J39*	**CLK** Colwick	**38A** Colwick	**38A** Colwick	**38A** Colwick	**40E** Colwick		
64975	*J39*	**ABD** Aberdeen Ferryhill	**61B** Aberdeen Ferryhill	**61B** Aberdeen Ferryhill	**61B** Aberdeen Ferryhill	**64A** St. Margarets		
64976	*J39*	**DON** Doncaster	**36A** Doncaster	**40D** Tuxford Junction	**38A** Colwick			
64977	*J39*	**DON** Doncaster	**36A** Doncaster	**40A** Lincoln	**40A** Lincoln	**40E** Colwick		
64978	*J39*	**DAR** Darlington	**51C** West Hartlepool	**51C** West Hartlepool	**51F** West Auckland	**52A** Gateshead		
64979	*J39*	**ARD** Ardsley	**37A** Ardsley	**37A** Ardsley	**56B** Ardsley	**56B** Ardsley		
64980	*J39*	**CLK** Colwick	**38A** Colwick	**38A** Colwick	**38A** Colwick			
64981	*J39*	**CLK** Colwick	**38A** Colwick	**35C** Spital Bridge	**35C** Spital Bridge	**36A** Doncaster		
64982	*J39*	**DAR** Darlington	**51A** Darlington	**51F** West Auckland	**51F** West Auckland	**51F** West Auckland		
64983	*J39*	**CLK** Colwick	**38A** Colwick	**38A** Colwick	**38A** Colwick			
64984	*J39*	**DON** Doncaster	**36A** Doncaster	**40A** Lincoln	**40A** Lincoln			
64985	*J39*	**ARD** Ardsley	**37A** Ardsley	**30A** Stratford	**35A** New England			
64986	*J39*	**CAR** Carlisle Canal	**64A** St. Margarets	**64A** St. Margarets	**64A** St. Margarets	**64C** Dalry Road		
64987	*J39*	**RET** Retford	**36E** Retford	**36A** Doncaster	**36A** Doncaster	**36A** Doncaster		
64988	*J39*	**CLK** Colwick	**38A** Colwick	**38A** Colwick	**38A** Colwick			
65002	*J1*	**NWE** New England	**35A** New England	**38A** Colwick				
65003	*J1*	**CLK** Colwick	**34D** Hitchin					
65004	*J1*	**NWE** New England	**35A** New England					
65005	*J1*	**NWE** New England	**35A** New England					
65006	*J1*	**NWE** New England	**35A** New England					
65007	*J1*	**LEI** Leicester Central	**38A** Colwick					
65008	*J1*	**CLK** Colwick	**38A** Colwick					
65009	*J1*	**LEI** Leicester Central	**38A** Colwick					
65010	*J1*	**CLK** Colwick	**34D** Hitchin					
65013	*J1*	**CLK** Colwick	**34D** Hitchin	**34D** Hitchin				
65014	*J1*	**CLK** Colwick	**38A** Colwick					
65015	*J2*	**LEI** Leicester Central	**38C** Leicester Central					
65016	*J2*	**BOS** Boston	**40F** Boston					
65017	*J2*	**BOS** Boston	**40F** Boston	**40F** Boston				
65018	*J2*	**LEI** Leicester Central	**38A** Colwick					
65019	*J2*	**LEI** Leicester Central	**38A** Colwick					
65020	*J2*	**BOS** Boston	**40F** Boston	**40F** Boston				
65021	*J2*	**LEI** Leicester Central						
65022	*J2*	**LEI** Leicester Central	**38A** Colwick					
65023	*J2*	**LEI** Leicester Central	**38A** Colwick					
65025	*J21*	**BLA** Blaydon	**52C** Blaydon					
65026	*J21*	**TWD** Tweedmouth						
65027	*J21*	**YK** York						
65028	*J21*	**KBY** Kirkby Stephen	**51H** Kirkby Stephen					
65029	*J21*	**BLA** Blaydon						
65030	*J21*	**HTN** Heaton	**51J** Northallerton					
65031	*J21*	**DAR** Darlington						
65032	*J21*	**AUK** West Auckland						
65033	*J21*	**DAR** Darlington	**51A** Darlington	**52F** South Blyth	**52C** Hexham	**52C** Blaydon		
65035	*J21*	**BLA** Blaydon	**52F** Rothbury	**52B** Heaton				
65036	*J21*	**NEV** Leeds Neville Hill						
65037	*J21*	**NEV** Leeds Neville Hill						
65038	*J21*	**DAR** Darlington	**51A** Darlington	**51J** Northallerton				
65039	*J21*	**TWD** Tweedmouth	**50C** Selby	**52B** Heaton	**52C** Blaydon			
65040	*J21*	**KBY** Kirkby Stephen	**51H** Kirkby Stephen					

		1948	1951	1954	1957	1960	1963	1966
65041	*J21*	**NEV** Leeds Neville Hill	**50B** Leeds Neville Hill					
65042	*J21*	**SEL** Selby	**50C** Selby	**52C** Blaydon				
65043	*J21*	**SEL** Selby	**50A** York					
65044	*J21*	**YK** York						
65047	*J21*	**KBY** Kirkby Stephen	**51H** Kirkby Stephen	**51H** Kirkby Stephen				
65049	*J21*	**NEV** Leeds Neville Hill						
65051	*J21*	**YK** York						
65052	*J21*	**SKN** Stockton on Tees						
65056	*J21*	**YK** York						
65057	*J21*	**SKN** Stockton on Tees						
65058	*J21*	**RET** Retford						
65059	*J21*	**YK** York						
65060	*J21*	**YK** York						
65061	*J21*	**AUK** West Auckland	**51F** West Auckland	**51F** West Auckland	**52B** Heaton			
65062	*J21*	**BLA** Blaydon	**51F** West Auckland	**51F** West Auckland				
65063	*J21*	**SBH** South Blyth						
65064	*J21*	**WHD** Wearhead	**51F** Wearhead	**51F** Wearhead	**51A** Darlington			
65066	*J21*	**SEL** Selby						
65067	*J21*	**TWD** Tweedmouth	**52F** North Blyth					
65068	*J21*	**YK** York	**51A** Darlington	**51A** Darlington				
65069	*J21*	**SBH** South Blyth						
65070	*J21*	**RET** Retford	**36E** Retford	**51A** Darlington	**52C** Blaydon	**52F** South Blyth		
65072	*J21*	**SEL** Selby						
65073	*J21*	**YK** York						
65075	*J21*	**SEL** Selby	**51J** Northallerton	**52B** Heaton				
65076	*J21*	**YK** York	**50B** Leeds Neville Hill					
65077	*J21*	**NEV** Leeds Neville Hill	**51F** West Auckland					
65078	*J21*	**DAR** Darlington	**51F** West Auckland	**51F** West Auckland	**52D** Tweedmouth			
65079	*J21*	**YK** York						
65080	*J21*	**BLA** Blaydon	**52F** South Blyth					
65081	*J21*	**HTN** Heaton						
65082	*J21*	**TWD** Tweedmouth	**52C** Blaydon	**52D** Tweedmouth				
65083	*J21*	**RBY** Rothbury						
65084	*J21*	**MID** Middlesbrough						
65086	*J21*	**HTN** Heaton						
65088	*J21*	**DAR** Darlington	**51F** West Auckland	**51F** West Auckland				
65089	*J21*	**SKN** Stockton on Tees	**51H** Kirkby Stephen	**51A** Darlington				
65090	*J21*	**DAR** Darlington	**51A** Darlington	**52C** Blaydon				
65091	*J21*	**DAR** Darlington	**51F** West Auckland	**51F** West Auckland	**52D** Tweedmouth			
65092	*J21*	**SKN** Stockton on Tees	**51F** West Auckland	**51F** West Auckland				
65093	*J21*	**SEL** Selby						
65094	*J21*	**NEV** Leeds Neville Hill						
65095	*J21*	**RET** Retford	**36A** Doncaster					
65097	*J21*	**NEV** Leeds Neville Hill	**51F** West Auckland	**51F** West Auckland				
65098	*J21*	**DAR** Darlington	**51A** Darlington	**51A** Darlington				
65099	*J21*	**ALN** Alnmouth	**52C** Blaydon	**52F** South Blyth	**52D** Tweedmouth	**52H** Tyne Dock		
65100	*J21*	**ALS** Alston	**51H** Kirkby Stephen	**51H** Kirkby Stephen				
65101	*J21*	**RMH** Reedsmouth						
65102	*J21*	**HTN** Heaton	**51F** West Auckland					
65103	*J21*	**KBY** Kirkby Stephen	**51H** Kirkby Stephen	**51A** Darlington	**52C** Blaydon			
65104	*J21*	**HTN** Heaton						
65105	*J21*	**SEL** Selby	**50C** Selby					
65107	*J21*	**NEV** Leeds Neville Hill						
65108	*J21*	**NMN** Normanton						
65109	*J21*	**NEV** Leeds Neville Hill						
65110	*J21*	**DAR** Darlington	**51A** Darlington	**52B** Heaton	**52B** Heaton	**52B** Heaton		
65111	*J21*	**BLA** Blaydon	**52C** Reedsmouth					
65112	*J21*	**BLA** Blaydon						
65114	*J21*	**HTN** Heaton						
65115	*J21*	**KBY** Kirkby Stephen						
65116	*J21*	**NEV** Leeds Neville Hill						
65117	*J21*	**RET** Retford	**36A** Doncaster	**51A** Darlington	**52C** Hexham			
65118	*J21*	**NEV** Leeds Neville Hill	**50B** Leeds Neville Hill					
65119	*J21*	**DAR** Darlington	**51A** Darlington	**52C** Hexham				
65120	*J21*	**SEL** Selby						
65121	*J21*	**YK** York						
65122	*J21*	**HTN** Heaton	**50B** Leeds Neville Hill					
65123	*J21*	**SBH** South Blyth						
65126	*J10*	**LIV** Brunswick	**8E** Brunswick					
65127	*J10*	**LIV** Brunswick						
65128	*J10*	**WIG** Wigan Lower Ince						
65130	*J10*	**WAL** Walton on the Hill	**27E** Walton on the Hill					
65131	*J10*	**NTH** Northwich	**10F** Wigan Lower Ince	**9G** Northwich	**10A** Wigan Springs Branch			
65132	*J10*	**STP** Heaton Mersey	**9F** Heaton Mersey	**9F** Heaton Mersey	**17E** Heaton Mersey			
65133	*J10*	**GOR** Gorton	**27E** Walton on the Hill	**27E** Walton on the Hill	**27E** Walton on the Hill			
65134	*J10*	**NTH** Northwich	**9G** Northwich	**9G** Northwich	**9G** Northwich			
65135	*J10*	**STP** Heaton Mersey	**9F** Heaton Mersey	**9F** Heaton Mersey	**17E** Heaton Mersey			
65136	*J10*	**LIV** Brunswick	**8E** Brunswick					
65137	*J10*	**STP** Heaton Mersey	**9E** Trafford Park					
65138	*J10*	**NTH** Northwich	**9G** Northwich	**9E** Trafford Park	**10A** Wigan Springs Branch			
65139	*J10*	**NTH** Northwich	**9G** Northwich	**9G** Northwich				
65140	*J10*	**NTH** Northwich	**9G** Northwich	**6D** Chester Northgate	**10A** Wigan Springs Branch			
65141	*J10*	**TFD** Trafford Park	**9E** Trafford Park					
65142	*J10*	**NTH** Northwich	**8E** Brunswick	**8E** Brunswick	**8E** Brunswick			
65143	*J10*	**CHR** Chester Northgate	**6D** Chester Northgate	**6D** Chester Northgate				
65144	*J10*	**LIV** Brunswick	**9F** Heaton Mersey	**9E** Trafford Park	**17F** Trafford Park			
65145	*J10*	**STP** Heaton Mersey	**9F** Heaton Mersey	**8E** Brunswick	**8E** Brunswick			
65146	*J10*	**NTH** Northwich	**9F** Heaton Mersey	**9E** Trafford Park	**10A** Wigan Springs Branch			
65147	*J10*	**NTH** Northwich	**9G** Northwich	**8E** Brunswick	**8E** Brunswick			
65148	*J10*	**STP** Heaton Mersey	**10F** Wigan Lower Ince	**10A** Wigan Springs Branch				
65149	*J10*	**LIV** Brunswick	**8E** Brunswick					
65151	*J10*	**WIG** Wigan Lower Ince	**9G** Northwich					
65153	*J10*	**WRX** Wrexham Rhosddu	**8E** Brunswick	**9E** Trafford Park				
65154	*J10*	**STP** Heaton Mersey	**9E** Trafford Park					
65155	*J10*	**NTH** Northwich	**8E** Brunswick					
65156	*J10*	**NTH** Northwich	**9G** Northwich	**9E** Trafford Park	**10A** Wigan Springs Branch			
65157	*J10*	**STP** Heaton Mersey	**9F** Heaton Mersey	**9E** Trafford Park	**8D** Widnes	**8F** Wigan Springs Branch		
65158	*J10*	**NTH** Northwich	**9G** Northwich	**9G** Northwich	**9G** Northwich			
65159	*J10*	**WIG** Wigan Lower Ince	**10F** Wigan Lower Ince	**10A** Wigan Springs Branch	**10A** Wigan Springs Branch			
65160	*J10*	**STP** Heaton Mersey	**9F** Heaton Mersey	**9F** Heaton Mersey	**17E** Heaton Mersey			
65161	*J10*	**TFD** Trafford Park	**9E** Trafford Park					
65162	*J10*	**WIG** Wigan Lower Ince	**10F** Wigan Lower Ince	**10A** Wigan Springs Branch				
65163	*J10*	**LIV** Brunswick	**8E** Brunswick					
65164	*J10*	**STP** Heaton Mersey	**10F** Wigan Lower Ince					
65165	*J10*	**NTH** Northwich	**9G** Northwich	**9G** Northwich				
65166	*J10*	**NTH** Northwich	**9G** Northwich	**8E** Brunswick	**8E** Brunswick			
65167	*J10*	**CHR** Chester Northgate	**6D** Chester Northgate	**9E** Trafford Park	**17F** Trafford Park			
65168	*J10*	**TFD** Trafford Park	**9E** Trafford Park					
65169	*J10*	**CHR** Chester Northgate	**9G** Northwich	**9G** Northwich	**9G** Northwich	**8E** Northwich		
65170	*J10*	**WIG** Wigan Lower Ince	**10F** Wigan Lower Ince	**9E** Trafford Park	**10A** Wigan Springs Branch			
65171	*J10*	**NTH** Northwich	**9G** Northwich	**9E** Trafford Park				
65172	*J10*	**LIV** Brunswick	**8E** Brunswick					
65173	*J10*	**WIG** Wigan Lower Ince	**10F** Wigan Lower Ince	**10A** Wigan Springs Branch				
65175	*J10*	**WIG** Wigan Lower Ince	**10F** Wigan Lower Ince	**10A** Wigan Springs Branch	**10A** Wigan Springs Branch			

No.	Class	1948	1951	1954	1957	1960	1963	1966
65176	*J10*	WIG Wigan Lower Ince	**10F** Wigan Lower Ince	**10A** Wigan Springs Branch				
65177	*J10*	WAL Walton on the Hill	**27E** Walton on the Hill	**27E** Walton on the Hill	**27E** Walton on the Hill			
65178	*J10*	STP Heaton Mersey	**9F** Heaton Mersey	**9F** Heaton Mersey	**17E** Heaton Mersey			
65179	*J10*	STP Heaton Mersey	**9E** Trafford Park					
65180	*J10*	WAL Walton on the Hill	**27E** Walton on the Hill	**27E** Walton on the Hill				
65181	*J10*	STP Heaton Mersey	**9F** Heaton Mersey	**9E** Trafford Park				
65182	*J10*	LIV Brunswick	**8E** Brunswick	**8E** Brunswick				
65183	*J10*	TFD Trafford Park	**9E** Trafford Park					
65184	*J10*	TFD Trafford Park	**9E** Trafford Park	**9E** Trafford Park	**8D** Widnes			
65185	*J10*	STP Heaton Mersey	**9F** Heaton Mersey	**8E** Brunswick				
65186	*J10*	STP Heaton Mersey	**9E** Trafford Park	**9E** Trafford Park	**9E** Trafford Park			
65187	*J10*	NTH Northwich	**9G** Northwich	**9E** Trafford Park	**17E** Heaton Mersey			
65188	*J10*	STP Heaton Mersey	**9F** Heaton Mersey					
65189	*J10*	WIG Wigan Lower Ince	**10F** Wigan Lower Ince					
65190	*J10*	NTH Northwich	**9G** Northwich					
65191	*J10*	NTH Northwich	**9G** Northwich	**9E** Trafford Park	**17F** Trafford Park			
65192	*J10*	WAL Walton on the Hill	**27E** Walton on the Hill	**27E** Walton on the Hill	**27E** Walton on the Hill	**8F** Wigan Springs Branch		
65193	*J10*	STP Heaton Mersey	**9F** Heaton Mersey					
65194	*J10*	STP Heaton Mersey	**9F** Heaton Mersey	**9F** Heaton Mersey	**17E** Heaton Mersey			
65195	*J10*	WAL Walton on the Hill						
65196	*J10*	WIG Wigan Lower Ince	**10F** Wigan Lower Ince	**8E** Brunswick	**8E** Brunswick			
65197	*J10*	STP Heaton Mersey	**9F** Heaton Mersey	**9E** Trafford Park				
65198	*J10*	STP Heaton Mersey	**9F** Heaton Mersey	**9E** Trafford Park	**8D** Widnes	**8F** Wigan Springs Branch		
65199	*J10*	WIG Wigan Lower Ince	**10F** Wigan Lower Ince	**10A** Wigan Springs Branch	**10A** Wigan Springs Branch			
65200	*J10*	STP Heaton Mersey	**9F** Heaton Mersey	**9F** Heaton Mersey	**17E** Heaton Mersey			
65201	*J10*	TFD Trafford Park	**9E** Trafford Park					
65202	*J10*	NTH Northwich	**9G** Northwich	**9G** Northwich	**9G** Northwich			
65203	*J10*	WIG Wigan Lower Ince	**10F** Wigan Lower Ince	**10A** Wigan Springs Branch				
65204	*J10*	TFD Trafford Park	**9E** Trafford Park					
65205	*J10*	NTH Northwich	**9G** Northwich	**9E** Trafford Park				
65208	*J10*	WIG Wigan Lower Ince	**9G** Northwich	**6D** Chester Northgate	**17F** Trafford Park			
65209	*J10*	STP Heaton Mersey	**9F** Heaton Mersey	**9E** Trafford Park	**17F** Trafford Park			
65210	*J36*	KPS Kipps	**65E** Kipps	**65E** Kipps	**65E** Kipps	**65E** Kipps		
65211	*J36*	BGT Bathgate	**64F** Bathgate	**64F** Bathgate	**64F** Bathgate	**65C** Parkhead		
65213	*J36*	PTH Perth South	**61B** Aberdeen Ferryhill	**61A** Kittybrewster	**61A** Kittybrewster			
65214	*J36*	PKD Parkhead	**65E** Kipps	**65E** Kipps	**65E** Kipps	**65E** Kipps	**67D** Ardrossan	
65215	*J36*	KPS Kipps						
65216	*J36*	CAR Carlisle Canal	**12B** Carlisle Canal	**68E** Carlisle Canal	**66A** Polmadie	**66A** Polmadie		
65217	*J36*	STM St. Margarets	**65E** Kipps	**65E** Kipps	**65E** Kipps	**65E** Kipps		
65218	*J36*	THJ Thornton Junction	**62A** Thornton Junction	**62A** Thornton Junction	**62A** Thornton Junction	**62A** Thornton Junction		
65220	*J36*	POL Polmont						
65221	*J36*	EFD Eastfield	**65A** Eastfield	**65A** Eastfield	**65A** Eastfield			
65222	*J36*	POL Polmont	**64E** Polmont	**64E** Polmont	**64E** Polmont	**64E** Polmont	**65F** Grangemouth	
65224	*J36*	STM St. Margarets	**64A** St. Margarets	**64A** St. Margarets	**64A** St. Margarets	**64A** St. Margarets	**64A** St. Margarets	
65225	*J36*	BGT Bathgate	**64F** Bathgate	**64F** Bathgate	**64F** Bathgate			
65226	*J36*	KPS Kipps	**65E** Kipps					
65227	*J36*	EFD Eastfield	**65I** Balloch	**65I** Balloch	**65I** Balloch	**61A** Kittybrewster		
65228	*J36*	EFD Eastfield	**65A** Eastfield	**65A** Eastfield	**65A** Eastfield	**65A** Eastfield		
65229	*J36*	BGT Bathgate	**64F** Bathgate	**64F** Bathgate	**64F** Bathgate	**64F** Bathgate		
65230	*J36*	BGT Bathgate	**64F** Bathgate	**64F** Bathgate	**64F** Bathgate	**65C** Parkhead		
65231	*J36*	BGT Bathgate	**64F** Bathgate					
65232	*J36*	HAW Hawick	**64G** Hawick	**64G** Hawick	**66A** Polmadie	**66A** Polmadie		
65233	*J36*	POL Polmont	**64E** Polmont	**64E** Polmont	**64E** Polmont	**64F** Bathgate		
65234	*J36*	BGT Bathgate	**64F** Bathgate	**64F** Bathgate	**64F** Bathgate	**64G** Hawick	**64G** Hawick	**64A** St. Margarets
65235	*J36*	BGT Bathgate	**64F** Bathgate	**64B** Haymarket	**64B** Haymarket	**64B** Haymarket		
65236	*J36*	KPS Kipps	**65E** Kipps	**65E** Kipps				
65237	*J36*	FW Fort William	**63D** Fort William	**63D** Fort William	**65J** Fort William	**12C** Carlisle Canal		
65238	*J36*	KPS Kipps	**65E** Kipps					
65239	*J36*	DFU Dunfermline Upper	**62C** Dunfermline Upper	**62C** Dunfermline Upper	**62C** Dunfermline Upper	**62C** Dunfermline Upper		
65240	*J36*	HAY Haymarket	**64B** Haymarket					
65241	*J36*	POL Polmont	**64E** Polmont	**64E** Polmont	**64E** Polmont	**65F** Grangemouth		
65242	*J36*	HAW Hawick	**64G** Hawick	**64A** St. Margarets	**61B** Aberdeen Ferryhill			
65243	*J36*	HAY Haymarket	**64B** Haymarket	**64B** Haymarket	**64B** Haymarket	**64B** Haymarket	**64B** Haymarket	**64F** Bathgate
65244	*J36*	POL Polmont	**64E** Polmont	**64E** Polmont	**64E** Polmont			
65245	*J36*	KPS Kipps	**65E** Kipps					
65246	*J36*	POL Polmont	**64E** Polmont	**64E** Polmont	**64E** Polmont	**65C** Parkhead		
65247	*J36*	KPS Kipps	**61A** Kittybrewster	**61B** Aberdeen Ferryhill	**61A** Kittybrewster			
65248	*J36*	BGT Bathgate	**64F** Bathgate	**64F** Bathgate				
65249	*J36*	KPS Kipps	**65E** Kipps	**65E** Kipps	**65E** Kipps	**65E** Kipps		
65250	*J36*	BGT Bathgate	**64F** Bathgate	**64F** Bathgate	**64F** Bathgate			
65251	*J36*	STM St. Margarets	**64A** St. Margarets	**64A** St. Margarets	**64A** St. Margarets	**61A** Kittybrewster	**64F** Bathgate	
65252	*J36*	DFU Dunfermline Upper	**62C** Dunfermline Upper	**62A** Thornton Junction	**62A** Thornton Junction	**62A** Thornton Junction		
65253	*J36*	DFU Dunfermline Upper	**62C** Dunfermline Upper	**62C** Dunfermline Upper	**62C** Dunfermline Upper	**62C** Dunfermline Upper	**62C** Dunfermline Upper	
65254	*J36*	BGT Bathgate	**64F** Bathgate					
65255	*J36*	KPS Kipps	**65E** Kipps					
65256	*J36*	KPS Kipps						
65257	*J36*	POL Polmont	**64E** Polmont	**64E** Polmont	**64E** Polmont	**64E** Polmont		
65258	*J36*	STM St. Margarets	**64A** St. Margarets	**64A** St. Margarets	**64A** St. Margarets	**64A** St. Margarets		
65259	*J36*	HAW Hawick	**64G** Hawick	**64G** Hawick	**64F** Bathgate			
65260	*J36*	KPS Kipps	**65E** Kipps	**65E** Kipps	**65E** Kipps	**65E** Kipps		
65261	*J36*	BGT Bathgate	**64F** Bathgate	**64F** Bathgate	**64F** Bathgate	**64F** Bathgate	**64F** Bathgate	
65264	*J36*	KPS Kipps	**65E** Kipps					
65265	*J36*	BGT Bathgate	**64F** Bathgate	**64F** Bathgate	**64F** Bathgate	**64F** Bathgate	**64F** Bathgate	
65266	*J36*	KPS Kipps	**65E** Kipps	**65E** Kipps	**65E** Kipps	**65E** Kipps		
65267	*J36*	STM St. Margarets	**64A** St. Margarets	**64A** St. Margarets	**61C** Keith	**61C** Keith	**64F** Bathgate	**64F** Bathgate
65268	*J36*	POL Polmont	**64E** Polmont	**64F** Bathgate	**64F** Bathgate	**64F** Bathgate		
65270	*J36*	EFD Eastfield	**65A** Eastfield	**65A** Eastfield	**65A** Eastfield			
65271	*J36*	BGT Bathgate	**64C** Dalry Road					
65273	*J36*	EFD Eastfield	**65A** Eastfield	**65A** Eastfield	**65A** Eastfield	**65C** Parkhead	**67D** Ardrossan	
65274	*J36*	PKD Parkhead						
65275	*J36*	POL Polmont	**64E** Polmont	**64E** Polmont	**64E** Polmont	**64G** Hawick		
65276	*J36*	BGT Bathgate	**64F** Bathgate	**64F** Bathgate	**64F** Bathgate	**64F** Bathgate		
65277	*J36*	BGT Bathgate	**64F** Bathgate	**64F** Bathgate	**64F** Bathgate	**61C** Keith	**64F** Bathgate	
65278	*J36*	BGT Bathgate	**64F** Bathgate					
65279	*J36*	HAW Hawick	**64G** Hawick					
65280	*J36*	BGT Bathgate	**64F** Bathgate	**64F** Bathgate	**64E** Polmont	**64E** Polmont		
65281	*J36*	STG Stirling Shore Road	**62C** Dunfermline Upper	**62C** Dunfermline Upper	**62C** Dunfermline Upper	**62C** Dunfermline Upper		
65282	*J36*	BGT Bathgate	**64F** Bathgate	**64F** Bathgate	**64F** Bathgate	**64F** Bathgate	**64F** Bathgate	**64F** Bathgate
65283	*J36*	PKD Parkhead	**65C** Parkhead					
65285	*J36*	KPS Kipps	**65E** Kipps	**65E** Kipps	**65E** Kipps	**65E** Kipps	**65B** St. Rollox	
65286	*J36*	STM St. Margarets	**64A** St. Margarets					
65287	*J36*	KPS Kipps	**65E** Kipps	**65E** Kipps	**65E** Kipps	**65E** Kipps	**65B** St. Rollox	
65288	*J36*	STM St. Margarets	**64A** St. Margarets	**64A** St. Margarets	**64A** St. Margarets	**64A** St. Margarets	**64A** St. Margarets	**62C** Dunfermline Upper
65289	*J36*	KPS Kipps						
65290	*J36*	POL Polmont	**64E** Polmont	**64E** Polmont	**64F** Bathgate	**64F** Bathgate	**64F** Bathgate	
65291	*J36*	THJ Thornton Junction						
65292	*J36*	STM St. Margarets	**64A** St. Margarets					
65293	*J36*	CAR Carlisle Canal	**12B** Carlisle Canal	**68E** Carlisle Canal	**68E** Carlisle Canal	**12C** Carlisle Canal		
65294	*J36*	KPS Kipps						
65295	*J36*	HEX Hexham	**52C** Hexham	**65C** Parkhead	**65C** Parkhead	**65C** Parkhead		
65296	*J36*	EFD Eastfield	**65A** Eastfield	**65A** Eastfield	**65A** Eastfield	**65A** Eastfield		
65297	*J36*	PTH Perth South	**61B** Aberdeen Ferryhill	**61B** Aberdeen Ferryhill	**61C** Keith	**61A** Kittybrewster	**67B** Hurlford	**64F** Bathgate
65298	*J36*	PKD Parkhead	**65C** Parkhead					
65300	*J36*	EFD Eastfield	**63D** Fort William	**63D** Fort William	**65J** Fort William	**65J** Fort William		

No.	Class	1948	1951	1954	1957	1960	1963	1966
65303	*J36*	**BGT** Bathgate	**64F** Bathgate	**64F** Bathgate	**61A** Kittybrewster	**61A** Kittybrewster		
65304	*J36*	**CAR** Carlisle Canal	**12B** Carlisle Canal	**68E** Carlisle Canal	**66A** Polmadie	**61C** Keith		
65305	*J36*	**STM** St. Margarets	**64A** St. Margarets	**64A** St. Margarets	**64A** St. Margarets	**61B** Aberdeen Ferryhill		
65306	*J36*	**POL** Polmont	**64E** Polmont	**64E** Polmont	**64E** Polmont	**64E** Polmont		
65307	*J36*	**STG** Stirling Shore Road	**62C** Dunfermline Upper	**62C** Dunfermline Upper	**62C** Dunfermline Upper	**62C** Dunfermline Upper	**62A** Thornton Junction	
65308	*J36*	**EFD** Eastfield	**65A** Eastfield					
65309	*J36*	**PTH** Perth South	**62B** Dundee Tay Bridge	**62B** Dundee Tay Bridge	**62B** Dundee Tay Bridge	**62B** Dundee Tay Bridge	**64F** Bathgate	
65310	*J36*	**STM** St. Margarets	**64A** St. Margarets	**64A** St. Margarets	**64A** St. Margarets	**61C** Keith		
65311	*J36*	**STM** St. Margarets	**64A** St. Margarets	**64A** St. Margarets	**64E** Polmont	**64E** Polmont	**65K** Polmont	
65312	*J36*	**CAR** Carlisle Canal	**12B** Carlisle Canal	**68E** Carlisle Canal	**68E** Carlisle Canal	**12C** Carlisle Canal		
65313	*J36*	**POL** Polmont	**63D** Fort William	**63D** Fort William	**65J** Fort William	**65J** Fort William		
65314	*J36*	**BGT** Bathgate	**64F** Bathgate	**64F** Bathgate				
65315	*J36*	**EFD** Eastfield	**65I** Balloch	**65I** Balloch	**65I** Balloch	**65I** Balloch		
65316	*J36*	**STM** St. Margarets	**64A** St. Margarets	**64G** Hawick	**64G** Hawick	**64E** Polmont		
65317	*J36*	**HAW** Hawick	**64G** Hawick	**64G** Hawick	**64G** Hawick	**64G** Hawick		
65318	*J36*	**BGT** Bathgate	**64F** Bathgate	**64F** Bathgate	**64F** Bathgate	**64F** Bathgate		
65319	*J36*	**DEE** Dundee Tay Bridge	**62B** Dundee Tay Bridge	**62B** Dundee Tay Bridge	**62B** Dundee Tay Bridge	**62B** Dundee Tay Bridge	**62B** Dundee Tay Bridge	**62B** Dundee Tay Bridge
65320	*J36*	**DFU** Dunfermline Upper	**62C** Dunfermline Upper	**62C** Dunfermline Upper	**62C** Dunfermline Upper	**62C** Dunfermline Upper		
65321	*J36*	**CAR** Carlisle Canal	**12B** Carlisle Canal	**68E** Carlisle Canal	**68E** Carlisle Canal	**12C** Carlisle Canal		
65322	*J36*	**STG** Stirling Shore Road	**62C** Dunfermline Upper					
65323	*J36*	**DFU** Dunfermline Upper	**62C** Dunfermline Upper	**62C** Dunfermline Upper	**62C** Dunfermline Upper	**62C** Dunfermline Upper	**62C** Dunfermline Upper	
65324	*J36*	**PKD** Parkhead	**65C** Parkhead	**65C** Parkhead	**65C** Parkhead			
65325	*J36*	**KPS** Kipps	**65E** Kipps	**65E** Kipps	**65E** Kipps	**65E** Kipps	**65E** Kipps	
65327	*J36*	**BGT** Bathgate	**64F** Bathgate	**64A** St. Margarets	**64A** St. Margarets	**64A** St. Margarets	**64A** St. Margarets	
65328	*J36*	**DEE** Dundee Tay Bridge						
65329	*J36*	**POL** Polmont	**64D** Carstairs	**64A** St. Margarets	**64A** St. Margarets	**64A** St. Margarets	**64A** St. Margarets	
65330	*J36*	**DEE** Dundee Tay Bridge	**62B** Dundee Tay Bridge	**62B** Dundee Tay Bridge	**62B** Dundee Tay Bridge	**62B** Dundee Tay Bridge		
65331	*J36*	**RMH** Reedsmouth	**52C** Reedsmouth	**64G** Hawick	**64G** Hawick	**64G** Hawick	**64G** Hawick	
65333	*J36*	**DEE** Dundee Tay Bridge	**62B** Dundee Tay Bridge	**62B** Dundee Tay Bridge	**62B** Dundee Tay Bridge			
65334	*J36*	**STM** St. Margarets	**64A** St. Margarets	**64A** St. Margarets	**64A** St. Margarets	**64A** St. Margarets		
65335	*J36*	**EFD** Eastfield	**65C** Parkhead	**65C** Parkhead	**65C** Parkhead	**65C** Parkhead	**65F** Grangemouth	
65337	*J36*	**EFD** Eastfield						
65338	*J36*	**POL** Polmont	**64E** Polmont	**64E** Polmont	**64A** St. Margarets	**61C** Keith	**62C** Dunfermline Upper	
65339	*J36*	**EFD** Eastfield	**65I** Balloch	**65I** Balloch	**65I** Balloch	**65I** Balloch		
65340	*J36*	**HAW** Hawick	**64G** Hawick					
65341	*J36*	**BGT** Bathgate	**64F** Bathgate	**64F** Bathgate	**64F** Bathgate	**64F** Bathgate	**64F** Bathgate	
65342	*J36*	**BGT** Bathgate	**64F** Bathgate	**64F** Bathgate	**64F** Bathgate	**64F** Bathgate		
65343	*J36*	**RMH** Reedsmouth	**52C** Blaydon	**65E** Kipps	**65E** Kipps	**65E** Kipps		
65344	*J36*	**BGT** Bathgate	**64F** Bathgate	**64F** Bathgate	**64F** Bathgate	**64F** Bathgate		
65345	*J36*	**THJ** Thornton Junction	**62A** Thornton Junction	**62A** Thornton Junction	**62A** Thornton Junction	**62A** Thornton Junction	**62A** Thornton Junction	**62A** Thornton Junction
65346	*J36*	**STG** Stirling Shore Road	**64F** Bathgate	**64F** Bathgate	**64F** Bathgate	**64F** Bathgate	**64F** Bathgate	
65350	*J15*	**CAM** Cambridge	**31A** Cambridge					
65351	*J15*	**LOW** Lowestoft						
65352	*J15*	**LOW** Lowestoft						
65353	*J15*	**LOW** Lowestoft						
65354	*J15*	**STR** Stratford	**30F** Parkeston					
65355	*J15*	**LOW** Lowestoft	**32C** Lowestoft					
65356	*J15*	**CAM** Cambridge	**31A** Cambridge	**31B** March	**31B** March			
65357	*J15*	**COL** Colchester						
65359	*J15*	**KL** Kings Lynn	**31C** Kings Lynn	**31C** Kings Lynn				
65361	*J15*	**STR** Stratford	**32B** Ipswich	**32B** Ipswich	**32B** Ipswich	**30A** Stratford		
65362	*J15*	**BSE** Bury St. Edmunds	**31E** Bury St. Edmunds					
65363	*J15*	**STR** Stratford						
65364	*J15*	**CAM** Cambridge						
65365	*J15*	**PKS** Parkeston						
65366	*J15*	**CAM** Cambridge	**31B** March					
65367	*J15*	**NOR** Norwich Thorpe						
65368	*J15*	**KL** Kings Lynn						
65369	*J15*	**CAM** Cambridge	**30E** Colchester					
65370	*J15*	**STR** Stratford	**30A** Stratford	**30A** Stratford				
65371	*J15*	**CAM** Cambridge						
65372	*J15*	**MAR** March						
65373	*J15*	**NOR** Norwich Thorpe						
65374	*J15*	**COL** Colchester						
65375	*J15*	**STR** Stratford						
65376	*J15*	**PKS** Parkeston						
65377	*J15*	**IPS** Ipswich	**32B** Ipswich					
65378	*J15*	**KL** Kings Lynn	**31C** Kings Lynn					
65379	*J15*	**CAM** Cambridge						
65380	*J15*	**CAM** Cambridge						
65381	*J15*	**STR** Stratford						
65382	*J15*	**KL** Kings Lynn	**32B** Ipswich					
65383	*J15*	**CAM** Cambridge						
65384	*J15*	**COL** Colchester	**30A** Stratford	**30A** Stratford				
65385	*J15*	**COL** Colchester						
65386	*J15*	**IPS** Ipswich						
65387	*J15*	**STR** Stratford						
65388	*J15*	**STR** Stratford	**32A** Norwich Thorpe	**32A** Norwich Thorpe	**32A** Norwich Thorpe			
65389	*J15*	**LOW** Lowestoft	**32C** Lowestoft	**32C** Lowestoft	**32B** Ipswich	**32B** Ipswich		
65390	*J15*	**NOR** Norwich Thorpe	**32A** Norwich Thorpe	**31A** Cambridge	**31A** Cambridge			
65391	*J15*	**CAM** Cambridge	**31A** Cambridge	**31E** Bury St. Edmunds	**31E** Bury St. Edmunds			
65392	*J15*	**STR** Stratford						
65393	*J15*	**STR** Stratford						
65394	*J15*	**NOR** Norwich Thorpe						
65395	*J15*	**STR** Stratford						
65396	*J15*	**KL** Kings Lynn	**32B** Ipswich					
65397	*J15*	**STR** Stratford						
65398	*J15*	**NOR** Norwich Thorpe	**32A** Norwich Thorpe					
65399	*J15*	**CAM** Cambridge						
65400	*J15*	**LOW** Lowestoft						
65401	*J15*	**NOR** Norwich Thorpe	**32C** Lowestoft					
65402	*J15*	**STR** Stratford						
65404	*J15*	**NOR** Norwich Thorpe	**32A** Norwich Thorpe	**32B** Ipswich				
65405	*J15*	**CAM** Cambridge	**31A** Cambridge	**31E** Bury St. Edmunds	**31E** Bury St. Edmunds			
65406	*J15*	**CAM** Cambridge	**31A** Cambridge					
65407	*J15*	**IPS** Ipswich	**32B** Ipswich					
65408	*J15*	**NOR** Norwich Thorpe	**32B** Ipswich					
65409	*J15*	**IPS** Ipswich						
65410	*J15*	**CAM** Cambridge						
65411	*J15*	**NOR** Norwich Thorpe						
65412	*J15*	**CAM** Cambridge						
65413	*J15*	**CAM** Cambridge						
65414	*J15*	**COL** Colchester						
65415	*J15*	**IPS** Ipswich						
65416	*J15*	**KL** Kings Lynn						
65417	*J15*	**NOR** Norwich Thorpe	**32A** Norwich Thorpe	**32A** Norwich Thorpe				
65418	*J15*	**STR** Stratford						
65419	*J15*	**MAR** March						
65420	*J15*	**BSE** Bury St. Edmunds	**31E** Bury St. Edmunds	**31E** Bury St. Edmunds	**31E** Bury St. Edmunds	**31B** March		
65421	*J15*	**IPS** Ipswich						
65422	*J15*	**NOR** Norwich Thorpe	**32A** Norwich Thorpe	**31B** March				
65423	*J15*	**IPS** Ipswich						
65424	*J15*	**COL** Colchester	**30E** Colchester	**30E** Colchester	**30E** Colchester			
65425	*J15*	**KL** Kings Lynn	**31A** Cambridge	**31A** Cambridge				

No.	Class	1948	1951	1954	1957	1960	1963	1966
65426	*J15*	**NOR** Norwich Thorpe	**32A** Norwich Thorpe					
65427	*J15*	**STR** Stratford						
65428	*J15*	**IPS** Ipswich						
65429	*J15*	**IPS** Ipswich						
65430	*J15*	**IPS** Ipswich	**32B** Ipswich	**32B** Ipswich				
65431	*J15*	**STR** Stratford	**30E** Colchester					
65432	*J15*	**COL** Colchester	**30E** Colchester	**30E** Colchester	**30E** Colchester			
65433	*J15*	**MAR** March	**32C** Lowestoft	**32C** Lowestoft	**32B** Ipswich			
65434	*J15*	**STR** Stratford	**30F** Parkeston	**30F** Parkeston	**30F** Parkeston			
65435	*J15*	**NOR** Norwich Thorpe	**32C** Lowestoft	**32C** Lowestoft				
65436	*J15*	**STR** Stratford						
65437	*J15*	**KL** Kings Lynn						
65438	*J15*	**CAM** Cambridge	**31A** Cambridge	**31A** Cambridge	**31A** Cambridge			
65439	*J15*	**MAR** March	**31B** March					
65440	*J15*	**COL** Colchester	**30A** Stratford	**30A** Stratford	**30A** Stratford	**30A** Stratford		
65441	*J15*	**STR** Stratford	**30E** Colchester	**30E** Colchester	**30E** Colchester			
65442	*J15*	**BSE** Bury St. Edmunds	**31E** Bury St. Edmunds	**31A** Cambridge	**31A** Cambridge			
65443	*J15*	**COL** Colchester	**30E** Colchester	**30A** Stratford	**30A** Stratford			
65444	*J15*	**STR** Stratford	**30A** Stratford	**30A** Stratford	**30A** Stratford			
65445	*J15*	**COL** Colchester	**30E** Colchester	**30E** Colchester	**30E** Colchester	**30F** Parkeston		
65446	*J15*	**STR** Stratford	**30A** Stratford	**30A** Stratford	**30A** Stratford	**30A** Stratford		
65447	*J15*	**IPS** Ipswich	**32B** Ipswich	**32B** Ipswich	**32B** Ipswich			
65448	*J15*	**COL** Colchester	**30E** Colchester	**30E** Colchester	**30E** Colchester	**30A** Stratford		
65449	*J15*	**STR** Stratford	**30A** Stratford	**30A** Stratford	**30A** Stratford			
65450	*J15*	**STR** Stratford	**30A** Stratford	**30A** Stratford	**30A** Stratford	**31A** Cambridge		
65451	*J15*	**CAM** Cambridge	**31A** Cambridge	**31A** Cambridge	**31A** Cambridge			
65452	*J15*	**STR** Stratford	**30A** Stratford	**30A** Stratford	**30A** Stratford			
65453	*J15*	**PKS** Parkeston	**30A** Stratford	**30F** Parkeston	**30F** Parkeston	**30F** Parkeston		
65454	*J15*	**STR** Stratford	**30A** Stratford	**30A** Stratford	**30A** Stratford			
65455	*J15*	**STR** Stratford	**30A** Stratford	**30A** Stratford	**30A** Stratford	**30A** Stratford		
65456	*J15*	**COL** Colchester	**30E** Colchester	**30E** Colchester	**30E** Colchester			
65457	*J15*	**CAM** Cambridge	**31A** Cambridge	**31A** Cambridge	**31A** Cambridge	**31A** Cambridge		
65458	*J15*	**PKS** Parkeston	**30F** Parkeston	**30F** Parkeston	**30F** Parkeston	**30F** Parkeston		
65459	*J15*	**IPS** Ipswich	**32B** Ipswich	**32B** Ipswich	**32B** Ipswich	**30A** Stratford		
65460	*J15*	**NOR** Norwich Thorpe	**32A** Norwich Thorpe	**32A** Norwich Thorpe	**32C** Lowestoft	**32C** Lowestoft		
65461	*J15*	**CAM** Cambridge	**31A** Cambridge	**31A** Cambridge	**31A** Cambridge	**31A** Cambridge		
65462	*J15*	**LOW** Lowestoft	**32C** Lowestoft	**32C** Lowestoft	**32C** Lowestoft	**32C** Lowestoft		
65463	*J15*	**STR** Stratford	**30A** Stratford	**30A** Stratford	**30A** Stratford			
65464	*J15*	**STR** Stratford	**30A** Stratford	**30A** Stratford	**30A** Stratford	**30A** Stratford		
65465	*J15*	**COL** Colchester	**30E** Colchester	**30E** Colchester	**30E** Colchester	**30A** Stratford		
65466	*J15*	**STR** Stratford	**30A** Stratford	**30E** Colchester	**30E** Colchester			
65467	*J15*	**IPS** Ipswich	**32B** Ipswich	**32B** Ipswich	**32B** Ipswich			
65468	*J15*	**STR** Stratford	**30E** Colchester	**30E** Colchester	**30E** Colchester			
65469	*J15*	**YB** Yarmouth Beach	**32A** Norwich Thorpe	**32A** Norwich Thorpe	**32A** Norwich Thorpe	**32A** Norwich Thorpe		
65470	*J15*	**NOR** Norwich Thorpe	**30E** Colchester	**30E** Colchester	**30E** Colchester			
65471	*J15*	**NOR** Norwich Thorpe	**32A** Norwich Thorpe	**32A** Norwich Thorpe	**32A** Norwich Thorpe	**32A** Norwich Thorpe		
65472	*J15*	**YB** Yarmouth Beach	**32A** Norwich Thorpe	**32A** Norwich Thorpe	**32A** Norwich Thorpe			
65473	*J15*	**COL** Colchester	**30E** Colchester	**30E** Colchester	**30E** Colchester	**30A** Stratford		
65474	*J15*	**CAM** Cambridge	**31A** Cambridge	**31A** Cambridge	**31B** March	**31B** March		
65475	*J15*	**STR** Stratford	**31A** Cambridge	**31A** Cambridge	**31A** Cambridge			
65476	*J15*	**STR** Stratford	**30A** Stratford	**30A** Stratford	**30A** Stratford	**30A** Stratford		
65477	*J15*	**CAM** Cambridge	**31A** Cambridge	**31A** Cambridge	**31A** Cambridge	**31A** Cambridge		
65478	*J15*	**NOR** Norwich Thorpe	**32C** Lowestoft	**32C** Lowestoft	**32C** Lowestoft	**32B** Ipswich		
65479	*J15*	**NOR** Norwich Thorpe	**30E** Colchester	**34D** Hitchin	**34D** Hitchin	**34D** Hitchin		
65480	*J5*	**CLK** Colwick	**38A** Colwick	**38A** Colwick				
65481	*J5*	**CLK** Colwick	**38A** Colwick					
65482	*J5*	**CLK** Colwick	**38A** Colwick					
65483	*J5*	**CLK** Colwick	**38A** Colwick	**38A** Colwick				
65484	*J5*	**CLK** Colwick	**38A** Colwick					
65485	*J5*	**CLK** Colwick	**38A** Colwick	**38C** Leicester Central				
65486	*J5*	**WFD** Woodford Halse	**38A** Colwick	**38A** Colwick				
65487	*J5*	**WFD** Woodford Halse	**38A** Colwick					
65488	*J5*	**WFD** Woodford Halse	**38A** Colwick					
65489	*J5*	**WFD** Woodford Halse	**38A** Colwick					
65490	*J5*	**CLK** Colwick	**38A** Colwick	**38A** Colwick				
65491	*J5*	**CLK** Colwick	**38A** Colwick					
65492	*J5*	**CLK** Colwick	**38A** Colwick					
65493	*J5*	**CLK** Colwick	**38A** Colwick	**38A** Colwick				
65494	*J5*	**CLK** Colwick	**38B** Annesley	**38A** Colwick				
65495	*J5*	**CLK** Colwick	**38C** Leicester Central	**38C** Leicester Central				
65496	*J5*	**CLK** Colwick	**38A** Colwick	**38A** Colwick				
65497	*J5*	**CLK** Colwick	**38A** Colwick					
65498	*J5*	**CLK** Colwick	**38A** Colwick	**38A** Colwick				
65499	*J5*	**CLK** Colwick	**38A** Colwick					
65500	*J17*	**STR** Stratford	**30A** Stratford	**30A** Stratford	**31A** Cambridge			
65501	*J17*	**CAM** Cambridge	**31A** Cambridge	**31C** Kings Lynn	**31C** Kings Lynn			
65502	*J17*	**CAM** Cambridge	**31A** Cambridge	**31A** Cambridge	**31A** Cambridge			
65503	*J17*	**CAM** Cambridge	**31A** Cambridge	**31B** March	**31B** March	**30A** Stratford		
65504	*J17*	**SL** South Lynn	**31D** South Lynn	**31A** Cambridge	**31A** Cambridge			
65505	*J17*	**SL** South Lynn	**31B** March	**31A** Cambridge	**31A** Cambridge			
65506	*J17*	**CAM** Cambridge	**31A** Cambridge	**31A** Cambridge	**31A** Cambridge	**30A** Stratford		
65507	*J17*	**STR** Stratford	**32A** Norwich Thorpe	**32C** Lowestoft	**32C** Lowestoft	**30A** Stratford		
65508	*J17*	**STR** Stratford	**30A** Stratford	**30A** Stratford	**30A** Stratford			
65509	*J17*	**MC** Melton Constable	**32G** Melton Constable	**32A** Norwich Thorpe	**32G** Melton Constable			
65510	*J17*	**IPS** Ipswich	**32A** Norwich Thorpe	**32B** Ipswich				
65511	*J17*	**STR** Stratford	**30A** Stratford	**30A** Stratford	**30A** Stratford	**30A** Stratford		
65512	*J17*	**MAR** March	**32A** Norwich Thorpe	**31A** Cambridge	**32B** Ipswich			
65513	*J17*	**MAR** March	**32A** Norwich Thorpe	**32A** Norwich Thorpe	**32B** Ipswich	**32B** Ipswich		
65514	*J17*	**MC** Melton Constable	**32A** Norwich Thorpe	**32A** Norwich Thorpe	**32G** Melton Constable	**30A** Stratford		
65515	*J17*	**MAR** March	**31B** March	**31B** March	**31B** March			
65516	*J17*	**NOR** Norwich Thorpe	**32G** Melton Constable	**32A** Norwich Thorpe				
65517	*J17*	**CAM** Cambridge	**31A** Cambridge	**31D** South Lynn				
65518	*J17*	**MAR** March	**31B** March	**31C** Kings Lynn	**31C** Kings Lynn			
65519	*J17*	**STR** Stratford	**31C** Kings Lynn	**31C** Kings Lynn	**32A** Norwich Thorpe	**32A** Norwich Thorpe		
65520	*J17*	**CAM** Cambridge	**31A** Cambridge	**31D** South Lynn	**31A** Cambridge	**31A** Cambridge		
65521	*J17*	**SL** South Lynn	**31B** March	**31C** Kings Lynn	**31C** Kings Lynn	**31C** Kings Lynn		
65522	*J17*	**COL** Colchester	**30E** Colchester	**30E** Colchester	**30E** Colchester			
65523	*J17*	**STR** Stratford	**30A** Stratford	**30A** Stratford	**30A** Stratford			
65524	*J17*	**MAR** March	**32A** Norwich Thorpe	**32A** Norwich Thorpe				
65525	*J17*	**MAR** March	**31A** Cambridge	**30A** Stratford	**30A** Stratford			
65526	*J17*	**SL** South Lynn	**31D** South Lynn	**31C** Kings Lynn	**31C** Kings Lynn			
65527	*J17*	**KL** Kings Lynn	**31C** Kings Lynn	**31C** Kings Lynn	**31C** Kings Lynn			
65528	*J17*	**STR** Stratford	**30A** Stratford	**30A** Stratford	**30A** Stratford	**31A** Cambridge		
65529	*J17*	**KL** Kings Lynn	**31A** Cambridge	**31C** Kings Lynn	**31C** Kings Lynn			
65530	*J17*	**KL** Kings Lynn	**31C** Kings Lynn	**31C** Kings Lynn	**31C** Kings Lynn	**31C** Kings Lynn		
65531	*J17*	**COL** Colchester	**30E** Colchester	**30E** Colchester	**30E** Colchester			
65532	*J17*	**SL** South Lynn	**31A** Cambridge	**31A** Cambridge	**31A** Cambridge	**31A** Cambridge		
65533	*J17*	**SL** South Lynn	**31D** South Lynn	**33A** Plaistow	**31C** Kings Lynn	**31C** Kings Lynn		
65534	*J17*	**NOR** Norwich Thorpe	**32A** Norwich Thorpe	**31A** Cambridge	**31A** Cambridge			
65535	*J17*	**CAM** Cambridge	**31A** Cambridge	**31A** Cambridge	**30A** Stratford			
65536	*J17*	**STR** Stratford	**30A** Stratford	**30A** Stratford	**30A** Stratford	**30A** Stratford		
65537	*J17*	**CAM** Cambridge	**31A** Cambridge	**31A** Cambridge	**32A** Norwich Thorpe			
65538	*J17*	**MAR** March	**31A** Cambridge	**30A** Stratford	**31B** March			
65539	*J17*	**COL** Colchester	**30E** Colchester	**30E** Colchester	**30E** Colchester	**30A** Stratford		

		1948	1951	1954	1957	1960	1963	1966
65540	*J17*	**STR** Stratford	**30A** Stratford	**30A** Stratford	**30A** Stratford			
65541	*J17*	**STR** Stratford	**30A** Stratford	**31B** March	**31A** Cambridge	**31A** Cambridge		
65542	*J17*	**STR** Stratford	**31C** Kings Lynn	**32A** Norwich Thorpe	**32A** Norwich Thorpe			
65543	*J17*	**STR** Stratford	**30A** Stratford	**30A** Stratford				
65544	*J17*	**KL** Kings Lynn	**31C** Kings Lynn	**31C** Kings Lynn	**31C** Kings Lynn			
65545	*J17*	**SL** South Lynn	**31D** South Lynn	**33C** Shoeburyness	**30A** Stratford			
65546	*J17*	**CAM** Cambridge	**31A** Cambridge	**30A** Stratford	**30A** Stratford	**30A** Stratford		
65547	*J17*	**MAR** March	**31A** Cambridge	**31A** Cambridge				
65548	*J17*	**KL** Kings Lynn	**31E** Bury St. Edmunds	**31A** Cambridge	**31A** Cambridge	**30A** Stratford		
65549	*J17*	**KL** Kings Lynn	**31C** Kings Lynn	**31C** Kings Lynn	**31C** Kings Lynn	**31C** Kings Lynn		
65551	*J17*	**MC** Melton Constable	**32G** Melton Constable	**32A** Norwich Thorpe	**32G** Melton Constable	**32A** Norwich Thorpe		
65552	*J17*	**MC** Melton Constable	**32G** Melton Constable	**33A** Plaistow				
65553	*J17*	**NOR** Norwich Thorpe	**32A** Norwich Thorpe	**32A** Norwich Thorpe	**32A** Norwich Thorpe			
65554	*J17*	**MAR** March	**31B** March	**31B** March	**31B** March	**31B** March		
65555	*J17*	**MAR** March	**31B** March	**30A** Stratford	**30A** Stratford	**30A** Stratford		
65556	*J17*	**MAR** March	**31B** March	**31B** March	**31B** March	**31A** Cambridge		
65557	*J17*	**MC** Melton Constable	**32G** Melton Constable	**32G** Melton Constable	**32G** Melton Constable			
65558	*J17*	**YB** Yarmouth Beach	**32F** Yarmouth Beach	**32C** Lowestoft	**32C** Lowestoft	**32C** Lowestoft		
65559	*J17*	**YB** Yarmouth Beach	**32F** Yarmouth Beach	**32C** Lowestoft	**32C** Lowestoft			
65560	*J17*	**IPS** Ipswich	**32B** Ipswich	**32B** Ipswich	**32B** Ipswich	**32B** Ipswich		
65561	*J17*	**SL** South Lynn	**31A** Cambridge	**31A** Cambridge	**31A** Cambridge			
65562	*J17*	**SL** South Lynn	**31D** South Lynn	**31D** South Lynn	**31C** Kings Lynn			
65563	*J17*	**CAM** Cambridge	**31A** Cambridge	**30A** Stratford	**30A** Stratford	**30A** Stratford		
65564	*J17*	**COL** Colchester	**30E** Colchester	**30E** Colchester	**30E** Colchester	**30A** Stratford		
65565	*J17*	**SL** South Lynn	**31A** Cambridge	**31A** Cambridge	**31A** Cambridge	**31C** Kings Lynn		
65566	*J17*	**MC** Melton Constable	**32C** Lowestoft	**33A** Plaistow	**32A** Norwich Thorpe	**32A** Norwich Thorpe		
65567	*J17*	**MC** Melton Constable	**32G** Melton Constable	**32A** Norwich Thorpe	**32G** Melton Constable	**32C** Lowestoft		
65568	*J17*	**MAR** March	**32A** Norwich Thorpe	**31C** Kings Lynn	**31C** Kings Lynn			
65569	*J17*	**NOR** Norwich Thorpe	**32A** Norwich Thorpe	**32A** Norwich Thorpe				
65570	*J17*	**NOR** Norwich Thorpe	**32C** Lowestoft	**32A** Norwich Thorpe	**32A** Norwich Thorpe	**32A** Norwich Thorpe		
65571	*J17*	**MAR** March	**31B** March	**31B** March	**31B** March			
65572	*J17*	**KL** Kings Lynn	**31C** Kings Lynn	**31B** March	**31B** March			
65573	*J17*	**MAR** March	**31A** Cambridge	**32A** Norwich Thorpe	**32A** Norwich Thorpe			
65574	*J17*	**YB** Yarmouth Beach	**32A** Norwich Thorpe	**32A** Norwich Thorpe				
65575	*J17*	**CAM** Cambridge	**31A** Cambridge	**31A** Cambridge	**31A** Cambridge			
65576	*J17*	**MAR** March	**31B** March	**31B** March	**31B** March	**31B** March		
65577	*J17*	**MAR** March	**31B** March	**31B** March	**31B** March	**31C** Kings Lynn		
65578	*J17*	**NOR** Norwich Thorpe	**32B** Ipswich	**32B** Ipswich	**32B** Ipswich	**31A** Cambridge		
65579	*J17*	**SL** South Lynn	**31D** South Lynn	**31D** South Lynn				
65580	*J17*	**KL** Kings Lynn	**31D** South Lynn	**31E** Bury St. Edmunds	**31A** Cambridge			
65581	*J17*	**YB** Yarmouth Beach	**32F** Yarmouth Beach	**32F** Yarmouth Beach	**32F** Yarmouth Beach	**32A** Norwich Thorpe		
65582	*J17*	**SL** South Lynn	**31D** South Lynn	**31C** Kings Lynn	**31C** Kings Lynn	**31C** Kings Lynn		
65583	*J17*	**MAR** March	**31B** March	**31E** Bury St. Edmunds	**31B** March	**31B** March		
65584	*J17*	**MAR** March	**31B** March	**31B** March	**31D** South Lynn	**31C** Kings Lynn		
65585	*J17*	**CAM** Cambridge	**31A** Cambridge	**31A** Cambridge				
65586	*J17*	**MC** Melton Constable	**32G** Melton Constable	**32F** Yarmouth Beach	**32F** Yarmouth Beach	**32A** Norwich Thorpe		
65587	*J17*	**MAR** March	**31A** Cambridge	**30A** Stratford	**31A** Cambridge			
65588	*J17*	**SL** South Lynn	**31D** South Lynn	**33A** Plaistow	**32A** Norwich Thorpe	**32C** Lowestoft		
65589	*J17*	**SL** South Lynn	**31A** Cambridge	**31A** Cambridge	**31A** Cambridge	**31A** Cambridge		
65600	*J24*	**BOR** Borough Gardens						
65601	*J24*	**NPT** Newport	**51B** Newport					
65602	*J24*	**TDK** Tyne Dock						
65603	*J24*	**BOR** Borough Gardens						
65604	*J24*	**BOR** Borough Gardens						
65606	*J24*	**TDK** Tyne Dock						
65607	*J24*	**MAL** Malton						
65608	*J24*	**NPT** Newport						
65609	*J24*	**WBY** Whitby						
65611	*J24*	**BOR** Borough Gardens						
65612	*J24*	**WBY** Whitby						
65614	*J24*	**DEE** Dundee Tay Bridge	**62B** Dundee Tay Bridge					
65615	*J24*	**MAL** Malton	**54C** Borough Gardens					
65617	*J24*	**STM** St. Margarets	**64A** St. Margarets					
65619	*J24*	**HLD** Hull Dairycoates	**50A** York					
65621	*J24*	**HLD** Hull Dairycoates						
65622	*J24*	**DEE** Dundee Tay Bridge	**62B** Dundee Tay Bridge					
65623	*J24*	**STM** St. Margarets	**64A** St. Margarets					
65624	*J24*	**BOR** Borough Gardens						
65625	*J24*	**STM** St. Margarets						
65626	*J24*	**NPT** Newport						
65627	*J24*	**BOR** Borough Gardens						
65628	*J24*	**MAL** Malton						
65629	*J24*	**WBY** Whitby						
65631	*J24*	**HLD** Hull Dairycoates						
65632	*J24*	**TDK** Tyne Dock						
65633	*J24*	**BOR** Borough Gardens						
65634	*J24*	**BOR** Borough Gardens						
65636	*J24*	**MAL** Malton						
65639	*J24*	**HLD** Hull Dairycoates						
65640	*J24*	**SBK** Starbeck	**50F** Malton					
65641	*J24*	**BOR** Borough Gardens						
65642	*J24*	**MAL** Malton						
65644	*J24*	**BOR** Borough Gardens	**50F** Malton					
65645	*J25*	**NLN** Northallerton	**51J** Northallerton	**51A** Darlington	**54C** Borough Gardens	**52H** Tyne Dock		
65646	*J25*	**DAR** Darlington						
65647	*J25*	**HLD** Hull Dairycoates	**53E** Cudworth	**50G** Whitby				
65648	*J25*	**DAR** Darlington	**51A** Darlington	**50F** Malton	**50B** Leeds Neville Hill			
65649	*J25*	**HTN** Heaton						
65650	*J25*	**DAR** Darlington	**51A** Darlington	**50A** York	**50B** Leeds Neville Hill			
65651	*J25*	**HLD** Hull Dairycoates						
65653	*J25*	**DAR** Darlington	**51H** Kirkby Stephen					
65654	*J25*	**HLS** Hull Springhead	**53A** Hull Dairycoates	**50A** York	**50B** Leeds Neville Hill			
65655	*J25*	**KBY** Kirkby Stephen	**51H** Kirkby Stephen	**51H** Kirkby Stephen	**53A** Hull Dairycoates			
65656	*J25*	**YK** York	**50F** Malton	**50F** Malton	**52B** Heaton			
65657	*J25*	**BOR** Borough Gardens	**54C** Borough Gardens	**54C** Borough Gardens	**54C** Borough Gardens			
65658	*J25*	**NLN** Northallerton						
65659	*J25*	**AUK** West Auckland	**51F** West Auckland					
65660	*J25*	**HLD** Hull Dairycoates	**51G** Haverton Hill					
65661	*J25*	**BOR** Borough Gardens	**54C** Borough Gardens	**54C** Borough Gardens				
65662	*J25*	**AUK** West Auckland	**51F** West Auckland	**51F** West Auckland	**54A** Sunderland	**52G** Sunderland		
65663	*J25*	**HLD** Hull Dairycoates	**53A** Hull Dairycoates	**50G** Whitby	**50G** Whitby	**52F** South Blyth		
65664	*J25*	**DAR** Darlington	**51A** Darlington					
65665	*J25*	**AUK** West Auckland						
65666	*J25*	**HLD** Hull Dairycoates	**54B** Tyne Dock	**54B** Tyne Dock	**54B** Tyne Dock	**52G** Sunderland		
65667	*J25*	**CUD** Cudworth	**53C** Hull Springhead	**52F** North Blyth				
65668	*J25*	**DAR** Darlington						
65669	*J25*	**KBY** Kirkby Stephen						
65670	*J25*	**TDK** Tyne Dock	**54B** Tyne Dock	**54B** Tyne Dock	**54B** Tyne Dock	**52H** Tyne Dock		
65671	*J25*	**HLD** Hull Dairycoates	**50F** Malton	**50F** Malton				
65672	*J25*	**DAR** Darlington	**51A** Darlington					
65673	*J25*	**KBY** Kirkby Stephen	**51H** Kirkby Stephen	**51H** Kirkby Stephen	**50D** Starbeck			
65674	*J25*	**NLN** Northallerton						
65675	*J25*	**AUK** West Auckland	**51F** West Auckland	**50C** Selby	**52B** Heaton			
65676	*J25*	**BOR** Borough Gardens	**54C** Borough Gardens	**54C** Borough Gardens				

		1948	1951	1954	1957	1960	1963	1966
65677	*J25*	AUK West Auckland	**51A** Darlington	**50A** York	**53A** Hull Dairycoates			
65679	*J25*	HLD Hull Dairycoates	**50A** York					
65680	*J25*	BOR Borough Gardens	**54C** Borough Gardens	**54C** Borough Gardens	**54B** Tyne Dock			
65681	*J25*	KBY Kirkby Stephen						
65683	*J25*	AUK West Auckland	**51F** West Auckland	**50C** Selby	**50B** Leeds Neville Hill			
65684	*J25*	KBY Kirkby Stephen						
65685	*J25*	BOR Borough Gardens	**54C** Borough Gardens	**50F** Malton	**52B** Heaton			
65686	*J25*	MID Middlesbrough	**54C** Borough Gardens	**54C** Borough Gardens				
65687	*J25*	AUK West Auckland	**51D** Middlesbrough	**50A** York	**52B** Heaton			
65688	*J25*	DAR Darlington	**51A** Darlington	**51A** Darlington				
65689	*J25*	AUK West Auckland	**51E** Stockton on Tees	**51E** Stockton on Tees				
65690	*J25*	HLD Hull Dairycoates	**53A** Hull Dairycoates	**50G** Whitby				
65691	*J25*	DAR Darlington	**51A** Darlington	**50A** York	**50A** York	**53A** Hull Dairycoates		
65692	*J25*	DAR Darlington	**51A** Darlington	**51A** Darlington				
65693	*J25*	NLN Northallerton	**51J** Northallerton	**51J** Northallerton	**53A** Hull Dairycoates	**53A** Hull Dairycoates		
65694	*J25*	TDK Tyne Dock	**54B** Tyne Dock	**54B** Tyne Dock				
65695	*J25*	DAR Darlington	**51H** Kirkby Stephen	**51H** Kirkby Stephen	**53A** Hull Dairycoates	**52H** Tyne Dock		
65696	*J25*	AUK West Auckland	**51F** West Auckland	**51F** West Auckland	**52F** South Blyth			
65697	*J25*	HTN Heaton	**52D** Tweedmouth	**51F** West Auckland	**54C** Borough Gardens			
65698	*J25*	HLD Hull Dairycoates	**53E** Cudworth	**50C** Selby	**50C** Selby			
65699	*J25*	HLD Hull Dairycoates	**53A** Hull Dairycoates	**54B** Tyne Dock	**54B** Tyne Dock			
65700	*J25*	YK York	**50A** York	**50A** York	**54C** Borough Gardens			
65702	*J25*	MID Middlesbrough	**51A** Darlington	**51A** Darlington	**54C** Borough Gardens			
65703	*J25*	CUD Cudworth						
65704	*J25*	HTN Heaton						
65705	*J25*	HLD Hull Dairycoates	**53C** Hull Springhead	**54C** Borough Gardens				
65706	*J25*	AUK West Auckland	**51F** West Auckland	**51F** West Auckland	**52F** South Blyth			
65707	*J25*	HLS Hull Springhead						
65708	*J25*	DAR Darlington	**50F** Malton	**51A** Darlington				
65710	*J25*	MID Middlesbrough	**51D** Middlesbrough	**51A** Darlington				
65712	*J25*	HLD Hull Dairycoates	**52B** Heaton	**51A** Darlington	**54C** Borough Gardens	**52A** Gateshead		
65713	*J25*	HLD Hull Dairycoates	**53A** Hull Dairycoates	**54B** Tyne Dock	**54B** Tyne Dock	**52H** Tyne Dock		
65714	*J25*	CUD Cudworth	**53E** Cudworth	**50F** Malton	**50A** York	**50A** York		
65715	*J25*	AUK West Auckland						
65716	*J25*	TDK Tyne Dock	**54B** Tyne Dock	**54B** Tyne Dock				
65717	*J25*	KBY Kirkby Stephen	**51H** Kirkby Stephen	**51H** Kirkby Stephen	**54B** Tyne Dock			
65718	*J25*	AUK West Auckland	**51E** Stockton on Tees					
65720	*J25*	HTN Heaton	**51A** Darlington	**51J** Northallerton	**51D** Middlesbrough	**51L** Thornaby		
65721	*J25*	TDK Tyne Dock						
65723	*J25*	YK York	**50A** York	**50F** Malton				
65724	*J25*	HLS Hull Springhead						
65725	*J25*	MID Middlesbrough						
65726	*J25*	MID Middlesbrough	**51D** Middlesbrough	**51J** Northallerton	**53A** Hull Dairycoates	**52G** Sunderland		
65727	*J25*	HTN Heaton	**52D** Tweedmouth	**52D** Tweedmouth	**52F** South Blyth	**52F** South Blyth		
65728	*J25*	HLS Hull Springhead	**53C** Hull Springhead	**54C** Borough Gardens	**54C** Borough Gardens	**52A** Gateshead		
65730	*J26*	NPT Newport	**51B** Newport	**51B** Newport	**51B** Newport			
65731	*J26*	NPT Newport	**51B** Newport	**51B** Newport	**51F** West Auckland	**51F** West Auckland		
65732	*J26*	WHL West Hartlepool	**51B** Newport	**51B** Newport	**51B** Newport			
65733	*J26*	MID Middlesbrough	**51D** Middlesbrough	**51B** Newport	**51F** West Auckland			
65734	*J26*	NPT Newport	**51B** Newport	**51B** Newport	**51B** Newport			
65735	*J26*	NPT Newport	**51B** Newport	**51B** Newport	**51F** West Auckland	**51F** West Auckland		
65736	*J26*	NPT Newport	**51B** Newport	**51B** Newport	**51B** Newport	**51L** Thornaby		
65737	*J26*	NPT Newport	**51B** Newport	**51D** Middlesbrough	**51D** Middlesbrough			
65738	*J26*	NPT Newport	**51B** Newport	**51B** Newport	**51B** Newport			
65739	*J26*	NPT Newport	**51B** Newport	**51E** Stockton on Tees	**51E** Stockton on Tees			
65740	*J26*	NPT Newport	**51B** Newport	**51B** Newport	**51B** Newport			
65741	*J26*	NPT Newport	**51B** Newport	**51B** Newport	**51B** Newport	**51L** Thornaby		
65742	*J26*	NPT Newport	**51B** Newport	**51B** Newport	**51B** Newport			
65743	*J26*	NPT Newport	**51B** Newport	**51B** Newport	**51B** Newport	**51L** Thornaby		
65744	*J26*	NPT Newport	**51B** Newport	**51B** Newport	**51B** Newport			
65745	*J26*	NPT Newport	**51B** Newport	**51B** Newport	**51B** Newport	**51L** Thornaby		
65746	*J26*	NPT Newport	**51B** Newport	**51B** Newport	**51B** Newport			
65747	*J26*	WHL West Hartlepool	**51C** West Hartlepool	**51C** West Hartlepool	**51C** West Hartlepool	**51L** Thornaby		
65748	*J26*	WHL West Hartlepool	**51C** West Hartlepool	**51C** West Hartlepool	**51C** West Hartlepool			
65749	*J26*	NPT Newport	**51B** Newport	**51B** Newport	**51B** Newport			
65750	*J26*	NPT Newport	**51B** Newport	**51B** Newport	**51B** Newport			
65751	*J26*	NPT Newport	**51B** Newport	**51B** Newport	**51B** Newport	**51L** Thornaby		
65752	*J26*	NPT Newport	**51B** Newport	**51B** Newport	**51B** Newport			
65753	*J26*	NPT Newport	**51B** Newport	**51B** Newport	**51B** Newport	**51L** Thornaby		
65754	*J26*	NPT Newport	**51B** Newport	**51B** Newport	**51B** Newport			
65755	*J26*	NPT Newport	**51B** Newport	**51B** Newport	**51B** Newport	**51L** Thornaby		
65756	*J26*	NPT Newport	**51B** Newport	**51B** Newport	**51B** Newport	**51L** Thornaby		
65757	*J26*	NPT Newport	**51B** Newport	**51B** Newport	**51B** Newport	**51L** Thornaby		
65758	*J26*	NPT Newport	**51B** Newport	**51B** Newport	**51B** Newport			
65759	*J26*	NPT Newport	**51B** Newport	**51B** Newport	**51B** Newport			
65760	*J26*	NPT Newport	**51B** Newport	**51B** Newport	**51B** Newport	**51L** Thornaby		
65761	*J26*	NPT Newport	**51B** Newport	**51B** Newport	**51B** Newport	**51L** Thornaby		
65762	*J26*	NPT Newport	**51B** Newport	**51B** Newport	**51B** Newport	**51L** Thornaby		
65763	*J26*	NPT Newport	**51B** Newport	**51B** Newport	**51B** Newport	**51L** Thornaby		
65764	*J26*	MID Middlesbrough	**51D** Middlesbrough	**51E** Stockton on Tees	**51E** Stockton on Tees			
65765	*J26*	NPT Newport	**51B** Newport	**51B** Newport	**51B** Newport			
65766	*J26*	NPT Newport	**51B** Newport	**51B** Newport	**51B** Newport			
65767	*J26*	NPT Newport	**51B** Newport	**51B** Newport	**51B** Newport			
65768	*J26*	NPT Newport	**51B** Newport	**51B** Newport	**51B** Newport	**51L** Thornaby		
65769	*J26*	NPT Newport	**51B** Newport	**51B** Newport	**51B** Newport	**51L** Thornaby		
65770	*J26*	NPT Newport	**51B** Newport	**51B** Newport	**51B** Newport			
65771	*J26*	MID Middlesbrough	**51D** Middlesbrough	**51E** Stockton on Tees	**51E** Stockton on Tees			
65772	*J26*	NPT Newport	**51B** Newport	**51B** Newport	**51B** Newport	**51L** Thornaby		
65773	*J26*	NPT Newport	**51B** Newport	**51B** Newport	**51B** Newport	**51L** Thornaby		
65774	*J26*	NPT Newport	**51B** Newport	**51B** Newport	**51B** Newport	**51L** Thornaby		
65775	*J26*	MID Middlesbrough	**51D** Middlesbrough	**51D** Middlesbrough	**51D** Middlesbrough			
65776	*J26*	MID Middlesbrough	**51D** Middlesbrough	**51D** Middlesbrough	**51D** Middlesbrough	**51L** Thornaby		
65777	*J26*	NPT Newport	**51B** Newport	**51B** Newport	**51B** Newport	**51L** Thornaby		
65778	*J26*	NPT Newport	**51B** Newport	**51B** Newport	**51B** Newport	**51L** Thornaby		
65779	*J26*	MID Middlesbrough	**51D** Middlesbrough	**51D** Middlesbrough	**51D** Middlesbrough	**51L** Thornaby		
65780	*J27*	PMN Percy Main	**52E** Percy Main	**52E** Percy Main	**52E** Percy Main			
65781	*J27*	HTN Heaton	**52F** South Blyth	**52F** South Blyth	**52F** South Blyth			
65782	*J27*	NMN Normanton	**51C** West Hartlepool	**51C** West Hartlepool	**51C** West Hartlepool	**51C** West Hartlepool		
65783	*J27*	NBH North Blyth	**52F** North Blyth	**52F** North Blyth	**52F** North Blyth			
65784	*J27*	PMN Percy Main	**52E** Percy Main	**52E** Percy Main	**52E** Percy Main			
65785	*J27*	SUN Sunderland	**54A** Sunderland	**54A** Sunderland	**54C** Borough Gardens			
65786	*J27*	NBH North Blyth	**52F** North Blyth	**52F** North Blyth	**52F** North Blyth	**52F** North Blyth		
65787	*J27*	HAV Haverton Hill	**51G** Haverton Hill	**51G** Haverton Hill	**51G** Haverton Hill	**51L** Thornaby		
65788	*J27*	SKN Stockton on Tees	**52B** Heaton	**51E** Stockton on Tees	**51E** Stockton on Tees	**51L** Thornaby	**52G** Sunderland	**52G** Sunderland
65789	*J27*	NBH North Blyth	**52F** North Blyth	**52F** North Blyth	**52F** North Blyth	**52F** North Blyth	**52F** North Blyth	**52F** North Blyth
65790	*J27*	WHL West Hartlepool	**51C** West Hartlepool	**51G** Haverton Hill	**51G** Haverton Hill	**51L** Thornaby	**52E** Percy Main	**52F** South Blyth
65791	*J27*	PMN Percy Main	**52E** Percy Main	**52E** Percy Main	**52E** Percy Main	**52E** Percy Main	**52E** Percy Main	
65792	*J27*	PMN Percy Main	**52F** North Blyth	**52F** North Blyth	**52F** North Blyth	**52F** North Blyth	**52F** North Blyth	
65793	*J27*	SUN Sunderland	**50C** Selby	**50C** Selby	**50A** York			
65794	*J27*	HTN Heaton	**52F** North Blyth	**52F** North Blyth	**52F** North Blyth	**52F** North Blyth	**52F** North Blyth	
65795	*J27*	HTN Heaton	**52E** Percy Main	**52E** Percy Main	**52E** Percy Main	**52E** Percy Main	**52E** Percy Main	**52F** South Blyth
65796	*J27*	PMN Percy Main	**52E** Percy Main	**52E** Percy Main	**52E** Percy Main	**52E** Percy Main	**52B** Heaton	**52F** North Blyth
65797	*J27*	NBH North Blyth	**52F** North Blyth	**52F** North Blyth	**52F** North Blyth	**52F** North Blyth		
65798	*J27*	SUN Sunderland	**54A** Sunderland	**54A** Sunderland	**54A** Sunderland			

No.	Class	1948		1951	1954	1957	1960	1963	1966
65799	J27	NBH	North Blyth	52F North Blyth	52E Percy Main	52E Percy Main	52F South Blyth		
65800	J27	SKN	Stockton on Tees	52B Heaton	52F North Blyth	52F North Blyth	52F North Blyth		
65801	J27	NBH	North Blyth	52F North Blyth	52F North Blyth	52F North Blyth	52F North Blyth	52F North Blyth	52F North Blyth
65802	J27	PMN	Percy Main	52E Percy Main	52E Percy Main	52E Percy Main	52E Percy Main	52E Percy Main	52F North Blyth
65803	J27	WHL	West Hartlepool	51C West Hartlepool	51C West Hartlepool	51C West Hartlepool			
65804	J27	NBH	North Blyth	52F North Blyth	52F North Blyth	52F North Blyth	52F North Blyth	52F North Blyth	52F North Blyth
65805	J27	SKN	Stockton on Tees	51G Haverton Hill	51G Haverton Hill	51G Haverton Hill	51C West Hartlepool	52E Percy Main	52F South Blyth
65806	J27	HTN	Heaton	52E Percy Main	52E Percy Main	52E Percy Main			
65807	J27	SKN	Stockton on Tees	52B Heaton	52E Percy Main	52E Percy Main	52E Percy Main		
65808	J27	SBH	South Blyth	52F South Blyth	52F South Blyth	52F South Blyth	52F South Blyth	52F South Blyth	
65809	J27	PMN	Percy Main	52E Percy Main	52E Percy Main	52E Percy Main	52E Percy Main	52E Percy Main	52F South Blyth
65810	J27	SBH	South Blyth	52F South Blyth	52F South Blyth	52F South Blyth	52F South Blyth	52F South Blyth	
65811	J27	NBH	North Blyth	52F North Blyth	52F North Blyth	52F North Blyth	52F North Blyth	52F North Blyth	52F North Blyth
65812	J27	PMN	Percy Main	52E Percy Main	52E Percy Main	52E Percy Main	52E Percy Main	52E Percy Main	52F South Blyth
65813	J27	PMN	Percy Main	52E Percy Main	52E Percy Main	52E Percy Main	52E Percy Main	52E Percy Main	52F South Blyth
65814	J27	PMN	Percy Main	52E Percy Main	52E Percy Main	52E Percy Main	52E Percy Main	52E Percy Main	52F South Blyth
65815	J27	PMN	Percy Main	52E Percy Main	52F North Blyth	52F North Blyth	52F North Blyth	52F North Blyth	52F North Blyth
65816	J27	WHL	West Hartlepool	51C West Hartlepool	51C West Hartlepool	51C West Hartlepool			
65817	J27	SUN	Sunderland	54A Sunderland	54A Sunderland	54A Sunderland	52G Sunderland	54A Sunderland	52G Sunderland
65818	J27	HAV	Haverton Hill	51C West Hartlepool	51C West Hartlepool	51C West Hartlepool	51C West Hartlepool		
65819	J27	NBH	North Blyth	52F North Blyth	52F North Blyth	52F North Blyth	52F North Blyth	52F North Blyth	52F South Blyth
65820	J27	SUN	Sunderland	51C West Hartlepool	51C West Hartlepool	51C West Hartlepool	51C West Hartlepool	51L Thornaby	
65821	J27	PMN	Percy Main	52E Percy Main	52E Percy Main	52E Percy Main	52E Percy Main	52E Percy Main	52F South Blyth
65822	J27	PMN	Percy Main	52E Percy Main	52F South Blyth	52F South Blyth	52F South Blyth	52F South Blyth	
65823	J27	SUN	Sunderland	54A Sunderland	54A Sunderland	54C Borough Gardens	52G Sunderland	52G Sunderland	50A York
65824	J27	HTN	Heaton	52F South Blyth	52F South Blyth	52F South Blyth			
65825	J27	PMN	Percy Main	52E Percy Main	52E Percy Main	52E Percy Main	52E Percy Main	52E Percy Main	52F South Blyth
65826	J27	PMN	Percy Main	52E Percy Main	52E Percy Main	52E Percy Main			
65827	J27	SEL	Selby	50C Selby	50A York	50F Malton			
65828	J27	NBH	North Blyth	52F North Blyth	52F North Blyth	52F North Blyth	52F North Blyth	52F North Blyth	
65829	J27	SBH	South Blyth	52F South Blyth	52F South Blyth	52F South Blyth			
65830	J27	HAV	Haverton Hill	51G Haverton Hill	51G Haverton Hill	51G Haverton Hill	51C West Hartlepool	52G Sunderland	
65831	J27	PMN	Percy Main	52E Percy Main	52E Percy Main	52E Percy Main	52E Percy Main	52E Percy Main	52G Sunderland
65832	J27	WHL	West Hartlepool	54A Sunderland	54A Sunderland	54A Sunderland	52G Sunderland	54A Sunderland	52G Sunderland
65833	J27	SUN	Sunderland	54A Sunderland	54A Sunderland	54A Sunderland	52G Sunderland	54A Sunderland	52G Sunderland
65834	J27	SBH	South Blyth	52F South Blyth	52F South Blyth	52F South Blyth	52F South Blyth	52F South Blyth	52F North Blyth
65835	J27	SUN	Sunderland	54A Sunderland	54A Sunderland	54A Sunderland	52G Sunderland	54A Sunderland	52G Sunderland
65836	J27	SEL	Selby	54A Sunderland	54A Sunderland	54A Sunderland			
65837	J27	PMN	Percy Main	52E Percy Main	52E Percy Main	52E Percy Main	52E Percy Main		
65838	J27	PMN	Percy Main	52E Percy Main	52F South Blyth	52F South Blyth	52F South Blyth	52F South Blyth	52F South Blyth
65839	J27	PMN	Percy Main	52E Percy Main	52E Percy Main	52E Percy Main	52E Percy Main		
65840	J27	SUN	Sunderland	54A Sunderland	54A Sunderland	54A Sunderland			
65841	J27	WHL	West Hartlepool	54A Sunderland	54A Sunderland	54A Sunderland	52G Sunderland	54A Sunderland	
65842	J27	HTN	Heaton	52B Heaton	52E Percy Main	52E Percy Main	52E Percy Main	52E Percy Main	52F South Blyth
65843	J27	SUN	Sunderland	54A Sunderland	54A Sunderland	54A Sunderland			
65844	J27	SEL	Selby	50C Selby	50A York	50F Malton	50F Malton	50F Malton	
65845	J27	SEL	Selby	50A York	50A York	50A York	50A York	52F North Blyth	
65846	J27	SUN	Sunderland	51C West Hartlepool	51C West Hartlepool	51C West Hartlepool	51C West Hartlepool	52G Sunderland	
65847	J27	SUN	Sunderland	54A Sunderland	54A Sunderland	54A Sunderland	52F South Blyth		
65848	J27	SEL	Selby	50C Selby	50A York	50F Malton			
65849	J27	SEL	Selby	50A York	50A York	50F Malton	50F Malton	50F Malton	
65850	J27	WHL	West Hartlepool	54A Sunderland	54A Sunderland	54A Sunderland	52G Sunderland	52E Percy Main	
65851	J27	NBH	North Blyth	52F North Blyth	52F North Blyth	52F North Blyth	52F North Blyth	52F North Blyth	
65852	J27	PMN	Percy Main	52E Percy Main	52E Percy Main	52E Percy Main	52E Percy Main	52B Heaton	
65853	J27	HAV	Haverton Hill	51G Haverton Hill	51G Haverton Hill	51G Haverton Hill	51L Thornaby	52G Sunderland	52G Sunderland
65854	J27	SUN	Sunderland	54A Sunderland	54A Sunderland	54A Sunderland	52G Sunderland	54A Sunderland	
65855	J27	HAV	Haverton Hill	51G Haverton Hill	51G Haverton Hill	51G Haverton Hill	51L Thornaby	51L Thornaby	52F South Blyth
65856	J27	SUN	Sunderland	54A Sunderland	54A Sunderland	54A Sunderland			
65857	J27	SKN	Stockton on Tees	50G Whitby	50C Selby	50A York	52F North Blyth	52F North Blyth	
65858	J27	PMN	Percy Main	52E Percy Main	52E Percy Main	52E Percy Main	52E Percy Main	52E Percy Main	
65859	J27	HAV	Haverton Hill	51G Haverton Hill	51G Haverton Hill	51G Haverton Hill	51L Thornaby	51L Thornaby	51A Darlington
65860	J27	SKN	Stockton on Tees	51E Stockton on Tees	51B Newport	51A Darlington	51A Darlington	52E Percy Main	52F South Blyth
65861	J27	NEV	Leeds Neville Hill	50A York	50A York	50C Selby	52F South Blyth	52F South Blyth	52F South Blyth
65862	J27	HTN	Heaton	52B Heaton	52F South Blyth	52F South Blyth	52F South Blyth	52F South Blyth	
65863	J27	HTN	Heaton	52B Heaton	52F North Blyth	52F North Blyth	52F North Blyth		
65864	J27	HTN	Heaton	52B Heaton	52F North Blyth	52B Heaton	52B Heaton	52B Heaton	
65865	J27	SUN	Sunderland	51G Haverton Hill	51C West Hartlepool	51C West Hartlepool	51L Thornaby	52G Sunderland	52G Sunderland
65866	J27	HAV	Haverton Hill	51C West Hartlepool	51C West Hartlepool	51C West Hartlepool			
65867	J27	NBH	North Blyth	52F North Blyth	52F North Blyth	52F North Blyth	52F North Blyth		
65868	J27	SAL	Saltburn	51E Stockton on Tees	51E Stockton on Tees	51E Stockton on Tees	51L Thornaby		
65869	J27	TWD	Tweedmouth	52B Heaton	52B Heaton	52B Heaton	52B Heaton	52G Sunderland	52F North Blyth
65870	J27	SKN	Stockton on Tees	52F North Blyth	52F North Blyth	51D Middlesbrough	51L Thornaby	52G Sunderland	
65871	J27	WHL	West Hartlepool	54A Sunderland	54A Sunderland	54A Sunderland	52G Sunderland	54A Sunderland	
65872	J27	SUN	Sunderland	54A Sunderland	54A Sunderland	54A Sunderland	52G Sunderland	54A Sunderland	52G Sunderland
65873	J27	TWD	Tweedmouth	52B Heaton	52B Heaton	54C Borough Gardens	52G Sunderland	52G Sunderland	52G Sunderland
65874	J27	SEL	Selby	50C Selby	50A York	50A York	50A York	52G Sunderland	52F South Blyth
65875	J27	SEL	Selby	50C Selby	50C Selby	50C Selby	52F North Blyth	52F North Blyth	
65876	J27	NBH	North Blyth	52F North Blyth	52F North Blyth	52B Heaton	52B Heaton	52F South Blyth	
65877	J27	NBH	North Blyth	52F North Blyth	52F North Blyth	52F South Blyth	52F South Blyth		
65878	J27	SUN	Sunderland	54A Sunderland	54A Sunderland	54A Sunderland	52G Sunderland	54A Sunderland	
65879	J27	NBH	North Blyth	52F North Blyth	52F North Blyth	52B Heaton	52F North Blyth	52F North Blyth	52F North Blyth
65880	J27	NBH	North Blyth	52F North Blyth	52F North Blyth	52F North Blyth	52F North Blyth	52F North Blyth	52F North Blyth
65881	J27	SEL	Selby	50C Selby	50C Selby	50C Selby	52F North Blyth	52B Heaton	
65882	J27	SEL	Selby	50C Selby	50C Selby	52B Heaton	52F North Blyth	52B Heaton	52F South Blyth
65883	J27	NEV	Leeds Neville Hill	50A York	50A York	50A York	50A York	52G Sunderland	
65884	J27	SUN	Sunderland	51K Saltburn	51K Saltburn	51E Stockton on Tees	51L Thornaby	51L Thornaby	
65885	J27	NEV	Leeds Neville Hill	50A York	50A York	50C Selby	50F Malton	52G Sunderland	52G Sunderland
65886	J27	HTN	Heaton	52B Heaton	52F North Blyth	52B Heaton			
65887	J27	SKN	Stockton on Tees	50G Whitby	50A York	50A York	50A York	52G Sunderland	
65888	J27	NEV	Leeds Neville Hill	50A York	50C Selby	50C Selby	50F Malton	50F Malton	
65889	J27	HTN	Heaton	52B Heaton	52F North Blyth	52F North Blyth	52F North Blyth	52F North Blyth	
65890	J27	SEL	Selby	50A York	50A York	50A York	50A York	52F South Blyth	
65891	J27	SEL	Selby	50C Selby	50C Selby	50C Selby	52F South Blyth	52F South Blyth	
65892	J27	NBH	North Blyth	52F North Blyth	52F North Blyth	54A Sunderland	52G Sunderland	54A Sunderland	52F North Blyth
65893	J27	HTN	Heaton	52B Heaton	52B Heaton	54A Sunderland	52F North Blyth	52F North Blyth	52F South Blyth
65894	J27	NEV	Leeds Neville Hill	50A York	50A York	50A York	50A York	50A York	50A York
65900	J38	DFU	Dunfermline Upper	62C Dunfermline Upper	62C Dunfermline Upper	62A Thornton Junction	62A Thornton Junction	62A Thornton Junction	
65901	J38	THJ	Thornton Junction	62A Thornton Junction	62A Thornton Junction	62A Thornton Junction	62A Thornton Junction	62A Thornton Junction	62A Thornton Junction
65902	J38	THJ	Thornton Junction	62A Thornton Junction	62A Thornton Junction	62A Thornton Junction	62A Thornton Junction	62A Thornton Junction	
65903	J38	THJ	Thornton Junction	62A Thornton Junction	62A Thornton Junction	62A Thornton Junction	62A Thornton Junction	62C Dunfermline Upper	62C Dunfermline Upper
65904	J38	THJ	Thornton Junction	62A Thornton Junction	62A Thornton Junction	62A Thornton Junction	62A Thornton Junction	62A Thornton Junction	
65905	J38	DFU	Dunfermline Upper	62C Dunfermline Upper	62C Dunfermline Upper	62A Thornton Junction	62A Thornton Junction	62A Thornton Junction	62A Thornton Junction
65906	J38	STM	St. Margarets	64A St. Margarets	64A St. Margarets	64A St. Margarets	64A St. Margarets	62C Dunfermline Upper	
65907	J38	THJ	Thornton Junction	62A Thornton Junction	62A Thornton Junction	62A Thornton Junction	62A Thornton Junction	62A Thornton Junction	62A Thornton Junction
65908	J38	THJ	Thornton Junction	62A Thornton Junction	62A Thornton Junction	62A Thornton Junction	62A Thornton Junction	62A Thornton Junction	
65909	J38	DFU	Dunfermline Upper	64E Polmont	64E Polmont	64E Polmont	64E Polmont	65K Polmont	62A Thornton Junction
65910	J38	THJ	Thornton Junction	62A Thornton Junction	62A Thornton Junction	62A Thornton Junction	62A Thornton Junction	62A Thornton Junction	62A Thornton Junction
65911	J38	THJ	Thornton Junction	62A Thornton Junction	62A Thornton Junction	62A Thornton Junction	62A Thornton Junction	62A Thornton Junction	62A Thornton Junction
65912	J38	STM	St. Margarets	64A St. Margarets	64A St. Margarets	64A St. Margarets	64A St. Margarets	64A St. Margarets	62C Dunfermline Upper
65913	J38	THJ	Thornton Junction	62A Thornton Junction	62A Thornton Junction	62A Thornton Junction	62A Thornton Junction	62A Thornton Junction	
65914	J38	STM	St. Margarets	64A St. Margarets	64A St. Margarets	64A St. Margarets	64A St. Margarets	64A St. Margarets	62A Thornton Junction
65915	J38	STM	St. Margarets	64A St. Margarets	64A St. Margarets	64A St. Margarets	64A St. Margarets	64A St. Margarets	62A Thornton Junction
65916	J38	DFU	Dunfermline Upper	62C Dunfermline Upper	62C Dunfermline Upper	64A St. Margarets	64A St. Margarets	62A Thornton Junction	
65917	J38	DFU	Dunfermline Upper	64E Polmont	64E Polmont	64E Polmont	64E Polmont	65K Polmont	62C Dunfermline Upper

		1948	1951	1954	1957	1960	1963	1966
65918	*J38*	**STM** St. Margarets	**64A** St. Margarets	**64A** St. Margarets	**64A** St. Margarets	**64A** St. Margarets	**64A** St. Margarets	**62C** Dunfermline Upper
65919	*J38*	**STM** St. Margarets	**64A** St. Margarets	**64A** St. Margarets	**64A** St. Margarets	**64A** St. Margarets	**64A** St. Margarets	
65920	*J38*	**STM** St. Margarets	**64A** St. Margarets	**64A** St. Margarets	**64A** St. Margarets	**64A** St. Margarets	**64A** St. Margarets	**62A** Thornton Junction
65921	*J38*	**THJ** Thornton Junction	**62A** Thornton Junction	**62A** Thornton Junction	**62A** Thornton Junction	**62A** Thornton Junction	**62A** Thornton Junction	**62A** Thornton Junction
65922	*J38*	**DFU** Dunfermline Upper	**62C** Dunfermline Upper	**62C** Dunfermline Upper	**64A** St. Margarets	**64A** St. Margarets	**64A** St. Margarets	**62A** Thornton Junction
65923	*J38*	**DFU** Dunfermline Upper	**62C** Dunfermline Upper	**62C** Dunfermline Upper	**62C** Dunfermline Upper	**62C** Dunfermline Upper		
65924	*J38*	**DFU** Dunfermline Upper	**62C** Dunfermline Upper	**62C** Dunfermline Upper	**62C** Dunfermline Upper	**62C** Dunfermline Upper	**62C** Dunfermline Upper	
65925	*J38*	**THJ** Thornton Junction	**62A** Thornton Junction	**62A** Thornton Junction	**62A** Thornton Junction	**62A** Thornton Junction	**62A** Thornton Junction	**62A** Thornton Junction
65926	*J38*	**DFU** Dunfermline Upper	**62C** Dunfermline Upper	**62C** Dunfermline Upper	**62C** Dunfermline Upper	**62C** Dunfermline Upper	**62C** Dunfermline Upper	
65927	*J38*	**STM** St. Margarets	**64A** St. Margarets	**64A** St. Margarets	**64A** St. Margarets	**64A** St. Margarets	**64A** St. Margarets	
65928	*J38*	**DFU** Dunfermline Upper	**62C** Dunfermline Upper	**62C** Dunfermline Upper	**62C** Dunfermline Upper	**62C** Dunfermline Upper		
65929	*J38*	**STM** St. Margarets	**64A** St. Margarets	**64A** St. Margarets	**64A** St. Margarets	**64A** St. Margarets	**64A** St. Margarets	**62C** Dunfermline Upper
65930	*J38*	**DFU** Dunfermline Upper	**62C** Dunfermline Upper	**62C** Dunfermline Upper	**62C** Dunfermline Upper	**62C** Dunfermline Upper	**62C** Dunfermline Upper	**62C** Dunfermline Upper
65931	*J38*	**THJ** Thornton Junction	**62A** Thornton Junction	**62A** Thornton Junction	**62A** Thornton Junction	**62A** Thornton Junction	**62C** Dunfermline Upper	**62C** Dunfermline Upper
65932	*J38*	**THJ** Thornton Junction	**62A** Thornton Junction	**62A** Thornton Junction	**62A** Thornton Junction	**62A** Thornton Junction	**62A** Thornton Junction	**62A** Thornton Junction
65933	*J38*	**DFU** Dunfermline Upper	**62C** Dunfermline Upper	**62C** Dunfermline Upper	**62C** Dunfermline Upper	**62C** Dunfermline Upper	**62C** Dunfermline Upper	
65934	*J38*	**DFU** Dunfermline Upper	**62C** Dunfermline Upper	**62C** Dunfermline Upper	**64A** St. Margarets	**64A** St. Margarets	**64A** St. Margarets	**62C** Dunfermline Upper
67093	*F7*	**STM** St. Margarets						
67094	*F7*	**STM** St. Margarets						
67097	*F1*	**GOR** Gorton						
67099	*F1*	**LIV** Brunswick						
67100	*F1*	**LIV** Brunswick						
67104	*F2*	**ARD** Ardsley						
67105	*F2*	**ANN** Annesley						
67106	*F2*	**KX** Kings Cross						
67107	*F2*	**ANN** Annesley						
67108	*F2*	**KX** Kings Cross						
67109	*F2*	**YAR** Yarmouth South Town						
67111	*F2*	**KX** Kings Cross						
67112	*F2*	**YB** Yarmouth Beach						
67113	*F2*	**KX** Kings Cross						
67114	*F3*	**LOW** Lowestoft						
67115	*F3*	**CAM** Cambridge						
67117	*F3*	**CAM** Cambridge						
67119	*F3*	**LOW** Lowestoft						
67124	*F3*	**BSE** Bury St. Edmunds						
67126	*F3*	**LOW** Lowestoft						
67127	*F3*	**NOR** Norwich Thorpe	**32C** Lowestoft					
67128	*F3*	**IPS** Ipswich						
67134	*F3*	**NOR** Norwich Thorpe						
67139	*F3*	**NOR** Norwich Thorpe						
67140	*F3*	**MC** Melton Constable						
67141	*F3*	**LOW** Lowestoft						
67143	*F3*	**IPS** Ipswich						
67149	*F3*	**KL** Kings Lynn						
67150	*F3*	**MC** Melton Constable						
67151	*F4*	**KIT** Kittybrewster	**61A** Kittybrewster					
67152	*F4*	**MC** Melton Constable	**32G** Melton Constable					
67153	*F4*	**MC** Melton Constable	**31B** March					
67154	*F4*	**YAR** Yarmouth South Town	**32D** Yarmouth South Town					
67155	*F4*	**MAL** Malton	**50F** Malton					
67156	*F4*	**NOR** Norwich Thorpe						
67157	*F4*	**YB** Yarmouth Beach	**61A** Kittybrewster	**61A** Kittybrewster				
67158	*F4*	**LOW** Lowestoft	**32C** Lowestoft					
67159	*F4*	**STR** Stratford						
67160	*F4*	**BSE** Bury St. Edmunds						
67161	*F4*	**STR** Stratford						
67162	*F4*	**YB** Yarmouth Beach	**32G** Melton Constable	**32E** Yarmouth Vauxhall				
67163	*F4*	**LOW** Lowestoft	**32C** Lowestoft					
67164	*F4*	**KIT** Kittybrewster	**61A** Kittybrewster					
67165	*F4*	**LOW** Lowestoft	**32C** Lowestoft					
67166	*F4*	**LOW** Lowestoft	**32C** Lowestoft					
67167	*F4*	**LOW** Lowestoft	**32C** Lowestoft					
67168	*F4*	**STR** Stratford						
67169	*F4*	**STR** Stratford						
67170	*F4*	**STR** Stratford						
67171	*F4*	**HLD** Hull Dairycoates	**53A** Hull Dairycoates					
67172	*F4*	**STR** Stratford						
67173	*F4*	**STR** Stratford						
67174	*F4*	**NOR** Norwich Thorpe	**32C** Lowestoft	**32C** Lowestoft				
67175	*F4*	**HLD** Hull Dairycoates	**53A** Hull Dairycoates					
67176	*F4*	**NOR** Norwich Thorpe	**32A** Norwich Thorpe					
67177	*F4*	**LOW** Lowestoft	**32C** Lowestoft					
67178	*F4*	**NOR** Norwich Thorpe	**32A** Norwich Thorpe					
67179	*F4*	**STR** Stratford						
67180	*F4*	**STR** Stratford						
67181	*F4*	**STR** Stratford						
67182	*F4*	**IPS** Ipswich	**32C** Lowestoft					
67183	*F4*	**STR** Stratford						
67184	*F4*	**NOR** Norwich Thorpe	**32C** Lowestoft					
67185	*F4*	**STR** Stratford						
67186	*F4*	**NOR** Norwich Thorpe	**32C** Lowestoft					
67187	*F4*	**BSE** Bury St. Edmunds	**31B** March	**32C** Lowestoft				
67188	*F5*	**COL** Colchester	**30E** Colchester	**30A** Stratford				
67189	*F5*	**COL** Colchester	**30E** Colchester	**30E** Colchester				
67190	*F5*	**COL** Colchester	**30E** Colchester	**32C** Lowestoft				
67191	*F5*	**STR** Stratford	**30E** Colchester	**30E** Colchester				
67192	*F5*	**STR** Stratford	**30A** Stratford	**30A** Stratford	**30E** Colchester			
67193	*F5*	**STR** Stratford	**30A** Stratford	**30A** Stratford	**30A** Stratford			
67194	*F5*	**STR** Stratford	**30E** Colchester	**30A** Stratford				
67195	*F5*	**STR** Stratford	**30E** Colchester	**32C** Lowestoft	**30A** Stratford			
67196	*F5*	**STR** Stratford	**30E** Colchester	**30E** Colchester				
67197	*F5*	**STR** Stratford	**30A** Stratford	**30A** Stratford				
67198	*F5*	**STR** Stratford	**30A** Stratford	**30A** Stratford				
67199	*F5*	**STR** Stratford	**32D** Yarmouth South Town	**32D** Yarmouth South Town	**32D** Yarmouth South Town			
67200	*F5*	**STR** Stratford	**30A** Stratford	**30A** Stratford	**30A** Stratford			
67201	*F5*	**STR** Stratford	**32C** Lowestoft	**32C** Lowestoft				
67202	*F5*	**STR** Stratford	**30A** Stratford	**30A** Stratford	**30A** Stratford			
67203	*F5*	**STR** Stratford	**30A** Stratford	**30A** Stratford	**30A** Stratford			
67204	*F5*	**PKS** Parkeston	**30E** Colchester	**32C** Lowestoft				
67205	*F5*	**STR** Stratford	**30A** Stratford	**30A** Stratford				
67206	*F5*	**PKS** Parkeston	**30A** Stratford	**32C** Lowestoft				
67207	*F5*	**COL** Colchester	**30A** Stratford	**32C** Lowestoft				
67208	*F5*	**STR** Stratford	**30A** Stratford	**30A** Stratford	**30A** Stratford			
67209	*F5*	**STR** Stratford	**30A** Stratford	**30A** Stratford	**30A** Stratford			
67210	*F5*	**STR** Stratford	**30A** Stratford	**30A** Stratford				
67211	*F5*	**STR** Stratford	**30A** Stratford	**30A** Stratford				
67212	*F5*	**STR** Stratford	**30A** Stratford	**30A** Stratford	**30A** Stratford			
67213	*F5*	**COL** Colchester	**30A** Stratford	**30A** Stratford				
67214	*F5*	**STR** Stratford	**30A** Stratford	**32C** Lowestoft	**30A** Stratford			
67215	*F5*	**STR** Stratford	**30E** Colchester	**30A** Stratford				
67216	*F5*	**STR** Stratford	**32C** Lowestoft	**32C** Lowestoft				
67217	*F5*	**STR** Stratford	**30E** Colchester	**30E** Colchester				
67218	*F6→F5*	**STR** Stratford	**32D** Yarmouth South Town	**32D** Yarmouth South Town	**30A** Stratford			

No.	Class	1948		1951	1954	1957	1960	1963	1966
67219	F6→F5	STR	Stratford	30E Colchester	30A Stratford				
67220	F6	STR	Stratford	32B Ipswich	32B Ipswich				
67221	F6	STR	Stratford	31E Bury St. Edmunds	31A Cambridge	30A Stratford			
67222	F6	STR	Stratford	31A Cambridge	31E Bury St. Edmunds				
67223	F6	YB	Yarmouth Beach	32F Yarmouth Beach	32C Lowestoft				
67224	F6	STR	Stratford	32A Norwich Thorpe	32G Melton Constable				
67225	F6	STR	Stratford	32G Melton Constable	32G Melton Constable				
67226	F6	YB	Yarmouth Beach	32F Yarmouth Beach	32C Lowestoft				
67227	F6	STR	Stratford	31D South Lynn	31A Cambridge	30E Colchester			
67228	F6	STR	Stratford	32G Melton Constable	32G Melton Constable	30E Colchester			
67229	F6	PKS	Parkeston	32A Norwich Thorpe	32G Melton Constable	32C Lowestoft			
67230	F6	STR	Stratford	32B Ipswich	32B Ipswich	30A Stratford			
67231	F6	STR	Stratford	32C Lowestoft	32C Lowestoft	32C Lowestoft			
67232	F6	STR	Stratford	32A Norwich Thorpe	32C Lowestoft				
67233	F6	YB	Yarmouth Beach	32F Yarmouth Beach	32C Lowestoft				
67234	F6	YB	Yarmouth Beach	32F Yarmouth Beach	32C Lowestoft				
67235	F6	YB	Yarmouth Beach	32F Yarmouth Beach	32D Yarmouth South Town				
67236	F6	KL	Kings Lynn	31E Bury St. Edmunds	31E Bury St. Edmunds				
67237	F6	BSE	Bury St. Edmunds	31E Bury St. Edmunds	31E Bury St. Edmunds				
67238	F6	BSE	Bury St. Edmunds	31E Bury St. Edmunds	31A Cambridge				
67239	F6	KL	Kings Lynn	32B Ipswich	32B Ipswich				
67240	G5	NEV	Leeds Neville Hill	50B Leeds Neville Hill	50G Whitby				
67241	G5	HTN	Heaton	52C Blaydon	52C Blaydon				
67242	G5	HLB	Hull Botanic Gardens	51E Stockton on Tees					
67243	G5	SUN	Sunderland	54A Sunderland	54A Sunderland				
67244	G5	SBH	South Blyth	52F South Blyth					
67245	G5	HEX	Hexham	52C Hexham					
67246	G5	HTN	Heaton	52F South Blyth	52F South Blyth	52C Blaydon			
67247	G5	SUN	Sunderland	54A Sunderland	54A Sunderland				
67248	G5	TWD	Tweedmouth	52D Tweedmouth	52C Blaydon	54A Durham			
67249	G5	HTN	Heaton	52C Hexham	52C Hexham				
67250	G5	DAR	Darlington	50C Selby	50C Selby	50C Selby			
67251	G5	SUN	Sunderland	54A Sunderland	54A Sunderland				
67252	G5	SUN	Sunderland	54A Sunderland					
67253	G5	PAT	Pateley Bridge	50D Pateley Bridge	53B Hull Botanic Gardens	53B Hull Botanic Gardens			
67254	G5	SKN	Stockton on Tees	53B Hull Botanic Gardens	53B Hull Botanic Gardens	54A Sunderland			
67255	G5	BLA	Blaydon	52C Blaydon					
67256	G5	HLB	Hull Botanic Gardens	53B Hull Botanic Gardens	53B Hull Botanic Gardens	53D Bridlington			
67257	G5	SUN	Sunderland	54A Sunderland	54A Sunderland				
67258	G5	DUR	Durham	54A Durham	54A Durham	54A Durham			
67259	G5	BLA	Blaydon	52C Blaydon	52C Blaydon	54A Sunderland			
67260	G5	SUN	Sunderland	54A Sunderland					
67261	G5	SBH	South Blyth	52F South Blyth	52F South Blyth	53B Hull Botanic Gardens			
67262	G5	WBY	Whitby	50B Leeds Neville Hill	50B Leeds Neville Hill	50B Leeds Neville Hill			
67263	G5	DUR	Durham	54A Durham	54A Durham	52F South Blyth			
67264	G5	SUN	Sunderland	54A Sunderland					
67265	G5	BLA	Blaydon	52C Hexham	52C Hexham	52C Hexham			
67266	G5	HLB	Hull Botanic Gardens	50B Leeds Neville Hill	50B Leeds Neville Hill				
67267	G5	SUN	Sunderland	54A Sunderland	54A Sunderland				
67268	G5	HEX	Hexham	52C Hexham	52C Hexham				
67269	G5	SBK	Starbeck	30A Stratford	31A Cambridge				
67270	G5	SUN	Sunderland	54A Sunderland	52D Tweedmouth	54A Sunderland			
67271	G5	WHL	West Hartlepool	51C West Hartlepool	51C West Hartlepool				
67272	G5	SKN	Stockton on Tees	51C West Hartlepool	51C West Hartlepool				
67273	G5	MAL	Malton	51A Darlington	53B Hull Botanic Gardens	50C Selby			
67274	G5	NEV	Leeds Neville Hill	50B Leeds Neville Hill	50B Leeds Neville Hill	50B Leeds Neville Hill			
67275	G5	MAL	Malton	50F Malton					
67276	G5	MAL	Malton	54A Sunderland					
67277	G5	BLA	Blaydon	52C Blaydon	52C Blaydon	52F South Blyth			
67278	G5	NEV	Leeds Neville Hill	51E Stockton on Tees	51E Stockton on Tees	54A Sunderland			
67279	G5	HLB	Hull Botanic Gardens	30A Stratford	31A Cambridge				
67280	G5	HLB	Hull Botanic Gardens	53B Hull Botanic Gardens	53B Hull Botanic Gardens	56C Copley Hill			
67281	G5	GUI	Guisborough	51D Guisborough	51D Guisborough	52F South Blyth			
67282	G5	HLB	Hull Botanic Gardens	53B Hull Botanic Gardens	53B Hull Botanic Gardens	53B Hull Botanic Gardens			
67283	G5	SUN	Sunderland	54A Sunderland	54A Sunderland				
67284	G5	MAL	Malton	51A Darlington	51A Darlington				
67285	G5	SBH	South Blyth						
67286	G5	SBK	Starbeck	50C Selby	50C Selby				
67287	G5	KIT	Kittybrewster	61A Kittybrewster					
67288	G5	SKN	Stockton on Tees	54B Tyne Dock	51E Stockton on Tees				
67289	G5	SBK	Starbeck	50D Starbeck	50B Leeds Neville Hill				
67290	G5	NEV	Leeds Neville Hill	50B Leeds Neville Hill	50B Leeds Neville Hill				
67291	G5	WHL	West Hartlepool	51F West Auckland					
67292	G5	KEI	Keith	61C Keith					
67293	G5	WBY	Whitby	50B Leeds Neville Hill	50C Selby				
67294	G5	SKN	Stockton on Tees	51C West Hartlepool	51C West Hartlepool	54A Durham			
67295	G5	SBH	South Blyth	52F South Blyth	52F South Blyth				
67296	G5	RBY	Rothbury	52F Rothbury	52A Gateshead				
67297	G5	SUN	Sunderland	54A Sunderland	54A Sunderland	54A Sunderland			
67298	G5	DUR	Durham	54A Durham	54A Durham				
67299	G5	SUN	Sunderland						
67300	G5	SUN	Sunderland	54A Sunderland	54A Sunderland				
67301	G5	HLB	Hull Botanic Gardens	53B Hull Botanic Gardens	53B Hull Botanic Gardens				
67302	G5	WBY	Whitby	50G Whitby	50G Whitby				
67303	G5	HTN	Heaton	52D Tweedmouth					
67304	G5	HTN	Heaton	52D Tweedmouth	52C Blaydon				
67305	G5	HLB	Hull Botanic Gardens	51E Stockton on Tees	51A Darlington	51A Darlington			
67306	G5	AUK	West Auckland						
67307	G5	DUR	Durham	54A Durham	54A Durham				
67308	G5	WBY	Whitby	50B Leeds Neville Hill	50F Pickering				
67309	G5	MIT	Middleton in Teesdale	52A Gateshead	52C Hexham				
67310	G5	SUN	Sunderland	54A Sunderland	54A Sunderland				
67311	G5	HLB	Hull Botanic Gardens	53B Hull Botanic Gardens	53B Hull Botanic Gardens	56C Copley Hill			
67312	G5	AUK	West Auckland	51F West Auckland	51J Northallerton				
67313	G5	BLA	Blaydon	52C Hexham					
67314	G5	WHL	West Hartlepool	51C West Hartlepool	51A Darlington				
67315	G5	ALS	Alston	52C Alston	52C Alston	50F Malton			
67316	G5	WHL	West Hartlepool	51A Darlington	52C Blaydon				
67317	G5	AUK	West Auckland	51E Stockton on Tees					
67318	G5	SKN	Stockton on Tees	51E Stockton on Tees	51J Northallerton	54A Sunderland			
67319	G5	NEV	Leeds Neville Hill	50B Leeds Neville Hill	50B Leeds Neville Hill	50F Malton			
67320	G5	SBH	South Blyth	52A Gateshead	52A Gateshead	52F South Blyth			
67321	G5	HLB	Hull Botanic Gardens	53B Hull Botanic Gardens	53B Hull Botanic Gardens	54A Sunderland			
67322	G5	STR	Stratford	30A Stratford	31A Cambridge				
67323	G5	BLA	Blaydon	52C Blaydon	52C Blaydon	51D Middlesbrough			
67324	G5	NLN	Northallerton	51J Northallerton	51C West Hartlepool	51C West Hartlepool			
67325	G5	BLA	Blaydon	52A Gateshead	52C Blaydon	50F Malton			
67326	G5	SBH	South Blyth	52F South Blyth	52F South Blyth	52C Blaydon			
67327	G5	KIT	Kittybrewster	61A Kittybrewster	61C Keith				
67328	G5	SUN	Sunderland	54A Sunderland	54A Sunderland				
67329	G5	HEX	Hexham	52A Gateshead	52A Gateshead	52C Hexham			
67330	G5	MAL	Malton	50F Malton					
67331	G5	WHL	West Hartlepool	51C West Hartlepool					
67332	G5	SBK	Starbeck	50F Malton	50F Malton				

No.	Class	1948	1951	1954	1957	1960	1963	1966
67333	G5	HTN Heaton	51A Darlington	51C West Hartlepool				
67334	G5	SBH South Blyth	52F South Blyth	52F South Blyth				
67335	G5	WBY Whitby	50G Whitby					
67336	G5	SUN Sunderland	54A Sunderland	54A Sunderland				
67337	G5	ILK Ilkley	50B Ilkley	53B Hull Botanic Gardens	53B Hull Botanic Gardens			
67338	G5	MID Middlesbrough	51D Middlesbrough	51D Middlesbrough	54A Sunderland			
67339	G5	BLA Blaydon	52C Blaydon	52C Blaydon	52F South Blyth			
67340	G5	HLB Hull Botanic Gardens	53B Hull Botanic Gardens	53B Hull Botanic Gardens	52F South Blyth			
67341	G5	SBH South Blyth	52F South Blyth	52F South Blyth	52F South Blyth			
67342	G5	DAR Darlington	51A Darlington	51J Northallerton	54A Sunderland			
67343	G5	WHL West Hartlepool	51C West Hartlepool	51E Stockton on Tees	54A Sunderland			
67344	G5	NLN Northallerton	51J Northallerton	54A Sunderland				
67345	G5	AUK West Auckland	51F West Auckland	51A Darlington				
67346	G5	LEY Leyburn	51J Leyburn	51C West Hartlepool	50F Malton			
67347	G5	SBH South Blyth	52F South Blyth	52F South Blyth				
67348	G5	SUN Sunderland	54A Sunderland					
67349	G5	MAL Malton	50F Malton	50F Malton				
67350	C12	LIN Lincoln	40F Boston	35A New England				
67351	C12	LNG Langwith Junction						
67352	C12	LTH Louth	40C Louth	53B Hull Botanic Gardens	35C Spital Bridge			
67353	C12	COP Copley Hill	37B Copley Hill	53B Hull Botanic Gardens				
67354	C12	MC Melton Constable	53B Hull Botanic Gardens					
67355	C12	LNG Langwith Junction						
67356	C12	COP Copley Hill	34A Kings Cross					
67357	C12	LNG Langwith Junction	35A New England	35A New England	35A New England			
67358	C12	TFD Trafford Park						
67359	C12	LTH Louth						
67360	C12	CAM Cambridge	31A Cambridge	31C Kings Lynn				
67361	C12	NWE New England	35A New England	35A New England				
67362	C12	NWE New England	35C Spital Bridge	35C Spital Bridge	35B Grantham			
67363	C12	NWE New England	38B Annesley	38B Annesley	33B Tilbury			
67364	C12	LIN Lincoln	40C Louth	40C Louth				
67365	C12	NWE New England	35A New England	35A New England	35A New England			
67366	C12	CHR Chester Northgate	9E Trafford Park	35C Spital Bridge	32D Yarmouth South Town			
67367	C12	CAM Cambridge	31A Cambridge	31C Kings Lynn	31A Cambridge			
67368	C12	NWE New England	35A New England	35C Spital Bridge				
67369	C12	TFD Trafford Park	9E Trafford Park	35A New England				
67370	C12	TFD Trafford Park						
67371	C12	HLB Hull Botanic Gardens	53B Hull Botanic Gardens	53B Hull Botanic Gardens				
67372	C12	COP Copley Hill	37B Copley Hill					
67373	C12	NWE New England	35A New England					
67374	C12	LTH Louth	34A Kings Cross	31C Kings Lynn	31C Kings Lynn			
67375	C12	CAM Cambridge	31A Cambridge	31E Bury St. Edmunds				
67376	C12	HSY Hornsey	34B Hornsey	35A New England	35A New England			
67377	C12	COP Copley Hill						
67378	C12	TFD Trafford Park						
67379	C12	LTH Louth	40C Louth	40C Louth	35A New England			
67380	C12	GRA Grantham	35B Grantham	35B Grantham	35A New England			
67381	C12	LIN Lincoln	40C Louth					
67382	C12	GRA Grantham	35B Grantham	35B Grantham				
67383	C12	COP Copley Hill	40C Louth	40C Louth				
67384	C12	LNG Langwith Junction	40C Louth	40C Louth				
67385	C12	CAM Cambridge	31A Cambridge	31E Bury St. Edmunds				
67386	C12	COP Copley Hill	37A Ardsley	31C Kings Lynn	31C Kings Lynn			
67387	C12	BOS Boston	38B Annesley	32D Yarmouth South Town				
67388	C12	COP Copley Hill						
67389	C12	LTH Louth	31A Cambridge	35A New England				
67390	C12	NWE New England	35A New England					
67391	C12	HLB Hull Botanic Gardens	53B Hull Botanic Gardens	53B Hull Botanic Gardens	35B Grantham			
67392	C12	HLB Hull Botanic Gardens	53B Hull Botanic Gardens	53B Hull Botanic Gardens				
67393	C12	HLB Hull Botanic Gardens	53B Hull Botanic Gardens					
67394	C12	HLB Hull Botanic Gardens	53B Hull Botanic Gardens	53B Hull Botanic Gardens	35A New England			
67395	C12	HLB Hull Botanic Gardens	53B Hull Botanic Gardens	53B Hull Botanic Gardens	31A Cambridge			
67397	C12	HLB Hull Botanic Gardens	53B Hull Botanic Gardens	53B Hull Botanic Gardens	31A Cambridge			
67398	C12	LTH Louth	40C Louth	40C Louth	40B Immingham			
67399	C12	HLB Hull Botanic Gardens						
67400	C13	CHR Chester Northgate	6D Chester Northgate	6D Chester Northgate				
67401	C13	GOR Gorton	39A Gorton	39A Gorton				
67402	C13	GOR Gorton	39A Gorton	39A Gorton				
67403	C13	GOR Gorton	39A Gorton	39A Gorton				
67404	C13	SHF Sheffield Darnall	39B Sheffield Darnall					
67405	C13	GOR Gorton	39A Gorton	39A Gorton				
67406	C13	SHF Sheffield Darnall	39B Sheffield Darnall					
67407	C13	GOR Gorton	39A Gorton	39A Gorton				
67408	C13	GOR Gorton	39A Gorton	38D Staveley				
67409	C13	BRN Barnsley	36D Barnsley	36D Barnsley				
67410	C13	GOR Gorton	39A Gorton					
67411	C13	BRN Barnsley	36D Barnsley	36D Barnsley				
67412	C13	GOR Gorton	39A Gorton	6E Wrexham Rhosddu				
67413	C13	CHR Chester Northgate	6D Chester Northgate	6D Chester Northgate	6D Chester Northgate			
67414	C13	CHR Chester Northgate	6D Chester Northgate	6D Chester Northgate				
67415	C13	GOR Gorton	39A Gorton	39A Gorton				
67416	C13	GOR Gorton	34A Kings Cross	34E Neasden	34E Neasden			
67417	C13	GOR Gorton	39A Gorton	39A Gorton	39A Gorton	9G Gorton		
67418	C13	NEA Neasden	34E Neasden	34E Neasden	34E Neasden			
67419	C13	GOR Gorton	39A Gorton	38D Staveley	39A Gorton			
67420	C13	NEA Neasden	34E Neasden	34E Neasden	34E Neasden			
67421	C13	GOR Gorton	39A Gorton	39A Gorton	39A Gorton			
67422	C13	GOR Gorton	39A Gorton	39A Gorton				
67423	C13	GOR Gorton	39A Gorton	39A Gorton	39A Gorton			
67424	C13	GOR Gorton	39A Gorton	39B Sheffield Darnall	41A Sheffield Darnall			
67425	C13	GOR Gorton	39A Gorton	39A Gorton				
67426	C13	GOR Gorton	39A Gorton	39A Gorton				
67427	C13	GOR Gorton	39A Gorton	39A Gorton	56B Ardsley			
67428	C13	WRX Wrexham Rhosddu	6E Wrexham Rhosddu	6E Wrexham Rhosddu	6E Wrexham Rhosddu			
67429	C13	WRX Wrexham Rhosddu	6E Wrexham Rhosddu	6E Wrexham Rhosddu				
67430	C13	CHR Chester Northgate	6E Wrexham Rhosddu	6E Wrexham Rhosddu				
67431	C13	GOR Gorton	39A Gorton	39A Gorton				
67432	C13	WRX Wrexham Rhosddu	6E Wrexham Rhosddu	6E Wrexham Rhosddu				
67433	C13	WRX Wrexham Rhosddu	6D Chester Northgate	6D Chester Northgate	56C Copley Hill			
67434	C13	BRN Barnsley	36D Barnsley	36D Barnsley	36D Barnsley			
67435	C13	WRX Wrexham Rhosddu	6E Wrexham Rhosddu					
67436	C13	CHR Chester Northgate	6D Chester Northgate	6D Chester Northgate				
67437	C13	GOR Gorton	39A Gorton	39A Gorton	39A Gorton			
67438	C13	NEA Neasden	39A Gorton	39A Gorton	56C Copley Hill			
67439	C13	GOR Gorton	39A Gorton	39B Sheffield Darnall	41A Sheffield Darnall			
67440	C14	ARD Ardsley	37A Ardsley	39A Gorton	39A Gorton			
67441	C14	ARD Ardsley	37A Ardsley	39A Gorton	39A Gorton			
67442	C14	ARD Ardsley	6E Wrexham Rhosddu	6E Wrexham Rhosddu	6E Wrexham Rhosddu			
67443	C14	ARD Ardsley	37A Ardsley	37A Ardsley	39A Gorton			
67444	C14	ARD Ardsley	37A Ardsley	39A Gorton	39A Gorton			
67445	C14	ARD Ardsley	37A Ardsley	39A Gorton	39A Gorton			
67446	C14	ARD Ardsley	37A Ardsley	37A Ardsley	39A Gorton			
67447	C14	IPS Ipswich	37C Bradford Hammerton St	39A Gorton	39A Gorton			

		1948		1951	1954	1957	1960	1963	1966
67448	*C14*	IPS	Ipswich	**37C** Bradford Hammerton St	**39A** Gorton	**39A** Gorton			
67449	*C14*	ARD	Ardsley	**6E** Wrexham Rhosddu	**6E** Wrexham Rhosddu	**6E** Wrexham Rhosddu			
67450	*C14*	IPS	Ipswich	**37C** Bradford Hammerton St	**39A** Gorton	**39A** Gorton	**9G** Gorton		
67451	*C14*	ARD	Ardsley	**37A** Ardsley	**39A** Gorton	**39A** Gorton			
67452	*C15*	THJ	Thornton Junction	**62A** Thornton Junction	**62A** Thornton Junction				
67453	*C15*	DFU	Dunfermline Upper	**62C** Dunfermline Upper	**62C** Dunfermline Upper				
67454	*C15*	PKD	Parkhead	**65C** Parkhead	**65A** Eastfield				
67455	*C15*	PTH	Perth South	**61B** Aberdeen Ferryhill	**61A** Kittybrewster				
67456	*C15*	EFD	Eastfield	**65A** Eastfield	**65F** Grangemouth				
67457	*C15*	HAW	Hawick	**64G** Hawick	**64G** Hawick				
67458	*C15*	CAR	Carlisle Canal	**12B** Carlisle Canal	**68E** Carlisle Canal				
67459	*C15*	HAW	Hawick	**64G** Hawick	**64G** Hawick				
67460	*C15*	EFD	Eastfield	**65A** Eastfield	**65A** Eastfield	**65A** Eastfield	**65A** Eastfield		
67461	*C15*	DEE	Dundee Tay Bridge	**62B** Dundee Tay Bridge	**62A** Thornton Junction				
67462	*C15*	STG	Stirling Shore Road	**63B** Stirling	**64E** Polmont				
67463	*C15*	POL	Polmont	**64E** Polmont	**64E** Polmont				
67464	*C15*	POL	Polmont	**64E** Polmont					
67465	*C15*	HAW	Hawick	**64G** Hawick	**64G** Hawick				
67466	*C15*	DFU	Dunfermline Upper	**62C** Dunfermline Upper	**62B** Dundee Tay Bridge				
67467	*C15*	EFD	Eastfield	**65E** Kipps	**65E** Kipps				
67468	*C15*	POL	Polmont	**64E** Polmont					
67469	*C15*	DFU	Dunfermline Upper	**62C** Dunfermline Upper	**62C** Dunfermline Upper				
67470	*C15*	PKD	Parkhead	**65C** Parkhead	**65C** Parkhead				
67471	*C15*	DEE	Dundee Tay Bridge	**62B** Dundee Tay Bridge					
67472	*C15*	HAW	Hawick	**64G** Hawick	**64G** Hawick				
67473	*C15*	HAW	Hawick	**64E** Polmont	**64E** Polmont				
67474	*C15*	CAR	Carlisle Canal	**12B** Carlisle Canal	**68E** Carlisle Canal	**65A** Eastfield	**65A** Eastfield		
67475	*C15*	KPS	Kipps	**65A** Eastfield	**65A** Eastfield				
67476	*C15*	THJ	Thornton Junction	**62A** Thornton Junction	**62A** Thornton Junction				
67477	*C15*	HAW	Hawick	**64G** Hawick	**64G** Hawick				
67478	*C15*	DFU	Dunfermline Upper	**61B** Aberdeen Ferryhill	**61B** Aberdeen Ferryhill				
67479	*C15*	PKD	Parkhead	**65C** Parkhead	**65C** Parkhead				
67480	*C15*	PKD	Parkhead	**65C** Parkhead	**65A** Eastfield				
67481	*C15*	CAR	Carlisle Canal	**12B** Carlisle Canal	**68E** Carlisle Canal				
67482	*C16*	EFD	Eastfield	**65A** Eastfield	**65C** Parkhead	**65C** Parkhead			
67483	*C16*	DEE	Dundee Tay Bridge	**62B** Dundee Tay Bridge	**62B** Dundee Tay Bridge				
67484	*C16*	DEE	Dundee Tay Bridge	**62B** Dundee Tay Bridge	**62B** Dundee Tay Bridge	**62B** Dundee Tay Bridge	**62B** Dundee Tay Bridge		
67485	*C16*	EFD	Eastfield	**65A** Eastfield	**65A** Eastfield	**65A** Eastfield	**65A** Eastfield		
67486	*C16*	DEE	Dundee Tay Bridge	**62B** Dundee Tay Bridge	**62B** Dundee Tay Bridge	**62B** Dundee Tay Bridge	**62B** Dundee Tay Bridge		
67487	*C16*	PKD	Parkhead	**65C** Parkhead	**65C** Parkhead	**65C** Parkhead			
67488	*C16*	PKD	Parkhead	**65A** Eastfield	**65A** Eastfield	**64E** Polmont			
67489	*C16*	DEE	Dundee Tay Bridge	**62B** Dundee Tay Bridge	**62B** Dundee Tay Bridge	**64G** Hawick	**64G** Hawick		
67490	*C16*	DEE	Dundee Tay Bridge	**62B** Dundee Tay Bridge	**62B** Dundee Tay Bridge	**62B** Dundee Tay Bridge	**62B** Dundee Tay Bridge		
67491	*C16*	DEE	Dundee Tay Bridge	**62B** Dundee Tay Bridge	**62B** Dundee Tay Bridge	**62B** Dundee Tay Bridge	**62B** Dundee Tay Bridge		
67492	*C16*	STM	St. Margarets	**64A** St. Margarets	**64A** St. Margarets	**64A** St. Margarets	**64A** St. Margarets		
67493	*C16*	STM	St. Margarets	**62B** Dundee Tay Bridge	**62B** Dundee Tay Bridge				
67494	*C16*	STM	St. Margarets	**64A** St. Margarets	**64E** Polmont	**64E** Polmont	**64E** Polmont		
67495	*C16*	STM	St. Margarets	**64A** St. Margarets	**64A** St. Margarets				
67496	*C16*	STM	St. Margarets	**64A** St. Margarets	**61B** Aberdeen Ferryhill	**61C** Keith	**62B** Dundee Tay Bridge		
67497	*C16*	STM	St. Margarets	**64A** St. Margarets	**64A** St. Margarets	**64A** St. Margarets			
67498	*C16*	DEE	Dundee Tay Bridge	**62B** Dundee Tay Bridge	**62B** Dundee Tay Bridge				
67499	*C16*	DEE	Dundee Tay Bridge	**62B** Dundee Tay Bridge	**62B** Dundee Tay Bridge				
67500	*C16*	EFD	Eastfield	**65A** Eastfield	**65C** Parkhead	**65C** Parkhead			
67501	*C16*	EFD	Eastfield	**65A** Eastfield	**61B** Aberdeen Ferryhill	**61B** Aberdeen Ferryhill	**62B** Dundee Tay Bridge		
67502	*C16*	EFD	Eastfield	**62B** Dundee Tay Bridge	**62B** Dundee Tay Bridge	**62B** Dundee Tay Bridge	**62B** Dundee Tay Bridge		
67600	*V1→V3*	EFD	Eastfield	**65A** Eastfield	**65A** Eastfield	**65A** Eastfield	**65A** Eastfield		
67601	*V1*	EFD	Eastfield	**65I** Balloch	**65I** Balloch	**65I** Balloch	**65I** Balloch		
67602	*V1*	EFD	Eastfield	**65A** Eastfield	**65A** Eastfield	**65A** Eastfield	**65A** Eastfield		
67603	*V1*	PKD	Parkhead	**65A** Eastfield	**65A** Eastfield	**65A** Eastfield	**65A** Eastfield		
67604	*V1→V3*	PKD	Parkhead	**65C** Parkhead	**65C** Parkhead	**65C** Parkhead	**65C** Parkhead		
67605	*V1→V3*	STM	St. Margarets	**64A** St. Margarets	**64A** St. Margarets	**64A** St. Margarets	**65E** Kipps		
67606	*V1→V3*	STM	St. Margarets	**64A** St. Margarets	**64A** St. Margarets	**64G** Hawick	**64A** St. Margarets		
67607	*V1→V3*	STM	St. Margarets	**64A** St. Margarets	**64A** St. Margarets	**64A** St. Margarets	**65C** Parkhead		
67608	*V1→V3*	STM	St. Margarets	**64A** St. Margarets	**64A** St. Margarets	**64A** St. Margarets	**65C** Parkhead		
67609	*V1→V3*	STM	St. Margarets	**64A** St. Margarets	**64A** St. Margarets	**64A** St. Margarets	**65E** Kipps		
67610	*V1*	HAY	Haymarket	**64B** Haymarket	**64B** Haymarket	**64B** Haymarket	**64B** Haymarket		
67611	*V1→V3*	PKD	Parkhead	**65C** Parkhead	**65C** Parkhead	**65C** Parkhead	**65C** Parkhead		
67612	*V1→V3*	PKD	Parkhead	**65C** Parkhead	**65C** Parkhead	**65C** Parkhead	**65C** Parkhead		
67613	*V1→V3*	PKD	Parkhead	**65H** Helensburgh	**65H** Helensburgh	**65H** Helensburgh	**65H** Helensburgh		
67614	*V1→V3*	PKD	Parkhead	**65H** Helensburgh	**65H** Helensburgh	**65H** Helensburgh	**65H** Helensburgh		
67615	*V1→V3*	HAY	Haymarket	**64B** Haymarket	**64B** Haymarket	**64B** Haymarket	**64B** Haymarket		
67616	*V1→V3*	PKD	Parkhead	**65H** Helensburgh	**65H** Helensburgh	**65H** Helensburgh	**65H** Helensburgh		
67617	*V1→V3*	STM	St. Margarets	**64A** St. Margarets	**64A** St. Margarets	**64A** St. Margarets	**64A** St. Margarets		
67618	*V1→V3*	STG	Stirling Shore Road	**65E** Kipps	**65E** Kipps	**65E** Kipps	**65E** Kipps		
67619	*V1→V3*	PKD	Parkhead	**65C** Parkhead	**65C** Parkhead	**65C** Parkhead	**65C** Parkhead		
67620	*V1→V3*	HAY	Haymarket	**64B** Haymarket	**64B** Haymarket	**64B** Haymarket	**64B** Haymarket	**52B** Heaton	
67621	*V1→V3*	PKD	Parkhead	**65C** Parkhead	**65C** Parkhead	**65C** Parkhead	**65C** Parkhead		
67622	*V1*	PKD	Parkhead	**65C** Parkhead	**65C** Parkhead	**65C** Parkhead	**65C** Parkhead		
67623	*V1→V3*	PKD	Parkhead	**65C** Parkhead	**65C** Parkhead	**65C** Parkhead	**65C** Parkhead		
67624	*V1→V3*	STM	St. Margarets	**64A** St. Margarets	**64A** St. Margarets	**64A** St. Margarets	**64A** St. Margarets		
67625	*V1→V3*	PKD	Parkhead	**65H** Helensburgh	**65H** Helensburgh	**65H** Helensburgh	**65H** Helensburgh		
67626	*V1→V3*	PKD	Parkhead	**65C** Parkhead	**65C** Parkhead	**65C** Parkhead	**65C** Parkhead		
67627	*V1→V3*	KPS	Kipps	**65E** Kipps	**65E** Kipps	**65E** Kipps	**65E** Kipps		
67628	*V1→V3*	PKD	Parkhead	**65C** Parkhead	**65C** Parkhead	**65C** Parkhead	**65C** Parkhead	**52A** Gateshead	
67629	*V1*	STM	St. Margarets	**64A** St. Margarets	**64A** St. Margarets	**64A** St. Margarets	**65C** Parkhead		
67630	*V1*	STM	St. Margarets	**64A** St. Margarets	**64A** St. Margarets	**64A** St. Margarets	**65C** Parkhead		
67631	*V1*	PKD	Parkhead	**65H** Helensburgh	**65H** Helensburgh	**65H** Helensburgh	**65H** Helensburgh		
67632	*V1→V3*	PKD	Parkhead	**65H** Helensburgh	**65H** Helensburgh	**65H** Helensburgh	**65H** Helensburgh		
67633	*V1→V3*	PKD	Parkhead	**65C** Parkhead	**65C** Parkhead	**65C** Parkhead	**65C** Parkhead		
67634	*V3*	GHD	Gateshead	**52A** Gateshead	**52A** Gateshead	**52C** Blaydon	**52C** Blaydon		
67635	*V1→V3*	HTN	Heaton	**52B** Heaton	**52B** Heaton	**52B** Heaton	**53A** Hull Dairycoates	**51L** Thornaby	
67636	*V1→V3*	BLA	Blaydon	**52C** Blaydon	**52C** Blaydon	**52C** Blaydon	**52C** Blaydon	**52C** Blaydon	
67637	*V1*	HTN	Heaton	**52B** Heaton	**52B** Heaton	**52B** Heaton	**52A** Gateshead		
67638	*V1→V3*	MID	Middlesbrough	**51D** Middlesbrough	**51D** Middlesbrough	**53B** Hull Botanic Gardens	**53A** Hull Dairycoates	**50B** Hull Dairycoates	
67639	*V1*	MID	Middlesbrough	**51D** Middlesbrough	**51D** Middlesbrough	**52C** Hexham	**52A** Gateshead		
67640	*V1→V3*	HTN	Heaton	**52B** Heaton	**52B** Heaton	**52B** Heaton	**53A** Hull Dairycoates	**51L** Thornaby	
67641	*V1*	HTN	Heaton	**52B** Heaton	**52B** Heaton	**52B** Heaton	**52B** Heaton		
67642	*V1→V3*	HTN	Heaton	**52B** Heaton	**52B** Heaton	**52B** Heaton	**52B** Heaton	**52B** Heaton	
67643	*V1→V3*	PKD	Parkhead	**65C** Parkhead	**65C** Parkhead	**65C** Parkhead	**65C** Parkhead	**52A** Gateshead	
67644	*V1→V3*	DFU	Dunfermline Upper	**65A** Eastfield	**65A** Eastfield	**65A** Eastfield	**65A** Eastfield		
67645	*V1→V3*	NEV	Leeds Neville Hill	**52B** Heaton	**52B** Heaton	**52B** Heaton	**52G** Sunderland	**52B** Heaton	
67646	*V1→V3*	NEV	Leeds Neville Hill	**52B** Heaton	**52B** Heaton	**52B** Heaton	**52B** Heaton	**52B** Heaton	
67647	*V1→V3*	NEV	Leeds Neville Hill	**52A** Gateshead	**52B** Heaton	**52B** Heaton	**52B** Heaton	**52B** Heaton	
67648	*V1→V3*	PKD	Parkhead	**65C** Parkhead	**65C** Parkhead	**65C** Parkhead	**65C** Parkhead		
67649	*V1*	STM	St. Margarets	**64A** St. Margarets	**64A** St. Margarets	**64A** St. Margarets	**64A** St. Margarets		
67650	*V1→V3*	STG	Stirling Shore Road	**63B** Stirling	**63B** Stirling	**63B** Stirling	**65C** Parkhead		
67651	*V1→V3*	HTN	Heaton	**52B** Heaton	**52B** Heaton	**52B** Heaton	**52B** Heaton	**52B** Heaton	
67652	*V1→V3*	HTN	Heaton	**52B** Heaton	**52B** Heaton	**52B** Heaton	**52B** Heaton	**52B** Heaton	
67653	*V1→V3*	HTN	Heaton	**52C** Blaydon	**52C** Blaydon	**52C** Blaydon	**52C** Blaydon	**52A** Gateshead	
67654	*V1→V3*	HTN	Heaton	**52B** Heaton	**52B** Heaton	**52B** Heaton	**52B** Heaton	**52B** Heaton	
67655	*V1*	PKD	Parkhead	**65C** Parkhead	**65C** Parkhead	**65C** Parkhead	**65C** Parkhead		
67656	*V1→V3*	NEV	Leeds Neville Hill	**52C** Blaydon	**52C** Blaydon	**52C** Blaydon	**52B** Heaton	**52B** Heaton	
67657	*V1→V3*	NEV	Leeds Neville Hill	**52C** Blaydon	**52C** Blaydon	**52C** Hexham	**65C** Parkhead		
67658	*V1→V3*	BLA	Blaydon	**52C** Blaydon	**52C** Blaydon	**52C** Hexham	**52B** Heaton	**52B** Heaton	

No.	Class	1948		1951	1954	1957	1960	1963	1966
67659	V1	STM	St. Margarets	64A St. Margarets	64A St. Margarets	64A St. Margarets	64A St. Margarets		
67660	V1→V3	KPS	Kipps	65E Kipps	65E Kipps	65E Kipps	65E Kipps		
67661	V1→V3	DFU	Dunfermline Upper	65C Parkhead	65C Parkhead	65C Parkhead	65C Parkhead		
67662	V1→V3	PKD	Parkhead	65C Parkhead	65C Parkhead	65C Parkhead	65C Parkhead	52A Gateshead	
67663	V1→V3	NOR	Norwich Thorpe	32A Norwich Thorpe	51D Middlesbrough	53B Hull Botanic Gardens	53A Hull Dairycoates	50B Hull Dairycoates	
67664	V1	NOR	Norwich Thorpe	32A Norwich Thorpe	65A Eastfield	65A Eastfield	65A Eastfield		
67665	V1	NOR	Norwich Thorpe	65E Kipps	65E Kipps	65E Kipps	65E Kipps		
67666	V1→V3	STM	St. Margarets	64A St. Margarets	64A St. Margarets	64A St. Margarets	64A St. Margarets		
67667	V1→V3	STR	Stratford	61A Kittybrewster	61A Kittybrewster	61A Kittybrewster	61A Kittybrewster		
67668	V1→V3	STR	Stratford	64A St. Margarets	64A St. Margarets	64A St. Margarets	64C Dalry Road		
67669	V3	STR	Stratford	62C Dunfermline Upper	62C Dunfermline Upper	62C Dunfermline Upper	62C Dunfermline Upper		
67670	V1→V3	STM	St. Margarets	64A St. Margarets	64A St. Margarets	64A St. Margarets	64A St. Margarets		
67671	V1	STR	Stratford	61A Kittybrewster	61A Kittybrewster	61A Kittybrewster	61A Kittybrewster		
67672	V3	STR	Stratford	62C Dunfermline Upper	62C Dunfermline Upper	62C Dunfermline Upper	62C Dunfermline Upper		
67673	V1	STR	Stratford	52B Heaton	52B Heaton	52C Blaydon	52G Sunderland		
67674	V1→V3	PKD	Parkhead	65E Kipps	65E Kipps	65E Kipps	65E Kipps		
67675	V3	STR	Stratford	63B Stirling	63B Stirling	63B Stirling	65C Parkhead		
67676	V1→V3	STR	Stratford	65C Parkhead	65C Parkhead	65C Parkhead	65C Parkhead		
67677	V1→V3	STR	Stratford	32A Norwich Thorpe	51D Middlesbrough	53B Hull Botanic Gardens	53A Hull Dairycoates		
67678	V1→V3	PKD	Parkhead	65C Parkhead	65C Parkhead	65C Parkhead	65C Parkhead	52A Gateshead	
67679	V1→V3	STR	Stratford	32A Norwich Thorpe	65C Parkhead	65C Parkhead	65C Parkhead		
67680	V1	STR	Stratford	65A Eastfield	65A Eastfield	65A Eastfield	65A Eastfield		
67681	V1→V3	STR	Stratford	65C Parkhead	65C Parkhead	65C Parkhead	65C Parkhead		
67682	V3	GHD	Gateshead	52A Gateshead	52A Gateshead	52C Hexham	53A Hull Dairycoates	51A Darlington	
67683	V3	GHD	Gateshead	52A Gateshead	52A Gateshead	52C Blaydon	52B Heaton	52B Heaton	
67684	V3	MID	Middlesbrough	51D Middlesbrough	51D Middlesbrough	53B Hull Botanic Gardens	53A Hull Dairycoates	50B Hull Dairycoates	
67685	V3	MID	Middlesbrough	51D Middlesbrough	51D Middlesbrough	53B Hull Botanic Gardens	52B Heaton		
67686	V3	MID	Middlesbrough	51D Middlesbrough	51D Middlesbrough	53B Hull Botanic Gardens	53A Hull Dairycoates	50B Hull Dairycoates	
67687	V3	GHD	Gateshead	52A Gateshead	52A Gateshead	52C Hexham	52A Gateshead		
67688	V3	GHD	Gateshead	52A Gateshead	52A Gateshead	52A Gateshead	52A Gateshead		
67689	V3	GHD	Gateshead	52A Gateshead	52A Gateshead	52A Gateshead	52A Gateshead		
67690	V3	GHD	Gateshead	52A Gateshead	52A Gateshead	52A Gateshead	52A Gateshead	52B Heaton	
67691	V3	MID	Middlesbrough	51D Middlesbrough	51D Middlesbrough	53B Hull Botanic Gardens	52B Heaton	52B Heaton	
67701	L1	(69000)		30A Stratford	30A Stratford	30A Stratford	30A Stratford		
67702	L1	→		32B Ipswich	32B Ipswich	32B Ipswich	30A Stratford		
67703	L1	→		32B Ipswich	32B Ipswich	32B Ipswich	30A Stratford		
67704	L1	→		32B Ipswich	32C Lowestoft	32C Lowestoft	30A Stratford		
67705	L1	→		32B Ipswich	32B Ipswich	32B Ipswich	30A Stratford		
67706	L1	→		32B Ipswich	32B Ipswich	32B Ipswich	30A Stratford		
67707	L1	→		34B Hornsey	32A Norwich Thorpe	32A Norwich Thorpe	32C Lowestoft		
67708	L1	→		32B Ipswich	32B Ipswich	32B Ipswich	30A Stratford		
67709	L1	→		32B Ipswich	32B Ipswich	32B Ipswich	30A Stratford		
67710	L1	→		32B Ipswich	32B Ipswich	32B Ipswich	32C Lowestoft		
67711	L1	→		32B Ipswich	32B Ipswich	32B Ipswich	30A Stratford		
67712	L1	→		30A Stratford	30A Stratford	30A Stratford	31A Cambridge		
67713	L1	→		30A Stratford	30A Stratford	30A Stratford	31A Cambridge		
67714	L1	→		34E Neasden	32C Lowestoft	32A Norwich Thorpe	30A Stratford		
67715	L1	→		34E Neasden	32B Ipswich	32B Ipswich	30A Stratford		
67716	L1	→		32B Ipswich	32B Ipswich	32B Ipswich	30A Stratford		
67717	L1	→		34E Neasden	32C Lowestoft	32A Norwich Thorpe	32A Norwich Thorpe		
67718	L1	→		34E Neasden	34A Kings Cross	30A Stratford	31A Cambridge		
67719	L1	→		32B Ipswich	32B Ipswich	32B Ipswich	32B Ipswich		
67720	L1	→		34E Neasden	34A Kings Cross	30A Stratford	31A Cambridge		
67721	L1	→		30A Stratford	30A Stratford	30A Stratford	31A Cambridge		
67722	L1	→		30A Stratford	30A Stratford	30A Stratford	31A Cambridge		
67723	L1	→		30A Stratford	30A Stratford	30A Stratford	31A Cambridge		
67724	L1	→		30A Stratford	30A Stratford	30A Stratford	30A Stratford		
67725	L1	→		30A Stratford	30A Stratford	30A Stratford	30A Stratford		
67726	L1	→		30A Stratford	30A Stratford	30A Stratford	30A Stratford		
67727	L1	→		30A Stratford	30A Stratford	30A Stratford	30A Stratford		
67728	L1	→		30A Stratford	30A Stratford	32D Yarmouth South Town	30A Stratford		
67729	L1	→		30A Stratford	30A Stratford	30A Stratford	30A Stratford		
67730	L1	→		30A Stratford	30A Stratford	30A Stratford	30A Stratford		
67731	L1	→		30A Stratford	30A Stratford	30A Stratford	30A Stratford		
67732	L1	→		30A Stratford	30A Stratford	30A Stratford	30A Stratford		
67733	L1	→		30A Stratford	30A Stratford	30A Stratford	32A Norwich Thorpe		
67734	L1	→		30A Stratford	30A Stratford	30A Stratford	31A Cambridge		
67735	L1	→		30A Stratford	30A Stratford	30A Stratford	30A Stratford		
67736	L1	→		30A Stratford	30A Stratford	32D Yarmouth South Town	30A Stratford		
67737	L1	→		30A Stratford	30A Stratford	30A Stratford	30A Stratford		
67738	L1	→		30A Stratford	30A Stratford	30A Stratford	32C Lowestoft		
67739	L1	→		30A Stratford	32A Norwich Thorpe	32B Ipswich	30A Stratford		
67740	L1	→		34D Hitchin	34E Neasden	34E Neasden	2F Woodford Halse		
67741	L1	→		34D Hitchin	34D Hitchin	34D Hitchin	40E Colwick		
67742	L1	→		51A Darlington	51A Darlington	51A Darlington	51A Darlington		
67743	L1	→		34D Hitchin	34D Hitchin	34E Neasden	9G Gorton		
67744	L1	→		34D Hitchin	34D Hitchin	34D Hitchin	34D Hitchin		
67745	L1	→		34D Hitchin	34D Hitchin	34D Hitchin	34D Hitchin		
67746	L1	→		34D Hitchin	34D Hitchin	34D Hitchin	34D Hitchin		
67747	L1	→		34E Neasden	34E Neasden	34E Neasden	9G Gorton		
67748	L1	→		34E Neasden	34E Neasden	34E Neasden	9G Gorton		
67749	L1	→		34E Neasden	34E Neasden	34A Kings Cross	34A Kings Cross		
67750	L1	→		51A Darlington	51A Darlington	51A Darlington	51A Darlington		
67751	L1	→		34E Neasden	34E Neasden	38A Colwick	9G Gorton		
67752	L1	→		34E Neasden	34E Neasden	34E Neasden	30A Stratford		
67753	L1	→		34E Neasden	34E Neasden	34E Neasden	40E Colwick		
67754	L1	→		51A Darlington	51A Darlington	51D Middlesbrough	51L Thornaby		
67755	L1	→		53B Hull Botanic Gardens	53B Hull Botanic Gardens	51D Middlesbrough	51A Darlington		
67756	L1	→		34B Hornsey	34A Kings Cross	34E Neasden	9G Gorton		
67757	L1	→		34B Hornsey	34A Kings Cross	34A Kings Cross	34A Kings Cross		
67758	L1	→		34E Neasden	34E Neasden	34E Neasden	40E Colwick		
67759	L1	→		53B Hull Botanic Gardens	53B Hull Botanic Gardens	51D Middlesbrough	51L Thornaby		
67760	L1	→		34E Neasden	34E Neasden	38A Colwick	40E Colwick		
67761	L1	→		34B Hornsey	34E Neasden	34A Kings Cross	34F Grantham		
67762	L1	→		34E Neasden	34E Neasden	34E Neasden	9G Gorton		
67763	L1	→		53B Hull Botanic Gardens	53B Hull Botanic Gardens	51D Middlesbrough	51A Darlington		
67764	L1	→		53B Hull Botanic Gardens	53B Hull Botanic Gardens	51D Middlesbrough	51L Thornaby		
67765	L1	→		53B Hull Botanic Gardens	53B Hull Botanic Gardens	51D Middlesbrough	51A Darlington		
67766	L1	→		53B Hull Botanic Gardens	53B Hull Botanic Gardens	51D Middlesbrough	51L Thornaby		
67767	L1	→		34E Neasden	34E Neasden	34E Neasden	34A Kings Cross		
67768	L1	→		34E Neasden	34E Neasden	34A Kings Cross	34A Kings Cross		
67769	L1	→		34E Neasden	34E Neasden	34E Neasden	40E Colwick		
67770	L1	→		34E Neasden	34E Neasden	32C Lowestoft	34A Kings Cross		
67771	L1	→		34E Neasden	34E Neasden	38A Colwick	2F Woodford Halse		
67772	L1	→		34E Neasden	34E Neasden	34A Kings Cross	34A Kings Cross		
67773	L1	→		34E Neasden	34E Neasden	34A Kings Cross	34A Kings Cross		
67774	L1	→		34E Neasden	34E Neasden	34A Kings Cross	34A Kings Cross		
67775	L1	→		34E Neasden	34A Kings Cross	32B Ipswich	32B Ipswich		
67776	L1	→		34E Neasden	34E Neasden	35B Grantham	34A Kings Cross		
67777	L1	→		51A Darlington	51A Darlington	51A Darlington	51A Darlington		
67778	L1	→		34E Neasden	34E Neasden	34E Neasden	30A Stratford		
67779	L1	→		34E Neasden	34E Neasden	34A Kings Cross	34A Kings Cross		
67780	L1	→		34E Neasden	34E Neasden	34A Kings Cross	34A Kings Cross		
67781	L1	→		34E Neasden	34E Neasden	34E Neasden	9G Gorton		

No.	Class	1948		1951	1954	1957	1960	1963	1966
67782	L1	→		**34E** Neasden	**34E** Neasden	**34E** Neasden	**9G** Gorton		
67783	L1	→		**34E** Neasden	**34E** Neasden	**34E** Neasden	**34A** Kings Cross		
67784	L1	→		**34E** Neasden	**34E** Neasden	**34A** Kings Cross	**34A** Kings Cross		
67785	L1	→		**34E** Neasden	**34D** Hitchin	**34D** Hitchin	**34F** Grantham		
67786	L1	→		**34E** Neasden	**34E** Neasden	**34D** Hitchin	**32A** Norwich Thorpe		
67787	L1	→		**32B** Ipswich	**34E** Neasden	**34E** Neasden	**34A** Kings Cross		
67788	L1	→		**32A** Norwich Thorpe	**34E** Neasden	**38A** Colwick	**40E** Colwick		
67789	L1	→		**32A** Norwich Thorpe	**34E** Neasden	**38E** Woodford Halse	**2F** Woodford Halse		
67790	L1	→		**34D** Hitchin	**34D** Hitchin	**34D** Hitchin	**40E** Colwick		
67791	L1	→		**34D** Hitchin	**34D** Hitchin	**34D** Hitchin	**34F** Grantham		
67792	L1	→		**34A** Kings Cross	**34E** Neasden	**34E** Neasden	**34A** Kings Cross		
67793	L1	→		**34A** Kings Cross	**34A** Kings Cross	**34A** Kings Cross	**34A** Kings Cross		
67794	L1	→		**32C** Lowestoft	**34E** Neasden	**34E** Neasden	**34A** Kings Cross		
67795	L1	→		**32A** Norwich Thorpe	**34E** Neasden	**34E** Neasden	**9G** Gorton		
67796	L1	→		**34A** Kings Cross	**34E** Neasden	**34E** Neasden	**9G** Gorton		
67797	L1	→		**34A** Kings Cross	**34A** Kings Cross	**34A** Kings Cross	**34A** Kings Cross		
67798	L1	→		**32A** Norwich Thorpe	**34E** Neasden	**38A** Colwick	**9G** Gorton		
67799	L1	→		**34A** Kings Cross	**34A** Kings Cross	**38A** Colwick	**40E** Colwick		
67800	L1	→		**34A** Kings Cross	**34A** Kings Cross	**35B** Grantham	**34A** Kings Cross		
68006	J94	IMM	Immingham	**6F** Bidston	**6F** Bidston	**17D** Rowsley	**17C** Rowsley	**17C** Rowsley	**9L** Buxton
68007	J94	NPT	Newport	**51B** Newport	**51B** Newport	**51A** Darlington	**51A** Darlington		
68008	J94	DAR	Darlington	**51A** Darlington	**51A** Darlington	**51A** Darlington	**51A** Darlington	**56B** Ardsley	
68009	J94	IMM	Immingham	**40B** Immingham	**40B** Immingham	**40B** Immingham	**40B** Immingham		
68010	J94	BLA	Blaydon	**52C** Blaydon	**52C** Blaydon	**52C** Blaydon	**52C** Blaydon	**51A** Darlington	
68011	J94	NPT	Newport	**51B** Newport	**51B** Newport	**51B** Newport	**53A** Hull Dairycoates	**56B** Ardsley	
68012	J94	IMM	Immingham	**39A** Gorton	**39A** Gorton	**39A** Gorton	**17C** Rowsley	**17C** Rowsley	**9L** Buxton
68013	J94	IMM	Immingham	**40B** Immingham	**6F** Bidston	**17D** Rowsley	**17C** Rowsley	**17C** Rowsley	
68014	J94	BLA	Blaydon	**52B** Heaton	**52B** Heaton	**52B** Heaton	**52C** Blaydon	**51A** Darlington	
68015	J94	BLA	Blaydon	**51A** Darlington	**51A** Darlington	**51A** Darlington	**51A** Darlington	**51C** West Hartlepool	
68016	J94	SUN	Sunderland	**54A** Sunderland	**54A** Sunderland	**54A** Sunderland	**52G** Sunderland	**52H** Tyne Dock	
68017	J94	SCA	Scarborough	**50A** York	**54A** Sunderland	**54A** Sunderland	**51A** Darlington		
68018	J94	IMM	Immingham	**40B** Immingham	**40B** Immingham	**40B** Immingham	**40B** Immingham		
68019	J94	BLA	Blaydon	**52C** Blaydon	**54D** Consett	**54D** Consett	**52H** Tyne Dock	**52H** Tyne Dock	
68020	J94	IMM	Immingham	**40B** Immingham	**40B** Immingham	**36A** Doncaster	**36A** Doncaster	**41J** Langwith Junction	
68021	J94	BLA	Blaydon	**52C** Blaydon	**52B** Heaton	**51C** West Hartlepool	**51C** West Hartlepool	**51C** West Hartlepool	
68022	J94	IMM	Immingham	**40B** Immingham	**40B** Immingham	**36A** Doncaster	**36A** Doncaster		
68023	J94	NPT	Newport	**51B** Newport	**51B** Newport	**51B** Newport	**51L** Thornaby	**51L** Thornaby	
68024	J94	BLA	Blaydon	**52C** Blaydon	**54A** Sunderland	**54A** Sunderland	**51A** Darlington	**51A** Darlington	
68025	J94	DAR	Darlington	**51A** Darlington	**51A** Darlington	**51A** Darlington	**51A** Darlington	**51A** Darlington	
68026	J94	IMM	Immingham	**40B** Immingham	**40B** Immingham	**40B** Immingham	**41J** Langwith Junction		
68027	J94	DAR	Darlington	**51A** Darlington	**51A** Darlington	**51A** Darlington	**51A** Darlington		
68028	J94	IMM	Immingham	**40B** Immingham	**40B** Immingham	**40B** Immingham	**40E** Colwick		
68029	J94	BLA	Blaydon	**52C** Blaydon	**50A** York	**50A** York	**52H** Tyne Dock	**52H** Tyne Dock	
68030	J94	IMM	Immingham	**40B** Immingham	**6F** Bidston	**17D** Rowsley	**17C** Rowsley		
68031	J94	YK	York	**50A** York	**50A** York	**50A** York	**52H** Tyne Dock	**52H** Tyne Dock	
68032	J94	YK	York	**50A** York	**50A** York	**50A** York	**51A** Darlington	**51C** West Hartlepool	
68033	J94	IMM	Immingham	**40B** Immingham	**40B** Immingham	**40B** Immingham	**34B** Hornsey		
68034	J94	IMM	Immingham	**40B** Immingham	**6F** Bidston	**6F** Bidston	**17C** Rowsley		
68035	J94	BLA	Blaydon	**52C** Blaydon	**52C** Blaydon	**52C** Blaydon	**52C** Blaydon	**51A** Darlington	
68036	J94	BLA	Blaydon	**52C** Blaydon	**52C** Blaydon	**52C** Blaydon	**52C** Blaydon	**51C** West Hartlepool	
68037	J94	BLA	Blaydon	**51B** Newport	**51B** Newport	**51A** Darlington	**51A** Darlington	**51A** Darlington	
68038	J94	BLA	Blaydon	**52C** Blaydon	**52C** Blaydon	**52C** Blaydon	**52H** Tyne Dock	**52H** Tyne Dock	
68039	J94	SEL	Selby	**51A** Darlington	**51A** Darlington	**51A** Darlington	**51A** Darlington	**51L** Thornaby	
68040	J94	SEL	Selby	**50A** York	**50A** York	**50A** York	**51A** Darlington	**51A** Darlington	
68041	J94	NPT	Newport	**52C** Blaydon	**54A** Sunderland	**54A** Sunderland	**52G** Sunderland	**51C** West Hartlepool	
68042	J94	YK	York	**51C** West Hartlepool	**50A** York	**50A** York	**53A** Hull Dairycoates	**50B** Hull Dairycoates	
68043	J94	YK	York	**51A** Darlington	**51A** Darlington	**51A** Darlington	**51A** Darlington	**51A** Darlington	
68044	J94	YK	York	**50A** York	**50A** York	**50A** York	**52G** Sunderland		
68045	J94	YK	York	**51A** Darlington	**51A** Darlington	**51A** Darlington	**51A** Darlington	**51C** West Hartlepool	
68046	J94	YK	York	**50A** York	**50A** York	**50A** York	**50A** York	**51A** Darlington	
68047	J94	DAR	Darlington	**51A** Darlington	**51A** Darlington	**51A** Darlington	**51A** Darlington	**51A** Darlington	
68048	J94	DAR	Darlington	**52C** Blaydon	**54A** Sunderland	**54A** Sunderland	**52G** Sunderland		
68049	J94	DAR	Darlington	**51B** Newport	**51B** Newport	**51B** Newport	**51L** Thornaby	**56B** Ardsley	
68050	J94	DAR	Darlington	**51A** Darlington	**51A** Darlington	**51A** Darlington	**51A** Darlington	**51A** Darlington	
68051	J94	DAR	Darlington	**51A** Darlington	**50A** York	**51C** West Hartlepool	**51C** West Hartlepool	**51C** West Hartlepool	
68052	J94	DAR	Darlington	**51A** Darlington	**51A** Darlington	**51A** Darlington	**51A** Darlington		
68053	J94	WHL	West Hartlepool	**51C** West Hartlepool	**51C** West Hartlepool	**51C** West Hartlepool	**51C** West Hartlepool	**52A** Gateshead	
68054	J94	WHL	West Hartlepool	**51C** West Hartlepool	**51C** West Hartlepool	**51C** West Hartlepool	**51C** West Hartlepool	**52H** Tyne Dock	
68055	J94	WHL	West Hartlepool	**51C** West Hartlepool	**51C** West Hartlepool	**51C** West Hartlepool	**51C** West Hartlepool		
68056	J94	WHL	West Hartlepool	**51C** West Hartlepool	**51C** West Hartlepool	**51C** West Hartlepool	**51C** West Hartlepool		
68057	J94	WHL	West Hartlepool	**51C** West Hartlepool	**51C** West Hartlepool	**51C** West Hartlepool	**51C** West Hartlepool		
68058	J94	BLA	Blaydon	**52C** Blaydon	**54A** Sunderland	**54A** Sunderland	**52G** Sunderland		
68059	J94	BLA	Blaydon	**52C** Hexham	**52C** Blaydon	**52C** Blaydon	**52H** Tyne Dock	**52A** Gateshead	
68060	J94	NPT	Newport	**51B** Newport	**51B** Newport	**51B** Newport	**51L** Thornaby	**51A** Darlington	
68061	J94	DAR	Darlington	**50A** York	**50A** York	**50A** York	**50A** York	**51C** West Hartlepool	
68062	J94	NPT	Newport	**51B** Newport	**51B** Newport	**51B** Newport	**51L** Thornaby	**56B** Ardsley	
68063	J94	GOR	Gorton	**6F** Bidston	**6F** Bidston	**6F** Bidston	**6F** Bidston		
68064	J94	GOR	Gorton	**39A** Gorton	**39A** Gorton	**39A** Gorton	**9G** Gorton		
68065	J94	GOR	Gorton	**6F** Bidston	**6F** Bidston	**6F** Bidston	**6F** Bidston		
68066	J94	GOR	Gorton	**6F** Bidston	**6F** Bidston	**6F** Bidston	**6F** Bidston		
68067	J94	GOR	Gorton	**39A** Gorton	**39A** Gorton	**40B** Immingham	**34B** Hornsey	**41J** Langwith Junction	
68068	J94	IMM	Immingham	**40B** Immingham	**40B** Immingham	**40B** Immingham	**9G** Gorton	**17C** Rowsley	
68069	J94	IMM	Immingham	**40B** Immingham	**40B** Immingham	**40B** Immingham	**36A** Doncaster		
68070	J94	IMM	Immingham	**40B** Immingham	**40B** Immingham	**40B** Immingham	**40B** Immingham	**41F** Mexborough	
68071	J94	IMM	Immingham	**8E** Brunswick	**39A** Gorton	**40B** Immingham	**36A** Doncaster	**51A** Darlington	
68072	J94	IMM	Immingham	**40B** Immingham	**40B** Immingham	**40B** Immingham	**40E** Colwick		
68073	J94	IMM	Immingham	**40B** Immingham	**40B** Immingham	**40B** Immingham	**34B** Hornsey		
68074	J94	IMM	Immingham	**40B** Immingham	**40B** Immingham	**40B** Immingham	**40B** Immingham		
68075	J94	IMM	Immingham	**40B** Immingham	**40B** Immingham	**40B** Immingham	**34B** Hornsey		
68076	J94	IMM	Immingham	**40B** Immingham	**40B** Immingham	**40B** Immingham	**40E** Colwick		
68077	J94	IMM	Immingham	**40B** Immingham	**40B** Immingham	**40B** Immingham	**34B** Hornsey		
68078	J94	IMM	Immingham	**40B** Immingham	**40B** Immingham	**40B** Immingham	**51L** Thornaby	**41J** Langwith Junction	
68079	J94	IMM	Immingham	**39A** Gorton	**39A** Gorton	**39A** Gorton	**9G** Gorton	**17C** Rowsley	**9L** Buxton
68080	J94	IMM	Immingham	**40B** Immingham	**40B** Immingham	**40B** Immingham	**41J** Langwith Junction		
68081	Y5		Stratford Works						
68082	Y6	KL	Kings Lynn	**31C** Kings Lynn					
68083	Y6	KL	Kings Lynn	**31C** Kings Lynn					
68088	Y7	TDK	Tyne Dock	Stratford Works	(34)				
68089	Y7	TDK	Tyne Dock	**52D** Tweedmouth					
68090	Y8	HLS	Hull Springhead						
68091	Y8	YK	York	**50A** York	**50A** York	(55)			
68092	Y9	STM	St. Margarets	**64A** St. Margarets					
68093	Y9	STM	St. Margarets	**64A** St. Margarets	**64A** St. Margarets				
68094	Y9	KPS	Kipps	**65E** Kipps	**65E** Kipps				
68095	Y9	STM	St. Margarets	**64A** St. Margarets	**64A** St. Margarets	**64A** St. Margarets	**64A** St. Margarets		
68096	Y9	STM	St. Margarets	**64A** St. Margarets	**64A** St. Margarets				
68097	Y9	STM	St. Margarets	**64A** St. Margarets	**64A** St. Margarets	**64A** St. Margarets			
68098	Y9	STM	St. Margarets	**64A** St. Margarets	**64A** St. Margarets				
68099	Y9	STM	St. Margarets	**64A** St. Margarets	**64A** St. Margarets				
68100	Y9	DEE	Dundee Tay Bridge	**62B** Dundee Tay Bridge	**62B** Dundee Tay Bridge	**62B** Dundee Tay Bridge	**65E** Kipps		
68101	Y9	DFU	Dunfermline Upper	**62C** Dunfermline Upper	**62C** Dunfermline Upper	**62C** Dunfermline Upper	**62C** Dunfermline Upper		
68102	Y9	STM	St. Margarets	**64A** St. Margarets	**64A** St. Margarets	**64A** St. Margarets			
68103	Y9	EFD	Eastfield	**65A** Eastfield	**64A** St. Margarets				
68104	Y9	POL	Polmont	**64E** Polmont	**64E** Polmont	**64E** Polmont	**64E** Polmont		

No.	Class	1948	1951	1954	1957	1960	1963	1966
68105	*Y9*	**STM** St. Margarets	**64A** St. Margarets	**64A** St. Margarets				
68106	*Y9*	**KPS** Kipps	**65E** Kipps		**65E** Kipps			
68107	*Y9*	**DEE** Dundee Tay Bridge	**62B** Dundee Tay Bridge					
68108	*Y9*	**DEE** Dundee Tay Bridge	**60A** Inverness	**62B** Dundee Tay Bridge	**62B** Dundee Tay Bridge			
68109	*Y9*	**EFD** Eastfield	**65A** Eastfield	**65A** Eastfield				
68110	*Y9*	**DEE** Dundee Tay Bridge	**62B** Dundee Tay Bridge	**62B** Dundee Tay Bridge	**65E** Kipps	**65E** Kipps		
68111	*Y9*	**STM** St. Margarets	**64A** St. Margarets					
68112	*Y9*	**KPS** Kipps	**65G** Yoker	**65G** Yoker				
68113	*Y9*	**POL** Polmont	**64E** Polmont	**64E** Polmont	**64E** Polmont			
68114	*Y9*	**DEE** Dundee Tay Bridge	**62B** Dundee Tay Bridge	**62B** Dundee Tay Bridge	**62B** Dundee Tay Bridge	**65E** Kipps		
68115	*Y9*	**STM** St. Margarets	**64A** St. Margarets	**64A** St. Margarets	**64A** St. Margarets			
68116	*Y9*	**KPS** Kipps	**65E** Kipps	**65E** Kipps	**65E** Kipps			
68117	*Y9*	**KPS** Kipps	**65E** Kipps	**65E** Kipps	**65E** Kipps	**65E** Kipps		
68118	*Y9*	**EFD** Eastfield	**65A** Eastfield	**65G** Yoker	**67C** Ayr			
68119	*Y9*	**STM** St. Margarets	**64A** St. Margarets	**64A** St. Margarets	**64A** St. Margarets	**64A** St. Margarets		
68120	*Y9*	**KPS** Kipps	**65E** Kipps	**65E** Kipps				
68121	*Y9*	**KPS** Kipps	**65E** Kipps	**65E** Kipps				
68122	*Y9*	**STM** St. Margarets	**64A** St. Margarets	**64A** St. Margarets				
68123	*Y9*	**DEE** Dundee Tay Bridge	**62B** Dundee Tay Bridge	**62B** Dundee Tay Bridge	**62B** Dundee Tay Bridge	**65E** Kipps		
68124	*Y9*	**EFD** Eastfield	**65A** Eastfield	**65A** Eastfield	**65E** Kipps			
68125	*Y4*	**STR** Stratford	**30A** Stratford	**30A** Stratford				
68126	*Y4*	**STR** Stratford	**30A** Stratford	**30A** Stratford	**30A** Stratford			
68127	*Y4*	**STR** Stratford	**30A** Stratford	**30A** Stratford				
68128	*Y4*	**STR** Stratford	**30A** Stratford	**30A** Stratford				
68129	*Y4*	Stratford Works	Stratford Works	(33)				
68130	*Y1*	Lowestoft Engineer's Dept	Lowestoft Engineer's Dept	(37)				
68131	*Y1*	Lowestoft Engineer's Dept	Lowestoft Engineer's Dept	(39)				
68132	*Y1*	Doncaster Works	Ranskill Wagon Works	(4)				
68133	*Y1*	Peterborough North Yard	Peterborough North Yard	(6)				
68134	*Y1*	Doncaster Works						
68135	*Y1*	Stratford Works						
68136	*Y1*	Faverdale Wagon Works	Faverdale Wagon Works	(51)				
68137	*Y1*	**HLD** Hull Dairycoates	**53A** Hull Dairycoates					
68138	*Y1*	**HAW** Hawick	**64G** Hawick	**64G** Hawick	**67C** Ayr			
68139	*Y1*	**HLD** Hull Dairycoates	**53A** Hull Dairycoates					
68140	*Y1*	**HLD** Hull Dairycoates	**53A** Hull Dairycoates	**53A** Hull Dairycoates				
68141	*Y1*	**GHD** Gateshead	**52A** Gateshead					
68142	*Y1*	**AUK** West Auckland	**51F** West Auckland	**51A** Darlington	**51E** Stockton on Tees			
68143	*Y1*	**SEL** Selby	**50C** Selby	**50C** Selby				
68144	*Y1*	**SKN** Stockton on Tees	**51E** Stockton on Tees	**51E** Stockton on Tees				
68145	*Y1*	**AUK** West Auckland	**51F** West Auckland	**51F** West Auckland	**53D** Bridlington			
68146	*Y1*	**GHD** Gateshead	**52A** Gateshead	**52A** Gateshead				
68147	*Y1*	**MAL** Malton	**50F** Malton					
68148	*Y1*	**BRI** Bridlington	**53D** Bridlington	**53D** Bridlington				
68149	*Y1*	**AUK** West Auckland	**51F** West Auckland	**51F** West Auckland	**51F** West Auckland			
68150	*Y1*	**MAL** Malton	**50F** Malton	**50F** Malton	**50C** Selby			
68151	*Y1*	**HLB** Hull Botanic Gardens	**53B** Hull Botanic Gardens	**53B** Hull Botanic Gardens				
68152	*Y1*	York Engineer's Yard	York Engineer's Yard	York Engineer's Yard	(53)			
68153	*Y1*	Darlington PW Depot	Darlington PW Depot	Darlington PW Depot	(54)			
68154	*Y3*	**GHD** Gateshead	**52A** Gateshead					
68155	*Y3*	**BRI** Bridlington	**53D** Bridlington	**53D** Bridlington				
68156	*Y3*	**SEL** Selby	**50C** Selby	**50C** Selby				
68157	*Y3*	**PKG** Pickering	**50F** Pickering					
68158	*Y3*	**NEV** Leeds Neville Hill	**50C** Selby	**50C** Selby				
68159	*Y3*	**NLN** Northallerton	**51J** Northallerton	**51J** Northallerton	**52A** Gateshead			
68160	*Y3*	**GHD** Gateshead	**52A** Gateshead	**52A** Gateshead	(57)			
68161	*Y3*	**SEL** Selby	**50C** Selby					
68162	*Y3*	**IMM** Immingham	**40B** Immingham	**6E** Wrexham Rhosddu	(21)			
68163	*Y3*	**WRX** Wrexham Rhosddu	**6E** Wrexham Rhosddu					
68164	*Y3*	**WRX** Wrexham Rhosddu	**6E** Wrexham Rhosddu	**6E** Wrexham Rhosddu	**84G** Shrewsbury			
68165	*Y3*	**RET** Retford	**36A** Doncaster	(5)				
68166	*Y3*	Boston Engineer's Dept.	Boston Engineer's Dept.	(7)				
68167	*Y3*	**SHF** Sheffield Darnall						
68168	*Y3*	**STR** Stratford	**32C** Lowestoft	(38)				
68169	*Y3*	**STR** Stratford	**39A** Gorton	**39A** Gorton				
68171	*Y3*	**IMM** Immingham	**40F** Boston					
68172	*Y3*	**NEA** Neasden	**34E** Neasden					
68173	*Y3*	**CAM** Cambridge	**32C** Lowestoft	(40)				
68174	*Y3*	**STR** Stratford	**30A** Stratford					
68175	*Y3*	**HAT** Hatfield	**34D** Hitchin					
68176	*Y3*	**WRX** Wrexham Rhosddu	**39B** Sheffield Darnall					
68177	*Y3*	Lowestoft Engineer's Dept	Lowestoft Engineer's Dept	(41)				
68178	*Y3*	Lowestoft Engineer's Dept	Lowestoft Engineer's Dept	(42)				
68179	*Y3*	**IMM** Immingham	**40B** Immingham					
68180	*Y3*	**GHD** Gateshead	**52A** Gateshead	**52A** Gateshead				
68181	*Y3*	**TDK** Tyne Dock	**54B** Tyne Dock	(3)				
68182	*Y3*	**AUK** West Auckland	**51F** West Auckland	**51A** Darlington	**50C** Selby			
68183	*Y3*	**TDK** Tyne Dock	**54B** Tyne Dock	**53A** Hull Dairycoates	(8)			
68184	*Y3*	**SHF** Sheffield Darnall	**39B** Sheffield Darnall	**39B** Sheffield Darnall				
68185	*Y3*	**HAT** Hatfield	**35A** New England	**40B** Immingham				
68186	*Y10*	**YAR** Yarmouth South Town	**32D** Yarmouth South Town					
68187	*Y10*	**YAR** Yarmouth South Town						
68190	*Z4*	**KIT** Kittybrewster	**61A** Kittybrewster	**61A** Kittybrewster	**61A** Kittybrewster	**61A** Kittybrewster		
68191	*Z4*	**KIT** Kittybrewster	**61A** Kittybrewster	**61A** Kittybrewster	**61A** Kittybrewster			
68192	*Z5*	**KIT** Kittybrewster	**61A** Kittybrewster	**61A** Kittybrewster	**61A** Kittybrewster	**61A** Kittybrewster		
68193	*Z5*	**KIT** Kittybrewster	**61A** Kittybrewster	**61A** Kittybrewster				
68200	*J62*	**WRX** Wrexham Rhosddu	**6E** Wrexham Rhosddu					
68201	*J62*	**WRX** Wrexham Rhosddu						
68203	*J62*	**IMM** Immingham						
68204	*J63*	**IMM** Immingham	**40B** Immingham	**40B** Immingham				
68205	*J63*	**BID** Bidston	**40B** Immingham	**40B** Immingham				
68206	*J63*	**IMM** Immingham	**40B** Immingham	**40B** Immingham				
68207	*J63*	**BID** Bidston	**40B** Immingham	**40B** Immingham				
68208	*J63*	**IMM** Immingham	**40B** Immingham					
68209	*J63*	**IMM** Immingham	**40B** Immingham	**6E** Wrexham Rhosddu				
68210	*J63*	**IMM** Immingham	**40B** Immingham	**40B** Immingham	**40B** Immingham			
68211	*J65*	**IPS** Ipswich	**32B** Ipswich					
68213	*J65*	**YB** Yarmouth Beach						
68214	*J65*	**CAM** Cambridge	**32F** Yarmouth Beach	**32F** Yarmouth Beach				
68215	*J65*	**STR** Stratford						
68216	*J70*	**IPS** Ipswich	**32B** Ipswich					
68217	*J70*	**KL** Kings Lynn	**31C** Kings Lynn					
68218	*J70*	**KL** Kings Lynn						
68219	*J70*	**IPS** Ipswich	**32D** Yarmouth South Town					
68220	*J70*	**KL** Kings Lynn	**31C** Kings Lynn					
68221	*J70*	**IPS** Ipswich	**32B** Ipswich					
68222	*J70*	**KL** Kings Lynn	**31C** Kings Lynn	**32B** Ipswich				
68223	*J70*	**KL** Kings Lynn	**31C** Kings Lynn	**32D** Yarmouth South Town				
68224	*J70*	**IPS** Ipswich	**32B** Ipswich					
68225	*J70*	**IPS** Ipswich	**31C** Kings Lynn	**32B** Ipswich				
68226	*J70*	**COL** Colchester	**30E** Colchester	**30E** Colchester				
68230	*J71*	**YK** York	**50A** York	**50A** York	**53A** Hull Dairycoates	**53A** Hull Dairycoates		
68231	*J71*	**YK** York	**51A** Darlington					
68232	*J71*	**HLD** Hull Dairycoates	**53A** Hull Dairycoates	**53A** Hull Dairycoates	**53A** Hull Dairycoates			

		1948	1951	1954	1957	1960	1963	1966
68233	*J71*	**WHL** West Hartlepool	**51C** West Hartlepool	**51C** West Hartlepool	**51C** West Hartlepool	**51C** West Hartlepool		
68234	*J71*	**GHD** Gateshead	**52B** Heaton	**52B** Heaton				
68235	*J71*	**DAR** Darlington	**51A** Darlington	**51A** Darlington	**51A** Darlington	**51F** West Auckland		
68236	*J71*	**DAR** Darlington	**51A** Darlington	**51A** Darlington				
68238	*J71*	**NMN** Normanton	**50A** Normanton	**20D** Normanton				
68239	*J71*	**DAR** Darlington	**51A** Darlington	**51A** Darlington				
68240	*J71*	**YK** York	**50A** York	**50A** York				
68242	*J71*	**HLD** Hull Dairycoates	**53A** Hull Dairycoates	**53A** Hull Dairycoates	**51F** West Auckland			
68243	*J71*	**HTN** Heaton						
68244	*J71*	**WHL** West Hartlepool	**51C** West Hartlepool	**51C** West Hartlepool	**51C** West Hartlepool			
68245	*J71*	**HTN** Heaton	**52B** Heaton	**52B** Heaton	**51D** Middlesbrough			
68246	*J71*	**YK** York	**50A** York	**50A** York	**50A** York			
68247	*J71*	**GHD** Gateshead	**52B** Heaton					
68248	*J71*	**WHL** West Hartlepool	**51C** West Hartlepool					
68249	*J71*	**AUK** West Auckland	**51F** West Auckland					
68250	*J71*	**YK** York	**50A** York	**50A** York	**50A** York			
68251	*J71*	**GHD** Gateshead	**52A** Gateshead	**52B** Heaton	**52B** Heaton			
68252	*J71*	**HLD** Hull Dairycoates	**53A** Hull Dairycoates	**53A** Hull Dairycoates	**53A** Hull Dairycoates			
68253	*J71*	**YK** York	**50A** York	**50A** York	**55E** Normanton			
68254	*J71*	**AUK** West Auckland	**51F** West Auckland	**51F** West Auckland	**51F** West Auckland	**51F** West Auckland		
68255	*J71*	**AUK** West Auckland	**51F** West Auckland					
68256	*J71*	**HTN** Heaton	**52B** Heaton	**52B** Heaton				
68258	*J71*	**WHL** West Hartlepool	**51C** West Hartlepool	**51C** West Hartlepool				
68259	*J71*	**DAR** Darlington	**51A** Darlington	**51A** Darlington				
68260	*J71*	**MID** Middlesbrough	**51D** Middlesbrough	**51D** Middlesbrough	**51D** Middlesbrough	**51L** Thornaby		
68262	*J71*	**GHD** Gateshead	**52B** Heaton	**52B** Heaton	**52B** Heaton	**52H** Tyne Dock		
68263	*J71*	**WHL** West Hartlepool	**51C** West Hartlepool	**51C** West Hartlepool	**52B** Heaton			
68264	*J71*	**HTN** Heaton	**52B** Heaton	**52B** Heaton	**52B** Heaton	**53A** Hull Dairycoates		
68265	*J71*	**GHD** Gateshead	**52C** Blaydon	**54B** Tyne Dock	**54B** Tyne Dock			
68266	*J71*	**TDK** Tyne Dock	**54B** Tyne Dock	**54B** Tyne Dock	**54B** Tyne Dock			
68267	*J71*	**GHD** Gateshead	**52B** Heaton	**52C** Blaydon	**52A** Gateshead			
68268	*J71*	**YK** York	**50C** Selby					
68269	*J71*	**AUK** West Auckland	**51F** West Auckland	**51F** West Auckland	**51F** West Auckland	**51F** West Auckland		
68270	*J71*	**GHD** Gateshead	**52A** Gateshead	**52A** Gateshead				
68271	*J71*	**HTN** Heaton	**52B** Heaton	**52B** Heaton				
68272	*J71*	**TDK** Tyne Dock	**54B** Tyne Dock	**52A** Gateshead	**52A** Gateshead	**51L** Thornaby		
68273	*J71*	**HTN** Heaton	**52B** Heaton	**52C** Blaydon	**52C** Blaydon			
68275	*J71*	**YK** York	**50A** York	**50A** York	**50C** Selby	**55E** Normanton		
68276	*J71*	**WHL** West Hartlepool	**51C** West Hartlepool	**51C** West Hartlepool				
68277	*J71*	**HLD** Hull Dairycoates						
68278	*J71*	**HTN** Heaton	**52B** Heaton	**52C** Hexham	**54C** Borough Gardens	**51L** Thornaby		
68279	*J71*	**DAR** Darlington	**51A** Darlington	**51A** Darlington	**51A** Darlington			
68280	*J71*	**YK** York	**50A** York	**50A** York	**50A** York			
68281	*J71*	**DAR** Darlington	**51A** Darlington					
68282	*J71*	**YK** York	**50A** York					
68283	*J71*	**GHD** Gateshead	**52A** Gateshead	**52A** Gateshead	**52A** Gateshead			
68284	*J71*	**BLA** Blaydon	**52D** Tweedmouth	**53C** Hull Springhead				
68285	*J71*	**SEL** Selby						
68286	*J71*	**YK** York	**50A** York					
68287	*J71*	**BOR** Borough Gardens	**54C** Borough Gardens	**54C** Borough Gardens				
68288	*J71*	**HLD** Hull Dairycoates						
68289	*J71*	**BOR** Borough Gardens	**54C** Borough Gardens	**54C** Borough Gardens				
68290	*J71*	**WHL** West Hartlepool	**51C** West Hartlepool	**51C** West Hartlepool	**51D** Middlesbrough			
68291	*J71*	**WHL** West Hartlepool	**51C** West Hartlepool	**51C** West Hartlepool				
68292	*J71*	**NMN** Normanton	**50A** Normanton	**20D** Normanton				
68293	*J71*	**YK** York	**50A** York	**50A** York				
68294	*J71*	**NMN** Normanton	**50A** Normanton	**20D** Normanton				
68295	*J71*	**WHL** West Hartlepool	**51C** West Hartlepool	**51C** West Hartlepool	**51C** West Hartlepool			
68296	*J71*	**HLB** Hull Botanic Gardens	**53A** Hull Dairycoates	**53A** Hull Dairycoates	**53A** Hull Dairycoates			
68297	*J71*	**YK** York	**50A** York	**50A** York				
68298	*J71*	**YK** York	**53A** Hull Dairycoates	**53A** Hull Dairycoates	**53A** Hull Dairycoates			
68299	*J71*	**BOR** Borough Gardens	**54C** Borough Gardens					
68300	*J71*	**DAR** Darlington	**51A** Darlington	**51A** Darlington				
68301	*J71*	**WHL** West Hartlepool	**51C** West Hartlepool	**51C** West Hartlepool				
68302	*J71*	**WHL** West Hartlepool	**51C** West Hartlepool					
68303	*J71*	**MID** Middlesbrough	**51D** Middlesbrough	**51D** Middlesbrough				
68304	*J71*	**HLD** Hull Dairycoates	**53A** Hull Dairycoates	**53A** Hull Dairycoates				
68305	*J71*	**SKN** Stockton on Tees	**51E** Stockton on Tees	**51E** Stockton on Tees	**51E** Stockton on Tees			
68306	*J71*	**WHL** West Hartlepool	**51C** West Hartlepool	**51C** West Hartlepool	**51C** West Hartlepool			
68307	*J71*	**MID** Middlesbrough	**51D** Middlesbrough	**51D** Middlesbrough				
68308	*J71*	**DAR** Darlington	**51A** Darlington	**51A** Darlington	**51A** Darlington			
68309	*J71*	**GHD** Gateshead	**52A** Gateshead	**52A** Gateshead	**52A** Gateshead	**50A** York		
68310	*J71*	**YK** York						
68311	*J71*	**HLD** Hull Dairycoates	**53A** Hull Dairycoates					
68312	*J71*	**MID** Middlesbrough	**51D** Middlesbrough	**51D** Middlesbrough	**51D** Middlesbrough			
68313	*J71*	**SEL** Selby	**50A** York	**50A** York				
68314	*J71*	**GHD** Gateshead	**52A** Gateshead	**52A** Gateshead	**52A** Gateshead	**52A** Gateshead		
68316	*J71*	**HLD** Hull Dairycoates	**53A** Hull Dairycoates	**54C** Borough Gardens	**54C** Borough Gardens	**51C** West Hartlepool		
68317	*J55*	**DON** Doncaster						
68319	*J55*	Doncaster Works						
68320	*J88*	**STM** St. Margarets	**64A** St. Margarets	**64A** St. Margarets	**64A** St. Margarets	**64A** St. Margarets		
68321	*J88*	**THJ** Thornton Junction	**62A** Thornton Junction	**62A** Thornton Junction	**62A** Thornton Junction			
68322	*J88*	**THJ** Thornton Junction	**62A** Thornton Junction	**62A** Thornton Junction	**62A** Thornton Junction			
68323	*J88*	**THJ** Thornton Junction	**62A** Thornton Junction	**62A** Thornton Junction				
68324	*J88*	**POL** Polmont	**64E** Polmont	**64E** Polmont	**64E** Polmont			
68325	*J88*	**STM** St. Margarets	**64A** St. Margarets	**64A** St. Margarets	**64A** St. Margarets	**65A** Eastfield		
68326	*J88*	**EFD** Eastfield	**65A** Eastfield	**65A** Eastfield	**65F** Grangemouth			
68327	*J88*	**EFD** Eastfield	**65A** Eastfield	**65A** Eastfield	**65A** Eastfield			
68328	*J88*	**HAY** Haymarket	**64B** Haymarket	**64B** Haymarket	**64B** Haymarket			
68329	*J88*	**KPS** Kipps	**65E** Kipps	**65E** Kipps	**65E** Kipps			
68330	*J88*	**EFD** Eastfield	**65A** Eastfield	**65A** Eastfield	**65A** Eastfield			
68331	*J88*	**EFD** Eastfield	**65E** Kipps	**65E** Kipps	**62A** Thornton Junction			
68332	*J88*	**THJ** Thornton Junction	**62A** Thornton Junction	**62A** Thornton Junction	**62A** Thornton Junction	**62A** Thornton Junction		
68333	*J88*	**EFD** Eastfield	**65D** Dawsholm	**65D** Dawsholm	**65D** Dawsholm			
68334	*J88*	**STM** St. Margarets	**64A** St. Margarets	**64A** St. Margarets	**62A** Thornton Junction			
68335	*J88*	**THJ** Thornton Junction	**62A** Thornton Junction	**62A** Thornton Junction	**62A** Thornton Junction	**64B** Haymarket		
68336	*J88*	**EFD** Eastfield	**65A** Eastfield	**65A** Eastfield	**65E** Kipps	**65E** Kipps		
68337	*J88*	**THJ** Thornton Junction	**62A** Thornton Junction	**62A** Thornton Junction				
68338	*J88*	**STM** St. Margarets	**64A** St. Margarets	**64A** St. Margarets	**64A** St. Margarets	**64A** St. Margarets		
68339	*J88*	**HAY** Haymarket	**64B** Haymarket	**64B** Haymarket	**64B** Haymarket			
68340	*J88*	**STM** St. Margarets	**64A** St. Margarets	**64A** St. Margarets	**64A** St. Margarets			
68341	*J88*	**THJ** Thornton Junction	hire NCB Bannockburn	**62A** Thornton Junction				
68342	*J88*	**STG** Stirling Shore Road	**64A** St. Margarets	**64A** St. Margarets	**64A** St. Margarets	**64A** St. Margarets		
68343	*J88*	**KPS** Kipps	**65E** Kipps	**65E** Kipps	**65E** Kipps	**65E** Kipps		
68344	*J88*	**KPS** Kipps	**65E** Kipps	**66B** Motherwell	**65E** Kipps	**65D** Dawsholm		
68345	*J88*	**EFD** Eastfield	**62C** Dunfermline Upper	**62C** Dunfermline Upper	**62C** Dunfermline Upper	**65A** Eastfield		
68346	*J88*	**STG** Stirling Shore Road	**62C** Dunfermline Upper	**62C** Dunfermline Upper	**62C** Dunfermline Upper	**62C** Dunfermline Upper		
68347	*J88*	**EFD** Eastfield	**65A** Eastfield	**65A** Eastfield	**65A** Eastfield			
68348	*J88*	**STM** St. Margarets	**64A** St. Margarets	**64A** St. Margarets	**64A** St. Margarets			
68349	*J88*	**EFD** Eastfield	**65A** Eastfield	**65A** Eastfield	**65A** Eastfield	**65F** Grangemouth		
68350	*J88*	**POL** Polmont	**64E** Polmont	**64E** Polmont	**64E** Polmont	**62C** Dunfermline Upper		
68351	*J88*	**STG** Stirling Shore Road	**62C** Dunfermline Upper	**62C** Dunfermline Upper	**62C** Dunfermline Upper			
68352	*J88*	**STM** St. Margarets	**64A** St. Margarets	**64A** St. Margarets	**64A** St. Margarets	**65A** Eastfield		
68353	*J88*	**THJ** Thornton Junction	**62A** Thornton Junction	**62A** Thornton Junction	**62A** Thornton Junction	**62A** Thornton Junction		

		1948	1951	1954	1957	1960	1963	1966
68354	*J88*	POL Polmont	**64E** Polmont	**64E** Polmont	**64E** Polmont	**64E** Polmont		
68355	*J73*	WHL West Hartlepool	**51C** West Hartlepool	**51C** West Hartlepool	**51C** West Hartlepool			
68356	*J73*	SEL Selby	**50C** Selby	**50C** Selby	**50C** Selby			
68357	*J73*	SEL Selby	**50C** Selby	**50C** Selby	**50C** Selby			
68358	*J73*	WHL West Hartlepool	**51C** West Hartlepool	**51C** West Hartlepool				
68359	*J73*	WHL West Hartlepool	**51C** West Hartlepool	**51J** Northallerton	**51C** West Hartlepool			
68360	*J73*	HLA Hull Alexandra Dock	**53C** Hull Alexandra Dock	**53C** Hull Alexandra Dock	**53C** Hull Alexandra Dock	**53A** Hull Dairycoates		
68361	*J73*	HLA Hull Alexandra Dock	**53C** Hull Alexandra Dock	**53C** Hull Alexandra Dock	**53C** Hull Springhead	**53A** Hull Dairycoates		
68362	*J73*	SEL Selby	**50C** Selby	**50C** Selby	**50C** Selby			
68363	*J73*	TWD Tweedmouth	**53C** Hull Alexandra Dock	**53C** Hull Alexandra Dock	**53B** Hull Botanic Gardens			
68364	*J73*	WHL West Hartlepool	**51C** West Hartlepool	**51C** West Hartlepool	**51C** West Hartlepool	**51C** West Hartlepool		
68365	*J75*	WAL Walton on the Hill						
68366	*J60*	WRX Wrexham Rhosddu						
68368	*J60*	WRX Wrexham Rhosddu						
68370	*J66*	Stratford Works	Stratford Works	(32)				
68371	*J66*	STV Staveley	**38D** Staveley	**38D** Staveley				
68372	*J66*	CAM Cambridge	**31A** Cambridge					
68373	*J66*	IPS Ipswich	**32B** Ipswich					
68374	*J66*	IPS Ipswich	**32B** Ipswich	**38D** Staveley				
68375	*J66*	IPS Ipswich	**32B** Ipswich					
68376	*J66*	LIN Lincoln	**40A** Lincoln					
68377	*J66*	NOR Norwich Thorpe	**32G** Melton Constable					
68378	*J66*	COL Colchester	**31D** South Lynn	(36)				
68379	*J66*	STV Staveley						
68380	*J66*	NWE New England	**30A** Stratford					
68381	*J66*	STR Stratford						
68382	*J66*	STV Staveley	**38D** Staveley	(31)				
68383	*J66*	MAR March	**31A** Cambridge	**38D** Staveley				
68384	*J66*	NOR Norwich Thorpe						
68385	*J66*	LIN Lincoln	**40A** Lincoln					
68386	*J66*	IPS Ipswich						
68387	*J66*	NWE New England	**35A** New England					
68388	*J66*	STR Stratford	**32A** Norwich Thorpe					
68390	*J77*	HLA Hull Alexandra Dock						
68391	*J77*	DAR Darlington	**51F** West Auckland	**51F** West Auckland	**51F** West Auckland			
68392	*J77*	SBK Starbeck	**50D** Starbeck	**50D** Starbeck	**50D** Starbeck	**50A** York		
68393	*J77*	SBK Starbeck	**50D** Starbeck	**50D** Starbeck				
68395	*J77*	HLA Hull Alexandra Dock	**50B** Leeds Neville Hill	**50B** Leeds Neville Hill				
68396	*J77*	NBH North Blyth						
68397	*J77*	NBH North Blyth	**52F** North Blyth	**52F** North Blyth	**52F** North Blyth			
68398	*J77*	NBH North Blyth	**52F** North Blyth					
68399	*J77*	YK York	**50C** Selby	**52F** North Blyth	**52F** North Blyth			
68400	*J77*	TWD Tweedmouth						
68401	*J77*	YK York	**53B** Hull Botanic Gardens	**53B** Hull Botanic Gardens				
68402	*J77*	HLA Hull Alexandra Dock	**53C** Hull Alexandra Dock	**53A** Hull Dairycoates	**52F** North Blyth			
68404	*J77*	SBK Starbeck	**50D** Starbeck					
68405	*J77*	NBH North Blyth	**52F** North Blyth	**52F** North Blyth	**52F** North Blyth			
68406	*J77*	HLA Hull Alexandra Dock	**50B** Leeds Neville Hill	**50C** Selby	**50C** Selby			
68407	*J77*	SKN Stockton on Tees	**51E** Stockton on Tees	**51E** Stockton on Tees				
68408	*J77*	DAR Darlington	**51A** Darlington	**51A** Darlington	**52F** South Blyth	**52F** South Blyth		
68409	*J77*	MID Middlesbrough	**51D** Middlesbrough	**51D** Middlesbrough	**51D** Middlesbrough			
68410	*J77*	DAR Darlington	**51A** Darlington	**51A** Darlington	**51A** Darlington	**51C** West Hartlepool		
68412	*J77*	SKN Stockton on Tees	**51E** Stockton on Tees	**51E** Stockton on Tees	**51E** Stockton on Tees			
68413	*J77*	HLA Hull Alexandra Dock	**53C** Hull Alexandra Dock	**53A** Hull Dairycoates				
68414	*J77*	MID Middlesbrough	**51D** Middlesbrough	**51D** Middlesbrough	**51D** Middlesbrough			
68415	*J77*	SBH South Blyth						
68416	*J77*	NEV Leeds Neville Hill						
68417	*J77*	DAR Darlington	**52F** North Blyth	**52F** North Blyth				
68420	*J77*	SKN Stockton on Tees	**51E** Stockton on Tees	**51E** Stockton on Tees				
68421	*J77*	DAR Darlington	**52D** Tweedmouth	**52D** Tweedmouth				
68422	*J77*	MID Middlesbrough	**51D** Middlesbrough	**51D** Middlesbrough				
68423	*J77*	MID Middlesbrough	**51A** Darlington	**51A** Darlington	**51G** Haverton Hill			
68424	*J77*	TWD Tweedmouth	**52F** South Blyth	**52F** South Blyth	**52F** South Blyth			
68425	*J77*	DAR Darlington	**51D** Middlesbrough	**51D** Middlesbrough	**51A** Darlington	**53A** Hull Dairycoates		
68426	*J77*	NBH North Blyth	**52F** North Blyth	**52F** North Blyth	**52F** North Blyth			
68427	*J77*	NPT Newport	**52F** North Blyth	**52F** North Blyth	**52F** North Blyth			
68428	*J77*	SBH South Blyth	**52F** South Blyth	**52B** Heaton				
68429	*J77*	HLA Hull Alexandra Dock	**53C** Hull Alexandra Dock	**53C** Hull Alexandra Dock				
68430	*J77*	HTN Heaton	**52B** Heaton	**52F** North Blyth				
68431	*J77*	NPT Newport	**52F** South Blyth	**52F** South Blyth	**52F** South Blyth	**50A** York		
68432	*J77*	AUK West Auckland	**51A** Darlington	**51A** Darlington				
68433	*J77*	SBK Starbeck	**50C** Selby					
68434	*J77*	SBK Starbeck	**50D** Starbeck	**50D** Starbeck	**50D** Starbeck			
68435	*J77*	HLA Hull Alexandra Dock	**53C** Hull Alexandra Dock	**53C** Hull Alexandra Dock	**50A** York			
68436	*J77*	NEV Leeds Neville Hill	**50A** York	**52D** Tweedmouth				
68437	*J77*	TWD Tweedmouth	**52D** Tweedmouth	**52D** Tweedmouth				
68438	*J77*	SBK Starbeck	**50D** Starbeck	**50C** Selby	**51E** Stockton on Tees			
68440	*J77*	YK York	**53C** Hull Alexandra Dock	**52B** Heaton				
68441	*J77*	NPT Newport						
68442	*J83*	KPS Kipps	**65E** Kipps	**65E** Kipps	**65E** Kipps	**65E** Kipps		
68443	*J83*	KPS Kipps	**65E** Kipps	**65E** Kipps	**65E** Kipps	**65E** Kipps		
68444	*J83*	KPS Kipps	**65E** Kipps	**65E** Kipps	**65E** Kipps	**65E** Kipps		
68445	*J83*	KPS Kipps	**65E** Kipps	**65E** Kipps	**65E** Kipps	**65E** Kipps		
68446	*J83*	DEE Dundee Tay Bridge	**62B** Dundee Tay Bridge	**62B** Dundee Tay Bridge				
68447	*J83*	EFD Eastfield	**65A** Eastfield	**65A** Eastfield	**65A** Eastfield	**65A** Eastfield		
68448	*J83*	STM St. Margarets	**64A** St. Margarets	**64A** St. Margarets	**64A** St. Margarets	**64A** St. Margarets		
68449	*J83*	STM St. Margarets	**64A** St. Margarets	**64A** St. Margarets	**64A** St. Margarets			
68450	*J83*	STM St. Margarets	**64A** St. Margarets	**64A** St. Margarets	**64A** St. Margarets			
68451	*J83*	THJ Thornton Junction	**62A** Thornton Junction	**62A** Thornton Junction	**62A** Thornton Junction			
68452	*J83*	DEE Dundee Tay Bridge	**62B** Dundee Tay Bridge	**62B** Dundee Tay Bridge	**62B** Dundee Tay Bridge			
68453	*J83*	THJ Thornton Junction	**62A** Thornton Junction	**62A** Thornton Junction	**62A** Thornton Junction	**64A** St. Margarets		
68454	*J83*	STM St. Margarets	**64A** St. Margarets	**64A** St. Margarets	**64A** St. Margarets	**64A** St. Margarets		
68455	*J83*	DEE Dundee Tay Bridge	**62B** Dundee Tay Bridge	**62B** Dundee Tay Bridge				
68456	*J83*	THJ Thornton Junction	**62A** Thornton Junction	**62A** Thornton Junction	**62A** Thornton Junction	**64E** Polmont		
68457	*J83*	HAY Haymarket	**64B** Haymarket	**64B** Haymarket	**64B** Haymarket	**64B** Haymarket		
68458	*J83*	THJ Thornton Junction	**62A** Thornton Junction	**62A** Thornton Junction	**62A** Thornton Junction	**62A** Thornton Junction		
68459	*J83*	THJ Thornton Junction	**62A** Thornton Junction	**62A** Thornton Junction	**62A** Thornton Junction	**62A** Thornton Junction		
68460	*J83*	HAY Haymarket	**64B** Haymarket	**64B** Haymarket	**64B** Haymarket			
68461	*J83*	KPS Kipps	**65E** Kipps	**65E** Kipps	**65E** Kipps			
68463	*J83*	STM St. Margarets	**64A** St. Margarets	**64A** St. Margarets	**64A** St. Margarets			
68464	*J83*	STM St. Margarets	**64A** St. Margarets	**64A** St. Margarets	**64A** St. Margarets			
68465	*J83*	DFU Dunfermline Upper	**62C** Dunfermline Upper	**62B** Dundee Tay Bridge	**62B** Dundee Tay Bridge			
68466	*J83*	DEE Dundee Tay Bridge	**62B** Dundee Tay Bridge	**62B** Dundee Tay Bridge	**62B** Dundee Tay Bridge			
68467	*J83*	THJ Thornton Junction	**62A** Thornton Junction	**62A** Thornton Junction	**64E** Polmont			
68468	*J83*	EFD Eastfield	**65A** Eastfield	**65A** Eastfield	**65A** Eastfield			
68469	*J83*	PTH Perth South	**64A** St. Margarets	**64A** St. Margarets				
68470	*J83*	STM St. Margarets	**62B** Dundee Tay Bridge	**62B** Dundee Tay Bridge	**62B** Dundee Tay Bridge	**64A** St. Margarets		
68471	*J83*	POL Polmont	**64E** Polmont	**64E** Polmont	**64E** Polmont	**64E** Polmont		
68472	*J83*	STM St. Margarets	**64A** St. Margarets	**64A** St. Margarets	**64A** St. Margarets	**64A** St. Margarets		
68473	*J83*	HAY Haymarket	**64B** Haymarket	**64B** Haymarket				
68474	*J83*	STM St. Margarets	**64A** St. Margarets	**64A** St. Margarets	**64A** St. Margarets			
68475	*J83*	EFD Eastfield	**65A** Eastfield	**65A** Eastfield	**65A** Eastfield			
68476	*J83*	EFD Eastfield	**65A** Eastfield	**65A** Eastfield				
68477	*J83*	STM St. Margarets	**64A** St. Margarets	**64A** St. Margarets	**64A** St. Margarets	**64A** St. Margarets		

No.	Class	1948		1951	1954	1957	1960	1963	1966
68478	*J83*	**HAY**	Haymarket	**64B** Haymarket	**64B** Haymarket	**64B** Haymarket			
68479	*J83*	**EFD**	Eastfield	**65A** Eastfield	**65A** Eastfield	**65A** Eastfield	**65A** Eastfield		
68480	*J83*	**EFD**	Eastfield	**65A** Eastfield	**65A** Eastfield	**65A** Eastfield			
68481	*J83*	**HAY**	Haymarket	**64B** Haymarket	**64B** Haymarket	**64B** Haymarket	**64B** Haymarket		
68484	*J93*	**SL**	South Lynn						
68488	*J93*	**SL**	South Lynn						
68489	*J93*	**MC**	Melton Constable						
68490	*J67→J69*	**KL**	Kings Lynn	**31C** Kings Lynn	**31C** Kings Lynn	**31C** Kings Lynn			
68491	*J69*	**LEI**	Leicester Central	**30A** Stratford	**31A** Cambridge	**35A** New England			
68492	*J67*	**STM**	St. Margarets	**64A** St. Margarets	**64A** St. Margarets				
68493	*J67*	**KL**	Kings Lynn	**31C** Kings Lynn	**32B** Ipswich				
68494	*J69*	**KL**	Kings Lynn	**31C** Kings Lynn	**31D** South Lynn	**31D** South Lynn			
68495	*J69*	**NOR**	Norwich Thorpe	**32A** Norwich Thorpe	**31C** Kings Lynn	**31C** Kings Lynn			
68496	*J67*	**STR**	Stratford	**30A** Stratford	**30A** Stratford				
68497	*J69*	**BSE**	Bury St. Edmunds	**31E** Bury St. Edmunds	**31E** Bury St. Edmunds	**31E** Bury St. Edmunds	**41F** Mexborough		
68498	*J69→J69*	**IPS**	Ipswich	**32B** Ipswich	**31C** Kings Lynn	**31C** Kings Lynn	(44)		
68499	*J69*	**CAR**	Carlisle Canal	**12B** Carlisle Canal	**40F** Boston	**31C** Kings Lynn	**31C** Kings Lynn		
68500	*J69*	**STR**	Stratford	**30A** Stratford	**30F** Parkeston	**30A** Stratford	**30A** Stratford		
68501	*J69*	**NOR**	Norwich Thorpe	**32A** Norwich Thorpe	**40F** Boston	**40F** Boston	**40A** Lincoln		
68502	*J69*	**KL**	Kings Lynn	**31C** Kings Lynn	**31C** Kings Lynn	**31C** Kings Lynn	**36E** Retford		
68503	*J69*	**PKD**	Parkhead	**65C** Parkhead	**65C** Parkhead	**65C** Parkhead			
68504	*J69*	**THJ**	Thornton Junction	**62A** Thornton Junction	**62A** Thornton Junction				
68505	*J69*	**STM**	St. Margarets	**64A** St. Margarets					
68507	*J69*	**STR**	Stratford	**30A** Stratford	**30A** Stratford	**36A** Doncaster	**36A** Doncaster		
68508	*J69*	**STR**	Stratford	**30A** Stratford	**30E** Colchester	**36E** Retford	**36A** Doncaster		
68509	*J67*	**STR**	Stratford	**31A** Cambridge	**32B** Ipswich				
68510	*J67→J69*	**IPS**	Ipswich	**30A** Stratford	**30A** Stratford	**30A** Stratford			
68511	*J67*	**STM**	St. Margarets	**64A** St. Margarets	**65D** Dawsholm				
68512	*J67→J69*	**HIT**	Hitchin	**34D** Hitchin	**40A** Lincoln	**38D** Staveley			
68513	*J67→J69*	**STR**	Stratford	**30A** Stratford	**30A** Stratford	**30A** Stratford	**30A** Stratford		
68514	*J67*	**KL**	Kings Lynn	**31C** Kings Lynn	**32A** Norwich Thorpe				
68515	*J67*	**KL**	Kings Lynn	**31C** Kings Lynn	**32G** Melton Constable	**32G** Melton Constable			
68516	*J67*	**CAM**	Cambridge	**31A** Cambridge	**32A** Norwich Thorpe	**30A** Stratford			
68517	*J67→J69*	**CAM**	Cambridge	**30A** Stratford	**30A** Stratford				
68518	*J67*	**IPS**	Ipswich	**32B** Ipswich	**32B** Ipswich	**32B** Ipswich			
68519	*J67→J69*	**PKS**	Parkeston	**30A** Stratford	**30A** Stratford	**36E** Retford			
68520	*J67→J69*	**STR**	Stratford	**30A** Stratford	**30A** Stratford	**36E** Retford			
68521	*J67*	**PKS**	Parkeston	**30A** Stratford	**30A** Stratford				
68522	*J67→J69*	**STR**	Stratford	**30E** Colchester	**30E** Colchester	**30E** Colchester	**40F** Boston		
68523	*J67*	**STR**	Stratford	**30A** Stratford	**32A** Norwich Thorpe				
68524	*J69*	**POL**	Polmont	**64E** Polmont	**64E** Polmont	**64E** Polmont			
68525	*J69*	**STM**	St. Margarets	**64A** St. Margarets					
68526	*J69*	**STR**	Stratford	**30A** Stratford	**30A** Stratford	**30A** Stratford	**30F** Parkeston		
68527	*J69*	**CLK**	Colwick	**30F** Parkeston	**30A** Stratford	**36E** Retford			
68528	*J69*	**BOS**	Boston	**40F** Boston	**40A** Lincoln	**40A** Lincoln			
68529	*J67→J69*	**LIN**	Lincoln	**40A** Lincoln	**34D** Hitchin	**30A** Stratford			
68530	*J69*	**CAM**	Cambridge	**31A** Cambridge	**31A** Cambridge	**31A** Cambridge	**36E** Retford		
68531	*J67*	**WRX**	Wrexham Rhosddu	**6E** Wrexham Rhosddu	**6E** Wrexham Rhosddu				
68532	*J69*	**STR**	Stratford	**30A** Stratford	**30A** Stratford	**30A** Stratford	(43)		
68533	*J69*	**POL**	Polmont	**64E** Polmont					
68534	*J69*	**STR**	Stratford	**30A** Stratford	**30A** Stratford				
68535	*J69*	**THJ**	Thornton Junction	**62A** Thornton Junction	**62A** Thornton Junction	**62B** Dundee Tay Bridge			
68536	*J67*	**CAM**	Cambridge	**32G** Melton Constable	**32G** Melton Constable	**32G** Melton Constable			
68537	*J69*	**LIN**	Lincoln	**40A** Lincoln	**40A** Lincoln	**40A** Lincoln			
68538	*J69*	**STR**	Stratford	**30A** Stratford	**30A** Stratford	**30A** Stratford	**30A** Stratford		
68540	*J67*	**TFD**	Trafford Park	**9E** Trafford Park	**34D** Hitchin				
68541	*J69*	**HIT**	Hitchin	**34D** Hitchin	**40A** Lincoln	**40A** Lincoln			
68542	*J69*	**KL**	Kings Lynn	**31D** South Lynn	**31D** South Lynn	**31D** South Lynn	**31C** Kings Lynn		
68543	*J69*	**BOS**	Boston	**40F** Boston	**40F** Boston	**40F** Boston	(45)		
68544	*J69*	**POL**	Polmont	**64E** Polmont	**64E** Polmont				
68545	*J69*	**STR**	Stratford	**31C** Kings Lynn	**31C** Kings Lynn	**31C** Kings Lynn	**40E** Colwick		
68546	*J69*	**NWE**	New England	**30A** Stratford	**30A** Stratford	**30A** Stratford			
68547	*J67*	**LIV**	Brunswick	**8D** Widnes	**8E** Brunswick				
68548	*J69*	**STR**	Stratford	**30A** Stratford					
68549	*J69*	**STR**	Stratford	**30A** Stratford	**30A** Stratford	**30A** Stratford	**30A** Stratford		
68550	*J69*	**THJ**	Thornton Junction	**62A** Thornton Junction	**30A** Stratford	**38A** Colwick	**40E** Colwick		
68551	*J69*	**EFD**	Eastfield	**65A** Eastfield	**65G** Yoker	**62B** Dundee Tay Bridge			
68552	*J69*	**EFD**	Eastfield	**65A** Eastfield	**30A** Stratford	**30E** Colchester	**30F** Parkeston		
68553	*J69*	**LIN**	Lincoln	**40A** Lincoln	**38D** Staveley	**40A** Lincoln			
68554	*J69*	**STR**	Stratford	**30A** Stratford	**30A** Stratford	**31A** Cambridge	**40A** Lincoln		
68555	*J69*	**THJ**	Thornton Junction	**62A** Thornton Junction	**31E** Bury St. Edmunds	**32A** Norwich Thorpe			
68556	*J69*	**STR**	Stratford	**30F** Parkeston	**30A** Stratford	**31C** Kings Lynn	**36A** Doncaster		
68557	*J69*	**STR**	Stratford	**30A** Stratford	**40F** Boston	**40F** Boston			
68558	*J69*	**LIN**	Lincoln	**40A** Lincoln	**40A** Lincoln	**40A** Lincoln	**36A** Doncaster		
68559	*J69*	**LIV**	Brunswick	**8E** Brunswick	**9E** Trafford Park				
68560	*J69*	**BOS**	Boston	**40F** Boston	**40F** Boston	**40F** Boston	**40A** Lincoln		
68561	*J69*	**STR**	Stratford	**30F** Parkeston	**30A** Stratford	**36E** Retford			
68562	*J69*	**STM**	St. Margarets	**64A** St. Margarets	**68B** Dumfries				
68563	*J69*	**STR**	Stratford	**30A** Stratford	**30A** Stratford	**30A** Stratford	**30F** Parkeston		
68565	*J69*	**HAT**	Hatfield	**34C** Hatfield	**30A** Stratford	**32C** Lowestoft	**30A** Stratford		
68566	*J69*	**SL**	South Lynn	**31D** South Lynn	**31D** South Lynn	**31D** South Lynn	**31C** Kings Lynn		
68567	*J69*	**PKD**	Parkhead	**65C** Parkhead	**31D** South Lynn	**31A** Cambridge			
68568	*J69*	**STM**	St. Margarets	**61B** Aberdeen Ferryhill	**30A** Stratford	**30A** Stratford			
68569	*J69*	**STR**	Stratford	**30A** Stratford	**30A** Stratford	**40F** Boston	**41J** Langwith Junction		
68570	*J69*	**MC**	Melton Constable	**32A** Norwich Thorpe	**40F** Boston	**40F** Boston	**40F** Boston		
68571	*J69*	**PKS**	Parkeston	**30A** Stratford	**30A** Stratford	**30A** Stratford	**30A** Stratford		
68572	*J67*	**HAT**	Hatfield	**34C** Hatfield	**32B** Ipswich				
68573	*J69*	**STR**	Stratford	**30A** Stratford	**30A** Stratford	**30A** Stratford	**30F** Parkeston		
68574	*J69*	**STR**	Stratford	**30A** Stratford	**30A** Stratford	**30A** Stratford			
68575	*J69*	**STR**	Stratford	**30A** Stratford	**30A** Stratford	**30A** Stratford	**30A** Stratford		
68576	*J69*	**STR**	Stratford	**30A** Stratford	**30A** Stratford	**30A** Stratford			
68577	*J69*	**STR**	Stratford	**30A** Stratford	**30A** Stratford	**30A** Stratford	**30A** Stratford		
68578	*J69*	**STR**	Stratford	**30E** Colchester	**30E** Colchester	**30A** Stratford	**30A** Stratford		
68579	*J69*	**BSE**	Bury St. Edmunds	**31A** Cambridge	**30A** Stratford	**30A** Stratford	**30A** Stratford		
68581	*J69*	**BOS**	Boston	**40F** Boston	**40F** Boston	**40F** Boston			
68583	*J67*	**CAM**	Cambridge	**9E** Trafford Park	**9E** Trafford Park	**17F** Trafford Park			
68584	*J67*	**WAL**	Walton on the Hill	**27E** Walton on the Hill	**6E** Wrexham Rhosddu				
68585	*J69*	**TFD**	Trafford Park	**27E** Walton on the Hill	**27E** Walton on the Hill	**6E** Wrexham Rhosddu			
68586	*J67*	**NOR**	Norwich Thorpe	**32A** Norwich Thorpe	**32B** Ipswich				
68587	*J69*	**LIN**	Lincoln	**40A** Lincoln	**40A** Lincoln	**40A** Lincoln			
68588	*J67→J69*	**NWE**	New England	**30A** Stratford	**30A** Stratford	**30A** Stratford			
68589	*J67*	**STR**	Stratford	**30A** Stratford	**30A** Stratford				
68590	*J67*	**STR**	Stratford	**30A** Stratford	**30A** Stratford				
68591	*J67→J69*	**STR**	Stratford	**30A** Stratford	**30A** Stratford	**30A** Stratford	**41J** Langwith Junction		
68592	*J67*	**STR**	Stratford	**30A** Stratford	**32A** Norwich Thorpe				
68593	*J67*	**STR**	Stratford	**32B** Ipswich	**32B** Ipswich	**32B** Ipswich			
68594	*J67*	**STR**	Stratford	**30A** Stratford	**30A** Stratford				
68595	*J67*	**NOR**	Norwich Thorpe	**9E** Trafford Park	**9E** Trafford Park	**6E** Wrexham Rhosddu			
68596	*J69*	**PKS**	Parkeston	**30F** Parkeston	**30A** Stratford	**30A** Stratford			
68597	*J67*	**SL**	South Lynn	**31D** South Lynn	**32A** Norwich Thorpe				
68598	*J69*	**GOR**	Gorton	**9E** Trafford Park	**9E** Trafford Park	**8E** Brunswick			
68599	*J69*	**LIN**	Lincoln	**40A** Lincoln	**40A** Lincoln	**40A** Lincoln			
68600	*J69*	**KL**	Kings Lynn	**31D** South Lynn	**31A** Cambridge	**31A** Cambridge	**30A** Stratford		
68601	*J69*	**STR**	Stratford	**30A** Stratford	**30A** Stratford	**38A** Colwick			

No.	Class	1948	1951	1954	1957	1960	1963	1966
68602	J69	LOW Lowestoft	32A Norwich Thorpe	40F Boston	40F Boston			
68603	J69	NOR Norwich Thorpe	32A Norwich Thorpe	31B March	31B March			
68605	J69	HIT Hitchin	34D Hitchin	40A Lincoln	40A Lincoln			
68606	J67	STR Stratford	30A Stratford	32B Ipswich				
68607	J69	STR Stratford	30A Stratford	30A Stratford	30A Stratford			
68608	J67	STR Stratford	30E Colchester	32A Norwich Thorpe	38D Staveley			
68609	J67→J69	CAM Cambridge	31A Cambridge	31A Cambridge	31A Cambridge	30A Stratford		
68610	J67	LIN Lincoln	40A Lincoln	34D Hitchin	34D Hitchin			
68611	J67	LOW Lowestoft	32C Lowestoft	32C Lowestoft				
68612	J69	STR Stratford	30A Stratford	30A Stratford	30A Stratford	30A Stratford		
68613	J69	STR Stratford	30A Stratford	30A Stratford	30A Stratford	30A Stratford		
68616	J67	COL Colchester	30E Colchester	32A Norwich Thorpe	38D Staveley			
68617	J69	STR Stratford	30A Stratford	30A Stratford	38D Staveley			
68618	J69	LIN Lincoln	40A Lincoln	40A Lincoln	40A Lincoln			
68619	J69	STR Stratford	30A Stratford	30A Stratford	30A Stratford	30A Stratford		
68621	J69	STR Stratford	30A Stratford	30A Stratford	36A Doncaster	36E Retford		
68623	J69	STM St. Margarets	64A St. Margarets	31D South Lynn	31D South Lynn	41F Mexborough		
68625	J69	YAR Yarmouth South Town	32D Yarmouth South Town	31A Cambridge	32G Melton Constable			
68626	J69	STR Stratford	30A Stratford	30A Stratford	35A New England	34F Grantham		
68628	J67	YAR Yarmouth South Town	32D Yarmouth South Town	32D Yarmouth South Town	32D Yarmouth South Town			
68629	J69	COL Colchester	30A Stratford	30A Stratford	38A Colwick			
68630	J69	STR Stratford	30A Stratford	30A Stratford	30A Stratford			
68631	J69	STR Stratford	30A Stratford	30A Stratford	30A Stratford			
68632	J69	NWE New England	35A New England	30A Stratford	30A Stratford			
68633	J69	STR Stratford	30A Stratford	30A Stratford	30A Stratford	30A Stratford		
68635	J69	DFU Dunfermline Upper	62C Dunfermline Upper	31C Kings Lynn	35A New England	34F Grantham		
68636	J69	COL Colchester	30E Colchester	30E Colchester	30A Stratford			
68638	J68	PKS Parkeston	30E Colchester	30E Colchester	34D Hitchin			
68639	J68	STR Stratford	30A Stratford	30A Stratford	30A Stratford			
68640	J68	LOW Lowestoft	32C Lowestoft	32C Lowestoft	32A Norwich Thorpe			
68641	J68	NOR Norwich Thorpe	32A Norwich Thorpe	32A Norwich Thorpe	32A Norwich Thorpe			
68642	J68	PKS Parkeston	30A Stratford	30A Stratford	32A Norwich Thorpe	30A Stratford		
68643	J68	STR Stratford	30F Parkeston	30F Parkeston	30F Parkeston			
68644	J68	STR Stratford	30A Stratford	30A Stratford	30A Stratford	30A Stratford		
68645	J68	CAM Cambridge	31A Cambridge	32A Norwich Thorpe	32A Norwich Thorpe			
68646	J68	STR Stratford	30A Stratford	30A Stratford	30A Stratford	30A Stratford		
68647	J68	STR Stratford	30A Stratford	30A Stratford	30A Stratford	30A Stratford		
68648	J68	STR Stratford	30A Stratford	30A Stratford	30A Stratford			
68649	J68	STR Stratford	30A Stratford	30A Stratford	30A Stratford	30A Stratford		
68650	J68	STR Stratford	30A Stratford	30A Stratford	30A Stratford	30A Stratford		
68651	J68	YB Yarmouth Beach	32F Yarmouth Beach	32F Yarmouth Beach	32F Yarmouth Beach			
68652	J68	STR Stratford	30A Stratford	30A Stratford	30A Stratford			
68653	J68	STR Stratford	30F Parkeston	30A Stratford	30A Stratford			
68654	J68	MAR March	31B March	30A Stratford	30A Stratford	36A Doncaster		
68655	J68	BOS Boston	40F Boston	30A Stratford	30A Stratford			
68656	J68	KL Kings Lynn	31C Kings Lynn	32D Yarmouth South Town	32D Yarmouth South Town	32C Lowestoft		
68657	J68	BOS Boston	40F Boston	30A Stratford	30A Stratford			
68658	J68	BOS Boston	40F Boston	30A Stratford	30A Stratford			
68659	J68	BOS Boston	40F Boston	30A Stratford	30A Stratford			
68660	J68	PKS Parkeston	30A Stratford	30A Stratford	30A Stratford	30A Stratford		
68661	J68	STR Stratford	30A Stratford	30A Stratford	34D Hitchin			
68662	J68	STR Stratford	30A Stratford	30A Stratford	30E Colchester			
68663	J68	STR Stratford	30A Stratford	30A Stratford	30A Stratford	30A Stratford		
68664	J68	MAR March	31B March	32A Norwich Thorpe	32C Lowestoft			
68665	J68	STR Stratford	30A Stratford	30A Stratford	30A Stratford			
68666	J68	STR Stratford	30A Stratford	30A Stratford	30E Colchester			
68667	J92	Stratford Works	Stratford Works					
68668	J92	Stratford Works	Stratford Works	(35)				
68669	J92	Stratford Works						
68670	J72	HLA Hull Alexandra Dock	53C Hull Alexandra Dock	53C Hull Alexandra Dock	53A Hull Dairycoates	53A Hull Dairycoates		
68671	J72	BID Bidston	6E Wrexham Rhosddu	6E Wrexham Rhosddu	6E Wrexham Rhosddu	6F Bidston		
68672	J72	NEV Leeds Neville Hill	50B Leeds Neville Hill	50B Leeds Neville Hill	50B Leeds Neville Hill	53A Hull Dairycoates		
68673	J72	HLD Hull Dairycoates	53C Hull Alexandra Dock	53C Hull Alexandra Dock	53C Hull Alexandra Dock	53C Hull Alexandra Dock		
68674	J72	GHD Gateshead	52A Gateshead	52A Gateshead	52A Gateshead	52A Gateshead		
68675	J72	HTN Heaton	52A Gateshead	52A Gateshead	52A Gateshead	52A Gateshead		
68676	J72	HLD Hull Dairycoates	53C Hull Alexandra Dock	53C Hull Alexandra Dock	53C Hull Alexandra Dock	53C Hull Alexandra Dock		
68677	J72	YK York	50A York	50A York	50A York	50A York		
68678	J72	AUK West Auckland	54A Sunderland	54A Sunderland	54A Sunderland	52G Sunderland		
68679	J72	BOR Borough Gardens	51A Darlington	51A Darlington	51A Darlington	51A Darlington		
68680	J72	GHD Gateshead	52A Gateshead	52A Gateshead	52A Gateshead	52A Gateshead		
68681	J72	NEV Leeds Neville Hill	50B Leeds Neville Hill	50B Leeds Neville Hill	55E Normanton	55E Normanton		
68682	J72	HTN Heaton	52B Heaton	52B Heaton	52D Tweedmouth			
68683	J72	HTN Heaton	51C West Hartlepool	51C West Hartlepool	51C West Hartlepool	51C West Hartlepool		
68684	J72	WHL West Hartlepool	51C West Hartlepool	51C West Hartlepool	51D Middlesbrough	51L Thornaby		
68685	J72	WHL West Hartlepool	51C West Hartlepool	51C West Hartlepool	51F West Auckland	51F West Auckland		
68686	J72	HLA Hull Alexandra Dock	53C Hull Alexandra Dock	53C Hull Alexandra Dock	50A York	50A York		
68687	J72	HTN Heaton	52B Heaton	54B Tyne Dock	54B Tyne Dock	50A York		
68688	J72	DAR Darlington	51D Middlesbrough	51D Middlesbrough	51D Middlesbrough	51L Thornaby		
68689	J72	WHL West Hartlepool	51D Middlesbrough	51D Middlesbrough	51D Middlesbrough	51L Thornaby		
68690	J72	MID Middlesbrough	51D Middlesbrough	51D Middlesbrough	51D Middlesbrough	51L Thornaby		
68691	J72	SUN Sunderland	51F West Auckland	51F West Auckland	51F West Auckland	51F West Auckland		
68692	J72	WHL West Hartlepool	51C West Hartlepool	51C West Hartlepool	51F West Auckland	51F West Auckland		
68693	J72	GHD Gateshead	52A Gateshead	52A Gateshead	52A Gateshead	52A Gateshead		
68694	J72	WHL West Hartlepool	51C West Hartlepool	51C West Hartlepool	54C Borough Gardens			
68695	J72	YK York	50A York	50A York	50A York	52A Gateshead		
68696	J72	AUK West Auckland	51F West Auckland	51F West Auckland	51E Stockton on Tees	51L Thornaby		
68697	J72	WHL West Hartlepool	51C West Hartlepool	51C West Hartlepool	54C Borough Gardens	52A Gateshead		
68698	J72	SUN Sunderland	54A Sunderland	54A Sunderland	54A Sunderland	51C West Hartlepool		
68699	J72	YK York	50A York	50A York	54C Borough Gardens			
68700	J72	KIT Kittybrewster	61A Kittybrewster	61A Kittybrewster	61C Keith			
68701	J72	BID Bidston	6F Bidston	6F Bidston	55E Normanton	55E Normanton		
68702	J72	GHD Gateshead	52A Gateshead	52B Heaton	52B Heaton	52B Heaton		
68703	J72	WHL West Hartlepool	51C West Hartlepool	51C West Hartlepool	51C West Hartlepool	51C West Hartlepool		
68704	J72	BOR Borough Gardens	54A Sunderland	54A Sunderland	54A Sunderland	52G Sunderland		
68705	J72	BOR Borough Gardens	54C Borough Gardens	54C Borough Gardens	54C Borough Gardens	53A Hull Dairycoates		
68706	J72	BOR Borough Gardens	54B Tyne Dock	54B Tyne Dock	54B Tyne Dock	52H Tyne Dock		
68707	J72	SUN Sunderland	51A Darlington	51F West Auckland	51C West Hartlepool	51C West Hartlepool		
68708	J72	BOR Borough Gardens	54C Borough Gardens	54C Borough Gardens	52B Heaton	52B Heaton		
68709	J72	EFD Eastfield	65A Eastfield	65A Eastfield	65A Eastfield	65E Kipps		
68710	J72	KIT Kittybrewster	61A Kittybrewster	61A Kittybrewster	61A Kittybrewster			
68711	J72	MID Middlesbrough	51C West Hartlepool	51C West Hartlepool	51C West Hartlepool	51C West Hartlepool		
68712	J72	MID Middlesbrough	51D Middlesbrough	51D Middlesbrough	51D Middlesbrough			
68713	J72	MID Middlesbrough	51D Middlesbrough	51D Middlesbrough	52B Heaton	52B Heaton		
68714	J72	BID Bidston	6F Bidston	6C Birkenhead	6C Birkenhead	6F Bidston		
68715	J72	YK York	50A York	51C West Hartlepool	51C West Hartlepool	51C West Hartlepool		
68716	J72	WHL West Hartlepool	51C West Hartlepool	51C West Hartlepool	52B Heaton	51A Darlington		
68717	J72	KIT Kittybrewster	61A Kittybrewster	61A Kittybrewster	61A Kittybrewster	61A Kittybrewster		
68718	J72	SUN Sunderland	54A Sunderland	53C Hull Alexandra Dock	53A Hull Dairycoates			
68719	J72	KIT Kittybrewster	61A Kittybrewster	61A Kittybrewster	61A Kittybrewster	61A Kittybrewster		
68720	J72	GHD Gateshead	52A Gateshead	52A Gateshead	52A Gateshead	52A Gateshead		
68721	J72	MID Middlesbrough	51D Middlesbrough	51D Middlesbrough	51D Middlesbrough	51L Thornaby		
68722	J72	YK York	50A York	50A York	50A York	51C West Hartlepool		
68723	J72	GHD Gateshead	52A Gateshead	52A Gateshead	52A Gateshead	52A Gateshead	52A Gateshead	
68724	J72	HLA Hull Alexandra Dock	53C Hull Alexandra Dock	50A York	50A York	51F West Auckland		

No.	Class	1948		1951	1954	1957	1960	1963	1966
68725	*J72*	**HTN**	Heaton	**52B** Heaton	**52B** Heaton	**52D** Tweedmouth	**52D** Tweedmouth		
68726	*J72*	**YK**	York	**50A** York	**50A** York	**50A** York	**55E** Normanton		
68727	*J72*	**BID**	Bidston	**6F** Bidston	**6F** Bidston	**6E** Wrexham Rhosddu	**6F** Bidston		
68728	*J72*	**TDK**	Tyne Dock	**54C** Borough Gardens	**54C** Borough Gardens	**54C** Borough Gardens	**52A** Gateshead		
68729	*J72*	**TDK**	Tyne Dock	**54B** Tyne Dock	**54B** Tyne Dock	**54B** Tyne Dock	**51L** Thornaby		
68730	*J72*	**SUN**	Sunderland	**54C** Borough Gardens	**54C** Borough Gardens	**54C** Borough Gardens	**52H** Tyne Dock		
68731	*J72*	**TDK**	Tyne Dock	**54B** Tyne Dock	**52C** Blaydon	**52C** Blaydon	**52H** Tyne Dock		
68732	*J72*	**HTN**	Heaton	**52A** Gateshead	**52A** Gateshead	**52A** Gateshead	**52B** Heaton		
68733	*J72*	**EFD**	Eastfield	**65A** Eastfield	**65A** Eastfield	**65A** Eastfield	**65E** Kipps		
68734	*J72*	**WHL**	West Hartlepool	**51C** West Hartlepool	**51C** West Hartlepool	**51C** West Hartlepool	**51C** West Hartlepool		
68735	*J72*	**YK**	York	**50A** York	**50A** York	**50A** York			
68736	*J72*	**BOR**	Borough Gardens	**54C** Borough Gardens	**54C** Borough Gardens	**54C** Borough Gardens	**50A** York	**52A** Gateshead	
68737	*J72*	**BOR**	Borough Gardens	**54C** Borough Gardens	**54C** Borough Gardens	**54C** Borough Gardens	**52A** Gateshead		
68738	*J72*	**DAR**	Darlington	**52B** Heaton	**52B** Heaton	**52B** Heaton	**52B** Heaton		
68739	*J72*	**YK**	York	**50A** York	**50A** York	**50A** York			
68740	*J72*	**MID**	Middlesbrough	**51D** Middlesbrough	**51D** Middlesbrough	**51D** Middlesbrough	**51L** Thornaby		
68741	*J72*	**YK**	York	**50A** York	**53C** Hull Alexandra Dock	**53A** Hull Dairycoates			
68742	*J72*	**WHL**	West Hartlepool	**52B** Heaton	**52B** Heaton	**52B** Heaton	**52B** Heaton		
68743	*J72*	**HTN**	Heaton	**53C** Hull Alexandra Dock	**53A** Hull Dairycoates	**54B** Tyne Dock	**52H** Tyne Dock		
68744	*J72*	**HTN**	Heaton	**52A** Gateshead	**52A** Gateshead	**52A** Gateshead	**51A** Darlington		
68745	*J72*	**YK**	York	**50A** York	**50A** York	**53C** Hull Alexandra Dock	**53C** Hull Alexandra Dock		
68746	*J72*	**NEV**	Leeds Neville Hill	**53C** Hull Alexandra Dock	**53C** Hull Alexandra Dock	**53C** Hull Alexandra Dock			
68747	*J72*	**HLA**	Hull Alexandra Dock	**53C** Hull Alexandra Dock	**53A** Hull Dairycoates	**52B** Heaton	**52B** Heaton		
68748	*J72*	**HLA**	Hull Alexandra Dock	**53A** Hull Dairycoates	**51A** Darlington	**51A** Darlington			
68749	*J72*	**KIT**	Kittybrewster	**61A** Kittybrewster	**61A** Kittybrewster	**61A** Kittybrewster	**61A** Kittybrewster		
68750	*J72*	**KIT**	Kittybrewster	**61A** Kittybrewster	**61A** Kittybrewster	**61A** Kittybrewster	**61A** Kittybrewster		
68751	*J72*	**HLA**	Hull Alexandra Dock	**53C** Hull Alexandra Dock	**53C** Hull Alexandra Dock	**53A** Hull Dairycoates			
68752	*J72*	**HLA**	Hull Alexandra Dock	**53C** Hull Alexandra Dock	**53C** Hull Alexandra Dock	**53C** Hull Alexandra Dock	**53A** Hull Dairycoates		
68753	*J72*	**HLA**	Hull Alexandra Dock	**53C** Hull Alexandra Dock	**53C** Hull Alexandra Dock	**53A** Hull Dairycoates	**53A** Hull Dairycoates		
68754	*J72*	**MID**	Middlesbrough	**51D** Middlesbrough	**51D** Middlesbrough	**51A** Darlington	**51A** Darlington		
68757	*J52*	**HSY**	Hornsey	**34B** Hornsey	**34A** Kings Cross				
68758	*J52*	**HSY**	Hornsey	**34B** Hornsey	**38A** Colwick				
68759	*J52*	**HSY**	Hornsey	**34B** Hornsey	**35C** Spital Bridge				
68760	*J52*	**HSY**	Hornsey	**34B** Hornsey	**35A** New England				
68761	*J52*	**HSY**	Hornsey	**34B** Hornsey	**36A** Doncaster	**36A** Doncaster			
68762	*J52*	**CLK**	Colwick	**38A** Colwick					
68763	*J52*	**DON**	Doncaster						
68764	*J52*	**KX**	Kings Cross	**34A** Kings Cross	**34A** Kings Cross				
68765	*J52*	**NWE**	New England	**35A** New England	**35A** New England				
68766	*J52*	**ARD**	Ardsley	**36E** Retford					
68767	*J52*	**CLK**	Colwick						
68768	*J52*	**CLK**	Colwick	**38A** Colwick	**38A** Colwick	**38A** Colwick			
68769	*J52*	**DON**	Doncaster	**36A** Doncaster	**36A** Doncaster				
68770	*J52*	**KX**	Kings Cross	**34A** Kings Cross					
68771	*J52*	**KX**	Kings Cross	**34A** Kings Cross	**35A** New England				
68772	*J52*	**KX**	Kings Cross	**34A** Kings Cross	**34A** Kings Cross				
68773	*J52*	**HSY**	Hornsey	**34B** Hornsey					
68774	*J52*	**HSY**	Hornsey	**34B** Hornsey					
68775	*J52*	**DON**	Doncaster	**36A** Doncaster					
68776	*J52*	**HSY**	Hornsey	**34B** Hornsey					
68777	*J52*	**HSY**	Hornsey	**34B** Hornsey	**38A** Colwick				
68778	*J52*	**HSY**	Hornsey	**34B** Hornsey	**36A** Doncaster	**36A** Doncaster			
68779	*J52*	**CLK**	Colwick	**38A** Colwick					
68780	*J52*	**KX**	Kings Cross	**34A** Kings Cross	**35B** Grantham				
68781	*J52*	**HSY**	Hornsey	**34B** Hornsey	**38A** Colwick				
68782	*J52*		Doncaster Works						
68783	*J52*	**HSY**	Hornsey	**34B** Hornsey	**35C** Spital Bridge				
68784	*J52*	**HSY**	Hornsey	**34B** Hornsey	**36A** Doncaster	**36A** Doncaster			
68785	*J52*	**HSY**	Hornsey	**34B** Hornsey	**36A** Doncaster	**38A** Colwick			
68786	*J52*	**DON**	Doncaster	**36A** Doncaster					
68787	*J52*	**HSY**	Hornsey	**34B** Hornsey	**38A** Colwick				
68788	*J52*	**HSY**	Hornsey	**34B** Hornsey	**38A** Colwick				
68789	*J52*	**NWE**	New England	**35A** New England					
68790	*J52*	**ARD**	Ardsley	**37A** Ardsley	**37A** Ardsley				
68791	*J52*	**HSY**	Hornsey	**34B** Hornsey	**38A** Colwick				
68792	*J52*	**CLK**	Colwick	**38A** Colwick					
68793	*J52*	**HSY**	Hornsey	**34B** Hornsey	**37A** Ardsley				
68794	*J52*	**HSY**	Hornsey	**34B** Hornsey					
68795	*J52*	**HSY**	Hornsey	**34B** Hornsey	**36A** Doncaster				
68796	*J52*	**HSY**	Hornsey	**34B** Hornsey	**36A** Doncaster				
68797	*J52*	**KX**	Kings Cross	**34A** Kings Cross	**35C** Spital Bridge				
68798	*J52*	**NWE**	New England	**35B** Grantham	**38A** Colwick				
68799	*J52*	**KX**	Kings Cross	**34A** Kings Cross	**34A** Kings Cross				
68800	*J52*	**DON**	Doncaster	**36A** Doncaster	**36A** Doncaster	**36A** Doncaster			
68801	*J52*	**GRA**	Grantham						
68802	*J52*	**KX**	Kings Cross	**34A** Kings Cross	**34A** Kings Cross				
68803	*J52*	**KX**	Kings Cross	**34A** Kings Cross					
68804	*J52*	**DON**	Doncaster	**36A** Doncaster	**36A** Doncaster				
68805	*J52*	**KX**	Kings Cross	**34A** Kings Cross	**34A** Kings Cross				
68806	*J52*	**DON**	Doncaster	**36A** Doncaster	**36A** Doncaster				
68807	*J52*	**CLK**	Colwick	**38A** Colwick	**38A** Colwick				
68808	*J52*	**HSY**	Hornsey	**34B** Hornsey	**34B** Hornsey	**34B** Hornsey			
68809	*J52*	**KX**	Kings Cross	**34A** Kings Cross	**35C** Spital Bridge				
68810	*J52*	**CLK**	Colwick	**38A** Colwick	**38A** Colwick				
68811	*J52*	**HSY**	Hornsey	**34B** Hornsey	**36A** Doncaster	**36A** Doncaster			
68812	*J52*	**CLK**	Colwick	**38A** Colwick	**38A** Colwick				
68813	*J52*	**DON**	Doncaster	**36A** Doncaster	**36A** Doncaster				
68814	*J52*	**CLK**	Colwick	**38A** Colwick	**38A** Colwick				
68815	*J52*	**HSY**	Hornsey	**34B** Hornsey	**35B** Grantham	**35A** New England			
68816	*J52*	**GRA**	Grantham	Doncaster Works	(2)				
68817	*J52*	**NWE**	New England	**35A** New England	**35A** New England	**36A** Doncaster			
68818	*J52*	**KX**	Kings Cross	**34A** Kings Cross	**34A** Kings Cross				
68819	*J52*	**NWE**	New England	**35A** New England	**35A** New England				
68820	*J52*	**NWE**	New England	**35A** New England	**35A** New England				
68821	*J52*	**NWE**	New England	**35A** New England	**35A** New England				
68822	*J52*	**KX**	Kings Cross	**34A** Kings Cross	**34A** Kings Cross				
68823	*J52*	**NWE**	New England	**35A** New England	**35A** New England	**35A** New England			
68824	*J52*	**NWE**	New England	**35A** New England	**34B** Hornsey	**34B** Hornsey			
68825	*J52*	**HSY**	Hornsey	**34B** Hornsey					
68826	*J52*	**HSY**	Hornsey	**34B** Hornsey	**35A** New England	**38A** Colwick			
68827	*J52*	**HSY**	Hornsey	**34B** Hornsey	**34A** Kings Cross				
68828	*J52*	**KX**	Kings Cross	**34A** Kings Cross	**35A** New England	**35A** New England			
68829	*J52*	**HSY**	Hornsey	**34B** Hornsey	**34A** Kings Cross	**38A** Colwick			
68830	*J52*	**KX**	Kings Cross	**34A** Kings Cross	**34A** Kings Cross				
68831	*J52*	**KX**	Kings Cross	**34A** Kings Cross	**35C** Spital Bridge	**35A** New England			
68832	*J52*	**KX**	Kings Cross	**34A** Kings Cross	**34A** Kings Cross	**34A** Kings Cross			
68833	*J52*	**HSY**	Hornsey	**34B** Hornsey	**36A** Doncaster				
68834	*J52*	**HSY**	Hornsey	**34B** Hornsey	**34B** Hornsey	**34B** Hornsey	**56B** Ardsley		
68835	*J52*	**DON**	Doncaster	**36A** Doncaster	**36A** Doncaster	**36A** Doncaster			
68836	*J52*	**DON**	Doncaster	**36A** Doncaster	**36A** Doncaster				
68837	*J52*	**DON**	Doncaster	**36A** Doncaster	**37A** Ardsley	**56B** Ardsley			
68838	*J52*	**KX**	Kings Cross	**34A** Kings Cross	**34A** Kings Cross				
68839	*J52*	**CLK**	Colwick	**38A** Colwick	**38C** Leicester Central	**38C** Leicester Central			
68840	*J52*	**NWE**	New England	**35A** New England	**35A** New England	**35A** New England	(9)		

		1948	1951	1954	1957	1960	1963	1966
68841	J52	DON Doncaster	36A Doncaster	36A Doncaster	36A Doncaster			
68842	J52	DON Doncaster	36A Doncaster	36A Doncaster	36A Doncaster			
68843	J52	DON Doncaster	36A Doncaster	36A Doncaster	36A Doncaster			
68844	J52	DON Doncaster	35A New England	35A New England				
68845	J52	DON Doncaster	Doncaster Works	(1)				
68846	J52	DON Doncaster	35A New England	35A New England	34B Hornsey			
68847	J52	DON Doncaster	36A Doncaster	36A Doncaster	36B Mexborough			
68848	J52	ARD Ardsley	37A Ardsley	37A Ardsley	56B Ardsley			
68849	J52	DON Doncaster	36A Doncaster	36A Doncaster	36A Doncaster			
68850	J52	NWE New England	35A New England	35A New England				
68851	J52	HSY Hornsey	34B Hornsey	38A Colwick	38A Colwick			
68852	J52	NWE New England	35A New England	35A New England				
68853	J52	HSY Hornsey	34B Hornsey	36A Doncaster				
68854	J52	KX Kings Cross	34A Kings Cross	34A Kings Cross				
68855	J52	KX Kings Cross	34A Kings Cross	34A Kings Cross				
68856	J52	HSY Hornsey	34B Hornsey	36A Doncaster				
68857	J52	DON Doncaster	36A Doncaster	37A Ardsley	56B Ardsley			
68858	J52	CLK Colwick	36A Doncaster	36A Doncaster	(2)			
68859	J52	CLK Colwick	38A Colwick	38A Colwick				
68860	J52	DON Doncaster	36A Doncaster	36A Doncaster	38A Colwick			
68861	J52	KX Kings Cross	34A Kings Cross	34A Kings Cross				
68862	J52	KX Kings Cross	34A Kings Cross	34A Kings Cross	34A Kings Cross			
68863	J52	CLK Colwick	38A Colwick	38A Colwick	38A Colwick			
68864	J52	KX Kings Cross	34A Kings Cross	34A Kings Cross				
68865	J52	DON Doncaster	36A Doncaster	36A Doncaster				
68866	J52	NWE New England	35A New England	34B Hornsey	34B Hornsey			
68867	J52	CLK Colwick	36A Doncaster	34C Hatfield	34C Hatfield			
68868	J52	NWE New England	35A New England	37A Ardsley				
68869	J52	DON Doncaster	36A Doncaster	36A Doncaster	36A Doncaster	56B Ardsley		
68870	J52	DON Doncaster	36A Doncaster	36A Doncaster	36B Mexborough			
68871	J52	ARD Ardsley	37A Ardsley	37A Ardsley	38A Colwick			
68872	J52	ARD Ardsley	37A Ardsley	37A Ardsley				
68873	J52	KX Kings Cross	34A Kings Cross	38A Colwick				
68874	J52	KX Kings Cross	34A Kings Cross	34A Kings Cross	34A Kings Cross			
68875	J52	CLK Colwick	38A Colwick	37A Ardsley	34B Hornsey	56B Ardsley		
68876	J52	NWE New England	35A New England	35A New England				
68877	J52	GRA Grantham	35B Grantham	35B Grantham				
68878	J52	KX Kings Cross	34A Kings Cross	34A Kings Cross				
68879	J52	NWE New England	35A New England	35A New England				
68880	J52	NWE New England	35A New England	35A New England				
68881	J52	KX Kings Cross	34A Kings Cross	34A Kings Cross				
68882	J52	CLK Colwick	38A Colwick	38A Colwick	38A Colwick			
68883	J52	HSY Hornsey	34B Hornsey	34B Hornsey				
68884	J52	KX Kings Cross	34A Kings Cross	35A New England				
68885	J52	DON Doncaster	36A Doncaster	34C Hatfield				
68886	J52	DON Doncaster	36A Doncaster	36A Doncaster	36A Doncaster			
68887	J52	CLK Colwick	38A Colwick	38A Colwick	38A Colwick			
68888	J52	KX Kings Cross	34A Kings Cross	34A Kings Cross	34A Kings Cross			
68889	J52	KX Kings Cross	34A Kings Cross	35C Spital Bridge				
68890	J50	DON Doncaster	36A Doncaster	37A Ardsley	56B Ardsley	56B Ardsley		
68891	J50	WFD Woodford Halse	38A Colwick	34B Hornsey	34B Hornsey	34B Hornsey		
68892	J50	BFD Bradford Hammerton St	37C Bradford Hammerton St	37C Bradford Hammerton St	56G Bradford Hammerton St	56B Ardsley	56C Copley Hill	
68893	J50	DON Doncaster	36A Doncaster	40B Immingham	38A Colwick			
68894	J50	WFD Woodford Halse	38A Colwick	34B Hornsey	34B Hornsey	34B Hornsey		
68895	J50	BFD Bradford Hammerton St	37C Bradford Hammerton St	37C Bradford Hammerton St	56G Bradford Hammerton St	56F Low Moor		
68896	J50	ARD Ardsley	37A Ardsley	38B Annesley	38B Annesley	34E New England		
68897	J50	BFD Bradford Hammerton St	37C Bradford Hammerton St	37C Bradford Hammerton St	56G Bradford Hammerton St	56A Wakefield		
68898	J50	BFD Bradford Hammerton St	37C Bradford Hammerton St	37C Bradford Hammerton St	56G Bradford Hammerton St	56A Wakefield		
68899	J50	DON Doncaster	32A Norwich Thorpe	32A Norwich Thorpe	32A Norwich Thorpe	32A Norwich Thorpe		
68900	J50	ARD Ardsley	37A Ardsley	37A Ardsley	56B Ardsley	56B Ardsley		
68901	J50	ARD Ardsley	37A Ardsley	37A Ardsley	56B Ardsley	56B Ardsley		
68902	J50	BFD Bradford Hammerton St	37C Bradford Hammerton St	37A Ardsley	56B Ardsley	56B Ardsley		
68903	J50	ARD Ardsley	37A Ardsley	34B Hornsey	34B Hornsey	34B Hornsey		
68904	J50	ARD Ardsley	37A Ardsley	37A Ardsley	56B Ardsley	56A Wakefield	56A Wakefield	
68905	J50	STR Stratford	32A Norwich Thorpe	32A Norwich Thorpe	32A Norwich Thorpe	32A Norwich Thorpe		
68906	J50	BFD Bradford Hammerton St	37C Bradford Hammerton St	34B Hornsey	34B Hornsey			
68907	J50	ARD Ardsley	37A Ardsley	34B Hornsey	34B Hornsey	34B Hornsey		
68908	J50	BFD Bradford Hammerton St	37C Bradford Hammerton St	37C Bradford Hammerton St	56G Bradford Hammerton St	56F Low Moor	56A Wakefield	
68909	J50	ARD Ardsley	37A Ardsley	37A Ardsley	56B Ardsley	56A Wakefield		
68910	J50	ARD Ardsley	37A Ardsley	37A Ardsley	56B Ardsley	56A Wakefield		
68911	J50	COP Copley Hill	37B Copley Hill	37B Copley Hill	56C Copley Hill	56C Copley Hill	(10)	
68912	J50	BFD Bradford Hammerton St	37C Bradford Hammerton St	37C Bradford Hammerton St	56G Bradford Hammerton St			
68913	J50	COP Copley Hill	37B Copley Hill	37B Copley Hill	56C Copley Hill	56C Copley Hill		
68914	J50	ARD Ardsley	37A Ardsley	37A Ardsley	56B Ardsley	56B Ardsley	(11)	
68915	J50	ARD Ardsley	37A Ardsley	37A Ardsley	56B Ardsley	56B Ardsley		
68916	J50	ARD Ardsley	37A Ardsley	37A Ardsley	56B Ardsley	56B Ardsley		
68917	J50	ARD Ardsley	36A Doncaster	34B Hornsey	34B Hornsey	34B Hornsey	(12)	
68918	J50	DON Doncaster	36A Doncaster	34B Hornsey	34B Hornsey	34B Hornsey		
68919	J50	ARD Ardsley	37A Ardsley	37A Ardsley	56B Ardsley			
68920	J50	WFD Woodford Halse	38A Colwick	34B Hornsey	34B Hornsey	34B Hornsey		
68921	J50	ARD Ardsley	37A Ardsley	34B Hornsey	34B Hornsey	34B Hornsey		
68922	J50	BFD Bradford Hammerton St	37C Bradford Hammerton St	37C Bradford Hammerton St	56G Bradford Hammerton St	56F Low Moor	56A Wakefield	
68923	J50	BFD Bradford Hammerton St	37C Bradford Hammerton St	37C Bradford Hammerton St	56G Bradford Hammerton St	56F Low Moor		
68924	J50	STR Stratford	32A Norwich Thorpe	32A Norwich Thorpe	32A Norwich Thorpe	32A Norwich Thorpe		
68925	J50	ARD Ardsley	37B Copley Hill	37B Copley Hill	56C Copley Hill	56C Copley Hill	56C Copley Hill	
68926	J50	DON Doncaster	36A Doncaster	40B Immingham	36A Doncaster	34B Hornsey		
68927	J50	ANN Annesley	38B Annesley	38B Annesley	38A Colwick	40E Colwick		
68928	J50	SHF Sheffield Darnall	39B Sheffield Darnall	34B Hornsey	34B Hornsey	34B Hornsey	(13)	
68929	J50	ANN Annesley	38B Annesley	34B Hornsey	34B Hornsey	34B Hornsey		
68930	J50	ARD Ardsley	37A Ardsley	34B Hornsey	34B Hornsey	34B Hornsey		
68931	J50	ARD Ardsley	37A Ardsley	34B Hornsey	34B Hornsey	34B Hornsey		
68932	J50	BFD Bradford Hammerton St	37C Bradford Hammerton St	37C Bradford Hammerton St	56G Bradford Hammerton St	56F Low Moor		
68933	J50	BFD Bradford Hammerton St	37C Bradford Hammerton St	37C Bradford Hammerton St	56G Bradford Hammerton St	56F Low Moor		
68934	J50	BFD Bradford Hammerton St	37C Bradford Hammerton St	37C Bradford Hammerton St	56G Bradford Hammerton St	56B Ardsley	56B Ardsley	
68935	J50	ANN Annesley	38A Colwick	37A Ardsley	56B Ardsley	56B Ardsley	56B Ardsley	
68936	J50	DON Doncaster	36A Doncaster	34B Hornsey	34B Hornsey	34B Hornsey		
68937	J50	COP Copley Hill	37B Copley Hill	37B Copley Hill	56C Copley Hill	56B Ardsley	56B Ardsley	
68938	J50	ARD Ardsley	37A Ardsley	37A Ardsley	56B Ardsley			
68939	J50	ARD Ardsley	37A Ardsley	37A Ardsley	56B Ardsley	56A Wakefield		
68940	J50	BFD Bradford Hammerton St	37C Bradford Hammerton St	37C Bradford Hammerton St	56G Bradford Hammerton St			
68941	J50	BFD Bradford Hammerton St	37C Bradford Hammerton St	37A Ardsley	56B Ardsley	56B Ardsley		
68942	J50	BFD Bradford Hammerton St	37C Bradford Hammerton St	37C Bradford Hammerton St	56G Bradford Hammerton St			
68943	J50	BFD Bradford Hammerton St	37C Bradford Hammerton St	37C Bradford Hammerton St	56G Bradford Hammerton St	56F Low Moor		
68944	J50	BFD Bradford Hammerton St	37C Bradford Hammerton St	37C Bradford Hammerton St	56G Bradford Hammerton St	56F Low Moor		
68945	J50	COP Copley Hill	36A Doncaster	34B Hornsey	34B Hornsey	34B Hornsey		
68946	J50	COP Copley Hill	36B Mexborough	40B Immingham	34B Hornsey	34B Hornsey		
68947	J50	ARD Ardsley	37A Ardsley	37A Ardsley	56B Ardsley	56B Ardsley		
68948	J50	ARD Ardsley	37A Ardsley	37A Ardsley	56B Ardsley	56F Low Moor		
68949	J50	ARD Ardsley	37A Ardsley	34B Hornsey	34B Hornsey			
68950	J50	STR Stratford	30A Stratford	30A Stratford	38A Colwick	40E Colwick		
68951	J50	ARD Ardsley	37A Ardsley	37A Ardsley	56B Ardsley	51C West Hartlepool		
68952	J50	STM St. Margarets	64A St. Margarets	65A Eastfield	65A Eastfield	65A Eastfield		
68953	J50	EFD Eastfield	65A Eastfield	65A Eastfield	65A Eastfield			
68954	J50	EFD Eastfield	65A Eastfield	65A Eastfield	65A Eastfield	65A Eastfield		

		1948	1951	1954	1957	1960	1963	1966
68955	*J50*	**EFD** Eastfield	**65A** Eastfield	**65A** Eastfield	**65A** Eastfield			
68956	*J50*	**EFD** Eastfield	**65A** Eastfield	**65A** Eastfield	**65A** Eastfield	**65A** Eastfield		
68957	*J50*	**EFD** Eastfield	**65A** Eastfield	**65A** Eastfield	**65A** Eastfield	**65A** Eastfield		
68958	*J50*	**EFD** Eastfield	**65A** Eastfield	**65A** Eastfield	**65A** Eastfield	**66A** Polmadie		
68959	*J50*	**BFD** Bradford Hammerton St	**37C** Bradford Hammerton St	**37C** Bradford Hammerton St	**56G** Bradford Hammerton St	**56A** Wakefield		
68960	*J50*	**ARD** Ardsley	**36A** Doncaster	**36C** Frodingham	**36C** Frodingham	**34B** Hornsey		
68961	*J50*	**BFD** Bradford Hammerton St	**36A** Doncaster	**34B** Hornsey	**34B** Hornsey	**34B** Hornsey	(14)	
68962	*J50*	**FRO** Frodingham	**36C** Frodingham	**36C** Frodingham	**36C** Frodingham	**36A** Doncaster		
68963	*J50*	**STR** Stratford	**30A** Stratford	**30A** Stratford	**36A** Doncaster	**36A** Doncaster		
68964	*J50*	**FRO** Frodingham	**36C** Frodingham	**36C** Frodingham	**36C** Frodingham	**36A** Doncaster		
68965	*J50*	**STR** Stratford	**30A** Stratford	**30A** Stratford	**36C** Frodingham	**36A** Doncaster	**56B** Ardsley	
68966	*J50*	**ARD** Ardsley	**37A** Ardsley	**37A** Ardsley	**34B** Hornsey	**34B** Hornsey		
68967	*J50*	**STR** Stratford	**30A** Stratford	**30A** Stratford	**38A** Colwick			
68968	*J50*	**FRO** Frodingham	**36C** Frodingham	**34B** Hornsey	**34B** Hornsey	**34B** Hornsey		
68969	*J50*	**BFD** Bradford Hammerton St	**37C** Bradford Hammerton St	**37C** Bradford Hammerton St	**56G** Bradford Hammerton St	**56F** Low Moor		
68970	*J50*	**FRO** Frodingham	**36C** Frodingham	**36C** Frodingham	**36C** Frodingham	**34B** Hornsey		
68971	*J50*	**FRO** Frodingham	**36C** Frodingham	**34B** Hornsey	**34B** Hornsey	**34B** Hornsey	(15)	
68972	*J50*	**ANN** Annesley	**38A** Colwick	**34B** Hornsey	**34B** Hornsey	**34B** Hornsey		
68973	*J50*	**FRO** Frodingham	**36C** Frodingham	**36A** Doncaster	**36C** Frodingham			
68974	*J50*	**DON** Doncaster	**36C** Frodingham	**36A** Doncaster	**36A** Doncaster			
68975	*J50*	**ANN** Annesley	**38B** Annesley	**38B** Annesley	**38A** Colwick	**40E** Colwick		
68976	*J50*	**ANN** Annesley	**38B** Annesley	**38B** Annesley	**38B** Annesley	**34E** New England	(16)	
68977	*J50*	**STR** Stratford	**30A** Stratford	**30A** Stratford	**40B** Immingham	**36A** Doncaster	**56A** Wakefield	
68978	*J50*	**COP** Copley Hill	**37B** Copley Hill	**37B** Copley Hill	**56C** Copley Hill			
68979	*J50*	**DON** Doncaster	**36B** Mexborough	**40B** Immingham	**34B** Hornsey	**34B** Hornsey		
68980	*J50*	**DON** Doncaster	**36A** Doncaster	**36C** Frodingham	**36A** Doncaster	**34B** Hornsey		
68981	*J50*	**CLK** Colwick	**38C** Leicester Central	**34B** Hornsey	**34B** Hornsey	**34B** Hornsey		
68982	*J50*	**CLK** Colwick	**38A** Colwick	**34B** Hornsey	**34B** Hornsey	**34B** Hornsey		
68983	*J50*	**SHF** Sheffield Darnall	**39B** Sheffield Darnall	**34B** Hornsey	**34B** Hornsey	**34B** Hornsey		
68984	*J50*	**COP** Copley Hill	**37B** Copley Hill	**37B** Copley Hill	**56C** Copley Hill	**56C** Copley Hill	**56C** Copley Hill	
68985	*J50*	**DON** Doncaster	**36A** Doncaster	**34B** Hornsey	**34B** Hornsey			
68986	*J50*	**DON** Doncaster	**36A** Doncaster	**34B** Hornsey	**34B** Hornsey	**34B** Hornsey		
68987	*J50*	**DON** Doncaster	**36A** Doncaster	**34B** Hornsey	**34B** Hornsey	**34B** Hornsey		
68988	*J50*	**COP** Copley Hill	**37B** Copley Hill	**37B** Copley Hill	**56C** Copley Hill	**56C** Copley Hill	**56C** Copley Hill	
68989	*J50*	**DON** Doncaster	**36A** Doncaster	**34B** Hornsey	**34B** Hornsey	**34B** Hornsey		
68990	*J50*	**SHF** Sheffield Darnall	**39B** Sheffield Darnall	**34B** Hornsey	**34B** Hornsey	**34B** Hornsey		
68991	*J50*	**DON** Doncaster	**36A** Doncaster	**34B** Hornsey	**34B** Hornsey	**34B** Hornsey		
69000	*L1*	**STR** Stratford	(67701)					
69001	*J72*	→	**53C** Hull Alexandra Dock	**53C** Hull Alexandra Dock	**52B** Heaton	**52A** Gateshead	**52A** Gateshead	
69002	*J72*	→	**53C** Hull Alexandra Dock	**54A** Sunderland	**54A** Sunderland	**52G** Sunderland		
69003	*J72*	→	**53C** Hull Alexandra Dock	**53C** Hull Alexandra Dock	**53C** Hull Alexandra Dock	**53C** Hull Alexandra Dock	**51C** West Hartlepool	
69004	*J72*	→	**51A** Darlington	**51A** Darlington	**51A** Darlington	**51A** Darlington	**52A** Gateshead	
69005	*J72*	→	**52A** Gateshead	**52A** Gateshead	**52A** Gateshead	**52A** Gateshead	**52A** Gateshead	(58)
69006	*J72*	→	**51D** Middlesbrough	**51D** Middlesbrough	**51D** Middlesbrough	**51L** Thornaby	**51A** Darlington	
69007	*J72*	→	**51F** West Auckland	**54A** Sunderland	**54A** Sunderland	**51F** West Auckland		
69008	*J72*	→	**54B** Tyne Dock	**54B** Tyne Dock	**54B** Tyne Dock	**53A** Hull Dairycoates	**52B** Heaton	
69009	*J72*	→	**53C** Hull Alexandra Dock	**53C** Hull Alexandra Dock	**53C** Hull Alexandra Dock	**53C** Hull Alexandra Dock	**50B** Hull Dairycoates	
69010	*J72*	→	**53A** Hull Dairycoates	**53C** Hull Alexandra Dock	**53C** Hull Alexandra Dock	**53C** Hull Alexandra Dock		
69011	*J72*	→	**53A** Hull Dairycoates	**53C** Hull Alexandra Dock	**53C** Hull Alexandra Dock	**53C** Hull Alexandra Dock	**50B** Hull Dairycoates	
69012	*J72*	→	**32B** Ipswich	**62A** Thornton Junction	**62A** Thornton Junction	**62A** Thornton Junction		
69013	*J72*	→	**32B** Ipswich	**62A** Thornton Junction	**62A** Thornton Junction	**64A** St. Margarets		
69014	*J72*	→	**36A** Doncaster	**64A** St. Margarets	**64A** St. Margarets	**64A** St. Margarets		
69015	*J72*	→	**36A** Doncaster	**65C** Parkhead	**65C** Parkhead	**65C** Parkhead		
69016	*J72*	→	**50E** Scarborough	**50E** Scarborough	**50E** Scarborough	**50A** York	**51L** Thornaby	
69017	*J72*	→	**54C** Borough Gardens	**54C** Borough Gardens	**54C** Borough Gardens	**51A** Darlington		
69018	*J72*	→	**54A** Sunderland	**51F** West Auckland	**51F** West Auckland	**51F** West Auckland		
69019	*J72*	→	**51D** Middlesbrough	**51D** Middlesbrough	**51D** Middlesbrough	**51L** Thornaby	**51C** West Hartlepool	
69020	*J72*	→	**50A** York	**50A** York	**50A** York	**50A** York	**51A** Darlington	
69021	*J72*	→	→	**51A** Darlington	**51A** Darlington	**51A** Darlington	**51C** West Hartlepool	
69022	*J72*	→	→	**51A** Darlington	**51A** Darlington	**51A** Darlington		
69023	*J72*	→	→	**52C** Blaydon	**52C** Blaydon	**52C** Blaydon	**52A** Gateshead	(59)
69024	*J72*	→	→	**52C** Blaydon	**52C** Blaydon	**52C** Blaydon	**52B** Heaton	
69025	*J72*	→	→	**52C** Blaydon	**52C** Blaydon	**52C** Blaydon	**52A** Gateshead	
69026	*J72*	→	→	**52C** Blaydon	**52C** Blaydon	**52C** Blaydon		
69027	*J72*	→	→	**52B** Heaton	**52B** Heaton	**52A** Gateshead		
69028	*J72*	→	→	**52B** Heaton	**52B** Heaton	**52B** Heaton	**52B** Heaton	
69050	*L3*	**WFD** Woodford Halse	**38E** Woodford Halse	**38E** Woodford Halse				
69051	*L3*	**MEX** Mexborough	**36C** Frodingham					
69052	*L3*	**NTH** Northwich	**9G** Northwich	**9G** Northwich				
69053	*L3*	**NEA** Neasden						
69054	*L3*	**NEA** Neasden						
69055	*L3*	**NEA** Neasden	**34E** Neasden					
69056	*L3*	**NEA** Neasden	**34E** Neasden					
69057	*L3*	**FRO** Frodingham						
69058	*L3*	**FRO** Frodingham						
69059	*L3*	**MEX** Mexborough						
69060	*L3*	**NEA** Neasden	**34E** Neasden	**36C** Frodingham				
69061	*L3*	**NEA** Neasden	**34E** Neasden					
69062	*L3*	**NTH** Northwich	**9G** Northwich					
69064	*L3*	**NWE** New England	**34E** Neasden	**36C** Frodingham				
69065	*L3*	**MEX** Mexborough	**34E** Neasden	**36C** Frodingham				
69066	*L3*	**MEX** Mexborough						
69067	*L3*	**NEA** Neasden	**34E** Neasden					
69068	*L3*	**NEA** Neasden						
69069	*L3*	**WFD** Woodford Halse	**38E** Woodford Halse	**38E** Woodford Halse				
69070	*L2*	**NEA** Neasden						
69071	*L2*	**NEA** Neasden						
69076	*M2*	**NEA** Neasden						
69077	*M2*	**NEA** Neasden						
69089	*N12*	**HLS** Hull Springhead						
69090	*N10*	**GHD** Gateshead	**52A** Gateshead	**52A** Gateshead				
69091	*N10*	**GHD** Gateshead	**52A** Gateshead	**52A** Gateshead				
69092	*N10*	**GHD** Gateshead	**52A** Gateshead	**52A** Gateshead	**52A** Gateshead			
69093	*N10*	**GHD** Gateshead	**53A** Hull Dairycoates	**53A** Hull Dairycoates	**54B** Tyne Dock			
69094	*N10*	**HLD** Hull Dairycoates	**53A** Hull Dairycoates	**53A** Hull Dairycoates	**53A** Hull Dairycoates			
69095	*N10*	**BLA** Blaydon	**52C** Blaydon	**52A** Gateshead				
69096	*N10*	**HLD** Hull Dairycoates	**53A** Hull Dairycoates	**53A** Hull Dairycoates	**53A** Hull Dairycoates			
69097	*N10*	**BOW** Bowes Bridge	**52A** Bowes Bridge	**52A** Bowes Bridge	**52A** Bowes Bridge	**52A** Bowes Bridge		
69098	*N10*	**HLD** Hull Dairycoates	**53A** Hull Dairycoates	**53A** Hull Dairycoates	**50B** Leeds Neville Hill			
69099	*N10*	**GHD** Gateshead	**53A** Hull Dairycoates	**53A** Hull Dairycoates	**53A** Hull Dairycoates			
69100	*N10*	**BOW** Bowes Bridge	**52A** Bowes Bridge	**52A** Bowes Bridge	**52A** Bowes Bridge			
69101	*N10*	**NLN** Northallerton	**51J** Northallerton	**54A** Sunderland	**54A** Sunderland	**52A** Gateshead		
69102	*N10*	**GHD** Gateshead	**53A** Hull Dairycoates	**53A** Hull Dairycoates	**54B** Tyne Dock			
69103	*N10*	**GHD** Gateshead						
69104	*N10*	**HLD** Hull Dairycoates	**53A** Hull Dairycoates	**53A** Hull Dairycoates	**53A** Hull Dairycoates			
69105	*N10*	**GHD** Gateshead	**54B** Tyne Dock	**54B** Tyne Dock	**54B** Tyne Dock	**52A** Gateshead		
69106	*N10*	**GHD** Gateshead	**53A** Hull Dairycoates	**53A** Hull Dairycoates	**54B** Tyne Dock			
69107	*N10*	**GHD** Gateshead	**53A** Hull Dairycoates	**53A** Hull Dairycoates	**53A** Hull Dairycoates			
69108	*N10*	**HLD** Hull Dairycoates	**53A** Hull Dairycoates	**53A** Hull Dairycoates	**53A** Hull Dairycoates			
69109	*N10*	**GHD** Gateshead	**52A** Gateshead	**52A** Gateshead	**52A** Gateshead	**52A** Gateshead		
69110	*N13*	**HLS** Hull Springhead						
69111	*N13*	**HLS** Hull Springhead	**53C** Hull Springhead					
69112	*N13*	**HLS** Hull Springhead	**53C** Hull Springhead					
69113	*N13*	**HLS** Hull Springhead	**53C** Hull Springhead					

No.	Class	1948	1951	1954	1957	1960	1963	1966
69114	N13	NEV Leeds Neville Hill	50B Leeds Neville Hill	50B Leeds Neville Hill				
69115	N13	NEV Leeds Neville Hill	50B Leeds Neville Hill	50B Leeds Neville Hill				
69116	N13	HLS Hull Springhead	53C Hull Springhead	50B Leeds Neville Hill				
69117	N13	NEV Leeds Neville Hill	50B Leeds Neville Hill	50B Leeds Neville Hill				
69118	N13	NEV Leeds Neville Hill	50B Leeds Neville Hill					
69119	N13	HLS Hull Springhead	50B Leeds Neville Hill	50B Leeds Neville Hill				
69120	N14	EFD Eastfield	65A Eastfield	65A Eastfield				
69124	N14	EFD Eastfield						
69125	N14	KIT Kittybrewster	61B Aberdeen Ferryhill	61B Aberdeen Ferryhill				
69126	N15	EFD Eastfield	65A Eastfield	65A Eastfield	65A Eastfield	65D Dawsholm		
69127	N15	EFD Eastfield	65A Eastfield	65A Eastfield	65A Eastfield			
69128	N15	ABD Aberdeen Ferryhill	61B Aberdeen Ferryhill	61B Aberdeen Ferryhill	61B Aberdeen Ferryhill	61B Aberdeen Ferryhill		
69129	N15	ABD Aberdeen Ferryhill	61B Aberdeen Ferryhill	61B Aberdeen Ferryhill	61B Aberdeen Ferryhill			
69130	N15	STM St. Margarets	64A St. Margarets	64A St. Margarets	64A St. Margarets			
69131	N15	EFD Eastfield	65A Eastfield	65A Eastfield	65A Eastfield	65A Eastfield		
69132	N15	THJ Thornton Junction	62A Thornton Junction	62A Thornton Junction	62A Thornton Junction	66B Motherwell		
69133	N15	STM St. Margarets	64A St. Margarets	64A St. Margarets	64A St. Margarets	64A St. Margarets		
69134	N15	STM St. Margarets	64A St. Margarets	64A St. Margarets	64A St. Margarets	64A St. Margarets		
69135	N15	DFU Dunfermline Upper	62C Dunfermline Upper	62C Dunfermline Upper	62C Dunfermline Upper	64A St. Margarets		
69136	N15	DFU Dunfermline Upper	62C Dunfermline Upper	62C Dunfermline Upper	62C Dunfermline Upper	62A Thornton Junction		
69137	N15	POL Polmont	64E Polmont	64E Polmont	64E Polmont	64E Polmont		
69138	N15	EFD Eastfield	65A Eastfield	65A Eastfield	65A Eastfield	61B Aberdeen Ferryhill		
69139	N15	CAR Carlisle Canal	12B Carlisle Canal	68E Carlisle Canal	68E Carlisle Canal			
69140	N15	STM St. Margarets	64A St. Margarets	64A St. Margarets	64A St. Margarets			
69141	N15	KPS Kipps	64A St. Margarets	64A St. Margarets	64A St. Margarets	64A St. Margarets		
69142	N15	BGT Bathgate	64F Bathgate	64F Bathgate	64F Bathgate			
69143	N15	PKD Parkhead	65C Parkhead	62A Thornton Junction	62A Thornton Junction	66B Motherwell		
69144	N15	STM St. Margarets	64A St. Margarets	64A St. Margarets	64A St. Margarets	64A St. Margarets		
69145	N15	PKD Parkhead	65E Kipps	65E Kipps	65E Kipps	66A Polmadie		
69146	N15	STM St. Margarets	64A St. Margarets	64A St. Margarets	64A St. Margarets			
69147	N15	STM St. Margarets	64A St. Margarets	64A St. Margarets	64A St. Margarets			
69148	N15	STM St. Margarets	64A St. Margarets	64A St. Margarets	64A St. Margarets			
69149	N15	STM St. Margarets	64A St. Margarets	64A St. Margarets	64A St. Margarets	64A St. Margarets		
69150	N15	THJ Thornton Junction	62A Thornton Junction	62A Thornton Junction	62A Thornton Junction	64A St. Margarets		
69151	N15	PKD Parkhead	65C Parkhead	65C Parkhead	65C Parkhead			
69152	N15	STM St. Margarets	64A St. Margarets	64A St. Margarets	64A St. Margarets			
69153	N15	THJ Thornton Junction	62A Thornton Junction	62A Thornton Junction	62A Thornton Junction			
69154	N15	DFU Dunfermline Upper	62C Dunfermline Upper	62C Dunfermline Upper	62C Dunfermline Upper			
69155	N15	CAR Carlisle Canal	12B Carlisle Canal	68E Carlisle Canal	68E Carlisle Canal	12C Carlisle Canal		
69156	N15	BGT Bathgate	64F Bathgate	64F Bathgate	64F Bathgate	64F Bathgate		
69157	N15	BGT Bathgate	65C Parkhead	65C Parkhead	65C Parkhead			
69158	N15	BGT Bathgate	64F Bathgate	64F Bathgate	64F Bathgate			
69159	N15	BGT Bathgate	64F Bathgate	64F Bathgate	64F Bathgate	64F Bathgate		
69160	N15	DFU Dunfermline Upper	62C Dunfermline Upper	62C Dunfermline Upper	62C Dunfermline Upper			
69161	N15	PKD Parkhead	65C Parkhead	65C Parkhead	65C Parkhead	65C Parkhead		
69162	N15	POL Polmont	64E Polmont	64E Polmont	64E Polmont			
69163	N15	EFD Eastfield	65D Dawsholm	65D Dawsholm	65A Eastfield	65A Eastfield		
69164	N15	DFU Dunfermline Upper	62C Dunfermline Upper	62C Dunfermline Upper	62C Dunfermline Upper			
69165	N15	EFD Eastfield	65C Parkhead	65C Parkhead	65C Parkhead	65C Parkhead		
69166	N15	EFD Eastfield	65C Parkhead	65C Parkhead	65C Parkhead			
69167	N15	STM St. Margarets	64A St. Margarets	64A St. Margarets	64A St. Margarets			
69168	N15	STM St. Margarets	64A St. Margarets	64A St. Margarets	64A St. Margarets	64A St. Margarets		
69169	N15	HAY Haymarket	64B Haymarket	64B Haymarket	64B Haymarket			
69170	N15	EFD Eastfield	65A Eastfield	65A Eastfield	65A Eastfield	65A Eastfield		
69171	N15	PKD Parkhead	65C Parkhead	65A Eastfield	65A Eastfield	65A Eastfield		
69172	N15	STM St. Margarets	64A St. Margarets	64A St. Margarets	64A St. Margarets			
69173	N15	STM St. Margarets	64A St. Margarets	64A St. Margarets	64A St. Margarets	64A St. Margarets		
69174	N15	CAR Carlisle Canal	12B Carlisle Canal	68E Carlisle Canal	68E Carlisle Canal			
69175	N15	STM St. Margarets	64A St. Margarets	64A St. Margarets	64A St. Margarets			
69176	N15	EFD Eastfield	65D Dawsholm	65D Dawsholm	65D Dawsholm			
69177	N15	EFD Eastfield	65D Dawsholm	65D Dawsholm	65D Dawsholm	65D Dawsholm		
69178	N15	EFD Eastfield	65A Eastfield	65A Eastfield	65A Eastfield	65A Eastfield		
69179	N15	EFD Eastfield	65A Eastfield	65A Eastfield	65A Eastfield	65A Eastfield		
69180	N15	EFD Eastfield	65A Eastfield	65A Eastfield	65A Eastfield	61A Kittybrewster		
69181	N15	EFD Eastfield	65A Eastfield	65A Eastfield	65A Eastfield	65A Eastfield		
69182	N15	EFD Eastfield	65A Eastfield	65A Eastfield	65A Eastfield			
69183	N15	EFD Eastfield	65A Eastfield	65A Eastfield	65A Eastfield	65A Eastfield		
69184	N15	EFD Eastfield	65D Dawsholm	65D Dawsholm	65D Dawsholm	65D Dawsholm		
69185	N15	CAR Carlisle Canal	12B Carlisle Canal	64A St. Margarets	64A St. Margarets			
69186	N15	STM St. Margarets	64A St. Margarets	64A St. Margarets	64A St. Margarets			
69187	N15	STM St. Margarets	64C Dalry Road	64C Dalry Road	64C Dalry Road			
69188	N15	EFD Eastfield	65A Eastfield	65A Eastfield	65A Eastfield	65A Eastfield		
69189	N15	EFD Eastfield	65A Eastfield	65A Eastfield	65A Eastfield			
69190	N15	PKD Parkhead	65C Parkhead	65C Parkhead	65C Parkhead	65C Parkhead		
69191	N15	EFD Eastfield	65A Eastfield	65A Eastfield	65A Eastfield	65A Eastfield		
69192	N15	DFU Dunfermline Upper	62C Dunfermline Upper	62C Dunfermline Upper	62C Dunfermline Upper			
69193	N15	PKD Parkhead	65C Parkhead	65C Parkhead	65C Parkhead			
69194	N15	PKD Parkhead	65C Parkhead	65C Parkhead	65C Parkhead	65C Parkhead		
69195	N15	PKD Parkhead	65C Parkhead	65C Parkhead	65C Parkhead			
69196	N15	KPS Kipps	65E Kipps	65E Kipps	65E Kipps	66C Hamilton		
69197	N15	CAR Carlisle Canal	12B Carlisle Canal	65A Eastfield	65A Eastfield			
69198	N15	PKD Parkhead	65C Parkhead	65C Parkhead	65C Parkhead	65C Parkhead		
69199	N15	PKD Parkhead	65C Parkhead	65C Parkhead	65C Parkhead	65C Parkhead		
69200	N15	POL Polmont	64E Polmont	64E Polmont	64E Polmont			
69201	N15	DFU Dunfermline Upper	61B Aberdeen Ferryhill	61B Aberdeen Ferryhill	61B Aberdeen Ferryhill			
69202	N15	DFU Dunfermline Upper	62C Dunfermline Upper	62C Dunfermline Upper	62C Dunfermline Upper	62C Dunfermline Upper		
69203	N15	EFD Eastfield	65D Dawsholm	65D Dawsholm	65D Dawsholm			
69204	N15	DFU Dunfermline Upper	62C Dunfermline Upper	62C Dunfermline Upper	62C Dunfermline Upper	62A Thornton Junction		
69205	N15	EFD Eastfield	65D Dawsholm	65D Dawsholm	65D Dawsholm	65D Dawsholm		
69206	N15	KPS Kipps	65E Kipps	65E Kipps	65E Kipps	65E Kipps		
69207	N15	KPS Kipps	65E Kipps	65E Kipps	65E Kipps	66A Polmadie		
69208	N15	EFD Eastfield	65D Dawsholm	65D Dawsholm	65D Dawsholm			
69209	N15	PKD Parkhead	65C Parkhead	65C Parkhead	65C Parkhead	65C Parkhead		
69210	N15	PKD Parkhead	65C Parkhead	65C Parkhead	65C Parkhead			
69211	N15	THJ Thornton Junction	62A Thornton Junction	62A Thornton Junction	62A Thornton Junction	64B Haymarket		
69212	N15	PKD Parkhead	65C Parkhead	65C Parkhead	65C Parkhead	65A Eastfield		
69213	N15	PKD Parkhead	65C Parkhead	65C Parkhead	65C Parkhead			
69214	N15	PKD Parkhead	65C Parkhead	65A Eastfield	65A Eastfield			
69215	N15	CAR Carlisle Canal	12B Carlisle Canal	68E Carlisle Canal	68E Carlisle Canal			
69216	N15	BGT Bathgate	64F Bathgate	64F Bathgate	64F Bathgate	64F Bathgate		
69217	N15	PKD Parkhead	65C Parkhead	65C Parkhead	65C Parkhead			
69218	N15	CAR Carlisle Canal	12B Carlisle Canal	65A Eastfield	65A Eastfield	65A Eastfield		
69219	N15	STM St. Margarets	64A St. Margarets	64A St. Margarets	64A St. Margarets	64A St. Margarets		
69220	N15	HAY Haymarket	64B Haymarket	64B Haymarket	64B Haymarket			
69221	N15	DFU Dunfermline Upper	62C Dunfermline Upper	62C Dunfermline Upper	62C Dunfermline Upper	62C Dunfermline Upper		
69222	N15	EFD Eastfield	65A Eastfield	64A St. Margarets	64A St. Margarets			
69223	N15	THJ Thornton Junction	62A Thornton Junction	62A Thornton Junction	62A Thornton Junction	66B Motherwell		
69224	N15	THJ Thornton Junction	62A Thornton Junction	62A Thornton Junction	62A Thornton Junction	61B Aberdeen Ferryhill		
69225	N4	MEX Mexborough	39B Sheffield Darnall	39B Sheffield Darnall				
69226	N4	SHF Sheffield Darnall						
69227	N4	SHF Sheffield Darnall	39B Sheffield Darnall					
69228	N4	SHF Sheffield Darnall	39B Sheffield Darnall	39B Sheffield Darnall				
69229	N4	SHF Sheffield Darnall	39B Sheffield Darnall					
69230	N4	SHF Sheffield Darnall	39B Sheffield Darnall	39B Sheffield Darnall				

No.	Class	1948		1951	1954	1957	1960	1963	1966
69231	N4	MEX	Mexborough	39B Sheffield Darnall	39B Sheffield Darnall				
69232	N4	SHF	Sheffield Darnall	39B Sheffield Darnall	39B Sheffield Darnall				
69233	N4	SHF	Sheffield Darnall	39B Sheffield Darnall	39B Sheffield Darnall				
69234	N4	SHF	Sheffield Darnall	39B Sheffield Darnall					
69235	N4	SHF	Sheffield Darnall	39B Sheffield Darnall	39B Sheffield Darnall				
69236	N4	SHF	Sheffield Darnall	39B Sheffield Darnall	39B Sheffield Darnall				
69237	N4	SHF	Sheffield Darnall						
69239	N4	MEX	Mexborough	39B Sheffield Darnall	39B Sheffield Darnall				
69240	N4	SHF	Sheffield Darnall	39B Sheffield Darnall					
69241	N4	SHF	Sheffield Darnall						
69242	N4	SHF	Sheffield Darnall	39B Sheffield Darnall					
69243	N4	SHF	Sheffield Darnall						
69244	N4	SHF	Sheffield Darnall	39B Sheffield Darnall					
69245	N4	SHF	Sheffield Darnall						
69246	N4	MEX	Mexborough	39B Sheffield Darnall					
69247	N4	SHF	Sheffield Darnall						
69250	N5	LIV	Brunswick	39A Gorton	39A Gorton				
69251	N5	STP	Heaton Mersey						
69252	N5	TFD	Trafford Park	9E Trafford Park					
69253	N5	BFD	Bradford Hammerton St	40A Lincoln	40A Lincoln				
69254	N5	GOR	Gorton	8E Brunswick	8E Brunswick				
69255	N5	TFD	Trafford Park	9E Trafford Park	9E Trafford Park				
69256	N5	BFD	Bradford Hammerton St	40F Boston	40F Boston				
69257	N5	NEA	Neasden	34E Neasden	34E Neasden	34E Neasden			
69258	N5	LIV	Brunswick	8E Brunswick	8E Brunswick	8E Brunswick	41A Sheffield Darnall		
69259	N5	NEA	Neasden	34E Neasden	34E Neasden	41A Sheffield Darnall			
69260	N5	GOR	Gorton	39A Gorton	39A Gorton				
69261	N5	BFD	Bradford Hammerton St	40F Boston	40F Boston	40B Immingham			
69262	N5	NTH	Northwich	9G Northwich	9F Heaton Mersey	17E Heaton Mersey			
69263	N5	CLK	Colwick	38E Woodford Halse	38A Colwick	38D Staveley	41J Langwith Junction		
69264	N5	MEX	Mexborough	36B Mexborough	36B Mexborough				
69265	N5	WAL	Walton on the Hill	27E Walton on the Hill	27E Walton on the Hill	27E Walton on the Hill			
69266	N5	COP	Copley Hill	37B Copley Hill	39B Sheffield Darnall	41A Sheffield Darnall	34E New England		
69267	N5	WRX	Wrexham Rhosddu	6E Wrexham Rhosddu	6E Wrexham Rhosddu	6E Wrexham Rhosddu	34E New England		
69268	N5	BRN	Barnsley	36D Barnsley	36D Barnsley	36D Barnsley	41J Langwith Junction		
69269	N5	WFD	Woodford Halse	38E Woodford Halse	38D Staveley	38D Staveley			
69270	N5	GOR	Gorton	39A Gorton	39A Gorton				
69271	N5	COP	Copley Hill	37B Copley Hill	38A Colwick	41A Sheffield Darnall			
69272	N5	GOR	Gorton	8E Brunswick	8E Brunswick				
69273	N5	NEA	Neasden	36E Retford	34E Neasden				
69274	N5	CHR	Chester Northgate	6D Chester Northgate	6D Chester Northgate	6D Chester Northgate	34E New England		
69275	N5	TUX	Tuxford Junction	40A Lincoln	40A Lincoln				
69276	N5	STP	Heaton Mersey	9F Heaton Mersey	9F Heaton Mersey	17E Heaton Mersey			
69277	N5	BRN	Barnsley	36E Retford	36E Retford				
69278	N5	BRN	Barnsley	36D Barnsley	36D Barnsley				
69279	N5	STV	Staveley	38D Staveley	38D Staveley				
69280	N5	BFD	Bradford Hammerton St	40C Louth	36B Mexborough				
69281	N5	CHR	Chester Northgate	6D Chester Northgate	6D Chester Northgate	6E Wrexham Rhosddu			
69282	N5	MEX	Mexborough	36E Retford	36E Retford				
69283	N5	NEA	Neasden	34E Neasden	36E Retford	36E Retford			
69284	N5	LNG	Langwith Junction	40E Langwith Junction	40E Langwith Junction	40F Boston			
69285	N5	BRN	Barnsley	36D Barnsley	39B Sheffield Darnall				
69286	N5	CLK	Colwick	38E Woodford Halse	38A Colwick	41A Sheffield Darnall	41J Langwith Junction		
69287	N5	TUX	Tuxford Junction	40A Lincoln	39B Sheffield Darnall				
69288	N5	LIV	Brunswick	6E Wrexham Rhosddu	6E Wrexham Rhosddu				
69289	N5	BID	Bidston	6F Bidston	6E Wrexham Rhosddu				
69290	N5	WRX	Wrexham Rhosddu	6E Wrexham Rhosddu	6E Wrexham Rhosddu	6E Wrexham Rhosddu			
69291	N5	BRN	Barnsley	36D Barnsley	36D Barnsley				
69292	N5	STV	Staveley	38D Staveley	39B Sheffield Darnall	41A Sheffield Darnall	34E New England		
69293	N5	NTH	Northwich	6D Chester Northgate	6D Chester Northgate	6D Chester Northgate	34E New England		
69294	N5	RET	Retford	36E Retford	39B Sheffield Darnall	41A Sheffield Darnall			
69295	N5	STV	Staveley	38D Staveley	39B Sheffield Darnall	41A Sheffield Darnall			
69296	N5	GOR	Gorton	39A Gorton	39A Gorton	41A Sheffield Darnall	41A Sheffield Darnall		
69297	N5	MEX	Mexborough	36B Mexborough	36B Mexborough	36D Barnsley			
69298	N5	WAL	Walton on the Hill	27E Walton on the Hill	27E Walton on the Hill	27E Walton on the Hill			
69299	N5	GOR	Gorton	39A Gorton	9F Heaton Mersey	17E Heaton Mersey	41J Langwith Junction		
69300	N5	NEA	Neasden	34E Neasden	36E Retford	36D Barnsley			
69301	N5	STV	Staveley	38D Staveley	38D Staveley				
69302	N5	NEA	Neasden	34E Neasden	34E Neasden	41A Sheffield Darnall			
69303	N5	BRN	Barnsley	36D Barnsley	36D Barnsley				
69304	N5	TFD	Trafford Park	9E Trafford Park	9E Trafford Park				
69305	N5	IMM	Immingham	40B Immingham	40B Immingham	36B Mexborough			
69306	N5	LTH	Louth	40C Louth	36B Mexborough				
69307	N5	GOR	Gorton	39A Gorton	39A Gorton	39A Gorton	9G Gorton		
69308	N5	GOR	Gorton	39A Gorton	39A Gorton	36B Mexborough	41F Mexborough		
69309	N5	IMM	Immingham	40B Immingham	40C Louth	38D Staveley	41H Staveley		
69310	N5	WFD	Woodford Halse	38E Woodford Halse	38A Colwick				
69311	N5	LIN	Lincoln	40A Lincoln					
69312	N5	CLK	Colwick	38A Colwick	39B Sheffield Darnall	41A Sheffield Darnall			
69313	N5	NEA	Neasden	36E Retford	36E Retford				
69314	N5	MEX	Mexborough	36B Mexborough	36E Retford	36E Retford	41A Sheffield Darnall		
69315	N5	NEA	Neasden	34E Neasden	34E Neasden	36D Barnsley			
69316	N5	MEX	Mexborough	36B Mexborough	36B Mexborough	41A Sheffield Darnall			
69317	N5	STP	Heaton Mersey	9F Heaton Mersey	9F Heaton Mersey				
69318	N5	NEA	Neasden	34E Neasden	34E Neasden				
69319	N5	LNG	Langwith Junction	40E Langwith Junction	40E Langwith Junction	40E Langwith Junction			
69320	N5	BRN	Barnsley	36D Barnsley	36D Barnsley	36D Barnsley			
69321	N5	RET	Retford	36E Retford	36E Retford				
69322	N5	IMM	Immingham	40B Immingham	40C Louth	40E Langwith Junction			
69323	N5	LNG	Langwith Junction	40E Langwith Junction	40E Langwith Junction				
69324	N5	CLK	Colwick	38A Colwick	39B Sheffield Darnall				
69325	N5	BRN	Barnsley	36D Barnsley	36D Barnsley				
69326	N5	WRX	Wrexham Rhosddu	9E Trafford Park	9E Trafford Park	17F Trafford Park			
69327	N5	LNG	Langwith Junction	40E Langwith Junction	40C Louth	41A Sheffield Darnall			
69328	N5	STP	Heaton Mersey	9F Heaton Mersey	39A Gorton	39A Gorton			
69329	N5	WRX	Wrexham Rhosddu	6E Wrexham Rhosddu	6E Wrexham Rhosddu	6E Wrexham Rhosddu			
69330	N5	WRX	Wrexham Rhosddu	6E Wrexham Rhosddu	6E Wrexham Rhosddu				
69331	N5	STP	Heaton Mersey	9F Heaton Mersey	9F Heaton Mersey	17E Heaton Mersey			
69332	N5	STP	Heaton Mersey	9F Heaton Mersey	6D Chester Northgate	6D Chester Northgate			
69333	N5	GOR	Gorton	39A Gorton	39A Gorton				
69334	N5	BRN	Barnsley	36D Barnsley	36D Barnsley				
69335	N5	NTH	Northwich	9G Northwich	9E Trafford Park	6E Wrexham Rhosddu			
69336	N5	TFD	Trafford Park	9E Trafford Park	9E Trafford Park				
69337	N5	LIV	Brunswick	37A Ardsley	36B Mexborough				
69338	N5	WAL	Walton on the Hill	39A Gorton	39A Gorton				
69339	N5	LIV	Brunswick	6F Bidston	6F Bidston				
69340	N5	WRX	Wrexham Rhosddu	6E Wrexham Rhosddu	6E Wrexham Rhosddu				
69341	N5	NEA	Neasden	34E Neasden	34E Neasden	34E Neasden			
69342	N5	LIV	Brunswick	6D Chester Northgate	6D Chester Northgate	6D Chester Northgate			
69343	N5	TFD	Trafford Park	9E Trafford Park	9E Trafford Park	17F Trafford Park	41G Barnsley		
69344	N5	WAL	Walton on the Hill	27E Walton on the Hill	27E Walton on the Hill	27E Walton on the Hill			
69345	N5	BRN	Barnsley	36D Barnsley	36D Barnsley				
69346	N5	WRX	Wrexham Rhosddu	6E Wrexham Rhosddu	6E Wrexham Rhosddu	6E Wrexham Rhosddu			
69347	N5	GOR	Gorton	9E Trafford Park	9E Trafford Park	9E Trafford Park			

		1948	1951	1954	1957	1960	1963	1966
69348	N5	BRN Barnsley	36D Barnsley	36D Barnsley	41A Sheffield Darnall			
69349	N5	NTH Northwich	6E Wrexham Rhosddu	6E Wrexham Rhosddu	6E Wrexham Rhosddu			
69350	N5	NEA Neasden	34E Neasden	34E Neasden	34E Neasden			
69351	N5	STV Staveley	38D Staveley	38D Staveley				
69352	N5	WRX Wrexham Rhosddu	6E Wrexham Rhosddu	6E Wrexham Rhosddu				
69353	N5	GOR Gorton	39A Gorton	39A Gorton				
69354	N5	NEA Neasden	36E Retford	34E Neasden	36D Barnsley	41G Barnsley		
69355	N5	BRN Barnsley	36D Barnsley	36D Barnsley	36D Barnsley			
69356	N5	WAL Walton on the Hill	27E Walton on the Hill	27E Walton on the Hill	27E Walton on the Hill			
69357	N5	BRN Barnsley	36D Barnsley	36D Barnsley				
69358	N5	NEA Neasden	34E Neasden	9E Trafford Park				
69359	N5	STP Heaton Mersey	9F Heaton Mersey	9F Heaton Mersey				
69360	N5	STV Staveley	38E Woodford Halse	38A Colwick	39A Gorton	9G Gorton		
69361	N5	TFD Trafford Park	9E Trafford Park	9E Trafford Park	17F Trafford Park			
69362	N5	WRX Wrexham Rhosddu	6E Wrexham Rhosddu	6E Wrexham Rhosddu	6E Wrexham Rhosddu			
69363	N5	STV Staveley	38D Staveley	38D Staveley				
69364	N5	TFD Trafford Park	9E Trafford Park	9E Trafford Park				
69365	N5	BRN Barnsley	36D Barnsley	36D Barnsley	36D Barnsley			
000CC	N5	WRX Wrexham Rhosddu	6E Wrexham Rhosddu	6E Wrexham Rhosddu				
69367	N5	BRN Barnsley	36D Barnsley	00D Darnsley				
69368	N5	BRN Barnsley	36D Barnsley	36D Barnsley				
69369	N5	NEA Neasden	34E Neasden	34E Neasden	40B Immingham			
69370	N5	TFD Trafford Park	9E Trafford Park	9E Trafford Park	17F Trafford Park	41G Barnsley		
69371	N8	HTN Heaton	52B Heaton					
69372	N8	HTN Heaton						
69373	N8	HLD Hull Dairycoates						
69374	N8	HLD Hull Dairycoates						
69375	N8	HLD Hull Dairycoates						
69376	N8	HLD Hull Dairycoates						
69377	N8	HLD Hull Dairycoates	53A Hull Dairycoates	52B Heaton				
69378	N8	TDK Tyne Dock	54B Tyne Dock	53D Bridlington				
69379	N8	HLD Hull Dairycoates	53A Hull Dairycoates					
69380	N8	HTN Heaton						
69381	N8	HLD Hull Dairycoates	53A Hull Dairycoates	53A Hull Dairycoates				
69382	N8	HLD Hull Dairycoates	53A Hull Dairycoates					
69383	N8	HLD Hull Dairycoates						
69384	N8	CON Consett						
69385	N8	HLD Hull Dairycoates	53A Hull Dairycoates	53A Hull Dairycoates				
69386	N8	HLD Hull Dairycoates	53A Hull Dairycoates	53A Hull Dairycoates				
69387	N8	HTN Heaton	52B Heaton					
69389	N8	HLD Hull Dairycoates	53A Hull Dairycoates					
69390	N8	HTN Heaton	52B Heaton	54D Consett				
69391	N8	HLD Hull Dairycoates	54C Borough Gardens					
69392	N8	HLD Hull Dairycoates	53A Hull Dairycoates	54A Sunderland				
69393	N8	HLD Hull Dairycoates	53A Hull Dairycoates					
69394	N8	CON Consett	54D Consett	54D Consett				
69395	N8	TDK Tyne Dock	54D Consett					
69396	N8	HLD Hull Dairycoates						
69397	N8	HLD Hull Dairycoates						
69398	N8	HLD Hull Dairycoates	53A Hull Dairycoates					
69399	N8	HLD Hull Dairycoates						
69400	N8	SUN Sunderland	54B Tyne Dock					
69401	N8	HLD Hull Dairycoates	53A Hull Dairycoates					
69410	N9	TDK Tyne Dock						
69411	N9	CON Consett						
69413	N9	SUN Sunderland						
69414	N9	CON Consett						
69415	N9	DAR Darlington						
69418	N9	DAR Darlington	54A Sunderland					
69419	N9	HAV Haverton Hill						
69420	N9	TDK Tyne Dock						
69421	N9	SUN Sunderland						
69422	N9	AUK West Auckland						
69423	N9	NLN Northallerton	54A Sunderland					
69424	N9	PEL Pelton Level	54A Sunderland	54B Tyne Dock				
69425	N9	SUN Sunderland						
69426	N9	DAR Darlington	51A Darlington					
69427	N9	SUN Sunderland	54A Sunderland	54B Tyne Dock				
69428	N9	SUN Sunderland						
69429	N9	SUN Sunderland	54B Tyne Dock	54B Tyne Dock				
69430	N1	COP Copley Hill	37B Copley Hill	37B Copley Hill				
69431	N1	HSY Hornsey	34B Hornsey	37A Ardsley				
69432	N1	HSY Hornsey	34B Hornsey	37C Bradford Hammerton St				
69433	N1	HSY Hornsey	34B Hornsey	37C Bradford Hammerton St				
69434	N1	KX Kings Cross	34B Hornsey	37C Bradford Hammerton St	56G Bradford Hammerton St			
69435	N1	HSY Hornsey	34B Hornsey	34B Hornsey				
69436	N1	COP Copley Hill	37B Copley Hill	37B Copley Hill				
69437	N1	BFD Bradford Hammerton St	37B Copley Hill	37B Copley Hill				
69439	N1	HSY Hornsey	34B Hornsey	37C Bradford Hammerton St				
69440	N1	COP Copley Hill	37B Copley Hill	37B Copley Hill	56B Ardsley			
69441	N1	HSY Hornsey	34B Hornsey	34B Hornsey				
69442	N1	HSY Hornsey	34B Hornsey					
69443	N1	BFD Bradford Hammerton St	37C Bradford Hammerton St	37C Bradford Hammerton St	56G Bradford Hammerton St			
69444	N1	COP Copley Hill	37B Copley Hill	37B Copley Hill				
69445	N1	HSY Hornsey	34B Hornsey	34B Hornsey				
69446	N1	COP Copley Hill	37B Copley Hill					
69447	N1	BFD Bradford Hammerton St	37C Bradford Hammerton St	37C Bradford Hammerton St				
69448	N1	BFD Bradford Hammerton St	37C Bradford Hammerton St					
69449	N1	BFD Bradford Hammerton St	37C Bradford Hammerton St	37C Bradford Hammerton St				
69450	N1	HSY Hornsey	34B Hornsey	37B Copley Hill	56C Copley Hill			
69451	N1	HSY Hornsey	34B Hornsey	34B Hornsey				
69452	N1	ARD Ardsley	37A Ardsley	37A Ardsley	56B Ardsley			
69453	N1	HSY Hornsey	34B Hornsey	34B Hornsey	56B Ardsley			
69454	N1	BFD Bradford Hammerton St	37C Bradford Hammerton St	37C Bradford Hammerton St				
69455	N1	HAT Hatfield	34B Hornsey	34B Hornsey				
69456	N1	HSY Hornsey	34B Hornsey	37A Ardsley				
69457	N1	HSY Hornsey	34B Hornsey	34B Hornsey	56G Bradford Hammerton St			
69458	N1	HSY Hornsey	34B Hornsey	34B Hornsey				
69459	N1	BFD Bradford Hammerton St	37C Bradford Hammerton St	37C Bradford Hammerton St				
69460	N1	HSY Hornsey	34B Hornsey	34B Hornsey				
69461	N1	ARD Ardsley	37A Ardsley	37A Ardsley				
69462	N1	KX Kings Cross	34B Hornsey	37B Copley Hill	34B Hornsey			
69463	N1	HSY Hornsey	34B Hornsey	37A Ardsley				
69464	N1	BFD Bradford Hammerton St	37C Bradford Hammerton St	37C Bradford Hammerton St				
69465	N1	HSY Hornsey	34B Hornsey	34B Hornsey				
69466	N1	KX Kings Cross	34B Hornsey	34B Hornsey				
69467	N1	KX Kings Cross	34B Hornsey	34B Hornsey				
69468	N1	KX Kings Cross	34B Hornsey	37B Copley Hill				
69469	N1	KX Kings Cross	34B Hornsey	34B Hornsey	56C Copley Hill			
69470	N1	HSY Hornsey	34B Hornsey	34B Hornsey				
69471	N1	COP Copley Hill	37B Copley Hill	37B Copley Hill				
69472	N1	COP Copley Hill	37B Copley Hill	37A Ardsley	56B Ardsley			
69473	N1	ARD Ardsley	37B Copley Hill					
69474	N1	BFD Bradford Hammerton St	37C Bradford Hammerton St	37C Bradford Hammerton St	56G Bradford Hammerton St			

No.	Class	1948	1951	1954	1957	1960	1963	1966
69475	N1	HSY Hornsey	34B Hornsey	37C Bradford Hammerton St				
69476	N1	KX Kings Cross	34B Hornsey	34B Hornsey				
69477	N1	HSY Hornsey	34B Hornsey	37B Copley Hill	34B Hornsey			
69478	N1	BFD Bradford Hammerton St	37C Bradford Hammerton St	37C Bradford Hammerton St				
69479	N1	BFD Bradford Hammerton St	37C Bradford Hammerton St					
69480	N1	KX Kings Cross	34B Hornsey					
69481	N1	KX Kings Cross	34B Hornsey	34B Hornsey				
69482	N1	BFD Bradford Hammerton St	37C Bradford Hammerton St	37C Bradford Hammerton St				
69483	N1	BFD Bradford Hammerton St	37C Bradford Hammerton St	37B Copley Hill				
69484	N1	KX Kings Cross	34C Hatfield	37A Ardsley	56B Ardsley			
69485	N1	BFD Bradford Hammerton St	37C Bradford Hammerton St	37C Bradford Hammerton St				
69490	N2	KX Kings Cross	34A Kings Cross	34A Kings Cross	34A Kings Cross			
69491	N2	KX Kings Cross	34A Kings Cross	34A Kings Cross	34A Kings Cross			
69492	N2	KX Kings Cross	34A Kings Cross	34A Kings Cross	34A Kings Cross			
69493	N2	KX Kings Cross	34C Hatfield	34A Kings Cross	34A Kings Cross			
69494	N2	KX Kings Cross	34C Hatfield	34C Hatfield	34C Hatfield			
69495	N2	KX Kings Cross	34A Kings Cross	34A Kings Cross	34A Kings Cross			
69496	N2	KX Kings Cross	34A Kings Cross	34A Kings Cross	34A Kings Cross			
69497	N2	KX Kings Cross	34A Kings Cross	34A Kings Cross	34A Kings Cross			
69498	N2	KX Kings Cross	34A Kings Cross	34A Kings Cross	34A Kings Cross	34A Kings Cross		
69499	N2	KX Kings Cross	34A Kings Cross	34A Kings Cross	34A Kings Cross			
69500	N2	PKD Parkhead	65C Parkhead	65C Parkhead	65C Parkhead			
69501	N2	CLK Colwick	38A Colwick	34A Kings Cross	34B Hornsey			
69502	N2	HAT Hatfield	34A Kings Cross	30F Parkeston	34A Kings Cross			
69503	N2	KPS Kipps	65E Kipps	65E Kipps	61B Aberdeen Ferryhill			
69504	N2	KX Kings Cross	34C Hatfield	34C Hatfield	34C Hatfield	34B Hornsey		
69505	N2	HSY Hornsey	34B Hornsey	34B Hornsey	34B Hornsey	34F Grantham		
69506	N2	KX Kings Cross	34A Kings Cross	34A Kings Cross	34A Kings Cross	34A Kings Cross		
69507	N2	PKD Parkhead	65C Parkhead	65C Parkhead	65C Parkhead	65C Parkhead		
69508	N2	KPS Kipps	65E Kipps	65C Parkhead	65C Parkhead			
69509	N2	KPS Kipps	65E Kipps	65D Dawsholm	65D Dawsholm	65C Parkhead		
69510	N2	PKD Parkhead	65C Parkhead	65C Parkhead	65C Parkhead			
69511	N2	KPS Kipps	65C Parkhead	65D Dawsholm	65D Dawsholm	65D Dawsholm		
69512	N2	KX Kings Cross	34A Kings Cross	34A Kings Cross	34A Kings Cross	34A Kings Cross		
69513	N2	HSY Hornsey	34B Hornsey	34B Hornsey	34B Hornsey	34E New England		
69514	N2	PKD Parkhead	65C Parkhead	65C Parkhead				
69515	N2	HIT Hitchin	34D Hitchin	34D Hitchin	34D Hitchin			
69516	N2	HSY Hornsey	34B Hornsey	34C Hatfield	34C Hatfield	34F Grantham		
69517	N2	KX Kings Cross	34A Kings Cross	34A Kings Cross	34A Kings Cross			
69518	N2	KPS Kipps	65E Kipps	65E Kipps	65E Kipps	65E Kipps		
69519	N2	NEA Neasden	34A Kings Cross	34A Kings Cross	34A Kings Cross			
69520	N2	KX Kings Cross	34A Kings Cross	34A Kings Cross	34A Kings Cross	34B Hornsey		
69521	N2	KX Kings Cross	34A Kings Cross	34A Kings Cross	34A Kings Cross	34E New England		
69522	N2	HSY Hornsey	34B Hornsey	34B Hornsey	34B Hornsey			
69523	N2	KX Kings Cross	34A Kings Cross	34A Kings Cross	34A Kings Cross	34A Kings Cross		
69524	N2	KX Kings Cross	34A Kings Cross	34A Kings Cross	34A Kings Cross			
69525	N2	KX Kings Cross	34A Kings Cross	34A Kings Cross	34A Kings Cross			
69526	N2	KX Kings Cross	34A Kings Cross	34A Kings Cross	34A Kings Cross			
69527	N2	KX Kings Cross	34A Kings Cross	34A Kings Cross	34A Kings Cross			
69528	N2	KX Kings Cross	34A Kings Cross	34A Kings Cross	34A Kings Cross			
69529	N2	KX Kings Cross	34A Kings Cross	34A Kings Cross	34A Kings Cross	34A Kings Cross		
69530	N2	HSY Hornsey	34B Hornsey	34B Hornsey	34B Hornsey			
69531	N2	HSY Hornsey	34B Hornsey	34B Hornsey	34B Hornsey	34C Hatfield		
69532	N2	KX Kings Cross	34A Kings Cross	34A Kings Cross	34A Kings Cross			
69533	N2	HSY Hornsey	34B Hornsey	34B Hornsey	34B Hornsey	34A Kings Cross		
69534	N2	HAT Hatfield	34C Hatfield	34C Hatfield	34C Hatfield			
69535	N2	KX Kings Cross	34A Kings Cross	34A Kings Cross	34A Kings Cross	34A Kings Cross		
69536	N2	KX Kings Cross	34A Kings Cross	34A Kings Cross	34A Kings Cross			
69537	N2	HAT Hatfield	34C Hatfield	34C Hatfield	34B Hornsey			
69538	N2	KX Kings Cross	34A Kings Cross	34A Kings Cross	34A Kings Cross	34A Kings Cross		
69539	N2	KX Kings Cross	34A Kings Cross	34A Kings Cross	34A Kings Cross			
69540	N2	KX Kings Cross	34A Kings Cross	34A Kings Cross	34A Kings Cross	34E New England		
69541	N2	KX Kings Cross	34A Kings Cross	34A Kings Cross	34A Kings Cross			
69542	N2	KX Kings Cross	34A Kings Cross	34A Kings Cross	34A Kings Cross			
69543	N2	KX Kings Cross	34A Kings Cross	34A Kings Cross	34A Kings Cross	34A Kings Cross		
69544	N2	KX Kings Cross	34A Kings Cross	34A Kings Cross	34A Kings Cross			
69545	N2	KX Kings Cross	34A Kings Cross	34A Kings Cross	34A Kings Cross			
69546	N2	KX Kings Cross	34A Kings Cross	34A Kings Cross	34A Kings Cross	34A Kings Cross		
69547	N2	HSY Hornsey	34B Hornsey	34B Hornsey	34C Hatfield			
69548	N2	KX Kings Cross	34A Kings Cross	34A Kings Cross	34A Kings Cross			
69549	N2	KX Kings Cross	34A Kings Cross	34A Kings Cross	34A Kings Cross	34A Kings Cross		
69550	N2	CLK Colwick	38A Colwick	30A Stratford	34A Kings Cross			
69551	N2	HAT Hatfield	34C Hatfield	30F Parkeston	34A Kings Cross			
69552	N2	CLK Colwick	38A Colwick	30F Parkeston	34A Kings Cross	34F Grantham		
69553	N2	KPS Kipps	65C Parkhead	65D Dawsholm	65D Dawsholm			
69554	N2	HAT Hatfield	34C Hatfield	34A Kings Cross	34B Hornsey			
69555	N2	CLK Colwick	38A Colwick	30E Colchester	34A Kings Cross			
69556	N2	HSY Hornsey	34B Hornsey	34B Hornsey	34B Hornsey			
69557	N2	HIT Hitchin	34D Hitchin	34D Hitchin	34D Hitchin			
69558	N2	HAT Hatfield	34C Hatfield	30E Colchester	34A Kings Cross			
69559	N2	HAT Hatfield	34C Hatfield	30A Stratford	34A Kings Cross			
69560	N2	CLK Colwick	38E Woodford Halse	34B Hornsey	34B Hornsey	34F Grantham		
69561	N2	NEA Neasden	34A Kings Cross	30F Parkeston	34A Kings Cross	34F Grantham		
69562	N2	PKD Parkhead	65C Parkhead	65C Parkhead				
69563	N2	KPS Kipps	65E Kipps	65C Parkhead	65C Parkhead	65C Parkhead		
69564	N2	PKD Parkhead	65C Parkhead	65C Parkhead	65C Parkhead	12C Carlisle Canal		
69565	N2	PKD Parkhead	65C Parkhead	65C Parkhead	65C Parkhead			
69566	N2	HSY Hornsey	34B Hornsey	30F Parkeston	34A Kings Cross			
69567	N2	KX Kings Cross	34B Hornsey	34B Hornsey	34B Hornsey			
69568	N2	KX Kings Cross	34A Kings Cross	34A Kings Cross	34A Kings Cross	34A Kings Cross		
69569	N2	KX Kings Cross	34A Kings Cross	34A Kings Cross	34A Kings Cross			
69570	N2	KX Kings Cross	34A Kings Cross	34A Kings Cross	34A Kings Cross			
69571	N2	KX Kings Cross	34A Kings Cross	34A Kings Cross	34A Kings Cross	34E New England		
69572	N2	KX Kings Cross	34A Kings Cross	34A Kings Cross	34A Kings Cross	34A Kings Cross		
69573	N2	KX Kings Cross	34A Kings Cross	34A Kings Cross	34A Kings Cross			
69574	N2	KX Kings Cross	34A Kings Cross	34A Kings Cross	34A Kings Cross	34A Kings Cross		
69575	N2	KX Kings Cross	34A Kings Cross	34A Kings Cross	34A Kings Cross	34A Kings Cross		
69576	N2	KX Kings Cross	34A Kings Cross	34A Kings Cross	34A Kings Cross			
69577	N2	KX Kings Cross	34A Kings Cross	34A Kings Cross	34A Kings Cross			
69578	N2	KX Kings Cross	34A Kings Cross	34A Kings Cross	34A Kings Cross			
69579	N2	KX Kings Cross	34A Kings Cross	34A Kings Cross	34A Kings Cross	34A Kings Cross		
69580	N2	HAT Hatfield	34C Hatfield	34A Kings Cross	34C Hatfield	34C Hatfield		
69581	N2	KX Kings Cross	34A Kings Cross	34A Kings Cross	34A Kings Cross	34A Kings Cross		
69582	N2	HAT Hatfield	34C Hatfield	34C Hatfield	34C Hatfield	34E New England		
69583	N2	KX Kings Cross	34A Kings Cross	34A Kings Cross	34A Kings Cross	34A Kings Cross		
69584	N2	KX Kings Cross	34A Kings Cross	34A Kings Cross	34A Kings Cross			
69585	N2	KX Kings Cross	34A Kings Cross	34A Kings Cross	34A Kings Cross	34A Kings Cross		
69586	N2	HAT Hatfield	34C Hatfield	34C Hatfield	34C Hatfield	34C Hatfield		
69587	N2	HAT Hatfield	34C Hatfield	34A Kings Cross	34B Hornsey	34B Hornsey		
69588	N2	HAT Hatfield	34C Hatfield	34C Hatfield	34C Hatfield	34C Hatfield		
69589	N2	KX Kings Cross	34A Kings Cross	34A Kings Cross	34A Kings Cross	34A Kings Cross		
69590	N2	HAT Hatfield	34A Kings Cross	34A Kings Cross	34A Kings Cross			
69591	N2	KX Kings Cross	34A Kings Cross	34A Kings Cross	34A Kings Cross			
69592	N2	KX Kings Cross	34A Kings Cross	34A Kings Cross	34A Kings Cross	34A Kings Cross		

		1948	1951	1954	1957	1960	1963	1966
69593	*N2*	**KX** Kings Cross	**34A** Kings Cross	**34A** Kings Cross	**34A** Kings Cross	**34A** Kings Cross		
69594	*N2*	**HAT** Hatfield	**34C** Hatfield	**34C** Hatfield	**34B** Hornsey	**34D** Hitchin		
69595	*N2*	**PKD** Parkhead	**65C** Parkhead	**65C** Parkhead	**65C** Parkhead			
69596	*N2*	**KPS** Kipps	**65E** Kipps	**65E** Kipps	**65E** Kipps	**65E** Kipps		
69600	*N7*	**STR** Stratford	**30A** Stratford	**30A** Stratford	**30A** Stratford			
69601	*N7*	**STR** Stratford	**30A** Stratford	**30A** Stratford	**30A** Stratford			
69602	*N7*	**STR** Stratford	**30A** Stratford	**30A** Stratford	**30A** Stratford			
69603	*N7*	**STR** Stratford	**30A** Stratford	**30A** Stratford	**30A** Stratford			
69604	*N7*	**STR** Stratford	**30A** Stratford	**30A** Stratford	**30A** Stratford			
69605	*N7*	**STR** Stratford	**30A** Stratford	**30A** Stratford	**30A** Stratford			
69606	*N7*	**STR** Stratford	**30A** Stratford	**30A** Stratford	**30A** Stratford			
69607	*N7*	**STR** Stratford	**30A** Stratford	**30A** Stratford	**30A** Stratford			
69608	*N7*	**STR** Stratford	**30A** Stratford	**30A** Stratford	**30A** Stratford			
69609	*N7*	**STR** Stratford	**30A** Stratford	**30A** Stratford	**30A** Stratford			
69610	*N7*	**STR** Stratford	**30A** Stratford	**30A** Stratford	**30A** Stratford			
69611	*N7*	**STR** Stratford	**30A** Stratford	**30A** Stratford	**30A** Stratford	**30A** Stratford		
69612	*N7*	**STR** Stratford	**30F** Parkeston	**30A** Stratford	**34B** Hornsey			
69613	*N7*	**STR** Stratford	**34C** Hatfield	**30A** Stratford	**30A** Stratford			
69614	*N7*	**STR** Stratford	**30F** Parkeston	**30A** Stratford	**30A** Stratford	**30A** Stratford		
69615	*N7*	**STR** Stratford	**34C** Hatfield	**38A** Colwick	**34B** Hornsey	**30A** Stratford		
69616	*N7*	**STR** Stratford	**30A** Stratford	**30A** Stratford	**30A** Stratford			
69617	*N7*	**STR** Stratford	**30A** Stratford	**30A** Stratford	**30A** Stratford	**30A** Stratford		
69618	*N7*	**STR** Stratford	**30A** Stratford	**30A** Stratford	**34B** Hornsey	**34C** Hatfield		
69619	*N7*	**STR** Stratford	**30A** Stratford	**30A** Stratford	**30A** Stratford			
69620	*N7*	**STR** Stratford	**34C** Hatfield	**38A** Colwick	**30A** Stratford	**30A** Stratford		
69621	*N7*	**STR** Stratford	**30F** Parkeston	**38A** Colwick	**30A** Stratford	**30A** Stratford		
69622	*N7*	**STR** Stratford	**30A** Stratford	**30A** Stratford	**30A** Stratford			
69623	*N7*	**STR** Stratford	**30A** Stratford	**30A** Stratford	**30A** Stratford			
69624	*N7*	**STR** Stratford	**30A** Stratford	**30A** Stratford	**30A** Stratford			
69625	*N7*	**STR** Stratford	**30A** Stratford	**30A** Stratford	**30A** Stratford			
69626	*N7*	**STR** Stratford	**30A** Stratford	**30A** Stratford	**30A** Stratford			
69627	*N7*	**STR** Stratford	**30A** Stratford	**30A** Stratford	**30A** Stratford			
69628	*N7*	**STR** Stratford	**30A** Stratford	**30A** Stratford	**30A** Stratford			
69629	*N7*	**STR** Stratford	**30A** Stratford	**30A** Stratford	**34B** Hornsey	**34C** Hatfield		
69630	*N7*	**STR** Stratford	**30A** Stratford	**30A** Stratford	**30A** Stratford	**30A** Stratford		
69631	*N7*	**STR** Stratford	**30A** Stratford	**30A** Stratford	**34C** Hatfield	**34C** Hatfield		
69632	*N7*	**STR** Stratford	**34C** Hatfield	**34C** Hatfield	**34C** Hatfield	**34C** Hatfield		
69633	*N7*	**STR** Stratford	**30A** Stratford	**30A** Stratford	**30A** Stratford			
69634	*N7*	**STR** Stratford	**30A** Stratford	**30A** Stratford	**30A** Stratford			
69635	*N7*	**STR** Stratford	**30F** Parkeston	**34C** Hatfield	**34C** Hatfield			
69636	*N7*	**STR** Stratford	**30A** Stratford	**30A** Stratford	**30A** Stratford	**30A** Stratford		
69637	*N7*	**STR** Stratford	**30A** Stratford	**30A** Stratford	**34C** Hatfield			
69638	*N7*	**STR** Stratford	**30A** Stratford	**34C** Hatfield	**34C** Hatfield			
69639	*N7*	**STR** Stratford	**34C** Hatfield	**34C** Hatfield	**34C** Hatfield			
69640	*N7*	**STR** Stratford	**34C** Hatfield	**34C** Hatfield	**34C** Hatfield	**34C** Hatfield		
69641	*N7*	**STR** Stratford	**30A** Stratford	**30A** Stratford	**30A** Stratford			
69642	*N7*	**STR** Stratford	**30A** Stratford	**30A** Stratford	**30A** Stratford	**30A** Stratford		
69643	*N7*	**STR** Stratford	**30A** Stratford	**30A** Stratford	**30A** Stratford			
69644	*N7*	**STR** Stratford	**34C** Hatfield	**34C** Hatfield	**34C** Hatfield			
69645	*N7*	**STR** Stratford	**30A** Stratford	**30A** Stratford	**30A** Stratford	**30A** Stratford		
69646	*N7*	**STR** Stratford	**30A** Stratford	**30A** Stratford	**30A** Stratford	**30A** Stratford		
69647	*N7*	**STR** Stratford	**30A** Stratford	**30A** Stratford	**30A** Stratford	**30A** Stratford		
69648	*N7*	**STR** Stratford	**30A** Stratford	**34C** Hatfield	**34C** Hatfield	**34C** Hatfield		
69649	*N7*	**STR** Stratford	**30A** Stratford	**34C** Hatfield	**34C** Hatfield			
69650	*N7*	**STR** Stratford	**30A** Stratford	**30A** Stratford	**34C** Hatfield			
69651	*N7*	**STR** Stratford	**30A** Stratford	**38B** Annesley	**31A** Cambridge	**30A** Stratford		
69652	*N7*	**STR** Stratford	**30A** Stratford	**30A** Stratford	**30A** Stratford	**30A** Stratford		
69653	*N7*	**STR** Stratford	**30A** Stratford	**30A** Stratford	**30A** Stratford	**30A** Stratford		
69654	*N7*	**STR** Stratford	**30A** Stratford	**38A** Colwick	**34C** Hatfield	**34C** Hatfield		
69655	*N7*	**STR** Stratford	**30A** Stratford	**30A** Stratford	**30A** Stratford			
69656	*N7*	**STR** Stratford	**30A** Stratford	**30A** Stratford	**30A** Stratford	**30A** Stratford		
69657	*N7*	**STR** Stratford	**30A** Stratford	**30A** Stratford	**30A** Stratford			
69658	*N7*	**STR** Stratford	**30A** Stratford	**30A** Stratford	**30A** Stratford	**30A** Stratford		
69659	*N7*	**STR** Stratford	**30A** Stratford	**30A** Stratford	**30A** Stratford			
69660	*N7*	**STR** Stratford	**30A** Stratford	**30A** Stratford	**30A** Stratford			
69661	*N7*	**STR** Stratford	**30A** Stratford	**30A** Stratford	**30A** Stratford			
69662	*N7*	**STR** Stratford	**30A** Stratford	**30A** Stratford	**30A** Stratford			
69663	*N7*	**STR** Stratford	**30A** Stratford	**30A** Stratford	**30A** Stratford	**30A** Stratford		
69664	*N7*	**STR** Stratford	**30A** Stratford	**30A** Stratford	**30A** Stratford	**30A** Stratford		
69665	*N7*	**STR** Stratford	**30A** Stratford	**30A** Stratford	**30A** Stratford	**30A** Stratford		
69666	*N7*	**STR** Stratford	**30A** Stratford	**30A** Stratford	**30A** Stratford			
69667	*N7*	**STR** Stratford	**30A** Stratford	**30A** Stratford	**30A** Stratford			
69668	*N7*	**STR** Stratford	**30A** Stratford	**30A** Stratford	**30A** Stratford	**30A** Stratford		
69669	*N7*	**STR** Stratford	**30A** Stratford	**30A** Stratford	**30A** Stratford			
69670	*N7*	**STR** Stratford	**30A** Stratford	**30A** Stratford	**30A** Stratford	**30A** Stratford		
69671	*N7*	**STR** Stratford	**30A** Stratford	**30A** Stratford	**30A** Stratford	**30A** Stratford		
69672	*N7*	**STR** Stratford	**30A** Stratford	**30E** Colchester	**30F** Parkeston			
69673	*N7*	**STR** Stratford	**30A** Stratford	**30E** Colchester	**30E** Colchester	**30F** Parkeston		
69674	*N7*	**STR** Stratford	**30A** Stratford	**30A** Stratford	**30A** Stratford	**30A** Stratford		
69675	*N7*	**STR** Stratford	**30A** Stratford	**30A** Stratford	**30F** Parkeston	**30F** Parkeston		
69676	*N7*	**STR** Stratford	**30A** Stratford	**30A** Stratford	**30A** Stratford			
69677	*N7*	**STR** Stratford	**30F** Parkeston	**30A** Stratford	**30A** Stratford	**30A** Stratford		
69678	*N7*	**STR** Stratford	**30A** Stratford	**34C** Hatfield	**34C** Hatfield	**34C** Hatfield		
69679	*N7*	**STR** Stratford	**32A** Norwich Thorpe	**32A** Norwich Thorpe	**32C** Lowestoft	**30A** Stratford		
69680	*N7*	**STR** Stratford	**30A** Stratford	**30A** Stratford	**30A** Stratford	**30A** Stratford		
69681	*N7*	**STR** Stratford	**30A** Stratford	**30A** Stratford	**30A** Stratford	**30A** Stratford		
69682	*N7*	**STR** Stratford	**30A** Stratford	**30A** Stratford	**30A** Stratford	**30A** Stratford		
69683	*N7*	**STR** Stratford	**30A** Stratford	**30A** Stratford	**30A** Stratford	**30A** Stratford		
69684	*N7*	**STR** Stratford	**30A** Stratford	**30A** Stratford	**30A** Stratford	**30A** Stratford		
69685	*N7*	**STR** Stratford	**30A** Stratford	**30A** Stratford	**30A** Stratford	**30A** Stratford		
69686	*N7*	**STR** Stratford	**30A** Stratford	**30A** Stratford	**30A** Stratford	**30A** Stratford		
69687	*N7*	**STR** Stratford	**30A** Stratford	**30A** Stratford	**30A** Stratford	**30A** Stratford		
69688	*N7*	**STR** Stratford	**30A** Stratford	**30A** Stratford	**30A** Stratford	**30A** Stratford		
69689	*N7*	**HAT** Hatfield	**34E** Neasden	**34A** Kings Cross	**32D** Yarmouth South Town			
69690	*N7*	**HAT** Hatfield	**34E** Neasden	**32A** Norwich Thorpe	**31A** Cambridge	**30A** Stratford		
69691	*N7*	**HAT** Hatfield	**34C** Hatfield	**38B** Annesley	**33B** Tilbury	**30A** Stratford		
69692	*N7*	**HAT** Hatfield	**34E** Neasden	**34A** Kings Cross	**31A** Cambridge	**34C** Hatfield		
69693	*N7*	**STR** Stratford	**30A** Stratford	**30A** Stratford	**30A** Stratford	**30A** Stratford		
69694	*N7*	**HAT** Hatfield	**34E** Neasden	**34A** Kings Cross	**33B** Tilbury	**31C** Kings Lynn		
69695	*N7*	**HAT** Hatfield	**34C** Hatfield	**38B** Annesley	**33B** Tilbury			
69696	*N7*	**HAT** Hatfield	**34C** Hatfield	**32A** Norwich Thorpe	**32D** Yarmouth South Town	**34C** Hatfield		
69697	*N7*	**STR** Stratford	**30A** Stratford	**30A** Stratford	**30A** Stratford	**30A** Stratford		
69698	*N7*	**HAT** Hatfield	**34E** Neasden	**34A** Kings Cross	**33B** Tilbury	**34C** Hatfield		
69699	*N7*	**STR** Stratford	**30A** Stratford	**30A** Stratford	**30A** Stratford	**30A** Stratford		
69700	*N7*	**STR** Stratford	**30A** Stratford	**30A** Stratford	**30A** Stratford	**30A** Stratford		
69701	*N7*	**STR** Stratford	**30E** Colchester	**30A** Stratford	**30A** Stratford	**30A** Stratford		
69702	*N7*	**STR** Stratford	**30A** Stratford	**30A** Stratford	**30A** Stratford	**30A** Stratford		
69703	*N7*	**STR** Stratford	**32B** Ipswich	**30A** Stratford	**30A** Stratford			
69704	*N7*	**STR** Stratford	**30A** Stratford	**34C** Hatfield	**34C** Hatfield	**34C** Hatfield		
69705	*N7*	**STR** Stratford	**30A** Stratford	**30A** Stratford	**30A** Stratford			
69706	*N7*	**STR** Stratford	**32A** Norwich Thorpe	**32A** Norwich Thorpe	**32A** Norwich Thorpe	**30A** Stratford		
69707	*N7*	**STR** Stratford	**32A** Norwich Thorpe	**32A** Norwich Thorpe	**32A** Norwich Thorpe	**30A** Stratford		
69708	*N7*	**STR** Stratford	**32G** Melton Constable	**32A** Norwich Thorpe	**32D** Yarmouth South Town	**30A** Stratford		
69709	*N7*	**STR** Stratford	**32A** Norwich Thorpe	**34C** Hatfield	**34C** Hatfield	**30A** Stratford		

		1948	1951	1954	1957	1960	1963	1966
69710	*N7*	STR Stratford	**30A** Stratford	**30A** Stratford	**30A** Stratford	**30A** Stratford		
69711	*N7*	STR Stratford	**30A** Stratford	**30A** Stratford	**30A** Stratford			
69712	*N7*	STR Stratford	**30A** Stratford	**30A** Stratford	**30A** Stratford	**30A** Stratford		
69713	*N7*	STR Stratford	**30A** Stratford	**30A** Stratford	**30A** Stratford	**30A** Stratford		
69714	*N7*	STR Stratford	**30A** Stratford	**30A** Stratford	**30A** Stratford	**30A** Stratford		
69715	*N7*	STR Stratford	**30A** Stratford	**30A** Stratford	**30A** Stratford	**30A** Stratford		
69716	*N7*	STR Stratford	**30A** Stratford	**30A** Stratford	**30A** Stratford			
69717	*N7*	STR Stratford	**30A** Stratford	**30A** Stratford	**30A** Stratford			
69718	*N7*	STR Stratford	**30A** Stratford	**30A** Stratford	**30A** Stratford	**30A** Stratford		
69719	*N7*	STR Stratford	**30A** Stratford	**30A** Stratford	**30A** Stratford	**30A** Stratford		
69720	*N7*	STR Stratford	**30A** Stratford	**30E** Colchester	**30A** Stratford	**30A** Stratford		
69721	*N7*	STR Stratford	**30A** Stratford	**30A** Stratford	**30F** Parkeston	**30A** Stratford		
69722	*N7*	STR Stratford	**30A** Stratford	**30A** Stratford	**30A** Stratford	**30A** Stratford		
69723	*N7*	STR Stratford	**30A** Stratford	**30A** Stratford	**30A** Stratford	**30A** Stratford		
69724	*N7*	STR Stratford	**30A** Stratford	**30A** Stratford	**30A** Stratford	**30A** Stratford		
69725	*N7*	STR Stratford	**30A** Stratford	**30A** Stratford	**30A** Stratford	**30A** Stratford		
69726	*N7*	STR Stratford	**30E** Colchester	**30A** Stratford	**30A** Stratford	**30A** Stratford		
69727	*N7*	STR Stratford	**30A** Stratford	**30A** Stratford	**30F** Parkeston	**30A** Stratford		
69728	*N7*	STR Stratford	**30A** Stratford	**30A** Stratford	**30A** Stratford	**30A** Stratford		
69729	*N7*	STR Stratford	**30A** Stratford	**30A** Stratford	**30A** Stratford	**30A** Stratford		
69730	*N7*	STR Stratford	**30A** Stratford	**30A** Stratford	**30A** Stratford	**30F** Parkeston		
69731	*N7*	STR Stratford	**30A** Stratford	**30A** Stratford	**30A** Stratford			
69732	*N7*	STR Stratford	**30A** Stratford	**30E** Colchester	**30E** Colchester	**30F** Parkeston		
69733	*N7*	STR Stratford	**30A** Stratford	**30A** Stratford	**30F** Parkeston	**30A** Stratford		
69770	*A7*	HLD Hull Dairycoates	**53A** Hull Dairycoates	**53A** Hull Dairycoates				
69771	*A7*	CUD Cudworth	**53A** Hull Dairycoates	**53A** Hull Dairycoates				
69772	*A7*	HLD Hull Dairycoates	**53A** Hull Dairycoates	**53A** Hull Dairycoates	**53C** Hull Springhead			
69773	*A7*	HLD Hull Dairycoates	**53A** Hull Dairycoates	**53A** Hull Dairycoates				
69774	*A7*	HLS Hull Springhead	**53C** Hull Springhead	**53C** Hull Springhead				
69775	*A7*	HLD Hull Dairycoates	**53A** Hull Dairycoates					
69776	*A7*	HLS Hull Springhead	**53C** Hull Springhead	**53C** Hull Springhead				
69777	*A7*	HLD Hull Dairycoates	**53A** Hull Dairycoates					
69778	*A7*	HLD Hull Dairycoates	**53A** Hull Dairycoates	**53A** Hull Dairycoates				
69779	*A7*	HLD Hull Dairycoates	**53A** Hull Dairycoates	**53A** Hull Dairycoates				
69780	*A7*	HLD Hull Dairycoates	**53A** Hull Dairycoates	**53C** Hull Springhead				
69781	*A7*	SKN Stockton on Tees	**51E** Stockton on Tees	**53A** Hull Dairycoates				
69782	*A7*	HLD Hull Dairycoates	**53A** Hull Dairycoates	**53A** Hull Dairycoates	**53C** Hull Springhead			
69783	*A7*	HLD Hull Dairycoates	**53A** Hull Dairycoates	**53C** Hull Springhead				
69784	*A7*	HLD Hull Dairycoates	**53A** Hull Dairycoates	**53C** Hull Springhead				
69785	*A7*	HLS Hull Springhead	**53C** Hull Springhead	**53C** Hull Springhead				
69786	*A7*	HLD Hull Dairycoates	**53A** Hull Dairycoates	**53A** Hull Dairycoates	**53C** Hull Springhead			
69787	*A7*	SKN Stockton on Tees	**51E** Stockton on Tees	**53C** Hull Springhead				
69788	*A7*	HLD Hull Dairycoates	**53A** Hull Dairycoates	**53A** Hull Dairycoates				
69789	*A7*	CUD Cudworth	**53C** Hull Springhead					
69791	*A6*	SBK Starbeck	**50D** Starbeck					
69792	*A6*	WBY Whitby						
69793	*A6*	SBK Starbeck	**50D** Starbeck					
69794	*A6*	SBK Starbeck	**50D** Starbeck					
69795	*A6*	HLB Hull Botanic Gardens						
69796	*A6*	HLB Hull Botanic Gardens	**53B** Hull Botanic Gardens					
69797	*A6*	SBK Starbeck	**50D** Starbeck					
69798	*A6*	HLB Hull Botanic Gardens	**53B** Hull Botanic Gardens					
69799	*A6*	SBK Starbeck						
69800	*A5*	NEA Neasden	**40B** Immingham	**40B** Immingham	**38A** Colwick			
69801	*A5*	NEA Neasden	**38A** Colwick	**38A** Colwick	**39A** Gorton	**9G** Gorton		
69802	*A5*	NEA Neasden	**51K** Saltburn	**53B** Hull Botanic Gardens	**53B** Hull Botanic Gardens			
69803	*A5*	NEA Neasden	**40F** Boston	**40F** Boston	**38D** Staveley			
69804	*A5*	NEA Neasden	**40A** Lincoln	**40A** Lincoln	**38A** Colwick			
69805	*A5*	NEA Neasden	**34E** Neasden	**34E** Neasden	**39A** Gorton			
69806	*A5*	NEA Neasden	**38A** Colwick	**38A** Colwick	**39A** Gorton	**9G** Gorton		
69807	*A5*	NEA Neasden	**38A** Colwick	**38A** Colwick	**38A** Colwick			
69808	*A5*	NEA Neasden	**40F** Boston	**40F** Boston	**40F** Boston	**40A** Lincoln		
69809	*A5*	NEA Neasden	**38A** Colwick	**38A** Colwick	**38B** Annesley			
69810	*A5*	NEA Neasden	**38A** Colwick	**38A** Colwick	**38A** Colwick			
69811	*A5*	NEA Neasden	**51K** Saltburn	**53B** Hull Botanic Gardens	**53B** Hull Botanic Gardens			
69812	*A5*	NEA Neasden	**40E** Langwith Junction	**40E** Langwith Junction	**38A** Colwick			
69813	*A5*	NEA Neasden	**40A** Lincoln	**40A** Lincoln	**40A** Lincoln	**9G** Gorton		
69814	*A5*	NEA Neasden	**38A** Colwick	**34E** Neasden	**35B** Grantham	**34A** Kings Cross		
69815	*A5*	NEA Neasden	**40E** Langwith Junction	**40E** Langwith Junction	**39A** Gorton			
69816	*A5*	NEA Neasden	**40F** Boston	**40F** Boston	**40B** Immingham			
69817	*A5*	NEA Neasden	**38A** Colwick	**38A** Colwick	**39A** Gorton	**9G** Gorton		
69818	*A5*	NEA Neasden	**40E** Langwith Junction	**38A** Colwick	**38B** Annesley			
69819	*A5*	NEA Neasden	**40F** Boston	**40F** Boston	**40F** Boston			
69820	*A5*	NEA Neasden	**40A** Lincoln	**40B** Immingham	**40A** Lincoln	**40A** Lincoln		
69821	*A5*	NEA Neasden	**38A** Colwick	**40E** Langwith Junction	**38A** Colwick	**40A** Lincoln		
69822	*A5*	NEA Neasden	**34E** Neasden	**38A** Colwick	**38A** Colwick			
69823	*A5*	NEA Neasden	**38A** Colwick	**38A** Colwick	**39A** Gorton	**9G** Gorton		
69824	*A5*	NEA Neasden	**40F** Boston	**32A** Norwich Thorpe	**32C** Lowestoft			
69825	*A5*	NEA Neasden	**38A** Colwick	**38A** Colwick	**38B** Annesley			
69826	*A5*	NEA Neasden	**38A** Colwick	**32A** Norwich Thorpe	**32C** Lowestoft			
69827	*A5*	NEA Neasden	**34E** Neasden	**34E** Neasden	**35B** Grantham			
69828	*A5*	NEA Neasden	**34E** Neasden	**40A** Lincoln	**39A** Gorton			
69829	*A5*	NEA Neasden	**34E** Neasden	**34E** Neasden	**32C** Lowestoft	**40B** Immingham		
69830	*A5*	DAR Darlington	**51A** Darlington	**51A** Darlington	**51A** Darlington			
69831	*A5*	DAR Darlington	**51K** Saltburn	**51K** Saltburn	**51A** Darlington			
69832	*A5*	DAR Darlington	**51A** Darlington	**51A** Darlington	**51A** Darlington			
69833	*A5*	DAR Darlington	**51A** Darlington	**51A** Darlington	**51A** Darlington			
69834	*A5*	DAR Darlington	**51K** Saltburn	**51K** Saltburn	**51A** Darlington			
69835	*A5*	DAR Darlington	**51A** Darlington	**51A** Darlington	**53B** Hull Botanic Gardens			
69836	*A5*	DAR Darlington	**51A** Darlington	**53B** Hull Botanic Gardens	**53B** Hull Botanic Gardens			
69837	*A5*	DAR Darlington	**51A** Darlington	**53B** Hull Botanic Gardens	**53B** Hull Botanic Gardens			
69838	*A5*	DAR Darlington	**51A** Darlington	**51A** Darlington	**51E** Stockton on Tees			
69839	*A5*	DAR Darlington	**51A** Darlington	**51A** Darlington	**51A** Darlington			
69840	*A5*	DAR Darlington	**51A** Darlington	**51A** Darlington	**51A** Darlington			
69841	*A5*	DAR Darlington	**51A** Darlington	**51A** Darlington	**51A** Darlington			
69842	*A5*	DAR Darlington	**51K** Saltburn	**51A** Darlington	**51E** Stockton on Tees			
69850	*A8*	SUN Sunderland	**54A** Sunderland	**54A** Sunderland	**54A** Sunderland	**52G** Sunderland		
69851	*A8*	BLA Blaydon	**51F** West Auckland	**51F** West Auckland	**51F** West Auckland			
69852	*A8*	WBY Whitby	**51C** West Hartlepool	**51D** Middlesbrough	**51K** Saltburn			
69853	*A8*	BLA Blaydon	**54A** Sunderland	**54A** Sunderland	**54A** Sunderland	**52G** Sunderland		
69854	*A8*	HLB Hull Botanic Gardens	**51D** Middlesbrough	**51D** Middlesbrough	**51D** Middlesbrough	**52G** Sunderland		
69855	*A8*	HLB Hull Botanic Gardens	**53B** Hull Botanic Gardens	**51K** Saltburn	**51K** Saltburn	**52G** Sunderland		
69856	*A8*	AUK West Auckland	**51F** West Auckland	**51F** West Auckland	**51F** West Auckland			
69857	*A8*	BLA Blaydon	**54A** Sunderland	**54A** Sunderland	**54A** Sunderland	**52G** Sunderland		
69858	*A8*	MID Middlesbrough	**50G** Whitby	**50G** Whitby	**53B** Hull Botanic Gardens	**52G** Sunderland		
69859	*A8*	MID Middlesbrough	**51D** Middlesbrough	**51D** Middlesbrough	**51K** Saltburn	**52G** Sunderland		
69860	*A8*	MID Middlesbrough	**50G** Whitby	**50G** Whitby	**53B** Hull Botanic Gardens	**51L** Thornaby		
69861	*A8*	SUN Sunderland	**50G** Whitby	**50G** Whitby	**50F** Malton	**50F** Malton		
69862	*A8*	WHL West Hartlepool	**51C** West Hartlepool	**51D** Middlesbrough	**51D** Middlesbrough			
69863	*A8*	WHL West Hartlepool	**51C** West Hartlepool	**54A** Sunderland	**54A** Sunderland			
69864	*A8*	WHL West Hartlepool	**50G** Whitby	**50G** Whitby	**50G** Whitby			
69865	*A8*	BLA Blaydon	**50G** Whitby	**50G** Whitby	**50G** Whitby			
69866	*A8*	HLB Hull Botanic Gardens	**51D** Middlesbrough	**51D** Middlesbrough	**51K** Saltburn			
69867	*A8*	HLB Hull Botanic Gardens	**50C** Selby	**50E** Scarborough	**50E** Scarborough			

No.	Class	1948	1951	1954	1957	1960	1963	1966
69868	*A8*	**SAL** Saltburn	**51F** West Auckland	**51F** West Auckland	**51F** West Auckland			
69869	*A8*	**MID** Middlesbrough	**51K** Saltburn	**51K** Saltburn	**51K** Saltburn	**51L** Thornaby		
69870	*A8*	**AUK** West Auckland	**51F** West Auckland	**51F** West Auckland	**51F** West Auckland	**52G** Sunderland		
69871	*A8*	**WHL** West Hartlepool	**51C** West Hartlepool	**51C** West Hartlepool	**51A** Darlington			
69872	*A8*	**SAL** Saltburn	**51F** West Auckland	**51F** West Auckland	**51F** West Auckland			
69873	*A8*	**HLB** Hull Botanic Gardens	**51D** Middlesbrough	**51D** Middlesbrough	**51C** West Hartlepool	**52G** Sunderland		
69874	*A8*	**SUN** Sunderland	**54A** Sunderland	**54A** Sunderland	**54A** Sunderland	**52G** Sunderland		
69875	*A8*	**SAL** Saltburn	**51F** West Auckland	**51F** West Auckland	**51F** West Auckland	**52G** Sunderland		
69876	*A8*	**SAL** Saltburn	**51D** Middlesbrough	**51D** Middlesbrough	**51D** Middlesbrough			
69877	*A8*	**AUK** West Auckland	**50C** Selby	**50F** Malton	**50A** York			
69878	*A8*	**MID** Middlesbrough	**51D** Middlesbrough	**51D** Middlesbrough	**51D** Middlesbrough	**52G** Sunderland		
69879	*A8*	**AUK** West Auckland	**50C** Selby	**50E** Scarborough	**53B** Hull Botanic Gardens			
69880	*A8*	**MID** Middlesbrough	**51D** Middlesbrough	**51D** Middlesbrough	**51K** Saltburn	**51C** West Hartlepool		
69881	*A8*	**SCA** Scarborough	**50E** Scarborough	**50E** Scarborough	**50B** Leeds Neville Hill			
69882	*A8*	**SAL** Saltburn	**50B** Leeds Neville Hill	**50B** Leeds Neville Hill	**53B** Hull Botanic Gardens			
69883	*A8*	**SAL** Saltburn	**51E** Stockton on Tees	**51D** Middlesbrough	**51C** West Hartlepool	**52G** Sunderland		
69884	*A8*	**SAL** Saltburn	**51K** Saltburn	**51K** Saltburn	**51K** Saltburn			
69885	*A8*	**SCA** Scarborough	**50E** Scarborough	**50E** Scarborough	**50B** Leeds Neville Hill	**50E** Scarborough		
69886	*A8*	**AUK** West Auckland	**50E** Scarborough	**50E** Scarborough	**53B** Hull Botanic Gardens	**50F** Malton		
69887	*A8*	**SUN** Sunderland	**54A** Sunderland	**54A** Sunderland	**51A** Darlington			
69888	*A8*	**MID** Middlesbrough	**50G** Whitby	**50G** Whitby	**53B** Hull Botanic Gardens			
69889	*A8*	**SAL** Saltburn	**51K** Saltburn	**51K** Saltburn	**51D** Middlesbrough	**52G** Sunderland		
69890	*A8*	**HLB** Hull Botanic Gardens	**50G** Whitby	**50G** Whitby	**50G** Whitby			
69891	*A8*	**SAL** Saltburn	**51K** Saltburn	**51K** Saltburn	**51D** Middlesbrough			
69892	*A8*	**SAL** Saltburn	**51K** Saltburn	**51K** Saltburn	**51K** Saltburn			
69893	*A8*	**WHL** West Hartlepool	**51C** West Hartlepool	**51C** West Hartlepool	**51C** West Hartlepool			
69894	*A8*	**SCA** Scarborough	**53B** Hull Botanic Gardens	**51K** Saltburn	**51K** Saltburn	**51C** West Hartlepool		
69900	*S1*	**MEX** Mexborough	**36B** Mexborough	**39B** Sheffield Darnall				
69901	*S1*	**MEX** Mexborough	**36B** Mexborough	**36B** Mexborough	**36C** Frodingham			
69902	*S1*	**MAR** March	**36C** Frodingham	**36B** Mexborough				
69903	*S1*	**MAR** March	**36B** Mexborough	**40B** Immingham				
69904	*S1*	**MEX** Mexborough	**36B** Mexborough	**36B** Mexborough				
69905	*S1*	**MEX** Mexborough	**36B** Mexborough	**36B** Mexborough	**36C** Frodingham			
69910	*T1*	**NPT** Newport	**51B** Newport	**51B** Newport	**50A** York			
69911	*T1*	**NPT** Newport	**51B** Newport	**51B** Newport	**51B** Newport			
69912	*T1*	**HLD** Hull Dairycoates	**53A** Hull Dairycoates	**51E** Stockton on Tees	**51E** Stockton on Tees			
69913	*T1*	**NPT** Newport	**51B** Newport	**51B** Newport	**50A** York			
69914	*T1*	**SEL** Selby	**53A** Hull Dairycoates	**54B** Tyne Dock				
69915	*T1*	**HLD** Hull Dairycoates	**53A** Hull Dairycoates	**51B** Newport	**50C** Selby			
69916	*T1*	**NPT** Newport	**51B** Newport	**51B** Newport	**50A** York			
69917	*T1*	**NPT** Newport	**51B** Newport	**51B** Newport	**54D** Consett			
69918	*T1*	**SKN** Stockton on Tees	**51E** Stockton on Tees	**51E** Stockton on Tees	**51E** Stockton on Tees			
69919	*T1*	**NPT** Newport	**51B** Newport	**51E** Stockton on Tees				
69920	*T1*	**HLD** Hull Dairycoates	**54B** Tyne Dock	**54B** Tyne Dock	**54B** Tyne Dock			
69921	*T1*	**NPT** Newport	**51B** Newport	**51B** Newport	**51E** Stockton on Tees	**52H** Tyne Dock		
69922	*T1*	**HLD** Hull Dairycoates	**53A** Hull Dairycoates	**51B** Newport				
69925	*Q1*	**EFD** Eastfield	**65A** Eastfield	**65A** Eastfield				
69926	*Q1*	**CAM** Cambridge	**31B** March	**36C** Frodingham	**36C** Frodingham			
69927	*Q1*	**EFD** Eastfield	**65A** Eastfield	**65A** Eastfield				
69928	*Q1*	**LNG** Langwith Junction	**40E** Langwith Junction	**40E** Langwith Junction	**40E** Langwith Junction			
69929	*Q1*	**LNG** Langwith Junction	**40E** Langwith Junction	**40E** Langwith Junction	**40E** Langwith Junction			
69930	*Q1*	**FRO** Frodingham	**36C** Frodingham	**36C** Frodingham	**36C** Frodingham			
69931	*Q1*	**GHD** Gateshead	**50C** Selby	**50C** Selby	**50C** Selby			
69932	*Q1*	**FRO** Frodingham	**36C** Frodingham	**36C** Frodingham	**36C** Frodingham			
69933	*Q1*	**GHD** Gateshead	**50C** Selby	**50C** Selby	**50C** Selby			
69934	*Q1*	**FRO** Frodingham	**36C** Frodingham	**36C** Frodingham	**36C** Frodingham			
69935	*Q1*	**FRO** Frodingham	**36C** Frodingham	**36C** Frodingham	**36C** Frodingham			
69936	*Q1*	**FRO** Frodingham	**36C** Frodingham	**36C** Frodingham	**36C** Frodingham			
69937	*Q1*	**FRO** Frodingham	**36C** Frodingham	**36C** Frodingham				
69999	*U1*	**MEX** Mexborough	**36B** Mexborough	**36B** Mexborough				
1	*J52*	(68845)	→	Doncaster Works	Doncaster Works			
2	*J52*	(68816)	→	Doncaster Works				
2	*J52*	(68858)	→	→	Doncaster Works	Doncaster Works		
3	*Y3*	(68181)	→	Ranskill Wagon Works	Ranskill Wagon Works			
4	*Y1*	(68132)	→	Ranskill Wagon Works	Ranskill Wagon Works			
5	*Y3*	(68165)	→	Doncaster	Doncaster			
6	*Y1*	(68133)	→	Peterborough Engineer's Yard				
7	*Y3*	(68166)	→	Boston Sleeper Depot	Boston Sleeper Depot	Boston Sleeper Depot	Boston Sleeper Depot	
8	*Y3*	(68183)	→	→	Peterborough Engineer's Yard			
9	*J52*	(68840)	→	→	→	Doncaster Works		
10	*J50*	(68911)	→	→	→	→	Doncaster Works	
11	*J50*	(68914)	→	→	→	→	Doncaster Works	
12	*J50*	(68917)	→	→	→	→	Doncaster Works	
13	*J50*	(68928)	→	→	→	→	Doncaster Works	
14	*J50*	(68961)	→	→	→	→	Doncaster Works	
15	*J50*	(68971)	→	→	→	→	Doncaster Works	
16	*J50*	(68976)	→	→	→	→	Doncaster Works	
17	*B1*	(61059)	→	→	→	→	→	Norwich
18	*B1*	(61181)						
19	*B1*	(61204)	→	→	→	→	→	Norwich
20	*B1*	(61205)						
21	*B1*	(61233)	→	→	→	→	→	Cambridge
22	*B1*	(61252)						
23	*B1*	(61300)						
24	*B1*	(61375)	→	→	→	→	→	Kings Lynn
25	*B1*	(61272)						
26	*B1*	(61138)	→	→	→	→	→	Norwich
27	*B1*	(61105)	→	→	→	→	→	Parkeston
28	*B1*	(61194)	→	→	→	→	→	Stratford
29	*B1*	(61264)	→	→	→	→	→	Norwich
30	*B1*	(61050)						
31	*B1*	(61051)						
32	*B1*	(61315)						
21	*Y3*	(68162)	→	→	Cambridge Engineer's Dept	Cambridge Engineer's Dept		
31	*J66*	(68382)	→	Stratford Works	Stratford Works			
32	*J66*	(68370)	→	Stratford Works	Stratford Works	Stratford Works		
33	*Y4*	(68129)	→	Stratford Works	Stratford Works	Stratford Works	Stratford Works	
34	*Y7*	(68088)						
35	*J92*	(68668)						
36	*J66*	(68378)	→	Stratford Works	Stratford Works			
37	*Y1*	(68130)	→	Lowestoft Engineer's Dept				
38	*Y3*	(68168)	→	Lowestoft Engineer's Dept	Lowestoft Engineer's Dept			
39	*Y1*	(68131)	→	Lowestoft Engineer's Dept	Lowestoft Engineer's Dept	Lowestoft Engineer's Dept	Lowestoft Engineer's Dept	
40	*Y3*	(68173)	→	Lowestoft Engineer's Dept	Lowestoft Engineer's Dept	Lowestoft Engineer's Dept	Lowestoft Engineer's Dept	
41	*Y3*	(68177)	→	Lowestoft Engineer's Dept	Lowestoft Engineer's Dept	Lowestoft Engineer's Dept	Lowestoft Engineer's Dept	
42	*Y3*	(68178)		Cambridge Engineer's Dept	Cambridge Engineer's Dept	Cambridge Engineer's Dept		
43	*J69*	(68532)						
44	*J69*	(68498)	→	→	→	Stratford Works		
45	*J69*	(68543)	→	→	→	Stratford Works		
51	*Y1*	(68136)	→	Faverdale Works Darlington				
53	*Y1*	(68152)	→	→	York Engineer's Yard			
54	*Y1*	(68153)	→	→	Darlington PW Depot	Darlington PW Depot		
55	*Y8*	(68091)						

		1948	1951	1954	1957	1960	1963	1966
57	*Y3*	(68160)	→	→	Faverdale Works Darlington	Faverdale Works Darlington		
58	*J72*	(69005)	→	→	→	→	→	Tyne Dock
59	*J72*	(69023)	→	→	→	→	→	Tyne Dock
49	*D40*	(62277)	→	→	→	**61C** Keith	**65D** Dawsholm	
256	*D34*	(62469)	→	→	→	**61C** Keith		
3	*J66*	Mersey Railway						
2136	*Railcar*	WBY Whitby						

Above: GCR Robinson 'B9' class 4-6-0 No 1470 at Brunswick on 13 June 1948. This engine did not receive its allocated number 61470 before withdrawal. *E. R. Wethersett*

Below: GCR Robinson 'B4' class 4-6-0 No 1482 *Immingham* at Ardsley on 26 September 1948. Allocated number 61482 not carried. *M. P. Mileham*

Left: Streamlined LNER Sandringham 'B17/5' class No 61659 *East Anglian* at Stratford on 31 April 1948. *A. F. Cook*

Below: LNER Gresley 'K4' class 2-6-0 No 61998 *Macleod of Macleod*.

Bottom: BR (LNER) Peppercorn 'K1' class 2-6-0 No 62028 at York on 1 May 1966. *P. J. Hughes*

Right: GNR Ivatt 'D3' class 4-4-0 No 2148 at Hitchin on 3 August 1948. This engine was withdrawn without carrying its allocated number 62148. *E. R. Wethersett*

Below: GNR Ivatt 'D2' class 4-4-0 No 62172 at Grantham on 8 July 1948. This was the only member of the class to carry its BR number. *H. C. Casserley*

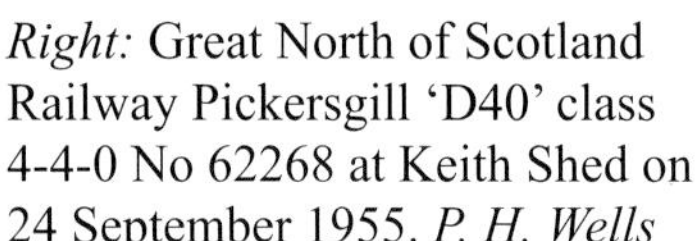

Right: Great North of Scotland Railway Pickersgill 'D40' class 4-4-0 No 62268 at Keith Shed on 24 September 1955. *P. H. Wells*

Left: NBR Holmes 'D31' class 4-4-0 No 62282 at Inverurie in June 1950. This was its second BR number as it was renumbered from 62060 to make space for newly built 'K1' engines. *J. Davenport*

Below: GCR Robinson 'D9' class 4-4-0 No 62307 *Queen Mary* at Trafford Park on 13 June 1949. *H. C. Casserley*

Bottom: NER Worsdell 'D20' class 4-4-0 No 62372 at Sunderland with a local train for Newcastle on 12 June 1954. *L. King*

Above: NBR Reid 'Scott' 'D30' class 4-4-0 No 62441 *Black Duncan* at Dunfermline on 21 April 1957. *R. E. Vincent*

Left: The last GNR Ivatt Atlantic 'C1' class 4-4-2 No 62822 on arrival at Doncaster on a special from Kings Cross on 26 November 1950. It was withdrawn at the end of this journey. *C. C. B. Herbert*

Below: GCR Robinson 'C4' class Atlantic No 2918 on a Spalding to Lincoln freight near Gosberton in June 1950. Allocated number 62918 not carried. *P. Ransome-Wallis*

Above: GCR Robinson 'Q4' class 0-8-0 No 63217. *P. Ransome-Wallis*

Right: NER Raven 'Q7' class 0-8-0 No 63463 based at 54B Tyne Dock shed is seen with its train loading at Tyne Dock. *P. Ransome-Wallis*

Below: LNER Thompson 'O1' class 2-8-0 No 63592 at Staveley GC shed on 27 July 1963. *N. E. Preedy*

Left: GNR Gresley 'O2/3' class 2-8-0 No 63947 at Doncaster on 5 September 1954. *A. R. Carpenter*

Above: GCR Robinson 'J11/3' class 0-6-0 No 64442 at its home shed 36B Mexborough on 17 June 1951. *R. E. Vincent*

Right: NBR Reid 'J37' class 0-6-0 No 64594 from 64A St. Margarets at Perth on 20 April 1957. *A .W. Martin*

Above: LNER Gresley 'J39' class 0-6-0 No 64735 at Grantham on 9 July 1958. *P. H. Groom*

Right: GNR Gresley 'J2' class 0-6-0 No 65016 at its home shed 40F Boston on 26 August 1950. *H. C. Casserley*

Below: NER Worsdell 'J21' class 0-6-0 No 65035 at its home shed 52B Heaton. *Brian Morrison*

Left: GER Holden 'J17' class 0-6-0 No 65554 at its home shed 31B March on 21 August 1958. *P. J. Sharpe*

Below: NER Worsdell 'J25' 0-6-0 No 65675 at its home shed 50C Selby. *Brian Morrison*

Left: NER Worsdell 'J26' 0-6-0 No 65743 at Thornaby on 8 July 1961. *A. Banting*

Right: NER Worsdell 'J27' 0-6-0 No 65846 at York shed in May 1965 (its home base from March 1965 until withdrawal). *K. R. Pirt*

Below: GCR Pollitt 'F2' class 2-4-2T No 7107 on an Alexandra Palace push-pull train. Allocated number 67107 not carried. *E. R. Wethersett*

Right: GER Holden 'F4' class 2-4-2T No 67174 at Stratford on 29 January 1955, just after withdrawal. *Brian Morrison*

Above: GER Holden 'F6' class 2-4-2T No 67227. *F. W. Day*

Right: NER Worsdell 'G5' class 0-4-4T No 67279 at Stratford on 28 January 1951. *R. E. Vincent*

Left: GCR Robinson 'C14' class 4-4-2T No 67442 based at 6E Wrexham Rhosddu. *Brian Morrison*

Right: NBR Reid 'C16' class 4-4-2T No 67489 at Dundee shed on 27 February 1950. *E. M. Patterson*

Below: LNER Gresley 'V3' class 2-6-2T No 67615 at Haymarket on 24 October 1954.

Right: GER Hill 'Y4' class 0-4-0T No 68127 at Stratford on 1 July 1951. *R. E. Vincent*

Left: LNER 'Y10' class Sentinel Tram 0-4-0T No 8186 at Yarmouth Vauxhall Yard on 21 June 1951. Allocated number 68186 not carried. *E. M. Patterson*

Below: Great North of Scotland Railway 'Z4' class Aberdeen Harbour shunter 0-4-2T No 69190 at Kittybrewster on 20 April 1957. *R. E. Vincent*

Left: Great North of Scotland Railway 'Z5' class Aberdeen Harbour shunter 0-4-2T No 69193. *J. N. Westwood*

Right: GCR Robinson 'J63' class 0-6-0ST No 68209 at Immingham on 17 June 1951. *R. E. Vincent*

Below: GER Holden 'J65' class 0-6-0T No 68211 at Ipswich in May 1953. With the front coupling rod removed it appears to be running as 2-4-0T.

Left: NBR Reid 'J88' class 0-6-0T No 68340 at Granton Quay in Edinburgh on 15 June 1956. *J. S. Swanson*

Right: Stovepipe chimney fitted GER Holden 'J67/1' class 0-6-0T No 68511 at St Margarets shed in Edinburgh on 7 March 1954. Attached to a tender for working on the Lauder Light Railway. *E. M. Patterson*

Left: GER Holden 'J69/1' class 0-6-0T No 68529 at Stratford Works in June 1954. *Brian Morrison*

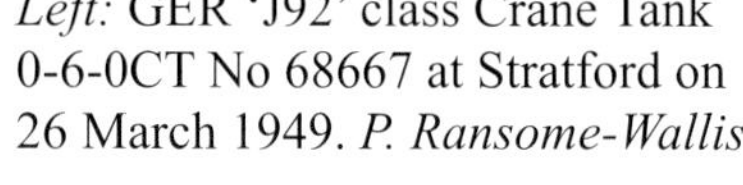

Left: GER 'J92' class Crane Tank 0-6-0CT No 68667 at Stratford on 26 March 1949. *P. Ransome-Wallis*

Right: GNR Ivatt 'J52/2' class 0-6-0ST No 68886 at Doncaster on 17 June 1951. *R. E. Vincent*

Right: Metropolitan Railway 'M2' class 0-6-4T No 9076 *Robert H. Selbie* at Neasden on 12 April 1947. Allocated number 69076.

Below: Manchester Sheffield & Lincolnshire Railway Parker 'N4' class 0-6-2T No 9241 based at SHF (Sheffield Darnall), at St James Bridge station in Doncaster on 31 May 1947. Allocated number 69241 not carried. *A. S. Whiteley*

Right: Manchester Sheffield & Lincolnshire Railway Parker/Pollitt 'N5' class 0-6-2T No 69315 at Marylebone on 21 July 1949. *A. B. Hubert*

Below: NER Worsdell 'A6' class 4-6-2T No 69798. *E. V. Fry*

Bottom: GCR Robinson 'A5/1' class 4-6-2T No 69827 with a Nottingham train at Grantham on 9 July 1958. *P. H. Groom*

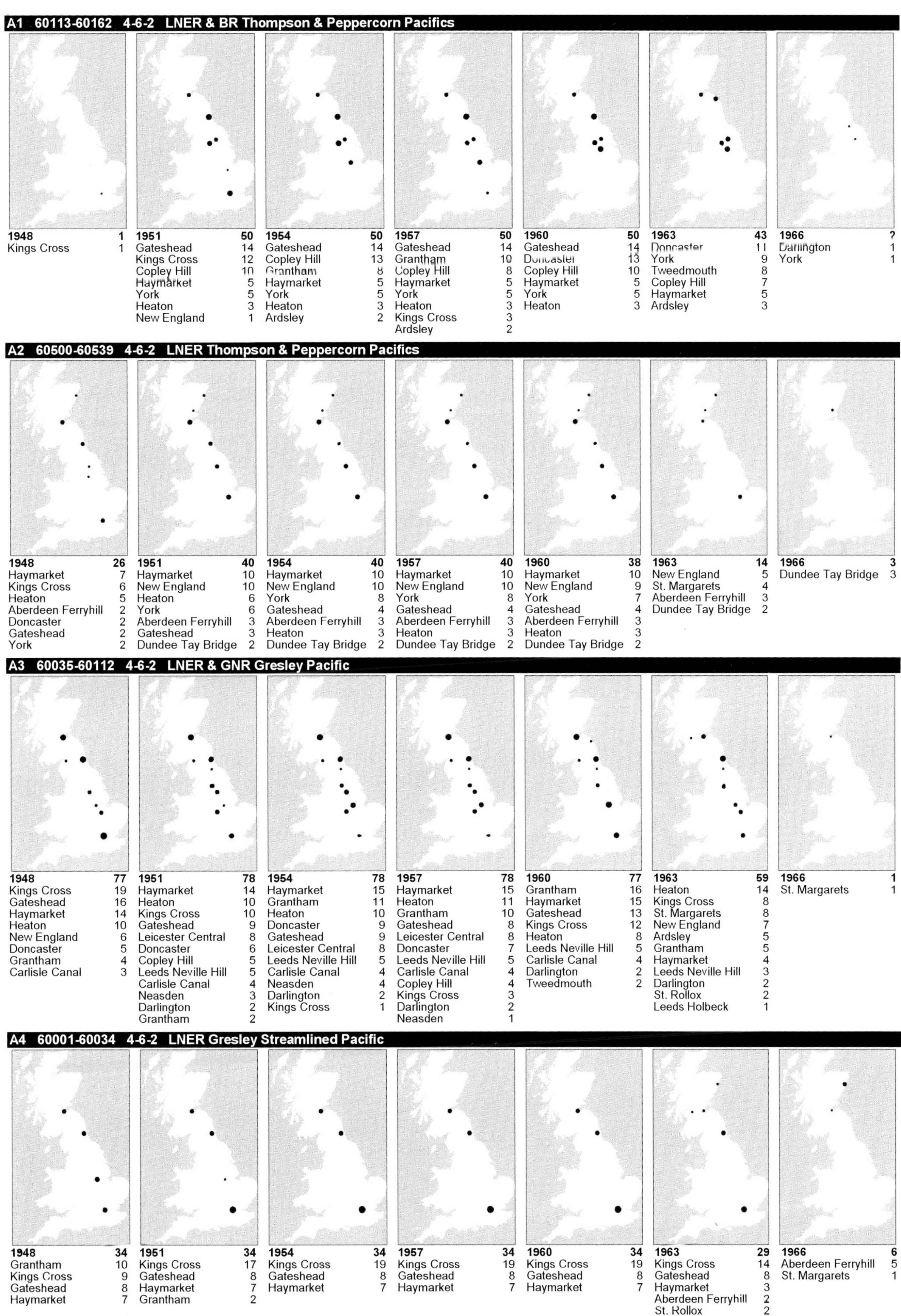

A1 60113-60162 4-6-2 LNER & BR Thompson & Peppercorn Pacifics

Year	Total	Shed	No.
1948	1	Kings Cross	1
1951	50	Gateshead	14
		Kings Cross	12
		Copley Hill	10
		Haymarket	5
		York	5
		Heaton	3
		New England	1
1954	50	Gateshead	14
		Copley Hill	13
		Grantham	8
		Haymarket	5
		York	5
		Heaton	3
		Ardsley	2
1957	50	Gateshead	14
		Grantham	10
		Copley Hill	8
		Haymarket	5
		York	5
		Heaton	3
		Kings Cross	3
		Ardsley	2
1960	50	Gateshead	14
		Doncaster	13
		Copley Hill	10
		Haymarket	5
		York	5
		Heaton	3
1963	43	Doncaster	11
		York	9
		Tweedmouth	8
		Copley Hill	7
		Haymarket	5
		Ardsley	3
1966	?	Darlington	1
		York	1

A2 60500-60539 4-6-2 LNER Thompson & Peppercorn Pacifics

Year	Total	Shed	No.
1948	26	Haymarket	7
		Kings Cross	6
		Heaton	5
		Aberdeen Ferryhill	2
		Doncaster	2
		Gateshead	2
		York	2
1951	40	Haymarket	10
		New England	10
		Heaton	6
		York	6
		Aberdeen Ferryhill	3
		Gateshead	3
		Dundee Tay Bridge	2
1954	40	Haymarket	10
		New England	10
		York	8
		Gateshead	4
		Aberdeen Ferryhill	3
		Heaton	3
		Dundee Tay Bridge	2
1957	40	Haymarket	10
		New England	10
		York	8
		Gateshead	4
		Aberdeen Ferryhill	3
		Heaton	3
		Dundee Tay Bridge	2
1960	38	Haymarket	10
		New England	9
		York	7
		Gateshead	4
		Aberdeen Ferryhill	3
		Heaton	3
		Dundee Tay Bridge	2
1963	14	New England	5
		St. Margarets	4
		Aberdeen Ferryhill	3
		Dundee Tay Bridge	2
1966	3	Dundee Tay Bridge	3

A3 60035-60112 4-6-2 LNER & GNR Gresley Pacific

Year	Total	Shed	No.
1948	77	Kings Cross	19
		Gateshead	16
		Haymarket	14
		Heaton	10
		New England	6
		Doncaster	5
		Grantham	4
		Carlisle Canal	3
1951	78	Haymarket	14
		Heaton	10
		Kings Cross	10
		Gateshead	9
		Leicester Central	8
		Doncaster	6
		Copley Hill	5
		Leeds Neville Hill	5
		Carlisle Canal	4
		Neasden	3
		Darlington	2
		Grantham	2
1954	78	Haymarket	15
		Grantham	11
		Heaton	10
		Doncaster	9
		Gateshead	9
		Leicester Central	8
		Leeds Neville Hill	5
		Carlisle Canal	4
		Neasden	4
		Darlington	2
		Kings Cross	1
1957	78	Haymarket	15
		Heaton	11
		Grantham	10
		Gateshead	8
		Leicester Central	8
		Doncaster	7
		Leeds Neville Hill	5
		Carlisle Canal	4
		Copley Hill	4
		Kings Cross	3
		Darlington	2
		Neasden	1
1960	77	Grantham	16
		Haymarket	15
		Gateshead	13
		Kings Cross	12
		Heaton	8
		Leeds Neville Hill	5
		Carlisle Canal	4
		Darlington	2
		Tweedmouth	2
1963	59	Heaton	14
		Kings Cross	8
		St. Margarets	8
		New England	7
		Ardsley	5
		Grantham	5
		Haymarket	4
		Leeds Neville Hill	3
		Darlington	2
		St. Rollox	2
		Leeds Holbeck	1
1966	1	St. Margarets	1

A4 60001-60034 4-6-2 LNER Gresley Streamlined Pacific

Year	Total	Shed	No.
1948	34	Grantham	10
		Kings Cross	9
		Gateshead	8
		Haymarket	7
1951	34	Kings Cross	17
		Gateshead	8
		Haymarket	7
		Grantham	2
1954	34	Kings Cross	19
		Gateshead	8
		Haymarket	7
1957	34	Kings Cross	19
		Gateshead	8
		Haymarket	7
1960	34	Kings Cross	19
		Gateshead	8
		Haymarket	7
1963	29	Kings Cross	14
		Gateshead	8
		Haymarket	3
		Aberdeen Ferryhill	2
		St. Rollox	2
1966	6	Aberdeen Ferryhill	5
		St. Margarets	1

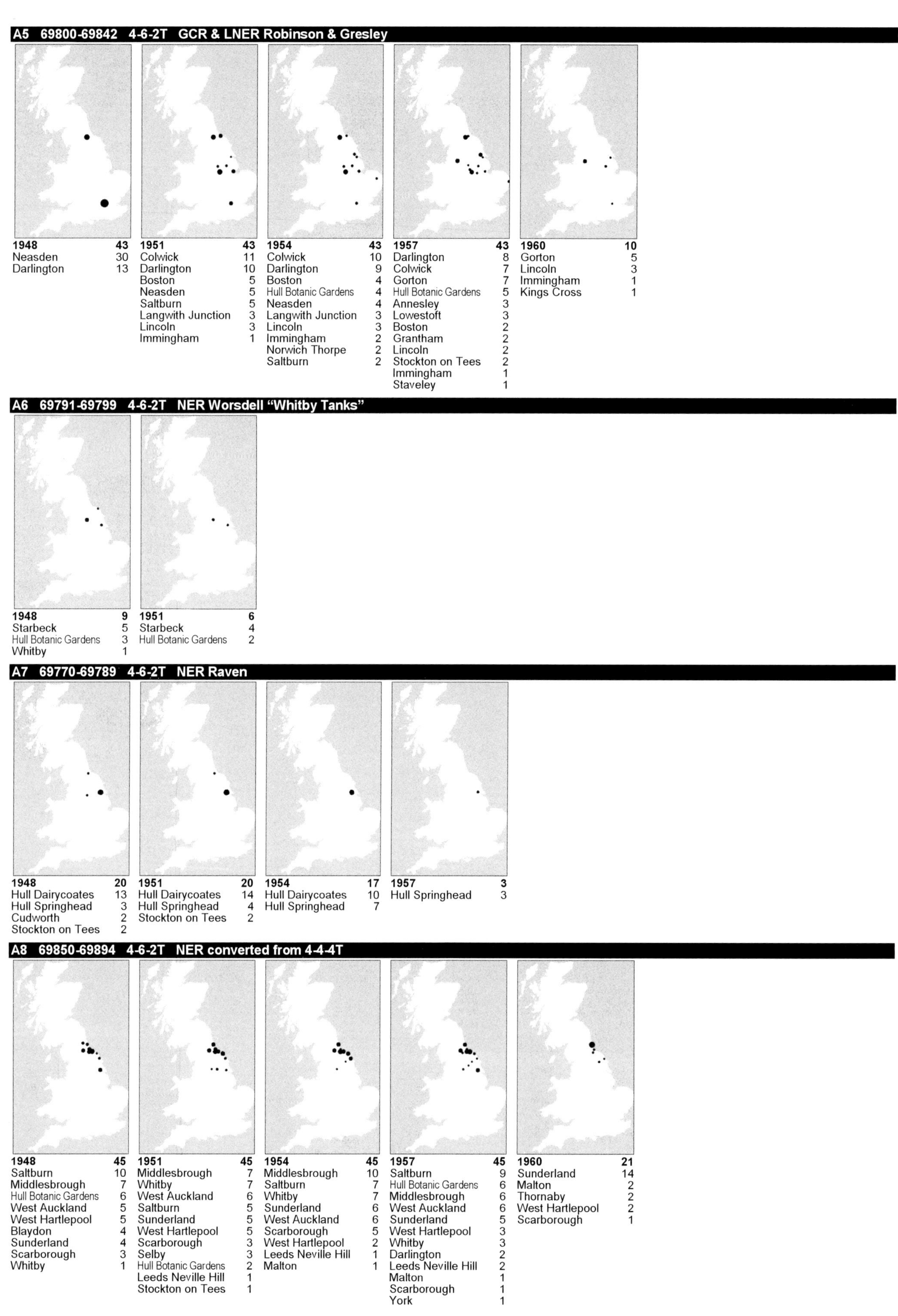

A5 69800-69842 4-6-2T GCR & LNER Robinson & Gresley

1948	43
Neasden	30
Darlington	13

1951	43
Colwick	11
Darlington	10
Boston	5
Neasden	5
Saltburn	5
Langwith Junction	3
Lincoln	3
Immingham	1

1954	43
Colwick	10
Darlington	9
Boston	4
Hull Botanic Gardens	4
Neasden	4
Langwith Junction	3
Lincoln	3
Immingham	2
Norwich Thorpe	2
Saltburn	2

1957	43
Darlington	8
Colwick	7
Gorton	7
Hull Botanic Gardens	5
Annesley	3
Lowestoft	3
Boston	2
Grantham	2
Lincoln	2
Stockton on Tees	2
Immingham	1
Staveley	1

1960	10
Gorton	5
Lincoln	3
Immingham	1
Kings Cross	1

A6 69791-69799 4-6-2T NER Worsdell "Whitby Tanks"

1948	9
Starbeck	5
Hull Botanic Gardens	3
Whitby	1

1951	6
Starbeck	4
Hull Botanic Gardens	2

A7 69770-69789 4-6-2T NER Raven

1948	20
Hull Dairycoates	13
Hull Springhead	3
Cudworth	2
Stockton on Tees	2

1951	20
Hull Dairycoates	14
Hull Springhead	4
Stockton on Tees	2

1954	17
Hull Dairycoates	10
Hull Springhead	7

1957	3
Hull Springhead	3

A8 69850-69894 4-6-2T NER converted from 4-4-4T

1948	45
Saltburn	10
Middlesbrough	7
Hull Botanic Gardens	6
West Auckland	5
West Hartlepool	5
Blaydon	4
Sunderland	4
Scarborough	3
Whitby	1

1951	45
Middlesbrough	7
Whitby	7
West Auckland	6
Saltburn	5
Sunderland	5
West Hartlepool	5
Scarborough	3
Selby	3
Hull Botanic Gardens	2
Leeds Neville Hill	1
Stockton on Tees	1

1954	45
Middlesbrough	10
Saltburn	7
Whitby	7
Sunderland	6
West Auckland	6
Scarborough	5
West Hartlepool	2
Leeds Neville Hill	1
Malton	1

1957	45
Saltburn	9
Hull Botanic Gardens	6
Middlesbrough	6
West Auckland	6
Sunderland	5
West Hartlepool	3
Whitby	3
Darlington	2
Leeds Neville Hill	2
Malton	1
Scarborough	1
York	1

1960	21
Sunderland	14
Malton	2
Thornaby	2
West Hartlepool	2
Scarborough	1

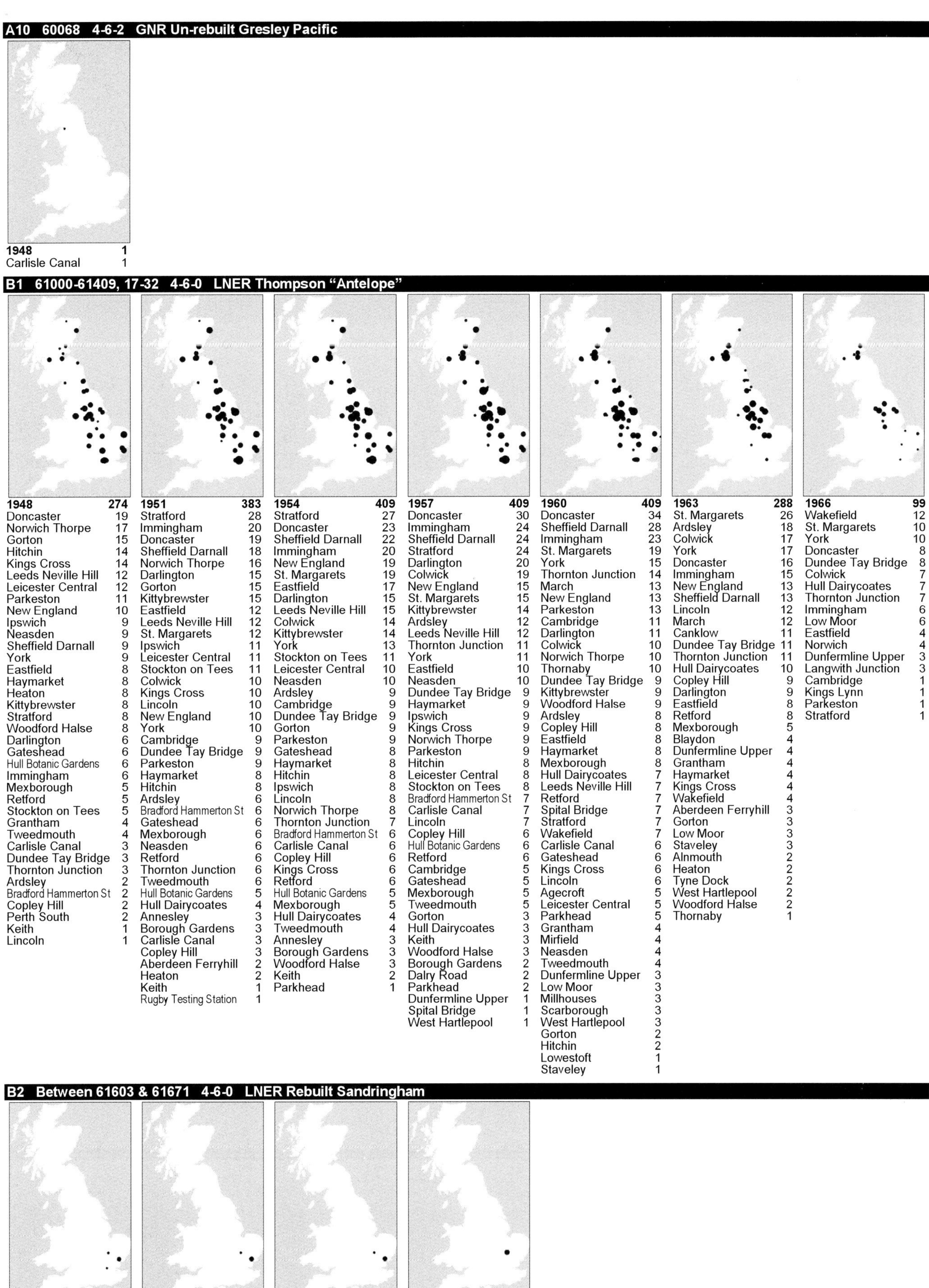

A10 60068 4-6-2 GNR Un-rebuilt Gresley Pacific

1948	1
Carlisle Canal	1

B1 61000-61409, 17-32 4-6-0 LNER Thompson "Antelope"

1948	274
Doncaster	19
Norwich Thorpe	17
Gorton	15
Hitchin	14
Kings Cross	14
Leeds Neville Hill	12
Leicester Central	12
Parkeston	11
New England	10
Ipswich	9
Neasden	9
Sheffield Darnall	9
York	9
Eastfield	8
Haymarket	8
Heaton	8
Kittybrewster	8
Stratford	8
Woodford Halse	8
Darlington	6
Gateshead	6
Hull Botanic Gardens	6
Immingham	6
Mexborough	5
Retford	5
Stockton on Tees	5
Grantham	4
Tweedmouth	4
Carlisle Canal	3
Dundee Tay Bridge	3
Thornton Junction	3
Ardsley	2
Bradford Hammerton St	2
Copley Hill	2
Perth South	2
Keith	1
Lincoln	1

1951	383
Stratford	28
Immingham	20
Doncaster	19
Sheffield Darnall	18
Norwich Thorpe	16
Darlington	15
Gorton	15
Kittybrewster	15
Eastfield	12
Leeds Neville Hill	12
St. Margarets	12
Ipswich	11
Leicester Central	11
Stockton on Tees	11
Colwick	10
Kings Cross	10
Lincoln	10
New England	10
York	10
Cambridge	9
Dundee Tay Bridge	9
Parkeston	9
Haymarket	8
Hitchin	8
Ardsley	6
Bradford Hammerton St	6
Gateshead	6
Mexborough	6
Neasden	6
Retford	6
Thornton Junction	6
Tweedmouth	6
Hull Botanic Gardens	5
Hull Dairycoates	4
Annesley	3
Borough Gardens	3
Carlisle Canal	3
Copley Hill	3
Aberdeen Ferryhill	2
Heaton	2
Keith	1
Rugby Testing Station	1

1954	409
Stratford	27
Doncaster	23
Sheffield Darnall	22
Immingham	20
New England	19
St. Margarets	19
Eastfield	17
Darlington	15
Leeds Neville Hill	15
Colwick	14
Kittybrewster	14
York	13
Stockton on Tees	11
Leicester Central	10
Neasden	10
Ardsley	9
Cambridge	9
Dundee Tay Bridge	9
Gorton	9
Parkeston	9
Gateshead	8
Haymarket	8
Hitchin	8
Ipswich	8
Lincoln	8
Norwich Thorpe	8
Thornton Junction	7
Bradford Hammerton St	6
Carlisle Canal	6
Copley Hill	6
Kings Cross	6
Retford	6
Hull Botanic Gardens	5
Mexborough	5
Hull Dairycoates	4
Tweedmouth	4
Annesley	3
Borough Gardens	3
Woodford Halse	3
Keith	2
Parkhead	1

1957	409
Doncaster	30
Immingham	24
Sheffield Darnall	24
Stratford	24
Darlington	20
Colwick	19
New England	15
St. Margarets	15
Kittybrewster	14
Ardsley	12
Leeds Neville Hill	12
Thornton Junction	11
York	11
Eastfield	10
Neasden	10
Dundee Tay Bridge	9
Haymarket	9
Ipswich	9
Kings Cross	9
Norwich Thorpe	9
Parkeston	9
Hitchin	8
Leicester Central	8
Stockton on Tees	8
Bradford Hammerton St	7
Carlisle Canal	7
Lincoln	7
Copley Hill	6
Hull Botanic Gardens	6
Retford	6
Cambridge	5
Gateshead	5
Mexborough	5
Tweedmouth	5
Gorton	5
Hull Dairycoates	3
Keith	3
Woodford Halse	3
Borough Gardens	2
Dalry Road	2
Parkhead	2
Dunfermline Upper	1
Spital Bridge	1
West Hartlepool	1

1960	409
Doncaster	34
Sheffield Darnall	28
Immingham	23
St. Margarets	19
York	15
Thornton Junction	14
March	13
New England	13
Parkeston	13
Cambridge	11
Darlington	11
Colwick	10
Norwich Thorpe	10
Thornaby	10
Dundee Tay Bridge	9
Kittybrewster	9
Woodford Halse	9
Ardsley	8
Copley Hill	8
Eastfield	8
Haymarket	8
Mexborough	8
Hull Dairycoates	7
Leeds Neville Hill	7
Retford	7
Spital Bridge	7
Stratford	7
Wakefield	7
Carlisle Canal	6
Gateshead	6
Kings Cross	6
Lincoln	6
Agecroft	5
Leicester Central	5
Parkhead	5
Grantham	4
Mirfield	4
Neasden	4
Tweedmouth	4
Dunfermline Upper	3
Low Moor	3
Millhouses	3
Scarborough	3
West Hartlepool	3
Gorton	2
Hitchin	2
Lowestoft	1
Staveley	1

1963	288
St. Margarets	26
Ardsley	18
Colwick	17
York	17
Doncaster	16
Immingham	15
New England	13
Sheffield Darnall	13
Lincoln	12
March	12
Canklow	11
Dundee Tay Bridge	11
Thornton Junction	11
Hull Dairycoates	10
Copley Hill	9
Darlington	9
Eastfield	8
Retford	8
Mexborough	5
Blaydon	4
Dunfermline Upper	4
Grantham	4
Haymarket	4
Kings Cross	4
Wakefield	4
Aberdeen Ferryhill	3
Gorton	3
Low Moor	3
Staveley	3
Alnmouth	2
Heaton	2
Tyne Dock	2
West Hartlepool	2
Woodford Halse	2
Thornaby	1

1966	99
Wakefield	12
St. Margarets	10
York	10
Doncaster	8
Dundee Tay Bridge	8
Colwick	7
Hull Dairycoates	7
Thornton Junction	7
Immingham	6
Low Moor	6
Eastfield	4
Norwich	4
Dunfermline Upper	3
Langwith Junction	3
Cambridge	1
Kings Lynn	1
Parkeston	1
Stratford	1

B2 Between 61603 & 61671 4-6-0 LNER Rebuilt Sandringham

1948	9
Colchester	6
Cambridge	2
Stratford	1

1951	10
Colchester	8
Cambridge	2

1954	10
Colchester	8
Cambridge	2

1957	10
Cambridge	10

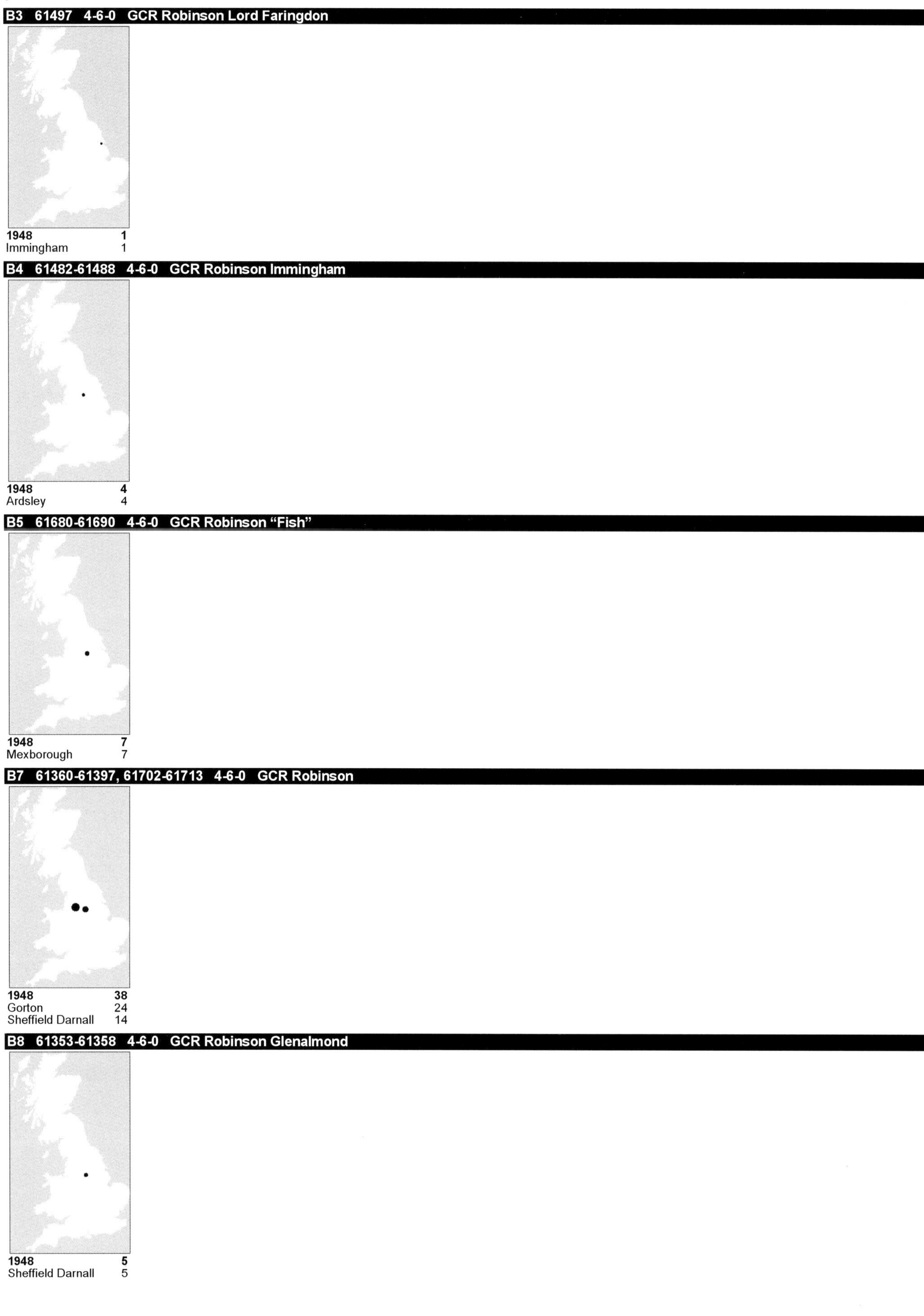
B3 61497 4-6-0 GCR Robinson Lord Faringdon
1948 1
Immingham 1
B4 61482-61488 4-6-0 GCR Robinson Immingham
1948 4
Ardsley 4
B5 61680-61690 4-6-0 GCR Robinson "Fish"
1948 7
Mexborough 7
B7 61360-61397, 61702-61713 4-6-0 GCR Robinson
1948 38
Gorton 24
Sheffield Darnall 14
B8 61353-61358 4-6-0 GCR Robinson Glenalmond
1948 5
Sheffield Darnall 5

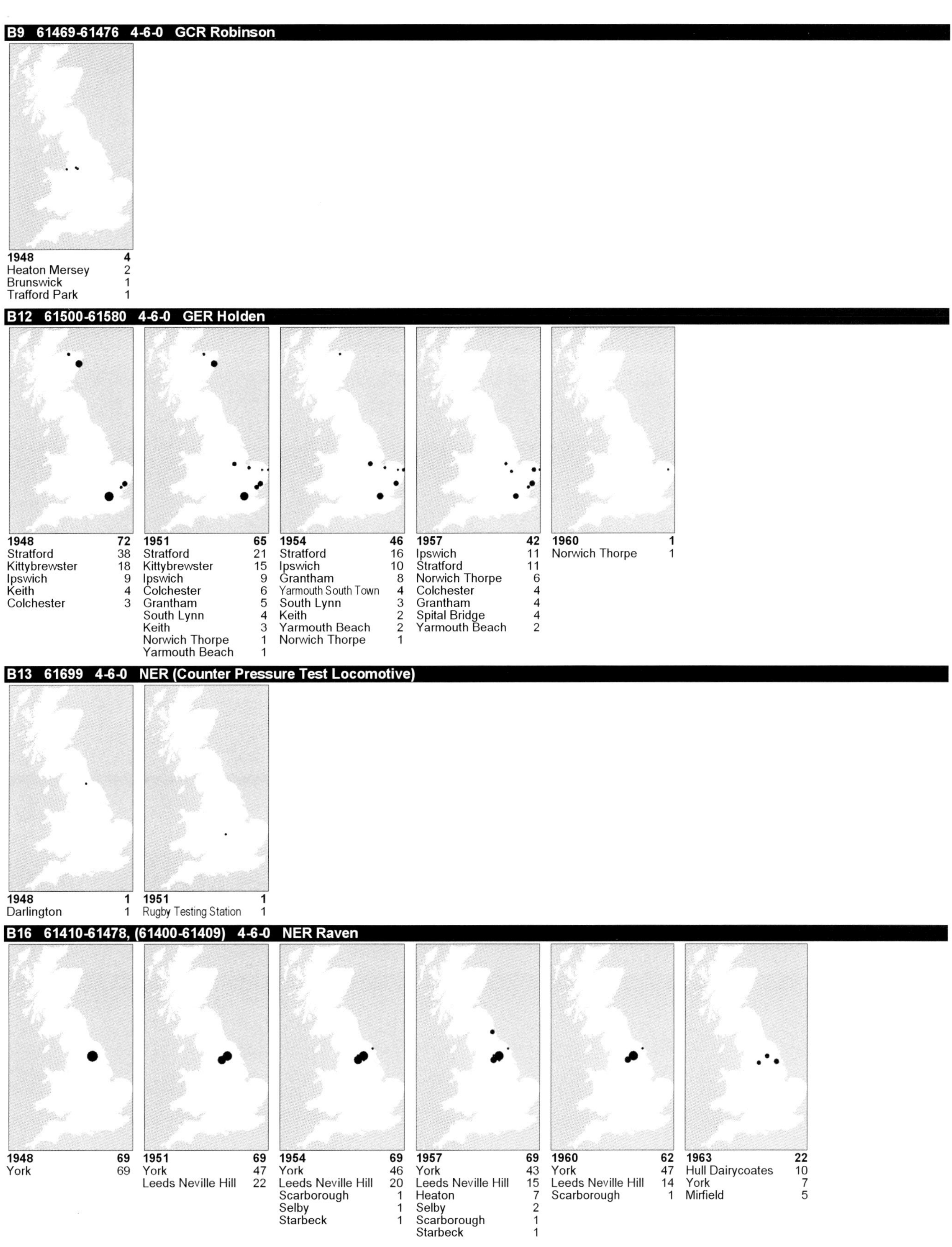

B9 61469-61476 4-6-0 GCR Robinson

1948	4
Heaton Mersey	2
Brunswick	1
Trafford Park	1

B12 61500-61580 4-6-0 GER Holden

1948	72
Stratford	38
Kittybrewster	18
Ipswich	9
Keith	4
Colchester	3

1951	65
Stratford	21
Kittybrewster	15
Ipswich	9
Colchester	6
Grantham	5
South Lynn	4
Keith	3
Norwich Thorpe	1
Yarmouth Beach	1

1954	46
Stratford	16
Ipswich	10
Grantham	8
Yarmouth South Town	4
South Lynn	3
Keith	2
Yarmouth Beach	2
Norwich Thorpe	1

1957	42
Ipswich	11
Stratford	11
Norwich Thorpe	6
Colchester	4
Grantham	4
Spital Bridge	4
Yarmouth Beach	2

1960	1
Norwich Thorpe	1

B13 61699 4-6-0 NER (Counter Pressure Test Locomotive)

1948	1
Darlington	1

1951	1
Rugby Testing Station	1

B16 61410-61478, (61400-61409) 4-6-0 NER Raven

1948	69
York	69

1951	69
York	47
Leeds Neville Hill	22

1954	69
York	46
Leeds Neville Hill	20
Scarborough	1
Selby	1
Starbeck	1

1957	69
York	43
Leeds Neville Hill	15
Heaton	7
Selby	2
Scarborough	1
Starbeck	1

1960	62
York	47
Leeds Neville Hill	14
Scarborough	1

1963	22
Hull Dairycoates	10
York	7
Mirfield	5

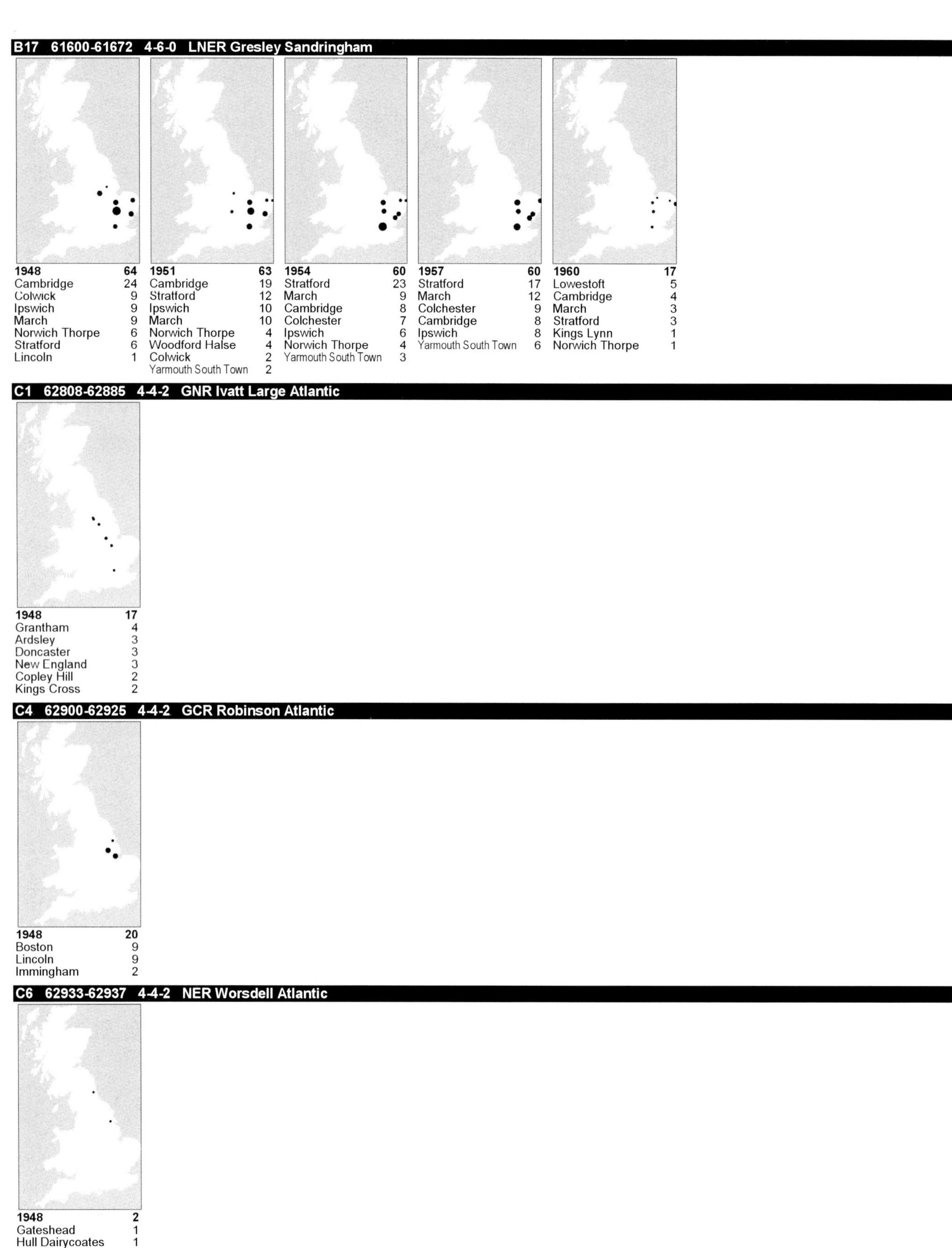

B17 61600-61672 4-6-0 LNER Gresley Sandringham

1948	64	1951	63	1954	60	1957	60	1960	17
Cambridge	24	Cambridge	19	Stratford	23	Stratford	17	Lowestoft	5
Colwick	9	Stratford	12	March	9	March	12	Cambridge	4
Ipswich	9	Ipswich	10	Cambridge	8	Colchester	9	March	3
March	9	March	10	Colchester	7	Cambridge	8	Stratford	3
Norwich Thorpe	6	Norwich Thorpe	4	Ipswich	6	Ipswich	8	Kings Lynn	1
Stratford	6	Woodford Halse	4	Norwich Thorpe	4	Yarmouth South Town	6	Norwich Thorpe	1
Lincoln	1	Colwick	2	Yarmouth South Town	3				
		Yarmouth South Town	2						

C1 62808-62885 4-4-2 GNR Ivatt Large Atlantic

1948	17
Grantham	4
Ardsley	3
Doncaster	3
New England	3
Copley Hill	2
Kings Cross	2

C4 62900-62925 4-4-2 GCR Robinson Atlantic

1948	20
Boston	9
Lincoln	9
Immingham	2

C6 62933-62937 4-4-2 NER Worsdell Atlantic

1948	2
Gateshead	1
Hull Dairycoates	1

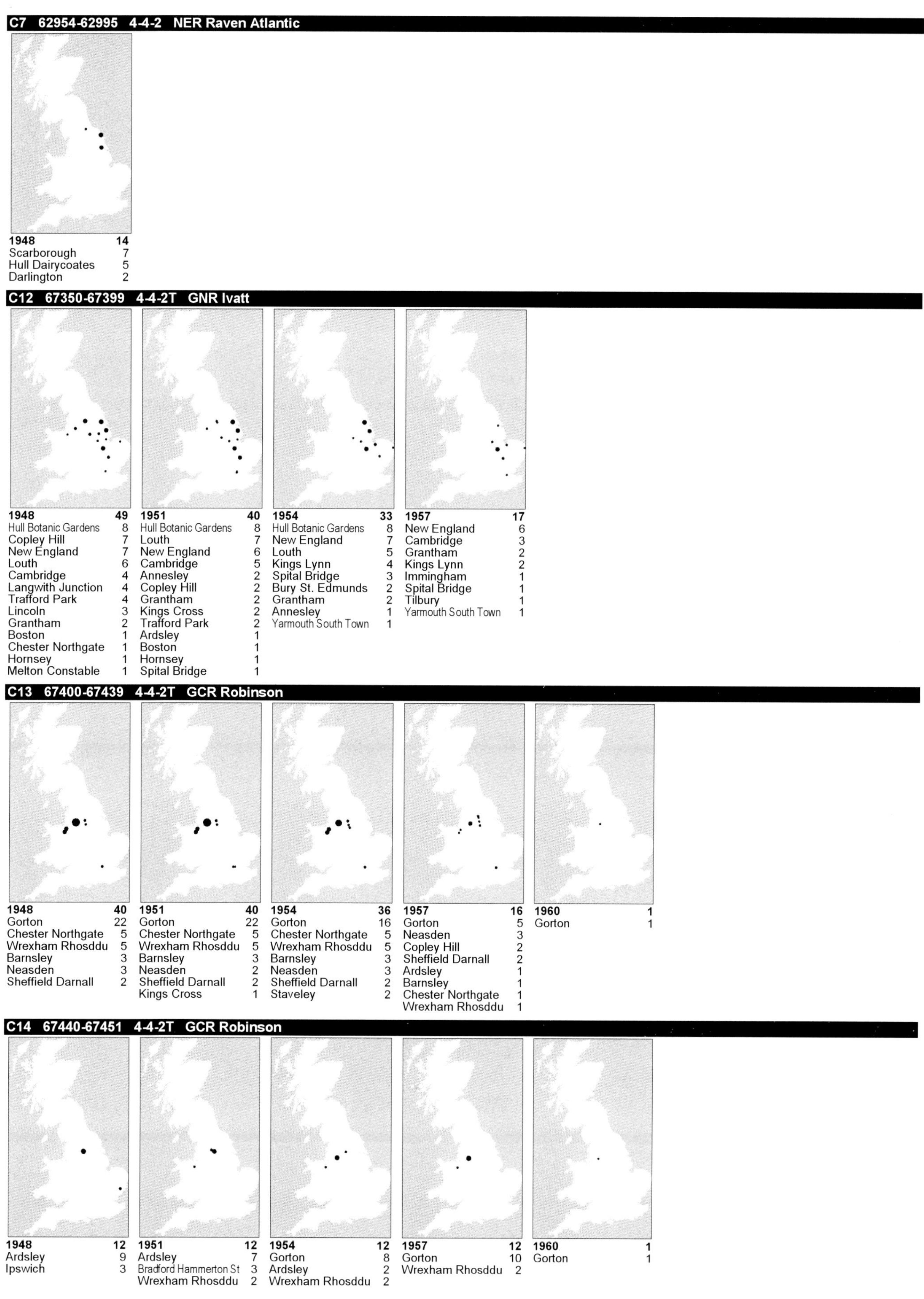

C7 62954-62995 4-4-2 NER Raven Atlantic

1948	14
Scarborough	7
Hull Dairycoates	5
Darlington	2

C12 67350-67399 4-4-2T GNR Ivatt

1948	49
Hull Botanic Gardens	8
Copley Hill	7
New England	7
Louth	6
Cambridge	4
Langwith Junction	4
Trafford Park	4
Lincoln	3
Grantham	2
Boston	1
Chester Northgate	1
Hornsey	1
Melton Constable	1

1951	40
Hull Botanic Gardens	8
Louth	7
New England	6
Cambridge	5
Annesley	2
Copley Hill	2
Grantham	2
Kings Cross	2
Trafford Park	2
Ardsley	1
Boston	1
Hornsey	1
Spital Bridge	1

1954	33
Hull Botanic Gardens	8
New England	7
Louth	5
Kings Lynn	4
Spital Bridge	3
Bury St. Edmunds	2
Grantham	2
Annesley	1
Yarmouth South Town	1

1957	17
New England	6
Cambridge	3
Grantham	2
Kings Lynn	2
Immingham	1
Spital Bridge	1
Tilbury	1
Yarmouth South Town	1

C13 67400-67439 4-4-2T GCR Robinson

1948	40
Gorton	22
Chester Northgate	5
Wrexham Rhosddu	5
Barnsley	3
Neasden	3
Sheffield Darnall	2

1951	40
Gorton	22
Chester Northgate	5
Wrexham Rhosddu	5
Barnsley	3
Neasden	2
Sheffield Darnall	2
Kings Cross	1

1954	36
Gorton	16
Chester Northgate	5
Wrexham Rhosddu	5
Barnsley	3
Neasden	3
Sheffield Darnall	2
Staveley	2

1957	16
Gorton	5
Neasden	3
Copley Hill	2
Sheffield Darnall	2
Ardsley	1
Barnsley	1
Chester Northgate	1
Wrexham Rhosddu	1

1960	1
Gorton	1

C14 67440-67451 4-4-2T GCR Robinson

1948	12
Ardsley	9
Ipswich	3

1951	12
Ardsley	7
Bradford Hammerton St	3
Wrexham Rhosddu	2

1954	12
Gorton	8
Ardsley	2
Wrexham Rhosddu	2

1957	12
Gorton	10
Wrexham Rhosddu	2

1960	1
Gorton	1

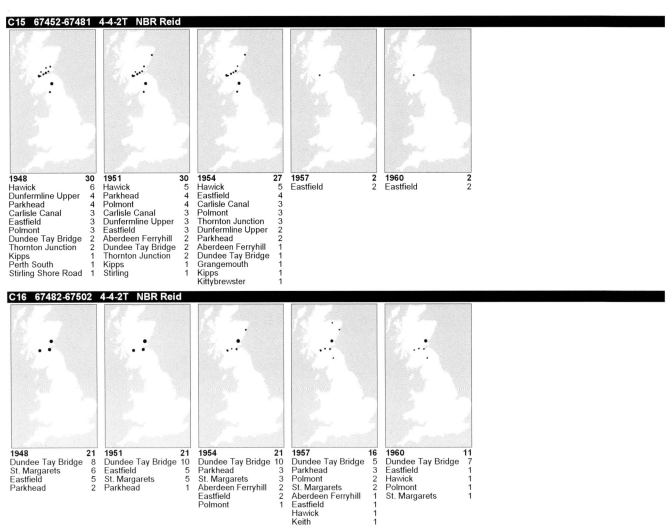

C15 67452-67481 4-4-2T NBR Reid

1948	30
Hawick	6
Dunfermline Upper	4
Parkhead	4
Carlisle Canal	3
Eastfield	3
Polmont	3
Dundee Tay Bridge	2
Thornton Junction	2
Kipps	1
Perth South	1
Stirling Shore Road	1

1951	30
Hawick	5
Parkhead	4
Polmont	4
Carlisle Canal	3
Dunfermline Upper	3
Eastfield	3
Aberdeen Ferryhill	2
Dundee Tay Bridge	2
Thornton Junction	2
Kipps	1
Stirling	1

1954	27
Hawick	5
Eastfield	4
Carlisle Canal	3
Polmont	3
Thornton Junction	3
Dunfermline Upper	2
Parkhead	2
Aberdeen Ferryhill	1
Dundee Tay Bridge	1
Grangemouth	1
Kipps	1
Kittybrewster	1

1957	2
Eastfield	2

1960	2
Eastfield	2

C16 67482-67502 4-4-2T NBR Reid

1948	21
Dundee Tay Bridge	8
St. Margarets	6
Eastfield	5
Parkhead	2

1951	21
Dundee Tay Bridge	10
Eastfield	5
St. Margarets	5
Parkhead	1

1954	21
Dundee Tay Bridge	10
Parkhead	3
St. Margarets	3
Aberdeen Ferryhill	2
Eastfield	2
Polmont	1

1957	16
Dundee Tay Bridge	5
Parkhead	3
Polmont	2
St. Margarets	2
Aberdeen Ferryhill	1
Eastfield	1
Hawick	1
Keith	1

1960	11
Dundee Tay Bridge	7
Eastfield	1
Hawick	1
Polmont	1
St. Margarets	1

D1 62203-62215 4-4-0 GNR Ivatt

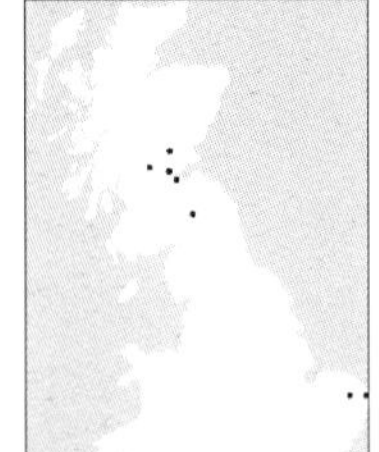

1948	7
Dunfermline Upper	1
Hawick	1
Haymarket	1
Norwich Thorpe	1
Perth South	1
Stirling Shore Road	1
Yarmouth Beach	1

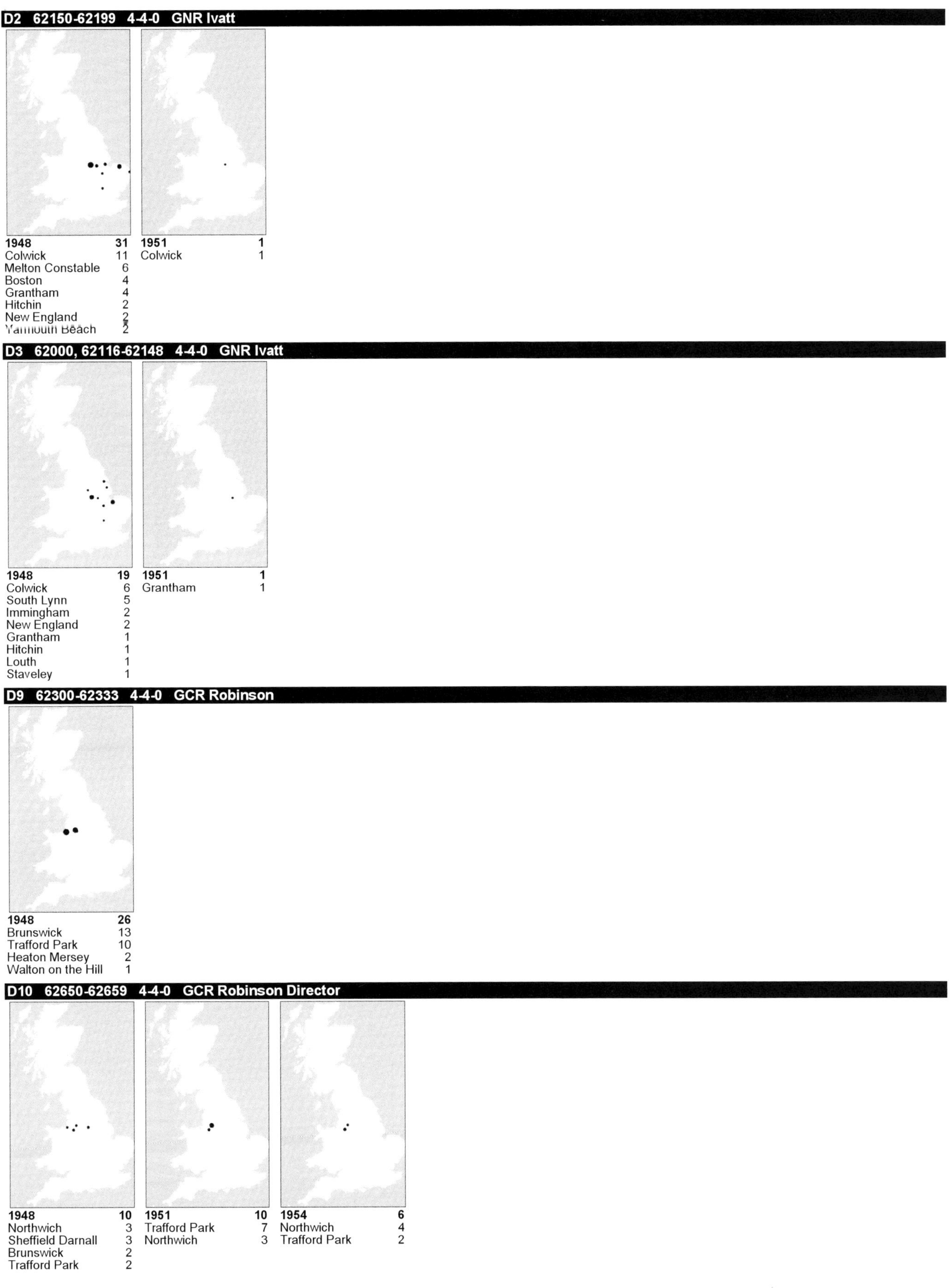

D2 62150-62199 4-4-0 GNR Ivatt

1948	31	1951	1
Colwick	11	Colwick	1
Melton Constable	6		
Boston	4		
Grantham	4		
Hitchin	2		
New England	2		
Yarmouth Beach	2		

D3 62000, 62116-62148 4-4-0 GNR Ivatt

1948	19	1951	1
Colwick	6	Grantham	1
South Lynn	5		
Immingham	2		
New England	2		
Grantham	1		
Hitchin	1		
Louth	1		
Staveley	1		

D9 62300-62333 4-4-0 GCR Robinson

1948	26
Brunswick	13
Trafford Park	10
Heaton Mersey	2
Walton on the Hill	1

D10 62650-62659 4-4-0 GCR Robinson Director

1948	10	1951	10	1954	6
Northwich	3	Trafford Park	7	Northwich	4
Sheffield Darnall	3	Northwich	3	Trafford Park	2
Brunswick	2				
Trafford Park	2				

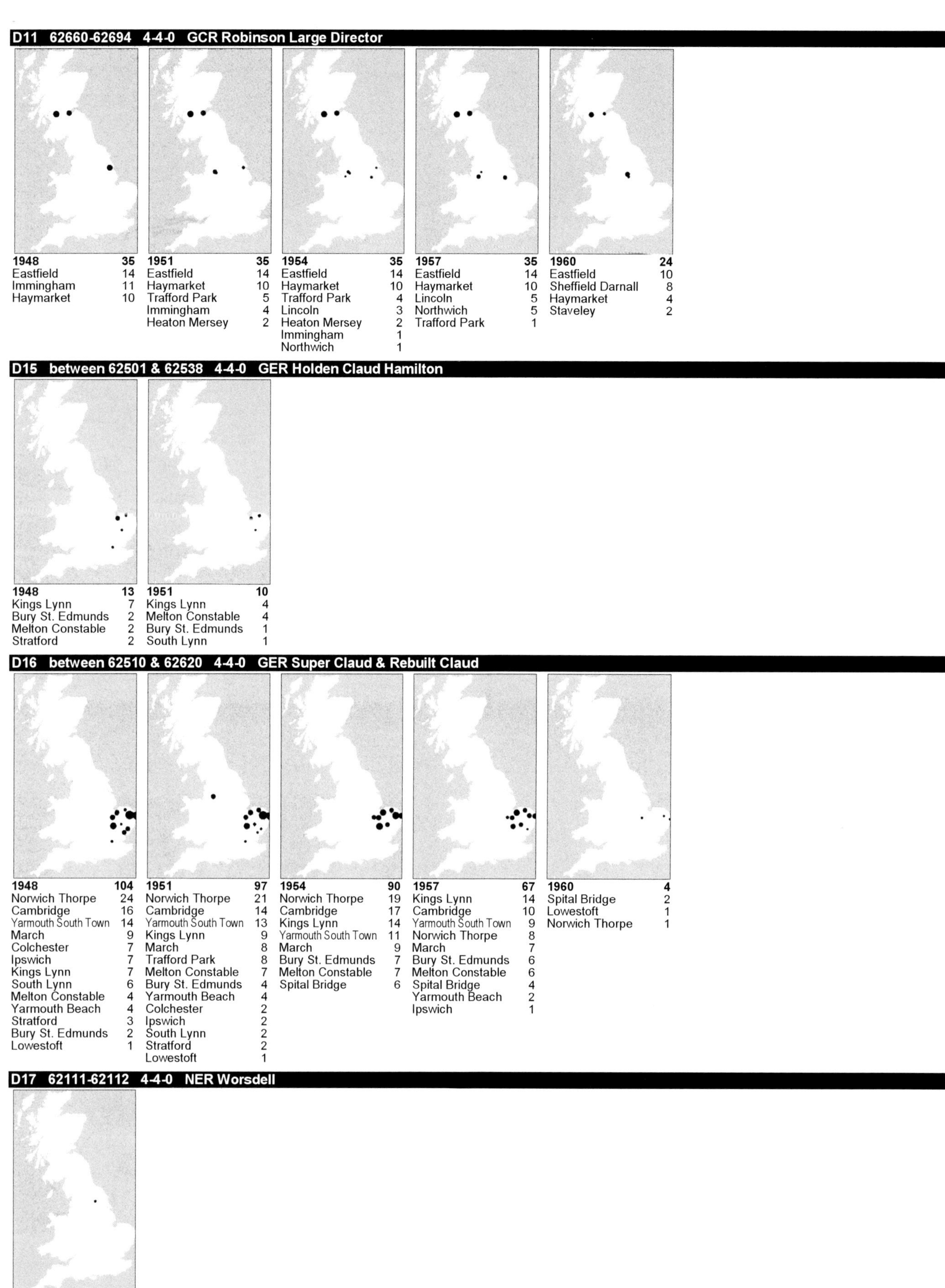

D11 62660-62694 4-4-0 GCR Robinson Large Director

1948	35	1951	35	1954	35	1957	35	1960	24
Eastfield	14	Eastfield	14	Eastfield	14	Eastfield	14	Eastfield	10
Immingham	11	Haymarket	10	Haymarket	10	Haymarket	10	Sheffield Darnall	8
Haymarket	10	Trafford Park	5	Trafford Park	4	Lincoln	5	Haymarket	4
		Immingham	4	Lincoln	3	Northwich	5	Staveley	2
		Heaton Mersey	2	Heaton Mersey	2	Trafford Park	1		
				Immingham	1				
				Northwich	1				

D15 between 62501 & 62538 4-4-0 GER Holden Claud Hamilton

1948	13	1951	10
Kings Lynn	7	Kings Lynn	4
Bury St. Edmunds	2	Melton Constable	4
Melton Constable	2	Bury St. Edmunds	1
Stratford	2	South Lynn	1

D16 between 62510 & 62620 4-4-0 GER Super Claud & Rebuilt Claud

1948	104	1951	97	1954	90	1957	67	1960	4
Norwich Thorpe	24	Norwich Thorpe	21	Norwich Thorpe	19	Kings Lynn	14	Spital Bridge	2
Cambridge	16	Cambridge	14	Cambridge	17	Cambridge	10	Lowestoft	1
Yarmouth South Town	14	Yarmouth South Town	13	Kings Lynn	14	Yarmouth South Town	9	Norwich Thorpe	1
March	9	Kings Lynn	9	Yarmouth South Town	11	Norwich Thorpe	8		
Colchester	7	March	8	March	9	March	7		
Ipswich	7	Trafford Park	8	Bury St. Edmunds	7	Bury St. Edmunds	6		
Kings Lynn	7	Melton Constable	7	Melton Constable	7	Melton Constable	6		
South Lynn	6	Bury St. Edmunds	4	Spital Bridge	6	Spital Bridge	4		
Melton Constable	4	Yarmouth Beach	4			Yarmouth Beach	2		
Yarmouth Beach	4	Colchester	2			Ipswich	1		
Stratford	3	Ipswich	2						
Bury St. Edmunds	2	South Lynn	2						
Lowestoft	1	Stratford	2						
		Lowestoft	1						

D17 62111-62112 4-4-0 NER Worsdell

1948	2
York	2

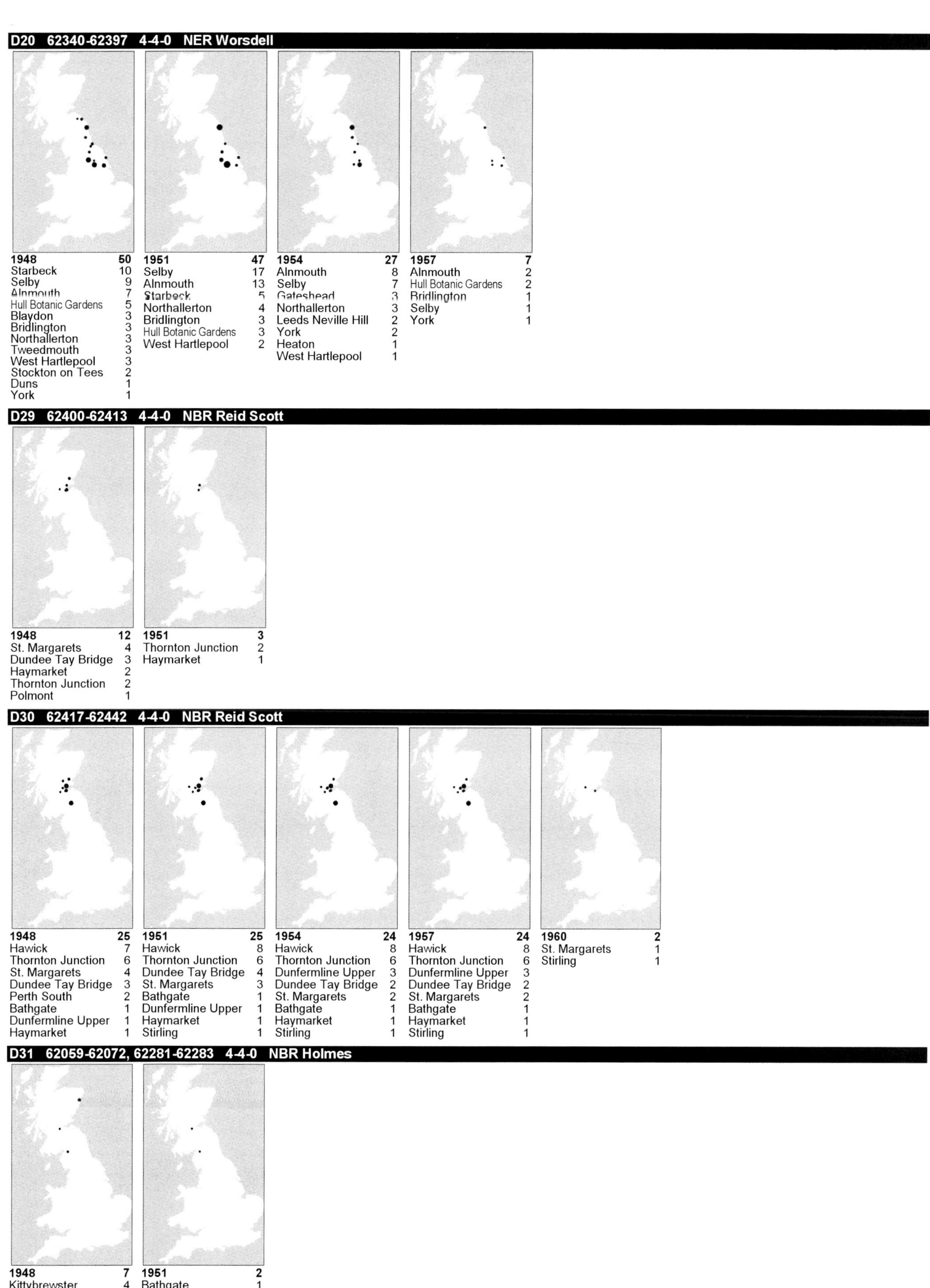

D20 62340-62397 4-4-0 NER Worsdell
1948 50
Starbeck 10
Selby 9
Alnmouth 7
Hull Botanic Gardens 5
Blaydon 3
Bridlington 3
Northallerton 3
Tweedmouth 3
West Hartlepool 3
Stockton on Tees 2
Duns 1
York 1
1951 47
Selby 17
Alnmouth 13
Starbeck 5
Northallerton 4
Bridlington 3
Hull Botanic Gardens 3
West Hartlepool 2
1954 27
Alnmouth 8
Selby 7
Gateshead 3
Northallerton 3
Leeds Neville Hill 2
York 2
Heaton 1
West Hartlepool 1
1957 7
Alnmouth 2
Hull Botanic Gardens 2
Bridlington 1
Selby 1
York 1
D29 62400-62413 4-4-0 NBR Reid Scott
1948 12
St. Margarets 4
Dundee Tay Bridge 3
Haymarket 2
Thornton Junction 2
Polmont 1
1951 3
Thornton Junction 2
Haymarket 1
D30 62417-62442 4-4-0 NBR Reid Scott
1948 25
Hawick 7
Thornton Junction 6
St. Margarets 4
Dundee Tay Bridge 3
Perth South 2
Bathgate 1
Dunfermline Upper 1
Haymarket 1
1951 25
Hawick 8
Thornton Junction 6
Dundee Tay Bridge 4
St. Margarets 3
Bathgate 1
Dunfermline Upper 1
Haymarket 1
Stirling 1
1954 24
Hawick 8
Thornton Junction 6
Dunfermline Upper 3
Dundee Tay Bridge 2
St. Margarets 2
Bathgate 1
Haymarket 1
Stirling 1
1957 24
Hawick 8
Thornton Junction 6
Dunfermline Upper 3
Dundee Tay Bridge 2
St. Margarets 2
Bathgate 1
Haymarket 1
Stirling 1
1960 2
St. Margarets 1
Stirling 1
D31 62059-62072, 62281-62283 4-4-0 NBR Holmes
1948 7
Kittybrewster 4
Carlisle Canal 2
Bathgate 1
1951 2
Bathgate 1
Carlisle Canal 1

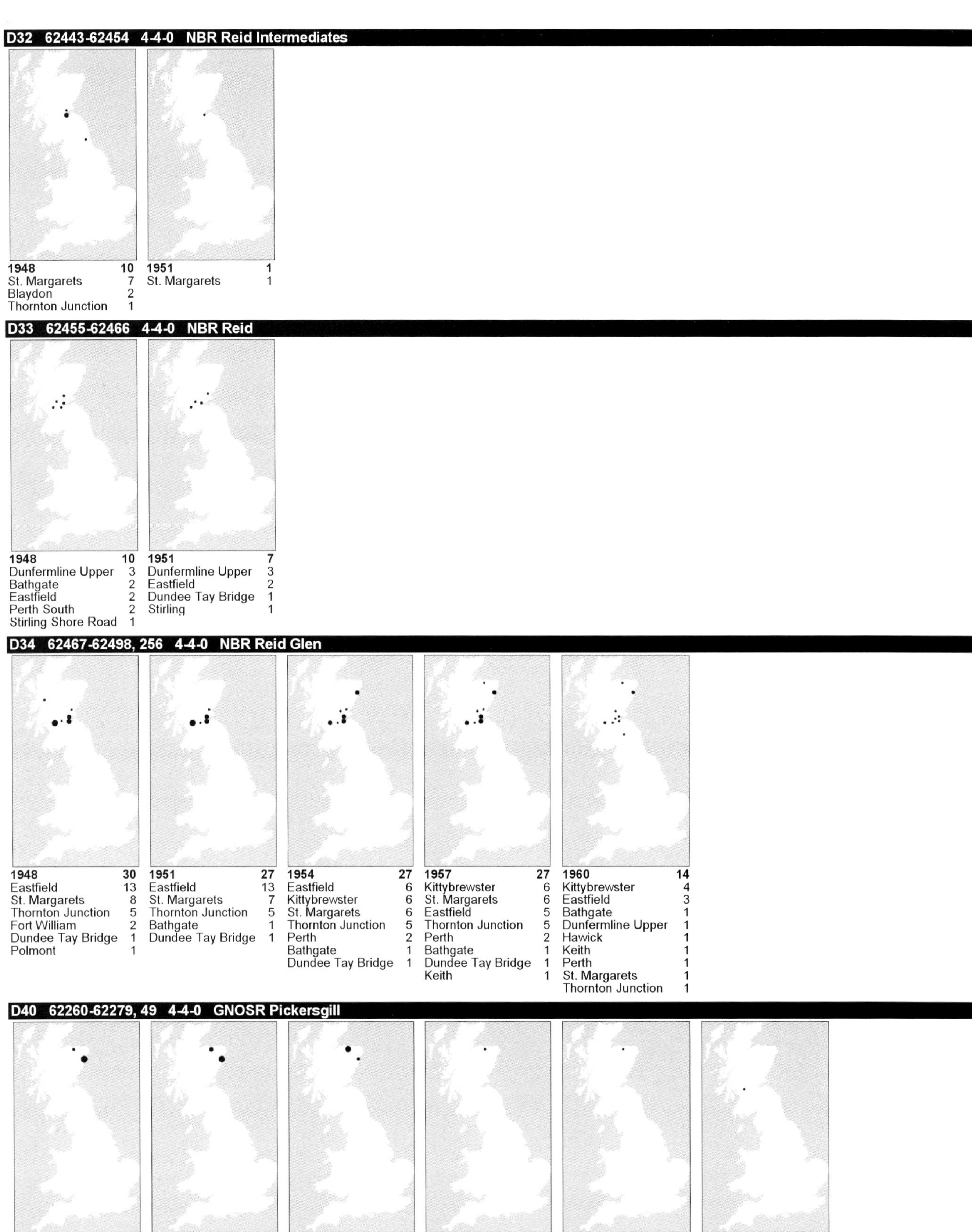

D32 62443-62454 4-4-0 NBR Reid Intermediates

1948	10	1951	1
St. Margarets	7	St. Margarets	1
Blaydon	2		
Thornton Junction	1		

D33 62455-62466 4-4-0 NBR Reid

1948	10	1951	7
Dunfermline Upper	3	Dunfermline Upper	3
Bathgate	2	Eastfield	2
Eastfield	2	Dundee Tay Bridge	1
Perth South	2	Stirling	1
Stirling Shore Road	1		

D34 62467-62498, 256 4-4-0 NBR Reid Glen

1948	30	1951	27	1954	27	1957	27	1960	14
Eastfield	13	Eastfield	13	Eastfield	6	Kittybrewster	6	Kittybrewster	4
St. Margarets	8	St. Margarets	7	Kittybrewster	6	St. Margarets	6	Eastfield	3
Thornton Junction	5	Thornton Junction	5	St. Margarets	6	Eastfield	5	Bathgate	1
Fort William	2	Bathgate	1	Thornton Junction	5	Thornton Junction	5	Dunfermline Upper	1
Dundee Tay Bridge	1	Dundee Tay Bridge	1	Perth	2	Perth	2	Hawick	1
Polmont	1			Bathgate	1	Bathgate	1	Keith	1
				Dundee Tay Bridge	1	Dundee Tay Bridge	1	Perth	1
						Keith	1	St. Margarets	1
								Thornton Junction	1

D40 62260-62279, 49 4-4-0 GNOSR Pickersgill

1948	18	1951	18	1954	15	1957	2	1960	1	1963	1
Kittybrewster	15	Kittybrewster	13	Keith	12	Keith	2	Keith	1	Dawsholm	1
Keith	3	Keith	5	Kittybrewster	3						

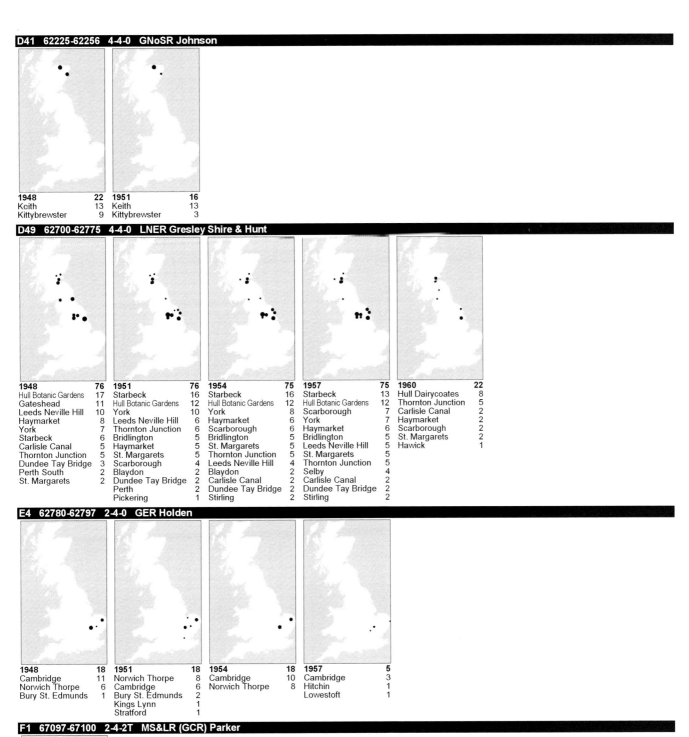

D41 62225-62256 4-4-0 GNoSR Johnson

1948	22
Kcith	13
Kittybrewster	9

1951	16
Keith	13
Kittybrewster	3

D49 62700-62775 4-4-0 LNER Gresley Shire & Hunt

1948	76
Hull Botanic Gardens	17
Gateshead	11
Leeds Neville Hill	10
Haymarket	8
York	7
Starbeck	6
Carlisle Canal	5
Thornton Junction	5
Dundee Tay Bridge	3
Perth South	2
St. Margarets	2

1951	76
Starbeck	16
Hull Botanic Gardens	12
York	10
Leeds Neville Hill	6
Thornton Junction	6
Bridlington	5
Haymarket	5
St. Margarets	5
Scarborough	4
Blaydon	2
Dundee Tay Bridge	2
Perth	2
Pickering	1

1954	75
Starbeck	16
Hull Botanic Gardens	12
York	8
Haymarket	6
Scarborough	6
Bridlington	5
St. Margarets	5
Thornton Junction	5
Leeds Neville Hill	4
Blaydon	2
Carlisle Canal	2
Dundee Tay Bridge	2
Stirling	2

1957	75
Starbeck	13
Hull Botanic Gardens	12
Scarborough	7
York	7
Haymarket	6
Bridlington	5
Leeds Neville Hill	5
St. Margarets	5
Thornton Junction	5
Selby	4
Carlisle Canal	2
Dundee Tay Bridge	2
Stirling	2

1960	22
Hull Dairycoates	8
Thornton Junction	5
Carlisle Canal	2
Haymarket	2
Scarborough	2
St. Margarets	2
Hawick	1

E4 62780-62797 2-4-0 GER Holden

1948	18
Cambridge	11
Norwich Thorpe	6
Bury St. Edmunds	1

1951	18
Norwich Thorpe	8
Cambridge	6
Bury St. Edmunds	2
Kings Lynn	1
Stratford	1

1954	18
Cambridge	10
Norwich Thorpe	8

1957	5
Cambridge	3
Hitchin	1
Lowestoft	1

F1 67097-67100 2-4-2T MS&LR (GCR) Parker

1948	3
Brunswick	2
Gorton	1

F2 67104-67113 2-4-2T GCR Pollitt
1948 9
Kings Cross 4
Annesley 2
Ardsley 1
Yarmouth Beach 1
Yarmouth South Town 1
F3 67114-67150 2-4-2T GER Holden
1948 15
Lowestoft 4
Norwich Thorpe 3
Cambridge 2
Ipswich 2
Melton Constable 2
Bury St. Edmunds 1
Kings Lynn 1
1951 1
Lowestoft 1
F4 67151-67187 2-4-2T GER Holden
1948 37
Stratford 12
Lowestoft 6
Norwich Thorpe 6
Bury St. Edmunds 2
Hull Dairycoates 2
Kittybrewster 2
Melton Constable 2
Yarmouth Beach 2
Ipswich 1
Malton 1
Yarmouth South Town 1
1951 23
Lowestoft 10
Kittybrewster 3
Hull Dairycoates 2
March 2
Melton Constable 2
Norwich Thorpe 2
Malton 1
Yarmouth South Town 1
1954 4
Lowestoft 2
Kittybrewster 1
Yarmouth Vauxhall 1
F5 67188-67219 2-4-2T GER Holden
1948 30
Stratford 23
Colchester 5
Parkeston 2
1951 32
Stratford 17
Colchester 11
Lowestoft 2
Yarmouth South Town 2
1954 32
Stratford 18
Lowestoft 8
Colchester 4
Yarmouth South Town 2
1957 12
Stratford 10
Colchester 1
Yarmouth South Town 1

F6 (67218-67219), 67220-67239 2-4-2T GER Holden

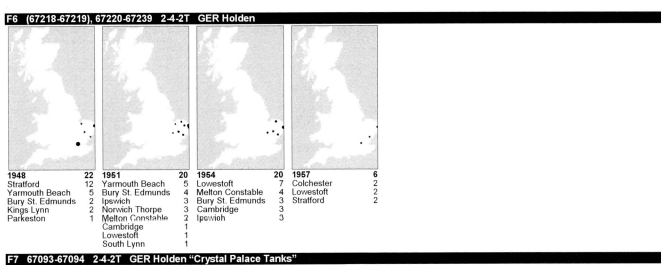

1948	22	1951	20	1954	20	1957	6
Stratford	12	Yarmouth Beach	5	Lowestoft	7	Colchester	2
Yarmouth Beach	5	Bury St. Edmunds	4	Melton Constable	4	Lowestoft	2
Bury St. Edmunds	2	Ipswich	3	Bury St. Edmunds	3	Stratford	2
Kings Lynn	2	Norwich Thorpe	3	Cambridge	3		
Parkeston	1	Melton Constable	2	Ipswich	3		
		Cambridge	1				
		Lowestoft	1				
		South Lynn	1				

F7 67093-67094 2-4-2T GER Holden "Crystal Palace Tanks"

1948	2
St. Margarets	2

G5 67240-67349 0-4-4T NER Worsdell

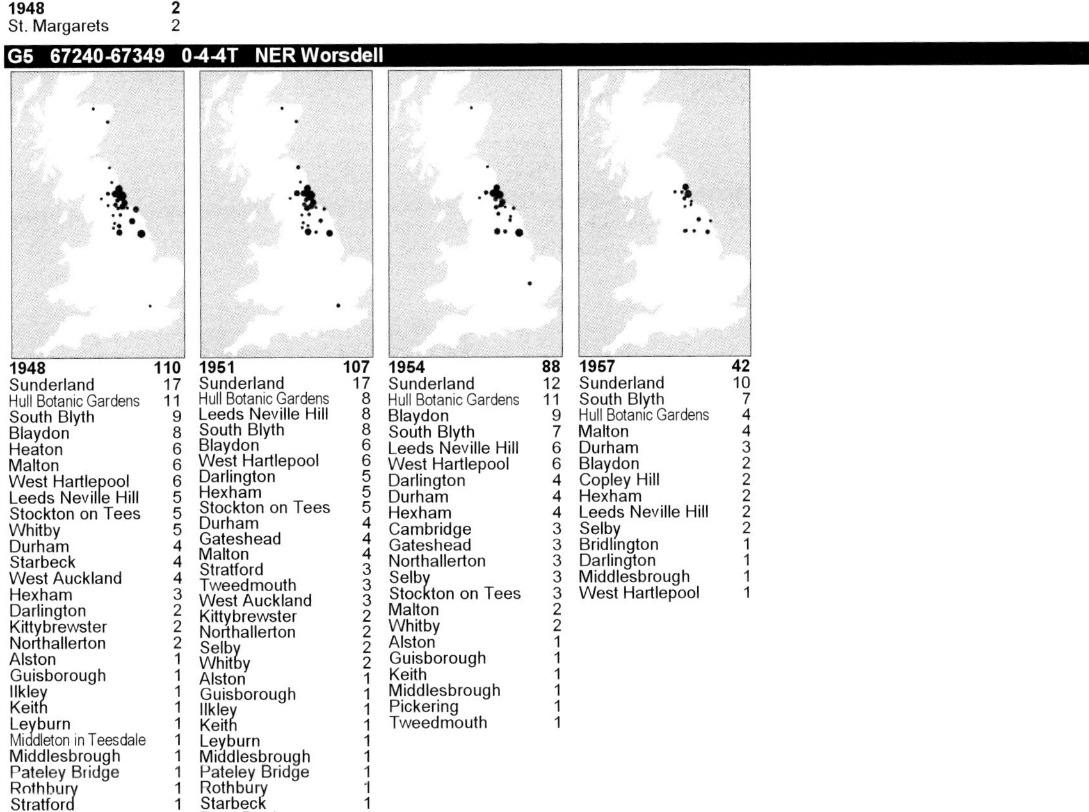

1948	110	1951	107	1954	88	1957	42
Sunderland	17	Sunderland	17	Sunderland	12	Sunderland	10
Hull Botanic Gardens	11	Hull Botanic Gardens	8	Hull Botanic Gardens	11	South Blyth	7
South Blyth	9	Leeds Neville Hill	8	Blaydon	9	Hull Botanic Gardens	4
Blaydon	8	South Blyth	8	South Blyth	7	Malton	4
Heaton	6	Blaydon	6	Leeds Neville Hill	6	Durham	3
Malton	6	West Hartlepool	6	West Hartlepool	6	Blaydon	2
West Hartlepool	6	Darlington	5	Darlington	4	Copley Hill	2
Leeds Neville Hill	5	Hexham	5	Durham	4	Hexham	2
Stockton on Tees	5	Stockton on Tees	5	Hexham	4	Leeds Neville Hill	2
Whitby	5	Durham	4	Cambridge	3	Selby	2
Durham	4	Gateshead	4	Gateshead	3	Bridlington	1
Starbeck	4	Malton	4	Northallerton	3	Darlington	1
West Auckland	4	Stratford	3	Selby	3	Middlesbrough	1
Hexham	3	Tweedmouth	3	Stockton on Tees	3	West Hartlepool	1
Darlington	2	West Auckland	3	Malton	2		
Kittybrewster	2	Kittybrewster	2	Whitby	2		
Northallerton	2	Northallerton	2	Alston	1		
Alston	1	Selby	2	Guisborough	1		
Guisborough	1	Whitby	2	Keith	1		
Ilkley	1	Alston	1	Middlesbrough	1		
Keith	1	Guisborough	1	Pickering	1		
Leyburn	1	Ilkley	1	Tweedmouth	1		
Middleton in Teesdale	1	Keith	1				
Middlesbrough	1	Leyburn	1				
Pateley Bridge	1	Middlesbrough	1				
Rothbury	1	Pateley Bridge	1				
Stratford	1	Rothbury	1				
Tweedmouth	1	Starbeck	1				
		Tyne Dock	1				

J1 65002-65014 0-6-0 GNR Ivatt

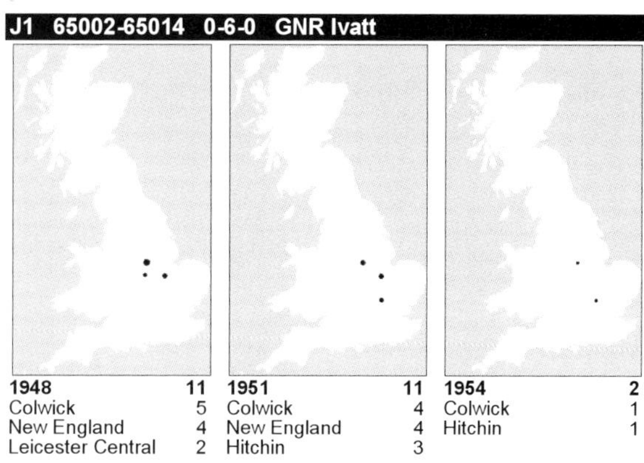

1948	11	1951	11	1954	2
Colwick	5	Colwick	4	Colwick	1
New England	4	New England	4	Hitchin	1
Leicester Central	2	Hitchin	3		

J2 65015-65023 0-6-0 GNR Gresley

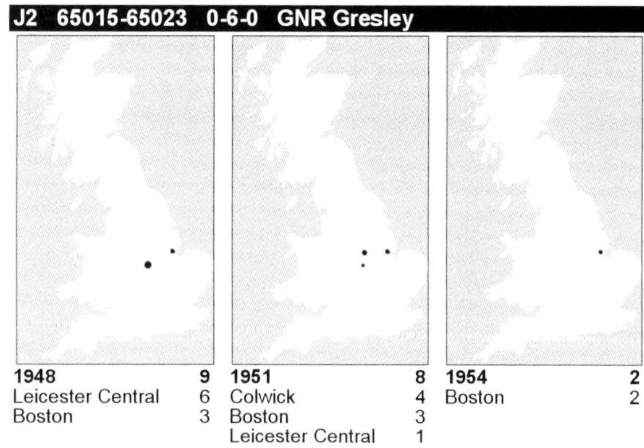

1948	9	1951	8	1954	2
Leicester Central	6	Colwick	4	Boston	2
Boston	3	Boston	3		
		Leicester Central	1		

J3 between 64105 & 64163 0-6-0 GNR & M&GNJR Stirling & Ivatt

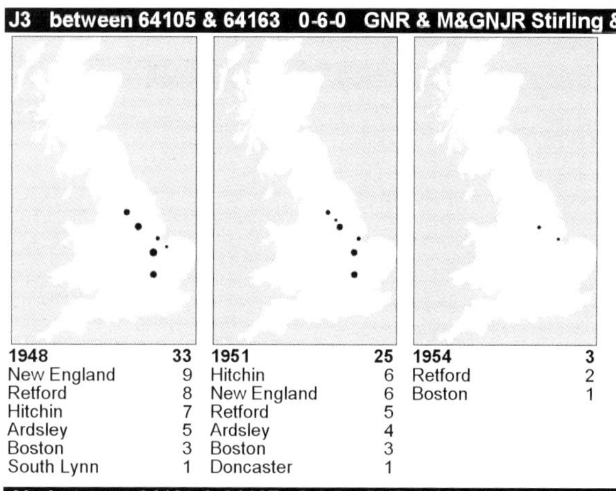

1948	33	1951	25	1954	3
New England	9	Hitchin	6	Retford	2
Retford	8	New England	6	Boston	1
Hitchin	7	Retford	5		
Ardsley	5	Ardsley	4		
Boston	3	Boston	3		
South Lynn	1	Doncaster	1		

J4 between 64109 & 64167 0-6-0 GNR & M&GNJR Stirling & Ivatt (Small Boilers)

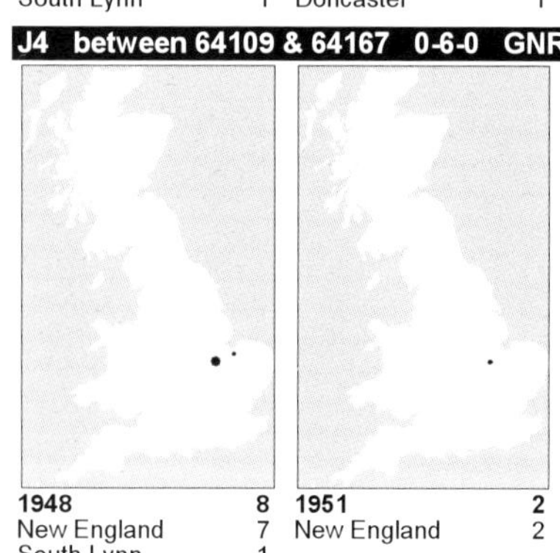

1948	8	1951	2
New England	7	New England	2
South Lynn	1		

GNR Ivatt/Gresley 'J3' class 0-6-0 No 64132 at Boston Goods in 1953.

J5 65480-65499 0-6-0 GNR Ivatt

1948	20
Colwick	16
Woodford Halse	4

1951	20
Colwick	18
Annesley	1
Leicester Central	1

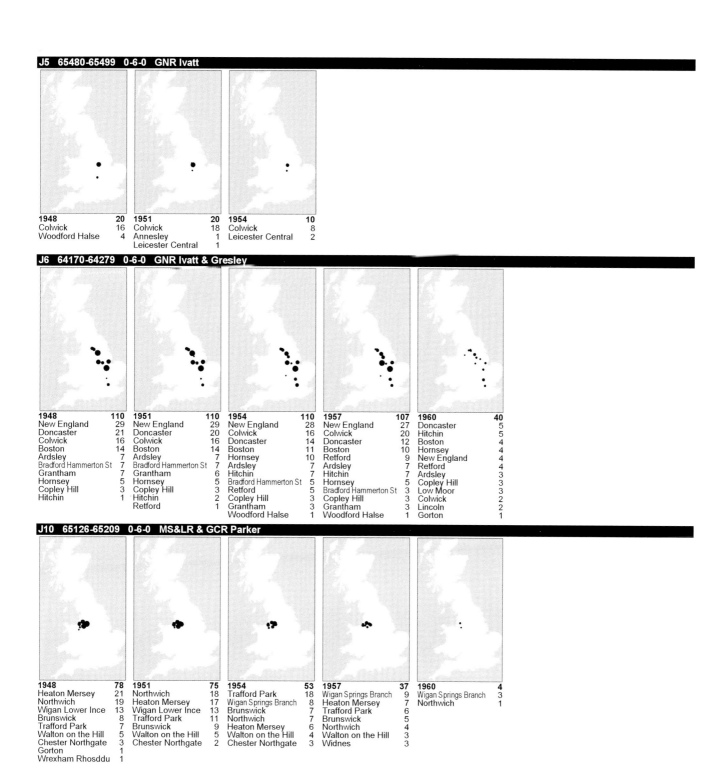

1954	10
Colwick	8
Leicester Central	2

J6 64170-64279 0-6-0 GNR Ivatt & Gresley

1948	110
New England	29
Doncaster	21
Colwick	16
Boston	14
Ardsley	7
Bradford Hammerton St	7
Grantham	7
Hornsey	5
Copley Hill	3
Hitchin	1

1951	110
New England	29
Doncaster	20
Colwick	16
Boston	14
Ardsley	7
Bradford Hammerton St	7
Grantham	6
Hornsey	5
Copley Hill	3
Hitchin	2
Retford	1

1954	110
New England	28
Colwick	16
Doncaster	14
Boston	11
Hornsey	10
Ardsley	7
Hitchin	7
Bradford Hammerton St	5
Retford	5
Copley Hill	3
Grantham	3
Woodford Halse	1

1957	107
New England	27
Colwick	20
Doncaster	12
Boston	10
Retford	9
Ardsley	7
Hitchin	7
Hornsey	5
Bradford Hammerton St	3
Copley Hill	3
Grantham	3
Woodford Halse	1

1960	40
Doncaster	5
Hitchin	5
Boston	4
Hornsey	4
New England	4
Retford	4
Ardsley	3
Copley Hill	3
Low Moor	3
Colwick	2
Lincoln	2
Gorton	1

J10 65126-65209 0-6-0 MS&LR & GCR Parker

1948	78
Heaton Mersey	21
Northwich	19
Wigan Lower Ince	13
Brunswick	8
Trafford Park	7
Walton on the Hill	5
Chester Northgate	3
Gorton	1
Wrexham Rhosddu	1

1951	75
Northwich	18
Heaton Mersey	17
Wigan Lower Ince	13
Trafford Park	11
Brunswick	9
Walton on the Hill	5
Chester Northgate	2

1954	53
Trafford Park	18
Wigan Springs Branch	8
Brunswick	7
Northwich	7
Heaton Mersey	6
Walton on the Hill	4
Chester Northgate	3

1957	37
Wigan Springs Branch	9
Heaton Mersey	7
Trafford Park	6
Brunswick	5
Northwich	4
Walton on the Hill	3
Widnes	3

1960	4
Wigan Springs Branch	3
Northwich	1

GNR Gresley 'J6' class 0-6-0 No 64259 at Newark on 30 March 1958. *R. K. Evans*

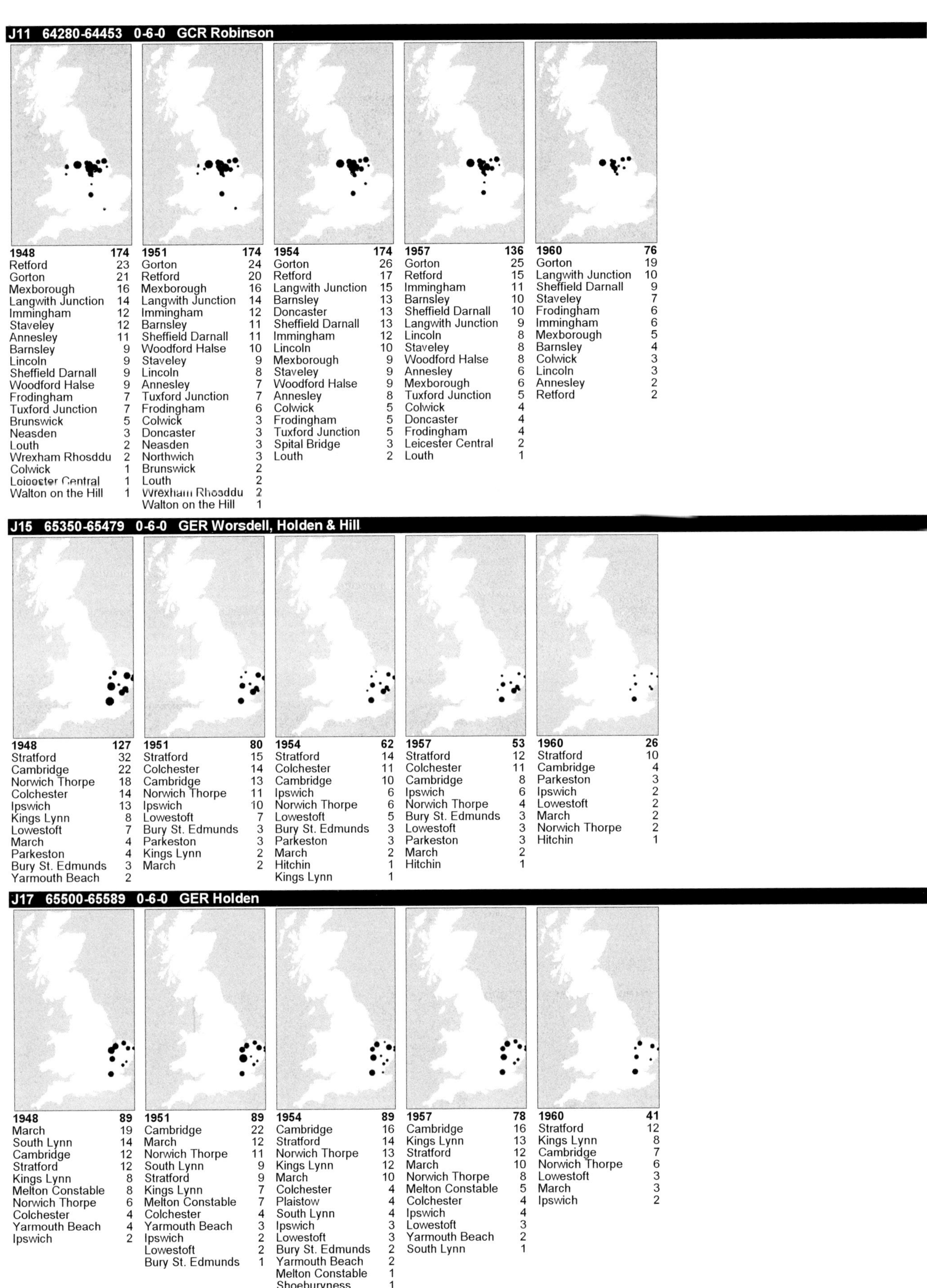

J11 64280-64453 0-6-0 GCR Robinson

1948	174
Retford	23
Gorton	21
Mexborough	16
Langwith Junction	14
Immingham	12
Staveley	12
Annesley	11
Barnsley	9
Lincoln	9
Sheffield Darnall	9
Woodford Halse	9
Frodingham	7
Tuxford Junction	7
Brunswick	5
Neasden	3
Louth	2
Wrexham Rhosddu	2
Colwick	1
Leicester Central	1
Walton on the Hill	1

1951	174
Gorton	24
Retford	20
Mexborough	16
Langwith Junction	14
Immingham	12
Barnsley	11
Sheffield Darnall	11
Woodford Halse	10
Staveley	9
Lincoln	8
Annesley	7
Tuxford Junction	7
Frodingham	6
Colwick	3
Doncaster	3
Neasden	3
Northwich	3
Brunswick	2
Louth	2
Wrexham Rhosddu	2
Walton on the Hill	1

1954	174
Gorton	26
Retford	17
Langwith Junction	15
Barnsley	13
Doncaster	13
Sheffield Darnall	13
Immingham	12
Lincoln	10
Mexborough	9
Staveley	9
Woodford Halse	9
Annesley	8
Colwick	5
Frodingham	5
Tuxford Junction	5
Spital Bridge	3
Louth	2

1957	136
Gorton	25
Retford	15
Immingham	11
Barnsley	10
Sheffield Darnall	10
Langwith Junction	9
Lincoln	8
Staveley	8
Woodford Halse	8
Annesley	6
Mexborough	6
Tuxford Junction	5
Colwick	4
Doncaster	4
Frodingham	4
Leicester Central	2
Louth	1

1960	76
Gorton	19
Langwith Junction	10
Sheffield Darnall	9
Staveley	7
Frodingham	6
Immingham	6
Mexborough	5
Barnsley	4
Colwick	3
Lincoln	3
Annesley	2
Retford	2

J15 65350-65479 0-6-0 GER Worsdell, Holden & Hill

1948	127
Stratford	32
Cambridge	22
Norwich Thorpe	18
Colchester	14
Ipswich	13
Kings Lynn	8
Lowestoft	7
March	4
Parkeston	4
Bury St. Edmunds	3
Yarmouth Beach	2

1951	80
Stratford	15
Colchester	14
Cambridge	13
Norwich Thorpe	11
Ipswich	10
Lowestoft	7
Bury St. Edmunds	3
Parkeston	3
Kings Lynn	2
March	2

1954	62
Stratford	14
Colchester	11
Cambridge	10
Ipswich	6
Norwich Thorpe	6
Lowestoft	5
Bury St. Edmunds	3
Parkeston	3
March	2
Hitchin	1
Kings Lynn	1

1957	53
Stratford	12
Colchester	11
Cambridge	8
Ipswich	6
Norwich Thorpe	4
Bury St. Edmunds	3
Lowestoft	3
Parkeston	3
March	2
Hitchin	1

1960	26
Stratford	10
Cambridge	4
Parkeston	3
Ipswich	2
Lowestoft	2
March	2
Norwich Thorpe	2
Hitchin	1

J17 65500-65589 0-6-0 GER Holden

1948	89
March	19
South Lynn	14
Cambridge	12
Stratford	12
Kings Lynn	8
Melton Constable	8
Norwich Thorpe	6
Colchester	4
Yarmouth Beach	4
Ipswich	2

1951	89
Cambridge	22
March	12
Norwich Thorpe	11
South Lynn	9
Stratford	9
Kings Lynn	7
Melton Constable	7
Colchester	4
Yarmouth Beach	3
Ipswich	2
Lowestoft	2
Bury St. Edmunds	1

1954	89
Cambridge	16
Stratford	14
Norwich Thorpe	13
Kings Lynn	12
March	10
Colchester	4
Plaistow	4
South Lynn	4
Ipswich	3
Lowestoft	3
Bury St. Edmunds	2
Yarmouth Beach	2
Melton Constable	1
Shoeburyness	1

1957	78
Cambridge	16
Kings Lynn	13
Stratford	12
March	10
Norwich Thorpe	8
Melton Constable	5
Colchester	4
Ipswich	4
Lowestoft	3
Yarmouth Beach	2
South Lynn	1

1960	41
Stratford	12
Kings Lynn	8
Cambridge	7
Norwich Thorpe	6
Lowestoft	3
March	3
Ipswich	2

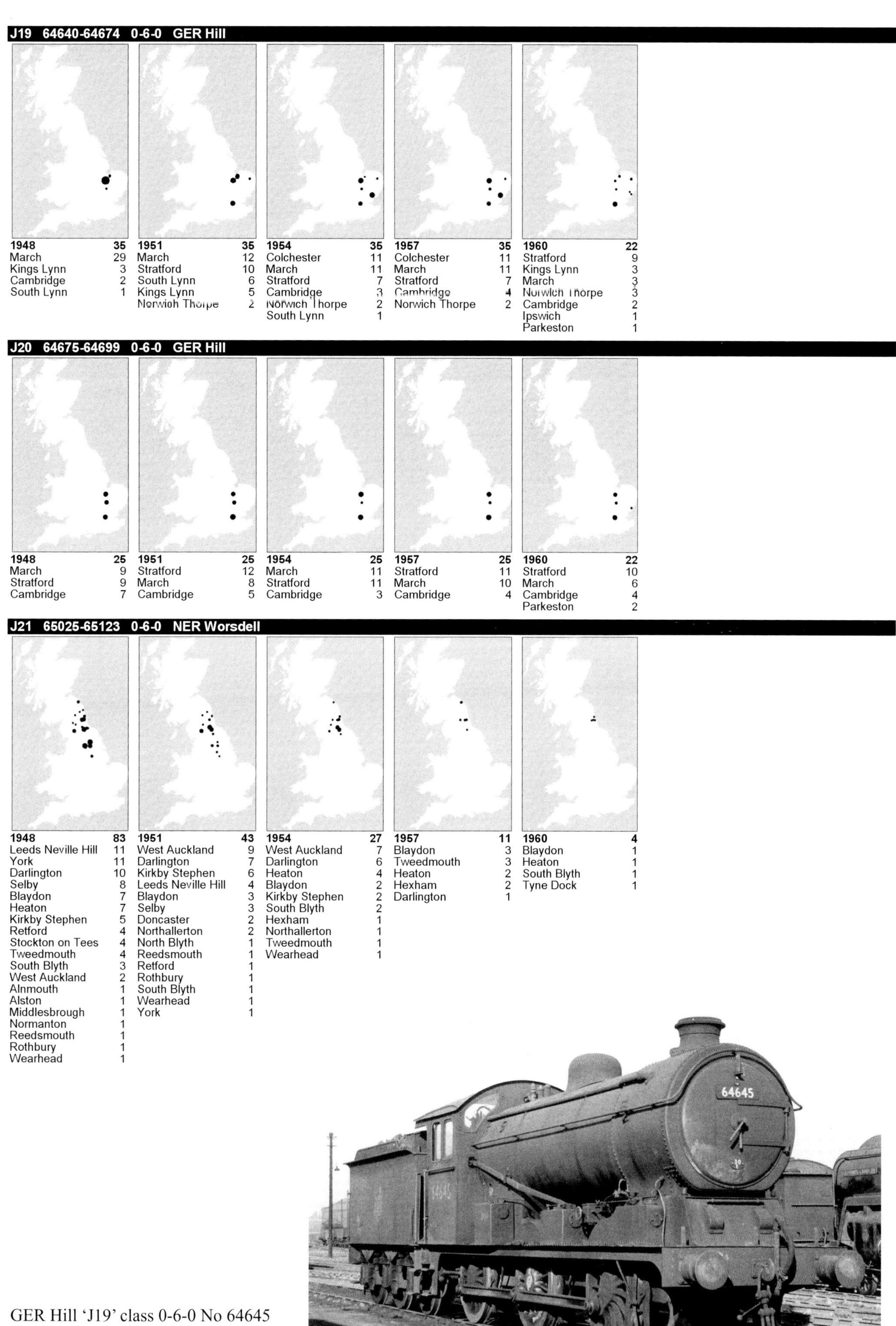

J19 64640-64674 0-6-0 GER Hill

1948	35	1951	35	1954	35	1957	35	1960	22
March	29	March	12	Colchester	11	Colchester	11	Stratford	9
Kings Lynn	3	Stratford	10	March	11	March	11	Kings Lynn	3
Cambridge	2	South Lynn	6	Stratford	7	Stratford	7	March	3
South Lynn	1	Kings Lynn	5	Cambridge	3	Cambridge	4	Norwich Thorpe	3
		Norwich Thorpe	2	Norwich Thorpe	2	Norwich Thorpe	2	Cambridge	2
				South Lynn	1			Ipswich	1
								Parkeston	1

J20 64675-64699 0-6-0 GER Hill

1948	25	1951	25	1954	25	1957	25	1960	22
March	9	Stratford	12	March	11	Stratford	11	Stratford	10
Stratford	9	March	8	Stratford	11	March	10	March	6
Cambridge	7	Cambridge	5	Cambridge	3	Cambridge	4	Cambridge	4
								Parkeston	2

J21 65025-65123 0-6-0 NER Worsdell

1948	83	1951	43	1954	27	1957	11	1960	4
Leeds Neville Hill	11	West Auckland	9	West Auckland	7	Blaydon	3	Blaydon	1
York	11	Darlington	7	Darlington	6	Tweedmouth	3	Heaton	1
Darlington	10	Kirkby Stephen	6	Heaton	4	Heaton	2	South Blyth	1
Selby	8	Leeds Neville Hill	4	Blaydon	2	Hexham	2	Tyne Dock	1
Blaydon	7	Blaydon	3	Kirkby Stephen	2	Darlington	1		
Heaton	7	Selby	3	South Blyth	2				
Kirkby Stephen	5	Doncaster	2	Hexham	1				
Retford	4	Northallerton	2	Northallerton	1				
Stockton on Tees	4	North Blyth	1	Tweedmouth	1				
Tweedmouth	4	Reedsmouth	1	Wearhead	1				
South Blyth	3	Retford	1						
West Auckland	2	Rothbury	1						
Alnmouth	1	South Blyth	1						
Alston	1	Wearhead	1						
Middlesbrough	1	York	1						
Normanton	1								
Reedsmouth	1								
Rothbury	1								
Wearhead	1								

GER Hill 'J19' class 0-6-0 No 64645 from 30E Colchester is seen at Stratford. *Brian Morrison*

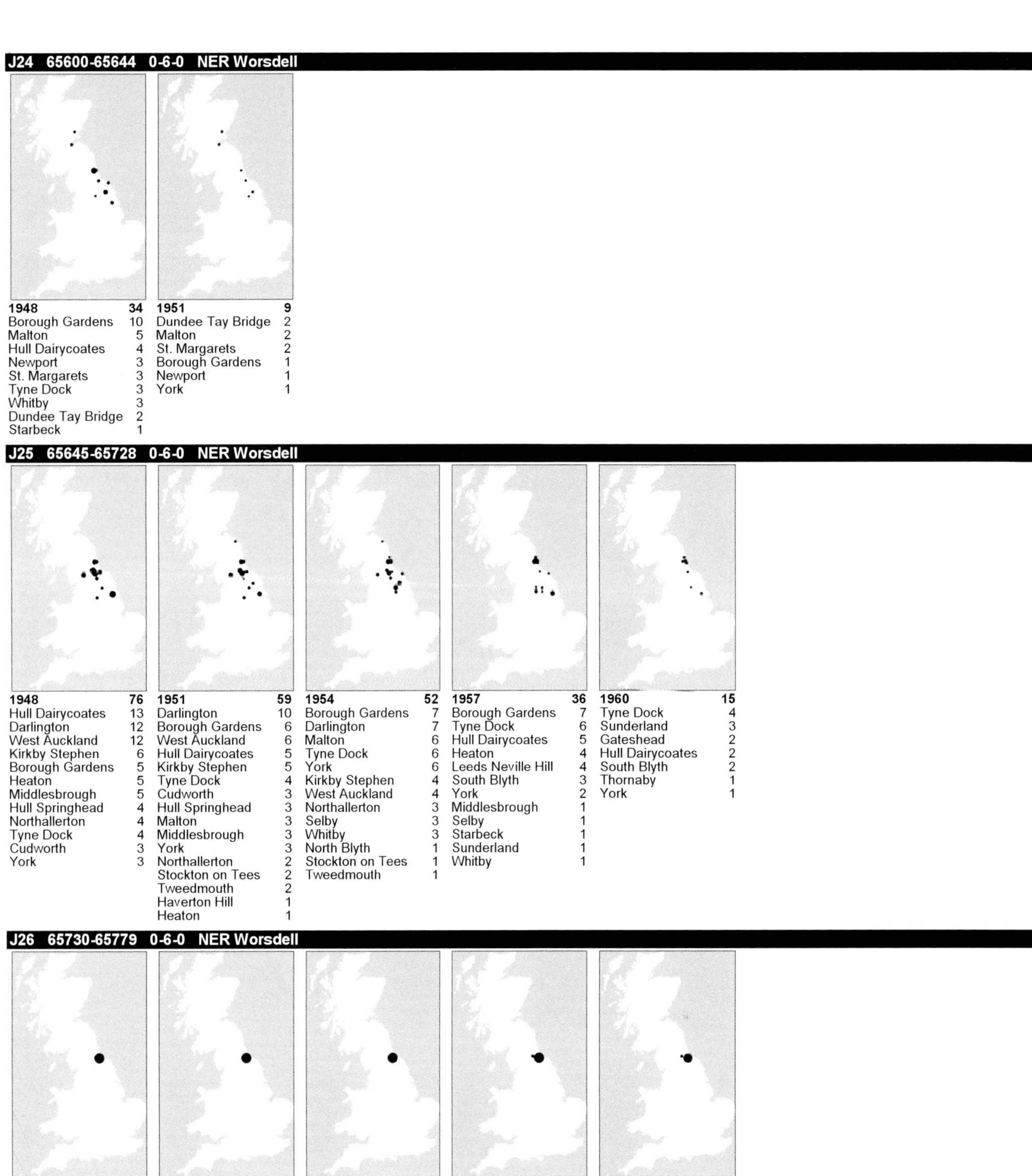

J24 65600-65644 0-6-0 NER Worsdell

1948	34
Borough Gardens	10
Malton	5
Hull Dairycoates	4
Newport	3
St. Margarets	3
Tyne Dock	3
Whitby	3
Dundee Tay Bridge	2
Starbeck	1

1951	9
Dundee Tay Bridge	2
Malton	2
St. Margarets	2
Borough Gardens	1
Newport	1
York	1

J25 65645-65728 0-6-0 NER Worsdell

1948	76
Hull Dairycoates	13
Darlington	12
West Auckland	12
Kirkby Stephen	6
Borough Gardens	5
Heaton	5
Middlesbrough	5
Hull Springhead	4
Northallerton	4
Tyne Dock	4
Cudworth	3
York	3

1951	59
Darlington	10
Borough Gardens	6
West Auckland	6
Hull Dairycoates	5
Kirkby Stephen	5
Tyne Dock	4
Cudworth	3
Hull Springhead	3
Malton	3
Middlesbrough	3
York	3
Northallerton	2
Stockton on Tees	2
Tweedmouth	2
Haverton Hill	1
Heaton	1

1954	52
Borough Gardens	7
Darlington	7
Malton	6
Tyne Dock	6
York	6
Kirkby Stephen	4
West Auckland	4
Northallerton	3
Selby	3
Whitby	3
North Blyth	1
Stockton on Tees	1
Tweedmouth	1

1957	36
Borough Gardens	7
Tyne Dock	6
Hull Dairycoates	5
Heaton	4
Leeds Neville Hill	4
South Blyth	3
York	2
Middlesbrough	1
Selby	1
Starbeck	1
Sunderland	1
Whitby	1

1960	15
Tyne Dock	4
Sunderland	3
Gateshead	2
Hull Dairycoates	2
South Blyth	2
Thornaby	1
York	1

J26 65730-65779 0-6-0 NER Worsdell

1948	50
Newport	41
Middlesbrough	6
West Hartlepool	3

1951	50
Newport	42
Middlesbrough	6
West Hartlepool	2

1954	50
Newport	41
Middlesbrough	4
Stockton on Tees	3
West Hartlepool	2

1957	50
Newport	38
Middlesbrough	4
Stockton on Tees	3
West Auckland	3
West Hartlepool	2

1960	25
Thornaby	23
West Auckland	2

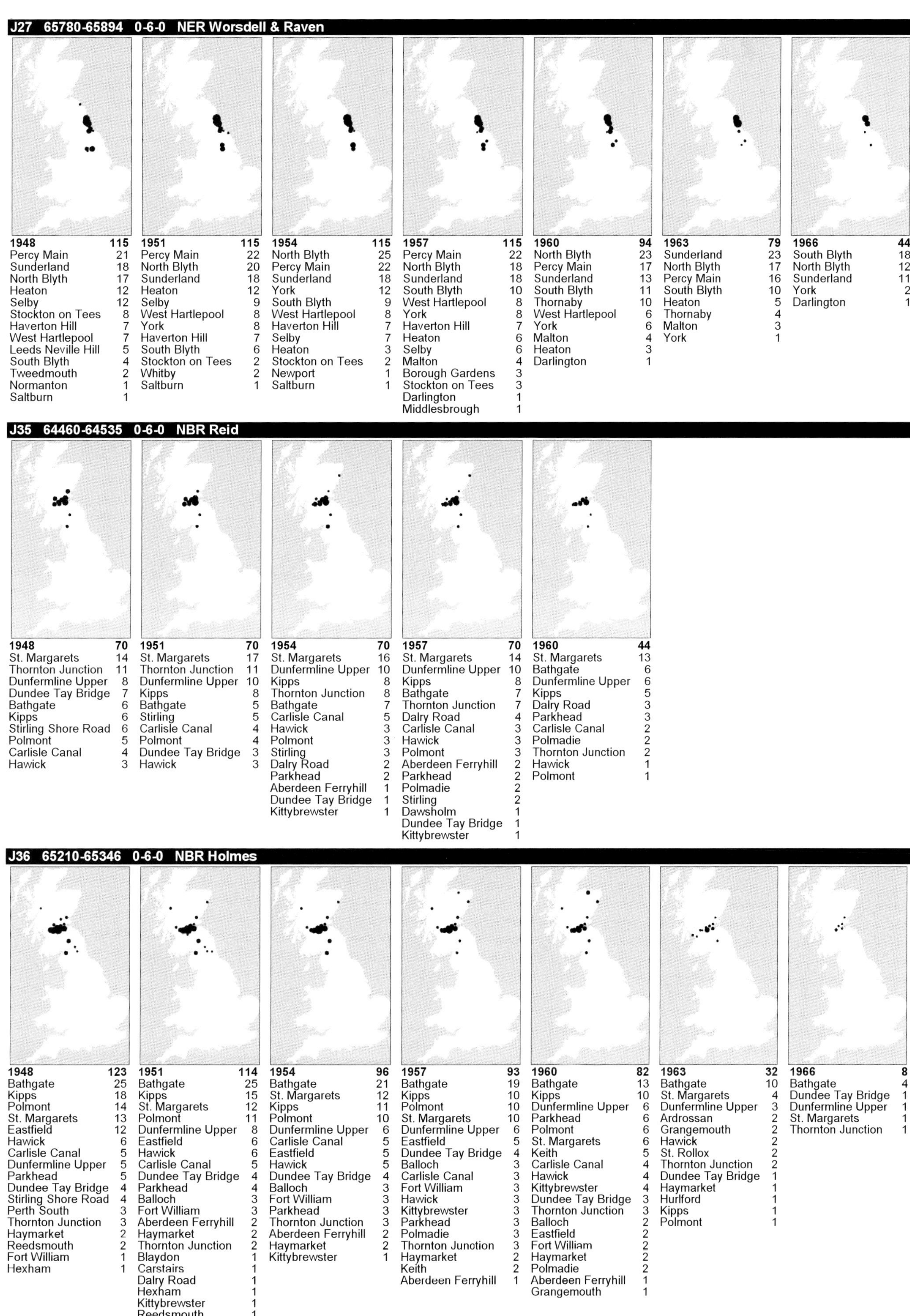

J27 65780-65894 0-6-0 NER Worsdell & Raven

1948 115
Percy Main 21
Sunderland 18
North Blyth 17
Heaton 12
Selby 12
Stockton on Tees 8
Haverton Hill 7
West Hartlepool 7
Leeds Neville Hill 5
South Blyth 4
Tweedmouth 2
Normanton 1
Saltburn 1

1951 115
Percy Main 22
North Blyth 20
Sunderland 18
Heaton 12
Selby 9
West Hartlepool 8
York 8
Haverton Hill 7
South Blyth 6
Stockton on Tees 2
Whitby 2
Saltburn 1

1954 115
North Blyth 25
Percy Main 22
Sunderland 18
York 12
South Blyth 9
West Hartlepool 8
Haverton Hill 7
Selby 7
Heaton 3
Stockton on Tees 2
Newport 1
Saltburn 1

1957 115
Percy Main 22
North Blyth 18
Sunderland 18
South Blyth 10
West Hartlepool 8
York 8
Haverton Hill 7
Heaton 6
Selby 6
Malton 4
Borough Gardens 3
Stockton on Tees 3
Darlington 1
Middlesbrough 1

1960 94
North Blyth 23
Percy Main 17
Sunderland 13
South Blyth 11
Thornaby 10
West Hartlepool 6
York 6
Malton 4
Heaton 3
Darlington 1

1963 79
Sunderland 23
North Blyth 17
Percy Main 16
South Blyth 10
Heaton 5
Thornaby 4
Malton 3
York 1

1966 44
South Blyth 18
North Blyth 12
Sunderland 11
York 2
Darlington 1

J35 64460-64535 0-6-0 NBR Reid

1948 70
St. Margarets 14
Thornton Junction 11
Dunfermline Upper 8
Dundee Tay Bridge 7
Bathgate 6
Kipps 6
Stirling Shore Road 6
Polmont 5
Carlisle Canal 4
Hawick 3

1951 70
St. Margarets 17
Thornton Junction 11
Dunfermline Upper 10
Kipps 8
Bathgate 5
Stirling 5
Carlisle Canal 4
Polmont 4
Dundee Tay Bridge 3
Hawick 3

1954 70
St. Margarets 16
Dunfermline Upper 10
Kipps 8
Thornton Junction 8
Bathgate 7
Carlisle Canal 5
Hawick 3
Polmont 3
Stirling 3
Dalry Road 2
Parkhead 2
Aberdeen Ferryhill 1
Dundee Tay Bridge 1
Kittybrewster 1

1957 70
St. Margarets 14
Dunfermline Upper 10
Kipps 8
Bathgate 7
Thornton Junction 7
Dalry Road 4
Carlisle Canal 3
Hawick 3
Polmont 3
Aberdeen Ferryhill 2
Parkhead 2
Polmadie 2
Stirling 2
Dawsholm 1
Dundee Tay Bridge 1
Kittybrewster 1

1960 44
St. Margarets 13
Bathgate 6
Dunfermline Upper 6
Kipps 5
Dalry Road 3
Parkhead 3
Carlisle Canal 2
Polmadie 2
Thornton Junction 2
Hawick 1
Polmont 1

J36 65210-65346 0-6-0 NBR Holmes

1948 123
Bathgate 25
Kipps 18
Polmont 14
St. Margarets 13
Eastfield 12
Hawick 6
Carlisle Canal 5
Dunfermline Upper 5
Parkhead 5
Dundee Tay Bridge 4
Stirling Shore Road 4
Perth South 3
Thornton Junction 3
Haymarket 2
Reedsmouth 2
Fort William 1
Hexham 1

1951 114
Bathgate 25
Kipps 15
St. Margarets 12
Polmont 11
Dunfermline Upper 8
Eastfield 6
Hawick 6
Carlisle Canal 5
Dundee Tay Bridge 4
Parkhead 4
Balloch 3
Fort William 3
Aberdeen Ferryhill 2
Haymarket 2
Thornton Junction 2
Blaydon 1
Carstairs 1
Dalry Road 1
Hexham 1
Kittybrewster 1
Reedsmouth 1

1954 96
Bathgate 21
St. Margarets 12
Kipps 11
Polmont 10
Dunfermline Upper 6
Carlisle Canal 5
Eastfield 5
Hawick 5
Dundee Tay Bridge 4
Balloch 3
Fort William 3
Parkhead 3
Thornton Junction 3
Aberdeen Ferryhill 2
Haymarket 2
Kittybrewster 1

1957 93
Bathgate 19
Kipps 10
Polmont 10
St. Margarets 10
Dunfermline Upper 6
Eastfield 5
Dundee Tay Bridge 4
Balloch 3
Carlisle Canal 3
Fort William 3
Hawick 3
Kittybrewster 3
Parkhead 3
Polmadie 3
Thornton Junction 3
Haymarket 2
Keith 2
Aberdeen Ferryhill 1

1960 82
Bathgate 13
Kipps 10
Dunfermline Upper 6
Parkhead 6
Polmont 6
St. Margarets 6
Keith 5
Carlisle Canal 4
Hawick 4
Kittybrewster 4
Dundee Tay Bridge 3
Thornton Junction 3
Balloch 2
Eastfield 2
Fort William 2
Haymarket 2
Polmadie 2
Aberdeen Ferryhill 1
Grangemouth 1

1963 32
Bathgate 10
St. Margarets 4
Dunfermline Upper 3
Ardrossan 2
Grangemouth 2
Hawick 2
St. Rollox 2
Thornton Junction 2
Dundee Tay Bridge 1
Haymarket 1
Hurlford 1
Kipps 1
Polmont 1

1966 8
Bathgate 4
Dundee Tay Bridge 1
Dunfermline Upper 1
St. Margarets 1
Thornton Junction 1

J37 64536-64639 0-6-0 NBR Reid

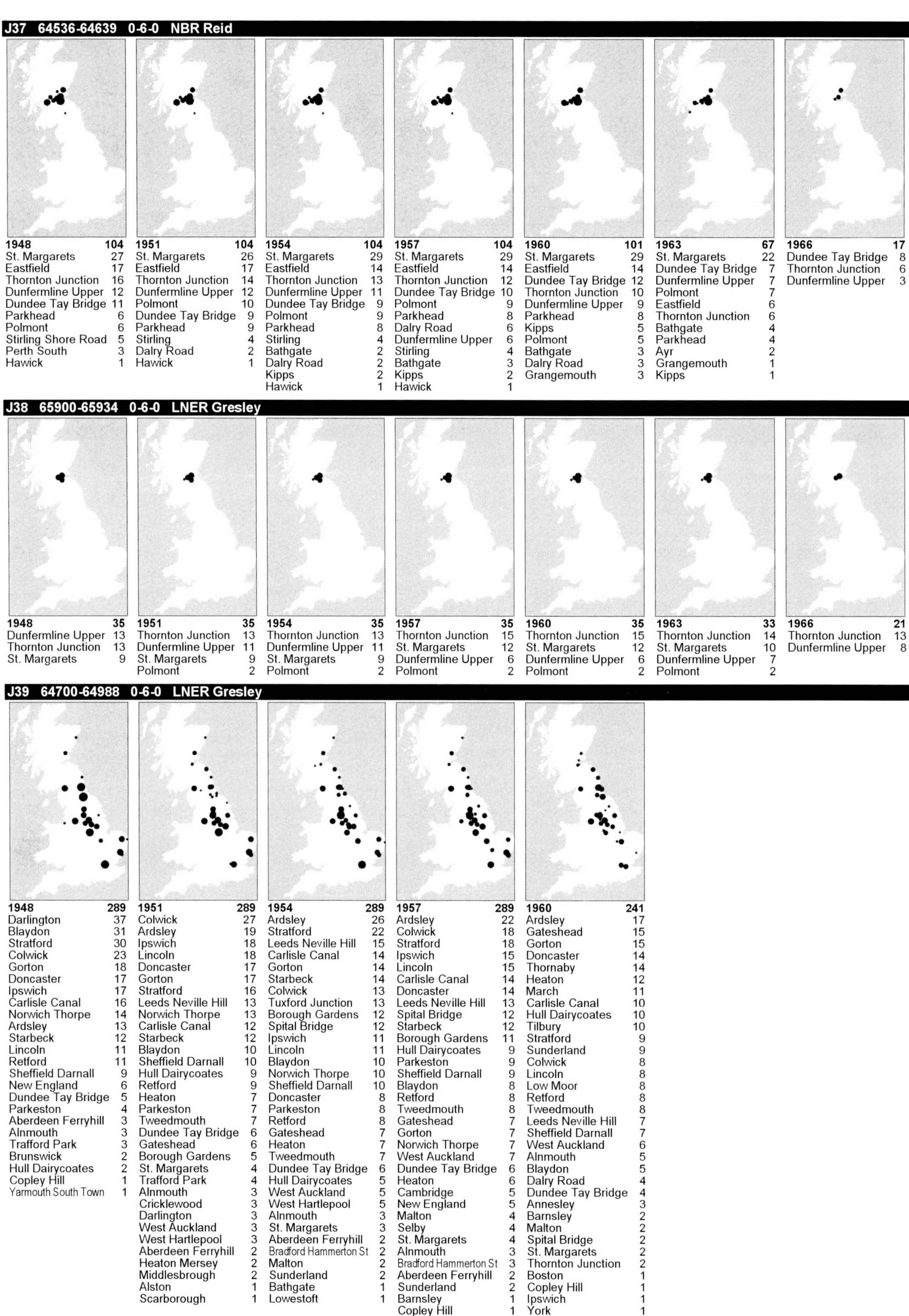

1948 104	1951 104	1954 104	1957 104	1960 101	1963 67	1966 17
St. Margarets 27	St. Margarets 26	St. Margarets 29	St. Margarets 29	St. Margarets 29	St. Margarets 22	Dundee Tay Bridge 8
Eastfield 17	Eastfield 17	Eastfield 14	Eastfield 14	Eastfield 14	Dundee Tay Bridge 7	Thornton Junction 6
Thornton Junction 16	Thornton Junction 14	Thornton Junction 13	Thornton Junction 12	Dundee Tay Bridge 12	Dunfermline Upper 7	Dunfermline Upper 3
Dunfermline Upper 12	Dunfermline Upper 12	Dunfermline Upper 11	Dundee Tay Bridge 10	Thornton Junction 10	Polmont 7	
Dundee Tay Bridge 11	Polmont 10	Dundee Tay Bridge 9	Polmont 9	Dunfermline Upper 9	Eastfield 6	
Parkhead 6	Dundee Tay Bridge 9	Polmont 9	Parkhead 8	Parkhead 8	Thornton Junction 6	
Polmont 6	Parkhead 9	Parkhead 8	Dalry Road 6	Kipps 5	Bathgate 4	
Stirling Shore Road 5	Stirling 4	Stirling 4	Dunfermline Upper 6	Polmont 5	Parkhead 4	
Perth South 3	Dalry Road 2	Bathgate 2	Stirling 4	Bathgate 3	Ayr 2	
Hawick 1	Hawick 1	Dalry Road 2	Bathgate 3	Dalry Road 3	Grangemouth 1	
		Kipps 2	Kipps 2	Grangemouth 3	Kipps 1	
		Hawick 1	Hawick 1			

J38 65900-65934 0-6-0 LNER Gresley

1948 35	1951 35	1954 35	1957 35	1960 35	1963 33	1966 21
Dunfermline Upper 13	Thornton Junction 13	Thornton Junction 13	Thornton Junction 15	Thornton Junction 15	Thornton Junction 14	Thornton Junction 13
Thornton Junction 13	Dunfermline Upper 11	Dunfermline Upper 11	St. Margarets 12	St. Margarets 12	St. Margarets 10	Dunfermline Upper 8
St. Margarets 9	St. Margarets 9	St. Margarets 9	Dunfermline Upper 6	Dunfermline Upper 6	Dunfermline Upper 7	
	Polmont 2	Polmont 2	Polmont 2	Polmont 2	Polmont 2	

J39 64700-64988 0-6-0 LNER Gresley

1948 289	1951 289	1954 289	1957 289	1960 241
Darlington 37	Colwick 27	Ardsley 26	Ardsley 22	Ardsley 17
Blaydon 31	Ardsley 19	Stratford 22	Colwick 18	Gateshead 15
Stratford 30	Ipswich 18	Leeds Neville Hill 15	Stratford 18	Gorton 15
Colwick 23	Lincoln 18	Carlisle Canal 14	Ipswich 15	Doncaster 14
Gorton 18	Doncaster 17	Gorton 14	Lincoln 15	Thornaby 14
Doncaster 17	Gorton 17	Starbeck 14	Carlisle Canal 14	Heaton 12
Ipswich 17	Stratford 16	Colwick 13	Doncaster 14	March 11
Carlisle Canal 16	Leeds Neville Hill 13	Tuxford Junction 13	Leeds Neville Hill 13	Carlisle Canal 10
Norwich Thorpe 14	Norwich Thorpe 13	Borough Gardens 12	Spital Bridge 12	Hull Dairycoates 10
Ardsley 13	Carlisle Canal 12	Spital Bridge 12	Starbeck 12	Tilbury 10
Starbeck 12	Starbeck 12	Ipswich 11	Borough Gardens 11	Stratford 9
Lincoln 11	Blaydon 10	Lincoln 11	Hull Dairycoates 9	Sunderland 9
Retford 11	Sheffield Darnall 10	Blaydon 10	Parkeston 9	Colwick 8
Sheffield Darnall 9	Hull Dairycoates 9	Norwich Thorpe 10	Sheffield Darnall 9	Lincoln 8
New England 6	Retford 9	Sheffield Darnall 10	Blaydon 8	Low Moor 8
Dundee Tay Bridge 5	Heaton 7	Doncaster 8	Retford 8	Retford 8
Parkeston 4	Parkeston 7	Parkeston 8	Tweedmouth 8	Tweedmouth 8
Aberdeen Ferryhill 3	Tweedmouth 7	Retford 8	Gateshead 7	Leeds Neville Hill 7
Alnmouth 3	Dundee Tay Bridge 6	Gateshead 7	Gorton 7	Sheffield Darnall 7
Trafford Park 3	Gateshead 6	Heaton 7	Norwich Thorpe 7	West Auckland 6
Brunswick 2	Borough Gardens 5	Tweedmouth 7	West Auckland 7	Alnmouth 5
Hull Dairycoates 2	St. Margarets 4	Dundee Tay Bridge 6	Dundee Tay Bridge 6	Blaydon 5
Copley Hill 1	Trafford Park 4	Hull Dairycoates 5	Heaton 6	Dalry Road 4
Yarmouth South Town 1	Alnmouth 3	West Auckland 5	Cambridge 5	Dundee Tay Bridge 4
	Cricklewood 3	West Hartlepool 5	New England 5	Annesley 3
	Darlington 3	Alnmouth 3	Malton 4	Barnsley 2
	West Auckland 3	St. Margarets 3	Selby 4	Malton 2
	West Hartlepool 3	Aberdeen Ferryhill 2	St. Margarets 4	Spital Bridge 2
	Aberdeen Ferryhill 2	Bradford Hammerton St 2	Alnmouth 3	St. Margarets 2
	Heaton Mersey 2	Malton 2	Bradford Hammerton St 3	Thornton Junction 2
	Middlesbrough 2	Sunderland 2	Aberdeen Ferryhill 2	Boston 1
	Alston 1	Bathgate 1	Sunderland 2	Copley Hill 1
	Scarborough 1	Lowestoft 1	Barnsley 1	Ipswich 1
			Copley Hill 1	York 1

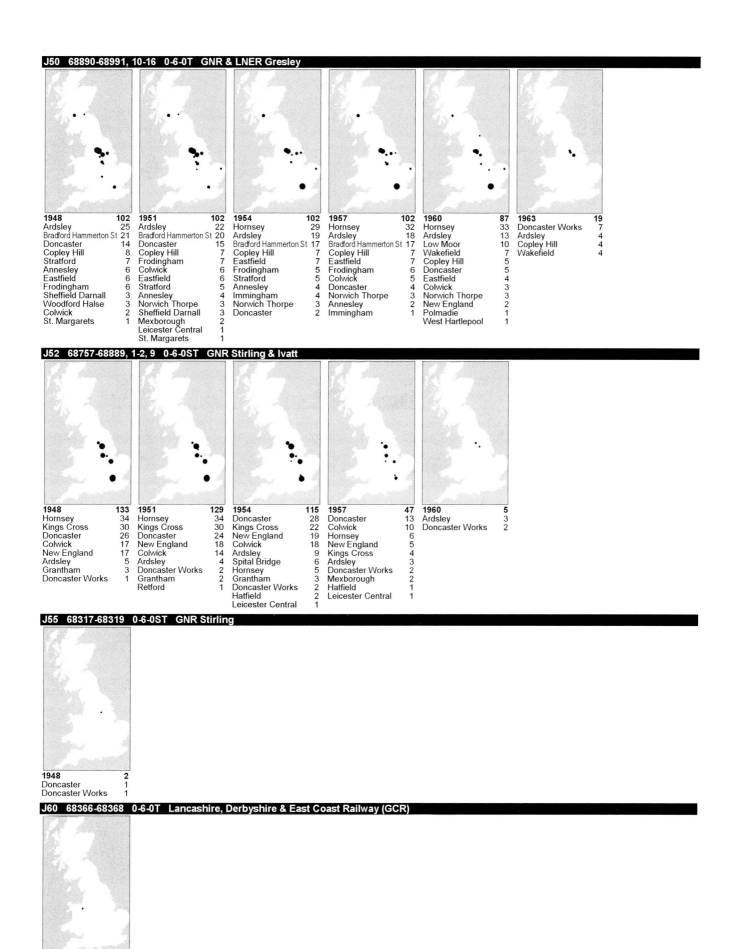

J50 68890-68991, 10-16 0-6-0T GNR & LNER Gresley

1948	102
Ardsley	25
Bradford Hammerton St	21
Doncaster	14
Copley Hill	8
Stratford	7
Annesley	6
Eastfield	6
Frodingham	6
Sheffield Darnall	3
Woodford Halse	3
Colwick	2
St. Margarets	1

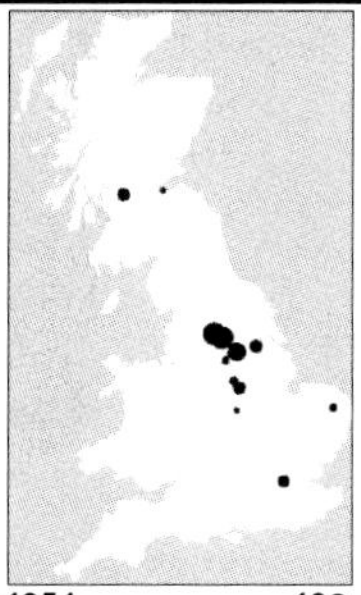

1951	102
Ardsley	22
Bradford Hammerton St	20
Doncaster	15
Copley Hill	7
Frodingham	7
Colwick	6
Eastfield	6
Stratford	5
Annesley	4
Norwich Thorpe	3
Sheffield Darnall	3
Mexborough	2
Leicester Central	1
St. Margarets	1

1954	102
Hornsey	29
Ardsley	19
Bradford Hammerton St	17
Copley Hill	7
Eastfield	7
Frodingham	5
Stratford	5
Annesley	4
Immingham	4
Norwich Thorpe	3
Doncaster	2

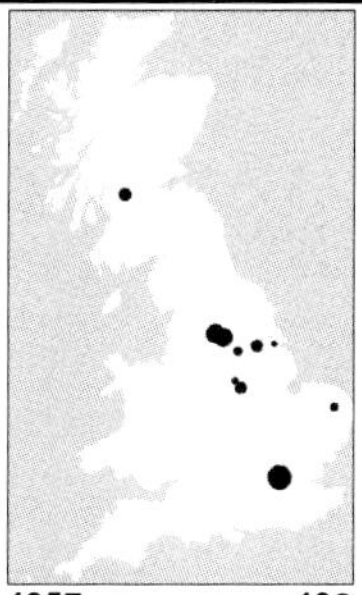

1957	102
Hornsey	32
Ardsley	18
Bradford Hammerton St	17
Copley Hill	7
Eastfield	7
Frodingham	6
Colwick	5
Doncaster	4
Norwich Thorpe	3
Annesley	2
Immingham	1

1960	87
Hornsey	33
Ardsley	13
Low Moor	10
Wakefield	7
Copley Hill	5
Doncaster	5
Eastfield	4
Colwick	3
Norwich Thorpe	3
New England	2
Polmadie	1
West Hartlepool	1

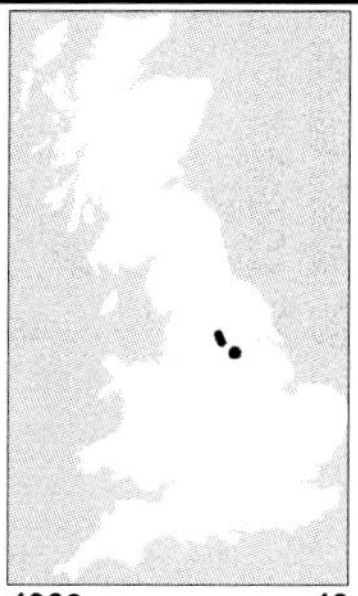

1963	19
Doncaster Works	7
Ardsley	4
Copley Hill	4
Wakefield	4

J52 68757-68889, 1-2, 9 0-6-0ST GNR Stirling & Ivatt

1948	133
Hornsey	34
Kings Cross	30
Doncaster	26
Colwick	17
New England	17
Ardsley	5
Grantham	3
Doncaster Works	1

1951	129
Hornsey	34
Kings Cross	30
Doncaster	24
New England	18
Colwick	14
Ardsley	4
Doncaster Works	2
Grantham	2
Retford	1

1954	115
Doncaster	28
Kings Cross	22
New England	19
Colwick	18
Ardsley	9
Spital Bridge	6
Hornsey	5
Grantham	3
Doncaster Works	2
Hatfield	2
Leicester Central	1

1957	47
Doncaster	13
Colwick	10
Hornsey	6
New England	5
Kings Cross	4
Ardsley	3
Doncaster Works	2
Mexborough	2
Hatfield	1
Leicester Central	1

1960	5
Ardsley	3
Doncaster Works	2

J55 68317-68319 0-6-0ST GNR Stirling

1948	2
Doncaster	1
Doncaster Works	1

J60 68366-68368 0-6-0T Lancashire, Derbyshire & East Coast Railway (GCR)

1948	2
Wrexham Rhosddu	2

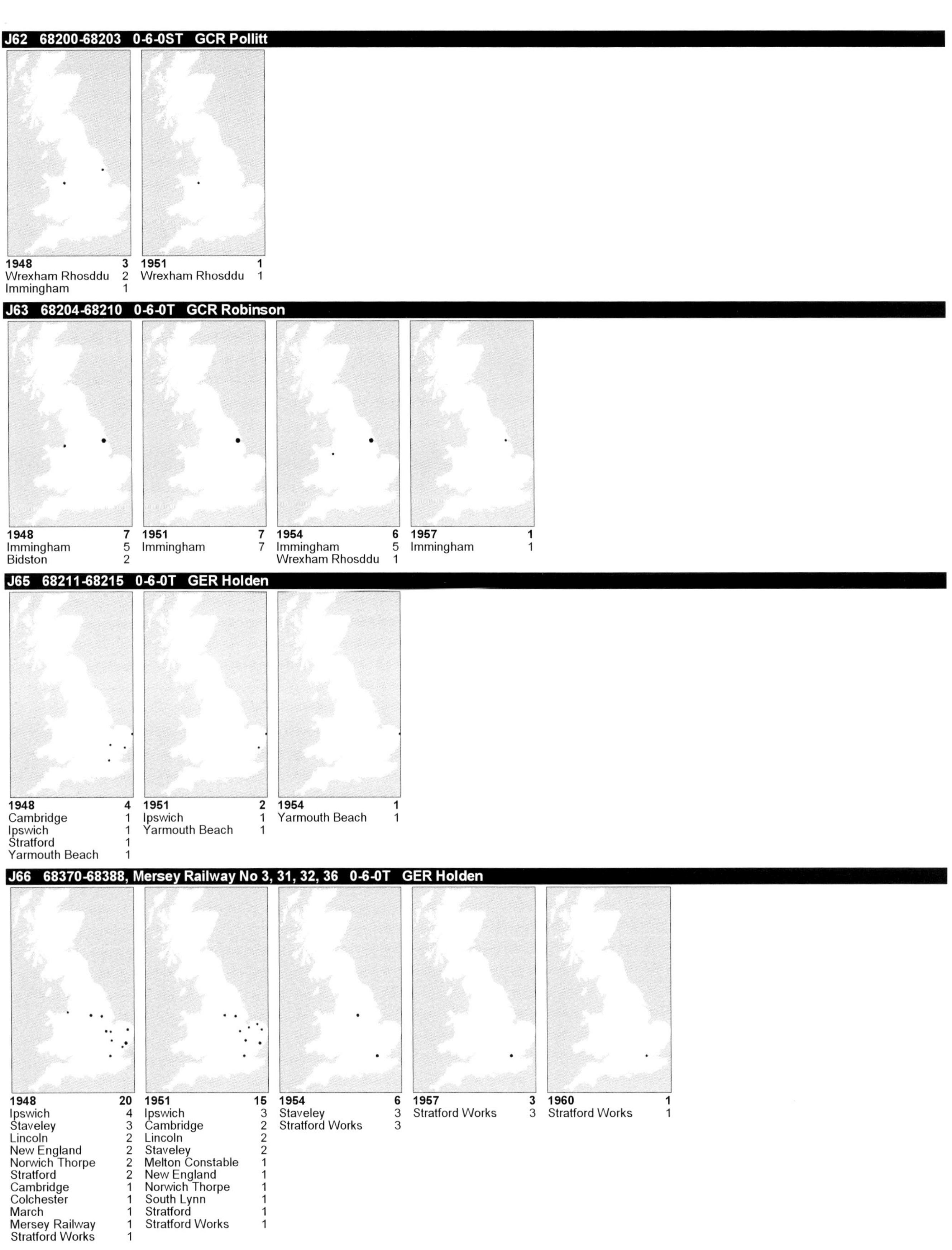

J62 68200-68203 0-6-0ST GCR Pollitt

1948	3
Wrexham Rhosddu	2
Immingham	1

1951	1
Wrexham Rhosddu	1

J63 68204-68210 0-6-0T GCR Robinson

1948	7
Immingham	5
Bidston	2

1951	7
Immingham	7

1954	6
Immingham	5
Wrexham Rhosddu	1

1957	1
Immingham	1

J65 68211-68215 0-6-0T GER Holden

1948	4
Cambridge	1
Ipswich	1
Stratford	1
Yarmouth Beach	1

1951	2
Ipswich	1
Yarmouth Beach	1

1954	1
Yarmouth Beach	1

J66 68370-68388, Mersey Railway No 3, 31, 32, 36 0-6-0T GER Holden

1948	20
Ipswich	4
Staveley	3
Lincoln	2
New England	2
Norwich Thorpe	2
Stratford	2
Cambridge	1
Colchester	1
March	1
Mersey Railway	1
Stratford Works	1

1951	15
Ipswich	3
Cambridge	2
Lincoln	2
Staveley	2
Melton Constable	1
New England	1
Norwich Thorpe	1
South Lynn	1
Stratford	1
Stratford Works	1

1954	6
Staveley	3
Stratford Works	3

1957	3
Stratford Works	3

1960	1
Stratford Works	1

J67 between 68490 & 68628 0-6-0T GER Holden

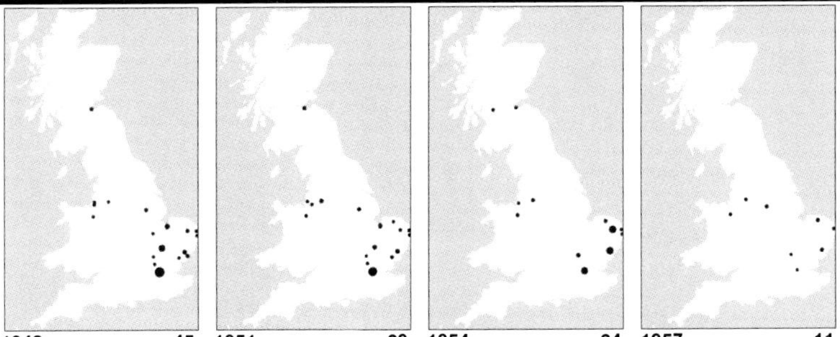

1948	45
Stratford	14
Cambridge	5
Kings Lynn	4
Ipswich	3
Lincoln	2
Norwich Thorpe	2
Parkeston	2
St. Margarets	2
Brunswick	1
Colchester	1
Hatfield	1
Hitchin	1
Lowestoft	1
New England	1
South Lynn	1
Trafford Park	1
Walton on the Hill	1
Wrexham Rhosddu	1
Yarmouth South Town	1

1951	39
Stratford	11
Cambridge	3
Ipswich	3
Kings Lynn	3
Trafford Park	3
Colchester	2
Lincoln	2
St. Margarets	2
Hatfield	1
Hitchin	1
Lowestoft	1
Melton Constable	1
Norwich Thorpe	1
South Lynn	1
Walton on the Hill	1
Widnes	1
Wrexham Rhosddu	1
Yarmouth South Town	1

1954	34
Ipswich	7
Norwich Thorpe	7
Stratford	6
Hitchin	3
Melton Constable	2
Trafford Park	2
Wrexham Rhosddu	2
Brunswick	1
Dawsholm	1
Lowestoft	1
St. Margarets	1
Yarmouth South Town	1

1957	11
Ipswich	2
Melton Constable	2
Staveley	2
Hitchin	1
Stratford	1
Trafford Park	1
Wrexham Rhosddu	1
Yarmouth South Town	1

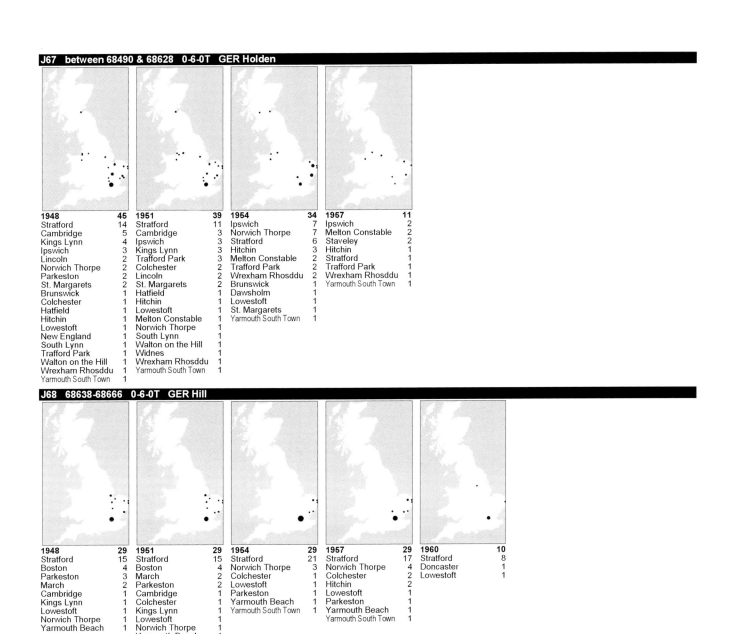

J68 68638-68666 0-6-0T GER Hill

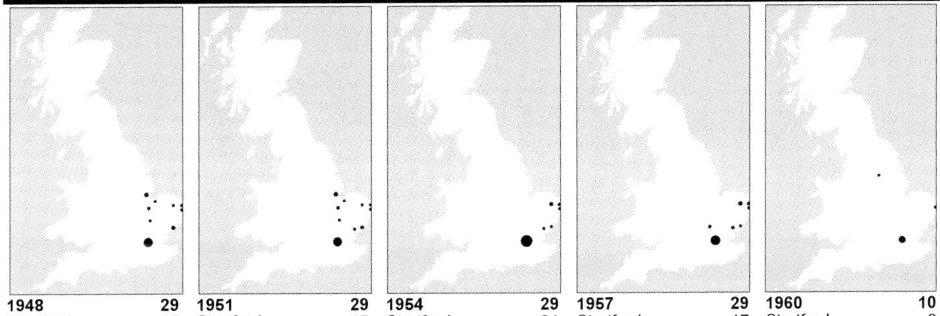

1948	29
Stratford	15
Boston	4
Parkeston	3
March	2
Cambridge	1
Kings Lynn	1
Lowestoft	1
Norwich Thorpe	1
Yarmouth Beach	1

1951	29
Stratford	15
Boston	4
March	2
Parkeston	2
Cambridge	1
Colchester	1
Kings Lynn	1
Lowestoft	1
Norwich Thorpe	1
Yarmouth Beach	1

1954	29
Stratford	21
Norwich Thorpe	3
Colchester	1
Lowestoft	1
Parkeston	1
Yarmouth Beach	1
Yarmouth South Town	1

1957	29
Stratford	17
Norwich Thorpe	4
Colchester	2
Hitchin	2
Lowestoft	1
Parkeston	1
Yarmouth Beach	1
Yarmouth South Town	1

1960	10
Stratford	8
Doncaster	1
Lowestoft	1

GER Hill 'J68' class 0-6-0T No 68662 at its home shed 30A Stratford.
Brian Morrison

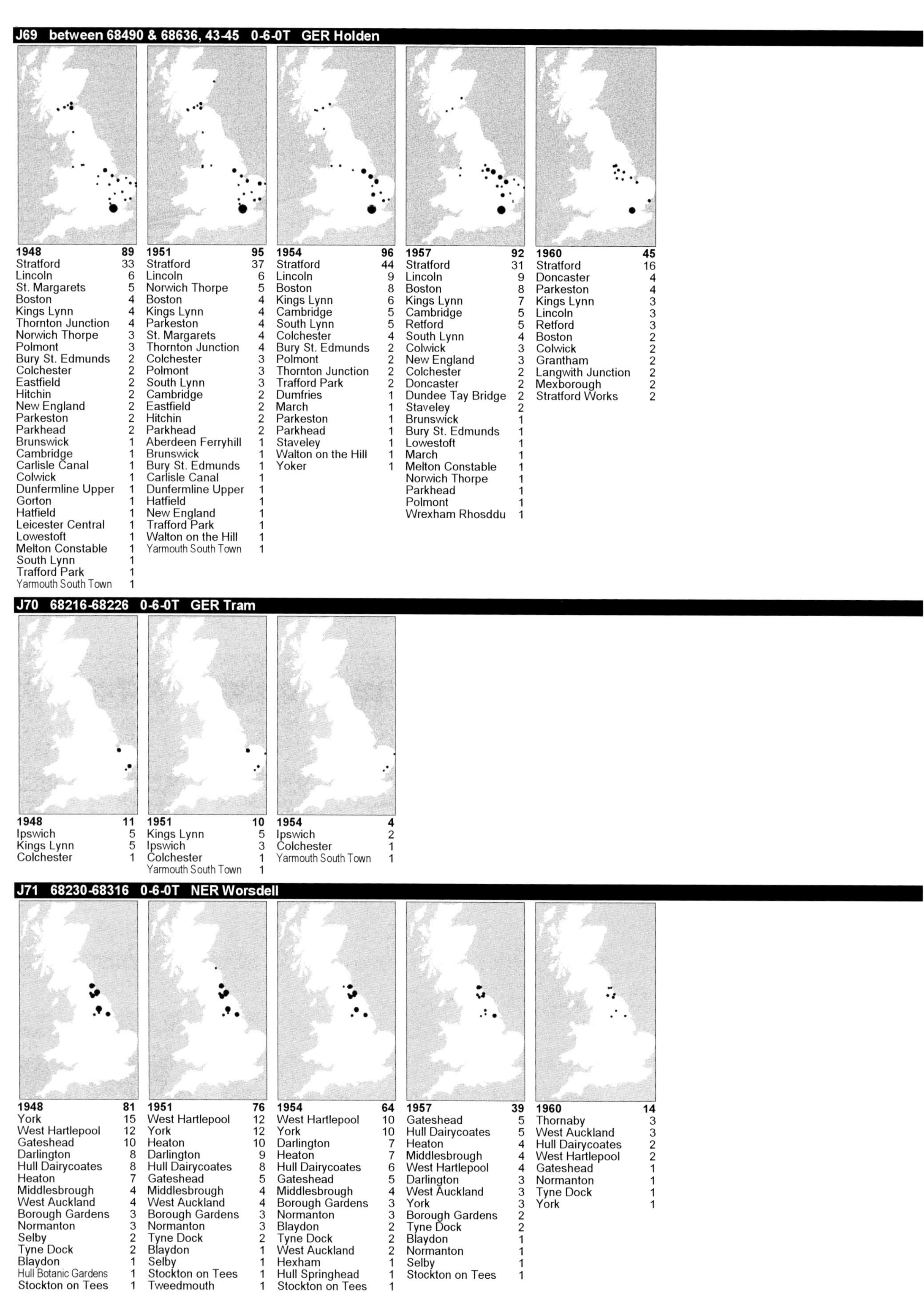

J69 between 68490 & 68636, 43-45 0-6-0T GER Holden

1948	89
Stratford	33
Lincoln	6
St. Margarets	5
Boston	4
Kings Lynn	4
Thornton Junction	4
Norwich Thorpe	3
Polmont	3
Bury St. Edmunds	2
Colchester	2
Eastfield	2
Hitchin	2
New England	2
Parkeston	2
Parkhead	2
Brunswick	1
Cambridge	1
Carlisle Canal	1
Colwick	1
Dunfermline Upper	1
Gorton	1
Hatfield	1
Leicester Central	1
Lowestoft	1
Melton Constable	1
South Lynn	1
Trafford Park	1
Yarmouth South Town	1

1951	95
Stratford	37
Lincoln	6
Norwich Thorpe	5
Boston	4
Kings Lynn	4
Parkeston	4
St. Margarets	4
Thornton Junction	4
Colchester	3
Polmont	3
South Lynn	3
Cambridge	2
Eastfield	2
Hitchin	2
Parkhead	2
Aberdeen Ferryhill	1
Brunswick	1
Bury St. Edmunds	1
Carlisle Canal	1
Dunfermline Upper	1
Hatfield	1
New England	1
Trafford Park	1
Walton on the Hill	1
Yarmouth South Town	1

1954	96
Stratford	44
Lincoln	9
Boston	8
Kings Lynn	6
Cambridge	5
South Lynn	5
Colchester	4
Bury St. Edmunds	2
Polmont	2
Thornton Junction	2
Trafford Park	2
Dumfries	1
March	1
Parkeston	1
Parkhead	1
Staveley	1
Walton on the Hill	1
Yoker	1

1957	92
Stratford	31
Lincoln	9
Boston	8
Kings Lynn	7
Cambridge	5
Retford	5
South Lynn	4
Colwick	3
New England	3
Colchester	2
Doncaster	2
Dundee Tay Bridge	2
Staveley	2
Brunswick	1
Bury St. Edmunds	1
Lowestoft	1
March	1
Melton Constable	1
Norwich Thorpe	1
Parkhead	1
Polmont	1
Wrexham Rhosddu	1

1960	45
Stratford	16
Doncaster	4
Parkeston	4
Kings Lynn	3
Lincoln	3
Retford	3
Boston	2
Colwick	2
Grantham	2
Langwith Junction	2
Mexborough	2
Stratford Works	2

J70 68216-68226 0-6-0T GER Tram

1948	11
Ipswich	5
Kings Lynn	5
Colchester	1

1951	10
Kings Lynn	5
Ipswich	3
Colchester	1
Yarmouth South Town	1

1954	4
Ipswich	2
Colchester	1
Yarmouth South Town	1

J71 68230-68316 0-6-0T NER Worsdell

1948	81
York	15
West Hartlepool	12
Gateshead	10
Darlington	8
Hull Dairycoates	8
Heaton	7
Middlesbrough	4
West Auckland	4
Borough Gardens	3
Normanton	3
Selby	2
Tyne Dock	2
Blaydon	1
Hull Botanic Gardens	1
Stockton on Tees	1

1951	76
West Hartlepool	12
York	12
Heaton	10
Darlington	9
Hull Dairycoates	8
Gateshead	5
Middlesbrough	4
West Auckland	4
Borough Gardens	3
Normanton	3
Tyne Dock	2
Blaydon	1
Selby	1
Stockton on Tees	1
Tweedmouth	1

1954	64
West Hartlepool	10
York	10
Darlington	7
Heaton	7
Hull Dairycoates	6
Gateshead	5
Middlesbrough	4
Borough Gardens	3
Normanton	3
Blaydon	2
Tyne Dock	2
West Auckland	2
Hexham	1
Hull Springhead	1
Stockton on Tees	1

1957	39
Gateshead	5
Hull Dairycoates	5
Heaton	4
Middlesbrough	4
West Hartlepool	4
Darlington	3
West Auckland	3
York	3
Borough Gardens	2
Tyne Dock	2
Blaydon	1
Normanton	1
Selby	1
Stockton on Tees	1

1960	14
Thornaby	3
West Auckland	3
Hull Dairycoates	2
West Hartlepool	2
Gateshead	1
Normanton	1
Tyne Dock	1
York	1

Right: NER Worsdell 'J71' class 0-6-0T No 68279 at Darlington on 17 May 1952. *R. E. Vincent*

J72 68670-68754, 69001-69028, 58-59 0-6-0T NER & BR Worsdell

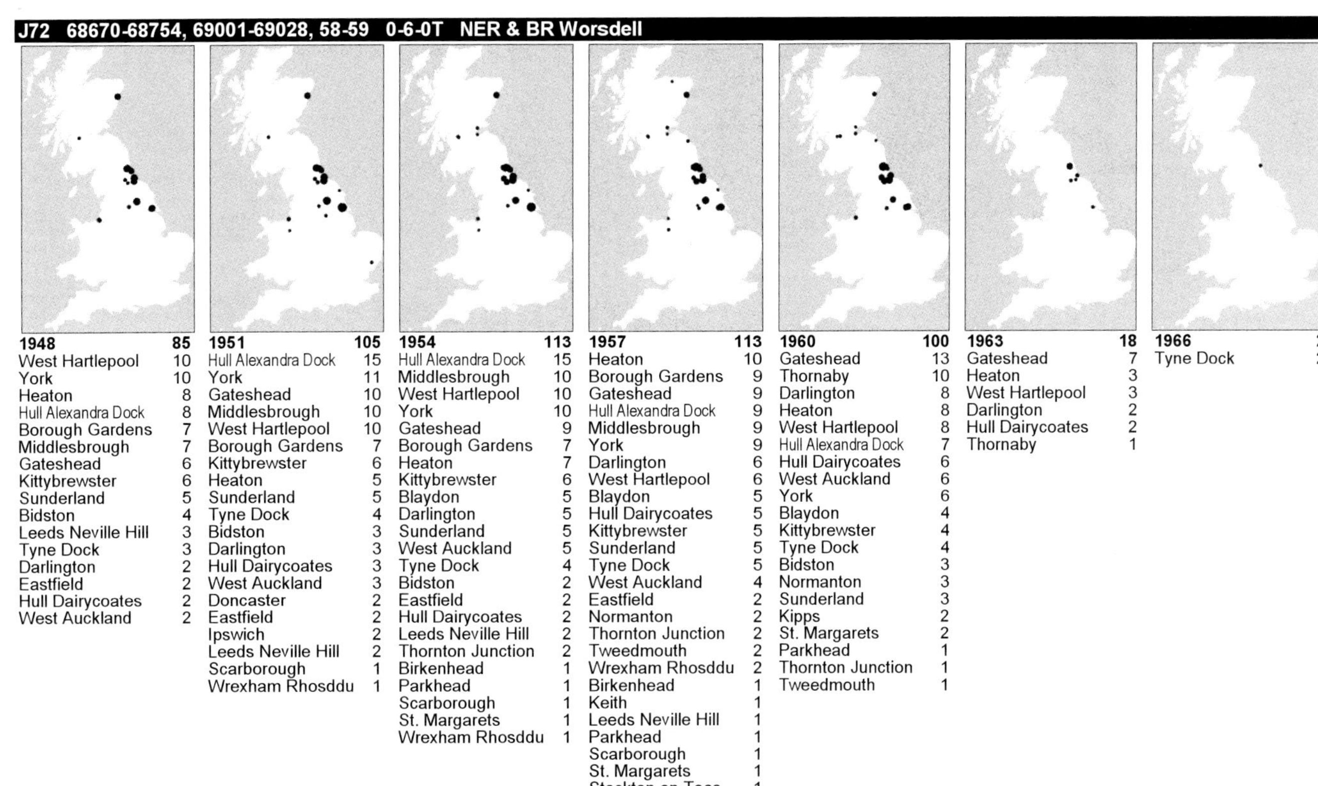

1948	85
West Hartlepool	10
York	10
Heaton	8
Hull Alexandra Dock	8
Borough Gardens	7
Middlesbrough	7
Gateshead	6
Kittybrewster	6
Sunderland	5
Bidston	4
Leeds Neville Hill	3
Tyne Dock	3
Darlington	2
Eastfield	2
Hull Dairycoates	2
West Auckland	2

1951	105
Hull Alexandra Dock	15
York	11
Gateshead	10
Middlesbrough	10
West Hartlepool	10
Borough Gardens	7
Kittybrewster	6
Heaton	5
Sunderland	5
Tyne Dock	4
Bidston	3
Darlington	3
Hull Dairycoates	3
West Auckland	3
Doncaster	2
Eastfield	2
Ipswich	2
Leeds Neville Hill	2
Scarborough	1
Wrexham Rhosddu	1

1954	113
Hull Alexandra Dock	15
Middlesbrough	10
West Hartlepool	10
York	10
Gateshead	9
Borough Gardens	7
Heaton	7
Kittybrewster	6
Blaydon	5
Darlington	5
Sunderland	5
West Auckland	5
Tyne Dock	4
Bidston	2
Eastfield	2
Hull Dairycoates	2
Leeds Neville Hill	2
Thornton Junction	2
Birkenhead	1
Parkhead	1
Scarborough	1
St. Margarets	1
Wrexham Rhosddu	1

1957	113
Heaton	10
Borough Gardens	9
Gateshead	9
Hull Alexandra Dock	9
Middlesbrough	9
York	9
Darlington	6
West Hartlepool	6
Blaydon	5
Hull Dairycoates	5
Kittybrewster	5
Sunderland	5
Tyne Dock	5
West Auckland	4
Eastfield	2
Normanton	2
Thornton Junction	2
Tweedmouth	2
Wrexham Rhosddu	2
Birkenhead	1
Keith	1
Leeds Neville Hill	1
Parkhead	1
Scarborough	1
St. Margarets	1
Stockton on Tees	1

1960	100
Gateshead	13
Thornaby	10
Darlington	8
Heaton	8
West Hartlepool	8
Hull Alexandra Dock	7
Hull Dairycoates	6
West Auckland	6
York	6
Blaydon	4
Kittybrewster	4
Tyne Dock	4
Bidston	3
Normanton	3
Sunderland	3
Kipps	2
St. Margarets	2
Parkhead	1
Thornton Junction	1
Tweedmouth	1

1963	18
Gateshead	7
Heaton	3
West Hartlepool	3
Darlington	2
Hull Dairycoates	2
Thornaby	1

1966	2
Tyne Dock	2

J73 68355-68364 0-6-0T NER Worsdell

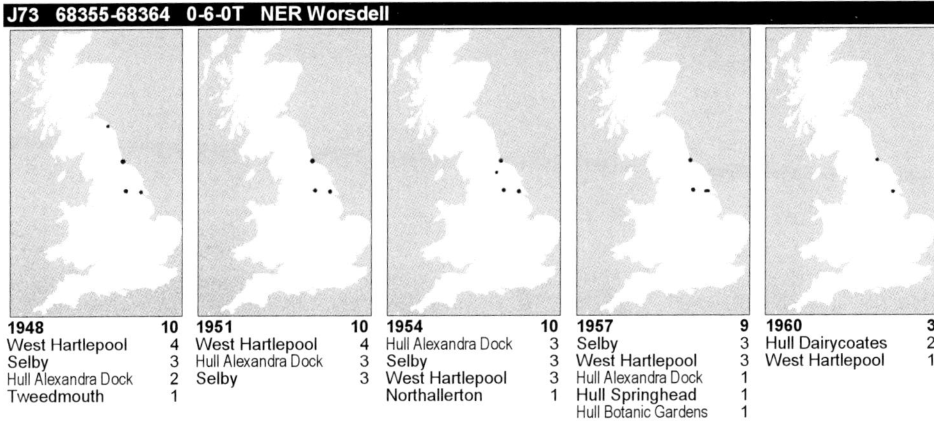

1948	10
West Hartlepool	4
Selby	3
Hull Alexandra Dock	2
Tweedmouth	1

1951	10
West Hartlepool	4
Hull Alexandra Dock	3
Selby	3

1954	10
Hull Alexandra Dock	3
Selby	3
West Hartlepool	3
Northallerton	1

1957	9
Selby	3
West Hartlepool	3
Hull Alexandra Dock	1
Hull Springhead	1
Hull Botanic Gardens	1

1960	3
Hull Dairycoates	2
West Hartlepool	1

J75 68365 0-6-0T H&BR

1948	1
Walton on the Hill	1

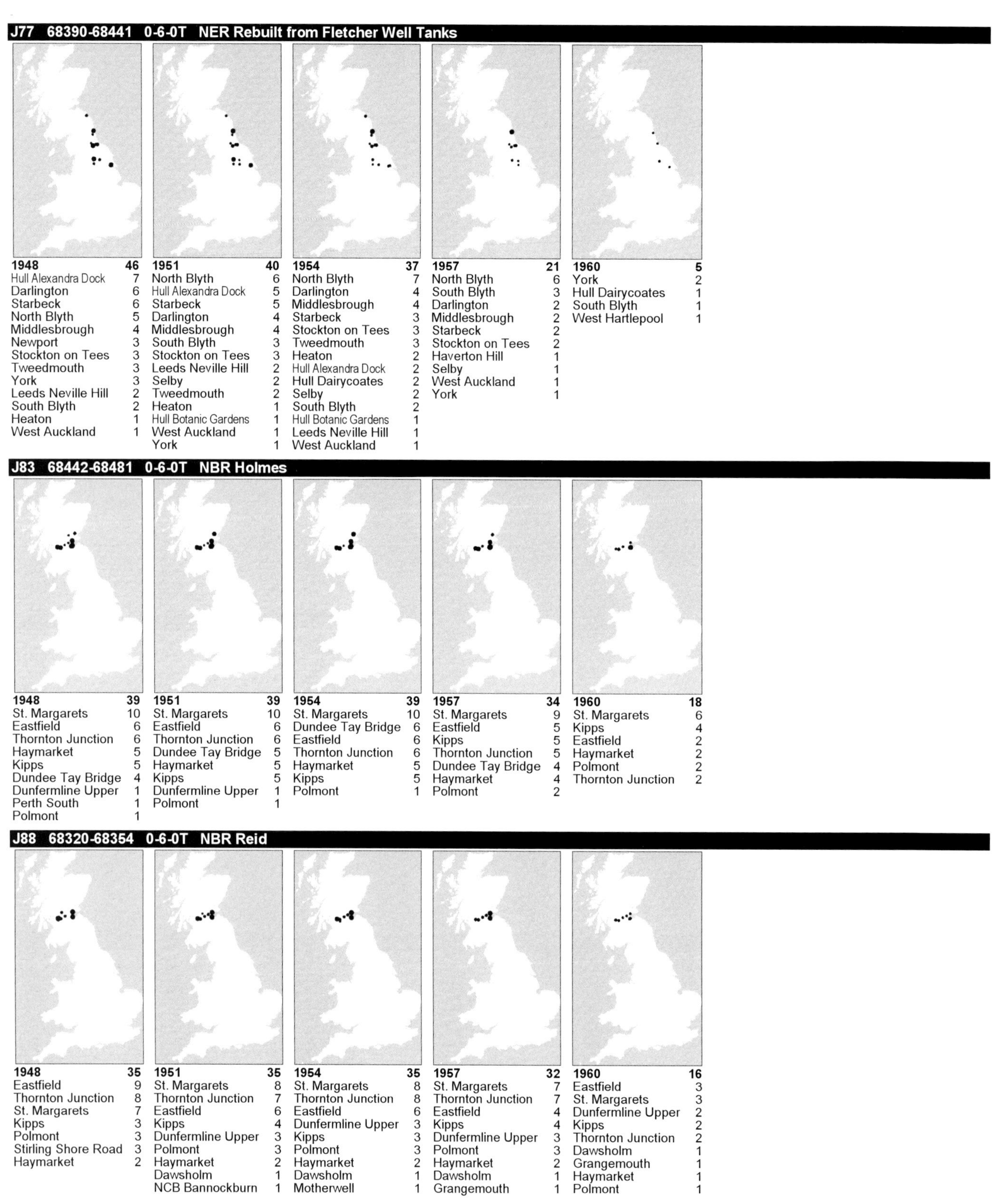

J77 68390-68441 0-6-0T NER Rebuilt from Fletcher Well Tanks

1948	46	1951	40	1954	37	1957	21	1960	5
Hull Alexandra Dock	7	North Blyth	6	North Blyth	7	North Blyth	6	York	2
Darlington	6	Hull Alexandra Dock	5	Darlington	4	South Blyth	3	Hull Dairycoates	1
Starbeck	6	Starbeck	5	Middlesbrough	4	Darlington	2	South Blyth	1
North Blyth	5	Darlington	4	Starbeck	3	Middlesbrough	2	West Hartlepool	1
Middlesbrough	4	Middlesbrough	4	Stockton on Tees	3	Starbeck	2		
Newport	3	South Blyth	3	Tweedmouth	3	Stockton on Tees	2		
Stockton on Tees	3	Stockton on Tees	3	Heaton	2	Haverton Hill	1		
Tweedmouth	3	Leeds Neville Hill	2	Hull Alexandra Dock	2	Selby	1		
York	3	Selby	2	Hull Dairycoates	2	West Auckland	1		
Leeds Neville Hill	2	Tweedmouth	2	Selby	2	York	1		
South Blyth	2	Heaton	1	South Blyth	2				
Heaton	1	Hull Botanic Gardens	1	Hull Botanic Gardens	1				
West Auckland	1	West Auckland	1	Leeds Neville Hill	1				
		York	1	West Auckland	1				

J83 68442-68481 0-6-0T NBR Holmes

1948	39	1951	39	1954	39	1957	34	1960	18
St. Margarets	10	St. Margarets	10	St. Margarets	10	St. Margarets	9	St. Margarets	6
Eastfield	6	Eastfield	6	Dundee Tay Bridge	6	Eastfield	5	Kipps	4
Thornton Junction	6	Thornton Junction	6	Eastfield	6	Kipps	5	Eastfield	2
Haymarket	5	Dundee Tay Bridge	5	Thornton Junction	6	Thornton Junction	5	Haymarket	2
Kipps	5	Haymarket	5	Haymarket	5	Dundee Tay Bridge	4	Polmont	2
Dundee Tay Bridge	4	Kipps	5	Kipps	5	Haymarket	4	Thornton Junction	2
Dunfermline Upper	1	Dunfermline Upper	1	Polmont	1	Polmont	2		
Perth South	1	Polmont	1						
Polmont	1								

J88 68320-68354 0-6-0T NBR Reid

1948	35	1951	35	1954	35	1957	32	1960	16
Eastfield	9	St. Margarets	8	St. Margarets	8	St. Margarets	7	Eastfield	3
Thornton Junction	8	Thornton Junction	7	Thornton Junction	8	Thornton Junction	7	St. Margarets	3
St. Margarets	7	Eastfield	6	Eastfield	6	Eastfield	4	Dunfermline Upper	2
Kipps	3	Kipps	4	Dunfermline Upper	3	Kipps	4	Kipps	2
Polmont	3	Dunfermline Upper	3	Kipps	3	Dunfermline Upper	3	Thornton Junction	2
Stirling Shore Road	3	Polmont	3	Polmont	3	Polmont	3	Dawsholm	1
Haymarket	2	Haymarket	2	Haymarket	2	Haymarket	2	Grangemouth	1
		Dawsholm	1	Dawsholm	1	Dawsholm	1	Haymarket	1
		NCB Bannockburn	1	Motherwell	1	Grangemouth	1	Polmont	1

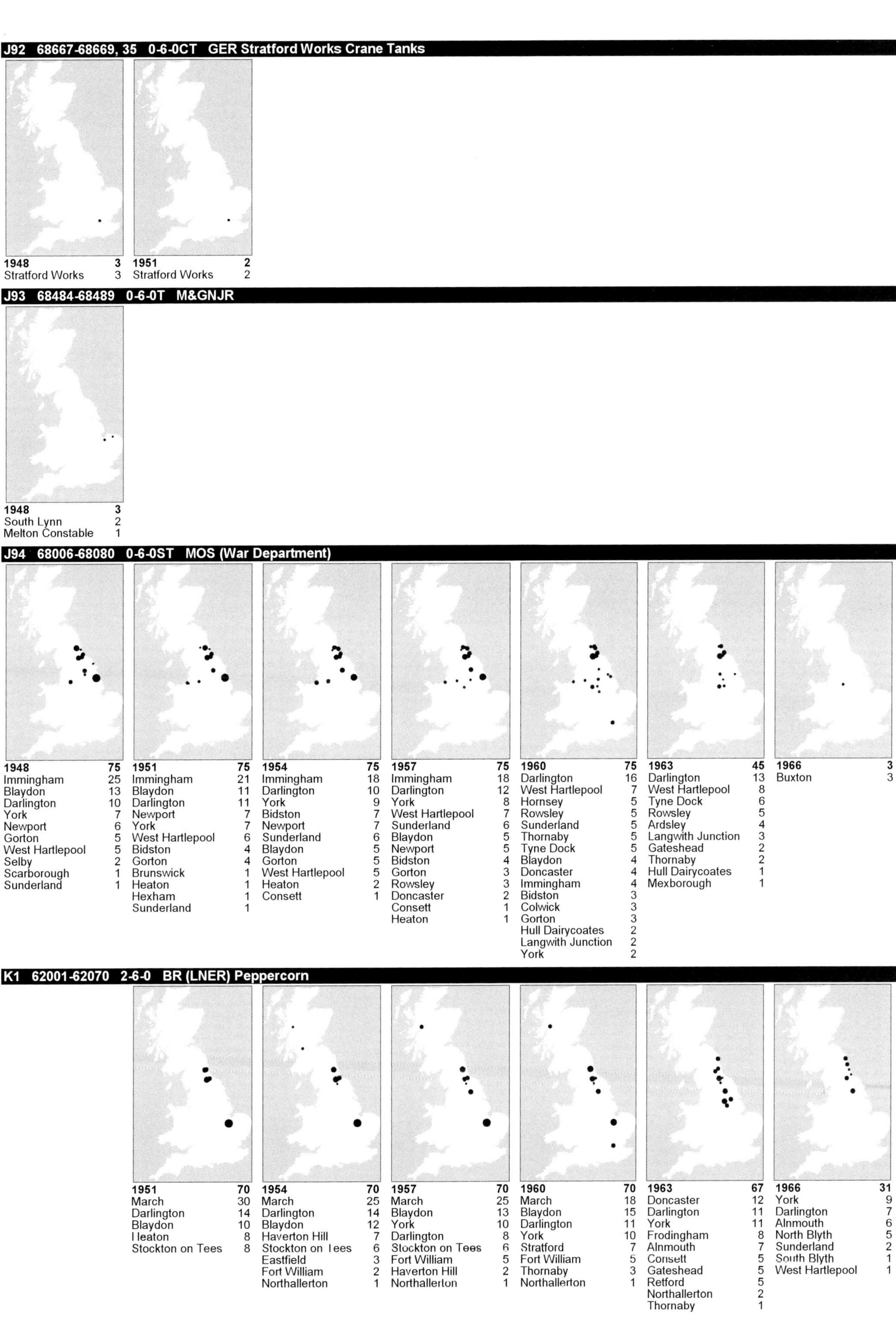

J92 68667-68669, 35 0-6-0CT GER Stratford Works Crane Tanks

1948	3
Stratford Works	3

1951	2
Stratford Works	2

J93 68484-68489 0-6-0T M&GNJR

1948	3
South Lynn	2
Melton Constable	1

J94 68006-68080 0-6-0ST MOS (War Department)

1948	75
Immingham	25
Blaydon	13
Darlington	10
York	7
Newport	6
Gorton	5
West Hartlepool	5
Selby	2
Scarborough	1
Sunderland	1

1951	75
Immingham	21
Blaydon	11
Darlington	11
Newport	7
York	7
West Hartlepool	6
Bidston	4
Gorton	4
Brunswick	1
Heaton	1
Hexham	1
Sunderland	1

1954	75
Immingham	18
Darlington	10
York	9
Bidston	7
Newport	7
Sunderland	6
Blaydon	5
Gorton	5
West Hartlepool	5
Heaton	2
Consett	1

1957	75
Immingham	18
Darlington	12
York	8
West Hartlepool	7
Sunderland	6
Blaydon	5
Newport	5
Bidston	4
Gorton	3
Rowsley	3
Doncaster	2
Consett	1
Heaton	1

1960	75
Darlington	16
West Hartlepool	7
Hornsey	5
Rowsley	5
Sunderland	5
Thornaby	5
Tyne Dock	5
Blaydon	4
Doncaster	4
Immingham	4
Bidston	3
Colwick	3
Gorton	3
Hull Dairycoates	2
Langwith Junction	2
York	2

1963	45
Darlington	13
West Hartlepool	8
Tyne Dock	6
Rowsley	5
Ardsley	4
Langwith Junction	3
Gateshead	2
Thornaby	2
Hull Dairycoates	1
Mexborough	1

1966	3
Buxton	3

K1 62001-62070 2-6-0 BR (LNER) Peppercorn

1951	70
March	30
Darlington	14
Blaydon	10
Heaton	8
Stockton on Tees	8

1954	70
March	25
Darlington	14
Blaydon	12
Haverton Hill	7
Stockton on Tees	6
Eastfield	3
Fort William	2
Northallerton	1

1957	70
March	25
Blaydon	13
York	10
Darlington	8
Stockton on Tees	6
Fort William	5
Haverton Hill	2
Northallerton	1

1960	70
March	18
Blaydon	15
Darlington	11
York	10
Stratford	7
Fort William	5
Thornaby	3
Northallerton	1

1963	67
Doncaster	12
Darlington	11
York	11
Frodingham	8
Alnmouth	7
Consett	5
Gateshead	5
Retford	5
Northallerton	2
Thornaby	1

1966	31
York	9
Darlington	7
Alnmouth	6
North Blyth	5
Sunderland	2
South Blyth	1
West Hartlepool	1

K1/1 61997 2-6-0 LNER Thompson K4 rebuilt as K1 prototype

1948	1	1951	1	1954	1	1957	1	1960	1
New England	1	Eastfield	1	Eastfield	1	Fort William	1	Fort William	1

K2 61720-61794 2-6-0 GNR Gresley

1948	75	1951	75	1954	75	1957	70	1960	24
Stratford	17	Stratford	15	Colwick	19	Boston	14	Immingham	7
Colwick	15	Colwick	12	Eastfield	11	Colwick	14	Sheffield Darnall	4
Eastfield	13	Eastfield	12	Boston	10	Eastfield	13	Eastfield	3
Immingham	8	Boston	9	Lincoln	8	Sheffield Darnall	7	Keith	3
Fort William	7	Fort William	7	Immingham	7	Keith	5	Fort William	2
Boston	6	Immingham	6	Fort William	5	Lincoln	4	New England	2
South Lynn	4	South Lynn	6	Parkhead	5	Parkhead	4	Boston	1
Colchester	2	New England	4	Kittybrewster	4	Dunfermline Upper	3	Kittybrewster	1
New England	2	Norwich Thorpe	2	Dunfermline Upper	3	Immingham	3	Parkhead	1
Parkhead	1	Grantham	1	Thornton Junction	2	Fort William	1		
		Parkhead	1	Aberdeen Ferryhill	1	Kittybrewster	1		
						Thornton Junction	1		

K3 61800-61992 2-6-0 GNR Gresley 3 cylinder

1948	192	1951	192	1954	192	1957	192	1960	180
New England	36	St. Margarets	24	March	43	Hull Dairycoates	25	Hull Dairycoates	24
March	23	Hull Dairycoates	21	Hull Dairycoates	24	St. Margarets	23	March	20
Hull Dairycoates	21	Gorton	20	St. Margarets	23	Stratford	18	Colwick	15
St. Margarets	20	March	18	Gorton	18	March	16	Doncaster	15
Immingham	11	New England	16	Stratford	18	Immingham	15	Norwich Thorpe	14
Colwick	10	Heaton	15	Immingham	14	Lincoln	13	Heaton	12
Heaton	10	Immingham	15	Tweedmouth	9	Colwick	12	Lincoln	11
Lincoln	10	Stratford	13	Carlisle Canal	8	Norwich Thorpe	12	St. Margarets	10
Norwich Thorpe	10	Norwich Thorpe	10	Heaton	8	Heaton	9	Woodford Halse	10
Gateshead	9	Colwick	9	Norwich Thorpe	8	Carlisle Canal	8	Immingham	8
Annesley	7	Lincoln	8	Lincoln	7	Tweedmouth	7	Tweedmouth	8
Carlisle Canal	7	Annesley	7	Lowestoft	7	Gorton	6	Parkeston	6
Woodford Halse	7	Carlisle Canal	7	Annesley	3	Lowestoft	5	Cambridge	5
Doncaster	6	Lowestoft	5	Colwick	2	Woodford Halse	5	New England	5
Lowestoft	5	Doncaster	4			Doncaster	4	Ardsley	4
						Sheffield Darnall	4	Sheffield Darnall	4
						Annesley	3	Carlisle Canal	3
						Mexborough	3	Gorton	2
						New England	3	Lowestoft	2
						Boston	1	Stratford	2

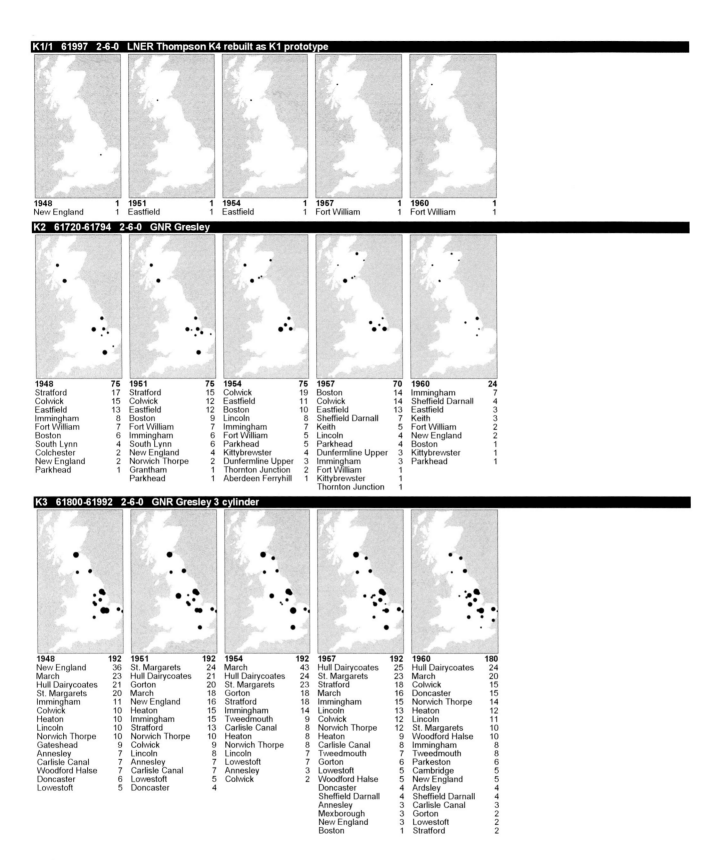

K4 61993-61998 2-6-0 LNER Gresley

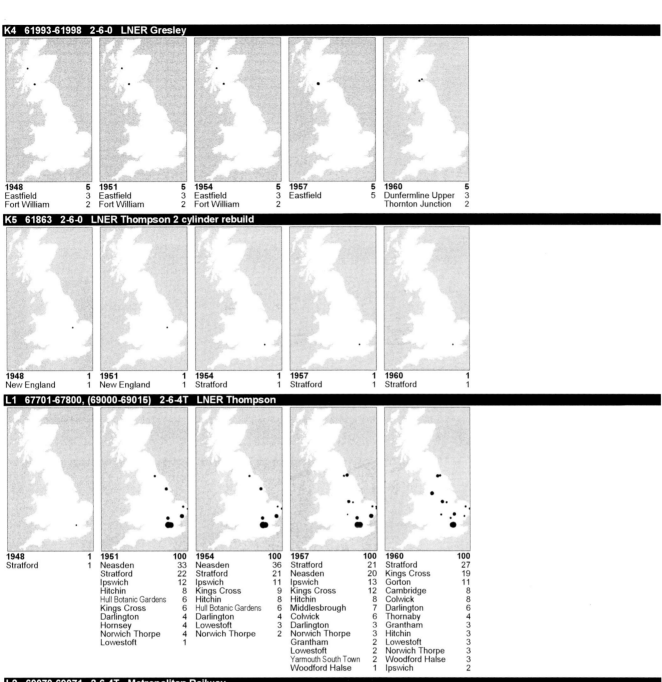

1948	5	1951	5	1954	5	1957	5	1960	5
Eastfield	3	Eastfield	3	Eastfield	3	Eastfield	5	Dunfermline Upper	3
Fort William	2	Fort William	2	Fort William	2			Thornton Junction	2

K5 61863 2-6-0 LNER Thompson 2 cylinder rebuild

1948	1	1951	1	1954	1	1957	1	1960	1
New England	1	New England	1	Stratford	1	Stratford	1	Stratford	1

L1 67701-67800, (69000-69015) 2-6-4T LNER Thompson

1948	1	1951	100	1954	100	1957	100	1960	100
Stratford	1	Neasden	33	Neasden	36	Stratford	21	Stratford	27
		Stratford	22	Stratford	21	Neasden	20	Kings Cross	19
		Ipswich	12	Ipswich	11	Ipswich	13	Gorton	11
		Hitchin	8	Kings Cross	9	Kings Cross	12	Cambridge	8
		Hull Botanic Gardens	6	Hitchin	8	Hitchin	8	Colwick	8
		Kings Cross	6	Hull Botanic Gardens	6	Middlesbrough	7	Darlington	6
		Darlington	4	Darlington	4	Colwick	6	Thornaby	4
		Hornsey	4	Lowestoft	3	Darlington	3	Grantham	3
		Norwich Thorpe	4	Norwich Thorpe	2	Norwich Thorpe	3	Hitchin	3
		Lowestoft	1			Grantham	2	Lowestoft	3
						Lowestoft	2	Norwich Thorpe	3
						Yarmouth South Town	2	Woodford Halse	3
						Woodford Halse	1	Ipswich	2

L2 69070-69071 2-6-4T Metropolitan Railway

1948	2
Neasden	2

GCR Robinson 'L3' class 2-6-4T No 69050 at its home shed 38E Woodford Halse on 2 August 1952 (see p408). *P H Wells*

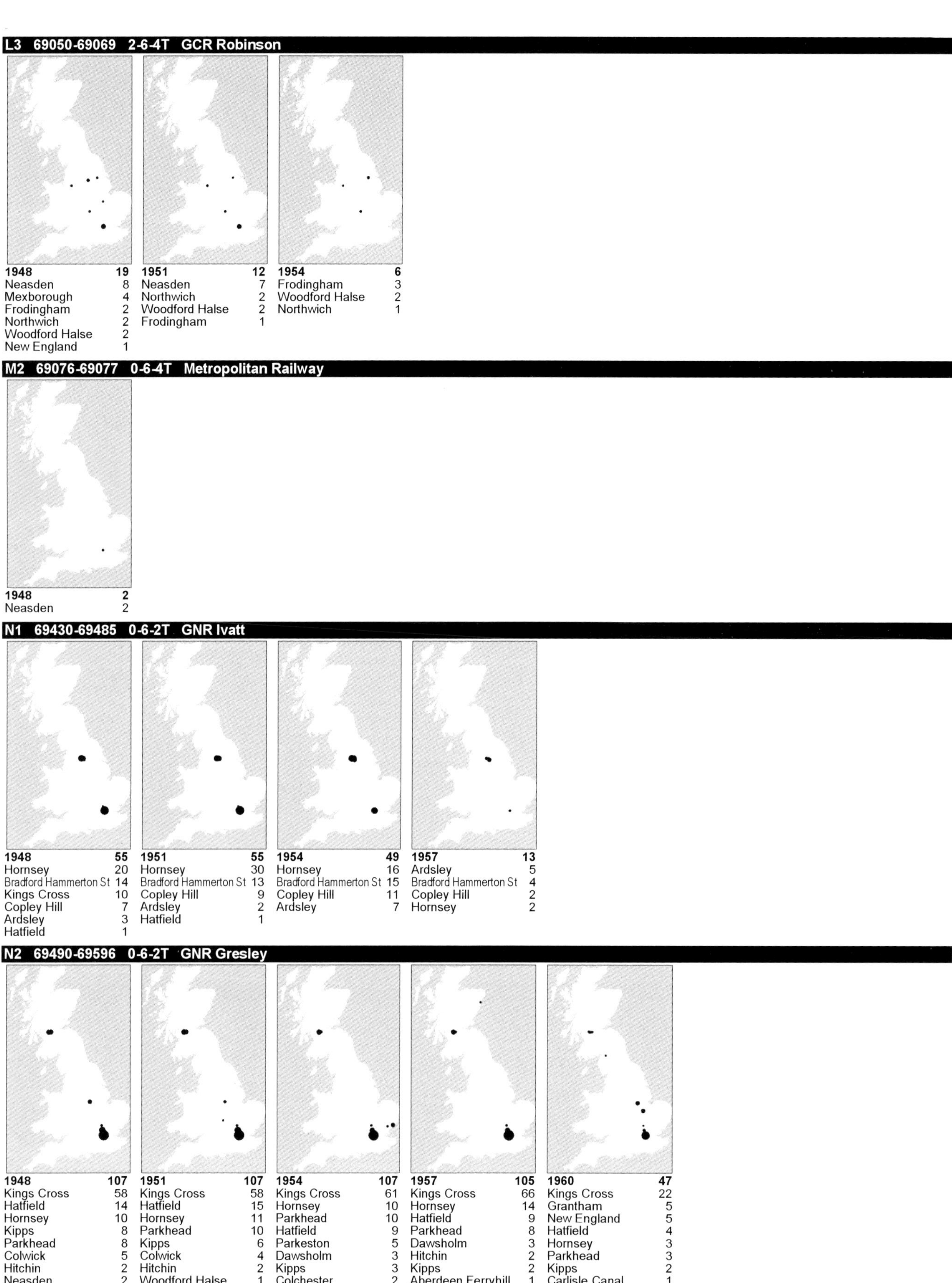

L3 69050-69069 2-6-4T GCR Robinson

1948	19
Neasden	8
Mexborough	4
Frodingham	2
Northwich	2
Woodford Halse	2
New England	1

1951	12
Neasden	7
Northwich	2
Woodford Halse	2
Frodingham	1

1954	6
Frodingham	3
Woodford Halse	2
Northwich	1

M2 69076-69077 0-6-4T Metropolitan Railway

1948	2
Neasden	2

N1 69430-69485 0-6-2T GNR Ivatt

1948	55
Hornsey	20
Bradford Hammerton St	14
Kings Cross	10
Copley Hill	7
Ardsley	3
Hatfield	1

1951	55
Hornsey	30
Bradford Hammerton St	13
Copley Hill	9
Ardsley	2
Hatfield	1

1954	49
Hornsey	16
Bradford Hammerton St	15
Copley Hill	11
Ardsley	7

1957	13
Ardsley	5
Bradford Hammerton St	4
Copley Hill	2
Hornsey	2

N2 69490-69596 0-6-2T GNR Gresley

1948	107
Kings Cross	58
Hatfield	14
Hornsey	10
Kipps	8
Parkhead	8
Colwick	5
Hitchin	2
Neasden	2

1951	107
Kings Cross	58
Hatfield	15
Hornsey	11
Parkhead	10
Kipps	6
Colwick	4
Hitchin	2
Woodford Halse	1

1954	107
Kings Cross	61
Hornsey	10
Parkhead	10
Hatfield	9
Parkeston	5
Dawsholm	3
Kipps	3
Colchester	2
Hitchin	2
Stratford	2

1957	105
Kings Cross	66
Hornsey	14
Hatfield	9
Parkhead	8
Dawsholm	3
Hitchin	2
Kipps	2
Aberdeen Ferryhill	1

1960	47
Kings Cross	22
Grantham	5
New England	5
Hatfield	4
Hornsey	3
Parkhead	3
Kipps	2
Carlisle Canal	1
Dawsholm	1
Hitchin	1

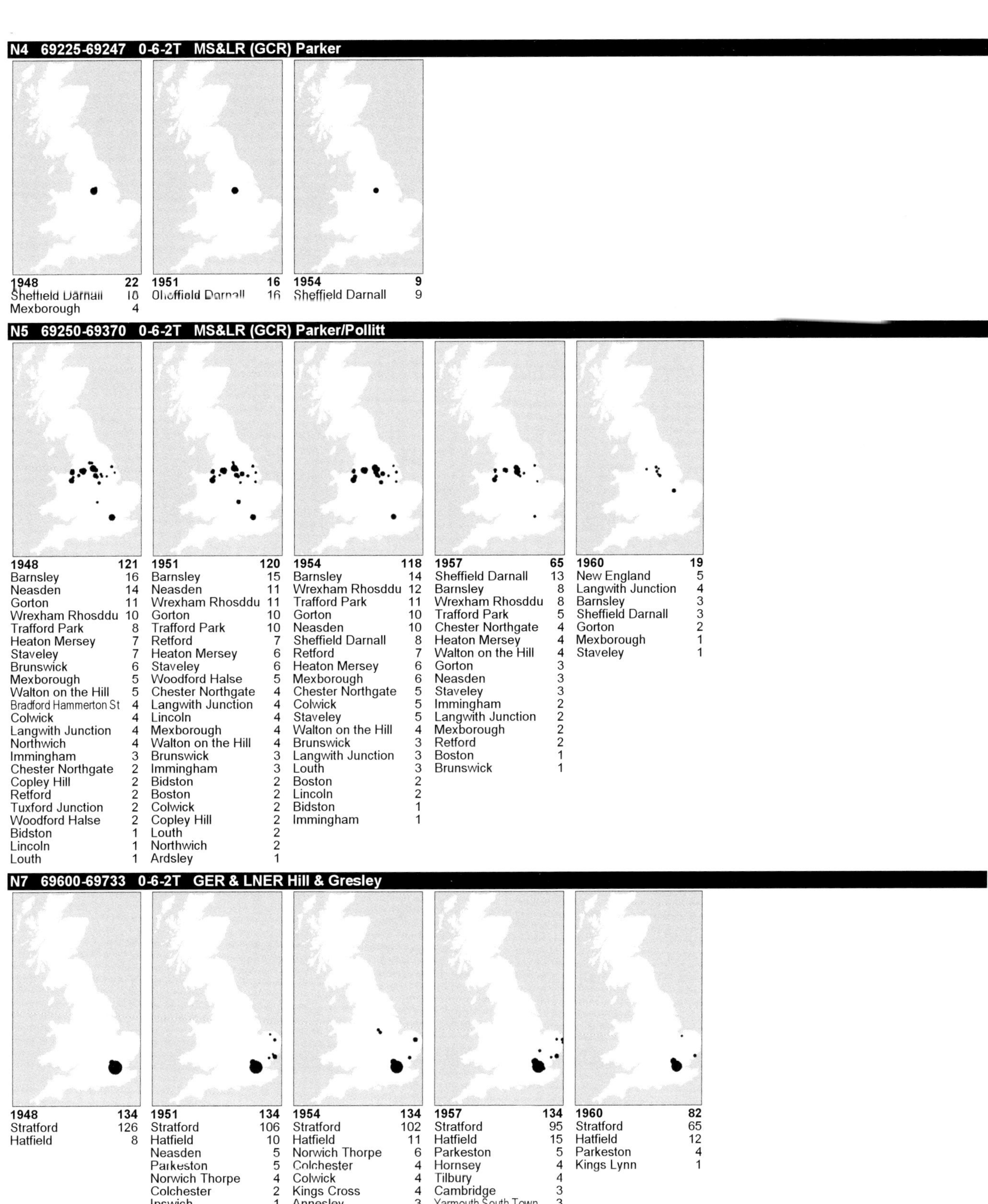

N4 69225-69247 0-6-2T MS&LR (GCR) Parker

1948	22
Sheffield Darnall	18
Mexborough	4

1951	16
Sheffield Darnall	16

1954	9
Sheffield Darnall	9

N5 69250-69370 0-6-2T MS&LR (GCR) Parker/Pollitt

1948	121
Barnsley	16
Neasden	14
Gorton	11
Wrexham Rhosddu	10
Trafford Park	8
Heaton Mersey	7
Staveley	7
Brunswick	6
Mexborough	5
Walton on the Hill	5
Bradford Hammerton St	4
Colwick	4
Langwith Junction	4
Northwich	4
Immingham	3
Chester Northgate	2
Copley Hill	2
Retford	2
Tuxford Junction	2
Woodford Halse	2
Bidston	1
Lincoln	1
Louth	1

1951	120
Barnsley	15
Neasden	11
Wrexham Rhosddu	11
Gorton	10
Trafford Park	10
Retford	7
Heaton Mersey	6
Staveley	6
Woodford Halse	5
Chester Northgate	4
Langwith Junction	4
Lincoln	4
Mexborough	4
Walton on the Hill	4
Brunswick	3
Immingham	3
Bidston	2
Boston	2
Colwick	2
Copley Hill	2
Louth	2
Northwich	2
Ardsley	1

1954	118
Barnsley	14
Wrexham Rhosddu	12
Trafford Park	11
Gorton	10
Neasden	10
Sheffield Darnall	8
Retford	7
Heaton Mersey	6
Mexborough	6
Chester Northgate	5
Colwick	5
Staveley	5
Walton on the Hill	4
Brunswick	3
Langwith Junction	3
Louth	3
Boston	2
Lincoln	2
Bidston	1
Immingham	1

1957	65
Sheffield Darnall	13
Barnsley	8
Wrexham Rhosddu	8
Trafford Park	5
Chester Northgate	4
Heaton Mersey	4
Walton on the Hill	4
Gorton	3
Neasden	3
Staveley	3
Immingham	2
Langwith Junction	2
Mexborough	2
Retford	2
Boston	1
Brunswick	1

1960	19
New England	5
Langwith Junction	4
Barnsley	3
Sheffield Darnall	3
Gorton	2
Mexborough	1
Staveley	1

N7 69600-69733 0-6-2T GER & LNER Hill & Gresley

1948	134
Stratford	126
Hatfield	8

1951	134
Stratford	106
Hatfield	10
Neasden	5
Parkeston	5
Norwich Thorpe	4
Colchester	2
Ipswich	1
Melton Constable	1

1954	134
Stratford	102
Hatfield	11
Norwich Thorpe	6
Colchester	4
Colwick	4
Kings Cross	4
Annesley	3

1957	134
Stratford	95
Hatfield	15
Parkeston	5
Hornsey	4
Tilbury	4
Cambridge	3
Yarmouth South Town	3
Colchester	2
Norwich Thorpe	2
Lowestoft	1

1960	82
Stratford	65
Hatfield	12
Parkeston	4
Kings Lynn	1

N8 69371-69401 0-6-2T NER Worsdell

1948	30	1951	19	1954	8
Hull Dairycoates	20	Hull Dairycoates	11	Hull Dairycoates	3
Heaton	5	Heaton	3	Consett	2
Consett	2	Consett	2	Bridlington	1
Tyne Dock	2	Tyne Dock	2	Heaton	1
Sunderland	1	Borough Gardens	1	Sunderland	1

N9 69410-69429 0-6-2T NER Worsdell

1948	17	1951	6	1954	3
Sunderland	6	Sunderland	4	Tyne Dock	3
Darlington	3	Darlington	1		
Consett	2	Tyne Dock	1		
Tyne Dock	2				
Haverton Hill	1				
Northallerton	1				
Pelton Level	1				
West Auckland	1				

N10 69090-69109 0-6-2T NER Worsdell

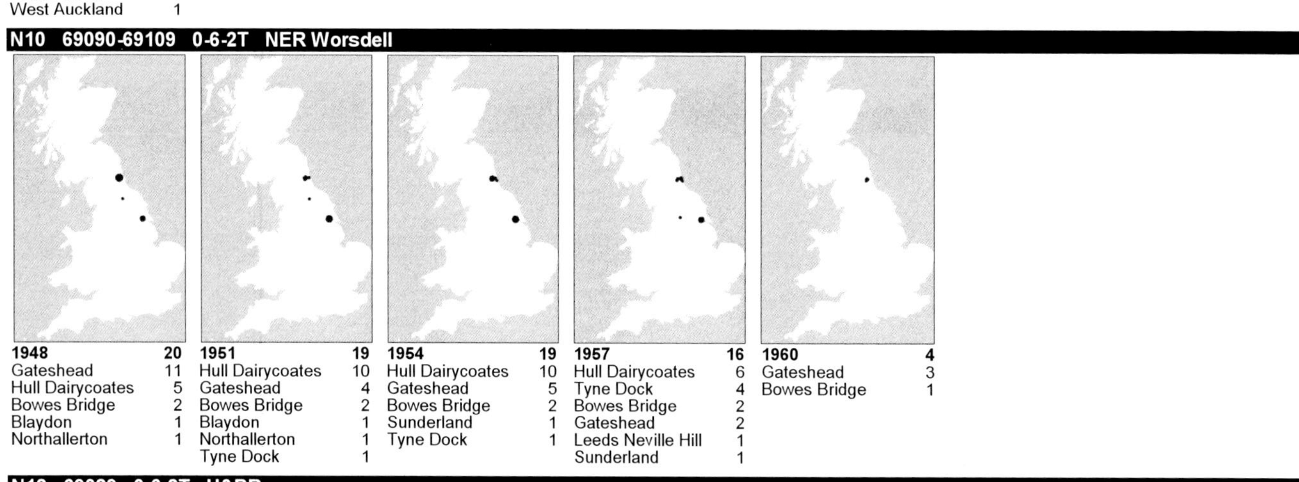

1948	20	1951	19	1954	19	1957	16	1960	4
Gateshead	11	Hull Dairycoates	10	Hull Dairycoates	10	Hull Dairycoates	6	Gateshead	3
Hull Dairycoates	5	Gateshead	4	Gateshead	5	Tyne Dock	4	Bowes Bridge	1
Bowes Bridge	2	Bowes Bridge	2	Bowes Bridge	2	Bowes Bridge	2		
Blaydon	1	Blaydon	1	Sunderland	1	Gateshead	2		
Northallerton	1	Northallerton	1	Tyne Dock	1	Leeds Neville Hill	1		
		Tyne Dock	1			Sunderland	1		

N12 69089 0-6-2T H&BR

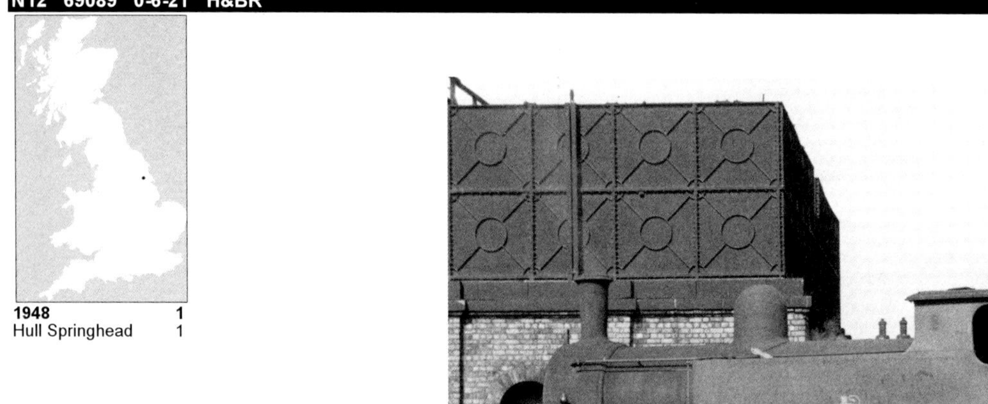

1948	1
Hull Springhead	1

Right: NER Worsdell 'N9' class 0-6-2T No 69427 at Tyne Dock. *Brian Morrison*

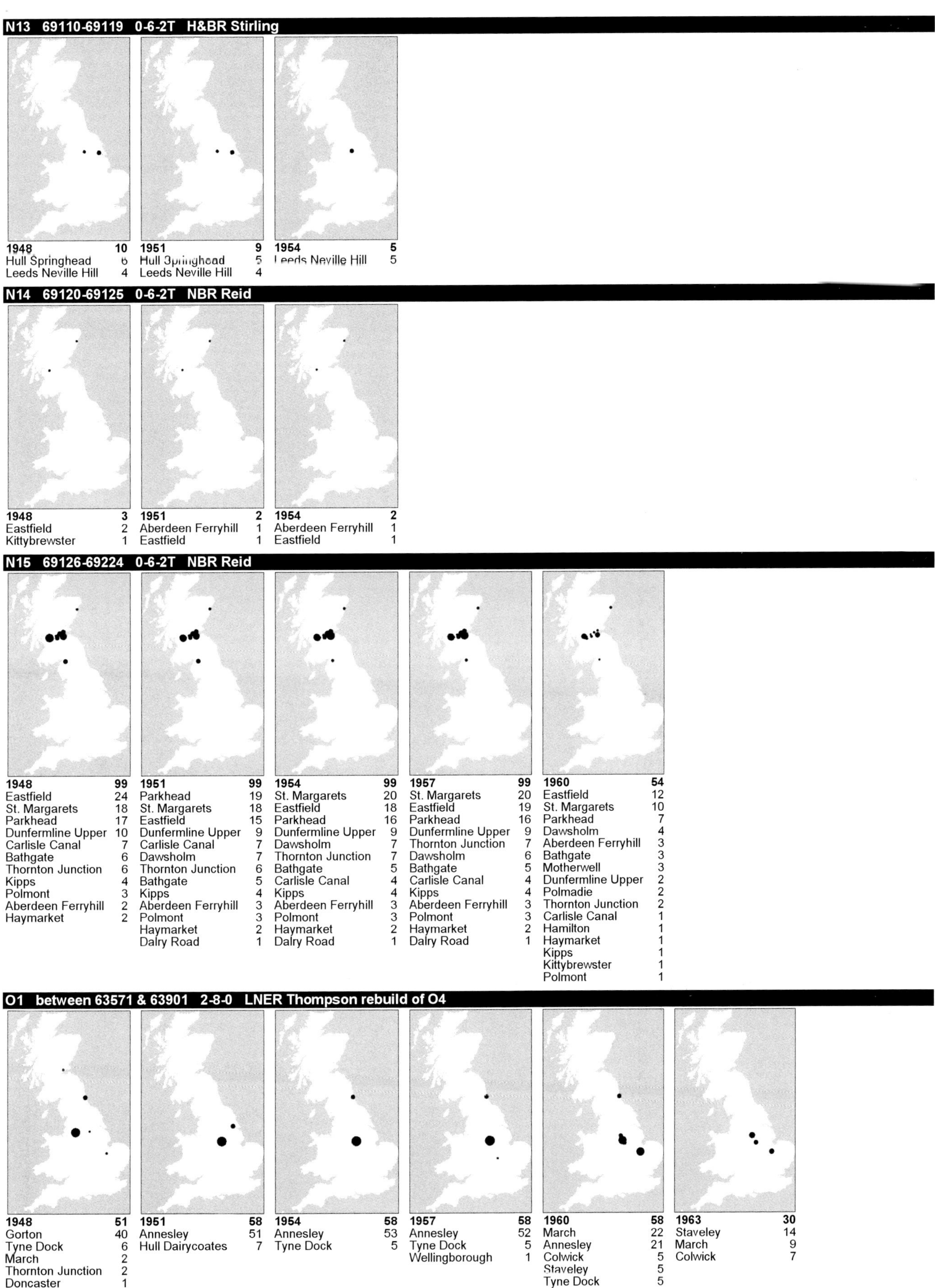

N13 69110-69119 0-6-2T H&BR Stirling

1948	10	1951	9	1954	5
Hull Springhead	6	Hull Springhead	5	Leeds Neville Hill	5
Leeds Neville Hill	4	Leeds Neville Hill	4		

N14 69120-69125 0-6-2T NBR Reid

1948	3	1951	2	1954	2
Eastfield	2	Aberdeen Ferryhill	1	Aberdeen Ferryhill	1
Kittybrewster	1	Eastfield	1	Eastfield	1

N15 69126-69224 0-6-2T NBR Reid

1948	99	1951	99	1954	99	1957	99	1960	54
Eastfield	24	Parkhead	19	St. Margarets	20	St. Margarets	20	Eastfield	12
St. Margarets	18	St. Margarets	18	Eastfield	18	Eastfield	19	St. Margarets	10
Parkhead	17	Eastfield	15	Parkhead	16	Parkhead	16	Parkhead	7
Dunfermline Upper	10	Dunfermline Upper	9	Dunfermline Upper	9	Dunfermline Upper	9	Dawsholm	4
Carlisle Canal	7	Carlisle Canal	7	Dawsholm	7	Thornton Junction	7	Aberdeen Ferryhill	3
Bathgate	6	Dawsholm	7	Thornton Junction	7	Dawsholm	6	Bathgate	3
Thornton Junction	6	Thornton Junction	6	Bathgate	5	Bathgate	5	Motherwell	3
Kipps	4	Bathgate	5	Carlisle Canal	4	Carlisle Canal	4	Dunfermline Upper	2
Polmont	3	Kipps	4	Kipps	4	Kipps	4	Polmadie	2
Aberdeen Ferryhill	2	Aberdeen Ferryhill	3	Aberdeen Ferryhill	3	Aberdeen Ferryhill	3	Thornton Junction	2
Haymarket	2	Polmont	3	Polmont	3	Polmont	3	Carlisle Canal	1
		Haymarket	2	Haymarket	2	Haymarket	2	Hamilton	1
		Dalry Road	1	Dalry Road	1	Dalry Road	1	Haymarket	1
								Kipps	1
								Kittybrewster	1
								Polmont	1

O1 between 63571 & 63901 2-8-0 LNER Thompson rebuild of O4

1948	51	1951	58	1954	58	1957	58	1960	58	1963	30
Gorton	40	Annesley	51	Annesley	53	Annesley	52	March	22	Staveley	14
Tyne Dock	6	Hull Dairycoates	7	Tyne Dock	5	Tyne Dock	5	Annesley	21	March	9
March	2					Wellingborough	1	Colwick	5	Colwick	7
Thornton Junction	2							Staveley	5		
Doncaster	1							Tyne Dock	5		

O2 63921-63987 2-8-0 GNR Gresley 3 cylinder

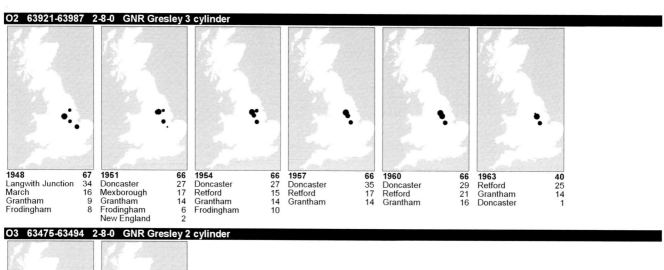

1948	67
Langwith Junction	34
March	16
Grantham	9
Frodingham	8

1951	66
Doncaster	27
Mexborough	17
Grantham	14
Frodingham	6
New England	2

1954	66
Doncaster	27
Retford	15
Grantham	14
Frodingham	10

1957	66
Doncaster	35
Retford	17
Grantham	14

1960	66
Doncaster	29
Retford	21
Grantham	16

1963	40
Retford	25
Grantham	14
Doncaster	1

O3 63475-63494 2-8-0 GNR Gresley 2 cylinder

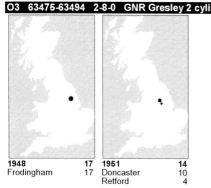

1948	17
Frodingham	17

1951	14
Doncaster	10
Retford	4

O4 63570-63920 2-8-0 GCR & ROD Robinson

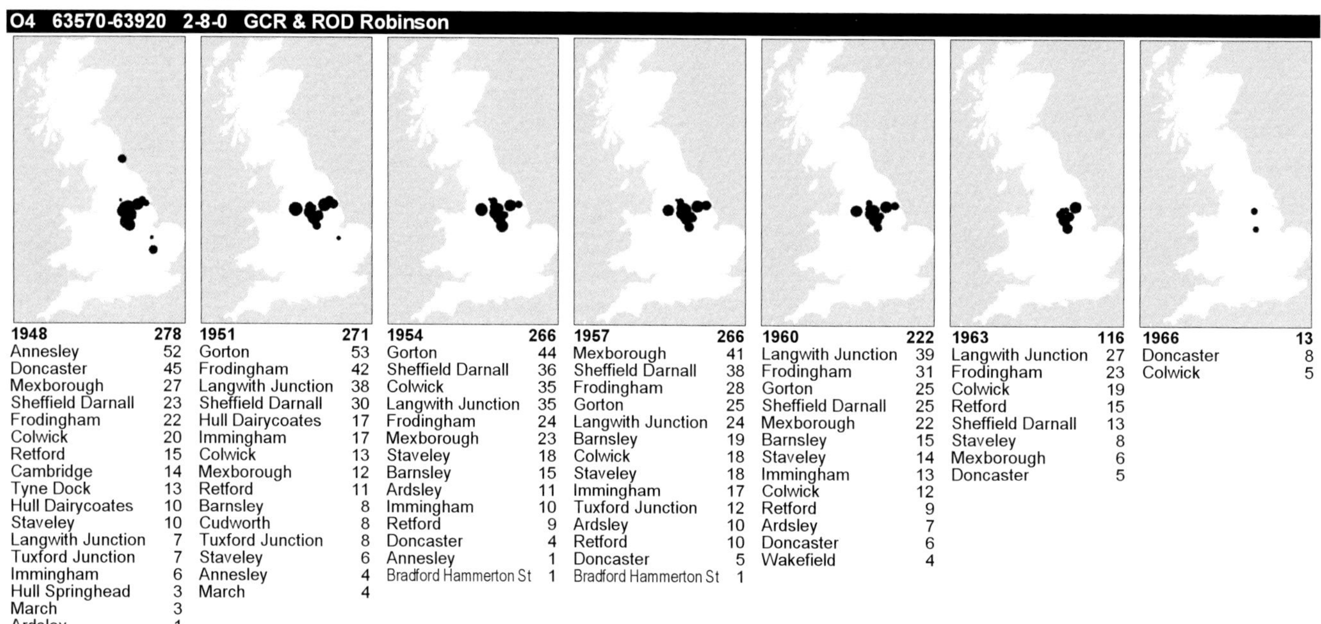

1948	278
Annesley	52
Doncaster	45
Mexborough	27
Sheffield Darnall	23
Frodingham	22
Colwick	20
Retford	15
Cambridge	14
Tyne Dock	13
Hull Dairycoates	10
Staveley	10
Langwith Junction	7
Tuxford Junction	7
Immingham	6
Hull Springhead	3
March	3
Ardsley	1

1951	271
Gorton	53
Frodingham	42
Langwith Junction	38
Sheffield Darnall	30
Hull Dairycoates	17
Immingham	17
Colwick	13
Mexborough	12
Retford	11
Barnsley	8
Cudworth	8
Tuxford Junction	8
Staveley	6
Annesley	4
March	4

1954	266
Gorton	44
Sheffield Darnall	36
Colwick	35
Langwith Junction	35
Frodingham	24
Mexborough	23
Staveley	18
Barnsley	15
Ardsley	11
Immingham	10
Retford	9
Doncaster	4
Annesley	1
Bradford Hammerton St	1

1957	266
Mexborough	41
Sheffield Darnall	38
Frodingham	28
Gorton	25
Langwith Junction	24
Barnsley	19
Colwick	18
Staveley	18
Immingham	17
Tuxford Junction	12
Ardsley	10
Retford	10
Doncaster	5
Bradford Hammerton St	1

1960	222
Langwith Junction	39
Frodingham	31
Gorton	25
Sheffield Darnall	25
Mexborough	22
Barnsley	15
Staveley	14
Immingham	13
Colwick	12
Retford	9
Ardsley	7
Doncaster	6
Wakefield	4

1963	116
Langwith Junction	27
Frodingham	23
Colwick	19
Retford	15
Sheffield Darnall	13
Staveley	8
Mexborough	6
Doncaster	5

1966	13
Doncaster	8
Colwick	5

O7 63000-63199 2-8-0 MOS (WD) Riddles Austerity

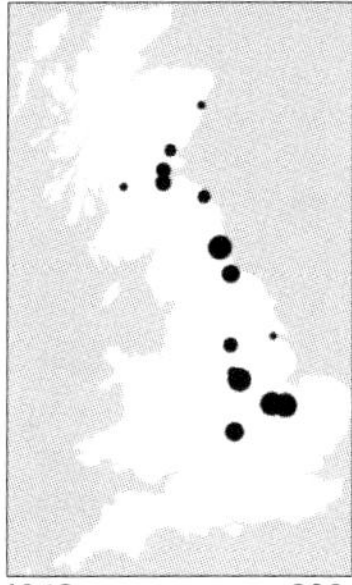

1948	200
March	30
Heaton	28
Colwick	27
New England	26
Woodford Halse	17
Newport	16
St. Margarets	11
Mexborough	10
Thornton Junction	9
Tweedmouth	7
Annesley	6
Dundee Tay Bridge	5
Aberdeen Ferryhill	3
Eastfield	3
Immingham	2

Q1 69925-69937 0-8-0T LNER Thompson rebuild of GCR Q4

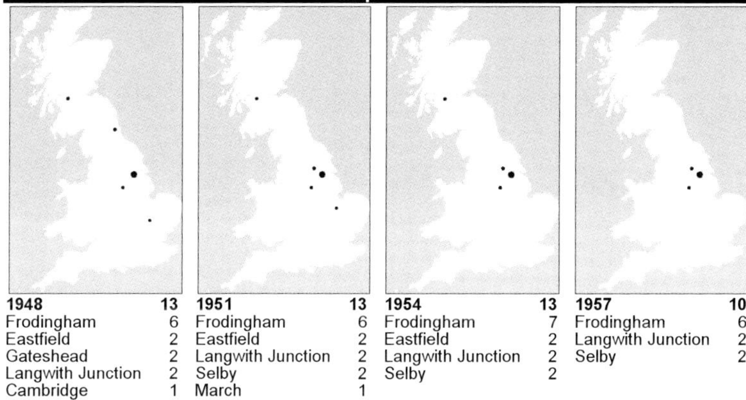

1948	13	1951	13	1954	13	1957	10
Frodingham	6	Frodingham	6	Frodingham	7	Frodingham	6
Eastfield	2	Eastfield	2	Eastfield	2	Langwith Junction	2
Gateshead	2	Langwith Junction	2	Langwith Junction	2	Selby	2
Langwith Junction	2	Selby	2	Selby	2		
Cambridge	1	March	1				

Q4 63200-63243 0-8-0 GCR Robinson

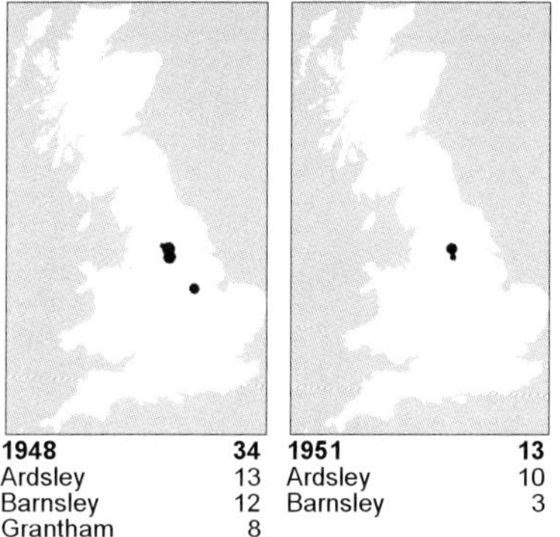

1948	34	1951	13
Ardsley	13	Ardsley	10
Barnsley	12	Barnsley	3
Grantham	8		
Bradford Hammerton St	1		

Right: LNER Thompson 'Q1/2' class 0-8-0T No 69933 at Selby on 16 April 1955. *L. Marshall*

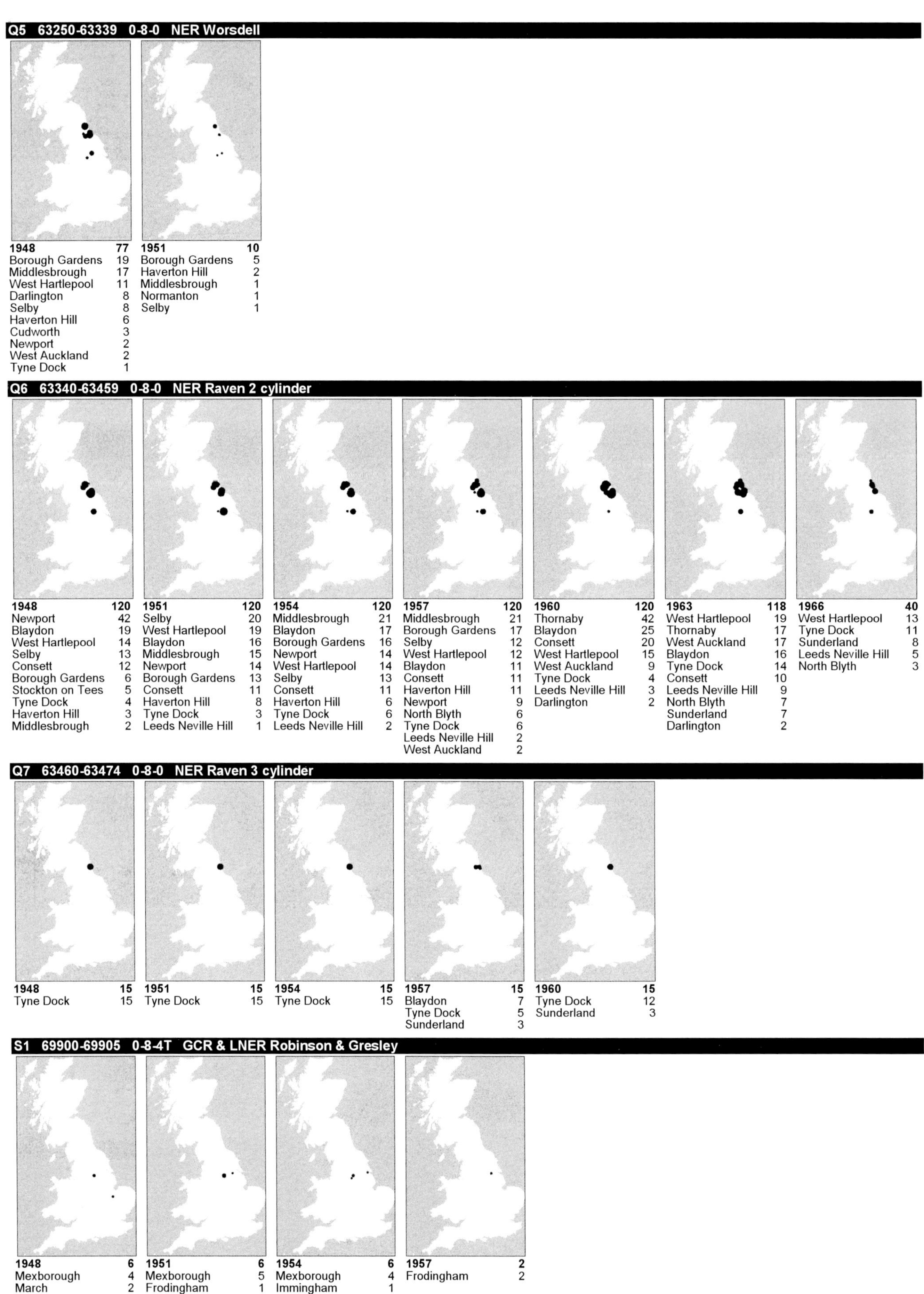

Q5 63250-63339 0-8-0 NER Worsdell

1948	77	1951	10
Borough Gardens	19	Borough Gardens	5
Middlesbrough	17	Haverton Hill	2
West Hartlepool	11	Middlesbrough	1
Darlington	8	Normanton	1
Selby	8	Selby	1
Haverton Hill	6		
Cudworth	3		
Newport	2		
West Auckland	2		
Tyne Dock	1		

Q6 63340-63459 0-8-0 NER Raven 2 cylinder

1948	120	1951	120	1954	120	1957	120	1960	120	1963	118	1966	40
Newport	42	Selby	20	Middlesbrough	21	Middlesbrough	21	Thornaby	42	West Hartlepool	19	West Hartlepool	13
Blaydon	19	West Hartlepool	19	Blaydon	17	Borough Gardens	17	Blaydon	25	Thornaby	17	Tyne Dock	11
West Hartlepool	14	Blaydon	16	Borough Gardens	16	Selby	12	Consett	20	West Auckland	17	Sunderland	8
Selby	13	Middlesbrough	15	Newport	14	West Hartlepool	12	West Hartlepool	15	Blaydon	16	Leeds Neville Hill	5
Consett	12	Newport	14	West Hartlepool	14	Blaydon	11	West Auckland	9	Tyne Dock	14	North Blyth	3
Borough Gardens	6	Borough Gardens	13	Selby	13	Consett	11	Tyne Dock	4	Consett	10		
Stockton on Tees	5	Consett	11	Consett	11	Haverton Hill	11	Leeds Neville Hill	3	Leeds Neville Hill	9		
Tyne Dock	4	Haverton Hill	8	Haverton Hill	6	Newport	9	Darlington	2	North Blyth	7		
Haverton Hill	3	Tyne Dock	3	Tyne Dock	6	North Blyth	6			Sunderland	7		
Middlesbrough	2	Leeds Neville Hill	1	Leeds Neville Hill	2	Tyne Dock	6			Darlington	2		
						Leeds Neville Hill	2						
						West Auckland	2						

Q7 63460-63474 0-8-0 NER Raven 3 cylinder

1948	15	1951	15	1954	15	1957	15	1960	15
Tyne Dock	15	Tyne Dock	15	Tyne Dock	15	Blaydon	7	Tyne Dock	12
						Tyne Dock	5	Sunderland	3
						Sunderland	3		

S1 69900-69905 0-8-4T GCR & LNER Robinson & Gresley

1948	6	1951	6	1954	6	1957	2
Mexborough	4	Mexborough	5	Mexborough	4	Frodingham	2
March	2	Frodingham	1	Immingham	1		
				Sheffield Darnall	1		

Right: LNER Gresley 'S1/3' class 0-8-4T No 69904 at Doncaster.
Brian Morrison

T1 69910-69922 4-8-0T NER Raven

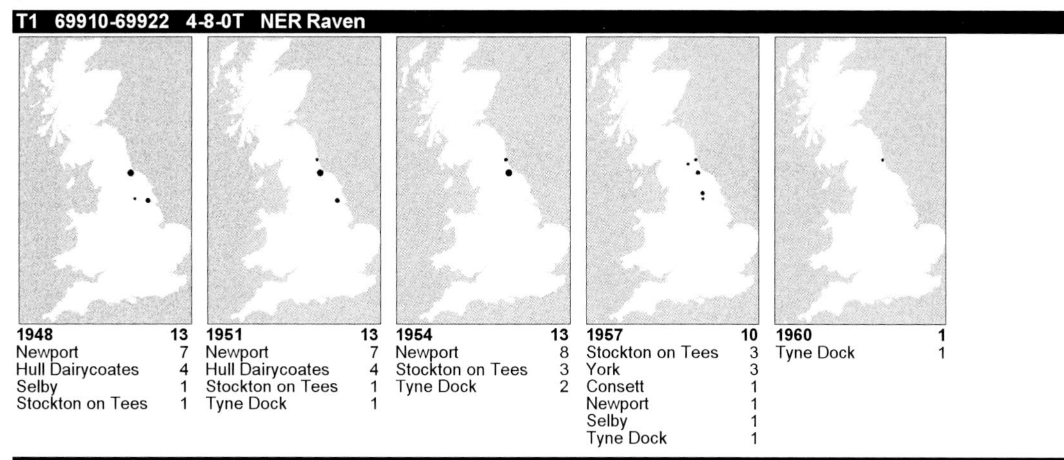

1948	13	1951	13	1954	13	1957	10	1960	1
Newport	7	Newport	7	Newport	8	Stockton on Tees	3	Tyne Dock	1
Hull Dairycoates	4	Hull Dairycoates	4	Stockton on Tees	3	York	3		
Selby	1	Stockton on Tees	1	Tyne Dock	2	Consett	1		
Stockton on Tees	1	Tyne Dock	1			Newport	1		
						Selby	1		
						Tyne Dock	1		

U1 69999 2-8-8-2T LNER Gresley Beyer Garratt

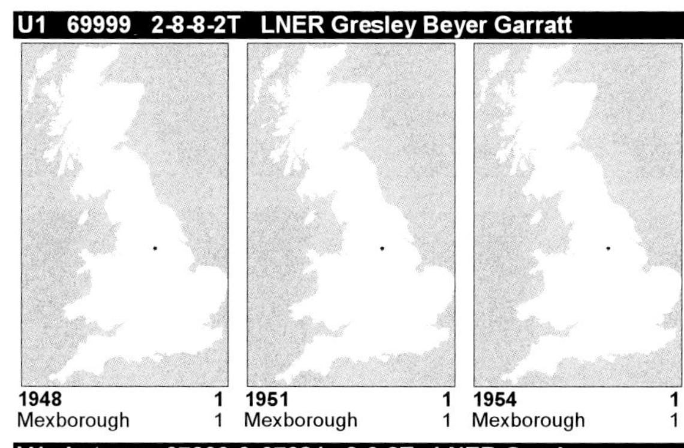

1948	1	1951	1	1954	1
Mexborough	1	Mexborough	1	Mexborough	1

V1 between 67600 & 67681 2-6-2T LNER Gresley

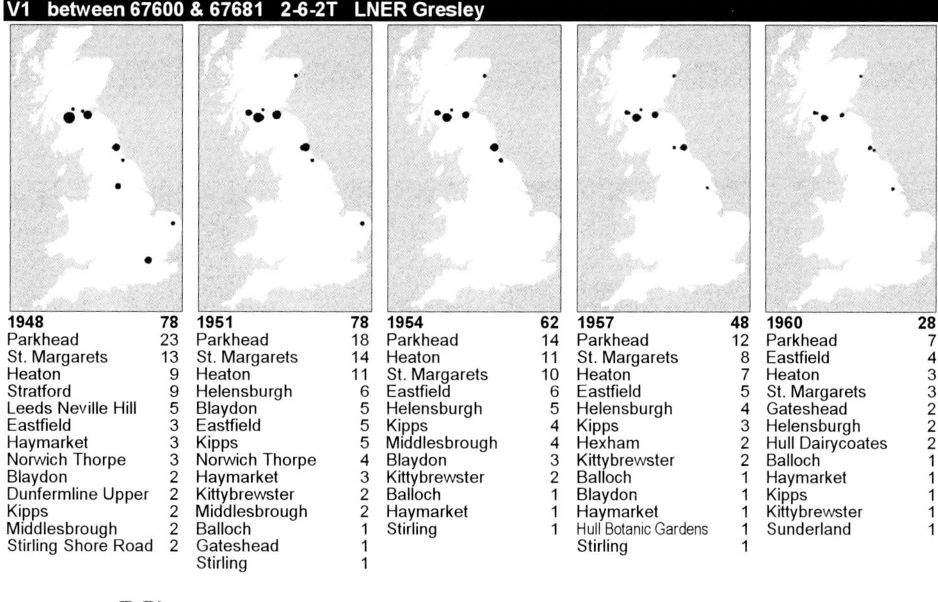

1948	78	1951	78	1954	62	1957	48	1960	28
Parkhead	23	Parkhead	18	Parkhead	14	Parkhead	12	Parkhead	7
St. Margarets	13	St. Margarets	14	Heaton	11	St. Margarets	8	Eastfield	4
Heaton	9	Heaton	11	St. Margarets	10	Heaton	7	Heaton	3
Stratford	9	Helensburgh	6	Eastfield	6	Eastfield	5	St. Margarets	3
Leeds Neville Hill	5	Blaydon	5	Helensburgh	5	Helensburgh	4	Gateshead	2
Eastfield	3	Eastfield	5	Kipps	4	Kipps	3	Helensburgh	2
Haymarket	3	Kipps	5	Middlesbrough	4	Hexham	2	Hull Dairycoates	2
Norwich Thorpe	3	Norwich Thorpe	4	Blaydon	3	Kittybrewster	2	Balloch	1
Blaydon	2	Haymarket	3	Kittybrewster	2	Balloch	1	Haymarket	1
Dunfermline Upper	2	Kittybrewster	2	Balloch	1	Blaydon	1	Kipps	1
Kipps	2	Middlesbrough	2	Haymarket	1	Haymarket	1	Kittybrewster	1
Middlesbrough	2	Balloch	1	Stirling	1	Hull Botanic Gardens	1	Sunderland	1
Stirling Shore Road	2	Gateshead	1			Stirling	1		
		Stirling	1						

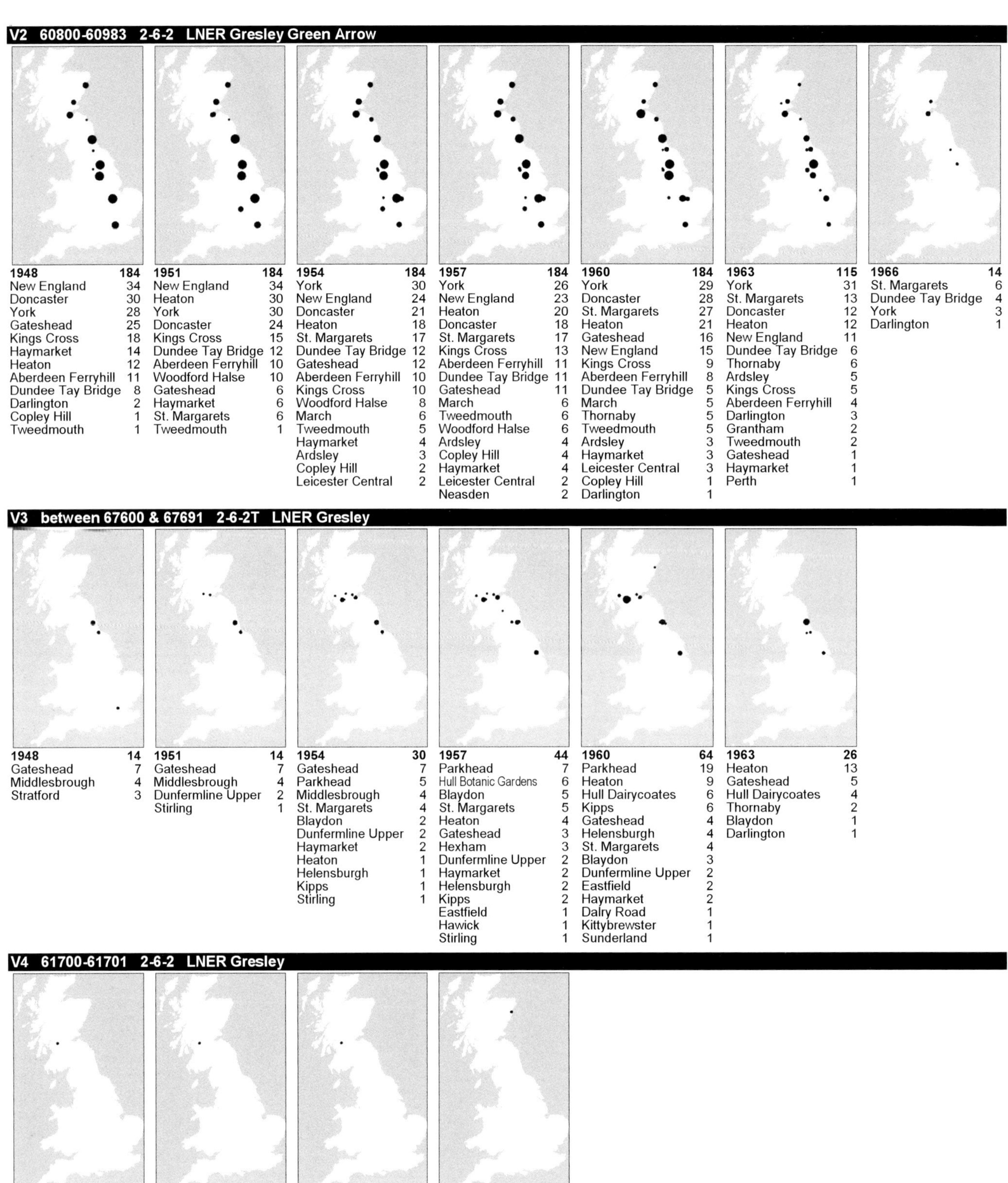

V2 60800-60983 2-6-2 LNER Gresley Green Arrow

1948	184
New England	34
Doncaster	30
York	28
Gateshead	25
Kings Cross	18
Haymarket	14
Heaton	12
Aberdeen Ferryhill	11
Dundee Tay Bridge	8
Darlington	2
Copley Hill	1
Tweedmouth	1

1951	184
New England	34
Heaton	30
York	30
Doncaster	24
Kings Cross	15
Dundee Tay Bridge	12
Aberdeen Ferryhill	10
Woodford Halse	10
Gateshead	6
Haymarket	6
St. Margarets	6
Tweedmouth	1

1954	184
York	30
New England	24
Doncaster	21
Heaton	18
St. Margarets	17
Dundee Tay Bridge	12
Gateshead	12
Aberdeen Ferryhill	10
Kings Cross	10
Woodford Halse	8
March	6
Tweedmouth	5
Haymarket	4
Ardsley	3
Copley Hill	2
Leicester Central	2

1957	184
York	26
New England	23
Heaton	20
Doncaster	18
St. Margarets	17
Kings Cross	13
Aberdeen Ferryhill	11
Dundee Tay Bridge	11
Gateshead	11
March	6
Tweedmouth	6
Woodford Halse	6
Ardsley	4
Copley Hill	4
Haymarket	4
Leicester Central	2
Neasden	2

1960	184
York	29
Doncaster	28
St. Margarets	27
Heaton	21
Gateshead	16
New England	15
Kings Cross	9
Aberdeen Ferryhill	8
Dundee Tay Bridge	5
March	5
Thornaby	5
Tweedmouth	5
Ardsley	3
Haymarket	3
Leicester Central	3
Copley Hill	1
Darlington	1

1963	115
York	31
St. Margarets	13
Doncaster	12
Heaton	12
New England	11
Dundee Tay Bridge	6
Thornaby	6
Ardsley	5
Kings Cross	5
Aberdeen Ferryhill	4
Darlington	3
Grantham	2
Tweedmouth	2
Gateshead	1
Haymarket	1
Perth	1

1966	14
St. Margarets	6
Dundee Tay Bridge	4
York	3
Darlington	1

V3 between 67600 & 67691 2-6-2T LNER Gresley

1948	14
Gateshead	7
Middlesbrough	4
Stratford	3

1951	14
Gateshead	7
Middlesbrough	4
Dunfermline Upper	2
Stirling	1

1954	30
Gateshead	7
Parkhead	5
Middlesbrough	4
St. Margarets	4
Blaydon	2
Dunfermline Upper	2
Haymarket	2
Heaton	1
Helensburgh	1
Kipps	1
Stirling	1

1957	44
Parkhead	7
Hull Botanic Gardens	6
Blaydon	5
St. Margarets	5
Heaton	4
Gateshead	3
Hexham	3
Dunfermline Upper	2
Haymarket	2
Helensburgh	2
Kipps	2
Eastfield	1
Hawick	1
Stirling	1

1960	64
Parkhead	19
Heaton	9
Hull Dairycoates	6
Kipps	6
Gateshead	4
Helensburgh	4
St. Margarets	4
Blaydon	3
Dunfermline Upper	2
Eastfield	2
Haymarket	2
Dalry Road	1
Kittybrewster	1
Sunderland	1

1963	26
Heaton	13
Gateshead	5
Hull Dairycoates	4
Thornaby	2
Blaydon	1
Darlington	1

V4 61700-61701 2-6-2 LNER Gresley

1948	2
Eastfield	2

1951	2
Eastfield	2

1954	2
Eastfield	2

1957	2
Aberdeen Ferryhill	2

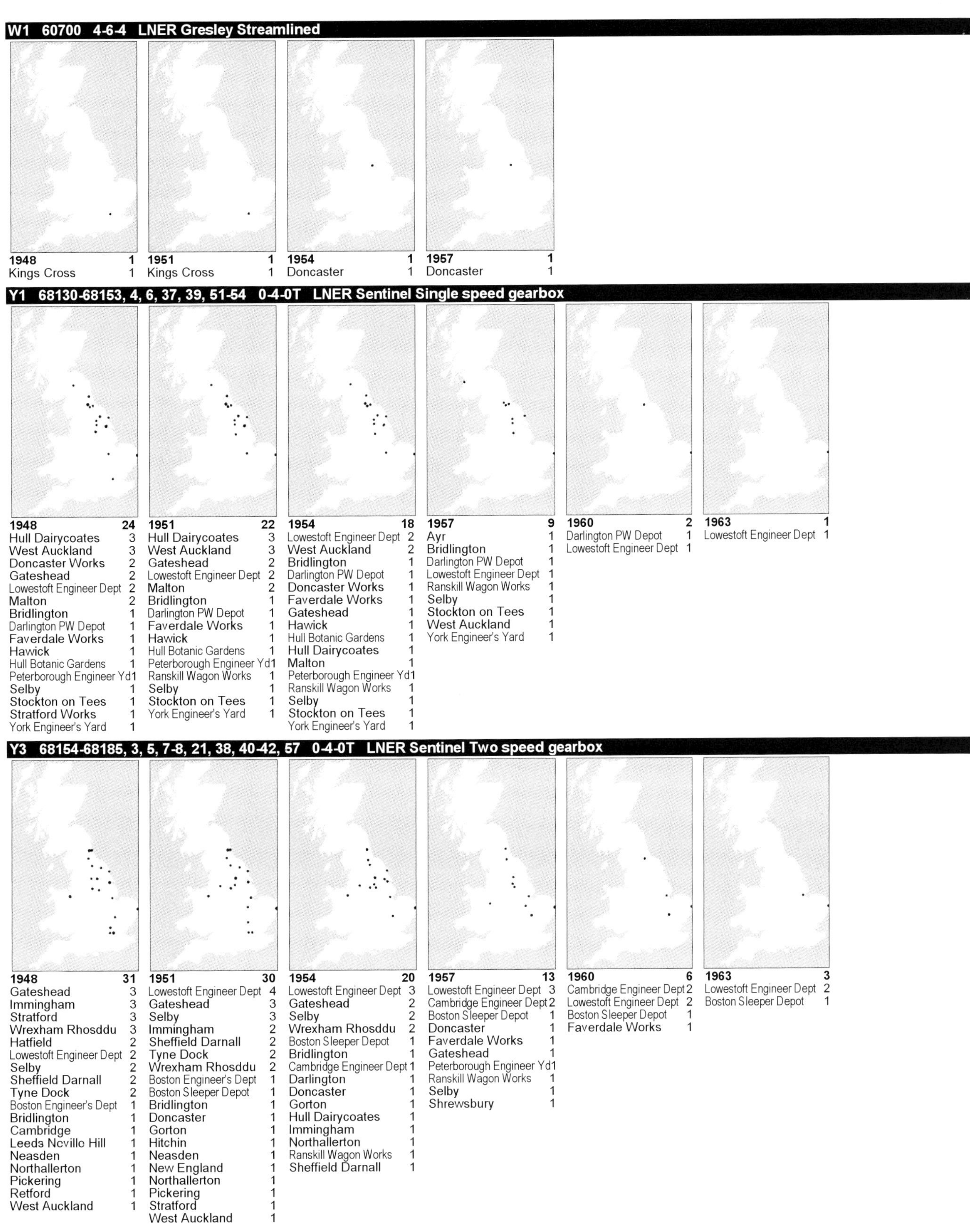

W1 60700 4-6-4 LNER Gresley Streamlined

1948	1
Kings Cross	1

1951	1
Kings Cross	1

1954	1
Doncaster	1

1957	1
Doncaster	1

Y1 68130-68153, 4, 6, 37, 39, 51-54 0-4-0T LNER Sentinel Single speed gearbox

1948	24
Hull Dairycoates	3
West Auckland	3
Doncaster Works	2
Gateshead	2
Lowestoft Engineer Dept	2
Malton	2
Bridlington	1
Darlington PW Depot	1
Faverdale Works	1
Hawick	1
Hull Botanic Gardens	1
Peterborough Engineer Yd	1
Selby	1
Stockton on Tees	1
Stratford Works	1
York Engineer's Yard	1

1951	22
Hull Dairycoates	3
West Auckland	3
Gateshead	2
Lowestoft Engineer Dept	2
Malton	2
Bridlington	1
Darlington PW Depot	1
Faverdale Works	1
Hawick	1
Hull Botanic Gardens	1
Peterborough Engineer Yd	1
Ranskill Wagon Works	1
Selby	1
Stockton on Tees	1
York Engineer's Yard	1

1954	18
Lowestoft Engineer Dept	2
West Auckland	2
Bridlington	1
Darlington PW Depot	1
Doncaster Works	1
Faverdale Works	1
Gateshead	1
Hawick	1
Hull Botanic Gardens	1
Hull Dairycoates	1
Malton	1
Peterborough Engineer Yd	1
Ranskill Wagon Works	1
Selby	1
Stockton on Tees	1
York Engineer's Yard	1

1957	9
Ayr	1
Bridlington	1
Darlington PW Depot	1
Lowestoft Engineer Dept	1
Ranskill Wagon Works	1
Selby	1
Stockton on Tees	1
West Auckland	1
York Engineer's Yard	1

1960	2
Darlington PW Depot	1
Lowestoft Engineer Dept	1

1963	1
Lowestoft Engineer Dept	1

Y3 68154-68185, 3, 5, 7-8, 21, 38, 40-42, 57 0-4-0T LNER Sentinel Two speed gearbox

1948	31
Gateshead	3
Immingham	3
Stratford	3
Wrexham Rhosddu	3
Hatfield	2
Lowestoft Engineer Dept	2
Selby	2
Sheffield Darnall	2
Tyne Dock	2
Boston Engineer's Dept	1
Bridlington	1
Cambridge	1
Leeds Neville Hill	1
Neasden	1
Northallerton	1
Pickering	1
Retford	1
West Auckland	1

1951	30
Lowestoft Engineer Dept	4
Gateshead	3
Selby	3
Immingham	2
Sheffield Darnall	2
Tyne Dock	2
Wrexham Rhosddu	2
Boston Engineer's Dept	1
Boston Sleeper Depot	1
Bridlington	1
Doncaster	1
Gorton	1
Hitchin	1
Neasden	1
New England	1
Northallerton	1
Pickering	1
Stratford	1
West Auckland	1

1954	20
Lowestoft Engineer Dept	3
Gateshead	2
Selby	2
Wrexham Rhosddu	2
Boston Sleeper Depot	1
Bridlington	1
Cambridge Engineer Dept	1
Darlington	1
Doncaster	1
Gorton	1
Hull Dairycoates	1
Immingham	1
Northallerton	1
Ranskill Wagon Works	1
Sheffield Darnall	1

1957	13
Lowestoft Engineer Dept	3
Cambridge Engineer Dept	2
Boston Sleeper Depot	1
Doncaster	1
Faverdale Works	1
Gateshead	1
Peterborough Engineer Yd	1
Ranskill Wagon Works	1
Selby	1
Shrewsbury	1

1960	6
Cambridge Engineer Dept	2
Lowestoft Engineer Dept	2
Boston Sleeper Depot	1
Faverdale Works	1

1963	3
Lowestoft Engineer Dept	2
Boston Sleeper Depot	1

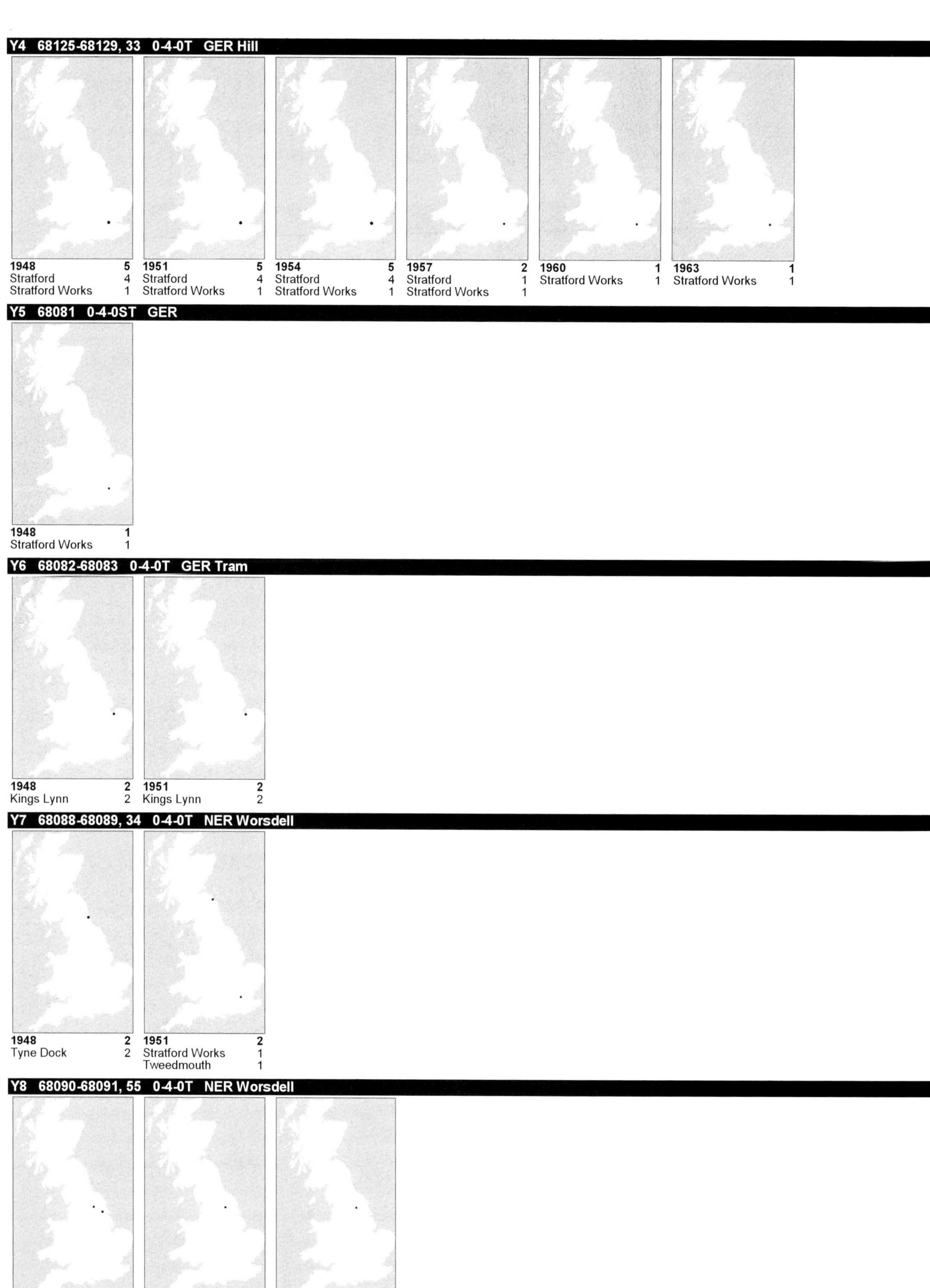
Y4 68125-68129, 33 0-4-0T GER Hill
1948 5
Stratford 4
Stratford Works 1
1951 5
Stratford 4
Stratford Works 1
1954 5
Stratford 4
Stratford Works 1
1957 2
Stratford 1
Stratford Works 1
1960 1
Stratford Works 1
1963 1
Stratford Works 1
Y5 68081 0-4-0ST GER
1948 1
Stratford Works 1
Y6 68082-68083 0-4-0T GER Tram
1948 2
Kings Lynn 2
1951 2
Kings Lynn 2
Y7 68088-68089, 34 0-4-0T NER Worsdell
1948 2
Tyne Dock 2
1951 2
Stratford Works 1
Tweedmouth 1
Y8 68090-68091, 55 0-4-0T NER Worsdell
1948 2
Hull Springhead 1
York 1
1951 1
York 1
1954 1
York 1

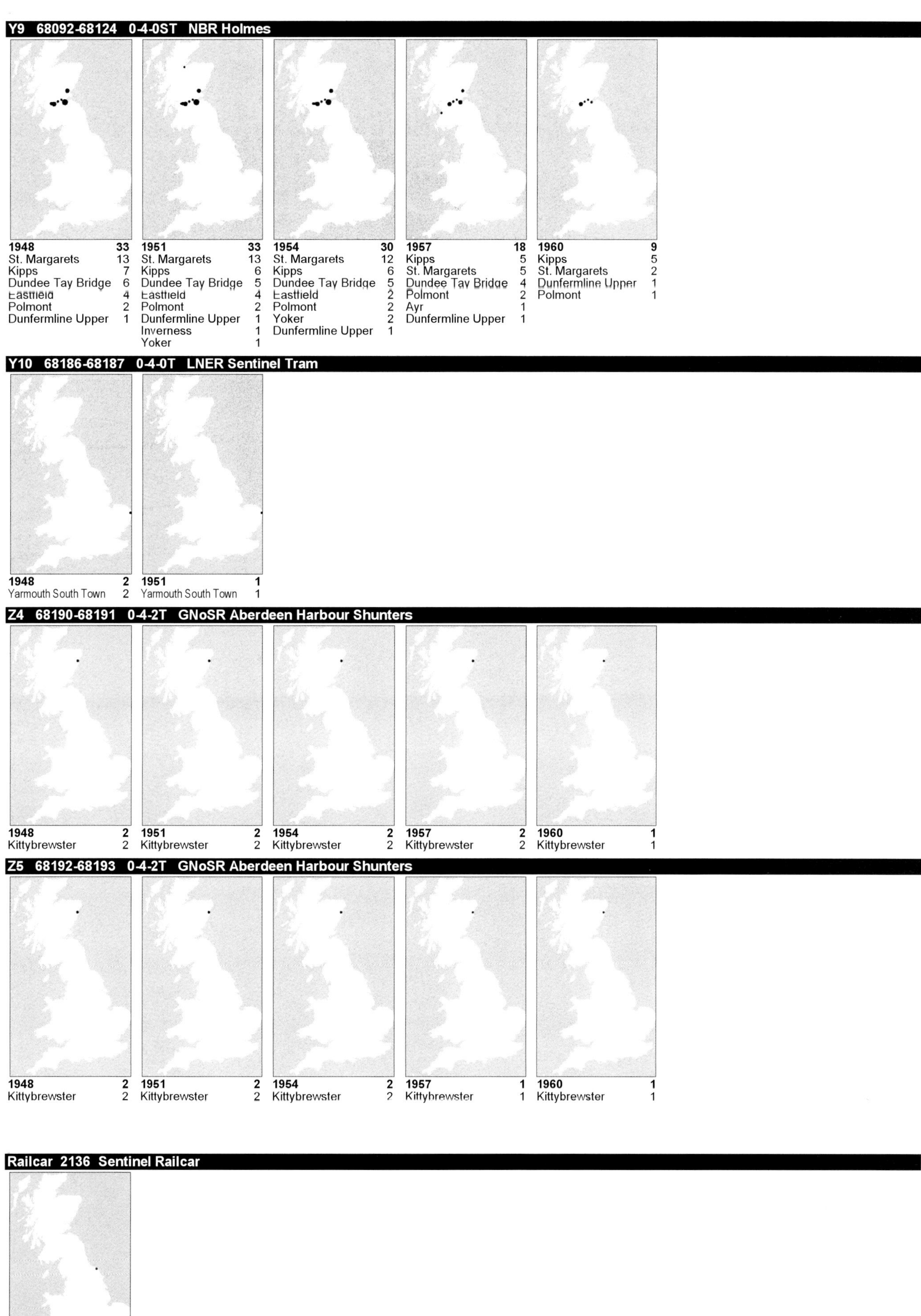

Y9 68092-68124 0-4-0ST NBR Holmes

1948	33	1951	33	1954	30	1957	18	1960	9
St. Margarets	13	St. Margarets	13	St. Margarets	12	Kipps	5	Kipps	5
Kipps	7	Kipps	6	Kipps	6	St. Margarets	5	St. Margarets	2
Dundee Tay Bridge	6	Dundee Tay Bridge	5	Dundee Tay Bridge	5	Dundee Tay Bridge	4	Dunfermline Upper	1
Eastfield	4	Eastfield	4	Eastfield	2	Polmont	2	Polmont	1
Polmont	2	Polmont	2	Polmont	2	Ayr	1		
Dunfermline Upper	1	Dunfermline Upper	1	Yoker	2	Dunfermline Upper	1		
		Inverness	1	Dunfermline Upper	1				
		Yoker	1						

Y10 68186-68187 0-4-0T LNER Sentinel Tram

1948	2	1951	1
Yarmouth South Town	2	Yarmouth South Town	1

Z4 68190-68191 0-4-2T GNoSR Aberdeen Harbour Shunters

1948	2	1951	2	1954	2	1957	2	1960	1
Kittybrewster	2	Kittybrewster	2	Kittybrewster	2	Kittybrewster	2	Kittybrewster	1

Z5 68192-68193 0-4-2T GNoSR Aberdeen Harbour Shunters

1948	2	1951	2	1954	2	1957	1	1960	1
Kittybrewster	2	Kittybrewster	2	Kittybrewster	2	Kittybrewster	1	Kittybrewster	1

Railcar 2136 Sentinel Railcar

1948	1
Whitby	1

Above: NER Raven 'T1' class 4-8-0T No 69922 at Newport. *D. Penney*

Below: LNER Gresley Beyer Garratt 'U1' class 2-8-8-2T No 9999 at Wentworth on 18 April 1947. Later renumbered 69999. *H. C. Casserley*

Right: 'Britannia' No 70054 *Dornoch Firth* at Carlisle Kingmoor, 9 August 1966. *J. L. McIvor*

BR Locomotives

Above: BR Standard '8P' class 4-6-2 No 71000 *Duke of Gloucester* as newly built on 5 June 1954. *BR*

Below: BR Standard 'Clan' '6P5F' class 4-6-2 No 72006 *Clan Mackenzie* from 12A Carlisle Kingmoor at Patricroft depot on 15 May 1964. *J. R. Carter*

		1948	1951	1954	1957	1960	1963	1966
70000	7P6F	→	→	30A Stratford	30A Stratford	32A Norwich Thorpe	31B March	5B Crewe South
70001	7P6F	→	→	30A Stratford	30A Stratford	32A Norwich Thorpe	31B March	12A Carlisle Kingmoor
70002	7P6F	→	→	30A Stratford	30A Stratford	32A Norwich Thorpe	31B March	12A Carlisle Kingmoor
70003	7P6F	→	→	30A Stratford	30A Stratford	32A Norwich Thorpe	31B March	12A Carlisle Kingmoor
70004	7P6F	→	→	73A Stewarts Lane	73A Stewarts Lane	9E Trafford Park	1A Willesden	9B Stockport Edgeley
70005	7P6F	→	→	30A Stratford	30A Stratford	32A Norwich Thorpe	31B March	12A Carlisle Kingmoor
70006	7P6F	→	→	32A Norwich Thorpe	32A Norwich Thorpe	32A Norwich Thorpe	31B March	12A Carlisle Kingmoor
70007	7P6F	→	→	32A Norwich Thorpe	32A Norwich Thorpe	32A Norwich Thorpe	31B March	
70008	7P6F	→	→	32A Norwich Thorpe	32A Norwich Thorpe	32A Norwich Thorpe	31B March	12A Carlisle Kingmoor
70009	7P6F	→	→	32A Norwich Thorpe	32A Norwich Thorpe	32A Norwich Thorpe	31B March	12A Carlisle Kingmoor
70010	7P6F	→	→	32A Norwich Thorpe	32A Norwich Thorpe	32A Norwich Thorpe	31B March	12A Carlisle Kingmoor
70011	7P6F	→	→	32A Norwich Thorpe	32A Norwich Thorpe	32A Norwich Thorpe	31B March	12B Carlisle Upperby
70012	7P6F	→	→	32A Norwich Thorpe	32A Norwich Thorpe	32A Norwich Thorpe	31B March	5B Crewe South
70013	7P6F	→	→	32A Norwich Thorpe	32A Norwich Thorpe	32A Norwich Thorpe	31B March	12B Carlisle Upperby
70014	7P6F	→	→	73A Stewarts Lane	73A Stewarts Lane	9E Trafford Park	6G Llandudno Junction	5B Crewe South
70015	7P6F	→	→	81A Old Oak Common	86C Cardiff Canton	9E Trafford Park	6G Llandudno Junction	9B Stockport Edgeley
70016	7P6F	→	→	83D Laira (Plymouth)	86C Cardiff Canton	86C Cardiff Canton	6G Llandudno Junction	12A Carlisle Kingmoor
70017	7P6F	→	→	81A Old Oak Common	86C Cardiff Canton	9E Trafford Park	2A Rugby	9D Newton Heath
70018	7P6F	→	→	81A Old Oak Common	86C Cardiff Canton	86C Cardiff Canton	5A Crewe North	5B Crewe South
70019	7P6F	→	→	83D Laira (Plymouth)	86C Cardiff Canton	86C Cardiff Canton	5A Crewe North	12B Carlisle Upperby
70020	7P6F	→	→	81A Old Oak Common	86C Cardiff Canton	86C Cardiff Canton	5A Crewe North	12B Carlisle Upperby
70021	7P6F	→	→	83D Laira (Plymouth)	83D Laira (Plymouth)	9E Trafford Park	1A Willesden	9D Newton Heath
70022	7P6F		→	83A Newton Abbot	86C Cardiff Canton	86C Cardiff Canton	2A Rugby	12B Carlisle Upperby
70023	7P6F	→	→	81A Old Oak Common	81A Old Oak Common	86C Cardiff Canton	2A Rugby	5B Crewe South
70024	7P6F	→	→	83D Laira (Plymouth)	86C Cardiff Canton	86C Cardiff Canton	2A Rugby	5B Crewe South
70025	7P6F	→	→	86C Cardiff Canton	86C Cardiff Canton	86C Cardiff Canton	21D Aston	5B Crewe South
70026	7P6F	→	→	86C Cardiff Canton	86C Cardiff Canton	86C Cardiff Canton	21D Aston	9B Stockport Edgeley
70027	7P6F	→	→	86C Cardiff Canton	86C Cardiff Canton	86C Cardiff Canton	21D Aston	5B Crewe South
70028	7P6F	→	→	86C Cardiff Canton	86C Cardiff Canton	86C Cardiff Canton	21D Aston	5B Crewe South
70029	7P6F	→	→	86C Cardiff Canton	86C Cardiff Canton	86C Cardiff Canton	21D Aston	12B Carlisle Upperby
70030	7P6F	→	→	32A Norwich Thorpe	32A Norwich Thorpe	32A Norwich Thorpe	31B March	12B Carlisle Upperby
70031	7P6F	→	→	9A Longsight	9A Longsight	9A Longsight	21D Aston	12B Carlisle Upperby
70032	7P6F	→	→	9A Longsight	9A Longsight	9A Longsight	1A Willesden	12B Carlisle Upperby
70033	7P6F	→	→	9A Longsight	9A Longsight	9A Longsight	6G Llandudno Junction	12A Carlisle Kingmoor
70034	7P6F	→	→	30A Stratford	30A Stratford	32A Norwich Thorpe	31B March	9D Newton Heath
70035	7P6F	→	→	32A Norwich Thorpe	32A Norwich Thorpe	32A Norwich Thorpe	40B Immingham	12A Carlisle Kingmoor
70036	7P6F	→	→	30A Stratford	30A Stratford	32A Norwich Thorpe	40B Immingham	12A Carlisle Kingmoor
70037	7P6F	→	→	30A Stratford	30A Stratford	32A Norwich Thorpe	40B Immingham	12A Carlisle Kingmoor
70038	7P6F	→	→	30A Stratford	30A Stratford	32A Norwich Thorpe	40B Immingham	12A Carlisle Kingmoor
70039	7P6F	→	→	30A Stratford	30A Stratford	32A Norwich Thorpe	40B Immingham	12A Carlisle Kingmoor
70040	7P6F	→	→	30A Stratford	30A Stratford	32A Norwich Thorpe	40B Immingham	12A Carlisle Kingmoor
70041	7P6F	→	→	30A Stratford	30A Stratford	32A Norwich Thorpe	40B Immingham	12A Carlisle Kingmoor
70042	7P6F	→	→	30A Stratford	30A Stratford	9E Trafford Park	1A Willesden	12A Carlisle Kingmoor
70043	7P6F	→	→	18A Toton	9A Longsight	9A Longsight	21D Aston	
70044	7P6F	→	→	9A Longsight	9A Longsight	55A Leeds Holbeck	5A Crewe North	9D Newton Heath
70045	7P6F	→	→	→	6J Holyhead	1B Camden	6J Holyhead	2D Banbury
70046	7P6F	→	→	→	6J Holyhead	5A Crewe North	6J Holyhead	2D Banbury
70047	7P6F	→	→	→	6J Holyhead	5A Crewe North	21D Aston	2D Banbury
70048	7P6F	→	→	→	6J Holyhead	1B Camden	6J Holyhead	12B Carlisle Upperby
70049	7P6F	→	→	→	6J Holyhead	1B Camden	6J Holyhead	12B Carlisle Upperby
70050	7P6F	→	→	→	66A Polmadie	66A Polmadie	6J Holyhead	2D Banbury
70051	7P6F	→	→	→	66A Polmadie	66A Polmadie	6J Holyhead	2D Banbury
70052	7P6F	→	→	→	66A Polmadie	66A Polmadie	5A Crewe North	2D Banbury
70053	7P6F	→	→	→	66A Polmadie	55A Leeds Holbeck	5A Crewe North	2D Banbury
70054	7P6F	→	→	→	66A Polmadie	55A Leeds Holbeck	5A Crewe North	2D Banbury
71000	8P	→	→	→	5A Crewe North	5A Crewe North		
72000	6P5F	→	→	66A Polmadie	66A Polmadie	64A St. Margarets		
72001	6P5F	→	→	66A Polmadie	66A Polmadie	64B Haymarket		
72002	6P5F	→	→	66A Polmadie	66A Polmadie	64B Haymarket		
72003	6P5F	→	→	66A Polmadie	66A Polmadie	64A St. Margarets		
72004	6P5F	→	→	66A Polmadie	66A Polmadie	64A St. Margarets		
72005	6P5F	→	→	68A Carlisle Kingmoor	68A Carlisle Kingmoor	12A Carlisle Kingmoor	12A Carlisle Kingmoor	
72006	6P5F	→	→	68A Carlisle Kingmoor	68A Carlisle Kingmoor	12A Carlisle Kingmoor	12A Carlisle Kingmoor	12A Carlisle Kingmoor
72007	6P5F	→	→	68A Carlisle Kingmoor	68A Carlisle Kingmoor	12A Carlisle Kingmoor	12A Carlisle Kingmoor	
72008	6P5F	→	→	68A Carlisle Kingmoor	68A Carlisle Kingmoor	12A Carlisle Kingmoor	12A Carlisle Kingmoor	12A Carlisle Kingmoor
72009	6P5F	→	→	68A Carlisle Kingmoor	68A Carlisle Kingmoor	12A Carlisle Kingmoor	12A Carlisle Kingmoor	
73000	5MT	→	→	16A Nottingham	16A Nottingham	41B Sheffield Grimesthorpe	2F Woodford Halse	6D Shrewsbury
73001	5MT	→	→	17A Derby	82C Swindon	82C Swindon	82C Swindon	
73002	5MT	→	→	16A Nottingham	16A Nottingham	41D Canklow	71A Eastleigh	70G Weymouth
73003	5MT	→	→	15C Leicester Midland	15C Leicester Midland	82E Bristol Barrow Road	82E Bristol Barrow Road	
73004	5MT	→	→	15C Leicester Midland	15C Leicester Midland	41C Millhouses	1A Willesden	6C Croes Newydd
73005	5MT	→	→	63A Perth	63A Perth	63A Perth	63A Perth	67A Corkerhill
73006	5MT	→	→	63A Perth	63A Perth	63A Perth	63A Perth	9H Patricroft
73007	5MT	→	→	63A Perth	63A Perth	63A Perth	63A Perth	65J Stirling
73008	5MT	→	→	63A Perth	63A Perth	63A Perth	63A Perth	
73009	5MT	→	→	63A Perth	63A Perth	63A Perth	63A Perth	67A Corkerhill
73010	5MT	→	→	20A Leeds Holbeck	55A Leeds Holbeck	15E Leicester Central	2F Woodford Halse	9H Patricroft
73011	5MT	→	→	19B Millhouses	19B Millhouses	41C Millhouses	6J Holyhead	9H Patricroft
73012	5MT	→	→	84G Shrewsbury	82C Swindon	82C Swindon	82C Swindon	
73013	5MT	→	→	84G Shrewsbury	84K Chester (GWR)	6A Chester	1A Willesden	2D Banbury
73014	5MT	→	→	84G Shrewsbury	86C Cardiff Canton	6E Chester (GWR)	1A Willesden	2D Banbury
73015	5MT	→	→	84G Shrewsbury	17A Derby	82E Bristol Barrow Road	82E Bristol Barrow Road	
73016	5MT	→	→	19B Millhouses	19B Millhouses	41C Millhouses	71A Eastleigh	70G Weymouth
73017	5MT	→	→	84G Shrewsbury	82C Swindon	71G Weymouth	71G Weymouth	
73018	5MT	→	→	84G Shrewsbury	82C Swindon	71G Weymouth	71G Weymouth	70G Weymouth
73019	5MT	→	→	82B St. Philips Marsh	82B St. Philips Marsh	82F Bath Green Park	85C Gloucester Barnwood	2B Oxley
73020	5MT	→	→	84K Chester (GWR)	82C Swindon	71G Weymouth	71G Weymouth	70G Weymouth
73021	5MT	→	→	84K Chester (GWR)	84K Chester (GWR)	86C Cardiff Canton	85C Gloucester Barnwood	
73022	5MT	→	→	87E Landore	82C Swindon	71G Weymouth	71G Weymouth	70C Guildford
73023	5MT	→	→	84K Chester (GWR)	84K Chester (GWR)	86C Cardiff Canton	87F Llanelly	
73024	5MT	→	→	84K Chester (GWR)	84G Shrewsbury	86C Cardiff Canton	85C Gloucester Barnwood	
73025	5MT	→	→	84G Shrewsbury	86C Cardiff Canton	84G Shrewsbury	89A Shrewsbury	6D Shrewsbury
73026	5MT	→	→	84G Shrewsbury	86C Cardiff Canton	84G Shrewsbury	89A Shrewsbury	2A Tyseley
73027	5MT	→	→	82B St. Philips Marsh	82C Swindon	82C Swindon	82C Swindon	
73028	5MT	→	→	82B St. Philips Marsh	82B St. Philips Marsh	82F Bath Green Park	82E Bristol Barrow Road	2B Oxley
73029	5MT	→	→	87G Carmarthen	82B St. Philips Marsh	71G Weymouth	71G Weymouth	70C Guildford
73030	5MT	→	→	17A Derby	17A Derby	26F Patricroft	26F Patricroft	
73031	5MT	→	→	17A Derby	17A Derby	Rugby Testing Station	85C Gloucester Barnwood	
73032	5MT	→	→	82B St. Philips Marsh	82B St. Philips Marsh	6C Birkenhead	2F Woodford Halse	
73033	5MT	→	→	84G Shrewsbury	84B Oxley	6A Chester	1A Willesden	9H Patricroft
73034	5MT	→	→	84G Shrewsbury	84B Oxley	84G Shrewsbury	89A Shrewsbury	6D Shrewsbury
73035	5MT	→	→	84G Shrewsbury	84B Oxley	84G Shrewsbury	89A Shrewsbury	9H Patricroft
73036	5MT	→	→	84G Shrewsbury	84E Tyseley	84G Shrewsbury	89A Shrewsbury	
73037	5MT	→	→	84G Shrewsbury	84E Tyseley	84G Shrewsbury	87F Llanelly	70C Guildford
73038	5MT	→		84K Chester (GWR)	84K Chester (GWR)	6E Chester (GWR)	6G Llandudno Junction	
73039	5MT	→	→	82B St. Philips Marsh	82B St. Philips Marsh	6C Birkenhead	1A Willesden	9H Patricroft
73040	5MT	→	→	6A Chester	6A Chester	6A Chester	6A Chester	6C Croes Newydd
73041	5MT	→	→	6A Chester	6A Chester	71G Weymouth	71G Weymouth	
73042	5MT	→	→	6A Chester	6A Chester	71G Weymouth	71G Weymouth	
73043	5MT	→	→	10C Patricroft	10C Patricroft	41B Sheffield Grimesthorpe	71A Eastleigh	70C Guildford
73044	5MT	→	→	10C Patricroft	10C Patricroft	26F Patricroft	26F Patricroft	
73045	5MT	→	→	20A Leeds Holbeck	55A Leeds Holbeck	15E Leicester Central	2F Woodford Halse	9H Patricroft
73046	5MT	→	→	15C Leicester Midland	15C Leicester Midland	41C Millhouses	70A Nine Elms	
73047	5MT	→	→	19B Millhouses	71G Bath Green Park	82F Bath Green Park	82F Bath Green Park	

		1948	1951	1954	1957	1960	1963	1966
73048	5MT	→	→	19B Millhouses	19B Millhouses	41C Millhouses	6A Chester	2D Banbury
73049	5MT	→	→	15C Leicester Midland	71G Bath Green Park	82F Bath Green Park	82F Bath Green Park	
73050	5MT	→	→	→	71G Bath Green Park	82F Bath Green Park	82F Bath Green Park	6D Shrewsbury
73051	5MT	→	→	→	71G Bath Green Park	82F Bath Green Park	82F Bath Green Park	
73052	5MT	→	→	→	71G Bath Green Park	82F Bath Green Park	82F Bath Green Park	
73053	5MT	→	→	→	55A Leeds Holbeck	15E Leicester Central	2F Woodford Halse	9H Patricroft
73054	5MT	→	→	→	17A Derby	82E Bristol Barrow Road	82F Bath Green Park	
73055	5MT	→	→	→	66A Polmadie	66A Polmadie	66A Polmadie	66A Polmadie
73056	5MT	→	→	→	66A Polmadie	66A Polmadie	66A Polmadie	
73057	5MT	→	→	→	66A Polmadie	66A Polmadie	66A Polmadie	67A Corkerhill
73058	5MT	→	→	→	66A Polmadie	66A Polmadie	66A Polmadie	
73059	5MT	→	→	→	66A Polmadie	66A Polmadie	66A Polmadie	66A Polmadie
73060	5MT	→	→	→	66B Motherwell	66A Polmadie	66A Polmadie	66A Polmadie
73061	5MT	→	→	→	66B Motherwell	66A Polmadie	66A Polmadie	
73062	5MT	→	→	→	66B Motherwell	66A Polmadie	66A Polmadie	
73063	5MT	→	→	→	66A Polmadie	66A Polmadie	66A Polmadie	66A Polmadie
73064	5MT	→	→	→	66A Polmadie	66A Polmadie	66A Polmadie	66A Polmadie
73065	5MT	→	→	→	19B Millhouses	41C Millhouses	71A Eastleigh	70C Guildford
73066	5MT	→	→	→	55A Leeds Holbeck	15E Leicester Central	15E Leicester Central	2A Tyseley
73067	5MT	→	→	→	16A Nottingham	41C Millhouses	6J Holyhead	6D Shrewsbury
73068	5MT	→	→	→	17A Derby	82E Bristol Barrow Road	85C Gloucester Barnwood	
73069	5MT	→	→	→	55A Leeds Holbeck	15E Leicester Central	15E Leicester Central	2A Tyseley
73070	5MT	→	→	→	6A Chester	6A Chester	6A Chester	6D Shrewsbury
73071	5MT	→	→	→	34A Kings Cross	6A Chester	6A Chester	9H Patricroft
73072	5MT	→	→	→	6A Chester	66A Polmadie	66A Polmadie	66A Polmadie
73073	5MT	→	→	→	15C Leicester Midland	41C Millhouses	6J Holyhead	9H Patricroft
73074	5MT	→	→	→	19B Millhouses	41B Sheffield Grimesthorpe	70A Nine Elms	
73075	5MT	→	→	→	66A Polmadie	66A Polmadie	66A Polmadie	
73076	5MT	→	→	→	66A Polmadie	66A Polmadie	66A Polmadie	
73077	5MT	→	→	→	65A Eastfield	65A Eastfield	65A Eastfield	
73078	5MT	→	→	→	65A Eastfield	65A Eastfield	65A Eastfield	65A Eastfield
73079	5MT	→	→	→	67A Corkerhill	67A Corkerhill	67A Corkerhill	67A Corkerhill
73080	5MT	→	→	→	73A Stewarts Lane	71G Weymouth	71G Weymouth	70G Weymouth
73081	5MT	→	→	→	73A Stewarts Lane	70A Nine Elms	70A Nine Elms	70C Guildford
73082	5MT	→	→	→	73A Stewarts Lane	70A Nine Elms	70A Nine Elms	70C Guildford
73083	5MT	→	→	→	73A Stewarts Lane	70A Nine Elms	70A Nine Elms	70G Weymouth
73084	5MT	→	→	→	73A Stewarts Lane	70A Nine Elms	70A Nine Elms	
73085	5MT	→	→	→	73A Stewarts Lane	70A Nine Elms	70A Nine Elms	70D Eastleigh
73086	5MT	→	→	→	73A Stewarts Lane	70A Nine Elms	70A Nine Elms	70A Nine Elms
73087	5MT	→	→	→	71A Eastleigh	82F Bath Green Park	70A Nine Elms	70C Guildford
73088	5MT	→	→	→	73A Stewarts Lane	70A Nine Elms	70A Nine Elms	70C Guildford
73089	5MT	→	→	→	73A Stewarts Lane	70A Nine Elms	70A Nine Elms	70C Guildford
73090	5MT	→	→	→	10C Patricroft	84G Shrewsbury	89A Shrewsbury	
73091	5MT	→	→	→	10C Patricroft	84G Shrewsbury	85C Gloucester Barnwood	
73092	5MT	→	→	→	10C Patricroft	84G Shrewsbury	85C Gloucester Barnwood	70C Guildford
73093	5MT	→	→	→	10C Patricroft	84G Shrewsbury	85C Gloucester Barnwood	70C Guildford
73094	5MT	→	→	→	10C Patricroft	84G Shrewsbury	85C Gloucester Barnwood	9H Patricroft
73095	5MT	→	→	→	10C Patricroft	84G Shrewsbury	89A Shrewsbury	6C Croes Newydd
73096	5MT	→	→	→	10C Patricroft	84G Shrewsbury	85C Gloucester Barnwood	9H Patricroft
73097	5MT	→	→	→	10C Patricroft	84G Shrewsbury	89A Shrewsbury	9H Patricroft
73098	5MT	→	→	→	10C Patricroft	66A Polmadie	66A Polmadie	66A Polmadie
73099	5MT	→	→	→	10C Patricroft	66A Polmadie	66A Polmadie	66A Polmadie
73100	5MT	→	→	→	67A Corkerhill	67A Corkerhill	67A Corkerhill	67A Corkerhill
73101	5MT	→	→	→	67A Corkerhill	67A Corkerhill	67A Corkerhill	67A Corkerhill
73102	5MT	→	→	→	67A Corkerhill	67A Corkerhill	67A Corkerhill	67A Corkerhill
73103	5MT	→	→	→	67A Corkerhill	67A Corkerhill	67A Corkerhill	
73104	5MT	→	→	→	67A Corkerhill	67A Corkerhill	67A Corkerhill	
73105	5MT	→	→	→	65A Eastfield	65A Eastfield	65A Eastfield	65J Stirling
73106	5MT	→	→	→	65A Eastfield	63A Perth	63A Perth	
73107	5MT	→	→	→	65A Eastfield	63A Perth	63A Perth	66B Motherwell
73108	5MT	→	→	→	65A Eastfield	65A Eastfield	65A Eastfield	65A Eastfield
73109	5MT	→	→	→	65A Eastfield	65A Eastfield	65A Eastfield	
73110	5MT	→	→	→	70A Nine Elms	70A Nine Elms	70A Nine Elms	70C Guildford
73111	5MT	→	→	→	70A Nine Elms	70A Nine Elms	70A Nine Elms	
73112	5MT	→	→	→	70A Nine Elms	70A Nine Elms	70A Nine Elms	
73113	5MT	→	→	→	70A Nine Elms	70A Nine Elms	70A Nine Elms	70G Weymouth
73114	5MT	→	→	→	70A Nine Elms	70A Nine Elms	70A Nine Elms	70G Weymouth
73115	5MT	→	→	→	70A Nine Elms	70A Nine Elms	70A Nine Elms	70D Eastleigh
73116	5MT	→	→	→	71A Eastleigh	82F Bath Green Park	70A Nine Elms	
73117	5MT	→	→	→	70A Nine Elms	70A Nine Elms	70A Nine Elms	70D Eastleigh
73118	5MT	→	→	→	70A Nine Elms	70A Nine Elms	70A Nine Elms	70D Eastleigh
73119	5MT	→	→	→	70A Nine Elms	70A Nine Elms	70A Nine Elms	70D Eastleigh
73120	5MT	→	→	→	63A Perth	63A Perth	63A Perth	67A Corkerhill
73121	5MT	→	→	→	67A Corkerhill	67A Corkerhill	67A Corkerhill	67A Corkerhill
73122	5MT	→	→	→	67A Corkerhill	67A Corkerhill	67A Corkerhill	
73123	5MT	→	→	→	67A Corkerhill	67A Corkerhill	67A Corkerhill	
73124	5MT	→	→	→	67A Corkerhill	67A Corkerhill	67A Corkerhill	
73125	5MT	→	→	→	84G Shrewsbury	26F Patricroft	26F Patricroft	9H Patricroft
73126	5MT	→	→	→	84G Shrewsbury	26F Patricroft	26F Patricroft	9H Patricroft
73127	5MT	→	→	→	84G Shrewsbury	26F Patricroft	26F Patricroft	9H Patricroft
73128	5MT	→	→	→	84G Shrewsbury	26F Patricroft	26F Patricroft	9H Patricroft
73129	5MT	→	→	→	84G Shrewsbury	26F Patricroft	26F Patricroft	9H Patricroft
73130	5MT	→	→	→	84G Shrewsbury	26F Patricroft	26F Patricroft	9H Patricroft
73131	5MT	→	→	→	84G Shrewsbury	26F Patricroft	26F Patricroft	9H Patricroft
73132	5MT	→	→	→	84G Shrewsbury	26F Patricroft	26F Patricroft	9H Patricroft
73133	5MT	→	→	→	84G Shrewsbury	26F Patricroft	26F Patricroft	9H Patricroft
73134	5MT	→	→	→	84G Shrewsbury	26F Patricroft	26F Patricroft	9H Patricroft
73135	5MT	→	→	→	6J Holyhead	17C Rowsley	17C Rowsley	9H Patricroft
73136	5MT	→	→	→	6J Holyhead	17C Rowsley	17C Rowsley	9H Patricroft
73137	5MT	→	→	→	6J Holyhead	17A Derby	17C Rowsley	9H Patricroft
73138	5MT	→	→	→	6J Holyhead	17C Rowsley	17C Rowsley	9H Patricroft
73139	5MT	→	→	→	6J Holyhead	17C Rowsley	17C Rowsley	9H Patricroft
73140	5MT	→	→	→	15C Leicester Midland	17C Rowsley	17C Rowsley	9H Patricroft
73141	5MT	→	→	→	15C Leicester Midland	17C Rowsley	17C Rowsley	9H Patricroft
73142	5MT	→	→	→	15C Leicester Midland	17C Rowsley	17C Rowsley	9H Patricroft
73143	5MT	→	→	→	15C Leicester Midland	17C Rowsley	17C Rowsley	9H Patricroft
73144	5MT	→	→	→	15C Leicester Midland	17C Rowsley	17C Rowsley	9H Patricroft
73145	5MT	→	→	→	→	65B St. Rollox	65B St. Rollox	65B St. Rollox
73146	5MT	→	→	→	→	65B St. Rollox	65B St. Rollox	65B St. Rollox
73147	5MT	→	→	→	→	65B St. Rollox	65B St. Rollox	
73148	5MT	→	→	→	→	65B St. Rollox	65B St. Rollox	
73149	5MT	→	→	→	→	65B St. Rollox	65B St. Rollox	65B St. Rollox
73150	5MT	→	→	→	→	65B St. Rollox	65B St. Rollox	65B St. Rollox
73151	5MT	→	→	→	→	65B St. Rollox	65B St. Rollox	65B St. Rollox
73152	5MT	→	→	→	→	65B St. Rollox	65B St. Rollox	
73153	5MT	→	→	→	→	65B St. Rollox	65B St. Rollox	65B St. Rollox
73154	5MT	→	→	→	→	65B St. Rollox	65B St. Rollox	65J Stirling
73155	5MT	→	→	→	34E Neasden	41C Millhouses	71A Eastleigh	70D Eastleigh
73156	5MT	→	→	→	34E Neasden	41B Sheffield Grimesthorpe	15E Leicester Central	2A Tyseley
73157	5MT	→	→	→	34E Neasden	17A Derby	14A Cricklewood	9H Patricroft
73158	5MT	→	→	→	34E Neasden	17A Derby	14A Cricklewood	9H Patricroft
73159	5MT	→	→	→	→	17A Derby	15E Leicester Central	9H Patricroft
73160	5MT	→	→	→	→	55E Normanton	55E Normanton	9H Patricroft
73161	5MT	→	→	→	→	55E Normanton	55H Leeds Neville Hill	

		1948	1951	1954	1957	1960	1963	1966
73162	5MT	→	→	→	→	**55G** Huddersfield	**55H** Leeds Neville Hill	
73163	5MT	→	→	→	→	**55G** Huddersfield	**55G** Huddersfield	
73164	5MT	→	→	→	→	**55G** Huddersfield	**55G** Huddersfield	
73165	5MT	→	→	→	→	**55G** Huddersfield	**55G** Huddersfield	
73166	5MT	→	→	→	→	**55A** Leeds Holbeck	**55D** Royston	
73167	5MT	→	→	→	→	**55E** Normanton	**55E** Normanton	
73168	5MT	→	→	→	→	**55A** Leeds Holbeck	**55H** Leeds Neville Hill	
73169	5MT	→	→	→	→	**55A** Leeds Holbeck	**55H** Leeds Neville Hill	**70D** Eastleigh
73170	5MT	→	→	→	→	**55A** Leeds Holbeck	**55D** Royston	**70D** Eastleigh
73171	5MT	→	→	→	→	**55A** Leeds Holbeck	**55D** Royston	**70D** Eastleigh
75000	4MT[1]	→	→	**82C** Swindon	**82C** Swindon	**84E** Tyseley	**84D** Leamington Spa	
75001	4MT[1]	→	→	**82C** Swindon	**81F** Oxford	**81F** Oxford	**81F** Oxford	
75002	4MT[1]	→	→	**82C** Swindon	**89A** Oswestry	**82C** Swindon	**89C** Machynlleth	**6F** Machynlleth
75003	4MT[1]	→	→	**82C** Swindon	**82C** Swindon	**85A** Worcester	**89C** Machynlleth	
75004	4MT[1]	→	→	**82C** Swindon	**86C** Cardiff Canton	**82E** Bristol Barrow Road	**89C** Machynlleth	**6F** Machynlleth
75005	4MT[1]	→	→	**86C** Cardiff Canton	**89A** Oswestry	**84E** Tyseley	**85A** Worcester	
75006	4MT[1]	→	→	**89A** Oswestry	**89A** Oswestry	**84E** Tyseley	**89C** Machynlleth	**6D** Shrewsbury
75007	4MT[1]	→	→	**86C** Cardiff Canton	**86C** Cardiff Canton	**81F** Oxford	**81F** Oxford	
75008	4MT[1]	→	→	**86C** Cardiff Canton	**86C** Cardiff Canton	**81F** Oxford	**81F** Oxford	
75009	4MT[1]	→	→	**86C** Cardiff Canton	**86C** Cardiff Canton	**85E** Gloucester Barnwood	**89C** Machynlleth	**6C** Croes Newydd
75010	4MT[1]	→	→	**6G** Llandudno Junction	**6G** Llandudno Junction	**6G** Llandudno Junction	**2B** Nuneaton	**6A** Chester
75011	4MT[1]	→	→	**6G** Llandudno Junction	**6G** Llandudno Junction	**6G** Llandudno Junction	**2B** Nuneaton	**10G** Skipton
75012	4MT[1]	→	→	**6G** Llandudno Junction	**6G** Llandudno Junction	**6G** Llandudno Junction	**2B** Nuneaton	**6A** Chester
75013	4MT[1]	→	→	**6G** Llandudno Junction	**6G** Llandudno Junction	**6A** Chester	**1E** Bletchley	**6F** Machynlleth
75014	4MT[1]	→	→	**6G** Llandudno Junction	**6G** Llandudno Junction	**6A** Chester	**1E** Bletchley	**6D** Shrewsbury
75015	4MT[1]	→	→	**27C** Southport	**27C** Southport	**27C** Southport	**27C** Southport	**10G** Skipton
75016	4MT[1]	→	→	**27C** Southport	**27C** Southport	**27C** Southport	**27C** Southport	**6D** Shrewsbury
75017	4MT[1]	→	→	**27C** Southport	**27C** Southport	**27C** Southport	**27C** Southport	**10G** Skipton
75018	4MT[1]	→	→	**27C** Southport	**27C** Southport	**27C** Southport	**27C** Southport	**5D** Stoke
75019	4MT[1]	→	→	**27C** Southport	**27C** Southport	**27C** Southport	**27C** Southport	**10G** Skipton
75020	4MT[1]	→	→	**89A** Oswestry	**89A** Oswestry	**89C** Machynlleth	**89C** Machynlleth	**5D** Stoke
75021	4MT[1]	→	→	**86C** Cardiff Canton	**86C** Cardiff Canton	**82E** Bristol Barrow Road	**89C** Machynlleth	**6C** Croes Newydd
75022	4MT[1]	→	→	**86C** Cardiff Canton	**86C** Cardiff Canton	**82E** Bristol Barrow Road	**81F** Oxford	
75023	4MT[1]	→	→	**89A** Oswestry	**82C** Swindon	**85E** Gloucester Barnwood	**89C** Machynlleth	**5D** Stoke
75024	4MT[1]	→	→	**89A** Oswestry	**89A** Oswestry	**84E** Tyseley	**89C** Machynlleth	**6J** Holyhead
75025	4MT[1]	→	→	→	**82C** Swindon	**85A** Worcester	**85A** Worcester	
75026	4MT[1]	→	→	→	**82C** Swindon	**89C** Machynlleth	**89C** Machynlleth	**8K** Bank Hall
75027	4MT[1]	→	→	→	**81F** Oxford	**82C** Swindon	**89C** Machynlleth	**8K** Bank Hall
75028	4MT[1]	→	→	→	**89A** Oswestry	**6E** Chester (GWR)	**1E** Bletchley	
75029	4MT[1]	→	→	→	**81F** Oxford	**82C** Swindon	**89C** Machynlleth	**6G** Llandudno Junction
75030	4MT[1]	→	→	**1E** Bletchley	**1E** Bletchley	**6D** Chester Northgate	**1A** Willesden	**5D** Stoke
75031	4MT[1]	→	→	**1E** Bletchley	**6A** Chester	**6A** Chester	**21D** Aston	**5D** Stoke
75032	4MT[1]	→	→	**1E** Bletchley	**6A** Chester	**6A** Chester	**2B** Nuneaton	**8K** Bank Hall
75033	4MT[1]	→	→	**1E** Bletchley	**6A** Chester	**6E** Chester (GWR)	**2B** Nuneaton	**8K** Bank Hall
75034	4MT[1]	→	→	**1E** Bletchley	**6A** Chester	**6A** Chester	**21D** Aston	**5D** Stoke
75035	4MT[1]	→	→	**1E** Bletchley	**6A** Chester	**6A** Chester	**2B** Nuneaton	**5E** Nuneaton
75036	4MT[1]	→	→	**1E** Bletchley	**1E** Bletchley	**1E** Bletchley	**2B** Nuneaton	**5D** Stoke
75037	4MT[1]	→	→	**1E** Bletchley	**1E** Bletchley	**1E** Bletchley	**21D** Aston	**5D** Stoke
75038	4MT[1]	→	→	**1E** Bletchley	**1E** Bletchley	**1E** Bletchley	**1E** Bletchley	
75039	4MT[1]	→	→	**1E** Bletchley	**6A** Chester	**6A** Chester	**1E** Bletchley	**10G** Skipton
75040	4MT[1]	→	→	**24A** Accrington	**15D** Bedford	**14E** Bedford	**17A** Derby	**5D** Stoke
75041	4MT[1]	→	→	**24A** Accrington	**15D** Bedford	**14E** Bedford	**17A** Derby	**10G** Skipton
75042	4MT[1]	→	→	**24A** Accrington	**15D** Bedford	**15C** Leicester Midland	**17A** Derby	**10G** Skipton
75043	4MT[1]	→	→	**24A** Accrington	**15D** Bedford	**14E** Bedford	**17A** Derby	**8L** Aintree
75044	4MT[1]	→	→	**24A** Accrington	**15D** Bedford	**14E** Bedford	**17A** Derby	**10G** Skipton
75045	4MT[1]	→	→	**24A** Accrington	**27A** Bank Hall	**27A** Bank Hall	**27A** Bank Hall	**5E** Nuneaton
75046	4MT[1]	→	→	**24A** Accrington	**27A** Bank Hall	**27A** Bank Hall	**27A** Bank Hall	**8K** Bank Hall
75047	4MT[1]	→	→	**24A** Accrington	**27A** Bank Hall	**27A** Bank Hall	**27A** Bank Hall	**8K** Bank Hall
75048	4MT[1]	→	→	**24A** Accrington	**27A** Bank Hall	**27A** Bank Hall	**27A** Bank Hall	**8K** Bank Hall
75049	4MT[1]	→	→	**24A** Accrington	**27A** Bank Hall	**27A** Bank Hall	**27A** Bank Hall	**8K** Bank Hall
75050	4MT[1]	→	→	→	**6G** Llandudno Junction	**6A** Chester	**2B** Nuneaton	**8K** Bank Hall
75051	4MT[1]	→	→	→	**6A** Chester	**6A** Chester	**1E** Bletchley	**10G** Skipton
75052	4MT[1]	→	→	→	**1E** Bletchley	**6D** Chester Northgate	**1A** Willesden	**6J** Holyhead
75053	4MT[1]	→	→	→	→	**6A** Chester	**21D** Aston	**6D** Shrewsbury
75054	4MT[1]	→	→	→	→	**6A** Chester	**1E** Bletchley	**5D** Stoke
75055	4MT[1]	→	→	→	→	**14E** Bedford	**17A** Derby	**6F** Machynlleth
75056	4MT[1]	→	→	→	→	**16A** Nottingham	**17A** Derby	**5D** Stoke
75057	4MT[1]	→	→	→	→	**15C** Leicester Midland	**17A** Derby	**10G** Skipton
75058	4MT[1]	→	→	→	→	**15C** Leicester Midland	**17A** Derby	**10G** Skipton
75059	4MT[1]	→	→	→	→	**15C** Leicester Midland	**17A** Derby	**10G** Skipton
75060	4MT[1]	→	→	→	→	**15C** Leicester Midland	**17A** Derby	**8A** Edge Hill
75061	4MT[1]	→	→	→	→	**15C** Leicester Midland	**17A** Derby	**8L** Aintree
75062	4MT[1]	→	→	→	→	**16A** Nottingham	**17A** Derby	**5D** Stoke
75063	4MT[1]	→	→	→	→	**16A** Nottingham	**17A** Derby	**6D** Shrewsbury
75064	4MT[1]	→	→	→	→	**16A** Nottingham	**17A** Derby	**8L** Aintree
75065	4MT[1]	→	→	→	**74C** Dover Marine	**71B** Bournemouth	**70D** Basingstoke	**70D** Eastleigh
75066	4MT[1]	→	→	→	**74C** Dover Marine	**71B** Bournemouth	**70D** Basingstoke	**70D** Eastleigh
75067	4MT[1]	→	→	→	**74C** Dover Marine	**71B** Bournemouth	**75A** Brighton	
75068	4MT[1]	→	→	→	**74C** Dover Marine	**71B** Bournemouth	**75A** Brighton	**70D** Eastleigh
75069	4MT[1]	→	→	→	**74C** Dover Marine	**73A** Stewarts Lane	**75D** Stewarts Lane	**70D** Eastleigh
75070	4MT[1]	→	→	→	**71G** Bath Green Park	**75A** Brighton	**75D** Stewarts Lane	**70D** Eastleigh
75071	4MT[1]	→	→	→	**71G** Bath Green Park	**82F** Bath Green Park	**82G** Templecombe	**6C** Croes Newydd
75072	4MT[1]	→	→	→	**71G** Bath Green Park	**82F** Bath Green Park	**82G** Templecombe	
75073	4MT[1]	→	→	→	**71A** Eastleigh	**82F** Bath Green Park	**82G** Templecombe	
75074	4MT[1]	→	→	→	**71A** Eastleigh	**73A** Stewarts Lane	**75D** Stewarts Lane	**70D** Eastleigh
75075	4MT[1]	→	→	→	**70D** Basingstoke	**75E** Three Bridges	**75D** Stewarts Lane	**70D** Eastleigh
75076	4MT[1]	→	→	→	**70D** Basingstoke	**70D** Basingstoke	**70D** Basingstoke	**70D** Eastleigh
75077	4MT[1]	→	→	→	**70D** Basingstoke	**70D** Basingstoke	**70D** Basingstoke	**70D** Eastleigh
75078	4MT[1]	→	→	→	**70D** Basingstoke	**70D** Basingstoke	**70D** Basingstoke	**70D** Eastleigh
75079	4MT[1]	→	→	→	**70D** Basingstoke	**70D** Basingstoke	**70D** Basingstoke	**70D** Eastleigh
76000	4MT[2]	→	→	**66B** Motherwell	**66B** Motherwell	**66B** Motherwell	**66B** Motherwell	**66B** Motherwell
76001	4MT[2]	→	→	**66B** Motherwell	**66B** Motherwell	**66B** Motherwell	**67A** Corkerhill	**67C** Ayr
76002	4MT[2]	→	→	**66B** Motherwell	**66B** Motherwell	**66B** Motherwell	**66B** Motherwell	**66B** Motherwell
76003	4MT[2]	→	→	**66B** Motherwell	**66B** Motherwell	**66B** Motherwell	**66B** Motherwell	**66B** Motherwell
76004	4MT[2]	→	→	**66B** Motherwell	**66B** Motherwell	**66B** Motherwell	**66B** Motherwell	**66A** Polmadie
76005	4MT[2]	→	→	**71A** Eastleigh	**72B** Salisbury	**72B** Salisbury	**70E** Salisbury	**70F** Bournemouth
76006	4MT[2]	→	→	**71A** Eastleigh	**72B** Salisbury	**72B** Salisbury	**71A** Eastleigh	**70F** Bournemouth
76007	4MT[2]	→	→	**71A** Eastleigh	**71A** Eastleigh	**72B** Salisbury	**70E** Salisbury	**70E** Salisbury
76008	4MT[2]	→	→	**71A** Eastleigh	**72B** Salisbury	**72B** Salisbury	**70E** Salisbury	**70E** Salisbury
76009	4MT[2]	→	→	**71A** Eastleigh	**75B** Redhill	**72B** Salisbury	**71A** Eastleigh	**70F** Bournemouth
76010	4MT[2]	→	→	**71A** Eastleigh	**71A** Eastleigh	**71A** Eastleigh	**71A** Eastleigh	**70F** Bournemouth
76011	4MT[2]	→	→	**71A** Eastleigh	**71A** Eastleigh	**71A** Eastleigh	**71A** Eastleigh	**70F** Bournemouth
76012	4MT[2]	→	→	**71A** Eastleigh	**71A** Eastleigh	**71A** Eastleigh	**71A** Eastleigh	**70D** Eastleigh
76013	4MT[2]	→	→	**71A** Eastleigh	**71A** Eastleigh	**71A** Eastleigh	**71A** Eastleigh	**70F** Bournemouth
76014	4MT[2]	→	→	**71A** Eastleigh	**75B** Redhill	**71A** Eastleigh	**71A** Eastleigh	**70F** Bournemouth
76015	4MT[2]	→	→	**71A** Eastleigh	**71A** Eastleigh	**71A** Eastleigh	**71B** Bournemouth	
76016	4MT[2]	→	→	**71A** Eastleigh	**71A** Eastleigh	**71A** Eastleigh	**71A** Eastleigh	**70D** Eastleigh
76017	4MT[2]	→	→	**71A** Eastleigh	**71A** Eastleigh	**71A** Eastleigh	**70E** Salisbury	
76018	4MT[2]	→	→	**71A** Eastleigh	**71A** Eastleigh	**71A** Eastleigh	**70E** Salisbury	**70D** Eastleigh
76019	4MT[2]	→	→	**71A** Eastleigh	**71A** Eastleigh	**71A** Eastleigh	**71B** Bournemouth	**70D** Eastleigh
76020	4MT[2]	→	→	**51A** Darlington	**51H** Kirkby Stephen	**8G** Sutton Oak	**5D** Stoke	**6A** Chester
76021	4MT[2]	→	→	**50F** Malton	**51F** West Auckland	**51F** West Auckland	**51F** West Auckland	**67B** Hurlford
76022	4MT[2]	→	→	**53A** Hull Dairycoates	**51H** Kirkby Stephen	**12D** Kirkby Stephen	**5D** Stoke	**2B** Oxley
76023	4MT[2]	→	→	**54A** Sunderland	**51H** Kirkby Stephen	**12D** Kirkby Stephen	**5D** Stoke	

		1948	1951	1954	1957	1960	1963	1966
76024	4MT[2]	→	→	**52D** Tweedmouth	**51F** West Auckland	**52B** Heaton	**51L** Thornaby	**67B** Hurlford
76025	4MT[2]	→	→	**71A** Eastleigh	**71A** Eastleigh	**71A** Eastleigh	**71B** Bournemouth	
76026	4MT[2]	→	→	**71A** Eastleigh	**71A** Eastleigh	**71A** Eastleigh	**71B** Bournemouth	**70F** Bournemouth
76027	4MT[2]	→	→	**71A** Eastleigh	**71A** Eastleigh	**71A** Eastleigh	**71B** Bournemouth	
76028	4MT[2]	→	→	**71A** Eastleigh	**71A** Eastleigh	**71A** Eastleigh	**71A** Eastleigh	
76029	4MT[2]	→	→	**71A** Eastleigh	**71A** Eastleigh	**71A** Eastleigh	**71A** Eastleigh	
76030	4MT[2]	→	→	**30A** Stratford	**30A** Stratford	**30A** Stratford	**75A** Brighton	
76031	4MT[2]	→	→	**30A** Stratford	**30A** Stratford	**30A** Stratford	**75A** Brighton	**70D** Eastleigh
76032	4MT[2]	→	→	**30A** Stratford	**30A** Stratford	**30A** Stratford	**75A** Brighton	
76033	4MT[2]	→	→	**30A** Stratford	**30A** Stratford	**30A** Stratford	**75A** Brighton	**70D** Eastleigh
76034	4MT[2]	→	→	**30A** Stratford	**30A** Stratford	**30A** Stratford	**75A** Brighton	
76035	4MT[2]	→	→	→	**38E** Woodford Halse	**14D** Neasden	**14A** Cricklewood	**6A** Chester
76036	4MT[2]	→	→	→	**34E** Neasden	**14D** Neasden	**14A** Cricklewood	**2C** Stourbridge
76037	4MT[2]	→	→	→	**34E** Neasden	**14D** Neasden	**14A** Cricklewood	**2B** Oxley
76038	4MT[2]	→	→	→	**34E** Neasden	**14D** Neasden	**14A** Cricklewood	**2E** Saltley
76039	4MT[2]	→	→	→	**34E** Neasden	**14D** Neasden	**14A** Cricklewood	**2B** Oxley
76040	4MT[2]	→	→	→	**34E** Neasden	**14D** Neasden	**14A** Cricklewood	**2E** Saltley
76041	4MT[2]	→	→	→	**34E** Neasden	**14D** Neasden	**14A** Cricklewood	**2B** Oxley
76042	4MT[2]	→	→	→	**34E** Neasden	**14D** Neasden	**14A** Cricklewood	**2C** Stourbridge
76043	4MT[2]	→	→	→	**34E** Neasden	**14D** Neasden	**14A** Cricklewood	**2E** Saltley
76044	4MT[2]	→	→	→	**34E** Neasden	**14D** Neasden	**2F** Woodford Halse	**5D** Stoke
76045	4MT[2]	→	→	→	**51F** West Auckland	**51F** West Auckland	**51F** West Auckland	**66E** Carstairs
76046	4MT[2]	→	→	→	**51F** West Auckland	**51F** West Auckland	**51F** West Auckland	**67A** Corkerhill
76047	4MT[2]	→	→	→	**51H** Kirkby Stephen	**12D** Kirkby Stephen	**14A** Cricklewood	**2F** Bescot
76048	4MT[2]	→	→	→	**51H** Kirkby Stephen	**9F** Heaton Mersey	**14A** Cricklewood	**2E** Saltley
76049	4MT[2]	→	→	→	**51F** West Auckland	**51F** West Auckland	**51F** West Auckland	**64A** St. Margarets
76050	4MT[2]	→	→	→	**51F** West Auckland	**51F** West Auckland	**51F** West Auckland	
76051	4MT[2]	→	→	→	**51H** Kirkby Stephen	**12D** Kirkby Stephen	**5D** Stoke	**5D** Stoke
76052	4MT[2]	→	→	→	**51H** Kirkby Stephen	**12D** Kirkby Stephen	**2F** Woodford Halse	**6A** Chester
76053	4MT[2]	→	→	→	**75B** Redhill	**75B** Redhill	**70E** Salisbury	**70D** Eastleigh
76054	4MT[2]	→	→	→	**75B** Redhill	**75B** Redhill	**70E** Salisbury	
76055	4MT[2]	→	→	→	**75B** Redhill	**75B** Redhill	**70E** Salisbury	
76056	4MT[2]	→	→	→	**75B** Redhill	**71B** Bournemouth	**71B** Bournemouth	
76057	4MT[2]	→	→	→	**75B** Redhill	**71B** Bournemouth	**71B** Bournemouth	**70F** Bournemouth
76058	4MT[2]	→	→	→	**75B** Redhill	**71B** Bournemouth	**71A** Eastleigh	**70D** Eastleigh
76059	4MT[2]	→	→	→	**75B** Redhill	**72B** Salisbury	**71A** Eastleigh	**70D** Eastleigh
76060	4MT[2]	→	→	→	**75B** Redhill	**72B** Salisbury	**71A** Eastleigh	
76061	4MT[2]	→	→	→	**75B** Redhill	**71A** Eastleigh	**71A** Eastleigh	**70D** Eastleigh
76062	4MT[2]	→	→	→	**75B** Redhill	**71A** Eastleigh	**71A** Eastleigh	
76063	4MT[2]	→	→	→	**71A** Eastleigh	**71A** Eastleigh	**71A** Eastleigh	**70D** Eastleigh
76064	4MT[2]	→	→	→	**71A** Eastleigh	**71A** Eastleigh	**71A** Eastleigh	**70D** Eastleigh
76065	4MT[2]	→	→	→	**71A** Eastleigh	**71A** Eastleigh	**71A** Eastleigh	
76066	4MT[2]	→	→	→	**71A** Eastleigh	**71A** Eastleigh	**70E** Salisbury	**70D** Eastleigh
76067	4MT[2]	→	→	→	**71A** Eastleigh	**71A** Eastleigh	**70E** Salisbury	**70E** Salisbury
76068	4MT[2]	→	→	→	**71A** Eastleigh	**71A** Eastleigh	**71A** Eastleigh	
76069	4MT[2]	→	→	→	**71A** Eastleigh	**71A** Eastleigh	**71A** Eastleigh	**70D** Eastleigh
76070	4MT[2]	→	→	→	**66B** Motherwell	**66B** Motherwell	**66B** Motherwell	**66A** Polmadie
76071	4MT[2]	→	→	→	**66B** Motherwell	**66B** Motherwell	**66B** Motherwell	**66A** Polmadie
76072	4MT[2]	→	→	→	**68B** Dumfries	**68B** Dumfries	**67E** Dumfries	
76073	4MT[2]	→	→	→	**68B** Dumfries	**68B** Dumfries	**67E** Dumfries	**67E** Dumfries
76074	4MT[2]	→	→	→	**65A** Eastfield	**65A** Eastfield	**65F** Grangemouth	**67E** Dumfries
76075	4MT[2]	→	→	→	**10D** Sutton Oak	**8G** Sutton Oak	**21B** Bescot	**5D** Stoke
76076	4MT[2]	→	→	→	**10D** Sutton Oak	**8G** Sutton Oak	**8G** Sutton Oak	**8G** Sutton Oak
76077	4MT[2]	→	→	→	**10D** Sutton Oak	**8G** Sutton Oak	**8G** Sutton Oak	**8G** Sutton Oak
76078	4MT[2]	→	→	→	**10D** Sutton Oak	**8G** Sutton Oak	**8G** Sutton Oak	**8G** Sutton Oak
76079	4MT[2]	→	→	→	→	**8G** Sutton Oak	**8G** Sutton Oak	**8G** Sutton Oak
76080	4MT[2]	→	→	→	→	**24D** Lower Darwen	**24D** Lower Darwen	**8G** Sutton Oak
76081	4MT[2]	→	→	→	→	**24D** Lower Darwen	**24D** Lower Darwen	**8G** Sutton Oak
76082	4MT[2]	→	→	→	→	**24D** Lower Darwen	**24D** Lower Darwen	**8G** Sutton Oak
76083	4MT[2]	→	→	→	→	**24D** Lower Darwen	**24D** Lower Darwen	**8G** Sutton Oak
76084	4MT[2]	→	→	→	→	**24D** Lower Darwen	**24D** Lower Darwen	**8G** Sutton Oak
76085	4MT[2]	→	→	→	→	**9F** Heaton Mersey	**14A** Cricklewood	**5D** Stoke
76086	4MT[2]	→	→	→	→	**9E** Trafford Park	**14A** Cricklewood	**2F** Bescot
76087	4MT[2]	→	→	→	→	**9F** Heaton Mersey	**2F** Woodford Halse	**2F** Bescot
76088	4MT[2]	→	→	→	→	**9E** Trafford Park	**14A** Cricklewood	**2F** Bescot
76089	4MT[2]	→	→	→	→	**9E** Trafford Park	**14A** Cricklewood	**5D** Stoke
76090	4MT[2]	→	→	→	→	**67A** Corkerhill	**66F** Beattock	**68D** Beattock
76091	4MT[2]	→	→	→	→	**67A** Corkerhill	**67A** Corkerhill	**67B** Hurlford
76092	4MT[2]	→	→	→	→	**67A** Corkerhill	**67A** Corkerhill	**67B** Hurlford
76093	4MT[2]	→	→	→	→	**67A** Corkerhill	**67A** Corkerhill	**67A** Corkerhill
76094	4MT[2]	→	→	→	→	**67A** Corkerhill	**67A** Corkerhill	**67B** Hurlford
76095	4MT[2]	→	→	→	→	**67A** Corkerhill	**67A** Corkerhill	**6A** Chester
76096	4MT[2]	→	→	→	→	**67A** Corkerhill	**67C** Ayr	**67C** Ayr
76097	4MT[2]	→	→	→	→	**67A** Corkerhill	**67C** Ayr	
76098	4MT[2]	→	→	→	→	**67A** Corkerhill	**67A** Corkerhill	**66F** Beattock
76099	4MT[2]	→	→	→	→	**67A** Corkerhill	**67C** Ayr	**5D** Stoke
76100	4MT[2]	→	→	→	→	**65D** Dawsholm	**65D** Dawsholm	**66F** Beattock
76101	4MT[2]	→	→	→	→	**65D** Dawsholm	**65D** Dawsholm	**67F** Stranraer
76102	4MT[2]	→	→	→	→	**65B** St. Rollox	**65D** Dawsholm	**67E** Dumfries
76103	4MT[2]	→	→	→	→	**65B** St. Rollox	**65F** Grangemouth	**66A** Polmadie
76104	4MT[2]	→	→	→	→	**61A** Kittybrewster	**61B** Aberdeen Ferryhill	**64F** Bathgate
76105	4MT[2]	→	→	→	→	**61A** Kittybrewster	**64C** Dalry Road	**64F** Bathgate
76106	4MT[2]	→	→	→	→	**61A** Kittybrewster	**64C** Dalry Road	
76107	4MT[2]	→	→	→	→	**61A** Kittybrewster	**61B** Aberdeen Ferryhill	
76108	4MT[2]	→	→	→	→	**61A** Kittybrewster	**61B** Aberdeen Ferryhill	**67B** Hurlford
76109	4MT[2]	→	→	→	→	**62A** Thornton Junction	**62C** Dunfermline Upper	**62C** Dunfermline Upper
76110	4MT[2]	→	→	→	→	**62A** Thornton Junction	**62C** Dunfermline Upper	**62C** Dunfermline Upper
76111	4MT[2]	→	→	→	→	**62A** Thornton Junction	**62A** Thornton Junction	**64F** Bathgate
76112	4MT[2]	→	→	→	→	**68C** Stranraer	**67F** Stranraer	
76113	4MT[2]	→	→	→	→	**65B** St. Rollox	**65F** Grangemouth	**66E** Carstairs
76114	4MT[2]	→	→	→	→	**65B** St. Rollox	**67A** Corkerhill	**67A** Corkerhill
77000	3MT[1]	→	→	→	**53D** Bridlington	**53A** Hull Dairycoates	**50B** Hull Dairycoates	**55B** Stourton
77001	3MT[1]	→	→	→	**53B** Hull Botanic Gardens	**53A** Hull Dairycoates	**51L** Thornaby	**50D** Goole
77002	3MT[1]	→	→	→	**51F** West Auckland	**51F** West Auckland	**51A** Darlington	**52D** Tweedmouth
77003	3MT[1]	→	→	→	**51F** West Auckland	**51F** West Auckland	**51F** West Auckland	**55B** Stourton
77004	3MT[1]	→	→	→	**51F** West Auckland	**50E** Scarborough	**50E** Scarborough	**52D** Tweedmouth
77005	3MT[1]	→	→	→	**66C** Hamilton	**66A** Polmadie	**66E** Carstairs	**66B** Motherwell
77006	3MT[1]	→	→	→	**66C** Hamilton	**66C** Hamilton	**66E** Carstairs	**66B** Motherwell
77007	3MT[1]	→	→	→	**66C** Hamilton	**66A** Polmadie	**66A** Polmadie	**67B** Hurlford
77008	3MT[1]	→	→	→	**66A** Polmadie	**66A** Polmadie	**66A** Polmadie	**66B** Motherwell
77009	3MT[1]	→	→	→	**66A** Polmadie	**66A** Polmadie	**66A** Polmadie	**66B** Motherwell
77010	3MT[1]	→	→	→	**53B** Hull Botanic Gardens	**53A** Hull Dairycoates	**51L** Thornaby	
77011	3MT[1]	→	→	→	**52C** Blaydon	**52A** Gateshead	**51L** Thornaby	**8E** Northwich
77012	3MT[1]	→	→	→	**50G** Whitby	**50A** York	**50A** York	**50D** Goole
77013	3MT[1]	→	→	→	**50G** Whitby	**50A** York	**50E** Scarborough	**55B** Stourton
77014	3MT[1]	→	→	→	**52C** Blaydon	**52A** Gateshead	**51L** Thornaby	**8E** Northwich
77015	3MT[1]	→	→	→	**67B** Hurlford	**67B** Hurlford	**67B** Hurlford	**67B** Hurlford
77016	3MT[1]	→	→	→	**67B** Hurlford	**67B** Hurlford	**67B** Hurlford	**67B** Hurlford
77017	3MT[1]	→	→	→	**67B** Hurlford	**67B** Hurlford	**67B** Hurlford	**67B** Hurlford
77018	3MT[1]	→	→	→	**67B** Hurlford	**67B** Hurlford	**67B** Hurlford	**67B** Hurlford
77019	3MT[1]	→	→	→	**67B** Hurlford	**67B** Hurlford	**67B** Hurlford	**67B** Hurlford
78000	2MT[1]	→	→	**89C** Machynlleth	**89C** Machynlleth	**89C** Machynlleth	**89C** Machynlleth	
78001	2MT[1]	→	→	**89C** Machynlleth	**85A** Worcester	**85A** Worcester	**85A** Worcester	
78002	2MT[1]	→	→	**89C** Machynlleth	**89C** Machynlleth	**89C** Machynlleth	**89C** Machynlleth	**10D** Lostock Hall

		1948	1951	1954	1957	1960	1963	1966
78003	2MT[1]	→	→	**89C** Machynlleth	**89C** Machynlleth	**89C** Machynlleth	**89C** Machynlleth	**5E** Nuneaton
78004	2MT[1]	→	→	**89C** Machynlleth	**82C** Swindon	**85C** Hereford	**86C** Hereford	
78005	2MT[1]	→	→	**89C** Machynlleth	**89C** Machynlleth	**89C** Machynlleth	**85C** Gloucester Barnwood	
78006	2MT[1]	→	→	**89C** Machynlleth	**89C** Machynlleth	**89C** Machynlleth	**85C** Gloucester Barnwood	
78007	2MT[1]	→	→	**89C** Machynlleth	**89C** Machynlleth	**89C** Machynlleth	**89C** Machynlleth	**9E** Trafford Park
78008	2MT[1]	→	→	**85A** Worcester	**85A** Worcester	**85A** Worcester	**84B** Oxley	**2B** Oxley
78009	2MT[1]	→	→	**85A** Worcester	**85A** Worcester	**85A** Worcester	**85A** Worcester	
78010	2MT[1]	→	→	**51F** West Auckland	**51J** Northallerton	**51J** Northallerton	**51J** Northallerton	**5B** Crewe South
78011	2MT[1]	→	→	**51F** West Auckland	**51J** Northallerton	**51J** Northallerton	**51J** Northallerton	
78012	2MT[1]	→	→	→	**50G** Whitby	**51J** Northallerton	**51J** Northallerton	**9E** Trafford Park
78013	2MT[1]	→	→	→	**51J** Northallerton	**12D** Kirkby Stephen	**16B** Kirkby in Ashfield	**15A** Leicester Midland
78014	2MT[1]	→	→	→	**51J** Northallerton	**51J** Northallerton	**51J** Northallerton	
78015	2MT[1]	→	→	→	**51J** Northallerton	**51J** Northallerton	**51J** Northallerton	
78016	2MT[1]	→	→	→	**51H** Kirkby Stephen	**51F** West Auckland	**51F** West Auckland	**67F** Stranraer
78017	2MT[1]	→	→	→	**51H** Kirkby Stephen	**12D** Kirkby Stephen	**5D** Stoke	**5D** Stoke
78018	2MT[1]	→	→	→	**51H** Kirkby Stephen	**12D** Kirkby Stephen	**6A** Chester	**5E** Nuneaton
78019	2MT[1]	→	→	→	**51H** Kirkby Stephen	**12D** Kirkby Stephen	**8E** Northwich	**5E** Nuneaton
78020	2MT[1]	→	→	→	**15B** Kettering	**16A** Nottingham	**16A** Nottingham	**16C** Derby
78021	2MT[1]	→	→	→	**15B** Kettering	**16A** Nottingham	**16A** Nottingham	**15A** Leicester Midland
78022	2MT[1]	→	→	→	**19B** Millhouses	**41C** Millhouses	**12E** Barrow	**10D** Lostock Hall
78023	2MT[1]	→	→	→	**19B** Millhouses	**41C** Millhouses	**12E** Barrow	**9E** Trafford Park
78024	2MT[1]	→	→	→	**19B** Millhouses	**41C** Millhouses	**51A** Darlington	
78025	2MT[1]	→	→	→	**19B** Millhouses	**41C** Millhouses	**51F** West Auckland	
78026	2MT[1]	→	→	→	**19C** Canklow	**41D** Canklow	**67C** Ayr	**67A** Corkerhill
78027	2MT[1]	→	→	→	**19C** Canklow	**41D** Canklow	**12E** Barrow	
78028	2MT[1]	→	→	→	**15C** Leicester Midland	**16A** Nottingham	**16A** Nottingham	**15A** Leicester Midland
78029	2MT[1]	→	→	→	**15C** Leicester Midland	**16A** Nottingham	**16A** Nottingham	
78030	2MT[1]	→	→	→	**5A** Crewe North	**5A** Crewe North	**5A** Crewe North	
78031	2MT[1]	→	→	→	**6D** Chester Northgate	**6K** Rhyl	**5B** Crewe South	**5B** Crewe South
78032	2MT[1]	→	→	→	**8D** Widnes	**8D** Widnes	**6A** Chester	
78033	2MT[1]	→	→	→	**8D** Widnes	**8D** Widnes	**6A** Chester	
78034	2MT[1]	→	→	→	**8D** Widnes	**8D** Widnes	**6H** Bangor	**5B** Crewe South
78035	2MT[1]	→	→	→	**8D** Widnes	**8D** Widnes	**8D** Widnes	
78036	2MT[1]	→	→	→	**10B** Preston	**24K** Preston	**24G** Skipton	**5B** Crewe South
78037	2MT[1]	→	→	→	**10B** Preston	**24K** Preston	**24G** Skipton	**10D** Lostock Hall
78038	2MT[1]	→	→	→	**6D** Chester Northgate	**8E** Northwich	**8E** Northwich	**6D** Shrewsbury
78039	2MT[1]	→	→	→	**8D** Widnes	**8D** Widnes	**8D** Widnes	**5E** Nuneaton
78040	2MT[1]	→	→	→	**27A** Bank Hall	**27D** Wigan	**27B** Aintree	**10D** Lostock Hall
78041	2MT[1]	→	→	→	**27A** Bank Hall	**27A** Bank Hall	**27A** Bank Hall	**10D** Lostock Hall
78042	2MT[1]	→	→	→	**27A** Bank Hall	**27A** Bank Hall	**27A** Bank Hall	
78043	2MT[1]	→	→	→	**27B** Aintree	**27A** Bank Hall	**27B** Aintree	
78044	2MT[1]	→	→	→	**27A** Bank Hall	**27A** Bank Hall	**27B** Aintree	**16A** Toton
78045	2MT[1]	→	→	→	**61A** Kittybrewster	**61A** Kittybrewster	**61B** Aberdeen Ferryhill	**64F** Bathgate
78046	2MT[1]	→	→	→	**64G** Hawick	**64G** Hawick	**64G** Hawick	**64F** Bathgate
78047	2MT[1]	→	→	→	**64G** Hawick	**64G** Hawick	**64G** Hawick	**64A** St. Margarets
78048	2MT[1]	→	→	→	**64A** St. Margarets	**64A** St. Margarets	**64G** Hawick	
78049	2MT[1]	→	→	→	**64A** St. Margarets	**64G** Hawick	**64G** Hawick	**64G** Hawick
78050	2MT[1]	→	→	→	**66B** Motherwell	**66B** Motherwell	**66B** Motherwell	**64F** Bathgate
78051	2MT[1]	→	→	→	**66B** Motherwell	**66B** Motherwell	**66B** Motherwell	**67E** Dumfries
78052	2MT[1]	→	→	→	**60A** Inverness	**60B** Aviemore	**63A** Perth	**64F** Bathgate
78053	2MT[1]	→	→	→	**61C** Keith	**61C** Keith	**61B** Aberdeen Ferryhill	
78054	2MT[1]	→	→	→	**61C** Keith	**61C** Keith	**61B** Aberdeen Ferryhill	
78055	2MT[1]	→	→	→	**6D** Chester Northgate	**6K** Rhyl	**5B** Crewe South	**16A** Toton
78056	2MT[1]	→	→	→	**6D** Chester Northgate	**6K** Rhyl	**5D** Stoke	**5D** Stoke
78057	2MT[1]	→	→	→	**6D** Chester Northgate	**8E** Northwich	**8E** Northwich	**10D** Lostock Hall
78058	2MT[1]	→	→	→	**6D** Chester Northgate	**6H** Bangor	**6H** Bangor	**6D** Shrewsbury
78059	2MT[1]	→	→	→	**6D** Chester Northgate	**6H** Bangor	**6H** Bangor	**5E** Nuneaton
78060	2MT[1]	→	→	→	**27D** Wigan	**27D** Wigan	**27B** Aintree	**6D** Shrewsbury
78061	2MT[1]	→	→	→	**27D** Wigan	**27D** Wigan	**27D** Wigan	**15A** Leicester Midland
78062	2MT[1]	→	→	→	**27D** Wigan	**27D** Wigan	**27D** Wigan	**9E** Trafford Park
78063	2MT[1]	→	→	→	**27D** Wigan	**27D** Wigan	**27D** Wigan	**5E** Nuneaton
78064	2MT[1]	→	→	→	**27D** Wigan	**27D** Wigan	**27D** Wigan	**16C** Derby
80000	4MT[3]	→	→	**67A** Corkerhill	**67A** Corkerhill	**67A** Corkerhill	**67D** Ardrossan	**67A** Corkerhill
80001	4MT[3]	→	→	**66A** Polmadie	**66A** Polmadie	**66A** Polmadie	**66F** Beattock	**66A** Polmadie
80002	4MT[3]	→	→	**66A** Polmadie	**66A** Polmadie	**66A** Polmadie	**66F** Beattock	**66A** Polmadie
80003	4MT[3]	→	→	**66A** Polmadie	**66A** Polmadie	**66A** Polmadie	**64A** St. Margarets	
80004	4MT[3]	→	→	**61A** Kittybrewster	**61A** Kittybrewster	**61A** Kittybrewster	**66F** Beattock	**67A** Corkerhill
80005	4MT[3]	→	→	**61A** Kittybrewster	**61A** Kittybrewster	**67A** Corkerhill	**67A** Corkerhill	**66A** Polmadie
80006	4MT[3]	→	→	**66A** Polmadie	**66A** Polmadie	**66A** Polmadie	**64A** St. Margarets	**64A** St. Margarets
80007	4MT[3]	→	→	**66A** Polmadie	**66A** Polmadie	**66A** Polmadie	**64A** St. Margarets	**66A** Polmadie
80008	4MT[3]	→	→	**67A** Corkerhill	**67A** Corkerhill	**67A** Corkerhill	**67A** Corkerhill	
80009	4MT[3]	→	→	**67A** Corkerhill	**67A** Corkerhill	**67A** Corkerhill	**67A** Corkerhill	
80010	4MT[3]	→	→	**75F** Tunbridge Wells West	**75A** Brighton	**75E** Three Bridges	**75E** Three Bridges	
80011	4MT[3]	→	→	**75F** Tunbridge Wells West	**75A** Brighton	**75E** Three Bridges	**75E** Three Bridges	**70F** Bournemouth
80012	4MT[3]	→	→	**75F** Tunbridge Wells West	**75F** Tunbridge Wells West	**75E** Three Bridges	**75E** Three Bridges	**70A** Nine Elms
80013	4MT[3]	→	→	**75F** Tunbridge Wells West	**75F** Tunbridge Wells West	**75A** Brighton	**75A** Brighton	**70F** Bournemouth
80014	4MT[3]	→	→	**75F** Tunbridge Wells West	**75F** Tunbridge Wells West	**75F** Tunbridge Wells West	**75F** Tunbridge Wells West	
80015	4MT[3]	→	→	**75F** Tunbridge Wells West	**75F** Tunbridge Wells West	**75F** Tunbridge Wells West	**75F** Tunbridge Wells West	**70A** Nine Elms
80016	4MT[3]	→	→	**75A** Brighton	**75F** Tunbridge Wells West	**75F** Tunbridge Wells West	**75F** Tunbridge Wells West	**70D** Eastleigh
80017	4MT[3]	→	→	**75F** Tunbridge Wells West	**75F** Tunbridge Wells West	**75F** Tunbridge Wells West	**75F** Tunbridge Wells West	
80018	4MT[3]	→	→	**75F** Tunbridge Wells West	**75F** Tunbridge Wells West	**75F** Tunbridge Wells West	**75F** Tunbridge Wells West	
80019	4MT[3]	→	→	**75A** Brighton	**75F** Tunbridge Wells West	**75F** Tunbridge Wells West	**75F** Tunbridge Wells West	**70F** Bournemouth
80020	4MT[3]	→	→	**61A** Kittybrewster	**61A** Kittybrewster	**61A** Kittybrewster	**67A** Corkerhill	
80021	4MT[3]	→	→	**61A** Kittybrewster	**61A** Kittybrewster	**61A** Kittybrewster	**67A** Corkerhill	
80022	4MT[3]	→	→	**66A** Polmadie	**66A** Polmadie	**66A** Polmadie	**64A** St. Margarets	
80023	4MT[3]	→	→	**66A** Polmadie	**66A** Polmadie	**66A** Polmadie	**67B** Hurlford	
80024	4MT[3]	→	→	**67A** Corkerhill	**67A** Corkerhill	**67A** Corkerhill	**67A** Corkerhill	**67A** Corkerhill
80025	4MT[3]	→	→	**67A** Corkerhill	**67A** Corkerhill	**67A** Corkerhill	**67A** Corkerhill	**67A** Corkerhill
80026	4MT[3]	→	→	**66A** Polmadie	**66A** Polmadie	**66A** Polmadie	**64A** St. Margarets	**64A** St. Margarets
80027	4MT[3]	→	→	**66A** Polmadie	**66A** Polmadie	**66A** Polmadie	**66A** Polmadie	**66A** Polmadie
80028	4MT[3]	→	→	**61A** Kittybrewster	**61A** Kittybrewster	**61A** Kittybrewster	**67B** Hurlford	**63A** Perth
80029	4MT[3]	→	→	**61A** Kittybrewster	**61A** Kittybrewster	**61A** Kittybrewster	**67B** Hurlford	
80030	4MT[3]	→	→	**67A** Corkerhill	**67A** Corkerhill	**67A** Corkerhill	**67A** Corkerhill	
80031	4MT[3]	→	→	**75A** Brighton	**75A** Brighton	**75A** Brighton	**75A** Brighton	
80032	4MT[3]	→	→	**75A** Brighton	**75A** Brighton	**75A** Brighton	**75A** Brighton	**70F** Bournemouth
80033	4MT[3]	→	→	**75A** Brighton	**75A** Brighton	**75A** Brighton	**75A** Brighton	**70B** Feltham
80034	4MT[3]	→	→	**1C** Watford	**1C** Watford	**73F** Ashford	**75D** Stewarts Lane	**70B** Feltham
80035	4MT[3]	→	→	**1C** Watford	**1C** Watford	**73F** Ashford	**72A** Exmouth Junction	
80036	4MT[3]	→	→	**1C** Watford	**1C** Watford	**73F** Ashford	**72A** Exmouth Junction	
80037	4MT[3]	→	→	**1C** Watford	**1C** Watford	**73F** Ashford	**72A** Exmouth Junction	**83G** Templecombe
80038	4MT[3]	→	→	**1C** Watford	**1C** Watford	**73F** Ashford	**72A** Exmouth Junction	
80039	4MT[3]	→	→	**1E** Bletchley	**1E** Bletchley	**73F** Ashford	**72A** Exmouth Junction	**83G** Templecombe
80040	4MT[3]	→	→	**1E** Bletchley	**1E** Bletchley	**73F** Ashford	**72A** Exmouth Junction	
80041	4MT[3]	→	→	**1E** Bletchley	**1E** Bletchley	**73F** Ashford	**72A** Exmouth Junction	**83G** Templecombe
80042	4MT[3]	→	→	**1E** Bletchley	**1E** Bletchley	**73F** Ashford	**72A** Exmouth Junction	
80043	4MT[3]	→	→	**1E** Bletchley	**1E** Bletchley	**73H** Dover Marine	**72A** Exmouth Junction	**83G** Templecombe
80044	4MT[3]	→	→	**15D** Bedford	**26A** Newton Heath	**26A** Newton Heath	**67A** Corkerhill	
80045	4MT[3]	→	→	**15D** Bedford	**6A** Chester	**6A** Chester	**67A** Corkerhill	**66A** Polmadie
80046	4MT[3]	→	→	**15D** Bedford	**26A** Newton Heath	**24E** Blackpool Central	**67A** Corkerhill	**67A** Corkerhill
80047	4MT[3]	→	→	**14B** Kentish Town	**6A** Chester	**6A** Chester	**67A** Corkerhill	**67A** Corkerhill
80048	4MT[3]	→	→	**14B** Kentish Town	**6A** Chester	**6A** Chester	**67A** Corkerhill	
80049	4MT[3]	→	→	**26A** Newton Heath	**6A** Chester	**6A** Chester	**67A** Corkerhill	
80050	4MT[3]	→	→	**26A** Newton Heath	**6A** Chester	**6A** Chester	**67A** Corkerhill	
80051	4MT[3]	→	→	**26A** Newton Heath	**6A** Chester	**6A** Chester	**67A** Corkerhill	**67A** Corkerhill

		1948	1951	1954	1957	1960	1963	1966
80052	$4MT^3$	→	→	**26A** Newton Heath	**6A** Chester	**6A** Chester	**67A** Corkerhill	
80053	$4MT^3$	→	→	**26A** Newton Heath	**6A** Chester	**6A** Chester	**67A** Corkerhill	
80054	$4MT^3$	→	→	→	**66A** Polmadie	**66A** Polmadie	**64A** St. Margarets	**66D** Greenock Ladyburn
80055	$4MT^3$	→	→	→	**66A** Polmadie	**66A** Polmadie	**64A** St. Margarets	**64A** St. Margarets
80056	$4MT^3$	→	→	→	**66A** Polmadie	**66A** Polmadie	**66A** Polmadie	
80057	$4MT^3$	→	→	→	**66A** Polmadie	**66A** Polmadie	**66A** Polmadie	**66A** Polmadie
80058	$4MT^3$	→	→	→	**66A** Polmadie	**66A** Polmadie	**66A** Polmadie	**66A** Polmadie
80059	$4MT^3$	→	→	**14B** Kentish Town	**6A** Chester	**73H** Dover Marine	**72A** Exmouth Junction	
80060	$4MT^3$	→	→	**15D** Bedford	**26A** Newton Heath	**26A** Newton Heath	**65J** Stirling	**66A** Polmadie
80061	$4MT^3$	→	→	**15D** Bedford	**26A** Newton Heath	**26A** Newton Heath	**65J** Stirling	**66A** Polmadie
80062	$4MT^3$	→	→	**14B** Kentish Town	**6A** Chester	**6C** Birkenhead	**65J** Stirling	
80063	$4MT^3$	→	→	**21A** Saltley	**6A** Chester	**6C** Birkenhead	**65J** Stirling	**67A** Corkerhill
80064	$4MT^3$	→	→	**1C** Watford	**1C** Watford	**73H** Dover Marine	**72A** Exmouth Junction	
80065	$4MT^3$	→	→	**1C** Watford	**1C** Watford	**73H** Dover Marine	**71A** Eastleigh	**70D** Eastleigh
80066	$4MT^3$	→	→	**1C** Watford	**1C** Watford	**73A** Stewarts Lane	**71A** Eastleigh	
80067	$4MT^3$	→	→	**1C** Watford	**1C** Watford	**73A** Stewarts Lane	**72A** Exmouth Junction	
80068	$4MT^3$	→	→	**1C** Watford	**1C** Watford	**73A** Stewarts Lane	**75D** Stewarts Lane	**70B** Feltham
80069	$4MT^3$	→	→	**33A** Plaistow	**33B** Tilbury	**33B** Tilbury	**87D** Swansea East Dock	**70A** Nine Elms
80070	$4MT^3$	→	→	**33A** Plaistow	**33B** Tilbury	**33B** Tilbury	**89A** Shrewsbury	
80071	$4MT^3$	→	→	**33A** Plaistow	**33B** Tilbury	**33B** Tilbury	**56B** Ardsley	
80072	$4MT^3$	→	→	**33A** Plaistow	**33B** Tilbury	**33B** Tilbury	**87D** Swansea East Dock	
80073	$4MT^3$	→	→	**33A** Plaistow	**33B** Tilbury	**33B** Tilbury	**56B** Ardsley	
80074	$4MT^3$	→	→	**33A** Plaistow	**33B** Tilbury	**33B** Tilbury	**56B** Ardsley	
80075	$4MT^3$	→	→	**33A** Plaistow	**33B** Tilbury	**33B** Tilbury	**56B** Ardsley	
80076	$4MT^3$	→	→	**33A** Plaistow	**33B** Tilbury	**33B** Tilbury	**56B** Ardsley	
80077	$4MT^3$	→	→	→	**33B** Tilbury	**33B** Tilbury	**56B** Ardsley	
80078	$4MT^3$	→	→	→	**33B** Tilbury	**33B** Tilbury	**89A** Shrewsbury	
80079	$4MT^3$	→	→	→	**33B** Tilbury	**33B** Tilbury	**89B** Croes Newydd	
80080	$4MT^3$	→	→	→	**33B** Tilbury	**33B** Tilbury	**89B** Croes Newydd	
80081	$4MT^3$	→	→	→	**1E** Bletchley	**73A** Stewarts Lane	**75D** Stewarts Lane	
80082	$4MT^3$	→	→	→	**1E** Bletchley	**73B** Bricklayers Arms	**71A** Eastleigh	**70D** Eastleigh
80083	$4MT^3$	→	→	→	**1E** Bletchley	**73B** Bricklayers Arms	**71A** Eastleigh	**70D** Eastleigh
80084	$4MT^3$	→	→	→	**1E** Bletchley	**73B** Bricklayers Arms	**75D** Stewarts Lane	
80085	$4MT^3$	→	→	→	**1E** Bletchley	**73B** Bricklayers Arms	**75D** Stewarts Lane	**70B** Feltham
80086	$4MT^3$	→	→	→	**6A** Chester	**6A** Chester	**66A** Polmadie	**66A** Polmadie
80087	$4MT^3$	→	→	→	**6H** Bangor	**75E** Three Bridges	**71A** Eastleigh	
80088	$4MT^3$	→	→	→	**6H** Bangor	**75E** Three Bridges	**75E** Three Bridges	
80089	$4MT^3$	→	→	→	**6H** Bangor	**75E** Three Bridges	**75E** Three Bridges	**70A** Nine Elms
80090	$4MT^3$	→	→	→	**6H** Bangor	**6C** Birkenhead	**62B** Dundee Tay Bridge	
80091	$4MT^3$	→	→	→	**6H** Bangor	**6A** Chester	**67B** Hurlford	**67B** Hurlford
80092	$4MT^3$	→	→	→	**1A** Willesden	**6A** Chester	**63A** Perth	**63A** Perth
80093	$4MT^3$	→	→	→	**26A** Newton Heath	**24E** Blackpool Central	**63A** Perth	**63A** Perth
80094	$4MT^3$	→	→	→	**6H** Bangor	**75E** Three Bridges	**75E** Three Bridges	**70B** Feltham
80095	$4MT^3$	→	→	→	**6H** Bangor	**75F** Tunbridge Wells West	**71A** Eastleigh	**70A** Nine Elms
80096	$4MT^3$	→	→	→	**33A** Plaistow	**33B** Tilbury	**89B** Croes Newydd	
80097	$4MT^3$	→	→	→	**33A** Plaistow	**33B** Tilbury	**87D** Swansea East Dock	
80098	$4MT^3$	→	→	→	**33A** Plaistow	**33B** Tilbury	**89B** Croes Newydd	
80099	$4MT^3$	→	→	→	**33A** Plaistow	**33B** Tilbury	**87D** Swansea East Dock	
80100	$4MT^3$	→	→	→	**33A** Plaistow	**33B** Tilbury	**89A** Shrewsbury	
80101	$4MT^3$	→	→	→	**33A** Plaistow	**33B** Tilbury	**89C** Machynlleth	
80102	$4MT^3$	→	→	→	**33A** Plaistow	**33B** Tilbury	**89A** Shrewsbury	
80103	$4MT^3$	→	→	→	**33A** Plaistow	**33B** Tilbury		
80104	$4MT^3$	→	→	→	**33A** Plaistow	**33B** Tilbury	**89B** Croes Newydd	
80105	$4MT^3$	→	→	→	**33A** Plaistow	**33B** Tilbury	**89C** Machynlleth	
80106	$4MT^3$	→	→	→	**61A** Kittybrewster	**66A** Polmadie	**66A** Polmadie	
80107	$4MT^3$	→	→	→	**61A** Kittybrewster	**66A** Polmadie	**66A** Polmadie	
80108	$4MT^3$	→	→	→	**61A** Kittybrewster	**66A** Polmadie	**66A** Polmadie	
80109	$4MT^3$	→	→	→	**61A** Kittybrewster	**66A** Polmadie	**66A** Polmadie	
80110	$4MT^3$	→	→	→	**61A** Kittybrewster	**66A** Polmadie	**66A** Polmadie	
80111	$4MT^3$	→	→	→	**66A** Polmadie	**61A** Kittybrewster	**67B** Hurlford	**67B** Hurlford
80112	$4MT^3$	→	→	→	**66A** Polmadie	**61A** Kittybrewster	**67B** Hurlford	**67A** Corkerhill
80113	$4MT^3$	→	→	→	**66A** Polmadie	**61A** Kittybrewster	**64G** Hawick	**64G** Hawick
80114	$4MT^3$	→	→	→	**66A** Polmadie	**61A** Kittybrewster	**64A** St. Margarets	**64A** St. Margarets
80115	$4MT^3$	→	→	→	**66A** Polmadie	**61A** Kittybrewster	**66A** Polmadie	
80116	$4MT^3$	→	→	→	**50G** Whitby	**50B** Leeds Neville Hill	**55H** Leeds Neville Hill	**66A** Polmadie
80117	$4MT^3$	→	→	→	**50G** Whitby	**50B** Leeds Neville Hill	**55H** Leeds Neville Hill	**66A** Polmadie
80118	$4MT^3$	→	→	→	**50G** Whitby	**50B** Leeds Neville Hill	**55H** Leeds Neville Hill	**66A** Polmadie
80119	$4MT^3$	→	→	→	**50G** Whitby	**50B** Leeds Neville Hill	**55H** Leeds Neville Hill	
80120	$4MT^3$	→	→	→	**50G** Whitby	**50B** Leeds Neville Hill	**55H** Leeds Neville Hill	**66A** Polmadie
80121	$4MT^3$	→	→	→	**61C** Keith	**61C** Keith	**66A** Polmadie	**66A** Polmadie
80122	$4MT^3$	→	→	→	**61C** Keith	**61C** Keith	**64A** St. Margarets	**66D** Greenock Ladyburn
80123	$4MT^3$	→	→	→	**62B** Dundee Tay Bridge	**62B** Dundee Tay Bridge	**62B** Dundee Tay Bridge	**66A** Polmadie
80124	$4MT^3$	→	→	→	**62B** Dundee Tay Bridge	**62B** Dundee Tay Bridge	**62B** Dundee Tay Bridge	**62B** Dundee Tay Bridge
80125	$4MT^3$	→	→	→	**63B** Stirling	**63B** Stirling	**65J** Stirling	
80126	$4MT^3$	→	→	→	**63A** Perth	**63A** Perth	**63A** Perth	**63A** Perth
80127	$4MT^3$	→	→	→	**67A** Corkerhill	**67A** Corkerhill	**67A** Corkerhill	
80128	$4MT^3$	→	→	→	**67A** Corkerhill	**67A** Corkerhill	**67A** Corkerhill	**67A** Corkerhill
80129	$4MT^3$	→	→	→	**66A** Polmadie	**66A** Polmadie	**66A** Polmadie	
80130	$4MT^3$	→	→	→	**66A** Polmadie	**66A** Polmadie	**66A** Polmadie	**66A** Polmadie
80131	$4MT^3$	→	→	→	**33A** Plaistow	**33B** Tilbury	**89A** Shrewsbury	
80132	$4MT^3$	→	→	→	**33A** Plaistow	**33B** Tilbury	**89A** Shrewsbury	**70D** Eastleigh
80133	$4MT^3$	→	→	→	**33A** Plaistow	**33C** Shoeburyness	**87D** Swansea East Dock	**70A** Nine Elms
80134	$4MT^3$	→	→	→	**33A** Plaistow	**33B** Tilbury	**87D** Swansea East Dock	**70F** Bournemouth
80135	$4MT^3$	→	→	→	**33A** Plaistow	**33B** Tilbury	**89A** Shrewsbury	
80136	$4MT^3$	→	→	→	**33A** Plaistow	**33B** Tilbury	**89A** Shrewsbury	
80137	$4MT^3$	→	→	→	**34E** Neasden	**75F** Tunbridge Wells West	**71A** Eastleigh	
80138	$4MT^3$	→	→	→	**34E** Neasden	**75F** Tunbridge Wells West	**75A** Brighton	**70F** Bournemouth
80139	$4MT^3$	→	→	→	**34E** Neasden	**75F** Tunbridge Wells West	**75F** Tunbridge Wells West	**70D** Eastleigh
80140	$4MT^3$	→	→	→	**34E** Neasden	**75F** Tunbridge Wells West	**75F** Tunbridge Wells West	**70B** Feltham
80141	$4MT^3$	→	→	→	**34E** Neasden	**75F** Tunbridge Wells West	**75F** Tunbridge Wells West	**70A** Nine Elms
80142	$4MT^3$	→	→	→	**34E** Neasden	**75F** Tunbridge Wells West	**75F** Tunbridge Wells West	**70E** Salisbury
80143	$4MT^3$	→	→	→	**34E** Neasden	**75A** Brighton	**75A** Brighton	**70A** Nine Elms
80144	$4MT^3$	→	→	→	**34E** Neasden	**75A** Brighton	**75A** Brighton	**70D** Eastleigh
80145	$4MT^3$	→	→	→	**75A** Brighton	**75A** Brighton	**75A** Brighton	**70E** Salisbury
80146	$4MT^3$	→	→	→	**75A** Brighton	**75A** Brighton	**75A** Brighton	**70F** Bournemouth
80147	$4MT^3$	→	→	→	**75A** Brighton	**75A** Brighton	**75A** Brighton	
80148	$4MT^3$	→	→	→	**75A** Brighton	**75A** Brighton	**75A** Brighton	
80149	$4MT^3$	→	→	→	**75A** Brighton	**75A** Brighton	**75A** Brighton	
80150	$4MT^3$	→	→	→	**75A** Brighton	**75A** Brighton	**75A** Brighton	
80151	$4MT^3$	→	→	→	→	**75A** Brighton	**75A** Brighton	**70E** Salisbury
80152	$4MT^3$	→	→	→	→	**75A** Brighton	**75A** Brighton	**70E** Salisbury
80153	$4MT^3$	→	→	→	→	**75A** Brighton	**75A** Brighton	
80154	$4MT^3$	→	→	→	→	**75A** Brighton	**75A** Brighton	**70A** Nine Elms
82000	$3MT^2$	→	→	**88F** Treherbert	**84G** Shrewsbury	**84K** Wrexham Rhosddu	**89C** Machynlleth	**9H** Patricroft
82001	$3MT^2$	→	→	**88C** Barry	**88F** Treherbert	**6E** Chester (GWR)	**86C** Hereford	
82002	$3MT^2$	→	→	**88C** Barry	**88F** Treherbert	**6E** Chester (GWR)	**86C** Hereford	
82003	$3MT^2$	→	→	**88C** Barry	**88C** Barry	**6E** Chester (GWR)	**89C** Machynlleth	**9H** Patricroft
82004	$3MT^2$	→	→	**88C** Barry	**84H** Wellington	**82F** Bath Green Park	**82F** Bath Green Park	
82005	$3MT^2$	→	→	**88C** Barry	**88F** Treherbert	**6E** Chester (GWR)	**89C** Machynlleth	
82006	$3MT^2$	→	→	**88C** Barry	**84H** Wellington	**84H** Wellington	**89C** Machynlleth	**70A** Nine Elms
82007	$3MT^2$	→	→	**88C** Barry	**84G** Shrewsbury	**82A** Bristol Bath Road	**82E** Bristol Barrow Road	
82008	$3MT^2$	→	→	**88C** Barry	**85D** Kidderminster	**85A** Worcester	**83B** Taunton	
82009	$3MT^2$	→	→	**88C** Barry	**84H** Wellington	**84H** Wellington	**89C** Machynlleth	**9H** Patricroft
82010	$3MT^2$	→	→	**72A** Exmouth Junction	**72A** Exmouth Junction	**72A** Exmouth Junction	**70A** Nine Elms	

		1948	1951	1954	1957	1960	1963	1966
82011	*3MT*[2]	→	→	**72A** Exmouth Junction	**72A** Exmouth Junction	**72A** Exmouth Junction	**70A** Nine Elms	
82012	*3MT*[2]	→	→	**71A** Eastleigh	**71A** Eastleigh	**71A** Eastleigh	**70A** Nine Elms	
82013	*3MT*[2]	→	→	**72A** Exmouth Junction	**72A** Exmouth Junction	**72A** Exmouth Junction	**70A** Nine Elms	
82014	*3MT*[2]	→	→	**71A** Eastleigh	**71A** Eastleigh	**71A** Eastleigh	**70A** Nine Elms	
82015	*3MT*[2]	→	→	**71A** Eastleigh	**71A** Eastleigh	**71A** Eastleigh	**70C** Guildford	
82016	*3MT*[2]	→	→	**71A** Eastleigh	**71A** Eastleigh	**71A** Eastleigh	**70C** Guildford	
82017	*3MT*[2]	→	→	**72A** Exmouth Junction	**72A** Exmouth Junction	**72A** Exmouth Junction	**70A** Nine Elms	
82018	*3MT*[2]	→	→	**72A** Exmouth Junction	**72A** Exmouth Junction	**72A** Exmouth Junction	**70A** Nine Elms	**70A** Nine Elms
82019	*3MT*[2]	→	→	**72A** Exmouth Junction	**72A** Exmouth Junction	**72A** Exmouth Junction	**70A** Nine Elms	**70A** Nine Elms
82020	*3MT*[2]	→	→	→	**6E** Wrexham Rhosddu	**84K** Wrexham Rhosddu	**89C** Machynlleth	
82021	*3MT*[2]	→	→	→	**6E** Wrexham Rhosddu	**84K** Wrexham Rhosddu	**89C** Machynlleth	
82022	*3MT*[2]	→	→	→	**72A** Exmouth Junction	**72A** Exmouth Junction	**70A** Nine Elms	
82023	*3MT*[2]	→	→	→	**72A** Exmouth Junction	**72A** Exmouth Junction	**70A** Nine Elms	**70A** Nine Elms
82024	*3MT*[2]	→	→	→	**72A** Exmouth Junction	**72A** Exmouth Junction	**70A** Nine Elms	**70A** Nine Elms
82025	*3MT*[2]	→	→	→	**72A** Exmouth Junction	**72A** Exmouth Junction	**70A** Nine Elms	
82026	*3MT*[2]	→	→	→	**51H** Kirkby Stephen	**50E** Scarborough	**56F** Low Moor	**70A** Nine Elms
82027	*3MT*[2]	→	→	→	**51H** Kirkby Stephen	**50F** Malton	**50F** Malton	**70A** Nine Elms
82028	*3MT*[2]	→	→	→	**51A** Darlington	**50E** Scarborough	**50F** Malton	**70A** Nine Elms
82029	*3MT*[2]	→	→	→	**51A** Darlington	**50F** Malton	**50F** Malton	**70A** Nine Elms
82030	*3MT*[2]	→	→	→	**85A** Worcester	**84H** Wellington	**83B** Taunton	
82031	*3MT*[2]	→	→	→	**84G** Shrewsbury	**84K** Wrexham Rhosddu	**89C** Machynlleth	**9H** Patricroft
82032	*3MT*[2]	→	→	→	**88F** Treherbert	**6E** Chester (GWR)	**89C** Machynlleth	
82033	*3MT*[2]	→	→	→	**88F** Treherbert	**82A** Bristol Bath Road	**89C** Machynlleth	
82034	*3MT*[2]	→	→	→	**88F** Treherbert	**6E** Chester (GWR)	**89C** Machynlleth	**9H** Patricroft
82035	*3MT*[2]	→	→	→	**88C** Barry	**82A** Bristol Bath Road	**82E** Bristol Barrow Road	
82036	*3MT*[2]	→	→	→	**88C** Barry	**6E** Chester (GWR)	**82E** Bristol Barrow Road	
82037	*3MT*[2]	→	→	→	**88C** Barry	**84K** Wrexham Rhosddu	**82E** Bristol Barrow Road	
82038	*3MT*[2]	→	→	→	**85A** Worcester	**84H** Wellington	**82E** Bristol Barrow Road	
82039	*3MT*[2]	→	→	→	**88C** Barry	**82G** Templecombe	**82E** Bristol Barrow Road	
82040	*3MT*[2]	→	→	→	**88C** Barry	**82A** Bristol Bath Road	**82E** Bristol Barrow Road	
82041	*3MT*[2]	→	→	→	**88C** Barry	**82F** Bath Green Park	**82F** Bath Green Park	
82042	*3MT*[2]	→	→	→	**88C** Barry	**82A** Bristol Bath Road	**83B** Taunton	
82043	*3MT*[2]	→	→	→	**88C** Barry	**82A** Bristol Bath Road	**82E** Bristol Barrow Road	
82044	*3MT*[2]	→	→	→	**88C** Barry	**82A** Bristol Bath Road	**83B** Taunton	
84000	*2MT*[2]	→	→	**10D** Plodder Lane	**6C** Birkenhead	**6C** Birkenhead	**8B** Warrington Dallam	
84001	*2MT*[2]	→	→	**10D** Plodder Lane	**6D** Chester Northgate	**6D** Chester Northgate	**6G** Llandudno Junction	
84002	*2MT*[2]	→	→	**10D** Plodder Lane	**1E** Bletchley	**1E** Bletchley	**1E** Bletchley	
84003	*2MT*[2]	→	→	**10D** Plodder Lane	**6C** Birkenhead	**6C** Birkenhead	**6K** Rhyl	
84004	*2MT*[2]	→	→	**10D** Plodder Lane	**1E** Bletchley	**1E** Bletchley	**1E** Bletchley	
84005	*2MT*[2]	→	→	**15D** Bedford	**15D** Bedford	**14E** Bedford	**14B** Kentish Town	
84006	*2MT*[2]	→	→	**17B** Burton	**17B** Burton	**15A** Wellingborough	**16D** Annesley	
84007	*2MT*[2]	→	→	**17B** Burton	**17B** Burton	**15A** Wellingborough	**16D** Annesley	
84008	*2MT*[2]	→	→	**17B** Burton	**17B** Burton	**15A** Wellingborough	**15C** Leicester Midland	
84009	*2MT*[2]	→	→	**20C** Royston	**55D** Royston	**53A** Hull Dairycoates	**6G** Llandudno Junction	
84010	*2MT*[2]	→	→	**25F** Low Moor	**24B** Rose Grove	**24F** Fleetwood	**24F** Fleetwood	
84011	*2MT*[2]	→	→	**25F** Low Moor	**24B** Rose Grove	**24D** Lower Darwen	**24F** Fleetwood	
84012	*2MT*[2]	→	→	**25F** Low Moor	**27A** Bank Hall	**24D** Lower Darwen	**24F** Fleetwood	
84013	*2MT*[2]	→	→	**25F** Low Moor	**26E** Lees Oldham	**26C** Bolton	**26C** Bolton	
84014	*2MT*[2]	→	→	**25F** Low Moor	**26E** Lees Oldham	**26C** Bolton	**26C** Bolton	
84015	*2MT*[2]	→	→	**25F** Low Moor	**24F** Fleetwood	**24G** Skipton	**24G** Skipton	
84016	*2MT*[2]	→	→	**26D** Bury	**24F** Fleetwood	**24F** Fleetwood	**24F** Fleetwood	
84017	*2MT*[2]	→	→	**26D** Bury	**24F** Fleetwood	**24F** Fleetwood	**24F** Fleetwood	
84018	*2MT*[2]	→	→	**26D** Bury	**24F** Fleetwood	**24F** Fleetwood	**24F** Fleetwood	
84019	*2MT*[2]	→	→	**26D** Bury	**26E** Lees Oldham	**26C** Bolton	**26C** Bolton	
84020	*2MT*[2]	→	→	→	→	**73F** Ashford	**6G** Llandudno Junction	
84021	*2MT*[2]	→	→	→	→	**73F** Ashford	Crewe Works	
84022	*2MT*[2]	→	→	→	→	**73F** Ashford	Crewe Works	
84023	*2MT*[2]	→	→	→	→	**73F** Ashford	Crewe Works	
84024	*2MT*[2]	→	→	→	→	**73F** Ashford	Crewe Works	
84025	*2MT*[2]	→	→	→	→	**73F** Ashford	**26C** Bolton	
84026	*2MT*[2]	→	→	→	→	**73F** Ashford	**26C** Bolton	
84027	*2MT*[2]	→	→	→	→	**73F** Ashford	**16D** Annesley	
84028	*2MT*[2]	→	→	→	→	**73F** Ashford	**24G** Skipton	
84029	*2MT*[2]	→	→	→	→	**73F** Ashford	**14B** Kentish Town	
90000	*WD*[1]	(63000)	**38A** Colwick	**38A** Colwick	**38A** Colwick	**34E** New England	**36C** Frodingham	
90001	*WD*[1]	(63001)	**52D** Tweedmouth	**38A** Colwick	**38A** Colwick	**31B** March	**36A** Doncaster	**36A** Doncaster
90002	*WD*[1]	(63002)	**38A** Colwick	**38A** Colwick	**38A** Colwick	**40E** Colwick	**40E** Colwick	**36A** Doncaster
90003	*WD*[1]	(63003)	**31B** March	**40B** Immingham	**40B** Immingham	**40B** Immingham	**36A** Doncaster	
90004	*WD*[1]	(63004)	**62A** Thornton Junction	**62A** Thornton Junction	**62A** Thornton Junction	**62A** Thornton Junction	**62A** Thornton Junction	
90005	*WD*[1]	(63005)	**31B** March	**36A** Doncaster	**38A** Colwick	**40E** Colwick	**40E** Colwick	
90006	*WD*[1]	(63006)	**53A** Hull Dairycoates	**53A** Hull Dairycoates	**53A** Hull Dairycoates	**53A** Hull Dairycoates	**50B** Hull Dairycoates	
90007	*WD*[1]	(63007)	**53A** Hull Dairycoates	**38A** Colwick	**38D** Staveley	**41H** Staveley	**36C** Frodingham	
90008	*WD*[1]	(63008)	**52D** Tweedmouth	**53A** Hull Dairycoates	**53A** Hull Dairycoates	**53A** Hull Dairycoates	**50B** Hull Dairycoates	**50B** Hull Dairycoates
90009	*WD*[1]	(63009)	**53A** Hull Dairycoates	**53A** Hull Dairycoates	**53A** Hull Dairycoates	**53A** Hull Dairycoates	**50B** Hull Dairycoates	**50B** Hull Dairycoates
90010	*WD*[1]	(63010)	**53C** Hull Springhead	**84G** Shrewsbury	**84G** Shrewsbury	**18B** Westhouses	**9G** Gorton	
90011	*WD*[1]	(63011)	**53C** Hull Springhead	**53C** Hull Springhead	**53C** Hull Springhead	**51A** Darlington	**51A** Darlington	**51A** Darlington
90012	*WD*[1]	(63012)	**51E** Stockton on Tees	**51E** Stockton on Tees	**51C** West Hartlepool	**55E** Normanton	**55E** Normanton	
90013	*WD*[1]	(63013)	**31B** March	**36C** Frodingham	**36C** Frodingham	**36C** Frodingham	**36C** Frodingham	**36C** Frodingham
90014	*WD*[1]	(63014)	**51B** Newport	**51B** Newport	**51B** Newport	**51L** Thornaby	**51A** Darlington	**51A** Darlington
90015	*WD*[1]	(63015)	**31B** March	**36B** Mexborough	**38A** Colwick	**34E** New England	**34E** New England	
90016	*WD*[1]	(63016)	**51B** Newport	**51B** Newport	**51B** Newport	**56A** Wakefield	**52H** Tyne Dock	**51C** West Hartlepool
90017	*WD*[1]	(63017)	**62B** Dundee Tay Bridge	**62C** Dunfermline Upper	**62C** Dunfermline Upper	**62C** Dunfermline Upper	**62C** Dunfermline Upper	
90018	*WD*[1]	(63018)	**31B** March	**31B** March	**31B** March	**31B** March	**36A** Doncaster	**36A** Doncaster
90019	*WD*[1]	(63019)	**62A** Thornton Junction	**62A** Thornton Junction	**62A** Thornton Junction	**62A** Thornton Junction	**62A** Thornton Junction	
90020	*WD*[1]	(63020)	**65A** Eastfield	**62A** Thornton Junction	**62A** Thornton Junction	**62A** Thornton Junction	**62A** Thornton Junction	**62A** Thornton Junction
90021	*WD*[1]	(63021)	**53A** Hull Dairycoates	**53A** Hull Dairycoates	**51A** Darlington	**55E** Normanton		
90022	*WD*[1]	(63022)	**53A** Hull Dairycoates	**53A** Hull Dairycoates	**53A** Hull Dairycoates	**53A** Hull Dairycoates		
90023	*WD*[1]	(63023)	**31B** March	**31B** March	**31B** March	**31F** Spital Bridge		
90024	*WD*[1]	(63024)	**31B** March	**36A** Doncaster	**38A** Colwick	**40E** Colwick	**36C** Frodingham	**36C** Frodingham
90025	*WD*[1]	(63025)	**38A** Colwick	**38A** Colwick	**38A** Colwick	**40E** Colwick	**36C** Frodingham	
90026	*WD*[1]	(63026)	**54B** Tyne Dock	**54B** Tyne Dock	**54B** Tyne Dock	**50A** York	**50A** York	
90027	*WD*[1]	(63027)	**51B** Newport	**51B** Newport	**51B** Newport	**51L** Thornaby	**51L** Thornaby	
90028	*WD*[1]	(63028)	**35A** New England	**35A** New England	**35A** New England	**30A** Stratford		
90029	*WD*[1]	(63029)	**30E** Colchester	**40B** Immingham	**40B** Immingham	**40B** Immingham	**40B** Immingham	
90030	*WD*[1]	(63030)	**52D** Tweedmouth	**53A** Hull Dairycoates	**53A** Hull Dairycoates	**53A** Hull Dairycoates	**50A** York	**50D** Goole
90031	*WD*[1]	(63031)	**35A** New England	**36C** Frodingham	**36C** Frodingham	**36C** Frodingham	**34E** New England	
90032	*WD*[1]	(63032)	**31B** March	**36C** Frodingham	**36C** Frodingham	**36C** Frodingham	**36C** Frodingham	**36C** Frodingham
90033	*WD*[1]	(63033)	**38E** Woodford Halse	**38E** Woodford Halse	**38E** Woodford Halse	**2F** Woodford Halse	**2F** Woodford Halse	
90034	*WD*[1]	(63034)	**35A** New England	**35A** New England	**35A** New England	**33B** Tilbury		
90035	*WD*[1]	(63035)	**31B** March	**40B** Immingham	**40B** Immingham	**40B** Immingham	**40B** Immingham	**36C** Frodingham
90036	*WD*[1]	(63036)	**38A** Colwick	**38A** Colwick	**38A** Colwick	**40B** Immingham	**40E** Colwick	
90037	*WD*[1]	(63037)	**31B** March	**36A** Doncaster	**38A** Colwick	**40E** Colwick	**40E** Colwick	**40B** Immingham
90038	*WD*[1]	(63038)	**64A** St. Margarets	**38A** Colwick	**38A** Colwick	**40E** Colwick	**40E** Colwick	
90039	*WD*[1]	(63039)	**38E** Woodford Halse	**38E** Woodford Halse	**38E** Woodford Halse	**64A** Polmadie	**66A** Polmadie	**62C** Dunfermline Upper
90040	*WD*[1]	(63040)	**38E** Woodford Halse	**38E** Woodford Halse	**38E** Woodford Halse	**2F** Woodford Halse	**2F** Woodford Halse	
90041	*WD*[1]	(63041)	**61B** Aberdeen Ferryhill	**61B** Aberdeen Ferryhill	**61B** Aberdeen Ferryhill	**61B** Aberdeen Ferryhill	**61B** Aberdeen Ferryhill	**61B** Aberdeen Ferryhill
90042	*WD*[1]	(63042)	**31B** March	**36A** Doncaster	**31B** March	**31B** March	**36A** Doncaster	
90043	*WD*[1]	(63043)	**38A** Colwick	**38A** Colwick	**40E** Langwith Junction	**41J** Langwith Junction	**41J** Langwith Junction	
90044	*WD*[1]	(63044)	**51B** Newport	**51B** Newport	**50D** Starbeck	**53E** Goole	**50D** Goole	**50B** Hull Dairycoates
90045	*WD*[1]	(63045)	**51B** Newport	**54D** Consett	**54B** Tyne Dock	**50A** York	**50A** York	
90046	*WD*[1]	(63046)	**38E** Woodford Halse	**38E** Woodford Halse	**38E** Woodford Halse	**2F** Woodford Halse	**9G** Gorton	
90047	*WD*[1]	(63047)	**53A** Hull Dairycoates	**50A** York	**51A** Darlington	**56A** Wakefield	**56A** Wakefield	**56A** Wakefield
90048	*WD*[1]	(63048)	**51E** Stockton on Tees	**51E** Stockton on Tees	**51C** West Hartlepool	**51L** Thornaby	**51L** Thornaby	
90049	*WD*[1]	(63049)	**64A** St. Margarets	**64A** St. Margarets	**65A** Eastfield	**65A** Eastfield	**62C** Dunfermline Upper	

No.	Class	1948	1951	1954	1957	1960	1963	1966
90050	WD[1]	(63050)	38A Colwick	38A Colwick	38A Colwick	40E Colwick	34E New England	
90051	WD[1]	(63051)	38A Colwick	38A Colwick	40E Langwith Junction	40E Colwick	40E Colwick	
90052	WD[1]	(63052)	53C Hull Springhead	38A Colwick	38A Colwick	41F Mexborough	36A Doncaster	
90053	WD[1]	(63053)	31B March	36A Doncaster	38A Colwick	40E Colwick	36C Frodingham	
90054	WD[1]	(63054)	51B Newport	54D Consett	54B Tyne Dock	56A Wakefield	56F Low Moor	56A Wakefield
90055	WD[1]	(63055)	31B March	40B Immingham	40E Langwith Junction	41H Staveley	40B Immingham	
90056	WD[1]	(63056)	50A York	50A York	51A Darlington	56A Wakefield	56B Ardsley	56A Wakefield
90057	WD[1]	(63057)	53A Hull Dairycoates	53A Hull Dairycoates	53A Hull Dairycoates	51A Darlington	52H Tyne Dock	50B Hull Dairycoates
90058	WD[1]	(63058)	62A Thornton Junction	62A Thornton Junction	62A Thornton Junction	62A Thornton Junction	62A Thornton Junction	
90059	WD[1]	(63059)	35A New England	36C Frodingham	36C Frodingham	36C Frodingham	36C Frodingham	
90060	WD[1]	(63060)	31B March	36A Doncaster	31B March	66A Polmadie		
90061	WD[1]	(63061)	51A Darlington	53A Hull Dairycoates	53C Hull Springhead	56A Wakefield	56A Wakefield	56A Wakefield
90062	WD[1]	(63062)	35A New England	35A New England	30A Stratford	30A Stratford		
90063	WD[1]	(63063)	35C Spital Bridge	35C Spital Bridge	35C Spital Bridge	31F Spital Bridge	36A Doncaster	36A Doncaster
90064	WD[1]	(63064)	31B March	36A Doncaster	38A Colwick	41F Mexborough	41D Canklow	
90065	WD[1]	(63065)	38E Woodford Halse	38E Woodford Halse	38E Woodford Halse	2F Woodford Halse	2F Woodford Halse	
90066	WD[1]	(63066)	31B March	36A Doncaster	38A Colwick	2F Woodford Halse	2F Woodford Halse	
90067	WD[1]	(63067)	51E Stockton on Tees	51E Stockton on Tees	51C West Hartlepool	51C West Hartlepool	51C West Hartlepool	
90068	WD[1]	(63068)	51B Newport	51B Newport	51B Newport	56F Low Moor	56D Mirfield	56A Wakefield
90069	WD[1]	(63069)	50A York	86A Ebbw Junction	86A Ebbw Junction	86C Cardiff Canton	36A Doncaster	41J Langwith Junction
90070	WD[1]	(63070)	31B March	36C Frodingham	36C Frodingham	36C Frodingham	36C Frodingham	
90071	WD[1]	(63071)	64A St. Margarets	66B Motherwell	66C Hamilton	66B Motherwell	66B Motherwell	62C Dunfermline Upper
90072	WD[1]	(63072)	52D Tweedmouth	53A Hull Dairycoates	53A Hull Dairycoates	53A Hull Dairycoates	51L Thornaby	
90073	WD[1]	(63073)	38A Colwick	38A Colwick	38A Colwick	34E New England	34E New England	36A Doncaster
90074	WD[1]	(63074)	51B Newport	51B Newport	51B Newport	51L Thornaby	52H Tyne Dock	56A Wakefield
90075	WD[1]	(63075)	31B March	38A Colwick	38A Colwick	40E Colwick	40B Immingham	36C Frodingham
90076	WD[1]	(63076)	51B Newport	51B Newport	51B Newport	56A Wakefield	56A Wakefield	56A Wakefield
90077	WD[1]	(63077)	62B Dundee Tay Bridge	62B Dundee Tay Bridge	62B Dundee Tay Bridge	66A Polmadie	61B Aberdeen Ferryhill	
90078	WD[1]	(63078)	51A Darlington	53A Hull Dairycoates	53A Hull Dairycoates	53A Hull Dairycoates	50A York	50A York
90079	WD[1]	(63079)	35A New England	35A New England	31B March	31B March	36C Frodingham	
90080	WD[1]	(63080)	38E Woodford Halse	38E Woodford Halse	38E Woodford Halse	2F Woodford Halse	9G Gorton	36C Frodingham
90081	WD[1]	(63081)	51B Newport	51B Newport	51B Newport	51L Thornaby	51L Thornaby	50D Goole
90082	WD[1]	(63082)	51E Stockton on Tees	53C Hull Springhead	50B Leeds Neville Hill	51A Darlington	51A Darlington	51C West Hartlepool
90083	WD[1]	(63083)	31B March	40B Immingham	31B March			
90084	WD[1]	(63084)	38A Colwick	38A Colwick	38A Colwick	40E Colwick	40E Colwick	
90085	WD[1]	(63085)	30E Colchester	36B Mexborough	38D Staveley	41H Staveley	41D Canklow	
90086	WD[1]	(63086)	51E Stockton on Tees	51E Stockton on Tees	51E Stockton on Tees	51L Thornaby	51L Thornaby	
90087	WD[1]	(63087)	31B March	40B Immingham	40E Langwith Junction	41H Staveley		
90088	WD[1]	(63088)	35A New England	35A New England	35A New England	41J Langwith Junction	41J Langwith Junction	
90089	WD[1]	(63089)	51G Haverton Hill	53A Hull Dairycoates	53A Hull Dairycoates	56A Wakefield	56A Wakefield	56A Wakefield
90090	WD[1]	(63090)	51B Newport	51B Newport	51B Newport	51L Thornaby	51L Thornaby	
90091	WD[1]	(63091)	51B Newport	51B Newport	51B Newport	51L Thornaby	51L Thornaby	50D Goole
90092	WD[1]	(63092)	51E Stockton on Tees	51E Stockton on Tees	51C West Hartlepool	51C West Hartlepool	51C West Hartlepool	
90093	WD[1]	(63093)	35A New England	35A New England	35A New England	33B Tilbury		
90094	WD[1]	(63094)	53C Hull Springhead	53C Hull Springhead	53C Hull Springhead	53E Goole	50D Goole	50D Goole
90095	WD[1]	(63095)	38E Woodford Halse	38E Woodford Halse	38E Woodford Halse	2F Woodford Halse	2F Woodford Halse	
90096	WD[1]	(63096)	35A New England	35A New England	35A New England	34E New England	34E New England	
90097	WD[1]	(63097)	61B Aberdeen Ferryhill	61B Aberdeen Ferryhill	61B Aberdeen Ferryhill	61B Aberdeen Ferryhill	61B Aberdeen Ferryhill	
90098	WD[1]	(63098)	51B Newport	51B Newport	51B Newport	51L Thornaby	51L Thornaby	
90099	WD[1]	(63099)	50A York	53A Hull Dairycoates	53A Hull Dairycoates	53A Hull Dairycoates	50B Hull Dairycoates	50D Goole
90100	WD[1]	(63100)	50A York	50A York	53A Hull Dairycoates	56A Wakefield	56B Ardsley	
90101	WD[1]	CDF Cardiff Canton	26A Newton Heath	25A Wakefield	27B Aintree	27B Aintree	27B Aintree	
90102	WD[1]	NA Newton Abbot	26B Agecroft	26B Agecroft	26B Agecroft	26C Bolton	26C Bolton	
90103	WD[1]	NEV Leeds Neville Hill	38A Colwick	38A Colwick	38A Colwick	40E Colwick	40E Colwick	
90104	WD[1]	HLS Hull Springhead	36B Mexborough	36B Mexborough	38A Colwick	40E Colwick	40E Colwick	40E Colwick
90105	WD[1]	PDN Old Oak Common	26A Newton Heath	26A Newton Heath	26A Newton Heath	26A Newton Heath		
90106	WD[1]	NPT Newport	35A New England	35A New England	35A New England	33B Tilbury		
90107	WD[1]	BTN Brighton	25D Mirfield	25D Mirfield	27B Aintree	27B Aintree	27B Aintree	
90108	WD[1]	MEX Mexborough	36B Mexborough	36A Doncaster	31B March	36A Doncaster	36C Frodingham	
90109	WD[1]	NPT Newport	24B Rose Grove	24B Rose Grove	24B Rose Grove	24B Rose Grove	24B Rose Grove	
90110	WD[1]	BAN Banbury	84G Shrewsbury	26C Bolton	26C Bolton	26C Bolton	26B Agecroft	
90111	WD[1]	NEV Leeds Neville Hill	31B March	36C Frodingham	36C Frodingham	36C Frodingham	36C Frodingham	
90112	WD[1]	BAN Banbury	26F Lees Oldham	24A Accrington	56D Mirfield	56A Wakefield	56A Wakefield	56A Wakefield
90113	WD[1]	PDN Old Oak Common	26A Newton Heath	26A Newton Heath	26A Newton Heath	56E Sowerby Bridge	56E Sowerby Bridge	56A Wakefield
90114	WD[1]	NPT Newport	64A St. Margarets	65D Dawsholm	65D Dawsholm	65D Dawsholm	65D Dawsholm	
90115	WD[1]	NWE New England	38D Staveley	38D Staveley	38A Colwick	40E Colwick	36C Frodingham	
90116	WD[1]	HLS Hull Springhead	53C Hull Springhead	53C Hull Springhead	53C Hull Springhead	56A Wakefield	56A Wakefield	56A Wakefield
90117	WD[1]	DFU Dunfermline Upper	62C Dunfermline Upper	62C Dunfermline Upper	62A Thornton Junction	62A Thornton Junction	62A Thornton Junction	62A Thornton Junction
90118	WD[1]	MEX Mexborough	31B March	36B Mexborough	38A Colwick	40E Colwick	40E Colwick	
90119	WD[1]	MEX Mexborough	31B March	36B Mexborough	31B March	41F Mexborough	36C Frodingham	
90120	WD[1]	MEX Mexborough	36B Mexborough	36B Mexborough	38A Colwick	40E Colwick	36C Frodingham	
90121	WD[1]	Stored	61B Aberdeen Ferryhill	27D Wigan	27D Wigan	27D Wigan	26C Bolton	
90122	WD[1]	Stored	38A Colwick	26G Belle Vue	56E Sowerby Bridge	56E Sowerby Bridge	56E Sowerby Bridge	
90123	WD[1]	BAN Banbury	26A Newton Heath	26D Bury	26D Bury	26E Lees Oldham	26E Lees Oldham	
90124	WD[1]	Stored	25A Wakefield	25D Mirfield	56D Mirfield	56A Wakefield	56A Wakefield	
90125	WD[1]	OXY Oxley	66B Motherwell	86A Ebbw Junction	86C Cardiff Canton	86C Cardiff Canton	8B Warrington Dallam	
90126	WD[1]	Stored	38A Colwick	26G Belle Vue	56F Low Moor	56D Mirfield	56B Ardsley	56A Wakefield
90127	WD[1]	FEL Feltham	73C Hither Green	25A Wakefield	55C Farnley Junction	55C Farnley Junction	55D Royston	
90128	WD[1]	THJ Thornton Junction	62A Thornton Junction	62A Thornton Junction	62A Thornton Junction	65A Eastfield		
90129	WD[1]	HLD Hull Dairycoates	38A Colwick	38A Colwick	31B March	30A Stratford	40B Immingham	
90130	WD[1]	NWE New England	35A New England	36B Mexborough	38A Colwick	40E Colwick	34E New England	
90131	WD[1]	MAR March	31B March	40B Immingham	40B Immingham	40B Immingham	40B Immingham	
90132	WD[1]	NPT Newport	51B Newport	51B Newport	51B Newport	51L Thornaby	51L Thornaby	50D Goole
90133	WD[1]	CLK Colwick	40B Immingham	36C Frodingham	36C Frodingham	36C Frodingham	36C Frodingham	
90134	WD[1]	DFU Dunfermline Upper	65F Grangemouth	66A Polmadie	66A Polmadie	66A Polmadie		
90135	WD[1]	OXY Oxley	24D Lower Darwen	25C Goole	53E Goole	56D Mirfield	56D Mirfield	56A Wakefield
90136	WD[1]	CLK Colwick	38A Colwick	38A Colwick	38A Colwick	41F Mexborough	41D Canklow	
90137	WD[1]	NEV Leeds Neville Hill	38E Woodford Halse	38E Woodford Halse	38E Woodford Halse	2F Woodford Halse		
90138	WD[1]	STM St. Margarets	24B Rose Grove	24B Rose Grove	24B Rose Grove	24B Rose Grove	24B Rose Grove	
90139	WD[1]	WFD Woodford Halse	38A Colwick	38A Colwick	38A Colwick	41F Mexborough	41D Canklow	
90140	WD[1]	Stored	38A Colwick	26G Belle Vue	26A Newton Heath	26E Lees Oldham	26F Patricroft	
90141	WD[1]	OXY Oxley	25A Wakefield	25A Wakefield	27B Aintree	26E Lees Oldham	26F Patricroft	
90142	WD[1]	FEL Feltham	73C Hither Green	25A Wakefield	26A Newton Heath	26A Newton Heath	26B Agecroft	
90143	WD[1]	OXY Oxley	24B Rose Grove	24B Rose Grove	24B Rose Grove	24B Rose Grove	24B Rose Grove	
90144	WD[1]	MEX Mexborough	36B Mexborough	36B Mexborough	31B March	36A Doncaster	36A Doncaster	
90145	WD[1]	THJ Thornton Junction	62A Thornton Junction	40B Immingham	40B Immingham	41D Canklow	41J Langwith Junction	
90146	WD[1]	MEX Mexborough	36B Mexborough	36B Mexborough	38A Colwick	40E Colwick	34E New England	
90147	WD[1]	Stored	38A Colwick	6B Mold Junction	6B Mold Junction	6B Mold Junction	8D Widnes	
90148	WD[1]	LA Laira (Plymouth)	83D Laira (Plymouth)	83A Newton Abbot	86C Cardiff Canton	84C Banbury	8F Wigan Springs Branch	36C Frodingham
90149	WD[1]	Stored	65A Eastfield	85B Gloucester	85B Gloucester	86C Cardiff Canton	41F Mexborough	41J Langwith Junction
90150	WD[1]	MEX Mexborough	36B Mexborough	36B Mexborough	31B March	31B March		
90151	WD[1]	NWE New England	35A New England	35A New England	35A New England	34E New England	34E New England	
90152	WD[1]	OXY Oxley	66B Motherwell	81C Southall	81C Southall	18B Westhouses	9G Gorton	
90153	WD[1]	MEX Mexborough	36B Mexborough	36B Mexborough	38A Colwick	41F Mexborough	41D Canklow	41J Langwith Junction
90154	WD[1]	HLS Hull Springhead	36B Mexborough	38A Colwick	38A Colwick	34E New England	34E New England	36A Doncaster
90155	WD[1]	SKN Stockton on Tees	51E Stockton on Tees	51E Stockton on Tees	51E Stockton on Tees	51A Darlington	51A Darlington	56A Wakefield
90156	WD[1]	NEV Leeds Neville Hill	35A New England	35C Spital Bridge	35A New England	30A Stratford	36A Doncaster	36A Doncaster
90157	WD[1]	Stored	38A Colwick	6B Mold Junction	6B Mold Junction	8D Widnes	8D Widnes	
90158	WD[1]	MAR March	35A New England	35A New England	35A New England	34E New England	34E New England	
90159	WD[1]	NPT Newport	24B Rose Grove	24B Rose Grove	24B Rose Grove	24B Rose Grove	24B Rose Grove	
90160	WD[1]	NEV Leeds Neville Hill	53A Hull Dairycoates	53A Hull Dairycoates	53A Hull Dairycoates	53A Hull Dairycoates	50D Goole	56A Wakefield
90161	WD[1]	MEX Mexborough	36B Mexborough	86K Abergavenny	38A Colwick	40E Colwick	36C Frodingham	
90162	WD[1]	CLK Colwick	40B Immingham	35A New England	40E Langwith Junction	40B Immingham	41D Canklow	
90163	WD[1]	Stored	38A Colwick	26G Belle Vue	26A Newton Heath	26A Newton Heath		

No.		1948		1951	1954	1957	1960	1963	1966
90164	WD[1]	BA	Bricklayers Arms	73B Bricklayers Arms	25A Wakefield	27B Aintree	27B Aintree	24B Rose Grove	
90165	WD[1]	CLK	Colwick	35A New England	35A New England	35A New England	34E New England	36C Frodingham	
90166	WD[1]	MEX	Mexborough	36B Mexborough	36B Mexborough	38A Colwick	40E Colwick	36C Frodingham	
90167	WD[1]	PDN	Old Oak Common	86A Ebbw Junction	86G Pontypool Road	86G Pontypool Road	87G Carmarthen		
90168	WD[1]	THJ	Thornton Junction	62A Thornton Junction	62A Thornton Junction	62A Thornton Junction	62A Thornton Junction	62A Thornton Junction	62A Thornton Junction
90169	WD[1]	MAR	March	35A New England	35A New England	35A New England	34E New England	40E Colwick	
90170	WD[1]	THJ	Thornton Junction	62A Thornton Junction	62A Thornton Junction	68A Carlisle Kingmoor	12A Carlisle Kingmoor	8G Sutton Oak	
90171	WD[1]		Stored	24B Rose Grove	24B Rose Grove	24B Rose Grove	24B Rose Grove	24B Rose Grove	
90172	WD[1]	SKN	Stockton on Tees	51E Stockton on Tees	51E Stockton on Tees	51E Stockton on Tees	51A Darlington	51A Darlington	50D Goole
90173	WD[1]	LA	Laira (Plymouth)	87K Swansea Victoria	6C Birkenhead	6C Birkenhead	6C Birkenhead	24J Lancaster	
90174	WD[1]	EFD	Eastfield	65A Eastfield	81C Southall	81C Southall	81C Southall		
90175	WD[1]	MAR	March	31B March	40B Immingham	40B Immingham	40B Immingham	40B Immingham	
90176	WD[1]	SPM	St. Philips Marsh	82B St. Philips Marsh	82B St. Philips Marsh	84G Shrewsbury	18B Westhouses	9G Gorton	
90177	WD[1]	THJ	Thornton Junction	62A Thornton Junction	62A Thornton Junction	62C Dunfermline Upper	62C Dunfermline Upper	62C Dunfermline Upper	
90178	WD[1]	OXY	Oxley	38A Colwick	6B Mold Junction	6B Mold Junction	8D Widnes	8G Sutton Oak	36C Frodingham
90179	WD[1]	GLO	Gloucester	85B Gloucester	86G Pontypool Road	86A Ebbw Junction	87G Carmarthen	9G Gorton	
90180	WD[1]	NWE	New England	35A New England	35A New England	35A New England	34E New England	40B Immingham	
90181	WD[1]	BA	Bricklayers Arms	25B Huddersfield	24B Rose Grove	24B Rose Grove	24B Rose Grove	24B Rose Grove	
90182	WD[1]	THJ	Thornton Junction	62A Thornton Junction	62A Thornton Junction	62A Thornton Junction	62A Thornton Junction	62A Thornton Junction	
90183	WD[1]	STM	St. Margarets	24B Rose Grove	24B Rose Grove	24B Rose Grove	24B Rose Grove	26F Patricroft	
90184	WD[1]	SKN	Stockton on Tees	51E Stockton on Tees	51E Stockton on Tees	51E Stockton on Tees	56D Mirfield	56D Mirfield	
90185	WD[1]	CLK	Colwick	38A Colwick	38A Colwick	38A Colwick	40E Colwick	40B Immingham	
90186	WD[1]	NA	Newton Abbot	26B Agecroft	25C Goole	53E Goole	53E Goole	50D Goole	
90187	WD[1]		Stored	38A Colwick	6B Mold Junction	6B Mold Junction	6B Mold Junction	24L Carnforth	36A Doncaster
90188	WD[1]	NA	Newton Abbot	87K Swansea Victoria	86C Cardiff Canton	86C Cardiff Canton	86C Cardiff Canton	41F Mexborough	
90189	WD[1]	MEX	Mexborough	36B Mexborough	36B Mexborough	38A Colwick	40E Colwick	36C Frodingham	
90190	WD[1]	HLS	Hull Springhead	36B Mexborough	36B Mexborough	36B Mexborough	41F Mexborough	36A Doncaster	40B Immingham
90191	WD[1]	NWE	New England	35A New England	35A New England	35A New England	31B March		
90192	WD[1]	EFD	Eastfield	65A Eastfield	86C Cardiff Canton	86G Pontypool Road	86G Pontypool Road	8D Widnes	
90193	WD[1]		Stored	65A Eastfield	65D Dawsholm	65D Dawsholm	65D Dawsholm	62A Thornton Junction	
90194	WD[1]	BA	Bricklayers Arms	73B Bricklayers Arms	26D Bury	26D Bury	26D Bury	26E Lees Oldham	
90195	WD[1]	MEX	Mexborough	36B Mexborough	36B Mexborough	36B Mexborough	41F Mexborough	36A Doncaster	
90196	WD[1]	MEX	Mexborough	36B Mexborough	36B Mexborough	33A Plaistow	33B Tilbury		
90197	WD[1]		Stored	38A Colwick	26G Belle Vue	26A Newton Heath	26A Newton Heath	26A Newton Heath	
90198	WD[1]	DEE	Dundee Tay Bridge	62B Dundee Tay Bridge	62B Dundee Tay Bridge	62B Dundee Tay Bridge	66A Polmadie		
90199	WD[1]	DFU	Dunfermline Upper	62C Dunfermline Upper	62C Dunfermline Upper	65F Grangemouth	66A Polmadie	66A Polmadie	62C Dunfermline Upper
90200	WD[1]	NEV	Leeds Neville Hill	50A York	50A York	51A Darlington	56F Low Moor	56E Sowerby Bridge	56A Wakefield
90201	WD[1]	OXY	Oxley	86E Severn Tunnel Junction	86E Severn Tunnel Junction	86C Cardiff Canton	86C Cardiff Canton	9G Gorton	
90202	WD[1]	WFD	Woodford Halse	38A Colwick	38A Colwick	38A Colwick	40E Colwick	41D Canklow	
90203	WD[1]		Stored	61B Aberdeen Ferryhill	40B Immingham	31B March	41F Mexborough	41F Mexborough	
90204	WD[1]		Stored	38A Colwick	26G Belle Vue	27B Aintree	27B Aintree	27B Aintree	
90205	WD[1]	NA	Newton Abbot	26C Bolton	26C Bolton	26D Bury	26D Bury	26D Bury	
90206	WD[1]		Stored	24A Accrington	26C Bolton	26C Bolton	26C Bolton	26C Bolton	
90207	WD[1]	SPM	St. Philips Marsh	82B St. Philips Marsh	81C Southall	81C Southall	87G Carmarthen	9G Gorton	
90208	WD[1]	HLD	Hull Dairycoates	35A New England	35A New England	31B March	31B March	36A Doncaster	
90209	WD[1]	MEX	Mexborough	36B Mexborough	36B Mexborough	36B Mexborough	41F Mexborough	41F Mexborough	
90210	WD[1]	TDK	Tyne Dock	54B Tyne Dock	53A Hull Dairycoates	51A Darlington	56E Sowerby Bridge	56E Sowerby Bridge	56A Wakefield
90211	WD[1]		Stored	36B Mexborough	36B Mexborough	36B Mexborough	41F Mexborough	41F Mexborough	
90212	WD[1]	LA	Laira (Plymouth)	38A Colwick	6B Mold Junction	6C Birkenhead	6C Birkenhead	8G Sutton Oak	
90213	WD[1]	BA	Bricklayers Arms	73C Hither Green	25C Goole	53E Goole	53E Goole	50D Goole	50B Hull Dairycoates
90214	WD[1]	CHR	Chester (GWR)	84K Chester (GWR)	84K Chester (GWR)	84K Chester (GWR)	6E Chester (GWR)	9G Gorton	
90215	WD[1]	MEX	Mexborough	38A Colwick	38A Colwick	38A Colwick	40E Colwick	40B Immingham	
90216	WD[1]	BA	Bricklayers Arms	73B Bricklayers Arms	27B Aintree	27B Aintree	27B Aintree	27B Aintree	
90217	WD[1]	NEV	Leeds Neville Hill	53C Hull Springhead	53C Hull Springhead	53C Hull Springhead	53A Hull Dairycoates	50A York	
90218	WD[1]	WFD	Woodford Halse	38E Woodford Halse	38E Woodford Halse	38E Woodford Halse	2F Woodford Halse	2F Woodford Halse	
90219	WD[1]	THJ	Thornton Junction	65F Grangemouth	26D Bury	26D Bury	26D Bury	24B Rose Grove	
90220	WD[1]	MEX	Mexborough	36B Mexborough	36A Doncaster	36B Mexborough	41F Mexborough	41F Mexborough	
90221	WD[1]	MAR	March	31B March	40B Immingham	40B Immingham	40B Immingham	40B Immingham	
90222	WD[1]		Stored	65A Eastfield	26A Newton Heath	26A Newton Heath	26A Newton Heath	26F Patricroft	
90223	WD[1]	NEV	Leeds Neville Hill	36B Mexborough	40B Immingham	40B Immingham	34E New England	40A Lincoln	
90224	WD[1]	MAR	March	31B March	40B Immingham	40B Immingham	40B Immingham	36A Doncaster	
90225	WD[1]	LLY	Llanelly	87K Swansea Victoria	86A Ebbw Junction	86A Ebbw Junction	86A Ebbw Junction	41F Mexborough	
90226	WD[1]	BA	Bricklayers Arms	73B Bricklayers Arms	26D Bury	26D Bury	26D Bury	26D Bury	
90227	WD[1]	STM	St. Margarets	24B Rose Grove	6C Birkenhead	6B Mold Junction	6B Mold Junction	8B Warrington Dallam	
90228	WD[1]	THJ	Thornton Junction	25C Goole	25C Goole	53E Goole	53E Goole	50D Goole	
90229	WD[1]	MEX	Mexborough	36B Mexborough	36B Mexborough	36B Mexborough	66A Polmadie	66A Polmadie	62C Dunfermline Upper
90230	WD[1]	NPT	Newport	51B Newport	51B Newport	51B Newport	56A Wakefield	56B Ardsley	51C West Hartlepool
90231	WD[1]	YK	York	24B Rose Grove	24B Rose Grove	24B Rose Grove	24B Rose Grove	24B Rose Grove	
90232	WD[1]	MEX	Mexborough	36B Mexborough	36C Frodingham	36C Frodingham	36C Frodingham	36C Frodingham	36C Frodingham
90233	WD[1]	NEV	Leeds Neville Hill	53C Hull Springhead	53C Hull Springhead	53C Hull Springhead	56D Mirfield	56E Sowerby Bridge	56A Wakefield
90234	WD[1]	BA	Bricklayers Arms	73B Bricklayers Arms	25A Wakefield	27B Aintree	66A Polmadie	65F Grangemouth	
90235	WD[1]	NEV	Leeds Neville Hill	50A York	38A Colwick	38A Colwick	40E Colwick	36A Doncaster	
90236	WD[1]	THJ	Thornton Junction	65F Grangemouth	25A Wakefield	56E Sowerby Bridge	56F Low Moor	56B Ardsley	56A Wakefield
90237	WD[1]	LA	Laira (Plymouth)	25A Wakefield	6C Birkenhead	6B Mold Junction	2F Woodford Halse	2F Woodford Halse	
90238	WD[1]	SPM	St. Philips Marsh	82B St. Philips Marsh	86C Cardiff Canton	86C Cardiff Canton	18B Westhouses	9G Gorton	
90239	WD[1]	MAR	March	35A New England	35A New England	35A New England	34E New England	36C Frodingham	
90240	WD[1]	SKN	Stockton on Tees	51E Stockton on Tees	51E Stockton on Tees	51E Stockton on Tees	51L Thornaby	56B Ardsley	50B Hull Dairycoates
90241	WD[1]	YK	York	24B Rose Grove	24B Rose Grove	24B Rose Grove	24B Rose Grove	24B Rose Grove	36C Frodingham
90242	WD[1]		Stored	38A Colwick	6B Mold Junction	6B Mold Junction	8D Widnes	8D Widnes	
90243	WD[1]		Stored	25A Wakefield	25A Wakefield	55G Huddersfield	55D Royston	55D Royston	55E Normanton
90244	WD[1]	WFD	Woodford Halse	35A New England	35A New England	35A New England	33B Tilbury		
90245	WD[1]		Stored	25G Farnley Junction	26A Newton Heath	26A Newton Heath	27B Aintree	27B Aintree	
90246	WD[1]	HLS	Hull Springhead	36B Mexborough	35A New England	35A New England	34E New England	34E New England	
90247	WD[1]	BTN	Brighton	75A Brighton	25A Wakefield	56A Wakefield	55E Normanton		
90248	WD[1]	NPT	Newport	64A St. Margarets	26A Newton Heath	26A Newton Heath	26A Newton Heath	26F Patricroft	
90249	WD[1]		Stored	25A Wakefield	25A Wakefield	55G Huddersfield	55E Normanton	55E Normanton	
90250	WD[1]	MEX	Mexborough	36B Mexborough	36B Mexborough	36B Mexborough	41F Mexborough	41F Mexborough	
90251	WD[1]	MAR	March	38A Colwick	82B St. Philips Marsh	81F Oxford	18B Westhouses	9G Gorton	
90252	WD[1]	MEX	Mexborough	36B Mexborough	36B Mexborough	36B Mexborough	41F Mexborough	41F Mexborough	
90253	WD[1]	HLS	Hull Springhead	35A New England	35A New England	35A New England	34E New England		
90254	WD[1]	BA	Bricklayers Arms	73B Bricklayers Arms	26B Agecroft	55C Farnley Junction	55E Normanton	55D Royston	50A York
90255	WD[1]	MEX	Mexborough	36B Mexborough	36B Mexborough	31B March	36A Doncaster	36A Doncaster	
90256	WD[1]	NWE	New England	35A New England	35A New England	33A Plaistow	33B Tilbury		
90257	WD[1]	FEL	Feltham	70B Feltham	6C Birkenhead	6B Mold Junction	6C Birkenhead	8F Wigan Springs Branch	
90258	WD[1]	STM	St. Margarets	24B Rose Grove	24C Lostock Hall	24C Lostock Hall	24C Lostock Hall	24C Lostock Hall	41J Langwith Junction
90259	WD[1]	MAR	March	35A New England	35A New England	40E Langwith Junction	41J Langwith Junction	40E Colwick	
90260	WD[1]		Stored	61B Aberdeen Ferryhill	25A Wakefield	53E Goole	53E Goole	50D Goole	
90261	WD[1]	RDG	Reading	86A Ebbw Junction	84G Shrewsbury	84G Shrewsbury	84C Banbury	8F Wigan Springs Branch	
90262	WD[1]	THJ	Thornton Junction	25C Goole	25C Goole	53E Goole	53E Goole	50D Goole	50B Hull Dairycoates
90263	WD[1]	NEV	Leeds Neville Hill	38E Woodford Halse	38A Colwick	38A Colwick	40E Colwick	40E Colwick	
90264	WD[1]		Stored	24B Rose Grove	24B Rose Grove	24B Rose Grove	24B Rose Grove	24B Rose Grove	
90265	WD[1]	EFD	Eastfield	65A Eastfield	25A Wakefield	55G Huddersfield	53E Goole	50D Goole	50B Hull Dairycoates
90266	WD[1]	RDG	Reading	24D Lower Darwen	24D Lower Darwen	24A Accrington	24C Lostock Hall	24B Rose Grove	
90267	WD[1]	FEL	Feltham	73C Hither Green	26C Bolton	26C Bolton	26C Bolton	26C Bolton	
90268	WD[1]	CDF	Cardiff Canton	86G Pontypool Road	81C Southall	81C Southall	84C Banbury	8F Wigan Springs Branch	
90269	WD[1]	STV	Staveley	38D Staveley	38D Staveley	38A Colwick	34E New England	34E New England	
90270	WD[1]	MEX	Mexborough	36B Mexborough	36A Doncaster	36B Mexborough	41F Mexborough		
90271	WD[1]	CDF	Cardiff Canton	86C Cardiff Canton	26C Bolton	26C Bolton	26A Newton Heath	26A Newton Heath	
90272	WD[1]	TDK	Tyne Dock	54B Tyne Dock	53A Hull Dairycoates	53A Hull Dairycoates	53A Hull Dairycoates	50B Hull Dairycoates	50B Hull Dairycoates
90273	WD[1]	NPT	Newport	51B Newport	51B Newport	51B Newport	51L Thornaby	51L Thornaby	
90274	WD[1]	RDG	Reading	24B Rose Grove	24B Rose Grove	24B Rose Grove	24B Rose Grove	24B Rose Grove	36C Frodingham
90275	WD[1]	MEX	Mexborough	31B March	40B Immingham	40E Langwith Junction	41J Langwith Junction	41J Langwith Junction	
90276	WD[1]	STV	Staveley	38D Staveley	38D Staveley	38D Staveley	41H Staveley	41D Canklow	
90277	WD[1]		Stored	25A Wakefield	25A Wakefield	24C Lostock Hall	24C Lostock Hall	24C Lostock Hall	

		1948	1951	1954	1957	1960	1963	1966
90278	*WD*[1]	Stored	**62C** Dunfermline Upper	**27B** Aintree	**27B** Aintree	**27B** Aintree		
90279	*WD*[1]	**MAR** March	**35A** New England	**35A** New England	**35A** New England	**31B** March	**36A** Doncaster	
90280	*WD*[1]	**MEX** Mexborough	**36B** Mexborough	**40B** Immingham	**40B** Immingham	**40B** Immingham	**40B** Immingham	
90281	*WD*[1]	**THJ** Thornton Junction	**25C** Goole	**25C** Goole	**53E** Goole	**56D** Mirfield	**56E** Sowerby Bridge	**56A** Wakefield
90282	*WD*[1]	**THJ** Thornton Junction	**62A** Thornton Junction	**27B** Aintree	**27B** Aintree	**27B** Aintree	**27B** Aintree	
90283	*WD*[1]	**LLY** Llanelly	**24B** Rose Grove	**26A** Newton Heath	**27B** Aintree	**27B** Aintree	**27B** Aintree	
90284	*WD*[1]	**BAN** Banbury	**85A** Worcester	**82B** St. Philips Marsh	**81F** Oxford	**18B** Westhouses	**9G** Gorton	
90285	*WD*[1]	**MEX** Mexborough	**36B** Mexborough	**40B** Immingham	**40B** Immingham	**40B** Immingham	**40B** Immingham	
90286	*WD*[1]	**MEX** Mexborough	**36B** Mexborough	**36B** Mexborough	**36B** Mexborough	**41F** Mexborough		
90287	*WD*[1]	**MAR** March	**35A** New England	**38A** Colwick	**40E** Langwith Junction	**41J** Langwith Junction		
90288	*WD*[1]	**MAR** March	**35A** New England	**38A** Colwick	**38A** Colwick	**40E** Colwick		
90289	*WD*[1]	**STM** St. Margarets	**64A** St. Margarets	**26A** Newton Heath	**26A** Newton Heath	**26A** Newton Heath	**26A** Newton Heath	
90290	*WD*[1]	**MEX** Mexborough	**36B** Mexborough	**36A** Doncaster	**36B** Mexborough	**41F** Mexborough	**41D** Canklow	
90291	*WD*[1]	**STM** St. Margarets	**64A** St. Margarets	**26A** Newton Heath	**26A** Newton Heath	**26A** Newton Heath	**26A** Newton Heath	
90292	*WD*[1]	**LA** Laira (Plymouth)	**25A** Wakefield	**25A** Wakefield	**26B** Agecroft	**26B** Agecroft	**26B** Agecroft	
90293	*WD*[1]	**THJ** Thornton Junction	**62C** Dunfermline Upper	**31B** March	**31B** March	**31B** March	**36A** Doncaster	
90294	*WD*[1]	**MAR** March	**31B** March	**40B** Immingham	**40B** Immingham	**40B** Immingham	**40B** Immingham	
90295	*WD*[1]	**STM** St. Margarets	**24C** Lostock Hall	**24C** Lostock Hall	**24C** Lostock Hall	**24C** Lostock Hall	**24B** Rose Grove	**40E** Colwick
90296	*WD*[1]	**MEX** Mexborough	**36B** Mexborough	**38A** Colwick	**38A** Colwick	**40E** Colwick	**36A** Doncaster	
90297	*WD*[1]	**LLY** Llanelly	**26C** Bolton	**26C** Bolton	**26C** Bolton	**26C** Bolton	**24D** Lower Darwen	
90298	*WD*[1]	**EFD** Eastfield	**65A** Eastfield	**40B** Immingham	**31B** March	**30A** Stratford		
90299	*WD*[1]	**MAR** March	**38D** Staveley	**38D** Staveley	**38E** Woodford Halse	**2F** Woodford Halse	**2F** Woodford Halse	
90300	*WD*[1]	**THJ** Thornton Junction	**25C** Goole	**25C** Goole	**53E** Goole	**56D** Mirfield	**56D** Mirfield	**56A** Wakefield
90301	*WD*[1]	**MEX** Mexborough	**36B** Mexborough	**36A** Doncaster	**36A** Doncaster	**41F** Mexborough	**41J** Langwith Junction	
90302	*WD*[1]	**MAR** March	**31B** March	**40B** Immingham	**40E** Langwith Junction	**41J** Langwith Junction	**41J** Langwith Junction	
90303	*WD*[1]	**NEV** Leeds Neville Hill	**38A** Colwick	**38A** Colwick	**38A** Colwick	**40E** Colwick		
90304	*WD*[1]	**MAR** March	**30E** Colchester	**36B** Mexborough	**36B** Mexborough	**41F** Mexborough	**40E** Colwick	
90305	*WD*[1]	**NPT** Newport	**35A** New England	**36A** Doncaster	**31B** March	**31B** March	**36A** Doncaster	**36A** Doncaster
90306	*WD*[1]	**DFU** Dunfermline Upper	**64A** St. Margarets	**26B** Agecroft	**26B** Agecroft	**26E** Lees Oldham	**26B** Agecroft	
90307	*WD*[1]	**PPRD** Pontypool Road	**26B** Agecroft	**26B** Agecroft	**26B** Agecroft	**26B** Agecroft		
90308	*WD*[1]	**FEL** Feltham	**25B** Huddersfield	**26D** Bury	**55C** Farnley Junction	**55C** Farnley Junction		
90309	*WD*[1]	**TDK** Tyne Dock	**54B** Tyne Dock	**54B** Tyne Dock	**54B** Tyne Dock	**55E** Normanton	**51A** Darlington	**51A** Darlington
90310	*WD*[1]	Stored	**25A** Wakefield	**25A** Wakefield	**56E** Sowerby Bridge	**56E** Sowerby Bridge	**56F** Low Moor	**56D** Mirfield
90311	*WD*[1]	**MEX** Mexborough	**36B** Mexborough	**36B** Mexborough	**36B** Mexborough	**41F** Mexborough	**41F** Mexborough	
90312	*WD*[1]	**SPM** St. Philips Marsh	**82C** Swindon	**81F** Oxford	**86C** Cardiff Canton	**86C** Cardiff Canton	**9G** Gorton	
90313	*WD*[1]	**EFD** Eastfield	**65A** Eastfield	**84C** Banbury	**81C** Southall	**84C** Banbury	**41F** Mexborough	
90314	*WD*[1]	**YK** York	**24B** Rose Grove	**24B** Rose Grove	**24B** Rose Grove	**24B** Rose Grove	**24B** Rose Grove	
90315	*WD*[1]	**CNYD** Croes Newydd	**87F** Llanelly	**87A** Neath	**86G** Pontypool Road	**86G** Pontypool Road	**8B** Warrington Dallam	
90316	*WD*[1]	Stored	**25G** Farnley Junction	**26C** Bolton	**26A** Newton Heath	**27B** Aintree	**24D** Lower Darwen	
90317	*WD*[1]	**AFD** Ashford	**75B** Redhill	**6B** Mold Junction	**6B** Mold Junction	**6C** Birkenhead	**8F** Wigan Springs Branch	
90318	*WD*[1]	Stored	**25G** Farnley Junction	**25G** Farnley Junction	**55C** Farnley Junction	**55E** Normanton	**55E** Normanton	**55D** Royston
90319	*WD*[1]	**THJ** Thornton Junction	**62A** Thornton Junction	**67C** Ayr	**67C** Ayr	**67C** Ayr	**67C** Ayr	
90320	*WD*[1]	Stored	**24C** Lostock Hall	**24C** Lostock Hall	**24C** Lostock Hall	**66A** Polmadie		
90321	*WD*[1]	Stored	**25D** Mirfield	**25D** Mirfield	**56D** Mirfield	**56A** Wakefield	**56A** Wakefield	**56A** Wakefield
90322	*WD*[1]	Stored	**25G** Farnley Junction	**25G** Farnley Junction	**55C** Farnley Junction	**56D** Mirfield	**56D** Mirfield	
90323	*WD*[1]	**HLD** Hull Dairycoates	**38A** Colwick	**86E** Severn Tunnel Junction	**86C** Cardiff Canton	**86C** Cardiff Canton	**9G** Gorton	
90324	*WD*[1]	**SPM** St. Philips Marsh	**26C** Bolton	**26B** Agecroft	**26B** Agecroft	**26B** Agecroft	**26B** Agecroft	
90325	*WD*[1]	Stored	**25G** Farnley Junction	**25B** Huddersfield	**55G** Huddersfield	**55G** Huddersfield	**55G** Huddersfield	
90326	*WD*[1]	**NEV** Leeds Neville Hill	**25G** Farnley Junction	**25D** Mirfield	**56D** Mirfield	**56A** Wakefield	**56A** Wakefield	
90327	*WD*[1]	**DID** Didcot	**26A** Newton Heath	**26A** Newton Heath	**26A** Newton Heath	**27B** Aintree	**24B** Rose Grove	
90328	*WD*[1]	Stored	**24C** Lostock Hall	**24C** Lostock Hall	**24C** Lostock Hall	**26A** Newton Heath	**26F** Patricroft	
90329	*WD*[1]	Stored	**25A** Wakefield	**25A** Wakefield	**56E** Sowerby Bridge	**56E** Sowerby Bridge	**56E** Sowerby Bridge	
90330	*WD*[1]	**MEX** Mexborough	**38D** Staveley	**36B** Mexborough	**36B** Mexborough	**41F** Mexborough	**41F** Mexborough	
90331	*WD*[1]	Stored	**24C** Lostock Hall	**24C** Lostock Hall	**24C** Lostock Hall	**24C** Lostock Hall	**26F** Patricroft	
90332	*WD*[1]	**HIT** Hither Green	**25B** Huddersfield	**25B** Huddersfield	**55G** Huddersfield	**55G** Huddersfield	**55G** Huddersfield	**55G** Huddersfield
90333	*WD*[1]	Stored	**25A** Wakefield	**25A** Wakefield	**56A** Wakefield	**56F** Low Moor	**56D** Mirfield	
90334	*WD*[1]	Stored	**25A** Wakefield	**25A** Wakefield	**56A** Wakefield	**55C** Farnley Junction	**55C** Farnley Junction	
90335	*WD*[1]	Stored	**24C** Lostock Hall	**24C** Lostock Hall	**24C** Lostock Hall	**24C** Lostock Hall	**24F** Fleetwood	
90336	*WD*[1]	Stored	**25G** Farnley Junction	**25G** Farnley Junction	**55C** Farnley Junction	**55D** Royston	**55D** Royston	**56A** Wakefield
90337	*WD*[1]	Stored	**25A** Wakefield	**25A** Wakefield	**56A** Wakefield	**55E** Normanton	**55E** Normanton	**55D** Royston
90338	*WD*[1]	Stored	**26A** Newton Heath	**26A** Newton Heath	**26A** Newton Heath	**26A** Newton Heath	**26A** Newton Heath	
90339	*WD*[1]	Stored	**25A** Wakefield	**25A** Wakefield	**56A** Wakefield	**56A** Wakefield	**56A** Wakefield	**56A** Wakefield
90340	*WD*[1]	**NWE** New England	**36B** Mexborough	**36B** Mexborough	**31B** March	**31B** March	**36A** Doncaster	
90341	*WD*[1]	Stored	**25A** Wakefield	**25A** Wakefield	**56A** Wakefield	**56A** Wakefield	**56A** Wakefield	
90342	*WD*[1]	Stored	**25A** Wakefield	**25A** Wakefield	**56A** Wakefield	**56A** Wakefield	**56A** Wakefield	
90343	*WD*[1]	**SPM** St. Philips Marsh	**26B** Agecroft	**26C** Bolton	**27B** Aintree	**27B** Aintree	**27B** Aintree	
90344	*WD*[1]	**SKN** Stockton on Tees	**51E** Stockton on Tees	**51E** Stockton on Tees	**51C** West Hartlepool	**51C** West Hartlepool	**51C** West Hartlepool	
90345	*WD*[1]	**BTN** Brighton	**25B** Huddersfield	**25B** Huddersfield	**55G** Huddersfield	**55G** Huddersfield	**55G** Huddersfield	**56A** Wakefield
90346	*WD*[1]	**NPT** Newport	**35A** New England	**38A** Colwick	**38E** Woodford Halse	**2F** Woodford Halse	**2F** Woodford Halse	
90347	*WD*[1]	**BTN** Brighton	**25B** Huddersfield	**25B** Huddersfield	**55G** Huddersfield	**55G** Huddersfield	**55G** Huddersfield	**56A** Wakefield
90348	*WD*[1]	**NPT** Newport	**24B** Rose Grove	**24A** Accrington	**56D** Mirfield	**56A** Wakefield	**56A** Wakefield	**56A** Wakefield
90349	*WD*[1]	**NWE** New England	**35A** New England	**35A** New England	**35A** New England	**34E** New England	**34E** New England	
90350	*WD*[1]	**THJ** Thornton Junction	**62A** Thornton Junction	**62A** Thornton Junction	**62A** Thornton Junction	**62A** Thornton Junction	**62A** Thornton Junction	**62A** Thornton Junction
90351	*WD*[1]	Stored	**25G** Farnley Junction	**25G** Farnley Junction	**55C** Farnley Junction	**56D** Mirfield	**56F** Low Moor	**56D** Mirfield
90352	*WD*[1]	**TDK** Tyne Dock	**54B** Tyne Dock	**53A** Hull Dairycoates	**53C** Hull Springhead	**53A** Hull Dairycoates	**50B** Hull Dairycoates	**50B** Hull Dairycoates
90353	*WD*[1]	Stored	**25A** Wakefield	**25A** Wakefield	**56A** Wakefield	**56A** Wakefield	**56A** Wakefield	
90354	*WD*[1]	**BTN** Brighton	**75A** Brighton	**26B** Agecroft	**26B** Agecroft	**26B** Agecroft	**26B** Agecroft	
90355	*WD*[1]	**CDF** Cardiff Canton	**86E** Severn Tunnel Junction	**86E** Severn Tunnel Junction	**81C** Southall	**81C** Southall		
90356	*WD*[1]	**SPM** St. Philips Marsh	**82B** St. Philips Marsh	**84G** Shrewsbury	**84G** Shrewsbury	**81C** Southall		
90357	*WD*[1]	**PDN** Old Oak Common	**24D** Lower Darwen	**24D** Lower Darwen	**24D** Lower Darwen	**55E** Normanton	**55E** Normanton	**56A** Wakefield
90358	*WD*[1]	**WFD** Woodford Halse	**38D** Staveley	**36B** Mexborough	**36B** Mexborough	**41F** Mexborough	**41F** Mexborough	
90359	*WD*[1]	**LA** Laira (Plymouth)	**26B** Agecroft	**26D** Bury	**26D** Bury	**26B** Agecroft	**26B** Agecroft	
90360	*WD*[1]	**AFD** Ashford	**75B** Redhill	**26A** Newton Heath	**56E** Sowerby Bridge	**56E** Sowerby Bridge	**56E** Sowerby Bridge	**56A** Wakefield
90361	*WD*[1]	**BAN** Banbury	**25A** Wakefield	**25A** Wakefield	**56A** Wakefield	**56A** Wakefield	**56B** Ardsley	**56A** Wakefield
90362	*WD*[1]	Stored	**25A** Wakefield	**25A** Wakefield	**56A** Wakefield	**55E** Normanton	**55E** Normanton	**55G** Huddersfield
90363	*WD*[1]	**NPT** Ebbw Junction	**25A** Wakefield	**25A** Wakefield	**56A** Wakefield	**56A** Wakefield	**56A** Wakefield	**56A** Wakefield
90364	*WD*[1]	**BAN** Banbury	**26D** Bury	**26D** Bury	**26D** Bury	**26D** Bury	**26D** Bury	
90365	*WD*[1]	**CLK** Colwick	**38E** Woodford Halse	**38E** Woodford Halse	**38E** Woodford Halse	**2F** Woodford Halse	**2F** Woodford Halse	
90366	*WD*[1]	**PDN** Old Oak Common	**26A** Newton Heath	**26A** Newton Heath	**26A** Newton Heath	**26A** Newton Heath	**26A** Newton Heath	
90367	*WD*[1]	**RDG** Reading	**24C** Lostock Hall	**24C** Lostock Hall	**24C** Lostock Hall	**24C** Lostock Hall	**24F** Fleetwood	**36C** Frodingham
90368	*WD*[1]	**CLK** Colwick	**38A** Colwick	**38A** Colwick	**38A** Colwick	**41D** Canklow	**41D** Canklow	
90369	*WD*[1]	**NEV** Leeds Neville Hill	**38A** Colwick	**38A** Colwick	**2E** Northampton	**6C** Birkenhead	**8B** Warrington Dallam	**36A** Doncaster
90370	*WD*[1]	Stored	**25A** Wakefield	**25A** Wakefield	**56A** Wakefield	**56A** Wakefield	**56A** Wakefield	**56A** Wakefield
90371	*WD*[1]	**STM** St. Margarets	**24B** Rose Grove	**24B** Rose Grove	**24B** Rose Grove	**24B** Rose Grove	**26F** Patricroft	
90372	*WD*[1]	Stored	**25G** Farnley Junction	**25G** Farnley Junction	**26B** Agecroft	**26B** Agecroft	**26B** Agecroft	
90373	*WD*[1]	**NPT** Newport	**51B** Newport	**51B** Newport	**51B** Newport	**51L** Thornaby	**51A** Darlington	**56A** Wakefield
90374	*WD*[1]	**STM** St. Margarets	**24D** Lower Darwen	**24D** Lower Darwen	**24A** Accrington	**24A** Accrington	**24B** Rose Grove	
90375	*WD*[1]	**BA** Bricklayers Arms	**25D** Mirfield	**25D** Mirfield	**27B** Aintree	**27B** Aintree	**24D** Lower Darwen	
90376	*WD*[1]	**STM** St. Margarets	**64A** St. Margarets	**26A** Newton Heath	**26A** Newton Heath	**26A** Newton Heath		
90377	*WD*[1]	**SKN** Stockton on Tees	**51E** Stockton on Tees	**51E** Stockton on Tees	**51E** Stockton on Tees	**51L** Thornaby	**55D** Royston	**55D** Royston
90378	*WD*[1]	**HLD** Hull Dairycoates	**53A** Hull Dairycoates	**53A** Hull Dairycoates	**53A** Hull Dairycoates	**53A** Hull Dairycoates	**50B** Hull Dairycoates	**50B** Hull Dairycoates
90379	*WD*[1]	Stored	**25A** Wakefield	**25A** Wakefield	**56A** Wakefield	**56A** Wakefield	**56A** Wakefield	**56A** Wakefield
90380	*WD*[1]	Stored	**25A** Wakefield	**25A** Wakefield	**56A** Wakefield	**56A** Wakefield	**56A** Wakefield	**56A** Wakefield
90381	*WD*[1]	Stored	**25A** Wakefield	**25A** Wakefield	**27B** Aintree	**27B** Aintree	**27B** Aintree	
90382	*WD*[1]	**HLD** Hull Dairycoates	**51G** Haverton Hill	**53A** Hull Dairycoates	**53A** Hull Dairycoates	**56A** Wakefield	**56A** Wakefield	**56A** Wakefield
90383	*WD*[1]	**NEV** Leeds Neville Hill	**31B** March	**36A** Doncaster	**36A** Doncaster	**40B** Immingham	**40E** Colwick	
90384	*WD*[1]	**MAR** March	**31B** March	**38A** Colwick	**38A** Colwick	**41F** Mexborough	**41F** Mexborough	**36C** Frodingham
90385	*WD*[1]	Stored	**25A** Wakefield	**25A** Wakefield	**56A** Wakefield	**56A** Wakefield	**56A** Wakefield	**56A** Wakefield
90386	*WD*[1]	**MAR** March	**66B** Motherwell	**66C** Hamilton	**66C** Hamilton	**66B** Motherwell	**66B** Motherwell	**62C** Dunfermline Upper
90387	*WD*[1]	**STM** St. Margarets	**24B** Rose Grove	**24B** Rose Grove	**24B** Rose Grove	**66A** Polmadie		
90388	*WD*[1]	Stored	**26A** Newton Heath	**26A** Newton Heath	**26A** Newton Heath	**26A** Newton Heath	**26A** Newton Heath	
90389	*WD*[1]	**BA** Bricklayers Arms	**73C** Hither Green	**26A** Newton Heath	**26A** Newton Heath	**26A** Newton Heath	**26A** Newton Heath	
90390	*WD*[1]	**HIT** Hither Green	**73C** Hither Green	**26A** Newton Heath	**26A** Newton Heath	**26A** Newton Heath	**26F** Patricroft	
90391	*WD*[1]	**YK** York	**38A** Colwick	**38A** Colwick	**38D** Staveley	**41D** Canklow		

		1948	1951	1954	1957	1960	1963	1966
90392	WD[1]	MAR March	31B March	38A Colwick	2E Northampton	6C Birkenhead	8B Warrington Dallam	
90393	WD[1]	MAR March	31B March	40B Immingham	40B Immingham	40B Immingham	40E Colwick	
90394	WD[1]	TDK Tyne Dock	38D Staveley	38D Staveley	38A Colwick	40E Colwick	40B Immingham	
90395	WD[1]	Stored	25G Farnley Junction	25G Farnley Junction	55C Farnley Junction	55C Farnley Junction	55D Royston	50A York
90396	WD[1]	BAN Banbury	25A Wakefield	25A Wakefield	56A Wakefield	56A Wakefield	56A Wakefield	56A Wakefield
90397	WD[1]	Stored	25A Wakefield	25A Wakefield	56F Low Moor	56D Mirfield	56F Low Moor	56D Mirfield
90398	WD[1]	Stored	24C Lostock Hall	24C Lostock Hall	24C Lostock Hall	24C Lostock Hall	24B Rose Grove	
90399	WD[1]	Stored	24B Rose Grove	24A Accrington	24A Accrington	24A Accrington	26F Patricroft	
90400	WD[1]	MEX Mexborough	36B Mexborough	36B Mexborough	36B Mexborough	41F Mexborough	41F Mexborough	
90401	WD[1]	MEX Mexborough	36B Mexborough	36B Mexborough	36B Mexborough	41F Mexborough	41F Mexborough	
90402	WD[1]	Stored	24A Accrington	26C Bolton	26C Bolton	26E Lees Oldham	26E Lees Oldham	
90403	WD[1]	HLD Hull Dairycoates	38D Staveley	38D Staveley	38E Woodford Halse	2F Woodford Halse	9G Gorton	
90404	WD[1]	Stored	25A Wakefield	25A Wakefield	56A Wakefield	56A Wakefield	56A Wakefield	56A Wakefield
90405	WD[1]	SKN Stockton on Tees	51E Stockton on Tees	51E Stockton on Tees	51E Stockton on Tees	56A Wakefield	56B Ardsley	56A Wakefield
90406	WD[1]	Stored	25A Wakefield	25A Wakefield	56F Low Moor	51L Thornaby	51L Thornaby	50D Goole
90407	WD[1]	Stored	25G Farnley Junction	25G Farnley Junction	55C Farnley Junction	55C Farnley Junction	55D Royston	56A Wakefield
90408	WD[1]	BA Bricklayers Arms	73B Bricklayers Arms	26D Bury	26D Bury	26D Bury	26D Bury	
90409	WD[1]	HLD Hull Dairycoates	53A Hull Dairycoates	53A Hull Dairycoates	51B Newport	51L Thornaby	56B Ardsley	56A Wakefield
90410	WD[1]	MEX Mexborough	36B Mexborough	36B Mexborough	36B Mexborough	41F Mexborough	41F Mexborough	36C Frodingham
90411	WD[1]	NEV Leeds Neville Hill	38A Colwick	38A Colwick	40E Langwith Junction	40B Immingham	41J Langwith Junction	
90412	WD[1]	Stored	25A Wakefield	25A Wakefield	56E Sowerby Bridge	56E Sowerby Bridge	56E Sowerby Bridge	
90413	WD[1]	GLO Gloucester	26A Newton Heath	26D Bury	26B Agecroft	24C Lostock Hall	24F Fleetwood	40E Colwick
90414	WD[1]	CDF Cardiff Canton	25A Wakefield	25A Wakefield	56A Wakefield	41D Canklow		
90415	WD[1]	Stored	25A Wakefield	25A Wakefield	56A Wakefield	56A Wakefield	56A Wakefield	56A Wakefield
90416	WD[1]	Stored	24A Accrington	26C Bolton	27B Aintree	27B Aintree	27B Aintree	
90417	WD[1]	Stored	25A Wakefield	25A Wakefield	56A Wakefield	56A Wakefield	56A Wakefield	56A Wakefield
90418	WD[1]	HLD Hull Dairycoates	38D Staveley	38D Staveley	38A Colwick	40E Colwick	41J Langwith Junction	41J Langwith Junction
90419	WD[1]	Stored	26D Bury	26D Bury	26D Bury	26D Bury	26D Bury	
90420	WD[1]	Stored	24B Rose Grove	24B Rose Grove	24B Rose Grove	24B Rose Grove	24B Rose Grove	
90421	WD[1]	MEX Mexborough	36B Mexborough	36B Mexborough	36B Mexborough	41F Mexborough	41F Mexborough	
90422	WD[1]	(63101)	31B March	36C Frodingham	36C Frodingham	36C Frodingham	36C Frodingham	
90423	WD[1]	(63102)	51A Darlington	38A Colwick	2E Northampton	8D Widnes	8D Widnes	
90424	WD[1]	(63103)	50A York	50C Selby	51B Newport	50A York	50A York	
90425	WD[1]	(63104)	31B March	36C Frodingham	36C Frodingham	36C Frodingham		
90426	WD[1]	(63105)	51B Newport	51B Newport	51B Newport	51L Thornaby	56A Wakefield	
90427	WD[1]	(63106)	52D Tweedmouth	53C Hull Springhead	53C Hull Springhead	53A Hull Dairycoates	50B Hull Dairycoates	50D Goole
90428	WD[1]	(63107)	35A New England	35A New England	35A New England	34E New England	34E New England	36A Doncaster
90429	WD[1]	(63108)	53C Hull Springhead	53C Hull Springhead	53C Hull Springhead	56A Wakefield	56A Wakefield	56A Wakefield
90430	WD[1]	(63109)	54B Tyne Dock	53A Hull Dairycoates	53A Hull Dairycoates	51A Darlington	51A Darlington	56A Wakefield
90431	WD[1]	(63110)	30E Colchester	40B Immingham	40E Langwith Junction	41J Langwith Junction		
90432	WD[1]	(63111)	50A York	38A Colwick	38A Colwick	40E Colwick	40E Colwick	
90433	WD[1]	(63112)	31B March	38A Colwick	38E Woodford Halse	2F Woodford Halse	2F Woodford Halse	
90434	WD[1]	(63113)	51B Newport	51B Newport	51B Newport	51L Thornaby	51L Thornaby	51C West Hartlepool
90435	WD[1]	(63114)	53A Hull Dairycoates	51B Newport	51B Newport	51L Thornaby	50B Hull Dairycoates	
90436	WD[1]	(63115)	64A St. Margarets	65D Dawsholm	65D Dawsholm	65D Dawsholm		
90437	WD[1]	(63116)	38A Colwick	38A Colwick	38A Colwick	40E Colwick	40E Colwick	36A Doncaster
90438	WD[1]	(63117)	35A New England	35A New England	35A New England	41J Langwith Junction	40E Colwick	
90439	WD[1]	(63118)	35A New England	35A New England	35A New England	34E New England	34E New England	
90440	WD[1]	(63119)	65D Dawsholm	65D Dawsholm	65D Dawsholm	65D Dawsholm	8F Wigan Springs Branch	
90441	WD[1]	(63120)	65A Eastfield	62A Thornton Junction	62A Thornton Junction	62A Thornton Junction	62A Thornton Junction	62A Thornton Junction
90442	WD[1]	(63121)	31B March	40B Immingham	33A Plaistow	33B Tilbury	36A Doncaster	
90443	WD[1]	(63122)	30E Colchester	31B March	40B Immingham	40B Immingham	40B Immingham	
90444	WD[1]	(63123)	62B Dundee Tay Bridge	62B Dundee Tay Bridge	62B Dundee Tay Bridge	62B Dundee Tay Bridge	62B Dundee Tay Bridge	62A Thornton Junction
90445	WD[1]	(63124)	54B Tyne Dock	54B Tyne Dock	54B Tyne Dock	56A Wakefield	51A Darlington	51C West Hartlepool
90446	WD[1]	(63125)	51B Newport	51B Newport	51B Newport	51L Thornaby	51L Thornaby	
90447	WD[1]	(63126)	35C Spital Bridge	35C Spital Bridge	35C Spital Bridge	31F Spital Bridge	36A Doncaster	
90448	WD[1]	(63127)	38A Colwick	38E Woodford Halse	38E Woodford Halse	2F Woodford Halse	2F Woodford Halse	
90449	WD[1]	(63128)	51A Darlington	38A Colwick	40E Langwith Junction	41J Langwith Junction	41J Langwith Junction	41J Langwith Junction
90450	WD[1]	(63129)	53A Hull Dairycoates	53A Hull Dairycoates	53A Hull Dairycoates	53A Hull Dairycoates	50B Hull Dairycoates	50B Hull Dairycoates
90451	WD[1]	(63130)	51B Newport	51B Newport	51B Newport	51L Thornaby	51L Thornaby	50D Goole
90452	WD[1]	(63131)	51B Newport	51B Newport	51B Newport	51L Thornaby	51L Thornaby	
90453	WD[1]	(63132)	31B March	40B Immingham	31B March	36A Doncaster	36C Frodingham	
90454	WD[1]	(63133)	35A New England	35A New England	35A New England	34E New England	34E New England	
90455	WD[1]	(63134)	61B Aberdeen Ferryhill	61B Aberdeen Ferryhill	61B Aberdeen Ferryhill	61B Aberdeen Ferryhill		
90456	WD[1]	(63135)	40B Immingham	36C Frodingham	36C Frodingham	36C Frodingham	36C Frodingham	36C Frodingham
90457	WD[1]	(63136)	51B Newport	51B Newport	51B Newport	56D Mirfield	56D Mirfield	56A Wakefield
90458	WD[1]	(63137)	54B Tyne Dock	53A Hull Dairycoates	53A Hull Dairycoates	53A Hull Dairycoates	50B Hull Dairycoates	50B Hull Dairycoates
90459	WD[1]	(63138)	51B Newport	51B Newport	51B Newport	51L Thornaby	51L Thornaby	51C West Hartlepool
90460	WD[1]	(63139)	40B Immingham	38D Staveley	38A Colwick	40B Immingham	40A Lincoln	
90461	WD[1]	(63140)	51B Newport	51B Newport	51B Newport	51L Thornaby	50D Goole	
90462	WD[1]	(63141)	51B Newport	51B Newport	51B Newport	51L Thornaby	51L Thornaby	50B Hull Dairycoates
90463	WD[1]	(63142)	62B Dundee Tay Bridge	62B Dundee Tay Bridge	62B Dundee Tay Bridge	67C Ayr	67D Ardrossan	
90464	WD[1]	(63143)	68A Carlisle Kingmoor	64A St. Margarets	68A Carlisle Kingmoor	12A Carlisle Kingmoor	8G Sutton Oak	
90465	WD[1]	(63144)	51B Newport	51B Newport	51B Newport	51L Thornaby	56B Ardsley	55E Normanton
90466	WD[1]	(63145)	38A Colwick	84D Leamington Spa	84C Banbury	81C Southall	8B Warrington Dallam	
90467	WD[1]	(63146)	51A Darlington	53C Hull Springhead	50B Leeds Neville Hill	50A York	50A York	
90468	WD[1]	(63147)	64A St. Margarets	66C Hamilton	66C Hamilton	66B Motherwell	66B Motherwell	62A Thornton Junction
90469	WD[1]	(63148)	64A St. Margarets	36A Doncaster	31B March	36C Frodingham	36C Frodingham	
90470	WD[1]	(63149)	53C Hull Springhead	53C Hull Springhead	53C Hull Springhead	56E Sowerby Bridge	56E Sowerby Bridge	56A Wakefield
90471	WD[1]	(63150)	30E Colchester	40B Immingham	40B Immingham	41D Canklow	41D Canklow	36C Frodingham
90472	WD[1]	(63151)	62A Thornton Junction	62A Thornton Junction	62A Thornton Junction	62A Thornton Junction	62A Thornton Junction	
90473	WD[1]	(63152)	31B March	38A Colwick	38A Colwick	40E Colwick		
90474	WD[1]	(63153)	31B March	38E Woodford Halse	38E Woodford Halse	2F Woodford Halse	2F Woodford Halse	
90475	WD[1]	(63154)	51B Newport	51B Newport	51B Newport	50A York	50D Goole	
90476	WD[1]	(63155)	31B March	38A Colwick	38A Colwick	40E Colwick	36A Doncaster	
90477	WD[1]	(63156)	30E Colchester	40B Immingham	31B March	31B March	36A Doncaster	40B Immingham
90478	WD[1]	(63157)	53C Hull Springhead	53C Hull Springhead	53C Hull Springhead	53E Goole	50D Goole	50B Hull Dairycoates
90479	WD[1]	(63158)	52D Tweedmouth	53A Hull Dairycoates	53A Hull Dairycoates	51L Thornaby	51L Thornaby	51C West Hartlepool
90480	WD[1]	(63159)	31B March	31B March	31B March	30A Stratford	36A Doncaster	
90481	WD[1]	(63160)	51B Newport	51B Newport	51B Newport	51L Thornaby	56B Ardsley	55E Normanton
90482	WD[1]	(63161)	54B Tyne Dock	53A Hull Dairycoates	53A Hull Dairycoates	53A Hull Dairycoates	50B Hull Dairycoates	56A Wakefield
90483	WD[1]	(63162)	53A Hull Dairycoates	84G Shrewsbury	84D Leamington Spa	84C Banbury	41J Langwith Junction	
90484	WD[1]	(63163)	38A Colwick	38E Woodford Halse	31B March	31B March	36A Doncaster	36A Doncaster
90485	WD[1]	(63164)	54B Tyne Dock	81C Southall	81C Southall	81D Reading	41F Mexborough	
90486	WD[1]	(63165)	38E Woodford Halse	38E Woodford Halse	38E Woodford Halse	2F Woodford Halse	2F Woodford Halse	
90487	WD[1]	(63166)	51B Newport	51B Newport	51B Newport	55E Normanton	55E Normanton	
90488	WD[1]	(63167)	51B Newport	51B Newport	51B Newport	55D Royston	55D Royston	
90489	WD[1]	(63168)	62A Thornton Junction	62A Thornton Junction	65A Eastfield	65A Eastfield	65D Dawsholm	62C Dunfermline Upper
90490	WD[1]	(63169)	35A New England	36C Frodingham	36C Frodingham	36C Frodingham	40B Immingham	
90491	WD[1]	(63170)	38A Colwick	38A Colwick	31B March	41F Mexborough	41F Mexborough	
90492	WD[1]	(63171)	38A Colwick	40B Immingham	40E Langwith Junction	41J Langwith Junction	40E Colwick	
90493	WD[1]	(63172)	64A St. Margarets	65D Dawsholm	65D Dawsholm	65D Dawsholm	8F Wigan Springs Branch	36C Frodingham
90494	WD[1]	(63173)	35A New England	35A New England	35A New England	33B Tilbury		
90495	WD[1]	(63174)	35A New England	36B Mexborough	36B Mexborough	41F Mexborough		
90496	WD[1]	(63175)	64A St. Margarets	38A Colwick	38A Colwick	40E Colwick	36A Doncaster	
90497	WD[1]	(63176)	53C Hull Springhead	53C Hull Springhead	53C Hull Springhead	56A Wakefield	56A Wakefield	
90498	WD[1]	(63177)	62A Thornton Junction	36A Doncaster	31B March	30A Stratford	36A Doncaster	36C Frodingham
90499	WD[1]	(63178)	38A Colwick	38A Colwick	38A Colwick	41F Mexborough	41F Mexborough	
90500	WD[1]	(63170)	51B Newport	50A York	51B Newport	51L Thornaby	51L Thornaby	
90501	WD[1]	(63180)	35C Spital Bridge	35C Spital Bridge	35C Spital Bridge	31F Spital Bridge	36A Doncaster	
90502	WD[1]	(63181)	31B March	35A New England	40E Langwith Junction	41H Staveley	34E New England	
90503	WD[1]	(63182)	51B Newport	51B Newport	51B Newport	53A Hull Dairycoates	55C Farnley Junction	55D Royston
90504	WD[1]	(63183)	38E Woodford Halse	38E Woodford Halse	38E Woodford Halse	2F Woodford Halse	2F Woodford Halse	
90505	WD[1]	(63184)	68A Carlisle Kingmoor	67C Ayr	67C Ayr	67C Ayr		

		1948	1951	1954	1957	1960	1963	1966
90506	WD[1]	(63185)	31B March	36A Doncaster	36B Mexborough	41F Mexborough	36A Doncaster	40B Immingham
90507	WD[1]	(63186)	38E Woodford Halse	38E Woodford Halse	38E Woodford Halse	2F Woodford Halse	8F Wigan Springs Branch	
90508	WD[1]	(63187)	30E Colchester	40B Immingham	30A Stratford	30A Stratford		
90509	WD[1]	(63188)	38E Woodford Halse	38E Woodford Halse	38E Woodford Halse	8F Wigan Springs Branch	8F Wigan Springs Branch	
90510	WD[1]	(63189)	31B March	40B Immingham	40B Immingham	40B Immingham	40E Colwick	
90511	WD[1]	(63190)	50A York	53C Hull Springhead	53C Hull Springhead	53A Hull Dairycoates	55D Royston	
90512	WD[1]	(63191)	35A New England	36C Frodingham	36C Frodingham	36C Frodingham		
90513	WD[1]	(63192)	62C Dunfermline Upper	62C Dunfermline Upper	62A Thornton Junction	62A Thornton Junction		
90514	WD[1]	(63193)	35A New England	35A New England	35A New England	33B Tilbury	34E New England	36C Frodingham
90515	WD[1]	(63194)	62B Dundee Tay Bridge	62B Dundee Tay Bridge	62B Dundee Tay Bridge	62B Dundee Tay Bridge	62B Dundee Tay Bridge	
90516	WD[1]	(63195)	38E Woodford Halse	38E Woodford Halse	38E Woodford Halse	2F Woodford Halse	2F Woodford Halse	
90517	WD[1]	(63196)	51B Newport	51B Newport	51B Newport	51L Thornaby	50A York	50A York
90518	WD[1]	(63197)	50A York	50A York	50D Starbeck	50A York	50A York	50A York
90519	WD[1]	(63198)	31B March	31B March	38A Colwick	41F Mexborough	41F Mexborough	
90520	WD[1]	(63199)	38E Woodford Halse	38E Woodford Halse	38E Woodford Halse	2F Woodford Halse	2F Woodford Halse	
90521	WD[1]	NEV Leeds Neville Hill	36B Mexborough	36B Mexborough	36B Mexborough	41F Mexborough	41F Mexborough	
90522	WD[1]	MAR March	30E Colchester	31B March	31B March	31B March	36A Doncaster	
90523	WD[1]	FEL Feltham	63A Perth	26A Newton Heath	26A Newton Heath	26A Newton Heath		
90524	WD[1]	CDF Cardiff Canton	85C Hereford	86C Cardiff Canton	86C Cardiff Canton	2F Woodford Halse	2F Woodford Halse	
90525	WD[1]	Stored	26A Newton Heath	26A Newton Heath	26A Newton Heath	26E Lees Oldham	26E Lees Oldham	
90526	WD[1]	TDK Tyne Dock	38D Staveley	35A New England	36B Mexborough	41F Mexborough		
90527	WD[1]	FEL Feltham	25B Huddersfield	25G Farnley Junction	27B Aintree	27B Aintree	27B Aintree	
90528	WD[1]	WFD Woodford Halse	35A New England	35A New England	35A New England	31F Spital Bridge	36A Doncaster	
90529	WD[1]	OXF	81F Oxford	81F Oxford	81C Southall	87G Carmarthen	41F Mexborough	
90530	WD[1]	FEL Feltham	63A Perth	26A Newton Heath	26A Newton Heath	26A Newton Heath	26F Patricroft	
90531	WD[1]	Stored	25C Goole	25C Goole	25C Goole	53E Goole	50D Goole	
90532	WD[1]	WFD Woodford Halse	38A Colwick	38A Colwick	2E Northampton	6B Mold Junction		
90533	WD[1]	FEL Feltham	73B Bricklayers Arms	26A Newton Heath	26A Newton Heath	26A Newton Heath	26A Newton Heath	40E Colwick
90534	WD[1]	THJ Thornton Junction	62A Thornton Junction	62A Thornton Junction	62A Thornton Junction	62A Thornton Junction	62A Thornton Junction	62C Dunfermline Upper
90535	WD[1]	OXY Oxley	26A Newton Heath	26A Newton Heath	27B Aintree	27B Aintree	27B Aintree	
90536	WD[1]	THJ Thornton Junction	65F Grangemouth	66A Polmadie	66A Polmadie	66A Polmadie	61B Aberdeen Ferryhill	
90537	WD[1]	HLS Hull Springhead	36B Mexborough	36A Doncaster	31B March	36A Doncaster	36C Frodingham	36A Doncaster
90538	WD[1]	MEX Mexborough	36B Mexborough	36A Doncaster	31B March	36A Doncaster	36A Doncaster	40B Immingham
90539	WD[1]	THJ Thornton Junction	62A Thornton Junction	62A Thornton Junction	62A Thornton Junction	65F Grangemouth	65F Grangemouth	
90540	WD[1]	MAR March	31B March	36C Frodingham	36C Frodingham	36C Frodingham	36C Frodingham	
90541	WD[1]	Stored	24C Lostock Hall	24C Lostock Hall	24C Lostock Hall	24C Lostock Hall	24C Lostock Hall	
90542	WD[1]	DFU Dunfermline Upper	62C Dunfermline Upper	62C Dunfermline Upper	62C Dunfermline Upper	62C Dunfermline Upper	62C Dunfermline Upper	
90543	WD[1]	FEL Feltham	25D Mirfield	25D Mirfield	56D Mirfield	56A Wakefield	56A Wakefield	
90544	WD[1]	HLS Hull Springhead	38A Colwick	86A Ebbw Junction	86A Ebbw Junction	86A Ebbw Junction	36C Frodingham	
90545	WD[1]	EFD Eastfield	65A Eastfield	38A Colwick	40E Langwith Junction	41J Langwith Junction	40E Colwick	
90546	WD[1]	TN Taunton	26B Agecroft	26B Agecroft	26B Agecroft	26B Agecroft	26B Agecroft	
90547	WD[1]	THJ Thornton Junction	62A Thornton Junction	64A St. Margarets	62C Dunfermline Upper	62C Dunfermline Upper	62C Dunfermline Upper	62C Dunfermline Upper
90548	WD[1]	OXY Oxley	26A Newton Heath	26A Newton Heath	26A Newton Heath	26A Newton Heath	26F Patricroft	
90549	WD[1]	Stored	65D Dawsholm	65D Dawsholm	65D Dawsholm	66A Polmadie		
90550	WD[1]	NEV Leeds Neville Hill	36B Mexborough	31B March	31B March	36A Doncaster		
90551	WD[1]	WFD Woodford Halse	38A Colwick	35A New England	30A Stratford	30A Stratford	36A Doncaster	36A Doncaster
90552	WD[1]	BA Bricklayers Arms	73B Bricklayers Arms	26G Belle Vue	26A Newton Heath	27B Aintree	27B Aintree	
90553	WD[1]	DFU Dunfermline Upper	62C Dunfermline Upper	62C Dunfermline Upper	62C Dunfermline Upper	62C Dunfermline Upper	62C Dunfermline Upper	
90554	WD[1]	MAR March	35A New England	35A New England	40E Langwith Junction	41J Langwith Junction		
90555	WD[1]	STM St. Margarets	64A St. Margarets	26D Bury	26D Bury	26D Bury	26D Bury	
90556	WD[1]	BA Bricklayers Arms	73C Hither Green	25A Wakefield	24F Fleetwood	24C Lostock Hall	24D Lower Darwen	
90557	WD[1]	Stored	24B Rose Grove	24B Rose Grove	24B Rose Grove	24B Rose Grove	24B Rose Grove	
90558	WD[1]	BA Bricklayers Arms	73B Bricklayers Arms	26A Newton Heath	26A Newton Heath	26B Agecroft	26B Agecroft	
90559	WD[1]	NPT Newport	35A New England	35A New England	35A New England	32A Norwich Thorpe		
90560	WD[1]	DFU Dunfermline Upper	62C Dunfermline Upper	64A St. Margarets	62C Dunfermline Upper	62C Dunfermline Upper	62C Dunfermline Upper	62C Dunfermline Upper
90561	WD[1]	TYS Tyseley	26A Newton Heath	26A Newton Heath	26A Newton Heath	27D Wigan	26A Newton Heath	
90562	WD[1]	FEL Feltham	70B Feltham	25G Farnley Junction	55C Farnley Junction	55C Farnley Junction		
90563	WD[1]	PPRD Pontypool Road	86G Pontypool Road	84D Leamington Spa	82B St. Philips Marsh	2F Woodford Halse	2F Woodford Halse	
90564	WD[1]	BA Bricklayers Arms	73B Bricklayers Arms	26B Agecroft	26B Agecroft	26B Agecroft	26B Agecroft	
90565	WD[1]	NPT Ebbw Junction	86A Ebbw Junction	86C Cardiff Canton	86C Cardiff Canton	85E Gloucester Barnwood		
90566	WD[1]	HIT Hither Green	73C Hither Green	6B Mold Junction	6B Mold Junction	6B Mold Junction	8B Warrington Dallam	
90567	WD[1]	HLS Hull Springhead	53A Hull Dairycoates	38A Colwick	31B March	41F Mexborough	41F Mexborough	
90568	WD[1]	CDF Cardiff Canton	26A Newton Heath	26D Bury	26D Bury	26D Bury	26F Patricroft	
90569	WD[1]	DFU Dunfermline Upper	64A St. Margarets	31B March	31B March	36A Doncaster	36A Doncaster	
90570	WD[1]	FEL Feltham	70B Feltham	27D Wigan	27D Wigan	27D Wigan	26F Patricroft	
90571	WD[1]	YK York	53C Hull Springhead	53C Hull Springhead	53C Hull Springhead	53A Hull Dairycoates	50A York	
90572	WD[1]	CHR Chester (GWR)	84K Chester (GWR)	86C Cardiff Canton	86C Cardiff Canton	86C Cardiff Canton	41F Mexborough	41J Langwith Junction
90573	WD[1]	SPM St. Philips Marsh	82B St. Philips Marsh	85B Gloucester	85B Gloucester	86C Cardiff Canton	36C Frodingham	
90574	WD[1]	WFD Woodford Halse	38A Colwick	38E Woodford Halse	38E Woodford Halse	2F Woodford Halse	8F Wigan Springs Branch	
90575	WD[1]	DFU Dunfermline Upper	62C Dunfermline Upper	62C Dunfermline Upper	62C Dunfermline Upper	62C Dunfermline Upper		
90576	WD[1]	NPT Newport	24B Rose Grove	26A Newton Heath	26A Newton Heath	26A Newton Heath	24B Rose Grove	
90577	WD[1]	NWE New England	35A New England	35A New England	40E Langwith Junction	41J Langwith Junction	40A Lincoln	
90578	WD[1]	FEL Feltham	25D Mirfield	25D Mirfield	56D Mirfield	50A York	50A York	
90579	WD[1]	CDF Cardiff Canton	87K Swansea Victoria	84C Banbury	86C Cardiff Canton	86C Cardiff Canton	41F Mexborough	
90580	WD[1]	MAR March	31B March	36B Mexborough	36B Mexborough	41F Mexborough	41F Mexborough	
90581	WD[1]	Stored	25A Wakefield	25A Wakefield	56A Wakefield	56A Wakefield	56A Wakefield	
90582	WD[1]	MAR March	31B March	36B Mexborough	36B Mexborough	41F Mexborough	41F Mexborough	
90583	WD[1]	HLS Hull Springhead	36B Mexborough	40B Immingham	40B Immingham	40B Immingham	40B Immingham	
90584	WD[1]	NPT Newport	24B Rose Grove	24B Rose Grove	27D Wigan	24C Lostock Hall	24B Rose Grove	
90585	WD[1]	PDN Old Oak Common	68A Carlisle Kingmoor	86A Ebbw Junction	84C Banbury	84C Banbury	8F Wigan Springs Branch	
90586	WD[1]	NEV Leeds Neville Hill	53C Hull Springhead	53C Hull Springhead	53C Hull Springhead	53A Hull Dairycoates	50B Hull Dairycoates	50B Hull Dairycoates
90587	WD[1]	HLS Hull Springhead	36B Mexborough	36B Mexborough	36B Mexborough	41F Mexborough	41F Mexborough	
90588	WD[1]	Stored	25G Farnley Junction	25G Farnley Junction	55C Farnley Junction	55C Farnley Junction	55C Farnley Junction	51C West Hartlepool
90589	WD[1]	SPM St. Philips Marsh	26A Newton Heath	26A Newton Heath	26A Newton Heath	26A Newton Heath	26F Patricroft	
90590	WD[1]	MEX Mexborough	36B Mexborough	36B Mexborough	36B Mexborough	41F Mexborough	41F Mexborough	
90591	WD[1]	Stored	25G Farnley Junction	25G Farnley Junction	55C Farnley Junction	55C Farnley Junction		
90592	WD[1]	STM St. Margarets	24B Rose Grove	24B Rose Grove	24B Rose Grove	24B Rose Grove	24D Lower Darwen	
90593	WD[1]	Stored	25D Mirfield	25D Mirfield	56D Mirfield	51L Thornaby	51L Thornaby	51C West Hartlepool
90594	WD[1]	HLS Hull Springhead	36B Mexborough	40B Immingham	40E Langwith Junction	41J Langwith Junction		
90595	WD[1]	Stored	24C Lostock Hall	24C Lostock Hall	24C Lostock Hall	24J Lancaster	24J Lancaster	
90596	WD[1]	MEX Mexborough	36B Mexborough	36C Frodingham	36C Frodingham	66A Polmadie	66A Polmadie	61B Aberdeen Ferryhill
90597	WD[1]	MEX Mexborough	36B Mexborough	36B Mexborough	36C Frodingham	36C Frodingham	36C Frodingham	
90598	WD[1]	MEX Mexborough	36B Mexborough	36B Mexborough	36C Frodingham	36C Frodingham	36C Frodingham	
90599	WD[1]	EFD Eastfield	24B Rose Grove	24B Rose Grove	27D Wigan	27D Wigan	27B Aintree	
90600	WD[1]	Stored	62B Dundee Tay Bridge	62B Dundee Tay Bridge	62B Dundee Tay Bridge	62C Dunfermline Upper	62C Dunfermline Upper	62A Thornton Junction
90601	WD[1]	MAR March	31B March	31B March	36C Frodingham	36C Frodingham	36C Frodingham	
90602	WD[1]	MAR March	31B March	31B March	31B March	36A Doncaster	36C Frodingham	
90603	WD[1]	SKN Stockton on Tees	51E Stockton on Tees	51E Stockton on Tees	51B Newport	51L Thornaby		
90604	WD[1]	FEL Feltham	70B Feltham	25A Wakefield	56A Wakefield	56A Wakefield	56A Wakefield	
90605	WD[1]	NPT Newport	51B Newport	51B Newport	51B Newport	55D Royston	55D Royston	55D Royston
90606	WD[1]	YK York	38D Staveley	6B Mold Junction	6B Mold Junction	6B Mold Junction	8G Sutton Oak	40E Colwick
90607	WD[1]	Stored	25A Wakefield	25A Wakefield	56A Wakefield	56A Wakefield		
90608	WD[1]	MAR March	31B March	31B March	31B March	41F Mexborough		
90609	WD[1]	NEV Leeds Neville Hill	50A York	53A Hull Dairycoates	53A Hull Dairycoates	53A Hull Dairycoates	50B Hull Dairycoates	
90610	WD[1]	Stored	24A Accrington	25A Wakefield	56A Wakefield	55E Normanton	55D Royston	56A Wakefield
90611	WD[1]	TDK Tyne Dock	54B Tyne Dock	54B Tyne Dock	54B Tyne Dock	55D Royston	55D Royston	56A Wakefield
90612	WD[1]	NEV Leeds Neville Hill	36B Mexborough	36B Mexborough	36B Mexborough	41F Mexborough	41F Mexborough	
90613	WD[1]	NWE New England	35A New England	35A New England	35A New England	34E New England	34E New England	
90614	WD[1]	THJ Thornton Junction	62A Thornton Junction	62A Thornton Junction	62A Thornton Junction	62A Thornton Junction	62A Thornton Junction	
90615	WD[1]	Stored	25A Wakefield	25A Wakefield	56A Wakefield	56A Wakefield	56A Wakefield	56A Wakefield
90616	WD[1]	THJ Thornton Junction	65F Grangemouth	66A Polmadie	66A Polmadie	66A Polmadie		
90617	WD[1]	Stored	25A Wakefield	25A Wakefield	56A Wakefield	55E Normanton	55E Normanton	55E Normanton
90618	WD[1]	NEV Leeds Neville Hill	36B Mexborough	38A Colwick	38A Colwick	40E Colwick	40B Immingham	
90619	WD[1]	BA Bricklayers Arms	25B Huddersfield	25B Huddersfield	55G Huddersfield	55G Huddersfield	55G Huddersfield	

		1948	1951	1954	1957	1960	1963	1966
90620	WD[1]	Stored	**25A** Wakefield	**25A** Wakefield	**56A** Wakefield	**56A** Wakefield	**56A** Wakefield	**56A** Wakefield
90621	WD[1]	**NEV** Leeds Neville Hill	**24B** Rose Grove	**25B** Huddersfield	**55G** Huddersfield	**55G** Huddersfield	**55G** Huddersfield	
90622	WD[1]	**BA** Bricklayers Arms	**25D** Mirfield	**25D** Mirfield	**56D** Mirfield	**56D** Mirfield	**56D** Mirfield	**56A** Wakefield
90623	WD[1]	**SKN** Stockton on Tees	**51E** Stockton on Tees	**53C** Hull Springhead	**53C** Hull Springhead	**53A** Hull Dairycoates	**50A** York	
90624	WD[1]	**LLY** Llanelly	**25A** Wakefield	**25A** Wakefield	**55G** Huddersfield	**55G** Huddersfield	**55G** Huddersfield	
90625	WD[1]	**NPT** Newport	**51B** Newport	**51B** Newport	**51B** Newport	**56A** Wakefield	**56B** Ardsley	**56A** Wakefield
90626	WD[1]	**STM** St. Margarets	**26F** Lees Oldham	**26D** Bury	**26D** Bury	**26D** Bury	**26B** Agecroft	
90627	WD[1]	**TDK** Tyne Dock	**54B** Tyne Dock	**53A** Hull Dairycoates	**53A** Hull Dairycoates	**53A** Hull Dairycoates	**50B** Hull Dairycoates	**50B** Hull Dairycoates
90628	WD[1]	**NEV** Leeds Neville Hill	**66B** Motherwell	**66B** Motherwell	**66B** Motherwell	**66B** Motherwell	**66B** Motherwell	**62A** Thornton Junction
90629	WD[1]	**YK** York	**38A** Colwick	**38A** Colwick	**38A** Colwick	**40E** Colwick	**40E** Colwick	
90630	WD[1]	**SPM** St. Philips Marsh	**82D** Westbury	**86C** Cardiff Canton	**81C** Southall	**81C** Southall		
90631	WD[1]	Stored	**25A** Wakefield	**25A** Wakefield	**56A** Wakefield	**56A** Wakefield	**56A** Wakefield	**56A** Wakefield
90632	WD[1]	Stored	**24A** Accrington	**26B** Agecroft	**26B** Agecroft	**26B** Agecroft	**26B** Agecroft	
90633	WD[1]	**PDN** Old Oak Common	**25A** Wakefield	**25A** Wakefield	**56A** Wakefield	**56A** Wakefield	**56A** Wakefield	**56A** Wakefield
90634	WD[1]	**STV** Staveley	**38D** Staveley	**38A** Colwick	**38A** Colwick	**40E** Colwick		
90635	WD[1]	Stored	**25A** Wakefield	**25A** Wakefield	**56A** Wakefield	**56A** Wakefield	**56A** Wakefield	
90636	WD[1]	**YK** York	**38A** Colwick	**38A** Colwick	**31B** March	**36A** Doncaster	**36A** Doncaster	**36A** Doncaster
90637	WD[1]	Stored	**25A** Wakefield	**25A** Wakefield	**56A** Wakefield	**55E** Normanton		
90638	WD[1]	**YK** York	**38A** Colwick	**38E** Woodford Halse	**38E** Woodford Halse	**2F** Woodford Halse		
90639	WD[1]	Stored	**25A** Wakefield	**25C** Goole	**56A** Wakefield	**56A** Wakefield	**56A** Wakefield	**56A** Wakefield
90640	WD[1]	Stored	**24C** Lostock Hall	**24C** Lostock Hall	**24C** Lostock Hall	**66A** Polmadie	**61B** Aberdeen Ferryhill	**61B** Aberdeen Ferryhill
90641	WD[1]	**AFD** Ashford	**75B** Redhill	**26C** Bolton	**26C** Bolton	**26C** Bolton	**26C** Bolton	
90642	WD[1]	**LA** Laira (Plymouth)	**25D** Mirfield	**25D** Mirfield	**56D** Mirfield	**56D** Mirfield	**56B** Ardsley	**56A** Wakefield
90643	WD[1]	Stored	**25A** Wakefield	**25A** Wakefield	**27B** Aintree	**27B** Aintree	**27B** Aintree	
90644	WD[1]	Stored	**25A** Wakefield	**25A** Wakefield	**56A** Wakefield	**56A** Wakefield	**56B** Ardsley	**55E** Normanton
90645	WD[1]	Stored	**25G** Farnley Junction	**25G** Farnley Junction	**55C** Farnley Junction	**55C** Farnley Junction	**55C** Farnley Junction	**55D** Royston
90646	WD[1]	**CLK** Colwick	**40B** Immingham	**36C** Frodingham	**36C** Frodingham	**36C** Frodingham	**36C** Frodingham	
90647	WD[1]	**CLK** Colwick	**40B** Immingham	**36C** Frodingham	**36C** Frodingham	**36C** Frodingham	**36C** Frodingham	
90648	WD[1]	**NEV** Leeds Neville Hill	**38A** Colwick	**38A** Colwick	**38A** Colwick	**40E** Colwick		
90649	WD[1]	Stored	**25G** Farnley Junction	**25G** Farnley Junction	**55C** Farnley Junction	**55G** Huddersfield	**55G** Huddersfield	**55G** Huddersfield
90650	WD[1]	**BA** Bricklayers Arms	**25B** Huddersfield	**25G** Farnley Junction	**55C** Farnley Junction	**55C** Farnley Junction	**55D** Royston	**55D** Royston
90651	WD[1]	Stored	**25A** Wakefield	**25A** Wakefield	**56A** Wakefield	**56A** Wakefield	**56A** Wakefield	**56A** Wakefield
90652	WD[1]	**OXY** Oxley	**25A** Wakefield	**25A** Wakefield	**56A** Wakefield	**55E** Normanton	**55E** Normanton	**55E** Normanton
90653	WD[1]	**MEX** Mexborough	**31B** March	**36B** Mexborough	**33A** Plaistow	**33B** Tilbury		
90654	WD[1]	Stored	**25A** Wakefield	**25A** Wakefield	**56A** Wakefield	**56A** Wakefield	**56A** Wakefield	**56A** Wakefield
90655	WD[1]	**AFD** Ashford	**25B** Huddersfield	**25B** Huddersfield	**56D** Mirfield	**56D** Mirfield	**56D** Mirfield	**56D** Mirfield
90656	WD[1]	**CNYD** Croes Newydd	**25A** Wakefield	**25A** Wakefield	**56A** Wakefield	**56A** Wakefield	**56A** Wakefield	
90657	WD[1]	**MEX** Mexborough	**35A** New England	**35A** New England	**35A** New England	**41J** Langwith Junction		
90658	WD[1]	**LA** Laira (Plymouth)	**24C** Lostock Hall	**24C** Lostock Hall	**24C** Lostock Hall	**24C** Lostock Hall	**24F** Fleetwood	
90659	WD[1]	**MEX** Mexborough	**35A** New England	**35A** New England	**35A** New England	**34E** New England	**34E** New England	
90660	WD[1]	**MAR** March	**31B** March	**40B** Immingham	**30A** Stratford	**30A** Stratford	**40B** Immingham	
90661	WD[1]	**TDK** Tyne Dock	**53C** Hull Springhead	**53C** Hull Springhead	**53C** Hull Springhead	**55E** Normanton	**55E** Normanton	
90662	WD[1]	**CLK** Colwick	**38A** Colwick	**38A** Colwick	**38A** Colwick	**40E** Colwick	**40B** Immingham	
90663	WD[1]	**HLD** Hull Dairycoates	**53A** Hull Dairycoates	**53C** Hull Springhead	**50B** Leeds Neville Hill	**50A** York	**50A** York	
90664	WD[1]	Stored	**25G** Farnley Junction	**25G** Farnley Junction	**55C** Farnley Junction	**55E** Normanton	**55E** Normanton	**56A** Wakefield
90665	WD[1]	**MEX** Mexborough	**35A** New England	**35A** New England	**35A** New England	**34E** New England	**36C** Frodingham	
90666	WD[1]	Stored	**25G** Farnley Junction	**25G** Farnley Junction	**55C** Farnley Junction	**55G** Huddersfield		
90667	WD[1]	Stored	**25A** Wakefield	**6C** Birkenhead	**6B** Mold Junction	**8F** Wigan Springs Branch	**8F** Wigan Springs Branch	
90668	WD[1]	**MAR** March	**31B** March	**31B** March	**36B** Mexborough	**41F** Mexborough	**41F** Mexborough	
90669	WD[1]	**HIT** Hither Green	**73C** Hither Green	**26A** Newton Heath	**26A** Newton Heath	**26A** Newton Heath	**26F** Patricroft	**40E** Colwick
90670	WD[1]	**TWD** Tweedmouth	**50A** York	**50A** York	**53A** Hull Dairycoates	**53A** Hull Dairycoates	**50B** Hull Dairycoates	**50B** Hull Dairycoates
90671	WD[1]	**HIT** Hither Green	**73C** Hither Green	**27D** Wigan	**27D** Wigan	**26E** Lees Oldham	**26E** Lees Oldham	
90672	WD[1]	**CLK** Colwick	**38A** Colwick	**38E** Woodford Halse	**38E** Woodford Halse	**2F** Woodford Halse	**2F** Woodford Halse	
90673	WD[1]	Stored	**25A** Wakefield	**25A** Wakefield	**56A** Wakefield	**55E** Normanton	**55E** Normanton	
90674	WD[1]	**TWD** Tweedmouth	**52D** Tweedmouth	**38A** Colwick	**36A** Doncaster	**40B** Immingham	**40E** Colwick	
90675	WD[1]	**FEL** Feltham	**63A** Perth	**26A** Newton Heath	**27B** Aintree	**24C** Lostock Hall	**24C** Lostock Hall	**36A** Doncaster
90676	WD[1]	**CLK** Colwick	**38A** Colwick	**83A** Newton Abbot	**86A** Ebbw Junction	**86A** Ebbw Junction	**9G** Gorton	
90677	WD[1]	**HLD** Hull Dairycoates	**53C** Hull Springhead	**53C** Hull Springhead	**53C** Hull Springhead	**53A** Hull Dairycoates	**50B** Hull Dairycoates	**50B** Hull Dairycoates
90678	WD[1]	**HIT** Hither Green	**73C** Hither Green	**25D** Mirfield	**56D** Mirfield	**56D** Mirfield	**56D** Mirfield	**56A** Wakefield
90679	WD[1]	Stored	**25A** Wakefield	**25C** Goole	**56A** Wakefield	**56A** Wakefield	**56A** Wakefield	**56A** Wakefield
90680	WD[1]	Stored	**25B** Huddersfield	**25B** Huddersfield	**55G** Huddersfield	**55G** Huddersfield	**55G** Huddersfield	**55G** Huddersfield
90681	WD[1]	Stored	**24C** Lostock Hall	**24C** Lostock Hall	**24C** Lostock Hall	**24C** Lostock Hall	**24F** Fleetwood	
90682	WD[1]	**OXY** Oxley	**25A** Wakefield	**25A** Wakefield	**56A** Wakefield	**55E** Normanton	**55E** Normanton	**55E** Normanton
90683	WD[1]	**NEV** Leeds Neville Hill	**35A** New England	**35A** New England	**35A** New England	**31B** March	**36A** Doncaster	**36A** Doncaster
90684	WD[1]	Stored	**25G** Farnley Junction	**25G** Farnley Junction	**55C** Farnley Junction	**55C** Farnley Junction	**55D** Royston	**56A** Wakefield
90685	WD[1]	**TYS** Tyseley	**84K** Chester (GWR)	**85B** Gloucester	**85B** Gloucester	**85E** Gloucester Barnwood	**36A** Doncaster	
90686	WD[1]	**OXY** Oxley	**84K** Chester (GWR)	**84K** Chester (GWR)	**84K** Chester (GWR)	**6E** Chester (GWR)	**8F** Wigan Springs Branch	
90687	WD[1]	**BHD** Birkenhead	**24B** Rose Grove	**27B** Aintree	**27B** Aintree	**27B** Aintree	**27B** Aintree	**36A** Doncaster
90688	WD[1]	**TDK** Tyne Dock	**53C** Hull Springhead	**53C** Hull Springhead	**53C** Hull Springhead	**53A** Hull Dairycoates	**50B** Hull Dairycoates	**50B** Hull Dairycoates
90689	WD[1]	Stored	**24C** Lostock Hall	**24C** Lostock Hall	**24C** Lostock Hall	**24C** Lostock Hall	**24F** Fleetwood	**40E** Colwick
90690	WD[1]	**THJ** Thornton Junction	**62A** Thornton Junction	**62A** Thornton Junction	**62A** Thornton Junction	**62A** Thornton Junction		
90691	WD[1]	**GLO** Gloucester	**85A** Worcester	**85B** Gloucester	**85B** Gloucester	**86C** Cardiff Canton		
90692	WD[1]	Stored	**25A** Wakefield	**25A** Wakefield	**56A** Wakefield	**56A** Wakefield	**56E** Sowerby Bridge	
90693	WD[1]	**PDN** Old Oak Common	**66B** Motherwell	**87A** Neath	**86C** Cardiff Canton	**86C** Cardiff Canton		
90694	WD[1]	**PPRD** Pontypool Road	**25B** Huddersfield	**25B** Huddersfield	**55G** Huddersfield	**55G** Huddersfield	**55G** Huddersfield	**55G** Huddersfield
90695	WD[1]	**HLD** Hull Dairycoates	**53G** Haverton Hill	**53A** Hull Dairycoates	**53A** Hull Dairycoates	**53A** Hull Dairycoates	**50B** Hull Dairycoates	**50B** Hull Dairycoates
90696	WD[1]	**MEX** Mexborough	**36B** Mexborough	**36A** Doncaster	**31B** March	**36A** Doncaster	**36C** Frodingham	
90697	WD[1]	**HLD** Hull Dairycoates	**38A** Colwick	**38E** Woodford Halse	**38E** Woodford Halse	**2F** Woodford Halse	**2F** Woodford Halse	
90698	WD[1]	Stored	**25G** Farnley Junction	**25G** Farnley Junction	**55C** Farnley Junction	**56D** Mirfield	**56F** Low Moor	**56A** Wakefield
90699	WD[1]	Stored	**25G** Farnley Junction	**25G** Farnley Junction	**55C** Farnley Junction	**55C** Farnley Junction	**55C** Farnley Junction	**55E** Normanton
90700	WD[1]	**MEX** Mexborough	**36B** Mexborough	**36B** Mexborough	**36B** Mexborough	**41F** Mexborough	**41F** Mexborough	
90701	WD[1]	**SPM** St. Philips Marsh	**82D** Westbury	**84G** Shrewsbury	**84G** Shrewsbury	**2F** Woodford Halse		
90702	WD[1]	**HIT** Hither Green	**73C** Hither Green	**6B** Mold Junction	**6B** Mold Junction	**6B** Mold Junction	**8G** Sutton Oak	
90703	WD[1]	**NEV** Leeds Neville Hill	**38A** Colwick	**38A** Colwick	**38A** Colwick	**40E** Colwick	**40E** Colwick	
90704	WD[1]	**TWD** Tweedmouth	**53A** Hull Dairycoates	**53A** Hull Dairycoates	**53A** Hull Dairycoates	**53E** Goole	**50D** Goole	**50B** Hull Dairycoates
90705	WD[1]	**DFU** Dunfermline Upper	**62C** Dunfermline Upper	**62C** Dunfermline Upper	**62A** Thornton Junction	**62A** Thornton Junction	**66B** Motherwell	
90706	WD[1]	Stored	**26A** Newton Heath	**26A** Newton Heath	**26A** Newton Heath	**24J** Lancaster	**24J** Lancaster	**40E** Colwick
90707	WD[1]	Stored	**25D** Mirfield	**25D** Mirfield	**56D** Mirfield	**56D** Mirfield	**56D** Mirfield	**56A** Wakefield
90708	WD[1]	Stored	**26A** Newton Heath	**26A** Newton Heath	**26A** Newton Heath	**26E** Lees Oldham	**26E** Lees Oldham	
90709	WD[1]	**MEX** Mexborough	**31B** March	**35A** New England	**35A** New England	**31B** March	**36A** Doncaster	**36A** Doncaster
90710	WD[1]	Stored	**25A** Wakefield	**25A** Wakefield	**56A** Wakefield	**56A** Wakefield	**56A** Wakefield	
90711	WD[1]	Stored	**25G** Farnley Junction	**25G** Farnley Junction	**55C** Farnley Junction	**56F** Low Moor	**56F** Low Moor	**56F** Low Moor
90712	WD[1]	**STJ** Severn Tunnel Junction	**26C** Bolton	**26C** Bolton	**27B** Aintree	**27B** Aintree	**27B** Aintree	
90713	WD[1]	Stored	**24A** Accrington	**26B** Agecroft	**26B** Agecroft	**26B** Agecroft	**24C** Lostock Hall	
90714	WD[1]	**MEX** Mexborough	**36B** Mexborough	**36C** Frodingham	**36C** Frodingham	**36C** Frodingham	**36C** Frodingham	
90715	WD[1]	**GLO** Gloucester	**26A** Newton Heath	**26A** Newton Heath	**26A** Newton Heath	**26A** Newton Heath	**26A** Newton Heath	
90716	WD[1]	Stored	**86E** Severn Tunnel Junction	**84G** Shrewsbury	**84C** Banbury	**18B** Westhouses	**9G** Gorton	
90717	WD[1]	Stored	**38A** Colwick	**38A** Colwick	**38A** Colwick	**40E** Colwick	**40E** Colwick	
90718	WD[1]	**HIT** Hither Green	**73C** Hither Green	**26D** Bury	**26D** Bury	**26E** Lees Oldham	**26E** Lees Oldham	**36A** Doncaster
90719	WD[1]	Stored	**25A** Wakefield	**25A** Wakefield	**56A** Wakefield	**41D** Canklow	**41D** Canklow	**41J** Langwith Junction
90720	WD[1]	Stored	**26F** Lees Oldham	**24C** Lostock Hall	**24C** Lostock Hall	**24C** Lostock Hall	**24C** Lostock Hall	
90721	WD[1]	Stored	**25D** Mirfield	**25D** Mirfield	**56D** Mirfield	**56D** Mirfield	**56F** Low Moor	**56A** Wakefield
90722	WD[1]	Stored	**25A** Wakefield	**25A** Wakefield	**56A** Wakefield	**55E** Normanton	**55E** Normanton	**55E** Normanton
90723	WD[1]	**SPM** St. Philips Marsh	**25D** Mirfield	**25D** Mirfield	**56D** Mirfield	**56D** Mirfield	**56F** Low Moor	**56F** Low Moor
90724	WD[1]	Stored	**25A** Wakefield	**25A** Wakefield	**27B** Aintree	**27B** Aintree	**24B** Rose Grove	
90725	WD[1]	**DID** Didcot	**25A** Wakefield	**26C** Bolton	**26C** Bolton	**26C** Bolton	**24F** Fleetwood	
90726	WD[1]	Stored	**25G** Farnley Junction	**25G** Farnley Junction	**55C** Farnley Junction	**55C** Farnley Junction		
90727	WD[1]	**DFU** Dunfermline Upper	**62B** Dundee Tay Bridge	**64A** St. Margarets	**62C** Dunfermline Upper	**62C** Dunfermline Upper	**62C** Dunfermline Upper	
90728	WD[1]	Stored	**25G** Farnley Junction	**25G** Farnley Junction	**55C** Farnley Junction	**55C** Farnley Junction	**55C** Farnley Junction	
90729	WD[1]	**SPM** St. Philips Marsh	**25A** Wakefield	**26C** Bolton	**26C** Bolton	**26C** Bolton	**26C** Bolton	
90730	WD[1]	**YK** York	**35A** New England	**35A** New England	**35A** New England	**34E** New England	**36C** Frodingham	
90731	WD[1]	Stored	**25D** Mirfield	**25D** Mirfield	**56D** Mirfield	**56D** Mirfield	**56D** Mirfield	**56F** Low Moor
90732	WD[1]	**MAR** March	**30E** Colchester	**31B** March	**31B** March	**36A** Doncaster		
90750	WD[2]	Stored	**66B** Motherwell	**66B** Motherwell	**66B** Motherwell	**66B** Motherwell		

		1948	1951	1954	1957	1960	1963	1966
90751	WD[2]	Stored	68A Carlisle Kingmoor	66A Polmadie	66A Polmadie	66A Polmadie		
90752	WD[2]	Stored	66B Motherwell	66B Motherwell	66B Motherwell	66B Motherwell		
90753	WD[2]	Stored	64D Carstairs	64D Carstairs	64D Carstairs	64D Carstairs		
90754	WD[2]	Stored	66B Motherwell	66B Motherwell	66B Motherwell	66B Motherwell		
90755	WD[2]	Stored	65F Grangemouth	65F Grangemouth	65F Grangemouth	65F Grangemouth		
90756	WD[2]	Stored	66B Motherwell	66B Motherwell	66B Motherwell	66B Motherwell		
90757	WD[2]	Stored	65F Grangemouth	65F Grangemouth	65F Grangemouth	65F Grangemouth		
90758	WD[2]	Stored	66B Motherwell	66B Motherwell	66B Motherwell	66B Motherwell		
90759	WD[2]	Stored	65F Grangemouth	65F Grangemouth	65F Grangemouth	65F Grangemouth		
90760	WD[2]	Stored	66B Motherwell	66B Motherwell	66B Motherwell	66B Motherwell		
90761	WD[2]	Stored	66B Motherwell	66B Motherwell	66B Motherwell	66B Motherwell		
90762	WD[2]	Stored	66B Motherwell	66B Motherwell	66B Motherwell	66B Motherwell		
90763	WD[2]	Stored	68A Carlisle Kingmoor	68A Carlisle Kingmoor	68A Carlisle Kingmoor	6F Bidston		
90764	WD[2]	Stored	Rugby Testing Station	66B Motherwell	66B Motherwell	66B Motherwell		
90765	WD[2]	Stored	65F Grangemouth	65F Grangemouth	65F Grangemouth	65F Grangemouth		
90766	WD[2]	Stored	66B Motherwell	66B Motherwell	66B Motherwell	65F Grangemouth		
90767	WD[2]	Stored	68A Carlisle Kingmoor	66A Polmadie	66A Polmadie	66A Polmadie		
90768	WD[2]	Stored	64D Carstairs	64D Carstairs	64D Carstairs	64D Carstairs		
90769	WD[2]	Stored	68A Carlisle Kingmoor	68A Carlisle Kingmoor	65F Grangemouth	65F Grangemouth		
90770	WD[2]	Stored	66B Motherwell	66B Motherwell	66B Motherwell	66B Motherwell		
90771	WD[2]	Stored	66B Motherwell	66B Motherwell	66B Motherwell	66B Motherwell		
90772	WD[2]	Stored	66B Motherwell	66B Motherwell	66B Motherwell	66C Hamilton		
90773	WD[2]	12A Carlisle Kingmoor	68A Carlisle Kingmoor	65F Grangemouth	65F Grangemouth	65F Grangemouth		
90774	WD[2]	12A Carlisle Kingmoor	68A Carlisle Kingmoor	68A Carlisle Kingmoor	65F Grangemouth	65F Grangemouth		
92000	9F	→	→	→	86A Ebbw Junction	86A Ebbw Junction	82E Bristol Barrow Road	
92001	9F	→	→	→	86A Ebbw Junction	86A Ebbw Junction	84E Tyseley	2A Tyseley
92002	9F	→	→	→	86A Ebbw Junction	86A Ebbw Junction	86A Ebbw Junction	2A Tyseley
92003	9F	→	→	→	86A Ebbw Junction	86C Cardiff Canton	88L Cardiff East Dock	
92004	9F	→	→	→	86A Ebbw Junction	86C Cardiff Canton	82E Bristol Barrow Road	2D Banbury
92005	9F	→	→	→	86A Ebbw Junction	86C Cardiff Canton	86A Ebbw Junction	
92006	9F	→	→	→	86A Ebbw Junction	86A Ebbw Junction	86A Ebbw Junction	50A York
92007	9F	→	→	→	86A Ebbw Junction	86A Ebbw Junction	82E Bristol Barrow Road	
92008	9F	→	→	→	15A Wellingborough	17C Rowsley	21A Saltley	8C Speke Junction
92009	9F	→	→	→	15A Wellingborough	17C Rowsley	18B Westhouses	12A Carlisle Kingmoor
92010	9F	→	→	→	31B March	16D Annesley	16D Annesley	12A Carlisle Kingmoor
92011	9F	→	→	→	35A New England	16D Annesley	16D Annesley	8H Birkenhead
92012	9F	→	→	→	35A New England	16D Annesley	16D Annesley	12A Carlisle Kingmoor
92013	9F	→	→	→	31B March	16D Annesley	16D Annesley	2D Banbury
92014	9F	→	→	→	31B March	16D Annesley	16D Annesley	8H Birkenhead
92015	9F	→	→	→	15A Wellingborough	26A Newton Heath	26A Newton Heath	12A Carlisle Kingmoor
92016	9F	→	→	→	15A Wellingborough	26A Newton Heath	26A Newton Heath	9D Newton Heath
92017	9F	→	→	→	15A Wellingborough	26A Newton Heath	26A Newton Heath	12A Carlisle Kingmoor
92018	9F	→	→	→	15A Wellingborough	15A Wellingborough	17C Rowsley	9D Newton Heath
92019	9F	→	→	→	15A Wellingborough	15A Wellingborough	15A Wellingborough	12A Carlisle Kingmoor
92020	9F	→	→	→	15A Wellingborough	15A Wellingborough	15A Wellingborough	8H Birkenhead
92021	9F	→	→	→	15A Wellingborough	15A Wellingborough	15A Wellingborough	8H Birkenhead
92022	9F	→	→	→	15A Wellingborough	15A Wellingborough	15A Wellingborough	9D Newton Heath
92023	9F	→	→	→	15A Wellingborough	15A Wellingborough	15A Wellingborough	8H Birkenhead
92024	9F	→	→	→	15A Wellingborough	15A Wellingborough	15A Wellingborough	8H Birkenhead
92025	9F	→	→	→	15A Wellingborough	15A Wellingborough	15A Wellingborough	8C Speke Junction
92026	9F	→	→	→	15A Wellingborough	15A Wellingborough	15A Wellingborough	8H Birkenhead
92027	9F	→	→	→	15A Wellingborough	15A Wellingborough	15A Wellingborough	8C Speke Junction
92028	9F	→	→	→	15A Wellingborough	15A Wellingborough	21A Saltley	2E Saltley
92029	9F	→	→	→	15A Wellingborough	15A Wellingborough	21A Saltley	2E Saltley
92030	9F	→	→	→	35A New England	16D Annesley	16D Annesley	2D Banbury
92031	9F	→	→	→	35A New England	16D Annesley	16D Annesley	9D Newton Heath
92032	9F	→	→	→	35A New England	16D Annesley	16D Annesley	8H Birkenhead
92033	9F	→	→	→	35A New England	16D Annesley	16D Annesley	
92034	9F	→	→	→	35A New England	34E New England	34E New England	
92035	9F	→	→	→	35A New England	34E New England	34E New England	40B Immingham
92036	9F	→	→	→	35A New England	34E New England	36A Doncaster	
92037	9F	→	→	→	35A New England	34E New England	34E New England	
92038	9F	→	→	→	35A New England	34E New England	34E New England	
92039	9F	→	→	→	35A New England	40B Immingham	36A Doncaster	
92040	9F	→	→	→	35A New England	34E New England	34E New England	
92041	9F	→	→	→	35A New England	34E New England	34E New England	
92042	9F	→	→	→	35A New England	34E New England	34E New England	
92043	9F	→	→	→	31B March	16D Annesley	16D Annesley	16F Burton
92044	9F	→	→	→	31B March	34E New England	36A Doncaster	
92045	9F	→	→	→	6F Bidston	6F Bidston	6F Bidston	8H Birkenhead
92046	9F	→	→	→	6F Bidston	6F Bidston	6F Bidston	8H Birkenhead
92047	9F	→	→	→	6F Bidston	6F Bidston	6F Bidston	8H Birkenhead
92048	9F	→	→	→	18A Toton	17C Rowsley	17C Rowsley	8H Birkenhead
92049	9F	→	→	→	18A Toton	17C Rowsley	17C Rowsley	8B Warrington Dallam
92050	9F	→	→	→	18A Toton	17C Rowsley	17C Rowsley	9D Newton Heath
92051	9F	→	→	→	18A Toton	17C Rowsley	17C Rowsley	12A Carlisle Kingmoor
92052	9F	→	→	→	18A Toton	15A Wellingborough	18A Toton	9D Newton Heath
92053	9F	→	→	→	18A Toton	15A Wellingborough	18A Toton	8B Warrington Dallam
92054	9F	→	→	→	18A Toton	15A Wellingborough	18B Westhouses	8C Speke Junction
92055	9F	→	→	→	18A Toton	15A Wellingborough	18A Toton	8B Warrington Dallam
92056	9F	→	→	→	18A Toton	15A Wellingborough	17C Rowsley	9D Newton Heath
92057	9F	→	→	→	18A Toton	18A Toton	16D Annesley	
92058	9F	→	→	→	18A Toton	15A Wellingborough	18B Westhouses	8B Warrington Dallam
92059	9F	→	→	→	18A Toton	15A Wellingborough	18A Toton	8H Birkenhead
92060	9F	→	→	→	54B Tyne Dock	52H Tyne Dock	52H Tyne Dock	52H Tyne Dock
92061	9F	→	→	→	54B Tyne Dock	52H Tyne Dock	52H Tyne Dock	52H Tyne Dock
92062	9F	→	→	→	54B Tyne Dock	52H Tyne Dock	52H Tyne Dock	52H Tyne Dock
92063	9F	→	→	→	54B Tyne Dock	52H Tyne Dock	52H Tyne Dock	52H Tyne Dock
92064	9F	→	→	→	54B Tyne Dock	52H Tyne Dock	52H Tyne Dock	52H Tyne Dock
92065	9F	→	→	→	54B Tyne Dock	52H Tyne Dock	52H Tyne Dock	52H Tyne Dock
92066	9F	→	→	→	54B Tyne Dock	52H Tyne Dock	52H Tyne Dock	
92067	9F	→	→	→	36A Doncaster	16D Annesley	16D Annesley	2D Banbury
92068	9F	→	→	→	36A Doncaster	16D Annesley	16D Annesley	16C Derby
92069	9F	→	→	→	36A Doncaster	16D Annesley	16D Annesley	8H Birkenhead
92070	9F	→	→	→	36A Doncaster	16D Annesley	18B Westhouses	8H Birkenhead
92071	9F	→	→	→	36A Doncaster	16D Annesley	16D Annesley	12A Carlisle Kingmoor
92072	9F	→	→	→	36A Doncaster	16D Annesley	16D Annesley	16E Kirkby in Ashfield
92073	9F	→	→	→	36A Doncaster	16D Annesley	16D Annesley	2D Banbury
92074	9F	→	→	→	36A Doncaster	16D Annesley	16D Annesley	2D Banbury
92075	9F	→	→	→	36A Doncaster	16D Annesley	16D Annesley	16E Kirkby in Ashfield
92076	9F	→	→	→	36A Doncaster	16D Annesley	16D Annesley	12A Carlisle Kingmoor
92077	9F	→	→	→	18A Toton	18A Toton	18A Toton	9D Newton Heath
92078	9F	→	→	→	18A Toton	18A Toton	18A Toton	8B Warrington Dallam
92079	9F	→	→	→	21C Bromsgrove	85F Bromsgrove	85D Bromsgrove	8H Birkenhead
92080	9F	→	→	→	18A Toton	15A Wellingborough	15A Wellingborough	9D Newton Heath
92081	9F	→	→	→	18A Toton	15A Wellingborough	15A Wellingborough	9D Newton Heath
92082	9F	→	→	→	15A Wellingborough	15A Wellingborough	15A Wellingborough	8H Birkenhead
92083	9F	→	→	→	15A Wellingborough	15A Wellingborough	15A Wellingborough	8H Birkenhead
92084	9F	→	→	→	15A Wellingborough	15A Wellingborough	15A Wellingborough	8H Birkenhead
92085	9F	→	→	→	15A Wellingborough	15A Wellingborough	21A Saltley	8H Birkenhead
92086	9F	→	→	→	15A Wellingborough	15A Wellingborough	15A Wellingborough	8H Birkenhead
92087	9F	→	→	→	36A Doncaster	16D Annesley	16D Annesley	2A Tyseley
92088	9F	→	→	→	36A Doncaster	16D Annesley	16D Annesley	8H Birkenhead
92089	9F	→	→	→	36A Doncaster	16D Annesley	16D Annesley	8H Birkenhead

		1948	1951	1954	1957	1960	1963	1966
92090	9F	→	→	→	36A Doncaster	16D Annesley	16D Annesley	8H Birkenhead
92091	9F	→	→	→	36A Doncaster	16D Annesley	16D Annesley	8C Speke Junction
92092	9F	→	→	→	36A Doncaster	16D Annesley	16D Annesley	8H Birkenhead
92093	9F	→	→	→	→	16D Annesley	16D Annesley	16E Kirkby in Ashfield
92094	9F	→	→	→	→	16D Annesley	16D Annesley	8H Birkenhead
92095	9F	→	→	→	→	16D Annesley	16D Annesley	16E Kirkby in Ashfield
92096	9F	→	→	→	→	16D Annesley	16D Annesley	16C Derby
92097	9F	→	→	→	54B Tyne Dock	52H Tyne Dock	52H Tyne Dock	52H Tyne Dock
92098	9F	→	→	→	54B Tyne Dock	52H Tyne Dock	52H Tyne Dock	52H Tyne Dock
92099	9F	→	→	→	54B Tyne Dock	52H Tyne Dock	52H Tyne Dock	52H Tyne Dock
92100	9F	→	→	→	18A Toton	18A Toton	18B Westhouses	8H Birkenhead
92101	9F	→	→	→	18A Toton	15C Leicester Midland	15C Leicester Midland	8H Birkenhead
92102	9F	→	→	→	18A Toton	15C Leicester Midland	15C Leicester Midland	8H Birkenhead
92103	9F	→	→	→	18A Toton	15C Leicester Midland	15C Leicester Midland	8H Birkenhead
92104	9F	→	→	→	18A Toton	15C Leicester Midland	18B Westhouses	8H Birkenhead
92105	9F	→	→	→	15B Kettering	15B Kettering	15B Kettering	8H Birkenhead
92106	9F	→	→	→	15B Kettering	15B Kettering	15B Kettering	8H Birkenhead
92107	9F	→	→	→	15A Wellingborough	15A Wellingborough	21A Saltley	8H Birkenhead
92108	9F	→	→	→	14A Cricklewood	15A Wellingborough	15C Leicester Midland	8H Birkenhead
92109	9F	→	→	→	18A Toton	15C Leicester Midland	15C Leicester Midland	8H Birkenhead
92110	9F	→	→	→	14A Cricklewood	15A Wellingborough	15C Leicester Midland	12A Carlisle Kingmoor
92111	9F	→	→	→	14A Cricklewood	15A Wellingborough	15C Leicester Midland	8H Birkenhead
92112	9F	→	→	→	14A Cricklewood	15A Wellingborough	15C Leicester Midland	8H Birkenhead
92113	9F	→	→	→	18B Westhouses	18B Westhouses	17C Rowsley	8H Birkenhead
92114	9F	→	→	→	18B Westhouses	18B Westhouses	17C Rowsley	12A Carlisle Kingmoor
92115	9F	→	→	→	18B Westhouses	18B Westhouses	18B Westhouses	8C Speke Junction
92116	9F	→	→	→	18B Westhouses	18B Westhouses	18B Westhouses	8B Warrington Dallam
92117	9F	→	→	→	18B Westhouses	18B Westhouses	15A Wellingborough	8C Speke Junction
92118	9F	→	→	→	18B Westhouses	15A Wellingborough	21A Saltley	2A Tyseley
92119	9F	→	→	→	→	15C Leicester Midland	15C Leicester Midland	8B Warrington Dallam
92120	9F	→	→	→	→	15A Wellingborough	15C Leicester Midland	8H Birkenhead
92121	9F	→	→	→	→	15C Leicester Midland	15C Leicester Midland	8H Birkenhead
92122	9F	→	→	→	→	15A Wellingborough	15C Leicester Midland	8H Birkenhead
92123	9F	→	→	→	→	15A Wellingborough	15C Leicester Midland	8H Birkenhead
92124	9F	→	→	→	→	15A Wellingborough	15A Wellingborough	8B Warrington Dallam
92125	9F	→	→	→	→	15A Wellingborough	15B Kettering	2E Saltley
92126	9F	→	→	→	→	15A Wellingborough	15A Wellingborough	8B Warrington Dallam
92127	9F	→	→	→	→	15A Wellingborough	15A Wellingborough	8H Birkenhead
92128	9F	→	→	→	→	15C Leicester Midland	21A Saltley	2D Banbury
92129	9F	→	→	→	→	15B Kettering	21A Saltley	2D Banbury
92130	9F	→	→	→	→	18A Toton	18A Toton	12A Carlisle Kingmoor
92131	9F	→	→	→	→	18A Toton	18B Westhouses	8H Birkenhead
92132	9F	→	→	→	→	15A Wellingborough	15A Wellingborough	2D Banbury
92133	9F	→	→	→	→	15A Wellingborough	15A Wellingborough	8H Birkenhead
92134	9F	→	→	→	→	15A Wellingborough	15A Wellingborough	8H Birkenhead
92135	9F	→	→	→	→	21A Saltley	21A Saltley	2E Saltley
92136	9F	→	→	→	→	21A Saltley	21A Saltley	2E Saltley
92137	9F	→	→	→	→	21A Saltley	21A Saltley	2E Saltley
92138	9F	→	→	→	→	21A Saltley	21A Saltley	2E Saltley
92139	9F	→	→	→	→	21A Saltley	21A Saltley	2E Saltley
92140	9F	→	→	→	→	34E New England	34E New England	
92141	9F	→	→	→	→	34E New England	36A Doncaster	
92142	9F	→	→	→	→	34E New England	34E New England	
92143	9F	→	→	→	→	34E New England	34E New England	
92144	9F	→	→	→	→	34E New England	40B Immingham	
92145	9F	→	→	→	→	34E New England	34E New England	40B Immingham
92146	9F	→	→	→	→	34E New England	34E New England	36A Doncaster
92147	9F	→	→	→	→	34E New England	34E New England	
92148	9F	→	→	→	→	34E New England	34E New England	
92149	9F	→	→	→	→	34E New England	34E New England	
92150	9F	→	→	→	→	21A Saltley	21A Saltley	2E Saltley
92151	9F	→	→	→	→	21A Saltley	21A Saltley	2E Saltley
92152	9F	→	→	→	→	21A Saltley	21A Saltley	2E Saltley
92153	9F	→	→	→	→	18A Toton	18A Toton	8C Speke Junction
92154	9F	→	→	→	→	15A Wellingborough	15A Wellingborough	8C Speke Junction
92155	9F	→	→	→	→	21A Saltley	21A Saltley	2E Saltley
92156	9F	→	→	→	→	18A Toton	18A Toton	8B Warrington Dallam
92157	9F	→	→	→	→	21A Saltley	21A Saltley	8H Birkenhead
92158	9F	→	→	→	→	18A Toton	18A Toton	8C Speke Junction
92159	9F	→	→	→	→	15A Wellingborough	15A Wellingborough	8H Birkenhead
92160	9F	→	→	→	→	15B Kettering	15B Kettering	8B Warrington Dallam
92161	9F	→	→	→	→	26A Newton Heath	26A Newton Heath	12A Carlisle Kingmoor
92162	9F	→	→	→	→	26A Newton Heath	26A Newton Heath	8H Birkenhead
92163	9F	→	→	→	→	15B Kettering	15B Kettering	8H Birkenhead
92164	9F	→	→	→	→	15B Kettering	21A Saltley	2E Saltley
92165	9F	→	→	→	→	21A Saltley	6F Bidston	8H Birkenhead
92166	9F	→	→	→	→	86A Ebbw Junction	6F Bidston	8H Birkenhead
92167	9F	→	→	→	→	21A Saltley	6F Bidston	8H Birkenhead
92168	9F	→	→	→	→	36A Doncaster	36A Doncaster	
92169	9F	→	→	→	→	36A Doncaster	36A Doncaster	
92170	9F	→	→	→	→	36A Doncaster	36A Doncaster	
92171	9F	→	→	→	→	36A Doncaster	36A Doncaster	
92172	9F	→	→	→	→	36A Doncaster	36A Doncaster	36A Doncaster
92173	9F	→	→	→	→	36A Doncaster	36A Doncaster	36A Doncaster
92174	9F	→	→	→	→	36A Doncaster	36A Doncaster	
92175	9F	→	→	→	→	36A Doncaster	36A Doncaster	
92176	9F	→	→	→	→	36A Doncaster	36A Doncaster	
92177	9F	→	→	→	→	36A Doncaster	36A Doncaster	
92178	9F	→	→	→	→	34E New England	34E New England	
92179	9F	→	→	→	→	34E New England	34E New England	
92180	9F	→	→	→	→	34E New England	34E New England	
92181	9F	→	→	→	→	34E New England	34E New England	
92182	9F	→	→	→	→	34E New England	34E New England	36A Doncaster
92183	9F	→	→	→	→	34E New England	34E New England	36A Doncaster
92184	9F	→	→	→	→	34E New England	34E New England	
92185	9F	→	→	→	→	34E New England	34E New England	
92186	9F	→	→	→	→	40E Colwick	34E New England	
92187	9F	→	→	→	→	34E New England	34E New England	
92188	9F	→	→	→	→	34E New England	34E New England	
92189	9F	→	→	→	→	36A Doncaster	36A Doncaster	
92190	9F	→	→	→	→	36A Doncaster	36A Doncaster	
92191	9F	→	→	→	→	36A Doncaster	36A Doncaster	
92192	9F	→	→	→	→	36A Doncaster	36A Doncaster	
92193	9F	→	→	→	→	40B Immingham	40B Immingham	
92194	9F	→	→	→	→	40B Immingham	40B Immingham	
92195	9F	→	→	→	→	40B Immingham	40B Immingham	
92196	9F	→	→	→	→	40B Immingham	40B Immingham	
92197	9F	→	→	→	→	36A Doncaster	40B Immingham	
92198	9F	→	→	→	→	36A Doncaster	36A Doncaster	
92199	9F	→	→	→	→	36A Doncaster	36A Doncaster	
92200	9F	→	→	→	→	36A Doncaster	36A Doncaster	
92201	9F	→	→	→	→	36A Doncaster	36A Doncaster	36A Doncaster
92202	9F	→	→	→	→	40B Immingham	40B Immingham	
92203	9F	→	→	→	→	82B St. Philips Marsh	81A Old Oak Common	2D Banbury

		1948	1951	1954	1957	1960	1963	1966
92204	*9F*	→	→	→	→	**82B** St. Philips Marsh	**81A** Old Oak Common	**2A** Tyseley
92205	*9F*	→	→	→	→	**82B** St. Philips Marsh	**71A** Eastleigh	**50A** York
92206	*9F*	→	→	→	→	**82B** St. Philips Marsh	**71A** Eastleigh	**50A** York
92207	*9F*	→	→	→	→	**82B** St. Philips Marsh	**81C** Southall	
92208	*9F*	→	→	→	→	**83D** Laira (Plymouth)	**88L** Cardiff East Dock	**12A** Carlisle Kingmoor
92209	*9F*	→	→	→	→	**86C** Cardiff Canton	**81A** Old Oak Common	
92210	*9F*	→	→	→	→	**86C** Cardiff Canton	**88L** Cardiff East Dock	
92211	*9F*	→	→	→	→	**81A** Old Oak Common	**71A** Eastleigh	**50A** York
92212	*9F*	→	→	→	→	**84C** Banbury	**84E** Tyseley	**2A** Tyseley
92213	*9F*	→	→	→	→	**84C** Banbury	**84C** Banbury	**2D** Banbury
92214	*9F*	→	→	→	→	**84C** Banbury	**86A** Ebbw Junction	
92215	*9F*	→	→	→	→	**84C** Banbury	**84C** Banbury	**2A** Tyseley
92216	*9F*	→	→	→	→	**86C** Cardiff Canton	**88L** Cardiff East Dock	
92217	*9F*	→	→	→	→	**86C** Cardiff Canton	**81A** Old Oak Common	**2A** Tyseley
92218	*9F*	→	→	→	→	→	**81A** Old Oak Common	**2D** Banbury
92219	*9F*	→	→	→	→	→	**88L** Cardiff East Dock	
92220	*9F*	→	→	→	→	→	**81F** Oxford	
92221	*9F*	→	→	→	→	**83D** Laira (Plymouth)	**82E** Bristol Barrow Road	
92222	*9F*	→	→	→	→	**83D** Laira (Plymouth)	**86A** Ebbw Junction	
92223	*9F*	→	→	→	→	**83D** Laira (Plymouth)	**86A** Ebbw Junction	**2A** Tyseley
92224	*9F*	→	→	→	→	**83D** Laira (Plymouth)	**81F** Oxford	**2D** Banbury
92225	*9F*	→	→	→	→	**83D** Laira (Plymouth)	**86A** Ebbw Junction	
92226	*9F*	→	→	→	→	**84C** Banbury	**86A** Ebbw Junction	
92227	*9F*	→	→	→	→	**84C** Banbury	**84C** Banbury	**2D** Banbury
92228	*9F*	→	→	→	→	**84C** Banbury	**84C** Banbury	**2D** Banbury
92229	*9F*	→	→	→	→	**81A** Old Oak Common	**86A** Ebbw Junction	
92230	*9F*	→	→	→	→	**81A** Old Oak Common	**86A** Ebbw Junction	
92231	*9F*	→	→	→	→	**86A** Ebbw Junction	**71A** Eastleigh	**50A** York
92232	*9F*	→	→	→	→	**84C** Banbury	**88L** Cardiff East Dock	
92233	*9F*	→	→	→	→	**84C** Banbury	**86A** Ebbw Junction	**12A** Carlisle Kingmoor
92234	*9F*	→	→	→	→	**84C** Banbury	**84E** Tyseley	**2D** Banbury
92235	*9F*	→	→	→	→	**86A** Ebbw Junction	**86A** Ebbw Junction	
92236	*9F*	→	→	→	→	**86C** Cardiff Canton	**88L** Cardiff East Dock	
92237	*9F*	→	→	→	→	**86C** Cardiff Canton	**88L** Cardiff East Dock	
92238	*9F*	→	→	→	→	**81A** Old Oak Common	**86A** Ebbw Junction	
92239	*9F*	→	→	→	→	**81A** Old Oak Common	**71A** Eastleigh	**50A** York
92240	*9F*	→	→	→	→	**81A** Old Oak Common	**81C** Southall	
92241	*9F*	→	→	→	→	**81A** Old Oak Common	**88L** Cardiff East Dock	
92242	*9F*	→	→	→	→	**86A** Ebbw Junction	**86A** Ebbw Junction	
92243	*9F*	→	→	→	→	**86A** Ebbw Junction	**81A** Old Oak Common	
92244	*9F*	→	→	→	→	**81A** Old Oak Common	**88L** Cardiff East Dock	
92245	*9F*	→	→	→	→	**81A** Old Oak Common	**81C** Southall	
92246	*9F*	→	→	→	→	**81A** Old Oak Common	**88L** Cardiff East Dock	
92247	*9F*	→	→	→	→	**81A** Old Oak Common	**84C** Banbury	**2D** Banbury
92248	*9F*	→	→	→	→	**21A** Saltley	**82E** Bristol Barrow Road	
92249	*9F*	→	→	→	→	**86A** Ebbw Junction	**86A** Ebbw Junction	**12A** Carlisle Kingmoor
92250	*9F*	→	→	→	→	**86A** Ebbw Junction	**86A** Ebbw Junction	

Right: BR Standard '3MT' class 2-6-2T No 82016 at its base 71A Eastleigh on 17 August 1961. *G. W. Morrison*

Below: MOS Riddles 'WD' class 2-10-0 No 90768 at Carstairs on 30 September 1962. *David C. Smith*

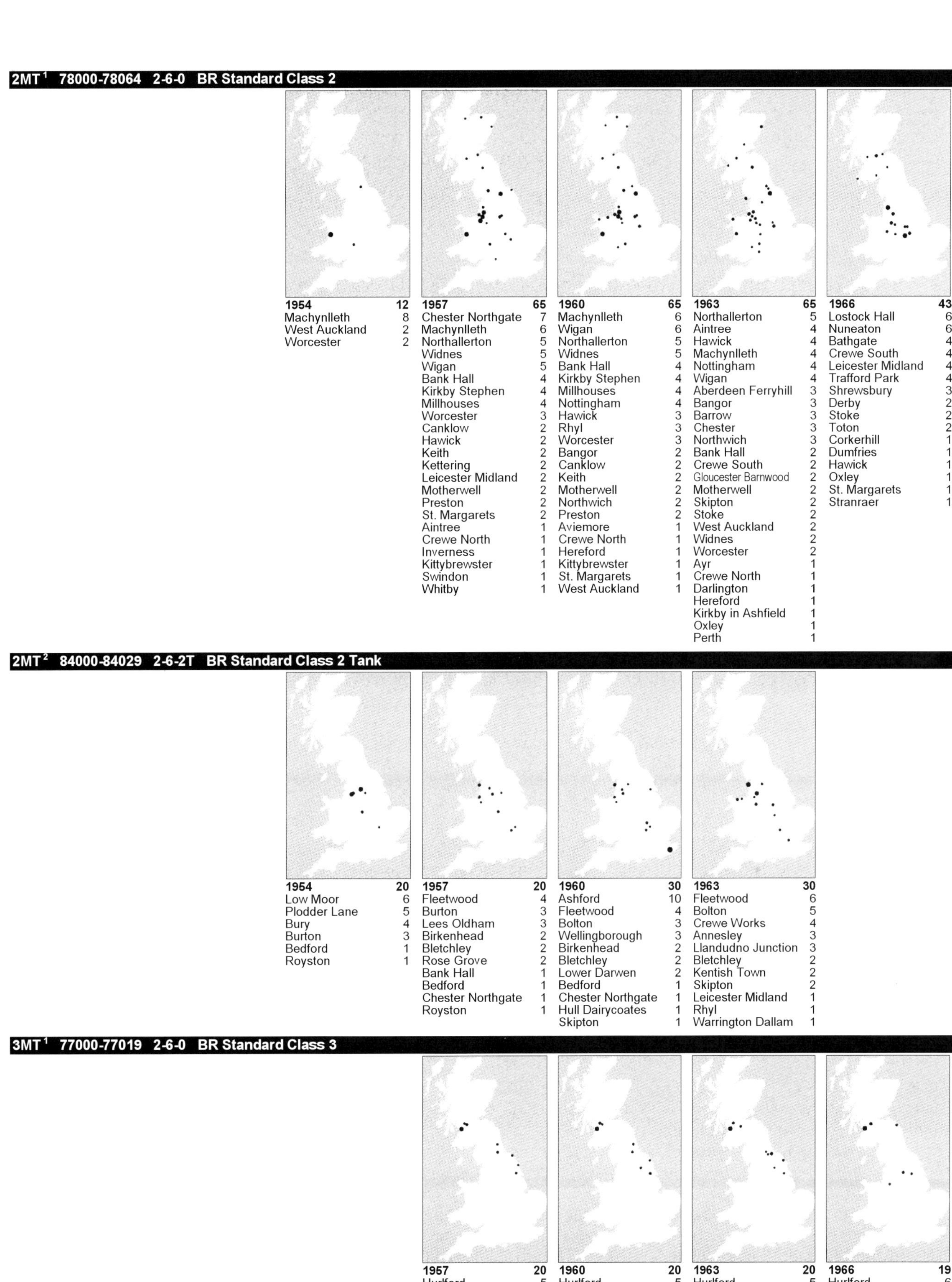

2MT[1] 78000-78064 2-6-0 BR Standard Class 2

1954	12
Machynlleth	8
West Auckland	2
Worcester	2

1957	65
Chester Northgate	7
Machynlleth	6
Northallerton	5
Widnes	5
Wigan	5
Bank Hall	4
Kirkby Stephen	4
Millhouses	4
Worcester	3
Canklow	2
Hawick	2
Keith	2
Kettering	2
Leicester Midland	2
Motherwell	2
Preston	2
St. Margarets	2
Aintree	1
Crewe North	1
Inverness	1
Kittybrewster	1
Swindon	1
Whitby	1

1960	65
Machynlleth	6
Wigan	6
Northallerton	5
Widnes	5
Bank Hall	4
Kirkby Stephen	4
Millhouses	4
Nottingham	4
Hawick	3
Rhyl	3
Worcester	3
Bangor	2
Canklow	2
Keith	2
Motherwell	2
Northwich	2
Preston	2
Aviemore	1
Crewe North	1
Hereford	1
Kittybrewster	1
St. Margarets	1
West Auckland	1

1963	65
Northallerton	5
Aintree	4
Hawick	4
Machynlleth	4
Nottingham	4
Wigan	4
Aberdeen Ferryhill	3
Bangor	3
Barrow	3
Chester	3
Northwich	3
Bank Hall	2
Crewe South	2
Gloucester Barnwood	2
Motherwell	2
Skipton	2
Stoke	2
West Auckland	2
Widnes	2
Worcester	2
Ayr	1
Crewe North	1
Darlington	1
Hereford	1
Kirkby in Ashfield	1
Oxley	1
Perth	1

1966	43
Lostock Hall	6
Nuneaton	6
Bathgate	4
Crewe South	4
Leicester Midland	4
Trafford Park	4
Shrewsbury	3
Derby	2
Stoke	2
Toton	2
Corkerhill	1
Dumfries	1
Hawick	1
Oxley	1
St. Margarets	1
Stranraer	1

2MT[2] 84000-84029 2-6-2T BR Standard Class 2 Tank

1954	20
Low Moor	6
Plodder Lane	5
Bury	4
Burton	3
Bedford	1
Royston	1

1957	20
Fleetwood	4
Burton	3
Lees Oldham	3
Birkenhead	2
Bletchley	2
Rose Grove	2
Bank Hall	1
Bedford	1
Chester Northgate	1
Royston	1

1960	30
Ashford	10
Fleetwood	4
Bolton	3
Wellingborough	3
Birkenhead	2
Bletchley	2
Lower Darwen	2
Bedford	1
Chester Northgate	1
Hull Dairycoates	1
Skipton	1

1963	30
Fleetwood	6
Bolton	5
Crewe Works	4
Annesley	3
Llandudno Junction	3
Bletchley	2
Kentish Town	2
Skipton	2
Leicester Midland	1
Rhyl	1
Warrington Dallam	1

3MT[1] 77000-77019 2-6-0 BR Standard Class 3

1957	20
Hurlford	5
Hamilton	3
West Auckland	3
Blaydon	2
Hull Botanic Gardens	2
Polmadie	2
Whitby	2
Bridlington	1

1960	20
Hurlford	5
Polmadie	4
Hull Dairycoates	3
Gateshead	2
West Auckland	2
York	2
Hamilton	1
Scarborough	1

1963	20
Hurlford	5
Thornaby	4
Polmadie	3
Carstairs	2
Scarborough	2
Darlington	1
Hull Dairycoates	1
West Auckland	1
York	1

1966	19
Hurlford	6
Motherwell	4
Stourton	3
Goole	2
Northwich	2
Tweedmouth	2

3MT[2] 82000-82044 2-6-2T BR Standard Class 3 Tank

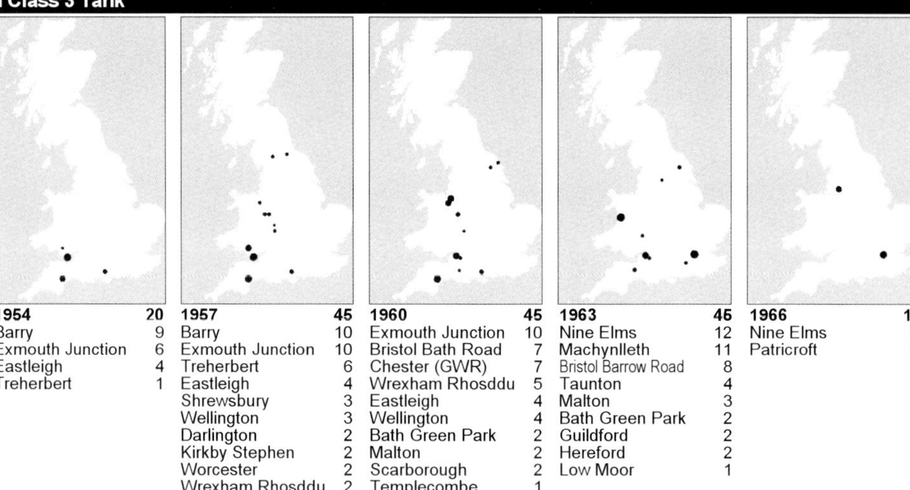

1954	20	1957	45	1960	45	1963	46	1966	14
Barry	9	Barry	10	Exmouth Junction	10	Nine Elms	12	Nine Elms	9
Exmouth Junction	6	Exmouth Junction	10	Bristol Bath Road	7	Machynlleth	11	Patricroft	5
Eastleigh	4	Treherbert	6	Chester (GWR)	7	Bristol Barrow Road	8		
Treherbert	1	Eastleigh	4	Wrexham Rhosddu	5	Taunton	4		
		Shrewsbury	3	Eastleigh	4	Malton	3		
		Wellington	3	Wellington	4	Bath Green Park	2		
		Darlington	2	Bath Green Park	2	Guildford	2		
		Kirkby Stephen	2	Malton	2	Hereford	2		
		Worcester	2	Scarborough	2	Low Moor	1		
		Wrexham Rhosddu	2	Templecombe	1				
		Kidderminster	1	Worcester	1				

4MT[1] 75000-75079 4-6-0 BR Standard Class 4

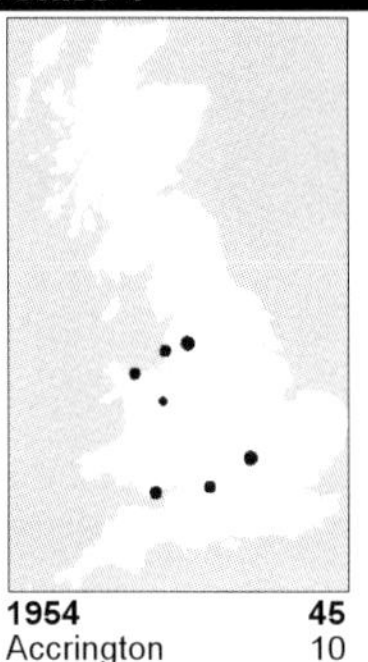
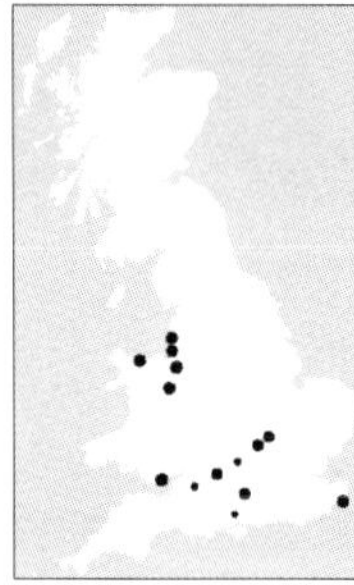

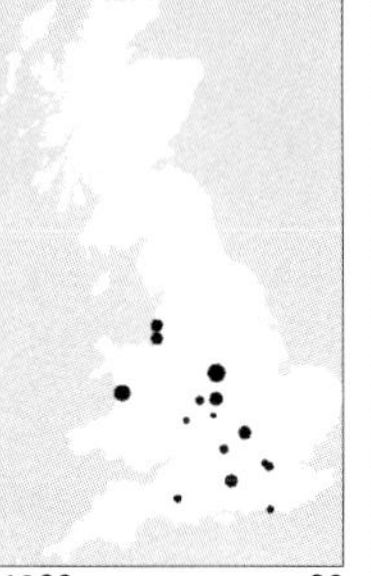
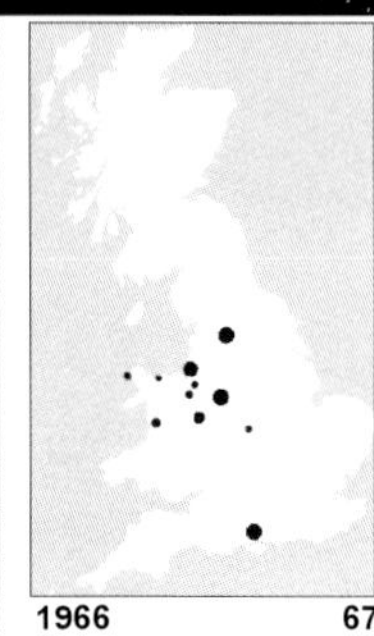

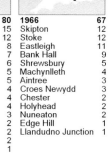

1954	45	1957	68	1960	80	1963	80	1966	67
Accrington	10	Chester	7	Chester	11	Derby	15	Skipton	12
Bletchley	10	Cardiff Canton	6	Leicester Midland	6	Machynlleth	12	Stoke	12
Cardiff Canton	6	Llandudno Junction	6	Bank Hall	5	Nuneaton	8	Eastleigh	11
Llandudno Junction	5	Oswestry	6	Bedford	5	Bletchley	7	Bank Hall	9
Southport	5	Bank Hall	5	Southport	5	Basingstoke	6	Shrewsbury	5
Swindon	5	Basingstoke	5	Basingstoke	4	Bank Hall	5	Machynlleth	4
Oswestry	4	Bedford	5	Bournemouth	4	Southport	5	Aintree	3
		Bletchley	5	Nottingham	4	Aston	4	Croes Newydd	3
		Dover Marine	5	Tyseley	4	Oxford	4	Chester	2
		Southport	5	Bath Green Park	3	Stewarts Lane	4	Holyhead	2
		Swindon	5	Bletchley	3	Templecombe	3	Nuneaton	2
		Bath Green Park	3	Bristol Barrow Road	3	Brighton	2	Edge Hill	1
		Oxford	3	Llandudno Junction	3	Willesden	2	Llandudno Junction	1
		Eastleigh	2	Oxford	3	Worcester	2		
				Swindon	3	Leamington Spa	1		
				Chester (GWR)	2				
				Chester Northgate	2				
				Gloucester Barnwood	2				
				Machynlleth	2				
				Stewarts Lane	2				
				Worcester	2				
				Brighton	1				
				Three Bridges	1				

BR Standard '4MT' class 4-6-0 No 75077 at its home depot 70D Basingstoke on 9 September 1962.
P. J. C. Skelton

4MT^2 76000-76114 2-6-0 BR Standard Class 4

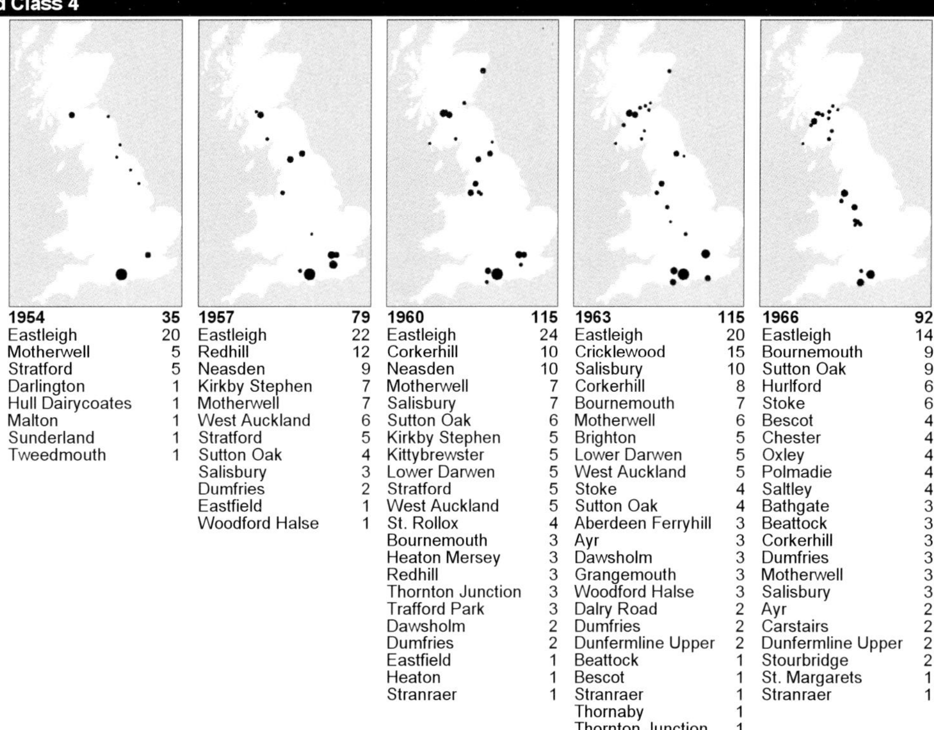

1954	35	1957	79	1960	115	1963	115	1966	92
Eastleigh	20	Eastleigh	22	Eastleigh	24	Eastleigh	20	Eastleigh	14
Motherwell	5	Redhill	12	Corkerhill	10	Cricklewood	15	Bournemouth	9
Stratford	5	Neasden	9	Neasden	10	Salisbury	10	Sutton Oak	9
Darlington	1	Kirkby Stephen	7	Motherwell	7	Corkerhill	8	Hurlford	6
Hull Dairycoates	1	Motherwell	7	Salisbury	7	Bournemouth	7	Stoke	6
Malton	1	West Auckland	6	Sutton Oak	6	Motherwell	6	Bescot	4
Sunderland	1	Stratford	5	Kirkby Stephen	5	Brighton	5	Chester	4
Tweedmouth	1	Sutton Oak	4	Kittybrewster	5	Lower Darwen	5	Oxley	4
		Salisbury	3	Lower Darwen	5	West Auckland	5	Polmadie	4
		Dumfries	2	Stratford	5	Stoke	4	Saltley	4
		Eastfield	1	West Auckland	5	Sutton Oak	4	Bathgate	3
		Woodford Halse	1	St. Rollox	4	Aberdeen Ferryhill	3	Beattock	3
				Bournemouth	3	Ayr	3	Corkerhill	3
				Heaton Mersey	3	Dawsholm	3	Dumfries	3
				Redhill	3	Grangemouth	3	Motherwell	3
				Thornton Junction	3	Woodford Halse	3	Salisbury	3
				Trafford Park	3	Dalry Road	2	Ayr	2
				Dawsholm	2	Dumfries	2	Carstairs	2
				Dumfries	2	Dunfermline Upper	2	Dunfermline Upper	2
				Eastfield	1	Beattock	1	Stourbridge	2
				Heaton	1	Bescot	1	St. Margarets	1
				Stranraer	1	Stranraer	1	Stranraer	1
						Thornaby	1		
						Thornton Junction	1		

4MT^3 80000-80154 2-6-4T BR Standard Class 4 Tank

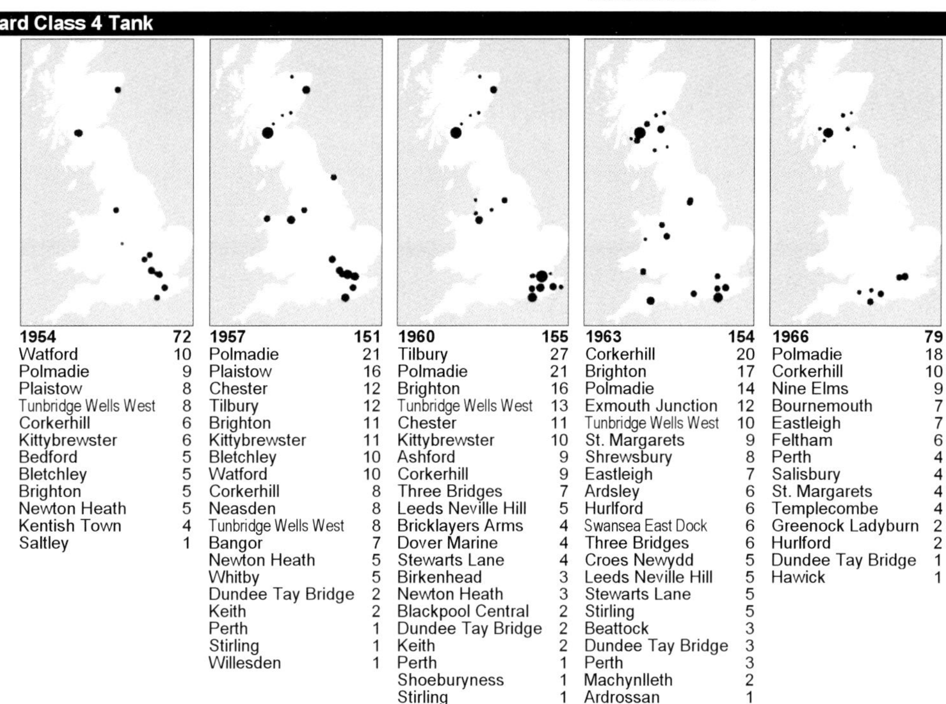

1954	72	1957	151	1960	155	1963	154	1966	79
Watford	10	Polmadie	21	Tilbury	27	Corkerhill	20	Polmadie	18
Polmadie	9	Plaistow	16	Polmadie	21	Brighton	17	Corkerhill	10
Plaistow	8	Chester	12	Brighton	16	Polmadie	14	Nine Elms	9
Tunbridge Wells West	8	Tilbury	12	Tunbridge Wells West	13	Exmouth Junction	12	Bournemouth	7
Corkerhill	6	Brighton	11	Chester	11	Tunbridge Wells West	10	Eastleigh	7
Kittybrewster	6	Kittybrewster	11	Kittybrewster	10	St. Margarets	9	Feltham	6
Bedford	5	Bletchley	10	Ashford	9	Shrewsbury	8	Perth	4
Bletchley	5	Watford	10	Corkerhill	9	Eastleigh	7	Salisbury	4
Brighton	5	Corkerhill	8	Three Bridges	7	Ardsley	6	St. Margarets	4
Newton Heath	5	Neasden	8	Leeds Neville Hill	5	Hurlford	6	Templecombe	4
Kentish Town	4	Tunbridge Wells West	8	Bricklayers Arms	4	Swansea East Dock	6	Greenock Ladyburn	2
Saltley	1	Bangor	7	Dover Marine	4	Three Bridges	6	Hurlford	2
		Newton Heath	5	Stewarts Lane	4	Croes Newydd	5	Dundee Tay Bridge	1
		Whitby	5	Birkenhead	3	Leeds Neville Hill	5	Hawick	1
		Dundee Tay Bridge	2	Newton Heath	3	Stewarts Lane	5		
		Keith	2	Blackpool Central	2	Stirling	5		
		Perth	1	Dundee Tay Bridge	2	Beattock	3		
		Stirling	1	Keith	2	Dundee Tay Bridge	3		
		Willesden	1	Perth	1	Perth	3		
				Shoeburyness	1	Machynlleth	2		
				Stirling	1	Ardrossan	1		
						Hawick	1		

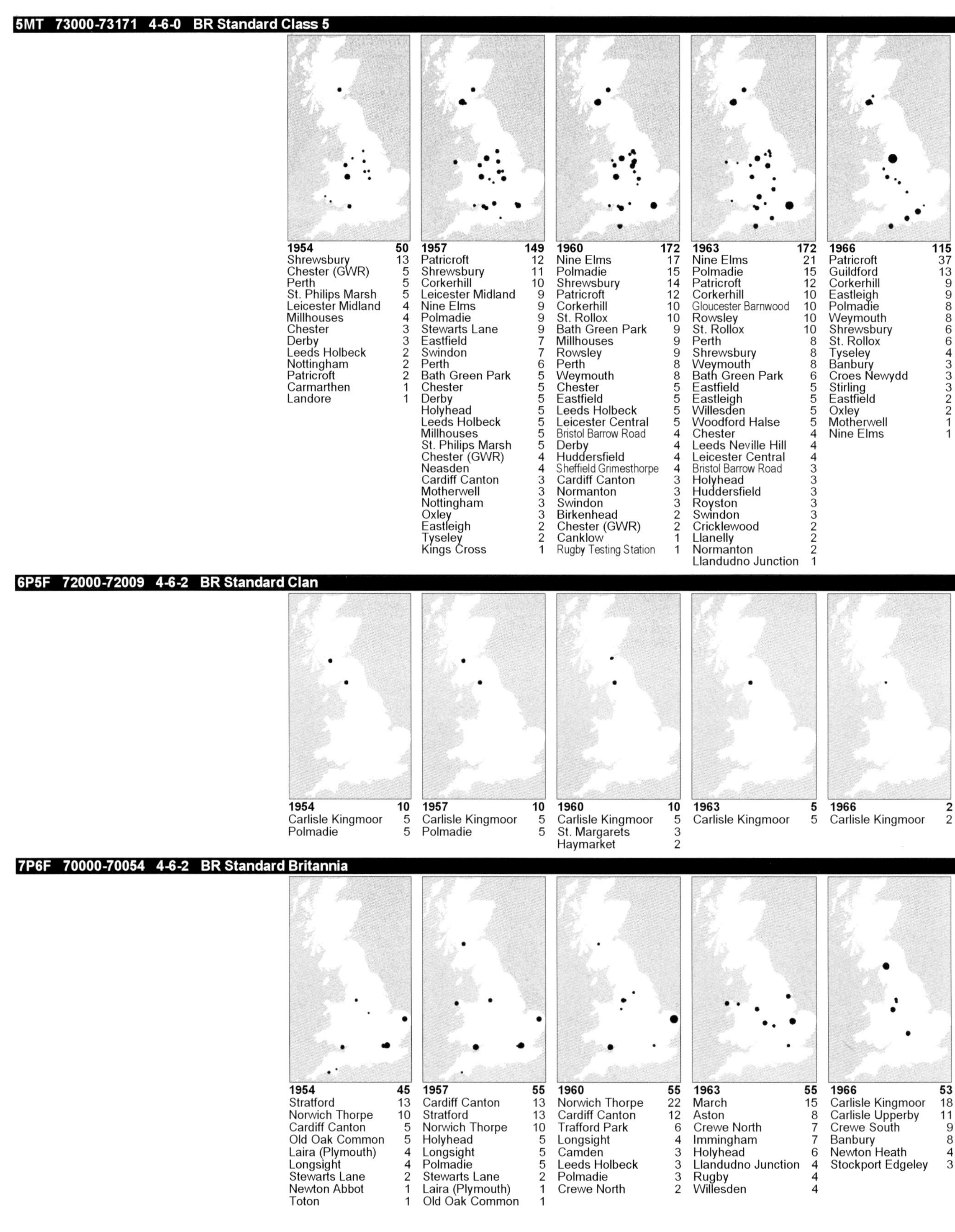

5MT 73000-73171 4-6-0 BR Standard Class 5

1954	50
Shrewsbury	13
Chester (GWR)	5
Perth	5
St. Philips Marsh	5
Leicester Midland	4
Millhouses	4
Chester	3
Derby	3
Leeds Holbeck	2
Nottingham	2
Patricroft	2
Carmarthen	1
Landore	1

1957	149
Patricroft	12
Shrewsbury	11
Corkerhill	10
Leicester Midland	9
Nine Elms	9
Polmadie	9
Stewarts Lane	9
Eastfield	7
Swindon	7
Perth	6
Bath Green Park	5
Chester	5
Derby	5
Holyhead	5
Leeds Holbeck	5
Millhouses	5
St. Philips Marsh	5
Chester (GWR)	4
Neasden	4
Cardiff Canton	3
Motherwell	3
Nottingham	3
Oxley	3
Eastleigh	2
Tyseley	2
Kings Cross	1

1960	172
Nine Elms	17
Polmadie	15
Shrewsbury	14
Patricroft	12
Corkerhill	10
St. Rollox	10
Bath Green Park	9
Millhouses	9
Rowsley	9
Perth	8
Weymouth	8
Chester	5
Eastfield	5
Leeds Holbeck	5
Leicester Central	5
Bristol Barrow Road	4
Derby	4
Huddersfield	4
Sheffield Grimesthorpe	4
Cardiff Canton	3
Normanton	3
Swindon	3
Birkenhead	2
Chester (GWR)	2
Canklow	1
Rugby Testing Station	1

1963	172
Nine Elms	21
Polmadie	15
Patricroft	12
Corkerhill	10
Gloucester Barnwood	10
Rowsley	10
St. Rollox	10
Perth	8
Shrewsbury	8
Weymouth	8
Bath Green Park	6
Eastfield	5
Eastleigh	5
Willesden	5
Woodford Halse	5
Chester	4
Leeds Neville Hill	4
Leicester Central	4
Bristol Barrow Road	3
Holyhead	3
Huddersfield	3
Royston	3
Swindon	3
Cricklewood	2
Llanelly	2
Normanton	2
Llandudno Junction	1

1966	115
Patricroft	37
Guildford	13
Corkerhill	9
Eastleigh	9
Polmadie	8
Weymouth	8
Shrewsbury	6
St. Rollox	6
Tyseley	4
Banbury	3
Croes Newydd	3
Stirling	3
Eastfield	2
Oxley	2
Motherwell	1
Nine Elms	1

6P5F 72000-72009 4-6-2 BR Standard Clan

1954	10
Carlisle Kingmoor	5
Polmadie	5

1957	10
Carlisle Kingmoor	5
Polmadie	5

1960	10
Carlisle Kingmoor	5
St. Margarets	3
Haymarket	2

1963	5
Carlisle Kingmoor	5

1966	2
Carlisle Kingmoor	2

7P6F 70000-70054 4-6-2 BR Standard Britannia

1954	45
Stratford	13
Norwich Thorpe	10
Cardiff Canton	5
Old Oak Common	5
Laira (Plymouth)	4
Longsight	4
Stewarts Lane	2
Newton Abbot	1
Toton	1

1957	55
Cardiff Canton	13
Stratford	13
Norwich Thorpe	10
Holyhead	5
Longsight	5
Polmadie	5
Stewarts Lane	2
Laira (Plymouth)	1
Old Oak Common	1

1960	55
Norwich Thorpe	22
Cardiff Canton	12
Trafford Park	6
Longsight	4
Camden	3
Leeds Holbeck	3
Polmadie	3
Crewe North	2

1963	55
March	15
Aston	8
Crewe North	7
Immingham	7
Holyhead	6
Llandudno Junction	4
Rugby	4
Willesden	4

1966	53
Carlisle Kingmoor	18
Carlisle Upperby	11
Crewe South	9
Banbury	8
Newton Heath	4
Stockport Edgeley	3

Right: 'Britannia' No 70031 *Byron* at Carlisle Upperby, December 1964.
P. J. Robinson

8P 71000 4-6-2 BR Standard Duke of Gloucester

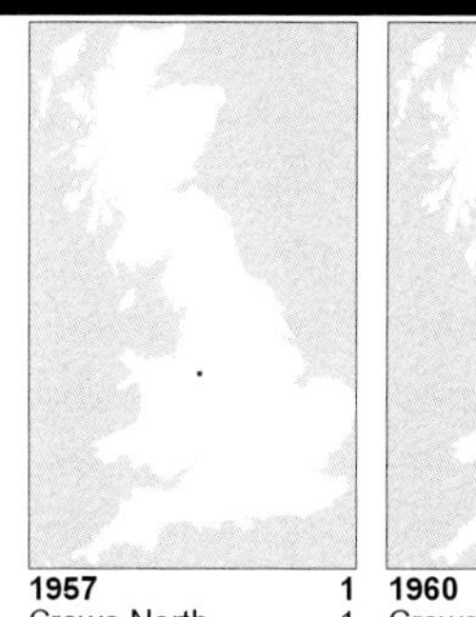

1957	1	1960	1
Crewe North	1	Crewe North	1

9F 92000-92250 2-10-0 BR Standard

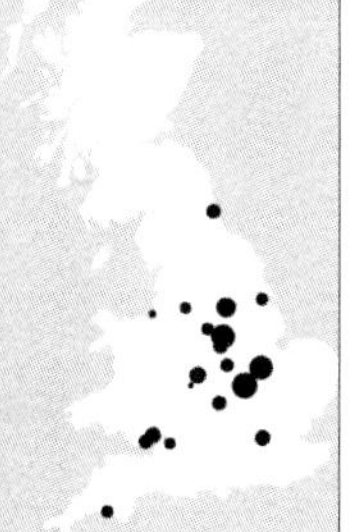

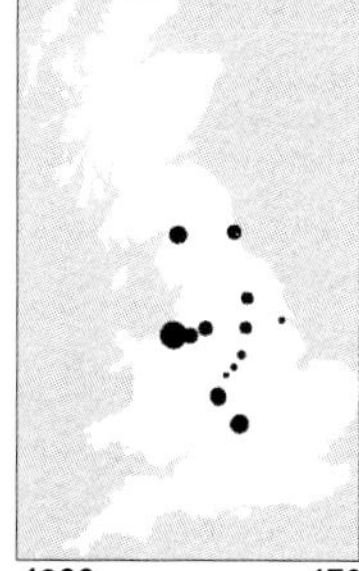

1957	115	1960	248	1963	251	1966	170
Wellingborough	23	Wellingborough	43	Annesley	30	Birkenhead	54
Toton	22	Annesley	30	New England	26	Banbury	17
Doncaster	16	New England	29	Wellingborough	24	Carlisle Kingmoor	16
New England	15	Doncaster	19	Doncaster	22	Saltley	13
Tyne Dock	10	Saltley	13	Saltley	19	Warrington Dallam	11
Ebbw Junction	8	Ebbw Junction	12	Ebbw Junction	16	Newton Heath	10
Westhouses	6	Old Oak Common	11	Leicester Midland	13	Speke Junction	10
March	5	Banbury	10	Cardiff East Dock	11	Tyne Dock	9
Cricklewood	4	Toton	10	Toton	10	Tyseley	9
Bidston	3	Tyne Dock	10	Tyne Dock	10	Doncaster	6
Kettering	2	Cardiff Canton	9	Westhouses	9	York	6
Bromsgrove	1	Leicester Midland	8	Rowsley	8	Kirkby in Ashfield	4
		Immingham	6	Immingham	7	Derby	2
		Kettering	6	Bidston	6	Immingham	2
		Laira (Plymouth)	6	Old Oak Common	6	Burton	1
		Rowsley	6	Banbury	5		
		Newton Heath	5	Bristol Barrow Road	5		
		St. Philips Marsh	5	Eastleigh	5		
		Westhouses	5	Kettering	5		
		Bidston	3	Newton Heath	5		
		Bromsgrove	1	Southall	3		
		Colwick	1	Tyseley	3		
				Oxford	2		
				Bromsgrove	1		

WD[1] 90000-90732 2-8-0 MOS (WD) Austerity

Totals include LNER O7 class in 1948

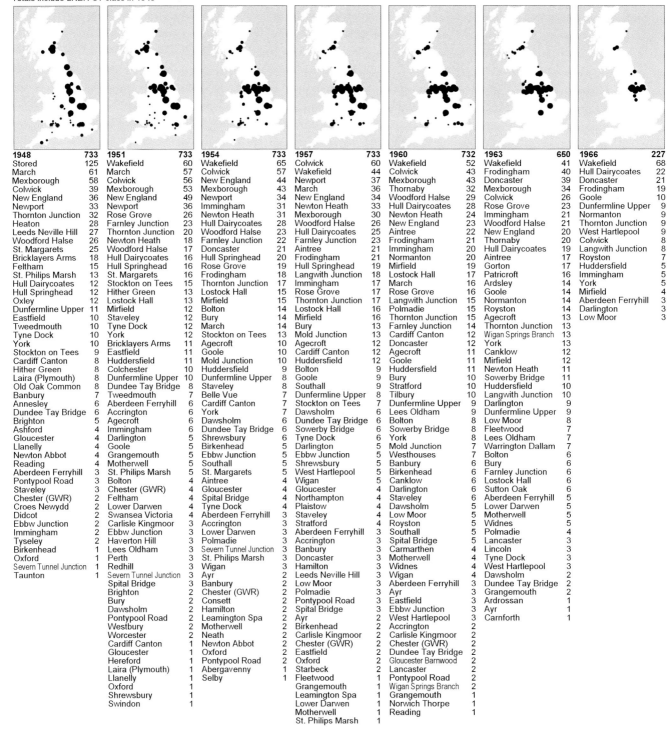

1948	733
Stored	125
March	61
Mexborough	58
Colwick	39
New England	36
Newport	33
Thornton Junction	32
Heaton	28
Leeds Neville Hill	27
Woodford Halse	26
St. Margarets	25
Bricklayers Arms	18
Feltham	15
St. Philips Marsh	13
Hull Dairycoates	12
Hull Springhead	12
Oxley	12
Dunfermline Upper	11
Eastfield	10
Tweedmouth	10
Tyne Dock	10
York	10
Stockton on Tees	9
Cardiff Canton	8
Hither Green	8
Laira (Plymouth)	8
Old Oak Common	8
Banbury	7
Annesley	6
Dundee Tay Bridge	6
Brighton	5
Ashford	4
Gloucester	4
Llanelly	4
Newton Abbot	4
Reading	4
Aberdeen Ferryhill	3
Pontypool Road	3
Staveley	3
Chester (GWR)	2
Croes Newydd	2
Didcot	2
Ebbw Junction	2
Immingham	2
Tyseley	2
Birkenhead	1
Oxford	1
Severn Tunnel Junction	1
Taunton	1

1951	733
Wakefield	60
March	57
Colwick	56
Mexborough	53
New England	49
Newport	36
Rose Grove	26
Farnley Junction	23
Thornton Junction	20
Newton Heath	18
Woodford Halse	17
Hull Dairycoates	16
Hull Springhead	16
St. Margarets	16
Stockton on Tees	15
Hither Green	13
Lostock Hall	13
Mirfield	12
Staveley	12
Tyne Dock	12
York	12
Bricklayers Arms	11
Eastfield	11
Huddersfield	11
Colchester	10
Dunfermline Upper	10
Dundee Tay Bridge	8
Tweedmouth	7
Aberdeen Ferryhill	6
Accrington	6
Agecroft	6
Immingham	6
Darlington	5
Goole	5
Grangemouth	5
Motherwell	5
St. Philips Marsh	5
Bolton	4
Chester (GWR)	4
Feltham	4
Lower Darwen	4
Swansea Victoria	4
Carlisle Kingmoor	3
Ebbw Junction	3
Haverton Hill	3
Lees Oldham	3
Perth	3
Redhill	3
Severn Tunnel Junction	3
Spital Bridge	3
Brighton	2
Bury	2
Dawsholm	2
Pontypool Road	2
Westbury	2
Worcester	2
Cardiff Canton	1
Gloucester	1
Hereford	1
Laira (Plymouth)	1
Llanelly	1
Oxford	1
Shrewsbury	1
Swindon	1

1954	733
Wakefield	65
Colwick	57
New England	44
Mexborough	43
Newport	34
Immingham	31
Newton Heath	31
Hull Dairycoates	28
Woodford Halse	23
Farnley Junction	22
Doncaster	21
Hull Springhead	20
Rose Grove	19
Frodingham	18
Thornton Junction	17
Lostock Hall	15
Mirfield	15
Bolton	14
Bury	14
March	14
Stockton on Tees	13
Agecroft	10
Goole	10
Mold Junction	10
Huddersfield	9
Dunfermline Upper	8
Staveley	8
Belle Vue	7
Cardiff Canton	7
York	7
Dawsholm	6
Dundee Tay Bridge	6
Shrewsbury	6
Birkenhead	5
Ebbw Junction	5
Southall	5
St. Margarets	5
Aintree	4
Gloucester	4
Spital Bridge	4
Tyne Dock	4
Aberdeen Ferryhill	4
Accrington	3
Lower Darwen	3
Polmadie	3
Severn Tunnel Junction	3
St. Philips Marsh	3
Wigan	3
Ayr	2
Banbury	2
Chester (GWR)	2
Consett	2
Hamilton	2
Leamington Spa	2
Motherwell	2
Neath	2
Newton Abbot	2
Oxford	2
Pontypool Road	2
Abergavenny	1
Selby	1

1957	733
Colwick	60
Wakefield	44
Newport	37
March	36
New England	34
Newton Heath	33
Mexborough	30
Woodford Halse	26
Hull Dairycoates	25
Farnley Junction	23
Aintree	21
Frodingham	21
Hull Springhead	19
Langwith Junction	18
Immingham	17
Rose Grove	17
Thornton Junction	17
Lostock Hall	16
Mirfield	16
Bury	13
Mold Junction	13
Agecroft	12
Cardiff Canton	12
Huddersfield	12
Bolton	9
Goole	9
Southall	9
Dunfermline Upper	8
Stockton on Tees	7
Dawsholm	6
Dundee Tay Bridge	6
Sowerby Bridge	6
Tyne Dock	6
Darlington	5
Ebbw Junction	5
Shrewsbury	5
West Hartlepool	5
Wigan	5
Gloucester	4
Northampton	4
Plaistow	4
Staveley	4
Stratford	4
Aberdeen Ferryhill	3
Accrington	3
Banbury	3
Doncaster	3
Hamilton	3
Leeds Neville Hill	3
Low Moor	3
Polmadie	3
Pontypool Road	3
Spital Bridge	3
Ayr	2
Birkenhead	2
Carlisle Kingmoor	2
Chester (GWR)	2
Eastfield	2
Oxford	2
Starbeck	2
Fleetwood	1
Grangemouth	1
Leamington Spa	1
Lower Darwen	1
Motherwell	1
St. Philips Marsh	1

1960	732
Wakefield	52
Colwick	43
Mexborough	43
Thornaby	32
Woodford Halse	29
Hull Dairycoates	28
Newton Heath	24
New England	23
Aintree	22
Frodingham	21
Immingham	20
Normanton	20
Mirfield	19
Lostock Hall	17
March	16
Rose Grove	16
Langwith Junction	15
Polmadie	15
Thornton Junction	15
Farnley Junction	14
Cardiff Canton	12
Doncaster	12
Agecroft	11
Goole	11
Huddersfield	11
Bury	10
Stratford	10
Tilbury	10
Dunfermline Upper	9
Lees Oldham	9
Bolton	8
Sowerby Bridge	8
York	8
Mold Junction	7
Westhouses	7
Banbury	6
Birkenhead	6
Canklow	6
Darlington	6
Staveley	6
Dawsholm	5
Low Moor	5
Royston	5
Southall	5
Spital Bridge	5
Carmarthen	4
Motherwell	4
Widnes	4
Wigan	4
Aberdeen Ferryhill	3
Ayr	3
Eastfield	3
Ebbw Junction	3
West Hartlepool	3
Accrington	2
Carlisle Kingmoor	2
Chester (GWR)	2
Dundee Tay Bridge	2
Gloucester Barnwood	2
Lancaster	2
Pontypool Road	2
Wigan Springs Branch	2
Grangemouth	1
Norwich Thorpe	1
Reading	1

1963	650
Wakefield	41
Frodingham	40
Doncaster	39
Mexborough	34
Colwick	26
Rose Grove	23
Immingham	21
Woodford Halse	21
New England	20
Thornaby	20
Hull Dairycoates	19
Aintree	17
Gorton	17
Patricroft	16
Ardsley	14
Goole	14
Normanton	14
Royston	14
Agecroft	13
Thornton Junction	13
Wigan Springs Branch	13
York	13
Canklow	12
Mirfield	12
Newton Heath	11
Sowerby Bridge	11
Huddersfield	10
Langwith Junction	10
Darlington	9
Dunfermline Upper	9
Low Moor	8
Fleetwood	7
Lees Oldham	7
Warrington Dallam	7
Bolton	6
Bury	6
Farnley Junction	6
Lostock Hall	6
Sutton Oak	6
Aberdeen Ferryhill	5
Lower Darwen	5
Motherwell	5
Widnes	5
Polmadie	4
Lancaster	3
Lincoln	3
Tyne Dock	3
West Hartlepool	3
Dawsholm	2
Dundee Tay Bridge	2
Grangemouth	2
Ardrossan	1
Ayr	1
Carnforth	1

1966	227
Wakefield	68
Hull Dairycoates	22
Doncaster	21
Frodingham	19
Goole	10
Dunfermline Upper	9
Normanton	9
Thornton Junction	9
West Hartlepool	9
Colwick	8
Langwith Junction	8
Royston	7
Huddersfield	5
Immingham	5
York	5
Mirfield	4
Aberdeen Ferryhill	3
Darlington	3
Low Moor	3

WD[2] 90750-90774 2-10-0 MOS (WD) Austerity

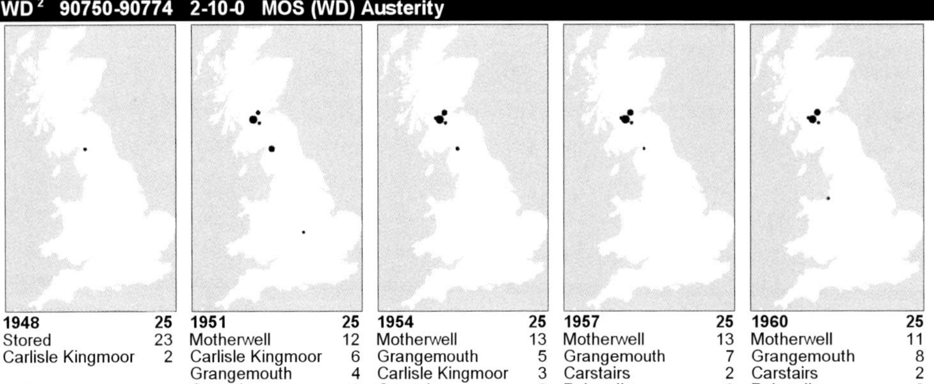

1948	25
Stored	23
Carlisle Kingmoor	2

1951	25
Motherwell	12
Carlisle Kingmoor	6
Grangemouth	4
Carstairs	2
Rugby Testing Station	1

1954	25
Motherwell	13
Grangemouth	5
Carlisle Kingmoor	3
Carstairs	2
Polmadie	2

1957	25
Motherwell	13
Grangemouth	7
Carstairs	2
Polmadie	2
Carlisle Kingmoor	1

1960	25
Motherwell	11
Grangemouth	8
Carstairs	2
Polmadie	2
Bidston	1
Hamilton	1

Right: Class N 2-6-0 No 31830 at Eastleigh, 24 April 1960. *C. P. Boocock*

Shed Lists

Right: GWR Dean & Armstrong '1901' class 0-6-0PT No 2008, carrying an 88C Barry shedplate, and fitted with an open backed cab.

Left: LNWR Webb 'Special Tank' '2F' class 0-6-0ST No 3323 (LNWR number) at Crewe works in August 1953. *Geoff Rixon*

Below: GER Holden 'J66' class 0-6-0T Departmental No 36 (ex 68378) at Stratford. *Brian Morrison*

Aberbeeg

1948 ABEEG
3612 5700
3616 5700
3640 5700
3670 5700
3680 5700
3683 5700
3729 5700
3776 5700
4217 4200
4222 4200
4231 4200
4243 4200
4267 4200
4287 4200
4514 4500
4522 4500
4597 4575
4682 5700
4685 5700
4686 5700
5259 5205
5733 5700
5786 5700
5788 5700
5789 5700
6621 5600
7703 5700
7720 5700
7740 5700
7778 5700
7789 5700
8723 5700
8724 5700
8739 5700
8776 5700
8794 5700
9723 5700

1951 86H
3640 5700
3680 5700
3711 5700
3716 5700
3776 5700
4214 4200
4217 4200
4223 4200
4238 4200
4267 4200
4271 4200
4514 4500
4522 4500
4597 4575
4637 5700
4652 5700
4682 5700
4685 5700
4686 5700
5207 5205
5236 5205
5520 4575
5733 5700
5777 5700
5789 5700
6642 5600
6685 5600
7703 5700
7721 5700
7775 5700
7778 5700
8402 9400
8724 5700
8776 5700
8794 5700
9796 5700

1954 86H
3711 5700
3716 5700
3747 5700
4214 4200
4215 4200
4227 4200
4238 4200
4287 4200
4593 4575
4643 5700
4652 5700
4682 5700
4685 5700
4686 5700
5202 4200
5241 5205
5520 4575
5602 5600
5645 5600
5750 5700
5777 5700
5785 5700
6638 5600
6663 5600
7703 5700
7775 5700
8402 9400
8436 9400
8493 9400
8494 9400
8786 5700
9427 9400
9450 9400
9459 9400
9460 9400

1957 86H
3647 5700
3674 5700
3711 5700
3747 5700
4200 4200
4238 4200
4250 4200
4259 4200
4269 4200
4277 4200
4287 4200
4643 5700
4652 5700
4682 5700
4685 5700
5206 5205
5241 5205
5539 4575
5544 4575
5564 4575
5645 5600
5685 5600
5729 5700
5785 5700
5794 5700
6663 5600
7703 5700
7774 5700
8436 9400
8439 9400
8494 9400
8705 5700
8778 5700
8786 5700
9450 9400
9458 9400
9460 9400

1960 86H
3647 5700
3683 5700
4237 4200
4250 4200
4277 4200
4285 4200
4287 4200
4291 4200
4627 5700
4652 5700
4685 5700
5206 5205
5241 5205
5257 5205
5516 4575
5544 4575
5568 4575
6621 5600
6629 5600
6644 5600
6663 5600
7755 5700
8429 9400
8436 9400
8437 9400
8444 9400
8489 9400
8705 5700
8778 5700
8786 5700
9458 9400
9460 9400

1963 86F
3647 5700
3686 5700
4237 4200
4277 4200
4285 4200
4604 5700
4650 5700
4693 5700
5202 4200
5206 5205
5218 5205
5231 5205
5252 5205
5260 5205
5264 5205
8437 9400
8444 9400
8786 5700
9444 9400
9482 9400
9494 9400
9682 5700

Abercynon

1948 AYN
219 TV[2]
236 TV[2]
281 TV[2]
287 TV[2]
288 TV[2]
295 TV[2]
304 TV[3]
337 TV[3]
351 TV[3]
356 TV[3]
380 TV[3]
397 TV[3]
1461 1400
2000 1901
5618 5600
5619 5600
5630 5600
5637 5600
5641 5600
5643 5600
5644 5600
5669 5600
5682 5600
5686 5600
6401 6400
6411 6400
6438 6400

1951 88E
218 TV[2]
219 TV[2]
236 TV[2]
295 TV[2]
304 TV[3]
337 TV[3]
351 TV[3]
356 TV[3]
380 TV[3]
386 TV[3]
397 TV[3]
1610 1600
1620 1600
5421 5400
5618 5600
5623 5600
5637 5600
5641 5600
5643 5600
5644 5600
5650 5600
5682 5600
5686 5600
5699 5600
6401 6400
6411 6400
6438 6400
6661 5600

1954 88E
304 TV[3]
316 TV[3]
322 TV[3]
351 TV[3]
356 TV[3]
370 TV[3]
379 TV[3]
380 TV[3]
385 TV[3]
386 TV[3]
397 TV[3]
1610 1600
1620 1600
5618 5600
5623 5600
5637 5600
5641 5600
5643 5600
5660 5600
5680 5600
5682 5600
5686 5600
5699 5600
6401 6400
6411 6400
6438 6400

1957 88E
304 TV[3]
349 TV[3]
370 TV[3]
373 TV[3]
390 TV[3]
393 TV[3]
397 TV[3]
1610 1600
1620 1600
3650 5700
3707 5700
5617 5600
5618 5600
5623 5600
5641 5600
5643 5600
5680 5600
5682 5600
5686 5600
5699 5600
6411 6400
6438 6400
7733 5700
7744 5700
9642 5700

1960 88E
1612 1600
1620 1600
3707 5700
3730 5700
3734 5700
3783 5700
5601 5600
5617 5600
5623 5600
5627 5600
5641 5600
5643 5600
5644 5600
5680 5600
5682 5600
5686 5600
5699 5600
6435 6400
6438 6400
7726 5700
7733 5700
7744 5700
8735 5700
9622 5700

1963 88E
1612 1600
1641 1600
3695 5700
3707 5700
3730 5700
3734 5700
5601 5600
5614 5600
5615 5600
5627 5600
5641 5600
5644 5600
5685 5600
5686 5600
5699 5600
8717 5700
9611 5700
9622 5700
9668 5700

Aberdare

1948 ABDR
65 RR[4]
204 TV[2]
206 TV[2]
282 TV[2]
284 TV[2]
362 TV[3]
374 TV[3]
1769 1854
2117 2021
2801 2800
2806 2800
2808 2800
2810 2800
2811 2800
2822 2800
2823 2800
2828 2800
2831 2800
2836 2800
2841 2800
2870 2800
2880 2800
3036 ROD
3605 5700
3610 5700
3655 5700
3747 5700
3753 5700
4228 4200
4257 4200
4264 4200
4285 4200
4297 4200
5237 5205
5245 5205
5258 5205
5263 5205
5520 4575
5770 5700
5787 5700
5796 5700
6410 6400
6413 6400
6437 6400
6605 5600
6628 5600
6652 5600
6692 5600
6693 5600
7205 7200
7213 7200
7221 7200
7242 7200
7423 7400
7748 5700
7773 5700
9607 5700
9609 5700
9712 5700

1951 86J
65 RR[4]
204 TV[2]
282 TV[2]
284 TV[2]
362 TV[3]
374 TV[3]
2159 2021
2808 2800
2828 2800
2831 2800
2836 2800
2870 2800
2880 2800
3605 5700
3610 5700
3655 5700
3747 5700
3753 5700
4228 4200
4257 4200
4264 4200
4297 4200
5237 5205
5245 5205
5258 5205
5263 5205
5649 5600
5770 5700
5787 5700
5796 5700
6410 6400
6413 6400
6437 6400
6605 5600
6622 5600
6628 5600
6651 5600
6652 5600
6692 5600
6693 5600
7213 7200
7221 7200
7242 7200
7423 7400
7720 5700
7748 5700
7773 5700
9607 5700
9609 5700
9712 5700

1954 86J
208 TV[2]
282 TV[2]
2808 2800
2810 2800
2828 2800
2831 2800
2836 2800
2863 2800
2870 2800
2876 2800
3605 5700
3610 5700
3647 5700
3655 5700
3680 5700
3695 5700
3699 5700
3753 5700
4228 4200
4257 4200
4264 4200
4272 4200
4297 4200
5237 5205
5245 5205
5258 5205
5263 5205
5644 5600
5649 5600
5698 5600
5741 5700
5787 5700
5797 5700
6410 6400
6413 6400
6417 6400
6437 6400
6605 5600
6622 5600
6628 5600
6649 5600
6651 5600
6652 5600
6661 5600
6687 5600
7213 7200
7216 7200
7221 7200
7423 7400
7720 5700
7773 5700
8724 5700
9607 5700
9609 5700
9712 5700
9731 5700

1957 86J
2810 2800
2828 2800
2831 2800
2836 2800
2863 2800
2870 2800
2876 2800
3605 5700
3610 5700
3655 5700
3695 5700
3699 5700
3716 5700
3753 5700
4228 4200
4255 4200
4257 4200
4272 4200
4297 4200
5237 5205
5245 5205
5258 5205
5263 5205
5264 5205
5624 5600
5644 5600
5649 5600
5698 5600
5797 5700
6361 4300
6410 6400
6413 6400
6417 6400
6431 6400
6437 6400
6605 5600
6622 5600
6628 5600
6649 5600
6651 5600
6652 5600
6661 5600
6687 5600
7216 7200
7221 7200
7423 7400
7720 5700
7773 5700
8444 9400
8445 9400
9607 5700
9609 5700
9712 5700
9731 5700

1960 86J
2813 2800
2831 2800
2873 2800
2876 2800
3603 5700
3610 5700
3655 5700
3695 5700
3699 5700
3716 5700
3753 5700
3850 2884
3866 2884
4228 4200
4257 4200
4262 4200
5237 5205
5249 5205
5258 5205
5263 5205
5624 5600
5633 5600
5642 5600
5649 5600
5698 5600
6361 4300
6431 6400
6437 6400
6605 5600
6622 5600
6628 5600
6651 5600
6652 5600
6661 5600
6687 5600
6750 6700
7203 7200
7214 7200
7216 7200
7221 7200
7224 7200
7237 7200
7423 7400
7720 5700
8445 9400
9607 5700
9712 5700
9731 5700

1963 88J
2876 2800
3603 5700
3627 5700
3699 5700
3753 5700
3816 2884
3839 2884
3843 2884
3847 2884
3850 2884
3853 2884
3860 2884
3866 2884
4252 4200
4257 4200
4279 4200
4688 5700
5237 5205
5240 5205
5249 5205
5263 5205
5624 5600
5633 5600
5647 5600
5649 5600
5680 5600
6361 4300
6605 5600
6622 5600
6628 5600
6651 5600
6661 5600
6664 5600
6673 5600
6690 5600
7209 7200
7214 7200
7234 7200
7247 7200
7423 7400
9600 5700
9607 5700
9731 5700

Aberdeen Ferryhill

1948 29B
41134 4P[1]
41176 4P[1]
41184 4P[1]
55220 2P[13]
55234 2P[13]
56240 3F[10]
56251 3F[10]
56278 3F[10]
56326 3F[10]
56348 3F[10]
56359 3F[10]
57283 2F[5]
57339 2F[5]
57345 2F[5]
57368 2F[5]
57400 2F[5]
60501 A2
60502 A2
60819 V2
60822 V2
60824 V2
60825 V2
60827 V2
60851 V2
60888 V2
60898 V2
60919 V2
60970 V2
60973 V2
63041 O7
63097 O7
63134 O7
64794 J39
64795 J39
64975 J39
69128 N15
69129 N15

1951 61B
41134 4P[1]
41176 4P[1]
41184 4P[1]
56240 3F[10]
56251 3F[10]
56278 3F[10]
56326 3F[10]
56348 3F[10]
60525 A2
60531 A2
60537 A2
60819 V2
60824 V2
60827 V2
60851 V2
60888 V2
60898 V2
60919 V2
60955 V2
60970 V2
60973 V2
61132 B1
61133 B1
64795 J39
64975 J39
65213 J36
65297 J36
67455 C15
67478 C15
68568 J69
69125 N14
69128 N15
69129 N15
69201 N15
90041 WD[1]
90097 WD[1]
90121 WD[1]
90203 WD[1]
90260 WD[1]
90455 WD[1]

1954 61B
41176 4P[1]
45245 5MT[3]
45367 5MT[3]
56240 3F[10]
56251 3F[10]
56278 3F[10]
56326 3F[10]
56348 3F[10]
60525 A2
60531 A2
60532 A2
60819 V2
60824 V2
60827 V2
60851 V2
60888 V2
60898 V2
60919 V2
60955 V2
60970 V2
60973 V2
61734 K2
64485 J35
64795 J39
64975 J39
65247 J36
65297 J36
67478 C15
67496 C16
67501 C16
69125 N14
69128 N15
69129 N15
69201 N15
90041 WD[1]
90097 WD[1]
90455 WD[1]

1957 61B
44703 5MT[3]
44794 5MT[3]
45162 5MT[3]
45167 5MT[3]
45469 5MT[3]
56240 3F[10]
56251 3F[10]
56278 3F[10]
56326 3F[10]
56348 3F[10]
60525 A2
60531 A2
60532 A2
60819 V2
60824 V2
60827 V2
60851 V2
60888 V2
60898 V2
60919 V2
60955 V2
60970 V2
60972 V2
60973 V2
61700 V4
61701 V4
64483 J35
64485 J35
64795 J39
64975 J39
65242 J36
67501 C16
69128 N15
69129 N15
69201 N15
69503 N2
90041 WD[1]
90097 WD[1]
90455 WD[1]

1960 61B
44703 5MT[3]
44794 5MT[3]
45162 5MT[3]
45167 5MT[3]
45469 5MT[3]
56240 3F[10]
56278 3F[10]
56325 3F[10]
56326 3F[10]
60525 A2
60531 A2
60532 A2
60851 V2
60888 V2
60898 V2
60919 V2
60955 V2
60970 V2
60972 V2
60973 V2
65305 J36
69128 N15
69138 N15
69224 N15
90041 WD[1]
90097 WD[1]
90455 WD[1]

1963 61B
44703 5MT[3]
44794 5MT[3]
45162 5MT[3]
60009 A4
60011 A4
60522 A2
60525 A2
60527 A2
60898 V2
60919 V2
60955 V2
60972 V2
61346 B1
61347 B1
61400 B1
76104 4MT[2]
76107 4MT[2]
76108 4MT[2]
78045 2MT[1]
78053 2MT[1]
78054 2MT[1]
90041 WD[1]
90077 WD[1]
90097 WD[1]
90536 WD[1]
90640 WD[1]

1966 61B
44703 5MT[3]
44794 5MT[3]
60004 A4
60007 A4
60009 A4
60019 A4
60034 A4
90041 WD[1]
90596 WD[1]
90640 WD[1]

Abergavenny

1948 4D
41202 2MT[1]
41203 2MT[1]
48899 7F[2]
48932 7F[2]
48948 7F[2]
49006 7F[2]
49019 7F[2]
49051 7F[2]
49113 7F[2]
49146 7F[2]
49148 7F[2]
49226 7F[2]
49243 7F[2]
49276 7F[2]
49403 7F[3]
58902 2F[14]
58905 2F[14]
58907 2F[14]
58911 2F[14]
58929 2F[14]
58933 2F[14]
58937 2F[14]
7812 2F[14]
7841 2F[14]

1951 86K
41201 2MT[1]
41202 2MT[1]
41203 2MT[1]
41204 2MT[1]
48899 7F[2]
48921 7F[2]
49006 7F[2]
49028 7F[2]
49046 7F[2]
49051 7F[2]
49064 7F[2]
49113 7F[2]
49121 7F[2]
49146 7F[2]
49161 7F[2]
49168 7F[2]
49174 7F[2]
49226 7F[2]
49243 7F[2]
49316 7F[2]
49345 7F[2]
49403 7F[3]
49409 7F[3]
49422 7F[3]
58880 2F[14]
58888 2F[14]
58889 2F[14]
58891 2F[14]
58895 2F[14]
58899 2F[14]
58902 2F[14]
58913 2F[14]
58915 2F[14]
58919 2F[14]
58924 2F[14]
58925 2F[14]
58933 2F[14]
58935 2F[14]

1954 86K
40091 3MT[2]
40097 3MT[2]
40098 3MT[2]
40105 3MT[2]
40141 3MT[2]
40161 3MT[2]
40171 3MT[2]
41201 2MT[1]
41202 2MT[1]
41203 2MT[1]
41204 2MT[1]
48899 7F[2]
48921 7F[2]
49028 7F[2]
49046 7F[2]
49051 7F[2]
49064 7F[2]
49113 7F[2]
49121 7F[2]
49146 7F[2]
49161 7F[2]
49168 7F[2]
49174 7F[2]
49226 7F[2]
49243 7F[2]
49316 7F[2]
49345 7F[2]
49403 7F[3]
49409 7F[3]
49422 7F[3]
49448 7F[3]
58888 2F[14]
58891 2F[14]
58902 2F[14]
58915 2F[14]
58924 2F[14]
58925 2F[14]
90161 WD[1]

Aberystwyth

1948 ABH
2200 2251
2223 2251
2260 2251
2283 2251
2298 2251
5560 4575
5570 4575
7406 7400
7802 7800
7803 7800
9002 9000
9013 9000
9017 9000
9021 9000
9025 9000
9087 3252

Aberystwyth (VoR)

1948 ABH sub
7 VoR
8 VoR
9 VoR

1951 89C sub
7 VoR
8 VoR
9 VoR

1954 89C sub
7 VoR
8 VoR
9 VoR

1957 89C sub
7 VoR
8 VoR
9 VoR

1960 89C sub
7 VoR
8 VoR
9 VoR

1963 89C sub
7 VoR
8 VoR
9 VoR

1966 6F sub
7 VoR
8 VoR
9 VoR

Accrington

1948 24A
40676 2P[3]
40682 2P[3]
40683 2P[3]
41100 4P[1]
41101 4P[1]
41102 4P[1]
41185 4P[1]
41187 4P[1]
41194 4P[1]
41198 4P[1]
42295 4MT[1]
42433 4MT[3]
42490 4MT[3]
42548 4MT[3]
42634 4MT[3]
44460 4F[2]
44479 4F[2]
45101 5MT[3]
45367 5MT[3]
45396 5MT[3]
48416 8F
48448 8F
48479 8F
48705 8F
51361 2F[2]
52216 3F[7]
52238 3F[7]
52288 3F[7]
52412 3F[7]
52441 3F[7]
52452 3F[7]
52524 3F[7]
52821 6F[3]
52822 6F[3]
52825 6F[3]
52831 6F[3]

1951 24A
40676 2P[3]
40677 2P[3]
40680 2P[3]
40681 2P[3]
42153 4MT[1]
42295 4MT[1]
42433 4MT[3]
42437 4MT[3]
42548 4MT[3]
42549 4MT[3]
42634 4MT[3]
42643 4MT[3]
42661 4MT[3]
42716 5MT[1]
42717 5MT[1]
42718 5MT[1]
42729 5MT[1]
42796 5MT[1]
42843 5MT[1]
44921 5MT[3]
45367 5MT[3]
45396 5MT[3]
51390 2F[2]
51410 2F[2]
51514 2F[2]
90206 WD[1]
90402 WD[1]
90416 WD[1]
90610 WD[1]
90632 WD[1]
90713 WD[1]

1954 24A
40937 4P[1]
41085 4P[1]
42153 4MT[1]
42294 4MT[1]
42295 4MT[1]
42433 4MT[3]
42437 4MT[3]
42548 4MT[3]
42549 4MT[3]
42634 4MT[3]
42643 4MT[3]
42661 4MT[3]
44932 5MT[3]
45226 5MT[3]
51390 2F[2]
51410 2F[2]
51464 2F[2]
75040 4MT[1]
75041 4MT[1]
75042 4MT[1]
75043 4MT[1]
75044 4MT[1]
75045 4MT[1]
75046 4MT[1]
75047 4MT[1]
75048 4MT[1]
75049 4MT[1]
90112 WD[1]
90348 WD[1]
90399 WD[1]

1957 24A
42110 4MT[1]
42153 4MT[1]
42294 4MT[1]
42295 4MT[1]
42433 4MT[3]
42437 4MT[3]
42548 4MT[3]
42549 4MT[3]
42619 4MT[3]
42620 4MT[3]
42634 4MT[3]
42643 4MT[3]
42661 4MT[3]
44689 5MT[3]
44692 5MT[3]
44889 5MT[3]
44932 5MT[3]
45068 5MT[3]
45078 5MT[3]
45226 5MT[3]
45227 5MT[3]
45415 5MT[3]
51497 2F[2]
90266 WD[1]
90374 WD[1]
90399 WD[1]

1960 24A
42110 4MT[1]
42153 4MT[1]
42294 4MT[1]
42295 4MT[1]
42433 4MT[3]
42619 4MT[3]
42620 4MT[3]
42643 4MT[3]
42661 4MT[3]
44689 5MT[3]
44692 5MT[3]
44889 5MT[3]
45068 5MT[3]
45078 5MT[3]
45226 5MT[3]
45227 5MT[3]
45415 5MT[3]
47201 3F[5]
47562 3F[6]
90374 WD[1]
90399 WD[1]

Agecroft

1948 26B
42645 4MT[3]
42646 4MT[3]
42647 4MT[3]
42648 4MT[3]
42715 5MT[1]
42716 5MT[1]
42717 5MT[1]
42718 5MT[1]
42719 5MT[1]
42720 5MT[1]
42721 5MT[1]
42722 5MT[1]
42723 5MT[1]
42724 5MT[1]
42725 5MT[1]
42734 5MT[1]
42750 5MT[1]
42753 5MT[1]
42755 5MT[1]
42796 5MT[1]
42819 5MT[1]
42838 5MT[1]
42860 5MT[1]
42864 5MT[1]
42868 5MT[1]
45104 5MT[3]
45219 5MT[3]
45220 5MT[3]
45223 5MT[3]
45337 5MT[3]

45338 5MT^3
47572 3F^6
47573 3F^6
47574 3F^6
47578 3F^6
47579 3F^6
47583 3F^6
47584 3F^6
47585 3F^6
48425 8F
48444 8F
48446 8F
48766 8F
49599 7F^4
49631 7F^4
51230 0F^4
51240 0F^4
51464 2F^2
51474 2F^2
51512 2F^2
52137 3F^7
52162 3F^7
52203 3F^7
52293 3F^7
52304 3F^7
52353 3F^7
52411 3F^7
52461 3F^7
52549 3F^9

1951 26B

41100 4P^1
41189 4P^1
41191 4P^1
41196 4P^1
42645 4MT^3
42646 4MT^3
42647 4MT^3
42648 4MT^3
42721 5MT^1
42722 5MT^1
42723 5MT^1
42724 5MT^1
42725 5MT^1
42730 5MT^1
42734 5MT^1
42753 5MT^1
42755 5MT^1
42819 5MT^1
42838 5MT^1
42860 5MT^1
42864 5MT^1
42868 5MT^1
44781 5MT^3
44782 5MT^3
44823 5MT^3
45337 5MT^3
45338 5MT^3
47574 3F^6
47578 3F^6
47579 3F^6
47583 3F^6
47584 3F^6
47585 3F^6
49502 7F^4
49511 7F^4
49532 7F^4
49538 7F^4
49544 7F^4
49555 7F^4
49578 7F^4
49627 7F^4
51230 0F^4
51464 2F^2
51500 2F^2
51512 2F^2
52140 3F^7
52219 3F^7
52279 3F^7
52293 3F^7
52333 3F^7
90102 WD^1
90186 WD^1
90307 WD^1
90343 WD^1
90359 WD^1
90546 WD^1

1954 26B

42645 4MT^3
42646 4MT^3
42647 4MT^3
42648 4MT^3
42721 5MT^1
42722 5MT^1
42723 5MT^1
42724 5MT^1
42725 5MT^1
42730 5MT^1
42734 5MT^1
42753 5MT^1
42755 5MT^1
42819 5MT^1
42838 5MT^1
42860 5MT^1
42864 5MT^1
42868 5MT^1
44781 5MT^3
44782 5MT^3
44823 5MT^3
44987 5MT^3
45337 5MT^3
45338 5MT^3
46412 2MT^2
46485 2MT^2
47574 3F^6
47578 3F^6
47579 3F^6
47583 3F^6
47584 3F^6
47585 3F^6
49555 7F^4
49578 7F^4
49603 7F^4
49627 7F^4
51207 0F^4
51230 0F^4
51500 2F^2
51512 2F^2
52124 3F^7
52293 3F^7
90102 WD^1
90254 WD^1
90306 WD^1
90307 WD^1
90324 WD^1
90354 WD^1
90546 WD^1
90564 WD^1
90632 WD^1
90713 WD^1

1957 26B

42645 4MT^3
42646 4MT^3
42647 4MT^3
42648 4MT^3
42721 5MT^1
42722 5MT^1
42723 5MT^1
42724 5MT^1
42725 5MT^1
42730 5MT^1
42734 5MT^1
42753 5MT^1
42755 5MT^1
42819 5MT^1
42838 5MT^1
42845 5MT^1
42860 5MT^1
42864 5MT^1
42868 5MT^1
44781 5MT^3
44782 5MT^3
44823 5MT^3
44987 5MT^3
45234 5MT^3
45337 5MT^3
45338 5MT^3
45450 5MT^3
46485 2MT^2
46486 2MT^2
47574 3F^6
47578 3F^6
47579 3F^6
47583 3F^6
47585 3F^6
49555 7F^4
49627 7F^4
49648 7F^4
51207 0F^4
51230 0F^4
51241 0F^4
51499 2F^2
51500 2F^2
90102 WD^1
90292 WD^1
90306 WD^1
90307 WD^1
90324 WD^1
90354 WD^1
90372 WD^1
90413 WD^1
90546 WD^1
90564 WD^1
90632 WD^1
90713 WD^1

1960 26B

42287 4MT^1
42461 4MT^3
42646 4MT^3
42647 4MT^3
42723 5MT^1
42724 5MT^1
42725 5MT^1
42734 5MT^1
42753 5MT^1
42755 5MT^1
42819 5MT^1
42838 5MT^1
42860 5MT^1
42868 5MT^1
44781 5MT^3
44782 5MT^3
44823 5MT^3
44929 5MT^3
44987 5MT^3
45261 5MT^3
45337 5MT^3
45338 5MT^3
46485 2MT^2
46486 2MT^2
47224 3F^5
47574 3F^6
47578 3F^6
47579 3F^6
47585 3F^6
49505 7F^4
49627 7F^4
49674 7F^4
51204 0F^4
51207 0F^4
51413 2F^2
51496 2F^2
61008 B1
61201 B1
61269 B1
61298 B1
61369 B1
90292 WD^1
90307 WD^1
90324 WD^1
90354 WD^1
90359 WD^1
90372 WD^1
90546 WD^1
90558 WD^1
90564 WD^1
90632 WD^1
90713 WD^1

1963 26B

42474 4MT^3
42647 4MT^3
42718 5MT^1
42723 5MT^1
42753 5MT^1
42755 5MT^1
42819 5MT^1
42838 5MT^1
42860 5MT^1
42901 5MT^1
44781 5MT^3
44782 5MT^3
44823 5MT^3
44928 5MT^3
44929 5MT^3
44987 5MT^3
45103 5MT^3
45195 5MT^3
45261 5MT^3
45337 5MT^3
45338 5MT^3
45590 6P5F^2
45654 6P5F^2
45664 6P5F^2
45716 6P5F^2
47230 3F^5
47428 3F^6
47578 3F^6
47579 3F^6
47631 3F^6
51232 0F^4
51237 0F^4
90110 WD^1
90142 WD^1
90292 WD^1
90306 WD^1
90324 WD^1
90354 WD^1
90359 WD^1
90372 WD^1
90546 WD^1
90558 WD^1
90564 WD^1
90626 WD^1
90632 WD^1

1966 9J

44781 5MT^3
44782 5MT^3
44817 5MT^3
44928 5MT^3
44929 5MT^3
44987 5MT^3
45062 5MT^3
45096 5MT^3
45368 5MT^3
45424 5MT^3
47202 3F^5
48011 8F
48026 8F
48164 8F
48224 8F
48250 8F
48397 8F
48521 8F
48536 8F
48539 8F
48708 8F
48743 8F

Aintree

1948 23B

44220 4F^2
44462 4F^2
44481 4F^2
44541 4F^2
48385 8F
48461 8F
48469 8F
48706 8F
48707 8F
49521 7F^4
49535 7F^4
49564 7F^4
49566 7F^4
49567 7F^4
49571 7F^4
49581 7F^4
49586 7F^4
49587 7F^4
49592 7F^4
49595 7F^4
49597 7F^4
49613 7F^4
50648 2P^8
50655 2P^8
50660 2P^8
51343 2F^2
51413 2F^2
51460 2F^2
51462 2F^2
51475 2F^2
51530 2F^2
51544 1F^3
52094 3F^7
52112 3F^7
52179 3F^7
52196 3F^7
52218 3F^7
52328 3F^7
52333 3F^7
52337 3F^7
52362 3F^7
52379 3F^7
52390 3F^7
52401 3F^7
52405 3F^7
52456 3F^7
52527 3F^7
52557 3F^9
52582 3F^9
52782 6F^3
52856 7F^5
52857 7F^5
52870 7F^5
52877 7F^5
52910 7F^5
52935 7F^5
52956 7F^5
52962 7F^5
52971 7F^5

1951 27B

42726 5MT^1
42727 5MT^1
42728 5MT^1
48515 8F
48523 8F
48713 8F
49503 7F^4
49505 7F^4
49506 7F^4
49510 7F^4
49515 7F^4
49523 7F^4
49524 7F^4
49545 7F^4
49547 7F^4
49552 7F^4
49554 7F^4
49563 7F^4
49566 7F^4
49571 7F^4
49582 7F^4
49586 7F^4
49589 7F^4
49592 7F^4
49595 7F^4
49600 7F^4
49603 7F^4
49617 7F^4
49623 7F^4
49624 7F^4
49631 7F^4
49640 7F^4
49671 7F^4
49672 7F^4
50648 2P^8
50655 2P^8
51343 2F^2
51413 2F^2
51460 2F^2
51462 2F^2
51530 2F^2
51544 1F^3
52093 3F^7
52112 3F^7
52179 3F^7
52196 3F^7
52218 3F^7
52244 3F^7
52312 3F^7
52362 3F^7
52381 3F^7
52405 3F^7
52412 3F^7
52557 3F^9

1954 27B

41102 4P^1
41186 4P^1
41187 4P^1
41188 4P^1
41283 2MT^1
41284 2MT^1
42726 5MT^1
42727 5MT^1
42728 5MT^1
42732 5MT^1
49503 7F^4
49505 7F^4
49515 7F^4
49545 7F^4
49547 7F^4
49552 7F^4
49554 7F^4
49566 7F^4
49582 7F^4
49586 7F^4
49620 7F^4
49637 7F^4
49638 7F^4
49640 7F^4
49659 7F^4
49664 7F^4
49672 7F^4
51343 2F^2
51413 2F^2
51460 2F^2
51462 2F^2
51530 2F^2
51535 1F^3
51537 1F^3
51544 1F^3
52135 3F^7
52136 3F^7
52171 3F^7
52258 3F^7
52278 3F^7
52299 3F^7
52311 3F^7
52378 3F^7
52379 3F^7
52381 3F^7
52412 3F^7
52416 3F^7
90216 WD^1
90278 WD^1
90282 WD^1
90687 WD^1

1957 27B

46405 2MT^2
46412 2MT^2
46439 2MT^2
49545 7F^4
49547 7F^4
49566 7F^4
49582 7F^4
49586 7F^4
49640 7F^4
49659 7F^4
49664 7F^4
49672 7F^4
51343 2F^2
51397 2F^2
51413 2F^2
51537 1F^3
52135 3F^7
52136 3F^7
52171 3F^7
52311 3F^7
52378 3F^7
52379 3F^7
52412 3F^7
78043 2MT^1
90101 WD^1
90107 WD^1
90141 WD^1
90164 WD^1
90204 WD^1
90216 WD^1
90234 WD^1
90278 WD^1
90282 WD^1
90283 WD^1
90343 WD^1
90375 WD^1
90381 WD^1
90416 WD^1
90527 WD^1
90535 WD^1
90643 WD^1
90675 WD^1
90687 WD^1
90712 WD^1
90724 WD^1

1960 27B

42711 5MT^1
42721 5MT^1
42727 5MT^1
42845 5MT^1
42864 5MT^1
42878 5MT^1
46405 2MT^2
46412 2MT^2
46439 2MT^2
47259 3F^5
47305 3F^6
47425 3F^6
49668 7F^4
51537 1F^3
52171 3F^7
52260 3F^7
52311 3F^7
52378 3F^7
90101 WD^1
90107 WD^1
90164 WD^1
90204 WD^1
90216 WD^1
90245 WD^1
90278 WD^1
90282 WD^1
90283 WD^1
90316 WD^1
90327 WD^1
90343 WD^1
90375 WD^1
90381 WD^1
90416 WD^1
90527 WD^1
90535 WD^1
90552 WD^1
90643 WD^1
90687 WD^1
90712 WD^1
90724 WD^1

1963 27B

42727 5MT^1
42730 5MT^1
42845 5MT^1
42878 5MT^1
44692 5MT^3
44729 5MT^3
44887 5MT^3
45061 5MT^3
45210 5MT^3
45228 5MT^3
47305 3F^6
47480 3F^6
47512 3F^6
47655 3F^6
78040 2MT^1
78043 2MT^1
78044 2MT^1
78060 2MT^1
90101 WD^1
90107 WD^1
90204 WD^1
90216 WD^1
90245 WD^1
90282 WD^1
90283 WD^1
90343 WD^1
90381 WD^1
90416 WD^1
90527 WD^1
90535 WD^1
90552 WD^1
90599 WD^1
90643 WD^1
90687 WD^1
90712 WD^1

1966 8L

44910 5MT^3
45147 5MT^3
45330 5MT^3
46439 2MT^2
46500 2MT^2
46502 2MT^2
46523 2MT^2
47279 3F^6
47289 3F^6
47327 3F^6
47367 3F^6
47453 3F^6
47566 3F^6
48017 8F
48050 8F
48108 8F
48139 8F
48268 8F
48301 8F
48340 8F
48363 8F
48421 8F
48605 8F
48648 8F
48676 8F
75043 4MT^1
75061 4MT^1
75064 4MT^1

Alnmouth

1948 ALN

62347 D20
62351 D20
62352 D20
62362 D20
62377 D20
62380 D20
62396 D20
64815 J39
64868 J39
64924 J39
65099 J21

1951 52D sub

62344 D20
62349 D20
62351 D20
62352 D20
62354 D20
62357 D20
62358 D20
62360 D20
62362 D20
62365 D20
62371 D20
62380 D20
62387 D20
64815 J39
64868 J39
64924 J39

1954 52D sub

62349 D20
62351 D20
62352 D20
62355 D20
62358 D20
62380 D20
62383 D20
62396 D20
64815 J39
64868 J39
64924 J39

1957 52D sub

62375 D20
62383 D20
64868 J39
64897 J39
64924 J39

1960 52D sub

64868 J39
64897 J39
64924 J39
64929 J39
64949 J39

1963 52D sub

61019 B1
61022 B1
62006 K1
62011 K1
62012 K1
62021 K1
62023 K1
62025 K1
62030 K1

1966 52D sub

62006 K1
62011 K1
62021 K1
62023 K1
62025 K1
62050 K1

Alsager

1948 5E

42348 4MT^2
42447 4MT^3
42471 4MT^3
42611 4MT^3
44063 4F^2
44301 4F^2
44384 4F^2
44450 4F^2
44452 4F^2
44494 4F^2
44595 4F^2
47392 3F^6
47595 3F^6
47661 3F^6
47662 3F^6
49198 7F^2

1951 5E

42447 4MT^3
42471 4MT^3
42611 4MT^3
44063 4F^2
44126 4F^2
44300 4F^2
44342 4F^2
44359 4F^2
44386 4F^2
44450 4F^2
44452 4F^2
44453 4F^2
44595 4F^2
47445 3F^6
47595 3F^6
47602 3F^6
47608 3F^6
47616 3F^6

1954 5E

42247 4MT^1
42471 4MT^3
42611 4MT^3
44063 4F^2
44079 4F^2
44125 4F^2
44126 4F^2
44300 4F^2
44342 4F^2
44386 4F^2
44450 4F^2
44453 4F^2
44503 4F^2
47445 3F^6
47595 3F^6
47598 3F^6
47608 3F^6
47633 3F^6

1957 5E

42247 4MT^1
42471 4MT^3
42611 4MT^3
44063 4F^2
44079 4F^2
44125 4F^2
44342 4F^2
44354 4F^2
44386 4F^2
44450 4F^2
44453 4F^2
44503 4F^2
47445 3F^6
47595 3F^6
47598 3F^6
47608 3F^6
47633 3F^6

1960 5E

43973 4F^1
44061 4F^2
44063 4F^2
44067 4F^2
44079 4F^2
44125 4F^2
44342 4F^2
44349 4F^2
44352 4F^2
44354 4F^2
44386 4F^2
44405 4F^2
44450 4F^2
44453 4F^2
44503 4F^2
47445 3F^6
47595 3F^6
47598 3F^6
47606 3F^6
47633 3F^6

Alston

1948 ALS

65100 J21
67315 G5

1951 52C sub

64851 J39
67315 G5

1954 52C sub

67315 G5

Annesley

1948 ANN

61895 K3
61974 K3
61975 K3
61976 K3
61977 K3
61979 K3
61980 K3
63000 O7
63002 O7
63010 O7
63014 O7
63026 O7
63079 O7
63571 O4
63575 O4
63580 O4
63582 O4
63589 O4
63596 O4
63614 O4
63618 O4
63631 O4
63633 O4
63635 O4
63638 O4
63662 O4
63674 O4
63681 O4
63685 O4
63694 O4
63699 O4
63700 O4
63706 O4
63716 O4
63720 O4
63722 O4
63723 O4
63735 O4
63739 O4
63742 O4
63743 O4
63748 O4
63756 O4
63759 O4
63761 O4
63762 O4
63767 O4
63794 O4
63799 O4
63801 O4
63804 O4
63805 O4
63809 O4
63829 O4
63841 O4
63851 O4
63853 O4
63859 O4
63862 O4
63873 O4
63876 O4
63893 O4
63894 O4
63899 O4
63912 O4
64292 J11
64294 J11
64300 J11
64318 J11
64354 J11
64365 J11
64370 J11
64375 J11
64386 J11
64409 J11
64431 J11
67105 F2
67107 F2
68927 J50
68929 J50
68935 J50
68972 J50
68975 J50
68976 J50

1951 38B

61063 B1
61066 B1
61209 B1
61943 K3
61974 K3
61975 K3
61976 K3
61977 K3
61979 K3
61980 K3
63571 O1
63578 O1
63579 O1
63589 O1
63590 O1
63591 O1
63592 O1
63594 O1
63596 O1
63610 O1
63619 O1
63630 O1
63639 O4
63646 O1
63650 O1
63652 O1
63663 O1
63670 O1
63674 O4
63678 O1
63687 O1
63689 O1
63711 O1
63725 O1
63746 O1
63752 O1
63768 O1
63773 O1
63777 O1
63780 O1
63784 O1
63786 O1
63789 O1
63792 O1
63795 O1
63796 O1
63798 O4
63803 O1
63806 O1
63808 O1
63817 O1
63838 O1
63851 O4
63854 O1
63863 O1
63865 O1
63867 O1
63868 O1
63869 O1
63872 O1
63879 O1
63886 O1
63887 O1
63890 O1
63901 O1
64292 J11
64300 J11
64318 J11
64354 J11
64361 J11
64370 J11
64431 J11
65494 J5
67363 C12
67387 C12
68927 J50
68929 J50
68975 J50
68976 J50

1954 38B

61063 B1
61066 B1
61209 B1
61974 K3
61975 K3
61980 K3
63571 O1
63578 O1
63579 O1
63589 O1
63590 O1
63591 O1
63592 O1
63594 O1
63596 O1
63610 O1
63619 O1
63630 O1
63646 O1
63650 O1
63652 O1
63663 O1
63670 O1
63676 O1
63678 O1
63687 O1
63689 O1
63711 O1
63725 O1
63740 O1
63746 O1
63751 O4
63752 O1
63768 O1
63773 O1
63777 O1
63780 O1
63784 O1
63786 O1
63789 O1
63792 O1
63795 O1
63796 O1
63803 O1
63806 O1
63808 O1
63817 O1
63838 O1
63854 O1
63863 O1
63865 O1
63867 O1
63868 O1
63869 O1
63872 O1
63879 O1
63886 O1
63887 O1
63890 O1
63901 O1
64292 J11
64300 J11
64318 J11
64354 J11
64361 J11
64370 J11
64406 J11
64431 J11
67363 C12
68896 J50
68927 J50
68975 J50
68976 J50
69651 N7
69691 N7
69695 N7

1957 38B

61856 K3
61975 K3
61980 K3
63571 O1
63578 O1
63579 O1
63589 O1
63590 O1
63591 O1
63592 O1
63594 O1
63596 O1
63610 O1
63619 O1
63630 O1
63646 O1
63650 O1
63652 O1
63663 O1
63670 O1
63676 O1
63678 O1
63687 O1
63689 O1
63711 O1
63740 O1
63746 O1
63752 O1
63768 O1
63773 O1
63777 O1
63780 O1
63784 O1
63786 O1
63789 O1
63792 O1
63795 O1
63796 O1
63803 O1
63806 O1
63808 O1
63817 O1
63838 O1
63854 O1
63863 O1
63865 O1
63867 O1
63868 O1
63869 O1
63872 O1
63879 O1
63886 O1
63887 O1
63890 O1
63901 O1
64318 J11
64324 J11
64354 J11
64364 J11
64386 J11
64406 J11
68896 J50
68976 J50
69809 A5
69818 A5
69825 A5

1960 16D

41320 2MT^1
42333 4MT^2
42339 4MT^2
42361 4MT^2
42769 5MT^1
42784 5MT^1
42847 5MT^1
42872 5MT^1
42897 5MT^1
63578 O1
63591 O1
63610 O1
63676 O1
63689 O1
63711 O1
63740 O1
63752 O1
63777 O1
63789 O1
63792 O1
63806 O1
63808 O1
63817 O1
63838 O1
63854 O1
63865 O1
63867 O1
63869 O1
63886 O1
63901 O1
64375 J11
64420 J11
64739 J39
64798 J39
64955 J39
92010 9F
92011 9F
92012 9F
92013 9F
92014 9F
92030 9F
92031 9F
92032 9F
92033 9F
92043 9F
92067 9F
92068 9F
92069 9F
92070 9F
92071 9F
92072 9F
92073 9F
92074 9F
92075 9F
92076 9F
92087 9F
92088 9F
92089 9F
92090 9F
92091 9F
92092 9F
92093 9F
92094 9F
92095 9F
92096 9F

1963 16D

44665 5MT^3
44717 5MT^3
44932 5MT^3
45116 5MT^3
45215 5MT^3
45217 5MT^3
45234 5MT^3
45267 5MT^3
45444 5MT^3
45450 5MT^3
45626 6P5F^2
46112 7P^{3}R
46122 7P^{3}R
46126 7P^{3}R
46143 7P^{3}R
46158 7P^{3}R
48002 8F
48007 8F
48011 8F
48024 8F
48057 8F
48064 8F
48079 8F
48099 8F
48117 8F
48141 8F
48142 8F
48168 8F
48293 8F
48304 8F
48324 8F
48333 8F
48378 8F
48615 8F
48700 8F
48770 8F
84006 2MT^2
84007 2MT^2
84027 2MT^2
92010 9F
92011 9F
92012 9F
92013 9F
92014 9F
92030 9F
92031 9F
92032 9F
92033 9F
92043 9F
92057 9F
92067 9F
92068 9F
92069 9F
92071 9F
92072 9F
92073 9F
92074 9F
92075 9F
92076 9F
92087 9F
92088 9F
92089 9F
92090 9F
92091 9F
92092 9F
92093 9F
92094 9F
92095 9F
92096 9F

1966 16B

44659 5MT^3
44665 5MT^3
44811 5MT^3
44825 5MT^3
44830 5MT^3
44835 5MT^3
44839 5MT^3
44847 5MT^3
44848 5MT^3
44920 5MT^3
44941 5MT^3
44984 5MT^3
45190 5MT^3
45267 5MT^3
45333 5MT^3
45406 5MT^3
45464 5MT^3
48000 8F
48060 8F
48107 8F
48132 8F
48137 8F
48142 8F
48167 8F
48170 8F
48180 8F
48192 8F
48193 8F
48197 8F
48212 8F
48258 8F
48279 8F
48282 8F
48313 8F
48315 8F
48342 8F
48361 8F
48380 8F

48382 8F
48384 8F
48388 8F
48393 8F
48414 8F
48432 8F
48507 8F
48510 8F
48552 8F
48614 8F
48617 8F
48645 8F
48687 8F
48696 8F
48698 8F
48699 8F
48750 8F

Ardrossan

1948 30C
40578 2P[3]
40579 2P[3]
40606 2P[3]
40607 2P[3]
40608 2P[3]
40609 2P[3]
40624 2P[3]
40625 2P[3]
40626 2P[3]
40667 2P[3]
40668 2P[3]
40669 2P[3]
42209 4MT[1]
42210 4MT[1]
42211 4MT[1]
42212 4MT[1]
56259 3F[10]
56279 3F[10]
56282 3F[10]
56311 3F[10]
56364 3F[10]
57263 2F[5]
57274 2F[5]
57276 2F[5]
57282 2F[5]
57304 2F[5]
57348 2F[5]
57355 2F[5]
57356 2F[5]
57357 2F[5]
57577 3F[12]
57579 3F[12]
57590 3F[12]
57627 3F[12]
57669 3F[14]
57673 3F[14]

1951 67D
40578 2P[3]
40579 2P[3]
40606 2P[3]
40607 2P[3]
40608 2P[3]
40609 2P[3]
40624 2P[3]
40625 2P[3]
40626 2P[3]
40667 2P[3]
40668 2P[3]
40669 2P[3]
42209 4MT[1]
42210 4MT[1]
42211 4MT[1]
42212 4MT[1]
56259 3F[10]
56279 3F[10]
56282 3F[10]
56311 3F[10]
56364 3F[10]
57263 2F[5]
57274 2F[5]
57276 2F[5]
57282 2F[5]
57348 2F[5]
57355 2F[5]
57356 2F[5]
57357 2F[5]
57577 3F[12]
57579 3F[12]
57590 3F[12]
57627 3F[12]
57669 3F[14]
57673 3F[14]

1954 67D
40578 2P[3]
40579 2P[3]
40606 2P[3]
40607 2P[3]
40608 2P[3]
40609 2P[3]
40624 2P[3]
40625 2P[3]
40626 2P[3]
40667 2P[3]
40668 2P[3]
40669 2P[3]
42209 4MT[1]
42210 4MT[1]
42211 4MT[1]
42212 4MT[1]
42742 5MT[1]
42911 5MT[1]
56259 3F[10]
56279 3F[10]
56282 3F[10]
56311 3F[10]
56364 3F[10]
57263 2F[5]
57274 2F[5]
57276 2F[5]
57282 2F[5]
57348 2F[5]
57355 2F[5]
57356 2F[5]
57357 2F[5]
57577 3F[12]
57590 3F[12]
57627 3F[12]
57669 3F[14]
57673 3F[14]

1957 67D
40578 2P[3]
40579 2P[3]
40606 2P[3]
40607 2P[3]
40608 2P[3]
40609 2P[3]
40624 2P[3]
40625 2P[3]
40626 2P[3]
40638 2P[3]
40666 2P[3]
40667 2P[3]
40668 2P[3]
40669 2P[3]
42209 4MT[1]
42210 4MT[1]
42211 4MT[1]
42212 4MT[1]
42697 4MT[1]
42742 5MT[1]
42806 5MT[1]
42911 5MT[1]
42912 5MT[1]
56259 3F[10]
56279 3F[10]
56282 3F[10]
56311 3F[10]
57254 2F[5]
57263 2F[5]
57266 2F[5]
57274 2F[5]
57309 2F[5]
57348 2F[5]
57355 2F[5]
57356 2F[5]
57357 2F[5]
57577 3F[12]
57590 3F[12]
57627 3F[12]
57669 3F[14]
57673 3F[14]

1960 67D
40578 2P[3]
40579 2P[3]
40624 2P[3]
40625 2P[3]
40638 2P[3]
40668 2P[3]
40669 2P[3]
42124 4MT[1]
42194 4MT[1]
42209 4MT[1]
42210 4MT[1]
42212 4MT[1]
42697 4MT[1]
42742 5MT[1]
42806 5MT[1]
42911 5MT[1]
45251 5MT[3]
45456 5MT[3]
45457 5MT[3]
45490 5MT[3]
56259 3F[10]
56282 3F[10]
57254 2F[5]
57263 2F[5]
57266 2F[5]
57274 2F[5]
57309 2F[5]
57348 2F[5]
57355 2F[5]
57356 2F[5]
57357 2F[5]
57566 3F[12]
57579 3F[12]
57590 3F[12]
57627 3F[12]
57669 3F[14]
57673 3F[14]

1963 67D
42123 4MT[1]
42124 4MT[1]
42190 4MT[1]
42740 5MT[1]
42806 5MT[1]
42911 5MT[1]
45167 5MT[3]
45251 5MT[3]
45456 5MT[3]
45457 5MT[3]
45463 5MT[3]
45479 5MT[3]
57309 2F[5]
57336 2F[5]
57348 2F[5]
57566 3F[12]
57590 3F[12]
57627 3F[12]
65214 J36
65273 J36
80000 4MT[3]
90463 WD[1]

Ardsley

1948 ARD
61267 B1
61268 B1
61482 B4
61483 B4
61485 B4
61488 B4
62828 C1
62829 C1
62849 C1
63200 Q4
63205 Q4
63210 Q4
63213 Q4
63221 Q4
63223 Q4
63224 Q4
63225 Q4
63226 Q4
63231 Q4
63232 Q4
63236 Q4
63241 Q4
63683 O4
64116 J3
64119 J3
64127 J3
64129 J3
64142 J3
64174 J6
64182 J6
64208 J6
64214 J6
64267 J6
64272 J6
64277 J6
64751 J39
64754 J39
64760 J39
64796 J39
64801 J39
64806 J39
64811 J39
64825 J39
64836 J39
64896 J39
64911 J39
64979 J39
64985 J39
67104 F2
67440 C14
67441 C14
67442 C14
67443 C14
67444 C14
67445 C14
67446 C14
67449 C14
67451 C14
68766 J52
68790 J52
68848 J52
68871 J52
68872 J52
68896 J50
68900 J50
68901 J50
68903 J50
68904 J50
68907 J50
68909 J50
68910 J50
68914 J50
68915 J50
68916 J50
68917 J50
68919 J50
68921 J50
68925 J50
68930 J50
68931 J50
68938 J50
68939 J50
68947 J50
68948 J50
68949 J50
68951 J50
68960 J50
68966 J50
69452 N1
69461 N1
69473 N1

1951 37A
61031 B1
61085 B1
61096 B1
61297 B1
61309 B1
61310 B1
63202 Q4
63204 Q4
63217 Q4
63223 Q4
63225 Q4
63227 Q4
63234 Q4
63236 Q4
63240 Q4
63243 Q4
64116 J3
64119 J3
64129 J3
64142 J3
64174 J6
64182 J6
64208 J6
64214 J6
64267 J6
64272 J6
64277 J6
64749 J39
64751 J39
64754 J39
64760 J39
64796 J39
64799 J39
64801 J39
64806 J39
64811 J39
64825 J39
64836 J39
64839 J39
64840 J39
64872 J39
64896 J39
64907 J39
64911 J39
64979 J39
64985 J39
67386 C12
67440 C14
67441 C14
67443 C14
67444 C14
67445 C14
67446 C14
67451 C14
68790 J52
68848 J52
68871 J52
68872 J52
68896 J50
68900 J50
68901 J50
68903 J50
68904 J50
68907 J50
68909 J50
68910 J50
68914 J50
68915 J50
68916 J50
68919 J50
68921 J50
68930 J50
68931 J50
68938 J50
68939 J50
68947 J50
68948 J50
68949 J50
68951 J50
68966 J50
69337 N5
69452 N1
69461 N1

1954 37A
60123 A1
60130 A1
60826 V2
60846 V2
60861 V2
61110 B1
61123 B1
61131 B1
61295 B1
61297 B1
61310 B1
61382 B1
61383 B1
61385 B1
63570 O4
63588 O4
63605 O4
63633 O4
63677 O4
63691 O4
63724 O4
63823 O4
63852 O4
63857 O4
63864 O4
63885 O4
64174 J6
64182 J6
64208 J6
64262 J6
64267 J6
64271 J6
64274 J6
64720 J39
64732 J39
64749 J39
64754 J39
64757 J39
64760 J39
64796 J39
64801 J39
64806 J39
64811 J39
64820 J39
64825 J39
64831 J39
64833 J39
64836 J39
64837 J39
64839 J39
64840 J39
64872 J39
64879 J39
64911 J39
64918 J39
64966 J39
64969 J39
64972 J39
64979 J39
67443 C14
67446 C14
68790 J52
68793 J52
68837 J52
68848 J52
68857 J52
68868 J52
68871 J52
68872 J52
68875 J52
68890 J50
68900 J50
68901 J50
68902 J50
68904 J50
68909 J50
68910 J50
68914 J50
68915 J50
68916 J50
68919 J50
68935 J50
68938 J50
68939 J50
68941 J50
68947 J50
68948 J50
68951 J50
68966 J50
69431 N1
69452 N1
69456 N1
69461 N1
69463 N1
69472 N1
69484 N1

1957 56B
60123 A1
60130 A1
60846 V2
60861 V2
60884 V2
60916 V2
61011 B1
61013 B1
61110 B1
61123 B1
61131 B1
61189 B1
61295 B1
61297 B1
61310 B1
61382 B1
61383 B1
61385 B1
63570 O4
63584 O4
63588 O4
63605 O4
63633 O4
63724 O4
63823 O4
63857 O4
63864 O4
63885 O4
64182 J6
64205 J6
64208 J6
64222 J6
64268 J6
64271 J6
64274 J6
64720 J39
64732 J39
64749 J39
64754 J39
64757 J39
64760 J39
64796 J39
64806 J39
64811 J39
64820 J39
64825 J39
64831 J39
64833 J39
64836 J39
64837 J39
64839 J39
64840 J39
64872 J39
64879 J39
64918 J39
64969 J39
64979 J39
67427 C13
68837 J52
68848 J52
68857 J52
68890 J50
68900 J50
68901 J50
68902 J50
68904 J50
68909 J50
68910 J50
68914 J50
68915 J50
68916 J50
68919 J50
68935 J50
68938 J50
68939 J50
68941 J50
68947 J50
68948 J50
68951 J50
69440 N1
69452 N1
69453 N1
69472 N1
69484 N1

1960 56B
47589 3F[6]
47640 3F[6]
48075 8F
48138 8F
60861 V2
60884 V2
60916 V2
61013 B1
61023 B1
61039 B1
61110 B1
61123 B1
61295 B1
61297 B1
61310 B1
61853 K3
61856 K3
61975 K3
61980 K3
63570 O4
63584 O4
63605 O4
63633 O4
63724 O4
63823 O4
63885 O4
64182 J6
64208 J6
64222 J6
64705 J39
64720 J39
64732 J39
64749 J39
64754 J39
64757 J39
64760 J39
64796 J39
64811 J39
64820 J39
64836 J39
64839 J39
64840 J39
64879 J39
64918 J39
64969 J39
64979 J39
68834 J52
68869 J52
68875 J52
68890 J50
68892 J50
68900 J50
68901 J50
68902 J50
68914 J50
68915 J50
68916 J50
68934 J50
68935 J50
68937 J50
68941 J50
68947 J50

1963 56B
43096 4MT[5]
60036 A3
60070 A3
60077 A3
60080 A3
60092 A3
60118 A1
60131 A1
60134 A1
60843 V2
60861 V2
60884 V2
60923 V2
60952 V2
61013 B1
61017 B1
61024 B1
61030 B1
61034 B1
61061 B1
61068 B1
61110 B1
61131 B1
61173 B1
61215 B1
61218 B1
61240 B1
61259 B1
61268 B1
61291 B1
61310 B1
61388 B1
68008 J94
68011 J94
68049 J94
68062 J94
68934 J50
68935 J50
68937 J50
68965 J50
80071 4MT[3]
80073 4MT[3]
80074 4MT[3]
80075 4MT[3]
80076 4MT[3]
80077 4MT[3]
90056 WD[1]
90100 WD[1]
90126 WD[1]
90230 WD[1]
90236 WD[1]
90240 WD[1]
90361 WD[1]
90405 WD[1]
90409 WD[1]
90465 WD[1]
90481 WD[1]
90625 WD[1]
90642 WD[1]
90644 WD[1]

Ashford

1948 AFD
30801 N15
30802 N15
30803 N15
30804 N15
30805 N15
30806 N15
31010 R1[1]
31069 R1[1]
31123 O1
31147 R1[1]
31158 H
31218 C
31239 H
31261 H
31268 C
31269 H
31271 C
31274 H
31305 H
31306 H
31322 H
31339 R1[1]
31390 O1
31400 N
31401 N
31402 N
31403 N
31404 N
31426 O1
31434 O1
31477 D
31549 D
31574 D
31577 D
31589 C
31595 J
31596 J
31597 J
31598 J
31599 J
31711 C
31721 C
31748 D
31770 L
31771 L
31772 L
31773 L
31774 L
31775 L
31776 L
32299 D1/M
32364 D3
32365 D3
32380 D3
32388 D3
90317 WD[1]
90360 WD[1]
90641 WD[1]
90655 WD[1]

1951 74A
30801 N15
30802 N15
30803 N15
30804 N15
30805 N15
30953 Z
31010 R1[1]
31041 O1
31048 O1
31069 R1[1]
31161 H
31218 C
31239 H
31260 C
31269 H
31271 C
31274 H
31305 H
31322 H
31339 R1[1]
31370 O1
31379 O1
31400 N
31401 N
31402 N
31403 N
31404 N
31405 N
31406 N
31477 D
31513 C
31514 E
31520 H
31547 E
31572 C
31577 D
31589 C
31591 D
31595 J
31596 J
31685 S
31710 R1[2]
31711 C
31721 C
31762 L
31763 L
31764 L
31770 L
31771 L
31772 L
31773 L
31774 L
31775 L
31860 N
31861 N
32640 A1X
32644 A1X
32659 A1X
32670 A1X
32678 A1X

1954 74A
30802 N15
30803 N15
30804 N15
30805 N15
30953 Z
31010 R1[1]
31048 O1
31064 O1
31065 O1
31147 R1[1]
31218 C
31276 H
31327 H
31339 R1[1]
31370 O1
31400 N
31401 N
31402 N
31403 N
31404 N
31405 N
31406 N
31407 N
31500 H
31512 H
31513 C
31521 H
31522 H
31549 D
31572 C
31574 D
31577 D
31589 C
31711 C
31756 L1
31757 L1
31758 L1
31759 L1
31772 L
31774 L
31775 L
31776 L
31777 L
31778 L
31782 L1
32655 A1X
32670 A1X
32678 A1X
42069 4MT[1]
42073 4MT[1]
42094 4MT[1]
42095 4MT[1]
42096 4MT[1]
42097 4MT[1]
42098 4MT[1]

1957 74A
30802 N15
30803 N15
30804 N15
30805 N15
30951 Z
30952 Z
30955 Z
31005 H
31037 C
31048 O1
31064 O1
31218 C
31219 C
31221 C
31223 C
31246 D1[1]
31263 H
31276 H
31307 H
31319 H
31370 O1
31400 N
31401 N
31402 N
31403 N
31404 N
31405 N
31406 N
31407 N
31522 H
31589 C
31593 C
31727 D1[1]
31756 L1
31757 L1
31758 L1
31759 L1
31772 L
31774 L
31775 L
31782 L1
31848 N
41294 2MT[1]
41303 2MT[1]
41317 2MT[1]
42092 4MT[1]
42095 4MT[1]
42096 4MT[1]
42097 4MT[1]
42098 4MT[1]
42099 4MT[1]
42100 4MT[1]

1960 73F
30932 V
30933 V
30934 V
30935 V
30936 V
30937 V
31005 H
31218 C
31223 C
31255 C
31256 C
31263 H
31307 H
31400 N
31401 N
31402 N
31403 N
31404 N
31405 N
31406 N
31407 N
31408 N
31409 N
31589 C
31848 N
31854 N
41308 2MT[1]
41309 2MT[1]
41310 2MT[1]
41311 2MT[1]
41312 2MT[1]
41313 2MT[1]
80034 4MT[3]
80035 4MT[3]
80036 4MT[3]
80037 4MT[3]
80038 4MT[3]
80039 4MT[3]
80040 4MT[3]
80041 4MT[3]
80042 4MT[3]
84020 2MT[2]
84021 2MT[2]
84022 2MT[2]
84023 2MT[2]
84024 2MT[2]
84025 2MT[2]
84026 2MT[2]
84027 2MT[2]
84028 2MT[2]
84029 2MT[2]

Ashford Works

1963
31271 C
31280 C
31592 C

1966
DS237 USA
DS238 USA
DS239 C
DS240 C

Aston

1948 3D
42440 4MT[3]
42441 4MT[3]
42449 4MT[3]
42470 4MT[3]
42538 4MT[3]
42552 4MT[3]
42578 4MT[3]
42616 4MT[3]
42782 5MT[1]
42811 5MT[1]
42891 5MT[1]
42892 5MT[1]
42894 5MT[1]
42921 5MT[1]
42929 5MT[1]
42963 5MT[2]
42966 5MT[2]
44058 4F[2]
44077 4F[2]
44219 4F[2]
44302 4F[2]
44350 4F[2]
44490 4F[2]
44517 4F[2]
44872 5MT[3]
45051 5MT[3]
45058 5MT[3]
45132 5MT[3]
45349 5MT[3]
45390 5MT[3]
45397 5MT[3]
45446 5MT[3]
47363 3F[6]
47364 3F[6]
47365 3F[6]
47366 3F[6]
49011 6F[2]
49017 6F[2]
49309 6F[2]
49362 6F[2]
58180 2F[8]
58182 2F[8]
58185 2F[8]
58243 2F[8]
58250 2F[9]
58409 2F[11]
58415 2F[11]
58886 2F[14]
58896 2F[14]
28586 2F[11]

1951 3D
40051 3MT[1]
42441 4MT[3]
42470 4MT[3]
42538 4MT[3]
42552 4MT[3]
42578 4MT[3]
42616 4MT[3]
42658 4MT[3]
42782 5MT[1]
42921 5MT[1]
42946 5MT[2]
42947 5MT[2]
42948 5MT[2]
42951 5MT[2]
42954 5MT[2]
42957 5MT[2]
42958 5MT[2]
42963 5MT[2]
42966 5MT[2]
42974 5MT[2]
43308 3F[3]
44219 4F[2]
44302 4F[2]
44350 4F[2]
44490 4F[2]
44517 4F[2]
44872 5MT[3]
44942 5MT[3]
45051 5MT[3]
45052 5MT[3]
45058 5MT[3]
45094 5MT[3]
45322 5MT[3]
45349 5MT[3]
45397 5MT[3]
45446 5MT[3]
45448 5MT[3]
47363 3F[6]
47364 3F[6]
47365 3F[6]
47366 3F[6]
49017 6F[2]
49261 6F[2]
49370 6F[2]
58117 2F[8]
58180 2F[8]
58182 2F[8]
58185 2F[8]
58279 2F[9]
58295 2F[9]

1954 3D
40206 3MT[2]
42441 4MT[3]
42470 4MT[3]
42489 4MT[3]
42552 4MT[3]
42616 4MT[3]
42658 4MT[3]
42782 5MT[1]
42921 5MT[1]
42946 5MT[2]
42947 5MT[2]
42948 5MT[2]
42951 5MT[2]
42954 5MT[2]
42957 5MT[2]
42958 5MT[2]
42963 5MT[2]
42966 5MT[2]
42974 5MT[2]
42979 5MT[2]
43308 3F[3]
43389 3F[3]
44120 4F[2]
44219 4F[2]
44302 4F[2]
44354 4F[2]
44360 4F[2]
44517 4F[2]
44525 4F[2]
44844 5MT[3]
44872 5MT[3]
44876 5MT[3]
44897 5MT[3]
45052 5MT[3]
45058 5MT[3]
45065 5MT[3]
45094 5MT[3]
45114 5MT[3]
45322 5MT[3]
45349 5MT[3]
45370 5MT[3]
45397 5MT[3]
45418 5MT[3]
45448 5MT[3]
46427 2MT[2]
46492 2MT[2]
49089 6F[2]
49189 7F[2]
49278 7F[2]
58182 2F[8]
58295 2F[9]

1957 3D
40180 3MT[2]
40206 3MT[2]
42470 4MT[3]
42616 4MT[3]
42782 5MT[1]
42921 5MT[1]
42946 5MT[2]
42947 5MT[2]
42951 5MT[2]
42954 5MT[2]
42957 5MT[2]
42958 5MT[2]
42974 5MT[2]
42979 5MT[2]
43389 3F[3]
44120 4F[2]
44302 4F[2]
44360 4F[2]
44517 4F[2]
44844 5MT[3]
44872 5MT[3]
44876 5MT[3]
44897 5MT[3]
44942 5MT[3]
45038 5MT[3]
45052 5MT[3]
45058 5MT[3]
45065 5MT[3]
45094 5MT[3]
45114 5MT[3]
45132 5MT[3]
45231 5MT[3]
45322 5MT[3]
45349 5MT[3]
45370 5MT[3]
45397 5MT[3]
45416 5MT[3]
45418 5MT[3]
45448 5MT[3]
46427 2MT[2]
46492 2MT[2]
49186 7F[2]
49189 7F[2]
49278 7F[2]
58182 2F[8]
58288 2F[9]
58295 2F[9]

1960 3D
40180 3MT[2]
40206 3MT[2]
42470 4MT[3]
42552 4MT[3]
42658 4MT[3]
42817 5MT[1]
42920 5MT[1]
42921 5MT[1]
42929 5MT[1]
42947 5MT[2]
42951 5MT[2]
42957 5MT[2]
42974 5MT[2]
42975 5MT[2]
42979 5MT[2]
44302 4F[2]
44439 4F[2]
44492 4F[2]
44872 5MT[3]
44876 5MT[3]
44897 5MT[3]
44942 5MT[3]
45051 5MT[3]
45058 5MT[3]
45065 5MT[3]
45094 5MT[3]
45114 5MT[3]
45231 5MT[3]
45322 5MT[3]
45327 5MT[3]
45349 5MT[3]
45353 5MT[3]
45395 5MT[3]
45418 5MT[3]
45430 5MT[3]
45448 5MT[3]
46423 2MT[2]
46427 2MT[2]
46492 2MT[2]
48718 8F
48719 8F
48726 8F
48752 8F

1963 21D
44710 5MT[3]
44837 5MT[3]
44865 5MT[3]
44872 5MT[3]
44876 5MT[3]
44942 5MT[3]
45038 5MT[3]
45052 5MT[3]
45058 5MT[3]
45065 5MT[3]
45114 5MT[3]
45231 5MT[3]
45322 5MT[3]
45349 5MT[3]
45353 5MT[3]
45374 5MT[3]
45418 5MT[3]
45430 5MT[3]
45448 5MT[3]
45593 6P5F[2]
45740 6P5F[2]
46427 2MT[2]
46492 2MT[2]
48718 8F
48719 8F
48752 8F
70025 7P6F
70026 7P6F
70027 7P6F
70028 7P6F
70029 7P6F
70031 7P6F
70043 7P6F
70047 7P6F
75031 4MT[1]
75034 4MT[1]
75037 4MT[1]
75053 4MT[1]

Aviemore

1948 32B
54363 2P[9]
54379 2P[10]
54398 2P[11]
54434 3P[4]
54493 3P[6]
54764 4P[4]
54767 4P[4]
55133 2P[12]
57597 3F[12]
57634 3F[13]

1951 60B
45018 5MT[3]
54455 3P[5]
54466 3P[6]
54488 3P[6]
54493 3P[6]
55174 2P[13]
57586 3F[12]
57625 3F[12]

1954 60B
45136 5MT[3]
54455 3P[5]
54466 3P[6]
54488 3P[6]
54493 3P[6]
55174 2P[13]
57586 3F[12]

1957 60B
40151 3MT[2]
45136 5MT[3]
54466 3P[6]
54488 3P[6]
55173 2P[13]
57586 3F[12]
57632 3F[13]

1960 60B
42202 4MT[1]
42269 4MT[1]
45136 5MT[3]
54466 3P[6]
54482 3P[6]
54488 3P[6]
55173 2P[13]
57586 3F[12]
57591 3F[12]
57597 3F[12]
57632 3F[13]
78052 2MT[1]

Ayr

1948 30D
40574 2P[3]
40575 2P[3]
40590 2P[3]
40610 2P[3]
40638 2P[3]
40640 2P[3]
40647 2P[3]
40648 2P[3]
40664 2P[3]
40670 2P[3]
40908 4P[1]
41132 4P[1]
41133 4P[1]
41138 4P[1]
41155 4P[1]
41183 4P[1]
42739 5MT[1]
42805 5MT[1]
42806 5MT[1]
42808 5MT[1]
42809 5MT[1]
42879 5MT[1]
42927 5MT[1]
47182 Sentinel[1]
55132 2P[12]
55262 2P[15]
55264 2P[15]
56257 3F[10]
56272 3F[10]
56273 3F[10]
56274 3F[10]
56363 3F[10]
56367 3F[10]
57234 2F[5]
57235 2F[5]
57261 2F[5]
57262 2F[5]
57271 2F[5]
57279 2F[5]
57284 2F[5]
57295 2F[5]
57312 2F[5]
57315 2F[5]
57351 2F[5]
57354 2F[5]
57364 2F[5]
57390 2F[5]
57392 2F[5]
57569 3F[12]
57611 3F[12]
57614 3F[12]
57615 3F[12]
57616 3F[12]
57628 3F[12]
57633 3F[13]
57640 3F[13]
57644 3F[13]
57684 3F[14]
57697 3F[15]

1951 67C
40574 2P[3]
40575 2P[3]
40590 2P[3]
40610 2P[3]
40638 2P[3]
40640 2P[3]
40647 2P[3]
40648 2P[3]
40664 2P[3]
40670 2P[3]
40908 4P[1]
40920 4P[1]
41132 4P[1]
41133 4P[1]
41138 4P[1]
41155 4P[1]
41183 4P[1]
42131 4MT[1]
42202 4MT[1]
42739 5MT[1]
42805 5MT[1]
42806 5MT[1]
42808 5MT[1]
42809 5MT[1]
42879 5MT[1]
42927 5MT[1]
47182 Sentinel[1]
55132 2P[12]
55240 2P[14]
55262 2P[15]
55264 2P[15]
56257 3F[10]
56272 3F[10]
56273 3F[10]
56274 3F[10]
56363 3F[10]
56367 3F[10]
57234 2F[5]
57235 2F[5]
57262 2F[5]
57279 2F[5]
57284 2F[5]
57295 2F[5]
57312 2F[5]
57315 2F[5]
57354 2F[5]
57364 2F[5]
57392 2F[5]
57569 3F[12]
57594 3F[12]
57611 3F[12]
57614 3F[12]
57615 3F[12]
57628 3F[12]
57633 3F[13]
57640 3F[13]
57644 3F[13]
57658 3F[14]
57684 3F[14]
57697 3F[15]

1954 67C
40574 2P[3]
40575 2P[3]
40590 2P[3]
40610 2P[3]
40638 2P[3]
40640 2P[3]
40647 2P[3]
40648 2P[3]
40664 2P[3]
40670 2P[3]
40920 4P[1]
41132 4P[1]
41138 4P[1]
41155 4P[1]
41183 4P[1]
42131 4MT[1]
42195 4MT[1]
42196 4MT[1]
42197 4MT[1]
42201 4MT[1]
42202 4MT[1]
42739 5MT[1]
42805 5MT[1]
42808 5MT[1]
42809 5MT[1]
42879 5MT[1]
42927 5MT[1]
45047 5MT[3]
45049 5MT[3]
47182 Sentinel[1]
55240 2P[14]
55262 2P[15]
56257 3F[10]
56272 3F[10]
56273 3F[10]
56274 3F[10]
56363 3F[10]
57234 2F[5]
57235 2F[5]
57262 2F[5]
57279 2F[5]
57284 2F[5]
57295 2F[5]
57315 2F[5]
57354 2F[5]
57364 2F[5]
57392 2F[5]
57569 3F[12]
57611 3F[12]
57614 3F[12]
57615 3F[12]
57628 3F[12]
57633 3F[13]
57640 3F[13]
57644 3F[13]
57658 3F[14]
57684 3F[14]
90319 WD[1]
90505 WD[1]

1957 67C
40574 2P[3]
40575 2P[3]
40590 2P[3]
40610 2P[3]
40640 2P[3]
40664 2P[3]
40670 2P[3]
42131 4MT[1]
42194 4MT[1]
42195 4MT[1]
42196 4MT[1]
42197 4MT[1]
42201 4MT[1]
42202 4MT[1]
42739 5MT[1]
42745 5MT[1]
42805 5MT[1]
42808 5MT[1]
42809 5MT[1]
42879 5MT[1]
42910 5MT[1]
42914 5MT[1]
42916 5MT[1]
42917 5MT[1]
42927 5MT[1]
44323 4F[2]
44330 4F[2]
44331 4F[2]
55231 2P[13]
55240 2P[14]
55262 2P[15]
56257 3F[10]
56272 3F[10]
56274 3F[10]
56363 3F[10]
57234 2F[5]
57262 2F[5]
57279 2F[5]
57284 2F[5]
57295 2F[5]
57354 2F[5]
57364 2F[5]
57392 2F[5]
57569 3F[12]
57611 3F[12]
57615 3F[12]
57628 3F[12]
57633 3F[13]
57640 3F[13]
57644 3F[13]
57658 3F[14]
57684 3F[14]
68118 Y9
68138 Y1
90319 WD[1]
90505 WD[1]

1960 67C
40640 2P[3]
40664 2P[3]
42122 4MT[1]
42196 4MT[1]
42745 5MT[1]
42800 5MT[1]
42801 5MT[1]
42805 5MT[1]
42808 5MT[1]
42809 5MT[1]
42879 5MT[1]
42910 5MT[1]
42912 5MT[1]
42914 5MT[1]
42916 5MT[1]
42917 5MT[1]
42927 5MT[1]
44323 4F[2]
44329 4F[2]
44331 4F[2]
45160 5MT[3]
45194 5MT[3]
55231 2P[13]
55262 2P[15]
56232 3F[10]
56363 3F[10]
56372 3F[10]
57262 2F[5]
57364 2F[5]
57392 2F[5]
57569 3F[12]
57580 3F[12]
57596 3F[12]
57611 3F[12]
57614 3F[12]
57615 3F[12]
57628 3F[12]
57633 3F[13]
57640 3F[13]
57644 3F[13]
57658 3F[14]
57684 3F[14]
90319 WD[1]
90463 WD[1]
90505 WD[1]

1963 67C
42736 5MT[1]
42737 5MT[1]
42780 5MT[1]
42800 5MT[1]
42801 5MT[1]
42803 5MT[1]
42805 5MT[1]
42910 5MT[1]
42912 5MT[1]
42916 5MT[1]
42917 5MT[1]
44977 5MT[3]
45160 5MT[3]
45164 5MT[3]
45194 5MT[3]
45384 5MT[3]
45460 5MT[3]
45486 5MT[3]
45490 5MT[3]
45497 5MT[3]
64541 J37
64626 J37
76096 4MT[2]
76097 4MT[2]
76099 4MT[2]
78026 2MT[1]
90319 WD[1]

1966 67C
42702 5MT[1]
42737 5MT[1]
42740 5MT[1]
42789 5MT[1]
42801 5MT[1]
42803 5MT[1]
42861 5MT[1]
42863 5MT[1]
42908 5MT[1]
42909 5MT[1]
42913 5MT[1]
42917 5MT[1]
42919 5MT[1]
44724 5MT[3]
44788 5MT[3]
44974 5MT[3]
44977 5MT[3]
45016 5MT[3]
45160 5MT[3]
45161 5MT[3]
45164 5MT[3]
45167 5MT[3]
45177 5MT[3]
45365 5MT[3]
45423 5MT[3]
45467 5MT[3]
45474 5MT[3]
46460 2MT[2]
76001 4MT[2]
76096 4MT[2]

Bacup

1948 26E
40580 2P[3]
40587 2P[3]
40681 2P[3]
40691 2P[3]
42649 4MT[3]
42650 4MT[3]
42651 4MT[3]
47577 3F[6]
47580 3F[6]
47582 3F[6]
50651 2P[8]
50652 2P[8]
52299 3F[7]
52388 3F[7]
52440 3F[7]
52442 3F[7]
52445 3F[7]

1951 26E
42619 4MT[3]
42620 4MT[3]
42649 4MT[3]
42650 4MT[3]
42651 4MT[3]
50650 2P[8]
50651 2P[8]
50652 2P[8]
50656 2P[8]
52299 3F[7]
52416 3F[7]
52440 3F[7]
52443 3F[7]

1954 26E
42619 4MT[3]
42620 4MT[3]
42649 4MT[3]
42650 4MT[3]
42651 4MT[3]
50647 2P[8]
50829 2P[8]
52443 3F[7]
52549 3F[9]

Balloch

1951 65I
65227 J36
65315 J36
65339 J36
67601 V1

1954 65I
65227 J36
65315 J36
65339 J36
67601 V1

1957 65I
65227 J36
65315 J36
65339 J36
67601 V1

1960 65I
65315 J36
65339 J36
67601 V1

Banbury

1948 BAN
1458 1400
1473 1400
2065 2021
2256 2251
2295 2251
2408 2301
2612 2600
2643 2600
2805 2800
2816 2800
2869 2800
2871 2800
2874 2800
2878 2800
2882 2800
2885 2884
2898 2884
2899 2884
2981 2900
3216 2251
3630 5700
3694 5700
3751 5700
3802 2884
3803 2884
3819 2884
3821 2884
3825 2884
3827 2884
3829 2884
3861 2884
4631 5700
4646 5700
4909 4900
5302 4300
5317 4300
5324 4300
5349 4300
5361 4300
5373 4300
5404 5400
5407 5400
5424 5400
5724 5700
5736 5700
5930 4900
5954 4900
5967 4900
5991 4900
5992 4900
6390 4300
6696 5600
6803 6800
6816 6800
6832 6800
6835 6800
6839 6800
6841 6800
6849 6800
6854 6800
6906 4900
6929 4900
6979 6959
7763 5700
7800 7800
7805 7800
7806 7800
7811 7800
8729 5700
8787 5700
9782 5700
90110 WD[1]
90112 WD[1]
90123 WD[1]
90284 WD[1]
90361 WD[1]
90364 WD[1]
90396 WD[1]

1951 84C
1401 1400
2256 2251
2295 2251
2805 2800
2816 2800
2847 2800
2853 2800
2863 2800
2883 2800
2886 2884
2897 2884
2898 2884
2899 2884
2981 2900
3020 ROD
3043 ROD
3216 2251
3218 2251
3630 5700
3694 5700
3802 2884
3819 2884
3820 2884
3829 2884
3831 2884
3849 2884
3861 2884
3863 2884
3865 2884
4149 5101
4631 5700
4646 5700
4918 4900
4960 4900
4980 4900
5317 4300
5324 4300
5332 4300
5361 4300
5391 4300
5404 5400
5407 5400
5417 5400
5424 5400
5724 5700
5930 4900
5967 4900
6342 4300
6354 4300
6390 4300
6418 6400
6696 5600
6803 6800
6816 6800
6819 6800
6835 6800
6839 6800
6854 6800
6901 4900
6906 4900
6929 4900
6979 6959
7763 5700
7800 7800
7811 7800
7823 7800
8400 9400
8405 9400
8407 9400
8459 9400
8729 5700
8787 5700
9426 9400
9782 5700

1954 84C
2202 2251
2209 2251
2246 2251
2256 2251
2259 2251
2270 2251
2297 2251
2812 2800
2816 2800
2817 2800
2823 2800
2827 2800
2834 2800
2835 2800
2847 2800
2850 2800
2857 2800
2886 2884
2897 2884
3020 ROD
3694 5700
3819 2884
3831 2884
3859 2884
4102 5101
4149 5101
4631 5700
4977 4900
4980 4900
4987 4900
5170 5101
5317 4300
5332 4300
5361 4300
5399 4300
5404 5400
5407 5400
5424 5400
5724 5700
5930 4900
5947 4900
5950 4900
5954 4900
5967 4900
6839 6800
6906 4900
6929 4900
6966 6959
6976 6959
6979 6959
7315 4300
7763 5700
7823 7800
8400 9400
8405 9400
8407 9400
8452 9400
8459 9400
8787 5700
9425 9400
9426 9400
9438 9400
9449 9400
90313 WD[1]
90579 WD[1]

1957 84C
2246 2251
2256 2251
2259 2251
2270 2251
2297 2251
2812 2800
2816 2800
2822 2800
2823 2800
2847 2800
2886 2884
3646 5700
3819 2884
3829 2884
3831 2884
3859 2884
4149 5101
4942 4900
5152 5101
5170 5101
5306 4300
5332 4300
5361 4300
5379 4300
5404 5400
5407 5400
5424 5400
5930 4900
5947 4900
6331 4300
6362 4300
6387 4300
6906 4900
6929 4900
6976 6959
6979 6959
7315 4300
8452 9400
9303 9300
9312 9300
9449 9400
48412 8F
48419 8F
48471 8F
90466 WD[1]
90585 WD[1]
90716 WD[1]

1960 84C
2256 2251
2297 2251
3646 5700
3816 2884
4078 4073
4149 5101
4942 4900
4964 4900
5057 4073
5152 5101
5407 5400
5420 5400
5921 4900
5989 4900
6311 4300
6364 4300
6387 4300
6429 6400
6906 4900
6911 4900
6929 4900
6949 4900
6976 6959
6979 6959
7011 4073
7305 4300
7308 4300
7315 4300
7761 5700
7905 6959
8452 9400
8498 9400
9449 9400
90148 WD[1]
90261 WD[1]
90268 WD[1]
90313 WD[1]
90483 WD[1]
90585 WD[1]
92212 9F
92213 9F
92214 9F
92215 9F
92226 9F
92227 9F
92228 9F
92232 9F
92233 9F
92234 9F

1963 84C
1440 1400
1455 1400
2289 2251
2845 2800
2851 2800
2866 2800
2875 2800
2888 2884
3806 2884
3809 2884
3817 2884
3821 2884
3825 2884
3828 2884
3845 2884
3849 2884
3852 2884
3855 2884
3857 2884
4105 5101
4149 5101
4154 5101
4998 4900
5990 4900
6129 6100
6317 4300
6367 4300
6904 4900
6906 4900
6911 4900
6929 4900
6952 4900
6976 6959
6979 6959
7207 7200
7218 7200
7236 7200
7905 6959
7912 6959
92213 9F
92215 9F
92227 9F
92228 9F
92247 9F

1966 2D
44710 5MT[3]
44860 5MT[3]
44869 5MT[3]
44872 5MT[3]
44936 5MT[3]
44942 5MT[3]
45089 5MT[3]
45114 5MT[3]
45288 5MT[3]
45299 5MT[3]
45308 5MT[3]
45331 5MT[3]
45392 5MT[3]
45418 5MT[3]
45426 5MT[3]
45454 5MT[3]
45493 5MT[3]
70045 7P6F
70046 7P6F
70047 7P6F
70050 7P6F
70051 7P6F
70052 7P6F
70053 7P6F
70054 7P6F
73013 5MT
73014 5MT
73048 5MT
92004 9F
92013 9F
92030 9F
92067 9F
92073 9F
92074 9F
92128 9F
92129 9F
92132 9F
92203 9F
92213 9F
92218 9F
92224 9F
92227 9F
92228 9F
92234 9F
92247 9F

Bangor

1948 7B
40072 3MT[2]
40073 3MT[2]
40083 3MT[2]
40124 3MT[2]
40133 3MT[2]
41200 2MT[1]
41201 2MT[1]
42258 4MT[1]
42259 4MT[1]
42260 4MT[1]
42261 4MT[1]
42460 4MT[3]
42628 4MT[3]
42948 5MT[2]
42951 5MT[2]
42984 5MT[2]
44305 4F[2]
44445 4F[2]
46643 1P[1]
46926 2P[7]
52176 3F[7]
52230 3F[7]
52407 3F[7]
58372 2F[11]
58374 2F[11]
58412 2F[11]
58888 2F[14]
58889 2F[14]
58932 2F[14]

1951 7B
40134 3MT[2]
40143 3MT[2]
40524 2P[2]
41200 2MT[1]
41223 2MT[1]
41224 2MT[1]
41233 2MT[1]
42156 4MT[1]
42157 4MT[1]
42258 4MT[1]
42259 4MT[1]
42260 4MT[1]
42261 4MT[1]
42460 4MT[3]
42588 4MT[3]
42617 4MT[3]
42628 4MT[3]
42677 4MT[1]
44305 4F[2]
44445 4F[2]
44913 5MT[3]
45144 5MT[3]
46899 2P[7]
46906 2P[7]
52119 3F[7]
52176 3F[7]
52230 3F[7]
52269 3F[7]
52407 3F[7]
58375 2F[11]
58381 2F[11]
58903 2F[14]

1954 6H
40102 3MT[2]
41200 2MT[1]
41212 2MT[1]
41223 2MT[1]
41230 2MT[1]
41233 2MT[1]
41287 2MT[1]
42156 4MT[1]
42157 4MT[1]
42258 4MT[1]
42259 4MT[1]
42260 4MT[1]
42261 4MT[1]
42444 4MT[3]
42455 4MT[3]
42460 4MT[3]
42588 4MT[3]
42617 4MT[3]
42628 4MT[3]
44305 4F[2]
44445 4F[2]
44913 5MT[3]
45144 5MT[3]
45417 5MT[3]
52119 3F[7]
52230 3F[7]
52269 3F[7]
58375 2F[11]
58903 2F[14]

1957 6H
40003 3MT[1]
40132 3MT[2]
41200 2MT[1]
41230 2MT[1]
41233 2MT[1]
41234 2MT[1]
41239 2MT[1]
42415 4MT[2]
42416 4MT[2]
44305 4F[2]
44445 4F[2]
44913 5MT[3]
45144 5MT[3]
45417 5MT[3]
51221 0F[4]
52119 3F[7]
52230 3F[7]
52269 3F[7]
80087 4MT[3]
80088 4MT[3]
80089 4MT[3]
80090 4MT[3]
80091 4MT[3]
80094 4MT[3]
80095 4MT[3]

1960 6H
40071 3MT[2]
40132 3MT[2]
40136 3MT[2]
41200 2MT[1]
41230 2MT[1]
41233 2MT[1]
41234 2MT[1]
41237 2MT[1]
41239 2MT[1]
41244 2MT[1]
42425 4MT[3]
42487 4MT[3]
42489 4MT[3]
42544 4MT[3]
44075 4F[2]
44355 4F[2]
44913 5MT[3]
45144 5MT[3]
45417 5MT[3]
47267 3F[6]
47511 3F[6]
78058 2MT[1]
78059 2MT[1]

1963 6H
41200 2MT[1]
41226 2MT[1]
41233 2MT[1]
41234 2MT[1]
42074 4MT[1]
42075 4MT[1]
42076 4MT[1]
42198 4MT[1]
42282 4MT[1]
42283 4MT[1]
42309 4MT[2]
42353 4MT[2]
42368 4MT[2]
42446 4MT[3]
42487 4MT[3]
42489 4MT[3]
42567 4MT[3]
42601 4MT[3]
44478 4F[2]
44504 4F[2]
44913 5MT[3]
45144 5MT[3]
45247 5MT[3]
45345 5MT[3]
45417 5MT[3]
47267 3F[6]
47511 3F[6]
78034 2MT[1]
78058 2MT[1]
78059 2MT[1]

Bank Hall

1948 23A
40581 2P[3]
40583 2P[3]
40937 4P[1]
41188 4P[1]
42639 4MT[3]
42643 4MT[3]
44946 5MT[3]
44982 5MT[3]
44990 5MT[3]
45216 5MT[3]
45217 5MT[3]
45225 5MT[3]
45226 5MT[3]
45227 5MT[3]
45228 5MT[3]
45229 5MT[3]
45335 5MT[3]
45336 5MT[3]
45698 6P5F[2]
46416 2MT[2]
46417 2MT[2]
47001 0F[3]
47002 0F[3]
49674 7F[4]
51206 0F[4]
51216 0F[4]
51227 0F[4]
51229 0F[4]
51231 0F[4]
51232 0F[4]
51237 0F[4]
51246 0F[4]
51253 0F[4]
51307 2F[2]
51325 2F[2]
51371 2F[2]
51375 2F[2]
51396 2F[2]
51535 1F[3]
51536 1F[3]
51537 1F[3]
51546 1F[3]
52102 3F[7]
52450 3F[7]

1951 27A
40581 2P[3]
40582 2P[3]
40584 2P[3]
40585 2P[3]
41187 4P[1]
41193 4P[1]
44688 5MT[3]
44689 5MT[3]
44690 5MT[3]
44691 5MT[3]
44692 5MT[3]
44767 5MT[3]
44982 5MT[3]
45068 5MT[3]
45216 5MT[3]
45227 5MT[3]
45228 5MT[3]
45229 5MT[3]
45698 6P5F[2]
45717 6P5F[2]
46406 2MT[2]
46414 2MT[2]
46415 2MT[2]
46416 2MT[2]
46417 2MT[2]
47001 0F[3]
47002 0F[3]
51206 0F[4]
51216 0F[4]
51227 0F[4]
51229 0F[4]
51231 0F[4]
51232 0F[4]
51234 0F[4]
51237 0F[4]
51240 0F[4]
51246 0F[4]
51253 0F[4]
51307 2F[2]
51371 2F[2]
51375 2F[2]
51396 2F[2]
51535 1F[3]
51536 1F[3]
51537 1F[3]
51546 1F[3]

1954 27A
40581 2P[3]
40584 2P[3]
40588 2P[3]
40684 2P[3]
41193 4P[1]
44688 5MT[3]
44689 5MT[3]
44690 5MT[3]
44691 5MT[3]
44692 5MT[3]
44767 5MT[3]
45068 5MT[3]
45216 5MT[3]
45227 5MT[3]
45228 5MT[3]
45229 5MT[3]
45698 6P5F[2]
45717 6P5F[2]
45719 6P5F[2]
46406 2MT[2]
46414 2MT[2]
46416 2MT[2]
46417 2MT[2]
46435 2MT[2]
46483 2MT[2]
47001 0F[3]
47002 0F[3]
51206 0F[4]
51216 0F[4]
51227 0F[4]
51229 0F[4]
51231 0F[4]
51232 0F[4]
51234 0F[4]
51237 0F[4]
51240 0F[4]
51246 0F[4]
51253 0F[4]
51307 2F[2]
51371 2F[2]
51375 2F[2]
51396 2F[2]
51546 1F[3]

1957 27A
40166 3MT[2]
40588 2P[3]
40684 2P[3]
40937 4P[1]
41085 4P[1]
41101 4P[1]
41283 2MT[1]
41284 2MT[1]
44688 5MT[3]
44690 5MT[3]
44691 5MT[3]
44767 5MT[3]
44928 5MT[3]
45077 5MT[3]
45201 5MT[3]
45210 5MT[3]
45216 5MT[3]
45261 5MT[3]
45698 6P5F[2]
45717 6P5F[2]
45719 6P5F[2]
47001 0F[3]
47002 0F[3]
51206 0F[4]
51227 0F[4]
51229 0F[4]
51231 0F[4]
51232 0F[4]
51234 0F[4]
51237 0F[4]
51246 0F[4]
51253 0F[4]
51307 2F[2]
51371 2F[2]
51481 2F[2]
51544 1F[3]
51546 1F[3]
75045 4MT[1]
75046 4MT[1]
75047 4MT[1]
75048 4MT[1]
75049 4MT[1]
78040 2MT[1]
78041 2MT[1]
78042 2MT[1]
78044 2MT[1]
84012 2MT[2]

1960 27A
40588 2P[3]
40684 2P[3]
41206 2MT[1]
41268 2MT[1]
41269 2MT[1]
44743 5MT[3]
44744 5MT[3]
44745 5MT[3]
44767 5MT[3]
44928 5MT[3]
45210 5MT[3]
45216 5MT[3]
45517 6P5F[1]
45698 6P5F[2]
45717 6P5F[2]
45719 6P5F[2]
47001 0F[3]
47002 0F[3]
47230 3F[5]
47303 3F[6]
47480 3F[6]
47550 3F[6]
47583 3F[6]
50721 2P[8]
51206 0F[4]
51227 0F[4]
51229 0F[4]
51232 0F[4]
51237 0F[4]
51246 0F[4]
51253 0F[4]
75045 4MT[1]
75046 4MT[1]
75047 4MT[1]
75048 4MT[1]
75049 4MT[1]
78041 2MT[1]
78042 2MT[1]
78043 2MT[1]
78044 2MT[1]

1963 27A
41205 2MT[1]
41237 2MT[1]

41268 2MT[1]
45627 6P5F[2]
45657 6P5F[2]
45698 6P5F[2]
45717 6P5F[2]
45719 6P5F[2]
47001 0F[3]
47306 3F[6]
47327 3F[6]
47583 3F[6]
75045 4MT[1]
75046 4MT[1]
75047 4MT[1]
75048 4MT[1]
75049 4MT[1]
78041 2MT[1]
78042 2MT[1]

1966 8K
41211 2MT[1]
41244 2MT[1]
41304 2MT[1]
45627 6P5F[2]
46405 2MT[2]
46414 2MT[2]
46496 2MT[2]
75026 4MT[1]
75027 4MT[1]
75032 4MT[1]
75033 4MT[1]
75046 4MT[1]
75047 4MT[1]
75048 4MT[1]
75049 4MT[1]
75050 4MT[1]

Barnsley

1948 BRN
63202 Q4
63203 Q4
63204 Q4
63212 Q4
63214 Q4
63216 Q4
63219 Q4
63220 Q4
63227 Q4
63233 Q4
63235 Q4
63238 Q4
64290 J11
64343 J11
64366 J11
64391 J11
64398 J11
64399 J11
64436 J11
64448 J11
64452 J11
67409 C13
67411 C13
67434 C13
69268 N5
69277 N5
69278 N5
69285 N5
69291 N5
69303 N5
69320 N5
69325 N5
69334 N5
69345 N5
69348 N5
69355 N5
69357 N5
69365 N5
69367 N5
69368 N5

1951 36D
63201 Q4
63220 Q4
63235 Q4
63623 O4
63625 O4
63656 O4
63697 O4
63727 O4
63883 O4
63904 O4
63913 O4
64290 J11
64343 J11
64362 J11
64366 J11
64391 J11
64398 J11
64399 J11
64425 J11
64436 J11
64448 J11
64452 J11
67409 C13
67411 C13
67434 C13
69268 N5
69278 N5
69285 N5
69291 N5
69303 N5
69320 N5
69325 N5
69334 N5
69345 N5
69348 N5
69355 N5
69357 N5
69365 N5
69367 N5
69368 N5

1954 36D
63623 O4
63625 O4
63656 O4
63669 O4
63697 O4
63718 O4
63726 O4
63727 O4
63731 O4
63763 O4
63824 O4
63883 O4
63904 O4
63907 O4
63913 O4
64290 J11
64302 J11
64343 J11
64362 J11
64366 J11
64391 J11
64398 J11
64399 J11
64417 J11
64425 J11
64436 J11
64448 J11
64452 J11
67409 C13
67411 C13
67434 C13
69268 N5
69278 N5
69291 N5
69303 N5
69320 N5
69325 N5
69334 N5
69345 N5
69348 N5
69355 N5
69357 N5
69365 N5
69367 N5
69368 N5

1957 36D
63612 O4
63623 O4
63625 O4
63656 O4
63659 O4
63669 O4
63697 O4
63704 O4
63718 O4
63726 O4
63727 O4
63731 O4
63763 O4
63824 O4
63883 O4
63904 O4
63907 O4
63911 O4
63913 O4
64290 J11
64302 J11
64343 J11
64362 J11
64399 J11
64417 J11
64425 J11
64442 J11
64448 J11
64452 J11
64902 J39
67434 C13
69268 N5
69297 N5
69300 N5
69315 N5
69320 N5
69354 N5
69355 N5
69365 N5

1960 41G
63622 O4
63623 O4
63632 O4
63656 O4
63659 O4
63669 O4
63722 O4
63726 O4
63727 O4
63802 O4
63883 O4
63904 O4
63907 O4
63911 O4
63913 O4
64417 J11
64425 J11
64442 J11
64452 J11
64828 J39
64902 J39
69343 N5
69354 N5
69370 N5

Barnstaple Junction

1948 BPL
30023 M7
30036 M7
30042 M7
30044 M7
30247 M7
30250 M7
30321 M7
30670 M7
32094 E1R
32095 E1R
32096 E1R
32608 E1R
32610 E1R
32696 E1R

1951 72E
30036 M7
30042 M7
30044 M7
30247 M7
30250 M7
30321 M7
30670 M7
31842 N
32095 E1R
32096 E1R
32608 E1R
32610 E1R
32696 E1R

1954 72E
30247 M7
30250 M7
30251 M7
30252 M7
30254 M7
30255 M7
30256 M7
31843 N
32096 E1R
32608 E1R
32610 E1R
32696 E1R
41298 2MT[1]

1957 72E
30247 M7
30250 M7
30251 M7
30252 M7
30253 M7
30254 M7
30255 M7
30256 M7
30671 M7
32608 E1R
41295 2MT[1]
41296 2MT[1]
41297 2MT[1]
41298 2MT[1]

1960 72E
30033 M7
30247 M7
30251 M7
30253 M7
30254 M7
30255 M7
41294 2MT[1]
41295 2MT[1]
41297 2MT[1]
41298 2MT[1]
41314 2MT[1]

1963 72E
30251 M7
30254 M7
30670 M7
41290 2MT[1]
41294 2MT[1]
41297 2MT[1]
41298 2MT[1]
41310 2MT[1]
41312 2MT[1]
41313 2MT[1]
41314 2MT[1]

Barrow

1948 11B
40067 3MT[1]
40068 3MT[1]
42321 4MT[2]
42359 4MT[2]
42386 4MT[2]
42392 4MT[2]
42393 4MT[2]
42427 4MT[3]
42430 4MT[3]
42462 4MT[3]
42493 4MT[3]
42570 4MT[3]
42571 4MT[3]
42573 4MT[3]
42581 4MT[3]
42594 4MT[3]
42602 4MT[3]
44059 4F[2]
44120 4F[2]
44306 4F[2]
44347 4F[2]
44351 4F[2]
44361 4F[2]
44368 4F[2]
44487 4F[2]
44594 4F[2]
47287 3F[6]
47322 3F[6]
47323 3F[6]
50643 2P[8]
50644 2P[8]
58021 1P[3]
58115 2F[8]
58120 2F[8]
58324 2F[10]
58330 2F[10]
58331 2F[10]
58335 2F[10]
58337 2F[10]
58339 2F[10]
58340 2F[10]
58344 2F[10]
58354 2F[10]
58356 2F[10]
58357 2F[10]
58360 2F[10]

1951 11B
40654 2P[3]
41221 2MT[1]
42179 4MT[1]
42321 4MT[2]
42359 4MT[2]
42372 4MT[2]
42392 4MT[2]
42393 4MT[2]
42395 4MT[2]
42401 4MT[2]
42402 4MT[2]
42462 4MT[3]
42493 4MT[3]
42571 4MT[3]
42581 4MT[3]
44059 4F[2]
44086 4F[2]
44347 4F[2]
44351 4F[2]
44368 4F[2]
44387 4F[2]
44487 4F[2]
44511 4F[2]
44594 4F[2]
45046 5MT[3]
45054 5MT[3]
45291 5MT[3]
45317 5MT[3]
45383 5MT[3]
45386 5MT[3]
47287 3F[6]
47322 3F[6]
47323 3F[6]
50643 2P[8]
58115 2F[8]
58120 2F[8]
58121 2F[8]
58187 2F[8]
58199 2F[9]
58291 2F[9]
58299 2F[9]
58309 2F[9]
58335 2F[10]
58340 2F[10]
58346 2F[10]
58349 2F[10]
58350 2F[10]
58352 2F[10]
58354 2F[10]
58360 2F[10]

1954 11B
40654 2P[3]
41217 2MT[1]
41221 2MT[1]
42179 4MT[1]
42321 4MT[2]
42359 4MT[2]
42364 4MT[2]
42372 4MT[2]
42376 4MT[2]
42392 4MT[2]
42395 4MT[2]
42401 4MT[2]
42402 4MT[2]
42493 4MT[3]
42571 4MT[3]
42581 4MT[3]
44059 4F[2]
44086 4F[2]
44347 4F[2]
44351 4F[2]
44368 4F[2]
44387 4F[2]
44487 4F[2]
44511 4F[2]
44594 4F[2]
45046 5MT[3]
45141 5MT[3]
45291 5MT[3]
45317 5MT[3]
45383 5MT[3]
45386 5MT[3]
47287 3F[6]
47322 3F[6]
47323 3F[6]
58115 2F[8]
58116 2F[8]
58120 2F[8]
58121 2F[8]
58139 2F[8]
58156 2F[8]
58177 2F[8]
58187 2F[8]
58199 2F[9]
58257 2F[9]
58273 2F[9]
58287 2F[9]
58291 2F[9]
58299 2F[9]
58309 2F[9]

1957 11B
40654 2P[3]
41217 2MT[1]
41221 2MT[1]
42179 4MT[1]
42320 4MT[2]
42332 4MT[2]
42359 4MT[2]
42364 4MT[2]
42372 4MT[2]
42376 4MT[2]
42392 4MT[2]
42395 4MT[2]
42401 4MT[2]
42402 4MT[2]
42427 4MT[3]
42571 4MT[3]
42581 4MT[3]
43904 4F[1]
44086 4F[2]
44347 4F[2]
44351 4F[2]
44366 4F[2]
44368 4F[2]
44443 4F[2]
44487 4F[2]
44511 4F[2]
44594 4F[2]
45141 5MT[3]
45383 5MT[3]
45386 5MT[3]
47287 3F[6]
47322 3F[6]
47323 3F[6]
47605 3F[6]
58115 2F[8]
58116 2F[8]
58120 2F[8]
58121 2F[8]
58123 2F[8]
58156 2F[8]
58177 2F[8]
58187 2F[8]
58199 2F[9]
58217 2F[9]
58221 2F[9]
58287 2F[9]
58291 2F[9]
58293 2F[9]
58299 2F[9]

1960 11A
40695 2P[3]
42119 4MT[1]
42120 4MT[1]
42179 4MT[1]
42233 4MT[1]
42320 4MT[2]
42332 4MT[2]
42364 4MT[2]
42376 4MT[2]
42392 4MT[2]
42395 4MT[2]
42397 4MT[2]
42401 4MT[2]
42402 4MT[2]
42427 4MT[3]
42432 4MT[3]
42440 4MT[3]
42478 4MT[3]
42581 4MT[3]
42591 4MT[3]
42666 4MT[3]
44086 4F[2]
44347 4F[2]
44351 4F[2]
44366 4F[2]
44443 4F[2]
44487 4F[2]
44511 4F[2]
44537 4F[2]
44594 4F[2]
44601 4F[2]
44837 5MT[3]
45141 5MT[3]
45383 5MT[3]
45386 5MT[3]
47287 3F[6]
47322 3F[6]
47323 3F[6]
47345 3F[6]
47356 3F[6]
47373 3F[6]
47503 3F[6]
47505 3F[6]
47517 3F[6]
47518 3F[6]
47520 3F[6]
47531 3F[6]
47564 3F[6]
47605 3F[6]
47675 3F[6]
47676 3F[6]
58115 2F[8]
58116 2F[8]
58293 2F[9]

1963 12E
42119 4MT[1]
42120 4MT[1]
42179 4MT[1]
42401 4MT[2]
42432 4MT[3]
42673 4MT[3]
44186 4F[2]
44345 4F[2]
44347 4F[2]
44351 4F[2]
44367 4F[2]
44443 4F[2]
44447 4F[2]
44601 4F[2]
44882 5MT[3]
45141 5MT[3]
45258 5MT[3]
45383 5MT[3]
45445 5MT[3]
46400 2MT[2]
47287 3F[6]
47503 3F[6]
47531 3F[6]
47564 3F[6]
47675 3F[6]
58182 2F[8]
78022 2MT[1]
78023 2MT[1]
78027 2MT[1]

1966 12C
42080 4MT[1]
42134 4MT[1]
42236 4MT[1]
42610 4MT[3]
42697 4MT[1]
44311 4F[2]
44394 4F[2]
44500 4F[2]
44882 5MT[3]
45141 5MT[3]
45182 5MT[3]
45294 5MT[3]
45383 5MT[3]
47675 3F[6]

Barry

1948 BRY
57 RR[4]
58 RR[4]
59 RR[4]
213 BR[1]
231 BR[1]
248 BR[2]
261 BR[2]
262 BR[2]
263 BR[2]
265 BR[2]
267 BR[2]
268 BR[2]
270 BR[2]
271 BR[2]
272 BR[2]
274 BR[2]
275 BR[2]
276 BR[2]
277 BR[2]
286 TV[2]
306 TV[3]
312 TV[3]
316 TV[3]
322 TV[3]
345 TV[3]
361 TV[3]
372 TV[3]
377 TV[3]
379 TV[3]
382 TV[3]
386 TV[3]
387 TV[3]
388 TV[3]
389 TV[3]
394 TV[3]
783 BR[3]
784 BR[3]
1993 1901
5195 5101
5609 5600
5621 5600
5622 5600
5627 5600
5632 5600
5648 5600
5662 5600
5664 5600
5665 5600
5667 5600
5693 5600
5699 5600
6602 5600
6614 5600
6619 5600
6620 5600
6637 5600
6641 5600
6643 5600
6647 5600
6653 5600
6658 5600
6662 5600
6668 5600
6669 5600
6712 6700
6722 6700
6723 6700
6724 6700
6733 6700
6736 6700
6738 6700
6740 6700
6745 6700
6746 6700
6747 6700
6748 6700
6750 6700
6752 6700
6753 6700
6754 6700
6758 6700
9631 5700

1951 88C
57 RR[4]
58 RR[4]
59 RR[4]
240 BR[2]
263 BR[2]
267 BR[2]
270 BR[2]
271 BR[2]
274 BR[2]
276 BR[2]
306 TV[3]
312 TV[3]
322 TV[3]
361 TV[3]
372 TV[3]
373 TV[3]
379 TV[3]
382 TV[3]
387 TV[3]
388 TV[3]
389 TV[3]
394 TV[3]
1600 1600
1615 1600
1993 1901
2008 1901
4160 5101
4161 5101
4163 5101
4177 5101
4601 5700
4692 5700
5195 5101
5609 5600
5614 5600
5619 5600
5621 5600
5627 5600
5632 5600
5648 5600
5664 5600
5665 5600
5667 5600
6614 5600
6615 5600
6619 5600
6620 5600
6637 5600
6641 5600
6643 5600
6653 5600
6658 5600
6668 5600
6669 5600
6712 6700
6722 6700
6723 6700
6724 6700
6733 6700
6736 6700
6738 6700
6745 6700
6746 6700
6747 6700
6748 6700
6750 6700
6752 6700
6753 6700
6754 6700
6758 6700
6769 6700
6774 6700
6775 6700
8451 9400
8458 9400
8460 9400
8461 9400
8735 5700
9631 5700
9676 5700
9776 5700

1954 88C
303 TV[3]
306 TV[3]
312 TV[3]
357 TV[3]
361 TV[3]
372 TV[3]
373 TV[3]
375 TV[3]
382 TV[3]
387 TV[3]
388 TV[3]
389 TV[3]
390 TV[3]
393 TV[3]
394 TV[3]
1600 1600
1615 1600
4177 5101
4224 4200
4267 4200
4578 4575
4601 5700
4692 5700
5183 5101
5527 4575
5529 4575
5609 5600
5614 5600
5619 5600
5621 5600
5627 5600
5632 5600
5648 5600
5664 5600
5665 5600
5667 5600
6615 5600
6619 5600
6637 5600
6641 5600
6643 5600
6658 5600
6712 6700
6722 6700
6723 6700
6724 6700
6733 6700
6736 6700
6738 6700
6740 6700
6745 6700
6746 6700
6747 6700
6748 6700
6750 6700
6752 6700
6753 6700
6754 6700
6758 6700
6769 6700
6774 6700
6775 6700
8455 9400
8735 5700
9470 9400
9631 5700
9676 5700
82001 3MT[2]
82002 3MT[2]
82003 3MT[2]
82004 3MT[2]
82005 3MT[2]
82006 3MT[2]
82007 3MT[2]
82008 3MT[2]
82009 3MT[2]

1957 88C
1600 1600
1615 1600
4578 4575
4601 5700
4692 5700
5527 4575
5529 4575
5609 5600
5614 5600
5619 5600
5621 5600
5648 5600
5664 5600
5667 5600
6615 5600
6637 5600
6641 5600
6643 5600
6658 5600
6712 6700
6722 6700
6723 6700
6724 6700
6733 6700
6738 6700
6740 6700
6745 6700
6746 6700
6747 6700
6748 6700
6750 6700
6752 6700
6753 6700
6754 6700
6758 6700
7230 7200
7241 7200
7252 7200
8446 9400
8450 9400
8459 9400
8465 9400
8735 5700
9453 9400
9622 5700
9631 5700
9676 5700
82003 3MT[2]
82035 3MT[2]
82036 3MT[2]
82037 3MT[2]
82039 3MT[2]
82040 3MT[2]
82041 3MT[2]
82042 3MT[2]
82043 3MT[2]
82044 3MT[2]

1960 88C
3727 5700
4618 5700
4667 5700
5609 5600
5614 5600
5619 5600
5621 5600
5664 5600
5667 5600
6637 5600
6643 5600
6658 5600
6752 6700
6754 6700
6765 6700
6775 6700
7241 7200
7717 5700
7766 5700
8419 9400
8446 9400
9425 9400

1963 88C
3615 5700
3668 5700
3689 5700
3690 5700
3710 5700
3727 5700
3748 5700
4618 5700
4667 5700
5619 5600
5621 5600
5637 5600
5643 5600
5653 5600
5667 5600
5668 5600
6619 5600
6643 5600
6655 5600
6696 5600
6697 5600
7202 7200
7208 7200
7221 7200
7228 7200
7231 7200
8446 9400
8481 9400
8728 5700
9425 9400
9472 9400
9603 5700
9648 5700
9681 5700
9713 5700
9780 5700
9794 5700

Basingstoke

1948 BAS
30265 G6
30278 G6
30307 T9
30348 G6
30368 700
30407 L11
30418 L12
30426 L12
30693 700
30706 T9
30708 T9
31627 U
31629 U
31632 U
31633 U
31634 U
32327 N15X
32328 N15X
32329 N15X
32330 N15X
32331 N15X
32332 N15X
32333 N15X
32408 E6

1951 70D
30258 G6
30266 G6
30302 T9
30355 700
30368 700
30418 L12
30693 700
30712 T9
30789 N15
30790 N15
31633 U
32045 B4X
32052 B4X
32067 B4X
32327 N15X
32328 N15X
32329 N15X
32330 N15X
32331 N15X
32332 N15X
32333 N15X

1954 70D
30258 G6
30266 G6
30368 700
30705 T9
30724 T9
30745 N15
30749 N15
30753 N15
31633 U
31634 U
32327 N15X
32328 N15X
32329 N15X
32330 N15X
32331 N15X
32332 N15X
32333 N15X
32568 E5
32587 E5
32591 E5

1957 70D
30160 G6
30258 G6
30368 700
30724 T9
30749 N15
30751 N15
30753 N15
30755 N15
31633 U
31806 U
32331 N15X
75075 4MT[1]
75076 4MT[1]
75077 4MT[1]
75078 4MT[1]
75079 4MT[1]

1960 70D
30258 G6
30368 700
30456 N15
30765 N15
30794 N15
30904 V
30905 V
30908 V
31611 U
31806 U
75076 4MT[1]
75077 4MT[1]
75078 4MT[1]
75079 4MT[1]

1963 70D
31611 U
31618 U
31806 U
75065 4MT[1]
75066 4MT[1]
75076 4MT[1]
75077 4MT[1]
75078 4MT[1]
75079 4MT[1]

Bath Green Park

1948 22C
40142 3MT[2]
40505 2P[2]
40568 2P[3]
40569 2P[3]
40601 2P[3]
40696 2P[3]
40697 2P[3]
40698 2P[3]
40700 2P[3]
41078 4P[1]
41900 2P[4]
41902 2P[4]
41903 2P[4]
41904 2P[4]
43875 4F[1]
44096 4F[2]
44422 4F[2]
44523 4F[2]
44535 4F[2]
44557 4F[2]
44558 4F[2]
44559 4F[2]
44560 4F[2]
44561 4F[2]
44585 4F[2]
44826 5MT[3]
44830 5MT[3]
44945 5MT[3]
45056 5MT[3]
45440 5MT[3]
47191 Sentinel[1]
47275 3F[6]
47316 3F[6]
47465 3F[6]
47496 3F[6]
47542 3F[6]
47557 3F[6]
51202 0F[4]
53800 7F[6]
53801 7F[6]
53802 7F[6]
53803 7F[6]
53804 7F[6]
53805 7F[6]
53806 7F[6]
53807 7F[6]
53808 7F[6]
53809 7F[6]
53810 7F[6]
58079 1P[6]

1951 71G
40505 2P[2]
40568 2P[3]
40569 2P[3]
40601 2P[3]
40696 2P[3]
40697 2P[3]
40698 2P[3]
40700 2P[3]
41240 2MT[1]
41241 2MT[1]
41242 2MT[1]
41243 2MT[1]
43013 4MT[5]
43017 4MT[5]
43036 4MT[5]
43875 4F[1]
44096 4F[2]
44235 4F[2]
44355 4F[2]
44422 4F[2]
44523 4F[2]
44535 4F[2]
44557 4F[2]
44558 4F[2]
44559 4F[2]
44560 4F[2]
44561 4F[2]
44826 5MT[3]
44830 5MT[3]
44839 5MT[3]
44945 5MT[3]
45440 5MT[3]
47191 Sentinel[1]
47275 3F[6]
47316 3F[6]
47465 3F[6]
47496 3F[6]
47542 3F[6]
47557 3F[6]
51202 0F[4]
53800 7F[6]
53801 7F[6]
53802 7F[6]
53803 7F[6]
53804 7F[6]
53805 7F[6]
53806 7F[6]
53807 7F[6]
53808 7F[6]
53809 7F[6]
53810 7F[6]

1954 71G
34040 WC
34041 WC
34042 WC
40696 2P[3]
40697 2P[3]
40698 2P[3]
40700 2P[3]
41241 2MT[1]
41242 2MT[1]
41243 2MT[1]
44096 4F[2]
44355 4F[2]
44422 4F[2]
44523 4F[2]
44557 4F[2]
44558 4F[2]
44559 4F[2]
44560 4F[2]
44561 4F[2]
44917 5MT[3]
45440 5MT[3]
47190 Sentinel[1]
47191 Sentinel[1]
47275 3F[6]
47316 3F[6]
47465 3F[6]
47496 3F[6]
47542 3F[6]
47557 3F[6]
53800 7F[6]
53801 7F[6]
53802 7F[6]
53803 7F[6]
53804 7F[6]
53805 7F[6]
53806 7F[6]
53807 7F[6]
53808 7F[6]
53809 7F[6]
53810 7F[6]

1957 71G
40509 2P[2]
40601 2P[3]
40696 2P[3]
40697 2P[3]
40698 2P[3]
40700 2P[3]
41241 2MT[1]
41242 2MT[1]
41243 2MT[1]
44096 4F[2]
44355 4F[2]
44422 4F[2]
44523 4F[2]
44557 4F[2]
44558 4F[2]
44559 4F[2]
44560 4F[2]
44561 4F[2]
44917 5MT[3]
45440 5MT[3]
47190 Sentinel[1]
47191 Sentinel[1]
47275 3F[6]
47316 3F[6]
47465 3F[6]
47496 3F[6]
47542 3F[6]
47557 3F[6]
53800 7F[6]
53801 7F[6]
53802 7F[6]
53803 7F[6]
53804 7F[6]
53805 7F[6]
53806 7F[6]
53807 7F[6]
53808 7F[6]
53809 7F[6]
53810 7F[6]
73047 5MT
73049 5MT
73050 5MT
73051 5MT
73052 5MT
75070 4MT[1]
75071 4MT[1]
75072 4MT[1]

1960 82F
3742 5700
40696 2P[3]

40697 2P[3]
40698 2P[3]
40700 2P[3]
41242 2MT[1]
41243 2MT[1]
44096 4F[2]
44146 4F[2]
44422 4F[2]
44523 4F[2]
44558 4F[2]
44559 4F[2]
44560 4F[2]
44561 4F[2]
47190 Sentinel[1]
47275 3F[6]
47316 3F[6]
47465 3F[6]
47496 3F[6]
47557 3F[6]
53801 7F[6]
53802 7F[6]
53803 7F[6]
53804 7F[6]
53805 7F[6]
53806 7F[6]
53807 7F[6]
53808 7F[6]
53809 7F[6]
53810 7F[6]
58086 1P[6]
73019 5MT
73028 5MT
73047 5MT
73049 5MT
73050 5MT
73051 5MT
73052 5MT
73087 5MT
73116 5MT
75071 4MT[1]
75072 4MT[1]
75073 4MT[1]
82004 3MT[2]
82041 3MT[2]

1963 82F
3742 5700
44146 4F[2]
44411 4F[2]
44558 4F[2]
44559 4F[2]
47465 3F[6]
47496 3F[6]
47539 3F[6]
47544 3F[6]
47557 3F[6]
48468 8F
48660 8F
48737 8F
53806 7F[6]
53807 7F[6]
53808 7F[6]
53809 7F[6]
53810 7F[6]
73047 5MT
73049 5MT
73050 5MT
73051 5MT
73052 5MT
73054 5MT
82004 3MT[2]
82041 3MT[2]

1966 82F
3681 5700
3758 5700
47276 3F[6]
47506 3F[6]
48309 8F
48444 8F
48706 8F
48760 8F

Bathgate

1948 BGT
62072 D31
62439 D30
62458 D33
62463 D33
64468 J35
64491 J35
64504 J35
64510 J35
64529 J35
64534 J35
65211 J36
65225 J36
65229 J36
65230 J36
65231 J36
65234 J36
65235 J36
65248 J36
65250 J36
65254 J36
65261 J36
65265 J36
65271 J36
65276 J36
65277 J36
65278 J36
65280 J36
65282 J36
65303 J36
65314 J36
65318 J36
65327 J36
65341 J36
65342 J36
65344 J36
69142 N15
69156 N15
69157 N15
69158 N15
69159 N15
69216 N15

1951 64F
62283 D31
62439 D30
62495 D34
64468 J35
64491 J35
64504 J35
64510 J35
64529 J35
65211 J36
65225 J36
65229 J36
65230 J36
65231 J36
65234 J36
65235 J36
65248 J36
65250 J36
65254 J36
65261 J36
65265 J36
65276 J36
65277 J36
65278 J36
65280 J36
65282 J36
65303 J36
65314 J36
65318 J36
65327 J36
65341 J36
65342 J36
65344 J36
65346 J36
69142 N15
69156 N15
69158 N15
69159 N15
69216 N15

1954 64F
62439 D30
62495 D34
64468 J35
64484 J35
64491 J35
64504 J35
64510 J35
64512 J35
64529 J35
64553 J37
64583 J37
64794 J39
65211 J36
65225 J36
65229 J36
65230 J36
65234 J36
65248 J36
65250 J36
65261 J36
65265 J36
65268 J36
65276 J36
65277 J36
65280 J36
65282 J36
65303 J36
65314 J36
65318 J36
65341 J36
65342 J36
65344 J36
65346 J36
69142 N15
69156 N15
69158 N15
69159 N15
69216 N15

1957 64F
43138 4MT[5]
62439 D30
62495 D34
64468 J35
64484 J35
64491 J35
64504 J35
64510 J35
64512 J35
64529 J35
64553 J37
64583 J37
64634 J37
65211 J36
65225 J36
65229 J36
65230 J36
65234 J36
65250 J36
65259 J36
65261 J36
65265 J36
65268 J36
65276 J36
65277 J36
65282 J36
65290 J36
65318 J36
65341 J36
65342 J36
65344 J36
65346 J36
69142 N15
69156 N15
69158 N15
69159 N15
69216 N15

1960 64F
43138 4MT[5]
62495 D34
64468 J35
64491 J35
64504 J35
64510 J35
64512 J35
64529 J35
64553 J37
64583 J37
64634 J37
65229 J36
65233 J36
65261 J36
65265 J36
65268 J36
65276 J36
65282 J36
65290 J36
65318 J36
65341 J36
65342 J36
65344 J36
65346 J36
69156 N15
69159 N15
69216 N15

1963 64F
64554 J37
64569 J37
64583 J37
64634 J37
65251 J36
65261 J36
65265 J36
65267 J36
65277 J36
65282 J36
65290 J36
65309 J36
65341 J36
65346 J36

1966 64F
65243 J36
65267 J36
65282 J36
65297 J36
76104 4MT[2]
76105 4MT[2]
76111 4MT[2]
78045 2MT[1]
78046 2MT[1]
78050 2MT[1]
78052 2MT[1]

Beattock

1948 12F
55164 2P[13]
55181 2P[13]
55232 2P[13]
55237 2P[14]
55239 2P[14]
55350 4P[5]
55351 4P[5]
55352 4P[5]
55353 4P[5]
55354 4P[5]
55356 4P[5]
55359 4P[5]
55360 4P[5]
55361 4P[5]
29988 Rail Motor[2]

1951 68D
46656 1P[1]
55181 2P[13]
55220 2P[13]
55232 2P[13]
55234 2P[13]
55237 2P[14]
55239 2P[14]
55350 4P[5]
55352 4P[5]
55353 4P[5]
55359 4P[5]
55360 4P[5]
55361 4P[5]

1954 68D
40021 3MT[1]
40030 3MT[1]
42192 4MT[1]
42213 4MT[1]
42214 4MT[1]
42215 4MT[1]
55187 2P[13]
55220 2P[13]
55232 2P[13]
55234 2P[13]
55237 2P[14]
55260 2P[15]

1957 68D
42130 4MT[1]
42192 4MT[1]
42205 4MT[1]
42213 4MT[1]
42214 4MT[1]
42215 4MT[1]
42688 4MT[1]
55232 2P[13]
55234 2P[13]
55260 2P[15]
57568 3F[12]

1960 68D
42130 4MT[1]
42192 4MT[1]
42205 4MT[1]
42213 4MT[1]
42214 4MT[1]
42215 4MT[1]
42688 4MT[1]
55234 2P[13]
55260 2P[15]
57568 3F[12]

1963 66F
42192 4MT[1]
42214 4MT[1]
42688 4MT[1]
42693 4MT[1]
76090 4MT[2]
80001 4MT[3]
80002 4MT[3]
80004 4MT[3]

1966 66F
42260 4MT[1]
42693 4MT[1]
76090 4MT[2]
76098 4MT[2]
76100 4MT[2]

Bedford

1948 15D
40453 2P[2]
40551 2P[2]
40762 3P[1]
41007 4P[2]
41009 4P[2]
41013 4P[2]
41017 4P[2]
41034 4P[2]
41038 4P[2]
41042 4P[2]
41044 4P[2]
41070 4P[1]
41091 4P[1]
41209 2MT[1]
43174 3F[2]
43185 3F[2]
43222 3F[3]
43428 3F[3]
43474 3F[3]
43721 3F[3]
43766 3F[4]
43777 3F[4]
43785 3F[4]
43888 4F[1]
43910 4F[1]
43967 4F[1]
43971 4F[1]
44362 4F[2]
44582 4F[2]
47252 3F[5]
47549 3F[6]
48177 8F
58037 1P[5]
58039 1P[6]
58040 1P[6]
58045 1P[6]
58053 1P[6]
58091 1P[6]
58131 2F[8]
58149 2F[8]
58239 2F[8]
58241 2F[8]
58305 2F[9]

1951 15D
40141 3MT[2]
40165 3MT[2]
40551 2P[2]
40762 3P[1]
41007 4P[2]
41009 4P[2]
41038 4P[2]
41044 4P[2]
41056 4P[1]
41070 4P[1]
41091 4P[1]
41094 4P[1]
41198 4P[1]
41209 2MT[1]
41269 2MT[1]
41270 2MT[1]
41271 2MT[1]
41272 2MT[1]
43174 3F[2]
43222 3F[3]
43428 3F[3]
43474 3F[3]
43721 3F[3]
43766 3F[4]
43777 3F[4]
43785 3F[4]
43888 4F[1]
43910 4F[1]
43923 4F[1]
43967 4F[1]
43971 4F[1]
47223 3F[5]
47252 3F[5]
47549 3F[6]
48177 8F
58091 1P[6]
58149 2F[8]
58241 2F[8]
58305 2F[9]

1954 15D
40165 3MT[2]
40411 2P[2]
41048 4P[1]
41049 4P[1]
41054 4P[1]
41079 4P[1]
41091 4P[1]
41199 4P[1]
41269 2MT[1]
41270 2MT[1]
41271 2MT[1]
41272 2MT[1]
41329 2MT[1]
43174 3F[2]
43222 3F[3]
43428 3F[3]
43454 3F[3]
43474 3F[3]
43665 3F[3]
43721 3F[3]
43766 3F[4]
43785 3F[4]
43873 4F[1]
43888 4F[1]
43923 4F[1]
43967 4F[1]
43971 4F[1]
44043 4F[2]
47223 3F[5]
47252 3F[5]
47549 3F[6]
48177 8F
58305 2F[9]
80044 4MT[3]
80045 4MT[3]
80046 4MT[3]
80060 4MT[3]
80061 4MT[3]
84005 2MT[2]

1957 15D
40165 3MT[2]
41269 2MT[1]
41270 2MT[1]
41271 2MT[1]
41272 2MT[1]
41329 2MT[1]
43174 3F[2]
43222 3F[3]
43428 3F[3]
43474 3F[3]
43529 3F[3]
43531 3F[3]
43665 3F[3]
43721 3F[3]
43766 3F[4]
43785 3F[4]
43808 3F[4]
43829 3F[4]
43873 4F[1]
43898 4F[1]
43967 4F[1]
43971 4F[1]
44043 4F[2]
44266 4F[2]
44317 4F[2]
44984 5MT[3]
45137 5MT[3]
45139 5MT[3]
45267 5MT[3]
45290 5MT[3]
45342 5MT[3]
47264 3F[6]
47549 3F[6]
48177 8F
50646 2P[6]
58215 2F[9]
75040 4MT[1]
75041 4MT[1]
75042 4MT[1]
75043 4MT[1]
75044 4MT[1]
84005 2MT[2]

1960 14E
40012 3MT[1]
40020 3MT[1]
41224 2MT[1]
41225 2MT[1]
41271 2MT[1]
41280 2MT[1]
43261 3F[3]
43333 3F[3]
43373 3F[3]
43428 3F[3]
43449 3F[3]
43456 3F[3]
43474 3F[3]
43529 3F[3]
43565 3F[3]
43766 3F[4]
43808 3F[4]
44984 5MT[3]
45137 5MT[3]
45139 5MT[3]
45221 5MT[3]
45267 5MT[3]
45342 5MT[3]
47264 3F[6]
47279 3F[6]
47549 3F[6]
58214 2F[9]
75040 4MT[1]
75041 4MT[1]
75043 4MT[1]
75044 4MT[1]
75055 4MT[1]
84005 2MT[2]

1963 14E
42680 4MT[1]
42682 4MT[1]
42686 4MT[1]
43342 3F[3]
43453 3F[3]
43521 3F[3]
43935 4F[1]
44171 4F[2]
44203 4F[2]
44433 4F[2]
44476 4F[2]
44540 4F[2]
44578 4F[2]
44774 5MT[3]
44985 5MT[3]
45416 5MT[3]
47264 3F[6]
47279 3F[6]
47485 3F[6]
47549 3F[6]

Beeston Creosote Works

1948
10 NG[2]

1951
10 NG[2]

1954
10 NG[2]

Belle Vue

1948 19E
41690 1F[1]
41702 1F[1]
41756 1F[1]
41814 1F[1]
42765 5MT[1]
42896 5MT[1]
43361 3F[3]
43612 3F[3]
43630 3F[3]
43638 3F[3]
43723 3F[3]
43756 3F[3]
43836 4F[1]
43927 4F[1]
43952 4F[1]
43985 4F[1]
44022 4F[1]
44025 4F[1]
44040 4F[2]
44114 4F[2]
44261 4F[2]
44371 4F[2]
44459 4F[2]
44802 5MT[3]
44803 5MT[3]
44845 5MT[3]
45031 5MT[3]
45284 5MT[3]
47336 3F[6]
47440 3F[6]
48330 8F
48348 8F
48349 8F

1951 26G
41690 1F[1]
41702 1F[1]
41814 1F[1]
42675 4MT[1]
43612 3F[3]
43630 3F[3]
43638 3F[3]
43756 3F[3]
43927 4F[1]
43952 4F[1]
44019 4F[1]
44022 4F[1]
44025 4F[1]
44040 4F[2]
44114 4F[2]
44119 4F[2]
44486 4F[2]
44803 5MT[3]
44845 5MT[3]
45031 5MT[3]
45226 5MT[3]
45284 5MT[3]
45450 5MT[3]
47336 3F[6]
47440 3F[6]
48188 8F
48348 8F
48349 8F
48531 8F
48714 8F
48715 8F
51484 2F[2]

1954 26G
41702 1F[1]
41814 1F[1]
43612 3F[3]
43630 3F[3]
43638 3F[3]
43756 3F[3]
43927 4F[1]
44022 4F[1]
44025 4F[1]
44040 4F[2]
44042 4F[2]
44114 4F[2]
44119 4F[2]
44486 4F[2]
44803 5MT[3]
44845 5MT[3]
45031 5MT[3]
45284 5MT[3]
45450 5MT[3]
47336 3F[6]
47440 3F[6]
51484 2F[2]
51510 2F[2]
90122 WD[1]
90126 WD[1]
90140 WD[1]
90163 WD[1]
90197 WD[1]
90204 WD[1]
90552 WD[1]

Bescot

1948 3A
42779 5MT[1]
42851 5MT[1]
42853 5MT[1]
44061 4F[2]
44913 5MT[3]
44914 5MT[3]
44942 5MT[3]
45144 5MT[3]
45322 5MT[3]
45417 5MT[3]
45418 5MT[3]
45433 5MT[3]
47382 3F[6]
47396 3F[6]
47519 3F[6]
48905 7F[2]
48909 7F[2]
48917 7F[2]
49022 7F[2]
49025 7F[2]
49034 7F[2]
49036 7F[2]
49039 7F[2]
49044 7F[2]
49045 7F[2]
49050 7F[2]
49063 7F[2]
49078 7F[2]
49081 7F[2]
49083 6F[2]
49084 7F[2]
49089 6F[2]
49096 7F[2]
49097 7F[2]
49099 7F[2]
49106 7F[2]
49131 6F[2]
49142 7F[2]
49160 7F[2]
49165 6F[2]
49175 6F[2]
49177 7F[2]
49180 7F[2]
49189 7F[2]
49195 6F[2]
49202 7F[2]
49211 7F[2]
49245 7F[2]
49259 6F[2]
49265 7F[2]
49266 7F[2]
49274 6F[2]
49279 6F[2]
49282 7F[2]
49286 6F[2]
49294 7F[2]
49301 7F[2]
49308 7F[2]
49313 7F[2]
49327 7F[2]
49328 7F[2]
49335 7F[2]
49354 7F[2]
49361 7F[2]
49367 7F[2]
49402 7F[3]
49425 7F[3]
49431 7F[3]
58122 2F[8]
58123 2F[8]
58157 2F[8]
58205 2F[9]
58288 2F[9]
58338 2F[10]
28097 2F[10]

1951 3A
42779 5MT[1]
42851 5MT[1]
42853 5MT[1]
42891 5MT[1]
42894 5MT[1]
42929 5MT[1]
44914 5MT[3]
45069 5MT[3]
45310 5MT[3]
45417 5MT[3]
45433 5MT[3]
46425 2MT[2]
46426 2MT[2]
47294 3F[6]
47382 3F[6]
47396 3F[6]
48120 8F
48175 8F
48318 8F
48335 8F
48375 8F
48556 8F
48674 8F
48905 7F[2]
48907 7F[2]
48917 7F[2]
48930 7F[2]
48950 7F[2]
48953 7F[2]
49009 7F[2]
49022 7F[2]
49025 7F[2]
49045 7F[2]
49063 7F[2]
49071 6F[2]
49077 7F[2]
49081 7F[2]
49088 7F[2]
49089 6F[2]
49093 7F[2]
49096 7F[2]
49098 6F[2]
49099 7F[2]
49106 7F[2]
49114 7F[2]
49142 7F[2]
49180 7F[2]
49189 7F[2]
49202 7F[2]
49212 7F[2]
49216 7F[2]
49223 7F[2]
49245 7F[2]
49246 7F[2]
49265 7F[2]
49266 7F[2]
49282 7F[2]
49308 7F[2]
49313 7F[2]
49327 7F[2]
49328 7F[2]
49354 7F[2]
49359 6F[2]
49361 7F[2]
49367 7F[2]
49371 6F[2]
58122 2F[8]
58257 2F[9]
58273 2F[9]
58277 2F[9]

1954 3A
42779 5MT[1]
42853 5MT[1]
42929 5MT[1]
44914 5MT[3]
45310 5MT[3]
45402 5MT[3]
45437 5MT[3]
45439 5MT[3]
46425 2MT[2]
46426 2MT[2]
46490 2MT[2]
47294 3F[6]
47382 3F[6]
47396 3F[6]
48120 8F
48175 8F
48250 8F
48297 8F
48310 8F
48318 8F
48335 8F
48366 8F
48375 8F
48453 8F
48477 8F
48514 8F
48556 8F
48602 8F
48674 8F
48705 8F
48713 8F
48722 8F
48725 8F
48727 8F
48733 8F
48752 8F
48755 8F
48762 8F
48766 8F
48767 8F
48769 8F
48930 7F[2]
48950 7F[2]
48964 7F[2]
49009 7F[2]
49021 7F[2]
49045 7F[2]
49063 7F[2]
49077 7F[2]
49099 7F[2]
49106 7F[2]
49202 7F[2]
49216 7F[2]
49223 7F[2]
49245 7F[2]
49246 7F[2]
49266 7F[2]
49308 7F[2]
49313 7F[2]
49327 7F[2]
49328 7F[2]
49361 7F[2]
49367 7F[2]
58169 2F[8]
58174 2F[8]
58277 2F[9]

1957 3A
42779 5MT[1]
42853 5MT[1]
42929 5MT[1]
44914 5MT[3]
45051 5MT[3]
46421 2MT[2]
46425 2MT[2]
46459 2MT[2]
46490 2MT[2]
47294 3F[6]
47382 3F[6]
47396 3F[6]
48120 8F
48175 8F
48250 8F
48297 8F
48310 8F
48318 8F
48335 8F
48366 8F
48375 8F
48453 8F
48477 8F
48514 8F
48556 8F
48602 8F
48674 8F
48705 8F
48713 8F
48722 8F
48725 8F
48733 8F
48752 8F
48755 8F
48762 8F
48766 8F
48767 8F
48769 8F
48930 7F[2]
48950 7F[2]
48964 7F[2]
49009 7F[2]
49021 7F[2]
49045 7F[2]
49063 7F[2]
49077 7F[2]
49099 7F[2]
49106 7F[2]
49125 7F[2]
49202 7F[2]
49216 7F[2]
49223 7F[2]
49246 7F[2]
49275 7F[2]
49308 7F[2]
49313 7F[2]
49327 7F[2]
49328 7F[2]
49361 7F[2]
49367 7F[2]
58135 2F[8]

1960 3A
40080 3MT[2]
40083 3MT[2]
40173 3MT[2]
40678 2P[3]
40692 2P[3]
42976 5MT[2]
43189 3F[2]
43760 3F[3]
43822 3F[4]
44027 4F[2]
44448 4F[2]
44488 4F[2]
44512 4F[2]
44873 5MT[3]
44914 5MT[3]
45385 5MT[3]
45419 5MT[3]
46421 2MT[2]
46425 2MT[2]
46459 2MT[2]
46490 2MT[2]
47294 3F[6]
47349 3F[6]
47354 3F[6]
47385 3F[6]
47396 3F[6]
48250 8F
48310 8F
48366 8F
48375 8F
48408 8F
48453 8F
48477 8F
48511 8F
48514 8F
48556 8F
48602 8F
48674 8F
48705 8F
48713 8F
48722 8F
48725 8F
48727 8F
48733 8F
48755 8F
48762 8F
48766 8F
48767 8F
48769 8F
48930 7F[2]
48964 7F[2]
49021 7F[2]
49045 7F[2]
49077 7F[2]
49099 7F[2]
49106 7F[2]
49114 7F[2]
49125 7F[2]
49216 7F[2]
49246 7F[2]
49275 7F[2]
49313 7F[2]
49328 7F[2]
49343 7F[2]
49361 7F[2]
49373 7F[3]
49411 7F[3]
58122 2F[8]
58169 2F[8]
58174 2F[8]
58181 2F[8]
58283 2F[9]

1963 21B
42957 5MT[2]
42974 5MT[2]
42979 5MT[2]
43001 4MT[5]
43002 4MT[5]
43003 4MT[5]
43005 4MT[5]
43112 4MT[5]
43115 4MT[5]
44027 4F[2]
44057 4F[2]
44302 4F[2]
44348 4F[2]
44358 4F[2]
44440 4F[2]
44442 4F[2]
44448 4F[2]
44484 4F[2]
44512 4F[2]
44766 5MT[3]
44840 5MT[3]
44873 5MT[3]
44875 5MT[3]
44910 5MT[3]
44914 5MT[3]
45146 5MT[3]
45180 5MT[3]
45387 5MT[3]
45410 5MT[3]
46421 2MT[2]
46425 2MT[2]
46429 2MT[2]
46430 2MT[2]
46456 2MT[2]
46457 2MT[2]
46459 2MT[2]
46490 2MT[2]
48256 8F
48269 8F
48375 8F
48477 8F
48514 8F
48522 8F
48529 8F
48556 8F
48602 8F
48674 8F
48680 8F
48705 8F
48713 8F
48725 8F
48726 8F
48733 8F
48734 8F
48747 8F
48762 8F
48766 8F
48767 8F
48769 8F
49173 7F[2]
49361 7F[2]
49406 7F[3]
49430 7F[3]
76075 4MT[2]

1966 2F
43002 4MT[5]
44766 5MT[3]
44840 5MT[3]
44875 5MT[3]
44914 5MT[3]
45048 5MT[3]
45064 5MT[3]
45067 5MT[3]
45222 5MT[3]
45324 5MT[3]
45410 5MT[3]
46421 2MT[2]
46427 2MT[2]
46429 2MT[2]
46445 2MT[2]
46490 2MT[2]
46522 2MT[2]
48035 8F
48061 8F
48101 8F
48203 8F
48256 8F
48335 8F
48336 8F
48375 8F
48449 8F
48477 8F
48514 8F
48517 8F
48522 8F
48529 8F
48556 8F
48659 8F
48674 8F
48680 8F
48705 8F
48713 8F
48724 8F
48725 8F
48726 8F
48729 8F
48747 8F
48752 8F
48766 8F
48767 8F
76047 4MT[2]
76086 4MT[2]
76087 4MT[2]
76088 4MT[2]

Bidston

1948 BID
68205 J63
68207 J63
68671 J72
68701 J72
68714 J72
68727 J72
69289 N5

1951 6F
68006 J94
68063 J94
68065 J94
68066 J94
68701 J72
68714 J72
68727 J72
69289 N5
69339 N5

1954 6F
47160 2F[1]
47164 2F[1]
47166 2F[1]
47627 3F[6]
47628 3F[6]
47672 3F[6]
47674 3F[6]
68006 J94
68013 J94
68030 J94
68034 J94
68063 J94
68065 J94
68066 J94
68701 J72
68727 J72
69339 N5

1957 6F
47160 2F[1]
47166 2F[1]
47622 3F[6]
47628 3F[6]
47674 3F[6]
48253 8F
48667 8F
68034 J94
68063 J94
68065 J94
68066 J94
92045 9F
92046 9F
92047 9F

1960 6F
47166 2F[1]
47343 3F[6]
47622 3F[6]
47628 3F[6]
68063 J94
68065 J94
68066 J94
68671 J72
68714 J72
68727 J72
90763 WD[2]
92045 9F
92046 9F
92047 9F

1963 6F
47160 2F[1]
47164 2F[1]
47343 3F[6]
47495 3F[6]
47622 3F[6]
47628 3F[6]
47674 3F[6]
92045 9F
92046 9F
92047 9F
92165 9F
92166 9F
92167 9F

Birkenhead

1948 BHD/6C
1917 1901
1949 1901
1968 1901
2004 1901

2006 1901
2052 2021
2089 2021
2104 2021
2106 2021
2108 2021
2129 2021
2833 2800
2895 2884
3169 3150
3626 5700
3742 5700
4120 5101
4121 5101
4122 5101
4123 5101
4124 5101
4125 5101
4126 5101
4127 5101
4128 5101
4129 5101
4337 4300
4353 4300
4386 4300
4704 4700
5316 4300
6346 4300
6350 4300
6376 4300
6404 6400
6405 6400
6819 6800
6878 6800
7714 5700
8393 8300
8725 5700
9651 5700
40101 3MT^{2}
40102 3MT^{2}
40104 3MT^{2}
40110 3MT^{2}
40121 3MT^{2}
40129 3MT^{2}
40131 3MT^{2}
40132 3MT^{2}
40136 3MT^{2}
41714 1F^{1}
41734 1F^{1}
41780 1F^{1}
41818 1F^{1}
41853 1F^{1}
42953 5MT^{2}
42967 5MT^{2}
42969 5MT^{2}
42970 5MT^{2}
47160 2F^{1}
47164 2F^{1}
47166 2F^{1}
47324 3F^{6}
47389 3F^{6}
47450 3F^{6}
47472 3F^{6}
47507 3F^{6}
47530 3F^{6}
47672 3F^{6}
47674 3F^{6}
49094 7F^{2}
49101 7F^{2}
49172 7F^{2}
49244 7F^{2}
49246 7F^{2}
49256 7F^{2}
49258 7F^{2}
49339 7F^{2}
51313 2F^{2}
52225 3F^{7}
52232 3F^{7}
52270 3F^{7}
52465 3F^{7}
58371 2F^{11}
58403 2F^{11}
58854 2F^{12}
58857 2F^{12}
58859 2F^{12}
58861 2F^{12}
58863 2F^{12}
90687 WD^{1}
27525 2F^{12}

1951 6C

1417 1400
1917 1901
1968 1901
2004 1901
2067 2021
2089 2021
2092 2021
2104 2021
2106 2021
2108 2021
2129 2021
2152 2021
2156 2021
3626 5700
3742 5700
4120 5101
4122 5101
4123 5101
4124 5101
4125 5101
4126 5101
4127 5101
4128 5101
4129 5101
4704 4700
5176 5101
5316 4300
5393 4300
6346 4300
6350 4300
6376 4300
6831 6800
6841 6800
6844 6800
6859 6800
6860 6800
6878 6800
7714 5700
8725 5700
9651 5700
9678 5700
40101 3MT^{2}
40102 3MT^{2}
40104 3MT^{2}
40110 3MT^{2}
40121 3MT^{2}
40129 3MT^{2}
40131 3MT^{2}
40132 3MT^{2}
40209 3MT^{2}
41734 1F^{1}
41780 1F^{1}
41853 1F^{1}
42953 5MT^{2}
42961 5MT^{2}
42967 5MT^{2}
42969 5MT^{2}
42970 5MT^{2}
42973 5MT^{2}
42981 5MT^{2}
47160 2F^{1}
47164 2F^{1}
47166 2F^{1}
47324 3F^{6}
47472 3F^{6}
47507 3F^{6}
47530 3F^{6}
47627 3F^{6}
47628 3F^{6}
47672 3F^{6}
47674 3F^{6}
48106 8F
48247 8F
48327 8F
48448 8F
48455 8F
48491 8F
48673 8F
48684 8F
48691 8F
48719 8F
48726 8F
51313 2F^{2}
51441 2F^{2}
52225 3F^{7}
52232 3F^{7}
52270 3F^{7}
52432 3F^{7}
58851 2F^{12}
58854 2F^{12}
58857 2F^{12}
58861 2F^{12}
58863 2F^{12}

1954 6C

1417 1400
1457 1400
2008 1901
2011 1901
2043 2021
2082 2021
2092 2021
2099 2021
2101 2021
2107 2021
2108 2021
2112 2021
2134 2021
2136 2021
3626 5700
3742 5700
4120 5101
4122 5101
4123 5101
4124 5101
4125 5101
4126 5101
4127 5101
4128 5101
4129 5101
5176 5101
5316 4300
5393 4300
6346 4300
6350 4300
6376 4300
6831 6800
6841 6800
6859 6800
6878 6800
7714 5700
8725 5700
9651 5700
40072 3MT^{2}
40088 3MT^{2}
40101 3MT^{2}
40103 3MT^{2}
40110 3MT^{2}
40121 3MT^{2}
40128 3MT^{2}
40131 3MT^{2}
40132 3MT^{2}
40144 3MT^{2}
40209 3MT^{2}
41734 1F^{1}
41753 1F^{1}
41853 1F^{1}
42961 5MT^{2}
42964 5MT^{2}
42967 5MT^{2}
42969 5MT^{2}
42970 5MT^{2}
42977 5MT^{2}
42978 5MT^{2}
42981 5MT^{2}
47005 0F^{3}
47006 0F^{3}
47007 0F^{3}
47324 3F^{6}
47507 3F^{6}
47530 3F^{6}
48249 8F
48448 8F
48455 8F
48479 8F
48491 8F
48673 8F
48684 8F
48691 8F
48718 8F
48719 8F
48726 8F
48764 8F
52232 3F^{7}
52270 3F^{7}
68714 J72
90173 WD^{1}
90227 WD^{1}
90237 WD^{1}
90257 WD^{1}
90667 WD^{1}

1957 6C

1417 1400
1457 1400
2008 1901
2012 1901
2069 2021
2134 2021
2160 2021
3626 5700
3742 5700
4120 5101
4122 5101
4123 5101
4124 5101
4125 5101
4126 5101
4127 5101
4128 5101
4129 5101
5176 5101
5393 4300
6346 4300
6350 4300
6376 4300
6831 6800
6841 6800
6859 6800
6878 6800
7714 5700
8725 5700
9651 5700
40101 3MT^{2}
40102 3MT^{2}
40121 3MT^{2}
40131 3MT^{2}
40135 3MT^{2}
40144 3MT^{2}
40209 3MT^{2}
41734 1F^{1}
41753 1F^{1}
42120 4MT^{1}
42303 4MT^{2}
42308 4MT^{2}
42447 4MT^{3}
42493 4MT^{3}
42597 4MT^{3}
42599 4MT^{3}
42608 4MT^{3}
42778 5MT^{1}
42941 5MT^{1}
42967 5MT^{2}
42969 5MT^{2}
42970 5MT^{2}
42977 5MT^{2}
42978 5MT^{2}
42981 5MT^{2}
47005 0F^{3}
47006 0F^{3}
47009 0F^{3}
47324 3F^{6}
47507 3F^{6}
47530 3F^{6}
48106 8F
48249 8F
48448 8F
48455 8F
48684 8F
48691 8F
48718 8F
48719 8F
48726 8F
48764 8F
52270 3F^{7}
68714 J72
84000 2MT^{2}
84003 2MT^{2}
90173 WD^{1}
90212 WD^{1}

1960 6C

40076 3MT^{2}
40078 3MT^{2}
40101 3MT^{2}
40102 3MT^{2}
40116 3MT^{2}
40121 3MT^{2}
40131 3MT^{2}
40202 3MT^{2}
40209 3MT^{2}
41226 2MT^{1}
41322 2MT^{1}
42077 4MT^{1}
42078 4MT^{1}
42441 4MT^{3}
42447 4MT^{3}
42493 4MT^{3}
42599 4MT^{3}
42602 4MT^{3}
42608 4MT^{3}
42778 5MT^{1}
42856 5MT^{1}
42888 5MT^{1}
42894 5MT^{1}
42941 5MT^{1}
42969 5MT^{2}
42970 5MT^{2}
42977 5MT^{2}
42978 5MT^{2}
45440 5MT^{3}
47005 0F^{3}
47009 0F^{3}
47324 3F^{6}
47338 3F^{6}
47372 3F^{6}
47497 3F^{6}
47507 3F^{6}
47530 3F^{6}
47565 3F^{6}
47627 3F^{6}
47674 3F^{6}
47677 3F^{6}
48260 8F
48348 8F
48349 8F
48441 8F
48448 8F
48455 8F
48684 8F
48691 8F
73032 5MT
73039 5MT
80062 4MT^{3}
80063 4MT^{3}
80090 4MT^{3}
84000 2MT^{2}
84003 2MT^{2}
90173 WD^{1}
90212 WD^{1}
90257 WD^{1}
90317 WD^{1}
90369 WD^{1}
90392 WD^{1}

1963 6C

42394 4MT^{2}
42441 4MT^{3}
42459 4MT^{3}
42493 4MT^{3}
42542 4MT^{3}
42583 4MT^{3}
42597 4MT^{3}
42602 4MT^{3}
42606 4MT^{3}
42608 4MT^{3}
42747 5MT^{1}
42783 5MT^{1}
42785 5MT^{1}
42810 5MT^{1}
42814 5MT^{1}
42828 5MT^{1}
42852 5MT^{1}
42853 5MT^{1}
42854 5MT^{1}
42859 5MT^{1}
42870 5MT^{1}
42885 5MT^{1}
42892 5MT^{1}
42923 5MT^{1}
42935 5MT^{1}
42936 5MT^{1}
42943 5MT^{1}
42944 5MT^{1}
45567 6P5F^{2}
47005 0F^{3}
47009 0F^{3}
47324 3F^{6}
47372 3F^{6}
47565 3F^{6}
47627 3F^{6}
47659 3F^{6}
48094 8F
48131 8F
48154 8F
48257 8F
48258 8F
48260 8F
48262 8F
48290 8F
48312 8F
48326 8F
48373 8F
48422 8F
48423 8F
48441 8F
48446 8F
48448 8F
48476 8F
48554 8F
48648 8F
48684 8F
48691 8F
48697 8F

1966 8H

42086 4MT^{1}
42121 4MT^{1}
42156 4MT^{1}
42581 4MT^{3}
42606 4MT^{3}
42700 5MT^{1}
42734 5MT^{1}
42765 5MT^{1}
42782 5MT^{1}
42812 5MT^{1}
42859 5MT^{1}
42924 5MT^{1}
47272 3F^{6}
47324 3F^{6}
47447 3F^{6}
47533 3F^{6}
47627 3F^{6}
47659 3F^{6}
47674 3F^{6}
92011 9F
92014 9F
92020 9F
92021 9F
92023 9F
92024 9F
92026 9F
92032 9F
92045 9F
92046 9F
92047 9F
92048 9F
92059 9F
92069 9F
92070 9F
92079 9F
92082 9F
92083 9F
92084 9F
92085 9F
92086 9F
92088 9F
92089 9F
92090 9F
92092 9F
92094 9F
92100 9F
92101 9F
92102 9F
92103 9F
92104 9F
92105 9F
92106 9F
92107 9F
92108 9F
92109 9F
92111 9F
92112 9F
92113 9F
92120 9F
92121 9F
92122 9F
92123 9F
92127 9F
92131 9F
92133 9F
92134 9F
92157 9F
92159 9F
92162 9F
92163 9F
92165 9F
92166 9F
92167 9F

Blackpool Central

1948 24E

41192 4P^{1}
41195 4P^{1}
41197 4P^{1}
42636 4MT^{3}
42637 4MT^{3}
42638 4MT^{3}
44778 5MT^{3}
44779 5MT^{3}
44927 5MT^{3}
44928 5MT^{3}
44929 5MT^{3}
44930 5MT^{3}
44932 5MT^{3}
44947 5MT^{3}
44950 5MT^{3}
44988 5MT^{3}
45571 6P5F^{2}
45574 6P5F^{2}
45588 6P5F^{2}
45653 6P5F^{2}
45695 6P5F^{2}
45697 6P5F^{2}
45707 6P5F^{2}
46410 2MT^{2}
46411 2MT^{2}
46412 2MT^{2}
46413 2MT^{2}
50412 5P
50423 5P
50429 5P
50432 5P
50442 5P
50448 5P
50455 5P
50721 2P^{8}
50725 2P^{8}
50749 2P^{8}
50750 2P^{8}
50766 2P^{8}
50799 2P^{8}
50889 2P^{8}
52174 3F^{7}
52194 3F^{7}
52215 3F^{7}
52275 3F^{7}
52415 3F^{7}
52430 3F^{7}
52447 3F^{7}
52459 3F^{7}
52542 3F^{9}
52558 3F^{9}
52572 3F^{9}

1951 28A

41192 4P^{1}
41195 4P^{1}
41263 2MT^{1}
41264 2MT^{1}
42148 4MT^{1}
42636 4MT^{3}
42637 4MT^{3}
42638 4MT^{3}
44730 5MT^{3}
44731 5MT^{3}
44732 5MT^{3}
44733 5MT^{3}
44778 5MT^{3}
44779 5MT^{3}
44927 5MT^{3}
44928 5MT^{3}
44929 5MT^{3}
44930 5MT^{3}
44932 5MT^{3}
44947 5MT^{3}
44950 5MT^{3}
44988 5MT^{3}
45043 5MT^{3}
45077 5MT^{3}
45571 6P5F^{2}
45574 6P5F^{2}
45588 6P5F^{2}
45653 6P5F^{2}
45695 6P5F^{2}
45697 6P5F^{2}
45707 6P5F^{2}
46410 2MT^{2}
46411 2MT^{2}
46412 2MT^{2}
46413 2MT^{2}
46435 2MT^{2}
50455 5P
50721 2P^{8}
50725 2P^{8}
50746 2P^{8}
50749 2P^{8}
50752 2P^{8}
50757 2P^{8}
50777 2P^{8}
50806 2P^{8}
52138 3F^{7}
52157 3F^{7}
52174 3F^{7}
52182 3F^{7}
52194 3F^{7}
52215 3F^{7}
52275 3F^{7}
52334 3F^{7}
52357 3F^{7}
52415 3F^{7}
52430 3F^{7}
52447 3F^{7}
52459 3F^{7}
52466 3F^{7}
52572 3F^{9}

1954 24E

41263 2MT^{1}
41264 2MT^{1}
42148 4MT^{1}
42473 4MT^{3}
42474 4MT^{3}
42476 4MT^{3}
42629 4MT^{3}
42636 4MT^{3}
42637 4MT^{3}
42638 4MT^{3}
44730 5MT^{3}
44731 5MT^{3}
44732 5MT^{3}
44733 5MT^{3}
44737 5MT^{3}
44778 5MT^{3}
44779 5MT^{3}
44889 5MT^{3}
44926 5MT^{3}
44927 5MT^{3}
44929 5MT^{3}
44930 5MT^{3}
44947 5MT^{3}
44950 5MT^{3}
44982 5MT^{3}
44988 5MT^{3}
45061 5MT^{3}
45077 5MT^{3}
45200 5MT^{3}
45318 5MT^{3}
45436 5MT^{3}
45571 6P5F^{2}
45574 6P5F^{2}
45580 6P5F^{2}
45584 6P5F^{2}
45588 6P5F^{2}
45653 6P5F^{2}
46413 2MT^{2}
46486 2MT^{2}
52215 3F^{7}
52240 3F^{7}
52415 3F^{7}
52437 3F^{7}
52466 3F^{7}

1957 24E

40072 3MT^{2}
40099 3MT^{2}
40103 3MT^{2}
40109 3MT^{2}
40164 3MT^{2}
40174 3MT^{2}
41102 4P^{1}
41189 4P^{1}
41193 4P^{1}
42148 4MT^{1}
42625 4MT^{3}
42636 4MT^{3}
42637 4MT^{3}
42638 4MT^{3}
44730 5MT^{3}
44731 5MT^{3}
44732 5MT^{3}
44733 5MT^{3}
44737 5MT^{3}
44778 5MT^{3}
44779 5MT^{3}
44926 5MT^{3}
44927 5MT^{3}
44929 5MT^{3}
44930 5MT^{3}
44947 5MT^{3}
44950 5MT^{3}
44982 5MT^{3}
44988 5MT^{3}
45200 5MT^{3}
45318 5MT^{3}
45436 5MT^{3}
45571 6P5F^{2}
45574 6P5F^{2}
45580 6P5F^{2}
45584 6P5F^{2}
45588 6P5F^{2}
45653 6P5F^{2}
45705 6P5F^{2}
52240 3F^{7}
52415 3F^{7}
52466 3F^{7}
52523 3F^{7}
52527 3F^{7}

1960 24E

40072 3MT^{2}
40091 3MT^{2}
40099 3MT^{2}
40103 3MT^{2}
40109 3MT^{2}
40164 3MT^{2}
40166 3MT^{2}
40174 3MT^{2}
42148 4MT^{1}
42455 4MT^{3}
42625 4MT^{3}
42638 4MT^{3}
42657 4MT^{3}
44730 5MT^{3}
44731 5MT^{3}
44732 5MT^{3}
44733 5MT^{3}
44737 5MT^{3}
44778 5MT^{3}
44779 5MT^{3}
44926 5MT^{3}
44927 5MT^{3}
44930 5MT^{3}
44947 5MT^{3}
44950 5MT^{3}
44982 5MT^{3}
44988 5MT^{3}
45077 5MT^{3}
45200 5MT^{3}
45201 5MT^{3}
45318 5MT^{3}
45436 5MT^{3}
45464 5MT^{3}
45571 6P5F^{2}
45574 6P5F^{2}
45580 6P5F^{2}
45584 6P5F^{2}
45653 6P5F^{2}
45705 6P5F^{2}
80046 4MT^{3}
80093 4MT^{3}

1963 24E

42148 4MT^{1}
42153 4MT^{1}
42206 4MT^{1}
42294 4MT^{1}
42455 4MT^{3}
42461 4MT^{3}
42558 4MT^{3}
42559 4MT^{3}
42625 4MT^{3}
42643 4MT^{3}
42657 4MT^{3}
44728 5MT^{3}
44730 5MT^{3}
44731 5MT^{3}
44732 5MT^{3}
44733 5MT^{3}
44737 5MT^{3}
44778 5MT^{3}
44779 5MT^{3}
44926 5MT^{3}
44927 5MT^{3}
44930 5MT^{3}
44947 5MT^{3}
44950 5MT^{3}
45077 5MT^{3}
45078 5MT^{3}
45102 5MT^{3}
45200 5MT^{3}
45201 5MT^{3}
45227 5MT^{3}
45318 5MT^{3}
45377 5MT^{3}
45415 5MT^{3}
45436 5MT^{3}
45442 5MT^{3}
45464 5MT^{3}
45571 6P5F^{2}
45574 6P5F^{2}
45580 6P5F^{2}
45584 6P5F^{2}
45653 6P5F^{2}
45681 6P5F^{2}
45697 6P5F^{2}
45703 6P5F^{2}
45705 6P5F^{2}
45732 6P5F^{2}

Blaydon

1948 BLA

62349 D20
62360 D20
62371 D20
62448 D32
62449 D32
63353 Q6
63356 Q6
63376 Q6
63381 Q6
63385 Q6
63390 Q6
63391 Q6
63394 Q6
63398 Q6
63399 Q6
63403 Q6
63412 Q6
63413 Q6
63428 Q6
63432 Q6
63437 Q6
63441 Q6
63444 Q6
63448 Q6
64700 J39
64701 J39
64703 J39
64704 J39
64705 J39
64707 J39
64709 J39
64711 J39
64813 J39
64814 J39
64816 J39
64817 J39
64842 J39
64843 J39
64844 J39
64846 J39
64849 J39
64852 J39
64853 J39
64854 J39
64856 J39
64871 J39
64915 J39
64917 J39
64920 J39
64923 J39
64926 J39
64927 J39
64934 J39
64941 J39
64947 J39
65025 J21
65029 J21
65035 J21
65062 J21
65080 J21
65111 J21
65112 J21
67255 G5
67259 G5
67265 G5
67277 G5
67313 G5
67323 G5
67325 G5
67339 G5
67636 V1
67658 V1
68010 J94
68014 J94
68015 J94
68019 J94
68021 J94
68024 J94
68029 J94
68035 J94
68036 J94
68037 J94
68038 J94
68058 J94
68059 J94
68284 J71
69095 N10
69851 A8
69853 A8
69857 A8
69865 A8

1951 52C

62021 K1
62022 K1
62023 K1
62024 K1
62025 K1
62026 K1
62027 K1
62028 K1
62029 K1
62030 K1
62747 D49
62771 D49
63353 Q6
63356 Q6
63376 Q6
63381 Q6
63385 Q6
63390 Q6
63391 Q6
63394 Q6
63398 Q6
63399 Q6
63403 Q6
63412 Q6
63413 Q6
63428 Q6
63432 Q6
63441 Q6
64700 J39
64703 J39
64705 J39
64812 J39
64814 J39
64816 J39
64842 J39
64849 J39
64852 J39
64858 J39
65025 J21
65082 J21
65099 J21
65343 J36
67241 G5
67255 G5
67259 G5
67277 G5
67323 G5
67339 G5
67636 V1
67653 V1
67656 V1
67657 V1
67658 V1
68010 J94
68019 J94
68021 J94
60024 J94
68029 J94
68035 J94
68036 J94
68038 J94
68041 J94
68048 J94
68058 J94
68265 J71
69095 N10

1954 52C

43126 4MT^{5}
43128 4MT^{5}
62002 K1
62010 K1
62021 K1
62022 K1
62023 K1
62024 K1
62025 K1
62026 K1
62027 K1
62028 K1
62029 K1
62030 K1
62747 D49
62771 D49
63353 Q6
63356 Q6
63363 Q6
63376 Q6
63381 Q6
63385 Q6
63390 Q6
63391 Q6
63394 Q6
63398 Q6
63399 Q6
63403 Q6
63412 Q6
63413 Q6
63428 Q6
63432 Q6
63441 Q6
64705 J39
64812 J39
64814 J39
64816 J39
64842 J39
64849 J39
64858 J39
64864 J39
64870 J39
64897 J39
65042 J21
65090 J21
67241 G5
67248 G5
67259 G5
67277 G5
67304 G5
67316 G5
67323 G5
67325 G5
67339 G5
67636 V3
67653 V1
67656 V3
67657 V1
67658 V1
68010 J94
68035 J94
68036 J94
68038 J94
68059 J94
68267 J71
68273 J71
68731 J72
69023 J72
69024 J72
69025 J72
69026 J72

1957 52C

62002 K1
62006 K1
62010 K1
62021 K1
62022 K1
62023 K1
62024 K1
62025 K1
62026 K1
62027 K1
62028 K1
62029 K1
62030 K1
63356 Q6
63363 Q6
63376 Q6
63381 Q6
63385 Q6
63390 Q6
63394 Q6
63412 Q6
63413 Q6
63432 Q6
63441 Q6
63461 Q7
63462 Q7
63464 Q7
63468 Q7
63470 Q7
63471 Q7
63472 Q7
64705 J39
64812 J39
64814 J39
64815 J39
64816 J39
64842 J39
64849 J39
64858 J39
65039 J21
65070 J21
65103 J21
67246 G5
67326 G5
67634 V3
67636 V3
67653 V3
67656 V3
67673 V1
67683 V3
68010 J94
68035 J94
68036 J94
68038 J94
68059 J94
68273 J71
68731 J72
69023 J72
69024 J72
69025 J72
69026 J72
77011 3MT^{1}
77014 3MT^{1}

1960 52C

62002 K1
62006 K1
62010 K1
62021 K1
62022 K1
62023 K1
62024 K1
62025 K1
62026 K1
62027 K1
62028 K1
62029 K1
62030 K1
62050 K1
62060 K1
63352 Q6
63356 Q6
63362 Q6
63363 Q6
63366 Q6
63368 Q6
63376 Q6
63377 Q6
63378 Q6
63381 Q6
63384 Q6
63385 Q6
63386 Q6
63390 Q6
63394 Q6
63400 Q6
63402 Q6
63408 Q6
63413 Q6
63431 Q6
63434 Q6
63441 Q6
63444 Q6
63453 Q6
63458 Q6
64815 J39
64816 J39
64842 J39
64849 J39
64858 J39
65033 J21
67634 V3
67636 V3
67653 V3
68010 J94
68014 J94
68035 J94
68036 J94
69023 J72
69024 J72
69025 J72
69026 J72

1963 52C

61035 B1
61038 B1
61199 B1
61237 B1
63362 Q6
63385 Q6
63387 Q6
63390 Q6
63394 Q6
63400 Q6
63402 Q6
63408 Q6
63429 Q6
63431 Q6
63434 Q6
63437 Q6
63441 Q6
63444 Q6
63453 Q6
63458 Q6
67636 V3

Bletchley

1948 2B

42442 4MT^{3}
42458 4MT^{3}
42566 4MT^{3}
42591 4MT^{3}
42600 4MT^{3}
42949 5MT^{2}
42957 5MT^{2}
43841 4F^{1}
43915 4F^{1}
44072 4F^{2}
44438 4F^{2}
44447 4F^{2}
44549 4F^{2}
44916 5MT^{3}
44968 5MT^{3}
45025 5MT^{3}
45130 5MT^{3}
45314 5MT^{3}
45316 5MT^{3}
45331 5MT^{3}
46604 1P^{1}
46909 2P^{7}
46912 2P^{7}
47288 3F^{6}
47298 3F^{6}
47452 3F^{6}
47521 3F^{6}
48894 6F^{2}
48902 6F^{2}
48913 6F^{2}
48925 7F^{2}
48931 6F^{2}
48935 6F^{2}
48951 7F^{2}
48952 7F^{2}
49005 7F^{2}
49007 7F^{2}
49037 7F^{2}
49076 6F^{2}
49093 7F^{2}
49100 6F^{2}
49117 7F^{2}
49127 7F^{2}
49154 7F^{2}
49173 7F^{2}
49179 6F^{2}
49193 6F^{2}
49201 6F^{2}
49208 6F^{2}
49213 6F^{2}
49237 7F^{2}
49300 7F^{2}
49307 7F^{2}
49332 6F^{2}
49359 6F^{2}
49371 6F^{2}
49372 7F^{2}
49391 7F^{2}
49401 7F^{3}
49406 7F^{3}
49416 7F^{3}
49427 7F^{3}
49443 7F^{3}
58881 2F^{14}
58919 2F^{14}
58934 2F^{14}
25722 4P^{6}
25827 4P^{6}

1951 4A

41222 2MT^{1}
41275 2MT^{1}
42303 4MT^{2}
42348 4MT^{2}
42378 4MT^{2}
42446 4MT^{3}
42566 4MT^{3}
42591 4MT^{3}
42600 4MT^{3}
42659 4MT^{3}
42666 4MT^{3}
42669 4MT^{3}
43000 4MT^{5}
43001 4MT^{5}
43002 4MT^{5}
43003 4MT^{5}
43005 4MT^{5}
43841 4F^{1}
44352 4F^{2}
44447 4F^{2}
44864 5MT^{3}
44865 5MT^{3}
44916 5MT^{3}
45057 5MT^{3}
45130 5MT^{3}
45314 5MT^{3}
45316 5MT^{3}
45353 5MT^{3}
46601 1P^{1}
47288 3F^{6}
47298 3F^{6}
47452 3F^{6}

47521 3F[6]
48207 8F
48373 8F
48535 8F
48549 8F
48550 8F
48688 8F
48693 8F
48951 7F[2]
48952 7F[2]
49005 7F[2]
49007 7F[2]
49014 7F[2]
49049 7F[2]
49061 7F[2]
49070 7F[2]
49144 7F[2]
49154 7F[2]
49155 7F[2]
49287 7F[2]
49288 7F[2]
49289 7F[2]
49292 7F[2]
49391 7F[2]
49406 7F[3]
49417 7F[3]
49427 7F[3]
49443 7F[3]
49448 7F[3]
58887 2F[14]
58908 2F[14]
58911 2F[14]

1954 1E
41222 2MT[1]
41275 2MT[1]
42061 4MT[1]
42062 4MT[1]
42155 4MT[1]
42582 4MT[3]
42659 4MT[3]
42669 4MT[3]
43841 4F[1]
44352 4F[2]
44364 4F[2]
44447 4F[2]
44593 4F[2]
44864 5MT[3]
44865 5MT[3]
47288 3F[6]
47298 3F[6]
47452 3F[6]
47521 3F[6]
48207 8F
48535 8F
48544 8F
48549 8F
48550 8F
48688 8F
48693 8F
48754 8F
48898 7F[2]
48951 7F[2]
48952 7F[2]
48953 7F[2]
49005 7F[2]
49049 7F[2]
49061 7F[2]
49287 7F[2]
49289 7F[2]
49310 7F[2]
49427 7F[3]
49443 7F[3]
58887 2F[14]
75030 4MT[1]
75031 4MT[1]
75032 4MT[1]
75033 4MT[1]
75034 4MT[1]
75035 4MT[1]
75036 4MT[1]
75037 4MT[1]
75038 4MT[1]
75039 4MT[1]
80039 4MT[3]
80040 4MT[3]
80041 4MT[3]
80042 4MT[3]
80043 4MT[3]

1957 1E
41222 2MT[1]
41275 2MT[1]
43841 4F[1]
44072 4F[2]
44352 4F[2]
44364 4F[2]
44447 4F[2]
44593 4F[2]
45004 5MT[3]
45020 5MT[3]
45195 5MT[3]
45307 5MT[3]
45331 5MT[3]
45388 5MT[3]
45393 5MT[3]
47500 3F[6]
47521 3F[6]
48207 8F
48446 8F
48535 8F
48544 8F
48549 8F
48550 8F
48688 8F
48754 8F
48898 7F[2]
48951 7F[2]
48952 7F[2]
48953 7F[2]
49005 7F[2]
49061 7F[2]
49094 7F[2]
49287 7F[2]
49289 7F[2]
49310 7F[2]
49330 7F[2]
49427 7F[3]
49443 7F[3]
75030 4MT[1]
75036 4MT[1]
75037 4MT[1]
75038 4MT[1]
75052 4MT[1]
80039 4MT[3]
80040 4MT[3]
80041 4MT[3]
80042 4MT[3]
80043 4MT[3]
80081 4MT[3]
80082 4MT[3]
80083 4MT[3]
80084 4MT[3]
80085 4MT[3]
84002 2MT[2]
84004 2MT[2]

1960 1E
41222 2MT[1]
41275 2MT[1]
42066 4MT[1]
42067 4MT[1]
42069 4MT[1]
42071 4MT[1]
42105 4MT[1]
42106 4MT[1]
44117 4F[2]
44364 4F[2]
44370 4F[2]
44397 4F[2]
44447 4F[2]
45020 5MT[3]
45089 5MT[3]
45331 5MT[3]
45388 5MT[3]
45393 5MT[3]
47348 3F[6]
47521 3F[6]
48207 8F
48446 8F
48544 8F
48549 8F
48550 8F
48610 8F
48688 8F
48898 7F[2]
48953 7F[2]
49061 7F[2]
49093 7F[2]
49094 7F[2]
49287 7F[2]
49310 7F[2]
49403 7F[3]
49443 7F[3]
75036 4MT[1]
75037 4MT[1]
75038 4MT[1]
84002 2MT[2]
84004 2MT[2]

1963 1E
41222 2MT[1]
41289 2MT[1]
42105 4MT[1]
42106 4MT[1]
42233 4MT[1]
42586 4MT[3]
45089 5MT[3]
45147 5MT[3]
45222 5MT[3]
45292 5MT[3]
45331 5MT[3]
45393 5MT[3]
47500 3F[6]
47521 3F[6]
48085 8F
48203 8F
48207 8F
48360 8F
48408 8F
48427 8F
48534 8F
48544 8F
48549 8F
48550 8F
48610 8F
48626 8F
48646 8F
48656 8F
48657 8F
48668 8F
48688 8F
48729 8F
48755 8F
75013 4MT[1]
75014 4MT[1]
75028 4MT[1]
75038 4MT[1]
75039 4MT[1]
75051 4MT[1]
75054 4MT[1]
84002 2MT[2]
84004 2MT[2]

Bolton

1948 26C
41103 4P[1]
41104 4P[1]
41190 4P[1]
41191 4P[1]
41199 4P[1]
42545 4MT[3]
42565 4MT[3]
42633 4MT[3]
42652 4MT[3]
42653 4MT[3]
42654 4MT[3]
42655 4MT[3]
42656 4MT[3]
42657 4MT[3]
48437 8F
48453 8F
48468 8F
48767 8F
49542 7F[4]
49573 7F[4]
49641 7F[4]
49664 7F[4]
50617 Rail Motor[1]
50642 2P[8]
50646 2P[8]
50697 2P[8]
50807 2P[8]
50815 2P[8]
50831 2P[8]
50859 2P[8]
51348 2F[2]
51511 2F[2]
51513 2F[2]
51519 2F[2]
52157 3F[7]
52212 3F[7]
52236 3F[7]
52348 3F[7]
52350 3F[7]
52357 3F[7]
52365 3F[7]
52404 3F[7]
52446 3F[7]
52528 3F[9]
52609 3F[9]

1951 26C
41085 4P[1]
41103 4P[1]
41104 4P[1]
41185 4P[1]
41186 4P[1]
41190 4P[1]
42472 4MT[3]
42545 4MT[3]
42565 4MT[3]
42633 4MT[3]
42652 4MT[3]
42653 4MT[3]
42654 4MT[3]
42655 4MT[3]
42656 4MT[3]
42657 4MT[3]
48453 8F
48710 8F
48711 8F
48762 8F
48765 8F
48767 8F
49664 7F[4]
50647 2P[8]
50660 2P[8]
50788 2P[8]
50807 2P[8]
50815 2P[8]
50818 2P[8]
50829 2P[8]
50831 2P[8]
50865 2P[8]
50872 2P[8]
51511 2F[2]
51513 2F[2]
51519 2F[2]
52136 3F[7]
52212 3F[7]
52231 3F[7]
52236 3F[7]
52311 3F[7]
52348 3F[7]
52350 3F[7]
52404 3F[7]
52427 3F[7]
52446 3F[7]
90205 WD[1]
90297 WD[1]
90324 WD[1]
90712 WD[1]

1954 26C
40585 2P[3]
40682 2P[3]
40685 2P[3]
41101 4P[1]
41189 4P[1]
42472 4MT[3]
42545 4MT[3]
42565 4MT[3]
42626 4MT[3]
42630 4MT[3]
42633 4MT[3]
42635 4MT[3]
42652 4MT[3]
42653 4MT[3]
42654 4MT[3]
42655 4MT[3]
42656 4MT[3]
42657 4MT[3]
49532 7F[4]
49538 7F[4]
49544 7F[4]
50646 2P[8]
50650 2P[8]
50660 2P[8]
50731 2P[8]
50765 2P[8]
50850 2P[8]
50855 2P[8]
50887 2P[8]
51511 2F[2]
51513 2F[2]
51519 2F[2]
52123 3F[7]
52132 3F[7]
52139 3F[7]
52312 3F[7]
52328 3F[7]
52348 3F[7]
52350 3F[7]
52413 3F[7]
52575 3F[9]
90110 WD[1]
90205 WD[1]
90206 WD[1]
90267 WD[1]
90271 WD[1]
90297 WD[1]
90316 WD[1]
90343 WD[1]
90402 WD[1]
90416 WD[1]
90641 WD[1]
90712 WD[1]
90725 WD[1]
90729 WD[1]

1957 26C
40586 2P[3]
40681 2P[3]
42289 4MT[1]
42472 4MT[3]
42545 4MT[3]
42565 4MT[3]
42626 4MT[3]
42629 4MT[3]
42630 4MT[3]
42633 4MT[3]
42635 4MT[3]
42653 4MT[3]
42654 4MT[3]
42655 4MT[3]
42656 4MT[3]
49538 7F[4]
49544 7F[4]
49674 7F[4]
50647 2P[8]
50660 2P[8]
50829 2P[8]
50850 2P[8]
50887 2P[8]
51408 2F[2]
51486 2F[2]
52132 3F[7]
52237 3F[7]
52348 3F[7]
52360 3F[7]
52389 3F[7]
52461 3F[7]
90110 WD[1]
90206 WD[1]
90267 WD[1]
90271 WD[1]
90297 WD[1]
90402 WD[1]
90641 WD[1]
90725 WD[1]
90729 WD[1]

1960 26C
42289 4MT[1]
42545 4MT[3]
42565 4MT[3]
42626 4MT[3]
42630 4MT[3]
42633 4MT[3]
42635 4MT[3]
42652 4MT[3]
42653 4MT[3]
42654 4MT[3]
42655 4MT[3]
42656 4MT[3]
49544 7F[4]
49618 7F[4]
50850 2P[8]
51408 2F[2]
51486 2F[2]
51498 2F[2]
52345 3F[7]
52393 3F[7]
52415 3F[7]
52523 3F[7]
84013 2MT[2]
84014 2MT[2]
84019 2MT[2]
90102 WD[1]
90110 WD[1]
90206 WD[1]
90267 WD[1]
90297 WD[1]
90641 WD[1]
90725 WD[1]
90729 WD[1]

1963 26C
42289 4MT[1]
42444 4MT[3]
42460 4MT[3]
42550 4MT[3]
42563 4MT[3]
42565 4MT[3]
42626 4MT[3]
42630 4MT[3]
42633 4MT[3]
42652 4MT[3]
42654 4MT[3]
42655 4MT[3]
42656 4MT[3]
42704 5MT[1]
42705 5MT[1]
42708 5MT[1]
42725 5MT[1]
44746 5MT[3]
45156 5MT[3]
45199 5MT[3]
45224 5MT[3]
45232 5MT[3]
45290 5MT[3]
45304 5MT[3]
45378 5MT[3]
47165 2F[1]
84013 2MT[2]
84014 2MT[2]
84019 2MT[2]
84025 2MT[2]
84026 2MT[2]
90102 WD[1]
90121 WD[1]
90206 WD[1]
90267 WD[1]
90641 WD[1]
90729 WD[1]

1966 9K
42133 4MT[1]
42159 4MT[1]
42183 4MT[1]
42240 4MT[1]
42249 4MT[1]
42252 4MT[1]
42484 4MT[3]
44664 5MT[3]
44728 5MT[3]
44736 5MT[3]
44737 5MT[3]
44816 5MT[3]
44893 5MT[3]
44927 5MT[3]
44947 5MT[3]
45104 5MT[3]
45110 5MT[3]
45239 5MT[3]
45252 5MT[3]
45258 5MT[3]
45260 5MT[3]
45290 5MT[3]
45304 5MT[3]
45318 5MT[3]
45377 5MT[3]
45381 5MT[3]
45409 5MT[3]
45411 5MT[3]
45415 5MT[3]
46416 2MT[2]
46417 2MT[2]
46436 2MT[2]
46504 2MT[2]
46506 2MT[2]
48106 8F
48166 8F
48205 8F
48469 8F
48511 8F
48523 8F
48547 8F
48652 8F
48702 8F
48740 8F
48773 8F

Borough Gardens

1948 BOR
63251 Q5
63254 Q5
63257 Q5
63259 Q5
63261 Q5
63264 Q5
63267 Q5
63271 Q5
63275 Q5
63282 Q5
63283 Q5
63284 Q5
63286 Q5
63287 Q5
63289 Q5
63296 Q5
63298 Q5
63321 Q5
63326 Q5
63342 Q6
63377 Q6
63388 Q6
63400 Q6
63402 Q6
63434 Q6
65600 J24
65603 J24
65604 J24
65611 J24
65624 J24
65627 J24
65633 J24
65634 J24
65641 J24
65644 J24
65657 J25
65661 J25
65676 J25
65680 J25
65685 J25
68287 J71
68289 J71
68299 J71
68679 J72
68704 J72
68705 J72
68706 J72
68708 J72
68736 J72
68737 J72

1951 54C
61319 B1
61320 B1
61321 B1
63259 Q5
63267 Q5
63284 Q5
63303 Q5
63326 Q5
63342 Q6
63350 Q6
63354 Q6
63358 Q6
63366 Q6
63377 Q6
63384 Q6
63386 Q6
63400 Q6
63402 Q6
63434 Q6
63444 Q6
63458 Q6
64846 J39
64864 J39
64929 J39
64936 J39
64939 J39
65615 J24
65657 J25
65661 J25
65676 J25
65680 J25
65685 J25
65686 J25
68287 J71
68289 J71
68299 J71
68705 J72
68708 J72
68728 J72
68730 J72
68736 J72
68737 J72
69017 J72
69391 N8

1954 54C
61319 B1
61320 B1
61321 B1
63342 Q6
63350 Q6
63354 Q6
63358 Q6
63366 Q6
63377 Q6
63384 Q6
63386 Q6
63400 Q6
63402 Q6
63408 Q6
63431 Q6
63434 Q6
63444 Q6
63456 Q6
63458 Q6
64700 J30
64707 J39
64710 J39
64713 J39
64846 J39
64851 J39
64854 J39
64921 J39
64926 J39
64927 J39
64931 J39
64936 J39
65657 J25
65661 J25
65676 J25
65680 J25
65686 J25
65705 J25
65728 J25
68287 J71
68289 J71
68316 J71
68705 J72
68708 J72
68728 J72
68730 J72
68736 J72
68737 J72
69017 J72

1957 54C
61319 B1
61321 B1
63342 Q6
63346 Q6
63350 Q6
63354 Q6
63358 Q6
63366 Q6
63377 Q6
63384 Q6
63386 Q6
63400 Q6
63402 Q6
63408 Q6
63431 Q6
63434 Q6
63444 Q6
63456 Q6
63458 Q6
64700 J39
64707 J39
64710 J39
64713 J39
64846 J39
64851 J39
64854 J39
64921 J39
64926 J39
64931 J39
64936 J39
65645 J25
65657 J25
65697 J25
65700 J25
65702 J25
65712 J25
65728 J25
65785 J27
65823 J27
65873 J27
68278 J71
68316 J71
68694 J72
68697 J72
68699 J72
68705 J72
68728 J72
68730 J72
68736 J72
68737 J72
69017 J72

Boston

1948 BOS
61725 K2
61731 K2
61744 K2
61755 K2
61760 K2
61762 K2
62154 D2
62179 D2
62180 D2
62181 D2
62900 C4
62901 C4
62919 C4
62920 C4
62921 C4
62922 C4
62923 C4
62924 C4
62925 C4
64115 J3
64132 J3
64137 J3
64180 J6
64181 J6
64190 J6
64196 J6
64198 J6
64201 J6
64204 J6
64210 J6
64229 J6
64242 J6
64244 J6
64247 J6
64248 J6
64276 J6
65016 J2
65017 J2
65020 J2
67387 C12
68528 J69
68543 J69
68560 J69
68581 J69
68655 J68
68657 J68
68658 J68
68659 J68

1951 40F
61725 K2
61731 K2
61744 K2
61750 K2
61755 K2
61756 K2
61760 K2
61762 K2
61770 K2
64115 J3
64132 J3
64137 J3
64180 J6
64181 J6
64190 J6
64196 J6
64198 J6
64201 J6
64204 J6
64210 J6
64229 J6
64242 J6
64244 J6
64247 J6
64248 J6
64276 J6
65016 J2
65017 J2
65020 J2
67350 C12
68171 Y3
68528 J69
68543 J69
68560 J69
68581 J69
68655 J68
68657 J68
68658 J68
68659 J68
69256 N5
69261 N5
69803 A5
69808 A5
69816 A5
69819 A5
69824 A5

1954 40F
61725 K2
61728 K2
61744 K2
61745 K2
61750 K2
61756 K2
61757 K2
61760 K2
61762 K2
61766 K2
64131 J3
64180 J6
64190 J6
64201 J6
64204 J6
64214 J6
64229 J6
64244 J6
64247 J6
64248 J6
64250 J6
64260 J6
65017 J2
65020 J2
68499 J69
68501 J69
68543 J69
68557 J69
68560 J69
68570 J69
68581 J69
68602 J69
69256 N5
69261 N5
69803 A5
69808 A5
69816 A5
69819 A5

1957 40F
61725 K2
61731 K2
61742 K2
61743 K2
61744 K2
61745 K2
61748 K2
61750 K2
61756 K2
61757 K2
61762 K2
61765 K2
61766 K2
61767 K2
61943 K3
64180 J6
64190 J6
64201 J6
64204 J6
64214 J6
64229 J6
64244 J6
64247 J6
64250 J6
64260 J6
68501 J69
68543 J69
68557 J69
68560 J69
68569 J69
68570 J69
68581 J69
68602 J69
69284 N5
69808 A5
69819 A5

1960 40F
43058 4MT[5]
43059 4MT[5]
43061 4MT[5]
43062 4MT[5]
43064 4MT[5]
43065 4MT[5]
43066 4MT[5]
43068 4MT[5]
43080 4MT[5]
43083 4MT[5]
43085 4MT[5]
43091 4MT[5]
43092 4MT[5]
43093 4MT[5]
43107 4MT[5]
43109 4MT[5]
43110 4MT[5]
43142 4MT[5]
43143 4MT[5]
43147 4MT[5]
43157 4MT[5]
61742 K2
64171 J6
64172 J6
64191 J6
64231 J6
64728 J39
68522 J69
68570 J69

1963 40F
43058 4MT[5]
43059 4MT[5]
43061 4MT[5]
43062 4MT[5]
43064 4MT[5]
43065 4MT[5]
43066 4MT[5]
43068 4MT[5]
43080 4MT[5]
43083 4MT[5]
43085 4MT[5]
43091 4MT[5]
43092 4MT[5]
43093 4MT[5]
43107 4MT[5]
43108 4MT[5]
43109 4MT[5]
43110 4MT[5]
43142 4MT[5]
43143 4MT[5]
43144 4MT[5]
43147 4MT[5]
43148 4MT[5]
43158 4MT[5]

Boston Engineer's Dept.

1948
68166 Y3

1951
68166 Y3

1954
7 Y3

1957
7 Y3

1960
7 Y3

1963
7 Y3

Bournemouth

1948 BM
30021 M7
30028 M7
30040 M7
30047 M7
30050 M7
30051 M7
30052 M7
30057 M7
30059 M7
30092 B4[1]
30093 B4[1]
30099 B4[1]
30100 B4[1]
30104 M7
30106 M7
30107 M7
30111 M7
30112 M7
30131 M7
30161 L11
30168 L11
30169 L11
30173 L11
30239 G6
30251 M7
30318 M7
30337 T9
30363 T1
30379 M7
30398 S11
30399 S11
30415 L12
30429 L12
30548 Q
30549 Q
30696 700
30700 700
30719 T9
30728 T9
30736 N15
30743 N15
30772 N15
30787 N15
30789 N15
30790 N15
30850 LN
30851 LN
30852 LN
30853 LN
30854 LN
30855 LN
30862 LN
30863 LN
30864 LN
30865 LN
31622 U
31624 U
31796 U

1951 71B
30028 M7
30040 M7
30051 M7
30052 M7
30057 M7
30059 M7
30086 B4[1]
30087 B4[1]
30093 B4[1]
30104 M7
30106 M7
30111 M7
30112 M7
30131 M7
30204 O2
30212 O2
30251 M7
30260 G6
30318 M7
30379 M7
30398 S11
30403 S11
30404 S11
30548 Q
30549 Q
30695 700
30705 T9
30708 T9
30728 T9
30733 T9
30736 N15
30737 N15
30738 N15
30739 N15
30740 N15
30741 N15
30742 N15
30743 N15
30861 LN
30862 LN
30863 LN
30864 LN
30865 LN
31622 U
31795 U
34093 WC
34094 WC
34095 WC
34105 WC
34106 WC
34107 WC
34108 WC
34109 BB

1954 71B
30056 M7
30057 M7
30058 M7
30059 M7
30060 M7
30086 B4[1]
30087 B4[1]
30093 B4[1]
30105 M7
30106 M7
30107 M7
30111 M7
30112 M7
30128 M7
30212 O2
30223 O2
30260 G6
30318 M7
30541 Q
30548 Q
30549 Q
30695 700
30728 T9
30729 T9
30736 N15
30737 N15
30738 N15
30739 N15
30740 N15
30741 N15
30742 N15
30743 N15
30782 N15
30783 N15
30861 LN
30862 LN
30863 LN
30864 LN
30865 LN
34043 WC
34044 WC
34093 WC
34094 WC
34095 WC
34105 WC
34106 WC
34107 WC
34108 WC
34109 BB
34110 BB

1957 71B
30040 M7
30057 M7
30058 M7
30059 M7
30060 M7
30087 B4[1]
30093 B4[1]
30104 M7
30105 M7
30106 M7
30107 M7
30108 M7
30111 M7
30112 M7
30127 M7
30128 M7
30260 G6
30306 700
30318 M7
30324 M7
30539 Q
30541 Q
30548 Q
30690 700
30695 700
30706 T9
30727 T9
30738 N15
30739 N15
30742 N15
30764 N15
30765 N15
30771 N15
30780 N15
30781 N15
30782 N15
30783 N15
30864 LN
30865 LN
31614 U
31615 U
31632 U
34040 WC
34041 WC
34042 WC
34043 WC
34044 WC
34093 WC
34094 WC
34105 WC
34106 WC
34107 WC
34108 WC
34109 BB
34110 BB
35010 MN
35022 MN R
35025 MN R
35027 MN

1960 71B
30040 M7
30057 M7
30058 M7
30059 M7
30060 M7
30093 B4[1]
30102 B4[1]
30104 M7
30105 M7
30106 M7
30107 M7
30108 M7
30111 M7
30112 M7
30127 M7
30128 M7
30274 G6
30539 Q
30541 Q
30548 Q
30690 700
30695 700
30707 T9
30764 N15
30771 N15
30772 N15
30781 N15
30782 N15
30783 N15
34028 WC R
34029 WC R
34039 WC R
34040 WC
34041 WC
34042 WC R
34043 WC
34044 WC
34045 WC R
34046 WC R
34047 WC R
34048 WC R
34102 WC
34105 WC
35002 MN R
35005 MN R
35010 MN R
35021 MN R
35022 MN R
35024 MN R
35025 MN R
35027 MN R
75065 4MT[1]
75066 4MT[1]
75067 4MT[1]
75068 4MT[1]
76056 4MT[2]
76057 4MT[2]
76058 4MT[2]

1963 71B
30024 M7
30031 M7
30056 M7
30057 M7
30105 M7
30107 M7
30108 M7
30110 M7
30111 M7
30127 M7
30328 M7
30379 M7
30535 Q
30539 Q

30541 Q
30548 Q
34029 WC R
34040 WC R
34041 WC
34042 WC R
34043 WC
34044 WC R
34045 WC R
34046 WC R
34047 WC R
34053 BB R
34085 BB R
34102 WC
34103 WC
34105 WC
35002 MN R
35005 MN R
35008 MN R
35011 MN R
35021 MN R
35023 MN R
35027 MN R
76015 4MT^{2}
76019 4MT^{2}
76025 4MT^{2}
76026 4MT^{2}
76027 4MT^{2}
76056 4MT^{2}
76057 4MT^{2}

1966 70F
34004 WC R
34005 WC R
34012 WC R
34024 WC R
34025 WC R
34040 WC R
34044 WC R
34047 WC R
35003 MN R
35008 MN R
35010 MN R
35011 MN R
35013 MN R
35023 MN R
35027 MN R
41224 2MT^{1}
41230 2MT^{1}
41295 2MT^{1}
41312 2MT^{1}
41316 2MT^{1}
41320 2MT^{1}
76005 4MT^{2}
76006 4MT^{2}
76009 4MT^{2}
76010 4MT^{2}
76011 4MT^{2}
76013 4MT^{2}
76014 4MT^{2}
76026 4MT^{2}
76057 4MT^{2}
80011 4MT^{3}
80013 4MT^{3}
80019 4MT^{3}
80032 4MT^{3}
80134 4MT^{3}
80138 4MT^{3}
80146 4MT^{3}

Bournville

1948 21B
40105 3MT^{2}
40162 3MT^{2}
40168 3MT^{2}
40173 3MT^{2}
40179 3MT^{2}
40439 2P^{2}
40517 2P^{2}
40917 4P^{1}
40934 4P^{1}
41061 4P^{1}
41064 4P^{1}
41073 4P^{1}
42327 4MT^{2}
42338 4MT^{2}
42339 4MT^{2}
42342 4MT^{2}
42373 4MT^{2}
43355 3F^{3}
43359 3F^{3}
43562 3F^{3}
43583 3F^{3}
43668 3F^{3}
43675 3F^{3}
43687 3F^{3}
43968 4F^{1}
44138 4F^{2}
44289 4F^{2}
44333 4F^{2}
58110 2F^{6}
58111 2F^{7}
58113 2F^{7}
58126 2F^{8}
58141 2F^{8}
58143 2F^{8}

1951 21B
40105 3MT^{2}
40168 3MT^{2}
40439 2P^{2}
40463 2P^{2}
40917 4P^{1}
41061 4P^{1}
41064 4P^{1}
41073 4P^{1}
42050 4MT^{1}
42186 4MT^{1}
42327 4MT^{2}
42338 4MT^{2}
42342 4MT^{2}
43203 3F^{3}
43263 3F^{3}
43355 3F^{3}
43359 3F^{3}
43583 3F^{3}
43668 3F^{3}
43675 3F^{3}
43687 3F^{3}
44138 4F^{2}
44333 4F^{2}
44366 4F^{2}
44811 5MT^{3}
44852 5MT^{3}
45236 5MT^{3}
45274 5MT^{3}
58126 2F^{8}
58138 2F^{8}
58143 2F^{8}

1954 21B
40439 2P^{2}
40463 2P^{2}
40917 4P^{1}
41064 4P^{1}
41073 4P^{1}
41117 4P^{1}
41156 4P^{1}
41194 4P^{1}
42050 4MT^{1}
42186 4MT^{1}
42338 4MT^{2}
43203 3F^{3}
43263 3F^{3}
43355 3F^{3}
43359 3F^{3}
43521 3F^{3}
43583 3F^{3}
43668 3F^{3}
43675 3F^{3}
43687 3F^{3}
44366 4F^{2}
44811 5MT^{3}
45236 5MT^{3}
48523 8F
58126 2F^{8}
58138 2F^{8}
58143 2F^{8}

1957 21B
40439 2P^{2}
41064 4P^{1}
41073 4P^{1}
41156 4P^{1}
41194 4P^{1}
42186 4MT^{1}
42334 4MT^{2}
42338 4MT^{2}
42340 4MT^{2}
43203 3F^{3}
43263 3F^{3}
43355 3F^{3}
43359 3F^{3}
43521 3F^{3}
43583 3F^{3}
43668 3F^{3}
43675 3F^{3}
43687 3F^{3}
43837 4F^{1}
43932 4F^{1}
43989 4F^{1}
44981 5MT^{3}
45236 5MT^{3}
48523 8F
58138 2F^{8}
58143 2F^{8}
58167 2F^{8}

1960 21B
40144 3MT^{2}
40439 2P^{2}
43012 4MT^{5}
43033 4MT^{5}
43521 3F^{3}
43583 3F^{3}
43668 3F^{3}
43687 3F^{3}
44463 4F^{2}
44516 4F^{2}
44571 4F^{2}
58138 2F^{8}
58143 2F^{8}
58168 2F^{8}

Bowes Bridge

1948 BOW
69097 N10
69100 N10

1951 52A sub
69097 N10
69100 N10

1954 52A sub
69097 N10
69100 N10

1957 52A sub
69097 N10
69100 N10

1960 52A sub
69097 N10

Bradford Hammerton Street

1948 BFD
61229 B1
61230 B1
63217 Q4
64170 J6
64203 J6
64205 J6
64226 J6
64268 J6
64271 J6
64274 J6
68892 J50
68895 J50
68897 J50
68898 J50
68902 J50
68906 J50
68908 J50
68912 J50
68922 J50
68923 J50
68932 J50
68933 J50
68934 J50
68940 J50
68941 J50
68942 J50
68943 J50
68944 J50
68959 J50
68961 J50
68969 J50
69253 N5
69256 N5
69261 N5
69280 N5
69437 N1
69443 N1
69447 N1
69448 N1
69449 N1
69454 N1
69459 N1
69464 N1
69474 N1
69478 N1
69479 N1
69482 N1
69483 N1
69485 N1

1951 37C
61229 B1
61230 B1
61267 B1
61268 B1
61294 B1
61296 B1
64170 J6
64203 J6
64205 Jo
64226 J6
64268 J6
64271 J6
64274 J6
67447 C14
67448 C14
67450 C14
68892 J50
68895 J50
68897 J50
68898 J50
68902 J50
68906 J50
68908 J50
68912 J50
68922 J50
68923 J50
68932 J50
68933 J50
68934 J50
68940 J50
68941 J50
68942 J50
68943 J50
68944 J50
68959 J50
68969 J50
69443 N1
69447 N1
69448 N1
69449 N1
69454 N1
69459 N1
69464 N1
69474 N1
69478 N1
69479 N1
69482 N1
69483 N1
69485 N1

1954 37C
61031 B1
61229 B1
61230 B1
61267 B1
61268 B1
61296 B1
63920 O4
64170 J6
64203 J6
64205 J6
64226 J6
64268 J6
64903 J39
64907 J39
68892 J50
68895 J50
68897 J50
68898 J50
68908 J50
68912 J50
68922 J50
68923 J50
68932 J50
68933 J50
68934 J50
68940 J50
68942 J50
68943 J50
68944 J50
68959 J50
68969 J50
69432 N1
69433 N1
69434 N1
69439 N1
69443 N1
69447 N1
69449 N1
69454 N1
69459 N1
69464 N1
69474 N1
69475 N1
69478 N1
69482 N1
69485 N1

1957 56G
61031 B1
61229 B1
61230 B1
61267 B1
61268 B1
61296 B1
61320 B1
63920 O4
64170 J6
64203 J6
64226 J6
64801 J39
64903 J39
64907 J39
68892 J50
68895 J50
68897 J50
68898 J50
68908 J50
68922 J50
68923 J50
68932 J50
68933 J50
68934 J50
68940 J50
68942 J50
68943 J50
68944 J50
68959 J50
68969 J50
69434 N1
69443 N1
69457 N1
69474 N1

Brecon

1948 BCN
2343 2301
2351 2301
2401 2301
2452 2301
2468 2301
2523 2301
2569 2301
3638 5700
3706 5700
3767 5700
5801 5800
9614 5700

1951 89B
2287 2251
2343 2301
2351 2301
2401 2301
2452 2301
2468 2301
2482 2301
2483 2301
3638 5700
3706 5700
3767 5700
3770 5700
5801 5800

1954 89B
2286 2251
2287 2251
3638 5700
3706 5700
3767 5700
3770 5700
5801 5800
46516 2MT^{2}
46517 2MT^{2}
46518 2MT^{2}
46521 2MT^{2}
46522 2MT^{2}
46523 2MT^{2}
46524 2MT^{2}

1957 89B
2235 2251
2287 2251
3638 5700
3706 5700
3767 5700
3770 5700
8438 9400
46508 2MT^{2}
46516 2MT^{2}
46517 2MT^{2}
46518 2MT^{2}
46521 2MT^{2}
46522 2MT^{2}
46524 2MT^{2}

Bricklayers Arms

1948 BA
30798 N15
30799 N15
30921 V
30922 V
30923 V
30928 V
30929 V
30930 V
30931 V
30932 V
30933 V
30934 V
30935 V
30936 V
30937 V
30938 V
30939 V
31033 C
31036 E
31090 C
31093 O1
31102 C
31159 E
31162 H
31166 E
31175 E
31176 E
31223 C
31275 E
31277 C
31280 C
31287 C
31294 C
31297 C
31315 E
31324 H
31326 H
31328 H
31388 O1
31389 O1
31395 O1
31397 O1
31398 O1
31425 O1
31428 O1
31429 O1
31460 C
31491 E
31500 H
31533 H
31541 H
31542 H
31546 H
31547 E
31550 H
31584 C
31685 S
31687 C
31693 C
31723 C
31724 C
31725 C
31758 L1
31759 L1
31782 L1
31783 L1
31784 L1
31785 L1
31786 L1
31787 L1
31788 L1
31789 L1
31824 N
31825 N
31826 N
31865 N
31901 U1
31902 U1
32075 I3
32076 I3
32077 I3
32085 I3
32087 I3
32089 I3
32097 E1^{2}
32128 E1^{2}
32141 E1^{2}
32142 E1^{2}
32151 E1^{2}
32165 E3
32166 E3
32168 E3
32170 E3
32410 E6
32412 E6
32413 E6
32415 E6
32442 C2X
32446 C2X
32448 C2X
32453 E3
32454 E3
32458 E3
32459 E3
32460 E3
32461 E3
32462 E3
32463 E4
32467 E4
32468 E4
32469 E4
32472 E4
32474 E4
32524 C2X
32525 C2X
32549 C2X
32551 C2X
32564 E4
32565 E4
32578 E4
90164 WD^{1}
90181 WD^{1}
90194 WD^{1}
90213 WD^{1}
90216 WD^{1}
90226 WD^{1}
90234 WD^{1}
90254 WD^{1}
90375 WD^{1}
90389 WD^{1}
90408 WD^{1}
90552 WD^{1}
90556 WD^{1}
90558 WD^{1}
90564 WD^{1}
90619 WD^{1}
90622 WD^{1}
90650 WD^{1}

1951 73B
30798 N15
30799 N15
30800 N15
30919 V
30920 V
30921 V
30928 V
30929 V
30930 V
30931 V
30932 V
30933 V
30934 V
30936 V
30937 V
30938 V
30939 V
31033 C
31036 E
31044 O1
31064 O1
31066 O1
31068 C
31071 C
31102 C
31160 E1^{1}
31162 H
31166 E
31175 E
31176 E
31227 C
31253 C
31273 E
31275 E
31278 H
31280 C
31293 C
31294 C
31297 C
31309 H
31315 E
31324 H
31326 H
31395 O1
31491 E
31507 E1^{1}
31508 C
31533 H
31541 H
31542 H
31543 H
31544 H
31546 H
31584 C
31687 C
31723 C
31725 C
31758 L1
31759 L1
31782 L1
31783 L1
31785 L1
31786 L1
31787 L1
31824 N
31825 N
31826 N
31827 N
31899 U1
31900 U1
31901 U1
31902 U1
32050 B4X
32056 B4X
32070 B4X
32075 I3
32113 E1^{2}
32151 E1^{2}
32165 E3
32166 E3
32168 E3
32170 E3
32408 E6
32410 E6
32413 E6
32415 E6
32442 C2X
32446 C2X
32448 C2X
32453 E3
32458 E3
32459 E3
32460 E3
32461 E3
32462 E3
32463 E4
32467 E4
32469 E4
32472 E4
32473 E4
32474 E4
32481 E4
32524 C2X
32525 C2X
32549 C2X
32551 C2X
32554 C2X
32564 E4
32565 E4
32585 E5
32587 E5
32590 E5
32602 I1X
90164 WD^{1}
90194 WD^{1}
90216 WD^{1}
90226 WD^{1}
90234 WD^{1}
90254 WD^{1}
90408 WD^{1}
90533 WD^{1}
90552 WD^{1}
90558 WD^{1}
90564 WD^{1}

1954 73B
30799 N15
30800 N15
30801 N15
30924 V
30925 V
30926 V
30927 V
30928 V
30929 V
30930 V
30931 V
30932 V
30933 V
30934 V
30935 V
30936 V
30937 V
30938 V
30939 V
31068 C
31071 C
31086 C
31102 C
31165 E1^{1}
31280 C
31287 C
31293 C
31294 C
31297 C
31408 N
31497 E1^{1}
31507 E1^{1}
31533 H
31540 H
31542 H
31544 H
31553 H
31720 C
31722 C
31723 C
31724 C
31725 C
31735 D1^{1}
31739 D1^{1}
31741 D1^{1}
31783 L1
31784 L1
31785 L1
31823 N
31824 N
31825 N
31826 N
31827 N
31828 N
31829 N
31853 N
31855 N
31870 N
31871 N
31872 N
31873 N
31874 N
31875 N
31890 U1
31891 U1
32408 E6
32409 E6
32410 E6
32412 E6
32415 E6
32453 E3
32455 E3
32458 E3
32459 E3
32460 E3
32461 E3
32462 E3
32471 E4
32472 E4
32473 E4
32474 E4
32524 C2X
32525 C2X
32551 C2X
32552 C2X
32553 C2X
32554 C2X
32564 E4
32565 E4
41299 2MT^{1}
41300 2MT^{1}
41301 2MT^{1}
41302 2MT^{1}
42080 4MT^{1}
42081 4MT^{1}
42082 4MT^{1}

1957 73B
30799 N15
30800 N15
30801 N15
30924 V
30925 V
30926 V
30927 V
30928 V
30929 V
30931 V
30932 V
30933 V
30934 V
30935 V
30936 V
30937 V
30938 V
30939 V
31068 C
31071 C
31086 C
31102 C
31165 E1^{1}
31267 C
31280 C
31287 C
31293 C
31297 C
31305 H
31306 H
31497 E1^{1}
31507 E1^{1}
31533 H
31540 H
31553 H
31735 D1^{1}
31739 D1^{1}
31741 D1^{1}
31783 L1
31784 L1
31823 N
31824 N
31825 N
31826 N
31827 N
31828 N
31829 N
31851 N
31853 N
31870 N
31871 N
31872 N
31873 N
31874 N
31875 N
31890 U1
31891 U1
31899 U1
31900 U1
31901 U1
31902 U1
32408 E6
32409 E6
32410 E6
32412 E6
32415 E6
32458 E3
32461 E3
32462 E3
32471 E4
32472 E4
32473 E4
32474 E4
32524 C2X
32525 C2X
32537 C2X
32538 C2X
32539 C2X
32551 C2X
32552 C2X
32553 C2X
32554 C2X
32564 E4
32565 E4
41299 2MT^{1}
41300 2MT^{1}
41302 2MT^{1}
42080 4MT^{1}
42081 4MT^{1}
42082 4MT^{1}

1960 73B
30924 V
30925 V
30926 V
30927 V
30928 V
30929 V
30930 V
30931 V
31068 C
31086 C
31102 C
31267 C
31293 C
31305 H
31480 C
31533 H
31540 H
31717 C
31739 D1^{1}
31743 D1^{1}
31749 D1^{1}
31823 N
31824 N
31825 N
31826 N
31827 N
31828 N
31829 N
31873 N
31874 N
31875 N
32408 E6
32410 E6
32415 E6
32416 E6
32417 E6
32418 E6
32472 E4
32473 E4
32474 E4
32525 C2X
32538 C2X
32539 C2X
32551 C2X
32552 C2X
32553 C2X
32554 C2X
32557 E4
32564 E4
32565 E4
34001 WC R
34003 WC R
34004 WC R
34005 WC R
34012 WC R
34013 WC R
34014 WC R
34016 WC R
34017 WC R
34021 WC R
34022 WC R
34025 WC R
34026 WC R
34027 WC R
34037 WC R
34078 BB
41299 2MT^{1}
41300 2MT^{1}
41301 2MT^{1}
41303 2MT^{1}
80082 4MT^{3}
80083 4MT^{3}
80084 4MT^{3}
80085 4MT^{3}

Bridlington

1948 BRI
62345 D20
62353 D20
62383 D20
68148 Y1
68155 Y3

1951 53D
62353 D20
62355 D20
62375 D20
62701 D49
62703 D49
62707 D49
62750 D49
62766 D49
68148 Y1
68155 Y3

1954 53D
62701 D49
62703 D49
62707 D49
62750 D49
62766 D49
68148 Y1
68155 Y3
69378 N8

1957 53D
62397 D20
62700 D49
62701 D49
62703 D49
62707 D49
62750 D49
67256 G5
68145 Y1
77000 3MT^{1}

Brighton

1948 BTN
31178 P
31557 P
31890 U1
31891 U1
31892 U1
31893 U1
31894 U1
31900 U1
32037 H1
32038 H1
32039 H1
32043 B4X
32056 B4X
32060 B4X
32071 B4X
32072 B4X
32084 I3
32086 I3
32088 I3
32122 E1^{2}
32127 E1^{2}
32139 E1^{2}
32235 D1/M
32339 K
32340 K
32341 K
32342 K
32343 K
32344 K
32345 K
32346 K
32347 K
32368 D3
32372 D3
32376 D3
32385 D3
32386 D3
32397 D3X
32437 C2X
32438 C2X
32443 C2X
32470 E4
32471 E4
32486 E4
32491 E4
32505 E4
32513 E4
32514 E4
32523 C2X
32528 C2X
32539 C2X
32543 C2X
32546 C2X
32558 E4
32566 E4
32567 E5
32576 E5X
32577 E4
32583 E5
32587 E5
32606 E1^{2}
90107 WD^{1}
90247 WD^{1}
90345 WD^{1}
90347 WD^{1}
90354 WD^{1}

1951 75A
31178 P
31556 P
31870 N
31871 N
31890 U1
31891 U1
31892 U1
31893 U1
31894 U1
32002 I1X
32005 I1X
32039 H1
32086 I3
32145 E1^{2}
32325 J1
32326 J2
32337 K
32339 K
32341 K
32342 K
32343 K
32344 K
32345 K
32346 K
32348 K
32368 D3
32372 D3
32376 D3
32386 D3
32393 D3
32400 E5
32406 E5
32425 H2
32426 H2
32434 C2X
32438 C2X
32443 C2X
32470 E4
32471 E4
32486 E4
32505 E4
32509 E4
32513 E4
32514 E4
32523 C2X
32528 C2X
32534 C2X
32538 C2X
32543 C2X
32566 E4
32573 E5
32575 E5
32576 E5X
32577 E4
32583 E5
32588 E5
32594 E5
32595 I1X
32689 E1^{2}
34037 WC
34038 WC
34039 WC
34040 WC
34041 WC
90247 WD^{1}
90354 WD^{1}

1954 75A
30052 M7
30053 M7
30129 M7
30950 Z
31310 H
31319 H
31320 H
31325 P
31556 P
32165 E3
32166 E3
32167 E3
32169 E3
32170 E3
32337 K
32338 K
32339 K
32340 K
32341 K
32342 K
32343 K
32344 K
32390 D3
32401 E5X
32421 H2
32425 H2
32426 H2
32434 C2X
32438 C2X
32440 C2X
32441 C2X
32442 C2X
32485 E4
32508 E4
32511 E4
32513 E4
32514 E4
32515 E4
32518 E4
32539 C2X
32540 C2X
32566 E4
32577 E4
32583 E5
32585 E5
32586 E5X
34039 WC
34045 WC
34046 WC
34047 WC
34048 WC
42086 4MT^{1}
42087 4MT^{1}
42088 4MT^{1}
42104 4MT^{1}
42105 4MT^{1}
80016 4MT^{3}
80019 4MT^{3}
80031 4MT^{3}
80032 4MT^{3}
80033 4MT^{3}

1957 75A
30031 M7
30052 M7
30053 M7
30054 M7
30055 M7
30056 M7
31325 P
31556 P
31724 C
31725 C
31776 L
31777 L
31778 L
32165 E3
32166 E3
32338 K
32339 K
32340 K
32341 K
32342 K
32343 K
32424 H2
32434 C2X
32437 C2X
32440 C2X
32441 C2X
32442 C2X
32449 C2X
32467 E4
32468 E4
32475 E4
32481 E4
32484 E4
32485 E4
32494 E4
32502 E4

32503 E4
32504 E4
32508 E4
32512 E4
32515 E4
32521 C2X
32536 C2X
32540 C2X
32562 E4
32566 E4
32577 E4
32655 A1X
32662 A1X
34039 WC
34045 WC
34046 WC
34047 WC
34048 WC
80010 4MT^3
80011 4MT^3
80031 4MT^3
80032 4MT^3
80033 4MT^3
80145 4MT^3
80146 4MT^3
80147 4MT^3
80148 4MT^3
80149 4MT^3
80150 4MT^3

1960 75A

30047 M7
30049 M7
30050 M7
30051 M7
30056 M7
30110 M7
30900 V
30901 V
30914 V
30915 V
30916 V
30917 V
31276 H
31308 H
31325 P
31530 H
31543 H
31556 P
31724 C
31725 C
31890 U1
31891 U1
32338 K
32339 K
32340 K
32341 K
32342 K
32343 K
32441 C2X
32442 C2X
32449 C2X
32468 E4
32475 E4
32484 E4
32503 E4
32504 E4
32508 E4
32512 E4
32515 E4
32562 E4
32580 E4
32635 A1X
32655 A1X
32662 A1X
32670 A1X
34008 WC
34019 WC
34097 WC
34098 WC
34099 WC
75070 4MT^1
80013 4MT^3
80031 4MT^3
80032 4MT^3
80033 4MT^3
80143 4MT^3
80144 4MT^3
80145 4MT^3
80146 4MT^3
80147 4MT^3
80148 4MT^3
80149 4MT^3
80150 4MT^3
80151 4MT^3
80152 4MT^3
80153 4MT^3
80154 4MT^3

1963 75A

31400 N
31401 N
31402 N
31403 N
31827 N
31828 N
31829 N
31830 N
31831 N
31832 N
31833 N
31873 N
31890 U1
31891 U1
31901 U1
31910 U1
32468 E4
32474 E4
32479 E4
32503 E4
32635 A1X
32636 A1X
32662 A1X
32670 A1X
34012 WC R
34013 WC R
34014 WC R
34019 WC
34027 WC R
34055 BB
34057 BB
34089 BB R
34100 WC R
34101 WC R
41223 2MT^1
41230 2MT^1
41260 2MT^1
41261 2MT^1
41276 2MT^1
41283 2MT^1
41287 2MT^1
41291 2MT^1
41300 2MT^1
41301 2MT^1
41303 2MT^1
41324 2MT^1
41325 2MT^1
41326 2MT^1
41327 2MT^1
75067 4MT^1
75068 4MT^1
76030 4MT^2
76031 4MT^2
76032 4MT^2
76033 4MT^2
76034 4MT^2
80013 4MT^3
80031 4MT^3
80032 4MT^3
80033 4MT^3
80138 4MT^3
80143 4MT^3
80144 4MT^3
80145 4MT^3
80146 4MT^3
80147 4MT^3
80148 4MT^3
80149 4MT^3
80150 4MT^3
80151 4MT^3
80152 4MT^3
80153 4MT^3
80154 4MT^3

Brighton Works

1948

DS377 A1X

1951

DS377 A1X

1954

DS377 A1X

1957

DS377 A1X

Bristol Barrow Road

1948 22A

40119 3MT^2
40174 3MT^2
40423 2P^2
40741 3P^1
40935 4P^1
41028 4P^2
41030 4P^2
41706 1F^1
41874 1F^1
43178 3F^2
43204 3F^3
43228 3F^3
43419 3F^3
43436 3F^3
43439 3F^3
43444 3F^3
43464 3F^3
43593 3F^3
43712 3F^3
43734 3F^3
43853 4F^1
43928 4F^1
43953 4F^1
44112 4F^2
44135 4F^2
44169 4F^2
44266 4F^2
44411 4F^2
44424 4F^2
44466 4F^2
44534 4F^2
44536 4F^2
44537 4F^2
44569 4F^2
44804 5MT^3
44812 5MT^3
44843 5MT^3
44855 5MT^3
45272 5MT^3
45561 6P5F^2
45570 6P5F^2
45572 6P5F^2
45662 6P5F^2
45663 6P5F^2
45682 6P5F^2
45685 6P5F^2
45690 6P5F^2
45694 6P5F^2
47190 Sentinel^1
47544 3F^6
47550 3F^6
47678 3F^6
51212 0F^4
58074 1P^6
58080 1P^6
58215 2F^9

1951 22A

40116 3MT^2
40163 3MT^2
40164 3MT^2
40174 3MT^2
40423 2P^2
40741 3P^1
40935 4P^1
41012 4P^2
41028 4P^2
41030 4P^2
41706 1F^1
43012 4MT^5
43046 4MT^5
43047 4MT^5
43427 3F^3
43436 3F^3
43444 3F^3
43462 3F^3
43464 3F^3
43593 3F^3
43712 3F^3
43734 3F^3
43853 4F^1
43926 4F^1
43928 4F^1
44135 4F^2
44169 4F^2
44266 4F^2
44267 4F^2
44269 4F^2
44411 4F^2
44424 4F^2
44466 4F^2
44534 4F^2
44536 4F^2
44537 4F^2
44553 4F^2
44569 4F^2
44743 5MT^3
44744 5MT^3
44745 5MT^3
44746 5MT^3
44747 5MT^3
44855 5MT^3
45561 6P5F^2
45570 6P5F^2
45572 6P5F^2
45660 6P5F^2
45662 6P5F^2
45663 6P5F^2
45682 6P5F^2
45685 6P5F^2
45690 6P5F^2
45699 6P5F^2
47190 Sentinel^1
47544 3F^6
47550 3F^6
47678 3F^6
51212 0F^4

1954 22A

40116 3MT^2
40120 3MT^2
40163 3MT^2
40164 3MT^2
40174 3MT^2
40426 2P^2
40486 2P^2
41240 2MT^1
41706 1F^1
43012 4MT^5
43427 3F^3
43462 3F^3
43464 3F^3
43593 3F^3
43712 3F^3
43734 3F^3
43926 4F^1
43928 4F^1
43932 4F^1
44135 4F^2
44169 4F^2
44266 4F^2
44269 4F^2
44296 4F^2
44317 4F^2
44411 4F^2
44424 4F^2
44466 4F^2
44534 4F^2
44536 4F^2
44537 4F^2
44553 4F^2
44569 4F^2
44743 5MT^3
44745 5MT^3
44747 5MT^3
45561 6P5F^2
45572 6P5F^2
45577 6P5F^2
45602 6P5F^2
45651 6P5F^2
45660 6P5F^2
45662 6P5F^2
45663 6P5F^2
45682 6P5F^2
45685 6P5F^2
45690 6P5F^2
45699 6P5F^2
47544 3F^6
47550 3F^6
47552 3F^6
47678 3F^6
51202 0F^4
51212 0F^4

1957 22A

40116 3MT^2
40426 2P^2
40486 2P^2
41207 2MT^1
41208 2MT^1
41240 2MT^1
41879 1F^1
43344 3F^3
43427 3F^3
43444 3F^3
43464 3F^3
43593 3F^3
43712 3F^3
43734 3F^3
43926 4F^1
44015 4F^2
44135 4F^2
44269 4F^2
44296 4F^2
44411 4F^2
44424 4F^2
44466 4F^2
44534 4F^2
44537 4F^2
44553 4F^2
44569 4F^2
44743 5MT^3
44744 5MT^3
44745 5MT^3
44746 5MT^3
44747 5MT^3
44966 5MT^3
45040 5MT^3
45280 5MT^3
45561 6P5F^2
45572 6P5F^2
45577 6P5F^2
45651 6P5F^2
45660 6P5F^2
45662 6P5F^2
45663 6P5F^2
45682 6P5F^2
45685 6P5F^2
45690 6P5F^2
45699 6P5F^2
47333 3F^6
47544 3F^6
47550 3F^6
47552 3F^6
47678 3F^6
51202 0F^4
51212 0F^4

1960 82E

2229 2251
3606 5700
3752 5700
6323 4300
6346 4300
6350 4300
6376 4300
8725 5700
40501 2P^2
40537 2P^2
41207 2MT^1
41208 2MT^1
41240 2MT^1
41304 2MT^1
41879 1F^1
43344 3F^3
43444 3F^3
43593 3F^3
44135 4F^2
44269 4F^2
44411 4F^2
44466 4F^2
44534 4F^2
44553 4F^2
44569 4F^2
45504 6P5F^1
45506 6P5F^1
45519 6P5F^1
45572 6P5F^2
45577 6P5F^2
45651 6P5F^2
45660 6P5F^2
45662 6P5F^2
45682 6P5F^2
45685 6P5F^2
45690 6P5F^2
45699 6P5F^2
47333 3F^6
47544 3F^6
47678 3F^6
51217 0F^4
51218 0F^4
51221 0F^4
73003 5MT
73015 5MT
73054 5MT
73068 5MT
75004 4MT^1
75021 4MT^1
75022 4MT^1

1963 82E

2217 2251
2221 2251
2251 2251
2277 2251
3218 2251
3643 5700
3675 5700
3677 5700
3696 5700
3702 5700
3752 5700
3765 5700
3795 5700
4103 5101
4131 5101
4619 5700
5203 4200
5215 5205
6147 6100
8795 5700
9623 5700
9626 5700
41207 2MT^1
41208 2MT^1
41245 2MT^1
41248 2MT^1
41249 2MT^1
41304 2MT^1
43924 4F^1
44135 4F^2
44209 4F^2
44264 4F^2
44269 4F^2
44466 4F^2
44523 4F^2
44534 4F^2
44569 4F^2
45682 6P5F^2
45685 6P5F^2
45690 6P5F^2
48110 8F
48431 8F
73003 5MT
73015 5MT
73028 5MT
82007 3MT^2
82035 3MT^2
82036 3MT^2
82037 3MT^2
82038 3MT^2
82039 3MT^2
82040 3MT^2
82043 3MT^2
92000 9F
92004 9F
92007 9F
92221 9F
92248 9F

Bristol Bath Road

1948 BRD

1002 1000
1005 1000
1007 1000
1011 1000
1013 1000
1014 1000
1028 1000
1415 1400
1430 1400
1463 1400
2072 2021
2444 2301
2462 2301
2929 2900
2931 2900
2939 2900
2942 2900
2950 2900
3950 4900
4019 4000
4020 4000
4030 4000
4033 4000
4034 4000
4035 4000
4041 4000
4042 4000
4043 4000
4047 4000
4080 4073
4084 4073
4089 4073
4093 4073
4096 4073
4142 5101
4143 5101
4151 5101
4152 5101
4155 5101
4535 4500
4536 4500
4539 4500
4563 4500
4577 4575
4580 4575
4595 4575
4942 4900
5019 4073
5024 4073
5025 4073
5048 4073
5074 4073
5076 4073
5082 4073
5083 4073
5084 4073
5091 4073
5096 4073
5169 5101
5325 4300
5327 4300
5343 4300
5506 4575
5511 4575
5512 4575
5514 4575
5523 4575
5527 4575
5528 4575
5535 4575
5536 4575
5539 4575
5546 4575
5547 4575
5548 4575
5553 4575
5555 4575
5558 4575
5559 4575
5561 4575
5564 4575
5572 4575
5803 5800
5809 5800
5813 5800
5949 4900
6958 4900
6971 6959
6972 6959
7809 7800
7812 7800
7814 7800

1951 82A

1002 1000
1005 1000
1007 1000
1011 1000
1014 1000
1028 1000
1415 1400
1430 1400
1463 1400
2072 2021
2534 2301
2931 2900
2948 2900
2950 2900
4020 4000
4033 4000
4035 4000
4041 4000
4042 4000
4043 4000
4047 4000
4056 4000
4060 4000
4073 4073
4075 4073
4084 4073
4091 4073
4096 4073
4142 5101
4143 5101
4151 5101
4152 5101
4155 5101
4535 4500
4539 4500
4563 4500
4577 4575
4580 4575
4595 4575
4914 4900
4942 4900
4954 4900
5000 4073
5019 4073
5025 4073
5037 4073
5048 4073
5064 4073
5067 4073
5074 4073
5076 4073
5082 4073
5094 4073
5096 4073
5311 4300
5325 4300
5327 4300
5506 4575
5511 4575
5512 4575
5514 4575
5523 4575
5527 4575
5528 4575
5535 4575
5536 4575
5539 4575
5546 4575
5547 4575
5548 4575
5553 4575
5555 4575
5558 4575
5559 4575
5561 4575
5564 4575
5572 4575
5809 5800
5813 5800
6000 6000
6102 6100
6107 6100
6351 4300
6954 4900
6958 4900
6965 6959
6972 6959
6977 6959
6981 6959
6997 6959
7011 4073
7014 4073
7019 4073
7034 4073
7901 6959

1954 82A

1005 1000
1007 1000
1011 1000
1014 1000
1026 1000
1028 1000
1415 1400
1430 1400
1454 1400
1463 1400
2203 2251
4056 4000
4073 4073
4075 4073
4084 4073
4091 4073
4094 4073
4096 4073
4139 5101
4157 5101
4159 5101
4166 5101
4532 4500
4535 4500
4558 4500
4577 4575
4582 4575
4592 4575
4595 4575
4597 4575
4603 5700
4660 5700
4909 4900
4914 4900
4942 4900
4961 4900
4972 4900
5000 4073
5019 4073
5025 4073
5037 4073
5048 4073
5064 4073
5067 4073
5069 4073
5074 4073
5076 4073
5085 4073
5094 4073
5096 4073
5182 5101
5197 5101
5506 4575
5512 4575
5514 4575
5523 4575
5525 4575
5528 4575
5532 4575
5535 4575
5546 4575
5548 4575
5553 4575
5559 4575
5561 4575
5565 4575
5809 5800
5813 5800
5904 4900
5919 4900
5934 4900
5949 4900
6351 4300
6900 4900
6972 6959
6977 6959
6981 6959
6982 6959
6997 6959
7011 4073
7014 4073
7019 4073
7034 4073
7782 5700
7901 6959
7907 6959
9016 9000
9020 9000
9026 9000
9604 5700
9610 5700

1957 82A

1000 1000
1005 1000
1009 1000
1011 1000
1014 1000
1028 1000
1412 1400
1454 1400
1463 1400
3692 5700
3748 5700
3759 5700
4056 4000
4073 4073
4075 4073
4080 4073
4084 4073
4096 4073
4139 5101
4524 4500
4577 4575
4582 4575
4595 4575
4597 4575
4918 4900
4924 4900
4927 4900
4947 4900
4956 4900
4958 4900
4983 4900
5019 4073
5027 4073
5048 4073
5057 4073
5063 4073
5064 4073
5067 4073
5076 4073
5085 4073
5096 4073
5197 5101
5512 4575
5523 4575
5525 4575
5528 4575
5532 4575
5535 4575
5546 4575
5547 4575
5553 4575
5559 4575
5561 4575
5565 4575
5813 5800
5910 4900
5919 4900
5949 4900
5950 4900
6107 6100
6137 6100
6163 6100
6360 4300
6900 4900
6908 4900
6915 4900
6936 4900
6951 4900
6954 4900
6957 4900
6958 4900
6972 6959
6977 6959
6981 6959
6986 6959
6997 6959
7011 4073
7014 4073
7015 4073
7018 4073
7019 4073
7034 4073
7035 4073
7901 6959
7907 6959
8491 9400
8714 5700
8747 5700
8795 5700
9610 5700
9623 5700
9729 5700
9771 5700
41202 2MT^1
41203 2MT^1
46527 2MT^2

1960 82A

1000 1000
1005 1000
1009 1000
1011 1000
1014 1000
1024 1000
1027 1000
1028 1000
1412 1400
1463 1400
3604 5700
3623 5700
3677 5700
3748 5700
4079 4073
4081 4073
4593 4575
4619 5700
4922 4900
5015 4073
5048 4073
5062 4073
5073 4073
5076 4073
5078 4073
5085 4073
5090 4073
5092 4073
5096 4073
5097 4073
5509 4575
5529 4575
5530 4575
5561 4575
5934 4900
5940 4900
5941 4900
5949 4900
6919 4900
6972 6959
6977 6959
6981 6959
6982 6959
6988 6959
6997 6959
7003 4073
7014 4073
7018 4073
7019 4073
7034 4073
7901 6959
7907 6959
8741 5700
9481 9400
9623 5700
9626 5700
9771 5700
41202 2MT^1
41203 2MT^1
41249 2MT^1
82007 3MT^2
82033 3MT^2
82035 3MT^2
82040 3MT^2
82042 3MT^2
82043 3MT^2
82044 3MT^2

Bromsgrove

1948 21C

47234 3F^5
47301 3F^6
47303 3F^6
47305 3F^6
47308 3F^6
47313 3F^6
47425 3F^6
47565 3F^6
58100 0-10-0
58261 2F^9
58271 2F^9

1951 21C

43186 3F^2
43667 3F^3
43686 3F^3
47234 3F^5
47276 3F^6
47301 3F^6
47303 3F^6
47305 3F^6
47308 3F^6
47425 3F^6
47565 3F^6
58100 0-10-0

1954 21C

43186 3F^2
43667 3F^3
47257 3F^5
47276 3F^6
47301 3F^6
47303 3F^6
47305 3F^6
47308 3F^6
47425 3F^6
47502 3F^6
47565 3F^6
56020 0F^5
58100 0-10-0

1957 21C

8400 9400
8401 9400
8402 9400
8403 9400
8404 9400
8405 9400
43186 3F^2
43762 3F^3
47276 3F^6
47308 3F^6
47502 3F^6
47565 3F^6
92079 9F

1960 85F

5226 5205
8400 9400
8401 9400
8402 9400
8403 9400
8404 9400
8405 9400
8406 9400
43762 3F^3
47276 3F^6
47308 3F^6
92079 9F

1963 85D

8400 9400
8401 9400
8402 9400
8403 9400
8405 9400
8409 9400
9401 9400
9430 9400
9493 9400
47276 3F^6
47308 3F^6
92079 9F

Brunswick

1948 LIV

61470 B9
62302 D9
62303 D9
62304 D9
62306 D9
62308 D9
62309 D9
62315 D9
62318 D9
62319 D9
62321 D9
62324 D9
62332 D9
62333 D9
62653 D10
62658 D10
64376 J11
64405 J11
64406 J11
64417 J11
64420 J11
64714 J39
64954 J39
65126 J10
65127 J10
65136 J10
65144 J10
65149 J10
65163 J10
65172 J10
65182 J10
67099 F1
67100 F1
68547 J67
68559 J69
69250 N5
69258 N5
69288 N5
69337 N5
69339 N5
69342 N5

1951 8E

40085 3MT^2
40127 3MT^2
40180 3MT^2
40203 3MT^2
40397 2P^2
40464 2P^2
40522 2P^2
40529 2P^2
40583 2P^3
40679 2P^3
40683 2P^3
40926 4P^1
41115 4P^1
41116 4P^1
41118 4P^1
41156 4P^1
41162 4P^1
41166 4P^1
42949 5MT^2
44308 4F^2
44392 4F^2
44421 4F^2
44494 4F^2
47309 3F^6
47320 3F^6
47327 3F^6
64405 J11
64420 J11
65126 J10
65136 J10
65142 J10
65149 J10
65153 J10
65155 J10
65163 J10
65172 J10
65182 J10
68071 J94
68559 J69
69254 N5
69258 N5
69272 N5

1954 8E

40093 3MT^2
40118 3MT^2
40127 3MT^2
40203 3MT^2
41116 4P^1
41118 4P^1
41151 4P^1
41170 4P^1
42349 4MT^2
42352 4MT^2
42448 4MT^3
42466 4MT^3
42479 4MT^3
42584 4MT^3
42597 4MT^3
42598 4MT^3
42612 4MT^3
42664 4MT^3
42949 5MT^2
43864 4F^1
44396 4F^2
44438 4F^2
44489 4F^2
44494 4F^2
45217 5MT^3
45333 5MT^3
45346 5MT^3
47309 3F^6
47320 3F^6
47327 3F^6
47566 3F^6
65142 J10
65145 J10
65147 J10
65166 J10
65182 J10
65185 J10
65196 J10
68547 J67
69254 N5
69258 N5
69272 N5

1957 8E

40127 3MT^2
42349 4MT^2
42352 4MT^2
42448 4MT^3
42466 4MT^3
42479 4MT^3
42580 4MT^3
42584 4MT^3
42596 4MT^3
42598 4MT^3
42612 4MT^3
42628 4MT^3
42949 5MT^2
43915 4F^1
44396 4F^2
44489 4F^2
44494 4F^2
45217 5MT^3
45333 5MT^3
45346 5MT^3
47320 3F^6
47325 3F^6
47327 3F^6
47367 3F^6
65142 J10
65145 J10
65147 J10
65166 J10
65196 J10
68598 J69
69258 N5

1960 27F

42183 4MT^1
42186 4MT^1
42423 4MT^2
42448 4MT^3
42490 4MT^3
42580 4MT^3
42584 4MT^3
42596 4MT^3
42598 4MT^3
42612 4MT^3
43915 4F^1
44127 4F^2
44232 4F^2
44396 4F^2
44489 4F^2
44494 4F^2
44587 4F^2
44589 4F^2
45217 5MT^3
45262 5MT^3
45346 5MT^3
45444 5MT^3
47320 3F^6
47325 3F^6
47327 3F^6
47367 3F^6
47611 3F^6

Burton

1948 17B

40364 2P^2
40395 2P^2
40432 2P^2
40436 2P^2
40456 2P^2
40500 2P^2
40525 2P^2
40526 2P^2
40631 2P^3
40633 2P^3
41516 0F^1
41523 0F^1
41533 0F^2
41536 0F^2
41718 1F^1
41770 1F^1
41839 1F^1
41859 1F^1
41865 1F^1
41878 1F^1
42336 4MT^2
42757 5MT^1
42763 5MT^1
42767 5MT^1
42768 5MT^1
42846 5MT^1
42898 5MT^1
43188 3F^2
43214 3F^3
43244 3F^3
43247 3F^3
43256 3F^3
43286 3F^3
43306 3F^3
43340 3F^3
43388 3F^3
43395 3F^3
43582 3F^3
43608 3F^3
43619 3F^3
43623 3F^3
43709 3F^3
43815 3F^4
43837 4F^1
43847 4F^1
43892 4F^1
43916 4F^1
43917 4F^1
43919 4F^1

43930 4F^1
43938 4F^1
43972 4F^1
43976 4F^1
43991 4F^1
44002 4F^1
44035 4F^2
44046 4F^2
44047 4F^2
44048 4F^2
44100 4F^2
44124 4F^2
44143 4F^2
44156 4F^2
44166 4F^2
44170 4F^2
44171 4F^2
44226 4F^2
44265 4F^2
44270 4F^2
44295 4F^2
44316 4F^2
44428 4F^2
44429 4F^2
44433 4F^2
44434 4F^2
44435 4F^2
44436 4F^2
44482 4F^2
44526 4F^2
44527 4F^2
44528 4F^2
44551 4F^2
44597 4F^2
44599 4F^2
44600 4F^2
47000 0F^3
47231 3F^5
47233 3F^5
47253 3F^5
47257 3F^5
47464 3F^6
47641 3F^6
47643 3F^6
51217 0F^4
51235 0F^4
56020 0F^5
58057 1P^6
58060 1P^6
58087 1P^6
58130 2F^8
58160 2F^8
58186 2F^8
58221 2F^9
58222 2F^9
58256 2F^9
58258 2F^9
58263 2F^9
58284 2F^9
58297 2F^9
58304 2F^9

1951 17B
40325 2P^1
40364 2P^2
40395 2P^2
40432 2P^2
40436 2P^2
40453 2P^2
40519 2P^2
40525 2P^2
40526 2P^2
40633 2P^3
41230 2MT^1
41516 0F^1
41523 0F^1
41536 0F^2
41748 1F^1
41770 1F^1
41839 1F^1
41865 1F^1
41878 1F^1
42336 4MT^2
42756 5MT^1
42761 5MT^1
42763 5MT^1
42767 5MT^1
42799 5MT^1
42846 5MT^1
42896 5MT^1
42922 5MT^1
43188 3F^2
43244 3F^3
43247 3F^3
43256 3F^3
43286 3F^3
43306 3F^3
43340 3F^3
43388 3F^3
43395 3F^3
43582 3F^3
43608 3F^3
43619 3F^3
43623 3F^3
43652 3F^3
43709 3F^3
43815 3F^4
43837 4F^1
43892 4F^1
43916 4F^1
43919 4F^1
43938 4F^1
43948 4F^1
43965 4F^1
43972 4F^1
43976 4F^1
43991 4F^1
44002 4F^1
44047 4F^2
44048 4F^2
44100 4F^2
44124 4F^2
44143 4F^2
44166 4F^2
44170 4F^2
44171 4F^2
44226 4F^2
44265 4F^2
44270 4F^2
44275 4F^2
44295 4F^2
44316 4F^2
44332 4F^2
44428 4F^2
44433 4F^2
44434 4F^2
44435 4F^2
44436 4F^2
44526 4F^2
44527 4F^2
44528 4F^2
44551 4F^2
44582 4F^2
44597 4F^2
44599 4F^2
44600 4F^2
47000 0F^3
47231 3F^5
47233 3F^5
47253 3F^5
47257 3F^5
47464 3F^6
47641 3F^6
47643 3F^6
51217 0F^4
56020 0F^5
58080 1P^6
58087 1P^6
58130 2F^8
58145 2F^8
58160 2F^8
58186 2F^8
58207 2F^9
58221 2F^9
58236 2F^8
58258 2F^9
58262 2F^9
58304 2F^9

1954 17B
40364 2P^2
40436 2P^2
40453 2P^2
40519 2P^2
40525 2P^2
40526 2P^2
40633 2P^3
41516 0F^1
41523 0F^1
41536 0F^2
41839 1F^1
41865 1F^1
41878 1F^1
42754 5MT^1
42756 5MT^1
42761 5MT^1
42763 5MT^1
42767 5MT^1
42791 5MT^1
42799 5MT^1
42826 5MT^1
42846 5MT^1
42890 5MT^1
42896 5MT^1
42922 5MT^1
43188 3F^2
43193 3F^3
43247 3F^3
43256 3F^3
43286 3F^3
43306 3F^3
43312 3F^3
43327 3F^3
43340 3F^3
43388 3F^3
43395 3F^3
43406 3F^3
43574 3F^3
43608 3F^3
43619 3F^3
43623 3F^3
43652 3F^3
43709 3F^3
43815 3F^4
43892 4F^1
43919 4F^1
43948 4F^1
43965 4F^1
43976 4F^1
43992 4F^1
44048 4F^2
44055 4F^2
44100 4F^2
44124 4F^2
44143 4F^2
44166 4F^2
44265 4F^2
44270 4F^2
44316 4F^2
44332 4F^2
44433 4F^2
44434 4F^2
44435 4F^2
44436 4F^2
44452 4F^2
44526 4F^2
44527 4F^2
44528 4F^2
44551 4F^2
44552 4F^2
44597 4F^2
44599 4F^2
44600 4F^2
46494 2MT^2
47231 3F^5
47233 3F^5
47253 3F^5
47464 3F^6
47485 3F^6
47641 3F^6
47643 3F^6
48002 8F
48401 8F
48547 8F
58087 1P^6
58130 2F^8
58160 2F^8
58186 2F^8
58236 2F^8
84006 2MT^2
84007 2MT^2
84008 2MT^2

1957 17B
40414 2P^2
40453 2P^2
40519 2P^2
40525 2P^2
40633 2P^3
41532 0F^2
41536 0F^2
41699 1F^1
41878 1F^1
42756 5MT^1
42763 5MT^1
42767 5MT^1
42799 5MT^1
42818 5MT^1
42822 5MT^1
42824 5MT^1
42825 5MT^1
42826 5MT^1
42829 5MT^1
42896 5MT^1
42922 5MT^1
43188 3F^2
43247 3F^3
43256 3F^3
43286 3F^3
43306 3F^3
43327 3F^3
43340 3F^3
43361 3F^3
43395 3F^3
43406 3F^3
43469 3F^3
43574 3F^3
43587 3F^3
43608 3F^3
43619 3F^3
43623 3F^3
43652 3F^3
43709 3F^3
43778 3F^4
43815 3F^4
43839 4F^1
43846 4F^1
43858 4F^1
43892 4F^1
43948 4F^1
43953 4F^1
43965 4F^1
43976 4F^1
44047 4F^2
44100 4F^2
44124 4F^2
44316 4F^2
44332 4F^2
44433 4F^2
44434 4F^2
44435 4F^2
44436 4F^2
44452 4F^2
44526 4F^2
44527 4F^2
44528 4F^2
44538 4F^2
44542 4F^2
44551 4F^2
44552 4F^2
44562 4F^2
44591 4F^2
44597 4F^2
44599 4F^2
44600 4F^2
44811 5MT^3
44843 5MT^3
45262 5MT^3
45264 5MT^3
47231 3F^5
47236 3F^5
47257 3F^5
47464 3F^6
47485 3F^6
47611 3F^6
47641 3F^6
47643 3F^6
48002 8F
48401 8F
48547 8F
51338 2F^2
58130 2F^8
58148 2F^8
58160 2F^8
58186 2F^8
84006 2MT^2
84007 2MT^2
84008 2MT^2

1960 17B
40396 2P^2
40453 2P^2
41277 2MT^1
41328 2MT^1
41532 0F^2
41536 0F^2
42756 5MT^1
42759 5MT^1
42763 5MT^1
42799 5MT^1
42818 5MT^1
42822 5MT^1
42824 5MT^1
42825 5MT^1
42826 5MT^1
42829 5MT^1
42839 5MT^1
42855 5MT^1
42896 5MT^1
42922 5MT^1
43188 3F^2
43256 3F^3
43340 3F^3
43570 3F^3
43574 3F^3
43608 3F^3
43621 3F^3
43652 3F^3
43679 3F^3
43709 3F^3
43789 3F^4
43839 4F^1
43843 4F^1
43989 4F^1
44100 4F^2
44124 4F^2
44241 4F^2
44332 4F^2
44380 4F^2
44433 4F^2
44434 4F^2
44435 4F^2
44436 4F^2
44452 4F^2
44526 4F^2
44527 4F^2
44528 4F^2
44538 4F^2
44541 4F^2
44542 4F^2
44551 4F^2
44552 4F^2
44562 4F^2
44591 4F^2
44597 4F^2
44599 4F^2
44600 4F^2
47236 3F^5
47458 3F^6
47464 3F^6
47485 3F^6
47502 3F^6
47638 3F^6
47641 3F^6
47643 3F^6
48182 8F
48662 8F
48694 8F
48728 8F
58128 2F^8
58148 2F^8
58160 2F^8
58165 2F^8
58186 2F^8
58305 2F^9

1963 17B
42082 4MT^1
44100 4F^2
44332 4F^2
44380 4F^2
44434 4F^2
44436 4F^2
44526 4F^2
44527 4F^2
44528 4F^2
44538 4F^2
44541 4F^2
44542 4F^2
44551 4F^2
44552 4F^2
44562 4F^2
44591 4F^2
44597 4F^2
44599 4F^2
44816 5MT^3
44817 5MT^3
44818 5MT^3
44822 5MT^3
44825 5MT^3
44839 5MT^3
44858 5MT^3
44941 5MT^3
45059 5MT^3
45062 5MT^3
45279 5MT^3
45407 5MT^3
45557 6P5F^2
45561 6P5F^2
45575 6P5F^2
45579 6P5F^2
45585 6P5F^2
45598 6P5F^2
45610 6P5F^2
45611 6P5F^2
45612 6P5F^2
45614 6P5F^2
45618 6P5F^2
45620 6P5F^2
45641 6P5F^2
45648 6P5F^2
45649 6P5F^2
45650 6P5F^2
45667 6P5F^2
45668 6P5F^2
45712 6P5F^2
47313 3F^6
47464 3F^6
47643 3F^6
48065 8F
48128 8F
48182 8F
48194 8F
48303 8F
48332 8F
48662 8F
48694 8F
48728 8F

1966 16F
44851 5MT^3
44962 5MT^3
45232 5MT^3
47313 3F^6
47629 3F^6
47643 3F^6
48056 8F
48064 8F
48117 8F
48128 8F
48194 8F
48254 8F
48266 8F
48271 8F
48332 8F
48367 8F
48368 8F
48606 8F
48635 8F
48651 8F
48662 8F
48672 8F
48681 8F
48690 8F
48700 8F
48728 8F
92043 9F

Bury

1948 26D
42473 4MT^3
42474 4MT^3
42476 4MT^3
42629 4MT^3
48768 8F
48769 8F
49557 7F^4
49590 7F^4
49591 7F^4
49594 7F^4
49665 7F^4
49666 7F^4
49667 7F^4
50823 2P^8
50872 2P^8
50875 2P^8
50892 2P^8
51338 2F^2
51419 2F^2
51481 2F^2
51486 2F^2
51487 2F^2
51489 2F^2
51504 2F^2
52129 3F^7
52139 3F^7
52159 3F^7
52164 3F^7
52165 3F^7
52245 3F^7
52246 3F^7
52382 3F^7
52455 3F^7
52554 3F^9
52579 3F^9
52580 3F^9
52581 3F^9
52608 3F^9
52615 3F^9

1951 26D
42473 4MT^3
42474 4MT^3
42476 4MT^3
42629 4MT^3
49508 7F^4
49557 7F^4
49591 7F^4
49594 7F^4
49666 7F^4
49667 7F^4
51376 2F^2
51419 2F^2
51486 2F^2
51489 2F^2
51504 2F^2
52129 3F^7
52159 3F^7
52164 3F^7
52165 3F^7
52245 3F^7
52246 3F^7
52271 3F^7
52328 3F^7
52382 3F^7
52554 3F^9
52580 3F^9
52581 3F^9
52615 3F^9
90364 WD^1
90419 WD^1

1954 26D
40586 2P^3
40690 2P^3
51376 2F^2
51419 2F^2
51486 2F^2
51489 2F^2
51504 2F^2
52094 3F^7
52129 3F^7
52164 3F^7
52179 3F^7
52237 3F^7
52239 3F^7
52245 3F^7
52268 3F^7
52405 3F^7
84016 2MT^2
84017 2MT^2
84018 2MT^2
84019 2MT^2
90123 WD^1
90194 WD^1
90219 WD^1
90226 WD^1
90308 WD^1
90359 WD^1
90364 WD^1
90408 WD^1
90413 WD^1
90419 WD^1
90555 WD^1
90568 WD^1
90626 WD^1
90718 WD^1

1957 26D
42444 4MT^3
42455 4MT^3
42460 4MT^3
42588 4MT^3
42652 4MT^3
42700 5MT^1
42712 5MT^1
42719 5MT^1
42731 5MT^1
42820 5MT^1
46406 2MT^2
46414 2MT^2
46416 2MT^2
46417 2MT^2
46436 2MT^2
47584 3F^6
52094 3F^7
52129 3F^7
52268 3F^7
52289 3F^7
52350 3F^7
52387 3F^7
52443 3F^7
90123 WD^1
90194 WD^1
90205 WD^1
90219 WD^1
90226 WD^1
90359 WD^1
90364 WD^1
90408 WD^1
90419 WD^1
90555 WD^1
90568 WD^1
90626 WD^1
90718 WD^1

1960 26D
42444 4MT^3
42460 4MT^3
42550 4MT^3
42700 5MT^1
42712 5MT^1
42719 5MT^1
42730 5MT^1
42731 5MT^1
42820 5MT^1
43880 4F^1
46406 2MT^2
46414 2MT^2
46416 2MT^2
46417 2MT^2
46436 2MT^2
47584 3F^6
52129 3F^7
52201 3F^7
52207 3F^7
90194 WD^1
90205 WD^1
90219 WD^1
90226 WD^1
90364 WD^1
90408 WD^1
90419 WD^1
90555 WD^1
90568 WD^1
90626 WD^1

1963 26D
42700 5MT^1
42712 5MT^1
42719 5MT^1
42820 5MT^1
43880 4F^1
43913 4F^1
44096 4F^2
44311 4F^2
44567 4F^2
46405 2MT^2
46406 2MT^2
46412 2MT^2
46414 2MT^2
46416 2MT^2
46417 2MT^2
46436 2MT^2
46439 2MT^2
47584 3F^6
90205 WD^1
90226 WD^1
90364 WD^1
90408 WD^1
90419 WD^1
90555 WD^1

Bury St. Edmunds

1948 BSE
62503 D15
62508 D15
62566 D16
62615 D16
62785 E4
65362 J15
65420 J15
65442 J15
67124 F3
67160 F4
67187 F4
67237 F6
67238 F6
68497 J69
68579 J69

1951 31E
62503 D15
62566 D16
62573 D16
62607 D16
62615 D16
62786 E4
62795 E4
65362 J15
65420 J15
65442 J15
65548 J17
67221 F6
67236 F6
67237 F6
67238 F6
68497 J69

1954 31E
62513 D16
62541 D16
62543 D16
62545 D16
62566 D16
62607 D16
62615 D16
65391 J15
65405 J15
65420 J15
65580 J17
65583 J17
67222 F6
67236 F6
67237 F6
67375 C12
67385 C12
68497 J69
68555 J69

1957 31E
62513 D16
62543 D16
62566 D16
62576 D16
62588 D16
62615 D16
65391 J15
65405 J15
65420 J15
68497 J69

Bushbury

1948 3B
40047 3MT^1
40049 3MT^1
40053 3MT^1
40054 3MT^1
40066 3MT^1
44027 4F^2
44439 4F^2
44492 4F^2
45287 5MT^3
45405 5MT^3
45434 5MT^3
45437 5MT^3
45514 7P^1
45528 7P^1
45529 7P^1
45531 7P^1
45540 7P^1
45733 6P5F^2
45734 6P5F^2
45738 6P5F^2
45742 6P5F^2
46654 1P^1
46881 2P^7
46931 2P^7
47397 3F^6
47398 3F^6
47399 3F^6
47413 3F^6
47473 3F^6
49110 7F^2
49196 7F^2
49204 6F^2
49233 6F^2
49295 6F^2
49356 7F^2
58333 2F^{10}
58341 2F^{10}
58345 2F^{10}
58378 2F^{11}
58414 2F^{11}
28230 2F^{10}

1951 3B
40049 3MT^1
40053 3MT^1
40066 3MT^1
41225 2MT^1
44027 4F^2
44439 4F^2
44492 4F^2
45015 5MT^3
45287 5MT^3
45405 5MT^3
45434 5MT^3
45437 5MT^3
45524 6P5F^1
45741 6P5F^2
46110 7P^3
46140 7P^3
46148 7P^3
46151 7P^3
46158 7P^3
46163 7P^3
46165 7P^3
47397 3F^6
47398 3F^6
47399 3F^6
47473 3F^6
48902 6F^2
48940 7F^2
49037 7F^2
49044 7F^2
49162 6F^2
49167 7F^2
49196 7F^2
49204 6F^2
49240 7F^2
49346 6F^2
58119 2F^8
58152 2F^8
58183 2F^8
58285 2F^9
58287 2F^9

1954 3B
40122 3MT^2
40125 3MT^2
40207 3MT^2
41225 2MT^1
44027 4F^2
44439 4F^2
44492 4F^2
44829 5MT^3
45015 5MT^3
45287 5MT^3
45405 5MT^3
45647 6P5F^2
45688 6P5F^2
45703 6P5F^2
45733 6P5F^2
45734 6P5F^2
45737 6P5F^2
45738 6P5F^2
45741 6P5F^2
45742 6P5F^2
47363 3F^6
47397 3F^6
47398 3F^6
47473 3F^6
48940 7F^2
49037 7F^2
49044 7F^2
49125 7F^2
49167 7F^2
49240 7F^2
49247 7F^2
58119 2F^8
58152 2F^8
58183 2F^8

1957 3B
41225 2MT^1
42428 4MT^3
42429 4MT^3
44027 4F^2
44439 4F^2
44829 5MT^3
45015 5MT^3
45287 5MT^3
45310 5MT^3
45403 5MT^3
45405 5MT^3
45439 5MT^3
45555 6P5F^2
45647 6P5F^2
45688 6P5F^2
45709 6P5F^2
45733 6P5F^2
45734 6P5F^2
45737 6P5F^2
45738 6P5F^2
45741 6P5F^2
45742 6P5F^2
47363 3F^6
47397 3F^6
47398 3F^6
47473 3F^6
48940 7F^2
49037 7F^2
49044 7F^2
49167 7F^2
49240 7F^2
49247 7F^2
58119 2F^8
58183 2F^8
58204 2F^9

1960 3B
41279 2MT^1
42582 4MT^3
42659 4MT^3
44829 5MT^3
45015 5MT^3
45287 5MT^3
45310 5MT^3
45405 5MT^3
45439 5MT^3
45540 7P^1
45647 6P5F^2
45709 6P5F^2
45737 6P5F^2
46122 7P^{3}R
46141 7P^{3}R
46143 7P^{3}R
46153 7P^{3}R
46158 7P^{3}R
47397 3F^6
47398 3F^6
47399 3F^6
47473 3F^6
48950 7F^2
49037 7F^2
49229 7F^2
49240 7F^2
49452 7F^3
58118 2F^8
58124 2F^8
58183 2F^8
58295 2F^9

1963 21C
42582 4MT^3
42659 4MT^3
42966 5MT^2
44829 5MT^3
45310 5MT^3
45405 5MT^3
45439 5MT^3
46428 2MT^2
46448 2MT^2
48895 7F^2
49407 7F^3
49446 7F^3

Buxton

1948 9D
40438 2P^2
40479 2P^2
40483 2P^2
40693 2P^3
42306 4MT^2
42315 4MT^2
42318 4MT^2
42365 4MT^2
42366 4MT^2
42367 4MT^2
42368 4MT^2
42370 4MT^2
42371 4MT^2
42942 5MT^1
42943 5MT^1
43268 3F^3
43269 3F^3
43271 3F^3
43274 3F^3
43278 3F^3
43282 3F^3
43296 3F^3
43387 3F^3
43842 4F^1
44019 4F^1
44080 4F^2
44309 4F^2
44360 4F^2
44365 4F^2
44382 4F^2
44548 4F^2
46738 1P^1
47936 7F^1
47954 7F^1
48326 8F
48451 8F
48464 8F
48558 8F
48712 8F
49009 7F^2
49059 6F^2
49132 7F^2
49212 7F^2
49214 7F^2
49216 7F^2
49224 7F^2
49225 6F^2
49240 7F^2
49305 6F^2
49315 7F^2
49326 6F^2
49331 7F^2
49347 7F^2
49376 7F^2
49386 7F^2
58042 1P^6
58084 1P^6
58092 1P^7

1951 9D
40655 2P^3
40692 2P^3
42306 4MT^2
42315 4MT^2
42365 4MT^2
42366 4MT^2
42367 4MT^2
42368 4MT^2
42370 4MT^2
42371 4MT^2
42942 5MT^1
42943 5MT^1
43268 3F^3
43271 3F^3
43274 3F^3
43278 3F^3
43296 3F^3
43387 3F^3
43562 3F^3
43842 4F^1
44339 4F^2
44382 4F^2
46616 1P^1
48090 8F
48166 8F
48278 8F
48322 8F
48326 8F
48421 8F
48451 8F
48465 8F
48519 8F
48712 8F
48731 8F
48734 8F
48740 8F
48741 8F
48742 8F
48745 8F
48746 8F
48749 8F
49057 7F^2
49132 7F^2
49214 7F^2
49347 7F^2
49348 7F^2
49387 7F^2
49450 7F^3
49454 7F^3
58042 1P^6
58084 1P^6
58092 1P^7

1954 9D
40433 2P^2
40536 2P^2
40655 2P^3
40692 2P^3
42306 4MT^2
42365 4MT^2
42366 4MT^2
42367 4MT^2
42368 4MT^2
42370 4MT^2
42371 4MT^2
42942 5MT^1
42943 5MT^1
43268 3F^3
43271 3F^3
43274 3F^3
43278 3F^3
43296 3F^3
43387 3F^3
43842 4F^1
44339 4F^2
44382 4F^2
48166 8F
48278 8F
48322 8F
48326 8F
48342 8F
48421 8F
48451 8F
48465 8F
48519 8F
48712 8F
48734 8F
48740 8F
48742 8F
48745 8F
48746 8F
48749 8F
49057 7F^2
49132 7F^2
49210 7F^2
49214 7F^2
49348 7F^2
49387 7F^2
49450 7F^3
58083 1P^6
58084 1P^6

1957 9D
41905 2P^4
41906 2P^4
42306 4MT^2
42365 4MT^2
42368 4MT^2
42370 4MT^2
42371 4MT^2
42942 5MT^1
42943 5MT^1
43268 3F^3
43274 3F^3
43278 3F^3
43300 3F^3
43387 3F^3
43836 4F^1
43842 4F^1
44339 4F^2
48165 8F
48166 8F
48278 8F
48322 8F
48326 8F
48421 8F
48451 8F
48465 8F
48479 8F
48519 8F
48679 8F
48712 8F
48740 8F
48745 8F
48746 8F
49057 7F^2
49132 7F^2
49210 7F^2
49214 7F^2
49348 7F^2
49387 7F^2
49450 7F^3
58083 1P^6

1960 9D
42306 4MT^2
42370 4MT^2
42371 4MT^2
42942 5MT^1
42943 5MT^1
43268 3F^3
43329 3F^3
43562 3F^3
44059 4F^2
44339 4F^2
44375 4F^2
48278 8F
48322 8F
48421 8F
48451 8F
48505 8F
48519 8F
48679 8F
48712 8F
48740 8F
48932 7F^2
49210 7F^2
49277 7F^2
49281 7F^2
49391 7F^2
49406 7F^3
49423 7F^3
49433 7F^3

1963 9D
42379 4MT^2
42391 4MT^2
42772 5MT^1
42926 5MT^1
42940 5MT^1
44059 4F^2
44083 4F^2
44110 4F^2
44247 4F^2
44271 4F^2
44315 4F^2
44339 4F^2
44364 4F^2
44497 4F^2
44524 4F^2
46465 2MT^2
46480 2MT^2
48062 8F
48165 8F
48275 8F
48278 8F
48322 8F
48389 8F
48421 8F
48428 8F
48451 8F
48465 8F
48519 8F
48558 8F
48679 8F
48712 8F
48727 8F

1966 9L
46401 2MT^2
46402 2MT^2
46465 2MT^2
46480 2MT^2
46484 2MT^2
48088 8F
48171 8F
48190 8F
48327 8F
48465 8F
48472 8F
48495 8F
48532 8F
48748 8F
68006 J94
68012 J94
68079 J94

BWL Renfrew

1951 On hire
56039 0F^5

Cambridge

1948 CAM
61608 B17
61610 B17
61611 B17
61613 B17
61617 B2
61619 B17
61620 B17
61621 B17
61622 B17
61623 B17
61624 B17
61627 B17
61628 B17
61631 B17

61633 B17
61637 B17
61638 B17
61640 B17
61641 B17
61642 B17
61643 B17
61654 B17
61663 B17
61665 B17
61666 B17
61671 B2
62516 D16
62525 D16
62527 D16
62530 D16
62531 D16
62536 D16
62549 D16
62551 D16
62557 D16
62567 D16
62571 D16
62574 D16
62601 D16
62606 D16
62607 D16
62618 D16
62780 E4
62781 E4
62783 E4
62784 E4
62786 E4
62788 E4
62790 E4
62791 E4
62794 E4
62795 E4
62796 E4
63704 O4
63705 O4
63708 O4
63718 O4
63724 O4
63730 O4
63779 O4
63836 O4
63839 O4
63880 O4
63897 O4
63898 O4
63904 O4
63913 O4
64649 J19
64658 J19
64676 J20
64678 J20
64679 J20
64680 J20
64683 J20
64684 J20
64687 J20
65350 J15
65356 J15
65364 J15
65366 J15
65369 J15
65371 J15
65379 J15
65380 J15
65383 J15
65391 J15
65399 J15
65405 J15
65406 J15
65410 J15
65412 J15
65413 J15
65438 J15
65451 J15
65457 J15
65461 J15
65474 J15
65477 J15
65501 J17
65502 J17
65503 J17
65506 J17
65517 J17
65520 J17
65535 J17
65537 J17
65546 J17
65563 J17
65575 J17
65585 J17
67115 F3
67117 F3
67360 C12
67367 C12
67375 C12
67385 C12
68173 Y3
68214 J65
68372 J66
68516 J67
68517 J67
68530 J69
68536 J67
68583 J67
68609 J67
68645 J68
69926 Q1

1951 31A
61121 B1
61285 B1
61286 B1
61287 B1
61300 B1
61301 B1
61302 B1
61333 B1
61334 B1
61617 B2
61619 B17
61620 B17
61622 B17
61623 B17
61624 B17
61625 B17
61627 B17
61628 B17
61631 B17
61636 B17
61637 B17
61638 B17
61640 B17
61642 B17
61643 B17
61652 B17
61653 B17
61655 B17
61663 B17
61671 B2
62516 D16
62525 D16
62527 D16
62530 D16
62531 D16
62543 D16
62549 D16
62551 D16
62557 D16
62567 D16
62571 D16
62574 D16
62603 D16
62618 D16
62781 E4
62783 E4
62784 E4
62785 E4
62788 E4
62794 E4
64678 J20
64679 J20
64683 J20
64684 J20
64687 J20
65350 J15
65356 J15
65391 J15
65405 J15
65406 J15
65425 J15
65438 J15
65451 J15
65457 J15
65461 J15
65474 J15
65475 J15
65477 J15
65501 J17
65502 J17
65503 J17
65506 J17
65517 J17
65520 J17
65525 J17
65529 J17
65532 J17
65535 J17
65537 J17
65538 J17
65546 J17
65547 J17
65561 J17
65563 J17
65565 J17
65573 J17
65575 J17
65585 J17
65587 J17
65589 J17
67222 F6
67360 C12
67367 C12
67375 C12
67385 C12
67389 C12
68372 J66
68383 J66
68509 J67
68516 J67
68530 J69
68579 J69
68609 J67
68645 J68

1954 31A
46465 2MT^2
46466 2MT^2
46467 2MT^2
61121 B1
61223 B1
61285 B1
61286 B1
61287 B1
61300 B1
61301 B1
61302 B1
61334 B1
61617 B2
61623 B17
61627 B17
61636 B17
61640 B17
61642 B17
61652 B17
61653 B17
61657 B17
61671 B2
62521 D16
62525 D16
62530 D16
62531 D16
62532 D16
62549 D16
62551 D16
62557 D16
62558 D16
62562 D16
62567 D16
62570 D16
62571 D16
62574 D16
62576 D16
62585 D16
62618 D16
62780 E4
62781 E4
62783 E4
62784 E4
62785 E4
62786 E4
62790 E4
62791 E4
62794 E4
62795 E4
64654 J19
64658 J19
64673 J19
64683 J20
64688 J20
64689 J20
65390 J15
65425 J15
65438 J15
65442 J15
65451 J15
65457 J15
65461 J15
65474 J15
65475 J15
65477 J15
65502 J17
65504 J17
65505 J17
65506 J17
65512 J17
65532 J17
65534 J17
65535 J17
65537 J17
65547 J17
65548 J17
65561 J17
65565 J17
65575 J17
65585 J17
65589 J17
67221 F6
67227 F6
67238 F6
67269 G5
67279 G5
67322 G5
68491 J69
68530 J69
68600 J69
68609 J69
68625 J69

1957 31A
43089 4MT^5
46465 2MT^2
46466 2MT^2
46467 2MT^2
61286 B1
61287 B1
61300 B1
61301 B1
61371 B1
61603 B2
61607 B2
61614 B2
61615 B2
61616 B2
61617 B2
61623 B17
61632 B2
61634 B17
61636 B17
61639 B2
61640 B17
61642 B17
61644 B2
61646 B17
61652 B17
61653 B17
61671 B2
62510 D16
62521 D16
62530 D16
62539 D16
62553 D16
62570 D16
62571 D16
62605 D16
62610 D16
62618 D16
62788 E4
62789 E4
62796 E4
64646 J19
64654 J19
64658 J19
64673 J19
64683 J20
64688 J20
64695 J20
64696 J20
64729 J39
64751 J39
64803 J39
64890 J39
64958 J39
65390 J15
65438 J15
65442 J15
65451 J15
65457 J15
65461 J15
65475 J15
65477 J15
65500 J17
65502 J17
65504 J17
65505 J17
65506 J17
65520 J17
65532 J17
65534 J17
65541 J17
65548 J17
65561 J17
65565 J17
65575 J17
65580 J17
65587 J17
65589 J17
67367 C12
67395 C12
67397 C12
68530 J69
68554 J69
68567 J69
68600 J69
68609 J69
69651 N7
69690 N7
69692 N7

1960 31A
46465 2MT^2
46466 2MT^2
46467 2MT^2
61066 B1
61171 B1
61182 B1
61203 B1
61236 B1
61280 B1
61283 B1
61286 B1
61287 B1
61301 B1
61371 B1
61608 B17
61610 B17
61618 B17
61626 B17
61801 K3
61817 K3
61834 K3
61849 K3
61880 K3
64646 J19
64654 J19
64684 J20
64695 J20
64696 J20
64698 J20
65450 J15
65457 J15
65461 J15
65477 J15
65520 J17
65528 J17
65532 J17
65541 J17
65556 J17
65578 J17
65589 J17
67712 L1
67713 L1
67718 L1
67720 L1
67721 L1
67722 L1
67723 L1
67734 L1

1966
21 B1

Cambridge Engineer's Dept

1954
42 Y3

1957
21 Y3
42 Y3

1960
21 Y3
42 Y3

Camden

1948 1B
45601 6P5F^2
45606 6P5F^2
45617 6P5F^2
45669 6P5F^2
45735 7P^2
45736 7P^2
46100 7P^3
46101 7P^{3}R
46116 7P^{3}R
46118 7P^{3}R
46119 7P^{3}R
46123 7P^3
46130 7P^3
46139 7P^{3}R
46140 7P^3
46141 7P^3
46142 7P^3
46148 7P^3
46151 7P^3
46152 7P^{3}R
46153 7P^3
46159 7P^{3}R
46168 7P^{3}R
46170 7P^{3}R
46202 8P^1
46225 8P^2
46237 8P^2
46239 8P^2
46240 8P^2
46241 8P^2
46243 8P^2
46244 8P^2
46245 8P^2
46246 8P^2
46247 8P^2
46248 8P^2
46253 8P^2
46254 8P^2
46255 8P^2
47354 3F^6
47356 3F^6
47358 3F^6
47359 3F^6
47467 3F^6
47522 3F^6
47527 3F^6
47529 3F^6
47667 3F^6
47668 3F^6
47669 3F^6
47671 3F^6

1951 1B
45514 7P^1
45522 7P^1
45532 7P^1
45541 6P5F^1
45545 7P^1
45601 6P5F^2
45669 6P5F^2
45672 6P5F^2
45676 6P5F^2
45735 7P^2
45736 7P^2
46100 7P^{3}R
46116 7P^{3}R
46126 7P^{3}R
46139 7P^{3}R
46141 7P^{3}R
46142 7P^3
46152 7P^{3}R
46154 7P^{3}R
46159 7P^{3}R
46162 7P^{3}R
46168 7P^{3}R
46170 7P^{3}R
46202 8P^1
46237 8P^2
46239 8P^2
46240 8P^2
46241 8P^2
46242 8P^2
46244 8P^2
46245 8P^2
46247 8P^2
46249 8P^2
46250 8P^2
46256 8P^2
46257 8P^2
47354 3F^6
47356 3F^6
47358 3F^6
47359 3F^6
47467 3F^6
47522 3F^6
47527 3F^6
47529 3F^6
47667 3F^6
47668 3F^6
47669 3F^6
47671 3F^6

1954 1B
45514 7P^1
45522 7P^1
45523 7P^1
45529 7P^1
45532 7P^1
45541 6P5F^1
45545 7P^1
45592 6P5F^2
45601 6P5F^2
45603 6P5F^2
45669 6P5F^2
45672 6P5F^2
45676 6P5F^2
45686 6P5F^2
45735 7P^2
45736 7P^2
45740 6P5F^2
46100 7P^{3}R
46116 7P^{3}R
46126 7P^{3}R
46139 7P^{3}R
46141 7P^{3}R
46142 7P^{3}R
46144 7P^{3}R
46146 7P^{3}R
46147 7P^{3}R
46154 7P^{3}R
46162 7P^{3}R
46168 7P^{3}R
46170 7P^{3}R
46229 8P^2
46236 8P^2
46237 8P^2
46239 8P^2
46240 8P^2
46241 8P^2
46244 8P^2
46245 8P^2
46247 8P^2
46249 8P^2
46250 8P^2
46253 8P^2
46254 8P^2
46256 8P^2
46257 8P^2
47350 3F^6
47354 3F^6
47356 3F^6
47358 3F^6
47359 3F^6
47467 3F^6
47522 3F^6
47527 3F^6
47529 3F^6
47667 3F^6
47668 3F^6
47669 3F^6
47671 3F^6

1957 1B
45514 7P^1
45522 7P^1
45523 7P^1
45532 7P^1
45541 6P5F^1
45592 6P5F^2
45601 6P5F^2
45606 6P5F^2
45669 6P5F^2
45672 6P5F^2
45676 6P5F^2
45686 6P5F^2
45735 7P^2
46100 7P^{3}R
46139 7P^{3}R
46144 7P^{3}R
46146 7P^{3}R
46154 7P^{3}R
46162 7P^{3}R
46168 7P^{3}R
46170 7P^{3}R
46229 8P^2
46236 8P^2
46237 8P^2
46239 8P^2
46240 8P^2
46241 8P^2
46242 8P^2
46244 8P^2
46245 8P^2
46247 8P^2
46250 8P^2
46253 8P^2
46254 8P^2
46256 8P^2
46257 8P^2
47354 3F^6
47356 3F^6
47358 3F^6
47467 3F^6
47522 3F^6
47527 3F^6
47529 3F^6
47667 3F^6
47668 3F^6
47669 3F^6
47671 3F^6

1960 1B
45514 7P^1
45523 7P^1
45592 6P5F^2
45606 6P5F^2
45632 6P5F^2
45676 6P5F^2
45686 6P5F^2
46101 7P^{3}R
46118 7P^{3}R
46144 7P^{3}R
46146 7P^{3}R
46207 8P^1
46221 8P^2
46229 8P^2
46239 8P^2
46240 8P^2
46242 8P^2
46245 8P^2
46247 8P^2
46254 8P^2
47495 3F^6
47514 3F^6
47522 3F^6
47529 3F^6
47668 3F^6
47669 3F^6
47671 3F^6
70045 7P6F
70048 7P6F
70049 7P6F

1963 1B
41239 2MT^1
46239 8P^2
46240 8P^2
46245 8P^2
46246 8P^2
46252 8P^2

Canklow

1948 19C
40726 3P^1
40727 3P^1
41797 1F^1
41813 1F^1
41835 1F^1
41869 1F^1
41917 2P^5
41926 2P^5
41958 3P^2
41962 3P^2
43180 3F^2
43181 3F^2
43208 3F^3
43243 3F^3
43300 3F^3
43325 3F^3
43660 3F^3
43664 3F^3
43669 3F^3
43747 3F^3
43813 3F^4
43814 3F^4
43906 4F^1
43950 4F^1
44013 4F^1
44015 4F^1
44036 4F^2
44071 4F^2
44127 4F^2
44128 4F^2
44173 4F^2
44232 4F^2
44457 4F^2
44477 4F^2
47546 3F^6
47547 3F^6
48026 8F
48065 8F
48209 8F
48407 8F
48430 8F
48434 8F
48450 8F
48548 8F
48682 8F
49055 7F^2
58114 2F^8
58127 2F^8
58147 2F^8
58150 2F^8
58154 2F^8
58170 2F^8
58175 2F^8
58198 2F^9
58204 2F^9
58233 2F^8
58244 2F^8
58266 2F^9

1951 19C
40726 3P^1
41797 1F^1
41805 1F^1
41835 1F^1
43037 4MT^5
43180 3F^2
43181 3F^2
43208 3F^3
43243 3F^3
43325 3F^3
43587 3F^3
43660 3F^3
43664 3F^3
43669 3F^3
43747 3F^3
43814 3F^4
43906 4F^1
43950 4F^1
44013 4F^1
44015 4F^1
44036 4F^2
44071 4F^2
44089 4F^2
44111 4F^2
44127 4F^2
44128 4F^2
44173 4F^2
44232 4F^2
44457 4F^2
44576 4F^2
47546 3F^6
47547 3F^6
48026 8F
48055 8F
48065 8F
48140 8F
48209 8F
48407 8F
48434 8F
48450 8F
48508 8F
48548 8F
48646 8F
58114 2F^8
58127 2F^8
58147 2F^8
58170 2F^8
58198 2F^9
58204 2F^9
58233 2F^8
58238 2F^8
58244 2F^8

1954 19C
41805 1F^1
41835 1F^1
43037 4MT^5
43180 3F^2
43181 3F^2
43208 3F^3
43225 3F^3
43243 3F^3
43325 3F^3
43463 3F^3
43587 3F^3
43660 3F^3
43664 3F^3
43669 3F^3
43814 3F^4
43872 4F^1
43950 4F^1
43978 4F^1
44002 4F^1
44013 4F^1
44015 4F^1
44036 4F^2
44037 4F^2
44071 4F^2
44089 4F^2
44111 4F^2
44127 4F^2
44128 4F^2
44232 4F^2
44576 4F^2
47238 3F^5
47546 3F^6
47547 3F^6
48026 8F
48055 8F
48065 8F
48083 8F
48140 8F
48209 8F
48216 8F
48391 8F
48397 8F
48402 8F
48407 8F
48434 8F
48450 8F
48470 8F
48508 8F
48548 8F
48646 8F
58114 2F^8
58127 2F^8
58170 2F^8
58198 2F^9
58204 2F^9
58233 2F^8
58238 2F^8
58244 2F^8

1957 19C
41835 1F^1
41875 1F^1
43037 4MT^5
43180 3F^2
43208 3F^3
43225 3F^3
43463 3F^3
43660 3F^3
43664 3F^3
43814 3F^4
43857 4F^1
43872 4F^1
43950 4F^1
43978 4F^1
44002 4F^1
44013 4F^1
44036 4F^2
44037 4F^2
44071 4F^2
44082 4F^2
44089 4F^2
44111 4F^2
44127 4F^2
44128 4F^2
44206 4F^2
44232 4F^2
44245 4F^2
44576 4F^2
47238 3F^5
47546 3F^6
47547 3F^6
48011 8F
48026 8F
48075 8F
48138 8F
48140 8F
48150 8F
48151 8F
48176 8F
48181 8F
48209 8F
48216 8F
48391 8F
48396 8F
48397 8F
48407 8F
48508 8F
48548 8F
48646 8F
58114 2F^8
58170 2F^8
58198 2F^9
58238 2F^8
78026 2MT^1
78027 2MT^1

1960 41D
41835 1F^1
41875 1F^1
43037 4MT^5
43225 3F^3
43371 3F^3
43664 3F^3
43814 3F^4
44002 4F^1
44037 4F^2
44071 4F^2
44082 4F^2
44089 4F^2
44111 4F^2
44128 4F^2
44206 4F^2
44245 4F^2
44576 4F^2
47620 3F^6
48011 8F
48026 8F
48140 8F
48150 8F
48151 8F
48176 8F
48181 8F
48209 8F
48216 8F
48391 8F
48396 8F
48397 8F
48407 8F
48508 8F
58170 2F^8
73002 5MT
78026 2MT^1
78027 2MT^1
90145 WD^1
90368 WD^1
90391 WD^1
90414 WD^1
90471 WD^1
90719 WD^1

1963 41D
48140 8F
48151 8F
48179 8F
48391 8F
48396 8F
48772 8F
61004 B1
61033 B1
61083 B1
61093 B1
61104 B1
61165 B1
61194 B1
61327 B1
61334 B1
61370 B1
61399 B1
90064 WD^1
90085 WD^1
90136 WD^1
90139 WD^1
90153 WD^1
90162 WD^1
90202 WD^1
90276 WD^1
90290 WD^1
90368 WD^1
90471 WD^1
90719 WD^1

Cardiff Canton

1948 CDF
200 TV^2
203 TV^2
205 TV^2
208 TV^2
209 TV^2
220 TV^2
238 BR^2
280 TV^2
335 TV^3
357 TV^3
381 TV^3
410 TV^4
411 TV^4
1889 1854
1891 1854
2484 2301
2537 2301
2538 2301
2570 2301
2667 2600
2820 2800
2821 2800
2837 2800
2860 2800
2864 2800
2877 2800
2889 2884
2890 2884
2891 2884
2905 2900
2906 2900
2940 2900
2943 2900
3038 ROD
3042 ROD
3044 ROD
3708 5700
3716 5700
3755 5700
3809 2884
3812 2884
3814 2884
3817 2884
3823 2884
3824 2884
4083 4073
4094 4073
4227 4200
4236 4200
4290 4200
4622 5700
4633 5700
4637 5700
4652 5700
4677 5700
4901 4900
4913 4900
4952 4900
4953 4900
4974 4900
4975 4900
4979 4900
5001 4073
5005 4073
5007 4073
5010 4073
5020 4073
5030 4073
5046 4073
5049 4073
5052 4073
5054 4073
5080 4073
5200 4200
5236 5205
5249 5205
5307 4300
5335 4300
5378 4300
5382 4300
5388 4300
5628 5600
5679 5600
5685 5600
5749 5700
5910 4900
5946 4900
5953 4900
5958 4900
5970 4900
5977 4900
6353 4300
6622 5600
6691 5600
6805 6800
6810 6800
6811 6800
6817 6800
6827 6800
6928 4900
6946 4900
6948 4900
6969 6959
7001 4073
7201 7200
7219 7200
8728 5700
8740 5700
9629 5700
9648 5700
9713 5700
9759 5700
9778 5700
9796 5700
90101 WD^1
90268 WD^1
90271 WD^1
90355 WD^1
90414 WD^1
90524 WD^1
90568 WD^1
90579 WD^1

1951 86C
203 TV^2
205 TV^2
208 TV^2
209 TV^2
220 TV^2
335 TV^3
357 TV^3
381 TV^3
425 BM^1
2407 2301
2537 2301
2806 2800
2820 2800
2837 2800
2877 2800
2891 2884
2892 2884
2906 2900
2940 2900
2943 2900
3036 ROD
3670 5700
3729 5700
3755 5700
3809 2884
3812 2884
3814 2884
3817 2884
3823 2884
3824 2884
4094 4073
4145 5101
4222 4200
4224 4200
4227 4200
4231 4200
4255 4200
4266 4200
4270 4200
4275 4200
4285 4200
4287 4200
4622 5700
4633 5700
4677 5700
4901 4900
4913 4900
4952 4900
4953 4900
4963 4900
4968 4900
4974 4900
4975 4900
4979 4900
5001 4073
5005 4073
5006 4073
5007 4073
5020 4073
5030 4073
5046 4073
5049 4073
5052 4073
5054 4073
5077 4073
5080 4073
5089 4073
5099 4073
5226 5205
5249 5205
5382 4300
5388 4300
5679 5600
5685 5600
5749 5700
5776 5700
5786 5700
5910 4900
5911 4900
5946 4900
5953 4900
5958 4900
5970 4900
5977 4900
6353 4300
6837 6800
6928 4900
6939 4900
6943 4900
6946 4900
6948 4900
6969 6959
6998 6959
6999 6959
7016 4073
7017 4073
7020 4073
7022 4073
7023 4073
7201 7200
7210 7200
7219 7200
7232 7200
8723 5700
8728 5700
9629 5700
9648 5700
9713 5700
9723 5700
9759 5700
90271 WD^1

1954 86C
205 TV^2
349 TV^3
371 TV^3
374 TV^3
381 TV^3
1205 AD^4
2806 2800
2820 2800
2837 2800
2877 2800
2891 2884
2892 2884
3024 ROD
3026 ROD
3043 ROD
3670 5700
3729 5700
3755 5700
3803 2884
3809 2884
3812 2884
3814 2884
3817 2884
3823 2884
3824 2884
3842 2884
3846 2884
4207 4200
4225 4200
4226 4200
4231 4200
4250 4200
4255 4200
4266 4200
4268 4200
4270 4200
4622 5700
4633 5700
4677 5700
4901 4900
4913 4900
4946 4900
4953 4900
4968 4900
4974 4900
5001 4073
5005 4073
5006 4073
5007 4073
5020 4073
5030 4073
5046 4073
5049 4073
5052 4073
5054 4073
5077 4073
5080 4073
5089 4073
5099 4073
5207 5205
5382 4300
5388 4300

5633 5600
5679 5600
5685 5600
5749 5700
5776 5700
5786 5700
5910 4900
5911 4900
5925 4900
5946 4900
5970 4900
5977 4900
6333 4300
6353 4300
6600 5600
6602 5600
6621 5600
6928 4900
6932 4900
6939 4900
6943 4900
6946 4900
6948 4900
6951 4900
6969 6959
6998 6959
6999 6959
7016 4073
7017 4073
7020 4073
7022 4073
7023 4073
8439 9400
8723 5700
8728 5700
8776 5700
9648 5700
9713 5700
9723 5700
9759 5700
9778 5700
70025 7P6F
70026 7P6F
70027 7P6F
70028 7P6F
70029 7P6F
75005 4MT[1]
75007 4MT[1]
75008 4MT[1]
75009 4MT[1]
75021 4MT[1]
75022 4MT[1]
90188 WD[1]
90192 WD[1]
90238 WD[1]
90524 WD[1]
90565 WD[1]
90572 WD[1]
90630 WD[1]

1957 86C
1508 1500
2805 2800
2821 2800
2837 2800
2874 2800
2877 2800
2891 2884
2892 2884
3670 5700
3755 5700
3801 2884
3803 2884
3809 2884
3810 2884
3816 2884
3817 2884
3842 2884
3843 2884
3846 2884
4207 4200
4225 4200
4226 4200
4231 4200
4254 4200
4266 4200
4270 4200
4622 5700
4633 5700
4901 4900
4913 4900
4934 4900
4946 4900
4964 4900
4968 4900
4973 4900
4974 4900
4996 4900
5001 4073
5005 4073
5007 4073
5020 4073
5030 4073
5046 4073
5049 4073
5052 4073
5054 4073
5072 4073
5074 4073
5099 4073
5207 5205
5218 5205
5334 4300
5602 5600
5633 5600
5679 5600
5749 5700
5776 5700
5786 5700
5911 4900
5923 4900
5925 4900
5946 4900
5970 4900
6308 4300
6333 4300
6352 4300
6353 4300
6600 5600
6621 5600
6644 5600
6928 4900
6932 4900
6939 4900
6943 4900
6946 4900
6948 4900
6969 6959
6998 6959
6999 6959
7020 4073
7022 4073
7023 4073
7775 5700
8447 9400
8723 5700
8728 5700
8776 5700
9300 9300
9306 9300
9426 9400
9459 9400
9461 9400
9493 9400
9494 9400
9603 5700
9648 5700
9713 5700
9723 5700
9759 5700
9778 5700
70015 7P6F
70016 7P6F
70017 7P6F
70018 7P6F
70019 7P6F
70020 7P6F
70022 7P6F
70024 7P6F
70025 7P6F
70026 7P6F
70027 7P6F
70028 7P6F
70029 7P6F
73014 5MT
73025 5MT
73026 5MT
75004 4MT[1]
75007 4MT[1]
75008 4MT[1]
75009 4MT[1]
75021 4MT[1]
75022 4MT[1]
90125 WD[1]
90148 WD[1]
90188 WD[1]
90201 WD[1]
90238 WD[1]
90312 WD[1]
90323 WD[1]
90524 WD[1]
90565 WD[1]
90572 WD[1]
90579 WD[1]
90693 WD[1]

1960 86C
1508 1500
2821 2800
2834 2800
2874 2800
2877 2800
2889 2884
2891 2884
2895 2884
3670 5700
3755 5700
3809 2884
3810 2884
3817 2884
3835 2884
3843 2884
3845 2884
3849 2884
3855 2884
3860 2884
4073 4073
4086 4073
4207 4200
4225 4200
4230 4200
4254 4200
4266 4200
4270 4200
4298 4200
4633 5700
4928 4900
4931 4900
4946 4900
4952 4900
4956 4900
4973 4900
4999 4900
5021 4073
5061 4073
5095 4073
5099 4073
5207 5205
5218 5205
5225 5205
5260 5205
5261 5205
5602 5600
5685 5600
5727 5700
5749 5700
5776 5700
5910 4900
5911 4900
5946 4900
5962 4900
6326 4300
6352 4300
6832 6800
6847 6800
6859 6800
6864 6800
6932 4900
6935 4900
6936 4900
6939 4900
6943 4900
6963 6959
6999 6959
7006 4073
7023 4073
7332 4300
7775 5700
7805 7800
7913 6959
7925 6959
8441 9400
8457 9400
8466 9400
8484 9400
8723 5700
8728 5700
8776 5700
9426 9400
9437 9400
9453 9400
9461 9400
9493 9400
9494 9400
9603 5700
9648 5700
9713 5700
9723 5700
9759 5700
9778 5700
48460 8F
70016 7P6F
70018 7P6F
70019 7P6F
70020 7P6F
70022 7P6F
70023 7P6F
70024 7P6F
70025 7P6F
70026 7P6F
70027 7P6F
70028 7P6F
70029 7P6F
73021 5MT
73023 5MT
73024 5MT
90069 WD[1]
90125 WD[1]
90149 WD[1]
90188 WD[1]
90201 WD[1]
90312 WD[1]
90323 WD[1]
90572 WD[1]
90573 WD[1]
90579 WD[1]
90691 WD[1]
90693 WD[1]
92003 9F
92004 9F
92005 9F
92209 9F
92210 9F
92216 9F
92217 9F
92236 9F
92237 9F

Cardiff Cathays

1948 CHYS
201 TV[2]
305 TV[3]
307 TV[3]
343 TV[3]
344 TV[3]
346 TV[3]
347 TV[3]
348 TV[3]
360 TV[3]
364 TV[3]
367 TV[3]
371 TV[3]
376 TV[3]
383 TV[3]
384 TV[3]
390 TV[3]
391 TV[3]
393 TV[3]
434 BM[2]
1420 1400
1425 1400
2066 2021
3597 3500
4616 5700
5605 5600
5614 5600
5617 5600
5623 5600
5624 5600
5646 5600
5651 5600
5658 5600
5659 5600
5661 5600
5672 5600
5681 5600
5687 5600
6402 6400
6416 6400
6423 6400
6433 6400
6435 6400
6436 6400
6615 5600
6626 5600
6627 5600
6635 5600
6648 5600
6655 5600
6659 5600
6660 5600
6661 5600

1951 88A
31 RR[1]
35 RR[3]
38 RR[3]
40 RR[3]
41 RR[3]
42 RR[3]
43 RR[3]
44 RR[3]
56 RR[4]
63 RR[4]
293 TV[2]
305 TV[3]
307 TV[3]
343 TV[3]
344 TV[3]
345 TV[3]
346 TV[3]
347 TV[3]
348 TV[3]
360 TV[3]
364 TV[3]
367 TV[3]
371 TV[3]
376 TV[3]
377 TV[3]
383 TV[3]
384 TV[3]
390 TV[3]
391 TV[3]
393 TV[3]
433 BM[2]
434 BM[2]
1420 1400
1425 1400
1461 1400
1629 1600
2066 2021
2140 2021
3672 5700
3734 5700
4618 5700
4667 5700
5411 5400
5601 5600
5630 5600
5636 5600
5640 5600
5653 5600
5654 5600
5669 5600
5670 5600
5678 5600
5681 5600
5683 5600
5687 5600
5692 5600
5697 5600
6402 6400
6416 6400
6423 6400
6433 6400
6435 6400
6436 6400
6603 5600
6607 5600
6608 5600
6612 5600
6618 5600
6626 5600
6634 5600
6635 5600
6647 5600
6659 5600
6660 5600
6664 5600
6665 5600
6682 5600
6684 5600
7202 7200
7205 7200
7445 7400
7738 5700
8780 5700

1954 88A
42 RR[3]
43 RR[3]
44 RR[3]
80 RR[6]
305 TV[3]
307 TV[3]
343 TV[3]
345 TV[3]
346 TV[3]
347 TV[3]
348 TV[3]
360 TV[3]
362 TV[3]
364 TV[3]
367 TV[3]
383 TV[3]
384 TV[3]
391 TV[3]
3672 5700
3734 5700
4580 4575
4581 4575
4589 4575
4618 5700
4667 5700
5511 4575
5534 4575
5568 4575
5572 4575
5601 5600
5630 5600
5636 5600
5650 5600
5653 5600
5654 5600
5659 5600
5663 5600
5669 5600
5670 5600
5678 5600
5681 5600
5683 5600
5687 5600
5692 5600
6402 6400
6416 6400
6423 6400
6603 5600
6607 5600
6608 5600
6612 5600
6618 5600
6626 5600
6635 5600
6647 5600
6659 5600
6660 5600
6665 5600
6682 5600
6684 5600
7202 7200
7205 7200
7242 7200
7445 7400
7726 5700
7738 5700
7779 5700
8470 9400
8471 9400
8478 9400
8481 9400
8482 9400
8484 9400
8495 9400
8780 5700

1957 88A
305 TV[3]
361 TV[3]
364 TV[3]
376 TV[3]
381 TV[3]
383 TV[3]
385 TV[3]
3672 5700
4101 5101
4177 5101
4580 4575
4589 4575
4618 5700
4634 5700
4667 5700
5511 4575
5534 4575
5568 4575
5572 4575
5574 4575
5601 5600
5626 5600
5627 5600
5630 5600
5636 5600
5637 5600
5653 5600
5654 5600
5663 5600
5669 5600
5670 5600
5683 5600
5687 5600
5692 5600
5710 5700
5724 5700
5793 5700
6402 6400
6416 6400
6435 6400
6603 5600
6606 5600
6607 5600
6608 5600
6612 5600
6614 5600
6618 5600
6626 5600
6633 5600
6635 5600
6638 5600
6647 5600
6648 5600
6659 5600
6660 5600
6665 5600
6682 5600
6684 5600
6689 5600
7202 7200
7205 7200
7242 7200
7445 7400
7726 5700
7751 5700
7772 5700
7779 5700
8469 9400
8470 9400
8471 9400
8478 9400
8481 9400
8482 9400
8484 9400
8489 9400
8495 9400
8780 5700

Cardiff East Dock

1948 CED
31 RR[1]
33 RR[2]
36 RR[3]
37 RR[3]
47 RR[2]
51 RR[2]
52 RR[4]
53 RR[4]
54 RR[4]
55 RR[4]
61 RR[4]
66 RR[4]
68 RR[4]
72 RR[4]
73 RR[4]
74 RR[4]
90 RR[8]
91 RR[8]
92 RR[8]
93 RR[9]
94 RR[9]
95 RR[9]
96 RR[9]
155 Car[1]
210 TV[2]
212 BR[1]
259 BR[2]
269 BR[2]
285 TV[2]
297 TV[2]
681 Car[2]
682 Car[2]
683 Car[2]
684 Car[2]
1705 1854
1884 1854
1888 1854
1897 1854
2008 1901
2022 2021
2048 2021
2086 2021
2123 2021
2124 2021
2130 2021
2140 2021
2141 2021
2147 2021
2724 2721
2754 2721
2781 2721
3707 5700
4618 5700
4630 5700
6700 6700
6701 6700
6702 6700
6703 6700
6704 6700
6705 6700
6706 6700
6707 6700
6708 6700
6709 6700
6721 6700
6744 6700
6751 6700
7751 5700
8743 5700

1951 88B
33 RR[2]
36 RR[3]
37 RR[3]
39 RR[3]
55 RR[4]
66 RR[4]
67 RR[4]
68 RR[4]
72 RR[4]
73 RR[4]
74 RR[4]
90 RR[8]
91 RR[8]
92 RR[8]
93 RR[9]
94 RR[9]
95 RR[9]
96 RR[9]
155 Car[1]
681 Car[2]
682 Car[2]
683 Car[2]
684 Car[2]
2048 2021
2086 2021
2123 2021
2147 2021
3681 5700
3707 5700
3783 5700
4616 5700
4630 5700
5710 5700
6700 6700
6701 6700
6702 6700
6703 6700
6704 6700
6705 6700
6706 6700
6707 6700
6708 6700
6709 6700
6721 6700
6744 6700
6751 6700
6765 6700
6767 6700
6770 6700
6771 6700
6773 6700
6778 6700
6779 6700
7751 5700
8414 9400
8416 9400
8455 9400
8457 9400
8743 5700
9677 5700
9679 5700

1964 88B
35 RR[3]
36 RR[3]
37 RR[3]
38 RR[3]
39 RR[3]
41 RR[3]
58 RR[4]
59 RR[4]
65 RR[4]
66 RR[4]
68 RR[4]
82 RR[7]
83 RR[7]
90 RR[8]
91 RR[8]
92 RR[8]
93 RR[9]
94 RR[9]
96 RR[9]
204 TV[2]
210 TV[2]
211 TV[2]
215 TV[2]
216 TV[2]
279 TV[2]
290 TV[2]
335 TV[3]
376 TV[3]
377 TV[3]
378 TV[3]
399 TV[3]
681 Car[2]
683 Car[2]
684 Car[2]
3650 5700
3681 5700
3707 5700
3783 5700
5710 5700
6700 6700
6701 6700
6702 6700
6703 6700
6704 6700
6705 6700
6706 6700
6707 6700
6708 6700
6709 6700
6721 6700
6744 6700
6751 6700
6765 6700
6767 6700
6770 6700
6771 6700
6773 6700
6778 6700
6779 6700
7722 5700
7751 5700
8414 9400
8416 9400
8429 9400
8457 9400
8464 9400
8743 5700
9677 5700
9679 5700
9776 5700

1957 88B
36 RR[3]
38 RR[3]
42 RR[3]
43 RR[3]
3400 9400
3401 9400
3402 9400
3403 9400
3404 9400
3405 9400
3406 9400
3407 9400
3408 9400
3409 9400
3681 5700
3694 5700
3730 5700
3734 5700
3783 5700
4626 5700
4631 5700
4686 5700
4698 5700
6700 6700
6701 6700
6702 6700
6703 6700
6704 6700
6705 6700
6706 6700
6707 6700
6708 6700
6709 6700
6736 6700
6744 6700
6751 6700
6765 6700
6767 6700
6769 6700
6770 6700
6771 6700
6773 6700
6774 6700
6775 6700
6778 6700
7722 5700
7738 5700
8414 9400
8416 9400
8424 9400
8429 9400
8437 9400
8441 9400
8457 9400
8464 9400
8722 5700
8743 5700
8787 5700
9437 9400
9443 9400
9477 9400
9677 5700
9679 5700
9769 5700
9776 5700

1963 88L
2887 2884
3784 5700
3804 2884
3810 2884
3862 2884
4080 4073
4090 4073
4242 4200
4272 4200
4633 5700
4918 4900
4936 4900
4953 4900
5015 4073
5029 4073
5043 4073
5073 4073
5074 4073
5081 4073
5091 4073
5092 4073
5096 4073
5097 4073
5220 5205
5224 5205
5225 5205
5261 5205
5749 5700
5937 4900
5962 4900
6326 4300
6345 4300
6681 5600
6808 6800
6847 6800
6859 6800
6875 6800
6912 4900
6918 4900
6931 4900
6932 4900
6935 4900
6936 4900
6939 4900
6944 4900
6945 4900
6950 4900
6957 4900
6987 6959
6995 6959
7303 4300
7317 4300
7805 7800
7820 7800
7913 6959
7925 6959
7927 6959
8425 9400
8452 9400
8466 9400
8471 9400
8484 9400
9426 9400
9437 9400
9461 9400
9629 5700
9651 5700
92003 9F
92208 9F
92210 9F
92216 9F
92219 9F
92232 9F
92236 9F
92237 9F
92241 9F
92244 9F
92246 9F

Carlisle Canal

1948 CAR
60068 A10
60091 A3
60093 A3
60095 A3
61217 B1
61219 B1
61222 B1
61851 K3
61854 K3
61858 K3
61882 K3
61898 K3
61936 K3
61937 K3
62059 D31
62060 D31
62730 D49
62731 D49
62732 D49
62734 D49
62735 D49
64478 J35
64499 J35
64511 J35
64526 J35
64875 J39
64877 J39
64880 J39
64884 J39
64888 J39
64892 J39
64895 J39
64899 J39
64912 J39
64930 J39
64932 J39
64946 J39
64948 J39
64963 J39
64964 J39
64986 J39
65216 J36
65293 J36
65304 J36
65312 J36
65321 J36
67458 C15
67474 C15
67481 C15
68499 J69
69139 N15
69155 N15
69174 N15
69185 N15
69197 N15
69215 N15
69218 N15

1951 12B
45014 5MT[3]
45096 5MT[3]
45454 5MT[3]
48074 8F
48323 8F
48544 8F
60068 A3
60079 A3
60093 A3
60095 A3
61217 B1
61219 B1
61222 B1
61851 K3
61854 K3
61858 K3
61882 K3
61898 K3
61936 K3
61937 K3
62281 D31
64478 J35
64499 J35
64511 J35
64526 J35
64875 J39
64877 J39
64880 J39
64884 J39
64888 J39
64895 J39
64899 J39
64912 J39
64930 J39
64932 J39
64948 J39
64964 J39
65216 J36
65293 J36
65304 J36
65312 J36
65321 J36
67458 C15
67474 C15
67481 C15
68499 J69
69139 N15
69155 N15
69174 N15
69185 N15
69197 N15
69215 N15
69218 N15

1954 68E
43139 4MT[5]
60068 A3
60079 A3
60093 A3
60095 A3
61217 B1
61219 B1
61222 B1
61239 B1
61290 B1
61395 B1
61851 K3
61854 K3
61858 K3
61882 K3
61898 K3
61916 K3
61936 K3
61937 K3
62732 D49
62734 D49
64471 J35
64478 J35
64499 J35
64511 J35
64526 J35
64727 J39
64733 J39
64875 J39
64877 J39
64880 J39
64884 J39
64888 J39
64895 J39
64899 J39
64912 J39
64930 J39
64932 J39
64948 J39
64964 J39
65216 J36
65293 J36
65304 J36
65312 J36
65321 J36
67458 C15
67474 C15
67481 C15
69139 N15
69155 N15
69174 N15
69215 N15

1957 68E
43139 4MT[5]
60068 A3
60079 A3
60093 A3
60095 A3
61064 B1
61217 B1
61219 B1
61222 B1
61239 B1
61290 B1
61395 B1
61851 K3
61854 K3
61858 K3
61882 K3
61898 K3
61916 K3
61936 K3
61937 K3
62732 D49
62734 D49
64478 J35
64499 J35
64526 J35
64727 J39
64733 J39
64875 J39
64877 J39
64880 J39
64884 J39
64888 J39
64895 J39
64899 J39
64912 J39
64930 J39
64932 J39
64948 J39
64964 J39
65293 J36
65312 J36
65321 J36
69139 N15
69155 N15
69174 N15
69215 N15

1960 12C
43139 4MT[5]
44157 4F[2]
60068 A3
60079 A3
60093 A3
60095 A3
61064 B1
61217 B1
61222 B1
61239 B1
61290 B1
61395 B1
61858 K3
61916 K3
61936 K3
62734 D49
62747 D49
64478 J35
64499 J35
64733 J39
64877 J39
64880 J39
64884 J39
64888 J39
64895 J39
64899 J39
64932 J39
64948 J39
64964 J39
65237 J36
65293 J36
65312 J36
65321 J36
69155 N15
69564 N2

1963 12C
42067 4MT[1]
42081 4MT[1]
42095 4MT[1]
42098 4MT[1]
42210 4MT[1]
42440 4MT[3]
42447 4MT[3]
42449 4MT[3]
42634 4MT[3]
43000 4MT[5]
43011 4MT[5]
43028 4MT[5]
43045 4MT[5]
43139 4MT[5]
44884 5MT[3]
47383 3F[6]
47388 3F[6]
47520 3F[6]

Carlisle Durran Hill

1951 68A sub
41971 3P[2]
41972 3P[2]
41973 3P[2]
41974 3P[2]

1954 68A sub
41971 3P[2]
41972 3P[2]
41973 3P[2]
41974 3P[2]

Carlisle Kingmoor

1948 12A
40602 2P[3]
40613 2P[3]
40615 2P[3]
41129 4P[1]
41139 4P[1]
41140 4P[1]
41141 4P[1]
41142 4P[1]
41143 4P[1]
41146 4P[1]
42742 5MT[1]
42743 5MT[1]
42744 5MT[1]
42745 5MT[1]
42746 5MT[1]
42748 5MT[1]
42749 5MT[1]
42751 5MT[1]
42752 5MT[1]
42780 5MT[1]
42802 5MT[1]
42803 5MT[1]
42830 5MT[1]
42831 5MT[1]
42832 5MT[1]
42833 5MT[1]
42834 5MT[1]
42835 5MT[1]
42836 5MT[1]
42837 5MT[1]
42875 5MT[1]
42876 5MT[1]
42877 5MT[1]
42878 5MT[1]
42880 5MT[1]
42881 5MT[1]
42882 5MT[1]
42883 5MT[1]
42884 5MT[1]
42905 5MT[1]
42906 5MT[1]
42907 5MT[1]
43868 4F[1]
43902 4F[1]
43922 4F[1]
43973 4F[1]
43996 4F[1]
44001 4F[1]
44008 4F[1]
44009 4F[1]
44016 4F[1]

44181 4F[2]
44183 4F[2]
44189 4F[2]
44199 4F[2]
44315 4F[2]
44324 4F[2]
44326 4F[2]
44795 5MT[3]
44877 5MT[3]
44878 5MT[3]
44879 5MT[3]
44882 5MT[3]
44883 5MT[3]
44884 5MT[3]
44886 5MT[3]
44898 5MT[3]
44899 5MT[3]
44900 5MT[3]
44901 5MT[3]
44902 5MT[3]
44903 5MT[3]
44993 5MT[3]
44994 5MT[3]
45005 5MT[3]
45006 5MT[3]
45009 5MT[3]
45013 5MT[3]
45014 5MT[3]
45015 5MT[3]
45017 5MT[3]
45022 5MT[3]
45023 5MT[3]
45081 5MT[3]
45082 5MT[3]
45083 5MT[3]
45084 5MT[3]
45096 5MT[3]
45100 5MT[3]
45118 5MT[3]
45119 5MT[3]
45126 5MT[3]
45127 5MT[3]
45151 5MT[3]
45152 5MT[3]
45169 5MT[3]
45241 5MT[3]
45266 5MT[3]
45363 5MT[3]
45364 5MT[3]
45429 5MT[3]
45432 5MT[3]
45443 5MT[3]
45454 5MT[3]
45455 5MT[3]
45482 5MT[3]
45564 6P5F[2]
45577 6P5F[2]
45579 6P5F[2]
45580 6P5F[2]
45581 6P5F[2]
45582 6P5F[2]
45713 6P5F[2]
45714 6P5F[2]
45715 6P5F[2]
45716 6P5F[2]
45727 6P5F[2]
45728 6P5F[2]
45729 6P5F[2]
45730 6P5F[2]
45731 6P5F[2]
45732 6P5F[2]
56231 3F[10]
56235 3F[10]
56248 3F[10]
56266 3F[10]
56310 3F[10]
56316 3F[10]
56317 3F[10]
56327 3F[10]
56332 3F[10]
56333 3F[10]
56340 3F[10]
56354 3F[10]
56355 3F[10]
56373 3F[10]
56374 3F[10]
56905 3F[11]
57592 3F[12]
57605 3F[12]
57626 3F[12]
90773 WD[2]
90774 WD[2]

1951 68A

40602 2P[3]
40613 2P[3]
40615 2P[3]
41129 4P[1]
41139 4P[1]
41140 4P[1]
41141 4P[1]
41142 4P[1]
41143 4P[1]
41146 4P[1]
42720 5MT[1]
42748 5MT[1]
42749 5MT[1]
42751 5MT[1]
42752 5MT[1]
42757 5MT[1]
42780 5MT[1]
42793 5MT[1]
42802 5MT[1]
42803 5MT[1]
42831 5MT[1]
42832 5MT[1]
42833 5MT[1]
42834 5MT[1]
42835 5MT[1]
42836 5MT[1]
42837 5MT[1]
42875 5MT[1]
42876 5MT[1]
42877 5MT[1]
42881 5MT[1]
42882 5MT[1]
42883 5MT[1]
42884 5MT[1]
42899 5MT[1]
42905 5MT[1]
42906 5MT[1]
42907 5MT[1]
42913 5MT[1]
43868 4F[1]
43902 4F[1]
43922 4F[1]
43973 4F[1]
44008 4F[1]
44009 4F[1]
44016 4F[1]
44181 4F[2]
44183 4F[2]
44189 4F[2]
44199 4F[2]
44315 4F[2]
44324 4F[2]
44326 4F[2]
44668 5MT[3]
44669 5MT[3]
44670 5MT[3]
44671 5MT[3]
44672 5MT[3]
44673 5MT[3]
44674 5MT[3]
44675 5MT[3]
44676 5MT[3]
44677 5MT[3]
44718 5MT[3]
44719 5MT[3]
44720 5MT[3]
44721 5MT[3]
44722 5MT[3]
44723 5MT[3]
44724 5MT[3]
44725 5MT[3]
44726 5MT[3]
44727 5MT[3]
44795 5MT[3]
44877 5MT[3]
44878 5MT[3]
44882 5MT[3]
44883 5MT[3]
44884 5MT[3]
44886 5MT[3]
44898 5MT[3]
44899 5MT[3]
44900 5MT[3]
44901 5MT[3]
44902 5MT[3]
44903 5MT[3]
44993 5MT[3]
44994 5MT[3]
45081 5MT[3]
45082 5MT[3]
45083 5MT[3]
45084 5MT[3]
45100 5MT[3]
45126 5MT[3]
45363 5MT[3]
45364 5MT[3]
45432 5MT[3]
45455 5MT[3]
45577 6P5F[2]
45580 6P5F[2]
45581 6P5F[2]
45582 6P5F[2]
45713 6P5F[2]
45714 6P5F[2]
45715 6P5F[2]
45716 6P5F[2]
45727 6P5F[2]
45728 6P5F[2]
45729 6P5F[2]
45730 6P5F[2]
45731 6P5F[2]
45732 6P5F[2]
48321 8F
48464 8F
48472 8F
48536 8F
48612 8F
56231 3F[10]
56235 3F[10]
56248 3F[10]
56266 3F[10]
56316 3F[10]
56317 3F[10]
56327 3F[10]
56332 3F[10]
56333 3F[10]
56340 3F[10]
56354 3F[10]
56355 3F[10]
56373 3F[10]
56374 3F[10]
57632 3F[13]
90464 WD[1]
90505 WD[1]
90585 WD[1]
90751 WD[2]
90763 WD[2]
90767 WD[2]
90769 WD[2]
90773 WD[2]
90774 WD[2]

1954 68A

40602 2P[3]
40613 2P[3]
40615 2P[3]
41141 4P[1]
41146 4P[1]
42720 5MT[1]
42748 5MT[1]
42751 5MT[1]
42752 5MT[1]
42757 5MT[1]
42780 5MT[1]
42793 5MT[1]
42802 5MT[1]
42803 5MT[1]
42831 5MT[1]
42832 5MT[1]
42833 5MT[1]
42834 5MT[1]
42835 5MT[1]
42836 5MT[1]
42837 5MT[1]
42875 5MT[1]
42876 5MT[1]
42877 5MT[1]
42881 5MT[1]
42882 5MT[1]
42883 5MT[1]
42884 5MT[1]
42899 5MT[1]
42905 5MT[1]
42906 5MT[1]
42907 5MT[1]
42913 5MT[1]
43241 3F[3]
43301 3F[3]
43351 3F[3]
43514 3F[3]
43622 3F[3]
43636 3F[3]
43678 3F[3]
43868 4F[1]
43902 4F[1]
43922 4F[1]
43973 4F[1]
44008 4F[1]
44009 4F[1]
44016 4F[1]
44181 4F[2]
44183 4F[2]
44189 4F[2]
44315 4F[2]
44324 4F[2]
44326 4F[2]
44668 5MT[3]
44669 5MT[3]
44670 5MT[3]
44671 5MT[3]
44672 5MT[3]
44673 5MT[3]
44674 5MT[3]
44675 5MT[3]
44676 5MT[3]
44703 5MT[3]
44725 5MT[3]
44726 5MT[3]
44727 5MT[3]
44790 5MT[3]
44792 5MT[3]
44795 5MT[3]
44877 5MT[3]
44878 5MT[3]
44882 5MT[3]
44883 5MT[3]
44884 5MT[3]
44886 5MT[3]
44898 5MT[3]
44899 5MT[3]
44900 5MT[3]
44901 5MT[3]
44902 5MT[3]
44903 5MT[3]
44921 5MT[3]
44958 5MT[3]
44993 5MT[3]
45007 5MT[3]
45012 5MT[3]
45013 5MT[3]
45018 5MT[3]
45081 5MT[3]
45082 5MT[3]
45083 5MT[3]
45100 5MT[3]
45112 5MT[3]
45118 5MT[3]
45120 5MT[3]
45122 5MT[3]
45126 5MT[3]
45138 5MT[3]
45163 5MT[3]
45281 5MT[3]
45330 5MT[3]
45334 5MT[3]
45363 5MT[3]
45364 5MT[3]
45432 5MT[3]
45455 5MT[3]
45466 5MT[3]
45481 5MT[3]
45491 5MT[3]
45640 6P5F[2]
45657 6P5F[2]
45679 6P5F[2]
45697 6P5F[2]
45704 6P5F[2]
45713 6P5F[2]
45714 6P5F[2]
45715 6P5F[2]
45716 6P5F[2]
45718 6P5F[2]
45724 6P5F[2]
45728 6P5F[2]
45729 6P5F[2]
45730 6P5F[2]
45731 6P5F[2]
45732 6P5F[2]
48321 8F
48464 8F
48472 8F
48536 8F
48612 8F
48708 8F
48756 8F
48758 8F
56231 3F[10]
56235 3F[10]
56316 3F[10]
56317 3F[10]
56332 3F[10]
56333 3F[10]
56340 3F[10]
56355 3F[10]
56373 3F[10]
56374 3F[10]
72005 6P5F
72006 6P5F
72007 6P5F
72008 6P5F
72009 6P5F
90763 WD[2]
90769 WD[2]
90774 WD[2]

1957 68A

40185 3MT[2]
40602 2P[3]
40613 2P[3]
40615 2P[3]
40651 2P[3]
42720 5MT[1]
42748 5MT[1]
42751 5MT[1]
42752 5MT[1]
42757 5MT[1]
42793 5MT[1]
42804 5MT[1]
42830 5MT[1]
42831 5MT[1]
42832 5MT[1]
42833 5MT[1]
42834 5MT[1]
42835 5MT[1]
42836 5MT[1]
42837 5MT[1]
42875 5MT[1]
42876 5MT[1]
42877 5MT[1]
42881 5MT[1]
42882 5MT[1]
42883 5MT[1]
42884 5MT[1]
42899 5MT[1]
42905 5MT[1]
42906 5MT[1]
42907 5MT[1]
42913 5MT[1]
43241 3F[3]
43301 3F[3]
43514 3F[3]
43622 3F[3]
43678 3F[3]
43868 4F[1]
43902 4F[1]
43922 4F[1]
43973 4F[1]
44008 4F[1]
44009 4F[1]
44016 4F[1]
44181 4F[2]
44183 4F[2]
44315 4F[2]
44324 4F[2]
44326 4F[2]
44668 5MT[3]
44669 5MT[3]
44670 5MT[3]
44671 5MT[3]
44672 5MT[3]
44673 5MT[3]
44674 5MT[3]
44675 5MT[3]
44676 5MT[3]
44725 5MT[3]
44726 5MT[3]
44727 5MT[3]
44790 5MT[3]
44792 5MT[3]
44795 5MT[3]
44877 5MT[3]
44878 5MT[3]
44882 5MT[3]
44883 5MT[3]
44884 5MT[3]
44886 5MT[3]
44898 5MT[3]
44899 5MT[3]
44900 5MT[3]
44901 5MT[3]
44902 5MT[3]
44903 5MT[3]
44958 5MT[3]
44993 5MT[3]
45007 5MT[3]
45012 5MT[3]
45013 5MT[3]
45018 5MT[3]
45081 5MT[3]
45082 5MT[3]
45083 5MT[3]
45100 5MT[3]
45112 5MT[3]
45118 5MT[3]
45120 5MT[3]
45122 5MT[3]
45126 5MT[3]
45138 5MT[3]
45163 5MT[3]
45281 5MT[3]
45330 5MT[3]
45334 5MT[3]
45363 5MT[3]
45364 5MT[3]
45432 5MT[3]
45455 5MT[3]
45466 5MT[3]
45481 5MT[3]
45491 5MT[3]
45640 6P5F[2]
45657 6P5F[2]
45679 6P5F[2]
45691 6P5F[2]
45696 6P5F[2]
45697 6P5F[2]
45704 6P5F[2]
45713 6P5F[2]
45714 6P5F[2]
45715 6P5F[2]
45716 6P5F[2]
45718 6P5F[2]
45724 6P5F[2]
45728 6P5F[2]
45729 6P5F[2]
45730 6P5F[2]
45731 6P5F[2]
45732 6P5F[2]
47332 3F[6]
47537 3F[6]
47540 3F[6]
48321 8F
48464 8F
48472 8F
48536 8F
48612 8F
48708 8F
48756 8F
48758 8F
56235 3F[10]
56316 3F[10]
56332 3F[10]
56333 3F[10]
56340 3F[10]
56373 3F[10]
56374 3F[10]
57653 3F[14]
72005 6P5F
72006 6P5F
72007 6P5F
72008 6P5F
72009 6P5F
90170 WD[1]
90464 WD[1]
90763 WD[2]

1960 12A

40602 2P[3]
40613 2P[3]
40615 2P[3]
40651 2P[3]
42449 4MT[3]
42542 4MT[3]
42720 5MT[1]
42751 5MT[1]
42752 5MT[1]
42757 5MT[1]
42793 5MT[1]
42804 5MT[1]
42830 5MT[1]
42831 5MT[1]
42832 5MT[1]
42833 5MT[1]
42834 5MT[1]
42835 5MT[1]
42836 5MT[1]
42837 5MT[1]
42875 5MT[1]
42876 5MT[1]
42877 5MT[1]
42881 5MT[1]
42882 5MT[1]
42883 5MT[1]
42884 5MT[1]
42899 5MT[1]
42905 5MT[1]
42906 5MT[1]
42907 5MT[1]
42913 5MT[1]
43240 3F[3]
43514 3F[3]
43902 4F[1]
43922 4F[1]
44008 4F[1]
44009 4F[1]
44181 4F[2]
44183 4F[2]
44324 4F[2]
44668 5MT[3]
44669 5MT[3]
44670 5MT[3]
44671 5MT[3]
44672 5MT[3]
44673 5MT[3]
44674 5MT[3]
44675 5MT[3]
44676 5MT[3]
44725 5MT[3]
44726 5MT[3]
44727 5MT[3]
44790 5MT[3]
44792 5MT[3]
44795 5MT[3]
44877 5MT[3]
44878 5MT[3]
44882 5MT[3]
44883 5MT[3]
44884 5MT[3]
44886 5MT[3]
44898 5MT[3]
44899 5MT[3]
44900 5MT[3]
44901 5MT[3]
44902 5MT[3]
44903 5MT[3]
44958 5MT[3]
44993 5MT[3]
45012 5MT[3]
45013 5MT[3]
45018 5MT[3]
45081 5MT[3]
45082 5MT[3]
45083 5MT[3]
45100 5MT[3]
45112 5MT[3]
45118 5MT[3]
45120 5MT[3]
45122 5MT[3]
45126 5MT[3]
45138 5MT[3]
45163 5MT[3]
45329 5MT[3]
45330 5MT[3]
45334 5MT[3]
45363 5MT[3]
45364 5MT[3]
45455 5MT[3]
45466 5MT[3]
45481 5MT[3]
45491 5MT[3]
45640 6P5F[2]
45657 6P5F[2]
45691 6P5F[2]
45697 6P5F[2]
45713 6P5F[2]
45714 6P5F[2]
45715 6P5F[2]
45716 6P5F[2]
45718 6P5F[2]
45724 6P5F[2]
45728 6P5F[2]
45729 6P5F[2]
45730 6P5F[2]
45731 6P5F[2]
45732 6P5F[2]
47332 3F[6]
47358 3F[6]
47492 3F[6]
47515 3F[6]
47527 3F[6]
47537 3F[6]
47540 3F[6]
47667 3F[6]
48321 8F
48464 8F
48472 8F
48536 8F
48612 8F
48708 8F
48729 8F
48756 8F
48758 8F
57653 3F[14]
72005 6P5F
72006 6P5F
72007 6P5F
72008 6P5F
72009 6P5F
90170 WD[1]
90464 WD[1]

1963 12A

42301 4MT[2]
42313 4MT[2]
42369 4MT[2]
42832 5MT[1]
42905 5MT[1]
42907 5MT[1]
43023 4MT[5]
43027 4MT[5]
43103 4MT[5]
43981 4F[1]
44009 4F[1]
44060 4F[2]
44181 4F[2]
44183 4F[2]
44305 4F[2]
44341 4F[2]
44451 4F[2]
44668 5MT[3]
44669 5MT[3]
44670 5MT[3]
44671 5MT[3]
44672 5MT[3]
44673 5MT[3]
44674 5MT[3]
44675 5MT[3]
44676 5MT[3]
44677 5MT[3]
44725 5MT[3]
44726 5MT[3]
44727 5MT[3]
44790 5MT[3]
44792 5MT[3]
44795 5MT[3]
44802 5MT[3]
44878 5MT[3]
44883 5MT[3]
44886 5MT[3]
44898 5MT[3]
44899 5MT[3]
44900 5MT[3]
44901 5MT[3]
44902 5MT[3]
44903 5MT[3]
44935 5MT[3]
44958 5MT[3]
44986 5MT[3]
44993 5MT[3]
45013 5MT[3]
45097 5MT[3]
45100 5MT[3]
45112 5MT[3]
45118 5MT[3]
45120 5MT[3]
45122 5MT[3]
45126 5MT[3]
45138 5MT[3]
45148 5MT[3]
45163 5MT[3]
45235 5MT[3]
45254 5MT[3]
45330 5MT[3]
45334 5MT[3]
45363 5MT[3]
45421 5MT[3]
45455 5MT[3]
45466 5MT[3]
45481 5MT[3]
45491 5MT[3]
45535 7P[1]
45588 6P5F[2]
45640 6P5F[2]
45680 6P5F[2]
45734 6P5F[2]
45738 6P5F[2]
45741 6P5F[2]
45742 6P5F[2]
46116 7P[3]R
46128 7P[3]R
46226 8P[2]
46236 8P[2]
46244 8P[2]
46247 8P[2]
46255 8P[2]
46257 8P[2]
47281 3F[6]
47471 3F[6]
47492 3F[6]
47515 3F[6]
48321 8F
48464 8F
48472 8F
48536 8F
48612 8F
48708 8F
48756 8F
48758 8F
72005 6P5F
72006 6P5F
72007 6P5F
72008 6P5F
72009 6P5F

1966 12A

43000 4MT[5]
43004 4MT[5]
43023 4MT[5]
43028 4MT[5]
43040 4MT[5]
43049 4MT[5]
43120 4MT[5]
43121 4MT[5]
43139 4MT[5]
44668 5MT[3]
44669 5MT[3]
44670 5MT[3]
44671 5MT[3]
44672 5MT[3]
44674 5MT[3]
44675 5MT[3]
44677 5MT[3]
44689 5MT[3]
44692 5MT[3]
44726 5MT[3]
44727 5MT[3]
44767 5MT[3]
44790 5MT[3]
44792 5MT[3]
44795 5MT[3]
44802 5MT[3]
44862 5MT[3]
44878 5MT[3]
44883 5MT[3]
44884 5MT[3]
44886 5MT[3]
44887 5MT[3]
44898 5MT[3]
44899 5MT[3]
44900 5MT[3]
44902 5MT[3]
44903 5MT[3]
44911 5MT[3]
44982 5MT[3]
44986 5MT[3]
44989 5MT[3]
44993 5MT[3]
45012 5MT[3]
45013 5MT[3]
45018 5MT[3]
45028 5MT[3]
45061 5MT[3]
45082 5MT[3]
45097 5MT[3]
45105 5MT[3]
45106 5MT[3]
45112 5MT[3]
45118 5MT[3]
45120 5MT[3]
45126 5MT[3]
45135 5MT[3]
45138 5MT[3]
45185 5MT[3]
45195 5MT[3]
45210 5MT[3]
45212 5MT[3]
45217 5MT[3]
45218 5MT[3]
45228 5MT[3]
45235 5MT[3]
45236 5MT[3]
45253 5MT[3]
45254 5MT[3]
45259 5MT[3]
45274 5MT[3]
45295 5MT[3]
45363 5MT[3]
45364 5MT[3]
45437 5MT[3]
45442 5MT[3]
45455 5MT[3]
45481 5MT[3]
47326 3F[6]
47471 3F[6]
47641 3F[6]
47667 3F[6]
70001 7P6F
70002 7P6F
70003 7P6F
70005 7P6F
70006 7P6F
70008 7P6F
70009 7P6F
70010 7P6F
70016 7P6F
70033 7P6F
70035 7P6F
70036 7P6F
70037 7P6F
70038 7P6F
70039 7P6F
70040 7P6F
70041 7P6F
70042 7P6F
72006 6P5F
72008 6P5F
92009 9F
92010 9F
92012 9F
92015 9F
92017 9F
92019 9F
92051 9F
92071 9F
92076 9F
92110 9F
92114 9F
92130 9F
92161 9F
92208 9F
92233 9F
92249 9F

Carlisle Upperby

1948 12B

40403 2P[2]
40446 2P[2]
40652 2P[3]
40654 2P[3]
40673 2P[3]
40699 2P[3]
44081 4F[2]
44086 4F[2]
44121 4F[2]
44346 4F[2]
44390 4F[2]
44783 5MT[3]
44784 5MT[3]
44785 5MT[3]
44786 5MT[3]
44787 5MT[3]
44868 5MT[3]
44869 5MT[3]
44876 5MT[3]
44905 5MT[3]
44906 5MT[3]
44907 5MT[3]
44936 5MT[3]
44939 5MT[3]
45046 5MT[3]
45106 5MT[3]
45129 5MT[3]
45133 5MT[3]
45139 5MT[3]
45184 5MT[3]
45193 5MT[3]
45230 5MT[3]
45243 5MT[3]
45244 5MT[3]
45246 5MT[3]
45258 5MT[3]
45293 5MT[3]
45295 5MT[3]
45296 5MT[3]
45299 5MT[3]
45307 5MT[3]
45311 5MT[3]
45323 5MT[3]
45327 5MT[3]
45348 5MT[3]
45354 5MT[3]
45368 5MT[3]
45371 5MT[3]
45378 5MT[3]
45388 5MT[3]
45393 5MT[3]
45409 5MT[3]
45414 5MT[3]
45416 5MT[3]
45428 5MT[3]
45439 5MT[3]
45450 5MT[3]
45451 5MT[3]
45494 5MT[3]
45506 6P5F[1]
45518 6P5F[1]
45541 6P5F[1]
45550 6P5F[1]
45553 6P5F[2]
45563 6P5F[2]
45595 6P5F[2]
45599 6P5F[2]
45624 6P5F[2]
45677 6P5F[2]
45678 6P5F[2]
45718 6P5F[2]
46110 7P[3]
46128 7P[3]R
46137 7P[3]
46158 7P[3]
46226 8P[2]
46228 8P[2]
46238 8P[2]
46249 8P[2]
46250 8P[2]
46251 8P[2]
46883 2P[7]
47295 3F[6]
47326 3F[6]
47340 3F[6]
47377 3F[6]
47391 3F[6]
47403 3F[6]
47408 3F[6]
47415 3F[6]
47556 3F[6]
47614 3F[6]
47618 3F[6]
47664 3F[6]
47666 3F[6]
52432 3F[7]

1951 12A

40356 2P[2]
40448 2P[2]
40652 2P[3]
40673 2P[3]
40699 2P[3]
44081 4F[2]
44121 4F[2]
44346 4F[2]
44390 4F[2]
44869 5MT[3]
44871 5MT[3]
44876 5MT[3]
44936 5MT[3]
44939 5MT[3]
45065 5MT[3]
45106 5MT[3]
45129 5MT[3]
45139 5MT[3]
45197 5MT[3]
45230 5MT[3]
45244 5MT[3]
45246 5MT[3]
45258 5MT[3]
45293 5MT[3]
45295 5MT[3]
45296 5MT[3]
45299 5MT[3]
45311 5MT[3]
45323 5MT[3]
45345 5MT[3]
45348 5MT[3]
45351 5MT[3]
45368 5MT[3]
45371 5MT[3]
45388 5MT[3]
45409 5MT[3]
45412 5MT[3]
45414 5MT[3]
45416 5MT[3]
45439 5MT[3]
45445 5MT[3]
45451 5MT[3]
45494 5MT[3]
45505 6P5F[1]
45512 7P[1]
45517 6P5F[1]
45518 6P5F[1]
45526 7P[1]
45542 6P5F[1]
45549 6P5F[1]
45550 6P5F[1]
45551 6P5F[1]
45552 6P5F[2]
45555 6P5F[2]
45578 6P5F[2]
45595 6P5F[2]
45624 6P5F[2]
45630 6P5F[2]
45677 6P5F[2]
45687 6P5F[2]
45718 6P5F[2]
45722 6P5F[2]
46136 7P[3]R
46147 7P[3]R
46225 8P[2]
46226 8P[2]
46228 8P[2]
46229 8P[2]
46238 8P[2]
46251 8P[2]
46253 8P[2]
46254 8P[2]
46255 8P[2]
47295 3F[6]
47326 3F[6]
47340 3F[6]
47377 3F[6]
47391 3F[6]
47403 3F[6]
47408 3F[6]
47415 3F[6]
47556 3F[6]
47614 3F[6]
47618 3F[6]
47664 3F[6]
47666 3F[6]
58376 2F[11]
58419 2F[11]

1954 12A

40356 2P[2]
40448 2P[2]
40582 2P[3]
40652 2P[3]
40699 2P[3]
43896 4F[1]
44060 4F[2]
44081 4F[2]
44121 4F[2]
44346 4F[2]
44936 5MT[3]
44939 5MT[3]
45070 5MT[3]
45106 5MT[3]
45129 5MT[3]
45139 5MT[3]
45140 5MT[3]
45146 5MT[3]
45197 5MT[3]
45230 5MT[3]
45244 5MT[3]
45246 5MT[3]
45248 5MT[3]
45258 5MT[3]
45286 5MT[3]
45288 5MT[3]
45293 5MT[3]
45295 5MT[3]
45296 5MT[3]
45299 5MT[3]
45311 5MT[3]
45315 5MT[3]
45316 5MT[3]
45323 5MT[3]
45345 5MT[3]
45348 5MT[3]
45351 5MT[3]
45368 5MT[3]
45409 5MT[3]
45412 5MT[3]
45414 5MT[3]
45416 5MT[3]
45438 5MT[3]
45445 5MT[3]
45451 5MT[3]
45494 5MT[3]
45502 6P5F[1]
45505 6P5F[1]
45508 6P5F[1]
45512 7P[1]
45526 7P[1]
45537 6P5F[1]
45542 6P5F[1]
45549 6P5F[1]
45551 6P5F[1]
45552 6P5F[2]
45583 6P5F[2]
45593 6P5F[2]
45599 6P5F[2]
45630 6P5F[2]
45643 6P5F[2]
45666 6P5F[2]
45722 6P5F[2]
46136 7P[3]R
46165 7P[3]R
46228 8P[2]
46238 8P[2]
46251 8P[2]
46255 8P[2]
47295 3F[6]
47326 3F[6]
47340 3F[6]
47377 3F[6]
47391 3F[6]
47403 3F[6]
47408 3F[6]
47415 3F[6]
47556 3F[6]
47614 3F[6]
47618 3F[6]
47664 3F[6]
47666 3F[6]

1957 12A

40356 2P[2]
40396 2P[2]
40412 2P[2]
40536 2P[2]
40628 2P[3]
40629 2P[3]
40652 2P[3]
40655 2P[3]
40656 2P[3]
40657 2P[3]
40692 2P[3]
40695 2P[3]
40699 2P[3]
42343 4MT[3]
42544 4MT[3]
43896 4F[1]
44060 4F[2]
44081 4F[2]
44121 4F[2]
44126 4F[2]
44346 4F[2]
44596 4F[2]
44678 5MT[3]
44714 5MT[3]
44770 5MT[3]
44936 5MT[3]
44939 5MT[3]
45071 5MT[3]
45106 5MT[3]
45140 5MT[3]
45184 5MT[3]
45197 5MT[3]
45244 5MT[3]
45246 5MT[3]
45248 5MT[3]
45258 5MT[3]
45259 5MT[3]
45286 5MT[3]
45293 5MT[3]
45295 5MT[3]
45296 5MT[3]
45304 5MT[3]
45315 5MT[3]
45316 5MT[3]
45317 5MT[3]
45323 5MT[3]
45329 5MT[3]
45348 5MT[3]
45351 5MT[3]
45368 5MT[3]
45371 5MT[3]
45382 5MT[3]
45394 5MT[3]
45402 5MT[3]
45409 5MT[3]
45412 5MT[3]
45414 5MT[3]
45431 5MT[3]
45438 5MT[3]
45445 5MT[3]
45451 5MT[3]
45494 5MT[3]
45500 6P5F[1]
45502 6P5F[1]
45504 6P5F[1]
45506 6P5F[1]
45508 6P5F[1]
45512 7P[1]
45513 6P5F[1]
45524 6P5F[1]
45526 7P[1]
45537 6P5F[1]
45542 6P5F[1]
45543 6P5F[1]
45546 6P5F[1]
45549 6P5F[1]
45551 6P5F[1]
45553 6P5F[2]
45593 6P5F[2]
45599 6P5F[2]
45613 6P5F[2]
45666 6P5F[2]
46116 7P[3]R
46126 7P[3]R
46130 7P[3]R
46136 7P[3]R
46141 7P[3]R
46165 7P[3]R
46167 7P[3]R
46226 8P[2]
46228 8P[2]
46238 8P[2]
46255 8P[2]
46449 2MT[2]
47292 3F[6]
47295 3F[6]
47326 3F[6]
47340 3F[6]
47377 3F[6]
47391 3F[6]
47408 3F[6]
47415 3F[6]
47602 3F[6]
47614 3F[6]
47618 3F[6]
47664 3F[6]
47666 3F[6]

1960 12B

40628 2P[3]
40629 2P[3]
42426 4MT[3]
42539 4MT[3]
42594 4MT[3]
42664 4MT[3]
44016 4F[1]
44060 4F[2]
44081 4F[2]
44121 4F[2]
44126 4F[2]
44346 4F[2]
44596 4F[2]
44770 5MT[3]
44936 5MT[3]
44939 5MT[3]
45025 5MT[3]
45070 5MT[3]
45106 5MT[3]
45140 5MT[3]
45185 5MT[3]
45197 5MT[3]
45236 5MT[3]
45244 5MT[3]
45246 5MT[3]
45258 5MT[3]
45259 5MT[3]
45286 5MT[3]
45293 5MT[3]
45295 5MT[3]
45296 5MT[3]
45297 5MT[3]
45315 5MT[3]
45316 5MT[3]
45317 5MT[3]
45323 5MT[3]
45344 5MT[3]
45351 5MT[3]
45368 5MT[3]
45371 5MT[3]
45394 5MT[3]
45397 5MT[3]
45402 5MT[3]
45412 5MT[3]
45414 5MT[3]
45437 5MT[3]
45438 5MT[3]
45445 5MT[3]
45451 5MT[3]
45512 7P[1]
45513 6P5F[1]
45524 6P5F[1]
45526 7P[1]
45544 6P5F[1]
45551 6P5F[1]
45555 6P5F[2]
45588 6P5F[2]
45593 6P5F[2]
45617 6P5F[2]
45672 6P5F[2]
45688 6P5F[2]
45703 6P5F[2]
45721 6P5F[2]
45723 6P5F[2]
45734 6P5F[2]
45738 6P5F[2]
45741 6P5F[2]
45742 6P5F[2]
46148 7P[3]R
46225 8P[2]
46226 8P[2]
46234 8P[2]
46236 8P[2]
46237 8P[2]
46238 8P[2]
46244 8P[2]
46250 8P[2]
46255 8P[2]
46256 8P[2]
46257 8P[2]
46449 2MT[2]
46457 2MT[2]
46488 2MT[2]
46489 2MT[2]
47288 3F[6]
47292 3F[6]
47295 3F[6]

47326 $3F^{6}$
47340 $3F^{6}$
47342 $3F^{6}$
47377 $3F^{6}$
47408 $3F^{6}$
47415 $3F^{6}$
47602 $3F^{6}$
47614 $3F^{6}$
47666 $3F^{6}$

1963 12B
43908 $4F^{1}$
44346 $4F^{2}$
44399 $4F^{2}$
44452 $4F^{2}$
44469 $4F^{2}$
44937 $5MT^{3}$
44939 $5MT^{3}$
45012 $5MT^{3}$
45025 $5MT^{3}$
45028 $5MT^{3}$
45072 $5MT^{3}$
45081 $5MT^{3}$
45082 $5MT^{3}$
45083 $5MT^{3}$
45092 $5MT^{3}$
45106 $5MT^{3}$
45185 $5MT^{3}$
45236 $5MT^{3}$
45244 $5MT^{3}$
45246 $5MT^{3}$
45259 $5MT^{3}$
45286 $5MT^{3}$
45293 $5MT^{3}$
45295 $5MT^{3}$
45296 $5MT^{3}$
45316 $5MT^{3}$
45317 $5MT^{3}$
45323 $5MT^{3}$
45351 $5MT^{3}$
45368 $5MT^{3}$
45371 $5MT^{3}$
45397 $5MT^{3}$
45402 $5MT^{3}$
45437 $5MT^{3}$
45451 $5MT^{3}$
45512 $7P^{1}$
45526 $7P^{1}$
45532 $7P^{1}$
45540 $7P^{1}$
45545 $7P^{1}$
46108 $7P^{3}R$
46118 $7P^{3}R$
46132 $7P^{3}R$
46136 $7P^{3}R$
46138 $7P^{3}R$
46141 $7P^{3}R$
46157 $7P^{3}R$
46160 $7P^{3}R$
46162 $7P^{3}R$
46166 $7P^{3}R$
46220 $8P^{2}$
46221 $8P^{2}$
46225 $8P^{2}$
46234 $8P^{2}$
46237 $8P^{2}$
46238 $8P^{2}$
46250 $8P^{2}$
46434 $2MT^{2}$
46455 $2MT^{2}$
46458 $2MT^{2}$
46489 $2MT^{2}$
47288 $3F^{6}$
47295 $3F^{6}$
47326 $3F^{6}$
47345 $3F^{6}$
47377 $3F^{6}$
47408 $3F^{6}$
47415 $3F^{6}$
47602 $3F^{6}$
47614 $3F^{6}$
47666 $3F^{6}$
47667 $3F^{6}$

1966 12B
41217 $2MT^{1}$
41222 $2MT^{1}$
41229 $2MT^{1}$
41264 $2MT^{1}$
41285 $2MT^{1}$
44937 $5MT^{3}$
45340 $5MT^{3}$
45371 $5MT^{3}$
45451 $5MT^{3}$
46426 $2MT^{2}$
46434 $2MT^{2}$
46455 $2MT^{2}$
46458 $2MT^{2}$
46513 $2MT^{2}$
70011 7P6F
70013 7P6F
70019 7P6F
70020 7P6F
70022 7P6F
70029 7P6F
70030 7P6F
70031 7P6F
70032 7P6F
70048 7P6F
70049 7P6F

Carmarthen

1948 CARM
1472 1400
1903 1901
1941 1901
2047 2021
2056 2021
2069 2021
2111 2021
2216 2251
2217 2251
2236 2251
2254 2251
2271 2251
2272 2251
2284 2251
2291 2251
2409 2301
2411 2301
2431 2301
2474 2301
3004 ROD
3006 ROD
3009 ROD
3010 ROD
3011 ROD
3015 ROD
3592 3500
4223 4200
4266 4200
4910 4900
4915 4900
4922 4900
4981 4900
4984 4900
5207 5205
5231 5205
5339 4300
5819 5800
5963 4900
5972 4900
6310 4300
6331 4300
6344 4300
6367 4300
6818 6800
6824 6800
6919 4900
7400 7400
7401 7400
7407 7400
7419 7400
7425 7400

1951 87G
1472 1400
1613 1600
1903 1901
2056 2021
2069 2021
2111 2021
2216 2251
2217 2251
2236 2251
2271 2251
2272 2251
2284 2251
2431 2301
2474 2301
3010 ROD
3011 ROD
3015 ROD
4178 5101
4910 4900
4915 4900
4922 4900
4937 4900
4981 4900
4984 4900
5339 4300
5819 5800
5963 4900
5972 4900
5984 4900
6304 4300
6310 4300
6331 4300
6344 4300
6367 4300
6818 6800
6919 4900
7400 7400
7401 7400
7407 7400
7419 7400
7425 7400
7444 7400

1954 87G
1472 1400
2069 2021
2216 2251
2217 2251
2271 2251
2272 2251
2273 2251
3010 ROD
3011 ROD
3015 ROD
3018 ROD
3025 ROD
4134 5101
4910 4900
4915 4900
4922 4900
4937 4900
4984 4900
5039 4073
5043 4073
5171 5101
5310 4300
5353 4300
5400 5400
5775 5700
5819 5800
5937 4900
5938 4900
5963 4900
5984 4900
6304 4300
6310 4300
6919 4900
7400 7400
7401 7400
7407 7400
7419 7400
7425 7400
7444 7400
7755 5700
7825 7800
7826 7800
7829 7800
8103 8100
9008 9000
9010 9000
9666 5700
73029 5MT

1957 87G
1659 1600
2216 2251
2224 2251
2272 2251
2273 2251
2290 2251
3011 ROD
3015 ROD
3018 ROD
3024 ROD
3036 ROD
3041 ROD
3642 5700
4074 4073
4134 5101
5039 4073
5080 4073
5171 5101
5310 4300
5353 4300
5400 5400
5819 5800
5937 4900
5938 4900
6310 4300
6329 4300
6935 4900
7002 4073
7028 4073
7400 7400
7401 7400
7402 7400
7407 7400
7419 7400
7425 7400
7439 7400
7444 7400
7804 7800
7825 7800
7826 7800
7829 7800
8103 8100
8777 5700
9310 9300
9632 5700
9666 5700

1960 87G
2216 2251
2274 2251
4090 4073
4134 5101
4213 4200
4935 4900
5006 4073
5030 4073
5067 4073
5080 4073
5180 5101
5353 4300
5937 4900
5938 4900
5953 4900
6329 4300
6377 4300
7012 4073
7016 4073
7400 7400
7402 7400
7407 7400
7419 7400
7422 7400
7425 7400
7444 7400
7804 7800
7825 7800
7826 7800
7829 7800
8102 8100
8103 8100
8777 5700
9606 5700
9645 5700
9787 5700
90167 WD^{1}
90179 WD^{1}
90207 WD^{1}
90529 WD^{1}

1963 87G
2248 2251
2287 2251
4081 4073
5039 4073
5098 4073
5938 4900
6114 6100
6118 6100
6151 6100
6965 6959
7306 4300
7405 7400
7407 7400
7439 7400
7444 7400
7445 7400
7448 7400
7815 7800
7826 7800
7829 7800
9606 5700
9632 5700
9787 5700

Carnforth

1948 11A
40001 $3MT^{1}$
40041 $3MT^{1}$
40103 $3MT^{2}$
42267 $4MT^{1}$
42428 $4MT^{3}$
42429 $4MT^{3}$
42431 $4MT^{3}$
42432 $4MT^{3}$
42544 $4MT^{3}$
42601 $4MT^{3}$
42613 $4MT^{3}$
42615 $4MT^{3}$
43189 $3F^{2}$
43237 $3F^{3}$
43329 $3F^{3}$
43570 $3F^{3}$
43757 $3F^{3}$
43760 $3F^{3}$
44060 $4F^{2}$
44118 $4F^{2}$
44126 $4F^{2}$
44374 $4F^{2}$
44375 $4F^{2}$
44510 $4F^{2}$
45039 $5MT^{3}$
45050 $5MT^{3}$
45291 $5MT^{3}$
45306 $5MT^{3}$
45333 $5MT^{3}$
45343 $5MT^{3}$
45392 $5MT^{3}$
45427 $5MT^{3}$
47317 $3F^{6}$
47339 $3F^{6}$
47406 $3F^{6}$
47407 $3F^{6}$
47409 $3F^{6}$
47410 $3F^{6}$
47503 $3F^{6}$
47605 $3F^{6}$
48934 $7F^{2}$
49109 $7F^{2}$
49151 $6F^{2}$
49188 $7F^{2}$
49269 $6F^{2}$
49314 $7F^{2}$
58329 $2F^{10}$
58334 $2F^{10}$

1951 11A
40041 $3MT^{1}$
40068 $3MT^{1}$
40070 $3MT^{1}$
42428 $4MT^{3}$
42429 $4MT^{3}$
42432 $4MT^{3}$
42544 $4MT^{3}$
42573 $4MT^{3}$
42601 $4MT^{3}$
44060 $4F^{2}$
44075 $4F^{2}$
44192 $4F^{2}$
44374 $4F^{2}$
44385 $4F^{2}$
44399 $4F^{2}$
44510 $4F^{2}$
44709 $5MT^{3}$
44874 $5MT^{3}$
44904 $5MT^{3}$
44905 $5MT^{3}$
45004 $5MT^{3}$
45039 $5MT^{3}$
45050 $5MT^{3}$
45072 $5MT^{3}$
45133 $5MT^{3}$
45193 $5MT^{3}$
45241 $5MT^{3}$
45306 $5MT^{3}$
45392 $5MT^{3}$
45427 $5MT^{3}$
47317 $3F^{6}$
47339 $3F^{6}$
47406 $3F^{6}$
47409 $3F^{6}$
47410 $3F^{6}$
47605 $3F^{6}$
49109 $7F^{2}$
49112 $7F^{2}$
49130 $7F^{2}$
49151 $6F^{2}$
49241 $6F^{2}$
49252 $7F^{2}$
49314 $7F^{2}$
49438 $7F^{3}$

1954 11A
40011 $3MT^{1}$
40041 $3MT^{1}$
40070 $3MT^{1}$
42428 $4MT^{3}$
42429 $4MT^{3}$
42432 $4MT^{3}$
42544 $4MT^{3}$
42573 $4MT^{3}$
42601 $4MT^{3}$
44192 $4F^{2}$
44306 $4F^{2}$
44399 $4F^{2}$
44510 $4F^{2}$
44709 $5MT^{3}$
44874 $5MT^{3}$
44892 $5MT^{3}$
44904 $5MT^{3}$
44905 $5MT^{3}$
45017 $5MT^{3}$
45019 $5MT^{3}$
45054 $5MT^{3}$
45072 $5MT^{3}$
45092 $5MT^{3}$
45133 $5MT^{3}$
45193 $5MT^{3}$
45241 $5MT^{3}$
45306 $5MT^{3}$
45326 $5MT^{3}$
45392 $5MT^{3}$
45427 $5MT^{3}$
47317 $3F^{6}$
47339 $3F^{6}$
47406 $3F^{6}$
47409 $3F^{6}$
47410 $3F^{6}$
47605 $3F^{6}$
49109 $7F^{2}$
49130 $7F^{2}$
49144 $7F^{2}$
49252 $7F^{2}$
49438 $7F^{3}$
49449 $7F^{3}$

1957 11A
40011 $3MT^{1}$
40041 $3MT^{1}$
42432 $4MT^{3}$
42542 $4MT^{3}$
42591 $4MT^{3}$
44192 $4F^{2}$
44306 $4F^{2}$
44399 $4F^{2}$
44454 $4F^{2}$
44510 $4F^{2}$
44709 $5MT^{3}$
44874 $5MT^{3}$
44892 $5MT^{3}$
44904 $5MT^{3}$
44905 $5MT^{3}$
45014 $5MT^{3}$
45017 $5MT^{3}$
45019 $5MT^{3}$
45037 $5MT^{3}$
45046 $5MT^{3}$
45054 $5MT^{3}$
45072 $5MT^{3}$
45092 $5MT^{3}$
45097 $5MT^{3}$
45193 $5MT^{3}$
45230 $5MT^{3}$
45241 $5MT^{3}$
45291 $5MT^{3}$
45306 $5MT^{3}$
45326 $5MT^{3}$
45327 $5MT^{3}$
45427 $5MT^{3}$
47317 $3F^{6}$
47339 $3F^{6}$
47373 $3F^{6}$
47406 $3F^{6}$
47409 $3F^{6}$
47410 $3F^{6}$
49130 $7F^{2}$
49252 $7F^{2}$
49438 $7F^{3}$
49449 $7F^{3}$
52501 $3F^{8}$

1960 24L
40011 $3MT^{1}$
40041 $3MT^{1}$
40081 $3MT^{2}$
43908 $4F^{1}$
44083 $4F^{2}$
44305 $4F^{2}$
44345 $4F^{2}$
44399 $4F^{2}$
44454 $4F^{2}$
44469 $4F^{2}$
44510 $4F^{2}$
44709 $5MT^{3}$
44874 $5MT^{3}$
44892 $5MT^{3}$
44904 $5MT^{3}$
44905 $5MT^{3}$
45014 $5MT^{3}$
45054 $5MT^{3}$
45072 $5MT^{3}$
45097 $5MT^{3}$
45193 $5MT^{3}$
45230 $5MT^{3}$
45241 $5MT^{3}$
45303 $5MT^{3}$
45306 $5MT^{3}$
45326 $5MT^{3}$
45427 $5MT^{3}$
45500 $6P5F^{1}$
45501 $6P5F^{1}$
45510 $6P5F^{1}$
45511 $6P5F^{1}$
45539 $6P5F^{1}$
45546 $6P5F^{1}$
45548 $6P5F^{1}$
47317 $3F^{6}$
47406 $3F^{6}$
47410 $3F^{6}$
49428 $7F^{3}$
49449 $7F^{3}$

1963 24L
42238 $4MT^{1}$
42319 $4MT^{2}$
42322 $4MT^{2}$
42359 $4MT^{2}$
42378 $4MT^{2}$
42464 $4MT^{3}$
42571 $4MT^{3}$
42594 $4MT^{3}$
42613 $4MT^{3}$
44081 $4F^{2}$
44390 $4F^{2}$
44709 $5MT^{3}$
44874 $5MT^{3}$
44892 $5MT^{3}$
44904 $5MT^{3}$
44905 $5MT^{3}$
45054 $5MT^{3}$
45230 $5MT^{3}$
45303 $5MT^{3}$
45306 $5MT^{3}$
45326 $5MT^{3}$
45340 $5MT^{3}$
45390 $5MT^{3}$
45394 $5MT^{3}$
45399 $5MT^{3}$
45592 $6P5F^{2}$
45604 $6P5F^{2}$
45606 $6P5F^{2}$
45613 $6P5F^{2}$
45625 $6P5F^{2}$
45629 $6P5F^{2}$
45633 $6P5F^{2}$
45696 $6P5F^{2}$
45714 $6P5F^{2}$
45730 $6P5F^{2}$
47322 $3F^{6}$
90187 WD^{1}

1966 10A
42154 $4MT^{1}$
42613 $4MT^{3}$
42616 $4MT^{3}$
42663 $4MT^{3}$
43027 $4MT^{5}$
43066 $4MT^{5}$
43095 $4MT^{5}$
43103 $4MT^{5}$
43105 $4MT^{5}$
44709 $5MT^{3}$
44733 $5MT^{3}$
44778 $5MT^{3}$
44874 $5MT^{3}$
44892 $5MT^{3}$
44894 $5MT^{3}$
44905 $5MT^{3}$
44948 $5MT^{3}$
45017 $5MT^{3}$
45054 $5MT^{3}$
45072 $5MT^{3}$
45092 $5MT^{3}$
45095 $5MT^{3}$
45209 $5MT^{3}$
45227 $5MT^{3}$
45326 $5MT^{3}$
45328 $5MT^{3}$
45342 $5MT^{3}$
45374 $5MT^{3}$
45390 $5MT^{3}$
45399 $5MT^{3}$
45495 $5MT^{3}$
46400 $2MT^{2}$
46499 $2MT^{2}$
48519 8F
48712 8F
48739 8F

Carstairs

1948 28C
40566 $2P^{3}$
40592 $2P^{3}$
40605 $2P^{3}$
40619 $2P^{3}$
40666 $2P^{3}$
40901 $4P^{1}$
40903 $4P^{1}$
40907 $4P^{1}$
40915 $4P^{1}$
41130 $4P^{1}$
41136 $4P^{1}$
41145 $4P^{1}$
41147 $4P^{1}$
41180 $4P^{1}$
44953 $5MT^{3}$
44955 $5MT^{3}$
48301 8F
48302 8F
48303 8F
48331 8F
54438 $3P^{5}$
54439 $3P^{5}$
54446 $3P^{5}$
54449 $3P^{5}$
54461 $3P^{6}$
54463 $3P^{6}$
54477 $3P^{6}$
54490 $3P^{6}$
54505 $3P^{6}$
54630 $4P^{3}$
55261 $2P^{15}$
57298 $2F^{5}$
57323 $2F^{5}$
57340 $2F^{5}$
57385 $2F^{5}$
57386 $2F^{5}$
57399 $2F^{5}$
57438 $2F^{5}$
57451 $2F^{5}$
57583 $3F^{12}$
57604 $3F^{12}$
57608 $3F^{12}$
57613 $3F^{12}$
57618 $3F^{12}$
57635 $3F^{13}$
57655 $3F^{14}$
57670 $3F^{14}$
57679 $3F^{14}$

1951 64D
40901 $4P^{1}$
40903 $4P^{1}$
40907 $4P^{1}$
41130 $4P^{1}$
41136 $4P^{1}$
41145 $4P^{1}$
41147 $4P^{1}$
41180 $4P^{1}$
42162 $4MT^{1}$
42163 $4MT^{1}$
42173 $4MT^{1}$
42177 $4MT^{1}$
42217 $4MT^{1}$
44700 $5MT^{3}$
44701 $5MT^{3}$
44952 $5MT^{3}$
44953 $5MT^{3}$
44955 $5MT^{3}$
45087 $5MT^{3}$
45161 $5MT^{3}$
54438 $3P^{5}$
54446 $3P^{5}$
54449 $3P^{5}$
54461 $3P^{6}$
54477 $3P^{6}$
54490 $3P^{6}$
54505 $3P^{6}$
55261 $2P^{15}$
57323 $2F^{5}$
57385 $2F^{5}$
57386 $2F^{5}$
57438 $2F^{5}$
57451 $2F^{5}$
57583 $3F^{12}$
57603 $3F^{12}$
57604 $3F^{12}$
57608 $3F^{12}$
57613 $3F^{12}$
57618 $3F^{12}$
57626 $3F^{12}$
57635 $3F^{13}$
57655 $3F^{14}$
57670 $3F^{14}$
57679 $3F^{14}$
65329 J36
90753 WD^{2}
90768 WD^{2}

1954 64D
40901 $4P^{1}$
40903 $4P^{1}$
40904 $4P^{1}$
41130 $4P^{1}$
42142 $4MT^{1}$
42145 $4MT^{1}$
42162 $4MT^{1}$
42163 $4MT^{1}$
42173 $4MT^{1}$
42177 $4MT^{1}$
42204 $4MT^{1}$
42216 $4MT^{1}$
42217 $4MT^{1}$
44700 $5MT^{3}$
44701 $5MT^{3}$
44952 $5MT^{3}$
44953 $5MT^{3}$
44955 $5MT^{3}$
45087 $5MT^{3}$
54446 $3P^{5}$
54461 $3P^{6}$
54477 $3P^{6}$
54490 $3P^{6}$
54505 $3P^{6}$
55261 $2P^{15}$
57385 $2F^{5}$
57386 $2F^{5}$
57451 $2F^{5}$
57583 $3F^{12}$
57604 $3F^{12}$
57608 $3F^{12}$
57613 $3F^{12}$
57618 $3F^{12}$
57626 $3F^{12}$
57635 $3F^{13}$
57655 $3F^{14}$
57670 $3F^{14}$
90753 WD^{2}
90768 WD^{2}

1957 64D
40904 $4P^{1}$
42142 $4MT^{1}$
42145 $4MT^{1}$
42162 $4MT^{1}$
42163 $4MT^{1}$
42173 $4MT^{1}$
42177 $4MT^{1}$
42204 $4MT^{1}$
42216 $4MT^{1}$
42217 $4MT^{1}$
44700 $5MT^{3}$
44701 $5MT^{3}$
44793 $5MT^{3}$
44952 $5MT^{3}$
44953 $5MT^{3}$
44955 $5MT^{3}$
45011 $5MT^{3}$
45087 $5MT^{3}$
45166 $5MT^{3}$
45173 $5MT^{3}$
45174 $5MT^{3}$
45175 $5MT^{3}$
54461 $3P^{6}$
54477 $3P^{6}$
54490 $3P^{6}$
54505 $3P^{6}$
55261 $2P^{15}$
57385 $2F^{5}$
57386 $2F^{5}$
57451 $2F^{5}$
57583 $3F^{12}$
57604 $3F^{12}$
57608 $3F^{12}$
57613 $3F^{12}$
57618 $3F^{12}$
57626 $3F^{12}$
57635 $3F^{13}$
57655 $3F^{14}$
57670 $3F^{14}$
90753 WD^{2}
90768 WD^{2}

1960 64D
42142 $4MT^{1}$
42145 $4MT^{1}$
42162 $4MT^{1}$
42163 $4MT^{1}$
42173 $4MT^{1}$
42177 $4MT^{1}$
42204 $4MT^{1}$
42216 $4MT^{1}$
42217 $4MT^{1}$
42271 $4MT^{1}$
44700 $5MT^{3}$
44701 $5MT^{3}$
44793 $5MT^{3}$
44952 $5MT^{3}$
44953 $5MT^{3}$
44955 $5MT^{3}$
45011 $5MT^{3}$
45087 $5MT^{3}$
45161 $5MT^{3}$
45166 $5MT^{3}$
45173 $5MT^{3}$
45174 $5MT^{3}$
45175 $5MT^{3}$
45245 $5MT^{3}$
45452 $5MT^{3}$
54477 $3P^{6}$
54490 $3P^{6}$
54505 $3P^{6}$
55261 $2P^{15}$
57385 $2F^{5}$
57386 $2F^{5}$
57451 $2F^{5}$
57583 $3F^{12}$
57604 $3F^{12}$
57608 $3F^{12}$
57613 $3F^{12}$
57618 $3F^{12}$
57626 $3F^{12}$
57635 $3F^{13}$
57655 $3F^{14}$
57670 $3F^{14}$
90753 WD^{2}
90768 WD^{2}

1963 66E
42055 $4MT^{1}$
42142 $4MT^{1}$
42145 $4MT^{1}$
42163 $4MT^{1}$
42165 $4MT^{1}$
42177 $4MT^{1}$
42204 $4MT^{1}$
42239 $4MT^{1}$
42271 $4MT^{1}$
44700 $5MT^{3}$
44701 $5MT^{3}$
44793 $5MT^{3}$
44952 $5MT^{3}$
44953 $5MT^{3}$
44954 $5MT^{3}$
44955 $5MT^{3}$
45011 $5MT^{3}$
45087 $5MT^{3}$
45161 $5MT^{3}$
45166 $5MT^{3}$
45172 $5MT^{3}$
45173 $5MT^{3}$
45175 $5MT^{3}$
45245 $5MT^{3}$
57670 $3F^{14}$
77005 $3MT^{1}$
77006 $3MT^{1}$

1966 66E
42058 $4MT^{1}$
42125 $4MT^{1}$
42169 $4MT^{1}$
42274 $4MT^{1}$
42694 $4MT^{1}$
44700 $5MT^{3}$
44707 $5MT^{3}$
44791 $5MT^{3}$
44952 $5MT^{3}$
44953 $5MT^{3}$
44954 $5MT^{3}$
44956 $5MT^{3}$
45309 $5MT^{3}$
45319 $5MT^{3}$
45478 $5MT^{3}$
45492 $5MT^{3}$
76045 $4MT^{2}$
76113 $4MT^{2}$

Cheltenham

1948 CHEL
1402 1400
3449 3300
4141 5101
4320 4300
4564 4500
4567 4500
4578 4575
5345 4300
5515 4575
5538 4575
5574 4575
6326 4300
6341 4300
7303 4300
7312 4300
7818 7800

Chester

1948 6A
40130 $3MT^{2}$
40900 $4P^{1}$
40926 $4P^{1}$
40933 $4P^{1}$
41098 $4P^{1}$
41106 $4P^{1}$
41107 $4P^{1}$
41108 $4P^{1}$
41120 $4P^{1}$
41121 $4P^{1}$
41157 $4P^{1}$
41158 $4P^{1}$
41162 $4P^{1}$
41163 $4P^{1}$
41164 $4P^{1}$
41169 $4P^{1}$
41170 $4P^{1}$
42425 $4MT^{3}$
42540 $4MT^{3}$
42568 $4MT^{3}$
42587 $4MT^{3}$
42617 $4MT^{3}$
42677 $4MT^{1}$
45042 $5MT^{3}$
45247 $5MT^{3}$
45275 $5MT^{3}$
45297 $5MT^{3}$
45382 $5MT^{3}$
45403 $5MT^{3}$
47297 $3F^{6}$
47373 $3F^{6}$
47374 $3F^{6}$
47375 $3F^{6}$
47383 $3F^{6}$
47504 $3F^{6}$
47600 $3F^{6}$
52417 $3F^{7}$
58010 $3P^{7}$
58011 $3P^{8}$
58012 $3P^{8}$
58428 $2F^{11}$
25321 $3P^{8}$

1951 6A
40430 $2P^{2}$
40658 $2P^{3}$
41098 $4P^{1}$
41106 $4P^{1}$
41107 $4P^{1}$
41108 $4P^{1}$
41120 $4P^{1}$
41121 $4P^{1}$
41153 $4P^{1}$
41157 $4P^{1}$
41158 $4P^{1}$
41163 $4P^{1}$
41164 $4P^{1}$
41169 $4P^{1}$
41170 $4P^{1}$
42425 $4MT^{3}$
42450 $4MT^{3}$
42451 $4MT^{3}$
42455 $4MT^{3}$
42540 $4MT^{3}$
42568 $4MT^{3}$
42584 $4MT^{3}$
42587 $4MT^{3}$
42595 $4MT^{3}$
42660 $4MT^{3}$
44840 $5MT^{3}$
44844 $5MT^{3}$
45045 $5MT^{3}$
45095 $5MT^{3}$
45247 $5MT^{3}$
45307 $5MT^{3}$
45385 $5MT^{3}$
47297 $3F^{6}$
47374 $3F^{6}$
47375 $3F^{6}$
47383 $3F^{6}$
47389 $3F^{6}$
47504 $3F^{6}$
47600 $3F^{6}$

1954 6A
40377 $2P^{2}$
40658 $2P^{3}$
41106 $4P^{1}$
41108 $4P^{1}$
41120 $4P^{1}$
41121 $4P^{1}$
41153 $4P^{1}$
41157 $4P^{1}$
41158 $4P^{1}$
41163 $4P^{1}$
41164 $4P^{1}$
41166 $4P^{1}$
41169 $4P^{1}$
42063 $4MT^{1}$
42159 $4MT^{1}$
42315 $4MT^{2}$
42425 $4MT^{3}$
42450 $4MT^{3}$
42451 $4MT^{3}$
42461 $4MT^{3}$
42540 $4MT^{3}$
42568 $4MT^{3}$
42587 $4MT^{3}$
42595 $4MT^{3}$
42660 $4MT^{3}$
44710 $5MT^{3}$
44910 $5MT^{3}$
45043 $5MT^{3}$
45132 $5MT^{3}$
45180 $5MT^{3}$
45247 $5MT^{3}$
47297 $3F^{6}$
47374 $3F^{6}$
47375 $3F^{6}$
47383 $3F^{6}$
47389 $3F^{6}$
47504 $3F^{6}$
47600 $3F^{6}$
73040 5MT
73041 5MT
73042 5MT

1957 6A
40559 $2P^{2}$
40580 $2P^{3}$
40658 $2P^{3}$
40675 $2P^{3}$
40679 $2P^{3}$
41106 $4P^{1}$
41120 $4P^{1}$
41153 $4P^{1}$
41157 $4P^{1}$
41158 $4P^{1}$
41164 $4P^{1}$
42315 $4MT^{2}$
42445 $4MT^{3}$
44710 $5MT^{3}$
44910 $5MT^{3}$
45312 $5MT^{3}$
45441 $5MT^{3}$
47297 $3F^{6}$
47374 $3F^{6}$
47375 $3F^{6}$
47383 $3F^{6}$
47389 $3F^{6}$
47504 $3F^{6}$
47600 $3F^{6}$
73040 5MT
73041 5MT
73042 5MT
73070 5MT
73072 5MT
75031 $4MT^{1}$
75032 $4MT^{1}$
75033 $4MT^{1}$
75034 $4MT^{1}$
75035 $4MT^{1}$
75039 $4MT^{1}$
75051 $4MT^{1}$
80045 $4MT^{3}$
80047 $4MT^{3}$
80048 $4MT^{3}$
80049 $4MT^{3}$
80050 $4MT^{3}$
80051 $4MT^{3}$
80052 $4MT^{3}$
80053 $4MT^{3}$
80059 $4MT^{3}$
80062 $4MT^{3}$
80063 $4MT^{3}$
80086 $4MT^{3}$

1960 6A
42431 $4MT^{3}$
42482 $4MT^{3}$
44710 $5MT^{3}$
44910 $5MT^{3}$
44911 $5MT^{3}$
45041 $5MT^{3}$
45312 $5MT^{3}$
47297 $3F^{6}$
47371 $3F^{6}$
47374 $3F^{6}$
47375 $3F^{6}$
47383 $3F^{6}$
47389 $3F^{6}$
47504 $3F^{6}$
47600 $3F^{6}$
73013 5MT
73033 5MT
73040 5MT
73070 5MT
73071 5MT
75013 $4MT^{1}$
75014 $4MT^{1}$
75031 $4MT^{1}$
75032 $4MT^{1}$
75034 $4MT^{1}$
75035 $4MT^{1}$
75039 $4MT^{1}$
75050 $4MT^{1}$
75051 $4MT^{1}$
75053 $4MT^{1}$
75054 $4MT^{1}$
80045 $4MT^{3}$
80047 $4MT^{3}$
80048 $4MT^{3}$
80049 $4MT^{3}$
80050 $4MT^{3}$
80051 $4MT^{3}$
80052 $4MT^{3}$
80053 $4MT^{3}$
80086 $4MT^{3}$
80091 $4MT^{3}$
80092 $4MT^{3}$

1963 6A
42202 $4MT^{1}$
42209 $4MT^{1}$
42212 $4MT^{1}$
42213 $4MT^{1}$
42229 $4MT^{1}$
42236 $4MT^{1}$
42240 $4MT^{1}$
42247 $4MT^{1}$
42270 $4MT^{1}$
42366 $4MT^{2}$
42431 $4MT^{3}$
42463 $4MT^{3}$
42482 $4MT^{3}$
42681 $4MT^{1}$
42933 $5MT^{1}$
42934 $5MT^{1}$
47297 $3F^{6}$
47371 $3F^{6}$
47389 $3F^{6}$
73040 5MT
73048 5MT
73070 5MT
73071 5MT
78018 $2MT^{1}$
78032 $2MT^{1}$
78033 $2MT^{1}$

1966 6A
44913 $5MT^{3}$
45000 $5MT^{3}$
45031 $5MT^{3}$
45044 $5MT^{3}$
45231 $5MT^{3}$
45250 $5MT^{3}$
45353 $5MT^{3}$
45403 $5MT^{3}$
45419 $5MT^{3}$
45427 $5MT^{3}$
45438 $5MT^{3}$
47389 $3F^{6}$
47437 $3F^{6}$
75010 $4MT^{1}$
75012 $4MT^{1}$
76020 $4MT^{2}$
76035 $4MT^{2}$
76052 $4MT^{2}$
76095 $4MT^{2}$

Chester (GWR)

1948 CHR
1434 1400
2262 2251
2513 2301
2662 2600
2812 2800
2883 2800
2886 2884
2915 2900
2926 2900
2930 2900
2953 2900
2989 2900
3366 3300
3665 5700
3762 5700
3786 5700
4013 4000
4159 5101
4918 4900
4976 4900
5033 4073
5117 5101
5174 5101
5176 5101
5179 5101
5181 5101
5184 5101
5186 5101
5344 4300
5399 4300
5647 5600
5690 5600
5723 5700
5725 5700
5791 5700
5912 4900
5923 4900
5966 4900
6308 4300
6311 4300
6337 4300
6339 4300
6380 4300
6392 4300
6624 5600
6859 6800
6941 4900
7313 4300
9728 5700
9774 5700
9794 5700
90214 WD^{1}
90572 WD^{1}

1951 84K
1434 1400
2513 2301
2810 2800
2812 2800
2869 2800
2882 2800
2890 2884
2926 2900
2953 2900

3619 5700
3646 5700
3665 5700
3762 5700
3786 5700
3858 2884
3859 2884
3860 2884
4076 4073
4905 4900
4976 4900
4987 4900
5027 4073
5033 4073
5075 4073
5103 5101
5129 5101
5141 5101
5174 5101
5179 5101
5181 5101
5184 5101
5186 5101
5331 4300
5344 4300
5399 4300
5647 5600
5690 5600
5723 5700
5725 5700
5791 5700
5912 4900
5923 4900
5966 4900
6308 4300
6337 4300
6339 4300
6380 4300
6392 4300
6624 5600
6941 4900
7827 7800
7921 6959
7922 6959
9425 9400
9728 5700
9774 5700
9794 5700
90214 WD[1]
90572 WD[1]
90685 WD[1]
90686 WD[1]

1954 84K

1000 1000
1008 1000
1022 1000
1024 1000
1434 1400
2513 2301
2822 2800
2890 2884
3630 5700
3646 5700
3665 5700
3762 5700
3786 5700
3858 2884
4076 4073
4115 5101
4165 5101
4602 5700
5033 4073
5061 4073
5075 4073
5103 5101
5174 5101
5177 5101
5179 5101
5186 5101
5311 4300
5326 4300
5331 4300
5344 4300
5647 5600
5690 5600
5723 5700
5725 5700
5791 5700
5968 4900
6331 4300
6337 4300
6344 4300
6345 4300
6367 4300
6380 4300
6392 4300
6833 6800
6835 6800
6901 4900
6941 4900
6963 6959
7800 7800
7801 7800
7807 7800
7820 7800
7827 7800
7921 6959
7922 6959
8729 5700
9728 5700
9794 5700
73020 5MT
73021 5MT
73023 5MT
73024 5MT
73038 5MT
90214 WD[1]
90686 WD[1]

1957 84K

1008 1000
1022 1000
1024 1000
2817 2800
2848 2800
2882 2800
3630 5700
3665 5700
3762 5700
3786 5700
3820 2884
3858 2884
4102 5101
4115 5101
4165 5101
4602 5700
5033 4073
5061 4073
5091 4073
5103 5101
5160 5101
5174 5101
5177 5101
5179 5101
5311 4300
5315 4300
5399 4300
5723 5700
5725 5700
5739 5700
5791 5700
5962 4900
6344 4300
6345 4300
6367 4300
6380 4300
6392 4300
6817 6800
6823 6800
6857 6800
6901 4900
6963 6959
7800 7800
7801 7800
7807 7800
7822 7800
7827 7800
7921 6959
7922 6959
8729 5700
8730 5700
9728 5700
9794 5700
73013 5MT
73021 5MT
73023 5MT
73038 5MT
90214 WD[1]
90686 WD[1]

1960 6E

3630 5700
3665 5700
3676 5700
3786 5700
4602 5700
5174 5101
5399 4300
6380 4300
7762 5700
8709 5700
8729 5700
8730 5700
9728 5700
9794 5700
40106 3MT[2]
73014 5MT
73038 5MT
75028 4MT[1]
75033 4MT[1]
82001 3MT[2]
82002 3MT[2]
82003 3MT[2]
82005 3MT[2]
82032 3MT[2]
82034 3MT[2]
82036 3MT[2]
90214 WD[1]
90686 WD[1]

Chester Northgate

1948 CHR

65143 J10
65167 J10
65169 J10
67366 C12
67400 C13
67413 C13
67414 C13
67430 C13
67436 C13
69274 N5
69281 N5

1951 6D

65143 J10
65167 J10
67400 C13
67413 C13
67414 C13
67433 C13
67436 C13
69274 N5
69281 N5
69293 N5
69342 N5

1954 6D

41215 2MT[1]
41216 2MT[1]
41234 2MT[1]
41235 2MT[1]
41239 2MT[1]
65140 J10
65143 J10
65208 J10
67400 C13
67413 C13
67414 C13
67433 C13
67436 C13
69274 N5
69281 N5
69293 N5
69332 N5
69342 N5

1957 6D

40002 3MT[1]
40004 3MT[1]
40069 3MT[1]
40070 3MT[1]
41215 2MT[1]
42417 4MT[2]
48135 8F
48296 8F
67413 C13
69274 N5
69293 N5
69332 N5
69342 N5
78031 2MT[1]
78038 2MT[1]
78055 2MT[1]
78056 2MT[1]
78057 2MT[1]
78058 2MT[1]
78059 2MT[1]
84001 2MT[2]

1960 6D

41215 2MT[1]
41323 2MT[1]
42303 4MT[2]
42317 4MT[2]
42417 4MT[2]
75030 4MT[1]
75052 4MT[1]
84001 2MT[2]

Coalville

1948 17C

40743 3P[1]
43429 3F[3]
43682 3F[3]
43779 3F[4]
43835 4F[1]
43865 4F[1]
43872 4F[1]
43921 4F[1]
44085 4F[2]
44087 4F[2]
44103 4F[2]
44109 4F[2]
44148 4F[2]
44227 4F[2]
44252 4F[2]
44260 4F[2]
44279 4F[2]
44539 4F[2]
45667 6P5F[2]
47449 3F[6]
48008 8F
48106 8F
48107 8F
48265 8F
48543 8F
58163 2F[8]
58174 2F[8]
58247 2F[8]
58251 2F[9]
58264 2F[9]

1951 17C

43429 3F[3]
43682 3F[3]
43779 3F[4]
43809 3F[4]
43835 4F[1]
43865 4F[1]
43872 4F[1]
43882 4F[1]
43894 4F[1]
43921 4F[1]
44085 4F[2]
44103 4F[2]
44109 4F[2]
44148 4F[2]
44156 4F[2]
44180 4F[2]
44227 4F[2]
44252 4F[2]
44260 4F[2]
44279 4F[2]
44539 4F[2]
44554 4F[2]
44572 4F[2]
47449 3F[6]
58163 2F[8]
58174 2F[8]
58247 2F[8]
58264 2F[9]

1954 17C

43429 3F[3]
43682 3F[3]
43809 3F[4]
43835 4F[1]
43894 4F[1]
43921 4F[1]
44085 4F[2]
44103 4F[2]
44109 4F[2]
44148 4F[2]
44156 4F[2]
44180 4F[2]
44252 4F[2]
44260 4F[2]
44279 4F[2]
44539 4F[2]
44554 4F[2]
44572 4F[2]
47449 3F[6]
58163 2F[8]
58247 2F[8]
58264 2F[9]

1957 17C

43809 3F[4]
43885 4F[1]
43921 4F[1]
43923 4F[1]
43933 4F[1]
44085 4F[2]
44103 4F[2]
44109 4F[2]
44113 4F[2]
44148 4F[2]
44156 4F[2]
44166 4F[2]
44180 4F[2]
44190 4F[2]
44260 4F[2]
44279 4F[2]
44539 4F[2]
44554 4F[2]
44572 4F[2]
47449 3F[6]
58163 2F[8]
58209 2F[9]
58247 2F[8]

1960 15D

43809 3F[4]
43854 4F[1]
43876 4F[1]
43975 4F[1]
44085 4F[2]
44109 4F[2]
44113 4F[2]
44148 4F[2]
44150 4F[2]
44156 4F[2]
44166 4F[2]
44180 4F[2]
44260 4F[2]
44278 4F[2]
44279 4F[2]
44539 4F[2]
48053 8F
48619 8F
48644 8F
58163 2F[8]
58209 2F[9]
58298 2F[9]

1963 15D

43854 4F[1]
43991 4F[1]
43995 4F[1]
44085 4F[2]
44109 4F[2]
44113 4F[2]
44150 4F[2]
44156 4F[2]
44260 4F[2]
44279 4F[2]
44539 4F[2]
44581 4F[2]
48053 8F
48315 8F
48382 8F
48619 8F
48644 8F
48687 8F
58143 2F[8]
58148 2F[8]

Colchester

1948 COL

61512 B12
61523 B12
61553 B12
61603 B2
61607 B2
61614 B2
61615 B2
61616 B2
61632 B2
61757 K2
61766 K2
62519 D16
62523 D16
62565 D16
62598 D16
62608 D16
62609 D16
62617 D16
65357 J15
65374 J15
65384 J15
65385 J15
65414 J15
65424 J15
65432 J15
65440 J15
65443 J15
65445 J15
65448 J15
65456 J15
65465 J15
65473 J15
65522 J17
65531 J17
65539 J17
65564 J17
67188 F5
67189 F5
67190 F5
67207 F5
67213 F5
68226 J70
68378 J66
68616 J67
68629 J69
68636 J69

1951 30E

61512 B12
61523 B12
61555 B12
61556 B12
61557 B12
61558 B12
61603 B2
61607 B2
61614 B2
61615 B2
61616 B2
61632 B2
61639 B2
61644 B2
62598 D16
62608 D16
65369 J15
65424 J15
65431 J15
65432 J15
65441 J15
65443 J15
65445 J15
65448 J15
65456 J15
65465 J15
65468 J15
65470 J15
65473 J15
65479 J15
65522 J17
65531 J17
65539 J17
65564 J17
67188 F5
67189 F5
67190 F5
67191 F5
67194 F5
67195 F5
67196 F5
67204 F5
67215 F5
67217 F5
67219 F5
68226 J70
68522 J69
68578 J69
68608 J67
68616 J67
68636 J69
68638 J68
69701 N7
69726 N7
90029 WD[1]
90085 WD[1]
90304 WD[1]
90431 WD[1]
90443 WD[1]
90471 WD[1]
90477 WD[1]
90508 WD[1]
90522 WD[1]
90732 WD[1]

1954 30E

46468 2MT[2]
46469 2MT[2]
61603 B2
61607 B2
61614 B2
61615 B2
61616 B2
61632 B2
61634 B17
61639 B2
61644 B2
61645 B17
61646 B17
61650 B17
61651 B17
61662 B17
61667 B17
64645 J19
64647 J19
64649 J19
64650 J19
64651 J19
64652 J19
64653 J19
64659 J19
64660 J19
64666 J19
64667 J19
65424 J15
65432 J15
65441 J15
65445 J15
65448 J15
65456 J15
65465 J15
65466 J15
65468 J15
65470 J15
65473 J15
65522 J17
65531 J17
65539 J17
65564 J17
67189 F5
67191 F5
67196 F5
67217 F5
68226 J70
68508 J69
68522 J69
68578 J69
68636 J69
68638 J68
69555 N2
69558 N2
69672 N7
69673 N7
69720 N7
69732 N7

1957 30E

41936 3P[2]
41949 3P[2]
41975 3P[2]
46468 2MT[2]
46469 2MT[2]
61555 B12
61556 B12
61557 B12
61558 B12
61606 B17
61608 B17
61611 B17
61650 B17
61651 B17
61658 B17
61662 B17
61666 B17
61667 B17
64645 J19
64647 J19
64649 J19
64650 J19
64651 J19
64652 J19
64653 J19
64659 J19
64660 J19
64666 J19
64667 J19
65424 J15
65432 J15
65441 J15
65445 J15
65448 J15
65456 J15
65465 J15
65466 J15
65468 J15
65470 J15
65473 J15
65522 J17
65531 J17
65539 J17
65564 J17
67192 F5
67227 F6
67228 F6
68522 J69
68552 J69
68662 J68
68666 J68
69673 N7
69732 N7

Colwick

1948 CLK

61650 B17
61651 B17
61652 B17
61653 B17
61657 B17
61662 B17
61664 B17
61667 B17
61669 B17
61723 K2
61726 K2
61732 K2
61741 K2
61749 K2
61750 K2
61751 K2
61756 K2
61758 K2
61763 K2
61768 K2
61769 K2
61770 K2
61771 K2
61773 K2
61801 K3
61802 K3
61808 K3
61816 K3
61821 K3
61824 K3
61826 K3
61865 K3
61894 K3
61905 K3
62116 D3
62123 D3
62125 D3
62126 D3
62135 D3
62140 D3
62150 D2
62151 D2
62153 D2
62169 D2
62177 D2
62187 D2
62188 D2
62193 D2
62194 D2
62198 D2
62199 D2
63008 O7
63021 O7
63022 O7
63025 O7
63027 O7
63036 O7
63050 O7
63051 O7
63068 O7
63069 O7
63073 O7
63084 O7
63100 O7
63102 O7
63128 O7
63129 O7
63136 O7
63138 O7
63145 O7
63157 O7
63163 O7
63170 O7
63171 O7
63178 O7
63184 O7
63191 O7
63192 O7
63573 O4
63574 O4
63599 O4
63605 O4
63636 O4
63639 O4
63641 O4
63695 O4
63713 O4
63721 O4
63729 O4
63750 O4
63781 O4
63787 O4
63797 O4
63798 O4
63827 O4
63848 O4
63858 O4
63895 O4
64194 J6
64197 J6
64199 J6
64200 J6
64202 J6
64212 J6
64213 J6
64215 J6
64222 J6
64223 J6
64224 J6
64230 J6
64231 J6
64233 J6
64253 J6
64269 J6
64317 J11
64716 J39
64719 J39
64720 J39
64732 J39
64735 J39
64739 J39
64747 J39
64750 J39
64757 J39
64762 J39
64763 J39
64805 J39
64827 J39
64828 J39
64831 J39
64832 J39
64837 J39
64955 J39
64974 J39
64980 J39
64981 J39
64983 J39
64988 J39
65003 J1
65008 J1
65010 J1
65013 J1
65014 J1
65480 J5
65481 J5
65482 J5
65483 J5
65484 J5
65485 J5
65490 J5
65491 J5
65492 J5
65493 J5
65494 J5
65495 J5
65496 J5
65497 J5
65498 J5
65499 J5
68527 J69
68762 J52
68767 J52
68768 J52
68779 J52
68792 J52
68807 J52
68810 J52
68812 J52
68814 J52
68839 J52
68858 J52
68859 J52
68863 J52
68867 J52
68875 J52
68882 J52
68887 J52
68981 J50
68982 J50
69263 N5
69286 N5
69312 N5
69324 N5
69501 N2
69550 N2
69552 N2
69555 N2
69560 N2
90133 WD[1]
90136 WD[1]
90162 WD[1]
90165 WD[1]
90185 WD[1]
90365 WD[1]
90368 WD[1]
90646 WD[1]
90647 WD[1]
90662 WD[1]
90672 WD[1]
90676 WD[1]

1951 38A

61078 B1
61110 B1
61111 B1
61122 B1
61123 B1
61131 B1
61283 B1
61367 B1
61368 B1
61369 D1
61657 B17
61662 B17
61723 K2
61726 K2
61732 K2
61741 K2
61749 K2
61751 K2
61758 K2
61763 K2
61768 K2
61769 K2
61771 K2
61773 K2
61812 K3
61816 K3
61821 K3
61822 K3
61824 K3
61826 K3
61833 K3
61864 K3
61982 K3
62172 D2
63599 O4
63618 O4
63636 O4
63699 O4
63723 O4
63729 O4
63735 O4
63756 O4
63762 O4
63801 O4
63804 O4
63893 O4
63894 O4
64194 J6
64197 J6
64199 J6
64200 J6
64202 J6
64212 J6
64213 J6
64215 J6
64222 J6
64223 J6
64224 J6
64230 J6
64231 J6
64233 J6
64253 J6
64269 J6
64301 J11
64406 J11
64417 J11
64716 J39
64719 J39
64720 J39
64729 J39
64735 J39
64739 J39
64747 J39
64750 J39
64757 J39
64762 J39
64763 J39
64798 J39
64805 J39
64807 J39
64827 J39
64828 J39
64831 J39
64832 J39
64837 J39
64838 J39
64955 J39
64965 J39
64974 J39
64980 J39
64981 J39
64983 J39
64988 J39
65007 J1
65008 J1
65009 J1
65014 J1
65018 J2
65019 J2
65022 J2
65023 J2
65480 J5
65481 J5
65482 J5
65483 J5
65484 J5
65485 J5
65486 J5
65487 J5
65488 J5
65489 J5
65490 J5
65491 J5
65492 J5
65493 J5
65496 J5
65497 J5
65498 J5
65499 J5
68762 J52
68768 J52
68779 J52
68792 J52
68807 J52
68810 J52
68812 J52
68814 J52
68839 J52
68859 J52
68863 J52
68875 J52
68882 J52
68887 J52
68891 J50
68894 J50
68920 J50
68935 J50
68972 J50
68982 J50
69312 N5
69324 N5
69501 N2
69550 N2
69552 N2
69555 N2
69801 A5
69806 A5
69807 A5
69809 A5
69810 A5
69814 A5
69817 A5
69821 A5
69823 A5
69825 A5
69826 A5
90000 WD[1]
90002 WD[1]
90025 WD[1]
90036 WD[1]
90043 WD[1]
90050 WD[1]
90051 WD[1]
90073 WD[1]
90084 WD[1]
90103 WD[1]
90122 WD[1]
90126 WD[1]
90129 WD[1]
90136 WD[1]
90139 WD[1]
90140 WD[1]
90147 WD[1]
90157 WD[1]
90163 WD[1]
90178 WD[1]
90185 WD[1]
90187 WD[1]
90197 WD[1]
90202 WD[1]
90204 WD[1]
90212 WD[1]
90215 WD[1]
90242 WD[1]
90251 WD[1]
90303 WD[1]
90323 WD[1]
90368 WD[1]
90369 WD[1]
90391 WD[1]
90411 WD[1]
90437 WD[1]
90448 WD[1]
90466 WD[1]
90484 WD[1]
90491 WD[1]
90492 WD[1]
90499 WD[1]
90532 WD[1]
90544 WD[1]
90551 WD[1]
90574 WD[1]
90629 WD[1]
90636 WD[1]
90638 WD[1]
90648 WD[1]
90662 WD[1]
90672 WD[1]
90676 WD[1]
90697 WD[1]
90703 WD[1]
90717 WD[1]

1954 38A

61033 B1
61056 B1
61111 B1
61186 B1
61188 B1
61192 B1
61201 B1
61269 B1
61271 B1
61272 B1
61283 B1
61367 B1
61376 B1
61390 B1
61723 K2
61726 K2
61729 K2
61732 K2
61737 K2
61738 K2
61747 K2
61749 K2
61751 K2
61752 K2
61753 K2
61754 K2
61759 K2
61763 K2
61768 K2
61771 K2
61773 K2
61777 K2
61780 K2
61821 K3
61833 K3
63599 O4
63602 O4
63618 O4
63628 O4
63639 O4
63647 O4
63649 O4
63657 O4
63658 O4
63673 O4
63674 O4
63684 O4
63699 O4
63723 O4
63729 O4
63735 O4
63745 O4
63754 O4
63756 O4
63766 O4
63798 O4
63804 O4
63807 O4
63812 O4
63816 O4
63832 O4
63835 O4
63839 O4
63845 O4
63851 O4
63877 O4
63881 O4
63894 O4
63908 O4
63912 O4
64183 J6
64194 J6
64199 J6
64200 J6
64202 J6
64212 J6
64213 J6
64215 J6
64218 J6
64225 J6
64230 J6
64235 J6
64249 J6
64257 J6
64269 J6
64273 J6
64301 J11
64369 J11
64375 J11
64420 J11
64438 J11
64716 J39
64739 J39
64747 J39
64762 J39
64798 J39
64823 J39
64827 J39
64832 J39
64955 J39
64974 J39
64980 J39
64983 J39
64988 J39
65002 J1
65480 J5
65483 J5
65486 J5
65490 J5
65493 J5
65494 J5
65496 J5
65498 J5
68758 J52
68768 J52
68777 J52
68781 J52
68787 J52
68788 J52
68791 J52
68798 J52
68807 J52
68810 J52
68812 J52
68814 J52
68851 J52
68859 J52
68863 J52
68873 J52
68882 J52
68887 J52
69263 N5
69271 N5
69286 N5
69310 N5
69360 N5
69615 N7
69620 N7
69621 N7
69654 N7
69801 A5
69806 A5
69807 A5
69809 A5
69810 A5
69817 A5
69818 A5
69822 A5
69823 A5
69825 A5
90000 WD[1]
90001 WD[1]
90002 WD[1]
90007 WD[1]
90025 WD[1]
90036 WD[1]
90038 WD[1]
90043 WD[1]
90050 WD[1]
90051 WD[1]
90052 WD[1]
90073 WD[1]
90075 WD[1]
90084 WD[1]
90103 WD[1]
90129 WD[1]
90136 WD[1]
90139 WD[1]
90154 WD[1]
90185 WD[1]
90202 WD[1]
90215 WD[1]
90235 WD[1]
90263 WD[1]
90287 WD[1]
90288 WD[1]
90296 WD[1]
90303 WD[1]
90346 WD[1]
90368 WD[1]
90369 WD[1]
90384 WD[1]
90391 WD[1]
90392 WD[1]
90411 WD[1]
90423 WD[1]
90432 WD[1]
90433 WD[1]
90437 WD[1]
90449 WD[1]
90473 WD[1]
90476 WD[1]
90491 WD[1]
90496 WD[1]
90499 WD[1]
90532 WD[1]
90545 WD[1]
90567 WD[1]
90618 WD[1]
90629 WD[1]
90634 WD[1]
90636 WD[1]
90648 WD[1]
90662 WD[1]
90674 WD[1]
90703 WD[1]
90717 WD[1]

1957 38A

61056 B1
61066 B1
61088 B1
61092 B1
61106 B1
61141 B1
61160 B1
61163 B1
61177 B1
61185 B1
61186 B1
61188 B1
61201 B1
61209 B1
61271 B1
61272 B1
61283 B1
61367 B1
61376 B1
61723 K2
61726 K2
61729 K2
61732 K2
61738 K2
61752 K2
61753 K2
61754 K2
61763 K2
61768 K2

61771 K2
61773 K2
61777 K2
61780 K2
61809 K3
61821 K3
61824 K3
61833 K3
61870 K3
61873 K3
61888 K3
61896 K3
61914 K3
61947 K3
61974 K3
61982 K3
63587 O4
63602 O4
63614 O4
63638 O4
63639 O4
63647 O4
63657 O4
63674 O4
63675 O4
63694 O4
63699 O4
63729 O4
63754 O4
63816 O4
63829 O4
63839 O4
63859 O4
63873 O4
64183 J6
64195 J6
64199 J6
64200 J6
64202 J6
64213 J6
64215 J6
64218 J6
64221 J6
64225 J6
64230 J6
64235 J6
64239 J6
64248 J6
64249 J6
64256 J6
64257 J6
64267 J6
64269 J6
64273 J6
64338 J11
64345 J11
64397 J11
64420 J11
64715 J39
64716 J39
64735 J39
64739 J39
64741 J39
64747 J39
64762 J39
64763 J39
64798 J39
64823 J39
64827 J39
64832 J39
64955 J39
64974 J39
64976 J39
64980 J39
64983 J39
64988 J39
67751 L1
67760 L1
67771 L1
67788 L1
67798 L1
67799 L1
68550 J69
68601 J69
68629 J69
68768 J52
68785 J52
68826 J52
68829 J52
68851 J52
68860 J52
68863 J52
68871 J52
68882 J52
68887 J52
68893 J50
68927 J50
68950 J50
68967 J50
68975 J50
69800 A5
69804 A5
69807 A5
69810 A5
69812 A5
69821 A5
69822 A5
90000 WD[1]
90001 WD[1]
90002 WD[1]
90005 WD[1]
90015 WD[1]
90024 WD[1]
90025 WD[1]
90036 WD[1]
90037 WD[1]
90038 WD[1]
90050 WD[1]
90052 WD[1]
90053 WD[1]
90064 WD[1]
90066 WD[1]
90073 WD[1]
90075 WD[1]
90084 WD[1]
90103 WD[1]
90104 WD[1]
90115 WD[1]
90118 WD[1]
90120 WD[1]
90130 WD[1]
90136 WD[1]
90139 WD[1]
90146 WD[1]
90153 WD[1]
90154 WD[1]
90161 WD[1]
90166 WD[1]
90185 WD[1]
90189 WD[1]
90202 WD[1]
90215 WD[1]
90235 WD[1]
90263 WD[1]
90269 WD[1]
90288 WD[1]
90296 WD[1]
90303 WD[1]
90368 WD[1]
90384 WD[1]
90394 WD[1]
90418 WD[1]
90432 WD[1]
90437 WD[1]
90460 WD[1]
90473 WD[1]
90476 WD[1]
90496 WD[1]
90499 WD[1]
90519 WD[1]
90618 WD[1]
90629 WD[1]
90634 WD[1]
90648 WD[1]
90662 WD[1]
90703 WD[1]
90717 WD[1]

1960 40E
43108 4MT[5]
43155 4MT[5]
61088 B1
61092 B1
61141 B1
61142 B1
61163 B1
61177 B1
61188 B1
61209 B1
61281 B1
61299 B1
61808 K3
61821 K3
61833 K3
61837 K3
61852 K3
61870 K3
61873 K3
61888 K3
61896 K3
61907 K3
61914 K3
61943 K3
61947 K3
61974 K3
61982 K3
63585 O4
63587 O4
63589 O1
63592 O1
63594 O1
63639 O4
63657 O4
63674 O4
63675 O4
63754 O4
63768 O1
63770 O4
63816 O4
63819 O4
63859 O4
63863 O1
63873 O4
64213 J6
64257 J6
64348 J11
64397 J11
64438 J11
64712 J39
64729 J39
64802 J39
64823 J39
64887 J39
64889 J39
64974 J39
64977 J39
67741 L1
67753 L1
67758 L1
67760 L1
67769 L1
67788 L1
67790 L1
67799 L1
68028 J94
68072 J94
68076 J94
68545 J69
68550 J69
68927 J50
68950 J50
68975 J50
90002 WD[1]
90005 WD[1]
90024 WD[1]
90025 WD[1]
90037 WD[1]
90038 WD[1]
90050 WD[1]
90051 WD[1]
90053 WD[1]
90075 WD[1]
90084 WD[1]
90103 WD[1]
90104 WD[1]
90115 WD[1]
90118 WD[1]
90120 WD[1]
90130 WD[1]
90146 WD[1]
90161 WD[1]
90166 WD[1]
90185 WD[1]
90189 WD[1]
90202 WD[1]
90215 WD[1]
90235 WD[1]
90263 WD[1]
90288 WD[1]
90296 WD[1]
90303 WD[1]
90394 WD[1]
90418 WD[1]
90432 WD[1]
90437 WD[1]
90473 WD[1]
90476 WD[1]
90496 WD[1]
90618 WD[1]
90629 WD[1]
90634 WD[1]
90648 WD[1]
90662 WD[1]
90703 WD[1]
90717 WD[1]
92186 9F

1963 40E
43032 4MT[5]
43060 4MT[5]
43145 4MT[5]
43152 4MT[5]
43154 4MT[5]
43155 4MT[5]
43156 4MT[5]
43160 4MT[5]
43161 4MT[5]
61088 B1
61092 B1
61141 B1
61142 B1
61160 B1
61175 B1
61177 B1
61188 B1
61227 B1
61232 B1
61264 B1
61281 B1
61285 B1
61299 B1
61336 B1
61361 B1
61390 B1
63585 O4
63589 O1
63592 O1
63594 O1
63607 O4
63615 O4
63639 O4
63644 O4
63651 O4
63652 O1
63663 O1
63674 O4
63675 O4
63692 O4
63707 O4
63738 O4
63750 O4
63754 O4
63768 O1
63770 O4
63816 O4
63819 O4
63859 O4
63863 O1
63873 O4
63878 O4
90002 WD[1]
90005 WD[1]
90036 WD[1]
90037 WD[1]
90038 WD[1]
90051 WD[1]
90084 WD[1]
90103 WD[1]
90104 WD[1]
90118 WD[1]
90169 WD[1]
90259 WD[1]
90263 WD[1]
90304 WD[1]
90383 WD[1]
90393 WD[1]
90432 WD[1]
90437 WD[1]
90438 WD[1]
90492 WD[1]
90510 WD[1]
90545 WD[1]
90629 WD[1]
90674 WD[1]
90703 WD[1]
90717 WD[1]

1966 40E
61089 B1
61092 B1
61145 B1
61232 B1
61281 B1
61302 B1
61390 B1
63644 O4
63674 O4
63675 O4
63816 O4
63873 O4
90104 WD[1]
90295 WD[1]
90413 WD[1]
90533 WD[1]
90606 WD[1]
90669 WD[1]
90689 WD[1]
90706 WD[1]

Consett

1948 CON
63346 Q6
63357 Q6
63359 Q6
63361 Q6
63365 Q6
63372 Q6
63379 Q6
63404 Q6
63418 Q6
63433 Q6
63439 Q6
63455 Q6
69384 N8
69394 N8
69411 N9
69414 N9

1951 54D
63346 Q6
63357 Q6
63359 Q6
63361 Q6
63365 Q6
63372 Q6
63404 Q6
63418 Q6
63433 Q6
63439 Q6
63455 Q6
69394 N8
69395 N8

1954 54D
63346 Q6
63357 Q6
63361 Q6
63365 Q6
63372 Q6
63404 Q6
63418 Q6
63427 Q6
63433 Q6
63439 Q6
63455 Q6
68019 J94
69390 N8
69394 N8
90045 WD[1]
90054 WD[1]

1957 54D
63357 Q6
63359 Q6
63361 Q6
63365 Q6
63372 Q6
63404 Q6
63418 Q6
63427 Q6
63433 Q6
63439 Q6
63455 Q6
68019 J94
69917 T1

1960 52K
63342 Q6
63345 Q6
63346 Q6
63354 Q6
63357 Q6
63359 Q6
63365 Q6
63372 Q6
63379 Q6
63387 Q6
63404 Q6
63406 Q6
63418 Q6
63427 Q6
63433 Q6
63437 Q6
63439 Q6
63448 Q6
63455 Q6
63456 Q6

1963 52K
62002 K1
62022 K1
62027 K1
62050 K1
62060 K1
63346 Q6
63357 Q6
63368 Q6
63379 Q6
63406 Q6
63427 Q6
63433 Q6
63439 Q6
63448 Q6
63455 Q6

Copley Hill

1948 COP
60853 V2
61031 B1
61033 B1
62875 C1
62881 C1
64173 J6
64250 J6
64260 J6
64749 J39
67353 C12
67356 C12
67372 C12
67377 C12
67383 C12
67386 C12
67388 C12
68911 J50
68913 J50
68937 J50
68945 J50
68946 J50
68978 J50
68984 J50
68988 J50
69266 N5
69271 N5
69430 N1
69436 N1
69440 N1
69444 N1
69446 N1
69471 N1
69472 N1

1951 37B
60044 A3
60046 A3
60056 A3
60061 A3
60062 A3
60114 A1
60117 A1
60118 A1
60119 A1
60120 A1
60123 A1
60125 A1
60133 A1
60134 A1
60141 A1
61029 B1
61033 B1
61295 B1
64173 J6
64250 J6
64260 J6
67353 C12
67372 C12
68911 J50
68913 J50
68925 J50
68937 J50
68978 J50
68984 J50
68988 J50
69266 N5
69271 N5
69430 N1
69436 N1
69437 N1
69440 N1
69444 N1
69446 N1
69471 N1
69472 N1
69473 N1

1954 37B
60117 A1
60118 A1
60119 A1
60120 A1
60122 A1
60125 A1
60131 A1
60133 A1
60134 A1
60139 A1
60141 A1
60148 A1
60158 A1
60865 V2
60913 V2
61129 B1
61309 B1
61377 B1
61386 B1
61387 B1
61388 B1
64173 J6
64276 J6
64277 J6
68911 J50
68913 J50
68925 J50
68937 J50
68978 J50
68984 J50
68988 J50
69430 N1
69436 N1
69437 N1
69440 N1
69444 N1
69450 N1
69462 N1
69468 N1
69471 N1
69477 N1
69483 N1

1957 56C
60051 A3
60052 A3
60053 A3
60058 A3
60117 A1
60118 A1
60120 A1
60131 A1
60133 A1
60134 A1
60141 A1
60148 A1
60859 V2
60865 V2
60885 V2
60913 V2
61129 B1
61214 B1
61309 B1
61386 B1
61387 B1
61388 B1
64173 J6
64276 J6
64277 J6
64911 J39
67280 G5
67311 G5
67433 C13
67438 C13
68911 J50
68913 J50
68925 J50
68937 J50
68978 J50
68984 J50
68988 J50
69450 N1
69469 N1

1960 56C
40074 3MT[2]
40112 3MT[2]
40114 3MT[2]
42649 4MT[3]
42650 4MT[3]
60117 A1
60118 A1
60120 A1
60123 A1
60130 A1
60131 A1
60133 A1
60134 A1
60141 A1
60148 A1
60859 V2
61115 B1
61129 B1
61189 B1
61214 B1
61309 B1
61320 B1
61339 B1
61386 B1
64173 J6
64268 J6
64277 J6
64911 J39
68911 J50
68913 J50
68925 J50
68984 J50
68988 J50

1963 56C
42073 4MT[1]
42411 4MT[2]
44912 5MT[3]
45219 5MT[3]
60117 A1
60120 A1
60130 A1
60133 A1
60141 A1
60145 A1
60148 A1
61016 B1
61023 B1
61115 B1
61123 B1
61129 B1
61214 B1
61309 B1
61320 B1
61385 B1
68892 J50
68925 J50
68984 J50
68988 J50

Corkerhill

1948 30A
40594 2P[3]
40595 2P[3]
40596 2P[3]
40598 2P[3]
40599 2P[3]
40603 2P[3]
40604 2P[3]
40620 2P[3]
40621 2P[3]
40622 2P[3]
40627 2P[3]
40636 2P[3]
40637 2P[3]
40641 2P[3]
40642 2P[3]
40649 2P[3]
40650 2P[3]
40651 2P[3]
40905 4P[1]
40906 4P[1]
40909 4P[1]
40913 4P[1]
40914 4P[1]
40919 4P[1]
40920 4P[1]
41110 4P[1]
41127 4P[1]
41148 4P[1]
41149 4P[1]
41182 4P[1]
42275 4MT[1]
42276 4MT[1]
42277 4MT[1]
42910 5MT[1]
42911 5MT[1]
42912 5MT[1]
42913 5MT[1]
42914 5MT[1]
42915 5MT[1]
42916 5MT[1]
42917 5MT[1]
45047 5MT[3]
45049 5MT[3]
45168 5MT[3]
45194 5MT[3]
45251 5MT[3]
45489 5MT[3]
45490 5MT[3]
45491 5MT[3]
45560 6P5F[2]
45575 6P5F[2]
45576 6P5F[2]
45643 6P5F[2]
45644 6P5F[2]
45645 6P5F[2]
45646 6P5F[2]
45693 6P5F[2]
47329 3F[6]
55135 2P[12]
55140 2P[12]
55143 2P[12]
55182 2P[13]
55193 2P[13]
55206 2P[13]
55211 2P[13]
55219 2P[13]
55225 2P[13]
55235 2P[13]
55266 2P[15]
55269 2P[15]
56249 3F[10]
56350 3F[10]
56361 3F[10]
56369 3F[10]
57241 2F[5]
57249 2F[5]
57255 2F[5]
57266 2F[5]
57300 2F[5]
57309 2F[5]
57359 2F[5]
57560 3F[12]
57561 3F[12]
57562 3F[12]
57566 3F[12]
57575 3F[12]
57580 3F[12]
57589 3F[12]
57594 3F[12]
57596 3F[12]
57624 3F[12]
57693 3F[15]
57694 3F[15]
57695 3F[15]
57698 3F[15]
57699 3F[15]
57702 3F[15]

1951 67A
40592 2P[3]
40594 2P[3]
40595 2P[3]
40596 2P[3]
40598 2P[3]
40599 2P[3]
40604 2P[3]
40620 2P[3]
40621 2P[3]
40627 2P[3]
40636 2P[3]
40637 2P[3]
40641 2P[3]
40642 2P[3]
40649 2P[3]
40651 2P[3]
40905 4P[1]
40906 4P[1]
40909 4P[1]
40914 4P[1]
40915 4P[1]
40919 4P[1]
42122 4MT[1]
42123 4MT[1]
42124 4MT[1]
42190 4MT[1]
42191 4MT[1]
42192 4MT[1]
42193 4MT[1]
42194 4MT[1]
42195 4MT[1]
42196 4MT[1]
42197 4MT[1]
42911 5MT[1]
42914 5MT[1]
42916 5MT[1]
42917 5MT[1]
43899 4F[1]
44159 4F[2]
44198 4F[2]
44329 4F[2]
44706 5MT[3]
44968 5MT[3]
45047 5MT[3]
45049 5MT[3]
45163 5MT[3]
45168 5MT[3]
45174 5MT[3]
45194 5MT[3]
45251 5MT[3]
45489 5MT[3]
45490 5MT[3]
45491 5MT[3]
45560 6P5F[2]
45576 6P5F[2]
45643 6P5F[2]
45645 6P5F[2]
45646 6P5F[2]
45693 6P5F[2]
47329 3F[6]
55135 2P[12]
55140 2P[12]
55143 2P[12]
55182 2P[13]
55206 2P[13]
55211 2P[13]
55219 2P[13]
55225 2P[13]
55235 2P[13]
55266 2P[15]
55269 2P[15]
56249 3F[10]
56329 3F[10]
56350 3F[10]
56361 3F[10]
56369 3F[10]
57241 2F[5]
57249 2F[5]
57255 2F[5]
57266 2F[5]
57300 2F[5]
57309 2F[5]
57359 2F[5]
57560 3F[12]
57562 3F[12]
57566 3F[12]
57575 3F[12]
57580 3F[12]
57589 3F[12]
57596 3F[12]
57695 3F[15]
57698 3F[15]

1954 67A
40594 2P[3]
40595 2P[3]
40596 2P[3]
40598 2P[3]
40599 2P[3]
40604 2P[3]
40620 2P[3]
40621 2P[3]
40627 2P[3]
40636 2P[3]
40637 2P[3]
40641 2P[3]
40642 2P[3]
40649 2P[3]
40651 2P[3]
40906 4P[1]
40908 4P[1]
40909 4P[1]
40914 4P[1]
40915 4P[1]
40919 4P[1]
41133 4P[1]
41134 4P[1]
41139 4P[1]
41142 4P[1]
42122 4MT[1]
42123 4MT[1]
42124 4MT[1]
42190 4MT[1]
42191 4MT[1]
42193 4MT[1]
42194 4MT[1]
42229 4MT[1]
42806 5MT[1]
42914 5MT[1]
42916 5MT[1]
42917 5MT[1]
43899 4F[1]
43996 4F[1]
44001 4F[1]
44198 4F[2]
44329 4F[2]
44706 5MT[3]
44791 5MT[3]
44968 5MT[3]
45160 5MT[3]
45166 5MT[3]
45174 5MT[3]
45194 5MT[3]
45251 5MT[3]
45362 5MT[3]
45489 5MT[3]
45490 5MT[3]
45621 6P5F[2]
45665 6P5F[2]
45687 6P5F[2]
45693 6P5F[2]
45711 6P5F[2]
45720 6P5F[2]
47329 3F[6]
55206 2P[13]
55211 2P[13]
55219 2P[13]
55225 2P[13]
55235 2P[13]
55266 2P[15]
55269 2P[15]
56249 3F[10]
56329 3F[10]
56350 3F[10]
56361 3F[10]
56369 3F[10]
57241 2F[5]
57249 2F[5]
57266 2F[5]
57300 2F[5]
57309 2F[5]
57359 2F[5]
57560 3F[12]
57562 3F[12]
57566 3F[12]
57575 3F[12]
57579 3F[12]
57580 3F[12]
57589 3F[12]
57594 3F[12]
57596 3F[12]
80000 4MT[3]
80008 4MT[3]
80009 4MT[3]
80024 4MT[3]
80025 4MT[3]
80030 4MT[3]

1957 67A
40594 2P[3]
40595 2P[3]
40596 2P[3]
40598 2P[3]
40599 2P[3]
40620 2P[3]
40621 2P[3]
40627 2P[3]
40636 2P[3]
40637 2P[3]
40641 2P[3]
40642 2P[3]
40647 2P[3]
40649 2P[3]
42122 4MT[1]
42123 4MT[1]
42124 4MT[1]
42190 4MT[1]
42191 4MT[1]
42193 4MT[1]
42229 4MT[1]
43899 4F[1]
43996 4F[1]
44001 4F[1]
44189 4F[2]
44198 4F[2]
44329 4F[2]
44706 5MT[3]
44791 5MT[3]
45160 5MT[3]
45194 5MT[3]
45251 5MT[3]
45362 5MT[3]
45489 5MT[3]
45490 5MT[3]
45621 6P5F[2]
45665 6P5F[2]
45677 6P5F[2]
45687 6P5F[2]
45693 6P5F[2]
45707 6P5F[2]
45711 6P5F[2]
45720 6P5F[2]
47329 3F[6]
55206 2P[13]
55211 2P[13]
55219 2P[13]
55225 2P[13]
55235 2P[13]
55266 2P[15]
55269 2P[15]
56267 3F[10]
56329 3F[10]
56350 3F[10]
56361 3F[10]
56364 3F[10]
56369 3F[10]
57241 2F[5]
57249 2F[5]
57300 2F[5]
57359 2F[5]
57560 3F[12]
57562 3F[12]
57566 3F[12]
57575 3F[12]
57579 3F[12]
57580 3F[12]
57594 3F[12]
57596 3F[12]
73079 5MT
73100 5MT
73101 5MT
73102 5MT
73103 5MT
73104 5MT
73121 5MT
73122 5MT
73123 5MT
73124 5MT
80000 4MT[3]
80008 4MT[3]
80009 4MT[3]
80024 4MT[3]
80025 4MT[3]
80030 4MT[3]
80127 4MT[3]
80128 4MT[3]

1960 67A
40596 2P[3]
40620 2P[3]
40621 2P[3]
40627 2P[3]
40637 2P[3]
42123 4MT[1]
42190 4MT[1]
42191 4MT[1]
42193 4MT[1]
42211 4MT[1]
42229 4MT[1]
42238 4MT[1]
42240 4MT[1]
42247 4MT[1]
42270 4MT[1]
43899 4F[1]
43996 4F[1]
44001 4F[1]
44159 4F[2]
44189 4F[2]
44198 4F[2]
44319 4F[2]
44330 4F[2]
44706 5MT[3]
44791 5MT[3]
45007 5MT[3]
45053 5MT[3]
45362 5MT[3]
45489 5MT[3]
45687 6P5F[2]
45693 6P5F[2]
55203 2P[13]
55206 2P[13]
55219 2P[13]
55225 2P[13]
55235 2P[13]
55264 2P[15]
55266 2P[15]
56031 0F[5]
56279 3F[10]
56361 3F[10]
56364 3F[10]
57249 2F[5]
57300 2F[5]
57359 2F[5]
57620 3F[12]
73079 5MT
73100 5MT
73101 5MT
73102 5MT
73103 5MT
73104 5MT
73121 5MT
73122 5MT
73123 5MT
73124 5MT
76090 4MT[2]
76091 4MT[2]
76092 4MT[2]
76093 4MT[2]
76094 4MT[2]
76095 4MT[2]
76096 4MT[2]
76097 4MT[2]
76098 4MT[2]
76099 4MT[2]
80000 4MT[3]
80005 4MT[3]
80008 4MT[3]
80009 4MT[3]
80024 4MT[3]
80025 4MT[3]
80030 4MT[3]
80127 4MT[3]
80128 4MT[3]

1963 67A
44699 5MT[3]
44706 5MT[3]
44723 5MT[3]
44784 5MT[3]
44785 5MT[3]
44791 5MT[3]
44798 5MT[3]
44801 5MT[3]
45171 5MT[3]
45361 5MT[3]
45362 5MT[3]
45365 5MT[3]
45366 5MT[3]
45467 5MT[3]
45488 5MT[3]
73079 5MT
73100 5MT
73101 5MT
73102 5MT
73103 5MT
73104 5MT
73121 5MT
73122 5MT
73123 5MT
73124 5MT
76001 4MT[2]
76091 4MT[2]
76092 4MT[2]
76093 4MT[2]
76094 4MT[2]
76095 4MT[2]
76098 4MT[2]
76114 4MT[2]
80005 4MT[3]
80008 4MT[3]
80009 4MT[3]
80020 4MT[3]
80021 4MT[3]
80024 4MT[3]
80025 4MT[3]
80030 4MT[3]
80044 4MT[3]
80045 4MT[3]
80046 4MT[3]
80047 4MT[3]
80048 4MT[3]
80049 4MT[3]
80050 4MT[3]
80051 4MT[1]
80052 4MT[3]
80053 4MT[3]
80127 4MT[3]
80128 4MT[3]

1966 67A
44798 5MT[3]
45488 5MT[3]
73005 5MT
73009 5MT
73057 5MT
73079 5MT
73100 5MT
73101 5MT
73102 5MT
73120 5MT
73121 5MT
76046 4MT[2]
76093 4MT[2]
76114 4MT[2]
78026 2MT[1]
80000 4MT[3]
80004 4MT[3]
80024 4MT[3]
80025 4MT[3]
80046 4MT[3]
80047 4MT[3]
80051 4MT[3]
80063 4MT[3]
80112 4MT[3]
80128 4MT[3]

Coventry

1948 2F
48892 6F[2]
49135 6F[2]
49167 7F[2]
49278 7F[2]
49340 7F[2]
49368 7F[2]
49423 7F[3]
49440 7F[3]
58187 2F[8]
58199 2F[9]
58211 2F[9]
58217 2F[9]
58293 2F[9]
58301 2F[9]

1951 2D
46445 2MT[2]
46446 2MT[2]
49330 7F[2]
49405 7F[3]
49441 7F[3]
49442 7F[3]
49444 7F[3]
49446 7F[3]
58217 2F[9]
58278 2F[9]
58293 2F[9]
58306 2F[9]

1954 2D
46445 2MT[2]
46446 2MT[2]
49330 7F[2]
49415 7F[3]
49425 7F[3]
49441 7F[3]
49442 7F[3]
49446 7F[3]
58217 2F[9]
58278 2F[9]
58293 2F[9]
58306 2F[9]

1957 2D
46420 2MT[2]
46446 2MT[2]
47338 3F[6]
49411 7F[3]
49415 7F[3]
49425 7F[3]
49441 7F[3]
49442 7F[3]

Crewe

1951 CME
49140 6F[2]

1954 CME
49140 6F[2]

Crewe North

1948 5A
40322 2P[1]
40471 2P[2]
40492 2P[2]
40529 2P[2]
40659 2P[3]
40660 2P[3]
41112 4P[1]
41115 4P[1]
41160 4P[1]
41167 4P[1]
41173 4P[1]
42266 4MT[1]
42309 4MT[2]
44758 5MT[3]
44759 5MT[3]
44760 5MT[3]
44761 5MT[3]
44762 5MT[3]
44763 5MT[3]
44764 5MT[3]
44765 5MT[3]
44766 5MT[3]
44767 5MT[3]
44788 5MT[3]
44789 5MT[3]
44790 5MT[3]
44801 5MT[3]
44807 5MT[3]
44808 5MT[3]
44832 5MT[3]
44833 5MT[3]
44834 5MT[3]
44835 5MT[3]
44836 5MT[3]
44837 5MT[3]
44838 5MT[3]
44862 5MT[3]
44863 5MT[3]
44864 5MT[3]
44865 5MT[3]
44874 5MT[3]
44875 5MT[3]
44908 5MT[3]
44952 5MT[3]
44954 5MT[3]
44967 5MT[3]
45369 5MT[3]
45374 5MT[3]
45412 5MT[3]
45422 5MT[3]
45436 5MT[3]
45493 5MT[3]
45503 6P5F[1]
45504 6P5F[1]
45507 6P5F[1]
45508 6P5F[1]
45511 6P5F[1]
45512 6P5F[1]
45522 6P5F[1]
45532 6P5F[1]
45539 6P5F[1]
45542 6P5F[1]
45546 6P5F[1]
45548 6P5F[1]
45549 6P5F[1]
45551 6P5F[1]
45555 6P5F[2]
45558 6P5F[2]
45578 6P5F[2]
45596 6P5F[2]
45600 6P5F[2]
45603 6P5F[2]
45630 6P5F[2]
45632 6P5F[2]
45637 6P5F[2]
45647 6P5F[2]
45674 6P5F[2]
45675 6P5F[2]
45676 6P5F[2]
45684 6P5F[2]
45686 6P5F[2]
45687 6P5F[2]
45688 6P5F[2]
45689 6P5F[2]
45709 6P5F[2]
45722 6P5F[2]
45737 6P5F[2]
45741 6P5F[2]
46113 7P[3]
46115 7P[3]R
46125 7P[3]R
46126 7P[3]R
46146 7P[3]R
46147 7P[3]R
46154 7P[3]R
46155 7P[3]
46161 7P[3]R
46162 7P[3]
46163 7P[3]
46165 7P[3]
46166 7P[3]R
46167 7P[3]
46200 8P[1]
46201 8P[1]
46203 8P[1]
46204 8P[1]
46205 8P[1]
46206 8P[1]
46207 8P[1]
46208 8P[1]
46209 8P[1]
46210 8P[1]
46211 8P[1]
46212 8P[1]
46227 8P[2]
46229 8P[2]
46233 8P[2]
46234 8P[2]
46235 8P[2]
46236 8P[2]
46252 8P[2]
46256 8P[2]
46605 1P[1]
46680 1P[1]
46711 1P[1]
28350 2F[11]

1951 5A
40332 2P[2]
40402 2P[2]
40425 2P[2]
40659 2P[3]
40660 2P[3]
40933 4P[1]
41112 4P[1]
41151 4P[1]
41160 4P[1]
41167 4P[1]
41229 2MT[1]
41288 2MT[1]
41289 2MT[1]
42308 4MT[2]
42318 4MT[2]
44678 5MT[3]
44679 5MT[3]
44680 5MT[3]
44681 5MT[3]
44682 5MT[3]
44683 5MT[3]
44684 5MT[3]
44685 5MT[3]
44717 5MT[3]
44758 5MT[3]
44761 5MT[3]
44762 5MT[3]
44763 5MT[3]
44764 5MT[3]
44765 5MT[3]
44766 5MT[3]
44770 5MT[3]
44771 5MT[3]
45217 5MT[3]
45305 5MT[3]
45502 6P5F[1]
45503 6P5F[1]
45504 6P5F[1]
45506 6P5F[1]
45507 6P5F[1]
45510 6P5F[1]
45511 6P5F[1]
45513 6P5F[1]
45523 7P[1]
45525 7P[1]
45528 7P[1]
45529 7P[1]
45535 7P[1]
45543 6P5F[1]
45548 6P5F[1]
45586 6P5F[2]
45592 6P5F[2]
45606 6P5F[2]
45634 6P5F[2]
45647 6P5F[2]
45666 6P5F[2]
45674 6P5F[2]
45678 6P5F[2]
45684 6P5F[2]
45686 6P5F[2]
45689 6P5F[2]
45703 6P5F[2]
45724 6P5F[2]
45733 6P5F[2]
45738 6P5F[2]
46101 7P[3]R
46113 7P[3]R
46118 7P[3]R
46128 7P[3]R
46130 7P[3]R
46146 7P[3]R
46155 7P[3]R
46157 7P[3]R
46206 8P[1]
46207 8P[1]
46208 8P[1]
46209 8P[1]
46210 8P[1]
46211 8P[1]
46212 8P[1]
46233 8P[2]
46234 8P[2]
46235 8P[2]
46236 8P[2]
46243 8P[2]
46246 8P[2]
46248 8P[2]
46252 8P[2]
46680 1P[1]

1954 5A
40332 2P[2]
40413 2P[2]
40419 2P[2]
40447 2P[2]
40529 2P[2]
40567 2P[3]
40659 2P[3]
40660 2P[3]
40926 4P[1]
41060 4P[1]
41076 4P[1]
41160 4P[1]
41167 4P[1]
41229 2MT[1]
41320 2MT[1]
42308 4MT[2]
42447 4MT[3]
42566 4MT[3]
42677 4MT[1]
44679 5MT[3]
44680 5MT[3]
44682 5MT[3]
44683 5MT[3]
44684 5MT[3]
44685 5MT[3]
44758 5MT[3]
44759 5MT[3]
44761 5MT[3]
44762 5MT[3]
44763 5MT[3]
44764 5MT[3]
44765 5MT[3]
44766 5MT[3]
44770 5MT[3]
44807 5MT[3]
44827 5MT[3]
44840 5MT[3]
44911 5MT[3]
45006 5MT[3]
45033 5MT[3]
45071 5MT[3]
45148 5MT[3]
45235 5MT[3]
45240 5MT[3]
45254 5MT[3]
45300 5MT[3]
45301 5MT[3]
45307 5MT[3]
45434 5MT[3]
45446 5MT[3]
45503 6P5F[1]
45504 6P5F[1]
45506 6P5F[1]
45507 6P5F[1]
45510 6P5F[1]
45513 6P5F[1]
45516 6P5F[1]
45524 6P5F[1]
45528 7P[1]
45535 7P[1]
45543 6P5F[1]
45544 6P5F[1]
45547 6P5F[1]
45548 6P5F[1]
45586 6P5F[2]
45604 6P5F[2]
45617 6P5F[2]
45634 6P5F[2]
45674 6P5F[2]
45678 6P5F[2]
45684 6P5F[2]
45726 6P5F[2]
46101 7P[3]R
46106 7P[3]R
46118 7P[3]R
46119 7P[3]R
46125 7P[3]R
46128 7P[3]R
46134 7P[3]R
46137 7P[3]
46138 7P[3]R
46140 7P[3]R
46148 7P[3]
46151 7P[3]R
46155 7P[3]R
46156 7P[3]
46159 7P[3]R
46163 7P[3]R
46166 7P[3]R
46167 7P[3]R
46201 8P[1]
46202 8P[1]
46203 8P[1]
46206 8P[1]
46209 8P[1]
46210 8P[1]
46211 8P[1]
46212 8P[1]
46225 8P[2]
46233 8P[2]
46234 8P[2]
46235 8P[2]
46242 8P[2]
46243 8P[2]
46246 8P[2]
46248 8P[2]
46252 8P[2]

1957 5A
40332 2P[2]
40402 2P[2]
40413 2P[2]
40447 2P[2]
40567 2P[3]
40659 2P[3]
40660 2P[3]
40926 4P[1]
41060 4P[1]
41167 4P[1]
41229 2MT[1]
41901 2P[4]
42321 4MT[2]
42566 4MT[3]
42677 4MT[1]
42955 5MT[2]
42961 5MT[2]
42963 5MT[2]
44679 5MT[3]
44680 5MT[3]
44682 5MT[3]
44683 5MT[3]
44684 5MT[3]
44685 5MT[3]
44758 5MT[3]
44759 5MT[3]
44761 5MT[3]
44762 5MT[3]
44763 5MT[3]
44764 5MT[3]
44765 5MT[3]
44766 5MT[3]
44807 5MT[3]
45033 5MT[3]
45113 5MT[3]
45148 5MT[3]
45150 5MT[3]
45235 5MT[3]
45240 5MT[3]
45254 5MT[3]
45282 5MT[3]
45289 5MT[3]
45300 5MT[3]
45302 5MT[3]
45369 5MT[3]
45373 5MT[3]
45379 5MT[3]
45434 5MT[3]
45446 5MT[3]
45503 6P5F[1]
45507 6P5F[1]
45528 7P[1]
45529 7P[1]
45545 7P[1]
45548 6P5F[1]
45556 6P5F[2]
45586 6P5F[2]
45591 6P5F[2]
45604 6P5F[2]
45617 6P5F[2]
45625 6P5F[2]
45630 6P5F[2]
45634 6P5F[2]
45674 6P5F[2]
45678 6P5F[2]
45684 6P5F[2]
45703 6P5F[2]
45721 6P5F[2]
45726 6P5F[2]
45736 7P[2]
46101 7P[3]R
46106 7P[3]R
46110 7P[3]R
46118 7P[3]R
46119 7P[3]R
46120 7P[3]R
46125 7P[3]R
46127 7P[3]R
46128 7P[3]R
46129 7P[3]R
46134 7P[3]R
46138 7P[3]R
46148 7P[3]R
46150 7P[3]R
46151 7P[3]R
46155 7P[3]R
46156 7P[3]R
46159 7P[3]R
46161 7P[3]R
46163 7P[3]R
46166 7P[3]R
46201 8P[1]
46203 8P[1]
46206 8P[1]
46209 8P[1]
46211 8P[1]
46212 8P[1]
46225 8P[2]
46233 8P[2]
46234 8P[2]
46235 8P[2]
46243 8P[2]
46246 8P[2]
46248 8P[2]
46249 8P[2]
46251 8P[2]
46252 8P[2]
71000 8P
78030 2MT[1]

1960 5A
41212 2MT[1]
41220 2MT[1]
41229 2MT[1]
42575 4MT[3]
42578 4MT[3]
42677 4MT[1]
42776 5MT[1]
42815 5MT[1]
42940 5MT[1]
42954 5MT[2]
42958 5MT[2]
42963 5MT[2]
42966 5MT[2]
42968 5MT[2]
44678 5MT[3]
44679 5MT[3]
44680 5MT[3]
44681 5MT[3]
44683 5MT[3]
44684 5MT[3]
44685 5MT[3]
44714 5MT[3]
44759 5MT[3]
44761 5MT[3]
44762 5MT[3]
44763 5MT[3]
44764 5MT[3]
44765 5MT[3]
44844 5MT[3]
45003 5MT[3]
45004 5MT[3]
45021 5MT[3]
45033 5MT[3]
45073 5MT[3]
45093 5MT[3]
45132 5MT[3]
45148 5MT[3]
45189 5MT[3]
45235 5MT[3]
45237 5MT[3]
45240 5MT[3]
45243 5MT[3]
45250 5MT[3]
45254 5MT[3]
45257 5MT[3]
45282 5MT[3]
45289 5MT[3]
45305 5MT[3]
45311 5MT[3]
45348 5MT[3]
45369 5MT[3]
45379 5MT[3]
45434 5MT[3]
45446 5MT[3]
45528 7P[1]
45529 7P[1]
45545 7P[1]
45553 6P5F[2]
45556 6P5F[2]
45591 6P5F[2]
45595 6P5F[2]
45604 6P5F[2]
45623 6P5F[2]
45625 6P5F[2]
45629 6P5F[2]
45630 6P5F[2]
45634 6P5F[2]
45643 6P5F[2]
45655 6P5F[2]
45666 6P5F[2]
45674 6P5F[2]
45679 6P5F[2]
45684 6P5F[2]
45689 6P5F[2]
45696 6P5F[2]
45726 6P5F[2]
45736 7P[2]
46110 7P[3]R
46116 7P[3]R
46120 7P[3]R
46125 7P[3]R
46128 7P[3]R
46134 7P[3]R
46135 7P[3]R
46147 7P[3]R
46152 7P[3]R
46155 7P[3]R
46159 7P[3]R
46164 7P[3]R
46169 7P[3]R
46200 8P[1]
46205 8P[1]
46206 8P[1]
46209 8P[1]
46212 8P[1]
46220 8P[2]
46228 8P[2]
46233 8P[2]
46235 8P[2]
46241 8P[2]
46243 8P[2]
46246 8P[2]
46248 8P[2]
46249 8P[2]
46251 8P[2]
46252 8P[2]
46253 8P[2]
70046 7P6F
70047 7P6F
71000 8P
78030 2MT[1]

1963 5A
41212 2MT[1]
41220 2MT[1]
41229 2MT[1]
42183 4MT[1]
44678 5MT[3]
44679 5MT[3]
44680 5MT[3]
44681 5MT[3]
44683 5MT[3]
44684 5MT[3]
44685 5MT[3]
44714 5MT[3]
44759 5MT[3]
44761 5MT[3]
44762 5MT[3]
44763 5MT[3]
44764 5MT[3]
44765 5MT[3]
44770 5MT[3]
45021 5MT[3]
45046 5MT[3]
45093 5MT[3]
45132 5MT[3]
45189 5MT[3]
45241 5MT[3]
45243 5MT[3]
45250 5MT[3]
45257 5MT[3]
45270 5MT[3]
45344 5MT[3]
45379 5MT[3]
45426 5MT[3]
45429 5MT[3]
45446 5MT[3]
45552 6P5F[2]
45553 6P5F[2]
45554 6P5F[2]
45556 6P5F[2]
45560 6P5F[2]
45591 6P5F[2]
45595 6P5F[2]
45617 6P5F[2]
45631 6P5F[2]
45647 6P5F[2]
45666 6P5F[2]
45674 6P5F[2]
45676 6P5F[2]
45689 6P5F[2]
45709 6P5F[2]
45721 6P5F[2]
45726 6P5F[2]
46228 8P[2]
46235 8P[2]
46248 8P[2]
46251 8P[2]
46253 8P[2]
46254 8P[2]
46256 8P[2]
70018 7P6F
70019 7P6F
70020 7P6F
70044 7P6F
70052 7P6F
70053 7P6F
70054 7P6F
78030 2MT[1]

Crewe South

1948 5B
40402 2P[2]
40405 2P[2]
40448 2P[2]
42785 5MT[1]
42856 5MT[1]
42920 5MT[1]
42939 5MT[1]
42944 5MT[1]
42947 5MT[2]
42950 5MT[2]
42952 5MT[2]
42955 5MT[2]
42956 5MT[2]
42960 5MT[2]
42961 5MT[2]
42962 5MT[2]
42968 5MT[2]
42977 5MT[2]
42980 5MT[2]
42982 5MT[2]
42983 5MT[2]
43000 4MT[5]
43001 4MT[5]
43002 4MT[5]
44300 4F[2]
44342 4F[2]
44344 4F[2]
44359 4F[2]
44387 4F[2]
44453 4F[2]
44461 4F[2]
44827 5MT[3]
44844 5MT[3]
45028 5MT[3]
45038 5MT[3]
45041 5MT[3]
45044 5MT[3]
45048 5MT[3]
45060 5MT[3]
45064 5MT[3]
45067 5MT[3]
45069 5MT[3]
45072 5MT[3]
45073 5MT[3]
45074 5MT[3]
45089 5MT[3]
45093 5MT[3]
45097 5MT[3]
45108 5MT[3]
45128 5MT[3]
45131 5MT[3]
45134 5MT[3]
45143 5MT[3]
45145 5MT[3]
45146 5MT[3]
45148 5MT[3]
45181 5MT[3]
45183 5MT[3]
45189 5MT[3]
45195 5MT[3]
45197 5MT[3]
45198 5MT[3]
45235 5MT[3]
45236 5MT[3]
45239 5MT[3]
45240 5MT[3]
45242 5MT[3]
45248 5MT[3]
45254 5MT[3]
45255 5MT[3]
45270 5MT[3]
45271 5MT[3]
45300 5MT[3]
45305 5MT[3]
45317 5MT[3]
47266 3F[6]
47280 3F[6]
47330 3F[6]
47344 3F[6]
47384 3F[6]
47414 3F[6]
47416 3F[6]
47431 3F[6]
47444 3F[6]
47445 3F[6]
47451 3F[6]
47523 3F[6]
47524 3F[6]
47526 3F[6]
47590 3F[6]
47602 3F[6]
47608 3F[6]
47616 3F[6]
47633 3F[6]
47665 3F[6]
47680 3F[6]
47681 3F[6]
48191 8F
48273 8F
48310 8F
48318 8F
48320 8F
48340 8F
48345 8F
48428 8F
48457 8F
48465 8F
48466 8F
48467 8F
48477 8F
48478 8F
48553 8F
48555 8F
48559 8F
48708 8F
48716 8F
48723 8F
48729 8F
48731 8F
48734 8F
48740 8F
48741 8F
48742 8F
48744 8F
48745 8F
48746 8F
48747 8F
48748 8F
48749 8F
48750 8F
48753 8F
48757 8F
48758 8F
48764 8F
48770 8F
48771 8F
48772 8F
48906 6F[2]
48962 6F[2]
49116 7F[2]
49184 6F[2]
49209 7F[2]
49210 7F[2]
49230 7F[2]
49232 6F[2]
49241 6F[2]
49263 6F[2]
49267 7F[2]
49272 6F[2]
49275 7F[2]
49296 7F[2]
49357 7F[2]
49369 7F[2]
49370 6F[2]
49373 7F[2]
49396 7F[3]
49415 7F[3]
49450 7F[3]
51221 0F[4]
58384 2F[11]
58386 2F[11]
58395 2F[11]
58396 2F[11]

1951 5B
42773 5MT[1]
42785 5MT[1]
42810 5MT[1]
42811 5MT[1]
42815 5MT[1]
42856 5MT[1]
42920 5MT[1]
42926 5MT[1]
42939 5MT[1]
42950 5MT[2]
42952 5MT[2]
42955 5MT[2]
42956 5MT[2]
42968 5MT[2]
42972 5MT[2]
42980 5MT[2]
42983 5MT[2]
42984 5MT[2]
43189 3F[2]
43207 3F[3]
44079 4F[2]
44125 4F[2]
44301 4F[2]
44341 4F[2]
44344 4F[2]
44708 5MT[3]
44807 5MT[3]
44827 5MT[3]
44832 5MT[3]
44911 5MT[3]
45006 5MT[3]
45013 5MT[3]
45028 5MT[3]
45030 5MT[3]
45038 5MT[3]
45041 5MT[3]
45044 5MT[3]
45048 5MT[3]
45060 5MT[3]
45067 5MT[3]
45073 5MT[3]
45074 5MT[3]
45093 5MT[3]
45108 5MT[3]
45128 5MT[3]
45131 5MT[3]
45134 5MT[3]
45148 5MT[3]
45185 5MT[3]
45189 5MT[3]
45195 5MT[3]
45198 5MT[3]
45239 5MT[3]
45240 5MT[3]
45254 5MT[3]
45270 5MT[3]
45271 5MT[3]
45294 5MT[3]
45300 5MT[3]
45301 5MT[3]
45369 5MT[3]
47266 3F[6]
47280 3F[6]
47330 3F[6]
47344 3F[6]
47384 3F[6]
47414 3F[6]
47431 3F[6]
47450 3F[6]
47523 3F[6]
47524 3F[6]
47526 3F[6]
47590 3F[6]
47633 3F[6]
47661 3F[6]
47662 3F[6]
47670 3F[6]
47680 3F[6]
48248 8F
48249 8F
48250 8F
48251 8F
48252 8F
48253 8F
48255 8F
48256 8F
48257 8F
48258 8F
48259 8F
48260 8F
48261 8F
48262 8F
48263 8F
48286 8F
48287 8F
48288 8F
48289 8F
48290 8F
48291 8F
48292 8F
48294 8F
48295 8F
48296 8F
48297 8F
48751 8F
48754 8F
48756 8F
48757 8F
49210 7F[2]
49230 7F[2]
49407 7F[3]
51204 0F[4]
51218 0F[4]
51221 0F[4]
58426 2F[11]
58429 2F[11]

1954 5B
42777 5MT[1]
42785 5MT[1]
42811 5MT[1]
42813 5MT[1]
42815 5MT[1]
42851 5MT[1]
42856 5MT[1]
42894 5MT[1]
42920 5MT[1]
42926 5MT[1]
42933 5MT[1]
42939 5MT[1]
42950 5MT[1]
42952 5MT[2]
42953 5MT[2]
42955 5MT[2]
42956 5MT[2]
42962 5MT[2]
42968 5MT[2]
42972 5MT[2]
42980 5MT[2]
42983 5MT[2]
42984 5MT[2]
43187 3F[2]
43189 3F[2]
43207 3F[3]
43330 3F[3]
43562 3F[3]
44301 4F[2]
44344 4F[2]
44359 4F[2]
44595 4F[2]
44832 5MT[3]
44834 5MT[3]
44971 5MT[3]
45028 5MT[3]
45038 5MT[3]
45041 5MT[3]
45044 5MT[3]
45048 5MT[3]
45060 5MT[3]
45067 5MT[3]
45073 5MT[3]
45074 5MT[3]
45093 5MT[3]
45108 5MT[3]
45128 5MT[3]
45131 5MT[3]
45134 5MT[3]
45189 5MT[3]
45195 5MT[3]
45198 5MT[3]
45270 5MT[3]
45353 5MT[3]
45369 5MT[3]
47184 Sentinel[2]
47266 3F[6]
47280 3F[6]
47330 3F[6]
47338 3F[6]
47384 3F[6]
47414 3F[6]
47431 3F[6]
47450 3F[6]
47523 3F[6]
47524 3F[6]
47526 3F[6]
47602 3F[6]
47616 3F[6]
47661 3F[6]
47662 3F[6]
47670 3F[6]
47680 3F[6]
48251 8F
48252 8F
48253 8F
48255 8F
48256 8F
48257 8F
48258 8F
48262 8F
48263 8F
48287 8F
48288 8F
48289 8F
48291 8F
48292 8F
48294 8F
48295 8F
48296 8F
48529 8F
48736 8F
48743 8F
49230 7F[2]
49318 7F[2]
49407 7F[3]
49454 7F[3]
51204 0F[4]
51218 0F[4]
51221 0F[4]
58196 2F[9]

1957 5B
42747 5MT[1]
42776 5MT[1]
42777 5MT[1]
42785 5MT[1]
42811 5MT[1]
42813 5MT[1]
42815 5MT[1]
42856 5MT[1]
42894 5MT[1]
42920 5MT[1]
42926 5MT[1]
42932 5MT[1]
42933 5MT[1]
42939 5MT[1]
42940 5MT[1]
42944 5MT[1]
42948 5MT[2]
42950 5MT[2]
42952 5MT[2]
42953 5MT[2]
42956 5MT[2]
42962 5MT[2]
42966 5MT[2]
42968 5MT[2]
42972 5MT[2]
42980 5MT[2]
42983 5MT[2]
42984 5MT[2]
43189 3F[2]
43207 3F[3]
43330 3F[3]
43562 3F[3]
44186 4F[2]
44301 4F[2]
44344 4F[2]
44359 4F[2]
44385 4F[2]
44592 4F[2]
44595 4F[2]
44827 5MT[3]
44832 5MT[3]
44834 5MT[3]
44868 5MT[3]
45000 5MT[3]
45003 5MT[3]
45041 5MT[3]
45044 5MT[3]
45045 5MT[3]
45048 5MT[3]
45060 5MT[3]
45067 5MT[3]
45073 5MT[3]
45074 5MT[3]
45093 5MT[3]
45108 5MT[3]
45111 5MT[3]
45128 5MT[3]
45131 5MT[3]
45134 5MT[3]
45180 5MT[3]
45188 5MT[3]
45189 5MT[3]
45198 5MT[3]
45270 5MT[3]
45301 5MT[3]
45305 5MT[3]
45311 5MT[3]
45353 5MT[3]
45390 5MT[3]
45391 5MT[3]
45426 5MT[3]
47280 3F[6]
47330 3F[6]
47384 3F[6]
47414 3F[6]
47431 3F[6]
47450 3F[6]
47516 3F[6]
47523 3F[6]
47524 3F[6]
47526 3F[6]
47661 3F[6]
47662 3F[6]
47670 3F[6]
47680 3F[6]
48248 8F
48251 8F
48252 8F
48255 8F
48256 8F
48257 8F
48262 8F
48287 8F
48289 8F
48291 8F
48292 8F
48294 8F
48295 8F
48411 8F
48505 8F
48529 8F
48626 8F
48630 8F
48734 8F
48736 8F
48743 8F
49025 7F[2]
49230 7F[2]
49407 7F[3]
49448 7F[3]
49454 7F[3]
51218 0F[4]
58196 2F[9]
58271 2F[9]

1960 5B
42946 5MT[2]
42948 5MT[2]
42949 5MT[2]
42950 5MT[2]
42952 5MT[2]
42953 5MT[2]
42955 5MT[2]
42956 5MT[2]
42959 5MT[2]
42961 5MT[2]
42962 5MT[2]
42964 5MT[2]
42972 5MT[2]
42980 5MT[2]
42983 5MT[2]
42984 5MT[2]
43464 3F[3]
44301 4F[2]
44359 4F[2]
44592 4F[2]
44595 4F[2]
44713 5MT[3]
44832 5MT[3]
44834 5MT[3]
44868 5MT[3]
44871 5MT[3]
45000 5MT[3]
45001 5MT[3]
45002 5MT[3]
45045 5MT[3]
45048 5MT[3]
45067 5MT[3]
45074 5MT[3]
45128 5MT[3]
45130 5MT[3]
45131 5MT[3]
45134 5MT[3]
45142 5MT[3]
45149 5MT[3]
45188 5MT[3]
45198 5MT[3]
45270 5MT[3]
45291 5MT[3]
45299 5MT[3]
45300 5MT[3]
45370 5MT[3]
45390 5MT[3]
45391 5MT[3]
45403 5MT[3]
45494 5MT[3]
47280 3F[6]
47330 3F[6]
47384 3F[6]
47391 3F[6]
47414 3F[6]
47450 3F[6]
47467 3F[6]
47516 3F[6]
47523 3F[6]
47524 3F[6]
47526 3F[6]
47608 3F[6]
47618 3F[6]
47661 3F[6]
47664 3F[6]
47670 3F[6]
47680 3F[6]
48174 8F
48248 8F
48255 8F
48256 8F
48257 8F
48262 8F
48292 8F
48294 8F
48297 8F
48516 8F
48548 8F
48626 8F
48630 8F
48633 8F
48655 8F
48659 8F
48692 8F
48693 8F
48734 8F
48743 8F
49130 7F[2]
49158 7F[2]
49407 7F[3]
49439 7F[3]
49454 7F[3]

1963 5B
42983 5MT[2]
42984 5MT[2]
43020 4MT[5]
43022 4MT[5]
43024 4MT[5]
43026 4MT[5]
43034 4MT[5]
43052 4MT[5]
43073 4MT[5]
43113 4MT[5]
44405 4F[2]
44450 4F[2]
44592 4F[2]
44832 5MT[3]
44834 5MT[3]
45000 5MT[3]
45001 5MT[3]
45002 5MT[3]
45004 5MT[3]
45033 5MT[3]
45048 5MT[3]
45067 5MT[3]
45128 5MT[3]
45142 5MT[3]
45248 5MT[3]
45297 5MT[3]
45299 5MT[3]
45300 5MT[3]
45315 5MT[3]
45391 5MT[3]
45403 5MT[3]
45494 5MT[3]
45555 6P5F[2]
45586 6P5F[2]
45634 6P5F[2]
45644 6P5F[2]
47330 3F[6]
47338 3F[6]
47354 3F[6]
47384 3F[6]
47391 3F[6]
47397 3F[6]
47399 3F[6]
47400 3F[6]
47445 3F[6]
47450 3F[6]
47467 3F[6]
47482 3F[6]
47494 3F[6]
47505 3F[6]
47524 3F[6]
47530 3F[6]
47615 3F[6]
47648 3F[6]
47677 3F[6]
47680 3F[6]
48248 8F
48255 8F
48292 8F
48305 8F
48502 8F
48505 8F
48516 8F
48548 8F
48555 8F
48630 8F
48633 8F
48659 8F
48736 8F
48743 8F
48757 8F
49448 7F[3]
49454 7F[3]
78031 2MT[1]
78055 2MT[1]

1966 5B
43001 4MT[5]
43020 4MT[5]
43024 4MT[5]
43026 4MT[5]
43034 4MT[5]
43052 4MT[5]
43088 4MT[5]
43113 4MT[5]
43151 4MT[5]
44680 5MT[3]
44681 5MT[3]
44683 5MT[3]
44684 5MT[3]
44685 5MT[3]
44715 5MT[3]
44759 5MT[3]
44761 5MT[3]
44765 5MT[3]
44829 5MT[3]
44832 5MT[3]
44833 5MT[3]
44834 5MT[3]
44844 5MT[3]
45021 5MT[3]
45033 5MT[3]
45056 5MT[3]
45243 5MT[3]
45248 5MT[3]
45297 5MT[3]
45391 5MT[3]
45393 5MT[3]
45434 5MT[3]
45446 5MT[3]
45494 5MT[3]
47391 3F[6]
47397 3F[6]
47445 3F[6]
47450 3F[6]
47482 3F[6]
47494 3F[6]
47521 3F[6]
47530 3F[6]
47565 3F[6]
47590 3F[6]
47649 3F[6]
48036 8F
48255 8F
48347 8F
48505 8F
48544 8F
48551 8F
48554 8F
48559 8F
48633 8F
48736 8F
70000 7P6F

70012 7P6F
70014 7P6F
70018 7P6F
70023 7P6F
70024 7P6F
70025 7P6F
70027 7P6F
70028 7P6F
78010 2MT[1]
78031 2MT[1]
78034 2MT[1]
78036 2MT[1]

Crewe Works

1948
47592 3F[6]
47862 1F[2]
47865 1F[2]
51412 2F[2]
51446 2F[2]
56032 0F[5]
58321 2F[10]
58323 2F[10]
58326 2F[10]
58328 2F[10]
58332 2F[10]
58336 2F[10]
58343 2F[10]
58347 2F[10]
58870 2F[13]
3323 2F[15]

1951
47592 3F[6]
47862 1F[2]
47865 1F[2]
51412 2F[2]
51444 2F[2]
51446 2F[2]
56032 0F[5]
58321 2F[10]
58323 2F[10]
58326 2F[10]
58328 2F[10]
58332 2F[10]
58336 2F[10]
58343 2F[10]
58347 2F[10]
3323 2F[15]

1954
47592 3F[6]
47862 1F[2]
51412 2F[2]
51444 2F[2]
51446 2F[2]
52093 3F[7]
52207 3F[7]
52212 3F[7]
52218 3F[7]
52345 3F[7]
52441 3F[7]
52459 3F[7]
52464 3F[7]
52517 3F[7]
56032 0F[5]
3323 2F[15]

1957
47592 3F[6]
51412 2F[2]
51444 2F[2]
51446 2F[2]
52093 3F[7]
52207 3F[7]
52212 3F[7]
52218 3F[7]
52312 3F[7]
52345 3F[7]
52441 3F[7]
52459 3F[7]
52464 3F[7]
52517 3F[7]
56032 0F[5]

1960
44363 4F[2]
44373 4F[2]
44374 4F[2]
47592 3F[6]
51412 2F[2]
51444 2F[2]
51446 2F[2]
52093 3F[7]
52218 3F[7]
52312 3F[7]
52441 3F[7]
52459 3F[7]
52464 3F[7]
56027 0F[5]
56032 0F[5]

1963
43957 4F[1]
44363 4F[2]
44373 4F[2]
44374 4F[2]
47380 3F[6]
47592 3F[6]
47597 3F[6]
47618 3F[6]
47658 3F[6]
47661 3F[6]
84021 2MT[2]
84022 2MT[2]
84023 2MT[2]
84024 2MT[2]

1966
44377 4F[2]
44405 4F[2]
44525 4F[2]
47384 3F[6]
47592 3F[6]
47615 3F[6]
47658 3F[6]
47661 3F[6]

Cricklewood

1948 14A
40023 3MT[1]
40025 3MT[1]
40026 3MT[1]
40029 3MT[1]
40030 3MT[1]
40031 3MT[1]
40032 3MT[1]
40033 3MT[1]
40038 3MT[1]
41712 1F[1]
41724 1F[1]
41811 1F[1]
41829 1F[1]
42794 5MT[1]
42855 5MT[1]
43246 3F[3]
43261 3F[3]
43265 3F[3]
43313 3F[3]
43400 3F[3]
43408 3F[3]
43440 3F[3]
43448 3F[3]
43565 3F[3]
43629 3F[3]
43782 3F[4]
43800 3F[4]
43806 3F[4]
43901 4F[1]
43926 4F[1]
43934 4F[1]
43947 4F[1]
44028 4F[2]
44029 4F[2]
44051 4F[2]
44210 4F[2]
44243 4F[2]
44298 4F[2]
44425 4F[2]
44581 4F[2]
44817 5MT[3]
44981 5MT[3]
45264 5MT[3]
45277 5MT[3]
45342 5MT[3]
47200 3F[5]
47201 3F[5]
47203 3F[5]
47204 3F[5]
47205 3F[5]
47206 3F[5]
47207 3F[5]
47208 3F[5]
47209 3F[5]
47210 3F[5]
47211 3F[5]
47212 3F[5]
47213 3F[5]
47214 3F[5]
47215 3F[5]
47216 3F[5]
47217 3F[5]
47218 3F[5]
47219 3F[5]
47220 3F[5]
47221 3F[5]
47222 3F[5]
47223 3F[5]
47224 3F[5]
47225 3F[5]
47226 3F[5]
47227 3F[5]
47228 3F[5]
47240 3F[5]
47243 3F[5]
47248 3F[5]
47250 3F[5]
47251 3F[5]
47433 3F[6]
47434 3F[6]
47435 3F[6]
47447 3F[6]
47548 3F[6]
47621 3F[6]
48410 8F
48414 8F
48415 8F
48533 8F
48541 8F
58065 1P[6]
58069 1P[6]
58070 1P[6]
58161 2F[8]
58200 2F[9]
58235 2F[8]
58260 2F[9]
58274 2F[9]
58296 2F[9]
1385 1P[6]

1951 14A
40023 3MT[1]
40025 3MT[1]
40030 3MT[1]
41207 2MT[1]
41208 2MT[1]
41695 1F[1]
41712 1F[1]
41811 1F[1]
42759 5MT[1]
42771 5MT[1]
42774 5MT[1]
42794 5MT[1]
42839 5MT[1]
42855 5MT[1]
43261 3F[3]
43307 3F[3]
43313 3F[3]
43400 3F[3]
43440 3F[3]
43448 3F[3]
43565 3F[3]
43629 3F[3]
43901 4F[1]
43905 4F[1]
43934 4F[1]
43935 4F[1]
43947 4F[1]
44028 4F[2]
44029 4F[2]
44033 4F[2]
44051 4F[2]
44139 4F[2]
44195 4F[2]
44259 4F[2]
44297 4F[2]
44298 4F[2]
44304 4F[2]
44529 4F[2]
44581 4F[2]
47203 3F[5]
47204 3F[5]
47205 3F[5]
47206 3F[5]
47207 3F[5]
47208 3F[5]
47209 3F[5]
47210 3F[5]
47211 3F[5]
47212 3F[5]
47213 3F[5]
47214 3F[5]
47215 3F[5]
47216 3F[5]
47217 3F[5]
47218 3F[5]
47219 3F[5]
47220 3F[5]
47221 3F[5]
47224 3F[5]
47225 3F[5]
47226 3F[5]
47227 3F[5]
47228 3F[5]
47240 3F[5]
47243 3F[5]
47248 3F[5]
47251 3F[5]
47433 3F[6]
47434 3F[6]
47435 3F[6]
48109 8F
48132 8F
48163 8F
48364 8F
48401 8F
48410 8F
48414 8F
48415 8F
48541 8F
58161 2F[8]
58235 2F[8]
58274 2F[9]
58310 2F[9]
64732 J39
64918 J39
64966 J39

1954 14A
40023 3MT[1]
40025 3MT[1]
41207 2MT[1]
41208 2MT[1]
41712 1F[1]
41826 1F[1]
42759 5MT[1]
42771 5MT[1]
42774 5MT[1]
42794 5MT[1]
42797 5MT[1]
42839 5MT[1]
42855 5MT[1]
43019 4MT[5]
43031 4MT[5]
43118 4MT[5]
43120 4MT[5]
43121 4MT[5]
43261 3F[3]
43307 3F[3]
43313 3F[3]
43440 3F[3]
43448 3F[3]
43901 4F[1]
43905 4F[1]
43934 4F[1]
43935 4F[1]
43947 4F[1]
44029 4F[2]
44051 4F[2]
44228 4F[2]
44259 4F[2]
44297 4F[2]
44529 4F[2]
44530 4F[2]
44581 4F[2]
47203 3F[5]
47206 3F[5]
47207 3F[5]
47208 3F[5]
47209 3F[5]
47210 3F[5]
47211 3F[5]
47212 3F[5]
47213 3F[5]
47214 3F[5]
47215 3F[5]
47216 3F[5]
47217 3F[5]
47218 3F[5]
47219 3F[5]
47220 3F[5]
47221 3F[5]
47224 3F[5]
47226 3F[5]
47240 3F[5]
47248 3F[5]
47251 3F[5]
47433 3F[6]
47434 3F[6]
47435 3F[6]
48062 8F
48109 8F
48132 8F
48163 8F
48219 8F
48410 8F
48414 8F
48415 8F
48541 8F
58234 2F[8]
58235 2F[8]

1957 14A
40023 3MT[1]
40025 3MT[1]
40030 3MT[1]
42759 5MT[1]
42839 5MT[1]
42855 5MT[1]
43019 4MT[5]
43031 4MT[5]
43118 4MT[5]
43120 4MT[5]
43121 4MT[5]
43261 3F[3]
43307 3F[3]
43440 3F[3]
43901 4F[1]
43905 4F[1]
43934 4F[1]
43935 4F[1]
43947 4F[1]
44029 4F[2]
44051 4F[2]
44228 4F[2]
44259 4F[2]
44297 4F[2]
44529 4F[2]
44530 4F[2]
44581 4F[2]
44774 5MT[3]
44777 5MT[3]
45059 5MT[3]
45335 5MT[3]
47203 3F[5]
47206 3F[5]
47207 3F[5]
47210 3F[5]
47211 3F[5]
47213 3F[5]
47214 3F[5]
47216 3F[5]
47217 3F[5]
47219 3F[5]
47224 3F[5]
47226 3F[5]
47240 3F[5]
47248 3F[5]
47251 3F[5]
47433 3F[6]
47434 3F[6]
47435 3F[6]
48062 8F
48109 8F
48132 8F
48163 8F
48180 8F
48381 8F
48414 8F
48750 8F
92108 9F
92110 9F
92111 9F
92112 9F

1960 14A
43019 4MT[5]
43031 4MT[5]
43118 4MT[5]
43120 4MT[5]
43121 4MT[5]
43905 4F[1]
43923 4F[1]
43935 4F[1]
43947 4F[1]
44029 4F[2]
44051 4F[2]
44228 4F[2]
44259 4F[2]
44297 4F[2]
44529 4F[2]
44530 4F[2]
44581 4F[2]
44774 5MT[3]
44777 5MT[3]
44816 5MT[3]
44941 5MT[3]
45059 5MT[3]
45062 5MT[3]
45238 5MT[3]
45274 5MT[3]
45335 5MT[3]
47211 3F[5]
47213 3F[5]
47223 3F[5]
47248 3F[5]
47432 3F[6]
47433 3F[6]
47434 3F[6]
47435 3F[6]
48142 8F
48301 8F
48304 8F
48306 8F
48313 8F
48324 8F
48367 8F
48378 8F
48517 8F
48616 8F
48678 8F

1963 14A
42070 4MT[1]
42086 4MT[1]
42090 4MT[1]
42092 4MT[1]
43964 4F[1]
44210 4F[2]
44259 4F[2]
44294 4F[2]
44381 4F[2]
44529 4F[2]
44531 4F[2]
44532 4F[2]
44572 4F[2]
47202 3F[5]
47223 3F[5]
47432 3F[6]
47434 3F[6]
47435 3F[6]
47437 3F[6]
47543 3F[6]
48367 8F
48517 8F
48627 8F
48678 8F
73157 5MT
73158 5MT
76035 4MT[2]
76036 4MT[2]
76037 4MT[2]
76038 4MT[2]
76039 4MT[2]
76040 4MT[2]
76041 4MT[2]
76042 4MT[2]
76043 4MT[2]
76047 4MT[2]
76048 4MT[2]
76085 4MT[2]
76086 4MT[2]
76088 4MT[2]
76089 4MT[2]

Croes Newydd

1948 CNYD
1401 1400
1411 1400
1416 1400
1428 1400
1457 1400
1532 1501
1706 1854
1747 655
1773 655
1780 655
2183 2181
2184 2181
2188 2181
2190 2181
2227 2251
2259 2251
2287 2251
2704 655
2713 655
2716 655
2717 655
3026 ROD
3028 ROD
3203 2251
3206 2251
4375 4300
5315 4300
5319 4300
5334 4300
5365 4300
5810 5800
5811 5800
6303 4300
6316 4300
6327 4300
6694 5600
6698 5600
7305 4300
7310 4300
7403 7400
7409 7400
7414 7400
7817 7800
9656 5700
90315 WD[1]
90656 WD[1]

1951 84J
1416 1400
1457 1400
1473 1400
1624 1600
2188 2181
2190 2181
2209 2251
2232 2251
2259 2251
2262 2251
2297 2251
2822 2800
2840 2800
2871 2800
2878 2800
3026 ROD
3028 ROD
3203 2251
3206 2251
3825 2884
4375 4300
4617 5700
4645 5700
5315 4300
5319 4300
5334 4300
5365 4300
5742 5700
5774 5700
5810 5800
5811 5800
6303 4300
6311 4300
6316 4300
6327 4300
6404 6400
6405 6400
6422 6400
6694 5600
6698 5600
7305 4300
7310 4300
7313 4300
7403 7400
7409 7400
7414 7400
7431 7400
7432 7400
7433 7400
7440 7400
7443 7400
7447 7400
7817 7800
7825 7800
7826 7800
9669 5700

1954 84J
1410 1400
1416 1400
1635 1600
1646 1600
2186 2181
2840 2800
2853 2800
2871 2800
2878 2800
4617 5700
4645 5700
4683 5700
5315 4300
5319 4300
5742 5700
5774 5700
5810 5800
5811 5800
6303 4300
6311 4300
6316 4300
6404 6400
6405 6400
6611 5600
6617 5600
6632 5600
6694 5600
6696 5600
7305 4300
7310 4300
7313 4300
7403 7400
7409 7400
7414 7400
7431 7400
7433 7400
7440 7400
7442 7400
7443 7400
7447 7400
7817 7800
9028 9000
9669 5700
9793 5700

1957 84J
1465 1400
1635 1600
1646 1600
1660 1600
2209 2251
2296 2251
2840 2800
2871 2800
2878 2800
4617 5700
4645 5700
4683 5700
5319 4300
5416 5400
5742 5700
5774 5700
5810 5800
5811 5800
6303 4300
6311 4300
6316 4300
6339 4300
6404 6400
6405 6400
6611 5600
6617 5600
6632 5600
6694 5600
6696 5600
7310 4300
7313 4300
7403 7400
7409 7400
7414 7400
7431 7400
7433 7400
7440 7400
7442 7400
7443 7400
7817 7800
8791 5700
9028 9000
9669 5700
9793 5700

1960 84J
1659 1600
1660 1600
2855 2800
2871 2800
3201 2251
3689 5700
3815 2884
3828 2884
4617 5700
4645 5700
5774 5700
6307 4300
6316 4300
6339 4300
6357 4300
6611 5600
6615 5600
6617 5600
6632 5600
6674 5600
6694 5600
6696 5600
7310 4300
7313 4300
7341 4300
7403 7400
7409 7400
7414 7400
7428 7400
7431 7400
7433 7400
7440 7400
7442 7400
7443 7400
7817 7800
8727 5700
8791 5700
9004 9000
9014 9000
9669 5700
9793 5700

1963 89B
1628 1600
1632 1600
1660 1600
3209 2251
3749 5700
3789 5700
3815 2884
3846 2884
4645 5700
4683 5700
5330 4300
5679 5600
6604 5600
6611 5600
6615 5600
6625 5600
6632 5600
6674 5600
6694 5600
6698 5600
7230 7200
7310 4300
7339 4300
7414 7400
7418 7400
7431 7400
7442 7400
7443 7400
7803 7800
7811 7800
7812 7800
7821 7800
7828 7800
9608 5700
9610 5700
9669 5700
9793 5700
80079 4MT[3]
80080 4MT[3]
80096 4MT[3]
80098 4MT[3]
80104 4MT[3]

1966 6C
1628 1600
1638 1600
1660 1600
3709 5700
5605 5600
6697 5600
9610 5700
9630 5700
9669 5700
45045 5MT[3]
45130 5MT[3]
45198 5MT[3]
45344 5MT[3]
46508 2MT[2]
48122 8F
48134 8F
48147 8F
48252 8F
48287 8F
48325 8F
48411 8F
48440 8F
48632 8F
48665 8F
48697 8F
73004 5MT
73040 5MT
73095 5MT
75009 4MT[1]
75021 4MT[1]
75071 4MT[1]

Cudworth

1948 CUD
63272 Q5
63311 Q5
63332 Q5
65667 J25
65703 J25
65714 J25
69771 A7
69789 A7

1951 53E
63620 O4
63667 O4
63751 O4
63754 O4
63843 O4
63845 O4
63849 O4
63857 O4
65647 J25
65698 J25
65714 J25

Dalry Road

1948 28B
40911 4P[1]
41177 4P[1]
41178 4P[1]
42268 4MT[1]
42269 4MT[1]
42270 4MT[1]
42271 4MT[1]
42272 4MT[1]
42273 4MT[1]
42804 5MT[1]
42807 5MT[1]
44318 4F[2]
44931 5MT[3]
45029 5MT[3]
47162 2F[1]
47163 2F[1]
48163 8F
48321 8F
54451 3P[5]
54452 3P[5]
54478 3P[6]
54507 3P[6]
54644 4P[3]
55125 2P[12]
55139 2P[12]
55165 2P[13]
55166 2P[13]
55177 2P[13]
55189 2P[13]
55202 2P[13]
55210 2P[13]
55229 2P[13]
55233 2P[13]
56236 3F[10]
56253 3F[10]
56283 3F[10]
56312 3F[10]
56313 3F[10]
56329 3F[10]
57550 3F[12]
57553 3F[12]
57559 3F[12]
57565 3F[12]
57576 3F[12]
57578 3F[12]
57645 3F[13]
57654 3F[14]
57659 3F[14]
57674 3F[14]

1951 64C
40911 4P[1]
41177 4P[1]
41178 4P[1]
42268 4MT[1]
42269 4MT[1]
42270 4MT[1]
42271 4MT[1]
42272 4MT[1]
42273 4MT[1]
42804 5MT[1]
42807 5MT[1]
42830 5MT[1]
45022 5MT[3]
45023 5MT[3]
45029 5MT[3]
45085 5MT[3]
45184 5MT[3]
45362 5MT[3]
47163 2F[1]
54451 3P[5]
54452 3P[5]
54478 3P[6]
55139 2P[12]
55165 2P[13]
55166 2P[13]
55177 2P[13]
55189 2P[13]
55202 2P[13]
55210 2P[13]
55229 2P[13]
55233 2P[13]
56253 3F[10]
56283 3F[10]
56312 3F[10]
56313 3F[10]
57550 3F[12]
57553 3F[12]
57559 3F[12]
57565 3F[12]
57576 3F[12]
57645 3F[13]
57654 3F[14]
64536 J37
64591 J37
65271 J36
69187 N15

1954 64C
41147 4P[1]
41177 4P[1]
42268 4MT[1]
42269 4MT[1]
42270 4MT[1]
42271 4MT[1]
42272 4MT[1]
42273 4MT[1]
42804 5MT[1]
42807 5MT[1]
42830 5MT[1]
44994 5MT[3]
45022 5MT[3]
45023 5MT[3]
45086 5MT[3]
45127 5MT[3]
45161 5MT[3]
45183 5MT[3]
45184 5MT[3]
47163 2F[1]
54451 3P[5]
54452 3P[5]
54478 3P[6]
55165 2P[13]
55177 2P[13]
55202 2P[13]
55210 2P[13]
55229 2P[13]
55233 2P[13]
56253 3F[10]
56283 3F[10]
56312 3F[10]
56313 3F[10]
57550 3F[12]
57559 3F[12]
57565 3F[12]
57576 3F[12]
57645 3F[13]
57654 3F[14]
57679 3F[14]
64495 J35
64500 J35
64536 J37
64591 J37
69187 N15

1957 64C
42268 4MT[1]
42269 4MT[1]
42270 4MT[1]
42271 4MT[1]
42272 4MT[1]
42273 4MT[1]
42695 4MT[1]
42807 5MT[1]
44994 5MT[3]
45022 5MT[3]
45023 5MT[3]
45030 5MT[3]
45036 5MT[3]
45086 5MT[3]
45127 5MT[3]
45161 5MT[3]
45183 5MT[3]
47163 2F[1]
54452 3P[5]
54478 3P[6]
55165 2P[13]
55202 2P[13]
55210 2P[13]
55229 2P[13]
55233 2P[13]
56253 3F[10]
56283 3F[10]
56312 3F[10]
56313 3F[10]
57550 3F[12]
57559 3F[12]
57565 3F[12]
57576 3F[12]
57645 3F[13]
57654 3F[14]
57679 3F[14]
61246 B1
61407 B1
64495 J35
64500 J35
64517 J35
64527 J35
64536 J37
64554 J37
64561 J37
64574 J37
64591 J37
64612 J37
69187 N15

1960 64C
42272 4MT[1]
42273 4MT[1]
42807 5MT[1]
44994 5MT[3]
45022 5MT[3]
45023 5MT[3]
45030 5MT[3]
45036 5MT[3]
45086 5MT[3]
45127 5MT[3]
45155 5MT[3]
45183 5MT[3]
47163 2F[1]
54478 3P[6]
55165 2P[13]
55202 2P[13]
55210 2P[13]
55229 2P[13]
55233 2P[13]
56312 3F[10]
56313 3F[10]
57550 3F[12]
57559 3F[12]
57560 3F[12]
57565 3F[12]
57645 3F[13]
57654 3F[14]
64497 J35
64500 J35
64527 J35
64554 J37
64561 J37
64569 J37
64794 J39
64946 J39
64963 J39
64986 J39
67668 V3

1963 64C
42168 4MT[1]
42273 4MT[1]
44975 5MT[3]
44976 5MT[3]
44994 5MT[3]
45022 5MT[3]
45023 5MT[3]
45053 5MT[3]
45127 5MT[3]
45155 5MT[3]
45170 5MT[3]
45183 5MT[3]
45360 5MT[3]
45367 5MT[3]
45469 5MT[3]
45476 5MT[3]
45477 5MT[3]
45483 5MT[3]
57634 3F[13]
76105 4MT[2]
76106 4MT[2]

Danygraig

1948 DG
60 RR[4]
71 RR[4]
359 LMM[1]
803 LMM[2]
1101 1101
1102 1101
1103 1101
1104 1101
1105 1101
1106 1101
1141 SHT[2]
1142 SHT[3]
1143 SHT[2]
1145 SHT[2]
1146 SHT[5]
1147 SHT[5]
1151 PM[1]
1153 PM[2]
1358 PT[2]
1945 1901
2082 2021
2134 2021
2798 2721
3661 5700
3781 5700
4299 4200
4694 5700
5730 5700
5775 5700
6713 6700
6734 6700
8720 5700

1951 87C
1 YTW
60 RR[4]
359 LMM[1]
803 LMM[2]
1101 1101
1102 1101
1103 1101
1104 1101
1105 1101
1106 1101
1141 SHT[2]
1142 SHT[3]
1143 SHT[2]
1145 SHT[2]
1147 SHT[5]
1151 PM[1]
1153 PM[2]
2055 2021
2082 2021
2134 2021
2151 2021
3781 5700
4299 4200
4666 5700
4694 5700
5730 5700
5775 5700
6713 6700
6734 6700
6762 6700
6763 6700
6766 6700
8408 9400
8720 5700

1954 87C
1 YTW
359 LMM[1]
1101 1101
1102 1101
1103 1101
1104 1101
1105 1101
1106 1101
1142 SHT[3]
1143 SHT[2]
1145 SHT[2]
1151 PM[1]
1634 1600
1640 1600
3781 5700
4299 4200
4666 5700
4694 5700
5703 5700
5730 5700
6713 6700
6762 6700
6763 6700
6766 6700
8408 9400
8475 9400
8476 9400
8483 9400
8720 5700
9485 9400

1957 87C
1101 1101
1102 1101
1103 1101
1104 1101
1105 1101
1106 1101
1142 SHT[3]
1143 SHT[2]
1145 SHT[2]
1151 PM[1]
1634 1600
1640 1600
1647 1600
1648 1600
3633 5700
3679 5700
3781 5700
4299 4200
4666 5700
4694 5700
5704 5700
5730 5700
5731 5700
5743 5700
6719 6700
6762 6700
6766 6700
8720 5700
8724 5700
9606 5700
9744 5700

1960 87C
1102 1101
1103 1101
1104 1101
1105 1101
1106 1101
1634 1600
1640 1600
1647 1600
1648 1600
5704 5700
5731 6700
6360 4300
6719 6700
7439 7400
7793 5700
9744 5700

Darlington

1948 DAR
60864 V2
60963 V2
61037 B1
61038 B1
61039 B1
61173 B1
61176 B1
61273 B1
61699 B13
62978 C7
62981 C7
63255 Q5
63277 Q5
63278 Q5
63307 Q5
63328 Q5
63330 Q5
63334 Q5
63335 Q5
64710 J39
64756 J39
64778 J39
64791 J39
64812 J39
64819 J39
64821 J39
64847 J39
64848 J39
64850 J39
64851 J39
64858 J39
64862 J39
64863 J39
64864 J39
64865 J39
64869 J39
64870 J39
64897 J39
64916 J39
64919 J39
64921 J39
64925 J39
64928 J39
64929 J39
64931 J39
64933 J39
64936 J39
64938 J39
64939 J39
64940 J39
64942 J39
64943 J39
64945 J39
64949 J39
64978 J39
64982 J39
65031 J21
65033 J21
65038 J21
65078 J21
65088 J21
65090 J21
65091 J21
65098 J21
65110 J21
65119 J21
65646 J25
65648 J25
65650 J25
65653 J25
65664 J25
65668 J25
65672 J25
65688 J25
65691 J25
65692 J25
65695 J25
65708 J25
67250 G5
67342 G5
68008 J94
68025 J94
68027 J94
68047 J94
68048 J94
68049 J94
68050 J94
68051 J94
68052 J94
68061 J94
68235 J71
68236 J71
68239 J71
68259 J71
68279 J71
68281 J71
68300 J71
68308 J71
68391 J77
68408 J77
68410 J77
68417 J77
68421 J77
68425 J77
68688 J72
68738 J72
69415 N9
69418 N9
69426 N9
69830 A5
69831 A5
69832 A5
69833 A5
69834 A5
69835 A5
69836 A5
69837 A5
69838 A5
69839 A5
69840 A5
69841 A5
69842 A5

1951 51A
43055 4MT^5
43056 4MT^5
43057 4MT^5
43071 4MT^5
43072 4MT^5
43073 4MT^5
43074 4MT^5
43075 4MT^5
60070 A3
60076 A3
61021 B1
61022 B1
61023 B1
61039 B1
61173 B1
61176 B1
61198 B1
61224 B1
61255 B1
61273 B1
61274 B1
61275 B1
61276 B1
61289 B1
61291 B1
62004 K1
62006 K1
62008 K1
62009 K1
62044 K1
62045 K1
62046 K1
62047 K1
62056 K1
62057 K1
62058 K1
62059 K1
62061 K1
62062 K1
64817 J39
64940 J39
64982 J39
65033 J21
65038 J21
65068 J21
65090 J21
65098 J21
65110 J21
65119 J21
65648 J25
65650 J25
65664 J25
65672 J25
65677 J25
65688 J25
65691 J25
65692 J25
65702 J25
65720 J25
67273 G5
67284 G5
67316 G5
67333 G5
67342 G5
67742 L1
67750 L1
67754 L1
67777 L1
68008 J94
68015 J94
68025 J94
68027 J94
68039 J94
68043 J94
68045 J94
68047 J94
68050 J94
68051 J94
68052 J94
68231 J71
68235 J71
68236 J71
68239 J71
68259 J71
68279 J71
68281 J71
68300 J71
68308 J71
68408 J77
68410 J77
68423 J77
68432 J77
68679 J72
68707 J72
69004 J72
69426 N9
69830 A5
69832 A5
69833 A5
69835 A5
69836 A5
69837 A5
69838 A5
69839 A5
69840 A5
69841 A5
90061 WD^1
90078 WD^1
90423 WD^1
90449 WD^1
90467 WD^1

1954 51A
42083 4MT^1
42084 4MT^1
42085 4MT^1
43056 4MT^5
43057 4MT^5
43071 4MT^5
43075 4MT^5
46472 2MT^2
46475 2MT^2
60040 A3
60070 A3
61021 B1
61023 B1
61024 B1
61039 B1
61040 B1
61049 B1
61061 B1
61198 B1
61255 B1
61273 B1
61274 B1
61276 B1
61289 B1
61291 B1
61353 B1
62001 K1
62003 K1
62004 K1
62005 K1
62006 K1
62007 K1
62008 K1
62009 K1
62045 K1
62046 K1
62047 K1
62049 K1
62062 K1
62063 K1
65068 J21
65070 J21
65089 J21
65098 J21
65103 J21
65117 J21
65645 J25
65688 J25
65692 J25
65702 J25
65708 J25
65710 J25
65712 J25
67284 G5
67305 G5
67314 G5
67345 G5
67742 L1
67750 L1
67754 L1
67777 L1
68008 J94
68015 J94
68025 J94
68027 J94
68039 J94
68043 J94
68045 J94
68047 J94
68050 J94
68052 J94
68142 Y1
68182 Y3
68235 J71
68236 J71
68239 J71
68259 J71
68279 J71
68300 J71
68308 J71
68408 J77
68410 J77
68423 J77
68432 J77
68679 J72
68748 J72
69004 J72
69021 J72
69022 J72
69830 A5
69832 A5
69833 A5
69835 A5
69838 A5
69839 A5
69840 A5
69841 A5
69842 A5
76020 4MT^2

1957 51A
43050 4MT^5
43124 4MT^5
43130 4MT^5
46473 2MT^2
46474 2MT^2
46475 2MT^2
46476 2MT^2
46477 2MT^2
46478 2MT^2
46479 2MT^2
60038 A3
60042 A3
61015 B1
61020 B1
61021 B1
61023 B1
61024 B1
61039 B1
61040 B1
61049 B1
61061 B1
61176 B1
61198 B1
61224 B1
61255 B1
61273 B1
61274 B1
61276 B1
61289 B1
61291 B1
61338 B1
61353 B1
62001 K1
62003 K1
62004 K1
62005 K1
62007 K1
62008 K1
62009 K1
62045 K1
65064 J21
65860 J27
67305 G5
67742 L1
67750 L1
67777 L1
68007 J94
68008 J94
68015 J94
68025 J94
68027 J94
68037 J94
68039 J94
68043 J94
68045 J94
68047 J94
68050 J94
68052 J94
68235 J71
68279 J71
68308 J71
68410 J77
68425 J77
68679 J72
68748 J72
68754 J72
69004 J72
69021 J72
69022 J72
69830 A5
69831 A5
69832 A5
69833 A5
69834 A5
69839 A5
69840 A5
69841 A5
69871 A8
69887 A8
82028 3MT^2
82029 3MT^2
90021 WD^1
90047 WD^1
90056 WD^1
90200 WD^1
90210 WD^1

1960 51A
43050 4MT^5
43099 4MT^5
43129 4MT^5
46473 2MT^2
46474 2MT^2
46475 2MT^2
46477 2MT^2
46479 2MT^2
60040 A3
60071 A3
60848 V2
61018 B1
61021 B1
61024 B1
61030 B1
61032 B1
61176 B1
61224 B1
61321 B1
61338 B1
61353 B1
61382 B1
62004 K1
62007 K1
62008 K1
62041 K1
62043 K1
62045 K1
62048 K1
62058 K1
62059 K1
62062 K1
62064 K1
63395 Q6
63423 Q6
65860 J27
67742 L1
67750 L1
67755 L1
67763 L1
67765 L1
67777 L1
68007 J94
68008 J94
68015 J94
68017 J94
68024 J94
68025 J94
68027 J94
68032 J94
68037 J94
68039 J94
68040 J94
68043 J94
68045 J94
68047 J94
68050 J94
68052 J94
68679 J72
68716 J72
68744 J72
68754 J72
69004 J72
69017 J72
69021 J72
69022 J72
90011 WD^1
90057 WD^1
90082 WD^1
90155 WD^1
90172 WD^1
90430 WD^1

1963 51A
42085 4MT^1
42405 4MT^2
42477 4MT^3
42639 4MT^3
43050 4MT^5
43056 4MT^5
43099 4MT^5
43102 4MT^5
43129 4MT^5
46482 2MT^2
60045 A3
60052 A3
60808 V2
60809 V2
60916 V2
61032 B1
61037 B1
61176 B1
61224 B1
61304 B1
61321 B1
61338 B1
61353 B1
61382 B1
62004 K1
62007 K1
62008 K1
62041 K1
62043 K1
62045 K1
62048 K1
62058 K1
62059 K1
62062 K1
62064 K1
63395 Q6
63423 Q6
67682 V3
68010 J94
68014 J94
68024 J94
68025 J94
68035 J94
68037 J94
68040 J94
68043 J94
68046 J94
68047 J94
68050 J94
68060 J94
68071 J94
69006 J72
69020 J72
77002 3MT^1
78024 2MT^1
90011 WD^1
90014 WD^1
90082 WD^1
90155 WD^1
90172 WD^1
90309 WD^1
90373 WD^1
90430 WD^1
90445 WD^1

1966 51A
42161 4MT^1
43050 4MT^5
43055 4MT^5
43056 4MT^5
43129 4MT^5
60124 A1
60806 V2
62001 K1
62008 K1
62041 K1
62044 K1
62045 K1
62048 K1
62059 K1
65859 J27
90011 WD^1
90014 WD^1
90309 WD^1

Darlington PW Depot

1948
68153 Y1

1951
68153 Y1

1954
68153 Y1

1957
54 Y1

1960
54 Y1

Dawsholm

1948 31E
40176 3MT^2
40177 3MT^2
40185 3MT^2
40186 3MT^2
40187 3MT^2
40188 3MT^2
40189 3MT^2
48153 8F
48155 8F
55129 2P^{12}
55136 2P^{12}
55145 2P^{12}
55168 2P^{13}
55174 2P^{13}
55240 2P^{14}
56026 0F^5
56030 0F^5
56038 0F^5
56039 0F^5
56154 2F^4
56158 2F^4
56161 2F^4
56168 2F^4
56169 2F^4
56170 2F^4
56171 2F^4
56238 3F^{10}
56250 3F^{10}
56297 3F^{10}
56302 3F^{10}
56315 3F^{10}
56339 3F^{10}
56344 3F^{10}
57245 2F^5
57258 2F^5
57259 2F^5
57296 2F^5
57306 2F^5
57314 2F^5
57322 2F^5
57336 2F^5
57341 2F^5
57346 2F^5
57366 2F^5
57371 2F^5
57372 2F^5
57426 2F^5
57427 2F^5
57429 2F^5
57452 2F^5
57456 2F^5
57469 2F^5
57470 2F^5
57471 2F^5
57472 2F^5
57607 3F^{12}
57612 3F^{12}
57652 3F^{14}

1951 65D
40152 3MT^2
40153 3MT^2
40154 3MT^2
40158 3MT^2
40176 3MT^2
40177 3MT^2
40185 3MT^2
40186 3MT^2
40187 3MT^2
40188 3MT^2
40189 3MT^2
43883 4F^1
55168 2P^{13}
56029 0F^5
56169 2F^4
56171 2F^4
56302 3F^{10}
56344 3F^{10}
57245 2F^5
57258 2F^5
57273 2F^5
57296 2F^5
57306 2F^5
57314 2F^5
57322 2F^5
57336 2F^5
57341 2F^5
57346 2F^5
57372 2F^5
57373 2F^5
57394 2F^5
57426 2F^5
57429 2F^5
57456 2F^5
57470 2F^5
57472 2F^5
57592 3F^{12}
57605 3F^{12}
57607 3F^{12}
57612 3F^{12}
57652 3F^{14}
68333 J88
69163 N15
69176 N15
69177 N15
69184 N15
69203 N15
69205 N15
69208 N15
90440 WD^1
90549 WD^1

1954 65D
40152 3MT^2
40153 3MT^2
40154 3MT^2
40158 3MT^2
40176 3MT^2
40177 3MT^2
40186 3MT^2
40187 3MT^2
40188 3MT^2
40189 3MT^2
56029 0F^5
56171 2F^4
56302 3F^{10}
56344 3F^{10}
57245 2F^5
57273 2F^5
57296 2F^5
57314 2F^5
57336 2F^5
57341 2F^5
57346 2F^5
57429 2F^5
57456 2F^5
57470 2F^5
57472 2F^5
57554 3F^{12}
57592 3F^{12}
57605 3F^{12}
57607 3F^{12}
57612 3F^{12}
57652 3F^{14}
68333 J88
68511 J67
69163 N15
69176 N15
69177 N15
69184 N15
69203 N15
69205 N15
69208 N15
69509 N2
69511 N2
69553 N2
90114 WD^1
90193 WD^1
90436 WD^1
90440 WD^1
90493 WD^1
90549 WD^1

1957 65D
40152 3MT^2
40153 3MT^2
40154 3MT^2
40158 3MT^2
40159 3MT^2
40176 3MT^2
40177 3MT^2
40186 3MT^2
40187 3MT^2
40188 3MT^2
40189 3MT^2
40200 3MT^2
56029 0F^5
56167 2F^4
56171 2F^4
56275 3F^{10}
56300 3F^{10}
56302 3F^{10}
56344 3F^{10}
57245 2F^5
57273 2F^5
57296 2F^5
57314 2F^5
57336 2F^5
57341 2F^5
57346 2F^5
57429 2F^5
57470 2F^5
57472 2F^5
57554 3F^{12}
57592 3F^{12}
57605 3F^{12}
57607 3F^{12}
57612 3F^{12}
57652 3F^{14}
64520 J35
68333 J88
69176 N15
69177 N15
69184 N15
69203 N15
69205 N15
69208 N15
69509 N2
69511 N2
69553 N2
90114 WD^1
90193 WD^1
90436 WD^1
90440 WD^1
90493 WD^1
90549 WD^1

1960 65D
40152 3MT^2
40153 3MT^2
40154 3MT^2
40158 3MT^2
40159 3MT^2
40176 3MT^2
40177 3MT^2
40186 3MT^2
40187 3MT^2
40188 3MT^2
40189 3MT^2
40200 3MT^2
42131 4MT^1
42195 4MT^1
42197 4MT^1
42201 4MT^1
42694 4MT^1
56171 2F^4
56336 3F^{10}
57245 2F^5
57273 2F^5
57296 2F^5
57314 2F^5
57341 2F^5
57429 2F^5
57470 2F^5
57472 2F^5
57554 3F^{12}
57592 3F^{12}
57607 3F^{12}
57652 3F^{14}
68344 J88
69126 N15
69177 N15
69184 N15
69205 N15
69511 N2
76100 4MT^2
76101 4MT^2
90114 WD^1
90193 WD^1
90436 WD^1
90440 WD^1
90493 WD^1
103 Jones Goods
123 CR Single

1963 65D
42131 4MT^1
42195 4MT^1
42197 4MT^1
42199 4MT^1
42201 4MT^1
42694 4MT^1
43135 4MT^5
43136 4MT^5
43140 4MT^5
57592 3F^{12}
57607 3F^{12}
57652 3F^{14}
76100 4MT^2
76101 4MT^2
76102 4MT^2
90114 WD^1
90489 WD^1
49 D40
103 Jones Goods
123 CR Single

Derby

1948 17A
40325 2P^1
40383 2P^2
40404 2P^2
40407 2P^2
40411 2P^2
40416 2P^2
40418 2P^2
40426 2P^2
40482 2P^2
40513 2P^2
40516 2P^2
40632 2P^3
40711 3P^1
40734 3P^1
40735 3P^1
40756 3P^1
40930 4P^1
41000 4P^2
41003 4P^2
41033 4P^2
41036 4P^2
41055 4P^1
41057 4P^1
41059 4P^1
41060 4P^1
41083 4P^1
41084 4P^1
41535 0F^2
41695 1F^1
41726 1F^1
41754 1F^1
41773 1F^1
41779 1F^1
41788 1F^1
41795 1F^1
41833 1F^1
41847 1F^1
42340 4MT^2
42341 4MT^2
42847 5MT^1
42872 5MT^1
42897 5MT^1
43191 3F^3
43200 3F^3
43273 3F^3
43308 3F^3
43312 3F^3
43315 3F^3
43318 3F^3
43323 3F^3
43324 3F^3
43364 3F^3
43368 3F^3
43370 3F^3
43402 3F^3
43406 3F^3
43459 3F^3
43469 3F^3
43482 3F^3
43496 3F^3
43510 3F^3
43548 3F^3
43550 3F^3
43572 3F^3
43574 3F^3
43578 3F^3
43584 3F^3
43598 3F^3
43658 3F^3
43735 3F^3
43745 3F^3
43759 3F^3
43763 3F^3
43776 3F^4
43838 4F^1
43839 4F^1
43840 4F^1
43881 4F^1
43955 4F^1
44023 4F^1
44031 4F^2
44101 4F^2
44142 4F^2
44177 4F^2
44195 4F^2
44214 4F^2
44263 4F^2
44402 4F^2
44409 4F^2
44419 4F^2
44420 4F^2
44430 4F^2
44432 4F^2
44542 4F^2
44565 4F^2
44566 4F^2
44601 4F^2
44602 4F^2
44605 4F^2
44809 5MT^3
44815 5MT^3
44818 5MT^3
44819 5MT^3
44839 5MT^3
44851 5MT^3
44962 5MT^3
45088 5MT^3
45261 5MT^3
45285 5MT^3
45585 6P5F^2
45602 6P5F^2
45610 6P5F^2
45639 6P5F^2
45656 6P5F^2
47417 3F^6
48157 8F
48322 8F
48390 8F
48404 8F
48432 8F
48640 8F
48647 8F
48654 8F
48677 8F
58035 1P^5
58077 1P^6
58090 1P^6
58125 2F^8
58132 2F^8
58144 2F^8
58145 2F^8
58148 2F^8
58158 2F^8
58188 2F^9
58216 2F^9
58227 2F^9
58230 2F^8
58246 2F^8
58253 2F^9

1951 17A
40383 2P^2
40404 2P^2
40407 2P^2
40411 2P^2
40416 2P^2
40418 2P^2
40426 2P^2
40513 2P^2
40632 2P^3
40927 4P^1
40934 4P^1
41000 4P^2
41003 4P^2
41014 4P^2
41023 4P^2
41043 4P^2
41057 4P^1
41059 4P^1
41060 4P^1
41084 4P^1
41088 4P^1
41247 2MT^1
41535 0F^2
41726 1F^1
41747 1F^1
41754 1F^1
41773 1F^1
41779 1F^1
41795 1F^1
41833 1F^1
41847 1F^1
41889 1F^1
41903 2P^4
42174 4MT^1
42340 4MT^2
42341 4MT^2
42847 5MT^1
42872 5MT^1
42897 5MT^1
43010 4MT^5
43031 4MT^5
43049 4MT^5
43137 3F^2
43185 3F^2
43191 3F^3
43200 3F^3
43226 3F^3
43259 3F^3
43312 3F^3
43315 3F^3
43318 3F^3
43323 3F^3
43324 3F^3
43361 3F^3
43364 3F^3
43368 3F^3
43402 3F^3
43406 3F^3
43459 3F^3
43469 3F^3
43482 3F^3
43496 3F^3
43510 3F^3
43548 3F^3
43550 3F^3
43572 3F^3
43574 3F^3
43578 3F^3
43584 3F^3
43598 3F^3
43658 3F^3
43735 3F^3
43745 3F^3
43763 3F^3
43776 3F^4
43838 4F^1
43839 4F^1
43840 4F^1
43847 4F^1
43859 4F^1
43862 4F^1
43955 4F^1
44031 4F^2
44101 4F^2
44142 4F^2
44164 4F^2
44177 4F^2
44214 4F^2
44402 4F^2
44409 4F^2
44419 4F^2
44420 4F^2
44432 4F^2
44542 4F^2
44555 4F^2
44565 4F^2
44566 4F^2
44601 4F^2
44602 4F^2
44667 5MT^3
44776 5MT^3
44809 5MT^3
44815 5MT^3
44818 5MT^3
44819 5MT^3
44820 5MT^3
44847 5MT^3
44848 5MT^3
44851 5MT^3
44917 5MT^3
45585 6P5F^2
45610 6P5F^2
45639 6P5F^2
45656 6P5F^2
45667 6P5F^2
45696 6P5F^2
46443 2MT^2
46444 2MT^2
46454 2MT^2
47250 3F^5
47417 3F^6
47660 3F^6
48079 8F
48121 8F
48153 8F
48302 8F
48390 8F
48404 8F
48432 8F
48640 8F
48647 8F
48654 8F
48677 8F
51235 0F^4
58058 1P^6
58110 2F^6
58125 2F^8
58132 2F^8
58144 2F^8
58148 2F^8
58203 2F^9
58216 2F^9
58246 2F^8

1954 17A
40326 2P^1
40404 2P^2
40407 2P^2
40416 2P^2
40418 2P^2
40513 2P^2
40927 4P^1
41069 4P^1
41084 4P^1
41088 4P^1
41143 4P^1
41192 4P^1
41247 2MT^1
41535 0F^2
41726 1F^1
41747 1F^1
41754 1F^1
41773 1F^1
41795 1F^1
41847 1F^1
41889 1F^1
42160 4MT^1
42174 4MT^1
42181 4MT^1
42336 4MT^2
42340 4MT^2
42342 4MT^2
42847 5MT^1
42872 5MT^1
42897 5MT^1
43010 4MT^5
43027 4MT^5
43049 4MT^5
43185 3F^2
43191 3F^3
43200 3F^3
43226 3F^3
43259 3F^3
43315 3F^3
43318 3F^3
43323 3F^3
43324 3F^3
43361 3F^3
43368 3F^3
43379 3F^3
43402 3F^3
43459 3F^3
43469 3F^3
43482 3F^3
43510 3F^3
43548 3F^3
43550 3F^3
43572 3F^3
43578 3F^3
43584 3F^3
43598 3F^3
43735 3F^3
43745 3F^3
43750 3F^2
43763 3F^3
43838 4F^1
43839 4F^1
43840 4F^1
43847 4F^1
43859 4F^1
43925 4F^1
43955 4F^1
43991 4F^1
44031 4F^2
44112 4F^2
44142 4F^2
44177 4F^2
44214 4F^2
44295 4F^2
44304 4F^2
44369 4F^2
44378 4F^2
44380 4F^2
44402 4F^2
44409 4F^2
44419 4F^2
44420 4F^2
44428 4F^2
44540 4F^2
44542 4F^2
44545 4F^2
44555 4F^2
44601 4F^2
44602 4F^2
44667 5MT^3
44809 5MT^3
44815 5MT^3
44818 5MT^3
44819 5MT^3
44839 5MT^3
44847 5MT^3
44856 5MT^3
44945 5MT^3
44963 5MT^3
44965 5MT^3
45186 5MT^3
45264 5MT^3
45272 5MT^3
45297 5MT^3
45509 6P5F^1
45570 6P5F^2
45585 6P5F^2
45610 6P5F^2
45626 6P5F^2
46443 2MT^2
46454 2MT^2
47250 3F^5
47417 3F^6
47629 3F^6
47660 3F^6
48011 8F
48079 8F
48121 8F
48153 8F
48302 8F
48390 8F
48432 8F
48510 8F
48654 8F
51217 0F^4
51235 0F^4
58132 2F^8
58144 2F^8
58148 2F^8
58216 2F^9
58219 2F^9
58246 2F^8
73001 5MT
73030 5MT
73031 5MT

1957 17A
40404 2P^2
40407 2P^2
40416 2P^2
40418 2P^2
40513 2P^2
40682 2P^3
40927 4P^1
41083 4P^1
41103 4P^1
41192 4P^1
41534 0F^2
41535 0F^2
41710 1F^1
41724 1F^1
41726 1F^1
41754 1F^1
41773 1F^1
41847 1F^1
42050 4MT^1
42146 4MT^1

42174 4MT[1]
42181 4MT[1]
42184 4MT[1]
42228 4MT[1]
42847 5MT[1]
42872 5MT[1]
42897 5MT[1]
43027 4MT[5]
43041 4MT[5]
43185 3F[2]
43200 3F[3]
43259 3F[3]
43292 3F[3]
43294 3F[3]
43312 3F[3]
43315 3F[3]
43318 3F[3]
43324 3F[3]
43368 3F[3]
43379 3F[3]
43402 3F[3]
43459 3F[3]
43510 3F[3]
43548 3F[3]
43572 3F[3]
43578 3F[3]
43584 3F[3]
43658 3F[3]
43735 3F[3]
43763 3F[3]
43840 4F[1]
43847 4F[1]
43855 4F[1]
43879 4F[1]
43881 4F[1]
43925 4F[1]
43955 4F[1]
43969 4F[1]
43991 4F[1]
44017 4F[1]
44020 4F[1]
44031 4F[2]
44042 4F[2]
44048 4F[2]
44049 4F[2]
44112 4F[2]
44142 4F[2]
44164 4F[2]
44169 4F[2]
44176 4F[2]
44177 4F[2]
44214 4F[2]
44295 4F[2]
44304 4F[2]
44334 4F[2]
44369 4F[2]
44378 4F[2]
44380 4F[2]
44402 4F[2]
44409 4F[2]
44419 4F[2]
44420 4F[2]
44425 4F[2]
44428 4F[2]
44501 4F[2]
44540 4F[2]
44545 4F[2]
44589 4F[2]
44601 4F[2]
44667 5MT[3]
44809 5MT[3]
44815 5MT[3]
44818 5MT[3]
44819 5MT[3]
44839 5MT[3]
44848 5MT[3]
44851 5MT[3]
44856 5MT[3]
45260 5MT[3]
45263 5MT[3]
45509 6P5F[1]
45570 6P5F[2]
45585 6P5F[2]
45602 6P5F[2]
45610 6P5F[2]
45626 6P5F[2]
46443 2MT[2]
46454 2MT[2]
47250 3F[5]
47563 3F[6]
47629 3F[6]
47660 3F[6]
48005 8F
48079 8F
48083 8F
48121 8F
48153 8F
48168 8F
48293 8F
48302 8F
48390 8F
48403 8F
48510 8F
51217 0F[4]
58132 2F[8]
58144 2F[8]
58158 2F[8]
58219 2F[9]
58246 2F[8]
73015 5MT
73030 5MT
73031 5MT
73054 5MT
73068 5MT

1960 17A
41157 4P[1]
41773 1F[1]
41847 1F[1]
42146 4MT[1]
42174 4MT[1]
42184 4MT[1]
42352 4MT[2]
43200 3F[3]
43306 3F[3]
43368 3F[3]
43435 3F[3]
43459 3F[3]
43510 3F[3]
43548 3F[3]
43658 3F[3]
43735 3F[3]
43778 3F[4]
43925 4F[1]
43955 4F[1]
43991 4F[1]
44020 4F[1]
44031 4F[2]
44048 4F[2]
44049 4F[2]
44112 4F[2]
44164 4F[2]
44169 4F[2]
44176 4F[2]
44214 4F[2]
44334 4F[2]
44419 4F[2]
44420 4F[2]
44425 4F[2]
44428 4F[2]
44465 4F[2]
44540 4F[2]
44545 4F[2]
44851 5MT[3]
45557 6P5F[2]
45559 6P5F[2]
45598 6P5F[2]
45610 6P5F[2]
45612 6P5F[2]
45618 6P5F[2]
45626 6P5F[2]
45627 6P5F[2]
45648 6P5F[2]
45649 6P5F[2]
45668 6P5F[2]
46402 2MT[2]
46440 2MT[2]
46443 2MT[2]
46497 2MT[2]
46499 2MT[2]
46500 2MT[2]
46502 2MT[2]
47000 0F[3]
47006 0F[3]
47429 3F[6]
47563 3F[6]
47629 3F[6]
47660 3F[6]
48002 8F
48005 8F
48079 8F
48083 8F
48121 8F
48124 8F
48153 8F
48168 8F
48198 8F
48270 8F
48293 8F
48302 8F
48390 8F
48403 8F
48510 8F
58144 2F[8]
58158 2F[8]
58219 2F[9]
73137 5MT
73157 5MT
73158 5MT
73159 5MT
1000 4P[2]

1963 17A
42181 4MT[1]
42335 4MT[2]
42339 4MT[2]
43620 3F[3]
43637 3F[3]
43658 3F[3]
43669 3F[3]
43855 4F[1]
43955 4F[1]
44023 4F[1]
44049 4F[2]
44176 4F[2]
44214 4F[2]
44241 4F[2]
44333 4F[2]
44420 4F[2]
44454 4F[2]
44517 4F[2]
44545 4F[2]
44664 5MT[3]
44776 5MT[3]
44777 5MT[3]
44819 5MT[3]
45253 5MT[3]
45262 5MT[3]
45274 5MT[3]
45346 5MT[3]
46402 2MT[2]
46440 2MT[2]
46495 2MT[2]
46497 2MT[2]
46499 2MT[2]
46500 2MT[2]
46502 2MT[2]
47000 0F[3]
47006 0F[3]
47236 3F[5]
47325 3F[6]
47441 3F[6]
47534 3F[6]
48060 8F
48083 8F
48121 8F
48124 8F
48153 8F
48198 8F
48270 8F
48510 8F
48530 8F
48636 8F
75040 4MT[1]
75041 4MT[1]
75042 4MT[1]
75043 4MT[1]
75044 4MT[1]
75055 4MT[1]
75056 4MT[1]
75057 4MT[1]
75058 4MT[1]
75059 4MT[1]
75060 4MT[1]
75061 4MT[1]
75062 4MT[1]
75063 4MT[1]
75064 4MT[1]

1966 16C
44690 5MT[3]
44858 5MT[3]
44932 5MT[3]
45224 5MT[3]
45262 5MT[3]
45289 5MT[3]
47000 0F[3]
47006 0F[3]
48083 8F
48103 8F
48153 8F
48270 8F
48350 8F
48359 8F
48370 8F
48604 8F
48666 8F
78020 2MT[1]
78064 2MT[1]
92068 9F
92096 9F

Derby Works

1948
41509 0F[1]

Devons Road

1948 13B
47302 3F[6]
47304 3F[6]
47306 3F[6]
47307 3F[6]
47310 3F[6]
47312 3F[6]
47314 3F[6]
47315 3F[6]
47348 3F[6]
47349 3F[6]
47350 3F[6]
47411 3F[6]
47482 3F[6]
47483 3F[6]
47486 3F[6]
47487 3F[6]
47488 3F[6]
47489 3F[6]
47490 3F[6]
47491 3F[6]
47492 3F[6]
47493 3F[6]
47494 3F[6]
47495 3F[6]
47497 3F[6]
47498 3F[6]
47499 3F[6]
47500 3F[6]
47501 3F[6]
47502 3F[6]
47505 3F[6]
47506 3F[6]
47511 3F[6]
47514 3F[6]
47515 3F[6]
47516 3F[6]
47517 3F[6]
47518 3F[6]
47558 3F[6]
47559 3F[6]
47560 3F[6]
47561 3F[6]
47562 3F[6]
47563 3F[6]
47564 3F[6]
58851 2F[12]
58852 2F[12]
58853 2F[12]
58855 2F[12]
58858 2F[12]
58860 2F[12]
58865 Crane

1951 1D
44348 4F[2]
44370 4F[2]
47302 3F[6]
47304 3F[6]
47306 3F[6]
47307 3F[6]
47310 3F[6]
47312 3F[6]
47314 3F[6]
47315 3F[6]
47348 3F[6]
47349 3F[6]
47350 3F[6]
47411 3F[6]
47482 3F[6]
47483 3F[6]
47486 3F[6]
47487 3F[6]
47488 3F[6]
47489 3F[6]
47490 3F[6]
47492 3F[6]
47493 3F[6]
47494 3F[6]
47495 3F[6]
47497 3F[6]
47498 3F[6]
47499 3F[6]
47500 3F[6]
47501 3F[6]
47506 3F[6]
47511 3F[6]
47514 3F[6]
47515 3F[6]
47516 3F[6]
47517 3F[6]
47518 3F[6]
47558 3F[6]
47559 3F[6]
47560 3F[6]
47561 3F[6]
47564 3F[6]
58852 2F[12]
58853 2F[12]
58855 2F[12]
58858 2F[12]
58859 2F[12]
58865 Crane

1954 1D
43000 4MT[5]
43001 4MT[5]
43020 4MT[5]
43021 4MT[5]
43022 4MT[5]
43024 4MT[5]
44348 4F[2]
44441 4F[2]
47302 3F[6]
47304 3F[6]
47307 3F[6]
47310 3F[6]
47314 3F[6]
47315 3F[6]
47348 3F[6]
47349 3F[6]
47482 3F[6]
47483 3F[6]
47486 3F[6]
47488 3F[6]
47493 3F[6]
47494 3F[6]
47495 3F[6]
47497 3F[6]
47499 3F[6]
47500 3F[6]
47501 3F[6]
47506 3F[6]
47511 3F[6]
47514 3F[6]
47515 3F[6]
47517 3F[6]
47518 3F[6]
47558 3F[6]
47559 3F[6]
47560 3F[6]
47561 3F[6]
47564 3F[6]
58851 2F[12]
58852 2F[12]
58853 2F[12]
58854 2F[12]
58855 2F[12]
58857 2F[12]
58859 2F[12]

1957 1D
43000 4MT[5]
43001 4MT[5]
43020 4MT[5]
43021 4MT[5]
43022 4MT[5]
43024 4MT[5]
44348 4F[2]
44381 4F[2]
44441 4F[2]
47007 0F[3]
47164 2F[1]
47302 3F[6]
47304 3F[6]
47307 3F[6]
47310 3F[6]
47314 3F[6]
47315 3F[6]
47348 3F[6]
47349 3F[6]
47482 3F[6]
47483 3F[6]
47486 3F[6]
47488 3F[6]
47494 3F[6]
47495 3F[6]
47497 3F[6]
47499 3F[6]
47501 3F[6]
47511 3F[6]
47514 3F[6]
47515 3F[6]
47517 3F[6]
47518 3F[6]
47558 3F[6]
47559 3F[6]
47560 3F[6]
47561 3F[6]
47564 3F[6]
58857 2F[12]
58859 2F[12]

Didcot

1948 DID
907 1854
1334 MSWJ
1861 1854
2202 2251
2221 2251
2222 2251
2226 2251
2240 2251
2252 2251
2289 2251
2532 2301
3210 2251
3211 2251
3212 2251
3376 3300
3396 3300
3408 3300
3419 3300
3448 3300
3622 5700
3709 5700
3721 5700
4318 4300
4326 4300
4601 5700
5330 4300
5380 4300
5381 4300
5397 4300
5710 5700
5735 5700
5744 5700
5752 5700
5903 4900
5935 4900
6329 4300
6359 4300
6379 4300
6923 4900
6952 4900
7204 7200
7214 7200
7228 7200
7252 7200
7710 5700
9006 9000
9015 9000
9083 3252
90327 WD[1]
90725 WD[1]

1951 81E
907 1854
1334 MSWJ
1502 1500
1861 1854
2202 2251
2221 2251
2222 2251
2226 2251
2240 2251
2252 2251
2289 2251
2532 2301
2579 2301
3024 ROD
3210 2251
3211 2251
3212 2251
3622 5700
3709 5700
3721 5700
4318 4300
4326 4300
4649 5700
4935 4900
5330 4300
5380 4300
5381 4300
5397 4300
5735 5700
5744 5700
5752 5700
5903 4900
5935 4900
6112 6100
6118 6100
6132 6100
6134 6100
6167 6100
6329 4300
6340 4300
6359 4300
6910 4900
6952 4900
7710 5700
9015 9000
9413 9400
9417 9400

1954 81E
1502 1500
2240 2251
2252 2251
2289 2251
2532 2301
2819 2800
3210 2251
3211 2251
3212 2251
3622 5700
3653 5700
3709 5700
3721 5700
3837 2884
3845 2884
4649 5700
4935 4900
4945 4900
4994 4900
5380 4300
5397 4300
5629 5600
5639 5600
5697 5600
5735 5700
5737 5700
5744 5700
5752 5700
5783 5700
5903 4900
5935 4900
6167 6100
6313 4300
6329 4300
6340 4300
6654 5600
6910 4900
6952 4900
6983 6959
7710 5700
8435 9400
9413 9400
9417 9400

1957 81E
1502 1500
2214 2251
2221 2251
2240 2251
2252 2251
3206 2251
3210 2251
3211 2251
3212 2251
3622 5700
3653 5700
3709 5700
3721 5700
3751 5700
4649 5700
4933 4900
4935 4900
4939 4900
4979 4900
4994 4900
5322 4300
5330 4300
5380 4300
5397 4300
5629 5600
5639 5600
5647 5600
5675 5600
5697 5600
5735 5700
5737 5700
5744 5700
5752 5700
5783 5700
5935 4900
5943 4900
6167 6100
6304 4300
6340 4300
6910 4900
6952 4900
6983 6959
7710 5700
8435 9400
8458 9400
9407 9400

1960 81E
1502 1500
2214 2251
2221 2251
2234 2251
2240 2251
2246 2251
2819 2800
2836 2800
2844 2800
2849 2800
3206 2251
3210 2251
3211 2251
3622 5700
3653 5700
3709 5700
3721 5700
3751 5700
4649 5700
4915 4900
4939 4900
4959 4900
4965 4900
4969 4900
4994 4900
5326 4300
5337 4300
5351 4300
5361 4300
5380 4300
5639 5600
5647 5600
5744 5700
5746 5700
5783 5700
5918 4900
5943 4900
5987 4900
6105 6100
6124 6100
6164 6100
6167 6100
6302 4300
6313 4300
6379 4300
6910 4900
6915 4900
6952 4900
6969 6959
6983 6959
6996 6959
7324 4300
7327 4300
7772 5700
8435 9400
8458 9400
8720 5700
9407 9400

1963 81E
1636 1600
2201 2251
2836 2800
2842 2800
2852 2800
2893 2884
2898 2884
3751 5700
3763 5700
3819 2884
3820 2884
3840 2884
4606 5700
4902 4900
4908 4900
4910 4900
4935 4900
4939 4900
4942 4900
4950 4900
4959 4900
4994 4900
5380 4300
5987 4900
6112 6100
6126 6100
6130 6100
6136 6100
6139 6100
6159 6100
6167 6100
6309 4300
6350 4300
6363 4300
6824 6800
6849 6800
6868 6800
6874 6800
6909 4900
6937 4900
6969 6959
6983 6959
6996 6959
7327 4300
7340 4300
8720 5700
9791 5700

Doncaster

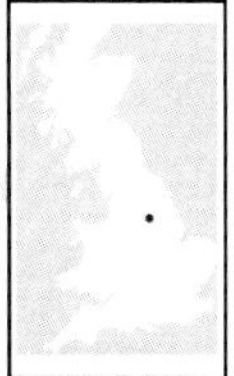

1948 DON
60048 A3
60049 A3
60058 A3
60063 A3
60103 A3
60520 A2
60525 A2
60815 V2
60826 V2
60830 V2
60831 V2
60832 V2
60845 V2
60846 V2
60849 V2
60852 V2
60857 V2
60861 V2
60867 V2
60870 V2
60872 V2
60875 V2
60877 V2
60880 V2
60881 V2
60889 V2
60890 V2
60896 V2
60902 V2
60906 V2
60917 V2
60928 V2
60930 V2
60935 V2
60943 V2
60948 V2
60956 V2
61026 B1
61120 B1
61124 B1
61125 B1
61126 B1
61127 B1
61170 B1
61190 B1
61191 B1
61193 B1
61194 B1
61196 B1
61201 B1
61246 B1
61247 B1
61248 B1
61249 B1
61250 B1
61265 B1
61856 K3
61861 K3
61907 K3
61910 K3
61918 K3
61978 K3
62854 C1
62877 C1
62885 C1
63572 O4
63586 O4
63587 O4
63593 O4
63594 O1
63598 O4
63600 O4
63601 O4
63607 O4
63616 O4
63617 O4
63621 O4
63623 O4
63624 O4
63627 O4
63643 O4
63647 O4
63657 O4
63659 O4
63660 O4
63668 O4
63671 O4
63682 O4
63684 O4
63693 O4
63697 O4
63698 O4
63719 O4
63728 O4
63731 O4
63738 O4
63741 O4
63745 O4
63757 O4
63758 O4
63765 O4
63800 O4
63832 O4
63847 O4
63864 O4
63883 O4
63884 O4
63891 O4
63900 O4
63911 O4
63915 O4
64179 J6
64183 J6
64185 J6
64193 J6
64195 J6
64209 J6
64218 J6
64219 J6
64232 J6
64236 J6
64241 J6
64243 J6
64255 J6
64258 J6
64259 J6
64261 J6
64262 J6
64263 J6
64264 J6
64270 J6
64279 J6
64713 J39
64721 J39
64737 J39
64758 J39
64835 J39
64885 J39
64891 J39
64893 J39
64902 J39
64909 J39
64910 J39
64951 J39
64952 J39
64967 J39
64976 J39
64977 J39
64984 J39
68317 J55
68763 J52
68769 J52
68775 J52
68786 J52
68800 J52
68804 J52
68806 J52
68813 J52
68835 J52
68836 J52
68837 J52
68841 J52
68842 J52
68843 J52
68844 J52
68845 J52
68846 J52
68847 J52
68849 J52
68857 J52
68860 J52
68865 J52
68869 J52
68870 J52
68885 J52
68886 J52
68890 J50
68893 J50
68899 J50
68918 J50
68926 J50
68936 J50
68974 J50
68979 J50
68980 J50
68985 J50
68986 J50
68987 J50
68989 J50
68991 J50

1951 36A
60047 A3
60055 A3
60058 A3
60064 A3
60066 A3
60112 A3
60846 V2
60849 V2
60852 V2
60857 V2
60861 V2
60867 V2
60870 V2
60872 V2
60875 V2
60877 V2
60880 V2
60881 V2
60889 V2
60890 V2
60896 V2
60902 V2
60917 V2
60921 V2
60928 V2
60930 V2
60935 V2
60943 V2
60948 V2
60956 V2
61026 B1
61036 B1
61086 B1
61087 B1
61107 B1
61120 B1
61124 B1
61125 B1
61127 B1
61128 B1
61170 B1
61193 B1
61196 B1
61246 B1
61247 B1
61248 B1
61249 B1
61250 B1
61265 B1
61861 K3
61907 K3
61918 K3
61978 K3
63476 O3
63477 O3
63479 O3
63480 O3
63481 O3
63483 O3
63484 O3
63485 O3
63486 O3
63493 O3
63925 O2
63926 O2
63928 O2
63941 O2
63942 O2
63943 O2
63945 O2
63946 O2
63947 O2
63951 O2
63952 O2
63953 O2
63954 O2
63955 O2
63956 O2
63957 O2
63958 O2
63959 O2
63961 O2
63962 O2
63964 O2
63967 O2
63968 O2
63973 O2
63974 O2
63986 O2
63987 O2
64124 J3
64179 J6
64183 J6
64185 J6
64193 J6
64195 J6
64209 J6
64218 J6
64219 J6
64232 J6
64236 J6
64243 J6
64255 J6
64258 J6
64259 J6
64261 J6
64262 J6
64263 J6
64264 J6
64270 J6
64279 J6
64285 J11
64349 J11
64410 J11
64713 J39
64721 J39
64737 J39
64758 J39
64835 J39
64885 J39
64891 J39
64893 J39
64902 J39
64909 J39
64910 J39
64951 J39
64952 J39
64967 J39
64976 J39
64977 J39
64984 J39
65095 J21
65117 J21
68165 Y3
68769 J52
68775 J52
68786 J52
68800 J52
68804 J52
68806 J52
68813 J52
68835 J52
68836 J52
68837 J52
68841 J52
68842 J52
68843 J52
68847 J52
68849 J52
68857 J52
68858 J52
68860 J52
68865 J52
68867 J52
68869 J52
68870 J52
68885 J52
68886 J52
68890 J50
68893 J50
68917 J50
68918 J50
68926 J50
68936 J50
68945 J50
68960 J50
68961 J50
68980 J50
68985 J50
68986 J50
68987 J50
68989 J50
68991 J50
69014 J72
69015 J72

1954 36A
60046 A3
60048 A3
60055 A3
60058 A3
60064 A3
60066 A3
60067 A3
60109 A3
60112 A3
60700 W1
60815 V2
60849 V2
60852 V2
60857 V2
60867 V2
60870 V2
60872 V2
60875 V2
60877 V2
60880 V2
60881 V2
60889 V2
60896 V2
60902 V2
60917 V2
60921 V2
60928 V2
60930 V2
60935 V2
60943 V2
60956 V2
61026 B1
61036 B1
61087 B1
61107 B1
61120 B1
61124 B1
61125 B1
61127 B1
61128 B1
61137 B1
61145 B1
61157 B1
61158 B1
61170 B1
61193 B1
61196 B1
61247 B1
61248 B1
61249 B1
61250 B1
61265 B1
61266 B1
61365 B1
63764 O4
63769 O4
63855 O4
63858 O4
63928 O2
63935 O2
63941 O2
63942 O2
63943 O2
63947 O2
63951 O2
63952 O2
63953 O2
63954 O2
63955 O2
63956 O2
63957 O2
63958 O2
63959 O2
63962 O2
63964 O2
63967 O2
63968 O2
63969 O2
63971 O2
63973 O2
63974 O2
63975 O2
63977 O2
63978 O2
63981 O2
64179 J6
64185 J6
64193 J6
64195 J6
64209 J6
64232 J6
64236 J6
64243 J6
64255 J6
64258 J6
64261 J6
64263 J6
64264 J6
64270 J6
64285 J11
64296 J11
64309 J11
64319 J11
64334 J11
64348 J11
64349 J11
64367 J11
64376 J11
64403 J11
64404 J11
64410 J11
64453 J11
64721 J39
64737 J39
64885 J39
64909 J39
64952 J39
64956 J39
64967 J39
64987 J39
68761 J52
68769 J52
68778 J52
68784 J52
68785 J52
68795 J52
68796 J52
68800 J52
68804 J52
68806 J52
68811 J52
68813 J52
68833 J52
68835 J52
68836 J52
68841 J52
68842 J52
68843 J52
68847 J52
68849 J52
68853 J52
68856 J52
68858 J52
68860 J52
68865 J52
68869 J52
68870 J52
68886 J52
68973 J50
68974 J50
90005 WD[1]
90024 WD[1]
90037 WD[1]
90042 WD[1]
90053 WD[1]
90060 WD[1]
90064 WD[1]
90066 WD[1]
90108 WD[1]
90220 WD[1]
90270 WD[1]
90290 WD[1]
90301 WD[1]
90305 WD[1]
90383 WD[1]
90469 WD[1]
90498 WD[1]
90506 WD[1]

90537 WD[1]
90538 WD[1]
90696 WD[1]
5 Y3

1957 36A
41779 1F[1]
60046 A3
60048 A3
60064 A3
60066 A3
60067 A3
60109 A3
60112 A3
60700 W1
60841 V2
60849 V2
60852 V2
60857 V2
60870 V2
60872 V2
60880 V2
60881 V2
60889 V2
60896 V2
60905 V2
60909 V2
60917 V2
60921 V2
60928 V2
60930 V2
60935 V2
60956 V2
61026 B1
61036 B1
61087 B1
61107 B1
61114 B1
61120 B1
61121 B1
61122 B1
61124 B1
61125 B1
61127 B1
61128 B1
61137 B1
61145 B1
61155 B1
61157 B1
61158 B1
61162 B1
61170 B1
61171 B1
61193 B1
61196 B1
61225 B1
61247 B1
61250 B1
61266 B1
61285 B1
61326 B1
61365 B1
61377 B1
61887 K3
61895 K3
61940 K3
61961 K3
63613 O4
63618 O4
63769 O4
63855 O4
63858 O4
63922 O2
63928 O2
63934 O2
63935 O2
63939 O2
63941 O2
63942 O2
63943 O2
63944 O2
63947 O2
63951 O2
63952 O2
63953 O2
63954 O2
63955 O2
63956 O2
63957 O2
63958 O2
63959 O2
63962 O2
63963 O2
63964 O2
63967 O2
63968 O2
63969 O2
63971 O2
63973 O2
63974 O2
63975 O2
63977 O2
63978 O2
63981 O2
63983 O2
63984 O2
63985 O2
64179 J6
64185 J6
64193 J6
64209 J6
64232 J6
64243 J6
64258 J6
64261 J6
64262 J6
64263 J6
64264 J6
64270 J6
64296 J11
64348 J11
64376 J11
64404 J11
64721 J39
64737 J39
64810 J39
64828 J39
64838 J39
64876 J39
64885 J39
64909 J39
64952 J39
64956 J39
64966 J39
64967 J39
64972 J39
64987 J39
68020 J94
68022 J94
68507 J69
68621 J69
68761 J52
68778 J52
68784 J52
68800 J52
68811 J52
68817 J52
68835 J52
68841 J52
68842 J52
68843 J52
68849 J52
68869 J52
68886 J52
68926 J50
68963 J50
68974 J50
68980 J50
90301 WD[1]
90383 WD[1]
90674 WD[1]
92067 9F
92068 9F
92069 9F
92070 9F
92071 9F
92072 9F
92073 9F
92074 9F
92075 9F
92076 9F
92087 9F
92088 9F
92089 9F
92090 9F
92091 9F
92092 9F
5 Y3

1960 36A
60113 A1
60114 A1
60119 A1
60122 A1
60125 A1
60128 A1
60136 A1
60139 A1
60144 A1
60149 A1
60156 A1
60157 A1
60158 A1
60817 V2
60826 V2
60841 V2
60849 V2
60850 V2
60852 V2
60857 V2
60866 V2
60870 V2
60872 V2
60875 V2
60880 V2
60881 V2
60889 V2
60896 V2
60899 V2
60905 V2
60908 V2
60909 V2
60912 V2
60917 V2
60921 V2
60928 V2
60930 V2
60935 V2
60936 V2
60943 V2
60956 V2
61000 B1
61001 B1
61003 B1
61036 B1
61055 B1
61087 B1
61107 B1
61121 B1
61122 B1
61124 B1
61125 B1
61127 B1
61128 B1
61135 B1
61145 B1
61155 B1
61157 B1
61158 B1
61170 B1
61193 B1
61196 B1
61225 B1
61247 B1
61250 B1
61266 B1
61270 B1
61279 B1
61285 B1
61314 B1
61326 B1
61360 B1
61365 B1
61377 B1
61390 B1
61800 K3
61803 K3
61812 K3
61829 K3
61836 K3
61839 K3
61850 K3
61867 K3
61868 K3
61887 K3
61895 K3
61925 K3
61940 K3
61961 K3
61964 K3
63613 O4
63618 O4
63677 O4
63693 O4
63698 O4
63858 O4
63922 O2
63928 O2
63934 O2
63935 O2
63939 O2
63941 O2
63942 O2
63943 O2
63951 O2
63952 O2
63953 O2
63954 O2
63955 O2
63956 O2
63958 O2
63962 O2
63964 O2
63967 O2
63968 O2
63969 O2
63973 O2
63974 O2
63975 O2
63977 O2
63978 O2
63981 O2
63983 O2
63984 O2
63985 O2
64179 J6
64185 J6
64209 J6
64232 J6
64270 J6
64716 J39
64721 J39
64722 J39
64723 J39
64810 J39
64827 J39
64838 J39
64874 J39
64883 J39
64885 J39
64909 J39
64967 J39
64981 J39
64987 J39
68020 J94
68022 J94
68069 J94
68071 J94
68507 J69
68508 J69
68556 J69
68558 J69
68654 J68
68962 J50
68963 J50
68964 J50
68965 J50
68977 J50
90108 WD[1]
90144 WD[1]
90255 WD[1]
90453 WD[1]
90537 WD[1]
90538 WD[1]
90550 WD[1]
90569 WD[1]
90602 WD[1]
90636 WD[1]
90696 WD[1]
90732 WD[1]
92168 9F
92169 9F
92170 9F
92171 9F
92172 9F
92173 9F
92174 9F
92175 9F
92176 9F
92177 9F
92189 9F
92190 9F
92191 9F
92192 9F
92197 9F
92198 9F
92199 9F
92200 9F
92201 9F

1963 36A
60114 A1
60119 A1
60125 A1
60128 A1
60136 A1
60139 A1
60144 A1
60149 A1
60156 A1
60157 A1
60158 A1
60852 V2
60853 V2
60870 V2
60872 V2
60889 V2
60897 V2
60899 V2
60905 V2
60921 V2
60924 V2
60935 V2
60966 V2
61001 B1
61003 B1
61087 B1
61121 B1
61125 B1
61135 B1
61145 B1
61157 B1
61158 B1
61196 B1
61270 B1
61279 B1
61326 B1
61329 B1
61360 B1
61365 B1
62014 K1
62015 K1
62036 K1
62037 K1
62038 K1
62040 K1
62051 K1
62053 K1
62055 K1
62066 K1
62068 K1
62069 K1
63593 O4
63613 O4
63618 O4
63818 O4
63858 O4
63935 O2
90001 WD[1]
90003 WD[1]
90018 WD[1]
90042 WD[1]
90052 WD[1]
90063 WD[1]
90069 WD[1]
90144 WD[1]
90156 WD[1]
90190 WD[1]
90195 WD[1]
90208 WD[1]
90224 WD[1]
90235 WD[1]
90255 WD[1]
90279 WD[1]
90293 WD[1]
90296 WD[1]
90305 WD[1]
90340 WD[1]
90442 WD[1]
90447 WD[1]
90476 WD[1]
90477 WD[1]
90480 WD[1]
90484 WD[1]
90496 WD[1]
90498 WD[1]
90501 WD[1]
90506 WD[1]
90522 WD[1]
90528 WD[1]
90538 WD[1]
90551 WD[1]
90569 WD[1]
90636 WD[1]
90683 WD[1]
90685 WD[1]
90709 WD[1]
92036 9F
92039 9F
92044 9F
92141 9F
92168 9F
92169 9F
92170 9F
92171 9F
92172 9F
92173 9F
92174 9F
92175 9F
92176 9F
92177 9F
92189 9F
92190 9F
92191 9F
92192 9F
92198 9F
92199 9F
92200 9F
92201 9F

1966 36A
61042 B1
61055 B1
61121 B1
61158 B1
61210 B1
61326 B1
61329 B1
61360 B1
63653 O4
63730 O4
63764 O4
63781 O4
63785 O4
63788 O4
63818 O4
63858 O4
90001 WD[1]
90002 WD[1]
90018 WD[1]
90063 WD[1]
90073 WD[1]
90154 WD[1]
90156 WD[1]
90187 WD[1]
90305 WD[1]
90369 WD[1]
90428 WD[1]
90437 WD[1]
90484 WD[1]
90537 WD[1]
90551 WD[1]
90636 WD[1]
90675 WD[1]
90683 WD[1]
90687 WD[1]
90709 WD[1]
90718 WD[1]
92146 9F
92172 9F
92173 9F
92182 9F
92183 9F
92201 9F

Doncaster Works

1948
68132 Y1
68134 Y1
68319 J55
68782 J52

1951
68816 J52
68845 J52

1954
1 J52
2 J52

1957
1 J52
2 J52

1960
2 J52
9 J52

1963
10 J50
11 J50
12 J50
13 J50
14 J50
15 J50
16 J50

Dorchester

1948 DOR
30146 K10
30156 L11
30162 G6
30177 O2
30221 O2
30223 O2
30229 O2
30233 O2
30281 T9
30284 T9
30300 T9
30410 L11
30695 700

1951 71C
30116 T9
30162 G6
30177 O2
30179 O2
30197 O2
30223 O2
30229 O2
30231 O2
30284 T9
30307 T9
30338 T9
30399 S11
30415 L12
31632 U

1954 71C
30162 G6
31618 U
31622 U
31631 U
31632 U

Dover Marine

1948 DOV
30083 B4[1]
30767 N15
30768 N15
30769 N15
30770 N15
30771 N15
30924 V
30925 V
30926 V
30927 V
31027 P
31065 O1
31108 O1
31161 H
31246 D1[1]
31252 C
31255 C
31276 H
31291 C
31325 P
31373 O1
31381 O1
31443 B1
31450 B1
31470 D1[1]
31512 H
31517 H
31520 H
31530 H
31531 H
31532 H
31545 D1[1]
31548 H
31555 P
31556 P
31673 R
31705 R1[2]
31708 R1[2]
31727 D1[1]
31735 D1[1]
31753 L1
31754 L1
31755 L1
31756 L1
31757 L1
31819 N
31820 N
31821 N
31823 N
32108 E2
32109 E2
32359 D1[2]
34056 BB
34057 BB

1951 74C
30767 N15
30768 N15
30769 N15
30770 N15
30771 N15
30781 N15
30794 N15
30795 N15
30796 N15
30806 N15
30924 V
30925 V
30926 V
30927 V
31027 P
31063 C
31108 O1
31113 C
31191 C
31243 C
31247 D1[1]
31276 H
31291 C
31306 H
31323 P
31373 O1
31381 O1
31383 O1
31425 O1
31430 O1
31434 O1
31470 D1[1]
31503 H
31512 H
31518 H
31530 H
31531 H
31540 H
31545 D1[1]
31555 P
31557 P
31673 R
31708 R1[2]
31735 D1[1]
31753 L1
31754 L1
31755 L1
31756 L1
31757 L1
31767 L
31819 N
31820 N
31821 N
31823 N
31859 N
32108 E2
32109 E2
32359 D1[2]
34072 BB
34073 BB
35029 MN
35030 MN
42075 4MT[1]
42076 4MT[1]
42077 4MT[1]
42078 4MT[1]

1954 74C
30084 B4[1]
30775 N15
30776 N15
30777 N15
30796 N15
30797 N15
30798 N15
30918 V
30919 V
30920 V
30921 V
30923 V
31027 P
31113 C
31145 D1[1]
31150 C
31178 P
31191 C
31243 C
31246 D1[1]
31258 O1
31278 H
31317 C
31323 P
31328 H
31329 H
31425 O1
31430 O1
31434 O1
31531 H
31661 R
31753 L1
31754 L1
31755 L1
31817 N
31818 N
31819 N
31820 N
31821 N
32108 E2
32109 E2
32593 E5
34072 BB
34073 BB
34074 BB
35029 MN
35030 MN
42074 4MT[1]
42075 4MT[1]
42076 4MT[1]
42078 4MT[1]
42079 4MT[1]

1957 74C
30084 B4[1]
30775 N15
30776 N15
30777 N15
30797 N15
30798 N15
30919 V
30921 V
31027 P
31065 O1
31113 C
31150 C
31178 P
31191 C
31243 C
31258 O1
31317 C
31323 P
31328 H
31425 O1
31430 O1
31434 O1
31542 H
31753 L1
31754 L1
31755 L1
31788 L1
31789 L1
31818 N
31819 N
31820 N
31821 N
34070 BB
34071 BB
34072 BB
34073 BB
34074 BB
34103 WC
34104 WC
42075 4MT[1]
42076 4MT[1]
42077 4MT[1]
42078 4MT[1]
42079 4MT[1]
75065 4MT[1]
75066 4MT[1]
75067 4MT[1]
75068 4MT[1]
75069 4MT[1]

1960 73H
30938 V
30939 V
31027 P
31065 O1
31112 C
31113 C
31150 C
31258 O1
31323 P
31326 H
31328 H
31413 N
31414 N
31481 C
31542 H
31720 C
31810 N
31818 N
31819 N
31820 N
31821 N
34070 BB
34071 BB
34073 BB
34082 BB
34083 BB
34084 BB
34103 WC
80043 4MT[3]
80059 4MT[3]
80064 4MT[3]
80065 4MT[3]

Dowlais Cae Harris

1948 CH
83 RR[7]
211 TV[2]
5652 5600
5653 5600
5666 5600
5671 5600
5674 5600
5694 5600
5698 5600

Duffryn Yard

1948 DYD
69 RR[4]
70 RR[4]
184 PT[1]
291 TV[2]
294 TV[2]
296 TV[2]
428 BM[1]
1754 1854
1867 1854
2079 2021
2715 655
2721 2721
2792 2721
3718 5700
3791 5700
4255 4200
4277 4200
4286 4200
4292 4200
4640 5700
4681 5700
4684 5700
5216 5205
5250 5205
5257 5205
5260 5205
5612 5600
5629 5600
5639 5600
5656 5600
5713 5700
5731 5700
5734 5700
5773 5700
6616 5600
6629 5600
6686 5600
6688 5600
6715 6700
6717 6700
6718 6700
6719 6700
6720 6700
6749 6700
7706 5700
7733 5700
7744 5700
9617 5700
9634 5700
9735 5700
9736 5700
9737 5700
9766 5700
9785 5700
9799 5700

1951 87B
69 RR[4]
70 RR[4]
1964 1901
2011 1901
2079 2021
2800 2800
3718 5700
3791 5700
4164 5101
4212 4200
4256 4200
4265 4200
4292 4200
4640 5700
4681 5700
4684 5700
5216 5205
5220 5205
5257 5205
5612 5600
5629 5600
5639 5600
5646 5600
5713 5700
5731 5700
5734 5700
5761 5700
5773 5700
6616 5600
6623 5600
6629 5600
6644 5600
6650 5600
6686 5600
6691 5600
6715 6700
6717 6700
6718 6700
6719 6700
6720 6700
6749 6700
6761 6700
6768 6700
6777 6700
7706 5700
7733 5700
7744 5700
8464 9400
8465 9400
9431 9400
9617 5700
9634 5700
9735 5700
9736 5700
9737 5700
9766 5700
9785 5700
9799 5700

1954 87B
69 RR[4]
70 RR[4]
2800 2800
2813 2800
2872 2800
2894 2884
3718 5700
3791 5700
4212 4200
4256 4200
4265 4200
4292 4200
4296 4200
4640 5700
4681 5700
4684 5700
5216 5205
5220 5205
5254 5205
5257 5205
5626 5600
5713 5700
5734 5700
5770 5700
5789 5700
6616 5600
6623 5600
6629 5600
6650 5600
6686 5600
6691 5600
6715 6700
6717 6700
6718 6700
6719 6700
6749 6700
6761 6700
6768 6700
6776 6700
6777 6700
7244 7200
7706 5700
7733 5700
7744 5700
8410 9400
8418 9400
8423 9400
8454 9400
8466 9400
8490 9400
9431 9400
9437 9400
9444 9400
9447 9400
9454 9400
9455 9400
9456 9400
9457 9400
9461 9400
9483 9400
9487 9400
9617 5700
9634 5700
9735 5700
9736 5700
9737 5700
9766 5700
9785 5700
9799 5700

1957 87B
3613 5700
3718 5700
3791 5700
4212 4200
4256 4200
4265 4200
4292 4200
4296 4200
4640 5700
4681 5700
4684 5700
5216 5205
5220 5205
5254 5205
5713 5700
5770 5700
5787 5700
5789 5700
6602 5600
6616 5600
6620 5600
6623 5600
6629 5600
6650 5600
6686 5600
6691 5600
6715 6700
6717 6700
6718 6700
6749 6700
6761 6700
6776 6700
6777 6700
7244 7200
7249 7200
7706 5700
8407 9400
8410 9400
8418 9400
8423 9400
8454 9400
8490 9400
9431 9400
9444 9400
9446 9400
9447 9400
9454 9400
9455 9400
9456 9400
9457 9400
9483 9400
9617 5700
9634 5700
9735 5700
9736 5700
9737 5700
9766 5700
9785 5700
9799 5700

1960 87B
3613 5700
3718 5700
3762 5700
3791 5700
4256 4200
4265 4200
4278 4200
4293 4200
4296 4200
4299 4200
4640 5700
4684 5700
4695 5700
5216 5205
5220 5205
5221 5205
5254 5205
5264 5205
5604 5600
5670 5600
5688 5600
5728 5700
5770 5700
5787 5700
6602 5600
6616 5600
6620 5600
6623 5600
6686 5600
6691 5600
6761 6700
6766 6700
7244 7200
7249 7200
7706 5700
7758 5700
8407 9400
8410 9400
8416 9400
8454 9400
8490 9400
8724 5700
9444 9400
9446 9400
9454 9400
9456 9400
9457 9400
9483 9400
9617 5700
9634 5700
9735 5700
9736 5700
9737 5700
9742 5700
9766 5700
9785 5700
9799 5700

1963 87B
3610 5700
3613 5700
3626 5700
3642 5700
3682 5700
3692 5700
3762 5700
3791 5700
4256 4200
4278 4200
4286 4200
4296 4200
4640 5700
4651 5700
4684 5700
4695 5700
4970 4900
4983 4900
5216 5205
5232 5205
5246 5205
5254 5205
5257 5205
5670 5600
5787 5700
6620 5600
6680 5600
6686 5600
6691 5600
6920 4900
7216 7200
7222 7200
7229 7200
7249 7200
7715 5700
8714 5700
9456 9400
9457 9400
9464 9400
9475 9400
9483 9400
9615 5700
9617 5700
9633 5700
9634 5700
9656 5700
9671 5700
9715 5700
9742 5700
9766 5700
9788 5700
9799 5700

Dumfries

1948 12G
40170 3MT[2]
40576 2P[3]
40577 2P[3]
40614 2P[3]
40902 4P[1]
40904 4P[1]
40912 4P[1]
41109 4P[1]
41135 4P[1]
41171 4P[1]
41175 4P[1]
41179 4P[1]
42908 5MT[1]
42909 5MT[1]
42918 5MT[1]
42919 5MT[1]
46635 1P[1]
46639 1P[1]
57230 2F[5]
57238 2F[5]
57286 2F[5]
57288 2F[5]
57302 2F[5]
57329 2F[5]
57337 2F[5]
57343 2F[5]
57349 2F[5]
57362 2F[5]
57378 2F[5]
57391 2F[5]
57405 2F[5]
57409 2F[5]
57563 3F[12]
57600 3F[12]
57601 3F[12]
57602 3F[12]
57621 3F[12]
57623 3F[12]
57636 3F[13]

1951 68B
40170 3MT[2]
40576 2P[3]
40577 2P[3]
40614 2P[3]
40902 4P[1]
40904 4P[1]
40912 4P[1]
41109 4P[1]
41135 4P[1]
41171 4P[1]
41175 4P[1]
41179 4P[1]
42908 5MT[1]
42909 5MT[1]
42915 5MT[1]
42918 5MT[1]
42919 5MT[1]
54443 3P[5]
54444 3P[5]
54507 3P[6]
55124 2P[12]
55164 2P[13]
57302 2F[5]
57329 2F[5]

57337 2F[5]
57344 2F[5]
57349 2F[5]
57362 2F[5]
57378 2F[5]
57397 2F[5]
57405 2F[5]
57563 3F[12]
57600 3F[12]
57601 3F[12]
57602 3F[12]
57621 3F[12]
57623 3F[12]

1954 68B
40170 3MT[2]
40185 3MT[2]
40576 2P[3]
40577 2P[3]
40614 2P[3]
40902 4P[1]
40912 4P[1]
41175 4P[1]
41179 4P[1]
42908 5MT[1]
42909 5MT[1]
42915 5MT[1]
42918 5MT[1]
42919 5MT[1]
44199 4F[2]
45169 5MT[3]
45480 5MT[3]
54438 3P[5]
54443 3P[5]
54502 3P[6]
54507 3P[6]
55124 2P[12]
55164 2P[13]
56327 3F[10]
57302 2F[5]
57329 2F[5]
57349 2F[5]
57362 2F[5]
57378 2F[5]
57405 2F[5]
57600 3F[12]
57601 3F[12]
57602 3F[12]
57621 3F[12]
57623 3F[12]
68562 J69

1957 68B
40170 3MT[2]
40576 2P[3]
40577 2P[3]
40614 2P[3]
41179 4P[1]
42908 5MT[1]
42909 5MT[1]
42915 5MT[1]
42918 5MT[1]
42919 5MT[1]
44995 5MT[3]
45169 5MT[3]
45480 5MT[3]
54502 3P[6]
54507 3P[6]
55124 2P[12]
55164 2P[13]
56243 3F[10]
56327 3F[10]
57302 2F[5]
57329 2F[5]
57349 2F[5]
57362 2F[5]
57378 2F[5]
57405 2F[5]
57600 3F[12]
57601 3F[12]
57602 3F[12]
57621 3F[12]
57623 3F[12]
76072 4MT[2]
76073 4MT[2]

1960 68B
40170 3MT[2]
40577 2P[3]
40614 2P[3]
40670 2P[3]
42908 5MT[1]
42909 5MT[1]
42915 5MT[1]
42918 5MT[1]
42919 5MT[1]
44995 5MT[3]
45169 5MT[3]
45432 5MT[3]
45480 5MT[3]
54502 3P[6]
54507 3P[6]
55124 2P[12]
55232 2P[13]
56302 3F[10]
56310 3F[10]
57302 2F[5]
57329 2F[5]
57349 2F[5]
57362 2F[5]
57378 2F[5]
57600 3F[12]
57601 3F[12]
57602 3F[12]
57621 3F[12]
57623 3F[12]
76072 4MT[2]
76073 4MT[2]

1963 67E
42194 4MT[1]
42196 4MT[1]
42269 4MT[1]
42689 4MT[1]
42699 4MT[1]
42908 5MT[1]
42909 5MT[1]
42913 5MT[1]
42914 5MT[1]
42919 5MT[1]
44885 5MT[3]
44995 5MT[3]
45432 5MT[3]
45480 5MT[3]
46450 2MT[2]
57296 2F[5]
57302 2F[5]
57600 3F[12]
57661 3F[14]
76072 4MT[2]
76073 4MT[2]

1966 67E
44699 5MT[3]
44723 5MT[3]
44995 5MT[3]
45115 5MT[3]
45432 5MT[3]
45463 5MT[3]
45480 5MT[3]
46450 2MT[2]
76073 4MT[2]
76074 4MT[2]
76102 4MT[2]
78051 2MT[1]

Dundee Tay Bridge

1948 DEE
60804 V2
60838 V2
60840 V2
60844 V2
60920 V2
60937 V2
60969 V2
60971 V2
61101 B1
61102 B1
61263 B1
62409 D29
62410 D29
62412 D29
62418 D30
62434 D30
62438 D30
62485 D34
62713 D49
62718 D49
62728 D49
63071 O7
63077 O7
63123 O7
63142 O7
63194 O7
64482 J35
64485 J35
64493 J35
64506 J35
64512 J35
64523 J35
64530 J35
64537 J37
64548 J37
64575 J37
64587 J37
64593 J37
64615 J37
64619 J37
64620 J37
64627 J37
64631 J37
64634 J37
64786 J39
64790 J39
64792 J39
64822 J39
64950 J39
65319 J36
65328 J36
65330 J36
65333 J36
65614 J24
65622 J24
67461 C15
67471 C15
67483 C16
67484 C16
67486 C16
67489 C16
67490 C16
67491 C16
67498 C16
67499 C16
68100 Y9
68107 Y9
68108 Y9
68110 Y9
68114 Y9
68123 Y9
68446 J83
68452 J83
68455 J83
68466 J83
90198 WD[1]

1951 62B
44954 5MT[3]
46463 2MT[2]
55173 2P[13]
55186 2P[13]
55217 2P[13]
55223 2P[13]
55226 2P[13]
55227 2P[13]
55231 2P[13]
56323 3F[10]
56325 3F[10]
57568 3F[12]
57653 3F[14]
60527 A2
60528 A2
60804 V2
60822 V2
60834 V2
60838 V2
60840 V2
60844 V2
60920 V2
60931 V2
60937 V2
60958 V2
60969 V2
60971 V2
61101 B1
61102 B1
61147 B1
61263 B1
61278 B1
61292 B1
61293 B1
61402 B1
61403 B1
62427 D30
62434 D30
62436 D30
62438 D30
62457 D33
62485 D34
62718 D49
62728 D49
64482 J35
64485 J35
64530 J35
64575 J37
64587 J37
64598 J37
64615 J37
64619 J37
64620 J37
64627 J37
64631 J37
64634 J37
64786 J39
64790 J39
64792 J39
64822 J39
64892 J39
64950 J39
65309 J36
65319 J36
65330 J36
65333 J36
65614 J24
65622 J24
67461 C15
67471 C15
67483 C16
67484 C16
67486 C16
67489 C16
67490 C16
67491 C16
67493 C16
67498 C16
67499 C16
67502 C16
68100 Y9
68107 Y9
68110 Y9
68114 Y9
68123 Y9
68446 J83
68452 J83
68455 J83
68466 J83
68470 J83
90017 WD[1]
90077 WD[1]
90198 WD[1]
90444 WD[1]
90463 WD[1]
90515 WD[1]
90600 WD[1]
90727 WD[1]

1954 62B
40600 2P[3]
42733 5MT[1]
42866 5MT[1]
44954 5MT[3]
45384 5MT[3]
46463 2MT[2]
46464 2MT[2]
55162 2P[13]
55169 2P[13]
55173 2P[13]
55217 2P[13]
55223 2P[13]
55227 2P[13]
56323 3F[10]
56325 3F[10]
57568 3F[12]
57653 3F[14]
60527 A2
60528 A2
60804 V2
60822 V2
60834 V2
60838 V2
60844 V2
60920 V2
60931 V2
60937 V2
60958 V2
60969 V2
60971 V2
60972 V2
61101 B1
61102 B1
61132 B1
61263 B1
61278 B1
61292 B1
61293 B1
61402 B1
61403 B1
62434 D30
62438 D30
62485 D34
62728 D49
62744 D49
64530 J35
64575 J37
64587 J37
64598 J37
64615 J37
64619 J37
64620 J37
64627 J37
64631 J37
64634 J37
64786 J39
64790 J39
64792 J39
64822 J39
64892 J39
64950 J39
65309 J36
65319 J36
65330 J36
65333 J36
67466 C15
67483 C16
67484 C16
67486 C16
67489 C16
67490 C16
67491 C16
67493 C16
67498 C16
67499 C16
67502 C16
68100 Y9
68108 Y9
68110 Y9
68114 Y9
68123 Y9
68446 J83
68452 J83
68455 J83
68465 J83
68466 J83
68470 J83
90077 WD[1]
90198 WD[1]
90444 WD[1]
90463 WD[1]
90515 WD[1]
90600 WD[1]

1957 62B
42690 4MT[1]
42691 4MT[1]
42692 4MT[1]
42693 4MT[1]
44954 5MT[3]
45164 5MT[3]
45384 5MT[3]
45486 5MT[3]
46463 2MT[2]
46464 2MT[2]
55227 2P[13]
56323 3F[10]
56325 3F[10]
60527 A2
60528 A2
60804 V2
60822 V2
60834 V2
60838 V2
60844 V2
60920 V2
60931 V2
60937 V2
60958 V2
60969 V2
60971 V2
61102 B1
61132 B1
61172 B1
61180 B1
61263 B1
61278 B1
61292 B1
61293 B1
61402 B1
62434 D30
62438 D30
62485 D34
62728 D49
62744 D49
64530 J35
64545 J37
64556 J37
64575 J37
64587 J37
64598 J37
64615 J37
64619 J37
64620 J37
64627 J37
64631 J37
64786 J39
64790 J39
64792 J39
64822 J39
64892 J39
64950 J39
65309 J36
65319 J36
65330 J36
65333 J36
67484 C16
67486 C16
67490 C16
67491 C16
67502 C16
68100 Y9
68108 Y9
68114 Y9
68123 Y9
68452 J83
68465 J83
68466 J83
68470 J83
68535 J69
68551 J69
80123 4MT[3]
80124 4MT[3]
90077 WD[1]
90198 WD[1]
90444 WD[1]
90463 WD[1]
90515 WD[1]
90600 WD[1]

1960 62B
42691 4MT[1]
42692 4MT[1]
44954 5MT[3]
45164 5MT[3]
45384 5MT[3]
45486 5MT[3]
46463 2MT[2]
46464 2MT[2]
60527 A2
60528 A2
60804 V2
60822 V2
60834 V2
60838 V2
60844 V2
61102 B1
61132 B1
61172 B1
61180 B1
61263 B1
61278 B1
61292 B1
61293 B1
61402 B1
64556 J37
64575 J37
64585 J37
64587 J37
64598 J37
64600 J37
64602 J37
64615 J37
64619 J37
64620 J37
64627 J37
64631 J37
64786 J39
64822 J39
64892 J39
64950 J39
65309 J36
65319 J36
65330 J36
67484 C16
67486 C16
67490 C16
67491 C16
67496 C16
67501 C16
67502 C16
80123 4MT[3]
80124 4MT[3]
90444 WD[1]
90515 WD[1]

1963 62B
46463 2MT[2]
46464 2MT[2]
60528 A2
60532 A2
60804 V2
60822 V2
60834 V2
60838 V2
60844 V2
60973 V2
61102 B1
61172 B1
61180 B1
61262 B1
61263 B1
61277 B1
61278 B1
61292 B1
61293 B1
61340 B1
61402 B1
64575 J37
64587 J37
64600 J37
64602 J37
64619 J37
64620 J37
64627 J37
65319 J36
80090 4MT[3]
80123 4MT[3]
80124 4MT[3]
90444 WD[1]
90515 WD[1]

1966 62B
46464 2MT[2]
60528 A2
60530 A2
60532 A2
60818 V2
60836 V2
60919 V2
60973 V2
61102 B1
61180 B1
61262 B1
61263 B1
61278 B1
61293 B1
61340 B1
61403 B1
64547 J37
64576 J37
64577 J37
64597 J37
64602 J37
64608 J37
64620 J37
64624 J37
65319 J36
80124 4MT[3]

Dundee West

1948 29C
41972 3P[2]
41973 3P[2]
55173 2P[13]
55180 2P[13]
55186 2P[13]
55196 2P[13]
55217 2P[13]
55223 2P[13]
55226 2P[13]
55231 2P[13]
56323 3F[10]
56325 3F[10]
57450 2F[5]
57568 3F[12]
57653 3F[14]

Dunfermline Upper

1948 DFU
62205 D1
62441 D30
62455 D33
62459 D33
62464 D33
64475 J35
64476 J35
64480 J35
64483 J35
64487 J35
64496 J35
64505 J35
64513 J35
64545 J37
64554 J37
64560 J37
64561 J37
64567 J37
64568 J37
64574 J37
64590 J37
64604 J37
64617 J37
64628 J37
64630 J37
65239 J36
65252 J36
65253 J36
65320 J36
65323 J36
65900 J38
65905 J38
65909 J38
65916 J38
65917 J38
65922 J38
65923 J38
65924 J38
65926 J38
65928 J38
65930 J38
65933 J38
65934 J38
67453 C15
67466 C15
67469 C15
67478 C15
67644 V1
67661 V1
68101 Y9
68465 J83
68635 J69
69135 N15
69136 N15
69154 N15
69160 N15
69164 N15
69192 N15
69201 N15
69202 N15
69204 N15
69221 N15
90117 WD[1]
90134 WD[1]
90199 WD[1]
90306 WD[1]
90542 WD[1]
90553 WD[1]
90560 WD[1]
90569 WD[1]
90575 WD[1]
90705 WD[1]
90727 WD[1]

1951 62C
62441 D30
62459 D33
62464 D33
62466 D33
64475 J35
64476 J35
64480 J35
64483 J35
64487 J35
64493 J35
64496 J35
64505 J35
64513 J35
64525 J35
64545 J37
64554 J37
64556 J37
64560 J37
64561 J37
64567 J37
64568 J37
64574 J37
64590 J37
64604 J37
64617 J37
64630 J37
65239 J36
65252 J36
65253 J36
65281 J36
65307 J36
65320 J36
65322 J36
65323 J36
65900 J38
65905 J38
65916 J38
65922 J38
65923 J38
65924 J38
65926 J38
65928 J38
65930 J38
65933 J38
65934 J38
67453 C15
67466 C15
67469 C15
67669 V3
67672 V3
68101 Y9
68345 J88
68346 J88
68351 J88
68465 J83
68635 J69
69135 N15
69136 N15
69154 N15
69160 N15
69164 N15
69192 N15
69202 N15
69204 N15
69221 N15
90117 WD[1]
90199 WD[1]
90278 WD[1]
90293 WD[1]
90513 WD[1]
90542 WD[1]
90553 WD[1]
90560 WD[1]
90575 WD[1]
90705 WD[1]

1954 62C
61721 K2
61758 K2
61770 K2
62427 D30
62436 D30
62441 D30
64475 J35
64476 J35
64480 J35
64483 J35
64487 J35
64493 J35
64496 J35
64505 J35
64513 J35
64525 J35
64545 J37
64554 J37
64556 J37
64560 J37
64561 J37
64567 J37
64568 J37
64574 J37
64604 J37
64617 J37
64630 J37
65239 J36
65253 J36
65281 J36
65307 J36
65320 J36
65323 J36
65900 J38
65905 J38
65916 J38
65922 J38
65923 J38
65924 J38
65926 J38
65928 J38
65930 J38
65933 J38
65934 J38
67453 C15
67469 C15
67669 V3
67672 V3
68101 Y9
68345 J88
68346 J88
68351 J88
69135 N15
69136 N15
69154 N15
69160 N15
69164 N15
69192 N15
69202 N15
69204 N15
69221 N15
90017 WD[1]
90117 WD[1]
90199 WD[1]
90513 WD[1]
90542 WD[1]
90553 WD[1]
90575 WD[1]
90705 WD[1]

1957 62C
61101 B1
61721 K2
61758 K2
61770 K2
62427 D30
62436 D30
62441 D30
64475 J35
64476 J35
64480 J35
64487 J35
64493 J35
64496 J35
64505 J35
64513 J35
64516 J35
64525 J35
64560 J37
64567 J37
64568 J37
64604 J37
64617 J37
64630 J37
65239 J36
65253 J36
65281 J36
65307 J36
65320 J36
65323 J36
65923 J38
65924 J38
65926 J38
65928 J38
65930 J38
65933 J38
67669 V3
67672 V3
68101 Y9
68345 J88
68346 J88
68351 J88
69135 N15
69136 N15
69154 N15
69160 N15
69164 N15
69192 N15
69202 N15
69204 N15
69221 N15
90017 WD[1]
90177 WD[1]
90542 WD[1]
90547 WD[1]
90553 WD[1]
90560 WD[1]
90575 WD[1]
90727 WD[1]

1960 62C
61072 B1
61101 B1
61407 B1
61994 K4
61995 K4
61998 K4
62485 D34
64476 J35
64480 J35
64487 J35
64493 J35
64505 J35
64525 J35
64543 J37
64545 J37
64560 J37
64567 J37
64568 J37
64597 J37
64604 J37
64617 J37
64630 J37
65239 J36
65253 J36
65281 J36
65307 J36
65320 J36
65323 J36
65923 J38
65924 J38
65926 J38
65928 J38
65930 J38
65933 J38
67669 V3
67672 V3
68101 Y9
68346 J88
68350 J88
69202 N15
69221 N15
90017 WD[1]
90177 WD[1]
90542 WD[1]
90547 WD[1]
90553 WD[1]
90560 WD[1]
90575 WD[1]
90600 WD[1]
90727 WD[1]

1963 62C
61072 B1
61101 B1
61403 B1
61407 B1
64550 J37
64552 J37
64568 J37
64573 J37
64579 J37
64585 J37
64597 J37
65253 J36
65323 J36
65338 J36
65903 J38
65906 J38
65924 J38
65926 J38
65930 J38
65931 J38
65933 J38
76109 4MT[2]
76110 4MT[2]
90017 WD[1]
90049 WD[1]
90177 WD[1]
90542 WD[1]
90547 WD[1]
90553 WD[1]
90560 WD[1]
90600 WD[1]
90727 WD[1]

1966 62C
61072 B1
61101 B1
61407 B1
64610 J37
64611 J37
64623 J37
65288 J36
65903 J38
65912 J38
65917 J38
65918 J38
65929 J38
65930 J38
65931 J38
65934 J38
76109 4MT[2]
76110 4MT[2]
90039 WD[1]
90071 WD[1]
90199 WD[1]
90229 WD[1]
90386 WD[1]
90489 WD[1]
90534 WD[1]
90547 WD[1]
90560 WD[1]

Duns

1948 DNS
62357 D20

Durham

1948 DUR
67258 G5
67263 G5
67298 G5
67307 G5

1951 54A sub
67258 G5
67263 G5
67298 G5
67307 G5

1954 54A sub
67258 G5
67263 G5
67298 G5
67307 G5

1957 54A sub
67248 G5
67258 G5
67294 G5

East Kent Railway

1948 on loan
30948 EKR
31371 O1
31372 O1
31383 O1

Eastbourne

1948 EBN
32005 I1X
32008 I1X
32009 I1X
32010 I1X
32044 B4[2]
32050 B4X
32052 B4X
32054 B4[2]
32062 B4[2]
32063 B4[2]
32068 B4[2]
32070 B4X
32073 B4X
32083 I3
32090 I3
32091 I3
32234 D1/M
32274 D1/M
32348 K
32349 K
32358 D1/M
32377 D3
32391 D3
32395 D3
32402 E5
32406 E5
32485 E4
32518 E4
32538 C2X
32574 E5
32575 E5
32588 E5
32595 I1X
32596 I1X
32605 D1/M

1951 75G
32009 I1X
32030 I3
32043 B4X
32054 B4[2]
32055 B4X
32060 B4X
32062 B4[2]
32063 B4[2]
32068 B4[2]
32071 B4X
32072 B4X
32073 B4X
32077 I3
32081 I3
32083 I3
32089 I3
32385 D3
32394 D3
32402 E5
32404 E5
32405 E5
32485 E4
32518 E4
32574 E5
32603 I1X

Eastfield

1948 EFD
61116 B1
61117 B1
61172 B1
61180 B1
61197 B1
61243 B1
61260 B1
61261 B1
61700 V4
61701 V4
61764 K2
61772 K2
61774 K2
61775 K2
61776 K2
61779 K2
61781 K2
61784 K2
61785 K2
61786 K2
61792 K2
61793 K2
61794 K2
61993 K4
61994 K4
61998 K4
62460 D33
62462 D33
62469 D34
62472 D34
62473 D34
62474 D34
62477 D34
62479 D34
62481 D34
62482 D34
62489 D34
62493 D34
62496 D34
62497 D34
62498 D34
62671 D11
62672 D11
62673 D11
62674 D11
62675 D11
62676 D11
62680 D11
62681 D11
62682 D11
62684 D11
62686 D11
62687 D11
62688 D11
62689 D11
63020 O7
63119 O7
63120 O7
64540 J37
64541 J37
64558 J37
64578 J37
64579 J37
64580 J37
64581 J37
64583 J37
64601 J37
64610 J37
64611 J37
64622 J37
64623 J37
64632 J37
64633 J37
64638 J37
64639 J37
65221 J36
65227 J36
65228 J36
65270 J36
65273 J36
65296 J36
65300 J36
65308 J36
65315 J36
65335 J36
65337 J36
65339 J36
67456 C15
67460 C15
67467 C15
67482 C16
67485 C16
67500 C16
67501 C16
67502 C16
67600 V1
67601 V1
67602 V1
68103 Y9
68109 Y9
68118 Y9
68124 Y9
68326 J88
68327 J88
68330 J88
68331 J88
68333 J88
68336 J88
68345 J88
68347 J88
68349 J88
68447 J83
68468 J83
68475 J83
68476 J83
68479 J83
68480 J83
68551 J69
68552 J69
68709 J72
68733 J72
68953 J50
68954 J50
68955 J50
68956 J50
68957 J50
68958 J50
69120 N14
69124 N14
69126 N15
69127 N15
69131 N15
69138 N15
69163 N15
69165 N15
69166 N15

69170 N15
69176 N15
69177 N15
69178 N15
69179 N15
69180 N15
69181 N15
69182 N15
69183 N15
69184 N15
69188 N15
69189 N15
69191 N15
69203 N15
69205 N15
69208 N15
69222 N15
69925 Q1
69927 Q1
90174 WD[1]
90192 WD[1]
90265 WD[1]
90298 WD[1]
90313 WD[1]
90545 WD[1]
90599 WD[1]

1951 65A

45010 5MT[3]
61064 B1
61116 B1
61117 B1
61172 B1
61180 B1
61197 B1
61243 B1
61260 B1
61261 B1
61340 B1
61342 B1
61344 B1
61700 V4
61701 V4
61764 K2
61774 K2
61775 K2
61776 K2
61779 K2
61781 K2
61784 K2
61785 K2
61786 K2
61792 K2
61793 K2
61794 K2
61993 K4
61994 K4
61997 K1/1
61998 K4
62460 D33
62462 D33
62469 D34
62470 D34
62472 D34
62474 D34
62477 D34
62479 D34
62480 D34
62482 D34
62489 D34
62493 D34
62496 D34
62497 D34
62498 D34
62671 D11
62672 D11
62673 D11
62674 D11
62675 D11
62676 D11
62680 D11
62681 D11
62682 D11
62684 D11
62686 D11
62687 D11
62688 D11
62689 D11
64540 J37
64541 J37
64558 J37
64578 J37
64579 J37
64580 J37
64581 J37
64583 J37
64601 J37
64611 J37
64622 J37
64623 J37
64628 J37
64632 J37
64633 J37
64638 J37
64639 J37
65221 J36
65228 J36
65270 J36
65273 J36
65296 J36
65308 J36
67456 C15
67460 C15
67475 C15
67482 C16
67485 C16
67488 C16
67500 C16
67501 C16
67600 V1
67602 V1
67603 V1
67644 V1
67680 V1
68103 Y9
68109 Y9
68118 Y9
68124 Y9
68326 J88
68327 J88
68330 J88
68336 J88
68347 J88
68349 J88
68447 J83
68468 J83
68475 J83
68476 J83
68479 J83
68480 J83
68551 J69
68552 J69
68709 J72
68733 J72
68953 J50
68954 J50
68955 J50
68956 J50
68957 J50
68958 J50
69120 N14
69126 N15
69127 N15
69131 N15
69138 N15
69170 N15
69178 N15
69179 N15
69180 N15
69181 N15
69182 N15
69183 N15
69188 N15
69189 N15
69191 N15
69222 N15
69925 Q1
69927 Q1
90020 WD[1]
90149 WD[1]
90174 WD[1]
90192 WD[1]
90193 WD[1]
90222 WD[1]
90265 WD[1]
90298 WD[1]
90313 WD[1]
90441 WD[1]
90545 WD[1]

1954 65A

43132 4MT[5]
43133 4MT[5]
43134 4MT[5]
43135 4MT[5]
43136 4MT[5]
43137 4MT[5]
43138 4MT[5]
44908 5MT[3]
45214 5MT[3]
45400 5MT[3]
61064 B1
61117 B1
61133 B1
61134 B1
61140 B1
61172 B1
61180 B1
61197 B1
61243 B1
61260 B1
61261 B1
61277 B1
61294 B1
61340 B1
61342 B1
61344 B1
61396 B1
61700 V4
61701 V4
61741 K2
61764 K2
61774 K2
61775 K2
61776 K2
61781 K2
61784 K2
61785 K2
61786 K2
61789 K2
61794 K2
61993 K4
61994 K4
61997 K1/1
61998 K4
62031 K1
62034 K1
62052 K1
62472 D34
62474 D34
62477 D34
62496 D34
62497 D34
62498 D34
62671 D11
62672 D11
62673 D11
62674 D11
62675 D11
62676 D11
62680 D11
62681 D11
62682 D11
62684 D11
62686 D11
62687 D11
62688 D11
62689 D11
64540 J37
64541 J37
64558 J37
64578 J37
64580 J37
64581 J37
64611 J37
64622 J37
64623 J37
64628 J37
64632 J37
64633 J37
64638 J37
64639 J37
65221 J36
65228 J36
65270 J36
65273 J36
65296 J36
67454 C15
67460 C15
67475 C15
67480 C15
67485 C16
67488 C16
67600 V1
67602 V1
67603 V1
67644 V1
67664 V1
67680 V1
68109 Y9
68124 Y9
68326 J88
68327 J88
68330 J88
68336 J88
68347 J88
68349 J88
68447 J83
68468 J83
68475 J83
68476 J83
68479 J83
68480 J83
68709 J72
68733 J72
68952 J50
68953 J50
68954 J50
68955 J50
68956 J50
68957 J50
68958 J50
69120 N14
69126 N15
69127 N15
69131 N15
69138 N15
69170 N15
69171 N15
69178 N15
69179 N15
69180 N15
69181 N15
69182 N15
69183 N15
69188 N15
69189 N15
69191 N15
69197 N15
69214 N15
69218 N15
69925 Q1
69927 Q1

1957 65A

43135 4MT[5]
43136 4MT[5]
43137 4MT[5]
44707 5MT[3]
44787 5MT[3]
44908 5MT[3]
44956 5MT[3]
44957 5MT[3]
44968 5MT[3]
44996 5MT[3]
56152 2F[4]
61140 B1
61197 B1
61243 B1
61260 B1
61261 B1
61277 B1
61340 B1
61342 B1
61344 B1
61396 B1
61741 K2
61764 K2
61774 K2
61775 K2
61776 K2
61781 K2
61784 K2
61785 K2
61786 K2
61787 K2
61788 K2
61789 K2
61794 K2
61993 K4
61994 K4
61995 K4
61996 K4
61998 K4
62472 D34
62474 D34
62477 D34
62496 D34
62497 D34
62671 D11
62672 D11
62673 D11
62674 D11
62675 D11
62676 D11
62680 D11
62681 D11
62682 D11
62684 D11
62686 D11
62687 D11
62688 D11
62689 D11
64540 J37
64541 J37
64558 J37
64578 J37
64580 J37
64581 J37
64611 J37
64622 J37
64623 J37
64628 J37
64632 J37
64633 J37
64638 J37
64639 J37
65221 J36
65228 J36
65270 J36
65273 J36
65296 J36
67460 C15
67474 C15
67485 C16
67600 V3
67602 V1
67603 V1
67644 V1
67664 V1
67680 V1
68327 J88
68330 J88
68347 J88
68349 J88
68447 J83
68468 J83
68475 J83
68479 J83
68480 J83
68709 J72
68733 J72
68952 J50
68953 J50
68954 J50
68955 J50
68956 J50
68957 J50
68958 J50
69126 N15
69127 N15
69131 N15
69138 N15
69163 N15
69170 N15
69171 N15
69178 N15
69179 N15
69180 N15
69181 N15
69182 N15
69183 N15
69188 N15
69189 N15
69191 N15
69197 N15
69214 N15
69218 N15
73077 5MT
73078 5MT
73105 5MT
73106 5MT
73107 5MT
73108 5MT
73109 5MT
76074 4MT[2]
90049 WD[1]
90489 WD[1]

1960 65A

43135 4MT[5]
43136 4MT[5]
43137 4MT[5]
44702 5MT[3]
44707 5MT[3]
44787 5MT[3]
44908 5MT[3]
44956 5MT[3]
44957 5MT[3]
44967 5MT[3]
44970 5MT[3]
44996 5MT[3]
61140 B1
61197 B1
61243 B1
61261 B1
61340 B1
61342 B1
61355 B1
61396 B1
61764 K2
61788 K2
61794 K2
62474 D34
62496 D34
62497 D34
62671 D11
62672 D11
62674 D11
62680 D11
62681 D11
62682 D11
62686 D11
62687 D11
62688 D11
62689 D11
64540 J37
64541 J37
64548 J37
64558 J37
64578 J37
64580 J37
64581 J37
64611 J37
64622 J37
64623 J37
64632 J37
64633 J37
64638 J37
64639 J37
65228 J36
65296 J36
67460 C15
67474 C15
67485 C16
67600 V3
67602 V1
67603 V1
67644 V3
67664 V1
67680 V1
68325 J88
68345 J88
68352 J88
68447 J83
68479 J83
68952 J50
68954 J50
68956 J50
68957 J50
69131 N15
69163 N15
69170 N15
69171 N15
69178 N15
69179 N15
69181 N15
69183 N15
69188 N15
69191 N15
69212 N15
69218 N15
73077 5MT
73078 5MT
73105 5MT
73108 5MT
73109 5MT
76074 4MT[2]
90049 WD[1]
90128 WD[1]
90489 WD[1]

1963 65A

44702 5MT[3]
44707 5MT[3]
44787 5MT[3]
44908 5MT[3]
44956 5MT[3]
44957 5MT[3]
44967 5MT[3]
44968 5MT[3]
44970 5MT[3]
44996 5MT[3]
61134 B1
61140 B1
61197 B1
61243 B1
61261 B1
61342 B1
61355 B1
61396 B1
64548 J37
64558 J37
64580 J37
64623 J37
64632 J37
64633 J37
73077 5MT
73078 5MT
73105 5MT
73108 5MT
73109 5MT

1966 65A

61008 B1
61116 B1
61140 B1
61342 B1
73078 5MT
73108 5MT

Eastleigh

1948 ELH

30001 T1
30002 T1
30005 T1
30008 T1
30029 M7
30048 M7
30053 M7
30082 B4[1]
30087 B4[1]
30088 B4[1]
30096 B4[1]
30102 B4[1]
30109 M7
30120 T9
30121 T9
30125 M7
30128 M7
30148 L11
30150 K10
30151 K10
30154 L11
30155 L11
30157 L11
30159 L11
30165 L11
30171 L11
30175 L11
30198 O2
30200 O2
30213 O2
30225 O2
30231 O2
30240 G6
30242 M7
30261 G6
30264 G6
30267 G6
30272 G6
30274 G6
30275 G6
30277 G6
30286 T9
30302 T9
30306 700
30313 T9
30316 700
30336 T9
30341 K10
30345 K10
30350 700
30351 G6
30357 M7
30366 T1
30367 T1
30393 K10
30394 K10
30395 S11
30397 S11
30411 L11
30420 L12
30422 L12
30423 L12
30428 L12
30430 L12
30437 L11
30463 D15
30464 D15
30465 D15
30466 D15
30467 D15
30468 D15
30469 D15
30470 D15
30471 D15
30472 D15
30473 H15
30474 H15
30478 H15
30479 M7
30521 H15
30522 H15
30523 H15
30524 H15
30530 Q
30532 Q
30535 Q
30536 Q
30566 0395
30571 0395
30581 0395
30588 C14
30589 C14
30627 A12
30629 A12
30636 A12
30674 M7
30705 T9
30707 T9
30713 T9
30722 T9
30737 N15
30739 N15
30740 N15
30741 N15
30745 N15
30748 N15
30749 N15
30750 N15
30751 N15
30752 N15
30754 N15
30756 756
30777 N15
30784 N15
30785 N15
30952 Z
31827 N
31829 N
31866 N
31867 N
31870 N
32133 E1[2]
32147 E1[2]
32160 E1[2]
32239 D1/M
32259 D1/M
32361 D1/M
32409 E6
32609 E1[2]
32699 D1/M
33014 Q1
33015 Q1
33016 Q1
33017 Q1
33018 Q1
33019 Q1
33020 Q1
33021 Q1
33022 Q1
33023 Q1
33024 Q1
33025 Q1
700S D1/M

1951 71A

30029 M7
30031 M7
30032 M7
30033 M7
30048 M7
30082 B4[1]
30083 B4[1]
30089 B4[1]
30096 B4[1]
30109 M7
30121 T9
30125 M7
30127 M7
30128 M7
30148 L11
30154 L11
30155 L11
30156 L11
30157 L11
30159 L11
30171 L11
30173 L11
30175 L11
30213 O2
30225 O2
30233 O2
30242 M7
30243 M7
30282 T9
30285 T9
30286 T9
30287 T9
30304 T9
30306 700
30313 T9
30316 700
30350 700
30357 M7
30367 T1
30378 M7
30401 S11
30411 L11
30414 L11
30421 L12
30422 L12
30423 L12
30429 L12
30430 L12
30431 L12
30437 L11
30463 D15
30464 D15
30465 D15
30466 D15
30467 D15
30468 D15
30469 D15
30470 D15
30471 D15
30472 D15
30473 H15
30474 H15
30475 H15
30476 H15
30477 H15
30478 H15
30479 M7
30522 H15
30523 H15
30524 H15
30530 Q
30531 Q
30532 Q
30535 Q
30536 Q
30542 Q
30543 Q
30544 Q
30565 0395
30566 0395
30571 0395
30588 C14
30589 C14
30667 M7
30673 M7
30674 M7
30700 700
30713 T9
30722 T9
30726 T9
30729 T9
30744 N15
30745 N15
30746 N15
30747 N15
30748 N15
30749 N15
30750 N15
30751 N15
30752 N15
30753 N15
30754 N15
30777 N15
30778 N15
30779 N15
30780 N15
30850 LN
30851 LN
30852 LN
30853 LN
30854 LN
30855 LN
30856 LN
30857 LN
30950 Z
30952 Z
30956 Z
31325 P
32133 E1[2]
32147 E1[2]
32409 E6
32412 E6
32416 E6
32491 E4
32492 E4
32510 E4
32557 E4
32558 E4
32559 E4
32562 E4
32563 E4
32579 E4
33017 Q1
33018 Q1
33019 Q1
33020 Q1
33021 Q1
33022 Q1
33023 Q1
33024 Q1
33025 Q1

1954 71A

30029 M7
30030 M7
30031 M7
30032 M7
30033 M7
30082 B4[1]
30083 B4[1]
30096 B4[1]
30117 T9
30120 T9
30125 M7
30127 M7
30133 M7
30177 O2
30225 O2
30229 O2
30233 O2
30282 T9
30283 T9
30284 T9
30285 T9
30287 T9
30288 T9
30289 T9
30300 T9
30306 700
30310 T9
30316 700
30375 M7
30376 M7
30378 M7
30379 M7
30467 D15
30473 H15
30474 H15
30475 H15
30476 H15
30477 H15
30478 H15
30479 M7
30480 M7
30481 M7
30530 Q
30531 Q
30532 Q
30535 Q
30536 Q
30542 Q
30543 Q
30566 0395
30588 C14
30589 C14
30746 N15
30748 N15
30784 N15
30785 N15
30786 N15
30787 N15
30788 N15
30789 N15
30790 N15
30850 LN
30851 LN
30852 LN
30853 LN
30854 LN
30855 LN
30856 LN
30857 LN
30952 Z
30955 Z
30956 Z
31558 P
31613 U
31621 U
31626 U
31786 L1
31787 L1
31788 L1
31789 L1
31801 U
32113 E1[2]
32151 E1[2]
32491 E4
32492 E4
32510 E4
32556 E4
32557 E4
32558 E4
32559 E4
32562 E4
32563 E4
32579 E4
33017 Q1
33020 Q1
33021 Q1
33023 Q1
33025 Q1
33038 Q1
41293 2MT[1]
41304 2MT[1]
41305 2MT[1]
76005 4MT[2]
76006 4MT[2]
76007 4MT[2]
76008 4MT[2]
76009 4MT[2]
76010 4MT[2]
76011 4MT[2]
76012 4MT[2]
76013 4MT[2]
76014 4MT[2]
76015 4MT[2]
76016 4MT[2]
76017 4MT[2]
76018 4MT[2]
76019 4MT[2]
76025 4MT[2]
76026 4MT[2]
76027 4MT[2]
76028 4MT[2]
76029 4MT[2]
82012 3MT[2]
82014 3MT[2]
82015 3MT[2]
82016 3MT[2]

1957 71A

30028 M7
30029 M7
30030 M7
30032 M7
30033 M7
30082 B4[1]
30083 B4[1]
30096 B4[1]
30117 T9
30120 T9
30125 M7
30130 M7
30212 O2
30223 O2
30229 O2
30233 O2
30283 T9
30284 T9
30285 T9
30287 T9
30288 T9
30289 T9
30300 T9
30310 T9
30316 700
30328 M7
30356 M7
30375 M7
30376 M7
30377 M7
30378 M7
30379 M7
30473 H15
30474 H15
30475 H15
30476 H15
30477 H15
30479 M7
30480 M7
30481 M7
30530 Q
30531 Q
30532 Q
30535 Q
30536 Q
30542 Q
30543 Q
30566 0395
30588 C14
30589 C14
30707 T9
30748 N15
30757 757
30763 N15
30770 N15
30784 N15
30785 N15
30786 N15
30787 N15
30788 N15
30789 N15
30790 N15
30791 N15
30850 LN
30851 LN
30852 LN
30853 LN
30854 LN
30855 LN
30856 LN
30857 LN
30861 LN
30862 LN
30863 LN
31613 U
31618 U
31619 U
31620 U
31629 U
31639 U
31801 U
31802 U
31803 U
32108 E2
32109 E2
32491 E4
32510 E4
32556 E4
32557 E4
32559 E4
32579 E4
33020 Q1
33021 Q1
33023 Q1
41293 2MT[1]
41305 2MT[1]
73087 5MT
73116 5MT
75073 4MT[1]
75074 4MT[1]
76007 4MT[2]
76010 4MT[2]
76011 4MT[2]
76012 4MT[2]
76013 4MT[2]
76015 4MT[2]
76016 4MT[2]
76017 4MT[2]
76018 4MT[2]
76019 4MT[2]
76025 4MT[2]
76026 4MT[2]
76027 4MT[2]
76028 4MT[2]
76029 4MT[2]
76063 4MT[2]
76064 4MT[2]
76065 4MT[2]
76066 4MT[2]
76067 4MT[2]
76068 4MT[2]
76069 4MT[2]
82012 3MT[2]
82014 3MT[2]
82015 3MT[2]
82016 3MT[2]

1960 71A

30028 M7
30029 M7
30039 M7
30053 M7
30096 B4[1]
30117 T9
30120 T9
30125 M7
30223 O2
30229 O2
30287 T9
30288 T9
30300 T9
30306 700
30316 700
30328 M7
30357 M7
30375 M7
30377 M7
30379 M7
30474 H15
30475 H15
30476 H15
30479 M7
30480 M7
30530 Q
30531 Q
30532 Q
30535 Q
30536 Q
30542 Q
30543 Q
30768 N15
30769 N15
30770 N15
30773 N15
30788 N15
30790 N15
30791 N15
30800 N15
30802 N15
30803 N15
30804 N15
30806 N15
30850 LN
30851 LN
30852 LN
30853 LN
30854 LN
30855 LN
30856 LN
30857 LN
30858 LN
30859 LN
30860 LN
30861 LN
30862 LN
30863 LN
30864 LN
30865 LN
31618 U
31619 U
31620 U
31629 U
31632 U
31639 U
31735 D1[1]
31792 U
31793 U
31794 U
31795 U
31801 U
31802 U
31803 U
31804 U
31808 U
31809 U
32491 E4
32510 E4
32556 E4
32559 E4
32636 A1X
32640 A1X
32646 A1X
32650 A1X
32661 A1X
32678 A1X
33020 Q1
33021 Q1
33023 Q1
41293 2MT[1]
41305 2MT[1]
41319 2MT[1]
76010 4MT[2]
76011 4MT[2]
76012 4MT[2]
76013 4MT[2]
76014 4MT[2]
76015 4MT[2]
76016 4MT[2]
76017 4MT[2]
76018 4MT[2]
76019 4MT[2]
76025 4MT[2]
76026 4MT[2]
76027 4MT[2]
76028 4MT[2]
76029 4MT[2]
76061 4MT[2]
76062 4MT[2]
76063 4MT[2]
76064 4MT[2]
76065 4MT[2]
76066 4MT[2]
76067 4MT[2]
76068 4MT[2]
76069 4MT[2]
82012 3MT[2]
82014 3MT[2]
82015 3MT[2]
82016 3MT[2]

1963 71A

30029 M7
30036 M7
30053 M7
30096 B4[1]
30102 B4[1]
30133 M7
30480 M7
30536 Q
31413 N
31791 U
31793 U
31794 U
31795 U
31801 U
31803 U
31804 U
31808 U
31809 U
31810 N
31816 N
32640 A1X
32646 A1X
32650 A1X
32661 A1X
32678 A1X
33020 Q1
33021 Q1
33023 Q1
33037 Q1
33039 Q1
34004 WC R
34008 WC R
34016 WC R
34021 WC R
34022 WC R
34025 WC R
34028 WC R
34034 WC R
34037 WC R
34038 WC
34039 WC R
34061 BB
34097 WC R
34098 WC R
34104 WC R
120 T9
41210 2MT[1]
41213 2MT[1]
41293 2MT[1]
41305 2MT[1]
41311 2MT[1]
41319 2MT[1]
41328 2MT[1]
41329 2MT[1]
73002 5MT
73016 5MT
73043 5MT
73065 5MT
73155 5MT
76006 4MT[2]
76009 4MT[2]
76010 4MT[2]
76011 4MT[2]
76012 4MT[2]
76013 4MT[2]
76014 4MT[2]
76016 4MT[2]
76028 4MT[2]
76029 4MT[2]
76058 4MT[2]
76059 4MT[2]
76060 4MT[2]
76061 4MT[2]
76062 4MT[2]
76063 4MT[2]
76064 4MT[2]
76065 4MT[2]
76068 4MT[2]
76069 4MT[2]
80065 4MT[3]
80066 4MT[3]
80082 4MT[3]
80083 4MT[3]
80087 4MT[3]
80095 4MT[3]
80137 4MT[3]
92205 9F
92206 9F
92211 9F
92231 9F
92239 9F

1966 70D

30064 USA
30067 USA
30069 USA
30071 USA
30073 USA
34008 WC R
34009 WC R
34017 WC R
34018 WC R
34019 WC
34023 WC R
34034 WC R

34036 WC R
34037 WC R
34041 WC
34060 BB R
34071 BB R
34077 BB R
34079 BB
34082 BB R
34086 BB
34087 BB R
34088 BB R
34090 BB R
34093 WC R
34095 WC R
34097 WC R
34098 WC R
34101 WC R
34102 WC
34104 WC R
41287 2MT[1]
41294 2MT[1]
41299 2MT[1]
41319 2MT[1]
73085 5MT
73115 5MT
73117 5MT
73118 5MT
73119 5MT
73155 5MT
73169 5MT
73170 5MT
73171 5MT
75065 4MT[1]
75066 4MT[1]
75068 4MT[1]
75069 4MT[1]
75070 4MT[1]
75074 4MT[1]
75075 4MT[1]
75076 4MT[1]
75077 4MT[1]
75078 4MT[1]
75079 4MT[1]
76012 4MT[2]
76016 4MT[2]
76018 4MT[2]
76019 4MT[2]
76031 4MT[2]
76033 4MT[2]
76053 4MT[2]
76058 4MT[2]
76059 4MT[2]
76061 4MT[2]
76063 4MT[2]
76064 4MT[2]
76066 4MT[2]
76069 4MT[2]
80016 4MT[3]
80065 4MT[3]
80082 4MT[3]
80083 4MT[3]
80132 4MT[3]
80139 4MT[3]
80144 4MT[3]

Ebbw Junction

1948 NPT

431 BM[2]
432 BM[2]
435 BM[2]
436 BM[2]
1421 1400
1713 1854
1720 1854
1862 1854
1894 1854
2063 2021
2073 2021
2122 2021
2218 2251
2239 2251
2280 2251
2407 2301
2794 2721
2795 2721
2842 2800
2851 2800
2865 2800
2866 2800
2876 2800
2879 2800
2894 2884
2896 2884
2936 2900
2979 2900
3103 3100
3634 5700
3636 5700
3647 5700
3662 5700
3700 5700
3712 5700
3714 5700
3726 5700
3796 5700
3800 2884
3801 2884
3804 2884
3805 2884
3807 2884
3810 2884
3816 2884
3830 2884
3833 2884
4203 4200
4206 4200
4224 4200
4225 4200
4230 4200
4242 4200
4247 4200
4248 4200
4260 4200
4263 4200
4268 4200
4270 4200
4271 4200
4276 4200
4289 4200
4294 4200
4518 4500
4593 4575
4599 4575
4671 5700
4857 2884
4941 4900
5201 4200
5206 5205
5208 5205
5217 5205
5218 5205
5222 5205
5224 5205
5229 5205
5233 5205
5234 5205
5238 5205
5243 5205
5251 5205
5255 5205
5256 5205
5264 5205
5364 4300
5516 4575
5545 4575
5550 4575
5602 5600
5603 5600
5638 5600
5709 5700
5732 5700
5741 5700
5906 4900
5911 4900
6409 6400
6415 6400
6426 6400
6428 6400
6439 6400
6612 5600
6649 5600
6654 5600
6663 5600
6672 5600
6821 6800
6837 6800
6868 6800
6870 6800
6874 6800
6926 4900
6927 4900
7203 7200
7212 7200
7217 7200
7231 7200
7241 7200
7245 7200
7247 7200
7249 7200
7253 7200
7712 5700
7736 5700
7753 5700
7768 5700
7771 5700
7781 5700
8710 5700
8711 5700
8778 5700
8786 5700
8796 5700
9632 5700
9637 5700
9644 5700
9731 5700
90363 WD[1]
90565 WD[1]

1951 86A

431 BM[2]
432 BM[2]
435 BM[2]
436 BM[2]
1509 1500
2063 2021
2073 2021
2122 2021
2218 2251
2227 2251
2239 2251
2280 2251
2815 2800
2817 2800
2819 2800
2821 2800
2834 2800
2842 2800
2851 2800
2861 2800
2865 2800
2866 2800
2876 2800
2879 2800
2889 2884
2894 2884
2896 2884
2936 2900
2979 2900
3103 3100
3634 5700
3636 5700
3647 5700
3662 5700
3700 5700
3712 5700
3714 5700
3726 5700
3796 5700
3798 5700
3800 2884
3801 2884
3804 2884
3805 2884
3807 2884
3810 2884
3816 2884
3830 2884
3833 2884
3836 2884
4130 5101
4137 5101
4148 5101
4156 5101
4168 5101
4203 4200
4206 4200
4225 4200
4230 4200
4242 4200
4247 4200
4248 4200
4268 4200
4289 4200
4294 4200
4671 5700
4941 4900
5201 4200
5206 5205
5208 5205
5212 5205
5217 5205
5218 5205
5222 5205
5224 5205
5229 5205
5233 5205
5234 5205
5238 5205
5243 5205
5251 5205
5255 5205
5256 5205
5259 5205
5264 5205
5364 4300
5545 4575
5550 4575
5602 5600
5709 5700
5732 5700
5741 5700
5906 4900
6415 6400
6426 6400
6428 6400
6439 6400
6654 5600
6672 5600
6820 6800
6821 6800
6834 6800
6870 6800
6874 6800
6927 4900
7203 7200
7214 7200
7215 7200
7217 7200
7231 7200
7241 7200
7245 7200
7247 7200
7249 7200
7252 7200
7253 7200
7736 5700
7753 5700
7768 5700
7771 5700
7781 5700
8406 9400
8453 9400
8710 5700
8711 5700
8778 5700
9616 5700
9632 5700
9637 5700
9644 5700
9662 5700
9664 5700
9667 5700
9731 5700
90167 WD[1]
90261 WD[1]
90565 WD[1]

1954 86A

435 BM[2]
436 BM[2]
1421 1400
1509 1500
2035 2021
2090 2021
2218 2251
2227 2251
2239 2251
2280 2251
2842 2800
2851 2800
2861 2800
2864 2800
2896 2884
3103 3100
3634 5700
3636 5700
3662 5700
3691 5700
3700 5700
3712 5700
3714 5700
3726 5700
3798 5700
3800 2884
3801 2884
3804 2884
3805 2884
3807 2884
3810 2884
3816 2884
3830 2884
3833 2884
3836 2884
4148 5101
4168 5101
4203 4200
4230 4200
4242 4200
4246 4200
4248 4200
4271 4200
4277 4200
4290 4200
4294 4200
4611 5700
4671 5700
4916 4900
4951 4900
4957 4900
4982 4900
5173 5101
5201 4200
5206 5205
5217 5205
5218 5205
5222 5205
5224 5205
5228 5205
5229 5205
5233 5205
5234 5205
5236 5205
5238 5205
5243 5205
5251 5205
5255 5205
5256 5205
5259 5205
5260 5205
5264 5205
5709 5700
5732 5700
5921 4900
6102 6100
6107 6100
6114 6100
6415 6400
6426 6400
6428 6400
6642 5600
6812 6800
6820 6800
6847 6800
6870 6800
7203 7200
7210 7200
7214 7200
7218 7200
7219 7200
7227 7200
7231 7200
7232 7200
7241 7200
7243 7200
7245 7200
7247 7200
7249 7200
7252 7200
7253 7200
7319 4300
7736 5700
7768 5700
7771 5700
7781 5700
8406 9400
8453 9400
8499 9400
8710 5700
8711 5700
8778 5700
8794 5700
9458 9400
9482 9400
9616 5700
9632 5700
9637 5700
9644 5700
9662 5700
9664 5700
9667 5700
9674 5700
90069 WD[1]
90125 WD[1]
90225 WD[1]
90544 WD[1]
90585 WD[1]

1957 86A

1421 1400
1509 1500
1653 1600
1656 1600
2218 2251
2227 2251
2280 2251
2800 2800
2814 2800
2820 2800
2842 2800
2845 2800
2858 2800
2861 2800
2868 2800
2894 2884
3103 3100
3170 3150
3634 5700
3636 5700
3662 5700
3691 5700
3712 5700
3714 5700
3726 5700
3798 5700
3800 2884
3804 2884
3805 2884
3807 2884
3808 2884
3827 2884
3830 2884
3833 2884
4119 5101
4130 5101
4168 5101
4203 4200
4227 4200
4246 4200
4248 4200
4267 4200
4271 4200
4283 4200
4286 4200
4290 4200
4294 4200
4611 5700
4671 5700
4916 4900
4951 4900
4957 4900
4982 4900
5173 5101
5201 4200
5205 5205
5217 5205
5227 5205
5228 5205
5229 5205
5233 5205
5234 5205
5238 5205
5251 5205
5255 5205
5256 5205
5259 5205
5318 4300
5382 4300
5414 5400
5657 5600
5709 5700
5732 5700
5772 5700
5916 4900
5921 4900
6102 6100
6114 6100
6318 4300
6370 4300
6401 6400
6409 6400
6412 6400
6415 6400
6425 6400
6426 6400
6428 6400
6430 6400
6838 6800
6847 6800
6849 6800
6865 6800
7210 7200
7212 7200
7214 7200
7218 7200
7219 7200
7222 7200
7227 7200
7229 7200
7231 7200
7232 7200
7243 7200
7245 7200
7246 7200
7251 7200
7253 7200
7319 4300
7736 5700
7755 5700
7768 5700
7771 5700
7781 5700
7787 5700
8406 9400
8440 9400
8453 9400
8493 9400
8499 9400
8710 5700
8711 5700
8766 5700
9427 9400
9468 9400
9482 9400
9490 9400
9499 9400
9616 5700
9644 5700
9662 5700
9664 5700
9667 5700
9674 5700
9746 5700
90069 WD[1]
90179 WD[1]
90225 WD[1]
90544 WD[1]
90676 WD[1]
92000 9F
92001 9F
92002 9F
92003 9F
92004 9F
92005 9F
92006 9F
92007 9F

1960 86A

1506 1500
1653 1600
1656 1600
2218 2251
2219 2251
2223 2251
2227 2251
2236 2251
2818 2800
2842 2800
2858 2800
2884 2884
2893 2884
2894 2884
2898 2884
3103 3100
3634 5700
3636 5700
3638 5700
3662 5700
3681 5700
3691 5700
3694 5700
3706 5700
3714 5700
3747 5700
3767 5700
3772 5700
3798 5700
3805 2884
3807 2884
3808 2884
3824 2884
3827 2884
3830 2884
3832 2884
3833 2884
3837 2884
3853 2884
4203 4200
4227 4200
4246 4200
4247 4200
4248 4200
4283 4200
4290 4200
4611 5700
4671 5700
5188 5101
5201 4200
5205 5205
5217 5205
5227 5205
5228 5205
5229 5205
5233 5205
5234 5205
5238 5205
5251 5205
5255 5205
5259 5205
5657 5600
5709 5700
6348 4300
6370 4300
6412 6400
6425 6400
6426 6400
6656 5600
6838 6800
6850 6800
6876 6800
7204 7200
7211 7200
7212 7200
7217 7200
7218 7200
7219 7200
7222 7200
7229 7200
7231 7200
7233 7200
7234 7200
7240 7200
7243 7200
7245 7200
7250 7200
7253 7200
7781 5700
7794 5700
8766 5700
9468 9400
9482 9400
9616 5700
9644 5700
9664 5700
9667 5700
9674 5700
9745 5700
9746 5700
90225 WD[1]
90544 WD[1]
90676 WD[1]
92000 9F
92001 9F
92002 9F
92006 9F
92007 9F
92166 9F
92231 9F
92235 9F
92242 9F
92243 9F
92249 9F
92250 9F

1963 86A

1614 1600
1656 1600
2218 2251
2243 2251
2247 2251
2298 2251
2818 2800
2867 2800
2885 2884
2891 2884
2894 2884
3201 2251
3634 5700
3662 5700
3681 5700
3691 5700
3700 5700
3706 5700
3714 5700
3729 5700
3747 5700
3764 5700
3767 5700
3772 5700
3800 2884
3805 2884
3807 2884
3808 2884
3818 2884
3824 2884
3830 2884
3832 2884
3833 2884
3837 2884
4227 4200
4258 4200
4265 4200
4283 4200
4290 4200
4297 4200
4299 4200
4611 5700
4627 5700
4657 5700
4671 5700
4679 5700
5213 5205
5217 5205
5227 5205
5228 5205
5229 5205
5233 5205
5234 5205
5236 5205
5238 5205
5251 5205
5255 5205
5259 5205
5306 4300
6412 6400
6434 6400
6800 6800
6813 6800
6820 6800
6829 6800
6850 6800
6852 6800
7219 7200
7223 7200
7233 7200
7238 7200
7240 7200
7245 7200
7253 7200
8702 5700
8766 5700
9488 9400
9616 5700
9644 5700
9662 5700
9664 5700
9667 5700
92002 9F
92005 9F
92006 9F
92214 9F
92222 9F
92223 9F
92225 9F
92226 9F
92229 9F
92230 9F
92233 9F
92235 9F
92238 9F
92242 9F
92249 9F
92250 9F

Edge Hill

1948 8A

40006 3MT[1]
40007 3MT[1]
40050 3MT[1]
40495 2P[2]
40628 2P[3]
42426 4MT[3]
42453 4MT[3]
42459 4MT[3]
42564 4MT[3]
42597 4MT[3]
42612 4MT[3]
42658 4MT[3]
44904 5MT[3]
44935 5MT[3]
44941 5MT[3]
45045 5MT[3]
45054 5MT[3]
45094 5MT[3]
45256 5MT[3]
45298 5MT[3]
45332 5MT[3]
45344 5MT[3]
45347 5MT[3]
45350 5MT[3]
45351 5MT[3]
45376 5MT[3]
45380 5MT[3]
45387 5MT[3]
45398 5MT[3]
45399 5MT[3]
45400 5MT[3]
45410 5MT[3]
45500 6P5F[1]
45501 6P5F[1]
45517 6P5F[1]
45520 6P5F[1]
45521 7P[1]
45523 6P5F[1]
45526 7P[1]
45527 6P5F[1]
45533 6P5F[1]
45543 6P5F[1]
45545 6P5F[1]
45547 6P5F[1]
45567 6P5F[2]
45586 6P5F[2]
45592 6P5F[2]
45613 6P5F[2]
45623 6P5F[2]
45634 6P5F[2]
45666 6P5F[2]
45672 6P5F[2]
45673 6P5F[2]
45681 6P5F[2]
45724 6P5F[2]
45725 6P5F[2]
46004 5XP
46106 7P[3]R
46111 7P[3]R
46124 7P[3]R
46134 7P[3]
46135 7P[3]R
46136 7P[3]
46138 7P[3]R
46144 7P[3]R
46156 7P[3]
46164 7P[3]
46900 2P[7]
46917 2P[7]
47309 3F[6]
47325 3F[6]
47385 3F[6]
47402 3F[6]
47404 3F[6]
47597 3F[6]
47603 3F[6]
47651 3F[6]
47930 7F[1]
47933 7F[1]
47938 7F[1]
47951 7F[1]
47956 7F[1]
47958 7F[1]
47959 7F[1]
48898 7F[2]
48908 6F[2]
48927 7F[2]
48933 7F[2]
48966 7F[2]
49016 7F[2]
49032 6F[2]
49130 7F[2]
49155 7F[2]
49239 7F[2]
49242 7F[2]
49287 7F[2]
49333 7F[2]
49355 7F[2]
49385 7F[2]
49449 7F[2]
51318 2F[2]
51353 2F[2]
51439 2F[2]
51445 2F[2]
52111 3F[7]
52170 3F[7]
58887 2F[14]
58897 2F[14]
58898 2F[14]
58900 2F[14]
58912 2F[14]
58915 2F[14]
58922 2F[14]
58924 2F[14]
58928 2F[14]
58930 2F[14]
58935 2F[14]

1951 8A

40001 3MT[1]
40003 3MT[1]
40007 3MT[1]
40103 3MT[2]
40144 3MT[2]
42426 4MT[3]
42459 4MT[3]
42564 4MT[3]
42570 4MT[3]
42583 4MT[3]
42596 4MT[3]
42597 4MT[3]
42602 4MT[3]
42612 4MT[3]
44768 5MT[3]
44769 5MT[3]
44772 5MT[3]
44773 5MT[3]
44906 5MT[3]
44907 5MT[3]
45005 5MT[3]
45017 5MT[3]
45113 5MT[3]
45181 5MT[3]
45242 5MT[3]
45243 5MT[3]
45248 5MT[3]
45256 5MT[3]
45276 5MT[3]
45303 5MT[3]
45333 5MT[3]
45343 5MT[3]
45347 5MT[3]
45350 5MT[3]
45352 5MT[3]
45380 5MT[3]
45393 5MT[3]
45398 5MT[3]
45399 5MT[3]
45515 6P5F[1]
45527 7P[1]
45531 7P[1]
45533 6P5F[1]
45538 6P5F[1]
45547 6P5F[1]
45567 6P5F[2]
45596 6P5F[2]
45613 6P5F[2]
45623 6P5F[2]
45637 6P5F[2]
45670 6P5F[2]
45673 6P5F[2]
45681 6P5F[2]
45721 6P5F[2]
45726 6P5F[2]
45737 6P5F[2]
46106 7P[3]R
46111 7P[3]R
46123 7P[3]R
46124 7P[3]R
46125 7P[3]R
46134 7P[3]
46135 7P[3]R
46137 7P[3]
46138 7P[3]R
46144 7P[3]R
46153 7P[3]R
46156 7P[3]
46164 7P[3]
46200 8P[1]
46201 8P[1]
46203 8P[1]
46204 8P[1]
46205 8P[1]
47325 3F[6]
47353 3F[6]
47357 3F[6]
47385 3F[6]
47392 3F[6]
47402 3F[6]
47404 3F[6]
47407 3F[6]
47416 3F[6]
47519 3F[6]
47597 3F[6]
47931 7F[1]
48457 8F
48510 8F
48512 8F
48513 8F
48898 7F[2]
48932 7F[2]
49082 7F[2]
49126 7F[2]
49137 7F[2]
49173 7F[2]
49200 7F[2]
49224 7F[2]
49239 7F[2]
49301 7F[2]
49355 7F[2]
49392 7F[2]
49394 7F[2]
49399 7F[3]
49404 7F[3]
49412 7F[3]
49419 7F[3]
49429 7F[3]
49437 7F[3]
49445 7F[3]
49449 7F[3]
51353 2F[2]
51445 2F[2]
52111 3F[7]
52118 3F[7]
52321 3F[7]
52330 3F[7]

1954 8A

42121 4MT[1]
42426 4MT[3]
42459 4MT[3]
42564 4MT[3]
42570 4MT[3]
42583 4MT[3]
42596 4MT[3]
42602 4MT[3]
44768 5MT[3]
44769 5MT[3]
44772 5MT[3]
44773 5MT[3]
44906 5MT[3]
44907 5MT[3]
45020 5MT[3]
45039 5MT[3]
45069 5MT[3]
45111 5MT[3]
45113 5MT[3]
45181 5MT[3]
45242 5MT[3]
45243 5MT[3]
45249 5MT[3]
45250 5MT[3]
45256 5MT[3]
45276 5MT[3]
45303 5MT[3]
45305 5MT[3]
45343 5MT[3]
45376 5MT[3]
45380 5MT[3]
45388 5MT[3]
45393 5MT[3]
45398 5MT[3]
45399 5MT[3]
45413 5MT[3]
45421 5MT[3]
45515 6P5F[1]
45518 6P5F[1]
45525 7P[1]
45527 7P[1]
45531 7P[1]
45533 6P5F[1]
45534 7P[1]
45538 6P5F[1]
45550 6P5F[1]
45567 6P5F[2]
45596 6P5F[2]
45606 6P5F[2]
45613 6P5F[2]
45623 6P5F[2]
45670 6P5F[2]
45681 6P5F[2]
45721 6P5F[2]
46123 7P[3]R
46124 7P[3]R
46135 7P[3]R
46149 7P[3]R
46152 7P[3]R
46153 7P[3]R
46158 7P[3]R
46164 7P[3]R
46200 8P[1]
46204 8P[1]
46205 8P[1]
46207 8P[1]
46208 8P[1]
46226 8P[2]
47325 3F[6]
47353 3F[6]
47357 3F[6]
47385 3F[6]
47392 3F[6]
47402 3F[6]
47404 3F[6]
47407 3F[6]
47411 3F[6]
47416 3F[6]
47487 3F[6]
47489 3F[6]
47498 3F[6]
47519 3F[6]
47597 3F[6]
48260 8F
48457 8F
48512 8F
48513 8F
48932 7F[2]
49082 7F[2]
49137 7F[2]
49173 7F[2]
49200 7F[2]
49224 7F[2]
49314 7F[2]
49355 7F[2]
49368 7F[2]
49375 7F[2]
49392 7F[2]
49394 7F[2]
49399 7F[3]
49404 7F[3]
49412 7F[3]
49419 7F[3]
49423 7F[3]
49429 7F[3]
49434 7F[3]
49437 7F[3]
49445 7F[3]
51313 2F[2]
51353 2F[2]
51445 2F[2]
52140 3F[7]
52321 3F[7]

1957 8A

41121 4P[1]
42121 4MT[1]
42155 4MT[1]
42426 4MT[3]
42459 4MT[3]
42564 4MT[3]
42570 4MT[3]
42583 4MT[3]
42602 4MT[3]
42664 4MT[3]
44768 5MT[3]
44769 5MT[3]
44772 5MT[3]
44773 5MT[3]
44906 5MT[3]
44907 5MT[3]
45005 5MT[3]
45039 5MT[3]
45069 5MT[3]
45181 5MT[3]
45242 5MT[3]
45243 5MT[3]
45249 5MT[3]
45250 5MT[3]
45256 5MT[3]
45276 5MT[3]
45303 5MT[3]
45343 5MT[3]
45376 5MT[3]
45380 5MT[3]
45398 5MT[3]
45399 5MT[3]
45401 5MT[3]
45410 5MT[3]
45413 5MT[3]
45421 5MT[3]
45515 6P5F[1]
45516 6P5F[1]
45518 6P5F[1]
45521 7P[1]
45525 7P[1]
45527 7P[1]
45531 7P[1]
45533 6P5F[1]
45534 7P[1]
45535 7P[1]
45538 6P5F[1]
45539 6P5F[1]
45544 6P5F[1]
45550 6P5F[1]
45552 6P5F[2]
45567 6P5F[2]
45583 6P5F[2]
45596 6P5F[2]
45623 6P5F[2]
45670 6P5F[2]
45681 6P5F[2]
46114 7P[3]R
46123 7P[3]R
46124 7P[3]R
46132 7P[3]R
46142 7P[3]R
46152 7P[3]R
46157 7P[3]R
46164 7P[3]R
46200 8P[1]
46204 8P[1]
46205 8P[1]
46207 8P[1]
46208 8P[1]
46210 8P[1]
47353 3F[6]
47357 3F[6]
47385 3F[6]
47392 3F[6]
47402 3F[6]
47404 3F[6]
47407 3F[6]
47411 3F[6]
47416 3F[6]
47487 3F[6]
47489 3F[6]
47519 3F[6]
47566 3F[6]
47597 3F[6]
48260 8F
48433 8F
48457 8F
48509 8F
48512 8F
48513 8F
49137 7F[2]
49173 7F[2]
49200 7F[2]
49224 7F[2]
49355 7F[2]
49375 7F[2]
49392 7F[2]
49394 7F[2]
49399 7F[3]
49404 7F[3]
49412 7F[3]
49419 7F[3]
49423 7F[3]
49429 7F[3]
49434 7F[3]
49437 7F[3]
49445 7F[3]
51353 2F[2]
51445 2F[2]
52140 3F[7]

1960 8A

42121 4MT[1]
42155 4MT[1]
42564 4MT[3]
42570 4MT[3]
44768 5MT[3]
44769 5MT[3]
44772 5MT[3]
44773 5MT[3]
44906 5MT[3]
44907 5MT[3]
45005 5MT[3]
45032 5MT[3]
45039 5MT[3]
45069 5MT[3]
45181 5MT[3]
45242 5MT[3]
45249 5MT[3]
45281 5MT[3]
45376 5MT[3]
45399 5MT[3]
45401 5MT[3]
45413 5MT[3]
45421 5MT[3]
45515 6P5F[1]
45516 6P5F[1]
45518 6P5F[1]
45521 7P[1]
45525 7P[1]
45527 7P[1]
45531 7P[1]
45535 7P[1]
45552 6P5F[2]
45554 6P5F[2]
45560 6P5F[2]
45567 6P5F[2]
45578 6P5F[2]
45583 6P5F[2]
45586 6P5F[2]
45596 6P5F[2]
45613 6P5F[2]
45670 6P5F[2]
45678 6P5F[2]
45681 6P5F[2]

45704 6P5F^2
45733 6P5F^2
46114 7P^{3}R
46119 7P^{3}R
46124 7P^{3}R
46203 8P^1
46204 8P^1
46208 8P^1
46211 8P^1
47285 3F^6
47289 3F^6
47336 3F^6
47353 3F^6
47357 3F^6
47402 3F^6
47404 3F^6
47412 3F^6
47416 3F^6
47487 3F^6
47488 3F^6
47498 3F^6
47519 3F^6
47566 3F^6
47594 3F^6
47597 3F^6
47656 3F^6
48152 8F
48249 8F
48280 8F
48318 8F
48433 8F
48457 8F
48479 8F
48509 8F
48512 8F
48513 8F
48683 8F
49064 7F^2
49082 7F^2
49137 7F^2
49173 7F^2
49224 7F^2
49243 7F^2
49375 7F^2
49392 7F^2
49394 7F^2
49399 7F^3
49404 7F^3
49405 7F^3
49412 7F^3
49416 7F^3
49434 7F^3
49437 7F^3
51445 2F^2

1963 8A
42155 4MT^1
42815 5MT^1
42848 5MT^1
42851 5MT^1
42886 5MT^1
42920 5MT^1
42924 5MT^1
42925 5MT^1
44768 5MT^3
44769 5MT^3
44772 5MT^3
44773 5MT^3
44838 5MT^3
44855 5MT^3
44906 5MT^3
44907 5MT^3
45005 5MT^3
45015 5MT^3
45039 5MT^3
45041 5MT^3
45091 5MT^3
45094 5MT^3
45139 5MT^3
45187 5MT^3
45196 5MT^3
45242 5MT^3
45249 5MT^3
45284 5MT^3
45307 5MT^3
45327 5MT^3
45376 5MT^3
45440 5MT^3
45531 7P^1
46110 7P^{3}R
46119 7P^{3}R
46229 8P^2
46233 8P^2
46241 8P^2
46243 8P^2
47166 2F^1
47285 3F^6
47289 3F^6
47336 3F^6
47357 3F^6
47412 3F^6
47416 3F^6
47487 3F^6
47519 3F^6
47566 3F^6
47594 3F^6
47656 3F^6
48078 8F
48152 8F
48188 8F
48249 8F
48280 8F
48318 8F
48323 8F
48425 8F
48433 8F
48457 8F
48469 8F
48509 8F
48512 8F
48513 8F
48532 8F
48652 8F
48702 8F
48742 8F
48746 8F

1966 8A
44688 5MT^3
44717 5MT^3
44768 5MT^3
44772 5MT^3
44773 5MT^3
44837 5MT^3
44838 5MT^3
44863 5MT^3
44864 5MT^3
44906 5MT^3
44907 5MT^3
44964 5MT^3
45005 5MT^3
45015 5MT^3
45039 5MT^3
45069 5MT^3
45094 5MT^3
45156 5MT^3
45187 5MT^3
45242 5MT^3
45249 5MT^3
45284 5MT^3
45307 5MT^3
45312 5MT^3
45376 5MT^3
45440 5MT^3
47357 3F^6
47406 3F^6
47415 3F^6
47416 3F^6
47493 3F^6
48129 8F
48151 8F
48152 8F
48188 8F
48200 8F
48249 8F
48280 8F
48293 8F
48433 8F
48512 8F
48513 8F
48742 8F
48746 8F
75060 4MT^1

Exeter

1948 EXE
1020 1000
1405 1400
1429 1400
1435 1400
1440 1400
1449 1400
1451 1400
1468 1400
1469 1400
2088 2021
2230 2251
2873 2800
3335 3300
3395 3300
3451 3300
3603 5700
3606 5700
3794 5700
3834 2884
4054 4000
4410 4400
4530 4500
4706 4700
5012 4073
5059 4073
5098 4073
5321 4300
5525 4575
5760 5700
5902 4900
6301 4300
6397 4300
7316 4300
7716 5700
7761 5700
9646 5700
9647 5700

1951 83C
1405 1400
1429 1400
1435 1400
1440 1400
1449 1400
1451 1400
1468 1400
1469 1400
2088 2021
2230 2251
3603 5700
3606 5700
3677 5700
3794 5700
4176 5101
4410 4400
4540 4500
5059 4073
5062 4073
5321 4300
5525 4575
5760 5700
5902 4900
5976 4900
6301 4300
6397 4300
6994 6959
7316 4300
7716 5700
7761 5700
8421 9400
8456 9400
9647 5700

1954 83C
1405 1400
1429 1400
1435 1400
1440 1400
1449 1400
1451 1400
1468 1400
1469 1400
2230 2251
3603 5700
3606 5700
3677 5700
3794 5700
4176 5101
4540 4500
4917 4900
4948 4900
5003 4073
5021 4073
5760 5700
5976 4900
6301 4300
6318 4300
6994 6959
7316 4300
7711 5700
7716 5700
7761 5700
8456 9400
9439 9400
9629 5700
9765 5700

1957 83C
1405 1400
1429 1400
1435 1400
1440 1400
1449 1400
1451 1400
1468 1400
1469 1400
2211 2251
2230 2251
3603 5700
3606 5700
3677 5700
3794 5700
4174 5101
4540 4500
4948 4900
4955 4900
5021 4073
5412 5400
5959 4900
5976 4900
6322 4300
6385 4300
6820 6800
7316 4300
7716 5700
7761 5700
8456 9400
9439 9400
9497 9400
9629 5700
9765 5700

1960 83C
1007 1000
1023 1000
1440 1400
1451 1400
1452 1400
1462 1400
1468 1400
1471 1400
3746 5700
3794 5700
4117 5101
4589 4575
4944 4900
4948 4900
4992 4900
5075 4073
5412 5400
5524 4575
6319 4300
6965 6959
7311 4300
7316 4300
9474 9400
9497 9400
9629 5700
9765 5700

1963 83C
1421 1400
1442 1400
1450 1400
1451 1400
1466 1400
1471 1400
3659 5700
3746 5700
3794 5700
4673 5700
5555 4575
6346 4300
9635 5700

Exmouth Junction

1948 EXJ
30024 M7
30025 M7
30030 M7
30032 M7
30034 M7
30037 M7
30039 M7
30046 M7
30049 M7
30055 M7
30105 M7
30124 M7
30133 M7
30135 K10
30137 K10
30192 O2
30193 O2
30199 O2
30207 O2
30224 O2
30230 O2
30232 O2
30245 M7
30252 M7
30253 M7
30255 M7
30256 M7
30282 T9
30283 T9
30301 T9
30320 M7
30323 M7
30329 K10
30356 M7
30374 M7
30375 M7
30376 M7
30377 M7
30408 L11
30409 L11
30436 L11
30439 L11
30564 0395
30582 0415
30583 0415
30584 0415
30668 M7
30669 M7
30671 M7
30723 T9
30724 T9
30725 T9
30730 T9
30747 N15
30823 S15
30824 S15
30825 S15
30826 S15
30827 S15
30843 S15
30844 S15
30845 S15
30846 S15
30847 S15
30954 Z
31407 N
31408 N
31409 N
31625 U
31635 U
31638 U
31828 N
31832 N
31833 N
31834 N
31835 N
31836 N
31837 N
31838 N
31839 N
31840 N
31841 N
31842 N
31845 N
31847 N
31853 N
31855 N
31856 N
31869 N
31871 N
31874 N
31875 N
32124 E1R
32135 E1R
32695 E1R
32697 E1R
34001 WC
34002 WC
34003 WC
34004 WC
34005 WC
34006 WC
34007 WC
34008 WC
34009 WC
34010 WC
34011 WC
34012 WC
34013 WC
34014 WC
34015 WC
34016 WC
34017 WC
34018 WC
34019 WC
34020 WC
34021 WC
34024 WC
34025 WC
34026 WC
34027 WC
34028 WC
34029 WC
34041 WC
34042 WC
34043 WC
34044 WC
34045 WC
34046 WC
34047 WC
35001 MN
35002 MN
35003 MN
35004 MN
35005 MN

1951 72A
30024 M7
30025 M7
30030 M7
30034 M7
30039 M7
30046 M7
30049 M7
30055 M7
30105 M7
30124 M7
30133 M7
30192 O2
30193 O2
30199 O2
30224 O2
30230 O2
30232 O2
30245 M7
30252 M7
30253 M7
30255 M7
30256 M7
30283 T9
30320 M7
30323 M7
30374 M7
30376 M7
30377 M7
30408 L11
30409 L11
30564 0395
30581 0395
30582 0415
30583 0415
30584 0415
30668 M7
30669 M7
30671 M7
30702 T9
30703 T9
30706 T9
30707 T9
30714 T9
30715 T9
30716 T9
30717 T9
30723 T9
30823 S15
30824 S15
30825 S15
30841 S15
30842 S15
30843 S15
30844 S15
30845 S15
30846 S15
30847 S15
30954 Z
31407 N
31408 N
31828 N
31829 N
31830 N
31831 N
31832 N
31833 N
31834 N
31835 N
31836 N
31837 N
31838 N
31839 N
31840 N
31841 N
31845 N
31846 N
31847 N
31853 N
31855 N
31856 N
31866 N
31867 N
31869 N
32124 E1R
32135 E1R
32695 E1R
32697 E1R
34001 WC
34002 WC
34003 WC
34004 WC
34005 WC
34006 WC
34007 WC
34008 WC
34009 WC
34010 WC
34014 WC
34015 WC
34016 WC
34017 WC
34018 WC
34019 WC
34020 WC
34021 WC
34024 WC
34025 WC
34026 WC
34027 WC
34028 WC
34029 WC
34030 WC
34044 WC
34045 WC
34046 WC
34047 WC
34048 WC
35001 MN
35002 MN
35003 MN
35004 MN
35021 MN
35022 MN
35023 MN
35024 MN

1954 72A
30021 M7
30023 M7
30024 M7
30025 M7
30041 M7
30042 M7
30044 M7
30045 M7
30046 M7
30199 O2
30232 O2
30323 M7
30564 0395
30575 0395
30580 0395
30582 0415
30583 0415
30584 0415
30668 M7
30669 M7
30670 M7
30671 M7
30676 M7
30708 T9
30709 T9
30710 T9
30711 T9
30712 T9
30715 T9
30717 T9
30727 T9
30841 S15
30842 S15
30843 S15
30844 S15
30845 S15
30846 S15
30954 Z
31830 N
31831 N
31832 N
31833 N
31834 N
31835 N
31836 N
31837 N
31838 N
31839 N
31840 N
31841 N
31842 N
31844 N
31845 N
31846 N
31847 N
31848 N
31849 N
31851 N
32124 E1R
32135 E1R
32695 E1R
32697 E1R
34001 WC
34002 WC
34003 WC
34004 WC
34013 WC
34014 WC
34015 WC
34016 WC
34017 WC
34021 WC
34022 WC
34023 WC
34024 WC
34025 WC
34026 WC
34027 WC
34028 WC
34029 WC
34030 WC
34031 WC
34032 WC
34033 WC
34034 WC
34056 BB
34057 BB
34058 BB
34059 BB
34060 BB
34061 BB
34062 BB
35001 MN
35002 MN
35003 MN
35004 MN
35005 MN
35023 MN
35024 MN
35025 MN
41313 2MT^1
41314 2MT^1
82010 3MT^2
82011 3MT^2
82013 3MT^2
82017 3MT^2
82018 3MT^2
82019 3MT^2

1957 72A
30021 M7
30023 M7
30024 M7
30044 M7
30045 M7
30046 M7
30183 O2
30193 O2
30199 O2
30232 O2
30315 700
30323 M7
30564 0395
30582 0415
30583 0415
30584 0415
30667 M7
30668 M7
30669 M7
30670 M7
30676 M7
30691 700
30708 T9
30709 T9
30710 T9
30711 T9
30712 T9
30715 T9
30717 T9
30841 S15
30842 S15
30843 S15
30844 S15
30845 S15
30846 S15
30950 Z
30956 Z
31804 U
31830 N
31831 N
31832 N
31833 N
31834 N
31835 N
31836 N
31837 N
31838 N
31839 N
31840 N
31841 N
31842 N
31843 N
31844 N
31845 N
31846 N
31847 N
31849 N
32124 E1R
32135 E1R
32695 E1R
32697 E1R
34001 WC
34002 WC
34003 WC
34004 WC
34013 WC
34014 WC
34015 WC
34016 WC
34021 WC
34022 WC
34023 WC
34024 WC
34025 WC
34026 WC
34027 WC
34028 WC
34029 WC
34030 WC
34031 WC
34032 WC
34033 WC
34034 WC
34056 BB
34057 BB
34058 BB
34060 BB
34061 BB
34062 BB
34069 BB
35001 MN
35002 MN
35003 MN
35004 MN
35008 MN
35013 MN R
35023 MN
35024 MN
41306 2MT^1
41307 2MT^1
82010 3MT^2
82011 3MT^2
82013 3MT^2
82017 3MT^2
82018 3MT^2
82019 3MT^2
82022 3MT^2
82023 3MT^2
82024 3MT^2
82025 3MT^2

1960 72A
3633 5700
3679 5700
9756 5700
30021 M7
30023 M7
30024 M7
30044 M7
30045 M7
30048 M7
30182 O2
30199 O2
30313 T9
30317 700
30327 700
30338 T9
30582 0415
30583 0415
30584 0415
30667 M7
30668 M7
30669 M7
30670 M7
30676 M7
30691 700
30709 T9
30715 T9
30717 T9
30718 T9
30719 T9
30841 S15
30842 S15
30843 S15
30844 S15
30845 S15
30846 S15
30950 Z
30951 Z
30952 Z
30953 Z
30954 Z
30955 Z
30956 Z
30957 Z
31830 N
31831 N
31832 N
31833 N
31834 N
31835 N
31836 N
31837 N
31838 N
31839 N
31840 N
31841 N
31842 N
31843 N
31844 N
31845 N
31846 N
31847 N
31849 N
31853 N
31860 N
34002 WC
34011 WC
34015 WC
34023 WC
34024 WC
34030 WC
34032 WC
34033 WC
34034 WC
34035 WC
34036 WC
34038 WC
34056 BB
34057 BB
34058 BB
34060 BB
34061 BB
34062 BB R
34063 BB
34064 BB
34065 BB
34069 BB
34072 BB
34074 BB
34075 BB
34076 BB
34079 BB
34080 BB
34081 BB
34096 WC
34104 WC
34106 WC
34107 WC
34108 WC
34109 BB
34110 BB
35003 MN R
35008 MN R
35009 MN R
35011 MN R
35013 MN R
35023 MN R
35026 MN R
41306 2MT^1
41307 2MT^1
41318 2MT^1
82010 3MT^2
82011 3MT^2
82013 3MT^2
82017 3MT^2
82018 3MT^2
82019 3MT^2
82022 3MT^2
82023 3MT^2
82024 3MT^2
82025 3MT^2

1963 72A
3679 5700
30048 M7
30530 Q
30531 Q
30667 M7
30841 S15
30842 S15
30843 S15
30844 S15
30845 S15
30846 S15
31406 N
31818 N
31834 N
31835 N
31836 N
31837 N
31838 N
31839 N
31840 N
31841 N
31842 N
31843 N
31844 N
31845 N
31846 N
31847 N
31848 N
31849 N
31853 N
31855 N
31856 N
31860 N
31874 N
31875 N
31911 W
31912 W
31913 W
31914 W
31915 W
31916 W
31917 W
31924 W
34002 WC
34011 WC
34015 WC
34020 WC
34023 WC
34024 WC R
34030 WC
34032 WC R
34033 WC
34035 WC
34036 WC R
34056 BB R
34058 BB R
34060 BB R
34062 BB R
34063 BB
34065 BB
34066 BB
34069 BB
34070 BB
34072 BB
34074 BB
34075 BB
34076 BB
34078 BB
34079 BB
34080 BB
34081 BB
34083 BB
34084 BB
34086 BB
34096 WC R
34106 WC
34107 WC
34108 WC R
34109 BB R
34110 BB
35003 MN R
35009 MN R
35010 MN R
35013 MN R
35022 MN R
35025 MN R
35026 MN R
41238 2MT^1
41270 2MT^1
41272 2MT^1
41284 2MT^1
41292 2MT^1
41299 2MT^1
41306 2MT^1
41307 2MT^1
41308 2MT^1
41309 2MT^1
41318 2MT^1
41320 2MT^1
41321 2MT^1
41322 2MT^1
41323 2MT^1
80035 4MT^3
80036 4MT^3
80037 4MT^3
80038 4MT^3
80039 4MT^3
80040 4MT^3
80041 4MT^3
80042 4MT^3
80043 4MT^3
80059 4MT^3
80064 4MT^3
80067 4MT^3

Farnley Junction

1948 25G
40195 3MT^2
40196 3MT^2
40197 3MT^2
42729 5MT^1
42730 5MT^1
42731 5MT^1
42821 5MT^1
42844 5MT^1
44896 5MT^3
45063 5MT^3
45075 5MT^3
45076 5MT^3
45077 5MT^3
45078 5MT^3
45080 5MT^3
45340 5MT^3
45341 5MT^3
45671 6P5F^2
45702 6P5F^2
45704 6P5F^2
45705 6P5F^2
45708 6P5F^2
46405 2MT^2
46406 2MT^2
47567 3F^6
47568 3F^6
47569 3F^6
47570 3F^6
47571 3F^6
48735 8F
48739 8F
48754 8F
48755 8F
49379 7F^2
49382 7F^2
49389 7F^2
49390 7F^2
49392 7F^2
49394 7F^2
49537 7F^4
49538 7F^4
49539 7F^4
49540 7F^4
49547 7F^4
49551 7F^4
49552 7F^4
49553 7F^4
49598 7F^4
49624 7F^4
49672 7F^4
49673 7F^4

1951 25G
41255 2MT^1
41256 2MT^1
41257 2MT^1
41258 2MT^1
41259 2MT^1
44896 5MT^3
45063 5MT^3
45075 5MT^3
45076 5MT^3
45078 5MT^3
45079 5MT^3
45080 5MT^3
45211 5MT^3
45341 5MT^3
45704 6P5F^2
45705 6P5F^2
45708 6P5F^2
45711 6P5F^2
47567 3F^6
47568 3F^6
47569 3F^6
47570 3F^6
47571 3F^6
48456 8F
90245 WD^1
90316 WD^1
90318 WD^1
90322 WD^1
90325 WD^1
90326 WD^1
90336 WD^1
90351 WD^1
90372 WD^1
90395 WD^1
90407 WD^1
90588 WD^1
90591 WD^1
90645 WD^1
90649 WD^1
90664 WD^1
90666 WD^1
90684 WD^1
90698 WD^1
90699 WD^1
90711 WD^1
90726 WD^1
90728 WD^1

1954 25G
40691 2P^3
41255 2MT^1
41256 2MT^1
41257 2MT^1
41258 2MT^1
42700 5MT^1
42712 5MT^1
42719 5MT^1
42731 5MT^1
44896 5MT^3
45063 5MT^3
45075 5MT^3
45076 5MT^3
45079 5MT^3
45080 5MT^3
45211 5MT^3
45341 5MT^3
45581 6P5F^2
45646 6P5F^2
45695 6P5F^2
45705 6P5F^2
45708 6P5F^2
47567 3F^6
47568 3F^6
47569 3F^6
47570 3F^6
47571 3F^6
48456 8F
90318 WD^1
90322 WD^1
90336 WD^1
90351 WD^1
90372 WD^1
90395 WD^1
90407 WD^1
90527 WD^1
90562 WD^1
90588 WD^1
90591 WD^1
90645 WD^1
90649 WD^1
90650 WD^1
90664 WD^1
90666 WD^1
90684 WD^1
90698 WD^1
90699 WD^1
90711 WD^1
90726 WD^1
90728 WD^1

1957 55C
40581 2P^3
40584 2P^3
41254 2MT^1
41255 2MT^1
41256 2MT^1
41257 2MT^1
41258 2MT^1
41259 2MT^1
42702 5MT^1
42713 5MT^1
42766 5MT^1
42789 5MT^1
42865 5MT^1
42866 5MT^1
44896 5MT^3
45063 5MT^3
45075 5MT^3
45079 5MT^3
45080 5MT^3
45204 5MT^3
45211 5MT^3
45581 6P5F^2
45646 6P5F^2
45695 6P5F^2
45708 6P5F^2
47567 3F^6
47568 3F^6
47569 3F^6
47570 3F^6
47571 3F^6
90127 WD^1
90254 WD^1
90308 WD^1
90318 WD^1
90322 WD^1
90336 WD^1
90351 WD^1
90395 WD^1
90407 WD^1
90562 WD^1
90588 WD^1
90591 WD^1
90645 WD^1
90649 WD^1
90650 WD^1
90664 WD^1
90666 WD^1
90684 WD^1
90698 WD^1
90699 WD^1
90711 WD^1
90726 WD^1
90728 WD^1

1960 55C
40584 2P^3
41254 2MT^1
41255 2MT^1
41256 2MT^1
41258 2MT^1
41259 2MT^1
42713 5MT^1
42766 5MT^1
42774 5MT^1
42789 5MT^1
42795 5MT^1
42865 5MT^1
42866 5MT^1
44896 5MT^3
45063 5MT^3
45075 5MT^3
45079 5MT^3
45080 5MT^3
45204 5MT^3
45211 5MT^3
45428 5MT^3
45581 6P5F^2
45646 6P5F^2
45695 6P5F^2
45708 6P5F^2
47568 3F^6
47569 3F^6
47570 3F^6
90127 WD^1
90308 WD^1
90334 WD^1
90395 WD^1
90407 WD^1
90562 WD^1
90588 WD^1
90591 WD^1
90645 WD^1
90650 WD^1
90684 WD^1
90699 WD^1
90726 WD^1
90728 WD^1

1963 55C
41281 2MT^1
41282 2MT^1
44896 5MT^3
45063 5MT^3
45075 5MT^3

45079 5MT[3]
45080 5MT[3]
45204 5MT[3]
45211 5MT[3]
45273 5MT[3]
45428 5MT[3]
45581 6P5F[2]
45646 6P5F[2]
45695 6P5F[2]
45708 6P5F[2]
47419 3F[6]
47581 3F[6]
47589 3F[6]
48542 8F
48664 8F
48689 8F
90334 WD[1]
90503 WD[1]
90588 WD[1]
90645 WD[1]
90699 WD[1]
90728 WD[1]

1966 55C
44826 5MT[3]
44896 5MT[3]
44943 5MT[3]
45080 5MT[3]
45428 5MT[3]
45562 6P5F[2]
45581 6P5F[2]
45647 6P5F[2]
48076 8F
48080 8F
48664 8F

Faverdale Wagon Works

1948
68136 Y1

1951
68136 Y1

1954
51 Y1

1957
57 Y3

1960
57 Y3

Faversham

1948 FAV
31046 O1
31106 O1
31229 C
31231 F1
31242 C
31260 C
31279 H
31309 H
31310 H
31369 O1
31379 O1
31438 O1
31440 B1
31448 B1
31481 C
31487 D1[1]
31489 D1[1]
31493 D
31495 C
31496 D
31501 D
31502 D1[1]
31505 D1[1]
31509 D1[1]
31631 U
31639 U
31667 R
31674 R
31691 C
31692 C
31699 R1[2]
31709 R1[2]
31715 C
31739 D1[1]
31741 D1[1]
31808 U

1951 73E
31157 E
31229 C
31242 C
31259 H
31268 C
31369 O1
31481 C
31489 D1[1]
31495 C
31502 D1[1]
31505 D1[1]
31532 H
31631 U
31638 U
31661 R
31674 R
31691 C
31692 C
31696 R1[2]
31698 R1[2]
31705 R1[2]
31715 C
31727 D1[1]
31734 D
31739 D1[1]
31806 U
31808 U
31850 N
31854 N
31868 N

1954 73E
31247 D1[1]
31253 C
31255 C
31256 C
31267 C
31268 C
31305 H
31470 D1[1]
31481 C
31487 D1[1]
31489 D1[1]
31492 D1[1]
31494 D1[1]
31503 H
31505 D1[1]
31714 C
31715 C
31803 U
31804 U
31806 U
31850 N
31852 N
31854 N
41308 2MT[1]
41309 2MT[1]
41310 2MT[1]
41311 2MT[1]
41312 2MT[1]

1957 73E
31242 C
31255 C
31256 C
31268 C
31481 C
31494 D1[1]
31503 H
31505 D1[1]
31509 D1[1]
31714 C
31715 C
31720 C
31765 L
31766 L
31767 L
31768 L
31850 N
31852 N
31892 U1
31893 U1
31903 U1
41308 2MT[1]
41309 2MT[1]
41310 2MT[1]
41311 2MT[1]
41312 2MT[1]
41313 2MT[1]

Feltham

1948 FEL
30009 T1
30031 M7
30139 K10
30140 K10
30144 K10
30153 K10
30158 L11
30167 L11
30174 L11
30254 M7
30383 K10
30385 K10
30492 G16
30493 G16
30494 G16
30495 G16
30496 S15
30497 S15
30498 S15
30499 S15
30500 S15
30501 S15
30502 S15
30503 S15
30504 S15
30505 S15
30506 S15
30507 S15
30508 S15
30509 S15
30510 S15
30511 S15
30512 S15
30513 S15
30514 S15
30515 S15
30516 H16
30517 H16
30518 H16
30519 H16
30520 H16
30567 0395
30569 0395
30570 0395
30572 0395
30573 0395
30579 0395
30687 700
30688 700
30689 700
30697 700
30698 700
30833 S15
30834 S15
30835 S15
30836 S15
30837 S15
30838 S15
30839 S15
30840 S15
30841 S15
30842 S15
31696 R1[2]
31698 R1[2]
33031 Q1
33032 Q1
33033 Q1
33034 Q1
33035 Q1
33036 Q1
33037 Q1
33038 Q1
33039 Q1
33040 Q1
90127 WD[1]
90142 WD[1]
90257 WD[1]
90267 WD[1]
90308 WD[1]
90523 WD[1]
90527 WD[1]
90530 WD[1]
90533 WD[1]
90543 WD[1]
90562 WD[1]
90570 WD[1]
90578 WD[1]
90604 WD[1]
90675 WD[1]

1951 70B
30043 M7
30164 L11
30174 L11
30254 M7
30309 700
30346 700
30352 700
30438 L11
30492 G16
30493 G16
30494 G16
30495 G16
30496 S15
30497 S15
30498 S15
30499 S15
30500 S15
30501 S15
30502 S15
30503 S15
30504 S15
30505 S15
30506 S15
30507 S15
30508 S15
30509 S15
30510 S15
30511 S15
30512 S15
30513 S15
30514 S15
30515 S15
30516 H16
30517 H16
30518 H16
30519 H16
30520 H16
30567 0395
30569 0395
30570 0395
30572 0395
30573 0395
30579 0395
30687 700
30688 700
30689 700
30696 700
30697 700
30698 700
30732 T9
30833 S15
30834 S15
30835 S15
30836 S15
30837 S15
30838 S15
30839 S15
30840 S15
33006 Q1
33007 Q1
33008 Q1
33009 Q1
33010 Q1
33011 Q1
33012 Q1
33013 Q1
90257 WD[1]
90562 WD[1]
90570 WD[1]
90604 WD[1]

1954 70B
30038 M7
30043 M7
30193 O2
30230 O2
30253 M7
30339 700
30346 700
30352 700
30355 700
30492 G16
30493 G16
30494 G16
30495 G16
30496 S15
30497 S15
30498 S15
30499 S15
30500 S15
30501 S15
30502 S15
30503 S15
30504 S15
30505 S15
30506 S15
30507 S15
30508 S15
30509 S15
30510 S15
30511 S15
30512 S15
30513 S15
30514 S15
30515 S15
30516 H16
30517 H16
30518 H16
30519 H16
30520 H16
30567 0395
30568 0395
30569 0395
30570 0395
30572 0395
30573 0395
30687 700
30688 700
30689 700
30833 S15
30834 S15
30838 S15
30839 S15
30840 S15
33006 Q1
33007 Q1
33008 Q1
33009 Q1
33010 Q1
33011 Q1
33012 Q1
33013 Q1
33026 Q1
33027 Q1

1957 70B
30038 M7
30041 M7
30042 M7
30043 M7
30177 O2
30179 O2
30339 700
30346 700
30352 700
30355 700
30492 G16
30493 G16
30494 G16
30495 G16
30496 S15
30497 S15
30498 S15
30499 S15
30500 S15
30501 S15
30502 S15
30503 S15
30504 S15
30505 S15
30506 S15
30507 S15
30508 S15
30509 S15
30510 S15
30511 S15
30512 S15
30513 S15
30514 S15
30515 S15
30516 H16
30517 H16
30518 H16
30519 H16
30520 H16
30567 0395
30568 0395
30572 0395
30687 700
30688 700
30689 700
30696 700
30833 S15
30834 S15
30838 S15
30839 S15
30840 S15
33006 Q1
33007 Q1
33008 Q1
33009 Q1
33010 Q1
33011 Q1
33012 Q1
33013 Q1
33016 Q1
33018 Q1
33026 Q1
33027 Q1

1960 70B
30031 M7
30032 M7
30043 M7
30339 700
30346 700
30355 700
30494 G16
30495 G16
30496 S15
30497 S15
30498 S15
30499 S15
30500 S15
30501 S15
30502 S15
30503 S15
30504 S15
30505 S15
30506 S15
30507 S15
30508 S15
30509 S15
30510 S15
30511 S15
30512 S15
30513 S15
30514 S15
30515 S15
30516 H16
30517 H16
30518 H16
30519 H16
30520 H16
30687 700
30689 700
30696 700
30775 N15
30777 N15
30793 N15
30795 N15
30833 S15
30834 S15
30838 S15
30839 S15
30840 S15
31033 C
31892 U1
31893 U1
32438 C2X
33006 Q1
33007 Q1
33008 Q1
33009 Q1
33010 Q1
33011 Q1
33012 Q1
33013 Q1
33016 Q1
33018 Q1
33026 Q1
33027 Q1

1963 70B
4610 5700
30032 M7
30035 M7
30496 S15
30497 S15
30498 S15
30499 S15
30500 S15
30501 S15
30503 S15
30506 S15
30507 S15
30508 S15
30509 S15
30510 S15
30511 S15
30512 S15
30513 S15
30514 S15
30515 S15
30833 S15
30834 S15
30837 S15
30838 S15
30839 S15
30840 S15
31922 W
31923 W
33001 Q1
33002 Q1
33003 Q1
33004 Q1
33006 Q1
33007 Q1
33008 Q1
33009 Q1
33010 Q1
33011 Q1
33012 Q1
33013 Q1
33027 Q1
33038 Q1
33040 Q1

1966 70B
80033 4MT[3]
80034 4MT[3]
80068 4MT[3]
80085 4MT[3]
80094 4MT[3]
80140 4MT[3]

Ferndale

1948 FDL
207 TV[2]
215 TV[2]
216 TV[2]
218 TV[2]
278 TV[2]
279 TV[2]
283 TV[2]
298 TV[2]
299 TV[2]
5600 5600
5610 5600
5668 5600

Fishguard Goodwick

1948 FGD
1419 1400
1423 1400
1431 1400
1452 1400
3637 5700
4982 4900
5395 4300
5716 5700
5905 4900
5928 4900
6823 6800
7413 7400
7747 5700
9602 5700
9603 5700
9760 5700

1951 87J
1423 1400
1431 1400
1452 1400
3637 5700
5395 4300
5716 5700
5905 4900
5908 4900
5928 4900
6823 6800
7747 5700
9602 5700
9603 5700
9760 5700

1954 87J
1423 1400
1431 1400
1452 1400
1456 1400
2223 2251
3637 5700
5716 5700
5905 4900
5908 4900
5928 4900
6909 4900
7747 5700
9602 5700
9603 5700
9760 5700

1957 87J
1423 1400
1431 1400
1452 1400
2223 2251
3637 5700
4677 5700
4981 4900
5716 5700
5905 4900
5908 4900
5928 4900
7747 5700
9602 5700
9760 5700

1960 87J
2271 2251
3637 5700
4677 5700
4981 4900
5713 5700
5905 4900
5908 4900
5928 4900
5947 4900
5969 4900
6347 4300
6869 6800
6909 4900
7747 5700
9602 5700
9666 5700
9677 5700
9760 5700

1963 87J
4644 5700
4962 4900
4981 4900
5905 4900
5972 4900
6116 6100
6900 4900
6968 6959
8739 5700
9602 5700
9645 5700
9666 5700
9677 5700
9760 5700

Fleetwood

1948 24F
42712 5MT[1]
42840 5MT[1]
42841 5MT[1]
42842 5MT[1]
42867 5MT[1]
44948 5MT[3]
45107 5MT[3]
45212 5MT[3]
45214 5MT[3]
47161 2F[1]
47165 2F[1]
50640 2P[8]
50675 2P[8]
50703 2P[8]
50705 2P[8]
50720 2P[8]
50732 2P[8]
50765 2P[8]
50802 2P[8]
50812 2P[8]
51321 2F[2]
51376 2F[2]
51477 2F[2]
51498 2F[2]
51514 2F[2]
52240 3F[7]
52439 3F[7]
52458 3F[7]

1951 28B
41260 2MT[1]
41261 2MT[1]
41262 2MT[1]
41280 2MT[1]
41281 2MT[1]
41282 2MT[1]
42840 5MT[1]
42841 5MT[1]
42842 5MT[1]
42844 5MT[1]
42867 5MT[1]
44948 5MT[3]
45107 5MT[3]
45212 5MT[3]
45214 5MT[3]
47161 2F[1]
47165 2F[1]
50640 2P[8]
50642 2P[8]
50646 2P[8]
50720 2P[8]
50766 2P[8]
50778 2P[8]
50802 2P[8]
50812 2P[8]
50840 2P[8]
50850 2P[8]
51321 2F[2]
51423 2F[2]
51477 2F[2]
51481 2F[2]
51498 2F[2]
52240 3F[7]
52290 3F[7]
52458 3F[7]
52588 3F[9]

1954 24F
41260 2MT[1]
41261 2MT[1]
41262 2MT[1]
41280 2MT[1]
41281 2MT[1]
41282 2MT[1]
42765 5MT[1]
42840 5MT[1]
42841 5MT[1]
42842 5MT[1]
42843 5MT[1]
42844 5MT[1]
42867 5MT[1]
44948 5MT[3]
45107 5MT[3]
45206 5MT[3]
45212 5MT[3]
47161 2F[1]
47165 2F[1]
50788 2P[8]
51321 2F[2]
51477 2F[2]
51481 2F[2]
51498 2F[2]
52290 3F[7]

1957 24F
41260 2MT[1]
41261 2MT[1]
42765 5MT[1]
42840 5MT[1]
42841 5MT[1]
42842 5MT[1]
42843 5MT[1]
42844 5MT[1]
42867 5MT[1]
45107 5MT[3]
45206 5MT[3]
45212 5MT[3]
47161 2F[1]
47165 2F[1]
51321 2F[2]
51419 2F[2]
51524 2F[2]
84015 2MT[2]
84016 2MT[2]
84017 2MT[2]
84018 2MT[2]
90556 WD[1]

1960 24F
41205 2MT[1]
41260 2MT[1]
41261 2MT[1]
42732 5MT[1]
42765 5MT[1]
42840 5MT[1]
42841 5MT[1]
42842 5MT[1]
42843 5MT[1]
42844 5MT[1]
42867 5MT[1]
45107 5MT[3]
45206 5MT[3]
45212 5MT[3]
47161 2F[1]
47165 2F[1]
51336 2F[2]
51419 2F[2]
51524 2F[2]
84010 2MT[2]
84016 2MT[2]
84017 2MT[2]
84018 2MT[2]

1963 24F
42722 5MT[1]
42765 5MT[1]
42840 5MT[1]
42841 5MT[1]
42842 5MT[1]
42843 5MT[1]
42844 5MT[1]
44889 5MT[3]
44894 5MT[3]
44982 5MT[3]
44988 5MT[3]
45107 5MT[3]
45206 5MT[3]
45212 5MT[3]
45226 5MT[3]
47161 2F[1]
84010 2MT[2]
84011 2MT[2]
84012 2MT[2]
84016 2MT[2]
84017 2MT[2]
84018 2MT[2]
90335 WD[1]
90367 WD[1]
90413 WD[1]
90658 WD[1]
90681 WD[1]
90689 WD[1]
90725 WD[1]

1966 10C
42224 4MT[1]
42431 4MT[1]
44729 5MT[3]
44940 5MT[3]
44988 5MT[3]
45107 5MT[3]
45200 5MT[3]
45347 5MT[3]
45421 5MT[3]
45444 5MT[3]
47317 3F[6]
47599 3F[6]
48005 8F
48199 8F
48223 8F
48310 8F
48319 8F
48338 8F
48377 8F

Folkestone Junction

1948 FOL
31047 R1[1]
31107 R1[1]
31127 R1[1]
31128 R1[1]
31154 R1[1]
31323 P
31337 R1[1]
31340 R1[1]
31558 P

1951 74C sub
31047 R1[1]
31107 R1[1]
31128 R1[1]
31147 R1[1]
31154 R1[1]
31337 R1[1]
31340 R1[1]

1954 74C sub
31047 R1[1]
31069 R1[1]
31107 R1[1]
31128 R1[1]
31154 R1[1]
31337 R1[1]
31340 R1[1]

1957 74C sub
31047 R1[1]
31069 R1[1]
31107 R1[1]
31128 R1[1]
31147 R1[1]
31337 R1[1]
31339 R1[1]
31340 R1[1]

1960 73H sub
4601 5700
4610 5700
4616 5700
4626 5700
4630 5700
4631 5700

Forfar

1948 29D
42738 5MT[1]
42800 5MT[1]
42801 5MT[1]
54450 3P[5]
54454 3P[5]
54486 3P[6]
55160 2P[13]
55161 2P[13]
55162 2P[13]
55172 2P[13]
55184 2P[13]
55185 2P[13]
55190 2P[13]
55194 2P[13]
55195 2P[13]
55198 2P[13]
55200 2P[13]
55214 2P[13]
55230 2P[13]
57324 2F[5]
57441 2F[5]
57642 3F[13]

1951 63C
42738 5MT[1]
42800 5MT[1]
42801 5MT[1]
54450 3P[5]
54454 3P[5]
55136 2P[12]
55161 2P[13]
55162 2P[13]
55169 2P[13]
55172 2P[13]
55185 2P[13]
55193 2P[13]
55194 2P[13]
55195 2P[13]
55200 2P[13]
55214 2P[13]
55230 2P[13]
57324 2F[5]
57368 2F[5]
57441 2F[5]

1954 63C
40939 4P[1]
42738 5MT[1]
42800 5MT[1]
42801 5MT[1]
44318 4F[2]
54450 3P[5]
54454 3P[5]
54486 3P[6]
55176 2P[13]
55193 2P[13]
55194 2P[13]
55198 2P[13]
55200 2P[13]
55230 2P[13]
57368 2F[5]

1957 63C
42738 5MT[1]
42800 5MT[1]
42801 5MT[1]
44314 4F[2]
54467 3P[6]
54486 3P[6]
55198 2P[13]
55220 2P[13]
55230 2P[13]
56290 3F[10]
57368 2F[5]
57424 2F[5]

1960 63C
57441 2F[5]

Forres

1948 32C
54385 2P[10]
54410 2P[11]
54473 3P[6]
54481 3P[6]
56301 3F[10]
57591 3F[12]
57620 3F[12]

1951 60E
54473 3P[6]
54481 3P[6]
54482 3P[6]
55178 2P[13]
56301 3F[10]
57620 3F[12]

1954 60E
54472 3P[6]
54473 3P[6]
54482 3P[6]
55178 2P[13]
56301 3F[10]
57620 3F[12]

1957 60E
54471 3P[6]
54472 3P[6]
54473 3P[6]
54482 3P[6]
55178 2P[13]
56301 3F[10]
57620 3F[12]

Fort William

1948 FW
61782 K2
61783 K2
61787 K2
61788 K2
61789 K2
61790 K2
61791 K2
61995 K4
61996 K4
62470 D34
62480 D34
65237 J36

1951 63D
61782 K2
61783 K2
61787 K2
61788 K2
61789 K2
61790 K2
61791 K2
61995 K4
61996 K4
65237 J36
65300 J36
65313 J36

1954 63D
61783 K2
61787 K2
61788 K2
61790 K2
61791 K2
61995 K4
61996 K4
62011 K1
62012 K1
65237 J36
65300 J36
65313 J36

1957 65J
44972 5MT[3]
44973 5MT[3]
44974 5MT[3]
44975 5MT[3]
44976 5MT[3]
44977 5MT[3]
61791 K2
61997 K1/1
62011 K1
62012 K1
62031 K1
62034 K1
62052 K1
65237 J36
65300 J36
65313 J36

1960 65J
44255 4F[2]
44972 5MT[3]
44973 5MT[3]
44974 5MT[3]
44975 5MT[3]
44976 5MT[3]
44977 5MT[3]
61784 K2
61791 K2
61997 K1/1
62011 K1
62012 K1
62031 K1
62034 K1
62052 K1
65300 J36
65313 J36

1963 63B
44960 5MT[3]

Fratton

1948 FRA
30020 T1
30027 M7
30045 M7
30054 M7
30113 T9
30114 T9
30115 T9
30118 T9
30164 L11
30166 L11
30170 L11
30172 L11
30280 T9
30287 T9
30303 T9
30304 T9
30305 T9
30314 T9
30338 T9
30384 K10
30396 S11
30400 S11
30401 S11
30402 S11
30403 S11
30404 S11
30413 L11
30414 L11
30417 L12
30424 L12
30425 L12
30441 L11
30480 M7
30731 T9
30732 T9
30733 T9
31797 U
31831 N
32153 E1[2]
32269 D1/M
32337 K
32338 K
32490 E4
32509 E4
32537 C2X
32548 C2X
32554 C2X
32559 E4
32562 E4
32640 A1X
32644 A1X
32655 A1X
32659 A1X
32661 A1X
32662 A1X
32690 E1[2]
32691 E1[2]
32694 E1[2]
701S D1/M

1951 71D
30020 T1
30045 M7
30050 M7
30053 M7
30054 M7
30113 T9
30114 T9
30115 T9
30118 T9
30120 T9
30170 L11
30172 L11
30280 T9
30303 T9
30305 T9
30310 T9
30314 T9
30395 S11
30396 S11
30397 S11
30400 S11
30402 S11
30416 L12
30417 L12
30419 L12
30426 L12
30427 L12
30441 L11
30480 M7
30711 T9
30731 T9
31612 U
31805 U
31809 U
32129 E1[2]
32139 E1[2]
32300 C3
32301 C3
32302 C3
32303 C3
32306 C3

32338 K
32340 K
32399 E5
32646 A1X
32655 A1X
32661 A1X
32662 A1X
32677 A1X
32691 E1[2]
32694 E1[2]
701S D1/M

1954 71D

30054 M7
30055 M7
30207 O2
30356 M7
30357 M7
30465 D15
30471 D15
30726 T9
30730 T9
30732 T9
31637 U
31638 U
31805 U
31807 U
31808 U
31809 U
32138 E1[2]
32139 E1[2]
32349 K
32479 E4
32495 E4
32505 E4
32509 E4
32548 C2X
32549 C2X
32550 C2X
32646 A1X
32650 A1X
32661 A1X
32677 A1X
32694 E1[2]

1957 70F

30022 M7
30039 M7
30207 O2
30357 M7
30726 T9
30729 T9
30730 T9
30732 T9
31611 U
31637 U
31638 U
31805 U
31807 U
31808 U
31809 U
32139 E1[2]
32337 K
32349 K
32479 E4
32495 E4
32509 E4
32548 C2X
32549 C2X
32550 C2X
32640 A1X
32646 A1X
32650 A1X
32661 A1X
32677 A1X
32694 E1[2]

Frodingham

1948 FRO

63475 O3
63476 O3
63477 O3
63478 O3
63479 O3
63480 O3
63481 O3
63482 O3
63483 O3
63484 O3
63485 O3
63486 O3
63488 O3
63489 O3
63491 O3
63493 O3
63494 O3
63584 O4
63595 O4
63602 O4
63606 O4
63626 O4
63640 O4
63642 O4
63645 O4
63649 O4
63655 O4
63669 O4
63690 O4
63696 O4
63726 O4
63744 O4
63778 O4
63788 O4
63793 O4
63802 O4
63818 O4
63824 O4
63920 O4
63922 O2
63934 O2
63937 O2
63939 O2
63941 O2
63944 O2
63963 O2
63975 O2
64308 J11
64309 J11
64339 J11
64362 J11
64395 J11
64407 J11
64429 J11
68962 J50
68964 J50
68968 J50
68970 J50
68971 J50
68973 J50
69057 L3
69058 L3
69930 Q1
69932 Q1
69934 Q1
69935 Q1
69936 Q1
69937 Q1

1951 36C

63572 O4
63576 O4
63584 O4
63587 O4
63595 O4
63601 O4
63602 O4
63606 O4
63617 O4
63626 O4
63640 O4
63642 O4
63645 O4
63649 O4
63653 O4
63655 O4
63659 O4
63660 O4
63669 O4
63671 O4
63684 O4
63690 O4
63696 O4
63718 O4
63726 O4
63728 O4
63731 O4
63741 O4
63744 O4
63745 O4
63747 O4
63778 O4
63788 O4
63793 O4
63818 O4
63824 O4
63832 O4
63847 O4
63906 O4
63911 O4
63917 O4
63920 O4
63922 O2
63934 O2
63937 O2
63939 O2
63944 O2
63963 O2
64308 J11
64309 J11
64339 J11
64395 J11
64407 J11
64429 J11
68962 J50
68964 J50
68968 J50
68970 J50
68971 J50
68973 J50
68974 J50
69051 L3
69902 S1
69930 Q1
69932 Q1
69934 Q1
69935 Q1
69936 Q1
69937 Q1

1954 36C

63572 O4
63576 O4
63595 O4
63606 O4
63617 O4
63626 O4
63642 O4
63653 O4
63655 O4
63659 O4
63660 O4
63671 O4
63690 O4
63696 O4
63728 O4
63741 O4
63744 O4
63747 O4
63788 O4
63793 O4
63818 O4
63906 O4
63911 O4
63917 O4
63922 O2
63934 O2
63939 O2
63944 O2
63945 O2
63961 O2
63963 O2
63983 O2
63984 O2
63985 O2
64308 J11
64339 J11
64395 J11
64407 J11
64429 J11
68960 J50
68962 J50
68964 J50
68970 J50
68980 J50
69060 L3
69064 L3
69065 L3
69926 Q1
69930 Q1
69932 Q1
69934 Q1
69935 Q1
69936 Q1
69937 Q1
90013 WD[1]
90031 WD[1]
90032 WD[1]
90059 WD[1]
90070 WD[1]
90111 WD[1]
90133 WD[1]
90232 WD[1]
90422 WD[1]
90425 WD[1]
90456 WD[1]
90490 WD[1]
90512 WD[1]
90540 WD[1]
90596 WD[1]
90646 WD[1]
90647 WD[1]
90714 WD[1]

1957 36C

63572 O4
63576 O4
63595 O4
63601 O4
63606 O4
63617 O4
63626 O4
63642 O4
63653 O4
63660 O4
63662 O4
63671 O4
63690 O4
63696 O4
63728 O4
63741 O4
63744 O4
63747 O4
63761 O4
63788 O4
63793 O4
63799 O4
63807 O4
63818 O4
63853 O4
63880 O4
63906 O4
63917 O4
64308 J11
64319 J11
64407 J11
64429 J11
68960 J50
68962 J50
68964 J50
68965 J50
68970 J50
68973 J50
69901 S1
69905 S1
69926 Q1
69930 Q1
69932 Q1
69934 Q1
69935 Q1
69936 Q1
90000 WD[1]
90013 WD[1]
90031 WD[1]
90032 WD[1]
90059 WD[1]
90070 WD[1]
90111 WD[1]
90133 WD[1]
90232 WD[1]
90422 WD[1]
90425 WD[1]
90456 WD[1]
90490 WD[1]
90512 WD[1]
90540 WD[1]
90596 WD[1]
90597 WD[1]
90598 WD[1]
90601 WD[1]
90646 WD[1]
90647 WD[1]
90714 WD[1]

1960 36C

63576 O4
63595 O4
63601 O4
63602 O4
63606 O4
63617 O4
63626 O4
63647 O4
63653 O4
63662 O4
63665 O4
63666 O4
63671 O4
63690 O4
63728 O4
63730 O4
63741 O4
63744 O4
63747 O4
63748 O4
63764 O4
63781 O4
63788 O4
63793 O4
63799 O4
63807 O4
63824 O4
63836 O4
63880 O4
63906 O4
63917 O4
64308 J11
64371 J11
64385 J11
64395 J11
64404 J11
64423 J11
90013 WD[1]
90031 WD[1]
90032 WD[1]
90059 WD[1]
90070 WD[1]
90111 WD[1]
90133 WD[1]
90232 WD[1]
90422 WD[1]
90425 WD[1]
90456 WD[1]
90469 WD[1]
90490 WD[1]
90512 WD[1]
90540 WD[1]
90597 WD[1]
90598 WD[1]
90601 WD[1]
90646 WD[1]
90647 WD[1]
90714 WD[1]

1963 36C

62013 K1
62016 K1
62017 K1
62018 K1
62020 K1
62032 K1
62033 K1
62035 K1
63576 O4
63586 O4
63601 O4
63606 O4
63628 O4
63653 O4
63671 O4
63728 O4
63730 O4
63741 O4
63744 O4
63781 O4
63788 O4
63791 O4
63793 O4
63802 O4
63807 O4
63836 O4
63880 O4
63884 O4
63897 O4
63898 O4
63906 O4
90007 WD[1]
90013 WD[1]
90024 WD[1]
90025 WD[1]
90032 WD[1]
90053 WD[1]
90059 WD[1]
90070 WD[1]
90079 WD[1]
90108 WD[1]
90111 WD[1]
90115 WD[1]
90119 WD[1]
90120 WD[1]
90133 WD[1]
90161 WD[1]
90165 WD[1]
90166 WD[1]
90189 WD[1]
90232 WD[1]
90239 WD[1]
90422 WD[1]
90453 WD[1]
90456 WD[1]
90469 WD[1]
90537 WD[1]
90540 WD[1]
90544 WD[1]
90573 WD[1]
90597 WD[1]
90598 WD[1]
90601 WD[1]
90602 WD[1]
90646 WD[1]
90647 WD[1]
90665 WD[1]
90696 WD[1]
90714 WD[1]
90730 WD[1]

1966 36C

90013 WD[1]
90024 WD[1]
90032 WD[1]
90035 WD[1]
90075 WD[1]
90080 WD[1]
90148 WD[1]
90178 WD[1]
90232 WD[1]
90241 WD[1]
90274 WD[1]
90367 WD[1]
90384 WD[1]
90410 WD[1]
90456 WD[1]
90471 WD[1]
90493 WD[1]
90498 WD[1]
90514 WD[1]

Gateshead

1948 GHD

60001 A4
60002 A4
60005 A4
60016 A4
60018 A4
60019 A4
60020 A4
60023 A4
60036 A3
60038 A3
60040 A3
60042 A3
60045 A3
60060 A3
60070 A3
60071 A3
60074 A3
60075 A3
60076 A3
60078 A3
60079 A3
60081 A3
60084 A3
60086 A3
60518 A2
60521 A2
60801 V2
60805 V2
60806 V2
60807 V2
60809 V2
60810 V2
60811 V2
60833 V2
60835 V2
60860 V2
60868 V2
60883 V2
60884 V2
60885 V2
60887 V2
60910 V2
60923 V2
60926 V2
60940 V2
60942 V2
60952 V2
60959 V2
60964 V2
60965 V2
60967 V2
61011 B1
61012 B1
61013 B1
61014 B1
61100 B1
61238 B1
61875 K3
61878 K3
61881 K3
61897 K3
61904 K3
61928 K3
61930 K3
61985 K3
61986 K3
62736 D49
62738 D49
62739 D49
62742 D49
62745 D49
62747 D49
62749 D49
62750 D49
62764 D49
62766 D49
62771 D49
62937 C6
67634 V3
67682 V3
67683 V3
67687 V3
67688 V3
67689 V3
67690 V3
68141 Y1
68146 Y1
68154 Y3
68160 Y3
68180 Y3
68234 J71
68247 J71
68251 J71
68262 J71
68265 J71
68267 J71
68270 J71
68283 J71
68309 J71
68314 J71
68674 J72
68680 J72
68693 J72
68702 J72
68720 J72
68723 J72
69090 N10
69091 N10
69092 N10
69093 N10
69099 N10
69102 N10
69103 N10
69105 N10
69106 N10
69107 N10
69109 N10
69931 Q1
69933 Q1

1951 52A

60001 A4
60002 A4
60005 A4
60016 A4
60018 A4
60019 A4
60020 A4
60023 A4
60038 A3
60040 A3
60042 A3
60045 A3
60060 A3
60071 A3
60075 A3
60078 A3
60082 A3
60115 A1
60124 A1
60129 A1
60132 A1
60135 A1
60137 A1
60142 A1
60143 A1
60145 A1
60147 A1
60150 A1
60151 A1
60154 A1
60155 A1
60518 A2
60521 A2
60538 A2
60883 V2
60923 V2
60940 V2
60964 V2
60965 V2
60967 V2
61011 B1
61012 B1
61013 B1
61014 B1
61100 B1
61238 B1
64701 J39
64704 J39
64707 J39
64853 J39
64869 J39
64871 J39
67309 G5
67320 G5
67325 G5
67329 G5
67634 V3
67647 V1
67682 V3
67683 V3
67687 V3
67688 V3
67689 V3
67690 V3
68141 Y1
68146 Y1
68154 Y3
68160 Y3
68180 Y3
68251 J71
68270 J71
68283 J71
68309 J71
68314 J71
68674 J72
68675 J72
68680 J72
68693 J72
68702 J72
68720 J72
68723 J72
68732 J72
68744 J72
69005 J72
69090 N10
69091 N10
69092 N10
69109 N10

1954 52A

60001 A4
60002 A4
60005 A4
60016 A4
60018 A4
60019 A4
60020 A4
60023 A4
60038 A3
60042 A3
60045 A3
60060 A3
60071 A3
60075 A3
60076 A3
60078 A3
60082 A3
60115 A1
60124 A1
60129 A1
60132 A1
60135 A1
60137 A1
60142 A1
60143 A1
60145 A1
60147 A1
60150 A1
60151 A1
60154 A1
60155 A1
60516 A2
60518 A2
60521 A2
60538 A2
60802 V2
60807 V2
60809 V2
60868 V2
60883 V2
60923 V2
60940 V2
60947 V2
60949 V2
60957 V2
60964 V2
60967 V2
61011 B1
61012 B1
61013 B1
61014 B1
61022 B1
61100 B1
61199 B1
61238 B1
62360 D20
62371 D20
62375 D20
64701 J39
64704 J39
64852 J39
64865 J39
64869 J39
64871 J39
64929 J39
67296 G5
67320 G5
67329 G5
67634 V3
67682 V3
67683 V3
67687 V3
67688 V3
67689 V3
67690 V3
68146 Y1
68160 Y3
68180 Y3
68270 J71
68272 J71
68283 J71
68309 J71
68314 J71
68674 J72
68675 J72
68680 J72
68693 J72
68720 J72
68723 J72
68732 J72
68744 J72
69005 J72
69090 N10
69091 N10
69092 N10
69095 N10
69109 N10

1957 52A

42072 4MT[1]
42073 4MT[1]
42093 4MT[1]
42094 4MT[1]
60001 A4
60002 A4
60005 A4
60016 A4
60018 A4
60019 A4
60020 A4
60023 A4
60040 A3
60045 A3
60060 A3
60070 A3
60071 A3
60075 A3
60076 A3
60078 A3
60115 A1
60124 A1
60129 A1
60132 A1
60135 A1
60137 A1
60142 A1
60143 A1
60145 A1
60147 A1
60150 A1
60151 A1
60154 A1
60155 A1
60516 A2
60518 A2
60521 A2
60538 A2
60807 V2
60833 V2
60848 V2
60868 V2
60887 V2
60923 V2
60940 V2
60947 V2
60949 V2
60964 V2
60967 V2
61012 B1
61019 B1
61022 B1
61100 B1
61238 B1
64701 J39
64704 J39
64852 J39
64865 J39
64869 J39
64871 J39
64929 J39
67688 V3
67689 V3
67690 V3
68159 Y3
68267 J71
68272 J71
68283 J71
68309 J71
68314 J71
68674 J72
68675 J72
68680 J72
68693 J72
68720 J72
68723 J72
68732 J72
68744 J72
69005 J72
69092 N10
69109 N10

1960 52A

60001 A4
60002 A4
60005 A4
60016 A4
60018 A4
60019 A4
60020 A4
60023 A4
60038 A3
60042 A3
60045 A3
60051 A3
60052 A3
60053 A3
60058 A3
60060 A3
60070 A3
60075 A3
60076 A3
60078 A3
60091 A3
60115 A1
60124 A1
60129 A1
60132 A1
60135 A1
60137 A1
60142 A1
60143 A1
60145 A1
60147 A1
60150 A1
60151 A1
60154 A1
60155 A1
60516 A2
60518 A2
60521 A2
60538 A2
60805 V2
60807 V2
60833 V2
60860 V2
60868 V2
60904 V2
60923 V2
60929 V2
60934 V2
60942 V2
60947 V2
60949 V2
60952 V2
60964 V2
60967 V2
60979 V2
61012 B1
61014 B1
61019 B1
61022 B1
61100 B1
61238 B1
64707 J39
64713 J39
64812 J39
64814 J39
64846 J39
64851 J39
64852 J39
64854 J39
64860 J39
64865 J39
64869 J39
64921 J39
64936 J39
64938 J39
64978 J39
65712 J25
65728 J25
67637 V1
67639 V1
67687 V3
67688 V3
67689 V3
67690 V3
68314 J71
68674 J72
68675 J72
68680 J72
68693 J72
68695 J72
68697 J72
68720 J72
68723 J72
68728 J72
68737 J72
69001 J72
69005 J72
69027 J72
69101 N10
69105 N10
69109 N10
77011 3MT[1]
77014 3MT[1]

1963 52A

60001 A4
60002 A4
60005 A4
60016 A4
60018 A4
60019 A4
60020 A4
60023 A4
60964 V2
62010 K1
62024 K1
62026 K1
62028 K1
62029 K1
67628 V3
67643 V3
67653 V3
67662 V3
67678 V3
68053 J94
68059 J94
68723 J72
68736 J72
69001 J72
69004 J72
69005 J72
69023 J72
69025 J72

Gillingham

1948 GIL

31002 F1
31003 O1
31007 O1
31013 B1
31014 O1
31039 O1
31051 O1
31064 O1
31066 O1
31092 D
31105 F1
31112 C
31215 F1
31234 C
31238 O1
31256 C
31267 C
31278 H
31308 H
31317 C
31378 O1
31384 O1
31391 O1
31430 O1
31439 O1
31449 B1
31510 C
31573 C
31579 C
31583 C
31585 C
31588 C
31658 R
31659 R
31660 R
31662 R
31663 R
31665 R
31666 R
31682 C
31684 C
31688 C
31697 R1[2]
31713 C
31746 D
31750 D

1951 73D

30951 Z
31086 C
31090 C
31092 D
31112 C
31221 C
31223 C
31225 C
31255 C
31256 C
31267 C
31287 C
31308 H
31317 C
31492 D1[1]
31494 D1[1]
31498 C
31501 D
31510 C
31516 E
31573 C
31579 C
31583 C
31585 C
31586 D
31588 C
31658 R
31659 R
31662 R
31663 R
31665 R
31666 R
31682 C
31688 C
31693 C
31697 R1[2]
31712 C
31713 C
31724 C
31729 D
31741 D1[1]
33026 Q1

1954 73D

31112 C
31158 H
31221 C
31223 C
31225 C
31227 C
31229 C
31242 C
31306 H
31307 H
31308 H
31495 C
31498 C
31508 C
31509 D1[1]
31510 C
31518 H
31545 D1[1]
31593 C
31671 R
31681 C
31682 C
31683 C
31684 C
31712 C
31713 C

1957 73D

31112 C
31161 H
31227 C
31229 C
31308 H
31322 H
31495 C
31508 C
31510 C
31512 H
31518 H
31681 C
31682 C
31683 C
31684 C
31711 C
31712 C
31785 L1
31786 L1
31787 L1
31815 N
31816 N

Gloucester

1948 GLO

1406 1400
1413 1400
1424 1400
1464 1400
1943 1901
1989 1901
2009 1901
2146 2021
2248 2251
2656 2600
2756 2721
2938 2900
2980 2900
3153 3150
3164 3150
3171 3150
3175 3150
3204 2251
3205 2251
3213 2251
3379 3300
3609 5700
4059 4000
4082 4073
4140 5101
4534 4500
4627 5700
4628 5700
4659 5700
4977 4900
5042 4073
5312 4300
5336 4300
5347 4300
5394 4300
5398 4300
5697 5600
5793 5700
5951 4900
5965 4900
5980 4900
5988 4900
5990 4900
6309 4300
6381 4300
6623 5600
6681 5600
6917 4900
6940 4900
7004 4073
7723 5700
7741 5700
7815 7800
8701 5700
8717 5700
8731 5700
8781 5700
9064 3252
9089 3252
9727 5700
9776 5700
90179 WD[1]
90413 WD[1]
90691 WD[1]
90715 WD[1]

1951 85B

1402 1400
1404 1400
1406 1400
1409 1400
1413 1400
1424 1400
1441 1400
1456 1400
1464 1400
1612 1600
1616 1600
1623 1600
1625 1600
1627 1600
1943 1901
2009 1901
2025 2021
2034 2021
2043 2021
2044 2021
2080 2021
2121 2021
2131 2021
2144 2021
2146 2021
2248 2251
2254 2251
2291 2251
2350 2301
2823 2800
2938 2900
2951 2900
3153 3150
3163 3150
3164 3150
3171 3150
3204 2251
3205 2251
3213 2251
3609 5700
4059 4000
4079 4073
4140 5101
4141 5101
4174 5101
4534 4500
4564 4500
4567 4500
4627 5700
4628 5700
4659 5700
4929 4900
4996 4900
5042 4073
5112 5101
5312 4300
5336 4300
5345 4300
5347 4300
5394 4300
5398 4300
5518 4575
5530 4575
5538 4575
5574 4575
5948 4900
5951 4900
5980 4900
5988 4900
5990 4900
6309 4300
6341 4300
6381 4300
6385 4300
6631 5600
6917 4900
6921 4900

6940 4900
6985 6959
6987 6959
6992 6959
7006 4073
7303 4300
7312 4300
7723 5700
7741 5700
7815 7800
7818 7800
7824 7800
7926 6959
8701 5700
8717 5700
8731 5700
8781 5700
9727 5700
90179 WD[1]

1954 85B
1401 1400
1402 1400
1404 1400
1406 1400
1409 1400
1413 1400
1424 1400
1441 1400
1464 1400
1612 1600
1616 1600
1623 1600
1625 1600
1627 1600
1630 1600
1631 1600
1632 1600
1639 1600
1642 1600
2248 2251
2254 2251
2291 2251
2292 2251
2295 2251
3022 ROD
3048 ROD
3163 3150
3164 3150
3171 3150
3180 3150
3203 2251
3204 2251
3205 2251
3213 2251
3609 5700
4140 5101
4141 5101
4174 5101
4521 4500
4564 4500
4586 4575
4627 5700
4628 5700
4659 5700
4929 4900
4934 4900
4996 4900
5017 4073
5018 4073
5042 4073
5312 4300
5345 4300
5347 4300
5394 4300
5398 4300
5408 5400
5417 5400
5530 4575
5538 4575
5907 4900
5951 4900
5980 4900
5990 4900
6309 4300
6330 4300
6341 4300
6349 4300
6355 4300
6373 4300
6381 4300
6385 4300
6631 5600
6690 5600
6917 4900
6921 4900
6938 4900
6985 6959
7006 4073
7035 4073
7312 4300
7723 5700
7741 5700
7926 6959
8487 9400
8488 9400
8717 5700
8781 5700
9441 9400
9445 9400
9464 9400
9471 9400
9475 9400
9727 5700
90149 WD[1]
90573 WD[1]
90685 WD[1]
90691 WD[1]

1957 85B
1401 1400
1406 1400
1409 1400
1424 1400
1428 1400
1430 1400
1441 1400
1464 1400
1616 1600
1623 1600
1627 1600
1630 1600
1631 1600
1632 1600
1639 1600
1642 1600
2207 2251
2248 2251
2254 2251
2278 2251
2291 2251
2809 2800
2854 2800
3163 3150
3171 3150
3180 3150
3203 2251
3609 5700
3740 5700
4141 5101
4358 4300
4553 4500
4564 4500
4573 4500
4627 5700
4628 5700
4659 5700
4929 4900
5017 4073
5018 4073
5042 4073
5094 4073
5157 5101
5162 5101
5182 5101
5398 4300
5417 5400
5418 5400
5514 4575
5530 4575
5538 4575
5907 4900
5951 4900
5980 4900
6330 4300
6341 4300
6349 4300
6365 4300
6373 4300
6381 4300
6631 5600
6669 5600
6690 5600
6917 4900
6985 6959
7006 4073
7312 4300
7700 5700
7723 5700
7741 5700
7808 7800
7810 7800
7926 6959
8487 9400
8488 9400
8717 5700
8731 5700
8781 5700
9438 9400
9441 9400
9445 9400
9464 9400
9471 9400
9475 9400
90149 WD[1]
90573 WD[1]
90685 WD[1]
90691 WD[1]

1960 85B
1409 1400
1424 1400
1426 1400
1427 1400
1441 1400
1454 1400
1472 1400
1605 1600
1623 1600
1627 1600
1630 1600
1631 1600
1632 1600
1639 1600
1642 1600
2207 2251
2248 2251
2253 2251
2854 2800
3203 2251
3609 5700
3803 2884
3848 2884
4085 4073
4100 5101
4101 5101
4116 5101
4123 5101
4141 5101
4165 5101
4573 4500
4628 5700
4929 4900
4989 4900
5017 4073
5094 4073
5173 5101
5177 5101
5182 5101
5198 5101
5418 5400
5421 5400
5514 4575
5538 4575
5763 5700
5914 4900
5951 4900
5977 4900
6137 6100
6304 4300
6330 4300
6363 4300
6365 4300
6368 4300
6373 4300
6381 4300
6394 4300
6415 6400
6669 5600
6690 5600
6917 4900
6985 6959
7000 4073
7312 4300
7319 4300
7338 4300
7700 5700
7741 5700
7926 6959
8487 9400
8488 9400
8491 9400
8701 5700
8717 5700
8731 5700
8743 5700
9441 9400
9445 9400
9464 9400
9471 9400
9475 9400
9477 9400

1963 85B
1409 1400
1424 1400
1453 1400
1472 1400
1608 1600
1623 1600
1631 1600
1650 1600
2232 2251
2245 2251
2253 2251
3203 2251
3721 5700
3745 5700
3775 5700
4100 5101
4101 5101
4109 5101
4141 5101
4142 5101
4161 5101
4614 5700
4929 4900
5000 4073
5058 4073
5099 4073
5154 5101
5184 5101
5420 5400
5944 4900
5951 4900
6137 6100
6304 4300
6344 4300
6365 4300
6381 4300
6394 4300
6437 6400
6943 4900
6947 4900
6948 4900
6956 4900
6985 6959
6989 6959
6993 6959
7000 4073
7003 4073
7034 4073
7335 4300
8491 9400
8701 5700
8743 5700
9453 9400
9471 9400

Gloucester Barnwood

1948 22B
40437 2P[2]
40523 2P[2]
40530 2P[2]
41001 4P[2]
41019 4P[2]
41025 4P[2]
41027 4P[2]
41039 4P[2]
41058 4P[1]
41074 4P[1]
41097 4P[1]
41530 0F[2]
41537 0F[2]
41720 1F[1]
41727 1F[1]
41870 1F[1]
42922 5MT[1]
43213 3F[3]
43257 3F[3]
43258 3F[3]
43263 3F[3]
43344 3F[3]
43373 3F[3]
43427 3F[3]
43506 3F[3]
43507 3F[3]
43604 3F[3]
43645 3F[3]
43754 3F[3]
43791 3F[4]
43846 4F[1]
43887 4F[1]
43924 4F[1]
43932 4F[1]
43978 4F[1]
44045 4F[2]
44167 4F[2]
44175 4F[2]
44229 4F[2]
44235 4F[2]
44269 4F[2]
44272 4F[2]
44553 4F[2]
44576 4F[2]
47237 3F[5]
47619 3F[6]
47620 3F[6]
47635 3F[6]
58034 1P[5]
58047 1P[6]
58059 1P[6]
58063 1P[6]
58206 2F[9]

1951 22B
40040 3MT[1]
40523 2P[2]
40530 2P[2]
41001 4P[2]
41025 4P[2]
41047 4P[1]
41058 4P[1]
41074 4P[1]
41078 4P[1]
41097 4P[1]
41530 0F[2]
41537 0F[2]
41720 1F[1]
41727 1F[1]
43213 3F[3]
43258 3F[3]
43337 3F[3]
43344 3F[3]
43373 3F[3]
43506 3F[3]
43645 3F[3]
43754 3F[3]
43846 4F[1]
43887 4F[1]
43924 4F[1]
43932 4F[1]
43978 4F[1]
44035 4F[2]
44045 4F[2]
44087 4F[2]
44123 4F[2]
44167 4F[2]
44175 4F[2]
44272 4F[2]
47237 3F[5]
47607 3F[6]
47619 3F[6]
47620 3F[6]
47635 3F[6]
58051 1P[6]
58054 1P[6]
58063 1P[6]
58206 2F[9]

1954 22B
40489 2P[2]
40540 2P[2]
40541 2P[2]
40930 4P[1]
40932 4P[1]
40934 4P[1]
41047 4P[1]
41078 4P[1]
41195 4P[1]
41530 0F[2]
41537 0F[2]
41720 1F[1]
41748 1F[1]
43213 3F[3]
43258 3F[3]
43337 3F[3]
43344 3F[3]
43373 3F[3]
43506 3F[3]
43645 3F[3]
43754 3F[3]
43837 4F[1]
43846 4F[1]
43853 4F[1]
43887 4F[1]
43924 4F[1]
44035 4F[2]
44045 4F[2]
44087 4F[2]
44123 4F[2]
44167 4F[2]
44175 4F[2]
44209 4F[2]
44272 4F[2]
44293 4F[2]
44567 4F[2]
44587 4F[2]
47237 3F[5]
47607 3F[6]
47619 3F[6]
47620 3F[6]
47635 3F[6]
58071 1P[6]
58206 2F[9]

1957 22B
40489 2P[2]
40540 2P[2]
40541 2P[2]
40930 4P[1]
40934 4P[1]
41049 4P[1]
41195 4P[1]
41530 0F[2]
41537 0F[2]
41748 1F[1]
43213 3F[3]
43258 3F[3]
43337 3F[3]
43373 3F[3]
43506 3F[3]
43520 3F[3]
43645 3F[3]
43754 3F[3]
43853 4F[1]
43887 4F[1]
43924 4F[1]
44035 4F[2]
44045 4F[2]
44087 4F[2]
44123 4F[2]
44167 4F[2]
44209 4F[2]
44272 4F[2]
44293 4F[2]
44567 4F[2]
44587 4F[2]
46401 2MT[2]
47417 3F[6]
47422 3F[6]
47506 3F[6]
47539 3F[6]
47623 3F[6]
58206 2F[9]

1960 85E
7723 5700
7756 5700
40489 2P[2]
40540 2P[2]
41535 0F[2]
41537 0F[2]
41900 2P[4]
43337 3F[3]
43645 3F[3]
43754 3F[3]
43853 4F[1]
43887 4F[1]
43924 4F[1]
44035 4F[2]
44045 4F[2]
44123 4F[2]
44167 4F[2]
44209 4F[2]
44272 4F[2]
44296 4F[2]
44567 4F[2]
47417 3F[6]
47422 3F[6]
47506 3F[6]
47539 3F[6]
47623 3F[6]
75009 4MT[1]
75023 4MT[1]
90565 WD[1]
90685 WD[1]

1963 85C
41535 0F[2]
41537 0F[2]
43853 4F[1]
43887 4F[1]
44045 4F[2]
44123 4F[2]
44296 4F[2]
47506 3F[6]
47623 3F[6]
48172 8F
48420 8F
48463 8F
73019 5MT
73021 5MT
73024 5MT
73031 5MT
73068 5MT
73091 5MT
73092 5MT
73093 5MT
73094 5MT
73096 5MT
78005 2MT[1]
78006 2MT[1]

Goole

1948 25C
40585 2P[3]
40586 2P[3]
40589 2P[3]
40685 2P[3]
41089 4P[1]
44105 4F[2]
44221 4F[2]
44485 4F[2]
44486 4F[2]
46407 2MT[2]
46408 2MT[2]
48429 8F
48441 8F
48449 8F
49582 7F[4]
49600 7F[4]
51207 0F[4]
51241 0F[4]
51244 0F[4]
51323 2F[2]
51432 2F[2]
51443 2F[2]
51458 2F[2]
51516 2F[2]
51521 2F[2]
52037 2F[3]
52041 2F[3]
52043 2F[3]
52044 2F[3]
52056 2F[3]
52133 3F[7]
52181 3F[7]
52454 3F[7]
52592 3F[9]

1951 25C
40586 2P[3]
40589 2P[3]
40685 2P[3]
42477 4MT[3]
42553 4MT[3]
46405 2MT[2]
46407 2MT[2]
46408 2MT[2]
46409 2MT[2]
46436 2MT[2]
46437 2MT[2]
48449 8F
51207 0F[4]
51222 0F[4]
51241 0F[4]
51244 0F[4]
51323 2F[2]
51361 2F[2]
51379 2F[2]
51432 2F[2]
51516 2F[2]
51521 2F[2]
52191 3F[7]
52273 3F[7]
52331 3F[7]
52448 3F[7]
52592 3F[9]
90228 WD[1]
90262 WD[1]
90281 WD[1]
90300 WD[1]
90531 WD[1]

1954 25C
42477 4MT[3]
42553 4MT[3]
46405 2MT[2]
46407 2MT[2]
46408 2MT[2]
46409 2MT[2]
46436 2MT[2]
46437 2MT[2]
46487 2MT[2]
51222 0F[4]
51241 0F[4]
51244 0F[4]
51323 2F[2]
51361 2F[2]
51379 2F[2]
51432 2F[2]
51479 2F[2]
51503 2F[2]
51516 2F[2]
51521 2F[2]
52121 3F[7]
52252 3F[7]
52273 3F[7]
52305 3F[7]
52309 3F[7]
52331 3F[7]
90135 WD[1]
90186 WD[1]
90213 WD[1]
90228 WD[1]
90262 WD[1]
90281 WD[1]
90300 WD[1]
90531 WD[1]
90639 WD[1]
90679 WD[1]

1957 53E
42311 4MT[2]
42324 4MT[2]
42407 4MT[2]
42411 4MT[2]
46407 2MT[2]
46408 2MT[2]
46409 2MT[2]
51222 0F[4]
51240 0F[4]
51244 0F[4]
51432 2F[2]
51503 2F[2]
52154 3F[7]
52244 3F[7]
52252 3F[7]
52305 3F[7]
90135 WD[1]
90186 WD[1]
90213 WD[1]
90228 WD[1]
90260 WD[1]
90262 WD[1]
90281 WD[1]
90300 WD[1]
90531 WD[1]

1960 53E
41855 1F[1]
43097 4MT[5]
43098 4MT[5]
43125 4MT[5]
46407 2MT[2]
46408 2MT[2]
46409 2MT[2]
46415 2MT[2]
47438 3F[6]
47462 3F[6]
47581 3F[6]
47634 3F[6]
51222 0F[4]
51241 0F[4]
51244 0F[4]
52154 3F[7]
52244 3F[7]
52252 3F[7]
52305 3F[7]
52319 3F[7]
90044 WD[1]
90094 WD[1]
90186 WD[1]
90213 WD[1]
90228 WD[1]
90260 WD[1]
90262 WD[1]
90265 WD[1]
90478 WD[1]
90531 WD[1]
90704 WD[1]

1963 50D
43098 4MT[5]
43125 4MT[5]
46409 2MT[2]
90044 WD[1]
90094 WD[1]
90160 WD[1]
90186 WD[1]
90213 WD[1]
90228 WD[1]
90260 WD[1]
90262 WD[1]
90265 WD[1]
90461 WD[1]
90475 WD[1]
90478 WD[1]
90531 WD[1]
90704 WD[1]

1966 50D
77001 3MT[1]
77012 3MT[1]
90030 WD[1]
90081 WD[1]
90091 WD[1]
90094 WD[1]
90099 WD[1]
90132 WD[1]
90172 WD[1]
90406 WD[1]
90427 WD[1]
90451 WD[1]

Gorton

1948 GOR
61036 B1
61155 B1
61156 B1
61157 B1
61158 B1
61159 B1
61160 B1
61161 B1
61162 B1
61182 B1
61184 B1
61223 B1
61225 B1
61227 B1
61228 B1
61364 B7
61366 B7
61367 B7
61368 B7
61369 B7
61370 B7
61371 B7
61373 B7
61374 B7
61375 B7
61376 B7
61380 B7
61381 B7
61382 B7
61385 B7
61388 B7
61389 B7
61390 B7
61391 B7
61392 B7
61393 B7
61394 B7
61395 B7
61396 B7
63578 O1
63590 O1
63591 O1
63592 O1
63619 O1
63630 O1
63646 O1
63650 O1
63652 O1
63663 O1
63670 O1
63678 O1
63687 O1
63689 O1
63711 O1
63725 O1
63752 O1
63768 O1
63773 O1
63777 O1
63780 O1
63784 O1
63786 O1
63789 O1
63795 O1
63796 O1
63803 O1
63808 O1
63817 O1
63854 O1
63863 O1
63865 O1
63868 O1
63869 O1
63872 O1
63879 O1
63886 O1
63887 O1
63890 O1
63901 O1
64298 J11
64304 J11
64311 J11
64316 J11
64322 J11
64326 J11
64332 J11
64346 J11
64357 J11
64363 J11
64367 J11
64368 J11
64382 J11
64383 J11
64401 J11
64415 J11
64434 J11
64435 J11
64437 J11
64440 J11
64453 J11
64712 J39
64717 J39
64718 J39
64740 J39
64741 J39
64742 J39
64743 J39
64744 J39
64745 J39
64755 J39
64807 J39
64810 J39
64824 J39
64879 J39
64918 J39
64962 J39
64966 J39
64972 J39
65133 J10
67097 F1
67401 C13
67402 C13
67403 C13
67405 C13
67407 C13
67408 C13
67410 C13
67412 C13
67415 C13
67416 C13
67417 C13
67419 C13
67421 C13
67422 C13
67423 C13
67424 C13
67425 C13
67426 C13
67427 C13
67431 C13
67437 C13
67439 C13
68063 J94
68064 J94
68065 J94
68066 J94
68067 J94
68598 J69
69254 N5
69260 N5
69270 N5
69272 N5
69296 N5
69299 N5
69307 N5
69308 N5
69333 N5
69347 N5
69353 N5

1951 39A
61114 B1
61155 B1
61156 B1
61157 B1
61158 B1
61159 B1
61160 B1
61161 B1
61162 B1
61182 B1
61184 B1
61223 B1
61225 B1
61228 B1
61326 B1
61808 K3
61809 K3
61828 K3
61829 K3
61832 K3
61839 K3
61848 K3
61852 K3
61856 K3
61865 K3
61870 K3
61877 K3
61896 K3
61908 K3
61910 K3
61913 K3
61914 K3
61919 K3
61950 K3
61956 K3
63573 O4
63575 O4
63580 O4
63582 O4
63598 O4
63600 O4
63614 O4
63631 O4
63633 O4
63635 O4
63638 O4
63641 O4
63662 O4
63681 O4
63686 O4
63695 O4
63700 O4
63702 O4
63705 O4
63706 O4
63708 O4
63713 O4
63716 O4
63719 O4
63721 O4
63722 O4
63739 O4
63742 O4
63743 O4
63748 O4
63761 O4
63781 O4
63787 O4
63794 O4
63799 O4
63805 O4
63829 O4
63839 O4
63841 O4
63848 O4
63853 O4
63858 O4
63859 O4
63862 O4
63864 O4
63873 O4
63876 O4
63880 O4
63891 O4
63895 O4
63899 O4
63912 O4
63915 O4
64294 J11
64298 J11
64304 J11
64311 J11
64316 J11
64322 J11
64326 J11
64332 J11
64333 J11
64342 J11
64346 J11
64357 J11
64363 J11
64368 J11
64382 J11
64383 J11
64401 J11
64409 J11
64415 J11
64434 J11
64435 J11
64437 J11
64440 J11
64450 J11
64712 J39
64714 J39
64717 J39
64718 J39
64740 J39
64741 J39
64742 J39
64743 J39
64744 J39
64745 J39
64748 J39
64755 J39
64810 J39
64824 J39
64879 J39
64962 J39
64972 J39
67401 C13
67402 C13
67403 C13
67405 C13
67407 C13
67408 C13
67410 C13
67412 C13
67415 C13
67417 C13
67419 C13
67421 C13
67422 C13
67423 C13
67424 C13
67425 C13
67426 C13
67427 C13
67431 C13
67437 C13
67438 C13
67439 C13
68012 J94
68064 J94
68067 J94
68079 J94
68169 Y3
69250 N5
69260 N5
69270 N5
69296 N5
69299 N5
69307 N5
69308 N5
69333 N5
69338 N5
69353 N5

1954 39A
61155 B1
61156 B1
61159 B1
61160 B1
61161 B1
61162 B1
61182 B1
61228 B1
61326 B1
61808 K3
61809 K3
61812 K3
61828 K3
61829 K3
61832 K3
61848 K3
61852 K3
61856 K3
61865 K3
61870 K3
61896 K3
61910 K3
61913 K3
61914 K3
61919 K3
61950 K3
61966 K3
63573 O4
63575 O4
63582 O4
63598 O4
63600 O4
63601 O4
63614 O4
63631 O4
63635 O4
63638 O4
63641 O4
63662 O4
63681 O4
63686 O4
63695 O4
63700 O4
63708 O4
63709 O4
63713 O4
63716 O4
63719 O4
63721 O4
63722 O4
63739 O4
63742 O4
63743 O4
63748 O4
63761 O4
63767 O4
63781 O4
63794 O4
63799 O4
63805 O4
63829 O4
63841 O4
63848 O4
63853 O4
63859 O4
63862 O4
63873 O4
63876 O4
63880 O4
63891 O4
63895 O4
64294 J11
64298 J11
64304 J11
64306 J11
64311 J11
64316 J11
64322 J11
64326 J11
64332 J11
64333 J11
64342 J11
64346 J11
64357 J11
64363 J11
64368 J11
64382 J11
64383 J11
64401 J11
64409 J11
64413 J11
64415 J11
64434 J11
64435 J11
64437 J11
64440 J11
64450 J11
64712 J39
64714 J39
64717 J39
64718 J39
64738 J39
64740 J39
64741 J39
64742 J39
64743 J39
64744 J39
64745 J39
64748 J39
64755 J39
64810 J39
67401 C13
67402 C13
67403 C13
67405 C13
67407 C13
67415 C13
67417 C13
67421 C13
67422 C13
67423 C13
67425 C13
67426 C13
67427 C13
67431 C13
67437 C13
67438 C13
67440 C14
67441 C14
67444 C14
67445 C14
67447 C14
67448 C14
67450 C14
67451 C14
68012 J94
68064 J94
68067 J94
68071 J94
68079 J94
68169 Y3
69250 N5
69260 N5
69270 N5
69296 N5
69307 N5
69308 N5
69328 N5
69333 N5
69338 N5
69353 N5

1957 39A
41702 1F[1]
43612 3F[3]
43630 3F[3]
43638 3F[3]
43927 4F[1]
44025 4F[1]
44114 4F[2]
47336 3F[6]
51484 2F[2]
51512 2F[2]
61156 B1
61161 B1
61265 B1
61808 K3
61832 K3
61865 K3
61910 K3
61913 K3
61966 K3
63573 O4
63575 O4
63582 O4
63598 O4
63600 O4
63631 O4
63641 O4
63649 O4
63681 O4
63686 O4
63700 O4
63709 O4
63713 O4
63716 O4
63719 O4
63721 O4
63743 O4
63766 O4
63767 O4
63794 O4
63805 O4
63848 O4
63862 O4
63895 O4
63915 O4
64288 J11
64294 J11
64298 J11
64304 J11
64306 J11
64311 J11
64316 J11
64317 J11
64322 J11
64332 J11
64333 J11
64346 J11
64349 J11
64357 J11
64363 J11
64368 J11
64382 J11
64383 J11
64401 J11
64409 J11
64434 J11
64435 J11
64437 J11
64440 J11

64450 J11
64717 J39
64718 J39
64740 J39
64742 J39
64743 J39
64745 J39
64748 J39
67417 C13
67419 C13
67421 C13
67423 C13
67437 C13
67440 C14
67441 C14
67443 C14
67444 C14
67445 C14
67446 C14
67447 C14
67448 C14
67450 C14
67451 C14
68012 J94
68064 J94
68079 J94
69307 N5
69328 N5
69360 N5
69801 A5
69805 A5
69806 A5
69815 A5
69817 A5
69823 A5
69828 A5

1960 9G

41321 2MT[1]
41702 1F[1]
42326 4MT[2]
42328 4MT[2]
42373 4MT[2]
42374 4MT[2]
42429 4MT[3]
42472 4MT[3]
42560 4MT[3]
42748 5MT[1]
42754 5MT[1]
42760 5MT[1]
42767 5MT[1]
42768 5MT[1]
42775 5MT[1]
42788 5MT[1]
42792 5MT[1]
42813 5MT[1]
42816 5MT[1]
42873 5MT[1]
42874 5MT[1]
42902 5MT[1]
43187 3F[2]
43207 3F[3]
43235 3F[3]
43457 3F[3]
43763 3F[3]
43773 3F[4]
43826 3F[4]
44015 4F[1]
44025 4F[1]
44114 4F[2]
44236 4F[2]
44275 4F[2]
61161 B1
61265 B1
61865 K3
61910 K3
63573 O4
63575 O4
63598 O4
63600 O4
63631 O4
63641 O4
63649 O4
63681 O4
63686 O4
63700 O4
63709 O4
63713 O4
63716 O4
63719 O4
63721 O4
63743 O4
63766 O4
63767 O4
63775 O4
63794 O4
63805 O4
63848 O4
63862 O4
63895 O4
63915 O4
64256 J6
64288 J11
64310 J11
64311 J11
64331 J11
64337 J11
64341 J11
64357 J11
64359 J11
64363 J11
64368 J11
64383 J11
64389 J11
64405 J11
64418 J11
64434 J11
64435 J11
64437 J11
64439 J11
64440 J11
64717 J39
64718 J39
64727 J39
64738 J39
64740 J39
64742 J39
64743 J39
64744 J39
64745 J39
64747 J39
64748 J39
64809 J39
64824 J39
64875 J39
64930 J39
67417 C13
67450 C14
67743 L1
67747 L1
67748 L1
67751 L1
67756 L1
67762 L1
67781 L1
67782 L1
67795 L1
67796 L1
67798 L1
68064 J94
68068 J94
68079 J94
69307 N5
69360 N5
69801 A5
69806 A5
69813 A5
69817 A5
69823 A5

1963 9G

42249 4MT[1]
42256 4MT[1]
42361 4MT[2]
42374 4MT[2]
42748 5MT[1]
42754 5MT[1]
42757 5MT[1]
42758 5MT[1]
42759 5MT[1]
42760 5MT[1]
42761 5MT[1]
42767 5MT[1]
42768 5MT[1]
42769 5MT[1]
42788 5MT[1]
42791 5MT[1]
42792 5MT[1]
42793 5MT[1]
42813 5MT[1]
42816 5MT[1]
42831 5MT[1]
42846 5MT[1]
42867 5MT[1]
42873 5MT[1]
42890 5MT[1]
42902 5MT[1]
43856 4F[1]
43915 4F[1]
43925 4F[1]
43929 4F[1]
43937 4F[1]
43950 4F[1]
43953 4F[1]
43972 4F[1]
44015 4F[1]
44025 4F[1]
44078 4F[2]
44114 4F[2]
44124 4F[2]
44151 4F[2]
44164 4F[2]
44169 4F[2]
44190 4F[2]
44195 4F[2]
44236 4F[2]
44275 4F[2]
44425 4F[2]
44602 4F[2]
47211 3F[5]
47248 3F[5]
47502 3F[6]
47641 3F[6]
61039 B1
61269 B1
61369 B1
90010 WD[1]
90046 WD[1]
90080 WD[1]
90152 WD[1]
90176 WD[1]
90179 WD[1]
90201 WD[1]
90207 WD[1]
90214 WD[1]
90238 WD[1]
90251 WD[1]
90284 WD[1]
90312 WD[1]
90323 WD[1]
90403 WD[1]
90676 WD[1]
90716 WD[1]

Grangemouth

1948 31D

42736 5MT[1]
42737 5MT[1]
43883 4F[1]
44320 4F[2]
48147 8F
48148 8F
48149 8F
48150 8F
48151 8F
48152 8F
55119 2P[12]
55142 2P[12]
55238 2P[14]
56152 2F[4]
56164 2F[4]
56230 3F[10]
56232 3F[10]
56243 3F[10]
56267 3F[10]
56275 3F[10]
56300 3F[10]
56336 3F[10]
56375 3F[10]
56376 3F[10]
57265 2F[5]
57285 2F[5]
57287 2F[5]
57294 2F[5]
57334 2F[5]
57338 2F[5]
57373 2F[5]
57442 2F[5]
57603 3F[12]
57658 3F[14]
57667 3F[14]
57689 3F[14]
57691 3F[14]

1951 65F

42736 5MT[1]
42737 5MT[1]
44320 4F[2]
54483 3P[6]
55119 2P[12]
55142 2P[12]
55238 2P[14]
56152 2F[4]
56164 2F[4]
56230 3F[10]
56243 3F[10]
56267 3F[10]
56275 3F[10]
56300 3F[10]
56336 3F[10]
56375 3F[10]
56376 3F[10]
57265 2F[5]
57285 2F[5]
57287 2F[5]
57334 2F[5]
57338 2F[5]
57366 2F[5]
57667 3F[14]
57689 3F[14]
57691 3F[14]
90134 WD[1]
90219 WD[1]
90236 WD[1]
90536 WD[1]
90616 WD[1]
90755 WD[2]
90757 WD[2]
90759 WD[2]
90765 WD[2]

1954 65F

42736 5MT[1]
42737 5MT[1]
44320 4F[2]
45011 5MT[3]
45119 5MT[3]
45396 5MT[3]
54483 3P[6]
55214 2P[13]
55238 2P[14]
56152 2F[4]
56164 2F[4]
56230 3F[10]
56243 3F[10]
56267 3F[10]
56275 3F[10]
56300 3F[10]
56336 3F[10]
56375 3F[10]
56376 3F[10]
57265 2F[5]
57285 2F[5]
57287 2F[5]
57338 2F[5]
57366 2F[5]
57667 3F[14]
57689 3F[14]
57691 3F[14]
67456 C15
90755 WD[2]
90757 WD[2]
90759 WD[2]
90765 WD[2]
90773 WD[2]

1957 65F

42736 5MT[1]
42737 5MT[1]
42780 5MT[1]
42802 5MT[1]
42803 5MT[1]
44320 4F[2]
55214 2P[13]
55238 2P[14]
56164 2F[4]
56230 3F[10]
56336 3F[10]
56376 3F[10]
57265 2F[5]
57285 2F[5]
57287 2F[5]
57338 2F[5]
57366 2F[5]
57689 3F[14]
57691 3F[14]
68326 J88
90199 WD[1]
90755 WD[2]
90757 WD[2]
90759 WD[2]
90765 WD[2]
90769 WD[2]
90773 WD[2]
90774 WD[2]

1960 65F

42736 5MT[1]
42737 5MT[1]
42780 5MT[1]
42802 5MT[1]
42803 5MT[1]
44234 4F[2]
44320 4F[2]
55204 2P[13]
55214 2P[13]
55238 2P[14]
56376 3F[10]
57265 2F[5]
57285 2F[5]
57287 2F[5]
57338 2F[5]
57366 2F[5]
57612 3F[12]
57691 3F[14]
64589 J37
64592 J37
64593 J37
65241 J36
68349 J88
90539 WD[1]
90755 WD[2]
90757 WD[2]
90759 WD[2]
90765 WD[2]
90766 WD[2]
90769 WD[2]
90773 WD[2]
90774 WD[2]

1963 65F

43137 4MT[5]
44788 5MT[3]
45177 5MT[3]
45178 5MT[3]
45319 5MT[3]
45482 5MT[3]
45487 5MT[3]
45496 5MT[3]
57269 2F[5]
64589 J37
65222 J36
65335 J36
76074 4MT[2]
76103 4MT[2]
76113 4MT[2]
90234 WD[1]
90539 WD[1]

Grantham

1948 GRA

60007 A4
60008 A4
60014 A4
60015 A4
60022 A4
60028 A4
60030 A4
60032 A4
60033 A4
60034 A4
60039 A3
60044 A3
60102 A3
60106 A3
61171 B1
61175 B1
61177 B1
61205 B1
62000 D3
62161 D2
62167 D2
62172 D2
62173 D2
62810 C1
62822 C1
62870 C1
62876 C1
63201 Q4
63206 Q4
63207 Q4
63228 Q4
63229 Q4
63234 Q4
63240 Q4
63243 Q4
63929 O2
63930 O2
63931 O2
63932 O2
63933 O2
63935 O2
63936 O2
63938 O2
63940 O2
64172 J6
64175 J6
64178 J6
64206 J6
64227 J6
64237 J6
64265 J6
67380 C12
67382 C12
68801 J52
68816 J52
68877 J52

1951 35B

60015 A4
60026 A4
60053 A3
60106 A3
61538 B12
61541 B12
61553 B12
61554 B12
61565 B12
61729 K2
62000 D3
63929 O2
63930 O2
63931 O2
63932 O2
63933 O2
63935 O2
63936 O2
63938 O2
63940 O2
63949 O2
63950 O2
63960 O2
63965 O2
63966 O2
64172 J6
64178 J6
64187 J6
64206 J6
64227 J6
64237 J6
67380 C12
67382 C12
68798 J52
68877 J52

1954 35B

43058 4MT[5]
60039 A3
60047 A3
60051 A3
60053 A3
60056 A3
60061 A3
60065 A3
60103 A3
60105 A3
60106 A3
60110 A3
60113 A1
60114 A1
60128 A1
60136 A1
60144 A1
60149 A1
60156 A1
60157 A1
61538 B12
61541 B12
61553 B12
61554 B12
61565 B12
61567 B12
61574 B12
61580 B12
63923 O2
63929 O2
63930 O2
63931 O2
63932 O2
63933 O2
63936 O2
63938 O2
63940 O2
63946 O2
63948 O2
63950 O2
63960 O2
63966 O2
64178 J6
64187 J6
64227 J6
67380 C12
67382 C12
68780 J52
68815 J52
68877 J52

1957 35B

47300 3F[6]
47429 3F[6]
47458 3F[6]
60044 A3
60047 A3
60050 A3
60056 A3
60061 A3
60063 A3
60065 A3
60103 A3
60105 A3
60110 A3
60113 A1
60114 A1
60119 A1
60122 A1
60125 A1
60128 A1
60136 A1
60139 A1
60144 A1
60158 A1
61541 B12
61553 B12
61574 B12
61580 B12
63923 O2
63929 O2
63930 O2
63931 O2
63932 O2
63933 O2
63936 O2
63938 O2
63940 O2
63946 O2
63948 O2
63950 O2
63960 O2
63966 O2
64178 J6
64187 J6
64227 J6
67362 C12
67391 C12
67776 L1
67800 L1
69814 A5
69827 A5

1960 34F

60046 A3
60047 A3
60048 A3
60049 A3
60050 A3
60054 A3
60056 A3
60063 A3
60064 A3
60065 A3
60102 A3
60105 A3
60106 A3
60107 A3
60111 A3
60112 A3
61251 B1
61367 B1
61389 B1
61392 B1
63923 O2
63929 O2
63930 O2
63931 O2
63932 O2
63933 O2
63936 O2
63938 O2
63940 O2
63946 O2
63948 O2
63950 O2
63957 O2
63960 O2
63963 O2
63966 O2
67761 L1
67785 L1
67791 L1
68626 J69
68635 J69
69505 N2
69516 N2
69552 N2
69560 N2
69561 N2

1963 34F

43087 4MT[5]
43090 4MT[5]
43111 4MT[5]
43159 4MT[5]
60054 A3
60056 A3
60105 A3
60106 A3
60112 A3
60814 V2
60830 V2
61251 B1
61367 B1
61389 B1
61392 B1
63928 O2
63931 O2
63932 O2
63938 O2
63940 O2
63941 O2
63942 O2
63943 O2
63949 O2
63956 O2
63960 O2
63963 O2
63974 O2
63981 O2

Greenock Ladyburn

1948 27B

42400 4MT[2]
42415 4MT[2]
42416 4MT[2]
42417 4MT[2]
42418 4MT[2]
42419 4MT[2]
42420 4MT[2]
42421 4MT[2]
42422 4MT[2]
42423 4MT[2]
42697 4MT[1]
47167 2F[1]
47168 2F[1]
47169 2F[1]
54440 3P[5]
54443 3P[5]
54444 3P[5]
54445 3P[5]
54457 3P[5]
54468 3P[6]
54479 3P[6]
54492 3P[6]
54497 3P[6]
54508 3P[6]
55355 4P[5]
56035 0F[5]
56156 2F[4]
56157 2F[4]
56163 2F[4]
56165 2F[4]
56166 2F[4]
56173 2F[4]
56288 3F[10]
57369 2F[5]
57463 2F[5]
57551 3F[12]
57552 3F[12]
57556 3F[12]
57639 3F[13]
57682 3F[14]

1951 66D

41148 4P[1]
41149 4P[1]
41182 4P[1]
42175 4MT[1]
42176 4MT[1]
42400 4MT[2]
42415 4MT[2]
42416 4MT[2]
42417 4MT[2]
42418 4MT[2]
42419 4MT[2]
42420 4MT[2]
42421 4MT[2]
42422 4MT[2]
42423 4MT[2]
42697 4MT[1]
47167 2F[1]
47168 2F[1]
47169 2F[1]
54440 3P[5]
54457 3P[5]
54468 3P[6]
54479 3P[6]
54492 3P[6]
54497 3P[6]
54498 3P[6]
54506 3P[6]
54508 3P[6]
55267 2P[15]
56028 0F[5]
56031 0F[5]
56035 0F[5]
56156 2F[4]
56157 2F[4]
56163 2F[4]
56165 2F[4]
56166 2F[4]
56173 2F[4]
56288 3F[10]
57369 2F[5]
57552 3F[12]
57556 3F[12]
57682 3F[14]

1954 66D

41149 4P[1]
42175 4MT[1]
42176 4MT[1]
42400 4MT[2]
42415 4MT[2]
42416 4MT[2]
42417 4MT[2]
42418 4MT[2]
42419 4MT[2]
42420 4MT[2]
42421 4MT[2]
42422 4MT[2]
42423 4MT[2]
42691 4MT[1]
42697 4MT[1]
42698 4MT[1]
47167 2F[1]
47168 2F[1]
47169 2F[1]
54440 3P[5]
54441 3P[5]
54453 3P[5]
54456 3P[5]
54468 3P[6]
54479 3P[6]
54492 3P[6]
54497 3P[6]
54498 3P[6]
54506 3P[6]
54508 3P[6]
55267 2P[15]
56028 0F[5]
56031 0F[5]
56035 0F[5]
56156 2F[4]
56157 2F[4]
56163 2F[4]
56165 2F[4]
56166 2F[4]
56173 2F[4]
56288 3F[10]
57552 3F[12]
57556 3F[12]
57682 3F[14]
57690 3F[14]

1957 66D

42175 4MT[1]
42176 4MT[1]
42236 4MT[1]
42238 4MT[1]
42239 4MT[1]
42240 4MT[1]
42241 4MT[1]
42258 4MT[1]
42259 4MT[1]
42260 4MT[1]
42261 4MT[1]
42262 4MT[1]
42263 4MT[1]
42264 4MT[1]
42265 4MT[1]
42266 4MT[1]
42698 4MT[1]
47167 2F[1]
47168 2F[1]
47169 2F[1]
54440 3P[5]
54441 3P[5]
54453 3P[5]
54456 3P[5]
54468 3P[6]
54479 3P[6]
54497 3P[6]
54498 3P[6]
54506 3P[6]
55267 2P[15]
56028 0F[5]
56031 0F[5]
56156 2F[4]
56157 2F[4]
56163 2F[4]
56165 2F[4]
56166 2F[4]
56173 2F[4]
56288 3F[10]
57552 3F[12]
57556 3F[12]
57682 3F[14]
57690 3F[14]

1960 66D

42175 4MT[1]
42176 4MT[1]
42236 4MT[1]
42241 4MT[1]
42258 4MT[1]
42259 4MT[1]
42260 4MT[1]
42261 4MT[1]
42262 4MT[1]
42263 4MT[1]
42264 4MT[1]
42265 4MT[1]
42266 4MT[1]
42698 4MT[1]
42740 5MT[1]
42741 5MT[1]
44011 4F[1]
47167 2F[1]
47168 2F[1]
54498 3P[6]
54506 3P[6]
55267 2P[15]
56035 0F[5]
56165 2F[4]
56167 2F[4]
56170 2F[4]
56173 2F[4]
57416 2F[5]
57619 3F[12]
57682 3F[14]
57690 3F[14]

1963 66D

42167 4MT[1]
42176 4MT[1]
42241 4MT[1]
42242 4MT[1]
42245 4MT[1]
42259 4MT[1]
42260 4MT[1]
42261 4MT[1]
42262 4MT[1]
42263 4MT[1]
42264 4MT[1]
42265 4MT[1]
42266 4MT[1]
42691 4MT[1]
43134 4MT[5]

1966 66D

42176 4MT[1]
42197 4MT[1]
42216 4MT[1]
42264 4MT[1]
42266 4MT[1]
80054 4MT[3]
80122 4MT[3]

Guildford

1948 GFD

30022 M7
30026 M7
30043 M7
30056 M7
30060 M7
30108 M7
30110 M7
30141 K10
30246 M7
30262 G6
30268 G6
30269 G6
30270 G6
30308 700
30309 700
30311 T9
30324 M7
30325 700
30326 700
30327 700
30328 M7
30343 K10
30346 700
30349 G6
30352 700
30378 M7
30416 L12
30419 L12
30433 L12
30434 L12
30438 L11
30458 0458
30481 M7
30565 0395
30568 0395
30574 0395
30575 0395
30578 0395
30580 0395
30618 A12
30704 T9
30726 T9
31614 U
31621 U
31623 U
31798 U
31799 U
31800 U
31801 U
31802 U
31803 U
31804 U
31805 U
31806 U
31809 U
32487 E4
32500 E4
32504 E4
33001 Q1
33002 Q1
33003 Q1
33004 Q1
33005 Q1
33006 Q1
33007 Q1
33008 Q1
33009 Q1
33010 Q1
33011 Q1
33012 Q1
33013 Q1

1951 70C

30021 M7
30022 M7
30026 M7
30056 M7
30060 M7
30108 M7
30110 M7
30238 G6
30246 M7
30281 T9
30308 700
30311 T9
30312 T9
30324 M7
30325 700
30326 700
30327 700
30328 M7
30336 T9
30349 G6
30384 K10
30420 L12
30424 L12
30425 L12
30428 L12
30432 L12
30433 L12
30434 L12
30436 L11
30442 L11
30458 0458
30481 M7
30568 0395
30574 0395
30575 0395
30577 0395
30578 0395
30580 0395
30710 T9
31620 U
31624 U
31627 U
31628 U
31629 U
31630 U
31635 U
31798 U
31800 U
31801 U
31802 U
31803 U
31804 U
32160 E1[2]
32487 E4
32490 E4
33001 Q1
33002 Q1
33003 Q1
33004 Q1
33005 Q1
33014 Q1
33015 Q1
33016 Q1

1954 70C

30026 M7
30027 M7
30028 M7
30109 M7
30110 M7
30238 G6
30246 M7
30277 G6
30308 700
30309 700
30313 T9
30324 M7
30325 700
30326 700
30327 700
30328 M7
30337 T9
30338 T9
30349 G6
30350 700
30400 S11
30434 L12
30458 0458
30574 0395
30577 0395
30578 0395
30579 0395
30675 M7
30693 700
31620 U
31624 U
31625 U
31627 U
31628 U
31629 U
31630 U
31797 U
31798 U
31799 U
31800 U
31802 U
32487 E4
32490 E4
33001 Q1
33002 Q1
33003 Q1
33004 Q1
33005 Q1
33019 Q1
33022 Q1

1957 70C

30026 M7
30027 M7
30086 B4[1]
30109 M7
30124 M7
30238 G6
30246 M7
30277 G6
30308 700
30325 700
30326 700
30337 T9
30349 G6
30350 700
30574 0395
30575 0395
30578 0395
30580 0395
30675 M7
30693 700
30697 700
30698 700
30700 700
30705 T9
31145 D1[1]
31247 D1[1]
31612 U
31616 U
31622 U
31625 U
31627 U
31628 U
31630 U
31631 U
31635 U
31636 U
31722 C
31723 C
31797 U
31798 U
31799 U
31800 U
32487 E4
32505 E4
32506 E4
33001 Q1
33002 Q1
33003 Q1
33004 Q1
33005 Q1
33019 Q1
33022 Q1
33025 Q1

1960 70C

30089 B4[1]
30124 M7
30132 M7
30238 G6
30246 M7
30277 G6
30308 700
30325 700
30326 700
30349 G6
30350 700
30378 M7
30693 700
30697 700
30698 700
30700 700
31037 C
31054 C
31612 U
31614 U
31615 U
31616 U
31622 U
31625 U
31627 U
31628 U
31630 U
31631 U
31635 U
31636 U
31637 U
31638 U
31722 C
31723 C
31797 U
31798 U
31799 U
31800 U
31805 U
31807 U
31811 N
31812 N
31815 N
31858 N
32505 E4
32506 E4
33005 Q1
33019 Q1
33022 Q1
33025 Q1

1963 70C

30055 M7
30089 B4[1]
30112 M7
30542 Q
31615 U
31622 U
31623 U
31625 U
31627 U
31628 U
31631 U
31633 U
31635 U
31638 U
31790 U
31797 U
31800 U
31811 N
31812 N
31815 N
31819 N
31820 N
31821 N
31857 N
31858 N
31859 N
33005 Q1
33019 Q1
33022 Q1
33025 Q1
33032 Q1
33033 Q1
33034 Q1
33035 Q1
33036 Q1
82015 3MT[2]
82016 3MT[2]

1966 70C

30072 USA
31405 N
31408 N
31411 N
31639 U
31791 U
31803 U
31809 U
31816 N
31866 N
31873 N
33006 Q1
33020 Q1
33027 Q1
73022 5MT
73029 5MT
73037 5MT
73043 5MT
73065 5MT
73081 5MT
73082 5MT
73087 5MT
73088 5MT
73089 5MT
73092 5MT
73093 5MT
73110 5MT

Guisborough

1948 GUI

67281 G5

1951 51D sub

67281 G5

1954 51D sub

67281 G5

Hamilton

1948 27C
40150 3MT^2
40151 3MT^2
40152 3MT^2
40153 3MT^2
40154 3MT^2
40158 3MT^2
42217 4MT^1
42735 5MT^1
42740 5MT^1
42741 5MT^1
46656 1P^1
54638 4P^3
54639 4P^3
54648 4P^3
55146 2P^{12}
56237 3F^{10}
56242 3F^{10}
56255 3F^{10}
56256 3F^{10}
56284 3F^{10}
56286 3F^{10}
56287 3F^{10}
56296 3F^{10}
56303 3F^{10}
56309 3F^{10}
56319 3F^{10}
56320 3F^{10}
56321 3F^{10}
56360 3F^{10}
56362 3F^{10}
56371 3F^{10}
57237 2F^5
57242 2F^5
57244 2F^5
57250 2F^5
57260 2F^5
57280 2F^5
57307 2F^5
57382 2F^5
57384 2F^5
57393 2F^5
57395 2F^5
57398 2F^5
57401 2F^5
57407 2F^5
57408 2F^5
57410 2F^5
57420 2F^5
57430 2F^5
57431 2F^5
57609 3F^{12}
57630 3F^{13}
57663 3F^{14}
57665 3F^{14}

1951 66C
40150 3MT^2
40151 3MT^2
42128 4MT^1
42129 4MT^1
42130 4MT^1
42164 4MT^1
42165 4MT^1
42166 4MT^1
42735 5MT^1
42740 5MT^1
42741 5MT^1
42850 5MT^1
42880 5MT^1
54638 4P^3
54639 4P^3
55146 2P^{12}
55221 2P^{13}
56237 3F^{10}
56242 3F^{10}
56255 3F^{10}
56256 3F^{10}
56284 3F^{10}
56286 3F^{10}
56296 3F^{10}
56303 3F^{10}
56309 3F^{10}
56319 3F^{10}
56320 3F^{10}
56321 3F^{10}
56360 3F^{10}
56362 3F^{10}
56371 3F^{10}
57237 2F^5
57242 2F^5
57244 2F^5
57250 2F^5
57260 2F^5
57280 2F^5
57307 2F^5
57384 2F^5
57395 2F^5
57398 2F^5
57407 2F^5
57410 2F^5
57413 2F^5
57430 2F^5
57431 2F^5
57609 3F^{12}
57630 3F^{13}
57663 3F^{14}
57665 3F^{14}

1954 66C
40150 3MT^2
40151 3MT^2
40159 3MT^2
42128 4MT^1
42129 4MT^1
42164 4MT^1
42165 4MT^1
42166 4MT^1
42735 5MT^1
42740 5MT^1
42741 5MT^1
42850 5MT^1
42880 5MT^1
55182 2P^{13}
56242 3F^{10}
56255 3F^{10}
56256 3F^{10}
56284 3F^{10}
56286 3F^{10}
56287 3F^{10}
56296 3F^{10}
56303 3F^{10}
56309 3F^{10}
56319 3F^{10}
56320 3F^{10}
56321 3F^{10}
56360 3F^{10}
56362 3F^{10}
56371 3F^{10}
57237 2F^5
57242 2F^5
57244 2F^5
57250 2F^5
57260 2F^5
57307 2F^5
57335 2F^5
57384 2F^5
57398 2F^5
57407 2F^5
57413 2F^5
57430 2F^5
57431 2F^5
57609 3F^{12}
57630 3F^{13}
57663 3F^{14}
57665 3F^{14}
90386 WD^1
90468 WD^1

1957 66C
42128 4MT^1
42129 4MT^1
42164 4MT^1
42165 4MT^1
42166 4MT^1
42167 4MT^1
42735 5MT^1
42740 5MT^1
42741 5MT^1
42850 5MT^1
42880 5MT^1
45433 5MT^3
47331 3F^6
55182 2P^{13}
56242 3F^{10}
56255 3F^{10}
56256 3F^{10}
56284 3F^{10}
56286 3F^{10}
56287 3F^{10}
56294 3F^{10}
56296 3F^{10}
56309 3F^{10}
56320 3F^{10}
56321 3F^{10}
56360 3F^{10}
56362 3F^{10}
56371 3F^{10}
57242 2F^5
57244 2F^5
57250 2F^5
57307 2F^5
57335 2F^5
57384 2F^5
57398 2F^5
57407 2F^5
57413 2F^5
57430 2F^5
57431 2F^5
57609 3F^{12}
57630 3F^{13}
57663 3F^{14}
57665 3F^{14}
77005 3MT^1
77006 3MT^1
77007 3MT^1
90071 WD^1
90386 WD^1
90468 WD^1

1960 66C
42128 4MT^1
42129 4MT^1
42164 4MT^1
42165 4MT^1
42166 4MT^1
42167 4MT^1
42735 5MT^1
42746 5MT^1
42880 5MT^1
56242 3F^{10}
56309 3F^{10}
56360 3F^{10}
56362 3F^{10}
56371 3F^{10}
57242 2F^5
57321 2F^5
57335 2F^5
57336 2F^5
57447 2F^5
57630 3F^{13}
57663 3F^{14}
69196 N15
77006 3MT^1
90772 WD^2

Hasland

1948 18C
40337 2P^2
40370 2P^2
40466 2P^2
40472 2P^2
40490 2P^2
40491 2P^2
40506 2P^2
40555 2P^2
40556 2P^2
40557 2P^2
41518 0F^1
41531 0F^2
41532 0F^2
41873 1F^1
41910 2P^5
41912 2P^5
41913 2P^5
41920 2P^5
41925 2P^5
43211 3F^3
43212 3F^3
43219 3F^3
43622 3F^3
43769 3F^4
43771 3F^4
43856 4F^1
43890 4F^1
43936 4F^1
43959 4F^1
44053 4F^2
44054 4F^2
44107 4F^2
44162 4F^2
44244 4F^2
44274 4F^2
44288 4F^2
44294 4F^2
44410 4F^2
47003 0F^3
47004 0F^3
47272 3F^6
47278 3F^6
47423 3F^6
47426 3F^6
47535 3F^6
47968 Garratt
47971 Garratt
47973 Garratt
47980 Garratt
47983 Garratt
47984 Garratt
47990 Garratt
47992 Garratt
47993 Garratt
47997 Garratt

1951 18C
40337 2P^2
40359 2P^2
40409 2P^2
40472 2P^2
40491 2P^2
40503 2P^2
40537 2P^2
40548 2P^2
40556 2P^2
40557 2P^2
41518 0F^1
41531 0F^2
41532 0F^2
41813 1F^1
41829 1F^1
43211 3F^3
43212 3F^3
43219 3F^3
43622 3F^3
43771 3F^4
43856 4F^1
43936 4F^1
43959 4F^1
43970 4F^1
44053 4F^2
44054 4F^2
44107 4F^2
44162 4F^2
44244 4F^2
44274 4F^2
44288 4F^2
44294 4F^2
44410 4F^2
47003 0F^3
47004 0F^3
47272 3F^6
47278 3F^6
47423 3F^6
47535 3F^6
47968 Garratt
47971 Garratt
47973 Garratt
47980 Garratt
47983 Garratt
47984 Garratt
47990 Garratt
47992 Garratt
47993 Garratt

1954 18C
40337 2P^2
40359 2P^2
40491 2P^2
40502 2P^2
40537 2P^2
40556 2P^2
40557 2P^2
41518 0F^1
41531 0F^2
41532 0F^2
41813 1F^1
43211 3F^3
43212 3F^3
43723 3F^3
43891 4F^1
43936 4F^1
43959 4F^1
44053 4F^2
44054 4F^2
44107 4F^2
44162 4F^2
44244 4F^2
44274 4F^2
44288 4F^2
44294 4F^2
44410 4F^2
44603 4F^2
46499 2MT^2
46500 2MT^2
47003 0F^3
47004 0F^3
47272 3F^6
47278 3F^6
47423 3F^6
47535 3F^6
47968 Garratt
47971 Garratt
47973 Garratt
47980 Garratt
47983 Garratt
47984 Garratt
47990 Garratt
47992 Garratt
58153 2F^8
58176 2F^8

1957 18C
40337 2P^2
40502 2P^2
40550 2P^2
40691 2P^3
43211 3F^3
43212 3F^3
43891 4F^1
43959 4F^1
44053 4F^2
44054 4F^2
44136 4F^2
44162 4F^2
44244 4F^2
44288 4F^2
44294 4F^2
44410 4F^2
44603 4F^2
46497 2MT^2
46499 2MT^2
46500 2MT^2
47003 0F^3
47004 0F^3
47218 3F^5
47272 3F^6
47278 3F^6
47423 3F^6
47535 3F^6
47967 Garratt
47968 Garratt
47969 Garratt
47972 Garratt
47973 Garratt
47978 Garratt
47979 Garratt
47980 Garratt
47982 Garratt
47986 Garratt
47994 Garratt
48065 8F
48082 8F
48095 8F
48212 8F
48371 8F

1960 18C
43967 4F^1
44053 4F^2
44054 4F^2
44122 4F^2
44244 4F^2
44288 4F^2
44410 4F^2
44603 4F^2
47003 0F^3
47004 0F^3
47218 3F^5
47272 3F^6
47278 3F^6
47423 3F^6
47535 3F^6
48056 8F
48065 8F
48082 8F
48089 8F
48095 8F
48116 8F
48125 8F
48187 8F
48205 8F
48212 8F
48284 8F
48359 8F
48371 8F
48494 8F
48527 8F
48547 8F

1963 18C
43967 4F^1
43982 4F^1
43986 4F^1
44053 4F^2
44054 4F^2
44261 4F^2
44288 4F^2
44463 4F^2
44603 4F^2
47003 0F^3
47004 0F^3
47272 3F^6
47278 3F^6
47423 3F^6
47535 3F^6
48116 8F
48187 8F
48205 8F
48359 8F
48371 8F
48527 8F
48547 8F

Hatfield

1948 HAT
68175 Y3
68185 Y3
68565 J69
68572 J67
69455 N1
69502 N2
69534 N2
69537 N2
69551 N2
69554 N2
69558 N2
69559 N2
69580 N2
69582 N2
69586 N2
69587 N2
69588 N2
69590 N2
69594 N2
69689 N7
69690 N7
69691 N7
69692 N7
69694 N7
69695 N7
69696 N7
69698 N7

1951 34C
68565 J69
68572 J67
69484 N1
69493 N2
69494 N2
69504 N2
69534 N2
69537 N2
69551 N2
69554 N2
69558 N2
69559 N2
69580 N2
69582 N2
69586 N2
69587 N2
69588 N2
69594 N2
69613 N7
69615 N7
69620 N7
69632 N7
69639 N7
69640 N7
69644 N7
69691 N7
69695 N7
69696 N7

1954 34C
68867 J52
68885 J52
69494 N2
69504 N2
69516 N2
69534 N2
69537 N2
69582 N2
69586 N2
69588 N2
69594 N2
69632 N7
69635 N7
69638 N7
69639 N7
69640 N7
69644 N7
69648 N7
69649 N7
69678 N7
69704 N7
69709 N7

1957 34C
68867 J52
69494 N2
69504 N2
69516 N2
69534 N2
69547 N2
69580 N2
69582 N2
69586 N2
69588 N2
69631 N7
69632 N7
69635 N7
69637 N7
69638 N7
69639 N7
69640 N7
69644 N7
69648 N7
69649 N7
69650 N7
69654 N7
69678 N7
69704 N7
69709 N7

1960 34C
69531 N2
69580 N2
69586 N2
69588 N2
69618 N7
69629 N7
69631 N7
69632 N7
69640 N7
69648 N7
69654 N7
69678 N7
69692 N7
69696 N7
69698 N7
69704 N7

Haverton Hill

1948 HAV
63252 Q5
63270 Q5
63299 Q5
63301 Q5
63306 Q5
63331 Q5
63340 Q6
63374 Q6
63416 Q6
65787 J27
65818 J27
65830 J27
65853 J27
65855 J27
65859 J27
65866 J27
69419 N9

1951 51G
63311 Q5
63314 Q5
63340 Q6
63367 Q6
63374 Q6
63405 Q6
63407 Q6
63416 Q6
63443 Q6
63446 Q6
65660 J25
65787 J27
65805 J27
65830 J27
65853 J27
65855 J27
65859 J27
65865 J27
90089 WD^1
90382 WD^1
90695 WD^1

1954 51G
62048 K1
62050 K1
62056 K1
62057 K1
62058 K1
62059 K1
62061 K1
63367 Q6
63374 Q6
63407 Q6
63416 Q6
63443 Q6
63446 Q6
65787 J27
65790 J27
65805 J27
65830 J27
65853 J27
65855 J27
65859 J27

1957 51G
62058 K1
62059 K1
63341 Q6
63343 Q6
63344 Q6
63345 Q6
63347 Q6
63367 Q6
63374 Q6
63407 Q6
63416 Q6
63443 Q6
63446 Q6
65787 J27
65790 J27
65805 J27
65830 J27
65853 J27
65855 J27
65859 J27
68423 J77

Hawick

1948 HAW
62208 D1
62417 D30
62422 D30
62423 D30
62425 D30
62428 D30
62432 D30
62440 D30
64463 J35
64494 J35
64509 J35
64539 J37
65232 J36
65242 J36
65259 J36
65279 J36
65317 J36
65340 J36
67457 C15
67459 C15
67465 C15
67472 C15
67473 C15
67477 C15
68138 Y1

1951 64G
62417 D30
62420 D30
62422 D30
62423 D30
62425 D30
62428 D30
62432 D30
62440 D30
64463 J35
64494 J35
64509 J35
64539 J37
65232 J36
65242 J36
65259 J36
65279 J36
65317 J36
65340 J36
67457 C15
67459 C15
67465 C15
67472 C15
67477 C15
68138 Y1

1954 64G
62420 D30
62422 D30
62423 D30
62425 D30
62428 D30
62432 D30
62435 D30
62440 D30
64463 J35
64494 J35
64509 J35
64539 J37
65232 J36
65259 J36
65316 J36
65317 J36
65331 J36
67457 C15
67459 C15
67465 C15
67472 C15
67477 C15
68138 Y1

1957 64G
62420 D30
62422 D30
62423 D30
62425 D30
62428 D30
62432 D30
62435 D30
62440 D30
64463 J35
64494 J35
64509 J35
64539 J37
65316 J36
65317 J36
65331 J36
67489 C16
67606 V3
78046 2MT^1
78047 2MT^1

1960 64G
43141 4MT^5
62488 D34
62719 D49
64494 J35
65234 J36
65275 J36
65317 J36
65331 J36
67489 C16
78046 2MT^1
78047 2MT^1
78049 2MT^1

1963 64G
43138 4MT^5
65234 J36
65331 J36
78046 2MT^1
78047 2MT^1
78048 2MT^1
78049 2MT^1
80113 4MT^3

1966 64G
78049 2MT^1
80113 4MT^3

Haymarket

1948 HAY
60004 A4
60009 A4
60011 A4
60012 A4
60024 A4
60027 A4
60031 A4
60035 A3
60037 A3
60041 A3
60043 A3
60057 A3
60064 A3
60065 A3
60066 A3
60067 A3
60087 A3
60094 A3
60099 A3
60100 A3
60101 A3
60503 A2
60504 A2
60505 A2
60506 A2
60509 A2
60510 A2
60519 A2
60816 V2
60834 V2
60836 V2
60848 V2
60882 V2
60894 V2
60927 V2
60931 V2
60951 V2
60953 V2
60955 V2
60958 V2
60972 V2
60980 V2
61007 B1
61072 B1
61076 B1
61081 B1
61178 B1
61221 B1
61244 B1
61245 B1
62214 D1
62403 D29
62413 D29
62437 D30
62677 D11
62678 D11
62679 D11
62683 D11
62685 D11
62690 D11
62691 D11
62692 D11
62693 D11
62694 D11
62705 D49
62706 D49
62709 D49
62711 D49
62712 D49
62719 D49
62721 D49
62733 D49
65240 J36
65243 J36
67610 V1
67615 V1
67620 V1
68328 J88
68339 J88
68457 J83
68460 J83
68473 J83
68478 J83
68481 J83
69169 N15
69220 N15

1951 64B
60004 A4
60009 A4
60011 A4
60012 A4
60024 A4
60027 A4
60031 A4
60035 A3
60037 A3
60041 A3
60043 A3
60057 A3
60087 A3
60090 A3
60094 A3
60096 A3
60097 A3
60098 A3
60099 A3
60100 A3
60101 A3
60152 A1
60159 A1
60160 A1
60161 A1
60162 A1
60507 A2
60509 A2
60510 A2
60519 A2
60529 A2
60530 A2
60532 A2
60534 A2
60535 A2
60536 A2
60816 V2
60882 V2
60927 V2
60951 V2
60959 V2
60972 V2
61007 B1
61076 B1
61081 B1
61178 B1
61221 B1
61244 B1
61245 B1
61404 B1
62405 D29
62437 D30
62677 D11
62678 D11
62679 D11
62683 D11
62685 D11
62690 D11
62691 D11
62692 D11
62693 D11
62694 D11
62705 D49
62706 D49
62709 D49
62719 D49
62733 D49
65240 J36
65243 J36
67610 V1
67615 V1
67620 V1
68328 J88
68339 J88
68457 J83
68460 J83
68473 J83
68478 J83
68481 J83
69169 N15
69220 N15

1954 64B
60004 A4
60009 A4
60011 A4
60012 A4
60024 A4
60027 A4
60031 A4
60035 A3
60037 A3
60041 A3
60043 A3
60057 A3
60087 A3
60089 A3
60090 A3
60094 A3
60096 A3
60097 A3
60098 A3
60099 A3
60100 A3
60101 A3
60152 A1
60159 A1
60160 A1
60161 A1
60162 A1
60507 A2
60509 A2
60510 A2
60519 A2
60529 A2
60530 A2
60534 A2
60535 A2
60536 A2
60537 A2
60816 V2
60927 V2
60951 V2
60959 V2
61007 B1
61076 B1
61081 B1
61178 B1
61221 B1
61244 B1
61245 B1
61404 B1
62437 D30
62677 D11
62678 D11
62679 D11
62683 D11
62685 D11
62690 D11
62691 D11
62692 D11
62693 D11
62694 D11
62705 D49
62706 D49
62709 D49
62719 D49
62733 D49
62743 D49
65235 J36
65243 J36
67610 V1
67615 V3
67620 V3
68328 J88
68339 J88
68457 J83
68460 J83
68473 J83
68478 J83
68481 J83
69169 N15
69220 N15

1957 64B
60004 A4
60009 A4
60011 A4
60012 A4
60024 A4
60027 A4
60031 A4
60035 A3
60037 A3
60041 A3
60043 A3
60057 A3
60087 A3
60089 A3
60090 A3
60094 A3
60096 A3
60097 A3
60098 A3
60099 A3
60100 A3
60101 A3
60152 A1
60159 A1
60160 A1
60161 A1
60162 A1
60507 A2
60509 A2
60510 A2
60519 A2
60529 A2
60530 A2
60534 A2
60535 A2
60536 A2
60537 A2
60816 V2
60927 V2
60951 V2
60959 V2
61007 B1
61076 B1
61081 B1
61178 B1
61221 B1
61244 B1
61245 B1
61355 B1
61404 B1
62437 D30
62677 D11
62678 D11
62679 D11
62683 D11
62685 D11
62690 D11
62691 D11
62692 D11
62693 D11
62694 D11
62705 D49
62706 D49
62709 D49
62719 D49
62733 D49
62743 D49
65235 J36
65243 J36
67610 V1
67615 V3
67620 V3
68328 J88
68339 J88
68457 J83
68460 J83
68478 J83
68481 J83
69169 N15
69220 N15

1960 64B
60004 A4
60009 A4
60011 A4
60012 A4
60024 A4
60027 A4
60031 A4
60035 A3
60037 A3
60041 A3
60043 A3
60057 A3
60087 A3
60089 A3
60090 A3
60094 A3
60096 A3
60097 A3
60098 A3
60099 A3
60100 A3
60101 A3
60152 A1
60159 A1
60160 A1
60161 A1
60162 A1
60507 A2
60509 A2
60510 A2
60519 A2
60529 A2
60530 A2
60534 A2
60535 A2
60536 A2
60537 A2
60927 V2
60951 V2
60959 V2
61007 B1
61076 B1
61081 B1
61178 B1
61219 B1
61221 B1
61244 B1
61245 B1
62685 D11
62690 D11
62691 D11
62693 D11
62709 D49
62743 D49
65235 J36
65243 J36
67610 V1
67615 V3
67620 V3
68335 J88
68457 J83
68481 J83
69211 N15
72001 6P5F
72002 6P5F

1963 64B
60004 A4
60012 A4
60024 A4
60098 A3
60099 A3
60100 A3
60101 A3
60152 A1
60159 A1
60160 A1
60161 A1
60162 A1
60957 V2
61081 B1
61178 B1
61221 B1
61245 B1
65243 J36

Heaton

1948 HTN
60069 A3
60072 A3
60073 A3
60077 A3
60080 A3
60082 A3
60083 A3
60085 A3
60088 A3
60092 A3
60511 A2
60512 A2
60515 A2
60516 A2
60517 A2
60802 V2
60808 V2
60812 V2
60886 V2
60891 V2
60895 V2
60939 V2
60944 V2
60947 V2
60949 V2
60957 V2
60966 V2
61019 B1
61020 B1
61021 B1
61022 B1
61023 B1
61224 B1
61241 B1
61255 B1
61818 K3
61884 K3
61901 K3
61906 K3
61917 K3
61952 K3
61962 K3
61969 K3
61984 K3

61987 K3
63012 O7
63045 O7
63048 O7
63061 O7
63067 O7
63076 O7
63078 O7
63082 O7
63086 O7
63092 O7
63099 O7
63103 O7
63105 O7
63109 O7
63111 O7
63113 O7
63124 O7
63137 O7
63141 O7
63146 O7
63158 O7
63161 O7
63162 O7
63164 O7
63166 O7
63167 O7
63182 O7
63197 O7
65030 J21
65081 J21
65086 J21
65102 J21
65104 J21
65114 J21
65122 J21
65649 J25
65697 J25
65704 J25
65720 J25
65727 J25
65781 J27
65794 J27
65795 J27
65806 J27
65824 J27
65842 J27
65862 J27
65863 J27
65864 J27
65886 J27
65889 J27
65893 J27
67241 G5
67246 G5
67249 G5
67303 G5
67304 G5
67333 G5
67635 V1
67637 V1
67640 V1
67641 V1
67642 V1
67651 V1
67652 V1
67653 V1
67654 V1
68243 J71
68245 J71
68256 J71
68264 J71
68271 J71
68273 J71
68278 J71
68430 J77
68675 J72
68682 J72
68683 J72
68687 J72
68725 J72
68732 J72
68743 J72
68744 J72
69371 N8
69372 N8
69380 N8
69387 N8
69390 N8

1951 52B
43070 4MT[5]
60069 A3
60072 A3
60073 A3
60077 A3
60080 A3
60083 A3
60085 A3
60088 A3
60091 A3
60092 A3
60116 A1
60126 A1
60127 A1
60511 A2
60512 A2
60515 A2
60516 A2
60517 A2
60539 A2
60801 V2
60802 V2
60805 V2
60806 V2
60807 V2
60808 V2
60809 V2
60810 V2
60811 V2
60812 V2
60833 V2
60835 V2
60860 V2
60868 V2
60884 V2
60885 V2
60886 V2
60887 V2
60891 V2
60895 V2
60910 V2
60926 V2
60939 V2
60942 V2
60944 V2
60945 V2
60947 V2
60949 V2
60952 V2
60957 V2
61065 B1
61338 B1
61818 K3
61875 K3
61884 K3
61901 K3
61904 K3
61906 K3
61917 K3
61930 K3
61952 K3
61962 K3
61969 K3
61984 K3
61985 K3
61986 K3
61987 K3
62002 K1
62003 K1
62005 K1
62007 K1
62010 K1
62048 K1
62049 K1
62050 K1
64709 J39
64856 J39
64865 J39
64915 J39
64923 J39
64945 J39
64947 J39
65712 J25
65788 J27
65800 J27
65807 J27
65842 J27
65862 J27
65863 J27
65864 J27
65869 J27
65873 J27
65886 J27
65889 J27
65893 J27
67635 V1
67637 V1
67640 V1
67641 V1
67642 V1
67645 V1
67646 V1
67651 V1
67652 V1
67654 V1
67673 V1
68014 J94
68234 J71
68245 J71
68247 J71
68256 J71
68262 J71
68264 J71
68267 J71
68271 J71
68273 J71
68278 J71
68430 J77
68682 J72
68687 J72
68725 J72
68738 J72
68742 J72
69371 N8
69387 N8
69390 N8

1954 52B
43016 4MT[5]
43030 4MT[5]
43043 4MT[5]
43070 4MT[5]
43125 4MT[5]
43129 4MT[5]
60069 A3
60072 A3
60073 A3
60077 A3
60080 A3
60083 A3
60085 A3
60088 A3
60091 A3
60092 A3
60116 A1
60126 A1
60127 A1
60511 A2
60517 A2
60539 A2
60801 V2
60805 V2
60806 V2
60810 V2
60811 V2
60812 V2
60833 V2
60835 V2
60885 V2
60886 V2
60887 V2
60891 V2
60910 V2
60939 V2
60942 V2
60944 V2
60945 V2
60952 V2
61818 K3
61875 K3
61904 K3
61906 K3
61927 K3
61984 K3
61986 K3
61987 K3
62387 D20
64703 J39
64853 J39
64856 J39
64904 J39
64915 J39
64923 J39
64945 J39
65035 J21
65039 J21
65075 J21
65110 J21
65869 J27
65873 J27
65893 J27
67635 V1
67637 V1
67640 V1
67641 V1
67642 V1
67645 V1
67646 V1
67647 V1
67651 V1
67652 V3
67654 V1
67673 V1
68014 J94
68021 J94
68234 J71
68245 J71
68251 J71
68256 J71
68262 J71
68264 J71
68271 J71
68428 J77
68440 J77
68682 J72
68702 J72
68725 J72
68738 J72
68742 J72
69027 J72
69028 J72
69377 N8

1957 52B
43016 4MT[5]
43030 4MT[5]
43043 4MT[5]
43055 4MT[5]
43056 4MT[5]
43070 4MT[5]
43075 4MT[5]
43101 4MT[5]
43126 4MT[5]
43129 4MT[5]
60069 A3
60072 A3
60073 A3
60077 A3
60080 A3
60082 A3
60083 A3
60085 A3
60088 A3
60091 A3
60092 A3
60116 A1
60126 A1
60127 A1
60511 A2
60517 A2
60539 A2
60802 V2
60806 V2
60809 V2
60810 V2
60811 V2
60812 V2
60835 V2
60886 V2
60891 V2
60901 V2
60910 V2
60922 V2
60939 V2
60942 V2
60944 V2
60945 V2
60952 V2
60962 V2
60978 V2
60979 V2
61410 B16
61413 B16
61440 B16
61451 B16
61456 B16
61458 B16
61469 B16
61818 K3
61844 K3
61869 K3
61875 K3
61906 K3
61927 K3
61984 K3
61986 K3
61987 K3
64703 J39
64853 J39
64856 J39
64915 J39
64923 J39
64945 J39
65061 J21
65110 J21
65656 J25
65675 J25
65685 J25
65687 J25
65864 J27
65869 J27
65876 J27
65879 J27
65882 J27
65886 J27
67635 V1
67637 V1
67640 V1
67641 V1
67642 V1
67645 V1
67646 V3
67647 V1
67651 V3
67652 V3
67654 V3
68014 J94
68251 J71
68262 J71
68263 J71
68264 J71
68702 J72
68708 J72
68713 J72
68716 J72
68738 J72
68742 J72
68747 J72
69001 J72
69027 J72
69028 J72

1960 52B
43126 4MT[5]
60073 A3
60077 A3
60080 A3
60082 A3
60083 A3
60085 A3
60088 A3
60092 A3
60116 A1
60126 A1
60127 A1
60511 A2
60517 A2
60539 A2
60802 V2
60806 V2
60808 V2
60809 V2
60810 V2
60811 V2
60812 V2
60835 V2
60846 V2
60886 V2
60891 V2
60901 V2
60910 V2
60922 V2
60932 V2
60940 V2
60944 V2
60945 V2
60962 V2
60976 V2
60978 V2
61818 K3
61844 K3
61869 K3
61875 K3
61884 K3
61906 K3
61923 K3
61927 K3
61962 K3
61984 K3
61986 K3
61987 K3
64806 J39
64837 J39
64856 J39
64864 J39
64866 J39
64871 J39
64915 J39
64923 J39
64926 J39
64931 J39
64939 J39
64945 J39
65110 J21
65864 J27
65869 J27
65876 J27
67641 V1
67642 V1
67646 V3
67647 V3
67651 V3
67652 V3
67654 V3
67656 V3
67658 V1
67683 V3
67685 V3
67691 V3
68702 J72
68708 J72
68713 J72
68732 J72
68738 J72
68742 J72
68747 J72
69028 J72
76024 4MT[2]

1963 52B
60040 A3
60042 A3
60051 A3
60053 A3
60058 A3
60060 A3
60071 A3
60073 A3
60075 A3
60082 A3
60083 A3
60085 A3
60088 A3
60091 A3
60802 V2
60812 V2
60835 V2
60868 V2
60891 V2
60904 V2
60910 V2
60922 V2
60940 V2
60944 V2
60962 V2
60976 V2
61216 B1
61322 B1
65796 J27
65852 J27
65864 J27
65881 J27
65882 J27
67620 V3
67642 V3
67645 V3
67646 V3
67647 V3
67651 V3
67652 V3
67654 V3
67656 V3
67658 V3
67683 V3
67690 V3
67691 V3
69008 J72
69024 J72
69028 J72

Heaton Mersey

1948 19D
40090 3MT[2]
40093 3MT[2]
40094 3MT[2]
40095 3MT[2]
40113 3MT[2]
43811 3F[4]
43908 4F[1]
43945 4F[1]
44010 4F[1]
44090 4F[2]
44110 4F[2]
44111 4F[2]
44117 4F[2]
44144 4F[2]
44178 4F[2]
44237 4F[2]
44271 4F[2]
44286 4F[2]
44407 4F[2]
44421 4F[2]
48089 8F
48099 8F
48135 8F
48154 8F
48179 8F
48190 8F
48208 8F
48220 8F
48275 8F
48315 8F
48316 8F
48329 8F
48406 8F
48667 8F
48676 8F
48683 8F
48697 8F
58128 2F[8]
58282 2F[9]
61469 B9
61475 B9
62314 D9
62322 D9
65132 J10
65135 J10
65137 J10
65145 J10
65148 J10
65154 J10
65157 J10
65160 J10
65164 J10
65178 J10
65179 J10
65181 J10
65185 J10
65186 J10
65188 J10
65193 J10
65194 J10
65197 J10
65198 J10
65200 J10
65209 J10
69251 N5
69276 N5
69317 N5
69328 N5
69331 N5
69332 N5
69359 N5

1951 9F
40089 3MT[2]
40113 3MT[2]
40118 3MT[2]
40124 3MT[2]
43811 3F[4]
43836 4F[1]
43945 4F[1]
44080 4F[2]
44090 4F[2]
44144 4F[2]
44178 4F[2]
44286 4F[2]
44407 4F[2]
44593 4F[2]
48089 8F
48099 8F
48127 8F
48134 8F
48154 8F
48155 8F
48190 8F
48208 8F
48220 8F
48275 8F
48315 8F
48316 8F
48329 8F
48406 8F
48503 8F
48527 8F
48557 8F
48676 8F
48682 8F
48683 8F
58128 2F[8]
58303 2F[9]
62663 D11
62665 D11
64727 J39
64733 J39
65132 J10
65135 J10
65144 J10
65145 J10
65146 J10
65157 J10
65160 J10
65178 J10
65181 J10
65185 J10
65188 J10
65193 J10
65194 J10
65197 J10
65198 J10
65200 J10
65209 J10
69276 N5
69317 N5
69328 N5
69331 N5
69332 N5
69359 N5

1954 9F
40089 3MT[2]
40094 3MT[2]
40113 3MT[2]
40124 3MT[2]
42775 5MT[1]
42788 5MT[1]
43854 4F[1]
43945 4F[1]
44080 4F[2]
44090 4F[2]
44144 4F[2]
44178 4F[2]
44286 4F[2]
44379 4F[2]
44407 4F[2]
48089 8F
48099 8F
48127 8F
48135 8F
48148 8F
48161 8F
48190 8F
48208 8F
48220 8F
48275 8F
48315 8F
48316 8F
48327 8F
48329 8F
48406 8F
48429 8F
48503 8F
48527 8F
48528 8F
48557 8F
48676 8F
48677 8F
48682 8F
48683 8F
58128 2F[8]
62663 D11
62665 D11
65132 J10
65135 J10
65160 J10
65178 J10
65194 J10
65200 J10
69262 N5
69276 N5
69299 N5
69317 N5
69331 N5
69359 N5

1957 17E
40001 3MT[1]
40067 3MT[1]
40089 3MT[2]
40094 3MT[2]
40113 3MT[2]
40124 3MT[2]
42775 5MT[1]
42788 5MT[1]
43854 4F[1]
43945 4F[1]
44090 4F[2]
44144 4F[2]
44178 4F[2]
44236 4F[2]
44261 4F[2]
44286 4F[2]
44361 4F[2]
44379 4F[2]
44387 4F[2]
44407 4F[2]
44421 4F[2]
48089 8F
48099 8F
48127 8F
48148 8F
48161 8F
48190 8F
48208 8F
48220 8F
48315 8F
48316 8F
48327 8F
48329 8F
48406 8F
48429 8F
48501 8F
48503 8F
48527 8F
48528 8F
48557 8F
48634 8F
48676 8F
48677 8F
48682 8F
48731 8F
65132 J10
65135 J10
65160 J10
65178 J10
65187 J10
65194 J10
65200 J10
69262 N5
69276 N5
69299 N5
69331 N5

1960 9F
40001 3MT[1]
40057 3MT[1]
40089 3MT[2]
40094 3MT[2]
40113 3MT[2]
40124 3MT[2]
43212 3F[3]
43245 3F[3]
43832 3F[4]
43945 4F[1]
44090 4F[2]
44250 4F[2]
44261 4F[2]
44286 4F[2]
44378 4F[2]
44379 4F[2]
44387 4F[2]
44407 4F[2]
44421 4F[2]
44501 4F[2]
44554 4F[2]
48161 8F
48190 8F
48191 8F
48208 8F
48316 8F
48327 8F
48329 8F
48406 8F
48429 8F
48501 8F
48503 8F
48543 8F
48557 8F
48613 8F
48634 8F
48676 8F
48677 8F
48682 8F
48695 8F
48731 8F
76048 4MT[2]
76085 4MT[2]
76087 4MT[2]

1963 9F
42133 4MT[1]
42134 4MT[1]
42159 4MT[1]
42469 4MT[3]
43042 4MT[5]
43046 4MT[5]
43048 4MT[5]
43049 4MT[5]
43063 4MT[5]
43945 4F[1]
44250 4F[2]
44286 4F[2]
44289 4F[2]
44379 4F[2]
44394 4F[2]
44501 4F[2]
44554 4F[2]
48089 8F
48161 8F
48190 8F
48191 8F
48208 8F
48302 8F
48316 8F
48327 8F
48329 8F
48338 8F
48390 8F
48403 8F
48406 8F
48429 8F
48501 8F
48503 8F
48523 8F
48543 8F
48557 8F
48613 8F
48634 8F
48676 8F
48677 8F
48682 8F
48695 8F
48731 8F

1966 9F
42945 5MT[2]
42951 5MT[2]
42955 5MT[2]
42957 5MT[2]
42960 5MT[2]
42967 5MT[2]
42968 5MT[2]
42975 5MT[2]
42977 5MT[2]
42978 5MT[2]
42980 5MT[2]
42981 5MT[2]
42983 5MT[2]
43012 4MT[5]
43031 4MT[5]
43042 4MT[5]
43047 4MT[5]
43048 4MT[5]
43063 4MT[5]
43106 4MT[5]
48089 8F
48115 8F
48161 8F
48176 8F
48191 8F
48208 8F
48316 8F
48322 8F
48329 8F
48365 8F
48390 8F
48428 8F
48464 8F
48501 8F
48503 8F
48515 8F
48546 8F
48613 8F
48677 8F
48695 8F
48701 8F
48731 8F

Helensburgh

1951 65H
67613 V1
67614 V1
67616 V1
67625 V1
67631 V1
67632 V1

1954 65H
67613 V1
67614 V1
67616 V1
67625 V3
67631 V1
67632 V1

1957 65H
67613 V3
67614 V1
67616 V1
67625 V3
67631 V1
67632 V1

1960 65H
67613 V3
67614 V3
67616 V1
67625 V3
67631 V1
67632 V3

Hellifield

1948 20G
40021 3MT[1]
40064 3MT[1]
40183 3MT[2]
40184 3MT[2]
40459 2P[2]
40470 2P[2]
40932 4P[1]
41006 4P[2]
41056 4P[1]
41080 4P[1]
41205 2MT[1]
41206 2MT[1]
42770 5MT[1]
42893 5MT[1]
43137 3F[2]
43186 3F[2]
43226 3F[3]
43231 3F[3]
43335 3F[3]
43585 3F[3]
43586 3F[3]
43781 3F[4]
44149 4F[2]
44282 4F[2]
44555 4F[2]
44579 4F[2]
48005 8F
48145 8F
48189 8F
50625 2P[8]
50686 2P[8]
50842 2P[8]
50896 2P[8]
50899 2P[8]

1951 23B
40021 3MT[1]
40064 3MT[1]
40162 3MT[2]
40183 3MT[2]
40184 3MT[2]
40470 2P[2]
41205 2MT[1]
41206 2MT[1]
42770 5MT[1]
42784 5MT[1]
43585 3F[3]
43586 3F[3]
44149 4F[2]
44276 4F[2]
44282 4F[2]
44579 4F[2]
48105 8F
48189 8F
48608 8F
48616 8F
50625 2P[8]
50686 2P[8]

1954 20G
40162 3MT[2]
40183 3MT[2]
40184 3MT[2]
40632 2P[3]
41205 2MT[1]
41206 2MT[1]
42770 5MT[1]
42784 5MT[1]
43585 3F[3]
43586 3F[3]
44149 4F[2]
44245 4F[2]
44276 4F[2]
44282 4F[2]
44579 4F[2]
48105 8F
48189 8F
48616 8F
58066 1P[6]

1957 20G
40120 3MT[2]
40162 3MT[2]
40163 3MT[2]
40183 3MT[2]
40685 2P[3]
41206 2MT[1]
42051 4MT[1]
42132 4MT[1]
43585 3F[3]
44149 4F[2]
44276 4F[2]
44282 4F[2]
44579 4F[2]
48105 8F
48189 8F
48616 8F

1960 24H
40685 2P[3]
42051 4MT[1]
42132 4MT[1]
42278 4MT[1]
42484 4MT[3]
42491 4MT[3]
42492 4MT[3]
42648 4MT[3]
43585 3F[3]
43756 3F[3]
44149 4F[2]
44276 4F[2]
44282 4F[2]
44579 4F[2]
48189 8F

1963 24H
42484 4MT[3]
42491 4MT[3]
42492 4MT[3]
44149 4F[2]
44276 4F[2]
44282 4F[2]

Helmsdale

1951 60C
54480 3P[6]
54495 3P[6]
55051 0P
55053 0P
57587 3F[12]

1954 60C
54480 3P[6]
54495 3P[6]
55051 0P
55053 0P
57587 3F[12]

1957 60C
54470 3P[6]
54480 3P[6]
54495 3P[6]
55053 0P
55236 2P[13]
57587 3F[12]

1960 60C
1646 1600
1649 1600
54480 3P[6]
54495 3P[6]
57587 3F[12]

Hereford

1948 HFD
1206 AD[4]
1404 1400
1445 1400
1455 1400
1460 1400
2026 2021
2029 2021
2040 2021
2096 2021
2099 2021
2138 2021
2243 2251
2286 2251
2349 2301
2541 2301
2680 2600
2714 655
2807 2800
2920 2900
2924 2900
2932 2900
2937 2900
2944 2900
2948 2900
2951 2900
2987 2900
3209 2251
3432 3300
3454 3300
3601 5700
3725 5700
3728 5700
3789 5700
4079 4073
4600 5700
4657 5700
4678 5700
5348 4300
5377 4300
5765 5700
5807 5800
5808 5800
5814 5800
5817 5800
6349 4300
6352 4300
6395 4300
6631 5600
6905 4900
6920 4900
6943 4900
7420 7400
7707 5700
9619 5700

1951 85C
1206 AD[4]
1445 1400
1455 1400
1460 1400
2026 2021
2040 2021
2099 2021
2138 2021
2160 2021
2243 2251
2281 2251
2286 2251
2349 2301
2515 2301
2541 2301
2807 2800
2920 2900
2937 2900
2944 2900
3209 2251
3406 3300
3728 5700
3789 5700
3848 2884
4600 5700
4657 5700
4678 5700
5348 4300
5377 4300
5765 5700
5807 5800
5808 5800
5814 5800
5817 5800
6326 4300
6349 4300
6352 4300
6395 4300
6681 5600
6905 4900
6916 4900
6936 4900
6951 4900
6984 6959
6989 6959
7307 4300
7308 4300
7314 4300
7416 7400
7420 7400
7707 5700
9619 5700
90524 WD[1]

1954 85C
1445 1400
1455 1400
1460 1400
1617 1600
2138 2021
2160 2021
2225 2251
2249 2251
2274 2251
2281 2251
2474 2301
2541 2301
3209 2251
3728 5700
3789 5700
4600 5700
4657 5700
4678 5700
4905 4900
4907 4900
4975 4900
4976 4900
5377 4300
5765 5700
5807 5800
5814 5800
5817 5800
5818 5800
6308 4300
6326 4300
6338 4300
6352 4300
6362 4300
6395 4300
6916 4900
6984 6959
6989 6959
6992 6959
7204 7200
7222 7200
7307 4300
7308 4300
7314 4300
7416 7400
7420 7400
7437 7400
7707 5700
7805 7800
8701 5700
9619 5700

1957 85C
1445 1400
1455 1400
1456 1400
1617 1600
1625 1600
1657 1600
1662 1600
1667 1600
2206 2251
2225 2251
2249 2251
2266 2251
2274 2251
2281 2251
2295 2251
3728 5700
4657 5700
4678 5700
4952 4900
4975 4900
5226 5205
5243 5205
5355 4300
5377 4300
5765 5700
5807 5800

5814 5800
5817 5800
5977 4900
5998 4900
6314 4300
6359 4300
6916 4900
6984 6959
6992 6959
7301 4300
7308 4300
7416 7400
7437 7400
7805 7800
8701 5700
9304 9300
9619 5700
9665 5700
9717 5700
49046 7F^2
49082 7F^2
49146 7F^2
49226 7F^2

1960 85C
1445 1400
1455 1400
1617 1600
1625 1600
1657 1600
1662 1600
1667 1600
2241 2251
2242 2251
2249 2251
2295 2251
3728 5700
4115 5101
4657 5700
4659 5700
4678 5700
4913 4900
4990 4900
5243 5205
5245 5205
5952 4900
5998 4900
7326 4300
7418 7400
7426 7400
7437 7400
7719 5700
8722 5700
8781 5700
8787 5700
9665 5700
9717 5700
78004 2MT^1

1963 86C
1420 1400
1447 1400
1617 1600
1657 1600
1662 1600
1667 1600
2241 2251
2242 2251
2249 2251
2286 2251
3728 5700
4115 5101
4135 5101
4623 5700
4659 5700
4907 4900
4916 4900
5952 4900
5970 4900
5998 4900
7413 7400
7437 7400
9665 5700
78004 2MT^1
82001 3MT^2
82002 3MT^2

Hexham

1951 HEX
65295 J36
67245 G5
67268 G5
67329 G5

1951 52C sub
65295 J36
67245 G5
67249 G5
67265 G5
67268 G5
67313 G5
68059 J94

1954 52C sub
65119 J21
67249 G5
67265 G5
67268 G5
67309 G5
68278 J71

1957 52C sub
65033 J21
65117 J21
67265 G5
67329 G5
67639 V1
67657 V3
67658 V1
67682 V3
67687 V3

Highbridge

1948 22E
43194 3F^3
43216 3F^3
43218 3F^3
58046 1P^6
58049 1P^6
58088 1P^6
1307 1P^6

1951 71J
43204 3F^3
43419 3F^3
43792 3F^4
58046 1P^6
58047 1P^6
58086 1P^6
58088 1P^6

1954 71J
43201 3F^3
43204 3F^3
43419 3F^3
58051 1P^6
58072 1P^6
58073 1P^6
58086 1P^6

1957 71J
43201 3F^3
43419 3F^3
43682 3F^3
58086 1P^6

Hitchin

1948 HIT
61089 B1
61090 B1
61091 B1
61092 B1
61093 B1
61094 B1
61095 B1
61096 B1
61097 B1
61098 B1
61099 B1
61105 B1
61106 B1
61107 B1
62148 D3
62160 D2
62163 D2
64105 J3
64114 J3
64117 J3
64122 J3
64140 J3
64145 J3
64153 J3
64240 J6
68512 J67
68541 J69
68605 J69
69515 N2
69557 N2

1951 34D
61090 B1
61091 B1
61093 B1
61094 B1
61095 B1
61097 B1
61099 B1
61105 B1
64105 J3
64114 J3
64117 J3
64122 J3
64140 J3
64153 J3
64175 J6
64240 J6
65003 J1
65010 J1
65013 J1
67740 L1
67741 L1
67743 L1
67744 L1
67745 L1
67746 L1
67790 L1
67791 L1
68175 Y3
68512 J67
68541 J69
68605 J69
69515 N2
69557 N2

1954 34D
61027 B1
61090 B1
61091 B1
61093 B1
61094 B1
61097 B1
61393 B1
61394 B1
64175 J6
64186 J6
64197 J6
64206 J6
64237 J6
64240 J6
64251 J6
65013 J1
65479 J15
67741 L1
67743 L1
67744 L1
67745 L1
67746 L1
67785 L1
67790 L1
67791 L1
68529 J67
68540 J67
68610 J67
69515 N2
69557 N2

1957 34D
42328 4MT^2
42374 4MT^2
61027 B1
61090 B1
61091 B1
61093 B1
61094 B1
61097 B1
61105 B1
61251 B1
62785 E4
64175 J6
64186 J6
64197 J6
64206 J6
64237 J6
64240 J6
64251 J6
65479 J15
67741 L1
67744 L1
67745 L1
67746 L1
67785 L1
67786 L1
67790 L1
67791 L1
68610 J67
68638 J68
68661 J68
69515 N2
69557 N2

1960 34D
61091 B1
61097 B1
64175 J6
64206 J6
64240 J6
64251 J6
64260 J6
65479 J15
67744 L1
67745 L1
67746 L1
69594 N2

Hither Green

1948 HIT
30800 N15
30950 Z
30951 Z
30953 Z
30955 Z
30956 Z
31018 C
31028 F1
31031 F1
31044 O1
31054 C
31059 C
31061 C
31068 C
31071 C
31109 O1
31113 C
31191 C
31243 C
31244 C
31245 C
31248 O1
31253 C
31257 C
31258 O1
31270 C
31298 C
31374 O1
31377 O1
31385 O1
31386 O1
31455 B1
31457 B1
31480 C
31486 C
31572 C
31581 C
31689 C
31695 C
31720 C
31878 N1
31879 N1
31880 N1
31911 W
31913 W
31921 W
31922 W
31923 W
31924 W
31925 W
90332 WD^1
90390 WD^1
90566 WD^1
90669 WD^1
90671 WD^1
90678 WD^1
90702 WD^1
90718 WD^1

1951 73C
30797 N15
31018 C
31054 C
31059 C
31061 C
31150 C
31159 E
31245 C
31248 O1
31258 O1
31270 C
31391 O1
31432 O1
31480 C
31486 C
31581 C
31616 U
31617 U
31639 U
31689 C
31694 C
31695 C
31720 C
31732 D
31822 N1
31876 N1
31877 N1
31878 N1
31879 N1
31880 N1
31911 W
31913 W
31921 W
31922 W
31923 W
31924 W
31925 W
90127 WD^1
90142 WD^1
90213 WD^1
90267 WD^1
90389 WD^1
90390 WD^1
90556 WD^1
90566 WD^1
90669 WD^1
90671 WD^1
90678 WD^1
90702 WD^1
90718 WD^1

1954 73C
30806 N15
31018 C
31033 C
31054 C
31059 C
31061 C
31063 C
31480 C
31686 C
31687 C
31688 C
31689 C
31690 C
31691 C
31692 C
31693 C
31694 C
31695 C
31822 N1
31856 N
31857 N
31858 N
31859 N
31860 N
31861 N
31876 N1
31877 N1
31878 N1
31879 N1
31880 N1
31892 U1
31893 U1
31911 W
31912 W
31913 W
31916 W
31921 W
31922 W
31923 W
31924 W
31925 W
33014 Q1
33015 Q1
33016 Q1
33018 Q1
33037 Q1

1957 73C
30772 N15
30806 N15
31018 C
31033 C
31054 C
31059 C
31061 C
31480 C
31498 C
31686 C
31688 C
31689 C
31690 C
31691 C
31692 C
31693 C
31694 C
31695 C
31721 C
31822 N1
31854 N
31855 N
31856 N
31857 N
31858 N
31859 N
31860 N
31861 N
31876 N1
31877 N1
31878 N1
31879 N1
31880 N1
31911 W
31912 W
31913 W
31916 W
31922 W
31923 W
31924 W
31925 W
33014 Q1
33037 Q1

1960 73C
31287 C
31498 C
31573 C
31686 C
31688 C
31689 C
31690 C
31691 C
31692 C
31693 C
31694 C
31695 C
31721 C
31816 N
31855 N
31856 N
31857 N
31859 N
31911 W
31912 W
31913 W
31916 W
31922 W
31923 W
31924 W
31925 W

Holyhead

1948 7C
41114 4P^1
41123 4P^1
41124 4P^1
45110 5MT^3
45111 5MT^3
45113 5MT^3
45249 5MT^3
45313 5MT^3
46112 7P^{3}R
46127 7P^{3}R
46132 7P^{3}R
46157 7P^{3}R
46899 2P^7
47321 3F^6
47368 3F^6
47476 3F^6

1951 7C
44868 5MT^3
45070 5MT^3
45110 5MT^3
45111 5MT^3
45249 5MT^3
45346 5MT^3
45376 5MT^3
45382 5MT^3
46112 7P^{3}R
46119 7P^{3}R
46127 7P^{3}R
46132 7P^{3}R
46161 7P^{3}R
46166 7P^{3}R
47321 3F^6
47368 3F^6
47476 3F^6

1954 6J
41115 4P^1
44678 5MT^3
44681 5MT^3
44868 5MT^3
44935 5MT^3
45045 5MT^3
45110 5MT^3
45292 5MT^3
45382 5MT^3
45385 5MT^3
46110 7P^{3}R
46127 7P^{3}R
46129 7P^{3}R
46132 7P^{3}R
46150 7P^{3}R
46157 7P^{3}R
47321 3F^6
47368 3F^6
47476 3F^6

1957 6J
41086 4P^1
44681 5MT^3
45110 5MT^3
45385 5MT^3
46147 7P^{3}R
46149 7P^{3}R
47321 3F^6
47368 3F^6
47439 3F^6
47476 3F^6
47627 3F^6
70045 7P6F
70046 7P6F
70047 7P6F
70048 7P6F
70049 7P6F
73135 5MT
73136 5MT
73137 5MT
73138 5MT
73139 5MT

1960 6J
44661 5MT^3
44802 5MT^3
44986 5MT^3
45056 5MT^3
45110 5MT^3
45382 5MT^3
45429 5MT^3
45441 5MT^3
46127 7P^{3}R
46129 7P^{3}R
46149 7P^{3}R
47321 3F^6
47368 3F^6
47439 3F^6
47476 3F^6

1963 6J
44807 5MT^3
45045 5MT^3
45110 5MT^3
45282 5MT^3
45527 7P^1
45736 7P^2
46114 7P^{3}R
46125 7P^{3}R
46150 7P^{3}R
46152 7P^{3}R
46156 7P^{3}R
46167 7P^{3}R
47321 3F^6
47368 3F^6
47439 3F^6
47476 3F^6
70045 7P6F
70046 7P6F
70048 7P6F
70049 7P6F
70050 7P6F
70051 7P6F
73011 5MT
73067 5MT
73073 5MT

1966 6J
44711 5MT^3
44712 5MT^3
44770 5MT^3
44807 5MT^3
45223 5MT^3
45247 5MT^3
45280 5MT^3
45447 5MT^3
47266 3F^6
47410 3F^6
75024 4MT^1
75052 4MT^1

Hornsey

1948 HSY
64188 J6
64234 J6
64239 J6
64251 J6
64256 J6
67376 C12
68757 J52
68758 J52
68759 J52
68760 J52
68761 J52
68773 J52
68774 J52
68776 J52
68777 J52
68778 J52
68781 J52
68783 J52
68784 J52
68785 J52
68787 J52
68788 J52
68791 J52
68793 J52
68794 J52
68795 J52
68796 J52
68808 J52
68811 J52
68815 J52
68825 J52
68826 J52
68827 J52
68829 J52
68833 J52
68834 J52
68851 J52
68853 J52
68856 J52
68883 J52
69431 N1
69432 N1
69433 N1
69435 N1
69439 N1
69441 N1
69442 N1
69445 N1
69450 N1
69451 N1
69453 N1
69456 N1
69457 N1
69458 N1
69460 N1
69463 N1
69465 N1
69470 N1
69475 N1
69477 N1
69505 N2
69513 N2
69516 N2
69522 N2
69530 N2
69531 N2
69533 N2
69547 N2
69556 N2
69566 N2

1951 34B
64188 J6
64234 J6
64239 J6
64251 J6
64256 J6
67376 C12
67707 L1
67756 L1
67757 L1
67761 L1
68757 J52
68758 J52
68759 J52
68760 J52
68761 J52
68773 J52
68774 J52
68776 J52
68777 J52
68778 J52
68781 J52
68783 J52
68784 J52
68785 J52
68787 J52
68788 J52
68791 J52
68793 J52
68794 J52
68795 J52
68796 J52
68808 J52
68811 J52
68815 J52
68825 J52
68826 J52
68827 J52
68829 J52
68833 J52
68834 J52
68851 J52
68853 J52
68856 J52
68883 J52
69431 N1
69432 N1
69433 N1
69434 N1
69435 N1
69439 N1
69441 N1
69442 N1
69445 N1
69450 N1
69451 N1
69453 N1
69455 N1
69456 N1
69457 N1
69458 N1
69460 N1
69462 N1
69463 N1
69465 N1
69466 N1
69467 N1
69468 N1
69469 N1
69470 N1
69475 N1
69476 N1
69477 N1
69480 N1
69481 N1
69505 N2
69513 N2
69516 N2
69522 N2
69530 N2
69531 N2
69533 N2
69547 N2
69556 N2
69566 N2
69567 N2

1954 34B
64196 J6
64221 J6
64222 J6
64223 J6
64233 J6
64239 J6
64242 J6
64253 J6
64256 J6
64266 J6
68808 J52
68824 J52
68834 J52
68866 J52
68883 J52
68891 J50
68894 J50
68903 J50
68906 J50
68907 J50
68917 J50
68918 J50
68920 J50
68921 J50
68928 J50
68929 J50
68930 J50
68931 J50
68936 J50
68945 J50
68949 J50
68961 J50
68968 J50
68971 J50
68972 J50
68981 J50
68982 J50
68983 J50
68985 J50
68986 J50
68987 J50
68989 J50
68990 J50
68991 J50
69435 N1
69441 N1
69445 N1
69451 N1
69453 N1
69455 N1
69457 N1
69458 N1
69460 N1
69465 N1
69466 N1
69467 N1
69469 N1
69470 N1
69476 N1
69481 N1
69505 N2
69513 N2
69522 N2
69530 N2
69531 N2
69533 N2
69547 N2
69556 N2
69560 N2
69567 N2

1957 34B
64196 J6
64223 J6
64233 J6
64253 J6
64266 J6
68808 J52
68824 J52
68834 J52
68846 J52
68866 J52
68875 J52
68891 J50
68894 J50
68903 J50
68906 J50
68907 J50
68917 J50
68918 J50
68920 J50
68921 J50
68928 J50
68929 J50
68930 J50
68931 J50
68936 J50
68945 J50
68946 J50
68949 J50
68961 J50
68966 J50
68968 J50
68971 J50
68972 J50
68979 J50
68981 J50
68982 J50
68983 J50
68985 J50
68986 J50
68987 J50
68989 J50
68090 J50
68991 J50
69462 N1
69477 N1
69501 N2
69505 N2
69513 N2
69522 N2
69530 N2
69531 N2
69533 N2
69537 N2
69554 N2
69556 N2
69560 N2
69567 N2
69587 N2
69594 N2
69612 N7
69615 N7
69618 N7
69629 N7

1960 34B
64196 J6
64223 J6
64233 J6
64253 J6
68033 J94
68067 J94
68073 J94
68075 J94
68077 J94
68891 J50
68894 J50
68903 J50
68907 J50
68917 J50
68918 J50
68920 J50
68921 J50
68926 J50
68928 J50
68929 J50
68930 J50
68931 J50
68936 J50
68945 J50
68946 J50
68960 J50
68961 J50
68966 J50
68968 J50
68970 J50
68971 J50
68972 J50
68979 J50
68980 J50
68981 J50
68982 J50
68983 J50
68986 J50
68987 J50
68989 J50
68990 J50
68991 J50
69504 N2
69520 N2
69587 N2

Horsham

1948 HOR
30540 Q
30543 Q
30544 Q
31157 E
31273 E
31730 D
32045 B4X
32051 B4^2
32055 B4X
32067 B4X
32074 B4^2
32252 D1/M
32283 D1/M
32286 D1^2
32289 D1/M
32300 C3
32301 C3
32306 C3
32307 C3
32308 C3
32366 D3
32373 D3
32384 D3
32387 D3
32389 D3
32399 E5
32401 E5X
32449 C2X
32464 E4
32496 E4
32501 E4
32511 E4
32515 E4
32521 C2X
32550 C2X
32556 E4
32557 E4
32570 E5X
32571 E5
32573 E5
32584 E5
32594 E5

1951 75D
30027 M7
30047 M7
30545 Q
30546 Q
32364 D3
32365 D3
32379 D3
32380 D3
32384 D3
32401 E5X
32464 E4
32482 E4
32511 E4
32515 E4
32521 C2X
32539 C2X
32544 C2X
32548 C2X
32556 E4
32570 E5X
32586 E5X

1954 75D
30047 M7
30048 M7
30049 M7
30050 M7
30051 M7
30108 M7
30544 Q
30545 Q
30546 Q
32463 E4
32464 E4
32465 E4
32467 E4
32468 E4
32469 E4
32470 E4
32521 C2X
32522 C2X
32523 C2X
32541 C2X
32570 E5X
32576 E5X

1957 75D
30047 M7
30048 M7
30049 M7
30050 M7
30051 M7
30544 Q
30545 Q
30546 Q
30547 Q
32463 E4
32469 E4
32470 E4
32480 E4
32522 C2X
32523 C2X
32541 C2X

Horwich Works

1948
11304 2F^2
11305 2F^2
11324 2F^2
11368 2F^2
11394 2F^2
Wren NG^1

1951
11304 2F^2
11305 2F^2
11324 2F^2
11368 2F^2
11394 2F^2
Wren NG^1

1954
51429 2F^4
11304 2F^2
11305 2F^2
11324 2F^2
11368 2F^2
11394 2F^2
Wren NG^1

1957
51429 2F^2
11304 2F^2
11305 2F^2
11324 2F^2
11368 2F^2
11394 2F^2
Wren NG^1

1960
51429 2F^2
11304 2F^2
11305 2F^2
11324 2F^2
11368 2F^2
11394 2F^2
Wren NG^1

1963
47429 3F^6
47550 3F^6
11305 2F^2
11324 2F^2
11368 2F^2

Huddersfield

1948 25B
42310 4MT^2
42311 4MT^2
42312 4MT^2
42324 4MT^2
42384 4MT^2
42408 4MT^2
42410 4MT^2
42411 4MT^2
42412 4MT^2
42413 4MT^2
42414 4MT^2
42733 5MT^1
42861 5MT^1
42862 5MT^1
42863 5MT^1
42866 5MT^1
42869 5MT^1
45099 5MT^3
45215 5MT^3
45218 5MT^3
45237 5MT^3
45238 5MT^3
48447 8F
48452 8F
48455 8F
48733 8F
48737 8F
49381 7F^2
49387 7F^2
49501 7F^4
49536 7F^4
49544 7F^4
49563 7F^4
49572 7F^4
49580 7F^4
49583 7F^4
49596 7F^4
51408 2F^2
51447 2F^2
51524 2F^2
52351 3F^7
52515 3F^7

1951 25B
42310 4MT^2
42311 4MT^2
42312 4MT^2
42384 4MT^2
42408 4MT^2
42409 4MT^2
42410 4MT^2
42412 4MT^2
42413 4MT^2
42414 4MT^2
42861 5MT^1
42862 5MT^1
42863 5MT^1
42866 5MT^1
42869 5MT^1
44780 5MT^3
44824 5MT^3
44949 5MT^3
45099 5MT^3
45215 5MT^3
45218 5MT^3
45222 5MT^3
45237 5MT^3
45340 5MT^3
49648 7F^4
50731 2P^8
50735 2P^8
50736 2P^8
50887 2P^8
51408 2F^2
51524 2F^2
90181 WD^1
90308 WD^1
90332 WD^1
90345 WD^1
90347 WD^1
90527 WD^1
90619 WD^1
90650 WD^1
90655 WD^1
90680 WD^1
90694 WD^1

1954 25B
42110 4MT^1
42310 4MT^2

42311 4MT[2]
42312 4MT[2]
42384 4MT[2]
42408 4MT[2]
42409 4MT[2]
42410 4MT[2]
42412 4MT[2]
42413 4MT[2]
42414 4MT[2]
42845 5MT[1]
42861 5MT[1]
42862 5MT[1]
42863 5MT[1]
44780 5MT[3]
44824 5MT[3]
44949 5MT[3]
45215 5MT[3]
45222 5MT[3]
45237 5MT[3]
45340 5MT[3]
49648 7F[4]
50865 2P[8]
51408 2F[2]
51524 2F[2]
90325 WD[1]
90332 WD[1]
90345 WD[1]
90347 WD[1]
90619 WD[1]
90621 WD[1]
90655 WD[1]
90680 WD[1]
90694 WD[1]

1957 55G
42310 4MT[2]
42312 4MT[2]
42384 4MT[2]
42408 4MT[2]
42409 4MT[2]
42410 4MT[2]
42412 4MT[2]
42413 4MT[2]
42414 4MT[2]
44824 5MT[3]
45215 5MT[3]
45222 5MT[3]
45237 5MT[3]
45339 5MT[3]
45340 5MT[3]
47403 3F[6]
47556 3F[6]
50725 2P[8]
50865 2P[8]
90243 WD[1]
90249 WD[1]
90265 WD[1]
90325 WD[1]
90332 WD[1]
90345 WD[1]
90347 WD[1]
90619 WD[1]
90621 WD[1]
90624 WD[1]
90680 WD[1]
90694 WD[1]

1960 55G
42310 4MT[2]
42384 4MT[2]
42410 4MT[2]
42412 4MT[2]
42413 4MT[2]
42414 4MT[2]
73162 5MT
73163 5MT
73164 5MT
73165 5MT
90325 WD[1]
90332 WD[1]
90345 WD[1]
90347 WD[1]
90619 WD[1]
90621 WD[1]
90624 WD[1]
90649 WD[1]
90666 WD[1]
90680 WD[1]
90694 WD[1]

1963 55G
42310 4MT[2]
42317 4MT[2]
42384 4MT[2]
42410 4MT[2]
42413 4MT[2]
73163 5MT
73164 5MT
73165 5MT
90325 WD[1]
90332 WD[1]
90345 WD[1]
90347 WD[1]
90619 WD[1]
90621 WD[1]
90624 WD[1]
90649 WD[1]
90680 WD[1]
90694 WD[1]

1966 55G
42141 4MT[1]
42213 4MT[1]
42410 4MT[2]
42689 4MT[1]
90332 WD[1]
90362 WD[1]
90649 WD[1]
90680 WD[1]
90694 WD[1]

Hull Alexandra Dock

1948 HLA
68360 J73
68361 J73
68390 J77
68395 J77
68402 J77
68406 J77
68413 J77
68429 J77
68435 J77
68670 J72
68686 J72
68724 J72
68747 J72
68748 J72
68751 J72
68752 J72
68753 J72

1951 53C sub
68360 J73
68361 J73
68363 J73
68402 J77
68413 J77
68429 J77
68435 J77
68440 J77
68670 J72
68673 J72
68676 J72
68686 J72
68724 J72
68743 J72
68746 J72
68747 J72
68751 J72
68752 J72
68753 J72
69001 J72
69002 J72
69003 J72
69009 J72

1954 53C sub
68360 J73
68361 J73
68363 J73
68429 J77
68435 J77
68670 J72
68673 J72
68676 J72
68686 J72
68718 J72
68741 J72
68746 J72
68751 J72
68752 J72
68753 J72
69001 J72
69003 J72
69009 J72
69010 J72
69011 J72

1957 53C sub
68360 J73
68673 J72
68676 J72
68745 J72
68746 J72
68752 J72
69003 J72
69009 J72
69010 J72
69011 J72

1960 53C
68673 J72
68676 J72
68745 J72
69003 J72
69009 J72
69010 J72
69011 J72

Hull Botanic Gardens

1948 HLB
61010 B1
61071 B1
61074 B1
61080 B1
61084 B1
61215 B1
62355 D20
62361 D20
62367 D20
62369 D20
62382 D20
62700 D49
62701 D49
62703 D49
62707 D49
62710 D49
62720 D49
62722 D49
62723 D49
62724 D49
62727 D49
62737 D49
62741 D49
62743 D49
62744 D49
62754 D49
62757 D49
62767 D49
67242 G5
67256 G5
67266 G5
67279 G5
67280 G5
67282 G5
67301 G5
67305 G5
67311 G5
67321 G5
67340 G5
67371 C12
67391 C12
67392 C12
67393 C12
67394 C12
67395 C12
67397 C12
67399 C12
68151 Y1
68296 J71
69795 A6
69796 A6
69798 A6
69854 A8
69855 A8
69866 A8
69867 A8
69873 A8
69890 A8

1951 53B
61010 B1
61215 B1
61304 B1
61305 B1
61306 B1
62345 D20
62383 D20
62396 D20
62700 D49
62710 D49
62720 D49
62722 D49
62723 D49
62724 D49
62737 D49
62741 D49
62743 D49
62754 D49
62757 D49
62767 D49
67254 G5
67256 G5
67280 G5
67282 G5
67301 G5
67311 G5
67321 G5
67340 G5
67354 C12
67371 C12
67391 C12
67392 C12
67393 C12
67394 C12
67395 C12
67397 C12
67755 L1
67759 L1
67763 L1
67764 L1
67765 L1
67766 L1
68151 Y1
68401 J77
69796 A6
69798 A6
69855 A8
69894 A8

1954 53B
61010 B1
61215 B1
61304 B1
61305 B1
61306 B1
62700 D49
62710 D49
62717 D49
62720 D49
62722 D49
62723 D49
62724 D49
62737 D49
62741 D49
62754 D49
62757 D49
62767 D49
67253 G5
67254 G5
67256 G5
67273 G5
67280 G5
67282 G5
67301 G5
67311 G5
67321 G5
67337 G5
67340 G5
67352 C12
67353 C12
67371 C12
67391 C12
67392 C12
67394 C12
67395 C12
67397 C12
67755 L1
67759 L1
67763 L1
67764 L1
67765 L1
67766 L1
68151 Y1
68401 J77
69802 A5
69811 A5
69836 A5
69837 A5

1957 53B
61010 B1
61068 B1
61215 B1
61304 B1
61305 B1
61306 B1
62381 D20
62396 D20
62710 D49
62717 D49
62720 D49
62722 D49
62723 D49
62724 D49
62737 D49
62741 D49
62754 D49
62757 D49
62766 D49
62767 D49
67253 G5
67261 G5
67282 G5
67337 G5
67638 V3
67663 V3
67677 V1
67684 V3
67685 V3
67686 V3
67691 V3
68363 J73
69802 A5
69811 A5
69835 A5
69836 A5
69837 A5
69858 A8
69860 A8
69879 A8
69882 A8
69886 A8
69888 A8
77001 3MT[1]
77010 3MT[1]

Hull Dairycoates

1948 HLD
61813 K3
61814 K3
61819 K3
61871 K3
61872 K3
61874 K3
61883 K3
61892 K3
61899 K3
61902 K3
61903 K3
61920 K3
61922 K3
61923 K3
61927 K3
61932 K3
61934 K3
61935 K3
61941 K3
61945 K3
61965 K3
62933 C6
62970 C7
62982 C7
62983 C7
62988 C7
62995 C7
63628 O4
63664 O4
63764 O4
63770 O4
63772 O4
63812 O4
63816 O4
63823 O4
63843 O4
63855 O4
64867 J39
64914 J39
65619 J24
65621 J24
65631 J24
65639 J24
65647 J25
65651 J25
65660 J25
65663 J25
65666 J25
65671 J25
65679 J25
65690 J25
65698 J25
65699 J25
65705 J25
65712 J25
65713 J25
67171 F4
67175 F4
68137 Y1
68139 Y1
68140 Y1
68232 J71
68242 J71
68252 J71
68277 J71
68288 J71
68304 J71
68311 J71
68316 J71
68673 J72
68676 J72
69094 N10
69096 N10
69098 N10
69104 N10
69108 N10
69373 N8
69374 N8
69375 N8
69376 N8
69377 N8
69379 N8
69381 N8
69382 N8
69383 N8
69385 N8
69386 N8
69389 N8
69391 N8
69392 N8
69393 N8
69396 N8
69397 N8
69398 N8
69399 N8
69401 N8
69770 A7
69772 A7
69773 A7
69775 A7
69777 A7
69778 A7
69779 A7
69780 A7
69782 A7
69783 A7
69784 A7
69786 A7
69788 A7
69912 T1
69915 T1
69920 T1
69922 T1
90129 WD[1]
90208 WD[1]
90323 WD[1]
90378 WD[1]
90382 WD[1]
90403 WD[1]
90409 WD[1]
90418 WD[1]
90663 WD[1]
90677 WD[1]
90695 WD[1]
90697 WD[1]

1951 53A
43053 4MT[5]
43076 4MT[5]
43077 4MT[5]
43078 4MT[5]
43079 4MT[5]
61060 B1
61068 B1
61074 B1
61080 B1
61813 K3
61814 K3
61819 K3
61871 K3
61872 K3
61874 K3
61883 K3
61892 K3
61899 K3
61902 K3
61903 K3
61920 K3
61922 K3
61923 K3
61927 K3
61932 K3
61934 K3
61935 K3
61941 K3
61945 K3
61965 K3
63603 O4
63628 O4
63664 O4
63673 O4
63676 O1
63712 O1
63732 O4
63740 O1
63753 O4
63755 O1
63760 O1
63764 O4
63769 O4
63770 O4
63772 O4
63812 O4
63816 O4
63823 O4
63828 O4
63835 O4
63855 O4
63856 O1
63874 O1
63881 O4
64867 J39
64870 J39
64897 J39
64914 J39
64926 J39
64927 J39
64928 J39
64931 J39
64941 J39
65654 J25
65660 J25
65690 J25
65699 J25
65713 J25
67171 F4
67175 F4
68137 Y1
68139 Y1
68140 Y1
68232 J71
68242 J71
68252 J71
68296 J71
68298 J71
68304 J71
68311 J71
68316 J71
68748 J72
69010 J72
69011 J72
69093 N10
69094 N10
69096 N10
69098 N10
69099 N10
69102 N10
69104 N10
69106 N10
69107 N10
69108 N10
69377 N8
69379 N8
69381 N8
69382 N8
69385 N8
69386 N8
69389 N8
69392 N8
69393 N8
69398 N8
69401 N8
69770 A7
69771 A7
69772 A7
69773 A7
69775 A7
69777 A7
69778 A7
69779 A7
69780 A7
69782 A7
69783 A7
69784 A7
69786 A7
69788 A7
69912 T1
69914 T1
69915 T1
69922 T1
90006 WD[1]
90007 WD[1]
90009 WD[1]
90021 WD[1]
90022 WD[1]
90047 WD[1]
90057 WD[1]
90160 WD[1]
90378 WD[1]
90409 WD[1]
90435 WD[1]
90450 WD[1]
90483 WD[1]
90567 WD[1]
90663 WD[1]
90704 WD[1]

1954 53A
43015 4MT[5]
43038 4MT[5]
43053 4MT[5]
43069 4MT[5]
43076 4MT[5]
43077 4MT[5]
43078 4MT[5]
43079 4MT[5]
43099 4MT[5]
43100 4MT[5]
43103 4MT[5]
43122 4MT[5]
43124 4MT[5]
43130 4MT[5]
43131 4MT[5]
61060 B1
61068 B1
61074 B1
61080 B1
61813 K3
61814 K3
61819 K3
61844 K3
61846 K3
61847 K3
61869 K3
61871 K3
61872 K3
61874 K3
61883 K3
61884 K3
61892 K3
61893 K3
61902 K3
61903 K3
61920 K3
61922 K3
61923 K3
61934 K3
61935 K3
61941 K3
61945 K3
61965 K3
64709 J39
64725 J39
64914 J39
64947 J39
64971 J39
68140 Y1
68183 Y3
68232 J71
68242 J71
68252 J71
68296 J71
68298 J71
68304 J71
68402 J77
68413 J77
68743 J72
68747 J72
69093 N10
69094 N10
69096 N10
69098 N10
69099 N10
69102 N10
69104 N10
69106 N10
69107 N10
69108 N10
69381 N8
69385 N8
69386 N8
69770 A7
69771 A7
69772 A7
69773 A7
69778 A7
69779 A7
69781 A7
69782 A7
69786 A7
69788 A7
76022 4MT[2]
90006 WD[1]
90008 WD[1]
90009 WD[1]
90021 WD[1]
90022 WD[1]
90030 WD[1]
90057 WD[1]
90061 WD[1]
90072 WD[1]
90078 WD[1]
90089 WD[1]
90099 WD[1]
90160 WD[1]
90210 WD[1]
90272 WD[1]
90352 WD[1]
90378 WD[1]
90382 WD[1]
90409 WD[1]
90430 WD[1]
90450 WD[1]
90458 WD[1]
90479 WD[1]
90482 WD[1]
90609 WD[1]
90627 WD[1]
90695 WD[1]
90704 WD[1]

1957 53A
43053 4MT[5]
43069 4MT[5]
43076 4MT[5]
43077 4MT[5]
43078 4MT[5]
43079 4MT[5]
43099 4MT[5]
43100 4MT[5]
43103 4MT[5]
43122 4MT[5]
43131 4MT[5]
61060 B1
61074 B1
61080 B1
61813 K3
61819 K3
61846 K3
61847 K3
61871 K3
61872 K3
61874 K3
61883 K3
61884 K3
61892 K3
61893 K3
61899 K3
61902 K3
61903 K3
61904 K3
61920 K3
61922 K3
61923 K3
61932 K3
61934 K3
61935 K3
61941 K3
61945 K3
61965 K3
64709 J39
64819 J39
64864 J39
64910 J39
64914 J39
64939 J39
64940 J39
64949 J39
64971 J39
65555 J25
65677 J25
65693 J25
65695 J25
65726 J25
68230 J71
68232 J71
68252 J71
68296 J71
68298 J71
68670 J72
68718 J72
68741 J72
68751 J72
68753 J72
69094 N10
69096 N10
69099 N10
69104 N10
69107 N10
69108 N10
90006 WD[1]
90008 WD[1]
90009 WD[1]
90022 WD[1]
90030 WD[1]
90057 WD[1]
90072 WD[1]
90078 WD[1]
90089 WD[1]
90099 WD[1]
90100 WD[1]
90160 WD[1]
90272 WD[1]
90378 WD[1]
90382 WD[1]
90430 WD[1]
90450 WD[1]
90458 WD[1]
90479 WD[1]
90482 WD[1]
90609 WD[1]
90627 WD[1]
90670 WD[1]
90695 WD[1]
90704 WD[1]

1960 53A
43069 4MT[5]
43076 4MT[5]
43077 4MT[5]
43078 4MT[5]
43079 4MT[5]
43123 4MT[5]
43131 4MT[5]
61010 B1
61065 B1
61080 B1
61215 B1
61256 B1
61289 B1
61306 B1
61813 K3
61814 K3
61819 K3
61846 K3
61847 K3
61857 K3
61871 K3
61872 K3
61874 K3
61883 K3
61892 K3
61893 K3
61897 K3
61899 K3
61902 K3
61903 K3
61904 K3
61920 K3
61922 K3
61932 K3
61935 K3
61941 K3
61945 K3
61965 K3
62710 D49
62717 D49
62723 D49
62727 D49
62740 D49
62759 D49
62763 D49
62765 D49
64709 J39
64819 J39
64831 J39
64904 J39
64910 J39
64914 J39
64940 J39
64943 J39
64947 J39
64971 J39
65691 J25
65693 J25
67635 V1
67638 V3
67640 V1
67663 V3
67677 V3
67682 V3
67684 V3
67686 V3
68011 J94
68042 J94
68230 J71
68264 J71
68360 J73
68361 J73
68425 J77
68670 J72
68672 J72
68705 J72
68752 J72
68753 J72
69008 J72
77000 3MT[1]
77001 3MT[1]
77010 3MT[1]
84009 2MT[2]
90006 WD[1]
90008 WD[1]
90009 WD[1]
90022 WD[1]
90030 WD[1]
90072 WD[1]
90078 WD[1]
90099 WD[1]
90160 WD[1]
90217 WD[1]
90272 WD[1]
90352 WD[1]
90378 WD[1]
90427 WD[1]
90450 WD[1]
90458 WD[1]
90482 WD[1]
90503 WD[1]
90511 WD[1]
90571 WD[1]
90586 WD[1]
90609 WD[1]
90623 WD[1]
90627 WD[1]
90670 WD[1]
90677 WD[1]
90688 WD[1]
90695 WD[1]

1963 50B
41262 2MT[1]
43069 4MT[5]
43076 4MT[5]
43077 4MT[5]
43078 4MT[5]
43079 4MT[5]
43131 4MT[5]
61010 B1
61012 B1
61065 B1
61080 B1
61255 B1
61256 B1
61289 B1
61303 B1
61305 B1
61306 B1
61418 B16
61420 B16
61435 B16
61437 B16
61438 B16
61444 B16
61453 B16
61463 B16
61467 B16
61472 B16
67638 V3
67663 V3
67684 V3
67686 V3
68042 J94
69009 J72
69011 J72
77000 3MT[1]
90006 WD[1]
90008 WD[1]
90009 WD[1]
90099 WD[1]
90272 WD[1]
90352 WD[1]
90378 WD[1]
90427 WD[1]
90435 WD[1]
90450 WD[1]
90458 WD[1]
90482 WD[1]
90586 WD[1]
90609 WD[1]
90627 WD[1]
90670 WD[1]
90677 WD[1]
90688 WD[1]
90695 WD[1]

1966 50B
61002 B1
61012 B1
61032 B1
61255 B1
61289 B1
61306 B1
61322 B1
90008 WD[1]
90009 WD[1]
90044 WD[1]
90057 WD[1]
90213 WD[1]
90240 WD[1]
90262 WD[1]
90265 WD[1]
90272 WD[1]
90352 WD[1]
90378 WD[1]
90450 WD[1]
90458 WD[1]
90462 WD[1]
90478 WD[1]
90586 WD[1]
90627 WD[1]
90670 WD[1]
90677 WD[1]
90688 WD[1]
90695 WD[1]
90704 WD[1]

Hull Springhead

1948 HLS
63673 O4
63732 O4
63849 O4
65654 J25
65707 J25
65724 J25
65728 J25
68090 Y8
69089 N12
69110 N13
69111 N13
69112 N13
69113 N13
69116 N13
69119 N13
69774 A7
69776 A7
69785 A7
90104 WD[1]
90116 WD[1]
90154 WD[1]
90190 WD[1]
90246 WD[1]
90253 WD[1]
90537 WD[1]
90544 WD[1]
90567 WD[1]
90583 WD[1]
90587 WD[1]
90594 WD[1]

1951 53C
65667 J25
65705 J25
65728 J25
69111 N13
69112 N13
69113 N13
69116 N13
69119 N13
69774 A7
69776 A7
69785 A7
69789 A7
90010 WD[1]
90011 WD[1]
90052 WD[1]
90094 WD[1]
90116 WD[1]
90217 WD[1]
90233 WD[1]
90429 WD[1]
90470 WD[1]
90478 WD[1]
90497 WD[1]
90571 WD[1]
90586 WD[1]
90661 WD[1]
90677 WD[1]
90688 WD[1]

1954 53C
68284 J71
69774 A7
69776 A7
69780 A7
69783 A7
69784 A7
69785 A7
69787 A7
90011 WD[1]
90082 WD[1]
90094 WD[1]
90116 WD[1]
90217 WD[1]
90233 WD[1]
90427 WD[1]
90429 WD[1]
90467 WD[1]
90470 WD[1]
90478 WD[1]
90497 WD[1]
90511 WD[1]
90571 WD[1]
90586 WD[1]
90623 WD[1]
90661 WD[1]
90663 WD[1]
90677 WD[1]
90688 WD[1]

1957 53C
68361 J73
69772 A7
69782 A7
69786 A7
90011 WD[1]
90061 WD[1]
90094 WD[1]
90116 WD[1]
90217 WD[1]
90233 WD[1]
90352 WD[1]
90427 WD[1]
90429 WD[1]
90470 WD[1]
90478 WD[1]
90497 WD[1]
90511 WD[1]
90571 WD[1]
90586 WD[1]
90623 WD[1]
90661 WD[1]
90677 WD[1]
90688 WD[1]

Hurlford

1948 30B
40570 2P[3]
40571 2P[3]
40572 2P[3]
40573 2P[3]
40593 2P[3]
40597 2P[3]
40612 2P[3]
40617 2P[3]
40618 2P[3]
40643 2P[3]
40644 2P[3]
40645 2P[3]
40661 2P[3]
40662 2P[3]
40663 2P[3]
40665 2P[3]
40686 2P[3]
40687 2P[3]
40688 2P[3]
40689 2P[3]
43899 4F[1]
44159 4F[2]
44198 4F[2]
44312 4F[2]
44319 4F[2]
44323 4F[2]
44325 4F[2]
44329 4F[2]
54456 3P[5]
54504 3P[6]
55203 2P[13]
55236 2P[13]
55260 2P[15]
56368 3F[10]
57236 2F[5]
57277 2F[5]
57331 2F[5]
57353 2F[5]
57383 2F[5]
57570 3F[12]
57571 3F[12]
57572 3F[12]
57573 3F[12]
57574 3F[12]
57637 3F[13]
57643 3F[13]
57650 3F[14]
57651 3F[14]
57671 3F[14]
57672 3F[14]
57688 3F[14]

1951 67B
40566 2P[3]
40570 2P[3]
40571 2P[3]
40572 2P[3]
40573 2P[3]
40593 2P[3]
40597 2P[3]
40605 2P[3]
40612 2P[3]
40617 2P[3]
40618 2P[3]
40619 2P[3]
40643 2P[3]
40644 2P[3]
40645 2P[3]
40661 2P[3]
40662 2P[3]
40663 2P[3]
40665 2P[3]
40666 2P[3]
40686 2P[3]
40687 2P[3]
40688 2P[3]
40689 2P[3]
41110 4P[1]
42744 5MT[1]
42745 5MT[1]
42910 5MT[1]
42912 5MT[1]
43996 4F[1]
44001 4F[1]
44281 4F[2]
44312 4F[2]

44319 4F[2]
44323 4F[2]
44325 4F[2]
54456 3P[5]
54504 3P[6]
55203 2P[13]
55236 2P[13]
55260 2P[15]
56236 3F[10]
56368 3F[10]
57236 2F[5]
57277 2F[5]
57331 2F[5]
57353 2F[5]
57383 2F[5]
57570 3F[12]
57571 3F[12]
57572 3F[12]
57573 3F[12]
57637 3F[13]
57643 3F[13]
57650 3F[14]
57651 3F[14]
57671 3F[14]
57672 3F[14]
57688 3F[14]

1954 67B

40566 2P[3]
40570 2P[3]
40571 2P[3]
40572 2P[3]
40573 2P[3]
40592 2P[3]
40593 2P[3]
40597 2P[3]
40605 2P[3]
40612 2P[3]
40617 2P[3]
40618 2P[3]
40619 2P[3]
40643 2P[3]
40644 2P[3]
40645 2P[3]
40661 2P[3]
40662 2P[3]
40663 2P[3]
40665 2P[3]
40666 2P[3]
40686 2P[3]
40687 2P[3]
40688 2P[3]
40689 2P[3]
41110 4P[1]
42743 5MT[1]
42744 5MT[1]
42745 5MT[1]
42910 5MT[1]
42912 5MT[1]
44159 4F[2]
44281 4F[2]
44312 4F[2]
44319 4F[2]
44323 4F[2]
44325 4F[2]
45010 5MT[3]
45266 5MT[3]
54504 3P[6]
55203 2P[13]
55264 2P[15]
56236 3F[10]
56368 3F[10]
57236 2F[5]
57331 2F[5]
57353 2F[5]
57383 2F[5]
57570 3F[12]
57571 3F[12]
57572 3F[12]
57573 3F[12]
57637 3F[13]
57643 3F[13]
57650 3F[14]
57651 3F[14]
57671 3F[14]
57672 3F[14]
57688 3F[14]

1957 67B

40566 2P[3]
40570 2P[3]
40571 2P[3]
40572 2P[3]
40573 2P[3]
40592 2P[3]
40593 2P[3]
40597 2P[3]
40605 2P[3]
40612 2P[3]
40617 2P[3]
40618 2P[3]
40619 2P[3]
40643 2P[3]
40644 2P[3]
40645 2P[3]
40661 2P[3]
40665 2P[3]
40686 2P[3]
40687 2P[3]
40688 2P[3]
40689 2P[3]
42743 5MT[1]
42744 5MT[1]
44159 4F[2]
44281 4F[2]
44312 4F[2]
44319 4F[2]
44325 4F[2]
45010 5MT[3]
45266 5MT[3]
55203 2P[13]
55264 2P[15]
56236 3F[10]
56368 3F[10]
57236 2F[5]
57331 2F[5]
57353 2F[5]
57383 2F[5]
57570 3F[12]
57571 3F[12]
57572 3F[12]
57573 3F[12]
57637 3F[13]
57643 3F[13]
57650 3F[14]
57651 3F[14]
57671 3F[14]
57672 3F[14]
57688 3F[14]
77015 3MT[1]
77016 3MT[1]
77017 3MT[1]
77018 3MT[1]
77019 3MT[1]

1960 67B

40151 3MT[2]
40570 2P[3]
40571 2P[3]
40572 2P[3]
40574 2P[3]
40575 2P[3]
40592 2P[3]
40593 2P[3]
40595 2P[3]
40597 2P[3]
40609 2P[3]
40612 2P[3]
40619 2P[3]
40626 2P[3]
40643 2P[3]
40645 2P[3]
40647 2P[3]
40661 2P[3]
40665 2P[3]
40686 2P[3]
40687 2P[3]
40689 2P[3]
42739 5MT[1]
42743 5MT[1]
42744 5MT[1]
44281 4F[2]
44312 4F[2]
44325 4F[2]
45010 5MT[3]
45266 5MT[3]
55211 2P[13]
56368 3F[10]
57236 2F[5]
57284 2F[5]
57295 2F[5]
57331 2F[5]
57353 2F[5]
57383 2F[5]
57562 3F[12]
57570 3F[12]
57572 3F[12]
57577 3F[12]
57637 3F[13]
57643 3F[13]
57650 3F[14]
57651 3F[14]
57671 3F[14]
57672 3F[14]
57689 3F[14]
77015 3MT[1]
77016 3MT[1]
77017 3MT[1]
77018 3MT[1]
77019 3MT[1]

1963 67B

42735 5MT[1]
42739 5MT[1]
42741 5MT[1]
42746 5MT[1]
42802 5MT[1]
42879 5MT[1]
42880 5MT[1]
43132 4MT[5]
43133 4MT[5]
44718 5MT[3]
44992 5MT[3]
45007 5MT[3]
45010 5MT[3]
45117 5MT[3]
45123 5MT[3]
45124 5MT[3]
45192 5MT[3]
45489 5MT[3]
46451 2MT[2]
46467 2MT[2]
57572 3F[12]
65297 J36
77015 3MT[1]
77016 3MT[1]
77017 3MT[1]
77018 3MT[1]
77019 3MT[1]
80023 4MT[3]
80028 4MT[3]
80029 4MT[3]
80091 4MT[3]
80111 4MT[3]
80112 4MT[3]

1966 67B

42736 5MT[1]
42739 5MT[1]
42795 5MT[1]
44972 5MT[3]
44992 5MT[3]
45124 5MT[3]
45489 5MT[3]
45490 5MT[3]
46451 2MT[2]
76021 4MT[2]
76024 4MT[2]
76091 4MT[2]
76092 4MT[2]
76094 4MT[2]
76108 4MT[2]
77007 3MT[1]
77015 3MT[1]
77016 3MT[1]
77017 3MT[1]
77018 3MT[1]
77019 3MT[1]
80091 4MT[3]
80111 4MT[3]

Ilkley

1948 ILK

67337 G5

1951 50B sub

67337 G5

Immingham

1948 IMM

61079 B1
61082 B1
61142 B1
61195 B1
61202 B1
61204 B1
61497 B3
61720 K2
61722 K2
61724 K2
61727 K2
61728 K2
61733 K2
61735 K2
61739 K2
61800 K3
61803 K3
61806 K3
61836 K3
61837 K3
61838 K3
61842 K3
61845 K3
61891 K3
61912 K3
61963 K3
62132 D3
62139 D3
62660 D11
62661 D11
62662 D11
62663 D11
62664 D11
62665 D11
62666 D11
62667 D11
62668 D11
62669 D11
62670 D11
62902 C4
62903 C4
63005 O7
63032 O7
63634 O4
63679 O4
63692 O4
63878 O4
63902 O4
63917 O4
64284 J11
64305 J11
64307 J11
64312 J11
64314 J11
64320 J11
64323 J11
64325 J11
64355 J11
64372 J11
64411 J11
64446 J11
68006 J94
68009 J94
68012 J94
68013 J94
68018 J94
68020 J94
68022 J94
68026 J94
68028 J94
68030 J94
68033 J94
68034 J94
68068 J94
68069 J94
68070 J94
68071 J94
68072 J94
68073 J94
68074 J94
68075 J94
68076 J94
68077 J94
68078 J94
68079 J94
68080 J94
68162 Y3
68171 Y3
68179 Y3
68203 J62
68204 J63
68206 J63
68208 J63
68209 J63
68210 J63
69305 N5
69309 N5
69322 N5

1951 40B

61079 B1
61082 B1
61142 B1
61190 B1
61191 B1
61195 B1
61202 B1
61204 B1
61284 B1
61318 B1
61325 B1
61328 B1
61365 B1
61366 B1
61372 B1
61373 B1
61406 B1
61407 B1
61408 B1
61409 B1
61720 K2
61722 K2
61724 K2
61727 K2
61728 K2
61733 K2
61800 K3
61802 K3
61803 K3
61806 K3
61825 K3
61827 K3
61836 K3
61837 K3
61838 K3
61842 K3
61845 K3
61891 K3
61905 K3
61912 K3
61963 K3
62660 D11
62661 D11
62664 D11
62667 D11
63586 O4
63593 O4
63607 O4
63616 O4
63621 O4
63624 O4
63647 O4
63651 O4
63657 O4
63692 O4
63693 O4
63698 O4
63738 O4
63802 O4
63819 O4
63836 O4
63878 O4
64284 J11
64305 J11
64307 J11
64312 J11
64314 J11
64323 J11
64325 J11
64355 J11
64372 J11
64411 J11
64439 J11
64446 J11
68009 J94
68013 J94
68018 J94
68020 J94
68022 J94
68026 J94
68028 J94
68030 J94
68033 J94
68034 J94
68068 J94
68069 J94
68070 J94
68072 J94
68073 J94
68074 J94
68075 J94
68076 J94
68077 J94
68078 J94
68080 J94
68162 Y3
68179 Y3
68204 J63
68205 J63
68206 J63
68207 J63
68208 J63
68209 J63
68210 J63
69305 N5
69309 N5
69322 N5
69800 A5
90133 WD[1]
90162 WD[1]
90456 WD[1]
90460 WD[1]
90646 WD[1]
90647 WD[1]

1954 40B

61079 B1
61082 B1
61098 B1
61130 B1
61142 B1
61144 B1
61168 B1
61175 B1
61190 B1
61195 B1
61284 B1
61318 B1
61325 B1
61328 B1
61366 B1
61374 B1
61379 B1
61406 B1
61408 B1
61409 B1
61720 K2
61724 K2
61727 K2
61730 K2
61736 K2
61739 K2
61740 K2
61800 K3
61802 K3
61803 K3
61806 K3
61825 K3
61827 K3
61836 K3
61837 K3
61838 K3
61839 K3
61891 K3
61905 K3
61912 K3
61956 K3
62670 D11
63616 O4
63651 O4
63692 O4
63738 O4
63770 O4
63802 O4
63819 O4
63836 O4
63878 O4
63900 O4
64284 J11
64305 J11
64307 J11
64312 J11
64314 J11
64323 J11
64325 J11
64355 J11
64372 J11
64411 J11
64439 J11
64446 J11
68009 J94
68018 J94
68020 J94
68022 J94
68026 J94
68028 J94
68033 J94
68068 J94
68069 J94
68070 J94
68072 J94
68073 J94
68074 J94
68075 J94
68076 J94
68077 J94
68078 J94
68080 J94
68185 Y3
68204 J63
68205 J63
68206 J63
68207 J63
68210 J63
68893 J50
68926 J50
68946 J50
68979 J50
69305 N5
69800 A5
69820 A5
69903 S1
90003 WD[1]
90029 WD[1]
90035 WD[1]
90055 WD[1]
90083 WD[1]
90087 WD[1]
90131 WD[1]
90145 WD[1]
90175 WD[1]
90203 WD[1]
90221 WD[1]
90223 WD[1]
90224 WD[1]
90275 WD[1]
90280 WD[1]
90285 WD[1]
90294 WD[1]
90298 WD[1]
90302 WD[1]
90393 WD[1]
90431 WD[1]
90442 WD[1]
90453 WD[1]
90471 WD[1]
90477 WD[1]
90492 WD[1]
90508 WD[1]
90510 WD[1]
90583 WD[1]
90594 WD[1]
90660 WD[1]

1957 40B

61079 B1
61082 B1
61098 B1
61130 B1
61142 B1
61144 B1
61159 B1
61168 B1
61175 B1
61182 B1
61190 B1
61195 B1
61281 B1
61284 B1
61318 B1
61325 B1
61328 B1
61366 B1
61374 B1
61379 B1
61390 B1
61406 B1
61408 B1
61409 B1
61730 K2
61736 K2
61740 K2
61800 K3
61803 K3
61806 K3
61825 K3
61827 K3
61836 K3
61837 K3
61838 K3
61839 K3
61852 K3
61891 K3
61905 K3
61912 K3
61950 K3
61956 K3
63615 O4
63616 O4
63644 O4
63651 O4
63692 O4
63708 O4
63738 O4
63750 O4
63759 O4
63770 O4
63802 O4
63819 O4
63836 O4
63837 O4
63860 O4
63878 O4
63900 O4
64284 J11
64305 J11
64312 J11
64314 J11
64320 J11
64325 J11
64355 J11
64372 J11
64411 J11
64439 J11
64446 J11
67398 C12
68009 J94
68018 J94
68026 J94
68028 J94
68033 J94
68067 J94
68068 J94
68069 J94
68070 J94
68071 J94
68072 J94
68073 J94
68074 J94
68075 J94
68076 J94
68077 J94
68078 J94
68080 J94
68210 J63
68977 J50
69261 N5
69369 N5
69816 A5
90003 WD[1]
90029 WD[1]
90035 WD[1]
90131 WD[1]
90145 WD[1]
90175 WD[1]
90221 WD[1]
90223 WD[1]
90224 WD[1]
90280 WD[1]
90285 WD[1]
90294 WD[1]
90393 WD[1]
90443 WD[1]
90471 WD[1]
90510 WD[1]
90583 WD[1]

1960 40B

61026 B1
61079 B1
61082 B1
61098 B1
61114 B1
61130 B1
61143 B1
61144 B1
61159 B1
61168 B1
61175 B1
61185 B1
61190 B1
61195 B1
61248 B1
61318 B1
61325 B1
61328 B1
61366 B1
61374 B1
61379 B1
61406 B1
61408 B1
61740 K2
61745 K2
61756 K2
61766 K2
61767 K2
61771 K2
61773 K2
61827 K3
61866 K3
61891 K3
61905 K3
61912 K3
61950 K3
61956 K3
61966 K3
63615 O4
63616 O4
63644 O4
63651 O4
63692 O4
63708 O4
63738 O4
63750 O4
63759 O4
63837 O4
63860 O4
63878 O4
63900 O4
64284 J11
64305 J11
64325 J11
64355 J11
64386 J11
64446 J11
68009 J94
68018 J94
68070 J94
68074 J94
69829 A5
90003 WD[1]
90029 WD[1]
90035 WD[1]
90036 WD[1]
90131 WD[1]
90162 WD[1]
90175 WD[1]
90221 WD[1]
90224 WD[1]
90280 WD[1]
90285 WD[1]
90294 WD[1]
90383 WD[1]
90393 WD[1]
90411 WD[1]
90443 WD[1]
90460 WD[1]
90510 WD[1]
90583 WD[1]
90674 WD[1]
92039 9F
92193 9F
92194 9F
92195 9F
92196 9F
92202 9F

1963 40B

61056 B1
61098 B1
61143 B1
61144 B1
61159 B1
61168 B1
61185 B1
61190 B1
61195 B1
61248 B1
61318 B1
61325 B1
61328 B1
61374 B1
61406 B1
70035 7P6F
70036 7P6F
70037 7P6F
70038 7P6F
70039 7P6F
70040 7P6F
70041 7P6F
90029 WD[1]
90035 WD[1]
90055 WD[1]
90075 WD[1]
90129 WD[1]
90131 WD[1]
90175 WD[1]
90180 WD[1]
90185 WD[1]
90215 WD[1]
90221 WD[1]
90280 WD[1]
90285 WD[1]
90294 WD[1]
90394 WD[1]
90443 WD[1]
90490 WD[1]
90583 WD[1]
90618 WD[1]
90660 WD[1]
90662 WD[1]
92144 9F
92193 9F
92194 9F
92195 9F
92196 9F
92197 9F
92202 9F

1966 40B

61026 B1
61058 B1
61223 B1
61250 B1
61384 B1
61406 B1
90037 WD[1]
90190 WD[1]
90477 WD[1]
90506 WD[1]
90538 WD[1]
92035 9F
92145 9F

Inverness

1948 32A

44771 5MT[3]
44772 5MT[3]
44773 5MT[3]
44798 5MT[3]
44799 5MT[3]
44991 5MT[3]
44992 5MT[3]
45053 5MT[3]
45066 5MT[3]
45090 5MT[3]
45098 5MT[3]
45122 5MT[3]
45123 5MT[3]
45124 5MT[3]
45136 5MT[3]
45138 5MT[3]
45160 5MT[3]
45192 5MT[3]
45319 5MT[3]
45320 5MT[3]
45360 5MT[3]
45361 5MT[3]
45476 5MT[3]
45477 5MT[3]
45478 5MT[3]
45479 5MT[3]
47541 3F[6]
54397 2P[11]
54399 2P[11]
54401 2P[11]
54403 2P[11]
54404 2P[11]
54409 2P[11]
54415 2P[11]
54416 2P[11]
54470 3P[6]
54471 3P[6]
54472 3P[6]
54480 3P[6]
54482 3P[6]
54484 3P[6]
54488 3P[6]
54495 3P[6]
55051 0P
55053 0P
55199 2P[13]
56010 0F[5]
56011 0F[5]
56262 3F[10]
56291 3F[10]
56293 3F[10]
56299 3F[10]
56341 3F[10]
57585 3F[12]
57586 3F[12]
57587 3F[12]
57622 3F[12]
57625 3F[12]
57629 3F[13]
57950 4F[4]
57951 4F[4]
57953 4F[4]
57954 4F[4]
57955 4F[4]
57956 4F[4]

1951 60A

44783 5MT[3]
44784 5MT[3]
44785 5MT[3]
44788 5MT[3]
44789 5MT[3]
44798 5MT[3]
44799 5MT[3]
44991 5MT[3]
44992 5MT[3]
45012 5MT[3]
45053 5MT[3]
45066 5MT[3]
45090 5MT[3]
45098 5MT[3]
45120 5MT[3]
45122 5MT[3]
45123 5MT[3]
45124 5MT[3]
45136 5MT[3]
45138 5MT[3]
45160 5MT[3]
45179 5MT[3]
45192 5MT[3]
45319 5MT[3]
45320 5MT[3]
45360 5MT[3]
45361 5MT[3]
45453 5MT[3]
45461 5MT[3]
45476 5MT[3]
45477 5MT[3]
45478 5MT[3]
45479 5MT[3]
54439 3P[5]
54458 3P[5]
54459 3P[5]
54463 3P[5]
54470 3P[6]
54471 3P[6]
54472 3P[6]
54484 3P[6]
54487 3P[6]
54491 3P[6]
54496 3P[6]
55160 2P[13]
55199 2P[13]
56011 0F[5]
56038 0F[5]
56262 3F[10]
56291 3F[10]
56293 3F[10]
56299 3F[10]
56341 3F[10]
57591 3F[12]
57597 3F[12]
57634 3F[13]
57642 3F[13]
57951 4F[4]
57954 4F[4]
57955 4F[4]
57956 4F[4]
68108 Y9

1954 60A

44718 5MT[3]
44719 5MT[3]
44722 5MT[3]
44723 5MT[3]
44724 5MT[3]
44783 5MT[3]
44784 5MT[3]
44785 5MT[3]
44788 5MT[3]
44789 5MT[3]
44798 5MT[3]
44799 5MT[3]
44991 5MT[3]
44992 5MT[3]
45066 5MT[3]
45090 5MT[3]
45098 5MT[3]
45123 5MT[3]
45124 5MT[3]
45179 5MT[3]
45192 5MT[3]
45319 5MT[3]
45360 5MT[3]
45361 5MT[3]
45453 5MT[3]
45461 5MT[3]
45476 5MT[3]
45477 5MT[3]
45478 5MT[3]
45479 5MT[3]
54439 3P[5]
54458 3P[5]
54463 3P[5]
54470 3P[6]
54471 3P[6]
54484 3P[6]
54487 3P[6]
54496 3P[6]
55160 2P[13]
55199 2P[13]
55216 2P[13]
55231 2P[13]
56011 0F[5]
56038 0F[5]
56262 3F[10]
56291 3F[10]
56293 3F[10]
56299 3F[10]
56341 3F[10]
57591 3F[12]
57597 3F[12]
57634 3F[13]
57642 3F[13]

1957 60A

44718 5MT[3]
44719 5MT[3]
44722 5MT[3]
44723 5MT[3]
44724 5MT[3]
44783 5MT[3]
44784 5MT[3]
44785 5MT[3]
44788 5MT[3]
44789 5MT[3]
44798 5MT[3]
44799 5MT[3]
44991 5MT[3]
44992 5MT[3]
45066 5MT[3]
45090 5MT[3]
45098 5MT[3]
45123 5MT[3]
45124 5MT[3]
45179 5MT[3]
45192 5MT[3]
45319 5MT[3]
45320 5MT[3]
45360 5MT[3]
45361 5MT[3]
45453 5MT[3]
45461 5MT[3]
45476 5MT[3]
45477 5MT[3]
45478 5MT[3]
45479 5MT[3]
54458 3P[5]
54463 3P[5]
54470 3P[6]
54484 3P[6]
54487 3P[6]
54493 3P[6]
54496 3P[6]
55160 2P[13]
55199 2P[13]
55216 2P[13]
56011 0F[5]
56038 0F[5]
56262 3F[10]
56291 3F[10]
56293 3F[10]
56299 3F[10]
56305 3F[10]
56341 3F[10]
57597 3F[12]
57642 3F[13]
57661 3F[14]
78052 2MT[1]

1960 60A

44718 5MT[3]
44719 5MT[3]
44722 5MT[3]
44723 5MT[3]
44724 5MT[3]
44783 5MT[3]
44784 5MT[3]
44785 5MT[3]
44788 5MT[3]
44789 5MT[3]
44798 5MT[3]
44799 5MT[3]
44991 5MT[3]
44992 5MT[3]
45066 5MT[3]
45090 5MT[3]
45098 5MT[3]
45117 5MT[3]
45123 5MT[3]
45124 5MT[3]
45179 5MT[3]
45192 5MT[3]
45319 5MT[3]
45320 5MT[3]
45360 5MT[3]
45361 5MT[3]
45453 5MT[3]
45460 5MT[3]
45461 5MT[3]
45476 5MT[3]
45477 5MT[3]
45478 5MT[3]
45479 5MT[3]
54463 3P[6]
54487 3P[6]
54493 3P[6]
55198 2P[13]
55199 2P[13]
55216 2P[13]
55227 2P[13]
55269 2P[15]
56300 3F[10]
56305 3F[10]
56341 3F[10]
57594 3F[12]
57605 3F[12]
57661 3F[14]

1963 60A

44719 5MT[3]
44783 5MT[3]

Ipswich

1948 IPS

61053 B1
61054 B1
61055 B1
61056 B1
61057 B1
61058 B1
61059 B1
61252 B1
61253 B1
61509 B12
61516 B12
61561 B12
61562 B12
61564 B12
61566 B12
61569 B12
61570 B12
61577 B12
61600 B17
61601 B17
61602 B17
61604 B17
61618 B17
61634 B17
61645 B17
61649 B17
61668 B17
62526 D16
62552 D16
62556 D16
62560 D16
62590 D16
62611 D16
62612 D16
64724 J39
64752 J39
64785 J39
64793 J39
64800 J39
64803 J39
64820 J39
64826 J39
64829 J39
64834 J39
64841 J39
64872 J39
64894 J39
64900 J39
64905 J39
64957 J39
64958 J39
65377 J15
65386 J15
65407 J15
65409 J15
65415 J15
65421 J15
65423 J15
65428 J15
65429 J15
65430 J15
65447 J15
65459 J15
65467 J15
65510 J17
65560 J17
67128 F3
67143 F3
67182 F4
67447 C14
67448 C14
67450 C14
68211 J65
68216 J70
68219 J70
68221 J70
68224 J70
68225 J70
68373 J66
68374 J66
68375 J66
68386 J66
68498 J67
68510 J67
68518 J67

1951 32B

61052 B1
61053 B1
61054 B1
61055 B1
61056 B1
61058 B1
61059 B1
61201 B1
61252 B1
61253 B1
61254 B1
61530 B12
61535 B12
61561 B12
61562 B12
61564 B12
61566 B12
61569 B12
61570 B12
61577 B12
61600 B17
61601 B17
61604 B17
61618 B17
61634 B17
61645 B17
61647 B17
61649 B17
61668 B17
61669 B17
62526 D16
62590 D16
64752 J39
64767 J39
64771 J39
64773 J39
64785 J39
64793 J39
64800 J39
64803 J39
64820 J39
64826 J39
64829 J39
64834 J39
64841 J39
64894 J39
64900 J39
64905 J39
64957 J39
64958 J39
65361 J15
65377 J15
65382 J15
65396 J15
65407 J15
65408 J15
65430 J15
65447 J15
65459 J15
65467 J15
65560 J17
65578 J17
67220 F6
67230 F6
67239 F6
67702 L1
67703 L1
67704 L1
67705 L1

67706 L1
67708 L1
67709 L1
67710 L1
67711 L1
67716 L1
67719 L1
67787 L1
68211 J65
68216 J70
68221 J70
68224 J70
68373 J66
68374 J66
68375 J66
68498 J67
68518 J67
68593 J67
69012 J72
69013 J72
69703 N7

1954 32B

61052 B1
61054 B1
61055 B1
61058 B1
61059 B1
61252 B1
61253 B1
61254 B1
61535 B12
61561 B12
61562 B12
61564 B12
61566 B12
61569 B12
61570 B12
61571 B12
61572 B12
61577 B12
61625 B17
61631 B17
61637 B17
61647 B17
61649 B17
61669 B17
64752 J39
64785 J39
64793 J39
64800 J39
64826 J39
64829 J39
64834 J39
64841 J39
64894 J39
64905 J39
64957 J39
65361 J15
65404 J15
65430 J15
65447 J15
65459 J15
65467 J15
65510 J17
65560 J17
65578 J17
67220 F6
67230 F6
67239 F6
67702 L1
67703 L1
67705 L1
67706 L1
67708 L1
67709 L1
67710 L1
67711 L1
67715 L1
67716 L1
67719 L1
68222 J70
68225 J70
68493 J67
68509 J67
68518 J67
68572 J67
68586 J67
68593 J67
68606 J67

1957 32B

61052 B1
61054 B1
61055 B1
61058 B1
61059 B1
61228 B1
61252 B1
61253 B1
61254 B1
61533 B12
61535 B12
61537 B12
61561 B12
61564 B12
61566 B12
61569 B12
61570 B12
61571 B12
61572 B12
61577 B12
61618 B17
61625 B17
61629 B17
61631 B17
61637 B17
61647 B17
61649 B17
61669 B17
62612 D16
64724 J39
64726 J39
64752 J39
64785 J39
64793 J39
64800 J39
64826 J39
64829 J39
64834 J39
64841 J39
64882 J39
64894 J39
64905 J39
64957 J39
64968 J39
65361 J15
65389 J15
65433 J15
65447 J15
65459 J15
65467 J15
65512 J17
65513 J17
65560 J17
65578 J17
67702 L1
67703 L1
67705 L1
67706 L1
67708 L1
67709 L1
67710 L1
67711 L1
67715 L1
67716 L1
67719 L1
67739 L1
67775 L1
68518 J67
68593 J67

1960 32B

64659 J19
64724 J39
65389 J15
65478 J15
65513 J17
65560 J17
67719 L1
67775 L1

Keith

1948 KEI

61064 B1
61500 B12
61501 B12
61502 B12
61503 B12
62234 D41
62235 D41
62238 D41
62240 D41
62243 D41
62246 D41
62247 D41
62248 D41
62249 D41
62251 D41
62252 D41
62255 D41
62256 D41
62262 D40
62264 D40
62267 D40
67292 G5

1951 61C

61308 B1
61501 B12
61502 B12
61503 B12
62225 D41
62227 D41
62230 D41
62231 D41
62232 D41
62242 D41
62243 D41
62246 D41
62248 D41
62251 D41
62252 D41
62255 D41
62256 D41
62262 D40
62264 D40
62267 D40
62269 D40
62271 D40
67292 G5

1954 61C

55185 2P^{13}
55221 2P^{13}
61242 B1
61308 B1
61502 B12
61539 B12
62262 D40
62264 D40
62265 D40
62267 D40
62268 D40
62269 D40
62271 D40
62272 D40
62273 D40
62274 D40
62275 D40
62277 D40
67327 G5

1957 61C

40600 2P^{3}
40602 2P^{3}
55185 2P^{13}
55221 2P^{13}
57591 3F^{12}
57634 3F^{13}
61242 B1
61307 B1
61308 B1
61779 K2
61782 K2
61783 K2
61792 K2
61793 K2
62264 D40
62277 D40
62469 D34
65267 J36
65297 J36
67496 C16
68700 J72
78053 2MT^{1}
78054 2MT^{1}
80121 4MT^{3}
80122 4MT^{3}

1960 61C

40603 2P^{3}
40604 2P^{3}
40618 2P^{3}
40622 2P^{3}
55185 2P^{13}
55221 2P^{13}
56348 3F^{10}
57634 3F^{13}
61779 K2
61782 K2
61792 K2
65267 J36
65277 J36
65304 J36
65310 J36
65338 J36
49 D40
256 D34
78053 2MT^{1}
78054 2MT^{1}
80121 4MT^{3}
80122 4MT^{3}

Kent & East Sussex Railway

1948 on loan

30576 0395

Kentish Town

1948 14B

40022 3MT^{1}
40027 3MT^{1}
40028 3MT^{1}
40035 3MT^{1}
40036 3MT^{1}
40037 3MT^{1}
40040 3MT^{1}
40079 3MT^{2}
40092 3MT^{2}
40096 3MT^{2}
40098 3MT^{2}
40099 3MT^{2}
40100 3MT^{2}
40111 3MT^{2}
40112 3MT^{2}
40114 3MT^{2}
40148 3MT^{2}
40149 3MT^{2}
40155 3MT^{2}
40160 3MT^{2}
40161 3MT^{2}
40164 3MT^{2}
40166 3MT^{2}
40167 3MT^{2}
40171 3MT^{2}
40172 3MT^{2}
40477 2P^{2}
40547 2P^{2}
41018 4P^{2}
41023 4P^{1}
41050 4P^{1}
41051 4P^{1}
41054 4P^{1}
41077 4P^{1}
41117 4P^{1}
41207 2MT^{1}
41208 2MT^{1}
41660 1F^{1}
41661 1F^{1}
41664 1F^{1}
41668 1F^{1}
41671 1F^{1}
41672 1F^{1}
41674 1F^{1}
41713 1F^{1}
42230 4MT^{1}
42325 4MT^{2}
42329 4MT^{2}
42331 4MT^{2}
42383 4MT^{2}
42683 4MT^{1}
42687 4MT^{1}
42839 5MT^{1}
43935 4F^{1}
43964 4F^{1}
44052 4F^{2}
44529 4F^{2}
44531 4F^{2}
44532 4F^{2}
44563 4F^{2}
44776 5MT^{3}
44777 5MT^{3}
44816 5MT^{3}
44822 5MT^{3}
44846 5MT^{3}
44917 5MT^{3}
44984 5MT^{3}
44985 5MT^{3}
45267 5MT^{3}
45279 5MT^{3}
45557 6P5F^{2}
45598 6P5F^{2}
45609 6P5F^{2}
45612 6P5F^{2}
45614 6P5F^{2}
45615 6P5F^{2}
45616 6P5F^{2}
45627 6P5F^{2}
45641 6P5F^{2}
45648 6P5F^{2}
45649 6P5F^{2}
45650 6P5F^{2}
45654 6P5F^{2}
45657 6P5F^{2}
45665 6P5F^{2}
47229 3F^{5}
47241 3F^{5}
47242 3F^{5}
47244 3F^{5}
47245 3F^{5}
47246 3F^{5}
47260 3F^{6}
47262 3F^{6}
47263 3F^{6}
47282 3F^{6}
47283 3F^{6}
47427 3F^{6}
47428 3F^{6}
47429 3F^{6}
47432 3F^{6}
47640 3F^{6}
47644 3F^{6}
47645 3F^{6}
58068 1P^{6}
58072 1P^{6}
58073 1P^{6}
58086 1P^{6}
58164 2F^{8}
58229 2F^{8}
58234 2F^{8}
58310 2F^{9}
3021 2F^{9}
23016 2F^{8}

1951 14B

40027 3MT^{1}
40028 3MT^{1}
40029 3MT^{1}
40031 3MT^{1}
40032 3MT^{1}
40033 3MT^{1}
40034 3MT^{1}
40035 3MT^{1}
40036 3MT^{1}
40037 3MT^{1}
40038 3MT^{1}
40079 3MT^{2}
40091 3MT^{2}
40092 3MT^{2}
40096 3MT^{2}
40098 3MT^{2}
40099 3MT^{2}
40100 3MT^{2}
40111 3MT^{2}
40112 3MT^{2}
40114 3MT^{2}
40119 3MT^{2}
40142 3MT^{2}
40148 3MT^{2}
40149 3MT^{2}
40155 3MT^{2}
40160 3MT^{2}
40161 3MT^{2}
40166 3MT^{2}
40167 3MT^{2}
40172 3MT^{2}
40477 2P^{2}
40547 2P^{2}
40930 4P^{1}
40932 4P^{1}
41020 4P^{2}
41050 4P^{1}
41051 4P^{1}
41054 4P^{1}
41071 4P^{1}
41077 4P^{1}
41083 4P^{1}
41117 4P^{1}
41199 4P^{1}
41248 2MT^{1}
41249 2MT^{1}
41661 1F^{1}
41664 1F^{1}
41671 1F^{1}
41672 1F^{1}
41713 1F^{1}
41724 1F^{1}
41826 1F^{1}
42051 4MT^{1}
42133 4MT^{1}
42138 4MT^{1}
42139 4MT^{1}
42237 4MT^{1}
42325 4MT^{2}
42329 4MT^{2}
42383 4MT^{2}
42791 5MT^{1}
43909 4F^{1}
43964 4F^{1}
44052 4F^{2}
44210 4F^{2}
44243 4F^{2}
44397 4F^{2}
44440 4F^{2}
44531 4F^{2}
44532 4F^{2}
44563 4F^{2}
44658 5MT^{3}
44777 5MT^{3}
44816 5MT^{3}
44817 5MT^{3}
44822 5MT^{3}
44846 5MT^{3}
44981 5MT^{3}
44984 5MT^{3}
44985 5MT^{3}
45221 5MT^{3}
45253 5MT^{3}
45267 5MT^{3}
45277 5MT^{3}
45279 5MT^{3}
45285 5MT^{3}
45557 6P5F^{2}
45598 6P5F^{2}
45602 6P5F^{2}
45612 6P5F^{2}
45614 6P5F^{2}
45615 6P5F^{2}
45616 6P5F^{2}
45627 6P5F^{2}
45641 6P5F^{2}
45648 6P5F^{2}
45649 6P5F^{2}
45650 6P5F^{2}
45657 6P5F^{2}
45665 6P5F^{2}
47200 3F^{5}
47202 3F^{5}
47229 3F^{5}
47241 3F^{5}
47242 3F^{5}
47244 3F^{5}
47245 3F^{5}
47246 3F^{5}
47260 3F^{6}
47262 3F^{6}
47282 3F^{6}
47283 3F^{6}
47428 3F^{6}
47429 3F^{6}
47644 3F^{6}
47645 3F^{6}
58131 2F^{8}
58158 2F^{8}
58200 2F^{9}
58215 2F^{9}
58229 2F^{8}
58234 2F^{8}

1954 14B

40027 3MT^{1}
40028 3MT^{1}
40029 3MT^{1}
40031 3MT^{1}
40032 3MT^{1}
40033 3MT^{1}
40034 3MT^{1}
40035 3MT^{1}
40036 3MT^{1}
40037 3MT^{1}
40038 3MT^{1}
40040 3MT^{1}
40092 3MT^{2}
40096 3MT^{2}
40100 3MT^{2}
40111 3MT^{2}
40114 3MT^{2}
40119 3MT^{2}
40142 3MT^{2}
40160 3MT^{2}
40166 3MT^{2}
40167 3MT^{2}
40172 3MT^{2}
41050 4P^{1}
41051 4P^{1}
41074 4P^{1}
41077 4P^{1}
41083 4P^{1}
41671 1F^{1}
41713 1F^{1}
41724 1F^{1}
42051 4MT^{1}
42133 4MT^{1}
42138 4MT^{1}
42139 4MT^{1}
42237 4MT^{1}
42325 4MT^{2}
42329 4MT^{2}
42383 4MT^{2}
43964 4F^{1}
44052 4F^{2}
44210 4F^{2}
44243 4F^{2}
44298 4F^{2}
44531 4F^{2}
44532 4F^{2}
44563 4F^{2}
44658 5MT^{3}
44816 5MT^{3}
44817 5MT^{3}
44822 5MT^{3}
44825 5MT^{3}
44846 5MT^{3}
44981 5MT^{3}
44984 5MT^{3}
44985 5MT^{3}
45253 5MT^{3}
45267 5MT^{3}
45277 5MT^{3}
45279 5MT^{3}
45285 5MT^{3}
45557 6P5F^{2}
45575 6P5F^{2}
45579 6P5F^{2}
45598 6P5F^{2}
45612 6P5F^{2}
45614 6P5F^{2}
45615 6P5F^{2}
45616 6P5F^{2}
45627 6P5F^{2}
45641 6P5F^{2}
45648 6P5F^{2}
45649 6P5F^{2}
45650 6P5F^{2}
47200 3F^{5}
47202 3F^{5}
47204 3F^{5}
47205 3F^{5}
47229 3F^{5}
47241 3F^{5}
47242 3F^{5}
47243 3F^{5}
47244 3F^{5}
47245 3F^{5}
47246 3F^{5}
47260 3F^{6}
47283 3F^{6}
47437 3F^{6}
47644 3F^{6}
47645 3F^{6}
58131 2F^{8}
58158 2F^{8}
58215 2F^{9}
80047 4MT^{3}
80048 4MT^{3}
80059 4MT^{3}
80062 4MT^{3}

1957 14B

40021 3MT^{1}
40027 3MT^{1}
40028 3MT^{1}
40029 3MT^{1}
40031 3MT^{1}
40032 3MT^{1}
40033 3MT^{1}
40034 3MT^{1}
40035 3MT^{1}
40036 3MT^{1}
40038 3MT^{1}
40040 3MT^{1}
40092 3MT^{2}
40100 3MT^{2}
40111 3MT^{2}
40119 3MT^{2}
40142 3MT^{2}
40160 3MT^{2}
40167 3MT^{2}
40172 3MT^{2}
42156 4MT^{1}
42157 4MT^{1}
42178 4MT^{1}
42237 4MT^{1}
42325 4MT^{2}
42329 4MT^{2}
42453 4MT^{3}
42540 4MT^{3}
42587 4MT^{3}
42595 4MT^{3}
42610 4MT^{3}
42617 4MT^{3}
42682 4MT^{1}
42685 4MT^{1}
43919 4F^{1}
43964 4F^{1}
43975 4F^{1}
44052 4F^{2}
44143 4F^{2}
44210 4F^{2}
44243 4F^{2}
44270 4F^{2}
44298 4F^{2}
44531 4F^{2}
44532 4F^{2}
44563 4F^{2}
44658 5MT^{3}
44806 5MT^{3}
44812 5MT^{3}
44816 5MT^{3}
44817 5MT^{3}
44822 5MT^{3}
44825 5MT^{3}
44846 5MT^{3}
44855 5MT^{3}
44985 5MT^{3}
45238 5MT^{3}
45253 5MT^{3}
45277 5MT^{3}
45279 5MT^{3}
45285 5MT^{3}
45407 5MT^{3}
45444 5MT^{3}
45447 5MT^{3}
45557 6P5F^{2}
45575 6P5F^{2}
45579 6P5F^{2}
45598 6P5F^{2}
45612 6P5F^{2}
45614 6P5F^{2}
45615 6P5F^{2}
45616 6P5F^{2}
45627 6P5F^{2}
45641 6P5F^{2}
45648 6P5F^{2}
45649 6P5F^{2}
45650 6P5F^{2}
47200 3F^{5}
47202 3F^{5}
47204 3F^{5}
47205 3F^{5}
47209 3F^{5}
47212 3F^{5}
47229 3F^{5}
47241 3F^{5}
47242 3F^{5}
47243 3F^{5}
47246 3F^{5}
47260 3F^{6}
47283 3F^{6}
47437 3F^{6}
47642 3F^{6}
47644 3F^{6}
47645 3F^{6}
58131 2F^{8}

1960 14B

40028 3MT^{1}
40029 3MT^{1}
40031 3MT^{1}
40032 3MT^{1}
40033 3MT^{1}
40034 3MT^{1}
40035 3MT^{1}
40036 3MT^{1}
40038 3MT^{1}
40053 3MT^{1}
40064 3MT^{1}
40092 3MT^{2}
40100 3MT^{2}
40111 3MT^{2}
40119 3MT^{2}
40142 3MT^{2}
40203 3MT^{2}
40548 2P^{2}
40580 2P^{3}
42156 4MT^{1}
42157 4MT^{1}
42178 4MT^{1}
42237 4MT^{1}
42325 4MT^{2}
42329 4MT^{2}
42334 4MT^{2}
42338 4MT^{2}
42342 4MT^{2}
42610 4MT^{3}
42617 4MT^{3}
42682 4MT^{1}
42685 4MT^{1}
43964 4F^{1}
44052 4F^{2}
44210 4F^{2}
44235 4F^{2}
44243 4F^{2}
44270 4F^{2}
44294 4F^{2}
44381 4F^{2}
44409 4F^{2}
44531 4F^{2}
44532 4F^{2}
44563 4F^{2}
44572 4F^{2}
44658 5MT^{3}
44817 5MT^{3}
44821 5MT^{3}
44822 5MT^{3}
44846 5MT^{3}
44855 5MT^{3}
44985 5MT^{3}
45277 5MT^{3}
45279 5MT^{3}
45285 5MT^{3}
45407 5MT^{3}
45522 7P^{1}
45561 6P5F^{2}
45575 6P5F^{2}
45579 6P5F^{2}
45585 6P5F^{2}
45614 6P5F^{2}
45615 6P5F^{2}
45622 6P5F^{2}
45628 6P5F^{2}
45652 6P5F^{2}
45712 6P5F^{2}
46103 7P^{3}R
46123 7P^{3}R
46132 7P^{3}R
46133 7P^{3}R
46139 7P^{3}R
46140 7P^{3}R
46142 7P^{3}R
46160 7P^{3}R
46162 7P^{3}R
47200 3F^{5}
47202 3F^{5}
47203 3F^{5}
47204 3F^{5}
47209 3F^{5}
47212 3F^{5}
47229 3F^{5}
47241 3F^{5}
47260 3F^{6}
47283 3F^{6}
47437 3F^{6}
47449 3F^{6}
47642 3F^{6}
47644 3F^{6}
47645 3F^{6}
58131 2F^{8}

1963 14B

45622 6P5F^{2}
47611 3F^{6}
84005 2MT^{2}
84029 2MT^{2}

Kettering

1948 15B

40454 2P^{2}
40537 2P^{2}
40550 2P^{2}
41010 4P^{2}
41047 4P^{1}
41071 4P^{1}
41889 1F^{1}
43889 4F^{1}
44278 4F^{2}
44465 4F^{2}
46400 2MT^{2}
46401 2MT^{2}
46402 2MT^{2}
46403 2MT^{2}
46404 2MT^{2}
47437 3F^{6}
48067 8F
48069 8F
48124 8F
48141 8F
48285 8F
48355 8F
48356 8F
48491 8F
48645 8F
48704 8F
49122 7F^{2}
49126 7F^{2}
58022 1P^{4}
58162 2F^{8}
58172 2F^{8}
58183 2F^{8}
58193 2F^{9}
58195 2F^{9}
58214 2F^{9}
3195 2F^{9}

1951 15B

40550 2P^{2}
43889 4F^{1}
43898 4F^{1}
44043 4F^{2}
44278 4F^{2}
44465 4F^{2}
46400 2MT^{2}
46401 2MT^{2}
46402 2MT^{2}
46403 2MT^{2}
46404 2MT^{2}
47437 3F^{6}
48069 8F
48124 8F
48141 8F
48143 8F
48285 8F
48301 8F
48355 8F
48356 8F
48391 8F
48471 8F
48611 8F
48645 8F
48704 8F
48759 8F
58162 2F^{8}
58164 2F^{8}
58172 2F^{8}
58193 2F^{9}
58195 2F^{9}
58214 2F^{9}

1954 15B

43244 3F^{3}
43889 4F^{1}
43898 4F^{1}
44278 4F^{2}
44465 4F^{2}
44535 4F^{2}
46400 2MT^{2}
46401 2MT^{2}
46402 2MT^{2}
46403 2MT^{2}
46404 2MT^{2}
46444 2MT^{2}
46495 2MT^{2}
46496 2MT^{2}
48024 8F
48035 8F
48061 8F
48069 8F
48124 8F
48131 8F
48133 8F
48141 8F
48143 8F
48285 8F
48301 8F
48355 8F
48356 8F
48380 8F
48467 8F
48471 8F
48609 8F
48611 8F
48645 8F
48690 8F
48704 8F
48759 8F
58162 2F^{8}
58164 2F^{8}
58172 2F^{8}
58193 2F^{9}
58195 2F^{9}
58214 2F^{9}

1957 15B

43367 3F^{3}
44122 4F^{2}
44278 4F^{2}
44418 4F^{2}
44465 4F^{2}
44535 4F^{2}
46403 2MT^{2}
46404 2MT^{2}
46444 2MT^{2}
46495 2MT^{2}
46496 2MT^{2}
48050 8F
48069 8F
48124 8F
48131 8F
48141 8F
48142 8F
48143 8F
48285 8F
48301 8F
48313 8F
48355 8F
48356 8F
48380 8F
48467 8F
48609 8F
48611 8F
48645 8F
48690 8F
48704 8F
48759 8F
58214 2F^{9}
78020 2MT^{1}
78021 2MT^{1}
92105 9F
92106 9F

1960 15B

43042 4MT^{5}
43048 4MT^{5}
43499 3F^{3}
43624 3F^{3}
43721 3F^{3}
46403 2MT^{2}
46404 2MT^{2}
46444 2MT^{2}
46495 2MT^{2}
46496 2MT^{2}
48050 8F
48069 8F
48180 8F
48285 8F
48355 8F
48356 8F
48376 8F
48380 8F
48467 8F
48609 8F
48611 8F
48645 8F
48690 8F
48704 8F
48759 8F
58215 2F^{9}
92105 9F
92106 9F
92129 9F
92160 9F
92163 9F
92164 9F

1963 15B

43947 4F^{1}
44051 4F^{2}
46403 2MT^{2}
46404 2MT^{2}
46444 2MT^{2}
46496 2MT^{2}
48008 8F
48050 8F
48069 8F
48107 8F
48127 8F
48132 8F
48163 8F
48180 8F
48183 8F
48285 8F
48336 8F
48355 8F
48356 8F
48376 8F
48380 8F
48388 8F
48467 8F
48545 8F
48607 8F
48609 8F
48611 8F
48645 8F
48690 8F
48704 8F
48759 8F
92105 9F
92106 9F
92125 9F
92160 9F
92163 9F

Kidderminster

1948 KDR

28 CMDP
29 CMDP
2093 2021
4153 5101
4584 4575
4586 4575
4594 4575
4625 5700
4641 5700
5110 5101
5303 4300
5518 4575
5573 4575
7700 5700
8101 8100
8718 5700
8727 5700

1951 85D

28 CMDP
29 CMDP
2051 2021
3601 5700
4100 5101
4153 5101
4175 5101
4578 4575
4584 4575
4586 4575
4594 4575
4599 4575
4625 5700
5110 5101
6382 4300
7700 5700
8101 8100
8718 5700
8727 5700

1954 85D

29 CMDP
2144 2021
2207 2251
3601 5700
4100 5101
4153 5101
4175 5101
4596 4575
4614 5700
4641 5700
5110 5101
5518 4575
7301 4300
7700 5700
8101 8100
8718 5700
8727 5700
8731 5700

1957 85D

1661 1600
3601 5700
4100 5101
4114 5101
4153 5101
4175 5101
4596 4575
4641 5700
5110 5101
5394 4300
5518 4575
6326 4300
6382 4300
6679 5600
8101 8100
8718 5700
8727 5700
82008 3MT^{2}

1960 85D

3601 5700
4114 5101
4153 5101
4175 5101
4629 5700
5333 4300
5518 4575
5791 5700
6314 4300
6382 4300
6388 4300
6679 5600
8101 8100
8718 5700

1963 84G

3601 5700
3607 5700
3619 5700
4114 5101
4147 5101
4153 5101
4173 5101
4175 5101
4629 5700
5153 5101
6314 4300
6364 4300
6679 5600
8718 5700

Kings Cross

1948 KX

60003 A4
60006 A4
60010 A4
60013 A4
60017 A4
60021 A4
60025 A4
60026 A4
60029 A4
60046 A3
60047 A3
60050 A3
60051 A3
60055 A3
60056 A3
60059 A3
60062 A3
60089 A3
60096 A3
60097 A3
60098 A3
60104 A3
60105 A3
60107 A3
60108 A3
60109 A3
60110 A3
60112 A3
60113 A1
60500 A2
60507 A2
60508 A2
60513 A2
60514 A2
60523 A2
60700 W1
60800 V2
60813 V2
60814 V2
60817 V2
60818 V2
60820 V2
60821 V2
60823 V2
60829 V2
60873 V2
60892 V2
60900 V2
60903 V2
60909 V2
60914 V2
60915 V2
60922 V2
60983 V2
61029 B1
61112 B1
61113 B1
61114 B1
61121 B1
61129 B1
61136 B1
61137 B1
61138 B1
61139 B1
61200 B1
61203 B1
61251 B1
61266 B1
62817 C1
62821 C1
67106 F2
67108 F2
67111 F2
67113 F2
68764 J52
68770 J52
68771 J52
68772 J52
68780 J52
68797 J52
68799 J52
68802 J52
68803 J52
68805 J52
68809 J52
68818 J52
68822 J52
68828 J52
68830 J52
68831 J52
68832 J52
68838 J52
68854 J52
68855 J52
68861 J52
68862 J52
68864 J52
68873 J52
68874 J52
68878 J52
68881 J52
68884 J52
68888 J52
68889 J52
69434 N1
69462 N1
69466 N1
69467 N1
69468 N1
69469 N1
69476 N1
69480 N1
69481 N1
69484 N1
69490 N2
69491 N2
69492 N2
69493 N2
69494 N2
69495 N2
69496 N2
69497 N2
69498 N2
69499 N2
69504 N2
69506 N2
69512 N2
69517 N2
69520 N2
69521 N2
69523 N2
69524 N2
69525 N2
69526 N2
69527 N2
69528 N2

69529 N2
69532 N2
69535 N2
69536 N2
69538 N2
69539 N2
69540 N2
69541 N2
69542 N2
69543 N2
69544 N2
69545 N2
69546 N2
69548 N2
69549 N2
69567 N2
69568 N2
69569 N2
69570 N2
69571 N2
69572 N2
69573 N2
69574 N2
69575 N2
69576 N2
69577 N2
69578 N2
69579 N2
69581 N2
69583 N2
69584 N2
69585 N2
69589 N2
69591 N2
69592 N2
69593 N2

1951 34A

60003 A4
60006 A4
60007 A4
60008 A4
60010 A4
60013 A4
60014 A4
60017 A4
60021 A4
60022 A4
60025 A4
60028 A4
60029 A4
60030 A4
60032 A4
60033 A4
60034 A4
60039 A3
60059 A3
60063 A3
60065 A3
60067 A3
60089 A3
60105 A3
60108 A3
60109 A3
60110 A3
60122 A1
60128 A1
60130 A1
60131 A1
60136 A1
60139 A1
60144 A1
60148 A1
60149 A1
60156 A1
60157 A1
60158 A1
60700 W1
60800 V2
60813 V2
60814 V2
60821 V2
60823 V2
60862 V2
60873 V2
60892 V2
60900 V2
60903 V2
60909 V2
60914 V2
60915 V2
60922 V2
60983 V2
61113 B1
61129 B1
61136 B1
61137 B1
61138 B1
61139 B1
61200 B1
61203 B1
61251 B1
61266 B1
67356 C12
67374 C12
67416 C13
67792 L1
67793 L1
67796 L1
67797 L1
67799 L1
67800 L1
68764 J52
68770 J52
68771 J52
68772 J52
68780 J52
68797 J52
68799 J52
68802 J52
68803 J52
68805 J52
68809 J52
68818 J52
68822 J52
68828 J52
68830 J52
68831 J52
68832 J52
68838 J52
68854 J52
68855 J52
68861 J52
68862 J52
68864 J52
68873 J52
68874 J52
68878 J52
68881 J52
68884 J52
68888 J52
68889 J52
69490 N2
69491 N2
69492 N2
69495 N2
69496 N2
69497 N2
69498 N2
69499 N2
69502 N2
69506 N2
69512 N2
69517 N2
69519 N2
69520 N2
69521 N2
69523 N2
69524 N2
69525 N2
69526 N2
69527 N2
69528 N2
69529 N2
69532 N2
69535 N2
69536 N2
69538 N2
69539 N2
69540 N2
69541 N2
69542 N2
69543 N2
69544 N2
69545 N2
69546 N2
69548 N2
69549 N2
69561 N2
69568 N2
69569 N2
69570 N2
69571 N2
69572 N2
69573 N2
69574 N2
69575 N2
69576 N2
69577 N2
69578 N2
69579 N2
69581 N2
69583 N2
69584 N2
69585 N2
69589 N2
69590 N2
69591 N2
69592 N2
69593 N2

1954 34A

60003 A4
60006 A4
60007 A4
60008 A4
60010 A4
60013 A4
60014 A4
60015 A4
60017 A4
60021 A4
60022 A4
60025 A4
60026 A4
60028 A4
60029 A4
60030 A4
60032 A4
60033 A4
60034 A4
60062 A3
60800 V2
60814 V2
60821 V2
60855 V2
60862 V2
60876 V2
60903 V2
60909 V2
60914 V2
60983 V2
61105 B1
61139 B1
61200 B1
61203 B1
61251 B1
61331 B1
67718 L1
67720 L1
67756 L1
67757 L1
67775 L1
67793 L1
67797 L1
67799 L1
67800 L1
68757 J52
68764 J52
68772 J52
68799 J52
68802 J52
68805 J52
68818 J52
68822 J52
68827 J52
68829 J52
68830 J52
68832 J52
68838 J52
68854 J52
68855 J52
68861 J52
68862 J52
68864 J52
68874 J52
68878 J52
68881 J52
68888 J52
69490 N2
69491 N2
69492 N2
69493 N2
69495 N2
69496 N2
69497 N2
69498 N2
69499 N2
69501 N2
69506 N2
69512 N2
69517 N2
69519 N2
69520 N2
69521 N2
69523 N2
69524 N2
69525 N2
69526 N2
69527 N2
69528 N2
69529 N2
69532 N2
69535 N2
69536 N2
69538 N2
69539 N2
69540 N2
69541 N2
69542 N2
69543 N2
69544 N2
69545 N2
69546 N2
69548 N2
69549 N2
69554 N2
69568 N2
69569 N2
69570 N2
69571 N2
69572 N2
69573 N2
69574 N2
69575 N2
69576 N2
69577 N2
69578 N2
69579 N2
69580 N2
69581 N2
69583 N2
69584 N2
69585 N2
69587 N2
69589 N2
69590 N2
69591 N2
69592 N2
69593 N2
69689 N7
69692 N7
69694 N7
69698 N7

1957 34A

44911 5MT[3]
60003 A4
60006 A4
60007 A4
60008 A4
60010 A4
60013 A4
60014 A4
60015 A4
60017 A4
60021 A4
60022 A4
60025 A4
60026 A4
60028 A4
60029 A4
60030 A4
60032 A4
60033 A4
60034 A4
60054 A3
60055 A3
60062 A3
60149 A1
60156 A1
60157 A1
60800 V2
60814 V2
60828 V2
60855 V2
60862 V2
60871 V2
60876 V2
60902 V2
60903 V2
60914 V2
60943 V2
60950 V2
60983 V2
61075 B1
61139 B1
61200 B1
61203 B1
61311 B1
61331 B1
61364 B1
61393 B1
61394 B1
67749 L1
67757 L1
67761 L1
67768 L1
67772 L1
67773 L1
67774 L1
67779 L1
67780 L1
67784 L1
67793 L1
67797 L1
68832 J52
68862 J52
68874 J52
68888 J52
69490 N2
69491 N2
69492 N2
69493 N2
69495 N2
69496 N2
69497 N2
69498 N2
69499 N2
69502 N2
69506 N2
69512 N2
69517 N2
69519 N2
69520 N2
69521 N2
69523 N2
69524 N2
69525 N2
69526 N2
69527 N2
69528 N2
69529 N2
69532 N2
69535 N2
69536 N2
69538 N2
69539 N2
69540 N2
69541 N2
69542 N2
69543 N2
69544 N2
69545 N2
69546 N2
69548 N2
69549 N2
69550 N2
69551 N2
69552 N2
69555 N2
69558 N2
69559 N2
69561 N2
69566 N2
69568 N2
69569 N2
69570 N2
69571 N2
69572 N2
69573 N2
69574 N2
69575 N2
69576 N2
69577 N2
69578 N2
69579 N2
69581 N2
69583 N2
69584 N2
69585 N2
69589 N2
69590 N2
69591 N2
69592 N2
69593 N2
73071 5MT

1960 34A

60003 A4
60006 A4
60007 A4
60008 A4
60010 A4
60013 A4
60014 A4
60015 A4
60017 A4
60021 A4
60022 A4
60025 A4
60026 A4
60028 A4
60029 A4
60030 A4
60032 A4
60033 A4
60034 A4
60039 A3
60044 A3
60055 A3
60059 A3
60061 A3
60062 A3
60066 A3
60067 A3
60103 A3
60108 A3
60109 A3
60110 A3
60800 V2
60814 V2
60854 V2
60862 V2
60871 V2
60902 V2
60903 V2
60950 V2
60983 V2
61075 B1
61174 B1
61179 B1
61331 B1
61364 B1
61394 B1
67749 L1
67757 L1
67767 L1
67768 L1
67770 L1
67772 L1
67773 L1
67774 L1
67776 L1
67779 L1
67780 L1
67783 L1
67784 L1
67787 L1
67792 L1
67793 L1
67794 L1
67797 L1
67800 L1
69498 N2
69506 N2
69512 N2
69523 N2
69529 N2
69533 N2
69535 N2
69538 N2
69543 N2
69546 N2
69549 N2
69568 N2
69572 N2
69574 N2
69575 N2
69579 N2
69581 N2
69583 N2
69585 N2
69589 N2
69592 N2
69593 N2
69814 A5

1963 34A

60006 A4
60007 A4
60008 A4
60010 A4
60013 A4
60015 A4
60017 A4
60021 A4
60022 A4
60025 A4
60026 A4
60029 A4
60032 A4
60034 A4
60039 A3
60044 A3
60061 A3
60063 A3
60066 A3
60103 A3
60107 A3
60110 A3
60854 V2
60862 V2
60871 V2
60902 V2
60903 V2
61075 B1
61179 B1
61393 B1
61394 B1

Kings Lynn

1948 KL

62501 D15
62502 D15
62504 D15
62505 D15
62506 D15
62507 D15
62512 D15
62513 D16
62514 D16
62518 D16
62569 D16
62575 D16
62582 D16
62614 D16
64642 J19
64668 J19
64670 J19
65359 J15
65368 J15
65378 J15
65382 J15
65396 J15
65416 J15
65425 J15
65437 J15
65527 J17
65529 J17
65530 J17
65544 J17
65548 J17
65549 J17
65572 J17
65580 J17
67149 F3
67236 F6
67239 F6
68082 Y6
68083 Y6
68217 J70
68218 J70
68220 J70
68222 J70
68223 J70
68490 J67
68493 J67
68494 J69
68502 J69
68514 J67
68515 J67
68542 J69
68600 J69
68656 J68

1951 31C

62501 D15
62502 D15
62505 D15
62506 D15
62513 D16
62514 D16
62518 D16
62559 D16
62569 D16
62575 D16
62582 D16
62601 D16
62614 D16
62790 E4
64640 J19
64642 J19
64654 J19
64668 J19
64672 J19
65359 J15
65378 J15
65519 J17
65527 J17
65530 J17
65542 J17
65544 J17
65549 J17
65572 J17
68082 Y6
68083 Y6
68217 J70
68220 J70
68222 J70
68223 J70
68225 J70
68490 J69
68493 J67
68494 J69
68502 J69
68514 J67
68515 J67
68545 J69
68656 J68

1954 31C

62514 D16
62516 D16
62518 D16
62534 D16
62559 D16
62565 D16
62569 D16
62573 D16
62575 D16
62579 D16
62582 D16
62601 D16
62606 D16
62614 D16
65359 J15
65501 J17
65518 J17
65519 J17
65521 J17
65526 J17
65527 J17
65529 J17
65530 J17
65544 J17
65549 J17
65568 J17
65582 J17
67360 C12
67367 C12
67374 C12
67386 C12
68490 J69
68495 J69
68498 J69
68502 J69
68545 J69
68635 J69

1957 31C

62514 D16
62516 D16
62518 D16
62522 D16
62534 D16
62545 D16
62558 D16
62565 D16
62575 D16
62582 D16
62584 D16
62601 D16
62606 D16
62614 D16
65501 J17
65518 J17
65521 J17
65526 J17
65527 J17
65529 J17
65530 J17
65533 J17
65544 J17
65549 J17
65562 J17
65568 J17
65582 J17
67374 C12
67386 C12
68490 J69
68495 J69
68498 J69
68499 J69
68502 J69
68545 J69
68556 J69

1960 31C

43087 4MT[5]
43089 4MT[5]
43090 4MT[5]
43094 4MT[5]
61620 B17
64647 J19
64655 J19
64673 J19
65521 J17
65530 J17
65533 J17
65549 J17
65565 J17
65577 J17
65582 J17
65584 J17
68499 J69
68542 J69
68566 J69
69694 N7

1966

24 B1

Kipps

1948 KPS

64460 J35
64470 J35
64472 J35
64473 J35
64498 J35
64507 J35
65210 J36
65215 J36
65226 J36
65236 J36
65238 J36
65245 J36
65247 J36
65249 J36
65255 J36
65256 J36
65260 J36
65264 J36
65266 J36
65285 J36
65287 J36
65289 J36
65294 J36
65325 J36
67475 C15
67627 V1
67660 V1
68094 Y9
68106 Y9
68112 Y9
68116 Y9
68117 Y9
68120 Y9
68121 Y9
68329 J88
68343 J88
68344 J88
68442 J83
68443 J83
68444 J83
68445 J83
68461 J83
69141 N15
69196 N15
69206 N15
69207 N15
69503 N2
69508 N2
69509 N2
69511 N2
69518 N2
69553 N2
69563 N2
69596 N2

1951 65E

64460 J35
64470 J35
64472 J35
64473 J35
64498 J35
64507 J35
64531 J35
64534 J35
65210 J36
65214 J36
65217 J36
65226 J36
65236 J36
65238 J36
65245 J36
65249 J36
65255 J36
65260 J36
65264 J36
65266 J36
65285 J36
65287 J36
65325 J36
67467 C15
67618 V1
67627 V1
67660 V1
67665 V1
67674 V1
68094 Y9
68106 Y9
68116 Y9
68117 Y9
68120 Y9
68121 Y9
68329 J88
68331 J88
68343 J88
68344 J88
68442 J83
68443 J83
68444 J83
68445 J83
68461 J83
69145 N15
69196 N15
69206 N15
69207 N15
69503 N2
69508 N2
69509 N2
69518 N2
69563 N2
69596 N2

1954 65E

56172 2F[4]
64460 J35
64470 J35
64472 J35
64473 J35
64498 J35
64507 J35
64531 J35
64534 J35
64548 J37
64579 J37
65210 J36
65214 J36
65217 J36
65236 J36
65249 J36
65260 J36
65266 J36
65285 J36
65287 J36
65325 J36
65343 J36
67467 C15
67618 V1
67627 V3
67660 V1
67665 V1
67674 V1
68094 Y9
68106 Y9
68116 Y9
68117 Y9
68120 Y9
68121 Y9
68329 J88
68331 J88
68343 J88
68442 J83
68443 J83
68444 J83
68445 J83
68461 J83
69145 N15
69196 N15
69206 N15
69207 N15
69503 N2
69518 N2
69596 N2

1957 65E

43132 4MT[5]
43133 4MT[5]
43134 4MT[5]
56172 2F[4]
64460 J35
64470 J35
64472 J35
64473 J35
64498 J35
64507 J35
64531 J35
64534 J35
64548 J37
64579 J37
65210 J36
65214 J36
65217 J36
65249 J36
65260 J36
65266 J36
65285 J36
65287 J36
65325 J36
65343 J36
67618 V1
67627 V3
67660 V3
67665 V1
67674 V1
68106 Y9
68110 Y9
68116 Y9
68117 Y9
68124 Y9
68329 J88
68336 J88
68343 J88
68344 J88
68442 J83
68443 J83
68444 J83
68445 J83
68461 J83
69145 N15
69196 N15
69206 N15
69207 N15
69518 N2
69596 N2

1960 65E

43132 4MT[5]
43133 4MT[5]
43134 4MT[5]
56029 0F[5]
64470 J35
64472 J35
64507 J35
64531 J35
64534 J35
64542 J37
64544 J37
64574 J37
64579 J37
64628 J37
65210 J36
65214 J36
65217 J36
65249 J36
65260 J36
65266 J36
65285 J36
65287 J36
65325 J36
65343 J36
67605 V3
67609 V3
67618 V3
67627 V3
67660 V3
67665 V1
67674 V3
68100 Y9
68110 Y9
68114 Y9
68117 Y9
68123 Y9
68336 J88
68343 J88
68442 J83
68443 J83
68444 J83
68445 J83
68709 J72
68733 J72
69206 N15
69518 N2
69596 N2

1963 65E

64593 J37
65325 J36

Kirkby in Ashfield

1948 16C

43494 3F[3]
43773 3F[4]
43894 4F[1]
43895 4F[1]
43907 4F[1]
44005 4F[1]
44021 4F[1]
44082 4F[2]
44113 4F[2]
44140 4F[2]
44202 4F[2]
44205 4F[2]
44206 4F[2]
44268 4F[2]
44415 4F[2]
44463 4F[2]
44472 4F[2]
44589 4F[2]
48000 8F
48006 8F
48007 8F
48009 8F
48027 8F
48029 8F
48036 8F
48074 8F
48092 8F
48096 8F
48097 8F
48098 8F
48100 8F
48101 8F
48104 8F
48108 8F
48109 8F
48114 8F
48139 8F
48166 8F
48193 8F
48214 8F
48215 8F
48223 8F
48224 8F
48225 8F
48267 8F
48268 8F
48270 8F
48272 8F
48283 8F
48378 8F
48379 8F
48382 8F
48383 8F
48392 8F
48393 8F
48409 8F
48413 8F
48421 8F
48442 8F
48530 8F
48552 8F
48608 8F
48616 8F
48641 8F
58137 2F[8]
3424 2F[9]

1951 16C

43242 3F[3]
43287 3F[3]
43305 3F[3]
43468 3F[3]
43494 3F[3]
43596 3F[3]
43773 3F[4]
43895 4F[1]
43903 4F[1]
43907 4F[1]
44005 4F[1]
44021 4F[1]
44082 4F[2]
44140 4F[2]
44202 4F[2]
44205 4F[2]
44206 4F[2]
44268 4F[2]
44463 4F[2]
44470 4F[2]
44547 4F[2]
44552 4F[2]
44589 4F[2]
48000 8F
48003 8F
48004 8F
48006 8F
48009 8F
48029 8F
48073 8F
48081 8F
48092 8F
48096 8F
48097 8F
48098 8F
48100 8F
48101 8F
48108 8F
48114 8F
48137 8F
48138 8F
48139 8F
48193 8F
48214 8F
48215 8F
48223 8F
48224 8F
48225 8F
48267 8F
48268 8F
48270 8F
48272 8F
48282 8F
48379 8F
48382 8F
48383 8F
48392 8F
48393 8F
48403 8F
48405 8F
48408 8F
48409 8F
48413 8F
48442 8F
48530 8F
48552 8F
58137 2F[8]

1954 16C

43242 3F[3]
43287 3F[3]
43305 3F[3]
43468 3F[3]
43596 3F[3]
43773 3F[4]
43779 3F[4]
43874 4F[1]
43895 4F[1]
43903 4F[1]
43907 4F[1]
43970 4F[1]
43997 4F[1]
44005 4F[1]
44021 4F[1]
44082 4F[2]
44140 4F[2]
44202 4F[2]
44205 4F[2]
44206 4F[2]
44268 4F[2]
44463 4F[2]
44470 4F[2]
44547 4F[2]
44589 4F[2]
48000 8F
48003 8F
48004 8F
48006 8F
48009 8F
48029 8F
48073 8F
48081 8F
48092 8F
48096 8F
48097 8F
48098 8F
48100 8F
48101 8F
48114 8F
48137 8F
48138 8F
48193 8F
48214 8F
48215 8F
48223 8F
48224 8F
48225 8F
48267 8F
48268 8F
48270 8F
48379 8F
48382 8F
48383 8F
48392 8F
48393 8F
48403 8F
48408 8F
48413 8F
48530 8F
48552 8F

1957 16B

43242 3F[3]
43287 3F[3]
43305 3F[3]
43468 3F[3]
43596 3F[3]
43773 3F[4]
43859 4F[1]
43903 4F[1]
43907 4F[1]
43970 4F[1]
43997 4F[1]
44005 4F[1]
44023 4F[1]
44088 4F[2]
44202 4F[2]
44268 4F[2]
44470 4F[2]
48000 8F
48003 8F
48004 8F
48006 8F
48008 8F
48009 8F
48029 8F
48073 8F
48081 8F
48092 8F
48096 8F
48097 8F
48098 8F
48100 8F
48101 8F
48102 8F
48114 8F
48137 8F
48193 8F
48214 8F
48215 8F
48223 8F
48224 8F
48225 8F
48267 8F
48268 8F
48270 8F
48334 8F
48379 8F
48382 8F
48383 8F
48392 8F
48393 8F
48408 8F
48413 8F
48552 8F
48770 8F

1960 16B

43885 4F[1]
43903 4F[1]
43933 4F[1]
44202 4F[2]
44268 4F[2]
44470 4F[2]
48003 8F
48004 8F
48006 8F
48009 8F
48029 8F
48063 8F
48073 8F
48092 8F
48096 8F
48097 8F
48098 8F
48100 0F
48102 8F
48114 8F
48137 8F
48177 8F
48192 8F
48214 8F
48215 8F
48223 8F
48224 8F

48225 8F
48267 8F
48317 8F
48334 8F
48379 8F
48383 8F
48392 8F
48395 8F
48413 8F
48432 8F
48447 8F
48528 8F
48552 8F
48673 8F

1963 16B
41712 1F[1]
41844 1F[1]
42080 4MT[1]
42089 4MT[1]
42222 4MT[1]
42231 4MT[1]
42232 4MT[1]
42618 4MT[3]
42629 4MT[3]
43885 4F[1]
43903 4F[1]
43923 4F[1]
43975 4F[1]
44091 4F[2]
44202 4F[2]
44252 4F[2]
44268 4F[2]
44416 4F[2]
44418 4F[2]
44470 4F[2]
48001 8F
48003 8F
48004 8F
48006 8F
48063 8F
48073 8F
48088 8F
48092 8F
48096 8F
48097 8F
48098 8F
48100 8F
48102 8F
48105 8F
48114 8F
48119 8F
48137 8F
48143 8F
48156 8F
48192 8F
48214 8F
48215 8F
48219 8F
48223 8F
48224 8F
48225 8F
48267 8F
48272 8F
48277 8F
48282 8F
48317 8F
48334 8F
48342 8F
48379 8F
48383 8F
48392 8F
48395 8F
48405 8F
48413 8F
48432 8F
48442 8F
48447 8F
48528 8F
48541 8F
48552 8F
48621 8F
48643 8F
48673 8F
48701 8F
78013 2MT[1]

1966 16E
48003 8F
48045 8F
48063 8F
48092 8F
48098 8F
48100 8F
48105 8F
48119 8F
48124 8F
48186 8F
48201 8F
48215 8F
48225 8F
48267 8F
48272 8F
48277 8F
48284 8F
48303 8F
48304 8F
48317 8F
48334 8F
48346 8F
48362 8F
48364 8F
48383 8F
48395 8F
48405 8F
48442 8F
48541 8F
48621 8F
48627 8F
48643 8F
48673 8F
48678 8F
48694 8F
92072 9F
92075 9F
92093 9F
92095 9F

Kirkby Stephen

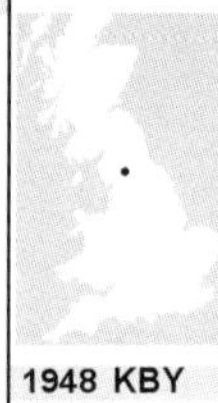

1948 KBY
65028 J21
65040 J21
65047 J21
65103 J21
65115 J21
65655 J25
65669 J25
65673 J25
65681 J25
65684 J25
65717 J25

1951 51H
65028 J21
65040 J21
65047 J21
65089 J21
65100 J21
65103 J21
65653 J25
65655 J25
65673 J25
65695 J25
65717 J25

1954 51H
46471 2MT[2]
46474 2MT[2]
46476 2MT[2]
46477 2MT[2]
46478 2MT[2]
46480 2MT[2]
46481 2MT[2]
65047 J21
65100 J21
65655 J25
65673 J25
65695 J25
65717 J25

1957 51H
46470 2MT[2]
46472 2MT[2]
76020 4MT[2]
76022 4MT[2]
76023 4MT[2]
76047 4MT[2]
76048 4MT[2]
76051 4MT[2]
76052 4MT[2]
78016 2MT[1]
78017 2MT[1]
78018 2MT[1]
78019 2MT[1]
82026 3MT[2]
82027 3MT[2]

1960 12D
46470 2MT[2]
76022 4MT[2]
76023 4MT[2]
76047 4MT[2]
76051 4MT[2]
76052 4MT[2]
78013 2MT[1]
78017 2MT[1]
78018 2MT[1]
78019 2MT[1]

Kittybrewster

1948 KIT
61067 B1
61132 B1
61133 B1
61134 B1
61146 B1
61147 B1
61148 B1
61242 B1
61504 B12
61505 B12
61507 B12
61508 B12
61511 B12
61513 B12
61521 B12
61524 B12
61526 B12
61528 B12
61529 B12
61532 B12
61536 B12
61539 B12
61543 B12
61552 B12
61560 B12
61563 B12
62062 D31
62064 D31
62065 D31
62066 D31
62225 D41
62227 D41
62228 D41
62229 D41
62230 D41
62231 D41
62232 D41
62241 D41
62242 D41
62260 D40
62261 D40
62265 D40
62268 D40
62269 D40
62270 D40
62271 D40
62272 D40
62273 D40
62274 D40
62275 D40
62276 D40
62277 D40
62278 D40
62279 D40
67151 F4
67164 F4
67287 G5
67327 G5
68190 Z4
68191 Z4
68192 Z5
68193 Z5
68700 J72
68710 J72
68717 J72
68719 J72
68749 J72
68750 J72
69125 N14

1951 61A
40603 2P[3]
40622 2P[3]
40650 2P[3]
61134 B1
61307 B1
61323 B1
61324 B1
61343 B1
61345 B1
61346 B1
61347 B1
61348 B1
61349 B1
61350 B1
61351 B1
61352 B1
61400 B1
61401 B1
61505 B12
61507 B12
61508 B12
61511 B12
61513 B12
61521 B12
61524 B12
61526 B12
61528 B12
61532 B12
61539 B12
61543 B12
61552 B12
61560 B12
61563 B12
62228 D41
62229 D41
62241 D41
62260 D40
62261 D40
62265 D40
62268 D40
62270 D40
62272 D40
62273 D40
62274 D40
62275 D40
62276 D40
62277 D40
62278 D40
62279 D40
65247 J36
67151 F4
67157 F4
67164 F4
67287 G5
67327 G5
67667 V1
67671 V1
68190 Z4
68191 Z4
68192 Z5
68193 Z5
68700 J72
68710 J72
68717 J72
68719 J72
68749 J72
68750 J72

1954 61A
40603 2P[3]
40622 2P[3]
40650 2P[3]
46460 2MT[2]
61307 B1
61323 B1
61324 B1
61343 B1
61345 B1
61346 B1
61347 B1
61348 B1
61349 B1
61350 B1
61351 B1
61352 B1
61400 B1
61401 B1
61779 K2
61782 K2
61792 K2
61793 K2
62276 D40
62278 D40
62279 D40
62469 D34
62479 D34
62480 D34
62482 D34
62489 D34
62493 D34
64482 J35
65213 J36
67157 F4
67455 C15
67667 V1
67671 V1
68190 Z4
68191 Z4
68192 Z5
68193 Z5
68700 J72
68710 J72
68717 J72
68719 J72
68749 J72
68750 J72
80004 4MT[3]
80005 4MT[3]
80020 4MT[3]
80021 4MT[3]
80028 4MT[3]
80029 4MT[3]

1957 61A
40603 2P[3]
40604 2P[3]
40648 2P[3]
40650 2P[3]
40663 2P[3]
46460 2MT[2]
61294 B1
61323 B1
61324 B1
61333 B1
61343 B1
61345 B1
61346 B1
61347 B1
61348 B1
61349 B1
61350 B1
61351 B1
61352 B1
61400 B1
61790 K2
62479 D34
62480 D34
62482 D34
62489 D34
62493 D34
62498 D34
64482 J35
65213 J36
65247 J36
65303 J36
67667 V1
67671 V1
68190 Z4
68191 Z4
68192 Z5
68710 J72
68717 J72
68719 J72
68749 J72
68750 J72
78045 2MT[1]
80004 4MT[3]
80005 4MT[3]
80020 4MT[3]
80021 4MT[3]
80028 4MT[3]
80029 4MT[3]
80106 4MT[3]
80107 4MT[3]
80108 4MT[3]
80109 4MT[3]
80110 4MT[3]

1960 61A
40648 2P[3]
40650 2P[3]
40663 2P[3]
46460 2MT[2]
61242 B1
61294 B1
61324 B1
61345 B1
61346 B1
61347 B1
61350 B1
61352 B1
61400 B1
61741 K2
62479 D34
62482 D34
62493 D34
62498 D34
65227 J36
65251 J36
65297 J36
65303 J36
67667 V3
67671 V1
68190 Z4
68192 Z5
68717 J72
68719 J72
68749 J72
68750 J72
69180 N15
76104 4MT[2]
76105 4MT[2]
76106 4MT[2]
76107 4MT[2]
76108 4MT[2]
78045 2MT[1]
80004 4MT[3]
80020 4MT[3]
80021 4MT[3]
80028 4MT[3]
80029 4MT[3]
80111 4MT[3]
80112 4MT[3]
80113 4MT[3]
80114 4MT[3]
80115 4MT[3]

Laira (Plymouth)

1948 LA
1004 1000
1006 1000
1009 1000
1361 1361
1363 1361
1364 1361
1365 1361
1799 1854
1973 1901
1990 1901
2776 2721
2857 2800
2867 2800
3186 3150
3187 3150
3391 3300
3401 3300
3431 3300
3441 3300
3445 3300
3446 3300
3629 5700
3639 5700
3675 5700
3686 5700
3705 5700
3787 5700
3790 5700
3811 2884
3864 2884
3901 4900
3902 4900
3904 4900
3955 4900
4032 4073
4087 4073
4088 4073
4090 4073
4402 4400
4407 4400
4517 4500
4524 4500
4528 4500
4531 4500
4542 4500
4583 4575
4591 4575
4653 5700
4656 5700
4658 5700
4679 5700
4693 5700
4703 4700
4807 2800
4808 2800
4811 2800
4855 2884
4966 1900
5009 4073
5026 4073
5041 4073
5050 4073
5057 4073
5060 4073
5079 4073
5090 4073
5095 4073
5148 5101
5318 4300
5376 4300
5412 5400
5540 4575
5567 4575
5569 4575
5998 4900
6000 6000
6002 6000
6004 6000
6010 6000
6012 6000
6016 6000
6017 6000
6019 6000
6020 6000
6022 6000
6026 6000
6029 6000
6319 4300
6406 6400
6414 6400
6417 6400
6419 6400
6421 6400
6907 4900
6913 4900
7762 5700
8709 5700
8719 5700
9711 5700
9716 5700
9765 5700
9770 5700
90148 WD[1]
90173 WD[1]
90212 WD[1]
90237 WD[1]
90292 WD[1]
90359 WD[1]
90642 WD[1]
90658 WD[1]

1951 83D
111 4073
1006 1000
1022 1000
1023 1000
1361 1361
1363 1361
1364 1361
1365 1361
2148 2021
2875 2800
3178 3150
3186 3150
3187 3150
3629 5700
3639 5700
3675 5700
3686 5700
3705 5700
3787 5700
3790 5700
3832 2884
3864 2884
4054 4000
4087 4073
4088 4073
4089 4073
4097 4073
4407 4400
4409 4400
4518 4500
4524 4500
4542 4500
4583 4575
4591 4575
4653 5700
4656 5700
4658 5700
4679 5700
4693 5700
4703 4700
4966 4900
4972 4900
4992 4900
5012 4073
5021 4073
5023 4073
5057 4073
5058 4073
5060 4073
5090 4073
5095 4073
5098 4073
5148 5101
5318 4300
5376 4300
5531 4575
5540 4575
5567 4575
5569 4575
5964 4900
5998 4900
6010 6000
6012 6000
6016 6000
6022 6000
6023 6000
6024 6000
6025 6000
6026 6000
6027 6000
6029 6000
6319 4300
6406 6400
6407 6400
6414 6400
6417 6400
6419 6400
6420 6400
6421 6400
6855 6800
6873 6800
6907 4900
6913 4900
6949 4900
7027 4073
7031 4073
7762 5700
7801 7800
7804 7800
7809 7800
7814 7800
7905 6959
7909 6959
8709 5700
8719 5700
9433 9400
9671 5700
9673 5700
9711 5700
9716 5700
9765 5700
9770 5700
90148 WD[1]

1954 83D
1006 1000
1010 1000
1012 1000
1015 1000
1021 1000
1363 1361
1364 1361
1365 1361
2097 2021
2843 2800
3186 3150
3187 3150
3629 5700
3639 5700
3675 5700
3686 5700
3787 5700
3790 5700
3862 2884
4086 4073
4089 4073
4410 4400
4524 4500
4530 4500
4534 4500
4542 4500
4583 4575
4590 4575
4591 4575
4653 5700
4656 5700
4658 5700
4679 5700
4693 5700
4950 4900
4963 4900
4966 4900
4978 4900
4992 4900
5057 4073
5058 4073
5098 4073
5148 5101
5175 5101
5356 4300
5376 4300
5531 4575
5567 4575
5569 4575
5913 4900
5961 4900
5964 4900
5998 4900
6008 6000
6010 6000
6012 6000
6014 6000
6017 6000
6022 6000
6023 6000
6024 6000
6025 6000
6026 6000
6027 6000
6029 6000
6319 4300
6406 6400
6407 6400
6414 6400
6419 6400
6420 6400
6421 6400
6802 6800
6816 6800
6821 6800
6838 6800
6855 6800
6869 6800
6873 6800
6907 4900
6912 4900
6913 4900
6933 4900
6940 4900
6965 6959
6978 6959
7031 4073
7762 5700
7804 7800
7809 7800
7814 7800
7815 7800
7824 7800
7905 6959
7909 6959
8422 9400
8425 9400
8426 9400
8709 5700
8719 5700
9433 9400
9467 9400
9671 5700
9711 5700
9716 5700
9770 5700
70016 7P6F
70019 7P6F
70021 7P6F
70024 7P6F

1957 83D
1010 1000
1015 1000
1021 1000
1361 1361
1363 1361
1364 1361
1408 1400
1434 1400
1650 1600
2843 2800
3186 3150
3187 3150
3629 5700
3639 5700
3675 5700
3686 5700
3787 5700
3790 5700
3862 2884
4077 4073
4086 4073
4087 4073
4088 4073
4583 4575
4590 4575
4591 4575
4592 4575
4653 5700
4656 5700
4658 5700
4679 5700
4693 5700
4936 4900
4950 4900
4976 4900
4992 4900
5003 4073
5023 4073
5028 4073
5058 4073
5069 4073
5098 4073
5148 5101
5175 5101
5193 5101
5336 4300
5356 4300
5376 4300
5506 4575
5531 4575
5551 4575
5567 4575
5569 4575
5934 4900
6004 6000
6008 6000
6010 6000
6017 6000
6021 6000
6025 6000
6026 6000
6027 6000
6029 6000
6301 4300
6319 4300
6328 4300
6406 6400
6407 6400
6414 6400
6419 6400
6420 6400
6421 6400
6802 6800
6816 6800
6821 6800
6848 6800
6855 6800
6858 6800
6873 6800
6913 4900
6921 4900
6940 4900
6941 4900
6965 6959
6978 6959
6988 6959
7029 4073
7031 4073
7762 5700
7809 7800
7812 7800
7820 7800
7824 7800
7905 6959
7909 6959
8422 9400
8425 9400
8426 9400
8709 5700
8719 5700
9433 9400
9467 9400
9711 5700
9716 5700
9770 5700
70021 7P6F

1960 83D
1361 1361
1363 1361
1364 1361
1420 1400
1421 1400
1434 1400
1650 1600
2809 2800
2899 2884
3675 5700
3686 5700
3787 5700
3790 5700
3862 2884
4087 4073
4174 5101
4591 4575
4592 4575
4658 5700
4679 5700
4705 4700
4950 4900
4967 4900
4976 4900
5028 4073
5029 4073
5053 4073
5058 4073
5069 4073
5098 4073
5106 5101
5175 5101
5511 4575
5519 4575
5531 4575
5532 4575
5567 4575
5569 4575
5572 4575
6013 6000
6016 6000
6026 6000
6166 6100
6301 4300
6400 6400
6406 6400
6408 6400
6410 6400
6413 6400
6419 6400
6421 6400
6863 6800
6873 6800
6913 4900
6921 4900
6938 4900
6941 4900
7022 4073
7333 4300
7335 4300
7921 6959
8422 9400
9433 9400
9467 9400
9711 5700
9716 5700
92208 9F
92221 9F
92222 9F
92223 9F
92224 9F
92225 9F

1963 83D
4087 4073
4555 4500
4570 4500
4574 4500
4591 4575
4658 5700
4920 4900
4978 4900
5564 4575
5568 4575
5569 4575
5645 5600
6400 6400
6421 6400
6430 6400
6921 4900
6988 6959
7022 4073
7916 6959

Lancaster

1948 20H
40488 2P[2]
40565 2P[3]
40931 4P[1]
41005 4P[2]
41022 4P[2]
41045 4P[1]
41053 4P[1]
41065 4P[1]
41081 4P[1]
41095 4P[1]
41901 2P[4]
42895 5MT[1]
42928 5MT[1]
43187 3F[2]
43293 3F[3]
43307 3F[3]
43330 3F[3]
44032 4F[2]
44201 4F[2]
44280 4F[2]
44405 4F[2]
44468 4F[2]
44554 4F[2]
44556 4F[2]
47381 3F[6]
47468 3F[6]
47469 3F[6]
47470 3F[6]
47471 3F[6]
47532 3F[6]
48055 8F

1951 23C
40362 2P[2]
41005 4P[2]
41045 4P[1]
41065 4P[1]
41081 4P[1]
41900 2P[4]
41901 2P[4]
41902 2P[4]
41904 2P[4]
42135 4MT[1]
42136 4MT[1]
42144 4MT[1]
42893 5MT[1]
42895 5MT[1]
42928 5MT[1]
43034 4MT[5]
43035 4MT[5]
43187 3F[2]
43293 3F[3]
43330 3F[3]
43890 4F[1]
43904 4F[1]
43933 4F[1]
44032 4F[2]
44280 4F[2]
44405 4F[2]
46441 2MT[2]
47201 3F[5]
47381 3F[6]
47468 3F[6]
47469 3F[6]
47470 3F[6]
47471 3F[6]
47532 3F[6]
47639 3F[6]
48001 8F
48148 8F
48161 8F

1954 11E
40362 2P[2]
41045 4P[1]
41065 4P[1]
41081 4P[1]
41107 4P[1]
41136 4P[1]
41152 4P[1]
41196 4P[1]
41197 4P[1]
41900 2P[4]
41901 2P[4]
41902 2P[4]
41903 2P[4]
41904 2P[4]
42135 4MT[1]
42136 4MT[1]
42589 4MT[3]
42893 5MT[1]
42895 5MT[1]
42928 5MT[1]
43034 4MT[5]
43035 4MT[5]
43890 4F[1]
43984 4F[1]
44032 4F[2]
46441 2MT[2]
47201 3F[5]
47381 3F[6]
47468 3F[6]
47469 3F[6]
47470 3F[6]
47471 3F[6]
47532 3F[6]
47639 3F[6]
48261 8F
48286 8F
48505 8F

1957 11E
41045 4P[1]
41098 4P[1]
41108 4P[1]
41112 4P[1]
41151 4P[1]
41152 4P[1]
41196 4P[1]
41197 4P[1]
41903 2P[4]
41904 2P[4]
42135 4MT[1]
42136 4MT[1]
42589 4MT[3]
42810 5MT[1]
42851 5MT[1]
42888 5MT[1]
42893 5MT[1]
42895 5MT[1]
42928 5MT[1]
43271 3F[3]
43502 3F[3]
43890 4F[1]
43984 4F[1]
46426 2MT[2]
46441 2MT[2]
47201 3F[5]
47381 3F[6]
47468 3F[6]
47469 3F[6]
47470 3F[6]
47471 3F[6]
47532 3F[6]
47639 3F[6]
48261 8F
48286 8F
48342 8F

1960 24J
42135 4MT[1]
42136 4MT[1]
42589 4MT[3]
42810 5MT[1]
42851 5MT[1]
42893 5MT[1]
42895 5MT[1]
42928 5MT[1]
43007 4MT[5]
43018 4MT[5]
43021 4MT[5]
43045 4MT[5]
43073 4MT[5]
43112 4MT[5]
43113 4MT[5]
43115 4MT[5]
46410 2MT[2]
46426 2MT[2]
46441 2MT[2]
47347 3F[6]
47369 3F[6]
47381 3F[6]
47468 3F[6]
47469 3F[6]
47470 3F[6]
47471 3F[6]
47481 3F[6]
47532 3F[6]
47639 3F[6]
90595 WD[1]
90706 WD[1]

1963 24J
41215 2MT[1]
41221 2MT[1]
42135 4MT[1]
42136 4MT[1]
42589 4MT[3]
42776 5MT[1]
42778 5MT[1]
42812 5MT[1]
42895 5MT[1]
42928 5MT[1]
42931 5MT[1]
42938 5MT[1]
44758 5MT[3]
44877 5MT[3]
45014 5MT[3]
45193 5MT[3]
46410 2MT[2]
46422 2MT[2]
46426 2MT[2]
46441 2MT[2]
47317 3F[6]
47375 3F[6]
47468 3F[6]
47469 3F[6]
47481 3F[6]
47532 3F[6]
47599 3F[6]
47662 3F[6]
90173 WD[1]
90595 WD[1]
90706 WD[1]

1966 10J
41207 2MT[1]
41251 2MT[1]
44667 5MT[3]
44758 5MT[3]
44889 5MT[3]
45014 5MT[3]
45025 5MT[3]
45193 5MT[3]
45373 5MT[3]
45394 5MT[3]
45445 5MT[3]
46422 2MT[2]
46431 2MT[2]
46433 2MT[2]
46441 2MT[2]
46486 2MT[2]
46514 2MT[2]
48077 8F
48079 8F
48211 8F

Lancing Carriage Works

1948
515S A1X
DS680 A1

1951
515S A1X
DS680 A1

1954
DS680 A1
DS681 A1X

1957
DS680 A1
DS681 A1X

1960
DS680 A1
DS681 A1X

1963
DS235 USA
DS681 A1X

Landore

1948 LDR
2273 2251
3678 5700
3701 5700
3713 5700
3768 5700
3785 5700
3797 5700
4003 4000
4023 4000
4039 4000
4048 4000
4050 4000
4074 4073
4078 4073
4081 4073
4095 4073
4134 5101

4207 4200
4212 4200
4250 4200
4256 4200
4265 4200
4295 4200
5002 4073
5006 4073
5013 4073
5016 4073
5051 4073
5072 4073
5089 4073
5093 4073
5211 5205
5219 5205
5341 4300
5400 5400
5408 5400
5604 5600
5631 5600
5759 5700
5913 4900
6304 4300
6412 6400
6425 6400
6431 6400
6604 5600
6679 5600
6680 5600
6695 5600
6800 6800
6806 6800
6828 6800
6857 6800
6872 6800
6903 4900
6918 4900
7002 4073
7003 4073
7225 7200
7244 7200
7787 5700
8789 5700
9738 5700
9761 5700
9775 5700
9777 5700

1951 87E

2273 2251
3678 5700
3701 5700
3713 5700
3768 5700
3785 5700
3797 5700
4003 4000
4023 4000
4048 4000
4050 4000
4074 4073
4078 4073
4081 4073
4095 4073
4134 5101
4207 4200
4250 4200
5002 4073
5013 4073
5016 4073
5051 4073
5072 4073
5093 4073
5162 5101
5211 5205
5219 5205
5400 5400
5408 5400
5604 5600
5631 5600
5656 5600
5759 5700
5913 4900
5929 4900
5955 4900
6412 6400
6425 6400
6431 6400
6604 5600
6680 5600
6695 5600
6903 4900
6918 4900
7002 4073
7003 4073
7009 4073
7012 4073
7018 4073
7021 4073
7028 4073
7211 7200
7225 7200
7244 7200
7787 5700
8789 5700
9738 5700
9761 5700
9775 5700
9777 5700

1954 87E

1428 1400
2284 2251
3678 5700
3701 5700
3713 5700
3768 5700
3785 5700
3797 5700
4074 4073
4078 4073
4081 4073
4093 4073
4095 4073
4106 5101
4107 5101
4981 4900
5002 4073
5013 4073
5016 4073
5051 4073
5072 4073
5604 5600
5631 5600
5656 5600
5673 5600
5759 5700
5929 4900
5955 4900
5988 4900
6412 6400
6425 6400
6431 6400
6604 5600
6680 5600
6688 5600
6695 5600
6903 4900
6905 4900
6918 4900
7002 4073
7003 4073
7009 4073
7012 4073
7018 4073
7021 4073
7028 4073
7200 7200
7207 7200
7209 7200
7217 7200
7236 7200
7787 5700
8463 9400
8789 5700
9484 9400
9738 5700
9761 5700
9775 5700
9777 5700
73022 5MT

1957 87E

2226 2251
2284 2251
3678 5700
3701 5700
3713 5700
3768 5700
3785 5700
3797 5700
4000 4073
4078 4073
4081 4073
4093 4073
4095 4073
4106 5101
4107 5101
4910 4900
4923 4900
4937 4900
5002 4073
5013 4073
5016 4073
5041 4073
5051 4073
5077 4073
5604 5600
5631 5600
5656 5600
5673 5600
5913 4900
5929 4900
5955 4900
5988 4900
5990 4900
6604 5600
6680 5600
6688 5600
6695 5600
6903 4900
6905 4900
6918 4900
7003 4073
7009 4073
7012 4073
7016 4073
7021 4073
7200 7200
7207 7200
7209 7200
7217 7200
7236 7200
7248 7200
8463 9400
8788 5700
8789 5700
8794 5700
9436 9400
9484 9400
9637 5700
9715 5700
9738 5700
9775 5700
9777 5700

1960 87E

3678 5700
3701 5700
3713 5700
3768 5700
3785 5700
3797 5700
4037 4073
4074 4073
4076 4073
4093 4073
4094 4073
4097 4073
4099 4073
4106 5101
4107 5101
4910 4900
4923 4900
5004 4073
5013 4073
5016 4073
5039 4073
5041 4073
5051 4073
5077 4073
5091 4073
5631 5600
5673 5600
5913 4900
5955 4900
5988 4900
5990 4900
6114 6100
6649 5600
6680 5600
6688 5600
6695 5600
6918 4900
6933 4900
7009 4073
7021 4073
7028 4073
7035 4073
7200 7200
7207 7200
7209 7200
7230 7200
7236 7200
8439 9400
8463 9400
8788 5700
8789 5700
8794 5700
9436 9400
9484 9400
9637 5700
9715 5700
9738 5700
9775 5700
9777 5700
42296 4MT^{1}
42305 4MT^{2}
42307 4MT^{2}
42385 4MT^{2}
42387 4MT^{2}
42388 4MT^{2}
42390 4MT^{2}
42394 4MT^{2}
42645 4MT^{3}
42651 4MT^{3}

Langwith Junction

1948 LNG

63597 O4
63615 O4
63644 O4
63651 O4
63665 O4
63677 O4
63837 O4
63921 O2
63923 O2
63924 O2
63925 O2
63926 O2
63927 O2
63928 O2
63942 O2
63943 O2
63945 O2
63946 O2
63964 O2
63965 O2
63966 O2
63967 O2
63968 O2
63969 O2
63970 O2
63971 O2
63972 O2
63973 O2
63974 O2
63976 O2
63977 O2
63978 O2
63979 O2
63980 O2
63981 O2
63982 O2
63983 O2
63984 O2
63985 O2
63986 O2
63987 O2
64281 J11
64289 J11
64297 J11
64321 J11
64333 J11
64358 J11
64378 J11
64379 J11
64389 J11
64414 J11
64418 J11
64426 J11
64427 J11
64450 J11
67351 C12
67355 C12
67357 C12
67384 C12
69284 N5
69319 N5
69323 N5
69327 N5
69928 Q1
69929 Q1

1951 40E

63577 O4
63585 O4
63597 O4
63615 O4
63627 O4
63632 O4
63643 O4
63644 O4
63648 O4
63658 O4
63665 O4
63679 O4
63682 O4
63683 O4
63703 O4
63707 O4
63709 O4
63715 O4
63717 O4
63724 O4
63750 O4
63758 O4
63759 O4
63765 O4
63776 O4
63800 O4
63807 O4
63809 O4
63833 O4
63837 O4
63840 O4
63842 O4
63870 O4
63877 O4
63884 O4
63900 O4
63902 O4
63908 O4
64281 J11
64286 J11
64289 J11
64297 J11
64310 J11
64321 J11
64358 J11
64378 J11
64379 J11
64389 J11
64414 J11
64418 J11
64426 J11
64427 J11
69284 N5
69319 N5
69323 N5
69327 N5
69812 A5
69815 A5
69818 A5
69928 Q1
69929 Q1

1954 40E

63577 O4
63585 O4
63597 O4
63603 O4
63615 O4
63632 O4
63634 O4
63636 O4
63643 O4
63644 O4
63664 O4
63665 O4
63667 O4
63679 O4
63683 O4
63703 O4
63707 O4
63715 O4
63717 O4
63732 O4
63750 O4
63758 O4
63759 O4
63765 O4
63776 O4
63800 O4
63833 O4
63837 O4
63840 O4
63842 O4
63861 O4
63870 O4
63893 O4
63902 O4
63915 O4
64281 J11
64289 J11
64293 J11
64297 J11
64310 J11
64321 J11
64337 J11
64358 J11
64378 J11
64379 J11
64389 J11
64408 J11
64414 J11
64426 J11
64427 J11
69284 N5
69319 N5
69323 N5
69812 A5
69815 A5
69821 A5
69928 Q1
69929 Q1

1957 40E

63577 O4
63585 O4
63603 O4
63632 O4
63634 O4
63636 O4
63664 O4
63667 O4
63679 O4
63703 O4
63707 O4
63715 O4
63717 O4
63732 O4
63739 O4
63765 O4
63776 O4
63800 O4
63833 O4
63840 O4
63842 O4
63861 O4
63870 O4
63902 O4
64281 J11
64293 J11
64297 J11
64310 J11
64337 J11
64379 J11
64389 J11
64414 J11
64427 J11
69319 N5
69322 N5
69928 Q1
69929 Q1
90043 WD^{1}
90051 WD^{1}
90055 WD^{1}
90087 WD^{1}
90162 WD^{1}
90259 WD^{1}
90275 WD^{1}
90287 WD^{1}
90302 WD^{1}
90411 WD^{1}
90431 WD^{1}
90449 WD^{1}
90492 WD^{1}
90502 WD^{1}
90545 WD^{1}
90554 WD^{1}
90577 WD^{1}
90594 WD^{1}

1960 41J

63577 O4
63597 O4
63603 O4
63607 O4
63612 O4
63634 O4
63635 O4
63636 O4
63643 O4
63664 O4
63679 O4
63683 O4
63691 O4
63697 O4
63703 O4
63704 O4
63707 O4
63715 O4
63717 O4
63718 O4
63731 O4
63732 O4
63739 O4
63758 O4
63763 O4
63765 O4
63776 O4
63800 O4
63801 O4
63829 O4
63833 O4
63840 O4
63842 O4
63853 O4
63861 O4
63870 O4
63893 O4
63902 O4
63912 O4
64314 J11
64316 J11
64317 J11
64324 J11
64332 J11
64333 J11
64352 J11
64364 J11
64379 J11
64427 J11
68026 J94
68080 J94
68569 J69
68591 J69
69263 N5
69268 N5
69286 N5
69299 N5
90043 WD^{1}
90088 WD^{1}
90259 WD^{1}
90275 WD^{1}
90287 WD^{1}
90302 WD^{1}
90431 WD^{1}
90438 WD^{1}
90449 WD^{1}
90492 WD^{1}
90545 WD^{1}
90554 WD^{1}
90577 WD^{1}
90594 WD^{1}
90657 WD^{1}

1963 41J

63577 O4
63622 O4
63636 O4
63679 O4
63683 O4
63691 O4
63697 O4
63703 O4
63715 O4
63717 O4
63720 O4
63722 O4
63731 O4
63732 O4
63739 O4
63763 O4
63765 O4
63800 O4
63801 O4
63828 O4
63829 O4
63840 O4
63842 O4
63853 O4
63861 O4
63893 O4
63902 O4
68020 J94
68067 J94
68078 J94
90043 WD^{1}
90088 WD^{1}
90145 WD^{1}
90275 WD^{1}
90301 WD^{1}
90302 WD^{1}
90411 WD^{1}
90418 WD^{1}
90449 WD^{1}
90483 WD^{1}

1966 41J

41528 0F^{2}
41533 0F^{2}
41708 1F^{1}
41734 1F^{1}
41763 1F^{1}
41804 1F^{1}
41835 1F^{1}
47001 0F^{3}
47005 0F^{3}
61050 B1
61051 B1
61315 B1
90069 WD^{1}
90149 WD^{1}
90153 WD^{1}
90258 WD^{1}
90418 WD^{1}
90449 WD^{1}
90572 WD^{1}
90719 WD^{1}

Law Junction

1951 CME

55134 2P^{12}

Leamington Spa

1948 LMTN

2772 2721
2902 2900
2933 2900
3631 5700
4102 5101
4112 5101
5104 5101
5109 5101
5130 5101
5144 5101
5161 5101
5163 5101
5185 5101
5187 5101
5192 5101
5194 5101
6625 5600
6632 5600
6644 5600
6650 5600
6657 5600
6697 5600
7218 7200
7702 5700
7810 7800
8100 8100
8109 8100
9740 5700

1951 84D

2933 2900
3631 5700
4102 5101
4112 5101
4171 5101
5104 5101
5144 5101
5161 5101
5163 5101
5185 5101
5192 5101
5194 5101
5634 5600
5954 4900
6625 5600
6632 5600
6657 5600
6697 5600
6833 6800
6924 4900
7208 7200
7218 7200
7237 7200
7702 5700
8100 8100
8109 8100
8454 9400
9740 5700

1954 84D

3619 5700
3624 5700
3631 5700
4112 5101
4171 5101
5104 5101
5161 5101
5184 5101
5185 5101
5192 5101
5194 5101
6624 5600
6657 5600
6697 5600
7702 5700
8100 8100
8109 8100
90466 WD^{1}
90563 WD^{1}

1957 84D

3619 5700
3624 5700
3631 5700
4112 5101
4118 5101
4171 5101
5104 5101
5161 5101
5184 5101
5185 5101
5194 5101
6624 5600
6657 5600
6697 5600
7702 5700
8100 8100
8109 8100
90483 WD^{1}

1960 84D

3619 5700
3624 5700
3631 5700
4112 5101
4118 5101
4162 5101
4171 5101
5101 5101
5184 5101
5194 5101
6657 5600
6697 5600
7702 5700
8100 8100
8109 8100
9614 5700
9733 5700
41228 2MT^{1}
42566 4MT^{3}

1963 84D

2210 2251
2211 2251
3217 2251
4120 5101
4125 5101
4133 5101
4171 5101
4176 5101
4178 5101
5101 5101
5640 5600
5658 5600
6618 5600
6663 5600
6668 5600
6671 5600
41231 2MT^{1}
41285 2MT^{1}
48412 8F
75000 4MT^{1}

Leeds Holbeck

1948 20A

40351 2P^{2}
40359 2P^{2}
40455 2P^{2}
40519 2P^{2}
40521 2P^{2}
40720 3P^{1}
40736 3P^{1}
40748 3P^{1}
40758 3P^{1}
40910 4P^{1}
40927 4P^{1}
41020 4P^{2}
41040 4P^{2}
41048 4P^{1}
41068 4P^{1}
41069 4P^{1}
41087 4P^{1}
41137 4P^{1}
41144 4P^{1}
41745 1F^{1}
43401 3F^{3}
43454 3F^{3}
43665 3F^{3}
43878 4F^{1}
44044 4F^{2}
44151 4F^{2}
44404 4F^{2}
44431 4F^{2}
44501 4F^{2}
44774 5MT^{3}
44775 5MT^{3}
44820 5MT^{3}
44821 5MT^{3}
44823 5MT^{3}
44824 5MT^{3}
44828 5MT^{3}
44847 5MT^{3}
44848 5MT^{3}
44849 5MT^{3}
44850 5MT^{3}
44853 5MT^{3}
44854 5MT^{3}
44856 5MT^{3}
44857 5MT^{3}
44943 5MT^{3}
44983 5MT^{3}
44986 5MT^{3}
45040 5MT^{3}
45043 5MT^{3}
45065 5MT^{3}
45068 5MT^{3}
45092 5MT^{3}
45187 5MT^{3}
45260 5MT^{3}
45276 5MT^{3}
45280 5MT^{3}
45289 5MT^{3}
45534 6P5F^{1}
45535 6P5F^{1}
45538 6P5F^{1}
45562 6P5F^{2}
45565 6P5F^{2}
45566 6P5F^{2}
45568 6P5F^{2}
45569 6P5F^{2}
45573 6P5F^{2}
45587 6P5F^{2}
45589 6P5F^{2}
45597 6P5F^{2}
45604 6P5F^{2}
45605 6P5F^{2}
45608 6P5F^{2}
45611 6P5F^{2}
45619 6P5F^{2}
45620 6P5F^{2}
45651 6P5F^{2}
45658 6P5F^{2}
45659 6P5F^{2}
45660 6P5F^{2}
45699 6P5F^{2}
46103 7P^{3}R
46108 7P^{3}R
46109 7P^{3}R
46117 7P^{3}R
46133 7P^{3}R
47254 3F^{5}
47418 3F^{6}
48001 8F
48073 8F
48090 8F
48110 8F
48121 8F
48126 8F
48127 8F
48129 8F
48137 8F
48138 8F
48143 8F
48176 8F
48306 8F
50622 2P^{8}
50689 2P^{8}
50880 2P^{8}
50903 3P^{3}
58032 1P^{5}
58048 1P^{6}

1951 20A

40075 3MT^{2}
40090 3MT^{2}
40169 3MT^{2}
40323 2P^{1}
40326 2P^{1}
40351 2P^{2}
40514 2P^{2}
40743 3P^{1}
40747 3P^{1}
40758 3P^{1}
41040 4P^{2}
41048 4P^{1}
41068 4P^{1}
41087 4P^{1}
41137 4P^{1}
41144 4P^{1}
41267 2MT^{1}
41745 1F^{1}
42795 5MT^{1}
42798 5MT^{1}
42816 5MT^{1}
43016 4MT^{5}
43030 4MT^{5}
43039 4MT^{5}
43665 3F^{3}
43931 4F^{1}
43953 4F^{1}
44044 4F^{2}
44207 4F^{2}
44404 4F^{2}
44431 4F^{2}
44501 4F^{2}
44584 4F^{2}
44662 5MT^{3}
44753 5MT^{3}
44754 5MT^{3}
44755 5MT^{3}
44756 5MT^{3}
44757 5MT^{3}
44774 5MT^{3}
44775 5MT^{3}
44821 5MT^{3}
44828 5MT^{3}
44843 5MT^{3}
44849 5MT^{3}
44850 5MT^{3}
44853 5MT^{3}
44854 5MT^{3}
44856 5MT^{3}
44857 5MT^{3}
44943 5MT^{3}
44983 5MT^{3}
45272 5MT^{3}
45562 6P5F^{2}
45565 6P5F^{2}
45566 6P5F^{2}
45568 6P5F^{2}
45569 6P5F^{2}
45573 6P5F^{2}
45587 6P5F^{2}
45589 6P5F^{2}
45597 6P5F^{2}
45604 6P5F^{2}
45605 6P5F^{2}
45608 6P5F^{2}
45619 6P5F^{2}
45626 6P5F^{2}
45651 6P5F^{2}
45658 6P5F^{2}
45659 6P5F^{2}
45675 6P5F^{2}
45694 6P5F^{2}
45739 6P5F^{2}
46103 7P^{3}R
46108 7P^{3}R
46109 7P^{3}R
46117 7P^{3}R
46133 7P^{3}R
47254 3F^{5}
47418 3F^{6}
47420 3F^{6}
48067 8F
48070 8F
48104 8F
48157 8F
48158 8F
48159 8F
48283 8F
48399 8F
48454 8F
48537 8F
58060 1P^{6}

1954 20A

40082 3MT^{2}
40148 3MT^{2}
40169 3MT^{2}
40323 2P^{1}
40518 2P^{2}
41068 4P^{1}
41087 4P^{1}
41100 4P^{1}
41103 4P^{1}
41104 4P^{1}
41137 4P^{1}
41267 2MT^{1}
42795 5MT^{1}
42798 5MT^{1}
42816 5MT^{1}
43039 4MT^{5}
43116 4MT^{5}
43117 4MT^{5}
43953 4F^{1}
43968 4F^{1}
44044 4F^{2}
44207 4F^{2}
44404 4F^{2}
44582 4F^{2}
44662 5MT^{3}
44744 5MT^{3}
44746 5MT^{3}
44753 5MT^{3}
44754 5MT^{3}
44755 5MT^{3}
44756 5MT^{3}
44757 5MT^{3}
44774 5MT^{3}
44777 5MT^{3}
44821 5MT^{3}
44826 5MT^{3}
44828 5MT^{3}
44843 5MT^{3}
44849 5MT^{3}
44852 5MT^{3}
44853 5MT^{3}
44854 5MT^{3}
44857 5MT^{3}
44943 5MT^{3}
44983 5MT^{3}
45447 5MT^{3}
45562 6P5F^{2}
45564 6P5F^{2}
45565 6P5F^{2}
45566 6P5F^{2}
45568 6P5F^{2}
45569 6P5F^{2}
45573 6P5F^{2}
45589 6P5F^{2}
45597 6P5F^{2}
45605 6P5F^{2}
45608 6P5F^{2}
45619 6P5F^{2}
45639 6P5F^{2}
45658 6P5F^{2}
45659 6P5F^{2}
45675 6P5F^{2}
45694 6P5F^{2}
45739 6P5F^{2}
46103 7P^{3}R
46108 7P^{3}R
46109 7P^{3}R
46112 7P^{3}R
46113 7P^{3}R
46117 7P^{3}R
46133 7P^{3}R
46145 7P^{3}R
46493 2MT^{2}
46497 2MT^{2}
46498 2MT^{2}
47254 3F^{5}
47418 3F^{6}
47420 3F^{6}
47436 3F^{6}
48001 8F
48067 8F
48070 8F
48104 8F
48145 8F
48157 8F
48158 8F
48159 8F
48266 8F
48283 8F
48399 8F
48404 8F
48454 8F
48537 8F
48750 8F
48770 8F
73010 5MT
73045 5MT

1957 55A

40140 3MT^{2}
40169 3MT^{2}
40193 3MT^{2}
40491 2P^{2}
40552 2P^{2}
40690 2P^{3}
41068 4P^{1}
41071 4P^{1}
41094 4P^{1}
41100 4P^{1}
41267 2MT^{1}
42377 4MT^{2}
42771 5MT^{1}
42774 5MT^{1}
42795 5MT^{1}
42798 5MT^{1}
43039 4MT^{5}
43117 4MT^{5}
43968 4F^{1}
44044 4F^{2}
44055 4F^{2}
44207 4F^{2}
44662 5MT^{3}
44753 5MT^{3}
44754 5MT^{3}
44755 5MT^{3}
44756 5MT^{3}
44757 5MT^{3}
44826 5MT^{3}
44828 5MT^{3}
44849 5MT^{3}
44852 5MT^{3}
44853 5MT^{3}
44854 5MT^{3}
44857 5MT^{3}
44943 5MT^{3}
44983 5MT^{3}
45273 5MT^{3}
45274 5MT^{3}
45428 5MT^{3}
45562 6P5F^{2}
45564 6P5F^{2}
45565 6P5F^{2}
45566 6P5F^{2}
45568 6P5F^{2}
45569 6P5F^{2}
45573 6P5F^{2}
45589 6P5F^{2}
45597 6P5F^{2}
45605 6P5F^{2}
45608 6P5F^{2}
45619 6P5F^{2}
45639 6P5F^{2}
45658 6P5F^{2}
45659 6P5F^{2}
45675 6P5F^{2}
45694 6P5F^{2}
45739 6P5F^{2}
46103 7P^{3}R
46108 7P^{3}R
46109 7P^{3}R
46112 7P^{3}R
46113 7P^{3}R
46117 7P^{3}R
46133 7P^{3}R
46145 7P^{3}R
46453 2MT^{2}
46493 2MT^{2}
46498 2MT^{2}
47254 3F^{5}
47418 3F^{6}
47420 3F^{6}
47436 3F^{6}
48067 8F
48104 8F
48157 8F
48158 8F
48159 8F
48283 8F
48399 8F
48454 8F
73010 5MT
73045 5MT
73053 5MT
73066 5MT
73069 5MT

1960 55A

40140 3MT^{2}
40193 3MT^{2}
40491 2P^{2}
40552 2P^{2}
40690 2P^{3}
41267 2MT^{1}
42052 4MT^{1}
42138 4MT^{1}
42377 4MT^{2}
42409 4MT^{2}
42771 5MT^{1}
42798 5MT^{1}
43039 4MT^{5}
43043 4MT^{5}
43117 4MT^{5}
43124 4MT^{5}
43130 4MT^{5}
44662 5MT^{3}
44753 5MT^{3}
44754 5MT^{3}
44755 5MT^{3}
44756 5MT^{3}
44757 5MT^{3}
44824 5MT^{3}
44826 5MT^{3}
44828 5MT^{3}
44849 5MT^{3}
44852 5MT^{3}
44853 5MT^{3}
44854 5MT^{3}
44857 5MT^{3}
44943 5MT^{3}
44983 5MT^{3}
45273 5MT^{3}
45562 6P5F^{2}
45564 6P5F^{2}
45565 6P5F^{2}
45566 6P5F^{2}
45568 6P5F^{2}
45569 6P5F^{2}
45573 6P5F^{2}
45589 6P5F^{2}
45597 6P5F^{2}
45605 6P5F^{2}
45608 6P5F^{2}
45619 6P5F^{2}
45639 6P5F^{2}
45658 6P5F^{2}
45659 6P5F^{2}
45675 6P5F^{2}
45694 6P5F^{2}
45739 6P5F^{2}
46109 7P^{3}R
46113 7P^{3}R
46117 7P^{3}R
46130 7P^{3}R
46145 7P^{3}R
46453 2MT^{2}
46493 2MT^{2}
46498 2MT^{2}
47420 3F^{6}
48067 8F
48104 8F
48157 8F
48158 8F
48159 8F
48283 8F
48399 8F
48443 8F
48454 8F
70044 7P6F
70053 7P6F
70054 7P6F
73166 5MT
73168 5MT
73169 5MT
73170 5MT
73171 5MT

1963 55A

42052 4MT^{1}
42138 4MT^{1}
42408 4MT^{2}
42409 4MT^{2}
42771 5MT^{1}
42798 5MT^{1}
43039 4MT^{5}
43043 4MT^{5}
43117 4MT^{5}
43124 4MT^{5}
43130 4MT^{5}
44662 5MT^{3}
44753 5MT^{3}
44756 5MT^{3}
44757 5MT^{3}
44824 5MT^{3}
44826 5MT^{3}
44828 5MT^{3}
44849 5MT^{3}

44852 5MT[3]
44853 5MT[3]
44854 5MT[3]
44857 5MT[3]
44943 5MT[3]
44983 5MT[3]
45562 6P5F[2]
45564 6P5F[2]
45568 6P5F[2]
45569 6P5F[2]
45573 6P5F[2]
45589 6P5F[2]
45597 6P5F[2]
45605 6P5F[2]
45608 6P5F[2]
45639 6P5F[2]
45658 6P5F[2]
45659 6P5F[2]
45675 6P5F[2]
45739 6P5F[2]
46498 2MT[2]
48104 8F
48157 8F
48158 8F
48283 8F
48399 8F
48454 8F
60038 A3

1966 55A
42052 4MT[1]
42145 4MT[1]
42271 4MT[1]
42394 4MT[2]
42622 4MT[3]
43039 4MT[5]
43069 4MT[5]
43124 4MT[5]
43130 4MT[5]
44662 5MT[3]
44824 5MT[3]
44828 5MT[3]
44852 5MT[3]
44853 5MT[3]
44854 5MT[3]
44857 5MT[3]
44983 5MT[3]
45063 5MT[3]
45075 5MT[3]
45079 5MT[3]
45204 5MT[3]
45211 5MT[3]
45273 5MT[3]
45574 6P5F[2]
45593 6P5F[2]
45643 6P5F[2]
45660 6P5F[2]
45675 6P5F[2]
45697 6P5F[2]
48104 8F
48157 8F
48158 8F
48283 8F
48399 8F
48454 8F
48542 8F

Leeds Neville Hill

1948 NEV
61034 B1
61060 B1
61062 B1
61065 B1
61068 B1
61069 B1
61218 B1
61237 B1
61256 B1
61257 B1
61258 B1
61259 B1
62746 D49
62748 D49
62756 D49
62758 D49
62765 D49
62769 D49
62770 D49
62772 D49
62774 D49
62775 D49
65036 J21
65037 J21
65041 J21
65049 J21
65077 J21
65094 J21
65097 J21
65107 J21
65109 J21
65116 J21
65118 J21
65861 J27
65883 J27
65885 J27
65888 J27
65894 J27
67240 G5
67274 G5
67278 G5
67290 G5
67319 G5
67645 V1
67646 V1
67647 V1
67656 V1
67657 V1
68158 Y3
68416 J77
68436 J77
68672 J72
68681 J72
68746 J72
69114 N13
69115 N13
69117 N13
69118 N13
90103 WD[1]
90111 WD[1]
90137 WD[1]
90156 WD[1]
90160 WD[1]
90200 WD[1]
90217 WD[1]
90223 WD[1]
90233 WD[1]
90235 WD[1]
90263 WD[1]
90303 WD[1]
90326 WD[1]
90369 WD[1]
90383 WD[1]
90411 WD[1]
90521 WD[1]
90550 WD[1]
90586 WD[1]
90609 WD[1]
90612 WD[1]
90618 WD[1]
90621 WD[1]
90628 WD[1]
90648 WD[1]
90683 WD[1]
90703 WD[1]

1951 50B
60036 A3
60074 A3
60081 A3
60084 A3
60086 A3
61035 B1
61062 B1
61069 B1
61216 B1
61218 B1
61237 B1
61240 B1
61256 B1
61257 B1
61258 B1
61259 B1
61339 B1
61410 B16
61411 B16
61412 B16
61413 B16
61414 B16
61415 B16
61425 B16
61427 B16
61428 B16
61429 B16
61431 B16
61432 B16
61433 B16
61440 B16
61442 B16
61445 B16
61446 B16
61447 B16
61469 B16
61470 B16
61471 B16
61478 B16
62739 D49
62742 D49
62746 D49
62748 D49
62756 D49
62775 D49
63450 Q6
64710 J39
64791 J39
64819 J39
64850 J39
64863 J39
64919 J39
64920 J39
64921 J39
64922 J39
64933 J39
64934 J39
64943 J39
64949 J39
65041 J21
65076 J21
65118 J21
65122 J21
67240 G5
67262 G5
67266 G5
67274 G5
67290 G5
67293 G5
67308 G5
67319 G5
68395 J77
68406 J77
68672 J72
68681 J72
69114 N13
69115 N13
69117 N13
69118 N13
69882 A8

1954 50B
60036 A3
60074 A3
60081 A3
60084 A3
60086 A3
61015 B1
61017 B1
61020 B1
61035 B1
61062 B1
61065 B1
61069 B1
61086 B1
61216 B1
61218 B1
61237 B1
61240 B1
61256 B1
61257 B1
61259 B1
61410 B16
61411 B16
61412 B16
61413 B16
61414 B16
61415 B16
61425 B16
61427 B16
61428 B16
61429 B16
61431 B16
61432 B16
61433 B16
61440 B16
61446 B16
61447 B16
61469 B16
61470 B16
61471 B16
61478 B16
62389 D20
62397 D20
62742 D49
62748 D49
62764 D49
62775 D49
63348 Q6
63436 Q6
64730 J39
64758 J39
64791 J39
64819 J39
64835 J39
64850 J39
64863 J39
64886 J39
64920 J39
64922 J39
64933 J39
64934 J39
64935 J39
64943 J39
64949 J39
67262 G5
67266 G5
67274 G5
67289 G5
67290 G5
67319 G5
68395 J77
68672 J72
68681 J72
69114 N13
69115 N13
69116 N13
69117 N13
69119 N13
69882 A8

1957 50B
60036 A3
60074 A3
60081 A3
60084 A3
60086 A3
61035 B1
61062 B1
61065 B1
61069 B1
61086 B1
61216 B1
61218 B1
61237 B1
61240 B1
61256 B1
61257 B1
61259 B1
61411 B16
61412 B16
61414 B16
61415 B16
61425 B16
61427 B16
61428 B16
61429 B16
61431 B16
61432 B16
61442 B16
61446 B16
61447 B16
61470 B16
61471 B16
62740 D49
62742 D49
62748 D49
62749 D49
62764 D49
63348 Q6
63436 Q6
64758 J39
64791 J39
64835 J39
64850 J39
64863 J39
64870 J39
64886 J39
64920 J39
64922 J39
64933 J39
64934 J39
64935 J39
64943 J39
65648 J25
65650 J25
65654 J25
65683 J25
67262 G5
67274 G5
68672 J72
69098 N10
69881 A8
69885 A8
90082 WD[1]
90467 WD[1]
90663 WD[1]

1960 50B
41252 2MT[1]
41281 2MT[1]
41282 2MT[1]
43051 4MT[5]
43054 4MT[5]
60036 A3
60074 A3
60081 A3
60084 A3
60086 A3
61016 B1
61035 B1
61038 B1
61216 B1
61218 B1
61237 B1
61259 B1
61411 B16
61412 B16
61414 B16
61415 B16
61425 B16
61427 B16
61428 B16
61429 B16
61431 B16
61432 B16
61442 B16
61446 B16
61447 B16
61471 B16
63348 Q6
63436 Q6
63449 Q6
64863 J39
64920 J39
64922 J39
64933 J39
64934 J39
64935 J39
64944 J39
80116 4MT[3]
80117 4MT[3]
80118 4MT[3]
80119 4MT[3]
80120 4MT[3]

1963 55H
42188 4MT[1]
43051 4MT[5]
43054 4MT[5]
44170 4F[2]
60074 A3
60084 A3
60086 A3
63348 Q6
63370 Q6
63417 Q6
63420 Q6
63424 Q6
63426 Q6
63436 Q6
63445 Q6
63449 Q6
73161 5MT
73162 5MT
73168 5MT
73169 5MT
80116 4MT[3]
80117 4MT[3]
80118 4MT[3]
80119 4MT[3]
80120 4MT[3]

1966 55H
42184 4MT[1]
42196 4MT[1]
42699 4MT[1]
43054 4MT[5]
63344 Q6
63387 Q6
63417 Q6
63420 Q6
63426 Q6

Lees Oldham

1948 26F
40012 3MT[1]
40056 3MT[1]
40057 3MT[1]
40059 3MT[1]
40060 3MT[1]
40061 3MT[1]
40062 3MT[1]
42550 4MT[3]
49509 7F[4]
49548 7F[4]
49593 7F[4]
49668 7F[4]
52248 3F[7]
52326 3F[7]
52378 3F[7]
52387 3F[7]
52389 3F[7]
52464 3F[7]
52545 3F[9]
52569 3F[9]
52586 3F[9]
52607 3F[9]

1951 26F
40012 3MT[1]
40014 3MT[1]
40056 3MT[1]
40057 3MT[1]
40059 3MT[1]
40060 3MT[1]
40061 3MT[1]
40062 3MT[1]
49509 7F[4]
49548 7F[4]
49590 7F[4]
49593 7F[4]
49668 7F[4]
52099 3F[7]
52248 3F[7]
52365 3F[7]
52378 3F[7]
52387 3F[7]
52389 3F[7]
52464 3F[7]
90112 WD[1]
90626 WD[1]
90720 WD[1]

1954 26F
40012 3MT[1]
40014 3MT[1]
40056 3MT[1]
40057 3MT[1]
40059 3MT[1]
40060 3MT[1]
40061 3MT[1]
40062 3MT[1]
42114 4MT[1]
42115 4MT[1]
42551 4MT[3]
49509 7F[4]
49536 7F[4]
49618 7F[4]
49662 7F[4]
49668 7F[4]
52099 3F[7]
52248 3F[7]
52365 3F[7]
52427 3F[7]
52569 3F[9]

1957 26E
41280 2MT[1]
42114 4MT[1]
42115 4MT[1]
42551 4MT[3]
42657 4MT[3]
49505 7F[4]
49509 7F[4]
49536 7F[4]
49578 7F[4]
49618 7F[4]
49662 7F[4]
49668 7F[4]
52248 3F[7]
52293 3F[7]
52388 3F[7]
52410 3F[7]
52427 3F[7]
84013 2MT[2]
84014 2MT[2]
84019 2MT[2]

1960 26E
42114 4MT[1]
42115 4MT[1]
52240 3F[7]
52248 3F[7]
52322 3F[7]
52410 3F[7]
52466 3F[7]
90123 WD[1]
90140 WD[1]
90141 WD[1]
90306 WD[1]
90402 WD[1]
90525 WD[1]
90671 WD[1]
90708 WD[1]
90718 WD[1]

1963 26E
42114 4MT[1]
42115 4MT[1]
42287 4MT[1]
46419 2MT[2]
46484 2MT[2]
46485 2MT[2]
46486 2MT[2]
90123 WD[1]
90194 WD[1]
90402 WD[1]
90525 WD[1]
90671 WD[1]
90708 WD[1]
90718 WD[1]

Leicester Central

1948 LEI
61086 B1
61110 B1
61111 B1
61122 B1
61123 B1
61128 B1
61130 B1
61185 B1
61186 B1
61187 B1
61188 B1
61192 B1
64361 J11
65007 J1
65009 J1
65015 J2
65018 J2
65019 J2
65021 J2
65022 J2
65023 J2
68491 J69

1951 38C
60048 A3
60049 A3
60052 A3
60054 A3
60102 A3
60103 A3
60104 A3
60107 A3
61088 B1
61092 B1
61106 B1
61108 B1
61141 B1
61185 B1
61186 B1
61187 B1
61188 B1
61298 B1
61299 B1
65015 J2
65495 J5
68981 J50

1954 38C
60044 A3
60049 A3
60052 A3
60054 A3
60059 A3
60102 A3
60104 A3
60107 A3
60820 V2
60863 V2
61088 B1
61092 B1
61106 B1
61141 B1
61185 B1
61187 B1
61298 B1
61299 B1
61369 B1
61380 B1
65485 J5
65495 J5
68839 J52

1957 38C
60039 A3
60049 A3
60059 A3
60102 A3
60104 A3
60106 A3
60107 A3
60111 A3
60863 V2
60878 V2
61008 B1
61063 B1
61269 B1
61298 B1
61299 B1
61369 B1
61380 B1
61381 B1
64375 J11
64453 J11
68839 J52

1960 15E
40165 3MT[2]
40167 3MT[2]
40182 3MT[2]
44932 5MT[3]
45116 5MT[3]
45223 5MT[3]
45234 5MT[3]
45450 5MT[3]
47442 3F[6]
60815 V2
60863 V2
60890 V2
61063 B1
61137 B1
61376 B1
61380 B1
61381 B1
73010 5MT
73045 5MT
73053 5MT
73066 5MT
73069 5MT

1963 15E
42437 4MT[3]
42453 4MT[3]
42556 4MT[3]
44690 5MT[3]
44821 5MT[3]
44830 5MT[3]
44847 5MT[3]
44848 5MT[3]
44984 5MT[3]
45223 5MT[3]
45277 5MT[3]
73066 5MT
73069 5MT
73156 5MT
73159 5MT

Leicester Midland

1948 15C
40116 3MT[2]
40120 3MT[2]
40141 3MT[2]
40145 3MT[2]
40146 3MT[2]
40165 3MT[2]
40182 3MT[2]
40400 2P[2]
40468 2P[2]
40485 2P[2]
40536 2P[2]
40538 2P[2]
40541 2P[2]
40542 2P[2]
40543 2P[2]
40549 2P[2]
40740 3P[1]
41008 4P[2]
41011 4P[2]
41031 4P[2]
41041 4P[2]
41088 4P[1]
41938 3P[2]
42330 4MT[2]
42334 4MT[2]
42792 5MT[1]
43183 3F[2]
43205 3F[3]
43232 3F[3]
43326 3F[3]
43333 3F[3]
43411 3F[3]
43653 3F[3]
43676 3F[3]
43710 3F[3]
43728 3F[3]
43748 3F[3]
43753 3F[3]
43790 3F[4]
43807 3F[4]
43829 3F[4]
43937 4F[1]
43965 4F[1]
43977 4F[1]
44034 4F[2]
44123 4F[2]
44231 4F[2]
44403 4F[2]
44423 4F[2]
47274 3F[6]
47441 3F[6]
47442 3F[6]
47533 3F[6]
47534 3F[6]
48132 8F
48211 8F
48397 8F
48398 8F
48399 8F
48531 8F
48619 8F
48668 8F
48709 8F
48728 8F
58051 1P[6]
58085 1P[6]
58142 2F[8]
58194 2F[9]
58242 2F[8]
58249 2F[9]
58298 2F[9]
58300 2F[9]

1951 15C
40145 3MT[2]
40146 3MT[2]
40173 3MT[2]
40182 3MT[2]
40485 2P[2]
40536 2P[2]
40538 2P[2]
40541 2P[2]
40542 2P[2]
40543 2P[2]
41006 4P[2]
41011 4P[2]
41041 4P[2]
41053 4P[1]
41075 4P[1]
41089 4P[1]
41095 4P[1]
41268 2MT[1]
41938 3P[2]
42137 4MT[1]
42181 4MT[1]
42182 4MT[1]
42183 4MT[1]
42330 4MT[2]
42331 4MT[2]
42792 5MT[1]
43045 4MT[5]
43183 3F[2]
43205 3F[3]
43232 3F[3]
43326 3F[3]
43333 3F[3]
43411 3F[3]
43454 3F[3]
43653 3F[3]
43676 3F[3]
43710 3F[3]
43728 3F[3]
43748 3F[3]
43753 3F[3]
43790 3F[4]
43806 3F[4]
43807 3F[4]
43829 3F[4]
43870 4F[1]
43876 4F[1]
43937 4F[1]
43977 4F[1]
44034 4F[2]
44160 4F[2]
44231 4F[2]
44287 4F[2]
44403 4F[2]
44423 4F[2]
44583 4F[2]
44663 5MT[3]
44806 5MT[3]
44812 5MT[3]
45088 5MT[3]
45263 5MT[3]
45280 5MT[3]
45342 5MT[3]
47274 3F[6]
47441 3F[6]
47442 3F[6]
47533 3F[6]
47534 3F[6]
48211 8F
48306 8F
48397 8F
48517 8F
48709 8F
48728 8F
58072 1P[6]
58073 1P[6]
58142 2F[8]
58194 2F[9]
58242 2F[8]
58249 2F[8]
58298 2F[9]
58300 2F[9]

1954 15C
40146 3MT[2]
40182 3MT[2]
40409 2P[2]
40485 2P[2]
40542 2P[2]
40543 2P[2]
41053 4P[1]
41059 4P[1]
41075 4P[1]
41089 4P[1]
41094 4P[1]
41095 4P[1]
41097 4P[1]
41198 4P[1]
41268 2MT[1]
41938 3P[2]
42137 4MT[1]
42182 4MT[1]
42183 4MT[1]
42330 4MT[2]
42331 4MT[2]
43018 4MT[5]
43045 4MT[5]
43205 3F[3]
43232 3F[3]
43326 3F[3]
43333 3F[3]
43411 3F[3]
43629 3F[3]
43676 3F[3]
43710 3F[3]
43728 3F[3]
43748 3F[3]
43753 3F[3]
43790 3F[4]
43799 3F[4]
43806 3F[4]
43829 3F[4]
43870 4F[1]
43876 4F[1]
43937 4F[1]
44034 4F[2]
44160 4F[2]
44231 4F[2]
44403 4F[2]
44423 4F[2]
44583 4F[2]
44663 5MT[3]
44806 5MT[3]
44812 5MT[3]
45221 5MT[3]
45263 5MT[3]
45280 5MT[3]
45342 5MT[3]
47227 3F[5]
47274 3F[6]
47441 3F[6]
47442 3F[6]
47533 3F[6]
47534 3F[6]
48211 8F
48306 8F
48517 8F
48619 8F
48728 8F
58142 2F[8]
58242 2F[8]
58298 2F[9]
58300 2F[9]
73003 5MT
73004 5MT
73046 5MT
73049 5MT

1957 15C
40182 3MT[2]
40452 2P[2]
40485 2P[2]
40543 2P[2]
40585 2P[3]
41078 4P[1]
41089 4P[1]
41095 4P[1]
41181 4P[1]
41268 2MT[1]
42137 4MT[1]
42160 4MT[1]
42182 4MT[1]
42183 4MT[1]
42330 4MT[2]
42331 4MT[2]
43018 4MT[5]
43045 4MT[5]
43205 3F[3]
43244 3F[3]
43326 3F[3]
43333 3F[3]
43411 3F[3]
43629 3F[3]
43710 3F[3]
43728 3F[3]
43753 3F[3]
43799 3F[4]
43806 3F[4]
43843 4F[1]
43870 4F[1]
43876 4F[1]
43930 4F[1]
43937 4F[1]
43995 4F[1]
44034 4F[2]
44175 4F[2]
44184 4F[2]
44231 4F[2]
44252 4F[2]
44403 4F[2]
44423 4F[2]
44663 5MT[3]
45221 5MT[3]
46402 2MT[2]
47227 3F[5]
47274 3F[6]
47441 3F[6]
47442 3F[6]
47533 3F[6]
47534 3F[6]
48007 8F
48010 8F
48061 8F
48107 8F
48133 8F
48149 8F
48211 8F
48266 8F
48306 8F
48507 8F
48517 8F
48619 8F
48728 8F
58142 2F[8]
58298 2F[9]
58305 2F[9]
73003 5MT
73004 5MT
73046 5MT
73073 5MT
73140 5MT
73141 5MT
73142 5MT
73143 5MT
73144 5MT
78028 2MT[1]
78029 2MT[1]

1960 15C
40402 2P[2]
40452 2P[2]
40543 2P[2]
42137 4MT[1]
42160 4MT[1]
42182 4MT[1]
42330 4MT[2]
42331 4MT[2]
42428 4MT[3]
43277 3F[3]
43326 3F[3]
43374 3F[3]
43405 3F[3]
43411 3F[3]
43793 3F[4]
43937 4F[1]
43969 4F[1]
44034 4F[2]
44231 4F[2]
44403 4F[2]
44667 5MT[3]
44690 5MT[3]
44811 5MT[3]
44815 5MT[3]
44843 5MT[3]
44848 5MT[3]
45264 5MT[3]
45333 5MT[3]
46454 2MT[2]
47231 3F[5]
47250 3F[5]
47257 3F[5]
47313 3F[6]
47441 3F[6]
47533 3F[6]
47534 3F[6]
47543 3F[6]
48007 8F
48010 8F
48061 8F
48107 8F
48133 8F
48149 8F
48211 8F
48266 8F
75042 4MT[1]
75057 4MT[1]
75058 4MT[1]
75059 4MT[1]
75060 4MT[1]
75061 4MT[1]
92101 9F
92102 9F
92103 9F
92104 9F
92109 9F
92119 9F
92121 9F
92128 9F

1963 15C
41225 2MT[1]
41228 2MT[1]
41279 2MT[1]
42087 4MT[1]
42174 4MT[1]
42184 4MT[1]
42279 4MT[1]
42333 4MT[2]
42334 4MT[2]
42338 4MT[2]
42355 4MT[2]
43969 4F[1]
43988 4F[1]
44013 4F[1]
44030 4F[2]
44034 4F[2]
44182 4F[2]
44231 4F[2]
44403 4F[2]
44414 4F[2]
44519 4F[2]
44530 4F[2]
44811 5MT[3]
44815 5MT[3]
44843 5MT[3]
45264 5MT[3]
45333 5MT[3]
84008 2MT[2]
92101 9F
92102 9F
92103 9F
92108 9F
92109 9F
92110 9F
92111 9F
92112 9F
92119 9F
92120 9F
92121 9F
92122 9F
92123 9F

1966 15A
48065 8F
48082 8F
48165 8F
48185 8F
48381 8F
48467 8F
48492 8F
48528 8F
48530 8F
48545 8F
48609 8F
48625 8F
48637 8F
48671 8F
48685 8F
78013 2MT[1]
78021 2MT[1]
78028 2MT[1]
78061 2MT[1]

Leyburn

1948 LEY
67346 G5

1951 51J sub
67346 G5

Lincoln

1948 LIN
61269 B1
61647 B17
61807 K3
61822 K3
61852 K3
61859 K3
61925 K3
61944 K3
61960 K3
61964 K3
61966 K3
61982 K3
62908 C4
62909 C4
62910 C4
62912 C4
62914 C4
62915 C4
62916 C4
62917 C4
62918 C4
64285 J11
64301 J11
64303 J11
64315 J11
64337 J11
64353 J11
64359 J11
64396 J11
64430 J11
64702 J39
64715 J39
64722 J39
64728 J39
64734 J39
64736 J39
64881 J39
64883 J39
64904 J39
64937 J39
64971 J39
67350 C12
67364 C12
67381 C12
68376 J66
68385 J66
68529 J67
68537 J69
68553 J69
68558 J69
68587 J69
68599 J69
68610 J67
68618 J69
69311 N5

1951 40A
61112 B1
61269 B1
61279 B1
61280 B1
61281 B1
61329 B1
61364 B1
61370 B1
61371 B1
61405 B1
61807 K3
61859 K3
61894 K3
61925 K3
61944 K3
61960 K3
61964 K3
61966 K3
64303 J11
64315 J11
64350 J11
64351 J11
64359 J11
64365 J11
64371 J11
64430 J11
64702 J39
64715 J39
64722 J39
64725 J39
64728 J39
64730 J39
64734 J39
64736 J39
64738 J39
64789 J39
64804 J39
64881 J39
64883 J39
64886 J39
64887 J39
64904 J39
64937 J39
64971 J39
68376 J66
68385 J66
68529 J67
68537 J69
68553 J69
68558 J69
68587 J69
68599 J69
68610 J67
68618 J69
69253 N5
69275 N5
69287 N5
69311 N5
69804 A5
69813 A5
69820 A5

1954 40A
41686 1F[1]
61171 B1
61177 B1
61202 B1
61258 B1
61279 B1
61281 B1
61371 B1
61405 B1
61742 K2

61743 K2
61746 K2
61748 K2
61761 K2
61765 K2
61767 K2
61778 K2
61807 K3
61859 K3
61894 K3
61925 K3
61944 K3
61960 K3
61964 K3
62660 D11
62666 D11
62667 D11
64303 J11
64315 J11
64350 J11
64351 J11
64359 J11
64365 J11
64371 J11
64381 J11
64405 J11
64430 J11
64702 J39
64715 J39
64722 J39
64728 J39
64736 J39
64804 J39
64887 J39
64937 J39
64959 J39
64977 J39
64984 J39
68512 J69
68528 J69
68537 J69
68541 J69
68558 J69
68587 J69
68599 J69
68605 J69
68618 J69
69253 N5
69275 N5
69804 A5
69813 A5
69828 A5

1957 40A

61085 B1
61143 B1
61202 B1
61248 B1
61258 B1
61279 B1
61405 B1
61746 K2
61751 K2
61759 K2
61778 K2
61802 K3
61804 K3
61807 K3
61828 K3
61848 K3
61859 K3
61889 K3
61894 K3
61919 K3
61925 K3
61944 K3
61960 K3
61964 K3
62660 D11
62663 D11
62666 D11
62667 D11
62670 D11
64303 J11
64315 J11
64351 J11
64359 J11
64365 J11
64371 J11
64381 J11
64430 J11
64702 J39
64712 J39
64714 J39
64722 J39
64728 J39
64734 J39
64755 J39
64804 J39
64881 J39
64887 J39
64937 J39
64959 J39
64960 J39
64977 J39
64984 J39
68528 J69
68537 J69
68541 J69
68553 J69
68558 J69
68587 J69
68599 J69
68605 J69
68618 J69
69813 A5
69820 A5

1960 40A

43060 4MT[5]
43095 4MT[5]
43104 4MT[5]
43154 4MT[5]
43158 4MT[5]
61009 B1
61202 B1
61258 B1
61284 B1
61405 B1
61409 B1
61802 K3
61806 K3
61807 K3
61828 K3
61848 K3
61859 K3
61889 K3
61894 K3
61919 K3
61944 K3
61960 K3
64219 J6
64278 J6
64318 J11
64346 J11
64362 J11
64726 J39
64741 J39
64890 J39
64896 J39
64937 J39
64959 J39
64960 J39
64966 J39
68501 J69
68554 J69
68560 J69
69808 A5
69820 A5
69821 A5

1963 40A

43086 4MT[5]
43095 4MT[5]
43104 4MT[5]
43105 4MT[5]
43149 4MT[5]
61006 B1
61026 B1
61042 B1
61058 B1
61089 B1
61107 B1
61113 B1
61223 B1
61258 B1
61348 B1
61384 B1
61409 B1
90223 WD[1]
90460 WD[1]
90577 WD[1]

Llandudno Junction

1948 7A

40002 3MT[1]
40087 3MT[2]
40123 3MT[2]
40134 3MT[2]
40137 3MT[2]
40209 3MT[2]
40396 2P[2]
40524 2P[2]
40658 2P[3]
40671 2P[3]
40675 2P[3]
40925 4P[1]
40936 4P[1]
41086 4P[1]
41093 4P[1]
41118 4P[1]
41119 4P[1]
41150 4P[1]
41156 4P[1]
41161 4P[1]
42954 5MT[2]
42971 5MT[2]
43877 4F[1]
44389 4F[2]
44860 5MT[3]
44911 5MT[3]
45112 5MT[3]
45253 5MT[3]
45301 5MT[3]
45303 5MT[3]
45346 5MT[3]
45370 5MT[3]
46681 1P[1]
46747 1P[1]
58364 2F[11]
58365 2F[11]
58392 2F[11]
7796 2F[14]

1951 7A

40083 3MT[2]
40095 3MT[2]
40123 3MT[2]
40130 3MT[2]
40133 3MT[2]
40207 3MT[2]
40208 3MT[2]
40925 4P[1]
41086 4P[1]
41093 4P[1]
41114 4P[1]
41119 4P[1]
41123 4P[1]
41124 4P[1]
41150 4P[1]
41161 4P[1]
41173 4P[1]
41232 2MT[1]
43877 4F[1]
44389 4F[2]
44738 5MT[3]
44739 5MT[3]
44740 5MT[3]
44741 5MT[3]
44742 5MT[3]
44808 5MT[3]
44941 5MT[3]
44971 5MT[3]
45292 5MT[3]
46604 1P[1]
47394 3F[6]
58364 2F[11]
58365 2F[11]
58398 2F[11]

1954 6G

40083 3MT[2]
40086 3MT[2]
40095 3MT[2]
40123 3MT[2]
40130 3MT[2]
40133 3MT[2]
40208 3MT[2]
40548 2P[2]
40559 2P[2]
40925 4P[1]
41086 4P[1]
41093 4P[1]
41111 4P[1]
41114 4P[1]
41119 4P[1]
41123 4P[1]
41124 4P[1]
41150 4P[1]
41232 2MT[1]
41236 2MT[1]
41237 2MT[1]
41238 2MT[1]
43877 4F[1]
44389 4F[2]
44738 5MT[3]
44739 5MT[3]
44740 5MT[3]
45331 5MT[3]
47394 3F[6]
75010 4MT[1]
75011 4MT[1]
75012 4MT[1]
75013 4MT[1]
75014 4MT[1]

1957 6G

40083 3MT[2]
40095 3MT[2]
40123 3MT[2]
40130 3MT[2]
40133 3MT[2]
40548 2P[2]
40925 4P[1]
41093 4P[1]
41111 4P[1]
41119 4P[1]
41236 2MT[1]
41238 2MT[1]
43981 4F[1]
44389 4F[2]
44525 4F[2]
44738 5MT[3]
44739 5MT[3]
44740 5MT[3]
44864 5MT[3]
44865 5MT[3]
45133 5MT[3]
45437 5MT[3]
47394 3F[6]
75010 4MT[1]
75011 4MT[1]
75012 4MT[1]
75013 4MT[1]
75014 4MT[1]
75050 4MT[1]

1960 6G

40095 3MT[2]
40123 3MT[2]
40128 3MT[2]
40130 3MT[2]
40133 3MT[2]
40635 2P[3]
41235 2MT[1]
41236 2MT[1]
41238 2MT[1]
44389 4F[2]
44525 4F[2]
44738 5MT[3]
44739 5MT[3]
44740 5MT[3]
44864 5MT[3]
44865 5MT[3]
45180 5MT[3]
45534 7P[1]
46138 7P[3]R
46150 7P[3]R
46156 7P[3]R
47558 3F[6]
47631 3F[6]
48046 8F
48253 8F
48667 8F
75010 4MT[1]
75011 4MT[1]
75012 4MT[1]

1963 6G

41244 2MT[1]
44389 4F[2]
44525 4F[2]
44661 5MT[3]
44686 5MT[3]
44687 5MT[3]
44738 5MT[3]
44739 5MT[3]
44740 5MT[3]
44760 5MT[3]
44780 5MT[3]
45149 5MT[3]
45197 5MT[3]
45289 5MT[3]
45311 5MT[3]
45348 5MT[3]
45369 5MT[3]
45525 7P[1]
45534 7P[1]
46120 7P[3]R
46144 7P[3]R
46148 7P[3]R
46155 7P[3]R
46165 7P[3]R
47361 3F[6]
47558 3F[6]
48246 8F
48771 8F
70014 7P6F
70015 7P6F
70016 7P6F
70033 7P6F
73038 5MT
84001 2MT[2]
84009 2MT[2]
84020 2MT[2]

1966 6G

45004 5MT[3]
45149 5MT[3]
45277 5MT[3]
45279 5MT[3]
45282 5MT[3]
45298 5MT[3]
45345 5MT[3]
47507 3F[6]
47673 3F[6]
75029 4MT[1]

Llanelly

1948 LLY

1907 1901
1957 1901
1967 1901
1991 1901
2002 1901
2012 1901
2019 1901
2027 2021
2042 2021
2059 2021
2081 2021
2083 2021
2085 2021
2098 2021
2126 2021
2137 2021
2150 2021
2162 BPGV[1]
2165 BPGV[1]
2167 BPGV[1]
2168 BPGV[1]
2176 BPGV[2]
2193 BPGV[3]
2197 BPGV[6]
2198 BPGV[7]
2707 655
2730 2721
2746 2721
2751 2721
3642 5700
3698 5700
3719 5700
3752 5700
3761 5700
3771 5700
3777 5700
4213 4200
4254 4200
4278 4200
4281 4200
4800 2800
4802 2800
4805 2800
4806 2800
4850 2884
4908 4900
5203 4200
5204 4200
5209 5205
5212 5205
5213 5205
5215 5205
5220 5205
5223 5205
5226 5205
5228 5205
5230 5205
5240 5205
5247 5205
5248 5205
5261 5205
5675 5600
5702 5700
5705 5700
5722 5700
5782 5700
5908 4900
7745 5700
7755 5700
7765 5700
7776 5700
7785 5700
8706 5700
8708 5700
8732 5700
8749 5700
8785 5700
9743 5700
9787 5700
9788 5700
90225 WD[1]
90283 WD[1]
90297 WD[1]
90624 WD[1]

1951 87F

1607 1600
1609 1600
1614 1600
1618 1600
1941 1901
1957 1901
1967 1901
1991 1901
2002 1901
2012 1901
2027 2021
2042 2021
2081 2021
2083 2021
2085 2021
2098 2021
2150 2021
2162 BPGV[1]
2165 BPGV[1]
2167 BPGV[1]
2168 BPGV[1]
2176 BPGV[2]
2193 BPGV[3]
2196 BPGV[5]
2197 BPGV[6]
2198 BPGV[7]
2803 2800
2824 2800
2850 2800
2855 2800
2872 2800
3642 5700
3661 5700
3698 5700
3719 5700
3752 5700
3761 5700
3771 5700
3777 5700
3811 2884
3851 2884
4213 4200
4254 4200
4278 4200
4281 4200
4283 4200
5203 4200
5204 4200
5209 5205
5213 5205
5215 5205
5223 5205
5230 5205
5240 5205
5247 5205
5248 5205
5261 5205
5335 4300
5378 4300
5675 5600
5702 5700
5705 5700
5722 5700
5782 5700
6688 5600
6810 6800
6824 6800
7228 7200
7745 5700
7755 5700
7765 5700
7776 5700
7785 5700
8424 9400
8706 5700
8708 5700
8732 5700
8738 5700
8749 5700
8785 5700
9743 5700
9787 5700
9788 5700
90315 WD[1]

1954 87F

1607 1600
1609 1600
1613 1600
1614 1600
1618 1600
1622 1600
1628 1600
1633 1600
1638 1600
1643 1600
1644 1600
2012 1901
2027 2021
2081 2021
2162 BPGV[1]
2165 BPGV[1]
2168 BPGV[1]
2176 BPGV[2]
2196 BPGV[5]
2198 BPGV[7]
2824 2800
3642 5700
3661 5700
3698 5700
3719 5700
3752 5700
3761 5700
3771 5700
3777 5700
3811 2884
3851 2884
4213 4200
4223 4200
4260 4200
4278 4200
4283 4200
5203 4200
5204 4200
5209 5205
5213 5205
5215 5205
5219 5205
5223 5205
5230 5205
5247 5205
5248 5205
5249 5205
5261 5205
5335 4300
5612 5600
5657 5600
5702 5700
5705 5700
5722 5700
5782 5700
6325 4300
6630 5600
6810 6800
6818 6800
6844 6800
6848 6800
7211 7200
7215 7200
7225 7200
7228 7200
7240 7200
7318 4300
7320 4300
7745 5700
7765 5700
7776 5700
7785 5700
8467 9400
8474 9400
8477 9400
8708 5700
8732 5700
8749 5700
8785 5700
9443 9400
9465 9400
9468 9400
9469 9400
9472 9400
9474 9400
9479 9400
9486 9400
9743 5700
9787 5700
9788 5700

1957 87F

1606 1600
1607 1600
1609 1600
1612 1600
1613 1600
1614 1600
1618 1600
1622 1600
1628 1600
1633 1600
1638 1600
1643 1600
1644 1600
1651 1600
1654 1600
1655 1600
1665 1600
1666 1600
2027 2021
2198 BPGV[7]
2808 2800
3661 5700
3698 5700
3719 5700
3752 5700
3761 5700
3771 5700
3777 5700
3811 2884
3851 2884
4213 4200
4223 4200
4260 4200
4278 4200
4941 4900
5203 4200
5204 4200
5209 5205
5213 5205
5215 5205
5219 5205
5223 5205
5230 5205
5247 5205
5248 5205
5249 5205
5261 5205
5335 4300
5392 4300
5612 5600
5702 5700
5703 5700
5705 5700
5722 5700
5782 5700
5902 4900
5961 4900
6389 4300
6396 4300
6810 6800
6818 6800
6843 6800
6844 6800
6909 4900
7203 7200
7211 7200
7215 7200
7225 7200
7228 7200
7240 7200
7307 4300
7314 4300
7320 4300
7718 5700
7745 5700
7765 5700
7776 5700
7785 5700
8467 9400
8474 9400
8477 9400
8708 5700
8732 5700
8749 5700
8785 5700
9465 9400
9472 9400
9474 9400
9479 9400
9486 9400
9743 5700
9787 5700
9788 5700

1960 87F

1606 1600
1607 1600
1609 1600
1611 1600
1614 1600
1615 1600
1622 1600
1633 1600
1638 1600
1643 1600
1651 1600
1654 1600
1655 1600
1665 1600
1666 1600
3642 5700
3719 5700
3761 5700
3771 5700
3777 5700
3811 2884
3834 2884
3851 2884
4272 4200
4286 4200
4292 4200
4676 5700
5204 4200
5209 5205
5213 5205
5219 5205
5223 5205
5240 5205
5247 5205
5248 5205
5262 5205
5332 4300
5370 4300
5612 5600
5656 5600
5702 5700
5902 4900
5903 4900
5909 4900
5961 4900
5984 4900
6310 4300
6345 4300
6653 5600
6810 6800
6818 6800
6843 6800
6844 6800
7228 7200
7232 7200
7235 7200
7307 4300
7314 4300
7321 4300
7718 5700
7745 5700
7765 5700
7776 5700
7785 5700
8467 9400
8474 9400
8477 9400
8706 5700
8708 5700
8736 5700
8749 5700
8785 5700
9465 9400
9485 9400
9652 5700
9743 5700
9788 5700
48309 8F
48328 8F
48330 8F
48400 8F
48409 8F
48419 8F
48438 8F
48452 8F
48461 8F
48463 8F
48470 8F
48524 8F
48525 8F
48706 8F
48707 8F
48730 8F
48732 8F
48735 8F
48760 8F
48761 8F

1963 87F

1607 1600
1611 1600
1643 1600
1651 1600
1655 1600
1665 1600
3678 5700
3701 5700
3719 5700
3761 5700
3771 5700
3777 5700
3781 5700
3811 2884
3851 2884
4076 4073
4225 4200
4292 4200
4295 4200
4298 4200
4676 5700
4927 4900
4928 4900
4988 4900
5080 4073
5087 4073
5201 4200
5209 5205
5241 5205
5242 5205
5247 5205
5262 5205
5602 5600
5612 5600
5692 5600
5903 4900
5976 4900
6347 4300
6349 4300
6357 4300
6395 4300
6652 5600
6653 5600
6804 6800
6815 6800
6818 6800
6837 6800
6843 6800
6844 6800
7028 4073
7200 7200
7211 7200
7232 7200
7235 7200
7237 7200
7239 7200
7244 7200
7307 4300
7312 4300
7315 4300
7319 4300
7804 7800
8103 8100
8474 9400
8749 5700
8785 5700
9408 9400
9429 9400
9485 9400
9621 5700
9637 5700
9652 5700
48307 8F
48309 8F
48328 8F
48400 8F
48409 8F
48419 8F
48434 8F
48438 8F
48444 8F
48452 8F
48461 8F
48470 8F
48524 8F
48525 8F
48706 8F
48707 8F
48730 8F
48732 8F
48735 8F
48760 8F
48761 8F
73023 5MT
73037 5MT

Llantrisant

1948 LTS

1205 AD[4]
1471 1400
3586 3500
3617 5700
3656 5700
3691 5700
3703 5700
4208 4200
4261 4200
4674 5700
5708 5700
5777 5700
7721 5700
9616 5700
9746 5700
9780 5700

1951 86D

1205 AD[4]
1421 1400
1471 1400
3612 5700
3617 5700
3644 5700
3656 5700
3691 5700
4208 4200
4261 4200
4620 5700
4674 5700
5241 5205
5708 5700
5788 5700
8739 5700
9746 5700
9780 5700

1954 86D

1471 1400
3612 5700
3617 5700
3644 5700
3656 5700
3776 5700
4208 4200
4261 4200
4620 5700
4637 5700
4674 5700
5708 5700
5788 5700
6439 6400
8739 5700
9746 5700
9780 5700

1957 86D

1471 1400
3612 5700
3617 5700
3644 5700
3656 5700
3680 5700
3776 5700
4208 4200
4261 4200
4268 4200
4620 5700
4637 5700
4662 5700
4674 5700
5708 5700
5788 5700
9780 5700

1960 86D

3612 5700
3617 5700
3644 5700
3656 5700
3663 5700
3680 5700
4252 4200
4267 4200
4268 4200
4273 4200
4620 5700
4637 5700
4662 5700
4674 5700
6600 5600
9780 5700

1963 88G

3612 5700
3617 5700
3644 5700
3661 5700
3680 5700
4268 4200
4620 5700
4662 5700
4674 5700
5248 5205
6639 5600
6670 5600
9778 5700

Longsight

1948 9A

40051 3MT[1]
40071 3MT[2]
40106 3MT[2]
40107 3MT[2]
40108 3MT[2]
40138 3MT[2]
40531 2P[2]
40539 2P[2]
40674 2P[3]
41113 4P[1]
41122 4P[1]
41159 4P[1]
41166 4P[1]
41168 4P[1]
42322 4MT[2]
42350 4MT[2]
42351 4MT[2]
42395 4MT[2]
42396 4MT[2]
42397 4MT[2]
42398 4MT[2]
42399 4MT[2]
42401 4MT[2]
42402 4MT[2]
42461 4MT[3]
42467 4MT[3]
42478 4MT[3]
42575 4MT[3]
42580 4MT[3]
42599 4MT[3]
42608 4MT[3]
42775 5MT[1]
42776 5MT[1]
42778 5MT[1]
42813 5MT[1]
42848 5MT[1]
42849 5MT[1]
42852 5MT[1]
42854 5MT[1]
42858 5MT[1]
42886 5MT[1]
42887 5MT[1]
42889 5MT[1]
42923 5MT[1]
42924 5MT[1]
42925 5MT[1]
42930 5MT[1]
42935 5MT[1]
42936 5MT[1]
42937 5MT[1]
43275 3F[3]
43457 3F[3]
43717 3F[3]
44078 4F[2]
44303 4F[2]
44308 4F[2]
44357 4F[2]
44870 5MT[3]
44871 5MT[3]
44937 5MT[3]
44938 5MT[3]
44969 5MT[3]
44970 5MT[3]
45294 5MT[3]
45530 7P[1]
45552 6P5F[2]
45556 6P5F[2]
45593 6P5F[2]
45631 6P5F[2]
45633 6P5F[2]
45638 6P5F[2]
45680 6P5F[2]
45703 6P5F[2]
45723 6P5F[2]
45740 6P5F[2]
46114 7P[3]R
46120 7P[3]R
46121 7P[3]R
46122 7P[3]R
46129 7P[3]R
46131 7P[3]R
46145 7P[3]R
46149 7P[3]R
46150 7P[3]R
46160 7P[3]R
46169 7P[3]R
47267 3F[6]
47341 3F[6]
47343 3F[6]
47345 3F[6]
47347 3F[6]
47369 3F[6]
47394 3F[6]
47400 3F[6]
47528 3F[6]
47673 3F[6]
49002 7F[2]
49054 6F[2]
49171 6F[2]
49183 6F[2]
49227 7F[2]
49284 7F[2]
49285 6F[2]
49298 7F[2]
49343 7F[2]
49363 7F[2]

1951 9A

40077 3MT[2]
40107 3MT[2]
40136 3MT[2]
40539 2P[2]
40674 2P[3]
40693 2P[3]
41113 4P[1]
41159 4P[1]
41168 4P[1]
41905 2P[4]
41906 2P[4]
41907 2P[4]
42322 4MT[2]
42350 4MT[2]
42351 4MT[2]
42397 4MT[2]
42398 4MT[2]
42399 4MT[2]
42427 4MT[3]
42430 4MT[3]
42461 4MT[3]
42467 4MT[3]
42478 4MT[3]
42542 4MT[3]
42575 4MT[3]
42580 4MT[3]
42594 4MT[3]
42599 4MT[3]
42608 4MT[3]
42772 5MT[1]
42775 5MT[1]
42776 5MT[1]
42778 5MT[1]
42788 5MT[1]
42848 5MT[1]
42854 5MT[1]
42858 5MT[1]
42886 5MT[1]
42887 5MT[1]
42889 5MT[1]
42923 5MT[1]
42924 5MT[1]
42925 5MT[1]
42930 5MT[1]
42935 5MT[1]
42936 5MT[1]
42937 5MT[1]
42938 5MT[1]
42978 5MT[2]
42979 5MT[2]
43275 3F[3]
43457 3F[3]
43717 3F[3]
44271 4F[2]
44303 4F[2]
44349 4F[2]
44357 4F[2]
44748 5MT[3]
44749 5MT[3]
44750 5MT[3]
44751 5MT[3]
44752 5MT[3]
44759 5MT[3]
44760 5MT[3]
44834 5MT[3]
44837 5MT[3]
44838 5MT[3]
44935 5MT[3]
44937 5MT[3]
45387 5MT[3]
45500 6P5F[1]
45501 6P5F[1]
45520 6P5F[1]
45530 7P[1]
45534 7P[1]
45536 7P[1]
45539 6P5F[1]
45540 7P[1]
45556 6P5F[2]
45593 6P5F[2]
45603 6P5F[2]
45617 6P5F[2]
45631 6P5F[2]
45632 6P5F[2]
45633 6P5F[2]
45638 6P5F[2]
45655 6P5F[2]
45680 6P5F[2]
45688 6P5F[2]
45709 6P5F[2]
45723 6P5F[2]
45734 6P5F[2]
45740 6P5F[2]
45742 6P5F[2]
46114 7P[3]R
46115 7P[3]R
46120 7P[3]R
46122 7P[3]R
46129 7P[3]R
46131 7P[3]R
46143 7P[3]R
46145 7P[3]R
46149 7P[3]R
46150 7P[3]R
46160 7P[3]R
46167 7P[3]R
46169 7P[3]R
47267 3F[6]
47341 3F[6]
47343 3F[6]
47345 3F[6]
47347 3F[6]
47369 3F[6]
47395 3F[6]
47400 3F[6]
47528 3F[6]
47673 3F[6]
48389 8F
48425 8F
48428 8F
48429 8F
48500 8F
48501 8F
48516 8F
48633 8F
49428 7F[3]
49439 7F[3]

1954 9A

40077 3MT[2]
40107 3MT[2]
40136 3MT[2]
40405 2P[3]
40482 2P[2]
40539 2P[2]
40674 2P[3]
40693 2P[3]
41159 4P[1]
41168 4P[1]
41905 2P[4]
41906 2P[4]
41907 2P[4]
42322 4MT[2]
42350 4MT[2]
42351 4MT[2]
42391 4MT[2]
42397 4MT[2]
42398 4MT[2]
42399 4MT[2]
42427 4MT[3]
42430 4MT[3]
42467 4MT[3]

42478 4MT[3]
42542 4MT[3]
42575 4MT[3]
42580 4MT[3]
42594 4MT[3]
42599 4MT[3]
42608 4MT[3]
42772 5MT[1]
42776 5MT[1]
42778 5MT[1]
42848 5MT[1]
42858 5MT[1]
42886 5MT[1]
42887 5MT[1]
42889 5MT[1]
42923 5MT[1]
42924 5MT[1]
42925 5MT[1]
42930 5MT[1]
42932 5MT[1]
42935 5MT[1]
42936 5MT[1]
42937 5MT[1]
42938 5MT[1]
42960 5MT[2]
43275 3F[3]
43457 3F[3]
43717 3F[3]
44069 4F[2]
44349 4F[2]
44357 4F[2]
44686 5MT[3]
44687 5MT[3]
44741 5MT[3]
44742 5MT[3]
44748 5MT[3]
44749 5MT[3]
44750 5MT[3]
44751 5MT[3]
44752 5MT[3]
44760 5MT[3]
44937 5MT[3]
44941 5MT[3]
45109 5MT[3]
45327 5MT[3]
45500 6P5F[1]
45501 6P5F[1]
45520 6P5F[1]
45530 7P[1]
45536 7P[1]
45539 6P5F[1]
45540 7P[1]
45553 6P5F[2]
45555 6P5F[2]
45556 6P5F[2]
45578 6P5F[2]
45587 6P5F[2]
45595 6P5F[2]
45624 6P5F[2]
45631 6P5F[2]
45632 6P5F[2]
45638 6P5F[2]
45644 6P5F[2]
45680 6P5F[2]
45689 6P5F[2]
45709 6P5F[2]
45723 6P5F[2]
46111 7P[3]R
46114 7P[3]R
46115 7P[3]R
46120 7P[3]R
46122 7P[3]R
46130 7P[3]R
46131 7P[3]R
46143 7P[3]R
46160 7P[3]R
46161 7P[3]R
46169 7P[3]R
47267 3F[6]
47341 3F[6]
47343 3F[6]
47345 3F[6]
47347 3F[6]
47369 3F[6]
47395 3F[6]
47400 3F[6]
47528 3F[6]
47673 3F[6]
48389 8F
48425 8F
48428 8F
48500 8F
48501 8F
48516 8F
48633 8F
48731 8F
48744 8F
49428 7F[3]
49439 7F[3]
70031 7P6F
70032 7P6F
70033 7P6F
70044 7P6F

1957 9A
40077 3MT[2]
40084 3MT[2]
40093 3MT[2]
40107 3MT[2]
40136 3MT[2]
40433 2P[2]
40482 2P[2]
40674 2P[3]
40693 2P[3]
41159 4P[1]
41168 4P[1]
41900 2P[4]
41907 2P[4]
41908 2P[4]
42304 4MT[2]
42319 4MT[2]
42322 4MT[2]
42350 4MT[2]
42351 4MT[2]
42381 4MT[2]
42397 4MT[2]
42398 4MT[2]
42399 4MT[2]
42430 4MT[3]
42478 4MT[3]
42594 4MT[3]
42772 5MT[1]
42848 5MT[1]
42858 5MT[1]
42886 5MT[1]
42887 5MT[1]
42889 5MT[1]
42923 5MT[1]
42924 5MT[1]
42925 5MT[1]
42930 5MT[1]
42935 5MT[1]
42936 5MT[1]
42938 5MT[1]
42960 5MT[2]
43325 3F[3]
43457 3F[3]
43717 3F[3]
44069 4F[2]
44349 4F[2]
44357 4F[2]
44686 5MT[3]
44687 5MT[3]
44741 5MT[3]
44742 5MT[3]
44748 5MT[3]
44749 5MT[3]
44750 5MT[3]
44751 5MT[3]
44752 5MT[3]
44760 5MT[3]
44840 5MT[3]
44935 5MT[3]
44937 5MT[3]
44938 5MT[3]
44941 5MT[3]
45109 5MT[3]
45146 5MT[3]
45299 5MT[3]
45501 6P5F[1]
45505 6P5F[1]
45519 6P5F[1]
45520 6P5F[1]
45530 7P[1]
45536 7P[1]
45540 7P[1]
45578 6P5F[2]
45587 6P5F[2]
45595 6P5F[2]
45624 6P5F[2]
45629 6P5F[2]
45631 6P5F[2]
45632 6P5F[2]
45638 6P5F[2]
45643 6P5F[2]
45644 6P5F[2]
45655 6P5F[2]
45680 6P5F[2]
45689 6P5F[2]
45723 6P5F[2]
46111 7P[3]R
46115 7P[3]R
46122 7P[3]R
46131 7P[3]R
46135 7P[3]R
46137 7P[3]R
46140 7P[3]R
46143 7P[3]R
46153 7P[3]R
46158 7P[3]R
46160 7P[3]R
46169 7P[3]R
47267 3F[6]
47341 3F[6]
47343 3F[6]
47345 3F[6]
47347 3F[6]
47369 3F[6]
47395 3F[6]
47400 3F[6]
47528 3F[6]
47673 3F[6]
48275 8F
48389 8F
48425 8F
48428 8F
48500 8F
48516 8F
48633 8F
48680 8F
48744 8F
49428 7F[3]
49439 7F[3]
70031 7P6F
70032 7P6F
70033 7P6F
70043 7P6F
70044 7P6F

1960 9A
40077 3MT[2]
40093 3MT[2]
40107 3MT[2]
40122 3MT[2]
41217 2MT[1]
41221 2MT[1]
42304 4MT[2]
42369 4MT[2]
42381 4MT[2]
42398 4MT[2]
42399 4MT[2]
42416 4MT[2]
42772 5MT[1]
42786 5MT[1]
42858 5MT[1]
42887 5MT[1]
42889 5MT[1]
42923 5MT[1]
42924 5MT[1]
42925 5MT[1]
42930 5MT[1]
42934 5MT[1]
42936 5MT[1]
42938 5MT[1]
44686 5MT[3]
44687 5MT[3]
44741 5MT[3]
44742 5MT[3]
44746 5MT[3]
44747 5MT[3]
44748 5MT[3]
44749 5MT[3]
44750 5MT[3]
44751 5MT[3]
44752 5MT[3]
44937 5MT[3]
45037 5MT[3]
45046 5MT[3]
45111 5MT[3]
45339 5MT[3]
45426 5MT[3]
45505 6P5F[1]
45520 6P5F[1]
45530 7P[1]
45536 7P[1]
45543 6P5F[1]
45587 6P5F[2]
45631 6P5F[2]
45638 6P5F[2]
45644 6P5F[2]
45671 6P5F[2]
45680 6P5F[2]
46106 7P[3]R
46111 7P[3]R
46115 7P[3]R
46131 7P[3]R
46137 7P[3]R
46151 7P[3]R
46166 7P[3]R
47341 3F[6]
47395 3F[6]
47400 3F[6]
47528 3F[6]
47673 3F[6]
48165 8F
48275 8F
48389 8F
48428 8F
48500 8F
48680 8F
48744 8F
70031 7P6F
70032 7P6F
70033 7P6F
70043 7P6F

1963 9A
42357 4MT[2]
42425 4MT[3]
44747 5MT[3]
44748 5MT[3]
44916 5MT[3]
45256 5MT[3]
45385 5MT[3]
46115 7P[3]R
46129 7P[3]R
46149 7P[3]R
48310 8F

Lostock Hall

1948 24C
40190 3MT[2]
40191 3MT[2]
40192 3MT[2]
40194 3MT[2]
40198 3MT[2]
40199 3MT[2]
42434 4MT[3]
42435 4MT[3]
42436 4MT[3]
42437 4MT[3]
42480 4MT[3]
42481 4MT[3]
42556 4MT[3]
42661 4MT[3]
48526 8F
48527 8F
48528 8F
48529 8F
48719 8F
48720 8F
49502 7F[4]
49503 7F[4]
49523 7F[4]
49524 7F[4]
49534 7F[4]
49585 7F[4]
49611 7F[4]
49612 7F[4]
49614 7F[4]
49615 7F[4]
49616 7F[4]
49617 7F[4]
49640 7F[4]
49649 7F[4]
51345 2F[2]
51423 2F[2]
51526 2F[2]
52160 3F[7]
52171 3F[7]
52244 3F[7]
52296 3F[7]
52317 3F[7]
52334 3F[7]
52336 3F[7]
52368 3F[7]
52399 3F[7]
52460 3F[7]
52467 3F[7]
52522 3F[7]
52541 3F[9]

1951 24C
42158 4MT[1]
42296 4MT[1]
42298 4MT[1]
42434 4MT[3]
42435 4MT[3]
42436 4MT[3]
42480 4MT[3]
42481 4MT[3]
42491 4MT[3]
42492 4MT[3]
42556 4MT[3]
50764 2P[8]
50781 2P[8]
50852 2P[8]
51345 2F[2]
51526 2F[2]
52160 3F[7]
52171 3F[7]
52216 3F[7]
52220 3F[7]
52238 3F[7]
52272 3F[7]
52296 3F[7]
52317 3F[7]
52336 3F[7]
52368 3F[7]
52399 3F[7]
52456 3F[7]
52522 3F[7]
52523 3F[7]
52524 3F[7]
52527 3F[7]
90295 WD[1]
90320 WD[1]
90328 WD[1]
90331 WD[1]
90335 WD[1]
90367 WD[1]
90398 WD[1]
90541 WD[1]
90595 WD[1]
90640 WD[1]
90658 WD[1]
90681 WD[1]
90689 WD[1]

1954 24C
42158 4MT[1]
42296 4MT[1]
42298 4MT[1]
42434 4MT[3]
42435 4MT[3]
42436 4MT[3]
42480 4MT[3]
42481 4MT[3]
42491 4MT[3]
42492 4MT[3]
42556 4MT[3]
50712 2P[8]
50725 2P[8]
51345 2F[2]
51423 2F[2]
51526 2F[2]
52174 3F[7]
52182 3F[7]
52203 3F[7]
52317 3F[7]
52368 3F[7]
52456 3F[7]
52458 3F[7]
52523 3F[7]
52524 3F[7]
90258 WD[1]
90295 WD[1]
90320 WD[1]
90328 WD[1]
90331 WD[1]
90335 WD[1]
90367 WD[1]
90398 WD[1]
90541 WD[1]
90595 WD[1]
90640 WD[1]
90658 WD[1]
90681 WD[1]
90689 WD[1]
90720 WD[1]

1957 24C
42158 4MT[1]
42296 4MT[1]
42298 4MT[1]
42434 4MT[3]
42435 4MT[3]
42436 4MT[3]
42476 4MT[3]
42480 4MT[3]
42481 4MT[3]
42491 4MT[3]
42492 4MT[3]
42556 4MT[3]
51423 2F[2]
51526 2F[2]
52182 3F[7]
52203 3F[7]
52290 3F[7]
52368 3F[7]
52445 3F[7]
52456 3F[7]
52458 3F[7]
90258 WD[1]
90277 WD[1]
90295 WD[1]
90320 WD[1]
90328 WD[1]
90331 WD[1]
90335 WD[1]
90367 WD[1]
90398 WD[1]
90541 WD[1]
90595 WD[1]
90640 WD[1]
90658 WD[1]
90681 WD[1]
90689 WD[1]
90720 WD[1]

1960 24C
40183 3MT[2]
40192 3MT[2]
42158 4MT[1]
42187 4MT[1]
42286 4MT[1]
42298 4MT[1]
42434 4MT[3]
42436 4MT[3]
42476 4MT[3]
42480 4MT[3]
42481 4MT[3]
42634 4MT[3]
52182 3F[7]
52290 3F[7]
52429 3F[7]
52445 3F[7]
52456 3F[7]
90258 WD[1]
90266 WD[1]
90277 WD[1]
90295 WD[1]
90331 WD[1]
90335 WD[1]
90367 WD[1]
90398 WD[1]
90413 WD[1]
90541 WD[1]
90556 WD[1]
90584 WD[1]
90658 WD[1]
90675 WD[1]
90681 WD[1]
90689 WD[1]
90720 WD[1]

1963 24C
42147 4MT[1]
42154 4MT[1]
42158 4MT[1]
42286 4MT[1]
42296 4MT[1]
42436 4MT[3]
42480 4MT[3]
42481 4MT[3]
46449 2MT[2]
46452 2MT[2]
46501 2MT[2]
47002 0F[3]
47008 0F[3]
47293 3F[6]
47360 3F[6]
47386 3F[6]
47413 3F[6]
47472 3F[6]
90258 WD[1]
90277 WD[1]
90541 WD[1]
90675 WD[1]
90713 WD[1]
90720 WD[1]

1966 10D
42096 4MT[1]
42105 4MT[1]
42187 4MT[1]
42251 4MT[1]
42297 4MT[1]
42436 4MT[3]
42546 4MT[3]
42625 4MT[3]
44915 5MT[3]
44958 5MT[3]
45197 5MT[3]
45226 5MT[3]
45402 5MT[3]
45450 5MT[3]
47293 3F[6]
47336 3F[6]
47472 3F[6]
48002 8F
48141 8F
48302 8F
48307 8F
48400 8F
48438 8F
48470 8F
48618 8F
48679 8F
48707 8F
48730 8F
78002 2MT[1]
78022 2MT[1]
78037 2MT[1]
78040 2MT[1]
78041 2MT[1]
78057 2MT[1]

Louth

1948 LTH
62143 D3
64328 J11
64439 J11
67352 C12
67359 C12
67374 C12
67379 C12
67389 C12
67398 C12
69306 N5

1951 40C
64320 J11
64328 J11
67352 C12
67364 C12
67379 C12
67381 C12
67383 C12
67384 C12
67398 C12
69280 N5
69306 N5

1954 40C
64320 J11
64328 J11
67364 C12
67379 C12
67383 C12
67384 C12
67398 C12
69309 N5
69322 N5
69327 N5

1957 40C
64328 J11

Low Moor

1948 25F
41186 4P[1]
41189 4P[1]
42187 4MT[1]
42188 4MT[1]
42189 4MT[1]
42296 4MT[1]
42297 4MT[1]
42298 4MT[1]
42299 4MT[1]
42406 4MT[2]
42407 4MT[2]
42409 4MT[2]
42644 4MT[3]
42726 5MT[1]
42727 5MT[1]
42728 5MT[1]
42732 5MT[1]
42828 5MT[1]
42843 5MT[1]
42865 5MT[1]
44912 5MT[3]
45062 5MT[3]
45201 5MT[3]
45207 5MT[3]
45208 5MT[3]
45209 5MT[3]
45210 5MT[3]
45211 5MT[3]
45221 5MT[3]
50665 2P[8]
50715 2P[8]
50762 2P[8]
50788 2P[8]
50840 2P[8]
50855 2P[8]
50886 2P[8]
50909 3P[3]
50952 3P[3]
52104 3F[7]
52127 3F[7]
52217 3F[7]
52237 3F[7]
52255 3F[7]
52403 3F[7]
52410 3F[7]
52422 3F[7]
52427 3F[7]

1951 25F
42107 4MT[1]
42108 4MT[1]
42109 4MT[1]
42110 4MT[1]
42111 4MT[1]
42112 4MT[1]
42113 4MT[1]
42114 4MT[1]
42115 4MT[1]
42116 4MT[1]
42188 4MT[1]
42189 4MT[1]
42732 5MT[1]
44693 5MT[3]
44694 5MT[3]
44695 5MT[3]
44912 5MT[3]
44946 5MT[3]
44951 5MT[3]
44990 5MT[3]
45201 5MT[3]
45207 5MT[3]
45208 5MT[3]
45210 5MT[3]
45219 5MT[3]
50909 3P[3]
51404 2F[2]
52092 3F[7]
52104 3F[7]
52237 3F[7]
52309 3F[7]
52410 3F[7]
52411 3F[7]
52461 3F[7]
52590 3F[9]
52857 7F[5]

1954 25F
42107 4MT[1]
42108 4MT[1]
42109 4MT[1]
42116 4MT[1]
42188 4MT[1]
42189 4MT[1]
44693 5MT[3]
44694 5MT[3]
44695 5MT[3]
44912 5MT[3]
44946 5MT[3]
44951 5MT[3]
44990 5MT[3]
45207 5MT[3]
45208 5MT[3]
45210 5MT[3]
45219 5MT[3]
50764 2P[8]
50807 2P[8]
50818 2P[8]
50831 2P[8]
50869 2P[8]
51404 2F[2]
52104 3F[7]
52166 3F[7]
52343 3F[7]
52351 3F[7]
52355 3F[7]
52461 3F[7]
52515 3F[7]
52521 3F[7]
52561 3F[9]
84010 2MT[2]
84011 2MT[2]
84012 2MT[2]
84013 2MT[2]
84014 2MT[2]
84015 2MT[2]

1957 56F
41250 2MT[1]
41262 2MT[1]
41263 2MT[1]
41264 2MT[1]
42107 4MT[1]
42108 4MT[1]
42109 4MT[1]
42116 4MT[1]
42188 4MT[1]
42189 4MT[1]
42622 4MT[3]
42649 4MT[3]
42650 4MT[3]
44693 5MT[3]
44694 5MT[3]
44695 5MT[3]
44912 5MT[3]
44946 5MT[3]
44951 5MT[3]
44990 5MT[3]
45207 5MT[3]
45208 5MT[3]
45219 5MT[3]
50757 2P[8]
50831 2P[8]
50855 2P[8]
51404 2F[2]
52120 3F[7]
52235 3F[7]
52355 3F[7]
52515 3F[7]
52521 3F[7]
90126 WD[1]
90397 WD[1]
90406 WD[1]

1960 56F
41250 2MT[1]
41253 2MT[1]
41262 2MT[1]
41263 2MT[1]
41274 2MT[1]
42084 4MT[1]
42107 4MT[1]
42108 4MT[1]
42109 4MT[1]
42116 4MT[1]
42188 4MT[1]
42189 4MT[1]
42311 4MT[2]
44062 4F[2]
44693 5MT[3]
44694 5MT[3]
44695 5MT[3]
44912 5MT[3]
44946 5MT[3]
44951 5MT[3]
44990 5MT[3]
45207 5MT[3]
45208 5MT[3]
45219 5MT[3]
46413 2MT[2]
46435 2MT[2]
47255 3F[5]
47405 3F[6]
47446 3F[6]
47635 3F[6]
48080 8F
48394 8F
48702 8F
52413 3F[7]
52461 3F[7]
61274 B1
61383 B1
61387 B1
64170 J6
64203 J6
64226 J6
64791 J39
64801 J39
64817 J39
64872 J39
64886 J39
64903 J39
64907 J39
64919 J39
68895 J50
68908 J50
68922 J50
68923 J50
68932 J50
68933 J50
68943 J50
68944 J50
68948 J50
68969 J50
90068 WD[1]
90200 WD[1]
90236 WD[1]
90333 WD[1]
90711 WD[1]

1963 56F
41250 2MT[1]
41264 2MT[1]
41274 2MT[1]
42084 4MT[1]
42107 4MT[1]
42108 4MT[1]
42109 4MT[1]
42116 4MT[1]
42151 4MT[1]
42285 4MT[1]
42311 4MT[2]
42622 4MT[3]
43072 4MT[5]
44693 5MT[3]
44694 5MT[3]
44695 5MT[3]
44946 5MT[3]
44951 5MT[3]
44990 5MT[3]
45207 5MT[3]
45208 5MT[3]
45565 6P5F[2]
45694 6P5F[2]
46435 2MT[2]
61189 B1
61383 B1
61386 B1
82026 3MT[2]
90054 WD[1]
90310 WD[1]
90351 WD[1]
90397 WD[1]
90698 WD[1]
90711 WD[1]
90721 WD[1]
90723 WD[1]

1966 56F
42055 4MT[1]
42073 4MT[1]
42074 4MT[1]
42107 4MT[1]
42116 4MT[1]
42142 4MT[1]
42177 4MT[1]
42664 4MT[3]
45565 6P5F[2]
61014 B1
61115 B1
61189 B1
61309 B1
61386 B1
61388 B1
90711 WD[1]
90723 WD[1]
90731 WD[1]

Lower Darwen

1948 24D
40677 2P[3]
40684 2P[3]
40690 2P[3]
42483 4MT[3]
42484 4MT[3]
42485 4MT[3]
42559 4MT[3]
43897 4F[1]
44225 4F[2]
44240 4F[2]
44291 4F[2]
44398 4F[2]
44483 4F[2]
48436 8F
48472 8F
48721 8F
50735 2P[8]
50781 2P[8]
50893 3P[3]
50945 3P[3]
50950 3P[3]
50951 3P[3]
50953 3P[3]
51336 2F[2]
51467 2F[2]
51499 2F[2]
51506 2F[2]
52253 3F[7]
52260 3F[7]
52289 3F[7]
52363 3F[7]
52431 3F[7]
52444 3F[7]
52526 3F[7]

1951 24D
40588 2P[3]
42147 4MT[1]
42154 4MT[1]
42439 4MT[3]
42483 4MT[3]
42484 4MT[3]
42485 4MT[3]
42490 4MT[3]
42558 4MT[3]
42559 4MT[3]
43897 4F[1]
44105 4F[2]
44220 4F[2]
44225 4F[2]
44240 4F[2]
44291 4F[2]
44398 4F[2]
44460 4F[2]
44479 4F[2]
44483 4F[2]
51415 2F[2]
51499 2F[2]
51506 2F[2]
52203 3F[7]
52260 3F[7]
52262 3F[7]
52268 3F[7]
52289 3F[7]
52363 3F[7]
52388 3F[7]
52431 3F[7]
52441 3F[7]
52444 3F[7]
52445 3F[7]
52460 3F[7]
52526 3F[7]
52529 3F[7]
52579 3F[9]
90135 WD[1]
90266 WD[1]
90357 WD[1]
90374 WD[1]

1954 24D
40681 2P[3]
42147 4MT[1]
42154 4MT[1]
42483 4MT[3]
42484 4MT[3]
42485 4MT[3]
42490 4MT[3]
42558 4MT[3]
42559 4MT[3]
42718 5MT[1]
42729 5MT[1]
42796 5MT[1]
42821 5MT[1]
43897 4F[1]
44398 4F[2]
44460 4F[2]
44479 4F[2]
44483 4F[2]
50746 2P[8]
51415 2F[2]
51499 2F[2]
51506 2F[2]
52160 3F[7]
52194 3F[7]
52216 3F[7]
52220 3F[7]
52260 3F[7]
52272 3F[7]
52300 3F[7]
52388 3F[7]
52399 3F[7]
52431 3F[7]
52445 3F[7]
52447 3F[7]
52522 3F[7]
52526 3F[7]
90266 WD[1]
90357 WD[1]
90374 WD[1]

1957 24D
42147 4MT[1]
42154 4MT[1]
42483 4MT[3]
42484 4MT[3]
42485 4MT[3]
42490 4MT[3]
42558 4MT[3]
42559 4MT[3]
42718 5MT[1]
42729 5MT[1]
42796 5MT[1]
42821 5MT[1]
43897 4F[1]
44398 4F[2]
44460 4F[2]
44479 4F[2]
44483 4F[2]
51415 2F[2]
51498 2F[2]
51506 2F[2]
52160 3F[7]
52216 3F[7]
52260 3F[7]
52413 3F[7]
52431 3F[7]
52526 3F[7]
90357 WD[1]

1960 24D
40120 3MT[2]
40162 3MT[2]
42147 4MT[1]
42154 4MT[1]
42483 4MT[3]
42485 4MT[3]
42551 4MT[3]
42558 4MT[3]
42559 4MT[3]
42718 5MT[1]
42722 5MT[1]
42729 5MT[1]
42796 5MT[1]
42821 5MT[1]
43897 4F[1]
44398 4F[2]
44460 4F[2]
44479 4F[2]
44483 4F[2]
76080 4MT[2]
76081 4MT[2]
76082 4MT[2]
76083 4MT[2]
76084 4MT[2]
84011 2MT[2]
84012 2MT[2]

1963 24D
42728 5MT[1]
42729 5MT[1]
42732 5MT[1]
42796 5MT[1]
43976 4F[1]
44119 4F[2]
44398 4F[2]
44460 4F[2]
44479 4F[2]
76080 4MT[2]
76081 4MT[2]
76082 4MT[2]
76083 4MT[2]
76084 4MT[2]
90297 WD[1]
90316 WD[1]
90375 WD[1]
90556 WD[1]
90592 WD[1]

1966 10H
43019 4MT[5]
43041 4MT[5]
43046 4MT[5]
43118 4MT[5]
43119 4MT[5]
48423 8F
48441 8F
48684 8F
48691 8F

Lowestoft

1948 LOW
61926 K3
61949 K3
61958 K3
61959 K3
61981 K3
62593 D16
65351 J15
65352 J15
65353 J15
65355 J15
65389 J15
65400 J15
65462 J15
67114 F3
67119 F3
67126 F3
67141 F3
67158 F4
67163 F4
67165 F4
67166 F4
67167 F4
67177 F4
68602 J69
68611 J67
68640 J68

1951 32C
61926 K3
61949 K3
61958 K3
61959 K3
61973 K3
62556 D16
65355 J15
65389 J15
65401 J15
65433 J15
65435 J15
65462 J15
65478 J15
65566 J17
65570 J17
67127 F3
67158 F4
67163 F4
67165 F4
67166 F4
67167 F4
67174 F4
67177 F4
67182 F4
67184 F4
67186 F4
67201 F5
67216 F5
67231 F6
67794 L1
68168 Y3
68173 Y3
68611 J67
68640 J68

1954 32C
61926 K3
61949 K3
61953 K3
61958 K3
61959 K3
61973 K3
61989 K3
64724 J39
65389 J15
65433 J15
65435 J15
65462 J15
65478 J15
65507 J17
65558 J17
65559 J17
67174 F4
67187 F4
67190 F5
67195 F5
67201 F5
67204 F5
67206 F5
67207 F5
67214 F5
67216 F5
67223 F6
67226 F6
67231 F6
67232 F6
67233 F6
67234 F6
67235 F6
67704 L1
67714 L1
67717 L1
68611 J67
68640 J68

1957 32C
61926 K3
61949 K3
61958 K3
61959 K3
61973 K3
62797 E4
65460 J15
65462 J15
65478 J15
65507 J17
65558 J17
65559 J17
67229 F6
67231 F6
67704 L1
67770 L1
68565 J69
68664 J68
69679 N7
69824 A5
69826 A5
69829 A5

1960 32C
61160 B1
61659 B17
61660 B17
61664 B17
61670 B17
61672 B17
61958 K3
61959 K3
62604 D16
65460 J15
65462 J15
65558 J17
65567 J17
65588 J17
67707 L1
67710 L1
67738 L1
68656 J68

Lowestoft Engineer's Dept.

1948
68130 Y1
68131 Y1
68177 Y3
68178 Y3

1951
68130 Y1
68131 Y1
68177 Y3
68178 Y3

1954
37 Y1
38 Y3
39 Y1
40 Y3
41 Y3

1957
38 Y3
39 Y1
40 Y3
41 Y3

1960
39 Y1

40 Y3
41 Y3

1963
39 Y1
40 Y3
41 Y3

Lydney

1948 LYD
1409 1400
1441 1400
1456 1400
2025 2021
2034 2021
2039 2021
2043 2021
2044 2021
2045 2021
2080 2021
2091 2021
2102 2021
2114 2021
2121 2021
2131 2021
2132 2021
2144 2021
2153 2021
2155 2021
2160 2021
2350 2301
2515 2301

Macclesfield

1948 9C
42305 4MT[2]
42319 4MT[2]
42323 4MT[2]
42349 4MT[2]
42355 4MT[2]
42356 4MT[2]
42357 4MT[2]
42369 4MT[2]
42382 4MT[2]

1951 9C
42319 4MT[2]
42355 4MT[2]
42356 4MT[2]
42357 4MT[2]
42360 4MT[2]
42362 4MT[2]
42363 4MT[2]
42369 4MT[2]
42381 4MT[2]
42382 4MT[2]
42386 4MT[2]

1954 9C
42318 4MT[2]
42319 4MT[2]
42355 4MT[2]
42356 4MT[2]
42357 4MT[2]
42362 4MT[2]
42363 4MT[2]
42369 4MT[2]
42381 4MT[2]
42382 4MT[2]
42386 4MT[2]

1957 9C
42318 4MT[2]
42355 4MT[2]
42356 4MT[2]
42357 4MT[2]
42362 4MT[2]
42363 4MT[2]
42369 4MT[2]
42382 4MT[2]
42386 4MT[2]

1960 9C
42318 4MT[2]
42347 4MT[2]
42348 4MT[2]
42355 4MT[2]
42363 4MT[2]
42382 4MT[2]

Machynlleth

1948 MCH
864 Cam[1]
894 Cam[1]
1465 1400
1474 1400
1965 1901
2151 2021
2204 2251
2219 2251
2323 2301
2356 2301
2464 2301
2572 2301
3200 2251
3201 2251
3207 2251
4501 4500
4511 4500
4512 4500
4513 4500
4549 4500
4555 4500
4560 4500
4571 4500
4575 4575
5507 4575
5517 4575
5524 4575
5541 4575
9000 9000
9004 9000
9005 9000
9009 9000
9012 9000
9014 9000
9027 9000
9054 3252
9072 3252
9091 3252

1951 89C
864 Cam[1]
892 Cam[1]
894 Cam[1]
1465 1400
1474 1400
1603 1600
2200 2251
2201 2251
2204 2251
2206 2251
2219 2251
2223 2251
2260 2251
2283 2251
2292 2251
2298 2251
2323 2301
3200 2251
3201 2251
3202 2251
3207 2251
4501 4500
4512 4500
4530 4500
4549 4500
4555 4500
4560 4500
4571 4500
4575 4575
4581 4575
5507 4575
5517 4575
5524 4575
5541 4575
5560 4575
5570 4575
7406 7400
7417 7400
7802 7800
7803 7800
9000 9000
9002 9000
9004 9000
9005 9000
9009 9000
9012 9000
9013 9000
9014 9000
9017 9000
9021 9000
9024 9000
9025 9000
9027 9000

1954 89C
849 Cam[1]
1465 1400
1603 1600
2200 2251
2204 2251
2233 2251
2260 2251
2298 2251
3201 2251
3202 2251
3207 2251
4549 4500
4555 4500
4560 4500
4575 4575
4599 4575
5395 4300
5507 4575
5517 4575
5541 4575
5556 4575
5570 4575
6371 4300
6383 4300
7402 7400
7406 7400
7417 7400
7802 7800
7803 7800
9000 9000
9002 9000
9004 9000
9005 9000
9009 9000
9012 9000
9013 9000
9014 9000
9017 9000
9018 9000
9021 9000
9024 9000
9025 9000
9027 9000
78000 2MT[1]
78001 2MT[1]
78002 2MT[1]
78003 2MT[1]
78004 2MT[1]
78005 2MT[1]
78006 2MT[1]
78007 2MT[1]

1957 89C
1636 1600
2200 2251
2202 2251
2204 2251
2217 2251
2232 2251
2233 2251
2237 2251
2244 2251
2255 2251
2260 2251
2264 2251
2267 2251
2271 2251
2285 2251
2286 2251
2289 2251
2298 2251
4377 4300
4549 4500
4555 4500
4560 4500
4575 4575
4599 4575
5507 4575
5517 4575
5541 4575
5556 4575
5570 4575
5801 5800
5803 5800
5809 5800
6335 4300
6371 4300
6378 4300
7406 7400
7417 7400
7802 7800
7803 7800
7806 7800
9004 9000
9008 9000
9009 9000
9012 9000
9013 9000
9014 9000
9015 9000
9016 9000
9017 9000
9018 9000
9020 9000
9021 9000
9022 9000
9024 9000
9025 9000
78000 2MT[1]
78002 2MT[1]
78003 2MT[1]
78005 2MT[1]
78006 2MT[1]
78007 2MT[1]

1960 89C
1449 1400
2200 2251
2201 2251
2202 2251
2204 2251
2217 2251
2232 2251
2233 2251
2244 2251
2255 2251
2260 2251
2264 2251
2275 2251
2286 2251
2294 2251
2298 2251
4549 4500
4575 4575
5540 4575
5541 4575
5553 4575
5565 4575
5570 4575
6335 4300
6371 4300
6378 4300
6392 4300
7406 7400
7417 7400
7434 7400
7802 7800
7803 7800
7814 7800
7815 7800
7823 7800
9015 9000
9017 9000
75020 4MT[1]
75026 4MT[1]
78000 2MT[1]
78002 2MT[1]
78003 2MT[1]
78005 2MT[1]
78006 2MT[1]
78007 2MT[1]

1963 89C
2236 2251
6368 4300
6378 4300
7814 7800
7818 7800
75002 4MT[1]
75003 4MT[1]
75004 4MT[1]
75006 4MT[1]
75009 4MT[1]
75020 4MT[1]
75021 4MT[1]
75023 4MT[1]
75024 4MT[1]
75026 4MT[1]
75027 4MT[1]
75029 4MT[1]
78000 2MT[1]
78002 2MT[1]
78003 2MT[1]
78007 2MT[1]
80101 4MT[3]
80105 4MT[3]
82000 3MT[2]
82003 3MT[2]
82005 3MT[2]
82006 3MT[2]
82009 3MT[2]
82020 3MT[2]
82021 3MT[2]
82031 3MT[2]
82032 3MT[2]
82033 3MT[2]
82034 3MT[2]

1966 6F
46446 2MT[2]
46521 2MT[2]
75002 4MT[1]
75004 4MT[1]
75013 4MT[1]
75055 4MT[1]

Maespoeth

1948 MCH sub
3 Cor
4 Cor

Malton

1948 MAL
65607 J24
65615 J24
65628 J24
65636 J24
65642 J24
67155 F4
67273 G5
67275 G5
67276 G5
67284 G5
67330 G5
67349 G5
68147 Y1
68150 Y1

1951 50F
65640 J24
65644 J24
65656 J25
65671 J25
65708 J25
67155 F4
67275 G5
67330 G5
67332 G5
67349 G5
68147 Y1
68150 Y1

1954 50F
64867 J39
64928 J39
65648 J25
65656 J25
65671 J25
65685 J25
65714 J25
65723 J25
67332 G5
67349 G5
68150 Y1
69877 A8
76021 4MT[2]

1957 50F
64867 J39
64928 J39
64938 J39
64947 J39
65827 J27
65844 J27
65848 J27
65849 J27
67315 G5
67319 G5
67325 G5
67346 G5
69861 A8

1960 50F
41247 2MT[1]
41251 2MT[1]
41265 2MT[1]
64867 J39
64928 J39
65844 J27
65849 J27
65885 J27
65888 J27
69861 A8
69886 A8
82027 3MT[2]
82029 3MT[2]

1963 50F
41251 2MT[1]
46413 2MT[2]
46473 2MT[2]
65844 J27
65849 J27
65888 J27
82027 3MT[2]
82028 3MT[2]
82029 3MT[2]

Manningham

1948 20E
40391 2P[2]
40489 2P[2]
40562 2P[2]
40567 2P[3]
41004 4P[2]
41043 4P[2]
41067 4P[1]
42377 4MT[2]
42380 4MT[2]
42682 4MT[1]
42762 5MT[1]
42791 5MT[1]
43351 3F[3]
43783 3F[4]
44400 4F[2]
47255 3F[5]
47419 3F[6]
50630 2P[8]
50631 2P[8]
50633 2P[8]
50634 2P[8]
50636 2P[8]
50681 2P[8]
50714 2P[8]
55130 2P[12]
55169 2P[13]
55192 2P[13]
55227 2P[13]
58036 1P[5]
58081 1P[6]
58155 2F[8]
58171 2F[8]
58212 2F[9]
58292 2F[9]

1951 20E
40069 3MT[1]
40455 2P[2]
40489 2P[2]
40562 2P[2]
40567 2P[3]
41004 4P[2]
41067 4P[1]
41069 4P[1]
41080 4P[1]
41197 4P[1]
41265 2MT[1]
41266 2MT[1]
42052 4MT[1]
42229 4MT[1]
42377 4MT[2]
42380 4MT[2]
42682 4MT[1]
42762 5MT[1]
43178 3F[2]
43351 3F[3]
43742 3F[3]
43770 3F[4]
44216 4F[2]
44400 4F[2]
44570 4F[2]
46452 2MT[2]
46453 2MT[2]
47222 3F[5]
47255 3F[5]
47419 3F[6]
50622 2P[8]
50623 2P[8]
50633 2P[8]
50634 2P[8]
50636 2P[8]
50671 2P[8]
50681 2P[8]
50689 2P[8]
50714 2P[8]
50795 2P[8]
50842 2P[8]
58069 1P[6]
58070 1P[6]

1954 20E
40074 3MT[2]
40090 3MT[2]
40112 3MT[2]
40117 3MT[2]
40147 3MT[2]
40149 3MT[2]
40155 3MT[2]
40178 3MT[2]
40455 2P[2]
40562 2P[2]
41061 4P[1]
41067 4P[1]
41080 4P[1]
41265 2MT[1]
41266 2MT[1]
42052 4MT[1]
42377 4MT[2]
42380 4MT[2]
42682 4MT[1]
42762 5MT[1]
43178 3F[2]
43686 3F[3]
43742 3F[3]
43770 3F[4]
44216 4F[2]
44400 4F[2]
46453 2MT[2]
47222 3F[5]
47255 3F[5]
47419 3F[6]
50636 2P[8]
50686 2P[8]
50795 2P[8]

1957 55F
40074 3MT[2]
40112 3MT[2]
40114 3MT[2]
40117 3MT[2]
40139 3MT[2]
40147 3MT[2]
40155 3MT[2]
40178 3MT[2]
41063 4P[1]
41075 4P[1]
41247 2MT[1]
41265 2MT[1]
41266 2MT[1]
41273 2MT[1]
42052 4MT[1]
42138 4MT[1]
42139 4MT[1]
42141 4MT[1]
42380 4MT[2]
42762 5MT[1]
42770 5MT[1]
43553 3F[3]
43586 3F[3]
43742 3F[3]
43784 3F[4]
43944 4F[1]
44216 4F[2]
44400 4F[2]
47222 3F[5]
47255 3F[5]
47419 3F[6]
50636 2P[8]
50795 2P[8]

1960 55F
41063 4P[1]
41257 2MT[1]
41266 2MT[1]
41273 2MT[1]
41325 2MT[1]
41326 2MT[1]
42072 4MT[1]
42093 4MT[1]
42139 4MT[1]
42141 4MT[1]
42702 5MT[1]
42762 5MT[1]
42770 5MT[1]
43016 4MT[5]
43030 4MT[5]
43178 3F[2]
43586 3F[3]
43784 3F[4]
43944 4F[1]
44055 4F[2]
44216 4F[2]
44400 4F[2]
47419 3F[6]

1963 55F
41253 2MT[1]
41273 2MT[1]
42072 4MT[1]
42093 4MT[1]
42139 4MT[1]
42141 4MT[1]
42189 4MT[1]
42774 5MT[1]
42789 5MT[1]
43016 4MT[5]
43030 4MT[5]
43074 4MT[5]
44039 4F[2]
44097 4F[2]
44400 4F[2]

1966 55F
42072 4MT[1]
42085 4MT[1]
42093 4MT[1]
42138 4MT[1]
42152 4MT[1]
42189 4MT[1]
43014 4MT[5]
43016 4MT[5]
43030 4MT[5]
43051 4MT[5]
43074 4MT[5]

Mansfield

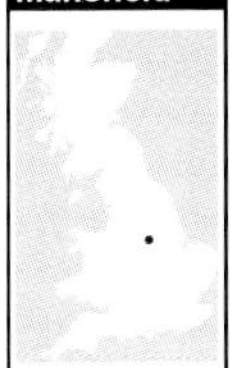

1948 16D
40424 2P[2]
40503 2P[2]
40630 2P[3]
41885 1F[1]
41940 3P[2]
41943 3P[2]
41947 3P[2]
41961 3P[2]
43193 3F[3]
43239 3F[3]
43341 3F[3]
43431 3F[3]
43522 3F[3]
43529 3F[3]
43558 3F[3]
43587 3F[3]
43634 3F[3]
43727 3F[3]
43762 3F[3]
43765 3F[4]
43802 3F[4]
43874 4F[1]
43983 4F[1]
43997 4F[1]
44004 4F[1]
44394 4F[2]
48035 8F
48088 8F
48621 8F
48622 8F
48643 8F
48701 8F
58054 1P[6]
58058 1P[6]
58133 2F[8]
58135 2F[8]

1951 16D
40424 2P[2]
40454 2P[2]
41885 1F[1]
41940 3P[2]
41943 3P[2]
41947 3P[2]
41958 3P[2]
41961 3P[2]
41962 3P[2]
43239 3F[3]
43251 3F[3]
43327 3F[3]
43431 3F[3]
43522 3F[3]
43529 3F[3]
43634 3F[3]
43727 3F[3]
43874 4F[1]
43983 4F[1]
43997 4F[1]
44004 4F[1]
44394 4F[2]
44415 4F[2]
44416 4F[2]
48088 8F
48119 8F
48156 8F
48277 8F
48621 8F
48643 8F
48701 8F

1954 16D
40079 3MT[2]
40168 3MT[2]
40175 3MT[2]
41885 1F[1]
41940 3P[2]
41943 3P[2]
41947 3P[2]
43239 3F[3]
43431 3F[3]
43494 3F[3]
43522 3F[3]
43529 3F[3]
43634 3F[3]
43711 3F[3]
43727 3F[3]
43983 4F[1]
44230 4F[2]
44394 4F[2]
44415 4F[2]
44416 4F[2]
46501 2MT[2]
48088 8F
48119 8F
48156 8F
48272 8F
48277 8F
48405 8F
48442 8F
48621 8F
48643 8F
48701 8F

1957 16C
40079 3MT[2]
40096 3MT[2]
40146 3MT[2]
40168 3MT[2]
40175 3MT[2]
40184 3MT[2]
41844 1F[1]
43239 3F[3]
43431 3F[3]
43522 3F[3]
43634 3F[3]
43727 3F[3]
44394 4F[2]
44415 4F[2]
44416 4F[2]
46501 2MT[2]
48001 8F
48024 8F
48088 8F
48119 8F
48156 8F
48272 8F
48277 8F
48405 8F
48442 8F
48447 8F
48541 8F
48621 8F
48643 8F
48701 8F

1960 16C
40050 3MT[1]
40054 3MT[1]
40073 3MT[2]
40079 3MT[2]
40115 3MT[2]
40146 3MT[2]
40156 3MT[2]
40168 3MT[2]
40175 3MT[2]
40184 3MT[2]
41712 1F[1]
41844 1F[1]
43972 4F[1]
44252 4F[2]
44415 4F[2]
44416 4F[2]
44441 4F[2]
46501 2MT[2]
48001 8F
48088 8F
48119 8F
48156 8F
48219 8F
48272 8F
48277 8F
48282 8F
48405 8F
48442 8F
48541 8F
48621 8F
48643 8F
48701 8F

March

1948 MAR
61630 B17
61635 B17
61636 B17
61646 B17
61648 B17
61656 B17
61660 B17
61661 B17
61672 B17
61805 K3
61812 K3
61815 K3
61817 K3
61820 K3
61830 K3
61831 K3
61835 K3
61846 K3
61847 K3
61849 K3
61860 K3
61866 K3
61873 K3
61886 K3
61887 K3
61888 K3
61889 K3
61893 K3
61914 K3
61919 K3
61940 K3
61948 K3
62539 D16
62542 D16
62547 D16
62548 D16
62579 D16
62584 D16
62589 D16
62603 D16
62605 D16
63003 O7
63013 O7
63015 O7
63018 O7
63023 O7
63024 O7
63028 O7
63029 O7
63035 O7
63037 O7
63042 O7
63053 O7
63083 O7
63085 O7
63087 O7
63096 O7
63101 O7
63104 O7
63107 O7
63110 O7
63112 O7
63122 O7
63133 O7
63150 O7
63152 O7
63155 O7
63156 O7
63159 O7
63185 O7
63187 O7
63653 O4
63658 O4
63701 O4
63792 O1
63867 O1
63947 O2
63948 O2
63949 O2
63950 O2
63951 O2
63952 O2
63953 O2
63954 O2
63955 O2
63956 O2
63957 O2
63958 O2
63959 O2
63960 O2
63961 O2
63962 O2
64640 J19
64641 J19
64643 J19
64644 J19
64646 J19
64647 J19
64648 J19
64650 J19
64651 J19
64652 J19
64653 J19
64654 J19
64655 J19
64656 J19
64657 J19
64659 J19
64660 J19
64661 J19
64662 J19
64663 J19
64664 J19
64665 J19
64666 J19
64667 J19
64669 J19
64671 J19
64672 J19
64673 J19
64674 J19
64688 J20
64689 J20
64690 J20
64692 J20
64693 J20
64694 J20
64697 J20
64698 J20
64699 J20
65372 J15
65419 J15
65433 J15
65439 J15
65512 J17
65513 J17
65515 J17
65518 J17
65524 J17
65525 J17
65538 J17
65547 J17
65554 J17
65555 J17
65556 J17
65568 J17
65571 J17
65573 J17
65576 J17
65577 J17
65583 J17
65584 J17
65587 J17
68383 J66
68654 J68
68664 J68
69902 S1
69903 S1
90131 WD[1]
90158 WD[1]
90169 WD[1]
90175 WD[1]
90221 WD[1]
90224 WD[1]
90239 WD[1]
90251 WD[1]
90259 WD[1]
90279 WD[1]
90287 WD[1]
90288 WD[1]
90294 WD[1]
90299 WD[1]
90302 WD[1]
90304 WD[1]
90384 WD[1]
90386 WD[1]
90392 WD[1]
90393 WD[1]
90522 WD[1]
90540 WD[1]
90554 WD[1]
90580 WD[1]
90582 WD[1]
90601 WD[1]
90602 WD[1]
90608 WD[1]
90660 WD[1]
90668 WD[1]
90732 WD[1]

1951 31B
61626 B17
61630 B17
61633 B17
61635 B17
61641 B17
61646 B17
61656 B17
61660 B17
61666 B17
61672 B17
61844 K3
61846 K3
61847 K3
61860 K3
61866 K3
61869 K3
61873 K3
61886 K3
61887 K3
61888 K3
61889 K3
61893 K3
61895 K3
61938 K3
61940 K3
61946 K3
61948 K3
61961 K3
62011 K1
62012 K1
62013 K1
62014 K1
62015 K1
62016 K1
62017 K1
62018 K1
62019 K1
62020 K1
62031 K1
62032 K1
62033 K1
62034 K1
62035 K1
62036 K1
62037 K1
62038 K1
62039 K1
62040 K1
62051 K1
62052 K1
62053 K1
62054 K1
62055 K1
62066 K1
62067 K1
62068 K1
62069 K1
62070 K1
62529 D16
62539 D16
62542 D16
62547 D16
62548 D16
62579 D16
62589 D16
62605 D16
63701 O4
63704 O4
63730 O4
63897 O4
64641 J19
64643 J19
64647 J19
64648 J19
64655 J19
64656 J19
64659 J19
64661 J19
64666 J19
64667 J19
64669 J19
64671 J19
64688 J20
64689 J20
64692 J20
64693 J20
64694 J20
64697 J20
64698 J20
64699 J20
65366 J15
65439 J15
65505 J17
65515 J17
65518 J17
65521 J17
65554 J17
65555 J17
65556 J17
65571 J17
65576 J17
65577 J17
65583 J17
65584 J17
67153 F4
67187 F4
68654 J68
68664 J68
69926 Q1
90003 WD[1]
90005 WD[1]
90013 WD[1]
90015 WD[1]
90018 WD[1]
90023 WD[1]
90024 WD[1]
90032 WD[1]
90035 WD[1]
90037 WD[1]
90042 WD[1]
90053 WD[1]
90055 WD[1]
90060 WD[1]
90064 WD[1]
90066 WD[1]
90070 WD[1]
90075 WD[1]
90083 WD[1]
90087 WD[1]
90111 WD[1]
90118 WD[1]
90119 WD[1]
90131 WD[1]
90175 WD[1]
90221 WD[1]
90224 WD[1]
90275 WD[1]
90294 WD[1]
90302 WD[1]
90383 WD[1]
90384 WD[1]
90392 WD[1]
90393 WD[1]
90422 WD[1]
90425 WD[1]
90433 WD[1]
90442 WD[1]
90453 WD[1]
90473 WD[1]
90474 WD[1]
90476 WD[1]
90480 WD[1]
90502 WD[1]
90506 WD[1]
90510 WD[1]
90519 WD[1]
90540 WD[1]
90580 WD[1]
90582 WD[1]
90601 WD[1]
90602 WD[1]
90608 WD[1]
90653 WD[1]
90660 WD[1]
90668 WD[1]
90709 WD[1]

1954 31B
60803 V2
60830 V2
60858 V2
60899 V2
60938 V2
60948 V2
61619 B17
61620 B17
61626 B17
61633 B17
61635 B17
61638 B17
61641 B17
61643 B17
61658 B17
61804 K3
61811 K3
61816 K3
61822 K3
61824 K3
61826 K3
61835 K3
61841 K3
61842 K3
61843 K3
61845 K3
61850 K3
61853 K3
61860 K3
61861 K3
61864 K3
61866 K3
61867 K3
61868 K3
61873 K3
61886 K3
61887 K3
61888 K3
61889 K3
61890 K3
61895 K3
61907 K3
61915 K3
61929 K3
61938 K3
61940 K3
61943 K3
61946 K3
61947 K3
61948 K3
61954 K3
61961 K3
61967 K3
61972 K3
61976 K3
61978 K3
61979 K3
61982 K3
62013 K1
62014 K1
62015 K1
62016 K1
62017 K1
62018 K1
62019 K1
62020 K1
62032 K1
62033 K1
62035 K1
62036 K1
62037 K1

62038 K1
62039 K1
62040 K1
62051 K1
62053 K1
62054 K1
62055 K1
62066 K1
62067 K1
62068 K1
62069 K1
62070 K1
62526 D16
62529 D16
62539 D16
62542 D16
62548 D16
62572 D16
62588 D16
62589 D16
62605 D16
64640 J19
64641 J19
64642 J19
64643 J19
64648 J19
64655 J19
64661 J19
64668 J19
64669 J19
64671 J19
64672 J19
64678 J20
64679 J20
64684 J20
64687 J20
64692 J20
64693 J20
64694 J20
64695 J20
64697 J20
64698 J20
64699 J20
65356 J15
65422 J15
65503 J17
65515 J17
65541 J17
65554 J17
65556 J17
65571 J17
65572 J17
65576 J17
65577 J17
65584 J17
68603 J69
90018 WD[1]
90023 WD[1]
90293 WD[1]
90443 WD[1]
90480 WD[1]
90519 WD[1]
90522 WD[1]
90550 WD[1]
90569 WD[1]
90601 WD[1]
90602 WD[1]
90608 WD[1]
90668 WD[1]
90732 WD[1]

1957 31B
60803 V2
60830 V2
60858 V2
60899 V2
60938 V2
60948 V2
61619 B17
61620 B17
61621 B17
61626 B17
61627 B17
61633 B17
61635 B17
61638 B17
61641 B17
61643 B17
61645 B17
61657 B17
61811 K3
61816 K3
61822 K3
61826 K3
61835 K3
61845 K3
61860 K3
61861 K3
61886 K3
61890 K3
61915 K3
61929 K3
61946 K3
61948 K3
61972 K3
61976 K3
62013 K1
62014 K1
62015 K1
62016 K1
62017 K1
62018 K1
62019 K1
62020 K1
62032 K1
62033 K1
62035 K1
62036 K1
62037 K1
62038 K1
62039 K1
62040 K1
62051 K1
62053 K1
62054 K1
62055 K1
62066 K1
62067 K1
62068 K1
62069 K1
62070 K1
62526 D16
62529 D16
62548 D16
62562 D16
62572 D16
62589 D16
62608 D16
64640 J19
64641 J19
64642 J19
64643 J19
64648 J19
64655 J19
64661 J19
64668 J19
64669 J19
64671 J19
64672 J19
64678 J20
64679 J20
64684 J20
64687 J20
64690 J20
64691 J20
64692 J20
64697 J20
64698 J20
64699 J20
65356 J15
65474 J15
65503 J17
65515 J17
65538 J17
65554 J17
65556 J17
65571 J17
65572 J17
65576 J17
65577 J17
65583 J17
68603 J69
90018 WD[1]
90023 WD[1]
90042 WD[1]
90060 WD[1]
90079 WD[1]
90083 WD[1]
90108 WD[1]
90119 WD[1]
90129 WD[1]
90144 WD[1]
90150 WD[1]
90203 WD[1]
90208 WD[1]
90255 WD[1]
90293 WD[1]
90298 WD[1]
90305 WD[1]
90340 WD[1]
90453 WD[1]
90469 WD[1]
90477 WD[1]
90480 WD[1]
90484 WD[1]
90491 WD[1]
90498 WD[1]
90522 WD[1]
90537 WD[1]
90538 WD[1]
90550 WD[1]
90567 WD[1]
90569 WD[1]
90602 WD[1]
90608 WD[1]
90636 WD[1]
90696 WD[1]
90732 WD[1]
92010 9F
92013 9F
92014 9F
92043 9F
92044 9F

1960 31B
41969 3P[2]
60803 V2
60830 V2
60858 V2
60938 V2
60948 V2
61004 B1
61005 B1
61006 B1
61042 B1
61052 B1
61056 B1
61058 B1
61059 B1
61252 B1
61253 B1
61254 B1
61300 B1
61363 B1
61641 B17
61653 B17
61657 B17
61810 K3
61811 K3
61822 K3
61831 K3
61835 K3
61840 K3
61845 K3
61851 K3
61860 K3
61861 K3
61886 K3
61890 K3
61915 K3
61929 K3
61937 K3
61946 K3
61948 K3
61954 K3
61972 K3
61976 K3
62016 K1
62017 K1
62018 K1
62020 K1
62032 K1
62033 K1
62035 K1
62037 K1
62038 K1
62039 K1
62040 K1
62051 K1
62054 K1
62055 K1
62066 K1
62067 K1
62068 K1
62069 K1
63571 O1
63579 O1
63596 O1
63619 O1
63630 O1
63646 O1
63650 O1
63652 O1
63670 O1
63678 O1
63687 O1
63725 O1
63746 O1
63780 O1
63786 O1
63796 O1
63803 O1
63868 O1
63872 O1
63879 O1
63887 O1
63890 O1
64642 J19
64669 J19
64671 J19
64687 J20
64690 J20
64691 J20
64692 J20
64697 J20
64699 J20
64764 J39
64769 J39
64770 J39
64771 J39
64772 J39
64774 J39
64779 J39
64782 J39
64800 J39
64826 J39
64891 J39
65420 J15
65474 J15
65554 J17
65576 J17
65583 J17
90001 WD[1]
90018 WD[1]
90042 WD[1]
90079 WD[1]
90150 WD[1]
90191 WD[1]
90208 WD[1]
90279 WD[1]
90293 WD[1]
90305 WD[1]
90340 WD[1]
90477 WD[1]
90484 WD[1]
90522 WD[1]
90683 WD[1]
90709 WD[1]

1963 31B
61059 B1
61095 B1
61119 B1
61156 B1
61204 B1
61205 B1
61233 B1
61252 B1
61300 B1
61323 B1
61375 B1
61378 B1
63687 O1
63725 O1
63746 O1
63780 O1
63803 O1
63868 O1
63872 O1
63879 O1
63890 O1
70000 7P6F
70001 7P6F
70002 7P6F
70003 7P6F
70005 7P6F
70006 7P6F
70007 7P6F
70008 7P6F
70009 7P6F
70010 7P6F
70011 7P6F
70012 7P6F
70013 7P6F
70030 7P6F
70034 7P6F

Market Harborough

1957 2F
42446 4MT[3]
44388 4F[2]
49431 7F[3]
49444 7F[3]
49446 7F[3]
49447 7F[3]

1960 15F
42446 4MT[3]
44388 4F[2]
49444 7F[3]
49447 7F[3]

Meldon Quarry

1948
500S T

1951
DS3152 G6

1954
DS3152 G6

1957
DS3152 G6

1960
DS3152 G6

1963
DS234 USA

1966
DS234 USA

Melton Constable

1948 MC
62155 D2
62156 D2
62157 D2
62189 D2
62195 D2
62197 D2
62515 D16
62520 D15
62528 D15
62533 D16
62562 D16
62578 D16
65509 J17
65514 J17
65551 J17
65552 J17
65557 J17
65566 J17
65567 J17
65586 J17
67140 F3
67150 F3
67152 F4
67153 F4
67354 C12
68489 J93
68570 J69

1951 32G
62509 D15
62515 D16
62519 D16
62520 D15
62523 D16
62528 D15
62533 D16
62538 D15
62562 D16
62578 D16
62620 D16
65509 J17
65516 J17
65551 J17
65552 J17
65557 J17
65567 J17
65586 J17
67152 F4
67162 F4
67225 F6
67228 F6
68377 J66
68536 J67
69708 N7

1954 32G
43145 4MT[5]
43146 4MT[5]
43147 4MT[5]
43148 4MT[5]
43149 4MT[5]
43150 4MT[5]
43151 4MT[5]
43152 4MT[5]
43153 4MT[5]
43154 4MT[5]
43155 4MT[5]
43156 4MT[5]
62515 D16
62519 D16
62533 D16
62578 D16
62596 D16
62617 D16
62620 D16
65557 J17
67224 F6
67225 F6
67228 F6
67229 F6
68515 J67
68536 J67

1957 32G
43145 4MT[5]
43146 4MT[5]
43147 4MT[5]
43148 4MT[5]
43149 4MT[5]
43150 4MT[5]
43151 4MT[5]
43152 4MT[5]
43153 4MT[5]
43154 4MT[5]
43155 4MT[5]
43156 4MT[5]
62515 D16
62519 D16
62533 D16
62561 D16
62578 D16
62617 D16
65509 J17
65514 J17
65551 J17
65557 J17
65567 J17
68515 J67
68536 J67
68625 J69

Mersey Railway

1948
No 3 J66

Merthyr

1948 MTHR
217 TV[2]
1878 1854
2760 2721
4632 5700
4635 5700
5654 5600
5677 5600
5678 5600
5711 5700
5721 5700
5769 5700
6408 6400
6427 6400
6434 6400
7717 5700
7766 5700
7772 5700
8736 5700
9618 5700
9622 5700
9638 5700
9643 5700

1951 88D
77 RR[5]
78 RR[6]
79 RR[6]
80 RR[6]
81 RR[6]
82 RR[7]
83 RR[7]
211 TV[2]
217 TV[2]
292 TV[2]
316 TV[3]
370 TV[3]
375 TV[3]
398 TV[3]
4632 5700
4635 5700
4690 5700
5603 5600
5605 5600
5617 5600
5622 5600
5635 5600
5652 5600
5655 5600
5659 5600
5660 5600
5661 5600
5662 5600
5666 5600
5671 5600
5672 5600
5674 5600
5677 5600
5694 5600
5696 5600
5698 5600
5711 5700
5721 5700
5769 5700
5793 5700
6408 6400
6427 6400
6434 6400
6627 5600
7717 5700
7766 5700
7772 5700
8736 5700
9618 5700
9622 5700
9638 5700
9643 5700
9675 5700

1954 88D
78 RR[6]
79 RR[6]
81 RR[6]
398 TV[3]
4101 5101
4143 5101
4152 5101
4160 5101
4161 5101
4162 5101
4163 5101
4164 5101
4616 5700
4630 5700
4632 5700
4635 5700
4690 5700
5603 5600
5605 5600
5617 5600
5622 5600
5635 5600
5640 5600
5652 5600
5655 5600
5661 5600
5662 5600
5666 5600
5671 5600
5672 5600
5674 5600
5677 5600
5694 5600
5696 5600
5711 5700
5769 5700
5793 5700
6408 6400
6427 0400
6433 6400
6434 6400
6435 6400
6436 6400
7717 5700
7766 5700
7772 5700
8736 5700
9618 5700
9622 5700
9638 5700
9643 5700
9675 5700

1957 88D
398 TV[3]
4143 5101
4152 5101
4160 5101
4161 5101
4162 5101
4163 5101
4164 5101
4616 5700
4630 5700
4632 5700
4635 5700
4690 5700
5603 5600
5605 5600
5615 5600
5622 5600
5635 5600
5640 5600
5650 5600
5652 5600
5655 5600
5660 5600
5661 5600
5662 5600
5666 5600
5671 5600
5672 5600
5674 5600
5677 5600
5681 5600
5696 5600
5711 5700
5769 5700
6408 6400
6423 6400
6427 6400
6433 6400
6434 6400
6436 6400
7717 5700
7766 5700
8736 5700
9618 5700
9638 5700
9643 5700
9675 5700
9747 5700

1960 88D
4632 5700
4635 5700
4690 5700
5603 5600
5605 5600
5622 5600
5626 5600
5630 5600
5635 5600
5636 5600
5650 5600
5652 5600
5655 5600
5660 5600
5661 5600
5662 5600
5666 5600
5671 5600
5672 5600
5674 5600
5677 5600
5681 5600
5696 5600
6416 6400
6433 6400
6436 6400
9618 5700
9631 5700
9638 5700
9643 5700
9675 5700
9676 5700
9679 5700
9747 5700
9776 5700

1963 88D
4635 5700
4690 5700
5603 5600
5605 5600
5610 5600
5618 5600
5622 5600
5626 5600
5650 5600
5655 5600
5660 5600
5662 5600
5666 5600
5671 5600
5677 5600
5681 5600
5687 5600
5696 5600
6416 6400
6433 6400
6658 5600
8723 5700
9618 5700
9631 5700
9638 5700
9675 5700
9676 5700
9679 5700
9747 5700
9776 5700

Mexborough

1948 MEX
61165 B1
61166 B1
61167 B1
61168 B1
61174 B1
61680 B5
61681 B5
61685 B5
61686 B5
61688 B5
61689 B5
61690 B5
63007 O7
63009 O7
63011 O7
63047 O7
63052 O7
63057 O7
63094 O7
63108 O7
63149 O7
63176 O7
63576 O4
63577 O4
63585 O4
63611 O4
63612 O4
63625 O4
63632 O4
63648 O4
63656 O4
63666 O4
63672 O4
63703 O4
63707 O4
63709 O4
63715 O4
63717 O4
63727 O4
63747 O4
63776 O4
63791 O4
63807 O4
63813 O4
63833 O4
63840 O4
63842 O4
63870 O4
63906 O4
64283 J11
64288 J11
64296 J11
64302 J11
64319 J11
64334 J11
64352 J11
64356 J11
64374 J11
64377 J11
64400 J11
64403 J11
64404 J11
64432 J11
64442 J11
64449 J11
69051 L3
69059 L3
69065 L3
69066 L3
69225 N4
69231 N4
69239 N4
69246 N4
69264 N5
69282 N5
69297 N5
69314 N5
69316 N5
69900 S1
69901 S1
69904 S1
69905 S1
69999 U1
90108 WD[1]
90118 WD[1]
90119 WD[1]
90120 WD[1]
90144 WD[1]
90146 WD[1]
90150 WD[1]
90153 WD[1]
90161 WD[1]
90166 WD[1]
90189 WD[1]
90195 WD[1]
90196 WD[1]
90209 WD[1]
90215 WD[1]
90220 WD[1]
90229 WD[1]
90232 WD[1]
90250 WD[1]
90252 WD[1]
90255 WD[1]
90270 WD[1]
90275 WD[1]
90280 WD[1]
90285 WD[1]
90286 WD[1]
90290 WD[1]
90296 WD[1]
90301 WD[1]
90311 WD[1]
90330 WD[1]
90400 WD[1]
90401 WD[1]
90410 WD[1]
90421 WD[1]
90538 WD[1]
90590 WD[1]
90596 WD[1]
90597 WD[1]
90598 WD[1]
90653 WD[1]
90657 WD[1]
90659 WD[1]
90665 WD[1]
90696 WD[1]
90700 WD[1]
90709 WD[1]
90714 WD[1]

1951 36B
61165 B1
61166 B1
61167 B1
61168 B1
61174 B1
61194 B1
63611 O4
63612 O4
63666 O4
63668 O4
63672 O4
63757 O4
63774 O4
63775 O4
63779 O4
63791 O4
63813 O4
63898 O4
63924 O2
63927 O2
63969 O2
63970 O2
63971 O2
63972 O2
63975 O2
63976 O2
63977 O2
63978 O2
63979 O2
63980 O2
63981 O2
63982 O2
63983 O2
63984 O2
63985 O2
64283 J11
64288 J11
64296 J11
64302 J11
64319 J11
64334 J11
64352 J11
64356 J11
64374 J11
64377 J11
64400 J11
64403 J11
64404 J11
64432 J11
64442 J11
64449 J11
68946 J50
68979 J50
69264 N5
69297 N5
69314 N5
69316 N5
69900 S1
69901 S1
69903 S1
69904 S1
69905 S1
69999 U1
90104 WD[1]
90108 WD[1]
90120 WD[1]
90144 WD[1]
90146 WD[1]
90150 WD[1]
90153 WD[1]
90154 WD[1]
90161 WD[1]
90166 WD[1]
90189 WD[1]
90190 WD[1]
90195 WD[1]
90196 WD[1]
90209 WD[1]
90211 WD[1]
90220 WD[1]
90223 WD[1]
90229 WD[1]
90232 WD[1]
90246 WD[1]
90250 WD[1]
90252 WD[1]
90255 WD[1]
90270 WD[1]
90280 WD[1]
90285 WD[1]
90286 WD[1]
90290 WD[1]
90296 WD[1]
90301 WD[1]
90311 WD[1]
90340 WD[1]
90400 WD[1]
90401 WD[1]
90410 WD[1]
90421 WD[1]
90521 WD[1]
90537 WD[1]
90538 WD[1]
90550 WD[1]
90583 WD[1]
90587 WD[1]
90590 WD[1]
90594 WD[1]
90596 WD[1]
90597 WD[1]
90598 WD[1]
90612 WD[1]
90618 WD[1]
90696 WD[1]
90700 WD[1]
90714 WD[1]

1954 36B
61112 B1
61165 B1
61166 B1
61167 B1
61194 B1
63586 O4
63593 O4
63611 O4
63612 O4
63666 O4
63668 O4
63672 O4
63693 O4
63698 O4
63701 O4
63704 O4
63730 O4
63753 O4
63757 O4
63774 O4
63775 O4
63779 O4
63791 O4
63813 O4
63828 O4
63843 O4
63897 O4
63898 O4
64283 J11
64352 J11
64356 J11
64374 J11
64377 J11
64400 J11
64432 J11
64442 J11
64449 J11
69264 N5
69280 N5
69297 N5
69306 N5
69316 N5
69337 N5
69901 S1
69902 S1
69904 S1
69905 S1
69999 U1
90015 WD[1]
90085 WD[1]
90104 WD[1]
90118 WD[1]
90119 WD[1]
90120 WD[1]
90130 WD[1]
90144 WD[1]
90146 WD[1]
90150 WD[1]
90153 WD[1]
90166 WD[1]
90189 WD[1]
90190 WD[1]
90195 WD[1]
90196 WD[1]
90209 WD[1]
90211 WD[1]
90229 WD[1]
90250 WD[1]
90252 WD[1]
90255 WD[1]
90286 WD[1]
90304 WD[1]
90311 WD[1]
90330 WD[1]
90340 WD[1]
90358 WD[1]
90400 WD[1]
90401 WD[1]
90410 WD[1]
90421 WD[1]
90495 WD[1]
90521 WD[1]
90580 WD[1]
90582 WD[1]
90587 WD[1]
90590 WD[1]
90597 WD[1]
90598 WD[1]
90612 WD[1]
90653 WD[1]
90700 WD[1]

1957 36B
61112 B1
61165 B1
61166 B1
61167 B1
61194 B1
61850 K3
61867 K3
61868 K3
63586 O4
63593 O4
63611 O4
63628 O4
63666 O4
63668 O4
63672 O4
63673 O4
63677 O4
63684 O4
63693 O4
63698 O4
63701 O4
63723 O4
63730 O4
63745 O4
63751 O4
63753 O4
63756 O4
63757 O4
63764 O4
63774 O4
63775 O4
63779 O4
63781 O4
63791 O4
63798 O4
63812 O4
63813 O4
63828 O4
63832 O4
63835 O4
63841 O4
63843 O4
63851 O4
63876 O4
63891 O4
63894 O4
63897 O4
63898 O4
63908 O4
64285 J11
64352 J11
64377 J11
64393 J11
64402 J11
64432 J11
68847 J52
68870 J52
69305 N5
69308 N5
90190 WD[1]
90195 WD[1]
90209 WD[1]
90211 WD[1]
90220 WD[1]
90229 WD[1]
90250 WD[1]
90252 WD[1]
90270 WD[1]
90286 WD[1]
90290 WD[1]
90304 WD[1]
90311 WD[1]
90330 WD[1]
90358 WD[1]
90400 WD[1]
90401 WD[1]
90410 WD[1]
90421 WD[1]
90495 WD[1]
90506 WD[1]
90521 WD[1]
90526 WD[1]
90580 WD[1]
90582 WD[1]
90587 WD[1]
90590 WD[1]
90612 WD[1]
90668 WD[1]
90700 WD[1]

1960 41F
43729 3F[3]
61083 B1
61090 B1
61093 B1
61104 B1
61165 B1
61166 B1
61167 B1
61194 B1
63586 O4
63593 O4
63611 O4
63628 O4
63672 O4
63684 O4
63701 O4
63757 O4
63774 O4
63779 O4
63791 O4
63798 O4
63813 O4
63828 O4
63832 O4
63841 O4
63843 O4
63891 O4
63894 O4
63897 O4
63898 O4
63908 O4
64377 J11
64393 J11
64402 J11
64403 J11
64406 J11
68497 J69
68623 J69
69308 N5
90052 WD[1]
90064 WD[1]
90119 WD[1]
90136 WD[1]
90139 WD[1]
90153 WD[1]
90190 WD[1]
90195 WD[1]
90203 WD[1]
90209 WD[1]
90211 WD[1]
90220 WD[1]
90250 WD[1]
90252 WD[1]
90270 WD[1]
90286 WD[1]
90290 WD[1]
90301 WD[1]
90304 WD[1]
90311 WD[1]
90330 WD[1]
90358 WD[1]
90384 WD[1]
90400 WD[1]
90401 WD[1]
90410 WD[1]
90421 WD[1]
90491 WD[1]
90495 WD[1]
90499 WD[1]
90506 WD[1]
90519 WD[1]
90521 WD[1]
90526 WD[1]
90567 WD[1]
90580 WD[1]
90582 WD[1]
90587 WD[1]
90590 WD[1]
90608 WD[1]
90612 WD[1]
90668 WD[1]
90700 WD[1]

1963 41F
61090 B1
61138 B1
61155 B1
61167 B1
61169 B1
63611 O4
63734 O4
63813 O4
63843 O4

63877 O4
63907 O4
68070 J94
90149 WD[1]
90188 WD[1]
90203 WD[1]
90209 WD[1]
90211 WD[1]
90220 WD[1]
90225 WD[1]
90250 WD[1]
90252 WD[1]
90311 WD[1]
90313 WD[1]
90330 WD[1]
90358 WD[1]
90384 WD[1]
90400 WD[1]
90401 WD[1]
90410 WD[1]
90421 WD[1]
90485 WD[1]
90491 WD[1]
90499 WD[1]
90519 WD[1]
90521 WD[1]
90529 WD[1]
90567 WD[1]
90572 WD[1]
90579 WD[1]
90580 WD[1]
90582 WD[1]
90587 WD[1]
90590 WD[1]
90612 WD[1]
90668 WD[1]
90700 WD[1]

Middlesbrough

1948 MID
63260 Q5
63263 Q5
63268 Q5
63273 Q5
63285 Q5
63291 Q5
63292 Q5
63295 Q5
63305 Q5
63308 Q5
63316 Q5
63317 Q5
63319 Q5
63322 Q5
63323 Q5
63333 Q5
63339 Q5
63364 Q6
63368 Q6
65084 J21
65686 J25
65702 J25
65710 J25
65725 J25
65726 J25
65733 J26
65764 J26
65771 J26
65775 J26
65776 J26
65779 J26
67338 G5
67638 V1
67639 V1
67684 V3
67685 V3
67686 V3
67691 V3
68260 J71
68303 J71
68307 J71
68312 J71
68409 J77
68414 J77
68422 J77
68423 J77
68690 J72
68711 J72
68712 J72
68713 J72
68721 J72
68740 J72
68754 J72
69858 A8
69859 A8
69860 A8
69869 A8
69878 A8
69880 A8
69888 A8

1951 51D
43050 4MT[5]
43051 4MT[5]
43054 4MT[5]
63328 Q5
63349 Q6
63351 Q6
63364 Q6
63368 Q6
63369 Q6
63373 Q6
63375 Q6
63380 Q6
63393 Q6
63409 Q6
63411 Q6
63417 Q6
63420 Q6
63442 Q6
63459 Q6
64821 J39
64847 J39
65687 J25
65710 J25
65726 J25
65733 J26
65764 J26
65771 J26
65775 J26
65776 J26
65779 J26
67338 G5
67638 V1
67639 V1
67684 V3
67685 V3
67686 V3
67691 V3
68260 J71
68303 J71
68307 J71
68312 J71
68409 J77
68414 J77
68422 J77
68425 J77
68688 J72
68689 J72
68690 J72
68712 J72
68713 J72
68721 J72
68740 J72
68754 J72
69006 J72
69019 J72
69854 A8
69859 A8
69866 A8
69873 A8
69876 A8
69878 A8
69880 A8

1954 51D
43050 4MT[5]
43051 4MT[5]
43054 4MT[5]
43072 4MT[5]
43073 4MT[5]
43074 4MT[5]
43101 4MT[5]
43102 4MT[5]
63340 Q6
63349 Q6
63351 Q6
63355 Q6
63364 Q6
63368 Q6
63369 Q6
63373 Q6
63375 Q6
63380 Q6
63393 Q6
63401 Q6
63405 Q6
63409 Q6
63411 Q6
63417 Q6
63420 Q6
63435 Q6
63442 Q6
63452 Q6
63459 Q6
65737 J26
65775 J26
65776 J26
65779 J26
67338 G5
67638 V1
67639 V1
67663 V1
67677 V1
67684 V3
67685 V3
67686 V3
67691 V3
68260 J71
68303 J71
68307 J71
68312 J71
68409 J77
68414 J77
68422 J77
68425 J77
68688 J72
68689 J72
68690 J72
68712 J72
68713 J72
68721 J72
68740 J72
68754 J72
69006 J72
69019 J72
69852 A8
69854 A8
69859 A8
69862 A8
69866 A8
69873 A8
69876 A8
69878 A8
69880 A8
69883 A8

1957 51D
43038 4MT[5]
43051 4MT[5]
43072 4MT[5]
43073 4MT[5]
43074 4MT[5]
43102 4MT[5]
63340 Q6
63349 Q6
63355 Q6
63364 Q6
63368 Q6
63369 Q6
63373 Q6
63375 Q6
63380 Q6
63393 Q6
63396 Q6
63401 Q6
63405 Q6
63409 Q6
63411 Q6
63417 Q6
63420 Q6
63424 Q6
63435 Q6
63442 Q6
63452 Q6
65720 J25
65737 J26
65775 J26
65776 J26
65779 J26
65870 J27
67323 G5
67754 L1
67755 L1
67759 L1
67763 L1
67764 L1
67765 L1
67766 L1
68245 J71
68260 J71
68290 J71
68312 J71
68409 J77
68414 J77
68684 J72
68688 J72
68689 J72
68690 J72
68712 J72
68721 J72
68740 J72
69006 J72
69019 J72
69854 A8
69862 A8
69876 A8
69878 A8
69889 A8
69891 A8

Middleton in Teesdale

1948 MIT
67309 G5

Millhouses

1948 19B
40075 3MT[2]
40082 3MT[2]
40139 3MT[2]
40487 2P[2]
40518 2P[2]
40544 2P[2]
40545 2P[2]
40731 3P[1]
41014 4P[2]
41016 4P[2]
41021 4P[2]
41024 4P[2]
41026 4P[2]
41037 4P[2]
41062 4P[1]
41063 4P[1]
41072 4P[1]
41075 4P[1]
41079 4P[1]
43463 3F[3]
44859 5MT[3]
44963 5MT[3]
44964 5MT[3]
44965 5MT[3]
44971 5MT[3]
45263 5MT[3]
45590 6P5F[2]
45594 6P5F[2]
45607 6P5F[2]
45621 6P5F[2]
45626 6P5F[2]
45679 6P5F[2]
45683 6P5F[2]
45696 6P5F[2]
58033 1P[5]
58067 1P[6]
58071 1P[6]
58076 1P[6]
58078 1P[6]
58209 2F[9]

1951 19B
40082 3MT[2]
40139 3MT[2]
40487 2P[2]
40493 2P[2]
40502 2P[2]
40518 2P[2]
40549 2P[2]
41016 4P[2]
41021 4P[2]
41037 4P[2]
41062 4P[1]
41063 4P[1]
41072 4P[1]
41079 4P[1]
41245 2MT[1]
41246 2MT[1]
43341 3F[3]
44664 5MT[3]
44665 5MT[3]
44859 5MT[3]
44962 5MT[3]
44963 5MT[3]
44964 5MT[3]
44965 5MT[3]
44986 5MT[3]
45260 5MT[3]
45264 5MT[3]
45297 5MT[3]
45590 6P5F[2]
45594 6P5F[2]
45607 6P5F[2]
45609 6P5F[2]
45621 6P5F[2]
45654 6P5F[2]
45664 6P5F[2]
45679 6P5F[2]
45683 6P5F[2]
45725 6P5F[2]
58067 1P[6]
58068 1P[6]
58071 1P[6]
58076 1P[6]
58209 2F[9]

1954 19B
40538 2P[2]
40907 4P[1]
41058 4P[1]
41062 4P[1]
41063 4P[1]
41070 4P[1]
41071 4P[1]
41072 4P[1]
41190 4P[1]
41191 4P[1]
41209 2MT[1]
41245 2MT[1]
41246 2MT[1]
43032 4MT[5]
44664 5MT[3]
44665 5MT[3]
44830 5MT[3]
44848 5MT[3]
44851 5MT[3]
44964 5MT[3]
44986 5MT[3]
45576 6P5F[2]
45590 6P5F[2]
45594 6P5F[2]
45607 6P5F[2]
45609 6P5F[2]
45654 6P5F[2]
45656 6P5F[2]
45664 6P5F[2]
45683 6P5F[2]
45725 6P5F[2]
58077 1P[6]
58080 1P[6]
58209 2F[9]
73011 5MT
73016 5MT
73047 5MT
73048 5MT

1957 19B
40148 3MT[2]
40538 2P[2]
40907 4P[1]
41062 4P[1]
41190 4P[1]
41199 4P[1]
41209 2MT[1]
41245 2MT[1]
41246 2MT[1]
43032 4MT[5]
44661 5MT[3]
44665 5MT[3]
44830 5MT[3]
44847 5MT[3]
44986 5MT[3]
45056 5MT[3]
45297 5MT[3]
45576 6P5F[2]
45590 6P5F[2]
45594 6P5F[2]
45607 6P5F[2]
45609 6P5F[2]
45654 6P5F[2]
45656 6P5F[2]
45664 6P5F[2]
45683 6P5F[2]
45725 6P5F[2]
46400 2MT[2]
46494 2MT[2]
73011 5MT
73016 5MT
73048 5MT
73065 5MT
73074 5MT
78022 2MT[1]
78023 2MT[1]
78024 2MT[1]
78025 2MT[1]

1960 41C
40907 4P[1]
41209 2MT[1]
41245 2MT[1]
41246 2MT[1]
43032 4MT[5]
45570 6P5F[2]
45576 6P5F[2]
45590 6P5F[2]
45594 6P5F[2]
45602 6P5F[2]
45607 6P5F[2]
45609 6P5F[2]
45654 6P5F[2]
45656 6P5F[2]
45664 6P5F[2]
45683 6P5F[2]
45725 6P5F[2]
46400 2MT[2]
46494 2MT[2]
61138 B1
61152 B1
61334 B1
73004 5MT
73011 5MT
73016 5MT
73046 5MT
73048 5MT
73065 5MT
73067 5MT
73073 5MT
73155 5MT
78022 2MT[1]
78023 2MT[1]
78024 2MT[1]
78025 2MT[1]

Mirfield

1948 25D
42405 4MT[2]
42553 4MT[3]
48738 8F
48751 8F
48752 8F
49500 7F[4]
49522 7F[4]
49555 7F[4]
49579 7F[4]
49601 7F[4]
49602 7F[4]
49618 7F[4]
49619 7F[4]
49620 7F[4]
49658 7F[4]
49659 7F[4]
49660 7F[4]
49661 7F[4]
49662 7F[4]
49663 7F[4]
50670 2P[8]
50712 2P[8]
50731 2P[8]
50798 2P[8]
50829 2P[8]
50850 2P[8]
50873 2P[8]
50898 2P[8]
51320 2F[2]
51453 2F[2]
52166 3F[7]
52191 3F[7]
52192 3F[7]
52231 3F[7]
52235 3F[7]
52273 3F[7]
52311 3F[7]
52331 3F[7]
52408 3F[7]
52448 3F[7]
52521 3F[7]
52583 3F[9]

1951 25D
42152 4MT[1]
42324 4MT[2]
42405 4MT[2]
42406 4MT[2]
42407 4MT[2]
42411 4MT[2]
42700 5MT[1]
42712 5MT[1]
42719 5MT[1]
42731 5MT[1]
42865 5MT[1]
44042 4F[2]
44056 4F[2]
44062 4F[2]
44462 4F[2]
44471 4F[2]
44474 4F[2]
44485 4F[2]
49598 7F[4]
49602 7F[4]
49618 7F[4]
49620 7F[4]
49660 7F[4]
51358 2F[2]
51453 2F[2]
52124 3F[7]
52166 3F[7]
52255 3F[7]
52408 3F[7]
52515 3F[7]
90107 WD[1]
90321 WD[1]
90375 WD[1]
90543 WD[1]
90578 WD[1]
90593 WD[1]
90622 WD[1]
90642 WD[1]
90707 WD[1]
90721 WD[1]
90723 WD[1]
90731 WD[1]

1954 25D
42152 4MT[1]
42324 4MT[2]
42405 4MT[2]
42406 4MT[2]
42407 4MT[2]
42411 4MT[2]
44056 4F[2]
44062 4F[2]
44462 4F[2]
44471 4F[2]
44474 4F[2]
44485 4F[2]
51358 2F[2]
51424 2F[2]
51453 2F[2]
52189 3F[7]
52236 3F[7]
52336 3F[7]
52452 3F[7]
52592 3F[9]
90107 WD[1]
90124 WD[1]
90321 WD[1]
90326 WD[1]
90375 WD[1]
90543 WD[1]
90578 WD[1]
90593 WD[1]
90622 WD[1]
90642 WD[1]
90678 WD[1]
90707 WD[1]
90721 WD[1]
90723 WD[1]
90731 WD[1]

1957 56D
42152 4MT[1]
42285 4MT[1]
42405 4MT[2]
42406 4MT[2]
42477 4MT[3]
42553 4MT[3]
44056 4F[2]
44062 4F[2]
44474 4F[2]
44485 4F[2]
51358 2F[2]
51424 2F[2]
51453 2F[2]
52121 3F[7]
52139 3F[7]
52236 3F[7]
52336 3F[7]
52576 3F[9]
90112 WD[1]
90124 WD[1]
90321 WD[1]
90326 WD[1]
90348 WD[1]
90543 WD[1]
90578 WD[1]
90593 WD[1]
90622 WD[1]
90642 WD[1]
90655 WD[1]
90678 WD[1]
90707 WD[1]
90721 WD[1]
90723 WD[1]
90731 WD[1]

1960 56D
41264 2MT[1]
42152 4MT[1]
42285 4MT[1]
42324 4MT[2]
42406 4MT[2]
42407 4MT[2]
44056 4F[2]
44474 4F[2]
44485 4F[2]
47266 3F[6]
47335 3F[6]
47443 3F[6]
47580 3F[6]
47632 3F[6]
48202 8F
48265 8F
48274 8F
48357 8F
52089 3F[7]
52121 3F[7]
52139 3F[7]
52515 3F[7]
61011 B1
61040 B1
61049 B1
61230 B1
90126 WD[1]
90135 WD[1]
90184 WD[1]
90233 WD[1]
90281 WD[1]
90300 WD[1]
90322 WD[1]
90351 WD[1]
90397 WD[1]
90457 WD[1]
90622 WD[1]
90642 WD[1]
90655 WD[1]
90678 WD[1]
90698 WD[1]
90707 WD[1]
90721 WD[1]
90723 WD[1]
90731 WD[1]

1963 56D
42152 4MT[1]
42406 4MT[2]
44056 4F[2]
48055 8F
48138 8F
48202 8F
48265 8F
48276 8F
48357 8F
48358 8F
48608 8F
61449 B16
61461 B16
61464 B16
61468 B16
61476 B16
90068 WD[1]
90135 WD[1]
90184 WD[1]
90300 WD[1]
90322 WD[1]
90333 WD[1]
90457 WD[1]
90622 WD[1]
90655 WD[1]
90678 WD[1]
90707 WD[1]
90731 WD[1]

1966 56D
44693 5MT[3]
44694 5MT[3]
44695 5MT[3]
44946 5MT[3]
44951 5MT[3]
44990 5MT[3]
45208 5MT[3]
48055 8F
48202 8F
48265 8F
48276 8F
48357 8F
48358 8F
48608 8F
90310 WD[1]
90351 WD[1]
90397 WD[1]
90655 WD[1]

Mold Junction

1948 6B
42945 5MT[2]
42965 5MT[2]
42975 5MT[2]
42976 5MT[2]
42979 5MT[2]
44065 4F[2]
44073 4F[2]
44367 4F[2]
44493 4F[2]
44800 5MT[3]
45286 5MT[3]
45288 5MT[3]
45328 5MT[3]
45383 5MT[3]
45385 5MT[3]
47353 3F[6]
47371 3F[6]
47372 3F[6]
47615 3F[6]
47646 3F[6]
47650 3F[6]
47656 3F[6]
48950 7F[2]
49047 7F[2]
49052 6F[2]
49072 7F[2]
49077 7F[2]
49105 7F[2]
49112 7F[2]
49115 7F[2]
49120 7F[2]
49143 7F[2]
49166 6F[2]
49220 7F[2]
49228 7F[2]
49235 7F[2]
49251 6F[2]
49261 6F[2]
49280 7F[2]
49291 7F[2]
49316 7F[2]
49322 7F[2]
49383 6F[2]
49447 7F[2]
58382 2F[11]

1951 6B
42945 5MT[2]
42959 5MT[2]
42975 5MT[2]
42976 5MT[2]
44065 4F[2]
44073 4F[2]
44367 4F[2]
44493 4F[2]
44800 5MT[3]
45132 5MT[3]
45275 5MT[3]
45286 5MT[3]
45288 5MT[3]
45315 5MT[3]
45402 5MT[3]
47371 3F[6]
47372 3F[6]
47615 3F[6]
47646 3F[6]
47650 3F[6]
47656 3F[6]
48017 8F
48094 8F
48142 8F
48246 8F
48342 8F
48444 8F
48446 8F
48447 8F
48452 8F
48458 8F
48459 8F
48467 8F
48470 8F
48477 8F
48744 8F
48750 8F
48770 8F
49278 7F[6]

1954 6B
42940 5MT[1]
42941 5MT[1]
42945 5MT[2]
42959 5MT[2]
42965 5MT[2]
42971 5MT[2]
42973 5MT[2]
42975 5MT[2]
42976 5MT[2]
42982 5MT[2]
43836 4F[1]
43904 4F[1]
43908 4F[1]
44065 4F[2]
44073 4F[2]
44117 4F[2]
44164 4F[2]
44493 4F[2]
44800 5MT[3]
45001 5MT[3]
45130 5MT[3]
45275 5MT[3]
47371 3F[6]
47372 3F[6]
47615 3F[6]
47646 3F[6]
47650 3F[6]
47656 3F[6]
48106 8F
48246 8F
48247 8F
48259 8F
48458 8F
90147 WD[1]
90157 WD[1]
90178 WD[1]
90187 WD[1]
90212 WD[1]
90242 WD[1]
90317 WD[1]
90566 WD[1]
90606 WD[1]
90702 WD[1]

1957 6B
42945 5MT[2]
42959 5MT[2]
42964 5MT[2]
42965 5MT[2]
42971 5MT[2]
42973 5MT[2]
42975 5MT[2]
42976 5MT[2]
42982 5MT[2]
43908 4F[1]
44065 4F[2]
44073 4F[2]
44117 4F[2]
44493 4F[2]
44800 5MT[3]
44971 5MT[3]
45001 5MT[3]
45002 5MT[3]
45028 5MT[3]
45043 5MT[3]
45055 5MT[3]
45130 5MT[3]
45142 5MT[3]
45247 5MT[3]
45275 5MT[3]
45325 5MT[3]
45345 5MT[3]
47371 3F[6]
47372 3F[6]
47615 3F[6]
47646 3F[6]
47650 3F[6]
47656 3F[6]
48174 8F
48246 8F
48259 8F
48458 8F
48749 8F
90147 WD[1]
90157 WD[1]
90178 WD[1]
90187 WD[1]
90227 WD[1]
90237 WD[1]
90242 WD[1]
90257 WD[1]
90317 WD[1]
90566 WD[1]
90606 WD[1]
90667 WD[1]
90702 WD[1]

1960 6B
42945 5MT[2]
42960 5MT[2]
42965 5MT[2]
42967 5MT[2]
42971 5MT[2]
42973 5MT[2]
42981 5MT[2]
42982 5MT[2]
44065 4F[2]
44445 4F[2]
44493 4F[2]
44800 5MT[3]
44917 5MT[3]
44935 5MT[3]
44971 5MT[3]
45028 5MT[3]
45042 5MT[3]
45043 5MT[3]
45055 5MT[3]
45247 5MT[3]
45275 5MT[3]
45325 5MT[3]
45345 5MT[3]
47269 3F[6]
47615 3F[6]
47646 3F[6]
47650 3F[6]
48054 8F
48074 8F
48166 8F
48175 8F
48246 8F
48259 8F
48264 8F
48323 8F
48458 8F
48697 8F
48749 8F
48753 8F
48754 8F
48771 8F
90147 WD[1]
90187 WD[1]
90227 WD[1]
90532 WD[1]
90566 WD[1]
90606 WD[1]
90702 WD[1]

1963 6B
44359 4F[2]
44595 4F[2]
44800 5MT[3]
44842 5MT[3]
44917 5MT[3]
44971 5MT[3]
45027 5MT[3]
45031 5MT[3]
45042 5MT[3]
45043 5MT[3]
45237 5MT[3]
45275 5MT[3]
45325 5MT[3]
45438 5MT[3]
47410 3F[6]
47646 3F[6]
47673 3F[6]
48175 8F
48253 8F
48259 8F
48348 8F
48455 8F
48458 8F
48655 8F
48667 8F
48749 8F

1966 6B
44800 5MT[3]
44842 5MT[3]
44897 5MT[3]
44917 5MT[3]
44971 5MT[3]
45042 5MT[3]
45043 5MT[3]
45111 5MT[3]
45116 5MT[3]
45275 5MT[3]
45325 5MT[3]
45369 5MT[3]
45395 5MT[3]
47598 3F[6]
48090 8F
48120 8F
48175 8F
48253 8F
48269 8F
48345 8F
48458 8F
48655 8F
48667 8F
48723 8F
48749 8F
48754 8F

Monument Lane

1948 3E
41111 4P[1]
41116 4P[1]
41153 4P[1]
41154 4P[1]
41172 4P[1]
42262 4MT[1]
42263 4MT[1]
42264 4MT[1]
42265 4MT[1]
42450 4MT[3]
42451 4MT[3]
42488 4MT[3]
42489 4MT[3]
42567 4MT[3]
42579 4MT[3]
42659 4MT[3]
44057 4F[2]
44514 4F[2]
44592 4F[2]
45495 5MT[3]
46878 2P[7]
46922 2P[7]
58117 2F[8]
58124 2F[8]
58177 2F[8]
58178 2F[8]
58179 2F[8]
58273 2F[9]
58429 2F[11]
58909 2F[14]
58916 2F[14]

1951 3E
42262 4MT[1]
42263 4MT[1]
42264 4MT[1]
42265 4MT[1]
42267 4MT[1]
42489 4MT[3]
42579 4MT[3]
43231 3F[3]
44057 4F[2]
44361 4F[2]
44506 4F[2]
44514 4F[2]
44592 4F[2]
44829 5MT[3]
45390 5MT[3]
45418 5MT[3]
46427 2MT[2]
46900 2P[7]
46912 2P[7]
46922 2P[7]
58124 2F[8]
58177 2F[8]
58178 2F[8]
58179 2F[8]
58286 2F[9]
58928 2F[14]

1954 3E
40129 3MT[2]
40933 4P[1]
40936 4P[1]
41090 4P[1]
42262 4MT[1]
42263 4MT[1]
42264 4MT[1]
42265 4MT[1]
42267 4MT[1]
42579 4MT[3]
43231 3F[3]
44057 4F[2]
44361 4F[2]
44490 4F[2]
44506 4F[2]
44512 4F[2]
44514 4F[2]
44592 4F[2]
44942 5MT[3]
45051 5MT[3]
45390 5MT[3]
58117 2F[8]
58124 2F[8]
58178 2F[8]
58179 2F[8]
58185 2F[8]
58286 2F[9]
58900 2F[14]

1957 3E
40108 3MT[2]
40118 3MT[2]
40933 4P[1]
40936 4P[1]
41090 4P[1]
42267 4MT[1]
42422 4MT[2]
42552 4MT[3]
42579 4MT[3]
42601 4MT[3]
42658 4MT[3]
43187 3F[3]
43231 3F[3]
44057 4F[2]
44490 4F[2]
44506 4F[2]
44514 4F[2]
45034 5MT[3]
45308 5MT[3]
58124 2F[8]
58178 2F[8]
58185 2F[8]
58220 2F[9]
58306 2F[9]

1960 3E
40108 3MT[2]
40129 3MT[2]
40936 4P[1]
41168 4P[1]
42267 4MT[1]
42488 4MT[3]
44057 4F[2]
44444 4F[2]
44490 4F[2]
44506 4F[2]
44514 4F[2]
44766 5MT[3]
44807 5MT[3]
44840 5MT[3]
45034 5MT[3]
45038 5MT[3]
45052 5MT[3]
45071 5MT[3]
45113 5MT[3]
45301 5MT[3]
45308 5MT[3]
47474 3F[6]
47494 3F[6]
47561 3F[6]
58135 2F[8]
58185 2F[8]
58220 2F[9]
58271 2F[9]

Moor Row

1948 12E
47337 3F[6]
47390 3F[6]
47525 3F[6]
52098 3F[7]
52110 3F[7]
52184 3F[7]
52201 3F[7]
52285 3F[7]
52418 3F[7]
52494 3F[8]
52499 3F[8]
52510 3F[8]
52551 3F[9]

1951 12E
44461 4F[2]
44549 4F[2]
47337 3F[6]
47390 3F[6]
47525 3F[6]
47604 3F[6]
52201 3F[7]
52285 3F[7]
52418 3F[7]
52494 3F[8]
52510 3F[8]

1954 12E
44461 4F[2]
47337 3F[6]
47390 3F[6]
47525 3F[6]
52201 3F[7]
52418 3F[7]
52494 3F[8]
52509 3F[8]
52510 3F[8]

Motherwell

1948 28A
40159 3MT[2]
40200 3MT[2]
43884 4F[1]
44011 4F[1]
44791 5MT[3]
44792 5MT[3]
45007 5MT[3]
45008 5MT[3]
45012 5MT[3]
45016 5MT[3]
45018 5MT[3]
45120 5MT[3]
45121 5MT[3]
45453 5MT[3]
45461 5MT[3]
45462 5MT[3]
45483 5MT[3]
45488 5MT[3]
45496 5MT[3]
45497 5MT[3]
45498 5MT[3]
45499 5MT[3]
48156 8F
48183 8F
48184 8F
48185 8F
48186 8F
48187 8F
48188 8F
54441 3P[5]
54453 3P[5]
54460 3P[5]
54462 3P[6]
54464 3P[6]
54465 3P[6]
54498 3P[6]
54506 3P[6]
54631 4P[3]
54634 4P[3]
54635 4P[3]
54636 4P[3]

54637 4P^3
54640 4P^3
54641 4P^3
54642 4P^3
54643 4P^3
54645 4P^3
54646 4P^3
54647 4P^3
54649 4P^3
54650 4P^3
54651 4P^3
54652 4P^3
54653 4P^3
54654 4P^3
55134 2P^{12}
55138 2P^{12}
55188 2P^{13}
55191 2P^{13}
56028 0F^5
56029 0F^5
56031 0F^5
56155 2F^4
56241 3F^{10}
56245 3F^{10}
56247 3F^{10}
56258 3F^{10}
56264 3F^{10}
56265 3F^{10}
56268 3F^{10}
56269 3F^{10}
56270 3F^{10}
56271 3F^{10}
56276 3F^{10}
56277 3F^{10}
56281 3F^{10}
56285 3F^{10}
56334 3F^{10}
56335 3F^{10}
56337 3F^{10}
56338 3F^{10}
56345 3F^{10}
56356 3F^{10}
56357 3F^{10}
56358 3F^{10}
57231 2F^5
57247 2F^5
57256 2F^5
57267 2F^5
57270 2F^5
57272 2F^5
57273 2F^5
57278 2F^5
57289 2F^5
57290 2F^5
57291 2F^5
57299 2F^5
57301 2F^5
57303 2F^5
57308 2F^5
57313 2F^5
57325 2F^5
57326 2F^5
57327 2F^5
57328 2F^5
57332 2F^5
57342 2F^5
57344 2F^5
57358 2F^5
57363 2F^5
57377 2F^5
57379 2F^5
57403 2F^5
57404 2F^5
57406 2F^5
57413 2F^5
57414 2F^5
57415 2F^5
57416 2F^5
57417 2F^5
57418 2F^5
57419 2F^5
57435 2F^5
57437 2F^5
57461 2F^5
57462 2F^5
57582 3F^{12}
57584 3F^{12}
57588 3F^{12}
57593 3F^{12}
57595 3F^{12}
57599 3F^{12}
57606 3F^{12}
57638 3F^{13}
57666 3F^{14}
57668 3F^{14}
57681 3F^{14}

1951 66B
42125 4MT^1
42126 4MT^1
42127 4MT^1
42200 4MT^1
42203 4MT^1
42208 4MT^1
44969 5MT^3
45008 5MT^3
45009 5MT^3
45121 5MT^3
45151 5MT^3
45152 5MT^3
45176 5MT^3
45462 5MT^3
45498 5MT^3
54441 3P^5
54453 3P^5
54460 3P^5
54462 3P^6
54464 3P^6
54465 3P^6
54630 4P^3
54634 4P^3
54635 4P^3
54636 4P^3
54640 4P^3
54647 4P^3
54648 4P^3
54649 4P^3
54650 4P^3
54654 4P^3
55138 2P^{12}
55188 2P^{13}
56155 2F^4
56172 2F^4
56241 3F^{10}
56245 3F^{10}
56247 3F^{10}
56258 3F^{10}
56264 3F^{10}
56265 3F^{10}
56268 3F^{10}
56269 3F^{10}
56271 3F^{10}
56276 3F^{10}
56277 3F^{10}
56285 3F^{10}
56334 3F^{10}
56335 3F^{10}
56337 3F^{10}
56338 3F^{10}
56345 3F^{10}
56356 3F^{10}
56357 3F^{10}
56358 3F^{10}
57247 2F^5
57256 2F^5
57267 2F^5
57270 2F^5
57272 2F^5
57278 2F^5
57289 2F^5
57291 2F^5
57299 2F^5
57303 2F^5
57325 2F^5
57326 2F^5
57328 2F^5
57332 2F^5
57335 2F^5
57363 2F^5
57377 2F^5
57379 2F^5
57404 2F^5
57414 2F^5
57416 2F^5
57417 2F^5
57418 2F^5
57419 2F^5
57435 2F^5
57436 2F^5
57437 2F^5
57461 2F^5
57462 2F^5
57582 3F^{12}
57588 3F^{12}
57593 3F^{12}
57595 3F^{12}
57599 3F^{12}
57638 3F^{13}
57659 3F^{14}
57666 3F^{14}
57668 3F^{14}
57681 3F^{14}
90125 WD^1
90152 WD^1
90386 WD^1
90628 WD^1
90693 WD^1
90750 WD^2
90752 WD^2
90754 WD^2
90756 WD^2
90758 WD^2
90760 WD^2
90761 WD^2
90762 WD^2
90766 WD^2
90770 WD^2
90771 WD^2
90772 WD^2

1954 66B
40200 3MT^2
42125 4MT^1
42126 4MT^1
42127 4MT^1
42200 4MT^1
42203 4MT^1
42208 4MT^1
42689 4MT^1
43883 4F^1
44850 5MT^3
44969 5MT^3
45008 5MT^3
45009 5MT^3
45029 5MT^3
45085 5MT^3
45099 5MT^3
45121 5MT^3
45151 5MT^3
45152 5MT^3
45176 5MT^3
45309 5MT^3
45433 5MT^3
45462 5MT^3
45498 5MT^3
54457 3P^5
54460 3P^5
54462 3P^6
54464 3P^6
54465 3P^6
55239 2P^{14}
56241 3F^{10}
56245 3F^{10}
56247 3F^{10}
56264 3F^{10}
56265 3F^{10}
56269 3F^{10}
56271 3F^{10}
56277 3F^{10}
56285 3F^{10}
56334 3F^{10}
56335 3F^{10}
56337 3F^{10}
56338 3F^{10}
56345 3F^{10}
56354 3F^{10}
56356 3F^{10}
56357 3F^{10}
56358 3F^{10}
56367 3F^{10}
57247 2F^5
57256 2F^5
57267 2F^5
57270 2F^5
57278 2F^5
57291 2F^5
57299 2F^5
57303 2F^5
57325 2F^5
57326 2F^5
57328 2F^5
57363 2F^5
57377 2F^5
57404 2F^5
57414 2F^5
57416 2F^5
57417 2F^5
57418 2F^5
57419 2F^5
57435 2F^5
57436 2F^5
57437 2F^5
57461 2F^5
57462 2F^5
57582 3F^{12}
57588 3F^{12}
57593 3F^{12}
57595 3F^{12}
57599 3F^{12}
57638 3F^{13}
57659 3F^{14}
57666 3F^{14}
57668 3F^{14}
57681 3F^{14}
68344 J88
76000 4MT^2
76001 4MT^2
76002 4MT^2
76003 4MT^2
76004 4MT^2
90071 WD^1
90628 WD^1
90750 WD^2
90752 WD^2
90754 WD^2
90756 WD^2
90758 WD^2
90760 WD^2
90761 WD^2
90762 WD^2
90764 WD^2
90766 WD^2
90770 WD^2
90771 WD^2
90772 WD^2

1957 66B
42125 4MT^1
42126 4MT^1
42127 4MT^1
42200 4MT^1
42203 4MT^1
42208 4MT^1
42689 4MT^1
42696 4MT^1
42699 4MT^1
43883 4F^1
44850 5MT^3
44969 5MT^3
45008 5MT^3
45009 5MT^3
45029 5MT^3
45085 5MT^3
45099 5MT^3
45121 5MT^3
45151 5MT^3
45152 5MT^3
45176 5MT^3
45309 5MT^3
45462 5MT^3
45484 5MT^3
45485 5MT^3
45498 5MT^3
54462 3P^6
54464 3P^6
54465 3P^6
56241 3F^{10}
56245 3F^{10}
56247 3F^{10}
56264 3F^{10}
56265 3F^{10}
56269 3F^{10}
56277 3F^{10}
56285 3F^{10}
56334 3F^{10}
56335 3F^{10}
56337 3F^{10}
56338 3F^{10}
56345 3F^{10}
56354 3F^{10}
56356 3F^{10}
56357 3F^{10}
56367 3F^{10}
57237 2F^5
57247 2F^5
57256 2F^5
57267 2F^5
57270 2F^5
57278 2F^5
57291 2F^5
57299 2F^5
57303 2F^5
57325 2F^5
57326 2F^5
57328 2F^5
57363 2F^5
57377 2F^5
57404 2F^5
57414 2F^5
57416 2F^5
57417 2F^5
57418 2F^5
57419 2F^5
57435 2F^5
57436 2F^5
57437 2F^5
57461 2F^5
57462 2F^5
57582 3F^{12}
57588 3F^{12}
57593 3F^{12}
57595 3F^{12}
57599 3F^{12}
57638 3F^{13}
57659 3F^{14}
57666 3F^{14}
57668 3F^{14}
57681 3F^{14}
73060 5MT
73061 5MT
73062 5MT
76000 4MT^2
76001 4MT^2
76002 4MT^2
76003 4MT^2
76004 4MT^2
76070 4MT^2
76071 4MT^2
78050 2MT^1
78051 2MT^1
90628 WD^1
90750 WD^2
90752 WD^2
90754 WD^2
90756 WD^2
90758 WD^2
90760 WD^2
90761 WD^2
90762 WD^2
90764 WD^2
90766 WD^2
90770 WD^2
90771 WD^2
90772 WD^2

1960 66B
42125 4MT^1
42126 4MT^1
42127 4MT^1
42200 4MT^1
42203 4MT^1
42208 4MT^1
42689 4MT^1
42696 4MT^1
42699 4MT^1
43883 4F^1
44196 4F^2
44850 5MT^3
44969 5MT^3
45008 5MT^3
45009 5MT^3
45029 5MT^3
45085 5MT^3
45099 5MT^3
45121 5MT^3
45151 5MT^3
45152 5MT^3
45176 5MT^3
45309 5MT^3
45433 5MT^3
45462 5MT^3
45484 5MT^3
45485 5MT^3
45498 5MT^3
54462 3P^6
54464 3P^6
54465 3P^6
56337 3F^{10}
56338 3F^{10}
56356 3F^{10}
56367 3F^{10}
57237 2F^5
57256 2F^5
57267 2F^5
57270 2F^5
57278 2F^5
57291 2F^5
57299 2F^5
57303 2F^5
57325 2F^5
57326 2F^5
57328 2F^5
57363 2F^5
57370 2F^5
57377 2F^5
57384 2F^5
57398 2F^5
57404 2F^5
57431 2F^5
57435 2F^5
57436 2F^5
57446 2F^5
57461 2F^5
57593 3F^{12}
57659 3F^{14}
57665 3F^{14}
57666 3F^{14}
57668 3F^{14}
57681 3F^{14}
57688 3F^{14}
69132 N15
69143 N15
69223 N15
76000 4MT^2
76001 4MT^2
76002 4MT^2
76003 4MT^2
76004 4MT^2
76070 4MT^2
76071 4MT^2
78050 2MT^1
78051 2MT^1
90071 WD^1
90386 WD^1
90468 WD^1
90628 WD^1
90750 WD^2
90752 WD^2
90754 WD^2
90756 WD^2
90758 WD^2
90760 WD^2
90761 WD^2
90762 WD^2
90764 WD^2
90770 WD^2
90771 WD^2

1963 66B
42125 4MT^1
42126 4MT^1
42127 4MT^1
42129 4MT^1
42169 4MT^1
42200 4MT^1
42208 4MT^1
42695 4MT^1
44786 5MT^3
44820 5MT^3
44850 5MT^3
44969 5MT^3
44991 5MT^3
45008 5MT^3
45009 5MT^3
45029 5MT^3
45099 5MT^3
45121 5MT^3
45168 5MT^3
45176 5MT^3
45309 5MT^3
45356 5MT^3
45433 5MT^3
45462 5MT^3
45484 5MT^3
45492 5MT^3
45498 5MT^3
57270 2F^5
57278 2F^5
57291 2F^5
57326 2F^5
57328 2F^5
57360 2F^5
57384 2F^5
57568 3F^{12}
57668 3F^{14}
57688 3F^{14}
57689 3F^{14}
57690 3F^{14}
76000 4MT^2
76002 4MT^2
76003 4MT^2
76004 4MT^2
76070 4MT^2
76071 4MT^2
78050 2MT^1
78051 2MT^1
90071 WD^1
90386 WD^1
90468 WD^1
90628 WD^1
90705 WD^1

1966 66B
44786 5MT^3
44820 5MT^3
44850 5MT^3
44880 5MT^3
44881 5MT^3
44908 5MT^3
44991 5MT^3
45029 5MT^3
45176 5MT^3
45433 5MT^3
46463 2MT^2
73107 5MT
76000 4MT^2
76002 4MT^2
76003 4MT^2
77005 3MT^1
77006 3MT^1
77008 3MT^1
77009 3MT^1

NCB Bannockburn

1951 on hire
68341 J88

NCB Blantyre

1951 on hire
56287 3F^{10}

Neasden

1948 NEA
61028 B1
61077 B1
61083 B1
61085 B1
61109 B1
61140 B1
61163 B1
61164 B1
61169 B1
64313 J11
64329 J11
64394 J11
67418 C13
67420 C13
67438 C13
68172 Y3
69053 L3
69054 L3
69055 L3
69056 L3
69060 L3
69061 L3
69067 L3
69068 L3
69070 L2
69071 L2
69076 M2
69077 M2
69257 N5
69259 N5
69273 N5
69283 N5
69300 N5
69302 N5
69313 N5
69315 N5
69318 N5
69341 N5
69350 N5
69354 N5
69358 N5
69369 N5
69519 N2
69561 N2
69800 A5
69801 A5
69802 A5
69803 A5
69804 A5
69805 A5
69806 A5
69807 A5
69808 A5
69809 A5
69810 A5
69811 A5
69812 A5
69813 A5
69814 A5
69815 A5
69816 A5
69817 A5
69818 A5
69819 A5
69820 A5
69821 A5
69822 A5
69823 A5
69824 A5
69825 A5
69826 A5
69827 A5
69828 A5
69829 A5

1951 34E
1411 1400
1426 1400
6129 6100
6166 6100
60050 A3
60051 A3
60111 A3
61028 B1
61077 B1
61083 B1
61140 B1
61163 B1
61164 B1
64313 J11
64329 J11
64394 J11
67418 C13
67420 C13
67714 L1
67715 L1
67717 L1
67718 L1
67720 L1
67747 L1
67748 L1
67749 L1
67751 L1
67752 L1
67753 L1
67758 L1
67760 L1
67762 L1
67767 L1
67768 L1
67769 L1
67770 L1
67771 L1
67772 L1
67773 L1
67774 L1
67775 L1
67776 L1
67778 L1
67779 L1
67780 L1
67781 L1
67782 L1
67783 L1
67784 L1
67785 L1
67786 L1
68172 Y3
69055 L3
69056 L3
69060 L3
69061 L3
69064 L3
69065 L3
69067 L3
69257 N5
69259 N5
69283 N5
69300 N5
69302 N5
69315 N5
69318 N5
69341 N5
69350 N5
69358 N5
69369 N5
69689 N7
69690 N7
69692 N7
69694 N7
69698 N7
69805 A5
69822 A5
69827 A5
69828 A5
69829 A5

1954 34E
1411 1400
1473 1400
43065 4MT^5
43066 4MT^5
43067 4MT^5
43068 4MT^5
43089 4MT^5
43107 4MT^5
43127 4MT^5
43144 4MT^5
43161 4MT^5
60050 A3
60063 A3
60108 A3
60111 A3
61001 B1
61009 B1
61028 B1
61077 B1
61083 B1
61116 B1
61136 B1
61163 B1
61164 B1
61206 B1
67416 C13
67418 C13
67420 C13
67740 L1
67747 L1
67748 L1
67749 L1
67751 L1
67752 L1
67753 L1
67758 L1
67760 L1
67761 L1
67762 L1
67767 L1
67768 L1
67769 L1
67770 L1
67771 L1
67772 L1
67773 L1
67774 L1
67776 L1
67778 L1
67779 L1
67780 L1
67781 L1
67782 L1
67783 L1
67784 L1
67786 L1
67787 L1
67788 L1
67789 L1
67792 L1
67794 L1
67795 L1
67796 L1
67798 L1
69257 N5
69259 N5
69273 N5
69302 N5
69315 N5
69318 N5
69341 N5
69350 N5
69354 N5
69369 N5
69805 A5
69814 A5
69827 A5
69829 A5

1957 34E
1473 1400
5409 5400
42222 4MT^1
42225 4MT^1
42230 4MT^1
42231 4MT^1
42232 4MT^1
42248 4MT^1
42249 4MT^1
42250 4MT^1
42251 4MT^1
42252 4MT^1
42253 4MT^1
42256 4MT^1
60108 A3
60820 V2
60877 V2
61001 B1
61028 B1
61077 B1
61083 B1
61111 B1
61116 B1
61136 B1
61164 B1
61187 B1
61206 B1
67416 C13
67418 C13
67420 C13
67740 L1
67743 L1
67747 L1
67748 L1
67752 L1
67753 L1
67756 L1
67758 L1
67762 L1
67767 L1
67769 L1
67778 L1
67781 L1
67782 L1
67783 L1
67787 L1
67792 L1
67794 L1
67795 L1
67796 L1
69257 N5
69341 N5
69350 N5
73155 5MT
73156 5MT
73157 5MT
73158 5MT
76036 4MT^2
76037 4MT^2
76038 4MT^2
76039 4MT^2
76040 4MT^2
76041 4MT^2
76042 4MT^2
76043 4MT^2
76044 4MT^2
80137 4MT^3
80138 4MT^3
80139 4MT^3
80140 4MT^3
80141 4MT^3
80142 4MT^3
80143 4MT^3
80144 4MT^3

1960 14D
1473 1400
5417 5400
41270 2MT^1
41272 2MT^1
41284 2MT^1
41329 2MT^1
42080 4MT^1
42081 4MT^1
42082 4MT^1
42086 4MT^1
42087 4MT^1
42088 4MT^1
42089 4MT^1
42090 4MT^1
42091 4MT^1
42092 4MT^1
42222 4MT^1
42225 4MT^1
42230 4MT^1
42231 4MT^1
42232 4MT^1
42248 4MT^1
42249 4MT^1
42250 4MT^1
42251 4MT^1
42252 4MT^1
42253 4MT^1
42256 4MT^1
42279 4MT^1
42281 4MT^1
42282 4MT^1
42283 4MT^1
42284 4MT^1
42291 4MT^1
42437 4MT^3
42450 4MT^3
42453 4MT^3
42540 4MT^3
42556 4MT^3
42562 4MT^3
42567 4MT^3
42568 4MT^3
42588 4MT^3
42595 4MT^3
42597 4MT^3
42601 4MT^3
42618 4MT^3
42629 4MT^3
42674 4MT^1
43010 4MT^5
44691 5MT^3
44819 5MT^3
44830 5MT^3
44847 5MT^3
45006 5MT^3
45215 5MT^3
45260 5MT^3
45416 5MT^3
61077 B1
61116 B1
61136 B1
61206 B1
76035 4MT^2
76036 4MT^2
76037 4MT^2
76038 4MT^2
76039 4MT^2
76040 4MT^2
76041 4MT^2
76042 4MT^2
76043 4MT^2
76044 4MT^2

Neath

1948 NEA
75 RR^4
906 1854
1715 1854
1855 1854
1858 1854
2192 BPGV^3
2722 2721
2797 2721
3455 3300
3611 5700
3621 5700
3757 5700
3774 5700
4132 5101
4221 4200
4232 4200
4252 4200
4259 4200
4272 4200
4274 4200
4279 4200
4284 4200
4288 4200
4293 4200
4621 5700
5225 5205
5239 5205
5242 5205
5254 5205
5703 5700
5720 5700
5746 5700
5778 5700
6613 5600
7701 5700
7737 5700
7739 5700
7742 5700
7743 5700
7757 5700
7767 5700
7769 5700
7786 5700
7799 5700
8104 8100
8715 5700
8775 5700
8782 5700
9627 5700
9734 5700
9750 5700
9756 5700
9779 5700
9783 5700
9786 5700
9792 5700

1951 87A
75 RR^4
1996 1901
2192 BPGV^3
2411 2301
3611 5700
3621 5700
3741 5700
3757 5700
3766 5700
3774 5700
4169 5101
4221 4200
4232 4200
4252 4200
4259 4200
4272 4200
4274 4200
4279 4200
4284 4200
4288 4200
4293 4200
4295 4200
4621 5700
5225 5205
5239 5205
5242 5205
5254 5205
5703 5700
5720 5700
5746 5700
5778 5700
6776 6700
7204 7200
7701 5700
7737 5700
7739 5700
7742 5700
7743 5700
7757 5700
7767 5700
7769 5700
7786 5700
7799 5700
7828 7800
7829 7800
8104 8100
8420 9400
8466 9400
8715 5700
8775 5700
8782 5700
9430 9400
9627 5700
9666 5700
9734 5700
9750 5700
9756 5700
9779 5700
9783 5700
9786 5700
9792 5700

1954 87A
1645 1600
3611 5700
3621 5700
3687 5700
3741 5700
3757 5700
3766 5700
3774 5700
4169 5101
4221 4200
4232 4200
4243 4200
4252 4200
4274 4200
4279 4200
4281 4200
4282 4200
4284 4200
4288 4200
4293 4200
4295 4200
4621 5700
5102 5101
5225 5205
5239 5205
5242 5205
5720 5700
5746 5700
5778 5700
7220 7200
7701 5700
7737 5700
7739 5700
7742 5700
7743 5700
7757 5700
7767 5700
7769 5700
7786 5700
7799 5700
8104 8100
8715 5700
8775 5700
8782 5700
8784 5700
9430 9400
9436 9400
9442 9400
9446 9400
9448 9400
9451 9400
9473 9400
9478 9400
9627 5700
9734 5700
9750 5700
9756 5700
9779 5700
9783 5700
9786 5700
9792 5700
90315 WD^1
90693 WD^1

1957 87A
1645 1600
3611 5700
3621 5700
3687 5700
3715 5700
3741 5700
3757 5700
3766 5700
3774 5700
4169 5101
4242 4200
4243 4200
4252 4200
4264 4200
4274 4200
4275 4200
4279 4200
4281 4200
4282 4200
4284 4200
4288 4200
4293 4200
4295 4200
4621 5700
5102 5101
5222 5205
5225 5205
5239 5205
5242 5205
5720 5700
5746 5700
5778 5700
7701 5700
7737 5700
7739 5700
7742 5700
7743 5700
7757 5700
7767 5700
7769 5700
7786 5700
7799 5700
8104 8100
8442 9400
8715 5700
8775 5700
8782 5700
8784 5700
9430 9400
9442 9400
9448 9400
9452 9400
9473 9400
9478 9400
9627 5700
9734 5700
9750 5700
9756 5700
9761 5700
9779 5700
9783 5700
9786 5700
9792 5700

1960 87A
1645 1600
3611 5700
3621 5700
3687 5700
3741 5700
3757 5700
3766 5700
3774 5700
4169 5101
4242 4200
4255 4200
4264 4200
4275 4200
4279 4200
4281 4200
4282 4200
4284 4200
4288 4200
4295 4200
4621 5700
4653 5700
5102 5101
5203 4200
5222 5205
5239 5205
5242 5205
5720 5700
5761 5700
5773 5700
5778 5700
6650 5600
7701 5700
7737 5700
7739 5700
7757 5700
7767 5700
7786 5700
7799 5700
8104 8100
8418 9400
8715 5700
8732 5700
8775 5700
8782 5700
8784 5700
9430 9400
9442 9400
9448 9400
9452 9400
9473 9400
9478 9400
9627 5700
9734 5700
9750 5700
9761 5700
9779 5700
9783 5700
9786 5700
9792 5700

1963 87A
1669 1600
2857 2800
2874 2800
3600 5700
3621 5700
3650 5700
3652 5700
3687 5700
3693 5700
3731 5700
3757 5700
3766 5700
3768 5700
3790 5700
3798 5700
3822 2884
4093 4073
4134 5101
4169 5101
4255 4200

4275 4200
4282 4200
4284 4200
4612 5700
4621 5700
4653 5700
4660 5700
4677 5700
4682 5700
4699 5700
4966 4900
5037 4073
5051 4073
5054 4073
5085 4073
5221 5205
5222 5205
5223 5205
5239 5205
5673 5600
5961 4900
6649 5600
6695 5600
6832 6800
6905 4900
6975 6959
7203 7200
7204 7200
7243 7200
7248 7200
8102 8100
8418 9400
8480 9400
8732 5700
8747 5700
8791 5700
9412 9400
9442 9400
9446 9400
9452 9400
9473 9400
9625 5700
9716 5700
9734 5700
9743 5700
9748 5700
9777 5700
9779 5700
9786 5700
9792 5700

New Cross Gate

1951 73B sub
32008 I1X
32596 I1X

New England

1948 NWE
60052 A3
60053 A3
60054 A3
60061 A3
60090 A3
60111 A3
60803 V2
60828 V2
60841 V2
60842 V2
60850 V2
60854 V2
60855 V2
60858 V2
60859 V2
60862 V2
60863 V2
60865 V2
60866 V2
60869 V2
60871 V2
60874 V2
60876 V2
60878 V2
60879 V2
60893 V2
60897 V2
60899 V2
60905 V2
60908 V2
60911 V2
60912 V2
60913 V2
60916 V2
60921 V2
60924 V2
60936 V2
60938 V2
60945 V2
60950 V2
61027 B1
61070 B1
61073 B1
61075 B1
61143 B1
61144 B1
61206 B1
61207 B1
61209 B1
61210 B1
61736 K2
61747 K2
61804 K3
61809 K3
61810 K3
61811 K3
61825 K3
61827 K3
61828 K3
61832 K3
61833 K3
61834 K3
61840 K3
61841 K3
61843 K3
61844 K3
61848 K3
61850 K3
61853 K3
61862 K3
61863 K5
61864 K3
61867 K3
61868 K3
61869 K3
61877 K3
61880 K3
61890 K3
61896 K3
61915 K3
61929 K3
61938 K3
61946 K3
61950 K3
61951 K3
61954 K3
61961 K3
61967 K3
61972 K3
61997 K1/1
62128 D3
62131 D3
62165 D2
62190 D2
62808 C1
62839 C1
62871 C1
63031 O7
63034 O7
63055 O7
63059 O7
63060 O7
63062 O7
63064 O7
63066 O7
63070 O7
63075 O7
63088 O7
63093 O7
63117 O7
63118 O7
63121 O7
63132 O7
63135 O7
63139 O7
63153 O7
63169 O7
63173 O7
63174 O7
63181 O7
63189 O7
63193 O7
63198 O7
64106 J3
64109 J4
64110 J4
64112 J4
64118 J3
64120 J4
64121 J4
64123 J3
64128 J3
64131 J3
64135 J3
64136 J3
64151 J3
64158 J3
64160 J4
64162 J4
64171 J6
64176 J6
64177 J6
64184 J6
64186 J6
64187 J6
64189 J6
64191 J6
64192 J6
64207 J6
64211 J6
64216 J6
64217 J6
64220 J6
64221 J6
64225 J6
64228 J6
64235 J6
64238 J6
64245 J6
64246 J6
64249 J6
64252 J6
64254 J6
64257 J6
64266 J6
64273 J6
64275 J6
64278 J6
64729 J39
64738 J39
64746 J39
64748 J39
64965 J39
64969 J39
65002 J1
65004 J1
65005 J1
65006 J1
67361 C12
67362 C12
67363 C12
67365 C12
67368 C12
67373 C12
67390 C12
68380 J66
68387 J66
68546 J69
68588 J67
68632 J69
68765 J52
68789 J52
68798 J52
68817 J52
68819 J52
68820 J52
68821 J52
68823 J52
68824 J52
68840 J52
68850 J52
68852 J52
68866 J52
68868 J52
68876 J52
68879 J52
68880 J52
69064 L3
90115 WD^1
90130 WD^1
90151 WD^1
90180 WD^1
90191 WD^1
90256 WD^1
90340 WD^1
90349 WD^1
90577 WD^1
90613 WD^1

1951 35A
43058 4MT^5
43059 4MT^5
43060 4MT^5
43061 4MT^5
43062 4MT^5
43063 4MT^5
43065 4MT^5
43066 4MT^5
43067 4MT^5
43068 4MT^5
43069 4MT^5
43080 4MT^5
43081 4MT^5
43082 4MT^5
43083 4MT^5
43084 4MT^5
43085 4MT^5
43086 4MT^5
43087 4MT^5
43088 4MT^5
43089 4MT^5
60113 A1
60500 A2
60504 A2
60505 A2
60506 A2
60508 A2
60513 A2
60514 A2
60520 A2
60523 A2
60533 A2
60803 V2
60828 V2
60829 V2
60841 V2
60842 V2
60850 V2
60854 V2
60855 V2
60858 V2
60859 V2
60863 V2
60865 V2
60866 V2
60869 V2
60871 V2
60874 V2
60876 V2
60878 V2
60879 V2
60893 V2
60897 V2
60899 V2
60905 V2
60906 V2
60908 V2
60911 V2
60912 V2
60913 V2
60916 V2
60924 V2
60936 V2
60938 V2
60950 V2
60966 V2
61027 B1
61070 B1
61073 B1
61075 B1
61143 B1
61206 B1
61207 B1
61210 B1
61330 B1
61331 B1
61735 K2
61736 K2
61739 K2
61740 K2
61804 K3
61811 K3
61841 K3
61843 K3
61850 K3
61853 K3
61862 K3
61863 K5
61867 K3
61868 K3
61890 K3
61915 K3
61929 K3
61951 K3
61954 K3
61967 K3
61972 K3
63923 O2
63948 O2
64112 J4
64118 J3
64123 J3
64131 J3
64135 J3
64151 J3
64158 J3
64160 J4
64171 J6
64176 J6
64177 J6
64184 J6
64186 J6
64189 J6
64191 J6
64192 J6
64207 J6
64211 J6
64216 J6
64217 J6
64220 J6
64221 J6
64225 J6
64228 J6
64235 J6
64238 J6
64245 J6
64246 J6
64249 J6
64252 J6
64254 J6
64257 J6
64265 J6
64266 J6
64273 J6
64275 J6
64278 J6
65002 J1
65004 J1
65005 J1
65006 J1
67357 C12
67361 C12
67365 C12
67368 C12
67373 C12
67390 C12
68185 Y3
68387 J66
68632 J69
68765 J52
68789 J52
68817 J52
68819 J52
68820 J52
68821 J52
68823 J52
68824 J52
68840 J52
68844 J52
68846 J52
68850 J52
68852 J52
68866 J52
68868 J52
68876 J52
68879 J52
68880 J52
90028 WD^1
90031 WD^1
90034 WD^1
90059 WD^1
90062 WD^1
90079 WD^1
90088 WD^1
90093 WD^1
90096 WD^1
90106 WD^1
90130 WD^1
90151 WD^1
90156 WD^1
90158 WD^1
90165 WD^1
90169 WD^1
90180 WD^1
90191 WD^1
90208 WD^1
90239 WD^1
90244 WD^1
90253 WD^1
90256 WD^1
90259 WD^1
90279 WD^1
90287 WD^1
90288 WD^1
90305 WD^1
90346 WD^1
90349 WD^1
90428 WD^1
90438 WD^1
90439 WD^1
90454 WD^1
90490 WD^1
90494 WD^1
90495 WD^1
90512 WD^1
90514 WD^1
90528 WD^1
90554 WD^1
90559 WD^1
90577 WD^1
90613 WD^1
90657 WD^1
90659 WD^1
90665 WD^1
90683 WD^1
90730 WD^1

1954 35A
43059 4MT^5
43060 4MT^5
43061 4MT^5
43062 4MT^5
43063 4MT^5
43080 4MT^5
43081 4MT^5
43082 4MT^5
43083 4MT^5
43084 4MT^5
43085 4MT^5
43086 4MT^5
43087 4MT^5
43088 4MT^5
60500 A2
60504 A2
60505 A2
60506 A2
60508 A2
60513 A2
60514 A2
60520 A2
60523 A2
60533 A2
60828 V2
60829 V2
60832 V2
60841 V2
60842 V2
60845 V2
60850 V2
60853 V2
60854 V2
60866 V2
60869 V2
60874 V2
60893 V2
60897 V2
60905 V2
60906 V2
60908 V2
60911 V2
60912 V2
60916 V2
60924 V2
60936 V2
60950 V2
60966 V2
61047 B1
61070 B1
61073 B1
61075 B1
61085 B1
61095 B1
61113 B1
61122 B1
61138 B1
61143 B1
61204 B1
61205 B1
61207 B1
61210 B1
61282 B1
61364 B1
61389 B1
61391 B1
61392 B1
64171 J6
64172 J6
64176 J6
64177 J6
64181 J6
64184 J6
64189 J6
64191 J6
64192 J6
64198 J6
64207 J6
64210 J6
64211 J6
64216 J6
64217 J6
64219 J6
64220 J6
64224 J6
64228 J6
64231 J6
64246 J6
64254 J6
64259 J6
64265 J6
64272 J6
64275 J6
64278 J6
64279 J6
67350 C12
67357 C12
67361 C12
67365 C12
67369 C12
67376 C12
67389 C12
68760 J52
68765 J52
68771 J52
68817 J52
68819 J52
68820 J52
68821 J52
68823 J52
68826 J52
68828 J52
68840 J52
68844 J52
68846 J52
68850 J52
68852 J52
68876 J52
68879 J52
68880 J52
68884 J52
90028 WD^1
90034 WD^1
90062 WD^1
90079 WD^1
90088 WD^1
90093 WD^1
90096 WD^1
90106 WD^1
90151 WD^1
90158 WD^1
90162 WD^1
90165 WD^1
90169 WD^1
90180 WD^1
90191 WD^1
90208 WD^1
90239 WD^1
90244 WD^1
90246 WD^1
90253 WD^1
90256 WD^1
90259 WD^1
90279 WD^1
90349 WD^1
90428 WD^1
90438 WD^1
90439 WD^1
90454 WD^1
90494 WD^1
90502 WD^1
90514 WD^1
90526 WD^1
90528 WD^1
90551 WD^1
90554 WD^1
90559 WD^1
90577 WD^1
90613 WD^1
90657 WD^1
90659 WD^1
90665 WD^1
90683 WD^1
90709 WD^1
90730 WD^1

1957 35A
43058 4MT^5
43059 4MT^5
43060 4MT^5
43061 4MT^5
43062 4MT^5
43064 4MT^5
43065 4MT^5
43066 4MT^5
43067 4MT^5
43080 4MT^5
43081 4MT^5
43082 4MT^5
43083 4MT^5
43084 4MT^5
43085 4MT^5
43086 4MT^5
43087 4MT^5
43088 4MT^5
60500 A2
60504 A2
60505 A2
60506 A2
60508 A2
60513 A2
60514 A2
60520 A2
60523 A2
60533 A2
60821 V2
60826 V2
60829 V2
60832 V2
60842 V2
60845 V2
60850 V2
60853 V2
60854 V2
60866 V2
60867 V2
60869 V2
60874 V2
60875 V2
60893 V2
60897 V2
60906 V2
60908 V2
60911 V2
60912 V2
60924 V2
60936 V2
60966 V2
61005 B1
61006 B1
61070 B1
61073 B1
61095 B1
61113 B1
61204 B1
61205 B1
61207 B1
61210 B1
61282 B1
61302 B1
61389 B1
61391 B1
61392 B1
61864 K3
61978 K3
61979 K3
64171 J6
64172 J6
64176 J6
64177 J6
64181 J6
64184 J6
64189 J6
64191 J6
64192 J6
64198 J6
64207 J6
64210 J6
64211 J6
64216 J6
64217 J6
64219 J6
64220 J6
64224 J6
64228 J6
64231 J6
64246 J6
64254 J6
64265 J6
64272 J6
64275 J6
64278 J6
64279 J6
64799 J39
64805 J39
64873 J39
64874 J39
64985 J39
67357 C12
67365 C12
67376 C12
67379 C12
67380 C12
67394 C12
68491 J69
68626 J69
68635 J69
68815 J52
68823 J52
68828 J52
68831 J52
68840 J52
90028 WD^1
90034 WD^1
90088 WD^1
90093 WD^1
90096 WD^1
90106 WD^1
90151 WD^1
90156 WD^1
90158 WD^1
90165 WD^1
90169 WD^1
90180 WD^1
90191 WD^1
90239 WD^1
90244 WD^1
90246 WD^1
90253 WD^1
90279 WD^1
90349 WD^1
90428 WD^1
90438 WD^1
90439 WD^1
90454 WD^1
90494 WD^1
90514 WD^1
90528 WD^1
90559 WD^1
90613 WD^1
90657 WD^1
90659 WD^1
90665 WD^1
90683 WD^1
90709 WD^1
90730 WD^1
92011 9F
92012 9F
92030 9F
92031 9F
92032 9F
92033 9F
92034 9F
92035 9F
92036 9F
92037 9F
92038 9F
92039 9F
92040 9F
92041 9F
92042 9F

1960 34E
43067 4MT^5
43081 4MT^5
43082 4MT^5
43084 4MT^5
43086 4MT^5
43088 4MT^5
60500 A2
60504 A2
60506 A2
60508 A2
60513 A2
60514 A2
60520 A2
60523 A2
60533 A2
60820 V2
60821 V2
60829 V2
60832 V2
60845 V2
60853 V2
60867 V2
60869 V2
60874 V2
60893 V2
60897 V2
60906 V2
60914 V2
60924 V2
60966 V2
61060 B1
61070 B1
61073 B1
61074 B1
61113 B1
61200 B1
61207 B1
61210 B1
61272 B1
61282 B1
61302 B1
61391 B1
61393 B1
61759 K2
61763 K2
61805 K3
61830 K3
61864 K3
61978 K3
61979 K3
64177 J6
64180 J6
64192 J6
64265 J6
68896 J50
68976 J50
69266 N5
69267 N5
69274 N5
69292 N5
69293 N5
69513 N2
69521 N2
69540 N2
69571 N2
69582 N2
90000 WD^1
90015 WD^1
90073 WD^1
90096 WD^1
90151 WD^1
90154 WD^1
90158 WD^1
90165 WD^1
90169 WD^1
90180 WD^1
90223 WD^1
90239 WD^1
90246 WD^1
90253 WD^1
90269 WD^1
90349 WD^1
90428 WD^1
90439 WD^1
90454 WD^1
90613 WD^1
90659 WD^1
90665 WD^1
90730 WD^1
92034 9F
92035 9F
92036 9F
92037 9F
92038 9F
92040 9F
92041 9F
92042 9F
92044 9F
92140 9F
92141 9F
92142 9F
92143 9F
92144 9F
92145 9F
92146 9F
92147 9F
92148 9F
92149 9F
92178 9F
92179 9F
92180 9F
92181 9F
92182 9F
92183 9F
92184 9F
92185 9F
92187 9F
92188 9F

1963 34E
43067 4MT^5
43081 4MT^5
43082 4MT^5
43084 4MT^5
43088 4MT^5
43089 4MT^5
43094 4MT^5
43146 4MT^5
43150 4MT^5
43151 4MT^5
43153 4MT^5
60046 A3
60047 A3
60048 A3
60050 A3
60062 A3
60065 A3
60108 A3
60500 A2
60513 A2
60520 A2
60523 A2
60533 A2
60803 V2
60817 V2
60841 V2
60858 V2
60869 V2
60880 V2
60881 V2
60906 V2
60912 V2
60948 V2
60950 V2
61070 B1
61073 B1
61074 B1
61097 B1
61122 B1
61174 B1
61207 B1
61210 B1
61250 B1
61272 B1
61302 B1
61314 B1
61331 B1
90015 WD^1
90031 WD^1
90050 WD^1
90073 WD^1
90096 WD^1
90130 WD^1
90146 WD^1
90151 WD^1
90154 WD^1
90158 WD^1
90246 WD^1
90269 WD^1
90349 WD^1
90428 WD^1
90439 WD^1
90454 WD^1
90502 WD^1
90514 WD^1
90613 WD^1
90659 WD^1
92034 9F
92035 9F
92037 9F
92038 9F
92040 9F
92041 9F
92042 9F
92140 9F
92142 9F
92143 9F
92145 9F
92146 9F
92147 9F
92148 9F
92149 9F
92178 9F
92179 9F
92180 9F
92181 9F
92182 9F
92183 9F
92184 9F
92185 9F
92186 9F
92187 9F
92188 9F

Newhaven

1948 NHN
32421 H2
32422 H2
32423 H2
32424 H2
32425 H2
32426 H2
32434 C2X
32475 E4
32482 E4
32492 E4
32494 E4
32499 E4
32508 E4
32533 C2
32534 C2X
32636 A1X
32647 A1X

1951 75A sub
32037 H1
32038 H1
32421 H2
32422 H2
32424 H2
32437 C2X
32475 E4
32494 E4
32496 E4
32504 E4
32508 E4
32537 C2X
32636 A1X
32647 A1X

1954 75A sub
32422 H2
32424 H2
32437 C2X
32475 E4
32494 E4
32496 E4
32504 E4
32636 A1X
32640 A1X
32662 A1X

Newport

1948 NPT
63016 O7
63044 O7
63054 O7
63074 O7
63081 O7
63091 O7
63098 O7
63125 O7
63130 O7
63131 O7
63140 O7
63144 O7
63154 O7
63160 O7
63179 O7
63196 O7
63327 Q5
63338 Q5
63341 Q6
63343 Q6
63344 Q6
63345 Q6
63347 Q6
63349 Q6
63350 Q6
63354 Q6
63355 Q6
63358 Q6
63360 Q6
63366 Q6
63370 Q6
63371 Q6
63373 Q6
63375 Q6
63384 Q6
63386 Q6
63389 Q6
63396 Q6
63397 Q6
63401 Q6
63405 Q6
63409 Q6
63411 Q6
63415 Q6
63417 Q6
63419 Q6
63420 Q6
63423 Q6
63425 Q6
63426 Q6
63430 Q6
63431 Q6
63438 Q6
63442 Q6
63443 Q6
63445 Q6
63446 Q6
63453 Q6
63458 Q6
63459 Q6
65601 J24
65608 J24
65626 J24
65730 J26
65731 J26
65734 J26
65735 J26
65736 J26
65737 J26
65738 J26
65739 J26
65740 J26
65741 J26
65742 J26
65743 J26
65744 J26
65745 J26
65746 J26
65749 J26
65750 J26
65751 J26
65752 J26
65753 J26
65754 J26
65755 J26
65756 J26
65757 J26
65758 J26
65759 J26
65760 J26
65761 J26
65762 J26
65763 J26
65765 J26
65766 J26
65767 J26
65768 J26
65769 J26
65770 J26
65772 J26
65773 J26
65774 J26
65777 J26
65778 J26
68007 J94
68011 J94
68023 J94
68041 J94
68060 J94
68062 J94
68427 J77
68431 J77
68441 J77
69910 T1
69911 T1
69913 T1
69916 T1
69917 T1
69919 T1
69921 T1
90106 WD^1
90109 WD^1
90114 WD^1
90132 WD^1
90159 WD^1
90230 WD^1
90248 WD^1
90273 WD^1
90305 WD^1
90346 WD^1
90348 WD^1
90373 WD^1
90559 WD^1
90576 WD^1
90584 WD^1
90605 WD^1
90625 WD^1

1951 51B
63341 Q6
63343 Q6
63344 Q6
63345 Q6
63347 Q6
63360 Q6
63370 Q6
63371 Q6
63388 Q6
63389 Q6
63426 Q6
63430 Q6
63445 Q6
63447 Q6
65601 J24
65730 J26
65731 J26
65732 J26
65734 J26
65735 J26
65736 J26
65737 J26
65738 J26
65739 J26
65740 J26
65741 J26
65742 J26
65743 J26
65744 J26
65745 J26
65746 J26
65749 J26
65750 J26
65751 J26
65752 J26
65753 J26
65754 J26
65755 J26
65756 J26
65757 J26
65758 J26
65759 J26
65760 J26
65761 J26
65762 J26
65763 J26
65765 J26
65766 J26
65767 J26
65768 J26
65769 J26
65770 J26
65772 J26
65773 J26
65774 J26
65777 J26
65778 J26
68007 J94
68011 J94
68023 J94
68037 J94
68049 J94
68060 J94
68062 J94
69910 T1
69911 T1
69913 T1
69916 T1
69917 T1
69919 T1
69921 T1
90014 WD^1
90016 WD^1
90027 WD^1
90044 WD^1
90045 WD^1
90054 WD^1
90068 WD^1
90074 WD^1
90076 WD^1
90081 WD^1
90090 WD^1
90091 WD^1
90098 WD^1
90132 WD^1
90230 WD^1
90273 WD^1
90373 WD^1
90426 WD^1
90434 WD^1
90446 WD^1
90451 WD^1
90452 WD^1
90457 WD^1
90459 WD^1
90461 WD^1
90462 WD^1
90465 WD^1
90475 WD^1

90481 WD[1]
90487 WD[1]
90488 WD[1]
90500 WD[1]
90503 WD[1]
90517 WD[1]
90605 WD[1]
90625 WD[1]

1954 51B
63341 Q6
63343 Q6
63344 Q6
63345 Q6
63347 Q6
63360 Q6
63370 Q6
63371 Q6
63388 Q6
63389 Q6
63426 Q6
63430 Q6
63445 Q6
63447 Q6
65730 J26
65731 J26
65732 J26
65733 J26
65734 J26
65735 J26
65736 J26
65738 J26
65740 J26
65741 J26
65742 J26
65743 J26
65744 J26
65745 J26
65746 J26
65749 J26
65750 J26
65751 J26
65752 J26
65753 J26
65754 J26
65755 J26
65756 J26
65757 J26
65758 J26
65759 J26
65760 J26
65761 J26
65762 J26
65763 J26
65765 J26
65766 J26
65767 J26
65768 J26
65769 J26
65770 J26
65772 J26
65773 J26
65774 J26
65777 J26
65778 J26
65860 J27
68007 J94
68011 J94
68023 J94
68037 J94
68049 J94
68060 J94
68062 J94
69910 T1
69911 T1
69913 T1
69915 T1
69916 T1
69917 T1
69921 T1
69922 T1
90014 WD[1]
90016 WD[1]
90027 WD[1]
90044 WD[1]
90068 WD[1]
90074 WD[1]
90076 WD[1]
90081 WD[1]
90090 WD[1]
90091 WD[1]
90098 WD[1]
90132 WD[1]
90230 WD[1]
90273 WD[1]
90373 WD[1]
90426 WD[1]
90434 WD[1]
90435 WD[1]
90446 WD[1]
90451 WD[1]
90452 WD[1]
90457 WD[1]
90459 WD[1]
90461 WD[1]
90462 WD[1]
90465 WD[1]
90475 WD[1]
90481 WD[1]
90487 WD[1]
90488 WD[1]
90503 WD[1]
90517 WD[1]
90605 WD[1]
90625 WD[1]

1957 51B
63360 Q6
63370 Q6
63371 Q6
63388 Q6
63389 Q6
63426 Q6
63430 Q6
63445 Q6
63447 Q6
65730 J26
65732 J26
65734 J26
65736 J26
65738 J26
65740 J26
65741 J26
65742 J26
65743 J26
65744 J26
65745 J26
65746 J26
65749 J26
65750 J26
65751 J26
65752 J26
65753 J26
65754 J26
65755 J26
65756 J26
65757 J26
65758 J26
65759 J26
65760 J26
65761 J26
65762 J26
65763 J26
65765 J26
65766 J26
65767 J26
65768 J26
65769 J26
65770 J26
65772 J26
65773 J26
65774 J26
65777 J26
65778 J26
68011 J94
68023 J94
68049 J94
68060 J94
68062 J94
69911 T1
90014 WD[1]
90016 WD[1]
90027 WD[1]
90068 WD[1]
90074 WD[1]
90076 WD[1]
90081 WD[1]
90090 WD[1]
90091 WD[1]
90098 WD[1]
90132 WD[1]
90230 WD[1]
90273 WD[1]
90373 WD[1]
90409 WD[1]
90424 WD[1]
90426 WD[1]
90434 WD[1]
90435 WD[1]
90446 WD[1]
90451 WD[1]
90452 WD[1]
90457 WD[1]
90459 WD[1]
90461 WD[1]
90462 WD[1]
90465 WD[1]
90475 WD[1]
90481 WD[1]
90487 WD[1]
90488 WD[1]
90500 WD[1]
90503 WD[1]
90517 WD[1]
90603 WD[1]
90605 WD[1]
90625 WD[1]

Newport IOW

1948 NPT
W1 E1[2]
W2 E1[2]
W3 E1[2]
W4 E1[2]
W8 A1X
W13 A1X
W25 O2
W26 O2
W27 O2
W28 O2
W29 O2
W30 O2
W31 O2
W32 O2
W33 O2
W34 O2
32510 E4

1951 71E
W1 E1[2]
W2 E1[2]
W3 E1[2]
W4 E1[2]
W26 O2
W27 O2
W28 O2
W29 O2
W30 O2
W31 O2
W32 O2
W33 O2
W34 O2
W35 O2
W36 O2

1954 71E
W1 E1[2]
W2 E1[2]
W3 E1[2]
W4 E1[2]
W26 O2
W27 O2
W28 O2
W29 O2
W30 O2
W31 O2
W32 O2
W33 O2
W34 O2
W35 O2
W36 O2

1957 70G
W1 E1[2]
W3 E1[2]
W4 E1[2]
W26 O2
W27 O2
W28 O2
W29 O2
W30 O2
W31 O2
W32 O2
W33 O2
W35 O2
W36 O2

Newport Pill

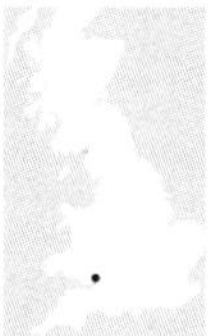

1948 PILL
62 RR[4]
190 AD[1]
421 BM[1]
424 BM[1]
425 BM[1]
426 BM[1]
666 AD[2]
667 AD[2]
1709 1854
1726 1854
1764 1854
1896 1854
2033 2021
2113 2021
2136 2021
2154 2021
2734 2721
2738 2721
2764 2721
2793 2721
4201 4200
4211 4200
4226 4200
4229 4200
4233 4200
4235 4200
4237 4200
4246 4200
4253 4200
4258 4200
4269 4200
4280 4200
4291 4200
4662 5700
5235 5205
5244 5205
5252 5205
5740 5700
5747 5700
5776 5700
6710 6700
6711 6700
6725 6700
6726 6700
6727 6700
6728 6700
6729 6700
6730 6700
6731 6700
6732 6700
6735 6700
6743 6700
6755 6700
6756 6700
6759 6700
7774 5700

1951 86B
666 AD[2]
667 AD[2]
1506 1500
1507 1500
2033 2021
2136 2021
2154 2021
3663 5700
4201 4200
4211 4200
4226 4200
4229 4200
4233 4200
4235 4200
4237 4200
4246 4200
4253 4200
4258 4200
4263 4200
4269 4200
4280 4200
4291 4200
5200 4200
5231 5205
5235 5205
5244 5205
5250 5205
5252 5205
5260 5205
5638 5600
5714 5700
5740 5700
5747 5700
5750 5700
6409 6400
6710 6700
6711 6700
6725 6700
6726 6700
6727 6700
6728 6700
6729 6700
6730 6700
6731 6700
6732 6700
6735 6700
6743 6700
6755 6700
6756 6700
6757 6700
6759 6700
6760 6700
6764 6700
6772 6700
7712 5700
7774 5700
7789 5700
8796 5700

1954 86B
666 AD[2]
667 AD[2]
1506 1500
1507 1500
2805 2800
3663 5700
4130 5101
4201 4200
4211 4200
4233 4200
4235 4200
4237 4200
4253 4200
4258 4200
4263 4200
4269 4200
4280 4200
4285 4200
4291 4200
5200 4200
5231 5205
5235 5205
5244 5205
5250 5205
5252 5205
5706 5700
5714 5700
5733 5700
5740 5700
5747 5700
6409 6400
6710 6700
6711 6700
6725 6700
6726 6700
6727 6700
6728 6700
6729 6700
6730 6700
6731 6700
6732 6700
6735 6700
6742 6700
6743 6700
6755 6700
6756 6700
6757 6700
6759 6700
6760 6700
6764 6700
6772 6700
7712 5700
7721 5700
7774 5700
8796 5700

1957 86B
1506 1500
1507 1500
3652 5700
3663 5700
3700 5700
4201 4200
4211 4200
4214 4200
4233 4200
4235 4200
4237 4200
4253 4200
4258 4200
4280 4200
4285 4200
4291 4200
5200 4200
5202 4200
5231 5205
5235 5205
5244 5205
5250 5205
5252 5205
5257 5205
5706 5700
5714 5700
5733 5700
5734 5700
5736 5700
5740 5700
5741 5700
5747 5700
5777 5700
6710 6700
6711 6700
6725 6700
6726 6700
6727 6700
6728 6700
6729 6700
6730 6700
6731 6700
6732 6700
6735 6700
6739 6700
6742 6700
6743 6700
6755 6700
6756 6700
6757 6700
6759 6700
6760 6700
6764 6700
6772 6700
7712 5700
7721 5700
8796 5700

1960 86B
1507 1500
3652 5700
3674 5700
4214 4200
4233 4200
4235 4200
4238 4200
4253 4200
4258 4200
4259 4200
4276 4200
4280 4200
4643 5700
4682 5700
5200 4200
5202 4200
5231 5205
5235 5205
5244 5205
5250 5205
5252 5205
5256 5205
5758 5700
5768 5700
6724 6700
6728 6700
6739 6700
6742 6700
6751 6700
6755 6700
6756 6700
6757 6700
6759 6700
6760 6700
6764 6700
6772 6700
7703 5700
8499 9400

1963 86B
3705 5700
4214 4200
4233 4200
4238 4200
4253 4200
4254 4200
4259 4200
4264 4200
4271 4200
4280 4200
4294 4200
4643 5700
5200 4200
5244 5205
5250 5205
5256 5205

Newton Abbot

1948 NA
1001 1000
1018 1000
1362 1361
1427 1400
1439 1400
1466 1400
1470 1400
2097 2021
2785 2721
3341 3300
3383 3300
3400 3300
3407 3300
3430 3300
4012 4000
4016 4073
4077 4073
4098 4073
4099 4073
4109 5101
4133 5101
4405 4400
4526 4500
4547 4500
4582 4575
4587 4575
4983 4900
5011 4073
5028 4073
5034 4073
5047 4073
5058 4073
5062 4073
5071 4073
5078 4073
5094 4073
5108 5101
5113 5101
5132 5101
5142 5101
5150 5101
5153 5101
5157 5101
5350 4300
5391 4300
5505 4575
5530 4575
5551 4575
5552 4575
5557 4575
5798 5700
6018 6000
6023 6000
6024 6000
6027 6000
6028 6000
6345 4300
6813 6800
6814 6800
6822 6800
6829 6800
6934 4900
7000 4073
7200 7200
7220 7200
7250 7200
7427 7400
9623 5700
9633 5700
9717 5700
90102 WD[1]
90186 WD[1]
90188 WD[1]
90205 WD[1]

1951 83A
1018 1000
1019 1000
1362 1361
1427 1400
1439 1400
1466 1400
1470 1400
1608 1600
2181 2181
2183 2181
2809 2800
2873 2800
2881 2800
3600 5700
3659 5700
3834 2884
4077 4073
4098 4073
4099 4073
4109 5101
4133 5101
4179 5101
4405 4400
4532 4500
4547 4500
4582 4575
4587 4575
5011 4073
5024 4073
5028 4073
5041 4073
5047 4073
5071 4073
5078 4073
5079 4073
5108 5101
5113 5101
5132 5101
5140 5101
5142 5101
5150 5101
5153 5101
5157 5101
5158 5101
5350 4300
5505 4575
5544 4575
5551 4575
5552 4575
5557 4575
5798 5700
5920 4900
6345 4300
6813 6800
6814 6800
6822 6800
6829 6800
6934 4900
7000 4073
7029 4073
7200 7200
7209 7200
7220 7200
7250 7200
7427 7400
7805 7800
7812 7800
7813 7800
8403 9400
8422 9400
9623 5700
9633 5700
9668 5700
9778 5700

1954 83A
1427 1400
1439 1400
1466 1400
1470 1400
1608 1600
1626 1600
2183 2181
2809 2800
2869 2800
2875 2800
2881 2800
3600 5700
3659 5700
3796 5700
3834 2884
3840 2884
3841 2884
3864 2884
4077 4073
4080 4073
4088 4073
4098 4073
4099 4073
4109 5101
4133 5101
4179 5101
4401 4400
4405 4400
4547 4500
4954 4900
5011 4073
5024 4073
5028 4073
5041 4073
5047 4073
5059 4073
5071 4073
5078 4073
5079 4073
5108 5101
5113 5101
5150 5101
5153 5101
5158 5101
5196 5101
5339 4300
5360 4300
5362 4300
5539 4575
5542 4575
5543 4575
5544 4575
5551 4575
5552 4575
5557 4575
5796 5700
5920 4900
6356 4300
6813 6800
6814 6800
6822 6800
6829 6800
7000 4073
7029 4073
7427 7400
7806 7800
7812 7800
7813 7800
7916 6959
8403 9400
8451 9400
8473 9400
9440 9400
9462 9400
9623 5700
9633 5700
9668 5700
9678 5700
70022 7P6F
90148 WD[1]
90676 WD[1]

1957 83A
1427 1400
1439 1400
1466 1400
1470 1400
1472 1400
1608 1600
1626 1600
2846 2800
2875 2800
2881 2800
3600 5700
3659 5700
3796 5700
3834 2884
3840 2884
3841 2884
3864 2884
4037 4073
4076 4073
4098 4073
4105 5101
4109 5101
4145 5101
4150 5101
4176 5101
4178 5101
4179 5101
4568 4500
4905 4900
4967 4900
5011 4073
5024 4073
5053 4073
5059 4073
5071 4073
5078 4073
5079 4073
5089 4073
5108 5101
5150 5101
5153 5101
5154 5101
5158 5101
5164 5101
5168 5101
5178 5101
5183 5101
5195 5101
5196 5101
5339 4300
5533 4575
5536 4575
5558 4575
5796 5700
5920 4900
5967 4900
6813 6800
6814 6800
6829 6800
6836 6800
6933 4900
6938 4900
7000 4073
7427 7400
7813 7800
7814 7800
7916 6959
8451 9400
8466 9400
9440 9400
9462 9400
9487 9400
9633 5700
9668 5700
9678 5700

1960 83A
1466 1400
1470 1400
1608 1600
1626 1600
2805 2800
2807 2800
2846 2800
2875 2800
2881 2800
3659 5700
3796 5700
3840 2884
3841 2884
3864 2884
4077 4073
4080 4073
4083 4073
4098 4073
4105 5101
4145 5101
4150 5101
4176 5101
4177 5101
4178 5101
4179 5101
4555 4500
4561 4500
4905 4900
4920 4900
4936 4900
4975 4900
5003 4073
5011 4073
5024 4073
5032 4073
5049 4073
5055 4073
5079 4073
5150 5101
5153 5101
5154 5101
5158 5101
5164 5101
5178 5101
5183 5101
5195 5101
5197 5101
5558 4575
5573 4575
5920 4900
5967 4900
6813 6800
6829 6800
6836 6800
6904 4900
6940 4900
7029 4073
7808 7800
7818 7800
7821 7800
7916 6959
9440 9400
9462 9400
9487 9400
9633 5700
9678 5700

1963 83A
3796 5700
5042 4073
5055 4073

Newton Heath

1948 26A
40013 3MT[1]
40014 3MT[1]
40015 3MT[1]
40063 3MT[1]
40065 3MT[1]
40582 2P[3]
40584 2P[3]
40588 2P[3]
42278 4MT[1]
42279 4MT[1]
42280 4MT[1]
42281 4MT[1]
42282 4MT[1]
42283 4MT[1]
42284 4MT[1]
42285 4MT[1]
42286 4MT[1]
42287 4MT[1]
42288 4MT[1]
42289 4MT[1]
42290 4MT[1]
42477 4MT[3]
42486 4MT[3]
42491 4MT[3]
42492 4MT[3]
42549 4MT[3]
42551 4MT[3]
42618 4MT[3]
42619 4MT[3]
42620 4MT[3]
42621 4MT[3]
42622 4MT[3]
42623 4MT[3]
42624 4MT[3]
42625 4MT[3]
42626 4MT[3]
42630 4MT[3]
42700 5MT[1]
42701 5MT[1]
42702 5MT[1]
42703 5MT[1]
42704 5MT[1]
42705 5MT[1]
42706 5MT[1]
42707 5MT[1]
42708 5MT[1]
42709 5MT[1]
42710 5MT[1]
42711 5MT[1]
42713 5MT[1]
42714 5MT[1]
42766 5MT[1]
42789 5MT[1]
42820 5MT[1]
42871 5MT[1]
42901 5MT[1]
44311 4F[2]
44543 4F[2]
44544 4F[2]
44781 5MT[3]
44782 5MT[3]
44888 5MT[3]
44889 5MT[3]
44890 5MT[3]
44891 5MT[3]
44893 5MT[3]
44894 5MT[3]
44895 5MT[3]
44933 5MT[3]
44934 5MT[3]
44940 5MT[3]
44951 5MT[3]
44987 5MT[3]
45079 5MT[3]
45102 5MT[3]
45103 5MT[3]
45105 5MT[3]
45202 5MT[3]
45203 5MT[3]
45222 5MT[3]
45224 5MT[3]
45232 5MT[3]
45233 5MT[3]
45234 5MT[3]
45635 6P5F[2]
45642 6P5F[2]
45661 6P5F[2]
45700 6P5F[2]
45701 6P5F[2]
45706 6P5F[2]
45710 6P5F[2]
45711 6P5F[2]
45712 6P5F[2]
45717 6P5F[2]
45719 6P5F[2]
46418 2MT[2]
46419 2MT[2]
47586 3F[6]
48460 8F
48462 8F
48756 8F
48760 8F
48761 8F
48762 8F
48763 8F
48765 8F
49510 7F[4]
49511 7F[4]
49512 7F[4]
49520 7F[4]
49533 7F[4]
49554 7F[4]
49556 7F[4]
49560 7F[4]
49565 7F[4]
49607 7F[4]
49608 7F[4]
49636 7F[4]
49637 7F[4]
49639 7F[4]
49642 7F[4]
49650 7F[4]
49651 7F[4]
49652 7F[4]
49653 7F[4]
49654 7F[4]
49655 7F[4]
49656 7F[4]
49657 7F[4]
50736 2P[8]
50738 2P[8]
50818 2P[8]
51222 0F[4]
51234 0F[4]
51379 2F[2]
51400 2F[2]
51404 2F[2]
51424 2F[2]
51425 2F[2]
51436 2F[2]
51438 2F[2]
51470 2F[2]
51472 2F[2]
51488 2F[2]
51496 2F[2]
51510 2F[2]
52120 3F[7]
52124 3F[7]
52132 3F[7]
52136 3F[7]
52138 3F[7]
52156 3F[7]
52207 3F[7]
52229 3F[7]
52239 3F[7]
52266 3F[7]
52279 3F[7]
52300 3F[7]
52343 3F[7]
52345 3F[7]
52355 3F[7]
52358 3F[7]
52437 3F[7]
52443 3F[7]
52466 3F[7]
52517 3F[7]
52518 3F[7]
52578 3F[9]

1951 26A
40013 3MT[1]
40015 3MT[1]
40063 3MT[1]
40065 3MT[1]
40682 2P[3]
40691 2P[3]
42278 4MT[1]
42279 4MT[1]
42280 4MT[1]
42281 4MT[1]
42282 4MT[1]
42283 4MT[1]
42284 4MT[1]
42285 4MT[1]
42286 4MT[1]
42287 4MT[1]
42288 4MT[1]
42289 4MT[1]
42290 4MT[1]
42486 4MT[3]
42550 4MT[3]
42551 4MT[3]
42618 4MT[3]
42621 4MT[3]
42622 4MT[3]
42623 4MT[3]
42624 4MT[3]
42625 4MT[3]
42626 4MT[3]
42630 4MT[3]
42635 4MT[3]
42701 5MT[1]
42702 5MT[1]
42703 5MT[1]
42704 5MT[1]
42705 5MT[1]
42707 5MT[1]
42708 5MT[1]
42709 5MT[1]
42710 5MT[1]
42711 5MT[1]
42713 5MT[1]
42714 5MT[1]
42715 5MT[1]
42750 5MT[1]
42766 5MT[1]
42789 5MT[1]
42820 5MT[1]
42845 5MT[1]
42871 5MT[1]
42878 5MT[1]
42901 5MT[1]
44311 4F[2]
44543 4F[2]
44696 5MT[3]
44697 5MT[3]
44734 5MT[3]
44735 5MT[3]
44736 5MT[3]
44889 5MT[3]
44890 5MT[3]
44891 5MT[3]
44893 5MT[3]
44894 5MT[3]
44895 5MT[3]
44933 5MT[3]
44934 5MT[3]
44940 5MT[3]
44987 5MT[3]
45102 5MT[3]
45103 5MT[3]
45104 5MT[3]
45105 5MT[3]
45202 5MT[3]
45203 5MT[3]
45220 5MT[3]
45223 5MT[3]
45224 5MT[3]
45225 5MT[3]
45232 5MT[3]
45233 5MT[3]
45234 5MT[3]
45336 5MT[3]
45635 6P5F[2]
45642 6P5F[2]
45661 6P5F[2]
45671 6P5F[2]
45700 6P5F[2]
45701 6P5F[2]
45702 6P5F[2]
45706 6P5F[2]
45710 6P5F[2]
45712 6P5F[2]
45719 6P5F[2]
46418 2MT[2]
46419 2MT[2]
47577 3F[6]
47586 3F[6]
48705 8F
48707 8F
48718 8F
48720 8F
48722 8F
48725 8F
48727 8F
48733 8F
48752 8F
48755 8F
48766 8F
48769 8F
49536 7F[4]
49558 7F[4]
49560 7F[4]
49570 7F[4]
49580 7F[4]
49608 7F[4]
49637 7F[4]
50855 2P[8]
50859 2P[8]
51338 2F[2]
51424 2F[2]
51425 2F[2]
51429 2F[2]
51436 2F[2]
51457 2F[2]
51458 2F[2]
51470 2F[2]
51472 2F[2]
51496 2F[2]
51510 2F[2]
52094 3F[7]
52102 3F[7]
52132 3F[7]
52137 3F[7]
52139 3F[7]
52156 3F[7]
52207 3F[7]
52239 3F[7]
52266 3F[7]
52300 3F[7]
52304 3F[7]
52343 3F[7]
52355 3F[7]
52358 3F[7]
52455 3F[7]
52517 3F[7]
52558 3F[9]
52569 3F[9]
52583 3F[9]
90101 WD[1]
90105 WD[1]
90113 WD[1]
90123 WD[1]
90327 WD[1]
90338 WD[1]
90366 WD[1]
90388 WD[1]
90413 WD[1]
90525 WD[1]
90535 WD[1]
90548 WD[1]
90561 WD[1]
90568 WD[1]
90589 WD[1]
90706 WD[1]
90708 WD[1]
90715 WD[1]

1954 26A
40013 3MT[1]
40015 3MT[1]
40063 3MT[1]
40065 3MT[1]
42278 4MT[1]
42279 4MT[1]
42280 4MT[1]
42281 4MT[1]
42282 4MT[1]
42283 4MT[1]
42284 4MT[1]
42285 4MT[1]
42286 4MT[1]
42287 4MT[1]
42288 4MT[1]
42289 4MT[1]
42290 4MT[1]
42486 4MT[3]
42550 4MT[3]
42618 4MT[3]
42621 4MT[3]
42622 4MT[3]
42623 4MT[3]
42624 4MT[3]
42625 4MT[3]
42701 5MT[1]
42702 5MT[1]
42703 5MT[1]
42704 5MT[1]
42705 5MT[1]
42707 5MT[1]
42708 5MT[1]
42709 5MT[1]
42710 5MT[1]
42711 5MT[1]
42713 5MT[1]
42714 5MT[1]

42715 5MT[1]
42750 5MT[1]
42766 5MT[1]
42789 5MT[1]
42820 5MT[1]
42871 5MT[1]
42878 5MT[1]
44311 4F[2]
44543 4F[2]
44696 5MT[3]
44697 5MT[3]
44734 5MT[3]
44735 5MT[3]
44736 5MT[3]
44890 5MT[3]
44891 5MT[3]
44893 5MT[3]
44894 5MT[3]
44895 5MT[3]
44933 5MT[3]
44934 5MT[3]
45102 5MT[3]
45103 5MT[3]
45104 5MT[3]
45105 5MT[3]
45202 5MT[3]
45203 5MT[3]
45220 5MT[3]
45223 5MT[3]
45224 5MT[3]
45225 5MT[3]
45232 5MT[3]
45233 5MT[3]
45234 5MT[3]
45336 5MT[3]
45635 6P5F[2]
45642 6P5F[2]
45661 6P5F[2]
45671 6P5F[2]
45700 6P5F[2]
45701 6P5F[2]
45702 6P5F[2]
45706 6P5F[2]
45710 6P5F[2]
45712 6P5F[2]
46410 2MT[2]
46411 2MT[2]
46418 2MT[2]
46419 2MT[2]
46484 2MT[2]
47577 3F[6]
47586 3F[6]
49508 7F[4]
49557 7F[4]
49560 7F[4]
49570 7F[4]
49666 7F[4]
49667 7F[4]
51436 2F[2]
51447 2F[2]
51457 2F[2]
51458 2F[2]
51470 2F[2]
51472 2F[2]
51496 2F[2]
52089 3F[7]
52108 3F[7]
52137 3F[7]
52159 3F[7]
52165 3F[7]
52271 3F[7]
52334 3F[7]
52358 3F[7]
52360 3F[7]
52389 3F[7]
52390 3F[7]
52455 3F[7]
80049 4MT[3]
80050 4MT[3]
80051 4MT[3]
80052 4MT[3]
80053 4MT[3]
90105 WD[1]
90113 WD[1]
90222 WD[1]
90245 WD[1]
90248 WD[1]
90283 WD[1]
90289 WD[1]
90291 WD[1]
90327 WD[1]
90338 WD[1]
90360 WD[1]
90366 WD[1]
90376 WD[1]
90388 WD[1]
90389 WD[1]
90390 WD[1]
90523 WD[1]
90525 WD[1]
90530 WD[1]
90533 WD[1]
90535 WD[1]
90548 WD[1]
90558 WD[1]
90561 WD[1]
90576 WD[1]
90589 WD[1]
90669 WD[1]
90675 WD[1]
90706 WD[1]
90708 WD[1]
90715 WD[1]

1957 26A
40013 3MT[1]
40014 3MT[1]
40015 3MT[1]
40062 3MT[1]
40063 3MT[1]
40065 3MT[1]
42063 4MT[1]
42278 4MT[1]
42279 4MT[1]
42280 4MT[1]
42281 4MT[1]
42282 4MT[1]
42283 4MT[1]
42284 4MT[1]
42286 4MT[1]
42287 4MT[1]
42288 4MT[1]
42290 4MT[1]
42450 4MT[3]
42451 4MT[3]
42461 4MT[3]
42486 4MT[3]
42550 4MT[3]
42568 4MT[3]
42618 4MT[3]
42621 4MT[3]
42623 4MT[3]
42624 4MT[3]
42651 4MT[3]
42660 4MT[3]
42701 5MT[1]
42703 5MT[1]
42704 5MT[1]
42705 5MT[1]
42707 5MT[1]
42708 5MT[1]
42709 5MT[1]
42710 5MT[1]
42711 5MT[1]
42714 5MT[1]
42715 5MT[1]
42726 5MT[1]
42727 5MT[1]
42728 5MT[1]
42732 5MT[1]
42733 5MT[1]
42750 5MT[1]
42871 5MT[1]
42878 5MT[1]
42901 5MT[1]
43756 3F[3]
44022 4F[1]
44119 4F[2]
44311 4F[2]
44543 4F[2]
44696 5MT[3]
44697 5MT[3]
44734 5MT[3]
44735 5MT[3]
44736 5MT[3]
44803 5MT[3]
44845 5MT[3]
44890 5MT[3]
44891 5MT[3]
44893 5MT[3]
44894 5MT[3]
44895 5MT[3]
44933 5MT[3]
44934 5MT[3]
45031 5MT[3]
45076 5MT[3]
45101 5MT[3]
45102 5MT[3]
45103 5MT[3]
45104 5MT[3]
45105 5MT[3]
45202 5MT[3]
45203 5MT[3]
45220 5MT[3]
45223 5MT[3]
45224 5MT[3]
45225 5MT[3]
45232 5MT[3]
45233 5MT[3]
45284 5MT[3]
45336 5MT[3]
45341 5MT[3]
45435 5MT[3]
45635 6P5F[2]
45642 6P5F[2]
45661 6P5F[2]
45671 6P5F[2]
45700 6P5F[2]
45701 6P5F[2]
45702 6P5F[2]
45706 6P5F[2]
45710 6P5F[2]
45712 6P5F[2]
46410 2MT[2]
46411 2MT[2]
46418 2MT[2]
46419 2MT[2]
46437 2MT[2]
46484 2MT[2]
46487 2MT[2]
47301 3F[6]
47303 3F[6]
47305 3F[6]
47425 3F[6]
47440 3F[6]
49508 7F[4]
49511 7F[4]
49515 7F[4]
49560 7F[4]
49624 7F[4]
49667 7F[4]
51336 2F[2]
51381 2F[2]
51447 2F[2]
51457 2F[2]
51458 2F[2]
51496 2F[2]
52089 3F[7]
52108 3F[7]
52141 3F[7]
52159 3F[7]
52165 3F[7]
52271 3F[7]
52275 3F[7]
52278 3F[7]
52328 3F[7]
52341 3F[7]
52455 3F[7]
58128 2F[5]
80044 4MT[3]
80046 4MT[3]
80060 4MT[3]
80061 4MT[3]
80093 4MT[3]
90105 WD[1]
90113 WD[1]
90140 WD[1]
90142 WD[1]
90163 WD[1]
90197 WD[1]
90222 WD[1]
90245 WD[1]
90248 WD[1]
90289 WD[1]
90291 WD[1]
90316 WD[1]
90327 WD[1]
90338 WD[1]
90366 WD[1]
90376 WD[1]
90388 WD[1]
90389 WD[1]
90390 WD[1]
90523 WD[1]
90525 WD[1]
90530 WD[1]
90533 WD[1]
90548 WD[1]
90552 WD[1]
90558 WD[1]
90561 WD[1]
90576 WD[1]
90589 WD[1]
90669 WD[1]
90706 WD[1]
90708 WD[1]
90715 WD[1]

1960 26A
40014 3MT[1]
40015 3MT[1]
40062 3MT[1]
40063 3MT[1]
42288 4MT[1]
42548 4MT[3]
42549 4MT[3]
42623 4MT[3]
42624 4MT[3]
42660 4MT[3]
42701 5MT[1]
42703 5MT[1]
42704 5MT[1]
42705 5MT[1]
42707 5MT[1]
42708 5MT[1]
42709 5MT[1]
42710 5MT[1]
42714 5MT[1]
42715 5MT[1]
42726 5MT[1]
42728 5MT[1]
42733 5MT[1]
42750 5MT[1]
42871 5MT[1]
42901 5MT[1]
44022 4F[1]
44311 4F[2]
44543 4F[2]
44696 5MT[3]
44697 5MT[3]
44734 5MT[3]
44735 5MT[3]
44736 5MT[3]
44803 5MT[3]
44845 5MT[3]
44890 5MT[3]
44891 5MT[3]
44893 5MT[3]
44894 5MT[3]
44895 5MT[3]
44933 5MT[3]
44934 5MT[3]
45031 5MT[3]
45076 5MT[3]
45101 5MT[3]
45102 5MT[3]
45103 5MT[3]
45104 5MT[3]
45105 5MT[3]
45154 5MT[3]
45156 5MT[3]
45202 5MT[3]
45203 5MT[3]
45220 5MT[3]
45224 5MT[3]
45225 5MT[3]
45232 5MT[3]
45233 5MT[3]
45284 5MT[3]
45290 5MT[3]
45336 5MT[3]
45341 5MT[3]
45435 5MT[3]
45509 6P5F[1]
45635 6P5F[2]
45642 6P5F[2]
45661 6P5F[2]
45700 6P5F[2]
45701 6P5F[2]
45702 6P5F[2]
45706 6P5F[2]
45710 6P5F[2]
46411 2MT[2]
46418 2MT[2]
46419 2MT[2]
46437 2MT[2]
46484 2MT[2]
46487 2MT[2]
47207 3F[5]
47217 3F[5]
47546 3F[6]
47547 3F[6]
48115 8F
48148 8F
48372 8F
48491 8F
48553 8F
48716 8F
48720 8F
48745 8F
49508 7F[4]
49624 7F[4]
51343 2F[2]
51371 2F[2]
52140 3F[7]
52141 3F[7]
52161 3F[7]
52230 3F[7]
52270 3F[7]
52271 3F[7]
52275 3F[7]
52341 3F[7]
80044 4MT[3]
80060 4MT[3]
80061 4MT[3]
90105 WD[1]
90142 WD[1]
90163 WD[1]
90197 WD[1]
90222 WD[1]
90248 WD[1]
90271 WD[1]
90289 WD[1]
90291 WD[1]
90328 WD[1]
90338 WD[1]
90366 WD[1]
90376 WD[1]
90388 WD[1]
90389 WD[1]
90390 WD[1]
90523 WD[1]
90530 WD[1]
90533 WD[1]
90548 WD[1]
90576 WD[1]
90589 WD[1]
90669 WD[1]
90715 WD[1]
92015 9F
92016 9F
92017 9F
92161 9F
92162 9F

1963 26A
42280 4MT[1]
42288 4MT[1]
42548 4MT[3]
42614 4MT[3]
42619 4MT[3]
42620 4MT[3]
42623 4MT[3]
42632 4MT[3]
42640 4MT[3]
42651 4MT[3]
42696 4MT[1]
42697 4MT[1]
42698 4MT[1]
42701 5MT[1]
42709 5MT[1]
42710 5MT[1]
42733 5MT[1]
42750 5MT[1]
42871 5MT[1]
43952 4F[1]
44022 4F[1]
44221 4F[2]
44431 4F[2]
44543 4F[2]
44696 5MT[3]
44697 5MT[3]
44734 5MT[3]
44735 5MT[3]
44736 5MT[3]
44803 5MT[3]
44845 5MT[3]
44890 5MT[3]
44891 5MT[3]
44893 5MT[3]
44895 5MT[3]
44933 5MT[3]
44934 5MT[3]
45076 5MT[3]
45101 5MT[3]
45104 5MT[3]
45154 5MT[3]
45202 5MT[3]
45203 5MT[3]
45220 5MT[3]
45233 5MT[3]
45255 5MT[3]
45336 5MT[3]
45339 5MT[3]
45341 5MT[3]
45435 5MT[3]
45522 7P[1]
45578 6P5F[2]
45601 6P5F[2]
45602 6P5F[2]
45623 6P5F[2]
45635 6P5F[2]
45642 6P5F[2]
45652 6P5F[2]
45661 6P5F[2]
45700 6P5F[2]
45701 6P5F[2]
45702 6P5F[2]
45706 6P5F[2]
45710 6P5F[2]
45737 6P5F[2]
46133 7P[3]R
46140 7P[3]R
46142 7P[3]R
46411 2MT[2]
46418 2MT[2]
46437 2MT[2]
46487 2MT[2]
47207 3F[5]
47284 3F[6]
47300 3F[6]
47547 3F[6]
47582 3F[6]
47640 3F[6]
48115 8F
48148 8F
48372 8F
48491 8F
48553 8F
48716 8F
48720 8F
48745 8F
90197 WD[1]
90271 WD[1]
90289 WD[1]
90291 WD[1]
90338 WD[1]
90366 WD[1]
90388 WD[1]
90389 WD[1]
90533 WD[1]
90561 WD[1]
90715 WD[1]
92015 9F
92016 9F
92017 9F
92161 9F
92162 9F

1966 9D
42079 4MT[1]
42087 4MT[1]
42115 4MT[1]
42283 4MT[1]
42548 4MT[3]
42656 4MT[3]
42676 4MT[1]
44696 5MT[3]
44697 5MT[3]
44734 5MT[3]
44803 5MT[3]
44818 5MT[3]
44822 5MT[3]
44845 5MT[3]
44846 5MT[3]
44861 5MT[3]
44890 5MT[3]
44891 5MT[3]
44926 5MT[3]
44933 5MT[3]
44934 5MT[3]
44938 5MT[3]
44949 5MT[3]
45076 5MT[3]
45083 5MT[3]
45101 5MT[3]
45133 5MT[3]
45202 5MT[3]
45203 5MT[3]
45206 5MT[3]
45246 5MT[3]
45255 5MT[3]
45271 5MT[3]
45336 5MT[3]
45339 5MT[3]
45341 5MT[3]
45343 5MT[3]
45382 5MT[3]
45420 5MT[3]
45435 5MT[3]
45654 6P5F[2]
46406 2MT[2]
46411 2MT[2]
46412 2MT[2]
46418 2MT[2]
46437 2MT[2]
46449 2MT[2]
46501 2MT[2]
47388 3F[6]
48136 8F
48174 8F
48318 8F
48321 8F
48331 8F
48369 8F
48372 8F
48426 8F
48533 8F
48543 8F
48557 8F
48602 8F
48612 8F
48744 8F
48756 8F
48758 8F
48775 8F
70017 7P6F
70021 7P6F
70034 7P6F
70044 7P6F
92016 9F
92018 9F
92022 9F
92031 9F
92050 9F
92052 9F
92056 9F
92077 9F
92080 9F
92081 9F

Neyland

1948 NEY
3447 3300
3654 5700
4358 4300
4654 5700
4937 4900
4957 4900
4997 4900
5310 4300
5353 4300
5357 4300
5368 4300
5372 4300
5392 4300
5929 4900
6347 4300
6355 4300
6371 4300
6389 4300
7306 4300
7816 7800
9652 5700

1951 87H
1001 1000
1009 1000
1020 1000
1027 1000
1601 1600
1602 1600
1606 1600
1611 1600
1628 1600
2010 1901
2288 2251
3654 5700
4132 5101
4358 4300
4506 4500
4515 4500
4519 4500
4553 4500
4556 4500
4576 4575
4579 4575
4654 5700
4957 4900
4982 4900
4997 4900
5310 4300
5353 4300
5357 4300
5368 4300
5372 4300
5392 4300
5513 4575
5549 4575
5568 4575
6347 4300
6355 4300
6371 4300
6389 4300
6602 5600
7306 4300
7413 7400
7816 7800
8102 8100
8107 8100
9652 5700

1954 87H
1001 1000
1009 1000
1020 1000
1027 1000
1029 1000
1601 1600
1602 1600
1606 1600
1611 1600
1637 1600
2220 2251
2226 2251
2228 2251
2229 2251
2283 2251
2288 2251
3654 5700
3657 5700
4132 5101
4358 4300
4506 4500
4519 4500
4541 4500
4553 4500
4556 4500
4557 4500
4576 4575
4579 4575
4654 5700
5324 4300
5357 4300
5372 4300
5392 4300
5513 4575
5549 4575
5550 4575
5646 5600
6347 4300
7306 4300
7413 7400
8102 8100
8107 8100
9452 9400
9652 5700

1957 87H
1001 1000
1020 1000
1027 1000
1029 1000
1601 1600
1611 1600
1637 1600
2220 2251
2228 2251
2229 2251
2263 2251
2283 2251
2288 2251
3654 5700
3657 5700
4132 5101
4519 4500
4550 4500
4556 4500
4557 4500
4558 4500
4576 4575
4579 4575
4594 4575
4654 5700
4699 5700
5324 4300
5357 4300
5372 4300
5513 4575
5520 4575
5549 4575
5550 4575
5748 5700
5903 4900
6347 4300
7306 4300
7318 4300
8102 8100
8107 8100
8738 5700
8739 5700
9318 9300
9652 5700
9714 5700

1960 87H
1001 1000
1020 1000
1029 1000
1601 1600
1613 1600
1637 1600
2220 2251
2251 2251
2283 2251
3639 5700
3654 5700
4122 5101
4132 5101
4550 4500
4556 4500
4557 4500
4558 4500
4594 4575
4654 5700
4699 5700
5357 4300
5520 4575
5527 4575
5549 4575
5550 4575
5560 4575
5748 5700
6306 4300
6389 4300
6627 5600
7306 4300
7318 4300
7320 4300
7340 4300
8107 8100
8738 5700
8739 5700
9714 5700

1963 87H
1001 1000
1008 1000
1014 1000
1027 1000
1613 1600
1648 1600
2283 2251
3214 2251
3639 5700
3654 5700
3712 5700
4107 5101
4122 5101
4132 5101
4569 4500
4654 5700
5508 4575
5545 4575
5554 4575
5571 4575
5573 4575
5634 5600
6610 5600
6623 5600
6627 5600
7318 4300
7320 4300
7825 7800
8738 5700

Nine Elms

1948 9E
30033 M7
30038 M7
30119 T9
30123 M7
30130 M7
30132 M7
30142 K10
30160 G6
30179 O2
30204 O2
30212 O2
30241 M7
30244 M7
30248 M7
30249 M7
30257 G6
30259 G6
30263 G6
30266 G6
30271 G6
30273 G6
30319 M7
30322 M7
30339 700
30353 G6
30354 G6
30380 K10
30386 K10
30390 K10
30391 K10
30392 K10
30406 L11
30427 L12
30431 L12
30435 L11
30440 L11
30442 L11
30443 T14
30444 T14
30445 T14
30446 T14
30447 T14
30459 T14
30460 T14
30461 T14
30462 T14
30477 H15
30482 H15
30483 H15
30484 H15
30485 H15
30486 H15
30487 H15
30488 H15
30489 H15
30490 H15
30491 H15
30667 M7
30672 M7
30673 M7
30676 M7
30692 700
30694 700
30699 700
30701 700
30718 T9
30738 N15
30742 N15
30753 N15
30755 N15
30766 N15
30773 N15
30774 N15
30779 N15
30782 N15
30783 N15
30786 N15
30788 N15
30791 N15
30792 N15
30856 LN
30857 LN
30858 LN
30859 LN
30860 LN
30861 LN
30949 KESR
31544 H
31551 H
31552 H
31553 H
31613 U
31616 U
31617 U
31619 U
31637 U
34022 WC
34023 WC
34058 BB
34059 BB
34060 BB
34061 BB
34064 BB
35011 MN
35012 MN
35013 MN
35014 MN
35015 MN
35016 MN
35017 MN
35018 MN
35019 MN
35020 MN

1951 70A
30038 M7
30119 T9
30123 M7
30130 M7
30132 M7
30160 G6
30163 L11
30165 L11
30221 O2
30241 M7
30244 M7
30248 M7
30249 M7
30319 M7
30322 M7
30339 700
30353 G6
30405 L11
30406 L11
30413 L11
30446 T14
30461 T14
30482 H15
30483 H15
30484 H15
30485 H15
30486 H15
30487 H15
30488 H15
30489 H15
30490 H15
30491 H15
30521 H15
30676 M7
30692 700
30694 700
30699 700
30701 700
30718 T9
30721 T9
30755 N15
30765 N15
30782 N15
30783 N15
30784 N15
30785 N15
30786 N15
30787 N15
30788 N15
30858 LN
30859 LN
30860 LN
30955 Z
31551 H
31552 H
31553 H
31554 H
31613 U
31619 U
31621 U
31625 U
31637 U
31807 U
32138 E1[2]
32468 E4
32493 E4
32498 E4
32499 E4
32500 E4
32501 E4
32502 E4
34031 WC
34049 BB
34050 BB
34051 BB
34052 BB
34053 BB
34054 BB
34055 BB
34056 BB
34057 BB
34058 BB
34059 BB
34060 BB
34061 BB
34062 BB
34063 BB
34064 BB
34065 BB
35005 MN
35010 MN
35011 MN
35012 MN
35013 MN
35014 MN
35015 MN
35016 MN
35017 MN
35018 MN
35019 MN
35020 MN

1954 70A
30124 M7
30130 M7
30132 M7
30179 O2
30224 O2
30241 M7
30242 M7
30243 M7
30244 M7
30248 M7
30249 M7
30319 M7
30320 M7
30321 M7
30322 M7
30455 N15
30456 N15
30457 N15
30464 D15
30482 H15
30483 H15
30484 H15
30485 H15
30486 H15
30487 H15
30488 H15
30489 H15
30490 H15
30491 H15
30521 H15
30522 H15
30523 H15
30524 H15
30692 700
30694 700
30697 700
30698 700
30699 700
30700 700
30701 700
30718 T9
30719 T9
30744 N15
30747 N15
30750 N15
30751 N15
30752 N15
30755 N15
30778 N15
30779 N15
30780 N15
30781 N15
30858 LN
30859 LN
30860 LN
31907 U1
31908 U1
31909 U1
31910 U1
32476 E4
32493 E4
32497 E4
32498 E4
32499 E4
32500 E4
34005 WC
34006 WC
34007 WC
34008 WC
34009 WC
34010 WC
34011 WC
34012 WC
34018 WC
34019 WC
34020 WC
34063 BB
34064 BB
34065 BB
35010 MN
35011 MN
35012 MN
35013 MN
35014 MN
35015 MN
35016 MN
35017 MN
35018 MN
35019 MN
35020 MN
35021 MN

1957 70A
30123 M7
30132 M7
30133 M7
30224 O2
30241 M7
30242 M7
30243 M7
30244 M7
30245 M7
30248 M7
30249 M7
30319 M7
30320 M7
30321 M7
30322 M7
30338 T9
30455 N15
30456 N15
30457 N15
30478 H15
30482 H15
30483 H15
30484 H15
30486 H15
30487 H15
30488 H15
30489 H15
30491 H15
30521 H15
30522 H15
30523 H15
30524 H15
30692 700
30694 700
30699 700
30701 700
30718 T9
30719 T9
30750 N15
30773 N15
30774 N15
30778 N15
30779 N15
30858 LN
30859 LN
30860 LN
31617 U
31621 U
31624 U
31634 U
32476 E4
32486 E4
32492 E4
32493 E4
32497 E4
32498 E4
32499 E4
32500 E4
32563 E4
33015 Q1
33017 Q1
33038 Q1
34005 WC
34006 WC
34007 WC
34008 WC
34009 WC
34010 WC
34011 WC
34012 WC
34018 WC
34019 WC
34020 WC
34063 BB
34064 BB
34065 BB
34095 WC
35005 MN
35011 MN
35012 MN
35014 MN R
35016 MN
35017 MN
35018 MN R
35019 MN
35020 MN R
35021 MN
35029 MN
35030 MN
73110 5MT
73111 5MT
73112 5MT
73113 5MT
73114 5MT
73115 5MT
73117 5MT
73118 5MT
73119 5MT

1960 70A
4634 5700
4672 5700
4681 5700
4692 5700
4698 5700
9770 5700
30133 M7
30241 M7
30245 M7
30248 M7
30249 M7
30319 M7
30320 M7
30321 M7
30457 N15
30489 H15
30491 H15
30521 H15
30694 700
30699 700
30701 700
30763 N15
30774 N15
30902 V
30903 V
30906 V
30907 V
30909 V
30910 V
30911 V
30912 V
30913 V
30918 V
30919 V
31004 C
31047 R1[1]
31048 O1
31061 C
31145 D1[1]
31229 C
31242 C
31246 D1[1]
31247 D1[1]
31268 C
31271 C
31298 C
31324 H
31337 R1[1]
31370 O1
31494 D1[1]
31495 C
31505 D1[1]
31509 D1[1]
31510 C
31545 D1[1]
31552 H
31553 H
31579 C
31592 C
31617 U
31621 U
31624 U
31634 U
31682 C
31727 D1[1]
31753 L1
31754 L1
31756 L1
31757 L1
31759 L1
31760 L
31762 L
31763 L
31764 L
31765 L
31766 L
31768 L
31771 L
31776 L
31780 L
31782 L1
31783 L1
31784 L1
31785 L1
31786 L1
31787 L1
31788 L1
31789 L1
31796 U
32487 E4
32498 E4
32500 E4
32563 E4
33015 Q1
33017 Q1
33038 Q1
34006 WC
34007 WC

34009 WC
34010 WC R
34018 WC R
34020 WC
34031 WC R
34090 BB
34093 WC
34094 WC
34095 WC
35001 MN R
35012 MN R
35014 MN R
35015 MN R
35016 MN R
35017 MN R
35018 MN R
35019 MN R
35020 MN R
35028 MN R
35029 MN R
35030 MN R
73081 5MT
73082 5MT
73083 5MT
73084 5MT
73085 5MT
73086 5MT
73088 5MT
73089 5MT
73110 5MT
73111 5MT
73112 5MT
73113 5MT
73114 5MT
73115 5MT
73117 5MT
73118 5MT
73119 5MT

1963 70A
4634 5700
4672 5700
4681 5700
4692 5700
4698 5700
9770 5700
30039 M7
30249 M7
30320 M7
31612 U
31613 U
31617 U
31621 U
31624 U
31634 U
31636 U
31796 U
34001 WC R
34006 WC
34007 WC
34009 WC R
34010 WC R
34017 WC R
34018 WC R
34031 WC R
34050 BB R
34064 BB
34071 BB R
34073 BB
34077 BB R
34082 BB R
34087 BB R
34088 BB R
34090 BB R
34093 WC R
34094 WC
34095 WC R
35001 MN R
35012 MN R
35014 MN R
35015 MN R
35016 MN R
35017 MN R
35018 MN R
35019 MN R
35020 MN R
35024 MN R
35028 MN R
35029 MN R
35030 MN R
73046 5MT
73074 5MT
73081 5MT
73082 5MT
73083 5MT
73084 5MT
73085 5MT
73086 5MT
73087 5MT
73088 5MT
73089 5MT
73110 5MT
73111 5MT
73112 5MT
73113 5MT
73114 5MT
73115 5MT
73116 5MT
73117 5MT
73118 5MT
73119 5MT
82010 3MT^{2}
82011 3MT^{2}
82012 3MT^{2}
82013 3MT^{2}
82014 3MT^{2}
82017 3MT^{2}
82018 3MT^{2}
82019 3MT^{2}
82022 3MT^{2}
82023 3MT^{2}
82024 3MT^{2}
82025 3MT^{2}

1966 70A
34001 WC R
34002 WC
34021 WC R
34038 WC
73086 5MT
80012 4MT^{3}
80015 4MT^{3}
80069 4MT^{3}
80089 4MT^{3}
80095 4MT^{3}
80133 4MT^{3}
80141 4MT^{3}
80143 4MT^{3}
80154 4MT^{3}
82006 3MT^{2}
82018 3MT^{2}
82019 3MT^{2}
82023 3MT^{2}
82024 3MT^{2}
82026 3MT^{2}
82027 3MT^{2}
82028 3MT^{2}
82029 3MT^{2}

Normanton

1948 20D/NMN
41793 1F^{1}
41844 1F^{1}
43301 3F^{3}
43497 3F^{3}
43514 3F^{3}
43639 3F^{3}
43656 3F^{3}
43714 3F^{3}
43742 3F^{3}
43903 4F^{1}
43913 4F^{1}
44098 4F^{2}
44099 4F^{2}
44153 4F^{2}
44179 4F^{2}
44216 4F^{2}
44217 4F^{2}
44290 4F^{2}
44335 4F^{2}
44336 4F^{2}
44337 4F^{2}
44338 4F^{2}
44562 4F^{2}
44570 4F^{2}
44586 4F^{2}
44603 4F^{2}
44604 4F^{2}
47334 3F^{6}
47335 3F^{6}
47405 3F^{6}
48084 8F
48123 8F
48130 8F
48131 8F
48146 8F
48159 8F
48160 8F
48164 8F
48266 8F
48271 8F
48274 8F
48352 8F
48357 8F
48394 8F
48395 8F
48396 8F
48670 8F
48702 8F
50621 2P^{8}
50901 3P^{3}
52089 3F^{7}
52095 3F^{7}
58238 2F^{8}
65108 J21
65782 J27
68238 J71
68292 J71
68294 J71

1951 20D/50A sub
40179 3MT^{2}
40406 2P^{2}
40480 2P^{2}
40630 2P^{3}
41793 1F^{1}
41844 1F^{1}
43301 3F^{3}
43497 3F^{3}
43509 3F^{3}
43514 3F^{3}
43639 3F^{3}
43656 3F^{3}
43714 3F^{3}
43851 4F^{1}
43852 4F^{1}
44098 4F^{2}
44099 4F^{2}
44151 4F^{2}
44217 4F^{2}
44336 4F^{2}
44337 4F^{2}
44338 4F^{2}
44586 4F^{2}
44603 4F^{2}
44604 4F^{2}
47239 3F^{5}
47334 3F^{6}
47335 3F^{6}
47405 3F^{6}
48084 8F
48130 8F
48146 8F
48160 8F
48164 8F
48266 8F
48271 8F
48274 8F
48352 8F
48357 8F
48394 8F
48395 8F
48396 8F
48507 8F
48547 8F
48670 8F
48702 8F
50621 2P^{8}
52089 3F^{7}
63270 Q5
68238 J71
68292 J71
68294 J71

1954 20D
40075 3MT^{2}
40179 3MT^{2}
40480 2P^{2}
40630 2P^{3}
41661 1F^{1}
41844 1F^{1}
42141 4MT^{1}
43183 3F^{2}
43449 3F^{3}
43497 3F^{3}
43509 3F^{3}
43639 3F^{3}
43656 3F^{3}
43714 3F^{3}
43852 4F^{1}
44098 4F^{2}
44099 4F^{2}
44170 4F^{2}
44171 4F^{2}
44217 4F^{2}
44336 4F^{2}
44337 4F^{2}
44338 4F^{2}
44604 4F^{2}
47239 3F^{5}
47334 3F^{6}
47335 3F^{6}
47405 3F^{6}
48076 8F
48084 8F
48130 8F
48146 8F
48160 8F
48202 8F
48274 8F
48313 8F
48352 8F
48357 8F
48394 8F
48395 8F
48396 8F
48670 8F
48702 8F
50621 2P^{8}
68238 J71
68292 J71
68294 J71

1957 55E
40075 3MT^{2}
40179 3MT^{2}
40630 2P^{3}
43114 4MT^{5}
43116 4MT^{5}
43183 3F^{2}
43321 3F^{3}
43449 3F^{3}
43509 3F^{3}
43639 3F^{3}
43656 3F^{3}
43714 3F^{3}
43852 4F^{1}
44098 4F^{2}
44099 4F^{2}
44170 4F^{2}
44336 4F^{2}
44337 4F^{2}
44338 4F^{2}
44408 4F^{2}
44458 4F^{2}
44604 4F^{2}
47239 3F^{5}
47334 3F^{6}
47335 3F^{6}
47405 3F^{6}
47446 3F^{6}
47607 3F^{6}
47635 3F^{6}
48055 8F
48076 8F
48084 8F
48130 8F
48160 8F
48202 8F
48274 8F
48352 8F
48357 8F
48394 8F
48702 8F
68253 J71
68681 J72
68701 J72

1960 55E
40075 3MT^{2}
40179 3MT^{2}
40630 2P^{3}
43074 4MT^{5}
43114 4MT^{5}
43116 4MT^{5}
43509 3F^{3}
43714 3F^{3}
44098 4F^{2}
44099 4F^{2}
44170 4F^{2}
44336 4F^{2}
44337 4F^{2}
44338 4F^{2}
44408 4F^{2}
44458 4F^{2}
44604 4F^{2}
68275 J71
68681 J72
68701 J72
68726 J72
73160 5MT
73161 5MT
73167 5MT
90012 WD^{1}
90021 WD^{1}
90247 WD^{1}
90249 WD^{1}
90254 WD^{1}
90309 WD^{1}
90318 WD^{1}
90337 WD^{1}
90357 WD^{1}
90362 WD^{1}
90487 WD^{1}
90610 WD^{1}
90617 WD^{1}
90637 WD^{1}
90652 WD^{1}
90661 WD^{1}
90664 WD^{1}
90673 WD^{1}
90682 WD^{1}
90722 WD^{1}

1963 55E
42083 4MT^{1}
42149 4MT^{1}
42702 5MT^{1}
42865 5MT^{1}
43114 4MT^{5}
43116 4MT^{5}
44336 4F^{2}
44337 4F^{2}
44408 4F^{2}
44457 4F^{2}
44458 4F^{2}
44604 4F^{2}
73160 5MT
73167 5MT
90012 WD^{1}
90249 WD^{1}
90318 WD^{1}
90337 WD^{1}
90357 WD^{1}
90362 WD^{1}
90487 WD^{1}
90617 WD^{1}
90652 WD^{1}
90661 WD^{1}
90664 WD^{1}
90673 WD^{1}
90682 WD^{1}
90722 WD^{1}

1966 55E
42083 4MT^{1}
42149 4MT^{1}
43043 4MT^{5}
43098 4MT^{5}
43099 4MT^{5}
43116 4MT^{5}
43125 4MT^{5}
43141 4MT^{5}
90243 WD^{1}
90465 WD^{1}
90481 WD^{1}
90617 WD^{1}
90644 WD^{1}
90652 WD^{1}
90682 WD^{1}
90699 WD^{1}
90722 WD^{1}

North Blyth

1948 NBH
65783 J27
65786 J27
65789 J27
65797 J27
65799 J27
65801 J27
65804 J27
65811 J27
65819 J27
65828 J27
65851 J27
65867 J27
65876 J27
65877 J27
65879 J27
65880 J27
65892 J27
68396 J77
68397 J77
68398 J77
68405 J77
68426 J77

1951 52F
65067 J21
65783 J27
65786 J27
65789 J27
65792 J27
65794 J27
65797 J27
65799 J27
65801 J27
65804 J27
65811 J27
65819 J27
65828 J27
65851 J27
65867 J27
65870 J27
65876 J27
65877 J27
65879 J27
65880 J27
65892 J27
68397 J77
68398 J77
68405 J77
68417 J77
68426 J77
68427 J77

1954 52F
65667 J25
65783 J27
65786 J27
65789 J27
65792 J27
65794 J27
65797 J27
65800 J27
65801 J27
65804 J27
65811 J27
65815 J27
65819 J27
65828 J27
65851 J27
65863 J27
65864 J27
65867 J27
65870 J27
65876 J27
65877 J27
65879 J27
65880 J27
65886 J27
65889 J27
65892 J27
68397 J77
68399 J77
68405 J77
68417 J77
68426 J77
68427 J77
68430 J77

1957 52F
63353 Q6
63391 Q6
63398 Q6
63399 Q6
63403 Q6
63428 Q6
65783 J27
65786 J27
65789 J27
65792 J27
65794 J27
65797 J27
65800 J27
65801 J27
65804 J27
65811 J27
65815 J27
65819 J27
65828 J27
65851 J27
65863 J27
65867 J27
65880 J27
65889 J27
68397 J77
68399 J77
68402 J77
68405 J77
68426 J77
68427 J77

1960 52F
65786 J27
65789 J27
65792 J27
65794 J27
65797 J27
65800 J27
65801 J27
65804 J27
65811 J27
65815 J27
65819 J27
65828 J27
65851 J27
65857 J27
65863 J27
65867 J27
65875 J27
65879 J27
65880 J27
65881 J27
65882 J27
65889 J27
65893 J27

1963 52F
63352 Q6
63354 Q6
63356 Q6
63359 Q6
63381 Q6
63386 Q6
63413 Q6
65789 J27
65792 J27
65794 J27
65801 J27
65804 J27
65811 J27
65815 J27
65819 J27
65828 J27
65845 J27
65851 J27
65857 J27
65875 J27
65879 J27
65880 J27
65889 J27
65893 J27

1966 52F
43101 4MT^{5}
43132 4MT^{5}
62017 K1
62022 K1
62024 K1
62027 K1
62067 K1
63381 Q6
63413 Q6
63429 Q6
65789 J27
65796 J27
65801 J27
65802 J27
65804 J27
65811 J27
65815 J27
65834 J27
65869 J27
65879 J27
65880 J27
65892 J27

Northallerton

1948 NLN
62388 D20
62391 D20
62397 D20
65645 J25
65658 J25
65674 J25
65693 J25
67324 G5
67344 G5
68159 Y3
69101 N10
69423 N9

1951 51J
62347 D20
62359 D20
62388 D20
62391 D20
65030 J21
65075 J21
65645 J25
65693 J25
67324 G5
67344 G5
68159 Y3
69101 N10

1954 51J
62044 K1
62347 D20
62372 D20
62388 D20
65038 J21
65693 J25
65720 J25
65726 J25
67312 G5
67318 G5
67342 G5
68159 Y3
68359 J73

1957 51J
62044 K1
78010 2MT^{1}
78011 2MT^{1}
78013 2MT^{1}
78014 2MT^{1}
78015 2MT^{1}

1960 51J
46471 2MT^{2}
62044 K1
78010 2MT^{1}
78011 2MT^{1}
78012 2MT^{1}
78014 2MT^{1}
78015 2MT^{1}

1963 51J
62003 K1
62044 K1
78010 2MT^{1}
78011 2MT^{1}
78012 2MT^{1}
78014 2MT^{1}
78015 2MT^{1}

Northampton

1948 2C
40412 2P^{2}
40420 2P^{2}
40421 2P^{2}
40534 2P^{2}
40653 2P^{3}
40657 2P^{3}
40692 2P^{3}
44076 4F^{2}
44366 4F^{2}
44491 4F^{2}
44596 4F^{2}
44915 5MT^{3}
45150 5MT^{3}
45191 5MT^{3}
45282 5MT^{3}
46616 1P^{1}
46666 1P^{1}
46742 1P^{1}
47299 3F^{6}
47318 3F^{6}
47612 3F^{6}
48422 8F
48423 8F
48426 8F
48445 8F
48550 8F
48557 8F
48693 8F
48914 7F^{2}
48929 6F^{2}
48936 7F^{2}
49004 7F^{2}
49042 7F^{2}
49103 6F^{2}
49153 7F^{2}
49157 7F^{2}
49158 7F^{2}
49169 7F^{2}
49203 7F^{2}
49205 7F^{2}
49270 7F^{2}
49271 7F^{2}
49321 7F^{2}
49324 6F^{2}
49395 7F^{3}
49414 7F^{3}
49426 7F^{3}
49444 7F^{3}
58121 2F^{8}
58218 2F^{9}
58270 2F^{9}
58299 2F^{9}

1951 4B
40412 2P^{2}
40420 2P^{2}
40421 2P^{2}
40527 2P^{2}
40531 2P^{2}
40534 2P^{2}
40653 2P^{3}
40657 2P^{3}
41218 2MT^{1}
41219 2MT^{1}
44061 4F^{2}
44072 4F^{2}
44076 4F^{2}
44448 4F^{2}
44491 4F^{2}
45021 5MT^{3}
45091 5MT^{3}
45191 5MT^{3}
45331 5MT^{3}
46666 1P^{1}
47299 3F^{6}
47318 3F^{6}
47612 3F^{6}
48422 8F
48423 8F
48426 8F
48445 8F
48914 7F^{2}
48936 7F^{2}
49105 7F^{2}
49203 7F^{2}
49270 7F^{2}
49271 7F^{2}
49321 7F^{2}
49357 7F^{2}
49366 7F^{2}
58218 2F^{9}
58281 2F^{9}

1954 2E
40412 2P^{2}
40420 2P^{2}
40421 2P^{2}
40464 2P^{2}
40534 2P^{2}
40653 2P^{3}
40657 2P^{3}
40683 2P^{3}
41218 2MT^{1}
41219 2MT^{1}
44061 4F^{2}
44076 4F^{2}
44186 4F^{2}
44242 4F^{2}
44391 4F^{2}
44491 4F^{2}
44524 4F^{2}
45014 5MT^{3}
45021 5MT^{3}
45091 5MT^{3}
45191 5MT^{3}
46666 1P^{1}
47299 3F^{6}
47318 3F^{6}
47612 3F^{6}
48090 8F
48422 8F
48423 8F
48441 8F
48445 8F
48446 8F
48534 8F
49105 7F^{2}
49203 7F^{2}
49270 7F^{2}
49321 7F^{2}
49357 7F^{2}
49366 7F^{2}
58281 2F^{9}

1957 2E
40464 2P^{2}
40534 2P^{2}
40653 2P^{3}
40677 2P^{3}
40683 2P^{3}
41218 2MT^{1}
41219 2MT^{1}
43399 3F^{3}
44061 4F^{2}
44076 4F^{2}
44219 4F^{2}
44242 4F^{2}
44391 4F^{2}
44524 4F^{2}
45021 5MT^{3}
45050 5MT^{3}
45091 5MT^{3}
45191 5MT^{3}
45292 5MT^{3}
45392 5MT^{3}
47318 3F^{6}
47612 3F^{6}
48090 8F
48147 8F
48422 8F
48423 8F
48445 8F
48534 8F
49105 7F^{2}
49270 7F^{2}
49321 7F^{2}
49357 7F^{2}
90369 WD^{1}
90392 WD^{1}
90423 WD^{1}
90532 WD^{1}

1960 2E
41218 2MT^{1}
41219 2MT^{1}
41278 2MT^{1}
42353 4MT^{2}
42467 4MT^{3}
42615 4MT^{3}
43399 3F^{3}
44076 4F^{2}
44219 4F^{2}
44242 4F^{2}
44353 4F^{2}
44391 4F^{2}
44491 4F^{2}
44524 4F^{2}
44712 5MT^{3}
44760 5MT^{3}
45050 5MT^{3}
45091 5MT^{3}
45147 5MT^{3}
45191 5MT^{3}
45222 5MT^{3}
45292 5MT^{3}
45307 5MT^{3}
45392 5MT^{3}
47318 3F^{6}
47499 3F^{6}
48090 8F
48147 8F
48269 8F
48290 8F
48305 8F
48360 8F
48422 8F
48445 8F
48529 8F
48534 8F
48736 8F

1963 2E
41218 2MT^{1}
41219 2MT^{1}
44682 5MT^{3}
44713 5MT^{3}
44869 5MT^{3}
44936 5MT^{3}
45050 5MT^{3}
45051 5MT^{3}
45064 5MT^{3}
45134 5MT^{3}
45287 5MT^{3}
45302 5MT^{3}
45308 5MT^{3}
45392 5MT^{3}
45398 5MT^{3}
45454 5MT^{3}
47286 3F^{6}
47499 3F^{6}
48090 8F
48147 8F
48349 8F
48658 8F

Northwich

1948 NTH
62650 D10
62652 D10
62655 D10
65131 J10
65134 J10
65138 J10
65139 J10
65140 J10
65142 J10
65146 J10
65147 J10
65155 J10
65156 J10
65158 J10
65165 J10
65166 J10
65171 J10
65187 J10
65190 J10
65191 J10
65202 J10
65205 J10
69052 L3
69062 L3
69262 N5
69293 N5
69335 N5
69349 N5

1951 9G
48011 8F
48045 8F
48046 8F
48135 8F
48254 8F
48340 8F
48555 8F
48605 8F
48613 8F
48667 8F
48697 8F
48717 8F
62650 D10
62652 D10
62655 D10
64367 J11
64376 J11
64453 J11
65134 J10
65138 J10
65139 J10
65140 J10
65147 J10
65151 J10
65156 J10
65158 J10
65165 J10
65166 J10
65169 J10
65171 J10
65187 J10
65190 J10
65191 J10
65202 J10
65205 J10
65208 J10
69052 L3
69062 L3
69262 N5
69335 N5

1954 9G
43538 3F^{3}
43651 3F^{3}
44155 4F^{2}
44341 4F^{2}
44456 4F^{2}
48045 8F
48046 8F
48155 8F
48254 8F
48340 8F
48426 8F
48521 8F
48555 8F
48605 8F
48613 8F
48667 8F
48697 8F
48711 8F
48717 8F
49405 7F^{3}
49435 7F^{3}
62650 D10
62652 D10
62656 D10
62659 D10
62669 D11
65131 J10
65134 J10
65139 J10
65158 J10
65165 J10
65169 J10
65202 J10
69052 L3

1957 9G
42467 4MT^{3}
42575 4MT^{3}
43538 3F^{3}
43651 3F^{3}
44155 4F^{2}
44341 4F^{2}
44456 4F^{2}
48045 8F
48046 8F
48155 8F
48254 8F
48340 8F
48368 8F
48426 8F
48506 8F
48521 8F
48555 8F
48605 8F
48613 8F
48697 8F
48711 8F
48717 8F
48742 8F
49304 7F^{2}
62661 D11
62662 D11
62664 D11
62665 D11
62669 D11
65134 J10
65158 J10
65169 J10
65202 J10

1960 8E
42319 4MT^{2}
42356 4MT^{2}
42359 4MT^{2}
42365 4MT^{2}
42386 4MT^{2}
42393 4MT^{2}
44155 4F^{2}
44341 4F^{2}
44456 4F^{2}
48017 8F
48045 8F
48135 8F
48139 8F
48155 8F
48254 8F
48295 8F
48340 8F
48368 8F
48426 8F
48462 8F
48465 8F
48521 8F
48555 8F
48605 8F
48632 8F
48711 8F
48717 8F
48742 8F
48764 8F
65169 J10
78038 2MT^{1}
78057 2MT^{1}

1963 8E
44155 4F^{2}
44456 4F^{2}
48017 8F
48039 8F
48118 8F
48135 8F
48155 8F
48166 8F
48254 8F
48295 8F
48340 8F
48426 8F
48462 8F
48511 8F
48521 8F
48605 8F
48631 8F
48683 8F
48693 8F
48717 8F
48740 8F
48764 8F
78019 2MT^{1}
78038 2MT^{1}
78057 2MT^{1}

1966 8E
48057 8F
48118 8F
48155 8F
48398 8F
48408 8F
48462 8F
48615 8F
48631 8F
48639 8F
48640 8F
48683 8F
48693 8F
48717 8F
48735 8F
77011 3MT^{1}
77014 3MT^{1}

Norwich

1966
17 B1
19 B1
26 B1
29 B1

Norwich Thorpe

1948 NOR
61040 B1
61041 B1
61042 B1
61043 B1
61044 B1
61045 B1
61046 B1
61047 B1
61048 B1
61049 B1
61050 B1
61051 B1
61052 B1
61254 B1
61270 B1
61271 B1
61272 B1
61625 B17
61626 B17
61629 B17
61644 B17
61659 B17
61670 B17
61921 K3
61939 K3
61942 K3
61947 K3
61953 K3
61957 K3
61970 K3
61971 K3
61973 K3
61989 K3
62203 D1
62510 D16
62511 D16
62522 D16
62529 D16
62535 D16
62541 D16
62545 D16
62554 D16
62555 D16
62563 D16
62564 D16
62568 D16
62570 D16
62576 D16
62577 D16
62581 D16
62583 D16
62585 D16
62599 D16
62600 D16
62610 D16
62616 D16
62619 D16
62620 D16
62782 E4
62787 E4
62789 E4
62792 E4
62793 E4
62797 E4
64726 J39
64731 J39
64761 J39
64784 J39
64797 J39
64798 J39
64802 J39
64833 J39
64838 J39
64882 J39
64889 J39
64913 J39
64959 J39
64968 J39
65367 J15
65373 J15
65390 J15
65394 J15
65398 J15
65401 J15
65404 J15
65408 J15
65411 J15
65417 J15
65422 J15
65426 J15
65435 J15
65460 J15
65470 J15
65471 J15
65478 J15
65479 J15
65516 J17
65534 J17
65553 J17
65569 J17
65570 J17
65578 J17
67127 F3
67134 F3
67139 F3
67156 F4
67174 F4
67176 F4
67178 F4
67184 F4
67186 F4
67663 V1
67664 V1
67665 V1
68377 J66
68384 J66
68495 J69
68501 J69
68586 J67
68595 J67
68603 J69
68641 J68

1951 32A
61040 B1
61041 B1
61042 B1
61043 B1
61044 B1
61045 B1
61046 B1
61047 B1
61048 B1
61049 B1
61050 B1
61051 B1
61270 B1
61271 B1
61272 B1
61332 B1
61545 B12
61609 B17
61629 B17
61659 B17
61670 B17
61730 K2
61747 K2
61921 K3
61939 K3
61942 K3
61947 K3
61953 K3
61957 K3
61970 K3
61971 K3
61981 K3
61989 K3
62510 D16
62522 D16
62540 D16
62541 D16
62545 D16
62552 D16
62553 D16
62554 D16
62555 D16
62570 D16
62577 D16
62581 D16
62584 D16
62585 D16
62593 D16
62606 D16
62610 D16
62612 D16
62616 D16
62617 D16
62619 D16
62780 E4
62782 E4
62787 E4
62789 E4
62792 E4
62793 E4
62796 E4
62797 E4
64644 J19
64674 J19
64724 J39
64726 J39
64731 J39
64761 J39
64784 J39
64797 J39
64802 J39
64833 J39
64882 J39
64889 J39
64913 J39
64959 J39
64968 J39
65388 J15
65390 J15
65398 J15
65404 J15
65417 J15
65422 J15
65426 J15
65460 J15
65469 J15
65471 J15
65472 J15
65507 J17
65510 J17
65512 J17
65513 J17
65514 J17
65524 J17
65534 J17
65553 J17
65568 J17
65569 J17
65574 J17
67176 F4
67178 F4
67224 F6
67229 F6
67232 F6
67663 V1
67664 V1
67677 V1
67679 V1
67788 L1
67789 L1
67795 L1
67798 L1
68388 J66
68495 J69
68501 J69
68570 J69
68586 J67
68602 J69
68603 J69
68641 J68
68899 J50
68905 J50
68924 J50
69679 N7
69706 N7
69707 N7
69709 N7

1954 32A
61042 B1
61043 B1
61045 B1
61046 B1
61048 B1
61050 B1
61051 B1
61270 B1
61530 B12
61629 B17
61656 B17
61664 B17
61665 B17
61877 K3
61908 K3
61918 K3
61939 K3
61957 K3
61970 K3
61971 K3
61981 K3
62510 D16
62522 D16
62523 D16
62540 D16
62552 D16
62553 D16
62554 D16
62555 D16
62556 D16
62561 D16
62564 D16
62577 D16
62584 D16
62592 D16
62593 D16
62608 D16
62610 D16
62612 D16
62619 D16
62782 E4
62787 E4
62788 E4
62789 E4
62792 E4
62793 E4
62796 E4
62797 E4
64644 J19
64674 J19
64726 J39
64731 J39
64761 J39
64797 J39
64802 J39
64882 J39
64889 J39
64900 J39
64913 J39
64968 J39
65388 J15
65417 J15
65460 J15
65469 J15
65471 J15
65472 J15
65509 J17
65513 J17
65514 J17
65516 J17
65524 J17
65542 J17
65551 J17
65553 J17
65567 J17
65569 J17
65570 J17
65573 J17
65574 J17
67707 L1
67739 L1
68514 J67
68516 J67
68523 J67
68592 J67
68597 J67
68608 J67
68616 J67
68641 J68
68645 J68
68664 J68
68899 J50
68905 J50
68924 J50
69679 N7
69690 N7
69696 N7
69706 N7
69707 N7
69708 N7
69824 A5
69826 A5
70006 7P6F
70007 7P6F
70008 7P6F
70009 7P6F
70010 7P6F
70011 7P6F
70012 7P6F
70013 7P6F
70030 7P6F
70035 7P6F

1957 32A
61042 B1
61043 B1
61045 B1
61046 B1
61048 B1
61223 B1
61270 B1
61312 B1
61317 B1
61514 B12
61520 B12
61540 B12
61542 B12
61547 B12
61568 B12
61812 K3
61829 K3
61877 K3
61908 K3
61918 K3
61939 K3
61953 K3
61957 K3
61970 K3
61971 K3
61981 K3
61989 K3
62540 D16
62555 D16
62556 D16
62564 D16
62592 D16
62593 D16
62596 D16
62619 D16
64644 J19
64674 J19
64731 J39
64761 J39
64797 J39
64802 J39
64889 J39
64900 J39
64913 J39
65388 J15
65469 J15
65471 J15
65472 J15
65519 J17
65537 J17
65542 J17
65553 J17
65566 J17
65570 J17
65573 J17
65588 J17
67707 L1
67714 L1
67717 L1
68555 J69
68640 J68
68641 J68
68642 J68
68645 J68
68899 J50
68905 J50
68924 J50
69706 N7
69707 N7
70006 7P6F
70007 7P6F
70008 7P6F
70009 7P6F
70010 7P6F
70011 7P6F
70012 7P6F
70013 7P6F
70030 7P6F
70035 7P6F

1960 32A
43145 4MT^5
43146 4MT^5
43156 4MT^5
43160 4MT^5
43161 4MT^5
61043 B1
61045 B1
61046 B1
61048 B1
61054 B1
61223 B1
61228 B1
61235 B1
61317 B1
61399 B1
61572 B12
61656 B17
61826 K3
61877 K3
61908 K3
61918 K3
61926 K3
61939 K3
61949 K3
61953 K3
61957 K3
61970 K3
61971 K3
61973 K3
61981 K3
61989 K3
62524 D16
64641 J19
64643 J19
64674 J19
65469 J15
65471 J15
65519 J17
65551 J17
65566 J17
65570 J17
65581 J17
65586 J17
67717 L1
67733 L1
67786 L1
68899 J50
68905 J50
68924 J50
70000 7P6F
70001 7P6F
70002 7P6F
70003 7P6F
70005 7P6F
70006 7P6F
70007 7P6F
70008 7P6F
70009 7P6F
70010 7P6F
70011 7P6F
70012 7P6F
70013 7P6F
70030 7P6F
70034 7P6F
70035 7P6F
70036 7P6F
70037 7P6F
70038 7P6F
70039 7P6F
70040 7P6F
70041 7P6F
90559 WD^1

Norwood Junction

1948 NOR
31814 N
31844 N
31916 W
31917 W
31918 W
31919 W
31920 W
32167 E3
32169 E3
32302 C3
32309 C3
32350 K
32351 K
32404 E5
32407 E6X
32411 E6X
32414 E6
32416 E6
32417 E6
32418 E6
32440 C2X
32444 C2X
32447 C2X
32455 E3
32456 E3
32457 E3
32466 E4X
32473 E4
32476 E4
32477 E4X
32478 E4X
32479 E4
32481 E4
32489 E4X
32493 E4
32495 E4
32498 E4
32502 E4
32506 E4
32526 C2X
32535 C2X
32536 C2X
32540 C2X
32544 C2X
32547 C2X
32561 E4
32563 E4
32579 E4

1951 75C
30533 Q
30534 Q
30537 Q
30538 Q
30539 Q
30547 Q
31916 W
31917 W
31918 W
31919 W
31920 W
32407 E6X
32411 E6X
32414 E6
32417 E6
32418 E6
32440 C2X
32444 C2X
32447 C2X
32466 E4X
32476 E4
32477 E4X
32478 E4X
32479 E4
32489 E4X
32495 E4
32506 E4
32526 C2X
32535 C2X
32536 C2X
32546 C2X
32547 C2X
32578 E4
32592 E5

1954 75C
30533 Q
30534 Q
30537 Q
30538 Q
30539 Q
30540 Q
30547 Q
31917 W
31918 W
31919 W
31920 W
32407 E6X
32411 E6X
32413 E6
32414 E6
32416 E6
32417 E6
32418 E6
32443 C2X
32444 C2X
32445 C2X
32446 C2X
32447 C2X
32466 E4X
32477 E4X
32478 E4X
32489 E4X
32543 C2X
32544 C2X
32545 C2X
32546 C2X
32547 C2X

1957 75C
30533 Q
30534 Q
30537 Q
30538 Q
30540 Q
30549 Q
31717 C
31719 C
31917 W
31918 W
31919 W
31920 W
32407 E6X
32411 E6X
32413 E6
32414 E6
32416 E6
32417 E6
32418 E6
32443 C2X
32444 C2X
32445 C2X
32446 C2X
32447 C2X
32466 E4X
32477 E4X
32543 C2X
32544 C2X
32545 C2X
32546 C2X
32547 C2X

1960 75C
30533 Q
30534 Q
30537 Q
30538 Q
30540 Q
30549 Q
31917 W
31918 W
31919 W
31920 W
32104 E2
32105 E2
32443 C2X
32444 C2X
32445 C2X
32446 C2X
32447 C2X
32448 C2X
32479 E4
32495 E4
32509 E4
32521 C2X
32541 C2X
32543 C2X
32544 C2X
32545 C2X
32546 C2X
32548 C2X
32549 C2X
32550 C2X

1963 75C
31616 U
31619 U
31620 U
31626 U
31629 U
31639 U
31799 U
31807 U
31918 W
31919 W
31920 W
31921 W
31925 W

Nottingham

1948 16A
40140 3MT^2
40163 3MT^2
40178 3MT^2
40193 3MT^2
40394 2P^2
40415 2P^2
40417 2P^2
40419 2P^2
40427 2P^2
40458 2P^2
40478 2P^2
40496 2P^2
40498 2P^2
40502 2P^2
40504 2P^2
40535 2P^2
40540 2P^2
40546 2P^2
40553 2P^2
40559 2P^2
40560 2P^2
40739 3P^1
40747 3P^1
40757 3P^1
40929 4P^1
41002 4P^2
41012 4P^2
41015 4P^2
41032 4P^2
41082 4P^1
41094 4P^1
41096 4P^1
41666 1F^1
41682 1F^1
41686 1F^1
41762 1F^1
41826 1F^1
41895 1F^1
41911 2P^5
41914 2P^5
41916 2P^5
41919 2P^5
41921 2P^5
41922 2P^5
42228 4MT^1
42229 4MT^1
42328 4MT^2
42333 4MT^2
42361 4MT^2
42678 4MT^1
42679 4MT^1
42680 4MT^1
42686 4MT^1
42823 5MT^1
42899 5MT^1
43192 3F^3
43249 3F^3
43369 3F^3
43378 3F^3
43399 3F^3
43458 3F^3
43538 3F^3
43637 3F^3
43711 3F^3
43724 3F^3
43729 3F^3
43869 4F^1
43933 4F^1
43948 4F^1
43954 4F^1
43956 4F^1
43958 4F^1
43962 4F^1
43969 4F^1
43994 4F^1
44030 4F^2
44039 4F^2
44055 4F^2
44095 4F^2
44131 4F^2
44132 4F^2
44158 4F^2
44164 4F^2
44180 4F^2
44215 4F^2
44223 4F^2
44230 4F^2
44247 4F^2
44264 4F^2
44267 4F^2
44275 4F^2
44313 4F^2
44401 4F^2
44408 4F^2
44412 4F^2
44414 4F^2
44416 4F^2
44480 4F^2
44533 4F^2
44546 4F^2
44577 4F^2
44578 4F^2
44598 4F^2
44825 5MT^3
44841 5MT^3
44861 5MT^3
44918 5MT^3
45059 5MT^3
45554 6P5F^2
45636 6P5F^2
45640 6P5F^2
47277 3F^6
47422 3F^6
47438 3F^6
47485 3F^6
47539 3F^6
47552 3F^6
47629 3F^6
47631 3F^6
47632 3F^6
47637 3F^6
48003 8F
48064 8F
48158 8F
48170 8F
48206 8F
48207 8F
48217 8F
48218 8F
48279 8F
48282 8F
48293 8F
48380 8F
48381 8F
48614 8F
48635 8F
48639 8F
48653 8F
48666 8F
48675 8F
48696 8F
52121 3F^7
52123 3F^7
52135 3F^7
58020 1P^2
58050 1P^6
58056 1P^6
58201 2F^9
58210 2F^9
58248 2F^8
58252 2F^9
58275 2F^9
3602 2F^9

1951 16A
40120 3MT^2
40140 3MT^2
40178 3MT^2
40415 2P^2
40417 2P^2
40419 2P^2
40452 2P^2
40458 2P^2
40504 2P^2
40535 2P^2
40540 2P^2
40546 2P^2
40552 2P^2
40553 2P^2
40560 2P^2
40929 4P^1
40931 4P^1
41015 4P^2
41019 4P^2
41032 4P^2
41082 4P^1
41096 4P^1
41682 1F^1
41686 1F^1
41846 1F^1
41917 2P^5
41919 2P^5
41921 2P^5
41922 2P^5
41925 2P^5
41926 2P^5
42140 4MT^1
42146 4MT^1
42184 4MT^1
42185 4MT^1
42228 4MT^1
42333 4MT^2
42339 4MT^2
42361 4MT^2
42373 4MT^2
42680 4MT^1
42686 4MT^1
42823 5MT^1
43018 4MT^5
43019 4MT^5
43033 4MT^5
43040 4MT^5
43192 3F^3
43240 3F^3
43249 3F^3
43300 3F^3
43369 3F^3
43371 3F^3
43378 3F^3
43399 3F^3
43401 3F^3
43538 3F^3
43558 3F^3
43637 3F^3
43711 3F^3
43723 3F^3
43724 3F^3
43729 3F^3
43954 4F^1
43956 4F^1
43958 4F^1
43962 4F^1
43982 4F^1
44030 4F^2
44039 4F^2
44055 4F^2
44095 4F^2
44113 4F^2
44131 4F^2
44132 4F^2
44158 4F^2
44215 4F^2
44223 4F^2
44230 4F^2
44247 4F^2
44264 4F^2
44313 4F^2
44401 4F^2
44408 4F^2
44412 4F^2
44414 4F^2
44425 4F^2
44472 4F^2
44480 4F^2
44533 4F^2
44546 4F^2
44577 4F^2
44578 4F^2
44585 4F^2
44598 4F^2
44825 5MT^3
44841 5MT^3
44861 5MT^3
44918 5MT^3
45059 5MT^3
45554 6P5F^2
45611 6P5F^2
45620 6P5F^2
45636 6P5F^2
45640 6P5F^2
47277 3F^6
47422 3F^6
47438 3F^6
47485 3F^6
47539 3F^6
47552 3F^6
47623 3F^6
47629 3F^6
47631 3F^6
47632 3F^6
47637 3F^6
48064 8F
48102 8F
48170 8F
48206 8F
48217 8F
48218 8F
48279 8F
48293 8F
48380 8F
48381 8F
48402 8F
48614 8F
48635 8F
48639 8F
48653 8F
48666 8F
48675 8F
48696 8F
52121 3F^7
52123 3F^7
52135 3F^7
58050 1P^6
58056 1P^6
58133 2F^8
58135 2F^8
58201 2F^9
58248 2F^8
58252 2F^9

1954 16A
40395 2P^2
40452 2P^2
40454 2P^2
40458 2P^2
40487 2P^2
40493 2P^2
40504 2P^2
40535 2P^2
40550 2P^2
40552 2P^2
40553 2P^2
40900 4P^1
40935 4P^1
41082 4P^1
41096 4P^1
41144 4P^1
41181 4P^1
41185 4P^1
41682 1F^1
41779 1F^1
42140 4MT^1
42146 4MT^1
42184 4MT^1
42185 4MT^1
42228 4MT^1
42333 4MT^2
42339 4MT^2
42361 4MT^2
42373 4MT^2
42680 4MT^1
42686 4MT^1
42769 5MT^1
42823 5MT^1
43033 4MT^5
43040 4MT^5
43119 4MT^5
43192 3F^3
43240 3F^3
43249 3F^3
43300 3F^3
43369 3F^3
43371 3F^3
43378 3F^3
43399 3F^3
43401 3F^3
43558 3F^3
43637 3F^3
43729 3F^3
43910 4F^1
43917 4F^1
43954 4F^1
43956 4F^1
43958 4F^1
43962 4F^1
43972 4F^1
43982 4F^1
44030 4F^2
44033 4F^2
44039 4F^2
44095 4F^2
44113 4F^2
44131 4F^2
44132 4F^2
44139 4F^2
44151 4F^2
44158 4F^2
44195 4F^2
44215 4F^2
44223 4F^2
44264 4F^2
44313 4F^2
44401 4F^2
44408 4F^2
44412 4F^2
44414 4F^2
44425 4F^2
44472 4F^2
44480 4F^2
44533 4F^2
44546 4F^2
44577 4F^2
44578 4F^2
44585 4F^2
44859 5MT^3
44861 5MT^3
44918 5MT^3
45088 5MT^3
45260 5MT^3
45554 6P5F^2
45560 6P5F^2
45611 6P5F^2
45620 6P5F^2
45636 6P5F^2
45667 6P5F^2
46502 2MT^2
47277 3F^6
47422 3F^6
47539 3F^6
47623 3F^6
47631 3F^6
48064 8F
48102 8F
48108 8F
48136 8F
48170 8F
48206 8F
48217 8F
48218 8F
48279 8F
48282 8F
48293 8F
48377 8F
48381 8F
48409 8F
48614 8F
48635 8F
48639 8F
48653 8F
48666 8F
48675 8F
48696 8F
48709 8F
48748 8F
58056 1P^6
58085 1P^6
58133 2F^8
58135 2F^8
58137 2F^8
58271 2F^9
73000 5MT
73002 5MT

1957 16A
40411 2P^2
40454 2P^2
40458 2P^2
40487 2P^2
40493 2P^2
40504 2P^2
40537 2P^2
40542 2P^2
40553 2P^2
40557 2P^2
40632 2P^3
40935 4P^1
41143 4P^1
41144 4P^1
41712 1F^1
42140 4MT^1
42161 4MT^1
42185 4MT^1
42333 4MT^2
42336 4MT^2
42339 4MT^2
42342 4MT^2
42361 4MT^2
42373 4MT^2
42769 5MT^1
42784 5MT^1
43033 4MT^5
43040 4MT^5
43192 3F^3
43240 3F^3
43249 3F^3
43369 3F^3
43371 3F^3
43378 3F^3
43401 3F^3
43729 3F^3
43856 4F^1
43888 4F^1
43910 4F^1
43917 4F^1
43918 4F^1
43928 4F^1
43954 4F^1
43958 4F^1
43962 4F^1
43972 4F^1
44018 4F^1
44021 4F^1
44030 4F^2
44033 4F^2
44095 4F^2
44131 4F^2
44132 4F^2
44139 4F^2
44151 4F^2
44158 4F^2
44195 4F^2
44215 4F^2
44223 4F^2
44264 4F^2
44313 4F^2
44401 4F^2
44412 4F^2
44414 4F^2
44472 4F^2
44480 4F^2
44533 4F^2
44546 4F^2
44555 4F^2
44577 4F^2
44578 4F^2
44585 4F^2
44861 5MT^3
44918 5MT^3
45088 5MT^3
45554 6P5F^2
45560 6P5F^2
45611 6P5F^2
45620 6P5F^2
45636 6P5F^2
45667 6P5F^2
46502 2MT^2
47277 3F^6
47631 3F^6
48053 8F
48064 8F
48108 8F
48111 8F
48117 8F
48136 8F
48170 8F
48206 8F
48217 8F
48218 8F
48279 8F
48282 8F
48377 8F
48409 8F
48614 8F
48635 8F
48639 8F
48653 8F
48666 8F
48675 8F
48696 8F
48709 8F
48748 8F
48763 8F
58137 2F^8
58175 2F^8
73000 5MT
73002 5MT
73067 5MT

1960 16A
40411 2P^2
40421 2P^2
40454 2P^2
40487 2P^2
40502 2P^2
40504 2P^2
40557 2P^2
40585 2P^3
40632 2P^3
40682 2P^3
40691 2P^3
42054 4MT^1
42140 4MT^1
42161 4MT^1
42185 4MT^1
42636 4MT^3
43856 4F^1
43859 4F^1
43870 4F^1
43888 4F^1
43917 4F^1
43918 4F^1
43928 4F^1
43953 4F^1
43954 4F^1
43958 4F^1
43962 4F^1
44030 4F^2
44033 4F^2
44047 4F^2
44131 4F^2
44132 4F^2
44139 4F^2
44151 4F^2
44158 4F^2
44190 4F^2
44195 4F^2
44215 4F^2
44223 4F^2
44248 4F^2
44264 4F^2
44304 4F^2
44394 4F^2
44401 4F^2
44412 4F^2
44414 4F^2
44418 4F^2
44472 4F^2
44480 4F^2
44533 4F^2
44546 4F^2
44555 4F^2
44577 4F^2
44578 4F^2
44585 4F^2
44664 5MT^3
44806 5MT^3
44861 5MT^3
44918 5MT^3
45532 7P^1
45611 6P5F^2
45616 6P5F^2
45620 6P5F^2
45636 6P5F^2
45641 6P5F^2
45650 6P5F^2
45667 6P5F^2
46100 7P^{3}R
46112 7P^{3}R
46157 7P^{3}R
47277 3F^6
48000 8F
48024 8F
48064 8F
48108 8F
48117 8F
48170 8F
48193 8F
48217 8F
48218 8F
48261 8F
48279 8F
48286 8F
48377 8F
48393 8F
48614 8F
48635 8F
48639 8F
48653 8F
48666 8F
48675 8F
48696 8F
48748 8F
48763 8F
58175 2F^8
75056 4MT^1
75062 4MT^1
75063 4MT^1
75064 4MT^1
78020 2MT^1
78021 2MT^1
78028 2MT^1
78029 2MT^1

1963 16A
42091 4MT^1
42140 4MT^1
42161 4MT^1
42185 4MT^1
42587 4MT^3
42588 4MT^3
42628 4MT^3
42636 4MT^3
42756 5MT^1
42763 5MT^1
42799 5MT^1
42826 5MT^1
42839 5MT^1
42855 5MT^1
42872 5MT^1
42896 5MT^1
42897 5MT^1
42922 5MT^1
43870 4F^1
43888 4F^1
43918 4F^1
43928 4F^1
43954 4F^1
44132 4F^2
44139 4F^2
44215 4F^2
44223 4F^2
44248 4F^2
44284 4F^2
44304 4F^2
44401 4F^2
44472 4F^2
44577 4F^2
44658 5MT^3
44806 5MT^3
44851 5MT^3
44856 5MT^3
44861 5MT^3
44918 5MT^3
47320 3F^6
47533 3F^6
48000 8F
48108 8F
48133 8F
48170 8F
48184 8F
48185 8F
48193 8F
48211 8F
48217 8F
48218 8F
48261 8F
48279 8F
48286 8F
48370 8F
48377 8F
48393 8F
48401 8F
48490 8F
48604 8F
48614 8F
48638 8F
48639 8F
48640 8F
48653 8F
48666 8F
48675 8F
48696 8F
48748 8F
48763 8F
78020 2MT^1
78021 2MT^1
78028 2MT^1
78029 2MT^1

Nuneaton

1948 2D
40018 3MT^1
40143 3MT^2
40201 3MT^2
40202 3MT^2
40204 3MT^2
40205 3MT^2
40206 3MT^2
40208 3MT^2
40430 2P^2
40433 2P^2
40447 2P^2
40464 2P^2

40508 2P[2]
42777 5MT[1]
42781 5MT[1]
42783 5MT[1]
42814 5MT[1]
42888 5MT[1]
42932 5MT[1]
42941 5MT[1]
42958 5MT[2]
42959 5MT[2]
42964 5MT[2]
42973 5MT[2]
42981 5MT[2]
47285 3F[6]
47286 3F[6]
47367 3F[6]
47594 3F[6]
48896 7F[2]
48911 6F[2]
49068 7F[2]
49080 7F[2]
49082 7F[2]
49114 7F[2]
49150 7F[2]
49181 7F[2]
49190 6F[2]
49191 7F[2]
49264 7F[2]
49268 7F[2]
49318 7F[2]
49342 7F[2]
49345 7F[2]
49346 6F[2]
49350 7F[2]
49351 7F[2]
49352 7F[2]
49366 7F[2]
49400 7F[3]
49412 7F[3]
49428 7F[3]
49429 7F[3]
49430 7F[3]
49432 7F[3]
49435 7F[3]
49436 7F[3]
49437 7F[3]
49439 7F[3]
52107 3F[7]
52141 3F[7]
52294 3F[7]
52321 3F[7]
52322 3F[7]
58116 2F[8]
58118 2F[8]
58213 2F[9]
58240 2F[8]
58363 2F[11]
58368 2F[11]
58405 2F[11]
58426 2F[11]

1951 2B
40137 3MT[2]
40201 3MT[2]
40202 3MT[2]
40205 3MT[2]
40413 2P[2]
40438 2P[2]
40447 2P[2]
40508 2P[2]
40528 2P[2]
41234 2MT[1]
41235 2MT[1]
41236 2MT[1]
41237 2MT[1]
41238 2MT[1]
42777 5MT[1]
42781 5MT[1]
42783 5MT[1]
42813 5MT[1]
42814 5MT[1]
42888 5MT[1]
42932 5MT[1]
42933 5MT[1]
42941 5MT[1]
42944 5MT[1]
42960 5MT[2]
43020 4MT[5]
43021 4MT[5]
43022 4MT[5]
43023 4MT[5]
43024 4MT[5]
43027 4MT[5]
47285 3F[6]
47286 3F[6]
47367 3F[6]
47594 3F[6]
48016 8F
48020 8F
48061 8F
48077 8F
48345 8F
48526 8F
48716 8F
48723 8F
48927 7F[2]
49068 7F[2]
49181 7F[2]
49186 7F[2]
49293 7F[2]
49304 7F[2]
49318 7F[2]
49339 7F[2]
49350 7F[2]
49368 7F[2]
49385 7F[2]
49397 7F[3]
49414 7F[3]
49418 7F[3]
49424 7F[3]
49432 7F[3]
49434 7F[3]
49435 7F[3]
49436 7F[3]
49453 7F[3]
52141 3F[7]
52322 3F[7]
52429 3F[7]
52465 3F[7]
58118 2F[8]
58240 2F[8]
58272 2F[9]

1954 2B
40003 3MT[1]
40087 3MT[2]
40104 3MT[2]
40109 3MT[2]
40135 3MT[2]
40204 3MT[2]
40583 2P[3]
40676 2P[3]
40677 2P[3]
41211 2MT[1]
41213 2MT[1]
42781 5MT[1]
42783 5MT[1]
42810 5MT[1]
42814 5MT[1]
42817 5MT[1]
42852 5MT[1]
42854 5MT[1]
42888 5MT[1]
42891 5MT[1]
42944 5MT[1]
43002 4MT[5]
43003 4MT[5]
43005 4MT[5]
43011 4MT[5]
43023 4MT[5]
43786 3F[4]
47285 3F[6]
47286 3F[6]
47367 3F[6]
47594 3F[6]
48016 8F
48020 8F
48077 8F
48154 8F
48320 8F
48343 8F
48345 8F
48372 8F
48449 8F
48526 8F
48716 8F
48723 8F
48751 8F
48927 7F[2]
49002 7F[2]
49068 7F[2]
49112 7F[2]
49142 7F[2]
49172 7F[2]
49181 7F[2]
49186 7F[2]
49212 7F[2]
49293 7F[2]
49304 7F[2]
49339 7F[2]
49342 7F[2]
49350 7F[2]
49414 7F[3]
49424 7F[3]
49430 7F[3]
49432 7F[3]
52141 3F[7]
52429 3F[7]
52465 3F[7]
58118 2F[8]
58221 2F[9]
58272 2F[9]

1957 2B
40087 3MT[2]
40104 3MT[2]
40122 3MT[2]
40138 3MT[2]
40156 3MT[2]
40157 3MT[2]
40204 3MT[2]
40207 3MT[2]
41226 2MT[1]
41322 2MT[1]
41323 2MT[1]
42781 5MT[1]
42783 5MT[1]
42814 5MT[1]
42817 5MT[1]
42854 5MT[1]
42891 5MT[1]
43002 4MT[5]
43003 4MT[5]
43011 4MT[5]
43023 4MT[5]
43034 4MT[5]
43308 3F[3]
43786 3F[4]
44157 4F[2]
47285 3F[6]
47286 3F[6]
47594 3F[6]
48016 8F
48020 8F
48077 8F
48154 8F
48258 8F
48312 8F
48320 8F
48343 8F
48345 8F
48372 8F
48398 8F
48449 8F
48456 8F
48526 8F
48658 8F
48686 8F
48716 8F
48723 8F
48751 8F
48927 7F[2]
49002 7F[2]
49068 7F[2]
49112 7F[2]
49120 7F[2]
49142 7F[2]
49172 7F[2]
49181 7F[2]
49293 7F[2]
49314 7F[2]
49342 7F[2]
49350 7F[2]
49414 7F[3]
49430 7F[3]
49432 7F[3]
52201 3F[7]
58118 2F[8]
58281 2F[9]

1960 2B
40087 3MT[2]
40104 3MT[2]
40135 3MT[2]
40138 3MT[2]
40157 3MT[2]
40185 3MT[2]
40207 3MT[2]
42781 5MT[1]
42783 5MT[1]
42811 5MT[1]
42814 5MT[1]
42853 5MT[1]
42891 5MT[1]
42926 5MT[1]
42933 5MT[1]
42935 5MT[1]
42939 5MT[1]
43000 4MT[5]
43001 4MT[5]
43002 4MT[5]
43003 4MT[5]
43005 4MT[5]
43020 4MT[5]
43022 4MT[5]
43023 4MT[5]
43024 4MT[5]
43026 4MT[5]
43034 4MT[5]
43052 4MT[5]
48016 8F
48020 8F
48077 8F
48111 8F
48154 8F
48251 8F
48258 8F
48263 8F
48287 8F
48289 8F
48291 8F
48312 8F
48320 8F
48343 8F
48398 8F
48449 8F
48456 8F
48504 8F
48623 8F
48658 8F
48686 8F
48723 8F
48751 8F
48927 7F[2]
49002 7F[2]
49079 7F[2]
49134 7F[2]
49142 7F[2]
49144 7F[2]
49293 7F[2]
49314 7F[2]
49342 7F[2]
49350 7F[2]
49414 7F[3]
49415 7F[3]
49425 7F[3]
49430 7F[3]
49431 7F[3]
49432 7F[3]
49440 7F[3]
49441 7F[3]

1963 2B
42945 5MT[2]
42946 5MT[2]
42947 5MT[2]
42950 5MT[2]
42951 5MT[2]
42954 5MT[2]
42955 5MT[2]
42958 5MT[2]
42960 5MT[2]
42962 5MT[2]
42964 5MT[2]
42967 5MT[2]
42968 5MT[2]
42969 5MT[2]
42970 5MT[2]
42971 5MT[2]
42973 5MT[2]
42975 5MT[2]
42976 5MT[2]
42978 5MT[2]
42981 5MT[2]
42982 5MT[2]
43977 4F[1]
45599 6P5F[2]
45624 6P5F[2]
45643 6P5F[2]
45669 6P5F[2]
45723 6P5F[2]
46420 2MT[2]
46447 2MT[2]
47396 3F[6]
47478 3F[6]
47653 3F[6]
48016 8F
48020 8F
48054 8F
48111 8F
48206 8F
48251 8F
48263 8F
48264 8F
48289 8F
48291 8F
48320 8F
48343 8F
48398 8F
48449 8F
48456 8F
48504 8F
48623 8F
48686 8F
48723 8F
48751 8F
48753 8F
75010 4MT[1]
75011 4MT[1]
75012 4MT[1]
75032 4MT[1]
75033 4MT[1]
75035 4MT[1]
75036 4MT[1]
75050 4MT[1]

1966 5E
44771 5MT[3]
44831 5MT[3]
44866 5MT[3]
45001 5MT[3]
45065 5MT[3]
45310 5MT[3]
45405 5MT[3]
45448 5MT[3]
46495 2MT[2]
46512 2MT[2]
46519 2MT[2]
46520 2MT[2]
48054 8F
48074 8F
48111 8F
48206 8F
48247 8F
48263 8F
48264 8F
48289 8F
48320 8F
48343 8F
48445 8F
48456 8F
48504 8F
48534 8F
48650 8F
48686 8F
48718 8F
48751 8F
48753 8F
75035 4MT[1]
75045 4MT[1]
78003 2MT[1]
78018 2MT[1]
78019 2MT[1]
78039 2MT[1]
78059 2MT[1]
78063 2MT[1]

Oban

1948 31C
55187 2P[13]
55215 2P[13]
55263 2P[15]
57396 2F[5]
57411 2F[5]

1951 63E
55187 2P[13]
55196 2P[13]
55198 2P[13]
55215 2P[13]
55263 2P[15]
57254 2F[5]
57396 2F[5]

1954 63E
55195 2P[13]
55196 2P[13]
55215 2P[13]
55263 2P[15]
57254 2F[5]
57424 2F[5]

1957 63D
55200 2P[13]
55208 2P[13]
55215 2P[13]
55263 2P[15]
57276 2F[5]
57667 3F[14]

1960 63C
55126 2P[12]
55208 2P[13]
55215 2P[13]
55220 2P[13]
55263 2P[15]
57571 3F[12]
57667 3F[14]

1963 63C
46460 2MT[2]

Old Oak Common

1948 PDN
100 A1 4073
111 4073
1000 1000
1003 1000
1008 1000
1010 1000
1012 1000
1015 1000
1021 1000
1026 1000
1912 1901
2276 2251
2282 2251
2826 2800
2835 2800
2840 2800
2850 2800
2855 2800
2856 2800
2868 2800
2875 2800
3600 5700
3618 5700
3619 5700
3635 5700
3644 5700
3646 5700
3648 5700
3658 5700
3659 5700
3669 5700
3672 5700
3685 5700
3688 5700
3710 5700
3723 5700
3734 5700
3738 5700
3754 5700
3766 5700
3832 2884
3851 2884
3852 2884
3853 2884
3903 4900
3952 4900
3953 4900
3954 4900
4037 4073
4073 4073
4075 4073
4076 4073
4091 4073
4606 5700
4609 5700
4615 5700
4642 5700
4644 5700
4665 5700
4666 5700
4667 5700
4680 5700
4691 5700
4698 5700
4699 5700
4700 4700
4701 4700
4702 4700
4705 4700
4707 4700
4809 2800
4853 2884
4854 2884
4856 2884
4900 4900
4935 4900
4943 4900
4951 4900
4958 4900
4961 4900
4962 4900
4978 4900
4985 4900
4998 4900
5000 4073
5004 4073
5008 4073
5014 4073
5022 4073
5023 4073
5027 4073
5029 4073
5035 4073
5036 4073
5037 4073
5038 4073
5039 4073
5040 4073
5043 4073
5044 4073
5045 4073
5055 4073
5056 4073
5065 4073
5066 4073
5069 4073
5081 4073
5085 4073
5087 4073
5099 4073
5717 5700
5764 5700
5922 4900
5931 4900
5932 4900
5936 4900
5937 4900
5938 4900
5939 4900
5940 4900
5941 4900
5952 4900
5962 4900
5987 4900
5996 4900
6001 6000
6003 6000
6007 6000
6009 6000
6013 6000
6014 6000
6015 6000
6021 6000
6025 6000
6112 6100
6120 6100
6129 6100
6132 6100
6134 6100
6135 6100
6137 6100
6141 6100
6142 6100
6144 6100
6149 6100
6155 6100
6158 6100
6159 6100
6166 6100
6168 6100
6865 6800
6869 6800
6900 4900
6910 4900
6959 6959
6960 6959
6961 6959
6962 6959
6973 6959
6974 6959
6977 6959
7713 5700
7734 5700
7738 5700
7754 5700
7760 5700
7791 5700
8707 5700
8735 5700
8738 5700
8750 5700
8751 5700
8754 5700
8756 5700
8757 5700
8759 5700
8760 5700
8761 5700
8762 5700
8763 5700
8765 5700
8767 5700
8768 5700
8769 5700
8770 5700
8771 5700
8772 5700
8773 5700
8780 5700
9302 9300
9306 9300
9308 9300
9310 9300
9401 9400
9402 9400
9403 9400
9404 9400
9405 9400
9406 9400
9407 9400
9409 9400
9658 5700
9659 5700
9661 5700
9700 9700
9701 9700
9702 9700
9703 9700
9704 9700
9705 9700
9706 9700
9707 9700
9708 9700
9709 9700
9710 9700
9725 5700
9726 5700
9751 5700
9754 5700
9758 5700
9784 5700
90105 WD[1]
90113 WD[1]
90167 WD[1]
90357 WD[1]
90366 WD[1]
90585 WD[1]
90633 WD[1]
90693 WD[1]

1951 81A
1000 1000
1003 1000
1008 1000
1010 1000
1012 1000
1015 1000
1021 1000
1026 1000
1500 1500
1503 1500
1504 1500
1505 1500
2276 2251
2282 2251
2826 2800
2835 2800
2868 2800
2895 2884
3017 ROD
3648 5700
3685 5700
3688 5700
3754 5700
3813 2884
3852 2884
3853 2884
4016 4073
4037 4073
4615 5700
4644 5700
4698 5700
4699 5700
4700 4700
4701 4700
4702 4700
4705 4700
4707 4700
4900 4900
4923 4900
4958 4900
4961 4900
5004 4073
5014 4073
5029 4073
5035 4073
5038 4073
5039 4073
5040 4073
5043 4073
5044 4073
5055 4073
5056 4073
5065 4073
5066 4073
5069 4073
5081 4073
5085 4073
5087 4073
5717 5700
5764 5700
5931 4900
5932 4900
5936 4900
5937 4900
5938 4900
5939 4900
5940 4900
5941 4900
5947 4900
5962 4900
5986 4900
5987 4900
5994 4900
5996 4900
6001 6000
6002 6000
6003 6000
6007 6000
6009 6000
6013 6000
6014 6000
6015 6000
6017 6000
6018 6000
6019 6000
6021 6000
6028 6000
6117 6100
6120 6100
6121 6100
6135 6100
6137 6100
6141 6100
6142 6100
6144 6100
6149 6100
6155 6100
6158 6100
6159 6100
6168 6100
6900 4900
6926 4900
6932 4900
6944 4900
6959 6959
6960 6959
6962 6959
6973 6959
6974 6959
6983 6959
7001 4073
7004 4073
7013 4073
7024 4073
7025 4073
7030 4073
7032 4073
7033 4073
7036 4073
7734 5700
7791 5700
7902 6959
7903 6959
7904 6959
7911 6959
8707 5700
8750 5700
8751 5700
8753 5700
8754 5700
8756 5700
8757 5700
8759 5700
8760 5700
8761 5700
8762 5700
8763 5700
8764 5700
8765 5700
8767 5700
8768 5700
8769 5700
8770 5700
8771 5700
8772 5700
8773 5700
9302 9300
9304 9300
9306 9300
9308 9300
9309 9300
9315 9300
9401 9400
9402 9400
9403 9400
9404 9400
9405 9400
9406 9400
9418 9400
9419 9400
9422 9400
9658 5700
9659 5700
9661 5700
9700 9700
9701 9700
9702 9700
9703 9700
9704 9700
9705 9700
9706 9700
9707 9700
9708 9700
9709 9700
9710 9700
9725 5700
9751 5700
9754 5700
9758 5700
9784 5700

1954 81A
1500 1500
1503 1500
1504 1500
1505 1500
2222 2251
2243 2251
2276 2251
2282 2251
3648 5700
3685 5700
3688 5700
3715 5700
3754 5700
4037 4073
4097 4073
4615 5700
4644 5700
4698 5700
4699 5700
4700 4700
4701 4700
4702 4700
4704 4700
4705 4700
4707 4700
4708 4700
4923 4900
4943 4900
4967 4900
4986 4900
5004 4073
5014 4073
5029 4073
5034 4073
5035 4073
5038 4073
5040 4073
5044 4073
5055 4073
5056 4073
5060 4073
5065 4073
5066 4073
5081 4073
5082 4073
5087 4073
5093 4073
5095 4073
5717 5700
5764 5700
5906 4900
5931 4900
5932 4900
5936 4900
5939 4900
5940 4900
5941 4900
5986 4900
5987 4900
5996 4900
6000 6000
6001 6000
6002 6000
6003 6000
6007 6000
6009 6000
6013 6000
6015 6000
6018 6000
6019 6000
6021 6000
6028 6000
6109 6100
6110 6100
6120 6100
6121 6100
6135 6100
6137 6100
6141 6100
6142 6100
6144 6100
6149 6100
6155 6100
6158 6100
6159 6100
6168 6100
6944 4900
6959 6959
6961 6959
6962 6959
6973 6959
6974 6959
6990 6959
6996 6959
7001 4073
7004 4073
7010 4073
7013 4073
7024 4073
7025 4073
7027 4073
7030 4073
7032 4073
7033 4073
7036 4073
7734 5700
7791 5700
7902 6959
7903 6959
7904 6959
8432 9400
8433 9400
8434 9400
8707 5700
8751 5700
8753 5700
8754 5700
8756 5700
8757 5700
8759 5700
8760 5700
8761 5700
8762 5700
8763 5700
8764 5700
8765 5700
8767 5700
8768 5700
8769 5700
8770 5700
8771 5700
8772 5700
8773 5700
9410 9400
9411 9400
9412 9400
9414 9400
9418 9400
9419 9400
9420 9400
9422 9400
9423 9400
9658 5700
9659 5700
9661 5700
9700 9700
9701 9700
9702 9700
9703 9700
9704 9700
9705 9700
9706 9700
9707 9700
9708 9700
9709 9700
9710 9700
9725 5700
9751 5700
9754 5700
9758 5700
9784 5700
70015 7P6F
70017 7P6F
70018 7P6F
70020 7P6F
70023 7P6F

1957 81A
1500 1500
1503 1500
1504 1500
1505 1500
2222 2251
2243 2251
2276 2251
2282 2251
3648 5700
3688 5700
3754 5700
4089 4073
4090 4073
4091 4073
4097 4073
4615 5700
4644 5700
4700 4700
4701 4700
4702 4700
4704 4700
4705 4700
4708 4700
4900 4900
4919 4900
4925 4900
4928 4900
4977 4900
5006 4073
5008 4073
5014 4073
5029 4073
5034 4073
5035 4073
5038 4073
5040 4073
5043 4073
5044 4073
5055 4073
5056 4073
5060 4073
5065 4073
5066 4073
5082 4073
5084 4073
5087 4073
5092 4073
5093 4073
5095 4073
5717 5700
5764 5700
5931 4900
5932 4900
5936 4900
5939 4900
5940 4900
5941 4900
5945 4900
5954 4900
5987 4900
5996 4900
6000 6000
6002 6000
6003 6000
6007 6000
6009 6000
6012 6000
6013 6000
6015 6000
6016 6000
6018 6000
6019 6000
6022 6000
6023 6000
6024 6000
6028 6000
6110 6100
6120 6100
6121 6100
6132 6100
6135 6100
6141 6100
6142 6100
6144 6100
6149 6100
6158 6100
6159 6100
6168 6100
6959 6959
6961 6959
6962 6959
6973 6959
6974 6959
6990 6959
7001 4073
7004 4073
7008 4073
7010 4073
7013 4073
7017 4073
7024 4073
7025 4073
7027 4073
7030 4073
7032 4073
7033 4073
7036 4073
7734 5700
7791 5700
7902 6959
7903 6959
7904 6959
8434 9400
8751 5700
8753 5700
8754 5700
8755 5700
8756 5700
8757 5700
8759 5700
8760 5700
8761 5700
8762 5700
8763 5700
8764 5700
8765 5700
8767 5700
8768 5700
8769 5700
8770 5700
8771 5700
8772 5700
8773 5700
9400 9400
9410 9400
9411 9400
9412 9400
9414 9400
9416 9400
9418 9400
9419 9400
9420 9400
9422 9400
9423 9400
9658 5700
9659 5700
9661 5700
9700 9700
9701 9700
9702 9700
9703 9700
9704 9700
9705 9700
9706 9700
9707 9700
9708 9700
9709 9700
9710 9700
9725 5700
9751 5700
9754 5700
9758 5700
9784 5700
70023 7P6F

1960 81A
1500 1500
1503 1500
1504 1500
1505 1500
2222 2251
2276 2251
2282 2251
3648 5700
3688 5700
3754 5700
4075 4073
4096 4073
4615 5700
4700 4700
4701 4700
4702 4700
4704 4700
4708 4700
4903 4900
4919 4900
4921 4900
5008 4073
5014 4073
5027 4073
5034 4073
5035 4073
5040 4073
5043 4073
5044 4073
5052 4073
5054 4073
5056 4073
5060 4073
5065 4073
5066 4073
5074 4073
5082 4073
5084 4073
5087 4073
5093 4073
5717 5700
5764 5700
5907 4900
5923 4900
5929 4900
5931 4900
5932 4900
5939 4900
5958 4900
5976 4900
6000 6000
6002 6000
6003 6000
6004 6000
6009 6000
6010 6000
6012 6000
6015 6000
6018 6000
6019 6000
6021 6000
6023 6000
6024 6000
6025 6000
6027 6000
6028 6000
6029 6000
6108 6100
6113 6100
6120 6100
6121 6100
6132 6100
6135 6100
6141 6100
6142 6100
6144 6100
6145 6100
6157 6100
6158 6100
6168 6100
6920 4900
6942 4900
6959 6959
6961 6959
6962 6959
6966 6959
6973 6959
6974 6959
6978 6959
6990 6959
7001 4073
7004 4073
7008 4073
7010 4073
7013 4073
7017 4073
7020 4073
7024 4073
7025 4073
7027 4073
7030 4073
7032 4073
7033 4073
7036 4073
7722 5700
7902 6959
7903 6959
7904 6959
7927 6959
8459 9400
8751 5700
8753 5700
8754 5700

8756 5700
8757 5700
8759 5700
8760 5700
8762 5700
8763 5700
8764 5700
8765 5700
8767 5700
8768 5700
8770 5700
8771 5700
8772 5700
8773 5700
9405 9400
9410 9400
9411 9400
9412 9400
9414 9400
9416 9400
9418 9400
9419 9400
9420 9400
9423 9400
9469 9400
9479 9400
9658 5700
9659 5700
9661 5700
9700 9700
9701 9700
9702 9700
9703 9700
9704 9700
9705 9700
9706 9700
9707 9700
9709 9700
9710 9700
9725 5700
9751 5700
9754 5700
9758 5700
9784 5700
92211 9F
92229 9F
92230 9F
92238 9F
92239 9F
92240 9F
92241 9F
92244 9F
92245 9F
92246 9F
92247 9F

1963 81A
1500 1500
1503 1500
1504 1500
1506 1500
1507 1500
3646 5700
3711 5700
3754 5700
4074 4073
4089 4073
4096 4073
4098 4073
4615 5700
4701 4700
4703 4700
4704 4700
4903 4900
5001 4073
5014 4073
5041 4073
5056 4073
5057 4073
5060 4073
5065 4073
5070 4073
5093 4073
5919 4900
5932 4900
5967 4900
5984 4900
5988 4900
6125 6100
6135 6100
6141 6100
6142 6100
6145 6100
6163 6100
6169 6100
6942 4900
6959 6959
6961 6959
6962 6959
6963 6959
6966 6959
6973 6959
6978 6959
6990 6959
6998 6959
7006 4073
7008 4073
7009 4073
7010 4073
7015 4073
7017 4073
7018 4073
7020 4073
7021 4073
7029 4073
7030 4073
7032 4073
7033 4073
7036 4073
7902 6959
7903 6959
7904 6959
7921 6959
8420 9400
8436 9400
8458 9400
8459 9400
8472 9400
8487 9400
8759 5700
8767 5700
8768 5700
9405 9400
9411 9400
9418 9400
9419 9400
9420 9400
9423 9400
9440 9400
9455 9400
9477 9400
9479 9400
9495 9400
9640 5700
9658 5700
9659 5700
9661 5700
9700 9700
9704 9700
9706 9700
9707 9700
9710 9700
9755 5700
9784 5700
92203 9F
92204 9F
92209 9F
92217 9F
92218 9F
92243 9F

Oswestry

1948 OSW
680 AD[3]
844 Cam[1]
849 Cam[1]
855 Cam[1]
873 Cam[1]
887 Cam[1]
892 Cam[1]
893 Cam[1]
895 Cam[1]
896 Cam[1]
1196 Cam[2]
1197 Cam[2]
1308 L&L
1331 W&C
1412 1400
1417 1400
1432 1400
1459 1400
2032 2021
2054 2021
2068 2021
2075 2021
2201 2251
2210 2251
2244 2251
2255 2251
2327 2301
2354 2301
2382 2301
2386 2301
2449 2301
2482 2301
2483 2301
2516 2301
2543 2301
2556 2301
3202 2251
3208 2251
5806 5800
7405 7400
7410 7400
7807 7800
7808 7800
7819 7800
8103 8100
9001 9000
9003 9000
9016 9000
9020 9000
9022 9000
9026 9000
9028 9000
9065 3252

1951 89A
844 Cam[1]
849 Cam[1]
855 Cam[1]
873 Cam[1]
887 Cam[1]
893 Cam[1]
895 Cam[1]
896 Cam[1]
1412 1400
1428 1400
1432 1400
1459 1400
1604 1600
2032 2021
2054 2021
2068 2021
2075 2021
2210 2251
2244 2251
2255 2251
2327 2301
2354 2301
2408 2301
2409 2301
2449 2301
2484 2301
2516 2301
2538 2301
2543 2301
2556 2301
2572 2301
3208 2251
5803 5800
5806 5800
5812 5800
7405 7400
7410 7400
7434 7400
7807 7800
7808 7800
7819 7800
7820 7800
7821 7800
7822 7800
8103 8100
9001 9000
9003 9000
9016 9000
9020 9000
9022 9000
9026 9000
9028 9000
9084 3252

1954 89A
844 Cam[1]
855 Cam[1]
873 Cam[1]
895 Cam[1]
1412 1400
1432 1400
1459 1400
1604 1600
1636 1600
2210 2251
2219 2251
2255 2251
2484 2301
2538 2301
3200 2251
3208 2251
4546 4500
5401 5400
5405 5400
5700 5700
5726 5700
5806 5800
5812 5800
7405 7400
7410 7400
7434 7400
7819 7800
7822 7800
9001 9000
9003 9000
9022 9000
46503 2MT[2]
46504 2MT[2]
46505 2MT[2]
46506 2MT[2]
46507 2MT[2]
46508 2MT[2]
46509 2MT[2]
46510 2MT[2]
46511 2MT[2]
46512 2MT[2]
46513 2MT[2]
46514 2MT[2]
46515 2MT[2]
46519 2MT[2]
46520 2MT[2]
75006 4MT[1]
75020 4MT[1]
75023 4MT[1]
75024 4MT[1]

1957 89A
822 W&L
823 W&L
1432 1400
1459 1400
1602 1600
1603 1600
1604 1600
2210 2251
2219 2251
2239 2251
2275 2251
2538 2301
3200 2251
3201 2251
3202 2251
3207 2251
3208 2251
3789 5700
4546 4500
5401 5400
5405 5400
5726 5700
5806 5800
5812 5800
7405 7400
7410 7400
7434 7400
7819 7800
9005 9000
9010 9000
9026 9000
9027 9000
9681 5700
46503 2MT[2]
46504 2MT[2]
46505 2MT[2]
46507 2MT[2]
46509 2MT[2]
46510 2MT[2]
46511 2MT[2]
46512 2MT[2]
46513 2MT[2]
46514 2MT[2]
46515 2MT[2]
46519 2MT[2]
46520 2MT[2]
46523 2MT[2]
46526 2MT[2]
75002 4MT[1]
75005 4MT[1]
75006 4MT[1]
75020 4MT[1]
75024 4MT[1]
75028 4MT[1]

1960 89A
822 W&L
823 W&L
1432 1400
1458 1400
1602 1600
1604 1600
1628 1600
1636 1600
2239 2251
2287 2251
2289 2251
3200 2251
3202 2251
3208 2251
3209 2251
3600 5700
3770 5700
3789 5700
5422 5400
6342 4300
7405 7400
7410 7400
7800 7800
7801 7800
7807 7800
7809 7800
7810 7800
7819 7800
7822 7800
7827 7800
9018 9000
9681 5700
41204 2MT[1]
46401 2MT[2]
46503 2MT[2]
46504 2MT[2]
46505 2MT[2]
46506 2MT[2]
46507 2MT[2]
46508 2MT[2]
46509 2MT[2]
46510 2MT[2]
46511 2MT[2]
46512 2MT[2]
46513 2MT[2]
46514 2MT[2]
46515 2MT[2]
46516 2MT[2]
46518 2MT[2]
46519 2MT[2]
46520 2MT[2]
46521 2MT[2]
46522 2MT[2]
46523 2MT[2]
46524 2MT[2]
46526 2MT[2]
46527 2MT[2]

1963 89D
1432 1400
1458 1400
1630 1600
1663 1600
1666 1600
1668 1600
2214 2251
3200 2251
3208 2251
3770 5700
7446 7400
7800 7800
7801 7800
7807 7800
7809 7800
7810 7800
7819 7800
7822 7800
7827 7800
46401 2MT[2]
46503 2MT[2]
46504 2MT[2]
46505 2MT[2]
46507 2MT[2]
46508 2MT[2]
46509 2MT[2]
46510 2MT[2]
46511 2MT[2]
46512 2MT[2]
46513 2MT[2]
46514 2MT[2]
46515 2MT[2]
46516 2MT[2]
46518 2MT[2]
46519 2MT[2]
46520 2MT[2]
46521 2MT[2]
46522 2MT[2]
46523 2MT[2]
46524 2MT[2]
46525 2MT[2]
46526 2MT[2]
46527 2MT[2]

Oxenholme

1948 11D
42301 4MT[2]
42313 4MT[2]
42314 4MT[2]
42317 4MT[2]
42457 4MT[3]
42464 4MT[3]
42595 4MT[3]

1951 11C
42301 4MT[2]
42313 4MT[2]
42314 4MT[2]
42317 4MT[2]
42457 4MT[3]
42464 4MT[3]
42613 4MT[3]
47503 3F[6]

1954 11C
42301 4MT[2]
42313 4MT[2]
42314 4MT[2]
42317 4MT[2]
42393 4MT[2]
42457 4MT[3]
42464 4MT[3]
42613 4MT[3]
47503 3F[6]

1957 11C
42301 4MT[2]
42313 4MT[2]
42314 4MT[2]
42317 4MT[2]
42457 4MT[3]
42464 4MT[3]
42613 4MT[3]
47503 3F[6]

1960 11C
42301 4MT[2]
42313 4MT[2]
42314 4MT[2]
42345 4MT[2]
42457 4MT[3]
42464 4MT[3]
42613 4MT[3]

Oxford

1948 OXF
1448 1400
1450 1400
1531 1501
1742 655
1935 1901
2249 2251
2579 2301
2827 2800
2861 2800
2881 2800
3585 3500
3588 3500
3589 3500
3608 5700
3687 5700
3722 5700
3741 5700
3835 2884
3836 2884
3838 2884
3847 2884
3848 2884
3866 2884
4004 4000
4021 4000
4049 4000
4052 4000
4645 5700
4676 5700
4902 4900
4903 4900
4921 4900
4928 4900
4938 4900
4973 4900
5323 4300
5616 5600
5904 4900
5960 4900
6103 6100
6122 6100
6138 6100
6300 4300
6682 5600
6925 4900
6933 4900
6937 4900
7404 7400
7411 7400
7412 7400
9316 9300
9317 9300
9611 5700
9654 5700
90529 WD[1]

1951 81F
1450 1400
1617 1600
1935 1901
2076 2021
2249 2251
2827 2800
2858 2800
2860 2800
3608 5700
3722 5700
3835 2884
3847 2884
3866 2884
4021 4000
4511 4500
4558 4500
4676 5700
4680 5700
4902 4900
4903 4900
4921 4900
4928 4900
4938 4900
5026 4073
5323 4300
5413 5400
5904 4900
5960 4900
5965 4900
6109 6100
6111 6100
6122 6100
6138 6100
6300 4300
6313 4300
6925 4900
6933 4900
6937 4900
6953 4900
6970 6959
6990 6959
7008 4073
7010 4073
7404 7400
7411 7400
7412 7400
7436 7400
7760 5700
9316 9300
9317 9300
9416 9400
9611 5700
9640 5700
9654 5700
90529 WD[1]

1954 81F
1420 1400
1425 1400
1442 1400
2236 2251
2579 2301
3608 5700
3722 5700
3835 2884
4147 5101
4676 5700
4902 4900
4903 4900
4921 4900
4928 4900
4933 4900
4938 4900
4969 4900
5012 4073
5026 4073
5323 4300
5413 5400
5803 5800
5808 5800
5960 4900
5965 4900
6106 6100
6111 6100
6112 6100
6113 6100
6122 6100
6138 6100
6920 4900
6937 4900
6953 4900
6970 6959
7008 4073
7212 7200
7238 7200
7239 7200
7246 7200
7404 7400
7411 7400
7412 7400
7436 7400
7760 5700
7900 6959
7911 6959
9015 9000
9302 9300
9311 9300
9316 9300
9403 9400
9416 9400
9611 5700
9640 5700
9653 5700
9654 5700
90312 WD[1]
90529 WD[1]

1957 81F
1420 1400
1437 1400
1442 1400
2236 2251
2294 2251
3608 5700
3722 5700
3854 2884
3857 2884
4147 5101
4676 5700
4902 4900
4903 4900
4907 4900
4921 4900
4938 4900
4954 4900
5012 4073
5026 4073
5190 5101
5413 5400
5808 5800
5960 4900
5965 4900
5966 4900
5969 4900
6106 6100
6111 6100
6112 6100
6113 6100
6138 6100
6336 4300
6854 6800
6864 6800
6920 4900
6922 4900
6924 4900
6937 4900
6970 6959
7238 7200
7239 7200
7404 7400
7411 7400
7412 7400
7436 7400
7760 5700
7900 6959
7911 6959
8432 9400
9302 9300
9403 9400
9611 5700
9640 5700
9653 5700
9654 5700
75001 4MT[1]
75027 4MT[1]
75029 4MT[1]
90251 WD[1]
90284 WD[1]

1960 81F
1435 1400
1442 1400
1444 1400
1450 1400
3722 5700
3814 2884
3823 2884
3857 2884
4103 5101
4125 5101
4147 5101
4148 5101
4979 4900
4995 4900
5012 4073
5025 4073
5033 4073
5190 5101
5697 5600
5957 4900
5960 4900
5966 4900
6106 6100
6111 6100
6133 6100
6138 6100
6139 6100
6163 6100
6664 5600
6822 6800
6854 6800
6858 6800
6927 4900
6937 4900
6970 6959
7238 7200
7239 7200
7404 7400
7412 7400
7445 7400
7760 5700
7900 6959
7911 6959
8424 9400
8494 9400
9450 9400
9611 5700
9640 5700
9653 5700
9654 5700
75001 4MT[1]
75007 4MT[1]
75008 4MT[1]

1963 81F
1444 1400
1627 1600
1630 1600
3653 5700
3814 2884
3823 2884
4649 5700
4919 4900
4951 4900
4979 4900
5025 4073
5922 4900
5923 4900
5933 4900
5945 4900
5955 4900
5956 4900
5957 4900
6106 6100
6111 6100
6124 6100
6144 6100
6149 6100
6150 6100
6154 6100
6156 6100
6910 4900
6927 4900
6970 6959
7035 4073
7404 7400
7412 7400
7900 6959
7911 6959
9653 5700
9654 5700
75001 4MT[1]
75007 4MT[1]
75008 4MT[1]
75022 4MT[1]
92220 9F
92224 9F

Oxley

1948 OXY
1762 1854
2623 2600
2665 2600
2825 2800
2830 2800
3016 ROD
3024 ROD
3031 ROD
3033 ROD
3039 ROD
3102 3100
3104 3100
3744 5700
3745 5700
3792 5700
3793 5700
4708 4700
4904 4900
4916 4900
4923 4900
4944 4900
4955 4900
4964 4900
4987 4900
4991 4900
4996 4900
5300 4300
5313 4300
5331 4300
5333 4300
5379 4300
5386 4300
5390 4300
5606 5600
5657 5600
5670 5600
5684 5600
5748 5700
5780 5700
5916 4900
5918 4900
5920 4900
5921 4900
5945 4900
5947 4900
5957 4900
5979 4900
5989 4900
6332 4300
6335 4300
6342 4300
6361 4300
6362 4300
6600 5600
6609 5600
6610 5600
6638 5600
6640 5600
6645 5600
6856 6800
6862 6800
6879 6800
6915 4900
6932 4900
6939 4900
6942 4900
6956 4900
6967 6959
6970 6959
6975 6959
7207 7200
7222 7200
7226 7200
7227 7200
7236 7200
7238 7200
7240 7200
7243 7200
7248 7200
7307 4300
7311 4300
7317 4300
7759 5700
7796 5700
7797 5700
7813 7800
8798 5700
9312 9300
9314 9300
9408 9400
9714 5700
9715 5700
9730 5700
9739 5700
9742 5700
9747 5700
9752 5700
9768 5700
9769 5700
90125 WD[1]
90135 WD[1]
90141 WD[1]
90143 WD[1]
90152 WD[1]
90178 WD[1]
90201 WD[1]
90535 WD[1]
90548 WD[1]
90652 WD[1]
90682 WD[1]
90686 WD[1]

1951 84B
2830 2800
2832 2800
2833 2800
2854 2800
3031 ROD
3033 ROD
3744 5700
3745 5700
3792 5700
3793 5700
4708 4700
4919 4900
4950 4900
4955 4900
4977 4900
4991 4900
5300 4300
5307 4300
5309 4300
5313 4300
5341 4300
5379 4300
5386 4300
5390 4300
5624 5600
5657 5600
5684 5600
5748 5700
5921 4900
5942 4900
5944 4900
5945 4900
5991 4900
5995 4900
6335 4300
6361 4300
6362 4300
6600 5600
6609 5600
6610 5600
6638 5600
6640 5600
6645 5600
6856 6800
6862 6800
6879 6800
6920 4900
6942 4900
6967 6959
6975 6959
7207 7200
7226 7200
7227 7200
7238 7200
7243 7200
7311 4300
7759 5700
7796 5700
7797 5700
8417 9400
8798 5700
9312 9300
9314 9300
9408 9400
9714 5700
9715 5700
9730 5700
9739 5700
9742 5700
9747 5700
9752 5700
9768 5700
9769 5700

1954 84B
2830 2800
2833 2800
2841 2800
2854 2800
2882 2800
3016 ROD
3028 ROD
3029 ROD
3031 ROD
3744 5700
3745 5700
3802 2884
3813 2884
3825 2884
3860 2884
3863 2884
3865 2884
4918 4900
4919 4900
4924 4900
4926 4900
4955 4900
4959 4900
5336 4300
5341 4300
5375 4300
5378 4300
5381 4300
5390 4300
5391 4300
5684 5600
5748 5700
5944 4900
5945 4900
5966 4900
5972 4900
5991 4900
5995 4900
6335 4300
6610 5600
6640 5600
6645 5600
6854 6800
6856 6800
6861 6800
6862 6800
6879 6800
6924 4900
6926 4900
6942 4900
6975 6959
7759 5700
7796 5700
7797 5700
7915 6959
8417 9400
8428 9400
9307 9300
9312 9300
9314 9300
9317 9300
9318 9300
9408 9400
9714 5700
9715 5700
9730 5700
9739 5700
9747 5700
9752 5700
9768 5700
9769 5700

1957 84B
2819 2800
2830 2800
2833 2800
2841 2800
2850 2800
3802 2884
3813 2884
3837 2884
3845 2884
3860 2884
3861 2884
3863 2884
3865 2884
4963 4900
4966 4900
4984 4900
4997 4900
5312 4300
5313 4300
5341 4300
5375 4300
5381 4300
5390 4300
5684 5600
5944 4900
5958 4900
5991 4900
5995 4900
6324 4300
6610 5600
6640 5600
6645 5600
6806 6800
6839 6800
6862 6800
6879 6800
6907 4900
6925 4900
6926 4900
6934 4900
6975 6959
7247 7200
7305 4300
7329 4300
7339 4300
7759 5700
7915 6959
8417 9400
8428 9400
8449 9400
9314 9300
9319 9300
9408 9400
9739 5700
9752 5700
9768 5700
73033 5MT
73034 5MT
73035 5MT

1960 84B
2850 2800
3698 5700
3802 2884
3813 2884
3820 2884
3829 2884
3842 2884
3854 2884
3861 2884
3865 2884
4146 5101
4912 4900
4957 4900
4963 4900
4966 4900
4984 4900
4997 4900
5916 4900
5919 4900
5944 4900
5965 4900
5985 4900
5991 4900
5995 4900
6353 4300
6640 5600
6645 5600
6806 6800
6817 6800
6839 6800
6857 6800
6862 6800
6907 4900
6925 4900
6934 4900
6975 6959
6980 6959
7247 7200
7339 4300
7759 5700
7915 6959
8428 9400
8464 9400
9408 9400
9739 5700
9752 5700
9768 5700

1963 84B
2856 2800
3605 5700
3631 5700
3698 5700
3813 2884
3831 2884
4923 4900
5606 5600
5995 4900
6631 5600
6644 5600
6803 6800
6823 6800
6828 6800
6830 6800
6831 6800
6833 6800
6839 6800
6851 6800
6854 6800
6855 6800
6857 6800
6858 6800
6862 6800
6864 6800
6870 6800
6871 6800
6907 4900
6917 4900
6925 4900
6933 4900
6980 6959
7213 7200
7806 7800
7824 7800
8464 9400
9768 5700
78008 2MT[1]

1966 2B
3605 5700
3744 5700
3776 5700
3782 5700
8767 5700
9640 5700
9658 5700
9776 5700
44691 5MT[3]
44805 5MT[3]
44808 5MT[3]
44812 5MT[3]
44841 5MT[3]
44843 5MT[3]
44856 5MT[3]
44876 5MT[3]
44919 5MT[3]
44944 5MT[3]
44945 5MT[3]
44965 5MT[3]
45006 5MT[3]
45040 5MT[3]
45186 5MT[3]
45263 5MT[3]
45283 5MT[3]
48415 8F
48474 8F
48475 8F
48628 8F
73019 5MT
73028 5MT
76022 4MT[2]
76037 4MT[2]
76039 4MT[2]
76041 4MT[2]
78008 2MT[1]

Pantyffynnon

1948 PANT
2787 2721

Parkeston

1948 PKS
61000 B1
61001 B1
61003 B1
61004 B1
61005 B1
61006 B1
61008 B1
61104 B1
61135 B1
61149 B1
61264 B1
64727 J39
64765 J39
64788 J39
64804 J39
65365 J15
65376 J15
65453 J15
65458 J15
67204 F5
67206 F5
67229 F6
68519 J67
68521 J67
68571 J69
68596 J69
68638 J68
68642 J68
68660 J68

1951 30F
61003 B1
61004 B1
61005 B1
61006 B1
61135 B1
61149 B1
61226 B1
61232 B1
61264 B1
64770 J39
64777 J39
64779 J39
64787 J39
64788 J39
64873 J39
64953 J39
65354 J15
65434 J15
65458 J15
68527 J69
68556 J69
68561 J69
68596 J69
68643 J68
68653 J68
69612 N7
69614 N7
69621 N7
69635 N7
69677 N7

1954 30F
61003 B1
61004 B1
61005 B1
61006 B1
61135 B1
61149 B1
61226 B1
61232 B1
61264 B1
64770 J39
64773 J39
64777 J39
64787 J39
64788 J39
64873 J39
64874 J39
64953 J39
65434 J15
65453 J15
65458 J15
68500 J69
68643 J68
69502 N2
69551 N2
69552 N2
69561 N2
69566 N2

1957 30F
61003 B1
61004 B1
61135 B1
61149 B1
61226 B1
61227 B1
61232 B1
61264 B1
61384 B1
64764 J39
64770 J39
64771 J39
64773 J39
64776 J39
64777 J39
64787 J39
64788 J39
64953 J39
65434 J15
65453 J15
65458 J15
68643 J68
69672 N7
69675 N7
69721 N7
69727 N7
69733 N7

1960 30F
46468 2MT^2
46469 2MT^2
61149 B1
61226 B1
61227 B1
61232 B1
61264 B1
61311 B1
61336 B1
61361 B1
61362 B1
61372 B1
61373 B1
61378 B1
61384 B1
61862 K3
61921 K3
61942 K3
61951 K3
61963 K3
61977 K3
64652 J19
64678 J20
64679 J20
65445 J15
65453 J15
65458 J15
68526 J69
68552 J69
68563 J69
68573 J69
69673 N7
69675 N7
69730 N7
69732 N7

1966
27 B1

Parkhead

1948 PKD
61729 K2
64559 J37
64563 J37
64573 J37
64584 J37
64609 J37
64626 J37
65214 J36
65274 J36
65283 J36
65298 J36
65324 J36
67454 C15
67470 C15
67479 C15
67480 C15
67487 C16
67488 C16
67603 V1
67604 V1
67611 V1
67612 V1
67613 V1
67614 V1
67616 V1
67619 V1
67621 V1
67622 V1
67623 V1
67625 V1
67626 V1
67628 V1
67631 V1
67632 V1
67633 V1
67643 V1
67648 V1
67655 V1
67662 V1
67674 V1
67678 V1
68503 J69
68567 J69
69143 N15
69145 N15
69151 N15
69161 N15
69171 N15
69190 N15
69193 N15
69194 N15
69195 N15
69198 N15
69199 N15
69209 N15
69210 N15
69212 N15
69213 N15
69214 N15
69217 N15
69500 N2
69507 N2
69510 N2
69514 N2
69562 N2
69564 N2
69565 N2
69595 N2

1951 65C
44791 5MT^3
61772 K2
64548 J37
64559 J37
64563 J37
64573 J37
64584 J37
64609 J37
64610 J37
64621 J37
64626 J37
65283 J36
65298 J36
65324 J36
65335 J36
67454 C15
67470 C15
67479 C15
67480 C15
67487 C16
67604 V1
67611 V1
67612 V1
67619 V1
67621 V1
67622 V1
67623 V1
67626 V1
67628 V1
67633 V1
67643 V1
67648 V1
67655 V1
67661 V1
67662 V1
67676 V1
67678 V1
67681 V1
68503 J69
68567 J69
69143 N15
69151 N15
69157 N15
69161 N15
69165 N15
69166 N15
69171 N15
69190 N15
69193 N15
69194 N15
69195 N15
69198 N15
69199 N15
69209 N15
69210 N15
69212 N15
69213 N15
69214 N15
69217 N15
69500 N2
69507 N2
69510 N2
69511 N2
69514 N2
69553 N2
69562 N2
69564 N2
69565 N2
69595 N2

1954 65C
61067 B1
61722 K2
61733 K2
61735 K2
61769 K2
61772 K2
64461 J35
64514 J35
64559 J37
64563 J37
64573 J37
64584 J37
64609 J37
64610 J37
64621 J37
64626 J37
65295 J36
65324 J36
65335 J36
67470 C15
67479 C15
67482 C16
67487 C16
67500 C16
67604 V3
67611 V3
67612 V3
67619 V1
67621 V1
67622 V1
67623 V1
67626 V3
67628 V1
67633 V1
67643 V1
67648 V1
67655 V1
67661 V1
67662 V1
67676 V1
67678 V1
67679 V3
67681 V1
68503 J69
69015 J72
69151 N15
69157 N15
69161 N15
69165 N15
69166 N15
69190 N15
69193 N15
69194 N15
69195 N15
69198 N15
69199 N15
69209 N15
69210 N15
69212 N15
69213 N15
69217 N15
69500 N2
69507 N2
69508 N2
69510 N2
69514 N2
69562 N2
69563 N2
69564 N2
69565 N2
69595 N2

1957 65C
61067 B1
61117 B1
61733 K2
61735 K2
61769 K2
61772 K2
64461 J35
64514 J35
64559 J37
64563 J37
64573 J37
64584 J37
64609 J37
64610 J37
64621 J37
64626 J37
65295 J36
65324 J36
65335 J36
67482 C16
67487 C16
67500 C16
67604 V3
67611 V3
67612 V3
67619 V1
67621 V1
67622 V1
67623 V1
67626 V3
67628 V1
67633 V1
67643 V3
67648 V1
67655 V1
67661 V1
67662 V3
67676 V1
67678 V1
67679 V3
67681 V1
68503 J69
69015 J72
69151 N15
69157 N15
69161 N15
69165 N15
69166 N15
69190 N15
69193 N15
69194 N15
69195 N15
69198 N15
69199 N15
69209 N15
69210 N15
69212 N15
69213 N15
69217 N15
69500 N2
69507 N2
69508 N2
69510 N2
69563 N2
69564 N2
69565 N2
69595 N2

1960 65C
61067 B1
61117 B1
61333 B1
61344 B1
61404 B1
61769 K2
64461 J35
64514 J35
64523 J35
64559 J37
64563 J37
64573 J37
64588 J37
64609 J37
64610 J37
64621 J37
64626 J37
65211 J36
65230 J36
65246 J36
65273 J36
65295 J36
65335 J36
67604 V3
67607 V3
67608 V1
67611 V3
67612 V3
67619 V3
67621 V3
67622 V1
67623 V3
67626 V3
67628 V3
67629 V1
67630 V1
67633 V1
67643 V3
67648 V3
67650 V3
67655 V1
67657 V3
67661 V3
67662 V3
67675 V3
67676 V1
67678 V3
67679 V3
67681 V3
69015 J72
69161 N15
69165 N15
69190 N15
69194 N15
69198 N15
69199 N15
69209 N15
69507 N2
69509 N2
69563 N2

1963 65C
64559 J37
64563 J37
64610 J37
64621 J37

Pateley Bridge

1948 PAT
67253 G5

1951 50D sub
67253 G5

Patricroft

1948 10C
40332 2P^2
40434 2P^2
40507 2P^2
40635 2P^3
42454 4MT^3
42542 4MT^3
42560 4MT^3
42561 4MT^3
42574 4MT^3
42596 4MT^3
42662 4MT^3
45037 5MT^3
45055 5MT^3
45135 5MT^3
45137 5MT^3
45147 5MT^3
45182 5MT^3
45188 5MT^3
45199 5MT^3
45231 5MT^3
45259 5MT^3
45290 5MT^3
45302 5MT^3
45304 5MT^3
45312 5MT^3
45315 5MT^3
45329 5MT^3
45377 5MT^3
45386 5MT^3
45401 5MT^3
45402 5MT^3
45408 5MT^3
45411 5MT^3
45420 5MT^3
45421 5MT^3
45424 5MT^3
45426 5MT^3
45438 5MT^3
45442 5MT^3
45444 5MT^3
45559 6P5F^2
45668 6P5F^2
45670 6P5F^2
45720 6P5F^2
45726 6P5F^2
47887 6F^1
47892 6F^1
48801 4F^3
48903 7F^2
48912 6F^2
48920 7F^2
48941 7F^2
49095 6F^2
49199 7F^2
49234 7F^2
49238 7F^2
49254 7F^2
49255 6F^2
49273 6F^2
49304 7F^2
49330 7F^2
49353 6F^2
49405 7F^3
52019 2F^3
52030 2F^3
52031 2F^3
52036 2F^3
52049 2F^3
52059 2F^3

1951 10C
40434 2P^2
40450 2P^2
40628 2P^3
40635 2P^3
42560 4MT^3
42561 4MT^3
42574 4MT^3
42662 4MT^3
45037 5MT^3
45042 5MT^3
45055 5MT^3
45135 5MT^3
45137 5MT^3
45142 5MT^3
45147 5MT^3
45182 5MT^3
45188 5MT^3
45199 5MT^3
45231 5MT^3
45259 5MT^3
45290 5MT^3
45302 5MT^3
45304 5MT^3
45312 5MT^3
45327 5MT^3
45329 5MT^3
45373 5MT^3
45377 5MT^3
45378 5MT^3
45401 5MT^3
45403 5MT^3
45408 5MT^3
45410 5MT^3
45411 5MT^3
45420 5MT^3
45421 5MT^3
45424 5MT^3
45426 5MT^3
45428 5MT^3
45438 5MT^3
45442 5MT^3
45444 5MT^3
45558 6P5F^2
45559 6P5F^2
45563 6P5F^2
45600 6P5F^2
45668 6P5F^2
45720 6P5F^2
48920 7F^2
48926 7F^2
49027 7F^2
49087 7F^2
49094 7F^2
49178 7F^2
49199 7F^2
49209 7F^2
49234 7F^2
49254 7F^2
49335 7F^2
49340 7F^2
49386 7F^2
49400 7F^3
49421 7F^3
49426 7F^3
52016 2F^3
52024 2F^3
52030 2F^3
52031 2F^3
52034 2F^3
52059 2F^3
52598 3F^9

1954 10C
40434 2P^2
40438 2P^2
40450 2P^2
40628 2P^3
40635 2P^3
42560 4MT^3
42561 4MT^3
42563 4MT^3
42574 4MT^3
42591 4MT^3
42662 4MT^3
44708 5MT^3
44808 5MT^3
45005 5MT^3
45037 5MT^3
45042 5MT^3
45057 5MT^3
45095 5MT^3
45137 5MT^3
45142 5MT^3
45147 5MT^3
45182 5MT^3
45188 5MT^3
45199 5MT^3
45231 5MT^3
45259 5MT^3
45290 5MT^3
45294 5MT^3
45302 5MT^3
45304 5MT^3
45312 5MT^3
45329 5MT^3
45352 5MT^3
45373 5MT^3
45377 5MT^3
45378 5MT^3
45401 5MT^3
45410 5MT^3
45411 5MT^3
45415 5MT^3
45420 5MT^3
45424 5MT^3
45426 5MT^3
45428 5MT^3
45442 5MT^3
45444 5MT^3
45558 6P5F^2
45559 6P5F^2
45563 6P5F^2
45600 6P5F^2
45645 6P5F^2
45668 6P5F^2
47364 3F^6
47365 3F^6
47399 3F^6
47430 3F^6
47621 3F^6
48926 7F^2
49027 7F^2
49087 7F^2
49094 7F^2
49199 7F^2
49209 7F^2
49234 7F^2
49254 7F^2
49335 7F^2
49340 7F^2
49386 7F^2
49400 7F^3
49421 7F^3
49426 7F^3
52016 2F^3
52024 2F^3
52031 2F^3
52045 2F^3
73043 5MT
73044 5MT

1957 10C
40450 2P^2
40635 2P^3
40676 2P^3
41287 2MT^1
42423 4MT^2
42442 4MT^3
42560 4MT^3
42561 4MT^3
42563 4MT^3
42574 4MT^3
42662 4MT^3
44708 5MT^3
44808 5MT^3
45042 5MT^3
45070 5MT^3
45095 5MT^3
45129 5MT^3
45182 5MT^3
45199 5MT^3
45294 5MT^3
45352 5MT^3
45377 5MT^3
45378 5MT^3
45411 5MT^3
45420 5MT^3
45424 5MT^3
45442 5MT^3
45558 6P5F^2
45559 6P5F^2
45563 6P5F^2
45600 6P5F^2
45645 6P5F^2
45668 6P5F^2
47309 3F^6
47364 3F^6
47365 3F^6
47399 3F^6
47401 3F^6
47430 3F^6
47621 3F^6
47672 3F^6
48926 7F^2
49027 7F^2
49034 7F^2
49087 7F^2
49147 7F^2
49149 7F^2
49199 7F^2
49209 7F^2
49234 7F^2
49254 7F^2
49335 7F^2
49340 7F^2
49386 7F^2
49400 7F^3
49421 7F^3
49426 7F^3
58279 2F^9
73043 5MT
73044 5MT
73090 5MT
73091 5MT
73092 5MT
73093 5MT
73094 5MT
73095 5MT
73096 5MT
73097 5MT
73098 5MT
73099 5MT

1960 26F
40631 2P^3
40671 2P^3
41283 2MT^1
41287 2MT^1
42442 4MT^3
42458 4MT^3
42468 4MT^3
42494 4MT^3
42561 4MT^3
42563 4MT^3
42574 4MT^3
42662 4MT^3
43976 4F^1
44708 5MT^3
44808 5MT^3
45095 5MT^3
45096 5MT^3
45129 5MT^3
45133 5MT^3
45182 5MT^3
45195 5MT^3
45199 5MT^3
45252 5MT^3
45255 5MT^3
45294 5MT^3
45304 5MT^3
45352 5MT^3
45377 5MT^3
45378 5MT^3
45409 5MT^3
45411 5MT^3
45420 5MT^3
45424 5MT^3
45442 5MT^3
45558 6P5F^2
45563 6P5F^2
45600 6P5F^2
45645 6P5F^2
45663 6P5F^2
47284 3F^6
47365 3F^6
47378 3F^6
47430 3F^6
47491 3F^6
47621 3F^6
47672 3F^6
49034 7F^2
49087 7F^2
49119 7F^2
49147 7F^2
49199 7F^2
49209 7F^2
49323 7F^2
49335 7F^2
49421 7F^3
49426 7F^3
73030 5MT
73044 5MT
73125 5MT
73126 5MT
73127 5MT
73128 5MT
73129 5MT
73130 5MT
73131 5MT
73132 5MT
73133 5MT
73134 5MT

1963 26F
42439 4MT^3
42442 4MT^3
42458 4MT^3
42468 4MT^3
42561 4MT^3
42574 4MT^3
42660 4MT^3
44708 5MT^3
44808 5MT^3
45095 5MT^3
45096 5MT^3
45129 5MT^3
45133 5MT^3
45182 5MT^3
45252 5MT^3
45294 5MT^3
45352 5MT^3
45409 5MT^3
45411 5MT^3
45420 5MT^3
45424 5MT^3
45558 6P5F^2
45563 6P5F^2
45600 6P5F^2
45645 6P5F^2
45663 6P5F^2
47365 3F^6
47378 3F^6
47430 3F^6
47458 3F^6
48037 8F
48103 8F
48164 8F
48178 8F
48181 8F
48213 8F
48346 8F
48397 8F
48546 8F
48663 8F
73030 5MT
73044 5MT
73125 5MT
73126 5MT
73127 5MT
73128 5MT
73129 5MT
73130 5MT
73131 5MT
73132 5MT
73133 5MT
73134 5MT
90140 WD^1
90141 WD^1
90183 WD^1
90222 WD^1
90248 WD^1
90328 WD^1
90331 WD^1
90371 WD^1
90390 WD^1
90399 WD^1
90530 WD^1
90548 WD^1
90568 WD^1
90570 WD^1
90589 WD^1
90669 WD^1

1966 9H
47662 3F^6
48168 8F
48181 8F
48213 8F
48324 8F
48491 8F
48502 8F
48553 8F
48636 8F
48663 8F
48714 8F
48720 8F
48745 8F
48770 8F
73006 5MT
73010 5MT
73011 5MT
73033 5MT
73035 5MT
73039 5MT
73045 5MT
73053 5MT
73071 5MT
73073 5MT
73094 5MT
73096 5MT
73097 5MT
73125 5MT
73126 5MT
73127 5MT
73128 5MT
73129 5MT
73130 5MT
73131 5MT
73132 5MT
73133 5MT
73134 5MT
73135 5MT
73136 5MT
73137 5MT
73138 5MT
73139 5MT
73140 5MT
73141 5MT
73142 5MT
73143 5MT
73144 5MT
73157 5MT
73158 5MT
73159 5MT
73160 5MT
82000 3MT^2
82003 3MT^2
82009 3MT^2
82031 3MT^2
82034 3MT^2

Pelton Level

1948 PEL
69424 N9

Penrith

1948 12C
58362 2F^{11}
58389 2F^{11}
58411 2F^{11}
58417 2F^{11}
58418 2F^{11}
58421 2F^{11}

1951 12C
44306 4F^2
46449 2MT^2
46455 2MT^2
46459 2MT^2
58409 2F^{11}
58412 2F^{11}

1954 12C
44390 4F^2
46449 2MT^2
46455 2MT^2
46459 2MT^2
58409 2F^{11}
58412 2F^{11}

Penzance

1948 PZ
1019 1000
1022 1000
2148 2021
2752 2721
4097 4073
4500 4500
4509 4500
4525 4500
4537 4500
4540 4500
4545 4500
4548 4500
4566 4500
4574 4500
4946 4900
4947 4900
4949 4900
4970 4900
5915 4900
6318 4300
6354 4300
6801 6800
6808 6800
6825 6800
6838 6800
6911 4900

1951 83G
1004 1000
2097 2021
4090 4073
4500 4500
4509 4500
4525 4500
4537 4500
4545 4500
4548 4500
4566 4500
4574 4500
4946 4900
4965 4900
5915 4900
5969 4900
6318 4300
6800 6800
6801 6800
6806 6800
6808 6800
6809 6800
6817 6800
6825 6800
6826 6800
6838 6800
6869 6800
6911 4900
7806 7800
7925 6959
8409 9400
9717 5700

1954 83G
1002 1000
4087 4073
4537 4500
4545 4500
4548 4500
4566 4500
4574 4500
4587 4575
4965 4900
5023 4073
5915 4900
5969 4900
6800 6800
6801 6800
6806 6800
6808 6800
6809 6800
6817 6800
6824 6800
6825 6800
6826 6800
6836 6800
6837 6800
6860 6800
6911 4900
7925 6959
8409 9400
9463 9400
9717 5700
9748 5700

1957 83G
1002 1000
1006 1000
1018 1000
4099 4073
4505 4500
4545 4500
4547 4500
4548 4500
4563 4500
4566 4500
4570 4500
4574 4500
4908 4900
4931 4900
4990 4900
5972 4900
5985 4900
6800 6800
6801 6800
6808 6800
6809 6800
6824 6800
6825 6800
6826 6800
6837 6800
6845 6800
6860 6800
7925 6959
8409 9400
8473 9400
9463 9400
9748 5700

1960 83G
1002 1000
1006 1000
1008 1000
1018 1000
4095 4073
4136 5101
4563 4500
4566 4500
4570 4500
4571 4500
4588 4575
4908 4900
5020 4073
6800 6800
6801 6800
6808 6800
6816 6800
6824 6800
6825 6800
6826 6800
6837 6800
6845 6800
6849 6800
6860 6800
6870 6800
6875 6800
6945 4900
8473 9400
9434 9400
9748 5700

Percy Main

1948 PMN
65780 J27
65784 J27
65791 J27
65792 J27
65796 J27
65802 J27
65809 J27
65812 J27
65813 J27
65814 J27
65815 J27
65821 J27
65822 J27
65825 J27
65826 J27
65831 J27
65837 J27
65838 J27
65839 J27
65852 J27
65858 J27

1951 52E
65780 J27
65784 J27
65791 J27
65795 J27
65796 J27
65802 J27
65806 J27
65809 J27
65812 J27
65813 J27
65814 J27
65815 J27
65821 J27
65822 J27
65825 J27
65826 J27
65831 J27
65837 J27
65838 J27
65839 J27
65852 J27
65858 J27

1954 52E
65780 J27
65784 J27
65791 J27
65795 J27
65796 J27
65799 J27
65802 J27
65806 J27
65807 J27
65809 J27
65812 J27
65813 J27
65814 J27
65821 J27
65825 J27
65826 J27
65831 J27
65837 J27
65839 J27
65842 J27
65852 J27
65858 J27

1957 52E
65780 J27
65784 J27
65791 J27
65795 J27
65796 J27
65799 J27
65802 J27
65806 J27
65807 J27
65809 J27
65812 J27
65813 J27
65814 J27
65821 J27
65825 J27
65826 J27
65831 J27
65837 J27
65839 J27

65842 J27
65852 J27
65858 J27

1960 52E
65791 J27
65795 J27
65796 J27
65802 J27
65807 J27
65809 J27
65812 J27
65813 J27
65814 J27
65821 J27
65825 J27
65831 J27
65837 J27
65839 J27
65842 J27
65852 J27
65858 J27

1963 52E
65790 J27
65791 J27
65795 J27
65802 J27
65805 J27
65809 J27
65812 J27
65813 J27
65814 J27
65821 J27
65825 J27
65831 J27
65842 J27
65850 J27
65858 J27
65860 J27

Perth

1948 29A
40921 4P^{1}
40922 4P^{1}
40923 4P^{1}
40924 4P^{1}
40938 4P^{1}
40939 4P^{1}
41099 4P^{1}
41125 4P^{1}
44193 4F^{2}
44196 4F^{2}
44251 4F^{2}
44258 4F^{2}
44314 4F^{2}
44322 4F^{2}
44328 4F^{2}
44768 5MT^{3}
44769 5MT^{3}
44770 5MT^{3}
44796 5MT^{3}
44797 5MT^{3}
44885 5MT^{3}
44924 5MT^{3}
44925 5MT^{3}
44958 5MT^{3}
44959 5MT^{3}
44960 5MT^{3}
44961 5MT^{3}
44972 5MT^{3}
44973 5MT^{3}
44974 5MT^{3}
44975 5MT^{3}
44976 5MT^{3}
44977 5MT^{3}
45010 5MT^{3}
45011 5MT^{3}
45036 5MT^{3}
45085 5MT^{3}
45086 5MT^{3}
45087 5MT^{3}
45125 5MT^{3}
45161 5MT^{3}
45162 5MT^{3}
45163 5MT^{3}
45164 5MT^{3}
45165 5MT^{3}
45166 5MT^{3}
45167 5MT^{3}
45170 5MT^{3}
45171 5MT^{3}
45172 5MT^{3}
45173 5MT^{3}
45174 5MT^{3}
45175 5MT^{3}
45213 5MT^{3}
45357 5MT^{3}
45365 5MT^{3}
45366 5MT^{3}
45389 5MT^{3}
45452 5MT^{3}
45456 5MT^{3}
45457 5MT^{3}
45458 5MT^{3}
45459 5MT^{3}
45460 5MT^{3}
45463 5MT^{3}
45464 5MT^{3}
45465 5MT^{3}
45466 5MT^{3}
45467 5MT^{3}
45469 5MT^{3}
45470 5MT^{3}
45472 5MT^{3}
45473 5MT^{3}
45474 5MT^{3}
45475 5MT^{3}
54447 3P^{5}
54448 3P^{5}
54458 3P^{5}
54459 3P^{5}
54467 3P^{6}
54469 3P^{6}
54476 3P^{6}
54489 3P^{6}
54499 3P^{6}
54500 3P^{6}
54501 3P^{6}
54502 3P^{6}
54503 3P^{6}
55144 2P^{12}
55171 2P^{13}
55175 2P^{13}
55176 2P^{13}
55208 2P^{13}
55209 2P^{13}
55213 2P^{13}
55216 2P^{13}
55218 2P^{13}
56246 3F^{10}
56290 3F^{10}
56328 3F^{10}
56331 3F^{10}
56347 3F^{10}
56352 3F^{10}
56353 3F^{10}
57397 2F^{5}
57449 2F^{5}
57473 2F^{5}

1951 63A
40159 3MT^{2}
40200 3MT^{2}
40921 4P^{1}
40922 4P^{1}
40923 4P^{1}
40938 4P^{1}
40939 4P^{1}
41125 4P^{1}
42742 5MT^{1}
42743 5MT^{1}
44193 4F^{2}
44194 4F^{2}
44251 4F^{2}
44253 4F^{2}
44254 4F^{2}
44257 4F^{2}
44258 4F^{2}
44314 4F^{2}
44318 4F^{2}
44328 4F^{2}
44698 5MT^{3}
44699 5MT^{3}
44704 5MT^{3}
44705 5MT^{3}
44796 5MT^{3}
44797 5MT^{3}
44801 5MT^{3}
44879 5MT^{3}
44885 5MT^{3}
44924 5MT^{3}
44925 5MT^{3}
44931 5MT^{3}
44958 5MT^{3}
44959 5MT^{3}
44960 5MT^{3}
44961 5MT^{3}
44972 5MT^{3}
44973 5MT^{3}
44974 5MT^{3}
44975 5MT^{3}
44976 5MT^{3}
44977 5MT^{3}
44978 5MT^{3}
44979 5MT^{3}
44980 5MT^{3}
44997 5MT^{3}
44998 5MT^{3}
44999 5MT^{3}
45007 5MT^{3}
45011 5MT^{3}
45086 5MT^{3}
45118 5MT^{3}
45119 5MT^{3}
45125 5MT^{3}
45127 5MT^{3}
45162 5MT^{3}
45164 5MT^{3}
45165 5MT^{3}
45166 5MT^{3}
45167 5MT^{3}
45169 5MT^{3}
45170 5MT^{3}
45171 5MT^{3}
45172 5MT^{3}
45173 5MT^{3}
45175 5MT^{3}
45213 5MT^{3}
45266 5MT^{3}
45309 5MT^{3}
45357 5MT^{3}
45365 5MT^{3}
45366 5MT^{3}
45389 5MT^{3}
45452 5MT^{3}
45456 5MT^{3}
45457 5MT^{3}
45458 5MT^{3}
45459 5MT^{3}
45460 5MT^{3}
45463 5MT^{3}
45464 5MT^{3}
45465 5MT^{3}
45466 5MT^{3}
45467 5MT^{3}
45469 5MT^{3}
45470 5MT^{3}
45472 5MT^{3}
45473 5MT^{3}
45474 5MT^{3}
45475 5MT^{3}
45483 5MT^{3}
45488 5MT^{3}
45492 5MT^{3}
45496 5MT^{3}
45497 5MT^{3}
45564 6P5F^{2}
45575 6P5F^{2}
45644 6P5F^{2}
54447 3P^{5}
54448 3P^{5}
54467 3P^{6}
54469 3P^{6}
54476 3P^{6}
54485 3P^{6}
54486 3P^{6}
54489 3P^{6}
54494 3P^{6}
54499 3P^{6}
54500 3P^{6}
54501 3P^{6}
54502 3P^{6}
54503 3P^{6}
55144 2P^{12}
55171 2P^{13}
55175 2P^{13}
55176 2P^{13}
55208 2P^{13}
55209 2P^{13}
55212 2P^{13}
55213 2P^{13}
55216 2P^{13}
55218 2P^{13}
56246 3F^{10}
56290 3F^{10}
56328 3F^{10}
56331 3F^{10}
56347 3F^{10}
56352 3F^{10}
56353 3F^{10}
56359 3F^{10}
57339 2F^{5}
57345 2F^{5}
57450 2F^{5}
57473 2F^{5}
62714 D49
62725 D49
90523 WD^{1}
90530 WD^{1}
90675 WD^{1}

1954 63A
40913 4P^{1}
40921 4P^{1}
40923 4P^{1}
40924 4P^{1}
42130 4MT^{1}
42205 4MT^{1}
44193 4F^{2}
44194 4F^{2}
44251 4F^{2}
44253 4F^{2}
44254 4F^{2}
44257 4F^{2}
44258 4F^{2}
44314 4F^{2}
44328 4F^{2}
44698 5MT^{3}
44699 5MT^{3}
44704 5MT^{3}
44705 5MT^{3}
44720 5MT^{3}
44721 5MT^{3}
44796 5MT^{3}
44797 5MT^{3}
44801 5MT^{3}
44879 5MT^{3}
44885 5MT^{3}
44924 5MT^{3}
44925 5MT^{3}
44931 5MT^{3}
44959 5MT^{3}
44960 5MT^{3}
44961 5MT^{3}
44972 5MT^{3}
44973 5MT^{3}
44974 5MT^{3}
44975 5MT^{3}
44976 5MT^{3}
44977 5MT^{3}
44978 5MT^{3}
44979 5MT^{3}
44980 5MT^{3}
44997 5MT^{3}
44998 5MT^{3}
44999 5MT^{3}
45053 5MT^{3}
45117 5MT^{3}
45125 5MT^{3}
45165 5MT^{3}
45167 5MT^{3}
45168 5MT^{3}
45170 5MT^{3}
45171 5MT^{3}
45172 5MT^{3}
45175 5MT^{3}
45213 5MT^{3}
45357 5MT^{3}
45365 5MT^{3}
45366 5MT^{3}
45389 5MT^{3}
45452 5MT^{3}
45456 5MT^{3}
45457 5MT^{3}
45458 5MT^{3}
45459 5MT^{3}
45460 5MT^{3}
45463 5MT^{3}
45464 5MT^{3}
45465 5MT^{3}
45467 5MT^{3}
45469 5MT^{3}
45470 5MT^{3}
45472 5MT^{3}
45473 5MT^{3}
45474 5MT^{3}
45475 5MT^{3}
45483 5MT^{3}
45488 5MT^{3}
45492 5MT^{3}
45496 5MT^{3}
45497 5MT^{3}
45673 6P5F^{2}
45727 6P5F^{2}
54448 3P^{5}
54467 3P^{6}
54469 3P^{6}
54476 3P^{6}
54485 3P^{6}
54489 3P^{6}
54494 3P^{6}
54499 3P^{6}
54500 3P^{6}
54503 3P^{6}
55208 2P^{13}
55209 2P^{13}
55212 2P^{13}
55213 2P^{13}
55218 2P^{13}
55226 2P^{13}
56246 3F^{10}
56290 3F^{10}
56328 3F^{10}
56331 3F^{10}
56347 3F^{10}
56352 3F^{10}
56353 3F^{10}
56359 3F^{10}
57345 2F^{5}
57473 2F^{5}
62470 D34
62484 D34
73005 5MT
73006 5MT
73007 5MT
73008 5MT
73009 5MT

1957 63A
42168 4MT^{1}
42169 4MT^{1}
44193 4F^{2}
44194 4F^{2}
44251 4F^{2}
44253 4F^{2}
44254 4F^{2}
44257 4F^{2}
44258 4F^{2}
44328 4F^{2}
44698 5MT^{3}
44699 5MT^{3}
44704 5MT^{3}
44705 5MT^{3}
44720 5MT^{3}
44721 5MT^{3}
44796 5MT^{3}
44797 5MT^{3}
44801 5MT^{3}
44820 5MT^{3}
44879 5MT^{3}
44885 5MT^{3}
44921 5MT^{3}
44924 5MT^{3}
44925 5MT^{3}
44931 5MT^{3}
44959 5MT^{3}
44960 5MT^{3}
44961 5MT^{3}
44978 5MT^{3}
44979 5MT^{3}
44980 5MT^{3}
44997 5MT^{3}
44998 5MT^{3}
44999 5MT^{3}
45047 5MT^{3}
45053 5MT^{3}
45117 5MT^{3}
45125 5MT^{3}
45165 5MT^{3}
45168 5MT^{3}
45170 5MT^{3}
45171 5MT^{3}
45172 5MT^{3}
45245 5MT^{3}
45365 5MT^{3}
45366 5MT^{3}
45367 5MT^{3}
45389 5MT^{3}
45452 5MT^{3}
45456 5MT^{3}
45457 5MT^{3}
45458 5MT^{3}
45459 5MT^{3}
45460 5MT^{3}
45463 5MT^{3}
45464 5MT^{3}
45465 5MT^{3}
45467 5MT^{3}
45470 5MT^{3}
45472 5MT^{3}
45473 5MT^{3}
45474 5MT^{3}
45475 5MT^{3}
45483 5MT^{3}
45487 5MT^{3}
45488 5MT^{3}
45492 5MT^{3}
45496 5MT^{3}
45497 5MT^{3}
45673 6P5F^{2}
45692 6P5F^{2}
45727 6P5F^{2}
54469 3P^{6}
54476 3P^{6}
54485 3P^{6}
54489 3P^{6}
54494 3P^{6}
54499 3P^{6}
54500 3P^{6}
54503 3P^{6}
55209 2P^{13}
55212 2P^{13}
55213 2P^{13}
55218 2P^{13}
55226 2P^{13}
56246 3F^{10}
56328 3F^{10}
56331 3F^{10}
56347 3F^{10}
56352 3F^{10}
56353 3F^{10}
56359 3F^{10}
57345 2F^{5}
57473 2F^{5}
62470 D34
62484 D34
73005 5MT
73006 5MT
73007 5MT
73008 5MT
73009 5MT
73120 5MT
80126 4MT^{3}

1960 63A
42168 4MT^{1}
42169 4MT^{1}
44194 4F^{2}
44253 4F^{2}
44254 4F^{2}
44257 4F^{2}
44258 4F^{2}
44314 4F^{2}
44328 4F^{2}
44698 5MT^{3}
44699 5MT^{3}
44704 5MT^{3}
44705 5MT^{3}
44720 5MT^{3}
44721 5MT^{3}
44796 5MT^{3}
44797 5MT^{3}
44801 5MT^{3}
44820 5MT^{3}
44879 5MT^{3}
44885 5MT^{3}
44921 5MT^{3}
44924 5MT^{3}
44925 5MT^{3}
44931 5MT^{3}
44959 5MT^{3}
44960 5MT^{3}
44961 5MT^{3}
44978 5MT^{3}
44979 5MT^{3}
44980 5MT^{3}
44997 5MT^{3}
44998 5MT^{3}
44999 5MT^{3}
45047 5MT^{3}
45165 5MT^{3}
45168 5MT^{3}
45170 5MT^{3}
45171 5MT^{3}
45172 5MT^{3}
45365 5MT^{3}
45366 5MT^{3}
45367 5MT^{3}
45463 5MT^{3}
45465 5MT^{3}
45467 5MT^{3}
45470 5MT^{3}
45472 5MT^{3}
45473 5MT^{3}
45474 5MT^{3}
45475 5MT^{3}
45483 5MT^{3}
45487 5MT^{3}
45488 5MT^{3}
45492 5MT^{3}
45496 5MT^{3}
45497 5MT^{3}
45621 6P5F^{2}
45673 6P5F^{2}
45677 6P5F^{2}
45692 6P5F^{2}
45727 6P5F^{2}
54485 3P^{6}
54486 3P^{6}
54489 3P^{6}
54494 3P^{6}
54499 3P^{6}
54500 3P^{6}
55200 2P^{13}
55209 2P^{13}
55217 2P^{13}
55218 2P^{13}
55226 2P^{13}
55230 2P^{13}
56246 3F^{10}
56331 3F^{10}
56347 3F^{10}
57345 2F^{5}
57473 2F^{5}
62484 D34
73005 5MT
73006 5MT
73007 5MT
73008 5MT
73009 5MT
73106 5MT
73107 5MT
73120 5MT
80126 4MT^{3}

1963 63A
44698 5MT^{3}
44704 5MT^{3}
44705 5MT^{3}
44720 5MT^{3}
44721 5MT^{3}
44722 5MT^{3}
44724 5MT^{3}
44796 5MT^{3}
44797 5MT^{3}
44799 5MT^{3}
44879 5MT^{3}
44921 5MT^{3}
44924 5MT^{3}
44925 5MT^{3}
44931 5MT^{3}
44959 5MT^{3}
44961 5MT^{3}
44978 5MT^{3}
44979 5MT^{3}
44980 5MT^{3}
44997 5MT^{3}
44998 5MT^{3}
44999 5MT^{3}
45047 5MT^{3}
45136 5MT^{3}
45461 5MT^{3}
45465 5MT^{3}
45472 5MT^{3}
45473 5MT^{3}
45474 5MT^{3}
45475 5MT^{3}
46468 2MT^{2}
60970 V2
73005 5MT
73006 5MT
73007 5MT
73008 5MT
73009 5MT
73106 5MT
73107 5MT
73120 5MT
78052 2MT^{1}
80092 4MT^{3}
80093 4MT^{3}
80126 4MT^{3}

1966 63A
44698 5MT^{3}
44704 5MT^{3}
44705 5MT^{3}
44720 5MT^{3}
44722 5MT^{3}
44797 5MT^{3}
44879 5MT^{3}
44960 5MT^{3}
44997 5MT^{3}
44998 5MT^{3}
45461 5MT^{3}
45472 5MT^{3}
45473 5MT^{3}
45475 5MT^{3}
80028 4MT^{3}
80092 4MT^{3}
80093 4MT^{3}
80126 4MT^{3}

Perth South

1948 PTH
61002 B1
61061 B1
62215 D1
62426 D30
62427 D30
62457 D33
62466 D33
62714 D49
62725 D49
64536 J37
64588 J37
64591 J37
65213 J36
65297 J36
65309 J36
67455 C15
68469 J83

Peterborough Engineer's Yard

1948
68133 Y1

1951
68133 Y1

1954
6 Y1

1957
8 Y3

Pickering

1948 PKG
68157 Y3

1951 50F sub
62774 D49
68157 Y3

1954 50F sub
67308 G5

Plaistow

1948 13A
41930 3P^{2}
41931 3P^{2}
41932 3P^{2}
41935 3P^{2}
41942 3P^{2}
41944 3P^{2}
41945 3P^{2}
41948 3P^{2}
41949 3P^{2}
41950 3P^{2}
41951 3P^{2}
41952 3P^{2}
41954 3P^{2}
41957 3P^{2}
41959 3P^{2}
41963 3P^{2}
41967 3P^{2}
41969 3P^{2}
41970 3P^{2}
41974 3P^{2}
41975 3P^{2}
41976 3P^{2}
41981 3F^{1}
41982 3F^{1}
41983 3F^{1}
41984 3F^{1}
41985 3F^{1}
41986 3F^{1}
41987 3F^{1}
41988 3F^{1}
41989 3F^{1}
41990 3F^{1}
41993 3F^{1}
42225 4MT^{1}
42226 4MT^{1}
42227 4MT^{1}
42248 4MT^{1}
42249 4MT^{1}
42250 4MT^{1}
42251 4MT^{1}
42252 4MT^{1}
42253 4MT^{1}
42254 4MT^{1}
42255 4MT^{1}
42256 4MT^{1}
42257 4MT^{1}
42522 4MT^{4}
42523 4MT^{4}
42524 4MT^{4}
42525 4MT^{4}
42526 4MT^{4}
42527 4MT^{4}
42528 4MT^{4}
42529 4MT^{4}
42530 4MT^{4}
42531 4MT^{4}
42532 4MT^{4}
42533 4MT^{4}
42534 4MT^{4}
42535 4MT^{4}
42536 4MT^{4}
43905 4F^{1}
44228 4F^{2}
44297 4F^{2}
44530 4F^{2}
47300 3F^{6}
47311 3F^{6}
47328 3F^{6}
47351 3F^{6}
47458 3F^{6}
47484 3F^{6}
47512 3F^{6}
58038 1P^{5}
58043 1P^{6}
58044 1P^{6}
58062 1P^{6}
58089 1P^{6}
58184 2F^{8}
58191 2F^{9}
58259 2F^{9}
58289 2F^{9}

1951 33A
41915 2P^{5}
41928 3P^{2}
41929 3P^{2}
41930 3P^{2}
41931 3P^{2}
41936 3P^{2}
41937 3P^{2}
41939 3P^{2}
41941 3P^{2}
41942 3P^{2}
41944 3P^{2}
41945 3P^{2}
41948 3P^{2}
41950 3P^{2}
41951 3P^{2}
41956 3P^{2}
41965 3P^{2}
41967 3P^{2}
41968 3P^{2}
41969 3P^{2}
41970 3P^{2}
41975 3P^{2}
41976 3P^{2}
41977 3P^{2}
41978 3P^{2}
41981 3F^{1}
41982 3F^{1}
41983 3F^{1}
41984 3F^{1}
41985 3F^{1}
41986 3F^{1}
41987 3F^{1}
41988 3F^{1}
41989 3F^{1}
41990 3F^{1}
41993 3F^{1}
42225 4MT^{1}
42226 4MT^{1}
42227 4MT^{1}
42231 4MT^{1}
42232 4MT^{1}
42248 4MT^{1}
42249 4MT^{1}
42250 4MT^{1}
42251 4MT^{1}
42252 4MT^{1}
42253 4MT^{1}
42254 4MT^{1}
42255 4MT^{1}
42256 4MT^{1}
42257 4MT^{1}
42328 4MT^{2}
42374 4MT^{2}
42530 4MT^{4}
42531 4MT^{4}
42532 4MT^{4}
42533 4MT^{4}
42534 4MT^{4}
42535 4MT^{4}
42536 4MT^{4}
42678 4MT^{1}
42679 4MT^{1}
42681 4MT^{1}
42684 4MT^{1}
42687 4MT^{1}
44228 4F^{2}
44530 4F^{2}
47300 3F^{6}
47311 3F^{6}
47328 3F^{6}
47351 3F^{6}
47458 3F^{6}
47484 3F^{6}
47512 3F^{6}
58038 1P^{5}
58043 1P^{6}
58045 1P^{6}
58062 1P^{6}
58065 1P^{6}
58089 1P^{6}
58184 2F^{8}
58191 2F^{9}
58259 2F^{9}
58289 2F^{9}

1954 33A
41928 3P^{2}
41939 3P^{2}
41941 3P^{2}
41942 3P^{2}
41948 3P^{2}
41951 3P^{2}
41976 3P^{2}
41977 3P^{2}
41978 3P^{2}
41980 3F^{1}
41981 3F^{1}
41983 3F^{1}
41984 3F^{1}
41985 3F^{1}
41986 3F^{1}
41987 3F^{1}
41988 3F^{1}
41989 3F^{1}
41991 3F^{1}
41992 3F^{1}
42226 4MT^{1}
42227 4MT^{1}
42230 4MT^{1}
42231 4MT^{1}
42232 4MT^{1}
42248 4MT^{1}
42249 4MT^{1}
42250 4MT^{1}
42251 4MT^{1}
42252 4MT^{1}
42253 4MT^{1}
42254 4MT^{1}
42255 4MT^{1}
42256 4MT^{1}
42257 4MT^{1}
42328 4MT^{2}
42374 4MT^{2}
42532 4MT^{4}
42533 4MT^{4}
42534 4MT^{4}
42535 4MT^{4}
42536 4MT^{4}
42678 4MT^{1}
42679 4MT^{1}
42681 4MT^{1}
42684 4MT^{1}
42687 4MT^{1}
47262 3F^{6}
47282 3F^{6}
47300 3F^{6}
47306 3F^{6}
47311 3F^{6}
47312 3F^{6}
47328 3F^{6}
47351 3F^{6}
47429 3F^{6}
47458 3F^{6}
47484 3F^{6}
47512 3F^{6}
47555 3F^{6}
58038 1P^{5}
58054 1P^{6}
58062 1P^{6}
58065 1P^{6}
58089 1P^{6}
58129 2F^{8}
58184 2F^{8}
58191 2F^{9}
58200 2F^{9}
65533 J17
65552 J17
65566 J17
65588 J17
80069 4MT^{3}
80070 4MT^{3}
80071 4MT^{3}
80072 4MT^{3}
80073 4MT^{3}
80074 4MT^{3}
80075 4MT^{3}
80076 4MT^{3}

1957 33A
41928 3P^{2}
41939 3P^{2}
41941 3P^{2}
41945 3P^{2}
41946 3P^{2}
41948 3P^{2}
41950 3P^{2}
41977 3P^{2}
41978 3P^{2}
41980 3F^{1}
41981 3F^{1}
41982 3F^{1}
41983 3F^{1}
41984 3F^{1}
41985 3F^{1}
41986 3F^{1}
41987 3F^{1}
41988 3F^{1}
41989 3F^{1}
41990 3F^{1}
41991 3F^{1}
41992 3F^{1}
41993 3F^{1}
42218 4MT^{1}
42219 4MT^{1}
42220 4MT^{1}
42221 4MT^{1}
42223 4MT^{1}
42224 4MT^{1}
42226 4MT^{1}
42227 4MT^{1}
42254 4MT^{1}
42255 4MT^{1}
42257 4MT^{1}
47262 3F^{6}
47312 3F^{6}
47328 3F^{6}
47351 3F^{6}
47484 3F^{6}
47512 3F^{6}
47555 3F^{6}
58191 2F^{9}
58197 2F^{9}
80096 4MT^{3}
80097 4MT^{3}
80098 4MT^{3}
80099 4MT^{3}
80100 4MT^{3}
80101 4MT^{3}
80102 4MT^{3}
80103 4MT^{3}
80104 4MT^{3}
80105 4MT^{3}
80131 4MT^{3}
80132 4MT^{3}
80133 4MT^{3}
80134 4MT^{3}
80135 4MT^{3}
80136 4MT^{3}
90196 WD^{1}
90256 WD^{1}
90442 WD^{1}
90653 WD^{1}

Plodder Lane

1948 10D
44079 4F^{2}
44119 4F^{2}
44341 4F^{2}
44352 4F^{2}
44356 4F^{2}
44379 4F^{2}
44386 4F^{2}
47401 3F^{6}
49147 7F^{2}
49378 7F^{2}
58890 2F^{14}
58904 2F^{14}
58908 2F^{14}
58914 2F^{14}
58918 2F^{14}
58923 2F^{14}
58926 2F^{14}
58927 2F^{14}

1951 10D
41210 2MT^{1}
41211 2MT^{1}
41212 2MT^{1}
41213 2MT^{1}
41214 2MT^{1}
41215 2MT^{1}
41216 2MT^{1}
41217 2MT^{1}
44237 4F^{2}
44261 4F^{2}
44356 4F^{2}
44384 4F^{2}
44454 4F^{2}
44473 4F^{2}
47401 3F^{6}
49034 7F^{2}
49147 7F^{2}
49315 7F^{2}
50644 2P^{8}

1954 10D
41210 2MT^{1}
41214 2MT^{1}
44237 4F^{2}
44261 4F^{2}
44356 4F^{2}
44384 4F^{2}
44473 4F^{2}
47401 3F^{6}
49034 7F^{2}
49147 7F^{2}
49149 7F^{2}
49315 7F^{2}
84000 2MT^{2}
84001 2MT^{2}
84002 2MT^{2}
84003 2MT^{2}
84004 2MT^{2}

Plymouth Friary

1948 PLY
30003 T1
30007 T1
30035 M7
30084 B4^{1}
30091 B4^{1}
30094 B4^{1}
30095 B4^{1}
30103 B4^{1}
30116 T9
30182 O2
30183 O2
30197 O2
30216 O2
30236 O2
30289 T9
30711 T9
30757 757
30758 757

1951 72D
30007 T1
30035 M7
30037 M7
30084 B4^{1}
30088 B4^{1}
30094 B4^{1}
30102 B4^{1}
30107 M7
30182 O2
30183 O2
30207 O2
30216 O2
30236 O2
30356 M7
30375 M7
30757 757
30758 757
32094 E1R
34011 WC
34012 WC
34013 WC
34034 WC
34035 WC
34036 WC

1954 72D
30034 M7
30035 M7
30036 M7
30037 M7
30039 M7
30040 M7
30088 B4^{1}
30089 B4^{1}
30094 B4^{1}
30102 B4^{1}
30183 O2
30192 O2
30216 O2
30236 O2
30757 757
30758 757
32094 E1R
32095 E1R
34035 WC
34036 WC
34037 WC
34038 WC
41315 2MT^{1}

1957 72D
30034 M7
30035 M7
30036 M7
30037 M7
30088 B4^{1}
30089 B4^{1}
30094 B4^{1}
30102 B4^{1}
30162 G6
30192 O2
30216 O2
30225 O2
34035 WC
34036 WC
34037 WC
34038 WC
41314 2MT^{1}
41315 2MT^{1}
41316 2MT^{1}

1960 83H
30034 M7
30035 M7
30036 M7
30183 O2
30192 O2
30193 O2
30225 O2
41302 2MT^{1}
41315 2MT^{1}
41316 2MT^{1}
41317 2MT^{1}

1963 83H
41206 2MT^{1}
41214 2MT^{1}
41216 2MT^{1}
41275 2MT^{1}
41295 2MT^{1}
41302 2MT^{1}
41315 2MT^{1}
41316 2MT^{1}
41317 2MT^{1}

Polmadie

1948 27A
40916 4P^{1}
41131 4P^{1}
42200 4MT^{1}
42201 4MT^{1}
42202 4MT^{1}
42203 4MT^{1}
42204 4MT^{1}
42205 4MT^{1}
42206 4MT^{1}
42207 4MT^{1}
42208 4MT^{1}
42213 4MT^{1}
42214 4MT^{1}
42215 4MT^{1}
42216 4MT^{1}
42238 4MT^{1}
42239 4MT^{1}
42240 4MT^{1}
42241 4MT^{1}
42242 4MT^{1}
42243 4MT^{1}
42244 4MT^{1}
42245 4MT^{1}
42246 4MT^{1}
42247 4MT^{1}
42274 4MT^{1}
42688 4MT^{1}
42689 4MT^{1}
42690 4MT^{1}
42691 4MT^{1}
42692 4MT^{1}
42693 4MT^{1}
42694 4MT^{1}
42695 4MT^{1}
42696 4MT^{1}
42698 4MT^{1}
42699 4MT^{1}
44234 4F^{2}
44281 4F^{2}
44793 5MT^{3}
44794 5MT^{3}
44978 5MT^{3}
44979 5MT^{3}
44980 5MT^{3}
45309 5MT^{3}
45484 5MT^{3}
45485 5MT^{3}
45486 5MT^{3}
45487 5MT^{3}
45583 6P5F^{2}
45584 6P5F^{2}
45691 6P5F^{2}
45692 6P5F^{2}
46102 7P^{3}
46104 7P^{3}R
46105 7P^{3}
46107 7P^{3}
46143 7P^{3}
46220 8P^{2}
46221 8P^{2}
46222 8P^{2}
46223 8P^{2}
46224 8P^{2}
46230 8P^{2}
46231 8P^{2}
46232 8P^{2}
46242 8P^{2}
47331 3F^{6}
47332 3F^{6}
47536 3F^{6}

47537 3F[6]
47540 3F[6]
55116 2P[12]
55123 2P[12]
55127 2P[12]
55141 2P[12]
55167 2P[13]
55170 2P[13]
55179 2P[13]
55183 2P[13]
55197 2P[13]
55201 2P[13]
55207 2P[13]
55221 2P[13]
55224 2P[13]
55228 2P[13]
55265 2P[15]
55267 2P[15]
55268 2P[15]
56153 2F[4]
56159 2F[4]
56160 2F[4]
56162 2F[4]
56167 2F[4]
56172 2F[4]
56239 3F[10]
56244 3F[10]
56260 3F[10]
56261 3F[10]
56263 3F[10]
56280 3F[10]
56292 3F[10]
56294 3F[10]
56295 3F[10]
56298 3F[10]
56304 3F[10]
56305 3F[10]
56306 3F[10]
56307 3F[10]
56308 3F[10]
56314 3F[10]
56318 3F[10]
56322 3F[10]
56324 3F[10]
56342 3F[10]
56346 3F[10]
56349 3F[10]
57239 2F[5]
57268 2F[5]
57275 2F[5]
57292 2F[5]
57310 2F[5]
57316 2F[5]
57317 2F[5]
57319 2F[5]
57320 2F[5]
57321 2F[5]
57330 2F[5]
57335 2F[5]
57347 2F[5]
57360 2F[5]
57361 2F[5]
57365 2F[5]
57367 2F[5]
57370 2F[5]
57381 2F[5]
57387 2F[5]
57388 2F[5]
57389 2F[5]
57412 2F[5]
57432 2F[5]
57433 2F[5]
57436 2F[5]
57439 2F[5]
57443 2F[5]
57444 2F[5]
57446 2F[5]
57447 2F[5]
57448 2F[5]
57459 2F[5]
57464 2F[5]
57465 2F[5]
57467 2F[5]
57555 3F[12]
57564 3F[12]
57581 3F[12]
57619 3F[12]
57632 3F[13]
57641 3F[13]
57661 3F[14]
57690 3F[14]

1951 66A

40916 4P[1]
41131 4P[1]
42055 4MT[1]
42056 4MT[1]
42057 4MT[1]
42058 4MT[1]
42059 4MT[1]
42060 4MT[1]
42167 4MT[1]
42168 4MT[1]
42169 4MT[1]
42170 4MT[1]
42171 4MT[1]
42172 4MT[1]
42201 4MT[1]
42204 4MT[1]
42205 4MT[1]
42206 4MT[1]
42207 4MT[1]
42213 4MT[1]
42214 4MT[1]
42215 4MT[1]
42216 4MT[1]
42238 4MT[1]
42239 4MT[1]
42240 4MT[1]
42241 4MT[1]
42242 4MT[1]
42243 4MT[1]
42244 4MT[1]
42245 4MT[1]
42246 4MT[1]
42247 4MT[1]
42274 4MT[1]
42275 4MT[1]
42276 4MT[1]
42277 4MT[1]
42688 4MT[1]
42689 4MT[1]
42690 4MT[1]
42691 4MT[1]
42692 4MT[1]
42693 4MT[1]
42694 4MT[1]
42695 4MT[1]
42696 4MT[1]
42698 4MT[1]
42699 4MT[1]
44196 4F[2]
44707 5MT[3]
44787 5MT[3]
44790 5MT[3]
44792 5MT[3]
44793 5MT[3]
44794 5MT[3]
45036 5MT[3]
45117 5MT[3]
45484 5MT[3]
45485 5MT[3]
45486 5MT[3]
45487 5MT[3]
45579 6P5F[2]
45583 6P5F[2]
45584 6P5F[2]
45691 6P5F[2]
45692 6P5F[2]
46102 7P[3]R
46104 7P[3]R
46105 7P[3]R
46107 7P[3]R
46121 7P[3]R
46220 8P[2]
46221 8P[2]
46222 8P[2]
46223 8P[2]
46224 8P[2]
46227 8P[2]
46230 8P[2]
46231 8P[2]
46232 8P[2]
47331 3F[6]
47332 3F[6]
47536 3F[6]
47537 3F[6]
47540 3F[6]
47541 3F[6]
55141 2P[12]
55167 2P[13]
55170 2P[13]
55179 2P[13]
55197 2P[13]
55201 2P[13]
55207 2P[13]
55224 2P[13]
55228 2P[13]
55265 2P[15]
55268 2P[15]
56153 2F[4]
56154 2F[4]
56159 2F[4]
56160 2F[4]
56162 2F[4]
56167 2F[4]
56239 3F[10]
56244 3F[10]
56260 3F[10]
56261 3F[10]
56263 3F[10]
56280 3F[10]
56281 3F[10]
56292 3F[10]
56294 3F[10]
56295 3F[10]
56298 3F[10]
56304 3F[10]
56305 3F[10]
56306 3F[10]
56307 3F[10]
56308 3F[10]
56314 3F[10]
56318 3F[10]
56322 3F[10]
56324 3F[10]
56342 3F[10]
56346 3F[10]
56349 3F[10]
57230 2F[5]
57238 2F[5]
57239 2F[5]
57268 2F[5]
57271 2F[5]
57275 2F[5]
57288 2F[5]
57292 2F[5]
57317 2F[5]
57319 2F[5]
57320 2F[5]
57321 2F[5]
57347 2F[5]
57360 2F[5]
57361 2F[5]
57365 2F[5]
57367 2F[5]
57370 2F[5]
57387 2F[5]
57388 2F[5]
57389 2F[5]
57412 2F[5]
57432 2F[5]
57433 2F[5]
57439 2F[5]
57443 2F[5]
57444 2F[5]
57446 2F[5]
57447 2F[5]
57448 2F[5]
57459 2F[5]
57463 2F[5]
57464 2F[5]
57465 2F[5]
57555 3F[12]
57564 3F[12]
57581 3F[12]
57619 3F[12]
57661 3F[14]
57674 3F[14]
57690 3F[14]

1954 66A

40916 4P[1]
41131 4P[1]
42055 4MT[1]
42056 4MT[1]
42057 4MT[1]
42058 4MT[1]
42059 4MT[1]
42060 4MT[1]
42143 4MT[1]
42144 4MT[1]
42167 4MT[1]
42168 4MT[1]
42169 4MT[1]
42170 4MT[1]
42171 4MT[1]
42172 4MT[1]
42238 4MT[1]
42239 4MT[1]
42240 4MT[1]
42241 4MT[1]
42242 4MT[1]
42243 4MT[1]
42244 4MT[1]
42245 4MT[1]
42246 4MT[1]
42274 4MT[1]
42275 4MT[1]
42276 4MT[1]
42277 4MT[1]
42688 4MT[1]
42690 4MT[1]
42692 4MT[1]
42693 4MT[1]
42694 4MT[1]
42695 4MT[1]
42696 4MT[1]
42699 4MT[1]
44196 4F[2]
44283 4F[2]
44707 5MT[3]
44787 5MT[3]
44793 5MT[3]
44794 5MT[3]
45030 5MT[3]
45036 5MT[3]
45162 5MT[3]
45164 5MT[3]
45173 5MT[3]
45484 5MT[3]
45485 5MT[3]
45677 6P5F[2]
45691 6P5F[2]
45692 6P5F[2]
45696 6P5F[2]
45707 6P5F[2]
46102 7P[3]R
46104 7P[3]R
46105 7P[3]R
46107 7P[3]R
46121 7P[3]R
46220 8P[2]
46221 8P[2]
46222 8P[2]
46223 8P[2]
46224 8P[2]
46227 8P[2]
46230 8P[2]
46231 8P[2]
46232 8P[2]
47331 3F[6]
47332 3F[6]
47536 3F[6]
47537 3F[6]
47540 3F[6]
47541 3F[6]
55141 2P[12]
55146 2P[12]
55167 2P[13]
55189 2P[13]
55197 2P[13]
55201 2P[13]
55207 2P[13]
55224 2P[13]
55228 2P[13]
55265 2P[15]
55268 2P[15]
56153 2F[4]
56154 2F[4]
56155 2F[4]
56159 2F[4]
56160 2F[4]
56162 2F[4]
56167 2F[4]
56239 3F[10]
56244 3F[10]
56248 3F[10]
56260 3F[10]
56261 3F[10]
56263 3F[10]
56266 3F[10]
56280 3F[10]
56281 3F[10]
56292 3F[10]
56294 3F[10]
56295 3F[10]
56298 3F[10]
56304 3F[10]
56305 3F[10]
56306 3F[10]
56307 3F[10]
56308 3F[10]
56314 3F[10]
56318 3F[10]
56322 3F[10]
56324 3F[10]
56342 3F[10]
56346 3F[10]
56349 3F[10]
57230 2F[5]
57238 2F[5]
57239 2F[5]
57268 2F[5]
57271 2F[5]
57275 2F[5]
57288 2F[5]
57292 2F[5]
57317 2F[5]
57319 2F[5]
57320 2F[5]
57321 2F[5]
57347 2F[5]
57360 2F[5]
57361 2F[5]
57365 2F[5]
57367 2F[5]
57369 2F[5]
57370 2F[5]
57389 2F[5]
57412 2F[5]
57432 2F[5]
57443 2F[5]
57444 2F[5]
57446 2F[5]
57447 2F[5]
57448 2F[5]
57459 2F[5]
57463 2F[5]
57465 2F[5]
57553 3F[12]
57555 3F[12]
57563 3F[12]
57564 3F[12]
57581 3F[12]
57603 3F[12]
57619 3F[12]
57622 3F[12]
57625 3F[12]
57632 3F[13]
57661 3F[14]
57674 3F[14]
72000 6P5F
72001 6P5F
72002 6P5F
72003 6P5F
72004 6P5F
80001 4MT[3]
80002 4MT[3]
80003 4MT[3]
80006 4MT[3]
80007 4MT[3]
80022 4MT[3]
80023 4MT[3]
80026 4MT[3]
80027 4MT[3]
90134 WD[1]
90536 WD[1]
90616 WD[1]
90751 WD[2]
90767 WD[2]

1957 66A

42055 4MT[1]
42056 4MT[1]
42057 4MT[1]
42058 4MT[1]
42059 4MT[1]
42060 4MT[1]
42143 4MT[1]
42144 4MT[1]
42170 4MT[1]
42171 4MT[1]
42172 4MT[1]
42242 4MT[1]
42243 4MT[1]
42244 4MT[1]
42245 4MT[1]
42246 4MT[1]
42274 4MT[1]
42275 4MT[1]
42276 4MT[1]
42277 4MT[1]
44196 4F[2]
44283 4F[2]
46102 7P[3]R
46104 7P[3]R
46105 7P[3]R
46107 7P[3]R
46121 7P[3]R
46220 8P[2]
46221 8P[2]
46222 8P[2]
46223 8P[2]
46224 8P[2]
46227 8P[2]
46230 8P[2]
46231 8P[2]
46232 8P[2]
47536 3F[6]
47541 3F[6]
55141 2P[12]
55167 2P[13]
55169 2P[13]
55189 2P[13]
55201 2P[13]
55207 2P[13]
55223 2P[13]
55224 2P[13]
55228 2P[13]
55237 2P[14]
55239 2P[14]
55265 2P[15]
55268 2P[15]
56153 2F[4]
56154 2F[4]
56155 2F[4]
56159 2F[4]
56160 2F[4]
56162 2F[4]
56239 3F[10]
56244 3F[10]
56260 3F[10]
56266 3F[10]
56280 3F[10]
56281 3F[10]
56292 3F[10]
56295 3F[10]
56298 3F[10]
56304 3F[10]
56306 3F[10]
56308 3F[10]
56314 3F[10]
56318 3F[10]
56322 3F[10]
56324 3F[10]
56342 3F[10]
56346 3F[10]
56349 3F[10]
57239 2F[5]
57268 2F[5]
57271 2F[5]
57275 2F[5]
57288 2F[5]
57292 2F[5]
57317 2F[5]
57319 2F[5]
57321 2F[5]
57347 2F[5]
57360 2F[5]
57361 2F[5]
57365 2F[5]
57367 2F[5]
57369 2F[5]
57370 2F[5]
57389 2F[5]
57432 2F[5]
57443 2F[5]
57444 2F[5]
57446 2F[5]
57447 2F[5]
57448 2F[5]
57463 2F[5]
57465 2F[5]
57553 3F[12]
57555 3F[12]
57563 3F[12]
57564 3F[12]
57581 3F[12]
57603 3F[12]
57619 3F[12]
57622 3F[12]
57625 3F[12]
57674 3F[14]
64471 J35
64511 J35
65216 J36
65232 J36
65304 J36
70050 7P6F
70051 7P6F
70052 7P6F
70053 7P6F
70054 7P6F
72000 6P5F
72001 6P5F
72002 6P5F
72003 6P5F
72004 6P5F
73055 5MT
73056 5MT
73057 5MT
73058 5MT
73059 5MT
73063 5MT
73064 5MT
73075 5MT
73076 5MT
77008 3MT[1]
77009 3MT[1]
80001 4MT[3]
80002 4MT[3]
80003 4MT[3]
80006 4MT[3]
80007 4MT[3]
80022 4MT[3]
80023 4MT[3]
80026 4MT[3]
80027 4MT[3]
80054 4MT[3]
80055 4MT[3]
80056 4MT[3]
80057 4MT[3]
80058 4MT[3]
80111 4MT[3]
80112 4MT[3]
80113 4MT[3]
80114 4MT[3]
80115 4MT[3]
80129 4MT[3]
80130 4MT[3]
90134 WD[1]
90536 WD[1]
90616 WD[1]
90751 WD[2]
90767 WD[2]

1960 66A

42055 4MT[1]
42056 4MT[1]
42057 4MT[1]
42058 4MT[1]
42059 4MT[1]
42060 4MT[1]
42143 4MT[1]
42144 4MT[1]
42170 4MT[1]
42171 4MT[1]
42172 4MT[1]
42239 4MT[1]
42242 4MT[1]
42243 4MT[1]
42244 4MT[1]
42245 4MT[1]
42246 4MT[1]
42268 4MT[1]
42274 4MT[1]
42275 4MT[1]
42276 4MT[1]
42277 4MT[1]
42695 4MT[1]
42738 5MT[1]
42850 5MT[1]
43848 4F[1]
43849 4F[1]
43884 4F[1]
44193 4F[2]
44251 4F[2]
44256 4F[2]
44283 4F[2]
44318 4F[2]
44322 4F[2]
45458 5MT[3]
45459 5MT[3]
45665 6P5F[2]
45707 6P5F[2]
45711 6P5F[2]
45720 6P5F[2]
46102 7P[3]R
46104 7P[3]R
46105 7P[3]R
46107 7P[3]R
46121 7P[3]R
46201 8P[1]
46210 8P[1]
46222 8P[2]
46223 8P[2]
46224 8P[2]
46227 8P[2]
46230 8P[2]
46231 8P[2]
46232 8P[2]
47336 3F[6]
47541 3F[6]
48773 8F
48774 8F
48775 8F
55167 2P[13]
55169 2P[13]
55189 2P[13]
55201 2P[13]
55207 2P[13]
55223 2P[13]
55224 2P[13]
55228 2P[13]
55237 2P[14]
55239 2P[14]
55265 2P[15]
55268 2P[15]
56158 2F[4]
56159 2F[4]
56172 2F[4]
56239 3F[10]
56241 3F[10]
56260 3F[10]
56292 3F[10]
56298 3F[10]
56304 3F[10]
56308 3F[10]
56324 3F[10]
56335 3F[10]
56349 3F[10]
57239 2F[5]
57244 2F[5]
57250 2F[5]
57268 2F[5]
57271 2F[5]
57275 2F[5]
57288 2F[5]
57292 2F[5]
57317 2F[5]
57319 2F[5]
57347 2F[5]
57360 2F[5]
57365 2F[5]
57367 2F[5]
57369 2F[5]
57389 2F[5]
57417 2F[5]
57418 2F[5]
57432 2F[5]
57448 2F[5]
57463 2F[5]
57555 3F[12]
57563 3F[12]
57564 3F[12]
57581 3F[12]
57603 3F[12]
57609 3F[12]
57622 3F[12]
57625 3F[12]
57674 3F[14]
64471 J35
64477 J35
65216 J36
65232 J36
68958 J50
69145 N15
69207 N15
70050 7P6F
70051 7P6F
70052 7P6F
73055 5MT
73056 5MT
73057 5MT
73058 5MT
73059 5MT
73060 5MT
73061 5MT
73062 5MT
73063 5MT
73064 5MT
73072 5MT
73075 5MT
73076 5MT
73098 5MT
73099 5MT
77005 3MT[1]
77007 3MT[1]
77008 3MT[1]
77009 3MT[1]
80001 4MT[3]
80002 4MT[3]
80003 4MT[3]
80006 4MT[3]
80007 4MT[3]
80022 4MT[3]
80023 4MT[3]
80026 4MT[3]
80027 4MT[3]
80054 4MT[3]
80055 4MT[3]
80056 4MT[3]
80057 4MT[3]
80058 4MT[3]
80106 4MT[3]
80107 4MT[3]
80108 4MT[3]
80109 4MT[3]
80110 4MT[3]
80129 4MT[3]
80130 4MT[3]
90039 WD[1]
90060 WD[1]
90077 WD[1]
90134 WD[1]
90198 WD[1]
90199 WD[1]
90229 WD[1]
90234 WD[1]
90320 WD[1]
90387 WD[1]
90536 WD[1]
90549 WD[1]
90596 WD[1]
90616 WD[1]
90640 WD[1]
90751 WD[2]
90767 WD[2]

1963 66A

42056 4MT[1]
42057 4MT[1]
42058 4MT[1]
42059 4MT[1]
42060 4MT[1]
42128 4MT[1]
42143 4MT[1]
42166 4MT[1]
42170 4MT[1]
42171 4MT[1]
42216 4MT[1]
42243 4MT[1]
42244 4MT[1]
42246 4MT[1]
42274 4MT[1]
42275 4MT[1]
42277 4MT[1]
43141 4MT[5]
44972 5MT[3]
44973 5MT[3]
44974 5MT[3]
45066 5MT[3]
45090 5MT[3]
45320 5MT[3]
45459 5MT[3]
45478 5MT[3]
46222 8P[2]
46223 8P[2]
46224 8P[2]
46230 8P[2]
46242 8P[2]
46249 8P[2]
57581 3F[12]
57625 3F[12]
57630 3F[13]
73055 5MT
73056 5MT
73057 5MT
73058 5MT
73059 5MT
73060 5MT
73061 5MT
73062 5MT
73063 5MT
73064 5MT
73072 5MT
73075 5MT
73076 5MT
73098 5MT
73099 5MT
77007 3MT[1]
77008 3MT[1]
77009 3MT[1]
80027 4MT[3]
80056 4MT[3]
80057 4MT[3]
80058 4MT[3]
80086 4MT[3]
80106 4MT[3]
80107 4MT[3]
80108 4MT[3]
80109 4MT[3]
80110 4MT[3]
80115 4MT[3]
80121 4MT[3]
80129 4MT[3]
80130 4MT[3]
90039 WD[1]
90199 WD[1]
90229 WD[1]
90596 WD[1]

1966 66A

42195 4MT[1]
42277 4MT[1]
42690 4MT[1]
44796 5MT[3]
73055 5MT
73059 5MT
73060 5MT
73063 5MT
73064 5MT
73072 5MT
73098 5MT
73099 5MT
76004 4MT[2]
76070 4MT[2]
76071 4MT[2]
76103 4MT[2]
80001 4MT[3]
80002 4MT[3]
80005 4MT[3]
80007 4MT[3]
80027 4MT[3]
80045 4MT[3]
80057 4MT[3]
80058 4MT[3]
80060 4MT[3]
80061 4MT[3]
80086 4MT[3]
80116 4MT[3]
80117 4MT[3]
80118 4MT[3]
80120 4MT[3]
80121 4MT[3]
80123 4MT[3]
80130 4MT[3]

Polmont

1948 POL

62411 D29
62476 D34
64484 J35
64490 J35
64502 J35
64528 J35
64531 J35
64551 J37
64570 J37
64571 J37
64589 J37
64613 J37
64621 J37
65220 J36
65222 J36
65233 J36
65241 J36
65244 J36
65246 J36
65257 J36
65268 J36
65275 J36
65290 J36
65306 J36
65313 J36
65329 J36
65338 J36
67463 C15
67464 C15
67468 C15
68104 Y9
68113 Y9
68324 J88
68350 J88
68354 J88
68471 J83
68524 J69
68533 J69
68544 J69
69137 N15
69162 N15
69200 N15

1951 64E

64484 J35
64490 J35
64502 J35
64528 J35
64537 J37
64551 J37
64553 J37
64570 J37
64571 J37
64588 J37
64589 J37
64592 J37
64593 J37
64613 J37
65222 J36
65233 J36
65241 J36
65244 J36
65246 J36
65257 J36
65268 J36
65275 J36
65290 J36
65306 J36
65338 J36
65909 J38
65917 J38
67463 C15
67464 C15
67468 C15
67473 C15
68104 Y9
68113 Y9
68324 J88
68350 J88
68354 J88
68471 J83
68524 J69
68533 J69
68544 J69
69137 N15
69162 N15
69200 N15

1954 64E

43140 4MT[5]
43141 4MT[5]
64490 J35
64502 J35
64528 J35
64537 J37
64551 J37
64570 J37
64571 J37
64588 J37
64589 J37
64592 J37
64593 J37
64636 J37
65222 J36
65233 J36
65241 J36
65244 J36
65246 J36
65257 J36
65275 J36
65290 J36
65306 J36
65338 J36
65909 J38
65917 J38
67462 C15
67463 C15
67473 C15
67494 C16
68104 Y9
68113 Y9
68324 J88
68350 J88
68354 J88
68471 J83
68524 J69
68544 J69
69137 N15
69162 N15
69200 N15

1957 64E

43140 4MT[5]
43141 4MT[5]
64490 J35
64502 J35
64528 J35
64537 J37
64551 J37
64570 J37
64571 J37
64588 J37
64589 J37
64592 J37
64593 J37
64636 J37
65222 J36
65233 J36
65241 J36
65244 J36
65246 J36
65257 J36
65275 J36
65280 J36
65306 J36
65311 J36
65909 J38
65917 J38
67488 C16
67494 C16
68104 Y9
68113 Y9
68324 J88
68350 J88
68354 J88
68467 J83
68471 J83
68524 J69
69137 N15
69162 N15
69200 N15

1960 64E

64502 J35
64537 J37
64551 J37
64570 J37
64571 J37
64636 J37
65222 J36
65257 J36
65280 J36
65306 J36
65311 J36
65316 J36
65909 J38
65917 J38
67494 C16
68104 Y9
68354 J88
68456 J83
68471 J83
69137 N15

1963 65K

64537 J37
64551 J37
64570 J37
64571 J37
64592 J37
64611 J37
64636 J37
65311 J36
65909 J38
65917 J38

Pontypool Road

1948 PPRD

349 TV[3]
385 TV[3]
1422 1400
2021 2021
2035 2021
2094 2021
2159 2021
2385 2301
2669 2600
2728 2721
2739 2721
2749 2721
2767 2721
2800 2800
2802 2800
2813 2800
2893 2884
3002 ROD
3012 ROD
3018 ROD
3023 ROD
3037 ROD
3040 ROD
3406 3300
3453 3300
3628 5700
3651 5700
3690 5700
3692 5700
3711 5700
3717 5700
3730 5700
3779 5700
3822 2884
3826 2884
3828 2884
3862 2884
4131 5101
4135 5101
4138 5101
4238 4200
4275 4200
4303 4300
4533 4500
4541 4500
4611 5700
4639 5700
4668 5700
4912 4900
4932 4900
4933 4900
5355 4300
5532 4575
5649 5600
5728 5700
5768 5700
5792 5700
5818 5800
5975 4900
6333 4300
6370 4300
6400 6400
6403 6400
6424 6400
6429 6400
6430 6400
6432 6400
6634 5600
6636 5600
6651 5600
6687 5600
6742 6700
6820 6800
6840 6800
6875 6800
7206 7200
7230 7200
7232 7200
7233 7200
7235 7200
7426 7400
7724 5700
8716 5700
8755 5700
8788 5700
9650 5700
9797 5700
90307 WD[1]
90563 WD[1]
90694 WD[1]

1951 86G

349 TV[3]
385 TV[3]
1422 1400
2021 2021
2035 2021
2094 2021
2117 2021
2385 2301
2801 2800
2802 2800
2811 2800
2813 2800
2862 2800
2864 2800
2884 2884
2888 2884
2893 2884
3012 ROD
3018 ROD
3023 ROD
3038 ROD
3040 ROD
3042 ROD
3044 ROD
3628 5700
3651 5700
3683 5700
3690 5700
3692 5700
3703 5700
3708 5700
3717 5700
3730 5700
3779 5700
3822 2884
3826 2884
3828 2884
3862 2884
4121 5101
4131 5101
4135 5101
4138 5101
4158 5101
4290 4200
4303 4300
4533 4500
4541 4500
4593 4575
4611 5700
4639 5700
4642 5700
4668 5700
5355 4300
5516 4575
5532 4575
5620 5600
5728 5700
5768 5700
5792 5700
5818 5800
6333 4300
6370 4300
6400 6400
6403 6400
6424 6400
6429 6400
6430 6400
6432 6400
6636 5600
6663 5600
6687 5600
6742 6700
6840 6800
6849 6800
6861 6800
7206 7200
7233 7200
7234 7200
7235 7200
7426 7400
7724 5700
7740 5700
8716 5700
8755 5700
8786 5700
8788 5700
9650 5700
9797 5700
90268 WD[1]
90563 WD[1]

1954 86G

1422 1400
2801 2800
2802 2800
2821 2800
2884 2884
3012 ROD
3023 ROD
3036 ROD
3038 ROD
3040 ROD
3042 ROD
3044 ROD
3628 5700
3640 5700
3651 5700
3683 5700
3703 5700
3708 5700
3717 5700
3730 5700
3779 5700
3822 2884
3826 2884
3828 2884
3855 2884
4131 5101
4135 5101
4138 5101
4142 5101
4229 4200
4522 4500
4533 4500
4639 5700
4642 5700
4668 5700
4990 4900
4991 4900
5318 4300
5334 4300
5355 4300
5516 4575
5573 4575
5620 5600
5638 5600
5728 5700
5756 5700
5768 5700
5792 5700
5916 4900
5948 4900
6317 4300
6361 4300
6393 4300
6400 6400
6403 6400
6424 6400
6429 6400
6430 6400
6432 6400
6634 5600
6636 5600
6653 5600
6675 5600

6685 5600
6693 5600
6819 6800
6840 6800
6849 6800
6871 6800
6872 6800
7206 7200
7233 7200
7234 7200
7235 7200
7426 7400
7724 5700
7740 5700
8716 5700
8755 5700
8777 5700
8788 5700
9650 5700
9796 5700
9797 5700
40145 3MT[2]
90167 WD[1]
90179 WD[1]

1957 86G

2801 2800
2802 2800
2884 2884
3628 5700
3640 5700
3651 5700
3683 5700
3685 5700
3703 5700
3708 5700
3717 5700
3779 5700
3822 2884
3824 2884
3826 2884
3828 2884
3855 2884
4135 5101
4138 5101
4229 4200
4230 4200
4593 4575
4600 5700
4639 5700
4642 5700
4668 5700
5388 4300
5516 4575
5573 4575
5625 5600
5638 5600
5659 5600
5728 5700
5750 5700
5756 5700
5759 5700
5768 5700
5775 5700
5948 4900
6325 4300
6368 4300
6400 6400
6403 6400
6424 6400
6429 6400
6432 6400
6634 5600
6636 5600
6653 5600
6675 5600
6685 5600
6693 5600
6812 6800
6819 6800
6840 6800
6872 6800
7201 7200
7204 7200
7206 7200
7213 7200
7220 7200
7233 7200
7234 7200
7235 7200
7724 5700
7740 5700
7796 5700
8707 5700
8716 5700
9650 5700
9730 5700
9796 5700
9797 5700
40091 3MT[2]
40145 3MT[2]
48415 8F
48417 8F
48418 8F
48424 8F
48444 8F
48460 8F
48470 8F
49113 7F[2]
49168 7F[2]
49174 7F[2]
49403 7F[3]
49422 7F[3]
90167 WD[1]
90192 WD[1]
90315 WD[1]

1960 86G

2839 2800
2845 2800
2857 2800
2859 2800
2866 2800
2867 2800
2883 2800
3628 5700
3640 5700
3651 5700
3685 5700
3703 5700
3708 5700
3717 5700
3779 5700
3804 2884
3818 2884
3822 2884
3826 2884
3844 2884
3859 2884
4135 5101
4600 5700
4639 5700
4642 5700
4668 5700
4916 4900
4926 4900
4937 4900
4943 4900
4958 4900
4983 4900
5103 5101
5306 4300
5318 4300
5322 4300
5330 4300
5625 5600
5638 5600
5645 5600
5659 5600
5679 5600
5750 5700
5756 5700
5759 5700
5775 5700
5789 5700
5948 4900
5970 4900
6393 4300
6634 5600
6636 5600
6675 5600
6676 5600
6685 5600
6693 5600
6802 6800
6812 6800
6819 6800
6821 6800
6840 6800
6848 6800
6867 6800
6872 6800
6901 4900
6903 4900
6928 4900
6946 4900
6958 4900
7201 7200
7210 7200
7213 7200
7220 7200
7227 7200
7246 7200
7251 7200
7325 4300
7334 4300
7712 5700
7724 5700
7740 5700
7796 5700
8440 9400
8493 9400
8495 9400
8707 5700
8716 5700
9650 5700
9730 5700
9796 5700
9797 5700
90192 WD[1]
90315 WD[1]

1963 86G

2839 2800
2859 2800
2897 2884
3628 5700
3651 5700
3683 5700
3685 5700
3708 5700
3717 5700
3779 5700
3826 2884
3841 2884
3844 2884
3861 2884
4600 5700
4603 5700
4639 5700
4642 5700
4668 5700
4678 5700
4943 4900
4958 4900
4964 4900
5164 5101
5322 4300
5369 4300
5620 5600
5638 5600
5659 5600
5775 5700
5948 4900
6115 6100
6335 4300
6370 4300
6634 5600
6636 5600
6675 5600
6676 5600
6685 5600
6693 5600
6810 6800
6819 6800
6821 6800
6822 6800
6836 6800
6838 6800
6840 6800
6848 6800
6867 6800
6872 6800
6876 6800
6901 4900
6903 4900
6928 4900
6946 4900
6958 4900
7201 7200
7210 7200
7220 7200
7227 7200
7246 7200
7251 7200
8461 9400
8493 9400
8495 9400
8707 5700
8716 5700
9650 5700
9655 5700
9730 5700
9796 5700

Preston

1948 10B

40356 2P[2]
40554 2P[2]
45021 5MT[3]
45091 5MT[3]
45142 5MT[3]
45185 5MT[3]
45345 5MT[3]
45373 5MT[3]
45502 6P5F[1]
45505 6P5F[1]
45513 6P5F[1]
45515 6P5F[1]
45516 6P5F[1]
45519 6P5F[1]
45524 6P5F[1]
45536 6P5F[1]
45537 6P5F[1]
45544 6P5F[1]
46762 2P[6]
47291 3F[6]
47293 3F[6]
47296 3F[6]
47319 3F[6]
49102 6F[2]
49119 7F[2]
49231 6F[2]
49250 6F[2]
49299 7F[2]
49348 7F[3]
49417 7F[3]
49419 7F[3]
49420 7F[3]
49421 7F[3]
49442 7F[3]
49451 7F[3]
50639 2P[8]
50676 2P[8]
50793 2P[8]
51218 0F[4]
52016 2F[3]
52034 2F[3]
52051 2F[3]
52341 3F[7]
52618 3F[9]
52619 3F[9]

1951 10B

40565 2P[3]
40631 2P[3]
44892 5MT[3]
45332 5MT[3]
45508 6P5F[1]
45516 6P5F[1]
45519 6P5F[1]
45537 6P5F[1]
45544 6P5F[1]
45599 6P5F[2]
46428 2MT[2]
46429 2MT[2]
46430 2MT[2]
46762 2P[6]
47291 3F[6]
47293 3F[6]
47296 3F[6]
47319 3F[6]
49104 7F[2]
49134 7F[2]
49141 7F[2]
49150 7F[2]
49160 7F[2]
49191 7F[2]
49267 7F[2]
49382 7F[2]
49390 7F[2]
50639 2P[8]
50678 2P[8]
50695 2P[8]
52105 3F[7]
52619 3F[9]
56027 0F[5]

1954 10B

40524 2P[2]
40565 2P[3]
40631 2P[3]
40673 2P[3]
45096 5MT[3]
45332 5MT[3]
45519 6P5F[1]
45582 6P5F[2]
45633 6P5F[2]
46429 2MT[2]
46430 2MT[2]
47008 0F[3]
47291 3F[6]
47293 3F[6]
47319 3F[6]
47360 3F[6]
47413 3F[6]
47472 3F[6]
47659 3F[6]
49104 7F[2]
49141 7F[2]
49150 7F[2]
49191 7F[2]
49196 7F[2]
49267 7F[2]
49382 7F[2]
49390 7F[2]
49391 7F[2]
49396 7F[3]
56027 0F[5]

1957 10B

40565 2P[3]
40631 2P[3]
40671 2P[3]
40673 2P[3]
40694 2P[3]
45096 5MT[3]
45332 5MT[3]
45582 6P5F[2]
45633 6P5F[2]
47008 0F[3]
47291 3F[6]
47293 3F[6]
47319 3F[6]
47360 3F[6]
47413 3F[6]
47472 3F[6]
47659 3F[6]
49104 7F[2]
49141 7F[2]
49150 7F[2]
49191 7F[2]
49196 7F[2]
49267 7F[2]
49382 7F[2]
49390 7F[2]
49391 7F[2]
49396 7F[3]
56027 0F[5]
78036 2MT[1]
78037 2MT[1]

1960 24K

40657 2P[3]
40683 2P[3]
40694 2P[3]
44682 5MT[3]
44827 5MT[3]
45150 5MT[3]
45248 5MT[3]
45302 5MT[3]
45332 5MT[3]
45454 5MT[3]
45502 6P5F[1]
45507 6P5F[1]
45508 6P5F[1]
45542 6P5F[1]
45582 6P5F[2]
45633 6P5F[2]
45735 7P[2]
46108 7P[3]R
46126 7P[3]R
46136 7P[3]R
46154 7P[3]R
46161 7P[3]R
46163 7P[3]R
46165 7P[3]R
46167 7P[3]R
46168 7P[3]R
46170 7P[3]R
47008 0F[3]
47293 3F[6]
47319 3F[6]
47360 3F[6]
47413 3F[6]
47472 3F[6]
49104 7F[2]
49196 7F[2]
49382 7F[2]
78036 2MT[1]
78037 2MT[1]

Radyr

1948 RYR

30 RR[1]
32 RR[1]
34 RR[1]
35 RR[3]
38 RR[3]
40 RR[3]
41 RR[3]
42 RR[3]
43 RR[3]
44 RR[3]
46 RR[3]
56 RR[4]
63 RR[4]
64 RR[4]
198 BR[1]
240 BR[2]
246 BR[2]
258 BR[2]
293 TV[2]
433 BM[2]
3599 3500
5640 5600
5655 5600
6603 5600
6607 5600
6608 5600
6618 5600
6664 5600

1960 88A

3401 9400
3402 9400
3403 9400
3404 9400
3405 9400
3406 9400
3407 9400
3408 9400
3409 9400
3672 5700
4143 5101
4160 5101
4163 5101
5615 5600
5618 5600
5640 5600
5648 5600
5663 5600
5669 5600
5683 5600
5692 5600
6411 6400
6434 6400
6603 5600
6606 5600
6607 5600
6608 5600
6612 5600
6614 5600
6618 5600
6624 5600
6626 5600
6633 5600
6635 5600
6638 5600
6647 5600
6648 5600
6659 5600
6660 5600
6665 5600
6682 5600
6684 5600
6689 5600
6699 5600
7202 7200
7205 7200
7242 7200
7252 7200
8420 9400
8438 9400
8455 9400
8469 9400
8470 9400
8471 9400
8478 9400
8481 9400
8780 5700

1963 88B

3400 9400
3401 9400
3402 9400
3403 9400
3405 9400
3406 9400
3409 9400
3672 5700
3716 5700
4160 5101
4166 5101
4177 5101
4637 5700
5625 5600
5635 5600
5648 5600
5651 5600
5669 5600
5672 5600
5683 5600
5697 5600
6603 5600
6606 5600
6607 5600
6608 5600
6612 5600
6614 5600
6621 5600
6624 5600
6626 5600
6635 5600
6637 5600
6638 5600
6648 5600
6656 5600
6657 5600
6659 5600
6660 5600
6665 5600
6682 5600
6684 5600
6688 5600
6689 5600
6699 5600
7205 7200
7242 7200
7250 7200
7252 7200
8469 9400
8478 9400
8479 9400
8497 9400
9480 9400
9711 5700

Ramsgate

1948 RAM

30911 V
30912 V
30913 V
30914 V
30915 V
30916 V
30917 V
30918 V
30919 V
30920 V
31004 C
31016 H
31080 O1
31151 F1
31164 H
31182 H
31265 H
31316 O1
31451 B1
31452 B1
31453 B1
31521 H
31522 H
31523 H
31592 C
31777 L
31778 L
31779 L
31780 L
31781 L
34030 WC
34031 WC
34032 WC
34062 BB
34063 BB
34065 BB
34066 BB
34067 BB
34068 BB
34069 BB
34070 BB

1951 74B

30911 V
30912 V
30913 V
30914 V
30915 V
30916 V
30917 V
30918 V
31004 C
31065 O1
31093 O1
31252 C
31298 C
31390 O1
31519 H
31521 H
31522 H
31592 C
31690 C
31737 D
31748 D
31776 L
31777 L
31780 L
31781 L
31788 L1
31789 L1
34077 BB
34078 BB
34079 BB
34080 BB
34081 BB
34082 BB
34086 BB
34087 BB
34088 BB
34089 BB
34090 BB
34096 WC
34097 WC
34098 WC
34099 WC
34100 WC
42066 4MT[1]
42067 4MT[1]
42068 4MT[1]
42069 4MT[1]
42106 4MT[1]

1954 74B

30911 V
30912 V
30913 V
30914 V
30916 V
30917 V
30922 V
31004 C
31245 C
31252 C
31271 C
31298 C
31324 H
31326 H
31592 C
31779 L
31780 L
31781 L
34075 BB
34076 BB
34077 BB
34078 BB
34079 BB
34080 BB
34081 BB
34082 BB
34083 BB
34084 BB
34085 BB
34086 BB
34096 WC
34097 WC
34098 WC
34099 WC
34100 WC
42067 4MT[1]
42070 4MT[1]
42071 4MT[1]
42072 4MT[1]

1957 74B

30796 N15
30911 V
30912 V
30913 V
30914 V
30915 V
30916 V
30917 V
30918 V
30922 V
31004 C
31245 C
31252 C
31271 C
31298 C
31324 H
31326 H
31500 H
31592 C
31764 L
31779 L
31780 L
31781 L
34075 BB
34076 BB
34077 BB
34078 BB
34079 BB
34080 BB
34081 BB
34082 BB
34083 BB
34084 BB
34085 BB
34086 BB
34096 WC
34097 WC
34098 WC
34099 WC
34100 WC
41301 2MT[1]
41304 2MT[1]
41318 2MT[1]
41319 2MT[1]
42074 4MT[1]

Ranskill Wagon Works

1951

68132 Y1

1954

3 Y3
4 Y1

1957

3 Y3
4 Y1

Reading

1948 RDG

1335 MSWJ
1336 MSWJ
1407 1400
1444 1400
1447 1400
2076 2021
2208 2251
2245 2251
2264 2251
2299 2251
2573 2301
3025 ROD
3047 ROD
3386 3300
3418 3300
3426 3300
3663 5700
3697 5700
3715 5700
3736 5700
3770 5700
3783 5700
3840 2884
3841 2884
3843 2884
3844 2884
3845 2884
3846 2884
4085 4073
4649 5700
4661 5700
4670 5700
4688 5700
4690 5700
4692 5700
4914 4900
4920 4900
4931 4900
4989 4900
4994 4900
4995 4900
5320 4300
5356 4300
5375 4300
5385 4300
5751 5700
5761 5700
5762 5700
5763 5700
5766 5700
5772 5700
5901 4900
5933 4900
5948 4900
5956 4900
5959 4900
5973 4900
6109 6100
6115 6100
6117 6100
6121 6100
6130 6100
6131 6100
6136 6100
6140 6100
6154 6100
6162 6100
6163 6100
6302 4300
6312 4300
6313 4300
6334 4300
6363 4300
6366 4300
6383 4300
6393 4300
6802 6800
6864 6800
6968 6959
7318 4300
7320 4300
7708 5700
7777 5700
7788 5700
9303 9300
9304 9300
9305 9300
9307 9300
9309 9300
9313 9300
9315 9300
9318 9300
9319 9300
9722 5700
9749 5700
9763 5700
9791 5700
90261 WD[1]
90266 WD[1]
90274 WD[1]
90367 WD[1]

1951 81D

1335 MSWJ
1336 MSWJ
1407 1400
1444 1400
1447 1400
1925 1901
2208 2251
2245 2251
2264 2251
2299 2251
2573 2301
2825 2800
2845 2800
3025 ROD
3047 ROD
3454 3300
3723 5700
3738 5700
3840 2884
3841 2884
3845 2884
3846 2884
4085 4073
4606 5700
4609 5700
4661 5700
4665 5700
4670 5700
4920 4900
4931 4900
4939 4900
4943 4900
4948 4900
4962 4900
4989 4900
4994 4900
4995 4900
4998 4900
5034 4073
5036 4073
5375 4300
5762 5700
5763 5700
5766 5700
5772 5700
5901 4900
5933 4900
5956 4900
5957 4900
5959 4900
5973 4900
5979 4900
6100 6100
6101 6100
6103 6100
6105 6100
6130 6100
6145 6100
6153 6100
6162 6100
6163 6100
6302 4300
6312 4300
6334 4300
6363 4300
6366 4300
6379 4300
6383 4300
6393 4300
6802 6800
6864 6800
6865 6800
6923 4900
6968 6959
6996 6959
7318 4300
7320 4300
7708 5700
7777 5700
7788 5700
7906 6959
7919 6959
7927 6959
9303 9300
9305 9300
9307 9300
9313 9300
9318 9300
9319 9300
9410 9400
9411 9400
9412 9400
9420 9400
9423 9400
9749 5700
9763 5700
9791 5700

1954 81D

1153 PM[2]
1336 MSWJ
1407 1400
1444 1400
1447 1400
2221 2251
2245 2251
2264 2251
2299 2251
2516 2301
3219 2251
3723 5700
3738 5700
4085 4073
4539 4500
4606 5700
4609 5700
4661 5700
4665 5700
4670 5700
4960 4900
4962 4900
4989 4900
4993 4900
4995 4900
4998 4900
5036 4073
5330 4300
5368 4300
5762 5700
5763 5700
5766 5700
5772 5700
5901 4900
5933 4900
5942 4900
5956 4900
5957 4900
5959 4900
5973 4900
5979 4900
5993 4900
6100 6100
6101 6100
6103 6100
6104 6100
6117 6100
6126 6100
6129 6100
6130 6100
6145 6100
6161 6100
6162 6100
6163 6100
6302 4300
6312 4300
6366 4300
6379 4300
6627 5600
6834 6800
6864 6800
6865 6800
6923 4900
6927 4900
6960 6959
6968 6959
7708 5700
7777 5700
7788 5700
7906 6959
7919 6959
7927 6959
8430 9400
9305 9300
9306 9300
9308 9300
9313 9300
9315 9300
9401 9400
9402 9400
9404 9400
9405 9400
9749 5700
9763 5700
9791 5700

1957 81D

1407 1400
1444 1400
1447 1400
2245 2251
2253 2251
2262 2251
2299 2251
2824 2800
2835 2800
2867 2800
3219 2251
3723 5700
3738 5700
3835 2884
4085 4073
4606 5700
4609 5700
4661 5700
4665 5700
4670 5700
4943 4900
4960 4900
4961 4900
4962 4900
4965 4900
4969 4900
4987 4900
4989 4900
4993 4900
4995 4900
4998 4900
5036 4073
5326 4300
5368 4300
5391 4300
5763 5700
5901 4900
5906 4900
5915 4900
5933 4900
5942 4900
5957 4900
5973 4900
5979 4900
5993 4900
6100 6100
6101 6100
6103 6100
6104 6100
6117 6100
6123 6100
6126 6100
6129 6100
6130 6100
6145 6100
6153 6100
6161 6100
6162 6100
6302 4300
6366 4300
6379 4300
6394 4300
6627 5600
6923 4900
6927 4900
6953 4900
6960 6959
6968 6959
7708 5700
7788 5700
7906 6959
7914 6959
7919 6959
7927 6959
8430 9400
9309 9300
9401 9400
9402 9400
9404 9400
9405 9400
9749 5700
9763 5700
9791 5700

1960 81D

1407 1400
2206 2251
2210 2251
2212 2251
2245 2251
2841 2800
2853 2800
3219 2251
3723 5700
3738 5700
3858 2884
4084 4073
4092 4073
4609 5700
4641 5700
4661 5700
4665 5700
4670 5700
4941 4900
4951 4900
4961 4900
4962 4900
4977 4900
4987 4900
4998 4900
5018 4073
5036 4073
5901 4900
5906 4900
5915 4900
5936 4900
5973 4900
5979 4900
5982 4900
5993 4900
6101 6100
6103 6100
6104 6100
6107 6100
6112 6100
6119 6100
6122 6100
6125 6100
6129 6100
6130 6100
6131 6100
6134 6100
6153 6100
6161 6100
6162 6100
6324 4300
6333 4300
6385 4300
6654 5600
6923 4900
6924 4900
6953 4900
6960 6959
6968 6959
7331 4300
7708 5700
7788 5700
7906 6959
7914 6959
7919 6959
8430 9400
9404 9400
9447 9400
9749 5700
9763 5700
90485 WD[1]

1963 81D

2257 2251
2261 2251
2841 2800
2889 2884
3219 2251
3715 5700
3858 2884
4609 5700
4661 5700
4670 5700
4915 4900
4975 4900
5018 4073
5038 4073
5076 4073
5901 4900
5914 4900
5936 4900
5977 4900
5979 4900
5993 4900
6103 6100
6107 6100
6119 6100
6122 6100
6131 6100
6134 6100
6138 6100
6161 6100
6164 6100
6337 4300
6379 4300
6385 4300
6812 6800
6825 6800
6826 6800
6863 6800
6913 4900
6923 4900
6924 4900
6938 4900
6953 4900
6960 6959
7808 7800
7813 7800
7816 7800
7817 7800
7906 6959
7914 6959
7919 6959
8430 9400
8496 9400
9404 9400
9450 9400
9763 5700
9789 5700

Reading South

1948 RDG
30258 G6
30260 G6
31042 F1
31078 F1
31217 B1
31446 B1
31459 B1
31610 U
31611 U
31615 U
31620 U
31628 U
31807 U
31850 N
31854 N
31857 N
31860 N
31861 N
31868 N

1951 70E
30270 G6
31057 D
31075 D
31443 B1
31515 E
31602 T
31610 U
31611 U
31614 U
31615 U
31740 D
31744 D
31750 D
31794 U
31796 U
31797 U
31799 U

1954 70E
30022 M7
30104 M7
30160 G6
30374 M7
30667 M7
31075 D
31488 D
31496 D
31586 D
31610 U
31611 U
31612 U
31614 U
31615 U
31616 U
31617 U
31619 U
31737 D
31746 D
32168 E3
32501 E4
32502 E4

1957 70E
32170 E3

Redbridge Sleeper Depot

1948
77S C14

1951
77S C14

1954
77S C14

1957
77S C14

1963
DS233 USA

1966
DS233 USA

Redhill

1948 RED
30533 Q
30537 Q
30538 Q
30539 Q
30545 Q
30546 Q
30547 Q
31406 N
31587 E
31728 D
31729 D
31815 N
31816 N
31817 N
31818 N
31843 N
31849 N
31851 N
31852 N
31858 N
31863 N
31864 N
31895 U1
31896 U1
31897 U1
31898 U1
31899 U1
32435 C2
32450 C2X
32507 E4
32517 E4
32541 C2X
32560 E4
32568 E5
32586 E5X
32592 E5

1951 75B
31488 D
31490 D
31843 N
31844 N
31848 N
31849 N
31851 N
31852 N
31857 N
31858 N
31862 N
31863 N
31864 N
31865 N
31895 U1
31896 U1
31897 U1
31898 U1
32449 C2X
32450 C2X
32507 E4
32512 E4
32517 E4
32540 C2X
32541 C2X
32550 C2X
32560 E4
32561 E4
32568 E5
32571 E5
32593 E5
90317 WD[1]
90360 WD[1]
90641 WD[1]

1954 75B
30123 M7
30245 M7
30377 M7
30835 S15
30836 S15
30837 S15
31309 H
31311 H
31550 H
31551 H
31591 D
31862 N
31863 N
31864 N
31865 N
31866 N
31867 N
31868 N
31869 N
31894 U1
31895 U1
31896 U1
31897 U1
31898 U1
31899 U1
31900 U1
32448 C2X
32449 C2X
32450 C2X
32451 C2X
32507 E4
32512 E4
32560 E4
32561 E4
42068 4MT[1]
42077 4MT[1]

1957 75B
30835 S15
30836 S15
30837 S15
31817 N
31862 N
31863 N
31864 N
31865 N
31866 N
31867 N
31868 N
31869 N
32450 C2X
32451 C2X
32507 E4
32560 E4
76009 4MT[2]
76014 4MT[2]
76053 4MT[2]
76054 4MT[2]
76055 4MT[2]
76056 4MT[2]
76057 4MT[2]
76058 4MT[2]
76059 4MT[2]
76060 4MT[2]
76061 4MT[2]
76062 4MT[2]

1960 75B
30835 S15
30836 S15
30837 S15
30847 S15
31817 N
31850 N
31851 N
31852 N
31861 N
31862 N
31863 N
31864 N
31865 N
31866 N
31867 N
31868 N
31869 N
31870 N
31871 N
31872 N
32450 C2X
32451 C2X
76053 4MT[2]
76054 4MT[2]
76055 4MT[2]

1963 75B
30835 S15
30836 S15
30847 S15
31817 N
31850 N
31851 N
31852 N
31861 N
31862 N
31863 N
31864 N
31865 N
31866 N
31867 N
31868 N
31869 N
31870 N
31871 N
31872 N

Reedsmouth

1948 RMH
65101 J21
65331 J36
65343 J36

1951 52C sub
65111 J21
65331 J36

Retford

1948 RET
61208 B1
61211 B1
61212 B1
61213 B1
61231 B1
63608 O4
63637 O4
63654 O4
63688 O4
63736 O4
63763 O4
63774 O4
63775 O4
63782 O4
63785 O4
63877 O4
63905 O4
63907 O4
63908 O4
63914 O4
64107 J3
64124 J3
64125 J3
64133 J3
64141 J3
64148 J3
64150 J3
64152 J3
64280 J11
64282 J11
64287 J11
64295 J11
64306 J11
64335 J11
64340 J11
64341 J11
64347 J11
64348 J11
64349 J11
64380 J11
64385 J11
64393 J11
64402 J11
64410 J11
64413 J11
64416 J11
64421 J11
64422 J11
64423 J11
64425 J11
64451 J11
64759 J39
64830 J39
64886 J39
64887 J39
64898 J39
64906 J39
64908 J39
64956 J39
64961 J39
64970 J39
64987 J39
65058 J21
65070 J21
65095 J21
65117 J21
68165 Y3
69294 N5
69321 N5

1951 36E
61126 B1
61208 B1
61211 B1
61212 B1
61213 B1
61231 B1
63475 O3
63478 O3
63482 O3
63488 O3
63608 O4
63637 O4
63654 O4
63688 O4
63736 O4
63763 O4
63782 O4
63785 O4
63905 O4
63907 O4
63914 O4
64125 J3
64133 J3
64141 J3
64148 J3
64150 J3
64241 J6
64280 J11
64282 J11
64287 J11
64295 J11
64306 J11
64335 J11
64340 J11
64341 J11
64347 J11
64348 J11
64380 J11
64385 J11
64393 J11
64402 J11
64413 J11
64416 J11
64421 J11
64422 J11
64423 J11
64451 J11
64759 J39
64830 J39
64898 J39
64906 J39
64908 J39
64956 J39
64961 J39
64970 J39
64987 J39
65070 J21
68766 J52
69273 N5
69277 N5
69282 N5
69294 N5
69313 N5
69321 N5
69354 N5

1954 36E
61126 B1
61208 B1
61211 B1
61212 B1
61213 B1
61231 B1
63608 O4
63637 O4
63654 O4
63688 O4
63736 O4
63782 O4
63785 O4
63905 O4
63914 O4
63924 O2
63925 O2
63926 O2
63927 O2
63937 O2
63949 O2
63965 O2
63970 O2
63972 O2
63976 O2
63979 O2
63980 O2
63982 O2
63986 O2
63987 O2
64132 J3
64140 J3
64188 J6
64234 J6
64241 J6
64245 J6
64252 J6
64280 J11
64282 J11
64287 J11
64295 J11
64335 J11
64340 J11
64341 J11
64347 J11
64380 J11
64385 J11
64393 J11
64402 J11
64416 J11
64421 J11
64422 J11
64423 J11
64451 J11
64759 J39
64830 J39
64893 J39
64898 J39
64906 J39
64908 J39
64961 J39
64970 J39
69277 N5
69282 N5
69283 N5
69300 N5
69313 N5
69314 N5
69321 N5

1957 36E
58065 1P[6]
58085 1P[6]
61126 B1
61208 B1
61211 B1
61212 B1
61213 B1
61231 B1
63608 O4
63637 O4
63654 O4
63655 O4
63688 O4
63736 O4
63782 O4
63785 O4
63905 O4
63914 O4
63924 O2
63925 O2
63926 O2
63927 O2
63937 O2
63945 O2
63949 O2
63961 O2
63965 O2
63970 O2
63972 O2
63976 O2
63979 O2
63980 O2
63982 O2
63986 O2
63987 O2
64174 J6
64188 J6
64234 J6
64236 J6
64241 J6
64245 J6
64252 J6
64255 J6
64259 J6
64280 J11
64283 J11
64287 J11
64295 J11
64321 J11
64340 J11
64341 J11
64385 J11
64395 J11
64403 J11
64416 J11
64421 J11
64422 J11
64423 J11
64451 J11
64759 J39
64830 J39
64893 J39
64898 J39
64906 J39
64908 J39
64961 J39
64970 J39
68508 J69
68519 J69
68520 J69
68527 J69
68561 J69
69283 N5
69314 N5

1960 36E
61120 B1
61126 B1
61208 B1
61211 B1
61212 B1
61213 B1
61231 B1
63608 O4
63637 O4
63655 O4
63688 O4
63736 O4
63782 O4
63785 O4
63818 O4
63914 O4
63924 O2
63925 O2
63926 O2
63927 O2
63937 O2
63944 O2
63945 O2
63947 O2
63949 O2
63959 O2
63961 O2
63965 O2
63970 O2
63971 O2
63972 O2
63976 O2
63979 O2
63980 O2
63982 O2
63986 O2
63987 O2
64174 J6
64178 J6
64236 J6
64245 J6
64315 J11
64450 J11
64759 J39
64830 J39
64882 J39
64893 J39
64898 J39
64906 J39
64908 J39
64970 J39
68502 J69
68530 J69
68621 J69

1963 36E
43037 4MT[5]
43127 4MT[5]
43157 4MT[5]
61055 B1
61120 B1
61126 B1
61127 B1
61208 B1
61212 B1
61213 B1
61225 B1
62019 K1
62039 K1
62054 K1
62067 K1
62070 K1
63632 O4
63647 O4
63665 O4
63672 O4
63688 O4
63702 O4
63704 O4
63726 O4
63727 O4
63736 O4
63764 O4
63785 O4
63824 O4
63908 O4
63914 O4
63924 O2
63925 O2
63926 O2
63927 O2
63936 O2
63937 O2
63939 O2
63945 O2
63946 O2
63962 O2
63964 O2
63968 O2
63969 O2
63972 O2
63973 O2
63975 O2
63976 O2
63977 O2
63978 O2
63980 O2
63983 O2
63984 O2
63985 O2
63986 O2
63987 O2

Rhyl

1948 7D
40494 2P[2]
40629 2P[3]
40646 2P[3]
43396 3F[3]
46632 1P[1]
46658 1P[1]
46687 1P[1]
46691 1P[1]
46701 1P[1]
46712 1P[1]
46727 1P[1]
52125 3F[7]
52167 3F[7]
52338 3F[7]
52356 3F[7]
58399 2F[11]
58427 2F[11]
58882 2F[14]
58884 2F[14]
58893 2F[14]
58903 2F[14]

1951 7D
40324 2P[1]
40377 2P[2]
40396 2P[2]
40433 2P[2]
40495 2P[2]
40629 2P[3]
40646 2P[3]
40671 2P[3]
40675 2P[3]
41231 2MT[1]
41276 2MT[1]
41277 2MT[1]
43396 3F[3]
52125 3F[7]
52167 3F[7]
52172 3F[7]
52233 3F[7]
52338 3F[7]
52356 3F[7]
52453 3F[7]
52608 3F[9]
58392 2F[11]
58420 2F[11]
58921 2F[14]

1954 6K
40396 2P[2]
40495 2P[2]
40580 2P[3]
40589 2P[3]
40629 2P[3]
40671 2P[3]
40675 2P[3]
40679 2P[3]
41224 2MT[1]
41231 2MT[1]
41244 2MT[1]
41276 2MT[1]
41324 2MT[1]
43396 3F[3]
44367 4F[2]
52162 3F[7]
52167 3F[7]
52172 3F[7]
52356 3F[7]
52453 3F[7]
52608 3F[9]

1957 6K
40420 2P[2]
40495 2P[2]
40589 2P[3]
41216 2MT[1]
41276 2MT[1]
43396 3F[3]
44367 4F[2]
46423 2MT[2]
46432 2MT[2]
46433 2MT[2]
46445 2MT[2]
47350 3F[6]
52162 3F[7]
52172 3F[7]
52356 3F[7]

1960 6K
41216 2MT[1]
41276 2MT[1]
43618 3F[3]
43981 4F[1]
44367 4F[2]
47350 3F[6]
52119 3F[7]
52162 3F[7]
52438 3F[7]
58287 2F[9]
78031 2MT[1]
78055 2MT[1]
78056 2MT[1]

1963 6K
47350 3F[6]
47507 3F[6]
47669 3F[6]
84003 2MT[2]

Rhymney

1948 RHY
39 RR[3]
67 RR[4]
76 RR[5]
77 RR[5]
78 RR[6]
79 RR[6]
80 RR[6]
81 RR[6]
82 RR[7]
292 TV[2]
370 TV[3]
375 TV[3]
398 TV[3]
5128 5101
5635 5600
5660 5600
5683 5600
5692 5600
5696 5600

Rolvenden

1948 KESR
32670 A1X
32678 A1X
KESR 4 0330

Rose Grove

1948 24B
42438 4MT[3]
42439 4MT[3]
42475 4MT[3]
42546 4MT[3]
42547 4MT[3]
42555 4MT[3]
42558 4MT[3]
42635 4MT[3]
47386 3F[6]
47575 3F[6]
47576 3F[6]
48312 8F
48319 8F
48339 8F
48408 8F
48435 8F
48456 8F
48458 8F
48459 8F
48463 8F
48470 8F
48471 8F
48475 8F
48523 8F
48524 8F
48525 8F
48710 8F
48711 8F
48713 8F
48714 8F
48715 8F
48718 8F
49549 7F[4]
49610 7F[4]
50653 2P[8]
50654 2P[8]
51410 2F[2]
51492 2F[2]
51497 2F[2]
52183 3F[7]
52220 3F[7]
52262 3F[7]
52268 3F[7]
52278 3F[7]
52309 3F[7]
52529 3F[7]
52841 7F[5]
52873 7F[5]
52886 7F[5]
52906 7F[5]
52913 7F[5]
52916 7F[5]
52945 7F[5]
52952 7F[5]

1951 24B
42187 4MT[1]
42438 4MT[3]
42475 4MT[3]
42546 4MT[3]
42547 4MT[3]
42555 4MT[3]
42706 5MT[1]
42733 5MT[1]
42765 5MT[1]
42821 5MT[1]
42828 5MT[1]
42898 5MT[1]
47386 3F[6]
47575 3F[6]
47576 3F[6]
48319 8F
48435 8F
50653 2P[8]
50654 2P[8]
51336 2F[2]
51497 2F[2]
90109 WD[1]
90138 WD[1]
90143 WD[1]
90159 WD[1]
90171 WD[1]
90183 WD[1]
90227 WD[1]
90231 WD[1]
90241 WD[1]
90258 WD[1]
90264 WD[1]
90274 WD[1]
90283 WD[1]
90314 WD[1]
90348 WD[1]
90371 WD[1]
90387 WD[1]
90399 WD[1]
90420 WD[1]
90557 WD[1]
90576 WD[1]
90584 WD[1]
90592 WD[1]
90599 WD[1]
90621 WD[1]
90687 WD[1]

1954 24B
42187 4MT[1]
42438 4MT[3]
42439 4MT[3]
42475 4MT[3]
42546 4MT[3]
42547 4MT[3]
42555 4MT[3]
42706 5MT[1]
42716 5MT[1]
42828 5MT[1]
42869 5MT[1]
42898 5MT[1]
44940 5MT[3]
45205 5MT[3]
45209 5MT[3]
47386 3F[6]
47575 3F[6]
47576 3F[6]
48319 8F
48435 8F
50648 2P[8]
50651 2P[8]
50652 2P[8]
50653 2P[8]
50655 2P[8]
50656 2P[8]
51336 2F[2]
51497 2F[2]
52138 3F[7]
52319 3F[7]
52369 3F[7]
52527 3F[7]
52529 3F[7]
52580 3F[9]
90109 WD[1]
90138 WD[1]
90143 WD[1]
90159 WD[1]
90171 WD[1]
90181 WD[1]
90183 WD[1]
90231 WD[1]
90241 WD[1]
90264 WD[1]
90274 WD[1]
90314 WD[1]
90371 WD[1]
90387 WD[1]
90420 WD[1]
90557 WD[1]
90584 WD[1]
90592 WD[1]
90599 WD[1]

1957 24B
42187 4MT[1]
42438 4MT[3]
42439 4MT[3]
42474 4MT[3]
42475 4MT[3]
42546 4MT[3]
42547 4MT[3]
42555 4MT[3]
42706 5MT[1]
42716 5MT[1]
42717 5MT[1]
42828 5MT[1]
42869 5MT[1]
42898 5MT[1]
44780 5MT[3]
44940 5MT[3]
44948 5MT[3]
44949 5MT[3]
45205 5MT[3]
45209 5MT[3]
45229 5MT[3]
47386 3F[6]
47575 3F[6]
47576 3F[6]
47577 3F[6]
47586 3F[6]
48435 8F
52095 3F[7]
52179 3F[7]
52319 3F[7]
52529 3F[7]
84010 2MT[2]
84011 2MT[2]
90109 WD[1]
90138 WD[1]
90143 WD[1]
90159 WD[1]
90171 WD[1]
90181 WD[1]
90183 WD[1]
90231 WD[1]
90241 WD[1]
90264 WD[1]
90274 WD[1]
90314 WD[1]
90371 WD[1]
90387 WD[1]
90420 WD[1]
90557 WD[1]
90592 WD[1]

1960 24B
42280 4MT[1]
42438 4MT[3]
42439 4MT[3]
42474 4MT[3]
42546 4MT[3]
42547 4MT[3]
42555 4MT[3]
42706 5MT[1]
42716 5MT[1]
42717 5MT[1]
42828 5MT[1]
42869 5MT[1]
42898 5MT[1]
44940 5MT[3]
44948 5MT[3]
44949 5MT[3]
45205 5MT[3]
45209 5MT[3]
45229 5MT[3]
47386 3F[6]
47575 3F[6]
47576 3F[6]
47577 3F[6]
47586 3F[6]
48435 8F
52179 3F[7]
52526 3F[7]
90109 WD[1]
90138 WD[1]
90143 WD[1]
90159 WD[1]
90171 WD[1]
90181 WD[1]
90183 WD[1]
90231 WD[1]
90241 WD[1]
90264 WD[1]
90274 WD[1]
90314 WD[1]
90371 WD[1]
90420 WD[1]
90557 WD[1]
90592 WD[1]

1963 24B
42110 4MT[1]
42295 4MT[1]
42546 4MT[3]
42547 4MT[3]
42703 5MT[1]
42706 5MT[1]
42716 5MT[1]
42717 5MT[1]
42869 5MT[1]
42898 5MT[1]
44940 5MT[3]
44948 5MT[3]
44949 5MT[3]
45068 5MT[3]
45205 5MT[3]
45209 5MT[3]
45216 5MT[3]
45229 5MT[3]
47201 3F[5]
47333 3F[6]
47660 3F[6]
90109 WD[1]
90138 WD[1]
90143 WD[1]
90159 WD[1]
90164 WD[1]
90171 WD[1]
90181 WD[1]
90219 WD[1]
90231 WD[1]
90241 WD[1]
90264 WD[1]
90266 WD[1]
90274 WD[1]
90295 WD[1]
90314 WD[1]
90327 WD[1]
90374 WD[1]
90398 WD[1]
90420 WD[1]
90557 WD[1]
90576 WD[1]
90584 WD[1]
90724 WD[1]

1966 10F
44870 5MT[3]
44909 5MT[3]
45196 5MT[3]
45205 5MT[3]
45215 5MT[3]
45216 5MT[3]
45234 5MT[3]
45397 5MT[3]
47383 3F[6]
47631 3F[6]
48024 8F
48053 8F
48062 8F
48081 8F
48154 8F
48218 8F
48257 8F
48323 8F
48348 8F
48386 8F
48435 8F
48448 8F
48451 8F
48506 8F
48668 8F

Rothbury

1948 RBY
65083 J21
67296 G5

1951 52F sub
65035 J21
67296 G5

Rowsley

1948 17D
40499 2P[2]
40520 2P[2]
41049 4P[1]
41875 1F[1]
42756 5MT[1]
42760 5MT[1]
42774 5MT[1]
42845 5MT[1]
42873 5MT[1]
42874 5MT[1]
42902 5MT[1]
43290 3F[3]
43338 3F[3]
43342 3F[3]
43918 4F[1]
43925 4F[1]
43929 4F[1]
44017 4F[1]
44018 4F[1]
44024 4F[1]
44050 4F[2]
44134 4F[2]
44163 4F[2]
44168 4F[2]
44172 4F[2]
44174 4F[2]
44209 4F[2]
44246 4F[2]
44249 4F[2]
44262 4F[2]
44327 4F[2]
44540 4F[2]
44564 4F[2]
44588 4F[2]
47457 3F[6]
47459 3F[6]
47460 3F[6]
47461 3F[6]
47679 3F[6]
58189 2F[9]
58197 2F[9]
58203 2F[9]
58219 2F[9]
58223 2F[9]
58224 2F[9]
58226 2F[9]
58228 2F[9]
58236 2F[9]
58254 2F[9]
58268 2F[9]
58850 2F[12]
58856 2F[12]
58862 2F[12]
3153 2F[8]

1951 17D
40499 2P[2]
40520 2P[2]
41049 4P[1]
41875 1F[1]
42760 5MT[1]
42768 5MT[1]
42873 5MT[1]
42874 5MT[1]
42902 5MT[1]
43273 3F[3]
43290 3F[3]
43342 3F[3]
43370 3F[3]
43881 4F[1]

43918 4F[1]
43925 4F[1]
43929 4F[1]
44017 4F[1]
44018 4F[1]
44024 4F[1]
44046 4F[2]
44050 4F[2]
44134 4F[2]
44163 4F[2]
44168 4F[2]
44172 4F[2]
44174 4F[2]
44209 4F[2]
44246 4F[2]
44262 4F[2]
44327 4F[2]
44429 4F[2]
44540 4F[2]
44564 4F[2]
44588 4F[2]
47447 3F[6]
47457 3F[6]
47459 3F[6]
47460 3F[6]
47461 3F[6]
47679 3F[6]
58189 2F[9]
58219 2F[9]
58224 2F[9]
58226 2F[9]
58228 2F[9]
58254 2F[9]
58850 2F[12]
58856 2F[12]
58860 2F[12]
58862 2F[12]

1954 17D
40520 2P[2]
40929 4P[1]
40931 4P[1]
41875 1F[1]
42760 5MT[1]
42768 5MT[1]
42792 5MT[1]
42873 5MT[1]
42874 5MT[1]
42902 5MT[1]
43273 3F[3]
43290 3F[3]
43342 3F[3]
43370 3F[3]
43400 3F[3]
43496 3F[3]
43658 3F[3]
43759 3F[3]
43776 3F[4]
43881 4F[1]
43918 4F[1]
43929 4F[1]
44017 4F[1]
44018 4F[1]
44028 4F[2]
44046 4F[2]
44050 4F[2]
44101 4F[2]
44134 4F[2]
44163 4F[2]
44168 4F[2]
44172 4F[2]
44262 4F[2]
44327 4F[2]
44429 4F[2]
44564 4F[2]
44565 4F[2]
44566 4F[2]
44588 4F[2]
47000 0F[3]
47447 3F[6]
47457 3F[6]
47459 3F[6]
47460 3F[6]
47461 3F[6]
47679 3F[6]
58189 2F[9]
58224 2F[9]
58228 2F[9]
58850 2F[12]
58856 2F[12]
58860 2F[12]
58862 2F[12]

1957 17D
40931 4P[1]
41077 4P[1]
41185 4P[1]
42760 5MT[1]
42768 5MT[1]
42792 5MT[1]
42873 5MT[1]
42874 5MT[1]
42902 5MT[1]
43290 3F[3]
43323 3F[3]
43342 3F[3]
43370 3F[3]
43400 3F[3]
43429 3F[3]
43496 3F[3]
43750 3F[2]
43759 3F[3]
43776 3F[4]
43982 4F[1]
44046 4F[2]
44050 4F[2]
44101 4F[2]
44134 4F[2]
44163 4F[2]
44168 4F[2]
44172 4F[2]
44241 4F[2]
44250 4F[2]
44262 4F[2]
44327 4F[2]
44429 4F[2]
44556 4F[2]
44564 4F[2]
44565 4F[2]
44566 4F[2]
44588 4F[2]
44602 4F[2]
47000 0F[3]
47447 3F[6]
47457 3F[6]
47459 3F[6]
47460 3F[6]
47461 3F[6]
47679 3F[6]
48192 8F
48432 8F
48654 8F
58189 2F[9]
58228 2F[9]
58850 2F[12]
58856 2F[12]
58860 2F[12]
68006 J94
68013 J94
68030 J94

1960 17C
42053 4MT[1]
42228 4MT[1]
42486 4MT[3]
43250 3F[3]
43342 3F[3]
43429 3F[3]
43496 3F[3]
43950 4F[1]
44042 4F[2]
44046 4F[2]
44101 4F[2]
44134 4F[2]
44163 4F[2]
44172 4F[2]
44262 4F[2]
44327 4F[2]
44429 4F[2]
44556 4F[2]
44564 4F[2]
44565 4F[2]
44566 4F[2]
44588 4F[2]
44602 4F[2]
47007 0F[3]
47447 3F[6]
47457 3F[6]
47459 3F[6]
47460 3F[6]
47461 3F[6]
47679 3F[6]
48008 8F
48081 8F
48364 8F
48654 8F
58137 2F[8]
58228 2F[9]
58850 2F[12]
68006 J94
68012 J94
68013 J94
68030 J94
68034 J94
73135 5MT
73136 5MT
73138 5MT
73139 5MT
73140 5MT
73141 5MT
73142 5MT
73143 5MT
73144 5MT
92008 9F
92009 9F
92048 9F
92049 9F
92050 9F
92051 9F

1963 17C
42053 4MT[1]
42156 4MT[1]
42225 4MT[1]
42228 4MT[1]
42230 4MT[1]
42284 4MT[1]
42291 4MT[1]
42486 4MT[3]
42595 4MT[3]
42610 4MT[3]
44042 4F[2]
44046 4F[2]
44080 4F[2]
44101 4F[2]
44134 4F[2]
44172 4F[2]
44262 4F[2]
44327 4F[2]
44334 4F[2]
44421 4F[2]
44428 4F[2]
44429 4F[2]
44556 4F[2]
44588 4F[2]
47007 0F[3]
47447 3F[6]
47459 3F[6]
47460 3F[6]
47461 3F[6]
47629 3F[6]
47679 3F[6]
48005 8F
48081 8F
48145 8F
48364 8F
48654 8F
68006 J94
68012 J94
68013 J94
68068 J94
68079 J94
73135 5MT
73136 5MT
73137 5MT
73138 5MT
73139 5MT
73140 5MT
73141 5MT
73142 5MT
73143 5MT
73144 5MT
92018 9F
92048 9F
92049 9F
92050 9F
92051 9F
92056 9F
92113 9F
92114 9F

Royston

1948 20C
40169 3MT[2]
40181 3MT[2]
40362 2P[2]
40444 2P[2]
40480 2P[2]
40514 2P[2]
43233 3F[3]
43250 3F[3]
43332 3F[3]
43446 3F[3]
43509 3F[3]
43553 3F[3]
43789 3F[4]
43942 4F[1]
44003 4F[1]
44141 4F[2]
44161 4F[2]
44446 4F[2]
47421 3F[6]
47448 3F[6]
47462 3F[6]
47581 3F[6]
47634 3F[6]
48062 8F
48078 8F
48079 8F
48080 8F
48085 8F
48095 8F
48103 8F
48113 8F
48161 8F
48162 8F
48169 8F
48376 8F
48377 8F
48412 8F
48419 8F
48431 8F
48439 8F
48443 8F
48532 8F
48540 8F
48542 8F
48545 8F
48546 8F
48547 8F
48700 8F
52108 3F[7]
52252 3F[7]
52258 3F[7]
52559 3F[9]
58052 1P[6]
58055 1P[6]
58066 1P[6]
58075 1P[6]
58134 2F[8]
58156 2F[8]
58207 2F[9]
58237 2F[8]
58265 2F[9]
3050 2F[9]

1951 20C
40074 3MT[2]
40147 3MT[2]
40181 3MT[2]
40193 3MT[2]
40444 2P[2]
40521 2P[2]
41273 2MT[1]
41274 2MT[1]
42142 4MT[1]
42143 4MT[1]
42145 4MT[1]
43233 3F[3]
43250 3F[3]
43332 3F[3]
43446 3F[3]
43553 3F[3]
43765 3F[4]
43789 3F[4]
43942 4F[1]
44003 4F[1]
44141 4F[1]
44161 4F[2]
44241 4F[2]
44290 4F[2]
44446 4F[2]
47421 3F[6]
47448 3F[6]
47462 3F[6]
47581 3F[6]
47634 3F[6]
48062 8F
48078 8F
48080 8F
48093 8F
48095 8F
48103 8F
48113 8F
48162 8F
48169 8F
48337 8F
48377 8F
48412 8F
48419 8F
48431 8F
48439 8F
48443 8F
48532 8F
48540 8F
48542 8F
52095 3F[7]
52108 3F[7]
52252 3F[7]
52258 3F[7]
52559 3F[9]
58052 1P[6]
58066 1P[6]
58075 1P[6]
58154 2F[8]
58156 2F[8]
58188 2F[9]
58237 2F[8]
58260 2F[9]
58265 2F[9]

1954 20C
40139 3MT[2]
40140 3MT[2]
40181 3MT[2]
40193 3MT[2]
40521 2P[2]
41273 2MT[1]
41274 2MT[1]
43233 3F[3]
43250 3F[3]
43267 3F[3]
43321 3F[3]
43332 3F[3]
43446 3F[3]
43476 3F[3]
43553 3F[3]
43705 3F[3]
43789 3F[4]
43906 4F[1]
43942 4F[1]
44003 4F[1]
44141 4F[2]
44290 4F[2]
44446 4F[2]
44501 4F[2]
47421 3F[6]
47438 3F[6]
47448 3F[6]
47462 3F[6]
47581 3F[6]
47634 3F[6]
48053 8F
48078 8F
48080 8F
48093 8F
48095 8F
48103 8F
48113 8F
48162 8F
48169 8F
48337 8F
48431 8F
48436 8F
48439 8F
48443 8F
48459 8F
48466 8F
48469 8F
48473 8F
48532 8F
48540 8F
48542 8F
48608 8F
48664 8F
48689 8F
48710 8F
58040 1P[6]
58154 2F[8]
58188 2F[9]
58212 2F[9]
58260 2F[9]
58265 2F[9]
84009 2MT[2]

1957 55D
40082 3MT[2]
40181 3MT[2]
40520 2P[2]
41274 2MT[1]
41281 2MT[1]
41282 2MT[1]
43233 3F[3]
43250 3F[3]
43267 3F[3]
43446 3F[3]
43476 3F[3]
43705 3F[3]
43789 3F[4]
43906 4F[1]
43914 4F[1]
43942 4F[1]
43983 4F[1]
44003 4F[1]
44107 4F[2]
44141 4F[2]
44274 4F[2]
44290 4F[2]
44446 4F[2]
44550 4F[2]
44582 4F[2]
47421 3F[6]
47438 3F[6]
47448 3F[6]
47462 3F[6]
47581 3F[6]
47634 3F[6]
48070 8F
48078 8F
48080 8F
48093 8F
48113 8F
48146 8F
48162 8F
48169 8F
48222 8F
48265 8F
48281 8F
48337 8F
48439 8F
48466 8F
48469 8F
48473 8F
48532 8F
48540 8F
48542 8F
48608 8F
48664 8F
48670 8F
48689 8F
48710 8F
58066 1P[6]
58188 2F[9]
58216 2F[9]
58260 2F[9]
84009 2MT[2]

1960 55D
40082 3MT[2]
40148 3MT[2]
40181 3MT[2]
40581 2P[3]
42408 4MT[2]
43267 3F[3]
43446 3F[3]
43906 4F[1]
43914 4F[1]
43942 4F[1]
43983 4F[1]
44141 4F[2]
44274 4F[2]
44290 4F[2]
44446 4F[2]
44550 4F[2]
44582 4F[2]
48070 8F
48078 8F
48093 8F
48113 8F
48123 8F
48130 8F
48146 8F
48162 8F
48169 8F
48222 8F
48281 8F
48337 8F
48439 8F
48466 8F
48469 8F
48473 8F
48532 8F
48537 8F
48540 8F
48542 8F
48608 8F
48664 8F
48670 8F
48689 8F
48710 8F
58197 2F[9]
58260 2F[9]
90243 WD[1]
90336 WD[1]
90488 WD[1]
90605 WD[1]
90611 WD[1]

1963 55D
42762 5MT[1]
42770 5MT[1]
42795 5MT[1]
43906 4F[1]
43942 4F[1]
43983 4F[1]
44098 4F[2]
44099 4F[2]
44274 4F[2]
44290 4F[2]
44446 4F[2]
44582 4F[2]
48067 8F
48070 8F
48076 8F
48093 8F
48113 8F
48123 8F
48130 8F
48146 8F
48159 8F
48162 8F
48169 8F
48222 8F
48281 8F
48337 8F
48439 8F
48443 8F
48466 8F
48473 8F
48537 8F
48540 8F
48670 8F
48710 8F
73166 5MT
73170 5MT
73171 5MT
90127 WD[1]
90243 WD[1]
90254 WD[1]
90336 WD[1]
90377 WD[1]
90395 WD[1]
90407 WD[1]
90488 WD[1]
90511 WD[1]
90605 WD[1]
90610 WD[1]
90611 WD[1]
90650 WD[1]
90684 WD[1]

1966 55D
43076 4MT[5]
43077 4MT[5]
43078 4MT[5]
43079 4MT[5]
44912 5MT[3]
45207 5MT[3]
45219 5MT[3]
48067 8F
48070 8F
48075 8F
48113 8F
48123 8F
48159 8F
48162 8F
48169 8F
48222 8F
48281 8F
48337 8F
48352 8F
48439 8F
48443 8F
48466 8F
48540 8F
48710 8F
90318 WD[1]
90337 WD[1]
90377 WD[1]
90503 WD[1]
90605 WD[1]
90645 WD[1]
90650 WD[1]

Rugby

1948 2A
40003 3MT[1]
40052 3MT[1]
40144 3MT[2]
40425 2P[2]
40450 2P[2]
40515 2P[2]
40522 2P[2]
40655 2P[3]
41090 4P[1]
41105 4P[1]
41152 4P[1]
41165 4P[1]
41174 4P[1]
42487 4MT[3]
42576 4MT[3]
42577 4MT[3]
44354 4F[2]
44392 4F[2]
44395 4F[2]
44455 4F[2]
44456 4F[2]
44511 4F[2]
44831 5MT[3]
44866 5MT[3]
44867 5MT[3]
44909 5MT[3]
44910 5MT[3]
44997 5MT[3]
44998 5MT[3]
44999 5MT[3]
45000 5MT[3]
45002 5MT[3]
45003 5MT[3]
45004 5MT[3]
45020 5MT[3]
45033 5MT[3]
45034 5MT[3]
45052 5MT[3]
45057 5MT[3]
45250 5MT[3]
45372 5MT[3]
45375 5MT[3]
45379 5MT[3]
45391 5MT[3]
45394 5MT[3]
45404 5MT[3]
45419 5MT[3]
45430 5MT[3]
45441 5MT[3]
45448 5MT[3]
47360 3F[6]
47378 3F[6]
47379 3F[6]
47677 3F[6]
48309 8F
48649 8F
48659 8F
48901 7F[2]
48926 7F[2]
49013 6F[2]
49049 7F[2]
49061 7F[2]
49069 7F[2]
49070 7F[2]
49107 6F[2]
49133 7F[2]
49137 7F[2]
49162 6F[2]
49200 7F[2]
49229 7F[2]
49319 7F[2]
49337 6F[2]
49397 7F[3]
49399 7F[3]
49404 7F[3]
49408 7F[3]
49410 7F[3]
49413 7F[3]
49433 7F[3]
49434 7F[3]
49441 7F[3]
49446 7F[3]
49452 7F[3]
58082 1P[6]
58083 1P[6]
58119 2F[8]
58152 2F[8]
58181 2F[8]
58269 2F[9]

1951 2A
41090 4P[1]
41105 4P[1]
41122 4P[1]
41152 4P[1]
41165 4P[1]
41172 4P[1]
41174 4P[1]
41278 2MT[1]
42487 4MT[3]
42541 4MT[3]
42576 4MT[3]
42577 4MT[3]
42585 4MT[3]
42615 4MT[3]
42673 4MT[1]
44058 4F[2]
44354 4F[2]
44395 4F[2]
44456 4F[2]
44710 5MT[3]
44711 5MT[3]
44712 5MT[3]
44713 5MT[3]
44714 5MT[3]
44715 5MT[3]
44716 5MT[3]
44831 5MT[3]
44833 5MT[3]
44836 5MT[3]
44860 5MT[3]
44862 5MT[3]
44863 5MT[3]
44866 5MT[3]
44867 5MT[3]
44870 5MT[3]
44909 5MT[3]
44910 5MT[3]
44915 5MT[3]
45000 5MT[3]
45002 5MT[3]
45003 5MT[3]
45020 5MT[3]
45033 5MT[3]
45034 5MT[3]
45150 5MT[3]
45187 5MT[3]
45250 5MT[3]
45282 5MT[3]
45372 5MT[3]
45375 5MT[3]
45379 5MT[3]
45391 5MT[3]
45394 5MT[3]
45404 5MT[3]
45419 5MT[3]
45429 5MT[3]
45430 5MT[3]
45431 5MT[3]
45441 5MT[3]
45493 5MT[3]
47360 3F[6]
47378 3F[6]
47379 3F[6]
47677 3F[6]
48039 8F
48085 8F
48165 8F
48173 8F
48320 8F
48343 8F
48372 8F
48398 8F
48427 8F
48437 8F
48479 8F
48505 8F
48509 8F
48559 8F
48686 8F
48729 8F
48736 8F
49401 7F[3]
49411 7F[3]
49413 7F[3]
49415 7F[3]
49416 7F[3]
49423 7F[3]
49425 7F[3]
49431 7F[3]
49433 7F[3]
49447 7F[3]
49452 7F[3]
58083 1P[6]
58181 2F[8]
58269 2F[9]
58280 2F[9]

1954 2A
41105 4P[1]
41113 4P[1]
41122 4P[1]
41162 4P[1]
41165 4P[1]
41172 4P[1]
41174 4P[1]
41278 2MT[1]
42446 4MT[3]
42487 4MT[3]
42541 4MT[3]
42576 4MT[3]
42577 4MT[3]
42585 4MT[3]
42615 4MT[3]
42673 4MT[1]
44064 4F[2]
44072 4F[2]
44395 4F[2]
44711 5MT[3]
44712 5MT[3]
44713 5MT[3]
44714 5MT[3]
44715 5MT[3]
44716 5MT[3]
44831 5MT[3]
44833 5MT[3]
44836 5MT[3]
44837 5MT[3]
44860 5MT[3]
44862 5MT[3]
44863 5MT[3]
44866 5MT[3]
44867 5MT[3]
44870 5MT[3]
44909 5MT[3]
44915 5MT[3]
45000 5MT[3]
45002 5MT[3]
45034 5MT[3]
45050 5MT[3]
45150 5MT[3]
45187 5MT[3]
45282 5MT[3]
45325 5MT[3]
45371 5MT[3]
45372 5MT[3]
45375 5MT[3]
45379 5MT[3]
45391 5MT[3]
45394 5MT[3]
45403 5MT[3]
45419 5MT[3]
45429 5MT[3]
45430 5MT[3]
45431 5MT[3]
45441 5MT[3]
45493 5MT[3]
46604 1P[1]
47269 3F[6]
47379 3F[6]
47622 3F[6]
47677 3F[6]
48085 8F
48165 8F
48173 8F
48248 8F
48398 8F
48427 8F
48437 8F
48509 8F
48559 8F
48686 8F
48729 8F
48757 8F
48914 7F[2]
49114 7F[2]
49397 7F[3]
49411 7F[3]
49413 7F[3]
49417 7F[3]
49431 7F[3]
49433 7F[3]
49444 7F[3]
49447 7F[3]
49452 7F[3]
58181 2F[8]
58218 2F[9]
58269 2F[9]
58290 2F[9]
58308 2F[9]

1957 2A
40012 3MT[1]
40017 3MT[1]
40045 3MT[1]
40056 3MT[1]
40057 3MT[1]
40059 3MT[1]
40060 3MT[1]
40061 3MT[1]
41105 4P[1]
41113 4P[1]
41122 4P[1]
41162 4P[1]
41165 4P[1]
41172 4P[1]
41214 2MT[1]
41278 2MT[1]
42061 4MT[1]
42062 4MT[1]
42489 4MT[3]
42541 4MT[3]
42573 4MT[3]
42576 4MT[3]
42577 4MT[3]
42585 4MT[3]
42615 4MT[3]
42669 4MT[3]
42673 4MT[1]
44064 4F[2]
44395 4F[2]
44711 5MT[3]
44712 5MT[3]
44715 5MT[3]
44716 5MT[3]
44831 5MT[3]
44833 5MT[3]
44836 5MT[3]
44837 5MT[3]
44860 5MT[3]
44862 5MT[3]
44863 5MT[3]
44866 5MT[3]
44867 5MT[3]
44870 5MT[3]
44909 5MT[3]
44915 5MT[3]
45419 5MT[3]
45429 5MT[3]
45493 5MT[3]
47269 3F[6]
47677 3F[6]
48085 8F
48173 8F
48427 8F
48437 8F
48559 8F
48757 8F
48914 7F[2]
49049 7F[2]
49114 7F[2]
49245 7F[2]
49249 7F[2]
49377 7F[2]
49397 7F[3]
49405 7F[3]
49413 7F[3]
49417 7F[3]
49433 7F[3]
49435 7F[3]
49452 7F[3]
58181 2F[8]
58218 2F[9]
58308 2F[9]

1960 2A
41162 4P[1]
41214 2MT[1]
41227 2MT[1]
42061 4MT[1]
42062 4MT[1]
42541 4MT[3]
42573 4MT[3]
42577 4MT[3]
42669 4MT[3]
42777 5MT[1]
42782 5MT[1]
42787 5MT[1]
44711 5MT[3]
44715 5MT[3]
44716 5MT[3]
44771 5MT[3]
44831 5MT[3]
44833 5MT[3]
44836 5MT[3]
44860 5MT[3]
44862 5MT[3]
44863 5MT[3]
44866 5MT[3]
44867 5MT[3]
44870 5MT[3]
44909 5MT[3]
44915 5MT[3]
44938 5MT[3]
45184 5MT[3]
45493 5MT[3]
45533 6P5F[1]
45537 6P5F[1]
45541 6P5F[1]
46420 2MT[2]
46445 2MT[2]
46446 2MT[2]
46472 2MT[2]
48012 8F
48018 8F
48035 8F
48085 8F
48120 8F
48131 8F
48136 8F
48173 8F
48203 8F
48252 8F
48345 8F
48365 8F
48411 8F
48423 8F
48427 8F
48437 8F
48526 8F
48559 8F
48646 8F
48668 8F
48757 8F
58218 2F[9]
58221 2F[9]

1963 2A
42062 4MT[1]
42079 4MT[1]
42103 4MT[1]
42104 4MT[1]
44711 5MT[3]
44712 5MT[3]
44715 5MT[3]
44716 5MT[3]
44771 5MT[3]
44831 5MT[3]
44833 5MT[3]
44836 5MT[3]
44860 5MT[3]
44862 5MT[3]
44863 5MT[3]
44866 5MT[3]
44870 5MT[3]
44897 5MT[3]
44909 5MT[3]
44915 5MT[3]
44938 5MT[3]
45056 5MT[3]
45113 5MT[3]
45130 5MT[3]
45184 5MT[3]
45324 5MT[3]
45419 5MT[3]
45493 5MT[3]
45670 6P5F[2]
45672 6P5F[2]
45684 6P5F[2]
45704 6P5F[2]
45733 6P5F[2]
46442 2MT[2]
46445 2MT[2]
46446 2MT[2]
48012 8F
48018 8F
48035 8F
48074 8F
48120 8F
48122 8F
48173 8F
48287 8F
48345 8F
48365 8F
48411 8F
48526 8F
48559 8F
48754 8F
70017 7P6F
70022 7P6F
70023 7P6F
70024 7P6F

Rugby Testing Station

1951
61353 B1
61699 B13
90764 WD[2]
10897 2P[8]

1954
35022 MN
10897 2P[8]

1957
45722 6P5F[2]

1960
73031 5MT

Ryde IOW

1948 RYD
W14 O2
W15 O2
W16 O2
W17 O2
W18 O2
W19 O2
W20 O2
W21 O2
W22 O2
W23 O2
W24 O2

1951 71F
W14 O2
W15 O2
W16 O2
W17 O2
W18 O2
W19 O2
W20 O2
W21 O2
W22 O2
W23 O2
W24 O2
W25 O2

1954 71F
W14 O2
W15 O2
W16 O2
W17 O2
W18 O2
W19 O2
W20 O2
W21 O2
W22 O2
W23 O2
W24 O2
W25 O2

1957 70H
W14 O2
W16 O2
W17 O2
W18 O2
W20 O2
W21 O2
W22 O2
W24 O2
W25 O2

1960 70H
W4 E1[2]
W14 O2
W16 O2
W17 O2
W18 O2
W20 O2
W21 O2
W22 O2
W24 O2
W25 O2
W26 O2
W27 O2
W28 O2
W29 O2
W30 O2
W31 O2
W32 O2
W33 O2
W35 O2
W36 O2

1963 70H
W14 O2
W16 O2
W17 O2
W18 O2
W20 O2
W21 O2
W22 O2
W24 O2
W26 O2
W27 O2
W28 O2
W29 O2
W30 O2
W31 O2
W32 O2
W33 O2
W35 O2
W36 O2

1966 70H
W14 O2
W16 O2
W17 O2
W20 O2
W21 O2
W22 O2
W24 O2
W26 O2
W27 O2
W28 O2
W29 O2
W31 O2
W33 O2
W35 O2

St. Albans

1948 14C
40024 3MT[1]
40034 3MT[1]
40039 3MT[1]
40091 3MT[2]
41854 1F[1]
42300 4MT[2]
42302 4MT[2]
42335 4MT[2]
42374 4MT[2]
42479 4MT[3]
42681 4MT[1]
42684 4MT[1]
43245 3F[3]
43801 3F[4]
47261 3F[6]

1951 14C
40022 3MT[1]
40024 3MT[1]
40026 3MT[1]
40039 3MT[1]
41854 1F[1]
42132 4MT[1]
42134 4MT[1]
42160 4MT[1]
42161 4MT[1]
42300 4MT[2]
42302 4MT[2]
42334 4MT[2]
42335 4MT[2]
43245 3F[3]
43782 3F[4]
43801 3F[4]
47261 3F[6]

1954 14C
40022 3MT[1]
40024 3MT[1]
40026 3MT[1]
40039 3MT[1]
41672 1F[1]
42132 4MT[1]
42134 4MT[1]
42161 4MT[1]
42300 4MT[2]
42302 4MT[2]
42334 4MT[2]
42335 4MT[2]
42341 4MT[2]
43245 3F[3]
43565 3F[3]
43782 3F[4]
47261 3F[6]

1957 14C
40022 3MT[1]
40024 3MT[1]
40026 3MT[1]
40037 3MT[1]

40039 3MT[1]
42133 4MT[1]
42134 4MT[1]
42159 4MT[1]
42300 4MT[2]
42302 4MT[2]
42335 4MT[2]
42341 4MT[2]
42680 4MT[1]
42686 4MT[1]
43119 4MT[5]
43245 3F[3]
43565 3F[3]
47261 3F[6]
47554 3F[6]

1960 14C
40022 3MT[1]
40024 3MT[1]
40026 3MT[1]
40037 3MT[1]
42133 4MT[1]
42134 4MT[1]
42159 4MT[1]
42181 4MT[1]
42300 4MT[2]
42302 4MT[2]
42587 4MT[3]
42680 4MT[1]
42686 4MT[1]
43119 4MT[5]
43846 4F[1]
43971 4F[1]
44043 4F[2]
47261 3F[6]
47554 3F[6]

St. Blazey

1948 SBZ
1900 1854
1930 1901
2050 2021
2181 2181
2182 2181
2780 2721
4215 4200
4298 4200
4503 4500
4505 4500
4516 4500
4529 4500
4552 4500
4559 4500
4565 4500
4568 4500
4570 4500
4598 4575
4940 4900
5140 5101
5158 5101
5502 4575
5519 4575
5531 4575
5926 4900
6330 4300
6356 4300
6420 6400
7709 5700
7715 5700
8783 5700
9655 5700

1951 83E
1419 1400
1626 1600
2050 2021
2182 2181
3635 5700
4215 4200
4298 4200
4503 4500
4505 4500
4516 4500
4517 4500
4526 4500
4529 4500
4552 4500
4559 4500
4565 4500
4568 4500
4569 4500
4570 4500
4598 4575
4940 4900
5502 4575
5519 4575
5926 4900
6330 4300
6356 4300
7446 7400
7709 5700
7715 5700
8783 5700
9655 5700
9755 5700

1954 83E
1419 1400
1624 1600
2182 2181
3635 5700
3705 5700
4167 5101
4206 4200
4247 4200
4505 4500
4508 4500
4523 4500
4526 4500
4552 4500
4559 4500
4565 4500
4568 4500
4569 4500
4584 4575
4585 4575
5193 5101
5502 4575
5519 4575
5521 4575
5926 4900
6300 4300
6305 4300
6397 4300
7446 7400
7709 5700
7715 5700
7816 7800
8733 5700
9655 5700
9673 5700
9755 5700

1957 83E
1419 1400
1624 1600
1664 1600
3635 5700
3705 5700
4167 5101
4206 4200
4247 4200
4526 4500
4552 4500
4559 4500
4565 4500
4569 4500
4584 4575
4585 4575
5378 4300
5502 4575
5519 4575
5521 4575
5557 4575
5926 4900
6305 4300
6397 4300
6942 4900
7446 7400
7709 5700
7715 5700
7816 7800
8702 5700
8733 5700
9655 5700
9673 5700
9755 5700

1960 83E
1419 1400
1624 1600
1664 1600
3635 5700
3705 5700
4167 5101
4294 4200
4547 4500
4552 4500
4559 4500
4565 4500
4569 4500
4906 4900
5193 5101
5523 4575
5539 4575
5551 4575
5557 4575
6814 6800
6931 4900
7446 7400
7709 5700
7715 5700
7806 7800
7816 7800
8409 9400
8702 5700
8719 5700
8733 5700
8737 5700
9655 5700
9673 5700
9755 5700

1963 83E
5518 4575
5531 4575

St. Leonards

1948 STL
30900 V
30901 V
30902 V
30903 V
30904 V
30905 V
30906 V
30907 V
30908 V
30909 V
30910 V
31037 C
31038 C
31041 O1
31075 D
31174 R1[1]
31335 R1[1]
31432 O1
31737 D
31738 D
31740 D
31744 D
31766 L
31767 L
31768 L
31822 N1
31876 N1
31877 N1
32371 D3
32379 D3
32383 D3
32394 D3

1951 74E
30900 V
30901 V
30902 V
30903 V
30904 V
30905 V
30906 V
30907 V
30908 V
30909 V
30910 V
30922 V
30923 V
30935 V
31037 C
31038 C
31164 H
31174 R1[1]
31279 H
31310 H
31319 H
31328 H
31335 R1[1]
31493 D
31587 E
31766 L
31768 L
31769 L
32378 D3
32388 D3
32390 D3
32391 D3
33039 Q1
33040 Q1

1954 74E
30900 V
30901 V
30902 V
30903 V
30904 V
30905 V
30906 V
30907 V
30908 V
30909 V
30910 V
31161 H
31162 H
31174 R1[1]
31269 H
31274 H
31279 H
31295 H
31335 R1[1]
31493 D
31519 H
31721 C
31767 L
31768 L
31769 L
33039 Q1
33040 Q1

1957 74E
30900 V
30901 V
30902 V
30903 V
30904 V
30905 V
30906 V
30907 V
30908 V
30909 V
30910 V
30920 V
30923 V
30930 V
31010 R1[1]
31162 H
31174 R1[1]
31269 H
31274 H
31279 H
31295 H
31519 H
31520 H
32636 A1X
32670 A1X
32678 A1X
33039 Q1
33040 Q1

St. Margarets

1948 STM
61823 K3
61855 K3
61857 K3
61876 K3
61879 K3
61885 K3
61900 K3
61909 K3
61911 K3
61916 K3
61924 K3
61931 K3
61933 K3
61955 K3
61968 K3
61983 K3
61988 K3
61990 K3
61991 K3
61992 K3
62400 D29
62402 D29
62404 D29
62405 D29
62420 D30
62421 D30
62424 D30
62435 D30
62443 D32
62444 D32
62445 D32
62450 D32
62451 D32
62453 D32
62454 D32
62471 D34
62483 D34
62484 D34
62487 D34
62488 D34
62490 D34
62494 D34
62495 D34
62702 D49
62715 D49
63038 O7
63063 O7
63089 O7
63090 O7
63115 O7
63126 O7
63147 O7
63148 O7
63172 O7
63175 O7
63180 O7
64462 J35
64479 J35
64486 J35
64489 J35
64492 J35
64515 J35
64517 J35
64518 J35
64519 J35
64524 J35
64527 J35
64532 J35
64533 J35
64535 J35
64538 J37
64543 J37
64547 J37
64552 J37
64555 J37
64557 J37
64562 J37
64566 J37
64572 J37
64576 J37
64577 J37
64582 J37
64586 J37
64592 J37
64594 J37
64595 J37
64599 J37
64603 J37
64605 J37
64606 J37
64607 J37
64608 J37
64614 J37
64624 J37
64625 J37
64636 J37
64637 J37
65217 J36
65224 J36
65251 J36
65258 J36
65267 J36
65286 J36
65288 J36
65292 J36
65305 J36
65310 J36
65311 J36
65316 J36
65334 J36
65617 J24
65623 J24
65625 J24
65906 J38
65912 J38
65914 J38
65915 J38
65918 J38
65919 J38
65920 J38
65927 J38
65929 J38
67093 F7
67094 F7
67492 C16
67493 C16
67494 C16
67495 C16
67496 C16
67497 C16
67605 V1
67606 V1
67607 V1
67608 V1
67609 V1
67617 V1
67624 V1
67629 V1
67630 V1
67649 V1
67659 V1
67666 V1
67670 V1
68092 Y9
68093 Y9
68095 Y9
68096 Y9
68097 Y9
68098 Y9
68099 Y9
68102 Y9
68105 Y9
68111 Y9
68115 Y9
68119 Y9
68122 Y9
68320 J88
68325 J88
68334 J88
68338 J88
68340 J88
68348 J88
68352 J88
68448 J83
68449 J83
68450 J83
68454 J83
68463 J83
68464 J83
68470 J83
68472 J83
68474 J83
68477 J83
68492 J67
68505 J69
68511 J67
68525 J69
68562 J69
68568 J69
68623 J69
68952 J50
69130 N15
69133 N15
69134 N15
69140 N15
69144 N15
69146 N15
69147 N15
69148 N15
69149 N15
69152 N15
69167 N15
69168 N15
69172 N15
69173 N15
69175 N15
69186 N15
69187 N15
69219 N15
90138 WD[1]
90183 WD[1]
90227 WD[1]
90258 WD[1]
90289 WD[1]
90291 WD[1]
90295 WD[1]
90371 WD[1]
90374 WD[1]
90376 WD[1]
90387 WD[1]
90555 WD[1]
90592 WD[1]
90626 WD[1]

1951 64A
46460 2MT[2]
46461 2MT[2]
46462 2MT[2]
46464 2MT[2]
47162 2F[1]
60825 V2
60836 V2
60848 V2
60894 V2
60953 V2
60980 V2
61002 B1
61061 B1
61067 B1
61242 B1
61277 B1
61341 B1
61354 B1
61355 B1
61356 B1
61357 B1
61358 B1
61359 B1
61823 K3
61855 K3
61857 K3
61876 K3
61878 K3
61879 K3
61881 K3
61885 K3
61897 K3
61900 K3
61909 K3
61911 K3
61916 K3
61924 K3
61928 K3
61931 K3
61933 K3
61955 K3
61968 K3
61983 K3
61988 K3
61990 K3
61991 K3
61992 K3
62421 D30
62424 D30
62435 D30
62451 D32
62471 D34
62483 D34
62484 D34
62487 D34
62488 D34
62490 D34
62494 D34
62702 D49
62711 D49
62712 D49
62715 D49
62721 D49
64462 J35
64479 J35
64486 J35
64489 J35
64492 J35
64506 J35
64512 J35
64515 J35
64517 J35
64518 J35
64519 J35
64523 J35
64524 J35
64527 J35
64532 J35
64533 J35
64535 J35
64538 J37
64543 J37
64547 J37
64552 J37
64555 J37
64557 J37
64562 J37
64566 J37
64572 J37
64576 J37
64577 J37
64582 J37
64586 J37
64594 J37
64595 J37
64599 J37
64603 J37
64605 J37
64606 J37
64607 J37
64608 J37
64614 J37
64624 J37
64625 J37
64636 J37
64637 J37
64794 J39
64946 J39
64963 J39
64986 J39
65224 J36
65251 J36
65258 J36
65267 J36
65286 J36
65288 J36
65292 J36
65305 J36
65310 J36
65311 J36
65316 J36
65334 J36
65617 J24
65623 J24
65906 J38
65912 J38
65914 J38
65915 J38
65918 J38
65919 J38
65920 J38
65927 J38
65929 J38
67492 C16
67494 C16
67495 C16
67496 C16
67497 C16
67605 V1
67606 V1
67607 V1
67608 V1
67609 V1
67617 V1
67624 V1
67629 V1
67630 V1
67649 V1
67659 V1
67666 V1
67668 V1
67670 V1
68092 Y9
68093 Y9
68095 Y9
68096 Y9
68097 Y9
68098 Y9
68099 Y9
68102 Y9
68105 Y9
68111 Y9
68115 Y9
68119 Y9
68122 Y9
68320 J88
68325 J88
68334 J88
68338 J88
68340 J88
68342 J88
68348 J88
68352 J88
68448 J83
68449 J83
68450 J83
68454 J83
68463 J83
68464 J83
68469 J83
68472 J83
68474 J83
68477 J83
68492 J67
68505 J69
68511 J67
68525 J69
68562 J69
68623 J69
68952 J50
69130 N15
69133 N15
69134 N15
69140 N15
69141 N15
69144 N15
69146 N15
69147 N15
69148 N15
69149 N15
69152 N15
69167 N15
69168 N15
69172 N15
69173 N15
69175 N15
69186 N15
69219 N15
90038 WD[1]
90049 WD[1]
90071 WD[1]
90114 WD[1]
90248 WD[1]
90289 WD[1]
90291 WD[1]
90306 WD[1]
90376 WD[1]
90436 WD[1]
90468 WD[1]
90469 WD[1]
90493 WD[1]
90496 WD[1]
90555 WD[1]
90569 WD[1]

1954 64A
42717 5MT[1]
42865 5MT[1]
42901 5MT[1]
44820 5MT[3]
45486 5MT[3]
45487 5MT[3]
46461 2MT[2]
46462 2MT[2]
47162 2F[1]
60813 V2
60818 V2
60823 V2
60825 V2
60836 V2
60840 V2
60848 V2
60873 V2
60882 V2
60892 V2
60894 V2
60900 V2
60922 V2
60933 V2
60953 V2
60965 V2
60980 V2
61029 B1
61099 B1
61108 B1
61184 B1
61191 B1
61246 B1
61330 B1
61332 B1
61333 B1
61341 B1
61354 B1
61355 B1
61356 B1
61357 B1
61358 B1
61359 B1
61397 B1
61398 B1
61407 B1
61823 K3
61855 K3
61857 K3
61876 K3
61878 K3
61879 K3
61881 K3
61885 K3
61897 K3
61900 K3
61909 K3
61911 K3
61924 K3
61928 K3
61931 K3
61933 K3
61955 K3
61968 K3
61983 K3
61988 K3
61990 K3
61991 K3
61992 K3
62421 D30
62424 D30
62471 D34
62483 D34
62487 D34
62488 D34
62490 D34
62494 D34
62711 D49
62712 D49
62715 D49
62718 D49
62721 D49
64462 J35
64479 J35
64486 J35
64489 J35
64492 J35
64506 J35
64515 J35
64517 J35
64518 J35
64519 J35
64523 J35
64524 J35
64527 J35
64532 J35
64533 J35
64535 J35
64538 J37
64543 J37
64547 J37
64552 J37
64555 J37
64557 J37
64562 J37
64566 J37
64572 J37
64576 J37
64577 J37
64582 J37
64586 J37
64590 J37
64594 J37
64595 J37
64597 J37
64599 J37
64601 J37
64603 J37
64605 J37
64606 J37
64607 J37
64608 J37
64613 J37
64614 J37
64624 J37
64625 J37
64637 J37
64946 J39
64963 J39
64986 J39
65224 J36
65242 J36
65251 J36
65258 J36
65267 J36
65288 J36
65305 J36
65310 J36
65311 J36
65327 J36
65329 J36
65334 J36
65906 J38
65912 J38
65914 J38
65915 J38
65918 J38
65919 J38
65920 J38
65927 J38
65929 J38
67492 C16
67495 C16
67497 C16
67605 V3
67606 V3
67607 V1
67608 V1
67609 V3
67617 V1
67624 V3
67629 V1
67630 V1
67649 V1
67659 V1
67666 V1
67668 V1
67670 V1
68093 Y9
68095 Y9
68096 Y9
68097 Y9
68098 Y9
68099 Y9
68102 Y9
68103 Y9
68105 Y9
68115 Y9
68119 Y9
68122 Y9
68320 J88
68325 J88
68334 J88
68338 J88
68340 J88
68342 J88
68348 J88
68352 J88
68448 J83
68449 J83
68450 J83
68454 J83
68463 J83
68464 J83
68469 J83
68472 J83
68474 J83
68477 J83
68492 J67
69014 J72
69130 N15
69133 N15
69134 N15
69140 N15
69141 N15
69144 N15
69146 N15
69147 N15
69148 N15
69149 N15
69152 N15
69167 N15
69168 N15
69172 N15
69173 N15
69175 N15
69185 N15
69186 N15
69219 N15
69222 N15
90049 WD[1]
90464 WD[1]
90547 WD[1]
90560 WD[1]
90727 WD[1]

1957 64A
46461 2MT[2]
46462 2MT[2]
47162 2F[1]
56035 0F[5]
60813 V2
60818 V2
60823 V2
60825 V2
60836 V2
60840 V2
60873 V2
60882 V2
60883 V2
60892 V2
60894 V2
60900 V2
60933 V2
60953 V2
60957 V2
60965 V2
60980 V2
61029 B1
61099 B1
61108 B1
61184 B1
61191 B1
61330 B1
61332 B1
61341 B1
61354 B1
61356 B1
61357 B1
61358 B1
61359 B1
61397 B1
61398 B1
61823 K3
61855 K3
61857 K3
61876 K3
61878 K3
61879 K3
61881 K3
61885 K3
61897 K3
61900 K3
61909 K3
61911 K3
61924 K3
61928 K3
61931 K3
61933 K3
61955 K3
61968 K3
61983 K3
61988 K3
61990 K3
61991 K3
61992 K3
62421 D30
62424 D30
62471 D34
62483 D34
62487 D34
62488 D34
62490 D34
62494 D34
62711 D49
62712 D49
62715 D49
62718 D49
62721 D49
64462 J35
64479 J35
64486 J35
64489 J35
64492 J35
64506 J35
64515 J35
64518 J35
64519 J35
64523 J35
64524 J35
64532 J35
64533 J35
64535 J35
64538 J37
64543 J37
64547 J37
64552 J37
64555 J37
64557 J37
64562 J37
64566 J37
64572 J37
64576 J37
64577 J37
64582 J37
64586 J37
64590 J37
64594 J37
64595 J37
64597 J37
64599 J37
64601 J37
64603 J37
64605 J37
64606 J37
64607 J37
64608 J37
64613 J37
64614 J37
64624 J37
64625 J37
64637 J37
64794 J39
64946 J39
64963 J39
64986 J39
65224 J36
65251 J36
65258 J36
65288 J36
65305 J36
65310 J36
65327 J36
65329 J36
65334 J36
65338 J36
65906 J38
65912 J38
65914 J38
65915 J38
65916 J38
65918 J38
65919 J38
65920 J38
65922 J38
65927 J38
65929 J38
65934 J38
67492 C16
67497 C16
67605 V3
67607 V1
67608 V1
67609 V3
67617 V1
67624 V3
67629 V1
67630 V1
67649 V1
67659 V1
67666 V1
67668 V3
67670 V3
68095 Y9
68097 Y9
68102 Y9
68115 Y9
68119 Y9
68320 J88
68325 J88
68338 J88
68340 J88
68342 J88
68348 J88
68352 J88
68448 J83
68449 J83
68450 J83
68454 J83
68463 J83
68464 J83
68472 J83
68474 J83
68477 J83
69014 J72
69130 N15
69133 N15
69134 N15
69140 N15
69141 N15
69144 N15
69146 N15
69147 N15
69148 N15
69149 N15
69152 N15
69167 N15
69168 N15
69172 N15
69173 N15
69175 N15
69185 N15
69186 N15
69219 N15
69222 N15
78048 2MT[1]
78049 2MT[1]

1960 64A
46461 2MT[2]
46462 2MT[2]
60813 V2
60816 V2
60818 V2
60819 V2
60823 V2
60824 V2
60825 V2
60827 V2
60836 V2
60840 V2
60873 V2
60882 V2
60883 V2
60892 V2
60894 V2
60900 V2
60920 V2
60931 V2
60933 V2
60937 V2
60953 V2
60957 V2
60958 V2
60965 V2
60969 V2
60971 V2
60980 V2
61029 B1
61099 B1
61108 B1
61184 B1
61191 B1
61246 B1
61260 B1
61307 B1
61308 B1
61332 B1
61341 B1
61349 B1
61351 B1
61354 B1
61356 B1
61357 B1
61359 B1
61397 B1
61398 B1
61881 K3
61900 K3
61909 K3
61924 K3
61928 K3
61933 K3
61955 K3
61968 K3
61990 K3
61992 K3
62421 D30
62471 D34
62711 D49
62718 D49
64462 J35
64463 J35
64479 J35
64482 J35
64483 J35
64489 J35
64515 J35
64518 J35
64519 J35
64524 J35
64532 J35
64533 J35
64535 J35
64539 J37
64547 J37
64552 J37
64555 J37
64557 J37
64562 J37
64566 J37
64572 J37
64576 J37
64577 J37
64582 J37
64586 J37
64590 J37
64591 J37
64594 J37
64595 J37
64599 J37
64601 J37
64603 J37
64605 J37
64606 J37
64607 J37
64608 J37
64612 J37
64613 J37
64614 J37
64624 J37
64625 J37
64637 J37
64795 J39
64975 J39
65224 J36
65258 J36
65288 J36
65327 J36
65329 J36
65334 J36
65906 J38
65912 J38
65914 J38
65915 J38
65916 J38
65918 J38
65919 J38
65920 J38

65922 J38
65927 J38
65929 J38
65934 J38
67492 C16
67606 V3
67617 V3
67624 V3
67649 V1
67659 V1
67666 V1
67670 V3
68095 Y9
68119 Y9
68320 J88
68338 J88
68342 J88
68448 J83
68453 J83
68454 J83
68470 J83
68472 J83
68477 J83
69013 J72
69014 J72
69133 N15
69134 N15
69135 N15
69141 N15
69144 N15
69149 N15
69150 N15
69168 N15
69173 N15
69219 N15
72000 6P5F
72003 6P5F
72004 6P5F
78048 2MT[1]

1963 64A
46461 2MT[2]
46462 2MT[2]
60037 A3
60041 A3
60043 A3
60057 A3
60087 A3
60089 A3
60096 A3
60097 A3
60512 A2
60524 A2
60530 A2
60535 A2
60813 V2
60816 V2
60818 V2
60824 V2
60825 V2
60836 V2
60882 V2
60883 V2
60892 V2
60900 V2
60931 V2
60959 V2
60969 V2
61007 B1
61029 B1
61076 B1
61099 B1
61117 B1
61191 B1
61219 B1
61242 B1
61244 B1
61294 B1
61307 B1
61308 B1
61324 B1
61341 B1
61344 B1
61345 B1
61349 B1
61350 B1
61351 B1
61354 B1
61356 B1
61357 B1
61359 B1
61397 B1
61398 B1
61404 B1
64547 J37
64555 J37
64557 J37
64561 J37
64562 J37
64572 J37
64576 J37
64577 J37
64582 J37
64586 J37
64588 J37
64591 J37
64595 J37
64599 J37
64603 J37
64605 J37
64606 J37
64608 J37
64613 J37
64614 J37
64624 J37
64625 J37
65224 J36
65288 J36
65327 J36
65329 J36
65912 J38
65914 J38
65915 J38
65918 J38
65919 J38
65920 J38
65922 J38
65927 J38
65929 J38
65934 J38
80003 4MT[3]
80006 4MT[3]
80007 4MT[3]
80022 4MT[3]
80026 4MT[3]
80054 4MT[3]
80055 4MT[3]
80114 4MT[3]
80122 4MT[3]

1966 64A
42128 4MT[1]
42273 4MT[1]
42691 4MT[1]
44925 5MT[3]
45047 5MT[3]
45053 5MT[3]
45127 5MT[3]
45162 5MT[3]
45168 5MT[3]
45469 5MT[3]
45477 5MT[3]
45483 5MT[3]
46462 2MT[2]
60024 A4
60052 A3
60813 V2
60824 V2
60868 V2
60955 V2
60970 V2
60976 V2
61029 B1
61099 B1
61307 B1
61308 B1
61344 B1
61345 B1
61347 B1
61349 B1
61350 B1
61354 B1
65234 J36
76049 4MT[2]
78047 2MT[1]
80006 4MT[3]
80026 4MT[3]
80055 4MT[3]
80114 4MT[3]

St. Philips Marsh

1948 SPM
5 WCP
6 WCP
1538 1501
2031 2021
2064 2021
2070 2021
2135 2021
2220 2251
2225 2251
2251 2251
2253 2251
2258 2251
2265 2251
2269 2251
2293 2251
2322 2301
2340 2301
2426 2301
2534 2301
2578 2301
2702 655
2709 655
2786 2721
2844 2800
2846 2800
2859 2800
3013 ROD
3017 ROD
3022 ROD
3034 ROD
3041 ROD
3046 ROD
3604 5700
3614 5700
3623 5700
3632 5700
3643 5700
3676 5700
3720 5700
3746 5700
3759 5700
3763 5700
3764 5700
3765 5700
3773 5700
3784 5700
3795 5700
3900 4900
3951 4900
4603 5700
4607 5700
4612 5700
4619 5700
4624 5700
4626 5700
4647 5700
4804 2800
4810 2800
4965 4900
4969 4900
4986 4900
4990 4900
5241 5205
5351 4300
5358 4300
5374 4300
5784 5700
5964 4900
5984 4900
6601 5600
6656 5600
6670 5600
6671 5600
6830 6800
6836 6800
6842 6800
6846 6800
6850 6800
6852 6800
6861 6800
6863 6800
6867 6800
6876 6800
6909 4900
6912 4900
6922 4900
6944 4900
6954 4900
7208 7200
7215 7200
7234 7200
7237 7200
7711 5700
7718 5700
7719 5700
7726 5700
7728 5700
7729 5700
7749 5700
7779 5700
7780 5700
7782 5700
7783 5700
7790 5700
7793 5700
7795 5700
7801 7800
7804 7800
8105 8100
8702 5700
8703 5700
8713 5700
8714 5700
8722 5700
8730 5700
8737 5700
8741 5700
8746 5700
8747 5700
8766 5700
8790 5700
8793 5700
8795 5700
9604 5700
9605 5700
9606 5700
9620 5700
9626 5700
9729 5700
9732 5700
9764 5700
90176 WD[1]
90207 WD[1]
90238 WD[1]
90312 WD[1]
90324 WD[1]
90343 WD[1]
90356 WD[1]
90573 WD[1]
90589 WD[1]
90630 WD[1]
90701 WD[1]
90723 WD[1]
90729 WD[1]

1951 82B
2031 2021
2070 2021
2135 2021
2215 2251
2220 2251
2225 2251
2251 2251
2253 2251
2258 2251
2265 2251
2269 2251
2293 2251
2322 2301
2340 2301
2426 2301
2445 2301
2462 2301
2578 2301
2818 2800
2839 2800
2844 2800
2846 2800
2859 2800
3014 ROD
3032 ROD
3034 ROD
3041 ROD
3215 2251
3604 5700
3614 5700
3623 5700
3632 5700
3643 5700
3676 5700
3720 5700
3731 5700
3746 5700
3759 5700
3763 5700
3764 5700
3765 5700
3773 5700
3784 5700
3795 5700
3842 2884
4262 4200
4603 5700
4607 5700
4619 5700
4624 5700
4626 5700
4655 5700
4660 5700
4688 5700
4706 4700
4907 4900
4909 4900
4912 4900
4916 4900
4932 4900
4934 4900
4947 4900
4967 4900
4969 4900
4986 4900
4990 4900
4999 4900
5351 4300
5358 4300
5784 5700
5919 4900
5924 4900
5949 4900
5982 4900
5992 4900
6601 5600
6656 5600
6670 5600
6671 5600
6804 6800
6805 6800
6811 6800
6827 6800
6830 6800
6832 6800
6836 6800
6842 6800
6845 6800
6846 6800
6850 6800
6852 6800
6863 6800
6867 6800
6876 6800
6908 4900
6909 4900
6914 4900
6922 4900
6957 4900
6986 6959
7711 5700
7718 5700
7719 5700
7726 5700
7728 5700
7729 5700
7749 5700
7779 5700
7780 5700
7782 5700
7783 5700
7790 5700
7793 5700
7795 5700
7900 6959
7907 6959
7908 6959
8105 8100
8413 9400
8702 5700
8703 5700
8713 5700
8714 5700
8730 5700
8737 5700
8741 5700
8746 5700
8747 5700
8766 5700
8790 5700
8795 5700
9604 5700
9605 5700
9606 5700
9626 5700
9665 5700
9729 5700
9764 5700
90176 WD[1]
90207 WD[1]
90238 WD[1]
90356 WD[1]
90573 WD[1]

1954 82B
1649 1600
2053 2021
2070 2021
2072 2021
2215 2251
2250 2251
2251 2251
2261 2251
2265 2251
2269 2251
2293 2251
2411 2301
2845 2800
2846 2800
2879 2800
2889 2884
2898 2884
3014 ROD
3017 ROD
3032 ROD
3215 2251
3604 5700
3614 5700
3623 5700
3632 5700
3643 5700
3676 5700
3720 5700
3731 5700
3748 5700
3758 5700
3759 5700
3763 5700
3764 5700
3765 5700
3773 5700
3784 5700
3795 5700
3854 2884
4262 4200
4619 5700
4624 5700
4626 5700
4655 5700
4688 5700
4703 4700
4706 4700
4947 4900
4958 4900
4983 4900
4999 4900
5306 4300
5307 4300
5325 4300
5350 4300
5351 4300
5367 4300
5675 5600
5784 5700
5924 4900
5958 4900
5982 4900
6322 4300
6363 4300
6370 4300
6374 4300
6601 5600
6656 5600
6670 5600
6671 5600
6804 6800
6811 6800
6827 6800
6830 6800
6842 6800
6845 6800
6846 6800
6852 6800
6863 6800
6867 6800
6876 6800
6908 4900
6925 4900
6936 4900
6954 4900
6957 4900
6958 4900
6986 6959
7201 7200
7250 7200
7303 4300
7718 5700
7719 5700
7728 5700
7729 5700
7749 5700
7780 5700
7783 5700
7790 5700
7793 5700
7795 5700
7808 7800
7908 6959
8413 9400
8491 9400
8492 9400
8702 5700
8703 5700
8713 5700
8714 5700
8730 5700
8737 5700
8741 5700
8746 5700
8747 5700
8766 5700
8790 5700
8795 5700
9453 9400
9481 9400
9488 9400
9605 5700
9606 5700
9626 5700
9665 5700
9729 5700
9771 5700
46525 2MT[2]
46526 2MT[2]
46527 2MT[2]
73019 5MT
73027 5MT
73028 5MT
73032 5MT
73039 5MT
90176 WD[1]
90251 WD[1]
90284 WD[1]

1957 82B
1649 1600
1669 1600
2201 2251
2213 2251
2215 2251
2250 2251
2251 2251
2261 2251
2265 2251
2269 2251
3215 2251
3604 5700
3623 5700
3632 5700
3643 5700
3676 5700
3720 5700
3731 5700
3758 5700
3764 5700
3765 5700
3773 5700
3784 5700
3795 5700
4131 5101
4262 4200
4603 5700
4619 5700
4655 5700
4660 5700
4688 5700
4703 4700
4706 4700
4909 4900
4914 4900
4922 4900
4980 4900
4999 4900
5323 4300
5345 4300
5360 4300
5367 4300
5642 5600
5904 4900
5924 4900
5975 4900
5981 4900
5982 4900
6306 4300
6312 4300
6327 4300
6351 4300
6356 4300
6363 4300
6374 4300
6391 4300
6601 5600
6630 5600
6656 5600
6670 5600
6671 5600
6804 6800
6811 6800
6827 6800
6830 6800
6833 6800
6834 6800
6835 6800
6842 6800
6846 6800
6852 6800
6863 6800
6867 6800
6869 6800
6870 6800
6876 6800
6982 6959
7250 7200
7303 4300
7323 4300
7719 5700
7728 5700
7729 5700
7749 5700
7780 5700
7783 5700
7790 5700
7703 5700
7795 5700
7929 6959
8413 9400
8492 9400
8703 5700
8737 5700
8741 5700
8746 5700
8790 5700
9313 9300
9481 9400
9488 9400
9495 9400
9626 5700
46506 2MT[2]
46525 2MT[2]
48404 8F
48410 8F
48420 8F
48430 8F
48431 8F
48434 8F
48436 8F
48450 8F
48459 8F
48461 8F
48475 8F
73019 5MT
73028 5MT
73029 5MT
73032 5MT
73039 5MT
90563 WD[1]

1960 82B
2203 2251
2213 2251
2215 2251
2224 2251
2261 2251
2265 2251
2277 2251
2288 2251
3215 2251
3632 5700
3643 5700
3650 5700
3692 5700
3726 5700
3731 5700
3764 5700
3765 5700
3773 5700
3776 5700
3784 5700
3795 5700
4129 5101
4131 5101
4603 5700
4655 5700
4660 5700
4688 5700
4703 4700
4706 4700
4909 4900
4914 4900
4947 4900
4949 4900
4960 4900
4968 4900
4980 4900
5104 5101
5215 5205
5311 4300
5385 4300
5769 5700
5771 5700
5924 4900
5950 4900
5954 4900
6312 4300
6327 4300
6341 4300
6351 4300
6356 4300
6374 4300
6601 5600
6630 5600
6641 5600
6670 5600
6671 5600
6681 5600
6804 6800
6809 6800
6811 6800
6827 6800
6830 6800
6831 6800
6833 6800
6834 6800
6835 6800
6841 6800
6842 6800
6846 6800
6852 6800
6865 6800
6878 6800
6900 4900
6908 4900
6954 4900
6957 4900
6986 6959
7301 4300
7323 4300
7728 5700
7729 5700
7749 5700
7783 5700
7790 5700
7929 6959
8714 5700
8746 5700
8747 5700
8790 5700
8795 5700
9488 9400
9495 9400
9601 5700
9651 5700
9729 5700
9769 5700
46517 2MT[2]
46525 2MT[2]
48404 8F
48410 8F
48412 8F
48420 8F
48431 8F
48434 8F
48436 8F
48450 8F
48459 8F
92203 9F
92204 9F
92205 9F
92206 9F
92207 9F

1963 82B
1000 1000
1005 1000
1009 1000
1011 1000
1020 1000
1021 1000
1024 1000
1028 1000
2224 2251
3604 5700
4905 4900
4914 4900
4922 4900
4933 4900
4949 4900
4980 4900
4991 4900
4992 4900
4993 4900
5040 4073
5049 4073
5050 4073
5071 4073
5900 4900
5904 4900
5908 4900
5924 4900
5934 4900
5954 4900
5958 4900
5975 4900
6814 6800
6816 6800
6835 6800
6846 6800
6860 6800
6873 6800
6878 6800
6908 4900
6919 4900
6954 4900
6972 6959
6981 6959
6982 6959
6997 6959
7901 6959
7907 6959
7924 6959
9601 5700
9729 5700

St. Rollox

1948 31A
40918 4P[1]
41126 4P[1]
41128 4P[1]
43848 4F[1]
43849 4F[1]
44194 4F[2]
44253 4F[2]
44254 4F[2]
44255 4F[2]
44256 4F[2]
44257 4F[2]
44880 5MT[3]
44881 5MT[3]
44922 5MT[3]
44923 5MT[3]
44956 5MT[3]
44957 5MT[3]
44995 5MT[3]
44996 5MT[3]
45115 5MT[3]
45116 5MT[3]
45117 5MT[3]
45153 5MT[3]
45154 5MT[3]
45155 5MT[3]
45156 5MT[3]
45157 5MT[3]
45158 5MT[3]
45159 5MT[3]
45176 5MT[3]
45177 5MT[3]
45178 5MT[3]
45179 5MT[3]
45355 5MT[3]
45356 5MT[3]
45358 5MT[3]
45359 5MT[3]
45362 5MT[3]
45423 5MT[3]
45468 5MT[3]
45471 5MT[3]
45480 5MT[3]
45481 5MT[3]
54474 3P[6]
54475 3P[6]
54483 3P[6]
54487 3P[6]
54494 3P[6]
55121 2P[12]
55124 2P[12]
55159 2P[13]
55178 2P[13]
55204 2P[13]
56151 2F[4]
56233 3F[10]
56234 3F[10]
56252 3F[10]
56289 3F[10]
56330 3F[10]
56370 3F[10]
57240 2F[5]
57251 2F[5]
57253 2F[5]
57254 2F[5]
57269 2F[5]
57305 2F[5]
57311 2F[5]
57318 2F[5]
57333 2F[5]
57350 2F[5]
57352 2F[5]
57374 2F[5]
57380 2F[5]
57394 2F[5]
57434 2F[5]
57453 2F[5]
57454 2F[5]
57455 2F[5]
57457 2F[5]
57554 3F[12]
57557 3F[12]
57558 3F[12]
57617 3F[12]
57631 3F[13]
57686 3F[14]

1951 65B
40918 4P[1]
41126 4P[1]
41128 4P[1]
42746 5MT[1]
43848 4F[1]
43849 4F[1]
44234 4F[2]
44255 4F[2]
44256 4F[2]
44702 5MT[3]
44703 5MT[3]
44786 5MT[3]
44880 5MT[3]
44881 5MT[3]
44922 5MT[3]
44923 5MT[3]
44956 5MT[3]
44957 5MT[3]
44967 5MT[3]
44970 5MT[3]
44995 5MT[3]
44996 5MT[3]
45115 5MT[3]
45116 5MT[3]
45153 5MT[3]
45154 5MT[3]
45155 5MT[3]
45156 5MT[3]
45157 5MT[3]
45158 5MT[3]
45159 5MT[3]
45177 5MT[3]
45178 5MT[3]
45355 5MT[3]
45356 5MT[3]
45423 5MT[3]
45443 5MT[3]
45468 5MT[3]
45471 5MT[3]
45480 5MT[3]
45481 5MT[3]
45482 5MT[3]
45499 5MT[3]
54474 3P[6]
54475 3P[6]
55121 2P[12]
55204 2P[13]
56151 2F[4]
56233 3F[10]
56252 3F[10]
56289 3F[10]
56310 3F[10]
56330 3F[10]
56370 3F[10]
57240 2F[5]
57251 2F[5]
57253 2F[5]
57261 2F[5]
57269 2F[5]
57311 2F[5]
57318 2F[5]
57350 2F[5]
57352 2F[5]
57411 2F[5]
57434 2F[5]
57454 2F[5]
57455 2F[5]
57457 2F[5]
57554 3F[12]
57557 3F[12]
57558 3F[12]
57617 3F[12]
57631 3F[13]
57686 3F[14]

1954 65B
41126 4P[1]
41128 4P[1]
42206 4MT[1]
42207 4MT[1]
42746 5MT[1]
43848 4F[1]
43849 4F[1]
44234 4F[2]
44255 4F[2]
44256 4F[2]
44677 5MT[3]
44702 5MT[3]
44786 5MT[3]
44880 5MT[3]
44881 5MT[3]
44922 5MT[3]
44923 5MT[3]
44956 5MT[3]
44957 5MT[3]
44967 5MT[3]
44970 5MT[3]
44995 5MT[3]
44996 5MT[3]
45115 5MT[3]
45116 5MT[3]
45153 5MT[3]
45154 5MT[3]
45155 5MT[3]
45156 5MT[3]
45157 5MT[3]
45158 5MT[3]
45159 5MT[3]
45177 5MT[3]
45178 5MT[3]
45355 5MT[3]
45356 5MT[3]
45423 5MT[3]
45443 5MT[3]
45468 5MT[3]
45471 5MT[3]
45482 5MT[3]
45499 5MT[3]
54474 3P[6]
54475 3P[6]
54501 3P[6]
55168 2P[13]
55204 2P[13]
56151 2F[4]
56169 2F[4]
56233 3F[10]
56252 3F[10]
56289 3F[10]
56310 3F[10]
56330 3F[10]
56370 3F[10]
57240 2F[5]
57251 2F[5]
57253 2F[5]
57258 2F[5]
57261 2F[5]
57269 2F[5]
57311 2F[5]
57350 2F[5]
57373 2F[5]
57411 2F[5]
57426 2F[5]
57434 2F[5]
57457 2F[5]
57557 3F[12]
57558 3F[12]
57617 3F[12]
57631 3F[13]
57686 3F[14]

1957 65B
42206 4MT[1]
42207 4MT[1]
42694 4MT[1]
42746 5MT[1]
43848 4F[1]
43849 4F[1]
44199 4F[2]
44234 4F[2]
44255 4F[2]
44256 4F[2]
44677 5MT[3]
44702 5MT[3]
44786 5MT[3]
44880 5MT[3]
44881 5MT[3]
44922 5MT[3]
44923 5MT[3]
44967 5MT[3]
44970 5MT[3]
45115 5MT[3]
45116 5MT[3]
45119 5MT[3]
45153 5MT[3]
45154 5MT[3]
45155 5MT[3]
45156 5MT[3]
45157 5MT[3]
45158 5MT[3]
45159 5MT[3]
45177 5MT[3]
45178 5MT[3]
45355 5MT[3]
45356 5MT[3]
45358 5MT[3]
45443 5MT[3]
45468 5MT[3]
45471 5MT[3]
45482 5MT[3]
45499 5MT[3]
54474 3P[6]
54475 3P[6]
54483 3P[6]
54501 3P[6]
55168 2P[13]
55204 2P[13]
56151 2F[4]
56169 2F[4]
56252 3F[10]
56289 3F[10]
56310 3F[10]
56330 3F[10]
56370 3F[10]
57240 2F[5]
57251 2F[5]
57253 2F[5]
57258 2F[5]
57261 2F[5]
57269 2F[5]
57311 2F[5]
57350 2F[5]
57373 2F[5]
57411 2F[5]
57426 2F[5]
57434 2F[5]
57557 3F[12]
57558 3F[12]
57617 3F[12]
57631 3F[13]
57686 3F[14]

1960 65B
42206 4MT[1]
42207 4MT[1]
43140 4MT[5]
44199 4F[2]
44677 5MT[3]
44786 5MT[3]
44880 5MT[3]
44881 5MT[3]
44922 5MT[3]
44923 5MT[3]
45115 5MT[3]
45119 5MT[3]
45125 5MT[3]
45153 5MT[3]
45157 5MT[3]
45158 5MT[3]
45159 5MT[3]
45177 5MT[3]
45178 5MT[3]
45355 5MT[3]
45356 5MT[3]
45358 5MT[3]
45443 5MT[3]
45468 5MT[3]
45471 5MT[3]
45482 5MT[3]
45499 5MT[3]
54475 3P[6]
54483 3P[6]
54501 3P[6]
56151 2F[4]
56169 2F[4]
56289 3F[10]
56370 3F[10]
57240 2F[5]
57251 2F[5]
57253 2F[5]
57258 2F[5]
57261 2F[5]
57269 2F[5]
57311 2F[5]
57350 2F[5]
57373 2F[5]
57411 2F[5]
57426 2F[5]
57434 2F[5]
57557 3F[12]
57558 3F[12]
57617 3F[12]
57631 3F[13]
57686 3F[14]
73145 5MT
73146 5MT
73147 5MT
73148 5MT
73149 5MT
73150 5MT
73151 5MT
73152 5MT
73153 5MT
73154 5MT
76102 4MT[2]
76103 4MT[2]
76113 4MT[2]
76114 4MT[2]

1963 65B
42690 4MT[1]
44880 5MT[3]
44881 5MT[3]
44922 5MT[3]
44923 5MT[3]
45115 5MT[3]
45153 5MT[3]
45158 5MT[3]
45358 5MT[3]
45443 5MT[3]
45468 5MT[3]
45471 5MT[3]
45499 5MT[3]
60027 A4
60031 A4
60090 A3
60094 A3
65285 J36
65287 J36
73145 5MT
73146 5MT
73147 5MT
73148 5MT
73149 5MT
73150 5MT
73151 5MT
73152 5MT
73153 5MT
73154 5MT

1966 65B
44718 5MT[3]
73145 5MT
73146 5MT
73149 5MT
73150 5MT
73151 5MT
73153 5MT

St. Rollox Works

1948
56025 0F[5]

1951
56025 0F[5]

1954
56025 0F[5]

1957
56025 0F[5]

1960
56025 0F[5]

Salisbury

1948 SAL
30010 T1
30013 T1
30041 M7
30117 T9
30122 T9
30127 M7
30237 G6
30243 M7
30279 G6
30285 T9
30288 T9
30312 T9
30315 700
30317 700
30330 H15
30331 H15
30332 H15
30333 H15
30334 H15
30335 H15
30355 700
30361 T1
30382 K10
30389 K10
30405 L11
30421 L12
30432 L12
30448 N15
30449 N15
30450 N15
30451 N15
30452 N15
30453 N15
30454 N15
30455 N15
30456 N15
30457 N15
30475 H15
30476 H15
30577 0395
30675 M7
30690 700
30691 700
30709 T9
30715 T9
30721 T9
30727 T9
30729 T9
30744 N15
30746 N15
30828 S15
30829 S15
30830 S15
30831 S15
30832 S15
30957 Z
31612 U
31618 U
31626 U
31630 U
31636 U
31846 N
31848 N
31872 N
31873 N
34048 WC
34049 BB
34050 BB
34051 BB
34052 BB
34053 BB
35006 MN
35007 MN
35008 MN
35009 MN
35010 MN

1951 72B
30023 M7
30041 M7
30122 T9
30288 T9
30289 T9
30300 T9
30301 T9
30315 700
30317 700
30330 H15
30331 H15
30332 H15
30333 H15
30334 H15
30335 H15
30448 N15
30449 N15
30450 N15
30451 N15
30452 N15
30453 N15
30454 N15
30455 N15
30456 N15
30457 N15
30675 M7
30690 700
30691 700
30709 T9
30719 T9
30724 T9
30725 T9
30727 T9
30730 T9
30826 S15
30827 S15
30828 S15
30829 S15
30830 S15
30831 S15
30832 S15
30957 Z
31618 U
31626 U
31872 N
31873 N
31874 N
31875 N
34022 WC
34023 WC
34032 WC
34042 WC
34043 WC
35006 MN
35007 MN
35008 MN
35009 MN

1954 72B
30270 G6
30301 T9
30304 T9
30315 700
30317 700
30330 H15
30331 H15
30332 H15
30333 H15
30334 H15
30335 H15
30448 N15
30449 N15
30450 N15
30451 N15
30452 N15
30453 N15
30454 N15
30673 M7
30674 M7
30690 700
30691 700
30702 T9
30721 T9
30823 S15
30824 S15
30825 S15
30826 S15
30827 S15
30828 S15
30829 S15
30830 S15
30831 S15
30832 S15
30847 S15
30957 Z
31635 U
31636 U
31639 U
31813 N
31814 N
32486 E4
32506 E4
34049 BB
34050 BB
34051 BB
34052 BB
34053 BB
34054 BB
34055 BB
35006 MN
35007 MN
35008 MN
35009 MN

1957 72B
30025 M7
30266 G6
30270 G6
30301 T9
30304 T9
30309 700
30313 T9
30317 700
30327 700
30330 H15
30331 H15
30333 H15
30334 H15
30335 H15
30374 M7
30448 N15
30449 N15
30450 N15
30451 N15
30452 N15
30453 N15
30454 N15
30673 M7
30674 M7
30702 T9
30721 T9
30823 S15
30824 S15
30825 S15
30826 S15
30827 S15
30828 S15
30829 S15
30830 S15
30831 S15
30832 S15
30847 S15
30954 Z
30957 Z
31813 N
31814 N
34049 BB
34050 BB
34051 BB
34052 BB
34053 BB
34054 BB
34055 BB
34059 BB
35006 MN
35007 MN
35009 MN
76005 4MT^2
76006 4MT^2
76008 4MT^2

1960 72B
30025 M7
30266 G6
30309 700
30315 700
30331 H15
30448 N15
30450 N15
30451 N15
30453 N15
30522 H15
30523 H15
30524 H15
30673 M7
30674 M7
30692 700
30729 T9
30796 N15
30798 N15
30799 N15
30823 S15
30824 S15
30825 S15
30826 S15
30827 S15
30828 S15
30829 S15
30830 S15
30831 S15
30832 S15
31019 E1^1
31067 E1^1
31497 E1^1
31507 E1^1
31813 N
31814 N
34049 BB
34050 BB R
34051 BB
34052 BB R
34053 BB R
34054 BB
34055 BB
34059 BB
35004 MN R
35006 MN R
35007 MN R
76005 4MT^2
76006 4MT^2
76007 4MT^2
76008 4MT^2
76009 4MT^2
76059 4MT^2
76060 4MT^2

1963 70E
4626 5700
4630 5700
30021 M7
30025 M7
30034 M7
30241 M7
30532 Q
30823 S15
30824 S15
30825 S15
30827 S15
30828 S15
30829 S15
30830 S15
30831 S15
30832 S15
31404 N
31408 N
31813 N
31814 N
34003 WC R
34005 WC R
34026 WC R
34048 WC R
34049 BB
34051 BB
34052 BB R
34054 BB
34059 BB R
34067 BB
34068 BB
34091 WC
34092 WC
34099 WC
35004 MN R
35006 MN R
35007 MN R
76005 4MT^2
76007 4MT^2
76008 4MT^2
76017 4MT^2
76018 4MT^2
76053 4MT^2
76054 4MT^2
76055 4MT^2
76066 4MT^2
76067 4MT^2

1966 70E
34006 WC
34013 WC R
34015 WC
34026 WC R
34032 WC R
34048 WC R
34052 BB R
34056 BB R
34057 BB
34059 BB R
34064 BB
34066 BB
34076 BB
34089 BB R
34100 WC R
34108 WC R
76007 4MT^2
76008 4MT^2
76067 4MT^2
80142 4MT^3
80145 4MT^3
80151 4MT^3
80152 4MT^3

Saltburn

1948 SAL
65868 J27
69868 A8
69872 A8
69875 A8
69876 A8
69882 A8
69883 A8
69884 A8
69889 A8
69891 A8
69892 A8

1951 51K
65884 J27
69802 A5
69811 A5
69831 A5
69834 A5
69842 A5
69869 A8
69884 A8
69889 A8
69891 A8
69892 A8

1954 51K
65884 J27
69831 A5
69834 A5
69855 A8
69869 A8
69884 A8
69889 A8
69891 A8
69892 A8
69894 A8

1957 51K
43054 4MT^5
69852 A8
69855 A8
69859 A8
69866 A8
69869 A8
69880 A8
69884 A8
69892 A8
69894 A8

Saltley

1948 21A
40097 3MT^2
40115 3MT^2
40117 3MT^2
40175 3MT^2
40385 2P^2
40463 2P^2
40486 2P^2
40493 2P^2
40511 2P^2
40512 2P^2
40715 3P^1
40745 3P^1
40928 4P^1
41029 4P^2
41035 4P^2
41046 4P^1
41699 1F^1
41777 1F^1
41856 1F^1
41879 1F^1
42326 4MT^2
42337 4MT^2
42685 4MT^1
42754 5MT^1
42758 5MT^1
42764 5MT^1
42784 5MT^1
42790 5MT^1
42793 5MT^1
42799 5MT^1
42818 5MT^1
42822 5MT^1
42824 5MT^1
42825 5MT^1
42826 5MT^1
42827 5MT^1
42829 5MT^1
42850 5MT^1
42857 5MT^1
42890 5MT^1
42900 5MT^1
42903 5MT^1
43201 3F^3
43203 3F^3
43210 3F^3
43223 3F^3
43225 3F^3
43284 3F^3
43321 3F^3
43336 3F^3
43339 3F^3
43374 3F^3
43433 3F^3
43435 3F^3
43441 3F^3
43443 3F^3
43484 3F^3
43490 3F^3
43491 3F^3
43531 3F^3
43540 3F^3
43544 3F^3
43594 3F^3
43620 3F^3
43621 3F^3
43624 3F^3
43627 3F^3
43644 3F^3
43667 3F^3
43673 3F^3
43674 3F^3
43680 3F^3
43684 3F^3
43686 3F^3
43690 3F^3
43698 3F^3
43812 3F^4
43843 4F^1
43845 4F^1
43858 4F^1
43879 4F^1
43891 4F^1
43911 4F^1
43912 4F^1
43940 4F^1
43941 4F^1
43946 4F^1
43949 4F^1
43951 4F^1
43986 4F^1
44026 4F^1
44049 4F^2
44084 4F^2
44088 4F^2
44092 4F^2
44108 4F^2
44137 4F^2
44139 4F^2
44145 4F^2
44176 4F^2
44184 4F^2
44185 4F^2
44186 4F^2
44190 4F^2
44200 4F^2
44203 4F^2
44207 4F^2
44213 4F^2
44224 4F^2
44248 4F^2
44304 4F^2
44317 4F^2
44406 4F^2
44413 4F^2
44427 4F^2
44475 4F^2
44515 4F^2
44516 4F^2
44520 4F^2
44524 4F^2
44525 4F^2
44538 4F^2
44545 4F^2
44567 4F^2
44571 4F^2
44580 4F^2
44583 4F^2
44584 4F^2
44591 4F^2
44805 5MT^3
44806 5MT^3
44810 5MT^3
44811 5MT^3
44813 5MT^3
44814 5MT^3
44840 5MT^3
44842 5MT^3
44852 5MT^3
44919 5MT^3
44920 5MT^3
44966 5MT^3
45186 5MT^3
45265 5MT^3
45268 5MT^3
45269 5MT^3
45273 5MT^3
45274 5MT^3
45447 5MT^3
47273 3F^6
47276 3F^6
47638 3F^6
47639 3F^6
48010 8F
48093 8F
48336 8F
48337 8F
48351 8F
48389 8F
48400 8F
48401 8F
48402 8F
48403 8F
48405 8F
48417 8F
48420 8F
48424 8F
48669 8F
48687 8F
49329 7F^2
49360 7F^2
49377 7F^2
58112 2F^7
58138 2F^8
58167 2F^8
58202 2F^9
58231 2F^8
58255 2F^9
58294 2F^9

1951 21A
40097 3MT^2
40115 3MT^2
40117 3MT^2
40171 3MT^2
40175 3MT^2
40486 2P^2
40511 2P^2
40928 4P^1
41035 4P^2
41046 4P^1
41699 1F^1
41856 1F^1
41879 1F^1
42053 4MT^1
42054 4MT^1
42141 4MT^1
42326 4MT^2
42337 4MT^2
42685 4MT^1
42754 5MT^1
42758 5MT^1
42764 5MT^1
42790 5MT^1
42818 5MT^1
42822 5MT^1
42824 5MT^1
42825 5MT^1
42826 5MT^1
42827 5MT^1
42829 5MT^1
42857 5MT^1
42890 5MT^1
42900 5MT^1
42903 5MT^1
43011 4MT^5
43014 4MT^5
43043 4MT^5
43044 4MT^5
43048 4MT^5
43201 3F^3
43210 3F^3
43214 3F^3
43223 3F^3
43225 3F^3
43246 3F^3
43257 3F^3
43284 3F^3
43321 3F^3
43336 3F^3
43339 3F^3
43374 3F^3
43433 3F^3
43435 3F^3
43441 3F^3
43443 3F^3
43484 3F^3
43490 3F^3
43491 3F^3
43507 3F^3
43531 3F^3
43540 3F^3
43544 3F^3
43594 3F^3
43620 3F^3
43621 3F^3
43624 3F^3
43627 3F^3
43644 3F^3
43673 3F^3
43674 3F^3
43680 3F^3
43684 3F^3
43690 3F^3
43698 3F^3
43759 3F^3
43762 3F^3
43791 3F^4
43800 3F^4
43812 3F^4
43843 4F^1
43845 4F^1
43855 4F^1
43858 4F^1
43869 4F^1
43879 4F^1
43891 4F^1
43911 4F^1
43912 4F^1
43939 4F^1
43940 4F^1
43941 4F^1
43946 4F^1
43949 4F^1
43951 4F^1
43968 4F^1
43985 4F^1
43986 4F^1
44010 4F^1
44023 4F^1
44026 4F^1
44049 4F^2
44084 4F^2
44088 4F^2
44092 4F^2
44108 4F^2
44112 4F^2
44137 4F^2
44145 4F^2
44150 4F^2
44165 4F^2
44176 4F^2
44179 4F^2
44184 4F^2
44185 4F^2
44187 4F^2
44190 4F^2
44200 4F^2
44201 4F^2
44203 4F^2
44213 4F^2
44224 4F^2
44248 4F^2
44263 4F^2
44289 4F^2
44317 4F^2
44362 4F^2
44406 4F^2
44413 4F^2
44418 4F^2
44427 4F^2
44475 4F^2
44515 4F^2
44516 4F^2
44520 4F^2
44525 4F^2
44538 4F^2
44545 4F^2
44567 4F^2
44571 4F^2
44580 4F^2
44591 4F^2
44659 5MT^3
44660 5MT^3
44661 5MT^3
44666 5MT^3
44804 5MT^3
44805 5MT^3
44810 5MT^3
44813 5MT^3
44814 5MT^3
44842 5MT^3
44888 5MT^3
44919 5MT^3
44920 5MT^3
44966 5MT^3
45040 5MT^3
45186 5MT^3
45265 5MT^3
45268 5MT^3
45269 5MT^3
45273 5MT^3
45447 5MT^3
47313 3F^6
47638 3F^6
48027 8F
48317 8F
48336 8F
48339 8F
48351 8F
48388 8F
48417 8F
48420 8F
48424 8F
48669 8F
48687 8F
48700 8F
48763 8F
58167 2F^8
58230 2F^8
58231 2F^8
58261 2F^9
58271 2F^9

1954 21A
40099 3MT^2
40115 3MT^2
40511 2P^2
40928 4P^1
41140 4P^1
41180 4P^1
41879 1F^1
42053 4MT^1
42054 4MT^1
42326 4MT^2
42327 4MT^2
42337 4MT^2
42685 4MT^1
42758 5MT^1
42764 5MT^1
42790 5MT^1
42818 5MT^1
42822 5MT^1
42824 5MT^1
42825 5MT^1
42827 5MT^1
42829 5MT^1
42857 5MT^1
42900 5MT^1
42903 5MT^1
43013 4MT^5
43017 4MT^5
43036 4MT^5
43046 4MT^5
43047 4MT^5
43048 4MT^5
43210 3F^3
43214 3F^3
43219 3F^3
43223 3F^3
43246 3F^3
43284 3F^3
43339 3F^3
43374 3F^3
43381 3F^3
43433 3F^3
43435 3F^3
43441 3F^3
43443 3F^3
43444 3F^3
43484 3F^3
43490 3F^3
43507 3F^3
43520 3F^3
43523 3F^3
43544 3F^3
43568 3F^3
43594 3F^3
43599 3F^3
43620 3F^3
43624 3F^3
43627 3F^3
43644 3F^3
43673 3F^3
43674 3F^3
43680 3F^3
43684 3F^3
43690 3F^3
43693 3F^3
43698 3F^3
43762 3F^3
43771 3F^4
43791 3F^4
43798 3F^4
43803 3F^4
43812 3F^4
43817 3F^4
43843 4F^1
43845 4F^1
43855 4F^1
43858 4F^1
43862 4F^1
43865 4F^1
43869 4F^1
43875 4F^1
43878 4F^1
43879 4F^1
43909 4F^1
43911 4F^1
43912 4F^1
43938 4F^1
43939 4F^1
43940 4F^1
43941 4F^1
43946 4F^1
43949 4F^1
43951 4F^1
43963 4F^1
43985 4F^1
43986 4F^1
44004 4F^1
44023 4F^1
44026 4F^1
44049 4F^2
44084 4F^2
44092 4F^2
44108 4F^2
44137 4F^2
44138 4F^2
44150 4F^2
44165 4F^2
44176 4F^2
44179 4F^2
44184 4F^2
44185 4F^2
44187 4F^2
44201 4F^2
44203 4F^2
44204 4F^2
44211 4F^2
44213 4F^2
44224 4F^2
44226 4F^2
44227 4F^2
44235 4F^2
44248 4F^2
44263 4F^2
44333 4F^2
44406 4F^2
44413 4F^2
44418 4F^2
44427 4F^2
44515 4F^2
44516 4F^2
44520 4F^2
44538 4F^2
44571 4F^2
44580 4F^2
44591 4F^2
44659 5MT^3
44660 5MT^3
44661 5MT^3
44666 5MT^3
44775 5MT^3
44776 5MT^3
44804 5MT^3
44805 5MT^3
44810 5MT^3
44813 5MT^3
44814 5MT^3
44841 5MT^3
44842 5MT^3
44888 5MT^3
44919 5MT^3
44920 5MT^3
44962 5MT^3
44966 5MT^3
45040 5MT^3
45265 5MT^3
45268 5MT^3
45269 5MT^3
45273 5MT^3
45274 5MT^3
47225 3F^5
47313 3F^6
47638 3F^6
48027 8F
48317 8F
48331 8F
48336 8F
48339 8F
48351 8F
48388 8F
48417 8F
48420 8F
48424 8F
48647 8F
48669 8F
48687 8F
48700 8F
48763 8F
58167 2F^8
58230 2F^8
58261 2F^9
80063 4MT^3

1957 21A
40115 3MT^2
40149 3MT^2
40511 2P^2
40928 4P^1
41140 4P^1
41180 4P^1
42053 4MT^1
42054 4MT^1
42326 4MT^2
42327 4MT^2
42337 4MT^2
42383 4MT^2
42754 5MT^1
42758 5MT^1
42761 5MT^1
42764 5MT^1
42790 5MT^1
42791 5MT^1
42816 5MT^1
42823 5MT^1
42827 5MT^1
42846 5MT^1
42857 5MT^1
42890 5MT^1
42900 5MT^1
42903 5MT^1
43010 4MT^5
43013 4MT^5
43017 4MT^5
43036 4MT^5
43046 4MT^5
43047 4MT^5
43048 4MT^5
43049 4MT^5
43210 3F^3
43214 3F^3
43219 3F^3
43223 3F^3
43284 3F^3
43339 3F^3
43374 3F^3
43381 3F^3
43433 3F^3
43435 3F^3
43441 3F^3
43443 3F^3
43482 3F^3
43484 3F^3
43490 3F^3
43507 3F^3
43523 3F^3
43558 3F^3
43594 3F^3
43599 3F^3
43620 3F^3
43627 3F^3
43644 3F^3
43673 3F^3
43674 3F^3
43680 3F^3
43684 3F^3
43690 3F^3
43693 3F^3
43771 3F^4
43798 3F^4
43812 3F^4
43878 4F^1
43911 4F^1
43912 4F^1
43938 4F^1
43939 4F^1
43940 4F^1
43949 4F^1
43951 4F^1
43963 4F^1
43985 4F^1
43986 4F^1
44004 4F^1
44026 4F^1
44084 4F^2
44092 4F^2
44108 4F^2
44137 4F^2
44138 4F^2
44160 4F^2
44165 4F^2
44171 4F^2
44179 4F^2
44185 4F^2
44187 4F^2
44201 4F^2
44203 4F^2
44211 4F^2
44213 4F^2
44226 4F^2
44227 4F^2
44230 4F^2
44235 4F^2
44248 4F^2
44263 4F^2
44333 4F^2
44406 4F^2
44413 4F^2
44463 4F^2
44516 4F^2
44520 4F^2
44571 4F^2
44580 4F^2
44583 4F^2
44659 5MT^3
44660 5MT^3
44664 5MT^3
44666 5MT^3
44775 5MT^3
44776 5MT^3
44804 5MT^3
44805 5MT^3
44810 5MT^3
44813 5MT^3
44814 5MT^3
44821 5MT^3
44841 5MT^3
44842 5MT^3
44859 5MT^3
44888 5MT^3
44919 5MT^3
44920 5MT^3
44945 5MT^3
44962 5MT^3
44963 5MT^3
44964 5MT^3
44965 5MT^3
45186 5MT^3
45265 5MT^3
45268 5MT^3
45269 5MT^3
45272 5MT^3
47225 3F^5
47313 3F^6
47638 3F^6
48027 8F
48035 8F
48152 8F
48269 8F
48317 8F
48336 8F
48338 8F
48339 8F
48351 8F
48388 8F
48647 8F
48668 8F
48669 8F
48687 8F
48692 8F
48700 8F
58168 2F^8
58261 2F^9

1960 21A
40149 3MT^2
40443 2P^2
40511 2P^2
42327 4MT^2
42337 4MT^2
42340 4MT^2
42383 4MT^2
42758 5MT^1
42761 5MT^1
42764 5MT^1
42790 5MT^1
42791 5MT^1
42823 5MT^1
42827 5MT^1
42846 5MT^1
42857 5MT^1
42890 5MT^1
42900 5MT^1
42903 5MT^1
43013 4MT^5
43017 4MT^5
43027 4MT^5
43036 4MT^5
43040 4MT^5
43041 4MT^5
43046 4MT^5
43047 4MT^5
43049 4MT^5
43103 4MT^5
43122 4MT^5
43214 3F^3
43242 3F^3
43263 3F^3
43284 3F^3
43309 3F^3
43321 3F^3
43359 3F^3
43389 3F^3
43453 3F^3
43468 3F^3
43482 3F^3
43484 3F^3
43507 3F^3
43523 3F^3
43594 3F^3
43599 3F^3
43620 3F^3
43627 3F^3
43639 3F^3
43644 3F^3
43673 3F^3
43680 3F^3
43812 3F^4
43855 4F^1
43911 4F^1
43932 4F^1
43938 4F^1
43940 4F^1
43948 4F^1
43949 4F^1
43951 4F^1
43963 4F^1
43985 4F^1
43986 4F^1
44004 4F^1
44013 4F^1
44026 4F^1
44091 4F^2
44092 4F^2
44137 4F^2
44143 4F^2
44160 4F^2
44165 4F^2
44168 4F^2
44171 4F^2
44179 4F^2
44184 4F^2
44185 4F^2
44187 4F^2
44203 4F^2
44211 4F^2
44213 4F^2
44226 4F^2
44263 4F^2
44333 4F^2
44406 4F^2
44515 4F^2
44520 4F^2
44580 4F^2
44583 4F^2
44659 5MT^3
44660 5MT^3
44663 5MT^3
44666 5MT^3
44775 5MT^3
44776 5MT^3
44804 5MT^3
44805 5MT^3
44810 5MT^3
44812 5MT^3
44813 5MT^3
44814 5MT^3
44818 5MT^3
44825 5MT^3
44839 5MT^3
44841 5MT^3
44856 5MT^3
44858 5MT^3
44859 5MT^3
44888 5MT^3
44919 5MT^3
44920 5MT^3
44944 5MT^3
44945 5MT^3
44962 5MT^3
44963 5MT^3
44965 5MT^3
44966 5MT^3
44981 5MT^3
45040 5MT^3
45088 5MT^3
45186 5MT^3
45253 5MT^3
45263 5MT^3
45265 5MT^3
45268 5MT^3
45269 5MT^3
45272 5MT^3
45280 5MT^3
45447 5MT^3
48027 8F
48101 8F
48105 8F
48220 8F
48315 8F
48336 8F
48339 8F
48342 8F
48351 8F
48388 8F
48523 8F
48647 8F
48669 8F
48687 8F
48700 8F
58261 2F^9
92135 9F
92136 9F
92137 9F
92138 9F
92139 9F
92150 9F
92151 9F
92152 9F
92155 9F
92157 9F
92165 9F
92167 9F
92248 9F

1963 21A
42400 4MT^2
42416 4MT^2
42417 4MT^2
42419 4MT^2
42421 4MT^2
42707 5MT^1
42790 5MT^1
42823 5MT^1
42827 5MT^1
42900 5MT^1
43017 4MT^5
43122 4MT^5
43940 4F^1
43949 4F^1
43951 4F^1
43958 4F^1
43963 4F^1
43979 4F^1
44038 4F^2
44040 4F^2
44047 4F^2
44092 4F^2
44112 4F^2
44131 4F^2
44137 4F^2
44160 4F^2
44165 4F^2
44168 4F^2
44179 4F^2
44180 4F^2
44184 4F^2
44185 4F^2
44211 4F^2
44218 4F^2
44226 4F^2
44263 4F^2

44413 4F[2]
44419 4F[2]
44516 4F[2]
44520 4F[2]
44571 4F[2]
44580 4F[2]
44583 4F[2]
44605 4F[2]
44659 5MT[3]
44660 5MT[3]
44663 5MT[3]
44666 5MT[3]
44775 5MT[3]
44804 5MT[3]
44805 5MT[3]
44810 5MT[3]
44812 5MT[3]
44813 5MT[3]
44814 5MT[3]
44841 5MT[3]
44859 5MT[3]
44888 5MT[3]
44919 5MT[3]
44920 5MT[3]
44944 5MT[3]
44945 5MT[3]
44962 5MT[3]
44963 5MT[3]
44965 5MT[3]
44966 5MT[3]
44981 5MT[3]
45006 5MT[3]
45040 5MT[3]
45088 5MT[3]
45186 5MT[3]
45221 5MT[3]
45260 5MT[3]
45263 5MT[3]
45268 5MT[3]
45269 5MT[3]
45272 5MT[3]
45280 5MT[3]
45447 5MT[3]
46443 2MT[2]
46454 2MT[2]
48101 8F
48109 8F
48220 8F
48339 8F
48351 8F
48669 8F
92008 9F
92028 9F
92029 9F
92085 9F
92107 9F
92118 9F
92128 9F
92129 9F
92135 9F
92136 9F
92137 9F
92138 9F
92139 9F
92150 9F
92151 9F
92152 9F
92155 9F
92157 9F
92164 9F

1966 2E

46443 2MT[2]
46448 2MT[2]
46454 2MT[2]
46492 2MT[2]
46505 2MT[2]
46526 2MT[2]
48085 8F
48109 8F
48133 8F
48220 8F
48339 8F
48351 8F
48385 8F
48603 8F
48629 8F
48646 8F
48669 8F
48755 8F
48762 8F
76038 4MT[2]
76040 4MT[2]
76043 4MT[2]
76048 4MT[2]
92028 9F
92029 9F
92125 9F
92135 9F
92136 9F
92137 9F
92138 9F
92139 9F
92150 9F
92151 9F
92152 9F
92155 9F
92164 9F

Scarborough

1948 SCA

62954 C7
62972 C7
62973 C7
62975 C7
62989 C7
62992 C7
62993 C7
68017 J94
69881 A8
69885 A8
69894 A8

1951 50E

43052 4MT[5]
62751 D49
62764 D49
62769 D49
62770 D49
64935 J39
69016 J72
69881 A8
69885 A8
69886 A8

1954 50E

61445 B16
62726 D49
62739 D49
62751 D49
62756 D49
62769 D49
62770 D49
69016 J72
69867 A8
69879 A8
69881 A8
69885 A8
69886 A8

1957 50E

42084 4MT[1]
42085 4MT[1]
61445 B16
62726 D49
62735 D49
62739 D49
62751 D49
62756 D49
62769 D49
62770 D49
69016 J72
69867 A8

1960 50E

47403 3F[6]
61068 B1
61304 B1
61305 B1
61445 B16
62739 D49
62762 D49
69885 A8
77004 3MT[1]
82026 3MT[2]
82028 3MT[2]

1963 50E

77004 3MT[1]
77013 3MT[1]

Selby

1948 SEL

62340 D20
62341 D20
62348 D20
62372 D20
62374 D20
62376 D20
62378 D20
62381 D20
62386 D20
63262 Q5
63276 Q5
63279 Q5
63280 Q5
63290 Q5
63310 Q5
63312 Q5
63313 Q5
63378 Q6
63382 Q6
63387 Q6
63406 Q6
63408 Q6
63429 Q6
63436 Q6
63440 Q6
63447 Q6
63449 Q6
63450 Q6
63451 Q6
63456 Q6
65042 J21
65043 J21
65066 J21
65072 J21
65075 J21
65093 J21
65105 J21
65120 J21
65827 J27
65836 J27
65844 J27
65845 J27
65848 J27
65849 J27
65874 J27
65875 J27
65881 J27
65882 J27
65890 J27
65891 J27
68039 J94
68040 J94
68143 Y1
68156 Y3
68161 Y3
68285 J71
68313 J71
68356 J73
68357 J73
68362 J73
69914 T1

1951 50C

43096 4MT[5]
62340 D20
62341 D20
62342 D20
62343 D20
62348 D20
62361 D20
62363 D20
62366 D20
62374 D20
62376 D20
62378 D20
62381 D20
62382 D20
62384 D20
62386 D20
62395 D20
62397 D20
63319 Q5
63348 Q6
63362 Q6
63363 Q6
63378 Q6
63382 Q6
63387 Q6
63395 Q6
63406 Q6
63408 Q6
63423 Q6
63425 Q6
63429 Q6
63431 Q6
63436 Q6
63440 Q6
63448 Q6
63449 Q6
63451 Q6
63453 Q6
63456 Q6
65039 J21
65042 J21
65105 J21
65793 J27
65827 J27
65844 J27
65848 J27
65874 J27
65875 J27
65881 J27
65882 J27
65891 J27
67250 G5
67286 G5
68143 Y1
68156 Y3
68158 Y3
68161 Y3
68268 J71
68356 J73
68357 J73
68362 J73
68399 J77
68433 J77
69867 A8
69877 A8
69879 A8
69931 Q1
69933 Q1

1954 50C

43052 4MT[5]
43096 4MT[5]
43097 4MT[5]
43098 4MT[5]
43123 4MT[5]
61422 B16
62374 D20
62378 D20
62381 D20
62384 D20
62386 D20
62392 D20
62395 D20
63362 Q6
63378 Q6
63382 Q6
63395 Q6
63406 Q6
63423 Q6
63425 Q6
63429 Q6
63440 Q6
63448 Q6
63449 Q6
63450 Q6
63451 Q6
65675 J25
65683 J25
65698 J25
65793 J27
65857 J27
65875 J27
65881 J27
65882 J27
65888 J27
65891 J27
67250 G5
67286 G5
67293 G5
68143 Y1
68156 Y3
68158 Y3
68356 J73
68357 J73
68362 J73
68406 J77
68438 J77
69931 Q1
69933 Q1
90424 WD[1]

1957 50C

43052 4MT[5]
43096 4MT[5]
43097 4MT[5]
43098 4MT[5]
43123 4MT[5]
43125 4MT[5]
61433 B16
61474 B16
62387 D20
62755 D49
62761 D49
62772 D49
62775 D49
63378 Q6
63382 Q6
63395 Q6
63406 Q6
63423 Q6
63425 Q6
63429 Q6
63440 Q6
63448 Q6
63449 Q6
63450 Q6
63451 Q6
64725 J39
64730 J39
64860 J39
64904 J39
65698 J25
65861 J27
65875 J27
65881 J27
65885 J27
65888 J27
65891 J27
67250 G5
67273 G5
68150 Y1
68182 Y3
68275 J71
68356 J73
68357 J73
68362 J73
68406 J77
69915 T1
69931 Q1
69933 Q1

Severn Tunnel Junction

1948 STJ

422 BM[1]
423 BM[1]
1752 1854
1870 1854
2414 2301
2460 2301
2804 2800
2809 2800
2815 2800
2819 2800
2824 2800
2829 2800
2838 2800
2884 2884
2887 2884
2892 2884
2952 2900
3150 3150
3154 3150
3157 3150
3159 3150
3161 3150
3163 3150
3165 3150
3167 3150
3168 3150
3170 3150
3172 3150
3174 3150
3176 3150
3177 3150
3178 3150
3182 3150
3183 3150
3184 3150
3185 3150
3188 3150
3189 3150
3190 3150
3575 3571
3806 2884
3808 2884
3815 2884
4119 5101
4130 5101
4137 5101
4144 5101
4148 5101
4156 5101
4158 5101
4200 4200
4262 4200
4801 2800
4803 2800
4851 2884
4852 2884
5183 5101
5205 5205
5262 5205
5362 4300
5620 5600
5625 5600
5626 5600
5645 5600
5706 5700
5714 5700
5729 5700
6386 4300
6639 5600
6666 5600
6673 5600
6676 5600
6689 5600
6757 6700
6815 6800
6834 6800
6871 6800
6873 6800
7202 7200
7209 7200
7210 7200
7216 7200
7223 7200
7224 7200
7229 7200
7239 7200
7246 7200
7251 7200
7429 7400
7764 5700
8799 5700
9745 5700
90712 WD[1]

1951 86E

1508 1500
2414 2301
2460 2301
2804 2800
2829 2800
2838 2800
2887 2884
2952 2900
3150 3150
3157 3150
3161 3150
3167 3150
3170 3150
3172 3150
3174 3150
3176 3150
3177 3150
3183 3150
3185 3150
3188 3150
3190 3150
3806 2884
3808 2884
3815 2884
3818 2884
3838 2884
3843 2884
3844 2884
3850 2884
4119 5101
4144 5101
4200 4200
4243 4200
4277 4200
4282 4200
4286 4200
4908 4900
5169 5101
5205 5205
5214 5205
5228 5205
5253 5205
5262 5205
5362 4300
5625 5600
5626 5600
5645 5600
5700 5700
5729 5700
6386 4300
6639 5600
6666 5600
6673 5600
6676 5600
6689 5600
6871 6800
6872 6800
7212 7200
7216 7200
7223 7200
7224 7200
7229 7200
7230 7200
7239 7200
7246 7200
7251 7200
7764 5700
8401 9400
8450 9400
8799 5700
9745 5700
90201 WD[1]
90355 WD[1]
90716 WD[1]

1954 86E

1508 1500
2460 2301
2803 2800
2811 2800
2815 2800
2829 2800
2838 2800
2839 2800
2844 2800
2859 2800
2860 2800
2862 2800
2866 2800
2873 2800
2883 2800
2887 2884
2888 2884
2893 2884
2895 2884
3150 3150
3170 3150
3172 3150
3174 3150
3176 3150
3177 3150
3183 3150
3185 3150
3190 3150
3806 2884
3808 2884
3815 2884
3818 2884
3832 2884
3838 2884
3843 2884
3844 2884
3847 2884
3849 2884
3850 2884
3852 2884
3853 2884
3866 2884
4119 5101
4121 5101
4137 5101
4144 5101
4145 5101
4151 5101
4156 5101
4200 4200
4275 4200
4286 4200
4289 4200
4298 4200
4941 4900
4952 4900
5155 5101
5169 5101
5205 5205
5212 5205
5214 5205
5253 5205
5262 5205
5625 5600
5729 5700
5902 4900
5923 4900
6369 4300
6375 4300
6386 4300
6639 5600
6666 5600
6672 5600
6673 5600
6676 5600
6689 5600
7208 7200
7223 7200
7229 7200
7230 7200
7237 7200
7251 7200
7764 5700
7789 5700
8401 9400
8450 9400
8799 5700
9745 5700
90201 WD[1]
90323 WD[1]
90355 WD[1]

1957 86E

2231 2251
2292 2251
2803 2800
2806 2800
2815 2800
2826 2800
2832 2800
2838 2800
2839 2800
2844 2800
2859 2800
2860 2800
2862 2800
2864 2800
2866 2800
2869 2800
2872 2800
2873 2800
2883 2800
2887 2884
2888 2884
2889 2884
2893 2884
2895 2884
2896 2884
3150 3150
3172 3150
3174 3150
3176 3150
3177 3150
3183 3150
3190 3150
3806 2884
3812 2884
3815 2884
3818 2884
3823 2884
3832 2884
3838 2884
3844 2884
3847 2884
3849 2884
3850 2884
3852 2884
3853 2884
3866 2884
4121 5101
4137 5101
4144 5101
4151 5101
4156 5101
4215 4200
4289 4200
4298 4200
5155 5101
5169 5101
5212 5205
5214 5205
5224 5205
5236 5205
5253 5205
5260 5205
5620 5600
6119 6100
6155 6100
6369 4300
6384 4300
6386 4300
6642 5600
6666 5600
6672 5600
7208 7200
7223 7200
7237 7200
7426 7400
7764 5700
7789 5700
9745 5700

1960 86E

2231 2251
2292 2251
2806 2800
2837 2800
2847 2800
2860 2800
2861 2800
2862 2800
2872 2800
2887 2884
2892 2884
2896 2884
3800 2884
3801 2884
3806 2884
3812 2884
3838 2884
3847 2884
3852 2884
3856 2884
3863 2884
4119 5101
4127 5101
4130 5101
4137 5101
4151 5101
4156 5101
4164 5101
4229 4200
4241 4200
4289 4200
4297 4200
4927 4900
4988 4900
5155 5101
5166 5101
5169 5101
5181 5101
5191 5101
5212 5205
5214 5205
5224 5205
5236 5205
5253 5205
5336 4300
5339 4300
5620 5600
5972 4900
5980 4900
6118 6100
6140 6100
6155 6100
6338 4300
6362 4300
6369 4300
6384 4300
6386 4300
6424 6400
6430 6400
6642 5600
6666 5600
6672 5600
6905 4900
6912 4900
7206 7200
7208 7200
7223 7200
7322 4300
7328 4300
7764 5700
9619 5700

1963 86E

2231 2251
2807 2800
2854 2800
2858 2800
2861 2800
2862 2800
2865 2800
2872 2800
2884 2884
2892 2884
2895 2884
2896 2884
3212 2251
3786 5700
3801 2884
3803 2884
3812 2884
3835 2884
3838 2884
3848 2884
3856 2884
3859 2884
3863 2884
3864 2884
4119 5101
4127 5101
4128 5101
4130 5101
4136 5101
4137 5101
4144 5101
4150 5101
4151 5101
4156 5101
4159 5101
4241 4200
4248 4200
5191 5101
5214 5205
5235 5205
5253 5205
5336 4300
6140 6100
6158 6100
6320 4300
6338 4300
6369 4300
6373 4300
6384 4300
6633 5600
6642 5600
6666 5600
6672 5600
7206 7200
7212 7200
7217 7200
7308 4300
7325 4300
7403 7400
7427 7400
9619 5700

Sheffield Darnall

1948 SHF

61145 B1
61150 B1
61151 B1
61152 B1
61153 B1
61154 B1
61181 B1
61183 B1
61353 B8
61354 B8
61355 B8
61357 B8
61358 B8
61360 B7
61361 B7
61362 B7
61363 B7
61365 B7
61372 B7
61377 B7
61378 B7
61379 B7
61383 B7
61384 B7
61386 B7
61387 B7
61397 B7
62654 D10
62657 D10
62659 D10
63579 O4
63581 O4
63583 O4
63588 O4
63622 O4
63629 O4
63661 O4
63680 O4
63686 O4
63710 O4
63714 O4
63733 O4
63737 O4
63766 O4
63771 O4
63783 O4
63790 O4
63821 O4
63822 O4
63846 O4
63860 O4
63882 O4
63888 O4
64291 J11
64360 J11
64387 J11
64412 J11
64419 J11
64441 J11
64443 J11
64445 J11
64447 J11
64725 J39
64753 J39
64808 J39
64809 J39
64878 J39
64890 J39
64903 J39
64960 J39
64973 J39
67404 C13
67406 C13
68167 Y3
68184 Y3
68928 J50
68983 J50
68990 J50
69226 N4
69227 N4
69228 N4
69229 N4
69230 N4
69232 N4
69233 N4
69234 N4
69235 N4
69236 N4
69237 N4
69240 N4
69241 N4
69242 N4
69243 N4
69244 N4
69245 N4
69247 N4

1951 39B

61145 B1
61150 B1
61151 B1
61152 B1
61153 B1
61154 B1
61169 B1
61179 B1
61181 B1
61183 B1
61311 B1
61312 B1
61313 B1
61314 B1
61315 B1
61316 B1
61317 B1
61327 B1
63574 O4
63581 O4
63583 O4
63604 O4
63605 O4
63609 O4
63622 O4
63629 O4
63661 O4
63675 O4
63680 O4
63685 O4
63710 O4
63714 O4
63733 O4
63734 O4
63737 O4
63766 O4
63771 O4
63783 O4
63790 O4
63797 O4
63821 O4
63822 O4
63846 O4
63850 O4
63860 O4
63882 O4
63888 O4
63889 O4
64291 J11
64336 J11
64360 J11
64373 J11
64387 J11
64412 J11
64419 J11
64441 J11
64443 J11
64445 J11
64447 J11
64746 J39
64753 J39
64808 J39
64809 J39
64878 J39
64890 J39
64903 J39
64960 J39
64969 J39
64973 J39
67404 C13
67406 C13
68176 Y3
68184 Y3
68928 J50
68983 J50
68990 J50
69225 N4
69227 N4
69228 N4
69229 N4
69230 N4
69231 N4
69232 N4
69233 N4
69234 N4
69235 N4
69236 N4
69239 N4
69240 N4
69242 N4
69244 N4
69246 N4

1954 39B

61041 B1
61044 B1
61096 B1
61150 B1
61151 B1
61152 B1
61153 B1
61154 B1
61169 B1
61174 B1
61179 B1
61181 B1
61183 B1
61225 B1
61311 B1
61312 B1
61313 B1
61314 B1
61315 B1
61316 B1
61317 B1
61327 B1
63574 O4
63581 O4
63583 O4
63584 O4
63604 O4
63605 O4
63607 O4
[illegible] O4
63620 O4
63621 O4
63622 O4
63624 O4
63629 O4
63640 O4
63645 O4
63661 O4
63680 O4
63682 O4
63685 O4
63710 O4
63714 O4
63733 O4
63734 O4
63737 O4
63771 O4
63783 O4
63790 O4
63797 O4
63821 O4
63822 O4
63846 O4
63850 O4
63860 O4
63882 O4
63888 O4
63889 O4
64286 J11
64291 J11
64329 J11
64360 J11
64373 J11
64387 J11
64394 J11
64412 J11
64419 J11
64441 J11
64443 J11
64445 J11
64447 J11
64746 J39
64753 J39
64808 J39
64809 J39
64824 J39
64878 J39
64890 J39
64960 J39
64962 J39
64973 J39
67424 C13
67439 C13
68184 Y3
69225 N4
69228 N4
69230 N4
69231 N4
69232 N4
69233 N4
69235 N4
69236 N4
69239 N4
69266 N5
69285 N5
69287 N5
69292 N5
69294 N5
69295 N5
69312 N5
69324 N5
69900 S1

1957 41A

61009 B1
61033 B1
61041 B1
61044 B1
61050 B1
61051 B1
61096 B1
61138 B1
61150 B1
61151 B1
61152 B1
61153 B1
61154 B1
61169 B1
61174 B1
61179 B1
61181 B1
61183 B1
61313 B1
61314 B1
61315 B1
61316 B1
61327 B1
61334 B1
61724 K2
61728 K2
61739 K2
61747 K2
61749 K2
61760 K2
61761 K2
61907 K3
61938 K3
61954 K3
61967 K3
63574 O4
63581 O4
63583 O4
63599 O4
63604 O4
63609 O4
63620 O4
63621 O4
63624 O4
63629 O4
63640 O4
63645 O4
63658 O4
63661 O4
63680 O4
63682 O4
63685 O4
63695 O4
63710 O4
63714 O4
63733 O4
63734 O4
63737 O4
63742 O4
63748 O4
63771 O4
63783 O4
63790 O4
63797 O4
63821 O4
63822 O4
63846 O4
63850 O4
63852 O4
63881 O4
63882 O4
63888 O4
63889 O4
64329 J11
64373 J11
64387 J11
64394 J11
64412 J11
64419 J11
64441 J11
64443 J11
64445 J11
64447 J11
64738 J39
64744 J39
64746 J39
64753 J39
64808 J39
64809 J39
64824 J39
64878 J39
64962 J39
67424 C13
67439 C13
69259 N5
69266 N5
69271 N5
69286 N5
69292 N5
69294 N5
69295 N5
69296 N5
69302 N5
69312 N5
69316 N5
69327 N5
69348 N5

1960 41A

61027 B1
61033 B1
61041 B1
61044 B1
61047 B1
61050 B1
61051 B1
61094 B1
61105 B1
61111 B1
61112 B1
61139 B1
61150 B1
61151 B1
61153 B1
61154 B1
61162 B1
61164 B1
61169 B1
61181 B1
61183 B1
61234 B1
61249 B1

61313 B1
61315 B1
61316 B1
61327 B1
61370 B1
61728 K2
61747 K2
61760 K2
61761 K2
61816 K3
61825 K3
61938 K3
61967 K3
62660 D11
62662 D11
62664 D11
62666 D11
62667 D11
62668 D11
62669 D11
62670 D11
63574 O4
63599 O4
63604 O4
63609 O4
63621 O4
63624 O4
63645 O4
63658 O4
63661 O4
63685 O4
63695 O4
63733 O4
63734 O4
63737 O4
63742 O4
63771 O4
63783 O4
63821 O4
63822 O4
63846 O4
63850 O4
63852 O4
63881 O4
63882 O4
63888 O4
64329 J11
64373 J11
64387 J11
64394 J11
64419 J11
64441 J11
64443 J11
64445 J11
64447 J11
64719 J39
64736 J39
64746 J39
64804 J39
64807 J39
64808 J39
64878 J39
69258 N5
69296 N5
69314 N5

1963 41A

61044 B1
61050 B1
61051 B1
61094 B1
61105 B1
61109 B1
61152 B1
61153 B1
61181 B1
61249 B1
61313 B1
61315 B1
61372 B1
63645 O4
63661 O4
63684 O4
63685 O4
63742 O4
63772 O4
63774 O4
63822 O4
63841 O4
63846 O4
63850 O4
63852 O4
63882 O4

Sheffield Grimesthorpe

1948 19A

40324 2P[1]
40401 2P[2]
40728 3P[1]
40729 3P[1]
41768 1F[1]
41855 1F[1]
41857 1F[1]
42761 5MT[1]
42769 5MT[1]
42797 5MT[1]
42904 5MT[1]
43241 3F[3]
43334 3F[3]
43468 3F[3]
43595 3F[3]
43596 3F[3]
43605 3F[3]
43607 3F[3]
43636 3F[3]
43661 3F[3]
43662 3F[3]
43683 3F[3]
43715 3F[3]
43731 3F[3]
43749 3F[3]
43755 3F[3]
43772 3F[4]
43775 3F[4]
43844 4F[1]
44006 4F[1]
44165 4F[2]
44211 4F[2]
44212 4F[2]
44284 4F[2]
44285 4F[2]
44334 4F[2]
44355 4F[2]
44418 4F[2]
44426 4F[2]
44437 4F[2]
44550 4F[2]
44568 4F[2]
44572 4F[2]
44573 4F[2]
44858 5MT[3]
44921 5MT[3]
45262 5MT[3]
45407 5MT[3]
47235 3F[5]
47236 3F[5]
47513 3F[6]
47545 3F[6]
47624 3F[6]
48017 8F
48105 8F
48116 8F
48216 8F
48219 8F
48284 8F
48314 8F
48642 8F
58139 2F[8]
58140 2F[8]
58151 2F[8]
58165 2F[8]
58190 2F[9]
58208 2F[9]
58220 2F[9]
58225 2F[9]
58232 2F[8]
58262 2F[9]
58276 2F[9]

1951 19A

40728 3P[1]
40729 3P[1]
41660 1F[1]
41781 1F[1]
41857 1F[1]
42769 5MT[1]
42797 5MT[1]
42904 5MT[1]
43015 4MT[5]
43032 4MT[5]
43038 4MT[5]
43041 4MT[5]
43042 4MT[5]
43241 3F[3]
43334 3F[3]
43335 3F[3]
43463 3F[3]
43595 3F[3]
43604 3F[3]
43605 3F[3]
43607 3F[3]
43636 3F[3]
43661 3F[3]
43662 3F[3]
43683 3F[3]
43715 3F[3]
43731 3F[3]
43749 3F[3]
43755 3F[3]
43775 3F[4]
43844 4F[1]
44211 4F[2]
44212 4F[2]
44284 4F[2]
44285 4F[2]
44334 4F[2]
44426 4F[2]
44437 4F[2]
44477 4F[2]
44550 4F[2]
44556 4F[2]
44568 4F[2]
44573 4F[2]
44802 5MT[3]
44858 5MT[3]
44944 5MT[3]
45056 5MT[3]
45062 5MT[3]
45238 5MT[3]
45262 5MT[3]
45335 5MT[3]
45407 5MT[3]
46450 2MT[2]
46451 2MT[2]
47235 3F[5]
47236 3F[5]
47432 3F[6]
47513 3F[6]
47548 3F[6]
47563 3F[6]
47611 3F[6]
47624 3F[6]
48116 8F
48179 8F
48216 8F
48219 8F
48284 8F
48314 8F
48642 8F
58139 2F[8]
58140 2F[8]
58151 2F[8]
58165 2F[8]
58175 2F[8]
58190 2F[9]
58192 2F[9]
58220 2F[9]
58225 2F[9]
58232 2F[8]
58276 2F[9]

1954 19A

41857 1F[1]
42904 5MT[1]
43041 4MT[5]
43042 4MT[5]
43114 4MT[5]
43115 4MT[5]
43252 3F[3]
43334 3F[3]
43335 3F[3]
43341 3F[3]
43595 3F[3]
43607 3F[3]
43661 3F[3]
43683 3F[3]
43715 3F[3]
43731 3F[3]
43749 3F[3]
43755 3F[3]
43775 3F[4]
43800 3F[4]
43844 4F[1]
43882 4F[1]
44174 4F[2]
44212 4F[2]
44284 4F[2]
44285 4F[2]
44287 4F[2]
44334 4F[2]
44426 4F[2]
44437 4F[2]
44457 4F[2]
44477 4F[2]
44550 4F[2]
44556 4F[2]
44568 4F[2]
44573 4F[2]
44802 5MT[3]
44855 5MT[3]
44858 5MT[3]
44944 5MT[3]
45056 5MT[3]
45059 5MT[3]
45062 5MT[3]
45238 5MT[3]
45262 5MT[3]
45335 5MT[3]
45407 5MT[3]
46450 2MT[2]
46451 2MT[2]
47228 3F[5]
47235 3F[5]
47236 3F[5]
47432 3F[6]
47513 3F[6]
47548 3F[6]
47563 3F[6]
47611 3F[6]
47624 3F[6]
48116 8F
48144 8F
48179 8F
48447 8F
48452 8F
48642 8F
48765 8F
58140 2F[8]
58165 2F[8]
58175 2F[8]
58190 2F[9]
58192 2F[9]
58220 2F[9]
58225 2F[9]
58232 2F[8]
58276 2F[9]

1957 19A

41795 1F[1]
41857 1F[1]
42794 5MT[1]
42797 5MT[1]
42904 5MT[1]
43012 4MT[5]
43042 4MT[5]
43115 4MT[5]
43181 3F[2]
43243 3F[3]
43254 3F[3]
43332 3F[3]
43335 3F[3]
43341 3F[3]
43388 3F[3]
43595 3F[3]
43637 3F[3]
43669 3F[3]
43715 3F[3]
43731 3F[3]
43745 3F[3]
43749 3F[3]
43800 3F[4]
43844 4F[1]
43882 4F[1]
44039 4F[2]
44174 4F[2]
44212 4F[2]
44265 4F[2]
44287 4F[2]
44426 4F[2]
44437 4F[2]
44457 4F[2]
44477 4F[2]
44547 4F[2]
44568 4F[2]
44573 4F[2]
44802 5MT[3]
44858 5MT[3]
44944 5MT[3]
45062 5MT[3]
46450 2MT[2]
46451 2MT[2]
47228 3F[5]
47235 3F[5]
47432 3F[6]
47513 3F[6]
47548 3F[6]
47624 3F[6]
47636 3F[6]
48116 8F
48144 8F
48179 8F
48452 8F
48642 8F
48765 8F
58140 2F[8]
58190 2F[9]
58192 2F[9]
58225 2F[9]

1960 41B

42794 5MT[1]
42797 5MT[1]
42904 5MT[1]
43111 4MT[5]
43159 4MT[5]
43174 3F[2]
43203 3F[3]
43234 3F[3]
43243 3F[3]
43254 3F[3]
43307 3F[3]
43361 3F[3]
43395 3F[3]
43406 3F[3]
43431 3F[3]
43634 3F[3]
43637 3F[3]
43669 3F[3]
43715 3F[3]
43749 3F[3]
43751 3F[3]
43800 3F[4]
43844 4F[1]
43872 4F[1]
43882 4F[1]
44036 4F[2]
44039 4F[2]
44087 4F[2]
44174 4F[2]
44212 4F[2]
44265 4F[2]
44287 4F[2]
44426 4F[2]
44437 4F[2]
44457 4F[2]
44477 4F[2]
44535 4F[2]
44547 4F[2]
44568 4F[2]
44573 4F[2]
46450 2MT[2]
46451 2MT[2]
47513 3F[6]
47548 3F[6]
47624 3F[6]
47636 3F[6]
48144 8F
48178 8F
48179 8F
48642 8F
48765 8F
73000 5MT
73043 5MT
73074 5MT
73156 5MT

Shoeburyness

1948 13D

41934 3P[2]
41937 3P[2]
41941 3P[2]
41968 3P[2]
41971 3P[2]
41978 3P[2]
41991 3F[1]
41992 3F[1]
42222 4MT[1]
42223 4MT[1]
42224 4MT[1]
42500 4MT[4]
42501 4MT[4]
42502 4MT[4]
42503 4MT[4]
42504 4MT[4]
42505 4MT[4]
42506 4MT[4]
42507 4MT[4]
42508 4MT[4]
42509 4MT[4]
42510 4MT[4]
42511 4MT[4]
42512 4MT[4]
42513 4MT[4]
42514 4MT[4]
42515 4MT[4]
42516 4MT[4]
42517 4MT[4]
42518 4MT[4]
42519 4MT[4]
42520 4MT[4]
42521 4MT[4]

1951 33C

41960 3P[2]
41963 3P[2]
41964 3P[2]
41966 3P[2]
41991 3F[1]
41992 3F[1]
42230 4MT[1]
42500 4MT[4]
42501 4MT[4]
42502 4MT[4]
42503 4MT[4]
42504 4MT[4]
42505 4MT[4]
42506 4MT[4]
42507 4MT[4]
42508 4MT[4]
42509 4MT[4]
42510 4MT[4]
42511 4MT[4]
42512 4MT[4]
42513 4MT[4]
42514 4MT[4]
42515 4MT[4]
42516 4MT[4]
42517 4MT[4]
42518 4MT[4]
42519 4MT[4]
42520 4MT[4]
42521 4MT[4]
42522 4MT[4]
42523 4MT[4]
42524 4MT[4]
42525 4MT[4]
42526 4MT[4]
42527 4MT[4]
42528 4MT[4]
42529 4MT[4]

1954 33C

41944 3P[2]
41990 3F[1]
42500 4MT[4]
42501 4MT[4]
42502 4MT[4]
42503 4MT[4]
42504 4MT[4]
42505 4MT[4]
42506 4MT[4]
42507 4MT[4]
42508 4MT[4]
42509 4MT[4]
42510 4MT[4]
42511 4MT[4]
42512 4MT[4]
42513 4MT[4]
42514 4MT[4]
42515 4MT[4]
42516 4MT[4]
42517 4MT[4]
42518 4MT[4]
42519 4MT[4]
42520 4MT[4]
42521 4MT[4]
42522 4MT[4]
42523 4MT[4]
42524 4MT[4]
42525 4MT[4]
42526 4MT[4]
42527 4MT[4]
42528 4MT[4]
42529 4MT[4]
42530 4MT[4]
42531 4MT[4]
65545 J17

1957 33C

41969 3P[2]
42500 4MT[4]
42501 4MT[4]
42502 4MT[4]
42503 4MT[4]
42504 4MT[4]
42505 4MT[4]
42506 4MT[4]
42507 4MT[4]
42508 4MT[4]
42509 4MT[4]
42510 4MT[4]
42511 4MT[4]
42512 4MT[4]
42513 4MT[4]
42514 4MT[4]
42515 4MT[4]
42516 4MT[4]
42517 4MT[4]
42518 4MT[4]
42519 4MT[4]
42520 4MT[4]
42521 4MT[4]
42522 4MT[4]
42523 4MT[4]
42524 4MT[4]
42525 4MT[4]
42526 4MT[4]
42527 4MT[4]
42528 4MT[4]
42529 4MT[4]
42530 4MT[4]
42531 4MT[4]
42532 4MT[4]
42533 4MT[4]
42534 4MT[4]
42535 4MT[4]
42536 4MT[4]
42678 4MT[1]
42679 4MT[1]
42681 4MT[1]
42684 4MT[1]
42687 4MT[1]

1960 33C

42218 4MT[1]
42219 4MT[1]
42220 4MT[1]
42221 4MT[1]
42223 4MT[1]
42224 4MT[1]
42226 4MT[1]
42227 4MT[1]
42500 4MT[4]
42501 4MT[4]
42502 4MT[4]
42503 4MT[4]
42504 4MT[4]
42505 4MT[4]
42506 4MT[4]
42507 4MT[4]
42508 4MT[4]
42509 4MT[4]
42510 4MT[4]
42511 4MT[4]
42512 4MT[4]
42513 4MT[4]
42514 4MT[4]
42515 4MT[4]
42516 4MT[4]
42517 4MT[4]
42518 4MT[4]
42519 4MT[4]
42520 4MT[4]
42521 4MT[4]
42522 4MT[4]
42523 4MT[4]
42524 4MT[4]
42525 4MT[4]
42526 4MT[4]
42527 4MT[4]
42528 4MT[4]
42529 4MT[4]
42530 4MT[4]
42531 4MT[4]
42532 4MT[4]
42533 4MT[4]
42534 4MT[4]
42535 4MT[4]
42536 4MT[4]
42678 4MT[1]
42679 4MT[1]
42681 4MT[1]
42684 4MT[1]
42687 4MT[1]
80133 4MT[3]

Shrewsbury

1948 SALOP/4A

2228 2251
2229 2251
2231 2251
2233 2251
2234 2251
2235 2251
2744 2721
2745 2721
2897 2884
3217 2251
3377 3300
3442 3300
3602 5700
3702 5700
3782 5700
3788 5700
4040 4000
4044 4000
4046 4000
4061 4000
4118 5101
4602 5700
4623 5700
4672 5700
4919 4900
5021 4073
5032 4073
5061 4073
5064 4073
5073 4073
5086 4073
5097 4073
5154 5101
5168 5101
5642 5600
5673 5600
5774 5700
5981 4900
5994 4900
6307 4300
6338 4300
6348 4300
6606 5600
6633 5600
6683 5600
6963 6959
6976 6959
6980 6959
7006 4073
7319 4300
9024 9000
9073 3252
9076 3252
9657 5700
9719 5700
40005 3MT[1]
40008 3MT[1]
40048 3MT[1]
40058 3MT[1]
41725 1F[1]
43394 3F[3]
43573 3F[3]
43581 3F[3]
43600 3F[3]
43618 3F[3]
43679 3F[3]
45180 5MT[3]
45190 5MT[3]
45245 5MT[3]
45281 5MT[3]
45283 5MT[3]
45292 5MT[3]
45318 5MT[3]
45330 5MT[3]
45384 5MT[3]
45406 5MT[3]
45445 5MT[3]
45492 5MT[3]
46601 1P[1]
47181 Sentinel[1]
48165 8F
48307 8F
48308 8F
48327 8F
48328 8F
48347 8F
48369 8F
48373 8F
48375 8F
48454 8F
48474 8F
48556 8F
48613 8F
48631 8F
48674 8F
48688 8F
48689 8F
48736 8F
48743 8F
48895 7F[2]
48945 7F[2]
49028 7F[2]
49046 7F[2]
49138 7F[2]
49445 7F[3]
52103 3F[7]
52105 3F[7]
52119 3F[7]
52233 3F[7]
52374 3F[7]
52414 3F[7]
52428 3F[7]
52429 3F[7]
52457 3F[7]
52525 3F[7]
56027 0F[5]
58355 2F[10]
58358 2F[10]
58367 2F[11]
58369 2F[11]
58397 2F[11]
58425 2F[11]
58894 2F[14]
58936 2F[14]
28153 2F[10]

1951 84G

1024 1000
1025 1000
2228 2251
2229 2251
2231 2251
2233 2251
2234 2251
2235 2251
2841 2800
3217 2251
3602 5700
3702 5700
3782 5700
3788 5700
4040 4000
4044 4000
4046 4000
4052 4000
4083 4073
4118 5101
4602 5700
4623 5700
4672 5700
4904 4900
5032 4073
5050 4073
5061 4073
5073 4073
5097 4073
5154 5101
5168 5101
5642 5600
5673 5600
5981 4900
6307 4300
6338 4300
6348 4300
6606 5600
6633 5600
6683 5600
6963 6959
6976 6959
6980 6959
7035 4073
7319 4300
7810 7800
9656 5700
9657 5700
9672 5700
9719 5700
40005 3MT[1]
40008 3MT[1]
40048 3MT[1]
40058 3MT[1]
41725 1F[1]
43357 3F[3]
43394 3F[3]
43570 3F[3]
43581 3F[3]
43600 3F[3]
43679 3F[3]
43757 3F[3]
43760 3F[3]
44835 5MT[3]
44908 5MT[3]
45112 5MT[3]
45143 5MT[3]
45145 5MT[3]
45180 5MT[3]
45183 5MT[3]
45190 5MT[3]
45245 5MT[3]
45281 5MT[3]
45283 5MT[3]
45298 5MT[3]
45318 5MT[3]
45330 5MT[3]
45384 5MT[3]
45400 5MT[3]
45406 5MT[3]
45422 5MT[3]
45436 5MT[3]
47183 Sentinel[1]
48110 8F
48172 8F
48307 8F
48308 8F
48309 8F
48328 8F
48344 8F
48347 8F
48354 8F
48369 8F
48438 8F
48468 8F
48474 8F
48478 8F
48660 8F
48735 8F
48760 8F
48901 7F[2]
48945 7F[2]
49138 7F[2]
49276 7F[2]
49440 7F[3]
52414 3F[7]
52428 3F[7]
52525 3F[7]
52551 3F[8]
58211 2F[9]
58213 2F[9]
58322 2F[10]
58327 2F[10]
58330 2F[10]
58333 2F[10]
58904 2F[14]
58926 2F[14]
90110 WD[1]

1954 84G

1003 1000
1013 1000
1016 1000
1017 1000
1025 1000
2206 2251
2231 2251
2232 2251
2234 2251
2235 2251
2244 2251
2832 2800
3041 ROD
3602 5700
3702 5700
3782 5700
3788 5700
3820 2884
4105 5101
4118 5101
4623 5700
4672 5700
4904 4900
5050 4073
5073 4073
5091 4073
5097 4073
5154 5101
5168 5101
5328 4300
5634 5600
5962 4900
5981 4900
6339 4300
6606 5600
6633 5600
6956 4900
6980 6959
7810 7800
7811 7800
7828 7800
9656 5700
9657 5700
9672 5700
9740 5700
40005 3MT[1]
40008 3MT[1]
40048 3MT[1]
40058 3MT[1]
41725 1F[1]
43277 3F[3]
43394 3F[3]
43491 3F[3]
43570 3F[3]
43581 3F[3]
43600 3F[3]
43621 3F[3]
43679 3F[3]
43757 3F[3]
43760 3F[3]
43822 3F[4]
44835 5MT[3]
45143 5MT[3]
45145 5MT[3]
45190 5MT[3]
45283 5MT[3]
45298 5MT[3]
45406 5MT[3]
45422 5MT[3]
47183 Sentinel[1]
48110 8F
48172 8F
48307 8F
48308 8F
48309 8F
48328 8F
48344 8F
48347 8F
48354 8F
48369 8F
48438 8F
48468 8F
48474 8F
48478 8F
48660 8F
48707 8F
48738 8F
48739 8F
48760 8F
48893 7F[2]
48945 7F[2]
49157 7F[2]
49260 7F[2]
49276 7F[2]
49440 7F[3]
58194 2F[9]
58203 2F[9]
58207 2F[9]
58213 2F[9]
58241 2F[8]
58258 2F[9]
58904 2F[14]
58926 2F[14]
73012 5MT
73013 5MT
73014 5MT
73015 5MT
73017 5MT
73018 5MT
73025 5MT
73026 5MT
73033 5MT
73034 5MT
73035 5MT
73036 5MT
73037 5MT
90010 WD[1]
90261 WD[1]
90356 WD[1]
90483 WD[1]
90701 WD[1]
90716 WD[1]

1957 84G

1003 1000
1013 1000
1016 1000
1017 1000
1025 1000
1026 1000
2234 2251
3602 5700
3782 5700
3788 5700
4623 5700
4672 5700
4915 4900
5004 4073
5050 4073
5073 4073
5097 4073
5328 4300
5331 4300
5347 4300
5362 4300
5634 5600
5690 5600
5968 4900
5986 4900
6317 4300
6944 4900
6980 6959
7309 4300
7797 5700
7811 7800
7828 7800
9308 9300
9470 9400
9656 5700
9657 5700
40005 3MT[1]
40008 3MT[1]
40048 3MT[1]
40058 3MT[1]
43277 3F[3]
43394 3F[3]
43491 3F[3]
43570 3F[3]
43621 3F[3]
43679 3F[3]
43757 3F[3]
43760 3F[3]
43822 3F[4]
44835 5MT[3]
45143 5MT[3]
45145 5MT[3]
45190 5MT[3]
45283 5MT[3]
45298 5MT[3]
45406 5MT[3]
45422 5MT[3]
48110 8F
48172 8F
48307 8F
48308 8F
48328 8F
48344 8F
48347 8F
48354 8F
48369 8F
48402 8F
48438 8F
48468 8F
48474 8F
48478 8F
48660 8F
48707 8F
48724 8F
48738 8F
48739 8F
48760 8F
48945 7F[2]
49051 7F[2]
49157 7F[2]
49243 7F[2]
49260 7F[2]
49276 7F[2]
49345 7F[2]
49424 7F[3]
49440 7F[3]
58213 2F[9]
58926 2F[14]
68164 Y3
73024 5MT
73125 5MT
73126 5MT
73127 5MT
73128 5MT
73129 5MT
73130 5MT
73131 5MT
73132 5MT
73133 5MT
73134 5MT
82000 3MT[2]
82007 3MT[2]
82031 3MT[2]
90010 WD[1]
90176 WD[1]
90261 WD[1]
90356 WD[1]
90701 WD[1]

1960 84G

1003 1000
1013 1000
1016 1000
1017 1000
1021 1000
1022 1000
1025 1000
1026 1000
1143 SHT[2]
3207 2251
3400 9400
3602 5700
3769 5700
3782 5700
3788 5700
3836 2884
4564 4500
4623 5700
4644 5700
4693 5700
5001 4073
5038 4073
5050 4073
5059 4073
5167 5101
5324 4300
5331 4300
5564 4575
5634 5600
5690 5600
5942 4900
5968 4900
5971 4900
6395 4300
6698 5600
6916 4900
6922 4900
6944 4900
6956 4900
6964 6959
6998 6959
7015 4073
7309 4300
7329 4300
7330 4300
7336 4300
7811 7800
7828 7800
7922 6959
8449 9400
9463 9400
9470 9400
9472 9400
9498 9400
9656 5700
9657 5700
44835 5MT[3]
45143 5MT[3]
45145 5MT[3]
45190 5MT[3]
45283 5MT[3]
45298 5MT[3]
45406 5MT[3]
45422 5MT[3]
48110 8F
48172 8F
48307 8F
48347 8F
48354 8F
48369 8F
48468 8F
48474 8F
48478 8F
48660 8F
48724 8F
48737 8F
48738 8F
48739 8F
48768 8F
73025 5MT
73026 5MT
73034 5MT
73035 5MT
73036 5MT
73037 5MT
73090 5MT
73091 5MT
73092 5MT
73093 5MT
73094 5MT
73095 5MT
73096 5MT
73097 5MT

1963 89A

1002 1000
1013 1000
1016 1000
1019 1000
1023 1000
1025 1000
3204 2251
3205 2251
3709 5700
3782 5700
3788 5700
3836 2884
4564 4500
4617 5700
4946 4900
5942 4900
5991 4900
5994 4900
6375 4300
6380 4300
6915 4900
6916 4900
6922 4900
6934 4900
6964 6959
7314 4300
7329 4300
9463 9400
9498 9400
9657 5700
41202 2MT[1]
41203 2MT[1]
41209 2MT[1]
41240 2MT[1]
44835 5MT[3]
45143 5MT[3]
45145 5MT[3]
45190 5MT[3]
45283 5MT[3]
45298 5MT[3]
45406 5MT[3]
45422 5MT[3]
45572 6P5F[2]
45577 6P5F[2]
45660 6P5F[2]
45699 6P5F[2]
48347 8F
48354 8F
48369 8F
48404 8F
48418 8F
48436 8F
48471 8F
48738 8F
48739 8F
48768 8F
73025 5MT
73026 5MT
73034 5MT
73035 5MT
73036 5MT
73090 5MT
73095 5MT
73097 5MT
80070 4MT[3]
80078 4MT[3]
80100 4MT[3]
80102 4MT[3]
80131 4MT[3]
80132 4MT[3]
80135 4MT[3]
80136 4MT[3]

1966 6D

9657 5700
44775 5MT[3]
44814 5MT[3]
44821 5MT[3]
44966 5MT[3]
44981 5MT[3]
45058 5MT[3]
45132 5MT[3]
45145 5MT[3]
45285 5MT[3]
45311 5MT[3]
45348 5MT[3]
45430 5MT[3]
48404 8F
48418 8F
48436 8F
48471 8F
73000 5MT
73025 5MT
73034 5MT
73050 5MT
73067 5MT
73070 5MT
75006 4MT[1]
75014 4MT[1]
75016 4MT[1]

75053 4MT[1]
75063 4MT[1]
78038 2MT[1]
78058 2MT[1]
78060 2MT[1]

Skipton

1948 20F

40323 2P[1]
40406 2P[2]
40409 2P[2]
40414 2P[2]
40422 2P[2]
40452 2P[2]
40484 2P[2]
41748 1F[1]
41767 1F[1]
41781 1F[1]
41805 1F[1]
41820 1F[1]
43251 3F[3]
43295 3F[3]
43337 3F[3]
43784 3F[4]
43893 4F[1]
43904 4F[1]
43944 4F[1]
43960 4F[1]
43984 4F[1]
43999 4F[1]
44000 4F[1]
44007 4F[1]
44041 4F[2]
44197 4F[2]
44222 4F[2]
44276 4F[2]
44277 4F[2]
44299 4F[2]
48081 8F
48317 8F
50623 2P[8]
50671 2P[8]
50795 2P[8]
58041 1P[6]
58061 1P[6]
58064 1P[6]
58192 2F[9]
58267 2F[9]
1361 1P[6]

1951 23A

40414 2P[2]
40422 2P[2]
40484 2P[2]
41767 1F[1]
41820 1F[1]
41855 1F[1]
43295 3F[3]
43784 3F[4]
43893 4F[1]
43913 4F[1]
43917 4F[1]
43944 4F[1]
43960 4F[1]
43984 4F[1]
43999 4F[1]
44000 4F[1]
44007 4F[1]
44041 4F[2]
44197 4F[2]
44222 4F[2]
44277 4F[2]
44468 4F[2]
46440 2MT[2]
46442 2MT[2]
47427 3F[6]
47562 3F[6]
48005 8F
48145 8F
48609 8F
58040 1P[6]
58077 1P[6]
58090 1P[6]

1954 20F

40414 2P[2]
40472 2P[2]
41325 2MT[1]
41326 2MT[1]
41327 2MT[1]
41855 1F[1]
43112 4MT[5]
43113 4MT[5]
43257 3F[3]
43295 3F[3]
43784 3F[4]
43893 4F[1]
43913 4F[1]
43916 4F[1]
43944 4F[1]
43960 4F[1]
43999 4F[1]
44000 4F[1]
44007 4F[1]
44041 4F[2]
44197 4F[2]
44222 4F[2]
44277 4F[2]
44431 4F[2]
44468 4F[2]
46440 2MT[2]
46442 2MT[2]
46452 2MT[2]
47427 3F[6]
47428 3F[6]
47454 3F[6]
47562 3F[6]

1957 20F

40409 2P[2]
41205 2MT[1]
41325 2MT[1]
41326 2MT[1]
41327 2MT[1]
41855 1F[1]
43112 4MT[5]
43113 4MT[5]
43178 3F
43257 3F[3]
43295 3F[3]
43893 4F[1]
43913 4F[1]
43916 4F[1]
43960 4F[1]
43992 4F[1]
43999 4F[1]
44000 4F[1]
44007 4F[1]
44041 4F[2]
44197 4F[2]
44222 4F[2]
44277 4F[2]
44431 4F[2]
44468 4F[2]
46442 2MT[2]
46452 2MT[2]
47427 3F[6]
47428 3F[6]
47454 3F[6]
47562 3F[6]

1960 24G

40586 2P[3]
41327 2MT[1]
43893 4F[1]
43913 4F[1]
43960 4F[1]
43999 4F[1]
44007 4F[1]
44041 4F[2]
44105 4F[2]
44119 4F[2]
44197 4F[2]
44220 4F[2]
44222 4F[2]
44277 4F[2]
44431 4F[2]
44468 4F[2]
46442 2MT[2]
46452 2MT[2]
47238 3F[5]
47427 3F[6]
47428 3F[6]
47454 3F[6]
84015 2MT[2]

1963 24G

43893 4F[1]
43960 4F[1]
43999 4F[1]
44007 4F[1]
44041 4F[2]
44197 4F[2]
44220 4F[2]
44277 4F[2]
44468 4F[2]
47427 3F[6]
47454 3F[6]
47577 3F[6]
78036 2MT[1]
78037 2MT[1]
84015 2MT[2]
84028 2MT[2]

1966 10G

41241 2MT[1]
47201 3F[5]
47427 3F[6]
47602 3F[6]
75011 4MT[1]
75015 4MT[1]
75017 4MT[1]
75019 4MT[1]
75039 4MT[1]
75041 4MT[1]
75042 4MT[1]
75044 4MT[1]
75051 4MT[1]
75057 4MT[1]
75058 4MT[1]
75059 4MT[1]

Slough

1948 SLO

1426 1400
1437 1400
1442 1400
2055 2021
2112 2021
2757 2721
2790 2721
3652 5700
3677 5700
3681 5700
3769 5700
3798 5700
4617 5700
4650 5700
5715 5700
5737 5700
5783 5700
6100 6100
6101 6100
6104 6100
6105 6100
6106 6100
6107 6100
6108 6100
6111 6100
6113 6100
6114 6100
6116 6100
6119 6100
6123 6100
6124 6100
6126 6100
6127 6100
6133 6100
6143 6100
6145 6100
6146 6100
6150 6100
6151 6100
6152 6100
6153 6100
6157 6100
6160 6100
6161 6100
6164 6100
6167 6100
9640 5700
9653 5700
9781 5700
9789 5700

1951 81B

1437 1400
1442 1400
1448 1400
2112 2021
3697 5700
3715 5700
4650 5700
4691 5700
5409 5400
5715 5700
5737 5700
5783 5700
6104 6100
6106 6100
6108 6100
6113 6100
6114 6100
6115 6100
6116 6100
6119 6100
6123 6100
6124 6100
6127 6100
6131 6100
6133 6100
6136 6100
6140 6100
6143 6100
6146 6100
6150 6100
6151 6100
6152 6100
6154 6100
6157 6100
6160 6100
6161 6100
6164 6100
7441 7400
7442 7400
8722 5700
9414 9400
9415 9400
9421 9400
9424 9400
9653 5700
9722 5700
9781 5700
9789 5700

1954 81B

1437 1400
1448 1400
1450 1400
3697 5700
3740 5700
4638 5700
4650 5700
4680 5700
4691 5700
5409 5400
5715 5700
6108 6100
6115 6100
6119 6100
6123 6100
6124 6100
6127 6100
6131 6100
6132 6100
6133 6100
6136 6100
6140 6100
6143 6100
6146 6100
6150 6100
6151 6100
6152 6100
6153 6100
6154 6100
6157 6100
6160 6100
6164 6100
8722 5700
9406 9400
9415 9400
9421 9400
9424 9400
9722 5700
9781 5700
9789 5700

1957 81B

1448 1400
1450 1400
3697 5700
4638 5700
4650 5700
4680 5700
4691 5700
5715 5700
5755 5700
5766 5700
6108 6100
6115 6100
6122 6100
6124 6100
6127 6100
6131 6100
6133 6100
6136 6100
6140 6100
6143 6100
6146 6100
6150 6100
6151 6100
6152 6100
6154 6100
6157 6100
6160 6100
6164 6100
6664 5600
9406 9400
9415 9400
9421 9400
9424 9400
9722 5700
9781 5700

1960 81B

1447 1400
1448 1400
3608 5700
3697 5700
4606 5700
4638 5700
4650 5700
4691 5700
5755 5700
5766 5700
6109 6100
6115 6100
6117 6100
6123 6100
6126 6100
6127 6100
6136 6100
6143 6100
6146 6100
6150 6100
6151 6100
6152 6100
6154 6100
6655 5600
9406 9400
9415 9400
9421 9400
9424 9400
9722 5700
9781 5700

1963 81B

1445 1400
1474 1400
1622 1600
3608 5700
3665 5700
4638 5700
6117 6100
6128 6100
6143 6100
6160 6100
8486 9400
9406 9400
9422 9400

South Blyth

1948 SBH

65003 J21
65069 J21
65123 J21
65808 J27
65810 J27
65829 J27
65834 J27
67244 G5
67261 G5
67285 G5
67295 G5
67320 G5
67326 G5
67334 G5
67341 G5
67347 G5
68415 J77
68428 J77

1951 52F sub

65080 J21
65781 J27
65808 J27
65810 J27
65824 J27
65829 J27
65834 J27
67244 G5
67246 G5
67261 G5
67295 G5
67326 G5
67334 G5
67341 G5
67347 G5
68424 J77
68428 J77
68431 J77

1954 52F sub

65033 J21
65099 J21
65781 J27
65808 J27
65810 J27
65822 J27
65824 J27
65829 J27
65834 J27
65838 J27
65862 J27
67246 G5
67261 G5
67295 G5
67326 G5
67334 G5
67341 G5
67347 G5
68424 J77
68431 J77

1957 52F sub

65696 J25
65706 J25
65727 J25
65781 J27
65808 J27
65810 J27
65822 J27
65824 J27
65829 J27
65834 J27
65838 J27
65862 J27
65877 J27
67263 G5
67277 G5
67281 G5
67320 G5
67339 G5
67340 G5
67341 G5
68408 J77
68424 J77
68431 J77

1960 52F sub

65070 J21
65663 J25
65727 J25
65799 J27
65808 J27
65810 J27
65822 J27
65834 J27
65838 J27
65847 J27
65861 J27
65862 J27
65877 J27
65891 J27
68408 J77

1963 52F sub

65808 J27
65810 J27
65822 J27
65834 J27
65838 J27
65861 J27
65862 J27
65876 J27
65890 J27
65891 J27

1966 52F sub

62002 K1
65790 J27
65795 J27
65805 J27
65809 J27
65812 J27
65813 J27
65814 J27
65819 J27
65821 J27
65825 J27
65838 J27
65842 J27
65855 J27
65860 J27
65861 J27
65874 J27
65882 J27
65893 J27

South Lynn

1948 SL

61738 K2
61742 K2
61743 K2
61748 K2
62122 D3
62124 D3
62137 D3
62144 D3
62145 D3
62534 D16
62543 D16
62558 D16
62559 D16
62572 D16
62573 D16
64163 J3
64167 J4
64645 J19
65504 J17
65505 J17
65521 J17
65526 J17
65532 J17
65533 J17
65545 J17
65561 J17
65562 J17
65565 J17
65579 J17
65582 J17
65588 J17
65589 J17
68484 J93
68488 J93
68566 J69
68597 J67

1951 31D

43090 4MT[5]
43091 4MT[5]
43092 4MT[5]
43093 4MT[5]
43094 4MT[5]
43095 4MT[5]
61533 B12
61537 B12
61540 B12
61547 B12
61738 K2
61742 K2
61743 K2
61748 K2
61757 K2
61766 K2
62507 D15
62534 D16
62558 D16
64645 J19
64646 J19
64649 J19
64653 J19
64658 J19
64673 J19
65504 J17
65526 J17
65533 J17
65545 J17
65562 J17
65579 J17
65580 J17
65582 J17
65588 J17
67227 F6
68378 J66
68542 J69
68566 J69
68597 J67
68600 J69

1954 31D

43090 4MT[5]
43091 4MT[5]
43092 4MT[5]
43093 4MT[5]
43094 4MT[5]
43095 4MT[5]
43104 4MT[5]
43105 4MT[5]
43106 4MT[5]
43108 4MT[5]
43109 4MT[5]
43110 4MT[5]
43111 4MT[5]
43142 4MT[5]
43143 4MT[5]
61537 B12
61540 B12
61547 B12
64646 J19
65517 J17
65520 J17
65562 J17
65579 J17
68494 J69
68542 J69
68566 J69
68567 J69
68623 J69

1957 31D

43068 4MT[5]
43090 4MT[5]
43091 4MT[5]
43092 4MT[5]
43093 4MT[5]
43094 4MT[5]
43095 4MT[5]
43104 4MT[5]
43105 4MT[5]
43107 4MT[5]
43108 4MT[5]
43109 4MT[5]
43110 4MT[5]
43111 4MT[5]
43142 4MT[5]
43143 4MT[5]
43144 4MT[5]
65584 J17
68494 J69
68542 J69
68566 J69
68623 J69

Southall

1948 SHL

1443 1400
1462 1400
1925 1901
1969 1901
2285 2251
2843 2800
2858 2800
3562 3500
3620 5700
3704 5700
3727 5700
3750 5700
3799 5700
3854 2884
3855 2884
3856 2884
3857 2884
3858 2884
3859 2884
3860 2884
4604 5700
4608 5700
4610 5700
4663 5700
4673 5700
4695 5700
5119 5101
5360 4300
5401 5400
5405 5400
5409 5400
5410 5400
5411 5400
5413 5400
5414 5400
5415 5400
5416 5400
5417 5400
5418 5400
5420 5400
5421 5400
5727 5700
5750 5700
5753 5700
5755 5700
5799 5700
6102 6100
6110 6100
6118 6100
6125 6100
6128 6100
6139 6100
6147 6100
6148 6100
6156 6100
6165 6100
6169 6100
6325 4300
6388 4300
6407 6400
6809 6800
6826 6800
7730 5700
7731 5700
7732 5700
8752 5700
8753 5700
8758 5700
8764 5700
8774 5700
9300 9300
9301 9300
9311 9300
9641 5700
9755 5700

1951 81C

1443 1400
1462 1400
1501 1500
1605 1600
2285 2251
2843 2800
3618 5700
3620 5700
3704 5700
3727 5700
3750 5700
3799 5700
3803 2884
3854 2884
3855 2884
3856 2884
3857 2884
4608 5700
4610 5700
4673 5700
4695 5700
4917 4900
4944 4900
4956 4900
4978 4900
5356 4300
5360 4300
5401 5400
5405 5400
5410 5400
5414 5400
5415 5400
5416 5400
5418 5400
5420 5400
5727 5700
5751 5700
5753 5700
5755 5700
5799 5700
5918 4900
5952 4900
5983 4900
5989 4900
6110 6100
6125 6100
6126 6100
6128 6100
6139 6100
6147 6100
6148 6100
6156 6100
6165 6100
6169 6100
6325 4300
6388 4300
6961 6959
7309 4300
7730 5700
7731 5700
7732 5700
7910 6959
8752 5700
8758 5700
8774 5700
9300 9300
9301 9300
9310 9300
9311 9300
9407 9400
9409 9400
9641 5700
9726 5700

1954 81C

1426 1400
1443 1400
1462 1400
1474 1400
1501 1500
2285 2251
2858 2800
2880 2800
2899 2884
3618 5700
3620 5700
3704 5700
3727 5700
3750 5700
3799 5700
3856 2884
3857 2884
4608 5700
4610 5700
4673 5700
4695 5700
4908 4900
4931 4900
4939 4900
4944 4900
4956 4900
4979 4900
5410 5400
5414 5400
5415 5400
5416 5400
5418 5400
5420 5400
5727 5700
5753 5700
5755 5700
5799 5700
5918 4900
5952 4900
5953 4900
5983 4900
5989 4900
6125 6100
6128 6100
6147 6100
6148 6100
6156 6100
6165 6100
6169 6100
6655 5600
6664 5600
6934 4900
7730 5700
7731 5700
7732 5700
7910 6959
8750 5700
8752 5700
8758 5700
8774 5700
9300 9300
9301 9300
9304 9300
9309 9300
9310 9300
9407 9400
9409 9400
9641 5700
9726 5700
90152 WD[1]
90174 WD[1]
90207 WD[1]
90268 WD[1]
90485 WD[1]

1957 81C

1415 1400
1426 1400
1436 1400
1443 1400
1446 1400
1474 1400
1501 1500
2853 2800
2880 2800
2890 2884
2899 2884
3618 5700
3620 5700
3704 5700
3727 5700
3750 5700
3799 5700
3814 2884
3836 2884
3856 2884
4608 5700
4610 5700
4673 5700
4695 5700
4707 4700
4944 4900
5410 5400
5415 5400
5420 5400
5727 5700
5753 5700
5799 5700
5918 4900
5953 4900
5983 4900
5989 4900
6109 6100
6125 6100
6128 6100
6147 6100
6148 6100
6156 6100
6165 6100
6169 6100
6313 4300
6654 5600
6655 5600
6991 6959
7730 5700
7731 5700
7910 6959
8750 5700
8752 5700
8758 5700
8774 5700
9305 9300
9409 9400
9413 9400
9417 9400
9469 9400
9641 5700
9726 5700
9789 5700
90152 WD[1]
90174 WD[1]
90207 WD[1]
90268 WD[1]
90313 WD[1]
90355 WD[1]
90485 WD[1]
90529 WD[1]
90630 WD[1]

1960 81C

1431 1400
1501 1500
3618 5700
3620 5700
3704 5700
3715 5700
3750 5700
3799 5700
4608 5700
4673 5700
4707 4700
4925 4900
4934 4900
5925 4900
5933 4900
6110 6100
6128 6100
6147 6100
6148 6100
6149 6100
6156 6100
6159 6100
6165 6100
6169 6100
6967 6959
6991 6959
7910 6959
7923 6959
8413 9400
8451 9400
8456 9400
8750 5700
8752 5700
8761 5700
8769 5700
8774 5700
9409 9400
9413 9400
9422 9400
9490 9400
9641 5700
9642 5700
9726 5700
9789 5700
9791 5700
90174 WD[1]
90355 WD[1]
90356 WD[1]
90466 WD[1]
90630 WD[1]

1963 81C

1654 1600
2873 2800
2899 2884
3618 5700
3620 5700
3622 5700
3834 2884
3854 2884
4608 5700
4705 4700
4706 4700
4707 4700
4976 4900
4989 4900
5929 4900
5971 4900
5985 4900
6108 6100
6110 6100
6132 6100
6133 6100
6165 6100
6809 6800
6834 6800
6841 6800
6869 6800
6967 6959
6974 6959
6986 6959
6991 6959
6994 6959
7910 6959
7922 6959
7923 6959
8456 9400
8465 9400
8752 5700
9413 9400
9415 9400
9641 5700
9642 5700
9726 5700
92207 9F
92210 9F
92245 9F

Southampton Docks

1948 SOT

30061 USA
30062 USA
30063 USA
30064 USA
30065 USA
30066 USA
30067 USA
30068 USA
30069 USA
30070 USA
30071 USA
30072 USA
30073 USA
30074 USA
30081 B4[1]
30085 B4[1]
30089 B4[1]
30097 B4[1]
30098 B4[1]
30101 B4[1]
30147 B4[1]
30176 B4[1]
32112 E1[2]
32156 E1[2]
32162 E1[2]
32689 E1[2]

1951 71I

30061 USA
30062 USA
30063 USA
30064 USA
30065 USA
30066 USA
30067 USA
30068 USA
30069 USA
30070 USA
30071 USA
30072 USA
30073 USA
30074 USA
32156 E1[2]
32606 E1[2]

1954 71I

30061 USA
30062 USA
30063 USA
30064 USA
30065 USA
30066 USA
30067 USA
30068 USA
30069 USA
30070 USA
30071 USA
30072 USA
30073 USA
30074 USA
32606 E1[2]
32689 E1[2]

1957 71I

30061 USA
30062 USA
30063 USA
30064 USA
30065 USA
30066 USA
30067 USA
30068 USA
30069 USA
30070 USA
30071 USA
30072 USA
30073 USA
30074 USA
32113 E1[2]
32151 E1[2]
32689 E1[2]

1960 71I

30061 USA
30062 USA
30063 USA
30064 USA
30065 USA
30066 USA
30067 USA
30068 USA
30069 USA
30070 USA
30071 USA
30072 USA
30073 USA
30074 USA
32101 E2
32108 E2
32109 E2
32151 E1[2]
32689 E1[2]
32694 E1[2]

1963 71I

30064 USA
30067 USA
30068 USA
30069 USA
30071 USA
30072 USA
30073 USA
30074 USA
32104 E2
32109 E2

Southport

1948 23C

41085 4P[1]
41193 4P[1]
41196 4P[1]
42291 4MT[1]
42292 4MT[1]
42293 4MT[1]
42294 4MT[1]
44056 4F[2]
44062 4F[2]
44471 4F[2]
44474 4F[2]
44887 5MT[3]
44989 5MT[3]
45061 5MT[3]
45200 5MT[3]
45334 5MT[3]
45415 5MT[3]
45435 5MT[3]
50678 2P[8]
50687 2P[8]
50696 2P[8]
50728 2P[8]
50743 2P[8]
50746 2P[8]
50752 2P[8]
50778 2P[8]
50849 2P[8]
50865 2P[8]
51490 2F[2]
52161 3F[7]
52197 3F[7]
52256 3F[7]
52271 3F[7]
52272 3F[7]
52381 3F[7]
52400 3F[7]
52523 3F[7]

1951 27C

40190 3MT[2]
40191 3MT[2]
40192 3MT[2]
40194 3MT[2]
40195 3MT[2]
40196 3MT[2]
40197 3MT[2]
40198 3MT[2]
42291 4MT[1]
42292 4MT[1]
42293 4MT[1]
42294 4MT[1]
44728 5MT[3]
44729 5MT[3]
44737 5MT[3]
44887 5MT[3]
44926 5MT[3]
44989 5MT[3]
45061 5MT[3]
45200 5MT[3]
45334 5MT[3]
45415 5MT[3]
45435 5MT[3]

51490 2F[2]
52161 3F[7]
52162 3F[7]
52183 3F[7]
52278 3F[7]
52582 3F[9]

1954 27C
40190 3MT[2]
40191 3MT[2]
40192 3MT[2]
40194 3MT[2]
40195 3MT[2]
40196 3MT[2]
40197 3MT[2]
40198 3MT[2]
42291 4MT[1]
42292 4MT[1]
42293 4MT[1]
44728 5MT[3]
44729 5MT[3]
44887 5MT[3]
44989 5MT[3]
45078 5MT[3]
50721 2P[8]
50777 2P[8]
50781 2P[8]
51425 2F[2]
52161 3F[7]
52183 3F[7]
52582 3F[9]
75015 4MT[1]
75016 4MT[1]
75017 4MT[1]
75018 4MT[1]
75019 4MT[1]

1957 27C
40090 3MT[2]
40190 3MT[2]
40191 3MT[2]
40192 3MT[2]
40194 3MT[2]
40195 3MT[2]
40196 3MT[2]
40197 3MT[2]
40198 3MT[2]
41186 4P[1]
42291 4MT[1]
42292 4MT[1]
42293 4MT[1]
42537 4MT[3]
44728 5MT[3]
44729 5MT[3]
44887 5MT[3]
44989 5MT[3]
45061 5MT[3]
45218 5MT[3]
45228 5MT[3]
50712 2P[8]
50721 2P[8]
50746 2P[8]
50781 2P[8]
52123 3F[7]
52161 3F[7]
52183 3F[7]
75015 4MT[1]
75016 4MT[1]
75017 4MT[1]
75018 4MT[1]
75019 4MT[1]

1960 27C
40090 3MT[2]
40145 3MT[2]
40178 3MT[2]
40191 3MT[2]
40194 3MT[2]
40195 3MT[2]
40196 3MT[2]
40197 3MT[2]
40198 3MT[2]
42063 4MT[1]
42290 4MT[1]
42292 4MT[1]
42293 4MT[1]
42435 4MT[3]
42451 4MT[3]
42537 4MT[3]
42637 4MT[3]
44728 5MT[3]
44729 5MT[3]
44887 5MT[3]
44989 5MT[3]
45061 5MT[3]
45218 5MT[3]
45228 5MT[3]
50746 2P[8]
75015 4MT[1]
75016 4MT[1]
75017 4MT[1]
75018 4MT[1]
75019 4MT[1]

1963 27C
42061 4MT[1]
42063 4MT[1]
42132 4MT[1]
42292 4MT[1]
42293 4MT[1]
42435 4MT[3]
42451 4MT[3]
42485 4MT[3]
42551 4MT[3]
42645 4MT[3]
42662 4MT[3]
44689 5MT[3]
44742 5MT[3]
44743 5MT[3]
44744 5MT[3]
44745 5MT[3]
44767 5MT[3]
44989 5MT[3]
45105 5MT[3]
45218 5MT[3]
75015 4MT[1]
75016 4MT[1]
75017 4MT[1]
75018 4MT[1]
75019 4MT[1]

1966 8M
42078 4MT[1]
42132 4MT[1]
42233 4MT[1]
42665 4MT[3]
44687 5MT[3]
44809 5MT[3]
45055 5MT[3]

Sowerby Bridge

1948 25E
44038 4F[2]
44042 4F[2]
44464 4F[2]
47508 3F[6]
47509 3F[6]
47510 3F[6]
49507 7F[4]
49508 7F[4]
49527 7F[4]
49528 7F[4]
49568 7F[4]
49569 7F[4]
49606 7F[4]
49628 7F[4]
50711 2P[8]
50835 3P[3]
50891 3P[3]
50925 3P[3]
50934 3P[3]
50943 3P[3]
51381 2F[2]
51429 2F[2]
51479 2F[2]
51482 2F[2]
52099 3F[7]
52243 3F[7]
52376 3F[7]
52416 3F[7]
52574 3F[9]
52575 3F[9]
52587 3F[9]
52590 3F[9]
52616 3F[9]

1951 25E
42149 4MT[1]
42150 4MT[1]
42151 4MT[1]
42639 4MT[3]
47508 3F[6]
47509 3F[6]
49540 7F[4]
49650 7F[4]
49657 7F[4]
49661 7F[4]
49662 7F[4]
49663 7F[4]
49673 7F[4]
49674 7F[4]
50712 2P[8]
50765 2P[8]
50892 2P[8]
50898 2P[8]
50925 3P[3]
51348 2F[2]
51381 2F[2]
51479 2F[2]
51488 2F[2]
51503 2F[2]
52189 3F[7]
52217 3F[7]
52243 3F[7]
52376 3F[7]
52400 3F[7]
52452 3F[7]
52575 3F[9]
52587 3F[9]

1954 25E
42149 4MT[1]
42150 4MT[1]
42151 4MT[1]
42639 4MT[3]
47508 3F[6]
47509 3F[6]
49511 7F[4]
49602 7F[4]
49624 7F[4]
49657 7F[4]
49674 7F[4]
50715 2P[8]
50752 2P[8]
50757 2P[8]
51381 2F[2]
51488 2F[2]
52154 3F[7]
52217 3F[7]
52400 3F[7]
52408 3F[7]
52410 3F[7]
52558 3F[9]

1957 56E
42149 4MT[1]
42150 4MT[1]
42151 4MT[1]
42639 4MT[3]
47266 3F[6]
47299 3F[6]
47379 3F[6]
47508 3F[6]
47509 3F[6]
49592 7F[4]
49657 7F[4]
50752 2P[8]
50777 2P[8]
50818 2P[8]
52217 3F[7]
52351 3F[7]
52399 3F[7]
52400 3F[7]
52411 3F[7]
52452 3F[7]
90122 WD[1]
90236 WD[1]
90310 WD[1]
90329 WD[1]
90360 WD[1]
90412 WD[1]

1960 56E
40147 3MT[2]
40190 3MT[2]
42083 4MT[1]
42094 4MT[1]
42149 4MT[1]
42150 4MT[1]
42151 4MT[1]
42380 4MT[2]
42405 4MT[2]
42411 4MT[2]
46438 2MT[2]
46483 2MT[2]
47379 3F[6]
47508 3F[6]
47509 3F[6]
52351 3F[7]
52400 3F[7]
52411 3F[7]
52452 3F[7]
90113 WD[1]
90122 WD[1]
90210 WD[1]
90310 WD[1]
90329 WD[1]
90360 WD[1]
90412 WD[1]
90470 WD[1]

1963 56E
44055 4F[2]
44094 4F[2]
44153 4F[2]
90113 WD[1]
90122 WD[1]
90200 WD[1]
90210 WD[1]
90233 WD[1]
90281 WD[1]
90329 WD[1]
90360 WD[1]
90412 WD[1]
90470 WD[1]
90692 WD[1]

Speke Junction

1948 8C
42788 5MT[1]
42810 5MT[1]
42815 5MT[1]
42926 5MT[1]
42933 5MT[1]
42934 5MT[1]
42946 5MT[2]
42972 5MT[2]
42974 5MT[2]
42978 5MT[2]
47284 3F[6]
47388 3F[6]
47439 3F[6]
47875 6F[1]
47877 6F[1]
47881 6F[1]
47884 6F[1]
48904 6F[2]
48942 7F[2]
49027 7F[2]
49057 7F[2]
49060 6F[2]
49065 7F[2]
49066 7F[2]
49086 7F[2]
49140 6F[2]
49218 7F[2]
49219 7F[2]
49253 7F[2]
49281 7F[2]
49293 7F[2]
49297 6F[2]
49341 7F[2]
49365 7F[2]
51342 2F[2]
51397 2F[2]
51405 2F[2]
51427 2F[2]
51441 2F[2]
51444 2F[2]
51469 2F[2]
52088 3F[7]
52143 3F[7]
52163 3F[7]
52219 3F[7]
52438 3F[7]
58883 2F[14]
58906 2F[14]

1951 8C
42786 5MT[1]
42849 5MT[1]
42852 5MT[1]
42892 5MT[1]
42962 5MT[2]
42964 5MT[2]
42965 5MT[2]
42971 5MT[2]
42977 5MT[2]
42982 5MT[2]
47284 3F[6]
47362 3F[6]
47373 3F[6]
47388 3F[6]
47439 3F[6]
47651 3F[6]
48054 8F
48520 8F
48521 8F
48522 8F
48528 8F
48529 8F
48630 8F
48631 8F
48743 8F
48747 8F
48748 8F
48942 7F[2]
48944 7F[2]
49120 7F[2]
49125 7F[2]
49143 7F[2]
49153 7F[2]
49172 7F[2]
49218 7F[2]
49244 7F[2]
49249 7F[2]
49253 7F[2]
49302 7F[2]
49395 7F[3]
49396 7F[3]
49398 7F[3]
49420 7F[3]
49451 7F[3]
51439 2F[2]
52100 3F[7]
52143 3F[7]
52163 3F[7]
52175 3F[7]
52438 3F[7]

1954 8C
42786 5MT[1]
42849 5MT[1]
42892 5MT[1]
47284 3F[6]
47373 3F[6]
47388 3F[6]
47439 3F[6]
47490 3F[6]
47516 3F[6]
47651 3F[6]
48039 8F
48054 8F
48094 8F
48323 8F
48373 8F
48522 8F
48630 8F
48631 8F
48747 8F
48942 7F[2]
48944 7F[2]
49134 7F[2]
49143 7F[2]
49153 7F[2]
49155 7F[2]
49395 7F[3]
49398 7F[3]
49406 7F[3]
49420 7F[3]
49451 7F[3]
51439 2F[2]
52163 3F[7]
52175 3F[7]
52438 3F[7]

1957 8C
42786 5MT[1]
42849 5MT[1]
42892 5MT[1]
47388 3F[6]
47493 3F[6]
47651 3F[6]
48039 8F
48054 8F
48323 8F
48373 8F
48522 8F
48631 8F
48747 8F
48942 7F[2]
48944 7F[2]
49109 7F[2]
49134 7F[2]
49143 7F[2]
49153 7F[2]
49266 7F[2]
49368 7F[2]
49395 7F[3]
49398 7F[3]
49406 7F[3]
49420 7F[3]
49451 7F[3]
52163 3F[7]
52175 3F[7]
52232 3F[7]
52438 3F[7]

1960 8C
42849 5MT[1]
42892 5MT[1]
47160 2F[1]
47164 2F[1]
47310 3F[6]
47314 3F[6]
47388 3F[6]
47493 3F[6]
47560 3F[6]
47612 3F[6]
47651 3F[6]
48039 8F
48247 8F
48268 8F
48506 8F
48522 8F
48531 8F
48535 8F
48631 8F
48714 8F
48747 8F

1963 8C
42078 4MT[1]
42121 4MT[1]
42389 4MT[2]
42445 4MT[3]
42584 4MT[3]
42598 4MT[3]
42612 4MT[3]
44741 5MT[3]
44749 5MT[3]
44750 5MT[3]
44751 5MT[3]
44754 5MT[3]
44827 5MT[3]
44864 5MT[3]
45032 5MT[3]
45034 5MT[3]
45069 5MT[3]
45071 5MT[3]
45131 5MT[3]
45137 5MT[3]
45181 5MT[3]
45312 5MT[3]
45329 5MT[3]
45332 5MT[3]
45370 5MT[3]
45375 5MT[3]
45386 5MT[3]
45404 5MT[3]
45412 5MT[3]
45413 5MT[3]
45441 5MT[3]
47651 3F[6]
48045 8F
48046 8F
48250 8F
48294 8F
48297 8F
48500 8F
48520 8F
48535 8F
48692 8F
48711 8F
48714 8F
48722 8F
51253 0F[4]

1966 8C
44678 5MT[3]
44679 5MT[3]
44725 5MT[3]
44732 5MT[3]
44743 5MT[3]
44806 5MT[3]
44877 5MT[3]
44950 5MT[3]
45034 5MT[3]
45057 5MT[3]
45059 5MT[3]
45071 5MT[3]
45131 5MT[3]
45137 5MT[3]
45154 5MT[3]
45181 5MT[3]
45188 5MT[3]
45201 5MT[3]
45329 5MT[3]
45332 5MT[3]
45338 5MT[3]
45370 5MT[3]
45386 5MT[3]
45388 5MT[3]
45407 5MT[3]
45412 5MT[3]
45417 5MT[3]
45441 5MT[3]
45466 5MT[3]
46410 2MT[2]
46440 2MT[2]
46503 2MT[2]
46515 2MT[2]
46516 2MT[2]
46518 2MT[2]
48029 8F
48163 8F
48292 8F
48294 8F
48296 8F
48305 8F
48308 8F
48374 8F
48425 8F
48457 8F
48476 8F
48493 8F
48509 8F
48520 8F
48692 8F
48709 8F
48711 8F
48722 8F
92008 9F
92025 9F
92027 9F
92054 9F
92091 9F
92115 9F
92117 9F
92153 9F
92154 9F
92158 9F

Spital Bridge

1948 16B
40180 3MT[2]
40408 2P[2]
40410 2P[2]
40497 2P[2]
40532 2P[2]
40533 2P[2]
40552 2P[2]
40558 2P[2]
41846 1F[1]
43253 3F[3]
43317 3F[3]
43319 3F[3]
43371 3F[3]
43651 3F[3]
43652 3F[3]
43854 4F[1]
43859 4F[1]
43864 4F[1]
43898 4F[1]
43920 4F[1]
43957 4F[1]
43980 4F[1]
43981 4F[1]
44097 4F[2]
44152 4F[2]
44155 4F[2]
44218 4F[2]
44238 4F[2]
44239 4F[2]
44273 4F[2]
44293 4F[2]
44296 4F[2]
44458 4F[2]
44476 4F[2]
44509 4F[2]
44518 4F[2]
44519 4F[2]
44521 4F[2]
44522 4F[2]
47202 3F[5]
47269 3F[6]
47270 3F[6]
47566 3F[6]
47622 3F[6]

1951 35C
40401 2P[2]
40410 2P[2]
40482 2P[2]
40497 2P[2]
40532 2P[2]
40558 2P[2]
40559 2P[2]
43064 4MT[5]
43651 3F[3]
43854 4F[1]
43864 4F[1]
43957 4F[1]
43980 4F[1]
43981 4F[1]
44097 4F[2]
44110 4F[2]
44117 4F[2]
44152 4F[2]
44155 4F[2]
44218 4F[2]
44238 4F[2]
44239 4F[2]
44273 4F[2]
44293 4F[2]
44296 4F[2]
44458 4F[2]
44476 4F[2]
44509 4F[2]
44518 4F[2]
44519 4F[2]
44521 4F[2]
44522 4F[2]
47269 3F[6]
47270 3F[6]
47566 3F[6]
47621 3F[6]
47622 3F[6]
47659 3F[6]
67362 C12
90063 WD[1]
90447 WD[1]
90501 WD[1]

1954 35C
43064 4MT[5]
43957 4F[1]
44097 4F[2]
44110 4F[2]
44152 4F[2]
44239 4F[2]
44247 4F[2]
44273 4F[2]
44458 4F[2]
44476 4F[2]
44509 4F[2]
44518 4F[2]
44519 4F[2]
44521 4F[2]
44522 4F[2]
62535 D16
62536 D16
62568 D16
62587 D16
62599 D16
62609 D16
64288 J11
64338 J11
64397 J11
64719 J39
64723 J39
64789 J39
64883 J39
64891 J39
64896 J39
64901 J39
64902 J39
64951 J39
64954 J39
64965 J39
64981 J39
67362 C12
67366 C12
67368 C12
68759 J52
68783 J52
68797 J52
68809 J52
68831 J52
68889 J52
90063 WD[1]
90156 WD[1]
90447 WD[1]
90501 WD[1]

1957 35C
43127 4MT[5]
43957 4F[1]
44097 4F[2]
44110 4F[2]
44152 4F[2]
44239 4F[2]
44247 4F[2]
44273 4F[2]
44476 4F[2]
44509 4F[2]
44518 4F[2]
44519 4F[2]
44521 4F[2]
44522 4F[2]
47282 3F[6]
47306 3F[6]
47311 3F[6]
61047 B1
61538 B12
61554 B12
61565 B12
61567 B12
62535 D16
62568 D16
62599 D16
62609 D16
64719 J39
64723 J39
64736 J39
64789 J39
64883 J39
64891 J39
64896 J39
64901 J39
64951 J39
64954 J39
64965 J39
64981 J39
67352 C12
90063 WD[1]
90447 WD[1]
90501 WD[1]

1960 31F
41949 3P[2]
43127 4MT[5]
43957 4F[1]
44097 4F[2]
44110 4F[2]
44152 4F[2]
44239 4F[2]
44247 4F[2]
44273 4F[2]
44476 4F[2]
44509 4F[2]
44518 4F[2]
44519 4F[2]
44521 4F[2]
44522 4F[2]
47300 3F[6]
61095 B1
61096 B1
61156 B1
61204 B1
61205 B1
61323 B1
61348 B1
62597 D16
62613 D16
64789 J39
64901 J39
90023 WD[1]
90063 WD[1]
90447 WD[1]
90501 WD[1]
90528 WD[1]

Stafford

1948 5C
40377 2P[2]
40443 2P[2]
40461 2P[2]
40528 2P[2]
41151 4P[1]
42345 4MT[2]
42346 4MT[2]
42347 4MT[2]
42391 4MT[2]
46876 2P[1]
47294 3F[6]
47588 3F[6]
47598 3F[6]
47606 3F[6]
47649 3F[6]
47653 3F[6]
47670 3F[6]
48940 7F[2]
49091 6F[2]
49098 6F[2]
49144 7F[2]
49194 6F[2]
49320 6F[2]
58000 4P[6]
58001 4P[6]
58002 4P[6]
58003 4P[6]

1951 5C
40322 2P[1]
40405 2P[2]
40443 2P[2]
40461 2P[2]
40471 2P[2]
40507 2P[2]
42309 4MT[2]
42320 4MT[2]
42345 4MT[2]
42346 4MT[2]
42347 4MT[2]
42391 4MT[2]
47588 3F[6]
47598 3F[6]
47606 3F[6]
47649 3F[6]
47653 3F[6]
47665 3F[6]
48922 7F[2]
49047 7F[2]
49115 7F[2]
49158 7F[2]
49229 7F[2]
49410 7F[3]

1954 5C
40443 2P[2]
40461 2P[2]
40522 2P[2]
40646 2P[3]
40678 2P[3]
42309 4MT[2]
42320 4MT[2]
42345 4MT[2]
42346 4MT[2]
42347 4MT[2]
47588 3F[6]
47590 3F[6]
47606 3F[6]
47649 3F[6]
47653 3F[6]
47665 3F[6]
49047 7F[2]
49115 7F[2]
49158 7F[2]
49229 7F[2]
49410 7F[3]

1957 5C
40443 2P[2]
40461 2P[2]
40583 2P[3]
40646 2P[3]
40678 2P[3]
42309 4MT[2]
42345 4MT[2]
42346 4MT[2]
42347 4MT[2]
42418 4MT[2]
42421 4MT[2]
42425 4MT[3]
42538 4MT[3]
42562 4MT[3]
42578 4MT[3]
47359 3F[6]
47588 3F[6]
47590 3F[6]
47606 3F[6]
47649 3F[6]
47653 3F[6]
47665 3F[6]
48263 8F
48727 8F
48922 7F[2]
49047 7F[2]
49048 7F[2]
49115 7F[2]
49158 7F[2]
49198 7F[2]
49229 7F[2]
49410 7F[3]

1960 5C
40583 2P[3]
40646 2P[3]
42309 4MT[2]
42389 4MT[2]
42400 4MT[2]
47359 3F[6]
47475 3F[6]
47588 3F[6]
47590 3F[6]
47649 3F[6]
47653 3F[6]
47665 3F[6]
49081 7F[2]
49126 7F[2]
49234 7F[2]
49357 7F[2]
49377 7F[2]
49446 7F[3]

1963 5C
42186 4MT[1]
42267 4MT[1]
42488 4MT[3]
47359 3F[6]
47451 3F[6]
47518 3F[6]
47590 3F[6]
47598 3F[6]
47649 3F[6]
47665 3F[5]
48174 8F
48366 8F
48453 8F

Stafford Road

1948 SRD
1016 1000
1017 1000
1024 1000
1025 1000
1029 1000
1863 1854
2061 2021
2067 2021
2095 2021
2109 2021
2110 2021
2156 2021
2232 2251
2791 2721
3008 ROD
3020 ROD
3043 ROD
3160 3150
3615 5700
3756 5700
3760 5700
3778 5700
4000 4073
4018 4000
4025 4000
4031 4000
4053 4000
4060 4000
4103 5101
4105 5101
4108 5101
4110 5101
4115 5101
4950 4900
4960 4900
5015 4073
5018 4073
5031 4073
5053 4073
5070 4073
5075 4073
5088 4073
5103 5101
5111 5101
5143 5101
5151 5101
5739 5700
5909 4900
5919 4900
5927 4900
5942 4900
5944 4900
5995 4900
6005 6000
6006 6000
6008 6000
6011 6000
6321 4300
6391 4300
6418 6400
6422 6400
6812 6800
6844 6800
6848 6800
6901 4900
6908 4900
6924 4900
6964 6959
7007 4073
7315 4300
8705 5700
8726 5700
8734 5700
9621 5700

1951 84A
1016 1000
1017 1000
1029 1000
2061 2021
2095 2021
2109 2021
3102 3100
3104 3100
3160 3150
3615 5700
3756 5700
3778 5700
4000 4073
4018 4000
4031 4000
4049 4000
4053 4000
4058 4000
4061 4000
4092 4073
4103 5101
4105 5101
4108 5101
4115 5101
5008 4073
5010 4073
5015 4073
5022 4073
5031 4073
5045 4073
5053 4073
5070 4073
5088 4073
5143 5101
5151 5101
5701 5700
5739 5700
5780 5700
6004 6000
6005 6000
6006 6000
6008 6000
6011 6000
6020 6000
6321 4300
6812 6800
6848 6800
6956 4900
6964 6959
7026 4073
7315 4300
7915 6959
8411 9400
8423 9400
8462 9400
8705 5700
8726 5700
8734 5700
9428 9400
9621 5700

1954 84A
1004 1000
1018 1000
1019 1000
3102 3100
3104 3100
3615 5700
3664 5700
3756 5700
3778 5700
3792 5700
3793 5700
4000 4073
4053 4000
4061 4000
4079 4073
4083 4073
4090 4073
4092 4073
4103 5101
4108 5101
4997 4900
5008 4073
5010 4073
5015 4073
5022 4073
5027 4073
5031 4073
5032 4073
5045 4073
5053 4073
5070 4073
5088 4073
5106 5101
5112 5101
5151 5101
5187 5101
5188 5101
5739 5700
5780 5700
6004 6000
6005 6000
6006 6000
6011 6000
6016 6000
6020 6000
6418 6400
6422 6400
6964 6959
7026 4073
7309 4300
8411 9400
8462 9400
8705 5700
8726 5700
8734 5700
8798 5700
9428 9400
9435 9400
9621 5700

1957 84A
3102 3100
3104 3100
3615 5700
3664 5700
3756 5700
3769 5700
3778 5700
3792 5700
3793 5700
4061 4000
4079 4073
4083 4073
4092 4073
4094 4073
4103 5101
4108 5101
4140 5101
4912 4900
4926 4900
4986 4900
5010 4073
5015 4073
5022 4073
5031 4073
5032 4073
5045 4073
5047 4073
5070 4073
5075 4073
5088 4073
5106 5101
5151 5101
5187 5101
5188 5101
5780 5700
5900 4900
6001 6000
6005 6000
6006 6000
6011 6000
6014 6000
6020 6000
6418 6400
6422 6400
6949 4900
6956 4900
6964 6959
7026 4073
8411 9400
8462 9400
8726 5700
8734 5700
8798 5700
9428 9400
9435 9400
9496 9400
9621 5700

1960 84A
3615 5700
3664 5700
3756 5700
3778 5700
3792 5700
4901 4900
4918 4900
4938 4900
4954 4900
4986 4900
5019 4073
5022 4073
5026 4073
5031 4073
5045 4073
5046 4073
5047 4073
5063 4073
5070 4073
5072 4073
5088 4073
5089 4073
5151 5101
5187 5101
5900 4900
5926 4900
6001 6000
6005 6000
6006 6000
6007 6000
6008 6000
6011 6000
6014 6000
6017 6000
6020 6000
6022 6000
6418 6400
6422 6400
6926 4900
6930 4900
6987 6959
7026 4073
8411 9400
8425 9400
8426 9400
8461 9400
8726 5700
8796 5700
8798 5700
9428 9400
9435 9400

1963 84A
3778 5700
3792 5700
4148 5101
4165 5101
4179 5101
5022 4073
5026 4073
5031 4073
5063 4073
5089 4073
5199 5101
7001 4073
7012 4073
7014 4073
7019 4073
7024 4073
7026 4073
8426 9400
8498 9400
9435 9400
9470 9400

Starbeck

1948 SBK
62342 D20
62343 D20
62363 D20
62366 D20
62370 D20
62373 D20
62375 D20
62389 D20
62392 D20
62395 D20
62726 D49
62752 D49
62753 D49
62762 D49
62768 D49
62773 D49
64706 J39
64818 J39
64845 J39
64855 J39
64857 J39
64859 J39
64860 J39
04001 J39
64866 J39
64922 J39
64935 J39
64944 J39
65640 J24
67269 G5
67286 G5
67289 G5
67332 G5
68392 J77
68393 J77
68404 J77
68433 J77
68434 J77
68438 J77
69791 A6
69793 A6
69794 A6
69797 A6
69799 A6

1951 50D
62369 D20
62370 D20
62373 D20
62389 D20
62392 D20
62727 D49
62736 D49
62738 D49
62740 D49
62749 D49
62752 D49
62753 D49
62755 D49
62758 D49
62761 D49
62762 D49
62763 D49
62765 D49
62768 D49
62772 D49
62773 D49
64706 J39
64818 J39
64845 J39
64855 J39
64857 J39
64859 J39
64860 J39
64861 J39
64866 J39
64938 J39
64942 J39
64944 J39
67289 G5
68392 J77
68393 J77
68404 J77
68434 J77
68438 J77
69791 A6
69793 A6
69794 A6
69797 A6

1954 50D
61442 B16
62727 D49
62736 D49
62738 D49
62740 D49
62746 D49
62749 D49
62752 D49
62753 D49
62755 D49
62758 D49
62761 D49
62762 D49
62763 D49
62765 D49
62772 D49
62773 D49
64706 J39
64818 J39
64821 J39
64845 J39
64847 J39
64855 J39
64857 J39
64859 J39
64860 J39
64861 J39
64866 J39
64938 J39
64942 J39
64944 J39
68392 J77
68393 J77
68434 J77

1957 50D
61478 B16
62727 D49
62736 D49
62738 D49
62746 D49
62752 D49
62753 D49
62758 D49
62759 D49
62762 D49
62763 D49
62765 D49
62773 D49
62774 D49
64706 J39
64818 J39
64821 J39
64845 J39
64847 J39
64855 J39
64857 J39
64859 J39
64861 J39
64866 J39
64942 J39
64944 J39
65673 J25
68392 J77
68434 J77
90044 WD^1
90518 WD^1

Staveley

1948 STV
62133 D3
63609 O4
63613 O4
63675 O4
63702 O4
63734 O4
63746 O4
63749 O4
63838 O4
63850 O4
63889 O4
64331 J11
64336 J11
64342 J11
64345 J11
64350 J11
64351 J11
64371 J11
64373 J11
64384 J11
64428 J11
64433 J11
64444 J11
68371 J66
68379 J66
68382 J66
69279 N5
69292 N5
69295 N5
69301 N5
69351 N5
69360 N5
69363 N5
90269 WD^1
90276 WD^1
90634 WD^1

1951 38D
63613 O4
63694 O4
63720 O4
63749 O4
63767 O4
63827 O4
64317 J11
64331 J11
64345 J11
64384 J11
64386 J11
64396 J11
64428 J11
64433 J11
64444 J11
68371 J66
68382 J66
69279 N5
69292 N5
69295 N5
69301 N5
69351 N5
69363 N5
90115 WD^1
90269 WD^1
90276 WD^1
90299 WD^1
90330 WD^1
90358 WD^1
90394 WD^1
90403 WD^1
90418 WD^1
90526 WD^1
90606 WD^1
90634 WD^1

1954 38D
63587 O4
63613 O4
63648 O4
63675 O4
63694 O4
63702 O4
63705 O4
63706 O4
63720 O4
63749 O4
63762 O4
63772 O4
63787 O4
63801 O4
63827 O4
63847 O4
63884 O4
63899 O4
64313 J11
64317 J11
64336 J11
64345 J11
64384 J11
64386 J11
64396 J11
64433 J11
64444 J11
67408 C13
67419 C13
68371 J66
68374 J66
68383 J66
68553 J69
69269 N5
69279 N5
69301 N5
69351 N5
69363 N5
90115 WD^1
90269 WD^1
90276 WD^1
90299 WD^1
90394 WD^1
90403 WD^1
90418 WD^1
90460 WD^1

1957 38D
63648 O4
63702 O4
63705 O4
63706 O4
63720 O4
63735 O4
63749 O4
63762 O4
63772 O4
63787 O4
63801 O4
63804 O4
63827 O4
63845 O4
63847 O4
63877 O4
63884 O4
63899 O4
64292 J11
64313 J11
64336 J11
64361 J11
64384 J11
64396 J11
64433 J11
64444 J11
68512 J69
68608 J67
68616 J67
68617 J69
69263 N5
69269 N5
69309 N5
69803 A5
90007 WD^1
90085 WD^1
90276 WD^1
90391 WD^1

1960 41H
61312 B1
62661 D11
62663 D11
63590 O1
63648 O4
63663 O1
63702 O4
63705 O4
63706 O4
63720 O4
63735 O4
63762 O4
63772 O4
63773 O1
63784 O1
63787 O4
63795 O1
63827 O4
63845 O4
63877 O4
63884 O4
63899 O4
64292 J11
64313 J11
64354 J11
64384 J11
64396 J11
64433 J11
64444 J11
69309 N5
90007 WD^1
90055 WD^1
90085 WD^1
90087 WD^1
90276 WD^1
90502 WD^1

1963 41H
61041 B1
61162 B1
61312 B1
63571 O1
63590 O1
63596 O1
63604 O4
63612 O4
63619 O1
63630 O1
63646 O1
63650 O1
63670 O1
63678 O1
63701 O4
63705 O4
63706 O4
63773 O1
63784 O1
63786 O1
63795 O1
63827 O4
63887 O1
63899 O4
63913 O4

Staveley Barrow Hill

1948 18D
41528 0F^2
41529 0F^2
41534 0F^2
41708 1F^1
41710 1F^1
41711 1F^1
41747 1F^1
41749 1F^1
41752 1F^1
41753 1F^1
41763 1F^1
41803 1F^1
41804 1F^1
43224 3F^3
43234 3F^3
43240 3F^3
43242 3F^3
43252 3F^3
43292 3F^3
43294 3F^3
43297 3F^3
43298 3F^3
43299 3F^3
43309 3F^3
43310 3F^3
43386 3F^3
43515 3F^3
43524 3F^3
43546 3F^3
43575 3F^3
43751 3F^3
43809 3F^4
43857 4F^1
43862 4F^1
43863 4F^1
43886 4F^1
43993 4F^1
44066 4F^2
44070 4F^2
44104 4F^2
44122 4F^2
44129 4F^2
44147 4F^2
44154 4F^2
44182 4F^2
44590 4F^2
47424 3F^6
47455 3F^6
47625 3F^6
47626 3F^6
47627 3F^6
47628 3F^6
48053 8F
48054 8F
48111 8F
48120 8F
48122 8F
48134 8F
48195 8F
48210 8F
48213 8F
48332 8F
48341 8F
48346 8F
48493 8F
48537 8F
48538 8F
48539 8F
48544 8F
48604 8F
48609 8F
48652 8F
48663 8F
48686 8F

1951 18D
41528 0F^2
41529 0F^2
41533 0F^2
41534 0F^2
41708 1F^1
41710 1F^1
41711 1F^1
41749 1F^1
41752 1F^1
41753 1F^1
41763 1F^1
41777 1F^1
41803 1F^1
41804 1F^1
43224 3F^3
43234 3F^3
43252 3F^3
43292 3F^3
43294 3F^3
43298 3F^3
43299 3F^3
43309 3F^3
43310 3F^3
43386 3F^3
43515 3F^3
43524 3F^3
43546 3F^3
43575 3F^3
43751 3F^3
43857 4F^1
43863 4F^1
43886 4F^1
43900 4F^1
43914 4F^1
43920 4F^1
43993 4F^1
44006 4F^1
44066 4F^2
44070 4F^2
44104 4F^2
44122 4F^2
44129 4F^2
44147 4F^2
44154 4F^2
44182 4F^2
44299 4F^2
44590 4F^2
47263 3F^6
47424 3F^6
47426 3F^6
47455 3F^6
47502 3F^6
47625 3F^6
47626 3F^6
48210 8F
48213 8F
48332 8F
48341 8F
48346 8F
48441 8F
48460 8F
48493 8F
48539 8F
48545 8F
48546 8F
48604 8F
48663 8F

1954 18D
41528 0F^2
41529 0F^2
41533 0F^2
41534 0F^2
41708 1F^1
41710 1F^1
41711 1F^1
41749 1F^1
41752 1F^1
41763 1F^1
41777 1F^1
41803 1F^1
41804 1F^1
43224 3F^3
43234 3F^3
43292 3F^3
43294 3F^3
43298 3F^3
43299 3F^3
43310 3F^3
43386 3F^3
43515 3F^3
43524 3F^3
43546 3F^3
43575 3F^3
43605 3F^3
43857 4F^1
43863 4F^1
43886 4F^1
43900 4F^1
43914 4F^1
43920 4F^1
43993 4F^1
44006 4F^1
44010 4F^1
44066 4F^2
44070 4F^2
44104 4F^2
44122 4F^2
44129 4F^2
44147 4F^2
44182 4F^2
44267 4F^2
44299 4F^2
44371 4F^2
44475 4F^2
44590 4F^2
44606 4F^2
47247 3F^5
47263 3F^6
47424 3F^6
47426 3F^6
47455 3F^6
47545 3F^6
47625 3F^6
47626 3F^6
47637 3F^6
48033 8F
48167 8F
48210 8F
48213 8F
48341 8F
48346 8F
48460 8F
48493 8F
48515 8F
48539 8F
48545 8F
48546 8F
48604 8F
48663 8F

1957 18D
41518 0F^1
41528 0F^2
41529 0F^2
41531 0F^2
41533 0F^2
41706 1F^1
41708 1F^1
41739 1F^1
41752 1F^1
41763 1F^1
41803 1F^1
41804 1F^1
43224 3F^3
43234 3F^3
43386 3F^3
43515 3F^3
43575 3F^3
43605 3F^3
43631 3F^3
43711 3F^3
43863 4F^1
43869 4F^1
43886 4F^1
43889 4F^1
43900 4F^1
43920 4F^1
43993 4F^1
44010 4F^1
44066 4F^2
44070 4F^2
44104 4F^2
44129 4F^2
44147 4F^2
44205 4F^2
44249 4F^2
44267 4F^2
44299 4F^2
44371 4F^2
44404 4F^2
44475 4F^2
44590 4F^2
44606 4F^2
47221 3F^5
47263 3F^6
47424 3F^6
47426 3F^6
47455 3F^6
47545 3F^6
47619 3F^6
47620 3F^6
47625 3F^6
47626 3F^6
47630 3F^6
47637 3F^6
48033 8F
48037 8F
48103 8F
48164 8F
48167 8F
48199 8F
48210 8F
48213 8F
48331 8F
48341 8F
48346 8F
48493 8F
48515 8F
48533 8F
48539 8F
48545 8F
48546 8F
48604 8F
48640 8F
48663 8F

1960 41E
41528 0F^2
41529 0F^2
41531 0F^2
41533 0F^2
41708 1F^1
41734 1F^1
41739 1F^1
41700 1F^1
41769 1F^1
41804 1F^1
43386 3F^3
43515 3F^3
43605 3F^3
43828 3F^4
43863 4F^1
43869 4F^1
43900 4F^1
43920 4F^1
44010 4F^1
44066 4F^2
44070 4F^2
44088 4F^2
44104 4F^2
44129 4F^2
44147 4F^2
44205 4F^2
44249 4F^2
44267 4F^2
44371 4F^2
44404 4F^2
44475 4F^2
44482 4F^2
44590 4F^2
44606 4F^2
47221 3F^5
47263 3F^6
47424 3F^6
47426 3F^6
47455 3F^6
47545 3F^6
47619 3F^6
47626 3F^6
47630 3F^6
47637 3F^6
48037 8F
48103 8F
48164 8F
48199 8F
48200 8F
48210 8F
48213 8F
48331 8F
48341 8F
48346 8F
48493 8F
48515 8F
48533 8F
48539 8F
48546 8F
48618 8F
48663 8F
48772 8F
58146 2F^8

1963 41E
41528 0F^2
41531 0F^2
41533 0F^2
41708 1F^1
41734 1F^1
41739 1F^1
41763 1F^1
41804 1F^1
41835 1F^1
41875 1F^1
43882 4F^1
44010 4F^1
44066 4F^2
44071 4F^2
44089 4F^2
44174 4F^2
44205 4F^2
44212 4F^2
44265 4F^2
44287 4F^2
44426 4F^2
44437 4F^2
44475 4F^2
44535 4F^2
44568 4F^2
48026 8F
48029 8F
48144 8F
48150 8F
48176 8F
48189 8F
48199 8F
48200 8F
48209 8F
48210 8F
48216 8F
48331 8F
48341 8F
48407 8F
48508 8F
48515 8F
48533 8F
48539 8F
48618 8F
48642 8F
48765 8F

Stewarts Lane

1948 BAT
30086 B4^1
30090 B4^1
30763 N15
30764 N15
30765 N15
30775 N15
30776 N15
30778 N15
30780 N15
30781 N15
30793 N15
30794 N15
30795 N15
30796 N15
30797 N15
31005 H
31019 E1^1
31067 E1^1
31145 D1^1
31160 E1^1
31163 E1^1
31165 E1^1
31177 H
31179 E1^1
31184 H
31247 D1^1
31259 H
31263 H
31266 H
31293 C
31295 H
31302 1302
31307 H
31311 H
31319 H
31321 H
31329 H
31405 N
31410 N
31411 N
31412 N
31413 N
31414 N
31445 B1
31454 B1
31492 D1^1
31494 D1^1
31497 E1^1
31498 C
31504 E1^1
31506 E1^1
31507 E1^1
31508 C
31511 E1^1
31514 E
31515 E
31516 E
31554 H
31575 C
31576 C
31578 C
31582 C
31602 T
31604 T
31661 R
31681 C
31683 C
31690 C
31694 C
31706 R1^2
31710 R1^2
31712 C
31714 C
31716 C
31717 C
31718 C
31719 C
31722 C
31736 D1^1
31743 D1^1
31745 D1^1
31749 D1^1
31760 L
31764 L
31765 L
31769 L
31810 N
31811 N
31812 N
31813 N
31903 U1
31904 U1
31905 U1
31906 U1
31907 U1
31908 U1
31909 U1
31910 U1
31912 W
31914 W
31915 W
32100 E2
32101 E2
32102 E2
32103 E2
32104 E2
32105 E2
32106 E2
32107 E2
34033 WC
34034 WC
34035 WC
34036 WC
34037 WC
34038 WC
34039 WC
34040 WC
34054 BB
34055 BB

1951 73A
30756 756
30763 N15
30764 N15
30766 N15
30772 N15
30773 N15
30774 N15
30775 N15
30776 N15
30791 N15
30792 N15
30793 N15
31005 H
31019 E1^1
31067 E1^1
31145 D1^1
31165 E1^1
31177 H
31184 H
31234 C
31261 H
31263 H
31266 H
31295 H
31307 H
31311 H
31321 H
31329 H
31409 N
31410 N
31411 N
31412 N
31413 N
31414 N
31487 D1^1
31497 E1^1
31500 H
31504 E1^1
31506 E1^1
31558 P
31575 C
31576 C
31578 C
31582 C
31623 U
31660 R
31681 C
31683 C
31714 C
31716 C
31717 C
31718 C
31719 C
31722 C
31743 D1^1
31749 D1^1
31810 N
31811 N
31812 N
31813 N
31814 N
31815 N
31816 N
31817 N
31818 N
31903 U1
31904 U1
31905 U1
31906 U1
31907 U1
31908 U1
31909 U1
31910 U1
31912 W
31914 W
31915 W
32100 E2
32101 E2
32102 E2
32103 E2
32104 E2
32105 E2
32106 E2
32107 E2
32128 E1^2
34033 WC
34066 BB
34067 BB
34068 BB
34069 BB
34070 BB
34071 BB
34074 BB
34075 BB
34076 BB
34083 BB
34084 BB
34085 BB
34091 WC
34092 WC
34101 WC
34102 WC
34103 WC
34104 WC
35025 MN
35026 MN
35027 MN
35028 MN
42070 4MT^1
42071 4MT^1
42072 4MT^1
42073 4MT^1
42074 4MT^1

1954 73A
30763 N15
30764 N15
30765 N15
30766 N15
30767 N15
30768 N15
30769 N15
30770 N15
30771 N15
30772 N15
30773 N15
30774 N15
30791 N15
30792 N15
30793 N15
30794 N15
30795 N15
30915 V
31005 H
31019 E1^1
31067 E1^1
31263 H
31265 H
31266 H
31315 E
31321 H
31409 N
31410 N
31411 N
31412 N
31413 N
31414 N
31461 C
31504 E1^1
31506 E1^1
31555 P
31557 P
31573 C
31575 C
31576 C
31578 C
31579 C
31581 C
31582 C
31583 C
31584 C
31718 C
31719 C
31743 D1^1
31749 D1^1
31810 N
31811 N
31812 N
31815 N
31816 N
31901 U1
31902 U1
31903 U1
31904 U1
31905 U1
31906 U1
31914 W
31915 W
32100 E2
32101 E2
32102 E2
32103 E2
32104 E2
32105 E2
32106 E2
32107 E2
34066 BB
34067 BB
34068 BB
34069 BB
34070 BB
34071 BB
34087 BB
34088 BB
34089 BB
34090 BB
34091 WC
34092 WC
34101 WC
34102 WC
34103 WC
34104 WC
35026 MN
35027 MN
35028 MN
41290 2MT^1
41291 2MT^1
41292 2MT^1
41294 2MT^1
41295 2MT^1
41296 2MT^1
42089 4MT^1
42090 4MT^1
42091 4MT^1
70004 7P6F
70014 7P6F

1957 73A
30766 N15
30767 N15
30768 N15
30769 N15
30792 N15
30793 N15
30794 N15
30795 N15
31019 E1^1
31067 E1^1
31253 C
31261 H
31265 H
31266 H
31321 H
31408 N
31409 N
31410 N
31411 N
31412 N
31413 N
31414 N
31461 C
31504 E1^1
31506 E1^1
31545 D1^1
31550 H
31551 H
31552 H
31557 P
31558 P
31573 C
31575 C
31576 C
31578 C
31579 C
31581 C
31582 C
31584 C
31743 D1^1
31749 D1^1
31810 N
31811 N
31812 N
31894 U1
31895 U1
31896 U1
31897 U1
31898 U1
31904 U1
31905 U1
31906 U1
31907 U1
31914 W
31915 W
31921 W
32100 E2
32101 E2
32102 E2
32103 E2
32104 E2
32105 E2
32106 E2
32107 E2
32448 C2X
32455 E3
34017 WC
34066 BB
34067 BB
34068 BB
34087 BB
34088 BB
34089 BB
34090 BB
34091 WC
34092 WC
34101 WC
34102 WC
35015 MN
35026 MN
35028 MN
41290 2MT^1
41291 2MT^1
41292 2MT^1
42086 4MT^1
42087 4MT^1
42088 4MT^1
42089 4MT^1
42090 4MT^1
42091 4MT^1
70004 7P6F
70014 7P6F
73080 5MT
73081 5MT
73082 5MT
73083 5MT
73084 5MT
73085 5MT
73086 5MT
73088 5MT
73089 5MT

1960 73A
30920 V
30921 V
30922 V
30923 V
31261 H
31265 H
31317 C
31410 N
31411 N
31412 N
31550 H
31551 H
31558 P
31575 C
31578 C
31581 C
31583 C
31584 C
31714 C
31715 C
31719 C
31894 U1
31895 U1
31896 U1
31897 U1
31898 U1
31899 U1
31900 U1
31914 W
31915 W
31921 W
32100 E2
32102 E2
32103 E2
32106 E2
32547 C2X
34066 BB
34067 BB
34068 BB
34077 BB
34085 BB
34086 BB
34087 BB
34088 BB
34089 BB
34091 WC
34092 WC
34100 WC
34101 WC
41290 2MT^1
41291 2MT^1
41292 2MT^1
75069 4MT^1
75074 4MT^1
80066 4MT^3
80067 4MT^3
80068 4MT^3
80081 4MT^3

1963 75D
30533 Q
30538 Q
30543 Q
30544 Q
31410 N
31411 N
31412 N
31823 N
31824 N
31825 N
31826 N
31854 N
75069 4MT^1
75070 4MT^1
75074 4MT^1
75075 4MT^1
80034 4MT^3
80068 4MT^3
80081 4MT^3
80084 4MT^3
80085 4MT^3

Stirling

1948 31B
44283 4F^2
44330 4F^2
44331 4F^2
54455 3P^5
54466 3P^6
54485 3P^6
54491 3P^6
54496 3P^6

55117 2P^{12}
55122 2P^{12}
55126 2P^{12}
55212 2P^{13}
55222 2P^{13}
56254 3F^{10}
56343 3F^{10}
56365 3F^{10}
56366 3F^{10}
57232 2F^{5}
57233 2F^{5}
57243 2F^{5}
57246 2F^{5}
57252 2F^{5}
57257 2F^{5}
57264 2F^{5}
57402 2F^{5}
57422 2F^{5}
57423 2F^{5}
57424 2F^{5}
57425 2F^{5}
57460 2F^{5}
57466 2F^{5}
57468 2F^{5}

1951 63B
40913 4P^{1}
40924 4P^{1}
42198 4MT^{1}
42199 4MT^{1}
43884 4F^{1}
44011 4F^{1}
44283 4F^{2}
44322 4F^{2}
44330 4F^{2}
44331 4F^{2}
45016 5MT^{3}
45358 5MT^{3}
45359 5MT^{3}
55122 2P^{12}
55126 2P^{12}
55145 2P^{12}
55222 2P^{13}
56232 3F^{10}
56254 3F^{10}
56343 3F^{10}
56365 3F^{10}
56366 3F^{10}
57232 2F^{5}
57233 2F^{5}
57243 2F^{5}
57246 2F^{5}
57252 2F^{5}
57257 2F^{5}
57264 2F^{5}
57283 2F^{5}
57423 2F^{5}
57424 2F^{5}
57460 2F^{5}
57468 2F^{5}
62426 D30
62461 D33
64461 J35
64471 J35
64497 J35
64501 J35
64520 J35
64542 J37
64544 J37
64569 J37
64585 J37
67462 C15
67650 V1
67675 V3

1954 63B
40938 4P^{1}
42198 4MT^{1}
42199 4MT^{1}
43884 4F^{1}
44011 4F^{1}
44322 4F^{2}
44330 4F^{2}
44331 4F^{2}
45016 5MT^{3}
45084 5MT^{3}
45358 5MT^{3}
45359 5MT^{3}
55126 2P^{12}
55145 2P^{12}
55222 2P^{13}
56232 3F^{10}
56254 3F^{10}
56343 3F^{10}
56365 3F^{10}
56366 3F^{10}
57232 2F^{5}
57233 2F^{5}
57243 2F^{5}
57246 2F^{5}
57252 2F^{5}
57257 2F^{5}
57264 2F^{5}
57324 2F^{5}
57339 2F^{5}
57396 2F^{5}
57441 2F^{5}
57460 2F^{5}
62426 D30
62714 D49
62725 D49
64497 J35
64501 J35
64520 J35
64542 J37
64544 J37
64569 J37
64585 J37
67650 V1
67675 V3

1957 63B
42198 4MT^{1}
42199 4MT^{1}
43884 4F^{1}
44011 4F^{1}
44318 4F^{2}
44322 4F^{2}
45016 5MT^{3}
45049 5MT^{3}
45084 5MT^{3}
45213 5MT^{3}
45214 5MT^{3}
45357 5MT^{3}
45359 5MT^{3}
45396 5MT^{3}
45400 5MT^{3}
45423 5MT^{3}
54504 3P^{6}
55126 2P^{12}
55176 2P^{13}
55195 2P^{13}
55222 2P^{13}
56232 3F^{10}
56254 3F^{10}
56343 3F^{10}
56365 3F^{10}
56375 3F^{10}
57232 2F^{5}
57233 2F^{5}
57243 2F^{5}
57246 2F^{5}
57252 2F^{5}
57257 2F^{5}
57264 2F^{5}
57324 2F^{5}
57339 2F^{5}
57396 2F^{5}
57441 2F^{5}
57460 2F^{5}
62426 D30
62714 D49
62725 D49
64497 J35
64501 J35
64542 J37
64544 J37
64569 J37
64585 J37
67650 V1
67675 V3
80125 4MT^{3}

1960 63B
42198 4MT^{1}
42199 4MT^{1}
42690 4MT^{1}
42693 4MT^{1}
45016 5MT^{3}
45049 5MT^{3}
45084 5MT^{3}
45213 5MT^{3}
45214 5MT^{3}
45357 5MT^{3}
45359 5MT^{3}
45389 5MT^{3}
45396 5MT^{3}
45400 5MT^{3}
45423 5MT^{3}
54476 3P^{6}
55195 2P^{13}
55222 2P^{13}
56343 3F^{10}
57232 2F^{5}
57233 2F^{5}
57246 2F^{5}
57252 2F^{5}
57257 2F^{5}
57264 2F^{5}
57324 2F^{5}
57576 3F^{12}
57642 3F^{13}
57679 3F^{14}
62426 D30
80125 4MT^{3}

1963 65J
45016 5MT^{3}
45049 5MT^{3}
45084 5MT^{3}
45213 5MT^{3}
45214 5MT^{3}
45357 5MT^{3}
45359 5MT^{3}
45389 5MT^{3}
45396 5MT^{3}
45400 5MT^{3}
45423 5MT^{3}
57261 2F^{5}
57679 3F^{14}
80060 4MT^{3}
80061 4MT^{3}
80062 4MT^{3}
80063 4MT^{3}
80125 4MT^{3}

1966 65J
45084 5MT^{3}
45213 5MT^{3}
45214 5MT^{3}
45357 5MT^{3}
45359 5MT^{3}
45396 5MT^{3}
73007 5MT
73105 5MT
73154 5MT

Stirling Shore Road

1948 STG
62209 D1
62461 D33
64461 J35
64471 J35
64497 J35
64501 J35
64520 J35
64525 J35
64542 J37
64544 J37
64556 J37
64569 J37
64585 J37
65281 J36
65307 J36
65322 J36
65346 J36
67462 C15
67618 V1
67650 V1
68342 J88
68346 J88
68351 J88

Stockport Edgeley

1948 9B
40055 3MT^{1}
40077 3MT^{2}
41905 2P^{4}
41906 2P^{4}
41907 2P^{4}
42332 4MT^{2}
42352 4MT^{2}
42353 4MT^{2}
42354 4MT^{2}
42463 4MT^{3}
42772 5MT^{1}
42773 5MT^{1}
42859 5MT^{1}
42938 5MT^{1}
43281 3F^{3}
44074 4F^{2}
44340 4F^{2}
44444 4F^{2}
47289 3F^{6}
47346 3F^{6}
47601 3F^{6}
49010 7F^{2}
49092 6F^{2}
49108 7F^{2}
49111 7F^{2}
49156 6F^{2}
49185 7F^{2}
49186 7F^{2}
49187 6F^{2}
58366 2F^{11}
58380 2F^{11}

1951 9B
40071 3MT^{2}
40106 3MT^{2}
40138 3MT^{2}
42332 4MT^{2}
42352 4MT^{2}
42353 4MT^{2}
42354 4MT^{2}
42379 4MT^{2}
42463 4MT^{3}
42859 5MT^{1}
42934 5MT^{1}
43281 3F^{3}
44069 4F^{2}
44074 4F^{2}
44340 4F^{2}
44444 4F^{2}
47289 3F^{6}
47346 3F^{6}
47601 3F^{6}
49002 7F^{2}
49010 7F^{2}
49024 7F^{2}
49108 7F^{2}
49156 6F^{2}
49187 6F^{2}
49281 7F^{2}
58377 2F^{11}
58427 2F^{11}

1954 9B
40071 3MT^{2}
40081 3MT^{2}
40106 3MT^{2}
40138 3MT^{2}
42120 4MT^{1}
42332 4MT^{2}
42353 4MT^{2}
42354 4MT^{2}
42379 4MT^{2}
42463 4MT^{3}
42773 5MT^{1}
42859 5MT^{1}
42934 5MT^{1}
43281 3F^{3}
43357 3F^{3}
44075 4F^{2}
44271 4F^{2}
44340 4F^{2}
44444 4F^{2}
47289 3F^{6}
47346 3F^{6}
47601 3F^{6}
49010 7F^{2}
49281 7F^{2}
49418 7F^{3}
49453 7F^{3}
58427 2F^{11}

1957 9B
40071 3MT^{2}
40081 3MT^{2}
42353 4MT^{2}
42354 4MT^{2}
42379 4MT^{2}
42391 4MT^{2}
42463 4MT^{3}
42773 5MT^{1}
42859 5MT^{1}
42934 5MT^{1}
43357 3F^{3}
44059 4F^{2}
44075 4F^{2}
44271 4F^{2}
44340 4F^{2}
44382 4F^{2}
47289 3F^{6}
47346 3F^{6}
47601 3F^{6}
49010 7F^{2}
49418 7F^{3}
49453 7F^{3}

1960 9B
42316 4MT^{2}
42322 4MT^{2}
42343 4MT^{2}
42357 4MT^{2}
42372 4MT^{2}
42379 4MT^{2}
42391 4MT^{2}
42415 4MT^{2}
42773 5MT^{1}
42779 5MT^{1}
42848 5MT^{1}
42854 5MT^{1}
42886 5MT^{1}
42932 5MT^{1}
42937 5MT^{1}
43305 3F^{3}
43410 3F^{3}
47431 3F^{6}
49191 7F^{2}
49453 7F^{3}

1963 9B
42316 4MT^{2}
42337 4MT^{2}
42343 4MT^{2}
42670 4MT^{3}
42817 5MT^{1}
42849 5MT^{1}
42904 5MT^{1}
42921 5MT^{1}
42932 5MT^{1}
42941 5MT^{1}
42942 5MT^{1}
44445 4F^{2}
44752 5MT^{3}
44755 5MT^{3}
44867 5MT^{3}
44868 5MT^{3}
44871 5MT^{3}
44911 5MT^{3}
45225 5MT^{3}
45291 5MT^{3}
45382 5MT^{3}
45596 6P5F^{2}
45632 6P5F^{2}
48437 8F
48744 8F

1966 9B
41202 2MT^{1}
41204 2MT^{1}
41220 2MT^{1}
41233 2MT^{1}
42712 5MT^{1}
42715 5MT^{1}
42727 5MT^{1}
42942 5MT^{1}
44836 5MT^{3}
44867 5MT^{3}
44868 5MT^{3}
44871 5MT^{3}
44916 5MT^{3}
45027 5MT^{3}
45046 5MT^{3}
45139 5MT^{3}
45225 5MT^{3}
45261 5MT^{3}
45596 6P5F^{2}
48182 8F
48373 8F
48392 8F
48437 8F
48447 8F
48549 8F
48626 0F
48765 8F
70004 7P6F
70015 7P6F
70026 7P6F

Stockton on Tees

1948 SKN
61030 B1
61032 B1
61189 B1
61214 B1
61220 B1
62365 D20
62390 D20
63367 Q6
63369 Q6
63380 Q6
63393 Q6
63407 Q6
65052 J21
65057 J21
65089 J21
65092 J21
65788 J27
65800 J27
65805 J27
65807 J27
65857 J27
65860 J27
65870 J27
65887 J27
67254 G5
67272 G5
67288 G5
67294 G5
67318 G5
68144 Y1
68305 J71
68407 J77
68412 J77
68420 J77
69781 A7
69787 A7
69918 T1
90155 WD^{1}
90172 WD^{1}
90184 WD^{1}
90240 WD^{1}
90344 WD^{1}
90377 WD^{1}
90405 WD^{1}
90603 WD^{1}
90623 WD^{1}

1951 51E
61017 B1
61018 B1
61030 B1
61032 B1
61034 B1
61037 B1
61189 B1
61214 B1
61220 B1
61290 B1
61303 B1
62001 K1
62041 K1
62042 K1
62043 K1
62060 K1
62063 K1
62064 K1
62065 K1
65689 J25
65718 J25
65860 J27
65868 J27
67242 G5
67278 G5
67305 G5
67317 G5
67318 G5
68144 Y1
68305 J71
68407 J77
68412 J77
68420 J77
69781 A7
69787 A7
69883 A8
69918 T1
90012 WD^{1}
90048 WD^{1}
90067 WD^{1}
90082 WD^{1}
90086 WD^{1}
90092 WD^{1}
90155 WD^{1}
90172 WD^{1}
90184 WD^{1}
90240 WD^{1}
90344 WD^{1}
90377 WD^{1}
90405 WD^{1}
90603 WD^{1}
90623 WD^{1}

1954 51E
61018 B1
61030 B1
61032 B1
61034 B1
61037 B1
61173 B1
61189 B1
61214 B1
61220 B1
61275 B1
61303 B1
62041 K1
62042 K1
62043 K1
62060 K1
62064 K1
62065 K1
65689 J25
65739 J26
65764 J26
65771 J26
65788 J27
65868 J27
67278 G5
67288 G5
67343 G5
68144 Y1
68305 J71
68407 J77
68412 J77
68420 J77
69912 T1
69918 T1
69919 T1
90012 WD^{1}
90048 WD^{1}
90067 WD^{1}
90086 WD^{1}
90092 WD^{1}
90155 WD^{1}
90172 WD^{1}
90184 WD^{1}
90240 WD^{1}
90344 WD^{1}
90377 WD^{1}
90405 WD^{1}
90603 WD^{1}

1957 51E
61018 B1
61030 B1
61032 B1
61034 B1
61037 B1
61173 B1
61220 B1
61303 B1
62041 K1
62042 K1
62043 K1
62060 K1
62064 K1
62065 K1
65739 J26
65764 J26
65771 J26
65788 J27
65868 J27
65884 J27
68142 Y1
68305 J71
68412 J77
68438 J77
68696 J72
69838 A5
69842 A5
69912 T1
69918 T1
69921 T1
90086 WD^{1}
90155 WD^{1}
90172 WD^{1}
90184 WD^{1}
90240 WD^{1}
90377 WD^{1}
90405 WD^{1}

Stoke

1948 5D
40076 3MT^{2}
40078 3MT^{2}
40122 3MT^{2}
40125 3MT^{2}
40126 3MT^{2}
40127 3MT^{2}
40128 3MT^{2}
40157 3MT^{2}
42231 4MT^{1}
42232 4MT^{1}
42233 4MT^{1}
42234 4MT^{1}
42235 4MT^{1}
42236 4MT^{1}
42237 4MT^{1}
42320 4MT^{2}
42343 4MT^{2}
42344 4MT^{2}
42360 4MT^{2}
42364 4MT^{2}
42375 4MT^{2}
42376 4MT^{2}
42378 4MT^{2}
42469 4MT^{3}
42494 4MT^{3}
42543 4MT^{3}
42584 4MT^{3}
42585 4MT^{3}
42603 4MT^{3}
42605 4MT^{3}
42607 4MT^{3}
42609 4MT^{3}
42663 4MT^{3}
42664 4MT^{3}
42665 4MT^{3}
42666 4MT^{3}
42667 4MT^{3}
42668 4MT^{3}
42669 4MT^{3}
42670 4MT^{3}
42671 4MT^{3}
42672 4MT^{3}
42673 4MT^{1}
42674 4MT^{1}
42675 4MT^{1}
42676 4MT^{1}
44067 4F^{2}
44068 4F^{2}
44093 4F^{2}
44310 4F^{2}
44343 4F^{2}
44349 4F^{2}
44353 4F^{2}
44363 4F^{2}
44369 4F^{2}
44373 4F^{2}
44377 4F^{2}
44378 4F^{2}
44380 4F^{2}
44383 4F^{2}
44388 4F^{2}
44391 4F^{2}
44393 4F^{2}
44448 4F^{2}
44478 4F^{2}
44484 4F^{2}
44489 4F^{2}
44496 4F^{2}
44498 4F^{2}
44499 4F^{2}
44500 4F^{2}
44502 4F^{2}
44503 4F^{2}
44508 4F^{2}
44513 4F^{2}
45114 5MT^{3}
45257 5MT^{3}
45278 5MT^{3}
45324 5MT^{3}
45325 5MT^{3}
45326 5MT^{3}
45352 5MT^{3}
45381 5MT^{3}
47320 3F^{6}
47338 3F^{6}
47370 3F^{6}
47587 3F^{6}
47596 3F^{6}
47599 3F^{6}
47609 3F^{6}
47610 3F^{6}
47647 3F^{6}
47648 3F^{6}
47658 3F^{6}
58379 2F^{11}
58385 2F^{11}

1951 5D
40088 3MT^{2}
40122 3MT^{2}
40126 3MT^{2}
40128 3MT^{2}
40157 3MT^{2}
42061 4MT^{1}
42062 4MT^{1}
42063 4MT^{1}
42064 4MT^{1}
42065 4MT^{1}
42155 4MT^{1}
42233 4MT^{1}
42234 4MT^{1}
42235 4MT^{1}
42236 4MT^{1}
42323 4MT^{2}
42343 4MT^{2}
42344 4MT^{2}
42349 4MT^{2}
42364 4MT^{2}
42375 4MT^{2}
42376 4MT^{2}
42431 4MT^{3}
42440 4MT^{3}
42443 4MT^{3}
42445 4MT^{3}
42449 4MT^{3}
42458 4MT^{3}
42479 4MT^{3}
42494 4MT^{3}
42543 4MT^{3}
42567 4MT^{3}
42582 4MT^{3}
42603 4MT^{3}
42605 4MT^{3}
42609 4MT^{3}
42664 4MT^{3}
42667 4MT^{3}
42668 4MT^{3}
42670 4MT^{3}
42672 4MT^{3}
42676 4MT^{1}
42683 4MT^{1}
43915 4F^{1}
44067 4F^{2}
44068 4F^{2}
44077 4F^{2}
44093 4F^{2}
44118 4F^{2}
44120 4F^{2}
44309 4F^{2}
44310 4F^{2}
44343 4F^{2}
44353 4F^{2}
44358 4F^{2}
44363 4F^{2}
44369 4F^{2}
44373 4F^{2}
44375 4F^{2}
44377 4F^{2}
44378 4F^{2}
44380 4F^{2}
44383 4F^{2}
44388 4F^{2}
44391 4F^{2}
44393 4F^{2}
44396 4F^{2}
44438 4F^{2}
44455 4F^{2}
44478 4F^{2}
44484 4F^{2}
44489 4F^{2}
44496 4F^{2}
44498 4F^{2}
44499 4F^{2}
44500 4F^{2}
44502 4F^{2}
44503 4F^{2}
44507 4F^{2}
44508 4F^{2}
44513 4F^{2}
44548 4F^{2}
44596 4F^{2}
45114 5MT^{3}
45257 5MT^{3}
45278 5MT^{3}
45324 5MT^{3}
45325 5MT^{3}
45326 5MT^{3}
45381 5MT^{3}
47281 3F^{6}
47338 3F^{6}
47370 3F^{6}
47587 3F^{6}
47596 3F^{6}
47599 3F^{6}
47609 3F^{6}
47610 3F^{6}
47647 3F^{6}
47648 3F^{6}
47658 3F^{6}
58382 2F^{11}
58389 2F^{11}
58400 2F^{11}

1954 5D
42233 4MT^{1}
42234 4MT^{1}
42235 4MT^{1}
42236 4MT^{1}
42303 4MT^{2}
42323 4MT^{2}
42343 4MT^{2}
42344 4MT^{2}
42348 4MT^{2}
42360 4MT^{2}
42378 4MT^{2}
42431 4MT^{3}
42440 4MT^{3}
42443 4MT^{3}
42445 4MT^{3}
42449 4MT^{3}
42458 4MT^{3}
42494 4MT^{3}
42543 4MT^{3}
42567 4MT^{3}
42590 4MT^{3}
42593 4MT^{3}
42600 4MT^{3}
42603 4MT^{3}
42609 4MT^{3}
42667 4MT^{3}
42668 4MT^{3}
42670 4MT^{3}
42671 4MT^{3}
42672 4MT^{3}
43980 4F^{1}
44024 4F^{1}
44068 4F^{2}
44074 4F^{2}
44077 4F^{2}
44093 4F^{2}
44246 4F^{2}
44308 4F^{2}
44309 4F^{2}
44310 4F^{2}
44353 4F^{2}
44358 4F^{2}
44373 4F^{2}
44374 4F^{2}
44375 4F^{2}
44377 4F^{2}
44383 4F^{2}
44385 4F^{2}
44388 4F^{2}
44393 4F^{2}
44405 4F^{2}
44421 4F^{2}
44432 4F^{2}
44455 4F^{2}
44478 4F^{2}
44484 4F^{2}
44496 4F^{2}
44498 4F^{2}
44499 4F^{2}
44500 4F^{2}
44502 4F^{2}
44507 4F^{2}
44508 4F^{2}
44513 4F^{2}
44548 4F^{2}
44596 4F^{2}
44871 5MT^{3}
45149 5MT^{3}
45257 5MT^{3}
45278 5MT^{3}
45324 5MT^{3}
45381 5MT^{3}
47270 3F^{6}
47281 3F^{6}
47344 3F^{6}
47370 3F^{6}
47451 3F^{6}
47587 3F^{6}
47596 3F^{6}
47599 3F^{6}
47609 3F^{6}
47610 3F^{6}
47647 3F^{6}
47648 3F^{6}
47658 3F^{6}
58376 2F^{11}
58382 2F^{11}

1957 5D
42119 4MT^{1}
42233 4MT^{1}
42234 4MT^{1}
42235 4MT^{1}
42323 4MT^{2}
42344 4MT^{2}
42348 4MT^{2}
42360 4MT^{2}
42366 4MT^{2}
42367 4MT^{2}
42378 4MT^{2}
42389 4MT^{2}
42400 4MT^{2}
42420 4MT^{2}
42431 4MT^{3}
42440 4MT^{3}
42443 4MT^{3}
42449 4MT^{3}
42458 4MT^{3}
42494 4MT^{3}
42543 4MT^{3}
42567 4MT^{3}
42582 4MT^{3}
42590 4MT^{3}
42593 4MT^{3}
42600 4MT^{3}
42603 4MT^{3}
42609 4MT^{3}
42659 4MT^{3}
42667 4MT^{3}
42668 4MT^{3}
42670 4MT^{3}
42671 4MT^{3}
42672 4MT^{3}
43864 4F^{1}
44032 4F^{2}
44068 4F^{2}
44074 4F^{2}
44077 4F^{2}
44093 4F^{2}
44246 4F^{2}
44308 4F^{2}
44309 4F^{2}
44310 4F^{2}
44353 4F^{2}
44358 4F^{2}
44373 4F^{2}
44374 4F^{2}
44375 4F^{2}
44377 4F^{2}
44383 4F^{2}
44393 4F^{2}
44405 4F^{2}
44432 4F^{2}
44455 4F^{2}
44478 4F^{2}
44484 4F^{2}
44496 4F^{2}
44498 4F^{2}
44499 4F^{2}
44500 4F^{2}
44502 4F^{2}
44507 4F^{2}
44508 4F^{2}
44513 4F^{2}
44548 4F^{2}
44871 5MT^{3}
45149 5MT^{3}
45185 5MT^{3}
45257 5MT^{3}
46429 2MT^{2}
46430 2MT^{2}
47270 3F^{6}
47281 3F^{6}
47344 3F^{6}
47370 3F^{6}
47451 3F^{6}
47587 3F^{6}
47596 3F^{6}
47599 3F^{6}
47609 3F^{6}
47610 3F^{6}
47647 3F^{6}
47648 3F^{6}
47658 3F^{6}

1960 5D
42315 4MT^{2}
42323 4MT^{2}
42344 4MT^{2}
42346 4MT^{2}
42362 4MT^{2}
42378 4MT^{2}
42418 4MT^{2}
42420 4MT^{2}
42421 4MT^{2}
42443 4MT^{3}
42454 4MT^{3}
42543 4MT^{3}
42590 4MT^{3}
42593 4MT^{3}
42600 4MT^{3}
42603 4MT^{3}
42609 4MT^{3}
42663 4MT^{3}
42667 4MT^{3}
42668 4MT^{3}
42670 4MT^{3}
42671 4MT^{3}
42672 4MT^{3}
43840 4F^{1}
44068 4F^{2}
44074 4F^{2}
44077 4F^{2}
44093 4F^{2}
44115 4F^{2}
44186 4F^{2}
44246 4F^{2}
44271 4F^{2}
44307 4F^{2}
44308 4F^{2}
44309 4F^{2}
44310 4F^{2}
44315 4F^{2}
44344 4F^{2}
44358 4F^{2}
44377 4F^{2}
44393 4F^{2}
44395 4F^{2}
44424 4F^{2}
44432 4F^{2}
44455 4F^{2}
44459 4F^{2}
44473 4F^{2}
44478 4F^{2}
44484 4F^{2}
44496 4F^{2}
44498 4F^{2}
44499 4F^{2}
44500 4F^{2}
44502 4F^{2}
44507 4F^{2}
44508 4F^{2}
44513 4F^{2}
44517 4F^{2}
44536 4F^{2}
44548 4F^{2}
44593 4F^{2}
45044 5MT^{3}
45060 5MT^{3}
46429 2MT^{2}
46430 2MT^{2}
47270 3F^{6}
47281 3F^{6}
47344 3F^{6}
47451 3F^{6}
47587 3F^{6}
47596 3F^{6}
47599 3F^{6}
47609 3F^{6}
47610 3F^{6}
47647 3F^{6}
47648 3F^{6}
47658 3F^{6}

1963 5D
42066 4MT^{1}
42160 4MT^{1}
42224 4MT^{1}
42226 4MT^{1}
42381 4MT^{2}
42392 4MT^{2}
42543 4MT^{3}
42590 4MT^{3}
42603 4MT^{3}
42609 4MT^{3}
42663 4MT^{3}
42667 4MT^{3}
42668 4MT^{3}
42782 5MT^{1}
42787 5MT^{1}
42856 5MT^{1}
42858 5MT^{1}
42888 5MT^{1}
42937 5MT^{1}
42948 5MT^{2}
42949 5MT^{2}
42952 5MT^{2}
42953 5MT^{2}
42956 5MT^{2}
42959 5MT^{2}
42961 5MT^{2}
42963 5MT^{2}
42965 5MT^{2}
42972 5MT^{2}
42977 5MT^{2}
42980 5MT^{2}
44068 4F^{2}
44074 4F^{2}
44079 4F^{2}
44115 4F^{2}
44126 4F^{2}
44208 4F^{2}
44242 4F^{2}
44299 4F^{2}
44308 4F^{2}
44309 4F^{2}
44310 4F^{2}
44342 4F^{2}
44344 4F^{2}
44349 4F^{2}
44352 4F^{2}
44354 4F^{2}
44370 4F^{2}
44395 4F^{2}
44424 4F^{2}
44432 4F^{2}
44455 4F^{2}
44499 4F^{2}
44500 4F^{2}
44536 4F^{2}
44548 4F^{2}
44593 4F^{2}
45003 5MT^{3}
45060 5MT^{3}
45074 5MT^{3}
45191 5MT^{3}
45240 5MT^{3}
45350 5MT^{3}
45395 5MT^{3}
47280 3F^{6}
47587 3F^{6}
47596 3F^{6}
47609 3F^{6}
47664 3F^{6}
76020 4MT^{2}
76022 4MT^{2}
76023 4MT^{2}
76051 4MT^{2}
78017 2MT^{1}
78056 2MT^{1}

1966 5D
43003 4MT^{5}
43007 4MT^{5}
43018 4MT^{5}
43021 4MT^{5}
43022 4MT^{5}
43112 4MT^{5}
43115 4MT^{5}
44682 5MT^{3}
44713 5MT^{3}
44714 5MT^{3}
44810 5MT^{3}
44813 5MT^{3}
45003 5MT^{3}
45050 5MT^{3}
45060 5MT^{3}
45191 5MT^{3}
45240 5MT^{3}
45241 5MT^{3}
45268 5MT^{3}
45270 5MT^{3}
45276 5MT^{3}
45322 5MT^{3}
45350 5MT^{3}
45422 5MT^{3}
47273 3F^{6}
47280 3F^{6}
47307 3F^{6}
48012 8F
48018 8F
48110 8F
48131 8F
48207 8F
48246 8F
48291 8F
48349 8F
48353 8F
48354 8F
48452 8F
48453 8F
48516 8F
48527 8F
48548 8F
48555 8F
48738 8F
48768 8F
75018 4MT^{1}
75020 4MT^{1}
75023 4MT^{1}
75030 4MT^{1}
75031 4MT^{1}
75034 4MT^{1}
75036 4MT^{1}
75037 4MT^{1}
75040 4MT^{1}
75054 4MT^{1}
75056 4MT^{1}
75062 4MT^{1}
76044 4MT^{2}
76051 4MT^{2}
76075 4MT^{2}
76085 4MT^{2}
76089 4MT^{2}
76099 4MT^{2}
78017 2MT^{1}
78056 2MT^{1}

Stourbridge

1948 STB
1410 1400
1414 1400
1438 1400
1745 655
1749 655
1835 1813
2090 2021
2092 2021
2107 2021
2185 2181
2186 2181
2187 2181
2189 2181
2246 2251
2270 2251
2279 2251
2281 2251
2620 2600
2655 2600
2706 655
2712 655
2771 2721
2852 2800
3450 3300
3649 5700
3667 5700
3740 5700
4104 5101
4146 5101
4149 5101
4150 5101
4638 5700
4687 5700
4696 5700
5101 5101
5105 5101
5107 5101
5122 5101
5131 5101
5134 5101
5136 5101
5138 5101
5141 5101
5146 5101
5147 5101
5155 5101
5160 5101
5165 5101
5167 5101
5170 5101
5180 5101
5189 5101
5191 5101
5193 5101
5196 5101
5197 5101
5719 5700
5726 5700
5754 5700
5794 5700
5795 5700
6617 5600

6646 5600
6665 5600
6667 5600
6674 5600
6677 5600
6678 5600
6684 5600
7402 7400
7428 7400
7705 5700
8704 5700
8742 5700
8791 5700
8792 5700
8797 5700
9084 3252
9613 5700
9636 5700
9741 5700
9767 5700

1951 84F
1410 1400
1414 1400
1430 1400
1458 1400
1621 1600
2090 2021
2107 2021
2185 2181
2186 2181
2187 2181
2246 2251
2270 2251
2279 2251
2852 2800
2856 2800
2857 2800
2874 2800
2885 2884
3649 5700
3667 5700
3710 5700
3740 5700
3821 2884
3827 2884
4104 5101
4146 5101
4150 5101
4173 5101
4337 4300
4638 5700
4687 5700
4696 5700
5101 5101
5105 5101
5107 5101
5134 5101
5136 5101
5147 5101
5155 5101
5160 5101
5165 5101
5167 5101
5170 5101
5180 5101
5189 5101
5191 5101
5193 5101
5196 5101
5197 5101
5199 5101
5606 5600
5651 5600
5658 5600
5719 5700
5726 5700
5754 5700
5794 5700
5795 5700
6332 4300
6391 4300
6617 5600
6646 5600
6667 5600
6674 5600
6677 5600
6678 5600
6828 6800
6857 6800
7402 7400
7428 7400
7429 7400
7430 7400
7435 7400
7448 7400
7449 7400
7705 5700
8418 9400
8419 9400
8704 5700
8742 5700
8791 5700
8792 5700
8797 5700
9427 9400
9613 5700
9636 5700
9741 5700
9767 5700

1954 84F
1414 1400
1438 1400
1458 1400
1619 1600
1621 1600
2279 2251
2804 2800
2874 2800
2885 2884
3206 2251
3216 2251
3217 2251
3218 2251
3649 5700
3658 5700
3667 5700
3710 5700
3743 5700
3751 5700
3821 2884
3827 2884
3861 2884
4104 5101
4146 5101
4173 5101
4326 4300
4375 4300
4646 5700
4687 5700
4696 5700
5101 5101
5105 5101
5107 5101
5160 5101
5165 5101
5167 5101
5180 5101
5189 5101
5191 5101
5199 5101
5313 4300
5371 4300
5379 4300
5606 5600
5642 5600
5651 5600
5658 5600
5719 5700
5754 5700
5794 5700
5795 5700
6327 4300
6332 4300
6391 4300
6609 5600
6646 5600
6667 5600
6674 5600
6677 5600
6678 5600
6681 5600
6683 5600
6692 5600
6698 5600
6803 6800
6823 6800
6828 6800
6857 6800
7428 7400
7429 7400
7430 7400
7432 7400
7435 7400
7441 7400
7448 7400
7449 7400
7705 5700
8419 9400
8437 9400
8438 9400
8704 5700
8742 5700
8791 5700
8792 5700
8797 5700
9477 9400
9613 5700
9636 5700
9719 5700
9767 5700
9782 5700

1957 84F
1414 1400
1438 1400
1458 1400
1619 1600
1621 1600
2804 2800
2829 2800
2834 2800
2885 2884
3649 5700
3658 5700
3667 5700
3710 5700
3729 5700
3743 5700
3745 5700
3821 2884
3825 2884
4104 5101
4146 5101
4173 5101
4326 4300
4375 4300
4646 5700
4687 5700
4696 5700
5101 5101
5105 5101
5107 5101
5109 5101
5165 5101
5180 5101
5186 5101
5189 5101
5191 5101
5199 5101
5371 4300
5606 5600
5651 5600
5658 5600
5719 5700
5754 5700
5795 5700
6332 4300
6393 4300
6609 5600
6646 5600
6667 5600
6674 5600
6677 5600
6678 5600
6681 5600
6683 5600
6692 5600
6698 5600
6803 6800
6828 6800
7420 7400
7428 7400
7429 7400
7430 7400
7432 7400
7435 7400
7441 7400
7447 7400
7448 7400
7449 7400
7705 5700
8704 5700
8742 5700
8792 5700
8797 5700
9613 5700
9624 5700
9636 5700
9719 5700
9767 5700
9782 5700

1960 84F
1619 1600
1621 1600
2856 2800
2885 2884
2888 2884
2897 2884
3649 5700
3658 5700
3667 5700
3710 5700
3729 5700
3743 5700
3745 5700
3821 2884
3825 2884
3831 2884
3839 2884
3846 2884
4104 5101
4110 5101
4140 5101
4161 5101
4168 5101
4173 5101
4646 5700
4687 5700
4696 5700
5176 5101
5199 5101
5754 5700
5795 5700
6317 4300
6332 4300
6340 4300
6349 4300
6367 4300
6401 6400
6403 6400
6604 5600
6609 5600
6646 5600
6667 5600
6677 5600
6678 5600
6683 5600
6692 5600
6803 6800
6855 6800
6879 6800
7429 7400
7430 7400
7432 7400
7435 7400
7441 7400
7448 7400
7449 7400
8704 5700
8742 5700
8792 5700
8797 5700
9613 5700
9624 5700
9636 5700
9719 5700
9767 5700
9782 5700

1963 84F
1619 1600
3658 5700
4140 5101
4168 5101
4602 5700
4646 5700
4665 5700
4687 5700
4696 5700
5192 5101
6403 6400
6424 6400
6646 5600
6667 5600
6677 5600
6678 5600
6683 5600
6692 5600
6811 6800
6827 6800
6842 6800
7430 7400
7432 7400
7435 7400
7441 7400
7449 7400
9613 5700
9614 5700
9624 5700
9646 5700
9733 5700
9782 5700
46506 $2MT^2$
46517 $2MT^2$
48330 8F
48402 8F
48410 8F
48415 8F
48417 8F
48424 8F
48430 8F
48450 8F
48459 8F
48460 8F
48474 8F
48475 8F
48478 8F
48724 8F

1966 2C
3607 5700
3619 5700
4646 5700
4696 5700
8718 5700
9608 5700
9614 5700
9641 5700
9724 5700
48121 8F
48402 8F
48410 8F
48412 8F
48417 8F
48424 8F
48450 8F
48459 8F
48460 8F
48468 8F
48526 8F
48531 8F
48550 8F
48757 8F
76036 $4MT^2$
76042 $4MT^2$

Stourton

1948 20B
41739 $1F^1$
41759 $1F^1$
41794 $1F^1$
41838 $1F^1$
41842 $1F^1$
41890 $1F^1$
42759 $5MT^1$
42771 $5MT^1$
42795 $5MT^1$
42798 $5MT^1$
42816 $5MT^1$
43267 $3F^3$
43392 $3F^3$
43449 $3F^3$
43456 $3F^3$
43476 $3F^3$
43579 $3F^3$
43678 $3F^3$
43681 $3F^3$
43705 $3F^3$
43737 $3F^3$
43770 $3F^4$
43851 $4F^1$
43852 $4F^1$
43855 $4F^1$
43871 $4F^1$
43931 $4F^1$
43963 $4F^1$
43987 $4F^1$
43989 $4F^1$
43998 $4F^1$
44020 $4F^1$
44037 $4F^2$
44094 $4F^2$
44245 $4F^2$
44467 $4F^2$
47239 $3F^5$
47271 $3F^6$
47420 $3F^6$
47443 $3F^6$
47463 $3F^6$
47538 $3F^6$
48140 8F
48276 8F
48277 8F
48354 8F
49018 $7F^2$
49087 $7F^2$
58136 $2F^8$
58245 $2F^8$

1951 20B
41666 $1F^1$
41739 $1F^1$
41794 $1F^1$
41838 $1F^1$
41859 $1F^1$
41869 $1F^1$
41890 $1F^1$
43267 $3F^3$
43392 $3F^3$
43449 $3F^3$
43456 $3F^3$
43476 $3F^3$
43579 $3F^3$
43678 $3F^3$
43681 $3F^3$
43705 $3F^3$
43737 $3F^3$
43781 $3F^4$
43871 $4F^1$
43878 $4F^1$
43963 $4F^1$
43987 $4F^1$
43989 $4F^1$
44020 $4F^1$
44094 $4F^2$
44153 $4F^2$
44245 $4F^2$
44335 $4F^2$
44467 $4F^2$
44562 $4F^2$
47249 $3F^5$
47271 $3F^6$
47443 $3F^6$
47463 $3F^6$
47538 $3F^6$
47589 $3F^6$
47640 $3F^6$
48123 8F
48126 8F
48149 8F
48276 8F
48311 8F
48622 8F
48641 8F
48652 8F
48703 8F
58136 $2F^8$
58212 $2F^9$

1954 20B
41739 $1F^1$
41797 $1F^1$
41811 $1F^1$
41838 $1F^1$
41859 $1F^1$
43014 $4MT^5$
43044 $4MT^5$
43392 $3F^3$
43456 $3F^3$
43579 $3F^3$
43681 $3F^3$
43737 $3F^3$
43781 $3F^4$
43851 $4F^1$
43871 $4F^1$
43931 $4F^1$
43987 $4F^1$
43989 $4F^1$
44094 $4F^2$
44153 $4F^2$
44238 $4F^2$
44241 $4F^2$
44335 $4F^2$
44467 $4F^2$
44562 $4F^2$
44570 $4F^2$
44584 $4F^2$
44586 $4F^2$
47249 $3F^5$
47271 $3F^6$
47443 $3F^6$
47463 $3F^6$
47538 $3F^6$
47589 $3F^6$
47632 $3F^6$
47640 $3F^6$
48005 8F
48123 8F
48126 8F
48149 8F
48276 8F
48311 8F
48314 8F
48358 8F
48622 8F
48641 8F
48652 8F
48703 8F
48721 8F
58136 $2F^8$

1957 55B
41661 $1F^1$
41797 $1F^1$
43014 $4MT^5$
43044 $4MT^5$
43392 $3F^3$
43456 $3F^3$
43579 $3F^3$
43681 $3F^3$
43737 $3F^3$
43851 $4F^1$
43871 $4F^1$
43931 $4F^1$
43987 $4F^1$
44028 $4F^2$
44094 $4F^2$
44153 $4F^2$
44238 $4F^2$
44335 $4F^2$
44467 $4F^2$
44570 $4F^2$
44584 $4F^2$
44586 $4F^2$
47249 $3F^5$
47271 $3F^6$
47443 $3F^6$
47463 $3F^6$
47538 $3F^6$
47589 $3F^6$
47632 $3F^6$
47640 $3F^6$
48123 8F
48126 8F
48276 8F
48311 8F
48358 8F
48443 8F
48537 8F
48622 8F
48641 8F
48652 8F
48703 8F
48721 8F
58136 $2F^8$

1960 55B
43038 $4MT^5$
43044 $4MT^5$
43681 $3F^3$
43737 $3F^3$
43871 $4F^1$
43931 $4F^1$
43968 $4F^1$
43987 $4F^1$
44003 $4F^1$
44028 $4F^2$
44044 $4F^2$
44094 $4F^2$
44107 $4F^2$
44153 $4F^2$
44207 $4F^2$
44238 $4F^2$
44335 $4F^2$
44368 $4F^2$
44467 $4F^2$
44570 $4F^2$
44584 $4F^2$
44586 $4F^2$
48055 8F
48076 8F
48084 8F
48126 8F
48160 8F
48276 8F
48311 8F
48352 8F
48358 8F
48622 8F
48641 8F
48652 8F
48703 8F
48721 8F

1963 55B
43038 $4MT^5$
43044 $4MT^5$
43871 $4F^1$
43931 $4F^1$
43968 $4F^1$
43987 $4F^1$
44003 $4F^1$
44028 $4F^2$
44044 $4F^2$
44207 $4F^2$
44238 $4F^2$
44335 $4F^2$
44467 $4F^2$
44485 $4F^2$
44570 $4F^2$
44584 $4F^2$
44586 $4F^2$
48075 8F
48080 8F
48084 8F
48126 8F
48160 8F
48274 8F
48311 8F
48352 8F
48394 8F
48622 8F
48641 8F
48703 8F
48721 8F

1966 55B
43044 $4MT^5$
43084 $4MT^5$
43096 $4MT^5$
43102 $4MT^5$
43117 $4MT^5$
43135 $4MT^5$
43140 $4MT^5$
48084 8F
48093 8F
48126 8F
48130 8F
48146 8F
48160 8F
48274 8F
48311 8F
48394 8F
48473 8F
48537 8F
48622 8F
48641 8F
48670 8F
48703 8F
48721 8F
77000 $3MT^1$
77003 $3MT^1$
77013 $3MT^1$

Stranraer

1948 12H
40600 $2P^3$
40611 $2P^3$
40616 $2P^3$
40623 $2P^3$
41092 $4P^1$
56351 $3F^{10}$
56372 $3F^{10}$
57375 $2F^5$
57421 $2F^5$
57440 $2F^5$
57445 $2F^5$
57458 $2F^5$

1951 68C
40600 $2P^3$
40611 $2P^3$
40616 $2P^3$
40623 $2P^3$
41092 $4P^1$
41099 $4P^1$
41127 $4P^1$
55125 $2P^{12}$
56234 $3F^{10}$
56372 $3F^{10}$
57340 $2F^5$
57375 $2F^5$
57445 $2F^5$
57458 $2F^5$

1954 68C
40611 $2P^3$
40616 $2P^3$
40623 $2P^3$
41127 $4P^1$
41129 $4P^1$
41135 $4P^1$
42749 $5MT^1$
55125 $2P^{12}$
56234 $3F^{10}$
56372 $3F^{10}$
57340 $2F^5$
57375 $2F^5$
57445 $2F^5$

1957 68C
40611 $2P^3$
40616 $2P^3$
40623 $2P^3$
40920 $4P^1$
41155 $4P^1$
42749 $5MT^1$
54492 $3P^6$
54508 $3P^6$
55125 $2P^{12}$
56234 $3F^{10}$
56372 $3F^{10}$
57238 $2F^5$
57340 $2F^5$
57375 $2F^5$
57445 $2F^5$

1960 68C
40566 $2P^3$
40623 $2P^3$
40641 $2P^3$
40642 $2P^3$
42749 $5MT^1$
54492 $3P^6$
55240 $2P^{14}$
57238 $2F^5$
57340 $2F^5$
57375 $2F^5$
57445 $2F^5$
76112 $4MT^2$

1963 67F
42738 $5MT^1$
44789 $5MT^3$
45470 $5MT^3$
45485 $5MT^3$
57365 $2F^5$
57375 $2F^5$
76112 $4MT^2$

1966 67F
44999 $5MT^3$
76101 $4MT^2$
78016 $2MT^1$

Stratford

1948 STR
61009 B1
61119 B1
61226 B1
61232 B1
61233 B1
61234 B1
61235 B1
61236 B1
61510 B12
61514 B12
61515 B12
61517 B12
61519 B12
61520 B12
61525 B12
61530 B12
61533 B12
61535 B12
61537 B12
61538 B12
61540 B12
61541 B12
61542 B12
61545 B12
61546 B12
61547 B12
61549 B12
61550 B12
61554 B12
61555 B12
61556 B12
61557 B12
61558 B12
61559 B12
61565 B12
61567 B12
61568 B12
61571 B12
61572 B12
61573 B12
61574 B12
61575 B12
61576 B12
61578 B12
61579 B12
61580 B12
61605 B17
61606 B17
61609 B17
61612 B17
61639 B2
61655 B17
61658 B17
61721 K2
61730 K2
61734 K2
61737 K2
61740 K2
61745 K2
61746 K2
61752 K2
61753 K2
61754 K2
61759 K2
61761 K2
61765 K2
61767 K2
61777 K2
61778 K2
61780 K2
62509 D15
62532 D16
62538 D15
62587 D16
62602 D16
64675 J20
64677 J20
64681 J20
64682 J20
64685 J20
64686 J20
64691 J20
64695 J20
64696 J20
64708 J39
64730 J39
64733 J39
64764 J39
64766 J39
64767 J39
64768 J39
64769 J39
64770 J39
64771 J39
64772 J39
64773 J39
64774 J39
64775 J39
64776 J39
64777 J39
64779 J39
64780 J39
64781 J39
64782 J39
64783 J39
64787 J39
64789 J39
64839 J39
64840 J39
64873 J39
64874 J39
64876 J39
64907 J39
64953 J39
65354 J15
65361 J15
65363 J15
65370 J15
65375 J15
65381 J15
65387 J15
65388 J15
65392 J15
65393 J15
65395 J15
65397 J15
65402 J15
65418 J15
65427 J15
65431 J15
65434 J15
65436 J15
65441 J15
65444 J15
65446 J15
65449 J15
65450 J15
65452 J15
65454 J15
65455 J15
65463 J15
65464 J15
65466 J15
65468 J15
65475 J15
65476 J15
65500 J17
65507 J17
65508 J17
65511 J17
65519 J17
65523 J17
65528 J17
65536 J17
65540 J17
65541 J17
65542 J17
65543 J17
67159 F4
67161 F4
67168 F4
67169 F4
67170 F4
67172 F4
67173 F4
67179 F4
67180 F4
67181 F4
67183 F4
67185 F4
67191 F5
67192 F5
67193 F5
67194 F5
67195 F5
67196 F5
67197 F5
67198 F5
67199 F5
67200 F5
67201 F5
67202 F5
67203 F5
67205 F5
67208 F5
67209 F5
67210 F5
67211 F5
67212 F5
67214 F5
67215 F5
67216 F5
67217 F5
67218 F6
67219 F6
67220 F6
67221 F6
67222 F6
67224 F6
67225 F6
67227 F6
67228 F6
67230 F6
67231 F6
67232 F6
67322 G5
67667 V1
67668 V1
67669 V3
67671 V1
67672 V3
67673 V1
67675 V3
67676 V1
67677 V1
67679 V1
67680 V1
67681 V1
68125 Y4
68126 Y4
68127 Y4
68128 Y4
68168 Y3
68169 Y3
68174 Y3
68215 J65
68381 J66
68388 J66
68496 J67
68500 J69
68507 J69
68508 J69
68509 J67
68513 J67
68520 J67
68522 J67
68523 J67
68526 J69
68532 J69
68534 J69
68538 J69
68545 J69
68548 J69
68549 J69
68554 J69
68556 J69
68557 J69
68561 J69
68563 J69
68569 J69
68573 J69
68574 J69
68575 J69
68576 J69
68577 J69
68578 J69
68589 J67
68590 J67
68591 J67
68592 J67
68593 J67
68594 J67
68601 J69
68606 J67
68607 J69
68608 J67
68612 J69
68613 J69
68617 J69
68619 J69
68621 J69
68626 J69
68630 J69
68631 J69
68633 J69
68639 J68
68643 J68
68644 J68
68646 J68
68647 J68
68648 J68
68649 J68
68650 J68
68652 J68
68653 J68
68661 J68
68662 J68
68663 J68
68665 J68
68666 J68
68905 J50
68924 J50
68950 J50
68963 J50
68965 J50
68967 J50
68977 J50
69000 L1
69600 N7
69601 N7
69602 N7
69603 N7
69604 N7
69605 N7
69606 N7
69607 N7
69608 N7
69609 N7
69610 N7
69611 N7
69612 N7
69613 N7
69614 N7
69615 N7
69616 N7
69617 N7
69618 N7
69619 N7
69620 N7
69621 N7
69622 N7
69623 N7
69624 N7
69625 N7
69626 N7
69627 N7
69628 N7
69629 N7
69630 N7
69631 N7
69632 N7
69633 N7
69634 N7
69635 N7
69636 N7
69637 N7
69638 N7
69639 N7
69640 N7
69641 N7
69642 N7
69643 N7
69644 N7
69645 N7
69646 N7
69647 N7
69648 N7
69649 N7
69650 N7
69651 N7
69652 N7
69653 N7
69654 N7
69655 N7
69656 N7
69657 N7
69658 N7
69659 N7
69660 N7
69661 N7
69662 N7
69663 N7
69664 N7
69665 N7
69666 N7
69667 N7
69668 N7
69669 N7
69670 N7
69671 N7
69672 N7
69673 N7
69674 N7
69675 N7
69676 N7
69677 N7
69678 N7
69679 N7
69680 N7
69681 N7
69682 N7
69683 N7
69684 N7
69685 N7
69686 N7
69687 N7
69688 N7
69693 N7
69697 N7
69699 N7
69700 N7
69701 N7
69702 N7
69703 N7
69704 N7
69705 N7
69706 N7
69707 N7
69708 N7
69709 N7
69710 N7
69711 N7
69712 N7
69713 N7
69714 N7
69715 N7
69716 N7
69717 N7
69718 N7
69719 N7
69720 N7
69721 N7
69722 N7
69723 N7
69724 N7
69725 N7
69726 N7
69727 N7
69728 N7
69729 N7
69730 N7
69731 N7
69732 N7
69733 N7

1951 30A
61000 B1
61001 B1
61008 B1
61009 B1
61089 B1
61098 B1
61104 B1
61109 B1
61119 B1
61130 B1
61144 B1
61171 B1
61175 B1
61177 B1
61192 B1
61205 B1
61227 B1
61233 B1
61234 B1
61235 B1
61236 B1
61282 B1
61335 B1
61336 B1
61360 B1
61361 B1
61362 B1
61363 B1
61514 B12
61515 B12
61516 B12
61519 B12
61525 B12
61542 B12
61546 B12
61549 B12
61550 B12
61559 B12
61567 B12
61568 B12
61571 B12
61572 B12
61573 B12
61574 B12
61575 B12
61576 B12
61578 B12
61579 B12
61580 B12
61602 B17
61605 B17
61606 B17
61608 B17
61610 B17
61611 B17
61612 B17
61613 B17
61621 B17
61648 B17
61654 B17
61658 B17
61721 K2
61734 K2
61737 K2
61745 K2
61746 K2
61752 K2
61753 K2
61754 K2
61759 K2
61761 K2
61765 K2
61767 K2
61777 K2
61778 K2
61780 K2
61801 K3
61805 K3
61810 K3
61815 K3
61817 K3
61820 K3
61830 K3
61831 K3
61834 K3
61835 K3
61840 K3
61849 K3
61880 K3
62565 D16
62572 D16
62791 E4
64650 J19
64651 J19
64652 J19
64657 J19
64660 J19
64662 J19
64663 J19
64664 J19
64665 J19

64670 J19
64675 J20
64676 J20
64677 J20
64680 J20
64681 J20
64682 J20
64685 J20
64686 J20
64690 J20
64691 J20
64695 J20
64696 J20
64708 J39
64764 J39
64765 J39
64766 J39
64768 J39
64769 J39
64772 J39
64774 J39
64775 J39
64776 J39
64780 J39
64781 J39
64782 J39
64783 J39
64874 J39
64876 J39
65370 J15
65384 J15
65440 J15
65444 J15
65446 J15
65449 J15
65450 J15
65452 J15
65453 J15
65454 J15
65455 J15
65463 J15
65464 J15
65466 J15
65476 J15
65500 J17
65508 J17
65511 J17
65523 J17
65528 J17
65536 J17
65540 J17
65541 J17
65543 J17
67192 F5
67193 F5
67197 F5
67198 F5
67200 F5
67202 F5
67203 F5
67205 F5
67206 F5
67207 F5
67208 F5
67209 F5
67210 F5
67211 F5
67212 F5
67213 F5
67214 F5
67269 G5
67279 G5
67322 G5
67701 L1
67712 L1
67713 L1
67721 L1
67722 L1
67723 L1
67724 L1
67725 L1
67726 L1
67727 L1
67728 L1
67729 L1
67730 L1
67731 L1
67732 L1
67733 L1
67734 L1
67735 L1
67736 L1
67737 L1
67738 L1
67739 L1
68125 Y4
68126 Y4
68127 Y4
68128 Y4
68174 Y3
68380 J66
68491 J69
68496 J67
68500 J69
68507 J69
68508 J69
68510 J69
68513 J67
68517 J67
68519 J69
68520 J69
68521 J67
68523 J67
68526 J69
68532 J69
68534 J69
68538 J69
68546 J69
68548 J69
68549 J69
68554 J69
68557 J69
68563 J69
68569 J69
68571 J69
68573 J69
68574 J69
68575 J69
68576 J69
68577 J69
68588 J67
68589 J67
68590 J67
68591 J69
68592 J67
68594 J67
68601 J69
68606 J67
68607 J69
68612 J69
68613 J69
68617 J69
68619 J69
68621 J69
68626 J69
68629 J69
68630 J69
68631 J69
68633 J69
68639 J68
68642 J68
68644 J68
68646 J68
68647 J68
68648 J68
68649 J68
68650 J68
68652 J68
68660 J68
68661 J68
68662 J68
68663 J68
68665 J68
68666 J68
68667 J92
68668 J92
68950 J50
68963 J50
68965 J50
68967 J50
68977 J50
69600 N7
69601 N7
69602 N7
69603 N7
69604 N7
69605 N7
69606 N7
69607 N7
69608 N7
69609 N7
69610 N7
69611 N7
69616 N7
69617 N7
69618 N7
69619 N7
69622 N7
69623 N7
69624 N7
69625 N7
69626 N7
69627 N7
69628 N7
69629 N7
69630 N7
69631 N7
69633 N7
69634 N7
69636 N7
69637 N7
69638 N7
69641 N7
69642 N7
69643 N7
69645 N7
69646 N7
69647 N7
69648 N7
69649 N7
69650 N7
69651 N7
69652 N7
69653 N7
69654 N7
69655 N7
69656 N7
69657 N7
69658 N7
69659 N7
69660 N7
69661 N7
69662 N7
69663 N7
69664 N7
69665 N7
69666 N7
69667 N7
69668 N7
69669 N7
69670 N7
69671 N7
69672 N7
69673 N7
69674 N7
69675 N7
69676 N7
69678 N7
69680 N7
69681 N7
69682 N7
69683 N7
69684 N7
69685 N7
69686 N7
69687 N7
69688 N7
69693 N7
69697 N7
69699 N7
69700 N7
69702 N7
69704 N7
69705 N7
69710 N7
69711 N7
69712 N7
69713 N7
69714 N7
69715 N7
69716 N7
69717 N7
69718 N7
69719 N7
69720 N7
69721 N7
69722 N7
69723 N7
69724 N7
69725 N7
69727 N7
69728 N7
69729 N7
69730 N7
69731 N7
69732 N7
69733 N7

1954 30A

41952 3P^2
41975 3P^2
61000 B1
61008 B1
61089 B1
61104 B1
61109 B1
61114 B1
61119 B1
61227 B1
61233 B1
61234 B1
61235 B1
61236 B1
61280 B1
61329 B1
61335 B1
61336 B1
61360 B1
61361 B1
61362 B1
61363 B1
61370 B1
61372 B1
61373 B1
61375 B1
61378 B1
61384 B1
61399 B1
61512 B12
61516 B12
61519 B12
61523 B12
61546 B12
61549 B12
61550 B12
61555 B12
61556 B12
61557 B12
61558 B12
61573 B12
61575 B12
61576 B12
61578 B12
61579 B12
61600 B17
61601 B17
61602 B17
61605 B17
61606 B17
61608 B17
61609 B17
61610 B17
61611 B17
61612 B17
61613 B17
61618 B17
61621 B17
61630 B17
61648 B17
61654 B17
61655 B17
61660 B17
61661 B17
61663 B17
61666 B17
61668 B17
61672 B17
61801 K3
61805 K3
61810 K3
61815 K3
61817 K3
61820 K3
61830 K3
61831 K3
61834 K3
61840 K3
61849 K3
61862 K3
61863 K5
61880 K3
61921 K3
61942 K3
61951 K3
61963 K3
61977 K3
64656 J19
64657 J19
64662 J19
64663 J19
64664 J19
64665 J19
64670 J19
64675 J20
64676 J20
64677 J20
64680 J20
64681 J20
64682 J20
64685 J20
64686 J20
64690 J20
64691 J20
64696 J20
64708 J39
64764 J39
64765 J39
64766 J39
64767 J39
64768 J39
64769 J39
64771 J39
64772 J39
64774 J39
64775 J39
64776 J39
64779 J39
64780 J39
64781 J39
64782 J39
64783 J39
64784 J39
64803 J39
64876 J39
64958 J39
64985 J39
65370 J15
65384 J15
65440 J15
65443 J15
65444 J15
65446 J15
65449 J15
65450 J15
65452 J15
65454 J15
65455 J15
65463 J15
65464 J15
65476 J15
65500 J17
65508 J17
65511 J17
65523 J17
65525 J17
65528 J17
65536 J17
65538 J17
65540 J17
65543 J17
65546 J17
65555 J17
65563 J17
65587 J17
67188 F5
67192 F5
67193 F5
67194 F5
67197 F5
67198 F5
67200 F5
67202 F5
67203 F5
67205 F5
67208 F5
67209 F5
67210 F5
67211 F5
67212 F5
67213 F5
67215 F5
67219 F5
67701 L1
67712 L1
67713 L1
67721 L1
67722 L1
67723 L1
67724 L1
67725 L1
67726 L1
67727 L1
67728 L1
67729 L1
67730 L1
67731 L1
67732 L1
67733 L1
67734 L1
67735 L1
67736 L1
67737 L1
67738 L1
68125 Y4
68126 Y4
68127 Y4
68128 Y4
68496 J67
68507 J69
68510 J69
68513 J69
68517 J67
68519 J69
68520 J69
68521 J67
68526 J69
68527 J69
68532 J69
68534 J69
68538 J69
68546 J69
68549 J69
68550 J69
68552 J69
68554 J69
68556 J69
68561 J69
68563 J69
68565 J69
68568 J69
68569 J69
68571 J69
68573 J69
68574 J69
68575 J69
68576 J69
68577 J69
68579 J69
68588 J69
68589 J67
68590 J67
68591 J69
68594 J67
68596 J69
68601 J69
68607 J69
68612 J69
68613 J69
68617 J69
68619 J69
68621 J69
68626 J69
68629 J69
68630 J69
68631 J69
68632 J69
68633 J69
68639 J68
68642 J68
68644 J68
68646 J68
68647 J68
68648 J68
68649 J68
68650 J68
68652 J68
68653 J68
68654 J68
68655 J68
68657 J68
68658 J68
68659 J68
68660 J68
68661 J68
68662 J68
68663 J68
68665 J68
68666 J68
68950 J50
68963 J50
68965 J50
68967 J50
68977 J50
69550 N2
69559 N2
69600 N7
69601 N7
69602 N7
69603 N7
69604 N7
69605 N7
69606 N7
69607 N7
69608 N7
69609 N7
69610 N7
69611 N7
69612 N7
69613 N7
69614 N7
69616 N7
69617 N7
69618 N7
69619 N7
69622 N7
69623 N7
69624 N7
69625 N7
69626 N7
69627 N7
69628 N7
69629 N7
69630 N7
69631 N7
69633 N7
69634 N7
69636 N7
69637 N7
69641 N7
69642 N7
69643 N7
69645 N7
69646 N7
69647 N7
69650 N7
69652 N7
69653 N7
69655 N7
69656 N7
69657 N7
69658 N7
69659 N7
69660 N7
69661 N7
69662 N7
69663 N7
69664 N7
69665 N7
69666 N7
69667 N7
69668 N7
69669 N7
69670 N7
69671 N7
69674 N7
69675 N7
69676 N7
69677 N7
69680 N7
69681 N7
69682 N7
69683 N7
69684 N7
69685 N7
69686 N7
69687 N7
69688 N7
69693 N7
69697 N7
69699 N7
69700 N7
69701 N7
69702 N7
69703 N7
69705 N7
69710 N7
69711 N7
69712 N7
69713 N7
69714 N7
69715 N7
69716 N7
69717 N7
69718 N7
69719 N7
69721 N7
69722 N7
69723 N7
69724 N7
69725 N7
69726 N7
69727 N7
69728 N7
69729 N7
69730 N7
69731 N7
69733 N7
70000 7P6F
70001 7P6F
70002 7P6F
70003 7P6F
70005 7P6F
70034 7P6F
70036 7P6F
70037 7P6F
70038 7P6F
70039 7P6F
70040 7P6F
70041 7P6F
70042 7P6F
76030 4MT^2
76031 4MT^2
76032 4MT^2
76033 4MT^2
76034 4MT^2

1957 30A

61000 B1
61089 B1
61104 B1
61109 B1
61119 B1
61233 B1
61234 B1
61235 B1
61236 B1
61249 B1
61280 B1
61329 B1
61335 B1
61336 B1
61360 B1
61361 B1
61362 B1
61363 B1
61370 B1
61372 B1
61373 B1
61375 B1
61378 B1
61399 B1
61512 B12
61516 B12
61519 B12
61546 B12
61549 B12
61550 B12
61573 B12
61575 B12
61576 B12
61578 B12
61579 B12
61600 B17
61601 B17
61602 B17
61605 B17
61609 B17
61610 B17
61612 B17
61613 B17
61630 B17
61648 B17
61654 B17
61655 B17
61660 B17
61661 B17
61663 B17
61668 B17
61672 B17
61801 K3
61805 K3
61810 K3
61815 K3
61817 K3
61820 K3
61830 K3
61831 K3
61834 K3
61840 K3
61849 K3
61862 K3
61863 K5
61880 K3
61921 K3
61942 K3
61951 K3
61963 K3
61977 K3
64656 J19
64657 J19
64662 J19
64663 J19
64664 J19
64665 J19
64670 J19
64675 J20
64676 J20
64677 J20
64680 J20
64681 J20
64682 J20
64685 J20
64686 J20
64689 J20
64693 J20
64694 J20
64708 J39
64750 J39
64765 J39
64766 J39
64767 J39
64768 J39
64769 J39
64772 J39
64774 J39
64775 J39
64779 J39
64780 J39
64781 J39
64782 J39
64783 J39
64784 J39
64807 J39
64973 J39
65440 J15
65443 J15
65444 J15
65446 J15
65449 J15
65450 J15
65452 J15
65454 J15
65455 J15
65463 J15
65464 J15
65476 J15
65508 J17
65511 J17
65523 J17
65525 J17
65528 J17
65535 J17
65536 J17
65540 J17
65545 J17
65546 J17
65555 J17
65563 J17
67193 F5
67195 F5
67200 F5
67202 F5
67203 F5
67208 F5
67209 F5
67212 F5
67214 F5
67218 F5
67221 F6
67230 F6
67701 L1
67712 L1
67713 L1
67718 L1
67720 L1
67721 L1
67722 L1
67723 L1
67724 L1
67725 L1
67726 L1
67727 L1
67729 L1
67730 L1
67731 L1
67732 L1
67733 L1
67734 L1
67735 L1
67737 L1
67738 L1
68126 Y4
68500 J69
68510 J69
68513 J69
68516 J67
68526 J69
68529 J69
68532 J69
68538 J69
68546 J69
68549 J69
68563 J69
68568 J69
68571 J69
68573 J69
68574 J69
68575 J69
68576 J69
68577 J69
68578 J69
68579 J69
68588 J69
68591 J69
68596 J69
68607 J69
68612 J69
68613 J69
68619 J69
68630 J69
68631 J69
68632 J69
68633 J69
68636 J69
68639 J68
68644 J68
68646 J68
68647 J68
68648 J68
68649 J68
68650 J68
68652 J68
68653 J68
68654 J68
68655 J68
68657 J68
68658 J68
68659 J68
68660 J68
68663 J68
68665 J68
69600 N7
69601 N7
69602 N7
69603 N7
69604 N7
69605 N7
69606 N7
69607 N7
69608 N7
69609 N7
69610 N7
69611 N7
69613 N7
69614 N7
69616 N7
69617 N7
69619 N7
69620 N7
69621 N7
69622 N7
69623 N7
69624 N7
69625 N7
69626 N7
69627 N7
69628 N7
69630 N7
69633 N7
69634 N7
69636 N7
69641 N7
69642 N7
69643 N7
69645 N7
69646 N7
69647 N7
69652 N7
69653 N7
69655 N7
69656 N7
69657 N7
69658 N7
69659 N7
69660 N7
69661 N7
69662 N7
69663 N7
69664 N7
69665 N7
69666 N7
69667 N7
69668 N7
69669 N7
69670 N7
69671 N7
69674 N7
69676 N7
69677 N7
69680 N7
69681 N7
69682 N7
69683 N7
69684 N7
69685 N7
69686 N7
69687 N7
69688 N7
69693 N7
69697 N7
69699 N7
69700 N7
69701 N7
69702 N7
69703 N7
69705 N7
69710 N7
69711 N7
69712 N7
69713 N7
69714 N7
69715 N7
69716 N7
69717 N7
69718 N7
69719 N7
69720 N7
69722 N7
69723 N7
69724 N7
69725 N7
69726 N7
69728 N7
69729 N7
69730 N7
69731 N7
70000 7P6F
70001 7P6F
70002 7P6F
70003 7P6F
70005 7P6F
70034 7P6F
70036 7P6F
70037 7P6F
70038 7P6F
70039 7P6F
70040 7P6F
70041 7P6F
70042 7P6F
76030 4MT^2
76031 4MT^2
76032 4MT^2
76033 4MT^2
76034 4MT^2
90062 WD^1
90508 WD^1
90551 WD^1
90660 WD^1

1960 30A

43105 4MT^5
43144 4MT^5
43148 4MT^5
43149 4MT^5
43150 4MT^5
43151 4MT^5
43152 4MT^5
43153 4MT^5
47282 3F^6
47306 3F^6
47311 3F^6
61089 B1
61109 B1
61119 B1
61233 B1
61329 B1
61335 B1
61375 B1
61663 B17
61666 B17
61668 B17
61815 K3
61820 K3
61863 K5
62013 K1
62014 K1
62015 K1
62019 K1
62036 K1
62053 K1
62070 K1
64650 J19
64653 J19
64656 J19
64657 J19
64660 J19
64663 J19
64664 J19
64666 J19
64667 J19
64676 J20
64677 J20
64680 J20
64681 J20
64682 J20
64685 J20
64686 J20
64689 J20
64693 J20
64694 J20
64708 J39
64765 J39
64767 J39
64775 J39
64777 J39
64780 J39
64781 J39
64783 J39
64784 J39
65361 J15
65440 J15
65446 J15
65448 J15
65455 J15
65459 J15
65464 J15
65465 J15
65473 J15
65476 J15
65503 J17
65506 J17
65507 J17
65511 J17
65514 J17
65536 J17
65539 J17
65546 J17
65548 J17
65555 J17
65563 J17
65564 J17
67701 L1
67702 L1
67703 L1
67704 L1
67705 L1
67706 L1
67708 L1
67709 L1
67711 L1
67714 L1
67715 L1
67716 L1
67724 L1
67725 L1
67726 L1
67727 L1
67728 L1
67729 L1
67730 L1
67731 L1
67732 L1
67735 L1
67736 L1
67737 L1
67739 L1
67752 L1
67778 L1
68500 J69
68513 J69
68538 J69
68549 J69
68565 J69
68571 J69
68575 J69
68577 J69
68578 J69
68579 J69
68600 J69
68609 J69
68612 J69
68613 J69
68619 J69
68633 J69
68642 J68
68644 J68
68646 J68
68647 J68
68649 J68
68650 J68
68660 J68
68663 J68
69611 N7
69614 N7
69615 N7
69617 N7
69620 N7
69621 N7
69630 N7
69636 N7
69642 N7
69645 N7
69646 N7
69647 N7
69651 N7
69652 N7
69653 N7
69656 N7
69658 N7
69663 N7
69664 N7
69665 N7
69668 N7
69670 N7
69671 N7
69674 N7
69677 N7
69679 N7
69680 N7
69681 N7
69682 N7
69683 N7
69684 N7
69685 N7
69686 N7
69687 N7
69688 N7
69690 N7
69691 N7
69693 N7
69697 N7
69699 N7
69700 N7
69701 N7
69702 N7
69706 N7
69707 N7
69708 N7
69709 N7
69710 N7
69712 N7
69713 N7
69714 N7
69715 N7
69718 N7
69719 N7
69720 N7
69721 N7
69722 N7
69723 N7
69724 N7
69725 N7
69726 N7
69727 N7
69728 N7
69729 N7
69733 N7
76030 4MT^2
76031 4MT^2
76032 4MT^2
76033 4MT^2
76034 4MT^2
90028 WD^1
90062 WD^1
90129 WD^1
90156 WD^1
90298 WD^1
90480 WD^1
90498 WD^1
90508 WD^1
90551 WD^1
90660 WD^1

1966

28 B1

Stratford Works

1948

68081 Y5
68129 Y4
68135 Y1
68370 J66
68667 J92
68668 J92
68669 J92

1951

68088 Y7
68129 Y4
68370 J66

1954

31 J66
32 J66
33 Y4
36 J66

1957

31 J66
32 J66
33 Y4
36 J66

1960

32 J66
33 Y4
44 J69
45 J69

1963

33 Y4

Stratford on Avon

1948 21D

43277 3F^3
43381 3F^3
43520 3F^3
43521 3F^3
43523 3F^3
43568 3F^3
43693 3F^3
43767 3F^4
43822 3F^4
43873 4F^1
44204 4F^2
44587 4F^2
44606 4F^2

1951 21D

43277 3F^3
43381 3F^3
43520 3F^3
43521 3F^3
43523 3F^3
43568 3F^3
43693 3F^3
43822 3F^4
43873 4F^1
44186 4F^2
44204 4F^2
44524 4F^2
44587 4F^2
44606 4F^2

Sunderland

1948 SUN

65785 J27
65793 J27
65798 J27
65817 J27
65820 J27
65823 J27
65833 J27
65835 J27
65840 J27
65843 J27
65846 J27
65847 J27
65854 J27
65856 J27
65865 J27
65872 J27
65878 J27
65884 J27
67243 G5
67247 G5
67251 G5
67252 G5
67257 G5
67260 G5
67264 G5
67267 G5
67270 G5
67283 G5
67297 G5
67299 G5
67300 G5
67310 G5
67328 G5
67336 G5
67348 G5
68016 J94
68691 J72
68698 J72
68707 J72
68718 J72
68730 J72
69400 N8
69413 N9
69421 N9

69425 N9
69427 N9
69428 N9
69429 N9
69850 A8
69861 A8
69874 A8
69887 A8

1951 54A
65785 J27
65798 J27
65817 J27
65823 J27
65832 J27
65833 J27
65835 J27
65836 J27
65840 J27
65841 J27
65843 J27
65847 J27
65850 J27
65854 J27
65856 J27
65871 J27
65872 J27
65878 J27
67243 G5
67247 G5
67251 G5
67252 G5
67257 G5
67260 G5
67264 G5
67267 G5
67270 G5
67276 G5
67283 G5
67297 G5
67300 G5
67310 G5
67328 G5
67336 G5
67348 G5
68016 J94
68678 J72
68698 J72
68704 J72
68718 J72
69018 J72
69418 N9
69423 N9
69424 N9
69427 N9
69850 A8
69853 A8
69857 A8
69874 A8
69887 A8

1954 54A
64919 J39
64939 J39
65785 J27
65798 J27
65817 J27
65823 J27
65832 J27
65833 J27
65835 J27
65836 J27
65840 J27
65841 J27
65843 J27
65847 J27
65850 J27
65854 J27
65856 J27
65871 J27
65872 J27
65878 J27
67243 G5
67247 G5
67251 G5
67257 G5
67267 G5
67283 G5
67297 G5
67300 G5
67310 G5
67328 G5
67336 G5
67344 G5
68016 J94
68017 J94
68024 J94
68041 J94
68048 J94
68058 J94
68678 J72
68698 J72
68704 J72
69002 J72
69007 J72
69101 N10
69392 N8
69850 A8
69853 A8
69857 A8
69863 A8
69874 A8
69887 A8
76023 4MT[2]

1957 54A
63466 Q7
63467 Q7
63474 Q7
64817 J39
64919 J39
65662 J25
65798 J27
65817 J27
65832 J27
65833 J27
65835 J27
65836 J27
65840 J27
65841 J27
65843 J27
65847 J27
65850 J27
65854 J27
65856 J27
65871 J27
65872 J27
65878 J27
65892 J27
65893 J27
67254 G5
67259 G5
67270 G5
67278 G5
67297 G5
67318 G5
67321 G5
67338 G5
67342 G5
67343 G5
68016 J94
68017 J94
68024 J94
68041 J94
68048 J94
68058 J94
68678 J72
68698 J72
68704 J72
69002 J72
69007 J72
69101 N10
69850 A8
69853 A8
69857 A8
69863 A8
69874 A8

1960 52G
63467 Q7
63469 Q7
63474 Q7
64700 J39
64701 J39
64703 J39
64704 J39
64710 J39
64825 J39
64833 J39
64847 J39
64853 J39
65662 J25
65666 J25
65726 J25
65817 J27
65823 J27
65832 J27
65833 J27
65835 J27
65841 J27
65850 J27
65854 J27
65871 J27
65872 J27
65873 J27
65878 J27
65892 J27
67645 V3
67673 V1
68016 J94
68041 J94
68044 J94
68048 J94
68058 J94
68678 J72
68704 J72
69002 J72
69850 A8
69853 A8
69854 A8
69855 A8
69857 A8
69858 A8
69859 A8
69870 A8
69873 A8
69874 A8
69875 A8
69878 A8
69883 A8
69889 A8

1963 52G
63342 Q6
63345 Q6
63365 Q6
63376 Q6
63404 Q6
63418 Q6
63456 Q6
65788 J27
65817 J27
65823 J27
65830 J27
65832 J27
65833 J27
65835 J27
65841 J27
65846 J27
65853 J27
65854 J27
65865 J27
65869 J27
65870 J27
65871 J27
65872 J27
65873 J27
65874 J27
65878 J27
65883 J27
65885 J27
65887 J27
65892 J27

1966 52G
62007 K1
62026 K1
63346 Q6
63395 Q6
63405 Q6
63406 Q6
63436 Q6
63437 Q6
63445 Q6
63458 Q6
65788 J27
65817 J27
65831 J27
65832 J27
65833 J27
65835 J27
65853 J27
65865 J27
65872 J27
65873 J27
65885 J27

Sutton Oak

1948 10E
44125 4F[2]
44358 4F[2]
44473 4F[2]
46628 1P[1]
46637 1P[1]
46676 1P[1]
46682 1P[1]
46692 1P[1]
47180 Sentinel[1]
47183 Sentinel[1]
47184 Sentinel[2]
47393 3F[6]
47453 3F[6]
48918 6F[2]
48954 7F[2]
49152 6F[2]
49303 6F[2]
49312 7F[2]
49317 7F[2]
51204 0F[4]
51316 2F[2]
51319 2F[2]
51471 2F[2]
51491 2F[2]
51495 2F[2]
52091 3F[7]
52126 3F[7]
52177 3F[7]
52280 3F[7]
52349 3F[7]
52366 3F[7]
52393 3F[7]
52397 3F[7]
52449 3F[7]
52453 3F[7]
58390 2F[11]
58394 2F[11]
58410 2F[11]
58419 2F[11]
58899 2F[14]
58913 2F[14]
58917 2F[14]

1951 10E
40080 3MT[2]
40084 3MT[2]
40108 3MT[2]
41285 2MT[1]
41286 2MT[1]
41287 2MT[1]
43025 4MT[5]
43026 4MT[5]
43028 4MT[5]
43029 4MT[5]
44379 4F[2]
46628 1P[1]
46643 1P[1]
46757 1P[1]
47180 Sentinel[1]
47181 Sentinel[1]
47393 3F[6]
47444 3F[6]
47451 3F[6]
47453 3F[6]
49205 7F[2]
49262 7F[2]
49312 7F[2]
49377 7F[2]
49389 7F[2]
51316 2F[2]
51319 2F[2]
51397 2F[2]
51471 2F[2]
51491 2F[2]
52091 3F[7]
52177 3F[7]
52280 3F[7]
52349 3F[7]
52366 3F[7]
52393 3F[7]
52397 3F[7]
52449 3F[7]
58378 2F[11]
58394 2F[11]
58418 2F[11]
58900 2F[14]
58932 2F[14]

1954 10E
41286 2MT[1]
41288 2MT[1]
41289 2MT[1]
43025 4MT[5]
43026 4MT[5]
43028 4MT[5]
43029 4MT[5]
44280 4F[2]
44303 4F[2]
47181 Sentinel[1]
47366 3F[6]
47393 3F[6]
47444 3F[6]
47453 3F[6]
49239 7F[2]
49262 7F[2]
49288 7F[2]
49377 7F[2]
49389 7F[2]
51316 2F[2]
51319 2F[2]
51397 2F[2]
51441 2F[2]
51471 2F[2]
51491 2F[2]
52125 3F[7]
52177 3F[7]
52196 3F[7]
52338 3F[7]
52349 3F[7]
52366 3F[7]
52393 3F[7]
52397 3F[7]

1957 10D
41286 2MT[1]
41288 2MT[1]
41289 2MT[1]
43025 4MT[5]
43026 4MT[5]
43028 4MT[5]
43029 4MT[5]
43035 4MT[5]
44280 4F[2]
44300 4F[2]
44303 4F[2]
44350 4F[2]
44438 4F[2]
47288 3F[6]
47298 3F[6]
47366 3F[6]
47393 3F[6]
47444 3F[6]
47452 3F[6]
47453 3F[6]
49239 7F[2]
49262 7F[2]
49281 7F[2]
49288 7F[2]
49318 7F[2]
51316 2F[2]
51319 2F[2]
51441 2F[2]
51491 2F[2]
52125 3F[7]
52196 3F[7]
52322 3F[7]
52338 3F[7]
52366 3F[7]
52429 3F[7]
76075 4MT[2]
76076 4MT[2]
76077 4MT[2]
76078 4MT[2]

1960 8G
41211 2MT[1]
41286 2MT[1]
41288 2MT[1]
41289 2MT[1]
43185 3F[2]
43213 3F[3]
44192 4F[2]
44266 4F[2]
44300 4F[2]
44350 4F[2]
47298 3F[6]
47366 3F[6]
47376 3F[6]
47393 3F[6]
47444 3F[6]
47452 3F[6]
47453 3F[6]
49262 7F[2]
49288 7F[2]
49352 7F[2]
49448 7F[3]
51441 2F[2]
58177 2F[8]
58182 2F[8]
58291 2F[9]
76020 4MT[2]
76075 4MT[2]
76076 4MT[2]
76077 4MT[2]
76078 4MT[2]
76079 4MT[2]

1963 8G
41286 2MT[1]
44075 4F[2]
44086 4F[2]
44117 4F[2]
44127 4F[2]
44192 4F[2]
44266 4F[2]
44300 4F[2]
44350 4F[2]
44493 4F[2]
44596 4F[2]
47298 3F[6]
47393 3F[6]
47452 3F[6]
47453 3F[6]
47490 3F[6]
47668 3F[6]
76076 4MT[2]
76077 4MT[2]
76078 4MT[2]
76079 4MT[2]
90170 WD[1]
90178 WD[1]
90212 WD[1]
90464 WD[1]
90606 WD[1]
90702 WD[1]

1966 8G
41234 2MT[1]
41286 2MT[1]
47298 3F[6]
47377 3F[6]
47393 3F[6]
47668 3F[6]
48033 8F
48251 8F
48326 8F
48422 8F
48479 8F
48623 8F
48647 8F
48727 8F
76076 4MT[2]
76077 4MT[2]
76078 4MT[2]
76079 4MT[2]
76080 4MT[2]
76081 4MT[2]
76082 4MT[2]
76083 4MT[2]
76084 4MT[2]

Swansea East Dock

1948 SED
289 TV[2]
308 TV[3]
309 TV[3]
1140 SHT[1]
1144 SHT[4]
1150 PM[1]
1152 PM[1]
2166 BPGV[1]
2789 2721
3577 3571
3633 5700
3641 5700
3679 5700
4282 4200
4283 4200
4296 4200
5210 5205
5214 5205
5221 5205
5227 5205
5232 5205
5246 5205
5253 5205
5704 5700
5743 5700
6714 6700
7211 7200
7704 5700
7756 5700
9625 5700
9645 5700
9744 5700

1951 87D
308 TV[3]
309 TV[3]
1140 SHT[1]
1144 SHT[4]
1146 SHT[5]
1150 PM[1]
1152 PM[1]
2166 BPGV[1]
3633 5700
3641 5700
3679 5700
4296 4200
5210 5205
5221 5205
5227 5205
5232 5205
5246 5205
5616 5600
5628 5600
5704 5700
5743 5700
6613 5600
6662 5600
6714 6700
7704 5700
7756 5700
9625 5700
9645 5700
9744 5700

1954 87D
308 TV[3]
1140 SHT[1]
1144 SHT[4]
1152 PM[1]
1641 1600
2166 BPGV[1]
3633 5700
3641 5700
3679 5700
4259 4200
5210 5205
5211 5205
5221 5205
5227 5205
5232 5205
5246 5205
5616 5600
5628 5600
5704 5700
5731 5700
5743 5700
6613 5600
6644 5600
6662 5600
6714 6700
6734 6700
7224 7200
7226 7200
7248 7200
7704 5700
7756 5700
8431 9400
9489 9400
9625 5700
9645 5700
9744 5700

1957 87D
1140 SHT[1]
1144 SHT[4]
1152 PM[1]
1641 1600
1652 1600
3641 5700
4221 4200
4232 4200
5210 5205
5211 5205
5221 5205
5232 5205
5240 5205
5246 5205
5262 5205
5616 5600
5628 5600
6613 5600
6662 5600
7224 7200
7226 7200
7704 5700
7756 5700
8408 9400
8431 9400
8443 9400
8475 9400
8476 9400
8483 9400
9485 9400
9489 9400
9491 9400
9492 9400
9625 5700
9645 5700

1960 87D
1144 SHT[4]
1151 PM[1]
1152 PM[1]
1641 1600
1652 1600
3641 5700
3661 5700
4232 4200
4271 4200
5210 5205
5211 5205
5230 5205
5232 5205
5246 5205
5616 5600
5628 5600
5675 5600
6613 5600
6662 5600
6700 6700
6702 6700
6712 6700
6714 6700
6720 6700
6738 6700
6749 6700
6753 6700
6762 6700
6763 6700
6767 6700
6768 6700
6770 6700
6776 6700
6777 6700
6778 6700
7215 7200
7225 7200
7226 7200
7248 7200
7408 7400
7704 5700
8414 9400
8431 9400
8475 9400
8476 9400
8483 9400
9431 9400
9489 9400
9625 5700

1963 87D
1151 PM[1]
1338 Car[3]
3635 5700
3797 5700
4232 4200
5210 5205
5211 5205
5230 5205
5609 5600
5616 5600
5623 5600
5628 5600
5656 5600
5675 5600
6602 5600
6613 5600
6650 5600
6662 5600
6714 6700
6724 6700
6741 6700
6742 6700
6760 6700
6762 6700
6763 6700
6764 6700
6765 6700
6768 6700
6772 6700
6777 6700
7215 7200
7225 7200
7226 7200
8414 9400
8431 9400
8475 9400
8488 9400
8794 5700
9431 9400
9441 9400
9484 9400
9489 9400
9744 5700
9746 5700
9752 5700
51218 0F[4]
80069 4MT[3]
80072 4MT[3]
80097 4MT[3]
80099 4MT[3]
80133 4MT[3]
80134 4MT[3]

Swansea Victoria

1948 4B
41676 1F[1]
42307 4MT[2]
42385 4MT[2]
42387 4MT[2]
42388 4MT[2]
42390 4MT[2]
42394 4MT[2]
46414 2MT[2]
46415 2MT[2]
46620 1P[1]
46740 1P[1]
47931 7F[1]
47932 7F[1]
47937 7F[1]
47948 7F[1]
48175 8F
48325 8F
48335 8F
48343 8F
48344 8F
48366 8F
48427 8F
48473 8F
48551 8F
48664 8F
48665 8F
48673 8F
48691 8F
48717 8F
48893 7F[2]
49033 7F[2]
49035 7F[2]
49260 7F[2]
49358 7F[2]
49407 7F[3]
49418 7F[3]
58406 2F[11]
58430 2F[11]
58891 2F[14]
58892 2F[14]
58910 2F[14]
7700 2F[14]
7715 2F[14]

1951 87K
1622 1600
7439 7400
41769 1F[1]
41824 1F[1]
41852 1F[1]
41860 1F[1]
42305 4MT[2]
42307 4MT[2]
42385 4MT[2]
42387 4MT[2]
42388 4MT[2]
42390 4MT[2]
42394 4MT[2]
46620 1P[1]
47230 3F[5]
47232 3F[5]
47256 3F[5]
47258 3F[5]
47259 3F[5]
47477 3F[6]
47478 3F[6]
47479 3F[6]
47480 3F[6]
47481 3F[6]
47655 3F[6]
47681 3F[6]
48330 8F
48524 8F
48525 8F
48706 8F
48724 8F
48730 8F
48732 8F
48737 8F
48738 8F
48739 8F
48761 8F
48768 8F
48893 7F[2]
49033 7F[2]
49035 7F[2]
49148 7F[2]
49177 7F[2]
49260 7F[2]
49358 7F[2]
49376 7F[2]
58892 2F[14]
58910 2F[14]
90173 WD[1]
90188 WD[1]
90225 WD[1]
90579 WD[1]

1954 87K
5761 5700
5773 5700
6720 6700
7439 7400
8706 5700
8738 5700
41699 1F[1]
41769 1F[1]
41860 1F[1]
42305 4MT[2]
42307 4MT[2]
42385 4MT[2]
42387 4MT[2]
42388 4MT[2]
42390 4MT[2]
42394 4MT[2]
46616 1P[1]
47230 3F[5]
47232 3F[5]
47256 3F[5]
47258 3F[5]
47259 3F[5]
47477 3F[6]
47478 3F[6]
47479 3F[6]
47480 3F[6]
47481 3F[6]
47655 3F[6]
47681 3F[6]
48330 8F
48524 8F
48525 8F
48706 8F
48724 8F
48730 8F
48732 8F
48735 8F
48737 8F
48761 8F
48768 8F
49033 7F[2]
49035 7F[2]
49117 7F[2]
49148 7F[2]
49177 7F[2]
49358 7F[2]
49376 7F[2]
58880 2F[14]
58899 2F[14]
58911 2F[14]
58921 2F[14]

1957 87K
5761 5700
5773 5700
6713 6700
6714 6700
6720 6700
6721 6700
6734 6700
6763 6700
6768 6700
6779 6700
7408 7400
8706 5700
40097 3MT[2]
40105 3MT[2]
40141 3MT[2]
41769 1F[1]
41860 1F[1]
42305 4MT[2]
42307 4MT[2]
42385 4MT[2]
42387 4MT[2]
42388 4MT[2]
42390 4MT[2]
42394 4MT[2]
47230 3F[5]
47258 3F[5]
47259 3F[5]
47477 3F[6]
47478 3F[6]
47479 3F[6]
47480 3F[6]
47481 3F[6]
47655 3F[6]
47681 3F[6]
48309 8F
48330 8F
48524 8F
48525 8F
48706 8F
48730 8F
48732 8F
48735 8F
48737 8F
48761 8F
48768 8F
49033 7F[2]
49035 7F[2]
49117 7F[2]
49148 7F[2]
49177 7F[2]
49358 7F[2]
49376 7F[2]

Swindon

1948 SDN
992 1901
1366 1366
1369 1366
1371 1366
1400 1400
1433 1400
1436 1400
1446 1400
1453 1400
1542 1501
1731 1854
1758 1854
2014 1901
2017 1901
2060 2021
2195 BPGV[4]
2224 2251
2250 2251
2568 2301
2908 2900
2913 2900
2927 2900
2934 2900
2935 2900
2945 2900
2947 2900
2949 2900
2954 2900
3215 2251
3421 3300
3452 3300
3561 3500
3645 5700
3666 5700
3682 5700
3684 5700
3724 5700
3737 5700
3739 5700
3748 5700
3780 5700
4015 4000
4017 4000
4022 4000
4036 4000
4055 4000
4057 4000
4062 4000
4381 4300
4502 4500
4507 4500
4510 4500
4521 4500
4538 4500
4543 4500
4544 4500
4550 4500
4551 4500
4585 4575
4590 4575
4592 4575
4651 5700
4697 5700
4905 4900
4925 4900
4945 4900
4956 4900
5067 4073
5068 4073
5322 4300
5367 4300
5371 4300
5396 4300
5510 4575
5534 4575
5563 4575
5566 4575
5800 5800
5802 5800
5804 5800
5805 5800
5934 4900
5943 4900
5978 4900
6320 4300
6322 4300
6340 4300
6357 4300
6358 4300
6360 4300
6374 4300
6384 4300
6387 4300
6716 6700
6737 6700
6739 6700
6741 6700
6902 4900
6935 4900
6965 6959
7321 4300
7415 7400
7418 7400
7424 7400
7792 5700
7794 5700
8733 5700
8779 5700
9011 9000
9018 9000
9023 9000
9400 9400
9600 5700
9720 5700
9721 5700
9772 5700
9773 5700
9790 5700
9795 5700

1951 82C
5 WCP
992 1901
1366 1366
1369 1366
1371 1366
1400 1400
1403 1400
1433 1400
1436 1400
1446 1400
1542 1501
2014 1901
2017 1901
2060 2021
2195 BPGV[4]
2224 2251
2250 2251
2568 2301
2927 2900
2934 2900
2945 2900
2947 2900
2949 2900
2954 2900
3444 3300
3449 3300
3451 3300
3453 3300
3645 5700
3666 5700
3682 5700
3684 5700
3724 5700
3737 5700
3739 5700
3748 5700
3780 5700
4015 4000
4022 4000
4036 4000
4055 4000
4057 4000
4062 4000
4381 4300
4502 4500
4521 4500
4536 4500
4538 4500
4544 4500
4550 4500
4551 4500
4585 4575
4590 4575
4592 4575
4612 5700
4651 5700
4697 5700
4925 4900
4945 4900
4951 4900
4973 4900
4983 4900
5009 4073
5018 4073
5068 4073
5083 4073
5084 4073
5091 4073
5322 4300
5367 4300
5371 4300
5396 4300
5510 4575
5534 4575
5563 4575
5566 4575
5800 5800
5802 5800
5804 5800
5805 5800
5922 4900
5934 4900
6320 4300
6322 4300
6357 4300
6358 4300
6360 4300
6374 4300
6384 4300
6387 4300
6716 6700
6737 6700
6739 6700
6741 6700
6915 4900
7015 4073
7037 4073
7321 4300
7415 7400
7418 7400
7424 7400
7792 5700
7794 5700
7914 6959
7916 6959
7923 6959
8733 5700
8779 5700
8793 5700
9011 9000
9018 9000
9023 9000
9089 3252
9400 9400
9600 5700
9720 5700
9721 5700
9772 5700
9773 5700
9790 5700
9795 5700
90312 WD[1]

1954 82C
5 WCP
1366 1366
1369 1366
1371 1366
1400 1400
1433 1400
1436 1400
1446 1400
1647 1600
1648 1600
2060 2021
2224 2251
2818 2800
2852 2800
2865 2800
2868 2800
3645 5700
3666 5700
3682 5700
3684 5700
3724 5700
3737 5700
3739 5700
3746 5700
3780 5700
4062 4000
4254 4200
4538 4500
4550 4500
4573 4500
4612 5700
4651 5700
4697 5700
4912 4900
4925 4900
4973 4900
5009 4073
5062 4073
5068 4073
5083 4073
5084 4073
5226 5205
5240 5205
5327 4300
5396 4300
5509 4575
5510 4575
5536 4575
5540 4575
5564 4575
5566 4575
5800 5800
5802 5800
5804 5800
5805 5800
5922 4900
5975 4900
5994 4900
5997 4900
6314 4300
6320 4300
6348 4300
6357 4300
6360 4300
6368 4300
6384 4300
6387 4300
6716 6700
6737 6700
6739 6700
6741 6700
6805 6800
6832 6800
6850 6800
6915 4900
6949 4900
6967 6959
7015 4073
7037 4073
7321 4300
7415 7400
7418 7400
7424 7400
7792 5700
7794 5700
7914 6959
7923 6959
8461 9400
8472 9400
8779 5700
8783 5700
8793 5700
9011 9000
9023 9000
9400 9400
9476 9400
9600 5700
9720 5700

9721 5700
9772 5700
9773 5700
9790 5700
9795 5700
75000 4MT[1]
75001 4MT[1]
75002 4MT[1]
75003 4MT[1]
75004 4MT[1]

1957 82C

1004 1000
1012 1000
1019 1000
1365 1361
1369 1366
1371 1366
1400 1400
1410 1400
1422 1400
1433 1400
1462 1400
1658 1600
2203 2251
2293 2251
2818 2800
2852 2800
2865 2800
2879 2800
3645 5700
3666 5700
3682 5700
3684 5700
3724 5700
3739 5700
3746 5700
3763 5700
3780 5700
4538 4500
4612 5700
4651 5700
4697 5700
4953 4900
4959 4900
4972 4900
5000 4073
5009 4073
5025 4073
5062 4073
5068 4073
5351 4300
5509 4575
5510 4575
5540 4575
5566 4575
5784 5700
5800 5800
5802 5800
5804 5800
5805 5800
5922 4900
6309 4300
6355 4300
6639 5600
6699 5600
6716 6700
6737 6700
6741 6700
6805 6800
6832 6800
6850 6800
6902 4900
6912 4900
6966 6959
6993 6959
7037 4073
7413 7400
7415 7400
7418 7400
7421 7400
7424 7400
7792 5700
7794 5700
7923 6959
8433 9400
8461 9400
8472 9400
8779 5700
8783 5700
8793 5700
9011 9000
9023 9000
9315 9300
9476 9400
9600 5700
9604 5700
9605 5700
9672 5700
9720 5700
9721 5700
9740 5700
9772 5700
9773 5700
9790 5700
9795 5700
73001 5MT
73012 5MT
73017 5MT
73018 5MT
73020 5MT
73022 5MT
73027 5MT
75000 4MT[1]
75003 4MT[1]
75023 4MT[1]
75025 4MT[1]
75026 4MT[1]
78004 2MT[1]

1960 82C

1004 1000
1010 1000
1012 1000
1015 1000
1019 1000
1365 1361
1369 1366
1371 1366
1410 1400
1433 1400
1438 1400
1464 1400
1658 1600
2230 2251
2250 2251
2291 2251
2835 2800
2852 2800
2865 2800
2879 2800
2890 2884
3645 5700
3666 5700
3682 5700
3684 5700
3711 5700
3724 5700
3739 5700
3758 5700
3763 5700
3780 5700
4102 5101
4612 5700
4651 5700
4697 5700
4953 4900
4972 4900
5000 4073
5002 4073
5005 4073
5007 4073
5009 4073
5023 4073
5064 4073
5068 4073
5510 4575
5536 4575
5547 4575
5815 5800
5922 4900
5945 4900
5964 4900
5978 4900
5981 4900
5983 4900
5986 4900
5997 4900
6309 4300
6336 4300
6366 4300
6391 4300
6639 5600
6741 6700
6758 6700
6769 6700
6902 4900
6993 6959
7031 4073
7037 4073
7337 4300
7413 7400
7421 7400
7427 7400
8433 9400
8465 9400
8472 9400
8779 5700
8783 5700
8793 5700
9476 9400
9600 5700
9604 5700
9605 5700
9672 5700
9720 5700
9721 5700
9740 5700
9773 5700
9790 5700
9795 5700
3440 City
73001 5MT
73012 5MT
73027 5MT
75002 4MT[1]
75027 4MT[1]
75029 4MT[1]

1963 82C

1006 1000
1010 1000
1012 1000
1621 1600
1658 1600
1664 1600
2244 2251
2291 2251
2879 2800
2890 2884
3739 5700
3758 5700
3842 2884
4079 4073
4088 4073
4697 5700
4924 4900
4930 4900
5002 4073
5023 4073
5570 4575
5939 4900
5943 4900
5978 4900
6769 6700
6940 4900
7037 4073
8433 9400
8793 5700
9605 5700
9672 5700
9680 5700
9754 5700
9773 5700
9790 5700
73001 5MT
73012 5MT
73027 5MT

Taunton

1948 TN

1338 Car[3]
1760 1854
1909 1901
2038 2021
2127 2021
2194 BPGV[4]
2211 2251
2212 2251
2213 2251
2214 2251
2215 2251
2261 2251
2266 2251
2267 2251
2268 2251
2275 2251
2708 655
2748 2721
2755 2721
2814 2800
3443 3300
3444 3300
3582 3500
4026 4000
4056 4000
4113 5101
4117 5101
4136 5101
4954 4900
5003 4073
5077 4073
5172 5101
5501 4575
5503 4575
5504 4575
5521 4575
5522 4575
5533 4575
5542 4575
5543 4575
5571 4575
5812 5800
5982 4900
5999 4900
6305 4300
6317 4300
6323 4300
6328 4300
6343 4300
6364 4300
6372 4300
6377 4300
6394 4300
6398 4300
7304 4300
7314 4300
7421 7400
9718 5700
9757 5700
90546 WD[1]

1951 83B

1338 Car[3]
2038 2021
2127 2021
2194 BPGV[4]
2211 2251
2212 2251
2213 2251
2214 2251
2261 2251
2266 2251
2267 2251
2268 2251
2275 2251
2814 2800
3669 5700
3736 5700
4032 4073
4113 5101
4117 5101
4136 5101
4604 5700
4663 5700
4949 4900
4970 4900
4971 4900
5003 4073
5172 5101
5412 5400
5501 4575
5503 4575
5504 4575
5521 4575
5522 4575
5533 4575
5542 4575
5543 4575
5571 4575
5779 5700
5999 4900
6305 4300
6317 4300
6323 4300
6328 4300
6343 4300
6364 4300
6372 4300
6377 4300
6394 4300
6398 4300
6815 6800
6868 6800
6875 6800
6995 6959
7304 4300
7421 7400
9646 5700
9663 5700
9670 5700
9718 5700
9757 5700

1954 83B

1338 Car[3]
1361 1361
1362 1361
1368 1366
2088 2021
2208 2251
2211 2251
2212 2251
2213 2251
2214 2251
2266 2251
2267 2251
2268 2251
2275 2251
2814 2800
3669 5700
3736 5700
4117 5101
4136 5101
4563 4500
4604 5700
4663 5700
4920 4900
4932 4900
4940 4900
4949 4900
4970 4900
4971 4900
4985 4900
5157 5101
5172 5101
5321 4300
5411 5400
5412 5400
5421 5400
5501 4575
5503 4575
5504 4575
5522 4575
5533 4575
5558 4575
5571 4575
5721 5700
5751 5700
5779 5700
5798 5700
5992 4900
5999 4900
6323 4300
6328 4300
6343 4300
6364 4300
6372 4300
6377 4300
6390 4300
6398 4300
6815 6800
6868 6800
6874 6800
6875 6800
6995 6959
7304 4300
7311 4300
9646 5700
9647 5700
9663 5700
9670 5700
9718 5700
9757 5700

1957 83B

1338 Car[3]
1362 1361
1366 1366
1668 1600
2212 2251
3669 5700
3736 5700
4117 5101
4136 5101
4157 5101
4159 5101
4604 5700
4663 5700
4920 4900
4932 4900
4940 4900
4949 4900
4970 4900
4971 4900
4978 4900
4985 4900
4991 4900
5172 5101
5321 4300
5344 4300
5411 5400
5421 5400
5501 4575
5503 4575
5504 4575
5522 4575
5542 4575
5543 4575
5571 4575
5721 5700
5751 5700
5760 5700
5779 5700
5798 5700
5992 4900
5999 4900
6323 4300
6337 4300
6343 4300
6364 4300
6375 4300
6377 4300
6390 4300
6398 4300
6815 6800
6856 6800
6868 6800
6874 6800
6875 6800
6995 6959
6996 6959
7304 4300
7311 4300
9646 5700
9647 5700
9663 5700
9670 5700
9671 5700
9718 5700
9757 5700

1960 83B

1338 Car[3]
1362 1361
1366 1366
1668 1600
2822 2800
2851 2800
2882 2800
3669 5700
3736 5700
4128 5101
4157 5101
4159 5101
4604 5700
4663 5700
4904 4900
4924 4900
4930 4900
4932 4900
4955 4900
4970 4900
4971 4900
4978 4900
4985 4900
4991 4900
5185 5101
5503 4575
5504 4575
5521 4575
5525 4575
5543 4575
5554 4575
5571 4575
5779 5700
5780 5700
5793 5700
5798 5700
5992 4900
5999 4900
6337 4300
6343 4300
6372 4300
6375 4300
6390 4300
6398 4300
6815 6800
6868 6800
6874 6800
6914 4900
6995 6959
7304 4300
7436 7400
7713 5700
7924 6959
9608 5700
9646 5700
9647 5700
9663 5700
9670 5700
9671 5700
9718 5700
9757 5700

1963 83B

2219 2251
2822 2800
2871 2800
2882 2800
3669 5700
3736 5700
4110 5101
4143 5101
4593 4575
4622 5700
4655 5700
4904 4900
4932 4900
4955 4900
4985 4900
4996 4900
5992 4900
6113 6100
6148 6100
6327 4300
6372 4300
6914 4900
6941 4900
7304 4300
7326 4300
7333 4300
7337 4300
7436 7400
7909 6959
8783 5700
9647 5700
9663 5700
9670 5700
82008 3MT[2]
82030 3MT[2]
82042 3MT[2]
82044 3MT[2]

Tebay

1948 11E

40016 3MT[1]
40070 3MT[1]
42308 4MT[2]
42403 4MT[2]
42404 4MT[2]
42424 4MT[2]
44083 4F[2]
44292 4F[2]
44469 4F[2]
49088 7F[2]
49104 7F[2]
49252 7F[2]

1951 11D

40067 3MT[1]
42396 4MT[2]
42403 4MT[2]
42404 4MT[2]
42424 4MT[2]
44083 4F[2]
44292 4F[2]
44459 4F[2]
44469 4F[2]

1954 11D

40064 3MT[1]
40067 3MT[1]
42396 4MT[2]
42403 4MT[2]
42404 4MT[2]
42424 4MT[2]
44083 4F[2]
44292 4F[2]
44459 4F[2]
44469 4F[2]

1957 11D

42393 4MT[2]
42396 4MT[2]
42403 4MT[2]
42404 4MT[2]
42424 4MT[2]
43980 4F[1]
44083 4F[2]
44292 4F[2]
44459 4F[2]
44469 4F[2]

1960 11D

42396 4MT[2]
42403 4MT[2]
42404 4MT[2]
42424 4MT[2]
43011 4MT[5]
43028 4MT[5]
43029 4MT[5]
43035 4MT[5]

1963 12H

42187 4MT[1]
42278 4MT[1]
42414 4MT[2]
42424 4MT[2]
43009 4MT[5]
43029 4MT[5]
43035 4MT[5]

1966 12E

42095 4MT[1]
42110 4MT[1]
42210 4MT[1]
42225 4MT[1]
42232 4MT[1]
43009 4MT[5]
43029 4MT[5]
43033 4MT[5]

Templecombe

1948 22D

40326 2P[1]
40509 2P[2]
40563 2P[3]
40564 2P[3]
40634 2P[3]
43248 3F[3]
43260 3F[3]
43356 3F[3]
43462 3F[3]
43792 3F[4]
44102 4F[2]
44146 4F[2]
44417 4F[2]

1951 71H

30274 G6
30277 G6
40509 2P[2]
40563 2P[3]
40564 2P[3]
40634 2P[3]
43194 3F[3]
43216 3F[3]
43218 3F[3]
43228 3F[3]
43248 3F[3]
43356 3F[3]
44102 4F[2]
44146 4F[2]
44417 4F[2]

1954 71H

30274 G6
40509 2P[2]
40527 2P[2]
40563 2P[3]
40564 2P[3]
40568 2P[3]
40569 2P[3]
40601 2P[3]
40634 2P[3]
41248 2MT[1]
41249 2MT[1]
43194 3F[3]
43216 3F[3]
43218 3F[3]
43248 3F[3]
43356 3F[3]
43436 3F[3]
44102 4F[2]
44146 4F[2]
44417 4F[2]

1957 71H

30274 G6
30953 Z
40563 2P[3]
40564 2P[3]
40568 2P[3]
40569 2P[3]
40634 2P[3]
41248 2MT[1]
41249 2MT[1]
43194 3F[3]
43216 3F[3]
43218 3F[3]
43248 3F[3]
43356 3F[3]
43436 3F[3]
44102 4F[2]
44146 4F[2]
44417 4F[2]

1960 82G

3720 5700
40563 2P[3]
40564 2P[3]
40569 2P[3]
40634 2P[3]
40652 2P[3]
41248 2MT[1]
41296 2MT[1]
43194 3F[3]
43216 3F[3]
43218 3F[3]
43427 3F[3]
43436 3F[3]
43682 3F[3]
43734 3F[3]
44102 4F[2]
44417 4F[2]
44557 4F[2]
47542 3F[6]
47552 3F[6]
82039 3MT[2]

1963 82G

2204 2251
3206 2251
3210 2251
3215 2251
3216 2251
3720 5700
4691 5700
41242 2MT[1]
41243 2MT[1]
41296 2MT[1]
44102 4F[2]
44167 4F[2]
44272 4F[2]
44422 4F[2]
44560 4F[2]
75071 4MT[1]
75072 4MT[1]
75073 4MT[1]

1966 83G

41206 2MT[1]
41216 2MT[1]
41223 2MT[1]
41249 2MT[1]
41283 2MT[1]
41290 2MT[1]
41291 2MT[1]
41296 2MT[1]
41307 2MT[1]
80037 4MT[3]
80039 4MT[3]
80041 4MT[3]
80043 4MT[3]

Thornaby

1960 51L

43072 4MT[5]
43102 4MT[5]
46478 2MT[2]
60885 V2
60911 V2
60915 V2
60946 V2
60960 V2
61031 B1
61034 B1
61037 B1
61062 B1
61173 B1
61220 B1
61240 B1
61255 B1
61257 B1
61303 B1
62001 K1
62003 K1
62042 K1
63341 Q6
63343 Q6
63344 Q6
63347 Q6
63349 Q6
63355 Q6
63360 Q6
63361 Q6
63364 Q6
63367 Q6
63369 Q6
63370 Q6
63371 Q6
63373 Q6
63374 Q6
63375 Q6
63380 Q6
63382 Q6
63388 Q6
63389 Q6
63393 Q6
63396 Q6
63399 Q6
63401 Q6
63405 Q6
63409 Q6
63411 Q6
63416 Q6
63417 Q6
63420 Q6
63424 Q6
63426 Q6
63428 Q6
63430 Q6
63432 Q6
63435 Q6
63442 Q6
63445 Q6
63447 Q6
63450 Q6
63451 Q6
63452 Q6
64706 J39
64725 J39
64730 J39
64758 J39
64818 J39
64821 J39
64835 J39
64845 J39
64850 J39
64855 J39
64857 J39
64859 J39
64861 J39
64870 J39
65720 J25
65736 J26
65741 J26
65743 J26
65745 J26
65747 J26
65751 J26
65753 J26
65755 J26
65756 J26
65757 J26
65760 J26
65761 J26
65762 J26
65763 J26
65768 J26
65769 J26
65772 J26
65773 J26
65774 J26
65776 J26
65777 J26
65778 J26
65779 J26
65787 J27
65788 J27
65790 J27
65853 J27
65855 J27
65859 J27
65865 J27
65868 J27
65870 J27
65884 J27
67754 L1
67759 L1
67764 L1
67766 L1
68023 J94
68049 J94
68060 J94
68062 J94
68078 J94
68260 J71
68272 J71
68278 J71
68684 J72
68688 J72
68689 J72
68690 J72
68696 J72
68721 J72
68729 J72
68740 J72
69006 J72
69019 J72
69860 A8
69869 A8
90014 WD[1]
90027 WD[1]
90048 WD[1]
90074 WD[1]
90081 WD[1]
90086 WD[1]
90090 WD[1]
90091 WD[1]
90098 WD[1]
90132 WD[1]
90240 WD[1]
90273 WD[1]
90373 WD[1]
90377 WD[1]
90406 WD[1]
90409 WD[1]
90426 WD[1]
90434 WD[1]
90435 WD[1]
90446 WD[1]
90451 WD[1]
90452 WD[1]
90459 WD[1]
90461 WD[1]
90462 WD[1]
90465 WD[1]
90479 WD[1]
90481 WD[1]
90500 WD[1]
90517 WD[1]
90593 WD[1]
90603 WD[1]

1963 51L

43057 4MT[5]
43075 4MT[5]
60806 V2
60846 V2
60859 V2
60885 V2
60901 V2
60946 V2
61220 B1
62001 K1
63349 Q6
63364 Q6
63367 Q6
63369 Q6
63371 Q6
63375 Q6
63388 Q6
63396 Q6
63401 Q6
63405 Q6
63416 Q6
63428 Q6
63430 Q6
63435 Q6
63442 Q6
63447 Q6
63452 Q6
65820 J27
65855 J27
65859 J27
65884 J27
67635 V3
67640 V3
68023 J94
68039 J94
69016 J72
76024 4MT[2]
77001 3MT[1]
77010 3MT[1]
77011 3MT[1]
77014 3MT[1]
90027 WD[1]
90048 WD[1]
90072 WD[1]
90081 WD[1]
90086 WD[1]
90090 WD[1]
90091 WD[1]
90098 WD[1]
90132 WD[1]
90273 WD[1]
90406 WD[1]
90434 WD[1]
90446 WD[1]
90451 WD[1]
90452 WD[1]
90459 WD[1]
90462 WD[1]
90479 WD[1]
90500 WD[1]
90593 WD[1]

Thornton Junction

1948 THJ

61103 B1
61118 B1
61262 B1
62401 D29
62406 D29
62419 D30
62429 D30
62430 D30
62431 D30
62436 D30
62442 D30
62446 D32
62467 D34
62468 D34
62475 D34
62478 D34
62492 D34
62704 D49
62708 D49
62716 D49
62717 D49
62729 D49
63004 O7
63017 O7
63019 O7
63049 O7
63058 O7
63143 O7
63151 O7
63168 O7
63177 O7
63610 O1
63806 O1
64464 J35
64466 J35
64474 J35
64477 J35
64488 J35
64495 J35
64500 J35
64514 J35
64516 J35
64521 J35
64522 J35
64546 J37
64549 J37
64550 J37
64553 J37
64564 J37
64565 J37
64596 J37
64597 J37
64598 J37
64600 J37
64602 J37
64612 J37
64616 J37
64618 J37
64629 J37
64635 J37
65218 J36
65291 J36
65345 J36
65901 J38
65902 J38
65903 J38
65904 J38
65907 J38
65908 J38
65910 J38
65911 J38
65913 J38
65921 J38
65925 J38
65931 J38
65932 J38
67452 C15
67476 C15
68321 J88
68322 J88
68323 J88
68332 J88
68335 J88
68337 J88
68341 J88
68353 J88
68451 J83
68453 J83
68456 J83
68458 J83
68459 J83
68467 J83
68504 J69
68535 J69
68550 J69
68555 J69
69132 N15
69150 N15
69153 N15
69211 N15
69223 N15
69224 N15
90128 WD[1]
90145 WD[1]
90168 WD[1]
90170 WD[1]
90177 WD[1]
90182 WD[1]
90219 WD[1]
90228 WD[1]
90236 WD[1]
90262 WD[1]
90281 WD[1]
90282 WD[1]
90293 WD[1]
90300 WD[1]
90319 WD[1]
90350 WD[1]
90534 WD[1]
90536 WD[1]
90539 WD[1]
90547 WD[1]
90614 WD[1]
90616 WD[1]
90690 WD[1]

1951 62A

61072 B1
61103 B1
61118 B1
61146 B1
61148 B1
61262 B1
62410 D29
62411 D29
62418 D30
62419 D30
62429 D30
62430 D30
62431 D30
62442 D30
62467 D34
62468 D34
62475 D34
62478 D34
62492 D34
62704 D49
62708 D49
62713 D49
62716 D49
62717 D49
62729 D49
64464 J35
64466 J35
64474 J35
64477 J35
64488 J35
64495 J35
64500 J35
64514 J35
64516 J35
64521 J35
64522 J35
64546 J37
64549 J37
64550 J37
64564 J37
64565 J37
64596 J37
64597 J37
64600 J37
64602 J37
64612 J37
64616 J37
64618 J37
64629 J37
64635 J37
65218 J36
65345 J36
65901 J38
65902 J38
65903 J38
65904 J38
65907 J38
65908 J38
65910 J38
65911 J38
65913 J38
65921 J38
65925 J38
65931 J38
65932 J38
67452 C15
67476 C15
68321 J88
68322 J88
68323 J88
68332 J88
68335 J88
68337 J88
68353 J88
68451 J83
68453 J83
68456 J83
68458 J83
68459 J83
68467 J83
68504 J69
68535 J69
68550 J69
68555 J69
69132 N15
69150 N15
69153 N15
69211 N15
69223 N15
69224 N15
90004 WD[1]
90019 WD[1]
90058 WD[1]
90128 WD[1]
90145 WD[1]
90168 WD[1]
90170 WD[1]
90177 WD[1]
90182 WD[1]
90282 WD[1]
90319 WD[1]
90350 WD[1]
90472 WD[1]
90489 WD[1]
90498 WD[1]
90534 WD[1]
90539 WD[1]
90547 WD[1]
90614 WD[1]
90690 WD[1]

1954 62A

61072 B1
61103 B1
61118 B1
61146 B1
61147 B1
61148 B1
61262 B1
61731 K2
61755 K2
62418 D30
62419 D30
62429 D30
62430 D30
62431 D30
62442 D30
62467 D34

62468 D34
62475 D34
62478 D34
62492 D34
62704 D49
62708 D49
62713 D49
62716 D49
62729 D49
64464 J35
64466 J35
64474 J35
64477 J35
64488 J35
64516 J35
64521 J35
64522 J35
64546 J37
64549 J37
64550 J37
64564 J37
64565 J37
64596 J37
64600 J37
64602 J37
64612 J37
64616 J37
64618 J37
64629 J37
64635 J37
65218 J36
65252 J36
65345 J36
65901 J38
65902 J38
65903 J38
65904 J38
65907 J38
65908 J38
65910 J38
65911 J38
65913 J38
65921 J38
65925 J38
65931 J38
65932 J38
67452 C15
67461 C15
67476 C15
68321 J88
68322 J88
68323 J88
68332 J88
68335 J88
68337 J88
68341 J88
68353 J88
68451 J83
68453 J83
68456 J83
68458 J83
68459 J83
68467 J83
68504 J69
68535 J69
69012 J72
69013 J72
69132 N15
69143 N15
69150 N15
69153 N15
69211 N15
69223 N15
69224 N15
90004 WD^1
90019 WD^1
90020 WD^1
90058 WD^1
90128 WD^1
90168 WD^1
90170 WD^1
90177 WD^1
90182 WD^1
90350 WD^1
90441 WD^1
90472 WD^1
90489 WD^1
90534 WD^1
90539 WD^1
90614 WD^1
90690 WD^1

1957 62A
55217 2P^{13}
61072 B1
61103 B1
61118 B1
61133 B1
61134 B1
61146 B1
61147 B1
61148 B1
61262 B1
61401 B1
61403 B1
61755 K2
62418 D30
62419 D30
62429 D30
62430 D30
62431 D30
62442 D30
62467 D34
62468 D34
62475 D34
62478 D34
62492 D34
62704 D49
62708 D49
62713 D49
62716 D49
62729 D49
64464 J35
64466 J35
64474 J35
64477 J35
64488 J35
64521 J35
64522 J35
64546 J37
64549 J37
64550 J37
64564 J37
64565 J37
64596 J37
64600 J37
64602 J37
64616 J37
64618 J37
64629 J37
64635 J37
65218 J36
65252 J36
65345 J36
65900 J38
65901 J38
65902 J38
65903 J38
65904 J38
65905 J38
65907 J38
65908 J38
65910 J38
65911 J38
65913 J38
65921 J38
65925 J38
65931 J38
65932 J38
68321 J88
68322 J88
68331 J88
68332 J88
68334 J88
68335 J88
68353 J88
68451 J83
68453 J83
68456 J83
68458 J83
68459 J83
69012 J72
69013 J72
69132 N15
69143 N15
69150 N15
69153 N15
69211 N15
69223 N15
69224 N15
90004 WD^1
90019 WD^1
90020 WD^1
90058 WD^1
90117 WD^1
90128 WD^1
90168 WD^1
90182 WD^1
90350 WD^1
90441 WD^1
90472 WD^1
90513 WD^1
90534 WD^1
90539 WD^1
90614 WD^1
90690 WD^1
90705 WD^1

1960 62A
61103 B1
61118 B1
61133 B1
61134 B1
61146 B1
61147 B1
61148 B1
61262 B1
61277 B1
61330 B1
61343 B1
61358 B1
61401 B1
61403 B1
61993 K4
61996 K4
62467 D34
62712 D49
62716 D49
62729 D49
62733 D49
62744 D49
64474 J35
64488 J35
64546 J37
64549 J37
64550 J37
64564 J37
64565 J37
64596 J37
64616 J37
64618 J37
64629 J37
64635 J37
64790 J39
64792 J39
65218 J36
65252 J36
65345 J36
65900 J38
65901 J38
65902 J38
65903 J38
65904 J38
65905 J38
65907 J38
65908 J38
65910 J38
65911 J38
65913 J38
65921 J38
65925 J38
65931 J38
65932 J38
68332 J88
68353 J88
68458 J83
68459 J83
69012 J72
69136 N15
69204 N15
76109 4MT^2
76110 4MT^2
76111 4MT^2
90004 WD^1
90019 WD^1
90020 WD^1
90058 WD^1
90117 WD^1
90168 WD^1
90182 WD^1
90350 WD^1
90441 WD^1
90472 WD^1
90513 WD^1
90534 WD^1
90614 WD^1
90690 WD^1
90705 WD^1

1963 62A
61103 B1
61118 B1
61132 B1
61133 B1
61146 B1
61147 B1
61148 B1
61330 B1
61343 B1
61358 B1
61401 B1
64546 J37
64549 J37
64564 J37
64616 J37
64618 J37
64629 J37
65307 J36
65345 J36
65900 J38
65901 J38
65902 J38
65904 J38
65905 J38
65907 J38
65908 J38
65910 J38
65911 J38
65913 J38
65916 J38
65921 J38
65925 J38
65932 J38
76111 4MT^2
90004 WD^1
90019 WD^1
90020 WD^1
90058 WD^1
90117 WD^1
90168 WD^1
90182 WD^1
90193 WD^1
90350 WD^1
90441 WD^1
90472 WD^1
90534 WD^1
90614 WD^1

1966 62A
61103 B1
61132 B1
61133 B1
61148 B1
61261 B1
61330 B1
61343 B1
64569 J37
64570 J37
64588 J37
64595 J37
64606 J37
64618 J37
65345 J36
65901 J38
65905 J38
65907 J38
65909 J38
65910 J38
65911 J38
65914 J38
65915 J38
65920 J38
65921 J38
65922 J38
65925 J38
65932 J38
90020 WD^1
90117 WD^1
90168 WD^1
90350 WD^1
90441 WD^1
90444 WD^1
90468 WD^1
90600 WD^1
90628 WD^1

Three Bridges

1948 3B
30541 Q
30542 Q
32002 I1X
32007 I1X
32078 I3
32079 I3
32080 I3
32081 I3
32082 I3
32303 C3
32352 K
32353 K
32400 E5
32405 E5
32436 C2
32441 C2X
32445 C2X
32451 C2X
32465 E4
32480 E4
32484 E4
32497 E4
32516 E4
32519 E4
32520 E4
32522 C2X
32527 C2X
32529 C2X
32532 C2X
32545 C2X
32552 C2X
32553 C2X
32572 E5
32585 E5
32593 E5
32598 I1X
32599 I1X
32601 I1X
32602 I1X
32604 I1X

1951 75E
30540 Q
30541 Q
32029 I3
32078 I3
32082 I3
32084 I3
32091 I3
32347 K
32349 K
32350 K
32351 K
32352 K
32353 K
32441 C2X
32445 C2X
32451 C2X
32465 E4
32480 E4
32484 E4
32497 E4
32516 E4
32519 E4
32520 E4
32522 C2X
32527 C2X
32529 C2X
32532 C2X
32545 C2X
32552 C2X
32553 C2X
32582 E4
32584 E5
32591 E5

1954 75E
30951 Z
32345 K
32346 K
32347 K
32348 K
32350 K
32351 K
32352 K
32353 K
32480 E4
32481 E4
32482 E4
32484 E4
32516 E4
32519 E4
32520 E4
32526 C2X
32527 C2X
32528 C2X
32529 C2X
32532 C2X
32534 C2X
32535 C2X
32536 C2X
32537 C2X
32538 C2X
32571 E5
41297 2MT^1
41303 2MT^1
41306 2MT^1
41307 2MT^1
42066 4MT^1
42092 4MT^1
42093 4MT^1
42106 4MT^1

1957 75E
31521 H
31530 H
32344 K
32345 K
32346 K
32347 K
32348 K
32350 K
32351 K
32352 K
32353 K
32438 C2X
32519 E4
32520 E4
32526 C2X
32527 C2X
32528 C2X
32529 C2X
32532 C2X
32534 C2X
32535 C2X
42066 4MT^1
42067 4MT^1
42068 4MT^1
42069 4MT^1
42070 4MT^1
42071 4MT^1

1960 75E
30052 M7
30055 M7
30109 M7
30544 Q
30545 Q
30546 Q
30547 Q
31161 H
31521 H
32107 E2
32337 K
32344 K
32345 K
32346 K
32347 K
32348 K
32349 K
32350 K
32351 K
32352 K
32353 K
32469 E4
32470 E4
32522 C2X
32523 C2X
32526 C2X
32527 C2X
32528 C2X
32532 C2X
32534 C2X
32535 C2X
32536 C2X
75075 4MT^1
80010 4MT^3
80011 4MT^3
80012 4MT^3
80087 4MT^3
80088 4MT^3
80089 4MT^3
80094 4MT^3

1963 75E
30545 Q
30546 Q
30547 Q
30549 Q
33014 Q1
33015 Q1
33016 Q1
33017 Q1
33018 Q1
33024 Q1
33026 Q1
33028 Q1
33029 Q1
33030 Q1
33031 Q1
80010 4MT^3
80011 4MT^3
80012 4MT^3
80088 4MT^3
80089 4MT^3
80094 4MT^3

Tilbury

1948 13C
41915 2P^5
41918 2P^5
41923 2P^5
41924 2P^5
41928 3P^2
41929 3P^2
41933 3P^2
41936 3P^2
41939 3P^2
41946 3P^2
41953 3P^2
41955 3P^2
41956 3P^2
41960 3P^2
41964 3P^2
41965 3P^2
41966 3P^2
41977 3P^2
41980 3F^1
42218 4MT^1
42219 4MT^1
42220 4MT^1
42221 4MT^1
44259 4F^2
58129 2F^8

1951 33B
41932 3P^2
41933 3P^2
41934 3P^2
41935 3P^2
41946 3P^2
41949 3P^2
41952 3P^2
41953 3P^2
41954 3P^2
41955 3P^2
41957 3P^2
41959 3P^2
41980 3F^1
42218 4MT^1
42219 4MT^1
42220 4MT^1
42221 4MT^1
42222 4MT^1
42223 4MT^1
42224 4MT^1
58129 2F^8

1954 33B
41936 3P^2
41945 3P^2
41946 3P^2
41949 3P^2
41950 3P^2
41969 3P^2
41970 3P^2
41982 3F^1
41993 3F^1
42218 4MT^1
42219 4MT^1
42220 4MT^1
42221 4MT^1
42222 4MT^1
42223 4MT^1
42224 4MT^1
42225 4MT^1
58310 2F^9

1957 33B
67363 C12
69691 N7
69694 N7
69695 N7
69698 N7
80069 4MT^3
80070 4MT^3
80071 4MT^3
80072 4MT^3
80073 4MT^3
80074 4MT^3
80075 4MT^3
80076 4MT^3
80077 4MT^3
80078 4MT^3
80079 4MT^3
80080 4MT^3

1960 33B
41981 3F^1
42254 4MT^1
42255 4MT^1
42257 4MT^1
47262 3F^6
47312 3F^6
47328 3F^6
47351 3F^6
47484 3F^6
47512 3F^6
47555 3F^6
64951 J39
64952 J39
64953 J39
64954 J39
64956 J39
64957 J39
64958 J39
64962 J39
64965 J39
64968 J39
80069 4MT^3
80070 4MT^3
80071 4MT^3
80072 4MT^3
80073 4MT^3
80074 4MT^3
80075 4MT^3
80076 4MT^3
80077 4MT^3
80078 4MT^3
80079 4MT^3
80080 4MT^3
80096 4MT^3
80097 4MT^3
80098 4MT^3
80099 4MT^3
80100 4MT^3
80101 4MT^3
80102 4MT^3
80103 4MT^3
80104 4MT^3
80105 4MT^3
80131 4MT^3
80132 4MT^3
80134 4MT^3
80135 4MT^3
80136 4MT^3
90034 WD^1
90093 WD^1
90106 WD^1
90196 WD^1
90244 WD^1
90256 WD^1
90442 WD^1
90494 WD^1
90514 WD^1
90653 WD^1

Tonbridge

1948 TON
31048 O1
31057 D
31063 C
31086 C
31150 C
31193 H
31219 C
31221 C
31225 C
31227 C
31272 C
31320 H
31327 H
31370 O1
31380 O1
31396 O1
31437 O1
31461 C
31488 D
31490 D
31503 H
31513 C
31518 H
31519 H
31540 H
31543 H
31580 C
31586 D
31590 C
31591 D
31593 C
31670 R
31671 R
31672 R
31675 R
31686 C
31700 R1^2
31703 R1^2
31704 R1^2
31707 R1^2
31731 D
31732 D
31733 D
31734 D
31761 L
31762 L
31763 L
31830 N
31859 N
31862 N
32113 E1^2
32129 E1^2
32138 E1^2
32145 E1^2
32164 E1^2
32367 D3
32370 D3
32374 D3
32378 D3
32488 E4
32503 E4
32580 E4
33026 Q1
33027 Q1
33028 Q1
33029 Q1
33030 Q1

1951 74D
31193 H
31219 C
31244 C
31246 D1^1
31265 H
31272 C
31277 C
31320 H
31327 H
31461 C
31496 D
31509 D1^1
31517 H
31523 H
31548 H
31549 D
31550 H
31574 D
31580 C
31590 C
31593 C
31667 R
31670 R
31671 R
31675 R
31684 C
31686 C
31700 R1^2
31703 R1^2
31704 R1^2
31706 R1^2
31728 D
31730 D
31731 D
31733 D
31745 D1^1
31746 D
31760 L
31761 L
31765 L
31778 L
31779 L
32167 E3
32169 E3
32454 E3
32455 E3
32456 E3
32488 E4
32503 E4
32580 E4
32581 E4
33027 Q1
33028 Q1
33029 Q1
33030 Q1
33031 Q1
33032 Q1
33033 Q1
33034 Q1
33035 Q1
33036 Q1
33037 Q1
33038 Q1

1954 74D
31037 C
31038 C
31164 H
31166 E
31177 H
31184 H
31193 H
31219 C
31239 H
31244 C
31259 H
31261 H
31270 C
31272 C
31277 C
31523 H
31530 H
31543 H
31548 H
31552 H
31554 H
31585 C
31588 C
31590 C
31666 R
31698 R1^2
31703 R1^2
31704 R1^2
31716 C
31717 C
31727 D1^1
31729 D
31734 D
31760 L
31761 L
31762 L
31763 L
31764 L
31765 L
31766 L
31770 L
31771 L
31773 L
32454 E3
32456 E3
32488 E4
32503 E4
32578 E4
32580 E4
33024 Q1
33028 Q1
33029 Q1
33030 Q1
33031 Q1
33032 Q1
33033 Q1
33034 Q1
33035 Q1
33036 Q1

1957 74D
31164 H
31177 H
31184 H
31193 H
31239 H
31244 C
31259 H
31270 C
31272 C
31470 D1^1
31487 D1^1
31489 D1^1
31492 D1^1
31517 H
31523 H
31543 H
31548 H
31554 H
31583 C
31585 C
31588 C
31590 C
31716 C
31760 L
31762 L
31763 L
31770 L
31771 L
31773 L
31908 U1
31909 U1
31910 U1
32454 E3
32456 E3
32488 E4
32578 E4
32580 E4
33024 Q1
33028 Q1
33029 Q1
33030 Q1
33031 Q1
33032 Q1
33033 Q1
33034 Q1
33035 Q1
33036 Q1

1960 73J
31177 H
31193 H
31239 H
31244 C
31280 C
31319 H
31322 H
31487 D1^1
31489 D1^1
31492 D1^1
31500 H
31512 H
31517 H
31518 H
31519 H
31520 H
31588 C
31590 C
31684 C
31716 C
31822 N1
31876 N1
31877 N1
31878 N1
31879 N1
31880 N1
31901 U1
31902 U1
31903 U1
31904 U1
31905 U1
31906 U1
31907 U1
31908 U1
31909 U1
31910 U1
32578 E4
33001 Q1
33002 Q1
33003 Q1
33004 Q1
33014 Q1
33024 Q1
33028 Q1
33029 Q1
33030 Q1
33031 Q1
33032 Q1
33033 Q1
33034 Q1
33035 Q1
33036 Q1
33037 Q1
33039 Q1
33040 Q1

Tondu

1948 TDU
1730 1854
2761 2721
2769 2721
3100 3100
3627 5700
3668 5700
3674 5700
3695 5700
3699 5700
3772 5700
4145 5101
4214 4200
4218 4200
4241 4200
4251 4200
4273 4200
4404 4400
4408 4400
4557 4500
4634 5700
4643 5700
4669 5700
4675 5700
5202 4200
5556 4575
5633 5600
5707 5700
5756 5700
5797 5700
6642 5600
6675 5600
6685 5600
7725 5700
7746 5700
7752 5700
7770 5700
7775 5700
7798 5700
8712 5700
8721 5700
8748 5700
8777 5700
9649 5700
9660 5700

1951 86F
3100 3100
3616 5700
3627 5700
3652 5700
3668 5700
3674 5700
3695 5700
3699 5700
3772 5700
4218 4200
4236 4200
4241 4200
4251 4200
4260 4200
4273 4200
4276 4200
4404 4400
4408 4400
4557 4500
4634 5700
4643 5700
4662 5700
4669 5700
4675 5700
5202 4200
5556 4575
5633 5600
5707 5700
5756 5700
5797 5700
6621 5600
6649 5600
6675 5600
6679 5600
7725 5700
7746 5700
7752 5700
7770 5700
7798 5700
8712 5700
8721 5700
8740 5700
8748 5700
8777 5700
9649 5700
9660 5700
9674 5700
9681 5700

1954 86F
3100 3100
3616 5700
3627 5700
3652 5700
3668 5700
3674 5700
3690 5700
3772 5700
4217 4200
4218 4200
4222 4200
4236 4200
4241 4200
4251 4200
4273 4200
4276 4200
4406 4400
4634 5700
4662 5700
4669 5700
4675 5700
5208 5205
5524 4575
5545 4575
5555 4575
5560 4575
5574 4575
5624 5600
5707 5700
6679 5600
7725 5700
7746 5700
7752 5700
7753 5700
7770 5700
7778 5700
7798 5700
8497 9400
8498 9400
8712 5700
8721 5700
8740 5700
8748 5700
9649 5700
9660 5700
9681 5700

1957 86F
3100 3100
3616 5700
3627 5700
3668 5700
3690 5700
3772 5700
4217 4200
4218 4200
4222 4200
4224 4200
4236 4200
4241 4200
4251 4200
4263 4200
4273 4200
4276 4200
4581 4575
4669 5700
4675 5700
5208 5205
5524 4575
5545 4575
5555 4575
5560 4575
5707 5700
6673 5600
6676 5600
7725 5700
7732 5700
7746 5700
7752 5700
7753 5700
7770 5700
7778 5700
7798 5700
8448 9400
8497 9400
8498 9400
8712 5700
8721 5700
8740 5700
8748 5700
9451 9400
9649 5700
9660 5700

1960 86F
3616 5700
3627 5700
3668 5700
3690 5700
3781 5700
4121 5101
4144 5101
4218 4200
4222 4200
4236 4200
4243 4200
4251 4200
4263 4200
4269 4200
4274 4200
4669 5700
4675 5700
5208 5205
5534 4575
5545 4575
5555 4575
5629 5600
5706 5700
6673 5600
7725 5700
7732 5700
7753 5700
7798 5700
8453 9400
8497 9400
8710 5700
8712 5700
8721 5700
8740 5700
8748 5700
9451 9400
9609 5700
9649 5700
9660 5700

1963 88H
3616 5700
3648 5700
3664 5700
3738 5700
3756 5700
4108 5101
4121 5101
4213 4200
4222 4200
4228 4200
4243 4200
4247 4200
4251 4200
4262 4200
4263 4200
4273 4200
4652 5700
4663 5700
4669 5700
4675 5700
5208 5205
5243 5205
5629 5600
5690 5600
6419 6400
6431 6400
6435 6400
8710 5700
8712 5700
9466 9400
9609 5700
9649 5700
9660 5700
9678 5700

Toton

1948 18A
43259 3F^3
43287 3F^3
43305 3F^3
43327 3F^3
43405 3F^3
43453 3F^3
43499 3F^3
43599 3F^3
43631 3F^3
43633 3F^3
43650 3F^3
43778 3F^4
43787 3F^4
43793 3F^4
43795 3F^4
43798 3F^4
43799 3F^4
43803 3F^4
43804 3F^4
43805 3F^4
43810 3F^4
43817 3F^4
43818 3F^4
43819 3F^4
43820 3F^4
43821 3F^4
43823 3F^4
43824 3F^4
43825 3F^4

43826 3F^4
43827 3F^4
43828 3F^4
43831 3F^4
43832 3F^4
43833 3F^4
43885 4F^1
43900 4F^1
43914 4F^1
43923 4F^1
43939 4F^1
43943 4F^1
43961 4F^1
43970 4F^1
43974 4F^1
43975 4F^1
43979 4F^1
43988 4F^1
43990 4F^1
43995 4F^1
44012 4F^1
44043 4F^2
44089 4F^2
44091 4F^2
44106 4F^2
44133 4F^2
44136 4F^2
44150 4F^2
44157 4F^2
44187 4F^2
44233 4F^2
44241 4F^2
44250 4F^2
44376 4F^2
44470 4F^2
44547 4F^2
44552 4F^2
44829 5MT^3
47247 3F^5
47249 3F^5
47436 3F^6
47454 3F^6
47551 3F^6
47555 3F^6
47623 3F^6
47630 3F^6
47967 Garratt
47969 Garratt
47970 Garratt
47972 Garratt
47974 Garratt
47975 Garratt
47976 Garratt
47977 Garratt
47978 Garratt
47979 Garratt
47981 Garratt
47982 Garratt
47985 Garratt
47986 Garratt
47987 Garratt
47988 Garratt
47989 Garratt
47991 Garratt
47994 Garratt
47995 Garratt
47996 Garratt
47998 Garratt
47999 Garratt
48002 8F
48004 8F
48033 8F
48037 8F
48070 8F
48075 8F
48112 8F
48117 8F
48119 8F
48133 8F
48142 8F
48144 8F
48168 8F
48178 8F
48182 8F
48194 8F
48196 8F
48197 8F
48199 8F
48200 8F
48201 8F
48202 8F
48203 8F
48204 8F
48205 8F
48221 8F
48304 8F
48311 8F
48313 8F
48323 8F
48324 8F
48350 8F
48361 8F
48362 8F
48367 8F
48370 8F
48384 8F
48387 8F
48388 8F
48418 8F
48490 8F
48606 8F
48607 8F
48611 8F
48615 8F
48618 8F
48636 8F
48637 8F
48638 8F
48655 8F
48662 8F
48672 8F
48681 8F
48685 8F
48690 8F
48703 8F
58146 2F^8
58153 2F^8
58159 2F^8
58166 2F^8
58173 2F^8
58176 2F^8

1951 18A

40370 2P^2
41911 2P^5
43405 3F^3
43453 3F^3
43499 3F^3
43599 3F^3
43631 3F^3
43650 3F^3
43767 3F^4
43778 3F^4
43793 3F^4
43795 3F^4
43798 3F^4
43799 3F^4
43803 3F^4
43804 3F^4
43810 3F^4
43817 3F^4
43819 3F^4
43820 3F^4
43821 3F^4
43823 3F^4
43824 3F^4
43825 3F^4
43826 3F^4
43828 3F^4
43832 3F^4
43833 3F^4
43943 4F^1
43961 4F^1
43969 4F^1
43974 4F^1
43979 4F^1
43988 4F^1
43990 4F^1
43994 4F^1
43995 4F^1
44012 4F^1
44091 4F^2
44106 4F^2
44133 4F^2
44136 4F^2
44157 4F^2
44233 4F^2
44250 4F^2
44371 4F^2
44376 4F^2
47247 3F^5
47436 3F^6
47454 3F^6
47545 3F^6
47551 3F^6
47555 3F^6
47630 3F^6
47967 Garratt
47969 Garratt
47970 Garratt
47972 Garratt
47974 Garratt
47975 Garratt
47976 Garratt
47977 Garratt
47978 Garratt
47979 Garratt
47981 Garratt
47982 Garratt
47985 Garratt
47986 Garratt
47987 Garratt
47988 Garratt
47989 Garratt
47991 Garratt
47994 Garratt
47995 Garratt
47996 Garratt
47997 Garratt
47998 Garratt
47999 Garratt
48002 8F
48007 8F
48033 8F
48037 8F
48053 8F
48075 8F
48112 8F
48117 8F
48144 8F
48152 8F
48168 8F
48176 8F
48178 8F
48182 8F
48184 8F
48185 8F
48186 8F
48187 8F
48194 8F
48195 8F
48196 8F
48197 8F
48199 8F
48200 8F
48201 8F
48202 8F
48203 8F
48204 8F
48205 8F
48221 8F
48273 8F
48303 8F
48304 8F
48313 8F
48324 8F
48331 8F
48350 8F
48361 8F
48362 8F
48367 8F
48370 8F
48384 8F
48387 8F
48400 8F
48418 8F
48461 8F
48463 8F
48490 8F
48538 8F
48553 8F
48606 8F
48607 8F
48615 8F
48618 8F
48636 8F
48637 8F
48638 8F
48655 8F
48662 8F
48672 8F
48681 8F
48685 8F
48690 8F
48694 8F
58146 2F^8
58153 2F^8
58159 2F^8
58169 2F^8
58171 2F^8
58173 2F^8
58176 2F^8
58197 2F^9
58268 2F^9
58296 2F^9

1954 18A

40402 2P^2
41966 3P^2
43251 3F^3
43309 3F^3
43405 3F^3
43453 3F^3
43499 3F^3
43631 3F^3
43650 3F^3
43751 3F^3
43778 3F^4
43793 3F^4
43795 3F^4
43810 3F^4
43819 3F^4
43821 3F^4
43823 3F^4
43825 3F^4
43826 3F^4
43828 3F^4
43832 3F^4
43933 4F^1
43943 4F^1
43961 4F^1
43969 4F^1
43974 4F^1
43988 4F^1
43990 4F^1
43994 4F^1
43995 4F^1
44012 4F^1
44020 4F^1
44047 4F^2
44088 4F^2
44091 4F^2
44106 4F^2
44133 4F^2
44136 4F^2
44145 4F^2
44154 4F^2
44157 4F^2
44161 4F^2
44190 4F^2
44200 4F^2
44233 4F^2
44250 4F^2
44289 4F^2
44362 4F^2
44376 4F^2
47234 3F^5
47551 3F^6
47630 3F^6
47967 Garratt
47969 Garratt
47970 Garratt
47972 Garratt
47975 Garratt
47976 Garratt
47978 Garratt
47979 Garratt
47981 Garratt
47985 Garratt
47986 Garratt
47987 Garratt
47988 Garratt
47989 Garratt
47991 Garratt
47993 Garratt
47996 Garratt
47997 Garratt
47998 Garratt
47999 Garratt
48007 8F
48037 8F
48075 8F
48112 8F
48117 8F
48128 8F
48139 8F
48152 8F
48168 8F
48176 8F
48178 8F
48182 8F
48184 8F
48185 8F
48186 8F
48187 8F
48194 8F
48195 8F
48196 8F
48197 8F
48199 8F
48200 8F
48201 8F
48203 8F
48204 8F
48205 8F
48221 8F
48271 8F
48273 8F
48284 8F
48303 8F
48304 8F
48324 8F
48332 8F
48350 8F
48361 8F
48362 8F
48367 8F
48370 8F
48384 8F
48387 8F
48400 8F
48412 8F
48418 8F
48419 8F
48461 8F
48463 8F
48490 8F
48507 8F
48538 8F
48543 8F
48553 8F
48606 8F
48607 8F
48615 8F
48618 8F
48636 8F
48637 8F
48638 8F
48640 8F
48655 8F
48662 8F
48672 8F
48681 8F
48685 8F
48694 8F
58146 2F^8
58159 2F^8
58171 2F^8
58173 2F^8
58197 2F^9
70043 7P6F

1957 18A

41947 3P^2
43251 3F^3
43309 3F^3
43405 3F^3
43453 3F^3
43499 3F^3
43650 3F^3
43751 3F^3
43793 3F^4
43795 3F^4
43823 3F^4
43826 3F^4
43828 3F^4
43832 3F^4
43845 4F^1
43865 4F^1
43941 4F^1
43946 4F^1
43961 4F^1
43988 4F^1
43990 4F^1
43994 4F^1
44012 4F^1
44091 4F^2
44106 4F^2
44133 4F^2
44140 4F^2
44145 4F^2
44154 4F^2
44161 4F^2
44200 4F^2
44217 4F^2
44224 4F^2
44289 4F^2
44362 4F^2
44376 4F^2
44427 4F^2
46440 2MT^2
47223 3F^5
47234 3F^5
47247 3F^5
47551 3F^6
47987 Garratt
47995 Garratt
48128 8F
48145 8F
48178 8F
48182 8F
48183 8F
48184 8F
48185 8F
48186 8F
48187 8F
48194 8F
48195 8F
48196 8F
48197 8F
48200 8F
48201 8F
48203 8F
48204 8F
48205 8F
48219 8F
48221 8F
48271 8F
48273 8F
48284 8F
48303 8F
48304 8F
48314 8F
48319 8F
48324 8F
48332 8F
48350 8F
48361 8F
48362 8F
48367 8F
48370 8F
48384 8F
48387 8F
48395 8F
48400 8F
48463 8F
48490 8F
48530 8F
48538 8F
48543 8F
48553 8F
48606 8F
48607 8F
48615 8F
48618 8F
48636 8F
48637 8F
48638 8F
48655 8F
48662 8F
48672 8F
48673 8F
48681 8F
48685 8F
48694 8F
48772 8F
58146 2F^8
58153 2F^8
58165 2F^8
58166 2F^8
58171 2F^8
58173 2F^8
92048 9F
92049 9F
92050 9F
92051 9F
92052 9F
92053 9F
92054 9F
92055 9F
92056 9F
92057 9F
92058 9F
92059 9F
92077 9F
92078 9F
92080 9F
92081 9F
92100 9F
92101 9F
92102 9F
92103 9F
92104 9F
92109 9F

1960 18A

41947 3P^2
43845 4F^1
43865 4F^1
43921 4F^1
43994 4F^1
44012 4F^1
44106 4F^2
44133 4F^2
44162 4F^2
44178 4F^2
44200 4F^2
44224 4F^2
44284 4F^2
44295 4F^2
44376 4F^2
44427 4F^2
47551 3F^6
48033 8F
48060 8F
48062 8F
48099 8F
48109 8F
48118 8F
48127 8F
48128 8F
48132 8F
48145 8F
48163 8F
48167 8F
48183 8F
48184 8F
48185 8F
48186 8F
48194 8F
48195 8F
48196 8F
48197 8F
48201 8F
48221 8F
48271 8F
48303 8F
48314 8F
48319 8F
48332 8F
48333 8F
48338 8F
48350 8F
48361 8F
48362 8F
48363 8F
48370 8F
48384 8F
48387 8F
48401 8F
48414 8F
48490 8F
48507 8F
48530 8F
48538 8F
48545 8F
48604 8F
48606 8F
48607 8F
48615 8F
48620 8F
48636 8F
48637 8F
48638 8F
48640 8F
48672 8F
48681 8F
48685 8F
48698 8F
48750 8F
48770 8F
58153 2F^8
58166 2F^8
58173 2F^8
92057 9F
92077 9F
92078 9F
92086 9F
92100 9F
92130 9F
92131 9F
92153 9F
92156 9F
92158 9F

1963 18A

43845 4F^1
43861 4F^1
43865 4F^1
43971 4F^1
43994 4F^1
44012 4F^1
44026 4F^1
44043 4F^2
44106 4F^2
44118 4F^2
44133 4F^2
44162 4F^2
44178 4F^2
44200 4F^2
44213 4F^2
44235 4F^2
44270 4F^2
44278 4F^2
44295 4F^2
44376 4F^2
44441 4F^2
44465 4F^2
44574 4F^2
47231 3F^5
47283 3F^6
47367 3F^6
47442 3F^6
47449 3F^6
47551 3F^6
47645 3F^6
48056 8F
48082 8F
48095 8F
48149 8F
48167 8F
48186 8F
48201 8F
48204 8F
48212 8F
48221 8F
48271 8F
48284 8F
48306 8F
48313 8F
48314 8F
48319 8F
48350 8F
48361 8F
48362 8F
48363 8F
48384 8F
48387 8F
48414 8F
48494 8F
48606 8F
48635 8F
48637 8F
48647 8F
48650 8F
48661 8F
48672 8F
48681 8F
48685 8F
48698 8F
92052 9F
92053 9F
92055 9F
92059 9F
92077 9F
92078 9F
92130 9F
92153 9F
92156 9F
92158 9F

1966 16A

78044 2MT^1
78055 2MT^1

Trafford Park

1948 19G/TFD

40074 3MT^2
40088 3MT^2
40089 3MT^2
40118 3MT^2
40147 3MT^2
41052 4P^1
41066 4P^1
41076 4P^1
41181 4P^1
43896 4F^1
44236 4F^2
44944 5MT^3
45618 6P5F^2
45622 6P5F^2
45628 6P5F^2
45629 6P5F^2
45652 6P5F^2
45655 6P5F^2
45664 6P5F^2
48411 8F
48440 8F
48680 8F
48698 8F
61476 B9
62300 D9
62301 D9
62305 D9
62307 D9
62312 D9
62313 D9
62317 D9
62325 D9
62329 D9
62330 D9
62651 D10
62656 D10
64723 J39
64823 J39
64901 J39
65141 J10
65161 J10
65168 J10
65183 J10
65184 J10
65201 J10
65204 J10
67358 C12
67369 C12
67370 C12
67378 C12
68540 J67
68585 J69
69252 N5
69255 N5
69304 N5
69336 N5
69343 N5
69361 N5
69364 N5
69370 N5

1951 9E

40093 3MT^2
40094 3MT^2
40900 4P^1
40910 4P^1
40936 4P^1
41052 4P^1
41055 4P^1
41066 4P^1
41076 4P^1
41111 4P^1
41154 4P^1
41181 4P^1
43896 4F^1
43908 4F^1
44236 4F^2
44938 5MT^3
45553 6P5F^2
45618 6P5F^2
45622 6P5F^2
45628 6P5F^2
45629 6P5F^2
45652 6P5F^2
48411 8F
48440 8F
48680 8F
48698 8F
62532 D16
62535 D16
62536 D16
62568 D16
62587 D16
62588 D16
62599 D16
62609 D16
62651 D10
62653 D10
62654 D10
62656 D10
62657 D10
62658 D10
62659 D10
62662 D11
62666 D11
62668 D11
62669 D11
62670 D11
64723 J39
64823 J39
64901 J39
64954 J39
65137 J10
65141 J10
65154 J10
65161 J10
65168 J10
65179 J10
65183 J10
65184 J10
65186 J10
65201 J10
65204 J10
67366 C12
67369 C12
68540 J67
68583 J67
68595 J67
68598 J69
69252 N5
69255 N5
69304 N5
69326 N5
69336 N5
69343 N5
69347 N5
69361 N5
69364 N5
69370 N5

1954 9E

40009 3MT^1
40017 3MT^1
40910 4P^1
41066 4P^1
41098 4P^1
41112 4P^1
41154 4P^1
41161 4P^1
41173 4P^1
42064 4MT^1
42065 4MT^1
42452 4MT^3
42469 4MT^3
42676 4MT^1
42683 4MT^1
44236 4F^2
44275 4F^2
44350 4F^2
44392 4F^2
44717 5MT^3
44938 5MT^3
45239 5MT^3
45347 5MT^3
45618 6P5F^2
45622 6P5F^2
45628 6P5F^2
45629 6P5F^2
45652 6P5F^2
45655 6P5F^2
48411 8F
48680 8F
48698 8F
48741 8F
62653 D10
62658 D10
62661 D11
62662 D11
62664 D11
62668 D11
65138 J10
65144 J10
65146 J10
65153 J10
65156 J10
65157 J10
65167 J10
65170 J10
65171 J10
65181 J10
65184 J10
65186 J10
65187 J10
65191 J10
65197 J10
65198 J10
65205 J10
65209 J10
68559 J69
68583 J67
68595 J67
68598 J69
69255 N5
69304 N5
69326 N5
69335 N5
69336 N5
69343 N5
69347 N5
69358 N5
69361 N5
69364 N5
69370 N5

1957 17F

40009 3MT^1
40018 3MT^1
40052 3MT^1
40055 3MT^1
40088 3MT^2
40208 3MT^2
41066 4P^1
41114 4P^1
41116 4P^1
41118 4P^1
41123 4P^1
41150 4P^1
41163 4P^1
41173 4P^1
42064 4MT^1
42065 4MT^1
42419 4MT^2
42452 4MT^3
42469 4MT^3
42675 4MT^1
42676 4MT^1
42683 4MT^1
44080 4F^2
44275 4F^2
44392 4F^2
44717 5MT^3
45006 5MT^3
45239 5MT^3
45618 6P5F^2
45622 6P5F^2
45628 6P5F^2
45652 6P5F^2
48288 8F
48698 8F
48741 8F
62668 D11
65144 J10
65167 J10
65186 J10
65191 J10
65208 J10
65209 J10
68583 J67
69326 N5
69343 N5
69347 N5
69361 N5
69370 N5

1960 9E

40009 3MT^1
40018 3MT^1
40088 3MT^2
40097 3MT^2
40105 3MT^2
40141 3MT^2
40208 3MT^2
42050 4MT^1
42064 4MT^1
42065 4MT^1
42111 4MT^1
42419 4MT^2
42445 4MT^3
42452 4MT^3
42466 4MT^3
42469 4MT^3
42479 4MT^3
42628 4MT^3
42675 4MT^1
42676 4MT^1
42683 4MT^1
43211 3F^3
43400 3F^3
43572 3F^3
43580 3F^3
43650 3F^3
44078 4F^2
44080 4F^2
44138 4F^2
44392 4F^2
44402 4F^2
44413 4F^2
44665 5MT^3
44688 5MT^3
44717 5MT^3
44809 5MT^3
44842 5MT^3
44964 5MT^3
45239 5MT^3
48273 8F
48288 8F
48344 8F
48741 8F
70004 7P6F
70014 7P6F
70015 7P6F
70017 7P6F
70021 7P6F
70042 7P6F
76086 4MT^2
76088 4MT^2
76089 4MT^2

1963 9E

42050 4MT^1
42051 4MT^1
42064 4MT^1
42065 4MT^1
42112 4MT^1
42113 4MT^1
42434 4MT^3
42466 4MT^3
42560 4MT^3
42675 4MT^1
42676 4MT^1
43033 4MT^5
43036 4MT^5
43040 4MT^5
43041 4MT^5
44378 4F^2
44392 4F^2
44396 4F^2
44402 4F^2
44489 4F^2
44533 4F^2
44564 4F^2
44565 4F^2
44566 4F^2
44587 4F^2
44809 5MT^3
44964 5MT^3
45239 5MT^3
48273 8F
48288 8F
48344 8F
48741 8F

1966 9E

42066 4MT^1
42069 4MT^1
42071 4MT^1
42076 4MT^1
42081 4MT^1
42267 4MT^1
42287 4MT^1
42455 4MT^3
42574 4MT^3
42583 4MT^3
42644 4MT^3
44708 5MT^3
44735 5MT^3
44804 5MT^3
44815 5MT^3
44855 5MT^3
44888 5MT^3
44895 5MT^3
44918 5MT^3
45073 5MT^3
45150 5MT^3
45220 5MT^3
45233 5MT^3
45269 5MT^3
45316 5MT^3
45346 5MT^3
45352 5MT^3
45404 5MT^3
48178 8F
48288 8F
48344 8F
48356 8F
48371 8F
48535 8F
48741 8F
78007 2MT^1
78012 2MT^1
78023 2MT^1
78062 2MT^1

Tredegar

1948 4E

41204 2MT^1
47939 7F^1
48921 7F^2
49064 7F^2
49161 7F^2
49168 7F^2
49174 7F^2
49409 7F^3
58880 2F^{14}
58885 2F^{14}
58895 2F^{14}
58920 2F^{14}
58921 2F^{14}
58931 2F^{14}
27648 2F^{14}

1957 86K

6439 6400
40098 3MT^2
40161 3MT^2
40171 3MT^2
41201 2MT^1
41204 2MT^1
48921 7F^2
49064 7F^2
49121 7F^2
49161 7F^2
49316 7F^2
49409 7F^3

1960 86K

3700 5700
3712 5700
6439 6400
7721 5700
7736 5700
7771 5700
7787 5700
8711 5700
9662 5700
40098 3MT^2
40161 3MT^2
40171 3MT^2

Treherbert

1948 THT

193 TV^1
194 TV^1
195 TV^1
202 TV^2
290 TV^2
303 TV^3
352 TV^3
365 TV^3
366 TV^3
368 TV^3
373 TV^3
378 TV^3
399 TV^3
5159 5101
5601 5600
5607 5600
5608 5600
5611 5600
5613 5600
5615 5600
5636 5600
5650 5600
5663 5600
5676 5600
5680 5600
5688 5600
5691 5600
5695 5600
7722 5700

1951 88F

193 TV^1
194 TV^1
195 TV^1
207 TV^2
210 TV^2
215 TV^2
216 TV^2
278 TV^2
279 TV^2
285 TV^2
290 TV^2
299 TV^2
303 TV^3
352 TV^3
365 TV^3
366 TV^3
368 TV^3
378 TV^3
399 TV^3
4162 5101
5159 5101
5183 5101
5600 5600
5607 5600
5608 5600
5610 5600
5611 5600
5613 5600
5615 5600
5663 5600
5668 5600
5676 5600
5680 5600
5688 5600
5691 5600
5693 5600
5695 5600
6648 5600
6655 5600
7722 5700

1954 88F

352 TV^3
365 TV^3
366 TV^3
368 TV^3
5159 5101
5162 5101
5195 5101
5600 5600
5607 5600
5608 5600
5610 5600
5611 5600
5613 5600
5615 5600
5668 5600
5676 5600
5688 5600
5691 5600
5693 5600
5695 5600
6648 5600
8420 9400
8424 9400
8460 9400
8465 9400
8469 9400
8489 9400
82000 3MT^2

1957 88F

5600 5600
5607 5600
5608 5600
5610 5600
5611 5600
5613 5600
5632 5600
5646 5600
5665 5600
5668 5600
5676 5600
5678 5600
5688 5600
5691 5600
5693 5600
5694 5600
5695 5600
6619 5600
8419 9400
8420 9400
8455 9400
8460 9400
9425 9400
82001 3MT^2
82002 3MT^2
82005 3MT^2
82032 3MT^2
82033 3MT^2
82034 3MT^2

1960 88F

5600 5600
5607 5600
5608 5600
5610 5600
5611 5600
5613 5600
5632 5600
5637 5600
5646 5600
5653 5600
5654 5600
5665 5600
5668 5600
5676 5600
5678 5600
5684 5600
5687 5600
5691 5600
5693 5600
5694 5600
5695 5600
6619 5600

1963 88F

5607 5600
5608 5600
5611 5600
5613 5600

5632 5600
5654 5600
5665 5600
5674 5600
5676 5600
5678 5600
5684 5600
5688 5600
5691 5600
5693 5600
5694 5600
6654 5600

Truro

1948 TR
1023 1000
1753 1854
1782 655
4523 4500
4532 4500
4554 4500
4561 4500
4569 4500
4581 4575
4588 4575
4589 4575
4906 4900
4929 4900
4936 4900
5500 4575
5526 4575
5537 4575
5562 4575
5779 5700
6373 4300
6931 4900
7422 7400

1951 83F
1013 1000
4167 5101
4504 4500
4523 4500
4554 4500
4561 4500
4588 4575
4589 4575
4906 4900
4936 4900
5500 4575
5515 4575
5526 4575
5537 4575
5562 4575
6373 4300
6931 4900
7422 7400
8404 9400
8412 9400

1954 83F
1023 1000
4554 4500
4561 4500
4570 4500
4588 4575
4598 4575
4906 4900
4936 4900
5500 4575
5505 4575
5515 4575
5526 4575
5537 4575
5562 4575
5985 4900
6931 4900
7422 7400
8404 9400
8412 9400
8421 9400
8485 9400
8486 9400
9434 9400

1957 83F
1007 1000
1023 1000
3702 5700
4508 4500
4554 4500
4561 4500
4587 4575
4588 4575
4906 4900
5500 4575
5505 4575
5515 4575
5526 4575
5537 4575
5552 4575
5562 4575
6300 4300
6871 6800
6911 4900
6931 4900
7422 7400
7823 7800
8412 9400
8421 9400
8485 9400
8486 9400
9311 9300
9434 9400

1960 83F
3702 5700
4108 5101
4574 4500
4587 4575
4622 5700
5376 4300
5515 4575
5537 4575
5546 4575
5552 4575
5559 4575
5562 4575
6300 4300
6806 6800
6823 6800
6828 6800
7812 7800
7813 7800
7820 7800
8486 9400

Tunbridge Wells West

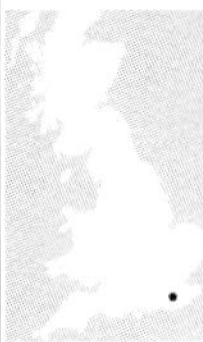

1948 TWW
30531 Q
30534 Q
32001 I1X
32003 I1X
32004 I1X
32006 I1X
32021 I3
32022 I3
32023 I3
32025 I3
32026 I3
32027 I3
32028 I3
32029 I3
32030 I3
32215 D1/M
32253 D1/M
32325 J1
32326 J2
32390 D3
32393 D3
32398 D3
32512 E4
32581 E4
32582 E4
32589 E5
32590 E5
32591 E5
32603 I1X

1951 75F
31016 H
31158 H
31182 H
32021 I3
32022 I3
32023 I3
32026 I3
32027 I3
32028 I3
42096 4MT^1
42097 4MT^1
42098 4MT^1
42099 4MT^1
42100 4MT^1
42101 4MT^1
42102 4MT^1
42103 4MT^1
42104 4MT^1
42105 4MT^1

1954 75F
31322 H
31517 H
31520 H
32517 E4
32581 E4
32582 E4
41316 2MT^1
41317 2MT^1
41318 2MT^1
41319 2MT^1
42099 4MT^1
42100 4MT^1
42101 4MT^1
42102 4MT^1
42103 4MT^1
80010 4MT^3
80011 4MT^3
80012 4MT^3
80013 4MT^3
80014 4MT^3
80015 4MT^3
80017 4MT^3
80018 4MT^3

1957 75F
31278 H
31310 H
31327 H
31329 H
31544 H
32517 E4
32581 E4
42101 4MT^1
42102 4MT^1
42103 4MT^1
42104 4MT^1
42105 4MT^1
42106 4MT^1
80012 4MT^3
80013 4MT^3
80014 4MT^3
80015 4MT^3
80016 4MT^3
80017 4MT^3
80018 4MT^3
80019 4MT^3

1960 75F
31162 H
31266 H
31278 H
31306 H
31310 H
31522 H
31544 H
32581 E4
80014 4MT^3
80015 4MT^3
80016 4MT^3
80017 4MT^3
80018 4MT^3
80019 4MT^3
80095 4MT^3
80137 4MT^3
80138 4MT^3
80139 4MT^3
80140 4MT^3
80141 4MT^3
80142 4MT^3

1963 75F
31005 H
31263 H
31518 H
31522 H
31543 H
31544 H
31551 H
80014 4MT^3
80015 4MT^3
80016 4MT^3
80017 4MT^3
80018 4MT^3
80019 4MT^3
80139 4MT^3
80140 4MT^3
80141 4MT^3
80142 4MT^3

Tuxford Junction

1948 TUX
63570 O4
63604 O4
63691 O4
63819 O4
63852 O4
63861 O4
63885 O4
64286 J11
64293 J11
64299 J11
64310 J11
64344 J11
64392 J11
64424 J11
69275 N5
69287 N5

1951 40D
63570 O4
63588 O4
63634 O4
63677 O4
63691 O4
63852 O4
63861 O4
63885 O4
64293 J11
64299 J11
64337 J11
64344 J11
64353 J11
64392 J11
64424 J11

1954 40D
64299 J11
64344 J11
64353 J11
64392 J11
64424 J11
64729 J39
64734 J39
64735 J39
64750 J39
64751 J39
64763 J39
64799 J39
64805 J39
64807 J39
64828 J39
64838 J39
64881 J39
64976 J39

1957 40D
63597 O4
63607 O4
63622 O4
63635 O4
63643 O4
63665 O4
63683 O4
63691 O4
63722 O4
63758 O4
63893 O4
63912 O4
64344 J11
64353 J11
64392 J11
64405 J11
64424 J11

Tweedmouth

1948 TWD
60932 V2
61024 B1
61025 B1
61198 B1
61199 B1
62344 D20
62354 D20
62358 D20
63001 O7
63006 O7
63030 O7
63072 O7
63106 O7
63114 O7
63190 O7
65026 J21
65039 J21
65067 J21
65082 J21
65869 J27
65873 J27
67248 G5
68363 J73
68400 J77
68424 J77
68437 J77
90670 WD^1
90674 WD^1
90704 WD^1

1951 52D
60932 V2
61019 B1
61024 B1
61025 B1
61199 B1
61241 B1
61322 B1
64711 J39
64813 J39
64843 J39
64844 J39
64854 J39
64917 J39
64925 J39
65697 J25
65727 J25
67248 G5
67303 G5
67304 G5
68089 Y7
68284 J71
68421 J77
68437 J77
90001 WD^1
90008 WD^1
90030 WD^1
90072 WD^1
90427 WD^1
90479 WD^1
90674 WD^1

1954 52D
60808 V2
60860 V2
60884 V2
60926 V2
60932 V2
61019 B1
61025 B1
61241 B1
61322 B1
61899 K3
61901 K3
61917 K3
61930 K3
61932 K3
61952 K3
61962 K3
61969 K3
61985 K3
64711 J39
64813 J39
64843 J39
64844 J39
64917 J39
64925 J39
64941 J39
65082 J21
65727 J25
67270 G5
68421 J77
68436 J77
68437 J77
76024 4MT^2

1957 52D
43057 4MT^5
43071 4MT^5
60801 V2
60805 V2
60808 V2
60860 V2
60926 V2
60932 V2
61014 B1
61025 B1
61199 B1
61241 B1
61322 B1
61901 K3
61917 K3
61930 K3
61952 K3
61962 K3
61969 K3
61985 K3
64711 J39
64813 J39
64843 J39
64844 J39
64916 J39
64917 J39
64925 J39
64941 J39
65078 J21
65091 J21
65099 J21
68682 J72
68725 J72

1960 52D
46476 2MT^2
46482 2MT^2
60069 A3
60072 A3
60801 V2
60843 V2
60865 V2
60913 V2
60926 V2
61025 B1
61199 B1
61241 B1
61322 B1
61854 K3
61901 K3
61917 K3
61930 K3
61934 K3
61952 K3
61969 K3
61985 K3
64711 J39
64813 J39
64843 J39
64844 J39
64916 J39
64917 J39
64925 J39
64941 J39
68725 J72

1963 52D
46474 2MT^2
46475 2MT^2
46479 2MT^2
60116 A1
60127 A1
60129 A1
60132 A1
60142 A1
60143 A1
60147 A1
60151 A1
60865 V2
60913 V2

1966 52D
77002 3MT^1
77004 3MT^1

Tyne Dock

1948 TDK
63274 Q5
63351 Q6
63352 Q6
63362 Q6
63363 Q6
63460 Q7
63461 Q7
63462 Q7
63463 Q7
63464 Q7
63465 Q7
63466 Q7
63467 Q7
63468 Q7
63469 Q7
63470 Q7
63471 Q7
63472 Q7
63473 Q7
63474 Q7
63603 O4
63620 O4
63667 O4
63676 O1
63712 O1
63740 O1
63751 O4
63753 O4
63754 O4
63755 O1
63760 O1
63769 O4
63828 O4
63835 O4
63845 O4
63856 O4
63857 O4
63874 O1
63881 O4
65602 J24
65606 J24
65632 J24
65670 J25
65694 J25
65716 J25
65721 J25
68088 Y7
68089 Y7
68181 Y3
68183 Y3
68266 J71
68272 J71
68728 J72
68729 J72
68731 J72
69378 N8
69395 N8
69410 N9
69420 N9
90210 WD^1
90272 WD^1
90309 WD^1
90352 WD^1
90394 WD^1
90526 WD^1
90611 WD^1
90627 WD^1
90661 WD^1
90688 WD^1

1951 54B
63352 Q6
63379 Q6
63437 Q6
63460 Q7
63461 Q7
63462 Q7
63463 Q7
63464 Q7
63465 Q7
63466 Q7
63467 Q7
63468 Q7
63469 Q7
63470 Q7
63471 Q7
63472 Q7
63473 Q7
63474 Q7
65666 J25
65670 J25
65694 J25
65716 J25
67288 G5
68181 Y3
68183 Y3
68266 J71
68272 J71
68706 J72
68729 J72
68731 J72
69008 J72
69105 N10
69378 N8
69400 N8
69429 N9
69920 T1
90026 WD^1
90210 WD^1
90272 WD^1
90309 WD^1
90352 WD^1
90430 WD^1
90445 WD^1
90458 WD^1
90482 WD^1
90485 WD^1
90611 WD^1
90627 WD^1

1954 54B
63352 Q6
63359 Q6
63379 Q6
63387 Q6
63437 Q6
63453 Q6
63460 Q7
63461 Q7
63462 Q7
63463 Q7
63464 Q7
63465 Q7
63466 Q7
63467 Q7
63468 Q7
63469 Q7
63470 Q7
63471 Q7
63472 Q7
63473 Q7
63474 Q7
63712 O1
63755 O1
63760 O1
63856 O1
63874 O1
65666 J25
65670 J25
65694 J25
65699 J25
65713 J25
65716 J25
68265 J71
68266 J71
68687 J72
68706 J72
68729 J72
69008 J72
69105 N10
69424 N9
69427 N9
69429 N9
69914 T1
69920 T1
90026 WD^1
90309 WD^1
90445 WD^1
90611 WD^1

1957 54B
63352 Q6
63362 Q6
63379 Q6
63387 Q6
63437 Q6
63453 Q6
63460 Q7
63463 Q7
63465 Q7
63469 Q7
63473 Q7
63712 O1
63755 O1
63760 O1
63856 O1
63874 O1
65666 J25
65670 J25
65680 J25
65699 J25
65713 J25
65717 J25
68265 J71
68266 J71
68687 J72
68706 J72
68729 J72
68743 J72
69008 J72
69093 N10
69102 N10
69105 N10
69106 N10
69920 T1
90026 WD^1
90045 WD^1
90054 WD^1
90309 WD^1
90445 WD^1
90611 WD^1
92060 9F
92061 9F
92062 9F
92063 9F
92064 9F
92065 9F
92066 9F
92097 9F
92098 9F
92099 9F

1960 52H
63350 Q6
63358 Q6
63425 Q6
63429 Q6
63460 Q7
63461 Q7
63462 Q7
63463 Q7
63464 Q7
63465 Q7
63466 Q7
63468 Q7
63470 Q7
63471 Q7
63472 Q7
63473 Q7
63712 O1
63755 O1
63760 O1
63856 O1
63874 O1
65099 J21
65645 J25
65670 J25
65695 J25
65713 J25
68019 J94
68029 J94
68031 J94
68038 J94
68059 J94
68262 J71
68706 J72
68730 J72
68731 J72
68743 J72
69921 T1
92060 9F
92061 9F
92062 9F
92063 9F
92064 9F
92065 9F
92066 9F
92097 9F
92098 9F
92099 9F

1963 52H
61014 B1
61238 B1
63350 Q6
63358 Q6
63360 Q6
63363 Q6
63366 Q6
63377 Q6
63378 Q6
63384 Q6
63389 Q6
63393 Q6
63399 Q6
63409 Q6
63411 Q6
63425 Q6
68016 J94
68019 J94
68029 J94
68031 J94
68038 J94
68054 J94
90016 WD^1
90057 WD^1
90074 WD^1
92060 9F
92061 9F
92062 9F
92063 9F
92064 9F
92065 9F
92066 9F
92097 9F
92098 9F
92099 9F

1966 52H
63360 Q6
63363 Q6
63366 Q6
63377 Q6
63379 Q6
63384 Q6
63409 Q6
63431 Q6
63453 Q6
63455 Q6
63459 Q6
92060 9F
92061 9F
92062 9F
92063 9F
92064 9F
92065 9F
92097 9F
92098 9F
92099 9F
58 J72
59 J72

Tyseley

1948 TYS
2071 2021
2152 2021
2203 2251
2206 2251
2209 2251
2238 2251
2257 2251
2292 2251
2296 2251
2297 2251
2719 655
2903 2900
2916 2900
2988 2900
3005 ROD
3049 ROD
3101 3100
3151 3150
3158 3150
3180 3150
3613 5700
3624 5700
3625 5700
3650 5700
3653 5700
3657 5700
3660 5700
3664 5700
3673 5700
3689 5700
3693 5700
3743 5700
4058 4000
4101 5101
4106 5101
4107 5101
4111 5101
4116 5101
4147 5101
4157 5101
4605 5700
4620 5700
4648 5700
4683 5700
4917 4900
4924 4900
4930 4900
4934 4900
4939 4900
4959 4900
4967 4900
4992 4900
4993 4900
4999 4900
5102 5101
5106 5101
5121 5101
5125 5101
5129 5101
5152 5101
5156 5101
5162 5101
5164 5101
5166 5101
5171 5101
5175 5101
5177 5101
5182 5101
5188 5101
5190 5101
5198 5101
5199 5101
5346 4300
5369 4300
5370 4300
5634 5600
5700 5700
5701 5700
5712 5700
5738 5700
5742 5700
5745 5700
5790 5700
5907 4900
5950 4900
5993 4900
5997 4900
6336 4300
6611 5600
6630 5600
6831 6800
6833 6800
6843 6800
6847 6800
6853 6800
6855 6800
6858 6800
6860 6800
6866 6800
6904 4900
6914 4900
7735 5700
7758 5700
8108 8100
8700 5700
8784 5700
9007 9000
9008 9000
9010 9000
9019 9000
9608 5700
9610 5700
9635 5700
9724 5700
9733 5700
9748 5700
9753 5700
9793 5700
9798 5700
90561 WD^1
90685 WD^1

1951 84E
2203 2251
2238 2251
2257 2251
2296 2251
2848 2800
2849 2800
2867 2800
2932 2900
3016 ROD
3101 3100
3151 3150
3180 3150
3624 5700
3625 5700
3650 5700
3653 5700
3657 5700
3658 5700
3660 5700
3664 5700
3673 5700
3689 5700
3693 5700
3743 5700
3751 5700
3769 5700
3837 2884
4101 5101
4106 5101
4107 5101
4110 5101
4111 5101
4116 5101
4147 5101
4157 5101
4159 5101
4165 5101
4166 5101
4170 5101
4172 5101
4605 5700
4648 5700
4683 5700
4924 4900
4959 4900
4964 4900
5102 5101
5106 5101
5152 5101
5156 5101
5164 5101
5166 5101
5171 5101
5175 5101
5177 5101
5182 5101
5187 5101
5188 5101
5190 5101
5198 5101
5333 4300
5346 4300
5369 4300
5370 4300
5700 5700
5712 5700
5736 5700
5738 5700
5745 5700
5790 5700
5907 4900
5909 4900
5916 4900
5927 4900
5950 4900
5993 4900
5997 4900
6336 4300
6611 5600
6630 5600
6843 6800
6847 6800
6853 6800
6858 6800
6866 6800
6904 4900
6971 6959
7317 4300
7438 7400
7713 5700
7735 5700
7758 5700
7912 6959
7913 6959
7918 6959
7929 6959
8108 8100
8410 9400
8415 9400
8452 9400
8463 9400
8700 5700
8784 5700
9008 9000
9010 9000
9432 9400
9608 5700
9610 5700
9614 5700
9635 5700
9680 5700
9682 5700
9724 5700
9733 5700
9748 5700
9753 5700
9793 5700
9798 5700

1954 84E
2238 2251
2257 2251
2296 2251
2826 2800
2848 2800
2849 2800
2856 2800
2867 2800
3101 3100
3625 5700
3660 5700
3673 5700
3689 5700
3693 5700
3769 5700
3829 2884
3839 2884
4110 5101
4111 5101
4116 5101
4170 5101
4172 5101
4648 5700
4964 4900
5152 5101
5156 5101
5163 5101
5164 5101
5166 5101
5181 5101
5198 5101
5322 4300
5333 4300
5369 4300
5370 4300
5386 4300
5736 5700
5738 5700
5790 5700
5900 4900
5909 4900
5912 4900
5927 4900
6105 6100
6116 6100
6118 6100
6134 6100
6139 6100
6166 6100
6307 4300
6321 4300
6336 4300
6342 4300
6394 4300
6614 5600
6620 5600
6668 5600
6669 5600
6843 6800
6853 6800
6858 6800
6866 6800
6904 4900
6971 6959
7317 4300
7438 7400
7713 5700
7735 5700
7758 5700
7818 7800
7821 7800
7912 6959
7913 6959
7918 6959
7929 6959
8108 8100
8415 9400
8468 9400
8700 5700
9303 9300
9319 9300
9432 9400
9608 5700
9614 5700
9635 5700
9680 5700
9682 5700
9724 5700
9733 5700
9753 5700
9798 5700

1957 84E
2238 2251
2257 2251
2279 2251
2849 2800
2851 2800
2856 2800
2857 2800
2897 2884
2898 2884
3101 3100
3625 5700
3660 5700
3673 5700
3689 5700
3693 5700
3839 2884
4111 5101
4116 5101
4155 5101
4170 5101
4172 5101
4648 5700
4904 4900
4988 4900
5156 5101
5163 5101
5166 5101
5181 5101
5192 5101
5198 5101
5325 4300
5333 4300
5369 4300
5370 4300
5386 4300
5738 5700
5745 5700
5790 5700
5912 4900
5927 4900
6105 6100
6116 6100
6118 6100
6134 6100
6139 6100
6166 6100
6307 4300
6342 4300
6668 5600
6853 6800
6861 6800
6866 6800
6904 4900
6971 6959
7317 4300
7438 7400
7713 5700
7735 5700
7758 5700
7763 5700
7818 7800
7821 7800
7908 6959
7912 6959
7913 6959
7918 6959
8108 8100
8415 9400
8468 9400
8700 5700
8713 5700
9432 9400
9498 9400
9608 5700
9614 5700
9635 5700
9680 5700
9682 5700
9724 5700
9727 5700
9733 5700
9753 5700
9798 5700
73036 5MT
73037 5MT

1960 84E
2211 2251
2257 2251
2267 2251
2886 2884
3625 5700
3657 5700
3660 5700
3673 5700
3693 5700
4111 5101
4126 5101
4155 5101
4170 5101
4172 5101
4648 5700
4902 4900
4974 4900
4982 4900
5192 5101
5369 4300
5658 5600

5912 4900
5927 4900
5930 4900
5959 4900
6116 6100
6160 6100
6631 5600
6668 5600
6853 6800
6861 6800
6866 6800
6871 6800
6971 6959
7317 4300
7424 7400
7824 7800
7908 6959
7912 6959
7918 6959
8108 8100
8415 9400
8468 9400
8700 5700
8713 5700
9635 5700
9680 5700
9682 5700
9724 5700
9727 5700
9753 5700
9798 5700
48402 8F
48415 8F
48417 8F
48418 8F
48424 8F
48430 8F
48444 8F
48471 8F
48475 8F
75000 4MT[1]
75005 4MT[1]
75006 4MT[1]
75024 4MT[1]

1963 84E
3625 5700
3660 5700
3673 5700
3802 2884
3829 2884
3865 2884
4111 5101
4155 5101
4158 5101
4167 5101
4172 5101
4648 5700
4954 4900
5927 4900
5983 4900
6609 5600
6845 6800
6853 6800
6861 6800
6866 6800
6879 6800
6926 4900
6930 4900
6971 6959
7424 7400
7426 7400
7802 7800
7823 7800
7908 6959
7915 6959
7918 6959
7929 6959
8109 8100
9724 5700
9753 5700
9798 5700
92001 9F
92212 9F
92234 9F

1966 2A
3625 5700
4635 5700
9774 5700
44661 5MT[3]
44663 5MT[3]
44666 5MT[3]
44760 5MT[3]
44762 5MT[3]
44774 5MT[3]
44776 5MT[3]
44777 5MT[3]
44780 5MT[3]
44859 5MT[3]
44865 5MT[3]
44985 5MT[3]
45038 5MT[3]
45051 5MT[3]
45052 5MT[3]
45134 5MT[3]
45264 5MT[3]
45287 5MT[3]
45292 5MT[3]
45302 5MT[3]
45349 5MT[3]
46428 2MT[2]
46442 2MT[2]
46457 2MT[2]
46470 2MT[2]
46509 2MT[2]
73026 5MT
73066 5MT
73069 5MT
73156 5MT
92001 9F
92002 9F
92087 9F
92118 9F
92204 9F
92212 9F
92215 9F
92217 9F
92223 9F

Upper Bank

1948 4C
41769 1F[1]
41824 1F[1]
41852 1F[1]
41860 1F[1]
41893 1F[1]
47230 3F[5]
47232 3F[5]
47256 3F[5]
47258 3F[5]
47259 3F[5]
47477 3F[6]
47478 3F[6]
47479 3F[6]
47480 3F[6]
47481 3F[6]
47655 3F[6]

Uttoxeter

1948 5F
40085 3MT[2]
40086 3MT[2]
40156 3MT[2]
42358 4MT[2]
42363 4MT[2]
42468 4MT[3]
44307 4F[2]
44504 4F[2]
10897 2P[8]

1951 5F
40086 3MT[2]
40156 3MT[2]
42358 4MT[2]
42663 4MT[3]
42665 4MT[3]
44307 4F[2]
44504 4F[2]

1954 5F
42304 4MT[2]
42358 4MT[2]
42375 4MT[2]
42468 4MT[3]
42605 4MT[3]
42665 4MT[3]
42675 4MT[1]
43915 4F[1]
44307 4F[2]
44504 4F[2]

1957 5F
42358 4MT[2]
42375 4MT[2]
42468 4MT[3]
42605 4MT[3]
42665 4MT[3]
44024 4F[1]
44504 4F[2]

1960 5F
42358 4MT[2]
42375 4MT[2]
42605 4MT[3]
42665 4MT[3]
44504 4F[2]

1963 5F
42069 4MT[1]
42137 4MT[1]
42564 4MT[3]
42605 4MT[3]
42665 4MT[3]
44048 4F[2]
44355 4F[2]

Wadebridge

1948 WAD
30181 O2
30203 O2
30585 0298
30586 0298
30587 0298
30703 T9
30717 T9

1951 72F
30200 O2
30203 O2
30585 0298
30586 0298
30587 0298

1954 72F
30200 O2
30203 O2
30585 0298
30586 0298
30587 0298

1957 72F
30200 O2
30236 O2
30585 0298
30586 0298
30587 0298

1960 72F
4666 5700
4694 5700
30200 O2
30236 O2
30585 0298
30586 0298
30587 0298

1963 72F
1367 1366
1368 1366
1369 1366
4666 5700
4694 5700

Wakefield

1948 25A
44780 5MT[3]
44949 5MT[3]
45204 5MT[3]
45205 5MT[3]
45206 5MT[3]
45339 5MT[3]
46409 2MT[2]
48386 8F
48500 8F
48501 8F
48502 8F
48503 8F
48504 8F
48505 8F
48506 8F
48507 8F
48508 8F
48509 8F
48510 8F
48511 8F
48512 8F
48513 8F
48514 8F
48515 8F
48516 8F
48517 8F
48518 8F
48519 8F
48520 8F
48521 8F
48522 8F
48722 8F
48724 8F
48725 8F
48726 8F
48727 8F
48730 8F
48732 8F
49504 7F[4]
49505 7F[4]
49506 7F[4]
49513 7F[4]
49514 7F[4]
49515 7F[4]
49516 7F[4]
49517 7F[4]
49518 7F[4]
49519 7F[4]
49525 7F[4]
49526 7F[4]
49529 7F[4]
49530 7F[4]
49531 7F[4]
49532 7F[4]
49541 7F[4]
49543 7F[4]
49545 7F[4]
49546 7F[4]
49550 7F[4]
49558 7F[4]
49559 7F[4]
49561 7F[4]
49562 7F[4]
49570 7F[4]
49574 7F[4]
49575 7F[4]
49576 7F[4]
49577 7F[4]
49578 7F[4]
49584 7F[4]
49588 7F[4]
49589 7F[4]
49603 7F[4]
49604 7F[4]
49605 7F[4]
49609 7F[4]
49621 7F[4]
49622 7F[4]
49623 7F[4]
49625 7F[4]
49626 7F[4]
49627 7F[4]
49629 7F[4]
49630 7F[4]
49632 7F[4]
49633 7F[4]
49634 7F[4]
49635 7F[4]
49638 7F[4]
49643 7F[4]
49644 7F[4]
49645 7F[4]
49646 7F[4]
49647 7F[4]
49648 7F[4]
49669 7F[4]
49670 7F[4]
49671 7F[4]
50647 2P[8]
50650 2P[8]
50656 2P[8]
50667 2P[8]
50695 2P[8]
50748 2P[8]
50755 2P[8]
50764 2P[8]
50777 2P[8]
50800 2P[8]
50801 2P[8]
50804 2P[8]
50806 2P[8]
50813 2P[8]
50852 2P[8]
50869 2P[8]
51358 2F[2]
51390 2F[2]
51415 2F[2]
51457 2F[2]
51468 2F[2]
51484 2F[2]
51500 2F[2]
51503 2F[2]
52046 2F[3]
52047 2F[3]
52092 3F[7]
52150 3F[7]
52154 3F[7]
52182 3F[7]
52186 3F[7]
52284 3F[7]
52305 3F[7]
52319 3F[7]
52369 3F[7]
52386 3F[7]
52433 3F[7]
52435 3F[7]
52561 3F[9]
52568 3F[9]
52576 3F[9]

1951 25A
41250 2MT[1]
41251 2MT[1]
41252 2MT[1]
41253 2MT[1]
41254 2MT[1]
41283 2MT[1]
41284 2MT[1]
45101 5MT[3]
45204 5MT[3]
45205 5MT[3]
45206 5MT[3]
45209 5MT[3]
45261 5MT[3]
45339 5MT[3]
46438 2MT[2]
46439 2MT[2]
47510 3F[6]
47572 3F[6]
47573 3F[6]
47580 3F[6]
47582 3F[6]
48502 8F
48504 8F
48506 8F
48511 8F
48514 8F
50715 2P[8]
50762 2P[8]
50799 2P[8]
50869 2P[8]
50873 2P[8]
50886 2P[8]
51447 2F[2]
52037 2F[3]
52043 2F[3]
52044 2F[3]
52056 2F[3]
52120 3F[7]
52133 3F[7]
52150 3F[7]
52154 3F[7]
52186 3F[7]
52235 3F[7]
52284 3F[7]
52305 3F[7]
52319 3F[7]
52345 3F[7]
52351 3F[7]
52353 3F[7]
52369 3F[7]
52386 3F[7]
52433 3F[7]
52435 3F[7]
52521 3F[7]
52561 3F[9]
52576 3F[9]
90124 WD[1]
90141 WD[1]
90237 WD[1]
90243 WD[1]
90249 WD[1]
90277 WD[1]
90292 WD[1]
90310 WD[1]
90329 WD[1]
90333 WD[1]
90334 WD[1]
90337 WD[1]
90339 WD[1]
90341 WD[1]
90342 WD[1]
90353 WD[1]
90361 WD[1]
90362 WD[1]
90363 WD[1]
90370 WD[1]
90379 WD[1]
90380 WD[1]
90381 WD[1]
90385 WD[1]
90396 WD[1]
90397 WD[1]
90404 WD[1]
90406 WD[1]
90412 WD[1]
90414 WD[1]
90415 WD[1]
90417 WD[1]
90581 WD[1]
90607 WD[1]
90615 WD[1]
90617 WD[1]
90620 WD[1]
90624 WD[1]
90631 WD[1]
90633 WD[1]
90635 WD[1]
90637 WD[1]
90639 WD[1]
90643 WD[1]
90644 WD[1]
90651 WD[1]
90652 WD[1]
90654 WD[1]
90656 WD[1]
90667 WD[1]
90673 WD[1]
90679 WD[1]
90682 WD[1]
90692 WD[1]
90710 WD[1]
90719 WD[1]
90722 WD[1]
90724 WD[1]
90725 WD[1]
90729 WD[1]

1954 25A
41250 2MT[1]
41251 2MT[1]
41252 2MT[1]
41253 2MT[1]
41254 2MT[1]
41259 2MT[1]
44019 4F[1]
44928 5MT[3]
45101 5MT[3]
45201 5MT[3]
45204 5MT[3]
45218 5MT[3]
45261 5MT[3]
45339 5MT[3]
45435 5MT[3]
46415 2MT[2]
46438 2MT[2]
46439 2MT[2]
47510 3F[6]
47572 3F[6]
47573 3F[6]
47580 3F[6]
47582 3F[6]
48502 8F
48504 8F
48506 8F
48511 8F
52044 2F[3]
52053 2F[3]
52120 3F[7]
52133 3F[7]
52150 3F[7]
52186 3F[7]
52235 3F[7]
52244 3F[7]
52376 3F[7]
52411 3F[7]
52435 3F[7]
52576 3F[9]
90101 WD[1]
90127 WD[1]
90141 WD[1]
90142 WD[1]
90164 WD[1]
90234 WD[1]
90236 WD[1]
90243 WD[1]
90247 WD[1]
90249 WD[1]
90260 WD[1]
90265 WD[1]
90277 WD[1]
90292 WD[1]
90310 WD[1]
90329 WD[1]
90333 WD[1]
90334 WD[1]
90337 WD[1]
90339 WD[1]
90341 WD[1]
90342 WD[1]
90353 WD[1]
90361 WD[1]
90362 WD[1]
90363 WD[1]
90370 WD[1]
90379 WD[1]
90380 WD[1]
90381 WD[1]
90385 WD[1]
90396 WD[1]
90397 WD[1]
90404 WD[1]
90406 WD[1]
90412 WD[1]
90414 WD[1]
90415 WD[1]
90417 WD[1]
90556 WD[1]
90581 WD[1]
90604 WD[1]
90607 WD[1]
90610 WD[1]
90615 WD[1]
90617 WD[1]
90620 WD[1]
90624 WD[1]
90631 WD[1]
90633 WD[1]
90635 WD[1]
90637 WD[1]
90643 WD[1]
90644 WD[1]
90651 WD[1]
90652 WD[1]
90654 WD[1]
90656 WD[1]
90673 WD[1]
90682 WD[1]
90692 WD[1]
90710 WD[1]
90719 WD[1]
90722 WD[1]
90724 WD[1]

1957 56A
41251 2MT[1]
41252 2MT[1]
41253 2MT[1]
42861 5MT[1]
42862 5MT[1]
42863 5MT[1]
44019 4F[1]
46413 2MT[2]
46415 2MT[2]
46435 2MT[2]
46438 2MT[2]
46483 2MT[2]
47510 3F[6]
47572 3F[6]
47573 3F[6]
47580 3F[6]
47582 3F[6]
48502 8F
48504 8F
48511 8F
52044 2F[3]
52133 3F[7]
52186 3F[7]
52376 3F[7]
90247 WD[1]
90333 WD[1]
90334 WD[1]
90337 WD[1]
90339 WD[1]
90341 WD[1]
90342 WD[1]
90353 WD[1]
90361 WD[1]
90362 WD[1]
90363 WD[1]
90370 WD[1]
90379 WD[1]
90380 WD[1]
90385 WD[1]
90396 WD[1]
90404 WD[1]
90414 WD[1]
90415 WD[1]
90417 WD[1]
90581 WD[1]
90604 WD[1]
90607 WD[1]
90610 WD[1]
90615 WD[1]
90617 WD[1]
90620 WD[1]
90631 WD[1]
90633 WD[1]
90635 WD[1]
90637 WD[1]
90639 WD[1]
90644 WD[1]
90651 WD[1]
90652 WD[1]
90654 WD[1]
90656 WD[1]
90673 WD[1]
90679 WD[1]
90682 WD[1]
90692 WD[1]
90710 WD[1]
90719 WD[1]
90722 WD[1]

1960 56A
40117 3MT[2]
40155 3MT[2]
42073 4MT[1]
42622 4MT[3]
42861 5MT[1]
42862 5MT[1]
42863 5MT[1]
43075 4MT[5]
43101 4MT[5]
43579 3F[3]
43705 3F[3]
44019 4F[1]
47271 3F[6]
47463 3F[6]
47510 3F[6]
47567 3F[6]
47571 3F[6]
47572 3F[6]
47573 3F[6]
47582 3F[6]
52133 3F[7]
52355 3F[7]
61015 B1
61017 B1
61020 B1
61131 B1
61268 B1
61296 B1
61385 B1
63588 O4
63857 O4
63864 O4
63920 O4
68897 J50
68898 J50
68904 J50
68909 J50
68910 J50
68939 J50
68959 J50
90016 WD[1]
90047 WD[1]
90054 WD[1]
90056 WD[1]
90061 WD[1]
90076 WD[1]
90089 WD[1]
90100 WD[1]
90112 WD[1]
90116 WD[1]
90124 WD[1]
90230 WD[1]
90321 WD[1]
90326 WD[1]
90339 WD[1]
90341 WD[1]
90342 WD[1]
90348 WD[1]
90353 WD[1]
90361 WD[1]
90363 WD[1]
90370 WD[1]
90379 WD[1]
90380 WD[1]
90382 WD[1]
90385 WD[1]
90396 WD[1]
90404 WD[1]
90405 WD[1]
90415 WD[1]
90417 WD[1]
90429 WD[1]
90445 WD[1]
90497 WD[1]
90543 WD[1]
90581 WD[1]
90604 WD[1]
90607 WD[1]
90615 WD[1]
90620 WD[1]
90625 WD[1]
90631 WD[1]
90633 WD[1]
90635 WD[1]
90639 WD[1]
90644 WD[1]
90651 WD[1]
90654 WD[1]
90656 WD[1]
90679 WD[1]
90692 WD[1]
90710 WD[1]

1963 56A
42150 4MT[1]
42649 4MT[3]
42650 4MT[3]
42861 5MT[1]
42863 5MT[1]
43070 4MT[5]
43101 4MT[5]
46438 2MT[2]
46483 2MT[2]
47266 3F[6]
47379 3F[6]
61040 B1
61161 B1
61274 B1
61387 B1
68904 J50
68908 J50
68922 J50
68977 J50
90047 WD[1]
90061 WD[1]
90076 WD[1]
90089 WD[1]
90112 WD[1]
90116 WD[1]
90124 WD[1]
90321 WD[1]
90326 WD[1]
90339 WD[1]
90341 WD[1]
90342 WD[1]
90348 WD[1]
90353 WD[1]
90363 WD[1]
90370 WD[1]
90379 WD[1]
90380 WD[1]
90382 WD[1]
90385 WD[1]
90396 WD[1]
90404 WD[1]
90415 WD[1]
90417 WD[1]
90426 WD[1]
90429 WD[1]
90497 WD[1]
90543 WD[1]
90581 WD[1]
90604 WD[1]
90615 WD[1]
90620 WD[1]
90631 WD[1]
90633 WD[1]
90635 WD[1]
90639 WD[1]
90651 WD[1]
90654 WD[1]
90656 WD[1]
90679 WD[1]
90710 WD[1]

1966 56A
42108 4MT[1]
42150 4MT[1]
42181 4MT[1]
42204 4MT[1]
42269 4MT[1]
42650 4MT[3]
43070 4MT[5]
43137 4MT[5]
45694 6P5F[2]
45739 6P5F[2]
61013 B1
61022 B1
61024 B1
61030 B1
61040 B1
61123 B1
61131 B1
61161 B1
61173 B1
61224 B1
61237 B1
61240 B1
90047 WD[1]
90054 WD[1]
90056 WD[1]
90061 WD[1]
90068 WD[1]
90074 WD[1]
90076 WD[1]
90089 WD[1]
90112 WD[1]
90113 WD[1]
90116 WD[1]
90126 WD[1]
90135 WD[1]
90155 WD[1]
90160 WD[1]
90200 WD[1]
90210 WD[1]
90233 WD[1]
90236 WD[1]
90281 WD[1]
90300 WD[1]
90321 WD[1]
90336 WD[1]
90339 WD[1]
90345 WD[1]
90347 WD[1]
90348 WD[1]
90357 WD[1]
90360 WD[1]
90361 WD[1]
90363 WD[1]
90370 WD[1]
90373 WD[1]
90379 WD[1]
90380 WD[1]
90382 WD[1]
90385 WD[1]
90396 WD[1]
90404 WD[1]
90405 WD[1]
90407 WD[1]
90409 WD[1]
90415 WD[1]
90417 WD[1]
90429 WD[1]
90430 WD[1]
90457 WD[1]
90470 WD[1]
90482 WD[1]
90610 WD[1]
90611 WD[1]
90615 WD[1]
90620 WD[1]
90622 WD[1]
90625 WD[1]
90631 WD[1]
90633 WD[1]
90639 WD[1]
90642 WD[1]
90651 WD[1]
90654 WD[1]
90664 WD[1]
90678 WD[1]
90679 WD[1]
90684 WD[1]
90698 WD[1]
90707 WD[1]
90721 WD[1]

Walsall

1948 3C
40011 3MT[1]
40017 3MT[1]
40019 3MT[1]
40042 3MT[1]
40045 3MT[1]
40069 3MT[1]
40413 2P[2]
40462 2P[2]
40501 2P[2]
42444 4MT[3]
42448 4MT[3]
42452 4MT[3]
42466 4MT[3]
42562 4MT[3]
42586 4MT[3]
42604 4MT[3]
42627 4MT[3]
42660 4MT[3]
43410 3F[3]
43502 3F[3]
43786 3F[4]
44069 4F[2]
44115 4F[2]
44339 4F[2]
44345 4F[2]
44454 4F[2]
44488 4F[2]
44506 4F[2]
44512 4F[2]
44873 5MT[3]
45308 5MT[3]
45395 5MT[3]
46661 1P[1]
46679 1P[1]
46757 1P[1]
49003 7F[2]
49015 6F[2]
49031 7F[2]
49040 6F[2]
49048 7F[2]
49056 6F[2]
49222 6F[2]
49236 6F[2]
49248 6F[2]
49283 6F[2]
49325 7F[2]
49349 6F[2]
49364 6F[2]
49388 7F[2]
58320 2F[10]
58322 2F[10]
58325 2F[10]
58348 2F[10]
58349 2F[10]
58350 2F[10]
58352 2F[10]
58359 2F[10]
58361 2F[10]
58423 2F[11]
28597 2F[11]

1951 3C
40011 3MT[1]
40019 3MT[1]
40045 3MT[1]
40047 3MT[1]
40462 2P[2]
40501 2P[2]
41226 2MT[1]
41279 2MT[1]
42444 4MT[3]
42448 4MT[3]
42452 4MT[3]
42466 4MT[3]
42469 4MT[3]
42482 4MT[3]
42488 4MT[3]
42562 4MT[3]
42586 4MT[3]
42604 4MT[3]
42627 4MT[3]
43410 3F[3]
43502 3F[3]
43786 3F[4]
44078 4F[2]
44115 4F[2]
44345 4F[2]
44360 4F[2]
44488 4F[2]
44512 4F[2]
44873 5MT[3]
45308 5MT[3]
45344 5MT[3]
45395 5MT[3]
46712 1P[1]
47413 3F[6]
48943 7F[2]
49031 7F[2]
49048 7F[2]
49066 7F[2]
49171 6F[2]
49193 6F[2]
49198 7F[2]
49208 6F[2]
49213 6F[2]
49222 6F[2]
49258 7F[2]
49300 7F[2]
49322 7F[2]
49326 6F[2]
49373 7F[2]
49388 7F[2]
58116 2F[8]
58123 2F[8]
58157 2F[8]
58283 2F[9]
58288 2F[9]
58302 2F[9]

1954 3C
40073 3MT[2]
40080 3MT[2]
40084 3MT[2]
40085 3MT[2]
40108 3MT[2]
40173 3MT[2]
40180 3MT[2]
40501 2P[2]
40531 2P[2]
41226 2MT[1]
41279 2MT[1]
42482 4MT[3]
42488 4MT[3]
42538 4MT[3]
42562 4MT[3]
42578 4MT[3]
42586 4MT[3]
42604 4MT[3]
42627 4MT[3]
43410 3F[3]
43502 3F[3]
44078 4F[2]
44115 4F[2]
44345 4F[2]
44448 4F[2]
44488 4F[2]
44873 5MT[3]
45308 5MT[3]
45344 5MT[3]
45395 5MT[3]
46712 1P[1]
47296 3F[6]
48905 7F[2]
48907 7F[2]
48917 7F[2]
48922 7F[2]
48943 7F[2]
49020 7F[2]
49048 7F[2]
49066 7F[2]
49108 7F[2]
49198 7F[2]
49271 7F[2]
49301 7F[2]
49354 7F[2]
49373 7F[2]
58122 2F[8]
58123 2F[8]
58125 2F[8]
58157 2F[8]
58279 2F[9]
58283 2F[9]
58288 2F[9]

1957 3C
40080 3MT[2]
40129 3MT[2]
40173 3MT[2]
40421 2P[2]
40501 2P[2]
41213 2MT[1]
41223 2MT[1]
41224 2MT[1]
41279 2MT[1]
42441 4MT[3]
42482 4MT[3]
42488 4MT[3]
42586 4MT[3]
42604 4MT[3]
42627 4MT[3]
43410 3F[3]
44078 4F[2]
44115 4F[2]
44345 4F[2]
44444 4F[2]
44448 4F[2]
44488 4F[2]
44512 4F[2]
44873 5MT[3]
45344 5MT[3]
45395 5MT[3]
47296 3F[6]
48905 7F[2]
48907 7F[2]
48917 7F[2]
48932 7F[2]
48943 7F[2]
49020 7F[2]
49066 7F[2]
49108 7F[2]
49271 7F[2]
49301 7F[2]
49373 7F[2]
58122 2F[8]
58157 2F[8]
58169 2F[8]
58174 2F[8]
58203 2F[9]
58283 2F[9]

Walton on the Hill

1948 WAL
62311 D9
64397 J11
65130 J10
65177 J10
65180 J10
65192 J10
65195 J10
68365 J75
68584 J67
69265 N5
69298 N5
69338 N5
69344 N5
69356 N5

1951 27E
40690 2P[3]
40937 4P[1]
41188 4P[1]
41194 4P[1]
44038 4F[2]
44221 4F[2]
44464 4F[2]
44481 4F[2]
44541 4F[2]
44544 4F[2]
52437 3F[7]
64397 J11
65130 J10
65133 J10
65177 J10
65180 J10
65192 J10
68584 J67
68585 J69
69265 N5
69298 N5
69344 N5
69356 N5

1954 27E
42111 4MT[1]
42112 4MT[1]
42113 4MT[1]
44038 4F[2]
44218 4F[2]
44481 4F[2]
44541 4F[2]
51338 2F[2]
65133 J10
65177 J10
65180 J10
65192 J10
68585 J69
69265 N5
69298 N5
69344 N5
69356 N5

1957 27E
42111 4MT[1]
42112 4MT[1]
42113 4MT[1]
44038 4F[2]
44040 4F[2]
44218 4F[2]
44291 4F[2]
44462 4F[2]
44471 4F[2]
44481 4F[2]
44541 4F[2]
65133 J10
65177 J10
65192 J10
69265 N5
69298 N5
69344 N5
69356 N5

1960 27E
42112 4MT[1]
42113 4MT[1]
43988 4F[1]
44023 4F[1]
44038 4F[2]
44040 4F[2]
44188 4F[2]
44218 4F[2]
44299 4F[2]
44462 4F[2]
44471 4F[2]
44481 4F[2]
44605 4F[2]
47225 3F[5]
47228 3F[5]
47235 3F[5]
47655 3F[6]
47681 3F[6]
50781 2P[8]

1963 27E
42054 4MT[1]
42617 4MT[3]
44177 4F[2]
44188 4F[2]
44462 4F[2]
44481 4F[2]
47225 3F[5]
47228 3F[5]
47681 3F[6]

Warrington Dallam

1948 8B
40080 3MT[2]
40081 3MT[2]
40084 3MT[2]
40207 3MT[2]
42583 4MT[3]
42606 4MT[3]
43207 3F[3]
43283 3F[3]
43314 3F[3]
43357 3F[3]
43389 3F[3]
43398 3F[3]
43615 3F[3]
43657 3F[3]
44897 5MT[3]
45001 5MT[3]
45026 5MT[3]
45032 5MT[3]
45035 5MT[3]
45095 5MT[3]
45109 5MT[3]
45149 5MT[3]
45196 5MT[3]
45252 5MT[3]
45321 5MT[3]
46603 1P[1]
46663 1P[1]
46688 1P[1]

46710 1P^1
46718 1P^1
46906 2P^7
46920 2P^7
46924 2P^7
47268 3F^6
47352 3F^6
47376 3F^6
47387 3F^6
47591 3F^6
47652 3F^6
47654 3F^6
47657 3F^6
48944 7F^2
49008 7F^2
49075 6F^2
49085 6F^2
49136 6F^2
49178 7F^2
49247 7F^2
49302 7F^2
49338 6F^2
49411 7F^3
52100 3F^7
52118 3F^7
52140 3F^7
52175 3F^7
52250 3F^7
52330 3F^7
58925 2F^{14}

1951 8B
40042 3MT^1
42606 4MT^3
42607 4MT^3
43237 3F^3
43282 3F^3
43283 3F^3
43314 3F^3
43329 3F^3
43389 3F^3
43398 3F^3
43615 3F^3
43618 3F^3
43633 3F^3
43657 3F^3
43787 3F^4
44897 5MT^3
45001 5MT^3
45032 5MT^3
45035 5MT^3
45109 5MT^3
45149 5MT^3
45196 5MT^3
45252 5MT^3
45255 5MT^3
45321 5MT^3
45328 5MT^3
45354 5MT^3
45370 5MT^3
45495 5MT^3
45521 7P^1
46603 1P^1
46654 1P^1
46688 1P^1
46701 1P^1
46727 1P^1
47268 3F^6
47352 3F^6
47376 3F^6
47387 3F^6
47591 3F^6
47603 3F^6
47652 3F^6
47654 3F^6
47657 3F^6
48366 8F
48436 8F
48466 8F
48469 8F
48473 8F
48664 8F
48689 8F
49008 7F^2
49119 7F^2
49149 7F^2
49247 7F^2
50687 2P^8
50697 2P^8
50703 2P^8
50705 2P^8
52088 3F^7

1954 8B
40143 3MT^2
40202 3MT^2
41321 2MT^1
41322 2MT^1
41323 2MT^1
42606 4MT^3
42607 4MT^3
43237 3F^3
43282 3F^3
43314 3F^3
43329 3F^3
43398 3F^3
43615 3F^3
43618 3F^3
43633 3F^3
43657 3F^3
43787 3F^4
45032 5MT^3
45035 5MT^3
45196 5MT^3
45252 5MT^3
45255 5MT^3
45271 5MT^3
45321 5MT^3
45328 5MT^3
45354 5MT^3
45495 5MT^3
45521 7P^1
47268 3F^6
47352 3F^6
47362 3F^6
47376 3F^6
47387 3F^6
47591 3F^6
47603 3F^6
47652 3F^6
47654 3F^6
47657 3F^6
48142 8F
48188 8F
48348 8F
48349 8F
48520 8F
48531 8F
48714 8F
48715 8F
49008 7F^2
49024 7F^2
49093 7F^2
49119 7F^2
49249 7F^2
50643 2P^8
50644 2P^8
50705 2P^8
52225 3F^7
52432 3F^7

1957 8B
40143 3MT^2
40202 3MT^2
41210 2MT^1
41211 2MT^1
41212 2MT^1
42606 4MT^3
42607 4MT^3
43237 3F^3
43282 3F^3
43314 3F^3
43329 3F^3
43398 3F^3
43615 3F^3
43618 3F^3
43657 3F^3
43787 3F^4
44237 4F^2
44356 4F^2
44384 4F^2
45032 5MT^3
45035 5MT^3
45196 5MT^3
45252 5MT^3
45255 5MT^3
45271 5MT^3
45321 5MT^3
45328 5MT^3
45354 5MT^3
45495 5MT^3
47268 3F^6
47352 3F^6
47362 3F^6
47376 3F^6
47387 3F^6
47591 3F^6
47603 3F^6
47652 3F^6
47654 3F^6
47657 3F^6
48094 8F
48188 8F
48247 8F
48348 8F
48349 8F
48441 8F
48491 8F
48520 8F
48531 8F
48683 8F
48693 8F
48714 8F
48715 8F
49008 7F^2
49119 7F^2
49323 7F^2
50643 2P^8
50644 2P^8
50705 2P^8
52225 3F^7
52432 3F^7

1960 8B
41210 2MT^1
41213 2MT^1
41324 2MT^1
42606 4MT^3
42607 4MT^3
43257 3F^3
43282 3F^3
43295 3F^3
43314 3F^3
43615 3F^3
43657 3F^3
44237 4F^2
44356 4F^2
44384 4F^2
45035 5MT^3
45196 5MT^3
45256 5MT^3
45271 5MT^3
45276 5MT^3
45321 5MT^3
45328 5MT^3
45343 5MT^3
45354 5MT^3
45380 5MT^3
45398 5MT^3
45410 5MT^3
45495 5MT^3
45503 6P5F^1
45549 6P5F^1
45550 6P5F^1
47268 3F^6
47352 3F^6
47362 3F^6
47392 3F^6
47401 3F^6
47591 3F^6
47603 3F^6
47652 3F^6
47654 3F^6
47657 3F^6
47659 3F^6
48094 8F
48106 8F
48188 8F
48296 8F
48373 8F
48520 8F
48715 8F
48746 8F
52225 3F^7

1963 8B
41211 2MT^1
41217 2MT^1
44061 4F^2
44063 4F^2
44219 4F^2
44232 4F^2
44237 4F^2
44239 4F^2
44353 4F^2
44356 4F^2
44377 4F^2
44384 4F^2
44494 4F^2
44522 4F^2
44589 4F^2
45018 5MT^3
45035 5MT^3
45150 5MT^3
45271 5MT^3
45321 5MT^3
45328 5MT^3
45343 5MT^3
45354 5MT^3
45380 5MT^3
45381 5MT^3
45414 5MT^3
45495 5MT^3
45583 6P5F^2
45638 6P5F^2
45655 6P5F^2
45671 6P5F^2
47362 3F^6
47654 3F^6
47657 3F^6
48106 8F
48268 8F
48715 8F
84000 2MT^2
90125 WD^1
90227 WD^1
90315 WD^1
90369 WD^1
90392 WD^1
90466 WD^1
90566 WD^1

1966 8B
44658 5MT^3
44730 5MT^3
44731 5MT^3
44779 5MT^3
44819 5MT^3
44930 5MT^3
44935 5MT^3
44963 5MT^3
45041 5MT^3
45070 5MT^3
45109 5MT^3
45129 5MT^3
45221 5MT^3
45238 5MT^3
45256 5MT^3
45303 5MT^3
45323 5MT^3
45375 5MT^3
45436 5MT^3
92049 9F
92053 9F
92055 9F
92058 9F
92078 9F
92116 9F
92119 9F
92124 9F
92126 9F
92156 9F
92160 9F

Warwick

1948 2E
40009 3MT^1
40044 3MT^1
40109 3MT^2
40135 3MT^2
40203 3MT^2
46669 1P^1
46673 1P^1
46683 1P^1
46749 1P^1
48897 7F^2
48910 6F^2
48922 7F^2
48924 6F^2
49384 6F^2
58308 2F^9
58388 2F^{11}
58404 2F^{11}

1951 2C
40002 3MT^1
40016 3MT^1
40076 3MT^2
40078 3MT^2
41227 2MT^1
41228 2MT^1
41239 2MT^1
42671 4MT^3
42674 4MT^1
46683 1P^1
46749 1P^1
48012 8F
48018 8F
49430 7F^3
58290 2F^9
58308 2F^9

1954 2C
40076 3MT^2
40078 3MT^2
40126 3MT^2
40156 3MT^2
40157 3MT^2
40205 3MT^2
41227 2MT^1
41228 2MT^1
41285 2MT^1
42674 4MT^1
48012 8F
48018 8F
49120 7F^2

1957 2C
40076 3MT^2
40078 3MT^2
40203 3MT^2
41227 2MT^1
41228 2MT^1
41285 2MT^1
41321 2MT^1
41902 2P^4
41909 2P^4
42316 4MT^2
42674 4MT^1
48012 8F
48018 8F
49024 7F^2

Watford

1948 1C
40004 3MT^1
40010 3MT^1
40020 3MT^1
40043 3MT^1
40046 3MT^1
40672 2P^3
41908 2P^4
41909 2P^4
42304 4MT^2
42389 4MT^2
42445 4MT^3
42446 4MT^3
42482 4MT^3
42541 4MT^3
42582 4MT^3
42589 4MT^3
42590 4MT^3
42593 4MT^3
42598 4MT^3
42610 4MT^3
44396 4F^2
44443 4F^2
46686 1P^1
48915 7F^2
48964 7F^2
49145 7F^2
49249 7F^2
49262 7F^2
49323 7F^2
49344 7F^2
49375 7F^2
58272 2F^9

1951 1C
40010 3MT^1
40020 3MT^1
40043 3MT^1
40072 3MT^2
40672 2P^3
41220 2MT^1
41908 2P^4
41909 2P^4
42119 4MT^1
42120 4MT^1
42121 4MT^1
42159 4MT^1
42178 4MT^1
42304 4MT^2
42389 4MT^2
42468 4MT^3
42589 4MT^3
42590 4MT^3
42593 4MT^3
42598 4MT^3
44441 4F^2
44443 4F^2
47355 3F^6
48915 7F^2
49078 7F^2
49145 7F^2
49157 7F^2
49323 7F^2
49375 7F^2

1954 1C
40010 3MT^1
40020 3MT^1
40043 3MT^1
40672 2P^3
41220 2MT^1
41908 2P^4
41909 2P^4
42119 4MT^1
42178 4MT^1
42389 4MT^2
44067 4F^2
44343 4F^2
44363 4F^2
44443 4F^2
47355 3F^6
48915 7F^2
49145 7F^2
49323 7F^2
80034 4MT^3
80035 4MT^3
80036 4MT^3
80037 4MT^3
80038 4MT^3
80064 4MT^3
80065 4MT^3
80066 4MT^3
80067 4MT^3
80068 4MT^3

1957 1C
40010 3MT^1
40020 3MT^1
40043 3MT^1
40672 2P^3
41220 2MT^1
41320 2MT^1
44343 4F^2
44363 4F^2
44442 4F^2
47355 3F^6
80034 4MT^3
80035 4MT^3
80036 4MT^3
80037 4MT^3
80038 4MT^3
80064 4MT^3
80065 4MT^3
80066 4MT^3
80067 4MT^3
80068 4MT^3

1960 1C
40659 2P^3
40672 2P^3
41223 2MT^1
42095 4MT^1
42096 4MT^1
42097 4MT^1
42098 4MT^1
42099 4MT^1
42100 4MT^1
42101 4MT^1
42102 4MT^1
42103 4MT^1
42104 4MT^1
43325 3F^3
44348 4F^2
44440 4F^2
44442 4F^2
46431 2MT^2
47307 3F^6
47355 3F^6

1963 1C
42096 4MT^1
42100 4MT^1
42102 4MT^1
42616 4MT^3
43007 4MT^5
43018 4MT^5
43021 4MT^5
46423 2MT^2
46431 2MT^2
46470 2MT^2
47355 3F^6
47606 3F^6

Wearhead

1948 WHD
65064 J21

1951 51F sub
65064 J21

1954 51F sub
65064 J21

Wellingborough

1948 15A
40353 2P^2
40510 2P^2
40548 2P^2
43367 3F^3
43796 3F^4
43797 3F^4
43808 3F^4
43830 3F^4
43861 4F^1
43870 4F^1
43876 4F^1
43909 4F^1
43982 4F^1
44033 4F^2
44160 4F^2
44242 4F^2
44287 4F^2
44332 4F^2
44574 4F^2
44575 4F^2
47238 3F^5
47264 3F^6
47265 3F^6
47279 3F^6
47333 3F^6
47446 3F^6
47543 3F^6
47554 3F^6
47636 3F^6
47642 3F^6
48024 8F
48050 8F
48082 8F
48128 8F
48167 8F
48180 8F
48181 8F
48192 8F
48198 8F
48222 8F
48264 8F
48269 8F
48281 8F
48305 8F
48334 8F
48338 8F
48359 8F
48360 8F
48363 8F
48364 8F
48365 8F
48371 8F
48374 8F
48492 8F
48617 8F
48625 8F
48627 8F
48644 8F
48646 8F
48651 8F
48671 8F
48678 8F
48692 8F
48694 8F
48695 8F
48699 8F
49121 7F^2
49123 7F^2
49217 7F^2
49223 7F^2
49288 7F^2
49289 7F^2
49290 7F^2
49292 7F^2
58030 1P^5
58031 1P^5

1951 15A
40353 2P^2
41244 2MT^1
41916 2P^5
43193 3F^3
43367 3F^3
43797 3F^4
43808 3F^4
43861 4F^1
43930 4F^1
43975 4F^1
44037 4F^2
44242 4F^2
44249 4F^2
44574 4F^2
44575 4F^2
47238 3F^5
47264 3F^6
47265 3F^6
47273 3F^6
47279 3F^6
47333 3F^6
47446 3F^6
47543 3F^6
47554 3F^6
47636 3F^6
47642 3F^6
48008 8F
48010 8F
48024 8F
48035 8F
48050 8F
48082 8F
48107 8F
48111 8F
48128 8F
48131 8F
48133 8F
48150 8F
48151 8F
48167 8F
48180 8F
48181 8F
48183 8F
48191 8F
48192 8F
48198 8F
48222 8F
48264 8F
48265 8F
48269 8F
48281 8F
48305 8F
48334 8F
48338 8F
48359 8F
48360 8F
48363 8F
48365 8F
48371 8F
48374 8F
48376 8F
48378 8F
48385 8F
48386 8F
48475 8F
48492 8F
48533 8F
48543 8F
48617 8F
48619 8F
48625 8F
48627 8F
48644 8F
48651 8F
48668 8F
48671 8F
48678 8F
48692 8F
48695 8F
48699 8F
48721 8F
58053 1P^6
58085 1P^6

1954 15A
41277 2MT^1
41328 2MT^1
43367 3F^3
43531 3F^3
43808 3F^4
43861 4F^1
43930 4F^1
43975 4F^1
43977 4F^1
43979 4F^1
44249 4F^2
44574 4F^2
44575 4F^2
47264 3F^6
47265 3F^6
47273 3F^6
47279 3F^6
47333 3F^6
47446 3F^6
47543 3F^6
47554 3F^6
47636 3F^6
47642 3F^6
47974 Garratt
47977 Garratt
47982 Garratt
47994 Garratt
47995 Garratt
48008 8F
48010 8F
48050 8F
48082 8F
48107 8F
48111 8F
48150 8F
48151 8F
48180 8F
48181 8F
48183 8F
48191 8F
48192 8F
48198 8F
48222 8F
40204 8F
48265 8F
48269 8F
48281 8F
48305 8F
48334 8F
48338 8F
48359 8F
48360 8F
48363 8F
48364 8F
48365 8F
48371 8F
48374 8F
48376 8F
48378 8F
48385 8F
48386 8F
48475 8F
48492 8F
48533 8F
48617 8F
48625 8F
48627 8F
48644 8F
48651 8F
48668 8F
48671 8F
48678 8F
48692 8F
48695 8F
48699 8F
48772 8F
58091 1P^6

1957 15A
41048 4P^1
41277 2MT^1
41328 2MT^1
43624 3F^3
43861 4F^1
43929 4F^1
43977 4F^1
43979 4F^1
44182 4F^2
44574 4F^2
44575 4F^2
47208 3F^5
47265 3F^6
47273 3F^6
47279 3F^6
47543 3F^6
48191 8F
48198 8F
48264 8F
48305 8F
48359 8F
48360 8F
48363 8F
48364 8F
48365 8F
48374 8F
48376 8F
48378 8F
48385 8F
48386 8F
48492 8F
48617 8F
48625 8F
48627 8F
48644 8F
48651 8F
48671 8F
48678 8F
48695 8F
48699 8F
63725 O1
92008 9F
92009 9F
92015 9F
92016 9F
92017 9F
92018 9F
92019 9F
92020 9F
92021 9F
92022 9F
92023 9F
92024 9F
92025 9F
92026 9F
92027 9F
92028 9F
92029 9F
92082 9F
92083 9F
92084 9F
92085 9F
92086 9F
92107 9F

1960 15A
43861 4F^1
43929 4F^1
43977 4F^1
43979 4F^1
43995 4F^1
44182 4F^2
44574 4F^2
44575 4F^2
47265 3F^6
47273 3F^6
48141 8F
48143 8F
48374 8F
48381 8F
48382 8F
48385 8F
48386 8F
48492 8F
48495 8F
48617 8F
48625 8F
48627 8F
48651 8F
48671 8F
48699 8F
84006 2MT^2
84007 2MT^2
84008 2MT^2
92018 9F
92019 9F
92020 9F
92021 9F
92022 9F
92023 9F
92024 9F
92025 9F
92026 9F
92027 9F
92028 9F
92029 9F
92052 9F
92053 9F
92054 9F
92055 9F
92056 9F
92058 9F
92059 9F
92080 9F
92081 9F
92082 9F
92083 9F
92084 9F
92085 9F
92107 9F
92108 9F
92110 9F
92111 9F
92112 9F
92118 9F
92120 9F
92122 9F
92123 9F
92124 9F
92125 9F
92126 9F
92127 9F
92132 9F
92133 9F
92134 9F
92154 9F
92159 9F

1963 15A
41224 2MT^1
41227 2MT^1
43010 4MT^5
43012 4MT^5
43013 4MT^5
43019 4MT^5
43031 4MT^5
43047 4MT^5
43106 4MT^5
43118 4MT^5
43119 4MT^5
43120 4MT^5
43121 4MT^5
44243 4F^2
44297 4F^2
44575 4F^2
47257 3F^5
47273 3F^6
48010 8F
48027 8F
48061 8F
48125 8F
48266 8F
40301 8F
48374 8F
48381 8F
48385 8F
48386 8F
48492 8F
48495 8F
48538 8F
48617 8F
48651 8F
48671 8F
48699 8F
92019 9F
92020 9F
92021 9F
92022 9F
92023 9F
92024 9F
92025 9F
92026 9F
92027 9F
92080 9F
92081 9F
92082 9F
92083 9F
92084 9F
92086 9F
92117 9F
92124 9F
92126 9F
92127 9F
92132 9F
92133 9F
92134 9F
92154 9F
92159 9F

Wellington

1948 WLN
2030 2021
3417 3300
3732 5700
3749 5700
3775 5700
4154 5101
4400 4400
4401 4400
4403 4400
4406 4400
4409 4400
5127 5101
5135 5101
5137 5101
5139 5101
5178 5101
5309 4300
5332 4300
5758 5700
9624 5700
9630 5700
9639 5700

1951 84H
1619 1600
2030 2021
3613 5700
3687 5700
3732 5700
3749 5700
3760 5700
3775 5700
4154 5101
4400 4400
4401 4400
4403 4400
4406 4400
5109 5101
5125 5101
5137 5101
5138 5101
5139 5101
5178 5101
5758 5700
7754 5700
9624 5700
9630 5700
9639 5700

1954 84H
2061 2021
3613 5700
3732 5700
3749 5700
3760 5700
4155 5101
4158 5101
4178 5101
4605 5700
5109 5101
5178 5101
5712 5700
5745 5700
5758 5700
7754 5700
9624 5700
9630 5700
9639 5700
9741 5700
9742 5700
9774 5700

1957 84H
1663 1600
3732 5700
3744 5700
3749 5700
3760 5700
4110 5101
4142 5101
4158 5101
4605 5700
5167 5101
5712 5700
5758 5700
7754 5700
9630 5700
9639 5700
9741 5700
9742 5700
9774 5700
82004 3MT^2
82006 3MT^2
82009 3MT^2

1960 84H
3626 5700
3732 5700
3744 5700
4120 5101
4158 5101
4605 5700
9621 5700
9630 5700
9639 5700
9741 5700
9774 5700
41201 2MT^1
41241 2MT^1
82006 3MT^2
82009 3MT^2
82030 3MT^2
82038 3MT^2

1963 84H
3744 5700
3776 5700
9630 5700
9636 5700
9639 5700
9774 5700
41201 2MT^1
41204 2MT^1
41232 2MT^1
41241 2MT^1

Welshpool (WLLR)

1948 OSW sub
822 W&L
823 W&L

1951 89A sub
822 W&L
823 W&L

1954 89A sub
822 W&L
823 W&L

West Auckland

1948 AUK
63314 Q5
63315 Q5
65032 J21
65061 J21
65659 J25
65662 J25
65665 J25
65675 J25
65677 J25
65683 J25
65687 J25
65689 J25
65696 J25
65706 J25
65715 J25
65718 J25
67306 G5
67312 G5
67317 G5
67345 G5
68142 Y1
68145 Y1
68149 Y1
68182 Y3
68249 J71
68254 J71
68255 J71
68269 J71
68432 J77
68678 J72
68696 J72
69422 N9
69856 A8
69870 A8
69877 A8
69879 A8
69886 A8

1951 51F
64756 J39
64778 J39
64848 J39
65061 J21
65062 J21
65077 J21
65078 J21
65088 J21
65091 J21
65092 J21
65097 J21
65102 J21
65659 J25
65662 J25
65675 J25
65683 J25
65696 J25
65706 J25
67291 G5
67312 G5
67345 G5
68142 Y1
68145 Y1
68149 Y1
68182 Y3
68249 J71
68254 J71
68255 J71
68269 J71
68391 J77
68691 J72
68696 J72
69007 J72
69851 A8
69856 A8
69868 A8
69870 A8
69872 A8
69875 A8

1954 51F
46470 2MT^2
46473 2MT^2
46479 2MT^2
46482 2MT^2
64756 J39
64778 J39
64848 J39
64940 J39
64982 J39
65061 J21
65062 J21
65078 J21
65088 J21
65091 J21
65092 J21
65097 J21
65662 J25
65696 J25
65697 J25
65706 J25
68145 Y1
68149 Y1
68254 J71
68269 J71
68391 J77
68691 J72
68692 J72
68696 J72
68707 J72
69018 J72
69851 A8
69856 A8
69868 A8
69870 A8
69872 A8
69875 A8
78010 2MT^1
78011 2MT^1

1957 51F
46471 2MT^2
46480 2MT^2
46481 2MT^2
46482 2MT^2
63351 Q6
63459 Q6
64756 J39
64778 J39
64848 J39
64862 J39
64927 J39
64978 J39
64982 J39
65731 J26
65733 J26
65735 J26
68149 Y1
68242 J71
68254 J71
68269 J71
68391 J77
68685 J72

68691 J72
68692 J72
69018 J72
69851 A8
69856 A8
69868 A8
69870 A8
69872 A8
69875 A8
76021 4MT^2
76024 4MT^2
76045 4MT^2
76046 4MT^2
76049 4MT^2
76050 4MT^2
77002 3MT^1
77003 3MT^1
77004 3MT^1

1960 51F

63340 Q6
63351 Q6
63353 Q6
63398 Q6
63403 Q6
63407 Q6
63443 Q6
63446 Q6
63459 Q6
64756 J39
64778 J39
64848 J39
64862 J39
64927 J39
64982 J39
65731 J26
65735 J26
68235 J71
68254 J71
68269 J71
68685 J72
68691 J72
68692 J72
68724 J72
69007 J72
69018 J72
76021 4MT^2
76045 4MT^2
76046 4MT^2
76049 4MT^2
76050 4MT^2
77002 3MT^1
77003 3MT^1
78016 2MT^1

1963 51F

63340 Q6
63341 Q6
63343 Q6
63344 Q6
63347 Q6
63351 Q6
63353 Q6
63355 Q6
63361 Q6
63373 Q6
63374 Q6
63398 Q6
63403 Q6
63407 Q6
63443 Q6
63446 Q6
63459 Q6
76021 4MT^2
76045 4MT^2
76046 4MT^2
76049 4MT^2
76050 4MT^2
77003 3MT^1
78016 2MT^1
78025 2MT^1

West Hartlepool

1948 WHL

62359 D20
62384 D20
62387 D20
63250 Q5
63253 Q5
63256 Q5
63281 Q5
63293 Q5
63294 Q5
63297 Q5
63300 Q5
63303 Q5
63318 Q5
63336 Q5
63348 Q6
63383 Q6
63392 Q6
63395 Q6
63410 Q6
63414 Q6
63421 Q6
63422 Q6
63424 Q6
63427 Q6
63435 Q6
63452 Q6
63454 Q6
63457 Q6
65732 J26
65747 J26
65748 J26
65790 J27
65803 J27
65816 J27
65832 J27
65841 J27
65850 J27
65871 J27
67271 G5
67291 G5
67314 G5
67316 G5
67331 G5
67343 G5
68053 J94
68054 J94
68055 J94
68056 J94
68057 J94
68233 J71
68244 J71
68248 J71
68258 J71
68263 J71
68276 J71
68290 J71
68291 J71
68295 J71
68301 J71
68302 J71
68306 J71
68355 J73
68358 J73
68359 J73
68364 J73
68684 J72
68685 J72
68689 J72
68692 J72
68694 J72
68697 J72
68703 J72
68716 J72
68734 J72
68742 J72
69862 A8
69863 A8
69864 A8
69871 A8
69893 A8

1951 51C

62372 D20
62379 D20
63355 Q6
63383 Q6
63392 Q6
63396 Q6
63397 Q6
63401 Q6
63410 Q6
63414 Q6
63415 Q6
63419 Q6
63421 Q6
63422 Q6
63424 Q6
63427 Q6
63435 Q6
63438 Q6
63452 Q6
63454 Q6
63457 Q6
64862 J39
64916 J39
64978 J39
65747 J26
65748 J26
65782 J27
65790 J27
65803 J27
65816 J27
65818 J27
65820 J27
65846 J27
65866 J27
67271 G5
67272 G5
67294 G5
67314 G5
67331 G5
67343 G5
68042 J94
68053 J94
68054 J94
68055 J94
68056 J94
68057 J94
68233 J71
68244 J71
68248 J71
68258 J71
68263 J71
68276 J71
68290 J71
68291 J71
68295 J71
68301 J71
68302 J71
68306 J71
68355 J73
68358 J73
68359 J73
68364 J73
68683 J72
68684 J72
68685 J72
68692 J72
68694 J72
68697 J72
68703 J72
68711 J72
68716 J72
68734 J72
69852 A8
69862 A8
69863 A8
69871 A8
69893 A8

1954 51C

43055 4MT^5
62359 D20
63383 Q6
63392 Q6
63396 Q6
63397 Q6
63410 Q6
63414 Q6
63415 Q6
63419 Q6
63421 Q6
63422 Q6
63424 Q6
63438 Q6
63454 Q6
63457 Q6
64817 J39
64862 J39
64910 J39
64916 J39
64978 J39
65747 J26
65748 J26
65782 J27
65803 J27
65816 J27
65818 J27
65820 J27
65846 J27
65865 J27
65866 J27
67271 G5
67272 G5
67294 G5
67324 G5
67333 G5
67346 G5
68053 J94
68054 J94
68055 J94
68056 J94
68057 J94
68233 J71
68244 J71
68258 J71
68263 J71
68276 J71
68290 J71
68291 J71
68295 J71
68301 J71
68306 J71
68355 J73
68358 J73
68364 J73
68683 J72
68684 J72
68694 J72
68697 J72
68703 J72
68711 J72
68715 J72
68716 J72
68734 J72
69871 A8
69893 A8

1957 51C

43015 4MT^5
43128 4MT^5
61275 B1
63383 Q6
63392 Q6
63397 Q6
63410 Q6
63414 Q6
63415 Q6
63419 Q6
63421 Q6
63422 Q6
63438 Q6
63454 Q6
63457 Q6
65747 J26
65748 J26
65782 J27
65803 J27
65816 J27
65818 J27
65820 J27
65846 J27
65865 J27
65866 J27
67324 G5
68021 J94
68051 J94
68053 J94
68054 J94
68055 J94
68056 J94
68057 J94
68233 J71
68244 J71
68295 J71
68306 J71
68355 J73
68359 J73
68364 J73
68683 J72
68703 J72
68707 J72
68711 J72
68715 J72
68734 J72
69873 A8
69883 A8
69893 A8
90012 WD^1
90048 WD^1
90067 WD^1
90092 WD^1
90344 WD^1

1960 51C

43015 4MT^5
43053 4MT^5
43100 4MT^5
43128 4MT^5
61061 B1
61267 B1
61275 B1
63383 Q6
63391 Q6
63392 Q6
63397 Q6
63410 Q6
63412 Q6
63414 Q6
63415 Q6
63419 Q6
63421 Q6
63422 Q6
63438 Q6
63440 Q6
63454 Q6
63457 Q6
65782 J27
65805 J27
65818 J27
65820 J27
65830 J27
65846 J27
68021 J94
68051 J94
68053 J94
68054 J94
68055 J94
68056 J94
68057 J94
68233 J71
68316 J71
68364 J73
68410 J77
68683 J72
68698 J72
68703 J72
68707 J72
68711 J72
68715 J72
68722 J72
68734 J72
68951 J50
69880 A8
69894 A8
90067 WD^1
90092 WD^1
90344 WD^1

1963 51C

43015 4MT^5
43053 4MT^5
43100 4MT^5
43123 4MT^5
43128 4MT^5
61257 B1
61275 B1
63380 Q6
63382 Q6
63383 Q6
63391 Q6
63392 Q6
63397 Q6
63410 Q6
63412 Q6
63414 Q6
63415 Q6
63419 Q6
63421 Q6
63422 Q6
63432 Q6
63438 Q6
63440 Q6
63450 Q6
63451 Q6
63454 Q6
68015 J94
68021 J94
68032 J94
68036 J94
68041 J94
68045 J94
68051 J94
68061 J94
69003 J72
69019 J72
69021 J72
90067 WD^1
90092 WD^1
90344 WD^1

1966 51C

43015 4MT^5
43057 4MT^5
43100 4MT^5
43123 4MT^5
62004 K1
63349 Q6
63368 Q6
63394 Q6
63397 Q6
63407 Q6
63410 Q6
63412 Q6
63421 Q6
63435 Q6
63440 Q6
63446 Q6
63450 Q6
63454 Q6
90016 WD^1
90082 WD^1
90230 WD^1
90434 WD^1
90445 WD^1
90459 WD^1
90479 WD^1
90588 WD^1
90593 WD^1

Westbury

1948 WES

1027 1000
2023 2021
2053 2021
2445 2301
2803 2800
2818 2800
2928 2900
2941 2900
2946 2900
3014 ROD
3019 ROD
3032 ROD
3035 ROD
3363 3300
3364 3300
3438 3300
3696 5700
3731 5700
3735 5700
3758 5700
3842 2884
3849 2884
3850 2884
3863 2884
4028 4000
4038 4000
4045 4000
4365 4300
4377 4300
4508 4500
4520 4500
4572 4500
4573 4500
4636 5700
4926 4900
4927 4900
4963 4900
5306 4300
5311 4300
5326 4300
5402 5400
5403 5400
5406 5400
5419 5400
5422 5400
5423 5400
5508 4575
5554 4575
5689 5600
5718 5700
5757 5700
5771 5700
5781 5700
5785 5700
5900 4900
5924 4900
5925 4900
5961 4900
5971 4900
5974 4900
5985 4900
6314 4300
6351 4300
6365 4300
6368 4300
6369 4300
6375 4300
6399 4300
6690 5600
6699 5600
6804 6800
6845 6800
6955 4900
6966 6959
6978 6959
7300 4300
7302 4300
7309 4300
7727 5700
7784 5700
8744 5700
8745 5700
9612 5700
9615 5700
9628 5700
9762 5700

1951 82D

2023 2021
2053 2021
2444 2301
3696 5700
3735 5700
3758 5700
4028 4000
4034 4000
4038 4000
4080 4073
4377 4300
4508 4500
4510 4500
4572 4500
4573 4500
4636 5700
4647 5700
4926 4900
4927 4900
4933 4900
4985 4900
5306 4300
5326 4300
5385 4300
5402 5400
5403 5400
5406 5400
5419 5400
5422 5400
5423 5400
5508 4575
5509 4575
5554 4575
5689 5600
5718 5700
5757 5700
5771 5700
5781 5700
5785 5700
5900 4900
5925 4900
5961 4900
5974 4900
5975 4900
5985 4900
6314 4300
6365 4300
6368 4300
6369 4300
6375 4300
6399 4300
6690 5600
6699 5600
6935 4900
6955 4900
6966 6959
6978 6959
6982 6959
6991 6959
7300 4300
7302 4300
7727 5700
7784 5700
7917 6959
7924 6959
8744 5700
9612 5700
9615 5700
9628 5700
9762 5700
90630 WD^1
90701 WD^1

1954 82D

2340 2301
3696 5700
3735 5700
4377 4300
4536 4500
4551 4500
4572 4500
4607 5700
4636 5700
4647 5700
4927 4900
4930 4900
5338 4300
5358 4300
5385 4300
5402 5400
5403 5400
5406 5400
5419 5400
5422 5400
5423 5400
5508 4575
5554 4575
5689 5600
5701 5700
5718 5700
5757 5700
5767 5700
5771 5700
5974 4900
6358 4300
6365 4300
6399 4300
6625 5600
6699 5600
6914 4900
6922 4900
6935 4900
6955 4900
6991 6959
7300 4300
7302 4300
7727 5700
7748 5700
7784 5700
7917 6959
7924 6959
8479 9400
8744 5700
9612 5700
9615 5700
9628 5700
9762 5700

1957 82D

2208 2251
2268 2251
2811 2800
2827 2800
3614 5700
3696 5700
3735 5700
4536 4500
4551 4500
4572 4500
4607 5700
4636 5700
4647 5700
4917 4900
4930 4900
4945 4900
5338 4300
5358 4300
5385 4300
5402 5400
5403 5400
5406 5400
5419 5400
5422 5400
5423 5400
5508 4575
5554 4575
5689 5600
5701 5700
5718 5700
5757 5700
5767 5700
5771 5700
5963 4900
5974 4900
6320 4300
6338 4300
6358 4300
6399 4300
6625 5600
6822 6800
6914 4900
6955 4900
6994 6959
7300 4300
7302 4300
7727 5700
7748 5700
7784 5700
7917 6959
7924 6959
8479 9400
8744 5700
9612 5700
9615 5700
9628 5700
9762 5700

1960 82D

2268 2251
3212 2251
3614 5700
3629 5700
3696 5700
3735 5700
3819 2884
4567 4500
4607 5700
4636 5700
4647 5700
4917 4900
4933 4900
4945 4900
5358 4300
5410 5400
5416 5400
5508 4575
5526 4575
5542 4575
5689 5600
5757 5700
5904 4900
5935 4900
5963 4900
5974 4900
5975 4900
6320 4300
6625 5600
6951 4900
6955 4900
6994 6959
7300 4300
7302 4300
7727 5700
7748 5700
7784 5700
7909 6959
7917 6959
8479 9400
8482 9400
8744 5700
9612 5700
9615 5700
9628 5700
9668 5700
9762 5700

1963 82D

2268 2251
2273 2251
2886 2884
3629 5700
3735 5700
3787 5700
4157 5101
4174 5101
4607 5700
4636 5700
4956 4900
4972 4900
5410 5400
5416 5400
5689 5600
5963 4900
5974 4900
5986 4900
6319 4300
6353 4300
6356 4300
6955 4900
6977 6959
6999 6959
7332 4300
7917 6959
9612 5700
9628 5700
9674 5700
9769 5700

Westhouses

1948 18B

43235 3F^3
43254 3F^3
43266 3F^3
43331 3F^3
43379 3F^3
43580 3F^3
43850 4F^1
43860 4F^1
43866 4F^1
43867 4F^1
43880 4F^1
43882 4F^1
43966 4F^1
43992 4F^1
44014 4F^1
44130 4F^2
44188 4F^2
44191 4F^2
44321 4F^2
47466 3F^6
48011 8F
48056 8F
48057 8F
48060 8F
48063 8F
48076 8F
48083 8F
48102 8F
48115 8F
48118 8F
48125 8F
48136 8F
48212 8F
48280 8F
48333 8F
48342 8F
48353 8F
48358 8F
48391 8F
48494 8F
48495 8F
48534 8F
48535 8F
48536 8F
48549 8F
48620 8F
48623 8F
48650 8F
48661 8F
58168 2F^8
58169 2F^8
58196 2F^9

1951 18B

43235 3F^3
43253 3F^3
43254 3F^3
43266 3F^3
43317 3F^3
43331 3F^3
43379 3F^3
43580 3F^3
43850 4F^1
43860 4F^1
43866 4F^1
43867 4F^1
43880 4F^1
43885 4F^1
43966 4F^1
43992 4F^1
43998 4F^1
44014 4F^1
44130 4F^2
44188 4F^2
44191 4F^2
44229 4F^2
44321 4F^2
44430 4F^2
44482 4F^2
44605 4F^2
47466 3F^6
48056 8F
48057 8F
48060 8F
48063 8F
48076 8F
48083 8F
48115 8F
48118 8F
48125 8F
48136 8F
48212 8F
48280 8F
48333 8F
48353 8F
48358 8F
48430 8F
48494 8F
48495 8F
48534 8F
48620 8F
48623 8F
48650 8F
48661 8F
58166 2F^8
58168 2F^8
58196 2F^9

1954 18B

43235 3F^3
43253 3F^3
43254 3F^3
43266 3F^3
43317 3F^3
43331 3F^3
43580 3F^3
43850 4F^1
43856 4F^1
43860 4F^1
43866 4F^1
43867 4F^1
43880 4F^1
43885 4F^1
43966 4F^1
43998 4F^1
44014 4F^1
44118 4F^2
44130 4F^2
44173 4F^2
44188 4F^2
44191 4F^2
44229 4F^2
44321 4F^2
44430 4F^2
44482 4F^2
44598 4F^2
44605 4F^2
47466 3F^6
48056 8F
48057 8F
48060 8F
48063 8F
48115 8F
48118 8F
48125 8F
48164 8F
48212 8F
48280 8F
48333 8F
48353 8F
48430 8F
48444 8F
48494 8F
48495 8F
48620 8F
48623 8F
48650 8F
48661 8F
58166 2F^8
58168 2F^8

1957 18B

43193 3F^3
43235 3F^3
43253 3F^3
43266 3F^3
43580 3F^3
43825 3F^4
43850 4F^1
43860 4F^1
43866 4F^1
43880 4F^1
43966 4F^1
43998 4F^1
44014 4F^1
44118 4F^2
44130 4F^2
44150 4F^2
44173 4F^2
44188 4F^2
44191 4F^2
44204 4F^2
44229 4F^2
44233 4F^2
44284 4F^2
44285 4F^2
44321 4F^2
44430 4F^2
44482 4F^2
44598 4F^2
44605 4F^2
47466 3F^6
48056 8F
48057 8F
48060 8F
48063 8F
48112 8F
48115 8F
48118 8F
48125 8F
48139 8F
48280 8F
48333 8F
48353 8F
48494 8F
48495 8F
48620 8F
48623 8F
48650 8F
48661 8F
92113 9F
92114 9F
92115 9F
92116 9F
92117 9F
92118 9F

1960 18B

43266 3F^3
43825 3F^4
43850 4F^1
43982 4F^1
44118 4F^2
44130 4F^2
44154 4F^2
44177 4F^2
44191 4F^2
44229 4F^2
44233 4F^2
44289 4F^2
44321 4F^2
44362 4F^2
44430 4F^2
44598 4F^2
47466 3F^6
48057 8F
48112 8F
48204 8F
48353 8F
48650 8F
48661 8F
90010 WD^1
90152 WD^1
90176 WD^1
90238 WD^1
90251 WD^1
90284 WD^1
90716 WD^1
92113 9F
92114 9F
92115 9F
92116 9F
92117 9F

1963 18B

43850 4F^1
43917 4F^1
44130 4F^2
44191 4F^2
44229 4F^2
44233 4F^2
44244 4F^2
44321 4F^2
44362 4F^2
44387 4F^2
44598 4F^2
47250 3F^5
47638 3F^6
48033 8F
48112 8F
48177 8F
48195 8F
48196 8F
48197 8F
48353 8F
48507 8F
48620 8F
48625 8F
48750 8F
92009 9F
92054 9F
92058 9F
92070 9F
92100 9F
92104 9F
92115 9F
92116 9F
92131 9F

1966 16G

44113 4F^2
44203 4F^2
44218 4F^2
44278 4F^2
47231 3F^5
47534 3F^6
47535 3F^6
47611 3F^6
48046 8F
48073 8F
48127 8F
48143 8F
48149 8F
48177 8F
48195 8F
48196 8F
48204 8F
48214 8F
48219 8F
48286 8F
48376 8F
48538 8F
48600 8F
48619 8F
48620 8F
48638 8F
48644 8F
48763 8F

Weymouth

1948 WEY

1367 1366
1368 1366
1370 1366
1403 1400
1454 1400
1467 1400
1789 655
2817 2800
2912 2900
2955 2900
4527 4500
4562 4500
4655 5700
4660 5700
4988 4900
5305 4300
5314 4300
5328 4300
5337 4300
5338 4300
5340 4300
5359 4300
5384 4300
5509 4575
5968 4900
5969 4900
6945 4900
7408 7400
9642 5700

1951 82F

1367 1366
1368 1366
1370 1366
1453 1400
1454 1400
1467 1400
2912 2900
4507 4500
4520 4500
4527 4500
4562 4500
4930 4900
4988 4900
5305 4300
5314 4300
5328 4300
5337 4300
5338 4300
5359 4300
5384 4300
5968 4900
5978 4900
6902 4900
6912 4900
6945 4900
6988 6959
6993 6959
7408 7400
9620 5700
9642 5700

1954 82F

1367 1366
1370 1366
1403 1400
1453 1400
1467 1400
3692 5700
4150 5101
4562 4500
4988 4900
5190 5101
5314 4300
5337 4300
5384 4300
5781 5700
5978 4900
6902 4900
6945 4900
6988 6959
6993 6959
7408 7400
7421 7400
9620 5700
9642 5700

1957 82F

1367 1366
1368 1366
1370 1366
1403 1400
1453 1400
1467 1400
3737 5700
4133 5101
4166 5101
4507 4500
4562 4500
4624 5700
5314 4300
5384 4300
5964 4900
5978 4900
5997 4900
6919 4900
6945 4900
6967 6959
7782 5700
8799 5700
9601 5700
9620 5700

1960 71G

1367 1366
1368 1366
1370 1366
1453 1400
1474 1400
3737 5700
3759 5700
4133 5101
4166 5101
4507 4500
4562 4500
4624 5700
4689 5700
5384 4300
6344 4300
7303 4300
7780 5700
7782 5700
8799 5700
9620 5700
73017 5MT
73018 5MT
73020 5MT
73022 5MT
73029 5MT
73041 5MT
73042 5MT
73080 5MT

1963 71G

3633 5700
3737 5700
3759 5700
4616 5700
4624 5700
4689 5700
7780 5700
7782 5700
9620 5700
31405 N
31407 N
73017 5MT
73018 5MT
73020 5MT
73022 5MT
73029 5MT
73041 5MT

73042 5MT
73080 5MT

1966 70G
35007 MN R
35012 MN R
35014 MN R
35017 MN R
35022 MN R
35026 MN R
35028 MN R
35029 MN R
35030 MN R
41284 2MT[1]
41298 2MT[1]
41301 2MT[1]
73002 5MT
73016 5MT
73018 5MT
73020 5MT
73080 5MT
73083 5MT
73113 5MT
73114 5MT

Whitby

1948 WBY
65609 J24
65612 J24
65629 J24
67262 G5
67293 G5
67302 G5
67308 G5
67335 G5
69792 A6
69852 A8
2136 Railcar

1951 50G
65857 J27
65887 J27
67302 G5
67335 G5
69858 A8
69860 A8
69861 A8
69864 A8
69865 A8
69888 A8
69890 A8

1954 50G
65647 J25
65663 J25
65690 J25
67240 G5
67302 G5
69858 A8
69860 A8
69861 A8
69864 A8
69865 A8
69888 A8
69890 A8

1957 50G
42083 4MT[1]
65663 J25
69864 A8
69865 A8
69890 A8
77012 3MT[1]
77013 3MT[1]
78012 2MT[1]
80116 4MT[3]
80117 4MT[3]
80118 4MT[3]
80119 4MT[3]
80120 4MT[3]

Whitland

1948 WTD
1964 1901
1979 1901
1996 1901
2010 1901
2011 1901
2013 1901
2018 1901
2288 2251
4506 4500
4515 4500
4519 4500
4553 4500
4556 4500
4576 4575
4579 4575
5513 4575
5549 4575
5568 4575
7417 7400
8102 8100
8107 8100

Wick

1951 60D
54398 2P[11]
54399 2P[11]
54445 3P[5]
57585 3F[12]
57622 3F[12]

1954 60D
54459 3P[5]
54491 3P[6]
55236 2P[13]
57585 3F[12]

1957 60D
40150 3MT[2]
54439 3P[5]
54491 3P[6]
57585 3F[12]

1960 60D
40150 3MT[2]
54491 3P[6]
55236 2P[13]
57585 3F[12]

Widnes

1948 8D
40527 2P[2]
48907 7F[2]
48939 6F[2]
49020 7F[2]
49038 6F[2]
49058 6F[2]
49067 6F[2]
49071 6F[2]
49073 7F[2]
49074 7F[2]
49079 7F[2]
49170 7F[2]
58327 2F[10]
58342 2F[10]
58346 2F[10]
58351 2F[10]
58353 2F[10]
58377 2F[11]
58383 2F[11]
58393 2F[11]
58402 2F[11]
58420 2F[11]
58424 2F[11]
28095 2F[10]

1951 8D
40125 3MT[2]
46420 2MT[2]
46421 2MT[2]
46422 2MT[2]
46423 2MT[2]
46424 2MT[2]
46434 2MT[2]
48462 8F
48554 8F
48558 8F
48708 8F
48753 8F
48764 8F
48771 8F
48772 8F
49020 7F[2]
49073 7F[2]
49079 7F[2]
49116 7F[2]
49343 7F[2]
58363 2F[11]
58383 2F[11]
58393 2F[11]
58413 2F[11]
58415 2F[11]
58430 2F[11]
68547 J67

1954 8D
40134 3MT[2]
40137 3MT[2]
40201 3MT[2]
46420 2MT[2]
46421 2MT[2]
46422 2MT[2]
46423 2MT[2]
46424 2MT[2]
48017 8F
48462 8F
48554 8F
48558 8F
48720 8F
48753 8F
48771 8F
49073 7F[2]
49079 7F[2]
49081 7F[2]
49116 7F[2]
49126 7F[2]
49343 7F[2]
49416 7F[3]
58394 2F[11]
58413 2F[11]
58400 2F[11]

1957 8D
40134 3MT[2]
40137 3MT[2]
40201 3MT[2]
47490 3F[6]
47616 3F[6]
48017 8F
48462 8F
48554 8F
48558 8F
48720 8F
48753 8F
48771 8F
49079 7F[2]
49081 7F[2]
49116 7F[2]
49126 7F[2]
49343 7F[2]
49366 7F[2]
49416 7F[3]
51204 0F[4]
65157 J10
65184 J10
65198 J10
78032 2MT[1]
78033 2MT[1]
78034 2MT[1]
78035 2MT[1]
78039 2MT[1]

1960 8D
40118 3MT[2]
40134 3MT[2]
40137 3MT[2]
40143 3MT[2]
40201 3MT[2]
47490 3F[6]
47601 3F[6]
47616 3F[6]
48206 8F
48308 8F
48326 8F
48425 8F
48502 8F
48554 8F
48558 8F
48709 8F
78032 2MT[1]
78033 2MT[1]
78034 2MT[1]
78035 2MT[1]
78039 2MT[1]
90157 WD[1]
90178 WD[1]
90242 WD[1]
90423 WD[1]

1963 8D
47349 3F[6]
47616 3F[6]
48129 8F
48136 8F
48139 8F
48296 8F
48308 8F
48709 8F
78035 2MT[1]
78039 2MT[1]
90147 WD[1]
90157 WD[1]
90192 WD[1]
90242 WD[1]
90423 WD[1]

Wigan

1948 23D
40678 2P[3]
40679 2P[3]
40680 2P[3]
42362 4MT[2]
42381 4MT[2]
42472 4MT[3]
42537 4MT[3]
42554 4MT[3]
42557 4MT[3]
42569 4MT[3]
42592 4MT[3]
42614 4MT[3]
42631 4MT[3]
42632 4MT[3]
42640 4MT[3]
42641 4MT[3]
42642 4MT[3]
50692 2P[8]
50757 2P[8]
50844 2P[8]
50887 2P[8]
52093 3F[7]
52152 3F[7]
52169 3F[7]
52189 3F[7]
52290 3F[7]
52312 3F[7]
52360 3F[7]
52413 3F[7]
52588 3F[9]
52598 3F[9]
52602 3F[9]
52727 6F[3]
52806 6F[3]
52827 6F[3]
52828 6F[3]
52834 6F[3]
52837 6F[3]
52839 6F[3]

1951 27D
40199 3MT[2]
40580 2P[3]
40587 2P[3]
40678 2P[3]
40684 2P[3]
41101 4P[1]
41102 4P[1]
42180 4MT[1]
42297 4MT[1]
42299 4MT[1]
42537 4MT[3]
42554 4MT[3]
42557 4MT[3]
42569 4MT[3]
42592 4MT[3]
42614 4MT[3]
42631 4MT[3]
42632 4MT[3]
42640 4MT[3]
42641 4MT[3]
42642 4MT[3]
42644 4MT[3]
49568 7F[4]
49585 7F[4]
49587 7F[4]
49610 7F[4]
49612 7F[4]
49625 7F[4]
49638 7F[4]
49659 7F[4]
51474 2F[2]
52169 3F[7]
52197 3F[7]
52288 3F[7]
52360 3F[7]
52379 3F[7]
52390 3F[7]
52413 3F[7]
52450 3F[7]
52549 3F[9]
52616 3F[9]
52831 6F[3]
52870 7F[5]
52945 7F[5]

1954 27D
40199 3MT[2]
40587 2P[3]
40680 2P[3]
42180 4MT[1]
42297 4MT[1]
42299 4MT[1]
42537 4MT[3]
42554 4MT[3]
42557 4MT[3]
42569 4MT[3]
42592 4MT[3]
42614 4MT[3]
42631 4MT[3]
42632 4MT[3]
42640 4MT[3]
42641 4MT[3]
42642 4MT[3]
42644 4MT[3]
43952 4F[1]
44105 4F[2]
44220 4F[2]
44221 4F[2]
44225 4F[2]
44240 4F[2]
44291 4F[2]
44464 4F[2]
44544 4F[2]
49592 7F[4]
49598 7F[4]
51474 2F[2]
52095 3F[7]
52197 3F[7]
52275 3F[7]
52289 3F[7]
52387 3F[7]
52450 3F[7]
90121 WD[1]
90570 WD[1]
90671 WD[1]

1957 27D
40199 3MT[2]
40587 2P[3]
40680 2P[3]
42180 4MT[1]
42297 4MT[1]
42299 4MT[1]
42473 4MT[3]
42554 4MT[3]
42557 4MT[3]
42569 4MT[3]
42592 4MT[3]
42614 4MT[3]
42631 4MT[3]
42632 4MT[3]
42640 4MT[3]
42641 4MT[3]
42642 4MT[3]
42644 4MT[3]
43952 4F[1]
44105 4F[2]
44220 4F[2]
44221 4F[2]
44225 4F[2]
44240 4F[2]
44464 4F[2]
44486 4F[2]
44544 4F[2]
49598 7F[4]
49637 7F[4]
51474 2F[2]
78060 2MT[1]
78061 2MT[1]
78062 2MT[1]
78063 2MT[1]
78064 2MT[1]
90121 WD[1]
90570 WD[1]
90584 WD[1]
90599 WD[1]
90671 WD[1]

1960 27D
40199 3MT[2]
40681 2P[3]
42180 4MT[1]
42297 4MT[1]
42299 4MT[1]
42473 4MT[3]
42475 4MT[3]
42554 4MT[3]
42557 4MT[3]
42569 4MT[3]
42592 4MT[3]
42614 4MT[3]
42621 4MT[3]
42631 4MT[3]
42632 4MT[3]
42640 4MT[3]
42641 4MT[3]
42642 4MT[3]
42644 4MT[3]
43952 4F[1]
44221 4F[2]
44240 4F[2]
44464 4F[2]
44486 4F[2]
44544 4F[2]
49637 7F[4]
78040 2MT[1]
78060 2MT[1]
78061 2MT[1]
78062 2MT[1]
78063 2MT[1]
78064 2MT[1]
90121 WD[1]
90561 WD[1]
90570 WD[1]
90599 WD[1]

1963 27D
42180 4MT[1]
42297 4MT[1]
42299 4MT[1]
42494 4MT[3]
42554 4MT[3]
42555 4MT[3]
42557 4MT[3]
42569 4MT[3]
42592 4MT[3]
42631 4MT[3]
42644 4MT[3]
42711 5MT[1]
42715 5MT[1]
42721 5MT[1]
42731 5MT[1]
42734 5MT[1]
42794 5MT[1]
42821 5MT[1]
44222 4F[2]
44240 4F[2]
44464 4F[2]
44486 4F[2]
44544 4F[2]
78061 2MT[1]
78062 2MT[1]
78063 2MT[1]
78064 2MT[1]

Wigan Lower Ince

1948 WIG
65128 J10
65151 J10
65159 J10
65162 J10
65170 J10
65173 J10
65175 J10
65176 J10
65189 J10
65196 J10
65199 J10
65203 J10
65208 J10

1951 10F
65131 J10
65148 J10
65159 J10
65162 J10
65164 J10
65170 J10
65173 J10
65175 J10
65176 J10
65189 J10
65196 J10
65199 J10
65203 J10

Wigan Springs Branch

1948 10A
40397 2P[2]
40561 2P[2]
42303 4MT[2]
42379 4MT[2]
42455 4MT[3]
42456 4MT[3]
42465 4MT[3]
42539 4MT[3]
42563 4MT[3]
42572 4MT[3]
42588 4MT[3]
44892 5MT[3]
45019 5MT[3]
45030 5MT[3]
45141 5MT[3]
45413 5MT[3]
45425 5MT[3]
45449 5MT[3]
47885 6F[1]
47888 6F[1]
47896 6F[1]
48824 4F[3]
48834 4F[3]
48930 7F[2]
49014 7F[2]
49023 7F[2]
49024 7F[2]
49026 7F[2]
49029 7F[2]
49030 6F[2]
49043 6F[2]
49053 6F[2]
49090 7F[2]
49124 6F[2]
49125 7F[2]
49129 7F[2]
49134 7F[2]
49141 7F[2]
49149 7F[2]
49159 6F[2]
49176 7F[2]
49192 7F[2]
49197 6F[2]
49207 7F[2]
49221 6F[2]
49257 7F[2]
49306 7F[2]
49310 7F[2]
49311 7F[2]
49422 7F[3]
49424 7F[3]
52021 2F[3]
52022 2F[3]
52023 2F[3]
52024 2F[3]
52032 2F[3]
52045 2F[3]
52053 2F[3]
52063 2F[3]
52064 2F[3]
52172 3F[7]
52208 3F[7]
52269 3F[7]
58373 2F[11]
58376 2F[11]
58381 2F[11]
58422 2F[11]
58901 2F[14]

1951 10A
42266 4MT[1]
42442 4MT[3]
42453 4MT[3]
42454 4MT[3]
42456 4MT[3]
42465 4MT[3]
42539 4MT[3]
42563 4MT[3]
42572 4MT[3]
42610 4MT[3]
45019 5MT[3]
45020 5MT[3]
45141 5MT[3]
45235 5MT[3]
45289 5MT[3]
45313 5MT[3]
45413 5MT[3]
45425 5MT[3]
45449 5MT[3]
47877 6F[1]
47881 6F[1]
47884 6F[1]
48895 7F[2]
48964 7F[2]
49018 7F[2]
49023 7F[2]
49030 6F[2]
49092 6F[2]
49129 7F[2]
49163 7F[2]
49228 7F[2]
49264 7F[2]
49268 7F[2]
49306 7F[2]
49310 7F[2]
49311 7F[2]
49341 7F[2]
49352 7F[2]
49378 7F[2]
49381 7F[2]
49393 7F[2]
49402 7F[3]
49408 7F[3]
52021 2F[3]
52045 2F[3]
52051 2F[3]
52053 2F[3]
52098 3F[7]
52107 3F[7]
52126 3F[7]
52250 3F[7]
52341 3F[7]
58368 2F[11]

1954 10A
42266 4MT[1]
42442 4MT[3]
42453 4MT[3]
42454 4MT[3]
42456 4MT[3]
42462 4MT[3]
42465 4MT[3]
42539 4MT[3]
42572 4MT[3]
42610 4MT[3]
42663 4MT[3]
42666 4MT[3]
45004 5MT[3]
45026 5MT[3]
45055 5MT[3]
45135 5MT[3]
45289 5MT[3]
45313 5MT[3]
45314 5MT[3]
45408 5MT[3]
45425 5MT[3]
45449 5MT[3]
45454 5MT[3]
46428 2MT[2]
46432 2MT[2]
46434 2MT[2]
46489 2MT[2]
48895 7F[7]
49007 7F[2]
49018 7F[2]
49023 7F[2]
49025 7F[2]
49129 7F[2]
49154 7F[2]
49160 7F[2]
49228 7F[2]
49268 7F[2]
49306 7F[2]
49311 7F[2]
49322 7F[2]
49341 7F[2]
49352 7F[2]
49378 7F[2]
49381 7F[2]
49385 7F[2]
49393 7F[2]
49401 7F[3]
49402 7F[3]
49408 7F[3]
49436 7F[3]
52021 2F[3]
52051 2F[3]
52118 3F[7]
52143 3F[7]
52322 3F[7]
52341 3F[7]
52449 3F[7]
52551 3F[9]
65148 J10
65159 J10
65162 J10
65173 J10
65175 J10
65176 J10
65199 J10
65203 J10

1957 10A
42454 4MT[3]
42456 4MT[3]
42462 4MT[3]
42465 4MT[3]
42539 4MT[3]
42572 4MT[3]
42663 4MT[3]
42666 4MT[3]
45026 5MT[3]
45057 5MT[3]
45135 5MT[3]
45313 5MT[3]
45314 5MT[3]
45347 5MT[3]
45408 5MT[3]
45425 5MT[3]
45449 5MT[3]
45454 5MT[3]
46422 2MT[2]
46428 2MT[2]
46434 2MT[2]
46448 2MT[2]
48895 7F[2]
48915 7F[2]
49007 7F[2]
49018 7F[2]
49023 7F[2]
49073 7F[2]
49093 7F[2]
49129 7F[2]
49144 7F[2]
49145 7F[2]
49154 7F[2]
49155 7F[2]
49160 7F[2]
49203 7F[2]
49228 7F[2]
49268 7F[2]
49306 7F[2]
49311 7F[2]
49315 7F[2]
49341 7F[2]
49352 7F[2]
49378 7F[2]
49381 7F[2]
49385 7F[2]
49393 7F[2]
49401 7F[3]
49402 7F[3]
49408 7F[3]
49436 7F[3]
52143 3F[7]
52393 3F[7]
52449 3F[7]
52551 3F[9]
65131 J10
65138 J10
65140 J10
65146 J10
65156 J10
65159 J10
65170 J10
65175 J10
65199 J10

1960 8F
42235 4MT[1]
42456 4MT[3]
42462 4MT[3]
42465 4MT[3]
42471 4MT[3]
42571 4MT[3]
42572 4MT[3]
44069 4F[2]
44280 4F[2]
44303 4F[2]
44438 4F[2]
44758 5MT[3]
44780 5MT[3]
45017 5MT[3]
45019 5MT[3]
45026 5MT[3]
45057 5MT[3]
45092 5MT[3]
45108 5MT[3]
45109 5MT[3]
45135 5MT[3]
45313 5MT[3]
45314 5MT[3]
45340 5MT[3]
45347 5MT[3]
45372 5MT[3]
45373 5MT[3]
45408 5MT[3]
45425 5MT[3]
45431 5MT[3]
45449 5MT[3]
46422 2MT[2]
46428 2MT[2]
46434 2MT[2]
46447 2MT[2]
46448 2MT[2]
48895 7F[2]
48915 7F[2]
48942 7F[2]
49007 7F[2]
49008 7F[2]
49020 7F[2]
49023 7F[2]
49025 7F[2]
49049 7F[2]
49129 7F[2]
49139 7F[2]
49141 7F[2]
49154 7F[2]
49155 7F[2]
49267 7F[2]
49321 7F[2]
49381 7F[2]
49401 7F[3]
49402 7F[3]
49408 7F[3]
49422 7F[3]
49438 7F[3]
49451 7F[3]
58120 2F[8]
58123 2F[8]
65157 J10
65192 J10
65198 J10
90509 WD[1]
90667 WD[1]

1963 8F
42235 4MT[1]
42327 4MT[2]
42426 4MT[3]
42456 4MT[3]
42462 4MT[3]
42465 4MT[3]
42572 4MT[3]
42607 4MT[3]
42664 4MT[3]
42751 5MT[1]
42777 5MT[1]
42894 5MT[1]
44069 4F[2]
44076 4F[2]
44121 4F[2]
44125 4F[2]
44246 4F[2]
44280 4F[2]
44301 4F[2]
44303 4F[2]
44444 4F[2]
44490 4F[2]
44492 4F[2]
44514 4F[2]
45017 5MT[3]
45019 5MT[3]
45024 5MT[3]
45026 5MT[3]
45055 5MT[3]
45057 5MT[3]
45070 5MT[3]
45073 5MT[3]
45108 5MT[3]
45109 5MT[3]
45135 5MT[3]
45140 5MT[3]
45188 5MT[3]
45278 5MT[3]
45281 5MT[3]
45313 5MT[3]
45314 5MT[3]
45347 5MT[3]
45372 5MT[3]
45373 5MT[3]
45388 5MT[3]
45408 5MT[3]
45425 5MT[3]
45431 5MT[3]
45449 5MT[3]
45521 7P[1]
46168 7P[3]R
47314 3F[6]
47395 3F[6]
47444 3F[6]
47493 3F[6]
47517 3F[0]
47603 3F[6]
47671 3F[6]
90148 WD[1]
90257 WD[1]
90261 WD[1]
90268 WD[1]
90317 WD[1]
90440 WD[1]
90493 WD[1]
90507 WD[1]
90509 WD[1]
90574 WD[1]
90585 WD[1]
90667 WD[1]
90686 WD[1]

1966 8F
42102 4MT[1]
42235 4MT[1]
42462 4MT[3]
42577 4MT[3]
42587 4MT[3]
42611 4MT[3]
42647 4MT[3]
42953 5MT[2]
42954 5MT[2]
42963 5MT[2]
44873 5MT[3]
45019 5MT[3]
45024 5MT[3]
45091 5MT[3]
45128 5MT[3]
45140 5MT[3]
45278 5MT[3]
45281 5MT[3]
45296 5MT[3]
45305 5MT[3]
45321 5MT[3]
45372 5MT[3]
45385 5MT[3]
45408 5MT[3]
45425 5MT[3]
45431 5MT[3]
45449 5MT[3]
46419 2MT[2]
46447 2MT[2]
46487 2MT[2]
46517 2MT[2]
47314 3F[6]
47444 3F[6]
47603 3F[6]
47671 3F[6]
48114 8F
48125 8F
48187 8F
48221 8F
48261 8F
48275 8F
48278 8F
48379 8F
48494 8F
48675 8F
48715 8F
48764 8F

Willesden

1948 1A
42316 4MT[2]
42372 4MT[2]
42443 4MT[3]
42747 5MT[1]
42786 5MT[1]
42787 5MT[1]
42812 5MT[1]
42817 5MT[1]
42870 5MT[1]
42885 5MT[1]
42931 5MT[1]
42940 5MT[1]
44116 4F[2]
44208 4F[2]
44348 4F[2]
44370 4F[2]
44372 4F[2]
44381 4F[2]
44397 4F[2]
44440 4F[2]
44441 4F[2]
44442 4F[2]
44451 4F[2]
44497 4F[2]
44507 4F[2]
45024 5MT[3]
45027 5MT[3]
45070 5MT[3]
45071 5MT[3]
45140 5MT[3]
45310 5MT[3]
45353 5MT[3]
45431 5MT[3]
45509 6P5F[1]
45510 6P5F[1]
45525 6P5F[1]
45591 6P5F[2]
45625 6P5F[2]
45721 6P5F[2]
45739 6P5F[2]
47281 3F[6]
47327 3F[6]
47342 3F[6]
47355 3F[6]
47357 3F[6]
47361 3F[6]
47362 3F[6]
47380 3F[6]
47395 3F[6]
47412 3F[6]
47430 3F[6]
47474 3F[6]
47475 3F[6]
47520 3F[6]
47531 3F[6]
47675 3F[6]
47676 3F[6]
48171 8F
48172 8F
48173 8F
48174 8F
48278 8F
48368 8F
48372 8F
48433 8F
48438 8F
48476 8F
48554 8F
48600 8F
48601 8F
48602 8F
48603 8F
48605 8F
48610 8F
48612 8F
48624 8F
48626 8F
48628 8F
48629 8F
48630 8F
48632 8F
48633 8F
48634 8F
48648 8F
48656 8F
48657 8F
48658 8F
48660 8F
48679 8F
48684 8F
48943 7F[2]
48953 7F[2]
49012 6F[2]
49021 7F[2]
49041 7F[2]
49062 7F[2]
49128 6F[2]
49139 7F[2]
49163 7F[2]
49164 7F[2]
49277 7F[2]
49334 6F[2]
49393 7F[2]
49398 7F[3]
49438 7F[3]
49448 7F[3]
49453 7F[3]
49454 7F[3]
58257 2F[9]
58277 2F[9]
58278 2F[9]
58279 2F[9]
58280 2F[9]
58281 2F[9]
58283 2F[9]
58285 2F[9]
58286 2F[9]
58287 2F[9]
58290 2F[9]
58291 2F[9]
58295 2F[9]
58302 2F[9]
58303 2F[9]
58306 2F[9]
58307 2F[9]
58309 2F[9]
3473 2F[9]

1951 1A
40004 3MT[1]
40006 3MT[1]
40009 3MT[1]
40017 3MT[1]
40018 3MT[1]
40044 3MT[1]
40046 3MT[1]
40050 3MT[1]
40052 3MT[1]
40054 3MT[1]
40055 3MT[1]
40073 3MT[2]
40081 3MT[2]
40087 3MT[2]
40109 3MT[2]
40135 3MT[2]
40204 3MT[2]
40206 3MT[2]
42117 4MT[1]
42118 4MT[1]
42316 4MT[2]
42747 5MT[1]
42787 5MT[1]
42812 5MT[1]
42817 5MT[1]
42870 5MT[1]
42885 5MT[1]
42931 5MT[1]
42940 5MT[1]
44116 4F[2]
44208 4F[2]
44372 4F[2]
44381 4F[2]
44442 4F[2]
44451 4F[2]
44497 4F[2]
44875 5MT[3]
45024 5MT[3]
45025 5MT[3]
45027 5MT[3]
45064 5MT[3]
45071 5MT[3]
45089 5MT[3]
45092 5MT[3]
45097 5MT[3]
45140 5MT[3]
45146 5MT[3]
45374 5MT[3]
45509 6P5F[1]
45546 6P5F[1]
45591 6P5F[2]
45625 6P5F[2]
46431 2MT[2]
46432 2MT[2]
46433 2MT[2]
47342 3F[6]
47361 3F[6]
47380 3F[6]
47412 3F[6]
47430 3F[6]
47474 3F[6]
47475 3F[6]
47491 3F[6]
47505 3F[6]
47520 3F[6]
47531 3F[6]
47675 3F[6]
47676 3F[6]
48036 8F
48122 8F
48129 8F
48147 8F
48171 8F
48174 8F
48310 8F
48312 8F
48325 8F
48368 8F
48416 8F
48433 8F
48476 8F
48518 8F
48551 8F
48600 8F
48601 8F
48602 8F
48603 8F
48610 8F
48624 8F
48626 8F
48628 8F
48629 8F
48632 8F
48634 8F
48648 8F
48649 8F
48656 8F
48657 8F
48658 8F
48659 8F
48665 8F
48679 8F
48758 8F
49021 7F[2]
49062 7F[2]
49117 7F[2]
49122 7F[2]
49139 7F[2]
49164 7F[2]
49275 7F[2]
49277 7F[2]
49296 7F[2]
49342 7F[2]
49344 7F[2]

1954 1A
40001 3MT[1]
40002 3MT[1]
40004 3MT[1]
40006 3MT[1]
40007 3MT[1]
40016 3MT[1]
40018 3MT[1]
40019 3MT[1]
40042 3MT[1]
40044 3MT[1]
40045 3MT[1]
40046 3MT[1]
40047 3MT[1]
40049 3MT[1]
40050 3MT[1]
40051 3MT[1]
40052 3MT[1]
40053 3MT[1]
40054 3MT[1]
40055 3MT[1]
40066 3MT[1]
40068 3MT[1]
40069 3MT[1]
42117 4MT[1]
42118 4MT[1]
42316 4MT[2]
42747 5MT[1]
42787 5MT[1]
42812 5MT[1]
42870 5MT[1]
42885 5MT[1]
42931 5MT[1]
44116 4F[2]
44208 4F[2]
44370 4F[2]
44372 4F[2]
44381 4F[2]
44397 4F[2]
44440 4F[2]
44442 4F[2]
44451 4F[2]
44497 4F[2]

44771 5MT^3
44838 5MT^3
44869 5MT^3
44875 5MT^3
44916 5MT^3
45003 5MT^3
45024 5MT^3
45025 5MT^3
45027 5MT^3
45064 5MT^3
45089 5MT^3
45097 5MT^3
45350 5MT^3
45374 5MT^3
45387 5MT^3
45404 5MT^3
45511 6P5F^1
45517 6P5F^1
45546 6P5F^1
45591 6P5F^2
45625 6P5F^2
46431 2MT^2
46433 2MT^2
47342 3F^6
47361 3F^6
47378 3F^6
47380 3F^6
47412 3F^6
47474 3F^6
47475 3F^6
47491 3F^6
47492 3F^6
47505 3F^6
47520 3F^6
47531 3F^6
47675 3F^6
47676 3F^6
48036 8F
48074 8F
48122 8F
48129 8F
48134 8F
48147 8F
48171 8F
48174 8F
48290 8F
48312 8F
48325 8F
48368 8F
48416 8F
48433 8F
48440 8F
48476 8F
48518 8F
48551 8F
48600 8F
48601 8F
48603 8F
48610 8F
48624 8F
48626 8F
48628 8F
48629 8F
48632 8F
48634 8F
48648 8F
48649 8F
48656 8F
48657 8F
48658 8F
48659 8F
48665 8F
48679 8F
49070 7F^2
49078 7F^2
49088 7F^2
49122 7F^2
49139 7F^2
49164 7F^2
49180 7F^2
49275 7F^2
49277 7F^2
49344 7F^2

1957 1A
40006 3MT^1
40007 3MT^1
40016 3MT^1
40019 3MT^1
40042 3MT^1
40044 3MT^1
40046 3MT^1
40047 3MT^1
40049 3MT^1
40050 3MT^1
40051 3MT^1
40053 3MT^1
40054 3MT^1
40064 3MT^1
40066 3MT^1
40068 3MT^1
40125 3MT^2
42117 4MT^1
42118 4MT^1
42487 4MT^3
42787 5MT^1
42812 5MT^1
42852 5MT^1
42870 5MT^1
42885 5MT^1
42931 5MT^1
42937 5MT^1
44067 4F^2
44116 4F^2
44208 4F^2
44370 4F^2
44372 4F^2
44397 4F^2
44440 4F^2
44451 4F^2
44473 4F^2
44491 4F^2
44492 4F^2
44497 4F^2
44713 5MT^3
44771 5MT^3
44838 5MT^3
44869 5MT^3
44875 5MT^3
44916 5MT^3
45024 5MT^3
45025 5MT^3
45027 5MT^3
45064 5MT^3
45089 5MT^3
45147 5MT^3
45187 5MT^3
45278 5MT^3
45288 5MT^3
45324 5MT^3
45350 5MT^3
45372 5MT^3
45374 5MT^3
45375 5MT^3
45381 5MT^3
45387 5MT^3
45404 5MT^3
45430 5MT^3
45510 6P5F^1
45511 6P5F^1
45517 6P5F^1
45547 6P5F^1
45603 6P5F^2
45740 6P5F^2
46424 2MT^2
46431 2MT^2
46458 2MT^2
47342 3F^6
47361 3F^6
47378 3F^6
47380 3F^6
47412 3F^6
47474 3F^6
47475 3F^6
47492 3F^6
47505 3F^6
47520 3F^6
47531 3F^6
47675 3F^6
47676 3F^6
48036 8F
48074 8F
48122 8F
48129 8F
48134 8F
48171 8F
48290 8F
48325 8F
48416 8F
48440 8F
48476 8F
48518 8F
48551 8F
48600 8F
48601 8F
48603 8F
48610 8F
48624 8F
48628 8F
48629 8F
48632 8F
48648 8F
48649 8F
48656 8F
48657 8F
48659 8F
48665 8F
48729 8F
49070 7F^2
49078 7F^2
49088 7F^2
49122 7F^2
49139 7F^2
49164 7F^2
49180 7F^2
49277 7F^2
49344 7F^2
80092 4MT^3

1960 1A
40003 3MT^1
40007 3MT^1
40010 3MT^1
40016 3MT^1
40042 3MT^1
40049 3MT^1
40051 3MT^1
40070 3MT^1
42068 4MT^1
42070 4MT^1
42074 4MT^1
42075 4MT^1
42076 4MT^1
42079 4MT^1
42117 4MT^1
42118 4MT^1
42234 4MT^1
42350 4MT^2
42351 4MT^2
42360 4MT^2
42366 4MT^2
42367 4MT^2
42368 4MT^2
42422 4MT^2
42430 4MT^2
42459 4MT^3
42463 4MT^3
42538 4MT^3
42576 4MT^3
42579 4MT^3
42583 4MT^3
42585 4MT^3
42586 4MT^3
42604 4MT^3
42611 4MT^3
42616 4MT^3
42627 4MT^3
42673 4MT^1
42747 5MT^1
42785 5MT^1
42812 5MT^1
42852 5MT^1
42859 5MT^1
42870 5MT^1
42885 5MT^1
42931 5MT^1
42944 5MT^1
44208 4F^2
44340 4F^2
44451 4F^2
44497 4F^2
44838 5MT^3
44869 5MT^3
44875 5MT^3
44916 5MT^3
45024 5MT^3
45027 5MT^3
45064 5MT^3
45146 5MT^3
45187 5MT^3
45278 5MT^3
45288 5MT^3
45324 5MT^3
45350 5MT^3
45374 5MT^3
45375 5MT^3
45381 5MT^3
45387 5MT^3
45404 5MT^3
45538 6P5F^1
45547 6P5F^1
45599 6P5F^2
45601 6P5F^2
45603 6P5F^2
45624 6P5F^2
45669 6P5F^2
45722 6P5F^2
45740 6P5F^2
46424 2MT^2
46458 2MT^2
47302 3F^6
47304 3F^6
47380 3F^6
47482 3F^6
47483 3F^6
47486 3F^6
47501 3F^6
47559 3F^6
48036 8F
48122 8F
48129 8F
48134 8F
48171 8F
48325 8F
48335 8F
48416 8F
48440 8F
48476 8F
48518 8F
48551 8F
48600 8F
48601 8F
48603 8F
48624 8F
48628 8F
48629 8F
48648 8F
48649 8F
48656 8F
48657 8F
48665 8F
49070 7F^2
49078 7F^2
49122 7F^2
49164 7F^2
49344 7F^2
49413 7F^3

1963 1A
42068 4MT^1
42071 4MT^1
42077 4MT^1
42099 4MT^1
42101 4MT^1
42118 4MT^1
42182 4MT^1
42218 4MT^1
42221 4MT^1
42234 4MT^1
42350 4MT^2
42430 4MT^3
42478 4MT^3
42562 4MT^3
42566 4MT^3
42573 4MT^3
42577 4MT^3
42581 4MT^3
42604 4MT^3
42611 4MT^3
44844 5MT^3
45020 5MT^3
45037 5MT^3
45044 5MT^3
45111 5MT^3
45198 5MT^3
45276 5MT^3
45288 5MT^3
45301 5MT^3
45305 5MT^3
45427 5MT^3
45434 5MT^3
45523 7P^1
45528 7P^1
45529 7P^1
45530 7P^1
45735 7P^2
46101 7P^{3}R
46111 7P^{3}R
46163 7P^{3}R
46169 7P^{3}R
46424 2MT^2
46472 2MT^2
47307 3F^6
47341 3F^6
47501 3F^6
48036 8F
48077 8F
48134 8F
48171 8F
48247 8F
48252 8F
48325 8F
48335 8F
48368 8F
48416 8F
48435 8F
48440 8F
48445 8F
48479 8F
48493 8F
48506 8F
48518 8F
48531 8F
48551 8F
48600 8F
48601 8F
48603 8F
48624 8F
48628 8F
48629 8F
48632 8F
48649 8F
48665 8F
70004 7P6F
70021 7P6F
70032 7P6F
70042 7P6F
73004 5MT
73013 5MT
73014 5MT
73033 5MT
73039 5MT
75030 4MT^1
75052 4MT^1

1966 1A
48010 8F

Wolverton Works

1948
CD3 2F^{15}
CD6 2F^{15}
CD7 2F^{15}
CD8 2F^{15}

1951
CD3 2F^{15}
CD6 2F^{15}
CD7 2F^{15}
CD8 2F^{15}

1954
CD3 2F^{15}
CD6 2F^{15}
CD7 2F^{15}
CD8 2F^{15}

1957
CD3 2F^{15}
CD6 2F^{15}
CD7 2F^{15}
CD8 2F^{15}

1960
40006 3MT^1
47286 3F^6
47478 3F^6
47479 3F^6
47500 3F^6

1963
47294 3F^6
47318 3F^6
47385 3F^6

1966
47318 3F^6
47341 3F^6
47396 3F^6
47435 3F^6

Woodford Halse

1948 WFD
61063 B1
61066 B1
61078 B1
61087 B1
61088 B1
61108 B1
61131 B1
61141 B1
61829 K3
61839 K3
61870 K3
61908 K3
61913 K3
61943 K3
61956 K3
63033 O7
63039 O7
63040 O7
63043 O7
63046 O7
63056 O7
63065 O7
63080 O7
63095 O7
63116 O7
63127 O7
63165 O7
63183 O7
63186 O7
63188 O7
63195 O7
63199 O7
64324 J11
64327 J11
64330 J11
64364 J11
64369 J11
64388 J11
64390 J11
64408 J11
64438 J11
65486 J5
65487 J5
65488 J5
65489 J5
68891 J50
68894 J50
68920 J50
69050 L3
69069 L3
69269 N5
69310 N5
90139 WD^1
90202 WD^1
90218 WD^1
90244 WD^1
90358 WD^1
90528 WD^1
90532 WD^1
90551 WD^1
90574 WD^1

1951 38E
60815 V2
60817 V2
60818 V2
60820 V2
60826 V2
60830 V2
60831 V2
60832 V2
60845 V2
60853 V2
61650 B17
61651 B17
61664 B17
61667 B17
64324 J11
64327 J11
64330 J11
64364 J11
64369 J11
64375 J11
64388 J11
64390 J11
64408 J11
64438 J11
69050 L3
69069 L3
69263 N5
69269 N5
69286 N5
69310 N5
69360 N5
69560 N2
90033 WD^1
90039 WD^1
90040 WD^1
90046 WD^1
90065 WD^1
90080 WD^1
90095 WD^1
90137 WD^1
90218 WD^1
90263 WD^1
90365 WD^1
90486 WD^1
90504 WD^1
90507 WD^1
90509 WD^1
90516 WD^1
90520 WD^1

1954 38E
60817 V2
60831 V2
60859 V2
60871 V2
60878 V2
60879 V2
60890 V2
60915 V2
61078 B1
61368 B1
61381 B1
64238 J6
64324 J11
64327 J11
64330 J11
64331 J11
64364 J11
64388 J11
64390 J11
64418 J11
64428 J11
69050 L3
69069 L3
90033 WD^1
90039 WD^1
90040 WD^1
90046 WD^1
90065 WD^1
90080 WD^1
90095 WD^1
90137 WD^1
90218 WD^1
90365 WD^1
90448 WD^1
90474 WD^1
90484 WD^1
90486 WD^1
90504 WD^1
90507 WD^1
90509 WD^1
90516 WD^1
90520 WD^1
90574 WD^1
90638 WD^1
90672 WD^1
90697 WD^1

1957 38E
43063 4MT^5
43106 4MT^5
60815 V2
60817 V2
60831 V2
60879 V2
60890 V2
60915 V2
61078 B1
61192 B1
61368 B1
61841 K3
61842 K3
61843 K3
61853 K3
61866 K3
64238 J6
64300 J11
64327 J11
64330 J11
64331 J11
64388 J11
64418 J11
64428 J11
64438 J11
67789 L1
76035 4MT^2
90033 WD^1
90039 WD^1
90040 WD^1
90046 WD^1
90065 WD^1
90080 WD^1
90095 WD^1
90137 WD^1
90218 WD^1
90299 WD^1
90346 WD^1
90365 WD^1
90403 WD^1
90433 WD^1
90448 WD^1
90474 WD^1
90486 WD^1
90504 WD^1
90507 WD^1
90509 WD^1
90516 WD^1
90520 WD^1
90574 WD^1
90638 WD^1
90672 WD^1
90697 WD^1

1960 2F
42335 4MT^2
42336 4MT^2
42349 4MT^2
43063 4MT^5
43106 4MT^5
43330 3F^3
43394 3F^3
61028 B1
61078 B1
61085 B1
61106 B1
61186 B1
61187 B1
61192 B1
61271 B1
61368 B1
61804 K3
61809 K3
61824 K3
61832 K3
61838 K3
61841 K3
61842 K3
61843 K3
61882 K3
61913 K3
67740 L1
67771 L1
67789 L1
90033 WD^1
90040 WD^1
90046 WD^1
90065 WD^1
90066 WD^1
90080 WD^1
90095 WD^1
90137 WD^1
90218 WD^1
90237 WD^1
90299 WD^1
90346 WD^1
90365 WD^1
90403 WD^1
90433 WD^1
90448 WD^1
90474 WD^1
90486 WD^1
90504 WD^1
90507 WD^1
90516 WD^1
90520 WD^1
90524 WD^1
90563 WD^1
90574 WD^1
90638 WD^1
90672 WD^1
90697 WD^1
90701 WD^1

1963 2F
42157 4MT^1
42178 4MT^1
42250 4MT^1
42251 4MT^1
42252 4MT^1
42253 4MT^1
42281 4MT^1
44667 5MT^3
44688 5MT^3
44691 5MT^3
44846 5MT^3
45238 5MT^3
45285 5MT^3
45335 5MT^3
45342 5MT^3
61008 B1
61116 B1
73000 5MT
73010 5MT
73032 5MT
73045 5MT
73053 5MT
76044 4MT^2
76052 4MT^2
76087 4MT^2
90033 WD^1
90040 WD^1
90065 WD^1
90066 WD^1
90095 WD^1
90218 WD^1
90237 WD^1
90299 WD^1
90346 WD^1
90365 WD^1
90433 WD^1
90448 WD^1
90474 WD^1
90486 WD^1
90504 WD^1
90516 WD^1
90520 WD^1
90524 WD^1
90563 WD^1
90672 WD^1
90697 WD^1

Worcester

1948 WOS
1408 1400
1418 1400
1919 1901
2001 1901
2007 1901
2016 1901
2037 2021
2051 2021
2100 2021
2101 2021
2115 2021
2205 2251
2207 2251
2237 2251
2241 2251
2242 2251
2247 2251
2263 2251
2274 2251
2277 2251
2278 2251
2290 2251
2294 2251
2339 2301
2458 2301
2551 2301
2651 2600
2743 2721
2774 2721
2799 2721
3021 ROD
3027 ROD
3029 ROD
3030 ROD
3048 ROD
3214 2251
3382 3300
3393 3300
3440 3300
3574 3571
3607 5700
4007 4000
4051 4000
4086 4073
4092 4073
4100 5101
4114 5101
4139 5101
4504 4500
4546 4500
4558 4500
4596 4575
4613 5700
4614 5700
4629 5700
4664 5700
4980 4900
5017 4073
5063 4073
5092 4073
5112 5101
5114 5101
5173 5101
5544 4575
5815 5800
5816 5800
5914 4900
5917 4900
5983 4900
6306 4300
6324 4300
6378 4300
6382 4300
6385 4300
6396 4300
6807 6800
6851 6800
6877 6800
6916 4900
6921 4900
6930 4900
6936 4900
6938 4900
6947 4900
6950 4900
6951 4900
7005 4073
7301 4300
7308 4300
7416 7400
7750 5700
8106 8100

1951 85A
1408 1400
1418 1400
2001 1901
2016 1901
2093 2021
2100 2021
2101 2021
2115 2021
2205 2251
2207 2251
2237 2251
2241 2251
2242 2251
2247 2251
2263 2251
2274 2251
2277 2251
2278 2251
2290 2251
2294 2251
2339 2301
2458 2301
2551 2301
3022 ROD
3029 ROD
3048 ROD
3214 2251
3219 2251
3377 3300
3447 3300
3607 5700
3725 5700
3839 2884
4007 4000
4082 4073
4086 4073
4093 4073
4114 5101
4139 5101
4546 4500
4596 4575
4613 5700
4614 5700
4629 5700
4641 5700
4664 5700
4993 4900
5017 4073
5063 4073
5086 4073
5092 4073
5173 5101
5303 4300
5573 4575
5815 5800
5816 5800
5914 4900
5917 4900
5943 4900
5971 4900
6306 4300
6324 4300
6378 4300
6396 4300
6807 6800
6851 6800
6877 6800
6930 4900
6938 4900
6947 4900
6950 4900
7005 4073
7007 4073
7222 7200
7236 7200
7240 7200
7248 7200
7301 4300
7437 7400
7750 5700
7920 6959
7928 6959
8106 8100
9429 9400
90284 WD^1
90691 WD^1

1954 85A
1408 1400
1418 1400
1461 1400
1605 1600
1629 1600
2034 2021
2040 2021
2201 2251
2205 2251
2237 2251
2241 2251
2242 2251
2247 2251
2253 2251
2258 2251
2262 2251
2263 2251
2277 2251
2278 2251
2290 2251
2294 2251
2458 2301
2807 2800
2825 2800
2855 2800
3214 2251
3607 5700
3725 5700
3775 5700
3848 2884
4082 4073
4113 5101
4114 5101
4154 5101
4567 4500
4571 4500
4594 4575
4613 5700
4625 5700
4629 5700
4664 5700
4900 4900
5063 4073
5086 4073
5090 4073
5092 4073
5815 5800
5816 5800
5914 4900
5917 4900
5943 4900
5971 4900
6306 4300
6324 4300
6334 4300
6354 4300
6359 4300
6378 4300
6382 4300
6388 4300
6389 4300
6396 4300
6807 6800
6851 6800
6877 6800
6930 4900
6947 4900
6950 4900
6987 6959
7005 4073
7007 4073
7750 5700
7920 6959
7928 6959
8105 8100
8106 8100
8427 9400
8458 9400
8480 9400
8496 9400
9429 9400
9466 9400
9480 9400
78008 2MT^1
78009 2MT^1

1957 85A
1418 1400
1461 1400
1605 1600
1629 1600
2205 2251
2241 2251
2242 2251
2247 2251
2258 2251
2277 2251
2807 2800
2813 2800
2825 2800
2855 2800
3204 2251
3205 2251
3209 2251
3213 2251
3214 2251
3216 2251
3217 2251
3218 2251
3607 5700
3725 5700
3775 5700
3848 2884
4082 4073
4113 5101
4148 5101
4154 5101
4567 4500
4571 4500
4613 5700
4614 5700
4625 5700
4629 5700
4664 5700
5037 4073
5081 4073
5083 4073
5086 4073
5090 4073
5337 4300
5350 4300
5396 4300
5815 5800
5816 5800
5818 5800
5909 4900
5914 4900
5917 4900
5952 4900
5956 4900
5971 4900
5984 4900
5994 4900
6334 4300
6348 4300
6354 4300
6357 4300
6388 4300
6395 4300
6807 6800
6851 6800
6877 6800
6930 4900
6947 4900
6950 4900
6987 6959
6989 6959
7005 4073
7007 4073
7321 4300
7707 5700
7750 5700
7777 5700
7815 7800
7920 6959
7928 6959
8105 8100
8106 8100
8427 9400
8480 9400
8496 9400
9316 9300
9429 9400
9466 9400
9480 9400
78001 2MT^1
78008 2MT^1
78009 2MT^1
82030 3MT^2
82038 3MT^2

1960 85A
1629 1600
1661 1600
2209 2251
2243 2251
2247 2251
2273 2251
3205 2251
3213 2251
3214 2251
3216 2251
3217 2251
3218 2251
3605 5700
3607 5700
3725 5700
3775 5700
4082 4073
4088 4073
4089 4073
4109 5101
4113 5101
4124 5101
4142 5101
4152 5101
4154 5101
4613 5700
4614 5700
4625 5700
4664 5700
4680 5700
4907 4900
4993 4900
4996 4900
5037 4073
5042 4073
5071 4073
5081 4073
5110 5101
5179 5101
5396 4300
5917 4900
5956 4900
5994 4900
5996 4900
6807 6800
6820 6800
6851 6800
6856 6800
6877 6800
6947 4900
6948 4900
6950 4900
6984 6959
6989 6959
6992 6959
7002 4073
7005 4073
7007 4073
7707 5700
7777 5700
7920 6959
7928 6959
8106 8100
8427 9400
8460 9400
8480 9400
8496 9400
9401 9400
9429 9400
9455 9400
9466 9400
9480 9400
9486 9400
75003 4MT^1
75025 4MT^1
78001 2MT^1
78008 2MT^1
78009 2MT^1
82008 3MT^2

1963 85A
1639 1600
1661 1600
2222 2251
2246 2251
3213 2251
3725 5700
4082 4073
4104 5101
4113 5101
4124 5101
4613 5700
4628 5700
4664 5700
4680 5700
5152 5101
5205 5205
5226 5205
5245 5205
6155 6100
6806 6800
6807 6800
6817 6800
6856 6800
6877 6800
6951 4900
6984 6959
6992 6959
7002 4073
7004 4073
7005 4073
7007 4073
7011 4073
7013 4073
7023 4073
7025 4073
7027 4073
7031 4073
7920 6959
7926 6959
7928 6959
8104 8100
8106 8100
8415 9400
9490 9400
75005 4MT^1
75025 4MT^1
78001 2MT^1
78009 2MT^1

Workington

1948 12D
40656 2P^3
40694 2P^3
40695 2P^3
44064 4F^2
44075 4F^2
44192 4F^2
44364 4F^2
44385 4F^2
44399 4F^2
44449 4F^2
44495 4F^2
44505 4F^2
44593 4F^2
47290 3F^6
47292 3F^6
47593 3F^6
47604 3F^6
52501 3F^8
52508 3F^8
52509 3F^8
58370 2F^{11}
58375 2F^{11}
58387 2F^{11}
58391 2F^{11}
58398 2F^{11}
58400 2F^{11}
58401 2F^{11}
58407 2F^{11}
58408 2F^{11}
58413 2F^{11}
58416 2F^{11}
28415 2F^{11}
28441 2F^{11}
28542 2F^{11}

1951 12D
40656 2P^3
40694 2P^3
40695 2P^3
43004 4MT^5
43006 4MT^5
43007 4MT^5
43008 4MT^5
43009 4MT^5
44064 4F^2
44364 4F^2
44365 4F^2
44449 4F^2
44495 4F^2
44505 4F^2
46447 2MT^2
46448 2MT^2

46456 2MT[2]
46457 2MT[2]
46458 2MT[2]
47290 3F[6]
47292 3F[6]
47593 3F[6]
52499 3F[8]
52501 3F[8]
52509 3F[8]
58362 2F[11]
58396 2F[11]
58421 2F[11]

1954 12D
40656 2P[3]
40694 2P[3]
40695 2P[3]
43004 4MT[5]
43006 4MT[5]
43007 4MT[5]
43008 4MT[5]
43009 4MT[5]
44365 4F[2]
44449 4F[2]
44454 4F[2]
44495 4F[2]
44505 4F[2]
44549 4F[2]
46447 2MT[2]
46448 2MT[2]
46456 2MT[2]
46457 2MT[2]
46458 2MT[2]
46488 2MT[2]
46491 2MT[2]
47290 3F[6]
47292 3F[6]
47593 3F[6]
47604 3F[6]
52499 3F[8]
52501 3F[8]

1957 12C
40582 2P[3]
43004 4MT[5]
43005 4MT[5]
43006 4MT[5]
43007 4MT[5]
43008 4MT[5]
43009 4MT[5]
44365 4F[2]
44390 4F[2]
44449 4F[2]
44461 4F[2]
44495 4F[2]
44505 4F[2]
44549 4F[2]
46447 2MT[2]
46455 2MT[2]
46456 2MT[2]
46457 2MT[2]
46488 2MT[2]
46489 2MT[2]
46491 2MT[2]
47290 3F[6]
47337 3F[6]
47390 3F[6]
47525 3F[6]
47593 3F[6]
47604 3F[6]
52418 3F[7]
52499 3F[8]
52510 3F[8]

1960 11B
43004 4MT[5]
43006 4MT[5]
43008 4MT[5]
43009 4MT[5]
43025 4MT[5]
43868 4F[1]
44292 4F[2]
44343 4F[2]
44360 4F[2]
44390 4F[2]
44449 4F[2]
44461 4F[2]
44495 4F[2]
44505 4F[2]
44549 4F[2]
46432 2MT[2]
46433 2MT[2]
46455 2MT[2]
46456 2MT[2]
46491 2MT[2]
47290 3F[6]
47361 3F[6]
47390 3F[6]
47525 3F[6]
47593 3F[6]
47604 3F[6]
47662 3F[6]

1963 12F
43004 4MT[5]
43006 4MT[5]
43008 4MT[5]
43025 4MT[5]
44035 4F[2]
44065 4F[2]
44157 4F[2]
44292 4F[2]
44386 4F[2]
44439 4F[2]
44449 4F[2]
44461 4F[2]
44505 4F[2]
44549 4F[2]
45364 5MT[3]
46432 2MT[2]
46433 2MT[2]
46488 2MT[2]
46491 2MT[2]
47344 3F[6]
47373 3F[6]
47390 3F[6]
47406 3F[6]
47612 3F[6]
47647 3F[6]
47676 3F[6]

1966 12D
43006 4MT[5]
43008 4MT[5]
43010 4MT[5]
43011 4MT[5]
43017 4MT[5]
43036 4MT[5]
43045 4MT[5]
43073 4MT[5]
43122 4MT[5]
44310 4F[2]
46424 2MT[2]
46432 2MT[2]
46452 2MT[2]
46485 2MT[2]
46491 2MT[2]
47373 3F[6]
47531 3F[6]
47612 3F[6]

Wrexham Rhosddu

1948 WRX
64338 J11
64381 J11
65153 J10
67428 C13
67429 C13
67432 C13
67433 C13
67435 C13
68163 Y3
68164 Y3
68176 Y3
68200 J62
68201 J62
68366 J60
68368 J60
68531 J67
69267 N5
69290 N5
69326 N5
69329 N5
69330 N5
69340 N5
69346 N5
69352 N5
69362 N5
69366 N5

1951 6E
47184 Sentinel[2]
64338 J11
64381 J11
67428 C13
67429 C13
67430 C13
67432 C13
67435 C13
67442 C14
67449 C14
68163 Y3
68164 Y3
68200 J62
68531 J67
68671 J72
69267 N5
69288 N5
69290 N5
69329 N5
69330 N5
69340 N5
69346 N5
69349 N5
69352 N5
69362 N5
69366 N5

1954 6E
43981 4F[1]
44058 4F[2]
67412 C13
67428 C13
67429 C13
67430 C13
67432 C13
67442 C14
67449 C14
68162 Y3
68164 Y3
68209 J63
68531 J67
68584 J67
68671 J72
69267 N5
69288 N5
69289 N5
69290 N5
69329 N5
69330 N5
69340 N5
69346 N5
69349 N5
69352 N5
69362 N5
69366 N5

1957 6E
40073 3MT[2]
40085 3MT[2]
40086 3MT[2]
40106 3MT[2]
40110 3MT[2]
40126 3MT[2]
40128 3MT[2]
40205 3MT[2]
41231 2MT[1]
41232 2MT[1]
41235 2MT[1]
41237 2MT[1]
41244 2MT[1]
41324 2MT[1]
43877 4F[1]
44058 4F[2]
44307 4F[2]
47284 3F[6]
47491 3F[6]
67428 C13
67442 C14
67449 C14
68585 J69
68595 J67
68671 J72
68727 J72
69267 N5
69281 N5
69290 N5
69329 N5
69335 N5
69346 N5
69349 N5
69362 N5
82020 3MT[2]
82021 3MT[2]

1960 84K
1618 1600
1663 1600
1669 1600
3204 2251
3749 5700
3760 5700
4683 5700
5606 5600
5651 5600
6610 5600
8734 5700
9610 5700
40085 3MT[2]
40086 3MT[2]
40110 3MT[2]
40126 3MT[2]
40205 3MT[2]
41231 2MT[1]
41232 2MT[1]
41285 2MT[1]
82000 3MT[2]
82020 3MT[2]
82021 3MT[2]
82031 3MT[2]
82037 3MT[2]

Yarmouth Beach

1948 YB
62152 D2
62175 D2
62207 D1
62561 D16
62592 D16
62596 D16
62613 D16
65469 J15
65472 J15
65558 J17
65559 J17
65574 J17
65581 J17
67112 F2
67157 F4
67162 F4
67223 F6
67226 F6
67233 F6
67234 F6
67235 F6
68213 J65
68651 J68

1951 32F
61520 B12
62561 D16
62564 D16
62592 D16
62596 D16
65558 J17
65559 J17
65581 J17
67223 F6
67226 F6
67233 F6
67234 F6
67235 F6
68214 J65
68651 J68

1954 32F
43157 4MT[5]
43158 4MT[5]
43159 4MT[5]
43160 4MT[5]
61520 B12
61545 B12
65581 J17
65586 J17
68214 J65
68651 J68

1957 32F
43157 4MT[5]
43158 4MT[5]
43159 4MT[5]
43160 4MT[5]
43161 4MT[5]
61530 B12
61545 B12
62517 D16
62597 D16
65581 J17
65586 J17
68651 J68

Yarmouth South Town

1948 YAR
62517 D16
62521 D16
62524 D16
62540 D16
62544 D16
62546 D16
62553 D16
62580 D16
62586 D16
62588 D16
62591 D16
62594 D16
62597 D16
62604 D16
64799 J39
67109 F2
67154 F4
68186 Y10
68187 Y10
68625 J69
68628 J67

1951 32D
61661 B17
61665 B17
62511 D16
62517 D16
62521 D16
62524 D16
62544 D16
62546 D16
62576 D16
62580 D16
62586 D16
62597 D16
62604 D16
62611 D16
62613 D16
67154 F4
67199 F5
67218 F5
68186 Y10
68219 J70
68625 J69
68628 J67

1954 32D
61514 B12
61533 B12
61542 B12
61568 B12
61622 B17
61659 B17
61670 B17
62511 D16
62517 D16
62524 D16
62544 D16
62546 D16
62580 D16
62586 D16
62597 D16
62604 D16
62611 D16
62613 D16
67199 F5
67218 F5
67387 C12
68223 J70
68628 J67
68656 J68

1957 32D
61622 B17
61656 B17
61659 B17
61664 B17
61665 B17
61670 B17
62511 D16
62524 D16
62544 D16
62546 D16
62580 D16
62586 D16
62604 D16
62611 D16
62613 D16
67199 F5
67366 C12
67728 L1
67736 L1
68628 J67
68656 J68
69689 N7
69696 N7
69708 N7

Yarmouth Vauxhall

1954 32E sub
67162 F4

Yeovil Pen Mill

1948 YEO
3671 5700
3733 5700
4689 5700
5529 4575
5565 4575
5767 5700
9601 5700
9771 5700

1951 82E
3671 5700
3733 5700
4689 5700
5529 4575
5565 4575
5767 5700
8745 5700
9601 5700
9732 5700
9771 5700

1954 82E
3671 5700
3733 5700
4507 4500
4689 5700
5563 4575
8745 5700
9601 5700
9732 5700
9764 5700

1957 82E
3671 5700
3733 5700
4689 5700
5548 4575
5563 4575
5781 5700
8745 5700
9732 5700
9764 5700

Yeovil Town

1948 YEO
30058 M7
30129 M7
30134 L11
30143 K10
30145 K10
30152 K10
30163 L11
30238 G6
30276 G6
30310 T9
30340 K10
30412 L11
30702 T9
30710 T9
30712 T9
30714 T9
30716 T9
31790 U
31791 U
31792 U
31793 U
31794 U
31795 U

1951 72C
30058 M7
30117 T9
30129 M7
30134 L11
30337 T9
30389 K10
30704 T9
31634 U
31636 U
31790 U
31791 U
31792 U
31793 U

1954 72C
30131 M7
30182 O2
30706 T9
30707 T9
31623 U
31790 U
31791 U
31792 U
31793 U
31794 U
31795 U
31796 U

1957 72C
30129 M7
30131 M7
30182 O2
31610 U
31623 U
31626 U
31790 U
31791 U
31792 U
31793 U
31794 U
31795 U
31796 U

1960 72C
3671 5700
3733 5700
4656 5700
5548 4575
5563 4575
8745 5700
9632 5700
9732 5700
9764 5700
30129 M7
30131 M7
31610 U
31613 U
31623 U
31626 U
31633 U
31790 U
31791 U

1963 72C
3671 5700
3733 5700
4507 4500
4631 5700
5548 4575
5563 4575
8745 5700
9732 5700
9764 5700
30052 M7
30129 M7
31614 U
31632 U
31637 U
31792 U
31798 U
31802 U
31805 U

Yoker

1951 65G
56030 0F[5]
56158 2F[4]
56161 2F[4]
56168 2F[4]
56170 2F[4]
56200 3F[10]
56250 3F[10]
56297 3F[10]
56315 3F[10]
56339 3F[10]
57259 2F[5]
68112 Y9

1954 65G
56030 0F[5]
56039 0F[5]
56158 2F[4]
56161 2F[4]
56168 2F[4]
56170 2F[4]
56238 3F[10]
56250 3F[10]
56297 3F[10]
56315 3F[10]
56339 3F[10]
57259 2F[5]
68112 Y9
68118 Y9
68551 J69

1957 65G
56030 0F[5]
56039 0F[5]
56158 2F[4]
56161 2F[4]
56168 2F[4]
56170 2F[4]
56238 3F[10]
56297 3F[10]
56315 3F[10]
57259 2F[5]

1960 65G
56039 0F[5]
56168 2F[4]
57259 2F[5]

York

1948 YK
60522 A2
60524 A2
60837 V2
60839 V2
60843 V2
60847 V2
60856 V2
60901 V2
60904 V2
60907 V2
60918 V2
60925 V2
60929 V2
60933 V2
60934 V2
60941 V2
60946 V2
60954 V2
60960 V2
60961 V2
60962 V2
60968 V2
60974 V2
60975 V2
60976 V2
60977 V2
60978 V2
60979 V2
60981 V2
60982 V2
61015 B1
61016 B1
61017 B1
61018 B1
61035 B1
61115 B1
61216 B1
61239 B1
61240 B1
61400 B16
61401 B16
61402 B16
61403 B16
61404 B16
61405 B16
61406 B16
61407 B16
61408 B16
61409 B16
61410 B16
61411 B16
61412 B16
61413 B16
61414 B16
61415 B16
61416 B16
61417 B16
61418 B16
61419 B16
61420 B16
61421 B16
61422 B16
61423 B16
61424 B16
61425 B16
61426 B16
61427 B16
61428 B16
61429 B16
61430 B16
61431 B16
61432 B16
61433 B16
61434 B16
61435 B16
61436 B16
61437 B16
61438 B16
61439 B16
61440 B16
61441 B16
61442 B16
61443 B16
61444 B16
61445 B16
61446 B16
61447 B16
61448 B16
61449 B16
61450 B16
61451 B16
61452 B16
61453 B16
61454 B16
61455 B16
61456 B16
61457 B16
61458 B16
61459 B16
61460 B16
61461 B16
61462 B16
61463 B16
61464 B16
61465 B16
61466 B16
61467 B16
61468 B16
62111 D17
62112 D17
62379 D20
62740 D49
62751 D49
62755 D49
62759 D49
62760 D49
62761 D49
62763 D49
65027 J21
65044 J21
65051 J21
65056 J21
65059 J21
65060 J21
65068 J21
65073 J21
65076 J21
65079 J21
65121 J21
65656 J25
65700 J25
65723 J25
68031 J94
68032 J94
68042 J94
68043 J94
68044 J94
68045 J94
68046 J94
68091 Y8
68230 J71
68231 J71
68240 J71
68246 J71
68250 J71
68253 J71
68268 J71
68275 J71
68280 J71
68282 J71
68286 J71
68293 J71
68297 J71
68298 J71
68310 J71
68399 J77
68401 J77
68440 J77
68677 J72
68695 J72
68699 J72
68715 J72
68722 J72
68726 J72
68735 J72
68739 J72
68741 J72
68745 J72
90231 WD[1]
90241 WD[1]
90314 WD[1]
90391 WD[1]
90571 WD[1]
90606 WD[1]
90629 WD[1]
90636 WD[1]
90638 WD[1]
90730 WD[1]

1951 50A
60121 A1
60138 A1
60140 A1
60146 A1
60153 A1
60501 A2
60502 A2
60503 A2
60522 A2
60524 A2
60526 A2
60837 V2
60839 V2
60843 V2
60847 V2
60856 V2
60864 V2
60901 V2
60904 V2
60907 V2
60918 V2
60925 V2
60929 V2
60933 V2
60934 V2
60941 V2
60946 V2
60954 V2
60960 V2
60961 V2
60962 V2
60963 V2
60968 V2
60974 V2
60975 V2
60976 V2
60977 V2
60978 V2
60979 V2
60981 V2
60982 V2
61015 B1
61016 B1
61020 B1
61038 B1
61071 B1
61084 B1
61115 B1
61239 B1
61288 B1
61337 B1
61416 B16
61417 B16
61418 B16
61419 B16
61420 B16
61421 B16
61422 B16
61423 B16
61424 B16
61426 B16
61430 B16
61434 B16
61435 B16
61436 B16
61437 B16
61438 B16
61439 B16
61441 B16
61443 B16
61444 B16
61448 B16
61449 B16
61450 B16
61451 B16
61452 B16
61453 B16
61454 B16
61455 B16
61456 B16
61457 B16
61458 B16
61459 B16
61460 B16
61461 B16
61462 B16
61463 B16
61464 B16
61465 B16
61466 B16
61467 B16
61468 B16
61472 B16
61473 B16
61474 B16
61475 B16
61476 B16
61477 B16
62726 D49
62730 D49
62731 D49
62732 D49
62734 D49
62735 D49
62744 D49
62745 D49
62759 D49
62760 D49
65043 J21
65619 J24
65679 J25
65700 J25
65723 J25
65845 J27
65849 J27
65861 J27
65883 J27
65885 J27
65888 J27
65890 J27
65894 J27
68017 J94
68031 J94
68032 J94
68040 J94
68044 J94
68046 J94
68061 J94
68091 Y8
68230 J71
68240 J71
68246 J71
68250 J71
68253 J71
68275 J71
68280 J71
68282 J71
68286 J71
68293 J71
68297 J71
68313 J71
68436 J77
68677 J72
68695 J72
68699 J72
68715 J72
68722 J72
68726 J72
68735 J72
68739 J72
68741 J72
68745 J72
69020 J72
90056 WD[1]
90069 WD[1]
90099 WD[1]
90100 WD[1]
90200 WD[1]
90235 WD[1]
90424 WD[1]
90432 WD[1]
90511 WD[1]
90518 WD[1]
90609 WD[1]
90670 WD[1]

1954 50A
60121 A1
60138 A1
60140 A1
60146 A1
60153 A1
60501 A2
60502 A2
60503 A2
60512 A2
60515 A2
60522 A2
60524 A2
60526 A2
60837 V2
60839 V2
60843 V2
60847 V2
60856 V2
60864 V2
60895 V2
60901 V2
60904 V2
60907 V2
60918 V2
60925 V2
60929 V2
60934 V2
60941 V2
60946 V2
60954 V2
60960 V2
60961 V2
60962 V2
60963 V2
60968 V2
60974 V2
60975 V2
60976 V2
60977 V2
60978 V2
60979 V2
60981 V2
60982 V2
61002 B1
61016 B1
61038 B1
61053 B1
61071 B1
61084 B1
61115 B1
61176 B1
61224 B1
61288 B1
61337 B1
61338 B1
61339 B1
61416 B16
61417 B16
61418 B16
61419 B16
61420 B16
61421 B16
61423 B16
61424 B16
61426 B16
61430 B16
61434 B16
61435 B16
61436 B16
61437 B16
61438 B16
61439 B16
61441 B16
61443 B16
61444 B16
61448 B16
61449 B16
61450 B16
61451 B16
61452 B16
61453 B16
61454 B16
61455 B16
61456 B16
61457 B16
61458 B16
61459 B16
61460 B16
61461 B16
61462 B16
61463 B16
61464 B16
61465 B16
61466 B16
61467 B16
61468 B16
61472 B16
61473 B16
61474 B16
61475 B16
61476 B16
61477 B16
62343 D20
62345 D20
62702 D49
62730 D49
62731 D49
62735 D49
62745 D49
62759 D49
62760 D49
62774 D49
65650 J25
65654 J25
65677 J25
65687 J25
65691 J25
65700 J25
65827 J27
65844 J27
65845 J27
65848 J27
65849 J27
65861 J27
65874 J27
65883 J27
65885 J27
65887 J27
65890 J27
65894 J27
68029 J94
68031 J94
68032 J94
68040 J94
68042 J94
68044 J94
68046 J94
68051 J94
68061 J94
68091 Y8
68230 J71
68240 J71
68246 J71
68250 J71
68253 J71
68275 J71
68280 J71
68293 J71
68297 J71
68313 J71
68677 J72
68695 J72
68699 J72
68722 J72
68724 J72
68726 J72
68735 J72
68739 J72
68745 J72
69020 J72
90047 WD[1]
90056 WD[1]
90100 WD[1]
90200 WD[1]
90500 WD[1]
90518 WD[1]
90670 WD[1]

1957 50A
51235 0F[4]
60121 A1
60138 A1
60140 A1
60146 A1
60153 A1
60501 A2
60502 A2
60503 A2
60512 A2
60515 A2
60522 A2
60524 A2
60526 A2
60837 V2
60839 V2
60843 V2
60847 V2
60856 V2
60864 V2
60895 V2
60904 V2
60907 V2
60918 V2
60925 V2
60929 V2
60934 V2
60941 V2
60946 V2
60954 V2
60960 V2
60961 V2
60963 V2
60968 V2
60974 V2
60975 V2
60976 V2
60977 V2
60981 V2
60982 V2
61002 B1
61016 B1
61017 B1
61038 B1
61053 B1
61071 B1
61084 B1
61115 B1
61288 B1
61337 B1
61339 B1
61416 B16
61417 B16
61418 B16
61419 B16
61420 B16
61421 B16
61422 B16
61423 B16
61424 B16
61426 B16
61430 B16
61434 B16
61435 B16
61436 B16
61437 B16
61438 B16
61439 B16
61441 B16
61443 B16
61444 B16
61448 B16
61449 B16
61450 B16
61452 B16
61453 B16
61454 B16
61455 B16
61457 B16
61459 B16
61460 B16
61461 B16
61462 B16
61463 B16
61464 B16
61465 B16
61466 B16
61467 B16
61468 B16
61472 B16
61473 B16
61475 B16
61476 B16
61477 B16
62046 K1

62047 K1
62048 K1
62049 K1
62050 K1
62056 K1
62057 K1
62061 K1
62062 K1
62063 K1
62395 D20
62702 D49
62730 D49
62731 D49
62745 D49
62747 D49
62760 D49
62771 D49
65691 J25
65714 J25
65793 J27
65845 J27
65857 J27
65874 J27
65883 J27
65887 J27
65890 J27
65894 J27
68029 J94
68031 J94
68032 J94
68040 J94
68042 J94
68044 J94
68046 J94
68061 J94
68246 J71
68250 J71
68280 J71
68435 J77
68677 J72
68686 J72
68695 J72
68722 J72
68724 J72
68726 J72
68735 J72
68739 J72
69020 J72
69877 A8
69910 T1
69913 T1
69916 T1

1960 50A

42085 4MT^1
42477 4MT^3
42553 4MT^3
42639 4MT^3
43014 4MT^5
43055 4MT^5
43056 4MT^5
43057 4MT^5
43070 4MT^5
43071 4MT^5
43096 4MT^5
46480 2MT^2
46481 2MT^2
47239 3F^5
47254 3F^5
47334 3F^6
47418 3F^6
47421 3F^6
47436 3F^6
47448 3F^6
47556 3F^6
47607 3F^6
60121 A1
60138 A1
60140 A1
60146 A1
60153 A1
60501 A2
60502 A2
60512 A2
60515 A2
60522 A2
60524 A2
60526 A2
60828 V2
60831 V2
60837 V2
60839 V2
60842 V2
60847 V2
60855 V2
60856 V2
60864 V2
60876 V2
60877 V2
60878 V2
60879 V2
60887 V2
60895 V2
60907 V2
60918 V2
60925 V2
60939 V2
60941 V2
60954 V2
60961 V2
60963 V2
60968 V2
60974 V2
60975 V2
60977 V2
60981 V2
60982 V2
61002 B1
61053 B1
61069 B1
61071 B1
61084 B1
61086 B1
61198 B1
61229 B1
61273 B1
61276 B1
61288 B1
61291 B1
61319 B1
61337 B1
61388 B1
61410 B16
61413 B16
61416 B16
61417 B16
61418 B16
61419 B16
61420 B16
61421 B16
61422 B16
61423 B16
61424 B16
61434 B16
61435 B16
61436 D10
61437 B16
61438 B16
61439 B16
61440 B16
61443 B16
61444 B16
61448 B16
61449 B16
61450 B16
61451 B16
61452 B16
61453 B16
61454 B16
61455 B16
61456 B16
61457 B16
61459 B16
61460 B16
61461 B16
61462 B16
61463 B16
61464 B16
61465 B16
61466 B16
61467 B16
61468 B16
61469 B16
61472 B16
61473 B16
61475 B16
61476 B16
61477 B16
61478 B16
62005 K1
62009 K1
62046 K1
62047 K1
62049 K1
62056 K1
62057 K1
62061 K1
62063 K1
62065 K1
64942 J39
65714 J25
65845 J27
65874 J27
65883 J27
65887 J27
65890 J27
65894 J27
68046 J94
68061 J94
68309 J71
68392 J77
68431 J77
68677 J72
68686 J72
68687 J72
68736 J72
69016 J72
69020 J72
77012 3MT^1
77013 3MT^1
90026 WD^1
90045 WD^1
90424 WD^1
90467 WD^1
90475 WD^1
90518 WD^1
90578 WD^1
90663 WD^1

1963 50A

43014 4MT^5
43055 4MT^5
43071 4MT^5
43097 4MT^5
43126 4MT^5
60121 A1
60124 A1
60126 A1
60138 A1
60140 A1
60146 A1
60150 A1
60154 A1
60155 A1
60805 V2
60810 V2
60828 V2
60831 V2
60833 V2
60837 V2
60847 V2
60855 V2
60856 V2
60864 V2
60876 V2
60877 V2
60886 V2
60887 V2
60895 V2
60925 V2
60929 V2
60932 V2
60939 V2
60941 V2
60942 V2
60945 V2
60954 V2
60961 V2
60963 V2
60967 V2
60968 V2
60974 V2
60975 V2
60981 V2
60982 V2
61002 B1
61018 B1
61021 B1
61031 B1
61049 B1
61053 B1
61062 B1
61069 B1
61071 B1
61084 B1
61198 B1
61229 B1
61273 B1
61276 B1
61288 B1
61319 B1
61337 B1
61421 B16
61434 B16
61448 B16
61454 B16
61455 B16
61457 B16
61475 B16
62005 K1
62009 K1
62042 K1
62046 K1
62047 K1
62049 K1
62056 K1
62057 K1
62061 K1
62063 K1
62065 K1
65894 J27
77012 3MT^1
90026 WD^1
90030 WD^1
90045 WD^1
90078 WD^1
90217 WD^1
90424 WD^1
90467 WD^1
90517 WD^1
90518 WD^1
90571 WD^1
90578 WD^1
90623 WD^1
90663 WD^1

1966 50A

43071 4MT^5
43097 4MT^5
43126 4MT^5
43133 4MT^5
43138 4MT^5
60145 A1
60831 V2
60877 V2
60886 V2
61017 B1
61019 B1
61021 B1
61035 B1
61199 B1
61216 B1
61238 B1
61303 B1
61319 B1
61337 B1
62005 K1
62012 K1
62028 K1
62042 K1
62046 K1
62057 K1
62060 K1
62062 K1
62065 K1
65823 J27
65894 J27
90078 WD^1
90254 WD^1
90395 WD^1
90517 WD^1
90518 WD^1
92006 9F
92205 9F
92206 9F
92211 9F
92231 9F
92239 9F

York Engineer's Yard

1948

68152 Y1

1951

68152 Y1

1954

68152 Y1

1957

53 Y1

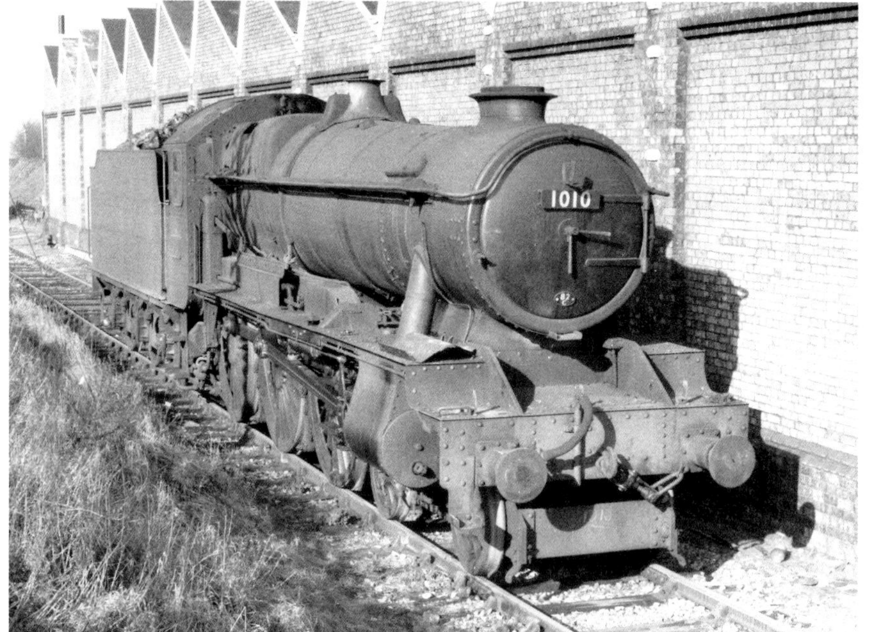

Right: GWR Hawksworth '1000' 'County' class 4-6-0 No 1010 *County of Caernarvon* standing outside the stock shed at Swindon on 7 June 1960. *Ivo Peters*

Photograph Locations (page numbers)

I *BR Steam Locomotives 1948-1968* II *BR Steam Locomotive Allocations 1948-1968 (this book)*